THE OLD TESTAMENT

Journal Edition

DESERET
BOOK

SALT LAKE CITY, UTAH

ISBN 978-1-62972-960-2 (paperbound)

Printed in China
RR Donnelley, Dongguan, China

10   9   8   7   6   5   4   3   2   1

THE BOOKS OF THE
OLD TESTAMENT

ABBREVIATIONS

Old Testament

Gen.	Genesis
Ex.	Exodus
Lev.	Leviticus
Num.	Numbers
Deut.	Deuteronomy
Josh.	Joshua
Judg.	Judges
Ruth	Ruth
1 Sam.	1 Samuel
2 Sam.	2 Samuel
1 Kgs.	1 Kings
2 Kgs.	2 Kings
1 Chr.	1 Chronicles
2 Chr.	2 Chronicles
Ezra	Ezra
Neh.	Nehemiah
Esth.	Esther
Job	Job
Ps.	Psalms
Prov.	Proverbs
Eccl.	Ecclesiastes
Song	Song of Solomon
Isa.	Isaiah
Jer.	Jeremiah
Lam.	Lamentations
Ezek.	Ezekiel
Dan.	Daniel
Hosea	Hosea
Joel	Joel
Amos	Amos
Obad.	Obadiah
Jonah	Jonah
Micah	Micah
Nahum	Nahum
Hab.	Habakkuk
Zeph.	Zephaniah
Hag.	Haggai
Zech.	Zechariah
Mal.	Malachi

New Testament

Matt.	Matthew
Mark	Mark
Luke	Luke
John	John
Acts	Acts
Rom.	Romans
1 Cor.	1 Corinthians
2 Cor.	2 Corinthians
Gal.	Galatians
Eph.	Ephesians
Philip.	Philippians
Col.	Colossians
1 Thes.	1 Thessalonians
2 Thes.	2 Thessalonians
1 Tim.	1 Timothy
2 Tim.	2 Timothy
Titus	Titus
Philem.	Philemon
Heb.	Hebrews
James	James
1 Pet.	1 Peter
2 Pet.	2 Peter
1 Jn.	1 John
2 Jn.	2 John
3 Jn.	3 John
Jude	Jude
Rev.	Revelation

Book of Mormon

1 Ne.	1 Nephi
2 Ne.	2 Nephi
Jacob	Jacob
Enos	Enos
Jarom	Jarom
Omni	Omni
W of M	Words of Mormon
Mosiah	Mosiah
Alma	Alma
Hel.	Helaman
3 Ne.	3 Nephi
4 Ne.	4 Nephi
Morm.	Mormon
Ether	Ether
Moro.	Moroni

Doctrine and Covenants

D&C	Doctrine and Covenants
OD	Official Declaration

Pearl of Great Price

Moses	Moses
Abr.	Abraham
JS—M	Joseph Smith—Matthew
JS—H	Joseph Smith—History
A of F	Articles of Faith

Other Abbreviations and Explanations

JST	Joseph Smith Translation
TG	Topical Guide
BD	Bible Dictionary
HEB	An alternate translation from the Hebrew
GR	An alternate translation from the Greek
IE	An explanation of idioms and difficult wording
OR	Alternate words that clarify the meaning of an archaic expression
HC	History of the Church

Italics in biblical text. Following the traditional format, italics in Bible verses indicate words that are not found in the original text (Hebrew, Aramaic, or Greek) but have been added for clarification in the translation.

THE
OLD TESTAMENT

TRANSLATED OUT OF THE
ORIGINAL TONGUES: AND WITH THE
FORMER TRANSLATIONS DILIGENTLY COMPARED
AND REVISED, BY HIS MAJESTY'S
SPECIAL COMMAND

AUTHORIZED KING JAMES VERSION
WITH EXPLANATORY NOTES AND
CROSS REFERENCES TO THE STANDARD WORKS
OF THE CHURCH OF JESUS CHRIST
OF LATTER-DAY SAINTS

JAMES

BY THE GRACE OF GOD

KING OF GREAT BRITAIN, FRANCE, AND IRELAND, DEFENDER OF THE FAITH, &C.

THE TRANSLATORS OF THE BIBLE WISH GRACE, MERCY, AND PEACE, THROUGH JESUS CHRIST OUR LORD

Great and manifold were the blessings, most dread Sovereign, which Almighty God, the Father of all mercies, bestowed upon us the people of *England,* when first he sent Your Majesty's Royal Person to rule and reign over us. For whereas it was the expectation of many, who wished not well unto our *Sion,* that upon the setting of that bright *Occidental Star,* Queen *Elizabeth* of most happy memory, some thick and palpable clouds of darkness would so have overshadowed this Land, that men should have been in doubt which way they were to walk; and that it should hardly be known, who was to direct the unsettled State; the appearance of Your Majesty, as of the *Sun* in his strength, instantly dispelled those supposed and surmised mists, and gave unto all that were well affected exceeding cause of comfort; especially when we beheld the Government established in Your Highness, and Your hopeful Seed, by an undoubted Title, and this also accompanied with peace and tranquillity at home and abroad.

But among all our joys, there was no one that more filled our hearts, than the blessed continuance of the preaching of God's sacred Word among us; which is that inestimable treasure, which excelleth all the riches of the earth; because the fruit thereof extendeth itself, not only to the time spent in this transitory world, but directeth and disposeth men unto that eternal happiness which is above in heaven.

Then not to suffer this to fall to the ground, but rather to take it up, and to continue it in that state, wherein the famous Predecessor of Your Highness did leave it: nay, to go forward with the confidence and resolution of a Man in maintaining the truth of Christ, and propagating it far and near, is that which hath so bound and firmly knit the hearts of all Your Majesty's loyal and religious people unto You, that Your very name is precious among them: their eye doth behold You with comfort, and they bless You in their hearts, as that sanctified Person, who, under God, is the immediate Author of their true happiness. And this their contentment doth not diminish or decay, but every day increaseth and taketh strength, when they observe, that the zeal of Your Majesty toward the house of God doth not slack or go backward, but is more and more kindled, manifesting itself abroad in the farthest parts of *Christendom,* by writing in defence of the Truth, (which hath given such a blow unto that man of sin, as will not be healed,) and every day at home, by religious and learned discourse, by frequenting the house of God, by hearing the Word preached, by cherishing the Teachers thereof, by caring for the Church, as a most tender and loving nursing Father.

There are infinite arguments of this right Christian and religious affection in Your Majesty; but none is more forcible to declare it to others than the vehement and perpetuated desire of accomplishing and publishing of this work, which now with all humility we present unto Your Majesty. For when Your Highness had once out of deep judgment apprehended how convenient it was, that out of the Original Sacred Tongues, together with comparing of the labours, both in our own, and other foreign Languages, of many worthy men who went before us, there should be one more exact Translation of the holy Scriptures into the *English Tongue*; Your Majesty did never desist to urge and to excite those to whom it was commended, that the work might be hastened, and that the business might be expedited in so decent a manner, as a matter of such importance might justly require.

And now at last, by the mercy of God, and the continuance of our labours, it being brought unto such a conclusion, as that we have great hopes that the Church of *England* shall reap good fruit thereby; we hold it our duty to offer it to Your Majesty, not only as to our King and Sovereign, but as to the principal Mover and Author of the work: humbly craving of Your most Sacred Majesty, that since things of this quality have ever been subject to the censures of illmeaning and discontented persons, it may receive approbation and patronage from so learned and judicious a Prince as Your Highness is, whose allowance and acceptance of our labours shall more honour and encourage us, than all the calumniations and hard interpretations of other men shall dismay us. So that if, on the one side, we shall be traduced by Popish Persons at home or abroad, who therefore will malign us, because we are poor instruments to make God's holy Truth to be yet more and more known unto the people, whom they desire still to keep in ignorance and darkness; or if, on the other side, we shall be maligned by selfconceited Brethren, who run their own ways, and give liking unto nothing, but what is framed by themselves, and hammered on their anvil; we may rest secure, supported within by the truth and innocency of a good conscience, having walked the ways of simplicity and integrity, as before the Lord; and sustained without by the powerful protection of Your Majesty's grace and favour, which will ever give countenance to honest and Christian endeavours against bitter censures and uncharitable imputations.

The Lord of heaven and earth bless Your Majesty with many and happy days, that, as his heavenly hand hath enriched Your Highness with many singular and extraordinary graces, so You may be the wonder of the world in this latter age for happiness and true felicity, to the honour of that great GOD, and the good of his Church, through Jesus Christ our Lord and only Saviour.

THE FIRST BOOK OF MOSES

CALLED

GENESIS

CHAPTER 1

God creates this earth and its heaven and all forms of life in six days—The creative acts of each day are described—God creates man, both male and female, in His own image—Man is given dominion over all things and is commanded to multiply and fill the earth.

IN the ªbeginning ᵇGod ᶜcreated the ᵈheaven and the ᵉearth.

2 And the earth was without ªform, and void; and ᵇdarkness *was* upon the face of the deep. And the ᶜSpirit of God ᵈmoved upon the face of the waters.

3 And God ªsaid, Let there be ᵇlight: and there was light.

4 And God saw the light, that *it was* ªgood: and God divided the light from the darkness.

5 And God called the light ªDay, and the ᵇdarkness he called Night. And the evening and the morning were the ᶜfirst ᵈday.

6 ¶ And God said, Let there be a ªfirmament in the midst of the waters, and let it divide the waters from the waters.

7 And God made the firmament, and divided the ªwaters which *were* under the firmament from the waters which *were* above the firmament: and it was so.

8 And God called the firmament ªHeaven. And the evening and the morning were the second ᵇday.

9 ¶ And God said, Let the ªwaters under the heaven be gathered together unto ᵇone place, and let the dry *land* appear: and it was so.

10 And God called the dry *land* ªEarth; and the gathering together of the waters called he Seas: and God saw that *it was* good.

11 And God said, Let the earth bring forth ªgrass, the herb yielding seed, *and* the fruit tree yielding fruit after his kind, whose seed *is* in itself, upon the earth: and it was so.

12 And the earth ªbrought forth grass, *and* herb yielding seed after his kind, and the tree yielding fruit, whose seed *was* in itself, after his ᵇkind: and God saw that *it was* good.

13 And the evening and the morning were the third day.

14 ¶ And God said, Let there be ªlights in the firmament of the heaven to divide the day from the

---

1 1a TG Time.
  b Mosiah 4:2;
    Morm. 9:11;
    D&C 14:9; 76:24 (20–24);
    Moses 2:1;
    Abr. 4:1.
  c HEB shaped, fashioned,
    created; always divine
    activity; see Abr. 4:1,
    organized, formed.
    TG Creation;
    God, Creator.
  d D&C 121:4;
    Moses 1:37 (36–38); 2:1;
    Abr. 4:1.
    TG Astronomy;
    Heaven.
  e TG Nature, Earth.

2a Abr. 4:2.
  b TG Darkness, Physical.
  c TG God, Spirit of.
  d Moses 2:2;
    Abr. 4:2.
3a Ps. 33:9.
  b TG Light [noun].
4a Alma 32:35;
    Moses 2:4;
    Abr. 4:4.
5a Moro. 7:15.
    TG Time.
  b TG Darkness, Physical.
  c TG Time.
  d Moses 2:5;
    Abr. 4:5.
6a HEB expanse.
    Moses 2:6 (6–8);

Abr. 4:6 (6–8);
    fac. 2, fig. 4.
7a Ps. 148:4 (3–5).
8a TG Heaven.
  b Abr. 4:8.
9a TG Earth, Dividing of.
  b Moses 2:9;
    Abr. 4:9.
10a Moses 1:29.
11a Moses 2:11 (11–12);
    Abr. 4:11 (11–12).
12a D&C 88:25.
  b Alma 32:31 (28–34);
    Moses 2:12 (11–12).
    TG Order.
14a Ps. 104:19;
    D&C 67:9.
    TG Astronomy.

night; and let them be for ᵇsigns, and for ᶜseasons, and for days, and years:

15 And let them be for lights in the firmament of the heaven to give light upon the earth: and it was so.

16 And God made two great lights; the ᵃgreater light to rule the day, and the lesser light to rule the night: *he made* the ᵇstars also.

17 And God set them in the ᵃfirmament of the heaven to give light upon the earth,

18 And to rule over the ᵃday and over the night, and to divide the light from the darkness: and God saw that *it was* good.

19 And the evening and the morning were the fourth day.

20 And God said, Let the ᵃwaters ᵇbring forth abundantly the moving creature that hath life, and ᶜfowl *that* may fly above the earth in the open firmament of heaven.

21 And God created ᵃgreat whales, and every living creature that moveth, which the waters brought forth abundantly, after their kind, and every winged fowl after his kind: and God saw that *it was* good.

22 And God blessed them, saying, Be fruitful, and ᵃmultiply, and fill the waters in the seas, and let fowl multiply in the earth.

23 And the evening and the morning were the fifth day.

24 ¶ And God said, Let the earth bring forth the living creature after his ᵃkind, cattle, and creeping thing, and beast of the earth after his kind: and it was so.

25 And God made the beast of the earth after his kind, and cattle after their kind, and every thing that creepeth upon the earth after his kind: and God saw that *it was* good.

26 ¶ And God said, Let ᵃus ᵇmake ᶜman in our ᵈimage, after our ᵉlikeness: and let them have ᶠdominion over the fish of the sea, and over the fowl of the air, and over the cattle, and over all the earth, and over every creeping thing that creepeth upon the earth.

27 So God created man in his *own* ᵃimage, in the image of God created he him; male and ᵇfemale created he them.

28 And God blessed them, and God said unto them, Be ᵃfruitful, and ᵇmultiply, and ᶜreplenish the ᵈearth, and subdue it: and have ᵉdominion over the fish of the sea, and over the fowl of the air, and over every living thing that moveth upon the earth.

29 ¶ And God said, Behold, I have given you every herb bearing seed, which *is* upon the face of all the earth, and every tree, in the which *is* the fruit of a tree yielding seed; to you it shall be for ᵃmeat.

30 And to every beast of the earth, and to every fowl of the air, and to every thing that creepeth upon the earth, wherein *there is* life, *I have*

14b D&C 29:14.
   TG Signs; Symbolism.
   c TG Order.
16a D&C 76:71 (70–71); 88:45;
   Moses 2:16; Abr. 4:16.
   b Abr. 3:2. TG Astronomy.
17a D&C 76:109.
18a Jer. 31:35.
20a D&C 61:14 (14–17).
   b HEB swarm with swarms
   of living creatures
   (souls).
   c 2 Ne. 2:15;
   D&C 49:19 (18–19).
21a HEB great sea monsters.
   Ether 2:24; 6:10;
   Moses 2:21; Abr. 4:21.
22a Moses 2:22; Abr. 4:22.
24a TG Order.
26a Abr. 4:27 (26–31); 5:7.

TG Godhead;
   Jesus Christ, Creator.
   b TG Creation.
   c TG Adam; Man, Physical
   Creation of.
   d Mosiah 7:27;
   Ether 3:15 (14–17);
   D&C 20:18 (17–18);
   Moses 1:6 (6, 13, 16);
   2:26 (26–29); 6:9 (8–10);
   Abr. 4:26 (26–31).
   e Gen. 5:3.
   f Prov. 12:10;
   D&C 49:19 (18–21);
   76:111 (110–12);
   121:37 (34–46);
   Moses 2:26 (26–28);
   Abr. 4:26 (26–28).
   TG Man, Potential to
   Become like Heavenly

Father.
27a TG God, Body of,
   Corporeal Nature.
   b TG Woman.
28a TG Children.
   b D&C 45:58;
   132:63 (55–56, 63).
   TG Birth Control;
   Marriage, Fatherhood;
   Marriage, Motherhood.
   c HEB fill; see same word
   in v. 22.
   1 Ne. 17:36.
   d TG Earth, Purpose of.
   e Gen. 9:2 (1–6).
29a HEB food.
   Moses 2:29 (29–30);
   Abr. 4:29 (29–30).
   TG Food;
   Word of Wisdom.

given every green herb for ^ameat: and it was so.

31 And God saw every thing that he had made, and, behold, *it was* very ^agood. And the evening and the morning were the ^bsixth day.

CHAPTER 2

The Creation is completed—God rests on the seventh day—The prior spirit creation is explained—Adam and Eve are placed in the Garden of Eden— They are forbidden to eat of the tree of knowledge of good and evil—Adam names every living creature—Adam and Eve are married by the Lord.

THUS the heavens and the ^aearth were finished, and all the ^bhost of them.

2 And on the seventh day God ended his work which he had ^amade; and he ^brested on the seventh day from all his ^cwork which he had made.

3 And God blessed the ^aseventh day, and ^bsanctified it: because that in it he had ^crested from all his work which God ^dcreated and made.

4 ¶ These *are* the generations of the heavens and of the earth when they were ^acreated, in the day that

the ^bLORD God made the earth and the heavens,

5 And every ^aplant of the field ^bbefore it was in the ^cearth, and every herb of the field before it grew: for the LORD God had not caused it to rain upon the earth, and *there was* not a ^dman to till the ^eground.

6 But there went up a ^amist from the earth, and watered the whole face of the ground.

7 And the LORD God ^aformed ^bman *of* the ^cdust of the ground, and breathed into his nostrils the ^dbreath of life; and ^eman became a living ^fsoul.

8 ¶ And the LORD God planted a garden eastward in ^aEden; and there he put the man whom he had formed.

9 And out of the ground made the LORD God to grow every tree that is pleasant to the ^asight, and good for ^bfood; the ^ctree of ^dlife also in the midst of the garden, and the tree of ^eknowledge of good and evil.

10 And a river went out of ^aEden to water the garden; and from thence it was ^bparted, and became into four heads.

11 The name of the first *is* Pison: that *is* it which ^acompasseth the

---

30a HEB food.
31a 1 Tim. 4:4; Moro. 7:12;
   D&C 59:17 (16–20);
   Moses 2:31.
   TG Body, Sanctity of.
  b Ex. 31:17; Mosiah 13:19;
   Moses 2:31; Abr. 4:31.
2 1a TG Creation.
  b Isa. 45:12;
   D&C 29:36; 38:1; 45:1;
   Moses 3:1; Abr. 5:1.
 2a OR done.
  b HEB stopped, ceased;
   from the verb *shavat*;
   the noun *shabbat* (Engl.
   Sabbath) means a
   stopping or cessation.
   D&C 77:12;
   Moses 3:2 (1–3);
   Abr. 5:2 (1–3).
   TG Rest.
  c TG Industry.
 3a TG Sabbath.
  b Ex. 20:11;
   Mosiah 13:19 (16–19);
   D&C 77:12;

Moses 3:3 (1–3);
Abr. 5:3 (1–3).
TG Sacred.
  c Ex. 31:17.
  d OR created through
   working.
 4a Moses 3:4 (4–5);
   Abr. 5:4 (4–5).
  b TG Jesus Christ, Jehovah.
 5a TG Nature, Earth.
  b TG Spirit Creation.
  c TG Creation.
  d TG Man, Physical
   Creation of.
  e Moses 3:5.
 6a HEB (also) flood, flow.
 7a TG Man, Physical
   Creation of.
  b TG Creation.
  c Gen. 18:27; Morm. 9:17;
   D&C 77:12; 93:35 (33–35);
   Moses 3:7;
   4:25 (25–29); 6:59;
   Abr. 5:7.
  d 2 Ne. 9:26;
   D&C 77:2; 93:33;

Abr. 5:7 (7–8).
   TG Breath of Life.
  e TG Adam.
  f D&C 88:15.
   TG Soul.
 8a TG Eden.
 9a TG Eden.
  b Moses 3:9; Abr. 5:9.
   TG Food.
  c Gen. 3:24;
   Rev. 2:7; 22:2 (2, 14);
   1 Ne. 8:10 (10–12);
   11:25 (21–22, 25);
   15:36 (22, 28, 36);
   2 Ne. 2:15;
   Alma 12:26 (21, 23, 26);
   32:40; 42:5 (2–6);
   Moses 3:9; 4:28 (28, 31);
   Abr. 5:9.
  d TG Immortality.
  e TG Knowledge;
   Opposition.
10a TG Eden.
  b HEB divided into four
   heads (branches).
11a HEB encircles.

whole land of *b*Havilah, where *there is* gold;

12 And the gold of that land *is* good: there *is* bdellium and *a*the onyx stone.

13 And the name of the second river *is* Gihon: the same *is* it that *a*compasseth the whole land of *b*Ethiopia.

14 And the name of the third river *is* Hiddekel: that *is* it which goeth toward the east of Assyria. And the fourth river *is* Euphrates.

15 And the LORD God took the man, and put him into the *a*garden of *b*Eden *c*to dress it and to *d*keep it.

16 And the LORD God *a*commanded the man, saying, Of every tree of the garden thou mayest *b*freely eat:

17 But of the *a*tree of the *b*knowledge of good and evil, thou shalt not eat of it: for in the *c*day that thou eatest thereof thou shalt surely *d*die.

18 ¶ And the LORD God said, *It is* not good that the man should be *a*alone; I will make him *b*an help meet for him.

19 And out of the ground the LORD God formed every beast of the field, and every fowl of the air; and brought *them* unto *a*Adam to see what he would call them: and whatsoever Adam called every living creature, that *was* the *b*name thereof.

20 And Adam gave names to all cattle, and to the fowl of the air, and to every beast of the field; but for Adam there was not found an help meet for him.

21 And the LORD God caused a deep sleep to fall upon Adam, and he slept: and he took one of his ribs, and closed up the flesh instead thereof;

22 And the rib, which the LORD God had taken from man, made he a *a*woman, and brought her unto the man.

23 And Adam said, This *is* now bone of my bones, and *a*flesh of my flesh: she shall be called *b*Woman, because she was taken out of Man.

24 Therefore shall a *a*man leave his *b*father and his mother, and shall *c*cleave unto his *d*wife: and they shall be *e*one flesh.

25 And they were both *a*naked, the man and his wife, and were not *b*ashamed.

CHAPTER 3

The serpent (Lucifer) deceives Eve—She and then Adam partake of the forbidden fruit—Her Seed (Christ) will bruise the serpent's head—The roles of woman and of man are explained—Adam and Eve are cast out of the Garden of Eden—Adam presides—Eve becomes the mother of all living.

Now the *a*serpent was more *b*subtil than any beast of the field which

---

11*b* Gen. 10:29 (7, 29); 25:18;
  Moses 3:11.
12*a* OR lapis lazuli, or
  cornelian (identity
  uncertain).
13*a* HEB encircles.
  b HEB Cush.
  Moses 3:13.
15*a* TG Earth, Purpose of.
  b TG Eden.
  c HEB to till it.
  d D&C 42:41.
16*a* TG Commandments
  of God.
  b TG Agency.
17*a* Gen. 3:3; 2 Ne. 2:15.
  b TG Knowledge.
  c Abr. 5:13.
  d Moses 3:17.
  TG Death; Death,
  Spiritual, First; Fall
  of Man; Man, Natural,

Not Spiritually Reborn;
  Mortality.
18*a* Moses 3:18;
  Abr. 5:14.
  TG Marriage, Celestial.
  b IE a helper suited
  to, worthy of, or
  corresponding to him.
  Moses 3:18;
  Abr. 5:14.
  TG Marriage, Wives.
19*a* Moses 1:34; 3:19;
  Abr. 1:3; 5:20.
  b TG Language.
22*a* TG Man, Physical
  Creation of.
23*a* Gen. 29:14; Jacob 2:21;
  Moses 3:23; Abr. 5:17.
  b TG Creation; Woman.
24*a* TG Marriage, Husbands.
  b TG Marriage,
  Fatherhood.

c D&C 42:22; 49:15 (15–16);
  Moses 3:24 (23–24);
  Abr. 5:18 (17–18).
  TG Chastity.
  d Mosiah 13:24;
  Alma 44:5; 3 Ne. 18:21.
  TG Family, Patriarchal;
  Marriage, Wives.
  e TG Divorce; Family,
  Eternal; Marriage,
  Celestial; Marriage,
  Marry; Unity.
25*a* Gen. 3:7;
  2 Ne. 9:14;
  Moses 4:13 (13, 16–17).
  b TG Shame.
3 1*a* TG Devil.
  b OR crafty, sly.
  2 Cor. 11:3;
  1 Jn. 3:8; Alma 12:4;
  D&C 123:12;
  Moses 4:5.

the LORD God had made. And he said unto the woman, ᶜYea, hath God said, Ye shall not eat of every tree of the garden?

2 And the woman said unto the serpent, We may eat of the fruit of the trees of the garden:

3 But of the fruit of the ᵃtree which is in the midst of the garden, God hath said, Ye shall not eat of it, neither shall ye touch it, lest ye die.

4 And the serpent said unto the woman, ᵃYe shall not surely die:

5 For God doth know that in the day ye eat thereof, then your ᵃeyes shall be opened, and ye shall be as gods, ᵇknowing good and ᶜevil.

6 And when the woman saw that the tree was good for ᵃfood, and that it was ᵇpleasant to the eyes, and a tree ᶜto be desired to make one wise, she took of the ᵈfruit thereof, and did ᵉeat, and gave also unto her husband with her; and he did ᶠeat.

7 And the eyes of them both were ᵃopened, and they knew that they were ᵇnaked; and they sewed fig leaves together, and made themselves ᶜaprons.

8 And they heard the voice of the LORD God ᵃwalking in the garden ᵇin the cool of the day: and Adam and his wife hid themselves from the presence of the LORD God amongst the trees of the garden.

9 And the LORD God called unto Adam, and said unto him, Where art thou?

10 And he said, I heard thy voice in the garden, and I was afraid, because I was naked; and I hid myself.

11 And he said, Who told thee that thou wast naked? Hast thou eaten of the tree, whereof I commanded thee that thou shouldest not eat?

12 And the man said, The woman whom thou gavest to be with me, she gave me of the tree, and I did eat.

13 And the LORD God said unto the woman, What is this that thou hast done? And the woman said, The serpent ᵃbeguiled me, and I did eat.

14 And the LORD God said unto the ᵃserpent, Because thou hast done this, thou art ᵇcursed above all cattle, and above every beast of the field; upon thy belly shalt thou go, and dust shalt thou eat all the days of thy life:

15 And I will put ᵃenmity between thee and the woman, and between thy seed and her seed; ᵇit shall ᶜbruise thy head, and thou shalt ᵈbruise his heel.

16 Unto the ᵃwoman he said, I will greatly ᵇmultiply thy ᶜsorrow and thy conception; in sorrow thou shalt

1c OR Has God actually said.
3a Gen. 2:17.
4a HEB (emphatic expression) Dying, ye shall not die. TG Death, Spiritual, First.
5a Mosiah 27:22; D&C 76:12 (12, 19); 88:11 (11–13); 110:1; 136:32; Moses 4:11 (10–13); 5:10.
b 2 Ne. 2:18 (18, 26); Mosiah 16:3; Alma 29:5; Moro. 7:16 (15–19). TG Earth, Purpose of; Knowledge.
c TG Evil.
6a TG Food.
b Hebrew idiom meaning "a desirable thing."
c OR desirable as a means to wisdom, insight. 1 Ne. 8:12 (10–15); 15:36;
Moses 4:12.
d 2 Ne. 2:15 (15–19); Mosiah 3:26; Alma 12:22 (21–23); D&C 29:40; Moses 4:12 (7–13).
e TG Fall of Man; Transgress.
f Rom. 5:12.
7a TG Fall of Man.
b Gen. 2:25.
c HEB things to gird about, or wrap around, the body. TG Apparel; Clothing; Modesty.
8a Moses 4:14.
b HEB at the wind of the day (i.e., at the time of the evening breeze).
13a 2 Ne. 9:9; Mosiah 16:3; Ether 8:25;
Moses 4:19 (5–19). TG Temptation.
14a TG Devil.
b Moses 4:20 (20–21). TG Curse.
15a Moses 4:21.
b HEB he.
c HEB crush, or grind. Rom. 16:20; Heb. 2:14; D&C 19:3 (2–3). TG Jesus Christ, Foreordained; Jesus Christ, Prophecies about; Redemption.
d Isa. 53:10 (10–12).
16a TG Marriage, Motherhood.
b HEB increase thy discomfort and thy size (i.e., in the condition and process of pregnancy).
c TG Suffering.

bring forth ^dchildren; and thy desire *shall be* to thy ^ehusband, and he shall rule over thee.

17 And unto Adam he said, Because thou hast hearkened unto the voice of thy ^awife, and hast eaten of the tree, of which I commanded thee, saying, Thou shalt not eat of it: ^bcursed *is* the ground for thy sake; in ^csorrow shalt thou eat *of it* all the days of thy life;

18 ^aThorns also and thistles shall it bring forth to thee; and thou shalt eat the herb of the field;

19 In the ^asweat of thy face shalt thou eat ^bbread, till thou return unto the ground; for out of it wast thou taken: for ^cdust thou *art,* and unto ^ddust shalt thou return.

20 And Adam called his wife's name Eve; because she was the ^amother of all living.

21 Unto Adam also and to his wife did the LORD God make ^acoats of skins, and ^bclothed them.

22 ¶ And the LORD God ^asaid, Behold, the ^bman is become as one of ^cus, to ^dknow good and ^eevil: and now, lest he put forth his hand, and take also of the tree of life, and eat, and live for ever:

23 Therefore the LORD God sent him forth from the garden of ^aEden, to till the ground from whence he was taken.

24 So he drove out the man; and he placed at the east of the garden of Eden ^aCherubims, and a flaming sword which turned every way, to keep the way of the ^btree of life.

CHAPTER 4

Eve bears Cain and Abel—They offer sacrifices—Cain slays Abel and is cursed by the Lord, who also sets a mark upon him—The children of men multiply—Adam begets Seth, and Seth begets Enos.

AND Adam knew Eve his wife; and she conceived, and bare ^aCain, and said, I have gotten a man from the LORD.

2 And she again bare his brother Abel. And Abel was a ^akeeper of sheep, but Cain was a tiller of the ground.

3 And in process of time it came to pass, that Cain brought of the fruit of the ground an offering unto the LORD.

4 And Abel, he also brought of the ^afirstlings of his flock and of the fat thereof. And the LORD had respect unto ^bAbel and to his ^coffering:

5 But unto ^aCain and to his ^boffering he had not ^crespect. And Cain was very wroth, and his countenance fell.

6 And the LORD said unto Cain, Why art thou wroth? and why is thy countenance fallen?

7 If thou doest well, shalt thou not be ^aaccepted? and if thou ^bdoest not

---

16*d* 2 Ne. 2:23;
　　Moses 4:22.
　　TG Children.
　e TG Marriage, Husbands;
　　Marriage, Wives.
17*a* TG Marriage, Wives.
　b TG Curse;
　　Earth, Curse of.
　c HEB travail, pain.
18*a* TG Opposition.
19*a* Moses 4:25 (23–25).
　　TG Industry;
　　Work, Value of.
　b TG Bread.
　c Gen. 18:27;
　　Eccl. 3:20.
　　TG Man, Physical
　　Creation of;
　　Mortality.
　d Job 10:9.

20*a* TG Marriage,
　　Motherhood.
21*a* OR garments, or tunics.
　b TG Apparel; Clothing.
22*a* Moses 4:28.
　b TG Man, Potential to
　　Become like Heavenly
　　Father.
　c TG Godhead;
　　Jesus Christ, Creator.
　d Alma 12:31.
　　TG Conscience;
　　Discernment, Spiritual;
　　Earth, Purpose of;
　　Knowledge;
　　Probation.
　e TG Evil.
23*a* TG Eden.
24*a* TG Cherubim.
　b Gen. 2:9;

　　Alma 42:5 (2–5).
4 1*a* Moses 5:2 (2–3), 16–17.
　2*a* Moses 5:17.
　4*a* Num. 18:17;
　　Mosiah 2:3;
　　Moses 5:20 (5, 19–23).
　　TG Jesus Christ, Types
　　of, in Anticipation.
　b Heb. 11:4.
　c TG Sacrifice.
　5*a* Jude 1:11 (7–21).
　b Prov. 15:8;
　　Moses 5:7 (4–8),
　　21 (20–26).
　c Num. 16:15.
　7*a* Mosiah 2:22;
　　D&C 52:15; 97:8; 132:50;
　　Moses 5:23.
　　TG Blessing.
　b TG Agency.

well, ^csin lieth at the door. And unto thee *shall be* ^dhis ^edesire, and thou shalt rule over him.

8 And Cain talked with Abel his brother: and it came to pass, when they were in the field, that Cain rose up against Abel his brother, and ^aslew him.

9 ¶ And the LORD said unto Cain, Where *is* Abel thy brother? And he said, I know not: Am I my ^abrother's ^bkeeper?

10 And he said, What hast thou done? the voice of thy brother's ^ablood crieth unto me from the ground.

11 And now *art* thou ^acursed from the ^bearth, which hath opened her mouth to receive thy brother's blood from thy hand;

12 When thou tillest the ground, it shall not henceforth yield unto thee her strength; a ^afugitive and a vagabond shalt thou be in the earth.

13 And Cain said unto the LORD, ^aMy punishment *is* greater than I can bear.

14 Behold, thou hast driven me out this day from the face of the earth; and from thy face shall I be hid; and I shall be a fugitive and a vagabond in the earth; and it shall come to pass, *that* every one that findeth me shall ^aslay me.

15 And the LORD said unto him, Therefore whosoever slayeth Cain, vengeance shall be taken on him sevenfold. And the LORD set a ^amark upon Cain, lest any finding him should kill him.

16 ¶ And Cain went out from the ^apresence of the LORD, and dwelt in the land of Nod, on the east of ^bEden.

17 And Cain knew his ^awife; and she conceived, and bare ^bEnoch: and he builded a city, and called the ^cname of the city, after the name of his son, Enoch.

18 And unto Enoch was born Irad: and Irad begat Mehujael: and Mehujael begat Methusael: and Methusael begat Lamech.

19 ¶ And Lamech took unto him two wives: the name of the one *was* Adah, and the name of the other Zillah.

20 And Adah bare Jabal: he was the father of such as dwell in tents, and *of such as have* cattle.

21 And his brother's name *was* Jubal: he was the father of all such as handle the ^aharp and organ.

22 And Zillah, she also bare Tubal-cain, an ^ainstructer of every ^bartificer in ^cbrass and iron: and the sister of Tubal-cain *was* Naamah.

23 And Lamech said unto his wives, Adah and Zillah, Hear my voice; ye wives of Lamech, hearken unto my speech: for I have ^aslain a man to my wounding, and a young man to my hurt.

24 If Cain shall be avenged sevenfold, truly ^aLamech seventy and sevenfold.

25 ¶ And Adam knew his wife again; and she bare a son, and called his name ^aSeth: For God, *said she,* hath appointed me another seed instead of ^bAbel, whom Cain slew.

26 And to Seth, to him also there

7c TG Sin.
  d Moses 5:23 (23–24).
  e Hel. 6:27 (26–30);
    Ether 8:15 (14–16).
8a TG Martyrdom; Murder.
9a TG Brotherhood and
    Sisterhood.
  b Moro. 10:21;
    Moses 5:34 (32–39).
10a 2 Ne. 26:3; 28:10;
    Morm. 8:27;
    D&C 136:36 (35–36).
    TG Life, Sanctity of.
11a TG Curse.
  b Num. 16:32.
12a Moses 5:37 (37–38).

13a OR My iniquity is too
    great to be forgiven.
    D&C 134:8 (6–8).
    TG Punish.
14a Moses 5:39 (38–41).
15a Alma 3:7 (7–16);
    Moses 5:40; 7:22.
16a Moses 5:41; 6:49.
  b TG Eden.
17a Moses 5:3 (2–3).
  b Do not confuse Enoch
    of Cain's lineage and
    the city of his name
    with the Enoch of Seth's
    lineage and the city
    (Zion) of his name. (See

Moses 6:21–7:69.)
  c Ps. 49:11.
21a Gen. 31:27.
22a HEB forger, sharpener.
  b TG Skill.
  c HEB bronze, brass, or
    copper.
    2 Ne. 5:15;
    Ether 10:23.
23a TG Secret Combinations.
24a Moses 5:49 (48–54).
25a HEB *Sheth;* i.e.,
    Appointed.
    D&C 107:42 (41–43);
    Moses 6:2 (2–3).
  b D&C 84:16.

was born a son; and he called his name Enos: then began men to ^acall upon the name of the ^bLORD.

CHAPTER 5

The generations of Adam are Adam, Seth, Enos, Cainan, Mahalaleel, Jared, Enoch (who walked with God), Methuselah, Lamech, and Noah (who begat Shem, Ham, and Japheth).

THIS *is* the ^abook of the ^bgenerations of Adam. In the day that God created man, in the ^clikeness of God ^dmade he him;

2 Male and female created he them; and blessed them, and called their name ^aAdam, in the day when they were created.

3 ¶ And Adam lived an hundred and thirty years, and begat *a son* in his own ^alikeness, after his image; and called his name Seth:

4 And the days of ^aAdam after he had begotten Seth were eight hundred years: and he begat sons and daughters:

5 And all the days that Adam lived were nine hundred and thirty years: and he died.

6 And Seth lived an hundred and five years, and begat Enos:

7 And Seth lived after he begat Enos eight hundred and seven years, and begat sons and daughters:

8 And all the days of Seth were nine hundred and twelve years: and he died.

9 ¶ And Enos lived ninety years, and begat Cainan:

10 And Enos lived after he begat Cainan eight hundred and fifteen years, and begat sons and daughters:

11 And all the days of Enos were nine hundred and five years: and he died.

12 ¶ And Cainan lived seventy years, and begat Mahalaleel:

13 And Cainan lived after he begat Mahalaleel eight hundred and forty years, and begat sons and daughters:

14 And all the days of ^aCainan were nine hundred and ten years: and he died.

15 ¶ And Mahalaleel lived sixty and five years, and begat Jared:

16 And Mahalaleel lived after he begat Jared eight hundred and thirty years, and begat sons and daughters:

17 And all the days of Mahalaleel were eight hundred ninety and five years: and he died.

18 ¶ And Jared lived an hundred sixty and two years, and he begat Enoch:

19 And Jared lived after he begat Enoch eight hundred years, and begat sons and daughters:

20 And all the days of Jared were nine hundred sixty and two years: and he died.

21 ¶ And Enoch lived sixty and five years, and begat Methuselah:

22 And ^aEnoch ^bwalked with God after he begat Methuselah three hundred years, and begat sons and daughters:

23 And all the days of ^aEnoch were three hundred sixty and five years:

24 And ^aEnoch ^bwalked with God: and he *was* not; for God ^ctook him.

26a Gen. 13:4;
    1 Chr. 16:8;
    Ps. 116:17;
    3 Ne. 4:30;
    Ether 4:15;
    Moro. 2:2;
    D&C 65:4.
    TG Prayer.
  b TG Jesus Christ, Jehovah.
5 1a 1 Ne. 19:23;
    3 Ne. 24:16;
    D&C 85:9 (7–9).
    TG Scriptures, Writing of.
  b TG Priesthood,
    History of.

  c TG God, Body of,
    Corporeal Nature.
  d TG Man, Physical
    Creation of.
 2a In Hebrew *adam* is also a
    common noun, meaning
    man, or mankind.
    TG Adam.
 3a Gen. 1:26 (26–28);
    D&C 107:43 (42–43).
 4a D&C 107:41 (41–50);
    Moses 5:2 (2–3).
    TG Adam.
14a D&C 107:45 (45, 53);
    Moses 6:19 (11–25).

22a Moses 6:21 (21–68);
    7:69; 8:1 (1–2).
  b D&C 107:49.
23a Jude 1:14;
    D&C 38:4; 76:57;
    107:57 (48–57); 133:54;
    Moses 7:68 (68–69); 8:1.
24a TG Translated Beings;
    Zion.
  b TG God, Access to;
    God, Manifestations of;
    Walking with God.
  c Moses 7:69 (68–69).

25 And Methuselah lived an hundred eighty and seven years, and begat Lamech:

26 And Methuselah lived after he begat Lamech seven hundred eighty and two years, and begat sons and daughters:

27 And all the days of Methuselah were nine hundred sixty and nine years: and he died.

28 ¶ And Lamech lived an hundred eighty and two years, and begat a son:

29 And he called his name *Noah, saying, This *same* shall *b*comfort us concerning our work and toil of our hands, because of the ground which the LORD hath *c*cursed.

30 And Lamech lived after he begat Noah five hundred ninety and five years, and begat sons and daughters:

31 And all the days of Lamech were seven hundred seventy and seven years: and he died.

32 And Noah was five hundred years old: and Noah *a*begat *b*Shem, Ham, and Japheth.

CHAPTER 6

The sons of God marry the daughters of men—Men turn to wickedness, the earth is filled with violence, and all flesh is corrupted—The Flood is promised—God establishes His covenant with Noah, who builds an ark to save his family and various living things.

AND it came to pass, when men began to multiply on the face of the earth, and daughters were born unto them,

2 That the *a*sons of God saw the daughters of men that they *were* fair; and they *b*took them *c*wives of all which they chose.

3 And the LORD said, My *a*spirit shall not always *b*strive with man, for that he also *is* *c*flesh: yet his days shall be an hundred and twenty years.

4 There were *a*giants in the earth in those days; and also after that, when the sons of God came in unto the daughters of men, and they bare *children* to them, the same *became* mighty men which *were* of old, men of renown.

5 ¶ And GOD saw that the *a*wickedness of man *was* great in the earth, and *that* *b*every imagination of the *c*thoughts of his *d*heart *was* only *e*evil continually.

6 *a*And it repented the LORD that he had made man on the earth, and it *b*grieved him at his heart.

7 And the LORD said, I will *a*destroy man whom I have created from the face of the earth; both man, and beast, and the creeping thing, and the fowls of the air; *b*for it repenteth me that I have made them.

8 But Noah found *a*grace in the eyes of the LORD.

9 ¶ These *are* the *a*generations of Noah: *b*Noah was a just man *and*

29*a* IE Rest or Repose.
    D&C 84:14 (14–15);
    133:54.
    TG Flood.
  b Moses 8:20 (16–20).
  c TG Curse;
    Earth, Curse of.
32*a* Gen. 9:18 (18–27); 10:1;
    Moses 8:12.
  b Luke 3:36 (36–38).
6 2*a* TG Sons and Daughters
    of God.
  b TG Marriage, Temporal.
  c TG Marriage, Interfaith;
    Marriage, Marry.
  3*a* TG God, Spirit of;
    Holy Ghost, Loss of.
  b TG God, Access to.
  c 2 Ne. 9:4 (4–8);

Mosiah 15:7; Moses 8:17.
4*a* Gen. 14:5; Num. 13:33;
    Deut. 3:11;
    Moses 8:18 (18–21).
5*a* Ps. 14:1; 3 Ne. 9:9;
    Morm. 4:12 (10–12);
    D&C 10:21 (20–23); 112:23;
    Moses 7:36 (36–37);
    8:22 (22, 28–30).
  b Matt. 15:19; Heb. 3:12;
    Alma 12:14 (3, 7, 14);
    Hel. 12:4;
    D&C 124:99; Moses 8:22.
  c Gen. 8:21.
    TG God, Omniscience of;
    Motivations.
  d TG Heart.
  e TG Evil.
6*a* JST Gen. 8:13 And it

repented *Noah, and his heart was pained,* that the Lord had made man . . .
    Ex. 32:12, 14; 1 Sam. 15:11;
    2 Sam. 24:16; Joel 2:13;
    Amos 7:3 (3, 6);
    3 Ne. 27:32; Moses 8:25.
  b Eph. 4:30; 1 Ne. 2:18;
    Alma 31:24;
    3 Ne. 7:16; Moses 8:25.
7*a* Gen. 7:23;
    Alma 10:22 (22–23).
  b JST Gen. 8:15 For it
    repenteth *Noah* that I
    have *created* them . . .
8*a* TG Grace.
9*a* IE genealogical lines.
  b Ezek. 14:14.

*c*perfect in his generations, *and* Noah *d*walked with God.

10 And Noah begat three sons, Shem, Ham, and Japheth.

11 The earth also was *a*corrupt before God, and the earth was filled with *b*violence.

12 And God looked upon the earth, and, behold, it was corrupt; for all *a*flesh had corrupted his *b*way upon the earth.

13 And God said unto Noah, The end of all flesh is come before me; for the earth is filled with *a*violence through them; and, behold, I will *b*destroy them *c*with the earth.

14 ¶ Make thee an *a*ark of gopher wood; *b*rooms shalt thou make in the ark, and shalt pitch it within and without with pitch.

15 And this *is the fashion* which thou shalt make it *of:* The length of the ark *shall be* three hundred cubits, the breadth of it fifty cubits, and the height of it thirty cubits.

16 A *a*window shalt thou make to the ark, and in a cubit shalt thou finish it above; and the door of the ark shalt thou set in the side thereof; *with* lower, second, and third *stories* shalt thou make it.

17 And, behold, I, even I, do bring a *a*flood of *b*waters upon the earth, to destroy all flesh, wherein *is* the *c*breath of life, from under heaven; *and* every thing that *is* in the earth shall die.

18 But with thee will I establish *a*my *b*covenant; and thou shalt come into the ark, thou, and thy sons, and thy wife, and thy sons' wives with thee.

19 And of every living thing of all flesh, two of every *sort* shalt thou bring into the ark, to keep *them* alive with thee; they shall be male and female.

20 Of fowls after their kind, and of cattle after their kind, of every creeping thing of the earth after his kind, two of every *sort* shall come unto thee, to keep *them* alive.

21 And take thou unto thee of all food that is eaten, and thou shalt gather *it* to thee; and it shall be for *a*food for thee, and for them.

22 Thus *a*did *b*Noah; according to all that God *c*commanded him, so did he.

CHAPTER 7

Noah's family and various beasts and fowl enter the ark—The Flood comes, and water covers the whole earth—All other life that breathes is destroyed.

AND the LORD said unto *a*Noah, Come thou and all thy house into the ark; for thee have I seen righteous before me in this generation.

2 Of every clean beast thou shalt take to thee by sevens, the male and his female: and of beasts that *are* not clean by two, the male and his female.

3 Of fowls also of the air by sevens, the male and the female; to keep seed alive upon the face of all the earth.

9*c* HEB complete, whole, having integrity.
  D&C 129:3 (3, 6);
  Moses 8:27.
  TG Integrity; Perfection.
  d TG Walking with God.
11*a* Ex. 32:7;
  Deut. 4:16 (14–19);
  D&C 10:21; 112:23;
  Moses 8:28 (28–30).
  TG Pollution.
  b D&C 88:18;
  Moses 7:33 (32–34);
  8:28 (28–30).
12*a* D&C 38:11.
  b 2 Ne. 28:11; Hel. 6:31;
  D&C 1:16; 82:6;
  132:25 (22–25);

Moses 8:29.
13*a* TG War.
  b 1 Ne. 17:31; 2 Ne. 1:17;
  Mosiah 12:8; 3 Ne. 9:9;
  D&C 56:3; 64:35;
  Moses 8:30 (26, 30).
  c Some Hebrew texts:
  from the earth.
14*a* Ether 6:7 (6–8);
  Moses 7:43.
  b HEB "nests,"
  compartments.
16*a* HEB *tsohar;* some
  rabbis believed it was
  a precious stone that
  shone in the ark.
  Ether 2:23 (23–24).
17*a* TG Flood.

  b TG Earth, Cleansing of.
  c 2 Ne. 9:26;
  Mosiah 2:21.
18*a* JST Gen. 8:23–24 . . . my
  covenant, *even as I have
  sworn unto thy father,
  Enoch, that of thy posterity
  shall come all nations.
  And thou . . .*
  b Gen. 9:9 (9, 12).
21*a* TG Food.
22*a* Gen. 7:5; Moses 7:43.
  TG Obedience.
  b Heb. 11:7.
  c TG Commandments
  of God.
7 1*a* Matt. 24:37 (36–38);
  1 Pet. 3:20.

4 For yet seven days, and I will cause it to ᵃrain upon the earth forty days and forty nights; and every living substance that I have made will I destroy from off the face of the earth.

5 And Noah ᵃdid according unto all that the LORD commanded him.

6 And Noah *was* ᵃsix hundred years old when the flood of waters was upon the earth.

7 ¶ And Noah went in, and his sons, and his wife, and his sons' wives with him, into the ark, because of the waters of the flood.

8 Of clean beasts, and of beasts that *are* not clean, and of fowls, and of every thing that creepeth upon the earth,

9 There went in two and two unto Noah into the ark, the male and the female, as God had commanded Noah.

10 And it came to pass after seven days, that the waters of the ᵃflood were upon the earth.

11 ¶ In the six hundredth year of Noah's life, in the second month, the seventeenth day of the month, the same day were all the ᵃfountains of the great deep ᵇbroken up, and the ᶜwindows of heaven were opened.

12 And the ᵃrain was upon the earth forty days and forty nights.

13 In the selfsame day entered Noah, and Shem, and Ham, and Japheth, the sons of Noah, and Noah's wife, and the three wives of his sons with them, into the ark;

14 They, and every beast after his kind, and all the cattle after their kind, and every creeping thing that creepeth upon the earth after his kind, and every fowl after his kind, every bird of every sort.

15 And they went in unto Noah into the ark, two and two of all flesh, wherein *is* the breath of life.

16 And they that went in, went in male and female of all flesh, as God had commanded him: and the LORD shut him in.

17 And the flood was forty days upon the earth; and the waters increased, and bare up the ark, and ᵃit was lift up above the earth.

18 And the waters prevailed, and were increased greatly upon the earth; and the ark went upon the face of the waters.

19 And the ᵃwaters prevailed exceedingly upon the earth; and ᵇall the high hills, that *were* under the whole heaven, were covered.

20 Fifteen cubits upward did the waters prevail; and the mountains were covered.

21 And all flesh died that moved upon the earth, both of fowl, and of cattle, and of beast, and of every creeping thing that creepeth upon the earth, and ᵃevery man:

22 All in whose nostrils *was* the ᵃbreath of life, of all that *was* in the dry *land,* died.

23 And every living substance was ᵃdestroyed which was upon the face of the ground, both man, and cattle, and the creeping things, and the fowl of the heaven; and they were destroyed from the earth: and ᵇNoah only remained ᶜalive, and they that *were* with him in the ark.

24 And the waters prevailed upon the earth an hundred and fifty days.

CHAPTER 8

The Flood ceases—Noah sends forth a dove, which returns with an olive leaf—He releases all living things from the ark—He offers sacrifices—Seedtime, harvest, and seasons are ensured.

4a TG Earth, Cleansing of.
5a Gen. 6:22;
    Moses 8:13.
6a Gen. 8:13.
10a TG Flood.
11a Gen. 8:2;
    D&C 133:20 (20, 23, 39).
  b OR burst open.
    Prov. 3:20;

1 Ne. 12:4;
    Hel. 14:21 (21–24).
  c 3 Ne. 24:10.
12a Ether 2:24.
    TG Nature, Earth.
17a OR it rose high above
    the ground.
19a Ps. 104:6;
    2 Pet. 3:6.

  b Ether 13:2.
21a OR the whole of
    mankind.
22a TG Breath of Life.
23a Gen. 6:7;
    Alma 10:22 (22–23);
    Moses 8:30 (26–30).
  b TG Earth, Cleansing of.
  c D&C 133:54 (52–54).

AND God remembered ᵃNoah, and every living thing, and all the cattle that *was* with him in the ark: and God made a wind to pass over the earth, and the waters ᵇassuaged;

2 The ᵃfountains also of the deep and the windows of heaven were stopped, and the rain from heaven was restrained;

3 And the waters ᵃreturned from off the earth continually: and after the end of the hundred and fifty days the ᵇwaters ᶜwere abated.

4 And the ark rested in the seventh month, on the seventeenth day of the month, upon the mountains of Ararat.

5 And the waters decreased continually until the tenth month: in the tenth *month*, on the first *day* of the month, were the tops of the mountains seen.

6 ¶ And it came to pass at the end of forty days, that Noah opened the window of the ark which he had made:

7 And he sent forth a raven, which went forth to and fro, until the waters were dried up from off the earth.

8 Also he sent forth a dove from him, to see if the waters were abated from off the face of the ground;

9 But the dove found no rest for the sole of her foot, and she returned unto him into the ark, for the waters *were* on the face of the whole earth: then he put forth his hand, and took her, and pulled her in unto him into the ark.

10 And he ᵃstayed yet other seven days; and again he sent forth the dove out of the ark;

11 And the dove came in to him in the evening; and, lo, in her mouth *was* an olive leaf plucked off: so Noah knew that the waters were abated from off the earth.

12 And he stayed yet other seven days; and sent forth the dove; which returned not again unto him any more.

13 ¶ And it came to pass in the ᵃsix hundredth and first year, in the first *month*, the first *day* of the month, the waters were dried up from off the earth: and Noah removed the covering of the ark, and looked, and, behold, the face of the ground was dry.

14 And in the second month, on the seven and twentieth day of the month, was the earth dried.

15 ¶ And God spake unto Noah, saying,

16 Go forth of the ark, thou, and thy ᵃwife, and thy sons, and thy sons' wives with thee.

17 Bring forth with thee every living thing that *is* with thee, of all flesh, *both* of fowl, and of cattle, and of every creeping thing that creepeth upon the earth; that they may breed abundantly in the earth, and be ᵃfruitful, and ᵇmultiply upon the earth.

18 And Noah went forth, and his sons, and his wife, and his sons' wives with him:

19 Every beast, every creeping thing, and every fowl, *and* whatsoever creepeth upon the earth, after their ᵃkinds, went forth out of the ark.

20 ¶ ᵃAnd Noah builded an altar unto the LORD; and took of every ᵇclean beast, and of every clean fowl, and offered burnt ᶜofferings on the altar.

21 And the LORD smelled a sweet ᵃsavour; and the LORD said in his heart, I will not again ᵇcurse the ground any more ᶜfor man's sake; for the ᵈimagination of man's heart *is* ᵉevil from his youth; neither will I again ᶠsmite any more every thing living, as I have done.

8 1*a* Heb. 11:7;
  1 Pet. 3:20 (20–21);
  2 Pet. 2:5.
  b OR subsided.
2*a* Gen. 7:11.
3*a* Ether 13:2.
  b TG Flood.
  c OR had decreased.
10*a* OR waited another.
13*a* Gen. 7:6.

16*a* Moses 7:42; 8:12.
  TG Family, Patriarchal.
17*a* Gen. 9:7, 28:3; 35:11.
  b Gen. 9:1.
19*a* HEB families.
20*a* JST Gen. 9:4–6
  (Appendix).
  b TG Food.
  c TG Sacrifice.
21*a* Ex. 29:18;

  Lev. 1:9;
  Eph. 5:2.
  b Enos 1:10;
  Alma 10:22;
  3 Ne. 22:9 (8–10).
  TG Curse; Earth, Curse of.
  c OR because of man.
  d Gen. 6:5.
  e TG Evil.
  f TG Earth, Cleansing of.

22 While the earth remaineth, ^aseedtime and harvest, and cold and heat, and summer and winter, and day and ^bnight shall not cease.

CHAPTER 9

Noah and his sons are commanded to multiply and fill the earth—They are given dominion over all forms of life—The death penalty is decreed for murder—God will not again destroy the earth by a flood—Canaan is cursed; Shem and Japheth are blessed.

AND God blessed Noah and his sons, and said unto them, ^aBe fruitful, and ^bmultiply, and ^creplenish the earth.

2 And the ^afear of you and the dread of you shall be upon every beast of the earth, and upon every fowl of the air, upon all that moveth *upon* the earth, and upon all the fishes of the sea; into your hand are they delivered.

3 Every moving thing that liveth shall be ^ameat for you; even as the green herb have I given you all things.

4 ^aBut flesh with the ^blife thereof, *which is* the ^cblood thereof, shall ye not eat.

5 And surely ^ayour blood of your lives will I ^brequire; at the hand of every beast will I require it, and at the hand of man; at the hand of every man's brother will I require the life of man.

6 Whoso ^asheddeth man's blood, by man shall his ^bblood be shed: for in the ^cimage of God made he man.

7 And you, be ye ^afruitful, and multiply; bring forth abundantly in the earth, and multiply therein.

8 ¶ And God spake unto Noah, and to his sons with him, saying,

9 And I, behold, ^aI establish my ^bcovenant with you, and with your seed after you;

10 And with every living creature that *is* with you, of the fowl, of the cattle, and of every beast of the earth with you; from all that go out of the ark, to every beast of the earth.

11 And I will establish my covenant with you; neither shall all flesh be cut off any more by the waters of a flood; neither shall there any more be a ^aflood to ^bdestroy the ^cearth.

12 And God said, This *is* the token of the covenant which I make between me and you and every living creature that *is* with you, for perpetual generations:

13 I do set my bow in the cloud, and it shall be for a token of a covenant between me and the earth.

14 And it shall come to pass, when I bring a cloud over the earth, that the bow shall be seen in the cloud:

15 And I will remember my ^acovenant, ^bwhich *is* between me and you and every living creature of all flesh; and the waters shall no more become a ^cflood to destroy all flesh.

16 ^aAnd the bow shall be in the cloud; and I will look upon it, that

---

22a Amos 9:13 (13–15).
  b Jer. 33:20 (20, 25).
9 1a Moses 5:2.
  b Gen. 8:17.
    TG Marriage,
    Fatherhood.
  c HEB fill.
 2a Gen. 1:28 (26–28).
 3a HEB food.
    TG Food;
    Meat;
    Word of Wisdom.
 4a JST Gen. 9:10–15
    (Appendix).
  b Lev. 17:11 (11–14).
  c TG Blood, Eating of.
 5a OR your life blood
    will . . .

  b Ps. 9:12.
 6a TG Blood, Shedding of;
    Murder.
  b TG Capital Punishment;
    Punish.
  c TG Body, Sanctity of;
    God, Body of, Corporeal
    Nature;
    Life, Sanctity of.
 7a Gen. 8:17; 28:3; 35:11.
 9a JST Gen. 9:15 . . . I *will*
    establish my covenant
    with you, *which I made
    unto your father Enoch,
    concerning* your seed
    after you.
  b Gen. 6:18.
    TG Priesthood, History of.

11a TG Flood.
  b TG Earth, Cleansing of.
  c JST Gen. 9:16–17 . . .
    earth. *And I will establish
    my covenant with you,
    which I made unto Enoch,
    concerning the remnants of
    your posterity.*
    Moses 7:51–52.
15a TG Covenants.
  b JST Gen. 9:20 . . . which
    I *have made* between me
    and you, *for every living
    creature* . . .
  c TG Flood.
16a JST Gen. 9:21–25
    (Appendix).

I may remember the ^beverlasting covenant between God and every living creature of all flesh that *is* upon the earth.

17 And God said unto Noah, This *is* the ^atoken of the covenant, which I have established between me and all flesh that *is* upon the earth.

18 ¶ And the ^asons of Noah, that went forth of the ark, were Shem, and Ham, and Japheth: and Ham *is* the father of Canaan.

19 These *are* the three sons of Noah: and of them was the whole ^aearth overspread.

20 And Noah began *to be* an husbandman, and he planted a vineyard:

21 And he drank of the wine, and was drunken; and he was uncovered within his tent.

22 And Ham, the father of Canaan, saw the nakedness of his father, and told his two brethren without.

23 And Shem and Japheth took a garment, and laid *it* upon both their shoulders, and went backward, and covered the nakedness of their father; and their faces *were* backward, and they saw not their father's nakedness.

24 And Noah awoke from his wine, and knew what his younger son had done unto him.

25 And he said, ^aCursed *be* ^bCanaan; a servant of servants shall he be unto his brethren.

26 And he said, Blessed *be* the Lord God of Shem; and Canaan shall be his ^aservant.

27 God shall enlarge Japheth, and he shall dwell in the tents of Shem; and Canaan shall be his servant.

28 ¶ And Noah lived after the flood three hundred and fifty years.

29 And all the days of Noah were nine hundred and fifty years: and he died.

CHAPTER 10

The descendants of Noah are Japheth, whose descendants are Gentiles; Ham, whose descendants include the Canaanites; and Shem, of whom came Peleg (in whose days the earth was divided).

Now these *are* the ^agenerations of the ^bsons of Noah, Shem, Ham, and Japheth: and unto them were sons born after the flood.

2 The sons of Japheth; ^aGomer, and ^bMagog, and Madai, and Javan, and Tubal, and ^cMeshech, and Tiras.

3 And the sons of Gomer; Ashkenaz, and Riphath, and ^aTogarmah.

4 And the sons of ^aJavan; ^bElishah, and Tarshish, Kittim, and ^cDodanim.

5 ^aBy these were the ^bisles of the ^cGentiles divided in their ^dlands; every one after his tongue, after their ^efamilies, in their nations.

6 ¶ And the sons of ^aHam; ^bCush, and ^cMizraim, and ^dPhut, and Canaan.

7 And the sons of Cush; Seba, and Havilah, and Sabtah, and Raamah, and Sabtecha: and the sons of Raamah; Sheba, and Dedan.

8 And Cush begat ^aNimrod: he began to be a mighty one in the earth.

9 He was a mighty hunter before the Lord: wherefore it is said, Even as ^aNimrod the mighty hunter before the Lord.

16*b* TG New and
    Everlasting Covenant.
17*a* TG Signs.
18*a* Gen. 5:32; Moses 8:12.
19*a* TG Nations.
25*a* TG Curse.
    b Moses 7:8 (7–12), 22;
     Abr. 1:22 (21–25).
26*a* JST Gen. 9:30 . . .
    servant, *and a veil of*
    darkness shall cover him,
    that he shall be known
    among all men.
10 1*a* IE genealogical lines.

    b Gen. 5:32.
2*a* Ezek. 38:6.
    b Ezek. 38:2; Rev. 20:8.
    c Ps. 120:5;
     Ezek. 27:13; 38:2.
3*a* Ezek. 27:14; 38:6.
4*a* 1 Chr. 1:7.
    b Ezek. 27:7.
    c Septuagint and 1 Chr.
     1:7: Rodanim.
5*a* HEB From these.
    b OR coasts, continents.
    c TG Gentiles.
    d TG Nations.

    e TG Family.
6*a* 1 Chr. 1:8 (8–10);
     Abr. 1:21, 25 (20–25).
    b IE Ethiopians,
     Egyptians, Libyans,
     and Canaanites. See
     1 Chr. 1:4–23.
    c IE Egypt.
     D&C 136:22;
     Abr. 1:23 (20–25); 2:21.
    d Nahum 3:9.
8*a* 1 Chr. 1:10;
     Ether 2:1 (1, 4).
9*a* Micah 5:6.

10 And the beginning of his kingdom was ^aBabel, and Erech, and Accad, and Calneh, in the land of ^bShinar.

11 Out of that land went forth Asshur, and builded Nineveh, and the city Rehoboth, and Calah,

12 And Resen between Nineveh and Calah: the same *is* a great city.

13 And ^aMizraim begat Ludim, and Anamim, and Lehabim, and Naphtuhim,

14 And Pathrusim, and Casluhim, (out of whom came ^aPhilistim,) and Caphtorim.

15 ¶ And ^aCanaan begat Sidon his firstborn, and Heth,

16 And the Jebusite, and the Amorite, and the Girgasite,

17 And the Hivite, and the Arkite, and the Sinite,

18 And the Arvadite, and the Zemarite, and the Hamathite: and afterward were the families of the ^aCanaanites spread abroad.

19 And the border of the Canaanites was from Sidon, as thou comest to ^aGerar, unto Gaza; as thou goest, unto Sodom, and Gomorrah, and Admah, and Zeboim, even unto Lasha.

20 These *are* the sons of Ham, after their families, after their tongues, in their countries, *and* in their nations.

21 ¶ Unto Shem also, the father of all the children of ^aEber, the brother of Japheth the elder, even to him were *children* born.

22 The children of ^aShem; Elam, and Asshur, and Arphaxad, and Lud, and Aram.

23 And the children of Aram; ^aUz, and Hul, and Gether, and Mash.

24 And Arphaxad begat Salah; and Salah begat Eber.

25 And unto Eber were born two sons: the name of one *was* ^aPeleg; for in his days was the earth ^bdivided; and his brother's name *was* Joktan.

26 And Joktan begat Almodad, and Sheleph, and Hazarmaveth, and Jerah,

27 And Hadoram, and Uzal, and Diklah,

28 And Obal, and Abimael, and Sheba,

29 And Ophir, and ^aHavilah, and Jobab: all these *were* the sons of Joktan.

30 And their dwelling was from Mesha, as thou goest unto Sephar a mount of the east.

31 These *are* the sons of Shem, after their families, after their tongues, in their lands, after their nations.

32 These *are* the families of the sons of Noah, after their generations, in their ^anations: and ^bby these were the ^cnations divided in the earth after the flood.

CHAPTER 11

All men speak the same language—They build the Tower of Babel—The Lord confounds their language and scatters them over all the earth—The generations of Shem include Abram, whose wife is Sarai—Abram leaves Ur and settles in Haran.

AND the whole earth was of one ^alanguage, and of one speech.

2 And it came to pass, as they journeyed from the east, that they found a plain in the land of ^aShinar; and they dwelt there.

3 And they said one to another, Go to, let us make brick, and burn them throughly. And they had brick for stone, and ^aslime had they for mortar.

4 And they said, Go to, let us build us a city and a tower, whose top *may*

10a OR (later) Babylon.
　b Gen. 11:2; 2 Ne. 21:11.
13a 1 Chr. 1:11 (11–16).
14a Gen. 21:34;
　　1 Chr. 1:12;
　　2 Ne. 12:6; 19:12.
15a Moses 7:7 (6–8);
　　Abr. 1:22 (21–22).
18a Gen. 12:6; 13:7.
19a Gen. 20:1.
21a Gen. 14:13.
22a 1 Chr. 1:17 (17–25).
23a Job 1:1.
25a IE Division.
　b TG Earth, Dividing of.
29a Gen. 2:11.
32a TG Nations.
　b HEB from.
　c TG Nations.
11 1a TG Language.
2a Gen. 10:10; 14:1;
　　Dan. 1:2.
3a OR bitumen.
　　Gen. 14:10.

reach unto heaven; and let us make us a ᵃname, lest we be scattered abroad upon the face of the whole earth.

5 And the Lᴏʀᴅ came down to see the city and the tower, which the children of men builded.

6 And the Lᴏʀᴅ said, Behold, the people *is one, and* they have all one language; and this they begin to do: and now nothing will be restrained from them, which they have imagined to do.

7 Go to, let us go down, and there confound their ᵃlanguage, that they may not understand one another's speech.

8 So the Lᴏʀᴅ scattered them abroad from thence upon the face of all the earth: and they left off to build the ᵃcity.

9 Therefore is the name of it called Babel; because the Lᴏʀᴅ did there ᵃconfound the ᵇlanguage of all the earth: and from thence did the Lᴏʀᴅ ᶜscatter them ᵈabroad upon the face of all the earth.

10 ¶ These *are* the generations of Shem: Shem *was* an hundred years old, and begat Arphaxad two years after the flood:

11 And Shem lived after he begat Arphaxad five hundred years, and begat sons and daughters.

12 And Arphaxad lived five and thirty years, and begat Salah:

13 And Arphaxad lived after he begat Salah four hundred and three years, and begat sons and daughters.

14 And Salah lived thirty years, and begat Eber:

15 And Salah lived after he begat Eber four hundred and three years, and begat sons and daughters.

16 And Eber lived four and thirty years, and begat ᵃPeleg:

17 And Eber lived after he begat Peleg four hundred and thirty years, and begat sons and daughters.

18 And Peleg lived thirty years, and begat Reu:

19 And Peleg lived after he begat Reu two hundred and nine years, and begat sons and daughters.

20 And Reu lived two and thirty years, and begat Serug:

21 And Reu lived after he begat Serug two hundred and seven years, and begat sons and daughters.

22 And Serug lived thirty years, and begat Nahor:

23 And Serug lived after he begat Nahor two hundred years, and begat sons and daughters.

24 And Nahor lived nine and twenty years, and begat ᵃTerah:

25 And Nahor lived after he begat Terah an hundred and nineteen years, and begat sons and daughters.

26 And ᵃTerah lived seventy years, and begat ᵇAbram, Nahor, and Haran.

27 ¶ Now these *are* the generations of Terah: Terah begat Abram, Nahor, and Haran; and Haran begat Lot.

28 And Haran died before his father Terah in the land of his nativity, in Ur of the ᵃChaldees.

29 And Abram and Nahor took them wives: the name of Abram's wife *was* ᵃSarai; and the name of Nahor's wife, ᵇMilcah, the daughter of Haran, the father of Milcah, and the father of Iscah.

30 But Sarai was ᵃbarren; she *had* no child.

31 And Terah took Abram his son, and Lot the son of Haran his son's son, and Sarai his daughter in law, his son Abram's wife; and they went forth with them from Ur of the

---

4ᵃ ᴛɢ Name.
7ᵃ Omni 1:22;
   Mosiah 28:17.
   ᴛɢ Communication.
8ᵃ ᴊsᴛ Gen. 11:6 . . . city,
   *and they hearkened not
   unto the Lord* . . .
9ᵃ ʜᴇʙ *balal,* "mix,"
   "confound" (a word
   play on Babel).

   b ᴛɢ Language.
   c 1 Ne. 10:13 (12–13).
     ᴛɢ Book of Mormon.
   d Ether 1:33 (33–43).
16ᵃ ᴛɢ Earth, Dividing of.
24ᵃ Abr. 2:1 (1–4).
26ᵃ Abr. 2:1 (1–2).
    b Luke 3:34 (34–36);
      Hel. 8:18 (16–19);
      D&C 136:37;

   Abr. 1:1.
28ᵃ Job 1:17;
    Abr. 1:1, 20 (20, 29–30);
    2:4 (1, 4).
29ᵃ Gen. 12:5;
    Abr. 2:2.
    b Gen. 22:20; 24:15;
      Abr. 2:2.
30ᵃ ᴛɢ Barren.

^aChaldees, to go into the land of ^bCanaan; and they came unto ^cHaran, and dwelt there.

32 And the days of Terah were two hundred and five years: and Terah died in Haran.

CHAPTER 12

Abram will become a great nation— He and his seed will bless all the families of the earth—He travels from Haran to the land of Canaan—Because of famine, he goes down into Egypt—Abram and Sarai are tested in Pharaoh's court.

Now the LORD had ^asaid unto ^bAbram, ^cGet thee out of thy ^dcountry, and from thy ^ekindred, and from thy ^ffather's house, unto a ^gland that I will shew thee:

2 And I will make of thee a ^agreat ^bnation, and I will ^cbless thee, and make thy ^dname great; and thou shalt be a blessing:

3 And I will ^abless them that bless thee, and ^bcurse him that ^ccurseth thee: and in thee shall all ^dfamilies of the earth be ^eblessed.

4 So Abram departed, as the LORD had spoken unto him; and Lot went with him: and Abram *was* ^aseventy and five years old when he departed out of Haran.

5 And Abram took ^aSarai his wife, and ^bLot his ^cbrother's son, and all their substance that they had gathered, and the souls that they had ^dgotten in ^eHaran; and they went forth to go into the land of Canaan; and into the land of Canaan they came.

6 ¶ And Abram passed through the land unto the place of Sichem, unto the plain of Moreh. And the ^aCanaanite *was* then in the land.

7 And the LORD appeared unto Abram, and said, ^aUnto thy ^bseed will I give this ^cland: and there builded he an ^daltar unto the LORD, who appeared unto him.

8 And he removed from thence unto a mountain on the east of ^aBeth-el, and pitched his tent, *having* ^bBeth-el on the west, and ^cHai on the east: and there he builded an altar unto the LORD, and ^dcalled upon the ^ename of the LORD.

9 And Abram journeyed, going on still toward the south.

10 ¶ And there was a ^afamine in the land: and Abram went down into Egypt to sojourn there; for the famine *was* grievous in the land.

11 And it came to pass, when he was come near to enter into Egypt, that he ^asaid unto Sarai his wife, Behold now, I know that thou *art* a fair woman to look upon:

12 Therefore it shall come to pass, when the Egyptians shall see thee, that they shall say, This *is* his wife:

31*a* Acts 7:4 (2, 4).
  b Abr. 2:3 (1–4),
    19 (6, 15–19).
  c Gen. 12:5; 24:4;
    Acts 7:2 (2–3);
    Abr. 2:4 (1–6, 14).
12 1*a* Acts 7:2 (1–8, 16);
    Abr. 2:3 (3–4).
  b Neh. 9:7; Heb. 11:8.
  c Gen. 20:13;
    1 Ne. 2:2;
    Ether 1:42;
    Abr. 2:3.
  d Isa. 51:2;
    Abr. 1:16.
  e Abr. 1:5 (1–7).
  f Gen. 24:7.
  g TG Promised Lands.
 2*a* Gen. 28:3 (3–4).
  b TG Israel, Blessings of;
    Israel, Origins of.
  c 1 Ne. 22:9;

3 Ne. 20:25 (25, 27).
  d Abr. 2:10 (8–11).
    TG Name.
 3*a* TG Blessing.
  b TG Curse.
  c Ex. 23:22 (20–23).
  d TG Abrahamic
    Covenant; Family;
    Family, Patriarchal;
    Israel, Mission of.
  e TG Election; Missionary
    Work; Mission of
    Early Saints; Mission
    of Latter-day Saints;
    Priesthood, History of;
    Seed of Abraham.
 4*a* Abr. 2:14.
 5*a* Gen. 11:29; Abr. 2:2.
  b Gen. 14:12; Abr. 2:15.
  c Gen. 13:8.
  d HEB made; i.e.,
    converted.

Abr. 2:15.
  e Gen. 11:31.
 6*a* Gen. 10:18 (15–19); 13:7;
    Moses 7:7 (7–8);
    Abr. 1:22 (21–25); 2:18.
 7*a* Gen. 33:1.
  b Neh. 9:8.
  c TG Israel, Land of;
    Lands of Inheritance;
    Promised Lands.
  d Gen. 13:4 (3–4); 26:25;
    1 Ne. 2:7; Abr. 2:17.
 8*a* Gen. 28:19 (16–19);
    Josh. 16:2 (1–2);
    2 Kgs. 2:2.
  b Gen. 13:3.
  c OR Ai.
  d Gen. 2:20.
    TG Prayer.
  e TG Name.
10*a* TG Famine.
11*a* Abr. 2:22.

and they will kill me, but they will save thee alive.

13 Say, I pray thee, thou *art* my *a*sister: that it may be well with me for thy sake; and my soul shall live because of thee.

14 ¶ And it came to pass, that, when Abram was come into Egypt, the Egyptians *a*beheld the woman that she *was* very fair.

15 The princes also of Pharaoh saw her, and commended her before Pharaoh: and the woman was taken into Pharaoh's house.

16 And he entreated Abram well for her sake: and he had sheep, and oxen, and he asses, and menservants, and maidservants, and she asses, and camels.

17 And the LORD *a*plagued Pharaoh and his house with great *b*plagues because of Sarai Abram's wife.

18 And Pharaoh called Abram, and said, What *is* this *that* thou hast *a*done unto me? why didst thou not tell me that she *was* thy wife?

19 Why saidst thou, She *is* my *a*sister? so I might have taken her to me to wife: now therefore behold thy wife, take *her*, and go thy way.

20 And Pharaoh commanded *his* men concerning him: and they sent him away, and his wife, and all that he had.

CHAPTER 13

Abram returns from Egypt—He and Lot part—The Lord will make Abram's seed as the dust of the earth in number—Abram settles in Hebron.

AND Abram went up out of Egypt, he, and his wife, and all that he had, and Lot with him, into the south.

2 And Abram *was* very *a*rich in cattle, in silver, and in gold.

3 And he went on his journeys from the south even to *a*Beth-el, unto the place where his tent had been at the beginning, between Beth-el and *b*Hai;

4 Unto the place of the *a*altar, which he had made there at the first: and there Abram *b*called on the name of the LORD.

5 ¶ And Lot also, which went with Abram, had flocks, and herds, and tents.

6 And the land was not able to bear them, that they might dwell together: for their substance was great, so that they could not dwell together.

7 And there was a strife between the herdmen of Abram's cattle and the herdmen of Lot's cattle: and the *a*Canaanite and the Perizzite dwelled then in the land.

8 And Abram said unto Lot, Let there be no *a*strife, I pray thee, between me and thee, and between my herdmen and thy herdmen; for we *be* *b*brethren.

9 *Is* not the whole land before thee? separate thyself, I pray thee, from me: if *thou wilt take* the left hand, then I will go to the right; or if *thou depart* to the right hand, then I will go to the left.

10 And Lot lifted up his eyes, and beheld all the plain of Jordan, that it *was* well watered every where, before the LORD destroyed *a*Sodom and Gomorrah, *even* as the garden of the LORD, like the land of Egypt, as thou comest unto *b*Zoar.

11 Then Lot chose him all the plain of Jordan; and Lot journeyed east: and they separated themselves the one from the other.

12 Abram dwelled in the land of Canaan, and *a*Lot dwelled in the

13*a* Gen. 20:5 (1–18);
    26:7 (6–11);
    Abr. 2:24 (21–25).
14*a* TG Covet.
17*a* Gen. 20:18;
    1 Chr. 16:21 (18–22);
    Ps. 105:14 (12–15).
  b TG Plague.
18*a* Gen. 20:9 (9–10).
19*a* Gen. 20:12;

    Abr. 2:25 (22–25).
13 2*a* Gen. 24:35.
  3*a* Gen. 12:8 (8–9).
    b OR Ai.
    Abr. 2:20.
  4*a* Gen. 12:7 (7–8).
    Abr. 2:20.
    b Gen. 4:26;
    Abr. 1:2; 2:20 (18–20).
  7*a* Gen. 10:18 (15–19); 12:6;

    Abr. 1:21 (21–22, 27).
  8*a* TG Contention;
    Strife.
    b Gen. 12:5.
10*a* Gen. 19:24 (24–25);
    Deut. 32:32;
    Isa. 3:9 (9–11).
    b Gen. 14:2 (2, 8);
    19:22 (20–25).
12*a* Gen. 19:9.

cities of the plain, and pitched *his* tent toward Sodom.

13 But the men of ªSodom *were* ᵇwicked and sinners before the LORD exceedingly.

14 ¶ And the LORD said unto Abram, after that Lot was separated from him, Lift up now thine eyes, and look from the place where thou art northward, and southward, and eastward, and ªwestward:

15 For all the ªland which thou seest, to thee will I give it, and to thy seed for ever.

16 And I will make thy ªseed as the ᵇdust of the earth: so that if a man can number the dust of the earth, *then* shall thy seed also be numbered.

17 Arise, walk through the land in the length of it and in the breadth of it; for I will give it unto thee.

18 Then Abram removed *his* tent, and came and dwelt ªin the plain of Mamre, which *is* in ᵇHebron, and built there an ᶜaltar unto the LORD.

CHAPTER 14

Lot is captured in the battles of the kings—He is rescued by Abram—Melchizedek administers bread and wine and blesses Abram—Abram pays tithes—He declines to accept the spoils of conquest.

AND it came to pass in the days of Amraphel king of ªShinar, Arioch king of Ellasar, Chedorlaomer king of Elam, and Tidal king of nations;

2 *That these* made war with Bera king of Sodom, and with Birsha king of Gomorrah, Shinab king of Admah, and Shemeber king of Zeboiim, and the king of Bela, which is ªZoar.

3 All these were joined together in the vale of Siddim, which is the ªsalt sea.

4 Twelve years they served Chedorlaomer, and in the thirteenth year they rebelled.

5 And in the fourteenth year came Chedorlaomer, and the kings that *were* with him, and smote the ªRephaims in Ashteroth Karnaim, and the ᵇZuzims in Ham, and the ᶜEmims in Shaveh Kiriathaim,

6 And the ªHorites in their mount Seir, unto El-paran, which *is* by the wilderness.

7 And they returned, and came to En-mishpat, which *is* Kadesh, and smote all the country of the Amalekites, and also the Amorites, that dwelt in Hazezon-tamar.

8 And there went out the king of Sodom, and the king of Gomorrah, and the king of Admah, and the king of Zeboiim, and the king of Bela (the same *is* Zoar;) and they joined battle with them in the vale of Siddim;

9 With Chedorlaomer the king of Elam, and with Tidal king of nations, and Amraphel king of Shinar, and Arioch king of Ellasar; four kings with five.

10 And the vale of Siddim *was* full of ªslimepits; and the kings of Sodom and Gomorrah fled, and fell there; and they that remained fled to the mountain.

11 And they took all the goods of Sodom and Gomorrah, and all their victuals, and went their way.

12 And they took ªLot, Abram's brother's son, who dwelt in Sodom, and his goods, and departed.

13 ¶ And there came one that had escaped, and told Abram the ªHebrew; for he dwelt ᵇin the plain

---

13*a* Ezek. 16:49.
  b TG Homosexual Behavior.
14*a* JST Gen. 13:12–13 . . .
    westward; *and remember the covenant which I make with thee; for it shall be an everlasting covenant; and thou shalt remember the days of Enoch thy father;*
15*a* Gen. 15:18 (18–21);
    Josh. 1:2 (2–4).
    TG Lands of Inheritance;

Promised Lands.
16*a* Gen. 22:17; D&C 132:30;
    Abr. 2:10; 3:14.
    TG Israel, Blessings of.
  b 1 Kgs. 3:8;
    Ps. 80:10 (10–11).
18*a* HEB by the
    terebinth(s) of.
  b Gen. 23:2.
  c Gen. 26:25.
14 1*a* Gen. 11:2.
  2*a* Gen. 13:10;

19:22 (20–25).
3*a* Num. 34:3 (2–3).
5*a* Gen. 6:4; Deut. 3:11.
  b Deut. 2:20 (20–21).
  c Deut. 2:10 (10–11).
6*a* Deut. 2:12.
10*a* OR bitumen pits.
    Gen. 11:3.
12*a* Gen. 12:5.
13*a* Gen. 10:21.
  b HEB by the terebinth(s) of Mamre.

of Mamre the Amorite, brother of Eshcol, and brother of Aner: and these *were* confederate with Abram.

14 And when Abram heard that his brother was taken captive, *ª*he armed his trained *servants,* *b*born in his own house, three hundred and eighteen, and pursued *them* unto Dan.

15 And he divided himself against them, he and his servants, by night, and smote them, and pursued them unto Hobah, which *is* on the *ª*left hand of Damascus.

16 And he brought back all the goods, and also brought again his *ª*brother Lot, and his goods, and the women also, and the people.

17 ¶ And the king of Sodom went out to meet him after his return from the slaughter of Chedorlaomer, and of the kings *were* with him, at the valley of Shaveh, which *is* the *ª*king's dale.

18 And *ª*Melchizedek king of *b*Salem brought forth *c*bread and wine: *d*and he *was* the *e*priest of the most high God.

19 And he blessed him, and said, *ª*Blessed *be* Abram of the most high *b*God, *c*possessor of heaven and earth:

20 And *ª*blessed be the most high God, which hath delivered thine enemies into thy hand. And he gave him *b*tithes of all.

21 And the king of Sodom said unto Abram, Give me the persons, and take the *ª*goods to thyself.

22 And Abram said to the king of Sodom, I have lift up mine hand unto the LORD, the most high God, the possessor of heaven and earth,

23 That I will not *take* from a thread even to a shoelatchet, and that I will not take any thing that *is* thine, lest thou shouldest say, I have made Abram *ª*rich:

24 Save only that which the young men have eaten, and the portion of the men which went with me, Aner, Eshcol, and Mamre; let them take their *ª*portion.

CHAPTER 15

Abram desires offspring—The Lord promises him seed in number as the stars—Abram believes the promise—His seed will be strangers in Egypt—Then, after four generations, they will inherit Canaan.

AFTER these things the word of the LORD came unto Abram in a *ª*vision, saying, *b*Fear not, Abram: I *am* thy *c*shield, *and* thy exceeding great reward.

2 And Abram said, Lord GOD, what wilt thou give me, seeing I go childless, and the *ª*steward of my house *is* this Eliezer of Damascus?

3 And Abram said, Behold, to me thou hast given no seed: and, lo, *ª*one born in my house is mine heir.

4 And, behold, the word of the LORD *came* unto him, saying, This shall not be thine heir; but he that shall come forth out of thine own bowels shall be thine heir.

5 And he brought him forth abroad, and said, Look now toward heaven, and *ª*tell the *b*stars, if thou be able to *c*number them: and he said unto him, So shall thy *d*seed be.

14*a* OR he led forth.
  b Gen. 15:3.
15*a* IE north.
16*a* TG Family, Love within.
17*a* 2 Sam. 18:18.
18*a* HEB King of righteousness.
  b TG Jerusalem.
  c Ex. 18:12.
    TG Bread.
  d JST Gen. 14:17 . . . and he *brake bread and blest it; and he blest the wine, he being* the priest of the most high God,
  e TG Church Organization;

High Priest, Melchizedek Priesthood; Priesthood, Melchizedek.
19*a* TG Blessing.
  b TG God the Father, Elohim.
  c OR creator.
20*a* Job 1:21;
    D&C 36:3.
  b Alma 13:15.
    TG Tithing.
21*a* 2 Kgs. 5:15.
23*a* 1 Sam. 2:7;
    4 Ne. 1:3;
    D&C 6:7; 38:16.
24*a* JST Gen. 14:25–40

(Appendix).
15 1*a* TG Vision.
  b Gen. 26:24;
    1 Ne. 22:17.
    TG Courage;
    Fearful.
  c TG Protection, Divine.
2*a* Gen. 24:2.
3*a* HEB a son of my house.
    Gen. 14:14.
5*a* HEB count.
  b Deut. 10:22;
    Neh. 9:23;
    D&C 132:30.
  c 1 Chr. 27:23.
  d TG Seed of Abraham.

6 *a*And he *b*believed in the LORD; and he counted it to him for *c*righteousness.

7 And he said unto him, I *am* the LORD that brought thee out of Ur of the Chaldees, to give thee this land to *a*inherit it.

8 And he said, Lord GOD, whereby shall I *a*know that I shall inherit it?

9 And he said unto him, Take me an heifer of three years old, and a she goat of three years old, and a ram of three years old, and a turtledove, and a young pigeon.

10 And he took unto him all these, and *a*divided them in the midst, and laid each piece one against another: but the birds divided he not.

11 And when the fowls came down upon the carcases, Abram drove them away.

12 And when the sun was going down, a deep sleep fell upon Abram; and, lo, an horror of great *a*darkness fell upon him.

13 And he said unto Abram, Know of a surety that thy seed shall be a *a*stranger in a land *that is* not theirs, and shall serve them; and they shall *b*afflict them four hundred years;

14 And also that nation, whom they shall serve, will I judge: and afterward shall they *a*come out with great *b*substance.

15 And thou shalt go to thy fathers in peace; thou shalt be buried in a good *a*old age.

16 But in the *a*fourth generation they shall come *b*hither again: for the iniquity of the Amorites *is* not yet *c*full.

17 And it came to pass, that, when the sun went down, and it was dark, behold a smoking furnace, and a burning lamp that *a*passed between those pieces.

18 In the same day the LORD made a *a*covenant with Abram, saying, Unto thy seed have I given this *b*land, from *c*the river of Egypt unto the great river, the river *d*Euphrates:

19 The Kenites, and the Kenizzites, and the Kadmonites,

20 And the Hittites, and the Perizzites, and the Rephaims,

21 And the Amorites, and the Canaanites, and the Girgashites, and the Jebusites.

CHAPTER 16

Sarai gives Hagar to Abram as his wife—Hagar flees from Sarai—An angel commands Hagar to return and submit herself to Sarai—Hagar bears Ishmael.

Now Sarai Abram's wife bare him no children: and she had an handmaid, an *a*Egyptian, whose name *was* *b*Hagar.

2 And Sarai said unto Abram, Behold now, the LORD hath restrained me from bearing: I pray thee, go in unto my *a*maid; it may be that I may obtain children by her. And Abram hearkened to the voice of Sarai.

3 And Sarai Abram's wife took Hagar her maid the Egyptian, after Abram had dwelt ten years in the

---

6*a* JST Gen. 15:9–12
  (Appendix).
 b TG Faith.
 c TG Righteousness.
7*a* Num. 32:18.
8*a* Judg. 6:17 (17–18);
  2 Kgs. 20:8 (8–9);
  Luke 1:18 (18–19).
10*a* Jer. 34:18 (18–19).
12*a* JS—H 1:15 (15–17).
13*a* TG Israel, Bondage of, in
  Egypt; Stranger.
 b Ex. 1:11 (10–11);
  1 Ne. 17:25 (23–25).
14*a* Ex. 2:24;
  1 Ne. 5:15; 19:10;
  Mosiah 12:34;
  Alma 36:28;

D&C 136:22.
 b Ex. 12:36.
15*a* TG Old Age.
16*a* Note in Ex. 6:16–20
  that four generations of
  Levi's descendants are
  named; they include
  (1) Levi, (2) Kohath,
  (3) Amram, (4) Moses.
  TG Israel, Bondage of, in
  Egypt.
 b Ex. 3:17.
 c 1 Ne. 17:35 (32–35);
  Alma 37:31;
  Hel. 13:14;
  Ether 2:9 (8–10);
  D&C 61:31; 101:11.
17*a* Jer. 34:18 (18–19).

18*a* TG Abrahamic
  Covenant.
 b Gen. 13:15 (14–17);
  Josh. 1:2 (2–4).
  TG Israel, Land of;
  Promised Lands.
 c IE the Wadi El Arish
  in northern Sinai.
  Ex. 23:31;
  1 Kgs. 4:21.
 d Deut. 11:24 (22–25).
16 1*a* Gen. 21:21;
  Abr. 1:22 (21–22); 2:21.
 b Gen. 21:9;
  Gal. 4:24;
  D&C 132:34 (34, 65).
2*a* Gal. 4:22 (21–31);
  D&C 132:34, 65.

land of Canaan, and gave her to her husband Abram to be his wife.

4 ¶ And he went in unto Hagar, and she conceived: and when she saw that she had conceived, her mistress was despised in her eyes.

5 And Sarai said unto Abram, My wrong *be* upon thee: I have given my maid into thy bosom; and when she saw that she had conceived, I was *a*despised in her eyes: the LORD judge between me and thee.

6 But Abram said unto Sarai, Behold, thy maid *is* in thy hand; do to her *a*as it pleaseth thee. And when Sarai dealt hardly with her, she fled from her face.

7 ¶ And the angel of the LORD found her by a fountain of water in the wilderness, by the fountain in the way to *a*Shur.

8 And he said, Hagar, Sarai's maid, whence camest thou? and whither wilt thou go? And she said, I flee from the face of my mistress Sarai.

9 And the *a*angel of the LORD said unto her, Return to thy mistress, and *b*submit thyself under her hands.

10 And the angel of the LORD said unto her, I will multiply thy *a*seed exceedingly, that it shall not be numbered for multitude.

11 And the angel of the LORD said unto her, Behold, thou *art* with child, and shalt bear a son, and shalt call his name *a*Ishmael; because the LORD hath heard thy affliction.

12 And he will be a *a*wild man; his hand *will be* against every man, and every man's hand against him; and he shall dwell in the presence of all his brethren.

13 And she called the name of the LORD that spake unto her, Thou God seest me: for she said, Have I also here looked after him that seeth me?

14 Wherefore the *a*well was called *b*Beer-lahai-roi; behold, *it is* between Kadesh and Bered.

15 ¶ And Hagar *a*bare Abram a son: and Abram called his son's name, which Hagar bare, *b*Ishmael.

16 And Abram *was* fourscore and six years old, when Hagar bare Ishmael to Abram.

CHAPTER 17

Abram is commanded to be perfect—He will be a father of many nations—His name is changed to Abraham—The Lord covenants to be a God unto Abraham and his seed forever—Also, the Lord gives Abraham the land of Canaan for an everlasting possession—Circumcision becomes a token of the everlasting covenant between God and Abraham—Sarai's name is changed to Sarah—She will bear Isaac, with whom the Lord will establish His covenant—Abraham and the men of his house are circumcised.

AND when Abram was ninety years old and nine, the LORD *a*appeared to *b*Abram, and said unto him, I *am* the *c*Almighty God; *d*walk before me, and be thou *e*perfect.

2 And I will make my *a*covenant between me and thee, and will multiply thee exceedingly.

3 *a*And Abram fell on his face: and God talked with him, saying,

4 As for me, behold, my *a*covenant *is* with thee, and thou shalt be a *b*father of many *c*nations.

5a Gen. 30:1;
   1 Sam. 1:6 (1–20).
6a HEB that which is good in thine eyes.
7a Gen. 20:1; 25:18;
   Ex. 15:22.
9a TG Angels.
 b TG Submissiveness.
10a TG Seed of Abraham.
11a IE God hears.
12a HEB wild ass (metaphorical here for freedom-loving; probably a nomad).

   Gen. 21:20;
   Moses 6:38.
14a Gen. 24:62.
 b IE The well of Him who liveth and seeth me.
15a Gen. 21:9; 25:12.
 b Gen. 21:3 (2–3);
   1 Chr. 1:28.
17 1a Abr. 2:6 (6, 8, 19); 3:11.
 b Ex. 6:3 (2–3).
 c TG God, Power of;
   Jesus Christ, Power of.
 d TG Walking with God.
 e TG Integrity; Perfection.

2a TG Abrahamic Covenant.
3a JST Gen. 17:3–12 (Appendix).
4a Ex. 6:4.
 b 2 Ne. 8:2;
   D&C 109:64; 132:49.
   TG Seed of Abraham.
 c JST Gen. 17:8–9 . . . nations. *And this covenant I make, that thy children may be known among all nations . . .*
   TG Nations.

5 Neither shall thy name any more be called Abram, but thy name shall be ᵃAbraham; for a father of many nations have I made thee.

6 And I will make thee exceeding ᵃfruitful, and I will make ᵇnations of thee, and ᶜkings shall come out of thee.

7 ᵃAnd I will establish my ᵇcovenant between me and thee and thy seed after thee in their generations for an ᶜeverlasting covenant, to be a ᵈGod unto thee, and to thy seed after thee.

8 And I will ᵃgive unto thee, and to thy seed after thee, the ᵇland wherein thou art a ᶜstranger, all the ᵈland of ᵉCanaan, for an everlasting ᶠpossession; and I will be their ᵍGod.

9 ¶ And God said unto Abraham, Thou shalt keep my covenant therefore, thou, and thy seed after thee in their generations.

10 This *is* my ᵃcovenant, which ye shall keep, between me and you and thy seed after thee; Every man child among you shall be ᵇcircumcised.

11 And ye shall ᵃcircumcise the flesh of your foreskin; and it shall be a ᵇtoken of the ᶜcovenant betwixt me and you.

12 And he that is ᵃeight days old shall be circumcised among you, every man child in your generations, he that is born in the house, or ᵇbought with money of any stranger, which *is* not of thy seed.

13 He that is born in thy house, and he that is bought with thy money, must needs be circumcised: and my covenant shall be in your flesh for an ᵃeverlasting covenant.

14 And the uncircumcised man child whose flesh of his foreskin is not circumcised, that soul shall be ᵃcut off from his people; he hath broken my covenant.

15 ¶ And God said unto Abraham, As for Sarai thy wife, thou shalt not call her name Sarai, but ᵃSarah *shall* her name *be.*

16 And I will bless her, and ᵃgive thee a son also of her: yea, I will bless her, and she shall be *a* ᵇ*mother* of nations; kings of people shall be of her.

17 ᵃThen Abraham fell upon his face, and ᵇlaughed, and said in his heart, Shall *a child* be born unto him that is an ᶜhundred years old? and shall Sarah, that is ninety years old, bear?

18 And Abraham said unto God, O that ᵃIshmael might live before thee!

19 And God said, ᵃSarah thy wife shall bear thee a son indeed; and thou shalt call his name Isaac: and I will establish my ᵇcovenant with him for an everlasting covenant, *and* with his seed after him.

20 And as for ᵃIshmael, I have heard thee: Behold, I have blessed him, and will make him fruitful, and will multiply him exceedingly; ᵇtwelve princes shall he beget, and I will make him a great nation.

21 But my ᵃcovenant will I establish with Isaac, which Sarah shall

---

5a 1 Chr. 1:27.
6a Gen. 26:22.
 b TG Israel, Blessings of.
 c TG Kings, Earthly.
7a JST Gen. 17:11–12 (Appendix).
 b TG Israel, Mission of; New and Everlasting Covenant.
 c 2 Ne. 29:14 (13–14).
 d Gen. 24:12.
8a TG God, Gifts of.
 b TG Promised Lands.
 c TG Stranger.
 d TG Israel, Land of.
 e Ex. 3:8 (1–10); Num. 34:2 (1–29); Abr. 2:19 (6, 19).

 f Gen. 48:4; Abr. 2:6.
 g Ex. 6:7.
10a TG Covenants.
 b TG Circumcision.
11a Acts 15:24; Moro. 8:8.
 b TG Signs.
 c 3 Ne. 20:12.
12a D&C 84:28 (27–28).
 b Ex. 12:44 (43–45).
13a The covenant is everlasting, but circumcision as a sign of such a covenant was later discontinued. See Acts 15:1, 24–29; Gal. 2:3–4; 5:12–15.
14a Ex. 4:24.
15a IE Princess.

16a TG God, Gifts of.
 b Gen. 24:60; 25:23. TG Marriage, Motherhood; Seed of Abraham.
17a JST Gen. 17:23–24 (Appendix).
 b HEB (also) rejoiced. JST Gen. 17:23 . . . *rejoiced* . . . TG Laughter.
 c Gen. 21:5.
18a Gen. 21:11.
19a Gen. 18:10 (10, 14); 21:1.
 b TG Seed of Abraham.
20a TG Seed of Abraham.
 b Gen. 25:16.
21a TG Abrahamic Covenant.

bear unto thee at this set *b*time in the next year.

22 And he left off talking with him, and God went up from Abraham.

23 ¶ And Abraham took Ishmael his son, and all that were born in his house, and all that were bought with his money, every male among the men of Abraham's house; and *a*circumcised the flesh of their foreskin in the selfsame day, as God had said unto him.

24 And Abraham *was* ninety years old and nine, when he was circumcised in the flesh of his foreskin.

25 And Ishmael his son *was* thirteen years old, when he was circumcised in the flesh of his foreskin.

26 In the selfsame day was Abraham circumcised, and Ishmael his son.

27 And all the men of his house, born in the house, and bought with money of the stranger, were circumcised with him.

CHAPTER 18

Abraham entertains three holy men— They promise that Sarah will have a son—Abraham will command his children to be just—The Lord appears to him—They discuss the destruction of Sodom and Gomorrah.

AND the LORD *a*appeared unto him in the plains of Mamre: and he sat in the tent door in the heat of the day;

2 And he lift up his eyes and looked, and, lo, three *a*men stood by him: and when he saw *them,* he ran to meet them from the tent door, and *b*bowed himself toward the ground,

3 And said, My *a*Lord, if now I have found favour in thy sight, pass not away, I pray thee, from thy servant:

4 Let a little water, I pray you, be fetched, and *a*wash your feet, and *b*rest yourselves under the tree:

5 And I will fetch a morsel of bread, and *a*comfort ye your hearts; after that ye shall pass on: for therefore are ye *b*come to your servant. And they said, So do, as thou hast said.

6 And Abraham hastened into the tent unto Sarah, and said, Make ready quickly three measures of fine meal, knead *it,* and make cakes upon the hearth.

7 And Abraham ran unto the herd, and fetcht a calf tender and good, and gave *it* unto a young man; and he hasted to dress it.

8 And he took butter, and milk, and the calf which he had dressed, and set *it* before them; and he stood by them under the tree, and they did eat.

9 ¶ And they said unto him, Where *is* Sarah thy wife? And he said, Behold, in the tent.

10 And he said, I will certainly return unto thee according to the time of life; and, lo, *a*Sarah thy wife shall have a *b*son. And Sarah heard *it* in the tent door, which *was* behind him.

11 Now Abraham and Sarah *were* *a*old *and* well stricken in age; *and* it *b*ceased to be with Sarah after the manner of women.

12 Therefore Sarah laughed within herself, saying, After I am waxed old shall I have pleasure, my lord being *a*old also?

13 And the LORD said unto Abraham, Wherefore did Sarah *a*laugh, saying, Shall I of a surety bear a child, which am *b*old?

14 Is any thing too *a*hard for the LORD? At the time appointed I will return unto thee, according to the

21*b* Gen. 21:2.
23*a* TG Circumcision.
18 1*a* TG Jesus Christ,
　　Appearances,
　　Antemortal.
　2*a* See JST Gen. 18:23
　　(Gen. 18:22 note *a*).
　　Josh. 5:13.
　　TG Angels.
　　b 3 Ne. 11:19;

　　Ether 6:12.
　　TG Courtesy.
　3*a* JST Gen. 18:3 . . .
　　brethren . . .
　4*a* TG Wash.
　　b TG Hospitality.
　5*a* OR sustain . . .
　　b Gen. 19:8.
10*a* Gen. 17:19; 21:1.
　　b TG Seed of Abraham.

11*a* TG Old Age.
　　b TG Barren.
12*a* Gen. 21:7;
　　Ether 7:3 (3–7, 26); 9:23.
13*a* TG Laughter.
　　b Luke 1:18.
14*a* Luke 1:37;
　　Rom. 4:21.
　　TG God, Power of.

^btime of life, and Sarah shall have a son.

15 Then Sarah denied, saying, I laughed not; for she was afraid. And he said, Nay; but thou didst laugh.

16 ¶ And the men rose up from thence, and looked toward Sodom: and Abraham went with them to bring them on the way.

17 And the LORD said, Shall I ^ahide from Abraham that thing which I do;

18 Seeing that Abraham shall surely become a great and mighty ^anation, and all the ^bnations of the earth shall be ^cblessed in him?

19 For I ^aknow him, that he will ^bcommand his ^cchildren and his ^dhousehold after him, and they shall ^ekeep the way of the LORD, to do justice and ^fjudgment; that the LORD may bring upon Abraham that which he hath spoken of him.

20 And the LORD said, Because the ^acry of Sodom and Gomorrah is great, and because their ^bsin is very grievous;

21 I will go down now, and see whether they have done altogether according to the cry of it, which is come unto me; and if not, I will ^aknow.

22 ^aAnd the men turned their faces from thence, and went toward Sodom: but Abraham ^bstood yet before the LORD.

23 ¶ And Abraham drew near, and said, Wilt thou also ^adestroy the ^brighteous with the ^cwicked?

24 Peradventure there be fifty righteous within the city: wilt thou also destroy and not ^aspare the place for the fifty righteous that *are* therein?

25 That be far from thee to do after this manner, to slay the righteous with the wicked: and that the righteous should be as the wicked, that be far from thee: Shall not the ^aJudge of all the earth do right?

26 And the LORD said, If I find in Sodom fifty ^arighteous within the city, then I will spare all the place for their sakes.

27 And Abraham answered and said, Behold now, I have taken upon me to speak unto the Lord, which *am but* ^adust and ashes:

28 Peradventure there shall lack five of the fifty righteous: wilt thou destroy all the city for *lack of* five? And he said, If I find there forty and five, I will not destroy *it*.

29 And he spake unto him yet again, and said, Peradventure there shall be forty found there. And he said, I will not do *it* for forty's sake.

30 And he said *unto him*, Oh let not the Lord be angry, and I will speak: Peradventure there shall thirty be found there. And he said, I will not do *it*, if I find thirty there.

31 And he said, Behold now, I have taken upon me to speak unto the Lord: Peradventure there shall be twenty found there. And he said, I will not destroy *it* for twenty's sake.

32 And he said, Oh let not the Lord be ^aangry, and I will speak yet but this once: Peradventure ten shall be

14 *b* 2 Kgs. 4:16.
17 *a* Abr. 3:15.
     TG Revelation.
18 *a* TG Nations.
  b TG Abrahamic
     Covenant.
  c Zech. 8:13;
     D&C 110:12; 115:5.
     TG Israel, Mission of.
19 *a* TG God, Omni-
     science of.
  b TG Family, Children,
     Responsibilities toward;
     Teaching.
  c TG Children;
     Family.

  d Alma 23:3.
  e TG Loyalty;
     Trustworthiness.
  f TG Judgment.
20 *a* Gen. 19:13;
     Mosiah 19:7 (1–9);
     Morm. 2:13 (10–15).
  b TG Homosexual
     Behavior.
21 *a* 2 Ne. 27:27.
22 *a* JST Gen. 18:23 And the
     angels which were holy
     men, and were sent forth
     after the order of God,
     turned their faces . . .
  b TG God, Access to.

23 *a* 1 Ne. 22:16;
     Omni 1:7 (6–7);
     Hel. 13:13 (12–14);
     D&C 64:24.
  b Gen. 20:4.
  c TG Wickedness.
24 *a* TG Worth of Souls.
25 *a* TG Jesus Christ, Judge.
26 *a* Jer. 5:1;
     Ezek. 22:30;
     3 Ne. 9:13.
     TG Righteousness.
27 *a* Gen. 2:7; 3:19;
     Mosiah 4:2 (1–3);
     Hel. 12:7.
32 *a* Judg. 6:39.

found there. And he said, I will *b*not destroy *it* for ten's sake.

33 And the LORD *a*went his way, as soon as he had left communing with Abraham: and Abraham returned unto his place.

CHAPTER 19

Lot entertains holy men—The men of Sodom seek to abuse Lot's guests and are smitten with blindness—Lot is sent out of Sodom—The Lord rains brimstone and fire upon Sodom and Gomorrah—Lot's daughters preserve his seed in the land.

AND there came *a*two *b*angels to Sodom at even; and Lot sat in the gate of Sodom: and Lot seeing *them* rose up to meet them; and he bowed himself with his face toward the ground;

2 And he said, Behold now, my lords, turn in, I pray you, into your servant's house, and tarry all night, and *a*wash your feet, and ye shall rise up early, and go on your ways. And they said, Nay; but we will abide in the street all night.

3 And he pressed upon them greatly; and they turned in unto him, and entered into his house; and he made them a *a*feast, and did bake *b*unleavened bread, and they did eat.

4 ¶ But before they lay down, the men of the city, *even* the men of Sodom, compassed the house round, both old and young, all the people from every quarter:

5 And they called unto Lot, and said unto him, Where *are* the men which came in to thee this night? bring them out unto us, that we may *a*know them.

6 And Lot went out at the door unto them, and shut the door after him,

7 And said, I pray you, brethren, do not so wickedly.

8 *a*Behold now, I have two *b*daughters which have not known man; let me, I pray you, bring them out unto you, and do ye to them as *is* good in your eyes: only unto these men do nothing; for therefore *c*came they under the shadow of my roof.

9 And they said, Stand back. And they said *again*, This one *fellow* came in to *a*sojourn, and he will needs be a judge: now will we deal worse with thee, than with them. And they pressed sore upon the man, *even* Lot, and came near to break the door.

10 But the men put forth their hand, and pulled Lot into the house to them, and shut to the door.

11 And they smote the men that *were* at the door of the house with *a*blindness, both small and great: so that they wearied themselves to find the door.

12 ¶ And *a*the men said unto Lot, Hast thou here any besides? son in law, and thy sons, and thy daughters, and whatsoever thou hast in the city, *b*bring *them* out of this place:

13 For we will destroy this place, because the *a*cry of them is waxen great before the face of the LORD; and the LORD hath sent us to destroy it.

14 And Lot went out, and spake unto his sons in law, which married his daughters, and said, Up, *a*get you *b*out of this place; for the LORD will destroy this city. But he seemed as one that *c*mocked unto his sons in law.

32b Isa. 65:8.
33a TG God, Body of, Corporeal Nature.
19 1a JST Gen. 19:1 . . . *three* . . .
 b HEB messengers. TG Angels.
2a TG Wash.
3a TG Hospitality.
 b TG Bread, Unleavened.
5a "Know" is used in both Hebrew and English in this kind of context as a euphemism in place of a sexual word. Judg. 19:22 (22–28); Isa. 3:9.
 TG Homosexual Behavior.
8a JST Gen. 19:9–15 (Appendix).
 b Judg. 19:24 (24–27).
 c Gen. 18:5.
9a Gen. 13:12.
11a 2 Kgs. 6:18; Acts 13:11 (8–12).
12a JST Gen. 19:18 . . . *these holy men* . . .
 b 1 Ne. 2:2 (1–4). Abr. 2:6.
13a Gen. 18:20.
14a 1 Ne. 5:8; D&C 133:5 (5–14).
 b Num. 16:21 (21–26, 45); Jer. 51:6; Rev. 18:4.
 c TG Mocking.

15 ¶ And when the morning arose, then the ^aangels hastened ^bLot, saying, Arise, take thy wife, and thy two daughters, which are here; lest thou be consumed in the iniquity of the city.

16 And while he lingered, the men laid hold upon his hand, and upon the hand of his wife, and upon the hand of his two daughters; the LORD being ^amerciful unto him: and they brought him forth, and set him without the city.

17 ¶ And it came to pass, when they had brought them forth abroad, that he said, Escape for thy life; ^alook not behind thee, neither stay thou in all the plain; escape to the ^bmountain, lest thou be consumed.

18 And Lot said unto them, Oh, not so, my Lord:

19 Behold now, thy servant hath found ^agrace in thy sight, and thou hast magnified thy mercy, which thou hast shewed unto me in saving my life; and I cannot escape to the mountain, lest some evil take me, and I die:

20 Behold now, this city *is* near to flee unto, and it *is* a little one: Oh, let me escape thither, (*is it not a little one?*) and my soul shall live.

21 And he said unto him, See, I have ^aaccepted thee concerning this thing also, that I will not overthrow this city, for the which thou hast spoken.

22 Haste thee, escape thither; for I cannot do any thing till thou be come thither. Therefore the name of the city was called ^aZoar.

23 ¶ The sun was risen upon the earth when Lot entered into Zoar.

24 Then the LORD rained upon ^aSodom and upon ^bGomorrah ^cbrimstone and fire from the LORD out of heaven;

25 And he overthrew those cities, and all the plain, and all the inhabitants of the cities, and that which grew upon the ground.

26 ¶ But his wife ^alooked back from behind him, and she became a ^bpillar of salt.

27 ¶ And Abraham gat up early in the morning to the place where he stood before the LORD:

28 And he looked toward Sodom and Gomorrah, and toward all the land of the plain, and beheld, and, lo, the ^asmoke of the country went up as the smoke of a furnace.

29 ¶ And it came to pass, when God destroyed the cities of the plain, that God remembered Abraham, and sent Lot out of the midst of the overthrow, when he overthrew the cities in the which Lot dwelt.

30 ¶ And Lot went up out of Zoar, and dwelt in the ^amountain, and his two daughters with him; for he feared to dwell in Zoar: and he dwelt in a cave, he and his two daughters.

31 And the ^afirstborn said unto the younger, Our father *is* old, and *there is* not a man in the earth to come in unto us after the manner of all the earth:

32 Come, let us make our father drink wine, and we will lie with him, that we may preserve seed of our father.

33 And they made their father drink wine that night: and the

15a TG Angels.
  b 2 Pet. 2:7.
16a Ps. 103:8; 2 Ne. 1:3;
    Alma 32:22; Moro. 10:3.
17a Gen. 19:26;
    Mosiah 8:13;
    D&C 133:15.
  b Gen. 19:30.
19a TG Grace.
21a Job 42:9 (8–9);
    D&C 96:6;
    124:75 (74–76).
22a IE Little (thing).

Gen. 13:10; 14:2 (2, 8).
24a Gen. 13:10;
    Isa. 13:19;
    Jer. 49:18 (18–22); 50:40;
    Amos 4:11; Zeph. 2:9;
    Luke 17:29;
    2 Pet. 2:6 (1–9);
    Jude 1:7 (4–7);
    2 Ne. 13:9; 23:19.
  b Deut. 29:23; Hosea 11:8.
  c HEB combustible
    materials (especially
    sulphur and pitch).

Deut. 29:23;
    Ezek. 16:50 (48–50).
26a Gen. 19:17.
  b Luke 17:32 (31–33).
28a Rev. 18:9 (9, 18); 19:3;
    1 Ne. 19:11;
    3 Ne. 10:13 (13–14);
    Morm. 8:29 (29–30);
    D&C 45:41 (40–41).
30a Gen. 19:17 (17–19).
31a JST Gen. 19:37 . . .
    firstborn *dealt wickedly,
    and* said . . .

firstborn went in, and lay with her father; and he perceived not when she lay down, nor when she arose.

34 And it came to pass on the morrow, that the firstborn said unto the younger, Behold, I lay yesternight with my father: let us make him drink wine this night also; and go thou in, *and* lie with him, that we may preserve seed of our father.

35 *a*And they made their father drink wine that night also: and the younger arose, and lay with him; and he perceived not when she lay down, nor when she arose.

36 Thus were both the daughters of Lot with child by their father.

37 And the firstborn bare a son, and called his name *a*Moab: the same *is* the father of the *b*Moabites unto this day.

38 And the younger, she also bare a son, and called his name Ben-ammi: the same *is* the father of the children of *a*Ammon unto this day.

CHAPTER 20

Abimelech desires Sarah, who is preserved by the Lord—Abraham prays for Abimelech, and the Lord blesses him and his household.

AND Abraham journeyed from thence toward the south country, and dwelled between Kadesh and *a*Shur, and sojourned in *b*Gerar.

2 And Abraham said of Sarah his wife, She *is* my sister: and *a*Abimelech king of Gerar sent, and took Sarah.

3 But *a*God came to Abimelech in a dream by night, and said to him, Behold, thou *art but* a dead man, for the woman which thou hast taken; for she *is* a man's wife.

4 But Abimelech had not come near her: and he said, Lord, wilt thou slay also *a*a righteous nation?

5 Said he not unto me, She *is* my *a*sister? and she, even she herself said, He *is* my *b*brother: in the *c*integrity of my heart and innocency of my hands have I done this.

6 And God said unto him in a dream, Yea, I know that thou didst this in the integrity of thy heart; for I also withheld thee from sinning against me: therefore suffered I thee not to touch her.

7 Now therefore restore the man *his* wife; for he *is* a prophet, and he shall *a*pray for thee, and thou shalt live: and if thou restore *her* not, know thou that thou shalt surely die, thou, and all that *are* thine.

8 Therefore Abimelech rose early in the morning, and called all his servants, and told all these things in their ears: and the men were sore afraid.

9 Then *a*Abimelech called Abraham, and said unto him, What hast thou *b*done unto us? and what have I offended thee, that thou hast brought on me and on my kingdom a great sin? thou hast *c*done deeds unto me that ought not to be done.

10 And Abimelech said unto Abraham, What sawest thou, that thou hast done this thing?

11 And Abraham said, Because I thought, Surely the *a*fear of God *is* not in this place; and they will slay me for my wife's sake.

12 And yet indeed *she is* my *a*sister; she *is* the daughter of my father, but not the daughter of my mother; and she became my wife.

13 And it came to pass, when God caused me to *a*wander from my father's house, that I said unto her, This *is* thy *b*kindness which thou

35a JST Gen. 19:39 And they *did wickedly, and* made . . .
37a Deut. 2:9; 2 Ne. 21:14.
   b 2 Kgs. 3:4; Isa. 15:1.
38a Deut. 2:19 (18–19); Ezek. 25:2.
20 1a Gen. 16:7 (7, 14).
   b Gen. 10:19; 26:6.
 2a Gen. 21:22; 26:1.

 3a Ps. 105:14.
 4a OR an innocent nation. Gen. 18:23.
 5a Gen. 12:13 (9–20); 26:7 (6–11).
   b Gen. 20:16.
   c TG Integrity; Sincere.
 7a 1 Sam. 7:5; Job 42:8; 2 Ne. 33:3; Enos 1:11 (11–12);

   W of M 1:8; Moro. 9:22.
 9a Gen. 26:10.
   b Gen. 12:18 (14–20).
   c Gen. 26:10.
11a TG Reverence.
12a Gen. 12:19 (9–20); Abr. 2:2, 25 (22–25).
13a Gen. 12:1; Abr. 2:3.
   b TG Kindness.

shalt shew unto me; at every place whither we shall come, say of me, He *is* my brother.

14 And Abimelech took sheep, and oxen, and menservants, and womenservants, and gave *them* unto Abraham, and restored him Sarah his wife.

15 And Abimelech said, Behold, my ªland *is* before thee: dwell where it pleaseth thee.

16 And unto Sarah he said, Behold, I have given thy ªbrother a thousand *pieces* of silver: behold, he *is* to thee a covering of the eyes, unto all that *are* with thee, and with all *other:* thus she was reproved.

17 ¶ So Abraham prayed unto God: and God healed Abimelech, and his wife, and his maidservants; and they bare *children.*

18 For the LORD had fast ªclosed up all the wombs of the house of Abimelech, because of Sarah Abraham's wife.

CHAPTER 21

Sarah bears Isaac—He is circumcised —Hagar and her son are cast out of Abraham's household—The Lord saves Hagar and Ishmael—Abraham and Abimelech deal honorably with each other.

AND the LORD ªvisited Sarah as he had said, and the LORD did unto ᵇSarah as he had spoken.

2 For Sarah conceived, and bare Abraham a ªson in his ᵇold age, at the set ᶜtime of which God had spoken to him.

3 And Abraham called the name of his ªson that was born unto

him, whom Sarah bare to him, Isaac.

4 And Abraham ªcircumcised his son Isaac being eight days old, as God had commanded him.

5 And Abraham was an ªhundred years old, when his son Isaac was born unto him.

6 ¶ And Sarah said, God hath made me to ªlaugh, *so that* all that hear will laugh with me.

7 And she said, Who would have said unto Abraham, that Sarah should have given children suck? for I have born *him* a son in his ªold age.

8 And the child grew, and was weaned: and Abraham made a great feast the *same* day that Isaac was weaned.

9 ¶ And Sarah saw the son of ªHagar the Egyptian, which she had ᵇborn unto Abraham, ᶜmocking.

10 Wherefore she said unto Abraham, ªCast out this bondwoman and her son: for the son of this bondwoman shall not be ᵇheir with my son, *even* with Isaac.

11 And the thing was very grievous in Abraham's sight because of his ªson.

12 ¶ And God said unto Abraham, Let it not be grievous in thy sight because of the lad, and because of thy bondwoman; in all that Sarah hath said unto thee, hearken unto her voice; for in ªIsaac shall thy ᵇseed be called.

13 And also of the son of the bondwoman will I make a ªnation, because he *is* thy seed.

14 And Abraham rose up early in the morning, and took bread, and a bottle of water, and gave *it* unto

---

15*a* Gen. 34:10.
16*a* Gen. 20:5.
18*a* Gen. 12:17.
21 1*a* Gen. 30:22 (22–23);
   1 Sam. 2:21.
   b Gen. 17:19;
     18:10 (10, 14).
   2*a* Gen. 24:36.
   b TG Old Age.
   c Gen. 17:21.
   3*a* Gen. 16:15 (11, 15);
     1 Chr. 1:28.
   TG Seed of Abraham.

4*a* TG Circumcision.
5*a* Gen. 17:17.
6*a* The Hebrew root
   tzachak means both "to
   laugh" and "to rejoice";
   thus there is double
   meaning implied in its
   use here.
   Gal. 4:27;
   D&C 132:56.
   TG Laughter.
7*a* Gen. 18:12 (11–12).
9*a* Gen. 16:1.

b Gen. 16:15.
c Gal. 4:29.
10*a* Gal. 4:30.
   b D&C 52:2.
11*a* Gen. 17:18.
12*a* 1 Ne. 17:40;
   D&C 27:10.
   b TG Abrahamic
     Covenant;
     Seed of Abraham.
13*a* TG Seed of Abraham.

Hagar, putting *it* on her shoulder, and the child, and ^asent her away: and she departed, and wandered in the wilderness of ^bBeer-sheba.

15 And the water was spent in the bottle, and she cast the child under one of the shrubs.

16 And she went, and sat her down over against *him* a good way off, as it were a bowshot: for she said, Let me not see the death of the child. And she sat over against *him*, and lift up her voice, and wept.

17 And God heard the voice of the lad; and the ^aangel of God called to Hagar out of heaven, and said unto her, What aileth thee, Hagar? fear not; for God hath heard the voice of the lad where he *is*.

18 Arise, lift up the lad, and hold him in thine hand; for I will make him a great ^anation.

19 And God ^aopened her eyes, and she saw a well of water; and she went, and filled the bottle with water, and gave the lad drink.

20 And God was with the lad; and he grew, and dwelt in the wilderness, and became an ^aarcher.

21 And he dwelt in the wilderness of Paran: and his mother took him a ^awife out of the land of ^bEgypt.

22 ¶ And it came to pass at that time, that ^aAbimelech and ^bPhichol the chief captain of his host spake unto Abraham, saying, ^cGod *is* with thee in all that thou doest:

23 Now therefore swear unto me here by God that thou wilt not deal falsely with me, nor with my son, nor with my son's son: *but* according to the kindness that I have done unto thee, thou shalt do unto me, and to the land wherein thou hast sojourned.

24 And Abraham said, I will swear.

25 And Abraham ^areproved Abimelech because of a well of water, which Abimelech's servants ^bhad violently taken away.

26 And Abimelech said, I wot not who hath done this thing: neither didst thou tell me, neither yet heard I *of it*, but to day.

27 And Abraham took sheep and oxen, and gave them unto Abimelech; and both of them ^amade a covenant.

28 And Abraham set seven ewe lambs of the flock by themselves.

29 And Abimelech said unto Abraham, What *mean* these seven ewe lambs which thou hast set by themselves?

30 And he said, For *these* seven ewe lambs shalt thou take of my hand, that they may be a witness unto me, that I have digged this ^awell.

31 Wherefore he called that place ^aBeer-sheba; because there they sware both of them.

32 Thus they made a covenant at Beer-sheba: ^athen Abimelech rose up, and Phichol the chief captain of his host, and they returned into the land of the Philistines.

33 ¶ And *Abraham* planted a ^agrove in Beer-sheba, and ^bcalled there on the name of the LORD, the ^ceverlasting God.

34 And Abraham sojourned in the ^aPhilistines' land many days.

CHAPTER 22

Abraham is commanded to sacrifice Isaac, his son—Both father and son yield to the will of God—Abraham's seed will be as the stars and the sand in number—In his seed, all nations will be blessed—Rebekah is born to Bethuel.

AND it came to pass after these

14a Gen. 25:6.
  b Gen. 21:31.
17a TG Angels.
18a TG Seed of Abraham.
19a 2 Kgs. 6:20.
20a Gen. 16:12.
21a TG Marriage, Interfaith.
  b Gen. 16:1.
22a Gen. 20:2 (1–16).

  b Gen. 26:26.
  c Gen. 26:28.
25a Gen. 26:20.
  b Gen. 26:15 (15–22).
27a Gen. 26:31 (26–33).
30a Gen. 26:15.
31a IE The well of the oath, or well of seven.
    Gen. 21:14 (14, 32); 26:18,

    33; 46:1.
32a JST Gen. 21:31–32 (Appendix).
33a OR tamarisk.
  b TG Prayer.
  c Isa. 40:28; Rom. 16:26; D&C 133:34.
34a Gen. 10:14; 26:1.

things, that God did ᵃtempt Abraham, and said unto him, Abraham: and he said, Behold, *here* I *am.*

2 And he said, ᵃTake now thy son, thine ᵇonly *son* Isaac, whom thou ᶜlovest, and get thee into the land of ᵈMoriah; and offer him there for a burnt offering upon one of the mountains which I will tell thee of.

3 ¶ And Abraham rose up early in the morning, and saddled his ass, and took two of his young men with him, and Isaac his son, and clave the ᵃwood for the burnt offering, and rose up, and went unto the place of which God had told him.

4 Then on the third day Abraham lifted up his eyes, and saw the place afar off.

5 And Abraham said unto his young men, Abide ye here with the ass; and I and the lad will go yonder and ᵃworship, and come again to you.

6 And Abraham took the wood of the burnt offering, and ᵃlaid *it* upon Isaac his son; and he took the fire in his hand, and a knife; and they went both of them together.

7 And Isaac spake unto Abraham his father, and said, My father: and he said, ᵃHere *am* I, my son. And he said, Behold the fire and the wood: but where *is* the lamb for a burnt offering?

8 And Abraham said, My son, God will provide himself a ᵃlamb for a burnt offering: so they went both of them together.

9 And they came to the place which God had told him of; and Abraham built an altar there, and ᵃlaid the wood in order, and bound Isaac his son, and laid him on the ᵇaltar upon the wood.

10 And Abraham stretched forth his hand, and took the knife to slay his son.

11 And the angel of the Lᴏʀᴅ called unto him out of heaven, and said, Abraham, Abraham: and he said, Here *am* I.

12 And he said, ᵃLay not thine hand upon the lad, neither do thou any thing unto him: for now I know that thou ᵇfearest God, seeing thou hast not ᶜwithheld thy son, thine only *son* from me.

13 And Abraham lifted up his eyes, and looked, and behold behind *him* a ram caught in a thicket by his horns: and Abraham went and took the ram, and offered him up for a burnt offering in the stead of his son.

14 And Abraham called the name of that place ᵃJehovah-jireh: as it is said *to* this day, ᵇIn the mount of the Lᴏʀᴅ it shall be seen.

15 ¶ And the angel of the Lᴏʀᴅ called unto Abraham out of heaven the second time,

16 And said, By myself have I ᵃsworn, saith the Lᴏʀᴅ, for because thou hast done this thing, and hast not withheld thy son, thine only *son:*

17 That in blessing I will bless thee, and in multiplying I will multiply thy ᵃseed as the stars of the heaven, and as the ᵇsand which *is* upon the sea shore; and thy seed shall possess the ᶜgate of his enemies;

18 And in thy ᵃseed shall all the nations of the earth be ᵇblessed;

---

22 1 *a* HEB test, or prove.
　　D&C 136:31.
　　ᴛɢ Test.
　2 *a* D&C 132:36.
　　b John 3:16 (16–21);
　　　Jacob 4:5.
　　c ᴛɢ Love.
　　d 2 Sam. 24:18;
　　　2 Chr. 3:1.
　3 *a* Neh. 10:34.
　5 *a* ᴛɢ Worship.
　6 *a* John 19:17.
　7 *a* ᴏʀ Yes, my son.
　8 *a* Isa. 53:7; John 8:56;
　　　1 Ne. 13:35; Hel. 8:17;

D&C 76:85.
　ᴛɢ Jesus Christ, Types
　　of, in Anticipation;
　　Passover.
　9 *a* James 2:21.
　　b ᴛɢ Sacrifice.
　12 *a* D&C 132:36.
　　b James 2:23 (21–23).
　　c ᴛɢ Loyalty.
　14 *a* ɪᴇ The Lᴏʀᴅ will see, or
　　　provide (v. 8).
　　ᴛɢ Jesus Christ, Jehovah.
　　b ᴏʀ In a mount the
　　　Lᴏʀᴅ shall be manifest
　　　(seen).

16 *a* Ex. 32:13; Deut. 1:11;
　　　Ps. 105:9.
　17 *a* Gen. 13:16 (14–16);
　　　Isa. 48:19 (18–22);
　　　1 Ne. 20:19 (18–22).
　　ᴛɢ Abrahamic Covenant.
　　b 1 Kgs. 4:20; 1 Ne. 12:1;
　　　2 Ne. 20:22;
　　　D&C 132:30.
　　c Gen. 24:60.
　18 *a* ᴛɢ Seed of Abraham.
　　b ᴛɢ Israel, Mission of;
　　　Mission of Early Saints;
　　　Mission of Latter-day
　　　Saints.

because thou hast ^cobeyed my voice.

19 So Abraham returned unto his young men, and they rose up and went together to Beer-sheba; and Abraham dwelt at Beer-sheba.

20 ¶ And it came to pass after these things, that it was told Abraham, saying, Behold, ^aMilcah, she hath also born children unto thy brother Nahor;

21 Huz his firstborn, and Buz his brother, and Kemuel the father of Aram,

22 And Chesed, and Hazo, and Pildash, and Jidlaph, and Bethuel.

23 And ^aBethuel begat ^bRebekah: these eight Milcah did bear to Nahor, Abraham's ^cbrother.

24 And his concubine, whose name *was* Reumah, she bare also Tebah, and Gaham, and Thahash, and Maachah.

CHAPTER 23

Sarah dies and is buried in the cave of Machpelah, which Abraham buys from Ephron the Hittite.

AND Sarah was an hundred and seven and twenty years old: *these were* the years of the life of Sarah.

2 And Sarah ^adied in Kirjath-arba; the same *is* ^bHebron in the land of Canaan: and Abraham came to mourn for Sarah, and to weep for her.

3 ¶ And Abraham stood up from before his dead, and spake unto the sons of Heth, saying,

4 I *am* ^aa stranger and a sojourner with you: give me a possession of a buryingplace with you, that I may bury my ^bdead out of my sight.

5 And the children of Heth answered Abraham, saying unto him,

6 Hear us, my lord: thou *art* ^aa mighty prince among us: in the choice of our sepulchres bury thy dead; none of us shall withhold from thee his sepulchre, but that thou mayest bury thy dead.

7 And Abraham stood up, and bowed himself to the people of the land, *even* to the children of Heth.

8 And he communed with them, saying, If it be your mind that I should bury my dead out of my sight; hear me, and entreat for me to Ephron the son of Zohar,

9 That he may give me the cave of ^aMachpelah, which he hath, which *is* in the end of his field; for as much money as it is worth he shall give it me for a possession of a burying-place amongst you.

10 And Ephron dwelt among the children of Heth: and Ephron the Hittite answered Abraham in the audience of the children of Heth, *even* of all that went in at the ^agate of his city, saying,

11 Nay, my lord, hear me: the field give I thee, and the cave that *is* therein, I give it thee; in the presence of the sons of my people give I it thee: bury thy dead.

12 And Abraham bowed down himself before the people of the land.

13 And he spake unto Ephron in the audience of the people of the land, saying, But if thou *wilt give it,* I pray thee, hear me: I will give thee money for the field; take *it* of me, and I will bury my dead there.

14 And Ephron answered Abraham, saying unto him,

15 My lord, hearken unto me: the land *is worth* four hundred ^ashekels of silver; what *is* that betwixt me and thee? bury therefore thy dead.

16 And Abraham hearkened unto ^aEphron; and Abraham ^bweighed to ^cEphron the silver, which he had named in the audience of the sons of Heth, four hundred shekels of silver, current *money* with the merchant.

18*c* TG Obedience.
20*a* Gen. 11:29; 24:15.
23*a* Gen. 24:15; 25:20; 28:2.
  b Gen. 24:47;
    Rom. 9:10.
  c Gen. 24:4;
    Abr. 2:2.

23 2*a* Gen. 24:67.
  b Gen. 13:18; 23:19.
  4*a* IE a resident alien.
    TG Stranger.
  b TG Death.
  6*a* HEB a prince of God.
  9*a* Gen. 25:9; 49:30.

10*a* Gen. 34:20; Ruth 4:1.
15*a* Ex. 30:13;
    Ezek. 45:12.
16*a* Gen. 49:30.
  b 1 Chr. 21:25;
    Jer. 32:9.
  c Gen. 25:10.

17 ¶ And the field of ^aEphron, which *was* in Machpelah, which *was* before Mamre, the field, and the cave which *was* therein, and all the trees that *were* in the field, that *were* in all the borders round about, were made sure

18 Unto Abraham for a possession in the presence of the children of Heth, before all that went in at the gate of his city.

19 And after this, Abraham buried Sarah his wife in the cave of the field of Machpelah before Mamre: the same *is* ^aHebron in the land of Canaan.

20 And the field, and the cave that *is* therein, were made sure unto Abraham for a possession of a buryingplace by the sons of Heth.

CHAPTER 24

Abraham commands that Isaac shall not marry a Canaanite—The Lord guides Abraham's servant in choosing Rebekah as a wife for Isaac—Rebekah is blessed to be the mother of thousands of millions—She marries Isaac.

AND Abraham was old, *and* well ^astricken in age: and the LORD had ^bblessed Abraham in all ^cthings.

2 And Abraham said unto his eldest ^aservant of his house, that ruled over all that he had, Put, I pray thee, thy hand under my ^bthigh:

3 And I will make thee ^aswear by the LORD, the God of heaven, and the God of the earth, that thou shalt ^bnot take a ^cwife unto my son of the daughters of the ^dCanaanites, among whom I dwell:

4 But thou shalt go unto my ^acountry, and to my ^bkindred, and take a wife unto my son Isaac.

5 And the servant said unto him, ^aPeradventure the woman will not be willing to follow me unto this land: must I needs bring thy son again unto the land from whence thou camest?

6 And Abraham said unto him, Beware thou that thou bring not my son thither again.

7 ¶ The ^aLORD God of heaven, which took me from my ^bfather's house, and from the land of my kindred, and which spake unto me, and that sware unto me, saying, Unto thy seed will I give this ^cland; he shall send his ^dangel before thee, and thou shalt take a wife unto my son from thence.

8 And if the woman will not be willing to follow thee, then thou shalt be clear from this my oath: only bring not my son thither again.

9 And the servant put his hand under the ^athigh of Abraham his master, and sware to him concerning that matter.

10 ¶ And the servant took ten camels of the camels of his master, and departed; for all the goods of his master *were* in his hand: and he arose, and went to ^aMesopotamia, unto the city of ^bNahor.

11 And he made his camels to kneel down without the city by a well of water at the time of the evening, *even* the time that women go out to draw *water.*

12 And he said, O ^aLORD God of my master Abraham, I pray thee, ^bsend me good speed this day, and shew kindness unto my master Abraham.

17a Gen. 50:13;
  Acts 7:16.
19a Gen. 23:2.
24 1a IE advanced in age.
  1 Ne. 18:17;
  Alma 1:9.
  b Isa. 51:2.
  c Prov. 28:10.
2a Gen. 15:2.
  b JST Gen. 24:2 ... hand ...
  Gen. 47:29.
3a Gen. 24:37;
  Alma 48:13; 51:6;

Hel. 1:11;
  3 Ne. 3:8;
  Ether 8:14 (13–14).
  TG Oath.
  b Moses 7:8 (7–8);
  Abr. 1:22 (21–24).
  c TG Marriage, Interfaith.
  d Gen. 28:1.
4a Gen. 11:31;
  Abr. 2:4 (2–5).
  b Gen. 22:23 (20–24); 24:38;
  27:43.
5a Gen. 24:39.

7a Gen. 24:40.
  b Gen. 12:1.
  c TG Promised Lands.
  d TG Angels.
9a JST Gen. 24:8 ... hand ...
10a HEB *Aram-naharaim*; i.e.,
  Aram of the two rivers.
  b Gen. 24:24; 27:43;
  Abr. 2:4 (4–6, 14–15).
12a Gen. 17:7; 24:27.
  b Gen. 24:21;
  Neh. 1:11.

13 Behold, I stand *here* by the well of water; and the daughters of the men of the city come out to draw *a*water:

14 And let it come to pass, that the damsel to whom I shall say, Let down thy pitcher, I pray thee, that I may drink; and she shall say, Drink, and I will give thy camels drink also: *let the same be* she *that* thou hast *a*appointed for thy servant Isaac; and thereby shall I know that thou hast shewed kindness unto my master.

15 ¶ And it came to pass, before he had done speaking, that, behold, Rebekah came out, who was born to *a*Bethuel, son of *b*Milcah, the wife of Nahor, Abraham's brother, with her pitcher upon her shoulder.

16 And the damsel *was* very *a*fair to look upon, a virgin, neither had any man *b*known her: and she went down to the well, and filled her pitcher, and came up.

17 And the servant ran to meet her, and said, Let me, I pray thee, drink a little water of thy pitcher.

18 And she said, Drink, my lord: and she hasted, and let down her pitcher upon her hand, and gave him drink.

19 And when she had done giving him drink, she said, I will draw *water* for thy camels also, until they have done drinking.

20 And she hasted, and emptied her pitcher into the trough, and ran again unto the well to draw *water*, and drew for all his camels.

21 And the man wondering at her held his peace, to wit whether the LORD had made his journey *a*prosperous or not.

22 And it came to pass, as the camels had done drinking, that the man took a golden *a*earring of half a shekel weight, and two bracelets for her hands of ten *shekels* weight of gold;

23 And said, Whose daughter *art* thou? tell me, I pray thee: is there room *in* thy father's house for us to lodge in?

24 And she said unto him, I *am* the daughter of Bethuel the son of Milcah, which she bare unto *a*Nahor.

25 She said moreover unto him, We have both straw and provender enough, and room to lodge in.

26 And the man *a*bowed down his head, and worshipped the LORD.

27 And he said, Blessed *be* the *a*LORD God of my master Abraham, who hath not left destitute my master of his *b*mercy and his truth: I *being* in the way, the LORD *c*led me to the house of my master's brethren.

28 And the damsel ran, and told *them of* her mother's house these things.

29 ¶ And Rebekah had a brother, and his name *was* Laban: and *a*Laban ran out unto the man, unto the well.

30 And it came to pass, when he saw the earring and bracelets upon his sister's hands, and when he heard the words of Rebekah his sister, saying, Thus spake the man unto me; that he came unto the man; and, behold, he stood by the camels at the well.

31 And he said, Come in, thou *a*blessed of the LORD; wherefore standest thou without? for I have prepared the house, and room for the camels.

32 ¶ And the man came into the house: and he ungirded his camels, and gave straw and *a*provender for the camels, and water to *b*wash his feet, and the men's feet that *were* with him.

33 And there was set *meat* before

13a Gen. 29:10 (8–10);
　　Ex. 2:16.
14a Gen. 24:51.
15a Gen. 22:23.
　b Gen. 11:29; 22:20.
16a Gen. 26:7;
　　1 Ne. 11:15; 13:15;
　　2 Ne. 5:21; 4 Ne. 1:10;
　　Morm. 9:6;

Abr. 2:22.
　b JST Gen. 24:16 . . . known
　　the like unto her . . .
21a Gen. 24:12, 56;
　　1 Ne. 20:15.
22a HEB ring.
24a Gen. 24:10.
26a Ex. 4:31.
27a Gen. 24:12.

　b Gen. 32:10; Ps. 98:3.
　c Alma 13:28; 22:1;
　　Morm. 5:17.
　　TG Guidance, Divine.
29a Gen. 29:5 (5, 13).
31a Gen. 26:29; Judg. 17:2;
　　Ps. 115:15.
32a Judg. 19:21.
　b TG Wash.

him to eat: but he said, I will not eat, until I have told mine errand. And he said, Speak on.

34 And he said, I *am* Abraham's servant.

35 And the Lord hath ªblessed my master greatly; and he is become ᵇgreat: and he hath given him flocks, and herds, and silver, and gold, and menservants, and maidservants, and camels, and asses.

36 And Sarah my master's wife bare a ªson to my master when she was ᵇold: and unto him hath he ᶜgiven all that he hath.

37 And my master made me ªswear, saying, Thou shalt not take a wife to my son of the daughters of the Canaanites, in whose land I dwell:

38 But thou shalt go unto my ªfather's house, and to my kindred, and take a wife unto my son.

39 And I said unto my master, ªPeradventure the woman will not follow me.

40 And he said unto me, The ªLord, before whom I ᵇwalk, will send his angel with thee, and prosper thy way; and thou shalt take a wife for my son of my kindred, and of my father's house:

41 Then shalt thou be clear from *this* my oath, when thou comest to my kindred; and if they give not thee *one,* thou shalt be clear from my oath.

42 And I came this day unto the well, and said, O Lord God of my master Abraham, if now thou do prosper my way which I go:

43 Behold, I stand by the well of water; and it shall come to pass, that when the virgin cometh forth to draw *water,* and I say to her, Give me, I pray thee, a little water of thy pitcher to drink;

44 And she say to me, Both drink thou, and I will also draw for thy camels: *let* the same *be* the woman whom the Lord hath ªappointed out for my master's son.

45 And before I had done speaking in mine ªheart, behold, Rebekah came forth with her pitcher on her shoulder; and she went down unto the well, and drew *water:* and I said unto her, Let me drink, I pray thee.

46 And she made haste, and let down her pitcher from her *shoulder,* and said, Drink, and I will give thy camels drink also: so I drank, and she made the camels drink also.

47 And I asked her, and said, Whose daughter *art* thou? And she said, The daughter of Bethuel, Nahor's son, whom Milcah bare unto him: and I put the ªearring upon her face, and the bracelets upon her hands.

48 And I ªbowed down my head, and worshipped the Lord, and blessed the Lord God of my master Abraham, which had led me in the right way to take my master's brother's ᵇdaughter unto his son.

49 And now if ye will deal kindly and truly with my master, tell me: and if not, tell me; that I may turn to the right hand, or to the left.

50 Then Laban and Bethuel answered and said, The thing proceedeth from the Lord: we cannot ªspeak unto thee bad or good.

51 Behold, Rebekah *is* before thee, take *her,* and go, and let her be thy master's son's ªwife, as the Lord hath spoken.

52 And it came to pass, that, when Abraham's servant heard their words, he worshipped the Lord, *bowing himself* to the earth.

53 And the servant brought forth ªjewels of silver, and jewels of gold, and raiment, and gave *them* to Rebekah: he gave also to her brother and to her mother precious things.

35a Gen. 13:2; 26:12.
  b Gen. 26:13 (12–15); 30:43.
36a Gen. 21:2.
  b 2 Ne. 8:2.
  c Gen. 25:5.
37a Gen. 24:3.
38a Gen. 24:4.

39a Gen. 24:5.
40a Gen. 24:7.
  b TG Walking with God.
44a Gen. 24:51.
45a 1 Ne. 4:10; 21:21;
    Alma 36:18; JS—H 1:25.
47a HEB ring on her nose.

48a TG Reverence.
  b Gen. 22:23.
50a Gen. 31:24.
51a Gen. 24:14 (13–15),
    44 (42–44).
53a HEB things of silver and
    gold.

54 And they did eat and drink, he and the men that *were* with him, and tarried all night; and they rose up in the morning, and he said, Send me away unto my master.

55 And her brother and her mother said, Let the damsel abide with us *a few* days, at the least ten; after that she shall go.

56 And he said unto them, Hinder me not, seeing the LORD hath *a*prospered my way; send me away that I may go to my master.

57 And they said, We will call the damsel, and inquire at her mouth.

58 And they called Rebekah, and said unto her, Wilt thou go with this man? And she said, I will go.

59 And they sent away Rebekah their sister, and her *a*nurse, and Abraham's servant, and his men.

60 And they blessed Rebekah, and said unto her, Thou *art* our sister, be thou the *a*mother of thousands of millions, and let thy seed possess the *b*gate of those which *c*hate them.

61 ¶ And Rebekah arose, and her damsels, and they rode upon the camels, and followed the man: and the servant took Rebekah, and went his way.

62 And Isaac came from the way of the *a*well Lahai-roi; for he dwelt in the south country.

63 And Isaac went out to *a*meditate in the field at the eventide: and he lifted up his eyes, and saw, and, behold, the camels *were* coming.

64 And Rebekah lifted up her eyes, and when she saw Isaac, *a*she lighted off the camel.

65 For she *had* said unto the servant, What man *is* this that walketh in the field to meet us? And the servant *had* said, It *is* my master:

therefore she took a veil, and covered herself.

66 And the servant told Isaac all things that he had done.

67 And Isaac brought her into his mother Sarah's tent, and took Rebekah, and she became his wife; and he loved her: and Isaac was *a*comforted after his mother's *b*death.

CHAPTER 25

Abraham marries, has descendants, dies, and is buried in the cave of Machpelah—His descendants through Ishmael are listed—Rebekah conceives, and Jacob and Esau struggle in her womb—The Lord reveals their destiny to Rebekah—Esau sells his birthright for a mess of pottage.

THEN again Abraham took a wife, and her name *was* Keturah.

2 And she bare him Zimran, and Jokshan, and *a*Medan, and *b*Midian, and Ishbak, and Shuah.

3 And Jokshan begat Sheba, and Dedan. And the sons of Dedan were Asshurim, and Letushim, and Leummim.

4 And the sons of *a*Midian; Ephah, and Epher, and Hanoch, and Abida, and Eldaah. All these *were* the children of *b*Keturah.

5 ¶ And *a*Abraham *b*gave all that he had unto Isaac.

6 But unto the sons of the *a*concubines, which Abraham had, Abraham gave gifts, and *b*sent them away from Isaac his son, while he yet lived, eastward, unto the *c*east country.

7 And these *are* the *a*days of the years of *b*Abraham's life which he lived, an hundred threescore and fifteen years.

8 Then Abraham gave up the

56*a* Gen. 24:21.
59*a* Gen. 35:8.
60*a* Gen. 17:16; 25:23;
     Moses 4:26.
   b Gen. 22:17.
   c TG Hate.
62*a* Gen. 16:14; 25:11.
63*a* D&C 76:19;
     JS—H 1:44.
     TG Meditation.

64*a* IE she dismounted.
67*a* TG Comfort.
   b Gen. 23:2.
25 2*a* 2 Ne. 20:26.
   b Ex. 2:16 (15–16);
     18:1 (1–11);
     1 Chr. 1:32 (32–33).
  4*a* Ex. 2:16 (16–22).
   b 1 Chr. 1:32 (32–33).
  5*a* TG Patriarch.

   b Gen. 24:36.
  6*a* Jacob 2:27 (23–30); 3:5;
     Mosiah 11:2 (2–14);
     Ether 10:5;
     D&C 132:1 (1, 37).
   b Gen. 21:14.
   c Judg. 6:3.
  7*a* Gen. 47:9.
   b Gen. 35:28; 47:28.

ghost, and died in a good *a*old age, an old man, and full *of years*; and was *b*gathered to his people.

9 And his sons Isaac and Ishmael *a*buried him in the cave of *b*Machpelah, in the field of Ephron the son of Zohar the Hittite, which *is* before Mamre;

10 The field which Abraham *a*purchased of the sons of Heth: there was Abraham *b*buried, and Sarah his wife.

11 ¶ And it came to pass after the death of Abraham, that God blessed his son Isaac; and Isaac dwelt by the *a*well Lahai-roi.

12 ¶ Now these *are* the *a*generations of Ishmael, Abraham's son, whom *b*Hagar the Egyptian, Sarah's handmaid, *c*bare unto Abraham:

13 And these *are* the names of the sons of *a*Ishmael, by their names, according to their generations: the firstborn of Ishmael, Nebajoth; and Kedar, and Adbeel, and Mibsam,

14 And Mishma, and Dumah, and Massa,

15 Hadar, and Tema, Jetur, Naphish, and Kedemah:

16 These *are* the sons of Ishmael, and these *are* their names, by their towns, and by their castles; *a*twelve princes according to their nations.

17 And these *are* the years of the life of Ishmael, an hundred and thirty and seven years: and he gave up the ghost and died; and was gathered unto his people.

18 And they dwelt from *a*Havilah unto *b*Shur, that *is* before Egypt, as thou goest toward Assyria: *and*

he died in the presence of all his brethren.

19 ¶ And these *are* the generations of Isaac, Abraham's son: *a*Abraham begat Isaac:

20 And Isaac was forty years old when he took Rebekah to wife, the daughter of *a*Bethuel the Syrian of *b*Padan-aram, the sister to Laban the Syrian.

21 And Isaac entreated the Lord for his *a*wife, because she *was* *b*barren: and the Lord was *c*entreated of him, and Rebekah his wife conceived.

22 And the children struggled together within her; and she said, If *it be* so, why *am* I thus? And she went to *a*inquire of the Lord.

23 And the Lord said unto her, *a*Two nations *are* in thy womb, and two manner of people shall be separated from thy bowels; and *the one* people shall be stronger than *the other* people; and the *b*elder shall serve the younger.

24 ¶ And when her days to be delivered were fulfilled, behold, *there were* twins in her womb.

25 And the first came out red, all over like an *a*hairy garment; and they called his name *b*Esau.

26 And after that came his brother out, and his hand took hold on Esau's *a*heel; and his *b*name was called *c*Jacob: and Isaac *was* threescore years old when she bare them.

27 And the boys grew: and Esau was a cunning *a*hunter, a man of the field; and Jacob *was* a *b*plain man, dwelling in *c*tents.

8*a* TG Old Age.
 b TG Family, Eternal.
9*a* Gen. 35:29.
 b Gen. 23:9 (9, 19); 49:30.
10*a* Gen. 23:16.
 b Gen. 49:31; 50:13.
11*a* Gen. 24:62.
12*a* TG Seed of Abraham.
 b D&C 132:34, 65.
 c Gen. 16:15.
13*a* Gen. 28:9;
  1 Chr. 1:29 (29–31).
16*a* Gen. 17:20.
18*a* Gen. 2:11.
 b Gen. 16:7; 1 Sam. 15:7.
19*a* Matt. 1:2.

20*a* Gen. 22:23.
 b Gen. 28:2.
21*a* TG Marriage, Husbands;
  Marriage, Wives.
 b TG Barren.
 c 1 Chr. 5:20;
  2 Chr. 33:13;
  Ezra 8:23.
22*a* TG Prayer.
23*a* Gen. 17:16; 24:60.
 b Gen. 27:40;
  Rom. 9:12;
  1 Ne. 3:29; 18:10.
25*a* Gen. 27:11.
 b Deut. 23:7.
26*a* Hosea 12:3.

 b Gen. 32:28 (24–32).
 c Gen. 27:36;
  1 Ne. 5:14;
  2 Ne. 20:21;
  Alma 7:25;
  D&C 27:10; 132:37;
  133:55.
27*a* Gen. 27:3 (3–5);
  Ether 2:1; 10:19.
 b HEB whole, complete,
  perfect, simple, plain.
 c Heb. 11:9;
  Enos 1:20;
  Hel. 3:9;
  Ether 2:13;
  D&C 61:25; Abr. 2:20.

28 And Isaac loved Esau, because he did eat of *his* [a]venison: but [b]Rebekah loved Jacob.

29 ¶ And Jacob sod pottage: and Esau came from the field, and he *was* faint:

30 And Esau said to Jacob, Feed me, I pray thee, with that same red *pottage*; for I *am* faint: therefore was his name called [a]Edom.

31 And Jacob said, Sell me this day thy [a]birthright.

32 And Esau said, Behold, I *am* at the point to die: and what profit shall this birthright do to me?

33 And Jacob said, Swear to me this day; and he sware unto him: and he sold his birthright unto Jacob.

34 Then Jacob gave Esau bread and pottage of lentiles; and he did eat and drink, and rose up, and went his way: thus Esau despised *his* birthright.

CHAPTER 26

The Lord promises Isaac posterity as the stars of heaven in number—In his seed, all nations will be blessed—The Lord prospers Isaac, temporally and spiritually, for Abraham's sake—Isaac offers sacrifices—Esau marries Hittite wives to the sorrow of his parents.

AND there was a [a]famine in the land, beside the first famine that was in the days of Abraham. And Isaac went unto [b]Abimelech king of the [c]Philistines unto Gerar.

2 And the LORD appeared unto him, and said, Go not down into Egypt; dwell in the land which I shall tell thee of:

3 [a]Sojourn in this land, and I will be with thee, and will [b]bless thee;

for unto thee, and unto thy seed, I will give all these [c]countries, and I will perform the [d]oath which I sware unto Abraham thy father;

4 And I will make thy [a]seed to multiply as the stars of heaven, and will give unto thy seed all these countries; and in thy seed shall all the [b]nations of the earth be blessed;

5 Because that Abraham [a]obeyed my voice, and kept my [b]charge, my commandments, my statutes, and my laws.

6 ¶ And Isaac dwelt in [a]Gerar:

7 And the men of the place asked *him* of his wife; and he said, She *is* my [a]sister: for he feared to say, *She is* my wife; lest, *said he,* the men of the place should kill me for Rebekah; because she *was* [b]fair to look upon.

8 And it came to pass, when he had been there a long time, that Abimelech king of the Philistines looked out at a window, and saw, and, behold, Isaac *was* sporting with Rebekah his wife.

9 And Abimelech called Isaac, and said, Behold, of a surety she *is* thy wife: and how saidst thou, She *is* my sister? And Isaac said unto him, Because I said, Lest I die for her.

10 And [a]Abimelech said, What *is* this thou hast done unto us? one of the people might lightly have [b]lien with thy wife, and thou shouldest have [c]brought guiltiness upon us.

11 And Abimelech charged all *his* people, saying, He that toucheth this man or his wife shall surely be put to death.

12 Then Isaac sowed in that land, and received in the same year an [a]hundredfold: and the LORD [b]blessed him.

28a Gen. 27:4 (4–31).
  b Gen. 27:6.
30a IE Red.
   Gen. 36:1 (1, 8).
31a TG Birthright.
26 1a TG Famine.
   b Gen. 20:2.
   c Gen. 21:34.
  3a Ps. 39:12;
   Acts 7:6 (2–8);
   Heb. 11:9;
   1 Ne. 17:4 (3–4);

Abr. 2:21.
  b Ether 1:43 (42–43).
  c TG Israel, Land of;
   Promised Lands.
  d TG Covenants.
 4a TG Seed of Abraham.
  b TG Abrahamic
   Covenant;
   Israel, Mission of.
 5a D&C 132:29.
   TG Good Works;
   Obedience.

 b TG Stewardship.
 6a Gen. 20:1.
 7a Gen. 12:13 (9–20);
   20:5 (1–18).
  b Gen. 24:16;
   Abr. 2:22 (21–25).
10a Gen. 20:9.
  b OR lain.
  c Gen. 20:9.
12a D&C 98:25.
  b Gen. 24:35; Job 42:12;
   D&C 136:11.

13 ^aAnd the man waxed ^bgreat, and went forward, and grew until he became very great:

14 For he had possession of flocks, and possession of herds, and great store of servants: and the Philistines ^aenvied him.

15 For all the ^awells which his father's servants had digged in the days of Abraham his father, the Philistines ^bhad stopped them, and filled them with earth.

16 And Abimelech said unto Isaac, Go from us; for thou art much ^amightier than we.

17 ¶ And Isaac departed thence, and pitched his tent in the valley of Gerar, and dwelt there.

18 And Isaac digged again the wells of water, which they had digged in the days of Abraham his father; for the Philistines had stopped them after the death of Abraham: and he called their ^anames after the names by which his father had called them.

19 And Isaac's servants digged in the valley, and found there a well of springing water.

20 And the herdmen of Gerar did ^astrive with Isaac's herdmen, saying, The water is ours: and he called the name of the well ^bEsek; because they strove with him.

21 And they digged another well, and strove for that also: and he called the name of it ^aSitnah.

22 And he ^aremoved from thence, and digged another well; and for that they ^bstrove not: and he called the name of it ^cRehoboth; and he said, For now the LORD hath made room for us, and we shall be ^dfruitful in the land.

23 And he went up from thence to ^aBeer-sheba.

24 And the ^aLORD appeared unto him the same night, and said, I am the God of Abraham thy father: ^bfear not, for ^cI am with thee, and will bless thee, and multiply thy ^dseed for my servant Abraham's sake.

25 And he builded an ^aaltar there, and called upon the ^bname of the LORD, and pitched his tent there: and there Isaac's servants digged a well.

26 ¶ Then Abimelech went to him from Gerar, and Ahuzzath one of his friends, and ^aPhichol the chief captain of his army.

27 And Isaac said unto them, Wherefore come ye to me, seeing ye ^ahate me, and have sent me away from you?

28 And they said, We saw certainly that the ^aLORD was with thee: and we said, Let there be now an oath betwixt us, even betwixt us and thee, and let us make a covenant with thee;

29 That thou wilt do us no hurt, as we have not touched thee, and as we have done unto thee nothing but good, and have sent thee away in ^apeace: thou art now the ^bblessed of the LORD.

30 And he made them a feast, and they did eat and drink.

31 And they ^arose up betimes in the morning, and ^bsware one to another: and Isaac sent them away, and they departed from him in peace.

32 And it came to pass the same day, that Isaac's servants came, and told him concerning the well which they had digged, and said unto him, We have found water.

13a HEB And the man continually increased in wealth until he was very wealthy.
  b Gen. 24:35 (34–35); 30:43.
14a Eccl. 4:4.
15a Gen. 21:30.
  b Gen. 21:25.
16a Ex. 1:9.
18a Gen. 21:31.
20a Gen. 21:25.
  b IE Strife.

21a IE Opposition.
22a TG Patience.
  b Prov. 15:1.
  c IE Broad open places.
  d Gen. 17:6; 28:3; 41:52;
    Ex. 1:7;
    Mosiah 25:24;
    Alma 62:51 (50–51).
23a Gen. 46:1.
24a Abr. 3:11.
  b Gen. 15:1; Isa. 41:10;
    D&C 68:6.

  c Gen. 28:15; 31:3.
  d TG Seed of Abraham.
25a Gen. 12:7; 13:18;
    1 Ne. 2:7.
  b TG Name.
26a Gen. 21:22.
27a TG Forbear.
28a Gen. 21:22.
29a TG Peacemakers.
  b Gen. 24:31.
31a HEB arose early.
  b Gen. 21:27 (27–32).

33 And he called it Shebah: therefore the name of the city *is* ᵃBeersheba unto this day.

34 ¶ And Esau was forty years old when he took to ᵃwife Judith the daughter of Beeri the Hittite, and Bashemath the daughter of Elon the Hittite:

35 Which were a ᵃgrief of mind unto Isaac and to Rebekah.

CHAPTER 27

Rebekah guides Jacob in seeking blessings—Jacob is blessed to have dominion and rule over peoples and nations—Esau hates Jacob and plans to slay him—Rebekah fears that Jacob may marry one of the daughters of Heth.

AND it came to pass, that when Isaac was old, and his eyes were ᵃdim, so that he could not see, he called Esau his eldest son, and said unto him, My son: and he said unto him, Behold, *here am* I.

2 And he said, Behold now, I am old, I know not the day of my death:

3 Now therefore take, I pray thee, thy weapons, thy ᵃquiver and thy bow, and go out to the field, and ᵇtake me *some* venison;

4 And make me ᵃsavoury meat, such as I love, and bring *it* to me, that I may eat; that my soul may bless thee before I die.

5 And Rebekah heard when Isaac spake to Esau his son. And Esau went to the field to hunt *for* venison, *and* to bring *it*.

6 ¶ And ᵃRebekah spake unto Jacob her son, saying, Behold, I heard thy father speak unto Esau thy brother, saying,

7 Bring me venison, and make me savoury meat, that I may eat, and bless thee before the LORD before my death.

8 Now therefore, my son, obey my voice according to that which I command thee.

9 Go now to the flock, and fetch me from thence two good kids of the goats; and I will make them savoury meat for thy father, such as he loveth:

10 And thou shalt bring *it* to thy father, that he may eat, and that he may bless thee before his death.

11 And Jacob said to Rebekah his mother, Behold, Esau my brother *is* a ᵃhairy man, and I *am* a smooth man:

12 My father peradventure will feel me, and I shall seem to him as a deceiver; and I shall bring a curse upon me, and not a blessing.

13 And his mother said unto him, Upon me *be* thy curse, my son: only obey my voice, and go fetch me *them*.

14 And he went, and fetched, and brought *them* to his mother: and his mother made savoury meat, such as his father loved.

15 And Rebekah took goodly raiment of her eldest son Esau, which *were* with her in the house, and put them upon Jacob her younger son:

16 And she put the ᵃskins of the kids of the goats upon his hands, and upon the smooth of his neck:

17 And she gave the savoury meat and the bread, which she had prepared, into the hand of her son Jacob.

18 ¶ And he came unto his father, and said, My father: and he said, Here *am* I; who *art* thou, my son?

19 And Jacob said unto his father, I *am* Esau thy firstborn; I have done according as thou badest me: arise, I pray thee, sit and eat of my venison, that thy soul may bless me.

20 And Isaac said unto his son, How *is it* that thou hast found *it* so quickly, my son? And he said, Because the LORD thy God brought *it* to me.

21 And Isaac said unto Jacob, Come near, I pray thee, that I may feel thee, my son, whether thou *be* my very son Esau or not.

33a IE Well of an oath.
    Gen. 21:31.
34a TG Marriage, Interfaith.
35a HEB bitterness of spirit
    (meaning great sorrow

    or grief).
27 1a Gen. 48:10.
    3a Gen. 25:27.
    b HEB hunt.
    4a Gen. 25:28.

    6a Gen. 25:28.
    11a Gen. 25:25.
    16a Alma 49:6;
        Moses 4:27.

22 And Jacob went near unto Isaac his father; and he felt him, and said, The voice *is* Jacob's voice, but the hands *are* the hands of Esau.

23 And he discerned him not, because his hands were hairy, as his brother Esau's hands: so he blessed him.

24 And he said, *Art* thou my very son Esau? And he said, I *am*.

25 And he said, Bring *it* near to me, and I will eat of my son's venison, that my soul may bless thee. And he brought *it* near to him, and he did eat: and he brought him wine, and he drank.

26 And his father Isaac said unto him, Come near now, and kiss me, my son.

27 And he came *ᵃ*near, and kissed him: and he smelled the smell of his raiment, and *ᵇ*blessed him, and said, See, the smell of my son *is* as the smell of a field which the LORD hath blessed:

28 Therefore God give thee of the *ᵃ*dew of heaven, and the fatness of the earth, and plenty of corn and wine:

29 Let people *ᵃ*serve thee, and nations bow down to thee: be lord over thy brethren, and let thy mother's sons *ᵇ*bow down to thee: cursed *be* every one that curseth thee, and *ᶜ*blessed *be* he that *ᵈ*blesseth thee.

30 ¶ And it came to pass, as soon as Isaac had made an end of blessing Jacob, and Jacob was yet scarce gone out from the presence of Isaac his father, that Esau his brother came in from his hunting.

31 And he also had made savoury meat, and brought it unto his father, and said unto his father, Let my father arise, and eat of his son's venison, that thy soul may bless me.

32 And Isaac his father said unto him, Who *art* thou? And he said, I *am* thy son, thy firstborn Esau.

33 And Isaac trembled very exceedingly, and said, Who? where *is* he that hath *ᵃ*taken venison, and brought *it* me, and I have eaten of all before thou camest, and have *ᵇ*blessed him? yea, *and* he shall be blessed.

34 And when Esau heard the words of his father, he cried with a great and exceeding bitter cry, and said unto his father, Bless me, *even* me also, O my father.

35 And he said, Thy brother came with subtilty, and hath taken away thy blessing.

36 And he said, Is not he rightly named *ᵃ*Jacob? for he hath supplanted me these two times: he took away my *ᵇ*birthright; and, behold, now he hath taken away my blessing. And he said, Hast thou not reserved a blessing for me?

37 And Isaac answered and said unto Esau, Behold, I have made him thy lord, and all his brethren have I given to him for *ᵃ*servants; and with corn and wine have I sustained him: and what shall I do now unto thee, my son?

38 And Esau said unto his father, Hast thou but one blessing, my father? bless me, *even* me also, O my father. And Esau lifted up his voice, and *ᵃ*wept.

39 And Isaac his father answered and said unto him, Behold, thy dwelling shall be the fatness of the earth, and of the dew of heaven from above;

40 And by thy sword shalt thou live, and shalt serve thy *ᵃ*brother; and it shall come to pass when thou shalt have the dominion, that thou shalt *ᵇ*break his *ᶜ*yoke from off thy neck.

41 ¶ And Esau hated Jacob because

27*a* Gen. 48:10.
  b Heb. 11:20.
28*a* Deut. 33:13, 28;
      D&C 121:45.
29*a* TG Israel, Blessings of.
  b Gen. 49:8;
      1 Ne. 7:20.
  c TG Abrahamic

Covenant.
  d TG Blessing.
33*a* HEB hunted game.
  b Gen. 28:3.
36*a* IE A supplanter.
      Gen. 25:26.
  b TG Birthright.
37*a* 2 Sam. 8:14.

38*a* Heb. 12:17;
      1 Ne. 17:7;
      Alma 31:26;
      3 Ne. 17:22 (21–22);
      Moses 7:44 (41–58).
40*a* Gen. 25:23.
  b 2 Kgs. 8:20 (20–22).
  c TG Bondage, Physical.

of the blessing wherewith his father blessed him: and Esau said in his heart, The days of mourning for my father are at hand; then will I slay my brother Jacob.

42 And these words of Esau her elder son were told to Rebekah: and she sent and called Jacob her younger son, and said unto him, Behold, thy brother Esau, as touching thee, doth comfort himself, *purposing* to kill thee.

43 Now therefore, my son, obey my voice; and arise, *a*flee thou to Laban my *b*brother to *c*Haran;

44 And tarry with him a few days, until thy brother's fury turn away;

45 Until thy brother's *a*anger turn away from thee, and he forget *that* which thou hast done to him: then I will send, and fetch thee from thence: why should I be deprived also of you both in one day?

46 And Rebekah said to Isaac, I am weary of my life because of the *a*daughters of Heth: if Jacob take a wife of the daughters of Heth, such as these *which are* of the daughters of the land, what good shall my life do me?

CHAPTER 28

Isaac forbids Jacob to marry a Canaanite—He blesses Jacob and his seed with the blessings of Abraham—Esau marries a daughter of Ishmael—Jacob sees in vision a ladder reaching up into heaven—The Lord promises him seed as the dust of the earth in number—The Lord also promises Jacob that in him and in his seed all the families of the earth will be blessed—Jacob covenants to pay tithes.

AND Isaac called Jacob, and blessed him, and charged him, and said unto him, Thou shalt not take a *a*wife of the daughters of *b*Canaan.

2 Arise, go to *a*Padan-aram, to the house of *b*Bethuel thy mother's father; and take thee a wife from thence of the daughters of *c*Laban thy mother's brother.

3 And God *a*Almighty *b*bless thee, and make thee *c*fruitful, and multiply thee, that thou mayest be a *d*multitude of people;

4 And give thee the blessing of Abraham, to thee, and to thy *a*seed with thee; that thou mayest inherit the land wherein thou art a stranger, which God gave unto Abraham.

5 And Isaac sent away Jacob: and he went to Padan-aram unto Laban, son of Bethuel the *a*Syrian, the brother of Rebekah, Jacob's and Esau's mother.

6 ¶ When Esau saw that Isaac had blessed Jacob, and sent him away to Padan-aram, to take him a wife from thence; and that as he blessed him he gave him a charge, saying, Thou shalt not take a wife of the daughters of Canaan;

7 And that Jacob obeyed his father and his mother, and was gone to Padan-aram;

8 And Esau seeing that the daughters of Canaan pleased not Isaac his father;

9 Then went Esau unto *a*Ishmael, and took unto the wives which he had Mahalath the daughter of Ishmael Abraham's son, the sister of Nebajoth, to be his *b*wife.

10 ¶ And Jacob went out from Beer-sheba, and went toward Haran.

11 And he lighted upon a certain place, and tarried there all night, because the sun was set; and he took of the stones of that place, and put *them for* his pillows, and lay down in that place to sleep.

12 And he *a*dreamed, and behold a

43*a* Gen. 35:1.
  b Gen. 24:4.
  c Gen. 24:10; 29:4.
45*a* TG Anger.
46*a* TG Marriage, Interfaith.
28 1*a* TG Marriage, Wives.
  b Gen. 24:3.
  2*a* Gen. 25:20.

  b Gen. 22:23.
  c Gen. 25:20.
3*a* TG God, Power of.
  b Gen. 27:33.
  c Gen. 8:17; 9:7; 26:22;
    35:11; 41:52.
  d Gen. 12:2.
4*a* TG Seed of Abraham.

5*a* HEB Aramean.
  Deut. 26:5;
  Hosea 12:12.
9*a* Gen. 25:13; 36:3 (1–8).
  b TG Marriage,
    Interfaith.
12*a* TG Dream.

ladder set up on the earth, and the top of it reached to heaven: and behold the *b*angels of God ascending and descending on it.

13 And, behold, the *a*LORD stood *b*above it, and said, I *am* the *c*LORD God of Abraham thy father, and the God of Isaac: the *d*land whereon thou liest, to thee will I give it, and to thy seed;

14 And thy seed shall be as the dust of the earth, and thou shalt spread abroad to the west, and to the east, and to the *a*north, and to the south: and in thee and in thy *b*seed shall all the *c*families of the earth be *d*blessed.

15 And, behold, *a*I *am* with thee, and will keep thee in all *places* whither thou goest, and will *b*bring thee again into this *c*land; for I will not leave thee, until I have done *that* which I have spoken to thee of.

16 ¶ And Jacob awaked out of his sleep, and he said, Surely the LORD is in this place; and I knew *it* not.

17 And he was afraid, and said, How dreadful *is* this place! this *is* none other but the house of God, and this *is* the gate of *a*heaven.

18 And Jacob rose up early in the morning, and took the stone that he had put *for* his pillows, and set it up *for* a *a*pillar, and poured oil upon the top of it.

19 And he called the name of that place *a*Beth-el: but the name of that city *was called* *b*Luz at the first.

20 And Jacob vowed a *a*vow, saying, If God will be with me, and will keep me in this way that I go, and will give me bread to eat, and raiment to put on,

21 So that I come again to my father's house in peace; then shall the *a*LORD be my God:

22 And this stone, which I have set *for* a pillar, shall be God's house: and of all that thou shalt give me I will surely give the *a*tenth unto thee.

CHAPTER 29

Jacob meets Rachel at the well—He serves Laban seven years for her—Laban gives to Jacob first Leah then Rachel in marriage—Jacob serves another seven years—Leah bears Reuben, Simeon, Levi, and Judah.

THEN Jacob went on his journey, and came into the land of the people of the east.

2 And he looked, and behold a well in the field, and, lo, there *were* three flocks of sheep lying by it; for out of that well they watered the flocks: and a great stone *was* upon the well's mouth.

3 And thither were all the flocks gathered: and they rolled the stone from the well's mouth, and watered the sheep, and put the stone again upon the well's mouth in his place.

4 And Jacob said unto them, My brethren, whence *be* ye? And they said, Of *a*Haran *are* we.

5 And he said unto them, Know ye *a*Laban the son of Nahor? And they said, We know *him*.

6 And he said unto them, *Is* he well? And they said, *He is* well: and, behold, Rachel his daughter cometh with the sheep.

7 And he said, Lo, *it is* yet high day, neither *is it* time that the cattle should be gathered together: water ye the sheep, and go *and* feed *them*.

---

12 *b* TG Angels.
13 *a* Hosea 12:4 (3–5).
  b OR beside him.
  c TG Jesus Christ, Jehovah.
  d TG Promised Lands.
14 *a* TG Israel, Ten Lost Tribes of.
  b TG Priesthood, History of; Seed of Abraham.
  c TG Abrahamic

Covenant.
  d TG Israel, Blessings of; Israel, Mission of.
15 *a* Gen. 26:24; 46:4.
  b TG Israel, Bondage of, in Egypt.
  c TG Israel, Land of.
17 *a* TG Heaven.
18 *a* Gen. 31:13 (13, 45); 35:14.
19 *a* IE House of God.

Gen. 12:8 (7–8);
Josh. 16:2 (1–2);
2 Kgs. 2:2;
Abr. 2:20.
  b Gen. 35:6; 48:3.
20 *a* TG Vow.
21 *a* Gen. 31:13;
Deut. 26:17 (16–19).
22 *a* TG Tithing.
29 4 *a* Gen. 27:43.
  5 *a* Gen. 24:29.

8 And they said, We cannot, until all *the flocks be gathered together, and *till* they roll the stone from the well's mouth; then we water the sheep.

9 ¶ And while he yet spake with them, Rachel came with her father's sheep: for she kept them.

10 And it came to pass, when Jacob saw Rachel the daughter of Laban his mother's brother, and the sheep of Laban his mother's brother, that Jacob went near, and rolled the stone from the well's mouth, and *watered the flock of Laban his mother's brother.

11 And Jacob kissed Rachel, and lifted up his voice, and wept.

12 And Jacob told Rachel that he *was* her father's brother, and that he *was* Rebekah's son: and she ran and told her father.

13 And it came to pass, when Laban heard the tidings of Jacob his sister's son, that he ran to meet him, and embraced him, and kissed him, and brought him to his house. And he told Laban all these things.

14 And Laban said to him, Surely thou *art* my bone and my *flesh. And he abode with him the space of a month.

15 ¶ And Laban said unto Jacob, Because thou *art* my brother, shouldest thou therefore serve me for nought? tell me, what *shall* thy wages *be?*

16 And Laban had two daughters: the name of the elder *was* Leah, and the name of the younger *was* Rachel.

17 Leah *was* tender eyed; but Rachel *was* *beautiful and well *favoured.

18 And Jacob loved Rachel; and said, I will *serve thee seven years for Rachel thy younger daughter.

19 And Laban said, *It is* better that I give her to thee, than that I should give her to another man: abide with me.

20 And Jacob served seven years for *Rachel; and they seemed unto him *but* a few days, for the *love he had to her.

21 ¶ And Jacob said unto Laban, Give *me* my wife, for my days are fulfilled, that I may go in unto her.

22 And Laban gathered together all the men of the place, and made a *feast.

23 And it came to pass in the evening, that he took Leah his daughter, and brought her to him; and he went in unto her.

24 And Laban gave unto his daughter Leah *Zilpah his maid *for* an handmaid.

25 And it came to pass, that in the morning, behold, it *was* Leah: and he said to Laban, What *is* this thou hast done unto me? did not I serve with thee for Rachel? wherefore then hast thou beguiled me?

26 And Laban said, It must not be so done in our country, to give the younger before the *firstborn.

27 Fulfil her week, and we will give thee this also for the service which thou shalt serve with me yet seven other years.

28 And Jacob did so, and fulfilled her week: and he gave him Rachel his daughter to wife also.

29 And Laban gave to Rachel his daughter *Bilhah his handmaid to be her maid.

30 And he went in also unto Rachel, and he *loved also Rachel more than Leah, and *served with him yet seven other years.

31 ¶ And when the LORD saw that Leah *was* hated, he opened her womb: but Rachel *was* *barren.

32 And *Leah conceived, and bare a son, and she called his name *Reuben: for she said, Surely the LORD

8*a* Samaritan and Septuagint: the shepherds.
10*a* Gen. 24:10.
14*a* Gen. 2:23.
17*a* TG Beauty.
  b Gen. 39:6.

18*a* Gen. 31:41.
20*a* Hosea 12:12.
  b TG Love.
22*a* Judg. 14:10.
24*a* Gen. 46:18.
26*a* TG Firstborn.
29*a* Gen. 46:25.

30*a* Gen. 30:15.
  b Gen. 30:26.
31*a* TG Barren.
32*a* Gen. 46:15.
  b IE Look, a son.
    Gen. 35:23 (2, 23); 49:3;
    1 Chr. 2:1; 5:1.

hath looked upon my affliction; now therefore my husband will love me.

33 And she conceived again, and bare a son; and said, Because the LORD hath heard that I *was* ᵃhated, he hath therefore given me this *son* also: and she called his name ᵇSimeon.

34 And she conceived again, and bare a son; and said, Now this time will my husband be joined unto me, because I have born him three sons: therefore was his name called ᵃLevi.

35 And she conceived again, and bare a son: and she said, Now will I ᵃpraise the LORD: therefore she called his name ᵇJudah; and left bearing.

CHAPTER 30

Jacob marries Bilhah, and she bears Dan and Naphtali—He marries Zilpah, and she bears Gad and Asher—Leah bears Issachar and Zebulun and a daughter, Dinah—Then Rachel conceives and bears Joseph—Jacob works for Laban for wages of cattle and sheep.

AND when Rachel saw that she bare Jacob no children, Rachel ᵃenvied her sister; and said unto Jacob, Give me children, or else I die.

2 And Jacob's anger was kindled against Rachel: and he said, *Am I* in ᵃGod's stead, who hath withheld from thee the fruit of the womb?

3 And she said, Behold my maid Bilhah, go in unto her; and she shall bear upon my knees, that I may also ᵃhave children by her.

4 And she gave him ᵃBilhah her handmaid to wife: and Jacob went in unto her.

5 And ᵃBilhah conceived, and bare Jacob a son.

6 And Rachel said, God hath judged me, and hath also heard my voice, and hath given me a son: therefore called she his name ᵃDan.

7 And Bilhah Rachel's maid conceived again, and bare Jacob a second son.

8 And Rachel said, ᵃWith great wrestlings have I wrestled with my sister, and I have prevailed: and she called his name ᵇNaphtali.

9 When Leah saw that she had left bearing, she took Zilpah her maid, and gave her Jacob to wife.

10 And Zilpah Leah's maid bare Jacob a son.

11 And Leah said, A ᵃtroop cometh: and she called his name ᵇGad.

12 And ᵃZilpah Leah's maid bare Jacob a second son.

13 And Leah said, Happy am I, for the daughters will call me ᵃblessed: and she called his name ᵇAsher.

14 ¶ And Reuben went in the days of wheat harvest, and found ᵃmandrakes in the field, and brought them unto his mother Leah. Then Rachel said to Leah, Give me, I pray thee, of thy son's mandrakes.

15 And she said unto her, *Is it* a small matter that thou hast ᵃtaken my husband? and wouldest thou take away my son's mandrakes also? And Rachel said, Therefore he shall lie with thee to night for thy son's mandrakes.

16 And Jacob came out of the field in the evening, and Leah went out to meet him, and said, Thou must come

---

33a Deut. 21:15.
  b IE Hearing.
    Gen. 49:5.
34a IE Joined, or Pledged.
    Num. 18:2 (2–4).
35a Gen. 49:8; 1 Ne. 18:16;
    Mosiah 2:20 (20–21);
    D&C 136:28.
  b IE Praise.
    TG Israel, Judah,
    People of.
30 1a Gen. 16:5 (4–16);
    1 Sam. 1:6 (1–20).

TG Envy.
2a 2 Kgs. 5:7.
3a HEB be built up by her
   (Gen. 16:2).
4a D&C 132:37.
5a Gen. 46:25.
6a IE He has judged, or
   vindicated.
   Gen. 49:16 (16–18);
   1 Chr. 2:2.
8a HEB The wrestlings of
   God have I wrestled
   with my sister.

  b IE My wrestling.
    Gen. 49:21; 2 Ne. 19:1.
11a Gen. 49:19.
  b IE Good fortune (word-
    play on the Hebrew
    words *gedud*, "troop,"
    and *gad*, "fortune").
12a Gen. 46:18.
13a TG Blessing.
  b IE Happy, Blessed.
    Gen. 49:20.
14a TG Superstitions.
15a Gen. 29:30.

in unto me; for surely I have hired thee with my son's mandrakes. And he lay with her that night.

17 And God hearkened unto Leah, and she conceived, and bare Jacob the fifth son.

18 And Leah said, God hath given me my *hire, because I have given my maiden to my husband: and she called his name *Issachar.

19 And Leah conceived again, and bare Jacob the sixth son.

20 And Leah said, God hath endued me *with* a good dowry; now will my husband *dwell with me, because I have born him six sons: and she called his name *Zebulun.

21 And afterwards she bare a daughter, and called her name Dinah.

22 ¶ And God *remembered Rachel, and God hearkened to her, and opened her womb.

23 And she conceived, and bare a son; and said, God hath taken away my *reproach:

24 And she called his name *Joseph; and said, The Lord shall add to me another son.

25 ¶ And it came to pass, when Rachel had born Joseph, that Jacob said unto Laban, Send me away, that I may go unto mine own place, and to my country.

26 Give *me* my wives and my children, for whom I have *served thee, and let me go: for thou knowest my service which I have done thee.

27 And Laban said unto him, I pray thee, if I have found favour in thine eyes, *tarry: for* I have learned by experience that the Lord hath *blessed me for thy *sake.

28 And he said, Appoint me thy wages, and I will give *it*.

29 And he said unto him, Thou knowest how I have served thee, and how thy cattle was with me.

30 For *it was* little which thou hadst before I *came,* and it is *now* increased unto a multitude; and the Lord hath blessed thee since my coming: and now when shall I provide for mine own house also?

31 And he said, What shall I give thee? And Jacob said, Thou shalt not give me any thing: if thou wilt do this thing for me, I will again feed *and* keep thy flock:

32 I will pass through all thy flock to day, removing from thence all the speckled and spotted *cattle, and all the brown cattle among the sheep, and the spotted and speckled among the goats: and *of such* shall be my hire.

33 So shall my *righteousness answer for me in time to come, when it shall come for my hire before thy face: every one that *is* not speckled and spotted among the goats, and brown among the sheep, that shall be counted stolen with me.

34 And Laban said, Behold, I would it might be according to thy word.

35 And he removed that day the he goats that were ringstraked and spotted, and all the she goats that were speckled and spotted, *and* every one that had *some* white in it, and all the brown among the sheep, and gave *them* into the hand of his sons.

36 And he set three days' journey betwixt himself and Jacob: and Jacob fed the rest of Laban's flocks.

37 ¶ And Jacob took him rods of green poplar, and of the *hazel and

---

18a OR recompense.
  b IE (perhaps) There is a
    recompense.
    Gen. 49:14 (14–15).
20a OR honor me, exalt me.
  b The Hebrew *zevul*
    means "exalted abode";
    see in Isa. 63:15.
    Gen. 49:13;
    2 Ne. 19:1.
22a Gen. 21:1 (1–3);
    1 Sam. 1:19 (19–20).

23a TG Barren;
    Reproach.
24a "Joseph" relates both to
    the Hebrew root *yasaph,*
    "to add," and to *asaph,*
    meaning both "to take
    away" and "to gather."
    The context plays upon
    all of these meanings.
    TG Israel, Joseph,
    People of.
26a Gen. 29:30 (20, 30).

27a TG Blessing.
  b Gen. 39:5 (3–5).
32a HEB sheep. "Cattle" is
    older English for "flock"
    or "herd" as part of one's
    property, or "stock."
    Enos 1:21;
    Ether 9:18;
    Abr. 5:21.
33a D&C 59:23.
37a OR almond.

chestnut tree; and *b*pilled white strakes in them, and made the white appear which *was* in the rods.

38 And he set the rods which he had pilled before the flocks in the gutters in the watering troughs when the flocks came to drink, that they should conceive when they came to drink.

39 And the flocks conceived before the *a*rods, and brought forth cattle ringstraked, speckled, and spotted.

40 And Jacob did separate the lambs, and set the faces of the flocks toward the ringstraked, and all the brown in the flock of Laban; and he put his own flocks by themselves, and put them not unto Laban's cattle.

41 And it came to pass, whensoever the stronger cattle did conceive, that Jacob laid the rods before the eyes of the cattle in the gutters, that they might conceive among the rods.

42 But when the cattle were feeble, he put *them* not in: so the feebler were Laban's, and the stronger Jacob's.

43 And the man *a*increased exceedingly, and had much cattle, and maidservants, and menservants, and camels, and asses.

CHAPTER 31

The Lord commands Jacob to return to Canaan, and Jacob departs secretly—Laban pursues him; they resolve their differences and make a covenant of peace—Laban blesses his descendants, and he and Jacob part company.

AND he heard the words of Laban's sons, saying, Jacob hath taken away all that *was* our father's; and of *that* which *was* our father's hath he gotten all this *a*glory.

2 And Jacob beheld the countenance of Laban, and, behold, it *was* not toward him as before.

3 And the LORD said unto Jacob, *a*Return unto the land of thy fathers, and to thy kindred; and *b*I will be with thee.

4 And *a*Jacob sent and called Rachel and Leah to the field unto his flock,

5 And said unto them, I see your father's countenance, that it *is* not toward me as before; but the God of my father hath been with me.

6 And ye know that with all my power I have served your father.

7 And your father hath deceived me, and changed my wages ten times; but God suffered him not to hurt me.

8 If he said thus, The speckled shall be thy wages; then all the cattle bare speckled: and if he said thus, The ringstraked shall be thy hire; then bare all the cattle ringstraked.

9 Thus God hath taken away the cattle of your father, and given *them* to me.

10 And it came to pass at the time that the *a*cattle conceived, that I lifted up mine eyes, and saw in a dream, and, behold, the rams which leaped upon the cattle *were* ringstraked, speckled, and grisled.

11 And the *a*angel of God spake unto me in a dream, *saying,* Jacob: And I said, Here *am* I.

12 And he said, Lift up now thine eyes, and see, all the rams which leap upon the *a*cattle *are* ringstraked, speckled, and grisled: for I have seen all that Laban doeth unto thee.

13 I *am* the *a*God of Beth-el, where thou anointedst the *b*pillar, *and* where thou vowedst a *c*vow unto me: now arise, get thee out from this land, and return unto the land of thy kindred.

14 And Rachel and Leah answered and said unto him, *Is there* yet any portion or *a*inheritance for us in our father's house?

37*b* HEB peeled.
39*a* TG Superstitions.
43*a* Gen. 24:35 (34–35);
    26:13 (12–15).
31 1*a* OR wealth.

3*a* Gen. 32:9.
  b Gen. 26:24.
4*a* TG Marriage, Husbands.
10*a* HEB flock.
11*a* TG Angels.

12*a* HEB flock.
13*a* Gen. 28:21 (16–22).
  b Gen. 28:18.
  c TG Vow.
14*a* TG Inheritance.

15 Are we not counted of him strangers? for he hath sold us, and hath quite devoured also our money.

16 For all the riches which God hath taken from our father, that *is* ours, and our children's: now then, whatsoever God hath said unto thee, do.

17 ¶ Then Jacob rose up, and set his sons and his wives upon camels;

18 And he carried away all his cattle, and all his goods which he had gotten, the cattle of his getting, which he had gotten in Padan-aram, for to go to Isaac his father in the land of Canaan.

19 And Laban went to shear his sheep: and Rachel had stolen the ^aimages that *were* her father's.

20 And Jacob stole away unawares to Laban the ^aSyrian, in that he told him not that he fled.

21 So he fled with all that he had; and he rose up, and passed over the river, and set his face *toward* the mount Gilead.

22 And it was told Laban on the third day that Jacob was fled.

23 And he took his brethren with him, and pursued after him seven days' journey; and they overtook him in the mount Gilead.

24 And God came to Laban the Syrian in a ^adream by night, and said unto him, Take heed that thou ^bspeak not to Jacob either good or bad.

25 ¶ Then Laban overtook Jacob. Now Jacob had pitched his tent in the mount: and Laban with his brethren pitched in the mount of Gilead.

26 And Laban said to Jacob, What hast thou done, that thou hast stolen away unawares to me, and carried away my daughters, as captives *taken* with the sword?

27 Wherefore didst thou flee away secretly, and steal away from me; and didst not tell me, that I might have sent thee away with mirth, and with songs, with tabret, and with ^aharp?

28 And hast not suffered me to kiss my sons and my daughters? thou hast now done foolishly in *so* doing.

29 It is in the power of my hand to do you hurt: but the God of your father spake unto me yesternight, saying, Take thou heed that thou speak not to Jacob either good or bad.

30 And now, *though* thou wouldest needs be gone, because thou sore longedst after thy father's house, *yet* wherefore hast thou stolen my gods?

31 And Jacob answered and said to Laban, Because I was afraid: for I said, Peradventure thou wouldest take by force thy daughters from me.

32 With whomsoever thou findest thy gods, let him not live: before our brethren discern thou what *is* thine with me, and take *it* to thee. For Jacob knew not that Rachel had stolen them.

33 And Laban went into Jacob's tent, and into Leah's tent, and into the two maidservants' tents; but he found *them* not. Then went he out of Leah's tent, and entered into Rachel's tent.

34 Now Rachel had taken the images, and put them in the camel's furniture, and sat upon them. And Laban searched all the tent, but found *them* not.

35 And she said to her father, Let it not displease my lord that I cannot rise up before thee; for the custom of women *is* upon me. And he searched, but found not the images.

36 ¶ And Jacob was wroth, and chode with Laban: and Jacob answered and said to Laban, What *is* my trespass? what *is* my sin, that thou hast so hotly pursued after me?

37 Whereas thou hast searched all my stuff, what hast thou found of all thy household stuff? set *it* here before my brethren and thy brethren, that they may judge betwixt us both.

38 This twenty years *have* I *been* with thee; thy ewes and thy she goats have not cast their young, and the rams of thy flock have I not eaten.

19a TG Idolatry.
20a HEB Aramean (also v. 24).
24a TG Dream.
  b Gen. 24:50.
27a Gen. 4:21;
  2 Sam. 6:5.

39 That which was ^atorn *of beasts* I brought not unto thee; I bare the loss of it; of my hand didst thou require it, *whether* stolen by day, or stolen by night.

40 *Thus* I was; in the day the ^adrought consumed me, and the frost by night; and my sleep departed from mine eyes.

41 Thus have I been twenty years in thy house; I ^aserved thee fourteen years for thy two daughters, and six years for thy cattle: and thou hast changed my wages ten times.

42 Except the God of my father, the God of Abraham, and the fear of Isaac, had been with me, surely thou hadst sent me away now empty. God hath seen mine affliction and the ^alabour of my hands, and rebuked *thee* yesternight.

43 ¶ And Laban answered and said unto Jacob, *These* daughters *are* my daughters, and *these* children *are* my children, and *these* cattle *are* my cattle, and all that thou seest *is* mine: and what can I do this day unto these my daughters, or unto their children which they have born?

44 Now therefore come thou, let us make a covenant, I and thou; and let it be for a witness between me and thee.

45 And Jacob took a stone, and set it up *for* a ^apillar.

46 And Jacob said unto his brethren, Gather stones; and they took stones, and made an heap: and they did eat there upon the heap.

47 And Laban called it ^aJegar-sahadutha: but Jacob called it ^bGaleed.

48 And Laban said, This heap *is* a witness between me and thee this day. Therefore was the name of it called Galeed;

49 And ^aMizpah; for he said, The LORD ^bwatch between me and thee,

when we are absent one from another.

50 If thou shalt afflict my daughters, or if thou shalt take *other* wives beside my daughters, no man *is* with us; see, God *is* witness betwixt me and thee.

51 And Laban said to Jacob, Behold this heap, and behold *this* pillar, which I have cast betwixt me and thee;

52 This heap *be* witness, and *this* pillar *be* witness, that I will not pass over this heap to thee, and that thou shalt not pass over this heap and this pillar unto me, for harm.

53 The God of Abraham, and the God of Nahor, the God of their father, judge betwixt us. And Jacob sware by the fear of his father Isaac.

54 Then Jacob offered sacrifice upon the mount, and called his brethren to eat bread: and they did eat ^abread, and tarried all night in the mount.

55 And early in the morning Laban rose up, and kissed his sons and his daughters, and blessed them: and Laban departed, and returned unto his place.

CHAPTER 32

Jacob sees angels—He asks God to preserve him from Esau, for whom he prepares presents—He wrestles all night with a messenger of God—Jacob's name is changed to Israel—He sees God face to face.

AND Jacob went on his way, and the angels of God met him.

2 And when Jacob saw them, he said, This *is* God's ^ahost: and he called the name of that place ^bMahanaim.

3 And Jacob sent messengers before him to Esau his brother unto the land of ^aSeir, the country of ^bEdom.

4 And he commanded them,

39a Ex. 22:13 (12–13).
40a TG Drought.
41a Gen. 29:18.
42a TG Industry.
45a Ex. 24:4.
47a IE The heap of witness (in Aramaic).

b IE The heap of witness (in Hebrew).
49a IE The lookout point.
  b TG Watch.
54a Ezek. 44:3 (1–3).
32 2a HEB *mahneh,* "camp."
  D&C 64:24.

b IE Two hosts, or camps.
3a Gen. 36:8 (8–9);
  Deut. 2:5 (4–6);
  Ezek. 35:2 (1–15).
  b Gen. 36:1 (1, 8).

saying, Thus shall ye speak unto my lord Esau; Thy servant Jacob saith thus, I have sojourned with Laban, and stayed there until now:

5 And I have oxen, and asses, and flocks, and menservants, and womenservants: and I have sent to tell my lord, that I may find grace in thy sight.

6 ¶ And the messengers returned to Jacob, saying, We came to thy brother Esau, and also he cometh to meet thee, and four hundred men with him.

7 Then Jacob was greatly afraid and *a*distressed: and he divided the people that *was* with him, and the flocks, and herds, and the camels, into two bands;

8 And said, If Esau come to the one company, and smite it, then the other company which is left shall escape.

9 ¶ And Jacob said, O *a*God of my father Abraham, and God of my father Isaac, the LORD which saidst unto me, *b*Return unto thy country, and to thy kindred, and I will deal well with thee:

10 *a*I am not worthy of the least of all the *b*mercies, and of all the truth, which thou hast shewed unto thy servant; for with my staff I passed over this Jordan; and now I am become two bands.

11 *a*Deliver me, I pray thee, from the hand of my brother, from the hand of Esau: for I fear him, lest he will come and smite me, *and* the mother with the children.

12 And thou saidst, I will surely do thee good, and make thy *a*seed as the *b*sand of the sea, which cannot be numbered for multitude.

13 ¶ And he lodged there that same night; and took of that which came to his hand a present for Esau his brother;

14 Two hundred she goats, and twenty he goats, two hundred ewes, and twenty rams,

15 Thirty milch camels with their colts, forty kine, and ten bulls, twenty she asses, and ten foals.

16 And he delivered *them* into the hand of his servants, every drove by themselves; and said unto his servants, Pass over before me, and put a space betwixt drove and drove.

17 And he commanded the foremost, saying, When Esau my brother meeteth thee, and asketh thee, saying, Whose *art* thou? and whither goest thou? and whose *are* these before thee?

18 Then thou shalt say, *They be* thy servant Jacob's; it *is* a present sent unto my lord Esau: and, behold, also he *is* behind us.

19 And so commanded he the second, and the third, and all that followed the droves, saying, On this manner shall ye speak unto Esau, when ye find him.

20 And say ye moreover, Behold, thy servant Jacob *is* behind us. For he said, I will appease him with the present that goeth before me, and afterward I will see his face; peradventure he will accept of me.

21 So went the present over before him: and himself lodged that night in the company.

22 And he rose up that night, and took his two wives, and his two womenservants, and his eleven sons, and passed over the ford Jabbok.

23 And he took them, and sent them over the brook, and sent over that he had.

24 ¶ And Jacob was left alone; and there *a*wrestled a man with him until the breaking of the day.

25 And when he saw that he prevailed not against him, he touched the hollow of his thigh; and the

7*a* Gen. 35:3.
9*a* Matt. 22:32;
  1 Ne. 19:10;
  D&C 136:21.
  b Gen. 31:3 (3, 13).
10*a* OR I am unworthy

of all the mercies . . .
  TG Worthiness.
  b Gen. 24:27;
  1 Ne. 1:20;
  Alma 34:38;
  D&C 46:15.

11*a* TG Deliver.
12*a* TG Seed of Abraham.
  b Hosea 1:10.
24*a* Enos 1:2 (1–12);
  Alma 8:10.

hollow of Jacob's thigh was out of joint, as he wrestled with him.

26 And he said, Let me go, for the day breaketh. And he said, I will not let thee go, except thou bless me.

27 And he said unto him, What *is* thy name? And he said, Jacob.

28 And he said, Thy *a*name shall be called no more Jacob, but *b*Israel: *c*for as a *d*prince hast thou *e*power with God and with men, and hast *f*prevailed.

29 And Jacob asked *him*, and said, Tell *me*, I pray thee, thy name. And he said, Wherefore *is* it *that* thou dost ask after my *a*name? And he *b*blessed him there.

30 And Jacob called the name of the place *a*Peniel: for I have *b*seen God *c*face to face, and my life is preserved.

31 And as he passed over *a*Penuel the sun rose upon him, and he halted upon his thigh.

32 Therefore the children of Israel eat not *of* the sinew which shrank, which *is* upon the hollow of the thigh, unto this day: because he touched the hollow of Jacob's thigh in the sinew that shrank.

CHAPTER 33

Jacob and Esau meet and are reconciled—Esau receives Jacob's presents—Jacob settles in Canaan, where he builds an altar.

AND Jacob lifted up his eyes, and looked, and, behold, Esau came, and with him four hundred men. And he divided the children unto Leah, and unto Rachel, and unto the two handmaids.

2 And he put the handmaids and their children foremost, and Leah and her children after, and Rachel and Joseph hindermost.

3 And he passed over before them, and *a*bowed himself to the ground seven times, until he came near to his brother.

4 And Esau ran to meet him, and embraced him, and fell on his neck, and kissed him: and they wept.

5 And he lifted up his eyes, and saw the women and the children; and said, Who *are* those with thee? And he said, The children which God hath graciously given thy servant.

6 Then the handmaidens came near, they and their children, and they bowed themselves.

7 And Leah also with her children came near, and bowed themselves: and after came Joseph near and Rachel, and they bowed themselves.

8 And he said, What *meanest* thou by all this drove which I met? And he said, *These are* to find grace in the sight of my lord.

9 And Esau said, I have enough, my brother; keep that thou hast unto thyself.

10 And Jacob said, Nay, I pray thee, if now I have found grace in thy sight, then receive my present at my hand: for therefore I have seen thy face, as though I had seen the face of God, and thou wast pleased with me.

11 Take, I pray thee, my blessing that is brought to thee; because God hath dealt graciously with me, and because I have enough. And he urged him, and he took *it*.

12 And he said, Let us take our journey, and let us go, and I will go before thee.

13 And he said unto him, My lord knoweth that the children *are* tender, and the flocks and herds with young *are* with me: and if men should

---

28 a Gen. 25:26. TG Name.
  b IE He perseveres (with) God; it may also mean, Let God prevail.
    TG Israel, Origins of.
  c OR for thou hast persevered with God . . .
  d Ps. 135:4; 3 Ne. 5:21 (21–26); D&C 49:24 (23–25); 52:2 (1–3); 132:37.

  e TG Priesthood, Power of.
  f Hosea 12:4.
29 a Judg. 13:18; Mosiah 5:12 (9–14); D&C 18:25; 130:11.
    TG Name.
  b Gen. 48:16.
30 a IE The face of God.
  b See JST Ex. 33:20, 23 (Appendix).

    TG God, Knowledge about; God, Privilege of Seeing.
  c Ether 12:39; D&C 17:1; Moses 1:11 (2, 11, 31); 7:4.
    TG God, Body of, Corporeal Nature; God, Manifestations of.
31 a Variant of Peniel.
33 3 a TG Courtesy.

overdrive them one day, all the flock will die.

14 Let my lord, I pray thee, pass over before his servant: and I will lead on softly, according as the cattle that goeth before me and the children be able to endure, until I come unto my lord unto Seir.

15 And Esau said, Let me now leave with thee *some* of the folk that *are* with me. And he said, What needeth it? let me find grace in the sight of my lord.

16 ¶ So Esau returned that day on his way unto Seir.

17 And Jacob journeyed to *a*Succoth, and built him an house, and made booths for his cattle: therefore the name of the place is called *b*Succoth.

18 ¶ And Jacob came to Shalem, a city of Shechem, which *is* in the land of Canaan, when he came from Padan-aram; and pitched his tent before the city.

19 And he bought a parcel of a field, where he had spread his tent, at the hand of the children of Hamor, Shechem's father, for an hundred pieces of money.

20 And he erected there an altar, and called it *a*El-elohe-Israel.

CHAPTER 34

Shechem defiles Dinah—The Hivites seek to arrange marriages with Jacob's family—Many, having been circumcised, are slain by Simeon and Levi— Jacob reproves his sons.

AND Dinah the daughter of Leah, which she bare unto Jacob, went out to see the daughters of the land.

2 And when Shechem the son of *a*Hamor the Hivite, prince of the country, saw her, he took her, and lay with her, and defiled her.

3 And his soul clave unto Dinah the daughter of Jacob, and he loved the damsel, and spake kindly unto the damsel.

4 And Shechem spake unto his father Hamor, saying, Get me this damsel to wife.

5 And Jacob heard that he had defiled Dinah his daughter: now his sons were with his cattle in the field: and Jacob held his peace until they were come.

6 ¶ And Hamor the father of Shechem went out unto Jacob to commune with him.

7 And the sons of Jacob came out of the field when they heard *it:* and the men were grieved, and they were very *a*wroth, because he had wrought folly in Israel in lying with Jacob's daughter; which thing ought not to be done.

8 And Hamor communed with them, saying, The soul of my son Shechem longeth for your daughter: I pray you give her him to wife.

9 And make ye marriages with us, *and* give your daughters unto us, and take our daughters unto you.

10 And ye shall dwell with us: and the *a*land shall be before you; dwell and *b*trade ye therein, and get you possessions therein.

11 And Shechem said unto her father and unto her brethren, Let me find grace in your eyes, and what ye shall say unto me I will give.

12 Ask me *a*never so much dowry and gift, and I will give according as ye shall say unto me: but give me the damsel to wife.

13 And the sons of Jacob answered Shechem and Hamor his father deceitfully, and said, because he had defiled Dinah their sister:

14 *a*And they said unto them, We cannot do this thing, to give our sister to one that is *b*uncircumcised; for that *were* a reproach unto us:

15 But in this will we consent unto you: If ye will be as we *be*, that every male of you be *a*circumcised;

17*a* IE Booths.
  b Josh. 13:27;
     Ps. 60:6.
20*a* IE El (God) is the God of Israel.
34 2*a* Judg. 9:28.

7*a* Gen. 49:7.
10*a* Gen. 20:15.
  b Mosiah 24:7;
     4 Ne. 1:46;
     Ether 10:22.
12*a* OR ever so high a dowry.

14*a* Septuagint: And Simeon and Levi, brothers of Dinah, sons of Leah, said . . .
  b Judg. 14:3.
15*a* TG Circumcision.

16 Then will we give our daughters unto you, and we will take your daughters to us, and we will dwell with you, and we will become one people.

17 But if ye will not hearken unto us, to be circumcised; then will we take our daughter, and we will be gone.

18 And their words pleased Hamor, and Shechem Hamor's son.

19 And the young man deferred not to do the thing, because he had delight in Jacob's daughter: and he *was* more honourable than all the house of his father.

20 ¶ And Hamor and Shechem his son came unto the *a*gate of their city, and communed with the men of their city, saying,

21 These men *are* peaceable with us; therefore let them dwell in the land, and trade therein; for the land, behold, *it is* large enough for them; let us take their daughters to us for wives, and let us give them our daughters.

22 Only herein will the men consent unto us for to dwell with us, to be one people, if every male among us be circumcised, as they *are* circumcised.

23 *Shall* not their cattle and their substance and every beast of theirs *be* ours? only let us consent unto them, and they will dwell with us.

24 And unto Hamor and unto Shechem his son hearkened all that went out of the gate of his city; and every male was circumcised, all that went out of the gate of his city.

25 ¶ And it came to pass on the third day, when they were sore, that two of the sons of Jacob, *a*Simeon and Levi, Dinah's brethren, took each man his sword, and came upon the city boldly, and slew all the males.

26 And they *a*slew Hamor and Shechem his son with the edge of the sword, and took Dinah out of Shechem's house, and went out.

27 The sons of Jacob came upon the slain, and spoiled the city, because they had defiled their sister.

28 They took their sheep, and their oxen, and their asses, and that which *was* in the city, and that which *was* in the field,

29 And all their wealth, and all their little ones, and their wives took they captive, and spoiled even all that *was* in the house.

30 And Jacob said to Simeon and Levi, Ye have troubled me to make me to stink among the inhabitants of the land, among the Canaanites and the Perizzites: and I *being* few in number, they shall gather themselves together against me, and slay me; and I shall be destroyed, I and my house.

31 And they said, Should he deal with our sister as with an harlot?

CHAPTER 35

God sends Jacob to Bethel, where he builds an altar and the Lord appears to him—God renews the promise that Jacob will be a great nation and that his name will be Israel—Jacob sets up an altar and pours a drink offering—Rachel bears Benjamin, dies in childbirth, and is buried near Bethlehem—Reuben sins with Bilhah—Isaac dies and is buried by Jacob and Esau.

AND God said unto Jacob, Arise, go up to Beth-el, and dwell there: and make there an altar unto God, that appeared unto thee when thou *a*fleddest from the face of Esau thy brother.

2 Then Jacob said unto his household, and to all that *were* with him, Put away the strange *a*gods that *are* among you, and be *b*clean, and change your garments:

3 And let us arise, and go up to Beth-el; and I will make there an altar unto God, who answered me in the day of my *a*distress, and was with me in the way which I went.

20*a* Gen. 23:10.
25*a* Gen. 49:5 (5–7).
26*a* Gen. 49:6.

35 1*a* Gen. 27:43 (41–45).
2*a* TG Idolatry.
b TG Purification.

3*a* Gen. 32:7 (7, 24);
Ps. 4:1.

4 And they gave unto Jacob all the strange gods which *were* in their hand, and *all their* earrings which *were* in their ears; and Jacob hid them under the oak which *was* by Shechem.

5 And they journeyed: and the terror of God was upon the cities that *were* round about them, and they did not pursue after the sons of Jacob.

6 ¶ So Jacob came to *a*Luz, which *is* in the land of Canaan, that *is*, Beth-el, he and all the people that *were* with him.

7 And he built there an altar, and called the place El-beth-el: because there God appeared unto him, when he fled from the face of his brother.

8 But Deborah Rebekah's *a*nurse died, and she was buried beneath Beth-el under an oak: and the name of it was called *b*Allon-bachuth.

9 ¶ And God appeared unto Jacob again, when he came out of Padan-aram, and blessed him.

10 And God said unto him, Thy name *is* Jacob: thy name shall not be called any more Jacob, but *a*Israel shall be thy name: and he called his name Israel.

11 And God said unto him, I *am* *a*God Almighty: be *b*fruitful and multiply; a nation and a company of *c*nations shall be of thee, and *d*kings shall come out of thy loins;

12 And the *a*land which I gave Abraham and Isaac, to thee I will give it, and to thy seed after thee will I give the land.

13 And God went up from him in the place where he talked with him.

14 And Jacob set up a *a*pillar in the place where he talked with him, *even* a pillar of stone: and he poured a *b*drink offering thereon, and he poured oil thereon.

15 And Jacob called the name of the place where God spake with him, Beth-el.

16 ¶ And they journeyed from Beth-el; and there was but a little way to come to Ephrath: and Rachel travailed, and she had hard labour.

17 And it came to pass, when she was in hard labour, that the midwife said unto her, Fear not; thou shalt have this son also.

18 And it came to pass, as her soul was in departing, (for she *a*died) that she called his name *b*Ben-oni: but his father called him *c*Benjamin.

19 And *a*Rachel died, and was buried in the way to *b*Ephrath, which *is* Beth-lehem.

20 And Jacob set a pillar upon her grave: that *is* the pillar of Rachel's grave unto this day.

21 ¶ And Israel journeyed, and spread his tent beyond the *a*tower of Edar.

22 And it came to pass, when Israel dwelt in that land, that Reuben went and *a*lay with Bilhah his father's concubine: and Israel heard *it*. Now the *b*sons of Jacob were *c*twelve:

23 The sons of Leah; *a*Reuben, Jacob's firstborn, and Simeon, and Levi, and Judah, and Issachar, and Zebulun:

24 The sons of Rachel; Joseph, and Benjamin:

25 And the sons of Bilhah, Rachel's handmaid; Dan, and Naphtali:

26 And the sons of Zilpah, Leah's handmaid; Gad, and Asher: these *are* the sons of Jacob, which were born to him in Padan-aram.

6a Gen. 28:19; 48:3;
   Josh. 18:13.
8a Gen. 24:59.
  b IE Oak of weeping.
10a TG Israel, Origins of.
11a HEB El Shaddai.
  b Gen. 8:17; 9:7; 28:3.
  c TG Israel, Blessings of;
   Seed of Abraham.
  d TG Kings, Earthly.
12a TG Israel, Land of;

Promised Lands.
14a Gen. 28:18.
  b Num. 28:7, 14 (7–24).
18a TG Death.
  b IE Son of my sorrow, or
   distress.
  c IE Son at the right
   (hand).
   Gen. 42:4; 43:29; 46:19.
19a Gen. 48:7.
  b Ruth 1:2.

21a Mosiah 2:7 (7–8);
   11:12 (12–13);
   Alma 50:4;
   Hel. 7:11 (10–14);
   Ether 1:33 (3–5, 33);
   D&C 101:45 (45–57).
22a TG Sexual Immorality.
  b Ex. 1:1 (1–4).
  c TG Israel, Twelve
   Tribes of.
23a Gen. 29:32; 42:22.

27 ¶ And Jacob came unto Isaac his father unto Mamre, unto the city of Arbah, which is Hebron, where Abraham and Isaac sojourned.

28 And the *a*days of *b*Isaac were an hundred and fourscore years.

29 And Isaac gave up the ghost, and died, and was *a*gathered unto his people, *being* old and full of days: and his sons Esau and Jacob *b*buried him.

CHAPTER 36

The descendants of Esau, who is Edom, are listed.

Now these *are* the generations of Esau, who *is* *a*Edom.

2 Esau took his wives of the daughters of Canaan; Adah the daughter of Elon the Hittite, and Aholibamah the daughter of Anah the daughter of Zibeon the Hivite;

3 And Bashemath *a*Ishmael's daughter, sister of Nebajoth.

4 And Adah bare to Esau Eliphaz; and Bashemath bare Reuel;

5 And Aholibamah bare Jeush, and Jaalam, and Korah: these *are* the sons of Esau, which were born unto him in the land of Canaan.

6 And Esau took his wives, and his sons, and his daughters, and all the persons of his house, and his cattle, and all his beasts, and all his substance, which he had got in the land of Canaan; and went into the country from the face of his brother Jacob.

7 For their riches were more than that they might dwell together; and the land wherein they were strangers could not bear them because of their cattle.

8 Thus dwelt Esau in mount *a*Seir: Esau *is* Edom.

9 ¶ And these *are* the *a*generations of *b*Esau the father of the Edomites in mount Seir:

10 These *are* the names of Esau's sons; Eliphaz the son of Adah the wife of Esau, Reuel the son of Bashemath the wife of Esau.

11 And the sons of Eliphaz were Teman, Omar, Zepho, and Gatam, and Kenaz.

12 And Timna was concubine to Eliphaz Esau's son; and she bare to Eliphaz Amalek: these *were* the sons of Adah Esau's wife.

13 And these *are* the sons of Reuel; Nahath, and Zerah, Shammah, and Mizzah: these were the sons of Bashemath Esau's wife.

14 ¶ And these were the sons of Aholibamah, the daughter of Anah the daughter of Zibeon, Esau's wife: and she bare to Esau Jeush, and Jaalam, and Korah.

15 ¶ These *were* *a*dukes of the sons of *b*Esau: the sons of Eliphaz the firstborn *son* of Esau; duke Teman, duke Omar, duke Zepho, duke Kenaz,

16 Duke Korah, duke Gatam, *and* duke Amalek: these *are* the dukes *that came* of Eliphaz in the land of Edom; these *were* the sons of Adah.

17 ¶ And these *are* the sons of Reuel Esau's son; duke Nahath, duke Zerah, duke Shammah, duke Mizzah: these *are* the dukes *that came* of Reuel in the land of Edom; these *are* the sons of Bashemath Esau's wife.

18 ¶ And these *are* the sons of Aholibamah Esau's wife; duke Jeush, duke Jaalam, duke Korah: these *were* the dukes *that came* of Aholibamah the daughter of Anah, Esau's wife.

19 These *are* the sons of Esau, who *is* Edom, and these *are* their dukes.

20 ¶ These *are* the sons of *a*Seir the Horite, who inhabited the land; Lotan, and Shobal, and Zibeon, and Anah,

21 And Dishon, and Ezer, and Dishan: these *are* the dukes of the Horites, the children of Seir in the land of Edom.

28*a* Gen. 47:9.
 b Gen. 25:7; 47:28.
29*a* TG Family, Eternal.
 b Gen. 25:9.
36 1*a* Gen. 25:30; 32:3;
 Jer. 49:7 (7–22);

Obad. 1:1.
3*a* Gen. 28:9.
8*a* Gen. 32:3;
 Isa. 21:11;
 Ezek. 35:2.
9*a* IE genealogical lines.

 b 1 Chr. 1:35 (35–37).
15*a* IE tribal chiefs.
 b Ex. 15:15.
20*a* 1 Chr. 1:38 (38–42).

22 And the children of Lotan were Hori and Hemam; and Lotan's sister *was* Timna.

23 And the children of Shobal *were* these; Alvan, and Manahath, and Ebal, Shepho, and Onam.

24 And these *are* the children of Zibeon; both Ajah, and Anah: this *was that* Anah that found the mules in the wilderness, as he fed the asses of Zibeon his father.

25 And the children of Anah *were* these; Dishon, and Aholibamah the daughter of Anah.

26 And these *are* the children of Dishon; Hemdan, and Eshban, and Ithran, and Cheran.

27 The children of Ezer *are* these; Bilhan, and Zaavan, and Akan.

28 The children of Dishan *are* these; Uz, and Aran.

29 These *are* the dukes *that came* of the Horites; duke Lotan, duke Shobal, duke Zibeon, duke Anah,

30 Duke Dishon, duke Ezer, duke Dishan: these *are* the dukes *that came* of Hori, among their dukes in the land of Seir.

31 ¶ And these *are* the kings that reigned in the land of ᵃEdom, before there reigned any king over the children of Israel.

32 And Bela the son of Beor reigned in Edom: and the name of his city *was* Dinhabah.

33 And Bela died, and Jobab the son of Zerah of Bozrah reigned in his stead.

34 And Jobab died, and Husham of the land of Temani reigned in his stead.

35 And Husham died, and Hadad the son of Bedad, who smote Midian in the field of Moab, reigned in his stead: and the name of his city *was* Avith.

36 And Hadad died, and Samlah of Masrekah reigned in his stead.

37 And Samlah died, and Saul of Rehoboth *by* the river reigned in his stead.

38 And Saul died, and Baal-hanan the son of Achbor reigned in his stead.

39 And Baal-hanan the son of Achbor died, and Hadar reigned in his stead: and the name of his city *was* Pau; and his wife's name *was* Mehetabel, the daughter of Matred, the daughter of Mezahab.

40 And these *are* the names of the dukes *that came* of Esau, according to their families, after their places, by their names; duke Timnah, duke Alvah, duke Jetheth,

41 Duke Aholibamah, duke Elah, duke Pinon,

42 Duke Kenaz, duke Teman, duke Mibzar,

43 Duke Magdiel, duke Iram: these *be* the dukes of Edom, according to their habitations in the land of their possession: he *is* ᵃEsau the father of the ᵇEdomites.

CHAPTER 37

Jacob loves and favors Joseph, who is hated by his brothers—Joseph dreams that his parents and brothers make obeisance to him—His brothers sell him into Egypt.

AND Jacob dwelt in the land ᵃwherein his father was a ᵇstranger, in the land of Canaan.

2 These *are* the ᵃgenerations of Jacob. ᵇJoseph, *being* seventeen years old, was feeding the flock with his brethren; and the lad *was* with the sons of Bilhah, and with the sons of Zilpah, his father's wives: and Joseph brought unto his father their evil report.

3 Now Israel loved ᵃJoseph more than all his children, because he *was* the son of his old age: and he made him a ᵇcoat of *many* ᶜcolours.

4 And when his brethren saw that

31*a* 1 Chr. 1:43 (43–54).
43*a* Jer. 49:10 (10–17).
   b 2 Kgs. 3:9.
37 1*a* HEB of his father's sojournings.
   b TG Stranger.

2*a* IE genealogical lines.
  b Gen. 41:46 (46–47, 54).
3*a* TG Israel, Joseph, People of.
  b Alma 46:23 (23–24).
  c The Septuagint word

indicates many colors, but the Hebrew term may indicate simply a long coat with sleeves.

their father loved him more than all his brethren, they hated him, and could not speak peaceably unto him.

5 ¶ And Joseph dreamed a ªdream, and he told *it* his brethren: and they hated him yet the more.

6 And he said unto them, Hear, I pray you, this dream which I have dreamed:

7 For, behold, we *were* binding sheaves in the field, and, lo, my sheaf arose, and also stood upright; and, behold, your sheaves stood round about, and made ªobeisance to my sheaf.

8 And his brethren said to him, Shalt thou indeed reign over us? or shalt thou indeed have dominion over us? And they hated him yet the more for his dreams, and for his words.

9 ¶ And he dreamed yet another dream, and told it his brethren, and said, Behold, I have dreamed a dream more; and, behold, the sun and the moon and the eleven stars made obeisance to me.

10 And he told *it* to his father, and to his brethren: and his father rebuked him, and said unto him, What *is* this dream that thou hast dreamed? Shall I and thy mother and thy brethren indeed come to ªbow down ourselves to thee to the earth?

11 And his brethren ªenvied him; but his father observed the saying.

12 ¶ And his brethren went to feed their father's ªflock in Shechem.

13 And Israel said unto Joseph, Do not thy brethren feed *the flock* in Shechem? come, and I will send thee unto them. And he said to him, Here *am* I.

14 And he said to him, Go, I pray thee, see whether it be well with thy brethren, and well with the flocks; and bring me word again. So he sent him out of the vale of Hebron, and he came to Shechem.

15 ¶ And a certain man found him, and, behold, *he was* wandering in the field: and the man asked him, saying, What seekest thou?

16 And he said, I seek my brethren: tell me, I pray thee, where they feed *their flocks.*

17 And the man said, They are departed hence; for I heard them say, Let us go to Dothan. And Joseph went after his brethren, and found them in Dothan.

18 And when they saw him afar off, even before he came near unto them, they ªconspired against him to slay him.

19 And they said one to another, Behold, this ªdreamer cometh.

20 Come now therefore, and let us slay him, and cast him into some pit, and we will say, Some evil beast hath devoured him: and we shall see what will become of his dreams.

21 And ªReuben heard *it,* and he delivered him out of their hands; and said, Let us not kill him.

22 And Reuben said unto them, Shed no blood, *but* cast him into this pit that *is* in the wilderness, and lay no hand upon him; that he might rid him out of their hands, to deliver him to his father again.

23 ¶ And it came to pass, when Joseph was come unto his brethren, that they stript Joseph out of his ªcoat, *his* coat of *many* colours that *was* on him;

24 And they took him, and cast him into a pit: and the pit *was* empty, *there was* no water in it.

25 And they sat down to eat bread: and they lifted up their eyes and looked, and, behold, a company of Ishmeelites came from Gilead with their camels bearing spicery and balm and myrrh, going to carry *it* down to Egypt.

26 And Judah said unto his brethren, What profit *is it* if we slay our brother, and conceal his blood?

27 Come, and let us sell him to the Ishmeelites, and let not our hand be upon him; for he *is* our brother *and*

5*a* TG Dream.
7*a* Gen. 42:6 (6, 9);
    43:26 (26–28); 44:14.
10*a* See JST Gen. 48:5–11

(Appendix).
    Gen. 50:18.
11*a* TG Envy.
12*a* Gen. 46:34.

18*a* TG Conspiracy.
19*a* HEB master of dreams.
21*a* Gen. 42:22.
23*a* Alma 46:24 (23–27).

our flesh. And his brethren *a*were content.

28 Then there passed by Midianites merchantmen; and they drew and lifted up Joseph out of the pit, and sold Joseph to the *a*Ishmeelites for twenty *pieces* of silver: and they brought Joseph into Egypt.

29 ¶ And Reuben returned unto the pit; and, behold, Joseph *was* not in the pit; and he rent his clothes.

30 And he returned unto his brethren, and said, The child *is* *a*not; and I, whither shall I go?

31 And they took Joseph's coat, and killed a kid of the goats, and dipped the coat in the blood;

32 And they sent the coat of *many* colours, and they brought *it* to their father; and said, This have we found: know now whether it *be* thy son's coat or no.

33 And he knew it, and said, *It is* my son's *a*coat; an evil beast hath devoured him; Joseph is without doubt *b*rent in pieces.

34 And Jacob rent his clothes, and put sackcloth upon his loins, and mourned for his son many days.

35 And all his *a*sons and all his daughters rose up to comfort him; but he refused to be *b*comforted; and he said, For I will go down into the grave unto my son *c*mourning. Thus his father wept for him.

36 And the Midianites *a*sold him into Egypt unto *b*Potiphar, an *c*officer of Pharaoh's, *and* *d*captain of the guard.

CHAPTER 38

Judah has three sons by a Canaanite woman—Er and Onan are slain by the Lord—Tamar, disguised as a harlot, bears twins by Judah.

AND it came to pass at that time,

that Judah went down from his brethren, and turned in to a certain Adullamite, whose name *was* Hirah.

2 And Judah saw there a *a*daughter of a certain Canaanite, whose name *was* Shuah; and he took her, and went in unto her.

3 And she conceived, and bare a son; and he called his name *a*Er.

4 And she conceived again, and bare a son; and she called his name Onan.

5 And she yet again conceived, and bare a son; and called his name Shelah: and he was at Chezib, when she bare him.

6 And Judah took a wife for Er his firstborn, whose name *was* Tamar.

7 And *a*Er, Judah's firstborn, was wicked in the sight of the LORD; and the LORD slew him.

8 And Judah said unto Onan, Go in unto thy brother's *a*wife, and marry her, and raise up seed to thy brother.

9 And Onan knew that the seed should not be his; and it came to pass, when he went in unto his brother's wife, that he spilled *it* on the ground, lest that he should give seed to his brother.

10 And the thing which he did displeased the LORD: wherefore he slew him also.

11 Then said Judah to Tamar his daughter in law, Remain a widow at thy father's house, till Shelah my son be grown: for he said, Lest peradventure he die also, as his brethren *did*. And Tamar went and dwelt in her father's house.

12 ¶ And in process of time the daughter of Shuah Judah's wife died; and Judah was comforted, and went up unto his sheepshearers to Timnath, he and his friend Hirah the Adullamite.

13 And it was told Tamar, saying,

27a HEB hearkened.
28a Gen. 39:1.
30a Gen. 42:13.
33a Alma 46:24 (23–24).
 b Gen. 44:28.
35a Gen. 46:7.
 b Ps. 77:2;
   Ether 15:3;
   Moses 7:44.

c Gen. 42:38.
 TG Mourning.
36a Ps. 105:17;
   1 Ne. 5:14;
   2 Ne. 3:4;
   Alma 10:3.
 b Gen. 39:1.
 c HEB eunuch (which
   often designates a

royal official).
 d HEB chief of the
   butchers, or the cooks;
   probably the chief
   steward.
38 2a TG Marriage, Interfaith.
 3a 1 Chr. 2:3 (3–4).
 7a Gen. 46:12.
 8a TG Widows.

Behold thy father in law goeth up to Timnath to shear his sheep.

14 And she put her widow's garments off from her, and covered her with a veil, and wrapped herself, and sat in an open place, which *is* by the way to Timnath; for she saw that Shelah was grown, and she was not given unto him to wife.

15 When Judah saw her, he thought her *to be* an harlot; because she had covered her face.

16 And he turned unto her by the way, and said, Go to, I pray thee, let me come in unto thee; (for he knew not that she *was* his daughter in law.) And she said, What wilt thou give me, that thou mayest come in unto me?

17 And he said, I will send *thee* a kid from the flock. And she said, Wilt thou give *me* a pledge, till thou send *it?*

18 And he said, What pledge shall I give thee? And she said, Thy *a*signet, and thy bracelets, and thy staff that *is* in thine hand. And he gave *it* her, and came in unto her, and she conceived by him.

19 And she arose, and went away, and laid by her veil from her, and put on the garments of her widowhood.

20 And Judah sent the kid by the hand of his friend the Adullamite, to receive *his* pledge from the woman's hand: but he found her not.

21 Then he asked the men of that place, saying, Where *is* the harlot, that *was* openly by the way side? And they said, There was no harlot in this *place.*

22 And he returned to Judah, and said, I cannot find her; and also the men of the place said, *that* there was no harlot in this *place.*

23 And Judah said, Let her take *it* to her, lest we be shamed: behold, I sent this kid, and thou hast not found her.

24 ¶ And it came to pass about three months after, that it was told Judah, saying, Tamar thy daughter in law hath played the harlot; and also, behold, she *is* with child by whoredom. And Judah said, Bring her forth, and let her be *a*burnt.

25 When she *was* brought forth, she sent to her father in law, saying, By the man, whose these *are, am* I with child: and she said, Discern, I pray thee, whose *are* these, the *a*signet, and bracelets, and staff.

26 And Judah acknowledged *them,* and said, She hath been more righteous than I; because that I gave her not to Shelah my son. And he knew her again no more.

27 ¶ And it came to pass in the time of her travail, that, behold, twins *were* in her womb.

28 And it came to pass, when she travailed, that *the one* put out *his* hand: and the midwife took and bound upon his hand a scarlet thread, saying, This came out first.

29 And it came to pass, as he drew back his hand, that, behold, his brother came out: and she said, How hast thou broken forth? *this* breach *be* upon thee: therefore his name was called *a*Pharez.

30 And afterward came out his brother, that had the scarlet thread upon his hand: and his name was called *a*Zarah.

CHAPTER 39

Joseph, prospered by the Lord, becomes ruler of Potiphar's house—He resists the advances of Potiphar's wife, is falsely accused, and is cast into prison—The keeper of the prison commits the prison's affairs into Joseph's hands.

AND Joseph was brought down to Egypt; and *a*Potiphar, an officer of Pharaoh, captain of the guard, an Egyptian, bought him of the hands of the *b*Ishmeelites, which had brought him down thither.

2 And the *a*LORD was with *b*Joseph,

18*a* Gen. 38:25.
24*a* Lev. 21:9.
25*a* Gen. 38:18.
29*a* Ruth 4:18 (18–22);
　　Luke 3:33 (23–38).

30*a* Gen. 46:12;
　　Neh. 11:24;
　　Matt. 1:3.
39 1*a* Gen. 37:36.
　　b Gen. 37:28.

2*a* Gen. 39:21.
　b 2 Ne. 3:4 (4–7);
　　4:1 (1–2).
　　TG God, Access to.

and he was a prosperous man; and he was in the house of his master the Egyptian.

3 And his master saw that the LORD *was* with him, and that the LORD made all that he did to ªprosper in his hand.

4 And Joseph found grace in his sight, and he served him: and he made him overseer over his house, and all *that* he had he put into his hand.

5 And it came to pass from the time *that* he had made him overseer in his house, and over all that he had, that the LORD blessed the Egyptian's house for Joseph's ªsake; and the blessing of the LORD was upon all that he had in the house, and in the field.

6 And he left all that he had in Joseph's hand; and he knew not ought he had, save the bread which he did eat. And Joseph was *a* ªgoodly *person,* and well ᵇfavoured.

7 ¶ And it came to pass after these things, that his master's wife cast her ªeyes upon Joseph; and she said, Lie with me.

8 But he ªrefused, and said unto his master's wife, Behold, my master ᵇwotteth not what *is* with me in the house, and he hath ᶜcommitted all that he hath to my hand;

9 *There is* none greater in this house than I; neither hath he kept back any thing from me but thee, because thou *art* his wife: how then can I do this great ªwickedness, and ᵇsin against God?

10 And it came to pass, as she spake to Joseph ªday by day, that he hearkened not unto her, to lie by her, *or* to be with her.

11 And it came to pass about this time, that *Joseph* went into the house to do his business; and *there*

was none of the men of the house there within.

12 And she caught him by his garment, saying, Lie with me: and he left his garment in her hand, and ªfled, and got him out.

13 And it came to pass, when she saw that he had left his garment in her hand, and was fled forth,

14 That she called unto the men of her house, and spake unto them, saying, See, he hath brought in an Hebrew unto us to mock us; he came in unto me to lie with me, and I cried with a loud voice:

15 And it came to pass, when he heard that I lifted up my voice and cried, that he left his garment with me, and fled, and got him out.

16 And she laid up his garment by her, until his lord came home.

17 And she spake unto him according to these words, saying, The Hebrew servant, which thou hast brought unto us, came in unto me to mock me:

18 And it came to pass, as I lifted up my voice and cried, that he left his garment with me, and fled out.

19 And it came to pass, when his master heard the words of his wife, which she spake unto him, saying, After this manner did thy servant to me; that his wrath was kindled.

20 And Joseph's master took him, and put him into the ªprison, a place where the king's prisoners *were* bound: and he was there in the prison.

21 ¶ But the ªLORD was with Joseph, and shewed him mercy, and gave him favour in the sight of the keeper of the prison.

22 And the keeper of the prison committed to Joseph's hand all the prisoners that *were* in the prison; and

---

3ª Ps. 1:3 (2–3);
   Matt. 10:31 (29–31);
   Mosiah 2:41.
5ª Gen. 30:27.
6ª TG Talents.
 ᵇ Gen. 29:17.
7ª TG Sensuality.
8ª TG Example.

ᵇ JST Gen. 39:8 . . .
   knoweth . . .
 ᶜ TG Trustworthiness.
9ª TG Adulterer;
   Fornication.
 ᵇ 2 Sam. 12:13.
10ª Judg. 16:16 (15–16).
12ª TG Chastity.

20ª Gen. 40:3 (3, 5); 41:14;
   Ps. 105:18;
   Mosiah 7:7;
   Alma 14:22; 20:3 (2–5);
   Hel. 9:14.
21ª Gen. 39:2.

whatsoever they did there, he was the ^adoer *of it.*

23 The keeper of the prison looked not to any thing *that was* under his hand; because the L<small>ORD</small> was with him, and *that* which he did, the L<small>ORD</small> made *it* to ^aprosper.

CHAPTER 40

Joseph interprets the dreams of Pharaoh's chief butler and chief baker—The butler fails to tell Pharaoh about Joseph.

A<small>ND</small> it came to pass after these things, *that* the butler of the king of Egypt and *his* baker had offended their lord the king of Egypt.

2 And Pharaoh was wroth against two *of* his officers, against the chief of the butlers, and against the chief of the bakers.

3 And he put them in ward in the house of the captain of the guard, into the ^aprison, the place where Joseph *was* bound.

4 And the captain of the guard charged Joseph with them, and he served them: and they continued a season in ward.

5 ¶ And they dreamed a dream both of them, each man his dream in one night, each man according to the interpretation of his dream, the butler and the baker of the king of Egypt, which *were* bound in the prison.

6 And Joseph came in unto them in the morning, and looked upon them, and, behold, they *were* sad.

7 And he asked Pharaoh's officers that *were* with him in the ward of his lord's house, saying, Wherefore look ye *so* sadly to day?

8 And they said unto him, We have dreamed a ^adream, and *there is* no interpreter of it. And Joseph said unto them, *Do* not ^binterpretations *belong* to God? tell me *them,* I pray you.

9 And the chief butler told his dream to Joseph, and said to him,

In my dream, behold, a vine *was* before me;

10 And in the vine *were* three branches: and it *was* as though it budded, *and* her blossoms shot forth; and the clusters thereof brought forth ripe grapes:

11 And Pharaoh's cup *was* in my hand: and I took the grapes, and pressed them into Pharaoh's cup, and I gave the cup into Pharaoh's hand.

12 And Joseph said unto him, This *is* the interpretation of it: The three branches *are* three days:

13 Yet within three days shall Pharaoh lift up thine head, and restore thee unto thy place: and thou shalt deliver Pharaoh's cup into his hand, after the former manner when thou wast his butler.

14 But think on me when it shall be well with thee, and shew kindness, I pray thee, unto me, and make mention of me unto Pharaoh, and bring me out of this house:

15 For indeed I was stolen away out of the land of the Hebrews: and here also have I done nothing that they should put me into the dungeon.

16 When the chief baker saw that the interpretation was good, he said unto Joseph, I also *was* in my dream, and, behold, *I had* three white baskets on my head:

17 And in the uppermost basket *there was* of all manner of bakemeats for Pharaoh; and the birds did eat them out of the basket upon my head.

18 And Joseph answered and said, This *is* the interpretation thereof: The three baskets *are* three days:

19 Yet within three days shall Pharaoh lift up thy head from off thee, and shall hang thee on a tree; and the birds shall eat thy flesh from off thee.

20 ¶ And it came to pass the third day, *which was* Pharaoh's birthday, that he made a feast unto all his

22a JST Gen. 39:22 . . .
    overseer . . .
23a TG Blessing.

40 3a Gen. 39:20.
    8a TG Dream.
    b Ps. 105:19;

Dan. 2:28;
2 Pet. 1:20 (20–21);
1 Ne. 11:11 (3–11).

servants: and he lifted up the head of the chief butler and of the chief baker among his servants.

21 And he restored the chief butler unto his butlership again; and he gave the cup into Pharaoh's hand:

22 But he hanged the chief baker: as Joseph had interpreted to them.

23 Yet did not the chief butler remember Joseph, but ^aforgat him.

CHAPTER 41

Pharaoh dreams of the cattle and the ears of grain—Joseph interprets the dreams as seven years of plenty and seven of famine—He proposes a grain storage program—Pharaoh makes him ruler of all Egypt—Joseph marries Asenath—He gathers grain as the sand upon the seashore—Asenath bears Manasseh and Ephraim—Joseph sells grain to Egyptians and others during the famine.

AND it came to pass at the end of two full years, that Pharaoh ^adreamed: and, behold, he stood by the river.

2 And, behold, there came up out of the river seven well favoured kine and fatfleshed; and they fed in a meadow.

3 And, behold, seven other kine came up after them out of the river, ill favoured and leanfleshed; and stood by the *other* kine upon the brink of the river.

4 And the ill favoured and leanfleshed kine did eat up the seven well favoured and fat kine. So Pharaoh awoke.

5 And he slept and dreamed the second time: and, behold, seven ears of corn came up upon one stalk, rank and good.

6 And, behold, seven thin ears and blasted with the east wind sprung up after them.

7 And the seven thin ears devoured the seven rank and full ears. And Pharaoh awoke, and, behold, *it was* a dream.

8 And it came to pass in the morning that his spirit was ^atroubled; and he sent and called for all the ^bmagicians of Egypt, and all the wise men thereof: and Pharaoh told them his dream; but *there was* none that could interpret them unto Pharaoh.

9 ¶ Then spake the chief butler unto Pharaoh, saying, I do remember my faults this day:

10 Pharaoh was wroth with his servants, and put me in ward in the captain of the guard's house, *both* me and the chief baker:

11 And we dreamed a dream in one night, I and he; we dreamed each man according to the interpretation of his dream.

12 And *there was* there with us a young man, an Hebrew, servant to the captain of the guard; and we told him, and he interpreted to us our dreams; to each man according to his dream he did interpret.

13 And it came to pass, as he interpreted to us, so it was; me he restored unto mine office, and him he hanged.

14 ¶ Then ^aPharaoh sent and called Joseph, and they brought him hastily out of the ^bdungeon: and he shaved *himself,* and changed his raiment, and came in unto Pharaoh.

15 And Pharaoh said unto Joseph, I have dreamed a dream, and *there is* none that can interpret it: and I have heard say of thee, *that* thou canst understand a dream to ^ainterpret it.

16 And Joseph answered Pharaoh, saying, *It is* not in me: ^aGod shall give Pharaoh an answer of ^bpeace.

17 And Pharaoh said unto Joseph, In my dream, behold, I stood upon the bank of the river:

18 And, behold, there came up out of the river seven kine, fatfleshed and well favoured; and they fed in a meadow:

19 And, behold, seven other kine came up after them, poor and very

---

23*a* TG Ingratitude.
41 1*a* TG Dream.
  8*a* Dan. 2:1 (1–3).
  b TG Sorcery.

14*a* Ps. 105:20; D&C 105:27;
  Abr. 1:20 (6–27).
  b Gen. 39:20.
15*a* Dan. 1:17 (6–20).

16*a* Dan. 2:30;
  Acts 3:12;
  Alma 26:35.
  b D&C 6:23.

ill favoured and leanfleshed, such as I never saw in all the land of Egypt for badness:

20 And the lean and the ill favoured kine did eat up the first seven fat kine:

21 And when they had eaten them up, it could not be known that they had eaten them; but they *were* still ill favoured, as at the beginning. So I awoke.

22 And I saw in my dream, and, behold, seven ears came up in one stalk, full and good:

23 And, behold, seven ears, withered, thin, *and* blasted with the *a*east *b*wind, sprung up after them:

24 And the thin ears devoured the seven good ears: and I told *this* unto the magicians; but *there was* none that could declare *it* to me.

25 ¶ And Joseph said unto Pharaoh, The dream of Pharaoh *is* one: God hath *a*shewed Pharaoh what he *is* about to do.

26 The seven good kine *are* seven years; and the seven good ears *are* seven years: the dream *is* one.

27 And the seven thin and ill favoured kine that came up after them *are* seven years; and the seven empty ears blasted with the east wind shall be seven years of *a*famine.

28 This *is* the thing which I have spoken unto Pharaoh: What God *is* about to do he sheweth unto Pharaoh.

29 Behold, there come seven years of great plenty throughout all the land of Egypt:

30 And there shall arise after them seven years of famine; and all the plenty shall be forgotten in the land of Egypt; and the *a*famine shall consume the land;

31 And the plenty shall not be known in the land by reason of that famine following; for it *shall be* very grievous.

32 And for that the dream was doubled unto Pharaoh twice; *it is* because the thing *is* established by God, and God will shortly bring it to pass.

33 Now therefore let Pharaoh look out a man discreet and wise, and set him over the land of Egypt.

34 Let Pharaoh do *this,* and let him appoint officers over the land, and take up the fifth part of the land of Egypt in the seven plenteous years.

35 And let them gather all the food of those good years that come, and lay up corn under the hand of Pharaoh, and let them keep food in the cities.

36 And that food shall be for *a*store to the land against the seven years of famine, which shall be in the land of Egypt; that the land perish not through the famine.

37 ¶ And the thing was *a*good in the eyes of Pharaoh, and in the eyes of all his servants.

38 And Pharaoh said unto his servants, Can we find *such a one* as this *is,* a man in whom the *a*Spirit of God *is?*

39 And Pharaoh said unto Joseph, Forasmuch as God hath *a*shewed thee all this, *there is* none so discreet and *b*wise as thou *art:*

40 Thou shalt be *a*over my house, and according unto thy word shall all my people be ruled: only in the throne will I be *b*greater than thou.

41 And Pharaoh said unto Joseph, See, I have *a*set thee over all the land of Egypt.

42 And Pharaoh took off his *a*ring from his hand, and put it upon Joseph's hand, and *b*arrayed him in *c*vestures of fine linen, and put a gold chain about his neck;

23*a* Ps. 78:26;
　　Ezek. 27:26;
　　Mosiah 7:31.
　 b Hosea 13:15 (15–16).
25*a* TG Dream.
27*a* TG Famine.
30*a* TG Famine.
36*a* 3 Ne. 4:18;
　　D&C 4:4.

37*a* Gen. 45:16;
　　TG Welfare.
　　Alma 20:28.
38*a* 1 Ne. 1:12; 17:47;
　　Mosiah 27:24;
　　Alma 18:16.
　　TG God, Spirit of.
39*a* TG Revelation.
　 b Alma 18:22; 48:11 (11–17);

　　Hel. 16:14.
　　TG Wisdom.
40*a* Ps. 105:21; Dan. 2:48;
　　JS—M 1:49 (49–50).
　 b Esth. 10:3.
41*a* Dan. 6:3.
42*a* Esth. 3:10; 8:2 (2, 8, 10).
　 b Dan. 5:29.
　 c Esth. 8:15.

43 And he made him to ride in the second chariot which he had; and they cried before him, Bow the knee: and he made him *aruler* over all the land of Egypt.

44 And Pharaoh said unto Joseph, I *am* Pharaoh, and without thee shall no man lift up his hand or foot in all the land of Egypt.

45 And Pharaoh called Joseph's name Zaphnath-paaneah; and he gave him to wife *a*Asenath the daughter of Poti-pherah *b*priest of On. And Joseph went out over *all* the land of Egypt.

46 ¶ And *a*Joseph *was* thirty years old when he stood before Pharaoh king of Egypt. And Joseph went out from the presence of Pharaoh, and went throughout all the land of Egypt.

47 And in the seven plenteous years the earth brought forth by handfuls.

48 And he gathered up all the *a*food of the seven years, which were in the land of Egypt, and laid up the food in the cities: the food of the field, which *was* round about every city, laid he up in the same.

49 And Joseph gathered corn as the sand of the sea, very much, until he left numbering; for *it was* without number.

50 And unto Joseph were born two sons before the years of famine came, which Asenath the daughter of Poti-pherah priest of On bare unto him.

51 And Joseph called the name of the firstborn *a*Manasseh: For God, *said he,* hath made me forget all my toil, and all my father's house.

52 And the name of the second called he *a*Ephraim: For God hath caused me to be *b*fruitful in the land of my affliction.

53 ¶ And the seven years of plen-teousness, that was in the land of Egypt, were ended.

54 And the seven years of *a*dearth began to come, according as Joseph had said: and the dearth was in all lands; but in all the land of Egypt there was bread.

55 And when all the land of Egypt was famished, the people cried to Pharaoh for bread: and Pharaoh said unto all the Egyptians, Go unto Joseph; what he saith to you, do.

56 And the famine was over all the face of the earth: And Joseph opened all the storehouses, and *a*sold unto the Egyptians; and the famine waxed sore in the land of Egypt.

57 And all countries came into Egypt to Joseph for to buy *corn;* because that the famine was *so* sore in all lands.

CHAPTER 42

Jacob sends his sons to buy grain in Egypt—They bow before Joseph—He makes harsh accusations against them, imprisons Simeon, and sends them back for Benjamin.

Now when Jacob saw that there was *a*corn in Egypt, Jacob said unto his sons, Why do ye look one upon another?

2 And he said, Behold, I have heard that there is corn in Egypt: get you down thither, and buy for us from thence; that we may live, and not die.

3 ¶ And Joseph's ten brethren went down to buy *a*corn in Egypt.

4 But *a*Benjamin, Joseph's brother, Jacob sent not with his brethren; for he said, Lest peradventure mischief befall him.

5 And the sons of Israel came to buy *corn* among those that came: for the famine was in the land of Canaan.

43a Gen. 42:6; 45:8, 26;
   1 Ne. 3:29;
   Mosiah 1:10;
   Alma 2:16.
45a Gen. 46:20 (19–20).
   b Gen. 47:22.
46a Gen. 37:2 (1–11); 50:26.
48a TG Food.
51a Gen. 46:20;

Ex. 29:42 (42–43);
Lev. 16:2;
Josh. 17:1 (1, 5);
Alma 10:3.
TG Israel, Joseph,
   People of.
52a D&C 113:4;
   133:34 (30–34).
   TG Israel, Joseph,

People of.
   b Gen. 26:22; 28:3.
54a TG Drought; Famine.
56a Gen. 47:14.
42 1a Acts 7:12.
   3a Gen. 43:20.
   4a Gen. 35:18; 44:29;
     49:27 (26–28);
     Josh. 18:11 (11–28).

6 And Joseph *was* the ᵃgovernor over the land, *and* he *it was* that sold to all the people of the land: and Joseph's brethren came, and ᵇbowed down themselves before him *with* their faces to the earth.

7 And Joseph saw his brethren, and he knew them, but made himself strange unto them, and spake roughly unto them; and he said unto them, Whence come ye? And they said, From the land of Canaan to buy food.

8 And Joseph knew his brethren, but they knew not him.

9 And Joseph remembered the ᵃdreams which he dreamed of them, and said unto them, Ye *are* spies; to see the nakedness of the land ye are come.

10 And they said unto him, Nay, my lord, but to buy food are thy servants come.

11 We *are* all one ᵃman's sons; we *are* true *men*, thy servants are no spies.

12 And he said unto them, Nay, but to see the nakedness of the land ye are come.

13 And they said, Thy servants *are* twelve brethren, the sons of one man in the land of Canaan; and, behold, the youngest *is* this day with our father, and one *is* ᵃnot.

14 And Joseph said unto them, That *is it* that I spake unto you, saying, Ye *are* spies:

15 Hereby ye shall be proved: By the life of Pharaoh ye shall not go forth hence, except your youngest brother come hither.

16 Send one of you, and let him fetch your brother, and ye shall be kept in prison, that your words may be proved, whether *there be any* truth in you: or else by the life of Pharaoh surely ye *are* spies.

17 And he put them all together into ward three days.

18 And Joseph said unto them the third day, This do, and live; *for* I ᵃfear God:

19 If ye *be* true *men*, let one of your brethren be bound in the house of your prison: go ye, carry corn for the famine of your houses:

20 But bring your youngest brother unto me; so shall your words be verified, and ye shall not die. And they did so.

21 ¶ And they said one to another, We *are* verily ᵃguilty concerning our brother, in that we saw the anguish of his soul, when he besought us, and we would not hear; therefore is this distress come upon us.

22 And ᵃReuben answered them, saying, Spake I not unto you, saying, Do not sin against the child; and ye would not hear? therefore, behold, also his ᵇblood is required.

23 And they knew not that Joseph understood *them*; for he spake unto them by an interpreter.

24 And he turned himself about from them, and ᵃwept; and returned to them again, and communed with them, and took from them Simeon, and bound him before their eyes.

25 ¶ Then Joseph commanded to fill their sacks with corn, and to restore every man's ᵃmoney into his sack, and to give them provision for the way: and thus did he unto them.

26 And they laded their asses with the corn, and departed thence.

27 And as one of them opened his sack to give his ass provender in the inn, he espied his ᵃmoney; for, behold, it *was* in his sack's mouth.

28 And he said unto his brethren, My money is restored; and, lo, *it is* even in my sack: and their heart failed *them*, and they were afraid, saying one to another, What *is* this *that* God hath done unto us?

29 ¶ And they came unto Jacob their father unto the land of Canaan, and told him all that befell unto them; saying,

---

6a Gen. 41:43 (41–43).
  b Gen. 37:7 (7, 9–10);
    43:26 (26–28); 44:14.
9a TG Dream.
11a Gen. 43:27; 44:20.

13a Gen. 37:30.
18a TG Reverence.
21a TG Guilt.
22a Gen. 35:23 (22–23);
    37:21; 42:37.

  b TG Capital Punishment.
24a Gen. 43:30.
25a Gen. 43:12.
27a Gen. 43:21.

30 The man, *who is* the lord of the land, spake roughly to us, and took us for spies of the country.

31 And we said unto him, We *are* true *men;* we are no spies:

32 We *be* twelve brethren, sons of our father; one *is* not, and the youngest *is* this day with our father in the land of Canaan.

33 And the man, the lord of the country, said unto us, Hereby shall I know that ye *are* true *men;* leave one of your brethren *here* with me, and take *food for* the famine of your households, and be gone:

34 And bring your youngest brother unto me: then shall I know that ye *are* no spies, but *that* ye *are* true *men: so* will I deliver you your brother, and ye shall traffick in the land.

35 ¶ And it came to pass as they emptied their sacks, that, behold, every man's bundle of money *was* in his sack: and when *both* they and their father saw the bundles of money, they were afraid.

36 And Jacob their father said unto them, Me have ye bereaved *of my children:* Joseph *is* not, and Simeon *is* not, and ye will take *a*Benjamin *away:* all these things are against me.

37 And *a*Reuben spake unto his father, saying, Slay my two sons, if I bring him not to thee: deliver him into my hand, and I will bring him to thee again.

38 And he said, My son shall not go down with you; for his brother is dead, and he is left alone: if mischief befall him by the way in the which ye go, then shall ye bring down my gray hairs with *a*sorrow to the grave.

CHAPTER 43

Jacob is persuaded to send Benjamin to Egypt—Joseph's brothers show respect to him—They all eat and drink together.

AND the famine *was* sore in the land.

2 And it came to pass, when they had eaten up the corn which they had brought out of Egypt, their father said unto them, Go again, buy us a little food.

3 And Judah spake unto him, saying, The man did solemnly protest unto us, saying, Ye shall not see my face, except your *a*brother *be* with you.

4 If thou wilt send our brother with us, we will go down and buy thee food:

5 But if thou wilt not send *him,* we will not go down: for the man said unto us, Ye shall not see my face, except your *a*brother *be* with you.

6 And Israel said, Wherefore dealt ye *so* ill with me, *as* to tell the man whether ye had yet a brother?

7 And they said, The man asked us straitly of our state, and of our kindred, saying, *Is* your father yet alive? have ye *another* brother? and we told him according to the tenor of these words: could we certainly know that he would say, Bring your brother down?

8 And Judah said unto Israel his father, Send the lad with me, and we will arise and go; that we may live, and not die, both we, and thou, *and* also our little ones.

9 I will be surety for him; of my hand shalt thou require him: if I bring him not unto thee, and set him before thee, then let me bear the *a*blame for ever:

10 For except we had lingered, surely now we had returned this second time.

11 And their father Israel said unto them, If *it must be* so now, do this; take of the best fruits in the land in your vessels, and carry down the man a present, a little balm, and a little honey, spices, and myrrh, nuts, and almonds:

12 And take double money in your hand; and the *a*money that was brought again in the mouth of your sacks, carry *it* again in your hand; peradventure it *was* an oversight:

36*a* Gen. 44:29.
37*a* Gen. 42:22;
    Num. 26:5.

38*a* Gen. 37:35; 44:31 (29, 31).
43 3*a* Gen. 44:26 (25–26).
    5*a* Gen. 44:23 (21–23).

9*a* Gen. 44:32.
12*a* Gen. 42:25 (25, 27, 35).

13 Take also your brother, and arise, go again unto the man:

14 And God Almighty give you mercy before the man, that he may send away your other brother, and Benjamin. If I be bereaved *of my children,* I am bereaved.

15 ¶ And the men took that present, and they took double money in their hand, and Benjamin; and rose up, and went down to Egypt, and stood before Joseph.

16 And when Joseph saw Benjamin with them, he said to the ruler of his house, Bring *these* men home, and slay, and make ready; for *these* men shall dine with me at noon.

17 And the man did as Joseph bade; and the man brought the men into Joseph's house.

18 And the men were afraid, because they were brought into Joseph's house; and they said, Because of the money that was returned in our sacks at the first time are we brought in; that he may seek occasion against us, and fall upon us, and take us for bondmen, and our asses.

19 And they came near to the steward of Joseph's house, and they communed with him at the door of the house,

20 And said, O *ª*sir, we came indeed down at the first time to buy *b*food:

21 And it came to pass, when we came to the inn, that we opened our sacks, and, behold, *every* man's *ª*money *was* in the mouth of his sack, our money in full weight: and we have brought it again in our hand.

22 And other money have we brought down in our hands to buy food: we cannot tell who put our money in our sacks.

23 And he said, Peace *be* to you, fear not: your God, and the God of your father, hath given you treasure in your sacks: I had your money. And he brought Simeon out unto them.

24 And the man brought the men into Joseph's house, and gave *them* water, and they *ª*washed their feet; and he gave their asses provender.

25 And they made ready the present against Joseph came at noon: for they heard that they should eat bread there.

26 ¶ And when Joseph came home, they brought him the present which *was* in their hand into the house, and *ª*bowed themselves to him to the earth.

27 And he asked them of *their* welfare, and said, *Is* your father well, the old *ª*man of whom ye spake? *Is* he yet alive?

28 And they answered, Thy servant our father *is* in good health, he *is* yet alive. And they bowed down their heads, and made obeisance.

29 And he lifted up his eyes, and saw his brother *ª*Benjamin, his mother's son, and said, *Is* this your younger brother, of whom ye spake unto me? And he said, God be gracious unto thee, my son.

30 And Joseph made haste; for his bowels did yearn upon his brother: and he sought *where* to weep; and he entered into *his* chamber, and *ª*wept there.

31 And he washed his face, and went out, and refrained himself, and said, Set on bread.

32 And they set on for him by himself, and for them by themselves, and for the Egyptians, which did eat with him, by themselves: because the Egyptians might not eat bread with the Hebrews; for that *is* an *ª*abomination unto the Egyptians.

33 And they sat before him, the firstborn according to his *ª*birthright, and the youngest according to his youth: and the men marvelled one at another.

34 And he took *and sent* *ª*messes unto them from before him: but

20*a* Gen. 44:18.
  b Gen. 42:3.
21*a* Gen. 42:27.
24*a* TG Wash.

26*a* Gen. 37:7 (7, 9–10); 42:6; 44:14.
27*a* Gen. 42:11 (11–13).
29*a* Gen. 35:18.

30*a* Gen. 42:24; 45:1 (1–2).
32*a* Gen. 46:34.
33*a* TG Birthright.
34*a* 2 Sam. 11:8.

*b*Benjamin's mess was five times so much as any of theirs. And they drank, and were merry with him.

CHAPTER 44

Joseph arranges to stop the return of his brothers to Canaan—Judah offers himself in place of Benjamin for their father's sake.

AND he commanded the steward of his house, saying, Fill the men's sacks *with* food, as much as they can carry, and put every man's money in his sack's mouth.

2 And put my cup, the silver cup, in the sack's mouth of the youngest, and his corn money. And he did according to the word that Joseph had spoken.

3 As soon as the morning was light, the men were sent away, they and their asses.

4 *And* when they were gone out of the city, *and* not *yet* far off, Joseph said unto his steward, Up, follow after the men; and when thou dost overtake them, say unto them, Wherefore have ye rewarded evil for good?

5 *Is* not this *it* in which my lord drinketh, and whereby indeed he divineth? ye have done evil in so doing.

6 ¶ And he overtook them, and he spake unto them these same words.

7 And they said unto him, Wherefore saith my lord these words? God forbid that thy servants should do according to this thing:

8 Behold, the money, which we found in our sacks' mouths, we brought again unto thee out of the land of Canaan: how then should we steal out of thy lord's house silver or gold?

9 With whomsoever of thy servants it be found, both let him die, and we also will be my lord's bondmen.

10 And he said, Now also *let it be* according unto your words: he with whom it is found shall be my servant; and ye shall be blameless.

11 Then they speedily took down every man his sack to the ground, and opened every man his sack.

12 And he searched, *and* began at the eldest, and left at the youngest: and the cup was found in Benjamin's sack.

13 Then they *a*rent their clothes, and laded every man his ass, and returned to the city.

14 ¶ And Judah and his brethren came to Joseph's house; for he *was* yet there: and they *a*fell before him on the ground.

15 And Joseph said unto them, What deed *is* this that ye have done? wot ye not that such a man as I can certainly divine?

16 And Judah said, What shall we say unto my lord? what shall we speak? or how shall we clear ourselves? God hath found out the iniquity of thy servants: behold, we *are* my lord's servants, both we, and *he* also with whom the cup is found.

17 And he said, God forbid that I should do so: *but* the man in whose hand the cup is found, he shall be my servant; and as for you, get you up in peace unto your father.

18 ¶ Then Judah came near unto him, and said, Oh my *a*lord, let thy servant, I pray thee, speak a word in my lord's ears, and let not thine *b*anger burn against thy servant: for thou *art* even as Pharaoh.

19 My lord asked his servants, saying, Have ye a father, or a brother?

20 And we said unto my lord, We have a father, an old *a*man, and a child of his old age, a little one; and his brother is dead, and he alone is left of his mother, and his father loveth him.

21 And thou saidst unto thy servants, Bring him down unto me, that I may set mine eyes upon him.

22 And we said unto my lord, The lad cannot leave his father: for *if* he

---

34*b* Gen. 45:22.
44 13*a* Job 1:20;
      Eccl. 3:7;

Alma 46:12 (12–23).
14*a* Gen. 37:7 (7, 9–10); 42:6;
      43:26 (26–28).

18*a* Gen. 43:20.
  b Ex. 32:22.
20*a* Gen. 42:11 (11–13).

should leave his father, *his father* would die.

23 And thou saidst unto thy servants, Except your youngest ^abrother come down with you, ye shall see my face no more.

24 And it came to pass when we came up unto thy servant my father, we told him the words of my lord.

25 And our father said, Go again, *and* buy us a little food.

26 And we said, We cannot go down: if our youngest brother be with us, then will we go down: for we may not see the man's face, except our ^ayoungest brother *be* with us.

27 And thy servant my father said unto us, Ye know that my wife bare me two *sons:*

28 And the one went out from me, and I said, Surely he is ^atorn in ^bpieces; and I saw him not since:

29 And if ye ^atake this also from me, and mischief befall ^bhim, ye shall bring down my gray hairs with sorrow to the grave.

30 Now therefore when I come to thy servant my father, and the lad *be* not with us; seeing that his life is ^abound up in the lad's life;

31 It shall come to pass, when he seeth that the lad *is* not *with us,* that he will die: and thy servants shall bring down the gray hairs of thy servant our father with ^asorrow to the grave.

32 For thy servant became surety for the lad unto my father, saying, If I bring him not unto thee, then I shall bear the ^ablame to my father for ever.

33 Now therefore, I pray thee, let thy servant abide instead of the lad a bondman to my lord; and let the lad go up with his brethren.

34 For how shall I go up to my father, and the lad *be* not with me? lest peradventure I see the evil that shall come on my father.

CHAPTER 45

Joseph makes himself known to his brothers—They rejoice together—Pharaoh invites Jacob and his family to dwell in Egypt and eat the fat of the land.

THEN Joseph could not ^arefrain himself before all them that stood by him; and he ^bcried, Cause every man to go out from me. And there stood no man with him, while Joseph made himself known unto his brethren.

2 And he wept aloud: and the Egyptians and the house of Pharaoh heard.

3 And Joseph said unto his brethren, I *am* ^aJoseph; doth my father yet live? And his brethren could not answer him; for they were ^btroubled at his presence.

4 And Joseph said unto his brethren, Come near to me, I pray you. And they came near. And he said, I *am* ^aJoseph your brother, whom ye sold into Egypt.

5 Now therefore be not ^agrieved, nor angry with yourselves, that ye sold me hither: for God did ^bsend me before you to preserve life.

6 For these two years *hath* the famine *been* in the land: and yet *there are* five years, in the which *there shall* neither *be* earing nor harvest.

7 And God sent me before you to ^apreserve you a ^bposterity in the earth, and to save your lives by a great deliverance.

8 So now *it was* not you *that* sent me hither, but God: and he hath made me a father to Pharaoh, and lord of all his house, and a ^aruler throughout all the land of Egypt.

---

23 a Gen. 43:5 (3–5).
26 a Gen. 43:3.
28 a Gen. 37:33.
  b Alma 46:24.
29 a Gen. 42:36 (36–38).
  b Gen. 42:4; 49:27 (26–28);
    Josh. 18:11 (11–28).
30 a 1 Sam. 18:1.
31 a Gen. 42:38.
32 a Gen. 43:9.
45 1 a Gen. 43:30 (30–31).
  b Gen. 46:29.
3 a Acts 7:13.
  b Job 23:15.
4 a 2 Ne. 3:4.
5 a TG Benevolence;
    Family, Love within.
  b Gen. 50:20;
    Ps. 105:17.
7 a Esth. 4:14; 2 Ne. 3:16;
    D&C 107:42.
  TG Protection, Divine.
  b 2 Ne. 3:3, 5 (3–7).
8 a Gen. 41:43 (41–44).

9 Haste ye, and go up to my father, and say unto him, Thus saith thy son Joseph, God hath made me lord of all Egypt: come down unto me, tarry not:

10 And thou shalt dwell in the land of ªGoshen, and thou shalt be near unto me, thou, and thy children, and thy children's children, and thy flocks, and thy herds, and all that thou hast:

11 And there will I ªnourish thee; for yet *there are* five years of famine; lest thou, and thy household, and all that thou hast, come to poverty.

12 And, behold, your eyes see, and the eyes of my brother Benjamin, that *it is* my mouth that speaketh unto you.

13 And ye shall tell my father of all my glory in Egypt, and of all that ye have seen; and ye shall haste and bring down my ªfather hither.

14 And he fell upon his brother Benjamin's neck, and wept; and Benjamin wept upon his neck.

15 Moreover he kissed all his brethren, and wept upon them: and after that his brethren talked with him.

16 ¶ And the fame thereof was heard in Pharaoh's house, saying, Joseph's brethren are come: and it ªpleased Pharaoh well, and his servants.

17 And Pharaoh said unto Joseph, Say unto thy brethren, This do ye; lade your beasts, and go, get you unto the land of Canaan;

18 And take your father and your households, and come unto me: and I will give you the good of the land of Egypt, and ye shall eat the fat of the land.

19 Now thou art commanded, this do ye; take you ªwagons out of the land of Egypt for your little ones, and for your wives, and bring your father, and come.

20 Also regard not your stuff; for the good of all the land of Egypt *is* yours.

21 And the children of Israel did so: and Joseph gave them wagons, according to the commandment of Pharaoh, and gave them provision for the way.

22 To all of them he gave each man changes of raiment; but to ªBenjamin he gave three hundred *pieces* of silver, and five changes of raiment.

23 And to his father he sent after this *manner;* ten asses laden with the good things of Egypt, and ten she asses laden with corn and bread and meat for his father by the way.

24 So he sent his brethren away, and they departed: and he said unto them, See that ye fall not out by the way.

25 ¶ And they went up out of Egypt, and came into the land of Canaan unto Jacob their father,

26 And told him, saying, Joseph *is* yet alive, and he *is* ªgovernor over all the land of Egypt. And Jacob's heart fainted, for he believed them not.

27 And they told him all the words of Joseph, which he had said unto them: and when he saw the ªwagons which Joseph had sent to carry him, the spirit of Jacob their father ᵇrevived:

28 And Israel said, *It is* enough; Joseph my son *is* yet alive: I will go and see him before I die.

CHAPTER 46

The Lord sends Jacob and his family of seventy souls to Egypt—The descendants of Jacob are named—Joseph meets Jacob.

AND Israel took his journey with all that he had, and came to ªBeersheba, and offered sacrifices unto the God of his father Isaac.

2 And God spake unto Israel in the ªvisions of the night, and said, Jacob, Jacob. And he said, Here *am* I.

10a Gen. 46:28 (28–34);
   47:1 (1, 11); 50:8.
11a Gen. 47:12.
13a Acts 7:14.
16a Gen. 41:37.

19a Gen. 46:5;
   D&C 136:5.
22a Gen. 43:34.
26a Gen. 41:43 (41–44).
27a Num. 7:3 (3, 5).

   b Gen. 46:5 (3–5).
46 1a Gen. 21:31 (31, 33);
   26:23 (23, 33).
2a TG Vision.

3 And he said, I *am* God, the God of thy ᵃfather: fear not to go down into ᵇEgypt; for I will there make of thee a great ᶜnation:

4 ᵃI will go down with thee into Egypt; and I will also surely ᵇbring thee up *again:* and ᶜJoseph shall put his hand upon thine eyes.

5 And Jacob ᵃrose up from Beersheba: and the sons of Israel carried Jacob their father, and their little ones, and their wives, in the ᵇwagons which Pharaoh had sent to carry him.

6 And they took their cattle, and their goods, which they had gotten in the land of Canaan, and came into ᵃEgypt, Jacob, and all his seed with him:

7 His sons, and his sons' sons with him, his daughters, and his sons' daughters, and all his ᵃseed brought he with him into Egypt.

8 ¶ And these *are* the ᵃnames of the ᵇchildren of Israel, which came into Egypt, Jacob and his sons: Reuben, Jacob's firstborn.

9 And the sons of ᵃReuben; Hanoch, and Phallu, and Hezron, and Carmi.

10 ¶ And the sons of Simeon; Jemuel, and Jamin, and Ohad, and Jachin, and Zohar, and Shaul the son of a Canaanitish woman.

11 ¶ And the sons of ᵃLevi; Gershon, Kohath, and Merari.

12 ¶ And the sons of Judah; ᵃEr, and ᵇOnan, and Shelah, and Pharez, and ᶜZerah: but Er and Onan died in the land of Canaan. And the sons of Pharez were Hezron and Hamul.

13 ¶ And the sons of ᵃIssachar; Tola, and Phuvah, and Job, and Shimron.

14 ¶ And the sons of Zebulun; Sered, and Elon, and Jahleel.

15 These *be* the sons of ᵃLeah, which she bare unto Jacob in Padan-aram, with his daughter Dinah: all the souls of his sons and his daughters *were* thirty and three.

16 ¶ And the sons of ᵃGad; Ziphion, and Haggi, Shuni, and Ezbon, Eri, and Arodi, and Areli.

17 ¶ And the sons of Asher; Jimnah, and Ishuah, and Isui, and Beriah, and Serah their sister: and the sons of Beriah; Heber, and Malchiel.

18 These *are* the sons of ᵃZilpah, whom Laban gave to Leah his daughter, and these she bare unto Jacob, *even* sixteen souls.

19 The sons of Rachel Jacob's wife; Joseph, and ᵃBenjamin.

20 ¶ And unto Joseph in the land of Egypt were born ᵃManasseh and Ephraim, which ᵇAsenath the daughter of Poti-pherah priest of On bare unto him.

21 ¶ And the sons of ᵃBenjamin *were* Belah, and Becher, and Ashbel, Gera, and Naaman, Ehi, and Rosh, Muppim, and Huppim, and Ard.

22 These *are* the sons of Rachel, which were born to Jacob: all the souls *were* fourteen.

23 ¶ And the sons of ᵃDan; Hushim.

24 ¶ And the sons of Naphtali; Jahzeel, and Guni, and Jezer, and Shillem.

25 These *are* the sons of ᵃBilhah, which Laban gave unto Rachel his daughter, and she bare these unto Jacob: all the souls *were* seven.

26 All the souls that came with Jacob into Egypt, which came out

3 *a* D&C 136:21.
  b TG Israel, Bondage of, in Egypt.
  c TG Israel, Origins of.
4 *a* Gen. 28:15; 48:21.
  b Ex. 2:24.
  c Gen. 50:1.
5 *a* Gen. 45:27 (26–28).
  b Gen. 45:19.
6 *a* Ps. 105:23; Isa. 52:4; Ether 13:7; Abr. 2:21.

7 *a* Gen. 37:35.
8 *a* Ex. 1:1 (1–5); 6:14 (14–25). TG Israel, Twelve Tribes of.
  b Alma 46:23; 3 Ne. 5:24; Morm. 7:10.
9 *a* Num. 26:5 (5–7).
11 *a* 1 Chr. 6:1.
12 *a* Gen. 38:7 (3, 7, 10).
  b 1 Chr. 2:3.
  c Gen. 38:30.

13 *a* 1 Chr. 7:1.
15 *a* Gen. 29:32.
16 *a* Num. 26:15 (15–17).
18 *a* Gen. 29:24; 30:12.
19 *a* Gen. 35:18.
20 *a* Gen. 41:51; Josh. 17:1 (1, 5).
  b Gen. 41:45.
21 *a* Num. 26:38; 1 Chr. 7:6 (6–12).
23 *a* Num. 26:42.
25 *a* Gen. 29:29; 30:5 (5–8).

of his loins, besides Jacob's sons' wives, all the souls *were* threescore and six;

27 And the sons of Joseph, which were born him in Egypt, *were* two souls: all the souls of the house of *a*Jacob, which came into Egypt, *were* *b*threescore and ten.

28 ¶ And he sent Judah before him unto Joseph, to direct his face unto Goshen; and they came into the land of *a*Goshen.

29 And Joseph made ready his chariot, and went up to meet Israel his father, to Goshen, and presented himself unto him; and he fell on his neck, and *a*wept on his neck a good while.

30 And Israel said unto Joseph, Now let me die, since I have seen thy face, because thou *art* yet alive.

31 And Joseph said unto his brethren, and unto his father's house, I will go up, and shew *a*Pharaoh, and say unto him, My brethren, and my father's house, which *were* in the land of Canaan, are come unto me;

32 And the men *are* shepherds, for their trade hath been to feed cattle; and they have brought their flocks, and their herds, and all that they have.

33 And it shall come to pass, when Pharaoh shall call you, and shall say, What *is* your *a*occupation?

34 That ye shall say, Thy servants' trade hath been about *a*cattle from our youth even until now, both we, *and* also our fathers: that ye may dwell in the land of Goshen; for every shepherd *is* an *b*abomination unto the Egyptians.

CHAPTER 47

The Israelites settle in Goshen—Jacob blesses Pharaoh—Joseph sells grain to the Egyptians—Pharaoh receives the Egyptians' cattle and lands—Jacob desires to be buried with his fathers in Canaan.

THEN Joseph came and told *a*Pharaoh, and said, My father and my brethren, and their flocks, and their herds, and all that they have, are come out of the land of Canaan; and, behold, they *are* in the land of *b*Goshen.

2 And he took some of his brethren, *even* five men, and presented them unto *a*Pharaoh.

3 And Pharaoh said unto his brethren, What *is* your *a*occupation? And they said unto Pharaoh, Thy servants *are* *b*shepherds, both we, *and* also our fathers.

4 They said moreover unto Pharaoh, For to *a*sojourn in the land are we come; for thy servants have no pasture for their flocks; for the famine *is* sore in the land of Canaan: now therefore, we pray thee, let thy servants dwell in the land of Goshen.

5 And Pharaoh spake unto Joseph, saying, Thy father and thy brethren are come unto thee:

6 The land of *a*Egypt *is* before thee; in the best of the land make thy father and brethren to dwell; in the land of Goshen let them dwell: and if thou knowest *any* men of activity among them, then make them rulers over my cattle.

7 And Joseph brought in Jacob his father, and set him before Pharaoh: and Jacob blessed Pharaoh.

8 And Pharaoh said unto Jacob, How old *art* thou?

9 And Jacob said unto Pharaoh, The days of the years of my *a*pilgrimage *are* an hundred and thirty years: few and *b*evil have the days of the years of my life been, and have not attained unto the *c*days of the years of the life of my fathers in the days of their pilgrimage.

27a TG Israel, Origins of.
  b Num. 1:46 (20–46).
28a Gen. 46:10.
29a Gen. 45:1.
31a Gen. 47:1.
33a Gen. 47:3.
34a Gen. 37:12; 47:3;

Abr. 2:5.
  b Gen. 43:32.
47 1a Gen. 46:31.
  b Gen. 45:10.
2a Acts 7:13.
3a Gen. 46:33.
  b Gen. 46:34.

4a Deut. 26:5.
6a Ether 13:7.
9a Ps. 119:54.
  b IE unpleasant.
  c Gen. 25:7; 35:28.

10 And Jacob blessed Pharaoh, and went out from before Pharaoh.

11 ¶ And Joseph placed his father and his brethren, and gave them a possession in the land of Egypt, in the best of the land, in the land of ᵃRameses, as Pharaoh had commanded.

12 And Joseph ᵃnourished his father, and his brethren, and all his father's household, with bread, according to *their* families.

13 ¶ And *there was* no bread in all the land; for the ᵃfamine *was* very sore, so that the land of Egypt and *all* the land of Canaan fainted by reason of the famine.

14 And Joseph gathered up all the ᵃmoney that was found in the land of Egypt, and in the land of Canaan, for the corn which they bought: and Joseph brought the money into Pharaoh's house.

15 And when money failed in the land of Egypt, and in the land of Canaan, all the Egyptians came unto Joseph, and said, Give us ᵃbread: for why should we die in thy presence? for the money faileth.

16 And Joseph said, Give your cattle; and I will give you for your cattle, if money fail.

17 And they brought their cattle unto Joseph: and Joseph gave them bread *in exchange* for horses, and for the flocks, and for the cattle of the herds, and for the asses: and he fed them with bread for all their cattle for that year.

18 When that year was ended, they came unto him the second year, and said unto him, We will not hide *it* from my lord, how that our money is spent; my lord also hath our herds of cattle; there is not ought left in the sight of my lord, but our bodies, and our lands:

19 Wherefore shall we die before thine eyes, both we and our land? buy us and our land for bread, and we and our land will be servants unto Pharaoh: and give *us* seed, that we may live, and not die, that the land be not desolate.

20 And Joseph bought all the land of Egypt for Pharaoh; for the Egyptians sold every man his field, because the famine prevailed over them: so the land became Pharaoh's.

21 And as for the people, ᵃhe removed them to cities from *one* end of the borders of Egypt even to the *other* end thereof.

22 Only the land of the ᵃpriests bought he not; for the priests had a portion *assigned them* of Pharaoh, and did eat their portion which Pharaoh gave them: wherefore they sold not their lands.

23 Then Joseph said unto the people, Behold, I have bought you this day and your land for Pharaoh: lo, *here is* seed for you, and ye shall sow the land.

24 And it shall come to pass ᵃin the increase, that ye shall give the ᵇfifth *part* unto Pharaoh, and four parts shall be your own, for seed of the field, and for your food, and for them of your households, and for food for your little ones.

25 And they said, Thou hast saved our lives: let us find grace in the sight of my lord, and we will be Pharaoh's servants.

26 And Joseph made it a law over the land of Egypt unto this day, *that* Pharaoh should have the fifth *part*; except the land of the ᵃpriests only, *which* became not Pharaoh's.

27 ¶ And Israel dwelt in the land of Egypt, in the country of Goshen; and they had possessions therein, and grew, and multiplied exceedingly.

28 And Jacob lived in the land of Egypt seventeen years: so the whole age of ᵃJacob was an hundred forty and seven years.

11*a* Ex. 1:11; 12:37;
        Num. 33:3 (3–5).
12*a* Gen. 45:11.
13*a* TG Famine.
14*a* Gen. 41:56.

15*a* TG Welfare.
21*a* Samaritan and
        Septuagint: he made
        them slaves, or serfs.
22*a* Gen. 41:45; 47:26.

24*a* HEB at the harvests.
    b Mosiah 11:3;
        Ether 10:5 (5–6).
26*a* Gen. 47:22.
28*a* Gen. 25:7; 35:28.

29 And the *a*time drew nigh that Israel must die: and he called his son Joseph, and said unto him, If now I have found grace in thy sight, put, I pray thee, thy hand under my *b*thigh, and deal kindly and truly with me; *c*bury me not, I pray thee, in Egypt:

30 But I will lie with my fathers, and thou shalt carry me out of Egypt, and *a*bury me in their buryingplace. And he said, I will do as thou hast said.

31 And he said, Swear unto me. And he sware unto him. And Israel *a*bowed himself *b*upon the *c*bed's head.

CHAPTER 48

Jacob tells of the appearance of God to him in Luz—He adopts Ephraim and Manasseh as his own children—Jacob blesses Joseph—He puts Ephraim before Manasseh—The seed of Ephraim will become a multitude of nations—The children of Israel will come again into the land of their fathers.

AND it came to pass after these things, that *one* told Joseph, Behold, thy father *is* sick: and he took with him his two sons, Manasseh and Ephraim.

2 And *one* told *a*Jacob, and said, Behold, thy son Joseph cometh unto thee: and Israel *b*strengthened himself, and sat upon the bed.

3 And Jacob said unto Joseph, God *a*Almighty *b*appeared unto me at *c*Luz in the land of Canaan, and blessed me,

4 And said unto me, Behold, I will make thee *a*fruitful, and multiply thee, and I will make of thee a multitude of people; and will give this *b*land to thy seed after thee *for* an everlasting *c*possession.

5 ¶ *a*And now thy two sons, *b*Ephraim and *c*Manasseh, which were born unto thee in the land of Egypt before I came unto thee into Egypt, *are* mine; as Reuben and Simeon, they shall be mine.

6 And thy issue, which thou begettest after them, shall be thine, *and* shall be called after the name of their brethren in their inheritance.

7 And as for me, when I came from Padan, *a*Rachel died by me in the land of Canaan in the way, when yet *there was* but a little way to come unto Ephrath: and I buried her there in the way of Ephrath; the same *is* Beth-lehem.

8 And Israel beheld Joseph's sons, and said, Who *are* these?

9 And Joseph said unto his father, They *are* my sons, whom God hath given me in this *place*. And he said, Bring them, I pray thee, unto me, and I will *a*bless them.

10 Now the eyes of Israel were *a*dim for age, *so that* he could not see. And he brought them *b*near unto him; and he kissed them, and embraced them.

11 And Israel said unto Joseph, I had not thought to see thy face: and, lo, God hath shewed me also thy seed.

12 And Joseph brought them out from between his knees, and he bowed himself with his face to the earth.

13 And Joseph took them both, Ephraim in his right hand toward Israel's left hand, and Manasseh in his left hand toward Israel's right hand, and brought *them* near unto him.

29*a* Deut. 31:14; 2 Ne. 1:14;
　　Jacob 1:9.
　b Gen. 24:2 (2, 8);
　　JST Gen. 24:2 (Gen. 24:2
　　note *b*).
　c Gen. 49:29; 50:25.
30*a* Gen. 50:5.
31*a* Gen. 48:2.
　b OR at the head of the
　　bed.
　c 1 Kgs. 1:47; Abr. 1:13.

48 2*a* Heb. 11:21.
　b Gen. 47:31.
　3*a* 1 Ne. 1:14; 2 Ne. 9:46;
　　3 Ne. 4:32;
　　D&C 76:106 (106–7); 87:6;
　　Moses 2:1; JS—H 1:29;
　　A of F 1:11.
　b D&C 107:54; Abr. 2:6.
　c Gen. 28:19; 35:6;
　　Josh. 18:13.
　4*a* TG Seed of Abraham.

　b TG Promised Lands.
　c Gen. 17:8; Abr. 2:6.
　5*a* JST Gen. 48:5–11
　　(Appendix).
　b TG Israel, Joseph,
　　People of.
　c Deut. 3:13.
　7*a* Gen. 35:19.
　9*a* Gen. 49:26.
10*a* Gen. 27:1.
　b Gen. 27:27.

14 And Israel stretched out his right hand, and laid *it* upon ᵃEphraim's head, who *was* the younger, and his left hand upon Manasseh's head, ᵇguiding his hands wittingly; for Manasseh *was* the firstborn.

15 ¶ And he blessed ᵃJoseph, and said, God, before whom my fathers Abraham and Isaac did ᵇwalk, the God which ᶜfed me all my life long unto this day,

16 The ᵃAngel which redeemed me from all evil, bless the lads; and let my ᵇname be named on them, and the name of my fathers Abraham and Isaac; and let them grow into a multitude in the midst of the earth.

17 And when Joseph saw that his father laid his right ᵃhand upon the head of ᵇEphraim, ᶜit displeased him: and he held up his father's hand, to remove it from Ephraim's head unto Manasseh's head.

18 And Joseph said unto his father, Not so, my father: for this *is* the firstborn; put thy right hand upon his head.

19 And his father refused, and said, I know *it,* my son, I know *it:* he also shall become a people, and he also shall be ᵃgreat: but truly his younger brother shall be greater than he, and his ᵇseed shall become a ᶜmultitude of ᵈnations.

20 And he blessed them that day, saying, ᵃIn thee shall Israel ᵇbless, saying, God make thee as Ephraim and as Manasseh: and he set ᶜEphraim before Manasseh.

21 And Israel said unto Joseph, Behold, I die: but ᵃGod shall be with you, and ᵇbring you again unto the ᶜland of your fathers.

22 Moreover I have given to thee one ᵃportion above thy brethren, which I took out of the hand of the Amorite with my sword and with my bow.

CHAPTER 49

Jacob blesses his sons and their seed— Reuben, Simeon, and Levi are chastened— Judah will rule until Shiloh (Christ) comes—Joseph is a fruitful bough by a well—His branches (the Nephites and Lamanites) will run over the wall—The Shepherd and Stone of Israel (Christ) will bless Joseph temporally and spiritually—Jacob chooses to be buried with his fathers in Canaan—He yields up the ghost and is gathered to his people.

AND ᵃJacob called unto his ᵇsons, and said, Gather yourselves together, that I may tell you *that* which shall befall you in the ᶜlast days.

2 Gather yourselves together, and hear, ye sons of Jacob; and hearken unto Israel your ᵃfather.

3 ¶ ᵃReuben, thou *art* my firstborn, my might, and the ᵇbeginning of my strength, the excellency of dignity, and the excellency of power:

4 Unstable as water, thou shalt not excel; because thou wentest up to thy father's ᵃbed; then ᵇdefiledst thou *it:* he went up to my couch.

5 ¶ ᵃSimeon and ᵇLevi *are* brethren;

14*a* Zech. 10:7 (6–12);
  D&C 109:60 (60–61);
  133:34.
  TG Israel, Joseph,
  People of.
 b Septuagint: crossing his
  hands.
15*a* Septuagint: them.
 b TG Walking with God.
 c HEB shepherded; i.e.,
  who was my shepherd.
16*a* Gen. 32:29 (24–30).
 b TG Israel, Joseph, People
  of; Name.
17*a* TG Hands, Laying on of.
 b TG Israel, Blessings of.
 c HEB it was wrong in his
  eyes.

19*a* Josh. 17:14.
 b TG Seed of Abraham.
 c Num. 1:33.
 d D&C 45:24 (24–25).
  TG Israel, Joseph,
  People of.
20*a* OR Through thee.
 b Septuagint: be blessed.
 c Jer. 31:9;
  D&C 133:34.
  TG Birthright.
21*a* Gen. 46:4.
 b TG Israel, Bondage of,
  in Egypt.
 c TG Israel, Land of;
  Promised Lands.
22*a* TG Inheritance.
49 1*a* 2 Ne. 4:12;

Alma 8:22; 45:15.
 b TG Patriarch.
 c TG Last Days.
2*a* TG Family, Patriarchal.
3*a* Gen. 29:32;
  Deut. 33:6;
  1 Chr. 5:1;
  2 Ne. 1:29 (28–29);
  D&C 68:17;
  Abr. 1:3.
 b Deut. 21:17.
4*a* TG Sexual Immorality.
 b TG Sensuality.
5*a* Gen. 29:33 (33–34);
  34:25 (25–31);
  D&C 128:24.
 b Deut. 33:8 (8–11);
  D&C 13.

instruments of ^ccruelty *are in* their habitations.

6 O my soul, come not thou into their secret; unto their assembly, mine honour, be not thou ^aunited: for in their ^banger they ^cslew a man, and in their selfwill they digged down a wall.

7 ^aCursed *be* their ^banger, for *it was* fierce; and their wrath, for it was ^ccruel: I will divide them in Jacob, and scatter them in Israel.

8 ¶ ^aJudah, thou *art he* whom thy brethren shall ^bpraise: thy hand *shall be* in the ^cneck of thine enemies; thy father's children shall ^dbow down before thee.

9 Judah *is* a ^alion's whelp: from the prey, my son, thou art gone up: he stooped down, he couched as a ^blion, and as an old lion; who shall rouse him up?

10 The sceptre shall not depart from ^aJudah, nor a ^blawgiver from between his feet, until ^cShiloh come; and unto him *shall* the ^dgathering of the people *be.*

11 Binding his foal unto the vine, and his ass's colt unto the choice ^avine; he ^bwashed his garments in wine, and his clothes in the ^cblood of grapes:

12 His eyes *shall be* red with wine, and his teeth white with milk.

13 ¶ ^aZebulun shall dwell at the haven of the sea; and he *shall be* for an haven of ships; and his border *shall be* unto Zidon.

14 ¶ ^aIssachar *is* a strong ass couching down between two burdens:

15 And he saw that rest *was* good, and the land that *it was* pleasant; and bowed his shoulder to bear, and became a servant unto tribute.

16 ¶ ^aDan shall ^bjudge his people, as one of the tribes of Israel.

17 Dan shall be a serpent by the way, an adder in the path, that biteth the horse heels, so that his rider shall fall backward.

18 I have ^awaited for thy salvation, O LORD.

19 ¶ ^aGad, a ^btroop shall overcome him: but he shall overcome at the last.

20 ¶ Out of ^aAsher his bread *shall be* fat, and he shall yield royal dainties.

21 ¶ ^aNaphtali *is* a hind let loose: he giveth goodly words.

22 ¶ ^aJoseph *is* a fruitful ^bbough, *even* a fruitful bough by a well; *whose* ^cbranches ^drun over the wall:

23 The archers have sorely grieved him, and shot *at him,* and hated him:

24 But his bow abode in strength, and the arms of his hands were made

5c TG Cruelty.
6a Eph. 5:11;
   Alma 5:57.
 b TG Retribution.
 c Gen. 34:26 (25–31).
7a TG Curse.
 b Gen. 34:7.
   TG Anger.
 c TG Cruelty.
8a TG Israel, Judah,
   People of.
 b Gen. 29:35.
 c 2 Sam. 22:41.
 d Gen. 27:29;
   1 Ne. 7:20; 21:23.
9a Deut. 33:22;
   Rev. 5:5.
 b Num. 24:9;
   3 Ne. 20:16 (15–16);
   Morm. 5:24.
10a TG Israel, Judah,
   People of.
 b Ps. 60:7;
   D&C 38:22; 45:59.

 c The Hebrew word *shiloh*
   may be a short form of
   asher-lo, which can be
   rendered "whose right
   it is." See JST Gen. 50:24
   (Appendix);
   Ezek. 21:27.
   TG Jesus Christ, Messiah;
   Jesus Christ, Prophecies
   about.
 d 2 Ne. 10:7 (7–8);
   25:17 (15–18).
   TG Israel, Mission of.
11a John 15:1 (1–6);
   1 Ne. 15:15.
 b D&C 133:35.
 c Isa. 63:2;
   D&C 76:107;
   133:48 (46–50).
13a Gen. 30:20;
   Deut. 33:18 (18–19);
   Josh. 19:10 (10–16).
14a Gen. 30:18;
   Deut. 33:18 (18–19).

16a Deut. 33:22.
 b Gen. 30:6.
18a Ps. 25:5;
   1 Ne. 21:23;
   2 Ne. 6:13;
   D&C 98:2; 133:45.
19a Deut. 33:20 (20–21);
   1 Chr. 5:26 (18, 26).
 b Gen. 30:11.
20a Gen. 30:13;
   Deut. 33:24 (24–25).
21a Gen. 30:8;
   Deut. 33:23.
22a 2 Ne. 3:4 (2–5).
 b TG Vineyard of the Lord.
 c 1 Ne. 15:12 (12, 16);
   19:24;
   2 Ne. 3:5 (4–5);
   Jacob 2:25;
   Alma 26:36.
   TG Book of Mormon.
 d TG Israel, Scattering of.

strong by the hands of the mighty God of Jacob; (from ^athence *is* the ^bshepherd, the ^cstone of Israel:)

25 *Even* by the God of thy father, who shall help thee; and by the ^aAlmighty, who shall bless thee with blessings of heaven above, blessings of the deep that lieth under, blessings of the breasts, and of the ^bwomb:

26 The ^ablessings of thy father have prevailed above the blessings of my progenitors unto the ^butmost bound of the everlasting ^chills: they shall be on the head of ^dJoseph, and on the crown of the head of him that was separate from his brethren.

27 ¶ ^aBenjamin shall ravin *as* a wolf: in the morning he shall devour the prey, and at night he shall divide the spoil.

28 ¶ All these *are* the ^atwelve tribes of Israel: and this *is it* that their father spake unto them, and ^bblessed them; every one according to his ^cblessing he blessed them.

29 And he charged them, and said unto them, I am to be gathered unto my ^apeople: ^bbury me with my fathers in the cave that *is* in the field of Ephron the Hittite,

30 In the cave that *is* in the field of ^aMachpelah, which *is* before Mamre, in the land of Canaan, which Abraham bought with the field of ^bEphron the Hittite for a possession of a buryingplace.

31 There they ^aburied Abraham and Sarah his wife; there they buried Isaac and Rebekah his wife; and there I buried Leah.

32 The purchase of the field and of the cave that *is* therein *was* from the children of Heth.

33 And when Jacob had made an end of commanding his sons, he gathered up his feet into the bed, and yielded up the ^aghost, and was ^bgathered unto his people.

CHAPTER 50

Jacob's body is embalmed—Joseph buries him in Canaan—Joseph comforts his brothers—The children of Israel multiply—Joseph promises that God will bring Israel out of Egypt into Canaan—Joseph dies in Egypt and is embalmed.

AND ^aJoseph fell upon his father's face, and ^bwept upon him, and kissed him.

2 And Joseph commanded his servants the physicians to ^aembalm his father: and the physicians embalmed Israel.

3 And forty days were fulfilled for him; for so are fulfilled the days of those which are embalmed: and the Egyptians mourned for him threescore and ten days.

4 And when the days of his mourning were past, Joseph spake unto the house of Pharaoh, saying, If now I have found grace in your eyes, speak, I pray you, in the ears of Pharaoh, saying,

5 My father made me swear, saying, Lo, I die: in my ^agrave which I have digged for me in the land of Canaan, there shalt thou bury me. Now therefore let me go up, I pray thee, and bury my father, and I will come again.

6 And Pharaoh said, Go up, and bury thy father, according as he made thee swear.

24a IE It is from the lineage of Jacob that the Messiah comes.
  b TG Jesus Christ, Good Shepherd; Shepherd.
  c D&C 50:44.
    TG Jesus Christ, Prophecies about; Rock.
25a TG God, Power of.
  b TG Birth Control.
26a Gen. 48:9; Abr. 2:9.
  b TG Lands of Inheritance.
  c Deut. 33:15;

2 Ne. 12:2 (2–3); D&C 49:25; 109:61; 133:31 (26–34).
  d TG Israel, Joseph, People of.
27a Gen. 42:4; 44:29; Deut. 33:12; Josh. 18:11 (11–28).
28a TG Israel, Twelve Tribes of.
  b Deut. 33:1 (1–25).
  c TG Israel, Blessings of.
29a Alma 5:24.

  b Gen. 47:29; 50:13.
30a Gen. 23:9 (9, 19); 25:9.
  b Gen. 23:16 (16–17).
31a Gen. 25:10.
33a Jacob 7:20 (20–21); Hel. 14:21.
    TG Spirits, Disembodied.
  b TG Family, Eternal.
50 1a Gen. 46:4.
  b D&C 42:45 (45–46).
2a Gen. 50:26.
5a Gen. 47:30; 2 Ne. 1:14.

7 ¶ And Joseph went up to bury his father: and with him went up all the servants of Pharaoh, the elders of his house, and all the elders of the land of Egypt,

8 And all the house of Joseph, and his brethren, and his father's house: only their little ones, and their flocks, and their herds, they left in the land of *a*Goshen.

9 And there went up with him both chariots and horsemen: and it was a very great company.

10 And they came to the threshingfloor of Atad, which *is* beyond Jordan, and there they *a*mourned with a great and very sore lamentation: and he made a *b*mourning for his father seven days.

11 And when the inhabitants of the land, the Canaanites, saw the mourning in the floor of Atad, they said, This *is* a grievous mourning to the Egyptians: wherefore the name of it was called *a*Abel-mizraim, which *is* beyond Jordan.

12 And his sons did unto him according as he commanded them:

13 For his sons *a*carried him into the land of Canaan, and buried him in the cave of the field of Machpelah, which Abraham bought with the field for a possession of a *b*buryingplace of *c*Ephron the Hittite, before Mamre.

14 ¶ And Joseph returned into Egypt, he, and his brethren, and all that went up with him to bury his father, after he had buried his father.

15 ¶ And when Joseph's brethren saw that their father was dead, they said, *a*Joseph will peradventure hate us, and will certainly requite us all the evil which we did unto him.

16 And they sent a messenger unto Joseph, saying, Thy father did command before he died, saying,

17 So shall ye say unto Joseph, *a*Forgive, I pray thee now, the trespass of thy brethren, and their sin; for they did unto thee evil: and now, we pray thee, forgive the trespass of the servants of the God of thy father. And Joseph *b*wept when they spake unto him.

18 And his brethren also went and fell down before his face; and they said, Behold, we *be* thy *a*servants.

19 And Joseph said unto them, Fear not: for *am* I in the place of God?

20 But as for you, ye thought *a*evil against me; *but* God *b*meant it unto *c*good, to bring to pass, as *it is* this day, to save much people alive.

21 Now therefore fear ye not: I will *a*nourish you, and your little ones. And he comforted them, and spake kindly unto them.

22 ¶ And *a*Joseph dwelt in Egypt, he, and his father's house: and Joseph lived an hundred and ten years.

23 And Joseph saw Ephraim's *a*children of the third *generation:* the children also of Machir the son of *b*Manasseh were brought up upon Joseph's knees.

24 *a*And Joseph said unto his brethren, I die: and God will surely visit you, and *b*bring you out of this land unto the *c*land which he sware to *d*Abraham, to Isaac, and to Jacob.

25 And Joseph took an *a*oath of the children of Israel, saying, God will surely visit you, and ye shall carry up my *b*bones from hence.

26 So *a*Joseph *b*died, *being* an hundred and ten years old: and they *c*embalmed him, and he was put in a coffin in Egypt.

8*a* Gen. 45:10.
10*a* Alma 28:12.
  b Job 2:13.
11*a* IE The mourning of the Egyptians.
13*a* Gen. 49:29.
  b Gen. 25:10.
  c Gen. 23:17.
15*a* OR If Joseph bears a grudge against us he will certainly repay us . . .

17*a* TG Forgive.
  b Morm. 2:12; D&C 18:16 (14–16).
18*a* Gen. 37:10 (5–11).
20*a* TG Evil.
  b Gen. 45:5.
  c D&C 100:15.
21*a* TG Family, Love within.
22*a* TG Israel, Joseph, People of.
23*a* TG Patriarch.
  b Num. 32:39.

24*a* JST Gen. 50:24–38 (Appendix).
  b TG Israel, Bondage of, in Egypt.
  c TG Promised Lands.
  d Deut. 11:9.
25*a* TG Oath.
  b Gen. 47:29; Ex. 13:19; Josh. 24:32.
26*a* Gen. 41:46 (46–47, 54).
  b Ex. 1:6.
  c Gen. 50:2.

THE SECOND BOOK OF MOSES

CALLED

EXODUS

CHAPTER 1

The children of Israel multiply—They are placed in bondage by the Egyptians—Pharaoh seeks to destroy the sons born to Hebrew women.

NOW these *are* the *a*names of the *b*children of Israel, which came *c*into *d*Egypt; every man and his household came with Jacob.
2 Reuben, Simeon, Levi, and Judah,
3 Issachar, Zebulun, and Benjamin,
4 Dan, and Naphtali, Gad, and Asher.
5 And all the souls that came out of the loins of *a*Jacob were seventy souls: for Joseph was in Egypt *already*.
6 And *a*Joseph died, and all his brethren, and all that generation.
7 ¶ And the children of Israel were *a*fruitful, and *b*increased abundantly, and multiplied, and *c*waxed exceeding mighty; and the land was filled with them.
8 Now there arose up a new *a*king over Egypt, which knew not Joseph.
9 And he said unto his people, Behold, the people of the children of Israel *are* *a*more and *b*mightier than we:

10 Come on, let us deal *a*wisely with them; lest they multiply, and it come to pass, that, when there *b*falleth out any war, they join also unto our enemies, and fight against us, and *so* get them up out of the land.
11 Therefore they did set over them *a*taskmasters to afflict them with their *b*burdens. And they built for Pharaoh *c*treasure cities, Pithom and *d*Raamses.
12 But the more they afflicted them, the more they *a*multiplied and grew. And they were *b*grieved because of the children of Israel.
13 And the Egyptians made the children of Israel to serve with rigour:
14 And they made their lives bitter with hard *a*bondage, in mortar, and in brick, and in all manner of service in the field: all their service, wherein they made them serve, *was* with rigour.
15 ¶ And the king of Egypt spake to the Hebrew midwives, of which the name of the one *was* Shiphrah, and the name of the other Puah:
16 And he said, When ye *a*do the office of a midwife to the Hebrew women, and see *them* upon the

---

1 1a Gen. 46:8.
  b Gen. 35:22 (22–26).
  c HEB into Egypt with Jacob.
  d Ps. 105:23.
5a TG Israel, Origins of.
6a Gen. 50:26.
7a Gen. 26:22;
   Deut. 26:5.
  b Ps. 105:24.
  c OR grew.
8a Acts 7:18 (17–19).
9a Ex. 12:37.

  b Gen. 26:16.
10a Ps. 105:25 (23–25).
  b OR breaks out, "happens."
11a Gen. 15:13 (13–14);
   Deut. 26:6.
  b Ex. 2:11;
   Ps. 81:6;
   1 Ne. 17:25; 20:10;
   Mosiah 21:3 (3–6); 24:9.
  c HEB storage cities; i.e., granaries.
  d OR Rameses (Zoan,

   Ps. 78:12); also the former Hyksos capital (Avaris or Tanis) of Joseph's time.
   Gen. 47:11.
12a Ex. 5:5.
  b OR apprehensive of.
14a HEB labor (same word).
   TG Bondage, Physical;
   Israel, Bondage of, in Egypt.
16a OR serve as.

*b*stools; if it *be* a son, then ye shall kill him: but if it *be* a daughter, then she shall live.

17 But the midwives *a*feared God, and did not as the king of Egypt *b*commanded them, but saved the men children alive.

18 And the king of Egypt called for the midwives, and said unto them, Why have ye done this thing, and have saved the men children alive?

19 And the midwives said unto Pharaoh, Because the Hebrew women *are* not as the Egyptian women; for they *are* lively, and are *a*delivered ere the midwives come in unto them.

20 Therefore God dealt *a*well with the midwives: and the people multiplied, and waxed very mighty.

21 And it came to pass, because the midwives *a*feared God, that he made them *b*houses.

22 And Pharaoh charged all his people, saying, Every son that is *a*born ye shall cast into the river, and every daughter ye shall save alive.

CHAPTER 2

Moses is born to Levite parents, is raised by Pharaoh's daughter, slays an Egyptian in defense of an Israelite, flees to Midian, and marries Zipporah—Israel in bondage cries to the Lord.

AND there went a man of the house of *a*Levi, and took *to wife* a daughter of Levi.

2 And the woman conceived, and bare a *a*son: and when she saw him that he *was a* goodly *child*, she hid him *b*three months.

3 And when she could not longer hide him, she took for him an ark of bulrushes, and daubed it with slime and with pitch, and put the child therein; and she laid *it* *a*in the flags by the river's brink.

4 And his *a*sister stood afar off, *b*to wit what would be done to him.

5 ¶ And the daughter of Pharaoh came down to wash *herself* at the river; and her maidens walked along by the river's side; and when she saw the ark among the flags, she sent her maid to fetch it.

6 And when she had opened *it*, she saw the child: and, behold, the babe wept. And she had compassion on him, and said, This *is one* of the Hebrews' children.

7 Then said his sister to Pharaoh's daughter, Shall I go and call to thee a nurse of the Hebrew women, that she may nurse the child for thee?

8 And Pharaoh's daughter said to her, Go. And the maid went and called the child's mother.

9 And Pharaoh's daughter said unto her, Take this child away, and nurse it for me, and I will give *thee* thy wages. And the woman took the child, and nursed it.

10 And the child grew, and she brought him unto Pharaoh's daughter, and he became her *a*son. And she called his name *b*Moses: and she said, Because I drew him out of the water.

11 ¶ And it came to pass in those days, when Moses was grown, that he went out unto his *a*brethren, and looked on their *b*burdens: and he spied an Egyptian smiting an Hebrew, one of his brethren.

12 And he looked this way and that way, and when he saw that *there was* no man, he *a*slew the Egyptian, and hid him in the sand.

13 And when he went out the second day, behold, two men of the Hebrews strove together: and he

---

16*b* OR birth-stools.
17*a* Prov. 16:6.
  b Dan. 3:18 (16–18);
     Acts 5:29 (27–29);
     Alma 47:2.
19*a* 1 Ne. 17:3 (1–3).
20*a* Eccl. 8:12.
21*a* OR revered God.
  b OR households
     (descendants).

1 Sam. 2:35 (35–36);
2 Sam. 7:11 (10–17).
22*a* IE to the Hebrews.
2 1*a* Ex. 6:20;
     Num. 26:59.
2*a* Heb. 11:23.
  b Acts 7:20.
3*a* HEB among the reeds.
4*a* Ex. 15:20 (20–21);
     Num. 26:59.

  b IE to know or learn.
10*a* Acts 7:21; Heb. 11:24.
  b IE in Egyptian "To
     beget a child" and in
     Hebrew "To draw out."
11*a* Acts 7:23 (22–36);
     Heb. 11:25 (24–27).
  b Ex. 1:11 (7–11); 5:4 (4–5);
     1 Ne. 17:25.
12*a* Acts 7:24 (23–25).

said to him that did the wrong, Wherefore *a*smitest thou thy fellow?

14 And he said, Who made thee a *a*prince and a judge over us? intendest thou to kill me, as thou killedst the Egyptian? And Moses feared, and said, Surely this thing is known.

15 Now when Pharaoh heard this thing, he sought to *a*slay Moses. But Moses *b*fled from *c*the face of Pharaoh, and dwelt in the land of Midian: and he sat down by a well.

16 Now the priest of *a*Midian had seven daughters: and they came and drew *b*water, and filled the troughs to water their father's flock.

17 And the shepherds came and drove them away: but Moses stood up and helped them, and watered their flock.

18 And when they came to *a*Reuel their father, he said, How *is it that* ye are come so soon to day?

19 And they said, An Egyptian delivered us out of the hand of the shepherds, and also drew *water* enough for us, and watered the flock.

20 And he said unto his daughters, And where *is* he? why *is it that* ye have left the man? call him, that he may eat bread.

21 And Moses was content to dwell with the man: and he gave Moses *a*Zipporah his daughter.

22 And she bare *him* a *a*son, and he called his name *b*Gershom: for he said, I have been a *c*stranger in a strange land.

23 ¶ And it came to pass in process of time, that the king of Egypt *a*died: and the children of Israel sighed by reason of the bondage, and they *b*cried, and their *c*cry came up unto God by reason of the bondage.

24 And God *a*heard their groaning, and God remembered his *b*covenant with Abraham, with Isaac, and with Jacob.

25 And God looked upon the children of Israel, *a*and God had respect unto *them*.

CHAPTER 3

The Lord appears to Moses at the burning bush—Moses is called to deliver Israel from bondage—The Lord identifies Himself as the God of Abraham, Isaac, and Jacob, and as the Great I AM—He promises to smite Egypt and bring His people out with great wealth.

NOW Moses kept the flock of *a*Jethro his father in law, the *b*priest of Midian: and he led the flock to the backside of the desert, and came to the *c*mountain of God, *even* to *d*Horeb.

2 And the *a*angel of the LORD appeared unto him in a flame of *b*fire out of the midst of a *c*bush: and he looked, and, behold, the bush burned with fire, and the bush *was* not consumed.

3 And Moses said, I will now turn aside, and see this great sight, why the bush is not burnt.

4 And when the LORD saw that he turned aside to see, God *a*called unto him out of the midst of the bush,

13*a* Acts 7:26 (26–28).
14*a* Ex. 3:13 (13–15); 4:1;
　　Num. 16:13;
　　Acts 7:25 (25–35).
15*a* Ex. 4:19.
　 b Acts 7:29.
　 c OR the presence of.
16*a* Gen. 25:2, 4 (1–6);
　　Ex. 18:1 (1–11).
　 b Gen. 24:13.
18*a* Ex. 3:1; 4:18;
　　Num. 10:29; D&C 84:6.
21*a* Ex. 18:2.
22*a* Acts 7:29.
　 b IE A sojourner there.
　　Ex. 18:3 (2–3);
　　1 Chr. 23:15.

　 c TG Stranger.
23*a* Ex. 4:19.
　 b Deut. 26:7;
　　1 Sam. 12:8 (1–8);
　　Mosiah 29:20;
　　Alma 43:49 (49–50).
　 c Ex. 3:9.
24*a* Ex. 6:5;
　　Mosiah 9:18 (17–18);
　　D&C 35:3;
　　Abr. 1:15 (15–16).
　 b Gen. 15:14 (13–14);
　　46:4 (2–4);
　　Ps. 105:8 (5–8).
25*a* HEB and God knew; i.e.,
　　He was cognizant of
　　them.

3 1*a* Ex. 2:18 (16–18).
　 b D&C 84:6 (6–16).
　 c Ex. 4:27; 18:5; 24:13;
　　Mosiah 13:5; Moses 1:42.
　 d 1 Kgs. 19:8; 3 Ne. 25:4.
2*a* JST Ex. 3:2 . . . *presence of the Lord* . . .
　　Acts 7:30.
　　TG Angels.
　 b Ex. 19:18;
　　Deut. 5:4 (4–5);
　　1 Ne. 1:6 (5–6);
　　D&C 29:12.
　 c Deut. 33:16;
　　Luke 20:37 (37–38);
　　Moses 1:17.
4*a* Acts 7:31 (31, 33).

and said, Moses, Moses. And he said, Here *am* I.

5 And he said, Draw not nigh hither: put off thy ^ashoes from off thy feet, for the place whereon thou standest *is* ^bholy ground.

6 Moreover he said, ^aI *am* the ^bGod of thy father, the God of Abraham, the God of Isaac, and the God of Jacob. And Moses hid his face; for he was ^cafraid to ^dlook upon God.

7 ¶ And the LORD said, I have surely seen the ^aaffliction of my people which *are* in ^bEgypt, and have heard their ^ccry by reason of their taskmasters; for I know their sorrows;

8 And I am come ^adown to ^bdeliver them out of the hand of the Egyptians, and to bring them up out of that land unto a good land and a large, unto a land ^cflowing with milk and honey; unto the place of the ^dCanaanites, and the Hittites, and the Amorites, and the Perizzites, and the Hivites, and the Jebusites.

9 Now therefore, behold, the ^acry of the children of Israel is come unto me: and I have also seen the oppression wherewith the Egyptians oppress them.

10 Come now therefore, and I will ^asend thee unto Pharaoh, that thou mayest ^bbring forth my people the ^cchildren of Israel ^dout of Egypt.

11 ¶ And Moses said unto God, ^aWho *am* I, that I should go unto ^bPharaoh, and that I should bring forth the children of Israel out of Egypt?

12 And he said, Certainly I will be ^awith thee; and this *shall be* ^ba token unto thee, that I have ^csent thee: When thou hast brought forth the people out of Egypt, ye shall serve God upon this ^dmountain.

13 And Moses said unto God, Behold, *when* I come unto the children of Israel, and shall say unto them, The God of your fathers hath sent me unto you; and they shall say to me, What *is* his name? ^awhat shall I say unto them?

14 And God said unto Moses, ^aI AM THAT I AM: and he said, Thus shalt thou say unto the children of Israel, I AM hath sent me unto you.

15 And God said moreover unto Moses, Thus shalt thou say unto the children of Israel, The ^aLORD God of your fathers, the God of Abraham, the God of Isaac, and the God of Jacob, hath sent me unto you: this *is* my ^bname for ever, and ^cthis *is* my ^dmemorial unto all generations.

16 Go, and gather the ^aelders of Israel together, and say unto them, The LORD God of your fathers, the God of Abraham, of Isaac, and of Jacob, appeared unto me, saying, I

5a Josh. 5:15.
  b D&C 45:32; 101:64; 115:7.
  TG Holiness; Reverence.
6a TG Jesus Christ, Jehovah.
  b Mark 12:26 (19–27);
    1 Ne. 19:10;
    Mosiah 7:19;
    Alma 29:11; 36:2;
    D&C 136:21.
  c Deut. 5:5;
    Matt. 17:6 (5–7);
    Ether 3:6 (6–8, 19).
  d TG God, Privilege of Seeing.
7a TG Affliction.
  b TG Israel, Bondage of, in Egypt.
  c D&C 38:16.
8a TG God, Access to.
  b TG Deliver;
    Israel, Deliverance of.
  c Deut. 8:7 (7–9);
    Jer. 11:5;

D&C 38:18.
  d Gen. 17:8 (1–27);
    Ex. 13:11 (1–16);
    Num. 34:2;
    Abr. 2:19 (4, 6, 18–19).
9a Ex. 2:23;
    2 Ne. 26:15;
    Mosiah 21:15;
    D&C 109:49.
10a TG Called of God;
    Priesthood, Keys of.
  b Ex. 13:14;
    1 Ne. 17:24 (24, 31, 40);
    19:10;
    2 Ne. 25:20;
    Mosiah 7:19;
    Alma 36:28;
    D&C 8:3 (2–3); 103:16.
  c TG Israel, Twelve Tribes of.
  d 1 Ne. 17:24.
11a Moses 6:31.
  b TG Courage; Fearful.

12a 1 Ne. 17:55;
    Mosiah 24:17;
    Alma 38:4.
    TG Walking with God.
  b OR the sign.
  c TG Authority.
  d Ex. 19:3 (3–6);
    Deut. 1:6 (5–8);
    4:10 (10–13);
    1 Kgs. 8:9.
13a Ex. 2:14; 4:1;
    Acts 7:25 (25–35).
14a TG Jesus Christ, Jehovah.
15a Acts 7:32.
  b Ps. 135:13; D&C 19:10;
    Moses 1:3; 7:35.
    TG Name.
  c OR thus shall I be remembered . . .
  d Hosea 12:5 (3–5).
16a Ex. 4:29.
    TG Elder, Melchizedek Priesthood.

have surely *b*visited you, and *seen* that which is done to you in Egypt:

17 And I have said, I will bring you up out of the *a*affliction of *b*Egypt unto the land of the *c*Canaanites, and the Hittites, and the Amorites, and the Perizzites, and the Hivites, and the *d*Jebusites, unto a *e*land flowing with milk and honey.

18 And they shall *a*hearken to thy voice: and thou shalt come, thou and the elders of Israel, unto the king of Egypt, and ye shall say unto him, The LORD *b*God of the Hebrews hath met with us: and now *c*let us go, we beseech thee, three days' journey into the wilderness, that we may *d*sacrifice to the LORD our God.

19 ¶ And *a*I am sure that the king of Egypt will not let you go, *b*no, not by a *c*mighty hand.

20 And I will stretch out my hand, and smite Egypt with all my *a*wonders which I will do in the midst thereof: and after that he will let you *b*go.

21 And I will give this people favour in the sight of the Egyptians: and it shall come to pass, that, when ye go, ye shall not go *a*empty:

22 But every woman shall *a*borrow of her neighbour, and of her that sojourneth in her house, jewels of silver, and jewels of gold, and raiment: and ye shall put *them* upon your sons, and upon your daughters; and ye shall *b*spoil the Egyptians.

CHAPTER 4

*The Lord gives signs to Moses—Aaron is chosen as a spokesman—Israel is the Lord's firstborn and must be released to serve Him—Moses' son is circum-*cised*—Moses and Aaron lead Israel in worship.*

AND Moses answered and said, But, behold, they will not *a*believe me, nor *b*hearken unto my voice: for they will say, The LORD hath not appeared unto thee.

2 And the LORD said unto him, What *is* that in thine hand? And he said, A rod.

3 And he said, Cast it on the ground. And he cast it on the ground, and it became a serpent; and Moses fled from before it.

4 And the LORD said unto Moses, Put forth thine hand, and take it by the tail. And he put forth his hand, and caught it, and it became a rod in his hand:

5 That they may believe that the LORD God of their fathers, the God of Abraham, the God of Isaac, and the God of Jacob, hath appeared unto thee.

6 ¶ And the LORD said furthermore unto him, Put now thine hand into thy bosom. And he put his hand into his bosom: and when he took it out, behold, his hand *was* *a*leprous as snow.

7 And he said, Put thine hand into thy bosom again. And he put his hand into his bosom again; and *a*plucked it out of his bosom, and, behold, it was *b*turned again as his *other* flesh.

8 And it shall come to pass, if they will not believe thee, neither hearken to the voice of the first sign, that they will believe the voice of the latter *a*sign.

9 And it shall come to pass, if they will not believe also these two signs,

---

16b Ex. 4:31;
    Luke 7:16;
    1 Ne. 13:34;
    2 Ne. 4:26;
    Mosiah 27:7;
    Alma 9:21;
    Morm. 1:15;
    D&C 124:8;
    Abr. 1:17.
17a TG Tribulation.
  b Gen. 15:16 (14–16).
  c Ex. 33:2.
  d 1 Chr. 11:4.

  e TG Israel, Land of.
18a Ex. 4:31.
  b Ex. 5:3.
  c Ex. 5:1.
  d Ex. 8:1.
19a HEB I know.
  b OR except by power.
  c Ex. 6:1.
20a TG Miracle.
  b Ex. 12:31.
21a Ex. 11:3 (2–3);
    12:36 (35–36).
22a HEB ask.

  b HEB despoil, make empty.
    Ex. 12:36 (35–36);
    2 Ne. 20:6.
4 1a Ex. 4:31.
    TG Doubt;
    Rebellion.
  b Ex. 2:14; 3:13 (13–15);
    Acts 7:25 (25–35).
6a TG Leprosy.
7a OR drew.
  b HEB restored like.
8a TG Signs.

neither hearken unto thy voice, that thou shalt take of the water of ^athe river, and pour *it* upon the dry *land:* and the water which thou takest out of the river shall become ^bblood upon the dry *land.*

10 ¶ And Moses said unto the LORD, O my Lord, I *am* not eloquent, neither heretofore, nor since thou hast spoken unto thy servant: but I *am* slow of ^aspeech, and of a ^bslow tongue.

11 And the LORD said unto him, Who hath made man's mouth? or who ^amaketh the dumb, or deaf, or the seeing, or the blind? have not I the LORD?

12 Now therefore go, and I will be with thy ^amouth, and ^bteach thee what thou shalt ^csay.

13 And he said, O my Lord, send, I pray thee, ^aby the hand *of him whom* thou wilt send.

14 And the ^aanger of the LORD was kindled against Moses, and he said, *Is* not Aaron the Levite thy brother? I know that he can speak well. And also, behold, he cometh forth to meet thee: and when he seeth thee, he will be glad in his heart.

15 And thou shalt speak unto him, and put words in his mouth: and I will be with thy ^amouth, and with his mouth, and will ^bteach you what ye shall do.

16 And he shall be thy ^aspokesman unto the people: and he shall be, *even* he shall be to thee instead of a mouth, and thou shalt be to him ^binstead of ^cGod.

17 And thou shalt take this ^arod in thine hand, wherewith thou shalt do signs.

18 ¶ And Moses went and returned to ^aJethro his father in law, and said unto him, Let me go, I pray thee, and return unto my brethren which *are* in Egypt, and see whether they be yet alive. And Jethro said to Moses, Go in peace.

19 And the LORD said unto Moses in Midian, Go, return into Egypt: for all the men are ^adead which sought thy ^blife.

20 And Moses took his wife and his sons, and set them upon an ass, and he returned to the land of Egypt: and Moses took the ^arod of God in his hand.

21 And the LORD said unto Moses, When thou goest to return into Egypt, see that thou do all those ^awonders before Pharaoh, which I have put in thine ^bhand: ^cbut I will ^dharden his heart, that he shall not let the people go.

22 And thou shalt say unto Pharaoh, Thus saith the LORD, ^aIsrael *is* my ^bson, *even* my ^cfirstborn:

23 And I say unto thee, Let my son go, that he may serve me: and if thou refuse to let him go, behold, I will slay thy ^ason, *even* thy firstborn.

24 ¶ ^aAnd it came to pass ^bby the way in the inn, that the LORD met him, and sought to ^ckill him.

25 Then Zipporah took a ^asharp stone, and cut off the foreskin of her son, and cast *it* at his feet, and said,

---

9a IE the Nile.
  b Ex. 7:19.
10a Jer. 1:6 (6–9);
     D&C 60:2 (2–3).
  b Ex. 6:12;
     Moses 6:31.
11a Ether 12:27.
12a Jer. 1:9 (6–9);
     Matt. 10:19 (19–20);
     Luke 12:12;
     D&C 24:6 (5–6); 28:4;
     Moses 6:8, 32.
  b TG Prophecy;
     Prophets, Mission of.
  c D&C 68:3 (3–4); 100:5.
13a OR through whomever
     thou wilt send.
14a TG Anger.

15a TG Authority.
  b 2 Ne. 32:3 (3, 5).
16a Ex. 16:9;
     2 Ne. 3:17 (17–18);
     D&C 100:9 (9–11);
     124:104.
     TG Prophecy.
  b A prophet is a spokes-
     man; hence he speaks
     for, or instead of, God.
     TG Prophets, Mission of.
  c Ex. 7:1; 18:19.
17a Ex. 7:15.
18a Ex. 2:18 (16–18).
19a Ex. 2:23.
  b Ex. 2:15.
20a Ex. 17:9;
     Num. 20:8 (8–9).

21a OR miracles.
  b OR power.
  c JST Ex. 4:21 . . . *and I will
     prosper thee; but Pharaoh
     will harden his heart,
     and he will* not let the
     people go.
  d TG Hardheartedness.
22a Jer. 2:14.
  b Hosea 11:1 (1–4).
  c TG Firstborn.
23a Ex. 11:5 (1–5).
24a JST Ex. 4:24–27
     (Appendix).
  b OR on the road by
     the inn.
  c Gen. 17:14.
25a HEB flint-stone.

Surely a *b*bloody husband *art* thou to me.

26 So he let him go: then she said, A bloody husband *thou art,* because of the *a*circumcision.

27 ¶ And the LORD said to Aaron, Go into the wilderness to meet Moses. And he went, and met him in the *a*mount of God, and kissed him.

28 And Moses told Aaron all the words of the LORD who had sent him, and all the signs which he had commanded him.

29 ¶ And Moses and Aaron went and gathered together all the *a*elders of the children of Israel:

30 And Aaron *a*spake all the words which the LORD had spoken unto Moses, and did the signs in the sight of the people.

31 And the people *a*believed: and when they heard that the LORD had *b*visited the children of Israel, and that he had looked upon their *c*affliction, then they *d*bowed their heads and worshipped.

CHAPTER 5

Moses and Aaron ask Pharaoh to free Israel—Pharaoh responds, Who is the Lord?—He places greater burdens upon the children of Israel.

AND afterward Moses and Aaron went in, and told Pharaoh, Thus saith the LORD God of Israel, *a*Let my people *b*go, that they may hold a *c*feast unto me in the wilderness.

2 And Pharaoh said, Who *is* the LORD, that I should *a*obey his voice to let Israel go? I *b*know not the LORD, neither will I let Israel go.

3 And they said, The *a*God of the Hebrews hath met with us: let us go, we pray thee, three days' journey into the desert, and sacrifice unto the LORD our God; lest he fall upon us with pestilence, or with the sword.

4 And the king of Egypt said unto them, Wherefore do ye, Moses and Aaron, *a*let the people from their works? get you unto your *b*burdens.

5 And Pharaoh said, Behold, the people of the land now *are* *a*many, and ye make them rest from their burdens.

6 And Pharaoh commanded the same day the taskmasters of the people, and their officers, saying,

7 Ye shall no more give the people straw to make brick, as heretofore: let them go and gather straw for themselves.

8 And the *a*tale of the bricks, which they did make heretofore, ye shall lay upon them; ye shall not diminish *ought* thereof: for *be* idle; therefore they cry, saying, Let us go *and* sacrifice to our God.

9 Let there more work be laid upon the men, that they may labour therein; and let them not regard vain words.

10 ¶ And the taskmasters of the people went out, and their officers, and they spake to the people, saying, Thus saith Pharaoh, I will not give you straw.

11 Go ye, get you straw where ye can find it: yet *a*not ought of your work shall be diminished.

12 So the people were scattered abroad throughout all the land of Egypt to gather stubble instead of straw.

13 And the taskmasters *a*hasted *them,* saying, Fulfil your works, *your* daily tasks, as when there was straw.

14 And the officers of the children of Israel, which Pharaoh's taskmasters had set over them, were beaten, *and* demanded, Wherefore

25*b* HEB bridegroom of blood. (There is some covenant significance in this.) Also v. 26.
26*a* TG Circumcision.
27*a* Ex. 3:1; 18:5; 1 Kgs. 19:8.
29*a* Ex. 3:16; 1 Ne. 4:22 (22, 27); Alma 6:1; Moro. 6:7.

30*a* TG Prophets, Mission of.
31*a* Ex. 3:18; 4:1 (1–9).
  b Ex. 3:16.
  c TG Israel, Deliverance of.
  d Gen. 24:26; Ex. 34:8.
5 1*a* Ex. 3:18.
  b 1 Ne. 17:25 (23–29).
  c Ex. 10:9; 12:14.
2*a* Ex. 9:17; 10:3; Alma 9:6;

Moses 5:16.
  b TG God, Knowledge about.
3*a* Ex. 3:18; 7:16.
4*a* HEB hinder, deter.
  b Ex. 2:11; 6:6 (6–7).
5*a* Ex. 1:12.
8*a* OR quota.
11*a* OR none of.
13*a* OR urged.

have ye not fulfilled your task in making brick both yesterday and to day, as heretofore?

15 ¶ Then the officers of the children of Israel came and cried unto Pharaoh, saying, Wherefore dealest thou thus with thy servants?

16 There is no straw given unto thy servants, and they say to us, Make brick: and, behold, thy servants *are* beaten; but the fault *is* in thine own people.

17 But he said, Ye *are* idle, *ye are* idle: therefore ye say, Let us go *and* do sacrifice to the LORD.

18 Go therefore now, *and* work; for there shall no straw be given you, yet shall ye deliver the tale of bricks.

19 And the officers of the children of Israel did see *that* they *ᵃwere* in evil *case,* after it was said, Ye shall not minish *ought* from your bricks of your daily task.

20 ¶ And they met Moses and Aaron, who stood in the way, as they came forth from Pharaoh:

21 And they said unto them, The LORD look upon you, and judge; because ye have made *ᵃ*our savour to be *ᵇ*abhorred in the eyes of Pharaoh, and in the eyes of his servants, to put a sword in their hand to slay us.

22 And Moses *ᵃ*returned unto the LORD, and said, Lord, wherefore hast thou so *ᵇ*evil entreated this people? why *is* it *that* thou hast sent me?

23 For since I came to Pharaoh to speak in thy name, he hath done evil to this people; neither hast thou delivered thy people at all.

CHAPTER 6

The Lord identifies Himself as Jehovah—The genealogies of Reuben, Simeon, and Levi are listed.

THEN the LORD said unto Moses, Now shalt thou see what I will do to Pharaoh: for *ᵃ*with a strong hand shall he let them go, and with a *ᵇ*strong hand shall he *ᶜ*drive them out of his land.

2 And God spake unto Moses, and said unto him, I *am* the LORD:

3 And I *ᵃ*appeared unto *ᵇ*Abraham, unto Isaac, *ᶜ*and unto Jacob, by *the name of* God Almighty, but by my *ᵈ*name JEHOVAH was I not known to them.

4 And I have also established my *ᵃ*covenant with them, to give them the land of Canaan, the land of their *ᵇ*pilgrimage, wherein they were *ᶜ*strangers.

5 And I have also *ᵃ*heard the groaning of the children of Israel, whom the Egyptians keep in *ᵇ*bondage; and I have remembered my covenant.

6 Wherefore say unto the children of Israel, I *am* the LORD, and I will *ᵃ*bring you out from under the *ᵇ*burdens of the Egyptians, and I will *ᶜ*rid you out of their bondage, and I will redeem you with a stretched out arm, and with great judgments:

7 And I will take you to me for a *ᵃ*people, and I will be to you a *ᵇ*God: and ye shall *ᶜ*know that I *am* the LORD your God, which bringeth you out from under the burdens of the Egyptians.

8 And I will bring you in unto the land, concerning the which I

19*a* Hebrew idiom meaning "found themselves in trouble."
21*a* HEB us as an offensive savor.
  b Ex. 14:12 (11–12).
22*a* D&C 121:2 (1–6).
  b OR badly treated.
6 1*a* HEB by a hand of strength; i.e., by reason of the power of the Lord.
  b Ex. 3:19.

c Ex. 12:31 (30–33).
3*a* TG God, Access to.
  b Gen. 17:1 (1–3); Abr. 2:6 (6–12).
  c JST Ex. 6:3 . . . and unto Jacob. *I am the Lord God Almighty; the Lord JEHOVAH. And was not my name known unto them?*
  d Jer. 16:21.
4*a* Gen. 17:4 (4–12); Abr. 2:6 (6–12).

  b HEB abode.
  c OR sojourners.
5*a* Ex. 2:24 (23–24).
  b TG Bondage, Physical.
6*a* 1 Ne. 19:10.
  b Ex. 5:4 (4–5); Ps. 81:6 (5–6).
  c HEB deliver.
7*a* TG Israel, Mission of.
  b Gen. 17:8; Ex. 29:45 (45–46); Deut. 29:13.
  c 1 Ne. 17:13.

did [a]swear to give it to Abraham, to Isaac, and to Jacob; and I will give it you for an heritage: I *am* the LORD.

9 ¶ And Moses spake so unto the children of Israel: but they hearkened not unto Moses for anguish of spirit, and for [a]cruel bondage.

10 And the LORD spake unto Moses, saying,

11 Go in, speak unto Pharaoh king of Egypt, that he let the children of Israel go out of his land.

12 And Moses spake before the LORD, saying, Behold, the children of Israel have not hearkened unto me; how then shall Pharaoh hear me, who *am* [a]of uncircumcised lips?

13 And the LORD spake unto Moses and unto Aaron, and gave them a [a]charge unto the children of Israel, and unto Pharaoh king of Egypt, to bring the children of Israel out of the land of Egypt.

14 ¶ These *be* the [a]heads of their fathers' houses: The sons of Reuben the firstborn of Israel; Hanoch, and Pallu, Hezron, and Carmi: these *be* the families of Reuben.

15 And the sons of Simeon; Jemuel, and Jamin, and Ohad, and Jachin, and Zohar, and Shaul the son of a Canaanitish woman: these *are* the families of Simeon.

16 ¶ And these *are* the names of the sons of [a]Levi according to their generations; Gershon, and Kohath, and Merari: and the years of the life of Levi *were* an hundred thirty and seven years.

17 The sons of [a]Gershon; Libni, and Shimi, according to their families.

18 And the sons of Kohath; Amram, and Izhar, and Hebron, and Uzziel: and the years of the life of Kohath *were* an hundred thirty and three years.

19 And the sons of [a]Merari; Mahali and Mushi: these *are* the [b]families of Levi according to their generations.

20 And [a]Amram took him Jochebed his father's sister to wife; and she bare him [b]Aaron and Moses: and the years of the life of Amram *were* an hundred and thirty and seven years.

21 ¶ And the sons of Izhar; Korah, and Nepheg, and Zichri.

22 And the sons of [a]Uzziel; Mishael, and Elzaphan, and Zithri.

23 And Aaron took him Elisheba, daughter of Amminadab, sister of Naashon, to wife; and she bare him [a]Nadab, and Abihu, Eleazar, and [b]Ithamar.

24 And the sons of Korah; Assir, and Elkanah, and Abiasaph: these *are* the families of the Korhites.

25 And [a]Eleazar Aaron's son took him *one* of the daughters of Putiel to wife; and she bare him Phinehas: these *are* the heads of the fathers of the Levites according to their families.

26 These *are* that Aaron and Moses, to whom the LORD said, Bring out the children of Israel from the land of Egypt according to their armies.

27 These *are* they which spake to Pharaoh king of Egypt, to bring out the children of Israel from Egypt: these *are* that Moses and Aaron.

28 ¶ And it came to pass on the day *when* the LORD spake unto Moses in the land of Egypt,

29 That the LORD spake unto Moses, saying, I *am* the LORD: speak thou unto Pharaoh king of Egypt all that I say unto thee.

30 And Moses said before the LORD, Behold, I *am* [a]of uncircumcised lips, and how shall Pharaoh hearken unto me?

8a Ex. 13:5.
9a TG Cruelty.
12a IE of impaired speech.
    Ex. 4:10.
13a TG Stewardship.
14a Gen. 46:8.
16a Num. 3:17; 4:4 (4–15);

1 Chr. 6:16 (16–19).
17a Num. 4:41.
19a Num. 4:42 (41–45).
    b Gen. 15:16 (13–16).
20a Ex. 2:1 (1–2);
    1 Chr. 23:13.
    b Ex. 7:7.

22a Lev. 10:4.
23a Ex. 24:1 (1–2).
    b Ex. 38:21.
25a Josh. 17:4.
30a JST Ex. 6:29 . . . of
    stammering lips, and *slow*
    of speech; how shall . . .

CHAPTER 7

Moses is appointed to give the word of the Lord to Pharaoh—The Lord will multiply signs and wonders in Egypt—Aaron's rod becomes a serpent—The river is turned into blood—The magicians imitate the miracles of Moses and Aaron.

AND the LORD said unto Moses, See, I have made thee *^a*a *^b*god to Pharaoh: and Aaron thy brother shall be thy *^c*prophet.

2 Thou shalt speak all that I *^a*command thee: and Aaron thy brother shall speak unto Pharaoh, that he send the children of Israel out of his land.

3 *^a*And I will harden Pharaoh's heart, and multiply my signs and my *^b*wonders in the land of Egypt.

4 *^a*But Pharaoh shall not hearken unto you, that I may lay my hand upon Egypt, and bring forth mine *^b*armies, *and* my people the children of Israel, out of the land of Egypt by great judgments.

5 And the Egyptians shall *^a*know that *^b*I *am* the *^c*LORD, when I stretch forth mine hand upon Egypt, and bring out the children of Israel from among them.

6 And Moses and Aaron did as the LORD commanded them, so did they.

7 And Moses *was* *^a*fourscore years old, and *^b*Aaron fourscore and three years old, when they spake unto Pharaoh.

8 ¶ And the LORD spake unto Moses and unto Aaron, saying,

9 When Pharaoh shall speak unto you, saying, *^a*Shew a *^b*miracle for you: then thou shalt say unto Aaron, Take thy rod, and cast *it* before Pharaoh, *and* it shall become a serpent.

10 ¶ And Moses and Aaron went in unto Pharaoh, and they did so as the LORD had commanded: and Aaron cast down his rod before Pharaoh, and before his servants, and it became a serpent.

11 Then Pharaoh also called the wise men and the *^a*sorcerers: now the *^b*magicians of Egypt, they also did in like manner with their enchantments.

12 For they cast down every man his rod, and they became serpents: but Aaron's rod swallowed up their rods.

13 *^a*And he hardened Pharaoh's heart, that he hearkened not unto them; as the LORD had said.

14 ¶ And the LORD said unto Moses, Pharaoh's heart *is* hardened, he refuseth to let the people go.

15 Get thee unto Pharaoh in the morning; lo, he goeth out unto the water; and thou shalt stand by the river's brink *^a*against he come; and the *^b*rod which was turned to a serpent shalt thou take in thine hand.

16 And thou shalt say unto him, The LORD *^a*God of the Hebrews hath sent me unto thee, saying, Let my people go, that they may *^b*serve me in the wilderness: and, behold, hitherto thou wouldest not hear.

17 Thus saith the LORD, In this thou shalt know that I *am* the LORD: behold, I will smite with the rod that *is* in mine hand upon the waters which *are* in the *^a*river, and they shall be *^b*turned to *^c*blood.

---

7 1a OR as God.
  b JST Ex. 7:1 . . . *prophet* . . .
    Ex. 4:16.
  c JST Ex. 7:1 . . . *spokesman.*
    TG Priesthood, Keys of;
    Prophecy;
    Prophets, Mission of.
 2a TG Authority.
 3a JST Ex. 7:3 And *Pharaoh will harden his heart, as I said unto thee;* and *thou shalt* multiply my signs . . .
  b TG Miracle.

4a OR But if Pharaoh will not hearken . . . then I will . . .
  b D&C 105:26.
 5a Ex. 14:4.
  b Neh. 9:10 (6–10).
  c Ex. 8:10.
 7a Deut. 31:2 (1–2); 34:7;
    Acts 7:23.
  b Ex. 6:20 (14–27);
    Num. 33:39.
 9a OR Prove yourselves by performing a miracle.
  b TG Sign Seekers.

11a TG False Prophets;
    Sorcery.
  b TG False Priesthoods.
13a JST Ex. 7:13 And *Pharaoh hardened his heart . . .*
15a HEB to meet him.
  b Ex. 4:17.
16a Ex. 5:3.
  b TG Service.
17a OR Nile (so also in vv. 18, 20–21, 24–25).
  b Rev. 11:6 (5–6).
  c TG Plague.

18 And the fish that *is* in the river shall die, and the river shall stink; and the Egyptians shall lothe to drink of the water of the river.

19 ¶ And the LORD spake unto Moses, Say unto Aaron, Take thy rod, and stretch out thine hand upon the waters of Egypt, upon their streams, upon their rivers, and upon their ponds, and upon all their pools of water, that they may become *a*blood; and *that* there may be blood throughout all the land of Egypt, both in *vessels of* wood, and in *vessels of* stone.

20 And Moses and Aaron did so, as the LORD commanded; and he lifted up the *a*rod, and smote the waters that *were* in the river, in the sight of Pharaoh, and in the sight of his servants; and all the waters that *were* in the river were turned to *b*blood.

21 And the fish that *was* in the river died; and the river stank, and the Egyptians could not drink of the water of the river; and there was blood throughout all the land of Egypt.

22 And the magicians of Egypt did so with their enchantments: and Pharaoh's heart was hardened, neither did he hearken unto them; as the LORD had said.

23 And Pharaoh turned and went into his house, *a*neither did he set his heart to this also.

24 And all the Egyptians digged round about the river for water to drink; for they could not drink of the water of the river.

25 And seven days were fulfilled, after that the LORD had smitten the river.

CHAPTER 8

The Lord sends plagues of frogs, lice, and flies upon Egypt—Pharaoh hardens his heart.

AND the LORD spake unto Moses, Go unto Pharaoh, and say unto him, Thus saith the LORD, Let my people go, that they may *a*serve me.

2 And if thou refuse to let *them* go, behold, I will smite *a*all thy borders with *b*frogs:

3 And the river shall bring forth frogs abundantly, which shall go up and come into thine house, and into thy bedchamber, and upon thy bed, and into the house of thy servants, and upon thy people, and into thine ovens, and into thy kneadingtroughs:

4 And the frogs shall come up both on thee, and upon thy people, and upon all thy servants.

5 ¶ And the LORD spake unto Moses, Say unto Aaron, Stretch forth thine hand with thy rod over the streams, over the *a*rivers, and over the ponds, and cause frogs to come up upon the land of Egypt.

6 And Aaron stretched out his hand over the waters of Egypt; and the *a*frogs came up, and covered the land of Egypt.

7 And the magicians did so with their enchantments, and brought up frogs upon the land of Egypt.

8 ¶ Then Pharaoh called for Moses and Aaron, and said, Entreat the LORD, that he may take away the frogs from me, and from my people; and I will let the people go, that they may do sacrifice unto the LORD.

9 And Moses said unto Pharaoh, *a*Glory over me: when shall I entreat for thee, and for thy servants, and for thy people, to destroy the frogs from thee and thy houses, *that* they may remain in the river only?

10 And he said, To morrow. And he said, *Be it* according to thy word: that thou mayest know that *there is* *a*none *b*like unto the *c*LORD our God.

11 And the frogs shall depart from thee, and from thy houses, and from

---

19a Ex. 4:9.
20a Ex. 14:16 (15–17); 17:5.
   b Ps. 105:29.
23a Hebrew idiom meaning "paying no regard even to this."
8 1a Ex. 3:18 (12, 18).

2a IE all within thy border.
   b TG Plague.
5a OR canals.
6a Ps. 105:30.
9a IE I grant you pre-eminence to declare: when . . .

10a D&C 76:1 (1–2).
   b 2 Sam. 7:22 (21–23); Isa. 46:9 (9–10); Jer. 10:7 (6–7).
   c Ex. 7:5.

thy servants, and from thy people; they shall remain in the river only.

12 And Moses and Aaron went out from Pharaoh: and Moses cried unto the LORD because of the frogs which he had brought against Pharaoh.

13 And the LORD did according to the word of Moses; and the frogs died out of the houses, out of the villages, and out of the fields.

14 And they gathered them together upon heaps: and the land stank.

15 But when Pharaoh saw that there was respite, he *a*hardened his heart, and hearkened not unto them; as the LORD had said.

16 ¶ And the LORD said unto Moses, Say unto Aaron, Stretch out thy rod, and smite the dust of the land, that it may become *a*lice throughout all the land of Egypt.

17 And they did so; for Aaron stretched out his hand with his rod, and smote the dust of the earth, and it became lice in man, and in beast; all the dust of the land became *a*lice throughout all the land of Egypt.

18 And the magicians did so with their enchantments to *a*bring forth lice, but they could not: so there were lice upon man, and upon beast.

19 Then the magicians said unto Pharaoh, This *is* the *a*finger of God: and Pharaoh's heart was hardened, and he hearkened not unto them; as the LORD had said.

20 ¶ And the LORD said unto Moses, Rise up early in the morning, and stand before Pharaoh; *a*lo, he cometh forth to the water; and say unto him, Thus saith the LORD, Let my people go, that they may serve me.

21 Else, if thou wilt not let my people go, behold, I will send swarms *of a*flies upon thee, and upon thy servants, and upon thy people, and into thy houses: and the houses of the Egyptians shall be full of swarms *of flies*, and also the ground whereon they *are*.

22 And I will *a*sever in that day the land of Goshen, in which my people dwell, that *b*no swarms *of flies* shall be there; to the end thou mayest know that I *am* the LORD in the midst of the earth.

23 And I will put a division between my people and thy people: to morrow shall this sign be.

24 And the LORD did so; and there came a grievous swarm *of flies* into the house of Pharaoh, and *into* his servants' houses, and into all the land of Egypt: the land was *a*corrupted by reason of the swarm *of flies*.

25 ¶ And Pharaoh called for Moses and for Aaron, and said, Go ye, sacrifice to your God in the land.

26 And Moses said, It *a*is not meet so to do; for we shall sacrifice *b*the abomination of the Egyptians to the LORD our God: lo, shall we sacrifice the abomination of the Egyptians before their eyes, and will they not stone us?

27 We will go three days' journey into the wilderness, and sacrifice to the LORD our God, as he shall command us.

28 And Pharaoh said, I will let you go, that ye may sacrifice to the LORD your God in the wilderness; only ye shall not go very far away: entreat for me.

29 And Moses said, Behold, I go out from thee, and I will entreat the LORD that the swarms *of flies* may depart from Pharaoh, from his servants, and from his people, to morrow: but let not Pharaoh deal deceitfully any more in not letting the people go to sacrifice to the LORD.

30 And Moses went out from Pharaoh, and entreated the LORD.

31 And the LORD did according to the word of Moses; and he removed

15*a* 1 Sam. 6:6; Eccl. 8:11.
16*a* TG Plague.
17*a* Ps. 105:31.
18*a* OR get rid of the lice.
19*a* Luke 11:20;
       John 3:2;

Acts 2:22; 10:38;
1 Ne. 19:22;
Alma 23:6;
D&C 84:3; 121:12.
20*a* OR as.
21*a* TG Plague.

22*a* OR separate, segregate.
    b D&C 38:18.
24*a* HEB ruined.
26*a* OR would not be right.
    b OR things abominable to.

the swarms *of flies* from Pharaoh, from his servants, and from his people; there remained not one.

32 And Pharaoh hardened his heart at this time also, neither would he let the people go.

CHAPTER 9

The Lord destroys the cattle of the Egyptians, but not of the Israelites—Boils and blains are sent upon the Egyptians—The Lord sends hail and fire upon the people of Pharaoh, but not upon the people of Israel.

THEN the LORD said unto Moses, Go in unto Pharaoh, and tell him, Thus saith the LORD God of the Hebrews, Let my people go, that they may serve me.

2 For if thou refuse to let *them* go, and wilt hold them still,

3 Behold, the hand of the LORD is upon thy cattle which *is* in the field, upon the horses, upon the asses, upon the camels, upon the oxen, and upon the sheep: *there shall be* a very *a*grievous *b*murrain.

4 And the LORD shall *a*sever between the cattle of Israel and the cattle of Egypt: and there shall nothing die of all *that is* the children's of Israel.

5 And the LORD appointed a set time, saying, To morrow the LORD shall do this thing in the land.

6 And the LORD did that thing on the morrow, and all the cattle of Egypt died: but of the cattle of the children of Israel died not one.

7 And Pharaoh sent, and, behold, there was not one of the cattle of the Israelites dead. And the heart of Pharaoh was hardened, and he did not let the people go.

8 ¶ And the LORD said unto Moses and unto Aaron, Take to you handfuls of ashes of the furnace, and let Moses sprinkle it toward the heaven in the sight of Pharaoh.

9 And it shall become small dust in all the land of Egypt, and shall be *a*a *b*boil breaking forth *with* *c*blains upon man, and upon beast, throughout all the land of Egypt.

10 And they took ashes of the furnace, and stood before Pharaoh; and Moses sprinkled it up toward heaven; and it became a boil breaking forth *with* blains upon man, and upon beast.

11 And the magicians could not stand before Moses because of the boils; for the boil was upon the magicians, and upon all the Egyptians.

12 *a*And the LORD hardened the heart of Pharaoh, and he hearkened not unto them; as the LORD had spoken unto Moses.

13 ¶ And the LORD said unto Moses, Rise up early in the morning, and stand before Pharaoh, and say unto him, Thus saith the LORD God of the Hebrews, Let my people go, that they may serve me.

14 For I will at this time send all my *a*plagues upon thine heart, and upon thy servants, and upon thy people; that thou mayest know that *there is* none like me in all the earth.

15 For now I will stretch out my hand, that I may smite thee and thy people with pestilence; and thou shalt be cut off from the earth.

16 And in very deed for this *a*cause have I *b*raised thee up, for to *c*shew *in* thee my power; and that my *d*name may be *e*declared throughout all the earth.

17 As yet *a*exaltest thou thyself against my people, that thou wilt not let them go?

18 Behold, to morrow about this time I will cause it to rain a very grievous *a*hail, such as hath not been

---

9 3*a* OR severe plague.
 b TG Plague.
 4*a* OR segregate,
  distinguish between.
 9*a* OR festering boils.
 b Deut. 28:27.
  TG Plague.
 c HEB blisters, pustules.

12*a* JST Ex. 9:12 And *Pharaoh hardened his* heart . . .
14*a* Deut. 28:60 (60–61).
16*a* Rom. 9:17.
 b OR let thee remain.
 c HEB show thee.
 d Neh. 9:10; Ps. 106:8; Isa. 63:14; Ezek. 20:9.

 TG Name.
 e TG Preaching.
17*a* Ex. 5:2; 10:3.
  TG Haughtiness.
18*a* Josh. 10:11; Ezek. 38:22; Rev. 16:21; Mosiah 12:6; D&C 29:16 (16–21); 109:30. TG Plague.

in Egypt since the foundation thereof even until now.

19 Send therefore now, *and* gather thy cattle, and all that thou hast in the field; *for upon* every man and beast which shall be found in the field, and shall not be brought home, the hail shall come down upon them, and they shall die.

20 He that feared the word of the LORD among the servants of Pharaoh made his servants and his cattle flee into the houses:

21 And he that regarded not the word of the LORD left his servants and his cattle in the field.

22 ¶ And the LORD said unto Moses, Stretch forth thine hand toward heaven, that there may be hail in all the land of Egypt, upon man, and upon beast, and upon every herb of the field, throughout the land of Egypt.

23 And Moses stretched forth his rod toward heaven: and the LORD sent thunder and ªhail, and the fire ran along upon the ground; and the LORD rained hail upon the land of Egypt.

24 So there was hail, and ªfire mingled with the hail, very grievous, such as there was none like it in all the land of Egypt since it became a nation.

25 And the ªhail smote throughout all the land of Egypt all that *was* in the field, both man and beast; and the hail smote every herb of the field, and brake every tree of the field.

26 Only in the land of Goshen, where the children of Israel *were*, was there no hail.

27 ¶ And Pharaoh sent, and called for Moses and Aaron, and said unto them, I have sinned this time: the LORD *is* righteous, and I and my people *are* wicked.

28 Entreat the LORD (for *it is* enough)

that there be no *more* mighty thunderings and hail; and I will let you go, and ye shall stay no longer.

29 And Moses said unto him, As soon as I am gone out of the city, I will ªspread abroad my hands unto the LORD; *and* the thunder shall cease, neither shall there be any more hail; that thou mayest know how that the ᵇearth *is* the ᶜLORD's.

30 But as for thee and thy servants, I know that ye will not yet fear the LORD God.

31 And the flax and the barley was smitten: for the barley *was* in the ear, and the flax *was* ªbolled.

32 But the ªwheat and the ᵇrie were not smitten: for they *were* not grown up.

33 And Moses went out of the city from Pharaoh, and spread abroad his hands unto the LORD: and the thunders and hail ceased, and the rain was not poured upon the earth.

34 And when Pharaoh saw that the rain and the hail and the thunders were ceased, he sinned yet more, and hardened his heart, he and his servants.

35 And the heart of Pharaoh was hardened, neither would he let the children of Israel go; as the LORD had spoken by Moses.

CHAPTER 10

The Lord sends a plague of locusts—This is followed by thick darkness in all Egypt for three days—Moses is cast out from the presence of Pharaoh.

AND the LORD said unto Moses, Go in unto Pharaoh: ªfor I have hardened his heart, and the heart of his servants, that I might shew these my signs before him:

2 And that thou mayest ªtell in the ears of thy son, and of thy son's son, what things I have wrought in

---

23ª Ps. 105:32.
24ª Rev. 8:7.
25ª Ps. 78:47 (47–48).
29ª 1 Kgs. 8:22.
  ᵇ Deut. 10:14; Ps. 24:1;
    1 Ne. 11:6; 3 Ne. 11:14;
    D&C 14:9; 15:2;

Abr. 4:12 (12, 24–25).
  ᶜ D&C 67:2.
31ª OR in bud.
32ª Ex. 10:5 (4–5).
  ᵇ HEB spelt (a type of
    wheat).
10 1ª JST Ex. 10:1 . . . for *he*

hath hardened his heart,
and the *hearts* of his
servants, *therefore* I *will*
show these my signs
before him;
2ª D&C 93:42 (42–43);
  Moses 6:58.

Egypt, and my signs which I have done among them; that ye may know how that I *am* the LORD.

3 And Moses and Aaron came in unto Pharaoh, and said unto him, Thus saith the LORD God of the Hebrews, How long wilt thou refuse to ^ahumble thyself before me? let my people go, that they may serve me.

4 Else, if thou refuse to let my people go, behold, to morrow will I bring the ^alocusts into thy coast:

5 And they shall cover the face of the earth, that one cannot be able to see the earth: and they shall eat the ^aresidue of that which is escaped, which remaineth unto you from the hail, and shall eat every tree which groweth for you out of the field:

6 And they shall fill thy houses, and the houses of all thy servants, and the houses of all the Egyptians; which neither thy fathers, nor thy fathers' fathers have seen, since the day that they were upon the earth unto this day. And he turned himself, and went out from Pharaoh.

7 And Pharaoh's servants said unto him, How long shall this man be a ^asnare unto us? let the men go, that they may serve the LORD their God: knowest thou not yet that Egypt is ^bdestroyed?

8 And Moses and Aaron were brought again unto Pharaoh: and he said unto them, Go, serve the LORD your God: *but* who *are* they that shall go?

9 And Moses said, We will go with our young and with our ^aold, with our sons and with our daughters, with our flocks and with our herds will we go; for we *must hold* a ^bfeast unto the LORD.

10 And he said unto them, Let the LORD be so with you, ^aas I will let you go, and your little ones: look *to it*; for ^bevil *is* before you.

11 Not so: go now ye *that are* men,

and serve the LORD; for that ye did desire. And they were driven out from Pharaoh's presence.

12 ¶ And the LORD said unto Moses, Stretch out thine hand over the land of Egypt for the locusts, that they may come up upon the land of Egypt, and eat every herb of the land, *even* all that the hail hath left.

13 And Moses stretched forth his rod over the land of Egypt, and the LORD brought an east wind upon the land all that day, and all *that* night; *and* when it was morning, the east wind brought the locusts.

14 And the ^alocusts went up over all the land of Egypt, and rested ^bin all the coasts of Egypt: very grievous *were they*; before them there were no such locusts as they, neither after them shall be such.

15 For they covered the face of the whole earth, so that the land was darkened; and they did eat every herb of the land, and all the fruit of the trees which the hail had left: and there remained not any green thing in the trees, or in the herbs of the field, through all the land of Egypt.

16 ¶ Then Pharaoh called for Moses and Aaron in haste; and he said, I have sinned against the LORD your God, and against you.

17 Now therefore forgive, I pray thee, my sin only this once, and entreat the LORD your God, that he may take away from me this death only.

18 And he went out from Pharaoh, and entreated the LORD.

19 And the LORD turned a mighty strong west wind, which took away the locusts, and cast them into the ^aRed sea; there remained not one locust in all the coasts of Egypt.

20 ^aBut the LORD hardened Pharaoh's heart, so that he would not let the children of Israel go.

21 ¶ And the LORD said unto

---

3 *a* Ex. 5:2; 9:17.
    TG Submissiveness.
4 *a* Ps. 105:34;
    Mosiah 12:6 (6–7).
    TG Plague.
5 *a* Ex. 9:32 (31–32).
7 *a* 2 Ne. 18:14; Mosiah 7:29.

b OR ruined.
9 *a* TG Old Age.
    b Ex. 5:1.
10 *a* OR if.
    b Hebrew idiom meaning "you are bent on mischief."

14 *a* Ps. 78:46.
    b HEB within the whole border.
19 *a* OR Reed Sea.
20 *a* JST Ex. 10:20 But *Pharaoh* hardened *his* heart . . .

Moses, Stretch out thine hand toward heaven, that there may be ªdarkness over the land of Egypt, even darkness *which* may be ᵇfelt.

22 And Moses stretched forth his hand toward heaven; and there was a thick ªdarkness in all the land of Egypt three days:

23 They saw not one another, neither rose any from his place for three days: but all the children of Israel had light in their dwellings.

24 ¶ And Pharaoh called unto Moses, and said, Go ye, serve the LORD; only let your flocks and your herds ªbe stayed: let your little ones also go with you.

25 And Moses said, Thou must ªgive us also sacrifices and burnt offerings, that we may sacrifice unto the LORD our God.

26 Our cattle also shall go with us; there shall not an hoof be left behind; for thereof must we take to serve the LORD our God; and we know not with what we must serve the LORD, until we come thither.

27 ¶ ªBut the LORD hardened Pharaoh's heart, and he would not let them go.

28 And Pharaoh said unto him, Get thee from me, take heed to thyself, see my face no more; for in *that* day thou seest my face thou shalt die.

29 And Moses said, ªThou hast spoken well, I will see thy face again no more.

CHAPTER 11

The departing Israelites are authorized to ask for jewels and gold from their neighbors—The Lord promises to slay the firstborn in every Egyptian home— He puts a difference between the Egyptians and the Israelites.

AND the LORD said unto Moses, Yet will I bring one plague *more* upon Pharaoh, and upon Egypt; afterwards he will let you go hence: when he shall let *you* go, he shall surely ªthrust you out hence altogether.

2 Speak now in the ears of the people, and let every man ªborrow of his neighbour, and every woman of her neighbour, ᵇjewels of silver, and jewels of gold.

3 And the LORD gave the people ªfavour in the sight of the Egyptians. Moreover the man Moses *was* very great in the land of Egypt, in the sight of Pharaoh's servants, and in the sight of the people.

4 And Moses said, Thus saith the LORD, About midnight will I go out into the midst of Egypt:

5 And all the ªfirstborn in the land of Egypt shall die, from the ᵇfirstborn of Pharaoh that sitteth upon his throne, even unto the firstborn of the maidservant that *is* behind the mill; and all the firstborn of beasts.

6 And there shall be a great cry throughout all the land of Egypt, such as there was none like it, nor shall be like it any more.

7 But against any of the children of Israel shall not a dog move his tongue, against man or beast: that ye may know how that the LORD doth put a ªdifference between the Egyptians and Israel.

8 And all these thy servants shall come down unto me, and bow down themselves unto me, saying, Get thee out, and all the people that follow thee: and after that I will go out. And he went out from Pharaoh in a great ªanger.

9 And the LORD said unto Moses, Pharaoh shall not hearken unto you; that my wonders may be multiplied in the land of Egypt.

10 And Moses and Aaron did all these wonders before Pharaoh: ªand the LORD hardened Pharaoh's heart,

---

21a TG Darkness, Physical.
  b 3 Ne. 8:20.
22a TG Plague.
24a OR remain behind.
25a HEB leave in our possession.
27a JST Ex. 10:27 But

Pharaoh hardened *his* heart . . .
29a HEB As you have spoken.
11 1a Ex. 12:39.
  2a HEB ask.
  b OR jewelry.
  3a Ex. 3:21 (21–22).

5a TG Plague.
  b Ex. 4:23 (21–23).
7a 1 Ne. 17:35 (33–38).
8a TG Anger.
10a JST Ex. 11:10 . . . And *Pharaoh* hardened *his* heart . . .

so that he would not let the children of Israel go out of his land.

CHAPTER 12

The Lord institutes the Passover and the Feast of Unleavened Bread—Lambs without blemish are slain—Israel is saved by their blood—The firstborn of all Egyptians are slain—Israel is thrust out of Egypt after 430 years—No bones of the paschal lambs are to be broken.

AND the LORD spake unto Moses and Aaron in the land of Egypt, saying,

2 This *a*month *shall be* unto you the *b*beginning of months: it *shall be* the first month of the year to you.

3 ¶ Speak ye unto all the congregation of Israel, saying, In the tenth *day* of this month they shall take to them every man a lamb, according to the house of *their* fathers, a lamb for an house:

4 And if the household be too little for the lamb, let him and his neighbour next unto his house take *it* according to the number of the souls; every man according to his *a*eating shall make your count for the lamb.

5 Your *a*lamb shall be without blemish, a male *b*of the first year: ye shall take *it* out from the sheep, or from the goats:

6 And ye shall keep it up until the *a*fourteenth day of the same month: and the whole assembly of the congregation of Israel shall kill it in the evening.

7 And they shall take of the blood, and strike *it* on the two side posts and on the upper door post of the houses, wherein they shall eat it.

8 And they shall eat the flesh in that night, roast with fire, and *a*unleavened bread; *and* with bitter *herbs* they shall eat it.

9 Eat not of it raw, nor *a*sodden at all with water, but roast *with* fire; his head with his legs, and with the *b*purtenance thereof.

10 And ye shall let nothing of it *a*remain until the morning; and that which remaineth of it until the morning ye shall burn with fire.

11 ¶ And thus shall ye eat it; *with* your loins *a*girded, your shoes on your feet, and your staff in your hand; and ye shall eat it in *b*haste: it *is* the LORD's passover.

12 For I will pass through the land of Egypt this night, and will smite all the *a*firstborn in the land of Egypt, both man and beast; and against all the *b*gods of Egypt I will execute *c*judgment: I *am* the LORD.

13 And the blood shall be to you for a *a*token upon the houses where ye *are:* and when I see the blood, I will pass over you, and the plague shall not be upon you to destroy *you,* when I smite the land of Egypt.

14 And this *a*day shall be unto you for a *b*memorial; and ye shall keep it a *c*feast to the LORD throughout your generations; ye shall keep it a *d*feast by an ordinance *e*for ever.

15 Seven days shall ye eat *a*unleavened bread; even the first day ye shall put away leaven out of your houses: for whosoever eateth leavened bread from the first day until the seventh day, that soul shall be *b*cut off from Israel.

16 And in the first day *there shall be* an holy *a*convocation, and in the

---

12 2*a* Ex. 34:18; 40:2.
　　b Ex. 13:4.
　　4*a* IE capacity to eat.
　　　Ex. 16:16.
　　5*a* TG Jesus Christ,
　　　Lamb of God; Jesus
　　　Christ, Types of, in
　　　Anticipation; Passover.
　　b HEB a year old.
　　6*a* Lev. 23:5;
　　　Num. 9:3 (1–5);
　　　2 Chr. 35:1 (1–19);
　　　Ezra 6:19.

8*a* Ex. 23:18 (18–19).
　　TG Bread, Unleavened.
9*a* HEB boiled . . . in.
　b IE edible inner parts.
10*a* Ex. 34:25.
11*a* Isa. 11:5;
　　D&C 27:15 (15–18).
　b Deut. 16:3.
　　TG Haste.
12*a* TG Firstborn.
　b Isa. 19:1; Jer. 43:12;
　　Alma 17:15;
　　Morm. 4:14 (14, 21);

Abr. 1:8 (6–14).
　c TG Judgment.
13*a* HEB sign.
14*a* John 19:31.
　b Ex. 13:9; D&C 124:39.
　c Ex. 5:1.
　d 1 Cor. 5:8.
　e 3 Ne. 9:19 (19–20).
15*a* Ex. 34:18; Acts 20:6.
　　TG Leaven.
　b TG Excommunication.
16*a* OR assembly.
　　TG Meetings.

*b*seventh day there shall be an holy convocation to you; no manner of work shall be done in them, save *that* which every man must eat, that only may be done of you.

17 And ye shall observe the *ªfeast of *b*unleavened bread; for in this selfsame day have I brought your *c*armies out of the land of Egypt: therefore shall ye observe this day in your generations *d*by an ordinance for ever.

18 ¶ In the first *month*, on the fourteenth day of the month at even, ye shall eat unleavened bread, until the one and twentieth day of the month at even.

19 Seven days shall there be no leaven found in your houses: for whosoever eateth that which is leavened, even that soul shall be cut off from the congregation of Israel, whether he be a *ª*stranger, or born in the land.

20 Ye shall eat nothing leavened; in all your habitations shall ye eat unleavened bread.

21 ¶ Then Moses called for all the elders of Israel, and said unto them, *ª*Draw out and take you a *b*lamb according to your *c*families, and kill the *d*passover.

22 And ye shall take a bunch of hyssop, and dip *it* in the blood that *is* in the basin, and strike the lintel and the two side posts with the *ª*blood that *is* in the basin; and none of you shall go out at the door of his house until the morning.

23 For the LORD will *ª*pass through to smite the Egyptians; and when he seeth the blood upon the lintel, and on the two side posts, the LORD will *b*pass over the door, and will not *c*suffer the *d*destroyer to come in unto your houses to smite *you.*

24 And ye shall observe this thing for an ordinance to thee and to thy sons for ever.

25 And it shall come to pass, when ye be come to the land which the LORD will give you, according as he hath promised, that ye shall keep this service.

26 And it shall come to pass, when your *ª*children shall say unto you, What mean ye by this service?

27 That ye shall say, It *is* the *ª*sacrifice of the LORD's *b*passover, who passed over the houses of the children of Israel in Egypt, when he smote the Egyptians, and *c*delivered our houses. And the people bowed the head and worshipped.

28 And the children of Israel went away, and did as the LORD had *ª*commanded Moses and Aaron, so did they.

29 ¶ And it came to pass, that at midnight the LORD *ª*smote all the *b*firstborn in the land of Egypt, from the firstborn of Pharaoh that sat on his throne unto the firstborn of the captive that *was* in the dungeon; and all the firstborn of cattle.

30 And Pharaoh rose up in the night, he, and all his servants, and all the Egyptians; and there was a great cry in Egypt; for *there was* not a house where *there was* not one *ª*dead.

31 ¶ And he called for Moses and Aaron by night, and said, Rise up, *and* get you *ª*forth from among my people, both ye and the children of Israel; and go, serve the LORD, as ye have said.

32 Also take your flocks and your

16*b* John 19:31.
17*a* TG Passover.
　b TG Bread, Unleavened.
　c OR hosts (also v. 51).
　d OR as a permanent law.
19*a* OR sojourner (also in vv. 43, 48–49).
21*a* OR Select.
　b Alma 34:14 (9–14).
　c TG Family, Patriarchal.
　d IE passover lamb.

22*a* TG Jesus Christ, Types of, in Anticipation; Passover.
22*a* 2 Chr. 30:16 (15–17); 35:11 (10–12); Heb. 11:28 (24–29).
23*a* D&C 89:21.
　b TG Passover.
　c OR allow.
　d TG Protection, Divine.
26*a* Ex. 13:14;

Deut. 6:21 (20–25).
27*a* TG Sacrifice.
　b Matt. 26:19 (17–19).
　c TG Deliver.
28*a* Heb. 11:28 (24–29).
29*a* Ex. 13:15.
　b Num. 8:17 (17–18); Ps. 105:36. TG Plague.
30*a* TG Death.
31*a* Ex. 3:20; 6:1.

herds, as ye have said, and be gone; and bless me also.

33 And the Egyptians were ^aurgent upon the people, that they might send them out of the land in haste; for they said, We *be* all dead *men.*

34 And the people took their dough before it was leavened, their kneadingtroughs being bound up in their clothes upon their shoulders.

35 And the children of Israel did according to the word of Moses; and they ^aborrowed of the Egyptians jewels of ^bsilver, and jewels of gold, and ^craiment:

36 And the LORD gave the people ^afavour in the sight of the Egyptians, so that they ^blent unto them *such things as they required.* And they ^cspoiled the Egyptians.

37 ¶ And the children of Israel ^ajourneyed from ^bRameses to Succoth, about ^csix hundred thousand on foot *that were* men, beside children.

38 And ^aa mixed multitude went up also with them; and flocks, and herds, *even* very much cattle.

39 And they baked ^aunleavened cakes of the dough which they brought forth out of Egypt, for it was not leavened; because they were ^bthrust out of Egypt, and could not tarry, neither had they prepared for themselves any ^cvictual.

40 ¶ Now the ^asojourning of the children of Israel, who dwelt in Egypt, *was* four hundred and thirty years.

41 And it came to pass at the end of the four hundred and thirty years, even the selfsame day it came to pass, that all the hosts of the LORD went out from the land of Egypt.

42 It *is* a night ^ato be much ^bobserved unto the LORD for bringing them out from the land of Egypt: this *is* that night of the LORD to be observed of all the children of ^cIsrael in their generations.

43 ¶ And the LORD said unto Moses and Aaron, This *is* the ordinance of the ^apassover: There shall no ^bstranger eat thereof:

44 But every man's servant that is ^abought for money, when thou hast circumcised him, then shall he eat thereof.

45 A foreigner and an hired servant shall not eat thereof.

46 In one house shall it be eaten; thou shalt not carry forth ^aought of the flesh ^babroad out of the house; neither shall ye ^cbreak a ^dbone thereof.

47 All the congregation of Israel shall keep it.

48 And when a stranger shall sojourn with thee, and will keep the passover to the LORD, let all his males be ^acircumcised, and then let him come near and keep it; and he shall be as one that is ^bborn in the land: for no uncircumcised person shall eat thereof.

49 One law shall be to him that is homeborn, and unto the stranger that sojourneth among you.

50 Thus did all the children of Israel; as the ^aLORD commanded Moses and Aaron, so did they.

51 And it came to pass the selfsame day, *that* the LORD did ^abring the children of Israel out of the land of Egypt by their armies.

33a Ps. 105:38 (37–38).
35a OR asked.
  b Ezra 7:18 (17–23);
    Ps. 105:37.
  c OR clothing.
36a Gen. 15:14 (13–14);
    Ex. 3:21 (21–22).
  b OR let them have.
  c OR despoiled.
    Ex. 3:22.
37a Deut. 26:8; Josh. 24:6.
  b Gen. 47:11.
  c Ex. 1:9.
38a HEB a blending of many;
    i.e., of other peoples.

Neh. 13:3.
39a TG Bread, Unleavened.
  b Ex. 11:1.
  c HEB provisions.
40a TG Israel, Bondage of, in
    Egypt.
42a HEB the LORD watched
    to bring them out.
  b Deut. 16:6.
  c Ex. 13:18 (3–22);
    Ps. 136:11.
43a TG Passover.
  b 3 Ne. 18:28 (28–30).
    TG Stranger.
44a Gen. 17:12 (12–13).

46a OR any.
  b OR outside.
  c TG Jesus Christ,
    Prophecies about.
  d John 19:36.
    TG Passover.
48a TG Circumcision.
  b Lev. 16:29;
    Ezek. 47:22.
50a Hosea 12:13 (12–14).
51a Deut. 26:8;
    Amos 2:10;
    Acts 7:36; 1 Ne. 17:40;
    Mosiah 7:19; 12:34;
    Alma 36:28.

CHAPTER 13

The firstborn of man and of beasts are to be sanctified unto the Lord—The Feast of Unleavened Bread is to be kept in the land of Canaan—Moses takes Joseph's bones out of Egypt—The Lord attends Israel in a pillar of cloud by day and a pillar of fire by night.

AND the LORD spake unto Moses, saying,

2 ^aSanctify unto me all the ^bfirstborn, whatsoever ^copeneth the ^dwomb among the children of Israel, *both* of man and of beast: it *is* mine.

3 ¶ And Moses said unto the people, Remember this day, in which ye came out from ^aEgypt, out of the house of bondage; for by strength of hand the LORD brought you out from this *place:* there shall no leavened bread be eaten.

4 This day ^acame ye out in ^bthe month ^cAbib.

5 ¶ And it shall be when the LORD shall ^abring thee into the land of the ^bCanaanites, and the Hittites, and the Amorites, and the Hivites, and the Jebusites, which he ^csware unto thy fathers to give thee, a land ^dflowing with milk and honey, that thou shalt keep this service in this month.

6 Seven days thou shalt eat unleavened bread, and in the seventh day *shall be* a feast to the LORD.

7 Unleavened bread shall be eaten seven days; and there shall no ^aleavened bread be seen with thee, neither shall there be ^bleaven seen with thee ^cin all thy quarters.

8 ¶ And thou shalt ^ashew thy son in that day, saying, *This is done* because of that *which* the LORD did unto me when I came forth out of Egypt.

9 And it shall be for a ^asign unto thee upon thine hand, and for a ^bmemorial between thine eyes, that the LORD's law may be in thy mouth: for with a strong hand hath the LORD brought thee out of Egypt.

10 Thou shalt therefore keep this ordinance ^ain his season from year to year.

11 ¶ And it shall be when the LORD shall bring thee into the land of the ^aCanaanites, as he ^bsware unto thee and to thy fathers, and shall give it thee,

12 That thou shalt set apart unto the LORD ^aall that openeth the matrix, and every ^bfirstling that cometh of a beast which thou hast; the males *shall be* the LORD's.

13 And every firstling of an ass thou shalt redeem with a lamb; and if thou wilt not redeem it, then thou shalt break his neck: and all the ^afirstborn of man among thy children shalt thou redeem.

14 ¶ And it shall be when thy ^ason ^basketh thee in time to come, saying, What *is* this? that thou shalt say unto him, By strength of hand the LORD ^cbrought us out from Egypt, from the house of ^dbondage:

15 And it came to pass, when Pharaoh would hardly let us go, that the LORD ^aslew all the firstborn in the land of Egypt, both the firstborn of man, and the firstborn of beast: therefore I sacrifice to the LORD all that openeth the matrix, being males; but all the firstborn of my children I redeem.

---

13 2*a* OR Consecrate.
  b Num. 3:41 (41, 45);
      Deut. 15:19.
      TG Firstborn.
  c Ex. 34:19.
  d Luke 2:23.
  3*a* Ps. 114:1.
  4*a* HEB you are to come out.
  b IE the first month of
      spring.
  c Ex. 12:2; Deut. 16:1.
  5*a* Ex. 34:11.
  b Ex. 33:2.

  c Ex. 6:8.
  d Ex. 33:3.
  7*a* Deut. 16:4.
  b TG Leaven.
  c OR within all your
      borders.
  8*a* HEB tell.
  9*a* TG Ex. 12:14 (14–17).
  b Deut. 6:8;
      Matt. 23:5 (1–22).
  10*a* HEB at the appointed
       time.
  11*a* Ex. 3:8 (1–10).

  b 1 Ne. 17:40.
  12*a* IE all the firstborn (see
       also v. 15).
  b Mosiah 2:3;
      Moses 5:5 (5–8).
  13*a* TG Firstborn.
  14*a* Ex. 12:26 (25–27).
  b Deut. 6:20.
  c Ex. 3:10 (2–10);
      Alma 36:28;
      D&C 8:3 (2–3).
  d TG Bondage, Physical.
  15*a* Ex. 12:29.

16 And it shall be for a token upon thine hand, and for *a*frontlets between thine eyes: for by strength of hand the LORD brought us forth out of Egypt.

17 ¶ And it came to pass, when Pharaoh had let the people go, that God led them not *through* the way of the land of the Philistines, although that *was* near; for God said, Lest *a*peradventure the people *b*repent when they see war, and they *c*return to Egypt:

18 But God *a*led the people about, *through* the way of the wilderness of the Red sea: and the children of *b*Israel went up *c*harnessed out of the land of Egypt.

19 And Moses took the bones of *a*Joseph with him: for he had straitly sworn the children of Israel, saying, God will surely visit you; and ye shall carry up my *b*bones away hence with you.

20 ¶ And they took their journey from *a*Succoth, and encamped in Etham, in the edge of the wilderness.

21 And the *a*LORD went before them by day in a pillar of a *b*cloud, to *c*lead them the way; and by night in a *d*pillar of fire, to give them light; to go by day and night:

22 He took not away the pillar of the cloud by day, nor the pillar of fire by night, *from* before the people.

CHAPTER 14

Israel goes out of Egypt—Israel passes through the Red Sea on dry ground— The Lord overthrows the Egyptians in the midst of the sea.

AND the LORD spake unto Moses, saying,

2 Speak unto the children of Israel, that they *a*turn and encamp before Pi-hahiroth, between *b*Migdol and the sea, over against Baal-zephon: before it shall ye encamp by the sea.

3 For Pharaoh will say of the children of Israel, They *are* entangled in the land, the wilderness hath shut them in.

4 *a*And I will harden Pharaoh's heart, that he shall follow after them; and I will be honoured *b*upon Pharaoh, and upon all his *c*host; that the Egyptians may *d*know that I *am* the LORD. And they did so.

5 ¶ And it was told the king of Egypt that the people fled: and the heart of Pharaoh and of his servants was turned against the people, and they said, Why have we done this, that we have let Israel go from serving us?

6 And he made ready his chariot, and took his people with him:

7 And he took six hundred chosen *a*chariots, and *b*all the chariots of Egypt, and captains over every one of them.

8 *a*And the LORD hardened the heart of Pharaoh king of Egypt, and he pursued after the children of Israel: and the children of Israel went out *b*with an *c*high hand.

9 But the Egyptians *a*pursued after them, all the horses *and* chariots of Pharaoh, and his horsemen, and his army, and overtook them encamping by the sea, beside *b*Pi-hahiroth, before Baal-zephon.

10 ¶ And when Pharaoh drew nigh,

16*a* Deut. 6:8 (6–9).
17*a* OR perhaps.
  b Ex. 14:12 (11–12);
     Num. 14:4 (1–4).
  c Deut. 17:16.
18*a* Ezek. 20:10;
     1 Ne. 17:30 (23–30);
     D&C 136:22 (21–22).
  b Ex. 12:42 (41–42);
     Ps. 136:11.
  c OR equipped for battle.
19*a* See JST Gen. 50:24–38
     (Appendix).
  b Gen. 50:25 (24–26);
     Josh. 24:32 (32–33).

20*a* Num. 33:5.
21*a* Ex. 14:19.
  b Ex. 24:15; 40:34;
     Num. 9:15;
     Ps. 78:14; 105:39;
     Ether 2:5.
     TG God, Presence of;
     Protection, Divine.
  c Ex. 32:1;
     D&C 103:17 (15–34).
     TG Guidance, Divine.
  d Neh. 9:12.
14 2*a* HEB return.
     Num. 33:7 (7–8).
  b Jer. 44:1.

4*a* JST Ex. 14:4 And *Pharaoh*
     will harden *his* heart . . .
  b OR by.
  c OR army (also
     vv. 17, 24, 28).
  d Ex. 7:5.
7*a* Ex. 15:4.
  b IE all the other chariots.
8*a* JST Ex. 14:8 And *Pharaoh*
     hardened *his* heart, and
     he pursued . . .
  b IE in defiance.
  c Num. 33:3.
9*a* Ex. 15:9.
  b Josh. 24:6.

the children of Israel lifted up their eyes, and, behold, the Egyptians marched after them; and they were sore afraid: and the children of Israel cried out unto the LORD.

11 And they said unto Moses, Because *there were* no graves in Egypt, hast thou taken us away to *a*die in the wilderness? wherefore hast thou *b*dealt thus with us, to carry us forth out of Egypt?

12 *Is* not this the *a*word that we did tell thee in Egypt, saying, Let us alone, that we may serve the Egyptians? For *it had been* better for us to *b*serve the Egyptians, than that we should die in the wilderness.

13 ¶ And Moses said unto the people, Fear ye not, stand still, and see the salvation of the LORD, which he will *a*shew to you to day: for the Egyptians whom ye have seen to day, ye shall see them again no more for ever.

14 The LORD shall *a*fight for you, and ye shall hold your *b*peace.

15 ¶ And the LORD said unto Moses, Wherefore criest thou unto me? speak unto the children of Israel, that they go forward:

16 But lift thou up thy *a*rod, and stretch out thine hand over the sea, and *b*divide it: and the children of Israel shall go on *c*dry *ground* through the midst of the sea.

17 *a*And I, behold, I will *b*harden the hearts of the Egyptians, and they shall follow them: and *c*I will get me honour upon Pharaoh, and upon all his host, upon his chariots, and upon his horsemen.

18 And the Egyptians shall know that I *am* the LORD, when I have gotten me honour upon Pharaoh, upon his chariots, and upon his horsemen.

19 ¶ And the *a*angel of God, which went before the camp of Israel, removed and went behind them; and the *b*pillar of the cloud went from before their face, and stood behind them:

20 And it came between the camp of the Egyptians and the camp of Israel; *a*and it was a cloud and *b*darkness *to them,* but it gave light by night *to these:* so that the one came not near the other all the night.

21 And Moses stretched out his hand over the *a*sea; and the LORD *b*caused the *c*sea to *d*go *back* by a strong east wind all *that* night, and made the sea *e*dry *land,* and the *f*waters were *g*divided.

22 And the children of Israel went into the midst of the sea upon the dry *ground:* and the waters *were* a wall unto them on their right hand, and on their left.

23 ¶ And the Egyptians pursued, and went in after them to the midst of the sea, *even* all Pharaoh's horses, his chariots, and his horsemen.

24 And it came to pass, that in the morning watch the LORD looked unto the host of the Egyptians through the pillar of fire and of the cloud, and troubled the host of the Egyptians,

25 And *a*took off their chariot wheels, that they drave them heavily: so that the Egyptians said,

---

11a Ps. 106:7.
  b Ex. 32:22.
12a OR thing.
  b Ex. 5:21 (20–23);
    13:17 (17–18).
13a HEB accomplish for you.
14a TG Protection, Divine.
  b D&C 10:37; 11:22.
16a See JST Gen. 50:34
    (Appendix).
    Ex. 7:20 (19–21).
  b See JST Gen. 14:26–31
    (Appendix).
    Isa. 43:16.
  c Mosiah 7:19;
    Hel. 8:11; D&C 8:3.
17a JST Ex. 14:17 And I *say*

unto thee the hearts of
the Egyptians *shall be
hardened,* and they . . .
  b TG Hardheartedness.
  c HEB I will be honored by
    Pharaoh and by all his
    army, etc.
19a Ex. 13:21 (21–22);
    16:10; 23:20 (20–23);
    1 Ne. 3:29 (28–31);
    D&C 103:20 (17–20).
  b Ex. 33:9; Num. 9:15.
20a JST Ex. 14:20 . . . and
    it was a cloud and
    darkness to *the Egyptians,*
    but it gave light by night
    to *the Israelites* . . .

  b Hel. 5:28 (28–43).
21a Ps. 106:9 (9–15);
    1 Ne. 4:2 (2–3);
    2 Ne. 7:2; D&C 133:68.
  b Ps. 78:13.
  c Josh. 2:10;
    3:16 (14–17); 4:23;
    2 Kgs. 2:8;
    1 Ne. 17:26 (24–34);
    2 Ne. 7:2; Moses 1:25.
    TG Nature, Earth.
  d Neh. 9:11; Isa. 63:12.
  e Isa. 51:10.
  f Ex. 15:8; Ps. 77:16.
  g 2 Kgs. 2:14;
    Ps. 114:3.
25a OR bound.

Let us flee from the face of Israel; for the Lord fighteth for them against the Egyptians.

26 ¶ And the Lord said unto Moses, Stretch out thine ᵃhand over the sea, that the waters may come again upon the Egyptians, upon their chariots, and upon their horsemen.

27 And Moses stretched forth his hand over the sea, and the sea returned to ᵃhis strength when the morning appeared; and the Egyptians fled ᵇagainst it; and the Lord overthrew the ᶜEgyptians in the midst of the sea.

28 And the ᵃwaters returned, and ᵇcovered the chariots, and the horsemen, *and* all the host of Pharaoh that came into the ᶜsea after them; there remained not so much as ᵈone of them.

29 But the children of Israel walked upon ᵃdry *land* in the midst of the sea; and the waters *were* a wall unto them on their right hand, and on their left.

30 Thus the Lord ᵃsaved Israel that day out of the hand of the Egyptians; and Israel saw the Egyptians dead upon the sea shore.

31 And Israel saw that great work which the Lord did upon the Egyptians: and the people feared the Lord, and ᵃbelieved the Lord, and his servant Moses.

CHAPTER 15

The children of Israel sing the song of Moses—They extol the Lord as a man of war and rejoice in their deliverance from Egypt—The waters of Marah are healed—The Lord promises to free Israel from the diseases of Egypt.

Then ᵃsang Moses and the children of Israel this song unto the Lord, and spake, saying, I will ᵇsing unto the Lord, for he hath triumphed gloriously: the horse and his rider hath he thrown into the sea.

2 The ᵃLord *is* my ᵇstrength and song, and he is become my ᶜsalvation: he *is* my God, and I will ᵈprepare him an habitation; my father's God, and I will ᵉexalt him.

3 The Lord *is* a man of ᵃwar: the Lord *is* his ᵇname.

4 Pharaoh's ᵃchariots and his host hath he ᵇcast into the sea: his chosen captains also are drowned in the ᶜRed sea.

5 The depths have covered them: they sank into the bottom as a ᵃstone.

6 Thy ᵃright ᵇhand, O Lord, is become glorious in power: thy right hand, O Lord, hath dashed in pieces the enemy.

7 And in the greatness of thine excellency thou hast overthrown them that rose up against thee: thou sentest forth thy wrath, *which* consumed them as ᵃstubble.

8 And with the blast of thy nostrils the ᵃwaters were gathered together, the floods stood upright as an ᵇheap, *and* the depths were congealed in the heart of the sea.

9 The enemy said, I will ᵃpursue, I will overtake, I will divide the spoil; my ᵇlust shall be satisfied upon them; I will draw my sword, my hand shall destroy them.

26a Isa. 10:26.
27a IE its normal condition.
  b HEB meeting it.
  c Isa. 10:26;
    2 Ne. 20:26 (25–26);
    Alma 36:28.
28a Ps. 78:53.
  b Ex. 15:4 (1–7).
  c Deut. 11:4.
  d Ps. 106:11 (10–11).
29a Isa. 11:16;
    2 Ne. 21:16;
    D&C 133:27.
30a Judg. 3:30 (13–31);
    10:11 (11–12).

  TG Israel, Deliverance of.
31a TG Faith.
15 1a TG Singing.
  b Hosea 2:15.
2a 2 Ne. 22:2.
  b TG Priesthood,
    Power of;
    Strength.
  c TG Jesus Christ, Savior.
  d HEB praise Him.
  e 2 Sam. 22:47.
3a TG War.
  b Jer. 16:21.
4a Ex. 14:7 (5–7).
  b Ex. 14:28 (27–30).

  c OR Reed Sea (also v. 22).
5a Neh. 9:11.
6a Ps. 98:1.
  b Ps. 118:16 (15–16).
7a Isa. 47:14;
    1 Ne. 22:23 (15, 23);
    D&C 29:9;
    JS—H 1:37.
8a Ex. 14:21 (21–22).
  b Josh. 3:13.
9a Ex. 14:9.
  b HEB soul; i.e., desire.
  TG Lust.

10 Thou didst blow with thy wind, the sea covered them: they sank as lead in the mighty waters.

11 Who is *a*like unto thee, O *b*LORD, among the gods? who is like thee, glorious in *c*holiness, *d*fearful in praises, doing wonders?

12 Thou stretchedst out thy right hand, the earth swallowed them.

13 Thou in thy mercy hast *a*led forth the people *which* thou hast redeemed: thou hast guided *them* in thy strength unto thy holy habitation.

14 The people shall *a*hear, *and* be afraid: sorrow shall take hold on the inhabitants of *b*Palestina.

15 Then the *a*dukes of *b*Edom shall be amazed; the mighty men of Moab, trembling shall take hold upon them; all the inhabitants of Canaan shall *c*melt away.

16 *a*Fear and *b*dread shall fall upon them; by the greatness of thine arm they shall be *as* still as a stone; till thy people pass over, O LORD, till the people pass over, *which* thou hast *c*purchased.

17 Thou shalt bring them in, and plant them in the mountain of thine inheritance, *in* the place, O LORD, *which* thou hast made for thee to dwell in, *in* the *a*Sanctuary, O Lord, *which* thy hands have established.

18 The *a*LORD shall reign for ever and ever.

19 For the horse of Pharaoh went in with his chariots and with his horsemen into the sea, and the LORD brought again the waters of the sea upon them; but the children of Israel went on dry *land* in the midst of the sea.

20 ¶ And *a*Miriam the *b*prophetess, the *c*sister of Aaron, took a *d*timbrel in her hand; and all the women went out after her with timbrels and with dances.

21 And Miriam answered them, *a*Sing ye to the LORD, for he hath triumphed gloriously; the horse and his rider hath he thrown into the sea.

22 So Moses brought Israel from the Red sea, and they went out into the wilderness of *a*Shur; and they went three days in the wilderness, and found no water.

23 ¶ And when they came to *a*Marah, they could not drink of the waters of Marah, for they *were* bitter: therefore the name of it was called Marah.

24 And the people *a*murmured against Moses, saying, What shall we drink?

25 And he cried unto the LORD; and the LORD shewed him a tree, *which* when he had cast into the waters, the *a*waters were made sweet: there he made for them a statute and an ordinance, and there he *b*proved them,

26 And said, If thou wilt *a*diligently *b*hearken to the voice of the LORD thy God, and wilt do that which is right in his sight, and wilt give ear to his commandments, and *c*keep all his statutes, I will put none of these *d*diseases upon thee, which I have brought upon the Egyptians: for I *am* the LORD that *e*healeth thee.

27 ¶ And they came to Elim, where *were* twelve wells of water, and *a*threescore and ten palm trees: and they encamped there by the waters.

11a 2 Sam. 7:22;
    D&C 76:2 (1–4).
  b Ps. 86:8.
  c TG Holiness.
  d OR to be praised
    with awe.
13a Ps. 77:20;
    1 Ne. 5:15;
    17:31 (23–31);
    D&C 103:16 (16–18).
14a Josh. 2:11; 5:1.
  b OR Philistia.
15a HEB chiefs.
  b Gen. 36:15 (15–43).

  c Josh. 2:9 (8–11).
16a Ex. 23:27 (27–30);
    Deut. 2:25.
  b Josh. 2:9.
  c Ps. 74:2;
    1 Cor. 6:20.
17a 1 Kgs. 8:13.
18a D&C 84:119.
20a Ex. 2:4.
  b Judg. 4:4; Alma 32:23.
  c Ex. 2:4; Num. 26:59.
  d 1 Sam. 18:6 (6–7).
21a TG Singing.
22a Gen. 16:7.

23a IE Bitterness.
24a TG Murmuring.
25a 2 Kgs. 2:21.
  b Deut. 8:2;
    D&C 98:14 (12–14);
    124:55; 132:51;
    Abr. 3:25.
26a TG Diligence;
    Perseverance.
  b TG Obedience.
  c D&C 5:35; 11:20.
  d Deut. 7:15.
  e TG Heal.
27a IE seventy palm trees.

CHAPTER 16

Israel murmurs for want of bread and lusts for the fleshpots of Egypt—The Lord rains bread from heaven and sends quail for meat—Israel is given manna each day, except the Sabbath, for forty years.

AND they took their journey from Elim, and all the congregation of the children of Israel came unto the wilderness of Sin, which *is* between Elim and Sinai, on the fifteenth day of the second month after their departing out of the land of Egypt.

2 And the whole congregation of the children of Israel *ᵃ*murmured against Moses and Aaron in the wilderness:

3 And the children of Israel said unto them, Would to God we had died by the hand of the LORD in the land of Egypt, when we sat by the *ᵃ*flesh pots, *and* when we did eat bread to the full; for ye have brought us forth into this wilderness, to kill this whole assembly with *ᵇ*hunger.

4 ¶ Then said the LORD unto Moses, Behold, I will rain *ᵃ*bread from heaven for you; and the people shall go out and gather a certain *ᵇ*rate every day, that I may *ᶜ*prove them, whether they will *ᵈ*walk in my law, or no.

5 And it shall come to pass, that on the sixth day they shall prepare *that* which they bring in; and it shall be twice as much as they gather daily.

6 And Moses and Aaron said unto all the children of Israel, At even, then ye shall know that the LORD hath brought you out from the land of Egypt:

7 And in the morning, then ye shall see the *ᵃ*glory of the LORD; for that he heareth your murmurings against the LORD: and what *are* we, that ye murmur against us?

8 And Moses said, *This shall be,* when the LORD shall give you in the evening flesh to eat, and in the morning bread to the full; for that the LORD heareth your murmurings which ye murmur against him: and what *are* we? your *ᵃ*murmurings *are* not against us, but *ᵇ*against the LORD.

9 ¶ And Moses *ᵃ*spake unto Aaron, Say unto all the congregation of the children of Israel, Come near before the LORD: for he hath heard your murmurings.

10 And it came to pass, as Aaron spake unto the whole congregation of the children of Israel, that they looked toward the wilderness, and, behold, the *ᵃ*glory of the LORD appeared in the *ᵇ*cloud.

11 ¶ And the LORD spake unto Moses, saying,

12 I have heard the *ᵃ*murmurings of the children of Israel: speak unto them, saying, At even ye shall eat flesh, and in the morning ye shall be filled with bread; and ye shall know that I *am* the LORD your God.

13 And it came to pass, that at even the *ᵃ*quails came up, and covered the camp: and in the morning the dew lay round about the *ᵇ*host.

14 And when the dew that lay was gone up, behold, upon the face of the wilderness *there lay* a small *ᵃ*round *ᵇ*thing, *as* small as the hoar frost on the ground.

15 And when the children of Israel saw *it,* they said one to another, *ᵃ*It is *ᵇ*manna: for they wist not what it

---

16 2*a* TG Murmuring; Rebellion.
  3*a* Ps. 78:18.
    b Ps. 78:19.
  4*a* OR food (also vv. 15, 22). TG Bread.
    b OR portion.
    c TG Test.
    d TG Walking with God.
  7*a* John 11:40.
  8*a* 1 Sam. 8:7 (7–9); Matt. 10:40–41.

  b Num. 16:11; 1 Ne. 16:22 (20–25); D&C 29:19.
  9*a* Ex. 4:16 (14–16).
  10*a* Ex. 14:19; 24:16; Num. 14:10. TG God, Manifestations of.
    b Ex. 40:38.
  12*a* Num. 14:27 (27–32); Mosiah 29:33.
  13*a* Num. 11:31;

  Ps. 78:27 (27–28); 105:40; 1 Ne. 17:2; 18:6.
    b IE of Israel.
  14*a* HEB fine, flake-like.
    b Neh. 9:15.
  15*a* OR What is it? (HEB *man-hu.*)
    b 1 Cor. 10:3 (1–6); 1 Ne. 17:28; Mosiah 7:19. TG Jesus Christ, Types of, in Anticipation.

was. And Moses said unto them, This *is* the ᶜbread which the Lord hath given you to eat.

16 ¶ This *is* the thing which the Lord hath commanded, Gather of it every man ᵃaccording to ᵇhis eating, an ᶜomer for every man, *according to* the number of your persons; take ye every man for *them* which *are* in his tents.

17 And the children of Israel did so, and gathered, some more, some less.

18 And when they did mete *it* with an omer, he that ᵃgathered much had nothing over, and he that gathered little had no lack; they gathered every man according to his eating.

19 And Moses said, Let no man leave of it till the morning.

20 Notwithstanding they ᵃhearkened not unto Moses; but some of them left of it until the morning, and it bred worms, and stank: and Moses was wroth with them.

21 And they gathered it every morning, every man according to his eating: and when the sun ᵃwaxed hot, it melted.

22 ¶ And it came to pass, *that* on the sixth day they gathered twice as much bread, two omers for one *man:* and all the rulers of the ᵃcongregation came and told Moses.

23 And he said unto them, This *is that* which the Lord hath said, To morrow *is* the rest of the holy ᵃsabbath unto the Lord: ᵇbake *that* which ye will bake *to day,* and ᶜseethe that ye will seethe; and that which remaineth over lay up for you to be kept until the morning.

24 And they laid it up till the morning, as Moses bade: and it did not stink, neither was there any worm therein.

25 And Moses said, Eat that to day; for to day *is* a sabbath unto the Lord: to day ye shall not find it in the field.

26 Six days ye shall gather it; but on the seventh day, *which is* the sabbath, in it there shall be none.

27 ¶ And it came to pass, *that* there went out *some* of the people on the seventh day for to gather, and they found none.

28 And the Lord said unto Moses, How long refuse ye to ᵃkeep my commandments and my laws?

29 See, for that the Lord hath given you the sabbath, therefore he giveth you on the sixth day the bread of two days; abide ye every man in his place, let no man go out of his place on the seventh day.

30 So the people rested on the seventh day.

31 And the house of Israel called the name thereof Manna: and it *was* like ᵃcoriander seed, white; and the taste of it *was* like wafers *made* with honey.

32 ¶ And Moses said, This *is* the thing which the Lord commandeth, Fill an omer of it to be kept for your ᵃgenerations; that they may see the bread wherewith I have fed you in the wilderness, when I brought you forth from the land of Egypt.

33 And Moses said unto Aaron, Take a ᵃpot, and put an omer full of manna therein, and lay it up before the Lord, to be kept for your generations.

34 As the Lord commanded Moses, so Aaron laid it up before the ᵃTestimony, to be kept.

35 And the children of Israel did eat ᵃmanna forty years, until they came to a land inhabited; they did eat manna, until they came unto the borders of the land of Canaan.

36 Now an ᵃomer *is* the tenth *part* of an ephah.

15c TG Bread.
16a Ex. 12:4.
  b OR what he could eat.
  c Ex. 16:36.
18a 2 Cor. 8:15.
20a Ex. 32:22.
21a OR became.
22a TG Church.

23a TG Sabbath.
  b Ex. 35:3.
  c OR cook what you will cook.
28a D&C 71:11.
31a Num. 11:7 (7–8).
32a OR posterity (also v. 33).
33a Heb. 9:4.

34a Ex. 25:21 (16, 21);
  30:6 (6–38).
35a Num. 11:7 (7–8);
  Josh. 5:12;
  1 Ne. 17:28 (15–43);
  Mosiah 7:19.
36a Ex. 16:16.

CHAPTER 17

Israel murmurs for want of water—Moses smites a rock in Horeb, and water gushes forth—Aaron and Hur uphold Moses' hands so that Joshua prevails against Amalek.

AND all the congregation of the children of Israel journeyed from the wilderness of ᵃSin, after their journeys, according to the commandment of the LORD, and ᵇpitched in Rephidim: and *there was* no water for the people to drink.

2 Wherefore the people ᵃdid chide with Moses, and said, Give us water that we may drink. And Moses said unto them, Why chide ye with me? wherefore do ye ᵇtempt the LORD?

3 And the people thirsted there for water; and the people ᵃmurmured against Moses, and said, Wherefore *is* this *that* thou hast brought us up out of Egypt, to kill us and our children and our cattle with thirst?

4 And Moses cried unto the LORD, saying, What shall I do unto this people? they be almost ready to stone me.

5 And the LORD said unto Moses, Go on before the people, and take with thee of the elders of Israel; and thy ᵃrod, ᵇwherewith thou smotest the river, take in thine hand, and go.

6 Behold, I will stand before thee there upon the rock in Horeb; and thou shalt ᵃsmite the ᵇrock, and there shall come ᶜwater out of it, that the people may drink. And Moses did so in the sight of the elders of Israel.

7 And he called the name of the place ᵃMassah, and ᵇMeribah, because of the ᶜchiding of the children of Israel, and because they tempted the LORD, saying, Is the LORD among us, or not?

8 ¶ Then came ᵃAmalek, and fought with Israel in Rephidim.

9 And Moses said unto ᵃJoshua, Choose us out men, and go out, fight with Amalek: to morrow I will stand on the top of the hill with the ᵇrod of God in mine hand.

10 So Joshua did as Moses had said to him, and fought with Amalek: and Moses, Aaron, and Hur went up to the top of the hill.

11 And it came to pass, when Moses held up his hand, that Israel prevailed: and when he let down his hand, Amalek prevailed.

12 But Moses' hands ᵃwere heavy; and they took a stone, and put *it* under him, and he sat thereon; and Aaron and Hur ᵇstayed up his hands, the one on the one side, and the other on the other side; and his hands were steady until the going down of the sun.

13 And Joshua ᵃdiscomfited Amalek and his people with the edge of the sword.

14 And the LORD said unto Moses, Write this *for* a memorial in a ᵃbook, and rehearse *it* in the ears of Joshua: for I will utterly put out the remembrance of ᵇAmalek from under heaven.

15 And Moses built an altar, and called the name of it ᵃJehovah-nissi:

---

17 1a Num. 33:12 (12–14).
    b OR encamped.
  2a HEB strove with, or
    complained to.
    Ex. 32:22.
    b HEB put the LORD to
    the test.
    TG Doubt; Test.
  3a TG Ingratitude;
    Murmuring.
  5a Ex. 7:20 (20–21).
    b OR with which you
    struck the Nile.
  6a Num. 20:8 (2–13);
    Ps. 74:15; 78:15 (15–16);
    1 Ne. 17:29;

D&C 133:26.
    b 1 Ne. 20:21;
    2 Ne. 25:20.
    TG Jesus Christ, Types
    of, in Anticipation.
    c Neh. 9:15; Ps. 114:8;
    Isa. 48:21.
  7a IE Testing, Trying, or
    Proving.
    b IE Strife, Complaint.
    Num. 20:13;
    Ps. 81:7.
    c OR complaints,
    contention.
    Deut. 9:22.
  8a Num. 24:20;

1 Sam. 15:2 (2–3).
  9a Ex. 24:13; 32:17; 33:11;
    Heb. 4:8.
    b Ex. 4:20.
 12a IE grew heavy with
    weariness.
    b OR supported.
 13a HEB weakened, disabled.
 14a Neh. 13:1 (1–3);
    1 Ne. 5:11; 19:23;
    Moses 1:41 (40–41).
    b Deut. 25:19 (17–19);
    2 Sam. 8:12 (11–12).
 15a IE The LORD is my
    banner.
    Judg. 6:24.

16 For he said, [a]Because the LORD hath sworn *that* the LORD *will have* war with Amalek from generation to generation.

CHAPTER 18

Jethro comes to Moses bringing Moses' wife and sons and offers sacrifices to the Lord—Moses sits in the judgment seat and hears all cases—Jethro counsels Moses to teach the law, to appoint lesser judges, and to delegate power to them.

WHEN [a]Jethro, the [b]priest of [c]Midian, Moses' father in law, heard of all that [d]God had done for Moses, and for Israel his people, *and* that the LORD had brought Israel out of Egypt;

2 Then Jethro, Moses' father in law, took [a]Zipporah, Moses' wife, after he had sent her back,

3 And her two [a]sons; of which the name of the one *was* [b]Gershom; for he said, [c]I have been an alien in a strange land:

4 And the name of the other *was* [a]Eliezer; for the God of my father, *said he, was* mine help, and delivered me from the sword of Pharaoh:

5 And Jethro, Moses' father in law, came with his sons and his wife unto Moses into the wilderness, where he encamped at the [a]mount of God:

6 And he [a]said unto Moses, I thy father in law Jethro am come unto thee, and thy wife, and her two sons with her.

7 ¶ And Moses went out to meet his father in law, and did obeisance, and kissed him; and they asked each other of *their* welfare; and they came into the tent.

8 And Moses told his father in law all that the LORD had done unto Pharaoh and to the Egyptians for Israel's sake, *and* all the travail that had come upon them by the way, and *how* the LORD delivered them.

9 And Jethro rejoiced for all the goodness which the LORD had done to Israel, whom he had delivered out of the hand of the Egyptians.

10 And Jethro said, Blessed *be* the LORD, who hath delivered you out of the hand of the Egyptians, and out of the hand of Pharaoh, who hath delivered the people from under the hand of the Egyptians.

11 Now I know that the LORD *is* greater than all gods: for in the thing wherein they dealt [a]proudly *he was* above them.

12 And Jethro, Moses' father in law, took a burnt offering and sacrifices for God: and Aaron came, and all the elders of Israel, to eat [a]bread with Moses' father in law before God.

13 ¶ And it came to pass on the morrow, that Moses sat to [a]judge the people: and the people stood by Moses from the morning unto the evening.

14 And when Moses' father in law saw all that he did to the people, he said, What *is* this thing that thou doest to the people? why sittest thou thyself alone, and all the people stand by thee from morning unto even?

15 And Moses said unto his father in law, Because the people come unto me to [a]inquire of God:

16 When they have a [a]matter, they come unto me; and I judge between one and another, and I do make *them* know the statutes of God, and his laws.

16*a* HEB A hand upon the throne of the LORD! (an oath, of strong affirmation).
18 1*a* TG Priesthood, Melchizedek.
b JST Ex. 18:1 . . . *high priest* . . . D&C 84:6 (6–16).
c Gen. 25:2 (1–6); Ex. 2:16 (15–16).
d Ps. 106:8.

2*a* Ex. 2:21.
3*a* Acts 7:29.
b Ex. 2:22 (21–22); 1 Chr. 23:15.
c HEB I have been a sojourner in a foreign land.
4*a* IE God of help.
5*a* Ex. 3:1; 4:27.
6*a* IE sent word.
11*a* Luke 1:51 (46–55).
12*a* Gen. 14:18.

13*a* Ezra 7:25; Mosiah 29:11 (11–44); Alma 46:4; D&C 107:74 (74, 78).
15*a* Amos 3:7; Mosiah 28:6; Alma 27:10 (7, 10); 43:23; D&C 102:23; JS—H 1:18. TG Priesthood, Authority.
16*a* 1 Cor. 6:1 (1–8).

17 And Moses' father in law said unto him, The thing that thou doest *is* not good.

18 Thou wilt surely wear away, both thou, and this people that *is* with thee: for this thing *is* ^atoo heavy for thee; thou art not able to perform it thyself alone.

19 Hearken now unto my voice, I will give thee counsel, and God shall be with thee: ^aBe thou for the people to ^bGod-ward, that thou mayest bring the causes unto God:

20 And thou shalt ^ateach them ^bordinances and ^claws, and shalt shew them the ^dway wherein they must ^ewalk, and the work that they must do.

21 Moreover thou shalt provide out of all the people ^aable men, such as ^bfear God, ^cmen of truth, hating ^dcovetousness; and place *such* over them, *to be* ^erulers of thousands, *and* rulers of ^fhundreds, rulers of fifties, and rulers of tens:

22 And let them ^ajudge the people at all seasons; and it shall be, *that* every great matter they shall bring unto thee, but every small matter they shall judge: so shall it be easier for thyself, and they shall bear the ^bburden with thee.

23 If thou shalt do this thing, and God command thee *so,* then thou shalt be able to endure, and all this people shall also go to their place in peace.

24 So Moses hearkened to the voice of his father in law, and did all that he had said.

25 And Moses chose able men out of all Israel, and made them ^aheads over the people, rulers of thousands, rulers of hundreds, rulers of fifties, and rulers of tens.

26 And they judged the people at all seasons: the hard causes they brought unto Moses, but every small matter they judged themselves.

27 ¶ And Moses let his father in law depart; and he went his way into his own land.

CHAPTER 19

The Lord covenants to make Israel a peculiar treasure, a kingdom of priests, and a holy nation—The people sanctify themselves—The Lord appears on Sinai amid fire, smoke, and earthquakes.

IN the third month, when the children of Israel were gone forth out of the land of Egypt, the same day came they *into* the ^awilderness of Sinai.

2 For they were departed from Rephidim, and were come to the desert of Sinai, and had ^apitched in the wilderness; and there Israel camped before the mount.

3 And Moses went up unto God, and the LORD ^acalled unto him out of the ^bmountain, saying, Thus shalt thou say to the house of Jacob, and tell the children of Israel;

4 Ye have seen what I did unto the Egyptians, and *how* I bare you on ^aeagles' wings, and brought you unto myself.

5 Now therefore, if ye will ^aobey my voice indeed, and keep my ^bcovenant, then ye shall be a ^cpeculiar ^dtreasure unto me above all people: for all the earth *is* mine:

18a Num. 11:14 (14–17);
  Deut. 1:9; D&C 10:4.
19a OR You represent the
  people before God.
  b Ex. 4:16.
20a Ezra 7:25; D&C 88:81.
  TG Teacher.
  b OR laws and doctrine.
  TG Ordinance.
  c TG Law of Moses.
  d John 14:6.
  e TG Walking with God.
21a Deut. 1:15 (12–18);
  2 Chr. 19:5 (5–10).
  b 2 Sam. 23:3;

2 Chr. 19:9 (7–9);
  Neh. 7:2;
  Mosiah 29:13.
  TG Reverence.
  c OR faithful or
  trustworthy men.
  d Deut. 16:19;
  1 Sam. 8:3 (1–4);
  2 Chr. 19:7 (5–10).
  e TG Church Organization.
  f D&C 136:3 (2–3).
22a TG Judgment.
  b TG Leadership.
25a TG Delegation of
  Responsibility.

19 1a Num. 10:12.
  2a OR encamped.
  3a Lev. 1:1; Moses 1:17.
  b Ex. 3:12;
  Moses 1:1 (1–3).
  4a Deut. 32:11;
  D&C 124:18 (18, 99).
  5a TG Obedience.
  b TG Abrahamic
  Covenant; Covenants.
  c TG Israel, Twelve
  Tribes of;
  Peculiar People.
  d TG Israel, Blessings of;
  Treasure.

6 And ye shall be unto me a ^akingdom of ^bpriests, and an ^choly ^dnation. These *are* the words which thou shalt speak unto the children of Israel.

7 ¶ And Moses came and called for the elders of the people, and laid before their faces all these words which the LORD ^acommanded him.

8 And all the people answered together, and said, All that the LORD hath spoken we will ^ado. And Moses returned the words of the people unto the LORD.

9 And the LORD said unto Moses, Lo, I come unto thee in a thick ^acloud, that the people may ^bhear when I speak with thee, and believe thee for ever. And Moses told the words of the people unto the LORD.

10 ¶ And the LORD said unto Moses, Go unto the people, and ^asanctify them to day and to morrow, and let them ^bwash their clothes,

11 And be ready against the third day: for the third day the LORD will come down in the ^asight of all the people upon mount Sinai.

12 And thou shalt set ^abounds unto the people round about, saying, Take heed to yourselves, *that ye* go *not* up into the ^bmount, or touch the border of it: whosoever toucheth the mount shall be surely put to death:

13 There shall not an hand touch it, but he shall surely be stoned, or shot through; whether *it be* beast or man, it shall not live: when the trumpet soundeth long, they shall come up to the mount.

14 ¶ And Moses went down from the mount unto the people, and sanctified the people; and they washed their clothes.

15 And he said unto the people, Be ready against the third day: ^acome not at *your* wives.

16 ¶ And it came to pass on the third day in the morning, that there were thunders and lightnings, and a thick cloud upon the mount, and the voice of the trumpet exceeding loud; so that all the people that *was* in the camp trembled.

17 And Moses brought forth the people out of the camp to ^ameet with God; and they stood at the ^bnether part of the mount.

18 And mount ^aSinai was ^baltogether on a ^csmoke, because the LORD ^ddescended upon it in ^efire: and the smoke thereof ascended as the smoke of a furnace, and the whole ^fmount quaked greatly.

19 And when the voice of the ^atrumpet sounded long, and waxed louder and louder, Moses spake, and God answered him by a ^bvoice.

20 And the LORD came down upon mount Sinai, on the top of the mount: and the LORD called Moses *up* to the ^atop of the mount; and Moses went up.

21 And the LORD said unto Moses, Go down, charge the people, lest they break through unto the LORD to ^agaze, and many of them ^bperish.

22 And let the priests also, which come near to the LORD, sanctify

---

6a TG Election.
  b TG Israel, Mission of; Priesthood; Priesthood, History of.
  c Ex. 22:31; 1 Pet. 2:9 (5–9). TG Holiness.
  d TG Separation.
7a Mal. 4:4.
8a Deut. 26:17 (16–19).
9a Ex. 24:15; Mosiah 27:11 (11–12); 3 Ne. 18:38 (38–39); Ether 2:5 (4–5, 14); D&C 45:44 (16, 44). TG God, Manifestations of.
  b Deut. 4:10 (10–12), 33 (33, 36); 5:23 (22–26); Jacob 7:5; 3 Ne. 17:25;

D&C 18:36 (35–36); 84:24 (23–24).
10a Josh. 3:5; 1 Sam. 16:5. TG Purification.
  b TG Cleanliness.
11a TG God, Privilege of Seeing; Sight.
12a Ex. 34:3.
  b Heb. 12:18 (18–19).
15a HEB do not go near any woman; i.e., with lust.
17a TG God, Presence of; Meetings.
  b OR foot of.
18a Deut. 4:10 (10–13); Ps. 81:7; Mosiah 12:33; 13:5; 3 Ne. 25:4.
  b IE covered with smoke

everywhere.
  c Isa. 6:4 (1–4); 1 Ne. 19:11; 3 Ne. 10:13.
  d TG God, Presence of.
  e Ex. 3:2 (2–4); Deut. 5:4 (4–5).
  f Hab. 3:10.
19a D&C 43:25 (18, 25).
  b TG God, Manifestations of.
20a Ex. 34:2.
21a See JST Ex. 33:20 (Appendix). 1 Sam. 6:19. TG God, Privilege of Seeing.
  b D&C 67:11 (11–13); Moses 1:11 (11, 14).

themselves, lest the LORD break forth upon them.

23 And Moses said unto the LORD, The people cannot come up to mount Sinai: for thou chargedst us, saying, Set bounds about the mount, and sanctify it.

24 And the LORD said unto him, Away, get thee down, and thou shalt come up, thou, and Aaron with thee: but let not the priests and the people break through to come up unto the LORD, lest he break forth upon them.

25 So Moses went down unto the people, and spake unto them.

CHAPTER 20

The Lord reveals the Ten Commandments—Israel is to bear witness that the Lord has spoken from heaven—The children of Israel are forbidden to make gods of silver or gold—They are to make altars of unhewn stones and sacrifice to the Lord thereon.

AND God ^aspake all these ^bwords, saying,

2 ^aI *am* the ^bLORD thy ^cGod, which have brought thee out of the land of ^dEgypt, out of the house of ^ebondage.

3 Thou shalt have ^ano other ^bgods before me.

4 Thou shalt ^anot make unto thee any ^bgraven ^cimage, or any likeness *of any thing* that *is* in heaven above, or that *is* in the earth beneath, or that *is* in the water under the earth:

5 Thou shalt not ^abow down thyself to them, nor serve them: for I the LORD thy God *am* a ^bjealous God, ^cvisiting the ^diniquity of the ^efathers upon the ^fchildren unto the third and fourth *generation* of them that ^ghate me;

6 And shewing ^amercy unto thousands of them that love me, and keep my ^bcommandments.

7 Thou shalt not take the ^aname of the LORD thy God in ^bvain; for the LORD will not hold him ^cguiltless that ^dtaketh his name in vain.

8 Remember the ^asabbath day, to keep it ^bholy.

9 ^aSix days shalt thou ^blabour, and do all thy work:

10 But the seventh day *is* the sabbath of the LORD thy God: *in it* thou shalt not do any work, thou, nor thy son, nor thy daughter, thy manservant, nor thy maidservant, nor thy cattle, nor thy ^astranger that *is* within thy gates:

11 For *in* ^asix days the LORD made heaven and earth, the sea, and all that in them *is,* and rested the seventh day: wherefore the LORD

20 1a TG Commandments of
      God; Law of Moses.
   b Deut. 5:2 (2–22);
      Mosiah 13:11 (11–14).
 2a Deut. 5:6 (6–21);
      Mosiah 13:12 (12–24).
   b Ezek. 20:5.
   c Ps. 50:7.
   d Ps. 80:8;
      1 Ne. 17:23 (23–25);
      Moses 1:26.
   e TG Israel, Bondage of,
      in Egypt; Liberty.
 3a Ex. 34:14;
      Deut. 6:14.
   b TG Idolatry; Worship.
 4a 2 Kgs. 17:12.
   b Ex. 32:8; Lev. 26:1;
      Mosiah 13:12;
      3 Ne. 21:17;
      D&C 1:16 (15–16).
   c Judg. 17:3;
      Ps. 97:7; 115:4 (3–8);
      3 Ne. 21:17.

 5a Ex. 23:24; Mosiah 13:13;
      Alma 31:1.
   b HEB *qannah,* "possessing
      sensitive and deep
      feelings."
      Ex. 34:14; Num. 25:11;
      Deut. 4:24; 6:15;
      Josh. 24:19;
      Mosiah 11:22.
   c TG Justice.
   d Ps. 109:14; Mosiah 13:13.
      TG Sin.
   e TG Marriage,
      Fatherhood.
   f IE insofar as the
      children learn and do
      the sinful things the
      parents do; but see v. 6
      concerning those who
      repent and serve the
      Lord.
      D&C 98:47 (46–47).
   g TG Accountability; Hate.
 6a TG God, Mercy of.

   b TG Commandments
      of God.
 7a Lev. 18:21.
      TG Name.
   b TG Profanity; Sacrilege;
      Swearing.
   c Josh. 2:17 (17–20);
      Mosiah 13:15;
      Morm. 7:7; D&C 58:30.
   d IE utters an oath or
      makes a promise using
      the Lord's name without
      valid purpose.
 8a HEB stopping, cessation,
      rest (from labor). See
      Ex. 31:17.
      TG Sabbath.
   b TG Holiness.
 9a Ex. 35:2.
   b TG Industry; Labor.
10a OR sojourner.
      TG Stranger.
11a Ex. 31:17;
      Moses 2:31 (24–31).

*b*blessed the sabbath day, and *c*hallowed it.

12 ¶ *a*Honour thy *b*father and thy *c*mother: that thy *d*days may be *e*long upon the *f*land which the LORD thy God giveth thee.

13 Thou shalt not *a*kill.

14 Thou shalt not commit *a*adultery.

15 Thou shalt not *a*steal.

16 Thou shalt not bear *a*false witness against thy *b*neighbour.

17 Thou shalt not *a*covet thy neighbour's house, thou shalt not covet thy neighbour's *b*wife, nor his manservant, nor his maidservant, nor his ox, nor his ass, nor any thing that *is* thy neighbour's.

18 ¶ And all the people *a*saw the thunderings, and the lightnings, and the noise of the trumpet, and the mountain smoking: and when the people *b*saw *it*, they *c*removed, and stood afar off.

19 And they said unto Moses, Speak thou with us, and we will hear: but let not God *a*speak with us, lest we die.

20 And Moses said unto the people, *a*Fear not: for *b*God is *c*come to *d*prove you, and *e*that his fear may be before your faces, that ye sin not.

21 And the people stood afar off, and Moses drew near unto the thick darkness where God *was*.

22 ¶ And the LORD said unto Moses, Thus thou shalt say unto the children of Israel, Ye have seen that I have *a*talked with you from heaven.

23 Ye shall not make *a*with me *b*gods of silver, neither shall ye make unto you gods of gold.

24 ¶ An altar of earth thou shalt make unto me, and shalt *a*sacrifice thereon thy burnt offerings, and thy peace offerings, thy sheep, and thine oxen: in all places where I record my name I will come unto thee, and I will bless thee.

25 And if thou wilt make me an altar of stone, thou shalt not build it of hewn *a*stone: for if thou lift up thy *b*tool upon it, thou hast polluted it.

26 Neither shalt thou go up by *a*steps unto mine altar, that thy nakedness be not *b*discovered thereon.

CHAPTER 21

The Lord reveals His laws pertaining to servants, marriage, the death penalty for various offenses, the giving of an eye for an eye and a tooth for a tooth, and the damage done by oxen.

Now these *are* the *a*judgments which thou shalt set before them.

2 If thou buy an Hebrew *a*servant, six years he shall serve: and in the

---

11*b* Gen. 2:3 (1–3);
    Mosiah 13:19;
    D&C 77:12;
    Moses 3:3.
  c OR sanctified or
    consecrated.
12*a* OR Respect or Value.
    TG Family, Children,
    Duties of; Family,
    Love within; Honor;
    Honoring Father and
    Mother; Respect.
  b TG Family, Patriarchal.
  c TG Marriage,
    Motherhood.
  d Prov. 4:10.
  e Deut. 11:9 (8–9),
    17 (16–17, 21);
    1 Ne. 17:55;
    Hel. 7:24;
    D&C 5:33.
  f TG Promised Lands.
13*a* HEB murder.

TG Blood, Shedding of;
    Life, Sanctity of;
    Murder.
14*a* TG Adulterer; Chastity;
    Fornication; Sensuality;
    Sexual Immorality.
15*a* TG Stealing.
16*a* TG Gossip; Honesty;
    Lying; Slander.
  b TG Neighbor.
17*a* HEB desire, take
    pleasure in.
    TG Covet.
  b TG Marriage, Husbands;
    Marriage, Wives.
18*a* Deut. 4:33.
  b TG God, Privilege of
    Seeing.
  c Deut. 5:5.
19*a* Deut. 5:25; 18:16;
    Heb. 12:19;
    D&C 84:22 (21–26);
    Moses 1:11 (11, 14).

20*a* TG Courage; Fearful.
  b Jer. 11:3 (1–23).
  c TG God, Presence of.
  d TG Test.
  e OR because respect for
    Him will always be
    present with you, you
    will not sin.
22*a* TG God, Manifesta-
    tions of.
23*a* IE in association
    with me.
  b Ex. 32:4; Deut. 9:16.
24*a* TG Sacrifice.
25*a* Josh. 8:31 (30–31);
    Isa. 65:3;
    1 Ne. 2:7.
  b Deut. 27:5.
26*a* IE A ramp was rather
    to be provided.
  b OR revealed.
21 1*a* OR ordinances.
  2*a* TG Bondage, Physical.

*b*seventh he shall go out *c*free for nothing.

3 If he came in *a*by himself, he shall go out by himself: if he were married, then his wife shall go out with him.

4 If his master have given him a wife, and she have born him sons or daughters; the wife and her children shall be her master's, and he shall go out by himself.

5 And if the servant shall plainly say, I love my master, my wife, and my children; I will not go out free:

6 Then his master shall bring him *a*unto the *b*judges; he shall also bring him to the door, or unto the door post; and his master shall bore his *c*ear through with an awl; and he shall serve him for ever.

7 ¶ And if a man sell his daughter to be a maidservant, she shall not go out as the menservants do.

8 If she please not her master, who hath betrothed her to himself, then shall he let her be redeemed: to sell her unto a strange nation he shall have no power, seeing he hath dealt deceitfully with her.

9 And if he have betrothed her unto his son, he shall deal with her after the manner of daughters.

10 If he take him another *wife*; her food, her raiment, and her *a*duty of marriage, shall he not diminish.

11 And if he do not these three unto her, then shall she go out free without money.

12 ¶ He that *a*smiteth a man, so that he die, shall be surely *b*put to death.

13 And if a man lie not in wait, but God deliver *him* into his hand; then I will appoint thee a *a*place whither he shall *b*flee.

14 But if a man come presumptuously upon his neighbour, to *a*slay him with *b*guile; thou shalt take him from mine altar, that he may die.

15 ¶ And he that smiteth his father, or his mother, shall be surely put to *a*death.

16 ¶ And he that *a*stealeth a man, and selleth him, or if he be found in his hand, he shall surely be put to death.

17 ¶ And he that *a*curseth his father, or his mother, shall surely be put to death.

18 ¶ And if men strive together, and one smite another with a stone, or with *his* fist, and he die not, but *a*keepeth *his* bed:

19 If he rise again, and walk abroad upon his staff, then shall he that smote *him* be quit: only he shall pay *for* the loss of his *a*time, and shall cause *him* to be thoroughly healed.

20 ¶ And if a man smite his servant, or his maid, with a rod, and he die under his hand; he shall be *a*surely punished.

21 Notwithstanding, if he *a*continue a day or two, he shall not be *b*punished: for he *is* his money.

22 ¶ If men strive, and hurt a woman with *a*child, so that *b*her fruit depart *from her*, and yet no *c*mischief follow: he shall be surely punished, according as the woman's husband will lay upon him; and he shall pay as the judges *determine*.

23 And if *any* mischief follow, then thou shalt give life for life,

24 *a*Eye for eye, tooth for tooth, hand for hand, foot for foot,

25 Burning for burning, wound for wound, stripe for stripe.

26 ¶ And if a man smite the eye of

2*b* TG Sabbatical Year.
  c TG Liberty.
3*a* OR singly.
6*a* HEB before God; i.e.,
    God's representatives in
    judicial matters.
  b Ex. 22:8 (8–9).
  c Deut. 15:17.
10*a* OR marital rights.
12*a* TG Murder.
  b See JST Gen. 9:12–13
    (Appendix).

TG Capital Punishment;
  Punish.
13*a* Deut. 19:2.
  b Deut. 19:3 (1–13);
    1 Kgs. 2:28.
14*a* Deut. 27:24.
  b TG Guile.
15*a* Mosiah 13:29 (29–30);
    D&C 84:27 (26–27).
16*a* TG Stealing.
17*a* TG Curse; Honoring
    Father and Mother.

18*a* OR is laid up in bed.
19*a* TG Time.
20*a* JST Ex. 21:20 . . . *put
    to death.*
21*a* TG remains alive.
  b JST Ex. 21:21 . . . *put
    to death . . .*
22*a* TG Birth Control.
  b IE she has a miscarriage.
  c OR other harm.
24*a* TG Punish;
    Retribution.

his servant, or the eye of his maid, that it perish; he shall let him go free for his eye's sake.

27 And if he smite out his manservant's tooth, or his maidservant's tooth; he shall let him go free for his tooth's sake.

28 ¶ If an ox gore a man or a woman, that they ^adie: then the ox shall be surely stoned, and his flesh shall not be eaten; but the owner of the ox *shall be* ^bquit.

29 But if the ox were ^awont to push with his horn in time past, and it hath been testified to his owner, and he hath not kept him in, but that he hath killed a man or a woman; the ox shall be stoned, and his owner also shall be put to ^bdeath.

30 If there be laid on him a sum of money, then he shall give for the ransom of his life whatsoever is laid upon him.

31 Whether he have gored a son, or have gored a daughter, according to this judgment shall it be done unto him.

32 If the ox shall push a manservant or a maidservant; he shall give unto their master ^athirty shekels of silver, and the ox shall be stoned.

33 ¶ And if a man shall open a pit, or if a man shall dig a pit, and not cover it, and an ox or an ass fall therein;

34 The owner of the pit shall make *it* good, *and* give money unto the owner of them; and the dead *beast* shall be his.

35 ¶ And if one man's ox hurt another's, that he die; then they shall sell the live ox, and divide the money of it; and the dead *ox* also they shall divide.

36 Or if it be known that the ox hath used to push in time past, and his owner hath not kept him in; he shall surely pay ox for ox; and the dead shall be his own.

CHAPTER 22

The Lord reveals His laws pertaining to stealing, destructions by fire, care of the property of others, borrowing, lascivious acts, sacrifices to false gods, afflicting widows, usury, reviling God, and the firstborn of men and of animals—The men of Israel are commanded to be holy.

IF a man shall ^asteal an ox, or a sheep, and kill it, or sell it; he shall ^brestore five oxen for an ox, and ^cfour sheep for a sheep.

2 ¶ If a thief be found ^abreaking ^bup, and be smitten that he die, *there shall* no blood *be shed* for him.

3 If the sun be risen upon him, *there shall be* blood *shed* for him; *for* he should make full restitution; if he have nothing, then he shall be sold for his theft.

4 If the theft be certainly found in his hand alive, whether it be ox, or ass, or sheep; he shall ^arestore double.

5 ¶ If a man shall cause a field or vineyard to be eaten, and shall ^aput in his beast, and shall feed in another man's field; of the best of his own field, and of the best of his own vineyard, shall he make restitution.

6 ¶ If fire break out, and catch in thorns, so that the stacks of ^acorn, or the standing corn, or the field, be consumed *therewith*; he that ^bkindled the fire shall surely make restitution.

7 ¶ If a man shall deliver unto his neighbour money or stuff to keep, and it be stolen out of the man's house; if the thief be found, let him pay double.

8 If the thief be not found, then the master of the house shall be brought unto the ^ajudges, *to see* whether he have put his hand unto his neighbour's goods.

9 For all manner of trespass, *whether it be* for ox, for ass, for sheep, for raiment, *or* for any manner of lost

28a TG Blood, Shedding of.
  b OR clear, innocent.
29a OR accustomed to gore (also vv. 32, 36).
  b TG Capital Punishment.
32a Matt. 26:15 (14–16).

22 1a TG Stealing.
  b TG Repent.
  c 2 Sam. 12:6.
2a Matt. 24:43.
  b OR in.
4a Prov. 6:31 (30–31).

5a HEB let his beast loose and it shall feed.
6a HEB grain.
  b Judg. 15:5.
8a Ex. 21:6.

thing, which *another* challengeth to be his, the cause of both parties shall come before the judges; *and* whom the judges shall condemn, he shall pay double unto his neighbour.

10 If a man deliver unto his neighbour an ass, or an ox, or a sheep, or any beast, to keep; and it die, or be hurt, or driven away, no man seeing *it:*

11 *Then* shall an ªoath of the LORD be between them both, that he hath not put his hand unto his neighbour's goods; and the owner of it shall accept *thereof,* and he shall not ᵇmake *it* good.

12 And if it be stolen from him, he shall make restitution unto the owner thereof.

13 If it be ªtorn in pieces, *then* let him bring it *for* witness, *and* he shall not make good that which was torn.

14 ¶ And if a man ªborrow ᵇought of his neighbour, and it be hurt, or die, the owner thereof *being* not with it, he shall surely make *it* good.

15 *But* if the owner thereof *be* with it, he shall not make *it* good: if it *be* an hired *thing,* it came for his hire.

16 ¶ And if a man entice a maid that is not betrothed, and lie with her, he shall surely endow her to be his ªwife.

17 If her father utterly refuse to give her unto him, he shall pay money according to the dowry of ªvirgins.

18 ¶ Thou shalt not suffer a ªwitch to live.

19 ¶ Whosoever lieth with a ªbeast shall surely be put to death.

20 ¶ He that ªsacrificeth unto *any* god, save unto the LORD only, he shall be utterly destroyed.

21 ¶ Thou shalt neither vex a ªstranger, nor ᵇoppress him: for ye were ᶜstrangers in the land of Egypt.

22 ¶ Ye shall not afflict any ªwidow, or fatherless child.

23 If thou afflict them in any wise, and they cry at all unto me, I will surely hear their cry;

24 And my ªwrath shall ᵇwax hot, and I will kill you with the sword; and your wives shall be widows, and your children fatherless.

25 ¶ If thou ªlend money to *any* of my people *that is* poor by thee, thou shalt not be to him as an usurer, neither shalt thou lay upon him ᵇusury.

26 If thou at all take thy neighbour's raiment to ªpledge, thou shalt deliver it unto him by that the sun goeth down:

27 For that *is* his ªcovering only, it *is* his raiment for his skin: wherein shall he sleep? and it shall come to pass, when he crieth unto me, that I will hear; for I *am* ᵇgracious.

28 ¶ Thou shalt not ªrevile ᵇthe gods, nor ᶜcurse the ᵈruler of thy people.

29 ¶ Thou shalt not delay *to offer* the ªfirst of thy ripe fruits, and of thy ᵇliquors: the ᶜfirstborn of thy sons shalt thou give unto me.

30 Likewise shalt thou do with thine oxen, *and* with thy sheep: ªseven days it shall be with his dam; on the eighth day thou shalt give it me.

11*a* 1 Kgs. 8:31;
　　1 Ne. 4:37 (35–37).
　b IE make restitution.
13*a* Gen. 31:39.
14*a* TG Borrow.
　b OR anything.
16*a* Deut. 22:29 (28–29).
17*a* Deut. 22:28.
18*a* IE a sorceress or a
　　sorcerer.
　　JST Ex. 22:18 . . .
　　murderer . . .
　　TG Sorcery.
19*a* D&C 59:6.
20*a* Num. 25:2 (2, 7–8);

Deut. 13:2 (1–2, 5, 7);
　　Ps. 1:3 (2–3);
　　D&C 9:13.
21*a* TG Stranger.
　b TG Love; Oppression.
　c Deut. 23:7.
22*a* TG Widows.
24*a* Ex. 32:10.
　b OR be aroused.
25*a* TG Debt.
　b OR interest.
　　TG Usury.
26*a* Deut. 24:13;
　　Ezek. 18:7.
27*a* OR only covering.

　b OR compassionate.
　　TG Grace.
28*a* TG Reviling.
　b JST Ex. 22:28 . . . *against*
　　God . . .
　c 2 Sam. 19:21 (21–22).
　　TG Curse.
　d TG Citizenship.
29*a* Neh. 10:35;
　　Prov. 3:9;
　　Ezek. 44:30.
　b OR outflow of the
　　presses.
　c TG Firstborn.
30*a* Lev. 22:27.

31 ¶ And ye shall be *a*holy men unto me: neither shall ye eat *any* flesh *that is* *b*torn of beasts in the field; ye shall cast it to the dogs.

CHAPTER 23

The Lord reveals His laws pertaining to integrity and godly conduct—The land is to rest during a sabbatical year—The children of Israel are to keep three annual feasts—An angel, bearing the Lord's name, will guide them—Sickness will be removed—The nations of Canaan will be driven out gradually.

THOU shalt not raise a *a*false report: put not thine hand with the wicked to be an unrighteous witness.

2 ¶ *a*Thou shalt not *b*follow a multitude to *do* evil; neither shalt thou speak in a cause to decline after many to wrest *c*judgment:

3 ¶ Neither shalt thou *a*countenance a *b*poor man in his cause.

4 ¶ If thou meet thine *a*enemy's ox or his ass going astray, thou shalt surely *b*bring it back to him again.

5 If thou see the ass of him that hateth thee lying under his burden, and wouldest forbear to help him, thou shalt surely *a*help with him.

6 Thou shalt not *a*wrest the *b*judgment of thy poor in his *c*cause.

7 Keep thee far from a false *a*matter; and the innocent and righteous slay thou not: for I will not *b*justify the wicked.

8 ¶ And thou shalt take no *a*gift: for the gift blindeth the wise, and perverteth the words of the righteous.

9 ¶ Also thou shalt not oppress a stranger: for ye know the heart of a stranger, seeing ye were strangers in the land of Egypt.

10 And six years thou shalt sow thy land, and shalt gather in the fruits thereof:

11 But the *a*seventh *year* thou shalt let it rest and lie still; that the *b*poor of thy people may eat: and what they leave the beasts of the field shall eat. In like manner thou shalt deal with thy vineyard, *and* with thy oliveyard.

12 Six days thou shalt do thy work, and on the *a*seventh day thou shalt *b*rest: that thine ox and thine ass may rest, and the son of thy handmaid, and the stranger, may be refreshed.

13 And in all *things* that I have said unto you *a*be circumspect: and make no mention of the name of other *b*gods, neither let it be heard out of thy mouth.

14 ¶ *a*Three times thou shalt keep a *b*feast unto me in the year.

15 Thou shalt keep the *a*feast of unleavened bread: (thou shalt eat unleavened bread seven days, as I commanded thee, in the time appointed of the month *b*Abib; for in it thou camest out from Egypt: and none shall appear before me *c*empty:)

16 And the *a*feast of harvest, the firstfruits of thy labours, which thou hast sown in the field: and the feast of *b*ingathering, *which is* in the end of the year, when thou hast gathered in *c*thy labours out of the field.

31*a* Ex. 19:6;
     W of M 1:17;
     Alma 13:26;
     D&C 49:8; 107:29;
     Moses 7:62.
   b Lev. 22:8; Ezek. 4:14.
23 1*a* TG Slander.
   2*a* OR Thou shalt not follow the crowd to do evil, neither speak up in a lawsuit, being influenced by the majority, to subvert justice.
   b TG Peer Influence.
   c TG Judgment.
   3*a* OR favor.
      Lev. 19:15.

   b JST Ex. 23:3 . . . *wicked man* . . .
      D&C 56:17 (17–18).
   4*a* Deut. 22:1.
      TG Enemies.
   b TG Honesty.
   5*a* TG Charity;
      Reconciliation; Service.
   6*a* TG Injustice.
   b TG Judgment.
   c OR charges or lawsuit.
   7*a* OR charge.
   b TG Justification.
   8*a* HEB bribe.
      TG Bribe.
   11*a* TG Sabbatical Year.
   b TG Almsgiving;

      Poor;
      Welfare.
   12*a* TG Sabbath.
   b TG Rest.
   13*a* OR take heed.
   b Josh. 23:7 (6–8);
      Hosea 2:17.
   14*a* Ex. 34:23; Deut. 16:16.
   b Ex. 34:18 (18–26);
      Deut. 16:16;
      Ezek. 46:9.
   15*a* TG Passover.
   b Ex. 34:18.
   c IE without offerings.
   16*a* Ex. 34:22.
   b Deut. 16:13.
   c IE the fruits thereof.

17 Three times in the year all thy *males shall appear before the Lord GOD.

18 Thou shalt not offer the *blood of my sacrifice with *leavened bread; neither shall the fat of my sacrifice remain until the morning.

19 The first of the *firstfruits of thy land thou shalt bring into the house of the LORD thy God. Thou shalt not *seethe a kid in his mother's milk.

20 ¶ Behold, I send an *Angel before thee, to keep thee in the way, and to bring thee into the place which I have prepared.

21 Beware of him, and obey his voice, *provoke him not; for he will not *pardon your *transgressions: for my name *is* in him.

22 But if thou shalt indeed obey his voice, and do all that I speak; then I will be an enemy unto thine *enemies, and an adversary unto thine adversaries.

23 For mine Angel shall go before thee, and bring thee in unto the Amorites, and the Hittites, and the Perizzites, and the Canaanites, the Hivites, and the Jebusites: and I will cut them off.

24 Thou shalt not *bow down to their gods, nor serve them, nor do after their works: but thou shalt utterly *overthrow them, and quite break down their images.

25 And ye shall serve the LORD your God, and he shall bless thy *bread, and thy water; and I will take *sickness away from the midst of thee.

26 ¶ *There shall nothing cast their young, nor be *barren, in thy land: the number of thy days I will fulfil.

27 I will send my *fear before thee, and will destroy all the people to whom thou shalt come, and I will make all thine enemies turn their backs unto thee.

28 And I will send *hornets before thee, which shall drive out the Hivite, the Canaanite, and the Hittite, from before thee.

29 I will not *drive them out from before thee in one year; lest the land become desolate, and the *beast of the field multiply against thee.

30 By little and little I will drive them out from before thee, until thou be increased, and inherit the land.

31 And I will set thy *bounds from the *Red sea even unto the sea of the Philistines, and from the desert unto *the *river: for I will *deliver the *inhabitants of the land into your hand; and thou shalt drive them out before thee.

32 Thou shalt make no *covenant with them, nor with their gods.

33 They shall not dwell in thy land, lest they make thee sin against me: for if thou serve their gods, it will surely be a *snare unto thee.

CHAPTER 24

Israel accepts the word of the Lord by covenant—Moses sprinkles the blood of the covenant—He, Aaron, Nadab, Abihu, and seventy of the elders of Israel see God—The Lord calls Moses on to the mount to receive the tables of stone and commandments.

17a Acts 2:1 (1–5).
18a Ex. 34:25.
  b Ex. 12:8.
19a Ex. 34:26; Lev. 2:12;
    Deut. 26:2.
  b OR cook . . . ; i.e., Israel
    must not do such
    fertility-cult practices.
    Ex. 34:26.
20a Ex. 14:19;
    Josh. 5:14 (13–15);
    Isa. 63:9.
21a TG Provoking.
  b TG Holy Ghost, Loss of.
  c TG Transgress.
22a Gen. 12:3;
    D&C 8:4; 105:15; 136:40.
24a Ex. 20:5.
  b Num. 33:52 (52–53);
    Deut. 6:19.
25a TG Bread.
  b TG Sickness.
26a OR None shall miscarry.
  b TG Barren.
27a Ex. 15:16;
    Josh. 2:9 (8–9); 24:12;
    Alma 14:26; D&C 64:43;
    Moses 7:17.
28a Josh. 24:12.
29a Deut. 7:22.
  b OR wild beasts.
31a Josh. 1:4 (3–4);
    1 Kgs. 4:24 (21, 24).
  b OR Reed Sea.
  c IE the Euphrates.
  d Gen. 15:18.
  e Josh. 2:24.
  f 1 Ne. 17:35 (32–38).
32a Ex. 34:12 (10–16);
    Deut. 7:2.
33a Judg. 2:3; 8:27;
    Mosiah 7:29.

AND he said unto Moses, Come up unto the LORD, thou, and Aaron, ^aNadab, and Abihu, and ^bseventy of the elders of Israel; and worship ye afar off.

2 And Moses alone shall come near the LORD: but they shall not come nigh; neither shall the people go up with him.

3 ¶ And Moses came and told the people all the words of the LORD, and all the ^ajudgments: and all the people answered with one ^bvoice, and said, All the words which the LORD hath said will we do.

4 And Moses ^awrote all the words of the LORD, and rose up early in the morning, and builded an ^baltar ^cunder the hill, and twelve ^dpillars, according to the twelve tribes of Israel.

5 And he sent young men of the children of Israel, which offered burnt offerings, and sacrificed ^apeace offerings of oxen unto the LORD.

6 And Moses took half of the ^ablood, and put it in basins; and half of the blood he sprinkled on the altar.

7 And he took the book of the ^acovenant, and ^bread in the audience of the people: and they said, All that the LORD hath said will we do, and be ^cobedient.

8 And Moses took the ^ablood, and ^bsprinkled it on the people, and said, Behold the ^cblood of the ^dcovenant, which the LORD hath made with you concerning all these words.

9 ¶ Then went up Moses, and Aaron, Nadab, and Abihu, and ^aseventy of the ^belders of Israel:

10 And they ^asaw the God of Israel: and there was under his ^bfeet as it were a paved work of a sapphire stone, and as ^cit were the body of heaven in his clearness.

11 And upon the nobles of the children of Israel he laid not his hand: also they ^asaw God, and did eat and drink.

12 ¶ And the LORD said unto Moses, Come up to me into the mount, and be there: and I will give thee ^atables of stone, and a ^blaw, and commandments which I have ^cwritten; that thou mayest teach them.

13 And Moses rose up, and his minister ^aJoshua: and Moses went up into the ^bmount of God.

14 And he said unto the elders, Tarry ye here for us, until we come again unto you: and, behold, Aaron and Hur are with you: if any man have any matters to do, let him come unto them.

15 And Moses went up into the mount, and a ^acloud covered the mount.

16 And the ^aglory of the LORD abode upon mount Sinai, and the cloud covered it six days: and the seventh day he called unto Moses out of the midst of the cloud.

17 And the ^asight of the ^bglory of the LORD was like devouring fire on the top of the mount in the eyes of the children of Israel.

24 1a Ex. 6:23; 28:1.
  b TG Seventy.
  3a OR ordinances.
  b TG Common Consent.
  4a TG Record Keeping; Scribe; Scriptures, Writing of.
  b 1 Ne. 2:7; Abr. 2:17.
  c HEB at the foot of the mountain.
  d Gen. 31:45.
  5a Ex. 32:6.
  6a Heb. 9:19 (18–22).
  7a TG Scriptures, Lost.
  b Heb. 9:19; Alma 31:5.
  c TG Obedience.
  8a 1 Pet. 1:2.
  b Heb. 9:19 (19–20).

  c Matt. 26:28 (26–28); Heb. 9:16 (15–22).
  TG Jesus Christ, Types of, in Anticipation; Redemption.
  d TG Covenants.
  9a TG Church Organization; Seventy.
  b TG Elder, Melchizedek Priesthood.
  10a TG God, Manifestations of; Jesus Christ, Appearances, Antemortal.
  b TG God, Body of, Corporeal Nature.
  c OR clear as the very heavens.

  11a TG God, Privilege of Seeing.
  12a Ex. 31:18; 32:15 (15–19); 34:1; 2 Cor. 3:3.
  b OR instruction.
  c TG Scriptures, Writing of.
  13a Ex. 17:9; 32:17; 33:11.
  b Ex. 3:1.
  15a Ex. 13:21; 19:9 (9, 16); Matt. 17:5.
  16a Ex. 16:10; Num. 14:10; 2 Ne. 1:15; D&C 45:56 (56, 67); 76:56.
  17a TG Sight.
  b TG Glory.

18 And Moses went into the midst of the cloud, and gat him up into the mount: and Moses was in the mount *forty days and forty nights.

CHAPTER 25

Israel is commanded to donate property and build a tabernacle, the ark of testimony (with the mercy seat and cherubims), a table (for the shewbread), and the candlestick, all according to patterns shown to Moses on the mount.

AND the LORD *spake unto Moses, saying,

2 *Speak unto the children of Israel, that they bring me an offering: of every man that giveth it *willingly with his heart ye shall take my offering.

3 And this *is* the offering which ye shall take of them; gold, and silver, and brass,

4 And *blue, and purple, and scarlet, and fine *linen, and goats' *hair,*

5 And *rams' skins dyed red, and badgers' skins, and *shittim wood,

6 *Oil for the light, *spices for *anointing oil, and for sweet *incense,

7 *Onyx stones, and stones to be set in the ephod, and in the *breastplate.

8 And let them make me a *sanctuary; that I may *dwell among them.

9 According to all that I shew thee, *after* the pattern of the *tabernacle, and the pattern of all the *instruments thereof, even so shall ye make *it.*

10 ¶ And they shall make an *ark *of* shittim wood: two cubits and a half *shall be* the length thereof, and a cubit and a half the breadth thereof, and a cubit and a half the height thereof.

11 And thou shalt overlay it with pure gold, within and without shalt thou overlay it, and shalt make upon it a crown of gold round about.

12 And thou shalt cast four rings of gold for it, and put *them* in the four corners thereof; and two rings *shall be* in the one side of it, and two rings in the other side of it.

13 And thou shalt make staves *of* shittim wood, and overlay them with gold.

14 And thou shalt put the staves into the rings by the sides of the *ark, that the ark may be borne with them.

15 The *staves shall be in the rings of the ark: they shall not be taken from it.

16 And thou shalt put into the ark the *testimony which I shall give thee.

17 And thou shalt make a *mercy seat *of* pure gold: two cubits and a half *shall be* the length thereof, and a cubit and a half the breadth thereof.

18 And thou shalt *make two *cherubims *of* gold, *of* beaten work shalt thou make them, in the two ends of the mercy seat.

19 And make one cherub on the one end, and the other cherub on the other end: *even* *of the mercy seat

18*a* Ex. 32:1; 34:28;
    Deut. 9:9;
    Matt. 4:2 (1–2).
25 1*a* Moses 1:2 (1–2).
  2*a* Ex. 35:4 (4–9);
    D&C 1:38.
   b Ezra 3:5; 2 Cor. 8:12;
    Hel. 6:36;
    D&C 59:15; 64:34; 97:8.
    TG Initiative.
  4*a* 1 Ne. 13:7 (7–8);
    Ether 10:24.
   b Ex. 35:23.
  5*a* Ex. 26:14.
   b OR acacia.
  6*a* Ex. 27:20.
   b Ex. 30:34 (34–38).
   c D&C 109:35 (35–36);

124:39 (38–40).
   d Ex. 31:11.
  7*a* Ex. 28:9 (6–14);
    Moses 3:12.
   b Mosiah 8:10 (10–11);
    D&C 17:1; JS—H 1:35.
  8*a* TG Temple.
   b 1 Kgs. 6:13;
    D&C 104:59;
    124:27 (26–28).
  9*a* Ex. 33:7;
    D&C 101:23;
    124:38 (38–41).
   b OR furniture,
    equipment, utensils.
10*a* Ex. 35:12;
    Num. 4:5 (5–15);
    Deut. 10:1; 1 Sam. 14:18;

D&C 85:8.
14*a* 1 Chr. 15:15.
15*a* 1 Kgs. 8:8 (7–8).
16*a* 2 Kgs. 11:12; Heb. 9:4.
    TG Scriptures,
    Preservation of.
17*a* HEB atonement-cover.
    Note that it was a
    golden slab of the same
    dimension as the top
    of the ark. A winged
    cherub was placed on
    each end.
    Ex. 37:6 (6–9);
    Heb. 9:5 (4–6).
18*a* TG Art.
   b TG Cherubim.
19*a* OR as part of it.

shall ye make the cherubims on the two ends thereof.

20 And the cherubims shall stretch forth *their* wings on high, covering the mercy seat with their wings, and ªtheir faces *shall look* one to another; toward the mercy seat shall the faces of the cherubims be.

21 And thou shalt put the ªmercy seat above upon the ark; and in the ark thou shalt put the ᵇtestimony that I shall give thee.

22 And there I will ªmeet with thee, and I will ᵇcommune with thee from above the ᶜmercy seat, from between the two ᵈcherubims which *are* upon the ark of the testimony, of all *things* which I will give thee in commandment unto the children of Israel.

23 ¶ Thou shalt also make a ªtable *of* shittim wood: two cubits *shall be* the length thereof, and a cubit the breadth thereof, and a cubit and a half the height thereof.

24 And thou shalt overlay it with pure gold, and make thereto a crown of gold round about.

25 And thou shalt make unto it a border of an hand breadth round about, and thou shalt make a golden crown to the border thereof round about.

26 And thou shalt make for it four rings of gold, and put the rings in the four corners that *are* on the four feet thereof.

27 Over against the border shall the rings be for places of the staves to bear the table.

28 And thou shalt make the staves *of* shittim wood, and overlay them with gold, that the table may be borne with them.

29 And thou shalt make the ªdishes thereof, and spoons thereof, and ᵇcovers thereof, and bowls thereof, ᶜto cover withal: *of* pure gold shalt thou make them.

30 And thou shalt set upon the table ªshewbread before me alway.

31 ¶ And thou shalt make a ªcandlestick *of* pure gold: *of* beaten work shall the candlestick be made: his shaft, and his branches, his bowls, his knops, and his flowers, shall be of ᵇthe same.

32 And six branches shall come out of the sides of it; three branches of the candlestick out of the one side, and three branches of the candlestick out of the other side:

33 Three bowls made like unto almonds, *with* ªa knop and a flower in one branch; and three bowls made like almonds in the other branch, *with* a knop and a flower: ᵇso in the six branches that come out of the candlestick.

34 And in the candlestick *shall be* four bowls made like unto almonds, *with* their knops and their flowers.

35 And *there shall be* a knop under two branches of the same, and a knop under two branches of the same, and a knop under two branches of the same, according to the six branches that proceed out of the candlestick.

36 Their knops and their branches shall be of the same: all it *shall be* one beaten work *of* pure gold.

37 And thou shalt make the seven ªlamps thereof: and they shall ᵇlight the ᶜlamps thereof, that they may give light over against it.

38 And the tongs thereof, and the

20a OR they shall face one
     another (see next line).
21a Ex. 26:34; 30:6 (6–10).
   b Ex. 16:34; Deut. 31:26;
     1 Kgs. 8:9.
     TG Record Keeping.
22a Ex. 29:43 (32, 43);
     30:36 (6, 36);
     Num. 17:4.
     TG God, Access to;
     Meetings.
   b Lev. 16:2;
     Num. 1:1; 7:89;

Ether 2:14.
   c TG Ark of the Covenant.
   d 2 Kgs. 19:15.
23a Ex. 35:13; 37:10 (10–16);
     Heb. 9:2.
29a Num. 4:7.
   b HEB Jugs, jars.
   c HEB wherewith to pour
     libations.
30a HEB bread of faces, or
     bread of the presence.
     1 Kgs. 7:48; Heb. 9:2.
     TG Bread, Shewbread.

31a Ex. 35:14; 37:17 (17–24);
     1 Kgs. 7:49;
     Heb. 9:2;
     Rev. 1:12.
   b OR one piece.
33a IE crown-shaped circlets
     (also vv. 34–36).
   b OR thus shall be the . . .
37a Num. 8:2 (1–4);
     1 Chr. 12:15.
   b HEB set up.
   c Ex. 40:25;
     Lev. 24:4 (3–4).

snuffdishes thereof, *shall be of* pure gold.

39 Of a talent of pure gold shall he make it, with all these vessels.

40 And look that thou make *them* after their *a*pattern, which was shewed thee in the mount.

CHAPTER 26

The tabernacle is to be built with ten curtains and with boards—A veil is to separate the holy place from the most holy place—The ark of testimony (with the mercy seat) is to be put in the most holy place.

MOREOVER thou shalt make the *a*tabernacle *with* ten *b*curtains *of* fine twined linen, and blue, and purple, and scarlet: *with* *c*cherubims of cunning work shalt thou make them.

2 The length of one curtain *shall be* eight and twenty cubits, and the breadth of one curtain four cubits: and every one of the curtains shall have one measure.

3 The five curtains shall be coupled together one to another; and *other* five curtains *shall be* coupled one to another.

4 And thou shalt make loops of blue upon the edge of the one curtain from the selvedge in the coupling; and likewise shalt thou make in the uttermost edge of *another* curtain, in the coupling of the second.

5 Fifty loops shalt thou make in the one curtain, and fifty loops shalt thou make in the edge of the curtain that *is* in the coupling of the second; that the loops may take hold one of another.

6 And thou shalt make fifty *a*taches of gold, and couple the curtains together with the taches: and *b*it shall be one tabernacle.

7 ¶ And thou shalt make curtains *of* goats' *hair* *a*to be a covering upon the tabernacle: eleven curtains shalt thou make.

8 The length of one curtain *shall*

be thirty cubits, and the breadth of one curtain four cubits: and the eleven curtains *shall be all* of one measure.

9 And thou shalt couple five curtains by themselves, and six curtains by themselves, and shalt double the sixth curtain in the forefront of the tabernacle.

10 And thou shalt make fifty loops on the edge of the one curtain *that is* outmost in the coupling, and fifty loops in the edge of the curtain which coupleth the second.

11 And thou shalt make fifty taches of brass, and put the taches into the loops, and couple the tent together, that it may be one.

12 And the remnant that remaineth of the curtains of the tent, the half curtain that remaineth, shall hang over the backside of the tabernacle.

13 And a cubit on the one side, and a cubit on the other side of that which remaineth in the length of the curtains of the tent, it shall hang over the sides of the tabernacle on this side and on that side, to cover it.

14 And thou shalt make a covering for the tent *of* *a*rams' skins dyed red, and a covering above *of* badgers' skins.

15 ¶ And thou shalt make *a*boards for the tabernacle *of* shittim *b*wood standing up.

16 Ten cubits *shall be* the length of a board, and a cubit and a half *shall be* the breadth of one board.

17 Two tenons *shall there be* in one board, set in order one against another: thus shalt thou make for all the boards of the tabernacle.

18 And thou shalt make the boards for the tabernacle, twenty boards on the south side southward.

19 And thou shalt make forty sockets of silver under the twenty boards; two sockets under one board for his two tenons, and two sockets under another board for his two tenons.

40*a* Ex. 26:30; 1 Ne. 17:8
   (7–14); Ether 2:16.
26 1*a* Ex. 35:11; Heb. 9:2.
  b Ex. 36:8 (8–19).

c TG Cherubim.
6*a* OR clasps (also v. 11).
  b OR the tabernacle shall
   be unified.

7*a* HEB as a tent.
14*a* Ex. 25:5.
15*a* Ex. 36:20 (20–34).
  b D&C 124:26.

20 And for the second side of the tabernacle on the north side *there shall be* twenty boards:

21 And their forty sockets *of* silver; two sockets under one board, and two sockets under another board.

22 And for the sides of the tabernacle westward thou shalt make six boards.

23 And two boards shalt thou make for the corners of the tabernacle in the two sides.

24 And they shall be coupled together beneath, and they shall be coupled together above the head of it unto one ring: thus shall it be for them both; they shall be for the two corners.

25 And they shall be eight boards, and their sockets *of* silver, sixteen sockets; two sockets under one board, and two sockets under another board.

26 ¶ And thou shalt make bars *of* shittim wood; five for the boards of the one side of the tabernacle,

27 And five bars for the boards of the other side of the tabernacle, and five bars for the boards of the side of the tabernacle, for the two sides westward.

28 And the middle bar in the midst of the boards shall reach from end to end.

29 And thou shalt overlay the boards with gold, and make their rings *of* gold *for* places for the bars: and thou shalt overlay the bars with gold.

30 And thou shalt rear up the tabernacle according to the ^afashion thereof which was shewed thee in the mount.

31 ¶ And thou shalt make a veil *of* blue, and purple, and scarlet, and fine twined linen of cunning work: with cherubims shall it be made:

32 And thou shalt hang it upon four pillars of shittim *wood* overlaid with gold: their hooks *shall be of* gold, upon the four sockets of silver.

33 ¶ And thou shalt hang up the veil under the taches, that thou mayest bring in thither within the veil the ^aark of the testimony: and the ^bveil shall divide unto you between the holy *place* and the most ^choly.

34 And thou shalt put the ^amercy seat upon the ark of the ^btestimony in the most holy *place*.

35 And thou shalt ^aset the table without the veil, and the ^bcandlestick ^cover against the table on the side of the tabernacle toward the south: and thou shalt put the table on the north side.

36 And thou shalt make ^aan ^bhanging for the door of the tent, *of* blue, and purple, and scarlet, and fine twined linen, wrought with ^cneedlework.

37 And thou shalt make for the hanging five pillars *of* shittim *wood,* and overlay them with gold, *and* their hooks *shall be of* gold: and thou shalt cast five sockets of ^abrass for them.

CHAPTER 27

The tabernacle is to contain an altar for burnt offerings and a court surrounded by pillars—A light is to burn always in the tabernacle of the congregation.

AND thou shalt make an ^aaltar *of* ^bshittim wood, five cubits long, and five cubits broad; the altar shall be foursquare: and the height thereof *shall be* three cubits.

2 And thou shalt make the ^ahorns of it upon the four corners thereof: his horns shall be ^bof the same: and thou shalt overlay it with ^cbrass.

3 And thou shalt make his ^apans to receive his ashes, and his shovels,

---

30*a* Ex. 25:40; 27:8.
33*a* 1 Kgs. 8:6.
  b TG Jesus Christ, Types of, in Anticipation; Veil.
  c 1 Kgs. 6:16; D&C 124:39.
34*a* Ex. 25:21.
  b TG Scriptures,

Preservation of.
35*a* Ex. 40:4.
  b Heb. 9:2.
  c OR opposite.
36*a* OR a screen, or curtain.
  b Ex. 27:16; 35:15.
  c TG Art.
37*a* OR bronze.

27 1*a* Ex. 35:16; 38:1 (1–7); Ezek. 9:2; Alma 15:17.
  b OR acacia.
2*a* 1 Kgs. 1:50; Jer. 17:1.
  b IE part of the altar.
  c OR bronze.
3*a* 2 Kgs. 25:14.

and his basins, and his fleshhooks, and his firepans: all the vessels thereof thou shalt make *of* brass.

4 And thou shalt make for it a grate of network *of* brass; and upon the net shalt thou make four brasen rings in the four corners thereof.

5 And thou shalt put it under the *a*compass of the altar beneath, that the net may be even to the midst of the altar.

6 And thou shalt make staves for the altar, staves *of* shittim wood, and overlay them with brass.

7 And the staves shall be put into the rings, and the staves shall be upon the two sides of the altar, to bear it.

8 Hollow with boards shalt thou make it: as it was *a*shewed thee in the mount, so shall they make *it*.

9 ¶ And thou shalt make the court of the tabernacle: for the south side southward *there shall be* hangings for the court *of* fine twined *a*linen of an hundred cubits long for one side:

10 And the twenty *a*pillars thereof and their twenty *b*sockets *shall be of* brass; the hooks of the pillars and their fillets *shall be of* silver.

11 And likewise for the north side in length *there shall be* hangings of an hundred *cubits* long, and his twenty pillars and their twenty sockets *of* brass; the hooks of the pillars and their fillets *of* silver.

12 ¶ And *for* the breadth of the court on the west side *shall be* hangings of fifty cubits: their pillars ten, and their sockets ten.

13 And the breadth of the court on the east side eastward *shall be* fifty cubits.

14 The hangings of one side *of the gate shall be* fifteen cubits: their pillars three, and their sockets three.

15 And on the other side *shall be* hangings fifteen *cubits:* their pillars three, and their sockets three.

16 ¶ And for the gate of the court *shall be* an *a*hanging of twenty cubits, *of* blue, and purple, and scarlet, and fine twined linen, wrought with needlework: *and* their pillars *shall be* four, and their sockets four.

17 All the pillars round about the court *shall be* filleted with silver; their hooks *shall be of* silver, and their sockets *of* brass.

18 ¶ The length of the court *shall be* an hundred cubits, and the breadth fifty every where, and the height five cubits *of* fine twined linen, and their sockets *of* brass.

19 All the vessels of the tabernacle in all the service thereof, and all the pins thereof, and all the pins of the court, *shall be of* brass.

20 ¶ And thou shalt command the children of Israel, that they bring thee pure *a*oil *b*olive beaten for the light, to cause the *c*lamp to burn always.

21 In the *a*tabernacle of the *b*congregation *c*without the *d*veil, which *is* before the testimony, *e*Aaron and his sons shall *f*order it from evening to morning before the LORD: *it shall be* a *g*statute for ever unto their *h*generations on the behalf of the children of Israel.

CHAPTER 28

Aaron and his sons are to be consecrated and anointed to minister in the priest's office—Aaron's garments are to include a breastplate, an ephod, a robe, a coat, a miter, and a girdle—The breastplate of judgment is to contain twelve precious stones with the names of the tribes of Israel thereon—The Urim and Thummim are to be carried in the breastplate.

AND take thou unto thee *a*Aaron

5*a* OR ledge.
8*a* Ex. 26:30;
     Num. 8:4.
9*a* Ex. 38:16 (9–20).
10*a* Ex. 38:10, 17 (9–20).
   b OR bases.
16*a* OR screen, or curtain.
     Ex. 26:36; 38:18 (9–20).
20*a* Ex. 35:14.

b Ex. 25:6.
c Lev. 24:2 (2–3);
   1 Sam. 3:3.
21*a* HEB tent of meeting.
   b TG Church.
   c OR outside of the veil.
   d TG Veil.
   e Ex. 30:8 (7–8);
     D&C 27:8; 84:34 (30–34);

107:13.
f OR keep it in order.
g Ex. 28:43 (40–43);
   29:9, 28.
h 1 Sam. 2:30.
28 1*a* 1 Chr. 23:13;
     Heb. 5:4;
     D&C 28:3.
     TG Called of God.

thy brother, and his sons with him, from among the children of Israel, that he may minister unto me in the *b*priest's *c*office, *even* Aaron, *d*Nadab and Abihu, Eleazar and *e*Ithamar, Aaron's *f*sons.

2 And thou shalt make holy *a*garments for Aaron thy brother for glory and for *b*beauty.

3 And thou shalt speak unto all *that are* *a*wise hearted, whom I have filled with the spirit of *b*wisdom, that they may make Aaron's garments to consecrate him, that he may minister unto me in the priest's office.

4 And these *are* the *a*garments which they shall make; a breastplate, and an *b*ephod, and a robe, and a broidered *c*coat, a *d*mitre, and a girdle: and they shall make holy garments for Aaron thy brother, and his sons, that he may minister unto me in the *e*priest's office.

5 And they shall take gold, and blue, and purple, and scarlet, and fine linen.

6 ¶ And they shall make the *a*ephod *of* gold, *of* blue, and *of* purple, *of* scarlet, and fine twined linen, with cunning work.

7 It shall have the two shoulderpieces thereof joined at the two edges thereof; and *so* it shall be joined together.

8 And the *a*curious girdle of the ephod, which *is* upon it, shall be of the same, according to the work thereof; *even of* gold, *of* blue, and purple, and scarlet, and fine twined linen.

9 And thou shalt take two *a*onyx stones, and grave on them the *b*names of the children of Israel:

10 Six of their names on one stone, and *the other* six names of the rest

on the other stone, according to their birth.

11 With the work of an *a*engraver in stone, *like* the engravings of a signet, shalt thou engrave the two stones with the names of the children of Israel: thou shalt make them to be set in *b*ouches of gold.

12 And thou shalt put the two stones upon the shoulders of the ephod *for* stones of memorial unto the children of Israel: and Aaron shall bear their names before the LORD upon his two shoulders for a memorial.

13 ¶ And thou shalt make ouches *of* gold;

14 And two chains *of* pure gold at the ends; *of* *a*wreathen work shalt thou make them, and fasten the wreathen chains to the ouches.

15 ¶ And thou shalt make the *a*breastplate of judgment with cunning work; *b*after the work of the ephod thou shalt make it; *of* gold, *of* blue, and *of* purple, and *of* scarlet, and *of* fine twined linen, shalt thou make it.

16 Foursquare it shall be *being* doubled; a span *shall be* the length thereof, and a span *shall be* the breadth thereof.

17 And thou shalt set in it settings of stones, *even* four rows of stones: *the first* row *shall be* a sardius, a topaz, and a carbuncle: *this shall be* the first row.

18 And the second row *shall be* an emerald, a sapphire, and a diamond.

19 And the third row a ligure, an agate, and an amethyst.

20 And the fourth row a beryl, and an onyx, and a jasper: they shall be set in gold in their inclosings.

21 And the stones shall be with the names of the children of Israel,

---

1b TG Priesthood, Aaronic.
  c D&C 107:61.
  d Ex. 24:1 (1–2).
  e Ex. 38:21.
  f 1 Chr. 24:1.
2a Ex. 29:5, 29; 39:1 (1–2).
  TG Clothing.
  b TG Beauty.
3a Ex. 35:10, 25.
  b TG Wisdom.

4a Ex. 39:1.
  b Judg. 8:27;
    1 Sam. 2:18, 28; 14:3;
    22:18.
  c Lev. 8:7.
  d HEB turban, bound cap.
  e TG Priest, Aaronic
    Priesthood.
    BD Priests.
6a Ex. 39:2 (2–7).

8a OR skillfully woven.
9a Ex. 25:7.
  b See JST Ps. 24:8
    (Appendix).
11a TG Art.
  b OR settings.
14a OR braided (also
    vv. 24–25).
15a TG Urim and Thummim.
  b OR similar to.

twelve, according to their names, *like* the engravings of a signet; every one with *a*his name shall they be according to the *b*twelve tribes.

22 ¶ And thou shalt make upon the breastplate chains at the ends *of* wreathen work *of* pure gold.

23 And thou shalt make upon the breastplate two rings of gold, and shalt put the two rings on the two ends of the breastplate.

24 And thou shalt put the two wreathen *chains* of gold in the two rings *which are* on the ends of the breastplate.

25 And *the other* two ends of the two wreathen *chains* thou shalt fasten in the two ouches, and put *them* on the shoulderpieces of the ephod before it.

26 ¶ And thou shalt make two rings of gold, and thou shalt put them upon the two ends of the breastplate in the border thereof, which *is* *a*in the side of the ephod inward.

27 And two *other* rings of gold thou shalt make, and shalt put them on the two sides of the ephod underneath, toward the forepart thereof, over against the *other* coupling thereof, above the curious girdle of the ephod.

28 And they shall bind the breastplate by the rings thereof unto the rings of the ephod with a lace of blue, that *it* may be above the curious girdle of the ephod, and that the breastplate be not loosed from the ephod.

29 And Aaron shall bear the names of the children of Israel in the breastplate of judgment upon his heart, when he goeth in unto the holy *place,* for a memorial before the Lord continually.

30 ¶ And thou shalt put in the breastplate of judgment the *a*Urim and the Thummim; and they shall be upon Aaron's heart, when he goeth in before the Lord: and Aaron shall bear the judgment of the children of Israel upon his heart before the Lord continually.

31 ¶ And thou shalt make the robe of the ephod all *of* blue.

32 And there shall be an *a*hole in the top of it, in the midst thereof: it shall have a binding of woven work round about the hole of it, as it were the *b*hole of an habergeon, that it be not rent.

33 ¶ And *beneath* upon the hem of it thou shalt make pomegranates *of* blue, and *of* purple, and *of* scarlet, round about the hem thereof; and bells of gold between them round about:

34 A golden bell and a pomegranate, a golden bell and a pomegranate, upon the hem of the robe round about.

35 And it shall be upon Aaron *a*to minister: and his sound shall be heard when he goeth in unto the holy *place* before the Lord, and when he cometh out, that he die not.

36 ¶ And thou shalt make a *a*plate *of* pure gold, and grave upon it, *like* the engravings of a signet, *b*HOLINESS TO THE LORD.

37 And thou shalt *a*put it on a blue lace, that it may be upon the *b*mitre; upon the forefront of the mitre it shall be.

38 And it shall be upon Aaron's forehead, that Aaron may *a*bear the iniquity of the holy things, which the children of Israel shall hallow in all their holy gifts; and it shall be always upon his forehead, that they may be *b*accepted before the Lord.

39 ¶ And thou shalt embroider the *a*coat of fine *b*linen, and thou shalt

---

21*a* OR its name.
  b TG Israel, Twelve Tribes of.
26*a* OR next to.
30*a* HEB Lights and Perfections.
  TG Urim and Thummim.
32*a* HEB opening for the head.
  b OR opening in a coat of mail.
35*a* OR when he ministers.
36*a* Lev. 8:9.
  b OR CONSECRATED . . . Ex. 39:30; Jer. 2:3 (1–4); Zech. 14:20.
TG Holiness.
37*a* OR attach it with.
  b HEB turban, cap.
38*a* OR atone for.
  TG Accountability.
  b Lev. 1:4 (1–4); 22:27.
39*a* Lev. 6:10.
  b Ex. 39:27; Ezek. 44:17.

make the mitre *of* fine linen, and thou shalt make the girdle *of* needlework.

40 ¶ And for Aaron's sons thou shalt make *ᵃ*coats, and thou shalt make for them girdles, and *ᵇ*bonnets shalt thou make for them, for glory and for beauty.

41 And thou shalt put them upon Aaron thy brother, and his sons with him; and shalt *ᵃ*anoint them, and *ᵇ*consecrate them, and sanctify them, that they may minister unto me in the priest's office.

42 And thou shalt make them linen breeches to cover their nakedness; from the loins even unto the thighs they shall reach:

43 And they shall be upon Aaron, and upon his sons, when they *ᵃ*come in unto the *ᵇ*tabernacle of the congregation, or when they come near unto the altar to minister in the holy *place;* that they *ᶜ*bear not iniquity, and die: *it shall be* a *ᵈ*statute for ever unto him and his seed after him.

CHAPTER 29

Aaron and his sons are to be washed, anointed, and consecrated—Various sacrificial rites are to be performed—Atonement is to be made for the sins of the people—The Lord promises to dwell among them.

AND this *is* the thing that thou shalt do unto them to *ᵃ*hallow them, to minister unto me in the *ᵇ*priest's office: Take one *ᶜ*young bullock, and two rams without blemish,

2 And *ᵃ*unleavened bread, and cakes unleavened *ᵇ*tempered with oil, and wafers unleavened *ᶜ*anointed with oil: *of* wheaten flour shalt thou make them.

3 And thou shalt put them into one basket, and bring them in the basket, with the bullock and the two rams.

4 And Aaron and his sons thou shalt bring unto the *ᵃ*door of the tabernacle of the congregation, and shalt *ᵇ*wash them with water.

5 And thou shalt take the *ᵃ*garments, and put upon Aaron the *ᵇ*coat, and the robe of the *ᶜ*ephod, and the ephod, and the breastplate, and gird him with the *ᵈ*curious girdle of the ephod:

6 And thou shalt put the *ᵃ*mitre upon his head, and put the holy crown upon the mitre.

7 Then shalt thou take the *ᵃ*anointing oil, and pour *it* upon his head, and anoint him.

8 And thou shalt bring his sons, and put coats upon them.

9 And thou shalt *ᵃ*gird them with girdles, Aaron and his sons, and *ᵇ*put the bonnets on them: and the *ᶜ*priest's office shall be theirs for a perpetual *ᵈ*statute: and thou shalt *ᵉ*consecrate Aaron and his sons.

10 And thou shalt cause a *ᵃ*bullock to be brought before the tabernacle of the congregation: and Aaron and his sons shall put their *ᵇ*hands upon the head of the bullock.

11 And thou shalt kill the bullock before the LORD, *by* the door of the tabernacle of the congregation.

12 And thou shalt take of the blood of the bullock, and put *it* upon the horns of the altar with thy

---

40*a* TG Clothing.
　b HEB hats, or headdresses.
41*a* TG Anointing.
　b TG Priesthood, Authority.
43*a* Ezek. 44:17.
　b HEB tent of meeting.
　c OR do not incur guilt.
　d Ex. 27:21.
29 1*a* OR consecrate or set apart.
　b Lev. 21:10 (10–15).
　c OR young bull (also

vv. 3, 10–12, 14, 36).
Lev. 8:2; 2 Chr. 13:9.
2*a* Lev. 2:4.
　b HEB mingled.
　c OR smeared.
4*a* HEB opening of the tent of meeting (also vv. 10–11, 30, 32, 42, 44).
　b Lev. 8:6; D&C 124:39.
5*a* Ex. 28:2 (1–5).
　b OR tunic. Lev. 8:7.
　c Ex. 35:9.
　d OR skillfully woven.

6*a* HEB turban.
7*a* Ex. 40:15 (12–15); D&C 124:39.
9*a* Lev. 8:13.
　b HEB bind headdresses.
　c TG Priest, Aaronic Priesthood; Priesthood, Aaronic. BD Priests.
　d Ex. 27:21.
　e TG Priesthood, Authority.
10*a* Ezek. 43:19.
　b TG Hands, Laying on of.

finger, and ^apour all the blood beside the bottom of the ^baltar.

13 And thou shalt take all the fat that covereth the inwards, and the ^acaul *that is* above the liver, and the two kidneys, and the fat that *is* upon them, and burn *them* upon the altar.

14 But the flesh of the ^abullock, and his skin, and his dung, shalt thou ^bburn with fire without the camp: it *is* a sin offering.

15 ¶ Thou shalt also take one ram; and Aaron and his sons shall put their hands upon the head of the ram.

16 And thou shalt slay the ram, and thou shalt take his blood, and sprinkle *it* round about upon the altar.

17 And thou shalt cut the ram in pieces, and wash the inwards of him, and his legs, and put *them* ^aunto his pieces, and unto his head.

18 And thou shalt burn the whole ram upon the altar: it *is* a burnt ^aoffering unto the LORD: it *is* a ^bsweet ^csavour, an offering made by fire unto the LORD.

19 ¶ And thou shalt take the other ^aram; and Aaron and his sons shall put their hands upon the head of the ram.

20 Then shalt thou kill the ram, and take of his blood, and put *it* upon the tip of the right ear of Aaron, and upon the tip of the right ear of his sons, and upon the thumb of their right hand, and upon the great toe of their right foot, and sprinkle the blood upon the altar round about.

21 And thou shalt take of the blood that *is* upon the altar, and of the anointing oil, and sprinkle *it* upon Aaron, and upon his garments, and upon his sons, and upon the garments of his sons with him: and ^ahe shall be hallowed, and his garments, and his sons, and his sons' garments with him.

22 Also thou shalt take of the ram

the fat and the ^arump, and the fat that covereth the inwards, and the caul *above* the liver, and the two kidneys, and the fat that *is* upon them, and the right ^bshoulder; for it *is* a ram of consecration:

23 And one loaf of bread, and one cake of oiled bread, and one wafer out of the basket of the ^aunleavened bread that *is* before the LORD:

24 And thou shalt put all in the hands of Aaron, and in the hands of his sons; and shalt ^awave them *for* a wave offering before the LORD.

25 And thou shalt receive them of their hands, and burn *them* upon the altar for a burnt offering, for a sweet savour before the LORD: it *is* an offering made by fire unto the LORD.

26 And thou shalt take the breast of the ram of Aaron's consecration, and wave it *for* a ^awave offering before the LORD: and it shall be thy part.

27 And thou shalt sanctify the breast of the wave offering, and the shoulder of the ^aheave offering, which is ^bwaved, and which is ^cheaved up, of the ram of the consecration, *even* of *that* which *is* for Aaron, and of *that* which is for his sons:

28 And it shall be Aaron's and his sons' by a ^astatute for ever from the children of Israel: for it *is* an heave offering: and it shall be an heave offering from the children of Israel of the sacrifice of their peace offerings, *even* their heave offering unto the LORD.

29 ¶ And the holy ^agarments of Aaron shall be his sons' after him, to be ^banointed therein, and to be consecrated in them.

30 *And* that son that is priest in his stead shall put them on seven days, when he cometh into the tabernacle of the congregation to minister in the holy *place*.

12*a* Lev. 4:7.
  b Lev. 8:15 (1–17).
13*a* HEB lobe.
14*a* Lev. 4:11 (3–12).
  b Ezek. 43:21.
17*a* OR by.
18*a* TG Sacrifice.
  b OR pleasing fragrance.

  c Gen. 8:21.
19*a* Lev. 8:22.
21*a* OR thus he shall be sanctified.
22*a* HEB fat tail.
  b 1 Sam. 9:24 (21–24).
23*a* TG Bread, Unleavened.
24*a* OR lift them up as an

  offering.
26*a* Lev. 10:14.
27*a* Num. 18:11.
  b OR lifted up.
  c OR elevated.
28*a* Ex. 27:21.
29*a* Ex. 28:2 (1–5).
  b Num. 18:8.

31 ¶ And thou shalt take the ram of the consecration, and ^aseethe his flesh in the holy place.

32 And Aaron and his sons shall eat the flesh of the ram, and the bread that *is* in the basket, *by* the door of the tabernacle of the congregation.

33 And they shall ^aeat those things wherewith the atonement was made, to consecrate *and* to sanctify them: but a ^bstranger shall not eat *thereof,* because they *are* holy.

34 And if ought of the flesh of the consecrations, or of the bread, remain unto the morning, then thou shalt burn the remainder with fire: it shall not be eaten, because it *is* holy.

35 And thus shalt thou do unto Aaron, and to his sons, according to all *things* which I have commanded thee: ^aseven days shalt thou ^bconsecrate them.

36 And thou shalt offer every day a bullock *for* a sin offering for atonement: and thou shalt cleanse the altar, when thou hast made an atonement for it, and thou shalt anoint it, to sanctify it.

37 Seven days thou shalt make an atonement for the altar, and sanctify it; and it shall be an altar most holy: whatsoever toucheth the altar shall be holy.

38 ¶ Now this *is that* which thou shalt ^aoffer upon the altar; two lambs ^bof the first year ^cday by day continually.

39 The one lamb thou shalt ^aoffer in the morning; and the other lamb thou shalt offer at even:

40 And with the one lamb a tenth ^adeal of flour mingled with the fourth part of an hin of beaten ^boil; and the fourth part of an hin of wine *for* a ^cdrink offering.

41 And the other lamb thou shalt offer at ^aeven, and shalt do thereto according to the ^bmeat offering of the morning, and according to the drink offering thereof, for a sweet savour, an offering made by fire unto the Lord.

42 *This shall be* a continual burnt ^aoffering throughout your generations *at* the door of the ^btabernacle of the congregation before the Lord: where I will meet you, to ^cspeak there unto thee.

43 And there I will ^ameet with the children of Israel, and *the* ^btabernacle shall be sanctified by my glory.

44 And I will sanctify the tabernacle of the congregation, and the altar: I will sanctify also both Aaron and his sons, to minister to me in the priest's office.

45 ¶ And ^aI will ^bdwell ^camong the children of Israel, and will be their ^dGod.

46 And they shall know that I *am* the Lord their God, that brought them forth out of the land of Egypt, that I may dwell among them: I *am* the Lord their God.

CHAPTER 30

An altar of incense is to be placed before the veil—Atonement is to be made with the blood of the sin offering—Atonement money is to be paid to ransom each male—Priests are to use holy anointing oil and perfume.

And thou shalt make an ^aaltar to burn ^bincense upon: of ^cshittim wood shalt thou make it.

31*a* OR cook its flesh.
　　Lev. 8:31 (31–32).
33*a* Lev. 10:14 (12–15);
　　24:9 (5–9);
　　Luke 6:4.
　b OR alien.
35*a* Lev. 8:33;
　　Ezek. 43:25.
　b OR engage in the ordinance of setting them apart.
38*a* Num. 28:3 (3–8);

　　1 Chr. 16:40; Dan. 8:11.
　b HEB a year old.
　c 2 Chr. 8:13 (12–13);
　　Ezek. 46:13;
　　Mosiah 13:30.
39*a* 2 Kgs. 3:20.
40*a* OR measure.
　b Ezek. 45:24.
　c Ezek. 45:17.
41*a* Ps. 141:2.
　b HEB cereal, meal, or flour.
42*a* Num. 28:6 (3–8).

　b Ex. 33:7.
　c Lev. 16:2.
43*a* Ex. 25:22.
　b TG Temple.
45*a* Ex. 6:7.
　b Hag. 2:5.
　c TG God, Presence of.
　d Ezek. 34:24 (20–31).
30 1*a* 1 Kgs. 6:22;
　　Ezek. 41:22; Rev. 11:1.
　b Ex. 35:15.
　c HEB acacia.

2 A cubit *shall be* the length thereof, and a cubit the breadth thereof; foursquare shall it be: and two cubits *shall be* the height thereof: the horns thereof *shall be* *a*of the same.

3 And thou shalt *a*overlay it with pure gold, the top thereof, and the sides thereof round about, and the horns thereof; and thou shalt make unto it a *b*crown of gold round about.

4 And two golden rings shalt thou make to it under the crown of it, *a*by the two corners thereof, upon the two sides of it shalt thou make *it*; and they shall be for places for the staves to *b*bear it withal.

5 And thou shalt make the staves *of* shittim wood, and overlay them with gold.

6 And thou shalt put it before the veil that *is* by the *a*ark of the testimony, before the *b*mercy seat that *is* over the testimony, where I will meet with thee.

7 And Aaron shall burn thereon sweet *a*incense every morning: when he dresseth the lamps, he shall burn incense upon it.

8 And when *a*Aaron lighteth the lamps at even, he shall burn incense upon it, a perpetual incense before the LORD throughout your generations.

9 Ye shall offer no *a*strange incense thereon, nor burnt sacrifice, nor *b*meat offering; neither shall ye pour drink offering thereon.

10 And Aaron shall make an atonement upon the horns of it *a*once in a year with the *b*blood of the sin offering of *c*atonements: once in the year shall he make atonement upon it throughout your generations: it *is* most holy unto the LORD.

11 ¶ And the LORD spake unto Moses, saying,

12 When thou takest the *a*sum of the children of Israel after their number, then shall they give every man a *b*ransom for his soul unto the LORD, when thou numberest them; that there be no plague among them, when *thou* numberest them.

13 This they shall *a*give, every one that passeth among them that are numbered, half a *b*shekel after the *c*shekel of the sanctuary: (a *d*shekel *is* twenty gerahs:) an half *e*shekel *shall be* the offering of the LORD.

14 Every one that passeth among them that are numbered, from twenty years old and above, shall give an offering unto the LORD.

15 The rich shall not give more, and the poor shall not give less than half a shekel, when *they* give an offering unto the LORD, to make an *a*atonement for your souls.

16 And thou shalt take the atonement *a*money of the children of Israel, and shalt appoint it for the service of the *b*tabernacle of the congregation; that it may be a memorial unto the children of Israel before the LORD, to make an atonement for your souls.

17 ¶ And the LORD spake unto Moses, saying,

18 Thou shalt also make a laver *of* brass, and his foot *also of* brass, *a*to wash *withal:* and thou shalt put it between the tabernacle of the congregation and the altar, and thou shalt put water therein.

19 For Aaron and his sons shall wash their hands and their feet thereat:

20 When they go into the tabernacle

2*a* IE of one piece with the altar.
3*a* 1 Kgs. 6:22.
  b HEB border.
4*a* HEB on two of its trusses, or supporting frames.
  b OR carry it.
6*a* Ex. 16:34.
  b Ex. 25:21 (16–22).
7*a* Ex. 31:11; 40:27; 1 Chr. 6:49;

    2 Chr. 26:18 (16–23); Ps. 141:2.
8*a* Ex. 27:21.
9*a* Lev. 10:1 (1–3).
  b OR meal offering.
10*a* Heb. 9:7.
  b TG Blood, Symbolism of.
  c Lev. 4:20; 1 Chr. 6:49.
12*a* OR census.
  b Num. 31:50 (44–54); 2 Kgs. 12:4.

13*a* Neh. 10:32.
  b Gen. 23:15.
  c Lev. 27:25.
  d Ezek. 45:12.
  e Ex. 38:26; Matt. 17:27 (24–27).
15*a* Num. 31:50.
16*a* 2 Chr. 24:6 (6–9).
  b HEB tent of meeting (also vv. 18, 20, 26, 36).
18*a* OR for washings.

of the congregation, they shall wash with water, that they die not; or when they come near to the altar to minister, to burn offering made by fire unto the LORD:

21 So they shall wash their hands and their feet, that they die not: and it shall be a statute for ever to them, *even* to him and to his seed throughout their generations.

22 ¶ Moreover the LORD spake unto Moses, saying,

23 Take thou also unto thee principal *a*spices, of pure myrrh five hundred *shekels,* and of sweet cinnamon half so much, *even* two hundred and fifty *shekels,* and of sweet calamus two hundred and fifty *shekels,*

24 And of cassia five hundred *shekels,* after the shekel of the sanctuary, and of *a*oil olive an hin:

25 And thou shalt make it an *a*oil of holy *b*ointment, an ointment compound after the art of the *c*apothecary: it shall be an holy *d*anointing oil.

26 And thou shalt anoint the tabernacle of the congregation therewith, and the ark of the testimony,

27 And the table and all *a*his vessels, and the candlestick and his vessels, and the altar of incense,

28 And the altar of burnt offering with all his vessels, and the laver and his foot.

29 And thou shalt *a*sanctify them, that they may be most holy: whatsoever toucheth them shall be holy.

30 And thou shalt *a*anoint Aaron and his sons, and consecrate them, that *they* may minister unto me in the priest's office.

31 And thou shalt speak unto the children of Israel, saying, This shall be an holy *a*anointing oil unto me throughout your generations.

32 Upon *a*man's flesh shall it not be poured, neither shall ye make

any other like it, after the composition of it: it *is* holy, *and* it shall be holy unto you.

33 Whosoever compoundeth *any* like it, or whosoever putteth *any* of it upon a stranger, shall even be cut off from his people.

34 ¶ And the LORD said unto Moses, Take unto thee sweet *a*spices, stacte, and onycha, and galbanum; *these* sweet spices with pure frankincense: of each shall there be a like *weight:*

35 And thou shalt make it a perfume, a confection after the art of the apothecary, tempered together, pure *and* holy:

36 And thou shalt beat *some* of it very small, and put of it before the testimony in the tabernacle of the congregation, where I will *a*meet with thee: it shall be unto you most holy.

37 And *as for* the perfume which thou shalt make, ye shall not make to yourselves according to the composition thereof: it shall be unto thee holy for the LORD.

38 Whosoever shall make like unto that, to smell thereto, shall even be cut off from his people.

CHAPTER 31

Artisans are inspired in building and furnishing the tabernacle—Israel is commanded to keep the Lord's Sabbaths—The death penalty is decreed for Sabbath desecration—Moses receives the stone tablets.

AND the LORD spake unto Moses, saying,

2 See, I have called by name *a*Bezaleel the son of Uri, the son of Hur, of the tribe of Judah:

3 And I have filled him with the *a*spirit of God, in *b*wisdom, and in understanding, and in *c*knowledge,

---

23*a* Ex. 35:28.
24*a* OR olive oil.
25*a* Ex. 31:11; 35:15;
       1 Kgs. 1:39.
   b OR anointing.
   c HEB perfumer.
   d TG Anointing.
27*a* OR its utensils.

29*a* OR consecrate.
30*a* Ex. 40:15 (12–15).
31*a* Ex. 31:11.
32*a* IE the common man
       who is not a priest.
34*a* Ex. 25:6 (1–9).
36*a* Ex. 25:22.
31 2*a* Ex. 35:30; 36:1 (1–4).

3*a* TG God, Spirit of;
       Holy Ghost, Gifts of;
       Teaching with the
       Spirit.
   b TG God, Wisdom of;
       Wisdom.
   c TG Knowledge.

and in all manner of [d]workman-ship,

4 To devise [a]cunning works, to work in [b]gold, and in silver, and in brass,

5 And in [a]cutting of stones, to set *them,* and in carving of timber, to work in all manner of workmanship.

6 And I, behold, I have given with him Aholiab, the son of Ahisamach, of the tribe of Dan: and in the hearts of all that are [a]wise hearted I have put [b]wisdom, that they may make all that I have commanded thee;

7 The [a]tabernacle of the congrega-tion, and the ark of the testimony, and the mercy seat that *is* there-upon, and all the furniture of the tabernacle,

8 And the table and [a]his furniture, and the pure candlestick with all his furniture, and the altar of incense,

9 And the altar of burnt offering with all his furniture, and the laver and his foot,

10 And the [a]cloths of service, and the holy garments for Aaron the priest, and the garments of his sons, to minister in the priest's office,

11 And the [a]anointing oil, and sweet [b]incense for the holy *place:* according to all that I have com-manded thee shall they do.

12 ¶ And the LORD spake unto Moses, saying,

13 Speak thou also unto the chil-dren of Israel, saying, Verily my [a]sabbaths ye shall keep: for it *is* a sign between me and you through-out your generations; that *ye* may know that I *am* the LORD that doth sanctify you.

14 Ye shall keep the sabbath there-fore; for it *is* [a]holy unto you: every one that defileth it shall surely be put to [b]death: for whosoever doeth *any* work therein, that soul shall be cut off from among his people.

15 Six days may work be done; but in the seventh *is* the sabbath of [a]rest, holy to the LORD: whosoever doeth *any* [b]work in the sabbath day, he shall surely be put to death.

16 Wherefore the children of Israel shall keep the sabbath, to observe the sabbath throughout their gen-erations, *for* a perpetual [a]covenant.

17 It *is* a sign between me and the children of Israel for ever: for *in* [a]six days the LORD [b]made heaven and earth, and on the [c]seventh day he [d]rested, and was [e]refreshed.

18 ¶ And he gave unto Moses, when he had made an end of commun-ing with him upon mount Sinai, two [a]tables of [b]testimony, tables of stone, [c]written with the finger of God.

CHAPTER 32

Aaron makes a golden calf, which Israel worships—Moses serves as a mediator between God and rebellious Israel—Moses breaks the tablets of stone—The Levites slay about 3,000 rebels—Moses pleads and intercedes for the people.

AND when the people saw that Moses [a]delayed to come down out of the mount, the people gathered them-selves together unto Aaron, and said unto him, Up, make us [b]gods, which shall [c]go before us; for *as for*

3*d* TG Art.
4*a* OR artistic designs.
  b 2 Ne. 5:15.
5*a* TG Skill.
6*a* Ex. 35:10.
  b TG Talents.
7*a* HEB tent of meeting.
8*a* HEB its utensils.
10*a* HEB officiating garments.
   Ex. 35:19.
11*a* Ex. 30:25, 31;
   Mark 6:13 (7–13);
   James 5:14 (14–15).
   b Ex. 25:6; 30:7.

13*a* TG Sabbath.
14*a* TG Holiness.
   b Ex. 35:2 (1–3);
   Num. 15:35 (32–36).
15*a* TG Rest.
   b Ex. 35:2;
   Mosiah 13:18 (16–19);
   Moses 3:3;
   Abr. 5:3.
16*a* TG Covenants.
17*a* Gen. 1:31 (1–31);
   Ex. 20:11 (8–11);
   Mosiah 13:19 (16–19);
   Moses 2:31 (24–31);
   Abr. 4:31 (1–31).

   b TG Creation.
   c TG Sabbath.
   d TG Rest.
   e Gen. 2:3 (1–3).
18*a* Ex. 24:12; 34:1;
   Deut. 4:13; 10:1 (1–5);
   2 Cor. 3:3.
   TG Law of Moses.
   b TG Testimony.
   c TG Scriptures,
   Writing of.
32 1*a* Ex. 24:18; 34:28;
   Deut. 9:9.
   b Ex. 32:23; Acts 7:40.
   c Ex. 13:21.

this Moses, the man that brought us up out of the land of Egypt, we ^dwot not what is become of him.

2 And Aaron said unto them, Break off the ^agolden earrings, which *are* in the ears of your wives, of your sons, and of your daughters, and bring *them* unto me.

3 And all the people brake off the golden earrings which *were* in their ears, and brought *them* unto Aaron.

4 And he received *them* at their hand, and fashioned it with a graving tool, after he had made it a ^amolten calf: and they said, ^bThese *be* thy ^cgods, O Israel, which brought thee up out of the land of Egypt.

5 And when Aaron saw *it*, he built an altar before it; and Aaron made proclamation, and said, To morrow *is* a feast to the LORD.

6 And they rose up early on the morrow, and offered burnt offerings, and brought ^apeace offerings; and the ^bpeople sat down to eat and to drink, and rose up to play.

7 ¶ And the LORD said unto Moses, Go, get thee down; for thy people, which thou broughtest out of the land of Egypt, have ^acorrupted *themselves:*

8 They have ^aturned aside ^bquickly out of the way which I commanded them: they have made them a ^cmolten calf, and have worshipped it, and have sacrificed thereunto, and said, These *be* thy gods, O Israel, which have brought thee up out of the land of Egypt.

9 And the LORD said unto Moses, I have seen this people, and, behold, it *is* a ^astiffnecked people:

10 Now therefore let me alone, that my ^awrath may wax hot against them, and that I may ^bconsume them: and I will make of thee a great ^cnation.

11 And Moses ^abesought the LORD his God, and said, LORD, why doth thy wrath wax hot against thy people, which thou hast brought forth out of the land of Egypt with great power, and with a mighty hand?

12 Wherefore should the ^aEgyptians speak, and say, For mischief did he bring them out, to slay them in the mountains, and to consume them from the face of the earth? Turn from thy fierce ^bwrath, and ^crepent of this evil against thy people.

13 Remember ^aAbraham, Isaac, and Israel, thy servants, to whom thou ^bswarest by thine own self, and saidst unto them, I will ^cmultiply your ^dseed as the stars of heaven, and all this ^eland that I have spoken of will I give unto your seed, and they shall inherit *it* for ever.

14 ^aAnd the LORD ^brepented of the evil which he thought to do unto his people.

15 ¶ And Moses turned, and went down from the mount, and the two ^atables of the testimony *were* in his hand: the tables *were* written on both their sides; on the one side and on the other *were* they written.

16 And the ^atables *were* the work of God, and the ^bwriting *was* the

---

1 d OR know (also v. 23).
2 a Judg. 8:26 (24–27).
4 a Neh. 9:18;
  Ps. 106:19;
  D&C 124:84.
  b Alma 30:53.
  c Ex. 20:23;
  Acts 7:41;
  Rom. 1:23 (18–25).
  TG Idolatry.
6 a Ex. 24:5 (5–8).
  b 1 Cor. 10:7.
7 a Gen. 6:11 (11–13);
  Deut. 4:16 (14–19);
  9:12 (11–15);
  Hosea 9:9 (7–9);
  D&C 38:11.

8 a Deut. 9:16;
  1 Ne. 17:30 (30–31, 42);
  D&C 84:24 (23–25).
  b Alma 46:8;
  Hel. 12:4 (2–7).
  c Ex. 20:4 (3–4, 23).
9 a TG Apostasy of Israel;
  Stiffnecked.
10 a Ex. 22:24;
  D&C 84:24.
  b Deut. 9:14 (13–14),
  19 (18–20);
  Ps. 106:23.
  c Num. 14:12.
11 a Deut. 9:18 (18, 26–29).
12 a Num. 14:13 (13–16);
  Deut. 9:28.

  b JST Ex. 32:12 . . . wrath.
  Thy people will repent of
  this evil; *therefore come*
  thou not out against them.
  c Gen. 6:6; Ex. 32:14;
  Deut. 9:19.
13 a 2 Kgs. 13:23.
  b Gen. 22:16 (15–19).
  c D&C 27:10; Abr. 1:2.
  d TG Seed of Abraham.
  e TG Promised Lands.
14 a JST Ex. 32:14 (Appendix).
  b Gen. 6:6; Ex. 32:12;
  Num. 23:19.
15 a Ex. 24:12; 34:29; Deut. 4:13.
16 a TG Law of Moses.
  b TG Scriptures, Writing of.

writing of God, graven upon the tables.

17 And when ^aJoshua heard the noise of the people as they ^bshouted, he said unto Moses, *There is* a noise of war in the camp.

18 And he said, *It is* not the voice of *them that* ^ashout for mastery, neither *is it* the voice of *them that* cry for being overcome: *but* the noise of *them that* sing do I hear.

19 ¶ And it came to pass, as soon as he came nigh unto the camp, that he ^asaw the calf, and the dancing: and Moses' ^banger waxed hot, and he cast the tables out of his hands, and ^cbrake them beneath the mount.

20 And he took the ^acalf which they had made, and burnt *it* in the fire, and ground *it* to powder, and ^bstrawed *it* upon the ^cwater, and made the children of Israel drink *of it*.

21 And Moses said unto Aaron, What did this people unto thee, that thou hast brought so great a sin upon them?

22 And Aaron said, Let not the ^aanger of my lord wax hot: thou knowest the people, that they *are* ^bset on ^cmischief.

23 For they said unto me, ^aMake us ^bgods, which shall go before us: for *as for* this Moses, the man that brought us up out of the land of Egypt, we wot not what is become of him.

24 And I said unto them, Whosoever hath any gold, let them break *it* off. So they gave *it* me: then I cast it into the fire, and there came out this calf.

25 ¶ And when Moses saw that the people *were* ^anaked; (for Aaron had made them ^bnaked unto *their* shame among their enemies:)

26 Then Moses stood in the gate of the camp, and said, Who *is* on the LORD's side? *let him come* unto me. And all the sons of Levi gathered themselves together unto him.

27 And he said unto them, Thus saith the LORD God of Israel, Put every man his sword by his side, *and* go in and out from gate to gate throughout the camp, and ^aslay every man his brother, and every man his companion, and every man his neighbour.

28 And the children of Levi did according to the word of Moses: and there fell of the people that day about three thousand men.

29 For Moses had said, ^aConsecrate yourselves to day to the LORD, even every man upon his ^bson, and upon his brother; that he may bestow upon you a ^rblessing this day.

30 ¶ And it came to pass on the morrow, that Moses said unto the people, Ye have ^asinned a great sin: and now I will go up unto the LORD; ^bperadventure I shall make an ^catonement for your sin.

31 And Moses returned unto the LORD, and said, Oh, this people have sinned a great sin, and have made them ^agods of gold.

32 Yet now, if thou wilt ^aforgive their sin—; and if not, ^bblot me, I pray thee, out of thy ^cbook which thou hast ^dwritten.

33 And the LORD said unto Moses, ^aWhosoever hath ^bsinned against me, him will I ^cblot out of my ^dbook.

17a Ex. 17:9; 24:13; 33:11.
  b TG Rioting and Reveling.
18a HEB call for courage.
19a Deut. 9:16 (16–17, 21).
  b TG Anger.
  c Ex. 34:1;
    D&C 84:23 (19–26).
20a Deut. 9:21.
  b OR strewed.
  c Deut. 9:21.
22a Gen. 44:18;
    Deut. 9:20.
  b Ex. 16:20 (19–21).
  c Ex. 14:11; 17:2 (2, 4).

23a Acts 7:40;
    1 Ne. 17:42.
  b Ex. 32:1.
25a OR riotous, let loose.
  b 2 Chr. 28:19;
    2 Ne. 9:14;
    Morm. 9:5.
27a Num. 25:5.
29a TG Dedication.
  b Deut. 13:6 (6–11).
  c D&C 130:20; 132:5.
30a 1 Sam. 12:20 (20–25).
  b OR perhaps.
  c Num. 25:13.

31a TG Worship.
32a Deut. 9:26 (18, 26–29).
  b Rom. 9:3.
  c Ps. 139:16.
  d Luke 10:20.
33a A of F 1:2.
  b TG Accountability.
  c Mosiah 26:36;
    Alma 1:24; 6:3;
    Moro. 6:7;
    D&C 20:83.
  d TG Book of Life;
    Book of Remembrance;
    Record Keeping.

34 Therefore now go, [a]lead the people unto *the place* of which I have spoken unto thee: behold, mine [b]Angel shall go before thee: nevertheless in the day when I visit I will visit their sin upon them.

35 And the LORD plagued the people, because they made the calf, which Aaron made.

CHAPTER 33

The Lord promises to be with Israel and drive out the people of the land— The tabernacle of the congregation is moved away from the camp—The Lord speaks to Moses face to face in the tabernacle—Later, Moses sees the glory of God but not His face.

AND the LORD said unto Moses, [a]Depart, *and* go up hence, thou and the people which thou hast brought up out of the land of Egypt, unto the land which I sware unto Abraham, to Isaac, and to Jacob, saying, Unto thy [b]seed will I give it:

2 And I will send an [a]angel before thee; and I will drive out the [b]Canaanite, the Amorite, and the Hittite, and the Perizzite, the Hivite, and the Jebusite:

3 Unto a land [a]flowing with milk and honey: for I will not go up in the midst of thee; for thou *art* a stiffnecked people: lest I consume thee in the way.

4 ¶ And when the people heard these evil tidings, they [a]mourned: and no man did put on him his [b]ornaments.

5 For the LORD had said unto Moses, Say unto the children of Israel, Ye *are* a [a]stiffnecked people: [b]I will come up into the midst of thee in a moment, and consume thee: therefore now put off thy ornaments from thee, that I may know what to do unto thee.

6 And the children of Israel stripped themselves of their ornaments by the mount Horeb.

7 And Moses took the tabernacle, and pitched it without the camp, afar off from the camp, and called it the [a]Tabernacle of the congregation. And it came to pass, *that* every one which sought the LORD went out unto the [b]tabernacle of the congregation, which *was* without the camp.

8 And it came to pass, when Moses went out unto the tabernacle, *that* all the people rose up, and stood every man *at* his [a]tent door, and looked after Moses, until he was gone into the tabernacle.

9 And it came to pass, as Moses entered into the tabernacle, the [a]cloudy pillar descended, and stood *at* the door of the tabernacle, and *the* LORD talked with Moses.

10 And all the people saw the cloudy pillar stand *at* the tabernacle door: and all the people rose up and worshipped, every man *in* his tent door.

11 And the LORD [a]spake unto Moses [b]face to face, as a man [c]speaketh unto his [d]friend. And he turned again into the camp: but his servant [e]Joshua, the son of [f]Nun, a young man, departed not out of the tabernacle.

12 ¶ And Moses said unto the LORD, See, thou sayest unto me, [a]Bring up this people: and thou hast not let me know whom thou wilt

---

34a Ex. 33:12.
  b Num. 20:16.
33 1a Deut. 10:11.
  b Gen. 12:7;
    Abr. 2:6 (3–6, 19).
    TG Seed of Abraham.
  2a TG Angels.
  b Ex. 3:17 (8, 17); 13:5.
  3a Ex. 13:5.
  4a Num. 14:39.
  b Ezek. 24:17 (17, 23).
  5a TG Stiffnecked.
  b OR if I came up . . . I

would consume . . .
  7a Ex. 25:9 (8–9, 22, 40);
    29:42 (42–43);
    D&C 124:38.
  b HEB tent of meeting
    (also vv. 9–11).
  8a Num. 16:27.
  9a Ex. 14:19 (19, 24);
    Ps. 99:7;
    D&C 84:5.
 11a TG Jesus Christ,
    Appearances,
    Antemortal.

  b TG God, Body of,
    Corporeal Nature;
    God, Privilege of Seeing.
  c TG Communication.
  d Ether 12:39;
    D&C 84:63; 88:62; 93:45.
  e Ex. 17:9; 24:13; 32:17.
  f Num. 11:28;
    1 Kgs. 16:34;
    Neh. 8:17.
 12a Ex. 32:34.

send with me. Yet thou hast said, I [b]know thee by [c]name, and thou hast also found grace in my sight.

13 Now therefore, I pray thee, if I have found [a]grace in thy sight, [b]shew me now thy [c]way, that I may know thee, that I may find grace in thy sight: and consider that this nation *is* [d]thy [e]people.

14 And he said, My [a]presence shall go *with thee,* and I will give thee [b]rest.

15 And he said unto him, If thy presence go not *with me,* carry us not up hence.

16 For wherein shall it be known here that I and thy people have found grace in thy sight? *is it* not in that thou [a]goest with us? so shall we be [b]separated, I and thy people, from all the people that *are* upon the face of the earth.

17 And the LORD said unto Moses, [a]I will [b]do this thing also that thou hast spoken: for thou hast found grace in my sight, and I know thee by name.

18 And he said, I beseech thee, [a]shew me thy [b]glory.

19 And he said, I will make all my [a]goodness pass before thee, and I will [b]proclaim the name of the LORD before thee; and will be gracious to whom I will be gracious, and will shew [c]mercy on whom I will shew mercy.

20 [a]And he said, Thou canst not see my face: for [b]there shall no man [c]see me, and live.

21 And the LORD said, Behold, *there is* a place by me, and thou shalt stand upon a rock:

22 And it shall come to pass, while my glory passeth by, that I will put thee in a clift of the rock, and will cover thee with my hand [a]while I pass by:

23 And I will take away mine hand, and thou shalt [a]see my [b]back parts: but my face shall not be [c]seen.

CHAPTER 34

Moses hews new tables of stone—He goes up into Mount Sinai for forty days—The Lord proclaims His name and attributes and reveals His law—He makes another covenant with Israel—The skin of Moses' face shines, and he wears a veil.

[a]AND the LORD said unto Moses, [b]Hew thee two [c]tables of stone like unto the first: and I will [d]write upon *these* tables the words that were in the first tables, which thou [e]brakest.

2 And be ready in the morning, and come up in the morning unto mount Sinai, and present thyself there to me in the [a]top of the mount.

3 And no man shall [a]come up with thee, neither let any man be seen throughout all the mount; neither let the flocks nor herds feed before that mount.

4 ¶ And he hewed two [a]tables of stone like unto the first; and Moses

---

12b John 10:14.
  c Isa. 45:3 (3–4);
    JS—H 1:33 (17, 33, 49).
13a TG Grace.
  b Ps. 119:33.
  c Ps. 25:4 (1–5);
    143:8 (5–12);
    John 14:6;
    2 Ne. 9:41; 31:21 (17–21);
    Alma 37:46;
    D&C 132:22 (22, 25).
  d Ex. 34:9.
  e Deut. 9:29; 1 Kgs. 8:51;
    Neh. 1:10; Joel 2:17.
14a Isa. 63:9 (8–9).
  b TG Rest.
16a Num. 14:14.
  b OR special, distinctive
    people.

    1 Kgs. 8:53.
    TG Separation.
17a James 5:16.
  b Hel. 10:5 (4–5).
18a TG God, Privilege of
    Seeing.
  b TG Jesus Christ, Glory of.
19a Ex. 34:6 (5–7);
    Jer. 31:14.
  b Ex. 34:5.
  c D&C 64:10 (9–11).
    TG Compassion.
20a JST Ex. 33:20 (Appendix).
  b Moses 1:11.
  c TG God, Privilege of
    Seeing; Jesus Christ, Ap-
    pearances, Antemortal.
22a HEB until I have gone
    past.

23a TG God, Knowledge
    about.
  b TG God, Body of,
    Corporeal Nature.
  c JST Ex. 33:23 . . . seen,
    *as at other times; for I
    am angry with my people
    Israel.*
34 1a JST Ex. 34:1–2
    (Appendix).
  b Ex. 34:29 (28–35).
  c Ex. 24:12; 31:18;
    Deut. 10:1 (1–2);
    2 Cor. 3:3.
  d Ex. 34:28.
  e Ex. 32:19.
2a Ex. 19:20.
3a Ex. 19:12 (12–13, 21).
4a Deut. 10:3 (1–4).

rose up early in the morning, and went up unto mount Sinai, as the LORD had commanded him, and took in his hand the two tables of stone.

5 And the LORD descended in the cloud, and stood with him there, and ^aproclaimed the name of the LORD.

6 And the LORD passed by before him, and proclaimed, The LORD, The LORD God, ^amerciful and ^bgracious, ^clongsuffering, and abundant in ^dgoodness and truth,

7 Keeping mercy for thousands, ^aforgiving iniquity and transgression and ^bsin, ^cand that will by no means ^dclear *the* ^e*guilty*; visiting the ^finiquity of the fathers upon the children, and upon the children's children, unto the third and to the fourth *generation.*

8 And Moses made haste, and ^abowed his head toward the earth, and worshipped.

9 And he said, If now I have found ^agrace in thy sight, O Lord, let my Lord, I pray thee, go among us; for it *is* a ^bstiffnecked people; and ^cpardon our iniquity and our sin, and take us for ^dthine ^einheritance.

10 ¶ And he said, Behold, I make a covenant: before all thy people I will do ^amarvels, such as have not been done in all the earth, nor in any nation: and all the people among which thou *art* shall see the work of the LORD: for it *is* a ^bterrible thing that I will do with thee.

11 ^aObserve thou that which I command thee this day: behold, I ^bdrive out before thee the Amorite, and the Canaanite, and the Hittite, and the Perizzite, and the Hivite, and the Jebusite.

12 Take heed to thyself, lest thou make a ^acovenant with the ^binhabitants of the land whither thou goest, lest it ^cbe for a snare in the midst of thee:

13 But ye shall ^adestroy their ^baltars, break their images, and cut down their ^cgroves:

14 For thou shalt worship ^ano other ^bgod: for the LORD, whose name *is* ^cJealous, *is* a ^djealous God:

15 Lest thou make a ^acovenant with the inhabitants of the land, and they go a ^bwhoring after their ^cgods, and do sacrifice unto their gods, and ^d*one* ^ecall thee, and thou ^feat of his sacrifice;

16 And thou ^atake of their ^bdaughters unto thy sons, and their daughters go a whoring after their gods, and make thy sons go a whoring after their gods.

17 Thou shalt make thee no molten ^agods.

18 ¶ The ^afeast of ^bunleavened bread shalt thou keep. Seven days

---

5a Ex. 33:19.
6a TG God, Mercy of;
   Mercy.
  b Ps. 145:8;
    D&C 76:5.
  c TG Forbear.
  d Ex. 33:19;
    2 Ne. 4:17; 9:10;
    Mosiah 4:11; 5:3;
    Moro. 8:3; D&C 86:11.
7a TG Forgive.
  b Moro. 10:33;
    D&C 84:61 (60–61).
  c OR but who.
  d Josh. 24:19;
    Alma 11:40 (40–41);
    D&C 56:14; 64:10.
  e JST Ex. 34:7 . . .
    rebellious . . .
    Micah 6:11 (10–15);
    Nahum 1:3;
    2 Ne. 23:11.
  f TG Accountability.

8a Ex. 4:31;
    2 Ne. 12:9;
    3 Ne. 11:19 (18–19);
    Moses 6:31.
9a TG Grace.
  b TG Stiffnecked.
  c TG Forgive.
  d Ex. 33:13.
  e TG Inheritance.
10a TG Miracle.
  b Deut. 10:21;
    Ps. 145:6; Isa. 64:3.
11a Deut. 6:25.
  b Ex. 13:5;
    1 Ne. 17:32 (32–38).
12a Ex. 23:32 (31–33);
    Judg. 2:2 (1–5).
  b TG Gentiles.
  c OR become a.
13a Deut. 7:5; 12:3.
  b Hosea 8:11.
  c HEB *asherim,* or cultic
    deities.

1 Kgs. 16:33;
    2 Kgs. 17:10 (10–12).
14a Ex. 20:3 (3, 5).
  b Ps. 16:4;
    2 Ne. 9:37 (37–38);
    Alma 7:6.
  c JST Ex. 34:14 . . .
    Jehovah . . .
    Mosiah 13:13.
  d Ex. 20:5.
15a TG Separation.
  b Deut. 31:16.
  c Judg. 2:17.
  d OR they.
  e Num. 25:2 (1–2).
  f Ps. 106:28;
    1 Cor. 10:27.
16a TG Marriage, Interfaith.
  b 1 Kgs. 16:31.
17a Deut. 27:15;
    2 Chr. 28:2.
18a Ex. 23:14 (14–19).
  b Ex. 12:15.

thou shalt eat unleavened bread, as I commanded thee, in the ᶜtime of the month ᵈAbib: for in the ᵉmonth Abib thou camest out from Egypt.

19 All that ᵃopeneth the ᵇmatrix *is* mine; and every firstling among thy cattle, *whether* ox or sheep, *that is male.*

20 But the firstling of an ass thou shalt redeem with a lamb: and if thou redeem *him* not, then shalt thou break his neck. All the ᵃfirstborn of thy sons thou shalt redeem. And none shall appear before me empty.

21 ¶ Six days thou shalt work, but on the seventh day thou shalt ᵃrest: in ᵇearing time and in harvest thou shalt rest.

22 ¶ And thou shalt observe the ᵃfeast of weeks, of the firstfruits of wheat harvest, and the feast of ingathering at the year's end.

23 ¶ ᵃThrice in the year shall all your men children appear before the Lord GOD, the God of Israel.

24 For I will ᵃcast out the nations before thee, and enlarge thy borders: neither shall any man ᵇdesire thy land, when thou shalt go up to appear before the LORD thy God thrice in the year.

25 Thou shalt not offer the ᵃblood of my sacrifice with ᵇleaven; neither shall the sacrifice of the feast of the passover be ᶜleft unto the morning.

26 The first of the ᵃfirstfruits of thy land thou shalt bring unto the house of the LORD thy God. Thou shalt not ᵇseethe a kid in his mother's milk.

27 And the LORD said unto Moses, ᵃWrite thou these words: for ᵇafter the tenor of these words I have made a covenant with thee and with Israel.

28 And he was there with the LORD ᵃforty days and forty nights; he did neither ᵇeat bread, nor drink water. And he ᶜwrote upon the tables the words of the ᵈcovenant, the ᵉten ᶠcommandments.

29 ¶ And it came to pass, when Moses came down from mount Sinai with the ᵃtwo ᵇtables of testimony in Moses' hand, when he came down from the mount, that Moses ᶜwist not that the skin of his face ᵈshone while he talked with him.

30 And when Aaron and all the children of Israel saw Moses, behold, the skin of his face shone; and they were afraid to come nigh him.

31 And Moses called unto them; and Aaron and all the ᵃrulers of the congregation returned unto him: and Moses talked with them.

32 And afterward all the children of Israel came nigh: and he gave them in commandment all that the LORD had spoken with him in mount Sinai.

33 And *till* Moses had done speaking with them, he put a ᵃveil on his face.

34 But when Moses went in before the LORD to speak with him, he took the veil off, until he came out. And he came out, and spake unto the children of Israel *that* which he was commanded.

35 And the children of Israel saw the face of Moses, that the skin of Moses' face shone: and Moses put the veil upon his face again, until he went in to speak with him.

18c OR appointed feast.
  d Ex. 23:15.
  e Ex. 12:2.
19a Ex. 13:2 (2, 12).
  b Luke 2:23.
20a TG Firstborn.
21a TG Rest.
  b HEB plowing.
22a Ex. 23:16; Acts 2:1.
23a Ex. 23:14 (14, 17).
24a Lev. 18:24.
  b Prov. 16:7.
25a Ex. 23:18.
  b TG Leaven.

  c Ex. 12:10; Deut. 16:4.
26a Ex. 23:19; Deut. 26:2;
     Neh. 10:35.
  b IE cook a young goat
     in its mother's milk—a
     ritual food of the
     fertility cults.
     Ex. 23:19; Deut. 14:21.
27a TG Scribe;
     Scriptures, Writing of.
  b OR according to.
28a Ex. 24:18; 32:1;
     Deut. 9:9 (9, 18).
  b Luke 18:12.

     TG Fast, Fasting.
  c Ex. 34:1.
  d Ps. 78:10.
  e Deut. 4:13.
  f TG Law of Moses.
29a Ex. 34:1 (1–2).
  b Ex. 32:15.
  c OR knew.
  d Mosiah 13:5 (5–6);
     Hel. 5:36; D&C 110:3;
     JS—H 1:32.
     TG Transfiguration.
31a OR leaders.
33a TG Veil.

CHAPTER 35

Israel is admonished to observe the Sabbath—Free gifts are offered for the tabernacle—The calls and inspiration of certain artisans are confirmed.

AND Moses gathered all the congregation of the children of Israel together, and said unto them, These *are* the words which the LORD hath commanded, that *ye* should do them.

2 *a*Six days shall *b*work be done, but on the seventh day there shall be to you an holy day, a *c*sabbath of rest to the LORD: whosoever doeth work therein shall be put to *d*death.

3 Ye shall *a*kindle no fire throughout your habitations upon the sabbath day.

4 ¶ And Moses spake unto all the congregation of the children of Israel, saying, This *is* the thing which the LORD *a*commanded, saying,

5 Take ye from among you an offering unto the LORD: whosoever *is* of a *a*willing heart, let him bring it, an offering of the LORD; gold, and silver, and brass,

6 And blue, and purple, and scarlet, and fine linen, and goats' *hair*,

7 And rams' skins dyed red, and badgers' skins, and *a*shittim wood,

8 And oil for the light, and spices for anointing oil, and for the sweet incense,

9 And onyx stones, and stones to be set for the *a*ephod, and for the breastplate.

10 And *a*every wise hearted among you shall come, and make all that the LORD hath commanded;

11 The *a*tabernacle, his tent, and his covering, *b*his taches, and his boards, his bars, his pillars, and his sockets,

12 The *a*ark, and the staves thereof, *with* the mercy seat, and the veil of the covering,

13 The *a*table, and his staves, and all *b*his vessels, and the *c*shewbread,

14 The *a*candlestick also for the light, and his furniture, and his lamps, with the *b*oil for the light,

15 And the *a*incense altar, and his staves, and the *b*anointing oil, and the sweet incense, and the *c*hanging for the door at the entering in of the tabernacle,

16 The *a*altar of burnt offering, with his brasen grate, his staves, and all his vessels, the laver and *b*his foot,

17 The hangings of the court, his pillars, and their sockets, and the hanging for the door of the court,

18 The *a*pins of the tabernacle, and the pins of the court, and their cords,

19 The *a*cloths of service, to do service in the holy *place,* the holy garments for Aaron the priest, and the garments of his sons, to minister in the priest's office.

20 ¶ And all the congregation of the children of Israel departed from the presence of Moses.

21 And they came, every one whose *a*heart stirred him up, and every one whom his spirit made *b*willing, *and* they brought the LORD's *c*offering *d*to the work of the *e*tabernacle of the congregation, and for all his service, and for the holy garments.

22 And they came, both men and women, as many as were willing

---

35 2*a* Ex. 20:9.
  b Ex. 31:15 (14–15).
  c Jarom 1:5;
    Mosiah 18:23;
    D&C 59:10 (9–12).
  d Ex. 31:14;
    Num. 15:35 (32–36).
    TG Capital Punishment.
  3*a* Ex. 16:23;
    D&C 59:13.
  4*a* Ex. 25:2 (1–7).
  5*a* D&C 59:15; 64:22, 34.
  7*a* HEB acacia (also v. 24).
  9*a* Ex. 29:5.

10*a* IE every one that is
    talented or skilled.
    Ex. 28:3; 31:6.
11*a* Ex. 26:1 (1–30);
    Heb. 8:5;
    D&C 124:38.
  b OR its hooks.
12*a* Ex. 25:10 (10–16).
13*a* Ex. 25:23 (23–29).
  b OR its utensils.
  c TG Bread, Shewbread.
14*a* Ex. 25:31 (31–39).
  b Ex. 27:20.
15*a* Ex. 30:1 (1–10).

  b Ex. 30:25 (23–38).
  c OR screen or curtain.
    Ex. 26:36.
16*a* Ex. 27:1 (1–8); 38:1 (1–7).
  b OR its base.
18*a* OR pegs.
19*a* HEB officiating
    garments.
    Ex. 31:10; 39:1 (1, 41).
21*a* Ex. 36:2.
  b TG Initiative.
  c TG Generosity.
  d OR for use in.
  e HEB tent of meeting.

hearted, *and* brought ^abracelets, and earrings, and rings, and tablets, all ^bjewels of gold: and every man that offered *offered* an ^coffering of gold unto the LORD.

23 And every man, with whom was found blue, and purple, and scarlet, and fine ^alinen, and goats' *hair,* and red skins of rams, and badgers' skins, brought *them.*

24 Every one that did offer an offering of silver and brass brought the LORD's ^aoffering: and every man, with whom was found shittim wood for any work of the service, brought *it.*

25 And all the women that were ^awise hearted did spin with their hands, and brought that which they had spun, *both* of blue, and of purple, *and* of scarlet, and of fine linen.

26 And all the women whose heart stirred them up ^ain wisdom spun goats' *hair.*

27 And the ^arulers brought onyx stones, and stones to be set, for the ephod, and for the breastplate;

28 And ^aspice, and oil for the light, and for the anointing oil, and for the sweet incense.

29 The children of Israel brought a ^awilling offering unto the LORD, every man and woman, whose heart made them willing to bring for all manner of work, which the LORD had commanded to be made by the hand of Moses.

30 ¶ And Moses said unto the children of Israel, See, the LORD hath called by name ^aBezaleel the son of Uri, the son of Hur, of the tribe of Judah;

31 And he hath filled him with the spirit of God, in ^awisdom, in understanding, and in knowledge, and in all manner of ^bworkmanship;

32 And to devise ^acurious works, to work in gold, and in silver, and in brass,

33 And in the cutting of stones, to set *them,* and in carving of wood, to ^amake any manner of cunning work.

34 And he hath put in his heart that he may ^ateach, *both* he, and Aholiab, the son of Ahisamach, of the tribe of Dan.

35 Them hath he filled with ^awisdom of heart, to ^bwork all manner of work, of the engraver, and of the ^ccunning workman, and of the embroiderer, in blue, and in purple, in scarlet, and in fine linen, and of the weaver, *even* of them that do any work, and of those that devise cunning work.

CHAPTER 36

Wise-hearted men are chosen to work on the tabernacle—Moses restrains the people from donating any more material.

THEN wrought ^aBezaleel and Aholiab, and ^bevery wise hearted man, in whom the LORD put ^cwisdom and understanding to know how to work all manner of work ^dfor the service of the sanctuary, according to all that the LORD had commanded.

2 And Moses called Bezaleel and Aholiab, and every wise hearted man, in whose ^aheart the LORD had put wisdom, *even* every one whose heart stirred him up to come unto the work to do it:

3 And they received of Moses all the ^aoffering, which the children of

22a Num. 31:50;
    Alma 31:28.
  b OR gold jewelry.
  c Ex. 38:24.
23a Ex. 25:4 (4–5).
24a Ex. 36:3.
25a Ex. 28:3.
26a IE unto skills.
27a OR presidents or
    presiding officers.
28a Ex. 30:23.
29a OR freewill.
30a Ex. 31:2 (2–6).

31a TG Wisdom.
  b TG Industry.
32a OR artistic things (also
    v. 35).
33a OR do . . . of skilled
    craftsmanship.
34a Moro. 10:9 (9–10);
    D&C 38:23; 42:14;
    88:77 (77–79, 118);
    107:85 (85–89).
35a Ex. 36:1 (1–2);
    1 Kgs. 7:14.
    TG Talents.

  b TG Art.
  c OR skilled craftsman.
36 1a Ex. 31:2 (1–6).
  b OR all the able men
    (see also v. 4).
  c Ex. 35:35;
    1 Kgs. 7:14.
    TG Holy Ghost,
    Gifts of.
  d IE in the construction
    of (see also vv. 2, 8).
2a Ex. 35:21.
3a Ex. 35:24 (21–29).

Israel had brought for the work of the service of the sanctuary, to make it *withal*. And they brought yet unto him ᵇfree offerings every morning.

4 And all the ᵃwise men, that wrought all the work of the sanctuary, came every man from his work which they made;

5 ¶ And they spake unto Moses, saying, The people ᵃbring much more than enough for the service of the work, which the LORD commanded to make.

6 And Moses gave commandment, and they caused it to be proclaimed throughout the camp, saying, Let neither man nor woman make any more work for the offering of the sanctuary. So the people were restrained from bringing.

7 For the ᵃstuff they had was sufficient for all the work to make it, and too much.

8 ¶ And every wise hearted man among them that wrought the work of the tabernacle ᵃmade ten ᵇcurtains *of* fine twined linen, and blue, and purple, and scarlet: *with* cherubims of cunning work made he them.

9 The length of ᵃone curtain *was* twenty and eight cubits, and the breadth of one curtain four cubits: the curtains *were* all of one size.

10 And he coupled the five curtains one unto another: and *the other* five curtains he coupled one unto another.

11 And he made loops of blue on the edge of one curtain ᵃfrom the selvedge in the coupling: likewise he made in the uttermost side of *another* curtain, in the coupling of the second.

12 Fifty loops made he in one curtain, and fifty loops made he in the edge of the curtain which *was* in the coupling of the second: the loops held one *curtain* to another.

13 And he made fifty ᵃtaches of gold, and coupled the curtains one unto another with the taches: so it became one tabernacle.

14 ¶ And he made curtains *of* goats' *hair* for the tent over the tabernacle: eleven curtains he made them.

15 The length of one curtain *was* thirty cubits, and four cubits *was* the breadth of one curtain: the eleven curtains *were* of one size.

16 And he coupled five curtains by themselves, and six curtains by themselves.

17 And he made fifty loops upon the uttermost edge of ᵃthe curtain in the coupling, and fifty loops made he upon the edge of the curtain which coupleth the second.

18 And he made fifty taches *of* brass to couple the tent together, that it might be one.

19 And he made a covering for the tent *of* rams' skins dyed red, and a covering *of* badgers' skins above *that*.

20 ¶ And he made ᵃboards for the tabernacle *of* ᵇshittim wood, standing up.

21 The length of a board *was* ten cubits, and the breadth of a board one cubit and a half.

22 One board had two tenons, ᵃequally distant one from another: thus did he make for all the boards of the tabernacle.

23 And he made boards for the tabernacle; twenty boards for the south side southward:

24 And forty ᵃsockets of silver he made under the twenty boards; two sockets under one board for his two tenons, and two sockets under another board for his two tenons.

25 And for the other side of the tabernacle, *which is* toward the north corner, he made twenty boards,

26 And their forty sockets of

3*b* OR freewill.
4*a* TG Wisdom.
5*a* TG Generosity.
7*a* OR materials.
8*a* TG Skill.
  b Ex. 26:1 (1–14).

9*a* OR each.
11*a* HEB on the outside of the first set.
13*a* OR clasps.
17*a* OR the other connecting curtain.

20*a* Ex. 26:15 (15–29).
  b HEB acacia.
22*a* HEB which made them fit one to another.
24*a* OR bases (also vv. 26, 30, 36, 38).

silver; two sockets under one board, and two sockets under another board.

27 And for the sides of the tabernacle westward he made six boards.

28 And two boards made he for the corners of the tabernacle in the *a*two sides.

29 And they were coupled beneath, and coupled together at the head thereof, to one ring: thus he did to both of them in both the corners.

30 And there were eight boards; and their sockets *were* sixteen sockets of silver, under every board two sockets.

31 ¶ And he made bars of shittim wood; five for the boards of the one side of the tabernacle,

32 And five bars for the boards of the other side of the tabernacle, and five bars for the boards of the tabernacle for the sides westward.

33 And he made the middle bar to *a*shoot through the boards from the one end to the other.

34 And he overlaid the boards with gold, and made their rings *of* gold *to be* places for the bars, and overlaid the bars with gold.

35 ¶ And he made a *a*veil *of* blue, and purple, and scarlet, and fine twined linen: *with* cherubims made he it of cunning work.

36 And he made thereunto four pillars *of* shittim *wood,* and overlaid them with gold: their hooks *were of* gold; and he cast for them four sockets of silver.

37 ¶ And he made *a*an hanging for the tabernacle door *of* blue, and purple, and scarlet, and fine twined linen, of needlework;

38 And the five pillars of it with their hooks: and he overlaid their *a*chapiters and their fillets with gold: but their five sockets *were of* brass.

CHAPTER 37

Bezaleel makes the ark, the mercy seat, and the cherubims—He makes the table, the vessels, the candlestick, the incense altar, the holy anointing oil, and the sweet incense.

AND Bezaleel *a*made the *b*ark *of* *c*shittim wood: two cubits and a half *was* the length of it, and a cubit and a half the breadth of it, and a cubit and a half the height of it:

2 And he overlaid it with pure gold within and without, and made a *a*crown of gold to it round about.

3 And he cast for it four rings of gold, *to be set* by the four corners of it; even two rings upon the one side of it, and two rings upon the other side of it.

4 And he made staves *of* shittim wood, and overlaid them with gold.

5 And he put the staves into the rings by the sides of the ark, to bear the ark.

6 ¶ And he made the *a*mercy seat *of* pure gold: two cubits and a half *was* the length thereof, and one cubit and a half the breadth thereof.

7 And he made two *a*cherubims *of* gold, beaten out of one piece made he them, on the two ends of the mercy seat;

8 One cherub on the end on this side, and another cherub on the *other* end on that side: *a*out of the mercy seat made he the cherubims on the two ends thereof.

9 And the *a*cherubims spread out *their* wings on high, *and* covered with their wings over the mercy seat, with their faces one to another; *even* to the mercy seatward were the faces of the cherubims.

10 ¶ And he made the *a*table *of* shittim wood: two cubits *was* the

---

28*a* IE those adjoining the west side.
33*a* OR pass.
35*a* TG Veil.
37*a* OR a screen or curtain.
38*a* OR capitals or tops of the pillars.

37 1*a* TG Skill.
  b TG Ark of the Covenant.
  c HEB acacia (also vv. 4, 10, 15, 25, 28).
  2*a* OR border (also vv. 11–12, 26–27).

6*a* Ex. 25:17 (17–21).
7*a* TG Cherubim.
8*a* OR of one piece with.
9*a* TG Symbolism.
10*a* Ex. 25:23 (23–29); 1 Kgs. 7:48.

length thereof, and a cubit the breadth thereof, and a cubit and a half the height thereof:

11 And he overlaid it with pure gold, and made thereunto a crown of gold round about.

12 Also he made thereunto a border of an handbreadth round about; and made a crown of gold for the border thereof round about.

13 And he cast for it four rings of gold, and put the rings upon the four corners that *were* in the four feet thereof.

14 *a*Over against the border were the rings, the places for the staves to bear the table.

15 And he made the staves *of* shittim wood, and overlaid them with gold, to bear the table.

16 And he made the *a*vessels which *were* upon the table, his dishes, and his spoons, and his bowls, and *b*his covers to cover withal, *of* pure gold.

17 ¶ And he made the *a*candlestick *of* pure gold: *of* beaten work made he the candlestick; his shaft, and *b*his branch, his bowls, *c*his knops, and his flowers, were of the same:

18 And six branches going out of the sides thereof; three branches of the candlestick out of the one side thereof, and three branches of the candlestick out of the other side thereof:

19 Three bowls made after the fashion of almonds in one branch, a knop and a flower; and three bowls made like almonds in another branch, a knop and a flower: so throughout the six branches going out of the candlestick.

20 And in the candlestick *were* four bowls made like almonds, his knops, and his flowers:

21 And a knop under two branches of the same, and a knop under two branches of the same, and a knop

under two branches of the same, according to the six branches going out of it.

22 Their knops and their branches were of the same: all of it *was* one beaten work *of* pure gold.

23 And he made his seven lamps, and his snuffers, and his snuffdishes, *of* pure gold.

24 *Of* a talent of pure gold made he it, and all the vessels thereof.

25 ¶ And he made the incense *a*altar *of* shittim wood: the length of it *was* a cubit, and the breadth of it a cubit; *it was* foursquare; and two cubits *was* the height of it; the horns thereof were of the same.

26 And he overlaid it with pure gold, *both* the top of it, and the sides thereof round about, and the horns of it: also he made unto it a crown of gold round about.

27 And he made two rings of gold for it under the crown thereof, by the two corners of it, upon the two sides thereof, to be places for the staves *a*to bear it withal.

28 And he made the staves *of* shittim wood, and overlaid them with gold.

29 ¶ And he made the holy anointing oil, and the pure *a*incense of sweet spices, according to the work of the *b*apothecary.

CHAPTER 38

Bezaleel and others make the altar of burnt offerings and all things pertaining to the tabernacle—Offerings are made by 603,550 men.

AND he *a*made the *b*altar of burnt offering *of* *c*shittim wood: five cubits *was* the length thereof, and five cubits the breadth thereof; *it was* foursquare; and three cubits the height thereof.

2 And he made the horns thereof on the four corners of it; the horns

---

14*a* OR Next to.
16*a* OR utensils.
  b HEB the jugs for pouring libations.
17*a* Ex. 25:31 (31–39); Zech. 4:2 (1–14);

Rev. 1:20.
  b OR its branches, its cups, etc.
  c OR its buds.
25*a* 1 Kgs. 7:48.
27*a* OR whereby to carry it.

29*a* Ps. 141:2.
  b OR perfumer.
38 1*a* TG Skill.
  b Ex. 27:1; 35:16.
  c HEB acacia (also v. 6).

thereof were of *the same: and he overlaid it with *brass.

3 And he made all the vessels of the altar, the pots, and the shovels, and the basins, *and* the fleshhooks, and the firepans: all the vessels thereof made he *of* brass.

4 And he made for the altar a brasen grate of network under *the compass thereof beneath unto the midst of it.

5 And he cast four rings for the four ends of the grate of brass, *to be* places for the staves.

6 And he made the staves *of* shittim wood, and overlaid them with brass.

7 And he put the staves into the rings on the sides of the altar, to bear it withal; he made the altar hollow with boards.

8 ¶ And he made the laver *of* brass, and the foot of it *of* brass, of the *lookingglasses of *the women* assembling, which assembled *at* the door of the tabernacle of the congregation.

9 ¶ And he made the court: on the south side southward the hangings of the court *were of* fine twined linen, an hundred cubits:

10 Their *pillars *were* twenty, and their brasen *sockets twenty; the hooks of the pillars and their fillets *were of* silver.

11 And for the north side *the hangings were* an hundred cubits, their pillars *were* twenty, and their sockets of brass twenty; the hooks of the pillars and their fillets *of* silver.

12 And for the west side *were* hangings of fifty cubits, their pillars ten, and their sockets ten; the hooks of the pillars and their fillets *of* silver.

13 And for the east side eastward fifty cubits.

14 The hangings of the one side *of* *the gate were* fifteen cubits; their pillars three, and their sockets three.

15 And for the other side of the court gate, on this hand and that hand, *were* hangings of fifteen cubits; their pillars three, and their sockets three.

16 All the hangings of the court round about *were* of fine twined *linen.

17 And the sockets for the pillars *were of* brass; the hooks of the pillars and their fillets *of* silver; and the overlaying of their *chapiters *of* silver; and all the *pillars of the court *were* filleted with silver.

18 And the *hanging for the gate of the court *was* needlework, *of* blue, and purple, and scarlet, and fine twined linen: and twenty cubits *was* the length, and the height in the breadth *was* five cubits, *answerable to the hangings of the court.

19 And their pillars *were* four, and their sockets *of* brass four; their hooks *of* silver, and the overlaying of their chapiters and their fillets *of* silver.

20 And all the pins of the tabernacle, and of the court round about, *were of* brass.

21 ¶ This is the *sum of the *tabernacle, *even* of the *tabernacle of testimony, as it was counted, according to the commandment of Moses, *for* the service of the *Levites, by the hand of *Ithamar, son to Aaron the priest.

22 And Bezaleel the son of Uri, the son of Hur, of the tribe of Judah, made all that the LORD commanded Moses.

23 And with him *was* Aholiab, son of Ahisamach, of the tribe of Dan, an engraver, and a cunning workman, and an embroiderer in blue, and in purple, and in scarlet, and fine linen.

2*a* OR one piece with it.
  b OR bronze (also
    vv. 3, 5–6).
    2 Chr. 1:5.
4*a* OR its rim or border.
8*a* OR mirrors.
10*a* Ex. 27:10 (10–11, 17).
  b OR bases (also vv. 11–12,

    14–15, etc.).
16*a* Ex. 27:9 (9–19).
17*a* OR capitals or headwork.
  b Ex. 27:10 (9–19).
18*a* OR screen or curtain.
    Ex. 27:16 (9–19).
  b OR corresponding.
21*a* IE of the items

connected with the tabernacle.
  b Num. 10:11.
  c Num. 17:7.
  d Num. 1:50 (47–53);
    3:41 (7–41);
    D&C 124:39.
  e Ex. 6:23; 28:1.

24 All the gold that was *occu-pied for the work in all the work of the holy *place*, even the gold of the *offering, was twenty and nine talents, and seven hundred and thirty shekels, after the shekel of the sanctuary.

25 And the silver of them that were numbered of the congregation *was* an hundred talents, and a thousand seven hundred and threescore and fifteen shekels, after the shekel of the sanctuary:

26 A bekah for every man, *that is,* half a shekel, after the *shekel of the sanctuary, for every one *that went to be numbered, from twenty years old and upward, for six hundred thousand and three thousand and five hundred and fifty *men.*

27 And of the hundred talents of silver were cast the sockets of the sanctuary, and the sockets of the veil; an hundred sockets of the hundred talents, a talent for a socket.

28 And of the thousand seven hundred seventy and five *shekels* he made hooks for the pillars, and overlaid their chapiters, and filleted them.

29 And the brass of the offering *was* seventy talents, and two thousand and four hundred shekels.

30 And therewith he made the sockets to the door of the tabernacle of the congregation, and the brasen altar, and the brasen grate for it, and all the vessels of the altar,

31 And the sockets of the court round about, and the sockets of the court gate, and all the pins of the tabernacle, and all the pins of the court round about.

CHAPTER 39

Holy garments are made for Aaron and the priests—The breastplate is made—

The tabernacle of the congregation is finished—Moses blesses the people.

AND of the blue, and purple, and scarlet, they *made *cloths of service, to do service in the holy *place*, and made the holy *garments for Aaron; as the LORD commanded Moses.

2 And he made the *ephod *of* gold, blue, and purple, and scarlet, and fine twined linen.

3 And they did beat the gold into thin plates, and cut *it into* *wires, to work *it* in the blue, and in the purple, and in the scarlet, and in the fine linen, *with* *cunning work.

4 They made shoulderpieces for it, to couple *it* together: by the two edges was it coupled together.

5 And the *curious girdle of his ephod, that *was* upon it, *was* of the same, according to the work thereof; *of* gold, blue, and purple, and scarlet, and fine twined linen; as the LORD commanded Moses.

6 ¶ And they wrought onyx stones inclosed in *ouches of gold, graven, as signets are graven, with the names of the children of Israel.

7 And he put them on the shoulders of the ephod, *that they should be* stones for a memorial to the children of Israel; as the LORD commanded Moses.

8 ¶ And he made the breastplate *of* cunning work, like the work of the ephod; *of* gold, blue, and purple, and scarlet, and fine twined linen.

9 It was foursquare; they made the breastplate double: a span *was* the length thereof, and a span the breadth thereof, *being* doubled.

10 And they set in it four rows of stones: *the first* row *was* a *sardius, a topaz, and a carbuncle: this *was* the first row.

11 And the second row, an emerald, a sapphire, and a diamond.

24a HEB used.
  b Ex. 35:22.
26a Ex. 30:13;
    Matt. 17:27 (24–27).
  b OR who was numbered in the census.
39 1a TG Skill.

  b HEB officiating garments.
    Ex. 35:19.
  c Ex. 28:2, 4 (1–5).
2a IE a special apron.
    Ex. 28:6 (6–14).
3a OR threads.

  b OR skillful design.
5a OR skillfully woven band (also vv. 20–21).
6a OR settings (also vv. 13, 16, 18).
10a OR ruby.

12 And the third row, a *a*ligure, an agate, and an amethyst.

13 And the fourth row, a beryl, an onyx, and a jasper: *they were* inclosed in ouches of gold in their inclosings.

14 And the stones *were* according to the names of the children of Israel, twelve, according to their names, *like* the engravings of a signet, every one with his name, according to the twelve tribes.

15 And they made upon the breastplate chains at the ends, of *a*wreathen work *of* pure gold.

16 And they made two ouches *of* gold, and two gold rings; and put the two rings in the two ends of the breastplate.

17 And they put the two wreathen chains of gold in the two rings on the ends of the breastplate.

18 And the two ends of the two wreathen chains they fastened in the two ouches, and put them on the shoulderpieces of the ephod, before it.

19 And they made two rings of gold, and put *them* on the two ends of the breastplate, upon the border of it, which *was* on the side of the ephod inward.

20 And they made two *other* golden rings, and put them on the two sides of the ephod underneath, toward the forepart of it, over against the *other* coupling thereof, above the curious girdle of the ephod.

21 And they did bind the breastplate by his rings unto the rings of the ephod with a lace of blue, that it might be above the curious girdle of the ephod, and that the breastplate might not be loosed from the ephod; as the LORD commanded Moses.

22 ¶ And he made the robe of the ephod *of* woven work, all *of* blue.

23 And *there was* an hole in the midst of the robe, as the hole of an *a*habergeon, *with* a band round about the hole, that it should not rend.

24 And they made upon the hems of the robe pomegranates *of* blue, and purple, and scarlet, *and* twined *linen.*

25 And they made bells *of* pure gold, and put the bells between the pomegranates upon the hem of the robe, round about between the pomegranates;

26 A bell and a pomegranate, a bell and a pomegranate, round about the hem of the robe to minister *in;* as the LORD commanded Moses.

27 ¶ And they made coats *of* fine *a*linen *of* woven work for Aaron, and for his sons,

28 And a *a*mitre *of* fine linen, and *b*goodly *c*bonnets *of* fine linen, and linen *d*breeches *of* fine twined linen,

29 And a girdle *of* fine twined linen, and blue, and purple, and scarlet, *of* *a*needlework; as the LORD commanded Moses.

30 ¶ And they made the plate of the holy crown *of* pure gold, and wrote upon it a writing, *like to* the engravings of a signet, *a*HOLINESS TO THE LORD.

31 And they tied unto it a lace of blue, to fasten *it* on high upon the mitre; as the LORD commanded Moses.

32 ¶ Thus was all the work of the tabernacle of the tent of the congregation finished: and the children of Israel did according to all that the LORD *a*commanded Moses, so did they.

33 ¶ And they brought the *a*tabernacle unto Moses, the tent, and all *b*his furniture, his taches, his boards, his bars, and his pillars, and his sockets,

34 And the covering of rams' skins dyed red, and the covering of badgers' skins, and the *a*veil of the covering,

---

12*a* HEB opal.
15*a* OR intertwined cords.
23*a* HEB garment of mail.
27*a* Ex. 28:39;
    Ezek. 44:17.
28*a* HEB turban.

b HEB caps.
c Ezek. 44:18.
d Lev. 6:10;
    Ezek. 44:18.
29*a* TG Art.
30*a* OR CONSECRATED.

    Ex. 28:36.
32*a* TG Commandments of
    God.
33*a* Heb. 9:2 (1–28).
b OR its implements.
34*a* OR screening veil.

35 The ark of the testimony, and the staves thereof, and the mercy seat,

36 The table, *and* all the vessels thereof, and the *a*shewbread,

37 The pure candlestick, *with* the lamps thereof, *even with* the lamps to be set in order, and all the vessels thereof, and the oil for light,

38 And the golden altar, and the anointing oil, and the sweet incense, and the *a*hanging for the tabernacle door,

39 The brasen altar, and his grate of brass, his staves, and all his vessels, the laver and *a*his foot,

40 The hangings of the court, his pillars, and his sockets, and the hanging for the court gate, his cords, and his pins, and all the vessels of the service of the tabernacle, for the tent of the congregation,

41 The cloths of service to do service in the holy *place*, and the holy garments for Aaron the priest, and his sons' garments, to minister in the priest's office.

42 According to all that the LORD commanded Moses, so the children of Israel made all the work.

43 And Moses did look upon all the work, and, behold, they had done it as the LORD had commanded, even so had they done it: and Moses blessed them.

CHAPTER 40

The tabernacle is reared—Aaron and his sons are washed and anointed and given an everlasting priesthood—The glory of the Lord fills the tabernacle—A cloud covers the tabernacle by day, and fire rests on it by night.

AND the LORD spake unto Moses, saying,

2 On the first day of the first *a*month shalt thou set up the *b*tabernacle of the tent of the *c*congregation.

3 And thou shalt put therein the *a*ark of the testimony, and cover the ark with the *b*veil.

4 And thou shalt bring in the table, and *a*set in order the things that are to be set in order upon it; and thou shalt bring in the candlestick, and light the lamps thereof.

5 And thou shalt set the altar of gold for the incense before the ark of the testimony, and *a*put the hanging of the door to the tabernacle.

6 And thou shalt set the altar of the burnt offering before the door of the tabernacle of the tent of the congregation.

7 And thou shalt set the laver between the tent of the congregation and the altar, and shalt put water therein.

8 And thou shalt set up the court round about, and hang up the *a*hanging at the court gate.

9 And thou shalt take the anointing oil, and anoint the *a*tabernacle, and all that *is* therein, and shalt hallow it, and all the vessels thereof: and it shall be holy.

10 And thou shalt anoint the altar of the burnt offering, and all his vessels, and sanctify the altar: and it shall be an altar most holy.

11 And thou shalt anoint the laver and *a*his foot, and sanctify it.

12 And thou shalt bring Aaron and his sons unto the door of the *a*tabernacle of the congregation, and wash them with water.

13 And thou shalt put upon Aaron the holy garments, and *a*anoint him, and sanctify him; that he may minister unto me in the priest's office.

14 And thou shalt bring his sons, and clothe them with coats:

15 And thou shalt *a*anoint them, as thou didst anoint their father, that they may minister unto me in the *b*priest's office: for their *c*anoint

---

36*a* OR bread of the
   presence.
   TG Bread, Shewbread.
38*a* HEB screen for the
   opening.
39*a* OR its base.
40 2*a* Ex. 12:2.
  b Heb. 8:2 (2–5).

  c TG Church.
3*a* TG Ark of the Covenant.
  b TG Veil.
4*a* Ex. 26:35; Lev. 24:6 (5–6).
5*a* HEB set up the screen for.
8*a* OR screen or curtain.
9*a* TG Temple.
11*a* OR its base.

12*a* HEB tent of meeting.
13*a* TG Called of God.
15*a* Ex. 29:7; 30:30;
   Lev. 7:36.
  TG Anointing.
  b TG Priesthood, Aaronic.
  c TG Priesthood,
   Ordination.

shall surely be ᵈan ᵉeverlasting ᶠpriesthood throughout their ᵍgenerations.

16 Thus did Moses: according to all that the LORD commanded him, so did he.

17 ¶ And it came to pass in the first month in the second year, on the first *day* of the month, *that* the tabernacle was ᵃreared up.

18 And Moses reared up the tabernacle, and fastened ᵃhis sockets, and set up the boards thereof, and put in the bars thereof, and reared up his pillars.

19 And he spread abroad the tent over the tabernacle, and put the covering of the tent above upon it; as the LORD commanded Moses.

20 ¶ And he took and put the ᵃtestimony into the ark, and set the ᵇstaves on the ark, and put the mercy seat above upon the ark:

21 And he brought the ark into the tabernacle, and set up the ᵃveil of the covering, and covered the ark of the testimony; as the LORD commanded Moses.

22 ¶ And he put the table in the tent of the congregation, upon the side of the tabernacle northward, without the veil.

23 And he set the bread in ᵃorder upon it before the LORD; as the LORD had commanded Moses.

24 ¶ And he put the candlestick in the tent of the congregation, ᵃover against the table, on the side of the tabernacle southward.

25 And he lighted the ᵃlamps before the LORD; as the LORD commanded Moses.

26 ¶ And he put the golden altar in the tent of the congregation before the veil:

27 And he burnt sweet ᵃincense

thereon; as the LORD commanded Moses.

28 ¶ And he set up the hanging *at* the door of the tabernacle.

29 And he put the altar of burnt offering *by* the door of the tabernacle of the tent of the congregation, and offered upon it the burnt offering and the ᵃmeat offering; as the LORD commanded Moses.

30 ¶ And he set the laver between the tent of the congregation and the altar, and put water there, ᵃto wash *withal.*

31 And Moses and Aaron and his sons washed their hands and their feet thereat:

32 When they went into the tent of the congregation, and when they came near unto the altar, they washed; as the LORD commanded Moses.

33 And he reared up the court round about the tabernacle and the altar, and set up the hanging of the court gate. So Moses finished the work.

34 ¶ Then a ᵃcloud covered the tent of the congregation, and the ᵇglory of the LORD ᶜfilled the ᵈtabernacle.

35 And Moses was not able to enter into the tent of the congregation, because the cloud abode thereon, and the glory of the LORD filled the tabernacle.

36 And when the ᵃcloud was taken up from over the tabernacle, the children of Israel went onward in all their journeys:

37 But if the cloud were not taken up, then they ᵃjourneyed not till the day that it was taken up.

38 For the ᵃcloud of the LORD *was* upon the tabernacle by day, and fire was on it by night, in the sight of all the house of Israel, throughout all their journeys.

15d OR for an.
  e TG Eternity.
  f TG Priesthood;
     Priesthood, History of.
  g TG Birthright.
17a Num. 7:1.
18a HEB its bases.
20a 1 Kgs. 8:9.
  b OR poles.
21a OR screening veil and

    screened the ark.
23a TG Order.
24a OR opposite.
25a Ex. 25:37.
27a Ex. 30:7 (7–8).
29a OR meal or cereal.
30a OR for washings.
34a Ex. 13:21;
     D&C 84:5.
  b Ezek. 44:4;

     Hag. 2:7 (7–9);
     D&C 109:12.
     TG Jesus Christ, Glory of.
  c Lev. 16:2.
  d TG Temple.
36a Num. 10:11 (11–13).
37a Num. 9:19 (19–23).
38a Ex. 16:10;
     Num. 9:15.

THE THIRD BOOK OF MOSES

LEVITICUS

CHAPTER 1

Animals without blemish are sacrificed as an atonement for sins—Burnt offerings are a sweet savor unto the Lord.

AND the LORD *a*called unto *b*Moses, and spake unto him out of the *c*tabernacle of the congregation, saying,

2 Speak unto the children of Israel, and say unto them, If any man of you bring an offering unto the LORD, ye shall bring your offering of the cattle, *even* of the herd, and of the flock.

3 If his offering *be* a *a*burnt *b*sacrifice of the herd, let him offer a male *c*without *d*blemish: he shall offer it of his own *e*voluntary will at the door of the tabernacle of the congregation before the LORD.

4 And he shall put his *a*hand upon the head of the burnt offering; and it shall be *b*accepted for him to make *c*atonement for him.

5 And he shall kill the *a*bullock before the LORD: and the priests, Aaron's sons, shall bring the blood, and *b*sprinkle the blood round about upon the altar that *is* by the door of the tabernacle of the congregation.

6 And he shall flay the burnt offering, and cut it into his pieces.

7 And the sons of *a*Aaron the priest shall put fire upon the altar, and lay the wood in *b*order upon the fire:

8 And the priests, Aaron's sons, shall lay the parts, the head, and the fat, in order upon the wood that *is* on the fire which *is* upon the altar:

9 But his inwards and his legs shall he wash in water: and the *a*priest shall burn all on the altar, *to be* a burnt sacrifice, an offering made by fire, of a *b*sweet savour unto the LORD.

10 ¶ And if his offering *be* of the flocks, *namely,* of the sheep, or of the goats, for a burnt sacrifice; he shall bring it a male *a*without blemish.

11 And he shall kill it on the side of the altar northward before the LORD: and the priests, Aaron's sons, shall sprinkle his blood round about upon the altar.

12 And he shall cut it into his pieces, with his head and his fat: and the priest shall lay them in order on the wood that *is* on the fire which *is* upon the altar:

13 But he shall wash the inwards and the legs with water: and the priest shall bring *it* all, and burn *it* upon the altar: it *is* a *a*burnt sacrifice, an offering made by fire, of a sweet savour unto the LORD.

14 ¶ And if the burnt sacrifice for his offering to the LORD *be* of fowls, then he shall bring his offering of *a*turtledoves, or of young pigeons.

---

1 1*a* Ex. 19:3.
  b D&C 28:2.
  c HEB tent of meeting.
  3*a* Ezek. 40:39.
  b TG Sacrifice.
  c HEB whole, sound.
  d Heb. 9:14;
    1 Pet. 1:19.
  e TG Initiative.
  4*a* TG Hands, Laying on of.

  b Ex. 28:38;
    Rom. 12:1.
  c Num. 15:25;
    2 Chr. 29:24 (23–24);
    Neh. 10:33.
  5*a* HEB offspring of the
    cattle, or calf.
  b Ezek. 43:18;
    Heb. 12:24;
    3 Ne. 20:45.

  7*a* D&C 68:15; 84:30;
    132:59.
  b TG Order.
  9*a* 1 Chr. 6:49.
  b Gen. 8:21;
    Eph. 5:2.
  10*a* HEB whole, sound.
  13*a* Deut. 12:27.
  14*a* Luke 2:24.

15 And the priest shall bring it unto the altar, and wring off his head, and burn *it* on the altar; and the blood thereof shall be wrung out at the side of the altar:

16 And he shall pluck away his crop with his feathers, and cast it beside the altar on the east part, by the place of the ashes:

17 And he shall cleave it with the wings thereof, *but* shall not divide *it* asunder: and the priest shall burn it upon the altar, upon the wood that *is* upon the fire: it *is* a burnt sacrifice, an offering made by fire, of a sweet savour unto the LORD.

CHAPTER 2

How offerings of flour with oil and incense are made.

AND when any will offer ᵃa meat offering unto the LORD, his offering shall be *of* fine flour; and he shall pour oil upon it, and put ᵇfrankincense thereon:

2 And he shall bring it to Aaron's sons the priests: and he shall take thereout his handful of the flour thereof, and of the oil thereof, with all the frankincense thereof; and the priest shall burn the memorial of it upon the altar, *to be* an offering made by fire, of a sweet savour unto the LORD:

3 And the remnant of the ᵃmeat offering *shall be* ᵇAaron's and his sons': it *is* a thing most holy of the offerings of the LORD made by fire.

4 ¶ And if thou bring an oblation of a meat offering ᵃbaken in the oven, it shall be ᵇunleavened cakes of fine flour mingled with oil, or unleavened wafers anointed with oil.

5 ¶ And if thy oblation *be* a meat offering *baken* in a pan, it shall be *of* fine flour unleavened, mingled with oil.

6 Thou shalt part it in pieces, and pour oil thereon: it *is* a meat offering.

7 ¶ And if thy oblation *be* a meat offering *baken* in the fryingpan, it shall be made *of* fine flour with oil.

8 And thou shalt bring the meat offering that is made of these things unto the LORD: and when it is presented unto the priest, he shall bring it unto the altar.

9 And the priest shall take from the meat offering a memorial thereof, and shall burn *it* upon the altar: *it is* an offering made by fire, of a sweet savour unto the LORD.

10 And that which is left of the meat offering *shall be* Aaron's and his sons': *it is* a thing most holy of the offerings of the LORD made by fire.

11 No meat offering, which ye shall bring unto the LORD, shall be made with ᵃleaven: for ye shall burn no leaven, nor any honey, in any offering of the LORD made by fire.

12 ¶ As for the oblation of the ᵃfirstfruits, ye shall offer them unto the LORD: but they shall not be burnt on the altar for a sweet savour.

13 And every oblation of thy meat offering shalt thou season with salt; neither shalt thou suffer the salt of the covenant of thy God to be lacking from thy meat offering: with all thine offerings thou shalt offer ᵃsalt.

14 And if thou offer a meat offering of thy firstfruits unto the LORD, thou shalt offer for the meat offering of thy firstfruits green ears of corn dried by the fire, *even* corn beaten out of full ears.

15 And thou shalt put oil upon it, and lay frankincense thereon: it *is* a meat offering.

16 And the priest shall burn the memorial of it, *part* of the beaten corn thereof, and *part* of the oil thereof, with all the frankincense thereof: *it is* an offering made by fire unto the LORD.

---

2 1a OR the evening sacrifice.
    Ezek. 42:13.
  b Matt. 2:11.
  3a Num. 18:9.

  b Lev. 6:16.
  4a Ezek. 46:20.
  b Ex. 29:2.
  11a TG Leaven.

  12a Ex. 23:19.
  13a TG Salt.

CHAPTER 3

Peace offerings are made with animals without blemish, whose blood is sprinkled on the altar—Israel is forbidden to eat fat or blood.

AND if his oblation be a *a*sacrifice of peace *b*offering, if he offer *it* of the herd; whether *it be* a male or female, he shall offer it *c*without blemish before the LORD.

2 And he shall lay his hand upon the head of his offering, and kill it *at* the door of the tabernacle of the congregation: and *a*Aaron's sons the priests shall *b*sprinkle the blood upon the altar round about.

3 And he shall offer of the sacrifice of the peace offering an offering made by fire unto the LORD; the fat that covereth the inwards, and all the fat that *is* upon the inwards,

4 And the two kidneys, and the fat that *is* on them, which *is* by the flanks, and the caul above the liver, with the kidneys, it shall he take away.

5 And Aaron's sons shall burn it on the altar upon the burnt sacrifice, which *is* upon the wood that *is* on the fire: *it is* an offering made by fire, of a sweet savour unto the LORD.

6 ¶ And if his offering for a sacrifice of peace offering unto the LORD *be* of the flock; male or female, he shall offer it without *a*blemish.

7 If he offer a lamb for his offering, then shall he offer it before the LORD.

8 And he shall lay his hand upon the head of his offering, and kill it before the tabernacle of the congregation: and Aaron's sons shall sprinkle the blood thereof round about upon the altar.

9 And he shall offer of the sacrifice of the peace offering an offering made by fire unto the LORD; the fat thereof, *and* the whole rump, it shall he take off hard by the backbone;

and the fat that covereth the inwards, and all the fat that *is* upon the inwards,

10 And the two kidneys, and the fat that *is* upon them, which *is* by the flanks, and the caul above the liver, with the kidneys, it shall he take away.

11 And the priest shall burn it upon the altar: *it is* the *a*food of the offering made by *b*fire unto the LORD.

12 ¶ And if his offering *be* a goat, then he shall offer it before the LORD.

13 And he shall lay his hand upon the head of it, and kill it before the tabernacle of the congregation: and the sons of Aaron shall sprinkle the blood thereof upon the altar round about.

14 And he shall offer thereof his offering, *even* an offering made by fire unto the LORD; the fat that covereth the inwards, and all the fat that *is* upon the inwards,

15 And the two kidneys, and the fat that *is* upon them, which *is* by the flanks, and the caul above the liver, with the kidneys, it shall he take away.

16 And the priest shall burn them upon the altar: *it is* the food of the offering made by fire for a sweet savour: all the fat *is* the LORD's.

17 *It shall be* a perpetual statute for your generations throughout all your dwellings, that ye eat neither *a*fat nor *b*blood.

CHAPTER 4

Sinners are forgiven through sin offerings of animals without blemish—Priests thereby make an atonement for the sins of the people.

AND the LORD spake unto Moses, saying,

2 Speak unto the children of Israel, saying, If a soul shall sin *a*through *b*ignorance against any of the commandments of the LORD *concerning*

---

3 1*a* TG Sacrifice.
  b 2 Chr. 29:35.
  c HEB whole, sound.
  2*a* TG Priesthood, Aaronic.
  b Num. 18:17.

6*a* Heb. 7:26 (26–27);
    1 Pet. 1:19 (18–19).
  11*a* Ezek. 44:7.
  b Lev. 21:6 (6, 21).
  17*a* Lev. 7:25; Ezek. 44:7.

  b TG Blood, Eating of.
4 2*a* IE in error or
    inadvertently.
  b TG Accountability;
    Ignorance.

things which ought not to be done, and shall do against any of them:

3 If the priest that is anointed do *a*sin according to the sin of the people; then let him bring for his sin, which he hath sinned, a *b*young bullock without blemish unto the LORD for a *c*sin *d*offering.

4 And he shall bring the bullock unto the door of the tabernacle of the congregation before the LORD; and shall lay his hand upon the bullock's head, and kill the bullock before the LORD.

5 And the priest that is anointed shall take of the bullock's *a*blood, and bring it to the tabernacle of the congregation:

6 And the priest shall dip his finger in the blood, and sprinkle of the blood seven times before the LORD, before the veil of the sanctuary.

7 And the priest shall put *some* of the blood upon the *a*horns of the altar of sweet incense before the LORD, which *is* in the tabernacle of the congregation; and shall *b*pour all the blood of the bullock at the bottom of the altar of the burnt offering, which *is at* the door of the tabernacle of the congregation.

8 And he shall take off from it all the fat of the bullock for the sin offering; the fat that covereth the inwards, and all the fat that *is* upon the inwards,

9 And the two kidneys, and the fat that *is* upon them, which *is* by the flanks, and the caul above the liver, with the kidneys, it shall he take away,

10 As it was taken off from the bullock of the sacrifice of peace offerings: and the priest shall burn them upon the altar of the burnt offering.

11 And the skin of the *a*bullock, and all his flesh, with his head, and with his legs, and his inwards, and his dung,

12 Even the whole bullock shall he carry forth *a*without the camp unto a clean place, where the ashes are poured out, and burn him on the wood with fire: where the ashes are poured out shall he be burnt.

13 ¶ And if the whole congregation of Israel sin through *a*ignorance, and the thing be hid from the eyes of the assembly, and they have done *somewhat against* any of the commandments of the LORD *concerning things* which should not be done, and are *b*guilty;

14 When the sin, which they have sinned against it, is known, then the congregation shall *a*offer a young bullock for the sin, and bring him before the tabernacle of the congregation.

15 And the elders of the *a*congregation shall lay their hands upon the head of the bullock before the LORD: and the bullock shall be killed before the LORD.

16 And the priest that is anointed shall bring of the bullock's blood to the tabernacle of the congregation:

17 And the priest shall dip his finger *in some* of the blood, and sprinkle *it* seven times before the LORD, *even* before the veil.

18 And he shall put *some* of the blood upon the horns of the altar which *is* before the LORD, that *is* in the tabernacle of the congregation, and shall pour out all the blood at the bottom of the altar of the burnt offering, which *is at* the door of the tabernacle of the congregation.

19 And he shall take all his fat from him, and burn *it* upon the altar.

20 And he shall do with the bullock as he did with the bullock for a sin offering, so shall he do with this: and the priest shall make an *a*atonement for them, and it shall be *b*forgiven them.

21 And he shall carry forth the

3*a* Heb. 5:3.
  b OR male calf.
  c Ezek. 40:39; 42:13.
  d TG Sacrifice.
5*a* Lev. 16:14; Num. 19:4;
    Heb. 9:13 (13–14).
7*a* Lev. 8:15; 9:9; 16:18.

  b Ex. 29:12; Lev. 8:15.
11*a* Ex. 29:14 (1–14).
12*a* Heb. 13:12 (11–12).
13*a* Mosiah 3:11.
  b TG Guilt.
14*a* 2 Chr. 29:21 (1–29).
15*a* TG Church.

20*a* Ex. 30:10; Num. 15:25;
    1 Chr. 6:49;
    Heb. 10:11 (10–12);
    2 Ne. 9:26;
    Mosiah 3:15;
    13:28 (28–32).
  b TG Forgive.

bullock without the camp, and burn him as he burned the first bullock: it *is* a sin offering for the congregation.

22 ¶ When a ^aruler hath sinned, and done *somewhat* through ignorance *against* any of the commandments of the LORD his God *concerning things* which should not be done, and is guilty;

23 Or if his ^asin, wherein he hath sinned, come to his knowledge; he shall bring his offering, a kid of the goats, a male without blemish:

24 And he shall lay his hand upon the head of the goat, and kill it in the place where they kill the burnt offering before the LORD: it *is* a ^asin offering.

25 And the priest shall take of the blood of the sin offering with his finger, and put *it* upon the horns of the altar of burnt offering, and shall pour out his blood at the bottom of the altar of burnt offering.

26 And he shall burn all his fat upon the altar, as the fat of the sacrifice of peace offerings: and the priest shall make an ^aatonement for him as concerning his sin, and it shall be forgiven him.

27 ¶ And if any one of the common people sin through ^aignorance, while he doeth *somewhat against* any of the commandments of the LORD *concerning things* which ought not to be done, and be guilty;

28 Or if his sin, which he hath sinned, come to his knowledge: then he shall bring his offering, a kid of the goats, a female without blemish, for his sin which he hath sinned.

29 And he shall lay his hand upon the head of the sin offering, and slay the sin offering in the place of the burnt offering.

30 And the priest shall take of the blood thereof with his finger, and put *it* upon the horns of the altar of burnt offering, and shall pour out

all the blood thereof at the bottom of the altar.

31 And he shall take away all the fat thereof, as the fat is taken away from off the sacrifice of peace offerings; and the priest shall burn *it* upon the altar for a sweet savour unto the LORD; and the priest shall make an ^aatonement for him, and it shall be forgiven him.

32 And if he bring a lamb for a sin offering, he shall bring it a female without blemish.

33 And he shall lay his hand upon the head of the sin offering, and slay it for a sin offering in the place where they kill the burnt offering.

34 And the priest shall take of the blood of the sin offering with his finger, and put *it* upon the horns of the altar of burnt offering, and shall pour out all the blood thereof at the bottom of the altar:

35 And he shall take away all the fat thereof, as the fat of the lamb is taken away from the sacrifice of the peace offerings; and the priest shall burn them upon the altar, according to the offerings made by fire unto the LORD: and the priest shall make an atonement for his sin that he hath committed, and it shall be forgiven him.

CHAPTER 5

The people are to confess and make amends for their sins—Forgiveness comes through a trespass offering—Priests thereby make an atonement for sin.

AND if a soul sin, and hear the voice of ^aswearing, and *is* a witness, whether he hath seen or known *of it*; if he do not utter *it*, then he shall ^bbear his iniquity.

2 Or if a soul touch any ^aunclean thing, whether *it be* a carcase of an unclean beast, or a carcase of unclean cattle, or the carcase of unclean creeping things, and *if it be*

---

22 *a* OR president or prince.
  D&C 63:55.
23 *a* 2 Kgs. 12:16.
24 *a* Num. 18:9.
26 *a* 2 Chr. 29:24.

27 *a* Ezek. 45:20.
31 *a* TG Jesus Christ,
  Atonement through.
5 1 *a* IE an oath or curse.
  b Lev. 7:18; 19:8.

2 *a* Lev. 11:24 (24–39);
  Num. 19:11 (11–16).
  TG Uncleanness.

hidden from him; he also shall be unclean, and *b*guilty.

3 Or if he touch the uncleanness of man, whatsoever uncleanness *it be* that a man shall be defiled withal, and it be hid from him; when he knoweth *of it,* then he shall be guilty.

4 Or if a soul *a*swear, pronouncing with *his* lips to do evil, or to do good, whatsoever *it be* that a man shall pronounce with an oath, and it be hid from him; when he knoweth *of it,* then he shall be guilty in one of these.

5 And it shall be, when he shall be guilty in one of these *things,* that he shall *a*confess that he hath sinned in that *thing:*

6 And he shall bring his *a*trespass offering unto the LORD for his sin which he hath sinned, a female from the flock, a lamb or a kid of the goats, for a sin offering; and the priest shall make an atonement for him concerning his sin.

7 And if he be not *a*able to bring a lamb, then he shall bring for his trespass, which he hath committed, two *b*turtledoves, or two young pigeons, unto the LORD; one for a sin offering, and the other for a burnt offering.

8 And he shall bring them unto the priest, who shall offer *that* which *is* for the sin offering first, and wring off his head from his neck, but shall not divide *it* asunder:

9 And he shall sprinkle of the blood of the sin offering upon the side of the altar; and the rest of the blood shall be wrung out at the bottom of the altar: it *is* a sin offering.

10 And he shall offer the second *for* a burnt offering, according to *a*the manner: and the priest shall make an atonement for him for his sin which he hath sinned, and it shall be forgiven him.

11 ¶ But if he be not able to bring two turtledoves, or two young pigeons, then he that sinned shall bring for his offering the tenth part of an ephah of fine flour for a sin offering; he shall put no oil upon it, neither shall he put *any* frankincense thereon: for it *is* a sin offering.

12 Then shall he bring it to the priest, and the priest shall take his handful of it, *even* a memorial thereof, and burn *it* on the altar, according to the offerings made by fire unto the LORD: it *is* a sin offering.

13 And the priest shall make an atonement for him as touching his sin that he hath sinned in one of these, and it shall be forgiven him: and *the remnant* shall be the priest's, as a *a*meat offering.

14 ¶ And the LORD spake unto Moses, saying,

15 If a soul commit a trespass, and sin through ignorance, in the holy things of the LORD; then he shall bring for his *a*trespass unto the LORD a ram without blemish out of the flocks, *b*with thy estimation by shekels of silver, after the shekel of the sanctuary, for a trespass offering:

16 And he shall make *a*amends for the harm that he hath done in the holy thing, and shall add the fifth part thereto, and give it unto the priest: and the priest shall make an atonement for him with the ram of the *b*trespass offering, and it shall be forgiven him.

17 ¶ And if a soul *a*sin, and commit any of these things which are forbidden to be done by the commandments of the LORD; though he wist *it* not, yet is he guilty, and shall *b*bear his iniquity.

18 And he shall bring a ram without blemish out of the flock, with thy estimation, for a trespass offering, unto the priest: and the priest shall make an atonement for him concerning his ignorance wherein he

---

2 *b* TG Guilt.
4 *a* 3 Ne. 12:34 (34–37).
5 *a* Num. 5:7 (6–10);
    2 Chr. 30:22 (2–27).
    TG Confession.
6 *a* HEB guilt sacrifice.

Ezek. 40:39.
7 *a* Lev. 12:8; 14:21.
  b Luke 2:24.
10 *a* HEB the statute.
13 *a* IE evening sacrifice.
15 *a* 2 Kgs. 12:16.

  b IE by your valuation in
    weights of silver.
16 *a* D&C 98:47.
  b 1 Sam. 6:3.
17 *a* D&C 1:31 (31–32).
  b TG Accountability.

erred and wist *it* not, and it shall be forgiven him.

19 It *is* a trespass offering: he hath certainly trespassed against the LORD.

CHAPTER 6

The people must first make restitution for sin, then offer a trespass offering, and thereby gain forgiveness through atonement made by the priests.

AND the LORD spake unto Moses, saying,

2 If a soul sin, and commit a trespass against the LORD, and *ª*lie unto his neighbour in that which was delivered him to keep, or in fellowship, or in a thing taken away by violence, or hath deceived his neighbour;

3 Or have found that which was lost, and lieth concerning it, and sweareth falsely; in any of all these that a man doeth, sinning therein:

4 Then it shall be, because he hath sinned, and is *ª*guilty, that he shall *b*restore that which he took violently away, or the thing which he hath *c*deceitfully gotten, or that which was delivered him to keep, or the *d*lost thing which he found,

5 Or all that about which he hath sworn falsely; he shall even restore it in the principal, and shall add the fifth part more thereto, *and* give it unto him to whom it appertaineth, in the day of his trespass offering.

6 And he shall bring his trespass offering unto the LORD, a ram without blemish out of the flock, with thy estimation, for a trespass offering, unto the priest:

7 And the priest shall make an atonement for him before the LORD: and it shall be forgiven him for any thing of all that he hath done in trespassing therein.

8 ¶ And the LORD spake unto Moses, saying,

9 Command Aaron and his sons, saying, This *is* the *ª*law of the burnt offering: It *is* the burnt offering, because of the burning upon the altar all night unto the morning, and the fire of the altar shall be burning in it.

10 And the priest shall put on his linen *ª*garment, and his linen *b*breeches shall he put upon his flesh, and take up the ashes which the fire hath consumed with the burnt offering on the altar, and he shall put them beside the altar.

11 And he shall put off his garments, and put on other *ª*garments, and carry forth the ashes without the camp unto a clean place.

12 And the fire upon the altar shall be burning in it; it shall not be put out: and the priest shall burn wood on it every morning, and lay the burnt offering in order upon it; and he shall burn thereon the fat of the peace *ª*offerings.

13 The fire shall ever be burning upon the altar; it shall never go out.

14 ¶ And this *is* the law of the *ª*meat offering: the sons of Aaron shall offer it before the LORD, before the altar.

15 And he shall take of it his handful, of the flour of the meat offering, and of the oil thereof, and all the frankincense which *is* upon the meat offering, and shall burn *it* upon the altar *for* a sweet savour, *even* the memorial of it, unto the LORD.

16 And the remainder thereof shall *ª*Aaron and his sons eat: with unleavened bread shall it be eaten in the holy *b*place; in the court of the tabernacle of the congregation they shall eat it.

17 It shall not be baken with *ª*leaven. I have given it *unto them for* their portion of my offerings made by fire; it *is* most holy, as *is* the sin offering, and as the trespass offering.

18 All the males among the

---

6 2*a* TG Lying.
4*a* TG Guilt.
  b D&C 98:47.
     TG Repent.
  c TG Deceit.
  d D&C 136:26.

9*a* 2 Ne. 25:24.
10*a* Ex. 28:39 (39–42).
     TG Apparel.
   b Ex. 39:28;
     Ezek. 44:18.
11*a* 1 Ne. 12:10 (10–11);

D&C 88:85.
12*a* TG Sacrifice.
14*a* Ezek. 44:29.
16*a* Lev. 2:3.
   b Num. 18:10.
17*a* TG Leaven.

children of Aaron shall eat of it. *It shall be* a statute for ever in your generations concerning the offerings of the LORD made by fire: every one that toucheth them shall be holy.

19 ¶ And the LORD spake unto Moses, saying,

20 This *is* the offering of Aaron and of his sons, which they shall offer unto the LORD in the day when he is anointed; the tenth part of an ephah of fine flour for [a]a meat offering perpetual, half of it in the morning, and half thereof at night.

21 In a pan it shall be made with oil; *and when it is* baken, thou shalt bring it in: *and* the baken pieces of the meat offering shalt thou offer *for* a sweet savour unto the LORD.

22 And the priest of his sons that is anointed in his stead shall offer it: *it is* a statute for ever unto the LORD; it shall be wholly burnt.

23 For every meat offering for the priest shall be wholly burnt: it shall not be eaten.

24 ¶ And the LORD spake unto Moses, saying,

25 Speak unto Aaron and to his sons, saying, This *is* the law of the sin offering: In the place where the burnt offering is killed shall the [a]sin offering be killed before the LORD: it *is* most holy.

26 The priest that offereth it for sin shall [a]eat it: in the holy place shall it be eaten, in the court of the tabernacle of the congregation.

27 Whatsoever shall touch the flesh thereof shall be holy: and when there is sprinkled of the blood thereof upon any garment, thou shalt wash that whereon it was sprinkled in the holy place.

28 But the earthen vessel wherein it is sodden shall be [a]broken: and if it be sodden in a brasen pot, it shall be both scoured, and rinsed in water.

29 All the males among the priests shall eat thereof: it *is* most holy.

30 And no sin offering, whereof *any* of the blood is brought into the tabernacle of the congregation to [a]reconcile *withal* in the holy *place,* shall be eaten: it shall be burnt in the fire.

CHAPTER 7

Laws governing various sacrifices are listed—The children of Israel are forbidden to eat fat or blood—They worship by sacrifice—Through sacrifice they gain forgiveness, make vows, consecrate their property, render thanks, and are reconciled to God.

LIKEWISE this *is* the [a]law of the trespass offering: it *is* most holy.

2 In the place where they kill the burnt offering shall they kill the trespass offering: and the blood thereof shall he sprinkle round about upon the altar.

3 And he shall offer of it all the fat thereof; the rump, and the fat that covereth the inwards,

4 And the two kidneys, and the fat that *is* on them, which *is* by the flanks, and the caul *that is* above the liver, with the kidneys, it shall he take away:

5 And the priest shall burn them upon the altar *for* an offering made by fire unto the LORD: it *is* a trespass offering.

6 Every male among the priests shall eat thereof: it shall be eaten [a]in the holy place: it *is* most holy.

7 As the [a]sin offering *is,* so *is* the [b]trespass offering: *there is* one law for them: the priest that maketh atonement therewith shall have *it.*

8 And the priest that offereth any man's burnt offering, *even* the priest shall have to himself the skin of the burnt offering which he hath offered.

9 And all the meat offering that is baken in the oven, and all that is dressed in the fryingpan, and in the pan, shall be the priest's that offereth it.

20a IE a continual meal offering.
25a Num. 18:9; Mosiah 15:10 (1–12).
26a Lev. 10:13; Ezek. 42:13.
28a Lev. 11:33; 15:12.
30a Jacob 4:11.
7 1a HEB teaching

concerning.
6a HEB in a holy place.
7a 2 Kgs. 12:16.
  b Num. 18:9.

10 And every meat offering, mingled with oil, and dry, shall all the sons of Aaron have, one *as much* as another.

11 And this *is* the law of the *a*sacrifice of peace offerings, which he shall offer unto the LORD.

12 If he offer it for a *a*thanksgiving, then he shall offer with the sacrifice of *b*thanksgiving unleavened cakes mingled with oil, and unleavened wafers anointed with oil, and cakes mingled with oil, of fine flour, fried.

13 Besides the cakes, he shall offer *for* his offering leavened bread with the sacrifice of thanksgiving of his peace offerings.

14 *a*And of it he shall offer one out of the whole oblation *for* an heave offering unto the LORD, *and* it shall be the priest's that sprinkleth the blood of the peace offerings.

15 And the flesh of the sacrifice of his peace offerings for thanksgiving shall be *a*eaten the same day that it is offered; he shall not leave any of it until the morning.

16 But if the sacrifice of his offering *be* a vow, or a *a*voluntary offering, it shall be eaten the same day that he offereth his sacrifice: and on the morrow also the remainder of it shall be eaten:

17 But the remainder of the flesh of the sacrifice on the third day shall be burnt with fire.

18 And if *any* of the flesh of the sacrifice of his peace offerings be eaten at all on the third day, it shall not be *a*accepted, neither shall it be imputed unto him that offereth it: it shall be an *b*abomination, and the soul that eateth of it shall *c*bear his iniquity.

19 And the flesh that toucheth any unclean *thing* shall not be eaten; it shall be burnt with fire: and as for the flesh, all that be clean shall eat thereof.

20 But the soul that eateth *of* the flesh of the sacrifice of peace offerings, that *pertain* unto the LORD, having his uncleanness upon him, even that soul shall be *a*cut off from his people.

21 Moreover the soul that shall touch any unclean *thing, as* the uncleanness of man, or *any* unclean beast, or any abominable unclean *thing,* and eat of the flesh of the sacrifice of peace offerings, which *pertain* unto the LORD, even that soul shall be *a*cut off from his people.

22 ¶ And the LORD *a*spake unto Moses, saying,

23 Speak unto the children of Israel, saying, Ye shall eat no manner of fat, of ox, or of sheep, or of goat.

24 And the fat of the beast that *a*dieth of itself, and the fat of that which is torn with beasts, may be used in any other use: but ye shall in no wise eat of it.

25 For whosoever eateth the *a*fat of the beast, of which men offer an offering made by fire unto the LORD, even the soul that eateth *it* shall be cut off from his people.

26 Moreover ye shall eat no manner of blood, *whether it be* of fowl or of beast, in any of your dwellings.

27 Whatsoever soul *it be* that eateth any manner of blood, even that soul shall be cut off from his people.

28 ¶ And the LORD spake unto Moses, saying,

29 Speak unto the children of Israel, saying, He that offereth the sacrifice of his peace offerings unto the LORD shall bring his oblation unto the LORD of the sacrifice of his peace offerings.

30 His own hands shall bring the offerings of the LORD made by fire, the fat with the breast, it shall he bring, that the breast may be waved *for* a wave offering before the LORD.

11a TG Sacrifice.
12a 2 Chr. 29:31.
    TG Thanksgiving.
  b Ps. 107:22.
14a HEB And of it he shall sacrifice one for every sacrifice that is due to

the LORD.
15a Lev. 22:30 (29–30).
16a Lev. 22:23; Ezek. 46:12;
    D&C 58:27 (26–28).
18a D&C 132:9 (7–12).
  b Lev. 19:7;
    Ezek. 4:14;

3 Ne. 18:28 (28–31).
  c Lev. 5:1 (1–6).
20a 2 Ne. 2:5; D&C 1:14.
21a TG Excommunication.
22a D&C 1:38.
24a Ezek. 4:14.
25a Lev. 3:17.

31 And the priest shall burn the fat upon the altar: but the breast shall be ^aAaron's and his sons'.

32 And the right shoulder shall ye give unto the priest for ^aan heave offering of the sacrifices of your peace offerings.

33 He among the sons of Aaron, that offereth the blood of the peace offerings, and the fat, shall have the right ^ashoulder ^bfor *his* part.

34 For the wave breast and the ^aheave shoulder have I taken of the children of Israel from off the sacrifices of their peace offerings, and have given them unto Aaron the priest and unto his sons by a statute for ever from among the children of Israel.

35 ¶ This *is the portion* of the anointing of Aaron, and of the anointing of his sons, out of the offerings of the LORD made by fire, in the day *when* he presented them to minister unto the LORD in the ^apriest's office;

36 Which the LORD commanded to be given them of the children of Israel, in the day that he ^aanointed them, *by* a statute for ever throughout their generations.

37 This *is* the law of the burnt offering, of the meat offering, and of the sin offering, and of the trespass offering, and of the consecrations, and of the sacrifice of the peace offerings;

38 Which the LORD commanded Moses in mount Sinai, in the day that he commanded the children of Israel to offer their oblations unto the LORD, in the wilderness of Sinai.

CHAPTER 8

Aaron and his sons are washed, anointed, clothed in their priesthood robes, and consecrated before all Israel—Moses and Aaron offer sacrifices to make reconciliation and atonement with the Lord.

AND the LORD spake unto Moses, saying,

2 Take Aaron and his sons with him, and the garments, and the anointing oil, and a ^abullock for the sin offering, and two rams, and a basket of unleavened bread;

3 And gather thou all the ^acongregation together unto the door of the tabernacle of the congregation.

4 And Moses did as the LORD commanded him; and the assembly was gathered together unto the door of the tabernacle of the congregation.

5 And Moses said unto the congregation, This *is* the thing which the LORD commanded to be done.

6 And Moses brought Aaron and his sons, and ^awashed them with water.

7 And he put upon him the ^acoat, and girded him with the girdle, and clothed him with the ^brobe, and put the ephod upon him, and he girded him with the curious girdle of the ephod, and bound *it* unto him therewith.

8 And he put the ^abreastplate upon him: also he put in the breastplate the ^bUrim and the Thummim.

9 And he put ^athe mitre upon his head; also upon the mitre, *even* upon his forefront, did he put the golden ^bplate, the holy crown; as the LORD commanded Moses.

10 And Moses took the anointing oil, and ^aanointed the tabernacle and all that *was* therein, and ^bsanctified them.

11 And he sprinkled thereof upon the altar seven times, and anointed the altar and all his vessels, both

31*a* Num. 18:8 (8–24);
    Deut. 18:3 (1–5).
32*a* IE a contribution.
    Mosiah 18:28 (25–29).
33*a* 1 Sam. 2:14.
  b HEB as a present.
34*a* Num. 18:11.
35*a* Luke 1:9;
    D&C 107:20.
36*a* Ex. 40:15 (13–15).

8 2*a* Ex. 29:1 (1–14).
  3*a* TG Church.
  6*a* Ex. 29:4;
    D&C 124:37 (37–39).
  7*a* Ex. 28:4; 29:5.
  b 2 Ne. 9:14;
    D&C 109:76.
  8*a* D&C 27:16 (15–18);
    JS—H 1:35.
  b TG Urim and Thummim.

9*a* HEB the cap (or turban)
    upon his head, and he
    put the golden diadem,
    the holy crown, upon
    the front face of the
    cap (or turban).
  b Ex. 28:36.
10*a* TG Anointing.
  b D&C 84:23.

the laver and his foot, to sanctify them.

12 And he poured of the ªanointing oil upon ᵇAaron's head, and anointed him, to sanctify him.

13 And Moses brought Aaron's ªsons, ᵇand put coats upon them, and ᶜgirded them with girdles, and put ᵈbonnets upon them; as the LORD commanded Moses.

14 And he brought the bullock for the ªsin offering: and Aaron and his sons laid their hands upon the head of the bullock for the sin offering.

15 And he slew it; and Moses took the blood, and put it upon the ªhorns of the altar round about with his finger, and purified the ᵇaltar, and ᶜpoured the blood at the bottom of the altar, and sanctified it, ᵈto make reconciliation upon it.

16 And he took all the fat that was upon the inwards, and the caul above the liver, and the two kidneys, and their fat, and Moses burned it upon the altar.

17 But the bullock, and his hide, his flesh, and his dung, he burnt with fire without the camp; as the LORD commanded Moses.

18 ¶ And he brought the ram for the burnt offering: and Aaron and his sons laid their hands upon the head of the ram.

19 And he killed it; and Moses sprinkled the blood upon the altar round about.

20 And he cut the ram into pieces; and Moses burnt the head, and the pieces, and the fat.

21 And he washed the inwards and the legs in water; and Moses burnt the whole ram upon the altar: it was a burnt sacrifice for a sweet savour, and an offering made by fire unto the LORD; as the LORD commanded Moses.

22 ¶ And he brought the other ªram, the ram of consecration: and Aaron and his sons laid their hands upon the head of the ram.

23 And he slew it; and Moses took of the blood of it, and put it upon the tip of Aaron's right ear, and upon the thumb of his right hand, and upon the great toe of his right foot.

24 And he brought Aaron's sons, and Moses put of the blood upon the tip of their right ear, and upon the thumbs of their right hands, and upon the great toes of their right feet: and Moses ªsprinkled the blood upon the altar round about.

25 And he took the fat, and the rump, and all the fat that was upon the inwards, and the caul above the liver, and the two kidneys, and their fat, and the right shoulder:

26 And out of the basket of unleavened bread, that was before the LORD, he took one unleavened cake, and a cake of oiled bread, and one wafer, and put them on the fat, and upon the right shoulder:

27 And he put all upon Aaron's hands, and upon his sons' hands, and waved them for a wave offering before the LORD.

28 And Moses took them from off their hands, and burnt them on the altar upon the burnt offering: they were consecrations for a sweet savour: it is an offering made by fire unto the LORD.

29 And Moses took the breast, and waved it for a wave offering before the LORD: for of the ram of consecration it was Moses' part; as the LORD commanded Moses.

30 And Moses took of the anointing oil, and of the blood which was upon the altar, and ªsprinkled it upon Aaron, and upon his garments, and upon his sons, and upon his sons' garments with him; and ᵇsanctified Aaron, and his garments, and his

---

12 a D&C 109:35.
   TG Priesthood, Ordination.
   b TG Priesthood, Aaronic.
13 a D&C 84:6, 18 (6–26),
      34 (33–41).
   b HEB and dressed them in
      shirts.

c Ex. 29:9 (8–9).
d HEB caps.
14 a Ezek. 43:19.
15 a Lev. 4:7.
   b Ex. 29:12 (1–14).
   c Lev. 4:7.
   d HEB to atone for it.

TG Reconciliation.
22 a Ex. 29:19.
24 a 2 Chr. 29:22 (1–29).
30 a Isa. 63:3 (2–4);
      D&C 133:51.
   b Alma 13:11 (11–13);
      Moses 6:60 (59–60).

sons, and his sons' garments with him.

31 ¶ And Moses said unto Aaron and to his sons, ªBoil the flesh *at* the door of the tabernacle of the congregation: and there eat it with the bread that *is* in the basket of consecrations, as I commanded, saying, Aaron and his sons shall eat it.

32 And that which remaineth of the flesh and of the bread shall ye burn with fire.

33 And ye shall not go out of the door of the tabernacle of the congregation *in* seven ªdays, until the days of your consecration be at an end: for ᵇseven days shall he consecrate you.

34 As he hath done this day, *so* the LORD hath commanded to do, to make an atonement for you.

35 Therefore ªshall ye abide *at* the door of the tabernacle of the congregation day and night seven days, and keep the ᵇcharge of the LORD, that ye die not: for so I am commanded.

36 So Aaron and his sons did all things which the LORD commanded by the hand of Moses.

CHAPTER 9

Aaron makes an atonement by sacrifice for himself and all Israel—He and his sons offer sacrifices—The glory of the Lord appears to all—Fire from the Lord consumes the offerings on the altar.

AND it came to pass on the ªeighth day, *that* Moses called Aaron and his sons, and the ᵇelders of Israel;

2 And he said unto Aaron, Take thee a young calf for a sin offering, and a ram for a burnt offering, without blemish, and offer *them* before the LORD.

3 And unto the children of Israel thou shalt speak, saying, Take ye a kid of the ªgoats for a sin offering;

and a calf and a lamb, *both* of the first year, without blemish, for a burnt offering;

4 Also a bullock and a ram for peace offerings, to sacrifice before the LORD; and a meat offering mingled with oil: for to day the LORD will ªappear unto you.

5 ¶ And they brought *that* which Moses commanded before the tabernacle of the congregation: and all the congregation drew ªnear and stood before the LORD.

6 And Moses said, This *is* the thing which the LORD commanded that ye should do: and the ªglory of the LORD shall appear unto you.

7 And Moses said unto Aaron, Go unto the altar, and offer thy sin offering, and thy burnt offering, and make an atonement for thyself, and for the people: and offer the offering of the people, and make an atonement for them; as the LORD commanded.

8 ¶ Aaron therefore went unto the altar, and slew the calf of the sin offering, which *was* for himself.

9 And the sons of Aaron brought the blood unto him: and he dipped his finger in the blood, and put *it* upon the ªhorns of the altar, and poured out the blood at the bottom of the altar:

10 But the fat, and the kidneys, and the caul above the liver of the sin offering, he burnt upon the altar; as the LORD commanded Moses.

11 And the flesh and the hide he burnt with fire without the camp.

12 And he slew the burnt offering; and Aaron's sons presented unto him the blood, which he sprinkled round about upon the altar.

13 And they presented the burnt offering unto him, with the pieces thereof, and the head: and he burnt *them* upon the altar.

14 And he did wash the inwards

31ª Ex. 29:31 (31–34).
33ª Luke 1:23.
    ᵇ Ex. 29:35 (35–36);
       Ezek. 43:25.
35ª HEB by the opening of
       the tent of meeting you

          shall sit.
        ᵇ Num. 3:7; Deut. 11:1.
9 1ª Ezek. 43:27.
        ᵇ Alma 6:1; D&C 46:2.
    3ª Lev. 10:16 (16–19).
    4ª D&C 67:10 (10–12);

        88:68; 93:1.
    5ª TG God, Access to.
    6ª Lev. 9:23;
        2 Ne. 1:15;
        Ether 12:6 (6–18).
    9ª Lev. 4:7.

and the legs, and burnt *them* upon the burnt offering on the altar.

15 ¶ And he brought the people's offering, and took the goat, which *was* the sin *^a*offering for the people, and slew it, and offered it for sin, as the first.

16 And he brought the burnt offering, and offered it according to the *^a*manner.

17 And he brought the meat offering, and took an handful thereof, and burnt *it* upon the altar, beside the burnt sacrifice of the morning.

18 He slew also the bullock and the ram *for* a sacrifice of peace offerings, which *was* for the people: and Aaron's sons presented unto him the blood, which he sprinkled upon the altar round about,

19 And the fat of the bullock and of the ram, the rump, and that which covereth *the inwards,* and the kidneys, and the caul *above* the liver:

20 And they put the fat upon the breasts, and he burnt the fat upon the altar:

21 And the breasts and the right shoulder Aaron waved *for* a wave offering before the LORD; as Moses commanded.

22 And Aaron lifted up his hand toward the people, and blessed them, and came down from offering of the sin offering, and the burnt offering, and peace offerings.

23 And Moses and Aaron went into the tabernacle of the congregation, and came out, and blessed the people: and the *^a*glory of the LORD appeared unto all the people.

24 And there came a *^a*fire out from before the LORD, and consumed upon the altar the burnt offering and the fat: *which* when all the people saw, they shouted, and fell on their faces.

CHAPTER 10

Nadab and Abihu perform unauthorized sacrifices and are slain by a fire from the Lord—Aaron and his other sons are forbidden to mourn for them—Aaron and his sons are to abstain from wine and strong drink—They are to teach all that the Lord revealed to Moses.

AND Nadab and Abihu, the *^a*sons of Aaron, took either of them his censer, and put fire therein, and put incense thereon, and offered *^b*strange fire before the LORD, which he commanded them not.

2 And there went out *^a*fire from the LORD, and *^b*devoured them, and they *^c*died before the LORD.

3 Then Moses said unto Aaron, This *is it* that the LORD spake, saying, I will be sanctified in them that come nigh me, and before all the people I will be glorified. And Aaron *^a*held his peace.

4 And Moses called Mishael and Elzaphan, the sons of *^a*Uzziel the uncle of Aaron, and said unto them, Come near, carry your brethren from before the sanctuary out of the camp.

5 So they went near, and carried them in their coats out of the camp; as Moses had said.

6 And Moses said unto Aaron, and unto Eleazar and unto Ithamar, his sons, Uncover not your *^a*heads, neither *^b*rend your clothes; lest ye die, and lest wrath come upon all the people: but let your brethren, the whole house of Israel, bewail the burning which the LORD hath kindled.

7 And ye shall not go out from the door of the tabernacle of the congregation, lest ye die: for the *^a*anointing oil of the LORD *is* upon you. And they did according to the word of Moses.

15a Judg. 13:19 (19–20).
16a HEB statute.
23a Lev. 9:6;
    2 Ne. 1:15;
    Ether 12:6 (6–18).
24a Lev. 10:2;
    Judg. 6:21;
    1 Chr. 21:26;

      2 Chr. 7:1; 1 Ne. 1:6.
10 1a Lev. 16:1.
    b Ex. 30:9 (6–10).
   2a Ezek. 9:24;
    2 Ne. 30:10.
    b Lev. 10:19.
    c Num. 3:4;
    1 Chr. 24:2;

      Acts 5:5 (1–10).
    3a D&C 101:5.
    4a Ex. 6:22 (18, 22).
    6a Ezek. 24:17.
    b Lev. 13:45;
    Alma 46:21.
    7a Lev. 21:12 (10–12);
    D&C 124:39 (38–40).

8 ¶ And the LORD spake unto Aaron, saying,

9 Do not drink ᵃwine nor ᵇstrong ᶜdrink, thou, nor thy sons with thee, when ye go into the tabernacle of the congregation, lest ye die: *it shall be* a statute for ever throughout your generations:

10 And ᵃthat ye may put difference between ᵇholy and unholy, and between ᶜunclean and ᵈclean;

11 And that ye may ᵃteach the children of Israel all the statutes which the LORD hath spoken unto them by the hand of Moses.

12 ¶ And Moses spake unto Aaron, and unto Eleazar and unto Ithamar, his sons that were left, Take the meat ᵃoffering that remaineth of the offerings of the LORD made by fire, and ᵇeat it without leaven beside the altar: for it *is* most holy:

13 And ye shall ᵃeat it in the holy place, because it *is* thy due, and thy sons' due, of the sacrifices of the LORD made by fire: for so I am commanded.

14 And the ᵃwave breast and heave shoulder shall ye ᵇeat in a clean place; thou, and thy sons, and thy daughters with thee: for *they be* thy due, and thy sons' due, *which are* given out of the sacrifices of peace offerings of the children of Israel.

15 ᵃThe heave shoulder and the wave breast shall they bring with the offerings made by fire of the fat, to wave *it for* a wave offering before the LORD; and it shall be thine, and thy sons' with thee, ᵇby a statute for ever; as the LORD hath commanded.

16 ¶ And Moses ᵃdiligently sought the ᵇgoat of the sin offering, and,

behold, it was burnt: and he was angry with Eleazar and Ithamar, the sons of Aaron *which were* left *alive,* saying,

17 Wherefore have ye not eaten the sin offering in the holy place, seeing it *is* most holy, and God hath given it you to ᵃbear the iniquity of the congregation, to make atonement for them before the LORD?

18 Behold, the blood of it was not brought in within the holy *place:* ye should indeed have eaten it in the holy *place,* as I commanded.

19 And Aaron said unto Moses, Behold, this day have they offered their sin offering and their burnt offering before the LORD; and such things have ᵃbefallen me: and *if* I had eaten the sin offering to day, should it have been ᵇaccepted in the sight of the LORD?

20 And when Moses heard *that,* he was content.

CHAPTER 11

The Lord reveals which living things may and may not be eaten, and which things are clean and unclean—He commands Israel: Be holy, for I am holy.

AND the LORD spake unto Moses and to Aaron, saying unto them,

2 Speak unto the children of Israel, saying, These *are* the beasts which ye shall ᵃeat among all the beasts that *are* on the earth.

3 Whatsoever parteth the hoof, and is clovenfooted, *and* cheweth the cud, among the beasts, that shall ye eat.

4 Nevertheless these shall ye not eat of them that chew the cud, or of

---

9a Ezek. 44:21.
  b HEB intoxicating drink.
  c TG Word of Wisdom.
10a HEB to distinguish between the holy and the profane, and between the impure and the pure. Ezek. 22:26; 44:23.
  b TG Holiness.
  c TG Uncleanness.
  d 3 Ne. 20:41.
11a D&C 20:46.

TG Teacher.
12a Num. 18:8 (8–19); 1 Sam. 2:28; Mosiah 2:3; 3 Ne. 9:19 (19–20); Moses 5:5.
  b HEB eat it with unleavened bread.
13a Lev. 6:26 (16, 26); Ezek. 42:13.
14a Ex. 29:26 (24–27).
  b Ex. 29:33 (31–34).
15a HEB The shoulder for

a contribution and the breast for a present.
  b HEB for a perpetual law.
16a HEB demanded the goat.
  b Lev. 9:3 (3, 15).
17a TG Accountability.
19a Lev. 10:2 (1–3).
  b Moro. 7:44.
11 2a Deut. 14:4 (4–21); Acts 10:14 (9–16); D&C 89:12.
  TG Food.

them that divide the hoof: *as* the camel, because he cheweth the cud, but divideth not the hoof; he *is* unclean unto you.

5 And the coney, because he cheweth the cud, but divideth not the hoof; he *is* unclean unto you.

6 And the hare, because he cheweth the cud, but divideth not the hoof; he *is* unclean unto you.

7 And the swine, though he divide the hoof, and be clovenfooted, yet he cheweth not the cud; he *is* unclean to you.

8 Of their flesh shall ye not eat, and their carcase shall ye not touch; they *are* unclean to you.

9 ¶ These shall ye eat of all that *are* in the waters: whatsoever hath fins and scales in the waters, in the seas, and in the rivers, them shall ye eat.

10 And all that have not fins and scales in the seas, and in the rivers, of all that move in the waters, and of any living thing which *is* in the waters, they *shall be* an abomination unto you:

11 They shall be even an abomination unto you; ye shall not eat of their flesh, but ye shall have their carcases in abomination.

12 Whatsoever hath no fins nor scales in the waters, that *shall be* an abomination unto you.

13 ¶ And these *are they which* ye shall have in abomination among the fowls; they shall not be eaten, they *are* an abomination: the eagle, and the ossifrage, and the ospray,

14 And the vulture, and the kite after his kind;

15 Every raven after his kind;

16 And the owl, and the night hawk, and the cuckow, and the hawk after his kind,

17 And the little owl, and the cormorant, and the great owl,

18 And the swan, and the pelican, and the gier eagle,

19 And the stork, the heron after her kind, and the lapwing, and the bat.

20 All fowls that creep, going upon *all* four, *shall be* an abomination unto you.

21 Yet these may ye eat of every flying creeping thing that goeth upon *all* four, which have legs above their feet, to leap withal upon the earth;

22 *Even* these of them ye may eat; the ᵃlocust after his kind, and the bald locust after his kind, and the beetle after his kind, and the grasshopper after his kind.

23 But all *other* flying creeping things, which have four feet, *shall be* an abomination unto you.

24 And for these ye shall be unclean: whosoever toucheth the carcase of them shall be ᵃunclean until the even.

25 And whosoever beareth *ought* of the carcase of them shall wash his clothes, and be unclean until the even.

26 *The carcases* of every beast which divideth the hoof, and *is* not clovenfooted, nor cheweth the cud, *are* unclean unto you: every one that toucheth them shall be unclean.

27 And whatsoever goeth upon his paws, among all manner of beasts that go on *all* four, those *are* unclean unto you: whoso toucheth their carcase shall be unclean until the even.

28 And he that beareth the carcase of them shall wash his clothes, and be unclean until the even: they *are* unclean unto you.

29 ¶ These also *shall be* ᵃunclean unto you among the creeping things that creep upon the earth; the weasel, and the mouse, and the tortoise after his kind,

30 And the ferret, and the chameleon, and the lizard, and the snail, and the mole.

31 These *are* unclean to you among all that creep: whosoever doth touch them, when they be dead, shall be unclean until the even.

32 And upon whatsoever *any* of them, when they are dead, doth fall, it shall be unclean; whether *it be* any vessel of wood, or raiment, or skin, or sack, whatsoever vessel *it be*, wherein *any* work is done, it must be put into water, and it shall

---

22*a* Matt. 3:4; Mark 1:6.   24*a* Lev. 5:2 (2–6).   29*a* Isa. 66:17.

be unclean until the even; so it shall be cleansed.

33 And every earthen vessel, whereinto *any* of them falleth, whatsoever *is* in it shall be unclean; and ye shall *a*break it.

34 Of all meat which may be eaten, *that* on which *such* water cometh shall be unclean: and all drink that may be drunk in every *such* vessel shall be unclean.

35 And every *thing* whereupon *any part* of their carcase falleth shall be unclean; *whether it be* *a*oven, or ranges for pots, they shall be broken down: *for* they *are* unclean, and shall be unclean unto you.

36 Nevertheless *a*a fountain or pit, *wherein there is* plenty of water, shall be clean: but that which toucheth their carcase shall be unclean.

37 And if *any part* of their carcase fall upon any sowing seed which is to be sown, it *shall be* clean.

38 But if *any* water be put upon the seed, and *any part* of their carcase fall thereon, it *shall be* unclean unto you.

39 And if any beast, of which ye may eat, die; he that toucheth the carcase thereof shall be unclean until the even.

40 And he that eateth of the *a*carcase of it shall wash his clothes, and be unclean until the even: he also that beareth the carcase of it shall wash his clothes, and be unclean until the even.

41 And every creeping thing that creepeth upon the earth *shall be* an abomination; it shall not be eaten.

42 Whatsoever goeth upon the belly, and whatsoever goeth upon *all* four, or *a*whatsoever hath more feet among all creeping things that creep upon the earth, them ye shall not eat; for they *are* an abomination.

43 Ye shall not make yourselves *a*abominable with any creeping thing that creepeth, neither shall ye make yourselves unclean with them, that ye should be defiled thereby.

44 For I *am* the LORD your God: ye shall therefore *a*sanctify yourselves, and ye shall be holy; for I *am* holy: neither shall ye defile yourselves with any manner of creeping thing that creepeth upon the earth.

45 For I *am* the LORD that bringeth you up out of the land of Egypt, to be your God: ye shall therefore be holy, for I *am* holy.

46 This *is* *a*the law of the beasts, and of the fowl, and of every living creature that moveth in the waters, and of every creature that creepeth upon the earth:

47 *a*To make a difference between the *b*unclean and the clean, and between the beast that may be eaten and the beast that may not be eaten.

CHAPTER 12

The Lord reveals the law of purification of women after childbirth, including a sin offering.

AND the LORD spake unto Moses, saying,

2 Speak unto the children of Israel, saying, If a woman have conceived seed, and born a man child: then she shall be unclean seven days; according to the days of the separation for her infirmity shall she be unclean.

3 And in the eighth day the flesh of his foreskin shall be *a*circumcised.

4 And she shall then continue in the blood of her purifying three and thirty days; she shall touch no hallowed thing, nor come into the sanctuary, until the days of her purifying be fulfilled.

5 But if she bear a maid child, then she shall be unclean two weeks, as in her separation: and she shall continue in the blood of her purifying threescore and six days.

6 And when the days of her *a*puri-

33*a* Lev. 6:28.
35*a* HEB stove and cooking ovens.
36*a* HEB a spring and a well.
40*a* Lev. 17:15.
42*a* OR every millipede

(or that which has numerous legs).
43*a* HEB detestable.
44*a* TG Sanctification.
46*a* HEB the teaching concerning the beast

and the fowl.
47*a* HEB To differentiate.
   b TG Uncleanness.
12 3*a* TG Circumcision.
   6*a* TG Purification.

fying are fulfilled, for a son, or for a daughter, she shall bring a lamb of the first year for a burnt offering, and a young pigeon, or a turtledove, for a sin offering, unto the door of the tabernacle of the congregation, unto the priest:

7 Who shall offer it before the LORD, and make an atonement for her; and she shall be cleansed from the issue of her blood. This *is* the law for her that hath born a male or a female.

8 And if she be not *a*able to bring a lamb, then she shall bring two turtles, or two young pigeons; the one for the burnt offering, and the other for a sin offering: and the priest shall make an *b*atonement for her, and she shall be clean.

CHAPTER 13

Laws and tokens are revealed for discerning and controlling leprosy—Leprous garments are to be burnt.

AND the LORD spake unto Moses and Aaron, saying,

2 When a man shall have in the skin of his flesh *a*a rising, a scab, or bright spot, and it be in the skin of his flesh *like* the plague of *b*leprosy; then he shall be brought unto Aaron the priest, or unto one of his sons the priests:

3 And the *a*priest shall look on the plague in the skin of the flesh: and *when* the hair in the plague is turned white, and the plague in sight *be* deeper than the skin of his flesh, it *is* a plague of leprosy: and the priest shall look on him, and pronounce him unclean.

4 If the bright spot *be* white in the skin of his flesh, and in sight *be* not deeper than the skin, and the hair thereof be not turned white; then the priest *a*shall shut up *him that hath* the plague seven days:

5 And the priest shall look on him the seventh day: and, behold, *if* the plague in his sight be at a stay, *and*

the plague spread not in the skin; then the priest shall shut him up seven days more:

6 And the priest shall look on him again the seventh day: and, behold, *if* the plague *be* somewhat dark, *and* the plague spread not in the skin, the priest shall pronounce him clean: it *is but* a scab: and he shall wash his clothes, and be clean.

7 But if the scab spread much abroad in the skin, after that he hath been seen of the priest for his *a*cleansing, he shall be seen of the priest again:

8 And *if* the priest see that, behold, the scab spreadeth in the skin, then the priest shall pronounce him unclean: it *is* a leprosy.

9 ¶ When the plague of leprosy is in a man, then he shall be brought unto the priest;

10 And the priest shall see *him:* and, behold, *if* the rising *be* white in the skin, and it have turned the hair white, and *there be* quick raw flesh in the rising;

11 It *is* an old leprosy in the skin of his flesh, and the priest shall pronounce him unclean, and shall not shut him up: for he *is* unclean.

12 And if a leprosy break out abroad in the skin, and the leprosy cover all the skin of *him that hath* the plague from his head even to his foot, wheresoever the priest looketh;

13 Then the priest shall *a*consider: and, behold, *if* the leprosy have covered all his flesh, he shall pronounce *him* clean *that hath* the plague: it is all turned white: he *is* clean.

14 But when raw flesh appeareth in him, he shall be unclean.

15 And the priest shall see the raw flesh, and pronounce him to be unclean: *for* the raw flesh *is* unclean: it *is* a leprosy.

16 Or if the raw flesh turn again, and be changed unto white, he shall come unto the priest;

17 And the priest shall see him:

8a Lev. 5:7.
  b Lev. 15:15 (14–15).
13 2a HEB a swelling.

b TG Leprosy.
3a TG Priest, Aaronic
  Priesthood. BD Priests.

4a OR shall quarantine.
7a TG Purification.
13a HEB look.

and, behold, *if* the plague be turned into white; then the priest shall pronounce *him* clean *that hath* the plague: he *is* clean.

18 ¶ The flesh also, in which, *even* in the skin thereof, was a boil, and is healed,

19 And in the place of the boil there be a white rising, or a bright spot, white, and somewhat reddish, and it be shewed to the priest;

20 And if, when the priest seeth it, behold, *a* it *be* in sight lower than the skin, and the hair thereof be turned white; the priest shall pronounce him unclean: it *is* a plague of leprosy broken out of the boil.

21 But if the priest look on it, and, behold, *there be* no white hairs therein, *a* and *if* it *be* not lower than the skin, but *be* somewhat dark; then the priest shall shut him up seven days:

22 And if it spread much abroad in the skin, then the priest shall pronounce him unclean: it *is* a plague.

23 But if the bright spot stay in his place, *and* spread not, it *is* a burning boil; and the priest shall pronounce him clean.

24 ¶ Or if there be *any* flesh, in the skin whereof *there is* a hot burning, and the quick *flesh* that burneth have a white bright spot, somewhat reddish, or white;

25 Then the priest shall look upon it: and, behold, *if* the hair in the bright spot be turned white, and it *be in* sight deeper than the skin; it *is* a leprosy broken out of *a* the burning: wherefore the priest shall pronounce him unclean: it *is* the plague of leprosy.

26 But if the priest look on it, and, behold, *there be* no white hair in the bright spot, and it *be* no lower than the *other* skin, but *be* somewhat dark; then the priest shall shut him up seven days:

27 And the priest shall look upon him the seventh day: *and* if it be spread much abroad in the skin, then the priest shall pronounce him unclean: it *is* the plague of leprosy.

28 And if the bright spot stay in his place, *and* spread not in the skin, but *be* somewhat dark; it *is* *a* rising of the burning, and the priest shall pronounce him clean: for it *is* an inflammation of the burning.

29 ¶ If a man or woman have a plague upon the head or the beard;

30 Then the priest shall see the plague: and, behold, if it *be* in sight deeper than the skin; *and there be* in it a yellow thin hair; then the priest shall pronounce him unclean: it *is* a dry scall, *even* a leprosy upon the head or beard.

31 And if the priest look on the plague of the scall, and, behold, it *be* not in sight deeper than the skin, and *that there is* no black hair in it; then the priest shall shut up *him that hath* the plague of the scall seven days:

32 And in the seventh day the priest shall look on the plague: and, behold, *if* the scall spread not, and there be in it no yellow hair, and the scall *be* not in sight deeper than the skin;

33 He shall be shaven, but the scall shall he not shave; and the priest shall shut up *him that hath* the scall seven days more:

34 And in the seventh day the priest shall look on the scall: and, behold, *if* the scall be not spread in the skin, nor *be* in sight deeper than the skin; then the priest shall pronounce him clean: and he shall wash his clothes, and be clean.

35 But if the scall spread much in the skin after his cleansing;

36 Then the priest shall look on him: and, behold, if the scall be spread in the skin, the priest shall not seek for yellow hair; he *is* unclean.

37 But *a* if the scall be in his sight at a stay, and *that* there is black hair grown up therein; the scall is healed,

---

20*a* HEB its appearance is of a depression in the skin.
21*a* HEB and there is no depression in the skin.
25*a* HEB the burn.
28*a* HEB a swelling of the burn.
37*a* IE if in his observation

the symptom remains as it was.

he *is* clean: and the priest shall pronounce him clean.

38 ¶ If a man also or a woman have in the skin of their flesh bright spots, *even* white bright spots;

39 Then the priest shall look: and, behold, *if* the bright spots in the skin of their flesh *be* darkish white; it *is* a *[a]*freckled spot *that* groweth in the skin; he *is* clean.

40 And the man whose hair is fallen off his head, he *is* bald; *yet is* he clean.

41 And he that hath his hair fallen off from the part of his head toward his face, he *is* forehead bald: *yet is* he clean.

42 And if there be in the bald head, or bald forehead, a white reddish sore; it *is* a leprosy sprung up in his bald head, or his bald forehead.

43 Then the priest shall look upon it: and, behold, *if* the rising of the sore *be* white reddish in his bald head, or in his bald forehead, as the leprosy appeareth in the skin of the flesh;

44 He is a leprous man, he *is* unclean: the priest shall pronounce him utterly unclean; his plague *is* in his head.

45 And the leper in whom the plague *is,* his clothes shall be *[a]*rent, and his head bare, and *[b]*he shall put a covering upon his upper lip, and shall cry, Unclean, unclean.

46 All the days wherein the plague *shall be* in him he shall be defiled; he *is* unclean: he shall dwell *[a]*alone; without the camp *shall* his habitation *be.*

47 ¶ The garment also that the plague of leprosy is in, *whether it be* a woollen garment, or a linen garment;

48 Whether *it be* in the warp, or woof; of linen, or of woollen; whether in a skin, or in any thing made of skin;

49 And if the plague be greenish or reddish in the garment, or in the skin, either in the warp, or in the woof, or in any thing of skin; it *is* a plague of leprosy, and shall be shewed unto the *[a]*priest:

50 And the priest shall look upon the plague, and shut up *it that hath* the plague seven days:

51 And he shall look on the plague on the seventh day: if the plague be spread in the garment, either in the warp, or in the woof, or in a skin, *or* in any work that is made of skin; the plague *is* a *[a]*fretting leprosy; it *is* unclean.

52 He shall therefore burn that garment, whether warp or woof, in woollen or in linen, or any thing of skin, wherein the plague is: for it *is* a fretting leprosy; it shall be burnt in the fire.

53 And if the priest shall look, and, behold, the plague be not spread in the garment, either in the warp, or in the woof, or in any thing of skin;

54 Then the priest shall command that they wash *the thing* wherein the plague *is,* and he shall *[a]*shut it up seven days more:

55 And the priest shall look on the plague, after that it is washed: and, behold, *if* the plague have not changed his colour, and the plague be not spread; it *is* unclean; thou shalt burn it in the fire; *[a]*it *is* fret inward, *whether* it *be* bare within or without.

56 And if the priest look, and, behold, the plague *be* somewhat dark after the washing of it; then he shall rend it out of the garment, or out of the skin, or out of the warp, or out of the woof:

57 And if it appear still in the garment, either in the warp, or in the woof, or in any thing of skin; it *is* a spreading *plague:* thou shalt burn that wherein the plague *is* with fire.

58 And the garment, either warp, or woof, or whatsoever thing of skin *it be,* which thou shalt wash, if the

---

39*a* HEB white.
45*a* Lev. 10:6;
    Alma 46:21.
   b HEB he shall cover his
    mouth.

Ezek. 24:17.
46*a* 2 Kgs. 15:5.
49*a* Luke 17:14.
51*a* HEB malignant leprosy.
54*a* HEB quarantine it seven

days the second time.
55*a* HEB it is a decay,
    whether it be bald in
    the head thereof, or in
    the forehead thereof.

plague be departed from them, then it shall be ^awashed the second time, and shall be clean.

59 This *is* the law of the plague of ^aleprosy in a garment of woollen or linen, either in the warp, or woof, or any thing of skins, to pronounce it clean, or to pronounce it unclean.

CHAPTER 14

Laws, rites, and sacrifices are revealed for cleansing lepers, their garments, and leprous houses.

AND the LORD spake unto Moses, saying,

2 This shall be the law of the ^aleper in the day of his cleansing: He shall be brought unto the ^bpriest:

3 And the priest shall go forth out of the camp; and the priest shall look, and, behold, *if* the plague of leprosy be ^ahealed in the leper;

4 Then shall the priest command to take for him that is to be cleansed two birds alive *and* clean, and cedar wood, and ^ascarlet, and hyssop:

5 And the priest shall command that one of the birds be killed in an earthen vessel over running water:

6 As for the living bird, he shall take it, and the cedar wood, and the scarlet, and the hyssop, and shall dip them and the living bird in the blood of the bird *that was* killed over the running water:

7 And he shall sprinkle upon him that is to be cleansed from the leprosy seven times, and shall pronounce him clean, and shall let the living bird loose into the open field.

8 And he that is to be cleansed shall wash his clothes, and ^ashave off all his hair, and wash himself in water, that he may be clean: and after that he shall come into the camp, and shall tarry abroad out of his tent seven days.

9 But it shall be on the seventh day, that he shall shave all his hair off his head and his beard and his eyebrows, even all his hair he shall shave off: and he shall wash his clothes, also he shall wash his flesh in water, and he shall be clean.

10 And on the eighth day he shall take two he lambs without blemish, and ^aone ewe lamb of the first year without blemish, and three tenth deals of fine flour *for* a meat offering, mingled with oil, and one log of oil.

11 And the priest that maketh *him* clean shall present the man that is to be made clean, and those things, before the LORD, *at* the door of the tabernacle of the congregation:

12 And the priest shall take one he lamb, and offer him for a trespass offering, and the log of oil, and wave them *for* a wave offering before the LORD:

13 And he shall slay the lamb in the place where he shall kill the sin ^aoffering and the burnt offering, in the holy place: for as the sin offering *is* the priest's, *so is* the trespass offering: it *is* most holy:

14 And the priest shall take *some* of the blood of the trespass offering, and the priest shall put *it* upon the tip of the right ear of him that is to be cleansed, and upon the thumb of his right hand, and upon the great toe of his right foot:

15 And the priest shall take *some* of the log of oil, and pour *it* into the palm of his own left hand:

16 And the priest shall dip his right finger in the oil that *is* in his left hand, and shall sprinkle of the oil with his finger seven times before the LORD:

17 And of the rest of the oil that *is* in his hand shall the priest put upon the tip of the right ear of him that is to be cleansed, and upon the thumb of his right hand, and upon the great toe of his right foot, upon the blood of the trespass offering:

18 And the remnant of the oil that *is* in the priest's hand he shall pour upon the head of him that is to be cleansed: and the priest shall make an atonement for him before the LORD.

58*a* TG Wash.
59*a* Lev. 14:55 (54–57).
14 2*a* TG Leprosy.

b Luke 5:14.
3*a* TG Heal.
4*a* IE scarlet dyed cloth.

8*a* Acts 21:24.
10*a* HEB a ewe, a year old.
13*a* TG Sacrifice.

19 And the priest shall offer the ^asin offering, and make an atonement for him that is to be cleansed from his uncleanness; and afterward he shall kill the burnt offering:

20 And the priest shall offer the burnt offering and the meat offering upon the altar: and the priest shall make an atonement for him, and he shall be clean.

21 And if he be ^apoor, and cannot get so much; then he shall take ^bone lamb for a trespass offering to be waved, to make an atonement for him, and one tenth deal of fine flour mingled with oil for a meat offering, and a log of oil;

22 And two turtledoves, or two young pigeons, such as he is able to get; and the one shall be a sin offering, and the other a burnt offering.

23 And he shall bring them on the eighth day for his cleansing unto the priest, unto the door of the tabernacle of the congregation, before the LORD.

24 And the priest shall take the lamb of the trespass offering, and the log of oil, and the priest shall wave them for a wave offering before the LORD:

25 And he shall kill the lamb of the trespass offering, and the priest shall take some of the blood of the trespass offering, and put it upon the tip of the right ear of him that is to be cleansed, and upon the thumb of his right hand, and upon the great toe of his right foot:

26 And the priest shall pour of the oil into the palm of his own left hand:

27 And the priest shall sprinkle with his right finger some of the oil that is in his left hand seven times before the LORD:

28 And the priest shall put of the ^aoil that is in his hand upon the tip of the right ear of him that is to be cleansed, and upon the thumb of his right hand, and upon the great toe of his right foot, upon the place of the blood of the trespass offering:

29 And the rest of the oil that is in the priest's hand he shall put upon the head of him that is to be cleansed, to make an atonement for him before the LORD.

30 And he shall offer the one of the turtledoves, or of the young pigeons, such as he can get;

31 Even such as he is able to get, the one for a sin offering, and the other for a burnt offering, with the meat offering: and the priest shall make an ^aatonement for him that is to be cleansed before the LORD.

32 This is the ^alaw of him in whom is the plague of leprosy, whose hand is not ^bable to get that which pertaineth to his cleansing.

33 ¶ And the LORD spake unto Moses and unto Aaron, saying,

34 When ye be come into the land of Canaan, which I give to you for a possession, and I put the plague of ^aleprosy in a house of the land of your possession;

35 And he that owneth the house shall come and tell the priest, saying, It seemeth to me there is as it were a plague in the house:

36 Then the priest shall command that they empty the house, before the priest go into it to see the plague, that all that is in the house be not made unclean: and afterward the priest shall go in to see the house:

37 And he shall look on the plague, and, behold, if the plague be in the walls of the house with ^ahollow strakes, greenish or reddish, ^bwhich in sight are lower than the wall;

38 Then the priest shall go out of the house to the door of the house, and shut up the house seven days:

39 And the priest shall come again the seventh day, and shall look: and,

---

19a Ezek. 45:17.
21a Lev. 5:7; 14:32.
    TG Poor.
  b HEB a sheep, a
    sin sacrifice for
    presentation, to atone

for him.
28a D&C 124:39.
31a Lev. 15:15 (14–15).
32a HEB teaching or
    instruction.
  b Lev. 14:21 (21–22).

34a Lev. 14:55 (54–57).
37a HEB sunken areas.
  b HEB whose appearance
    is depressed from (the
    rest of) the wall.

behold, *if* the plague be spread in the walls of the house;

40 Then the priest shall command that they take away the stones in which the plague *is*, and they shall cast them into an unclean place without the city:

41 And he shall cause the house to be scraped within round about, and they shall pour out the dust that they scrape off without the city into an unclean place:

42 And they shall take other stones, and put *them* in the place of those stones; and he shall take other mortar, and shall plaster the house.

43 And if the plague come again, and break out in the house, after that he hath *a*taken away the stones, and after he hath scraped the house, and after it is plastered;

44 Then the priest shall come and look, and, behold, *if* the plague be spread in the house, it *is* a *a*fretting leprosy in the house: it *is* unclean.

45 And he shall break down the house, the stones of it, and the timber thereof, and all the mortar of the house; and he shall carry *them* forth out of the city into an unclean place.

46 Moreover he that goeth into the house all the while that it is shut up shall be unclean until the even.

47 And he that lieth in the house shall wash his clothes; and he that eateth in the house shall wash his clothes.

48 And if the priest shall come in, and look *upon it,* and, behold, the plague hath not spread in the house, after the house was plastered: then the priest shall pronounce the house clean, because the plague is healed.

49 And he shall take to *a*cleanse the house two birds, and cedar wood, and scarlet, and hyssop:

50 And he shall kill the one of the birds in an earthen vessel over running water:

51 And he shall take the cedar wood, and the hyssop, and the scarlet, and the living bird, and dip them in the blood of the slain bird, and in the running water, and sprinkle the house seven times:

52 And he shall cleanse the house with the blood of the bird, and with the running water, and with the living bird, and with the cedar wood, and with the hyssop, and with the scarlet:

53 But he shall let go the living bird out of the city into the open fields, and make an atonement for the house: and it shall be clean.

54 This *is* the law for all manner of plague of leprosy, and *a*scall,

55 And for the *a*leprosy of a garment, and of a *b*house,

56 And for a rising, and for a scab, and for a bright spot:

57 To teach when *it is* unclean, and when *it is* clean: this *is* the law of leprosy.

CHAPTER 15

Laws, rites, and sacrifices are revealed for cleansing those who have a discharge and other types of uncleanness.

AND the LORD spake unto Moses and to Aaron, saying,

2 Speak unto the children of Israel, and say unto them, When any man hath a running *a*issue out of his flesh, *because of* his issue he *is* unclean.

3 And this shall be his uncleanness in his issue: whether his flesh run with his issue, or his flesh be stopped from his issue, it *is* his uncleanness.

4 Every bed, whereon he lieth that hath the issue, is unclean: and every thing, whereon he sitteth, shall be unclean.

5 And whosoever toucheth his bed shall wash his clothes, and bathe *himself* in water, and be unclean until the even.

6 And he that sitteth on *any* thing whereon he sat that hath the issue shall wash his clothes, and bathe *himself* in water, and be unclean until the even.

7 And he that toucheth the flesh of

43*a* HEB extracted.
44*a* HEB malignant.
49*a* TG Purification.

54*a* HEB tinea or other scaly symptoms.
55*a* Lev. 13:59 (47–59).

b Lev. 14:34 (33–53).
15 2*a* Num. 5:2 (2–4).

him that hath the issue shall wash his clothes, and bathe *himself* in water, and be unclean until the even.

8 And if he that hath the issue spit upon him that is clean; then he shall wash his clothes, and bathe *himself* in water, and be unclean until the even.

9 And what saddle soever he rideth upon that hath the issue shall be unclean.

10 And whosoever toucheth any thing that was under him shall be unclean until the even: and he that beareth *any of* those things shall wash his clothes, and bathe *himself* in water, and be unclean until the even.

11 And whomsoever he toucheth that hath the issue, and hath not rinsed his hands in water, he shall wash his clothes, and bathe *himself* in water, and be unclean until the even.

12 And the vessel of earth, that he toucheth which hath the issue, shall be *a*broken: and every vessel of wood shall be rinsed in water.

13 And when he that hath an issue is cleansed of his issue; then he shall number to himself seven days for his cleansing, and wash his clothes, and bathe his flesh in running water, and shall be clean.

14 And on the eighth day he shall take to him two turtledoves, or two young pigeons, and come before the LORD unto the door of the tabernacle of the congregation, and give them unto the priest:

15 And the priest shall offer them, the one *for* a sin offering, and the other *for* a burnt offering; and the priest shall make an *a*atonement for him before the LORD for his issue.

16 And if any man's seed of copulation go out from him, then he shall wash all his flesh in water, and be unclean until the even.

17 And every garment, and every skin, whereon is the seed of copulation, shall be washed with water, and be unclean until the even.

18 The woman also with whom man shall lie *with* seed of copulation, they shall *both* bathe *themselves* in water, and be unclean until the even.

19 ¶ And if a woman have an issue, *and* her issue in her flesh be blood, she shall be put apart seven days: and whosoever toucheth her shall be unclean until the even.

20 And every thing that she lieth upon in her separation shall be unclean: every thing also that she sitteth upon shall be unclean.

21 And whosoever toucheth her bed shall wash his clothes, and bathe *himself* in water, and be unclean until the even.

22 And whosoever toucheth any thing that she sat upon shall wash his clothes, and bathe *himself* in water, and be unclean until the even.

23 And if it *be* on *her* bed, or on any thing whereon she sitteth, when he toucheth it, he shall be unclean until the even.

24 And if any man lie with her at all, and her flowers be upon him, he shall be unclean seven days; and all the bed whereon he lieth shall be unclean.

25 And if a woman have an issue of her *a*blood many days out of the time of her separation, or if it run beyond the time of her separation; all the days of the issue of her uncleanness shall be as the days of her separation: she *shall be* unclean.

26 Every bed whereon she lieth all the days of her issue shall be unto her as the bed of her separation: and whatsoever she sitteth upon shall be unclean, as the uncleanness of her separation.

27 And whosoever toucheth those things shall be unclean, and shall wash his clothes, and bathe *himself* in water, and be unclean until the even.

28 But if she be cleansed of her issue, then she shall number to

---

12*a* Lev. 6:28.   14:31 (30–31).   Luke 8:43.
15*a* Lev. 12:8 (7–8);   25*a* Matt. 9:20;

herself seven days, and after that she shall be clean.

29 And on the eighth day she shall take unto her two turtles, or two young pigeons, and bring them unto the priest, to the door of the tabernacle of the congregation.

30 And the priest shall offer the one *for* a sin offering, and the other *for* a burnt offering; and the priest shall make an atonement for her before the LORD for the issue of her uncleanness.

31 Thus shall ye separate the children of Israel from their *a*uncleanness; that they die not in their uncleanness, when they defile my *b*tabernacle that *is* among them.

32 This *is* the law of him that hath an issue, and *of him* whose seed goeth from him, and is defiled therewith;

33 And of her that is sick of her flowers, and of him that hath an issue, of the man, and of the woman, and of him that lieth with her that is unclean.

CHAPTER 16

How and when Aaron must enter the holy place is explained—Sacrifices are offered to reconcile Israel to God—The scapegoat carries away the sins of the people—The sins of all Israel are forgiven on the Day of Atonement.

AND the LORD spake unto Moses after the death of the two *a*sons of Aaron, when they offered before the LORD, and died;

2 And the LORD said unto Moses, Speak unto Aaron thy brother, that he come not at all times into the *a*holy *place* within the *b*veil before the mercy seat, which *is* upon the ark; that he die not: for I will *c*appear in the cloud upon the mercy seat.

3 Thus shall Aaron come into the holy *place:* with a young bullock

for a sin offering, and a ram for a burnt offering.

4 He shall put on the holy linen coat, and he shall have the linen breeches upon his flesh, and shall be girded with a linen girdle, and with the linen *a*mitre shall he be attired: these *are* holy garments; therefore shall he wash his flesh in water, and *so* put them on.

5 And he shall take of the congregation of the children of Israel two kids of the goats for a sin offering, and one ram for a burnt offering.

6 And Aaron shall offer his bullock of the sin offering, which *is* for himself, and make an atonement for himself, and for his house.

7 And he shall take the two goats, and present them before the LORD *at* the door of the tabernacle of the congregation.

8 And Aaron shall cast lots upon the two goats; one lot for the LORD, and the other lot for the scapegoat.

9 And Aaron shall bring the goat upon which the LORD's lot fell, and offer him *for* a sin *a*offering.

10 But the goat, on which the lot fell to be the scapegoat, shall be presented alive before the LORD, to make an atonement with him, *and* to let him go for a scapegoat into the wilderness.

11 And Aaron shall bring the bullock of the sin offering, which *is* for himself, and shall make an atonement for himself, and for his house, and shall kill the bullock of the sin offering which *is* for himself:

12 And he shall take a *a*censer full of burning coals of fire from off the altar before the LORD, and his hands full of sweet incense beaten small, and bring *it* within the veil:

13 And he shall put the *a*incense upon the fire before the LORD, that the cloud of the incense may cover

---

31*a* Num. 5:3;
    D&C 94:9;
    Moses 6:57.
  b Mosiah 2:37.
16 1*a* Lev. 10:1 (1–2).
  2*a* Heb. 9:12 (7, 12, 24–25);

    10:19 (19–22).
  b TG Veil.
  c Ex. 25:22; 29:42 (42–43);
    40:34 (34–35);
    D&C 97:16 (15–17);
    109:5 (5, 12–13);

    Abr. 2:19 (19–20).
  4*a* HEB cap.
  9*a* 3 Ne. 9:22 (15–22);
    D&C 21:9.
 12*a* HEB shovel.
 13*a* Rev. 8:3 (2–4).

the mercy seat that *is* [b]upon the testimony, that he die not:

14 And he shall take of the [a]blood of the bullock, and sprinkle *it* with his finger upon the mercy seat eastward; and before the mercy seat shall he sprinkle of the blood with his finger seven times.

15 ¶ Then shall he kill the goat of the sin offering, that *is* for the people, and bring his blood within the veil, and do with that blood as he did with the blood of the bullock, and sprinkle it upon the mercy seat, and before the mercy seat:

16 And he shall make an atonement for the holy *place*, because of the uncleanness of the children of Israel, and because of their [a]transgressions in all their sins: and so shall he do for the tabernacle of the congregation, that remaineth among them in the midst of their uncleanness.

17 And there shall be no man in the tabernacle of the congregation when he goeth in to make an atonement in the holy *place*, until he come out, and have made an atonement for himself, and for his household, and for all the congregation of Israel.

18 And he shall go out unto the altar that *is* before the LORD, and make an atonement for it; and shall take of the blood of the bullock, and of the blood of the goat, and put *it* upon the [a]horns of the altar round about.

19 And he shall sprinkle of the blood upon it with his finger seven times, and cleanse it, and hallow it from the uncleanness of the children of Israel.

20 ¶ And when he hath made an end of reconciling the holy *place*, and the tabernacle of the congregation, and the altar, he shall bring the live goat:

21 And Aaron shall lay both his [a]hands upon the head of the live goat, and [b]confess over him all the iniquities of the children of Israel, and all their transgressions in all their sins, putting them upon the head of the goat, and shall send *him* away by the hand of a [c]fit man into the wilderness:

22 And the goat shall [a]bear upon him all their [b]iniquities unto a land not inhabited: and he shall let go the goat in the wilderness.

23 And Aaron shall come into the tabernacle of the congregation, and shall put off the linen garments, which he put on when he went into the holy [a]*place*, and shall leave them there:

24 And he shall wash his flesh with water [a]in the holy place, and put on his garments, and come forth, and offer his burnt offering, and the burnt offering of the people, and make an atonement for himself, and for the people.

25 And the fat of the sin offering shall he burn upon the altar.

26 And he that let go the goat for the scapegoat shall wash his clothes, and bathe his flesh in water, and afterward come into the camp.

27 And the bullock *for* the sin offering, and the goat *for* the sin offering, whose blood was brought in to make atonement in the holy *place*, shall *one* carry forth without the camp; and they shall burn in the fire their skins, and their flesh, and their dung.

28 And he that burneth them shall wash his clothes, and bathe his flesh in water, and afterward he shall come into the camp.

29 ¶ And *this* shall be a statute for ever unto you: *that* in the seventh month, on the tenth *day* of the month, ye shall [a]afflict your souls, and do no work at all, *whether it be* one of your own [b]country, or a stranger that sojourneth among you:

13*b* IE upon the ark containing the stone tablets and other written revelations.
14*a* Lev. 4:5 (5–6).
16*a* TG Transgress.
18*a* Lev. 4:7.

21*a* TG Hands, Laying on of.
  b Heb. 10:3.
    TG Confession.
  c HEB appointed.
22*a* Mosiah 14:11.
  b TG Jesus Christ, Types of, in Anticipation.

23*a* D&C 109:13.
24*a* HEB in a holy place.
29*a* OR humble.
  b Ex. 12:48 (19, 48–49); Ezek. 47:22.

30 For on that day shall *the priest* make an atonement for you, to cleanse you, *that* ye may be clean from all your sins before the LORD.

31 It *shall be* a *a*sabbath of rest unto you, and ye shall afflict your souls, by a statute for ever.

32 And the *a*priest, whom he shall *b*anoint, and whom he shall *c*consecrate to minister in the priest's office in his father's stead, shall make the atonement, and shall put on the linen clothes, *even* the holy garments:

33 And he shall make an atonement for the holy sanctuary, and he shall make an atonement for the tabernacle of the *a*congregation, and for the altar, and he shall make an atonement for the priests, and for all the people of the congregation.

34 And this shall be an everlasting statute unto you, to make an atonement for the children of Israel for all their sins once a year. And he did as the LORD commanded Moses.

CHAPTER 17

Sacrifices are to be offered only to the Lord at the tabernacle of the congregation—Israel is forbidden to sacrifice to devils—All eating of blood is forbidden—Shedding of blood is required for an atonement for sins.

AND the LORD spake unto Moses, saying,

2 Speak unto Aaron, and unto his sons, and unto all the children of Israel, and say unto them; This *is* the thing which the LORD hath commanded, saying,

3 What man soever *there be* of the house of Israel, that killeth an ox, or lamb, or goat, in the camp, or that killeth *it* out of the camp,

4 And bringeth it not unto the door of the *a*tabernacle of the congregation, to offer an offering unto the LORD before the tabernacle of the LORD; blood shall be imputed unto that man; he hath shed blood; and that man shall be cut off from among his people:

5 To the end that the children of Israel may bring their sacrifices, which they offer in the open field, even that they may bring them unto the LORD, unto the door of the tabernacle of the congregation, unto the priest, and offer them *for* peace *a*offerings unto the LORD.

6 And the priest shall sprinkle the blood upon the altar of the LORD *at* the door of the tabernacle of the congregation, and burn the fat for a sweet savour unto the LORD.

7 And they shall no more offer their sacrifices unto devils, after whom they have gone a *a*whoring. This shall be a statute for ever unto them throughout their generations.

8 ¶ And thou shalt say unto them, Whatsoever man *there be* of the house of Israel, or of the strangers which sojourn among you, that *a*offereth a burnt offering or sacrifice,

9 And bringeth it not unto the door of the tabernacle of the congregation, to offer it unto the LORD; even that man shall be cut off from among his people.

10 ¶ And whatsoever man *there be* of the house of Israel, or of the strangers that sojourn among you, that eateth any manner of blood; I will even set my *a*face against that soul that eateth *b*blood, and will cut him off from among his people.

11 For the *a*life of the *b*flesh *is* in the blood: and I have given it to you upon the altar to make an atonement for your souls: for it *is* the *c*blood *that* maketh an *d*atonement for the soul.

12 Therefore I said unto the children of Israel, No soul of you shall eat blood, neither shall any stranger

31 *a* Mosiah 13:18 (18–19).
32 *a* Num. 27:21.
   b TG Priesthood, Aaronic.
   c 2 Ne. 5:26;
      Mosiah 23:17.
33 *a* TG Church.

17 4 *a* Deut. 12:14 (13–14).
   5 *a* TG Sacrifice.
   7 *a* Jer. 3:9 (8–9); Ezek. 23:37.
   8 *a* Moro. 7:6 (5–6);
      D&C 132:9.
 10 *a* Ezek. 14:8.

   b TG Blood, Eating of.
11 *a* Gen. 9:4.
   b TG Mortality.
   c TG Blood, Symbolism of.
   d TG Jesus Christ,
      Atonement through.

that sojourneth among you eat blood.

13 And whatsoever man *there be* of the children of Israel, or of the strangers that sojourn among you, which hunteth and catcheth any beast or fowl that may be eaten; he shall even pour out the blood thereof, and *a*cover it with dust.

14 For *it is* the life of all flesh; the blood of it *is* for the life thereof: therefore I said unto the children of Israel, Ye shall eat the *a*blood of no manner of flesh: for the life of all flesh *is* the *b*blood thereof: whosoever eateth it shall be cut off.

15 And every soul that eateth that which *a*died *of itself,* or that which was torn *with beasts, whether it be* one of your own country, or a stranger, he shall both wash his clothes, and bathe *himself* in water, and be unclean until the even: then shall he be clean.

16 But if he wash *them* not, nor bathe his flesh; then he shall bear his iniquity.

CHAPTER 18

Israel shall not live as the Egyptians and the Canaanites—Marriages to many close relatives and others are forbidden—Homosexual behavior and other sexual perversions are an abomination—The land expels those nations that practice sexual abominations.

AND the LORD spake unto Moses, saying,

2 Speak unto the children of Israel, and say unto them, I am the LORD your God.

3 After the *a*doings of the land of Egypt, wherein ye dwelt, shall ye not do: and after the doings of the land of Canaan, whither I bring you, shall ye not do: neither shall ye *b*walk in their ordinances.

4 Ye shall do my *a*judgments, and keep mine *b*ordinances, to *c*walk therein: I *am* the LORD your God.

5 Ye shall therefore keep my *a*statutes, and my judgments: which if a man do, he shall *b*live *c*in them: I *am* the LORD.

6 ¶ None of you shall approach to any that is near of kin to him, to uncover *their* *a*nakedness: I *am* the LORD.

7 The *a*nakedness of thy father, or the nakedness of thy mother, shalt thou not uncover: she *is* thy mother; thou shalt not uncover her nakedness.

8 The *a*nakedness of thy father's wife shalt thou not uncover: it *is* thy father's nakedness.

9 The nakedness of thy sister, the daughter of thy father, or daughter of thy mother, *whether she be* born at home, or born abroad, *even* their nakedness thou shalt not *a*uncover.

10 The nakedness of thy son's daughter, or of thy daughter's daughter, *even* their nakedness thou shalt not uncover: for theirs *is* thine own nakedness.

11 The nakedness of thy father's wife's daughter, begotten of thy father, she *is* thy sister, thou shalt not uncover her nakedness.

12 Thou shalt not uncover the nakedness of thy father's sister: she *is* thy father's near kinswoman.

13 Thou shalt not uncover the nakedness of thy mother's sister: for she *is* thy mother's near kinswoman.

14 Thou shalt not uncover the nakedness of thy father's brother, thou shalt not approach to his wife: she *is* thine aunt.

15 Thou shalt not uncover the nakedness of thy daughter in law: she *is* thy son's wife; thou shalt not uncover her nakedness.

16 Thou shalt not uncover the

13*a* Ezek. 24:7.
14*a* TG Blood, Eating of.
  b 1 Cor. 15:50.
15*a* Lev. 11:40.
18 3*a* TG Apostasy of Israel.
  b TG Walking in
    Darkness.

4*a* TG Judgment.
  b TG Ordinance.
  c TG Walking with God.
5*a* Ezek. 33:15.
  b Luke 10:28;
    3 Ne. 15:9;
    D&C 84:44.

  c OR by them.
6*a* TG Sensuality;
    Sexual Immorality.
7*a* Ezek. 22:10.
8*a* Lev. 20:11 (11–21).
9*a* 2 Sam. 13:12.

nakedness of thy brother's ^awife: it *is* thy brother's nakedness.

17 Thou shalt not uncover the nakedness of a ^awoman and her daughter, neither shalt thou take her son's daughter, or her daughter's daughter, to uncover her nakedness; *for* they *are* her near kinswomen: it *is* wickedness.

18 Neither shalt thou take a wife to her sister, to vex *her*, to uncover her nakedness, beside the other in her life *time*.

19 Also thou shalt not approach unto a ^awoman to uncover her nakedness, as long as she is put ^bapart for her uncleanness.

20 Moreover thou shalt not lie carnally with thy neighbour's wife, to defile thyself with her.

21 And thou shalt not let any of thy seed pass through *the* ^afire to ^bMolech, neither shalt thou ^cprofane the ^dname of thy God: I *am* the LORD.

22 ^aThou shalt not lie with mankind, as with womankind: it *is* ^babomination.

23 Neither shalt thou lie with any beast to defile thyself therewith: neither shall any woman stand before a beast to lie down thereto: it *is* confusion.

24 ^aDefile not ye yourselves in any of these things: for in all these the nations are ^bdefiled which I ^ccast out before you:

25 And the ^aland is ^bdefiled: therefore I do visit the iniquity thereof upon it, and the land itself vomiteth out her inhabitants.

26 Ye shall therefore ^akeep my statutes and my judgments, and shall not commit *any* of these

abominations; *neither* any of your own nation, nor any stranger that sojourneth among you:

27 (For all these ^aabominations have the men of the land done, which *were* before you, and the land is defiled;)

28 That the ^aland spue not you out also, when ye defile it, as it spued out the nations that *were* before you.

29 For whosoever shall commit any of these abominations, even the souls that commit *them* shall be ^acut off from among their people.

30 Therefore shall ye keep mine ordinance, that *ye* commit not *any one* of these abominable ^acustoms, which were committed before you, and that ye defile not yourselves therein: I *am* the LORD your God.

CHAPTER 19

Israel is commanded: Be holy, live righteously, love your neighbor, and keep the commandments—The Lord reveals and reaffirms sundry laws and commandments—Enchantments, wizardry, prostitution, and all evil practices are forbidden.

AND the LORD spake unto Moses, saying,

2 Speak unto all the congregation of the children of Israel, and say unto them, Ye shall be ^aholy: for I the LORD your God *am* holy.

3 ¶ Ye shall fear every man his mother, and his father, and keep my ^asabbaths: I *am* the ^bLORD your God.

4 ¶ Turn ye not unto ^aidols, nor make to yourselves molten gods: I *am* the LORD your God.

16*a* Lev. 20:21;
    Matt. 14:4 (3–4).
17*a* TG Woman.
19*a* Ezek. 18:6.
  b Ezek. 22:10.
21*a* Deut. 12:31; 18:10;
    2 Kgs. 16:3 (3–4); 21:6;
    Jer. 7:31; 19:5; 32:35.
  b 2 Kgs. 23:10.
  c TG Swearing.
  d Ex. 20:7.
22*a* OR With the male you
    shall not lie as one lies

with the woman.
  b TG Homosexual
    Behavior.
24*a* Deut. 18:12.
    TG Virtue.
  b Num. 35:34 (33–34).
  c Ex. 34:24;
    Josh. 24:13 (8–13).
25*a* TG Israel, Land of.
  b Ezek. 36:17.
    TG Pollution.
26*a* TG Obedience.
27*a* TG Apostasy of Israel; Sin.

28*a* Deut. 18:9.
29*a* TG Excommunication.
30*a* TG Traditions of Men.
19 2*a* OR saints or holy ones.
    Josh. 24:19; Isa. 5:16;
    D&C 82:14.
    TG God, the Standard
    of Righteousness;
    Holiness.
3*a* D&C 59:9.
  b Lev. 20:8.
4*a* Judg. 17:3 (3–4);
    2 Ne. 9:37; D&C 1:16.

5 ¶ And if ye offer a sacrifice of peace offerings unto the LORD, ye shall ªoffer it at your own ᵇwill.

6 It shall be eaten the same day ye offer it, and on the morrow: and if ought remain until the third day, it shall be burnt in the fire.

7 And if it be eaten at all on the third day, it is ªabominable; it shall not be accepted.

8 Therefore *every one* that eateth it shall ªbear his iniquity, because he hath profaned the hallowed thing of the LORD: and that soul shall be cut off from among his people.

9 ¶ And when ye reap the ªharvest of your land, thou shalt not wholly ᵇreap the corners of thy field, neither shalt thou gather the ᶜgleanings of thy harvest.

10 And thou shalt not glean thy vineyard, neither shalt thou gather *every* grape of thy vineyard; thou shalt leave them for the ªpoor and stranger: I *am* the LORD your God.

11 ¶ Ye shall not ªsteal, neither ᵇdeal falsely, neither ᶜlie one to another.

12 ¶ And ye shall not ªswear by my name ᵇfalsely, neither shalt thou ᶜprofane the name of thy God: I *am* the LORD.

13 ¶ Thou shalt not ªdefraud thy ᵇneighbour, neither rob *him:* the ᶜwages of him that is hired shall not abide with thee all night until the morning.

14 ¶ Thou shalt not ªcurse the ᵇdeaf, nor put a ᶜstumblingblock before the ᵈblind, but shalt fear thy God: I *am* ᵉthe LORD.

15 ¶ Ye shall do no ªunrighteousness in ᵇjudgment: thou shalt not ᶜrespect the person of the poor, nor honour the person of the mighty: *but* in ᵈrighteousness shalt thou judge thy neighbour.

16 ¶ Thou shalt not go up and down *as* a ªtalebearer among thy people: neither shalt thou stand against the blood of thy neighbour: I *am* the LORD.

17 ¶ ªThou shalt not hate thy brother in thine ᵇheart: thou shalt in any wise rebuke thy neighbour, and not suffer sin upon him.

18 ¶ Thou shalt not ªavenge, nor bear any ᵇgrudge against the children of thy people, but thou shalt ᶜlove thy ᵈneighbour as thyself: I *am* the LORD.

19 ¶ Ye shall keep my statutes. ªThou shalt not let thy cattle gender with a diverse kind: thou shalt not sow thy field with ᵇmingled seed: neither shall a garment ᶜmingled of linen and woollen come upon thee.

20 ¶ And whosoever lieth carnally with a woman, that *is* a bondmaid, betrothed to ªan husband, and not at all redeemed, nor freedom given

5a TG Sacrifice.
  b Moro. 7:6.
7a Lev. 7:18;
    Ezek. 14:14.
8a Lev. 5:1 (1–6).
9a TG Harvest.
  b Ruth 2:2 (2, 12).
  c Ruth 2:8 (2–9);
    Mosiah 4:26;
    D&C 42:31.
10a TG Charity; Poor;
    Welfare.
11a TG Stealing.
  b D&C 136:25.
  c TG Lying.
12a TG Swearing.
  b TG Honesty.
  c TG Profanity.
13a Deut. 24:15.
    TG Fraud.
  b TG Neighbor.

  c TG Wages.
14a TG Curse.
  b TG Compassion.
  c Rom. 14:13.
  d Deut. 27:18.
  e HEB Jehovah. Note
    that this phrase occurs
    fifteen times like a seal
    of authority upon each
    of these statutes.
15a HEB injustice.
    Ex. 23:3 (1–3).
  b TG Judgment.
  c IE show unjust
    favoritism either to the
    humble or the mighty.
    Deut. 1:17;
    D&C 38:25 (25–27).
  d TG Righteousness.
16a TG Gossip; Honesty.
17a IE Though you may

reprove a neighbor and
not tolerate his sin, do
not hate him.
  Jacob 2:7;
  D&C 121:43.
  b TG Hardheartedness.
18a TG Forbear;
    Retribution.
  b TG Malice.
  c TG Charity; Love.
  d TG Fellowshipping;
    Neighbor.
19a Note that these laws
    are in harmony with
    the other admonitions
    to keep things pure
    and in proper use.
    TG Separation.
  b Deut. 22:9.
  c Deut. 22:11.
20a HEB a man.

her; *b*she shall be scourged; they shall not be put to death, because she was not free.

21 And he shall bring his trespass offering unto the LORD, unto the door of the tabernacle of the congregation, *even* a ram for a trespass offering.

22 And the priest shall make an atonement for him with the ram of the trespass offering before the LORD for his sin which he hath done: and the sin which he hath done shall be *a*forgiven him.

23 ¶ And when ye shall come into the land, and shall have planted all manner of trees for food, then ye shall count the fruit thereof as uncircumcised: three years shall it be as uncircumcised unto you: it shall not be eaten of.

24 But in the fourth year all the fruit thereof shall be holy to praise the LORD *withal.*

25 And in the fifth year shall ye eat of the fruit thereof, that it may yield unto you the increase thereof: I *am* the LORD your God.

26 ¶ Ye shall not eat *any thing* with the *a*blood: *b*neither shall ye use *c*enchantment, nor *d*observe times.

27 Ye shall not *a*round the corners of your heads, neither shalt thou mar the corners of thy beard.

28 Ye shall not make any *a*cuttings in your *b*flesh for the dead, nor print any marks upon you: I *am* the LORD.

29 ¶ Do not *a*prostitute thy daughter, to cause her to be a whore; lest the land fall to *b*whoredom, and the land become full of *c*wickedness.

30 ¶ Ye shall keep my *a*sabbaths, and *b*reverence my sanctuary: I *am* the LORD.

31 ¶ *a*Regard not them that have *b*familiar *c*spirits, neither seek after *d*wizards, to be defiled by them: I *am* the LORD your God.

32 ¶ Thou shalt *a*rise up before the *b*hoary head, and *c*honour the face of the old man, and fear thy God: I *am* the LORD.

33 ¶ And if a stranger sojourn with thee in your land, ye shall not *a*vex him.

34 *But* the *a*stranger that dwelleth with you shall be unto you *b*as one born among you, and thou shalt *c*love him as thyself; for ye were strangers in the land of Egypt: I *am* the LORD your God.

35 ¶ Ye shall do no *a*unrighteousness in judgment, in meteyard, in weight, or in measure.

36 Just balances, just *a*weights, a just *b*ephah, and a just hin, shall ye have: I *am* the LORD your God, which brought you out of the land of Egypt.

37 Therefore shall ye observe all my statutes, and all my judgments, and do them: I *am* the LORD.

CHAPTER 20

The death penalty is prescribed for sacrificing children to Molech, cursing father and mother, adultery, homosexual behavior, bestiality, spiritualism, and other abominations—Various laws and ordinances are listed.

AND the LORD spake unto Moses, saying,

20*b* HEB there shall be an investigation or inquisition.
22*a* TG Forgive.
26*a* TG Blood, Eating of.
  b HEB you shall not divine or use sorcery.
  c 2 Kgs. 21:6; 2 Ne. 10:15; 26:22 (22–23).
  d Deut. 18:14; Isa. 47:13 (13–15).
27*a* IE by cutting the forelocks of the hair of the head. Lev. 21:5.
28*a* 1 Kgs. 18:28. TG Mourning.
  b TG Body, Sanctity of.
29*a* Deut. 23:17 (17–18).
  b TG Whore.
  c HEB lewdness.
30*a* Lev. 23:3.
  b TG Reverence.
31*a* HEB Do not turn to magic or necromancy.
  b TG Spirits, Evil or Unclean.
  c TG Sorcery.
  d TG Superstitions.
32*a* HEB rise before the face of old age.
  b Prov. 20:29.
  c TG Courtesy; Family, Children, Duties of; Respect.
33*a* HEB oppress.
34*a* TG Fellowshipping; Stranger.
  b HEB as a citizen of yours.
  c Deut. 10:19. TG Love.
35*a* HEB injustice.
36*a* Deut. 25:13.
  b Deut. 25:15 (14–15); Ezek. 45:10; Amos 8:5.

2 Again, thou shalt say to the children of Israel, Whosoever *he be* of the children of Israel, or of the strangers that sojourn in Israel, that giveth *any* of his seed unto *a*Molech; he shall surely be put to death: the people of the land shall stone him with stones.

3 And I will set my face against that man, and will cut him off from among his people; because he hath given of his seed unto Molech, to *a*defile my sanctuary, and to *b*profane my holy name.

4 And if the people of the land do any ways hide their eyes from the man, when he giveth of his seed unto Molech, and *a*kill him not:

5 Then I will set my *a*face against that man, and against his family, and will cut him off, and all that go a whoring after him, to commit *b*whoredom with Molech, from among their people.

6 ¶ And the soul that turneth *a*after such as have *b*familiar *c*spirits, and after *d*wizards, to go a whoring after them, I will even set my face against that soul, and will *e*cut him off from among his people.

7 ¶ *a*Sanctify yourselves therefore, and be ye *b*holy: for I *am* the LORD your God.

8 And ye shall keep my statutes, and do them: I *am* the *a*LORD which sanctify you.

9 ¶ For every one that *a*curseth his *b*father or his mother shall be surely put to death: he hath cursed his father or his mother; his *c*blood *shall be* upon him.

10 ¶ And the man that committeth adultery with *another* man's wife, *even he* that committeth adultery with his *a*neighbour's wife, the *b*adulterer and the *c*adulteress shall surely be put to *d*death.

11 And the man that lieth with his *a*father's wife hath uncovered his father's *b*nakedness: both of them shall surely be put to death; their blood *shall be* upon them.

12 And if a man lie with his daughter in law, both of them shall surely be put to death: they have *a*wrought confusion; their blood *shall be* upon them.

13 If a man *a*also lie with mankind, as he lieth with a *b*woman, both of them have committed an *c*abomination: they shall surely be put to death; their blood *shall be* upon them.

14 And if a man take a wife and her mother, it *is* *a*wickedness: they shall be burnt with fire, both he and they; that there be no wickedness among you.

15 And if a man lie with a *a*beast, he shall surely be put to death: and ye shall slay the beast.

16 And if a woman approach unto any beast, and lie down thereto, thou shalt kill the woman, and the beast: they shall surely be put to death; their blood *shall be* upon them.

17 And if a man shall take his sister, his father's daughter, or his mother's daughter, and see her *a*nakedness, and she see his nakedness; it *is* a *b*wicked thing; and they shall be *c*cut off in the sight of their people: he hath uncovered his sister's nakedness; he shall bear his iniquity.

---

20 2*a* TG Superstitions.
   3*a* TG Sacrilege.
     b TG Profanity.
   4*a* Deut. 17:5 (2–3, 5).
   5*a* Jer. 21:10; 44:11.
     b Jer. 3:9 (8–9);
        Ezek. 23:37.
   6*a* HEB to magic or
        necromancy.
     b TG Spirits, Evil or
        Unclean.
     c TG Sorcery.
     d 2 Ne. 18:19.
     e TG Excommunication.

   7*a* Lev. 21:8; 22:32;
        D&C 88:74.
     b OR saints.
   8*a* Lev. 19:3.
   9*a* TG Curse.
     b TG Family, Children,
        Duties of.
     c TG Accountability.
  10*a* Ezek. 18:11.
     b TG Adulterer;
        Sexual Immorality.
     c John 8:5.
     d TG Capital Punishment.
  11*a* Deut. 22:30.

     b Lev. 18:8 (7–8).
  12*a* OR done lewdness.
  13*a* HEB lies with a male.
     b TG Woman.
     c TG Homosexual
        Behavior.
  14*a* OR lewdness or an evil
        device.
  15*a* Deut. 27:21.
  17*a* Deut. 27:22.
     b OR disgrace
        (Aramaism).
     c IE publicly
        excommunicated.

18 And if a man shall lie with a woman having her sickness, and shall uncover her nakedness; he hath discovered her fountain, and she hath uncovered the fountain of her blood: and both of them shall be cut off from among their people.

19 And thou shalt not uncover the nakedness of thy mother's sister, nor of thy father's sister: for he uncovereth his near kin: they shall bear their iniquity.

20 And if a man shall lie with his uncle's wife, he hath uncovered his uncle's nakedness: they shall bear their sin; they shall die childless.

21 And if a man shall take his brother's wife, it *is* *a*an unclean thing: he hath uncovered his brother's nakedness; they shall be childless.

22 ¶ Ye shall therefore keep all my statutes, and all my judgments, and do them: that the land, whither I bring you to dwell therein, *a*spue you not out.

23 And ye shall not *a*walk in the manners of the *b*nation, which I cast out before you: for they committed all these things, and therefore I abhorred them.

24 But I have said unto you, Ye shall inherit their land, and I will give it unto you to possess it, a land that floweth with *a*milk and honey: I *am* the LORD your God, which have *b*separated you from *other* people.

25 Ye shall therefore *a*put difference between clean beasts and unclean, and between unclean fowls and clean: and ye shall not make your souls abominable by beast, or by fowl, or by any manner of living thing that creepeth on the ground,

which I have *b*separated from you as *c*unclean.

26 And ye shall be *a*holy unto me: for I the LORD *am* *b*holy, and have *c*severed you from *other* people, that ye should be *d*mine.

27 ¶ A man also or woman that hath a *a*familiar spirit, or that is a wizard, shall surely be put to death: they shall stone them with stones: their *b*blood *shall be* upon them.

CHAPTER 21

The priests are to be holy—The high priest is not to marry a widow, a divorced person, or a harlot—Descendants of Aaron with physical blemishes may not offer the bread of God upon the altar.

AND the LORD said unto Moses, Speak unto the priests the sons of Aaron, and say unto them, There shall none be defiled for the *a*dead *b*among his people:

2 But for his kin, that is near unto him, *that is,* for his mother, and for his father, and for his son, and for his daughter, and for his brother,

3 And for his sister a virgin, that is nigh unto him, which hath had no husband; for her may he be defiled.

4 But he shall not defile himself, *being* a chief man among his people, to profane himself.

5 They shall not make *a*baldness upon their head, neither shall they shave off the corner of their beard, nor make any cuttings in their *b*flesh.

6 They shall be *a*holy unto their God, and not *b*profane the name of their God: for the offerings of the LORD made by *c*fire, *and* the bread of their God, they do offer: therefore they shall be holy.

---

21 *a* HEB impurity; i.e.,
  repulsive.
  Lev. 18:16;
  Matt. 14:4 (3–4).
22 *a* 1 Ne. 17:38 (37–38).
23 *a* TG Walking in Darkness.
  b Deut. 7:1 (1–2).
24 *a* D&C 38:18.
  b 1 Kgs. 8:53.
25 *a* HEB distinguish between.
  b HEB distinguished for
  you as impure.

  c Acts 10:15.
26 *a* TG Peculiar People.
  b TG Holiness.
  c HEB distinguished
  you from the nations.
  TG Separation.
  d 3 Ne. 24:17.
27 *a* This is in Hebrew
  ov, a skin bottle used
  as an instrument of
  necromancy.
  TG Spirits, Evil or

  Unclean.
  b Jacob 1:19.
21 1 *a* Ezek. 44:25.
  b IE among the family of
  Aaron.
5 *a* Lev. 19:27;
  Ezek. 44:20.
  b TG Body, Sanctity of.
6 *a* D&C 38:42.
  TG Holiness.
  b TG Profanity.
  c Lev. 3:11.

7 They shall not take a wife *that is* a *a*whore, or profane; neither shall they take a woman put away from her husband: for he *is* holy unto his God.

8 Thou shalt sanctify him therefore; for he offereth the bread of thy God: he shall be holy unto thee: for I the LORD, which *a*sanctify you, *am* holy.

9 ¶ And the daughter of any priest, if she profane herself by playing the whore, she profaneth her father: she shall be *a*burnt with fire.

10 And *he that is* the *a*high priest among his brethren, upon whose head the *b*anointing oil was poured, and *c*that is consecrated to put on the garments, shall not uncover his head, nor rend his clothes;

11 Neither shall he go in to any dead body, nor defile himself for his father, or for his mother;

12 Neither shall he go out of the *a*sanctuary, nor profane the sanctuary of his God; for the *b*crown of the *c*anointing oil of his God *is* upon him: I *am* the LORD.

13 And he shall take a wife in her virginity.

14 A *a*widow, or a divorced woman, or profane, *or* an harlot, these shall he not take: but he shall take a virgin of his own people to wife.

15 Neither shall he profane his seed among his people: for I the LORD do sanctify him.

16 ¶ And the LORD spake unto Moses, saying,

17 Speak unto Aaron, saying, Whosoever *he be* of thy seed in their generations that hath *any* *a*blemish, let him not approach to offer the bread of his God.

18 For whatsoever man *he be* that hath a blemish, he shall not approach: a blind man, or a lame,

or he that hath a flat nose, or any thing *a*superfluous,

19 Or a man that is brokenfooted, or brokenhanded,

20 Or crookbackt, or a dwarf, or that hath a blemish in his eye, or be scurvy, or scabbed, or hath his stones broken;

21 No man that hath a blemish of the seed of Aaron the priest shall come nigh to offer the offerings of the LORD made by fire: he hath a blemish; he shall not come nigh to offer the bread of his God.

22 He shall eat the bread of his God, *both* of the most holy, and of the holy.

23 Only he shall not go in unto the *a*veil, nor come nigh unto the altar, because he hath a blemish; that he profane not my sanctuaries: for I the LORD do sanctify them.

24 And Moses told *it* unto Aaron, and to his sons, and unto all the children of Israel.

CHAPTER 22

Those of the priests and their families who may eat of the holy things are described—Sacrificial animals are to be perfect and without blemish.

AND the LORD spake unto Moses, saying,

2 Speak unto Aaron and to his sons, that they separate themselves from the *a*holy things of the children of Israel, and that they *b*profane not my holy name *in those things* *c*which they hallow unto me: I *am* the LORD.

3 Say unto them, Whosoever *he be* of all your seed among your generations, that goeth unto the holy things, which the children of Israel hallow unto the LORD, *a*having his *b*uncleanness upon him, that soul

---

7*a* TG Whore.
8*a* Lev. 20:7.
9*a* Gen. 38:24.
10*a* Ex. 29:1 (1–46);
     Num. 35:25.
  b TG Priesthood, Aaronic.
  c HEB (literally) whose
     hand is filled; i.e.,
     who is equipped or
     authorized.

12*a* OR temple.
  b OR consecration.
  c Lev. 10:7.
     TG Anointing.
14*a* Ezek. 44:22.
17*a* Deut. 23:1.
18*a* HEB too long; i.e.,
     deformed.
23*a* TG Veil.
22 2*a* Ezra 2:63.

  b D&C 88:74.
  c HEB which they
     sanctify for me.
     Deut. 15:19.
3*a* HEB and any impurity
     is upon him.
  b Num. 18:11;
     Morm. 9:29.

shall be ^ccut off from my presence: I *am* the LORD.

4 What man soever of the seed of Aaron *is* a ^aleper, or hath a running issue; he shall not eat of the holy things, until he be clean. And whoso toucheth any thing *that is* unclean *by* the dead, or a man whose seed goeth from him;

5 Or whosoever toucheth any creeping thing, whereby he may be made unclean, or a man ^aof whom he may take uncleanness, whatsoever uncleanness he hath;

6 The soul which hath touched any such shall be unclean until even, and shall not eat of the holy things, unless he wash his flesh with water.

7 And when the sun is down, he shall be clean, and shall afterward eat of the holy things; because it *is* his food.

8 That which ^adieth of itself, or is torn *with beasts,* he shall not eat to defile himself therewith: I *am* the LORD.

9 They shall therefore keep mine ordinance, lest they bear sin for it, and die therefore, if they profane it: I the LORD do sanctify them.

10 ^aThere shall no stranger eat *of* the holy thing: a sojourner of the priest, or an hired servant, shall not eat *of* the holy thing.

11 But ^aif the priest buy *any* soul with his money, he shall eat of it, and he that is born in his house: they shall eat of his ^bmeat.

12 If the priest's daughter also be *married* unto a stranger, she may not eat of an offering of the holy things.

13 But if the priest's daughter be a widow, or divorced, and have no child, and is returned unto her father's house, as in her youth, she shall eat of her father's meat: but there shall no stranger eat thereof.

14 ¶ And if a man eat *of* the holy thing unwittingly, then he shall put the fifth *part* thereof unto it, and shall give *it* unto the priest with the holy thing.

15 And they shall not profane the holy things of the children of Israel, which they offer unto the LORD;

16 ^aOr suffer them to bear the iniquity of trespass, when they eat their holy things: for I the LORD do sanctify them.

17 ¶ And the LORD spake unto Moses, saying,

18 Speak unto Aaron, and to his sons, and unto all the children of Israel, and say unto them, Whatsoever *he be* of the house of Israel, or of the strangers in Israel, that will ^aoffer his oblation for all his vows, and for all his ^bfreewill offerings, which they will offer unto the LORD for a burnt offering;

19 *Ye shall* ^a*offer* at your own will a male without blemish, of the beeves, of the sheep, or of the goats.

20 *But* whatsoever hath a ^ablemish, *that* shall ye not offer: for it shall not be ^bacceptable for you.

21 And whosoever offereth a sacrifice of peace offerings unto the LORD to accomplish *his* ^avow, or a freewill offering in beeves or sheep, ^bit shall be perfect to be accepted; there shall be no blemish therein.

22 ^aBlind, or ^bbroken, or maimed, or having a ^cwen, or scurvy, or scabbed, ye shall not offer these unto the LORD, nor make an offering by fire of them upon the altar unto the LORD.

23 Either a bullock or a lamb that hath any thing superfluous or lacking in his parts, that mayest thou

---

3c TG Death, Spiritual, First.
4a TG Leprosy.
5a HEB by whom he may become unclean.
8a Ex. 22:31; Ezek. 44:31.
10a HEB Any alien shall not eat a sacred thing.
11a IE if he purchase a servant, the servant may partake of the sacred food.

b HEB bread or food.
16a HEB And cause them to bear the iniquity of guilt in their eating of their holy things.
18a HEB sacrifice his sacrifice.
b Amos 4:5.
19a TG Sacrifice.
20a Deut. 15:21; 17:1; Heb. 9:14;

1 Pet. 1:19.
b Mal. 1:13; D&C 132:10; Moses 5:21.
21a Eccl. 5:4 (4–5).
b IE it must be whole, or without blemish, to be acceptable.
22a Mal. 1:8.
b Mal. 1:13 (8–13).
c HEB wart.

offer *for* a *ª*freewill offering; but for a vow it shall not be accepted.

24 Ye shall not offer unto the LORD that which is bruised, or crushed, or broken, or cut; neither shall ye make *any offering thereof* in your land.

25 Neither from a stranger's hand shall ye offer the bread of your God of any of these; because their corruption *is* in them, *and* blemishes *be* in them: they shall not be accepted for you.

26 ¶ And the LORD spake unto Moses, saying,

27 When a bullock, or a sheep, or a goat, is *ª*brought forth, then it shall be *b*seven days under *c*the dam; and from the eighth day and thenceforth it shall be *d*accepted for an offering made by fire unto the LORD.

28 And *whether it be* cow or ewe, ye shall not kill *ª*it and her young both in one day.

29 And when ye will offer a sacrifice of *ª*thanksgiving unto the LORD, offer *it* at your own will.

30 On the same day it shall be *ª*eaten up; ye shall leave none of it until the morrow: I *am* the LORD.

31 Therefore shall ye keep my commandments, and do them: I *am* the LORD.

32 Neither shall ye profane my holy name; but I will be *ª*hallowed among the children of Israel: I *am* the LORD which *b*hallow you,

33 That brought you out of the land of Egypt, to be your God: I *am* the LORD.

CHAPTER 23

Israel is to hold a holy convocation on each weekly Sabbath—Israel is to keep the Feasts of the Passover, of Unleavened Bread, of Pentecost or Firstfruits, of Trumpets, of the Day of Atonement, and of Tabernacles.

AND the LORD spake unto Moses, saying,

2 Speak unto the children of Israel, and say unto them, *Concerning* the feasts of the LORD, which ye shall proclaim *to be* holy convocations, *even* these *are* my feasts.

3 Six days shall work be done: but the *ª*seventh day *is* the *b*sabbath of rest, an holy *c*convocation; ye shall do no work *therein:* it *is* the *d*sabbath of the LORD in all your dwellings.

4 ¶ These *are* the feasts of the LORD, *even* holy convocations, which ye shall proclaim in their seasons.

5 In the *ª*fourteenth *day* of the first month *b*at even *is* the LORD's *c*passover.

6 And on the fifteenth day of the same month *is* the feast of unleavened bread unto the LORD: seven days ye must eat *ª*unleavened bread.

7 In the first day ye shall have an holy *ª*convocation: ye shall do no servile work therein.

8 But ye shall offer an offering made by fire unto the LORD seven days: in the seventh day *is* an holy convocation: ye shall do no servile work *therein.*

9 ¶ And the LORD spake unto Moses, saying,

10 Speak unto the children of Israel, and say unto them, When ye be come into the land which I give unto you, and shall reap the harvest thereof, then ye shall bring a sheaf of the *ª*firstfruits of your harvest unto the priest:

11 And he shall wave the sheaf before the LORD, to be accepted for you: on the morrow after the sabbath the priest shall wave it.

12 And ye shall offer that day when

23*a* Lev. 7:16;
   Ezek. 46:12.
27*a* HEB born.
  b Ex. 22:30.
  c HEB its mother.
  d Ex. 28:38.
28*a* Deut. 22:6.
29*a* TG Thanksgiving.

30*a* Lev. 7:15.
32*a* HEB sanctified.
  b Lev. 20:7.
23 3*a* Lev. 19:30.
  b TG Sabbath.
  c TG Meetings.
  d D&C 59:9 (9–13).
5*a* Ex. 12:6 (1–14);

Ezek. 45:21.
  b IE between daytime and nighttime.
  c TG Passover.
6*a* TG Bread, Unleavened.
7*a* TG Meetings.
10*a* Num. 28:26 (26–31);
   Mosiah 2:3.

ye wave the sheaf an he ᵃlamb without blemish of the first year for a burnt offering unto the LORD.

13 And the meat offering thereof *shall be* two tenth deals of fine flour mingled with oil, an offering made by fire unto the LORD *for* a sweet savour: and the drink offering thereof *shall be* of wine, the fourth *part* of an hin.

14 And ye shall eat neither bread, nor parched corn, nor green ears, until the selfsame day that ye have brought an offering unto your God: *it shall be* a statute for ever throughout your generations in all your dwellings.

15 ¶ And ye shall count unto you from the morrow after the sabbath, from the day that ye brought the sheaf of the wave offering; ᵃseven sabbaths shall be complete:

16 Even unto the morrow after the seventh sabbath shall ye number ᵃfifty days; and ye shall offer a new meat offering unto the LORD.

17 Ye shall bring out of your habitations two wave ᵃloaves of two tenth deals: they shall be of fine flour; they shall be baken with ᵇleaven; *they are* the firstfruits unto the LORD.

18 And ye shall offer with the bread seven ᵃlambs without blemish of the first year, and one young bullock, and two rams: they shall be *for* a burnt offering unto the LORD, with their meat offering, and their drink offerings, *even* an offering made by fire, of sweet savour unto the LORD.

19 Then ye shall sacrifice one kid of the goats for a sin offering, and two lambs of the first year for a sacrifice of peace offerings.

20 And the priest shall wave them with the bread of the firstfruits *for* a wave offering before the LORD, with the two lambs: they shall be holy to the LORD for the priest.

21 And ye shall proclaim on the selfsame day, *that* it may be an holy convocation unto you: ye shall do no servile work *therein: it shall be* a statute for ever in all your dwellings throughout your generations.

22 ¶ And when ye reap the harvest of your land, thou shalt not make clean riddance of the corners of thy field when thou reapest, neither shalt thou gather any gleaning of thy harvest: thou shalt leave them unto the ᵃpoor, and to the stranger: I *am* the LORD your God.

23 ¶ And the LORD spake unto Moses, saying,

24 Speak unto the children of Israel, saying, In the seventh month, in the first *day* of the month, shall ye have a sabbath, a memorial of ᵃblowing of ᵇtrumpets, an holy ᶜconvocation.

25 Ye shall do no servile ᵃwork *therein:* but ye shall offer an offering made by fire unto the LORD.

26 ¶ And the LORD spake unto Moses, saying,

27 Also on the tenth *day* of this seventh month *there shall be* a day of atonement: it shall be an holy ᵃconvocation unto you; and ye shall ᵇafflict your souls, and offer an offering made by fire unto the LORD.

28 And ye shall do no work in that same day: for it *is* a day of atonement, to make an atonement for you before the LORD your God.

29 For whatsoever soul *it be* that shall not be afflicted in that same day, he shall be cut off from among his people.

30 And whatsoever soul *it be* that doeth any work in that same day, the same soul will I destroy from among his people.

31 Ye shall do no manner of work: *it shall be* a statute for ever throughout your generations in all your dwellings.

12a TG Passover.
15a Deut. 16:10 (9–12).
16a Acts 2:1.
17a Neh. 10:37.
  b TG Leaven.
18a HEB sheep, whole, a
    year old.
22a TG Poor;
    Welfare.
24a IE a blast, or a trill, of
    the ram's horn.
  b Num. 10:10; 29:1 (1–6);
Ps. 81:3.
  c TG Meetings.
25a D&C 59:10.
27a TG Meetings.
  b IE humble.
    Acts 27:9.

32 It *shall be* unto you a sabbath of rest, and ye shall afflict your souls: in the ninth *day* of the month at even, from even unto even, shall ye [a]celebrate your sabbath.

33 ¶ And the LORD spake unto Moses, saying,

34 Speak unto the children of Israel, saying, The fifteenth day of this [a]seventh month *shall be* the [b]feast of [c]tabernacles *for* seven days unto the LORD.

35 On the first day *shall be* an holy [a]convocation: ye shall do no servile work *therein.*

36 Seven days ye shall offer an offering made by fire unto the LORD: on the eighth day shall be an holy convocation unto you; and ye shall offer an offering made by fire unto the LORD: it *is* a [a]solemn assembly; *and* ye shall do no servile work *therein.*

37 These *are* the feasts of the LORD, which ye shall proclaim *to be* holy convocations, to offer an offering made by fire unto the LORD, a burnt offering, and a meat offering, a sacrifice, and drink offerings, [a]every thing upon his day:

38 Beside the sabbaths of the LORD, and beside your gifts, and beside all your vows, and beside all your freewill offerings, which ye give unto the LORD.

39 Also in the fifteenth day of the seventh month, when ye have gathered in the fruit of the land, ye shall keep a feast unto the LORD seven days: on the first day *shall be* a sabbath, and on the eighth day *shall be* a sabbath.

40 And ye shall take you on the first day the boughs of goodly trees, branches of palm trees, and the boughs of thick trees, and willows of the brook; and ye shall rejoice before the LORD your God seven days.

41 And ye shall keep it a [a]feast unto the LORD seven days in the year. *It shall be* a statute for ever in your generations: ye shall celebrate it in the seventh month.

42 Ye shall dwell in booths seven days; all that are Israelites born shall dwell in booths:

43 That your generations may know that I made the children of Israel to dwell in [a]booths, when I brought them out of the land of Egypt: I *am* the LORD your God.

44 And Moses declared unto the children of Israel the feasts of the LORD.

CHAPTER 24

A perpetual fire is to burn outside the veil in the tabernacle—A blasphemer is put to death by stoning—Israel's law is one of an eye for an eye and a tooth for a tooth.

AND the LORD spake unto Moses, saying,

2 Command the children of Israel, that they bring unto thee pure oil olive beaten for the light, to cause the [a]lamps to burn continually.

3 Without the veil of the testimony, [a]in the tabernacle of the congregation, shall Aaron [b]order it from the evening unto the morning before the LORD continually: *it shall be* a statute for ever in your generations.

4 He shall order the [a]lamps upon the pure candlestick before the LORD continually.

5 ¶ And thou shalt take fine flour, and bake twelve [a]cakes thereof: two tenth deals shall be in one cake.

6 And thou shalt [a]set them in two rows, six on a row, upon the pure [b]table before the LORD.

7 And thou shalt put pure frankincense upon *each* row, that it may

---

32a OR observe.
34a Ezek. 45:25.
  b 1 Kgs. 8:2, 65; 12:32;
    Ezra 3:4; John 7:2.
  c OR booths.
    Num. 29:12 (12–38).
    Deut. 16:13;
    Hosea 12:9 (8–9);
    Zech. 14:16.

35a TG Meetings.
36a TG Solemn Assembly.
37a OR every one
    according to its day.
41a Num. 29:12 (12–38).
43a Neh. 8:14.
24 2a Ex. 27:20 (20–21);
    1 Sam. 3:3;
    Matt. 25:1 (1–13).

3a HEB in the tent of
    meeting shall Aaron set
    it in order.
  b TG Order.
4a Ex. 25:37.
5a Hosea 7:8.
    TG Bread, Shewbread.
6a Ex. 40:4.
  b Heb. 9:2.

be on the bread for a memorial, *even* an offering made by fire unto the LORD.

8 Every sabbath he shall set it in order before the LORD continually, *being taken* from the children of Israel by an everlasting covenant.

9 And it shall be Aaron's and his sons'; and they shall *a*eat it in the holy place: for it *is* most holy unto him of the offerings of the LORD made by fire by a perpetual statute.

10 ¶ And the son of an Israelitish woman, whose father *was* an Egyptian, went out among the children of Israel: and this son of the Israelitish *woman* and a man of Israel strove together in the camp;

11 And the Israelitish woman's son *a*blasphemed the name *of the* LORD, and cursed. And they brought him unto Moses: (and his mother's name *was* Shelomith, the daughter of Dibri, of the tribe of Dan:)

12 And they put him *a*in ward, that the *b*mind of the LORD might be shewed them.

13 And the LORD spake unto Moses, saying,

14 Bring forth him that hath cursed without the camp; and let all that heard *him* lay their hands upon his head, and let all the congregation stone him.

15 And thou shalt speak unto the children of Israel, saying, Whosoever *a*curseth his God shall bear his sin.

16 And he that *a*blasphemeth the name of the LORD, he shall surely be put to death, *and* all the congregation shall certainly stone him: as well the stranger, as he that is born in the land, when he blasphemeth the name *of the* LORD, shall be put to death.

17 ¶ And he that *a*killeth any man shall surely be put to *b*death.

18 And he that killeth a beast shall make it good; *a*beast for beast.

19 And if a man cause a *a*blemish in his neighbour; as he hath done, so shall it be done to him;

20 Breach for breach, *a*eye for eye, tooth for tooth: as he hath caused a blemish in a man, so shall it be done to him *again*.

21 And he that killeth a beast, he shall *a*restore it: and he that killeth a man, he shall be put to death.

22 Ye shall have one manner of *a*law, as well for the stranger, as for one of your own country: for I *am* the LORD your God.

23 ¶ And Moses spake to the children of Israel, that they should bring forth him that had cursed out of the camp, and stone him with stones. And the children of Israel did as the LORD commanded Moses.

CHAPTER 25

Each seventh year is to be kept as a sabbath year—Each fiftieth year is to be one of jubilee, in which liberty is proclaimed throughout the land—Laws are revealed for the sale and redemption of lands, houses, and servants—The land is the Lord's, as are the servants—Usury is forbidden.

AND the LORD spake unto Moses in mount Sinai, saying,

2 Speak unto the children of Israel, and say unto them, When ye come into the land which I give you, then shall the land keep a *a*sabbath unto the LORD.

3 Six years thou shalt sow thy field, and six years thou shalt prune thy vineyard, and gather in the fruit thereof;

4 But in the seventh year shall be a sabbath of rest unto the land, a sabbath for the LORD: thou shalt neither sow thy field, nor prune thy vineyard.

5 That which groweth of its own accord of thy harvest thou shalt not

---

9*a* Ex. 29:33 (32–33);
   Luke 6:4.
11*a* TG Profanity.
12*a* HEB under guard.
   b D&C 102:23.
   TG Mind.
15*a* TG Curse.

16*a* John 19:7 (6–8).
   TG Blaspheme.
17*a* TG Murder.
   b TG Punish.
18*a* HEB a soul for a soul; i.e.,
   life for life.
19*a* HEB defect; i.e.,

   maims him.
20*a* Matt. 5:38 (38–42);
   3 Ne. 12:38 (38–40).
21*a* D&C 98:47.
22*a* HEB judging or
   judgment.
25 2*a* TG Sabbatical Year.

reap, neither gather the grapes ^aof thy vine undressed: *for* it is a year of rest unto the land.

6 And the sabbath of the land shall be meat for you; for thee, and for thy servant, and for thy maid, and for thy hired servant, and for thy stranger that sojourneth with thee,

7 And for thy cattle, and for the beast that *are* in thy land, shall all the increase thereof be ^ameat.

8 ¶ And thou shalt number seven sabbaths of years unto thee, seven times seven years; and the space of the seven sabbaths of years shall be unto thee forty and nine years.

9 Then shalt thou ^acause the trumpet of the jubilee to sound on the tenth *day* of the seventh month, in the day of atonement shall ye make the trumpet sound throughout all your land.

10 And ye shall ^ahallow the fiftieth year, and proclaim ^bliberty throughout *all* the land unto all the inhabitants thereof: it shall be a jubilee unto you; and ye shall return every man unto his possession, and ye shall return every man unto his ^cfamily.

11 A ^ajubilee shall that fiftieth year be unto you: ye shall not sow, neither reap that which groweth of itself in it, nor gather *the grapes* in it of ^bthy vine undressed.

12 For it *is* the jubilee; it shall be holy unto you: ye shall eat the increase thereof out of the field.

13 In the year of this jubilee ye shall return every man unto his possession.

14 And if thou sell ought unto thy neighbour, or buyest *ought* of thy neighbour's hand, ye shall not ^aoppress ^bone another:

15 According to the number of years after the jubilee thou shalt buy of thy neighbour, *and* according unto the number of years of the fruits he shall sell unto thee:

16 According to the ^amultitude of years thou shalt increase the price thereof, and according to the fewness of years thou shalt diminish the price of it: for *according* to the number *of the years* of the fruits doth he sell unto thee.

17 Ye shall not therefore ^aoppress ^bone another; but thou shalt fear thy God: for I *am* the LORD your God.

18 ¶ Wherefore ye shall ^ado my statutes, and keep my ^bjudgments, and do them; and ye shall dwell in the land in safety.

19 And the land shall yield her fruit, and ye shall eat your fill, and dwell therein in safety.

20 And if ye shall say, What shall we eat the ^aseventh year? behold, we shall not sow, nor gather in our increase:

21 Then I will command my ^ablessing upon you in the sixth year, and it shall bring forth fruit for three years.

22 And ye shall sow the eighth year, and eat *yet* of old fruit until the ninth year; until her fruits come in ye shall eat *of* the old *store.*

23 ¶ The land shall not be sold for ever: for the land *is* mine; for ye *are* ^astrangers and sojourners with me.

24 And in all the land of your possession ye shall grant a redemption for the land.

25 ¶ If thy brother be waxen poor, and hath sold away *some* of his possession, and if any of his kin come to ^aredeem it, then shall he redeem that which his brother sold.

26 And if the man have none to redeem it, and himself be able to redeem it;

27 Then let him count the years

5*a* HEB of thy separation; i.e., of the time "set apart" as a sabbatical year.
7*a* HEB to eat.
9*a* HEB sound the trill of the ram's horn.
10*a* HEB sanctify.
 b TG Liberty.
c TG Family, Patriarchal.
11*a* Num. 36:4.
 b HEB (the time of) its separation or consecration.
14*a* TG Love.
 b Lev. 25:17.
16*a* OR amount, number.
17*a* TG Oppression.
 b Lev. 25:14.
18*a* Mosiah 1:7; 2:22; Alma 50:20 (20–22).
 b HEB decrees or laws.
20*a* TG Sabbatical Year.
21*a* 1 Ne. 3:7.
23*a* OR proselytes. TG Stranger.
25*a* Ruth 4:4.

of the sale thereof, and restore the overplus unto the man to whom he sold it; that he may return unto his possession.

28 But if he be not able to restore *it* to him, then that which is sold shall remain in the hand of him that hath bought it until the year of jubilee: and in the jubilee it shall *a*go out, and he shall *b*return unto his possession.

29 And if a man sell a dwelling house in a walled city, then he may redeem it within a whole year after it is sold; *within* a full year may he redeem it.

30 And if it be not redeemed within the space of a full year, then the house that *is* in the walled city shall be established for ever to him that bought it throughout his generations: it shall not go out in the jubilee.

31 But the houses of the villages which have no wall round about them shall be counted as the fields of the country: they may be redeemed, and they shall go out in the jubilee.

32 Notwithstanding the cities of the Levites, *and* the houses of the cities of their possession, may the Levites redeem at any time.

33 And if a man purchase of the Levites, then the house that was sold, and the city of his possession, shall go out in *the year of* jubilee: for the houses of the cities of the Levites *are* their possession among the children of Israel.

34 But the *a*field of the *b*suburbs of their cities may not be sold; for it *is* their perpetual possession.

35 ¶ And if thy brother be waxen poor, and *a*fallen in decay with thee; then thou shalt relieve him: *yea, though he be* a stranger, or a sojourner; that he may live with thee.

36 Take thou no *a*usury of him, or increase: but fear thy God; that thy brother may live with thee.

37 Thou shalt not give him thy money upon *a*usury, nor lend him thy victuals for increase.

38 I *am* the LORD your God, which brought you forth out of the land of Egypt, to give you the land of Canaan, *and* to be your God.

39 ¶ And if thy brother *that dwelleth* by thee be waxen poor, and be *a*sold unto thee; thou shalt not compel him to serve as a *b*bondservant:

40 *But* as an hired servant, *and* as a sojourner, he shall be with thee, *and* shall serve thee unto the year of jubilee:

41 And *then* shall he depart from thee, *both* he and his children with him, and shall return unto his own family, and unto the possession of his fathers shall he return.

42 For they *are* my servants, which I brought forth out of the land of Egypt: they shall not be sold as bondmen.

43 Thou shalt not rule over him with rigour; but shalt *a*fear thy God.

44 Both thy bondmen, and thy bondmaids, which thou shalt have, *shall be* of the *a*heathen that are round about you; of them shall ye buy bondmen and bondmaids.

45 Moreover of the children of the strangers that do sojourn among you, of them shall ye buy, and of their families that *are* with you, which they begat in your land: and they shall be your possession.

46 And ye shall take them as an *a*inheritance for your children after you, to inherit *them for* a possession; they shall be your bondmen *b*for ever: but over your brethren the children of Israel, ye shall not rule one over another with rigour.

47 ¶ And if a sojourner or stranger wax rich by thee, and thy brother *that dwelleth* by him wax poor, and sell himself unto the stranger *or* sojourner by thee, or to the stock of the stranger's family:

28*a* HEB release; i.e., be
  released.
  b Lev. 27:24.
34*a* 2 Chr. 31:19.
  b Num. 35:2 (2–7);
  2 Chr. 11:14.

35*a* HEB his hand slips or
  fails.
36*a* TG Usury.
37*a* TG Debt.
39*a* Deut. 15:12 (12–18).
  b TG Bondage, Physical.

43*a* Morm. 9:27.
44*a* HEB nations, or
  Gentiles.
46*a* Num. 36:4;
  D&C 38:20.
  b HEB perpetually.

48 After that he is sold he may be redeemed again; one of his brethren may redeem him:

49 Either his uncle, or his uncle's son, may redeem him, or *any* that is nigh of kin unto him of his family may redeem him; or if he be able, he may redeem himself.

50 And he shall reckon with him that bought him from the year that he was sold to him unto the year of jubilee: and the price of his sale shall be according unto the number of years, according to the time of an hired servant shall it be with him.

51 If *there be* yet many years *behind,* according unto them he shall give again the price of his redemption out of the money that he was bought for.

52 And if there remain but few years unto the year of jubilee, then he shall count with him, *and* according unto his years shall he give him again the price of his redemption.

53 *And* as a yearly hired servant shall he be with him: *and the other* shall not rule with rigour over him in thy sight.

54 And if he be not redeemed in these *years,* then he shall go out in the year of jubilee, *both* he, and his children with him.

55 For unto me the children of Israel *are* ᵃservants; they *are* my servants whom I brought forth out of the land of Egypt: I *am* the LORD your God.

CHAPTER 26

Temporal and spiritual blessings will abound in Israel if the people keep the commandments—Cursing, scourging, and desolation will be theirs if they disobey the Lord—When His people repent, the Lord will show mercy unto them.

YE shall make you no ᵃidols nor ᵇgraven image, neither rear you up a ᶜstanding image, neither shall ye set up *any* image of stone in your land, to bow down unto it: for I *am* the LORD your God.

2 ¶ Ye shall keep my sabbaths, and ᵃreverence my sanctuary: I *am* the LORD.

3 ¶ If ye ᵃwalk in my statutes, and ᵇkeep my commandments, and do them;

4 Then I will ᵃgive you ᵇrain in due season, and the land shall yield her increase, and the trees of the field shall yield their fruit.

5 And your threshing shall reach unto the vintage, and the vintage shall reach unto the sowing time: and ye shall eat your bread to the full, and dwell in your land safely.

6 And I will ᵃgive ᵇpeace in the land, and ye shall lie down, and none shall make *you* afraid: and I will rid evil beasts out of the land, neither shall the sword go through your land.

7 And ye shall chase your ᵃenemies, and they shall fall before you by the sword.

8 And five of you shall chase an hundred, and an hundred of you shall put ten thousand to flight: and your enemies shall fall before you by the sword.

9 For I will ᵃhave respect unto you, and make you fruitful, and multiply you, and establish my covenant with you.

10 And ye shall eat old store, and ᵃbring forth the old because of the new.

11 And I will set my tabernacle among you: and my soul shall not abhor you.

12 And I will ᵃwalk ᵇamong you,

55a 1 Ne. 21:3 (3–6);
       D&C 93:46 (45–46).
26 1a D&C 52:39.
    b Ex. 20:4 (4–6);
       Mosiah 12:36 (35–36).
    c OR pillar.
  2a TG Reverence.
  3a Joel 2:25 (23–26);
       2 Ne. 1:20.
       TG Obedience;

       Walking with God.
    b Judg. 2:15.
  4a TG God, Gifts of.
    b Deut. 28:12;
       Jer. 3:3;
       Joel 2:23;
       Acts 14:17;
       2 Ne. 15:6.
  6a TG God, Gifts of.
    b Ps. 66:12.

  7a 2 Ne. 4:33 (16–35);
       D&C 44:5.
  9a HEB turn unto you.
 10a HEB put out.
 12a Deut. 23:14;
       Zech. 2:10.
       TG Walking with God.
    b Josh. 22:31.

and will be your *c*God, and ye shall be my *d*people.

13 I *am* the Lord your God, which brought you forth out of the land of Egypt, that ye should not be their bondmen; and I have broken the bands of your *a*yoke, and made you go upright.

14 ¶ But if ye will not *a*hearken unto me, and will not do all these *b*commandments;

15 And if ye shall despise my statutes, or if your soul abhor my judgments, so that ye will not do all my commandments, *but* that ye *a*break my covenant:

16 I also will *a*do this unto you; I will even appoint over you terror, *b*consumption, and *c*the burning ague, that shall consume the eyes, and cause sorrow of heart: and ye shall sow your seed in vain, for your enemies shall eat it.

17 And I will set my face against you, and ye shall be *a*slain before your *b*enemies: they that hate you shall *c*reign over you; and ye shall *d*flee when none pursueth you.

18 And if ye will not yet for all this hearken unto me, then I will *a*punish you seven times more for your sins.

19 And I will break the *a*pride of your power; and I will make your heaven as iron, and your earth as brass:

20 And your strength shall be *a*spent in vain: for your land shall not yield her increase, neither shall the trees of the land yield their fruits.

21 ¶ And if ye walk *a*contrary unto me, and will not hearken unto me; I will bring seven times more

*b*plagues upon you according to your sins.

22 I will also send wild beasts among you, which shall rob you of your children, and destroy your cattle, and make you few in number; and your *a*high ways shall be desolate.

23 And if ye will not be reformed by me by these things, but will walk contrary unto me;

24 Then will I also walk contrary unto you, and will punish you yet *a*seven times for your sins.

25 And I will bring a *a*sword upon you, that shall *b*avenge the quarrel of *my* covenant: and when ye are gathered together within your cities, I will send the pestilence among you; and ye shall be delivered into the hand of the *c*enemy.

26 *And* when I have *a*broken the *b*staff of your bread, ten women shall bake your bread in one oven, and they shall deliver *you* your bread again by weight: and ye shall eat, and not be *c*satisfied.

27 And if ye will not for all this hearken unto me, but walk contrary unto me;

28 Then I will walk contrary unto you also in fury; and I, even I, will *a*chastise you seven times for your sins.

29 And ye shall *a*eat the *b*flesh of your sons, and the flesh of your daughters shall ye eat.

30 And I will destroy your high places, and cut down your images, and cast your carcases upon the carcases of your idols, and my soul shall abhor you.

31 And I will make your cities

12*c* Ezek. 34:24 (20–31);
　　 2 Cor. 6:16.
　d 3 Ne. 20:19; D&C 63:1 (1–6).
　　 TG Israel, Blessings of;
　　 Israel, Mission of.
13*a* TG Bondage, Physical.
14*a* Deut. 28:15 (15–68);
　　 Jer. 26:4; Amos 2:4;
　　 Alma 5:38 (38–42);
　　 D&C 101:7.
　b Dan. 9:13.
15*a* TG Apostasy of Israel.
16*a* Mosiah 7:29;
　　 Hel. 12:3 (2–4);

　　 D&C 43:25.
　b Deut. 28:22.
　c IE fever.
17*a* 1 Kgs. 8:33.
　b Josh. 7:4.
　c D&C 103:8.
　d Ps. 53:5; Prov. 28:1.
18*a* OR chastise.
19*a* TG Pride.
20*a* TG Waste.
21*a* TG Obedience.
　b Deut. 9:8 (7–29);
　　 Ps. 66:11 (10–12).
　　 TG Plague.

22*a* Judg. 5:6; Hel. 14:24;
　　 3 Ne. 21:14 (14–15).
24*a* Joel 1:4.
25*a* Ezek. 14:17.
　b HEB execute the vengeance of the covenant.
　c Ezek. 39:23 (23–24).
26*a* Ezek. 14:13.
　b Ps. 105:16.
　c Micah 6:14.
28*a* TG Chastening.
29*a* Deut. 28:53; Jer. 19:9;
　　 Lam. 4:10.
　b 1 Ne. 21:26; Moro. 9:8.

^{a}waste, and bring your sanctuaries unto desolation, and ^{b}I will not smell the savour of your sweet odours.

32 And I will bring the ^{a}land into desolation: and your enemies which dwell therein shall be astonished at it.

33 And I will ^{a}scatter you among the heathen, and will draw out a sword after you: and your land shall be ^{b}desolate, and your cities waste.

34 Then shall the land enjoy her ^{a}sabbaths, as long as it lieth desolate, and ye *be* in your enemies' land; *even* then shall the land rest, and enjoy her sabbaths.

35 As long as it lieth desolate it shall rest; because it did not rest in your sabbaths, when ye dwelt upon it.

36 And upon them that are left *alive* of you I will send a faintness into their hearts in the lands of their enemies; and the sound of a shaken leaf shall chase them; and they shall flee, as fleeing from a sword; and they shall fall when none pursueth.

37 And they shall fall one upon another, as it were before a sword, when none pursueth: and ye shall have no power to stand before your enemies.

38 And ye shall perish among the heathen, and the land of your ^{a}enemies shall eat you up.

39 And they that are left of you shall ^{a}pine away in their iniquity in your enemies' lands; and also in the iniquities of their fathers shall they pine away with them.

40 If they shall ^{a}confess their iniquity, and the iniquity of their fathers, with their trespass which they trespassed against me, and that also they have walked contrary unto me;

41 And *that* I also have walked contrary unto them, and have brought them into the land of their enemies; if then their uncircumcised hearts be ^{a}humbled, and they then accept of the ^{b}punishment of their iniquity:

42 Then will I remember my ^{a}covenant with Jacob, and also my covenant with Isaac, and also my covenant with ^{b}Abraham will I remember; and I will remember the land.

43 The land also shall be left of them, and shall enjoy her sabbaths, while she lieth desolate without them: and they shall accept of the punishment of their iniquity: because, even because they despised my judgments, and because their soul abhorred my statutes.

44 And yet for all that, when they be in the land of their ^{a}enemies, I will not cast them away, neither will I abhor them, to ^{b}destroy them utterly, and to break my ^{c}covenant with them: for I *am* the LORD their God.

45 But I will for their sakes remember the covenant of their ancestors, whom I brought forth out of the land of Egypt in the ^{a}sight of the heathen, that I might be their God: I *am* the LORD.

46 These *are* the statutes and judgments and laws, which the LORD made between him and the children of Israel in mount Sinai by the hand of Moses.

CHAPTER 27

How properties are consecrated unto the Lord is explained—Israel is commanded to pay tithes of their crops, flocks, and herds.

AND the LORD spake unto Moses, saying,

2 Speak unto the children of Israel, and say unto them, When a man shall make a singular vow, the

---

31*a* Ezek. 5:14.
  b IE I will not accept your burnt offerings.
32*a* Isa. 3:1.
33*a* TG Israel, Scattering of.
  b 2 Kgs. 22:19.
34*a* TG Sabbatical Year.

38*a* Ps. 106:42 (42–43).
39*a* HEB decay or waste away.
40*a* TG Confession.
41*a* TG Contrite Heart.
  b TG Punish.
42*a* TG Covenants.

  b D&C 84:34; 132:30 (30–32).
44*a* 1 Kgs. 8:46.
  b Enos 1:13 (11–18).
  c TG Promise.
45*a* Ps. 98:2.

persons *shall be* for the LORD by thy estimation.

3 And thy estimation shall be of the male from twenty years old even unto sixty years old, even thy estimation shall be fifty shekels of silver, after the shekel of the sanctuary.

4 And if it *be* a female, then thy estimation shall be thirty shekels.

5 And if *it be* from five years old even unto twenty years old, then thy estimation shall be of the male twenty shekels, and for the female ten shekels.

6 And if *it be* from a month old even unto five years old, then thy estimation shall be of the male five shekels of silver, and for the female thy estimation *shall be* three shekels of silver.

7 And if *it be* from sixty years old and above; if *it be* a male, then thy estimation shall be fifteen shekels, and for the female ten shekels.

8 But if he be poorer than thy estimation, then he shall present himself before the priest, and the priest shall value him; according to his ability that vowed shall the priest value him.

9 And if *it be* a beast, whereof men bring an offering unto the LORD, all that *any man* giveth of such unto the LORD shall be holy.

10 He shall not alter it, nor change it, a good for a bad, or a bad for a good: and if he shall at all change beast for beast, then it and the exchange thereof shall be holy.

11 And if *it be* any unclean beast, of which they do not offer a sacrifice unto the LORD, then he shall present the beast before the priest:

12 And the priest shall value it, whether it be good or bad: as thou valuest it, *who art* the priest, so shall it be.

13 But if he will at all redeem it, then he shall add a fifth *part* thereof unto thy estimation.

14 ¶ And when a man shall sanctify his house *to be* holy unto the LORD, then the priest shall estimate it, whether it be good or bad: as the priest shall estimate it, so shall it stand.

15 And if he that sanctified it will redeem his house, then he shall add the fifth *part* of the money of thy estimation unto it, and it shall be his.

16 And if a man shall sanctify unto the LORD *some part* of a field of his possession, then thy estimation shall be according to the seed thereof: an ᵃhomer of barley seed *shall be valued* at fifty shekels of silver.

17 If he sanctify his field from the year of jubilee, according to thy estimation it shall stand.

18 But if he sanctify his field after the jubilee, then the priest shall reckon unto him the money according to the years that remain, even unto the year of the jubilee, and it shall be abated from thy estimation.

19 And if he that sanctified the field will in any wise redeem it, then he shall add the fifth *part* of the money of thy estimation unto it, and it shall be assured to him.

20 And if he will not redeem the field, or if he have sold the field to another man, it shall not be redeemed any more.

21 But the field, when it goeth out in the jubilee, shall be holy unto the LORD, as a field ᵃdevoted; the possession thereof shall be the priest's.

22 And if *a man* sanctify unto the LORD a field which he hath bought, which *is* not of the fields of his possession;

23 Then the priest shall reckon unto him the worth of thy estimation, *even* unto the year of the jubilee: and he shall give thine estimation in that day, *as a holy thing* unto the LORD.

24 In the year of the jubilee the field shall ᵃreturn unto him of whom it was bought, *even* to him to whom the possession of the land *did belong.*

25 And all thy estimations shall be according to the ᵃshekel of the sanctuary: twenty gerahs shall be the shekel.

---

27 16a Ezek. 45:11.   24a Lev. 25:28.
     21a Num. 18:14 (11–14).   25a Ex. 30:13.

26 ¶ Only the *firstling of the beasts, which should be the LORD's firstling, no man shall sanctify it; whether *it be* ox, or sheep: it *is* the LORD's.

27 And if *it be* of an unclean beast, then he shall redeem *it* according to thine estimation, and shall add a fifth *part* of it thereto: or if it be not redeemed, then it shall be sold according to thy estimation.

28 Notwithstanding no devoted thing, that a man shall devote unto the LORD of all that he hath, *both* of man and beast, and of the field of his possession, shall be *sold or redeemed: every devoted thing *is* most holy unto the LORD.

29 None devoted, which shall be devoted of men, shall be redeemed; *but* shall surely be put to death.

30 And all the *tithe of the land, *whether* of the seed of the land, *or* of the fruit of the tree, *is* the LORD's: *it is* holy unto the LORD.

31 And if a man will at all redeem *ought* of his tithes, he shall add thereto the fifth *part* thereof.

32 And concerning the tithe of the herd, or of the flock, *even* of whatsoever passeth under the *rod, the tenth shall be holy unto the LORD.

33 He shall not search whether it be good or bad, neither shall he change it: and if he change it at all, then both it and the change thereof shall be holy; it shall not be redeemed.

34 These *are* the commandments, which the LORD commanded Moses for the children of Israel in mount Sinai.

THE FOURTH BOOK OF MOSES

CALLED

NUMBERS

CHAPTER 1

Moses and the princes in Israel count from each tribe (except Levi) those males twenty years of age and older—They total 603,550—The Levites are appointed to attend the tabernacle.

AND the LORD *spake unto Moses in the *wilderness of Sinai, in the tabernacle of the congregation, on the first *day* of the second month, in the *second year after they were come out of the land of Egypt, saying,

2 Take ye the *sum of all the congregation of the children of Israel, after their *families, by the house of their *fathers, with the number of *their* names, every male by *their polls;

3 From twenty years old and upward, all that are able to go forth to war in Israel: thou and Aaron shall number them by their armies.

26a TG Firstborn.
28a Ezek. 48:14.
30a TG Tithing.
32a Ezek. 20:37 (23–38).

[NUMBERS]

1 1a Ex. 25:22.
  b The lessons of this

period of wilderness wandering are reviewed in Ps. 105–7 and in Heb. 3:7–19.
  Num. 10:12;
  Mosiah 12:33;
  D&C 84:23 (23–34).
c Num. 9:1.

2a Num. 26:2 (1–51).
  b Mosiah 6:3;
  Ether 1:41;
  D&C 48:6.
c TG Family, Patriarchal.
d OR a head count.

4 And with you there shall be a man of every tribe; every one ᵃhead of the house of his fathers.

5 ¶ And these *are* the names of the men that shall stand with you: of *the tribe of* Reuben; Elizur the son of Shedeur.

6 Of Simeon; Shelumiel the son of Zurishaddai.

7 Of Judah; ᵃNahshon the son of Amminadab.

8 Of Issachar; Nethaneel the son of Zuar.

9 Of Zebulun; Eliab the son of Helon.

10 Of the children of Joseph: of Ephraim; Elishama the son of Ammihud: of Manasseh; Gamaliel the son of Pedahzur.

11 Of Benjamin; Abidan the son of Gideoni.

12 Of Dan; Ahiezer the son of Ammishaddai.

13 Of Asher; Pagiel the son of Ocran.

14 Of Gad; Eliasaph the son of ᵃDeuel.

15 Of Naphtali; Ahira the son of Enan.

16 These *were* the renowned of the congregation, princes of the tribes of their fathers, heads of thousands in Israel.

17 ¶ And Moses and Aaron took these men which are expressed by *their* names:

18 And they assembled all the congregation together on the first *day* of the second month, and they declared their ᵃpedigrees after their families, by the house of their fathers, according to the number of the names, from twenty years old and upward, by their polls.

19 As the Lᴏʀᴅ commanded Moses, so he ᵃnumbered them in the wilderness of Sinai.

20 And the children of Reuben, Israel's eldest son, by their generations, after their families, by the house of their fathers, according to the number of the names, by their

polls, every male from twenty years old and upward, all that were able to go forth to war;

21 Those that were ᵃnumbered of them, *even* of the tribe of Reuben, *were* forty and six thousand and five hundred.

22 ¶ Of the children of Simeon, by their generations, after their families, by the house of their fathers, those that were numbered of them, according to the number of the names, by their ᵃpolls, every male from twenty years old and upward, all that were able to go forth to war;

23 Those that were numbered of them, *even* of the tribe of Simeon, *were* fifty and nine thousand and three hundred.

24 ¶ Of the children of Gad, by their generations, after their families, by the house of their fathers, according to the number of the names, from twenty years old and upward, all that were able to go forth to war;

25 Those that were numbered of them, *even* of the tribe of Gad, *were* forty and five thousand six hundred and fifty.

26 ¶ Of the children of Judah, by their generations, after their families, by the house of their fathers, according to the number of the names, from twenty years old and upward, all that were able to go forth to war;

27 Those that were numbered of them, *even* of the tribe of Judah, *were* threescore and fourteen thousand and six hundred.

28 ¶ Of the children of ᵃIssachar, by their generations, after their families, by the house of their fathers, according to the number of the names, from twenty years old and upward, all that were able to go forth to war;

29 Those that were numbered of them, *even* of the tribe of Issachar, *were* fifty and four thousand and four hundred.

4*a* Num. 7:2.
7*a* Matt. 1:4.
14*a* Num. 2:14.

18*a* D&C 128:24.
19*a* 2 Sam. 24:1 (1–4).
21*a* Num. 26:7; Deut. 33:6.

22*a* 1 Chr. 23:24.
28*a* Num. 26:23 (23–26);
1 Chr. 7:1.

30 ¶ Of the children of Zebulun, by their generations, after their families, by the house of their fathers, according to the number of the names, from twenty years old and upward, all that were able to go forth to war;

31 Those that were numbered of them, *even* of the tribe of Zebulun, *were* fifty and seven thousand and four hundred.

32 ¶ Of the children of *a*Joseph, *namely*, of the children of Ephraim, by their generations, after their families, by the house of their fathers, according to the number of the names, from twenty years old and upward, all that were able to go forth to war;

33 Those that were numbered of them, *even* of the tribe of Ephraim, *were* forty *a*thousand and five hundred.

34 ¶ Of the children of Manasseh, by their generations, after their families, by the house of their fathers, according to the number of the names, from twenty years old and upward, all that were able to go forth to war;

35 Those that were numbered of them, *even* of the tribe of *a*Manasseh, *were* thirty and two thousand and two hundred.

36 ¶ Of the children of Benjamin, by their generations, after their families, by the house of their fathers, according to the number of the names, from twenty years old and upward, all that were able to go forth to war;

37 Those that were numbered of them, *even* of the tribe of Benjamin, *were* thirty and five thousand and four hundred.

38 ¶ Of the children of Dan, by their generations, after their families, by the house of their fathers, according to the number of the names, from twenty years old and upward, all that were able to go forth to war;

39 Those that were numbered of them, *even* of the tribe of Dan, *were* threescore and two thousand and seven hundred.

40 ¶ Of the children of Asher, by their generations, after their families, by the house of their fathers, according to the number of the names, from twenty years old and upward, all that were able to go forth to war;

41 Those that were numbered of them, *even* of the tribe of Asher, *were* forty and one thousand and five hundred.

42 ¶ Of the children of Naphtali, throughout their generations, after their families, by the house of their fathers, according to the number of the names, from twenty years old and upward, all that were able to go forth to war;

43 Those that were numbered of them, *even* of the tribe of Naphtali, *were* fifty and three thousand and four hundred.

44 These *are* those that were numbered, which Moses and Aaron numbered, and the princes of Israel, *being* *a*twelve men: each one was for the house of his fathers.

45 So were all those that were numbered of the children of Israel, by the house of their fathers, from twenty years old and upward, all that were able to go forth to war in Israel;

46 Even all they that were *a*numbered were *b*six hundred thousand and three thousand and five hundred and fifty.

47 ¶ But the Levites after the tribe of their fathers were not numbered among them.

48 For the Lord had spoken unto Moses, saying,

49 Only thou shalt not number the tribe of Levi, neither take the sum of them among the children of Israel:

50 But thou shalt appoint the

32*a* TG Israel, Joseph,
  People of.
33*a* Gen. 48:19.

35*a* TG Israel, Joseph,
  People of.
44*a* TG Israel, Twelve

Tribes of.
46*a* Gen. 46:27 (26–27).
  b Num. 26:51.

*a*Levites over the *b*tabernacle of testimony, and over all the vessels thereof, and over all things that *belong* to it: they shall bear the tabernacle, and all the vessels thereof; and they shall minister unto it, and shall encamp round about the tabernacle.

51 And when the tabernacle setteth forward, the Levites shall take it down: and when the tabernacle is to be pitched, the Levites shall set it up: and *a*the *b*stranger that cometh nigh shall be *c*put to death.

52 And the children of Israel shall pitch their tents, every man by his own camp, and every man by his own standard, throughout their hosts.

53 But the Levites shall pitch round about the *a*tabernacle of testimony, that there be no wrath upon the congregation of the children of Israel: and the Levites shall keep the charge of the *b*tabernacle of testimony.

54 And the children of Israel did according to all that the LORD commanded Moses, so did they.

CHAPTER 2

The order and leaders of the tribes and armies of Israel in their tents are given.

AND the LORD spake unto Moses and unto Aaron, saying,

2 Every man of the children of Israel shall pitch by his own standard, with the ensign of their *a*father's house: *b*far off about the tabernacle of the congregation shall they pitch.

3 And on the east side toward the rising of the sun shall they of the standard of the camp of Judah pitch throughout their armies: and Nahshon the son of Amminadab *shall be* captain of the children of Judah.

4 And his host, and those that

were numbered of them, *were* threescore and fourteen thousand and six hundred.

5 And those that do pitch next unto him *shall be* the tribe of Issachar: and Nethaneel the son of Zuar *shall be* captain of the children of Issachar.

6 And his host, and those that were numbered thereof, *were* fifty and four thousand and four hundred.

7 *Then* the tribe of Zebulun: and Eliab the son of Helon *shall be* captain of the children of Zebulun.

8 And his host, and those that were numbered thereof, *were* fifty and seven thousand and four hundred.

9 All that were numbered in the camp of *a*Judah *were* an hundred thousand and fourscore thousand and six thousand and four hundred, throughout their armies. These shall first set forth.

10 ¶ On the south side *shall be* the standard of the camp of Reuben according to their armies: and the captain of the children of Reuben *shall be* Elizur the son of Shedeur.

11 And his host, and those that were numbered thereof, *were* forty and six thousand and five hundred.

12 And those which pitch by him *shall be* the tribe of Simeon: and the captain of the children of Simeon *shall be* Shelumiel the son of Zurishaddai.

13 And his host, and those that were numbered of them, *were* fifty and nine thousand and three hundred.

14 Then the tribe of Gad: and the captain of the sons of Gad *shall be* Eliasaph the son of *a*Reuel.

15 And his host, and those that were numbered of them, *were* forty and five thousand and six hundred and fifty.

16 All that were numbered in the camp of Reuben *were* an hundred

---

50*a* Ex. 38:21 (21–26);
    Num. 3:41 (7–41).
    TG Priesthood,
    Authority.
  b Num. 3:8 (6–8);
    1 Chr. 23:32.
51*a* IE anyone
    unauthorized.

  b Num. 18:22.
  c Num. 3:38 (10–38);
    1 Sam. 6:19 (19–20);
    2 Sam. 6:7 (6–7);
    D&C 85:8.
53*a* 1 Chr. 23:32.
  b 2 Chr. 24:6.
2 2*a* Num. 24:2.

  b OR facing the tent of
    meeting on all sides.
 9*a* Num. 10:14.
14*a* Deuel in Num. 1:14;
    7:42, 47; 10:20. Hebrew
    "r" and "d" look much
    alike.

thousand and fifty and one thousand and four hundred and fifty, throughout their armies. And they shall set forth in the second rank.

17 ¶ Then the tabernacle of the congregation shall set forward with the camp of the Levites in the midst of the camp: as they encamp, so shall they set forward, every man in his place by their standards.

18 ¶ On the west side *shall be* the standard of the camp of Ephraim according to their armies: and the captain of the sons of Ephraim *shall be* Elishama the son of Ammihud.

19 And his host, and those that were numbered of them, *were* forty thousand and five hundred.

20 And by him *shall be* the tribe of Manasseh: and the captain of the children of Manasseh *shall be* Gamaliel the son of Pedahzur.

21 And his host, and those that were numbered of them, *were* thirty and two thousand and two hundred.

22 Then the tribe of Benjamin: and the captain of the sons of Benjamin *shall be* Abidan the son of Gideoni.

23 And his host, and those that were numbered of them, *were* thirty and five thousand and four hundred.

24 All that were numbered of the camp of ᵃEphraim *were* an hundred thousand and eight thousand and an hundred, throughout their armies. And they shall go forward in the third rank.

25 ¶ The standard of the camp of ᵃDan *shall be* on the north side by their armies: and the captain of the children of Dan *shall be* Ahiezer the son of Ammishaddai.

26 And his host, and those that were numbered of them, *were* threescore and two thousand and seven hundred.

27 And those that encamp by him *shall be* the tribe of Asher: and the captain of the children of Asher *shall be* Pagiel the son of Ocran.

28 And his host, and those that were numbered of them, *were* forty and one thousand and five hundred.

29 ¶ Then the tribe of Naphtali: and the captain of the children of Naphtali *shall be* Ahira the son of Enan.

30 And his host, and those that were numbered of them, *were* fifty and three thousand and four hundred.

31 All they that were numbered in the camp of Dan *were* an hundred thousand and fifty and seven thousand and six hundred. They shall go hindmost with their standards.

32 ¶ These *are* those which were numbered of the children of Israel by the house of their fathers: all those that were numbered of the camps throughout their hosts *were* six hundred thousand and three thousand and five hundred and fifty.

33 But the Levites were not numbered among the children of Israel; as the Lᴏʀᴅ commanded Moses.

34 And the children of Israel did according to all that the Lᴏʀᴅ commanded Moses: so they ᵃpitched by their ᵇstandards, and so they set forward, every one after their families, according to the house of their fathers.

CHAPTER 3

Aaron and his sons minister in the priest's office—The Levites are chosen to do the service of the tabernacle—They are the Lord's, replacing the firstborn of all families of Israel—Their number, charge, and service are given.

Tʜᴇsᴇ also *are* the generations of Aaron and Moses in the day *that* the Lᴏʀᴅ spake with Moses in mount Sinai.

2 And these *are* the names of the sons of ᵃAaron; Nadab the firstborn, and Abihu, Eleazar, and Ithamar.

3 These *are* the names of the sons of Aaron, the ᵃpriests which were anointed, whom he ᵇconsecrated to minister in the priest's office.

4 And Nadab and Abihu ᵃdied

24a Num. 10:22 (22–24).
25a Ezek. 48:1.
34a D&C 61:25 (24–25).
  b OR flags.

3 2a 1 Chr. 23:24 (24–32).
3a TG Priest, Aaronic
  Priesthood.
  BD Priests.

  b OR ordained.
4a Lev. 10:2 (1–2).

before the LORD, when they offered strange fire before the LORD, in the wilderness of Sinai, and they had no children: and Eleazar and Ithamar ministered in the priest's office in the sight of Aaron their father.

5 ¶ And the LORD spake unto Moses, saying,

6 Bring the tribe of *a*Levi near, and present them before Aaron the priest, that they may minister unto him.

7 And they shall keep his *a*charge, and the charge of the whole *b*congregation before the tabernacle of the congregation, to do the service of the tabernacle.

8 And they shall keep all the *a*instruments of the tabernacle of the congregation, and the charge of the children of Israel, to do the *b*service of the *c*tabernacle.

9 And thou shalt give the *a*Levites unto *b*Aaron and to his sons: they *are* wholly given unto him out of the children of Israel.

10 And thou shalt appoint *a*Aaron and his *b*sons, and they shall wait on their priest's office: and *c*the stranger that cometh nigh shall be put to death.

11 And the LORD spake unto Moses, saying,

12 And I, behold, I have taken the Levites from among the children of Israel instead of all the *a*firstborn that openeth the matrix among the children of Israel: therefore the Levites shall be mine;

13 Because all the firstborn *are* mine; *for* on the day that I smote all the firstborn in the land of Egypt I *a*hallowed unto me all the firstborn in Israel, both man and beast: mine shall they be: I *am* the LORD.

14 ¶ And the LORD spake unto Moses in the wilderness of Sinai, saying,

15 Number the children of *a*Levi after the house of their fathers, by their families: every male from a month old and upward shalt thou number them.

16 And Moses numbered them according to the word of the LORD, as he was commanded.

17 And these were the sons of *a*Levi by their names; Gershon, and Kohath, and Merari.

18 And these *are* the names of the sons of Gershon by their families; Libni, and Shimei.

19 And the sons of Kohath by their families; Amram, and Izehar, Hebron, and Uzziel.

20 And the sons of Merari by their families; Mahli, and Mushi. These *are* the families of the Levites according to the house of their fathers.

21 Of Gershon *was* the family of the Libnites, and the family of the Shimites: these *are* the families of the Gershonites.

22 Those that were numbered of them, according to the number of all the males, from a month old and upward, *even* those that were numbered of them *were* seven thousand and five hundred.

23 The families of the Gershonites shall pitch behind the tabernacle westward.

24 And the chief of the house of the father of the Gershonites *shall be* Eliasaph the son of Lael.

25 And the *a*charge of the sons of Gershon in the tabernacle of the congregation *shall be* the tabernacle, and the tent, the covering thereof, and the hanging for the *b*door of the tabernacle of the congregation,

26 And the hangings of the court, and the curtain for the door of the court, which *is* by the tabernacle, and by the altar round about, and

---

6a Deut. 10:8.
7a Lev. 8:35.
  b TG Church.
8a OR vessels, implements, furniture.
  b 1 Chr. 25:1.
     TG Service.
  c Num. 1:50 (50–53).

9a TG Priesthood, Aaronic.
  b Num. 16:40;
     1 Chr. 23:32.
10a TG Bishop.
  b TG Birthright.
  c IE the unauthorized person who presumes to officiate.

12a TG Firstborn.
13a OR consecrated.
15a Num. 26:57 (57–62).
17a Ex. 6:16 (16, 18);
     Num. 4:4 (4–15).
25a Num. 18:3 (2–3).
  b HEB opening into the courtyard.

the cords of it *a*for all the service thereof.

27 ¶ And of Kohath *was* the family of the Amramites, and the family of the Izeharites, and the family of the Hebronites, and the family of the Uzzielites: these *are* the families of the Kohathites.

28 In the number of all the males, from a month old and upward, *were* eight thousand and six hundred, keeping the charge of the sanctuary.

29 The families of the sons of Kohath shall pitch on the side of the tabernacle southward.

30 And the chief of the house of the father of the families of the Kohathites *shall be* Elizaphan the son of Uzziel.

31 And their charge *shall be* the *a*ark, and the table, and the candlestick, and the altars, and the vessels of the sanctuary wherewith they minister, and the hanging, and all the service thereof.

32 And Eleazar the son of *a*Aaron the priest *shall be* chief over the chief of the Levites, *and have* the oversight of them that keep the charge of the sanctuary.

33 ¶ Of Merari *was* the family of the Mahlites, and the family of the Mushites: these *are* the families of Merari.

34 And those that were numbered of them, according to the number of all the males, from a month old and upward, *were* six thousand and two hundred.

35 And the chief of the house of the father of the families of Merari *was* Zuriel the son of Abihail: *these* shall pitch on the side of the tabernacle northward.

36 And *under* the custody and charge of the sons of Merari *shall be* the boards of the tabernacle, and the bars thereof, and the pillars thereof, and the *a*sockets thereof, and all the vessels thereof, and all that serveth thereto,

37 And the pillars of the court round about, and their sockets, and their pins, and their cords.

38 ¶ But those that encamp before the tabernacle toward the east, *even* before the tabernacle of the congregation eastward, *shall be* Moses, and Aaron and his sons, keeping the *a*charge of the sanctuary for the charge of the children of Israel; and the stranger that cometh nigh shall be *b*put to death.

39 All that were numbered of the Levites, which Moses and Aaron numbered at the commandment of the LORD, throughout their families, all the males from a month old and upward, *were* twenty and two thousand.

40 ¶ And the LORD said unto Moses, Number all the firstborn of the males of the children of Israel from a month old and upward, and take the number of their names.

41 And thou shalt take the *a*Levites for me (I *am* the LORD) instead of all the *b*firstborn among the children of Israel; and the cattle of the Levites instead of all the firstlings among the cattle of the children of Israel.

42 And Moses numbered, as the LORD commanded him, all the firstborn among the children of Israel.

43 And all the firstborn males by the number of names, from a month old and upward, of those that were numbered of them, were twenty and two thousand two hundred and *a*threescore and thirteen.

44 ¶ And the LORD spake unto Moses, saying,

45 Take the Levites instead of all the firstborn among the children of Israel, and the cattle of the Levites instead of their cattle; and the Levites shall be mine: I *am* the LORD.

46 And for those that are to be redeemed of the two hundred and threescore and thirteen of the

---

26*a* OR according to their functions.
31*a* TG Ark of the Covenant.
32*a* 1 Chr. 6:50.

36*a* OR bases.
38*a* Num. 18:5 (2–7).
    b Num. 1:51.
41*a* Ex. 38:21 (21–26);

Num. 1:50 (47–53).
    b Ex. 13:2.
43*a* HEB seventy-three.

firstborn of the children of Israel, which are more than the Levites;

47 Thou shalt even take five shekels apiece *by the poll, after the shekel of the sanctuary shalt thou take *them:* (the shekel *is* twenty gerahs:)

48 And thou shalt give the money, wherewith the *odd number of them is to be redeemed, unto Aaron and to his sons.

49 And Moses took the redemption money of them that were over and above them that were redeemed by the Levites:

50 Of the firstborn of the children of Israel took he the money; a thousand three hundred and threescore and five *shekels,* after the shekel of the sanctuary:

51 And Moses gave the money of them that were redeemed unto Aaron and to his sons, according to the word of the LORD, as the LORD commanded Moses.

CHAPTER 4

When the camps of Israel move, Aaron and his sons cover the holy things in the tabernacle—The Levites of the families of Kohath, Gershon, and Merari carry the burden of the tabernacle.

AND the LORD spake unto Moses and unto Aaron, saying,

2 Take the sum of the sons of Kohath from among the sons of Levi, after their families, by the house of their fathers,

3 From *thirty years old and upward even until fifty years old, all that enter into the host, to do the work in *the tabernacle of the congregation.

4 This *shall be* the *service of the sons of *Kohath in the tabernacle of the congregation, *about* the most holy things:

5 ¶ And when the camp setteth forward, Aaron shall come, and his sons, and they shall take down the covering veil, and cover the *ark of testimony with it:

6 And shall put thereon the covering of badgers' skins, and shall spread over *it* a cloth wholly of blue, and shall put in the staves thereof.

7 And upon the table of *shewbread they shall spread a cloth of blue, and put thereon the *dishes, and the spoons, and the bowls, and *covers to cover withal: and the continual bread shall be thereon:

8 And they shall spread upon them a cloth of scarlet, and cover the same with a covering of badgers' skins, and shall put in the staves thereof.

9 And they shall take a cloth of blue, and cover the candlestick of the light, and his lamps, and his tongs, and his snuffdishes, and all the oil vessels thereof, wherewith they minister unto it:

10 And they shall put it and all the vessels thereof within a covering of badgers' skins, and shall put *it* upon a *bar.

11 And upon the golden altar they shall spread a cloth of blue, and cover it with a covering of badgers' skins, and shall put to the staves thereof:

12 And they shall take all the instruments of ministry, wherewith they minister in the sanctuary, and put *them* in a cloth of blue, and cover them with a covering of badgers' skins, and shall put *them* on a bar:

13 And they shall take away the ashes from the altar, and spread a purple cloth thereon:

14 And they shall put upon it all the vessels thereof, wherewith they minister about it, *even* the censers, the fleshhooks, and the shovels, and the basins, all the vessels of the

---

47a HEB per head, or each.
48a OR excess.
4 3a 1 Chr. 23:3;
  Luke 3:23.
  b HEB the tent of meeting (also as found in vv. 4–47).

4a TG Stewardship.
  b Ex. 6:16 (16, 18);
  Num. 3:17.
5a Ex. 25:10 (10–22).
7a OR the bread of the presence.
  TG Bread, Shewbread.

b Ex. 25:29.
c HEB jars for pouring (drink offering).
10a OR yoke, or carrying frame (also v. 12).

altar; and they shall spread upon it a covering of badgers' skins, and put to the staves of it.

15 And when Aaron and his sons have made an end of covering the sanctuary, and all the vessels of the sanctuary, as the camp is to set forward; after that, the sons of *Kohath shall come to *bear *it:* but they shall not *touch *any *holy thing, lest they die. These *things are* the burden of the sons of Kohath in the tabernacle of the congregation.

16 ¶ And to the office of Eleazar the son of Aaron the priest *pertaineth* the oil for the light, and the sweet incense, and the *daily meat offering, and the anointing oil, *and* the oversight of all the tabernacle, and of all that therein *is,* in the sanctuary, and in the vessels thereof.

17 ¶ And the LORD spake unto Moses and unto Aaron, saying,

18 Cut ye not off the tribe of the families of the Kohathites from among the Levites:

19 But thus do unto them, that they may live, and not die, when they approach unto the most holy things: Aaron and his sons shall go in, and appoint them every one to his service and to his burden:

20 But they shall not go in to see when the holy things are covered, lest they die.

21 ¶ And the LORD spake unto Moses, saying,

22 Take also the sum of the sons of Gershon, throughout the houses of their fathers, by their families;

23 From thirty years old and upward until fifty years old shalt thou number them; all that enter in to perform the service, to do the work in the tabernacle of the congregation.

24 This *is* the service of the families of the Gershonites, to serve, and for burdens:

25 And they shall bear the curtains of the tabernacle, and the tabernacle of the congregation, his covering, and the covering of the badgers' skins that *is* above upon it, and the hanging for the door of the tabernacle of the congregation,

26 And the hangings of the court, and the hanging for the door of the gate of the court, which *is* by the tabernacle and by the altar round about, and their cords, and all the instruments of their service, and all that is made for them: so shall they serve.

27 At the appointment of Aaron and his sons shall be all the service of the sons of the Gershonites, in all their burdens, and in all their service: and ye shall appoint unto them in charge all their burdens.

28 This *is* the service of the families of the sons of Gershon in the tabernacle of the congregation: and their charge *shall be* under the hand of Ithamar the son of Aaron the priest.

29 ¶ As for the sons of Merari, thou shalt number them after their families, by the house of their fathers;

30 From thirty years old and upward even unto fifty years old shalt thou number them, every one that entereth into the service, to do the work of the tabernacle of the congregation.

31 And this *is* the charge of their burden, according to all their service in the tabernacle of the congregation; the boards of the tabernacle, and the bars thereof, and the pillars thereof, and sockets thereof,

32 And the pillars of the court round about, and their sockets, and their pins, and their cords, with all their instruments, and with all their service: and by name ye shall reckon the instruments of the charge of their burden.

33 This *is* the service of the families of the sons of Merari, according to all their service, in the tabernacle of the congregation, under the

---

15a 1 Kgs. 8:3.
 b Deut. 10:8;
   1 Chr. 15:2.
 c 1 Chr. 13:10.

d IE of the sanctuary (more particularly the ark).
e Num. 18:3 (2–3).

16a HEB continual cereal offering.

hand of Ithamar the son of Aaron the priest.

34 ¶ And Moses and Aaron and the chief of the [a]congregation numbered the sons of the Kohathites after their families, and after the house of their fathers,

35 From thirty years old and upward even unto fifty years old, every one that entereth into the service, for the work in the tabernacle of the congregation:

36 And those that were numbered of them by their families were two thousand seven hundred and fifty.

37 These *were* they that were numbered of the families of the Kohathites, all that might do service in the tabernacle of the congregation, which Moses and Aaron did number according to the commandment of the LORD by the hand of Moses.

38 And those that were numbered of the sons of Gershon, throughout their families, and by the house of their fathers,

39 From thirty years old and upward even unto fifty years old, every one that entereth into the service, for the work in the tabernacle of the congregation,

40 Even those that were numbered of them, throughout their families, by the house of their fathers, were two thousand and six hundred and thirty.

41 These *are* they that were numbered of the families of the sons of [a]Gershon, of all that might do service in the tabernacle of the congregation, whom Moses and Aaron did number according to the commandment of the LORD.

42 ¶ And those that were numbered of the families of the sons of [a]Merari, throughout their families, by the house of their fathers,

43 From thirty years old and upward even unto fifty years old, every one that entereth into the service,

for the work in the tabernacle of the congregation,

44 Even those that were numbered of them after their families, were three thousand and two hundred.

45 These *be* those that were numbered of the families of the sons of Merari, whom Moses and Aaron numbered according to the word of the LORD by the hand of Moses.

46 All those that were numbered of the Levites, whom Moses and Aaron and the chief of Israel numbered, after their families, and after the house of their fathers,

47 From thirty years old and upward even unto fifty years old, every one that came to do the service of the [a]ministry, and the service of the burden in the tabernacle of the congregation,

48 Even those that were numbered of them, were eight thousand and five hundred and fourscore.

49 According to the commandment of the LORD they were numbered by the hand of Moses, every one according to his service, and according to his burden: thus were they numbered of him, as the LORD commanded Moses.

CHAPTER 5

Lepers are put out of the camp—Sinners must confess and make restitution to gain forgiveness—Women believed to be immoral undergo a trial of jealousy before the priests.

AND the LORD spake unto Moses, saying,

2 Command the children of Israel, that they [a]put out of the camp every [b]leper, and every one that hath [c]an issue, and whosoever is [d]defiled by the dead:

3 Both male and female shall ye put out, without the camp shall ye put them; that they [a]defile not their camps, in the midst whereof I dwell.

34a TG Church.
41a Ex. 6:17.
42a Ex. 6:19.
47a TG Priest, Aaronic
Priesthood.

BD Priests.
5 2a Details on the clean and
unclean are in
Lev. 12:1–15:33.
b TG Leprosy.

c HEB any discharge.
Lev. 15:2 (2–5).
d Num. 9:6 (6–8).
3a Lev. 15:31.

4 And the children of Israel did so, and put them out without the camp: as the LORD spake unto Moses, so did the children of Israel.

5 ¶ And the LORD spake unto Moses, saying,

6 Speak unto the children of Israel, When a man or woman shall commit any ^asin that men commit, to do a trespass against the LORD, and that person be guilty;

7 Then they shall ^aconfess their sin which they have done: and he shall ^brecompense his trespass with the principal thereof, and add unto it the fifth *part* thereof, and give *it* unto *him* against whom he hath trespassed.

8 But if the man have no ^akinsman to recompense the trespass unto, let the trespass be recompensed unto the LORD, *even* to the priest; beside the ram of the atonement, whereby an atonement shall be made for him.

9 And every offering of all the holy things of the children of Israel, which they bring unto the priest, shall be his.

10 And every man's hallowed things shall be his: whatsoever any man giveth the priest, it shall be his.

11 ¶ And the LORD spake unto Moses, saying,

12 Speak unto the children of Israel, and say unto them, If any man's wife go aside, and commit a trespass against him,

13 And a man lie with her carnally, and it be hid from the eyes of her husband, and ^abe kept close, and she be defiled, and *there be* no witness against her, neither she be ^btaken *with the manner;*

14 And the spirit of jealousy come upon him, and he be jealous of his wife, and she be defiled: or if the spirit of jealousy come upon him, and he be jealous of his wife, and she be not defiled:

15 Then shall the man bring his wife unto the priest, and he shall bring her offering for her, the tenth *part* of an ephah of barley meal; he shall pour no oil upon it, nor put frankincense thereon; for it *is* an offering of jealousy, an offering of memorial, bringing iniquity to remembrance.

16 And the priest shall bring her near, and set her before the LORD:

17 And the priest shall take ^aholy water in an earthen vessel; and of the dust that is in the floor of the tabernacle the priest shall take, and put *it* into the water:

18 And the priest shall set the woman before the LORD, and uncover the woman's head, and put the offering of memorial in her hands, which *is* the jealousy offering: and the priest shall have in his hand the bitter water that causeth the curse:

19 And the priest shall charge her by an oath, and say unto the woman, If no man have lain with thee, and if thou hast not gone aside to uncleanness *with another* instead of thy husband, be thou free from this bitter water that causeth the curse:

20 But if thou hast gone aside *to another* instead of thy husband, and if thou be defiled, and some man have lain with thee beside thine husband:

21 Then the priest shall charge the woman with an oath of cursing, and the priest shall say unto the woman, The LORD make thee a curse and an oath among thy people, when the LORD doth make thy thigh to ^arot, and thy belly to swell;

22 And this water that causeth the curse shall go into thy bowels, to make *thy* belly to swell, and *thy* thigh to rot: And the woman shall say, Amen, amen.

23 And the priest shall write these

6a TG Sin.
7a Lev. 5:5 (1–10);
   Mosiah 26:29 (29, 35);
   Alma 17:4;
   3 Ne. 1:25;
   D&C 19:20; 58:43; 64:7.

b TG Repent.
8a HEB redeemer.
13a HEB secret.
   b HEB apprehended,
      caught in the act.
17a OR consecrated water;

i.e., for use in
purifications.
21a HEB diminish, or fall
   away (also vv. 22, 27).

curses in a book, and he shall blot *them* out with the bitter water:

24 And he shall cause the woman to drink the bitter water that causeth the curse: and the water that causeth the curse shall enter into her, *and become* bitter.

25 Then the priest shall take the jealousy offering out of the woman's hand, and shall wave the offering before the LORD, and offer it upon the altar:

26 And the priest shall take an handful of the offering, *even* the memorial thereof, and burn *it* upon the altar, and afterward shall cause the woman to drink the water.

27 And when he hath made her to drink the water, then it shall come to pass, *that*, if she be defiled, and have done trespass against her husband, that the water that causeth the curse shall enter into her, *and become* bitter, and her belly shall swell, and her thigh shall rot: and the woman shall be a curse among her people.

28 And if the woman be not defiled, but be clean; then she shall be free, and shall conceive seed.

29 This *is* the law of jealousies, when a wife goeth aside *to another* instead of her husband, and is defiled;

30 Or when the spirit of jealousy cometh upon him, and he be jealous over his wife, and shall set the woman before the LORD, and the priest shall execute upon her all this law.

31 Then shall the man be guiltless from iniquity, and this woman shall bear her iniquity.

CHAPTER 6

The law of the Nazarite is explained, whereby the children of Israel may consecrate themselves to the Lord by a vow—They drink no wine nor strong drink and if defiled must shave their heads—The Lord reveals the blessing to be used by Aaron and his sons in blessing Israel.

AND the LORD spake unto Moses, saying,

2 Speak unto the children of Israel, and say unto them, When either man or woman shall separate *themselves* to vow a *a*vow of a *b*Nazarite, to separate *themselves* unto the LORD:

3 He shall separate *himself* from *a*wine and *b*strong *c*drink, and shall drink no vinegar of wine, or vinegar of strong drink, neither shall he drink any *d*liquor of grapes, nor eat moist grapes, or dried.

4 All the days of his separation shall he eat nothing that is made of the *a*vine tree, from the kernels even to the husk.

5 All the days of the vow of his separation there shall no *a*razor come upon his head: until the days be fulfilled, in the which he separateth *himself* unto the LORD, he shall be holy, *and* shall let the locks of the hair of his head grow.

6 All the days that he separateth *himself* unto the LORD he shall come at no dead body.

7 He shall not make himself unclean for his father, or for his mother, for his brother, or for his sister, when they die: because the consecration of his God *is* upon his head.

8 All the days of his separation he *is* holy unto the LORD.

9 And if any man die very suddenly by him, and he hath defiled the head of his consecration; then he shall shave his head in the day of his cleansing, on the *a*seventh day shall he shave it.

10 And on the eighth day he shall bring two turtles, or two young pigeons, to the priest, to the door of the *a*tabernacle of the congregation:

11 And the priest shall offer the one for a sin *a*offering, and the other

---

6 2*a* TG Vow.
   b Amos 2:11 (11–12).
  3*a* Luke 1:15.
     TG Drunkenness.
   b IE alcoholic drinks.

   c TG Word of Wisdom.
   d OR juice.
  4*a* OR grapevine.
  5*a* Judg. 13:5;
     1 Sam. 1:11.

  9*a* Acts 21:27.
 10*a* HEB tent of meeting
    (also vv. 13, 18).
 11*a* Acts 21:26.

for a burnt offering, and make an atonement for him, for that he sinned by [b]the dead, and shall hallow his head that same day.

12 And he shall consecrate unto the LORD the days of his separation, and shall bring a lamb of the first year for a trespass offering: but the days that were before shall be lost, because his separation was defiled.

13 ¶ And this *is* the law of the Nazarite, when the days of his separation are [a]fulfilled: he shall be brought unto the door of the tabernacle of the congregation:

14 And he shall offer his offering unto the LORD, one he lamb of the first year without blemish for a burnt offering, and one ewe lamb of the first year without blemish for a sin offering, and one ram without blemish for peace [a]offerings,

15 And a basket of [a]unleavened bread, cakes of fine flour mingled with oil, and wafers of unleavened bread anointed with oil, and their [b]meat offering, and their drink offerings.

16 And the priest shall bring *them* before the LORD, and shall offer his sin offering, and his burnt offering:

17 And he shall offer the ram *for* a sacrifice of peace offerings unto the LORD, with the basket of unleavened bread: the priest shall offer also his meat offering, and his drink offering.

18 And the Nazarite shall [a]shave the head of his [b]separation *at* the door of the tabernacle of the congregation, and shall take the hair of the head of his separation, and put *it* in the fire which *is* under the sacrifice of the peace offerings.

19 And the priest shall take the [a]sodden shoulder of the ram, and one unleavened cake out of the basket, and one unleavened wafer,

and shall put *them* upon the hands of the Nazarite, after *the hair of* his separation is shaven:

20 And the priest shall wave them *for* a wave offering before the LORD: this *is* holy for the priest, with the [a]wave breast and [b]heave shoulder: and after that the Nazarite may drink wine.

21 This *is* the law of the Nazarite who hath vowed, *and of* his offering unto the LORD for his [a]separation, beside [b]*that* that his hand shall get: according to the vow which he vowed, so he must do after the law of his separation.

22 ¶ And the LORD spake unto Moses, saying,

23 Speak unto Aaron and unto his sons, saying, On this wise ye shall [a]bless the children of Israel, saying unto them,

24 The LORD bless thee, and keep thee:

25 The LORD make his face [a]shine upon thee, and be gracious unto thee:

26 The LORD lift up his countenance upon thee, and give thee [a]peace.

27 And they shall put my [a]name upon the children of Israel; and I will bless them.

CHAPTER 7

The princes of Israel make offerings for the tabernacle at its dedication—The Lord speaks to Moses from the mercy seat, between the cherubim, upon the ark.

AND it came to pass on the day that Moses had fully [a]set up the tabernacle, and had anointed it, and sanctified it, and all the instruments thereof, both the altar and all the vessels thereof, and had anointed them, and sanctified them;

11 *b* IE being near a dead body.
13 *a* Acts 21:26.
14 *a* TG Sacrifice.
15 *a* TG Bread, Unleavened.
   b OR meal or cereal (also v. 17).
18 *a* Acts 21:24.
   b OR consecration (also vv. 19, 21).

19 *a* OR cooked.
20 *a* OR breast that is waved.
   b OR shoulder that is lifted up.
21 *a* TG Setting Apart.
   b IE that which he can afford to give.
23 *a* Deut. 10:8;
   1 Sam. 2:20;
   1 Chr. 23:13;

2 Chr. 30:27 (2–27).
25 *a* Ps. 31:16; 119:135;
   Dan. 9:17.
26 *a* TG Peace of God.
27 *a* Deut. 28:10;
   Mosiah 5:12 (8–13).
   TG Name.
7 1 *a* Ex. 40:17 (17–38).

2 That the princes of Israel, ^aheads of the house of their fathers, who *were* the princes of the tribes, and were over them that were numbered, offered:

3 And they brought their offering before the LORD, six covered ^awagons, and twelve oxen; a wagon for two of the princes, and for each one an ox: and they brought them before the tabernacle.

4 And the LORD spake unto Moses, saying,

5 Take *it* of them, that they may be to do the service of the ^atabernacle of the congregation; and thou shalt give them unto the Levites, to every man according to his service.

6 And Moses took the wagons and the oxen, and gave them unto the Levites.

7 Two wagons and four oxen he gave unto the sons of Gershon, according to their service:

8 And four wagons and eight oxen he gave unto the sons of Merari, according unto their service, under the hand of Ithamar the son of Aaron the priest.

9 But unto the sons of Kohath he gave none: because the service of the sanctuary belonging unto them *was that* they should bear upon their shoulders.

10 ¶ And the princes offered for dedicating of the altar in the day that it was anointed, even the princes offered their offering before the altar.

11 And the LORD said unto Moses, They shall offer their offering, ^aeach prince on his day, for the dedicating of the altar.

12 ¶ And he that offered his offering the first day was Nahshon the son of Amminadab, of the tribe of Judah:

13 And his offering *was* one silver charger, the weight thereof *was* an hundred and thirty *shekels*, one silver bowl of seventy shekels, after the shekel of the sanctuary; both of them *were* full of fine flour mingled with oil for a ^ameat offering:

14 One ^aspoon of ten *shekels* of gold, full of incense:

15 One young bullock, one ram, one lamb of the first year, for a burnt offering:

16 One kid of the goats for a sin offering:

17 And for a sacrifice of peace offerings, two oxen, five rams, five he goats, five lambs of the first year: this *was* the offering of Nahshon the son of Amminadab.

18 ¶ On the second day Nethaneel the son of Zuar, ^aprince of Issachar, did offer:

19 He offered *for* his offering one silver charger, the weight whereof *was* an hundred and thirty *shekels*, one silver bowl of seventy shekels, after the shekel of the sanctuary; both of them full of fine flour mingled with oil for a meat offering:

20 One spoon of gold of ten *shekels*, full of incense:

21 One young bullock, one ram, one lamb of the first year, for a burnt offering:

22 One kid of the goats for a sin offering:

23 And for a sacrifice of peace offerings, two oxen, five rams, five he goats, five lambs of the first year: this *was* the offering of Nethaneel the son of Zuar.

24 ¶ On the third day Eliab the son of Helon, prince of the children of Zebulun, *did offer:*

25 His offering *was* one silver charger, the weight whereof *was* an hundred and thirty *shekels*, one silver bowl of seventy shekels, after the shekel of the sanctuary; both of them full of fine flour mingled with oil for a meat offering:

26 One golden spoon of ten *shekels*, full of incense:

27 One young bullock, one ram, one lamb of the first year, for a burnt offering:

2*a* Num. 1:4 (4–16).
3*a* Gen. 45:27.
5*a* HEB tent of meeting

(also v. 89).
11*a* OR one leader per day.
13*a* HEB meal or cereal.

14*a* OR scoop or pan.
18*a* HEB leader or president.

28 One kid of the goats for a sin offering:

29 And for a sacrifice of peace offerings, two oxen, five rams, five he goats, five lambs of the first year: this *was* the offering of Eliab the son of Helon.

30 ¶ On the fourth day Elizur the son of Shedeur, prince of the children of Reuben, *did offer:*

31 His offering *was* one silver charger of the weight of an hundred and thirty *shekels,* one silver bowl of seventy shekels, after the shekel of the sanctuary; both of them full of fine flour mingled with oil for a meat offering:

32 One golden spoon of ten *shekels,* full of incense:

33 One young bullock, one ram, one lamb of the first year, for a burnt offering:

34 One kid of the goats for a sin offering:

35 And for a sacrifice of peace offerings, two oxen, five rams, five he goats, five lambs of the first year: this *was* the offering of Elizur the son of Shedeur.

36 ¶ On the fifth day Shelumiel the son of Zurishaddai, prince of the children of Simeon, *did offer:*

37 His offering *was* one silver charger, the weight whereof *was* an hundred and thirty *shekels,* one silver bowl of seventy shekels, after the shekel of the sanctuary; both of them full of fine flour mingled with oil for a meat offering:

38 One golden spoon of ten *shekels,* full of incense:

39 One young bullock, one ram, one lamb of the first year, for a burnt offering:

40 One kid of the goats for a sin offering:

41 And for a sacrifice of peace offerings, two oxen, five rams, five he goats, five lambs of the first year: this *was* the offering of Shelumiel the son of Zurishaddai.

42 ¶ On the sixth day Eliasaph the son of Deuel, prince of the children of Gad, *offered:*

43 His offering *was* one silver charger of the weight of an hundred

and thirty *shekels,* a silver bowl of seventy shekels, after the shekel of the sanctuary; both of them full of fine flour mingled with oil for a meat offering:

44 One golden spoon of ten *shekels,* full of incense:

45 One young bullock, one ram, one lamb of the first year, for a burnt offering:

46 One kid of the goats for a sin offering:

47 And for a sacrifice of peace offerings, two oxen, five rams, five he goats, five lambs of the first year: this *was* the offering of Eliasaph the son of Deuel.

48 ¶ On the seventh day Elishama the son of Ammihud, prince of the children of Ephraim, *offered:*

49 His offering *was* one silver charger, the weight whereof *was* an hundred and thirty *shekels,* one silver bowl of seventy shekels, after the shekel of the sanctuary; both of them full of fine flour mingled with oil for a meat offering:

50 One golden spoon of ten *shekels,* full of incense:

51 One young bullock, one ram, one lamb of the first year, for a burnt offering:

52 One kid of the goats for a sin offering:

53 And for a sacrifice of peace offerings, two oxen, five rams, five he goats, five lambs of the first year: this *was* the offering of Elishama the son of Ammihud.

54 ¶ On the eighth day *offered* Gamaliel the son of Pedahzur, prince of the children of Manasseh:

55 His offering *was* one silver charger of the weight of an hundred and thirty *shekels,* one silver bowl of seventy shekels, after the shekel of the sanctuary; both of them full of fine flour mingled with oil for a meat offering:

56 One golden spoon of ten *shekels,* full of incense:

57 One young bullock, one ram, one lamb of the first year, for a burnt offering:

58 One kid of the goats for a sin offering:

59 And for a sacrifice of peace offerings, two oxen, five rams, five he goats, five lambs of the first year: this *was* the offering of Gamaliel the son of Pedahzur.

60 ¶ On the ninth day Abidan the son of Gideoni, prince of the children of Benjamin, *offered:*

61 His offering *was* one silver charger, the weight whereof *was* an hundred and thirty *shekels,* one silver bowl of seventy shekels, after the shekel of the sanctuary; both of them full of fine flour mingled with oil for a meat offering:

62 One golden spoon of ten *shekels,* full of incense:

63 One young bullock, one ram, one lamb of the first year, for a burnt offering:

64 One kid of the goats for a sin offering:

65 And for a sacrifice of peace offerings, two oxen, five rams, five he goats, five lambs of the first year: this *was* the offering of Abidan the son of Gideoni.

66 ¶ On the tenth day Ahiezer the son of Ammishaddai, prince of the children of Dan, *offered:*

67 His offering *was* one silver charger, the weight whereof *was* an hundred and thirty *shekels,* one silver bowl of seventy shekels, after the shekel of the sanctuary; both of them full of fine flour mingled with oil for a meat offering:

68 One golden spoon of ten *shekels,* full of incense:

69 One young bullock, one ram, one lamb of the first year, for a burnt offering:

70 One kid of the goats for a sin offering:

71 And for a sacrifice of peace offerings, two oxen, five rams, five he goats, five lambs of the first year: this *was* the offering of Ahiezer the son of Ammishaddai.

72 ¶ On the eleventh day Pagiel the son of Ocran, prince of the children of Asher, *offered:*

73 His offering *was* one silver charger, the weight whereof *was*

an hundred and thirty *shekels,* one silver bowl of seventy shekels, after the shekel of the sanctuary; both of them full of fine flour mingled with oil for a meat offering:

74 One golden spoon of ten *shekels,* full of incense:

75 One young bullock, one ram, one lamb of the first year, for a burnt offering:

76 One kid of the goats for a sin offering:

77 And for a sacrifice of peace offerings, two oxen, five rams, five he goats, five lambs of the first year: this *was* the offering of Pagiel the son of Ocran.

78 ¶ On the twelfth day Ahira the son of Enan, prince of the children of Naphtali, *offered:*

79 His offering *was* one silver charger, the weight whereof *was* an hundred and thirty *shekels,* one silver bowl of seventy shekels, after the shekel of the sanctuary; both of them full of fine flour mingled with oil for a meat offering:

80 One golden spoon of ten *shekels,* full of incense:

81 One young bullock, one ram, one lamb of the first year, for a burnt offering:

82 One kid of the goats for a sin offering:

83 And for a sacrifice of peace offerings, two oxen, five rams, five he goats, five lambs of the first year: this *was* the offering of Ahira the son of Enan.

84 This *was* the dedication of the altar, in the day when it was anointed, by the [a]princes of Israel: twelve chargers of silver, twelve silver bowls, twelve spoons of gold:

85 Each charger of silver *weighing* an hundred and thirty *shekels,* each bowl seventy: all the silver vessels *weighed* two thousand and four hundred *shekels,* after the shekel of the sanctuary:

86 The golden spoons *were* twelve, full of incense, *weighing* ten *shekels* apiece, after the shekel of the

---

84*a* HEB leaders or presidents.

sanctuary: all the gold of the spoons *was* an hundred and twenty *shekels.*

87 All the oxen for the burnt offering *were* twelve bullocks, the rams twelve, the lambs of the first year twelve, with their meat offering: and the kids of the goats for sin offering twelve.

88 And all the oxen for the sacrifice of the peace offerings *were* twenty and four bullocks, the rams sixty, the he goats sixty, the lambs of the first year sixty. This *was* the dedication of the altar, after that it was anointed.

89 And when Moses was gone into the tabernacle of the congregation to speak with him, then he heard the voice of one [a]speaking unto him from off the mercy seat that *was* upon the ark of testimony, from between the two [b]cherubims: and he spake unto him.

CHAPTER 8

The Levites are washed, consecrated, and set apart by the laying on of hands—They are the Lord's in place of the firstborn of every family—They are a gift to Aaron and his sons to do the service of the tabernacle.

AND the LORD spake unto Moses, saying,

2 Speak unto Aaron, and say unto him, When thou lightest the [a]lamps, the seven lamps shall give light over against the candlestick.

3 And Aaron did so; he lighted the lamps thereof over against the candlestick, as the LORD commanded Moses.

4 And this work of the candlestick *was of* beaten gold, unto the shaft thereof, unto the flowers thereof, *was* beaten work: according unto the [a]pattern which the LORD had shewed Moses, so he made the candlestick.

5 ¶ And the LORD spake unto Moses, saying,

6 Take the Levites from among the children of Israel, and [a]cleanse them.

7 And thus shalt thou do unto them, to [a]cleanse them: Sprinkle water of [b]purifying upon them, and let them shave all their flesh, and let them wash their clothes, and *so* make themselves clean.

8 Then let them take a young bullock with his [a]meat offering, *even* fine flour mingled with oil, and another young bullock shalt thou take for a sin offering.

9 And thou shalt bring the Levites before the [a]tabernacle of the congregation: and thou shalt gather the whole assembly of the children of Israel together:

10 And thou shalt bring the Levites before the LORD: and the children of Israel shall put their [a]hands upon the [b]Levites:

11 And Aaron shall offer the Levites before the LORD *for* an offering of the children of Israel, that they may execute the service of the LORD.

12 And the Levites shall lay their hands upon the heads of the bullocks: and thou shalt offer the one *for* a sin offering, and the other *for* a burnt offering, unto the LORD, to make an atonement for the Levites.

13 And thou shalt set the Levites before Aaron, and before his sons, and offer them *for* an offering unto the LORD.

14 Thus shalt thou [a]separate the Levites from among the children of Israel: and the Levites shall be mine.

15 And after that shall the Levites go in to do the service of the tabernacle of the congregation: and thou shalt cleanse them, and offer them *for* an offering.

16 For they *are* wholly given unto me from among the children of Israel; instead of such as open every womb, *even instead of* the firstborn of all the children of Israel, have I taken them unto me.

89*a* Ex. 25:22 (17–22).
  b TG Cherubim.
8 2*a* Ex. 25:37 (31–40).
  4*a* Ex. 27:8;
    1 Chr. 28:19 (11, 19);
    D&C 52:14; 94:2; 97:10;

115:14 (14–16).
6*a* HEB (ritually) purify.
7*a* Neh. 12:30.
  b TG Purification.
8*a* HEB meal or cereal.
9*a* HEB tent of meeting.

10*a* JS—H 1:68;
    A of F 1:5.
  b TG Priest, Aaronic
    Priesthood.
    BD Priests.
14*a* TG Setting Apart.

17 For all the *a*firstborn of the children of Israel *are* mine, *both* man and beast: on the day that I smote every firstborn in the land of Egypt I *b*sanctified them for myself.

18 And I have taken the *a*Levites for all the *b*firstborn of the children of Israel.

19 And I have given the Levites *as* a gift to *a*Aaron and to his sons from among the children of Israel, to do the service of the children of Israel in the tabernacle of the congregation, and to make an atonement for the children of Israel: that there be no plague among the children of Israel, when the children of Israel come nigh unto the sanctuary.

20 And Moses, and Aaron, and all the congregation of the children of Israel, did to the Levites according unto all that the Lord commanded Moses concerning the Levites, so did the children of Israel unto them.

21 And the Levites were *a*purified, and they washed their clothes; and Aaron offered them *as* an offering before the Lord; and Aaron made an atonement for them to cleanse them.

22 And after that went the Levites in to do their service in the tabernacle of the congregation before Aaron, and before his sons: as the Lord had commanded Moses concerning the Levites, so did they unto them.

23 ¶ And the Lord spake unto Moses, saying,

24 This *is it* that *belongeth* unto the Levites: from twenty and five years old and upward they shall go in to wait upon the service of the tabernacle of the congregation:

25 And from the age of fifty years they shall cease waiting upon the service *thereof,* and shall serve no more:

26 But shall minister with their brethren in the tabernacle of the congregation, to keep the charge, and shall do no service. Thus shalt thou do unto the Levites touching their charge.

CHAPTER 9

Israel is again commanded to keep the Passover—A cloud rests upon the tabernacle by day and by night, plus a fire by night—When the cloud rests, Israel camps; when it lifts, they journey.

And the Lord spake unto Moses in the wilderness of Sinai, in the first month of the *a*second year after they were come out of the land of Egypt, saying,

2 Let the children of Israel also keep the passover at his appointed season.

3 In the *a*fourteenth day of this month, at even, ye shall keep it in his appointed season: according to all the rites of it, and according to all the ceremonies thereof, shall ye keep it.

4 And Moses spake unto the children of Israel, that they should keep the passover.

5 And they kept the passover on the fourteenth day of the first month at even in the wilderness of Sinai: according to all that the Lord commanded Moses, so did the children of Israel.

6 ¶ And there were certain men, who were *a*defiled by the dead body of a man, that they could not keep the passover on that day: and they came before Moses and before Aaron on that day:

7 And those men said unto him, We *are* defiled by *a*the dead body of a man: wherefore are we kept back, that we may not offer an offering of the Lord in his appointed season among the children of Israel?

8 And Moses said unto them, Stand still, and I will *a*hear what the Lord will command concerning you.

9 ¶ And the Lord spake unto Moses, saying,

17*a* Ex. 12:29.
  b TG Sanctification.
18*a* TG Priesthood,
    History of.

  b TG Firstborn.
19*a* TG Priesthood, Aaronic.
21*a* TG Purification.
 9 1*a* Num. 1:1.

3*a* Ex. 12:6 (3–17).
6*a* Num. 5:2 (1–4).
7*a* IE having touched it.
8*a* D&C 102:23.

10 Speak unto the children of Israel, saying, If any man of you or of your posterity shall be unclean by reason of a dead body, or *be* in a journey afar off, yet he shall keep the passover unto the LORD.

11 The fourteenth day of the *a*second month at even they shall keep it, *and* eat it with *b*unleavened bread and bitter *herbs.*

12 They shall leave none of it unto the morning, nor *a*break any bone of it: according to all the ordinances of the passover they shall keep it.

13 But the man that *is* clean, and is not in a journey, and forbeareth to keep the passover, even the same soul shall be cut off from among his people: because he brought not the offering of the LORD in his appointed season, that man shall bear his sin.

14 And if a stranger shall sojourn among you, and will keep the *a*passover unto the LORD; according to the ordinance of the passover, and according to the manner thereof, so shall he do: ye shall have one ordinance, both for the *b*stranger, and for him that was born in the land.

15 ¶ And on the day that the tabernacle was reared up the *a*cloud covered the tabernacle, *namely,* the tent of the testimony: and at even there was upon the tabernacle as it were the appearance of fire, until the morning.

16 So it was alway: the cloud covered it *by day,* and the appearance of fire by night.

17 And when the cloud was taken up from the tabernacle, then after that the children of Israel journeyed: and in the place where the cloud abode, there the children of Israel pitched their tents.

18 At the commandment of the LORD the children of Israel journeyed, and at the commandment of the LORD they pitched: as long as the cloud abode upon the tabernacle they rested in their tents.

19 And when the cloud tarried long upon the tabernacle many days, then the children of Israel kept the charge of the LORD, and *a*journeyed not.

20 And *so* it was, when the cloud was a few days upon the tabernacle; according to the commandment of the LORD they abode in their tents, and according to the commandment of the LORD they journeyed.

21 And *so* it was, when the cloud abode from even unto the morning, and *that* the cloud was taken up in the morning, then they journeyed: whether *it was* by day or by night that the cloud was taken up, they journeyed.

22 Or *whether it were* two days, or a month, or *a*a year, that the cloud tarried upon the tabernacle, remaining thereon, the children of Israel abode in their tents, and journeyed not: but when it was taken up, they journeyed.

23 At the commandment of the LORD they rested in the tents, and at the commandment of the LORD they journeyed: they kept the charge of the LORD, at the commandment of the LORD by the hand of Moses.

CHAPTER 10

Silver trumpets are used to call assemblies and to blow alarms—The cloud is taken from the tabernacle, and the children of Israel march forth in their prescribed order—The ark of the covenant goes before them in their journeyings.

AND the LORD spake unto Moses, saying,

2 Make thee two trumpets of silver; of *a*a whole piece shalt thou make them: that thou mayest use them for the calling of the assembly, and for the journeying of the camps.

11*a* 2 Chr. 30:2 (2–27).
  b TG Bread, Unleavened.
12*a* John 19:36.
   TG Jesus Christ, Types
   of, in Anticipation.
14*a* TG Passover.
  b TG Stranger.
15*a* Ex. 13:21;
   14:19 (19, 24); 40:38;
   Num. 10:34;
19*a* Ex. 40:37.
22*a* HEB an extended
   period of time.
10 2*a* HEB hammered work.

3 And when they shall blow with them, all the assembly shall assemble themselves to thee at the door of the *a*tabernacle of the congregation.

4 And if they blow *but* with one *trumpet*, then the princes, *which are* heads of the thousands of Israel, shall gather themselves unto thee.

5 When ye blow an alarm, then the camps that lie on the east parts shall go forward.

6 When ye blow an alarm the second time, then the camps that lie on the south side shall take their journey: they shall blow an alarm for their journeys.

7 But when the congregation is to be gathered together, ye shall blow, but ye shall not sound an alarm.

8 And the sons of Aaron, the priests, shall blow with the *a*trumpets; and they shall be to you for an ordinance for ever throughout your generations.

9 And if ye go to war in your land against the enemy that oppresseth you, then ye shall blow an alarm with the trumpets; and ye shall be remembered before the Lord your God, and ye shall be saved from your enemies.

10 Also in the day of your gladness, and in your *a*solemn days, and in the beginnings of your months, ye shall blow with the *b*trumpets over your burnt offerings, and over the sacrifices of your peace offerings; that they may be to you for a memorial before your God: I *am* the Lord your God.

11 ¶ And it came to pass on the twentieth *day* of the second month, in the second year, that the *a*cloud was taken up from off the *b*tabernacle of the testimony.

12 And the children of Israel took their journeys out of the *a*wilderness of Sinai; and the cloud rested in the wilderness of Paran.

13 And they first took their journey according to the commandment of the Lord by the hand of Moses.

14 ¶ In the first *place* went the standard of the camp of the children of *a*Judah according to their armies: and over his host *was* Nahshon the son of Amminadab.

15 And over the host of the tribe of the children of Issachar *was* Nethaneel the son of Zuar.

16 And over the host of the tribe of the children of Zebulun *was* Eliab the son of Helon.

17 And the tabernacle was taken down; and the sons of *a*Gershon and the sons of Merari set forward, bearing the tabernacle.

18 ¶ And the standard of the camp of Reuben set forward according to their armies: and over his host *was* Elizur the son of Shedeur.

19 And over the host of the tribe of the children of Simeon *was* Shelumiel the son of Zurishaddai.

20 And over the host of the tribe of the children of Gad *was* Eliasaph the son of Deuel.

21 And the Kohathites set forward, bearing the sanctuary: and *a*the other* did set up the tabernacle against they came.

22 ¶ And the standard of the camp of the children of *a*Ephraim set forward according to their armies: and over his host *was* Elishama the son of Ammihud.

23 And over the host of the tribe of the children of Manasseh *was* Gamaliel the son of Pedahzur.

24 And over the host of the tribe of the children of Benjamin *was* Abidan the son of Gideoni.

25 ¶ And the standard of the camp of the children of Dan set forward, *which was* the rearward of all the camps throughout their hosts: and over his host *was* Ahiezer the son of Ammishaddai.

26 And over the host of the tribe of

3*a* HEB tent of meeting.
8*a* 1 Chr. 15:24.
10*a* HEB appointed feast
    days.
  b Lev. 23:24; Ps. 81:3.

11*a* Ex. 40:36.
  b Ex. 38:21.
12*a* Ex. 19:1;
    Num. 1:1.
14*a* Num. 2:9.

17*a* 1 Chr. 23:24.
21*a* HEB the tabernacle
    was set up before their
    arrival.
22*a* Num. 2:24.

the children of Asher *was* Pagiel the son of Ocran.

27 And over the host of the tribe of the children of Naphtali *was* Ahira the son of Enan.

28 Thus *were* the journeyings of the children of Israel according to their armies, when they set forward.

29 ¶ And Moses said unto Hobab, the son of *ª*Raguel the Midianite, Moses' father in law, We are journeying unto the place of which the LORD said, I will give it you: come thou with us, and we will do thee good: for the LORD hath spoken good concerning Israel.

30 And he said unto him, I will not go; but I will depart to mine own land, and to my kindred.

31 And he said, Leave us not, I pray thee; forasmuch as thou knowest how we are to encamp in the wilderness, and thou mayest be to us *ª*instead of eyes.

32 And it shall be, if thou go with us, yea, it shall be, that what goodness the LORD shall do unto us, the same will we do unto thee.

33 ¶ And they departed from the mount of the LORD three days' journey: and the *ª*ark of the covenant of the LORD went before them in the three days' journey, to search out a resting place for them.

34 And the *ª*cloud of the LORD *was* upon them by day, when they went out of the camp.

35 And it came to pass, when the ark set forward, that Moses said, Rise up, LORD, and let thine enemies be *ª*scattered; and let them that *ᵇ*hate thee flee before thee.

36 And when it rested, he said, Return, O LORD, unto the many thousands of Israel.

CHAPTER 11

Fire from the Lord consumes the rebels in Israel—Israel murmurs and lusts for meat instead of manna—Moses complains that he cannot bear the burden alone—He is commanded to choose seventy elders to assist him—The Lord promises meat until it becomes loathsome to the Israelites—The seventy elders are chosen, they prophesy, the Lord comes down, and Eldad and Medad prophesy in the camp—Israel is provided with quail—The people lust, a great plague follows, and many die.

AND *when* the people *ª*complained, it displeased the LORD: and the LORD heard *it*; and his anger was kindled; and the *ᵇ*fire of the LORD burnt among them, and consumed *them that were* in the uttermost parts of the camp.

2 And the people cried unto Moses; and when Moses prayed unto the LORD, the fire was quenched.

3 And he called the name of the place Taberah: because the fire of the LORD burnt among them.

4 ¶ And the mixed multitude that *was* among them fell a *ª*lusting: and the children of Israel also wept again, and said, Who shall give us flesh to eat?

5 We remember the fish, which we did eat in Egypt freely; the cucumbers, and the melons, and the leeks, and the onions, and the garlick:

6 But now our soul *is* dried away: *there is* nothing at all, beside this manna, *before* our eyes.

7 And the *ª*manna *was* as *ᵇ*coriander seed, and the colour thereof as the colour of bdellium.

8 *And* the people went about, and gathered *it*, and ground *it* in mills, or beat *it* in a mortar, and baked *it* in pans, and made cakes of it: and the taste of it was as the taste of fresh oil.

29*a* Ex. 2:18;
    D&C 84:6 (6–7).
31*a* HEB for eyes; i.e., as a
    guide.
33*a* TG Ark of the Covenant.
34*a* Num. 9:15; 14:14.
35*a* Ps. 68:1.

    b TG Hate.
11 1*a* Deut. 9:22;
    1 Ne. 16:22; 17:2;
    D&C 75:7 (7–8).
    b Deut. 32:22;
    Ps. 78:21; 1 Ne. 15:30;
    2 Ne. 26:6;

    D&C 35:14; 128:24;
    Moses 7:34.
4*a* TG Lust.
7*a* Ex. 16:35;
    1 Ne. 17:28 (15–43);
    Mosiah 7:19.
    b Ex. 16:31.

9 And when the dew fell upon the camp in the night, the manna fell ^aupon it.

10 ¶ Then Moses heard the people weep throughout their families, every man in the door of his tent: and the anger of the LORD was kindled greatly; Moses also was displeased.

11 And Moses said unto the LORD, Wherefore hast thou afflicted thy servant? and wherefore have I not found favour in thy sight, that thou layest the burden of all this people upon me?

12 Have I conceived all this people? have I begotten them, that thou shouldest say unto me, Carry them in thy bosom, as a nursing father beareth the sucking child, unto the land which thou swarest unto their fathers?

13 Whence should I have flesh to give unto all this people? for they weep unto me, saying, Give us flesh, that we may eat.

14 I am not able to bear all this people alone, because *it is* too ^aheavy for me.

15 And if thou deal thus with me, kill me, I pray thee, ^aout of hand, if I have found favour in thy sight; and let me not see my wretchedness.

16 ¶ And the LORD said unto Moses, Gather unto me ^aseventy men of the elders of Israel, whom thou knowest to be the elders of the people, and ^bofficers over them; and bring them unto the ^ctabernacle of the congregation, that they may stand there with thee.

17 And I will come down and talk with thee there: and I will take of the spirit which *is* upon thee, and will put *it* upon them; and they shall ^abear the burden of the people with thee, that thou bear *it* not thyself alone.

18 And say thou unto the people, Sanctify yourselves against to morrow, and ye shall eat flesh: for ye have wept in the ears of the LORD, saying, Who shall give us flesh to eat? for *it was* well with us in Egypt: therefore the LORD will give you flesh, and ye shall eat.

19 Ye shall not eat one day, nor two days, nor five days, neither ten days, nor twenty days;

20 *But* even a whole month, until it come out at your nostrils, and it be loathsome unto you: because that ye have despised the LORD which *is* among you, and have wept before him, saying, Why came we forth out of Egypt?

21 And Moses said, The people, among whom I *am, are* six hundred thousand footmen; and thou hast said, I will give them flesh, that they may eat a whole month.

22 Shall the flocks and the herds be slain for them, to suffice them? or shall all the fish of the sea be gathered together for them, to suffice them?

23 And the LORD said unto Moses, Is the LORD's hand waxed short? thou shalt see now whether my word shall come to pass unto thee or not.

24 ¶ And Moses went out, and told the people the words of the LORD, and gathered the ^aseventy men of the elders of the people, and set them round about the tabernacle.

25 And the LORD came down in a ^acloud, and spake unto him, and took of the spirit that *was* upon him, and gave *it* unto the seventy ^belders: and it came to pass, *that,* when the spirit rested upon them, they ^cprophesied, and did not cease.

26 But there remained two *of the* men in the camp, the name of the one *was* Eldad, and the name of the other Medad: and the spirit

---

9a OR with it.
14a Ex. 18:18.
15a OR immediately.
16a TG Church Organization; Seventy.
  b Deut. 16:18; D&C 88:127; 107:21.

TG Delegation of Responsibility.
  c HEB tent of meeting.
17a TG Leadership.
24a TG Seventy.
25a Num. 12:5; Ether 2:4 (4–5, 14);

D&C 34:7 (7–9); JS—H 1:68 (68–71).
  b TG Elder, Melchizedek Priesthood.
  c TG Holy Ghost, Gifts of.

rested upon them; and they *were* of them that were written, but went not out unto the tabernacle: and they prophesied in the camp.

27 And there ran a young man, and told Moses, and said, Eldad and Medad do prophesy in the camp.

28 And *a*Joshua the son of *b*Nun, the servant of Moses, *one* of his young men, answered and said, My lord Moses, forbid them.

29 And Moses said unto him, Enviest thou for my sake? would God that all the LORD's people were *a*prophets, *and* that the LORD would put his spirit upon them!

30 And Moses gat him into the camp, he and the elders of Israel.

31 ¶ And there went forth a wind from the LORD, and brought *a*quails from the sea, and let *them* fall by the camp, as it were a day's journey on this side, and as it were a day's journey on the other side, round about the camp, and as it were two cubits *high* upon the face of the earth.

32 And the people stood up all that day, and all *that* night, and all the next day, and they gathered the quails: he that gathered least gathered ten homers: and they spread *them* all abroad for themselves round about the camp.

33 And while the flesh *was* yet between their teeth, ere it was chewed, the wrath of the LORD was kindled against the people, and the LORD smote the people with a very great *a*plague.

34 And he called the name of that place *a*Kibroth-hattaavah: because there they buried the people that *b*lusted.

35 *And* the people journeyed from Kibroth-hattaavah unto Hazeroth; and abode at Hazeroth.

CHAPTER 12

Aaron and Miriam complain against Moses, the most meek of all men—The Lord promises to speak to Moses mouth to mouth and to reveal to him the similitude of the Lord—Miriam becomes leprous for a week.

AND Miriam and Aaron spake against Moses because of the *a*Ethiopian woman whom he had married: for he had married an Ethiopian woman.

2 And they said, Hath the LORD indeed spoken only by Moses? hath he not spoken also by us? And the LORD heard *it*.

3 (Now the man Moses *was* very *a*meek, above all the men which *were* upon the face of the earth.)

4 And the LORD spake suddenly unto Moses, and unto Aaron, and unto Miriam, Come out ye three unto the tabernacle of the congregation. And they three came out.

5 And the LORD came down in the *a*pillar of the cloud, and stood *in* the door of the tabernacle, and called Aaron and Miriam: and they both came forth.

6 And he said, Hear now my words: If there be a *a*prophet among you, *I* the LORD will make myself known unto him in a *b*vision, *and* will speak unto him in a *c*dream.

7 My servant Moses *is* not so, who *is* faithful in all mine house.

8 With him will I *a*speak *b*mouth to mouth, even apparently, and not in dark speeches; and the similitude of the LORD shall he *c*behold: wherefore then were ye not afraid to speak against my servant Moses?

9 And the anger of the LORD was kindled against them; and he departed.

10 And the cloud departed from

28a Num. 13:16;
   1 Chr. 7:27.
   b Ex. 33:11;
   Num. 27:18;
   Josh. 14:1;
   1 Kgs. 16:34;
   Neh. 8:17.
29a TG Prophecy;
   Prophets, Mission of.

31a Ex. 16:13.
33a TG Plague.
34a IE The graves of lust.
   b Deut. 9:22.
12 1a HEB Cushite.
 3a TG Meek.
 5a Num. 11:25.
 6a TG Prophets, Mission of.
   b TG Vision.

   c TG Dream.
 8a TG God, Privilege of
   Seeing.
   b Judg. 6:22;
   Ether 12:39;
   D&C 17:1;
   Moses 1:2.
   c TG Jesus Christ, Appearances, Antemortal.

off the tabernacle; and, behold, Miriam *became* ^aleprous, *white* as snow: and Aaron looked upon Miriam, and, behold, *she was* leprous.

11 And Aaron said unto Moses, Alas, my lord, I beseech thee, lay not the sin upon us, wherein we have done foolishly, and wherein we have sinned.

12 Let her not be as one dead, of whom the flesh is half consumed when he cometh out of his mother's womb.

13 And Moses cried unto the LORD, saying, ^aHeal her now, O God, I beseech thee.

14 ¶ And the LORD said unto Moses, If her father had but spit in her face, should she not be ashamed seven days? let her be shut out from the camp seven days, and after that let her be received in *again*.

15 And Miriam was shut out from the camp seven days: and the people journeyed not till Miriam was brought in *again*.

16 And afterward the people removed from Hazeroth, and pitched in the wilderness of Paran.

CHAPTER 13

Moses sends twelve spies to search the land of Canaan—Ten of them bring an evil report, telling only of the strength of the inhabitants.

AND the LORD spake unto Moses, saying,

2 ^aSend thou men, that they may ^bsearch the land of Canaan, which I give unto the children of Israel: of every tribe of their fathers shall ye send a man, every one a ruler among them.

3 And Moses by the commandment of the LORD sent them from the wilderness of Paran: all those men *were* heads of the children of Israel.

4 And these *were* their names: of the tribe of Reuben, Shammua the son of Zaccur.

5 Of the tribe of Simeon, Shaphat the son of Hori.

6 Of the tribe of Judah, ^aCaleb the son of Jephunneh.

7 Of the tribe of Issachar, Igal the son of Joseph.

8 Of the tribe of Ephraim, Oshea the son of Nun.

9 Of the tribe of Benjamin, Palti the son of Raphu.

10 Of the tribe of Zebulun, Gaddiel the son of Sodi.

11 Of the tribe of Joseph, *namely,* of the tribe of Manasseh, Gaddi the son of Susi.

12 Of the tribe of Dan, Ammiel the son of Gemalli.

13 Of the tribe of Asher, Sethur the son of Michael.

14 Of the tribe of Naphtali, Nahbi the son of Vophsi.

15 Of the tribe of Gad, Geuel the son of Machi.

16 These *are* the names of the men which Moses sent to spy out the ^aland. And Moses called ^bOshea the son of ^cNun ^dJehoshua.

17 ¶ And Moses sent them to spy out the land of Canaan, and said unto them, Get you up ^athis *way* southward, and go up into the mountain:

18 And see the land, what it *is*; and the people that dwelleth therein, whether they *be* strong or weak, few or many;

19 And what the land *is* that they dwell in, whether it *be* good or bad; and what cities *they be* that they dwell in, whether in tents, or in strong holds;

20 And what the land *is*, whether it *be* fat or lean, whether there be wood therein, or not. And be ye of good courage, and bring of the fruit of the land. Now the time *was* the time of the firstripe grapes.

21 ¶ So they went up, and searched the land from the wilderness of Zin unto Rehob, ^aas men come to Hamath.

22 And they ^aascended by the

10*a* TG Leprosy.
13*a* TG Heal.
13 2*a* Josh. 14:7.
  b Deut. 1:23.
  6*a* Deut. 1:36 (34–36);

Josh. 15:13.
16*a* TG Israel, Land of.
  b Num. 11:28.
  c Deut. 34:9; Judg. 2:8.
  d Num. 14:6;

1 Chr. 7:27.
17*a* HEB through the Negev.
21*a* OR by the access to.
22*a* HEB went up through the Negev.

south, and came unto *b*Hebron; where Ahiman, Sheshai, and Talmai, the children of Anak, *were*. (Now Hebron was built seven years before *c*Zoan in Egypt.)

23 And they came unto the *a*brook of Eshcol, and cut down from thence a branch with one cluster of grapes, and they bare it between two upon a staff; and *they brought* of the pomegranates, and of the figs.

24 The place was called the brook Eshcol, because of the cluster of grapes which the children of Israel cut down from thence.

25 And they returned from searching of the land after forty days.

26 ¶ And they went and came to Moses, and to Aaron, and to all the congregation of the children of Israel, unto the wilderness of Paran, to Kadesh; and brought back word unto them, and unto all the congregation, and shewed them the fruit of the land.

27 And they told him, and said, We came unto the land whither thou sentest us, and surely it *a*floweth with milk and honey; and this *is* the fruit of it.

28 Nevertheless the people *be* strong that dwell in the land, and the cities *are* *a*walled, *and* very great: and moreover we saw the children of Anak there.

29 The *a*Amalekites dwell in the land of the *b*south: and the Hittites, and the Jebusites, and the Amorites, dwell in the mountains: and the Canaanites dwell by the sea, and by the coast of Jordan.

30 And *a*Caleb stilled the people before Moses, and said, Let us go up at once, and possess it; for we are well able to overcome it.

31 But the *a*men that went up with him said, We be not able to go up against the people; for they *are* stronger than we.

32 And they brought up an evil report of the land which they had searched unto the children of Israel, saying, The land, through which we have gone to search it, *is* a land that eateth up the inhabitants thereof; and all the people that we saw in it *are* men of a great stature.

33 And there we saw the *a*giants, the sons of Anak, *which come* of the *b*giants: and we were in our own sight as grasshoppers, and so we were in their sight.

CHAPTER 14

Israel murmurs and speaks of returning to Egypt—Joshua and Caleb give a good report of Canaan—Moses mediates between Israel and the Lord—The adults of Israel will not enter the promised land—The Lord slays the false spies by a plague—Some rebels try to go alone and are slain by the Amalekites and Canaanites.

AND all the congregation lifted up their voice, and cried; and the people wept that night.

2 And all the children of Israel *a*murmured against Moses and against Aaron: and the whole congregation said unto them, Would God that we had died in the land of Egypt! or would God we had died in this wilderness!

3 And wherefore hath the LORD brought us unto this land, to fall by the sword, that our wives and our children should be a prey? were it not better for us to return into Egypt?

4 And they said one to another, Let us make a captain, and let us *a*return into Egypt.

5 Then Moses and Aaron fell on their faces before all the assembly of the congregation of the children of Israel.

6 ¶ And *a*Joshua the son of Nun,

22*b* Josh. 14:9.
  c Ps. 78:12;
     Isa. 19:11.
23*a* OR wadi or valley.
27*a* Neh. 9:25.
28*a* Deut. 1:28; 9:1 (1–2);
     Alma 55:20.

29*a* Num. 14:25, 43.
  b HEB Negev.
30*a* Num. 14:24.
31*a* Josh. 14:8.
33*a* Deut. 2:11 (10–11); 3:11.
  b HEB *nephilim*.
     Gen. 6:4 (2–4);

Moses 7:15 (14–15);
     8:18.
14 2*a* Deut. 9:23.
     TG Murmuring.
  4*a* Ex. 13:17 (17–18);
     Neh. 9:17.
  6*a* Num. 13:16.

and Caleb the son of Jephunneh, *which were* of them that searched the land, rent their clothes:

7 And they spake unto all the company of the children of Israel, saying, The land, which we passed through to search it, *is* an exceeding good land.

8 If the LORD delight in us, then he will bring us into this land, and give it us; a land which floweth with milk and honey.

9 Only ^arebel not ye against the LORD, neither fear ye the people of the land; for they *are* bread for us: their defence is departed from them, and the LORD *is* with us: ^bfear them not.

10 But all the congregation bade stone them with stones. And the ^aglory of the LORD appeared in the tabernacle of the congregation before all the children of Israel.

11 ¶ And the LORD said unto Moses, How long will this people ^aprovoke me? and how long will it be ere they ^bbelieve me, for all the signs which I have shewed among them?

12 I will smite them with the pestilence, and disinherit them, and will make of thee a greater ^anation and mightier than they.

13 ¶ And Moses said unto the LORD, Then the ^aEgyptians shall hear *it,* (for thou broughtest up this people in thy might from among them;)

14 And they will tell *it* to the inhabitants of this land: *for* they have heard that thou LORD *art* ^aamong this people, that thou LORD art seen face to face, and *that* thy ^bcloud standeth over them, and *that* thou ^cgoest before them, by day time in a ^dpillar of a ^ecloud, and in a pillar of fire by night.

15 ¶ Now *if* thou shalt kill *all* this people as one man, then the nations which have heard the fame of thee will speak, saying,

16 Because the LORD was not able to bring this people into the land which he sware unto them, therefore he hath slain them in the wilderness.

17 And now, I beseech thee, let the power of my Lord be great, according as thou hast spoken, saying,

18 The ^aLORD *is* longsuffering, and of great mercy, ^bforgiving iniquity and transgression, and by no means clearing *the guilty,* visiting the iniquity of the fathers upon the children unto the third and fourth *generation.*

19 Pardon, I beseech thee, the iniquity of this people according unto the greatness of thy mercy, and as thou hast forgiven this people, from Egypt even until now.

20 And the LORD said, ^aI have pardoned according to thy word:

21 But *as* truly *as* I live, all the earth shall be ^afilled with the glory of the LORD.

22 Because all those men which have seen my glory, and my ^amiracles, which I did in Egypt and in the wilderness, and have ^btempted me now these ten times, and have not hearkened to my voice;

23 Surely they shall not ^asee the ^bland which I sware unto their fathers, neither shall any of them that ^cprovoked me see it:

24 But my servant ^aCaleb, because he had another spirit with him, and hath ^bfollowed me fully, him will I ^cbring into the land whereinto he went; and his seed shall possess it.

25 (Now the ^aAmalekites and the Canaanites dwelt in the valley.) To morrow turn you, and get you into

---

9*a* TG Rebellion.
  b TG Protection, Divine.
10*a* Ex. 16:10; 24:16.
11*a* Isa. 63:10;
       1 Ne. 17:30 (23–31);
       Jacob 1:8;
       Alma 12:37 (36–37);
       Hel. 7:18.
  b TG Faith.
12*a* Ex. 32:10.
13*a* Ex. 32:12.

14*a* TG God, Presence of.
  b Ps. 99:7; D&C 84:5.
  c Ex. 33:16.
  d Deut. 1:33.
  e Num. 10:34.
18*a* Ps. 86:15.
  b TG Forgive.
20*a* See JST Ex. 32:14
       (Appendix).
21*a* Ps. 72:19; D&C 65:2.
22*a* TG Miracle.

  b TG Test.
23*a* Num. 32:11 (11–12);
       Jacob 1:7 (7–8);
       D&C 84:24 (23–25).
  b Josh. 5:6.
  c Heb. 3:8 (7–11, 15).
24*a* Num. 13:30.
  b Josh. 14:8 (6–8).
       TG Commitment.
  c Josh. 14:10.
25*a* Num. 13:29.

the wilderness by the way of the Red sea.

26 ¶ And the LORD spake unto Moses and unto Aaron, saying,

27 How long *shall I bear with* this evil congregation, which *a*murmur against me? I have heard the murmurings of the children of Israel, which they murmur against me.

28 Say unto them, *As truly as* I live, saith the LORD, as ye have spoken in mine ears, so will I do to you:

29 Your *a*carcases shall fall in this *b*wilderness; and all that were numbered of you, according to your whole number, from twenty years old and upward, which have murmured against me,

30 Doubtless ye shall not come into the land, *concerning* which I sware to make you dwell therein, save Caleb the son of Jephunneh, and Joshua the son of Nun.

31 But your little ones, which ye said should be a prey, them will I bring in, and they shall know the land which ye have despised.

32 But *as for* you, your carcases, they shall fall in this wilderness.

33 And your children shall wander in the wilderness *a*forty years, and *b*bear your whoredoms, until your carcases be wasted in the wilderness.

34 After the number of the days in which ye searched the land, *even* forty days, each day for a year, shall ye bear your iniquities, *even* forty years, and ye shall *a*know my breach of promise.

35 I the LORD have said, I will surely do it unto all this evil congregation, that are gathered together against me: in this wilderness they shall be consumed, and there they shall *a*die.

36 And the men, which Moses sent to search the land, who returned, and made all the congregation to murmur against him, by bringing up a slander upon the land,

37 Even those men that did bring up the evil report upon the land, *a*died by the *b*plague before the LORD.

38 But Joshua the son of Nun, and Caleb the son of Jephunneh, *which were* of the men that went to search the land, lived *still.*

39 And Moses told these sayings unto all the children of Israel: and the people *a*mourned greatly.

40 ¶ And they rose up early in the morning, and gat them up into the top of the mountain, saying, Lo, we *be here,* and will go up unto the place which the LORD hath promised: for we have *a*sinned.

41 And Moses said, Wherefore now do ye transgress the commandment of the LORD? but it shall not prosper.

42 Go not up, for the LORD *is* not among you; that ye be not smitten before your enemies.

43 For the *a*Amalekites and the Canaanites *are* there before you, and ye shall fall by the sword: because ye are turned away from the LORD, therefore the LORD will not be with you.

44 But they *a*presumed to go up unto the hill top: nevertheless the ark of the covenant of the LORD, and Moses, departed not out of the camp.

45 Then the Amalekites came down, and the Canaanites which dwelt in that hill, and smote them, and discomfited them, *even* unto Hormah.

CHAPTER 15

Various sacrificial ordinances bring forgiveness to repentant Israel—Those who sin willfully are cut off from among the people—A man is stoned for gathering sticks on the Sabbath day—The Israelites are to look on the fringes of their garments and remember the commandments.

27*a* Ex. 16:12.
29*a* Heb. 3:17.
   b Num. 26:65;
     Ezek. 20:13 (13, 15).
33*a* Ps. 95:10; Amos 2:10.

b OR suffer for your
   faithlessness.
34*a* HEB feel my displeasure.
35*a* Deut. 2:14 (14–15).
37*a* 1 Cor. 10:10.

b TG Plague.
39*a* Ex. 33:4.
40*a* Deut. 1:41.
43*a* Num. 13:29.
44*a* Deut. 1:43.

AND the LORD spake unto Moses, saying,

2 Speak unto the children of Israel, and say unto them, When ye be come into the land of your habitations, which I give unto you,

3 And will make an ᵃoffering by fire unto the LORD, a burnt offering, or a sacrifice in performing a vow, or in a freewill offering, or in your solemn feasts, to make a sweet savour unto the LORD, of the herd, or of the flock:

4 Then shall he that offereth his offering unto the LORD bring a meat offering of a tenth deal of flour mingled with the fourth *part* of an hin of oil.

5 And the fourth *part* of an hin of wine for a drink ᵃoffering shalt thou prepare with the burnt offering or sacrifice, for one lamb.

6 Or for a ram, thou shalt prepare *for* a meat offering two tenth deals of flour mingled with the third *part* of an hin of oil.

7 And for a drink offering thou shalt offer the third *part* of an hin of wine, *for* a sweet savour unto the LORD.

8 And when thou preparest a bullock *for* a burnt offering, or *for* a sacrifice in performing a vow, or peace offerings unto the LORD:

9 Then shall he bring with a bullock a meat offering of three tenth deals of flour mingled with half an hin of oil.

10 And thou shalt bring for a drink offering half an hin of wine, *for* an offering made by fire, of a sweet savour unto the LORD.

11 Thus shall it be done for one bullock, or for one ram, or for a lamb, or a kid.

12 According to the number that ye shall prepare, so shall ye do to every one according to their number.

13 All that are born of the country shall do these things after this manner, in offering an offering made by fire, of a sweet savour unto the LORD.

14 And if a stranger sojourn with you, or whosoever *be* among you in your generations, and will offer an offering made by fire, of a sweet savour unto the LORD; as ye do, so he shall do.

15 ᵃOne ordinance *shall be both* for you of the congregation, and also for the stranger that sojourneth *with you*, an ordinance for ever in your generations: as ye *are*, so shall the ᵇstranger be before the LORD.

16 ᵃOne law and one manner shall be for you, and for the stranger that sojourneth with you.

17 ¶ And the LORD spake unto Moses, saying,

18 Speak unto the children of Israel, and say unto them, When ye come into the land whither I bring you,

19 Then it shall be, that, when ye eat of the bread of the land, ye shall offer up an heave offering unto the LORD.

20 Ye shall offer up a cake of the first of your ᵃdough *for* an heave offering: as *ye do* the heave offering of the threshingfloor, so shall ye ᵇheave it.

21 Of the first of your dough ye shall give unto the LORD an heave offering in your generations.

22 ¶ And if ye have erred, and not observed all these commandments, which the LORD hath spoken unto Moses,

23 *Even* all that the LORD hath commanded you by the hand of Moses, from the day that the LORD commanded *Moses*, and henceforward among your generations;

24 Then it shall be, if *ought* be committed by ignorance without the knowledge of the congregation, that all the congregation shall offer one young bullock for a burnt offering, for a sweet savour unto the LORD, with his meat offering, and his drink offering, according to the ᵃmanner,

---

15 3*a* TG Sacrifice.
5*a* 2 Chr. 29:35.
15*a* TG Unity.

b Num. 35:15 (15–34).
16*a* OR The same doctrine and ordinances.

20*a* Ezek. 44:30.
b HEB elevate.
24*a* HEB ordinance.

and one kid of the goats for a sin offering.

25 And the priest shall make an *a*atonement for all the congregation of the children of Israel, and it shall be *b*forgiven them; for it *is* ignorance: and they shall bring their offering, a sacrifice made by fire unto the LORD, and their sin offering before the LORD, for their ignorance:

26 And it shall be forgiven all the congregation of the children of Israel, and the stranger that sojourneth among them; seeing all the people *were* in ignorance.

27 ¶ And if any soul sin through *a*ignorance, then he shall bring a she goat of the first year for a sin offering.

28 And the priest shall make an atonement for the soul that sinneth ignorantly, when he sinneth by ignorance before the LORD, to make an atonement for him; and it shall be forgiven him.

29 Ye shall have one law for him that sinneth through ignorance, *both for* him that is born among the children of Israel, and for the stranger that sojourneth among them.

30 ¶ But the soul that doeth *ought* *a*presumptuously, *whether he be* born in the land, or a stranger, the same reproacheth the LORD; and that soul shall be *b*cut off from among his people.

31 Because he hath *a*despised the word of the LORD, and hath broken his commandment, that soul shall utterly be cut off; his iniquity *shall be* upon him.

32 ¶ And while the children of Israel were in the wilderness, they found a man that gathered sticks upon the *a*sabbath day.

33 And they that found him gathering sticks brought him unto Moses and Aaron, and unto all the congregation.

34 And they put him in ward, because it was not declared what should be done to him.

35 And the LORD said unto Moses, The man shall be surely put to *a*death: all the congregation shall stone him with stones without the camp.

36 And all the congregation brought him without the camp, and stoned him with stones, and he died; as the LORD commanded Moses.

37 ¶ And the LORD spake unto Moses, saying,

38 Speak unto the children of Israel, and bid them that they make them *a*fringes in the *b*borders of their garments throughout their generations, and that they put upon the fringe of the borders a ribband of blue:

39 And it shall be unto you for a fringe, that ye may look upon it, and remember all the commandments of the LORD, and do them; and that ye seek not after your own heart and your own eyes, after which ye use to go a whoring:

40 That ye may remember, and do all my commandments, and be holy unto your God.

41 I *am* the LORD your God, which brought you out of the land of Egypt, to be your God: I *am* the LORD your God.

CHAPTER 16

Korah, Dathan, Abiram, and 250 leaders rebel and seek priestly offices—The earth swallows the three rebels and their families—Fire from the Lord consumes the 250 rebels—Israel murmurs against Moses and Aaron for slaying the people—The Lord sends a plague, from which 14,700 die.

Now Korah, the son of Izhar, the son of Kohath, the son of Levi, and

---

25a Lev. 1:4; 4:20 (20–26);
   2 Chr. 29:24 (23–24).
   b TG Forgive.
27a Mosiah 3:11;
   3 Ne. 6:18.
30a TG Accountability.

b TG Excommunication.
31a 2 Sam. 12:9 (7–9);
   1 Ne. 19:7;
   2 Ne. 33:2;
   Jacob 4:14;
   D&C 3:7 (4–13).

32a TG Sabbath.
35a Ex. 31:14; 35:2 (1–3).
38a Deut. 22:12.
   b Matt. 23:5.

*a*Dathan and Abiram, the sons of Eliab, and On, the son of Peleth, sons of Reuben, took *men:*

2 And they *a*rose up before Moses, with certain of the children of Israel, two hundred and fifty princes of the assembly, famous in the congregation, men of renown:

3 And they gathered themselves together against *a*Moses and against Aaron, and said unto them, *Ye take* too much upon you, seeing all the congregation *are* holy, every one of them, and the LORD *is* *b*among them: wherefore then lift ye up yourselves above the congregation of the LORD?

4 And when Moses heard *it*, he fell upon his face:

5 And he spake unto Korah and unto all his company, saying, Even to morrow the LORD will shew who *are* his, and *who is* *a*holy; and will cause *him* to come near unto him: even *him* whom he hath *b*chosen will he cause to *c*come near unto him.

6 This do; Take you censers, Korah, and all his company;

7 And put fire therein, and put incense in them before the LORD to morrow: and it shall be *that* the man whom the LORD doth choose, he *shall be* holy: *ye take* too much upon you, ye sons of Levi.

8 And Moses said unto Korah, Hear, I pray you, ye sons of Levi:

9 *Seemeth it but* a small thing unto you, that the God of Israel hath separated you from the congregation of Israel, to bring you near to himself to do the *a*service of the tabernacle of the LORD, and to stand before the congregation to minister unto them?

10 And he hath brought thee near *to him*, and all thy brethren the sons of Levi with thee: and seek ye the *a*priesthood also?

11 For which cause *both* thou and

all thy company *are* gathered together *a*against the LORD: and what *is* Aaron, that ye *b*murmur against him?

12 ¶ And Moses sent to call *a*Dathan and Abiram, the sons of Eliab: which said, We will not come up:

13 *Is it* a small thing that thou hast brought us up out of a land that floweth with milk and honey, to kill us in the wilderness, except thou make thyself altogether a *a*prince over us?

14 Moreover thou hast not brought us into a land that floweth with milk and honey, or given us inheritance of fields and vineyards: wilt thou put out the eyes of these men? we will not come up.

15 And Moses was very wroth, and said unto the LORD, *a*Respect not thou their offering: I have not taken one ass from them, neither have I hurt one of them.

16 And Moses said unto Korah, Be thou and all thy company before the LORD, thou, and they, and Aaron, to morrow:

17 And take every man his censer, and put incense in them, and bring ye before the LORD every man his censer, two hundred and fifty censers; thou also, and Aaron, each *of you* his censer.

18 And they took every man his censer, and put fire in them, and laid incense thereon, and stood in the door of the tabernacle of the congregation with Moses and Aaron.

19 And Korah gathered all the congregation against them unto the door of the tabernacle of the congregation: and the glory of the LORD appeared unto all the congregation.

20 And the LORD spake unto Moses and unto Aaron, saying,

21 *a*Separate yourselves from

16 1*a* Deut. 11:6.
  2*a* TG Ingratitude.
  3*a* 3 Jn. 1:10 (9–10).
   b TG God, Presence of.
  5*a* TG Holiness.
   b TG Priesthood, Authority.
   c Ezek. 40:46;

    44:15 (15–16).
  9*a* TG Priesthood, Aaronic.
 10*a* JST Num. 16:10 . . . *high priesthood* . . .
   TG Priesthood, Melchizedek.
 11*a* Ex. 16:8.
   b D&C 121:16.

 12*a* Num. 26:9;
   Deut. 11:6.
 13*a* Ex. 2:14;
   1 Ne. 16:37 (37–38);
   2 Ne. 5:3 (3, 19).
 15*a* Gen. 4:5 (4–5).
 21*a* Gen. 19:14.

among this congregation, that I may consume them in a moment.

22 And they fell upon their faces, and said, O God, the ^aGod of the ^bspirits of all flesh, shall one man sin, and wilt thou be wroth with all the congregation?

23 ¶ And the LORD spake unto Moses, saying,

24 Speak unto the congregation, saying, Get you up from about the ^atabernacle of Korah, Dathan, and Abiram.

25 And Moses rose up and went unto Dathan and Abiram; and the elders of Israel followed him.

26 And he spake unto the congregation, saying, Depart, I pray you, from the tents of these wicked men, and touch nothing of theirs, lest ye be consumed in all their sins.

27 So they gat up from the tabernacle of Korah, Dathan, and Abiram, on every side: and Dathan and Abiram came out, and stood in the door of their ^atents, and their wives, and their sons, and their little children.

28 And Moses said, Hereby ye shall know that the LORD hath sent me to do all these works; for I *have* not *done them* of mine own ^amind.

29 If these men die the common death of all men, or if they be visited ^aafter the visitation of all men; *then* the LORD hath not sent me.

30 But if the LORD make a new thing, and the earth open her mouth, and swallow them up, with all that *appertain* unto them, and they go down quick into the ^apit; then ye shall understand that these men have provoked the LORD.

31 ¶ And it came to pass, as he had made an end of speaking all these words, that the ground clave asunder that *was* under them:

32 And the ^aearth ^bopened her mouth, and swallowed them up, and their ^chouses, and all the men that *appertained* unto Korah, and all *their* goods.

33 They, and all that *appertained* to them, went down alive into the ^apit, and the earth closed upon them: and they perished from among the congregation.

34 And all Israel that *were* round about them fled at the cry of them: for they said, Lest the earth swallow us up *also*.

35 And there came out a ^afire from the LORD, and consumed the two hundred and fifty men that offered incense.

36 ¶ And the LORD spake unto Moses, saying,

37 Speak unto Eleazar the son of Aaron the priest, that he take up the censers out of the burning, and scatter thou the fire yonder; for they are hallowed.

38 The censers of these ^asinners against their own souls, let them make them broad plates *for* a covering of the altar: for they offered them before the LORD, therefore they are hallowed: and they shall be a sign unto the children of Israel.

39 And Eleazar the priest took the brasen censers, wherewith they that were burnt had offered; and they were made broad *plates for* a covering of the altar:

40 *To be* a memorial unto the children of Israel, that no ^astranger, which *is* not of the seed of ^bAaron, come near to offer ^cincense before the LORD; that he be not as Korah, and as his company: as the LORD said to him by the hand of Moses.

41 ¶ But on the morrow all the congregation of the children of Israel ^amurmured against Moses and

---

22a TG God the Father, Elohim.
  b TG Man, Antemortal Existence of; Man, a Spirit Child of Heavenly Father; Spirit Body; Spirit Creation.
24a OR dwelling places (see v. 26).

27a Ex. 33:8.
28a TG Mind.
29a IE by death as all men are.
30a Ps. 55:15.
32a Gen. 4:11; 1 Ne. 19:11; 2 Ne. 26:5; 3 Ne. 9:8; 10:14.
  b Ps. 106:17.

c HEB households.
33a Ps. 69:15.
35a Ps. 106:18.
38a Jer. 44:7.
40a IE unauthorized person. 2 Chr. 26:18 (16–23).
  b Num. 3:9; D&C 84:18.
  c Rev. 8:3 (2–4).
41a TG Murmuring.

against Aaron, saying, Ye have killed the people of the LORD.

42 And it came to pass, when the congregation was gathered against Moses and against Aaron, that they looked toward the tabernacle of the congregation: and, behold, the cloud covered it, and the glory of the LORD appeared.

43 And Moses and Aaron came before the tabernacle of the congregation.

44 ¶ And the LORD spake unto Moses, saying,

45 ªGet you up from among this congregation, that I may consume them as in a moment. And they fell upon their faces.

46 ¶ And Moses said unto Aaron, Take a censer, and put fire therein from off the altar, and put on incense, and go quickly unto the congregation, and make an atonement for them: for there is wrath gone out from the LORD; the ªplague is begun.

47 And Aaron took as Moses commanded, and ran into the midst of the congregation; and, behold, the plague was begun among the people: and he put on incense, and made an atonement for the people.

48 And he stood between the ªdead and the living; and the ᵇplague was stayed.

49 Now they that died in the plague were fourteen thousand and seven hundred, beside them that died about the matter of Korah.

50 And Aaron returned unto Moses unto the door of the tabernacle of the congregation: and the plague was stayed.

CHAPTER 17

As a test, a rod for each tribe is placed in the tabernacle of witness—Aaron's rod buds and blossoms and brings forth almonds—It is kept as a token against rebels.

AND the LORD spake unto Moses, saying,

2 Speak unto the children of Israel, and take of every one of them ªa rod according to the house of *their* fathers, of all their princes according to the house of their fathers twelve rods: write thou every man's name upon his rod.

3 And thou shalt write Aaron's name upon the rod of Levi: for one rod *shall be* for the head of the house of their fathers.

4 And thou shalt lay them up in the ªtabernacle of the congregation before the testimony, where I will ᵇmeet with you.

5 And it shall come to pass, *that* the man's rod, whom I shall ªchoose, shall blossom: and I will make to cease from me the murmurings of the children of Israel, whereby they murmur against you.

6 ¶ And Moses spake unto the children of Israel, and every one of their ªprinces gave him a rod apiece, for each prince one, according to their fathers' houses, *even* twelve rods: and the rod of Aaron *was* among their rods.

7 And Moses laid up the rods before the LORD in the ªtabernacle of witness.

8 And it came to pass, that on the morrow Moses went into the tabernacle of witness; and, behold, the rod of Aaron for the house of Levi was budded, and brought forth buds, and bloomed blossoms, and yielded almonds.

9 And Moses brought out all the rods from before the LORD unto all the children of Israel: and they looked, and took every man his rod.

10 ¶ And the LORD said unto Moses, Bring ªAaron's rod again before the testimony, to be kept for a token against the rebels; and thou shalt quite take away their murmurings from me, that they die not.

45ª Gen. 19:14.
46ª TG Plague.
48ª TG Death.
  ᵇ Num. 18:5 (2–7).
17 2ª Ezek. 37:16.

4ª HEB tent of meeting.
  ᵇ Ex. 25:22.
5ª TG Priesthood,
  Authority.
6ª HEB leaders, heads,

rulers.
7ª Ex. 38:21.
10ª Heb. 9:4.

11 And Moses did *so:* as the LORD commanded him, so did he.

12 And the children of Israel spake unto Moses, saying, Behold, we die, we perish, we all perish.

13 Whosoever cometh *a*any thing near unto the tabernacle of the LORD shall *b*die: *c*shall we be consumed with dying?

CHAPTER 18

Aaron and his sons are called to minister in the priest's office—Levites are called to minister in the service of the tabernacle—Levites receive no land inheritance but are supported by the tithes of the people.

AND the LORD said unto Aaron, Thou and thy sons and thy father's house with thee shall bear the iniquity of the sanctuary: and thou and thy sons with thee shall *a*bear the iniquity of your priesthood.

2 And thy brethren also of the tribe of Levi, the tribe of thy father, bring thou with thee, that they may be *a*joined unto thee, and minister unto thee: but thou and thy sons with thee *shall minister* before the tabernacle of witness.

3 And they shall keep thy charge, and the *a*charge of all the tabernacle: only they shall not come *b*nigh the *c*vessels of the sanctuary and the altar, that neither they, nor ye also, *d*die.

4 And they shall be joined unto thee, and *a*keep the charge of the tabernacle of the congregation, for all the service of the tabernacle: and *b*a stranger shall not come nigh unto you.

5 And ye shall *a*keep the *b*charge of the sanctuary, and the charge of the altar: that there be no *c*wrath any more upon the children of Israel.

6 And I, behold, I have taken your brethren the *a*Levites from among the children of Israel: to you *they are* given *as* a gift for the LORD, to do the service of the tabernacle of the congregation.

7 Therefore thou and thy sons with thee shall keep your *a*priest's office for every thing of the altar, and within the *b*veil; and ye shall serve: I have given your priest's office *unto you as* a service of gift: and the stranger that cometh nigh shall be put to death.

8 ¶ And the LORD spake unto Aaron, Behold, I also have given thee the charge of mine heave *a*offerings of all the hallowed things of the children of Israel; unto thee have I *b*given them by reason of the *c*anointing, and to thy sons, by an ordinance for ever.

9 This shall be thine of the most holy things, *reserved* from the fire: every oblation of theirs, every *a*meat offering of theirs, and every *b*sin offering of theirs, and every *c*trespass offering of theirs, which they shall render unto me, *shall be* most holy for thee and for thy sons.

10 In the most *a*holy *place* shalt thou *b*eat it; every male shall eat it: it shall be holy unto thee.

11 And this *is* thine; the *a*heave offering of their gift, with all the wave offerings of the children of Israel: I have given them unto thee, and to thy sons and to thy daughters

---

13*a* OR anywhere.
　b Num. 18:3 (2–7).
　c OR are we all to die?
18 1*a* IE bear any guilt incurred in failure to bear the full responsibility thereof.
　2*a* Gen. 29:34.
　3*a* Num. 3:25 (25, 31, 36).
　b Ezek. 44:13 (9–14).
　c Num. 4:15;
　　　Dan. 5:2.
　d Num. 17:13.
　4*a* OR attend to the

duties of.
　b OR any unauthorized person.
　5*a* Num. 3:38.
　b Ezek. 40:46;
　　　D&C 107:20.
　c Num. 16:48 (46–48).
　6*a* TG Priesthood, Aaronic.
　7*a* TG Priest, Aaronic Priesthood; Priesthood, History of.
　　　BD Priests.
　b TG Veil.
　8*a* Lev. 10:12 (12–15);

1 Sam. 2:28.
　b Lev. 7:31 (30–34);
　　　Deut. 18:3 (1–5).
　c Ex. 29:29;
　　　D&C 68:21; 124:39.
　9*a* HEB meal or cereal.
　　　Lev. 2:3 (2–3).
　b Lev. 4:24 (22–35);
　　　6:25 (25–26).
　c Lev. 7:7.
　10*a* Lev. 6:16 (16, 18, 26).
　b Deut. 18:1.
　11*a* Ex. 29:27 (27–28);
　　　Lev. 7:34.

with thee, by a statute for ever: every one that is [b]clean in thy house shall eat of it.

12 All the best of the oil, and all the best of the wine, and of the wheat, the [a]firstfruits of them which they shall offer unto the LORD, them have I given thee.

13 *And* whatsoever is [a]first ripe in the land, which they shall bring unto the LORD, shall be thine; every one that is clean in thine house shall eat *of* it.

14 Every thing [a]devoted in Israel shall be thine.

15 Every thing that openeth the [a]matrix in all flesh, which they bring unto the LORD, *whether it be* of men or beasts, shall be thine: nevertheless the [b]firstborn of man shalt thou surely redeem, and the firstling of unclean beasts shalt thou redeem.

16 And those that are to be redeemed from a month old shalt thou redeem, according to thine estimation, for the money of five shekels, after the shekel of the sanctuary, which *is* twenty gerahs.

17 But the [a]firstling of a cow, or the firstling of a sheep, or the firstling of a goat, thou shalt not redeem; they *are* holy: thou shalt [b]sprinkle their blood upon the altar, and shalt burn their fat *for* an offering made by fire, for a sweet savour unto the LORD.

18 And the flesh of them shall be thine, as the wave breast and as the right shoulder are thine.

19 All the heave offerings of the holy things, which the children of Israel offer unto the LORD, have I given thee, and thy sons and thy daughters with thee, by a statute for ever: it *is* a [a]covenant of [b]salt for ever before the LORD unto thee and to thy seed with thee.

20 ¶ And the LORD spake unto Aaron, Thou shalt have no [a]inheritance in their land, neither shalt thou have any [b]part among them: I *am* thy part and thine [c]inheritance among the children of Israel.

21 And, behold, I have given the children of Levi all the tenth in Israel for an [a]inheritance, for their service which they serve, *even* the service of the tabernacle of the congregation.

22 Neither must the [a]children of Israel henceforth come nigh the tabernacle of the congregation, lest they bear sin, and die.

23 But the [a]Levites shall do the service of the tabernacle of the congregation, and they shall bear their iniquity: *it shall be* a statute for ever throughout your generations, that among the children of Israel they have no inheritance.

24 But the tithes of the children of Israel, which they offer *as* an heave offering unto the LORD, I have given to the Levites to inherit: therefore I have said unto them, Among the children of Israel they shall have no [a]inheritance.

25 ¶ And the LORD spake unto Moses, saying,

26 Thus speak unto the Levites, and say unto them, When ye take of the children of Israel the tithes which I have given you from them for your inheritance, then ye shall offer up an heave offering of it for the LORD, *even* a [a]tenth *part* of the tithe.

27 And *this* your heave offering shall be reckoned unto you, as though *it were* the corn of the threshingfloor, and as the fulness of the winepress.

28 Thus ye also shall offer an heave offering unto the LORD of all your tithes, which ye receive of the children of Israel; and ye shall give

11b Lev. 22:3 (2–3, 11–13).
12a Deut. 18:4.
13a Deut. 26:2.
14a Lev. 27:21 (17–21, 28).
15a OR womb.
 b TG Firstborn.
17a Gen. 4:4;

 Moses 5:5 (5–8).
 b Lev. 3:2 (2, 5);
 D&C 133:51 (50–52).
19a 2 Chr. 13:5.
 b TG Salt.
20a Deut. 10:9; 18:1;
 Josh. 13:14.

 b Deut. 18:1 (1–2).
 c Ezek. 44:28.
21a TG Birthright.
22a Num. 1:51.
23a Num. 35:2 (1–8).
24a TG Inheritance.
26a TG Tithing.

thereof the LORD's heave offering to Aaron the priest:

29 Out of all your gifts ye shall offer every heave offering of the LORD, of all the best thereof, *even* the hallowed part thereof out of it.

30 Therefore thou shalt say unto them, When ye have heaved the best thereof from it, then it shall be counted unto the Levites as the increase of the threshingfloor, and as the increase of the winepress.

31 And ye *a*shall eat it in every place, ye and your households: for it *is* your *b*reward for your service in the tabernacle of the congregation.

32 And ye shall bear no sin by reason of it, when ye have heaved from it the best of it: neither shall ye *a*pollute the holy things of the children of Israel, lest ye die.

CHAPTER 19

Directions are given for the sacrifice of a red heifer—The water of separation is used for purification from sin—Ceremonially unclean persons are sprinkled with the water of separation.

AND the LORD spake unto Moses and unto Aaron, saying,

2 This *is* the ordinance of the law which the LORD hath commanded, saying, Speak unto the children of Israel, that they bring thee a red heifer without *a*spot, wherein *is* no blemish, *and* upon which never came yoke:

3 And ye shall give her unto Eleazar the priest, that he may bring her forth without the camp, and *one* shall slay her before his face:

4 And Eleazar the priest shall take of her *a*blood with his finger, and sprinkle of her blood directly before the *b*tabernacle of the congregation seven times:

5 And *one* shall burn the heifer in his sight; her skin, and her flesh, and her blood, with her dung, shall he burn:

6 And the priest shall take cedar wood, and hyssop, and scarlet, and cast *it* into the midst of the burning of the heifer.

7 Then the priest shall *a*wash his clothes, and he shall bathe his flesh in water, and afterward he shall come into the camp, and the priest shall be unclean until the even.

8 And he that burneth her shall wash his clothes in water, and bathe his flesh in water, and shall be unclean until the even.

9 And a man *that is* clean shall gather up the ashes of the heifer, and lay *them* up without the camp in a clean place, and it shall be kept for the congregation of the children of Israel for a *a*water of separation: it *is* a purification for sin.

10 And he that gathereth the ashes of the heifer shall wash his clothes, and be unclean until the even: and it shall be unto the children of Israel, and unto the stranger that sojourneth among them, for a statute for ever.

11 ¶ He that toucheth the dead body of any man shall be *a*unclean seven days.

12 He shall purify himself with it on the third day, and on the seventh day he shall be clean: but if he purify not himself the third day, then the seventh day he shall not be clean.

13 Whosoever toucheth the dead body of any man that is dead, and purifieth not himself, defileth the tabernacle of the LORD; and that soul shall be *a*cut off from Israel: because the water of separation was not sprinkled upon him, he shall be unclean; his uncleanness *is* yet upon him.

14 This *is* the law, when a man dieth in a tent: all that come into the tent, and all that *is* in the tent, shall be unclean seven days.

31*a* OR may eat it in any place.
  b Matt. 10:10; Luke 10:7.
32*a* TG Pollution.

19 2*a* HEB defect.
  4*a* Lev. 4:5 (5–6).
    b HEB tent of meeting.
  7*a* TG Wash.
  9*a* IE water for removal

of impurity.
11*a* Lev. 5:2 (2–6); Ezek. 44:26.
13*a* TG Excommunication.

15 And every open vessel, which hath no covering bound upon it, *is* unclean.

16 And whosoever toucheth one that is slain with a sword in the open fields, or a dead body, or a bone of a man, or a grave, shall be unclean seven days.

17 And for an unclean *person* they shall take of the ashes of the burnt heifer of *a*purification for sin, and running water shall be put thereto in a vessel:

18 And a clean person shall take *a*hyssop, and dip *it* in the water, and sprinkle *it* upon the tent, and upon all the vessels, and upon the persons that were there, and upon him that touched a bone, or one slain, or one dead, or a grave:

19 And the clean *person* shall sprinkle upon the unclean on the third day, and on the seventh day: and on the seventh day he shall purify himself, and wash his clothes, and bathe himself in water, and shall be clean at even.

20 But the man that shall be unclean, and shall not purify himself, that soul shall be cut off from among the congregation, because he hath defiled the sanctuary of the LORD: the water of separation hath not been sprinkled upon him; he *is* unclean.

21 And it shall be a perpetual statute unto them, that he that sprinkleth the water of separation shall wash his clothes; and he that toucheth the water of separation shall be unclean until even.

22 And whatsoever the unclean *person* toucheth shall be unclean; and the soul that toucheth *it* shall be unclean until even.

CHAPTER 20

Miriam dies—Moses smites a rock at Meribah and brings forth water—The king of Edom refuses to let Israel pass peacefully through his land—Aaron dies, and Eleazar becomes the high priest.

THEN came the children of Israel, *even* the whole congregation, into the desert of Zin in the first month: and the people abode in *a*Kadesh; and Miriam died there, and was buried there.

2 And there was no water for the congregation: and they gathered themselves together against Moses and against Aaron.

3 And the people *a*chode with Moses, and spake, saying, Would God that we had died when our brethren died before the LORD!

4 And why have ye brought up the congregation of the LORD into this wilderness, that we and our cattle should die there?

5 And wherefore have ye made us to come up out of Egypt, to bring us in unto this evil place? it *is* no place of seed, or of figs, or of vines, or of pomegranates; neither *is* there any water to drink.

6 And Moses and Aaron went from the presence of the assembly unto the door of the *a*tabernacle of the congregation, and they fell upon their faces: and the glory of the LORD appeared unto them.

7 ¶ And the LORD spake unto Moses, saying,

8 Take the *a*rod, and gather thou the assembly together, thou, and Aaron thy brother, and *b*speak ye unto the rock before their eyes; and it shall give forth his water, and thou shalt bring forth to them water out of the rock: so thou shalt give the congregation and their beasts drink.

9 And Moses took the rod from before the LORD, as he commanded him.

10 And Moses and Aaron gathered the congregation together before the rock, and he said unto them, *a*Hear now, ye rebels; must *b*we fetch you water out of this rock?

17*a* TG Purification.
18*a* Ps. 51:7.
20 1*a* Num. 27:14 (12–14);
    33:36.
  3*a* OR contended (also

v. 13, for "strove").
Deut. 33:8.
6*a* HEB tent of meeting.
8*a* See JST Gen. 50:34
    (Appendix).

Ex. 4:20.
  b Ex. 17:6 (6–7).
10*a* Ps. 106:33.
  b TG Rashness.

11 And Moses lifted up his hand, and with his rod he ^asmote the ^brock twice: and the ^cwater came out abundantly, and the congregation drank, and their beasts *also.*

12 ¶ And the LORD spake unto Moses and Aaron, Because ye ^abelieved me not, to ^bsanctify me in the eyes of the children of Israel, therefore ye shall not ^cbring this congregation into the ^dland which I have given them.

13 This *is* the water of ^aMeribah; because the children of Israel ^bstrove with the LORD, and he was sanctified in them.

14 ¶ And Moses ^asent messengers from Kadesh unto the king of Edom, Thus saith thy brother Israel, Thou knowest all the travail that hath befallen us:

15 How our fathers went down into Egypt, and we have dwelt in Egypt a long time; and the Egyptians vexed us, and our fathers:

16 And when we cried unto the LORD, he heard our voice, and sent an ^aangel, and hath brought us forth out of Egypt: and, behold, we *are* in Kadesh, a city in the uttermost of thy border:

17 Let us pass, I pray thee, through thy country: we will not pass through the fields, or through the vineyards, neither will we drink *of* the water of the wells: we will go by the king's *high* way, we will not turn to the right hand nor to the left, until we have passed thy borders.

18 And Edom said unto him, Thou shalt not pass ^aby me, lest I come out against thee with the sword.

19 And the children of Israel said unto him, We will go by the high way: and if I and my cattle drink of thy water, then I will ^apay for it: I will only, without *doing* any thing *else,* go through on my feet.

20 And he said, Thou shalt not go through. And Edom came out against him with much people, and with a strong hand.

21 Thus Edom refused to give Israel passage through his border: wherefore Israel turned away from him.

22 ¶ And the children of Israel, *even* the whole congregation, journeyed from Kadesh, and came unto mount Hor.

23 And the LORD spake unto Moses and Aaron in mount Hor, by the ^acoast of the land of Edom, saying,

24 Aaron shall be gathered unto his people: for he shall not enter into the land which I have given unto the children of Israel, because ye ^arebelled against my word at the water of Meribah.

25 Take Aaron and Eleazar his son, and bring them up unto mount Hor:

26 And strip Aaron of his garments, and put them upon Eleazar his son: and Aaron shall be gathered *unto his people,* and shall die there.

27 And Moses did as the LORD commanded: and they went up into mount Hor in the sight of all the congregation.

28 And Moses stripped Aaron of his garments, and put them upon Eleazar his son; and ^aAaron died there in the top of the mount: and Moses and Eleazar came down from the mount.

29 And when all the congregation saw that Aaron was dead, they mourned for Aaron thirty days, *even* all the house of Israel.

11a Ps. 78:15 (15–16, 20).
  b 1 Ne. 17:29; 20:21;
     2 Ne. 25:20.
  c Isa. 48:21.
12a IE in not speaking to
     the rock, striking it
     instead.
   TG Unbelief.
  b TG Sanctification.
  c Deut. 31:2.

    d Deut. 4:26 (24–28);
       32:51.
13a IE Quarrel, Strife,
       Contention.
       Ex. 17:7;
       Deut. 33:8;
       Ezek. 47:19.
  b Ezek. 48:28.
       TG Strife.
14a Judg. 11:17.

16a Ex. 32:34.
    TG Angels.
18a HEB through me (i.e.,
       through my land).
19a Deut. 2:28.
23a HEB border.
24a TG Rebellion.
28a Num. 33:38 (37–39);
       Deut. 10:6; 32:50.

CHAPTER 21

The children of Israel destroy those Canaanites who fight against them—The Israelites are plagued with fiery serpents—Moses lifts up a serpent of brass to save those who look thereon—Israel defeats the Amorites, destroys the people of Bashan, and occupies their lands.

AND *when* [a]king [b]Arad the Canaanite, which dwelt in the [c]south, heard tell that Israel came by the way of [d]the spies; then he fought against Israel, and took *some* of them prisoners.

2 And Israel vowed a [a]vow unto the LORD, and said, If thou wilt indeed deliver this people into my hand, then I will utterly destroy their cities.

3 And the LORD hearkened to the voice of Israel, and delivered up the Canaanites; and they utterly [a]destroyed them and their cities: and he called the name of the place [b]Hormah.

4 ¶ And they journeyed from mount [a]Hor by the way of the [b]Red sea, to [c]compass the land of Edom: and the soul of the people was much discouraged because of the way.

5 And the people [a]spake against God, and against Moses, Wherefore have ye brought us up out of Egypt to die in the wilderness? for *there is* no bread, neither *is there any* water; and our soul loatheth this light bread.

6 And the LORD sent [a]fiery [b]serpents among the people, and they bit the people; and much people of Israel died.

7 ¶ Therefore the people came to Moses, and said, We have [a]sinned, for we have spoken against the LORD, and against thee; pray unto the LORD, that he take away the serpents from us. And Moses [b]prayed for the people.

8 And the LORD said unto Moses, [a]Make thee a fiery serpent, and set it upon a pole: and it shall come to pass, that every one that is bitten, when he looketh upon it, shall [b]live.

9 And Moses made a [a]serpent of brass, and put it upon a pole, and it came to pass, that if a serpent had bitten any man, when he beheld the serpent of brass, he lived.

10 ¶ And the children of Israel set forward, and [a]pitched in Oboth.

11 And they journeyed from Oboth, and pitched at Ije-abarim, in the wilderness which *is* [a]before Moab, toward the sunrising.

12 ¶ From thence they removed, and pitched in the valley of Zared.

13 From thence they removed, and pitched on the other side of Arnon, which *is* in the wilderness that [a]cometh out of the coasts of the Amorites: for [b]Arnon *is* the border of Moab, between Moab and the Amorites.

14 Wherefore it is said in the [a]book of the wars of the LORD, What he did in the Red sea, and in the brooks of Arnon,

15 And at the [a]stream of the brooks that goeth down to the dwelling of Ar, and lieth upon the border of Moab.

16 And from thence *they went* to [a]Beer: that *is* the well whereof the LORD spake unto Moses, Gather the people together, and I will give them water.

---

21 1a Num. 33:40.
  b HEB of Arad.
  c HEB Negev.
  d HEB Atharim (a place).
 2a TG Vow.
 3a Ps. 80:8 (8–10);
    Acts 13:19 (17–19);
    1 Ne. 17:35 (32–35).
  b IE Destruction.
    Josh. 12:14.
 4a Num. 33:41 (41–42).
  b HEB Reed Sea (also
    v. 14).

 c OR go around.
 5a 1 Cor. 10:5 (5–10).
 6a OR poisonous.
  b Deut. 8:15 (1–20);
    1 Ne. 17:41 (40–42).
 7a TG Confession.
  b 1 Sam. 7:5; Jer. 42:4;
    2 Ne. 33:3; Enos 1:9.
    TG Prayer.
 8a TG Jesus Christ, Types
    of, in Anticipation;
    Symbolism.
  b TG Heal.

 9a 1 Ne. 17:41;
    Alma 33:19 (18–22).
10a OR encamped (also
    vv. 11–13).
11a OR opposite.
13a OR extends from the
    boundary of.
  b Judg. 11:13;
    Isa. 16:2.
14a TG Scriptures, Lost.
15a HEB slopes of the
    valleys.
16a Judg. 9:21; Isa. 15:8.

17 ¶ Then Israel sang this song, Spring up, O well; sing ye unto it:

18 The princes digged the well, the nobles of the people digged it, by *the direction of* the lawgiver, with their staves. And from the wilderness *they went* to Mattanah:

19 And from Mattanah to Nahaliel: and from Nahaliel to Bamoth:

20 And from Bamoth *in the* valley, that *is* in the country of Moab, to the top of Pisgah, which *a*looketh toward Jeshimon.

21 ¶ And Israel sent messengers unto *a*Sihon king of the *b*Amorites, saying,

22 Let me pass through thy land: we will not turn into the fields, or into the vineyards; we will not drink *of* the waters of the well: *but* we will go along by the king's *high* way, until we be past thy borders.

23 And *a*Sihon would not suffer Israel to pass through his *b*border: but Sihon gathered all his people together, and went out against Israel into the wilderness: and he came to Jahaz, and fought against Israel.

24 And Israel *a*smote him with the edge of the sword, and possessed his land from *b*Arnon unto Jabbok, even unto the children of Ammon: for the border of the children of Ammon *was* strong.

25 And Israel took all these *a*cities: and Israel dwelt in all the cities of the Amorites, in Heshbon, and in all the villages thereof.

26 For Heshbon *was* the city of Sihon the king of the Amorites, who had fought against the former king of Moab, and taken all his land out of his hand, even unto Arnon.

27 Wherefore they that speak in proverbs say, Come into Heshbon, let the city of Sihon be built and *a*prepared:

28 For there is a fire gone out of *a*Heshbon, a flame from the city of Sihon: it hath consumed Ar of Moab, *and* the lords of the high places of Arnon.

29 Woe to thee, Moab! thou art undone, O people of *a*Chemosh: he hath given his sons that escaped, and his daughters, into captivity unto Sihon king of the Amorites.

30 We have shot at them; Heshbon is perished even unto Dibon, and we have laid them waste even unto Nophah, which *reacheth* unto Medeba.

31 ¶ Thus Israel dwelt in the land of the Amorites.

32 And Moses sent to spy out *a*Jaazer, and they took the villages thereof, and drove out the Amorites that *were* there.

33 ¶ And they turned and went up by the way of Bashan: and *a*Og the king of Bashan went out against them, he, and all his people, to the battle at Edrei.

34 And the LORD said unto Moses, Fear him not: for I have delivered him into thy hand, and all his people, and his land; and thou shalt do to him as thou didst unto Sihon king of the *a*Amorites, which dwelt at Heshbon.

35 So they *a*smote him, and his sons, and all his people, until there was none left him alive: and they possessed his land.

CHAPTER 22

Balak offers money, cattle, and great honors to Balaam to curse Israel—The Lord forbids Balaam to do so—An angel opposes Balaam on the way.

AND the children of Israel set forward, and *a*pitched in the plains of Moab *b*on this side Jordan *by* Jericho.

---

20 *a* HEB overlooks the desert.
21 *a* Josh. 12:2.
   b Josh. 24:8.
23 *a* Deut. 1:4.
   b OR territory (also v. 22).
24 *a* Deut. 2:33; 29:7 (7–8);
   Judg. 11:21;
   Ps. 135:11;

Amos 2:9.
   b Deut. 3:16 (15–17);
   4:48 (47–49);
   Josh. 13:9 (7–12).
25 *a* Deut. 2:19 (16–19);
   Judg. 11:13 (13–23).
27 *a* OR established.
28 *a* Jer. 48:45.
29 *a* 1 Kgs. 11:7.

32 *a* Isa. 16:8.
33 *a* Deut. 1:4; 3:11 (10–11).
34 *a* Josh. 2:10.
35 *a* Deut. 3:3;
   Ps. 135:11.
22 1 *a* OR encamped.
   b IE across the Jordan from Jericho.

2 ¶ And ^aBalak the son of Zippor saw all that Israel had done to the Amorites.

3 And Moab was sore afraid of the people, because they *were* many: and Moab was distressed because of the children of Israel.

4 And Moab said unto the elders of Midian, Now shall this company lick up all *that are* round about us, as the ox licketh up the grass of the field. And Balak the son of Zippor *was* king of the Moabites at that time.

5 He sent messengers therefore unto ^aBalaam the son of Beor to Pethor, which *is* by the river of the land of the children of his people, to call him, saying, Behold, there is a people come out from Egypt: behold, they cover the face of the earth, and they abide over against me:

6 Come now therefore, I pray thee, curse me this people; for they *are* too mighty for me: peradventure I shall prevail, *that* we may smite them, and *that* I may drive them out of the land: for I ^awot that he whom thou blessest *is* blessed, and he whom thou cursest is cursed.

7 And the elders of Moab and the elders of Midian departed with the ^arewards of ^bdivination in their hand; and they came unto Balaam, and spake unto him the words of Balak.

8 And he said unto them, Lodge here this night, and I will bring you word again, as the LORD shall speak unto me: and the ^aprinces of Moab abode with Balaam.

9 And God came unto Balaam, and said, What men *are* these with thee?

10 And Balaam said unto God, Balak the son of Zippor, king of Moab, hath sent unto me, *saying,*

11 Behold, *there is* a people come out of Egypt, which covereth the face of the earth: come now, curse me them; peradventure I shall be able to overcome them, and drive them out.

12 And God said unto Balaam, Thou shalt not go with them; thou shalt not curse the people: for they *are* blessed.

13 And Balaam rose up in the morning, and said unto the princes of Balak, Get you into your land: for the LORD refuseth to give me leave to go with you.

14 And the princes of Moab rose up, and they went unto Balak, and said, Balaam refuseth to come with us.

15 ¶ And Balak sent yet again princes, more, and more honourable than they.

16 And they came to Balaam, and said to him, Thus saith Balak the son of Zippor, Let nothing, I pray thee, hinder thee from coming unto me:

17 For I will promote thee unto very great honour, and I will do whatsoever thou sayest unto me: come therefore, I pray thee, curse me this people.

18 And Balaam answered and said unto the servants of Balak, If Balak would give me his house full of silver and gold, I cannot go beyond the word of the LORD my God, to do less or more.

19 Now therefore, I pray you, tarry ye also here this night, that I may know what the LORD will say unto me more.

20 And God came unto Balaam at night, and said unto him, If the men come to call thee, rise up, *and* go with them; but yet the word which I shall say unto thee, that shalt thou do.

21 And Balaam rose up in the morning, and saddled his ass, and went with the princes of Moab.

22 ¶ And God's anger was kindled because he went: and the angel of the LORD stood in the way for an adversary against him. Now he was riding upon his ass, and his two servants *were* with him.

23 And the ass ^asaw the angel of

---

2 *a* Judg. 11:25;
  Micah 6:5.
5 *a* Deut. 23:4;
  Neh. 13:2;

2 Pet. 2:15.
6 *a* OR know.
7 *a* TG Selfishness.
  b Deut. 18:10.

8 *a* HEB leaders, rulers (also
  vv. 13–15, 21, 35, 40).
23 *a* 2 Kgs. 6:17.

the LORD standing in the way, and his sword drawn in his hand: and the ass turned aside out of the way, and went into the field: and Balaam smote the ass, to turn her into the way.

24 But the angel of the LORD stood in a path of the vineyards, a wall *being* on this side, and a wall on that side.

25 And when the ass saw the angel of the LORD, she thrust herself unto the wall, and crushed Balaam's foot against the wall: and he smote her again.

26 And the angel of the LORD went further, and stood in a narrow place, where *was* no way to turn either to the right hand or to the left.

27 And when the ass saw the angel of the LORD, she fell down under Balaam: and Balaam's anger was kindled, and he smote the ass with a staff.

28 And the LORD opened the mouth of the ass, and she said unto Balaam, What have I done unto thee, that thou hast smitten me these three times?

29 And Balaam said unto the ass, Because thou hast mocked me: I would there were a sword in mine hand, for now would I *a*kill thee.

30 And the *a*ass said unto Balaam, *Am* not I thine ass, upon which thou hast ridden ever since *I was* thine unto this day? was I ever *b*wont to do so unto thee? And he said, Nay.

31 Then the LORD opened the eyes of Balaam, and he saw the angel of the LORD standing in the way, and his sword drawn in his hand: and he bowed down his head, and fell flat on his face.

32 And the angel of the LORD said unto him, Wherefore hast thou smitten thine ass these three times? behold, I went out to withstand thee, because *thy* way is *a*perverse before me:

33 And the ass saw me, and turned from me these three times: unless she had turned from me, surely now also I had slain thee, and saved her alive.

34 And Balaam said unto the angel of the LORD, I have sinned; for I knew not that thou stoodest in the way against me: now therefore, if it displease thee, I will get me back again.

35 And the angel of the LORD said unto Balaam, Go with the men: but only the word that I shall speak unto thee, that thou shalt speak. So Balaam went with the princes of Balak.

36 ¶ And when Balak heard that Balaam was come, he went out to meet him unto a city of Moab, which *is* in the border of Arnon, which *is* in the utmost *a*coast.

37 And Balak said unto Balaam, Did I not earnestly send unto thee to call thee? wherefore camest thou not unto me? am I not able indeed to promote thee to honour?

38 And Balaam said unto Balak, Lo, I am come unto thee: have I now any power at all to say any thing? the word that God putteth in my mouth, that shall I speak.

39 And Balaam went with Balak, and they came unto Kirjath-huzoth.

40 And Balak offered oxen and sheep, and sent to Balaam, and to the princes that *were* with him.

41 And it came to pass on the morrow, that Balak took Balaam, and brought him up into the high places of Baal, that thence he might see the utmost *part* of the people.

CHAPTER 23

The Lord commands Balaam to bless Israel—He does so, saying, Who can count the dust of Jacob? and, What hath God wrought!

AND Balaam said unto Balak, Build me here seven altars, and prepare me here *a*seven oxen and seven rams.

2 And Balak did as Balaam had spoken; and Balak and Balaam offered on *every* altar a bullock and a ram.

3 And Balaam said unto Balak,

29*a* TG Rashness.
30*a* 2 Pet. 2:16.

b OR accustomed.
32*a* TG Stiffnecked.

36*a* OR boundary.
23 1*a* 1 Chr. 15:26.

Stand by thy burnt offering, and I will go: peradventure the LORD will come to meet me: and whatsoever he sheweth me I will tell thee. And he went to *an high place.

4 And God met Balaam: and he said unto him, I have prepared seven altars, and I have offered upon *every* altar a bullock and a ram.

5 And the LORD put a word in Balaam's mouth, and said, Return unto Balak, and thus thou shalt speak.

6 And he returned unto him, and, lo, he stood by his burnt sacrifice, he, and all the princes of Moab.

7 And he took up his parable, and said, Balak the king of Moab hath brought me from Aram, out of the mountains of the east, *saying,* Come, curse me Jacob, and come, *defy Israel.

8 How shall I curse, whom God hath not cursed? or how shall I defy, *whom* the LORD hath not defied?

9 For from the top of the rocks I see him, and from the hills I behold him: lo, the people shall dwell alone, and shall not be reckoned among the nations.

10 Who can count the dust of Jacob, and the number of the fourth *part* of Israel? Let me die the *death of the righteous, and let my last end be like his!

11 And Balak said unto *Balaam, What hast thou done unto me? I took thee to *curse mine enemies, and, behold, thou hast blessed *them* altogether.

12 And he answered and said, Must I not take heed to speak that which the LORD hath put in my mouth?

13 And Balak said unto him, Come, I pray thee, with me unto another place, from whence thou mayest see them: thou shalt see but the utmost part of them, and shalt not see them all: and curse me them from thence.

14 ¶ And he brought him into *the field of Zophim, to *the top of Pisgah, and built seven altars, and offered a bullock and a ram on *every* altar.

15 And he said unto Balak, Stand here by thy burnt offering, while I meet *the* LORD yonder.

16 And the LORD met Balaam, and put a word in his mouth, and said, Go again unto Balak, and say thus.

17 And when he came to him, behold, he stood by his burnt offering, and the princes of Moab with him. And Balak said unto him, What hath the LORD spoken?

18 And he took up his parable, and said, Rise up, Balak, and hear; hearken unto me, thou son of Zippor:

19 God *is* not a man, that he should *lie; neither the son of man, that he should *repent: hath he said, and shall he not do *it?* or hath he *spoken, and shall he not make it good?

20 Behold, I have received *commandment* to bless: and he hath blessed; and I cannot reverse it.

21 He hath not beheld iniquity in Jacob, neither hath he seen perverseness in Israel: the LORD his God *is* with him, and the shout of a king *is* among them.

22 God brought them out of Egypt; he hath as it were the strength of *an unicorn.

23 Surely *there is* no enchantment against Jacob, neither *is there* any divination against Israel: according to this time it shall be said of Jacob and of Israel, What hath God wrought!

24 Behold, the people shall rise up as a great lion, and lift up himself as a young lion: he shall not lie down until he eat *of* the prey, and drink the blood of the slain.

25 ¶ And Balak said unto Balaam, Neither curse them at all, nor bless them at all.

3*a* HEB a bare hill.
7*a* HEB denounce (also v. 8).
10*a* TG Death.
11*a* Neh. 13:2.
  b Deut. 23:5.

14*a* HEB a lookout point.
  b HEB the summit.
19*a* TG Lying.
  b Ex. 32:14;
     Deut. 32:36;

Isa. 31:2;
Amos 7:3 (3, 6).
TG God, Perfection of.
c Isa. 46:11.
22*a* HEB a wild ox.

26 But Balaam answered and said unto Balak, Told not I thee, saying, All that the LORD speaketh, that I must do?

27 ¶ And Balak said unto Balaam, Come, I pray thee, I will bring thee unto another place; peradventure it will please God that thou mayest curse me them from thence.

28 And Balak brought Balaam unto the top of Peor, that *looketh toward Jeshimon.

29 And Balaam said unto Balak, Build me here seven altars, and prepare me here seven bullocks and seven rams.

30 And Balak did as Balaam had said, and offered a bullock and a ram on *every* altar.

CHAPTER 24

Balaam sees in vision and prophesies of the destiny of Israel—He prophesies of the Messiah: There will come a Star out of Jacob, and a Sceptre will rise out of Israel.

AND when Balaam saw that it *pleased the LORD to bless Israel, he went not, as at other times, to seek for enchantments, but he set his face toward the wilderness.

2 And Balaam lifted up his eyes, and he saw Israel abiding *in his tents* according to their *tribes; and the spirit of God came upon him.

3 And he took up his *parable, and said, Balaam the son of Beor hath said, and the man whose eyes are open hath said:

4 He hath said, which heard the words of God, which saw the *vision of the Almighty, falling *into a trance,* but having his eyes open:

5 How goodly are thy tents, O Jacob, *and* thy *tabernacles, O Israel!

6 As the valleys are they spread forth, as gardens by the river's side,

as the *trees of lign aloes which the LORD hath planted, *and* as cedar trees beside the waters.

7 *He shall pour the water out of his buckets, and his seed *shall be* in many waters, and his king shall be higher than *Agag, and his kingdom shall be exalted.

8 God brought him forth out of Egypt; he hath as it were the strength of an unicorn: he shall eat up the nations his enemies, and shall *break their bones, and *pierce *them* through with his arrows.

9 He couched, he lay down as a *lion, and as a great lion: who shall stir him up? Blessed *is* he that blesseth thee, and cursed *is* he that curseth thee.

10 ¶ And Balak's anger was kindled against Balaam, and he smote his hands together: and Balak said unto Balaam, I called thee to curse mine enemies, and, behold, thou hast altogether blessed *them* these three times.

11 Therefore now flee thou to thy place: I thought to promote thee unto great honour; but, lo, the LORD hath kept thee back from honour.

12 And Balaam said unto Balak, Spake I not also to thy messengers which thou sentest unto me, saying,

13 If Balak would give me his house full of silver and gold, I cannot go beyond the commandment of the LORD, to do *either* good or bad of mine own *mind; *but* what the LORD saith, that will I *speak?

14 And now, behold, I go unto my people: come *therefore, and* I will *advertise thee what this people shall do to thy people in the latter days.

15 ¶ And he took up his parable, and said, Balaam the son of Beor hath said, and the man whose eyes are open hath said:

16 He hath said, which heard the

28*a* HEB overlooks the desert.
24 1*a* D&C 41:1; 76:5.
   2*a* Num. 2:2 (2–31).
   3*a* IE figurative discourse.
   4*a* TG Vision.

5*a* OR dwellings.
6*a* Ps. 104:16 (16–17).
7*a* HEB Water shall flow from his branches.
   b IE the Amalekites.
8*a* Jer. 50:17.

b Jer. 50:9.
9*a* Gen. 49:9.
13*a* TG Mind.
   b Ezek. 2:7 (6–8).
14*a* HEB tell.

words of God, and knew the knowledge of the most High, *which* saw the vision of the Almighty, falling *into a trance,* but having his eyes open:

17 I shall see him, but *a*not now: I shall behold him, but not nigh: there shall come a *b*Star out of Jacob, and a Sceptre shall rise out of Israel, and shall smite the corners of *c*Moab, and destroy all the children of Sheth.

18 And *a*Edom shall be a possession, Seir also shall be a possession for his enemies; and Israel shall do valiantly.

19 Out of Jacob shall come he that shall have dominion, and shall destroy him that remaineth of the city.

20 ¶ And when he looked on Amalek, he took up his parable, and said, *a*Amalek *was* the first of the nations; but his latter end *shall be* that he perish for ever.

21 And he looked on the Kenites, and took up his parable, and said, Strong is thy dwellingplace, and thou puttest thy nest in a rock.

22 Nevertheless the Kenite shall be wasted, until Asshur shall carry thee away captive.

23 And he took up his parable, and said, Alas, who shall live when God doeth this!

24 And ships *shall come* from the coast of *a*Chittim, and shall afflict Asshur, and shall afflict Eber, and he also shall perish for ever.

25 And Balaam rose up, and went and returned to his place: and Balak also went his way.

CHAPTER 25

The Israelites who worship false gods are slain—Phinehas slays the adulterers and stays the plague—Israel is commanded to vex the Midianites who beguiled them.

AND Israel abode in Shittim, and the people began to commit *a*whoredom with the daughters of Moab.

2 And they *a*called the people unto the *b*sacrifices of their gods: and the people did eat, and bowed down to their gods.

3 And Israel joined himself unto *a*Baal-peor: and the anger of the LORD was kindled against Israel.

4 And the LORD said unto Moses, Take all the *a*heads of the people, and hang them up before the LORD *b*against the sun, that the *c*fierce anger of the LORD may be turned away from Israel.

5 And Moses said unto the judges of Israel, *a*Slay ye every one his men that were joined unto *b*Baal-peor.

6 ¶ And, behold, one of the children of Israel came and brought unto his brethren a Midianitish woman in the sight of Moses, and in the sight of all the congregation of the children of Israel, who *were* weeping *before* the door of the *a*tabernacle of the congregation.

7 And when *a*Phinehas, the son of Eleazar, the son of Aaron the priest, saw *it,* he rose up from among the congregation, and took a javelin in his hand;

8 And he went after the man of Israel into the tent, and thrust both of them through, the man of Israel, and the woman through her belly. So the plague was stayed from the children of Israel.

9 And those that died in the plague were twenty and four thousand.

10 ¶ And the LORD spake unto Moses, saying,

11 Phinehas, the son of Eleazar, the son of Aaron the priest, hath turned my wrath away from the children of Israel, while he was zealous for my sake among them, that I

17*a* IE His coming was to be in the future, long after Moses' time.
 b TG Jesus Christ, Prophecies about.
 c 2 Sam. 8:2; Jer. 48:45.
18*a* 2 Sam. 8:14.

20*a* Ex. 17:8 (8–16).
24*a* Dan. 11:30.
25 1*a* TG Sexual Immorality; Whore.
 2*a* Ex. 34:15.
 b Ex. 22:20.
3*a* IE The idol at Peor (a mountain in Moab).

Hosea 9:10.
4*a* OR chief men.
 b OR facing.
 c Deut. 13:17.
5*a* Ex. 32:27.
 b Deut. 4:3 (3–4).
6*a* HEB tent of meeting.
7*a* Ps. 106:30.

consumed not the children of Israel in my ᵃjealousy.

12 Wherefore say, Behold, I give unto him my ᵃcovenant of peace:

13 And he shall have it, and his ᵃseed after him, *even* the ᵇcovenant of an everlasting ᶜpriesthood; because he was ᵈzealous for his God, and made an ᵉatonement for the children of Israel.

14 Now the name of the Israelite that was slain, *even* that was slain with the Midianitish woman, *was* Zimri, the son of Salu, ᵃa prince of a chief house among the Simeonites.

15 And the name of the Midianitish woman that was slain *was* Cozbi, the daughter of Zur; he *was* head over a people, *and* of a chief house in Midian.

16 ¶ And the Lᴏʀᴅ spake unto Moses, saying,

17 Vex the Midianites, and ᵃsmite them:

18 For they vex you with their wiles, wherewith they have beguiled you in the matter of Peor, and in the matter of Cozbi, the daughter of a prince of Midian, their sister, which was slain in the day of the plague ᵃfor Peor's sake.

CHAPTER 26

Moses and Eleazar count the Israelites on the plains of Moab near Jericho— The males twenty years and older, excluding Levites, total 601,730—Only Caleb and Joshua remain from those numbered at Sinai.

Aɴᴅ it came to pass after the plague, that the Lᴏʀᴅ spake unto Moses and unto Eleazar the son of Aaron the priest, saying,

2 Take ᵃthe sum of all the congregation of the children of Israel, from twenty years old and upward, throughout their fathers' house, all that are able to go to war in Israel.

3 And Moses and Eleazar the priest spake with them in the plains of Moab by Jordan *near* Jericho, saying,

4 *Take the sum of the people*, from twenty years old and upward; as the Lᴏʀᴅ commanded Moses and the children of Israel, which went forth out of the land of Egypt.

5 ¶ ᵃReuben, the eldest son of Israel: the children of Reuben; Hanoch, *of whom cometh* the family of the Hanochites: of Pallu, the family of the Palluites:

6 Of Hezron, the family of the Hezronites: of Carmi, the family of the Carmites.

7 These *are* the families of the Reubenites: and they that were ᵃnumbered of them were forty and three thousand and seven hundred and thirty.

8 And the sons of Pallu; Eliab.

9 And the sons of Eliab; Nemuel, and Dathan, and Abiram. This *is* that ᵃDathan and Abiram, *which were* ᵇfamous in the congregation, who strove against Moses and against Aaron in the company of Korah, when they strove against the Lᴏʀᴅ:

10 And the earth opened her mouth, and swallowed them up together with Korah, when that company died, what time the fire devoured two hundred and fifty men: and they became a ᵃsign.

11 Notwithstanding the children of Korah died not.

12 ¶ The sons of Simeon after their families: of Nemuel, the family of

---

11a Ex. 20:5;
　　Deut. 32:16 (16, 21);
　　Mosiah 13:13.
12a Mal. 2:5.
13a ᴛɢ Birthright.
　 b ᴛɢ Covenants; New and
　　Everlasting Covenant;
　　Priesthood, Oath and
　　Covenant.
　 c ᴛɢ Priesthood;
　　Priesthood, Aaronic.

　 d ᴛɢ Zeal.
　 e Ex. 32:30.
14a ʜᴇʙ the head of a
　　father's house, i.e.,
　　a patriarchal clan
　　(also v. 15).
17a 1 Ne. 4:13.
18a ᴏʀ on account of the
　　Peor incident.
26 2a ᴏʀ a census by their
　　fathers' houses.

　　Num. 1:2 (2–46).
 5a Gen. 42:37; 46:9;
　　Josh. 13:15 (15–23).
 7a Num. 1:21;
　　Deut. 33:6.
 9a Num. 16:12 (1–32);
　　Deut. 11:6.
　 b ʜᴇʙ chosen men of.
10a Ezek. 14:8;
　　Jacob 7:14 (1–22);
　　D&C 124:53 (50–53).

the Nemuelites: of Jamin, the family of the Jaminites: of Jachin, the family of the Jachinites:

13 Of Zerah, the family of the Zarhites: of Shaul, the family of the Shaulites.

14 These *are* the families of the Simeonites, twenty and two thousand and two hundred.

15 ¶ The children of *a*Gad after their families: of Zephon, the family of the Zephonites: of Haggi, the family of the Haggites: of Shuni, the family of the Shunites:

16 Of Ozni, the family of the Oznites: of Eri, the family of the Erites:

17 Of Arod, the family of the Arodites: of Areli, the family of the Arelites.

18 These *are* the families of the children of Gad according to those that were numbered of them, forty thousand and five hundred.

19 ¶ The sons of Judah *were* Er and Onan: and Er and Onan died in the land of Canaan.

20 And the sons of Judah after their families were; of Shelah, the family of the Shelanites: of Pharez, the family of the Pharzites: of Zerah, the family of the Zarhites.

21 And the sons of Pharez were; of Hezron, the family of the Hezronites: of Hamul, the family of the Hamulites.

22 These *are* the families of Judah according to those that were numbered of them, threescore and sixteen thousand and five hundred.

23 ¶ *Of* the sons of *a*Issachar after their families: *of* Tola, the family of the Tolaites: of Pua, the family of the Punites:

24 Of Jashub, the family of the Jashubites: of Shimron, the family of the Shimronites.

25 These *are* the families of Issachar according to those that were numbered of them, threescore and four thousand and three hundred.

26 ¶ *Of* the sons of Zebulun after their families: of Sered, the family of the Sardites: of Elon, the family of the Elonites: of Jahleel, the family of the Jahleelites.

27 These *are* the families of the Zebulunites according to those that were numbered of them, threescore thousand and five hundred.

28 ¶ The sons of Joseph after their families *were* Manasseh and Ephraim.

29 Of the sons of *a*Manasseh: of Machir, the family of the Machirites: and Machir begat Gilead: of Gilead *come* the family of the Gileadites.

30 These *are* the sons of Gilead: *of* Jeezer, the family of the Jeezerites: of Helek, the family of the Helekites:

31 And *of* Asriel, the family of the Asrielites: and *of* Shechem, the family of the Shechemites:

32 And *of* Shemida, the family of the Shemidaites: and *of* Hepher, the family of the Hepherites.

33 ¶ And Zelophehad the son of Hepher had no sons, but daughters: and the names of the daughters of Zelophehad *were* Mahlah, and Noah, Hoglah, Milcah, and Tirzah.

34 These *are* the families of Manasseh, and those that were numbered of them, fifty and two thousand and seven hundred.

35 ¶ These *are* the sons of Ephraim after their families: of Shuthelah, the family of the Shuthalhites: of Becher, the family of the Bachrites: of Tahan, the family of the Tahanites.

36 And these *are* the sons of Shuthelah: of Eran, the family of the Eranites.

37 These *are* the families of the sons of Ephraim according to those that were numbered of them, thirty and two thousand and five hundred. These *are* the sons of Joseph after their families.

38 ¶ The sons of *a*Benjamin after their families: of Bela, the family of the Belaites: of Ashbel, the family of the Ashbelites: of Ahiram, the family of the Ahiramites:

15*a* Gen. 46:16.
23*a* Num. 1:28 (28–29);
    1 Chr. 7:1.

29*a* Josh. 17:2;
    1 Chr. 7:14.
38*a* Gen. 46:21;

1 Chr. 7:6 (6–12).

39 Of Shupham, the family of the Shuphamites: of Hupham, the family of the Huphamites.

40 And the sons of Bela were Ard and Naaman: *of Ard,* the family of the Ardites: *and* of Naaman, the family of the Naamites.

41 These *are* the sons of Benjamin after their families: and they that were numbered of them *were* forty and five thousand and six hundred.

42 ¶ These *are* the sons of *a*Dan after their families: of Shuham, the family of the Shuhamites. These *are* the families of Dan after their families.

43 All the families of the Shuhamites, according to those that were numbered of them, *were* threescore and four thousand and four hundred.

44 ¶ *Of* the children of Asher after their families: of Jimna, the family of the Jimnites: of Jesui, the family of the Jesuites: of Beriah, the family of the Beriites.

45 Of the sons of Beriah: of Heber, the family of the Heberites: of Malchiel, the family of the Malchielites.

46 And the name of the daughter of Asher *was* Sarah.

47 These *are* the families of the sons of Asher according to those that were numbered of them; *who were* fifty and three thousand and four hundred.

48 ¶ *Of* the sons of Naphtali after their families: of Jahzeel, the family of the Jahzeelites: of Guni, the family of the Gunites:

49 Of Jezer, the family of the Jezerites: of Shillem, the family of the Shillemites.

50 These *are* the families of Naphtali according to their families: and they that were numbered of them *were* forty and five thousand and four hundred.

51 These *were* the numbered of the children of Israel, *a*six hundred thousand and a thousand seven hundred and thirty.

52 ¶ And the LORD spake unto Moses, saying,

53 Unto these the land shall be divided for an inheritance according to the number of names.

54 To *a*many thou shalt give the more inheritance, and to *b*few thou shalt give the less inheritance: to every one shall his inheritance be given according to those that were numbered of him.

55 Notwithstanding the land shall be divided by lot: according to the names of the tribes of their fathers they shall inherit.

56 According to the lot shall the possession thereof be divided between many and few.

57 ¶ And these *are* they that were numbered of the *a*Levites after their families: of Gershon, the family of the Gershonites: of Kohath, the family of the Kohathites: of Merari, the family of the Merarites.

58 These *are* the families of the Levites: the family of the Libnites, the family of the Hebronites, the family of the Mahlites, the family of the Mushites, the family of the Korathites. And Kohath begat Amram.

59 And the name of *a*Amram's wife *was* Jochebed, the daughter of Levi, whom *her mother* bare to Levi in Egypt: and she bare unto Amram Aaron and Moses, and Miriam their *b*sister.

60 And unto Aaron was born Nadab, and Abihu, Eleazar, and Ithamar.

61 And Nadab and Abihu died, when they offered *a*strange fire before the LORD.

62 And those that were numbered of them were twenty and three thousand, all males from a month old and upward: for they were not numbered among the children of Israel, because there was no *a*inheritance given them among the children of Israel.

63 ¶ These *are* they that were numbered by Moses and Eleazar the

42*a* Gen. 46:23.
51*a* Num. 1:46.
54*a* IE a large tribe (also v. 56).

b IE a small tribe.
57*a* Num. 3:15 (14–39).
59*a* Ex. 2:1 (1–2).
b Ex. 2:4; 15:20 (20–21).

61*a* OR unauthorized.
62*a* Deut. 18:1.

priest, who numbered the children of Israel in the plains of Moab by Jordan *near* Jericho.

64 But among these there was not a man of them whom Moses and Aaron the priest numbered, when they numbered the children of Israel in the wilderness of Sinai.

65 For the LORD had said of them, They shall surely die in the *a*wilderness. And there was not left a man of them, save Caleb the son of Jephunneh, and Joshua the son of Nun.

CHAPTER 27

The law of inheritances to sons, daughters, and kinsmen is explained—Moses will see but not enter the promised land—Joshua is called and set apart to lead Israel.

THEN came the daughters of Zelophehad, the son of Hepher, the son of Gilead, the son of Machir, the son of Manasseh, of the families of Manasseh the son of Joseph: and these *are* the names of his daughters; Mahlah, Noah, and Hoglah, and Milcah, and Tirzah.

2 And they stood before Moses, and before Eleazar the priest, and before the *a*princes and all the congregation, *by* the door of the *b*tabernacle of the congregation, saying,

3 Our father died in the wilderness, and he was not in the company of them that gathered themselves together against the LORD in the company of Korah; but died in his own sin, and had no sons.

4 Why should the name of our father be done away from among his family, because he hath no son? Give unto us *therefore* a possession among the brethren of our father.

5 And Moses brought their cause before the LORD.

6 ¶ And the LORD spake unto Moses, saying,

7 The daughters of Zelophehad speak right: thou shalt surely give them a possession of an *a*inheritance among their father's brethren; and thou shalt cause the inheritance of their father to pass unto them.

8 And thou shalt speak unto the children of Israel, saying, If a man die, and have no son, then ye shall cause his inheritance to pass unto his daughter.

9 And if he have no daughter, then ye shall give his inheritance unto his brethren.

10 And if he have no brethren, then ye shall give his inheritance unto his father's brethren.

11 And if his father have no brethren, then ye shall give his inheritance unto his kinsman that is next to him of his family, and he shall possess it: and it shall be unto the children of Israel a *a*statute of judgment, as the LORD commanded Moses.

12 ¶ And the LORD said unto Moses, Get thee up into this mount *a*Abarim, and see the *b*land which I have given unto the children of Israel.

13 And when thou hast seen it, thou also shalt be gathered unto thy people, as Aaron thy brother was gathered.

14 For ye rebelled against my commandment in the desert of Zin, in the *a*strife of the congregation, to sanctify me at the water before their eyes: that *is* the water of *b*Meribah in *c*Kadesh in the wilderness of Zin.

15 ¶ And Moses spake unto the LORD, saying,

16 Let the LORD, the *a*God of the *b*spirits of all flesh, *c*set a man over the congregation,

---

65a Num. 14:29;
    Ezek. 20:13 (13, 15);
    1 Cor. 10:5;
    1 Ne. 17:31 (23–31);
    Jacob 1:7;
    D&C 84:24 (23–25).
27 2a HEB leaders, rulers.
   b HEB tent of meeting.

7a Num. 36:2 (1–13);
    Josh. 17:4.
11a HEB statutory law.
12a Deut. 32:49 (48–52).
   b TG Promised Lands.
14a TG Strife.
   b HEB Contention.
   c Num. 20:1 (1–29);

    Deut. 32:51 (48–52).
16a TG God the Father,
    Elohim.
   b TG Man, Antemortal
    Existence of;
    Spirit Body.
   c A of F 1:5.

17 Which may go out before them, and which may go in before them, and which may lead them out, and which may bring them in; that the *a*congregation of the LORD be not as *b*sheep which have no *c*shepherd.

18 ¶ And the LORD said unto Moses, Take thee *a*Joshua the son of *b*Nun, a man in whom *is* the *c*spirit, and *d*lay thine hand upon him;

19 And *a*set him before Eleazar the priest, and before all the congregation; and give him a charge in their sight.

20 And thou shalt *a*put *some* of thine *b*honour upon him, that all the congregation of the children of Israel may be obedient.

21 And he shall stand before Eleazar the *a*priest, who shall ask *b*counsel for him *c*after the judgment of *d*Urim before the LORD: at his word shall they go out, and at his word they shall come in, *both* he, and all the children of Israel with him, even all the congregation.

22 And Moses did as the LORD commanded him: and he took Joshua, and set him before Eleazar the priest, and before all the congregation:

23 And he *a*laid his *b*hands upon him, and gave him a *c*charge, as the LORD commanded by the hand of Moses.

CHAPTER 28

Sacrifices are to be offered each morning and evening, on the Sabbath, on the first day of each month, at Passover, on each day of the Feast of Unleavened Bread, and at the Feast of Firstfruits.

AND the LORD spake unto Moses, saying,

2 Command the children of Israel, and say unto them, My offering, *and* my bread for my sacrifices made by fire, *for* a sweet savour unto me, shall ye observe to offer unto me in their due season.

3 And thou shalt say unto them, This *is* the *a*offering made by fire which ye shall offer unto the LORD; two lambs *b*of the first year without *c*spot day by day, *for* a continual *d*burnt offering.

4 The one lamb shalt thou offer in the morning, and the other lamb shalt thou offer at even;

5 And a tenth *part* of an ephah of flour for a *a*meat offering, mingled with the fourth *part* of an hin of beaten oil.

6 *It is* a continual burnt *a*offering, which was ordained in mount Sinai for a sweet savour, a sacrifice made by fire unto the LORD.

7 And the drink offering thereof *shall be* the fourth *part* of an hin for *a*the one lamb: in the holy *place* shalt thou cause the strong wine to be poured unto the LORD *for* a *b*drink offering.

8 And the other lamb shalt thou offer at even: as the *a*meat offering of the morning, and as the drink offering thereof, thou shalt offer *it,* a sacrifice made by fire, of a sweet savour unto the LORD.

9 ¶ And on the *a*sabbath day two

17*a* TG Church Organization.
b TG Sheep.
c TG Shepherd.
18*a* Deut. 3:21.
b Num. 11:28; Josh. 14:1.
c TG God, Spirit of.
d TG Church Organization.
19*a* TG Common Consent; Setting Apart; Sustaining Church Leaders.
20*a* OR invest him with some of your authority.

b TG Delegation of Responsibility.
21*a* Lev. 16:32 (1–34).
b Josh. 9:14.
c OR as revealed through the Urim and Thummim.
d TG Urim and Thummim.
23*a* TG Priesthood, Ordination.
b TG Hands, Laying on of.
c TG Called of God; Priesthood, Authority; Priesthood, History of; Stewardship.

28 3*a* Ex. 29:38 (38–46). TG Sacrifice.
b HEB a year old (also vv. 9, 11, 19, 27).
c OR blemish, defect (also vv. 9, 11).
d 2 Chr. 31:3 (2–19).
5*a* HEB meal, cereal (also vv. 8–9, 12, 20, 24, 26, 28, 31).
6*a* Ex. 29:42 (38–44).
7*a* HEB each (also v. 13).
b Gen. 35:14.
8*a* Neh. 10:33.
9*a* Matt. 12:5.

lambs of the first year without spot, and two tenth deals of flour *for a* meat offering, mingled with oil, and the drink offering thereof:

10 *This is* the burnt offering of every *a*sabbath, beside the continual burnt offering, and *b*his drink offering.

11 ¶ And in the *a*beginnings of your months ye shall offer a burnt offering unto the LORD; two young bullocks, and one ram, seven lambs of the first year without spot;

12 And three tenth deals of flour *for* a meat offering, mingled with oil, for one bullock; and two tenth deals of flour *for* a meat offering, mingled with oil, for one ram;

13 And *a*a several tenth deal of flour mingled with oil *for* a meat offering unto one lamb; *for* a burnt offering of a sweet savour, a sacrifice made by fire unto the LORD.

14 And their *a*drink offerings shall be half an hin of wine unto a bullock, and the third *part* of an hin unto a ram, and a fourth *part* of an hin unto a lamb: this *is* the burnt offering of every month throughout the months of the year.

15 And one *a*kid of the goats for a sin offering unto the LORD shall be offered, beside the continual burnt offering, and his drink offering.

16 And in the fourteenth day of the first month *is* the *a*passover of the LORD.

17 And in the fifteenth day of this month *is* the *a*feast: seven days shall unleavened bread be eaten.

18 In the first day *shall be* *a*an holy convocation; ye shall do no manner of servile work *therein:*

19 But ye shall offer a sacrifice made by fire *for* a burnt offering unto the LORD; two young bullocks, and one ram, and seven lambs of the first year: they shall be unto you without blemish:

20 And their meat offering *shall be of* flour mingled with oil: three tenth deals shall ye offer for a bullock, and two tenth deals for a ram;

21 A several tenth deal shalt thou offer for every lamb, throughout the seven lambs:

22 And one goat *for* a sin offering, to make an atonement for you.

23 Ye shall offer these beside the burnt offering in the morning, which *is* for a continual burnt offering.

24 After this manner ye shall offer daily, throughout the seven days, the meat of the sacrifice made by fire, of a sweet savour unto the LORD: it shall be offered beside the continual burnt offering, and his drink offering.

25 And on the seventh day ye shall have an holy *a*convocation; ye shall do no servile work.

26 ¶ Also in the day of the *a*firstfruits, when ye bring a new meat offering unto the LORD, after your weeks *be out,* ye shall have an holy convocation; ye shall do no servile work:

27 But ye shall offer the burnt offering for a sweet savour unto the LORD; two young bullocks, one ram, seven lambs of the first year;

28 And their meat offering of flour mingled with oil, three tenth deals unto one bullock, two tenth deals unto one ram,

29 A several tenth deal unto one lamb, throughout the seven lambs;

30 *And* one kid of the goats, to make an atonement for you.

31 Ye shall offer *them* beside the continual burnt offering, and his meat offering, (they shall be unto you without blemish) and their drink offerings.

CHAPTER 29

Sacrifices are to be offered during the seventh month, including at the Feast of Trumpets and at the Feast of Tabernacles.

10*a* 2 Chr. 31:3 (2–19); Ezek. 46:4.
  b OR the drink offering thereof (also vv. 15, 24, 31).
11*a* 2 Chr. 31:3 (2–19);
Ezek. 45:17 (17–18).
13*a* OR for each a tenth of a measure (also vv. 21, 29).
14*a* Gen. 35:14.
15*a* Ezek. 45:23.
16*a* Deut. 16:1 (1–8).
17*a* 2 Chr. 31:3 (2–19).
18*a* OR a sacred meeting (also vv. 25, 26).
25*a* TG Meetings.
26*a* Lev. 23:10 (9–22).

AND in the seventh month, on the first *day* of the month, ye shall have an holy ^aconvocation; ye shall do no servile work: it is a day of blowing the ^btrumpets unto you.

2 And ye shall offer a burnt offering for a sweet savour unto the LORD; one young bullock, one ram, *and* seven lambs of the first year without blemish:

3 And their ^ameat ^boffering *shall be of* flour mingled with oil, three tenth deals for a bullock, *and* two tenth deals for a ram,

4 And one tenth deal for one lamb, throughout the seven lambs:

5 And one kid of the goats *for* a sin offering, to make an atonement for you:

6 Beside the burnt offering of the month, and his meat offering, and the daily burnt offering, and his meat offering, and their drink offerings, according unto their ^amanner, for a sweet savour, a sacrifice made by fire unto the LORD.

7 ¶ And ye shall have on the tenth *day* of this seventh month an holy convocation; and ye shall afflict your souls: ye shall not do any work *therein:*

8 But ye shall offer a burnt offering unto the LORD *for* a sweet savour; one young bullock, one ram, *and* seven lambs of the first year; they shall be unto you without blemish:

9 And their meat offering *shall be of* flour mingled with oil, three tenth deals to a bullock, *and* two tenth deals to one ram,

10 A several tenth deal for one lamb, throughout the seven lambs:

11 One kid of the goats *for* a sin offering; beside the sin offering of atonement, and the continual burnt offering, and the meat offering of it, and their drink offerings.

12 ¶ And on the fifteenth day of the seventh month ye shall have an holy convocation; ye shall do no servile work, and ye shall keep a ^afeast unto the LORD seven days:

13 And ye shall offer a burnt offering, a sacrifice made by fire, of a sweet savour unto the LORD; thirteen young bullocks, two rams, *and* fourteen lambs of the first year; they shall be without blemish:

14 And their meat offering *shall be of* flour mingled with oil, three tenth deals unto every bullock of the thirteen bullocks, two tenth deals to each ram of the two rams,

15 And a several tenth deal to each lamb of the fourteen lambs:

16 And one kid of the goats *for* a sin offering; beside the continual burnt offering, his meat offering, and his drink offering.

17 ¶ And on the second day *ye shall offer* twelve young bullocks, two rams, fourteen lambs of the first year without ^aspot:

18 And their meat offering and their drink offerings for the bullocks, for the rams, and for the lambs, *shall be* according to their number, after the manner:

19 And one kid of the goats *for* a sin offering; beside the continual burnt offering, and the meat offering thereof, and their drink offerings.

20 ¶ And on the third day eleven bullocks, two rams, fourteen lambs of the first year without blemish;

21 And their meat offering and their drink offerings for the bullocks, for the rams, and for the lambs, *shall be* according to their number, after the manner:

22 And one goat *for* a sin offering; beside the continual burnt offering, and his meat offering, and his drink offering.

23 ¶ And on the fourth day ten bullocks, two rams, *and* fourteen lambs of the first year without blemish:

24 Their meat offering and their drink offerings for the bullocks, for the rams, and for the lambs, *shall be*

29 1a TG Meetings.
  b Lev. 23:24 (23–25).
  3a HEB meal, cereal (also vv. 6–39).
  b TG Sacrifice.
  6a HEB ordinances (also vv. 18, 21, 24, 27, 30, 33, 37).
  12a Lev. 23:34, 41 (33–43).
  17a OR blemish, defect (also v. 26).

according to their number, after the manner:

25 And one kid of the goats *for* a sin offering; beside the continual burnt offering, his meat offering, and his drink offering.

26 ¶ And on the fifth day nine bullocks, two rams, *and* fourteen lambs of the first year without spot:

27 And their meat offering and their drink offerings for the bullocks, for the rams, and for the lambs, *shall be* according to their number, after the manner:

28 And one goat *for* a sin offering; beside the continual burnt offering, and his meat offering, and his drink offering.

29 ¶ And on the sixth day eight bullocks, two rams, *and* fourteen lambs of the first year without blemish:

30 And their meat offering and their drink offerings for the bullocks, for the rams, and for the lambs, *shall be* according to their number, after the manner:

31 And one goat *for* a sin offering; beside the continual burnt offering, his meat offering, and his drink offering.

32 ¶ And on the seventh day seven bullocks, two rams, *and* fourteen lambs of the first year without blemish:

33 And their meat offering and their drink offerings for the bullocks, for the rams, and for the lambs, *shall be* according to their number, after the manner:

34 And one goat *for* a sin offering; beside the continual burnt offering, his meat offering, and his drink offering.

35 ¶ On the eighth day ye shall have a *a*solemn assembly: ye shall do no servile work *therein:*

36 But ye shall offer a burnt offering, a sacrifice made by fire, of a sweet savour unto the LORD: one bullock, one ram, seven lambs of the first year without blemish:

37 Their meat offering and their drink offerings for the bullock, for the ram, and for the lambs, *shall be* according to their number, after the manner:

38 And one goat *for* a sin offering; beside the continual burnt offering, and his meat offering, and his drink offering.

39 These *things* ye shall do unto the LORD in your set *a*feasts, beside your vows, and your freewill offerings, for your burnt offerings, and for your meat offerings, and for your drink offerings, and for your peace offerings.

40 And Moses told the children of Israel according to all that the LORD commanded Moses.

CHAPTER 30

Vows and oaths must be kept—Fathers may disallow vows of daughters, and husbands may disallow vows of wives.

AND Moses spake unto the heads of the tribes concerning the children of Israel, saying, This *is* the thing which the LORD hath commanded.

2 If a man vow a *a*vow unto the LORD, or swear an *b*oath to bind his soul with a bond; he shall not *c*break his word, he shall do according to all that proceedeth out of his mouth.

3 If a *a*woman also vow a vow unto the LORD, and bind *herself* by a bond, *being* in her father's house in her youth;

4 And her father hear her vow, and her *a*bond wherewith she hath bound her soul, and her father shall hold his peace at her: then all her vows shall stand, and every bond wherewith she hath bound her soul shall stand.

5 But if her father disallow her in the day that he heareth; not any of her vows, or of her bonds wherewith she hath bound her soul, shall stand: and the LORD shall forgive her, because her father disallowed her.

35*a* TG Solemn Assembly.
39*a* 1 Chr. 23:31;
    Ezra 3:5.

30 2*a* TG Vow.
    b TG Oath.
    c TG Integrity.

3*a* TG Woman.
4*a* OR pledge (also vv. 5, 7, 10–12).

6 And if she had at all an husband, when she vowed, or uttered ought out of her lips, wherewith she bound her soul;

7 And her husband heard *it*, and held his peace at her in the day that he heard *it*: then her vows shall stand, and her bonds wherewith she bound her soul shall stand.

8 But if her husband disallowed her on the day that he heard *it*; then he shall make her vow which she vowed, and that which she uttered with her lips, wherewith she bound her soul, of none effect: and the LORD shall forgive her.

9 But every vow of a widow, and of her that is divorced, wherewith they have bound their souls, shall stand against her.

10 And if she vowed in her husband's house, or bound her soul by a bond with an oath;

11 And her husband heard *it*, and held his peace at her, *and* disallowed her not: then all her vows shall stand, and every bond wherewith she bound her soul shall stand.

12 But if her husband hath utterly made them void on the day he heard *them; then* whatsoever proceeded out of her lips concerning her vows, or concerning the bond of her soul, shall not stand: her husband hath made them void; and the LORD shall forgive her.

13 Every vow, and every binding oath to afflict the soul, her husband may establish it, or her husband may make it void.

14 But if her husband altogether hold his peace at her from day to day; then he establisheth all her vows, or all her bonds, which *are* upon her: he confirmeth them, because he held his peace at her in the day that he heard *them.*

15 But if he shall any ways make them void after that he hath heard *them;* then he shall bear her iniquity.

16 These *are* the statutes, which the LORD commanded Moses, between a man and his wife, between the father and his daughter, *being yet* in her youth in her father's house.

CHAPTER 31

Moses sends forth 12,000 warriors who destroy the Midianites—The prey is divided in Israel—None in the armies of Israel are lost.

AND the LORD spake unto Moses, saying,

2 ªAvenge the children of Israel of the ᵇMidianites: afterward shalt thou be gathered unto thy people.

3 And Moses spake unto the people, saying, Arm some of yourselves unto the war, and let them go against the Midianites, and avenge the LORD of Midian.

4 Of every tribe a thousand, throughout all the tribes of Israel, shall ye send to the war.

5 So there were delivered out of the thousands of Israel, a thousand of *every* tribe, twelve thousand armed for war.

6 And Moses sent them to the war, a thousand of *every* tribe, them and Phinehas the son of Eleazar the priest, to the war, with the holy instruments, and the trumpets to blow in his hand.

7 And they warred against the Midianites, as the LORD commanded Moses; and they slew all the males.

8 And they slew the ªkings of Midian, beside the rest of them that were slain; *namely,* Evi, and Rekem, and Zur, and Hur, and Reba, five kings of Midian: Balaam also the son of Beor they slew with the sword.

9 And the children of Israel took *all* the women of Midian captives, and their little ones, and took the spoil of all their cattle, and all their flocks, and all their goods.

10 And they burnt all their cities wherein they dwelt, and all their ªgoodly castles, with fire.

11 And they took all the spoil, and all the prey, *both* of men and of beasts.

12 And they brought the captives,

31 2a Luke 18:7;
   D&C 101:58.
   b Hab. 3:7.
   8a Josh. 13:21.
   10a HEB closed
   encampments.

and the prey, and the spoil, unto Moses, and Eleazar the priest, and unto the congregation of the children of Israel, unto the camp at the plains of Moab, which *are* by Jordan *near* Jericho.

13 ¶ And Moses, and Eleazar the priest, and all the *a*princes of the congregation, went forth to meet them without the camp.

14 And Moses was wroth with the officers of the host, *with* the captains over thousands, and captains over hundreds, which came from the battle.

15 And Moses said unto them, Have ye saved all the women alive?

16 Behold, these caused the children of Israel, through the counsel of Balaam, to commit *a*trespass against the LORD in the matter of Peor, and there was a plague among the congregation of the LORD.

17 Now therefore kill every male among the little ones, and kill every woman that hath known man by lying with him.

18 But all the *a*women children, that have not known a man by lying with him, keep alive for yourselves.

19 And do ye abide without the camp seven days: whosoever hath killed any person, and whosoever hath touched any slain, purify *both* yourselves and your captives on the third day, and on the seventh day.

20 And purify all *your* raiment, and all that is made of skins, and all work of goats' *hair,* and all things made of wood.

21 ¶ And Eleazar the priest said unto the men of war which went to the battle, This *is* the ordinance of the law which the LORD commanded Moses;

22 Only the gold, and the silver, the brass, the iron, the tin, and the lead,

23 Every thing that may abide the fire, ye shall make *it* go through the fire, and it shall be clean: nevertheless it shall be purified with the water of *a*separation: and all that abideth not the fire ye shall make go through the water.

24 And ye shall wash your clothes on the seventh day, and ye shall be clean, and afterward ye shall come into the camp.

25 ¶ And the LORD spake unto Moses, saying,

26 Take the sum of the prey that was taken, *both* of man and of beast, thou, and Eleazar the priest, and the chief fathers of the congregation:

27 And divide the prey into two parts; between them that *a*took the war upon them, who went out to battle, and between all the congregation:

28 And levy a tribute unto the LORD of the men of war which went out to battle: one soul of five hundred, *both* of the persons, and of the beeves, and of the asses, and of the sheep:

29 Take *it* of their half, and give *it* unto Eleazar the priest, *for* an *a*heave offering of the LORD.

30 And of the children of Israel's half, thou shalt take one portion of fifty, of the persons, of the beeves, of the asses, and of the flocks, of all manner of beasts, and give them unto the Levites, which keep the charge of the tabernacle of the LORD.

31 And Moses and Eleazar the priest did as the LORD commanded Moses.

32 And the booty, *being* the rest of the prey which the men of war had caught, was six hundred thousand and seventy thousand and five thousand sheep,

33 And threescore and twelve thousand beeves,

34 And threescore and one thousand asses,

35 And thirty and two thousand persons in all, of women that had not known man by lying with him.

36 And the half, *which was* the portion of them that went out to war,

---

13*a* HEB leaders, presidents.
16*a* 2 Pet. 2:15.
18*a* OR young girls.

23*a* HEB impurity; i.e., water for cleansing impurity.
27*a* OR took part in the war.

29*a* HEB contribution (also v. 41).

was in number three hundred thousand and seven and thirty thousand and five hundred sheep:

37 And the LORD's tribute of the sheep was six hundred and threescore and fifteen.

38 And the beeves *were* thirty and six thousand; of which the LORD's tribute *was* threescore and twelve.

39 And the asses *were* thirty thousand and five hundred; of which the LORD's tribute *was* threescore and one.

40 And the persons *were* sixteen thousand; of which the LORD's tribute *was* thirty and two persons.

41 And Moses gave the tribute, *which was* the LORD's heave offering, unto Eleazar the priest, as the LORD commanded Moses.

42 And of the children of Israel's half, which Moses divided from the men that warred,

43 (Now the half *that pertained unto* the congregation was three hundred thousand and thirty thousand *and* seven thousand and five hundred sheep,

44 And thirty and six thousand beeves,

45 And thirty thousand asses and five hundred,

46 And sixteen thousand persons;)

47 Even of the children of Israel's half, Moses took one portion of fifty, *both* of man and of beast, and gave them unto the Levites, which kept the charge of the tabernacle of the LORD; as the LORD commanded Moses.

48 ¶ And the officers which *were* over thousands of the host, the captains of thousands, and captains of hundreds, came near unto Moses:

49 And they said unto Moses, Thy servants have taken the sum of the men of war which *are* under our charge, and there lacketh not one man of us.

50 We have therefore brought an ᵃoblation for the LORD, what every man hath gotten, of ᵇjewels of gold, chains, and bracelets, rings, earrings,

and tablets, to make an ᶜatonement for our souls before the LORD.

51 And Moses and Eleazar the priest took the gold of them, *even* all wrought ᵃjewels.

52 And all the gold of the offering that they offered up to the LORD, of the captains of thousands, and of the captains of hundreds, was sixteen thousand seven hundred and fifty shekels.

53 (*For* the men of war had taken spoil, every man for himself.)

54 And Moses and Eleazar the priest took the gold of the captains of thousands and of hundreds, and brought it into the tabernacle of the congregation, *for* a memorial for the children of Israel before the LORD.

CHAPTER 32

Reuben, Gad, and half the tribe of Manasseh receive their inheritances east of the Jordan—They covenant to join other tribes in conquering Canaan.

NOW the children of Reuben and the children of Gad had a very great multitude of cattle: and when they saw the land of Jazer, and the land of Gilead, that, behold, the place *was* a place for cattle;

2 The children of ᵃGad and the children of ᵇReuben came and spake unto Moses, and to Eleazar the priest, and unto the princes of the congregation, saying,

3 Ataroth, and Dibon, and Jazer, and Nimrah, and Heshbon, and Elealeh, and Shebam, and Nebo, and Beon,

4 *Even* the country which the LORD smote before the congregation of Israel, *is* a land for cattle, and thy servants have cattle:

5 Wherefore, said they, if we have found grace in thy sight, let this land be given unto thy servants for a possession, *and* bring us not over Jordan.

6 ¶ And Moses said unto the children of Gad and to the children of

---

50*a* Ex. 30:12 (11–16).
  b Ex. 35:22.

c Ex. 30:15 (12, 15–16).
51*a* OR ornaments.

32 2*a* Deut. 33:21.
  b Deut. 3:12.

Reuben, Shall your brethren go to war, and shall ye sit here?

7 And wherefore discourage ye the heart of the children of Israel from going over into the land which the LORD hath given them?

8 Thus did your fathers, when I sent them from Kadesh-barnea to see the land.

9 For when they went up unto the valley of Eshcol, and saw the land, they discouraged the heart of the children of Israel, that they should not go into the land which the LORD had given them.

10 And the LORD's anger was kindled the same time, and he sware, saying,

11 Surely none of the men that came up out of Egypt, from twenty years old and upward, shall ᵃsee the land which I sware unto Abraham, unto Isaac, and unto Jacob; because they have not wholly followed me:

12 Save ᵃCaleb the son of Jephunneh the Kenezite, and Joshua the son of Nun: for they have wholly followed the LORD.

13 And the LORD's anger was kindled against Israel, and he made them wander in the wilderness forty years, until all the generation, that had done evil in the sight of the LORD, was consumed.

14 And, behold, ye are risen up in your fathers' stead, an increase of sinful men, to augment yet the fierce anger of the LORD toward Israel.

15 For if ye turn away from after him, he will yet again leave them in the wilderness; and ye shall destroy all this people.

16 ¶ And they came near unto him, and said, We will build sheepfolds here for our cattle, and cities for our little ones:

17 But we ourselves will go ready armed before the children of Israel, until we have brought them unto their place: and our little ones shall dwell in the fenced cities because of the inhabitants of the land.

18 We will not return unto our houses, until the children of Israel have inherited every man his ᵃinheritance.

19 For we will not inherit with them on ᵃyonder side Jordan, or forward; because our inheritance is fallen to us on this side Jordan eastward.

20 ¶ And Moses said unto them, If ye will ᵃdo this thing, if ye will go armed before the LORD to war,

21 And will go all of you armed over Jordan before the LORD, until he hath driven out his enemies from before him,

22 And the land be subdued before the LORD: then afterward ye shall return, and be guiltless before the LORD, and before Israel; and this land shall be your possession before the LORD.

23 But if ye will not do so, behold, ye have sinned against the LORD: and be sure your sin will find you out.

24 Build you cities for your little ones, and folds for your sheep; and do that which hath proceeded out of your mouth.

25 And the children of Gad and the children of Reuben spake unto Moses, saying, Thy servants will do as my lord commandeth.

26 Our little ones, our wives, our flocks, and all our cattle, shall be there in the cities of Gilead:

27 But thy servants will pass over, every man armed for war, before the LORD to battle, as my lord saith.

28 So concerning them Moses commanded Eleazar the priest, and Joshua the son of Nun, and the chief fathers of the tribes of the children of Israel:

29 And Moses said unto them, If the children of Gad and the children of Reuben will pass with you over Jordan, every man armed to battle, before the LORD, and the land shall be subdued before you; then ye shall give them the land of Gilead for a possession:

30 But if they will not pass over

11a Num. 14:23.
12a Josh. 15:17.

18a Gen. 15:7; D&C 52:42.
19a OR the other side of the

Jordan and beyond.
20a Josh. 1:13.

with you armed, they shall have possessions among you in the land of Canaan.

31 And the children of Gad and the children of Reuben answered, saying, As the LORD hath said unto thy servants, so will we do.

32 We will pass over armed before the LORD into the land of Canaan, that the possession of our *inheritance on this side Jordan *may be* ours.

33 And Moses *gave unto them, *even* to the children of Gad, and to the children of Reuben, and unto half the tribe of Manasseh the son of Joseph, the kingdom of Sihon king of the Amorites, and the kingdom of Og king of Bashan, the land, with the cities thereof *in the coasts, *even* the cities of the country round about.

34 ¶ And the children of Gad *built Dibon, and Ataroth, and Aroer,

35 And Atroth, Shophan, and Jaazer, and Jogbehah,

36 And Beth-nimrah, and Beth-haran, *fenced cities: and folds for sheep.

37 And the children of Reuben built Heshbon, and Elealeh, and Kirjathaim,

38 And Nebo, and Baal-meon, (their names being changed,) and Shibmah: and gave other names unto the cities which they builded.

39 And the children of *Machir the son of *Manasseh went to Gilead, and took it, and dispossessed the Amorite which *was* in it.

40 And Moses gave *Gilead unto Machir the son of Manasseh; and he dwelt therein.

41 And Jair the son of Manasseh went and took the small *towns thereof, and called them Havoth-jair.

42 And Nobah went and took Kenath, and the villages thereof, and called it Nobah, after his own name.

CHAPTER 33

Israel's journeys from Egypt to Canaan are reviewed—The people are commanded to drive out the inhabitants of the land—Any remaining inhabitants will vex Israel.

THESE *are* the journeys of the children of Israel, which went forth out of the land of Egypt with their armies under the hand of Moses and Aaron.

2 And Moses wrote their goings out according to their journeys by the commandment of the LORD: and these *are* their journeys according to their goings out.

3 And they departed from *Rameses in the first month, on the fifteenth day of the first month; on the morrow after the passover the children of Israel went out *with an *high hand in the sight of all the Egyptians.

4 For the Egyptians buried all *their* firstborn, which the LORD had smitten among them: upon their gods also the LORD executed judgments.

5 And the children of Israel removed from Rameses, and pitched in *Succoth.

6 And they departed from Succoth, and pitched in Etham, which *is* in the edge of the wilderness.

7 And they removed from Etham, and *turned again unto Pi-hahiroth, which *is* before Baal-zephon: and they pitched before Migdol.

8 And they departed from before Pi-hahiroth, and passed through the midst of the sea into the wilderness, and went three days' journey in the wilderness of Etham, and pitched in Marah.

9 And they removed from Marah, and came unto Elim: and in Elim *were* twelve *fountains of water, and threescore and ten palm trees; and they pitched there.

32*a* Num. 34:14 (13–15).
33*a* Josh. 12:6; 22:4.
  b HEB with their borders.
34*a* OR rebuilt.
36*a* HEB fortified.
39*a* Gen. 50:23.

b TG Israel, Joseph,
  People of.
40*a* Josh. 17:1;
  Judg. 5:14.
41*a* Josh. 13:30.
33 3*a* Gen. 47:11.

b OR triumphantly.
c Ex. 14:8 (8–9).
5*a* Ex. 13:20.
7*a* Ex. 14:2 (1–3).
9*a* HEB springs.

10 And they removed from Elim, and encamped by the *a*Red sea.

11 And they removed from the Red sea, and encamped in the wilderness of Sin.

12 And they took their *a*journey out of the wilderness of Sin, and encamped in Dophkah.

13 And they departed from Dophkah, and encamped in Alush.

14 And they removed from Alush, and encamped at Rephidim, where was no water for the people to drink.

15 And they departed from Rephidim, and pitched in the wilderness of Sinai.

16 And they removed from the desert of Sinai, and pitched at Kibroth-hattaavah.

17 And they departed from Kibroth-hattaavah, and encamped at Hazeroth.

18 And they departed from Hazeroth, and pitched in Rithmah.

19 And they departed from Rithmah, and pitched at Rimmon-parez.

20 And they departed from Rimmon-parez, and pitched in Libnah.

21 And they removed from Libnah, and pitched at Rissah.

22 And they journeyed from Rissah, and pitched in Kehelathah.

23 And they went from Kehelathah, and pitched in mount Shapher.

24 And they removed from mount Shapher, and encamped in Haradah.

25 And they removed from Haradah, and pitched in Makheloth.

26 And they removed from Makheloth, and encamped at Tahath.

27 And they departed from Tahath, and pitched at Tarah.

28 And they removed from Tarah, and pitched in Mithcah.

29 And they went from Mithcah, and pitched in Hashmonah.

30 And they departed from Hashmonah, and encamped at Moseroth.

31 And they departed from Moseroth, and pitched in Bene-jaakan.

32 And they removed from Bene-jaakan, and encamped at Hor-hagidgad.

33 And they went from Hor-hagidgad, and pitched in *a*Jotbathah.

34 And they removed from Jotbathah, and encamped at Ebronah.

35 And they departed from Ebronah, and encamped at Ezion-gaber.

36 And they removed from *a*Ezion-gaber, and pitched in the wilderness of Zin, which is *b*Kadesh.

37 And they removed from Kadesh, and pitched in mount Hor, in the edge of the land of Edom.

38 And *a*Aaron the priest went up into mount Hor at the commandment of the Lord, and died there, in the *b*fortieth year after the children of Israel were come out of the land of Egypt, in the first *day* of the fifth month.

39 And *a*Aaron *was* an hundred and twenty and three years old when he died in mount Hor.

40 And *a*king Arad the Canaanite, which dwelt in the *b*south in the land of Canaan, heard of the coming of the children of Israel.

41 And they departed from mount *a*Hor, and pitched in Zalmonah.

42 And they departed from Zalmonah, and pitched in Punon.

43 And they departed from Punon, and pitched in Oboth.

44 And they departed from Oboth, and pitched in Ije-abarim, in the border of Moab.

45 And they departed from Iim, and pitched in Dibon-gad.

46 And they removed from Dibon-gad, and encamped in Almon-diblathaim.

47 And they removed from Almon-diblathaim, and pitched in the mountains of Abarim, before *a*Nebo.

48 And they departed from the mountains of Abarim, and pitched in the plains of Moab by Jordan *near* Jericho.

10*a* or Reed Sea.
12*a* Ex. 17:1.
33*a* Deut. 10:7.
36*a* 1 Kgs. 9:26; 22:48.
  b Num. 20:1 (1-29).
38*a* Num. 20:28 (22-29).
  b Deut. 1:3.
39*a* Ex. 7:7.
40*a* heb the king of Arad.
    Num. 21:1 (1-3).
  b heb Negev.
41*a* Num. 21:4 (4-9).
47*a* Deut. 32:49 (48-52).

49 And they pitched by Jordan, from Beth-jesimoth *even* unto Abel-shittim in the plains of Moab.

50 ¶ And the LORD spake unto Moses in the plains of Moab by Jordan *near* Jericho, saying,

51 Speak unto the children of Israel, and say unto them, When ye are passed over Jordan into the land of Canaan;

52 Then ye shall *a*drive out all the inhabitants of the land from before you, and destroy all their *b*pictures, and destroy all their molten images, and quite pluck down all their *c*high places:

53 And ye shall dispossess *the inhabitants of* the land, and dwell therein: for I have given you the land to possess it.

54 And ye shall divide the *a*land by *b*lot for an *c*inheritance among your families: *and* to the more ye shall give the more inheritance, and to the fewer ye shall give the less inheritance: every man's *inheritance* shall be in the place where his lot falleth; according to the tribes of your fathers ye shall inherit.

55 But if ye will not drive out the inhabitants of the land from before you; then it shall come to pass, that those which ye let remain of them *shall be* *a*pricks in your eyes, and thorns in your sides, and shall vex you in the land wherein ye dwell.

56 Moreover it shall come to pass, *that* I shall do unto you, as I thought to do unto them.

CHAPTER 34

Moses specifies the borders of Israel's inheritance in Canaan and names the princes of the tribes who will divide the land.

AND the LORD spake unto Moses, saying,

2 Command the children of Israel, and say unto them, When ye come into the land of *a*Canaan; (this *is* the *b*land that shall fall unto you for an *c*inheritance, *even* the land of Canaan *d*with the coasts thereof:)

3 Then your south quarter shall be from the wilderness of *a*Zin along by the *b*coast of Edom, and your south border shall be the outmost coast of the *c*salt sea eastward:

4 And your border shall turn from the south to the ascent of Akrabbim, and pass on to Zin: and the going forth thereof shall be from the south to Kadesh-barnea, and shall go on to Hazar-addar, and pass on to Azmon:

5 And the border shall *a*fetch a compass from Azmon unto the river of Egypt, and *b*the goings out of it shall be at the sea.

6 And *as for* the *a*western border, ye shall even have *b*the *c*great sea for a border: this shall be your west border.

7 And this shall be your north border: from the great sea ye shall point out for you mount Hor:

8 From mount Hor ye shall point out *your border* unto the entrance of Hamath; and the goings forth of the border shall be to Zedad:

9 ¶ And the border shall go on to Ziphron, and the goings out of it shall be at Hazar-enan: this shall be your north border.

10 And ye shall point out your east border from Hazar-enan to Shepham:

11 And the *a*coast shall go down from Shepham to Riblah, on the east side of Ain; and the border shall descend, and shall reach unto the side of *b*the sea of Chinnereth eastward:

52*a* Ex. 23:24;
      Deut. 6:19;
      1 Ne. 17:32 (32–38).
   b HEB stone figures.
   c OR hill shrines.
54*a* TG Israel, Land of.
  · *b* D&C 85:7.
   c Deut. 9:1 (1–6).
55*a* Josh. 23:13;
      Ezek. 28:24.

34 2*a* Gen. 17:8 (1–27);
       Ex. 3:8;
       Abr. 2:19 (15–16, 19).
    b TG Promised Lands.
    c Josh. 13:6;
       Ezek. 47:14 (14–21);
       48:29 (1–29);
       1 Ne. 2:4; 3:16.
    d HEB and all its
       territory.

3*a* Josh. 15:1 (1–4).
  b OR side.
  c Gen. 14:3.
5*a* OR turn from.
  b OR it shall terminate at.
6*a* Josh. 15:12.
  b IE the Mediterranean.
  c Josh. 1:4 (3–4); 9:1.
11*a* OR boundary.
   b IE the Sea of Galilee.

12 And the border shall go down to Jordan, and the goings out of it shall be at the ᵃsalt ᵇsea: this shall be your land with the coasts thereof round about.

13 And Moses commanded the children of Israel, saying, This *is* the ᵃland which ye shall ᵇinherit by lot, which the LORD commanded to give unto the nine tribes, and to the half tribe:

14 For the tribe of the children of Reuben according to the ᵃhouse of their fathers, and the tribe of the children of Gad according to the house of their fathers, have received *their* ᵇinheritance; and half the tribe of Manasseh have received their inheritance:

15 The two tribes and the half tribe have received their inheritance on this side Jordan ᵃnear Jericho eastward, toward the sunrising.

16 And the LORD spake unto Moses, saying,

17 These *are* the names of the men which shall divide the ᵃland unto you: Eleazar the priest, and ᵇJoshua the son of Nun.

18 And ye shall take one ᵃprince of every ᵇtribe, to divide the land by inheritance.

19 And the names of the men *are* these: Of the tribe of Judah, Caleb the son of Jephunneh.

20 And of the tribe of the children of Simeon, Shemuel the son of Ammihud.

21 Of the tribe of Benjamin, Elidad the son of Chislon.

22 And the prince of the tribe of the children of Dan, Bukki the son of Jogli.

23 The prince of the children of Joseph, for the tribe of the children of Manasseh, Hanniel the son of Ephod.

24 And the prince of the tribe of the children of Ephraim, Kemuel the son of Shiphtan.

25 And the prince of the tribe of the children of Zebulun, Elizaphan the son of Parnach.

26 And the prince of the tribe of the children of Issachar, Paltiel the son of Azzan.

27 And the prince of the tribe of the children of Asher, Ahihud the son of Shelomi.

28 And the prince of the tribe of the children of Naphtali, Pedahel the son of Ammihud.

29 These *are they* whom the LORD commanded to divide the inheritance unto the children of Israel in the land of Canaan.

CHAPTER 35

The Levites are to possess their own cities—Cities of refuge are established for those guilty of manslaughter—Murderers are to be executed by the revenger of blood.

AND the LORD spake unto Moses in the plains of Moab by Jordan *near* Jericho, saying,

2 Command the children of Israel, that they give unto the ᵃLevites of the inheritance of their possession cities to dwell in; and ye shall give *also* unto the Levites ᵇsuburbs for the cities round about them.

3 And the cities shall they have to ᵃdwell in; and the suburbs of them shall be for their cattle, and for their ᵇgoods, and for all their beasts.

4 And the suburbs of the cities, which ye shall give unto the Levites, *shall reach* from the wall of the city and outward a thousand cubits round about.

5 And ye shall measure from ᵃwithout the city on the east side

12a Josh. 3:16.
  b Deut. 3:17; 4:49 (47–49).
13a TG Israel, Land of.
  b D&C 85:3 (3, 7).
14a OR houses, clans.
  b Num. 32:32 (1–42).
15a OR east of Jericho.
17a Josh. 14:1.
  b Josh. 19:51.

18a HEB leader, president
     (also vv. 23, 25–28).
  b TG Israel, Twelve
     Tribes of.
35 2a Num. 18:23 (1, 20–32);
       Josh. 21:1 (1–3).
  b IE open areas for
     fields and pasture
     (also vv. 3–7).

     Lev. 25:34 (32–34);
     Josh. 14:4;
     2 Chr. 11:14;
     Ezek. 48:15 (15–17).
3a Deut. 18:6.
  b HEB property, livestock,
     etc.
5a HEB the outside of.

two thousand cubits, and on the south side two thousand cubits, and on the west side two thousand cubits, and on the north side two thousand cubits; and the city *shall be* in the midst: this shall be to them the suburbs of the cities.

6 And among the cities which ye shall give unto the Levites *there shall be* six cities for *a*refuge, which ye shall appoint for the manslayer, that he may flee thither: and to them ye shall add forty and two cities.

7 *So* all the cities which ye shall give to the *a*Levites *shall be* forty and eight cities: them *shall ye give* with their suburbs.

8 And the cities which ye shall give *shall be* of the possession of the children of Israel: from *them that have* many ye shall give many; but from *them that have* few ye shall give few: every one shall give of his cities unto the Levites according to his inheritance which he inheriteth.

9 ¶ And the LORD spake unto Moses, saying,

10 Speak unto the children of Israel, and say unto them, When ye be come over Jordan into the land of Canaan;

11 Then ye shall appoint you cities to be cities of refuge for you; that the slayer may flee thither, which killeth any person *a*at unawares.

12 And they shall be unto you cities for refuge from the *a*avenger; that the manslayer die not, until he stand before the congregation in judgment.

13 And of these cities which ye shall give six cities shall ye have for refuge.

14 Ye shall give three cities on this side Jordan, and three cities shall ye give in the land of Canaan, *which* shall be cities of refuge.

15 These six cities shall be a refuge, *both* for the children of Israel, and for the *a*stranger, and for the sojourner among them: that every one that killeth any person unawares may flee thither.

16 And if he smite him with an instrument of iron, so that he die, he *is* a murderer: the *a*murderer shall surely be put to *b*death.

17 And if he smite him with throwing a stone, wherewith he may die, and he die, he *is* a murderer: the murderer shall surely be put to death.

18 Or *if* he smite him with an hand weapon of wood, wherewith he may die, and he die, he *is* a murderer: the murderer shall surely be put to death.

19 The *a*revenger of blood himself shall slay the murderer: when he meeteth him, he shall slay him.

20 But if he *a*thrust him of hatred, or hurl at him by laying of wait, that he die;

21 Or in enmity smite him with his hand, that he die: he that smote *him* shall surely be put to death; *for* he *is* a murderer: the revenger of blood shall slay the murderer, when he meeteth him.

22 But if he thrust him suddenly without enmity, or *a*have cast upon him any thing without laying of wait,

23 Or with any stone, wherewith a man may die, seeing *him* not, and cast *it* upon him, that he die, and *was* not his enemy, neither sought his harm:

24 Then the congregation shall judge between the slayer and the revenger of blood according to these judgments:

25 And the congregation shall deliver the slayer out of the hand of the revenger of blood, and the congregation shall restore him to the city of his refuge, whither he was fled: and he shall abide in it unto the death of the *a*high priest, which was anointed with the holy oil.

6a TG Refuge.
7a Josh. 21:41.
11a OR unintentionally.
12a Josh. 20:5 (3–6).
15a Num. 15:15 (15–16);
　　Josh. 20:9.

16a See JST Gen. 9:10–13
　　(Appendix).
　　Deut. 19:11 (11–13);
　　2 Ne. 9:35.
　b TG Capital Punishment.
19a 2 Sam. 14:11.

20a OR stabs.
22a OR hurls at him.
25a Lev. 21:10 (10–15);
　　Josh. 20:6.

26 But if the slayer shall at any time come *a*without the border of the city of his refuge, whither he was fled;

27 And the revenger of blood find him without the borders of the city of his refuge, and the revenger of blood *a*kill the slayer; he shall not be *b*guilty of blood:

28 Because he should have remained in the city of his refuge until the death of the high priest: but after the death of the high priest the slayer shall return into the land of his possession.

29 So these *things* shall be for a statute of judgment unto you throughout your generations in all your dwellings.

30 Whoso killeth any person, the *a*murderer shall be put to *b*death by the mouth of *c*witnesses: but one witness shall not testify against any person *to cause him* to die.

31 Moreover ye shall take no *a*satisfaction for the life of a murderer, which *is* *b*guilty of death: but he shall be surely put to death.

32 And ye shall take no satisfaction for him that is fled to the city of his refuge, that he should come again to dwell in the land, until the death of the priest.

33 So ye shall not *a*pollute the land wherein ye *are:* for blood it defileth the land: and *b*the land cannot be cleansed of the blood that is shed therein, but by the blood of him that shed it.

34 *a*Defile not therefore the land which ye shall inhabit, wherein I dwell: for I the LORD dwell *b*among the children of Israel.

CHAPTER 36

Some daughters in Israel are directed to marry within their own tribe—Inheritances are not to move from tribe to tribe.

AND the chief fathers of the families of the children of Gilead, the son of Machir, the son of Manasseh, of the families of the sons of Joseph, came near, and spake before Moses, and before the princes, the chief fathers of the children of Israel:

2 And they said, The LORD commanded my lord to give the land for an inheritance by lot to the children of Israel: and my lord was commanded by the LORD to give the *a*inheritance of Zelophehad our brother unto his daughters.

3 And if they be married to any of the sons of the *other* tribes of the children of Israel, then shall their inheritance be taken from the inheritance of our fathers, and shall be *a*put to the inheritance of the tribe whereunto they are received: so shall it be taken from the lot of our inheritance.

4 And when the *a*jubilee of the children of Israel shall be, then shall their *b*inheritance be put unto the inheritance of the tribe whereunto they are received: so shall their inheritance be taken away from the inheritance of the tribe of our fathers.

5 And Moses commanded the children of Israel according to the word of the LORD, saying, The tribe of the sons of Joseph hath said well.

6 This *is* the thing which the LORD doth command concerning the daughters of Zelophehad, saying, Let them marry to whom they think best; only to the family of the tribe of their father shall they marry.

7 So shall not the inheritance of the children of Israel remove from tribe to tribe: for every one of the children of Israel shall keep himself to the inheritance of the tribe of his fathers.

8 And every daughter, that

26*a* OR outside of.
27*a* TG Capital Punishment.
  b TG Guilt.
30*a* See JST Gen. 9:10–13 (Appendix).
  TG Murder.
  b TG Capital Punishment.
  c TG Witness.

31*a* HEB ransom, fine (also v. 32).
  b TG Guilt.
33*a* TG Pollution.
  b HEB atonement cannot be made for blood shed in the land except by the blood of him who shed it.

  TG Accountability.
34*a* Lev. 18:24 (24–30).
  b TG God, Presence of.
36 2*a* Num. 27:7 (1–11).
  3*a* HEB added (also v. 4).
  4*a* Lev. 25:11 (1–55).
  b Lev. 25:46.

possesseth an inheritance in any tribe of the children of Israel, shall be wife unto one of the family of the tribe of her father, that the children of Israel may enjoy every man the inheritance of his fathers.

9 Neither shall the inheritance remove from *one* tribe to another tribe; but every one of the tribes of the children of Israel shall keep himself to his own inheritance.

10 Even as the LORD commanded Moses, so did the daughters of Zelophehad:

11 For Mahlah, Tirzah, and Hoglah, and Milcah, and Noah, the daughters of Zelophehad, were married unto their father's brothers' sons:

12 *And* they were married into the families of the sons of Manasseh the son of Joseph, and their inheritance remained in the tribe of the family of their father.

13 These *are* the commandments and the judgments, which the LORD commanded by the hand of Moses unto the children of Israel in the plains of Moab by Jordan *near* Jericho.

THE FIFTH BOOK OF MOSES
CALLED
DEUTERONOMY

CHAPTER 1

Moses begins the recitation of all that befell Israel during forty years in the wilderness—The children of Israel are commanded to go into and possess Canaan—Judges and rulers are chosen to assist Moses—Israel's spies bring an evil report—The adults of Israel will perish—The Amorites defeat the armies of Israel.

THESE *be* the words which Moses spake unto all Israel ^aon this side Jordan in the wilderness, in the ^bplain over against the ^cRed sea, between Paran, and Tophel, and Laban, and Hazeroth, and Dizahab.

2 (*There are* eleven days' *journey* from Horeb by the way of mount Seir unto Kadesh-barnea.)

3 And it came to pass in the ^afortieth year, in the eleventh month, on the first *day* of the month, *that* Moses spake unto the children of Israel, according unto all that the LORD had given him in commandment unto them;

4 After he had slain ^aSihon the king of the Amorites, which dwelt in Heshbon, and ^bOg the king of Bashan, which dwelt at Astaroth in Edrei:

5 On this side Jordan, in the land of Moab, began Moses to ^adeclare ^bthis law, saying,

6 The LORD our God spake unto us in Horeb, saying, Ye have dwelt long enough in this ^amount:

7 Turn you, and take your journey, and go to the mount of the

1 1a HEB beyond the Jordan.
  b HEB Arabah.
  c HEB Reed Sea.
3a Num. 33:38 (38–39).
4a Num. 21:23 (21–30).

b Num. 21:33 (33–35);
  Deut. 3:11 (10–11);
  Josh. 9:10.
5a HEB explain, clarify,
  expound.

b HEB this "teaching."
6a Ex. 3:12 (1, 12);
  Deut. 4:10 (10–13);
  1 Kgs. 8:9.

Amorites, and unto all *the places* nigh thereunto, in the plain, in the hills, and [a]in the vale, and in the [b]south, and by the sea side, to the land of the Canaanites, and unto Lebanon, unto the great river, the river Euphrates.

8 Behold, I have set the land before you: go in and [a]possess the [b]land which the LORD sware unto your fathers, Abraham, Isaac, and Jacob, to give unto them and to their seed after them.

9 ¶ And I spake unto you at that time, saying, I am not able to [a]bear you myself alone:

10 The LORD your God hath multiplied you, and, behold, ye *are* this day as the [a]stars of heaven for [b]multitude.

11 (The LORD God of your fathers make you a thousand times so many [a]more as ye *are,* and bless you, as he hath [b]promised you!)

12 How can I myself alone bear your [a]cumbrance, and your burden, and your [b]strife?

13 Take you wise men, and understanding, and known among your tribes, and I will [a]make them [b]rulers over you.

14 And ye answered me, and said, The thing which thou hast spoken *is* good *for us* to do.

15 So I took the chief of your tribes, [a]wise men, and known, and made them [b]heads over you, captains over thousands, and captains over hundreds, and captains over fifties, and captains over tens, and officers among your tribes.

16 And I charged your judges at that time, saying, Hear *the causes* between your brethren, and [a]judge righteously between *every* man and his brother, and the [b]stranger *that is* with him.

17 Ye shall not [a]respect persons in [b]judgment; *but* ye shall hear the small as well as the great; ye shall not [c]afraid of the face of man; for the judgment *is* God's: and the cause that is too hard for you, bring *it* unto me, and I will hear it.

18 And I commanded you at that time all the things which ye should do.

19 ¶ And when we departed from Horeb, we went through all that great and terrible wilderness, which ye saw by the way of the mountain of the Amorites, as the LORD our God commanded us; and we came to Kadesh-barnea.

20 And I said unto you, Ye are come unto the mountain of the Amorites, which the LORD our God doth give unto us.

21 Behold, the LORD thy God hath set the land before thee: go up *and* possess *it,* as the LORD God of thy fathers hath said unto thee; fear not, neither be discouraged.

22 ¶ And ye came near unto me every one of you, and said, We will send men before us, and they shall search us out the land, and bring us word again by what way we must go up, and into what cities we shall come.

23 And the saying pleased me well: and I took [a]twelve men of you, one of a tribe:

24 And they turned and went up into the mountain, and came unto the valley of Eshcol, and searched it out.

25 And they took of the fruit of the land in their hands, and brought *it* down unto us, and brought us word

---

7a HEB in the lowlands.
 b HEB Negev.
8a Neh. 9:15;
   1 Ne. 17:36 (35–38);
   D&C 69:8 (6–8).
 b TG Israel, Land of;
   Promised Lands.
9a Ex. 18:18 (17–26).
10a D&C 132:30.
 b TG Seed of Abraham.
11a Ps. 115:14.

 b Gen. 22:16 (15–18).
12a HEB troubles.
 b TG Strife.
13a HEB appoint them as
   your heads.
 b TG Delegation of
   Responsibility.
15a Ex. 18:21.
 b D&C 136:15 (12–18).
16a TG Citizenship; Justice.
 b HEB alien, proselyte.

17a HEB acknowledge
   faces. The idiom
   means to favor some
   unjustifiably.
   Lev. 19:15;
   Prov. 24:23;
   James 2:9 (1–9);
   D&C 1:35 (34–35); 38:16.
 b TG Judgment.
 c 2 Ne. 8:7.
23a Num. 13:2 (1–33).

again, and said, *It is* a good land which the LORD our God doth give us.

26 Notwithstanding ye would not go up, but ^arebelled against the commandment of the LORD your God:

27 And ye ^amurmured in your tents, and said, Because the LORD hated us, he hath brought us forth out of the land of Egypt, to deliver us into the hand of the Amorites, to destroy us.

28 Whither shall we go up? our brethren have discouraged our heart, saying, The people *is* greater and taller than we; the cities *are* great and ^awalled up to heaven; and moreover we have seen the sons of the Anakims there.

29 Then I said unto you, Dread not, neither be afraid of them.

30 The LORD your God which goeth before you, he shall ^afight for you, according to all that he did for you in Egypt before your eyes;

31 And in the wilderness, where thou hast seen how that the LORD thy God bare thee, as a man doth bear his son, in all the way that ye went, until ye came into this place.

32 Yet in this thing ye did not ^abelieve the LORD your God,

33 Who went in the way before you, to search you out a place to pitch your tents *in*, in fire by night, to shew you by what way ye should go, and in a ^acloud by day.

34 And the LORD heard the voice of your words, and ^awas wroth, and sware, saying,

35 Surely there shall not one of these men of this ^aevil generation ^bsee that good land, which I sware to give unto your fathers,

36 Save ^aCaleb the son of Jephunneh; he shall see it, and to him will I give the land that he hath trodden upon, and to his children, because he hath wholly followed the LORD.

37 Also the LORD was ^aangry with me for your ^bsakes, saying, Thou also shalt not go in thither.

38 *But* ^aJoshua the son of Nun, which standeth before thee, he shall go in thither: encourage him: for he shall cause Israel to inherit it.

39 Moreover your little ones, which ye said should be a prey, and your children, which in that day had no ^aknowledge between good and evil, they shall go in thither, and unto them will I give it, and they shall possess it.

40 But *as for* you, turn you, and take your journey into the wilderness by the way of the Red sea.

41 Then ye answered and said unto me, We have ^asinned against the LORD, we will go up and fight, according to all that the LORD our God commanded us. And when ye had girded on every man his weapons of war, ye were ready to go up into the hill.

42 And the LORD said unto me, Say unto them, Go not up, neither fight; for I *am* not among you; lest ye be smitten before your enemies.

43 So I spake unto you; and ye would not hear, but rebelled against the commandment of the LORD, and ^awent presumptuously up into the hill.

44 And the Amorites, which dwelt in that mountain, came out against you, and chased you, as ^abees do, and ^bdestroyed you in Seir, *even* unto Hormah.

45 And ye returned and wept before the LORD; but the LORD would not hearken to your voice, nor give ear unto you.

26a TG Rebellion.
27a TG Murmuring.
28a HEB fortified.
    Num. 13:28.
30a Josh. 10:14 (12–14);
    1 Ne. 3:7.
32a TG Doubt; Unbelief.
33a Num. 14:14;
    Neh. 9:12 (12, 19);
    Isa. 4:5 (3–6).

34a HEB was angered, and
    made an oath.
35a Jude 1:5.
    b Jacob 1:7.
36a Num. 13:6 (1–16);
    Josh. 15:13.
37a TG Anger.
    b Deut. 3:26;
    Ps. 106:32.
38a Deut. 31:7 (7, 23);

    Josh. 12:7 (7–21).
39a TG Man, Natural, Not
    Spiritually Reborn.
41a Num. 14:40.
43a HEB ye were
    presumptuous and
    went up.
    Num. 14:44.
44a Ps. 118:12.
    b HEB beat.

46 So ye abode in Kadesh many days, according unto the days that ye abode *there*.

CHAPTER 2

The children of Israel press forward to their promised land—They pass through the lands of Esau and of Ammon in peace but destroy the Amorites.

THEN we turned, and took our journey into the wilderness by the way of the Red sea, as the LORD spake unto me: and we compassed mount [a]Seir many days.

2 And the LORD spake unto me, saying,

3 Ye have [a]compassed this mountain long enough: turn you northward.

4 And command thou the people, saying, Ye *are* to pass through the coast of your brethren the children of Esau, which dwell in Seir; and they shall be afraid of you: take ye good heed unto yourselves therefore:

5 Meddle not with them; for I will not give you of their [a]land, no, not so much as a foot [b]breadth; because I have given mount [c]Seir unto Esau *for* a possession.

6 Ye [a]shall buy meat of them for money, that ye may eat; and ye shall also buy water of them for money, that ye may drink.

7 For the LORD thy God hath blessed thee in all the works of thy hand: he [a]knoweth thy walking through this great wilderness: these forty years the LORD thy God *hath been* with thee; thou hast lacked nothing.

8 And when we passed by from our brethren the children of Esau, which dwelt in Seir, through the way of the plain from Elath, and from Ezion-gaber, we turned and passed by the way of the wilderness of Moab.

9 And the LORD said unto me, Distress not the [a]Moabites, neither contend with them in battle: for I will not give thee of their land *for* a possession; because I have given [b]Ar unto the children of Lot *for* a possession.

10 The [a]Emims dwelt therein in times past, a people great, and many, and tall, as the [b]Anakims;

11 Which also were accounted [a]giants, as the [b]Anakims; but the Moabites call them Emims.

12 The [a]Horims also dwelt in Seir beforetime; but the children of Esau [b]succeeded them, when they had destroyed them from before them, and dwelt in their stead; as Israel did unto the land of his possession, which the LORD gave unto them.

13 Now rise up, *said I*, and get you over the brook Zered. And we went over the brook Zered.

14 And the [a]space in which we came from Kadesh-barnea, until we were come over the brook Zered, *was* thirty and eight years; until all the generation of the [b]men of war [c]were wasted out from among the host, as the LORD sware unto them.

15 For indeed the hand of the LORD was against them, to destroy them from among the host, until they were consumed.

16 ¶ So it came to pass, when all the men of war were consumed and dead from among the people,

17 That the LORD spake unto me, saying,

18 Thou art to pass over through Ar, the [a]coast of Moab, this day:

19 And *when* thou comest nigh over against the children of [a]Ammon,

---

2 1a Ezek. 35:2 (1–15).
3a HEB gone around this mountain region, or hill country.
5a TG Lands of Inheritance.
  b HEB tread, step.
  c Gen. 32:3.
6a HEB may buy food.
7a Hosea 13:5 (5–8).

9a Gen. 19:37 (30–38); Judg. 11:15.
  b Isa. 15:1.
10a Gen. 14:5.
  b IE an ancient race of large people; sometimes translated as "giants" (also vv. 11, 21).
11a Num. 13:33; Deut. 3:11.

  b Deut. 9:2.
12a Gen. 14:6.
  b HEB dispossessed.
14a HEB time.
  b Num. 14:35 (33–35); Ps. 95:10 (10–11).
  c HEB had perished from the camp.
18a HEB territory (also v. 4).
19a Gen. 19:38 (30–38).

distress them not, nor meddle with them: for I will not give thee of the *b*land of the children of Ammon *any* possession; because I have given it unto the children of Lot *for* a possession.

20 (That also was accounted a land of *a*giants: giants dwelt therein in old time; and the Ammonites call them *b*Zamzummims;

21 A people great, and many, and tall, as the Anakims; but the LORD destroyed them before them; and they succeeded them, and dwelt in their stead:

22 As he did to the children of Esau, which dwelt in Seir, when he destroyed the Horims from before them; and they succeeded them, and dwelt in their stead even unto this day:

23 And the Avims which dwelt in *a*Hazerim, *even* unto Azzah, the Caphtorims, which came forth out of *b*Caphtor, destroyed them, and dwelt in their stead.)

24 ¶ Rise ye up, take your journey, and pass over the river Arnon: behold, I have given into thine hand Sihon the Amorite, king of Heshbon, and his land: begin to possess *it*, and contend with him in battle.

25 This day will I begin to put the dread of thee and the *a*fear of thee upon the nations *that are* under the whole heaven, who shall hear report of thee, and shall tremble, and be in anguish because of thee.

26 ¶ And I sent messengers out of the wilderness of Kedemoth unto Sihon king of Heshbon with words of peace, saying,

27 Let me pass through thy land: I will go along by the high way, I will neither turn unto the right hand nor to the left.

28 Thou shalt *a*sell me *b*meat for money, that I may eat; and give me water for money, that I may drink: only *c*I will pass through on my feet;

29 (As the children of Esau which dwell in Seir, and the Moabites which dwell in Ar, did unto me;) until I shall pass over Jordan into the land which the LORD our God giveth us.

30 But Sihon king of Heshbon would not let us pass by him: for the LORD thy God *a*hardened his spirit, and made his heart *b*obstinate, that he might deliver him into thy hand, as *appeareth* this day.

31 And the LORD said unto me, Behold, I have begun to give Sihon and his land before thee: begin to possess, that thou mayest inherit his land.

32 Then *a*Sihon came out against us, he and all his people, to fight at Jahaz.

33 And the LORD our God delivered him before us; and we *a*smote him, and his sons, and all his people.

34 And we took all his cities at that time, and utterly *a*destroyed the men, and the women, and the little ones, of every city, we left none to remain:

35 Only the cattle we took for a prey unto ourselves, and the spoil of the cities which we took.

36 From *a*Aroer, which *is* by the brink of the river of Arnon, and *from* the city that *is* by the river, even unto Gilead, there was not one city too strong for us: the LORD our God *b*delivered all unto us:

37 Only unto the land of the children of Ammon thou camest not, *nor* unto any place of the river Jabbok, nor unto the cities in the mountains, nor unto whatsoever the LORD our God forbad us.

19*b* Num. 21:25 (21–35);
  Judg. 11:13 (13–23).
20*a* Moses 8:18.
  b Gen. 14:5.
23*a* HEB villages.
  b IE Crete, from which early Philistines (Caphtorim) migrated to Canaan.

25*a* Ex. 15:16 (14–16, 18).
28*a* Num. 20:19.
  b HEB food.
  c HEB let me pass through on foot.
30*a* Rom. 9:18.
  b TG Stubbornness.
32*a* Deut. 29:7 (7–8).
33*a* Num. 21:24 (21–24);

Deut. 29:7 (7–8).
34*a* Deut. 7:2;
  1 Sam. 15:3.
36*a* Deut. 3:12;
  2 Kgs. 10:33;
  Jer. 48:19.
  b Ps. 44:3.

CHAPTER 3

The children of Israel destroy the people of Bashan—Their lands, on the east of the Jordan, are given to Reuben and Gad—Moses sees Canaan from Pisgah but is denied entrance thereto—He counsels and strengthens Joshua.

THEN we turned, and went up the way to Bashan: and Og the king of Bashan came out against us, he and all his people, to battle at Edrei.

2 And the LORD said unto me, Fear him not: for I will deliver him, and all his people, and his land, into thy hand; and thou shalt do unto him as thou didst unto Sihon king of the Amorites, which dwelt at Heshbon.

3 So the LORD our God delivered into our hands Og also, the king of Bashan, and all his people: and we *ᵃsmote him until none was left to him remaining.

4 And we took all his cities at that time, there was not a city which we took not from them, threescore cities, all the region of Argob, the kingdom of Og in Bashan.

5 All these cities *were* fenced with high *ᵃwalls, gates, and bars; beside unwalled towns a great many.

6 And we utterly destroyed them, as we did unto Sihon king of Heshbon, utterly destroying the men, women, and children, of every city.

7 But all the cattle, and the spoil of the cities, we took for a prey to ourselves.

8 And we took at that time out of the hand of the two kings of the Amorites the land that *was* *ᵃon this side Jordan, from the river of Arnon unto mount Hermon;

9 (*Which* *ᵃHermon the Sidonians call Sirion; and the Amorites call it *ᵇShenir;)

10 All the cities of the *ᵃplain, and all Gilead, and all Bashan, unto Salchah and Edrei, cities of the kingdom of Og in Bashan.

11 For only *ᵃOg king of Bashan remained of the remnant of *ᵇgiants; behold, his bedstead *was* a bedstead of iron; *is* it not in Rabbath of the children of Ammon? nine *ᶜcubits *was* the length thereof, and four cubits the breadth of it, after the *ᵈcubit of a man.

12 And this land, *which* we possessed at that time, from *ᵃAroer, which *is* by the river Arnon, and half *ᵇmount Gilead, and the cities thereof, gave I unto the *ᶜReubenites and to the Gadites.

13 And the rest of Gilead, and all Bashan, *being* the kingdom of Og, gave I unto the half tribe of *ᵃManasseh; all the region of Argob, with all Bashan, which was called the land of giants.

14 Jair the son of Manasseh took all the country of Argob unto the *ᵃcoasts of *ᵇGeshuri and Maachathi; and called *ᶜthem after his own name, Bashan-havoth-jair, unto this day.

15 And I gave Gilead unto Machir.

16 And unto the Reubenites and unto the Gadites I gave from Gilead even unto the river *ᵃArnon *ᵇhalf the valley, and the border even unto the river *ᶜJabbok, *which is* the border of the children of Ammon;

17 The *ᵃplain also, *ᵇand Jordan, and the coast *thereof,* from Chinnereth even unto the *ᶜsea of the

---

3 3*a* Num. 21:35 (33–35).
  5*a* Alma 48:8.
  8*a* HEB beyond the Jordan.
  9*a* Deut. 4:48 (47–49);
       Ps. 133:3 (1–3).
    b Ezek. 27:5.
 10*a* Deut. 4:43.
 11*a* Num. 21:33 (33–35);
       Deut. 1:4;
       Josh. 9:10 (9–10).
    b Gen. 6:4; 14:5;
       Num. 13:33;
       Deut. 2:11 (10–11);

      Josh. 12:4.
    c 1 Sam. 17:4.
    d OR common cubit;
       about 18 inches or 45
       centimeters.
 12 *a* Deut. 2:36.
    b OR the hill country of.
    c Num. 32:2 (2–6);
       Josh. 12:6 (4–6).
 13 *a* Gen. 48:5.
 14 *a* HEB border.
    b Josh. 13:2 (1–5); 2 Sam. 3:3.
    c IE the villages.

 16*a* Num. 21:24;
       Deut. 4:48 (47–49);
       Josh. 13:9 (7–12);
       Judg. 11:13.
    b HEB with the middle of
       the valley as the border.
    c Num. 21:24.
 17*a* HEB Arabah.
    b HEB with the Jordan as
       the border.
    c Num. 34:12;
       Deut. 4:49 (47–49);
       Ezek. 47:8 (8–11).

plain, *even* the salt sea, under Ashdoth-pisgah eastward.

18 ¶ And I commanded you at that time, saying, The LORD your God hath given you this land to possess it: ye shall pass over armed before your brethren the children of Israel, *a*all *that are* meet for the war.

19 But your wives, and your little ones, and your cattle, (*for* I know that ye have much cattle,) shall abide in your cities which I have given you;

20 Until the LORD have given *a*rest unto your brethren, as well as unto you, and *until* they also possess the land which the LORD your God hath given them beyond Jordan: and *then* shall ye return every man unto his possession, which I have given you.

21 ¶ And I commanded *a*Joshua at that time, saying, Thine eyes have seen all that the LORD your God hath done unto these two kings: so shall the LORD do unto all the kingdoms whither thou passest.

22 Ye shall not fear them: for the LORD your God he shall *a*fight for you.

23 And I besought the LORD at that time, saying,

24 O Lord GOD, thou hast begun to shew thy servant thy greatness, and thy mighty *a*hand: for what God *is there* in heaven or in earth, that can do according to thy works, and according to thy might?

25 I pray thee, let me go over, and see the good land that *is* beyond Jordan, that goodly mountain, and *a*Lebanon.

26 But the LORD was *a*wroth with me for your *b*sakes, and would not hear me: and the LORD said unto me, Let it suffice thee; speak no more unto me of this matter.

27 Get thee up into the top of Pisgah, and lift up thine eyes westward,

and northward, and southward, and eastward, and behold *it* with thine eyes: for thou shalt not go over this Jordan.

28 But *a*charge Joshua, and encourage him, and *b*strengthen him: for he shall *c*go over before this people, and he shall cause them to inherit the land which thou shalt see.

29 So we abode in the valley over against Beth-peor.

CHAPTER 4

Moses exhorts the children of Israel to keep the commandments, to teach them to their children, and to be exemplary before all nations—They are forbidden to make graven images or worship other gods—They are to witness that they have heard the voice of God—They will be scattered among all nations when they worship other gods—They will be gathered again in the latter days when they seek the Lord their God—Moses extols the mercy and goodness of God to Israel.

NOW therefore hearken, O Israel, unto the *a*statutes and unto the *b*judgments, which I teach you, for to do *them*, that ye may live, and go in and possess the land which the LORD God of your fathers giveth you.

2 Ye shall not *a*add unto the word which I command you, neither shall ye diminish *ought* from it, that ye may keep the commandments of the LORD your God which I command you.

3 Your eyes have seen what the LORD did *a*because of *b*Baal-peor: for all the men that followed Baal-peor, the LORD thy God hath destroyed them from among you.

4 But ye that did cleave unto the LORD your God *are* alive every one of you this day.

5 Behold, I have taught you statutes and judgments, even as the

18*a* HEB all the men of valor.
20*a* Josh. 21:44.
21*a* Num. 27:18.
22*a* TG Protection, Divine.
24*a* 1 Kgs. 8:42.
25*a* Josh. 1:4.
26*a* TG God, Indignation of.

b Deut. 1:37; Ps. 106:32.
28*a* Deut. 31:23.
  b D&C 108:7.
  c Josh. 4:11 (7–17).
4 1*a* Hosea 8:12 (11–12).
  b HEB ordinances (also vv. 5, 8, 14, 45).

TG Judgment.
2*a* Rev. 22:18 (18–20).
  TG False Doctrine; Scriptures, Preservation of.
3*a* HEB at.
  b Num. 25:5 (1–18).

LORD my God commanded me, that ye should do so in the land whither ye go to possess it.

6 Keep therefore and do *them;* for this *is* your ªwisdom and your ᵇunderstanding in the sight of the ᶜnations, which shall hear all these ᵈstatutes, and say, Surely this great nation *is* a wise and understanding people.

7 For what ªnation *is there so* great, who *hath* God so ᵇnigh unto them, as the LORD our God *is* in all *things that* we call upon him *for?*

8 And what nation *is there so* great, that hath ªstatutes and judgments *so* righteous as all this law, which I set before you this day?

9 Only take ªheed to thyself, and keep thy soul diligently, lest thou ᵇforget the things which thine eyes have seen, and lest they depart from thy heart all the days of thy life: but ᶜteach them thy ᵈsons, and thy sons' sons;

10 *Specially* the day that thou stoodest before the LORD thy God in ªHoreb, when the LORD said unto me, ᵇGather me the people together, and I will make them ᶜhear my words, that they may learn to ᵈfear me all the days that they shall live upon the earth, and *that* they may teach their ᵉchildren.

11 And ye came near and stood ªunder the mountain; and the mountain burned with fire unto the midst of heaven, with darkness, clouds, and thick darkness.

12 And the LORD spake unto you out of the midst of the fire: ye heard the ªvoice of the words, but saw no ᵇsimilitude; only *ye heard* a voice.

13 And he declared unto you his ªcovenant, which he commanded you to perform, *even* ᵇten ᶜcommandments; and he ᵈwrote them upon two ᵉtables of stone.

14 ¶ And the LORD commanded me at that time to ªteach you statutes and judgments, that ye might do them in the land whither ye go over to possess it.

15 Take ye therefore good heed unto yourselves; for ye saw no manner of similitude on the day *that* the LORD spake unto you in Horeb out of the midst of the fire:

16 Lest ye ªcorrupt *yourselves,* and make you a graven ᵇimage, the similitude of any figure, the likeness of male or female,

17 The likeness of any beast that *is* on the earth, the likeness of any winged fowl that flieth in the air,

18 The likeness of any thing that creepeth on the ground, the likeness of any fish that *is* in the waters beneath the earth:

19 And lest thou lift up thine eyes unto heaven, and when thou seest the sun, and the moon, and the ªstars, *even* all the host of heaven, shouldest be driven to ᵇworship them, and serve ᶜthem, which the LORD thy God hath divided unto all nations under the whole heaven.

20 But the LORD hath taken you, and brought you forth out of the iron furnace, *even* out of Egypt, to be unto him a people of ªinheritance, as *ye are* this day.

6a TG Israel, Blessings of; Wisdom.
  b TG Understanding.
  c TG Israel, Mission of.
  d Hosea 8:12 (11–12).
7a 2 Sam. 7:23.
  b D&C 88:63.
8a Neh. 9:13; Ezek. 20:11; Mosiah 29:25.
9a Mosiah 4:30; D&C 84:43 (43–44).
  b 1 Ne. 7:10 (10–12).
  c Eph. 6:4 (1–4). TG Family, Children, Responsibilities toward; Teaching.

d Ps. 78:3 (3–4); 145:4 (1–21); 2 Tim. 3:15 (14–17).
10a Ex. 3:12 (1, 12); 19:18 (9, 16–20); Deut. 1:6 (5–8); 1 Kgs. 8:9; Mal. 4:4.
  b Deut. 9:10.
  c Ex. 19:9 (7–13); Deut. 4:33 (33, 36); 5:23 (22–26).
  d OR revere, worship.
  e TG Children.
11a IE at the foot of.
12a TG God, Manifestations of.

b OR form (also vv. 15–16).
13a TG Covenants.
  b Ex. 34:28.
  c TG Commandments of God.
  d TG Scriptures, Writing of.
  e Ex. 31:18; 32:15 (15–19); 2 Cor. 3:3.
14a D&C 84:23 (19–23).
16a Gen. 6:11 (11–13); Ex. 32:7.
  b TG Idolatry.
19a TG Astronomy.
  b TG Idolatry.
  c OR those things.
20a TG Inheritance.

21 Furthermore the LORD was *angry with me for your sakes, and sware that I should not go over Jordan, and that I should not go in unto that good land, which the LORD thy God giveth thee *for* an inheritance:

22 But I must die in this land, I must not go over Jordan: but ye shall go over, and possess that good land.

23 Take heed unto yourselves, lest ye *forget the *covenant of the LORD your God, which he made with you, and make you a graven image, *or* the likeness of any *thing*, which the LORD thy God hath forbidden thee.

24 For the LORD thy God *is* a consuming *fire, *even* a *jealous God.

25 ¶ When thou shalt beget children, and children's children, and ye shall have remained long in the land, and shall corrupt *yourselves*, and make a graven image, *or* the likeness of any *thing*, and shall do *evil in the sight of the LORD thy God, to provoke him to *anger:

26 I call *heaven and earth to witness against you this day, that ye shall soon utterly perish from off the land whereunto ye go over *Jordan to possess it; ye shall not prolong *your* days upon it, but shall *utterly be destroyed.

27 And the LORD shall *scatter you among the nations, and ye shall be left few in number *among the heathen, whither the LORD shall lead you.

28 And there ye shall serve *gods, the work of men's hands, wood and stone, which neither *see, nor hear, nor eat, nor smell.

29 But if from thence thou shalt *seek the LORD thy God, thou shalt *find *him,* if thou seek him with all thy heart and with all thy soul.

30 When thou art in *tribulation, and all these things are come upon thee, *even* in the *latter days, if thou *turn to the LORD thy God, and shalt be obedient unto his voice;

31 (For the LORD thy God *is* a *merciful God;) he will not forsake thee, neither destroy thee, nor forget the *covenant of thy fathers which he sware unto them.

32 For ask now of the days that are past, which were before thee, since the day that God created man upon the earth, and *ask* from the one side of heaven unto the other, whether there hath been *any such thing* as this great thing *is*, or hath been heard like it?

33 Did *ever* people *hear the *voice of God speaking out of the midst of the fire, as thou hast heard, and live?

34 Or hath God *assayed to go *and* take him a *nation from the midst of *another* nation, by *temptations, by signs, and by *wonders, and by war, and by a *mighty hand, and by a *stretched out arm, and by great terrors, according to all that the LORD your God did for you in Egypt before your eyes?

35 Unto thee it was shewed, that thou mightest know that the LORD he *is* a *God; *there is* *none else beside him.

36 Out of heaven he made thee to hear his voice, that he might *instruct thee: and upon earth he *shewed thee his great fire; and thou

---

21a TG God, Indignation of.
23a 2 Kgs. 17:38.
  b TG Covenants;
    Obedience.
24a 3 Ne. 24:2.
  b Ex. 20:5;
    Josh. 24:19;
    Ezek. 36:5.
25a TG Evil.
  b TG Anger.
26a Ps. 50:4.
  b Num. 20:12 (7–12).
  c IE as a nation (see v. 31).
27a TG Israel, Scattering of.
  b HEB among the Gentiles
    (see v. 34).

28a TG Idolatry.
  b TG God, Body of,
    Corporeal Nature.
29a TG God, Access to.
  b TG Israel, Gathering of.
30a TG Tribulation.
  b TG Last Days.
  c HEB return, repent.
    TG Israel, Restoration of.
31a TG God, Mercy of;
    Mercy.
  b 1 Ne. 22:9 (6–10).
    TG Dispensations.
33a Ex. 19:9 (7–13); 20:18;
    Deut. 4:10 (10–12);
    5:23 (22–26).

  b Hel. 5:29 (28–36);
    3 Ne. 11:3 (3–14).
34a OR attempted.
  b 1 Ne. 17:34 (33–35).
  c HEB trials, tests.
    TG Test.
  d 1 Ne. 17:30 (26–32).
  e Ps. 136:12.
  f Jer. 21:5.
35a 1 Kgs. 8:60.
  b 1 Sam. 2:2 (1–10).
36a TG Edification.
  b TG God, Manifestations of.

heardest his words out of the midst of the fire.

37 And because he [a]loved thy fathers, therefore he chose their seed after them, and brought thee out in his sight with his mighty power out of [b]Egypt;

38 To [a]drive out nations from before thee greater and mightier than thou *art*, to bring thee in, to give thee their land *for* an [b]inheritance, as *it is* this day.

39 Know therefore this day, and consider *it* in thine heart, that the LORD he *is* [a]God in heaven above, and upon the earth beneath: *there is* none else.

40 Thou shalt [a]keep therefore his statutes, and his commandments, which I command thee this day, that it may go well with thee, and with thy children after thee, and that thou mayest [b]prolong *thy* [c]days upon the [d]earth, which the LORD thy God giveth thee, for ever.

41 ¶ Then Moses [a]severed three cities on this side Jordan [b]toward the sunrising;

42 That the slayer might flee thither, which should kill his neighbour [a]unawares, and hated him not in times past; and that fleeing unto one of these cities he might [b]live:

43 *Namely*, Bezer in the wilderness, [a]in the [b]plain country, of the Reubenites; and Ramoth in Gilead, of the Gadites; and Golan in Bashan, of the Manassites.

44 ¶ And this *is* the law which Moses set before the children of Israel:

45 These *are* the testimonies, and the statutes, and the judgments, which Moses spake unto the children of Israel, after they came forth out of Egypt,

46 On this side Jordan, in the valley over against Beth-peor, in the land of Sihon king of the Amorites, who dwelt at Heshbon, whom Moses and the children of Israel smote, after they were come forth out of Egypt:

47 And they possessed his land, and the land of Og king of Bashan, two kings of the Amorites, which *were* on this side Jordan toward the sunrising;

48 From Aroer, which *is* by the bank of the river [a]Arnon, even unto mount [b]Sion, which *is* [c]Hermon,

49 And all [a]the plain on this side Jordan eastward, even unto [b]the sea of the plain, [c]under the springs of Pisgah.

CHAPTER 5

Moses tells of the covenant God made with Israel in Horeb—He reviews the Ten Commandments—Sabbath observance also commemorates the deliverance from Egypt—God talks with man—Blessings flow from obedience.

AND Moses called all Israel, and said unto them, Hear, O Israel, the [a]statutes and [b]judgments which I speak in your ears this day, that ye may learn them, and keep, and do them.

2 The LORD our God made a [a]covenant with us in Horeb.

3 The LORD made not this [a]covenant with our fathers, but with us, *even* us, who *are* all of us here alive this day.

4 The LORD talked with you [a]face

37a TG God, Love of.
  b 1 Ne. 17:40 (23–40).
38a D&C 101:80 (77–80).
  b TG Lands of Inheritance.
39a Josh. 2:11;
    1 Kgs. 8:23;
    Mosiah 4:9.
40a TG Obedience.
  b Deut. 22:7; 25:15;
    D&C 5:33.
  c TG Mortality.
  d HEB land.
41a OR set apart.

  b OR in the east.
42a HEB unintentionally.
  b TG Refuge.
43a HEB on the plateau.
  b Deut. 3:10.
48a Num. 21:24;
    Deut. 3:16 (15–17);
    Josh. 13:9 (7–12).
  b Some Hebrew texts:
    Sirion.
  c Deut. 3:9 (8–9).
49a HEB the Arabah beyond
    Jordan.

  b IE the Dead Sea.
    Num. 34:12; Deut. 3:17.
  c HEB at the foot of the
    slopes of Pisgah.
5 1a TG Commandments
    of God.
  b HEB the ordinances
    (also v. 31).
2a Ex. 20:1 (1–17).
3a Deut. 29:1.
4a Moses 1:31; 7:4;
    Abr. 3:11.
    TG God, Presence of.

to face in the mount out of the midst of the [b]fire,

5 (I stood between the LORD and you at that time, to [a]shew you the word of the LORD: for ye were [b]afraid by reason of the fire, and went not up into the mount;) saying,

6 ¶ [a]I *am* the LORD thy God, which brought thee out of the land of Egypt, from the house of bondage.

7 Thou shalt have none other gods before me.

8 Thou shalt not make thee *any* graven image, *or* any likeness *of any thing* that *is* in heaven above, or that *is* in the earth beneath, or that *is* in the waters beneath the earth:

9 Thou shalt not bow down thyself unto them, nor serve them: for I the LORD thy God *am* a jealous God, visiting [a]the iniquity of the fathers upon the children unto the third and fourth [b]*generation* of them that [c]hate me,

10 And shewing [a]mercy unto thousands of them that [b]love me and keep my commandments.

11 Thou shalt not take the name of the LORD thy God in vain: for the LORD will not hold *him* guiltless that taketh his name in vain.

12 Keep the [a]sabbath day to sanctify it, as the LORD thy God hath commanded thee.

13 Six days thou shalt labour, and do all thy work:

14 But the seventh day *is* the sabbath of the LORD thy God: *in it* thou shalt not do any work, thou, nor thy son, nor thy daughter, nor thy manservant, nor thy maidservant, nor thine ox, nor thine ass, nor any of thy cattle, nor thy stranger that *is* within thy gates; that thy man-

servant and thy maidservant may rest as well as thou.

15 And remember that thou wast a servant in the land of Egypt, and *that* the LORD thy God brought thee out thence through a mighty hand and by a stretched out arm: therefore the LORD thy God commanded thee to keep the sabbath day.

16 ¶ [a]Honour thy father and thy mother, as the LORD thy God hath commanded thee; that thy days may be prolonged, and that it may go well with thee, in the land which the LORD thy God giveth thee.

17 Thou shalt not [a]kill.

18 Neither shalt thou commit [a]adultery.

19 Neither shalt thou [a]steal.

20 Neither shalt thou bear [a]false witness against thy neighbour.

21 Neither shalt thou [a]desire thy neighbour's wife, neither shalt thou [b]covet thy neighbour's house, his field, or his manservant, or his maidservant, his ox, or his ass, or any *thing* that *is* thy neighbour's.

22 ¶ These words the LORD spake unto all your assembly in the mount out of the midst of the fire, of the cloud, and of the thick darkness, with a great voice: and he added no more. And he [a]wrote them in two [b]tables of stone, and delivered them unto me.

23 And it came to pass, when ye [a]heard the voice out of the midst of the darkness, (for the mountain did burn with fire,) that ye came near unto me, *even* all the heads of your tribes, and your elders;

24 And ye said, Behold, the LORD our God hath [a]shewed us his [b]glory and his greatness, and we have heard his [c]voice out of the midst of

4b Ex. 3:2 (2–4); 19:18.
5a HEB declare to.
  b Ex. 3·6; 20:18 (18–21);
    Matt. 17:6 (5–7).
6a Ex. 20:2 (2–17);
    Mosiah 13:12 (12–24).
9a IE the effects of sin.
  b D&C 124:50.
  c TG Accountability;
    Hate.
10a TG Mercy.

    b TG God, Love of.
12a TG Sabbath.
16a TG Honoring Father and
    Mother.
17a TG Murder.
18a TG Adulterer.
19a TG Stealing.
20a TG Lying.
21a TG Covet.
  b HEB desire.
22a TG Scriptures,

    Writing of.
  b TG Law of Moses.
23a Ex. 19:9 (7–13);
    Deut. 4:10 (10–12),
    33 (33, 36).
24a TG Jesus Christ,
    Appearances,
    Antemortal.
  b TG Glory.
  c TG God, Manifesta-
    tions of.

the fire: we have seen this day that God doth talk with man, and he ^dliveth.

25 Now therefore why should we die? for this great fire will consume us: if we hear the ^avoice of the LORD our God any more, then we shall die.

26 For who *is there of* all flesh, that hath heard the voice of the living God speaking out of the midst of the fire, as we *have,* and lived?

27 Go thou near, and hear all that the LORD our God shall say: and ^aspeak thou unto us all that the LORD our God shall speak unto thee; and we will hear *it,* and ^bdo *it.*

28 And the LORD heard the voice of your words, when ye spake unto me; and the LORD said unto me, I have heard the voice of the words of this people, which they have spoken unto thee: they have well said all that they have spoken.

29 O that there were such an ^aheart in them, that they would ^bfear me, and keep all my commandments always, that it might be well with them, and with their children for ever!

30 Go say to them, Get you into your tents again.

31 But as for thee, stand thou here by me, and I will speak unto thee all the ^acommandments, and the ^bstatutes, and the judgments, which thou shalt teach them, that they may do *them* in the land which I give them to possess it.

32 Ye shall ^aobserve to do therefore as the LORD your God hath commanded you: ye shall not ^bturn aside to the right hand or to the left.

33 Ye shall ^awalk in all the ways which the LORD your God hath commanded you, that ye may live, and *that it may be* well with you, and *that* ye may prolong *your* days in the land which ye shall possess.

CHAPTER 6

Moses proclaims, The Lord our God is one Lord, and, Thou shalt love the Lord thy God—The children of Israel are commanded to teach their children—Moses exhorts them to keep the commandments, testimonies, and statutes of the Lord that they may prosper.

Now these *are* the commandments, the ^astatutes, and the ^bjudgments, which the LORD your God commanded to teach you, that ye might do *them* in the land whither ye go to possess it:

2 That thou mightest fear the LORD thy God, to keep all his statutes and his commandments, which I command thee, thou, and thy son, and thy son's son, all the days of thy life; and that thy days may be ^aprolonged.

3 ¶ Hear therefore, O Israel, and ^aobserve to do *it;* that it may be well with thee, and that ye may increase mightily, as the LORD God of thy fathers hath promised thee, in the land that floweth with milk and honey.

4 ^aHear, O Israel: The LORD our God *is* ^bone LORD:

5 And thou shalt ^alove the LORD thy God with all thine ^bheart, and with all thy soul, and with all thy ^cmight.

6 And these ^awords, which I command thee this day, shall be in thine ^bheart:

24*d* Ps. 18:46.
25*a* Ex. 20:19;
     Deut. 18:16.
27*a* D&C 1:38.
  b TG Obedience.
29*a* 1 Chr. 29:19.
  b Job 1:1;
     Mosiah 15:26 (26–27);
     D&C 1:7.
31*a* TG Commandments of
     God.
  b Ezek. 20:19.

32*a* TG Duty.
  b Deut. 17:20; 28:14.
33*a* TG Walking with God.
6 1*a* Ezek. 20:19.
  b HEB ordinances (also
     v. 20).
  2*a* Alma 9:18 (16–18).
  3*a* TG Obedience.
  4*a* Mark 12:29.
  b 1 Ne. 13:41;
     2 Ne. 31:21;
     Mosiah 15:4 (2–4).

5*a* Deut. 11:1; 2 Kgs. 23:25;
     Mark 12:30;
     D&C 11:20.
     TG God, Love of; Love.
  b TG Commitment; Heart.
  c D&C 20:31.
6*a* Deut. 11:18;
     2 Chr. 34:21;
     1 Ne. 15:24 (23–24);
     Mosiah 1:5;
     D&C 88:62.
  b Deut. 32:46; Moro. 10:3.

7 And thou shalt ^ateach them diligently unto thy children, and shalt ^btalk of them when thou sittest in thine house, and when thou walkest by the way, and when thou liest down, and when thou risest up.

8 And thou shalt ^abind them for a ^bsign upon thine hand, and they shall be as ^cfrontlets between thine eyes.

9 And thou shalt write them upon the ^aposts of thy house, and on thy gates.

10 And it shall be, when the LORD thy God shall have brought thee into the land which he sware unto thy fathers, to Abraham, to Isaac, and to Jacob, to give thee great and goodly cities, which thou buildedst not,

11 And houses full of all good *things,* which thou filledst not, and wells digged, which thou diggedst not, vineyards and olive trees, which thou plantedst not; when thou shalt have eaten and be full;

12 *Then* beware lest thou ^aforget the LORD, which brought thee forth out of the land of Egypt, from the house of bondage.

13 Thou shalt ^afear the LORD thy God, and ^bserve him, and shalt ^cswear by his name.

14 Ye shall not go after ^aother ^bgods, of the gods of the people which *are* round about you;

15 (For the LORD thy God *is* a ^ajealous God among you) lest the ^banger of the LORD thy God be kindled against thee, and destroy thee from off the face of the earth.

16 ¶ Ye shall not ^atempt the LORD your God, as ye tempted *him* in Massah.

17 Ye shall ^adiligently keep the ^bcommandments of the LORD your God, and his testimonies, and his statutes, which he hath commanded thee.

18 And thou shalt do *that which is* ^aright and good in the sight of the LORD: that it may be well with thee, and that thou mayest go in and possess the good land which the LORD ^bsware unto thy fathers,

19 To ^acast out all thine enemies from before thee, as the LORD hath spoken.

20 *And* when thy son ^aasketh thee in time to come, saying, What *mean* the ^btestimonies, and the statutes, and the judgments, which the LORD our God hath commanded you?

21 Then thou shalt say unto thy ^ason, We were Pharaoh's bondmen in Egypt; and the LORD brought us out of Egypt with a mighty hand:

22 And the LORD shewed signs and wonders, great and ^asore, upon Egypt, upon Pharaoh, and upon all his household, before our eyes:

23 And he brought us out from thence, that he might bring us in, to

7a Eph. 6:4 (1–4).
   TG Family, Children, Responsibilities toward; Teaching.
  b 1 Chr. 16:9; D&C 19:29 (29–31).
8a Prov. 3:3; 6:21; 7:3 (1–4).
  b IE phylacteries: passages of the law written on scrolls of parchment enclosed in tiny boxes, bound on the left arm and on the forehead, as an ordinance of remembrance of the Mosaic law, and worn by Jews during the morning prayers.
  c Ex. 13:9, 16; Deut. 11:18; Matt. 23:5 (1–22).

9a IE *mezuzot*: passages of the law written on tiny scrolls, enclosed in a small container and nailed to the right door post or gate, as an ordinance of remembrance. Deut. 11:20.
12a Alma 46:8 (8–9).
13a Josh. 4:24; D&C 76:5.
   TG Worship.
  b Deut. 7:4; 1 Sam. 7:3; D&C 4:2; 20:19.
   TG Service.
  c IE make oaths. Isa. 45:23.
14a Ex. 20:3.
  b D&C 20:19.

15a Ex. 20:5; Mosiah 11:22.
  b TG God, Indignation of.
16a HEB put to the test. TG Doubt; Jesus Christ, Temptation of; Test.
17a TG Diligence.
  b TG Commandments of God.
18a D&C 58:27 (26–28).
  b OR promised (also v. 23).
19a Ex. 23:24; Num. 33:52 (52–53).
20a Ex. 13:14.
  b TG Testimony.
21a Ex. 12:26 (25–27).
22a OR grievous.

give us the land which he sware unto our fathers.

24 And the L**ORD** *a*commanded us to do all these statutes, to *b*fear the L**ORD** our God, for our *c*good always, that he might *d*preserve us alive, as *it is* at this day.

25 And it shall be our *a*righteousness, if we *b*observe to do all these commandments before the L**ORD** our God, as he hath commanded us.

CHAPTER 7

Israel is to destroy the seven nations of Canaan—Marriages with them are forbidden lest apostasy result—Israel has a mission as a holy and chosen people—The Lord shows mercy unto those who love Him and keep His commandments—He promises to remove sickness from the children of Israel if they obey.

W**HEN** the L**ORD** thy God shall bring thee into the land whither thou goest to possess it, and hath cast out many nations before thee, the Hittites, and the Girgashites, and the Amorites, and the Canaanites, and the Perizzites, and the Hivites, and the Jebusites, seven *a*nations greater and mightier than thou;

2 And when the L**ORD** thy God shall deliver them before thee; thou shalt smite them, *and* utterly *a*destroy them; thou shalt *b*make no *c*covenant with them, nor shew mercy unto them:

3 Neither shalt thou make *a*marriages with them; thy daughter thou shalt not give unto his son,

nor his daughter shalt thou take unto thy son.

4 For they will *a*turn away thy son from following me, that they may *b*serve other gods: so will the *c*anger of the L**ORD** be kindled against you, and destroy thee suddenly.

5 But thus shall ye deal with them; ye shall *a*destroy their altars, and break down their *b*images, and cut down their *c*groves, and burn their graven images with fire.

6 For thou *art* *a*an *b*holy people unto the L**ORD** thy God: the L**ORD** thy God hath *c*chosen thee to be a *d*special people unto himself, above all people that *are* upon the face of the earth.

7 The L**ORD** did not set his love upon you, nor choose you, because ye were more in number than any people; for ye *were* the fewest of all people:

8 But because the L**ORD** *a*loved you, and because he would keep the *b*oath which he had sworn unto your fathers, hath the L**ORD** brought you out with a mighty hand, and *c*redeemed you out of the house of bondmen, from the hand of Pharaoh king of Egypt.

9 Know therefore that the L**ORD** thy God, he *is* God, the faithful God, which *a*keepeth covenant and *b*mercy with them that love him and keep his commandments to a thousand generations;

10 And *a*repayeth them that hate him to their face, to *b*destroy them: he will not be slack to him that *c*hateth him, he will repay him to his face.

24*a* TG Commandments
    of God.
 b TG Reverence.
 c Deut. 10:13;
    Jer. 32:39;
    D&C 130:21.
 d Ps. 41:2 (1–2);
    Alma 11:37.
25*a* TG Righteousness.
 b Ex. 34:11.
    TG Watch.
7 1*a* Lev. 20:23.
 2*a* Deut. 2:34;
    Josh. 6:21; 9:24.
 b Alma 5:57.
 c Ex. 23:32 (31–33).

3*a* TG Marriage, Interfaith;
    Marriage, Temporal.
4*a* TG Apostasy of Israel.
 b Deut. 6:13 (13–15);
    D&C 4:2.
 c TG God, Indignation of.
5*a* Ex. 34:13.
 b HEB pillars.
    TG Idolatry.
 c HEB *asherim*; i.e.,
    fertility deities.
    Judg. 6:25.
6*a* OR a nation consecrated to.
 b Ezra 9:2;
    Isa. 63:18.

 c TG Israel, Blessings of;
    Israel, Mission of.
 d TG Peculiar People;
    Separation.
8*a* TG God, Love of;
    Love.
 b TG Covenants;
    Oath.
 c Ps. 107:2.
9*a* 1 Kgs. 8:23;
    Neh. 1:5; 9:32;
    Dan. 9:4.
 b TG God, Mercy of.
10*a* TG Punish.
 b 1 Ne. 17:35 (32–38).
 c TG Hate.

11 Thou shalt therefore keep the commandments, and the statutes, and the ^ajudgments, which I ^bcommand thee this day, to do them.

12 ¶ Wherefore it shall come to pass, if ye ^ahearken to these ^bjudgments, and keep, and do them, that the LORD thy God shall keep unto thee the ^ccovenant and the mercy which he sware unto thy fathers:

13 And he will ^alove thee, and bless thee, and ^bmultiply thee: he will also bless the fruit of thy womb, and the ^cfruit of thy land, thy ^dcorn, and thy wine, and thine oil, the increase of thy kine, and the flocks of thy sheep, in the land which he sware unto thy fathers to give thee.

14 Thou shalt be blessed above all people: there shall not be male or female ^abarren among you, or among your cattle.

15 And the LORD will take away from thee all ^asickness, and will put none of the evil ^bdiseases of Egypt, which thou knowest, upon thee; but will lay them upon all *them* that hate thee.

16 And thou shalt consume all the people which the LORD thy God shall deliver thee; thine eye shall have no pity upon them: neither shalt thou serve their ^agods; for that *will be* a snare unto thee.

17 If thou shalt say in thine heart, These nations *are* more than I; how can I dispossess them?

18 Thou shalt not be afraid of them: *but* shalt well remember what the LORD thy God did unto Pharaoh, and unto all Egypt;

19 The great ^atemptations which thine eyes saw, and the signs, and the ^bwonders, and the mighty hand, and the stretched out arm, whereby the LORD thy God brought thee out: so shall the LORD thy God do unto all the people of whom thou art afraid.

20 Moreover the LORD thy God will send the hornet among them, until they that are left, and hide themselves from thee, be destroyed.

21 Thou shalt not be affrighted at them: for the LORD thy God *is* among you, a mighty God and ^aterrible.

22 And the LORD thy God will ^aput out those nations before thee by little and little: thou mayest not consume them at once, lest the ^bbeasts of the field increase upon thee.

23 But the LORD thy God shall ^adeliver them unto thee, and shall ^bdestroy them with a mighty destruction, until they be destroyed.

24 And he shall deliver their kings into thine hand, and thou shalt destroy their name from under heaven: there shall no man be able to stand before thee, until thou have destroyed them.

25 The graven images of their gods shall ye burn with fire: thou shalt not desire the silver or gold *that is* on them, nor take *it* unto thee, lest thou be snared therein: for it *is* an abomination to the LORD thy God.

26 Neither shalt thou bring an abomination into thine house, lest thou be a cursed thing like it: *but* thou shalt utterly detest it, and thou shalt utterly abhor it; for it *is* a cursed thing.

CHAPTER 8

The Lord tested the children of Israel in the wilderness for forty years—Eating manna taught them that man lives by the word of God—Their clothing did not wear out—The Lord chastened them—If they serve other gods, they will perish.

ALL the commandments which I ^acommand thee this day shall ye

---

11 a HEB ordinances.
  b TG Duty.
12 a TG Obedience.
  b 2 Sam. 22:23.
  c Jer. 11:5.
13 a TG God, Love of.
  b TG Birth Control.
  c Hosea 2:8.
  d HEB grain.

14 a TG Barren.
15 a TG Sickness.
  b Ex. 15:26.
16 a 2 Kgs. 17:35 (33–36).
19 a HEB trials.
  TG Test.
  b Deut. 29:3.
21 a OR awesome.
  Ps. 47:2.

22 a Ex. 23:29 (27–30).
  b HEB wild animals become too numerous for you.
23 a D&C 98:29.
  b HEB throw them into great tumults.
8 1 a D&C 93:20.

observe to do, that ye may live, and multiply, and go in and possess the land which the LORD sware unto your fathers.

2 And thou shalt remember all the way which the LORD thy God led thee these forty years in the wilderness, to ᵃhumble thee, *and* to ᵇprove thee, to know what *was* in thine heart, whether thou wouldest keep his commandments, or no.

3 And he ᵃhumbled thee, and suffered thee to hunger, and fed thee with ᵇmanna, which thou knewest not, neither did thy fathers know; that he might make thee know that ᶜman doth not live by ᵈbread only, but by every ᵉ*word* that proceedeth out of the mouth of the LORD doth man live.

4 ᵃThy raiment waxed not old upon thee, neither did thy foot swell, these forty years.

5 Thou shalt also consider in thine heart, that, as a man ᵃchasteneth his son, *so* the LORD thy God chasteneth thee.

6 Therefore thou shalt keep the commandments of the LORD thy God, to ᵃwalk in his ways, and to fear him.

7 For the LORD thy God bringeth thee into a ᵃgood ᵇland, a land of brooks of water, of ᶜfountains and depths that spring out of valleys and hills;

8 A land of wheat, and barley, and vines, and fig trees, and pomegranates; a land of ᵃoil olive, and honey;

9 A land wherein thou shalt eat bread without scarceness, thou shalt not lack any *thing* in it; a land

whose stones *are* iron, and out of whose hills thou mayest dig ᵃbrass.

10 When thou hast eaten and art full, then thou shalt bless the LORD thy God for the good land which he hath given thee.

11 Beware that thou ᵃforget not the LORD thy God, in not keeping his commandments, and his ᵇjudgments, and his statutes, which I command thee this day:

12 Lest *when* thou hast eaten and art full, and hast built goodly houses, and dwelt *therein*;

13 And *when* thy herds and thy flocks multiply, and thy silver and thy gold is multiplied, and all that thou hast is multiplied;

14 Then thine ᵃheart be ᵇlifted up, and thou ᶜforget the LORD thy God, which brought thee forth out of the land of Egypt, from the house of bondage;

15 Who led thee through that great and terrible wilderness, *wherein were* fiery ᵃserpents, and scorpions, and ᵇdrought, where *there was* no water; who brought thee forth ᶜwater out of the rock of flint;

16 Who fed thee in the wilderness with ᵃmanna, which thy fathers knew not, that he might humble thee, and that he might ᵇprove thee, to do thee good at thy latter end;

17 And thou say in thine heart, My power and the might of *mine* hand hath gotten me this wealth.

18 But thou shalt remember the LORD thy God: for *it is* he that giveth thee power to get ᵃwealth, that he may establish his covenant which he sware unto thy fathers, as *it is* this day.

2a TG Humility.
 b Ex. 15:25 (23–26);
   2 Chr. 32:31 (20, 22, 31).
   TG Test.
3a TG Humility.
 b Neh. 9:20;
   1 Ne. 17:28.
   TG Jesus Christ, Types of, in Anticipation.
 c Matt. 4:4; Luke 4:4;
   D&C 84:44 (43–44).
 d TG Bread; Bread of Life.
 e TG Revelation;

   Scriptures, Study of.
4a OR Your clothing did not wear out.
5a TG Chastening.
6a TG Walking with God.
7a Ex. 3:8.
 b TG Israel, Land of.
 c OR springs and water recesses.
   Deut. 33:28.
8a IE olive trees.
9a HEB bronze, copper, brass.

11a Hel. 12:2 (1–6).
 b HEB ordinances.
14a TG Pride.
 b 2 Kgs. 14:10.
 c TG Ingratitude.
15a Num. 21:6 (4–9);
   1 Ne. 17:41;
   Ether 9:33 (31–33).
 b TG Drought.
 c 1 Ne. 17:29.
16a Hosea 13:6 (5–8).
 b TG Test.
18a TG Treasure.

19 And it shall be, if thou do at all forget the LORD thy God, and *a*walk after other *b*gods, and serve them, and worship them, I testify against you this day that ye shall surely *c*perish.

20 As the nations which the LORD destroyeth before your face, so shall ye perish; because ye would not be *a*obedient unto the voice of the LORD your God.

CHAPTER 9

Other nations are driven out of Canaan because of their wickedness—Moses rehearses the rebellions of Israel and tells how he mediated between the people and the Lord—On two occasions he went without food and water for forty days.

HEAR, O Israel: Thou *art* to pass over Jordan this day, to go in to *a*possess nations greater and mightier than thyself, cities great and *b*fenced up to heaven,

2 A people great and tall, the children of the *a*Anakims, whom thou knowest, and *of whom* thou hast heard *say*, Who can stand before the children of Anak!

3 Understand therefore this day, that the LORD thy God *is* he which goeth over *a*before thee; *as* a consuming fire he shall destroy them, and he shall *b*bring them down before thy face: so shalt thou drive them out, and destroy them quickly, as the LORD hath said unto thee.

4 Speak not thou in thine heart, after that the LORD thy God hath cast them out from before thee, saying, For my *a*righteousness the LORD hath *b*brought me in to possess this land: but for the *c*wickedness of these nations the LORD doth drive them out from before thee.

5 Not for thy *a*righteousness, or for the uprightness of thine heart, dost thou go to possess their land: but for the wickedness of these nations the LORD thy God doth drive them out from before thee, and that he may perform the word which the LORD sware unto thy fathers, Abraham, Isaac, and Jacob.

6 Understand therefore, that the LORD thy God giveth thee not this good land to possess it for thy righteousness; for thou *art* a *a*stiffnecked people.

7 ¶ Remember, *and* forget not, how thou provokedst the LORD thy God to wrath in the wilderness: from the day that thou didst depart out of the land of Egypt, until ye came unto this place, ye have been *a*rebellious against the LORD.

8 Also in Horeb ye provoked the LORD to wrath, so that the LORD was angry with you *a*to have *b*destroyed you.

9 When I was gone up into the mount to receive the tables of stone, *even* the tables of the covenant which the LORD made with you, then I abode in the mount *a*forty days and forty nights, I neither did eat bread nor drink water:

10 And the LORD delivered unto me two tables of stone *a*written with the finger of God; and on them *was written* according to all the words, which the LORD *b*spake with you in the mount out of the midst of the fire in the *c*day of the assembly.

11 And it came to pass at the end of forty days and forty nights, *that* the LORD gave me the two tables of stone, *even* the tables of the covenant.

19*a* TG Walking in Darkness.
 b TG Idolatry.
 c Ezek. 5:11 (5–17).
20*a* TG Disobedience.
9 1*a* Num. 33:54 (50–56); Deut. 12:10 (10–19).
 b Num. 13:28.
2*a* Deut. 2:11 (10–11).
3*a* Judg. 4:14.

 b HEB subdue them before you.
4*a* TG Blessing.
 b 1 Ne. 17:38 (32–38).
 c TG Sin.
5*a* Ezek. 36:22.
 TG Righteousness.
6*a* TG Stiffnecked.
7*a* TG Apostasy of Israel.
8*a* OR and would have.

 b Lev. 26:21 (14–33); Ps. 66:11 (10–12).
9*a* Ex. 24:18; 32:1; 34:28.
10*a* 2 Cor. 3:3.
 TG Scriptures, Writing of.
 b TG God, Manifestations of.
 c Deut. 4:10.

12 And the LORD said unto me, Arise, get thee down quickly from hence; for thy people which thou hast brought forth out of Egypt have ᵃcorrupted *themselves*; they are quickly turned aside out of the way which I commanded them; they have made them a molten image.

13 Furthermore the LORD spake unto me, saying, I have seen this people, and, behold, it *is* a ᵃstiffnecked people:

14 Let me alone, that I may ᵃdestroy them, and ᵇblot out their name from under heaven: and I will make of thee a nation mightier and greater than they.

15 So I turned and came down from the mount, and the mount burned with fire: and the two tables of the covenant *were* in my two hands.

16 And I ᵃlooked, and, behold, ye had ᵇsinned against the LORD your God, *and* had made you a molten calf: ye had turned aside quickly out of the way which the LORD had commanded you.

17 And I took the two tables, and cast them out of my two hands, and brake them before your eyes.

18 And I ᵃfell down before the LORD, as at the first, forty days and forty nights: I did neither eat bread, nor drink water, because of all your sins which ye sinned, in doing ᵇwickedly in the sight of the LORD, to provoke him to ᶜanger.

19 For I was afraid of the anger and hot displeasure, wherewith the LORD was wroth against you to ᵃdestroy you. But the LORD ᵇhearkened unto me at that time also.

20 And the LORD was very ᵃangry with Aaron to have destroyed him: and I prayed for Aaron also the same time.

21 And I took your ᵃsin, the calf which ye had made, and burnt it with fire, and ᵇstamped it, *and* ground *it* very small, *even* until it was as small as dust: and I cast the dust thereof into the brook that descended out of the mount.

22 And at Taberah, and at Massah, and at Kibroth-hattaavah, ye ᵃprovoked the LORD to wrath.

23 Likewise when the LORD sent you from Kadesh-barnea, saying, Go up and possess the land which I have given you; then ye ᵃrebelled against the commandment of the LORD your God, and ye believed him not, nor hearkened to his voice.

24 Ye have been ᵃrebellious against the LORD from the day that I knew you.

25 Thus I fell down before the LORD forty days and forty nights, as I fell down *at the first*; because the LORD had said he would destroy you.

26 I ᵃprayed therefore unto the LORD, and said, O Lord GOD, destroy not thy people and thine ᵇinheritance, which thou hast redeemed through thy greatness, which thou hast brought forth out of Egypt with a mighty hand.

27 Remember thy servants, Abraham, Isaac, and Jacob; look not unto the ᵃstubbornness of this people, nor to their wickedness, nor to their sin:

28 Lest the ᵃland whence thou broughtest us out say, Because the LORD was not able to bring them into the land which he promised them, and because he hated them, he hath brought them out to slay them in the wilderness.

12a Ex. 32:7 (7–10).
13a 2 Kgs. 17:14;
　　Jacob 4:14.
14a Ex. 32:10 (9–10).
　b Ps. 9:5;
　　Alma 5:57;
　　D&C 20:83 (82–83).
16a Ex. 32:19 (19–20).
　b Ex. 20:23; 32:8;
　　Neh. 9:18.

18a HEB lay prostrate (also
　　v. 25).
　　Ex. 32:11.
　b TG Evil.
　c TG Anger.
19a Ex. 32:10 (10–11).
　b Ex. 32:12.
20a Ex. 32:22 (21–24).
21a Ex. 32:20.
　b OR crushed.

22a Ex. 17:7 (4–7);
　　Num. 11:1 (1–2),
　　34 (21–34).
23a Num. 14:2 (1–45);
　　D&C 84:24.
24a TG Rebellion.
26a Ex. 32:32 (31–32).
　b TG Inheritance.
27a TG Stubbornness.
28a Ex. 32:12.

29 Yet they *are* thy ᵃpeople and thine ᵇinheritance, which thou broughtest out by thy mighty power and by thy stretched out arm.

CHAPTER 10

The tables of stone containing the Ten Commandments are placed in the ark— All that God requires is that Israel love and serve Him—How great and mighty is the Lord!

AT that time the LORD said unto me, Hew thee two ᵃtables of stone like unto the first, and come up unto me into the mount, and make thee an ᵇark of wood.

2 And I will ᵃwrite on the tables the words that were in the first tables ᵇwhich thou brakest, and thou shalt put them in the ark.

3 And I made an ark *of* ᵃshittim wood, and hewed two ᵇtables of stone like unto the first, and went up into the mount, having the two tables in mine hand.

4 And he ᵃwrote on the tables, according to the first writing, the ten commandments, which the LORD spake unto you in the mount out of the midst of the fire in the day of the assembly: and the LORD gave them unto me.

5 And I turned myself and came down from the mount, and put the tables in the ark which I had made; and there they be, as the LORD commanded me.

6 ¶ And the children of Israel took their journey from Beeroth of the children of Jaakan to Mosera: there ᵃAaron died, and there he was buried; and Eleazar his son ministered in the priest's office in his stead.

7 From thence they journeyed unto Gudgodah; and from Gudgodah to ᵃJotbath, a land of ᵇrivers of waters.

8 ¶ At that time the LORD ᵃseparated the tribe of ᵇLevi, to ᶜbear the ark of the covenant of the LORD, to stand before the LORD to minister unto him, and to ᵈbless in his name, unto this day.

9 Wherefore ᵃLevi hath no ᵇpart nor inheritance with his brethren; the LORD *is* his ᶜinheritance, according as the LORD thy God promised him.

10 And I stayed in the mount, according to the first time, forty days and forty nights; and the LORD hearkened unto me at that time also, *and* the LORD would not destroy thee.

11 And the LORD said unto me, Arise, take *thy* ᵃjourney before the people, that they may go in and possess the land, which I sware unto their fathers to give unto them.

12 ¶ And now, Israel, what doth the LORD thy God ᵃrequire of thee, but to ᵇfear the LORD thy God, to walk in all his ways, and to love him, and to ᶜserve the LORD thy God with all thy ᵈheart and with all thy soul,

13 To keep the ᵃcommandments of the LORD, and his statutes, which I command thee this day for thy ᵇgood?

14 Behold, the heaven and the ᵃheaven of heavens *is* the LORD's

---

29a Ex. 33:13.
   b TG Inheritance.
10 1a Ex. 31:18; 34:1 (1–2);
     JST Ex. 34:1–2
     (Appendix).
   b OR cabinet, chest (also
     vv. 3, 5).
     Ex. 25:10.
  2a 2 Ne. 3:17;
     Morm. 8:4 (4–5);
     D&C 76:80; Moses 2:1.
   b JST Deut. 10:2 . . .
     which thou brakest,
     save the words of the
     everlasting covenant of
     the holy priesthood, and

thou shalt . . .
3a OR acacia.
  b Ex. 34:4 (1–5).
4a TG Scriptures,
   Writing of.
6a Num. 20:28 (22–29).
7a Num. 33:33 (33–34).
  b HEB streams, brooks.
8a OR set apart.
   TG Setting Apart.
  b Num. 3:6 (5–13);
   Ezek. 44:15;
   3 Ne. 24:3;
   D&C 13; 107:6;
   124:39; 128:24;
   JS—H 1:69.

c Num. 4:15 (2–15);
  1 Chr. 15:2.
d Num. 6:23 (23–27).
9a Deut. 12:19.
  b OR portion.
  c Num. 18:20 (20–24).
11a Ex. 33:1 (1–3).
12a TG Duty.
  b TG Reverence.
  c TG Service; Worship.
  d TG Commitment.
13a TG Commandments
   of God.
  b Deut. 6:24; Jer. 32:39;
   D&C 21:6; 61:13.
14a TG Heaven.

thy God, the *b*earth *also*, with *c*all that therein *is*.

15 *a*Only the LORD had a delight in thy fathers to *b*love them, and he *c*chose their seed after them, *even* you above all people, as *it is* this day.

16 *a*Circumcise therefore the foreskin of your *b*heart, and be no more *c*stiffnecked.

17 For the LORD your *a*God *is* *b*God of gods, and *c*Lord of lords, a great God, a mighty, and a terrible, *d*which *e*regardeth not persons, nor taketh *f*reward:

18 He *a*doth execute the judgment of the fatherless and widow, and *b*loveth the *c*stranger, in giving him *d*food and raiment.

19 *a*Love ye therefore the *b*stranger: for ye were strangers in the land of Egypt.

20 Thou shalt fear the LORD thy God; him shalt thou serve, and to him shalt thou *a*cleave, and *b*swear by his name.

21 He *is* thy praise, and he *is* thy God, that hath done for thee these *a*great and terrible things, which thine eyes have seen.

22 Thy *a*fathers went down into Egypt with threescore and ten persons; and now the LORD thy God hath made thee as the *b*stars of heaven for multitude.

CHAPTER 11

Thou shalt love and obey the Lord thy God—If the children of Israel obey, they will be blessed with rain and harvests and will drive out mighty nations—Israel must learn God's laws and teach them—Blessings flow from obedience; cursings attend disobedience.

THEREFORE thou shalt *a*love the LORD thy God, and keep his *b*charge, and his statutes, and his *c*judgments, and his commandments, alway.

2 And know ye this day: for *I speak* not with your children which have not known, and which have not seen the *a*chastisement of the LORD your God, his greatness, his mighty hand, and his stretched out arm,

3 And his miracles, and his acts, which he did in the midst of Egypt unto Pharaoh the king of Egypt, and unto all his land;

4 And what he did unto the army of Egypt, unto their horses, and to their chariots; how he made the water of the *a*Red sea to overflow them as they pursued after you, and *how* the LORD hath destroyed them unto this day;

5 And what he did unto you in the wilderness, until ye came into this place;

6 And what he did unto *a*Dathan and Abiram, the sons of Eliab, the son of Reuben: how the earth opened her mouth, and swallowed them up, and their households, and their tents, and *b*all the substance that *was* in their possession, in the midst of all Israel:

7 But your eyes have seen all the

14*b* Ex. 9:29;
　Ps. 24:1;
　1 Ne. 11:6; 2 Ne. 29:7;
　D&C 55:1;
　Moses 6:44.
　c TG God, Works of.
15*a* HEB Yet (see context of
　previous verse).
　b TG God, Love of.
　c TG Peculiar People.
16*a* IE Purify your hearts.
　TG Circumcision.
　b Mosiah 4:2.
　c OR stubborn.
　TG Stiffnecked.
17*a* Ps. 136:2 (1–3);
　D&C 76:58;
　121:32 (28–32).
　b Josh. 22:22; Dan. 11:36.

c Rev. 17:14; 19:16 (11–16).
d OR who is not partial.
e 2 Chr. 19:7; Rom. 2:11;
　Alma 1:30; 16:14;
　D&C 1:35;
　Moses 5:21 (20–21).
f OR bribes.
18*a* OR deals justly with.
　b TG God, Love of.
　c OR alien, sojourner (also
　v. 19).
　d TG Food.
19*a* Lev. 19:34 (33–34).
　b TG Stranger.
20*a* Jacob 6:5.
　b OR make an oath in.
21*a* Ex. 34:10;
　D&C 133:43.
22*a* TG Israel, Origins of.

b Gen. 15:5.
11 1*a* Deut. 6:5;
　Mosiah 2:4;
　Moro. 10:32;
　D&C 20:19; 59:5 (5–6).
　b Lev. 8:35; Zech. 3:7;
　D&C 107:99.
　c HEB ordinances (also
　v. 32).
2*a* Mosiah 23:21;
　Hel. 12:3;
　D&C 95:1; 98:21; 105:6.
4*a* HEB Reed Sea.
　Ex. 14:28 (27–28);
　D&C 8:3; 17:1.
6*a* Num. 16:1, 12 (1–32);
　26:9.
　b HEB every living thing
　that followed them.

great acts of the LORD which he did.

8 Therefore shall ye keep all the commandments which I command you this day, that ye may be ^astrong, and go in and ^bpossess the land, whither ye go to possess it;

9 And that ye may ^aprolong *your* days in the land, which the LORD sware unto your ^bfathers to give unto them and to their seed, a land that floweth with milk and honey.

10 ¶ For the land, whither thou goest in to possess it, *is* not as the land of Egypt, from whence ye came out, where thou sowedst thy seed, and wateredst *it* with thy foot, as a garden of ^aherbs:

11 But the ^aland, whither ye go to possess it, *is* a land of hills and valleys, *and* drinketh water of the rain of heaven:

12 A land which the LORD thy God careth for: the eyes of the LORD thy God *are* always upon it, from the beginning of the year even unto the end of the year.

13 ¶ And it shall come to pass, if ye shall hearken diligently unto my commandments which I command you this day, to ^alove the LORD your God, and to ^bserve him with all your heart and with all your soul,

14 That I will give *you* the ^arain of your land in his due season, the ^bfirst rain and the ^clatter rain, that thou mayest gather in thy ^dcorn, and thy wine, and thine oil.

15 And I will send grass in thy fields for thy cattle, that thou mayest eat and be full.

16 Take heed to yourselves, that your heart be not ^adeceived, and ye turn aside, and serve other gods, and worship them;

17 And *then* the LORD's wrath be kindled against you, and he ^ashut up the heaven, that there be no rain, and that the land yield not her fruit; and lest ye ^bperish quickly from off the good land which the LORD giveth you.

18 ¶ Therefore shall ye ^alay up these my ^bwords in your ^cheart and in your soul, and bind them for a sign upon your ^dhand, that they may be as ^efrontlets between your eyes.

19 And ye shall ^ateach them your ^bchildren, speaking of them when thou sittest in thine house, and when thou walkest by the way, when thou liest down, and when thou risest up.

20 And thou shalt write them upon the ^adoor posts of thine house, and upon thy gates:

21 That your days may be multiplied, and the days of your ^achildren, in the land which the LORD sware unto your fathers to give them, ^bas the days of heaven upon the earth.

22 ¶ For if ye shall diligently keep all these commandments which I command you, to do them, to love the LORD your God, to ^awalk in all his ways, and to cleave unto him;

23 Then will the LORD drive out all these nations from before you, and ye shall ^apossess greater nations and mightier than yourselves.

24 Every place whereon the soles of your feet shall tread shall be yours: from the wilderness and Lebanon, from the river, the river

8*a* 1 Ne. 4:2;
  Ether 12:27;
  D&C 38:15.
 b Josh. 1:6 (6–7);
  1 Ne. 10:3;
  Abr. 2:6.
9*a* Ex. 20:12;
  Deut. 11:17 (16–17, 21);
  Alma 9:16;
  Hel. 15:11 (10–11);
  D&C 5:33.
 b Gen. 50:24;
  D&C 27:10; 98:32.
10*a* OR vegetables.
11*a* 3 Ne. 20:33.

13*a* 2 Thes. 3:5.
 b TG Service.
14*a* Deut. 28:12;
  Hel. 11:13.
 b OR early.
 c Joel 2:23;
  Zech. 10:1.
 d HEB grain.
16*a* TG Deceit.
17*a* 1 Kgs. 8:35;
  Job 12:15.
 b Ex. 20:12;
  Deut. 11:9 (8–9).
18*a* Moro. 10:3;
  D&C 11:26; 58:5.

 b Deut. 6:6;
  D&C 8:5.
 c TG Heart.
 d OR arm.
 e Deut. 6:8.
19*a* Eph. 6:4 (1–4).
 b TG Children;
  Family, Children,
  Responsibilities toward.
20*a* Deut. 6:9.
21*a* Ps. 89:29.
 b OR as long as there is a
  heaven above.
22*a* TG Walking with God.
23*a* OR dispossess.

*a*Euphrates, even unto the uttermost sea shall *b*your coast be.

25 There shall no man be able to *a*stand before you: *for the* LORD your God shall lay the fear of you and the dread of you upon all the land that ye shall tread upon, as he hath said unto you.

26 ¶ Behold, I set before you this day a *a*blessing and a *b*curse;

27 A *a*blessing, if ye obey the commandments of the LORD your God, which I command you this day:

28 And a *a*curse, if ye will not *b*obey the commandments of the LORD your God, but turn aside out of the way which I command you this day, to go after other gods, which ye have not known.

29 And it shall come to pass, when the LORD thy God hath brought thee in unto the land whither thou goest to possess it, that thou shalt put the *a*blessing upon mount *b*Gerizim, and the curse upon mount Ebal.

30 *Are* they not on the other side Jordan, by the way where the sun goeth down, in the land of the Canaanites, which dwell in the *a*champaign over against Gilgal, beside the *b*plains of Moreh?

31 For ye shall pass over Jordan to go in to possess the land which the LORD your God giveth you, and ye shall possess it, and dwell therein.

32 And ye shall observe to do all the statutes and judgments which I set before you this day.

CHAPTER 12

Israel is to destroy the Canaanite gods and places of worship—The Lord will designate where His people will worship—The eating of blood is forbid- *den—Israel's worship must conform to the divine standard.*

THESE *are* the statutes and *a*judgments, which ye shall observe to do in the land, which the LORD God of thy fathers giveth thee to possess it, all the days that ye live upon the earth.

2 Ye shall utterly destroy all the *a*places, wherein the nations which ye shall *b*possess served their *c*gods, upon the high mountains, and upon the hills, and under every green tree:

3 And ye shall *a*overthrow their altars, and break their pillars, and burn their *b*groves with fire; and ye shall hew down the graven images of their gods, and destroy the names of them out of that place.

4 Ye shall not do so unto the LORD your God.

5 But unto the *a*place which the LORD your God shall *b*choose out of all your tribes to put his name there, *even* unto his habitation shall ye seek, and thither thou shalt *c*come:

6 And thither ye shall bring your burnt *a*offerings, and your sacrifices, and your *b*tithes, and *c*heave offerings of your hand, and your *d*vows, and your freewill offerings, and the *e*firstlings of your herds and of your flocks:

7 And there ye shall eat before the LORD your God, and ye shall *a*rejoice in all that ye put your hand unto, ye and your households, wherein the LORD thy God hath blessed thee.

8 Ye shall not do after all *the things* that we do here this day, every man whatsoever *is* *a*right in his own eyes.

9 For ye are not as yet come to the rest and to the inheritance, which the LORD your God giveth you.

24*a* Gen. 15:18.
  b HEB be your territory.
25*a* Deut. 28:10 (7–10).
26*a* TG Agency; Blessing.
  b TG Curse.
27*a* Deut. 12:25;
      D&C 130:20 (20–21).
28*a* 1 Ne. 2:23; D&C 41:1.
  b TG Disobedience.
29*a* Deut. 27:12 (12–13);
      Josh. 8:33 (33–35).
  b Judg. 9:7;

John 4:20.
30*a* HEB Arabah (desert descent).
  b HEB oaks.
12 1*a* HEB ordinances.
 2*a* 2 Kgs. 12:3.
  b HEB dispossess.
  c TG Idolatry.
 3*a* Ex. 34:13.
  b HEB *asherim*; i.e., idols, fertility goddesses.
 5*a* Deut. 15:20; 26:2;

1 Kgs. 8:29 (26–30);
 2 Chr. 7:12.
  b 1 Kgs. 11:36.
  c 1 Kgs. 12:27.
 6*a* Ezra 3:2.
  b TG Tithing.
  c HEB given contributions (also vv. 11, 17).
  d OR vowed offerings.
  e Mosiah 2:3.
 7*a* Deut. 26:11.
 8*a* Judg. 17:6; 21:25.

10 But *when* ye go over Jordan, and dwell in the land which the LORD your God giveth you to *a*inherit, and *when* he giveth you *b*rest from all your enemies round about, so that ye dwell in safety;

11 Then there shall be a place which the LORD your God shall choose to cause his name to dwell there; thither shall ye bring all that I command you; your burnt offerings, and your sacrifices, your tithes, and the heave offering of your hand, and all your choice vows which ye vow unto the LORD:

12 And ye shall rejoice before the LORD your God, ye, and your sons, and your daughters, and your menservants, and your maidservants, and the Levite that *is* within your gates; forasmuch as he hath no part nor inheritance with you.

13 Take heed to thyself that thou offer not thy burnt offerings in every place that thou seest:

14 But in the *a*place which the LORD shall choose in one of thy tribes, there thou shalt offer thy burnt offerings, and there thou shalt do all that I command thee.

15 Notwithstanding thou mayest kill and eat *a*flesh in all thy gates, *b*whatsoever thy soul lusteth after, according to the blessing of the LORD thy God which he hath given thee: the *c*unclean and the clean may eat thereof, as of the *d*roebuck, and as of the *e*hart.

16 Only ye shall not eat the blood; ye shall pour it upon the earth as water.

17 ¶ Thou mayest not eat within thy gates the tithe of thy *a*corn, or of thy wine, or of thy oil, or the firstlings of thy herds or of thy flock, nor any of thy vows which thou vowest, nor thy freewill offerings, or heave offering of thine hand:

18 But thou must eat them before the LORD thy God in the place which the LORD thy God shall choose, thou, and thy son, and thy daughter, and thy manservant, and thy maidservant, and the Levite that *is* within thy gates: and thou shalt rejoice before the LORD thy God in all that thou puttest thine hands unto.

19 Take heed to thyself that thou forsake not the *a*Levite as long as thou livest upon the earth.

20 ¶ When the LORD thy God shall enlarge thy *a*border, as he hath promised thee, and thou shalt say, I will eat flesh, because thy soul longeth to eat flesh; thou mayest eat flesh, whatsoever thy soul lusteth after.

21 If the place which the LORD thy God hath chosen to put his name there be too far from thee, then thou shalt kill of thy herd and of thy flock, which the LORD hath given thee, as I have commanded thee, and thou shalt eat in thy gates whatsoever thy soul lusteth after.

22 Even as the roebuck and the hart is eaten, so thou shalt eat them: the unclean and the clean shall eat *of* them alike.

23 Only be sure that thou eat not the blood: for the *a*blood *is* the life; and thou mayest not eat the life with the flesh.

24 Thou shalt not eat it; thou shalt pour it upon the earth as water.

25 Thou shalt not eat it; that it may go *a*well with thee, and with thy children after thee, when thou shalt do *that which is* right in the sight of the LORD.

26 Only thy holy things which thou hast, and thy vows, thou shalt take, and go unto the place which the LORD shall choose:

27 And thou shalt offer thy *a*burnt offerings, the *b*flesh and the blood, upon the altar of the LORD thy God: and the blood of thy sacrifices shall be poured out upon the altar of the

---

10*a* Deut. 9:1 (1–6);
　　Josh. 1:11 (1–18).
　b TG Rest.
14*a* Lev. 17:4 (1–7).
15*a* TG Food;
　　Meat.

b HEB of whatever meat you desire.
c Deut. 15:22.
d OR gazelle.
e OR male deer.
17*a* HEB grain.

19*a* Deut. 10:9 (8–9).
20*a* OR territory.
23*a* TG Blood, Eating of.
25*a* Deut. 11:27 (26–28).
27*a* Lev. 1:13 (11, 13).
　b TG Flesh and Blood.

LORD thy God, and thou shalt eat the flesh.

28 Observe and hear all these words which I command thee, that it may go ^awell with thee, and with thy children after thee for ever, when thou doest *that which is* good and right in the sight of the LORD thy God.

29 ¶ When the LORD thy God shall ^acut off the nations from before thee, whither thou goest to possess them, and thou ^bsucceedest them, and dwellest in their land;

30 Take heed to thyself that thou be not snared by following them, after that they be destroyed from before thee; and that thou inquire not after their gods, saying, How did these nations serve their gods? even so will I do likewise.

31 Thou shalt not do so unto the LORD thy God: for every ^aabomination to the LORD, which he hateth, have they done unto their gods; for even their sons and their daughters they have ^bburnt in the ^cfire to their gods.

32 What thing soever I command you, observe to do it: thou shalt not ^aadd thereto, nor ^bdiminish from it.

CHAPTER 13

The Lord tests His people to see if they will worship false gods—Prophets, dreamers, relatives, or friends who advocate worship of false gods will be put to death—Idolatrous cities will be destroyed.

IF there arise among you a ^aprophet, or a dreamer of ^bdreams, and giveth thee a ^csign or a wonder,

2 And the sign or the wonder come to pass, whereof he spake unto thee, saying, Let us go after other ^agods, which thou hast not known, and let us serve them;

3 Thou shalt not hearken unto the words of that ^aprophet, or that dreamer of dreams: for the LORD your God ^bproveth you, to know whether ye love the LORD your God with all your heart and with all your soul.

4 Ye shall ^awalk after the LORD your God, and fear him, and keep his commandments, and obey his voice, and ye shall serve him, and cleave unto him.

5 And that prophet, or that dreamer of dreams, shall be put to ^adeath; because he hath spoken to ^bturn *you* away from the LORD your God, which brought you out of the land of Egypt, and redeemed you out of the house of bondage, to ^cthrust thee out of the way which the LORD thy God commanded thee to walk in. So shalt thou put the evil away from the midst of thee.

6 ¶ If thy brother, the son of thy mother, or thy ^ason, or thy daughter, or the wife of thy bosom, or thy friend, which *is* as thine own soul, ^bentice thee secretly, saying, Let us go and serve other gods, which thou hast not known, thou, nor thy fathers;

7 *Namely*, of the gods of the people which *are* round about you, nigh unto thee, or far off from thee, from the *one* end of the earth even unto the *other* end of the earth;

8 Thou shalt not ^aconsent unto him, nor hearken unto him; neither shall thine eye pity him, neither shalt thou spare, neither shalt thou conceal him:

9 But thou shalt surely kill him; thine hand shall be ^afirst upon him to put him to death, and afterwards the hand of all the people.

28a 2 Ne. 13:10.
29a 1 Ne. 4:13.
  b HEB dispossessest.
31a Ezra 9:1;
    Jer. 44:4 (4–5).
  b Abr. 1:8.
  c Lev. 18:21;
    Deut. 18:10;
    Jer. 7:31.

32a TG False Doctrine.
  b TG Scriptures,
    Preservation of.
13 1a TG False Prophets.
  b TG Dream.
  c TG Signs.
2a Ex. 22:20.
3a TG False Prophets.
  b TG Test.

4a TG Walking with God.
5a TG Capital Punishment.
  b TG False Doctrine.
  c HEB seduce (also v. 10).
6a Ex. 32:29.
  b TG Peer Influence;
    Temptation.
8a Matt. 10:28.
9a Deut. 17:7.

10 And thou shalt stone him with stones, that he die; because he hath sought to thrust thee away from the LORD thy God, which brought thee out of the land of Egypt, from the house of bondage.

11 And all Israel shall hear, and *a*fear, and shall do no more any such wickedness as this is among you.

12 ¶ If thou shalt hear *say* in one of thy cities, which the LORD thy God hath given thee to dwell there, saying,

13 *Certain* men, the children of *a*Belial, are gone out from among you, and have *b*withdrawn the inhabitants of their city, saying, Let us go and serve other gods, which ye have not known;

14 Then shalt thou inquire, and make search, and ask diligently; and, behold, *if it be* truth, *and* the thing certain, *that* such abomination is wrought among you;

15 Thou shalt surely smite the inhabitants of that city with the edge of the sword, destroying it utterly, and all that *is* therein, and the cattle thereof, with the edge of the sword.

16 And thou shalt gather all the spoil of it into the midst of the street thereof, and shalt burn with fire the city, and all the spoil thereof every whit, for the LORD thy God: and it shall be an heap for ever; it shall not be built again.

17 And *a*there shall cleave nought of the cursed thing to thine hand: that the LORD may turn from the fierceness of his *b*anger, and shew thee mercy, and have compassion upon thee, and multiply thee, as he hath sworn unto thy fathers;

18 When thou shalt hearken to the voice of the LORD thy God, to keep all his commandments which I command thee this day, to do *that which is* right in the eyes of the LORD thy God.

CHAPTER 14

The Israelites are children of the Lord Jehovah—Unclean beasts, fish, and fowl are not to be eaten—The Israelites are to tithe all the increase of their seed annually.

YE *are* the *a*children of the LORD your God: ye shall *b*not *c*cut yourselves, nor make any baldness *d*between your eyes for the dead.

2 For thou *art* an *a*holy people unto the LORD thy God, and the LORD hath chosen thee to be a *b*peculiar people unto himself, above all the nations that *are* upon the earth.

3 ¶ Thou shalt not *a*eat any abominable thing.

4 These *are* the beasts which ye shall *a*eat: the ox, the sheep, and the goat,

5 The hart, and the *a*roebuck, and the fallow deer, and the wild goat, and the pygarg, and the wild ox, and the chamois.

6 And every beast that parteth the hoof, and *a*cleaveth the cleft into two claws, *and* cheweth the cud among the beasts, that ye shall eat.

7 Nevertheless these ye shall not eat of them that chew the cud, or of them that divide the cloven hoof; *as* the camel, and the hare, and the coney: for they chew the cud, but divide not the hoof; *therefore* they *are* unclean unto you.

8 And the swine, because it divideth the hoof, yet cheweth not the cud, it *is* unclean unto you: ye shall not eat of their flesh, nor touch their dead carcase.

9 ¶ These ye shall eat of all that *are* in the waters: all that have fins and scales shall ye eat:

10 And whatsoever hath not fins and scales ye may not eat; it *is* unclean unto you.

11 ¶ Of all clean birds ye shall eat.

12 But these *are they* of which ye

11*a* Deut. 17:13.
13*a* Judg. 20:13;
　　1 Sam. 1:16; 2:12;
　　2 Sam. 16:7; 20:1; Jude 1:19.
　 b HEB seduced.
17*a* HEB you shall not retain any of the confiscated property.

　 b Num. 25:4.
14 1*a* TG Sons and Daughters of God.
　 b Jer. 16:6.
　 c 1 Kgs. 18:28.
　　 TG Body, Sanctity of.
　 d IE on the forehead.
2*a* TG Holiness.

　 b TG Abrahamic Covenant; Peculiar People.
3*a* TG Meat; Word of Wisdom.
4*a* Lev. 11:2 (2–47).
5*a* HEB gazelle.
6*a* IE has a divided hoof, with two "toes."

shall not eat: the eagle, and the ªos-sifrage, and the ospray,

13 And the ªglede, and the kite, and the ᵇvulture after his kind,

14 And every raven after his kind,

15 And the owl, and the night hawk, and the ªcuckow, and the hawk after his kind,

16 The little owl, and the great owl, and the ªswan,

17 And the pelican, and the ªgier eagle, and the cormorant,

18 And the stork, and the heron after her kind, and the ªlapwing, and the bat.

19 And every ªcreeping thing that flieth *is* unclean unto you: they shall not be eaten.

20 *But of* all clean fowls ye may eat.

21 ¶ Ye shall not eat *of* any thing that dieth of itself: thou shalt ªgive it unto the stranger that *is* in thy gates, that he may eat it; or thou mayest ᵇsell it unto an alien: for thou *art* an holy people unto the LORD thy God. Thou shalt not ᶜseethe a kid in his mother's milk.

22 Thou shalt truly ªtithe all the increase of thy seed, that the field bringeth forth year by year.

23 And thou shalt eat before the LORD thy God, in the place which he shall choose to place his name there, the tithe of thy corn, of thy wine, and of thine oil, and the first-lings of thy herds and of thy flocks; that thou mayest learn to fear the LORD thy God always.

24 And if the way be too long for thee, so that thou art not able to carry it; *or* if the place be too far from thee, which the LORD thy God shall choose to set his name there, when the LORD thy God hath blessed thee:

25 Then shalt thou turn *it* into money, and bind up the money in thine hand, and shalt go unto the place which the LORD thy God shall choose:

26 And thou shalt bestow that money for whatsoever thy soul lust-eth after, for oxen, or for sheep, or for wine, or for strong drink, or for whatsoever thy soul desireth: and thou shalt eat there before the LORD thy God, and thou shalt rejoice, thou, and thine household,

27 And the Levite that *is* within thy gates; thou shalt not forsake him; for he hath no part nor inheri-tance with thee.

28 ¶ At the end of three years thou shalt bring forth all the ªtithe of thine increase the same year, and shalt lay *it* up within thy gates:

29 And the Levite, (because he hath no part nor inheritance with thee,) and the stranger, and the fatherless, and the ªwidow, which *are* within thy gates, shall come, and shall eat and be satisfied; that the LORD thy God may bless thee in all the work of thine hand which thou doest.

CHAPTER 15

Every seven years, all debts are to be released—The people are admonished to care for the poor—Hebrew servants are to be released and given gifts during the seventh year—The firstling males of herds and flocks are the Lord's.

AT the end of *every* ªseven years thou shalt make a ᵇrelease.

2 And this *is* the manner of the ªrelease: Every creditor that lend-eth *ought* unto his neighbour shall release *it*; he shall not exact *it* of his neighbour, or of his brother; because it is called the LORD's release.

3 Of a foreigner thou mayest ex-act *it again*: but *that* which is thine with thy brother thine hand shall release;

4 ªSave when there shall be no

12*a* HEB vulture.
13*a* HEB buzzard.
  b HEB falcon.
15*a* HEB seagull.
16*a* HEB barn owl.
17*a* HEB vulture.
18*a* HEB hoopoe bird.
19*a* OR winged insect.

21*a* JST Deut. 14:21 . . . *not give* . . .
  b JST Deut. 14:21 . . . *not sell* . . .
  c Ex. 34:26.
22*a* TG Tithing.
28*a* Amos 4:4.
29*a* D&C 83:6 (5–6).

15 1*a* TG Sabbatical Year.
  b IE pardoning or cancellation of debts.
2*a* Deut. 31:10.
4*a* HEB To the end that there may be no needy.

poor among you; for the LORD shall greatly bless thee in the land which the LORD thy God giveth thee *for* an inheritance to possess it:

5 Only if thou carefully hearken unto the voice of the LORD thy God, to observe to do all these commandments which I command thee this day.

6 For the LORD thy God blesseth thee, as he promised thee: and thou shalt lend unto many nations, but thou shalt not *a*borrow; and thou shalt reign over many nations, but they shall not reign over thee.

7 ¶ If there be among you a poor man of one of thy brethren within any of thy *a*gates in thy land which the LORD thy God giveth thee, thou shalt not *b*harden thine heart, nor shut thine hand from thy *c*poor *d*brother:

8 But thou shalt open thine *a*hand wide unto him, and shalt surely lend him sufficient for his need, *in that* which he *b*wanteth.

9 Beware that there be not a thought in thy wicked heart, saying, The seventh year, the year of release, is at hand; and thine *a*eye be evil against thy poor brother, and thou givest him nought; and he *b*cry unto the LORD against thee, and it be sin unto thee.

10 Thou shalt surely give him, and thine heart shall not be grieved when thou givest unto him: because that for this thing the LORD thy God shall bless thee in all thy works, and in all that thou puttest thine hand unto.

11 For the poor shall never cease out of the land: therefore I command thee, saying, Thou shalt open thine *a*hand wide unto thy brother, to thy poor, and to thy needy, in thy land.

12 ¶ *And* if thy brother, an Hebrew man, or an Hebrew woman, be *a*sold unto thee, and serve thee six years; then in the seventh year thou shalt let him go free from thee.

13 And when thou sendest him out free from thee, thou shalt not let him go away empty:

14 Thou shalt furnish him liberally out of thy flock, and out of thy *a*floor, and out of thy winepress: *of that* wherewith the LORD thy God hath blessed thee thou shalt give unto him.

15 And thou shalt *a*remember that thou wast a bondman in the land of Egypt, and the LORD thy God redeemed thee: therefore I command thee this thing to day.

16 And it shall be, if he say unto thee, I will not go away from thee; because he loveth thee and thine house, because he is well with thee;

17 Then thou shalt take an awl, and thrust *it* through his *a*ear unto the door, and he shall be thy servant for ever. And also unto thy maidservant thou shalt do likewise.

18 It shall not seem hard unto thee, when thou sendest him away free from thee; for he hath been *a*worth a double hired servant *to thee*, in serving thee six years: and the LORD thy God shall bless thee in all that thou *doest*.

19 ¶ All the *a*firstling males that come of thy herd and of thy flock thou shalt *b*sanctify unto the LORD thy God: thou shalt do no work with the firstling of thy *c*bullock, nor shear the firstling of thy sheep.

20 Thou shalt eat *it* before the LORD thy God year by year in the *a*place which the LORD shall choose, thou and thy household.

21 And if there be *any* *a*blemish therein, *as if it be* lame, or blind, *or*

6*a* TG Borrow.
7*a* IE cities, towns (also v. 22).
  b TG Hardheartedness.
  c TG Poor; Welfare.
  d TG Brotherhood and Sisterhood.
8*a* TG Almsgiving.

  b HEB needs.
9*a* D&C 88:67 (67–68).
  b Deut. 24:15.
11*a* TG Generosity.
12*a* Lev. 25:39 (39–43).
14*a* OR threshing floor.
15*a* Matt. 7:12.
17*a* Ex. 21:6.
18*a* IE at half the cost of a

hired worker.
19*a* Ex. 13:2; Mosiah 2:3.
  b Lev. 22:2.
  c HEB cattle.
20*a* Deut. 12:5 (5–6); 1 Kgs. 8:29 (26–30).
21*a* Lev. 22:20; 1 Pet. 1:19 (18–20).

have any ᵇill blemish, thou shalt not ᶜsacrifice it unto the LORD thy God.

22 Thou shalt eat it within thy gates: the ᵃunclean and the clean *person shall eat it* alike, as the roebuck, and as the hart.

23 Only thou shalt not eat the blood thereof; thou shalt pour it upon the ground as water.

CHAPTER 16

Israel is to keep the Passover, the Feast of Unleavened Bread, the Feast of Weeks, and the Feast of Tabernacles— All males are to appear annually before the Lord at these three feasts—Judges are not to make dishonest judgments nor take gifts.

OBSERVE the month of ᵃAbib, and keep the ᵇpassover unto the LORD thy God: for in the month of Abib the LORD thy God brought thee forth out of Egypt by night.

2 Thou shalt therefore sacrifice the ᵃpassover unto the LORD thy God, of the flock and the herd, in the ᵇplace which the LORD shall choose to place his name there.

3 Thou shalt eat no ᵃleavened bread with it; seven days shalt thou eat ᵇunleavened bread therewith, *even* the bread of affliction; for thou camest forth out of the land of Egypt in ᶜhaste: that thou mayest remember the day when thou camest forth out of the land of Egypt all the days of thy life.

4 And there shall be no ᵃleavened bread seen with thee in all thy ᵇcoast seven days; neither shall there *any thing* of the flesh, which thou sacrificedst the first day at even, ᶜremain all night until the morning.

5 Thou mayest not sacrifice the passover within any of thy ᵃgates,

which the LORD thy God giveth thee:

6 But at the place which the LORD thy God shall choose to place his name in, there thou shalt sacrifice the ᵃpassover at even, at the going down of the sun, at the ᵇseason that thou camest forth out of Egypt.

7 And thou shalt ᵃroast and eat *it* in the place which the LORD thy God shall choose: and thou shalt turn in the morning, and go unto thy tents.

8 Six days thou shalt eat ᵃunleavened bread: and on the seventh day *shall be* a ᵇsolemn assembly to the LORD thy God: thou shalt do no work *therein*.

9 ¶ Seven weeks shalt thou number unto thee: begin to number the seven weeks from *such time as* thou beginnest *to put* the sickle to the ᵃcorn.

10 And thou shalt keep the feast of ᵃweeks unto the LORD thy God with a tribute of a freewill offering of thine hand, which thou shalt give *unto the LORD thy God*, according as the LORD thy God hath ᵇblessed thee:

11 And thou shalt rejoice before the LORD thy God, thou, and thy son, and thy daughter, and thy manservant, and thy maidservant, and the Levite that *is* within thy gates, and the stranger, and the fatherless, and the widow, that *are* among you, in the place which the LORD thy God hath chosen to place his name there.

12 And thou shalt remember that thou wast a ᵃbondman in Egypt: and thou shalt observe and do these statutes.

13 ¶ Thou shalt observe the feast of ᵃtabernacles seven days, ᵇafter that thou hast gathered in thy corn and thy wine:

21ᵇ OR serious.
  ᶜ TG Sacrifice.
22ᵃ Deut. 12:15.
16 1ᵃ Ex. 13:4.
  ᵇ Num. 28:16 (16–25);
     Luke 2:41;
     John 13:1 (1–3).
2ᵃ 2 Kgs. 23:21.
  ᵇ 2 Chr. 7:12.
3ᵃ TG Leaven.

  ᵇ TG Bread, Unleavened.
  ᶜ Ex. 12:11.
4ᵃ Ex. 13:7.
  ᵇ OR territory.
  ᶜ Ex. 34:25.
5ᵃ IE cities, towns (also
     vv. 11, 14, 18).
6ᵃ Ex. 12:42.
  ᵇ OR time.
7ᵃ HEB boil, cook.

8ᵃ TG Bread, Unleavened.
  ᵇ TG Solemn Assembly.
9ᵃ HEB standing grain.
10ᵃ Lev. 23:15 (15–21).
  ᵇ 1 Cor. 16:2.
12ᵃ OR slave.
13ᵃ Ex. 23:16;
     Lev. 23:34.
  ᵇ HEB when you gather
     your grain.

14 And thou shalt rejoice in thy feast, thou, and thy son, and thy daughter, and thy manservant, and thy maidservant, and the Levite, the stranger, and the fatherless, and the widow, that *are* within thy gates.

15 Seven days shalt thou keep a solemn feast unto the LORD thy God in the place which the LORD shall choose: because the LORD thy God shall bless thee in all thine increase, and in all the works of thine hands, therefore thou shalt surely rejoice.

16 ¶ *a*Three times in a year shall all thy males *b*appear before the LORD thy God in the place which he shall choose; in the *c*feast of unleavened bread, and in the feast of weeks, and in the feast of tabernacles: and they shall not appear before the LORD empty:

17 Every man *shall* *a*give as he is able, according to the blessing of the LORD thy God which he hath given thee.

18 ¶ *a*Judges and *b*officers shalt thou make thee in all thy gates, which the LORD thy God giveth thee, throughout thy tribes: and they shall judge the people with just judgment.

19 Thou shalt not *a*wrest *b*judgment; thou shalt not respect persons, neither take a *c*gift: for a gift doth *d*blind the eyes of the wise, and pervert the words of the righteous.

20 That which is altogether just shalt thou follow, that thou mayest live, and inherit the land which the LORD thy God giveth thee.

21 ¶ *a*Thou shalt not plant thee a grove of any trees near unto the altar of the LORD thy God, which thou shalt make thee.

22 Neither shalt thou set thee up any *a*image; which the LORD thy God hateth.

CHAPTER 17

Those who worship false gods will be put to death—Priests and judges are to determine the hard cases—Kings are not to acquire horses, wives, or gold for themselves—The king must study the laws of God daily.

THOU shalt not sacrifice unto the LORD thy God *any* bullock, or sheep, wherein is *a*blemish, *or* any *b*evilfavouredness: for that *is* an abomination unto the LORD thy God.

2 ¶ If there be found among you, within any of thy *a*gates which the LORD thy God giveth thee, man or woman, that hath wrought wickedness in the sight of the LORD thy God, in *b*transgressing his covenant,

3 And hath gone and served other gods, and worshipped them, either the sun, or moon, or any of the host of heaven, which I have not commanded;

4 And it be told thee, and thou hast heard *of it*, and inquired diligently, and, behold, *it be* true, *and* the thing certain, *that* such abomination is wrought in Israel:

5 Then shalt thou bring forth that man or that woman, which have committed that wicked thing, unto thy gates, *even* that man or that woman, and shalt *a*stone them with stones, till they *b*die.

6 *a*At the mouth of *b*two witnesses, or three witnesses, shall he that is

---

16*a* Ex. 23:14 (14–17);
      2 Chr. 8:13 (12–13).
   b Ps. 84:7.
   c Ex. 23:14 (1–17);
      Ezek. 46:9.
17*a* Mark 12:42 (41–43);
      Mosiah 4:24 (24–25).
18*a* 1 Chr. 23:4;
      Mosiah 29:11 (11–25);
      D&C 58:17 (14–20).
   b Num. 11:16.
19*a* OR pervert justice, nor
      show partiality nor take

a bribe.
   b TG Judgment.
   c Ex. 18:21 (21–22).
   d TG Spiritual Blindness.
21*a* HEB Thou shalt not
      plant thee an *asherah* of
      any kind of tree beside
      the altar (an *asherah* was
      a fertility idol made of
      a tree trunk).
      1 Kgs. 14:15;
      2 Kgs. 17:16 (15–16).
22*a* HEB pillar (for idol

worship).
17 1*a* Lev. 22:20.
    b HEB defect.
  2*a* IE cities, towns (also
      v. 8).
    b Josh. 23:16.
  5*a* Lev. 20:4.
    b TG Capital
      Punishment.
  6*a* IE On the evidence.
    b TG Witness.

worthy of death be put to ^cdeath; *but* at the mouth of one witness he shall not be put to death.

7 The hands of the witnesses shall be ^afirst upon him to put him to death, and afterward the hands of all the people. So thou shalt put the evil away from among you.

8 ¶ If there arise a matter too hard for thee in ^ajudgment, ^bbetween blood and blood, between plea and plea, and between stroke and stroke, *being* matters of ^ccontroversy within thy gates: then shalt thou arise, and get thee up into the ^dplace which the Lord thy God shall choose;

9 And thou shalt come unto the ^apriests the Levites, and unto the judge that shall be in those days, and inquire; and they shall ^bshew thee the sentence of judgment:

10 And thou shalt do according to the sentence, which they of that place which the Lord shall choose shall shew thee; and thou shalt observe to do according to all that they inform thee:

11 According to the sentence of the law which they shall teach thee, and according to the judgment which they shall tell thee, thou shalt do: thou shalt not decline from the sentence which they shall shew thee, *to* the right hand, nor *to* the left.

12 And the man that will do presumptuously, and will not hearken unto the priest that standeth to minister there before the Lord thy God, or unto the judge, even that man shall die: and thou shalt put away the evil from Israel.

13 And all the people shall hear,

and ^afear, and do no more presumptuously.

14 ¶ When thou art come unto the land which the Lord thy God giveth thee, and shalt possess it, and shalt dwell therein, and shalt say, I will set a king over me, like as all the nations that *are* about me;

15 ^aThou shalt in any wise set *him* ^bking over thee, whom the Lord thy God shall choose: *one* from among thy brethren shalt thou set king over thee: thou mayest not set a ^cstranger over thee, which *is* not thy brother.

16 But he shall not multiply ^ahorses to himself, nor cause the people to return to Egypt, to the end that he should multiply horses: forasmuch as the Lord hath said unto you, Ye shall henceforth ^breturn no more that way.

17 Neither shall he multiply ^awives to himself, that his heart turn not away: neither shall he greatly ^bmultiply to himself silver and gold.

18 And it shall be, when he sitteth upon the throne of his kingdom, that he shall write him a copy of this law in a book out of *that which is* before the priests the Levites:

19 And it shall be with him, and he shall ^aread therein all the days of his life: that he may learn to fear the Lord his God, to keep all the words of this law and these statutes, to do them:

20 That his heart be not lifted up above his ^abrethren, and that he ^bturn not aside from the commandment, *to* the right hand, or *to* the left: to the end that he may prolong *his* days in his kingdom, he, and his ^cchildren, in the midst of Israel.

6c TG Capital Punishment.
7a Deut. 13:9;
   John 8:7 (3–11).
8a Mosiah 29:28 (28–29).
 b IE regarding degrees of manslaughter, etc.
 c Ezek. 44:24.
   TG Disputations.
 d 1 Kgs. 8:29 (26–30).
9a Ezek. 43:19; 44:15.
 b HEB pronounce to you

(also vv. 10–11).
13a Deut. 13:11.
15a OR You may indeed.
 b TG Governments; Kings, Earthly.
 c OR alien.
16a 1 Kgs. 4:26;
   2 Chr. 9:28.
 b Ex. 13:17;
   Jer. 42:19 (15–19).
17a 2 Sam. 5:13;

1 Kgs. 11:1;
   Jacob 1:15; 2:24 (24, 30).
 b Mosiah 2:14.
19a TG Scriptures, Study of; Scriptures, Value of.
20a D&C 38:24.
 b Deut. 5:32;
   1 Kgs. 15:5.
 c TG Family.

CHAPTER 18

How priests are supported—Divination, spiritualism, and the like are abominations—A Prophet (Christ) will arise like unto Moses.

THE priests the Levites, *and* all the tribe of Levi, shall have no *a*part nor *b*inheritance with Israel: they shall *c*eat the offerings of the LORD made by fire, and his inheritance.

2 Therefore shall they have no inheritance among their brethren: the LORD *is* their *a*inheritance, as he hath said unto them.

3 ¶ And this shall be the priest's *a*due from the people, from them that offer a sacrifice, whether *it be* ox or sheep; and they shall give unto the priest the shoulder, and the two cheeks, and the *b*maw.

4 The *a*firstfruit *also* of thy *b*corn, of thy wine, and of thine oil, and the first of the fleece of thy sheep, shalt thou give him.

5 For the LORD thy God hath chosen him out of all thy tribes, to stand to *a*minister in the *b*name of the LORD, him and his sons for ever.

6 ¶ And if a Levite come from any of thy *a*gates out of all Israel, where he *b*sojourned, and come with all the desire of his mind unto the *c*place which the LORD shall choose;

7 Then he shall minister in the name of the LORD his God, as all his brethren the Levites *do*, which stand there before the LORD.

8 They shall have like portions to eat, beside that which cometh of the sale of his patrimony.

9 ¶ When thou art come into the *a*land which the LORD thy God giveth thee, thou shalt not learn to do after the *b*abominations of those nations.

10 There shall not be found among you *any one* that maketh his son or his daughter *a*to pass through the *b*fire, *or* that useth *c*divination, *or* an observer of times, or an *d*enchanter, or a witch,

11 Or a charmer, or a consulter with *a*familiar spirits, or a wizard, or a necromancer.

12 For all that do these things *are* an *a*abomination unto the LORD: and because of these *b*abominations the LORD thy God doth drive them out from before thee.

13 Thou shalt be *a*perfect with the LORD thy God.

14 For these nations, which thou shalt *a*possess, hearkened unto *b*observers of times, and unto diviners: but as for thee, the LORD thy God hath not suffered thee so *to do*.

15 ¶ The LORD thy God will *a*raise up unto thee a *b*Prophet from the midst of thee, of thy brethren, like unto me; unto him ye shall hearken;

16 According to all that thou desiredst of the LORD thy God in Horeb in the day of the assembly, saying, Let me not *a*hear again the voice of the LORD my God, neither let me see this great fire any more, that I die not.

17 And the LORD said unto me, They have well *spoken that* which they have spoken.

---

18 1*a* Num. 18:20.
　　b Num. 26:62.
　　c Num. 18:10 (8–10);
　　　　1 Cor. 9:13.
　　2*a* Ps. 16:5.
　　3*a* Lev. 7:31 (30–34);
　　　　Num. 18:8 (8–24);
　　　　1 Sam. 2:14.
　　b OR stomach.
　　4*a* Num. 18:12.
　　b HEB grain.
　　5*a* D&C 107:6.
　　b TG Name.
　　6*a* IE of the cities, or towns.
　　b Num. 35:3 (2–3).

　　c 2 Chr. 7:12.
　　9*a* Lev. 18:28 (26–30);
　　　　Isa. 65:9; Ezek. 34:13.
　　b 2 Kgs. 23:24.
　10*a* IE to be burnt as an idolatrous sacrifice.
　　b Lev. 18:21;
　　　　Deut. 12:31;
　　　　Jer. 7:31.
　　TG Superstitions.
　　c Num. 22:7 (7–18);
　　　　1 Sam. 6:2.
　　d TG Sorcery.
　11*a* TG Spirits, Evil or Unclean.
　12*a* 2 Chr. 33:6.

　　b Lev. 18:24 (24–25);
　　　　1 Ne. 17:37 (33–40).
　13*a* TG Perfection.
　14*a* OR dispossess.
　　b Lev. 19:26.
　15*a* Deut. 34:10.
　　b Acts 3:22 (22–23); 7:37;
　　　　1 Ne. 22:21;
　　　　3 Ne. 20:23;
　　　　JS—H 1:40.
　　TG Jesus Christ,
　　　Mission of; Jesus Christ,
　　　Prophecies about.
　16*a* Ex. 20:19;
　　　　Deut. 5:25.
　　TG Hardheartedness.

18 I will raise them up a ^aProphet from among their brethren, like unto thee, and will put my ^bwords in his mouth; and he shall ^cspeak unto them all that I shall command him.

19 And it shall come to pass, *that* whosoever will not hearken unto my words which he shall speak in my name, I will require *it* of him.

20 But the ^aprophet, which shall ^bpresume to speak a word in my name, which I have not commanded him to speak, or that shall speak in the name of other gods, even that prophet shall die.

21 And if thou say in thine heart, How shall we ^aknow the word which the LORD hath not spoken?

22 When a ^aprophet ^bspeaketh in the name of the LORD, if the thing follow not, nor come to pass, that *is* the thing which the LORD hath not spoken, *but* the prophet hath spoken it presumptuously: thou shalt not be afraid of him.

CHAPTER 19

Cities of refuge are appointed for cases of manslaughter—Murderers will be put to death—Two or three witnesses are required in court cases—False witnesses will be punished.

WHEN the LORD thy God hath cut off the nations, whose land the LORD thy God giveth thee, and ^athou succeedest them, and dwellest in their cities, and in their houses;

2 Thou shalt ^aseparate three ^bcities for thee in the midst of thy land, which the LORD thy God giveth thee to possess it.

3 Thou shalt prepare thee ^aa way, and divide the ^bcoasts of thy land, which the LORD thy God giveth thee to inherit, into three parts, that every slayer may ^cflee thither.

4 ¶ And this *is* the case of the slayer, which shall flee thither, that he may live: Whoso killeth his neighbour ^aignorantly, whom he hated not in time past;

5 As when a man goeth into the wood with his neighbour to hew wood, and his hand fetcheth a stroke with the axe to cut down the tree, and the head slippeth from the helve, and lighteth upon his neighbour, that he die; he shall flee unto one of those cities, and live:

6 Lest the ^aavenger of the blood pursue the slayer, while his heart is hot, and overtake him, because the way is long, and slay him; whereas he *was* not worthy of death, inasmuch as he hated him not in time past.

7 Wherefore I command thee, saying, Thou shalt separate three cities for thee.

8 And if the LORD thy God enlarge thy ^acoast, as he hath sworn unto thy fathers, and give thee all the land which he promised to give unto thy fathers;

9 If thou shalt keep all these commandments to do them, which I command thee this day, to love the LORD thy God, and to ^awalk ever in his ways; then shalt thou add three cities more for thee, beside these three:

10 That innocent blood be not shed in thy land, which the LORD thy God giveth thee *for* an inheritance, and *so* blood be upon thee.

11 ¶ But if any man hate his ^aneighbour, and ^blie in wait for him, and rise up against him, and smite him mortally that he die, and fleeth into one of these cities:

12 Then the elders of his city shall send and fetch him thence, and deliver him into the hand of the avenger of blood, that he may die.

18a TG Jesus Christ,
   Prophecies about.
  b John 8:28;
    12:49 (49–50); 17:8;
    D&C 1:38.
  c John 4:25; 12:50.
20a TG False Prophets.
  b Zech. 10:2.
21a Jer. 28:9 (8–9);

D&C 64:39.
22a TG Prophets, Mission of.
  b Jer. 28:9.
19 1a HEB you dispossess.
  2a OR set apart (also v. 7).
  b Ex. 21:13.
  3a HEB roads.
  b HEB area, territory
    (also v. 8).

c Ex. 21:13 (12–14).
4a HEB unintentionally.
6a D&C 98:23.
8a 1 Chr. 4:10.
9a TG Walking with God.
11a Deut. 27:24;
    2 Ne. 9:35;
    Mosiah 13:21.
  b Num. 35:16 (16–25).

13 Thine eye shall not pity him, but thou shalt ^aput away *the* ^b*guilt of* innocent blood from Israel, that it may go well with thee.

14 ¶ Thou shalt not remove thy neighbour's ^alandmark, which they of old time have set in thine inheritance, which thou shalt inherit in the land that the LORD thy God giveth thee to possess it.

15 ¶ One ^awitness shall not rise up against a man for any iniquity, or for any sin, in any sin that he sinneth: at the mouth of two ^bwitnesses, or at the mouth of three witnesses, shall the matter be established.

16 ¶ If a ^afalse witness rise up against any man to testify against him *that which is* wrong;

17 Then both the men, between whom the ^acontroversy *is,* shall stand before the LORD, before the priests and the judges, which shall be in those days;

18 And the ^ajudges shall make diligent inquisition: and, behold, *if* the witness *be* a false witness, *and* hath testified falsely against his brother;

19 Then shall ye ^ado unto him, as he had thought to have done unto his brother: so shalt thou put the evil away from among you.

20 And those which remain shall hear, and fear, and shall henceforth commit no more any such evil among you.

21 And thine eye shall not pity; *but* life *shall go* for life, ^aeye for eye, tooth for tooth, hand for hand, foot for foot.

CHAPTER 20

Laws are revealed for selecting soldiers and making war—Hittites, Amorites, Canaanites, Perizzites, Hivites, and Jebusites will be utterly destroyed.*

WHEN thou goest out to ^abattle against thine enemies, and seest horses, and ^bchariots, *and* a people more than thou, be not ^cafraid of them: for the ^dLORD thy God *is* with thee, which brought thee up out of the land of Egypt.

2 And it shall be, when ye are come nigh unto the battle, that the priest shall approach and speak unto the people,

3 And shall say unto them, Hear, O Israel, ye approach this day unto battle against your enemies: let not your hearts faint, fear not, and do not tremble, neither be ye terrified because of them;

4 For the LORD your God *is* he that goeth with you, to ^afight for you against your enemies, to save you.

5 ¶ And the officers shall speak unto the people, saying, What man *is there* that hath built a new house, and hath not dedicated it? let him go and return to his house, lest he die in the battle, and another man dedicate it.

6 And what man *is he* that hath planted a ^avineyard, and hath not *yet* eaten of it? let him *also* go and return unto his house, lest he die in the battle, and another man eat of it.

7 And what man *is there* that hath betrothed a ^awife, and hath not taken her? let him go and return unto his house, lest he die in the battle, and another man take her.

8 And the officers shall speak further unto the people, and they shall say, What man *is there that is* ^afearful and fainthearted? let him go and return unto his house, lest his brethren's heart ^bfaint as well as his heart.

13*a* HEB purge.
  b 1 Kgs. 2:31.
    TG Guilt.
14*a* Deut. 27:17; Job 24:2;
    Prov. 22:28;
    Hosea 5:10.
15*a* Matt. 26:60;
    1 Tim. 5:19.
  b 2 Cor. 13:1;
    2 Ne. 27:12 (12, 14);

D&C 6:28.
16*a* TG Lying.
17*a* TG Disputations.
18*a* Ezra 7:25.
19*a* TG Retribution.
21*a* IE not literally; interpreted by the Rabbis to be symbolic of equal compensation.
20 1*a* D&C 98:37; 105:14.

  b Josh. 17:18.
  c TG Courage.
  d 2 Sam. 22:3.
4*a* Josh. 23:10.
6*a* 1 Cor. 9:7.
7*a* Deut. 24:5.
8*a* Judg. 7:3.
  b HEB melt like his; i.e., lest they all lost their courage.

9 And it shall be, when the officers have made an end of speaking unto the people, that they shall make captains of the armies to lead the people.

10 ¶ When thou comest nigh unto a city to ᵃfight against it, then proclaim ᵇpeace unto it.

11 And it shall be, if it make thee answer of peace, and open unto thee, then it shall be, *that* all the people *that is* found therein shall be ᵃtributaries unto thee, and they shall serve thee.

12 And if it will make no peace with thee, but will make war against thee, then thou shalt besiege it:

13 And when the LORD thy God hath delivered it into thine hands, thou shalt smite every male thereof with the edge of the sword:

14 But the women, and the little ones, and the cattle, and all that is in the city, *even* all the spoil thereof, shalt thou take unto thyself; and thou shalt ᵃeat the spoil of thine enemies, which the LORD thy God hath given thee.

15 Thus shalt thou do unto all the cities *which are* very far off from thee, which *are* not of the cities of these nations.

16 But of the ᵃcities of these people, which the LORD thy God doth give thee *for* an inheritance, thou shalt save alive nothing that breatheth:

17 But thou shalt utterly ᵃdestroy them; *namely,* the Hittites, and the Amorites, the Canaanites, and the Perizzites, the Hivites, and the Jebusites; as the LORD thy God hath commanded thee:

18 That they teach you not to do after all their abominations, which they have done unto their gods; so should ye sin against the LORD your God.

19 ¶ When thou shalt besiege a city a long time, in making war against it to take it, thou shalt not destroy the trees thereof by forcing an axe against them: for thou mayest eat of them, and thou shalt not cut them down (ᵃfor the tree of the field *is* man's *life*) to employ *them* in the siege:

20 Only the trees which thou knowest that they *be* not trees for ᵃmeat, thou shalt destroy and cut them down; and thou shalt build bulwarks against the city that maketh war with thee, until it be subdued.

CHAPTER 21

How amends are made for murders by unknown persons—Equity is required in dealing with wives and children—Stubborn and rebellious sons will be put to death.

IF *one* be found slain in the land which the LORD thy God giveth thee to possess it, lying in the field, *and* it be not known who hath slain him:

2 Then thy elders and thy judges shall come forth, and they shall measure ᵃunto the cities which *are* round about him that is slain:

3 And it shall be, *that* the city *which is* next unto the slain man, even the elders of that city shall take an heifer, which hath not been ᵃwrought with, *and* which hath not drawn in the yoke;

4 And the elders of that city shall bring down the heifer unto a rough valley, which is neither ᵃeared nor sown, and shall ᵇstrike off the heifer's neck there in the valley:

5 And the priests the sons of Levi shall come near; for them the LORD thy God hath chosen to minister unto him, and to bless in the name of the LORD; and by their word shall every controversy and every ᵃstroke be *tried:*

6 And all the elders of that city, *that are* next unto the slain *man,* shall

---

10a TG War.
 b TG Peace;
   Peacemakers.
11a OR servants, in tribute.
14a IE consume, enjoy.
16a Josh. 11:14.

17a Josh. 10:40 (40–43);
   11:12 (11–12).
19a HEB for are the trees in
   the field men, that you
   should besiege them?
20a HEB food.

21 2a OR the distance to.
  3a OR worked.
  4a HEB plowed, worked.
   b OR break.
  5a OR case of assault.

wash their hands over the heifer
^athat is beheaded in the valley:

7 And they shall answer and say,
Our hands have not shed this blood,
neither have our eyes seen *it.*

8 ^aBe merciful, O LORD, unto thy
people Israel, whom thou hast ^bre-
deemed, and lay not innocent blood
unto thy people of Israel's charge.
And the blood shall be forgiven
them.

9 So shalt thou put away the *guilt
of* innocent blood from among you,
when thou shalt do *that which is*
right in the sight of the LORD.

10 ¶ When thou goest forth to war
against thine enemies, and the LORD
thy God hath delivered them into
thine hands, and thou hast taken
them captive,

11 And seest among the captives a
beautiful woman, and hast a desire
unto her, that thou wouldest have
her to thy wife;

12 Then thou shalt bring her home
to thine house; and she shall shave
her head, and pare her nails;

13 And she shall put the ^araiment
of her captivity from off her, and
shall remain in thine house, and
bewail her father and her mother
a full month: and after that thou
shalt go in unto her, and be her
husband, and she shall be thy wife.

14 And it shall be, if thou have no
delight in her, then thou shalt let
her go whither she will; but thou
shalt not ^asell her at all for money,
thou shalt not ^bmake merchandise of
her, because thou hast humbled her.

15 ¶ If a man have two wives, one
beloved, and another ^ahated, and
they have born him children, *both*
the beloved and the hated; and *if*

the firstborn son be hers that was
hated:

16 Then it shall be, when he maketh his sons to inherit *that* which
he hath, *that* he may not ^amake the
son of the beloved firstborn before
the son of the hated, *which is indeed*
the firstborn:

17 But he shall acknowledge the
son of the hated *for* the firstborn,
by giving him a ^adouble portion of
all that he hath: for he *is* ^bthe ^cbe-
ginning of his strength; the right
of the ^dfirstborn *is* his.

18 ¶ If a man have a ^astubborn
and rebellious son, which will not
^bobey the voice of his father, or the
voice of his mother, and *that,* when
they have chastened him, will not
hearken unto them:

19 Then shall his father and his
mother lay hold on him, and bring
him out unto the elders of his city,
and unto ^athe gate of his place;

20 And they shall say unto the
elders of his city, This our son *is*
stubborn and rebellious, he will
not obey our voice; *he is* a glutton,
and a drunkard.

21 And all the men of his city shall
stone him with stones, that he die: so
shalt thou put evil away from among
you; and all Israel shall hear, and fear.

22 ¶ And if a man have committed
a sin worthy of death, and he be
to be put to death, and thou hang
him on a tree:

23 His ^abody shall not ^bremain all
night upon the ^ctree, but thou shalt
in any wise bury him that day; (for
he that is hanged *is* ^daccursed of
God;) that thy land be not defiled,
which the LORD thy God giveth thee
for an ^einheritance.

6*a* OR whose neck is
   broken.
8*a* HEB Let atonement be
   made for.
   b Ps. 25:22;
      D&C 84:99 (99–100).
13*a* OR captive garb.
14*a* Deut. 24:7.
   b HEB treat her harshly.
15*a* OR despised, disliked
   (also vv. 16–17).
   Gen. 29:33.

16*a* HEB prefer.
17*a* 2 Kgs. 2:9.
   b OR his first issue.
   c Gen. 49:3.
   d TG Firstborn.
18*a* TG Stubbornness.
   b TG Disobedience; Honor-
      ing Father and Mother.
19*a* IE the gate of the city
      nearest his house.
23*a* According to Rabbinical
      commentaries, to

leave a body hanging
was a degradation of
the human body and
therefore an affront to
God, in whose image
man's body was made.
   b John 19:31 (31–33).
   c Gal. 3:13.
      TG Jesus Christ,
      Crucifixion of.
   d Gal. 3:13.
   e TG Lands of Inheritance.

CHAPTER 22

Moses sets forth laws pertaining to lost property, wearing of proper clothes, caring for interests of others, marrying virgins, and sexual immorality.

THOU shalt not see thy ^abrother's ox or his sheep go ^bastray, and hide thyself from them: thou shalt in any case bring them again unto thy brother.

2 And if thy brother ^abe not nigh unto thee, or if thou know him not, then thou shalt bring it unto thine own house, and it shall be with thee until thy brother seek after it, and thou shalt restore it to him again.

3 In like manner shalt thou do with his ass; and so shalt thou do with his raiment; and with all ^alost thing of thy brother's, which he hath lost, and thou hast found, shalt thou do likewise: thou mayest not hide thyself.

4 ¶ Thou shalt not see thy brother's ass or his ox fall down by the way, and hide thyself from them: thou shalt surely ^ahelp him to lift *them* up again.

5 ¶ The woman shall not ^awear that which pertaineth unto a man, neither shall a man put on a woman's garment: for all that do so *are* abomination unto the LORD thy God.

6 ¶ If a bird's nest chance to be before thee in the way in any tree, or on the ground, *whether they be* young ones, or eggs, and the ^adam sitting upon the young, or upon the eggs, thou shalt not take the ^bdam with the young:

7 *But* thou shalt in any wise let the dam go, and take the young to thee; that it may be well with thee, and *that* thou mayest ^aprolong *thy* days.

8 ¶ When thou buildest a new house, then thou shalt make a ^abat-tlement for thy roof, that thou bring not blood upon thine house, if any man fall from thence.

9 ¶ Thou shalt not sow thy vineyard with ^adivers seeds: lest the fruit of thy seed which thou hast sown, and the fruit of thy vineyard, be defiled.

10 ¶ Thou shalt not plow with an ox and an ass together.

11 ¶ Thou shalt not wear a garment of ^adivers sorts, *as* of woollen and linen together.

12 ¶ Thou shalt make thee ^afringes upon the four quarters of thy vesture, wherewith thou coverest *thyself.*

13 ¶ If any man take a wife, and go in unto her, and ^ahate her,

14 And ^agive occasions of speech against her, and bring up an evil name upon her, and say, I took this woman, and when I came to her, I found her not a ^bmaid:

15 Then shall the father of the damsel, and her mother, take and bring forth *the tokens of* the damsel's virginity unto the elders of the city in the gate:

16 And the damsel's father shall say unto the elders, I gave my daughter unto this man to wife, and he hateth her;

17 And, lo, he hath given occasions of speech *against her,* saying, I found not thy daughter a maid; and yet these *are the tokens of* my daughter's virginity. And they shall spread the cloth before the elders of the city.

18 And the elders of that city shall take that man and chastise him;

19 And they shall ^aamerce him in an hundred *shekels* of silver, and give *them* unto the father of the damsel, because he hath brought up an evil ^bname upon a virgin of Israel: and she shall be his wife; he may not put her away all his days.

20 But if this thing be true, *and the*

---

22 1*a* TG Brotherhood and
    Sisterhood.
  b Ex. 23:4.
  2*a* OR does not live near.
  3*a* D&C 136:26.
  4*a* D&C 58:28 (27–29).
  5*a* TG Apparel;

    Clothing.
  6*a* OR mother (also v. 7).
  b Lev. 22:28.
  7*a* Deut. 4:40.
  8*a* OR parapet, railing.
  9*a* Lev. 19:19.
 11*a* Lev. 19:19.

 12*a* Num. 15:38 (37–40).
 13*a* OR then despise.
 14*a* OR charge her with
    misconduct (also v. 17).
  b HEB virgin (also v. 17).
 19*a* OR fine.
  b TG Name.

tokens of virginity be not found for the damsel:

21 Then they shall bring out the damsel to the door of her father's house, and the men of her city shall stone her with stones that she *^adie:* because she hath wrought folly in Israel, to play the whore in her father's house: so shalt thou put evil away from among you.

22 ¶ If a man be found lying with a woman *^amarried* to an husband, then they shall both of them die, *both* the man that lay with the woman, and the woman: so shalt thou put away evil from Israel.

23 ¶ If a damsel *that is* a virgin be betrothed unto *^aan* husband, and a man find her in the city, and lie with her;

24 Then ye shall bring them both out unto the gate of that city, and ye shall stone them with stones that they die; the damsel, because she *^acried* not, *being* in the city; and the man, because he hath humbled his neighbour's wife: so thou shalt put away evil from among you.

25 ¶ But if a man find a betrothed damsel in the field, and the man force her, and *^alie* with her: then the man only that lay with her shall die:

26 But unto the damsel thou shalt do nothing; *there is* in the damsel no sin *worthy* of death: for as when a man riseth against his neighbour, and slayeth him, *^aeven* so *is* this matter:

27 For he found her in the field, *and* the betrothed damsel cried, and *there was* none to save her.

28 ¶ If a man find a damsel *that is* a *^avirgin,* which is not betrothed, and lay hold on her, and lie with her, and they be found;

29 Then the man that lay with her shall give unto the damsel's father fifty *shekels* of silver, and she shall be his *^awife;* because he hath humbled her, he may not put her away all his days.

30 ¶ A man shall not take his *^afather's* wife, nor *^bdiscover* his father's skirt.

CHAPTER 23

Moses specifies those who may and may not enter the congregation—He sets forth laws concerning sanitation, servants, usury, and vows.

HE that is *^awounded* in the stones, or hath his privy member cut off, shall not enter into the congregation of the LORD.

2 A bastard shall not enter into the congregation of the LORD; even to his tenth generation shall he not enter into the congregation of the LORD.

3 An *^aAmmonite* or Moabite shall not enter into the congregation of the LORD; even to their tenth generation shall they not enter into the congregation of the LORD for ever:

4 Because they met you not with *^abread* and with water in the way, when ye came forth out of Egypt; and because they hired against thee *^bBalaam* the son of Beor of Pethor of Mesopotamia, to curse thee.

5 Nevertheless the LORD thy God would not hearken unto Balaam; but the LORD thy God turned the *^acurse* into a *^bblessing* unto thee, because the LORD thy God *^cloved* thee.

6 Thou shalt not seek their peace nor their prosperity all thy days for ever.

7 ¶ Thou shalt not abhor an *^aEdom*ite; for he *is* thy brother: thou shalt not abhor an Egyptian; because thou wast a *^bstranger* in his land.

8 The children that are begotten of them shall enter into the congregation of the LORD in their third generation.

21*a* TG Capital Punishment.
22*a* TG Adulterer.
23*a* HEB a man.
24*a* IE did not cry for help.
25*a* TG Sexual Immorality.
26*a* IE in gravity.
28*a* Ex. 22:17 (16–17).
29*a* Ex. 22:16 (16–17).

30*a* Lev. 20:11.
   b IE uncover her who is his father's.
23 1*a* Lev. 21:17 (17–23).
  3*a* Neh. 13:1.
  4*a* OR food.
   b Num. 22:5; 2 Pet. 2:15.

5*a* Num. 23:11.
   TG Curse.
   b D&C 90:24.
   c TG God, Love of.
7*a* Gen. 25:25 (24–27).
   b HEB sojourner.
   Ex. 22:21.

9 ¶ When *a*the host goeth forth against thine enemies, then keep thee from every wicked thing.

10 ¶ If there be among you any man, that is not clean by reason of uncleanness that chanceth him by night, then shall he go abroad out of the camp, he shall not come within the camp:

11 But it shall be, when evening cometh on, he shall wash *himself* with water: and when the sun is down, he shall come into the camp *again*.

12 ¶ Thou shalt have a place also without the camp, whither thou shalt go forth abroad:

13 And thou shalt have a paddle upon thy weapon; and it shall be, when thou wilt ease thyself abroad, thou shalt dig therewith, and shalt turn back and cover *a*that which cometh from thee:

14 For the LORD thy God *a*walketh in the *b*midst of thy camp, to deliver thee, and to give up thine enemies before thee; therefore shall thy camp be holy: that he see no unclean thing in thee, and turn away from thee.

15 ¶ Thou shalt not deliver unto his *a*master the servant which is escaped from his master unto thee:

16 He shall dwell with thee, *even* among you, in that place which he shall choose in one of thy *a*gates, where it liketh him best: thou shalt not oppress him.

17 ¶ There shall be no *a*whore of the daughters of Israel, nor *b*a sodomite of the sons of Israel.

18 Thou shalt not bring the hire of a whore, or the price of a dog, into the house of the LORD thy God for any vow: for even both these *are* abomination unto the LORD thy God.

19 ¶ Thou shalt not lend upon *a*usury to thy brother; usury of money, usury of victuals, usury of any thing that is lent upon usury:

20 Unto a *a*stranger thou mayest lend upon usury; but unto thy brother thou shalt not *b*lend upon usury: that the LORD thy God may bless thee in all that thou settest thine hand to in the land whither thou goest to possess it.

21 ¶ When thou shalt *a*vow a *b*vow unto the LORD thy God, thou shalt not slack to pay it: for the LORD thy God will surely require it of thee; and it would be sin in thee.

22 But if thou shalt forbear to vow, it shall be no sin in thee.

23 That which is gone out of thy lips thou shalt keep and perform; *even* a freewill offering, according as thou hast vowed unto the LORD thy God, which thou hast promised with thy mouth.

24 ¶ When thou comest into thy neighbour's vineyard, then thou mayest eat grapes thy fill at thine own pleasure; but thou shalt not put *any* in thy vessel.

25 When thou comest into the standing *a*corn of thy neighbour, then thou mayest pluck the *b*ears with thine hand; but thou shalt not move a sickle unto thy neighbour's standing corn.

CHAPTER 24

Laws are given concerning divorce, newly married persons, making merchandise of men, taking pledges, leprosy, oppression of servants, and leaving gleanings of crops.

WHEN a man hath taken a *a*wife, and married her, and it come to pass that she find no favour in his eyes, because he hath found some *b*uncleanness in her: then let him write her a bill of *c*divorcement, and give

---

9*a* HEB you are out and encamped.
13*a* HEB your excrement.
14*a* Lev. 26:12.
  b Ps. 46:5; Isa. 12:6.
15*a* 1 Sam. 30:15.
16*a* IE of the cities or towns.
17*a* Lev. 19:29.
  b HEB a professional male

or female prostitute or cultist.
  2 Kgs. 23:7.
  TG Homosexual Behavior.
19*a* OR interest (also v. 20).
  TG Usury.
20*a* HEB foreigner.
  b TG Debt.

21*a* TG Vow.
  b Matt. 5:33.
25*a* HEB grain.
  b Matt. 12:1.
24 1*a* TG Marriage, Wives.
  b IE from unchastity, indecency.
  c Matt. 1:19.
  TG Divorce.

it in her hand, and send her out of his house.

2 And when she is departed out of his house, she may go and be another man's *wife.*

3 And *if* the latter husband hate her, and write her a bill of divorcement, and giveth *it* in her hand, and sendeth her out of his house; or if the latter husband die, which took her *to be* his wife;

4 Her former husband, which sent her away, may not take her again to be his wife, after that she is defiled; for that *is* abomination before the LORD: and thou shalt not *a*cause the land to sin, which the LORD thy God giveth thee *for* an inheritance.

5 ¶ When a man hath taken a new *a*wife, he shall not go out to war, neither shall he be charged with any business: *but* he shall be free at home one year, and shall *b*cheer up his wife which he hath taken.

6 ¶ No man shall take the *a*nether or the upper millstone to pledge: for *b*he taketh *a man's* life to pledge.

7 ¶ If a man be found *a*stealing any of his brethren of the children of Israel, and maketh *b*merchandise of him, or selleth him; then that thief shall die; and thou shalt put evil away from among you.

8 ¶ Take heed in the plague of *a*leprosy, that thou observe diligently, and do according to all that the priests the Levites shall *b*teach you: as I commanded them, *so* ye shall observe to do.

9 Remember what the LORD thy God did unto Miriam by the way, after that ye were come forth out of Egypt.

10 ¶ When thou dost lend thy brother any thing, thou shalt not go into his house to fetch his pledge.

11 Thou shalt stand *a*abroad, and the man to whom thou dost lend shall bring out the pledge abroad unto thee.

12 And if the man *be* poor, thou shalt not *a*sleep with his pledge:

13 In any case thou shalt deliver him the *a*pledge again when the sun goeth down, that he may sleep in his own *b*raiment, and bless thee: and it shall be righteousness unto thee before the LORD thy God.

14 ¶ Thou shalt not *a*oppress an hired servant *that is* poor and needy, *whether he be* of thy brethren, or of thy strangers that *are* in thy land within thy *b*gates:

15 *a*At his day thou shalt give *him* his *b*hire, neither shall the sun go down upon it; for he *is* poor, and setteth his heart upon it: lest he *c*cry against thee unto the LORD, and it be sin unto thee.

16 The *a*fathers shall not be put to *b*death for the children, neither shall the *c*children be put to death for the fathers: every man shall be put to death for his *d*own *e*sin.

17 ¶ Thou shalt not *a*pervert the *b*judgment of the stranger, *nor* of the fatherless; nor take a widow's raiment to pledge:

18 But thou shalt remember that thou wast a *a*bondman in Egypt, and the LORD thy God redeemed thee thence: therefore I command thee to do this thing.

19 ¶ When thou cuttest down thine harvest in thy field, and hast forgot a sheaf in the field, thou shalt not go again to fetch it: it shall be for the stranger, for the fatherless,

---

4*a* HEB bring guilt upon the land.
5*a* Deut. 20:7.
  b HEB be happy with.
   TG Family, Love within; Marriage, Husbands.
6*a* HEB lower.
  b OR it is as if he took.
7*a* TG Stealing.
  b Deut. 21:14.
8*a* TG Leprosy.

b TG Teacher.
11*a* OR outside.
12*a* IE keep it overnight.
13*a* Ex. 22:26; Ezek. 18:7.
  b OR garment (also v. 17).
14*a* Prov. 14:31.
  b IE of the cities, towns.
15*a* HEB The same day.
  b Lev. 19:13.
  c Deut. 15:9.

16*a* TG Marriage, Fatherhood.
  b TG Punish.
  c 2 Sam. 21:6 (1–14); Isa. 14:21.
  d TG Accountability; Justice.
  e TG Sin.
17*a* Deut. 27:19.
  b TG Judgment.
18*a* HEB slave.

and for the ^awidow: that the LORD thy God may bless thee in all the work of thine hands.

20 When thou beatest thine olive tree, thou shalt not go over the boughs again: it shall be for the stranger, for the fatherless, and for the widow.

21 When thou gatherest the grapes of thy vineyard, thou shalt not glean *it* afterward: it shall be for the stranger, for the fatherless, and for the widow.

22 And thou shalt remember that thou wast a bondman in the land of Egypt: therefore I command thee to do this thing.

CHAPTER 25

Judges prescribe punishment for the wicked—The marriage law provides for a brother's widow—Just weights and measures are required—Israel is commanded to blot out the Amalekites from under heaven.

IF there be a ^acontroversy between men, and they come unto ^bjudgment, that *the judges* may judge them; then they shall ^cjustify the righteous, and condemn the wicked.

2 And it shall be, if the wicked man *be* worthy to be ^abeaten, that the judge shall cause him to lie down, and to be beaten before his face, according to his fault, by a certain ^bnumber.

3 ^aForty stripes he may give him, *and* not exceed: lest, *if* he should exceed, and beat him above these with many stripes, then thy brother should seem ^bvile unto thee.

4 ¶ Thou shalt not ^amuzzle the ox when he treadeth out *the* ^bcorn.

5 ¶ If brethren dwell together, and one of them die, and have no child, the ^awife of the dead shall not marry ^bwithout unto a stranger: her ^chusband's ^dbrother shall go in unto her, and take her to him to wife, and perform the duty of an ^ehusband's brother unto her.

6 And it shall be, *that* the firstborn which she beareth shall succeed in the ^aname of his brother *which is* dead, that his ^bname be not ^cput out of Israel.

7 And if the man like not to take his brother's wife, then let his brother's wife go up to the gate unto the elders, and say, My husband's brother refuseth to raise up unto his brother a name in Israel, he will not perform the duty of my husband's brother.

8 Then the elders of his city shall call him, and speak unto him: and *if* he ^astand *to it*, and say, I like not to take her;

9 Then shall his brother's wife come unto him in the presence of the elders, and loose his ^ashoe from off his foot, and spit in his face, and shall answer and say, So shall it be done unto that man that will not build up his brother's house.

10 And his name shall be called in Israel, The house of him that hath his shoe loosed.

11 ¶ When men strive together one with another, and the wife of the one draweth near for to deliver her husband out of the hand of him that smiteth him, and putteth forth her hand, and taketh him by the secrets:

12 Then thou shalt cut off her hand, thine eye shall not pity *her*.

13 ¶ Thou shalt not have in thy bag ^adivers ^bweights, a great and a small.

14 Thou shalt not have in thine house divers measures, a great and a small.

19a Ruth 2:2.
   TG Poor;
   Welfare.
25 1a TG Disputations.
   b Ezek. 44:24.
   c TG Justification.
   2a Luke 12:48.
   b IE of stripes (see next verse).
   3a 2 Cor. 11:24.
   b OR degraded.

4a 1 Cor. 9:9;
   1 Tim. 5:18.
   b IE grain.
5a TG Widows.
   b OR outside the family.
   c Ruth 1:11; 3:12.
   d Ruth 4:5;
   Matt. 22:24 (23–33);
   Mark 12:19;
   Luke 20:28 (27–38).
   e TG Marriage,

Fatherhood.
6a Ruth 4:6.
   TG Name.
   b Ruth 4:10.
   c HEB blotted.
8a OR persists.
9a Ruth 4:7 (6–8).
13a OR two kinds of (also v. 14).
   b Lev. 19:36.

15 *But* thou shalt have a *a*perfect and just weight, a perfect and just *b*measure shalt thou have: that thy days may be *c*lengthened in the land which the LORD thy God giveth thee.

16 For all that do such things, *and* all that do unrighteously, *are* an abomination unto the LORD thy God.

17 ¶ Remember what Amalek did unto thee by the way, when ye were come forth out of Egypt;

18 How he met thee by the way, and *a*smote the hindmost of thee, *even* all *that were* feeble behind thee, when thou *wast* faint and weary; and he feared not God.

19 Therefore it shall be, when the LORD thy God hath given thee rest from all thine enemies round about, in the land which the LORD thy God giveth thee *for* an inheritance to possess it, *that* thou shalt *a*blot out the remembrance of *b*Amalek from under heaven; thou shalt not forget *it.*

CHAPTER 26

The children of Israel are to offer to the Lord a basket of the firstfruits of Canaan—They are commanded to keep the law of tithing—They covenant to keep the commandments, and the Lord promises to make them a holy people and a great nation.

AND it shall be, when thou *art* come in unto the land which the LORD thy God giveth thee *for* an inheritance, and possessest it, and dwellest therein;

2 That thou shalt take of the first of all the *a*fruit of the earth, which thou shalt bring of thy land that the LORD thy God giveth thee, and shalt put *it* in a basket, and shalt go unto the *b*place which the LORD thy God shall choose to place his name there.

3 And thou shalt go unto the priest that shall be in those days, and say unto him, I profess this day unto the LORD thy God, that I am come unto the country which the LORD sware unto our fathers for to give us.

4 And the priest shall take the basket out of thine hand, and set it down before the altar of the LORD thy God.

5 And thou shalt speak and say before the LORD thy God, A *a*Syrian ready to perish *was* my father, and he went down into *b*Egypt, and sojourned there with a few, and became there a *c*nation, great, mighty, and *d*populous:

6 And the *a*Egyptians *b*evil entreated us, and afflicted us, and laid upon us hard bondage:

7 And when we *a*cried unto the LORD God of our fathers, the LORD *b*heard our voice, and looked on our affliction, and our labour, and our *c*oppression:

8 And the LORD *a*brought us forth out of Egypt with a mighty hand, and with an outstretched arm, and with great terribleness, and with *b*signs, and with wonders:

9 And he hath brought us into this place, and hath given us this land, *even* a *a*land that floweth with milk and honey.

10 And now, behold, I have brought the firstfruits of the land, which thou, O LORD, hast given me. And thou shalt set it before the LORD thy God, and worship before the LORD thy God:

11 And thou shalt *a*rejoice in every good *thing* which the LORD thy God hath given unto thee, and unto thine

---

15a HEB full, whole.
 b Lev. 19:36;
   Ezek. 45:10;
   Amos 8:5.
 c Deut. 4:40.
18a HEB attacked your
   rear.
19a Alma 5:57.
 b Ex. 17:14 (8–16).
26 2a Ex. 23:19; 34:26;
   Num. 18:13.

 b Deut. 12:5;
   1 Kgs. 8:29 (26–30).
5a HEB Aramean. Abraham
   migrated to Aram and
   from there to the land
   of promise.
   Gen. 28:5;
   Hosea 12:12.
 b Gen. 47:4.
 c TG Israel, Origins of.
 d Ex. 1:7.

6a Ex. 1:11.
 b OR treated us harshly.
7a Ex. 2:23 (23–25).
 b Alma 9:26.
 c TG Oppression.
8a Ex. 12:37, 51;
   Alma 36:2.
 b Mosiah 3:15 (14–15).
9a 1 Ne. 2:20.
11a Deut. 12:7;
   2 Ne. 9:52.

house, thou, and the Levite, and the *b*stranger that *is* among you.

12 ¶ When thou hast made an end of tithing all the *a*tithes of thine increase the third year, *which is* the year of tithing, and hast given *it* unto the Levite, the stranger, the fatherless, and the widow, that they may eat within thy *b*gates, and be filled;

13 Then thou shalt say before the LORD thy God, I have brought away the *a*hallowed things out of *mine* house, and also have given them unto the Levite, and unto the stranger, to the *b*fatherless, and to the widow, according to all thy commandments which thou hast commanded me: I have not transgressed thy commandments, neither have I forgotten *them:*

14 I have not eaten thereof in my mourning, neither have I taken away *ought* thereof for *any* unclean *use,* nor given *ought* thereof for the dead: *but* I have hearkened to the voice of the LORD my God, *and* have done according to all that thou hast commanded me.

15 *a*Look down from thy holy habitation, from heaven, and bless thy people Israel, and the land which thou hast given us, as thou swarest unto our fathers, a land that floweth with milk and honey.

16 ¶ This day the LORD thy God hath commanded thee to do these statutes and *a*judgments: thou shalt therefore keep and do them with all thine *b*heart, and with all thy soul.

17 Thou hast *a*avouched the *b*LORD this day to be thy God, and to walk in his ways, and to keep his statutes, and his commandments, and his judgments, and to hearken unto his voice:

18 And the LORD hath avouched thee this day to be his *a*peculiar people, as he hath promised thee, and that *thou* shouldest keep all his commandments;

19 And to make thee *a*high above all nations which he hath made, in praise, and in name, and in honour; and that thou mayest be an *b*holy people unto the LORD thy God, as he hath spoken.

CHAPTER 27

The children of Israel are to cross the Jordan, build an altar, and worship the Lord—They are the Lord's people but will be cursed if they do not obey Him.

AND Moses with the *a*elders of Israel commanded the people, saying, *b*Keep all the commandments which I command you this day.

2 And it shall be on the day when ye shall pass over Jordan unto the land which the LORD thy God giveth thee, that thou shalt set thee up great *a*stones, and plaster them with plaster:

3 And thou shalt write upon them all the words of this law, when thou art passed over, that thou mayest go in unto the land which the LORD thy God giveth thee, a land that floweth with milk and honey; as the LORD God of thy fathers hath promised thee.

4 Therefore it shall be when ye be gone over Jordan, *that* ye shall set up these stones, which I command you this day, in mount Ebal, and thou shalt plaster them with plaster.

5 And there shalt thou build an altar unto the LORD thy God, an altar of *a*stones: thou shalt not lift up *any* *b*iron *tool* upon them.

6 Thou shalt build the *a*altar of the LORD thy God of whole stones: and

---

11*b* HEB sojourner, proselyte (also vv. 12–13).
12*a* TG Tithing.
  b IE of the cities, towns.
13*a* HEB consecrated.
  b James 1:27.
15*a* Isa. 63:15.
16*a* HEB ordinances (also v. 17).

b TG Commitment.
17*a* OR declared, testified. Ex. 19:8.
  b Gen. 28:21.
18*a* OR treasured. TG Israel, Mission of; Peculiar People.
19*a* Deut. 28:1.
  b TG Israel, Blessings of.

27 1*a* TG Church Organization.
  b Mosiah 12:33 (33–37).
2*a* Josh. 4:3.
5*a* 1 Ne. 2:7.
  b Ex. 20:25.
6*a* Josh. 8:31 (30–32).

thou shalt offer burnt offerings thereon unto the LORD thy God:

7 And thou shalt offer peace ᵃofferings, and shalt eat there, and rejoice before the LORD thy God.

8 And thou shalt write upon the stones all the words of this law very plainly.

9 ¶ And Moses and the priests the Levites spake unto all Israel, saying, Take heed, and hearken, O Israel; this day thou art become the people of the ᵃLORD thy God.

10 Thou shalt therefore obey the voice of the LORD thy God, and do his commandments and his statutes, which I command thee this day.

11 ¶ And Moses charged the people the same day, saying,

12 These shall stand upon mount Gerizim to ᵃbless the people, when ye are come over Jordan; Simeon, and Levi, and Judah, and Issachar, and Joseph, and Benjamin:

13 And these shall stand upon mount Ebal to curse; Reuben, Gad, and Asher, and Zebulun, Dan, and Naphtali.

14 ¶ And the Levites shall ᵃspeak, and say unto all the men of Israel with a loud voice,

15 ᵃCursed *be* the man that maketh *any* graven or molten ᵇimage, an abomination unto the LORD, the work of the hands of the craftsman, and putteth *it* in *a* secret *place*. And all the people shall answer and say, Amen.

16 Cursed *be* he that ᵃsetteth light by his ᵇfather or his mother. And all the people shall say, Amen.

17 Cursed *be* he that removeth his neighbour's ᵃlandmark. And all the people shall say, Amen.

18 Cursed *be* he that ᵃmaketh the ᵇblind to wander out of the way. And all the people shall say, Amen.

19 Cursed *be* he that ᵃperverteth the ᵇjudgment of the stranger, fatherless, and widow. And all the people shall say, Amen.

20 Cursed *be* he that lieth with his father's wife; because he uncovereth ᵃhis father's skirt. And all the people shall say, Amen.

21 Cursed *be* he that lieth with any manner of ᵃbeast. And all the people shall say, Amen.

22 ᵃCursed *be* he that lieth with his sister, the daughter of his father, or the daughter of his mother. And all the people shall say, Amen.

23 Cursed *be* he that lieth with his mother in law. And all the people shall say, Amen.

24 Cursed *be* he that ᵃsmiteth his ᵇneighbour ᶜsecretly. And all the people shall say, Amen.

25 Cursed *be* he that taketh ᵃreward to slay an innocent person. And all the people shall say, Amen.

26 ᵃCursed *be* he that confirmeth not *all* the words of this law to do them. And all the people shall say, Amen.

CHAPTER 28

If the children of Israel are obedient, they will be blessed temporally and spiritually—If they are disobedient, they will be cursed, smitten, and destroyed; diseases, plagues, and oppression will come upon them; they will serve false gods and become a byword among all nations; fierce nations will enslave them; and they will eat their own children and be scattered among all nations.

AND it shall come to pass, if thou shalt ᵃhearken diligently unto the voice of the LORD thy God, to

---

7a TG Sacrifice.
9a Mosiah 5:8 (5–15).
12a Deut. 11:29;
   Josh. 8:33 (33–35);
   Alma 45:16 (15–17);
   D&C 130:21.
14a Deut. 33:10.
15a TG Curse.
   b Ex. 34:17;
   Hosea 13:2;
   Mosiah 13:12 (12–14).

16a HEB esteems lightly, disgraces.
   b TG Honoring Father and Mother.
17a Deut. 19:14.
18a OR misleads.
   b Lev. 19:14.
19a Deut. 24:17.
   b OR justice due to.
20a OR her who is his father's.

21a Lev. 20:15 (15–16).
22a Lev. 20:17.
24a Ex. 21:14.
   b Deut. 19:11.
   c Moses 5:31 (29–41).
25a HEB bribe.
   Ezek. 22:12;
   Moses 5:31 (29–41).
26a TG Curse.
28 1a TG Obedience.

observe *and* to do all his commandments which I command thee this day, that the LORD thy God will set thee on *b*high above all nations of the earth:

2 And all these *a*blessings shall come on thee, and overtake thee, if thou shalt hearken unto the voice of the LORD thy God.

3 Blessed *shalt* thou *be* in the city, and blessed *shalt* thou *be* in the field.

4 Blessed *shall be* the *a*fruit of thy body, and the fruit of thy ground, and the fruit of thy *b*cattle, the increase of thy kine, and the *c*flocks of thy sheep.

5 Blessed *shall be* thy basket and thy *a*store.

6 Blessed *shalt* thou *be* when thou *a*comest in, and blessed *shalt* thou *be* when thou goest out.

7 The LORD shall cause thine enemies that rise up against thee to be smitten before thy face: they shall come out against thee one way, and flee before thee seven ways.

8 The LORD shall *a*command the blessing upon thee in thy storehouses, and in *b*all that thou settest thine hand unto; and he shall bless thee in the *c*land which the LORD thy God giveth thee.

9 The LORD shall establish thee an *a*holy people unto himself, as he hath sworn unto thee, if thou shalt keep the commandments of the LORD thy God, and walk in his ways.

10 And all people of the earth shall see that thou art called by the *a*name of the LORD; and they shall be *b*afraid of thee.

11 And the LORD shall make thee *a*plenteous in goods, in the *b*fruit of thy body, and in the fruit of thy cattle, and in the fruit of thy ground,

in the land which the LORD sware unto thy fathers to give thee.

12 The LORD shall open unto thee his good *a*treasure, the heaven to give the *b*rain unto thy land in his season, and to bless all the work of thine hand: and thou shalt lend unto many nations, and thou shalt not *c*borrow.

13 And the LORD shall make thee the head, and not the tail; and thou shalt be above only, and thou shalt not be beneath; if that thou hearken unto the commandments of the LORD thy God, which I command thee this day, to observe and to do *them:*

14 And thou shalt not go *a*aside from any of the words which I command thee this day, *to* the right hand, or *to* the left, to go after other *b*gods to serve them.

15 ¶ But it shall come to pass, if thou wilt not *a*hearken unto the voice of the LORD thy God, to observe to do all his commandments and his statutes which I command thee this day; that all these *b*curses shall come upon thee, and overtake thee:

16 Cursed *shalt* thou *be* in the city, and cursed *shalt* thou *be* in the field.

17 Cursed *shall be* thy basket and thy store.

18 Cursed *shall be* the *a*fruit of thy body, and the fruit of thy land, the increase of thy kine, and the flocks of thy sheep.

19 Cursed *shalt* thou *be* when thou comest in, and cursed *shalt* thou *be* when thou goest out.

20 The LORD shall send upon thee cursing, vexation, and rebuke, in all that thou settest thine hand unto for to do, until thou be destroyed, and

1 *b* Deut. 26:19.
2 *a* TG Blessing;
    Israel, Blessings of.
4 *a* TG Birth Control.
  b HEB beasts (also v. 11).
  c HEB increase of thy
    flocks (also vv. 18, 51).
5 *a* HEB kneading trough.
6 *a* Ps. 121:8.
8 *a* Ps. 133:3 (1–3).
  b Luke 12:31;

    D&C 24:3 (3–4).
  c Ether 1:43 (42–43).
9 *a* TG Holiness.
10 *a* Num. 6:27;
    Mosiah 26:18.
  b Deut. 11:25.
11 *a* Deut. 30:9 (8–10).
  b TG Birth Control.
12 *a* TG Treasure.
  b Lev. 26:4;
    Deut. 11:14.

  c TG Borrow.
14 *a* D&C 124:120.
  b Deut. 5:32 (32–33).
15 *a* Lev. 26:14 (14–45);
    Jer. 26:4;
    Ezek. 11:21;
    Mal. 2:2;
    D&C 97:26 (25–26);
    133:63.
  b TG Curse; Plague.
18 *a* Hag. 1:10.

until thou perish quickly; because of the wickedness of thy doings, whereby thou hast forsaken me.

21 The LORD shall make the pestilence cleave unto thee, until he have consumed thee from off the land, whither thou goest to possess it.

22 The LORD shall *a*smite thee with a *b*consumption, and with a fever, and with an inflammation, and with an extreme burning, and with the sword, and with blasting, and with mildew; and they shall pursue thee until thou perish.

23 And thy heaven that *is* over thy head shall be brass, and the earth that *is* under thee *shall be* iron.

24 The LORD shall make the rain of thy land powder and dust: from heaven shall it come down upon thee, until thou be destroyed.

25 The LORD shall cause thee to be smitten before thine enemies: thou shalt go out one way against them, and flee seven ways before them: and shalt be removed into all the kingdoms of the earth.

26 And thy *a*carcase shall be meat unto all fowls of the air, and unto the beasts of the earth, and no man shall fray *them* away.

27 The LORD will *a*smite thee with the *b*botch of Egypt, and with *c*the *d*emerods, and with the scab, and with the itch, whereof thou canst not be healed.

28 The LORD shall smite thee with madness, and blindness, and astonishment of heart:

29 And thou shalt grope at noonday, as the *a*blind gropeth in darkness, and thou shalt not *b*prosper in thy ways: and thou shalt be only oppressed and *c*spoiled evermore, and no man shall save *thee*.

30 Thou shalt betroth a wife, and another man shall lie with her: thou shalt build an house, and thou shalt not *a*dwell therein: thou shalt *b*plant a vineyard, and shalt not gather the grapes thereof.

31 Thine ox *shall be* slain before thine eyes, and thou shalt not eat thereof: thine ass *shall be* violently taken away from before thy face, and shall not be restored to thee: thy sheep *shall be* given unto thine enemies, and thou shalt have none to rescue *them*.

32 Thy sons and thy daughters *shall be* given unto another people, and thine eyes shall look, and fail *with longing* for them all the day long: and *there shall be* no *a*might in thine hand.

33 The fruit of thy land, and all thy labours, shall a nation which thou knowest not eat up; and thou shalt be only oppressed and crushed alway:

34 So that thou shalt be *a*mad for the sight of thine eyes which thou shalt see.

35 The LORD shall smite thee in the knees, and in the legs, with a sore botch that cannot be healed, from the sole of thy foot unto the top of thy head.

36 The LORD shall bring thee, and thy king which thou shalt set over thee, unto a nation which neither thou nor thy fathers have known; and there shalt thou serve other *a*gods, wood and stone.

37 And thou shalt become an *a*astonishment, a *b*proverb, and a *c*byword, among all nations whither the LORD shall lead thee.

38 Thou shalt carry much *a*seed out into the field, and shalt gather *but* little in; for the locust shall consume it.

39 Thou shalt plant vineyards, and dress *them*, but shalt neither

---

22*a* Hag. 2:17.
  b Lev. 26:16.
26*a* Jer. 16:4;
    Mosiah 12:2;
    JS—M 1:27.
27*a* TG Punish.
  b OR boils.
    Ex. 9:9 (8–10).
  c HEB hemorrhoids or

tumors.
  d 1 Sam. 5:6.
29*a* Isa. 59:10 (9–10);
    D&C 95:6.
  b Omni 1:6.
  c HEB robbed continually.
30*a* Amos 5:11.
  b Zeph. 1:13.
32*a* OR power to prevent it.

34*a* OR driven mad by the sight your eyes shall see.
36*a* TG Idolatry.
37*a* Isa. 65:15.
  b Jer. 24:9.
  c 1 Ne. 19:14.
38*a* Micah 6:15;
    Hag. 1:6 (5–11).

drink *of* the wine, nor gather *the grapes*; for the worms shall eat them.

40 Thou shalt have olive trees throughout all thy coasts, but thou shalt not *a*anoint *thyself* with the oil; for thine olive shall cast *his fruit*.

41 Thou shalt beget *a*sons and daughters, but thou shalt not enjoy them; for they shall go into captivity.

42 All thy trees and fruit of thy land shall the locust consume.

43 The stranger that *is* within thee shall get up above thee very high; and thou shalt come down very low.

44 He shall lend to thee, and thou shalt not lend to him: he shall be the head, and thou shalt be the tail.

45 Moreover all these curses shall come upon thee, and shall pursue thee, and overtake thee, till thou be destroyed; because thou hearkenedst not unto the voice of the LORD thy God, to keep his commandments and his statutes which he commanded thee:

46 And they shall be upon thee for a sign and for a wonder, and upon thy seed for ever.

47 Because thou servedst not the LORD thy God with *a*joyfulness, and with *b*gladness of heart, for the abundance of all *things;*

48 Therefore shalt thou serve thine enemies which the LORD shall send against thee, in hunger, and in thirst, and in nakedness, and in want of all *things:* and he shall put a *a*yoke of iron upon thy neck, until he have destroyed thee.

49 The LORD shall bring a nation against thee from *a*far, from the *b*end of the earth, *as swift* as the *c*eagle flieth; a nation whose *d*tongue thou shalt not understand;

50 A nation of fierce countenance, which shall not *a*regard the person

of the *b*old, nor shew favour to the young:

51 And he shall *a*eat the fruit of thy cattle, and the fruit of thy *b*land, until thou be destroyed: which *also* shall not leave thee *either* corn, wine, or oil, *or* the increase of thy *c*kine, or flocks of thy sheep, until he have destroyed thee.

52 And he shall *a*besiege thee in all thy gates, until thy high and fenced walls come down, wherein thou trustedst, throughout all thy land: and he shall besiege thee in all thy gates throughout all thy land, which the LORD thy God hath given thee.

53 And thou shalt *a*eat the fruit of thine own body, the *b*flesh of thy sons and of thy daughters, which the LORD thy God hath given thee, in the siege, and in the *c*straitness, wherewith thine enemies shall distress thee:

54 *So that* the man *that is* tender among you, and very delicate, his eye shall be evil toward his brother, and toward the wife of his bosom, and toward the remnant of his children which he shall leave:

55 So that he will not give to any of them of the flesh of his children whom he shall eat: because he hath nothing left him in the siege, and in the straitness, wherewith thine enemies shall distress thee in all thy gates.

56 The tender and delicate woman among you, which would not adventure to set the sole of her foot upon the ground for delicateness and tenderness, her eye shall be evil toward the husband of her bosom, and toward her son, and toward her daughter,

57 And toward her young one that cometh out from between her feet, and toward her children which she shall bear: for she shall *a*eat them

40*a* TG Anointing.
41*a* Job 27:14 (13–15).
47*a* TG Joy.
  b TG Cheerful.
48*a* TG Bondage, Physical.
49*a* Jer. 6:22 (22–24).
  b Isa. 5:26 (26–30).
  c Hosea 8:1.

d Isa. 33:19.
  TG Language.
50*a* Jer. 21:7.
  b Isa. 3:5;
    Lam. 4:16 (16–17).
51*a* Jer. 5:17.
  b Isa. 1:7.
  c HEB cattle.

52*a* Luke 19:43 (43–44).
53*a* Lev. 26:29;
    Jer. 19:9;
    2 Ne. 19:20.
  b 2 Kgs. 6:29 (28–29).
  c OR distress (also
    vv. 55, 57).
57*a* Lam. 4:10.

for want of all *things* secretly in the siege and straitness, wherewith thine enemy shall distress thee in thy gates.

58 If thou wilt not ^aobserve to do all the words of this law that are written in this book, that thou mayest fear this glorious and fearful ^bname, ^cTHE LORD THY GOD;

59 Then the LORD will make thy ^aplagues ^bwonderful, and the plagues of thy seed, *even* great plagues, and of long continuance, and sore ^csicknesses, and of long continuance.

60 Moreover he will bring upon thee all the ^adiseases of Egypt, which thou wast afraid of; and they shall cleave unto thee.

61 Also every sickness, and every plague, which *is* not written in the book of this law, them will the LORD bring upon thee, until thou be destroyed.

62 And ye shall be left few in number, whereas ye were as the stars of heaven for multitude; because thou wouldest not ^aobey the voice of the LORD thy God.

63 And it shall come to pass, *that* as the LORD rejoiced over you to do you good, and to multiply you; so the LORD will rejoice over you to destroy you, and to bring you to nought; and ye shall be plucked from off the land whither thou goest to possess it.

64 And the LORD shall ^ascatter thee among all people, from the one end of the earth even unto the other; and there thou shalt serve other gods, which neither thou nor thy fathers have known, *even* wood and stone.

65 And among these nations shalt thou find no ease, neither shall the sole of thy foot have rest: but the LORD shall give thee there a trembling heart, and failing of eyes, and ^asorrow of mind:

66 And thy life shall hang in ^adoubt before thee; and thou shalt fear day and night, and shalt have none assurance of thy life:

67 In the morning thou shalt say, Would God it were even! and at even thou shalt say, Would God it were morning! for the fear of thine heart wherewith thou shalt fear, and for the sight of thine eyes which thou shalt see.

68 And the LORD shall bring thee ^ainto Egypt again with ships, by the way whereof I spake unto thee, Thou shalt see it no more again: and there ye shall be sold unto your enemies for bondmen and bondwomen, and no man shall buy *you*.

CHAPTER 29

The children of Israel make a covenant with the Lord under which they will be blessed if they are obedient, and cursed if they are disobedient—If they are disobedient, their land will be as brimstone and salt.

THESE *are* the words of the ^acovenant, which the LORD commanded Moses to make with the children of Israel in the land of Moab, beside the covenant which he made with them in Horeb.

2 ¶ And Moses called unto all Israel, and said unto them, Ye have seen all that the LORD did before your eyes in the land of Egypt unto Pharaoh, and unto all his servants, and unto all his land;

3 The great ^atemptations which thine eyes have seen, the signs, and those great ^bmiracles:

4 Yet the LORD hath not given you an heart to perceive, and eyes to see, and ears to hear, unto this day.

5 And I have led you forty years in the wilderness: your clothes are not ^awaxen old upon you, and thy shoe is not waxen old upon thy foot.

58*a* TG Obedience.
  b Ps. 48:10.
    TG Name.
  c HEB Jehovah.
59*a* TG Plague.
  b HEB extraordinary.
  c TG Sickness.

60*a* Ex. 9:14.
62*a* TG Disobedience.
64*a* TG Israel, Scattering of.
65*a* HEB anguish of soul.
    TG Sorrow.
66*a* TG Doubt.
68*a* IE into captivity,

symbolized by "Egypt."
    Hosea 8:13.
29 1*a* Deut. 5:3 (2–3).
  3*a* HEB trials, tests.
    TG Test.
  b Deut. 7:19.
  5*a* OR become worn.

6 Ye have not eaten bread, neither have ye drunk wine or strong drink: that ye might know that I *am* the LORD your God.

7 And when ye came unto this place, ^aSihon the king of Heshbon, and Og the king of Bashan, came out against us unto battle, and we ^bsmote them:

8 And we took their land, and gave it for an inheritance unto the Reubenites, and to the Gadites, and to the half tribe of Manasseh.

9 Keep therefore the words of this covenant, and do them, that ye may ^aprosper in all that ye do.

10 ¶ Ye stand this day all of you before the LORD your God; your captains of your tribes, your elders, and your officers, *with* all the men of Israel,

11 Your little ones, your wives, and thy stranger that *is* in thy camp, from the ^ahewer of thy wood unto the drawer of thy water:

12 That thou shouldest enter into ^acovenant with the LORD thy God, and into his ^boath, which the LORD thy God maketh with thee this day:

13 That he may establish thee to day for a people unto himself, and *that* he may be unto thee a ^aGod, as he hath said unto thee, and as he hath sworn unto thy fathers, to Abraham, to Isaac, and to Jacob.

14 Neither with you only do I make this covenant and this oath;

15 But with *him* that standeth here with us this day before the LORD our God, and also with *him* that *is* not here with us this day:

16 (For ye know how we have dwelt in the land of Egypt; and how we came through the nations which ye passed by;

17 And ye have seen their abominations, and their idols, wood and stone, silver and gold, which *were* among them:)

18 Lest there should be among you man, or woman, or family, or tribe, whose heart ^aturneth away this day from the LORD our God, to go *and* serve the gods of these nations; lest there should be among you a root that beareth ^bgall and wormwood;

19 And it come to pass, when he heareth the words of this ^acurse, that he ^bbless himself in his heart, saying, I shall have peace, though I walk in the imagination of mine heart, to add ^cdrunkenness to thirst:

20 The LORD will not spare him, but then the anger of the LORD and his jealousy shall smoke against that man, and all the ^acurses that are written in this book shall lie upon him, and the LORD shall ^bblot out his name from under heaven.

21 And the LORD shall separate him unto evil out of all the tribes of Israel, according to all the curses of the covenant that are written in this book of the law:

22 So that the generation to come of your children that shall rise up after you, and the stranger that shall come from a far land, shall say, when they see the plagues of that land, and the sicknesses which the LORD hath laid upon it;

23 *And that* the whole land thereof *is* ^abrimstone, and ^bsalt, *and* burning, *that* it is not sown, nor beareth, nor any grass groweth therein, like the overthrow of Sodom, and Gomorrah, ^cAdmah, and Zeboim, which the LORD overthrew in his anger, and in his wrath:

24 Even all nations shall say, ^aWherefore hath the LORD ^bdone thus unto this land? what *meaneth* the heat of this great anger?

25 Then men shall say, Because

7a Deut. 2:32 (32–33).
  b Num. 21:24 (21–24);
    Deut. 2:33.
9a Josh. 1:7; 1 Kgs. 2:3;
    2 Ne. 1:9; D&C 9:13.
11a Josh. 9:21.
12a TG Covenants.
  b TG Oath.
13a Ex. 6:7.

18a TG Apostasy of
    Individuals.
  b HEB poisonous and
    bitter fruit.
19a OR oath; i.e., the
    covenant is a blessing to
    those who keep it, but
    a curse to those who
    don't.

  b Ps. 49:18 (16–20).
  c TG Drunkenness.
20a TG Curse.
  b Alma 5:57.
23a Gen. 19:24 (24–25).
  b Jer. 17:6.
  c Hosea 11:8.
24a Jer. 16:10.
  b 1 Kgs. 9:8.

they have ^aforsaken the ^bcovenant of the LORD God of their fathers, which he made with them when he brought them forth out of the land of Egypt:

26 For they went and served other gods, and worshipped them, gods whom they knew not, and *whom* he had not given unto them:

27 And the anger of the LORD was kindled against this land, to bring upon it all the curses that are written in this book:

28 And the LORD ^arooted them out of their ^bland in anger, and in wrath, and in great ^cindignation, and cast them into another land, as *it is* this day.

29 The ^asecret *things belong* unto the LORD our God: but those *things which are* ^brevealed *belong* unto us and to our children for ever, that *we* may do all the words of this law.

CHAPTER 30

The scattered Israelites will be gathered from all nations when they remember the covenant—Moses places life or death, blessing or cursing, before the people.

AND it shall come to pass, when all these things are come upon thee, the ^ablessing and the curse, which I have set before thee, and thou shalt call *them* to mind among all the nations, whither the LORD thy God hath driven thee,

2 And shalt ^areturn unto the LORD thy God, and shalt obey his voice according to all that I command thee this day, thou and thy children, with all thine heart, and with all thy soul;

3 That then the LORD thy God will turn thy ^acaptivity, and have ^bcompassion upon thee, and will return and ^cgather thee from all the nations, whither the LORD thy God hath scattered thee.

4 If *any* of thine be driven out unto the outmost *parts* of ^aheaven, from thence will the LORD thy God gather thee, and from thence will he fetch thee:

5 And the LORD thy God will bring thee into the land which thy fathers possessed, and thou shalt possess it; and he will do thee good, and multiply thee above thy fathers.

6 And the LORD thy God will ^acircumcise thine heart, and the heart of thy seed, to ^blove the LORD thy God with all thine heart, and with all thy soul, that thou mayest live.

7 And the LORD thy God will put all these ^acurses upon thine ^benemies, and on them that hate thee, which persecuted thee.

8 And thou shalt return and obey the voice of the LORD, and do all his commandments which I command thee this day.

9 And the LORD thy God will make thee ^aplenteous in every work of thine hand, in the fruit of thy body, and in the fruit of thy cattle, and in the fruit of thy land, for good: for the LORD will again rejoice over thee for good, as he rejoiced over thy fathers:

10 If thou shalt hearken unto the voice of the LORD thy God, to keep his commandments and his statutes which are written in this book of the law, *and* if thou ^aturn unto the LORD thy God with all thine heart, and with all thy soul.

11 ¶ For this commandment which I command thee this day, it *is* not ^ahidden from thee, neither *is* it far off.

25*a* Jer. 22:9 (8–9).
    TG Apostasy of Israel.
  b TG Covenants.
28*a* 2 Chr. 7:20.
  b Ether 11:21 (20–21).
  c TG God, Indignation of.
29*a* TG Mysteries of Godliness.
  b TG Revelation.
30 1*a* TG Agency.
  2*a* 1 Sam. 7:3;

Zech. 10:9.
  TG Israel, Restoration of.
3*a* Zeph. 2:7; 3:20.
  b Jer. 12:15.
  c Neh. 1:9;
    Ps. 147:2;
    Ezek. 20:34;
    D&C 33:6; 45:69; 101:13.
    TG Israel, Gathering of.
4*a* Matt. 24:31.

6*a* TG Circumcision.
  b TG Love.
7*a* TG Curse.
  b D&C 103:25 (24–26); 136:30.
9*a* Deut. 28:11 (9–12); 2 Ne. 1:9.
10*a* Mosiah 7:33.
11*a* OR too hard for you.
    1 Ne. 20:16;
    D&C 84:23; 93:31.

12 It *is* not in heaven, that thou shouldest say, Who shall go up for us to heaven, and bring it unto us, that we may hear it, and do it?

13 Neither *is* it beyond the sea, that thou shouldest say, Who shall go over the sea for us, and bring it unto us, that we may hear it, and do it?

14 But the word *is* very nigh unto thee, in thy mouth, and in thy ᵃheart, that thou mayest do it.

15 ¶ See, I have set before thee this day ᵃlife and good, and death and ᵇevil;

16 In that I command thee this day to love the Lᴏʀᴅ thy God, to ᵃwalk in his ways, and to keep his commandments and his statutes and his ᵇjudgments, that thou mayest live and multiply: and the Lᴏʀᴅ thy God shall bless thee in the land whither thou goest to possess it.

17 But if thine heart turn away, so that thou wilt not hear, but shalt be drawn away, and worship other gods, and serve them;

18 I ᵃdenounce unto you this day, that ye shall surely perish, *and that* ye shall not prolong *your* days upon the land, whither thou passest over Jordan to go to possess it.

19 I call heaven and earth to record this day against you, *that* I have set before you life and death, blessing and ᵃcursing: therefore ᵇchoose life, that both thou and thy seed may live:

20 That thou mayest love the Lᴏʀᴅ thy God, *and* that thou mayest ᵃobey his voice, and that thou mayest cleave unto him: for he *is* thy ᵇlife, and the length of thy days: that thou mayest dwell in the land which the Lᴏʀᴅ sware unto thy fathers, to Abraham, to Isaac, and to Jacob, to give them.

CHAPTER 31

Moses counsels Joshua and all Israel to be strong and of good courage—The law is to be read to all Israel every seven years—The children of Israel will follow false gods and corrupt themselves.

Aɴᴅ Moses went and spake these words unto all Israel.

2 And he said unto them, I *am* an ᵃhundred and twenty years old this day; I can no more go out and come in: also the Lᴏʀᴅ hath said unto me, Thou shalt not ᵇgo over this Jordan.

3 The Lᴏʀᴅ thy God, he will go over before thee, *and* he will destroy these nations from before thee, and thou shalt ᵃpossess them: *and* Joshua, he shall go over before thee, as the Lᴏʀᴅ hath said.

4 And the Lᴏʀᴅ shall do unto them as he did to Sihon and to Og, kings of the Amorites, and unto the land of them, whom he ᵃdestroyed.

5 And the Lᴏʀᴅ shall give them up before your face, that ye may do unto them according unto all the commandments which I have commanded you.

6 Be strong and of a good ᵃcourage, fear not, nor be afraid of them: for the ᵇLᴏʀᴅ thy God, he *it is* that doth go with thee; he will not ᶜfail thee, nor ᵈforsake thee.

7 ¶ And Moses called unto ᵃJoshua, and said unto him in the sight of all Israel, Be strong and of a good courage: for thou must go with this people unto the land which the Lᴏʀᴅ hath sworn unto their fathers to give them; and thou shalt cause them to inherit it.

8 And the Lᴏʀᴅ, he *it is* that doth go before thee; he will be ᵃwith thee, he will not fail thee, neither forsake thee: fear not, neither be dismayed.

9 ¶ And Moses ᵃwrote this law,

14*a* TG Heart.
15*a* Jer. 21:8; 2 Ne. 2:27.
  b TG Evil.
16*a* D&C 25:2.
  b HEB ordinances.
18*a* HEB declare.
19*a* TG Curse.
  b TG Agency; Justice.
20*a* TG Obedience.

  b Acts 17:28;
     D&C 88:13 (7, 13).
31 2*a* Ex. 7:7;
     Deut. 34:7;
     Acts 7:23.
  b Num. 20:12.
 3*a* OR dispossess.
 4*a* Ether 9:20.
 6*a* TG Courage.

  b Isa. 41:10; D&C 68:6.
  c Alma 2:28.
  d 1 Kgs. 6:13;
     Ps. 94:14.
 7*a* Deut. 1:38.
 8*a* Josh. 1:5.
 9*a* TG Record Keeping;
     Scribe;
     Scriptures, Writing of.

and delivered it unto the priests the sons of Levi, which bare the ark of the covenant of the LORD, and unto all the *b*elders of Israel.

10 And Moses commanded them, saying, At the end of *every* seven years, *a*in the solemnity of the year of *b*release, in the feast of tabernacles,

11 When all Israel is *a*come to appear before the LORD thy God in the *b*place which he shall choose, thou shalt *c*read this *d*law before all Israel in their hearing.

12 Gather the people together, men, and women, and children, and thy *a*stranger that *is* within thy gates, that they may hear, and that they may learn, and fear the LORD your God, and observe to do all the words of this law:

13 And *that* their children, which have not known *any thing*, may hear, and *a*learn to fear the LORD your God, as long as ye live in the land whither ye go over Jordan to possess it.

14 ¶ And the LORD said unto Moses, Behold, thy *a*days approach that thou must die: call Joshua, and present yourselves in the *b*tabernacle of the congregation, that I may give him a charge. And Moses and Joshua went, and presented themselves in the tabernacle of the congregation.

15 And the LORD appeared in the tabernacle in a pillar of a cloud: and the pillar of the cloud stood over the door of the tabernacle.

16 ¶ And the LORD said unto Moses, Behold, thou shalt sleep with thy fathers; and this people will rise up, and go a *a*whoring after the *b*gods of the strangers of the land, whither they go *to be* among them, and will forsake me, and *c*break my covenant which I have made with them.

17 Then my anger shall be kindled against them in that day, and I will forsake them, and I will *a*hide my face from them, and they shall be devoured, and many evils and troubles shall befall them; so that they will say in that day, Are not these evils come upon us, because our God *is* not among us?

18 And I will surely hide my *a*face in that day for all the evils which they shall have wrought, in that they are turned unto other gods.

19 Now therefore *a*write ye this *b*song for you, and teach it the children of Israel: put it in their mouths, that this song may be a witness for me against the children of Israel.

20 For when I shall have brought them into the land which I sware unto their fathers, that floweth with milk and honey; and they shall have eaten and filled themselves, and waxen fat; then will they turn unto other gods, and serve them, and *a*provoke me, and break my covenant.

21 And it shall come to pass, when many evils and troubles are befallen them, that this *a*song shall testify against them as a witness; for it shall not be forgotten out of the mouths of their seed: for I know *b*their imagination which they go about, even now, before I have brought them into the land which I sware.

22 ¶ Moses therefore wrote this song the same day, and taught it the children of Israel.

23 And he gave Joshua the son of Nun a *a*charge, and said, Be strong and of a good courage: for thou shalt bring the children of Israel into the land which I sware unto them: and I will be with thee.

24 ¶ And it came to pass, when

9*b* TG Elder, Melchizedek Priesthood.
10*a* HEB at the appointed time.
   b Deut. 15:2 (1–2, 9).
11*a* TG Meetings.
   b Josh. 9:27 (24–27);
      2 Chr. 7:12.
   c TG Scriptures, Study of.
   d Neh. 8:2 (2–3).

12*a* OR sojourners, proselytes.
13*a* TG Learn.
14*a* Gen. 47:29 (28–29).
   b HEB tent of meeting.
16*a* Ex. 34:15;
      Jer. 3:2 (1–10);
      Hosea 9:1.
   b 2 Ne. 9:37; Alma 7:6.
   c Judg. 2:1.

17*a* Ezek. 39:23.
18*a* 3 Ne. 9:11.
19*a* 3 Ne. 16:4.
   b Deut. 32:1 (1–43).
20*a* TG Provoking.
21*a* TG Singing.
   b HEB their inclinations which are already forming.
23*a* Deut. 3:28.

Moses had made an end of writing the words of this law in a book, until they were finished,

25 That Moses commanded the Levites, which bare the ark of the covenant of the LORD, saying,

26 Take this ªbook of the ᵇlaw, and put it in the side of the ᶜark of the covenant of the LORD your God, that it may be there for a ᵈwitness against thee.

27 For I know thy ªrebellion, and thy ᵇstiff neck: behold, while I am yet alive with you this day, ye have been rebellious against the LORD; and how much more after my death?

28 ¶ Gather unto me all the elders of your tribes, and your officers, that I may speak these words in their ears, and call heaven and earth to record against them.

29 For I know that after my death ye will utterly ªcorrupt *yourselves*, and turn aside from the way which I have commanded you; and evil will befall you in the ᵇlatter days; because ye will do evil in the sight of the LORD, to provoke him to anger through the work of your hands.

30 And Moses spake in the ears of all the congregation of Israel the words of this song, until they were ended.

CHAPTER 32

Israel will sing the song of Moses and acclaim: God speaks to heaven and earth; the children of Israel were known in the premortal life; God chose them in this life; they forgot the Rock of their salvation; He sent terror, a sword, and vengeance upon them; there is no God beside Him—Moses will be gathered to his people.

ªGIVE ear, O ye heavens, and I will speak; and ᵇhear, O earth, the ᶜwords of my mouth.

2 My doctrine shall drop as the ªrain, my ᵇspeech shall distil as the ᶜdew, as the small rain upon the tender herb, and as the showers upon the grass:

3 Because I will ªpublish the name of the LORD: ascribe ye greatness unto our God.

4 *He is* the ªRock, his work *is* ᵇperfect: for all his ways *are* ᶜjudgment: a God of truth and without iniquity, ᵈjust and right *is* he.

5 They have corrupted themselves, ªtheir spot *is* not *the spot* of his ᵇchildren: *they are* a ᶜperverse and crooked ᵈgeneration.

6 Do ye thus ªrequite the LORD, O foolish people and unwise? *is* not he thy ᵇfather *that* hath ᶜbought thee? hath he not ᵈmade thee, and established thee?

7 ¶ ªRemember the days of old, consider the years of many generations: ᵇask thy father, and he will shew thee; thy elders, and they will tell thee.

8 When the most High divided to the ªnations their ᵇinheritance, when he separated the sons of Adam, he set the ᶜbounds of the people according to the number of the children of Israel.

9 For the LORD's portion *is* his people; Jacob *is* the lot of his ªinheritance.

26ª TG Scriptures,
    Preservation of.
  b 1 Kgs. 8:21.
  c TG Ark of the Covenant.
  d Ex. 25:21.
27ª TG Rebellion.
  b TG Stiffnecked.
29ª Jer. 44:23.
  b Hosea 3:5 (1–5).
32 1ª Isa. 1:2;
    D&C 1:1 (1–2).
  b D&C 41:1.
  c Deut. 31:19.
 2ª TG Nature, Earth.
  b Isa. 55:11.

  c Hosea 14:5 (4–6);
    D&C 121:45; 128:19.
 3ª HEB proclaim.
 4ª TG Rock.
  b TG God, Perfection of;
    Perfection.
  c HEB just, justice.
  d TG God, Justice of;
    Justice.
 5ª HEB they are no longer
    His children because of
    their blemish.
  b Alma 5:25 (24–25).
  c Matt. 17:17; D&C 33:2.
  d Prov. 30:12 (11–14).

 6ª TG Ingratitude.
  b 1 Chr. 29:10;
    Isa. 63:16; 64:8.
  c HEB created.
  d Isa. 27:11;
    1 Ne. 2:12;
    D&C 43:23.
 7ª Isa. 46:9.
  b Ps. 44:1.
 8ª TG Nations.
  b Acts 17:26 (26–27).
  c D&C 122:9.
    TG Foreordination;
    God, Foreknowledge of.
 9ª TG Inheritance.

10 He found him in a desert land, and in the waste howling wilderness; he [a]led him about, he instructed him, he kept him as the [b]apple of his eye.

11 As an [a]eagle stirreth up her nest, fluttereth over her young, spreadeth abroad her wings, taketh them, beareth them on her wings:

12 *So* the LORD alone did lead him, and *there was* no strange god with him.

13 He made him ride on the [a]high places of the earth, that he might eat the increase of the fields; and he made him to suck honey out of the rock, and oil out of the flinty rock;

14 Butter of kine, and milk of sheep, with fat of lambs, and rams of the breed of Bashan, and goats, with the fat of kidneys of wheat; and thou didst drink the pure [a]blood of the [b]grape.

15 ¶ But [a]Jeshurun waxed fat, and kicked: thou art waxen [b]fat, thou art grown thick, thou art covered *with fatness;* then he [c]forsook God *which* made him, and lightly esteemed the [d]Rock of his salvation.

16 They [a]provoked him to [b]jealousy with strange [c]*gods,* with abominations provoked they him to anger.

17 They [a]sacrificed unto devils, [b]not to God; to [c]gods whom they knew not, to new [d]*gods that* came newly up, whom your fathers feared not.

18 Of the Rock *that* begat thee thou art unmindful, and hast forgotten God that [a]formed thee.

19 And when the LORD saw *it,* he [a]abhorred *them,* because of the [b]provoking of his sons, and of his daughters.

20 And he said, I will [a]hide my face from them, I will see what their end *shall be:* for they *are* a [b]very froward generation, children in whom *is* no [c]faith.

21 They have moved me to [a]jealousy with *that which is* not God; they have [b]provoked me to [c]anger with their vanities: and I will move them to [d]jealousy with *those which are* not a people; I will provoke them to anger with a foolish nation.

22 For a [a]fire is kindled in mine anger, and shall burn unto the lowest hell, and shall consume the earth with her increase, and set on fire the foundations of the mountains.

23 I will heap [a]mischiefs upon them; I will spend mine arrows upon them.

24 *They shall be* [a]burnt with hunger, and devoured with burning heat, and with bitter destruction: I will also send the teeth of beasts upon them, with the poison of serpents of the dust.

25 The [a]sword without, and terror within, shall destroy both the young man and the virgin, the suckling *also* with the man of gray hairs.

26 I said, I would [a]scatter them into corners, I would make the remembrance of them to cease from among men:

27 Were it not that I feared the wrath of the enemy, lest their adversaries should behave themselves strangely, *and* lest they should say,

---

10a HEB encircled him, cared for him.
  b Prov. 7:2.
11a Ex. 19:4.
13a Deut. 33:29;
    Isa. 58:14;
    Hab. 3:19.
14a Matt. 26:28 (26–29).
  b D&C 27:5 (2–5).
15a Deut. 33:26.
  b Jer. 5:7 (7, 28).
  c TG Ingratitude.
  d TG Cornerstone; Rock.
16a Ps. 78:58.
  b Num. 25:11.
  c TG Idolatry.

17a 1 Cor. 10:20;
    Abr. 1:8.
  b HEB which were not gods.
  c Judg. 5:8.
  d D&C 52:39;
    Moses 1:6.
18a HEB gave you birth.
19a Alma 37:29.
  b Isa. 1:2.
20a Isa. 8:17.
  b HEB perverse.
  c OR faithfulness.
    TG Faith.
21a Mosiah 11:22; 13:13.
  b TG Provoking.
  c 2 Ne. 15:25;

D&C 63:32;
    Moses 6:27.
  d Rom. 10:19 (17–21).
22a Num. 11:1 (1, 10);
    2 Ne. 26:6.
23a HEB evils.
24a HEB exhausted, spent.
25a Ezek. 7:15;
    1 Ne. 1:13;
    Alma 10:22;
    JS—H 1:45.
26a HEB put an end to them.
    1 Ne. 10:12 (12–14);
    2 Ne. 25:15 (15–16);
    3 Ne. 16:8;
    Morm. 5:15.

Our hand *is* ^ahigh, and the LORD hath not done all this.

28 For they *are* a nation void of counsel, neither *is there any* understanding in them.

29 O that they were ^awise, *that* they understood this, *that* they would consider their latter ^bend!

30 How should one chase a thousand, and two put ten thousand to ^aflight, except their Rock had sold them, and the LORD had shut them up?

31 For their rock *is* not as our ^aRock, even our enemies themselves *being* judges.

32 For their vine *is* of the vine of ^aSodom, and of the fields of Gomorrah: their grapes *are* grapes of gall, their clusters *are* bitter:

33 Their ^awine *is* the poison of ^bdragons, and the cruel venom of asps.

34 *Is* not this laid up in store with me, *and* sealed up among my treasures?

35 To me *belongeth* ^avengeance, and ^brecompence; their foot shall slide in *due* time: for the day of their ^ccalamity *is* at hand, and the things that shall come upon them make haste.

36 For the LORD shall ^ajudge his people, and ^brepent himself for his servants, when he seeth that *their* power is gone, and *there is* none ^cshut up, or left.

37 And he shall say, Where *are* their ^agods, *their* rock in whom they ^btrusted,

38 Which did eat the fat of their sacrifices, *and* drank the wine of their drink offerings? let them rise up and help you, *and* be your protection.

39 See now that I, *even* I, ^a*am* he, and *there is* no god ^bwith me: ^cI kill, and I make ^dalive; I wound, and I heal: neither *is there any* that can deliver out of my hand.

40 For I lift up my hand to heaven, and say, I ^alive for ever.

41 If I whet my glittering ^asword, and mine hand take hold on judgment; I will render vengeance to mine enemies, and will reward them that hate me.

42 I will make mine arrows drunk with blood, and my sword shall devour flesh; *and that* with the blood of the slain and of the captives, from the beginning of revenges upon the enemy.

43 Rejoice, O ye nations, *with* his people: for he will ^aavenge the blood of his servants, and will render vengeance to his adversaries, and will be ^bmerciful unto his land, *and* to his people.

44 ¶ And Moses came and spake all the words of this ^asong in the ears of the people, he, and ^bHoshea the son of Nun.

45 And Moses made an end of speaking all these words to ^aall Israel:

46 And he said unto them, Set your ^ahearts unto all the words which I testify among you this day, which ye shall command your ^bchildren to observe to do, all the words of this law.

47 For it *is* not a vain thing for you; because it *is* your life: and through this thing ye shall ^aprolong *your* days in the land, whither ye go over Jordan to possess it.

48 And the LORD spake unto Moses that selfsame day, saying,

27*a* OR victorious.
29*a* Ps. 81:13; D&C 111:11.
  b Lam. 1:9.
30*a* D&C 133:58.
31*a* 2 Sam. 22:32.
32*a* Gen. 13:10 (10–13);
    Isa. 3:9 (9–11).
33*a* TG Word of Wisdom.
  b HEB serpents.
35*a* TG Retribution;
    Vengeance.
  b Joel 3:4.

c 2 Pet. 2:3 (3–4).
36*a* TG Jesus Christ, Judge.
  b Num. 23:19.
  c HEB left, bond or free.
37*a* TG Idolatry.
  b Judg. 10:14.
39*a* D&C 38:1.
  b OR beside me.
  c HEB I bring about death,
    and I bring about life.
    Ps. 68:20.
  d TG Resurrection.

40*a* D&C 110:4 (2–4).
41*a* Isa. 66:16;
    D&C 87:6.
43*a* Rev. 6:10.
  b Ps. 85:1.
44*a* TG Singing.
  b OR Joshua.
45*a* IE of all generations.
46*a* Deut. 6:6;
    D&C 64:34.
  b Eph. 6:4 (1–4).
47*a* Alma 9:16 (16–18).

49 Get thee up into this mountain Abarim, *unto* mount *ª*Nebo, which *is* in the land of Moab, that *is* *ᵇ*over against Jericho; and behold the land of Canaan, which I give unto the children of Israel for a possession:

50 And *ª*die in the mount whither thou goest up, and be gathered unto thy people; as *ᵇ*Aaron thy brother died in mount Hor, and was gathered unto his people:

51 Because ye *ª*trespassed against me among the children of Israel at the waters of *ᵇ*Meribah-Kadesh, in the wilderness of Zin; because ye sanctified me not in the midst of the children of Israel.

52 Yet thou shalt see the land before *thee*; but thou shalt not go thither unto the land which I give the children of Israel.

CHAPTER 33

Moses blesses the tribes of Israel—Levi is blessed to teach the Lord's judgments and His law—Joseph is blessed above all; the Lord will gather Israel in the latter days—Israel will triumph.

AND this *is* the blessing, wherewith *ª*Moses the *ᵇ*man of God *ᶜ*blessed the children of *ᵈ*Israel before his death.

2 And he said, The LORD came from Sinai, and rose up from Seir unto them; he *ª*shined forth from mount *ᵇ*Paran, and he came with ten thousands of saints: from his right hand *went* a fiery law for them.

3 Yea, he loved the people; all his *ª*saints *are* in thy hand: and they sat down at thy *ᵇ*feet; *every one* shall receive of thy words.

4 Moses commanded us a *ª*law, *even* the inheritance of the congregation of Jacob.

5 And he was king in Jeshurun, when the heads of the people *and* the tribes of Israel were gathered together.

6 ¶ Let *ª*Reuben live, and not die; and let *not* his men be *ʰ*few.

7 ¶ And this *is the* blessing of *ª*Judah: and he said, Hear, LORD, the voice of Judah, and bring him unto his people: let his hands be sufficient for him; and be thou an *ᵇ*help *to him* from his enemies.

8 ¶ And of *ª*Levi he said, *Let* thy Thummim and thy *ᵇ*Urim *be* with thy holy one, whom thou didst prove at Massah, *and with* whom thou didst *ᶜ*strive at the waters of *ᵈ*Meribah;

9 Who said *ª*unto his father and to his mother, I *ᵇ*have not seen him; neither did he acknowledge his brethren, nor knew his own children: for they have observed thy word, and kept thy covenant.

10 They shall *ª*teach Jacob thy *ᵇ*judgments, and Israel thy law: they shall put incense before thee, and whole burnt sacrifice upon thine altar.

11 Bless, LORD, his substance, and accept the work of his hands: smite through the loins of them that rise against him, and of them that hate him, that they rise not again.

12 ¶ And of *ª*Benjamin he said, The beloved of the LORD shall dwell in safety by him; *and the* LORD shall cover him all the day long, and he shall dwell between his shoulders.

13 ¶ And of *ª*Joseph he said, Blessed

49*a* Num. 27:12 (12–14);
    33:47.
  b OR opposite.
50*a* Deut. 34:5 (1–8);
    Josh. 1:1.
  b Num. 20:28 (24–28).
51*a* Num. 20:12 (11–13).
  b Num. 27:14 (12–14).
33 1*a* 1 Chr. 23:14.
  b Ezra 3:2;
    D&C 107:91 (91–92).
  c Gen. 49:28 (1–33).
  d TG Israel, Twelve

Tribes of.
2*a* Ps. 50:2.
  b Hab. 3:3.
3*a* TG Saints.
  b Acts 22:3.
4*a* TG Law of Moses.
6*a* Gen. 49:3 (3–4);
    1 Chr. 5:1 (1–2);
    Ezek. 48:31.
  b Num. 1:21; 26:7.
7*a* TG Israel, Judah,
    People of.
  b Judg. 1:19 (17–19).

8*a* Gen. 49:5 (5–7).
  b TG Urim and Thummim.
  c Num. 20:3 (1–13).
  d Num. 20:13; Ezek. 47:19.
9*a* HEB of.
  b HEB regard them not.
10*a* Deut. 27:14;
    2 Chr. 15:3 (1–4);
    17:9; 35:3;
    2 Ne. 9:48.
  b HEB ordinances.
12*a* Gen. 49:27.
13*a* TG Book of Mormon.

of the LORD *be* his ^bland, for the ^cprecious things of heaven, for the dew, and for the deep that coucheth beneath,

14 And for the precious fruits *brought forth* by the sun, and for the precious things put forth by the moon,

15 And for the chief things of the ancient mountains, and for the precious things of the lasting ^ahills,

16 And for the precious things of the earth and fulness thereof, and *for* the good will of him that dwelt in the ^abush: let *the* ^bblessing come upon the head of Joseph, and upon the top of the head of him *that was* separated from his brethren.

17 His ^aglory *is like* the firstling of his bullock, and his horns *are like* the horns of ^bunicorns: with them he shall ^cpush the people together to the ends of the earth: and they *are* the ten thousands of ^dEphraim, and they *are* the thousands of Manasseh.

18 ¶ And of ^aZebulun he said, Rejoice, Zebulun, in thy going out; and, ^bIssachar, in thy tents.

19 They shall call the people unto the mountain; there they shall offer sacrifices of righteousness: for they shall suck *of* the abundance of the seas, and *of* treasures hid in the sand.

20 ¶ And of ^aGad he said, Blessed *be* he that enlargeth Gad: he dwelleth as a lion, and teareth the arm ^bwith the crown of the head.

21 And he provided the ^afirst part for himself, because there, *in* a portion of the lawgiver, *was* he seated; and he came ^bwith the heads of the people, he executed the justice of

the LORD, and his judgments with Israel.

22 ¶ And of ^aDan he said, Dan *is* a ^blion's whelp: he shall leap from Bashan.

23 ¶ And of ^aNaphtali he said, O Naphtali, satisfied with favour, and full with the blessing of the LORD: possess thou the ^bwest and the south.

24 ¶ And of ^aAsher he said, *Let* Asher *be* blessed with children; let him be acceptable to his brethren, and let him dip his foot in oil.

25 Thy ^ashoes *shall be* iron and brass; and as thy days, *so shall* thy strength *be*.

26 ¶ *There is* none like unto the God of ^aJeshurun, *who* rideth upon the heaven in thy help, and in his ^bexcellency on the sky.

27 The ^aeternal God *is thy* ^brefuge, and underneath *are* the everlasting arms: and he shall thrust out the ^cenemy from before thee; and shall say, Destroy *them*.

28 ^aIsrael then shall dwell in ^bsafety alone: the ^cfountain of Jacob *shall be* upon a land of corn and wine; also his ^dheavens shall drop down dew.

29 ^aHappy *art* thou, O Israel: who *is* like unto thee, O people saved by the LORD, the ^bshield of thy help, and who *is* the sword of thy ^cexcellency! and thine enemies shall ^dbe found liars unto thee; and thou shalt tread upon their ^ehigh places.

CHAPTER 34

Moses sees the promised land and is taken by the Lord—Joshua leads Israel— Moses was Israel's greatest prophet.

13*b* TG Lands of
    Inheritance.
  c Gen. 27:28.
15*a* Gen. 49:26.
16*a* Ex. 3:2 (2, 4).
  b D&C 133:32 (30–33).
17*a* D&C 133:32 (32–34).
  b HEB the wild ox.
  c D&C 58:45 (44–45).
  d TG Israel, Joseph,
    People of.
18*a* Gen. 49:13.
  b Gen. 49:14 (14–15).
20*a* Gen. 49:19.
  b HEB as well as.

21*a* Num. 32:2 (1–5, 16–19).
  b HEB to.
22*a* Gen. 49:16 (16–17).
  b Gen. 49:9.
23*a* Gen. 49:21.
  b HEB sea; i.e., Galilee as
    an inheritance.
24*a* Gen. 49:20.
25*a* OR bars (locks).
26*a* HEB the upright,
    righteous.
    Deut. 32:15;
    Isa. 44:2.
  b OR majesty through.
27*a* TG Eternity;

God, Eternal Nature of.
  b TG Refuge.
  c D&C 103:6 (6, 25).
28*a* TG Israel, Origins of.
  b Jer. 23:6.
  c Deut. 8:7 (7–8).
  d Gen. 27:28.
29*a* TG Happiness.
  b Ps. 33:20.
  c OR victory, triumph.
  d HEB diminish before.
  e Deut. 32:13;
    Hab. 3:19.

AND Moses went up from the plains of Moab unto the mountain of Nebo, to the top of Pisgah, that *is* ^{*a*}over against Jericho. And the LORD shewed him all the land of Gilead, unto Dan,

2 And all Naphtali, and the land of Ephraim, and Manasseh, and all the land of Judah, unto ^{*a*}the utmost sea,

3 And the ^{*a*}south, and the plain of the valley of ^{*b*}Jericho, the city of palm trees, unto Zoar.

4 And the LORD said unto him, This *is* the land which I ^{*a*}sware unto Abraham, unto Isaac, and unto Jacob, saying, I will give it unto thy seed: I have caused thee to see *it* with thine eyes, but thou shalt not go over thither.

5 ¶ So ^{*a*}Moses the servant of the LORD ^{*b*}died there in the land of Moab, according to the word of the LORD.

6 And he ^{*a*}buried him in a valley in the land of Moab, over against Beth-peor: but no man knoweth ^{*b*}of his ^{*c*}sepulchre unto this day.

7 ¶ And Moses *was* an ^{*a*}hundred and twenty years old when he died: his eye was not dim, nor his natural force abated.

8 ¶ And the children of Israel wept for Moses in the plains of Moab thirty days: so the days of weeping *and* ^{*a*}mourning for Moses were ended.

9 ¶ And Joshua the son of ^{*a*}Nun was full of the spirit of wisdom; for Moses had ^{*b*}laid his hands upon him: and the children of Israel ^{*c*}hearkened unto him, and did as the LORD commanded Moses.

10 ¶ And there arose not a ^{*a*}prophet since in Israel like unto Moses, whom the LORD knew ^{*b*}face to face,

11 In all the signs and the wonders, which the LORD sent him to do in the land of Egypt to Pharaoh, and to all his servants, and to all his land,

12 And in all that mighty ^{*a*}hand, and in all the great ^{*b*}terror which Moses shewed in the sight of all Israel.

THE BOOK OF

JOSHUA

CHAPTER 1

The Lord speaks to Joshua—He is commanded to be of good courage, to meditate upon the law, and to keep the commandments—He prepares Israel to enter Canaan.

NOW after the ^{*a*}death of Moses the servant of the LORD it came to pass, that the LORD spake unto Joshua the son of Nun, Moses' minister, saying,

2 Moses my servant is dead; now therefore arise, go over this Jordan,

---

34 1*a* OR opposite.
  2*a* IE the Mediterranean.
  3*a* HEB Negev.
   b Judg. 1:16.
  4*a* TG Promised Lands.
  5*a* D&C 84:25.
   b Deut. 32:50 (48–50);
    Josh. 1:1.
  6*a* Alma 45:19 (18–19).
   b OR the place of his
    burial.

   c TG Translated Beings.
  7*a* Ex. 7:7;
    Deut. 31:2 (1–2);
    Acts 7:23.
  8*a* TG Mourning.
  9*a* Num. 13:16; Judg. 2:8.
   b TG Church Organization;
    Hands, Laying on of;
    Priesthood, Authority;
    Priesthood, Ordination.
   c TG Sustaining Church

Leaders.
  10*a* Deut. 18:15 (15, 18).
   b TG God, Privilege of
    Seeing; Jesus Christ, Appearances, Antemortal.
  12*a* IE power.
   b OR awesome acts.

[JOSHUA]

1 1*a* Deut. 32:50 (48–50);
   34:5 (1–8).

thou, and all this people, unto the ªland which I do give to them, *even* to the children of Israel.

3 Every place that the sole of your foot shall tread upon, that have I given unto you, as I said unto Moses.

4 From the wilderness and this ªLebanon even unto the great river, the river Euphrates, all the land of the Hittites, and unto the ᵇgreat sea toward the going down of the sun, shall be your ᶜcoast.

5 There shall not any man be able to stand before thee all the days of thy life: as I was with ªMoses, *so* I will be ᵇwith thee: I will not fail thee, nor ᶜforsake thee.

6 Be strong and of a good ªcourage: for unto this people shalt thou ᵇdivide for an ᶜinheritance the ᵈland, which I sware unto their fathers to give them.

7 Only be thou strong and very ªcourageous, that thou mayest ob serve to do according to all the law, which Moses my servant commanded thee: ᵇturn not from it *to* the right hand or *to* the left, that thou mayest ᶜprosper whithersoever thou goest.

8 This book of the ªlaw shall not depart out of thy mouth; but thou shalt ᵇmeditate therein day and night, that thou mayest observe to do according to all that is written therein: for then thou shalt make thy way prosperous, and then thou shalt have good success.

9 Have not I commanded thee? Be strong and of a good courage; be not afraid, neither be thou dismayed: for the ªLORD thy God *is* with thee whithersoever thou goest.

10 ¶ Then Joshua commanded ªthe officers of the people, saying,

11 Pass through ªthe host, and command the people, saying, Prepare you ᵇvictuals; for within three days ye shall pass over this Jordan, to go in to ᶜpossess the land, which the LORD your God giveth you to possess it.

12 ¶ And to the Reubenites, and to the Gadites, and to half the tribe of Manasseh, spake Joshua, saying,

13 Remember the ªword which Moses the servant of the LORD commanded you, saying, The LORD your God hath given you ᵇrest, and hath given you this land.

14 Your wives, your little ones, and your cattle, shall remain in the land which Moses gave you on this side Jordan; but ye shall pass before your brethren armed, all the mighty men of valour, and help them;

15 Until the LORD have given your brethren rest, as *he hath given* you, and they also have possessed the land which the LORD your God giveth them: then ye shall return unto the land of your possession, and enjoy it, which Moses the LORD's servant gave you on this side Jordan toward the sunrising.

16 ¶ And they answered Joshua, saying, All that thou commandest us we will do, and whithersoever thou sendest us, we will go.

17 According as we hearkened unto Moses in all things, so will we hearken unto thee: only the LORD thy God be with thee, as he was with Moses.

18 Whosoever *he be* that doth ªrebel

2a Gen. 13:15 (14–17);
   15:18 (18–21).
4a Deut. 3:25.
  b Ex. 23:31 (31–33);
   Num. 34:6 (2–12).
  c IE boundary, border.
5a D&C 107:91 (91–92).
  b Deut. 31:8 (6–8, 23);
   Josh. 6:27;
   Judg. 6:16.
  c 1 Kgs. 6:13;
   Heb. 13:5;
   D&C 88:83.
6a D&C 52:17; 66:8; 133:58.
  b Ezek. 47:22.

  c Deut. 11:8.
  d TG Israel, Land of.
7a TG Courage.
  b 3 Ne. 18:13 (12–14);
   D&C 3:2.
  c Deut. 29:9;
   1 Ne. 2:20;
   Jarom 1:9; Mosiah 1:7;
   D&C 90:24;
   97:18 (18–20); 100:15.
8a 1 Ne. 4:16;
   Mosiah 3:14 (14–15);
   13:29 (29–32);
   Alma 25:15 (15–16);
   D&C 41:5 (4–5); 42:59.

  b TG Meditation;
   Scriptures, Study of.
9a D&C 38:7.
10a IE the heads of the
   families and the tribes.
11a HEB the camp,
   encampment.
  b HEB bread or food,
   provisions.
   Judg. 7:8; 20:10.
  c Deut. 12:10 (10–19).
13a Num. 32:20 (20–28).
  b 2 Ne. 24:3 (1–3);
   D&C 84:24.
18a TG Rebellion.

against thy commandment, and will not hearken unto thy words in all that thou commandest him, he shall be put to ᵇdeath: only be strong and of a good courage.

CHAPTER 2

Joshua sends spies to Jericho—They are received and concealed by Rahab—They promise to preserve Rahab and her household.

AND Joshua the son of Nun sent out of Shittim two men to spy secretly, saying, Go view the land, even Jericho. And they went, and came into an harlot's house, named ᵃRahab, and lodged there.

2 And it was told the king of Jericho, saying, Behold, there came men in hither to night of the children of Israel to search out the country.

3 And the king of Jericho sent unto Rahab, saying, Bring forth the men that are come to thee, which are entered into thine house: for they be come to search out all the country.

4 And the woman took the two men, and hid them, and said thus, There came men unto me, but I wist not whence they *were:*

5 And it came to pass *about the time* of shutting of the gate, when it was dark, that the men went out: whither the men went I ᵃwot not: pursue after them quickly; for ye shall overtake them.

6 But she had brought them up to the roof of the house, and hid them with the stalks of flax, which she had laid in order upon the roof.

7 And the men pursued after them the way to Jordan unto the fords: and as soon as they which pursued after them were gone out, they shut the gate.

8 ¶ And before they were laid down, she came up unto them upon the roof;

9 And she said unto the men, I know that the LORD hath given you the land, and that your ᵃterror is fallen upon us, and that all the inhabitants of the land ᵇfaint because of you.

10 For we have ᵃheard how the LORD dried up the water of the ᵇRed sea for you, when ye came out of Egypt; and what ye did unto the two kings of the ᶜAmorites, that *were* on the other side Jordan, Sihon and Og, whom ye utterly destroyed.

11 And as soon as we had ᵃheard *these things,* our ᵇhearts did melt, neither did there remain any more courage in any man, because of you: for the LORD your God, he *is* ᶜGod in ᵈheaven above, and in earth beneath.

12 Now therefore, I pray you, ᵃswear unto me by the LORD, since I have shewed you ᵇkindness, that ye will also shew kindness unto my father's house, and give me a true token:

13 And *that* ye will save alive my father, and my mother, and my brethren, and my sisters, and all that they have, and deliver our lives from death.

14 And the men answered her, Our life for yours, if ye utter not this our business. And it shall be, when the LORD hath given us the land, that we will deal kindly and truly with thee.

15 Then she let them down by a ᵃcord through the window: for her house *was* upon the town wall, and she dwelt upon the wall.

16 And she said unto them, Get you to the mountain, lest the pursuers meet you; and hide yourselves there three days, until the pursuers be returned: and afterward may ye go your way.

18b TG Capital Punishment.
2 1a Heb. 11:31;
   James 2:25.
 5a JST Josh. 2:5 . . . know . . .
 9a Ex. 15:16 (14–16); 23:27.
   b HEB melt away; i.e., with fear.
   Ex. 15:15.

10a Josh. 6:27; 9:9.
   b Ex. 14:21;
   1 Ne. 4:2; 17:26;
   Mosiah 7:19;
   Hel. 8:11;
   D&C 8:3.
   c Num. 21:34 (21, 33–35).
11a Ex. 15:14 (14–15).

   b Josh. 5:1.
   c Deut. 4:39;
   2 Ne. 10:14;
   D&C 20:17; 65:6.
   d TG Heaven.
12a OR covenant.
   b TG Benevolence.
15a Acts 9:25.

17 And the men said unto her, We *will be* ^ablameless of this thine oath which thou hast made us swear.

18 Behold, *when* we come into the land, thou shalt bind this line of scarlet thread in the window which thou didst let us down by: and thou shalt bring thy ^afather, and thy mother, and thy brethren, and all thy father's household, home unto thee.

19 And it shall be, *that* whosoever shall go out of the doors of thy house into the street, his blood *shall be* upon his head, and we *will be* guiltless: and whosoever shall be with thee in the house, his blood *shall be* on our head, if *any* hand be upon him.

20 And if thou utter this our business, then we will be quit of thine oath which thou hast made us to swear.

21 And she said, According unto your words, so *be* it. And she sent them away, and they departed: and she bound the scarlet line in the window.

22 And they went, and came unto the mountain, and abode there three days, until the pursuers were returned: and the pursuers sought *them* throughout all the way, but found *them* not.

23 ¶ So the two men returned, and descended from the mountain, and passed over, and came to Joshua the son of Nun, and told him all *things* that befell them:

24 And they said unto Joshua, Truly the Lord hath ^adelivered into our hands all the land; for even all the inhabitants of the country do faint because of us.

CHAPTER 3

Joshua leads Israel to the Jordan—The Lord cuts off the water of the Jordan; it stands up as a heap, and Israel passes over on dry ground.

And Joshua rose early in the morning; and they removed from Shittim, and came to Jordan, he and all the children of Israel, and lodged there before they passed over.

2 And it came to pass after three days, that the officers went through the host;

3 And they commanded the people, saying, When ye see the ^aark of the covenant of the Lord your God, and the priests the Levites bearing it, then ye shall remove from your place, and go after it.

4 Yet there shall be a space between you and it, about two thousand cubits by measure: come not near unto it, that ye may know the ^away by which ye must go: for ye have not passed *this* way heretofore.

5 And Joshua said unto the people, ^aSanctify yourselves: for to morrow the Lord will do wonders among you.

6 And Joshua spake unto the priests, saying, Take up the ark of the covenant, and pass over before the people. And they took up the ark of the covenant, and went before the people.

7 ¶ And the Lord said unto Joshua, This day will I begin to ^amagnify thee in the sight of all Israel, that they may know that, as I was with Moses, *so* I will be with thee.

8 And thou shalt command the priests that bear the ark of the covenant, saying, When ye are come to the brink of the water of Jordan, ye shall stand still in Jordan.

9 ¶ And Joshua said unto the children of Israel, Come hither, and hear the words of the Lord your God.

10 And Joshua said, Hereby ye shall know that the ^aliving God *is*

17a HEB pure; i.e., innocent, free from blame in this covenant. Ex. 20:7.
18a Josh. 6:23.
24a Ex. 23:31; 1 Ne. 17:35 (32–35).

3 3a TG Ark of the Covenant.
4a 1 Ne. 16:10.
5a IE Make yourselves clean, holy, by ritual washings and proper behavior. Ex. 19:10;

Josh. 7:13; D&C 43:16 (11–16).
7a Josh. 4:14; 1 Chr. 29:25.
10a Ps. 42:2; Hosea 1:10; D&C 50:1; 76:22.

among you, and *that* he will without fail drive out from before you the *b*Canaanites, and the Hittites, and the Hivites, and the Perizzites, and the Girgashites, and the Amorites, and the Jebusites.

11 Behold, the ark of the covenant of the Lord of all the earth passeth over before you into Jordan.

12 Now therefore take you twelve men out of the tribes of Israel, out of every tribe a man.

13 And it shall come to pass, as soon as the soles of the feet of the priests that bear the ark of the LORD, the Lord of all the earth, shall rest in the waters of Jordan, *that* the waters of Jordan shall be cut off *from* the waters that come down from above; and they shall stand upon an *a*heap.

14 ¶ And it came to pass, when the people removed from their tents, to pass over Jordan, and the priests bearing the ark of the covenant before the people;

15 And as they that bare the ark were come unto Jordan, and the feet of the priests that bare the ark were dipped in the brim of the water, (for Jordan overfloweth all his banks all the time of harvest,)

16 That the *a*waters which came down from *b*above *c*stood *and* rose up upon an *d*heap very far from the city Adam, that *is* beside Zaretan: and those that came down toward the sea of the plain, *even* the *e*salt sea, failed, *and* were cut off: and the people passed over right against Jericho.

17 And the priests that bare the ark of the covenant of the LORD stood firm on *a*dry ground in the midst of Jordan, and all the Israelites passed over on dry ground, until all the people were passed clean over Jordan.

CHAPTER 4

Joshua places twelve stones to commemorate the crossing of the Jordan—Joshua is magnified before the children of Israel as they cross the Jordan—After the priests bearing the ark pass over, the river returns to its course.

AND it came to pass, when all the people were *a*clean passed over Jordan, that the LORD spake unto Joshua, saying,

2 Take you twelve men out of the people, out of every tribe a man,

3 And command ye them, saying, Take you hence out of the midst of Jordan, out of the place where the priests' feet stood firm, *a*twelve *b*stones, and ye shall carry them over with you, and leave them in the lodging place, where ye shall lodge this night.

4 Then Joshua called the *a*twelve men, whom he had prepared of the children of Israel, out of every tribe a man:

5 And Joshua said unto them, Pass over before the ark of the LORD your God into the midst of Jordan, and take ye up every man of you a stone upon his shoulder, according unto the number of the tribes of the children of Israel:

6 That this may be a sign among you, *that* when your *a*children ask *their fathers* in time to come, saying, What *mean* ye by these stones?

7 Then ye shall answer them, That the waters of Jordan were cut off before the *a*ark of the covenant of the LORD; when it passed over Jordan, the waters of Jordan were cut off: and these stones shall be for a *b*memorial unto the children of Israel for ever.

8 And the children of Israel did so as Joshua commanded, and took up twelve stones out of the midst of

---

10*b* 1 Ne. 17:35 (32–38).
13*a* Ex. 15:8.
16*a* Ex. 14:21;
    2 Kgs. 2:8.
  b IE up the river.
  c OR stopped.
  d Hab. 3:15.

  e IE Dead Sea.
    Num. 34:12 (3, 12);
    Josh. 15:2.
17*a* Ps. 66:6; 74:15;
    D&C 133:68.
4 1*a* HEB completely.
  3*a* 1 Kgs. 18:31.

  b Deut. 27:2.
4*a* TG Church
    Organization.
6*a* TG Children.
7*a* TG Ark of the Covenant.
  b TG Symbolism.

Jordan, as the LORD spake unto Joshua, according to the number of the tribes of the children of Israel, and carried them over with them unto the place where they lodged, and laid them down there.

9 And Joshua set up twelve stones in the midst of Jordan, in the place where the feet of the priests which bare the ark of the covenant stood: and they are there unto this day.

10 ¶ For the priests which bare the ark stood in the midst of Jordan, until every thing was finished that the LORD commanded Joshua to speak unto the people, according to all that Moses commanded Joshua: and the people hasted and passed over.

11 And it came to pass, when all the people were clean *passed over, that the ark of the LORD passed over, and the priests, in the presence of the people.

12 And the children of Reuben, and the children of Gad, and half the tribe of Manasseh, passed over armed before the children of Israel, as Moses spake unto them:

13 About forty thousand prepared for war passed over before the LORD unto battle, to the plains of Jericho.

14 ¶ On that day the LORD *magnified Joshua in the sight of all Israel; and they feared him, as they feared Moses, all the days of his life.

15 And the LORD spake unto Joshua, saying,

16 Command the priests that bear the ark of the *testimony, that they come up out of Jordan.

17 Joshua therefore commanded the priests, saying, Come ye up out of Jordan.

18 And it came to pass, when the priests that bare the ark of the covenant of the LORD were come up out of the midst of Jordan, *and the soles of the priests' feet were lifted up unto the dry land, that the waters of Jordan returned unto their place, and flowed over all his banks, as *they did before.

19 ¶ And the people came up out of Jordan on the tenth *day of the first month, and encamped in *Gilgal, in the east border of Jericho.

20 And those twelve stones, which they took out of Jordan, did Joshua pitch in Gilgal.

21 And he spake unto the children of Israel, saying, When your children shall ask their fathers in time to come, saying, What *mean these stones?

22 Then ye shall let your *children *know, saying, Israel came over this Jordan on dry land.

23 For the LORD your God dried up the waters of Jordan from before you, until ye were passed over, as the LORD your God did to the Red sea, which he *dried up from before us, until we were gone over:

24 That all the people of the earth might *know the hand of the LORD, that it *is mighty: that ye might *fear the LORD your God for ever.

CHAPTER 5

The inhabitants of Canaan fear Israel— The males of Israel are circumcised— Israel keeps the Passover, eats the fruit of the land, and manna ceases—The captain of the Lord's host appears to Joshua.

AND it came to pass, when all the kings of the Amorites, which *were* on the side of Jordan westward, and all the kings of the Canaanites, which *were* by the sea, *heard that the LORD had dried up the waters of Jordan from before the children of Israel, until we were passed over, that their *heart melted, neither was there spirit in them any more, because of the children of Israel.

2 ¶ At that time the LORD said unto Joshua, Make thee *sharp knives, and *circumcise again the children of Israel the second time.

11a Deut. 3:28.
14a Josh. 3:7.
16a OR covenant.
19a Josh. 5:9.
22a TG Children.

b TG Teaching.
23a Ex. 14:21.
24a 1 Kgs. 8:43.
  b Deut. 6:13;
    D&C 76:5.

5 1a Ex. 15:14–16.
  b Josh. 2:11.
2a HEB flint knives.
  b TG Circumcision.

3 And Joshua made him sharp knives, and circumcised the children of Israel at the hill of the foreskins.

4 And this *is* the cause why Joshua did circumcise: All the people that came out of Egypt, *that were* males, *even* all the men of war, died in the wilderness by the way, after they came out of Egypt.

5 Now all the people that came out were circumcised: but all the people *that were* born in the wilderness by the way as they came forth out of Egypt, *them* they had not circumcised.

6 For the children of Israel walked forty years in the wilderness, till all the people *that were* men of war, which came out of Egypt, were consumed, because they [a]obeyed not the voice of the Lord: unto whom the Lord sware that he would not shew them the [b]land, which the Lord [c]sware unto their fathers that he would give us, a land that floweth with milk and honey.

7 And their children, *whom* he raised up [a]in their stead, them Joshua circumcised: for they were uncircumcised, because they had not circumcised them by the way.

8 And it came to pass, when they had done circumcising all the people, that they abode in their places in the camp, till they were [a]whole.

9 And the Lord said unto Joshua, This day have I rolled away the reproach of Egypt from off you. Wherefore the name of the place is called [a]Gilgal unto this day.

10 ¶ And the children of Israel encamped in Gilgal, and kept the [a]passover on the fourteenth day of the month at even in the plains of Jericho.

11 And they did eat of the [a]old corn of the land on the morrow after the passover, [b]unleavened cakes, and parched *corn* in the selfsame day.

12 ¶ And the [a]manna ceased on the morrow after they had eaten of the old corn of the land; neither had the children of Israel manna any more; but they did eat of the fruit of the land of Canaan that year.

13 ¶ And it came to pass, when Joshua was by Jericho, that he lifted up his eyes and looked, and, behold, there stood a [a]man over against him with his sword drawn in his hand: and Joshua went unto him, and said unto him, Art thou for us, or for our adversaries?

14 And he said, Nay; but *as* captain of the [a]host of the Lord am I now come. And Joshua fell on his face to the earth, and did worship, and said unto him, What saith my lord unto his servant?

15 And the captain of the Lord's host said unto Joshua, Loose thy [a]shoe from off thy foot; for the place whereon thou standest *is* [b]holy. And Joshua did so.

CHAPTER 6

Jericho is taken and destroyed—Only Rahab and her household are saved.

Now [a]Jericho was straitly shut up because of the children of Israel: none went out, and none came in.

2 And the Lord said unto Joshua, See, I have given into thine hand Jericho, and the king thereof, *and* the mighty men of valour.

3 And ye shall [a]compass the city, all *ye* men of war, *and* go round about the city once. Thus shalt thou do six days.

4 And seven priests shall bear before the ark seven trumpets of rams' horns: and the seventh day ye shall compass the city seven times,

---

6a TG Disobedience.
  b Num. 14:23.
  c OR covenanted.
7a IE in the place of their fathers.
8a IE completely healed.
9a IE Rolling.
  Josh. 4:19;

2 Sam. 19:15;
  2 Kgs. 2:1.
10a TG Passover.
11a IE grain from the previous year.
  b TG Bread, Unleavened.
12a Ex. 16:35;
  Mosiah 7:19.

13a Gen. 18:2.
14a Ex. 23:20 (20–23).
15a Ex. 3:5.
  b D&C 115:7.
6 1a Josh. 24:11.
3a HEB go around (also vv. 4, 7, 11, 14–15).
  Judg. 11:18; 16:2.

and the priests shall blow with the trumpets.

5 And it shall come to pass, that when they make a long *blast* with the ram's horn, *and* when ye hear the sound of the trumpet, all the people shall shout with a great shout; and the wall of the city shall fall down flat, and the people shall ascend up every man straight before him.

6 ¶ And Joshua the son of Nun called the priests, and said unto them, Take up the ªark of the covenant, and let seven priests bear seven trumpets of rams' horns before the ark of the LORD.

7 And he said unto the people, Pass on, and compass the city, and let him that is armed pass on before the ark of the LORD.

8 ¶ And it came to pass, when Joshua had spoken unto the people, that the seven priests bearing the seven trumpets of rams' horns passed on before the LORD, and blew with the trumpets: and the ark of the covenant of the LORD followed them.

9 ¶ And the armed men went before the priests that blew with the trumpets, and ªthe rearward came after the ark, *the priests* going on, and blowing with the trumpets.

10 And Joshua had commanded the people, saying, Ye shall not shout, nor make any noise with your voice, neither shall *any* word proceed out of your mouth, until the day I bid you shout; then shall ye shout.

11 So the ark of the LORD compassed the city, going about *it* once: and they came into the camp, and lodged in the camp.

12 ¶ And Joshua rose early in the morning, and the priests took up the ark of the LORD.

13 And seven priests bearing seven trumpets of rams' horns before the ark of the LORD went on continually, and blew with the trumpets: and the

armed men went before them; but the rearward came after the ark of the LORD, *the priests* going on, and blowing with the trumpets.

14 And the second day they compassed the city once, and returned into the camp: so they did six days.

15 And it came to pass on the seventh day, that they rose early about the dawning of the day, and compassed the city after the same manner seven times: only on that day they compassed the city seven times.

16 And it came to pass at the seventh time, when the priests blew with the trumpets, Joshua said unto the people, Shout; for the LORD hath given you the city.

17 ¶ And the city shall be accursed, *even* it, and all that *are* therein, to the LORD: only Rahab the harlot shall live, she and all that *are* with her in the house, because she hid the messengers that we sent.

18 And ye, in any wise keep *yourselves* from ªthe accursed thing, lest ye make *yourselves* accursed, when ye take of the accursed thing, and make the camp of Israel a curse, and trouble it.

19 But all the silver, and gold, and vessels of brass and iron, *are* consecrated unto the LORD: they shall come into the treasury of the LORD.

20 So the people shouted when *the priests* blew with the trumpets: and it came to pass, when the people heard the sound of the trumpet, and the people shouted with a great shout, that the ªwall fell down flat, so that the people went up into the city, every man straight before him, and they took the city.

21 And they utterly ªdestroyed all that *was* in the city, both man and woman, young and old, and ox, and sheep, and ass, with the edge of the sword.

22 But Joshua had said unto the two men that had spied out the

---

6*a* TG Ark of the Covenant.
9*a* IE those bringing up the rear.
18*a* IE those things under

a ban for the people to take, or dedicated for a sacrifice to the Lord. Josh. 7:1;

1 Chr. 2:7.
20*a* Heb. 11:30;
        D&C 101:57.
21*a* Deut. 7:2.

country, Go into the harlot's house, and bring out thence the woman, and all that she hath, as ye sware unto her.

23 And the young men that were spies went in, and brought out ªRahab, and her father, and her mother, and her brethren, and all that she had; and they brought out all her kindred, and left them without the camp of Israel.

24 And they burnt the city with fire, and all that *was* therein: only the silver, and the gold, and the vessels of brass and of iron, they put into the treasury of the house of the LORD.

25 And Joshua saved Rahab the harlot alive, and her father's household, and all that she had; and she dwelleth in Israel *even* unto this day; because she hid the messengers, which Joshua sent to spy out Jericho.

26 ¶ And Joshua ªadjured *them* at that time, saying, Cursed *be* the man before the LORD, that riseth up and buildeth this city ᵇJericho: he shall lay the foundation thereof in his firstborn, and in his youngest *son* shall he set up the gates of it.

27 So the LORD was ªwith ᵇJoshua; and his fame was ᶜnoised throughout all the country.

CHAPTER 7

Israel is defeated by the people of Ai—Joshua complains to the Lord—Achan and his household are destroyed because he disobeyed the Lord by taking the spoils of Jericho.

BUT the children of Israel committed a trespass in the accursed thing: for ªAchan, the son of Carmi, the son of Zabdi, the son of Zerah, of the tribe of Judah, took of the ᵇaccursed thing: and the anger of

the LORD was kindled against the children of Israel.

2 And Joshua sent men from Jericho to Ai, which *is* beside ªBeth-aven, on the east side of Beth-el, and spake unto them, saying, Go up and view the country. And the men went up and viewed Ai.

3 And they returned to Joshua, and said unto him, Let not all the people go up; but let about two or three thousand men go up and smite Ai; *and* make not all the people to labour thither; for they *are but* few.

4 So there went up thither of the people about three thousand men: and they ªfled before the men of Ai.

5 And the men of Ai smote of them about thirty and six men: for they chased them *from* before the gate *even* unto ªShebarim, and smote them in the ᵇgoing down: wherefore the hearts of the people melted, and became as water.

6 ¶ And Joshua ªrent his clothes, and fell to the earth upon his face before the ark of the LORD until the eventide, he and the elders of Israel, and put dust upon their heads.

7 And Joshua said, Alas, O Lord GOD, wherefore hast thou at all brought this people over Jordan, to deliver us into the hand of the Amorites, to destroy us? would to God we had been content, and dwelt on the other side Jordan!

8 O Lord, what shall I say, when Israel turneth their backs before their enemies!

9 For the Canaanites and all the inhabitants of the land shall hear *of it,* and shall ªenviron us round, and cut off our name from the earth: and what wilt thou do unto thy great ᵇname?

10 ¶ And the LORD said unto Joshua, Get thee up; wherefore liest thou thus upon thy face?

23*a* Josh. 2:18.
26*a* IE charged, as by an oath.
  b 1 Kgs. 16:34 (29–34).
27*a* Josh. 1:5.
  b Josh. 9:3; 1 Sam. 3:19.
  c Josh. 2:10.

7 1*a* HEB *achar* means "trouble."
  b Josh. 6:18; 22:20; 1 Chr. 2:7.
2*a* Josh. 18:12.
4*a* Lev. 26:17 (14–17); Alma 53:9;

    D&C 136:42.
5*a* HEB the quarries.
  b HEB descent, or pass.
6*a* 1 Sam. 4:12; Alma 46:12 (12–23).
9*a* HEB surround.
  b Isa. 48:9.

11 Israel hath ^asinned, and they have also transgressed my covenant which I commanded them: for they have even taken of the accursed thing, and have also stolen, and ^bdissembled also, and they have put *it* even among their own stuff.

12 Therefore the children of Israel could not stand before their enemies, *but* turned *their* backs before their enemies, because they were accursed: neither will I be with you any more, except ye destroy the accursed from among you.

13 Up, ^asanctify the people, and say, ^bSanctify yourselves against to morrow: for thus saith the LORD God of Israel, *There is* an accursed thing in the midst of thee, O Israel: thou canst not stand before thine enemies, until ye take away the accursed thing from among you.

14 In the morning therefore ye shall be brought according to your tribes: and it shall be, *that* the tribe which the LORD taketh shall come according to the families *thereof;* and the ^afamily which the LORD shall take shall come by households; and the household which the LORD shall take shall come man by man.

15 And it shall be, *that* he that is taken with the accursed thing shall be burnt with fire, he and all that he hath: because he hath transgressed the covenant of the LORD, and because he hath ^awrought folly in Israel.

16 ¶ So Joshua rose up early in the morning, and brought Israel by their tribes; and the tribe of Judah was taken:

17 And he brought the family of Judah; and he took the family of the Zarhites: and he brought the family of the Zarhites man by man; and Zabdi was taken:

18 And he brought his household man by man; and Achan, the son of Carmi, the son of Zabdi, the son of Zerah, of the tribe of Judah, was taken.

19 And Joshua said unto Achan, My son, give, I pray thee, ^aglory to the LORD God of Israel, and make ^bconfession unto him; and ^ctell me now what thou hast done; hide *it* not from me.

20 And Achan answered Joshua, and said, Indeed I have sinned against the LORD ^aGod of Israel, and thus and thus have I done:

21 When I saw among the spoils a goodly ^aBabylonish garment, and two hundred shekels of silver, and a wedge of gold of fifty shekels weight, then I ^bcoveted them, and took them; and, behold, they *are* hid in the earth in the midst of my tent, and the silver under it.

22 ¶ So Joshua sent messengers, and they ran unto the tent; and, behold, *it was* hid in his tent, and the silver under it.

23 And they took them out of the midst of the tent, and brought them unto Joshua, and unto all the children of Israel, and laid them out before the LORD.

24 And Joshua, and all Israel with him, took Achan the son of Zerah, and the silver, and the garment, and the wedge of gold, and his sons, and his daughters, and his oxen, and his asses, and his sheep, and his tent, and all that he had: and they brought them unto the valley of Achor.

25 And Joshua said, Why hast thou troubled us? the LORD shall trouble thee this day. And all Israel stoned him with stones, and burned them with fire, after they had stoned them with stones.

26 And they raised over him a great heap of stones unto this day. So the LORD turned from the fierceness of his anger. Wherefore the name of that place was called, The valley of ^aAchor, unto this day.

11*a* Eccl. 9:18; 10:1.
　b HEB deceived, been false.
13*a* Josh. 3:5.
　b Hel. 3:35;
　　D&C 88:68.
14*a* TG Family, Patriarchal.
15*a* OR done a foolish thing.
19*a* 1 Sam. 6:5.
　b TG Confession.
　c TG Accountability.
20*a* Acts 5:4 (1–10).
21*a* HEB Shinar (area of biblical Babylon, famous for fine weaving).
　b Acts 5:2 (1–11).
26*a* Hosea 2:15.

CHAPTER 8

Joshua uses an ambush, takes Ai, and slays its inhabitants—He builds an altar in Mount Ebal—The words of the law, both blessings and cursings, are read to the people.

AND the LORD said unto Joshua, Fear not, neither be thou dismayed: take all the people of war with thee, and arise, go up to Ai: see, I have given into thy hand the king of Ai, and his people, and his city, and his land:

2 And thou shalt do to Ai and her king as thou didst unto *a*Jericho and her king: only the spoil thereof, and the cattle thereof, shall ye take for a prey unto yourselves: lay thee an ambush for the city behind it.

3 ¶ So Joshua arose, and all the people of war, to go up against Ai: and Joshua chose out thirty thousand mighty men of valour, and sent them away by night.

4 And he commanded them, saying, Behold, ye shall lie in wait against the city, *even* behind the city: go not very far from the city, but be ye all ready:

5 And I, and all the people that *are* with me, will approach unto the city: and it shall come to pass, when they come out against us, as at the first, that we will flee before them,

6 (For they will come out after us) till we have drawn them from the city; for they will say, They flee before us, as at the first: therefore we will flee before them.

7 Then ye shall rise up from the ambush, and seize upon the city: for the LORD your God will deliver it into your hand.

8 And it shall be, when ye have taken the city, *that* ye shall set the city on fire: according to the commandment of the LORD shall ye do. See, I have commanded you.

9 ¶ Joshua therefore sent them forth: and they went to lie in ambush,

and abode between Beth-el and Ai, on the west side of Ai: but Joshua lodged that night among the people.

10 And Joshua rose up early in the morning, and numbered the people, and went up, he and the elders of Israel, before the people to Ai.

11 And all the people, *even the people* of war that *were* with him, went up, and drew nigh, and came before the city, and *a*pitched on the north side of Ai: now *there was* a valley between them and Ai.

12 And he took about five thousand men, and set them to lie in ambush between Beth-el and Ai, on the west side of the city.

13 And when they had set the people, *even* all the host that *was* on the north of the city, and *a*their liers in wait on the west of the city, Joshua went that night into the midst of the valley.

14 ¶ And it came to pass, when the king of Ai saw *it*, that they hasted and rose up early, and the men of the city went out against Israel to battle, he and all his people, at a time appointed, before the plain; but he *a*wist not that *there were* liers in ambush against him behind the city.

15 And Joshua and all Israel made as if they were beaten before them, and fled by the way of the wilderness.

16 And all the people that *were* in Ai were called together to pursue after them: and they pursued after Joshua, and were drawn away from the city.

17 And there was not a man left in Ai or *a*Beth-el, that went not out after Israel: and they left the city open, and pursued after Israel.

18 And the LORD said unto Joshua, Stretch out the spear that *is* in thy hand toward Ai; for I will give it into thine hand. And Joshua stretched out the spear that *he had* in his hand toward the city.

---

8 2*a* Morm. 7:4;
    D&C 98:33.
11*a* OR set camp.
13*a* IE those in the ambush.

Judg. 9:25 (25, 32, 35);
16:12; 20:29 (29, 33);
21:20;
Alma 43:31 (30–43);

52:21 (21–31);
58:16 (15–21).
14*a* OR knew.
17*a* Josh. 12:16.

19 And the ambush arose quickly out of their place, and they ran as soon as he had stretched out his hand: and they entered into the city, and took it, and hasted and set the city on fire.

20 And when the men of Ai looked behind them, they saw, and, behold, the smoke of the city ascended up to heaven, and they had no power to flee this way or that way: and the people that fled to the wilderness turned back upon the pursuers.

21 And when Joshua and all Israel saw that the ambush had taken the city, and that the smoke of the city ascended, then they turned again, and slew the men of Ai.

22 And the other issued out of the city against them; so they were in the midst of Israel, some on this side, and some on that side: and they smote them, so that they let none of them remain or escape.

23 And the king of Ai they took alive, and brought him to Joshua.

24 And it came to pass, when Israel had made an end of slaying all the inhabitants of Ai in the field, in the wilderness wherein they chased them, and when they were all fallen on the edge of the sword, until they were consumed, that all the Israelites returned unto Ai, and smote it with the edge of the sword.

25 And *so* it was, *that* all that fell that day, both of men and women, *were* twelve thousand, *even* all the men of Ai.

26 For Joshua drew not his hand back, wherewith he stretched out the spear, until he had utterly destroyed all the inhabitants of Ai.

27 Only the cattle and the spoil of that city Israel took for *a* prey unto themselves, according unto the word of the LORD which he commanded Joshua.

28 And Joshua burnt Ai, and made it an heap for ever, *even* a desolation unto this day.

29 And the king of Ai he hanged on a tree until eventide: and as soon as the sun was down, Joshua commanded that they should take his carcase down from the tree, and cast it at the entering of the gate of the city, and raise thereon a great heap of stones, *that remaineth* unto this day.

30 ¶ Then Joshua built an altar unto the LORD God of Israel in mount Ebal,

31 As Moses the servant of the LORD commanded the children of Israel, as it is written in the book of the law of Moses, an *a*altar of whole *b*stones, over which no man hath lift up *any* *c*iron: and they offered thereon burnt offerings unto the LORD, and sacrificed peace offerings.

32 ¶ And he *a*wrote there upon the stones a copy of the law of Moses, which he wrote in the presence of the children of Israel.

33 And all Israel, and their elders, and officers, and their judges, stood on this side the ark and on that side before the priests the Levites, which bare the ark of the covenant of the LORD, as well the stranger, as he that was born among them; half of them over against mount *a*Gerizim, and half of them over against mount Ebal; as Moses the servant of the LORD had commanded before, that they should bless the people of Israel.

34 And afterward he *a*read all the words of the law, the blessings and *b*cursings, according to all that is written in the book of the law.

35 There was not a word of all that Moses commanded, which Joshua read not before all the *a*congregation of Israel, with the women, and the little ones, and the strangers that *b*were conversant among them.

27*a* OR spoil, booty.
31*a* Deut. 27:6 (1–8).
  b Ex. 20:25 (24–25);
    1 Ne. 2:7.
  c 2 Ne. 5:15;

Ether 10:23;
  Moses 5:46.
32*a* TG Scriptures,
    Writing of.
33*a* Deut. 11:29;

27:12 (12–13).
34*a* TG Scriptures, Study of.
  b TG Curse.
35*a* TG Church.
  b HEB went, walked.

CHAPTER 9

The Gibeonites by craft obtain a league with Israel—Joshua makes them servants to the congregation of Israel.

AND it came to pass, when all the kings which *were* on this side Jordan, in the hills, and in the valleys, and in all the coasts of the *a*great sea over against Lebanon, the Hittite, and the Amorite, the Canaanite, the Perizzite, the Hivite, and the Jebusite, heard *thereof*;

2 That they gathered themselves together, to fight with Joshua and with Israel, with one accord.

3 ¶ And when the inhabitants of *a*Gibeon heard what *b*Joshua had done unto Jericho and to Ai,

4 They did work *a*wilily, and went and *b*made as if they had been ambassadors, and took old sacks upon their asses, and wine bottles, old, and rent, and bound up;

5 And *a*old shoes and clouted upon their feet, and old garments upon them; and all the bread of their provision was dry *and* *b*mouldy.

6 And they went to Joshua unto the camp at Gilgal, and said unto him, and to the men of Israel, We be come from a far country: now therefore make ye a league with us.

7 And the men of Israel said unto the Hivites, Peradventure ye dwell among us; and how shall we make a *a*league with you?

8 And they said unto Joshua, We *are* thy servants. And Joshua said unto them, Who *are* ye? and from whence come ye?

9 And they said unto him, From a very far country thy servants are come because of the name of the LORD thy God: for we have *a*heard the fame of him, and all that he did in Egypt,

10 And all that he did to the two kings of the Amorites, that *were* beyond Jordan, to Sihon king of Heshbon, and to *a*Og king of Bashan, which *was* at Ashtaroth.

11 Wherefore our elders and all the inhabitants of our country spake to us, saying, Take *a*victuals with you for the journey, and go to meet them, and say unto them, We *are* your servants: therefore now make ye a league with us.

12 This our bread we took hot *for* our provision out of our houses on the day we came forth to go unto you; but now, behold, it is dry, and it is mouldy:

13 And these bottles of wine, which *were* new; and, behold, they be rent: and these our garments and our shoes are become old by reason of the very long journey.

14 And the men took of their victuals, and asked not *a*counsel at the mouth of the LORD.

15 And Joshua made peace with them, and made a league with them, to let them live: and the princes of the congregation *a*sware unto them.

16 ¶ And it came to pass at the end of three days after they had made a league with them, that they heard that they *were* their neighbours, and *that* they dwelt among them.

17 And the children of Israel journeyed, and came unto their cities on the third day. Now their cities *were* *a*Gibeon, and Chephirah, and Beeroth, and Kirjath-jearim.

18 And the children of Israel smote them not, because the princes of the congregation had sworn unto them by the LORD God of Israel. And all the congregation *a*murmured against the princes.

19 But all the princes said unto all the congregation, We have sworn

---

9 1*a* Num. 34:6.
3*a* Josh. 10:2;
　　1 Kgs. 3:4.
　b Josh. 6:27.
4*a* OR craftily, with
　　cunning.
　b Other Hebrew texts:
　　made ready provisions.
　　(See v. 12.)

5*a* OR old, patched shoes
　　upon.
　b OR had become crumbs.
7*a* OR covenant, treaty
　　(also vv. 11, 15–16).
　　Judg. 2:2;
　　Alma 44:15 (6–15, 20);
　　3 Ne. 6:3.
9*a* Josh. 2:10.

10*a* Deut. 1:4; 3:11 (10–11).
11*a* HEB bread, or
　　provisions (also v. 14).
14*a* Num. 27:21; Jacob 4:10;
　　Alma 37:37;
　　D&C 3:4.
15*a* OR covenanted.
17*a* 2 Sam. 21:2.
18*a* TG Murmuring.

unto them by the LORD God of Israel: now therefore we may not touch them.

20 This we will do to them; we will even let them live, lest wrath be upon us, because of the oath which we sware unto them.

21 And the princes said unto them, Let them live; but let them be *hewers of wood and drawers of water unto all the congregation; as the princes had promised them.

22 ¶ And Joshua called for them, and he spake unto them, saying, Wherefore have ye *beguiled us, saying, We *are* very far from you; when ye dwell among us?

23 Now therefore ye *are* cursed, and there shall none of you be freed from being bondmen, and hewers of wood and drawers of water for the house of my God.

24 And they answered Joshua, and said, Because it was certainly told thy servants, how that the LORD thy God commanded his servant Moses to give you all the land, and to *destroy all the inhabitants of the land from before you, therefore we were sore afraid of our lives because of you, and have done this thing.

25 And now, behold, we *are* in thine hand: as it seemeth good and right unto thee to do unto us, do.

26 And so did he unto them, and delivered them out of the hand of the children of Israel, that they slew them not.

27 And Joshua made them that day hewers of wood and drawers of water for the congregation, and for the altar of the LORD, even unto this day, in the *place which he should choose.

CHAPTER 10

Israel defeats the Amorites and their allies, and the Lord casts stones from heaven upon them—The sun and moon stand still—Many kings and cities are destroyed—The Lord fought for Israel.

Now it came to pass, when *Adoni-zedek king of Jerusalem had heard how Joshua had taken Ai, and had utterly destroyed it; as he had done to Jericho and her king, so he had done to Ai and her king; and how the inhabitants of Gibeon had made peace with Israel, and were among them;

2 That they feared greatly, because *Gibeon *was* a great city, as one of the royal cities, and because it *was* greater than Ai, and all the men thereof *were* mighty.

3 Wherefore Adoni-zedek king of Jerusalem sent unto Hoham king of Hebron, and unto Piram king of Jarmuth, and unto Japhia king of Lachish, and unto Debir king of Eglon, saying,

4 Come up unto me, and help me, that we may smite Gibeon: for it hath made peace with Joshua and with the children of Israel.

5 Therefore the five kings of the Amorites, the king of Jerusalem, the king of Hebron, the king of Jarmuth, the king of Lachish, the king of Eglon, gathered themselves together, and went up, they and all their hosts, and encamped before Gibeon, and made war against it.

6 ¶ And the men of Gibeon sent unto Joshua to the camp to Gilgal, saying, Slack not thy hand from thy servants; come up to us quickly, and save us, and help us: for all the kings of the Amorites that dwell in the mountains are gathered together against us.

7 So Joshua ascended from Gilgal, he, and all the people of war with him, and all the mighty men of valour.

8 ¶ And the LORD said unto Joshua, Fear them not: for I have *delivered them into thine hand; there shall not a man of them stand before thee.

9 Joshua therefore came unto them suddenly, *and* went up from Gilgal all night.

21a Deut. 29:11 (10–13).
22a OR deceived.
　　Alma 18:23.
24a Deut. 7:2 (1–4).

27a Deut. 31:11 (9–13).
10 1a HEB Lord of
　　righteousness.
2a Josh. 9:3.

8a Josh. 10:42; 21:44;
　　D&C 98:37.

10 And the LORD *discomfited them before Israel, and slew them with a great slaughter at *Gibeon, and chased them along the way that goeth up to Beth-horon, and smote them to Azekah, and unto Makkedah.

11 And it came to pass, as they fled from before Israel, *and* were in the going down to Beth-horon, that the LORD cast down great *stones from heaven upon them unto Azekah, and they died: *they were* more which died with hailstones than *they* whom the children of Israel slew with the sword.

12 ¶ Then spake Joshua to the LORD in the day when the LORD delivered up the Amorites before the children of Israel, and he said in the sight of Israel, *Sun, stand thou still upon Gibeon; and thou, Moon, in the valley of Ajalon.

13 And the *sun stood still, and the moon stayed, until the people had avenged themselves upon their enemies. *Is* not this written in the book of *Jasher? So the sun stood still in the midst of heaven, and hasted not to go down about a whole day.

14 And there was no day like that before it or after it, that the LORD hearkened unto the voice of a man: for the LORD *fought for Israel.

15 ¶ And Joshua returned, and all Israel with him, unto the camp to Gilgal.

16 But these five kings fled, and hid themselves in a cave at Makkedah.

17 And it was told Joshua, saying, The five kings are found hid in a cave at Makkedah.

18 And Joshua said, Roll great stones upon the mouth of the cave, and set men by it for to keep them:

19 And stay ye not, *but* pursue after your enemies, and smite the hindmost of them; suffer them not to enter into their cities: for the LORD your God hath delivered them into your hand.

20 And it came to pass, when Joshua and the children of Israel had made an end of slaying them with a very great slaughter, till they were consumed, that the rest *which* remained of them entered into fenced cities.

21 And all the people returned to the camp to Joshua at Makkedah in peace: none moved his tongue against any of the children of Israel.

22 Then said Joshua, Open the mouth of the cave, and bring out those five kings unto me out of the cave.

23 And they did so, and brought forth those five kings unto him out of the cave, the *king of Jerusalem, the king of Hebron, the king of Jarmuth, the king of Lachish, *and* the king of Eglon.

24 And it came to pass, when they brought out those kings unto Joshua, that Joshua called for all the men of Israel, and said unto the captains of the men of war which went with him, Come near, put your feet upon the necks of these kings. And they came near, and *put their feet upon the necks of them.

25 And Joshua said unto them, Fear not, nor be dismayed, be strong and of good courage: for thus shall the LORD do to all your enemies against whom ye fight.

26 And afterward Joshua smote them, and slew them, and hanged them on five trees: and they were hanging upon the trees until the evening.

27 And it came to pass at the time of the going down of the sun, *that* Joshua commanded, and they took them down off the trees, and cast them into the cave wherein they had been hid, and laid great stones

---

10a OR put them to flight.
  b Isa. 28:21.
11a Ex. 9:18 (13–35);
  Ezek. 38:22;
  Rev. 16:21.
12a 2 Kgs. 20:11 (8–11);

Isa. 38:8 (7–8);
  Hab. 3:11;
  Hel. 12:14.
13a 3 Ne. 1:15 (13–16).
  TG Astronomy.
  b TG Scriptures, Lost.

14a Deut. 1:30 (29–30);
  D&C 105:14.
23a Josh. 12:10 (10–12).
24a This symbolized triumph of one people over another.

in the cave's mouth, *which remain* until this very day.

28 ¶ And that day Joshua took ᵃMakkedah, and smote it with the edge of the sword, and the king thereof he utterly destroyed, them, and all the souls that *were* therein; he let none remain: and he did to the king of Makkedah as he did unto the king of Jericho.

29 Then Joshua passed from Makkedah, and all Israel with him, unto Libnah, and fought against ᵃLibnah:

30 And the Lord delivered it also, and the king thereof, into the hand of Israel; and he smote it with the edge of the sword, and all the souls that *were* therein; he let none remain in it; but did unto the king thereof as he did unto the king of Jericho.

31 ¶ And Joshua passed from Libnah, and all Israel with him, unto Lachish, and encamped against it, and fought against it:

32 And the Lord delivered Lachish into the hand of Israel, which took it on the second day, and smote it with the edge of the sword, and all the souls that *were* therein, according to all that he had done to Libnah.

33 ¶ Then Horam king of ᵃGezer came up to help Lachish; and Joshua smote him and his people, until he had left him none remaining.

34 ¶ And from Lachish Joshua passed unto Eglon, and all Israel with him; and they encamped against it, and fought against it:

35 And they took it on that day, and smote it with the edge of the sword, and all the souls that *were* therein he utterly destroyed that day, according to all that he had done to Lachish.

36 And Joshua went up from Eglon, and all Israel with him, unto Hebron; and they fought against it:

37 And they took it, and smote it with the edge of the sword, and the king thereof, and all the cities thereof, and all the souls that *were* therein; he left none remaining, according to all that he had done to Eglon; but destroyed it utterly, and all the souls that *were* therein.

38 ¶ And Joshua returned, and all Israel with him, to ᵃDebir; and fought against it:

39 And he took it, and the king thereof, and all the cities thereof; and they smote them with the edge of the sword, and utterly destroyed all the souls that *were* therein; he left none remaining: as he had done to Hebron, so he did to Debir, and to the king thereof; as he had done also to Libnah, and to her king.

40 ¶ So Joshua smote all the country of the hills, and of the south, and of the ᵃvale, and of the springs, and all their kings: he left none remaining, but utterly ᵇdestroyed all that breathed, as the Lord God of Israel commanded.

41 And Joshua smote them from Kadesh-barnea even unto Gaza, and all the country of Goshen, even unto Gibeon.

42 And all these kings and their land did Joshua take at one time, because the Lord God of Israel ᵃfought for Israel.

43 And Joshua returned, and all Israel with him, unto the camp to Gilgal.

CHAPTER 11

Joshua and Israel conquer the whole land, destroying many cities and nations.

And it came to pass, when Jabin king of Hazor had heard *those things*, that he sent to Jobab ᵃking of Madon, and to the king of Shimron, and to the king of Achshaph,

2 And to the kings that *were* on the north of the mountains, and of the plains south of Chinneroth, and in the valley, and in the borders of ᵃDor on the west,

3 *And to* the Canaanite on the east

28a Josh. 12:16.
29a Josh. 12:15.
33a Josh. 12:12.
38a Josh. 12:13.

40a OR lowland, foothill area.
 b Deut. 20:17 (17–18).
42a Josh. 10:8;

D&C 98:37.
11 1a Josh. 12:19 (19–20).
 2a Josh. 12:23.

and on the west, and *to* the Amorite, and the Hittite, and the Perizzite, and the Jebusite in the mountains, and *to* the Hivite under Hermon in the land of Mizpeh.

4 And they went out, they and all their hosts with them, much people, even as the sand that *is* upon the sea shore in multitude, with horses and chariots very many.

5 And when all these kings were met together, they came and pitched together at the waters of Merom, to fight against Israel.

6 ¶ And the LORD said unto Joshua, Be not afraid because of them: for to morrow about this time will I *a*deliver them up all slain before Israel: thou shalt *b*hough their horses, and burn their chariots with fire.

7 So Joshua came, and all the people of war with him, against them by the waters of Merom suddenly; and they fell upon them.

8 And the LORD delivered them into the hand of Israel, who smote them, and chased them unto great Zidon, and unto Misrephoth-maim, and unto the valley of Mizpeh eastward; and they smote them, until they left them none remaining.

9 And Joshua did unto them as the LORD bade him: he houghed their horses, and burnt their chariots with fire.

10 ¶ And Joshua at that time turned back, and took Hazor, and smote the king thereof with the sword: for Hazor beforetime was the head of all those kingdoms.

11 And they smote all the souls that *were* therein with the edge of the sword, utterly destroying *them:* there was not any left to breathe: and he burnt Hazor with fire.

12 And all the cities of those kings, and all the kings of them, did Joshua take, and smote them with the edge of the sword, *and* he utterly *a*destroyed them, as Moses the servant of the LORD commanded.

13 But *as for* the cities that stood still in their strength, Israel burned none of them, save Hazor only; *that* did Joshua burn.

14 And all the spoil of these *a*cities, and the cattle, the children of Israel took for *b*a prey unto themselves; but every man they smote with the edge of the sword, until they had destroyed them, neither left they any to breathe.

15 ¶ As the LORD commanded Moses his servant, so did Moses command Joshua, and so did Joshua; he left nothing undone of all that the LORD commanded Moses.

16 So Joshua took all that land, the hills, and all the south country, and all the land of Goshen, and the valley, and the plain, and the mountain of Israel, and the valley of the same;

17 *Even* from the mount Halak, that goeth up to Seir, even unto Baal-gad in the valley of Lebanon under mount Hermon: and all their kings he took, and smote them, and slew them.

18 Joshua made war a long time with all those kings.

19 There was not a city that made peace with the children of Israel, save the Hivites the inhabitants of Gibeon: all *other* they took in battle.

20 For it was of the *a*LORD to harden their hearts, that they should come against Israel in battle, that he might destroy them utterly, *and* that they might have no favour, but that he might destroy them, as the LORD commanded Moses.

21 ¶ And at that time came Joshua, and cut off the Anakims from the mountains, from Hebron, from Debir, from Anab, and from all the mountains of Judah, and from all the mountains of Israel: Joshua destroyed them utterly with their cities.

22 There was none of the Anakims left in the land of the children of Israel: only in Gaza, in *a*Gath, and in Ashdod, there remained.

6a 1 Ne. 17:32 (32–38); D&C 105:14.
b OR hock, cut the hamstring of.
12a Deut. 20:17 (17–18).
14a Deut. 20:16.
b OR booty, plunder.
20a Judg. 14:4.
22a 1 Sam. 17:4.

23 So Joshua took the whole land, according to all that the LORD said unto Moses; and Joshua gave it for an inheritance unto Israel according to their divisions by their tribes. And the land rested from war.

CHAPTER 12

Two kings on the east of the Jordan and thirty-one on the west are conquered by Israel.

Now these *are* the kings of the land, which the children of Israel smote, and possessed their land on the other side Jordan toward the rising of the sun, from the river Arnon unto mount Hermon, and all the plain on the east:

2 *a*Sihon king of the Amorites, who dwelt in Heshbon, *and* ruled from Aroer, which *is* upon the bank of the river Arnon, and from the middle of the river, and from half Gilead, even unto the river Jabbok, *which is* the border of the children of Ammon;

3 And from the plain to the sea of Chinneroth on the east, and unto the sea of the plain, *even* the *a*salt sea on the east, the way to *b*Beth-jeshimoth; and from the south, under *c*Ashdoth-pisgah:

4 ¶ And the coast of Og king of Bashan, *which was* of the remnant of the *a*giants, that dwelt at Ashta-roth and at Edrei,

5 And reigned in mount Hermon, and in Salcah, and in all Bashan, unto the border of the Geshurites and the Maachathites, and half Gilead, the border of Sihon king of Heshbon.

6 Them did Moses the servant of the LORD and the children of Israel smite: and Moses the servant of the LORD gave it *for* a *a*possession unto the *b*Reubenites, and the Gadites, and the half tribe of Manasseh.

7 ¶ And these *are* the *a*kings of the country which *b*Joshua and the children of Israel smote on this side Jordan on the west, from Baal-gad in the valley of Lebanon even unto the mount Halak, that goeth up to Seir; which Joshua gave unto the tribes of Israel *for* a possession according to their divisions;

8 In the mountains, and in the valleys, and in the plains, and in the springs, and in the wilderness, and in the south country; the Hittites, the Amorites, and the Canaanites, the Perizzites, the Hivites, and the Jebusites:

9 ¶ The king of Jericho, one; the king of Ai, which *is* beside Beth-el, one;

10 The *a*king of Jerusalem, one; the king of Hebron, one;

11 The king of Jarmuth, one; the king of Lachish, one;

12 The king of Eglon, one; the king of *a*Gezer, one;

13 The *a*king of Debir, one; the king of Geder, one;

14 The king of *a*Hormah, one; the king of Arad, one;

15 The *a*king of Libnah, one; the king of Adullam, one;

16 The *a*king of Makkedah, one; the *b*king of Beth-el, one;

17 The king of Tappuah, one; the king of Hepher, one;

18 The king of *a*Aphek, one; the king of Lasharon, one;

19 The *a*king of Madon, one; the king of Hazor, one;

20 The king of Shimron-meron, one; the king of Achshaph, one;

21 The king of Taanach, one; the king of Megiddo, one;

22 The king of Kedesh, one; the king of Jokneam of Carmel, one;

23 The *a*king of Dor in the coast of Dor, one; the king of the nations of Gilgal, one;

24 The king of Tirzah, one: all the kings thirty and one.

12 2*a* Num. 21:21 (21–24).
  3*a* OR Dead Sea.
    b Ezek. 25:9.
    c OR the slopes of Pisgah.
  4*a* Deut. 3:11.
  6*a* Num. 32:33 (29–33).
    b Deut. 3:12.

  7*a* Ps. 135:11.
    b Deut. 1:38.
  10*a* Josh. 10:23 (23–25).
  12*a* Josh. 10:33.
  13*a* Josh. 10:38 (38–39).
  14*a* Num. 21:3 (1–3).
  15*a* Josh. 10:29 (29–30).

  16*a* Josh. 10:28.
    b Josh. 8:17 (12, 17).
  18*a* 1 Sam. 4:1.
  19*a* Josh. 11:1 (1, 8).
  23*a* Josh. 11:2.

CHAPTER 13

There remain some lands yet to be possessed—Some inhabitants are not expelled—The inheritances of Reuben, Gad, and one half of Manasseh are confirmed.

Now ᵃJoshua was old *and* stricken in years; and the LORD said unto him, Thou art old *and* stricken in years, and there remaineth yet very much land to be possessed.

2 This *is* the land that yet remaineth: all the borders of the Philistines, and all ᵃGeshuri,

3 From Sihor, which *is* before Egypt, even unto the borders of Ekron northward, *which* is counted to the Canaanite: ᵃfive lords of the Philistines; the Gazathites, and the Ashdothites, the Eshkalonites, the Gittites, and the Ekronites; also the Avites:

4 From the south, all the land of the Canaanites, and Mearah that *is* beside the Sidonians, unto Aphek, to the borders of the Amorites:

5 And the land of the ᵃGiblites, and all Lebanon, toward the sunrising, from Baal-gad under mount Hermon unto the entering into Hamath.

6 All the inhabitants of the hill country from Lebanon unto Misrephoth-maim, *and* all the Sidonians, them will I drive out from before the children of Israel: only ᵃdivide thou it by lot unto the Israelites for an inheritance, as I have commanded thee.

7 Now therefore divide this land for an ᵃinheritance unto the nine tribes, and the half tribe of Manasseh,

8 With whom the ᵃReubenites and the Gadites have received their inheritance, which Moses gave them, beyond Jordan eastward, *even* as Moses the servant of the LORD gave them;

9 From Aroer, that *is* upon the bank of the river ᵃArnon, and the city that *is* in the midst of the river, and all the plain of ᵇMedeba unto Dibon;

10 And all the cities of Sihon king of the Amorites, which reigned in Heshbon, unto the border of the children of Ammon;

11 And Gilead, and the border of the Geshurites and Maachathites, and all mount Hermon, and all Bashan unto Salcah;

12 All the kingdom of Og in Bashan, which reigned in Ashtaroth and in Edrei, who remained of the remnant of the giants: for these did Moses smite, and cast them out.

13 Nevertheless the children of Israel expelled not the Geshurites, nor the Maachathites: but the Geshurites and the Maachathites dwell among the Israelites until this day.

14 Only unto the tribe of Levi he gave none ᵃinheritance; the sacrifices of the LORD God of Israel made by fire *are* their inheritance, as he said unto them.

15 ¶ And Moses gave unto the tribe of the children of ᵃReuben *inheritance* according to their families.

16 And their ᵃcoast was from Aroer, that *is* on the bank of the river Arnon, and the city that *is* in the midst of the river, and all the plain by Medeba;

17 Heshbon, and all her cities that *are* in the plain; Dibon, and Bamoth-baal, and Beth-baal-meon,

18 And Jahazah, and Kedemoth, and Mephaath,

19 And Kirjathaim, and Sibmah, and Zareth-shahar in the mount of the valley,

20 And Beth-peor, and Ashdoth-pisgah, and Beth-jeshimoth,

21 And all the cities of the plain, and all the kingdom of Sihon king of the Amorites, which reigned in

---

13 1*a* Josh. 23:1.
2*a* Deut. 3:14.
3*a* Judg. 3:3.
5*a* 1 Kgs. 5:18.
6*a* Num. 34:2;
Ps. 135:12.

7*a* TG Lands of Inheritance.
8*a* Josh. 14:3.
9*a* Num. 21:24;
Deut. 3:16 (15–17);
4:48 (47–49).
b 1 Chr. 19:7.

14*a* Num. 18:20.
15*a* Num. 26:5.
16*a* OR border (also vv. 25, 30).

Heshbon, whom Moses smote with the *a*princes of Midian, Evi, and Rekem, and Zur, and Hur, and Reba, *which were* *b*dukes of Sihon, dwelling in the country.

22 ¶ Balaam also the son of Beor, the *a*soothsayer, did the children of Israel slay with the sword among them that were slain by them.

23 And the border of the children of Reuben was Jordan, and the border *thereof*. This *was* the inheritance of the children of Reuben after their families, the cities and the villages thereof.

24 And Moses gave *inheritance* unto the tribe of Gad, *even* unto the children of Gad according to their families.

25 And their coast was Jazer, and all the cities of Gilead, and half the land of the children of Ammon, unto Aroer that *is* before Rabbah;

26 And from Heshbon unto Ramath-mizpeh, and Betonim; and from Mahanaim unto the border of Debir;

27 And in the valley, Beth-aram, and Beth-nimrah, and *a*Succoth, and Zaphon, the rest of the kingdom of Sihon king of Heshbon, Jordan and *his* border, *even* unto the edge of the sea of Chinnereth on the other side Jordan eastward.

28 This *is* the inheritance of the children of Gad after their families, the cities, and their villages.

29 ¶ And Moses gave *inheritance* unto the half tribe of Manasseh: and *this* was *the possession* of the half tribe of the children of Manasseh by their families.

30 And their coast was from Mahanaim, all Bashan, all the kingdom of Og king of Bashan, and all the *a*towns of Jair, which *are* in Bashan, threescore cities:

31 And half Gilead, and Ashtaroth, and Edrei, cities of the kingdom of Og in Bashan, *were pertaining* unto the children of Machir the son of Manasseh, *even* to the one half of the children of Machir by their families.

32 These *are the countries* which Moses did distribute for inheritance in the plains of Moab, on the other side Jordan, by Jericho, eastward.

33 But unto the tribe of Levi Moses gave not *any* *a*inheritance: the LORD God of Israel *was* their inheritance, as he said unto them.

CHAPTER 14

The land is divided by lot among 9½ tribes—Caleb inherits Hebron as a special reward for his faithfulness.

AND these *are the* *a*countries which the children of Israel inherited in the land of Canaan, which Eleazar the priest, and Joshua the son of *b*Nun, and the heads of the fathers of the tribes of the children of Israel, distributed for inheritance to them.

2 By *a*lot *was* their inheritance, as the LORD commanded by the hand of Moses, for the nine tribes, and *for* the half tribe.

3 For Moses had given the inheritance of two *a*tribes and an half tribe on the other side Jordan: but unto the Levites he gave none inheritance among them.

4 For the children of *a*Joseph were two tribes, Manasseh and Ephraim: therefore they gave no part unto the Levites in the land, save cities to dwell *in*, with their *b*suburbs for their cattle and for their substance.

5 As the LORD commanded Moses, so the children of Israel did, and they divided the land.

6 ¶ Then the children of Judah came unto Joshua in Gilgal: and Caleb the son of Jephunneh the Kenezite said unto him, Thou knowest the thing that the LORD said unto Moses the man of God concerning me and thee in Kadesh-barnea.

21*a* Num. 31:8.
  b OR vassal princes.
22*a* TG Sorcery.
27*a* Gen. 33:17.
30*a* Num. 32:41.

33*a* TG Inheritance.
14 1*a* Num. 34:17.
  b Num. 11:28; 27:18.
2*a* Josh. 18:6;
    D&C 102:34.

3*a* Josh. 13:8 (7–8).
4*a* 1 Chr. 5:1 (1–2);
    Ezek. 47:13.
  b Num. 35:2 (2–5).

7 Forty years old *was* I when Moses the servant of the LORD ^asent me from Kadesh-barnea to espy out the land; and I brought him word again as *it was* in mine heart.

8 Nevertheless my ^abrethren that went up with me made the heart of the people melt: but I wholly ^bfollowed the LORD my God.

9 And Moses sware on that day, saying, Surely the ^aland whereon thy feet have trodden shall be thine inheritance, and thy children's for ever, because thou hast wholly followed the LORD my God.

10 And now, behold, the LORD hath kept me alive, ^aas he said, these forty and five years, even since the LORD spake this word unto Moses, while *the children of* Israel wandered in the wilderness: and now, lo, I *am* this day fourscore and five years old.

11 As yet I *am as* strong this day as *I was* in the day that Moses sent me: as my strength *was* then, even so *is* my strength now, for war, both to go out, and to come in.

12 Now therefore give me this mountain, whereof the LORD spake in that day; for thou heardest in that day how the Anakims *were* there, and *that* the cities *were* great and ^afenced: if so be the LORD *will be* with me, then I shall be able to drive them out, as the LORD said.

13 And Joshua blessed him, and gave unto Caleb the son of Jephunneh Hebron for an inheritance.

14 Hebron therefore became the inheritance of ^aCaleb the son of Jephunneh the Kenezite unto this day, because that he wholly followed the LORD God of Israel.

15 And the name of Hebron before *was* Kirjath-arba; *which* ^aArba *was* a great man among the Anakims. And the land had rest from war.

CHAPTER 15

Judah is given an inheritance in Canaan—The Jebusites dwell with Judah at Jerusalem.

THIS then was the lot of the tribe of the children of Judah by their families; *even* to the border of Edom the wilderness of ^aZin southward *was* the uttermost part of the south coast.

2 And their south border was from the shore of the ^asalt sea, from the bay that ^blooketh southward:

3 And it went out to the south side to Maaleh-acrabbim, and passed along to Zin, and ascended up on the south side unto Kadesh-barnea, and passed along to Hezron, and went up to Adar, and ^afetched a compass to Karkaa:

4 *From thence* it passed toward Azmon, and went out unto the river of Egypt; and the goings out of that ^acoast were at the sea: this shall be your south coast.

5 And the east border *was* the salt sea, *even* unto the end of Jordan. And *their* border in the north quarter *was* from the bay of the sea at the uttermost part of Jordan:

6 And the border went up to Beth-hogla, and passed along by the north of Beth-arabah; and the border went up to the ^astone of Bohan the son of Reuben:

7 And the border went up toward Debir from the valley of Achor, and so northward, looking toward Gilgal, that *is* before the going up to Adummim, which *is* on the south side of the river: and the border passed toward the waters of En-shemesh, and the goings out thereof were at En-rogel:

8 And the border went up by the valley of the son of Hinnom unto the south side of the ^aJebusite; the same *is* Jerusalem: and the border went

---

7a Num. 13:2 (2–3, 6).
8a Num. 13:31 (30–33).
  b Num. 14:24.
9a Num. 13:22.
10a Num. 14:24.
12a OR fortified.

14a Josh. 21:12.
15a Josh. 21:11.
15 1a Num. 34:3 (2–8).
  2a Josh. 3:16.
  b OR faces.
  3a HEB circled about.

4a HEB border
    (also vv. 12, 21).
6a HEB thumb rock;
    apparently a landmark.
    Josh. 18:17.
8a Josh. 15:63; 18:28.

up to the top of the mountain that *lieth* before the valley of Hinnom westward, which *is* at the end of the valley of the giants northward:

9 And the border was ᵃdrawn from the top of the hill unto the fountain of the water of Nephtoah, and went out to the cities of mount Ephron; and the border was drawn to Baalah, which *is* Kirjath-jearim:

10 And the border ᵃcompassed from Baalah westward unto mount Seir, and passed along unto the side of mount Jearim, which *is* Chesalon, on the north side, and went down to Beth-shemesh, and passed on to Timnah:

11 And the border went out unto the side of Ekron northward: and the border was drawn to Shicron, and passed along to mount Baalah, and went out unto Jabneel; and the goings out of the border were at the sea.

12 And the ᵃwest border *was* to ᵇthe great sea, and the coast *thereof.* This *is* the coast of the children of Judah round about according to their families.

13 ¶ And unto ᵃCaleb the son of Jephunneh he gave a part among the children of Judah, according to the commandment of the LORD to Joshua, *even* the city of Arba the father of Anak, which *city is* Hebron.

14 And Caleb drove thence the three sons of Anak, Sheshai, and Ahiman, and Talmai, the children of Anak.

15 And he went up thence to the inhabitants of Debir: and the name of Debir before *was* Kirjath-sepher.

16 ¶ And Caleb said, He that smiteth Kirjath-sepher, and taketh it, to him will I give Achsah my daughter to wife.

17 And Othniel the son of Kenaz, the brother of ᵃCaleb, took it: and he gave him Achsah his daughter to wife.

18 And it came to pass, as she came *unto him,* that she moved him to ask of her father a field: and she lighted off *her* ass; and Caleb said unto her, What wouldest thou?

19 Who answered, Give me a blessing; for thou hast given me a south land; give me also springs of water. And he gave her the upper springs, and the ᵃnether springs.

20 This *is* the inheritance of the tribe of the children of Judah according to their families.

21 And the uttermost cities of the tribe of the children of Judah toward the coast of Edom southward were Kabzeel, and Eder, and Jagur,

22 And Kinah, and Dimonah, and Adadah,

23 And Kedesh, and Hazor, and Ithnan,

24 Ziph, and Telem, and Bealoth,

25 And Hazor, Hadattah, and ᵃKerioth, *and* Hezron, which *is* Hazor,

26 Amam, and Shema, and Moladah,

27 And Hazar-gaddah, and Heshmon, and Beth-palet,

28 And Hazar-shual, and Beersheba, and Bizjothjah,

29 Baalah, and Iim, and Azem,

30 And Eltolad, and Chesil, and Hormah,

31 And Ziklag, and Madmannah, and Sansannah,

32 And Lebaoth, and Shilhim, and Ain, and Rimmon: all the cities *are* twenty and nine, with their villages:

33 *And* in the valley, Eshtaol, and Zoreah, and Ashnah,

34 And Zanoah, and En-gannim, Tappuah, and Enam,

35 Jarmuth, and Adullam, Socoh, and Azekah,

36 And Sharaim, and Adithaim, and Gederah, and Gederothaim; fourteen cities with their villages:

37 Zenan, and Hadashah, and Migdal-gad,

38 And Dilean, and Mizpeh, and Joktheel,

9ᵃ HEB inclined.
10ᵃ IE turned about from.
12ᵃ Num. 34:6 (6–7).
  ᵇ IE the Mediterranean

(also v. 47).
Josh. 23:4.
13ᵃ Num. 13:6 (1–16);
  Deut. 1:36 (34–36).

17ᵃ Num. 32:12.
19ᵃ OR lower.
  Judg. 1:15.
25ᵃ Luke 6:16.

39 Lachish, and Bozkath, and Eglon,

40 And Cabbon, and Lahmam, and Kithlish,

41 And Gederoth, Beth-dagon, and Naamah, and Makkedah; sixteen cities with their villages:

42 Libnah, and Ether, and Ashan,

43 And Jiphtah, and Ashnah, and Nezib,

44 And *a*Keilah, and Achzib, and Mareshah; nine cities with their villages:

45 Ekron, with her towns and her villages:

46 From Ekron even unto the sea, all that *lay* near Ashdod, with their villages:

47 Ashdod with her towns and her villages, Gaza with her towns and her villages, unto the river of Egypt, and the great sea, and the border *thereof:*

48 ¶ And in the mountains, Shamir, and Jattir, and Socoh,

49 And Dannah, and Kirjath-sannah, which *is* Debir,

50 And Anab, and Eshtemoh, and Anim,

51 And Goshen, and Holon, and Giloh; eleven cities with their villages:

52 Arab, and Dumah, and Eshean,

53 And Janum, and Beth-tappuah, and Aphekah,

54 And Humtah, and Kirjath-arba, which *is* Hebron, and Zior; nine cities with their villages:

55 Maon, Carmel, and Ziph, and Juttah,

56 And Jezreel, and Jokdeam, and Zanoah,

57 Cain, Gibeah, and Timnah; ten cities with their villages:

58 Halhul, Beth-zur, and Gedor,

59 And Maarath, and Beth-anoth, and Eltekon; six cities with their villages:

60 Kirjath-baal, which *is* *a*Kirjath-jearim, and Rabbah; two cities with their villages:

61 In the wilderness, Beth-arabah, Middin, and Secacah,

62 And Nibshan, and the city of Salt, and En-gedi; six cities with their villages.

63 ¶ As for the *a*Jebusites the inhabitants of Jerusalem, the children of Judah could not drive them out: but the *b*Jebusites dwell with the children of Judah at Jerusalem unto this day.

CHAPTER 16

The children of Joseph (Ephraim and Manasseh) receive their inheritances— Some Canaanites continue to dwell among the Ephraimites.

AND the lot of the children of *a*Joseph fell from Jordan by Jericho, unto the water of Jericho on the east, to the wilderness that goeth up from Jericho throughout mount Beth-el,

2 And goeth out from *a*Beth-el to Luz, and passeth along unto the borders of Archi to Ataroth,

3 And goeth down westward to the *a*coast of Japhleti, unto the coast of Beth-horon the *b*nether, and to Gezer: and the goings out thereof are at the sea.

4 So the children of Joseph, Manasseh and Ephraim, took their *a*inheritance.

5 ¶ And the border of the children of Ephraim according to their families was *thus:* even the border of their inheritance on the east side was Ataroth-addar, unto Beth-horon the upper;

6 And the border went out toward the sea to Michmethah on the north side; and the border went about eastward unto Taanath-shiloh, and passed by it on the east to Janohah;

7 And it went down from Janohah to Ataroth, and to Naarath, and came to Jericho, and went out at Jordan.

8 The border went out from Tappuah westward unto the river Kanah;

44*a* 1 Sam. 23:1 (1–2).
60*a* Judg. 18:12.
63*a* Josh. 15:8; 1 Chr. 11:4.
  b Judg. 1:21; 2 Sam. 5:6.

16 1*a* TG Israel, Joseph,
        People of.
    2*a* Gen. 12:8 (7–8);
        28:19 (16–19);

2 Kgs. 2:2.
3*a* OR border.
  b OR lower.
4*a* Josh. 17:4 (4, 14).

and the goings out thereof were at the sea. This *is* the inheritance of the tribe of the children of Ephraim by their families.

9 And the separate cities for the children of Ephraim *were* among the inheritance of the children of Manasseh, all the cities with their villages.

10 And they drave not out the *a*Canaanites that dwelt in Gezer: but the Canaanites dwell among the Ephraimites unto this day, and serve *b*under tribute.

CHAPTER 17

Manasseh and Ephraim both receive an additional inheritance—Ephraim is to drive out the Canaanites from the hill country.

THERE was also a lot for the tribe of *a*Manasseh; for he *was* the firstborn of Joseph; *to wit,* for *b*Machir the firstborn of Manasseh, the father of Gilead: because he was a man of war, therefore he had Gilead and Bashan.

2 There was also *a lot* for the rest of the children of *a*Manasseh by their families; for the children of Abiezer, and for the children of Helek, and for the children of Asriel, and for the children of Shechem, and for the children of Hepher, and for the children of Shemida: these *were* the male children of Manasseh the son of Joseph by their families.

3 ¶ But Zelophehad, the son of Hepher, the son of Gilead, the son of Machir, the son of Manasseh, had no sons, but daughters: and these *are* the names of his daughters, Mahlah, and Noah, Hoglah, Milcah, and Tirzah.

4 And they came near before *a*Eleazar the priest, and before Joshua the son of Nun, and before the princes, saying, The LORD commanded Moses to give us an *b*inheritance among our brethren. Therefore according to the commandment of the LORD

he gave them an inheritance among the brethren of their father.

5 And there fell ten portions to Manasseh, beside the land of Gilead and Bashan, which *were* on the other side Jordan;

6 Because the daughters of Manasseh had an inheritance among his sons: and the rest of Manasseh's sons had the land of Gilead.

7 ¶ And the *a*coast of Manasseh was from Asher to Michmethah, that *lieth* before Shechem; and the border went along on the right hand unto the inhabitants of En-tappuah.

8 *Now* Manasseh had the land of Tappuah: but Tappuah on the border of Manasseh *belonged* to the children of Ephraim;

9 And the coast descended unto the river Kanah, southward of the river: these cities of Ephraim *are* among the cities of Manasseh: the coast of Manasseh also *was* on the north side of the river, and the outgoings of it were at the sea:

10 Southward *it was* Ephraim's, and northward *it was* Manasseh's, and the sea is his border; and they met together in Asher on the north, and in Issachar on the east.

11 And Manasseh had in Issachar and in Asher Beth-shean and her towns, and Ibleam and her towns, and the inhabitants of Dor and her towns, and the inhabitants of En-dor and her towns, and the inhabitants of Taanach and her towns, and the inhabitants of Megiddo and her towns, *even* three countries.

12 Yet the children of Manasseh could not drive out *the inhabitants of* those cities; but the Canaanites would dwell in that land.

13 Yet it came to pass, when the children of Israel were waxen strong, that they put the Canaanites to *a*tribute; but did not utterly drive them out.

14 And the children of Joseph spake unto Joshua, saying, Why

10*a* Judg. 1:29 (28–30).
  b HEB as task servants.
17 1*a* Gen. 41:51; 46:20;
  Alma 10:3.

b Num. 32:40;
  Judg. 5:14.
2*a* Num. 26:29 (29–32).
4*a* Ex. 6:25.

b Num. 27:7 (6–7);
  Josh. 16:4.
7*a* OR border (also v. 9).
13*a* Judg. 1:28.

hast thou given me *but* one lot and one portion to inherit, seeing I *am* a *a*great people, forasmuch as the LORD hath blessed me hitherto?

15 And Joshua answered them, If thou *be* a great people, *then* get thee up to the wood *country,* and *a*cut down for thyself there in the land of the Perizzites and of the *b*giants, if mount Ephraim be too narrow for thee.

16 And the children of Joseph said, The hill is not enough for us: and all the Canaanites that dwell in the land of the valley have *a*chariots of iron, *both they* who *are* of Beth-shean and her towns, and *they* who *are* of the valley of Jezreel.

17 And Joshua spake unto the house of Joseph, *even* to Ephraim and to Manasseh, saying, Thou *art* a great people, and hast great power: thou shalt not have one lot *only:*

18 But the mountain shall be thine; for it *is* a *a*wood, and thou shalt cut it down: and the outgoings of it shall be thine: for thou shalt drive out the Canaanites, though they have iron *b*chariots, *and* though they *be* strong.

CHAPTER 18

The tabernacle of the congregation is set up at Shiloh—Benjamin receives an inheritance by lot.

AND the whole congregation of the children of Israel assembled together at *a*Shiloh, and set up the *b*tabernacle of the congregation there. And the land was subdued before them.

2 And there remained among the children of Israel seven tribes, which had not yet received their inheritance.

3 And Joshua said unto the children of Israel, How long *are* ye slack to go to possess the land, which the LORD God of your fathers hath given you?

4 Give out from among you three men for *each* tribe: and I will send them, and they shall rise, and go through the land, and describe it according to the inheritance of them; and they shall come *again* to me.

5 And they shall divide it into seven parts: Judah shall abide in their *a*coast on the south, and the house of Joseph shall abide in their coasts on the north.

6 Ye shall therefore describe the land *into* seven parts, and bring *the* description hither to me, that I may cast *a*lots for you here before the LORD our God.

7 But the *a*Levites have no part among you; for the priesthood of the LORD *is* their *b*inheritance: and Gad, and *c*Reuben, and half the tribe of Manasseh, have received their inheritance beyond Jordan on the east, which Moses the servant of the LORD gave them.

8 ¶ And the men arose, and went away: and Joshua charged them that went to describe the land, saying, Go and walk through the land, and describe it, and come again to me, that I may here cast lots for you before the LORD in Shiloh.

9 And the men went and passed through the land, and described it by cities into seven parts in a book, and came *again* to Joshua to the host at Shiloh.

10 ¶ And Joshua cast lots for them in Shiloh before the LORD: and there Joshua divided the land unto the children of Israel according to their divisions.

11 ¶ And the lot of the tribe of the children of *a*Benjamin came up according to their families: and the coast of their lot came forth between the children of Judah and the children of Joseph.

14a Gen. 48:19.
15a IE clear forest lands for yourselves.
   b HEB Rephaim.
     Moses 8:18.
16a Judg. 1:19; 4:3.
18a 2 Sam. 18:6.
   b Deut. 20:1.

18 1a Judg. 20:26 (26–27);
     1 Sam. 1:3 (3–18); 3:21;
     Jer. 7:12.
   b HEB tent.
     TG Temple.
5a HEB border (also
     vv. 11, 19–20).
     Judg. 11:22.

6a Josh. 14:2.
7a TG Priesthood, Aaronic.
   b TG Priesthood,
     History of.
   c Josh. 22:1 (1–6).
11a Gen. 42:4; 44:29;
     49:27 (26–28).

12 And their border on the north side was from Jordan; and the border went up to the side of Jericho on the north side, and went up through the mountains westward; and the goings out thereof were at the wilderness of ᵃBeth-aven.

13 And the border went over from thence toward Luz, to the side of ᵃLuz, which is Beth-el, southward; and the border descended to Ataroth-adar, near the hill that lieth on the south side of the ᵇnether Beth-horon.

14 And the border was drawn thence, and ᵃcompassed the corner of the sea southward, from the hill that lieth before Beth-horon southward; and the goings out thereof were at Kirjath-baal, which is Kirjath-jearim, a city of the children of Judah: this was the west quarter.

15 And the south quarter was from the end of Kirjath-jearim, and the border went out on the west, and went out to the well of waters of Nephtoah:

16 And the border came down to the end of the mountain that lieth before the valley of the son of ᵃHinnom, and which is in the valley of the giants on the north, and descended to the valley of ᵇHinnom, to the side of Jebusi on the south, and descended to En-rogel,

17 And was drawn from the north, and went forth to En-shemesh, and went forth toward Geliloth, which is over against the going up of Adummim, and descended to the ᵃstone of Bohan the son of Reuben,

18 And passed along toward the side over against Arabah northward, and went down unto Arabah:

19 And the border passed along to the side of Beth-hoglah northward: and the outgoings of the border were at the north bay of ᵃthe salt sea at the south end of Jordan: this was the south coast.

20 And Jordan was the border of it on the east side. This was the inheritance of the children of Benjamin, by the coasts thereof round about, according to their families.

21 Now the cities of the tribe of the children of Benjamin according to their families were Jericho, and Beth-hoglah, and the valley of Keziz,

22 And Beth-arabah, and Zemaraim, and Beth-el,

23 And Avim, and Parah, and Ophrah,

24 And Chephar-haammonai, and Ophni, and Gaba; twelve cities with their villages:

25 Gibeon, and Ramah, and Beeroth,

26 And Mizpeh, and Chephirah, and Mozah,

27 And Rekem, and Irpeel, and Taralah,

28 And Zelah, Eleph, and ᵃJebusi, which is Jerusalem, ᵇGibeath, and Kirjath; fourteen cities with their villages. This is the ᶜinheritance of the children of Benjamin according to their families.

CHAPTER 19

Simeon, Zebulun, Issachar, Asher, Naphtali, and Dan receive their inheritances by lot.

AND the second lot came forth to Simeon, even for the tribe of the children of Simeon according to their families: and their inheritance was within the inheritance of the children of Judah.

2 And they had in their inheritance Beer-sheba, or Sheba, and Moladah,

3 And Hazar-shual, and Balah, and Azem,

4 And Eltolad, and Bethul, and Hormah,

5 And Ziklag, and Beth-marcaboth, and Hazar-susah,

6 And Beth-lebaoth, and Sharuhen; thirteen cities and their villages:

12a Josh. 7:2.
13a Gen. 35:6; 48:3.
  b OR lower.
14a OR turned.

16a Jer. 19:2 (2, 6).
  b 2 Kgs. 23:10;
    Jer. 7:31 (31–32).
17a Josh. 15:6.

19a IE the Dead Sea.
28a Josh. 15:8.
  b 2 Sam. 21:6.
  c Judg. 1:21; 19:14.

7 Ain, Remmon, and Ether, and Ashan; four cities and their villages:

8 And all the villages that *were* round about these cities to Baalath-beer, Ramath of the south. This *is* the inheritance of the tribe of the children of Simeon according to their families.

9 Out of the portion of the children of Judah *was* the inheritance of the children of Simeon: for the part of the children of Judah was too much for them: therefore the children of Simeon had their inheritance within the inheritance of them.

10 ¶ And the third lot came up for the children of ᵃZebulun according to their families: and the border of their inheritance was unto Sarid:

11 And their border went up toward the sea, and Maralah, and reached to Dabbasheth, and reached to the river that *is* before Jokneam;

12 And turned from Sarid eastward toward the sunrising unto the border of Chisloth-tabor, and then goeth out to Daberath, and goeth up to Japhia,

13 And from thence passeth on along on the east to Gittah-hepher, to Ittah-kazin, and goeth out to Remmon-methoar to Neah;

14 And the border compasseth it on the north side to Hannathon: and the outgoings thereof are in the valley of Jiphthah-el:

15 And Kattath, and Nahallal, and Shimron, and Idalah, and Beth-lehem: twelve cities with their villages.

16 This *is* the inheritance of the children of Zebulun according to their families, these cities with their villages.

17 ¶ *And* the fourth lot came out to Issachar, for the children of Issachar according to their families.

18 And their border was toward Jezreel, and Chesulloth, and ᵃShunem,

19 And Hapharaim, and Shion, and Anaharath,

20 And Rabbith, and Kishion, and Abez,

21 And Remeth, and En-gannim, and En-haddah, and Beth-pazzez;

22 And the ᵃcoast reacheth to Tabor, and Shahazimah, and Beth-shemesh; and the outgoings of their border were at Jordan: sixteen cities with their villages.

23 This *is* the inheritance of the tribe of the children of Issachar according to their families, the cities and their villages.

24 ¶ And the fifth lot came out for the tribe of the children of Asher according to their families.

25 And their border was Helkath, and Hali, and Beten, and Achshaph,

26 And Alammelech, and Amad, and Misheal; and reacheth to Carmel westward, and to Shihor-libnath;

27 And turneth toward the sunrising to Beth-dagon, and reacheth to Zebulun, and to the valley of Jiphthah-el toward the north side of Beth-emek, and Neiel, and goeth out to Cabul on the left hand,

28 And Hebron, and Rehob, and Hammon, and Kanah, *even* unto great Zidon;

29 And *then* the coast turneth to Ramah, and to the strong city Tyre; and the coast turneth to Hosah; and the outgoings thereof are at the sea from the coast to Achzib:

30 Ummah also, and Aphek, and Rehob: twenty and two cities with their villages.

31 This *is* the inheritance of the tribe of the children of Asher according to their families, these cities with their villages.

32 ¶ The sixth lot came out to the children of Naphtali, *even* for the children of Naphtali according to their families.

33 And their coast was from Heleph, from Allon to Zaanannim, and Adami, Nekeb, and Jabneel, unto Lakum; and the outgoings thereof were at Jordan:

34 And *then* the coast turneth westward to Aznoth-tabor, and goeth out from thence to Hukkok, and reacheth to Zebulun on the south

---

19 10*a* Gen. 49:13.
18*a* 2 Kgs. 4:8.

22*a* HEB border (also vv. 29, 33–34, 41, 47, 49).

side, and reacheth to Asher on the west side, and to Judah upon Jordan toward the sunrising.

35 And the [a]fenced cities are Ziddim, Zer, and Hammath, Rakkath, and Chinnereth,

36 And Adamah, and Ramah, and Hazor,

37 And Kedesh, and Edrei, and En-hazor,

38 And Iron, and Migdal-el, Horem, and Beth-anath, and Beth-shemesh; nineteen cities with their villages.

39 This is the inheritance of the tribe of the children of Naphtali according to their families, the cities and their villages.

40 ¶ And the seventh lot came out for the tribe of the children of Dan according to their families.

41 And the coast of their inheritance was Zorah, and Eshtaol, and Ir-shemesh,

42 And Shaalabbin, and Ajalon, and Jethlah,

43 And Elon, and Thimnathah, and Ekron,

44 And Eltekeh, and Gibbethon, and Baalath,

45 And Jehud, and Bene-berak, and Gath-rimmon,

46 And Me-jarkon, and Rakkon, with the border before Japho.

47 And the coast of the children of Dan went out too little for them: therefore the children of Dan went up to fight against Leshem, and took it, and smote it with the edge of the sword, and possessed it, and dwelt therein, and called Leshem, Dan, after the name of Dan their father.

48 This is the inheritance of the tribe of the children of Dan according to their families, these cities with their villages.

49 ¶ When they had made an end of dividing the land for inheritance by their coasts, the children of Israel gave an inheritance to Joshua the son of Nun among them:

50 According to the word of the LORD they gave him the city which he asked, even Timnath-serah in mount [a]Ephraim: and he built the city, and dwelt therein.

51 These are the [a]inheritances, which Eleazar the priest, and [b]Joshua the son of Nun, and the heads of the fathers of the tribes of the children of Israel, divided for an inheritance by lot in Shiloh before the LORD, at the door of the tabernacle of the congregation. So they made an end of dividing the country.

CHAPTER 20

Six cities of refuge are appointed for those guilty of manslaughter.

THE LORD also spake unto Joshua, saying,

2 Speak to the children of Israel, saying, Appoint out for you cities of [a]refuge, whereof I spake unto you by the hand of Moses:

3 That the [a]slayer that killeth any person [b]unawares and unwittingly may flee thither: and they shall be your refuge from the avenger of blood.

4 And when he that doth flee unto one of those cities shall stand at the entering of the [a]gate of the city, and shall declare his cause in the ears of the [b]elders of that city, they shall take him into the city unto them, and give him a place, that he may dwell among them.

5 And if the [a]avenger of blood pursue after him, then they shall not deliver the slayer up into his hand; because he smote his neighbour unwittingly, and hated him not beforetime.

6 And he shall dwell in that city, until he stand before the congregation for judgment, and until the death of the [a]high priest that shall be

---

35a HEB fortified.
50a Josh. 24:30 (29–30).
51a TG Inheritance.
  b Num. 34:17.
20 2a TG Refuge.

3a D&C 134:2 (2–5).
  b HEB by mistake, or by accident.
4a Ruth 4:1; Mosiah 7:10.
  b Ruth 4:2 (1–2);

1 Ne. 4:22 (22, 27);
  Alma 4:16 (7, 16);
  Moro. 6:7.
5a Num. 35:12 (11–34).
6a Num. 35:25.

in those days: then shall the slayer return, and come unto his own city, and unto his own house, unto the city from whence he fled.

7 ¶ And they appointed Kedesh in Galilee in mount Naphtali, and Shechem in mount Ephraim, and Kirjath-arba, which *is* Hebron, in the mountain of Judah.

8 And on the other side Jordan by Jericho eastward, they assigned Bezer in the wilderness upon the plain out of the tribe of Reuben, and Ramoth in *a*Gilead out of the tribe of Gad, and Golan in Bashan out of the tribe of Manasseh.

9 These were the cities appointed for all the children of Israel, and for the *a*stranger that *b*sojourneth among them, that whosoever killeth *any* person at unawares might flee thither, and not die by the hand of the avenger of blood, until he stood before the congregation.

CHAPTER 21

The Levites receive forty-eight cities with their suburbs—The Lord fulfills all His promises and gives Israel rest.

THEN came near the heads of the fathers of the *a*Levites unto Eleazar the priest, and unto Joshua the son of Nun, and unto the heads of the fathers of the tribes of the children of Israel;

2 And they spake unto them at Shiloh in the land of Canaan, saying, The LORD commanded by the hand of Moses to give us cities to dwell in, with the suburbs thereof for our cattle.

3 And the children of Israel gave unto the Levites out of their inheritance, at the commandment of the LORD, these cities and their suburbs.

4 And the lot came out for the families of the *a*Kohathites: and the children of Aaron the priest, *which were* of the Levites, had by lot out of the tribe of Judah, and out of the

tribe of Simeon, and out of the tribe of Benjamin, thirteen cities.

5 And the rest of the children of Kohath *had* by lot out of the families of the tribe of Ephraim, and out of the tribe of Dan, and out of the half tribe of Manasseh, ten cities.

6 And the children of Gershon *had* by lot out of the families of the tribe of Issachar, and out of the tribe of Asher, and out of the tribe of Naphtali, and out of the half tribe of Manasseh in Bashan, thirteen cities.

7 The children of Merari by their families *had* out of the tribe of Reuben, and out of the tribe of Gad, and out of the tribe of Zebulun, twelve cities.

8 And the children of Israel gave by lot unto the Levites these cities with their suburbs, as the LORD commanded by the hand of Moses.

9 ¶ And they gave out of the tribe of the children of Judah, and out of the tribe of the children of Simeon, these *a*cities which are *here* mentioned by name,

10 Which the children of Aaron, *being* of the families of the Kohathites, *who were* of the children of Levi, had: for theirs was the first lot.

11 And they gave them the city of *a*Arba the father of Anak, which *city is* Hebron, in the hill *country* of Judah, with the suburbs thereof round about it.

12 But the fields of the city, and the villages thereof, gave they to *a*Caleb the son of Jephunneh for his possession.

13 ¶ Thus they gave to the children of *a*Aaron the priest Hebron with her suburbs, *to be a* city of refuge for the slayer; and Libnah with her suburbs,

14 And Jattir with her suburbs, and Eshtemoa with her suburbs,

15 And Holon with her suburbs, and Debir with her suburbs,

16 And Ain with her suburbs, and Juttah with her suburbs, *and* Beth-

---

8*a* Josh. 21:38.
9*a* Num. 35:15.
  b Judg. 17:8 (7–9); 19:16.

21 1*a* Num. 35:2.
  4*a* 1 Chr. 6:54.
  9*a* 2 Chr. 31:15.

11*a* Josh. 14:15.
12*a* Josh. 14:14.
13*a* 1 Chr. 6:57 (55–60).

shemesh with her suburbs; nine cities out of those two tribes.

17 And out of the tribe of Benjamin, Gibeon with her suburbs, Geba with her suburbs,

18 *a*Anathoth with her suburbs, and Almon with her suburbs; four cities.

19 All the cities of the children of Aaron, the priests, *were* thirteen cities with their suburbs.

20 ¶ And the families of the children of *a*Kohath, the Levites which remained of the children of Kohath, even they had the cities of their lot out of the tribe of Ephraim.

21 For they gave them Shechem with her suburbs in mount Ephraim, *to be* a city of refuge for the slayer; and Gezer with her suburbs,

22 And Kibzaim with her suburbs, and Beth-horon with her suburbs; four cities.

23 And out of the tribe of Dan, Eltekeh with her suburbs, Gibbethon with her suburbs,

24 Aijalon with her suburbs, Gathrimmon with her suburbs; four cities.

25 And out of the half tribe of Manasseh, Tanach with her suburbs, and Gath-rimmon with her suburbs; two cities.

26 All the cities *were* ten with their suburbs for the families of the children of Kohath that remained.

27 ¶ And unto the children of Gershon, of the families of the Levites, out of the *other* half tribe of Manasseh *they gave* Golan in Bashan with her suburbs, *to be* a city of refuge for the slayer; and Beeshterah with her suburbs; two cities.

28 And out of the tribe of Issachar, Kishon with her suburbs, Dabareh with her suburbs,

29 Jarmuth with her suburbs, Engannim with her suburbs; four cities.

30 And out of the tribe of Asher, Mishal with her suburbs, Abdon with her suburbs,

31 Helkath with her suburbs, and Rehob with her suburbs; four cities.

32 And out of the tribe of Naphtali, Kedesh in Galilee with her suburbs, *to be* a city of refuge for the slayer; and Hammoth-dor with her suburbs, and Kartan with her suburbs; three cities.

33 All the cities of the Gershonites according to their families *were* thirteen cities with their suburbs.

34 ¶ And unto the families of the children of *a*Merari, the rest of the Levites, out of the tribe of Zebulun, Jokneam with her suburbs, and Kartah with her suburbs,

35 Dimnah with her suburbs, Nahalal with her suburbs; four cities.

36 And out of the tribe of Reuben, Bezer with her suburbs, and Jahazah with her suburbs,

37 Kedemoth with her suburbs, and Mephaath with her suburbs; four cities.

38 And out of the tribe of Gad, Ramoth in *a*Gilead with her suburbs, *to be* a city of refuge for the slayer; and Mahanaim with her suburbs,

39 Heshbon with her suburbs, Jazer with her suburbs; four cities in all.

40 So all the cities for the children of Merari by their families, which were remaining of the families of the Levites, were *by* their lot twelve cities.

41 All the cities of the *a*Levites within the *b*possession of the children of Israel *were* forty and eight cities with their suburbs.

42 These cities were every one with their suburbs round about them: thus *were* all these cities.

43 ¶ And the LORD gave unto Israel all the *a*land which he *b*sware to give unto their fathers; and they possessed it, and dwelt therein.

44 And the LORD gave them *a*rest round about, according to all that he sware unto their fathers: and there *b*stood not a man of all their

---

18*a* 1 Kgs. 2:26.
20*a* 1 Chr. 6:66 (66–70).
34*a* 1 Chr. 6:77 (77–81).
38*a* Josh. 20:8.
41*a* Num. 35:7.

b 2 Chr. 11:14.
43*a* TG Israel, Land of; Promised Lands.
b OR covenanted (also v. 44).

44*a* Deut. 3:20; Josh. 22:4.
b Josh. 23:9.

^{c}enemies before them; the Lord ^{d}delivered all their enemies into their hand.

45 There ^{a}failed not ought of any good thing which the Lord had ^{b}spoken unto the house of Israel; all came to pass.

CHAPTER 22

The 2½ tribes are dismissed with a blessing—They build an altar of testimony by the Jordan to show they are the Lord's people—It is not an altar for sacrifices or burnt offerings.

THEN Joshua called the ^{a}Reubenites, and the Gadites, and the half tribe of Manasseh,

2 And said unto them, Ye have kept all that Moses the servant of the Lord commanded you, and have obeyed my voice in all that I commanded you:

3 Ye have not left your brethren these many days unto this day, but have kept the charge of the commandment of the Lord your God.

4 And now the Lord your God hath given ^{a}rest unto your brethren, as he promised them: therefore now return ye, and get you unto your tents, *and* unto the ^{b}land of your possession, which Moses the servant of the Lord gave you on the other side Jordan.

5 But take ^{a}diligent heed to do the ^{b}commandment and the law, which Moses the servant of the Lord charged you, to ^{c}love the Lord your God, and to ^{d}walk in all his ways, and to keep his commandments, and to cleave unto him, and to ^{e}serve him with all your ^{f}heart and with all your soul.

6 So Joshua blessed them, and sent them away: and they went unto their tents.

7 ¶ Now to the *one* half of the tribe of Manasseh Moses had given *possession* in Bashan: but unto the *other* half thereof gave Joshua among their brethren on this side Jordan westward. And when Joshua sent them away also unto their tents, then he blessed them,

8 And he spake unto them, saying, Return with much riches unto your tents, and with very much cattle, with silver, and with gold, and with brass, and with iron, and with very much raiment: divide the spoil of your enemies with your brethren.

9 ¶ And the children of Reuben and the children of Gad and the half tribe of Manasseh returned, and departed from the children of Israel out of Shiloh, which *is* in the land of Canaan, to go unto the country of ^{a}Gilead, to the land of their possession, whereof they were possessed, according to the word of the Lord by the hand of Moses.

10 ¶ And when they came unto the borders of Jordan, that *are* in the land of Canaan, the children of Reuben and the children of Gad and the half tribe of Manasseh built there an altar by Jordan, a great altar to see to.

11 ¶ And the children of Israel heard say, Behold, the children of Reuben and the children of Gad and the half tribe of Manasseh have built an altar over against the land of Canaan, in the borders of Jordan, at the passage of the children of Israel.

12 And when the children of Israel heard *of it,* the whole congregation of the children of Israel gathered themselves together at Shiloh, to go up to war against them.

13 And the children of Israel sent unto the children of Reuben, and to the children of Gad, and to the half tribe of Manasseh, into the land of Gilead, Phinehas the son of Eleazar the priest,

14 And with him ten princes, of

44c Josh. 10:8.
  d Mosiah 9:17;
    Alma 46:7.
45a 1 Kgs. 8:56;
    Matt. 24:35.
  b Josh. 23:15.

22 1a Josh. 18:7;
     1 Chr. 5:3 (1, 3, 18).
  4a Josh. 21:44; 23:1.
   b Num. 32:33 (1–33).
  5a TG Diligence.
   b D&C 84:27 (25–27).

  c Moro. 7:47–48.
  d TG Walking with God.
  e TG Commitment.
  f Morm. 9:27;
    D&C 4:2; 64:34 (22, 34).
9a 1 Chr. 5:9 (4–9).

each chief house a prince throughout all the tribes of Israel; and each one *was* an head of the house of their fathers among the thousands of Israel.

15 ¶ And they came unto the children of Reuben, and to the children of Gad, and to the half tribe of Manasseh, unto the land of Gilead, and they spake with them, saying,

16 Thus saith the whole ᵃcongregation of the LORD, What trespass *is* this that ye have committed against the God of Israel, to turn away this day from following the LORD, in that ye have builded you an altar, that ye might ᵇrebel this day against the LORD?

17 *Is* the ᵃiniquity of Peor too little for us, from which we are not cleansed until this day, although there was a plague in the congregation of the LORD,

18 But that ye must turn away this day from following the LORD? and it will be, *seeing* ye ᵃrebel to day against the LORD, that to morrow he will be wroth with the whole congregation of Israel.

19 Notwithstanding, if the land of your possession *be* unclean, *then* pass ye over unto the land of the possession of the LORD, wherein the LORD's tabernacle dwelleth, and take possession among us: but rebel not against the LORD, nor rebel against us, in building you an altar beside the altar of the LORD our God.

20 Did not ᵃAchan the son of Zerah commit a trespass in the accursed thing, and wrath fell on all the congregation of Israel? and that man perished not alone in his iniquity.

21 ¶ Then the children of Reuben and the children of Gad and the half tribe of Manasseh answered, and said unto the heads of the thousands of Israel,

22 The LORD ᵃGod of gods, the LORD God of gods, he knoweth, and Israel he shall know; if *it be* in rebel-

lion, or if in transgression against the LORD, (save us not this day,)

23 That we have built us an altar to turn from following the LORD, or if to offer thereon burnt offering or meat offering, or if to offer peace offerings thereon, let the LORD himself require *it*;

24 And if we have not *rather* done it for fear of *this* thing, saying, In time to come your children might speak unto our children, saying, What have ye to do with the LORD God of Israel?

25 For the LORD hath made Jordan a border between us and you, ye children of Reuben and children of Gad; ye have no part in the LORD: so shall your children make our children cease from fearing the LORD.

26 Therefore we said, Let us now prepare to build us an altar, not for burnt offering, nor for sacrifice:

27 But *that it may be* a witness between us, and you, and our generations after us, that we might do the service of the LORD before him with our burnt offerings, and with our sacrifices, and with our peace offerings; that your children may not say to our children in time to come, Ye have no part in the LORD.

28 Therefore said we, that it shall be, when they should *so* say to us or to our generations in time to come, that we may say *again*, Behold the pattern of the altar of the LORD, which our fathers made, not for burnt offerings, nor for sacrifices; but it *is* a witness between us and you.

29 God forbid that we should rebel against the LORD, and turn this day from following the LORD, to build an altar for burnt offerings, for meat offerings, or for sacrifices, beside the altar of the LORD our God that *is* before his tabernacle.

30 ¶ And when Phinehas the priest, and the princes of the congregation and heads of the thousands of Israel which *were* with him, heard

---

16a TG Church.
  b 1 Ne. 2:23 (21–24);
    Mosiah 15:26.

17a TG Sexual Immorality.
18a Alma 3:18;
    4 Ne. 1:38.

20a Josh. 7:1 (1–5).
22a Deut. 10:17.

the words that the children of Reuben and the children of Gad and the children of Manasseh spake, it pleased them.

31 And Phinehas the son of Eleazar the priest said unto the children of Reuben, and to the children of Gad, and to the children of Manasseh, This day we perceive that the LORD is *among us, because ye have not committed this trespass against the LORD: now ye have delivered the children of Israel out of the hand of the LORD.

32 ¶ And Phinehas the son of Eleazar the priest, and the princes, returned from the children of Reuben, and from the children of Gad, out of the land of Gilead, unto the land of Canaan, to the children of Israel, and brought them word again.

33 And the thing pleased the children of Israel; and the children of Israel blessed God, and did not intend to go up against them in battle, to destroy the land wherein the children of Reuben and Gad dwelt.

34 And the children of Reuben and the children of Gad called the altar *Ed:* for it *shall be* a witness between us that the LORD *is* *God.

CHAPTER 23

Joshua exhorts Israel to be courageous, keep the commandments, love the Lord, and neither marry among nor cleave unto the remnants of the Canaanites who remain in the land—When the children of Israel serve other gods, they will be cursed and dispossessed.

AND it came to pass a long time after that the LORD had given *rest unto Israel from all their enemies round about, that *Joshua waxed old *and* stricken in age.

2 And Joshua called for all Israel, *and* for their elders, and for their heads, and for their judges, and for their officers, and said unto them, I am old *and* stricken in age:

3 And ye have seen all that the LORD your God hath done unto all these nations because of you; for the LORD your God *is* he that hath fought for you.

4 Behold, I have divided unto you by lot these nations that remain, to be an inheritance for your tribes, from Jordan, with all the nations that I have cut off, even unto the *great sea westward.

5 And the LORD your God, he shall *expel them from before you, and drive them from out of your sight; and ye shall possess their land, as the LORD your God hath promised unto you.

6 Be ye therefore very *courageous to keep and to do all that is written in the book of the law of Moses, that ye turn not aside therefrom *to the right hand or *to the left;

7 That ye come not among these nations, these that remain among you; neither make mention of the name of their *gods, nor cause to swear *by them,* neither serve them, nor bow yourselves unto them:

8 But *cleave unto the LORD your God, as ye have done unto this day.

9 For the LORD hath driven out from before you great nations and strong: but *as for* you, no man hath been able to *stand before you unto this day.

10 One man of you shall chase a thousand: for the LORD your God, he *it is* that *fighteth for you, as he hath *promised you.

11 Take good heed therefore unto yourselves, that ye love the LORD your God.

12 Else if ye do in any wise go back, and cleave unto the remnant of these nations, *even* these that remain among you, and shall make

---

31a Lev. 26:12 (11–12);
    D&C 101:18 (16–18).
34a Jer. 10:1;
    D&C 76:1.
23 1a Josh. 22:4.
    b Josh. 13:1.

4a Josh. 15:12.
5a D&C 98:37 (33–38).
6a TG Courage.
7a Ex. 23:13.
8a 2 Kgs. 18:6;
    Jacob 6:5;

Hel. 4:25;
    D&C 11:19.
9a Josh. 21:44.
10a Deut. 20:4.
    b TG Promise.

*a*marriages with them, and go in unto them, and they to you:

13 Know for a certainty that the LORD your God will no more drive out *any of* these nations from before you; but they shall be snares and traps unto you, and *a*scourges in your sides, and *b*thorns in your eyes, until ye *c*perish from off this good land which the LORD your God hath given you.

14 And, behold, this day I *am* going the *a*way of all the earth: and ye know in all your hearts and in all your souls, that not one thing hath failed of all the *b*good things which the LORD your God spake concerning you; all are come to pass unto you, *and* not one thing hath failed thereof.

15 Therefore it shall come to pass, *that* as all good things are come upon you, which the LORD your God *a*promised you; so shall the LORD bring upon you all evil things, until he have destroyed you from off this good land which the LORD your God hath given you.

16 When ye have *a*transgressed the covenant of the LORD your God, which he commanded you, and have gone and served other gods, and bowed yourselves to them; then shall the anger of the LORD be kindled against you, and ye shall perish quickly from off the *b*good land which he hath given unto you.

CHAPTER 24

Joshua recites how the Lord has blessed and led Israel—Joshua and all the people covenant to choose the Lord and serve Him only—Joshua and Eleazar die—The bones of Joseph, taken from Egypt, are buried in Shechem.

AND Joshua gathered all the tribes of Israel to Shechem, and called for the elders of Israel, and for their heads, and for their judges, and for their officers; and they presented themselves before God.

2 And Joshua said unto all the people, Thus saith the LORD God of Israel, Your fathers dwelt on the other side of the flood in old time, *even* Terah, the father of Abraham, and the father of Nachor: and they served other *a*gods.

3 And I took your father Abraham from the other side of the flood, and led him throughout all the land of Canaan, and multiplied his *a*seed, and gave him Isaac.

4 And I gave unto Isaac Jacob and Esau: and I gave unto Esau mount Seir, to possess it; but Jacob and his children went down into Egypt.

5 I sent Moses also and Aaron, and I *a*plagued Egypt, according to that which I did among them: and afterward I brought you out.

6 And I *a*brought your fathers out of Egypt: and ye came unto the sea; and the Egyptians pursued after your fathers with chariots and horsemen unto the *b*Red sea.

7 And when they cried unto the LORD, he put *a*darkness between you and the Egyptians, and brought the sea upon them, and covered them; and your eyes have seen what I have done in Egypt: and ye dwelt in the wilderness a long season.

8 And I brought you into the land of the *a*Amorites, which dwelt on the other side Jordan; and they fought with you: and I gave them into your hand, that ye might possess their land; and I *b*destroyed them from before you.

9 Then Balak the son of Zippor,

12*a* TG Marriage, Interfaith.
13*a* Judg. 1:27 (27–36).
   b Num. 33:55;
      Ezek. 28:24;
      1 Ne. 2:24;
      3 Ne. 20:28 (27–28).
   c 1 Ne. 2:21 (20–21).
14*a* 1 Kgs. 2:2;
      2 Ne. 1:14.
      TG Death.

   b D&C 82:10.
15*a* Josh. 21:45.
16*a* Deut. 17:2;
      D&C 1:15; 3:6 (6–8);
      54:4 (3–6); 104:52.
   b 1 Kgs. 14:15.
24 2*a* Abr. 2:5 (1–5).
      TG Idolatry.
   3*a* TG Seed of Abraham.
   5*a* TG Plague.

6*a* Ex. 12:37;
      1 Ne. 17:26 (23–26).
   b Ex. 14:9;
      1 Ne. 17:27 (26–27).
7*a* TG Darkness, Physical.
8*a* Num. 21:21 (21–31).
   b Amos 2:9;
      1 Ne. 17:32 (32–35).

king of Moab, arose and warred against Israel, and sent and called Balaam the son of Beor to curse you:

10 But I would not hearken unto Balaam; therefore he blessed you still: so I delivered you out of his hand.

11 And ye went over Jordan, and came unto ^aJericho: and the men of Jericho fought against you, the Amorites, and the Perizzites, and the Canaanites, and the Hittites, and the Girgashites, the Hivites, and the Jebusites; and I delivered them into your hand.

12 And I sent the ^ahornet before you, which drave them out from before you, *even* the two kings of the Amorites; *but* not with thy ^bsword, nor with thy bow.

13 And I have ^agiven you a land for which ye did not labour, and cities which ye built not, and ye dwell in them; of the vineyards and oliveyards which ye planted not do ye eat.

14 ¶ Now therefore ^afear the LORD, and serve him in ^bsincerity and in truth: and put away the ^cgods which your fathers served on the other side of the flood, and in Egypt; and serve ye the LORD.

15 And if it seem evil unto you to serve the LORD, ^achoose you ^bthis day whom ye will ^cserve; whether the gods which your fathers served that *were* on the other side of the flood, or the gods of the Amorites, in whose land ye dwell: but as for me and my ^dhouse, we will ^eserve the LORD.

16 And the people answered and said, God forbid that we should forsake the LORD, to serve other gods;

17 For the LORD our God, he *it is*

that brought us up and our fathers out of the land of Egypt, from the house of bondage, and which did those great signs in our sight, and preserved us in all the way wherein we went, and among all the people through whom we passed:

18 And the LORD drave out from before us all the people, even the Amorites which dwelt in the land: *therefore* will we also serve the LORD; for he *is* our God.

19 And Joshua said unto the people, Ye cannot serve the LORD: for he *is* an ^aholy God; he *is* a ^bjealous God; he will not ^cforgive your transgressions nor your sins.

20 If ye forsake the LORD, and serve strange ^agods, then he will turn and do you ^bhurt, and consume you, after that he hath done you good.

21 And the people said unto Joshua, Nay; but we will ^aserve the LORD.

22 And Joshua said unto the people, Ye *are* witnesses against yourselves that ye have chosen you the LORD, to ^aserve him. And they said, We *are* witnesses.

23 Now therefore put away, *said he,* the strange ^agods which *are* among you, and incline your heart unto the LORD God of Israel.

24 And the people said unto Joshua, The LORD our God will we serve, and his voice will we obey.

25 So Joshua made a covenant with the people that day, and set them a statute and an ordinance in Shechem.

26 ¶ And Joshua wrote these words in the book of the law of God, and took a great ^astone, and set it up there under an oak, that *was* by the sanctuary of the LORD.

27 And Joshua said unto all the

11*a* Josh. 6:1 (1–27).
12*a* Ex. 23:27–28.
  b Ps. 44:3.
13*a* Lev. 18:24.
14*a* TG Reverence.
  b TG Sincere.
  c Abr. 1:5 (5–7).
15*a* TG Agency;
    Commitment.
  b TG Procrastination.
  c TG Service.

  d TG Family, Children,
    Responsibilities toward.
  e TG Example;
    Loyalty;
    Objectives; Service;
    Sustaining Church
    Leaders.
19*a* Lev. 19:2;
    Isa. 5:16;
    D&C 20:11.
  b IE desiring exclusive

    devotion.
    Ex. 20:5;
    Deut. 4:24;
    Mosiah 13:13.
  c Ex. 34:7.
20*a* TG Idolatry.
  b Mosiah 7:29; Hel. 12:3.
21*a* TG Service.
22*a* D&C 4:2 (2–5).
23*a* TG Idolatry.
26*a* 1 Sam. 7:12.

people, Behold, this stone shall be a witness unto us; for it hath heard all the words of the LORD which he spake unto us: it shall be therefore a witness unto you, lest ye deny your God.

28 So Joshua let the people depart, every man unto his inheritance.

29 ¶ And it came to pass after these things, that Joshua the son of Nun, the servant of the LORD, died, *being* an hundred and ten years old.

30 And they *a*buried him in the border of his inheritance in Timnathserah, which *is* in mount Ephraim, on the north side of the hill of Gaash.

31 And Israel *a*served the LORD all the days of Joshua, and all the days of the elders that overlived Joshua, and which had known all the works of the LORD, that he had done for Israel.

32 ¶ And the *a*bones of Joseph, which the children of Israel brought up out of Egypt, buried they in Shechem, in a parcel of ground which Jacob bought of the sons of Hamor the father of Shechem for an hundred pieces of silver: and it became the inheritance of the children of Joseph.

33 And Eleazar the son of Aaron died; and they buried him in a hill *that pertained to* Phinehas his son, which was given him in *a*mount Ephraim.

THE BOOK OF
JUDGES

CHAPTER 1

Judah, Simeon, and Joseph continue to conquer the Canaanites—Remnants of the Canaanites remain in the lands of Judah, Manasseh, Ephraim, Zebulun, Asher, Naphtali, and Dan.

NOW after the death of Joshua it came to pass, that the children of Israel asked the LORD, saying, Who shall go up for us against the Canaanites first, to fight against them?

2 And the LORD said, Judah shall go up: behold, I have delivered the land into his hand.

3 And Judah said unto Simeon his brother, Come up with me into my lot, that we may fight against the Canaanites; and I likewise will go with thee into thy lot. So Simeon went with him.

4 And Judah went up; and the LORD delivered the Canaanites and the Perizzites into their hand: and they slew of them in Bezek *a*ten thousand men.

5 And they found Adoni-bezek in Bezek: and they fought against him, and they slew the Canaanites and the Perizzites.

6 But Adoni-bezek fled; and they pursued after him, and caught him, and cut off his thumbs and his great toes.

7 And Adoni-bezek said, *a*Threescore and ten kings, having their thumbs and their great toes cut off, gathered *their meat* under my table: as I have done, so God hath requited

---

30*a* Josh. 19:50 (49–50).
31*a* Judg. 2:7.
32*a* Gen. 50:25;

33*a* Judg. 17:1.

Ex. 13:19.

[JUDGES]
1 4*a* Morm. 6:10 (9–16).
    7*a* OR Seventy kings.

me. And they brought him to Jerusalem, and there he died.

8 Now the children of Judah had fought against Jerusalem, and had taken it, and smitten it with the edge of the sword, and set the city on fire.

9 ¶ And afterward the children of Judah went down to fight against the Canaanites, that dwelt in the mountain, and in the south, and in the valley.

10 And Judah went against the Canaanites that dwelt in Hebron: (now the name of Hebron before was Kirjath-arba:) and they slew Sheshai, and Ahiman, and Talmai.

11 And from thence he went against the inhabitants of Debir: and the name of Debir before was Kirjath-sepher:

12 And Caleb said, He that smiteth Kirjath-sepher, and taketh it, to him will I give Achsah my daughter to wife.

13 And Othniel the son of Kenaz, Caleb's younger brother, took it: and he gave him Achsah his daughter to wife.

14 And it came to pass, when she came to him, that she moved him to ask of her father a field: and she lighted from off her ass; and Caleb said unto her, What wilt thou?

15 And she said unto him, Give me a blessing: for thou hast given me a south land; give me also springs of water. And Caleb gave her the upper springs and the *nether springs.

16 ¶ And the children of the *Kenite, Moses' father in law, went up out of the *city of palm trees with the children of Judah into the wilderness of Judah, which lieth in the south of Arad; and they went and dwelt among the people.

17 And Judah went with Simeon his brother, and they slew the Canaanites that inhabited Zephath, and utterly destroyed it. And the name of the city was called Hormah.

18 Also Judah took Gaza with the *coast thereof, and Askelon with the coast thereof, and Ekron with the coast thereof.

19 And the Lord was with *Judah; and he drave out the inhabitants of the mountain; but could not drive out the inhabitants of the valley, because they had *chariots of iron.

20 And they gave Hebron unto Caleb, as Moses said: and he expelled thence the three sons of Anak.

21 And the children of Benjamin did not *drive out the *Jebusites that inhabited Jerusalem; but the *Jebusites dwell with the children of Benjamin in Jerusalem unto this day.

22 ¶ And the house of Joseph, they also went up against Beth-el: and the Lord was with them.

23 And the house of Joseph sent to descry Beth-el. (Now the name of the city before was Luz.)

24 And the spies saw a man come forth out of the city, and they said unto him, Shew us, we pray thee, the entrance into the city, and we will shew thee mercy.

25 And when he shewed them the entrance into the city, they smote the city with the edge of the sword; but they let go the *man and all his family.

26 And the man went into the land of the Hittites, and built a city, and called the name thereof Luz: which is the name thereof unto this day.

27 ¶ Neither did Manasseh *drive out the inhabitants of Beth-shean and her towns, nor Taanach and her towns, nor the inhabitants of Dor and her towns, nor the inhabitants of Ibleam and her towns, nor the inhabitants of Megiddo and her towns: but the Canaanites would dwell in that land.

15a Josh. 15:19.
16a 1 Sam. 15:6;
   1 Chr. 2:55.
   b Deut. 34:3.
18a HEB border (also v. 36).
19a Deut. 33:7.

b Josh. 17:16;
   Judg. 4:3.
21a Ps. 106:34.
   b Josh. 18:28;
   Judg. 19:14.
   c Josh. 15:63;

2 Sam. 5:6;
1 Chr. 11:4;
Zech. 9:7.
25a Josh. 6:17.
27a Josh. 23:13 (1–16).

28 And it came to pass, when Israel was strong, that they put the Canaanites to *a*tribute, and did not utterly drive them out.

29 ¶ Neither did Ephraim drive out the *a*Canaanites that dwelt in Gezer; but the Canaanites dwelt in Gezer among them.

30 ¶ Neither did Zebulun drive out the inhabitants of Kitron, nor the inhabitants of Nahalol; but the Canaanites dwelt among them, and became tributaries.

31 ¶ Neither did Asher drive out the inhabitants of Accho, nor the inhabitants of Zidon, nor of Ahlab, nor of Achzib, nor of Helbah, nor of Aphik, nor of Rehob:

32 But the Asherites dwelt among the Canaanites, the inhabitants of the land: for they did not drive them out.

33 ¶ Neither did Naphtali drive out the inhabitants of Beth-shemesh, nor the inhabitants of Beth-anath; but he dwelt among the Canaanites, the inhabitants of the land: nevertheless the inhabitants of Beth-shemesh and of Beth-anath became tributaries unto them.

34 And the Amorites forced the children of Dan into the mountain: for they would not suffer them to come down to the valley:

35 But the Amorites would dwell in mount Heres in Aijalon, and in Shaalbim: yet the hand of the house of Joseph prevailed, so that they became tributaries.

36 And the coast of the Amorites *was* from the going up to Akrabbim, from the rock, and upward.

CHAPTER 2

An angel rebukes Israel for not serving the Lord—As a pattern of future events, a new generation arises that forsakes the Lord and serves Baal and Ashtaroth—The Lord is angry with the children of Israel and ceases to preserve them—He raises up judges to guide and lead them—The Canaanites are left in the land to test Israel.

AND an angel of the LORD came up from Gilgal to Bochim, and said, I made you to go up out of Egypt, and have brought you unto the land which I sware unto your fathers; and I said, I will never *a*break my *b*covenant with you.

2 And ye shall make no *a*league with the inhabitants of this land; ye shall throw down their altars: but ye have not *b*obeyed my voice: why have ye done this?

3 Wherefore I also said, I will not drive them out from before you; but they shall be *as thorns* in your sides, and their gods shall be a *a*snare unto you.

4 And it came to pass, when the angel of the LORD spake these words unto all the children of Israel, that the people lifted up their voice, and wept.

5 And they called the name of that place Bochim: and they sacrificed there unto the LORD.

6 ¶ And when Joshua had let the people go, the children of Israel went every man unto his inheritance to possess the land.

7 And the people *a*served the LORD all the days of Joshua, and all the days of the elders that outlived Joshua, who had seen all the great works of the LORD, that he did for Israel.

8 And Joshua the son of *a*Nun, the servant of the LORD, died, *being* an hundred and ten years old.

9 And they buried him in the border of his inheritance in Timnath-heres, in the mount of Ephraim, on the north side of the hill Gaash.

10 And also all that generation were gathered unto their fathers: and there arose another generation after them, which *a*knew not the LORD, nor yet the works which he had done for Israel.

28*a* Josh. 17:13 (12–13).
29*a* Josh. 16:10.
2 1*a* Deut. 31:16.
  b TG Abrahamic Covenant; Covenants.

2*a* Ex. 34:12;
     Josh. 9:7.
  b TG Disobedience.
3*a* Ex. 23:33.
7*a* Josh. 24:31.

8*a* Num. 13:16;
     Deut. 34:9.
10*a* TG God, Knowledge about.

11 ¶ And the children of Israel did evil in the sight of the LORD, and served Baalim:

12 And they forsook the LORD God of their fathers, which brought them out of the land of Egypt, and followed other gods, of the gods of the people that *were* round about them, and bowed themselves unto them, and provoked the LORD to *a*anger.

13 And they forsook the LORD, and served *a*Baal and Ashtaroth.

14 ¶ And the *a*anger of the LORD was hot against Israel, and he delivered them into the hands of *b*spoilers that spoiled them, and he sold them into the hands of their enemies round about, so that they could not any longer stand before their enemies.

15 Whithersoever they went out, the *a*hand of the LORD was against them for evil, as the LORD had said, and as the LORD had sworn unto them: and they were greatly distressed.

16 ¶ Nevertheless the LORD raised up *a*judges, which *b*delivered them out of the hand of those that spoiled them.

17 And yet they would not hearken unto their judges, but they went a *a*whoring after other *b*gods, and bowed themselves unto them: they turned *c*quickly out of the way which their fathers walked in, obeying the commandments of the LORD; *but* they did not so.

18 And when the LORD raised them up judges, then the LORD was with the judge, and delivered them out of the hand of their enemies all the days of the judge: *a*for it repented the LORD because of their groanings by reason of them that oppressed them and *b*vexed them.

19 And it came to pass, when the judge was dead, *that* they returned, and corrupted *themselves* more than their *a*fathers, in following other gods to serve them, and to bow down unto them; they ceased not from their own doings, nor from their *b*stubborn way.

20 ¶ And the anger of the LORD was hot against Israel; and he said, Because that this people hath transgressed my covenant which I commanded their fathers, and have not hearkened unto my voice;

21 I also will not henceforth drive out any from before them of the nations which Joshua left when he died:

22 That through them I may *a*prove Israel, whether they will keep the way of the LORD to *b*walk therein, as their fathers did keep *it*, or not.

23 Therefore the LORD left those nations, without driving them out hastily; neither delivered he them into the hand of Joshua.

CHAPTER 3

The children of Israel intermarry with the Canaanites, worship false gods, and are cursed—Othniel judges the Israelites—They serve Moab and are delivered by Ehud, who slays Eglon.

NOW these *are* the nations which the LORD left, to prove Israel by them, *even* as many *of* Israel as had not known all the wars of Canaan;

2 Only that the generations of the children of Israel might know, to teach them war, at the least such as before knew nothing thereof;

3 *Namely, *a*five lords of the Philistines, and all the Canaanites, and the Sidonians, and the Hivites that dwelt in mount Lebanon, from

---

12*a* TG Anger.
13*a* 1 Sam. 7:4.
14*a* D&C 95:2 (1–3); 98:21.
    TG God, Indignation of.
  b Neh. 9:27.
15*a* Lev. 26:3 (3–46).
16*a* Ruth 1:1;
    2 Sam. 7:11;
    Mosiah 29:41 (41, 44).
  b TG Deliver.
17*a* 2 Ne. 9:37;

Alma 7:6;
Hel. 6:31.
  b Ex. 34:15.
  c Alma 46:8;
    Hel. 12:4 (2–5).
18*a* The Hebrew root means
    "to be sorry," "moved
    to pity," or "have
    compassion."
    Ps. 106:45.
    JST Judg. 2:18 . . . for the

Lord *hearkened* because
    of . . .
  b HEB crushed.
19*a* Matt. 23:32 (30–32).
  b TG Stubbornness.
22*a* 1 Ne. 2:24 (23–24).
    TG Test.
  b TG Walking with God.
3 3*a* Josh. 13:3.

mount Baal-hermon unto the entering in of Hamath.

4 And they were to prove Israel by them, to know whether they would hearken unto the commandments of the LORD, which he commanded their fathers by the hand of Moses.

5 ¶ And the children of Israel *dwelt among the Canaanites, Hittites, and Amorites, and Perizzites, and Hivites, and Jebusites:

6 And they took their daughters to be their wives, and *gave their daughters to their sons, and served their gods.

7 And the children of Israel did *evil in the sight of the LORD, and forgat the LORD their God, and *served *Baalim and the *groves.

8 ¶ Therefore the anger of the LORD was hot against Israel, and he sold them into the hand of Chushan-rishathaim king of Mesopotamia: and the children of Israel served Chushan-rishathaim eight years.

9 And when the children of Israel cried unto the LORD, the LORD raised up a *deliverer to the children of Israel, who delivered them, *even* Othniel the son of Kenaz, Caleb's younger brother.

10 And the *Spirit of the LORD came upon him, and he judged Israel, and went out to war: and the LORD delivered Chushan-rishathaim king of Mesopotamia into his hand; and his hand prevailed against *Chushan-rishathaim.

11 And the land had rest forty years. And Othniel the son of Kenaz died.

12 ¶ And the children of Israel did evil again in the sight of the LORD: and the LORD strengthened Eglon the king of Moab against Israel, because they had done evil in the sight of the LORD.

13 And he gathered unto him the children of Ammon and Amalek, and went and smote Israel, and possessed the city of palm trees.

14 So the children of Israel served Eglon the king of Moab eighteen years.

15 But when the children of Israel cried unto the LORD, the LORD raised them up a deliverer, Ehud the son of Gera, a Benjamite, a man left-handed: and by him the children of Israel sent a present unto Eglon the king of Moab.

16 But Ehud made him a dagger which had two edges, of a cubit length; and he did gird it under his raiment upon his right thigh.

17 And he brought the present unto Eglon king of Moab: and Eglon *was* a very fat man.

18 And when he had made an end to offer the present, he sent away the people that bare the present.

19 But he himself turned again from the quarries that *were* by Gilgal, and said, I have a secret *errand unto thee, O king: who said, Keep silence. And all that stood by him went out from him.

20 And Ehud came unto him; and he was sitting in a summer parlour, which he had for himself alone. And Ehud said, I have a message from God unto thee. And he arose out of *his* seat.

21 And Ehud put forth his left hand, and took the dagger from his right thigh, and thrust it into his belly:

22 And the *haft also went in after the blade; and the fat closed upon the blade, so that he could not draw the dagger out of his belly; and the dirt came out.

23 Then Ehud went forth through the porch, and shut the doors of the *parlour upon him, and locked them.

24 When he was gone out, his servants came; and when they saw that, behold, the doors of the parlour

---

5a Ps. 106:35.
6a TG Marriage, Interfaith.
7a TG Apostasy of Israel.
  b Judg. 4:1.
  c Hosea 2:13.
  d HEB *asheroth*; fertility

cult goddesses.
  TG Idolatry.
9a Neh. 9:27.
  TG Deliver.
10a TG God, Spirit of.
  b Hab. 3:7.

19a OR message.
22a OR handle.
23a HEB upper, or roof,
  chamber.

were locked, they said, Surely he covereth his feet in his summer chamber.

25 And they tarried till they were ashamed: and, behold, he opened not the doors of the parlour; therefore they took a key, and opened *them:* and, behold, their lord *was* fallen down dead on the earth.

26 And Ehud escaped while they tarried, and passed beyond the quarries, and escaped unto Seirath.

27 And it came to pass, when he was come, that he blew a trumpet in the mountain of Ephraim, and the children of Israel went down with him from the mount, and he before them.

28 And he said unto them, Follow after me: for the Lord hath delivered your enemies the Moabites into your hand. And they went down after him, and took the fords of Jordan toward Moab, and suffered not a man to pass over.

29 And they slew of Moab at that time about ten thousand men, all *a*lusty, and all men of valour; and there escaped not a man.

30 So *a*Moab was *b*subdued that day under the hand of Israel. And the land had rest *c*fourscore years.

31 ¶ And after him was Shamgar the son of Anath, which slew of the Philistines six hundred men with an ox goad: and he also delivered Israel.

CHAPTER 4

Deborah, a prophetess, judges Israel— She and Barak deliver Israel from the Canaanites—Jael, a woman, slays Sisera, the Canaanite.

AND the children of Israel again did *a*evil in the sight of the Lord, when Ehud was dead.

2 And the Lord *a*sold them into the hand of Jabin king of Canaan, that reigned in Hazor; the captain of whose host *was* Sisera, which dwelt in Harosheth of the Gentiles.

3 And the children of Israel cried unto the Lord: for he had nine hundred *a*chariots of iron; and twenty years he *b*mightily *c*oppressed the children of Israel.

4 ¶ And Deborah, a *a*prophetess, the wife of Lapidoth, she judged Israel at that time.

5 And she *a*dwelt under the palm tree of Deborah between Ramah and Beth-el in mount Ephraim: and the children of Israel came up to her for judgment.

6 And she sent and called *a*Barak the son of Abinoam out of Kedesh-naphtali, and said unto him, Hath not the Lord God of Israel commanded, *saying,* Go and draw toward mount Tabor, and take with thee ten thousand men of the children of Naphtali and of the children of Zebulun?

7 And I will draw unto thee to the river Kishon Sisera, the captain of Jabin's army, with his chariots and his multitude; and I will deliver him into thine hand.

8 And Barak said unto her, If thou wilt go with me, then I will go: but if thou wilt not go with me, *then* I will not go.

9 And she said, I will surely go with thee: notwithstanding the journey that thou takest shall not be for thine honour; for the Lord shall sell Sisera into the hand of a woman. And Deborah arose, and went with Barak to Kedesh.

10 ¶ And Barak called Zebulun and Naphtali to Kedesh; and he went up with ten thousand men at his feet: and Deborah went up with him.

11 Now Heber the Kenite, *which was* of the children of Hobab the father in law of Moses, had severed himself from the Kenites, and pitched

---

29a HEB fat or hardy.
30a 2 Kgs. 3:18.
  b Ex. 14:30 (1–30);
    Judg. 10:11 (11–12).
  c OR eighty.
4 1a Judg. 3:7 (5–7);

3 Ne. 30:2;
  Abr. 1:6 (5–7).
2a 2 Ne. 7:1.
3a Josh. 17:16; Judg. 1:19.
  b HEB forcibly, violently.
  c Ps. 106:42 (42–43).

4a Ex. 15:20 (20–21);
  Acts 21:9 (8–9).
  TG Woman.
5a HEB used to sit or
  remain.
6a Heb. 11:32.

his tent unto the plain of Zaanaim, which *is* by Kedesh.

12 And they shewed Sisera that Barak the son of Abinoam was gone up to mount Tabor.

13 And Sisera gathered together all his chariots, *even* nine hundred chariots of iron, and all the people that *were* with him, from Harosheth of the Gentiles unto the river of Kishon.

14 And Deborah said unto Barak, Up; for this *is* the day in which the LORD hath delivered Sisera into thine hand: is not the LORD gone out *a*before thee? So Barak went down from mount Tabor, and ten thousand men after him.

15 And the LORD *a*discomfited *b*Sisera, and all *his* chariots, and all *his* host, with the edge of the sword before Barak; so that Sisera lighted down off *his* chariot, and fled away on his feet.

16 But Barak pursued after the chariots, and after the host, unto Harosheth of the Gentiles: and all the host of Sisera fell upon the edge of the sword; *and* there was not a man left.

17 Howbeit Sisera fled away on his feet to the tent of Jael the wife of Heber the Kenite: for *there was* peace between Jabin the king of Hazor and the house of Heber the Kenite.

18 ¶ And Jael went out to meet Sisera, and said unto him, Turn in, my lord, turn in to me; fear not. And when he had turned in unto her into the tent, she covered him with a *a*mantle.

19 And he said unto her, Give me, I pray thee, a little water to drink; for I am thirsty. And she opened a bottle of milk, and gave him drink, and covered him.

20 Again he said unto her, Stand in the door of the tent, and it shall be, when any man doth come and inquire of thee, and say, Is there any man here? that thou shalt say, No.

21 Then Jael Heber's wife took a nail of the tent, and took an hammer in her hand, and went softly unto him, and smote the *a*nail into his *b*temples, and fastened it into the ground: for he was fast asleep and weary. So he died.

22 And, behold, as Barak pursued Sisera, Jael came out to meet him, and said unto him, Come, and I will shew thee the man whom thou seekest. And when he came into her *tent*, behold, Sisera lay dead, and the nail *was* in his temples.

23 So God subdued on that day Jabin the king of Canaan before the children of Israel.

24 And the hand of the children of Israel prospered, and prevailed against Jabin the king of Canaan, until they had destroyed Jabin king of Canaan.

CHAPTER 5

Deborah and Barak sing a song of praise because Israel is delivered from Canaanite bondage.

THEN *a*sang Deborah and Barak the son of Abinoam on that day, saying,

2 Praise ye the LORD for the avenging of Israel, when the people willingly offered themselves.

3 Hear, O ye kings; give ear, O ye princes; I, *even* I, will sing unto the LORD; I will sing *praise* to the LORD God of Israel.

4 LORD, when thou wentest out of Seir, when thou *a*marchedst out of the field of Edom, the earth trembled, and the heavens dropped, the clouds also dropped water.

5 The mountains *a*melted from before the LORD, *even* that *b*Sinai from before the LORD God of Israel.

14*a* Deut. 9:3;
   Ether 1:42 (42–43);
   D&C 84:88 (87–88).
15*a* OR panicked, put to
   flight.
   b Ps. 83:9.
18*a* HEB rug, thick coverlet,

or blanket.
21*a* HEB tent peg or pin.
   b Judg. 5:26 (25–27).
5 1*a* TG Singing.
4*a* Ps. 68:7.
5*a* OR quaked.
   Ps. 97:5;

Micah 1:4;
Hel. 12:9;
3 Ne. 22:10;
D&C 109:74;
133:22 (21–22, 40);
Moses 6:34.
b Ps. 68:8.

6 In the days of Shamgar the son of Anath, in the days of Jael, the ^ahighways were unoccupied, and the travellers walked through byways.

7 *The inhabitants of* the villages ceased, they ceased in Israel, until that I Deborah arose, that I arose a ^amother in Israel.

8 They chose new ^agods; then *was* war in the gates: was there a shield or spear seen among forty thousand in Israel?

9 My heart *is* toward the governors of Israel, that offered themselves willingly among the people. Bless ye the LORD.

10 Speak, ye that ride ^aon white asses, ye that sit ^bin judgment, and walk by the way.

11 ^a*They that are delivered* from the noise of archers in the places of drawing water, there shall they rehearse the righteous acts of the LORD, *even* the righteous acts *toward the inhabitants* of his villages in Israel: then shall the people of the LORD go down to the gates.

12 Awake, awake, Deborah: awake, awake, utter a song: arise, Barak, and lead thy captivity captive, thou son of Abinoam.

13 ^aThen he made him that remaineth have dominion over the nobles among the people: the LORD made me have dominion over the mighty.

14 Out of Ephraim *was there* a root of them against Amalek; after thee, Benjamin, among thy people; out of ^aMachir came down governors, and out of Zebulun they that ^bhandle the pen of the ^cwriter.

15 And the princes of Issachar *were* with Deborah; even Issachar, and also Barak: he was sent on foot into the valley. For the divisions of Reuben *there were* great thoughts of heart.

16 Why abodest thou among the sheepfolds, to hear the bleatings of the flocks? For the divisions of Reuben *there were* great searchings of heart.

17 Gilead abode beyond Jordan: and why did Dan remain in ships? Asher continued on the sea shore, and abode in his breaches.

18 Zebulun and Naphtali *were* a people *that* jeoparded their lives unto the death in the high places of the field.

19 The kings came *and* fought, then fought the kings of Canaan in Taanach by the waters of Megiddo; they took no gain of money.

20 They fought from heaven; the stars in their courses fought against Sisera.

21 The river of Kishon swept them away, that ancient river, the river Kishon. O my soul, ^athou hast trodden down strength.

22 ^aThen were the horsehoofs broken by the means of the pransings, the pransings of their mighty ones.

23 Curse ye Meroz, said the angel of the LORD, curse ye bitterly the inhabitants thereof; because they ^acame not to the help of the LORD, to the help of the LORD against the mighty.

24 Blessed above ^awomen shall Jael the wife of Heber the Kenite be, blessed shall she be above women in the tent.

25 He asked water, *and* she gave

6a Lev. 26:22 (21–22).
7a TG Marriage, Motherhood.
8a Deut. 32:17.
10a IE on animals used by rich merchants, leaders.
  b Hebrew meaning uncertain; perhaps "on rich cloths, carpets."
11a HEB By the voices of archers down among the watering places, there they rehearse the righteousness of Jehovah, even the righteousness of His rulers in Israel. Then the people of the LORD went down to the gates.
13a HEB Then a remnant descended against the nobles; the people of the LORD descended for me against the mighty.
14a Num. 32:40; Josh. 17:1.

  b HEB hold the sceptre of the muster-officer, the marshal's staff.
  c TG Scribe.
21a HEB (perhaps) tread (them) down with might.
22a OR Then did the horse hooves stamp.
23a Judg. 21:5 (5–6).
24a TG Woman.

him milk; she brought forth ^abutter in a ^blordly dish.

26 She put her hand to the ^anail, and her right hand to the workmen's hammer; and with the hammer she smote Sisera, she smote off his head, when she had pierced and stricken through his ^btemples.

27 At her feet he bowed, he fell, he lay down: at her feet he bowed, he fell: where he bowed, there he fell down dead.

28 The mother of Sisera looked out at a window, and cried through the lattice, Why is his chariot *so* long in coming? why tarry the wheels of his chariots?

29 Her wise ladies answered her, yea, she returned answer to herself,

30 ^aHave they not sped? have they *not* divided the prey; to every man a damsel *or* two; to Sisera ^ba prey of divers colours, a prey of divers colours of needlework, of divers colours of needlework on both sides, *meet* for the necks of *them that take* the spoil?

31 So let all thine enemies perish, O LORD: but *let* them that love him *be* as the sun when he goeth forth in his might. And the land had rest forty years.

CHAPTER 6

Israel is in bondage to the Midianites—An angel appears to Gideon and calls him to deliver Israel—He overthrows the altar of Baal, the Spirit of the Lord rests upon him, and the Lord gives him a sign to show he is called to deliver Israel.

AND the children of Israel did evil in the sight of the LORD: and the LORD delivered them into the hand of Midian seven years.

2 And the hand of Midian prevailed against Israel: *and* because of the Midianites the children of Israel made them the dens which *are* in the mountains, and caves, and strong holds.

3 And *so* it was, when Israel had sown, that the Midianites came up, and the Amalekites, and the children of the ^aeast, even they came up against them;

4 And they encamped against them, and destroyed the ^aincrease of the earth, till thou come unto Gaza, and left no sustenance for Israel, neither sheep, nor ox, nor ass.

5 For they came up with their cattle and their tents, and they came as grasshoppers for multitude; *for* both they and their camels were without number: and they entered into the land to destroy it.

6 And Israel was greatly impoverished because of the Midianites; and the children of Israel cried unto the LORD.

7 ¶ And it came to pass, when the children of Israel cried unto the LORD because of the Midianites,

8 That the LORD sent a prophet unto the children of Israel, which said unto them, Thus saith the LORD God of Israel, I brought you up from Egypt, and brought you forth out of the house of bondage;

9 And I delivered you out of the hand of the Egyptians, and out of the hand of all that oppressed you, and drave them out from before you, and gave you their land;

10 And I said unto you, I *am* the LORD your God; ^afear not the gods of the Amorites, in whose land ye dwell: but ye have not ^bobeyed my voice.

11 ¶ And there came an angel of the LORD, and sat under an oak which *was* in Ophrah, that ^apertained unto Joash the Abi-ezrite: and his son Gideon threshed wheat ^bby the winepress, to hide *it* from the Midianites.

25*a* HEB curds, curdled milk.
  b HEB bowl of nobles.
26*a* HEB tent peg or pin.
  b Judg. 4:21 (17–21).
30*a* HEB Are they not

finding, dividing spoil?
  b OR a spoil of dyed stuffs.
6 3*a* Gen. 25:6.
  4*a* OR produce.
  10*a* HEB (also) do not

reverence, honor.
  2 Kgs. 17:35.
  b TG Disobedience.
11*a* OR belonged.
  b HEB in the winepress.

12 And the angel of the LORD appeared unto him, and said unto him, The LORD *is* with thee, thou mighty man of valour.

13 And Gideon said unto him, Oh my Lord, if the LORD be with us, why then is all this befallen us? and where *be* all his *a*miracles which our fathers told us of, saying, Did not the LORD bring us up from Egypt? but now the LORD hath forsaken us, and delivered us into the hands of the Midianites.

14 And the LORD looked upon him, and said, Go in this thy *a*might, and thou shalt save Israel from the hand of the Midianites: have not I sent thee?

15 And he said unto him, Oh my Lord, wherewith shall I save Israel? behold, my family *is* poor in Manasseh, and I *am* the *a*least in my father's house.

16 And the LORD said unto him, Surely I will be *a*with thee, and thou shalt smite the Midianites as one man.

17 And he said unto him, If now I have found *a*grace in thy sight, then shew me a *b*sign that thou talkest with me.

18 Depart not hence, I pray thee, until I come unto thee, and bring forth my present, and set *it* before thee. And he said, I will tarry until thou come again.

19 ¶ And Gideon went in, and made ready a kid, and unleavened cakes of an ephah of flour: the flesh he put in a basket, and he put the broth in a pot, and brought *it* out unto him under the oak, and presented *it.*

20 And the angel of God said unto him, Take the flesh and the unleavened cakes, and lay *them* upon this rock, and pour out the broth. And he did so.

21 ¶ Then the angel of the LORD put forth the end of the staff that *was* in his hand, and touched the flesh and the unleavened cakes; and there rose up *a*fire out of the rock, and consumed the flesh and the unleavened cakes. Then the angel of the LORD departed out of his sight.

22 And when Gideon perceived that he *was* an angel of the LORD, Gideon said, Alas, O Lord GOD! for because I have seen an *a*angel of the LORD face to *b*face.

23 And the LORD said unto him, Peace *be* unto thee; fear not: thou shalt not die.

24 Then Gideon built an altar there unto the LORD, and called it *a*Jehovah-shalom: unto this day it *is* yet in Ophrah of the Abi-ezrites.

25 ¶ And it came to pass the same night, that the LORD said unto him, Take thy father's young bullock, even the second bullock of seven years old, and throw down the altar of *a*Baal that thy father hath, and cut down the *b*grove that *is* by it:

26 And build an altar unto the LORD thy God upon the top of this *a*rock, in the ordered place, and take the second bullock, and offer a burnt sacrifice with the wood of the grove which thou shalt cut down.

27 Then Gideon took ten men of his servants, and did as the LORD had said unto him: and *so* it was, because he feared his father's household, and the men of the city, that he could not do *it* by day, that he did *it* by night.

28 ¶ And when the men of the city arose early in the morning, behold, the altar of Baal was cast down, and the grove was cut down that *was* by it, and the second bullock was offered upon the altar *that was* built.

29 And they said one to another, Who hath done this thing? And when they inquired and asked, they

13 *a* Morm. 9:20 (15–20).
14 *a* D&C 4:2.
15 *a* 1 Sam. 9:21.
16 *a* Josh. 1:5.
17 *a* TG Grace.
  b Gen. 15:8 (7–9).
21 *a* Lev. 9:24; 1 Ne. 1:6.
22 *a* TG Angels.
  b Num. 12:8.
24 *a* Ex. 17:15.
25 *a* 2 Kgs. 3:2.
  b HEB *asherah*—a pole
or tree representing a fertility goddess (also vv. 26, 28, 30).
Deut. 7:5;
2 Kgs. 18:4.
26 *a* HEB stronghold.

said, Gideon the son of Joash hath done this thing.

30 Then the men of the city said unto Joash, Bring out thy son, that he may die: because he hath cast down the altar of Baal, and because he hath cut down the grove that *was* by it.

31 And Joash said unto all that stood against him, Will ye plead for Baal? will ye save him? he that will plead for him, let him be put to death *a*whilst *it is yet* morning: if he *be* a god, let him plead for himself, because *one* hath cast down his altar.

32 Therefore on that day he called him *a*Jerubbaal, saying, Let Baal plead against him, because he hath thrown down his altar.

33 ¶ Then all the Midianites and the Amalekites and the children of the east were gathered together, and went over, and pitched in the valley of Jezreel.

34 But the Spirit of the LORD came upon Gideon, and he blew a trumpet; and Abi-ezer was gathered after him.

35 And he sent messengers throughout all Manasseh; who also was gathered after him: and he sent messengers unto Asher, and unto Zebulun, and unto Naphtali; and they came up to meet them.

36 ¶ And Gideon said unto God, If thou wilt save Israel by mine hand, as thou hast said,

37 Behold, I will put a fleece of wool in the floor; *and* if the dew be on the fleece only, and *it be* dry upon all the earth *beside,* then shall I know that thou wilt save Israel by mine hand, as thou hast said.

38 And it was so: for he rose up early on the morrow, and thrust the fleece together, and wringed the dew out of the fleece, a bowl full of water.

39 And Gideon said unto God, Let not thine *a*anger be hot against me, and I will speak but this once: let me *b*prove, I pray thee, but this once with the fleece; let it now be dry only upon the fleece, and upon all the ground let there be dew.

40 And God did so that night: for it was dry upon the fleece only, and there was dew on all the ground.

CHAPTER 7

Gideon's army is reduced to 300—They frighten the Midianite armies with trumpets and lights—The Midianites fight among themselves, flee, and are defeated by Israel.

THEN Jerubbaal, who *is* Gideon, and all the people that *were* with him, rose up early, and pitched beside the well of Harod: so that the host of the Midianites were on the north side of them, by the hill of Moreh, in the valley.

2 And the LORD said unto Gideon, The people that *are* with thee *are* too many for me to give the Midianites into their hands, lest Israel vaunt themselves against me, saying, Mine own hand hath saved me.

3 Now therefore go to, proclaim in the ears of the people, saying, Whosoever *is* *a*fearful and afraid, let him return and depart early from *b*mount Gilead. And there returned of the people twenty and two thousand; and there remained ten thousand.

4 And the LORD said unto Gideon, The people *are* yet *too* *a*many; bring them down unto the water, and I will *b*try them for thee there: and it shall be, *that* of whom I say unto thee, This shall go with thee, the same shall go with thee; and of whomsoever I say unto thee, This shall not go with thee, the same shall not go.

5 So he brought down the people unto the water: and the LORD said unto Gideon, Every one that lappeth of the water with his tongue, as a dog lappeth, him shalt thou set by himself; likewise every one that boweth down upon his knees to drink.

6 And the number of them that

---

31 *a* OR before morning.
32 *a* 1 Sam. 12:11.
39 *a* Gen. 18:32.

b HEB try or test.
7 3 *a* Deut. 20:8.
  b OR Mount Gilboa.

4 *a* 1 Sam. 14:6.
  b OR test.
  Alma 27:15; D&C 98:12.

lapped, *putting* their hand to their mouth, were three hundred men: but all the rest of the people bowed down upon their knees to drink water.

7 And the Lord said unto Gideon, By the three hundred men that lapped will I save you, and deliver the Midianites into thine hand: and let all the *other* people go every man unto his place.

8 So the people took ᵃvictuals in their hand, and their trumpets: and he sent all *the rest of* Israel every man unto his tent, and retained those three hundred men: and the host of Midian was beneath him in the valley.

9 ¶ And it came to pass the same night, that the Lord said unto him, Arise, get thee down unto the host; for I have delivered it into thine hand.

10 But if thou fear to go down, go thou with Phurah thy servant down to the host:

11 And thou shalt hear what they say; and afterward shall thine hands be strengthened to go down unto the host. Then went he down with Phurah his servant unto the outside of the armed men that *were* in the host.

12 And the Midianites and the Amalekites and all the children of the east lay along in the valley like grasshoppers for multitude; and their camels *were* without number, as the sand by the sea side for multitude.

13 And when Gideon was come, behold, *there was* a man that told a dream unto his fellow, and said, Behold, I dreamed a ᵃdream, and, lo, a cake of barley bread tumbled into the ᵇhost of Midian, and came unto a tent, and smote it that it fell, and overturned it, that ᶜthe tent lay along.

14 And his fellow answered and said, This *is* nothing else save the sword of Gideon the son of Joash, a man of Israel: *for* into his hand

hath God delivered Midian, and all the host.

15 ¶ And it was *so,* when Gideon heard the telling of the dream, and the interpretation thereof, that he worshipped, and returned into the host of Israel, and said, Arise; for the Lord hath delivered into your hand the host of Midian.

16 And he divided the three hundred men *into* three companies, and he put a trumpet in every man's hand, with empty pitchers, and lamps within the pitchers.

17 And he said unto them, Look on me, and do likewise: and, behold, when I come to the outside of the camp, it shall be *that,* as I do, so shall ye do.

18 When I blow with a trumpet, I and all that *are* with me, then blow ye the trumpets also on every side of all the camp, and say, *The sword of the Lord, and of Gideon.*

19 ¶ So Gideon, and the hundred men that *were* with him, came unto the outside of the camp in the beginning of the middle watch; and they had but newly set the watch: and they blew the trumpets, and brake the pitchers that *were* in their hands.

20 And the three companies blew the trumpets, and brake the pitchers, and held the lamps in their left hands, and the trumpets in their right hands to blow *withal:* and they cried, The sword of the Lord, and of Gideon.

21 And they stood every man in his place round about the camp: and all the host ran, and cried, and fled.

22 And the three hundred blew the trumpets, and the Lord set every man's sword against his ᵃfellow, even throughout all the host: and the host fled to Beth-shittah in Zererath, *and* to the border of Abel-meholah, unto Tabbath.

23 And the men of Israel gathered themselves together out of Naphtali, and out of Asher, and out of all

---

8*a* Josh. 1:11.
13*a* TG Dream.

b HEB camp.
c IE the tent lay flat.

22*a* 1 Sam. 14:20;
2 Chr. 20:23.

Manasseh, and pursued after the ^aMidianites.

24 ¶ And Gideon sent messengers throughout all mount Ephraim, saying, Come down against the Midianites, and take before them the waters unto Beth-barah and Jordan. Then all the men of Ephraim gathered themselves together, and took the waters unto Beth-barah and Jordan.

25 And they took two princes of the Midianites, Oreb and Zeeb; and they slew ^aOreb upon the rock Oreb, and Zeeb they slew at the winepress of Zeeb, and pursued Midian, and brought the heads of Oreb and Zeeb to Gideon on the other side Jordan.

CHAPTER 8

Gideon pursues and destroys the Midianites—He frees the children of Israel but refuses their invitation to reign as king over them—Gideon dies, and Israel returns to idolatry.

AND the men of Ephraim said unto him, Why hast thou served us thus, that thou calledst us not, when thou wentest to fight with the Midianites? And they did chide with him sharply.

2 And he said unto them, What have I done now in comparison of you? *Is* not the gleaning of the grapes of Ephraim better than the vintage of Abi-ezer?

3 God hath delivered into your hands the princes of Midian, Oreb and Zeeb: and what was I able to do in comparison of you? Then their anger was abated toward him, when he had said that.

4 ¶ And Gideon came to Jordan, *and* passed over, he, and the three hundred men that *were* with him, faint, yet pursuing *them.*

5 And he said unto the men of Succoth, Give, I pray you, loaves of bread unto the people that follow me; for they *be* faint, and I am pursuing after ^aZebah and Zalmunna, kings of Midian.

6 ¶ And the princes of Succoth

said, *Are* the hands of Zebah and Zalmunna now in thine hand, that we should give bread unto thine army?

7 And Gideon said, Therefore when the Lord hath delivered Zebah and Zalmunna into mine hand, then I will tear your flesh with the thorns of the wilderness and with briers.

8 ¶ And he went up thence to Penuel, and spake unto them likewise: and the men of Penuel answered him as the men of Succoth had answered *him.*

9 And he spake also unto the men of Penuel, saying, When I come again in peace, I will break down this tower.

10 ¶ Now Zebah and Zalmunna *were* in Karkor, and their hosts with them, about fifteen thousand *men,* all that were left of all the hosts of the children of the east: for there fell an hundred and twenty thousand men that drew sword.

11 ¶ And Gideon went up by the way of them that dwelt in tents on the east of Nobah and Jogbehah, and smote the host: for the host was ^asecure.

12 And when Zebah and Zalmunna fled, he pursued after them, and took the two kings of Midian, Zebah and Zalmunna, and discomfited all the host.

13 ¶ And Gideon the son of Joash returned from battle before the sun *was up,*

14 And caught a young man of the men of Succoth, and inquired of him: and he described unto him the princes of Succoth, and the elders thereof, *even* threescore and seventeen men.

15 And he came unto the men of Succoth, and said, Behold Zebah and Zalmunna, with whom ye did upbraid me, saying, *Are* the hands of Zebah and Zalmunna now in thine hand, that we should give bread unto thy men *that are* weary?

16 And he took the elders of the city, and thorns of the wilderness and briers, and with them he taught the men of Succoth.

23*a* Isa. 9:4.
25*a* Isa. 10:26.

8 5*a* Ps. 83:11.
11*a* Judg. 18:10.

17 And he beat down the tower of Penuel, and slew the men of the city.

18 ¶ Then said he unto Zebah and Zalmunna, What manner of men *were they* whom ye slew at Tabor? And they answered, As thou *art*, so *were* they; each one resembled the children of a king.

19 And he said, They *were* my brethren, *even* the sons of my mother: *as* the LORD liveth, if ye had saved them alive, I would not slay you.

20 And he said unto Jether his firstborn, Up, *and* slay them. But the youth drew not his sword: for he feared, because he *was* yet a youth.

21 Then Zebah and Zalmunna said, Rise thou, and fall upon us: for as the man *is, so is* his strength. And Gideon arose, and slew Zebah and Zalmunna, and took away the ornaments that *were* on their camels' necks.

22 ¶ Then the men of Israel said unto Gideon, Rule thou over us, both thou, and thy son, and thy son's son also: for thou hast delivered us from the hand of Midian.

23 And Gideon said unto them, I will not *ᵃ*rule over you, neither shall my son rule over you: the LORD shall *ᵇ*rule over you.

24 ¶ And Gideon said unto them, I would desire a request of you, that ye would give me every man the earrings of his prey. (For they had golden earrings, because they *were* Ishmaelites.)

25 And they answered, We will willingly give *them*. And they spread a garment, and did cast therein every man the earrings of his prey.

26 And the weight of the *ᵃ*golden earrings that he requested was a thousand and seven hundred *ᵇ*shekels of gold; beside *ᶜ*ornaments, and collars, and purple raiment that *was* on the kings of Midian, and beside the chains that *were* about their camels' necks.

27 And Gideon made an *ᵃ*ephod thereof, and put it in his city, *even* in Ophrah: and all Israel went thither a whoring after it: which thing became a *ᵇ*snare unto Gideon, and to his house.

28 ¶ Thus was Midian subdued before the children of Israel, so that they lifted up their heads no more. And the country was in quietness forty years in the days of Gideon.

29 ¶ And Jerubbaal the son of Joash went and dwelt in his own house.

30 And Gideon had threescore and ten sons of his body begotten: for he had many wives.

31 And his concubine that *was* in Shechem, she also bare him a son, whose name he called Abimelech.

32 ¶ And Gideon the son of Joash died in a good old age, and was buried in the sepulchre of Joash his father, in Ophrah of the Abi-ezrites.

33 And it came to pass, as soon as Gideon was dead, that the children of Israel turned again, and went a whoring after Baalim, and made Baal-berith their god.

34 And the children of Israel remembered not the LORD their God, who had delivered them out of the hands of all their enemies on every side:

35 Neither shewed they kindness to the house of Jerubbaal, *namely*, Gideon, according to all the goodness which he had shewed unto Israel.

CHAPTER 9

Gideon's son Abimelech is made king—He slays his seventy brothers—Jotham tells a fable of trees choosing a king—The Shechemites conspire against Abimelech—He is slain at Thebez.

AND Abimelech the son of Jerubbaal went to Shechem unto his mother's brethren, and communed with

---

23*a* TG Governments.
  b Hel. 12:6;
    D&C 60:4.
26*a* Ex. 32:2.
  b Hebrew for "shekels"
    implied but not

expressed here.
  c HEB crescents and
    pendants.
27*a* IE probably here a
    medallion of gold
    to adorn the priest's

ephod. Later it was at
    times revered.
    Ex. 28:4 (4–35);
    Judg. 17:5.
  b Ex. 23:33.

them, and with all the family of the house of his mother's father, saying,

2 Speak, I pray you, in the ears of all the men of Shechem, Whether *is* better for you, either that all the sons of Jerubbaal, *which are* threescore and ten persons, reign over you, or that one reign over you? remember also that I *am* your bone and your flesh.

3 And his mother's brethren spake of him in the ears of all the men of Shechem all these words: and their hearts inclined to follow Abimelech; for they said, He *is* our brother.

4 And they gave him threescore and ten *pieces* of silver out of the house of Baal-berith, wherewith Abimelech ^ahired ^bvain and light persons, which followed him.

5 And he went unto his father's house at Ophrah, and slew his brethren the sons of Jerubbaal, *being* threescore and ten persons, upon one stone: notwithstanding yet Jotham the youngest son of Jerubbaal was left; for he hid himself.

6 And all the men of Shechem gathered together, and all the house of Millo, and went, and made Abimelech king, by the ^aplain of the pillar that *was* in Shechem.

7 ¶ And when they told *it* to Jotham, he went and stood in the top of mount ^aGerizim, and lifted up his voice, and cried, and said unto them, Hearken unto me, ye men of Shechem, that God may hearken unto you.

8 The trees went forth *on a time* to anoint a king over them; and they said unto the olive tree, Reign thou over us.

9 But the olive tree said unto them, Should I leave my fatness, wherewith by me they honour ^aGod and man, and go to be promoted over the trees?

10 And the trees said to the fig tree, Come thou, *and* reign over us.

11 But the fig tree said unto them, Should I forsake my sweetness, and my good fruit, and go to be promoted over the trees?

12 Then said the trees unto the ^avine, Come thou, *and* reign over us.

13 And the vine said unto them, Should I leave my ^awine, which cheereth God and man, and go to be promoted over the trees?

14 Then said all the trees unto the ^abramble, Come thou, *and* reign over us.

15 And the bramble said unto the trees, If in truth ye anoint me king over you, *then* come *and* put your trust in my shadow: and if not, let ^afire come out of the bramble, and devour the cedars of Lebanon.

16 Now therefore, if ye have done truly and sincerely, in that ye have made Abimelech king, and if ye have dealt well with Jerubbaal and his house, and have done unto him according to the deserving of his hands;

17 (For my father fought for you, and adventured his life far, and delivered you out of the hand of Midian:

18 And ye are risen up against my father's house this day, and have slain his sons, threescore and ten persons, upon one stone, and have made Abimelech, the son of his maidservant, king over the men of Shechem, because he *is* your brother;)

19 If ye then have dealt truly and sincerely with Jerubbaal and with his house this day, *then* rejoice ye in Abimelech, and let him also rejoice in you:

20 But if not, let fire come out from Abimelech, and devour the men of Shechem, and the house of Millo; and let fire come out from the men of Shechem, and from the house of Millo, and devour Abimelech.

21 And Jotham ran away, and

---

9 4*a* TG Tyranny.
  b HEB empty (or idle) and reckless (or violent).
  6*a* HEB terebinth tree.
  7*a* Deut. 11:29.

9*a* HEB gods and men; i.e., in ritual services.
12*a* TG Vineyard of the Lord.
13*a* HEB *tirosh*—fresh or

new wine.
14*a* OR thistle (also v. 15).
15*a* Ezek. 19:14 (10–14).

fled, and went to ^aBeer, and dwelt there, for fear of Abimelech his brother.

22 ¶ When Abimelech had reigned three years over Israel,

23 Then God ^asent an evil spirit between Abimelech and the men of Shechem; and the men of Shechem dealt treacherously with Abimelech:

24 That the cruelty *done* to the threescore and ten sons of Jerubbaal might come, and their blood be laid upon Abimelech their brother, which slew them; and upon the men of Shechem, which aided him in the killing of his brethren.

25 And the men of Shechem set ^aliers in wait for him in the top of the mountains, and they robbed all that came along that way by them: and it was told Abimelech.

26 And Gaal the son of Ebed came with his brethren, and went over to Shechem: and the men of Shechem put their confidence in him.

27 And they went out into the fields, and gathered their vineyards, and trode *the grapes,* and made merry, and went into the house of their god, and did eat and drink, and cursed Abimelech.

28 And Gaal the son of Ebed said, Who *is* Abimelech, and who *is* Shechem, that we should serve him? *is* not *he* the son of Jerubbaal? and Zebul his officer? serve the men of ^aHamor the father of Shechem: for why should we serve him?

29 And would to God this people were under my hand! then would I remove Abimelech. And he said to Abimelech, Increase thine army, and come out.

30 ¶ And when Zebul the ruler of the city heard the words of Gaal the son of Ebed, his anger was kindled.

31 And he sent messengers unto Abimelech privily, saying, Behold, Gaal the son of Ebed and his brethren be come to Shechem; and, behold, they ^afortify the city against thee.

32 Now therefore up by night, thou and the people that *is* with thee, and lie in wait in the field:

33 And it shall be, *that* in the morning, as soon as the sun is up, thou shalt rise early, and set upon the city: and, behold, *when* he and the people that *is* with him come out against thee, then mayest thou do to them as thou shalt find occasion.

34 ¶ And Abimelech rose up, and all the people that *were* with him, by night, and they laid wait against Shechem in four companies.

35 And Gaal the son of Ebed went out, and stood in the entering of the gate of the city: and Abimelech rose up, and the people that *were* with him, from lying in wait.

36 And when Gaal saw the people, he said to Zebul, Behold, there come people down from the top of the mountains. And Zebul said unto him, Thou seest the shadow of the mountains as *if they were* men.

37 And Gaal spake again and said, See there come people down by the middle of the land, and another company come along by ^athe plain of Meonenim.

38 Then said Zebul unto him, Where *is* now thy mouth, wherewith thou saidst, Who *is* Abimelech, that we should serve him? *is* not this the people that thou hast despised? go out, I pray now, and fight with them.

39 And Gaal went out before the men of Shechem, and fought with Abimelech.

40 And Abimelech chased him, and he fled before him, and many were overthrown *and* wounded, *even* unto the entering of the gate.

41 And Abimelech dwelt at Arumah: and Zebul thrust out Gaal and his brethren, that they should not dwell in Shechem.

42 And it came to pass on the morrow, that the people went out into the field; and they told Abimelech.

43 And he took the people, and divided them into three companies, and laid wait in the field, and looked,

---

21*a* Num. 21:16.
23*a* Judg. 9:57 (56–57).
25*a* Josh. 8:13.

28*a* Gen. 34:2 (2, 6).
31*a* HEB (probably) incite the city.

37*a* HEB the oak of the diviners.

and, behold, the people *were* come forth out of the city; and he rose up against them, and smote them.

44 And Abimelech, and the company that *was* with him, rushed forward, and stood in the entering of the gate of the city: and the two *other* companies ran upon all *the people* that *were* in the fields, and slew them.

45 And Abimelech fought against the city all that day; and he took the city, and slew the people that *was* therein, and beat down the city, and *a*sowed it with salt.

46 ¶ And when all the men of the tower of Shechem heard *that,* they entered into an hold of the house of the god Berith.

47 And it was told Abimelech, that all the men of the tower of Shechem were gathered together.

48 And Abimelech gat him up to mount Zalmon, he and all the people that *were* with him; and Abimelech took an axe in his hand, and cut down a bough from the trees, and took it, and laid *it* on his shoulder, and said unto the people that *were* with him, What ye have seen me do, make haste, *and* do as I *have done.*

49 And all the people likewise cut down every man his bough, and followed Abimelech, and put *them* to the hold, and set the hold on fire upon them; so that all the men of the tower of Shechem died also, about a thousand men and women.

50 ¶ Then went Abimelech to Thebez, and encamped against Thebez, and took it.

51 But there was a strong tower within the city, and thither fled all the men and women, and all they of the city, and shut *it* to them, and gat them up to the top of the tower.

52 And Abimelech came unto the tower, and fought against it, and went hard unto the door of the tower to burn it with fire.

53 And a certain woman cast a piece of a millstone upon *a*Abimelech's head, and all to brake his skull.

54 Then he called hastily unto the young man his armourbearer, and said unto him, Draw thy sword, and slay me, that men say not of me, A woman slew him. And his young man thrust him through, and he died.

55 And when the men of Israel saw that Abimelech was dead, they departed every man unto his place.

56 ¶ Thus God rendered the wickedness of Abimelech, which he did unto his father, in slaying his seventy brethren:

57 And all the *a*evil of the men of Shechem did God render upon their heads: and upon them came the curse of Jotham the son of Jerubbaal.

CHAPTER 10

Tola and then Jair judge Israel—The children of Israel worship false gods, are forsaken by the Lord, and are distressed by their enemies—They repent and ask the Lord for deliverance.

AND after Abimelech there arose to *a*defend Israel Tola the son of Puah, the son of Dodo, a man of Issachar; and he dwelt in Shamir in mount Ephraim.

2 And he judged Israel twenty and three years, and died, and was buried in Shamir.

3 ¶ And after him arose Jair, a Gileadite, and judged Israel twenty and two years.

4 And he had thirty sons that rode on thirty ass colts, and they had thirty cities, which are called Havoth-jair unto this day, which *are* in the land of Gilead.

5 And Jair died, and was buried in Camon.

6 ¶ And the children of Israel did evil again in the sight of the LORD, and served Baalim, and Ashtaroth, and the gods of Syria, and the gods of Zidon, and the gods of Moab, and the gods of the children of Ammon, and the gods of the Philistines, and

---

45*a* IE covered the soil with salt, supposed to ensure | desolation.
53*a* 2 Sam. 11:21. | 57*a* Judg. 9:23.
10 1*a* HEB deliver, save.

forsook the LORD, and served not him.

7 And the anger of the LORD was hot against Israel, and he *sold them into the hands of the Philistines, and into the hands of the children of Ammon.

8 And that year they vexed and oppressed the children of Israel: eighteen years, all the children of Israel that *were* on the other side Jordan in the land of the Amorites, which *is* in Gilead.

9 Moreover the children of Ammon passed over Jordan to fight also against Judah, and against Benjamin, and against the house of Ephraim; so that Israel was sore distressed.

10 ¶ And the children of Israel cried unto the LORD, saying, We have *sinned against thee, both because we have forsaken our God, and also served Baalim.

11 And the LORD said unto the children of Israel, *Did* not I *deliver you* from the Egyptians, and from the Amorites, from the children of Ammon, and from the Philistines?

12 The Zidonians also, and the Amalekites, and the Maonites, did oppress you; and ye cried to me, and I delivered you out of their hand.

13 Yet ye have forsaken me, and served other gods: wherefore I will *deliver you no more.

14 *Go and cry unto the *gods which ye have *chosen; let them deliver you in the time of your *tribulation.

15 ¶ And the children of Israel said unto the LORD, We have sinned: do thou unto us whatsoever seemeth good unto thee; deliver us only, we pray thee, this day.

16 And they *put away the strange gods from among them, and served the LORD: and his soul was *grieved for the misery of Israel.

17 Then the children of Ammon were gathered together, and encamped in Gilead. And the children of Israel assembled themselves together, and encamped in Mizpeh.

18 And the people *and* princes of Gilead said one to another, What man *is he* that will begin to fight against the children of Ammon? he shall be head over all the inhabitants of Gilead.

CHAPTER 11

Jephthah is chosen as the captain of the armies of Israel—The Ammonites assail Israel in war—Jephthah is guided by the Spirit and defeats Ammon with a great slaughter—He makes a rash vow, which leads to the sacrifice of his only daughter.

NOW *Jephthah the Gileadite was a mighty man of valour, and he *was* the son of an harlot: and Gilead begat Jephthah.

2 And Gilead's wife bare him sons; and his wife's sons grew up, and they thrust out Jephthah, and said unto him, Thou shalt not inherit in our father's house; for thou *art* the son of a strange woman.

3 Then Jephthah fled from his brethren, and dwelt in the land of Tob: and there were gathered *vain men to Jephthah, and went out with him.

4 ¶ And it came to pass in process of time, that the children of Ammon made war against Israel.

5 And it was so, that when the children of Ammon made war against Israel, the elders of Gilead went to fetch Jephthah out of the land of Tob:

6 And they said unto *Jephthah, Come, and be our captain, that we may fight with the children of Ammon.

7 And Jephthah said unto the elders of Gilead, Did not ye hate me, and expel me out of my father's

---

7a Hel. 12:3 (2–6).
10a 1 Sam. 7:6.
11a Ex. 14:30 (1–30);
    Judg. 3:30 (13–31).
13a TG Deliver.
14a 2 Kgs. 3:13;

Prov. 1:28 (27–28);
    Jer. 2:28 (26–37).
b TG Idolatry.
c Deut. 32:37 (37–38).
d TG Tribulation.
16a 1 Sam. 7:3.

b HEB at the end of
    patience, exasperated.
11 1a 1 Sam. 12:11.
3a HEB empty, idle,
    worthless.
6a Heb. 11:32 (32–35).

house? and why are ye come unto me now when ye are in distress?

8 And the elders of Gilead said unto Jephthah, Therefore we turn again to thee now, that thou mayest go with us, and fight against the children of Ammon, and be our head over all the inhabitants of Gilead.

9 And Jephthah said unto the elders of Gilead, If ye bring me home again to fight against the children of Ammon, and the LORD deliver them before me, ªshall I be your head?

10 And the elders of Gilead said unto Jephthah, The LORD be witness between us, if we do not so according to thy words.

11 Then Jephthah went with the elders of Gilead, and the people made him head and captain over them: and Jephthah uttered all his words before the LORD in Mizpeh.

12 ¶ And Jephthah sent messengers unto the king of the children of Ammon, saying, What hast thou to do with me, that thou art come against me to fight in my land?

13 And the king of the children of Ammon answered unto the messengers of Jephthah, Because Israel took away my ªland, when they came up out of Egypt, from ᵇArnon even unto Jabbok, and unto Jordan: now therefore restore those *lands* again peaceably.

14 And Jephthah sent messengers again unto the king of the children of Ammon:

15 And said unto him, Thus saith Jephthah, Israel took not away the land of ªMoab, nor the land of the children of Ammon:

16 But when Israel came up from Egypt, and walked through the wilderness unto the Red sea, and came to Kadesh;

17 Then Israel ªsent messengers unto the king of Edom, saying, Let me, I pray thee, pass through thy land: but the king of Edom would

not hearken *thereto.* And in like manner they sent unto the king of Moab: but he would not *consent:* and Israel abode in Kadesh.

18 Then they went along through the wilderness, and ªcompassed the land of Edom, and the land of Moab, and came by the east side of the land of Moab, and pitched on the other side of Arnon, but came not within the border of Moab: for Arnon *was* the border of Moab.

19 And Israel sent messengers unto Sihon king of the Amorites, the king of Heshbon; and Israel said unto him, Let us pass, we pray thee, through thy land into my place.

20 But Sihon trusted not Israel to pass through his ªcoast: but Sihon gathered all his people together, and pitched in Jahaz, and fought against Israel.

21 And the LORD God of Israel delivered Sihon and all his people into the hand of Israel, and they ªsmote them: so Israel possessed all the land of the Amorites, the inhabitants of that country.

22 And they possessed all the ªcoasts of the Amorites, from Arnon even unto Jabbok, and from the wilderness even unto Jordan.

23 So now the LORD God of Israel hath dispossessed the Amorites from before his people Israel, and shouldest thou possess it?

24 Wilt not thou possess that which Chemosh thy god giveth thee to possess? So whomsoever the LORD our God shall drive out from before us, them will we possess.

25 And now *art* thou any thing better than ªBalak the son of Zippor, king of Moab? did he ever strive against Israel, or did he ever fight against them,

26 While Israel dwelt in Heshbon and her towns, and in Aroer and her towns, and in all the cities that *be* along by the coasts of Arnon, three

---

9 a HEB I shall be your head.
13 a Num. 21:25 (21–35); Deut. 2:19 (16–19).
  b Num. 21:13;

Deut. 3:16 (15–17).
15 a Deut. 2:9 (9, 19).
17 a Num. 20:14.
18 a HEB went around. Josh. 6:3.

20 a HEB border(s).
21 a Num. 21:24 (24–25).
22 a Josh. 18:5.
25 a Num. 22:2.

hundred years? why therefore did ye not recover *them* within that time?

27 Wherefore I have not sinned against thee, but thou doest me wrong to war against me: the LORD the ᵃJudge be judge this day between the children of Israel and the children of Ammon.

28 Howbeit the king of the children of Ammon hearkened not unto the words of Jephthah which he sent him.

29 ¶ Then the Spirit of the LORD came upon Jephthah, and he passed over Gilead, and Manasseh, and passed over Mizpeh of Gilead, and from Mizpeh of Gilead he passed over *unto* the children of Ammon.

30 And Jephthah ᵃvowed a vow unto the LORD, and said, If thou shalt without fail deliver the children of Ammon into mine hands,

31 Then it shall be, that whatsoever cometh forth of the doors of my house to meet me, when I return in peace from the children of Ammon, shall surely be the LORD's, and I will offer it up for a burnt offering.

32 ¶ So Jephthah passed over unto the children of Ammon to fight against them; and the LORD delivered them into his hands.

33 And he smote them from Aroer, even till thou come to ᵃMinnith, *even* twenty cities, and unto the plain of the vineyards, with a very great slaughter. Thus the children of Ammon were subdued before the children of Israel.

34 ¶ And Jephthah came to Mizpeh unto his house, and, behold, his ᵃdaughter came out to meet him with ᵇtimbrels and with dances: and she *was his* only child; beside her he had neither son nor daughter.

35 And it came to pass, when he saw her, that he rent his clothes, and said, Alas, my daughter! ᵃthou hast brought me very low, and thou art one of them that trouble me: for I have ᵇopened my mouth unto the LORD, and I cannot go back.

36 And she said unto him, My father, *if* thou hast opened thy mouth unto the LORD, do to me according to that which hath proceeded out of thy mouth; forasmuch as the LORD hath taken vengeance for thee of thine enemies, *even* of the children of Ammon.

37 And she said unto her father, Let this thing be done for me: let me alone two months, that I may go up and down upon the mountains, and bewail my virginity, I and my fellows.

38 And he said, Go. And he sent her away *for* two months: and she went with her companions, and bewailed her virginity upon the mountains.

39 And it came to pass at the end of two months, that she returned unto her father, who did with her *according* to his vow which he had vowed: and she knew no man. And it was a custom in Israel,

40 *That* the daughters of Israel went yearly to lament the daughter of Jephthah the Gileadite four days in a year.

CHAPTER 12

The Gileadites slay 42,000 Ephraimites—Jephthah, Ibzan, Elon, and Abdon each in turn judge Israel.

AND the men of Ephraim gathered themselves together, and went northward, and said unto Jephthah, Wherefore passedst thou over to fight against the children of Ammon, and didst not call us to go with thee? we will burn thine house upon thee with fire.

2 And Jephthah said unto them, I and my people were at great ᵃstrife with the children of Ammon; and when I called you, ye delivered me not out of their hands.

3 And when I saw that ye delivered *me* not, I put my ᵃlife in my hands,

---

27a TG Jesus Christ, Judge.
30a 1 Sam. 1:11 (10–12).
33a Ezek. 27:17.
34a 1 Sam. 18:6.

b IE small hand drums.
35a HEB thou hast indeed
  brought me to my
  knees, and thou art one

bringing trouble to me.
  b IE made a promise.
12 2a TG Strife.
  3a Ps. 119:109.

and passed over against the children of Ammon, and the LORD delivered them into my hand: wherefore then are ye come up unto me this day, to fight against me?

4 Then Jephthah gathered together all the men of Gilead, and fought with Ephraim: and the men of Gilead smote Ephraim, because they said, Ye Gileadites *are* fugitives of Ephraim among the Ephraimites, *and* among the Manassites.

5 And the Gileadites took the passages of Jordan before the Ephraimites: and it was *so*, that when those Ephraimites which were escaped said, Let me go over; that the men of Gilead said unto him, *Art* thou an Ephraimite? If he said, Nay;

6 Then said they unto him, Say now *a*Shibboleth: and he said Sibboleth: for he could not frame to pronounce *it* right. Then they took him, and slew him at the passages of Jordan: and there fell at that time of the Ephraimites forty and two thousand.

7 And Jephthah judged Israel six years. Then died Jephthah the Gileadite, and was buried in *one of* the cities of Gilead.

8 ¶ And after him Ibzan of Bethlehem judged Israel.

9 And he had thirty sons, and thirty daughters, *whom* he sent *a*abroad, and took in thirty daughters from abroad for his sons. And he judged Israel seven years.

10 Then died Ibzan, and was buried at Beth-lehem.

11 ¶ And after him Elon, a Zebulonite, judged Israel; and he judged Israel ten years.

12 And Elon the Zebulonite died, and was buried in Aijalon in the country of Zebulun.

13 ¶ And after him Abdon the son of Hillel, a Pirathonite, judged Israel.

14 And he had forty sons and thirty *a*nephews, that rode on threescore and ten ass colts: and he judged Israel eight years.

15 And Abdon the son of Hillel the Pirathonite died, and was buried in Pirathon in the land of Ephraim, in the mount of the Amalekites.

CHAPTER 13

Israel is in Philistine bondage for forty years—An angel comes to Manoah's wife and promises a son who will begin to deliver Israel—The angel comes again; he ascends in a flame from the altar—Samson is born, and the Spirit of the Lord moves upon him.

AND the children of Israel did *a*evil again in the sight of the LORD; and the LORD delivered them into the *b*hand of the Philistines forty years.

2 ¶ And there was a certain man of Zorah, of the family of the Danites, whose name *was* Manoah; and his wife *was* barren, and bare not.

3 And the *a*angel of the LORD appeared unto the woman, and said unto her, Behold now, thou *art* *b*barren, and bearest not: but thou shalt conceive, and bear a son.

4 Now therefore beware, I pray thee, and *a*drink not wine nor strong drink, and eat not any *b*unclean *thing*:

5 For, lo, thou shalt conceive, and bear a son; and no *a*razor shall come on his head: for the child shall be a Nazarite unto God from the womb: and he shall begin to *b*deliver Israel out of the hand of the Philistines.

6 ¶ Then the woman came and told her husband, saying, A man of God came unto me, and his countenance *was* like the countenance of an *a*angel of God, very terrible: but I asked him not whence he *was*, neither told he me his name:

7 But he said unto me, Behold,

6*a* TG Language.
9*a* OR outside the family (as in marriage).
14*a* HEB grandsons.
13 1*a* Mosiah 1:17; Hel. 12:3 (2–3).

b 1 Sam. 4:9.
3*a* Moro. 7:29 (29–32).
  b TG Barren.
4*a* TG Word of Wisdom.
  b TG Uncleanness.
5*a* Num. 6:5 (1–8);

Judg. 16:17; 1 Sam. 1:11.
  b TG Deliver.
6*a* TG Angels.

thou shalt conceive, and bear a son; and now drink no wine nor strong drink, neither eat any unclean *thing:* for the child shall be a Nazarite to God from the womb to the day of his death.

8 ¶ Then Manoah entreated the LORD, and said, O my Lord, let the man of God which thou didst send come again unto us, and teach us what we shall do unto the child that shall be born.

9 And God hearkened to the voice of Manoah; and the angel of God came again unto the woman as she sat in the field: but Manoah her husband *was* not with her.

10 And the woman made haste, and ran, and shewed her husband, and said unto him, Behold, the man hath appeared unto me, that came unto me the *other* day.

11 And Manoah arose, and went after his wife, and came to the man, and said unto him, *Art* thou the man that spakest unto the woman? And he said, I *am.*

12 And Manoah said, Now let thy words come to pass. How shall we order the child, and *how* shall we do unto him?

13 And the angel of the LORD said unto Manoah, Of all that I said unto the woman let her beware.

14 She may not eat of any *thing* that cometh of the vine, neither let her drink wine or strong drink, nor eat any unclean *thing:* all that I commanded her let her observe.

15 ¶ And Manoah said unto the angel of the LORD, I pray thee, let us detain thee, until we shall have made ready a kid for thee.

16 And the angel of the LORD said unto Manoah, Though thou detain me, I will not eat of thy bread: and if thou wilt offer a burnt offering, thou must offer it unto the LORD. For Manoah knew not that he *was* an angel of the LORD.

17 And Manoah said unto the angel of the LORD, What *is* thy name, that when thy sayings come to pass we may do thee honour?

18 And the angel of the LORD said unto him, Why askest thou thus after my name, seeing it *is* ᵃsecret?

19 So Manoah took a kid with a ᵃmeat ᵇoffering, and offered *it* upon a rock unto the LORD: and *the angel* did wondrously; and Manoah and his wife looked on.

20 For it came to pass, when the flame went up toward heaven from off the altar, that the angel of the LORD ascended in the flame of the altar. And Manoah and his wife looked on *it,* and fell on their faces to the ground.

21 But the angel of the LORD did no more appear to Manoah and to his wife. Then Manoah knew that he *was* an angel of the LORD.

22 And Manoah said unto his wife, We shall surely die, because we have ᵃseen God.

23 But his wife said unto him, If the LORD were pleased to kill us, he would not have received a burnt offering and a meat offering at our hands, neither would he have shewed us all these *things,* nor would as at this time have told us *such things* as these.

24 ¶ And the woman bare a son, and called his name Samson: and the child grew, and the LORD blessed him.

25 And the Spirit of the LORD began to move him at times in the camp of Dan between Zorah and Eshtaol.

CHAPTER 14

Samson slays a young lion with his bare hands—He marries a Philistine wife, propounds a riddle, is deceived by his wife, and slays thirty Philistines.

AND Samson went down to Timnath, and saw a woman in Timnath of the daughters of the Philistines.

2 And he came up, and told his father and his mother, and said, I

18*a* Gen. 32:29.
19*a* HEB gift, or offering; actually this part was

made of meal (also v. 23).
b Lev. 9:15 (7–24).

22*a* TG God, Privilege of Seeing.

have seen a woman in Timnath of the daughters of the Philistines: now therefore get her for me to wife.

3 Then his father and his mother said unto him, *Is there* never a woman among the daughters of thy brethren, or among all my people, that thou goest to take a *a*wife of the *b*uncircumcised Philistines? And Samson said unto his father, Get her for me; for she pleaseth me well.

4 But his father and his mother knew not that it *was* of the *a*LORD, that he sought an occasion against the Philistines: for at that time the Philistines had *b*dominion over Israel.

5 ¶ Then went Samson down, and his father and his mother, to Timnath, and came to the vineyards of Timnath: and, behold, a young lion roared against him.

6 And the *a*Spirit of the LORD came mightily upon him, and he rent him as he would have rent a kid, and *he had* nothing in his hand: but he told not his father or his mother what he had done.

7 And he went down, and talked with the woman; and she pleased Samson well.

8 ¶ And after a time he returned to take her, and he turned aside to see the carcase of the lion: and, behold, *there was* a swarm of bees and honey in the carcase of the lion.

9 And he took thereof in his hands, and went on eating, and came to his father and mother, and he gave them, and they did eat: but he told not them that he had taken the honey out of the carcase of the lion.

10 ¶ So his father went down unto the woman: and Samson made there a *a*feast; for so used the young men to do.

11 And it came to pass, when they saw him, that they brought thirty companions to be with him.

12 ¶ And Samson said unto them,

I will now put forth a riddle unto you: if ye can certainly declare it me within the seven days of the feast, and find *it* out, then I will give you thirty *a*sheets and thirty change of garments:

13 But if ye cannot declare *it* me, then shall ye give me thirty sheets and thirty change of garments. And they said unto him, Put forth thy riddle, that we may hear it.

14 And he said unto them, Out of the eater came forth meat, and out of the strong came forth sweetness. And they could not in three days expound the riddle.

15 And it came to pass on the seventh day, that they said unto Samson's wife, *a*Entice thy husband, that he may declare unto us the riddle, lest we *b*burn thee and thy father's house with fire: have ye called us to take that we have? is it not *so?*

16 And Samson's wife wept before him, and said, Thou dost but hate me, and lovest me not: thou hast put forth a *a*riddle unto the children of my people, and hast not told *it* me. And he said unto her, Behold, I have not told *it* my father nor my mother, and shall I tell *it* thee?

17 And she wept before him the seven days, while their feast lasted: and it came to pass on the seventh day, that he told her, because she *a*lay sore upon him: and she told the riddle to the children of her people.

18 And the men of the city said unto him on the seventh day before the sun went down, What *is* sweeter than honey? and what *is* stronger than a lion? And he said unto them, If ye had not plowed with my heifer, ye had not found out my riddle.

19 ¶ And the Spirit of the LORD came upon him, and he went down to Ashkelon, and slew thirty men of them, and took their spoil, and gave change of garments unto them which

---

14 3*a* TG Marriage,
     Interfaith.
   b Gen. 34:14.
4*a* Josh. 11:20.
   b Judg. 15:11.

6*a* 1 Ne. 7:17 (17–18).
10*a* Gen. 29:22.
12*a* HEB linen garments or
      tunics (also v. 13).
15*a* Judg. 16:5.

b Judg. 15:6.
16*a* Judg. 16:15.
17*a* IE pressed him hard.

expounded the riddle. And his anger was kindled, and he went up to his father's house.

20 But Samson's wife was *given* to his companion, whom he had used as his friend.

CHAPTER 15

Samson burns the grain of the Philistines—They burn his wife and father-in-law—Samson slays a thousand Philistines at Lehi with the jawbone of an ass.

BUT it came to pass within a while after, in the time of wheat harvest, that Samson visited his wife with a kid; and he said, I will go in to my wife into the chamber. But her father would not suffer him to go in.

2 And her father said, I verily thought that thou hadst utterly hated her; therefore I gave her to thy companion: *is* not her younger sister fairer than she? take her, I pray thee, instead of her.

3 ¶ And Samson said concerning them, Now shall I be more blameless than the Philistines, though I do them a displeasure.

4 And Samson went and caught three hundred foxes, and took firebrands, and turned tail to tail, and put a firebrand in the midst between two tails.

5 And when he had set the brands on fire, he let *them* go into the standing corn of the Philistines, and *a*burnt up both the shocks, and also the standing *b*corn, with the vineyards *and* *c*olives.

6 ¶ Then the Philistines said, Who hath done this? And they answered, Samson, the son in law of the Timnite, because he had taken his wife, and given her to his companion. And the Philistines came up, and *a*burnt her and *b*her father with fire.

7 ¶ And Samson said unto them, *a*Though ye have done this, yet will I be avenged of you, and after that I will cease.

8 And he smote them hip and thigh with a great slaughter: and he went down and dwelt in the top of the rock Etam.

9 ¶ Then the Philistines went up, and pitched in Judah, and spread themselves in Lehi.

10 And the men of Judah said, Why are ye come up against us? And they answered, To bind Samson are we come up, to do to him as he hath done to us.

11 Then three thousand men of Judah went to the top of the rock Etam, and said to Samson, Knowest thou not that the Philistines *are* *a*rulers over us? what *is* this *that* thou hast done unto us? And he said unto them, As they did unto me, so have I done unto them.

12 And they said unto him, We are come down to bind thee, that we may deliver thee into the hand of the Philistines. And Samson said unto them, Swear unto me, that ye will not fall upon me yourselves.

13 And they spake unto him, saying, No; but we will bind thee fast, and deliver thee into their hand: but surely we will not kill thee. And they bound him with two new cords, and brought him up from the rock.

14 ¶ *And* when he came unto Lehi, the Philistines shouted against him: and the Spirit of the LORD came mightily upon him, and the cords that *were* upon his arms became as flax that was burnt with fire, and his bands *a*loosed from off his hands.

15 And he found a new jawbone of an ass, and put forth his hand, and took it, and slew a thousand men therewith.

16 And Samson said, With the jawbone of an ass, heaps upon heaps, with the jaw of an ass have I slain a thousand men.

17 And it came to pass, when he had made an end of speaking, that he cast away the jawbone out of his hand, and called that place Ramath-lehi.

---

15 5a Ex. 22:6.
   b OR grain.
   c IE olive trees.
   6a Judg. 14:15.

   b Septuagint, Syriac, and many Hebrew texts: her father's house.
   7a OR If you act in this

way.
11a Judg. 14:4.
14a Alma 2:28 (26–36);
   14:26.

18 ¶ And he was [a]sore athirst, and called on the LORD, and said, Thou hast given this great deliverance into the hand of thy servant: and now shall I die for thirst, and fall into the hand of the uncircumcised?

19 [a]But God clave an hollow place that *was* in the jaw, and there came water thereout; and when he had drunk, his spirit came again, and he revived: wherefore he called the name thereof [b]En-hakkore, which *is* in Lehi unto this day.

20 And he judged Israel in the days of the Philistines twenty years.

CHAPTER 16

Samson carries away the doors of the gate of Gaza—He loves Delilah, who delivers him to the Philistines—He destroys a building, killing himself and 3,000 others.

THEN went Samson to Gaza, and saw there an harlot, and went in unto her.

2 *And it was told* the Gazites, saying, Samson is come hither. And they [a]compassed *him* in, and laid wait for him all night in the gate of the city, and were quiet all the night, saying, In the morning, when it is day, we shall kill him.

3 And Samson lay till midnight, and arose at midnight, and took the doors of the gate of the city, and the two posts, and went away with them, bar and all, and put *them* upon his shoulders, and carried them up to the top of an hill that *is* before Hebron.

4 ¶ And it came to pass afterward, that he loved a woman in the valley of Sorek, whose name *was* Delilah.

5 And the lords of the Philistines came up unto her, and said unto her, [a]Entice him, and see wherein his great strength *lieth,* and by what *means* we may prevail against him, that we may bind him to afflict him:

and we will give thee every one of us [b]eleven hundred *pieces* of silver.

6 ¶ And Delilah said to Samson, Tell me, I pray thee, wherein thy great strength *lieth,* and wherewith thou mightest be bound to afflict thee.

7 And Samson said unto her, If they bind me with seven [a]green withs that were never dried, then shall I be weak, and be as another man.

8 Then the lords of the Philistines brought up to her seven green withs which had not been dried, and she bound him with them.

9 Now *there were* men lying in wait, abiding with her in the chamber. And she said unto him, The Philistines *be* upon thee, Samson. And he brake the withs, as a thread of tow is broken when it toucheth the fire. So his strength was not known.

10 And Delilah said unto Samson, Behold, thou hast [a]mocked me, and told me lies: now tell me, I pray thee, wherewith thou mightest be bound.

11 And he said unto her, If they bind me fast with new ropes that never were occupied, then shall I be weak, and be as another man.

12 Delilah therefore took new ropes, and bound him therewith, and said unto him, The Philistines *be* upon thee, Samson. And *there were* [a]liers in wait abiding in the chamber. And he brake them from off his arms like a thread.

13 And Delilah said unto Samson, Hitherto thou hast mocked me, and told me lies: tell me wherewith thou mightest be bound. And he said unto her, If thou weavest the seven locks of my head with the [a]web.

14 And she fastened *it* with the pin, and said unto him, The Philistines *be* upon thee, Samson. And he awaked out of his sleep, and went away with the pin of the beam, and with the web.

18a OR very thirsty.
19a OR But God opened up the basin that was at Lehi.
 b IE The spring of him

who calls.
16 2a Josh. 6:3.
 5a Judg. 14:15.
 b Judg. 16:18.
 7a OR new cords; e.g.,

fresh or moist sinews from animals.
10a TG Mocking.
12a Josh. 8:13.
13a IE the web of the loom.

15 ¶ And she said unto him, How canst thou say, I love thee, when thine heart *is* not with me? thou hast *a*mocked me these three times, and hast not told me wherein thy great strength *lieth*.

16 And it came to pass, when she pressed him *a*daily with her words, and urged him, *so* that his soul was *b*vexed unto death;

17 That he told her all his heart, and said unto her, There hath not come a *a*razor upon mine head; for I *have been* a Nazarite unto God from my mother's womb: if I be shaven, then my strength will go from me, and I shall become weak, and be like any *other* man.

18 And when Delilah saw that he had told her all his heart, she sent and called for the lords of the Philistines, saying, Come up this once, for he hath shewed me all his heart. Then the lords of the Philistines came up unto her, and brought *a*money in their hand.

19 And she made him sleep upon her knees; and she called for a man, and she caused him to shave off the seven locks of his head; and she began to afflict him, and his strength went from him.

20 And she said, The Philistines *be* upon thee, Samson. And he awoke out of his sleep, and said, I will go out as at other times before, and shake myself. And he *a*wist not that the LORD was departed from him.

21 ¶ But the Philistines took him, and put out his eyes, and brought him down to Gaza, and bound him with fetters of brass; and he did grind in the prison house.

22 Howbeit the hair of his head began to grow again after he was shaven.

23 Then the lords of the Philistines gathered them together for to offer a great sacrifice unto *a*Dagon their god, and to rejoice: for they said, Our god hath delivered Samson our enemy into our hand.

24 And when the people saw him, they praised their god: for they said, Our god hath delivered into our hands our enemy, and the destroyer of our country, which slew many of us.

25 And it came to pass, when their hearts were merry, that they said, Call for Samson, that he may make us sport. And they called for Samson out of the prison house; and he made them sport: and they set him between the pillars.

26 And Samson said unto the lad that held him by the hand, Suffer me that I may feel the pillars whereupon the house standeth, that I may lean upon them.

27 Now the house was full of men and women; and all the lords of the Philistines *were* there; and *there were* upon the roof about three thousand men and women, that beheld while Samson made sport.

28 And Samson called unto the LORD, and said, O Lord GOD, remember me, I pray thee, and strengthen me, I pray thee, only this once, O God, that I may be at once avenged of the Philistines for my two eyes.

29 And Samson took hold of the two middle pillars upon which the house stood, and on which it was borne up, of the one with his right hand, and of the other with his left.

30 And Samson said, Let me die with the Philistines. And he bowed himself with *all his* might; and the house fell upon the lords, and upon all the people that *were* therein. So the dead which he slew at his death were more than *they* which he slew in his life.

31 Then his brethren and all the house of his father came down, and took him, and brought *him* up, and buried him between Zorah and Eshtaol in the buryingplace of Manoah his father. And he judged Israel twenty years.

15*a* Judg. 14:16.
16*a* Gen. 39:10 (7–10).
  b Judg. 2:18.

17*a* Judg. 13:5.
18*a* Judg. 16:5.
20*a* OR knew.

23*a* 1 Sam. 5:2.

CHAPTER 17

Micah has a house of gods (images) and consecrates his own priests.

AND there was a man of [a]mount Ephraim, whose name *was* Micah.

2 And he said unto his mother, The eleven hundred *shekels* of silver that were taken from thee, about which thou cursedst, and spakest of also in mine ears, behold, the silver *is* with me; I took it. And his mother said, [a]Blessed *be thou* of the LORD, my son.

3 And when he had restored the eleven hundred *shekels* of silver to his mother, his mother said, I had wholly dedicated the silver unto the LORD from my hand for my son, to make a [a]graven image and a molten image: now therefore I will restore it unto thee.

4 Yet he restored the money unto his mother; and his mother took two hundred *shekels* of silver, and gave them to the founder, who made thereof a graven image and a molten image: and they were in the house of Micah.

5 And the man Micah had an house of gods, and made an [a]ephod, and [b]teraphim, and consecrated one of his sons, who became his [c]priest.

6 In those days *there was* no [a]king in Israel, *but* every man did *that which was* [b]right in his [c]own eyes.

7 ¶ And there was a young man out of Beth-lehem-judah of the family of Judah, who *was* a Levite, and he sojourned there.

8 And the man departed out of the city from Beth-lehem-judah to [a]sojourn where he could find *a place:* and he came to mount Ephraim to the house of Micah, as he journeyed.

9 And Micah said unto him, Whence comest thou? And he said unto him, I *am* a [a]Levite of Beth-lehem-judah, and I go to sojourn where I may find *a place.*

10 And Micah said unto him, Dwell with me, and be unto me a father and a priest, and I will give thee ten *shekels* of silver by the year, and a suit of [a]apparel, and thy victuals. So the Levite went in.

11 And the Levite was content to dwell with the man; and the young man was unto him as one of his sons.

12 And Micah consecrated the Levite; and the young man became his priest, and was in the house of Micah.

13 Then said Micah, Now know I that the LORD will do me good, seeing I have a Levite to *my* priest.

CHAPTER 18

The Danites send men to seek an inheritance—They take Micah's images and priest, burn the city of Laish, and set up idolatry.

IN those days *there was* no [a]king in Israel: and in those days the tribe of the Danites sought them an inheritance to dwell in; for unto that day *all their* inheritance had not fallen unto them among the tribes of Israel.

2 And the children of Dan sent of their family five men from their coasts, men of valour, from Zorah, and from Eshtaol, to spy out the land, and to search it; and they said unto them, Go, search the land: who when they came to mount Ephraim, to the house of Micah, they lodged there.

3 When they *were* by the house of Micah, they knew the voice of the young man the Levite: and they turned in thither, and said unto him, Who brought thee hither? and what makest thou in this *place?* and what hast thou here?

4 And he said unto them, Thus and thus dealeth Micah with me, and hath hired me, and I am his priest.

5 And they said unto him, Ask

---

17 1a Josh. 24:33.
  2a Gen. 24:31.
  3a Ex. 20:4 (4, 23);
    Lev. 19:4; Mosiah 12:36.
  5a Judg. 8:27.
    b IE domestic idols,

perhaps in size and shape of a man.
    Judg. 18:18 (18, 20);
    1 Sam. 19:13 (13, 16).
  c Judg. 18:19 (1, 19–20).
  6a Judg. 18:1; 21:25.

    b Deut. 12:8.
    c Prov. 16:2.
  8a Josh. 20:9.
  9a Judg. 19:1 (1, 18).
  10a TG Apparel.
18 1a Judg. 17:6; 21:25.

counsel, we pray thee, of God, that we may know whether our way which we go shall be prosperous.

6 And the priest said unto them, Go in peace: before the LORD *is* your way wherein ye go.

7 ¶ Then the five men departed, and came to Laish, and saw the people that *were* therein, how they dwelt ªcareless, after the manner of the Zidonians, ᵇquiet and secure; and *there was* no magistrate in the land, that might put *them* to shame in *any* thing; and they *were* far from the Zidonians, and had no business with *any* man.

8 And they came unto their brethren to Zorah and Eshtaol: and their brethren said unto them, What *say* ye?

9 And they said, Arise, that we may go up against them: for we have seen the land, and, behold, it *is* very good: and *are* ye ªstill? be not ᵇslothful to go, *and* to enter to possess the land.

10 When ye go, ye shall come unto a people ªsecure, and to a large land: for God hath given it into your hands; a place where *there is* no want of any thing that *is* in the earth.

11 ¶ And there went from thence of the family of the Danites, out of Zorah and out of Eshtaol, six hundred men ªappointed with weapons of war.

12 And they went up, and pitched in ªKirjath-jearim, in Judah: wherefore they called that place ᵇMahaneh-dan unto this day: behold, *it is* behind Kirjath-jearim.

13 And they passed thence unto mount Ephraim, and came unto the house of Micah.

14 ¶ Then answered the five men that went to spy out the country of Laish, and said unto their brethren, Do ye know that there is in these houses an ephod, and teraphim, and a graven image, and a molten image? now therefore consider what ye have to do.

15 And they turned thitherward, and came to the house of the young man the Levite, *even* unto the house of Micah, and ªsaluted him.

16 And the six hundred men appointed with their weapons of war, which *were* of the children of Dan, stood by the entering of the gate.

17 And the five men that went to spy out the land went up, *and* came in thither, *and* took the graven image, and the ephod, and the teraphim, and the molten image: and the priest stood in the entering of the gate with the six hundred men *that were* appointed with weapons of war.

18 And these went into Micah's house, and fetched the carved image, the ephod, and the ªteraphim, and the molten image. Then said the priest unto them, What do ye?

19 And they said unto him, Hold thy peace, lay thine ªhand upon thy mouth, and go with us, and be to us a father and a ᵇpriest: *is it* better for thee to be a priest unto the house of one man, or that thou be a priest unto a tribe and a family in Israel?

20 And the priest's heart was glad, and he took the ephod, and the teraphim, and the graven image, and went in the midst of the people.

21 So they turned and departed, and put the little ones and the cattle and the carriage before them.

22 ¶ *And* when they were a good way from the house of Micah, the men that *were* in the houses near to Micah's house were gathered together, and overtook the children of Dan.

23 And they cried unto the children of Dan. And they turned their faces, and said unto Micah, What aileth thee, that thou comest with such a company?

24 And he said, Ye have taken away my gods which I made, and

7a HEB securely.
  b Judg. 18:27 (27–28).
9a HEB inactive, quiet.
  b TG Laziness.
10a Judg. 8:11.

11a HEB girded.
12a Josh. 15:60.
  b IE Camp of Dan.
15a HEB asked him
    concerning his welfare.

1 Sam. 10:4; 13:10.
18a Judg. 17:5.
19a Job 21:5.
  b Judg. 17:5.

the priest, and ye are gone away: and what have I more? and what *is* this *that* ye say unto me, What aileth thee?

25 And the children of Dan said unto him, Let not thy voice be heard among us, lest angry fellows run upon thee, and thou lose thy life, with the lives of thy household.

26 And the children of Dan went their way: and when Micah saw that they *were* too strong for him, he turned and went back unto his house.

27 And they took *the things* which Micah had made, and the priest which he had, and came unto Laish, unto a people *that were* at ªquiet and secure: and they smote them with the edge of the sword, and burnt the city with fire.

28 And *there was* no deliverer, because it *was* far from Zidon, and they had no business with *any* man; and it was in the valley that *lieth* by Beth-rehob. And they built a city, and dwelt therein.

29 And they called the name of the city Dan, after the name of Dan their father, who was born unto Israel: howbeit the name of the city *was* Laish at the first.

30 ¶ And the children of Dan set up the graven image: and Jonathan, the son of Gershom, the son of ªManasseh, he and his sons were priests to the tribe of Dan until the day of the captivity of the land.

31 And they set them up Micah's graven image, which he made, all the time that the ªhouse of God was in ᵇShiloh.

CHAPTER 19

A Levite's concubine returns to her father—Her husband takes her back, and they lodge overnight in Gibeah— The men of Gibeah abuse the concubine and she dies—The Levite husband cuts her into twelve pieces and sends them to the tribes of Israel.

AND it came to pass in those days, when *there was* no king in Israel, that there was a certain ªLevite sojourning on the side of mount Ephraim, who took to him a concubine out of Beth-lehem-judah.

2 And his concubine played the whore against him, and went away from him unto her father's house to Beth-lehem-judah, and was there four whole months.

3 And her husband arose, and went after her, to speak friendly unto her, *and* to bring her again, having his servant with him, and a couple of asses: and she brought him into her father's house: and when the father of the damsel saw him, he rejoiced to meet him.

4 And his father in law, the damsel's father, retained him; and he abode with him three days: so they did eat and drink, and lodged there.

5 ¶ And it came to pass on the fourth day, when they arose early in the morning, that he rose up to depart: and the damsel's father said unto his son in law, ªComfort thine heart with a morsel of bread, and afterward go your way.

6 And they sat down, and did eat and drink both of them together: for the damsel's father had said unto the man, Be content, I pray thee, and tarry all night, and let thine heart be merry.

7 And when the man rose up to depart, his father in law urged him: therefore he lodged there again.

8 And he arose early in the morning on the fifth day to depart: and the damsel's father said, Comfort thine heart, I pray thee. And they tarried until afternoon, and they did eat both of them.

9 And when the man rose up to depart, he, and his concubine, and his servant, his father in law, the damsel's father, said unto him, Behold, now the day draweth toward evening, I pray you tarry all night: behold, the day groweth to an end,

---

27ª Judg. 18:7.
30ª HEB Moses, altered
　　to Manasseh. See

Ex. 2:22; 18:3.
31ª TG Temple.
　ᵇ Ps. 78:60.

19 1ª Judg. 17:9.
5ª OR Sustain (also v. 8).

lodge here, that thine heart may be merry; and to morrow get you early on your way, that thou mayest go home.

10 But the man would not tarry that night, but he rose up and departed, and came over against Jebus, which *is* Jerusalem; and *there were* with him two asses saddled, his concubine also *was* with him.

11 *And* when they *were* by Jebus, the day was far spent; and the servant said unto his master, Come, I pray thee, and let us turn in into this city of the Jebusites, and lodge in it.

12 And his master said unto him, We will not turn aside hither into the city of a stranger, that *is* not of the children of Israel; we will pass over to Gibeah.

13 And he said unto his servant, Come, and let us draw near to one of these places to lodge all night, in Gibeah, or in Ramah.

14 And they passed on and went their way; and the sun went down upon them *when they were* by ᵃGibeah, which *belongeth* to ᵇBenjamin.

15 And they turned aside thither, to go in *and* to lodge in Gibeah: and when he went in, he sat him down in a street of the city: for *there was* no man that took them into his house to lodging.

16 ¶ And, behold, there came an old man from his work out of the field at even, which *was* also of mount Ephraim; and he ᵃsojourned in Gibeah: but the men of the place *were* Benjamites.

17 And when he had lifted up his eyes, he saw a wayfaring man in the street of the city: and the old man said, Whither goest thou? and whence comest thou?

18 And he said unto him, We *are* passing from Beth-lehem-judah toward the side of mount Ephraim; from thence *am* I: and I went to Beth-lehem-judah, but I *am now* going to the house of the LORD; and there *is* no man that receiveth me to house.

19 Yet there is both straw and ᵃprovender for our asses; and there is bread and wine also for me, and for thy handmaid, and for the young man *which is* with thy servants: *there is* no want of any thing.

20 And the old man said, Peace *be* with thee; howsoever *let* all thy wants *lie* upon me; only lodge not in the street.

21 So he brought him into his house, and gave ᵃprovender unto the asses: and they washed their feet, and did eat and drink.

22 ¶ *Now* as they were making their hearts merry, behold, the men of the city, certain sons of Belial, beset the house round about, *and* beat at the door, and spake to the master of the house, the old man, saying, Bring forth the man that came into thine house, that we may ᵃknow him.

23 And the man, the master of the house, went out unto them, and said unto them, Nay, my brethren, *nay,* I pray you, do not *so* wickedly; seeing that this man is come into mine house, do not this folly.

24 Behold, *here is* my ᵃdaughter a maiden, and his concubine; them I will bring out now, and humble ye them, and do with them what seemeth good unto you: but unto this man do not so vile a thing.

25 But the men would not hearken to him: so the man took his concubine, and brought her forth unto them; and they knew her, and abused her all the night until the morning: and when the day began to spring, they let her go.

26 Then came the woman in the dawning of the day, and fell down at the door of the man's house where her lord *was,* till it was light.

27 And her lord rose up in the morning, and opened the doors of the house, and went out to go his way: and, behold, the woman his

14*a* Hosea 9:9.
  b Josh. 18:28;
    Judg. 1:21.
16*a* Josh. 20:9.

19*a* OR food, fodder (also
    v. 21).
21*a* Gen. 24:32.
22*a* Gen. 19:5;

Rom. 1:26 (26–27).
24*a* Gen. 19:8.

concubine was fallen down *at* the door of the house, and her hands *were* upon the threshold.

28 And he said unto her, Up, and let us be going. But none answered. Then the man took her *up* upon an ass, and the man rose up, and gat him unto his place.

29 ¶ And when he was come into his house, he took a knife, and laid hold on his concubine, and divided her, *together* with her bones, into twelve pieces, and *ª*sent her into all the coasts of Israel.

30 And it was so, that all that saw it said, There was no such deed done nor seen from the day that the children of Israel came up out of the land of Egypt unto this day: consider of it, take advice, and speak *your minds.*

CHAPTER 20

All Israel arises against the Benjamites, who refuse to deliver up the men of Gibeah—The Benjamites are smitten and destroyed.

THEN all the children of Israel went out, and the congregation was gathered together as one man, from Dan even to Beer-sheba, with the land of Gilead, unto the LORD in *ª*Mizpeh.

2 And the chief of all the people, *even* of all the tribes of Israel, presented themselves in the assembly of the people of God, four hundred thousand footmen that drew sword.

3 (Now the children of Benjamin heard that the children of Israel were gone up to Mizpeh.) Then said the children of Israel, Tell *us,* how was this wickedness?

4 And the Levite, the husband of the woman that was slain, answered and said, I came into *ª*Gibeah that *belongeth* to Benjamin, I and my concubine, to lodge.

5 And the men of Gibeah rose against me, and beset the house

round about upon me by night, *and* thought to have slain me: and my concubine have they *ª*forced, that she is dead.

6 And I took my concubine, and cut her in pieces, and sent her throughout all the country of the inheritance of Israel: for they have committed lewdness and *ª*folly in Israel.

7 Behold, ye *are* all children of Israel; give here your advice and counsel.

8 ¶ And all the people arose as one man, saying, We will not any *of us* go to his tent, neither will we any *of us* turn into his house.

9 But now this *shall be* the thing which we will do to Gibeah; *we will go up* by lot against it;

10 And we will take ten men of an hundred throughout all the tribes of Israel, and an hundred of a thousand, and a thousand out of ten thousand, to fetch *ª*victual for the people, that they may do, when they come to Gibeah of Benjamin, according to all the folly that they have wrought in Israel.

11 So all the men of Israel were gathered against the city, *ª*knit together as one man.

12 ¶ And the tribes of Israel sent men through all the tribe of Benjamin, saying, What wickedness *is* this that is done among you?

13 Now therefore deliver *us* the men, the children of *ª*Belial, which *are* in Gibeah, that we may put them to death, and put away evil from Israel. But the children of Benjamin would not hearken to the voice of their brethren the children of Israel:

14 But the children of Benjamin gathered themselves together out of the cities unto Gibeah, to go out to battle against the children of Israel.

15 And the children of Benjamin were *ª*numbered at that time out of the cities twenty and six thousand men that drew sword, beside the

---

29*a* 1 Sam. 11:7.
20 1*a* 1 Sam. 7:5.
  4*a* Hosea 10:9.
  5*a* IE assaulted.

6*a* OR disgrace,
    wantonness.
10*a* Josh. 1:11.
11*a* OR united.

13*a* Deut. 13:13;
    Jude 1:19.
15*a* HEB mustered.

inhabitants of Gibeah, which were numbered seven hundred chosen men.

16 Among all this people *there were* seven hundred chosen men *a*left-handed; every one could sling stones at an hair *breadth*, and not miss.

17 And the men of Israel, beside Benjamin, were numbered four hundred thousand men that drew sword: all these *were* men of war.

18 ¶ And the children of Israel arose, and went up to *a*the house of God, and asked counsel of God, and said, Which of us shall go up first to the battle against the children of Benjamin? And the LORD said, Judah *shall go up* first.

19 And the children of Israel rose up in the morning, and *a*encamped against Gibeah.

20 And the men of Israel went out to battle against Benjamin; and the men of Israel put themselves in array to fight against them at Gibeah.

21 And the children of Benjamin came forth out of Gibeah, and destroyed down to the ground of the Israelites that day twenty and two thousand men.

22 And the people the men of Israel encouraged themselves, and set their battle again in array in the place where they put themselves in array the first day.

23 (And the children of Israel went up and wept before the LORD until even, and asked counsel of the LORD, saying, Shall I go up again to battle against the children of Benjamin my brother? And the LORD said, Go up against him.)

24 And the children of Israel came near against the children of Benjamin the second day.

25 And Benjamin went forth against them out of Gibeah the second day, and destroyed down to the ground of the children of Israel again eighteen thousand men; all these drew the sword.

26 ¶ Then all the children of Israel,

and all the people, went up, and came unto the *a*house of God, and wept, and sat there before the LORD, and fasted that day until even, and offered burnt offerings and peace offerings before the LORD.

27 And the children of Israel inquired of the LORD, (for the ark of the covenant of God *was* there in those days,

28 And Phinehas, the son of Eleazar, the son of Aaron, stood before it in those days,) saying, Shall I yet again go out to battle against the children of Benjamin my brother, or shall I cease? And the LORD said, Go up; for to morrow I will deliver them into thine hand.

29 And Israel set *a*liers in wait round about Gibeah.

30 And the children of Israel went up against the children of Benjamin on the third day, and put themselves in array against Gibeah, as at other times.

31 And the children of Benjamin went out against the people, *and* were drawn away from the city; and they began to smite of the people, *and* kill, as at other times, in the highways, of which one goeth up to the house of God, and the other to Gibeah in the field, about thirty men of Israel.

32 And the children of Benjamin said, They *are* smitten down before us, as at the first. But the children of Israel said, Let us flee, and draw them from the city unto the highways.

33 And all the men of Israel rose up out of their place, and put themselves in array at Baal-tamar: and the liers in wait of Israel came forth out of their places, *even* out of the meadows of Gibeah.

34 And there came against Gibeah ten thousand chosen men out of all Israel, and the battle was *a*sore: but they knew not that evil *was* near them.

35 And the LORD smote Benjamin

16*a* 1 Chr. 12:2.
18*a* OR Bethel (also Judg. 21:2).

19*a* Hosea 10:9.
26*a* Josh. 18:1.
29*a* Josh. 8:13.

34*a* OR heavy, hard.

before Israel: and the children of Israel destroyed of the Benjamites that day twenty and five thousand and an hundred men: all these drew the sword.

36 So the children of Benjamin saw that they were smitten: for the men of Israel gave place to the Benjamites, because they trusted unto the liers in wait which they had set beside Gibeah.

37 And the liers in wait hasted, and rushed upon Gibeah; and the liers in wait drew *themselves* along, and smote all the city with the edge of the sword.

38 Now there was an appointed sign between the men of Israel and the liers in wait, that they should make a great flame with smoke rise up out of the city.

39 And when the men of Israel retired in the battle, Benjamin began to smite *and* kill of the men of Israel about thirty persons: for they said, Surely they are smitten down before us, as *in* the first battle.

40 But when the flame began to arise up out of the city with a pillar of smoke, the Benjamites looked behind them, and, behold, the flame of the city ascended up to heaven.

41 And when the men of Israel turned again, the men of Benjamin were amazed: for they saw that evil was come upon them.

42 Therefore they turned *their backs* before the men of Israel unto the way of the wilderness; but the battle overtook them; and them which *came* out of the cities they destroyed in the midst of them.

43 *Thus* they inclosed the Benjamites round about, *and* chased them, *and* ᵃtrode them down with ease over against Gibeah toward ᵇthe sunrising.

44 And there fell of Benjamin eighteen thousand men; all these *were* men of valour.

45 And they turned and fled toward the wilderness unto the rock of Rimmon: and they ᵃgleaned of

them in the highways five thousand men; and pursued hard after them unto Gidom, and slew two thousand men of them.

46 So that all which fell that day of Benjamin were twenty and five thousand men that drew the sword; all these *were* men of valour.

47 But six hundred men turned and fled to the wilderness unto the rock Rimmon, and abode in the rock Rimmon four months.

48 And the men of Israel turned again upon the children of Benjamin, and smote them with the edge of the sword, as well the men of *every* city, as the beast, and all that came to hand: also they set on fire all the cities that they came to.

CHAPTER 21

The people lament the desolation of Benjamin—The inhabitants of Jabesh-gilead are destroyed for not engaging in the war with Benjamin—Wives are provided for the remnant of Benjamin.

Now the men of Israel had sworn in Mizpeh, saying, There shall not any of us give his daughter unto Benjamin to wife.

2 And the people came to the house of God, and abode there till even before God, and lifted up their voices, and wept sore;

3 And said, O LORD God of Israel, why is this come to pass in Israel, that there should be to day one tribe lacking in Israel?

4 And it came to pass on the morrow, that the people rose early, and built there an altar, and offered burnt offerings and peace offerings.

5 And the children of Israel said, Who *is there* among all the tribes of Israel that ᵃcame not up with the ᵇcongregation unto the LORD? For they had made a great oath concerning him that came not up to the LORD to Mizpeh, saying, He shall surely be put to death.

6 And the children of Israel repented them for Benjamin their brother,

---

43*a* HEB overtook.   45*a* IE killed the fugitives.   *b* TG Church.
b IE the east.   **21** 5*a* Judg. 5:23.

and said, There is one tribe cut off from Israel this day.

7 How shall we do for wives for them that remain, seeing we have sworn by the LORD that we will not give them of our daughters to wives?

8 ¶ And they said, What one *is there* of the tribes of Israel that came not up to Mizpeh to the LORD? And, behold, there came none to the camp from Jabesh-gilead to the assembly.

9 For the people were numbered, and, behold, *there were* none of the inhabitants of Jabesh-gilead there.

10 And the congregation sent thither twelve thousand men of the valiantest, and commanded them, saying, Go and smite the inhabitants of Jabesh-gilead with the edge of the sword, with the women and the children.

11 And this *is* the thing that ye shall do, Ye shall utterly destroy every male, and every woman that hath lain by man.

12 And they found among the inhabitants of Jabesh-gilead four hundred young virgins, that had known no man by lying with any male: and they brought them unto the camp to Shiloh, which *is* in the land of Canaan.

13 And the whole congregation sent *some* to speak to the children of Benjamin that *were* in the rock Rimmon, and to call peaceably unto them.

14 And Benjamin came again at that time; and they gave them wives which they had saved alive of the women of Jabesh-gilead: and yet so they sufficed them not.

15 And the people repented them for Benjamin, because that the LORD had made a breach in the tribes of Israel.

16 ¶ Then the elders of the congregation said, How shall we do for wives for them that remain, seeing the women are destroyed out of Benjamin?

17 And they said, *There must be* an inheritance for them that be escaped of Benjamin, that a tribe be not destroyed out of Israel.

18 Howbeit we may not give them wives of our daughters: for the children of Israel have sworn, saying, Cursed *be* he that giveth a wife to Benjamin.

19 Then they said, Behold, *there is* a feast of the LORD in Shiloh yearly *in a place* which *is* on the north side of Beth-el, on the east side of the highway that goeth up from Beth-el to Shechem, and on the south of Lebonah.

20 Therefore they commanded the children of Benjamin, saying, Go and ᵃlie in wait in the vineyards;

21 And see, and, behold, if the daughters of Shiloh come out to ᵃdance in dances, then come ye out of the vineyards, and catch you every man his wife of the daughters of Shiloh, and go to the land of Benjamin.

22 And it shall be, when their fathers or their brethren come unto us to complain, that we will say unto them, Be favourable unto them for our sakes: because we reserved not to each man his wife in the war: for ye did not give unto them at this time, *that* ye should be ᵃguilty.

23 And the children of Benjamin did so, and took *them* wives, according to their number, of them that danced, whom they caught: and they went and returned unto their inheritance, and repaired the cities, and dwelt in them.

24 And the children of Israel departed thence at that time, every man to his tribe and to his family, and they went out from thence every man to his inheritance.

25 In those days *there was* no ᵃking in Israel: every man did *that which was* ᵇright in his own eyes.

20*a* Josh. 8:13.
21*a* Mosiah 20:1 (1–5).

22*a* TG Guilt.
25*a* Judg. 17:6; 18:1.

b Deut. 12:8;
Judg. 17:6.

THE BOOK OF

RUTH

CHAPTER 1

Elimelech and his family go to Moab because of famine—His sons marry—The father and sons die—Ruth, the Moabitess, her husband having died, remains constant to Naomi—They come to Bethlehem.

NOW it came to pass in the days when the ªjudges ruled, that there was a famine in the land. And a certain man of Beth-lehem-judah went to sojourn in the country of Moab, he, and his wife, and his two sons.

2 And the name of the man *was* ªElimelech, and the name of his wife Naomi, and the name of his two sons Mahlon and Chilion, ᵇEphrath-ites of Beth-lehem-judah. And they came into the country of Moab, and continued there.

3 And Elimelech Naomi's husband died; and she was left, and her two sons.

4 And they took them wives of the women of Moab; the name of the one *was* Orpah, and the name of the other Ruth: and they dwelled there about ten years.

5 And Mahlon and Chilion died also both of them; and the woman was left of her two sons and her husband.

6 ¶ Then she arose with her daughters in law, that she might return from the country of Moab: for she had heard in the country of Moab how that the LORD had visited his people in giving them bread.

7 Wherefore she went forth out of the place where she was, and her two daughters in law with her; and they went on the way to return unto the land of Judah.

8 And Naomi said unto her two daughters in law, Go, return each to her mother's house: the LORD deal kindly with you, as ye have dealt with the dead, and with me.

9 The LORD grant you that ye may find rest, each *of you* in the house of her husband. Then she kissed them; and they lifted up their voice, and wept.

10 And they said unto her, Surely we will return with thee unto thy people.

11 And Naomi said, Turn again, my daughters: why will ye go with me? *are* there yet *any more* ªsons in my womb, that they may be your husbands?

12 Turn again, my daughters, go *your way*; for I am too old to have an husband. If I should say, I have hope, *if* I should have an husband also to night, and should also bear sons;

13 Would ye tarry for them till they were grown? would ye stay for them from having husbands? nay, my daughters; for it grieveth me much for your sakes that the hand of the LORD is gone out against me.

14 And they lifted up their voice, and wept again: and Orpah kissed her mother in law; but Ruth ªclave unto her.

15 And she said, Behold, thy sister in law is gone back unto her people, and unto her gods: return thou after thy sister in law.

16 And Ruth said, Entreat me not to leave thee, *or* to return from ªfollowing after thee: for whither thou goest, I will ᵇgo; and where thou

---

1 1*a* Judg. 2:16;
　　Mosiah 29:44 (11–44).
　2*a* HEB My God is king.

b Gen. 35:19.
11*a* Deut. 25:5.
14*a* IE held fast to.

16*a* TG Example.
16*a* TG Family, Love within.
　b TG Loyalty.

lodgest, I will lodge: thy ^cpeople *shall be* my people, and thy God my ^dGod:

17 Where thou diest, will I die, and there will I be buried: the Lord do so to me, and more also, *if ought* but death part thee and me.

18 When she saw that she was ^asteadfastly minded to go with her, then she left speaking unto her.

19 ¶ So they two went until they came to Beth-lehem. And it came to pass, when they were come to Beth-lehem, that all the city was moved about them, and they said, *Is* this Naomi?

20 And she said unto them, Call me not ^aNaomi, call me ^bMara: for the Almighty hath dealt very bitterly with me.

21 I went out full, and the Lord hath brought me home again empty: why *then* call ye me Naomi, seeing the Lord hath ^atestified against me, and the Almighty hath afflicted me?

22 So Naomi returned, and Ruth the Moabitess, her daughter in law, with her, which returned out of the country of Moab: and they came to Beth-lehem in the beginning of barley harvest.

CHAPTER 2

Ruth gleans in the fields of Boaz, a near relative of Naomi—He treats Ruth kindly.

And Naomi had a kinsman of her husband's, a mighty man of wealth, of the family of Elimelech; and his name *was* ^aBoaz.

2 And Ruth the Moabitess said unto Naomi, Let me now go to the field, and ^aglean ears of ^bcorn after *him* in whose sight I shall find grace. And she said unto her, Go, my daughter.

3 And she went, and came, and gleaned in the field after the reapers: and her ^ahap was to light on a part of the field *belonging* unto Boaz, who *was* of the kindred of Elimelech.

4 ¶ And, behold, Boaz came from Beth-lehem, and said unto the reapers, The Lord *be* with you. And they answered him, The Lord bless thee.

5 Then said Boaz unto his servant that was set over the reapers, Whose damsel *is* this?

6 And the servant that was set over the reapers answered and said, It *is* the Moabitish damsel that came back with Naomi out of the country of Moab:

7 And she said, I pray you, let me glean and gather after the reapers among the sheaves: so she came, and hath continued even from the morning until now, that she tarried a little in the house.

8 Then said Boaz unto Ruth, Hearest thou not, my daughter? Go not to ^aglean in another field, neither go from hence, but abide here ^bfast by my maidens:

9 *Let* thine eyes *be* on the field that they do reap, and go thou after them: have I not charged the young men that they shall not touch thee? and when thou art athirst, go unto the vessels, and drink of *that* which the young men have drawn.

10 Then she fell on her face, and bowed herself to the ground, and said unto him, Why have I found grace in thine eyes, that thou shouldest take ^aknowledge of me, seeing I *am* a stranger?

11 And Boaz answered and said unto her, It hath fully been shewed me, all that thou hast done unto thy mother in law since the death of thine husband: and *how* thou hast left thy father and thy mother, and the land of thy nativity, and art come unto a people which thou knewest not heretofore.

16c TG Brotherhood and Sisterhood.
 d TG Conversion.
18a TG Commitment; Courage; Perseverance; Steadfastness.
20a IE Pleasant.
 b IE a name given to Naomi by herself, which means "bitter," or "very sad."
21a OR humbled me (so also in the Septuagint and the Latin Vulgate).
2 1a HEB In him is strength, swiftness, quickness.
2a Lev. 19:9; Deut. 24:19.
 b OR grain.
3a OR chance, good fortune.
8a Lev. 19:9.
 b OR close.
10a OR notice.

12 The LORD recompense thy work, and a full [a]reward be given thee of the LORD God of Israel, under whose [b]wings thou art come to trust.

13 Then she said, Let me find favour in thy sight, my lord; for that thou hast comforted me, and for that thou hast spoken [a]friendly unto thine handmaid, though I be not like unto one of thine handmaidens.

14 And Boaz said unto her, At mealtime come thou hither, and eat of the bread, and dip thy morsel in the vinegar. And she sat beside the reapers: and he reached her parched [a]corn, and she did eat, and was sufficed, and [b]left.

15 And when she was risen up to glean, Boaz commanded his young men, saying, Let her glean even among the sheaves, and reproach her not:

16 And let fall also *some* of the handfuls of purpose for her, and leave *them*, that she may glean *them*, and rebuke her not.

17 So she gleaned in the field until even, and beat out that she had gleaned: and it was about an ephah of barley.

18 ¶ And she took *it* up, and went into the city: and her mother in law saw what she had gleaned: and she brought forth, and gave to her that she had reserved after she was sufficed.

19 And her mother in law said unto her, Where hast thou gleaned to day? and where wroughtest thou? blessed be he that did take knowledge of thee. And she [a]shewed her mother in law with whom she had [b]wrought, and said, The man's name with whom I wrought to day *is* Boaz.

20 And Naomi said unto her daughter in law, Blessed *be* he of the LORD, who hath not [a]left off his kindness to the living and to the dead. And

Naomi said unto her, The man *is* near of kin unto us, one of our [b]next [c]kinsmen.

21 And Ruth the Moabitess said, He said unto me also, Thou shalt keep [a]fast by my young men, until they have ended all my harvest.

22 And Naomi said unto Ruth her daughter in law, *It is* good, my daughter, that thou go out with his maidens, that they [a]meet thee not in any other field.

23 So she kept fast by the maidens of Boaz to glean unto the end of barley harvest and of wheat harvest; and dwelt with her mother in law.

CHAPTER 3

By Naomi's instruction, Ruth lies at the feet of Boaz—He promises as a relative to take her as his wife.

THEN Naomi her mother in law said unto her, My daughter, shall I not seek [a]rest for thee, that it may be well with thee?

2 And now *is* not Boaz of our kindred, with whose maidens thou wast? Behold, he winnoweth barley to night in the threshingfloor.

3 Wash thyself therefore, and anoint thee, and put thy raiment upon thee, and get thee down to the [a]floor: *but* make not thyself known unto the man, until he shall have done eating and drinking.

4 And it shall be, when he lieth down, that thou shalt mark the place where he shall lie, and thou shalt go in, and uncover his feet, and lay thee down; and he will tell thee what thou shalt do.

5 And she said unto her, All that thou sayest unto me I will do.

6 ¶ And she went down unto the floor, and did according to all that her mother in law bade her.

7 And when Boaz had eaten and drunk, and his heart was merry,

---

12a D&C 70:15.
  b Ps. 57:1.
13a TG Friendship.
14a OR grain.
  b IE left some food.
19a OR told.

  b OR worked.
20a OR ceased.
  b OR redeemers; one of those having the right to redeem.
  c Ruth 3:9 (9, 12–13);

4:1 (1, 3, 6, 8).
  TG Redemption.
21a OR close.
22a OR find.
3 1a Implying marriage.
  3a IE threshing floor.

he went to lie down at the end of the heap of ᵃcorn: and she came softly, and uncovered his feet, and laid her down.

8 ¶ And it came to pass at midnight, that the man was afraid, and turned himself: and, behold, a woman lay at his feet.

9 And he said, Who *art* thou? And she answered, I *am* Ruth thine handmaid: spread therefore thy skirt over thine handmaid; for thou *art* a near ᵃkinsman.

10 And he said, Blessed *be* thou of the LORD, my daughter: *for* thou hast shewed more kindness in the latter end than at the beginning, inasmuch as thou followedst not young men, whether poor or rich.

11 And now, my daughter, fear not; I will do to thee all that thou requirest: for all the city of my people doth know that thou *art* a ᵃvirtuous woman.

12 And now it is true that I *am thy* ᵃnear kinsman: howbeit there is a kinsman nearer than I.

13 Tarry this night, and it shall be in the morning, *that* if he will perform unto thee the ᵃpart of a kinsman, well; let him do the kinsman's part: but if he will not do the part of a kinsman to thee, then will I do the part of a kinsman to thee, *as* the LORD liveth: lie down until the morning.

14 ¶ And she lay at his feet until the morning: and she rose up before one could know another. And he said, Let it not be known that a woman came into the floor.

15 Also he said, Bring the ᵃveil that *thou hast* upon thee, and hold it. And when she held it, he measured six *measures* of barley, and laid *it* on her: and she went into the city.

16 And when she came to her mother in law, she said, Who *art* thou, my daughter? And she told her all that the man had done to her.

17 And she said, These six *measures* of barley gave he me; for he said to me, Go not empty unto thy mother in law.

18 Then said she, Sit still, my daughter, until thou know how the matter will fall: for the man will not be in rest, until he have finished the thing this day.

CHAPTER 4

The nearest relative declines, and Boaz takes Ruth to wife—Ruth bears Obed, through whom came David the king.

THEN went Boaz up to the ᵃgate, and sat him down there: and, behold, the ᵇkinsman of whom Boaz spake came by; unto whom he said, ᶜHo, such a one! turn aside, sit down here. And he turned aside, and sat down.

2 And he took ten men of the ᵃelders of the city, and said, Sit ye down here. And they sat down.

3 And he said unto the kinsman, Naomi, that is come again out of the country of Moab, selleth a parcel of land, which *was* our brother Elimelech's:

4 And I thought to advertise thee, saying, ᵃBuy *it* before the inhabitants, and before the elders of my people. If thou wilt ᵇredeem *it,* redeem *it:* but if thou wilt not redeem *it, then* tell me, that I may know: for *there is* none to redeem *it* beside thee; and I *am* after thee. And he said, I will redeem *it.*

5 Then said Boaz, What day thou buyest the field of the hand of Naomi, thou must buy *it* also of Ruth the Moabitess, the ᵃwife of the dead, to raise up the ᵇname of the dead upon his inheritance.

6 ¶ And the kinsman said, I cannot

7ᵃ OR grain.
9ᵃ Ruth 2:20.
11ᵃ Prov. 12:4;
    Moro. 9:9.
12ᵃ Deut. 25:5.
13ᵃ Matt. 22:24.
15ᵃ OR cloak, mantle;

a square piece of cloth
    used as an outer robe.
4 1ᵃ Gen. 23:10; Josh. 20:4.
    b Ruth 2:20.
    c In Hebrew a manner
    of address to a certain
    unnamed person as

"Mr. So & So."
2ᵃ Josh. 20:4.
4ᵃ Lev. 25:25.
    b TG Redemption.
5ᵃ TG Widows.
    b Deut. 25:5 (5–6).
    TG Name.

^aredeem *it* for myself, lest I ^bmar mine own inheritance: redeem thou my right to thyself; for I cannot redeem *it*.

7 Now this *was the manner* in former time in Israel concerning redeeming and concerning ^achanging, for to confirm all things; a man plucked off his ^bshoe, and gave *it* to his neighbour: and this *was* a testimony in Israel.

8 Therefore the kinsman said unto Boaz, Buy *it* for thee. So he drew off his shoe.

9 ¶ And Boaz said unto the elders, and *unto* all the people, Ye *are* witnesses this day, that I have bought all that *was* Elimelech's, and all that *was* Chilion's and Mahlon's, of the hand of Naomi.

10 Moreover Ruth the Moabitess, the wife of Mahlon, have I purchased to be my wife, to raise up the name of the dead upon his inheritance, that the ^aname of the dead be not cut off from among his brethren, and from the gate of his place: ye *are* witnesses this day.

11 And all the people that *were* in the gate, and the elders, said, We *are* witnesses. The LORD make the woman that is come into thine house like Rachel and like Leah, which two did build the house of Israel: and ^ado thou worthily in Ephratah, and be famous in Beth-lehem:

12 And let thy house be like the house of Pharez, whom Tamar bare unto Judah, of the seed which the LORD shall give thee of this young woman.

13 ¶ So Boaz took Ruth, and she was his wife: and when he went in unto her, the LORD gave her conception, and she bare a son.

14 And the women said unto Naomi, Blessed *be* the LORD, which hath not left thee this day without a kinsman, that his name may be famous in Israel.

15 And he shall be unto thee a restorer of *thy* life, and a nourisher of thine ^aold age: for thy daughter in law, which loveth thee, which is better to thee than seven sons, hath born him.

16 And Naomi took the child, and laid it in her bosom, and became nurse unto it.

17 And the women her neighbours gave it a name, saying, There is a son born to Naomi; and they called his name Obed: he *is* the father of Jesse, the father of David.

18 ¶ Now these *are* the generations of ^aPharez: Pharez begat Hezron,

19 And Hezron begat Ram, and Ram begat Amminadab,

20 And Amminadab begat Nahshon, and Nahshon begat Salmon,

21 And Salmon begat ^aBoaz, and Boaz begat Obed,

22 And Obed begat Jesse, and Jesse begat David.

6*a* TG Selfishness.
  b Deut. 25:6 (5–6).
7*a* OR exchanging, doing business.
  b Deut. 25:9 (5–10).
10*a* Deut. 25:6.
11*a* OR may you do well.
15*a* TG Old Age.
18*a* Gen. 38:29 (1–30);
    1 Chr. 2:4 (4–15);
Matt. 1:3 (3–6);
Luke 3:33 (23–38).
21*a* Matt. 1:5.

THE FIRST BOOK OF
SAMUEL

OTHERWISE CALLED
THE FIRST BOOK OF THE KINGS

CHAPTER 1

Hannah prays for a son and vows to give him to the Lord—Eli the priest blesses her—Samuel is born—Hannah loans him to the Lord.

NOW there was a certain man of *a*Ramathaim-zophim, of mount Ephraim, and his name *was* *b*Elkanah, the son of Jeroham, the son of Elihu, the son of Tohu, the son of Zuph, an Ephrathite:

2 And he had two wives; the name of the one *was* Hannah, and the name of the other Peninnah: and Peninnah had children, but Hannah had *a*no children.

3 And this man went up out of his city *a*yearly to worship and to sacrifice unto the LORD of hosts in *b*Shiloh. And the two sons of Eli, Hophni and Phinehas, the priests of the LORD, *were* there.

4 ¶ And when the time was that Elkanah offered, he gave to Peninnah his wife, and to all her sons and her daughters, portions:

5 But unto Hannah he gave a worthy portion; for he loved Hannah: but the LORD had shut up her womb.

6 And her adversary also *a*provoked her sore, for to make her fret, because the LORD had shut up her womb.

7 And *as* he did so year by year, when she went up to the *a*house of the LORD, so she provoked her; therefore she wept, and did not eat.

8 Then said Elkanah her husband to her, Hannah, why weepest thou? and why eatest thou not? and why is thy heart grieved? *am* not I better to thee than ten sons?

9 ¶ So Hannah rose up after they had eaten in Shiloh, and after they had drunk. Now Eli the priest sat upon a *a*seat by a post of the temple of the LORD.

10 And she *was* in *a*bitterness of soul, and prayed unto the LORD, and wept sore.

11 And she *a*vowed a *b*vow, and said, O LORD of hosts, if thou wilt indeed look on the affliction of thine *c*handmaid, and remember me, and not forget thine handmaid, but wilt give unto thine handmaid a man child, then I will give him unto the LORD all the days of his life, and there shall no *d*razor come upon his head.

12 And it came to pass, as she continued praying before the LORD, that Eli *a*marked her mouth.

13 Now Hannah, she spake in her heart; only her lips moved, but her voice was not heard: therefore Eli thought she had been drunken.

14 And Eli said unto her, How long wilt thou be drunken? put away thy wine from thee.

15 And Hannah answered and said, No, my lord, I *am* a woman of a sorrowful spirit: I have drunk neither

---

1 1*a* 1 Sam. 1:19.
  b 1 Chr. 6:23 (16–28).
2*a* TG Barren.
3*a* 1 Sam. 1:21.
  b Josh. 18:1;
     Jer. 7:12.

6*a* Gen. 16:5 (4–16); 30:1.
7*a* TG Temple.
9*a* 1 Sam. 4:18.
10*a* OR sadness, grief.
11*a* Judg. 11:30 (30–31).
  b TG Vow.

c Luke 1:48 (48–49).
d Num. 6:5 (1–8);
   Judg. 13:5.
12*a* IE saw.

wine nor strong drink, but have ^apoured out my soul before the LORD.

16 Count not thine handmaid for a ^adaughter of ^bBelial: for out of the abundance of my complaint and grief have I spoken hitherto.

17 Then Eli answered and said, Go in peace: and the God of Israel grant *thee* thy petition that thou hast asked of him.

18 And she said, Let thine handmaid find grace in thy sight. So the woman went her way, and did eat, and her countenance was no more *sad*.

19 ¶ And they rose up in the morning early, and worshipped before the LORD, and returned, and came to their house to ^aRamah: and Elkanah knew Hannah his wife; and the LORD ^bremembered her.

20 Wherefore it came to pass, when the time was come about after Hannah had conceived, that she bare a ^ason, and called his name Samuel, *saying*, Because I have asked him of the LORD.

21 And the man Elkanah, and all his house, went up to offer unto the LORD the ^ayearly sacrifice, and his vow.

22 But Hannah went not up; for she said unto her husband, *I will not go up* until the child be weaned, and *then* I will bring him, that he may appear before the LORD, and there abide for ever.

23 And Elkanah her husband said unto her, Do what seemeth thee good; tarry until thou have weaned him; only the LORD establish his word. So the woman abode, and gave her son suck until she weaned him.

24 ¶ And when she had weaned him, she took him up with her, with three bullocks, and one ephah of flour, and a bottle of wine, and brought him unto the house of the LORD in Shiloh: and the child *was* young.

25 And they slew a bullock, and brought the child to Eli.

26 And she said, Oh my lord, *as* thy soul liveth, my lord, I *am* the woman that stood by thee here, praying unto the LORD.

27 For this ^achild I prayed; and the LORD hath given me my petition which I asked of him:

28 Therefore also I have lent him to the LORD; as long as he liveth he shall be ^alent to the LORD. And he worshipped the LORD there.

CHAPTER 2

Hannah sings praises to the Lord—Samuel ministers before the Lord—Eli blesses Elkanah and Hannah, and they have sons and daughters—The sons of Eli reject the Lord and live in wickedness—The Lord rejects the house of Eli.

AND Hannah ^aprayed, and said, My heart ^brejoiceth in the LORD, mine ^chorn is exalted in the LORD: my mouth is enlarged over mine enemies; because I rejoice in thy ^dsalvation.

2 *There is* ^anone holy as the LORD: for *there is* none beside thee: neither *is there* any ^brock like our God.

3 Talk no more so exceeding proudly; let *not* arrogancy come out of your mouth: for the LORD *is* a God of ^aknowledge, and by him ^bactions are weighed.

4 The bows of the mighty men *are*

15*a* Enos 1:9;
 Alma 34:26 (26–27).
16*a* Deut. 13:13.
 b HEB worthlessness;
 good-for-nothing, base
 wickedness.
 1 Sam. 2:12.
19*a* 1 Sam. 1:1.
 b Gen. 30:22 (22–23).
20*a* TG Marriage,
 Motherhood.

21*a* 1 Sam. 1:3.
27*a* TG Marriage,
 Motherhood.
28*a* 1 Sam. 2:20.
2 1*a* TG Singing.
 b Luke 1:46 (46–55).
 TG Thanksgiving.
 c HEB horn; used
 figuratively, means
 "power," "capacity."
 Ps. 75:10; 89:17 (17, 24).

d Ps. 9:14; 13:5.
2*a* Deut. 4:35;
 1 Kgs. 8:23;
 2 Ne. 2:7.
 b TG Cornerstone;
 Rock.
3*a* TG God, Intelligence
 of; God, Omniscience
 of; Intelligence;
 Knowledge.
 b 3 Ne. 27:15 (11–15).

broken, and they that stumbled are girded with strength.

5 *They that were* full have hired out themselves for bread; and *they that were* hungry ceased: so that the ᵃbarren hath born seven; and she that hath many children is waxed feeble.

6 The LORD killeth, and maketh alive: he ᵃbringeth down to the grave, and bringeth up.

7 The LORD ᵃmaketh ᵇpoor, and maketh ᶜrich: he bringeth low, and lifteth up.

8 He ᵃraiseth up the ᵇpoor out of the dust, *and* lifteth up the beggar from the dunghill, to set *them* among princes, and to make them inherit the throne of glory: for the ᶜpillars of the earth *are* the LORD's, and he hath set the world upon them.

9 He will keep the feet of his saints, and the wicked shall be ᵃsilent in darkness; for by ᵇstrength shall no man prevail.

10 The adversaries of the LORD shall be broken to pieces; out of heaven shall he thunder upon them: the LORD shall ᵃjudge the ends of the earth; and he shall give strength unto his king, and exalt the horn of his ᵇanointed.

11 And Elkanah went to Ramah to his house. ᵃAnd the child did minister unto the LORD before Eli the priest.

12 ¶ Now the ᵃsons of Eli *were* ᵇsons of ᶜBelial; they knew not the LORD.

13 And the priests' custom with the people *was, that,* when any man offered sacrifice, the priest's ser-vant came, while the flesh was ᵃin seething, with a fleshhook of three teeth in his hand;

14 And he struck *it* into the pan, or kettle, or caldron, or pot; all that the fleshhook brought up the priest ᵃtook for himself. So they did in Shiloh unto all the Israelites that came thither.

15 Also before they burnt the fat, the priest's servant came, and said to the man that sacrificed, Give flesh to roast for the priest; for he will not have ᵃsodden flesh of thee, but raw.

16 And *if* any man said unto him, Let them not fail to burn the fat ᵃpresently, and *then* take *as much* as thy soul desireth; then he would answer him, *Nay*; but thou shalt give *it me* now: and if not, I will take *it* by force.

17 Wherefore the sin of the young men was very great before the LORD: for men ᵃabhorred the offering of the LORD.

18 ¶ But Samuel ministered before the LORD, *being* a child, girded with a linen ᵃephod.

19 Moreover his ᵃmother made him a little coat, and brought *it* to him from year to year, when she came up with her husband to offer the yearly sacrifice.

20 ¶ And Eli ᵃblessed Elkanah and his wife, and said, The LORD give thee seed of this woman for ᵇthe loan which is ᶜlent to the LORD. And they went unto their own home.

21 And the LORD ᵃvisited Hannah, so that she conceived, and bare three sons and two daughters. And

---

5a TG Barren.
6a TG Jesus Christ, Resurrection; Resurrection.
7a Ps. 75:7.
  b TG Poor.
  c Gen. 14:23; D&C 38:16.
8a Ps. 113:7 (7–8).
  b TG Poor.
  c Ps. 75:3.
9a TG Silence.
  b TG Strength.
10a TG Jesus Christ, Judge;

Judgment, the Last.
  b In the Septuagint Greek version, the noun is *christos*.
11a HEB And the youth served the LORD in the presence of Eli, the priest.
12a TG Family, Children, Responsibilities toward.
  b 1 Sam. 3:13.
  c Deut. 13:13; 1 Sam. 1:16.
13a OR boiling.

14a Lev. 7:33 (30–34); Deut. 18:3.
15a OR cooked, boiled.
16a IE first of all.
17a Mal. 2:8.
18a Ex. 28:4.
19a TG Marriage, Motherhood.
20a Num. 6:23; Alma 8:22; 10:11.
  b HEB the petition which she asked.
  c 1 Sam. 1:28.
21a Gen. 21:1 (1–2).

the child Samuel grew before the LORD.

22 ¶ Now Eli was very old, and heard all that his sons did unto all Israel; and how they lay with the women that assembled *at* the door of the tabernacle of the congregation.

23 And he said unto them, Why do ye such things? for I hear of your evil dealings by all this people.

24 Nay, my sons; for *it is* no good report that I hear: ye make the LORD's people to ªtransgress.

25 If one man sin against another, the judge shall ªjudge him: but if a man sin against the LORD, who shall entreat for him? Notwithstanding they hearkened not unto the voice of their father, because the LORD would slay them.

26 And the child Samuel ªgrew on, and was in ᵇfavour both with the LORD, and also with men.

27 ¶ And there came a man of God unto Eli, and said unto him, Thus saith the LORD, Did I plainly appear unto the house of thy father, when they were in Egypt in Pharaoh's house?

28 And did I ªchoose him out of all the tribes of Israel *to be* my priest, to offer upon mine altar, to burn incense, to wear an ᵇephod before me? and did I give unto the house of thy father all the ᶜofferings made by fire of the children of Israel?

29 Wherefore ªkick ye at my sacrifice and at mine offering, which I have commanded *in my* habitation; and ᵇhonourest thy sons above me, to make yourselves fat with the chiefest of all the offerings of Israel my people?

30 Wherefore the LORD God of Israel saith, I said indeed *that* thy house, and the ªhouse of thy father, should ᵇwalk before me for ever: but now the LORD saith, Be it far from me; for them that ᶜhonour me I will honour, and they that despise me shall be lightly ᵈesteemed.

31 Behold, the ªdays come, that I will ᵇcut off thine arm, and the arm of thy father's house, that there shall not be an old man in thine house.

32 And thou shalt see an enemy *in my* habitation, in all *the wealth* which *God* shall give Israel: and there shall not be an old man in thine house for ever.

33 And the man of thine, *whom* I shall not cut off from mine altar, *shall be* to consume thine eyes, and to grieve thine heart: and all the increase of thine house shall die in the flower of their age.

34 And this *shall be* a sign unto thee, that shall come upon thy two sons, on Hophni and Phinehas; in one day they shall ªdie both of them.

35 And I will ªraise me up a faithful ᵇpriest, *that* shall do according to *that* which *is* in mine heart and in my mind: and ᶜI will build him a sure house; and he shall walk before mine anointed for ever.

36 And it shall come to pass, *that* every one that is left in thine house shall come *and* crouch to him for a piece of silver and a morsel of bread, and shall say, Put me, I pray thee, into one of the priests' offices, that I may eat a piece of bread.

CHAPTER 3

The Lord calls Samuel—The house of Eli will not be purged by sacrifices and offerings—Samuel is recognized as a prophet by all Israel—The Lord appears to him.

24a Alma 39:11 (1–11).
25a TG Judgment.
26a 1 Sam. 3:19;
  Luke 2:52.
  b Prov. 3:4.
28a TG Priesthood, Authority.
  b Ex. 28:4 (2–4);
  1 Sam. 14:3; 22:18.
  c Lev. 10:12 (12–15);
  Num. 18:8 (8–19).
29a IE treat with scorn.

b Matt. 10:37.
30a Ex. 27:21.
  b TG Walking with God.
  c Acts 10:35 (34–35);
  1 Ne. 17:35.
  TG Honor;
  Priesthood, Magnifying
  Callings within;
  Respect.
  d Mal. 2:9.
31a 1 Kgs. 2:27.

b 1 Sam. 3:12.
34a 1 Sam. 4:11.
35a D&C 114:2.
  b 1 Kgs. 2:35;
  1 Chr. 29:22.
  c IE his progeny shall be
  perpetuated.
  Ex. 1:21 (15–22);
  1 Sam. 25:28;
  2 Sam. 7:11 (10–17);
  1 Kgs. 11:38.

AND the child Samuel ministered unto the LORD before Eli. And the word of the LORD was precious in those days; *there was* no open ªvision.

2 And it came to pass at that time, when Eli *was* laid down in his place, and his ªeyes began to wax dim, *that* he could not see;

3 And ere the ªlamp of God went out in the temple of the LORD, where the ark of God *was*, and Samuel was laid down *to sleep*;

4 That the LORD called Samuel: and he answered, Here *am* I.

5 And he ran unto Eli, and said, Here *am* I; for thou calledst me. And he said, I called not; lie down again. And he went and lay down.

6 And the LORD called yet again, Samuel. And Samuel arose and went to Eli, and said, Here *am* I; for thou didst call me. And he answered, I called not, my son; lie down again.

7 Now Samuel did not yet know the LORD, neither was the word of the LORD yet revealed unto him.

8 And the LORD called Samuel again the third time. And he arose and went to Eli, and said, Here *am* I; for thou didst call me. And Eli perceived that the LORD had called the child.

9 Therefore Eli said unto Samuel, Go, lie down: and it shall be, if he call thee, that thou shalt say, Speak, LORD; for thy servant heareth. So Samuel went and lay down in his place.

10 And the LORD came, and ªstood, and called as at other times, Samuel, Samuel. Then Samuel answered, Speak; for thy ᵇservant heareth.

11 ¶ And the LORD said to Samuel,

Behold, I will do a thing in Israel, at which both the ears of every one that heareth it shall ªtingle.

12 In that day I will perform ªagainst Eli all *things* which I have spoken concerning his house: when I begin, I will also make an end.

13 For I have told him that I will ªjudge his house for ever for the iniquity which he knoweth; because his ᵇsons made themselves vile, and he ᶜrestrained them not.

14 And therefore I have sworn unto the house of Eli, that the iniquity of Eli's house shall not be purged with sacrifice nor offering for ever.

15 ¶ And Samuel lay until the morning, and opened the doors of the house of the LORD. And Samuel ªfeared to shew Eli the vision.

16 Then Eli called Samuel, and said, Samuel, my son. And he answered, Here *am* I.

17 And he said, What *is* the thing that *the* LORD hath said unto thee? I pray thee hide *it* not from me: God do so to thee, and more also, if thou hide *any* thing from me of all the things that he said unto thee.

18 And Samuel told him every whit, and hid nothing from him. And he said, It *is* the LORD: let him do what seemeth him good.

19 ¶ And Samuel ªgrew, and the ᵇLORD was ᶜwith him, and did let none of his words ᵈfall to the ground.

20 And all Israel from Dan even to Beer-sheba knew that Samuel *was* ªestablished *to be* a prophet of the LORD.

21 And the LORD ªappeared again in ᵇShiloh: for the LORD revealed himself to Samuel in Shiloh by the ᶜword of the LORD.

3 1 *a* Ps. 74:9; Amos 8:11;
    Morm. 1:14 (13–14);
    JS—H 1:21.
    TG Revelation; Vision.
  2 *a* 1 Sam. 4:15.
  3 *a* Ex. 27:20 (20–21);
    Lev. 24:2 (2–3).
10 *a* 1 Ne. 1:11 (8–15);
    D&C 110:2 (2–3);
    JS—H 1:17.
   b TG Servant.
11 *a* 2 Kgs. 21:12; Jer. 19:3;

    3 Ne. 11:3;
    D&C 1:2 (1–2).
12 *a* 1 Sam. 2:31 (30–36).
13 *a* Ezek. 7:3 (3–8).
   b 1 Sam. 2:12;
    1 Ne. 2:12 (12–13);
    Mosiah 27:8 (7–37);
    Moses 5:16.
   c D&C 68:25; 93:42 (40–50).
    TG Family, Children,
    Responsibilities toward.
15 *a* D&C 60:2 (2–3).

19 *a* 1 Sam. 2:26; Luke 2:52.
   b 1 Sam. 9:15 (15–20).
   c Josh. 6:27.
   d 2 Kgs. 10:10.
20 *a* TG Called of God;
    Priesthood, Authority.
21 *a* Ether 3:13 (6–16);
    D&C 107:54 (53–54);
    Abr. 2:19 (6, 19).
   b Josh. 18:1.
   c TG Jesus Christ, Messenger of the Covenant.

CHAPTER 4

The Israelites are smitten and defeated by the Philistines, who also capture the ark of God—Eli's sons are slain, Eli dies in an accident, and his daughter-in-law dies in childbirth.

AND the word of Samuel came to all Israel. Now Israel went out against the Philistines to battle, and pitched beside *a*Eben-ezer: and the Philistines pitched in *b*Aphek.

2 And the Philistines put themselves in array against Israel: and when they joined battle, Israel was smitten before the Philistines: and they slew of the army in the field about four thousand men.

3 ¶ And when the people were come into the camp, the elders of Israel said, Wherefore hath the LORD smitten us to day before the Philistines? Let us fetch the *a*ark of the covenant of the LORD out of Shiloh unto us, that, when it cometh among us, it may save us out of the hand of our enemies.

4 So the people sent to Shiloh, that they might bring from thence the ark of the covenant of the LORD of hosts, which dwelleth *between* the *a*cherubims: and the two sons of Eli, Hophni and Phinehas, *were* there with the ark of the covenant of God.

5 And when the ark of the covenant of the LORD came into the camp, all Israel shouted with a great shout, so that the earth rang again.

6 And when the Philistines heard the noise of the shout, they said, What *meaneth* the noise of this great shout in the camp of the Hebrews? And they understood that the ark of the LORD was come into the camp.

7 And the Philistines were afraid, for they said, God is come into the camp. And they said, Woe unto us! for there hath not been such a thing heretofore.

8 Woe unto us! who shall deliver us out of the hand of these *a*mighty Gods? these *are* the Gods that smote the Egyptians with all the plagues in the wilderness.

9 Be strong, and *a*quit yourselves like *b*men, O ye Philistines, that ye be not *c*servants unto the Hebrews, as they have been to you: quit yourselves like men, and fight.

10 ¶ And the Philistines fought, and Israel was smitten, and they fled every man into his tent: and there was a very great slaughter; for there fell of Israel thirty thousand footmen.

11 And the ark of God was taken; and the two sons of Eli, Hophni and Phinehas, were *a*slain.

12 ¶ And there ran a man of Benjamin out of the army, and came to Shiloh the same day with his clothes *a*rent, and with earth upon his head.

13 And when he came, lo, Eli sat upon a seat by the wayside watching: for his heart trembled for the ark of God. And when the man came into the city, and told *it,* all the city cried out.

14 And when Eli heard the noise of the crying, he said, What *meaneth* the noise of this tumult? And the man came in hastily, and told Eli.

15 Now Eli was ninety and eight years old; and his *a*eyes were dim, that he could not see.

16 And the man said unto Eli, I *am* he that came out of the army, and I fled to day out of the army. And he said, What is there done, my son?

17 And the messenger answered and said, Israel is fled before the Philistines, and there hath been also a great slaughter among the people, and thy two sons also, Hophni and Phinehas, are dead, and the ark of God is taken.

18 And it came to pass, when he made mention of the ark of God, that he fell from off the *a*seat backward by the side of the gate, and his

---

4 1*a* 1 Sam. 5:1; 7:12.
   b Josh. 12:18.
  3*a* TG Ark of the Covenant.
  4*a* TG Cherubim.
  8*a* 1 Ne. 7:11 (10–12).

9*a* OR be men.
  b 2 Sam. 10:12;
    Isa. 46:8;
    1 Cor. 16:13;
    2 Ne. 1:21.

c Judg. 13:1.
11*a* 1 Sam. 2:34 (31–34).
12*a* Josh. 7:6.
15*a* 1 Sam. 3:2.
18*a* 1 Sam. 1:9.

neck brake, and he died: for he was an old man, and heavy. And he had judged Israel forty years.

19 ¶ And his daughter in law, Phinehas' wife, was with child, *near* to be delivered: and when she heard the tidings that the ark of God was taken, and that her father in law and her husband were dead, she bowed herself and travailed; for her pains came upon her.

20 And about the time of her death the women that stood by her said unto her, Fear not; for thou hast born a son. But she answered not, neither did she regard *it*.

21 And she named the child ᵃI-chabod, saying, The glory is departed from Israel: because the ark of God was taken, and because of her father in law and her husband.

22 And she said, The glory is departed from Israel: for the ark of God is taken.

CHAPTER 5

The Philistines place the ark in the house of Dagon, their god—The Philistines in Ashdod, then Gath, and then Ekron are plagued and slain because the ark is lodged with them.

AND the Philistines took the ᵃark of God, and brought it from ᵇEbenezer unto Ashdod.

2 When the Philistines took the ᵃark of God, they brought it into the house of ᵇDagon, and set it by Dagon.

3 ¶ And when they of Ashdod arose early on the morrow, behold, Dagon *was* fallen upon his face to the earth before the ark of the LORD. And they took Dagon, and set him in his place again.

4 And when they arose early on the morrow morning, behold, Dagon *was* fallen upon his face to the ground before the ark of the LORD; and the head of Dagon and both the palms of his hands *were* cut off upon the threshold; only *the stump of* Dagon was left to him.

5 Therefore neither the priests of Dagon, nor any that come into Dagon's house, tread on the threshold of Dagon in Ashdod unto this day.

6 But the hand of the LORD was heavy upon them of Ashdod, and he destroyed them, and smote them with ᵃemerods, *even* Ashdod and the coasts thereof.

7 And when the men of Ashdod saw that *it was* so, they said, The ark of the God of Israel shall not abide with us: for his hand is sore upon us, and upon Dagon our god.

8 They sent therefore and gathered all the lords of the Philistines unto them, and said, What shall we do with the ark of the God of Israel? And they answered, Let the ark of the God of Israel be carried about unto ᵃGath. And they carried the ark of the God of Israel about *thither*.

9 And it was *so*, that, after they had carried it about, the ᵃhand of the LORD was against the city with a very great destruction: and he smote the men of the city, both small and great, and they had emerods in their secret parts.

10 ¶ Therefore they sent the ark of God to Ekron. And it came to pass, as the ark of God came to Ekron, that the Ekronites cried out, saying, They have brought about the ark of the God of Israel to us, to slay us and our people.

11 So they sent and gathered together all the lords of the Philistines, and said, Send away the ark of the God of Israel, and let it go again to his own place, that it slay us not, and our people: for there was a deadly destruction throughout all the city; the hand of God was very heavy there.

12 And the men that died not were smitten with the emerods: and the cry of the city went up to heaven.

21*a* IE Where is the glory?
5 1*a* 1 Chr. 13:3.
  b 1 Sam. 4:1; 7:12.
2*a* TG Sacrilege.
  b Judg. 16:23.

6*a* OR tumors, boils (also vv. 9, 12).
  Deut. 28:27;
  1 Sam. 6:11 (5, 11, 17).
8*a* 1 Sam. 17:4.

9*a* 1 Sam. 7:13;
  Morm. 5:23;
  Ether 1:1;
  D&C 87:6 (6–7).

CHAPTER 6

The Philistines send back the ark with an offering—The Lord smites and slays the Israelites in Beth-shemesh who look into the ark.

AND the ark of the LORD was in the country of the Philistines seven months.

2 And the Philistines called for the priests and the *a*diviners, saying, What shall we do to the ark of the LORD? tell us wherewith we shall send it to his place.

3 And they said, If ye send away the ark of the God of Israel, send it not empty; but in any wise return him a *a*trespass offering: then ye shall be healed, and it shall be known to you why his hand is not removed from you.

4 Then said they, What *shall be* the trespass offering which we shall return to him? They answered, Five golden emerods, and five golden mice, *according to* the number of the lords of the Philistines: for one plague *was* on you all, and on your lords.

5 Wherefore ye shall make images of your emerods, and images of your mice that mar the land; and ye shall give *a*glory unto the God of Israel: peradventure he will lighten his hand from off you, and from off your gods, and from off your land.

6 Wherefore then do ye *a*harden your hearts, as the Egyptians and Pharaoh *b*hardened their hearts? when he had wrought wonderfully among them, did they not let the people go, and they departed?

7 Now therefore make a new cart, and take two *a*milch kine, on which there hath come no yoke, and tie the kine to the cart, and bring their calves home from them:

8 And take the ark of the LORD, and lay it upon the cart; and put the jewels of gold, which ye return him *for* a trespass offering, in a *a*coffer by the side thereof; and send it away, that it may go.

9 And see, if it goeth up by the way of his own coast to Beth-shemesh, *then* he hath done us this great evil: but if not, then we shall know that *it is* not his hand *that* smote us; it *was* a chance *that* happened to us.

10 ¶ And the men did so; and took two milch kine, and tied them to the cart, and shut up their calves at home:

11 And they laid the ark of the LORD upon the cart, and the coffer with the mice of gold and the images of their *a*emerods.

12 And the kine took the straight way to the way of Beth-shemesh, *and* went along the highway, lowing as they went, and turned not aside *to* the right hand or *to* the left; and the lords of the Philistines went after them unto the border of Beth-shemesh.

13 And *they of* Beth-shemesh *were* reaping their wheat harvest in the valley: and they lifted up their eyes, and saw the ark, and rejoiced to see *it*.

14 And the cart came into the field of Joshua, a Beth-shemite, and stood there, where *there was* a great stone: and they *a*clave the wood of the cart, and offered the kine a burnt offering unto the LORD.

15 And the Levites took down the ark of the LORD, and the coffer that *was* with it, wherein the jewels of gold *were*, and put *them* on the great stone: and the men of Beth-shemesh offered burnt offerings and sacrificed sacrifices the same day unto the LORD.

16 And when the five lords of the Philistines had seen *it*, they returned to Ekron the same day.

17 And these *are* the golden emerods which the Philistines returned *for* a trespass offering unto the LORD; for Ashdod one, for Gaza one, for Askelon one, for Gath one, for Ekron one;

18 And the golden mice, *according*

---

6 2*a* Deut. 18:10.
　3*a* Lev. 5:16 (15–16).
　5*a* Josh. 7:19.
　6*a* TG Hardheartedness.

b Ex. 8:15.
7*a* OR milk cows.
8*a* OR basket, chest, trunk,
　　especially for valuables

(also vv. 11, 15).
11*a* 1 Sam. 5:6.
14*a* OR split, cut up.

to the number of all the cities of the Philistines *belonging* to the five lords, *both* of ^afenced cities, and of country villages, even unto the great *stone of* Abel, whereon they set down the ark of the LORD: *which stone remaineth* unto this day in the field of Joshua, the Beth-shemite.

19 ¶ And he ^asmote the men of Beth-shemesh, because they had ^blooked into the ark of the LORD, even he smote of the people fifty thousand and threescore and ten men: and the people lamented, because the LORD had smitten *many* of the people with a great slaughter.

20 And the men of Beth-shemesh said, Who is able to stand before this holy LORD God? and to whom shall he go up from us?

21 ¶ And they sent messengers to the inhabitants of Kirjath-jearim, saying, The Philistines have brought again the ^aark of the LORD; come ye down, *and* fetch it up to you.

CHAPTER 7

Samuel exhorts Israel to forsake Ashtaroth and Baalim and serve the Lord—Israel fasts and seeks the Lord—The Philistines are subdued—Samuel judges Israel.

AND the men of Kirjath-jearim came, and fetched up the ^aark of the LORD, and brought it into the house of Abinadab in the hill, and sanctified Eleazar his son to keep the ark of the LORD.

2 And it came to pass, while the ark abode in Kirjath-jearim, that the time was long; for it was twenty years: and all the house of Israel lamented after the LORD.

3 ¶ And Samuel spake unto all the house of Israel, saying, If ye do ^areturn unto the LORD with all your hearts, *then* ^bput away the strange ^cgods and ^dAshtaroth from among you, and prepare your ^ehearts unto the LORD, and ^fserve him only: and he will deliver you out of the hand of the Philistines.

4 Then the children of Israel did put away ^aBaalim and Ashtaroth, and served the LORD only.

5 And Samuel said, Gather all Israel to ^aMizpeh, and I will ^bpray for you unto the LORD.

6 And they gathered together to Mizpeh, and drew water, and poured *it* out before the LORD, and fasted on that day, and said there, We have ^asinned against the LORD. And Samuel judged the children of Israel in Mizpeh.

7 And when the Philistines heard that the children of Israel were gathered together to Mizpeh, the lords of the Philistines went up against Israel. And when the children of Israel heard *it,* they were afraid of the Philistines.

8 And the children of Israel said to Samuel, ^aCease not to cry unto the LORD our God for us, that he will save us out of the hand of the Philistines.

9 ¶ And Samuel took a sucking lamb, and offered *it for* a burnt offering wholly unto the LORD: and Samuel ^acried unto the LORD for Israel; and the LORD ^bheard him.

10 And as Samuel was offering up the burnt offering, the Philistines drew near to battle against Israel: but the LORD thundered with a great thunder on that day upon the Philistines, and ^adiscomfited them; and they were smitten before Israel.

18a OR fortified.
19a Num. 1:51;
  2 Sam. 6:7.
  b Ex. 19:21.
21a TG Ark of the Covenant.
7 1a TG Ark of the Covenant.
3a Deut. 30:2 (2–10);
  Hel. 13:11;
  3 Ne. 10:6 (5–7); 24:7;
  Moro. 9:22.
  b Judg. 10:16.

c TG Idolatry.
d IE the images of the fertility goddess.
e TG Heart.
f Deut. 6:13; 3 Ne. 13:24;
  D&C 4:2;
  59:10 (9–14); 76:5;
  Moses 1:15.
4a Judg. 2:13 (11–13).
5a Judg. 20:1.
  b Gen. 20:7; Num. 21:7;

Jer. 42:4; 2 Ne. 33:3;
  Enos 1:9, 11.
6a Judg. 10:10;
  1 Kgs. 8:47;
  D&C 95:3.
8a 2 Ne. 32:9;
  3 Ne. 20:1.
9a Alma 10:22.
  b HEB answered.
10a HEB caused them confusion.

11 And the men of Israel went out of Mizpeh, and pursued the Philistines, and smote them, until *they came* under Beth-car.

12 Then Samuel took a *a*stone, and set *it* between Mizpeh and Shen, and called the name of it *b*Ebenezer, saying, Hitherto hath the LORD helped us.

13 ¶ So the Philistines were *a*subdued, and they came no more into the coast of Israel: and the *b*hand of the LORD was against the Philistines all the days of Samuel.

14 And the cities which the Philistines had taken from Israel were restored to Israel, from Ekron even unto Gath; and the coasts thereof did Israel deliver out of the hands of the Philistines. And there was peace between Israel and the Amorites.

15 And Samuel judged Israel all the days of his life.

16 And he went from year to year in circuit to Beth-el, and Gilgal, and Mizpeh, and judged Israel in all those places.

17 And his return *was* to Ramah; for there *was* his house; and there he judged Israel; and there he built an altar unto the LORD.

CHAPTER 8

Samuel's sons take bribes and pervert judgment—The Israelites seek for a king to rule over them—Samuel rehearses the nature and evils of kingly rule— The Lord consents to give them a king.

AND it came to pass, when *a*Samuel was old, that he made his sons judges over Israel.

2 Now the name of his firstborn was Joel; and the name of his second, Abiah: *they were* judges in Beer-sheba.

3 And his sons walked not in his ways, but turned aside after lucre, and took *a*bribes, and perverted judgment.

4 Then all the elders of Israel gathered themselves together, and came to Samuel unto Ramah,

5 And said unto him, Behold, thou art old, and thy sons *a*walk not in thy ways: now make us a *b*king to judge us like all the nations.

6 ¶ But the thing displeased Samuel, when they said, Give us a king to judge us. And Samuel prayed unto the LORD.

7 And the LORD said unto Samuel, Hearken unto the *a*voice of the people in all that they say unto thee: for they have not rejected thee, but they have *b*rejected me, that I should not *c*reign over them.

8 According to all the works which they have done since the day that I brought them up out of Egypt even unto this day, wherewith they have forsaken me, and served other gods, so do they also unto thee.

9 Now therefore hearken unto their voice: howbeit yet *a*protest solemnly unto them, and shew them the manner of the *b*king that shall *c*reign over them.

10 ¶ And Samuel told all the words of the LORD unto the people that asked of him a king.

11 And he said, This will be the manner of the king that shall reign over you: He will take your sons, and appoint *them* for himself, for his chariots, and *to be* his horsemen; and *some* shall run before his chariots.

12 And he will appoint him captains over thousands, and captains over fifties; and *will set them* to *a*ear his ground, and to reap his harvest, and to make his instruments of war, and instruments of his chariots.

13 And he will take your daughters

12*a* Josh. 24:26.
  b IE The stone of help.
    1 Sam. 4:1; 5:1.
13*a* Alma 36:28.
  b 1 Sam. 5:9.
8 1*a* 1 Chr. 6:28.
  3*a* Ex. 18:21 (20–22);
    Hel. 9:20;
    Ether 9:11.

5*a* TG Walking in Darkness.
  b Hosea 13:10 (9–14);
    Mosiah 23:6 (6–14);
    29:16 (10–39);
    3 Ne. 6:30;
    D&C 38:21.
7*a* Mosiah 29:26;
    Alma 29:4;
    D&C 26:2.

  b Ex. 16:8;
    Hosea 13:11;
    D&C 38:21.
  c Hel. 12:6 (3–6).
    TG Governments.
9*a* Jacob 1:19; Moro. 9:6.
  b Mosiah 29:21 (21–23).
  c TG Tyranny.
12*a* OR cultivate.

to be ᵃconfectionaries, and to be cooks, and to be bakers.

14 And he will take your fields, and your vineyards, and your olive-yards, even the best of them, and give them to his servants.

15 And he will take the ᵃtenth of your seed, and of your vineyards, and give to his officers, and to his servants.

16 And he will take your menser-vants, and your maidservants, and your goodliest young men, and your asses, and put them to his work.

17 He will take the tenth of your sheep: and ye shall be his servants.

18 And ye shall cry out in that day because of your ᵃking which ye shall have ᵇchosen you; and the Lᴏʀᴅ will not ᶜhear you in that day.

19 ¶ Nevertheless the people re-fused to ᵃobey the voice of Samuel; and they said, Nay; but we will have a king over us;

20 That we also may be like all the ᵃnations; and that our king may judge us, and go out before us, and fight our battles.

21 And Samuel heard all the words of the people, and he rehearsed them in the ears of the Lᴏʀᴅ.

22 And the Lᴏʀᴅ said to Samuel, Hearken unto their voice, and make them a king. And Samuel said unto the men of Israel, Go ye every man unto his city.

CHAPTER 9

Saul, the son of Kish, a Benjamite, is a choice and goodly person—He is sent to seek his father's asses—The Lord reveals to Samuel the seer that Saul is to be king—Saul goes to Samuel and is entertained by him.

Now there was a man of Benjamin, whose name was ᵃKish, the son of Abiel, the son of Zeror, the son of Bechorath, the son of Aphiah, a Benjamite, a mighty man of power.

2 And he had a son, whose name was ᵃSaul, a choice young man, and a ᵇgoodly: and there was not among the children of Israel a goodlier per-son than he: from his shoulders and upward he was ᶜhigher than any of the people.

3 And the asses of Kish Saul's father were lost. And Kish said to Saul his son, Take now one of the servants with thee, and arise, go seek the asses.

4 And he passed through mount Ephraim, and passed through the land of Shalisha, but they found them not: then they passed through the land of Shalim, and there they were not: and he passed through the land of the Benjamites, but they found them not.

5 And when they were come to the land of Zuph, Saul said to his servant that was with him, Come, and let us return; lest my father leave caring for the asses, and take thought for us.

6 And he said unto him, Behold now, there is in this city a man of God, and he is an honourable man; all that he saith cometh surely to pass: now let us go thither; perad-venture he can shew us our way that we should go.

7 Then said Saul to his servant, But, behold, if we go, what shall we bring the man? for the bread is spent in our vessels, and there is not a ᵃpresent to bring to the man of God: what have we?

8 And the servant answered Saul again, and said, Behold, I have here at hand the fourth part of a shekel of silver: that will I give to the man of God, to tell us our way.

9 (Beforetime in Israel, when a man went to ᵃinquire of God, thus he

---

13a ᴏʀ perfumers, ointment makers.
15a 1 Kgs. 4:22 (22–23).
18a ᴛɢ Kings, Earthly.
 b ᴛɢ Agency.
 c Isa. 1:15;
  Ezek. 20:3;

Mosiah 21:15;
 D&C 101:7 (7–9).
19a ᴛɢ Disobedience.
20a D&C 1:16.
9 1a 1 Sam. 14:51;
  1 Chr. 8:33.
2a 1 Chr. 12:29.

 b ᴛɢ Talents.
 c 1 Sam. 10:23.
7a 2 Kgs. 4:42; 5:5.
9a 1 Ne. 15:3;
  Alma 27:7;
  D&C 6:11; 46:7; 102:23;
  JS—H 1:18 (18, 26).

spake, Come, and let us go to the *b*seer: for *he that is* now *called* a *c*Prophet was beforetime called a *d*Seer.)

10 Then said Saul to his servant, Well said; come, let us go. So they went unto the city where the man of God *was*.

11 ¶ *And* as they went up the hill to the city, they found young maidens going out to draw water, and said unto them, Is the seer here?

12 And they answered them, and said, He is; behold, *he is* *a*before you: make haste now, for he came to day to the city; for *there is* a sacrifice of the people to day in the high place:

13 As soon as ye be come into the city, ye shall straightway find him, before he go up to the high place to eat: for the people will not eat until he come, because he doth bless the sacrifice; *and* afterwards they eat that be bidden. Now therefore get you up; for about this time ye shall find him.

14 And they went up into the city: *and* when they were come into the city, behold, Samuel came out *a*against them, for to go up to the high place.

15 ¶ Now the *a*LORD had *b*told Samuel in his ear a day before Saul came, saying,

16 To morrow about this time I will send thee a man out of the land of Benjamin, and thou shalt *a*anoint him *to be* captain over my people Israel, that he may save my people out of the hand of the Philistines: for I have looked upon my people, because their *b*cry is come unto me.

17 And when Samuel saw Saul, the LORD said unto him, Behold the man whom I spake to thee of! this same shall reign over my people.

18 Then Saul drew near to Samuel in the gate, and said, Tell me, I pray thee, where the seer's house *is*.

19 And Samuel answered Saul, and said, I *am* the *a*seer: go up before me unto the high place; for ye shall eat with me to day, and to morrow I will let thee go, and will tell thee all that *is* in thine heart.

20 And as for thine asses that were lost three days ago, set not thy mind on them; for they are found. And on whom *is* all the desire of Israel? *Is it* not on thee, and on all thy father's house?

21 And Saul answered and said, *Am* not I a Benjamite, of the smallest of the tribes of Israel? and my family the *a*least of all the families of the tribe of Benjamin? wherefore then speakest thou *b*so to me?

22 And Samuel took Saul and his servant, and brought them into the *a*parlour, and made them sit in the chiefest place among them that were bidden, which *were* about thirty persons.

23 And Samuel said unto the cook, Bring the portion which I gave thee, of which I said unto thee, *a*Set it by thee.

24 And the cook took up the *a*shoulder, and *that* which *was* upon it, and set *it* before Saul. And *Samuel* said, Behold that which is left! set *it* before thee, *and* eat: for unto this time hath it been kept for thee since I said, I have invited the people. So Saul did eat with Samuel that day.

25 ¶ And when they were come down from the high place into the city, *Samuel* communed with Saul upon the *a*top of the house.

26 And they arose early: and it came to pass *a*about the spring of the day, that Samuel called Saul to the top of the house, saying, Up, that I may send thee away. And Saul arose, and they went out both of them, he and Samuel, abroad.

27 *And* as they were going down to

9*b* TG Priesthood, Authority.
  c TG Prophets, Mission of.
  d TG Seer.
12*a* IE just ahead.
14*a* OR towards them, to meet them.
15*a* 1 Sam. 3:19 (19–21).

b D&C 88:66.
16*a* TG Anointing; Called of God.
  b D&C 88:63 (63–65).
19*a* TG Seer.
21*a* Judg. 6:15.
  b HEB this way to me

according to this manner.
22*a* OR dining area.
23*a* OR Set it aside.
24*a* Ex. 29:22 (22, 27).
25*a* Acts 10:9 (9–35).
26*a* OR at dawn.

the end of the city, Samuel said to Saul, Bid the servant pass on before us, (and he passed on,) but ^astand thou still a while, that I may shew thee the word of God.

CHAPTER 10

Samuel anoints Saul to be captain over the Lord's inheritance—Samuel manifests the gift of seership—Saul prophesies among the prophets, and the Lord gives him a new heart—He is chosen king at Mizpeh.

THEN Samuel took a vial of oil, and poured *it* upon his head, and kissed him, and said, *Is it* not because the LORD hath ^aanointed thee *to be* captain over his inheritance?

2 When thou art departed from me to day, then thou shalt find two men by Rachel's sepulchre in the border of Benjamin at Zelzah; and they will say unto thee, The asses which thou wentest to seek are found: and, lo, thy father hath left the care of the asses, and sorroweth for you, saying, What shall I do for my son?

3 Then shalt thou go on forward from thence, and thou shalt come to the plain of Tabor, and there shall meet thee three men going up to God to Beth-el, one carrying three kids, and another carrying three loaves of bread, and another carrying a bottle of wine:

4 And they will ^asalute thee, and give thee two *loaves* of bread; which thou shalt receive of their hands.

5 After that thou shalt come to the hill of God, where *is* the garrison of the Philistines: and it shall come to pass, when thou art come thither to the city, that thou shalt meet a company of prophets coming down from the high place with a psaltery, and a tabret, and a ^apipe, and a harp, before them; and they shall prophesy:

6 And the Spirit of the LORD will come upon thee, and thou shalt ^aprophesy with them, and shalt be ^bturned into another man.

7 And let it be, when these signs are come unto thee, *that* thou do ^aas occasion serve thee; for God *is* with thee.

8 And thou shalt go down before me to Gilgal; and, behold, I will come down unto thee, to offer ^aburnt offerings, *and* to sacrifice sacrifices of peace offerings: seven days shalt thou tarry, till I come to thee, and shew thee what thou shalt do.

9 ¶ And it was *so,* that when he had turned his back to go from Samuel, God gave him another ^aheart: and all those signs came to pass that day.

10 And when they came thither to the hill, behold, a company of ^aprophets met him; and the ^bSpirit of God came upon him, and he prophesied among them.

11 And it came to pass, when all that knew him beforetime saw that, behold, he prophesied among the prophets, then the people said one to another, What *is* this *that* is come unto the son of Kish? *Is* Saul also among the prophets?

12 And one of the same place answered and said, But who *is* their father? Therefore it became a proverb, *Is* ^aSaul also among the prophets?

13 And when he had made an end of prophesying, he came to the high place.

14 ¶ And Saul's uncle said unto him and to his servant, Whither went ye? And he said, To seek the asses: and when we saw that *they were* no where, we came to Samuel.

15 And Saul's uncle said, Tell me, I pray thee, what Samuel said unto you.

16 And Saul said unto his uncle, He told us plainly that the asses

---

27*a* D&C 5:34.
10 1*a* 1 Kgs. 1:34.
  4*a* Judg. 18:15.
  5*a* 2 Kgs. 3:15.
  6*a* TG Holy Ghost, Gifts of.

b 2 Pet. 1:4.
7*a* IE whatever occasion demands.
8*a* 1 Sam. 13:9.
9*a* TG Man, New,

  Spiritually Reborn.
10*a* 1 Sam. 19:20.
  b TG Man, New,
  Spiritually Reborn.
12*a* 1 Sam. 19:24.

were found. But of the matter of the kingdom, whereof Samuel spake, he told him not.

17 ¶ And Samuel called the people together unto the LORD to Mizpeh;

18 And said unto the children of Israel, Thus saith the LORD God of Israel, I brought up Israel out of Egypt, and delivered you out of the hand of the Egyptians, and out of the hand of all kingdoms, *and* of them that oppressed you:

19 And ye have this day rejected your God, who himself saved you out of all your *a*adversities and your *b*tribulations; and ye have said unto him, *Nay,* but set a *c*king over us. Now therefore present yourselves before the LORD by your tribes, and by your thousands.

20 And when Samuel had caused all the tribes of Israel to come near, the tribe of Benjamin was taken.

21 When he had caused the tribe of Benjamin to come near by their families, the family of Matri was taken, and Saul the son of Kish was taken: and when they sought him, he could not be found.

22 Therefore they *a*inquired of the LORD further, if the man should yet come thither. And the LORD answered, Behold, he hath hid himself among the stuff.

23 And they ran and fetched him thence: and when he stood among the people, he was *a*higher than any of the people from his shoulders and upward.

24 And Samuel said to all the people, See ye him whom the LORD hath chosen, that *there is* none like him among all the people? And all the people shouted, and said, God save the king.

25 Then Samuel told the people the manner of the *a*kingdom, and *b*wrote *it* in a *c*book, and laid *it* up before the LORD. And Samuel sent all the people away, every man to his house.

26 ¶ And Saul also went home to Gibeah; and there went with him a band of men, whose hearts God had touched.

27 But the children of Belial said, How shall this man *a*save us? And they despised him, and brought him no presents. But he *b*held his peace.

CHAPTER 11

The Ammonites encamp against the Israelites of Jabesh-gilead—Saul rescues them and defeats the Ammonites—His kingship is renewed in Gilgal.

THEN Nahash the Ammonite came up, and encamped against Jabesh-gilead: and all the men of Jabesh said unto Nahash, Make a covenant with us, and we will serve thee.

2 And Nahash the Ammonite answered them, On this *condition* will I make *a covenant* with you, that I may thrust out all your right eyes, and lay it *for* a reproach upon all Israel.

3 And the elders of Jabesh said unto him, Give us seven days' respite, that we may send messengers unto all the coasts of Israel: and then, if *there be* no man to save us, we will come out to thee.

4 ¶ Then came the messengers to Gibeah of Saul, and told the tidings in the ears of the people: and all the people lifted up their voices, and wept.

5 And, behold, Saul came after the herd out of the field; and Saul said, What *aileth* the people that they weep? And they told him the tidings of the men of Jabesh.

6 And the Spirit of God came upon Saul when he heard those tidings, and his anger was kindled greatly.

7 And he took a yoke of oxen, and *a*hewed them in pieces, and *b*sent *them* throughout all the coasts of Israel by the hands of messengers, saying, Whosoever cometh not forth

---

19*a* TG Adversity.
  b TG Tribulation.
  c TG Kings, Earthly.
22*a* TG Prayer.
23*a* 1 Sam. 9:2.

25*a* TG Governments.
  b TG Scribe;
    Scriptures, Writing of.
  c TG Scriptures, Lost.
27*a* 1 Sam. 11:12 (8–15).

  b IE ignored them.
11 7*a* OR cut.
  b Judg. 19:29.

after Saul and after Samuel, so shall it be done unto his oxen. And the fear of the LORD fell on the people, and they came out with one consent.

8 And when he numbered them in Bezek, the children of Israel were three hundred thousand, and the men of Judah thirty thousand.

9 And they said unto the messengers that came, Thus shall ye say unto the men of Jabesh-gilead, To morrow, by *that time* the sun be hot, ye shall have help. And the messengers came and shewed *it* to the men of Jabesh; and they were glad.

10 Therefore the men of Jabesh said, To morrow we will come out unto you, and ye shall do with us all that seemeth good unto you.

11 And it was *so* on the morrow, that Saul put the people in three companies; and they came into the midst of the host in the morning watch, and slew the Ammonites until the heat of the day: and it came to pass, that they which remained were scattered, so that two of them were not left together.

12 ¶ And the people said unto Samuel, Who *is* he that said, Shall Saul ᵃreign over us? bring the men, that we may put them to death.

13 And Saul said, There shall not a man be put to death this day: for to day the LORD hath wrought salvation in Israel.

14 Then said Samuel to the people, Come, and let us go to Gilgal, and renew the kingdom there.

15 And all the people went to Gilgal; and there they made Saul king before the LORD in Gilgal; and there they sacrificed sacrifices of peace offerings before the LORD; and there Saul and all the men of Israel rejoiced greatly.

CHAPTER 12

Samuel testifies of his own just dealings in Israel—He reproves the people for their ingratitude—He exhorts them to keep the commandments lest the Lord consume them and their king.

AND Samuel said unto all Israel, Behold, I have hearkened unto your voice in all that ye said unto me, and have made a king over you.

2 And now, behold, the king walketh before you: and I am old and gray-headed; and, behold, my sons *are* with you: and I have ᵃwalked before you from my childhood unto this day.

3 Behold, here I *am:* witness against me before the LORD, and before his anointed: whose ox have I taken? or whose ass have I taken? or whom have I ᵃdefrauded? whom have I oppressed? or of whose hand have I received *any* ᵇbribe to blind mine eyes therewith? and I will restore it you.

4 And they said, Thou hast not defrauded us, nor oppressed us, neither hast thou taken ought of any man's hand.

5 And he said unto them, The LORD *is* witness against you, and his anointed *is* witness this day, that ye have not found ought in my hand. And they answered, He *is* witness.

6 ¶ And Samuel said unto the people, *It is* the LORD that ᵃadvanced Moses and Aaron, and that brought your fathers up out of the land of Egypt.

7 Now therefore stand still, that I may ᵃreason with you before the LORD of all the righteous acts of the LORD, which he did to you and to your fathers.

8 When Jacob was come into Egypt, and your fathers ᵃcried unto the LORD, then the LORD sent Moses and Aaron, which brought forth your fathers out of Egypt, and made them dwell in this place.

9 And when they forgat the LORD their God, he sold them into the hand of Sisera, captain of the host of Hazor, and into the hand of the Philistines, and into the hand of the king of Moab, and they fought against them.

12*a* 1 Sam. 10:27.
12 2*a* Mosiah 2:12 (9–41).
   3*a* TG Fraud.

b TG Bribe.
6*a* HEB made; i.e., established or appointed.

7*a* TG Teachable.
8*a* Ex. 2:23.

10 And they cried unto the Lord, and said, We have sinned, because we have forsaken the Lord, and have served Baalim and Ashtaroth: but now deliver us out of the hand of our enemies, and we will serve thee.

11 And the Lord sent ªJerubbaal, and Bedan, and ᵇJephthah, and Samuel, and delivered you out of the hand of your enemies on every side, and ye dwelled safe.

12 And when ye saw that Nahash the king of the children of Ammon came against you, ye said unto me, Nay; but a king shall reign over us: when the Lord your God *was* your ªking.

13 Now therefore behold the king whom ye have chosen, *and* whom ye have desired! and, behold, the Lord hath set a king over you.

14 If ye will fear the Lord, and serve him, and obey his voice, and not ªrebel against the commandment of the Lord, then shall both ye and also the king that reigneth over you continue following the Lord your God:

15 But if ye will not ªobey the voice of the Lord, but rebel against the commandment of the Lord, then shall the ᵇhand of the Lord be against you, as *it was* against your fathers.

16 ¶ Now therefore stand and see this great thing, which the Lord will do before your eyes.

17 *Is it* not wheat harvest to day? I will call unto the Lord, and he shall send thunder and rain; that ye may perceive and see that your wickedness *is* great, which ye have done in the sight of the Lord, in asking you a ªking.

18 So Samuel called unto the Lord; and the Lord sent thunder and rain that day: and all the people greatly feared the Lord and Samuel.

19 And all the people said unto Samuel, Pray for thy servants unto the Lord thy God, that we die not: for we have added unto all our sins *this* evil, to ask us a king.

20 ¶ And Samuel said unto the people, Fear not: ye have done all this wickedness: yet ªturn not aside from following the Lord, but serve the Lord with all your heart;

21 And turn ye not aside: for *then* should ye go after vain *things,* which cannot ªprofit nor deliver; for they *are* vain.

22 For the Lord will not forsake his people for his great ªname's sake: because it hath pleased the Lord to make you his people.

23 Moreover as for me, God forbid that I should sin against the Lord in ceasing to pray for you: but I will teach you the good and the right ªway:

24 Only ªfear the Lord, and ᵇserve him in truth with all your heart: for ᶜconsider how great *things* he hath done for you.

25 But if ye shall still do wickedly, ye shall be consumed, both ye and your king.

CHAPTER 13

Saul offers a burnt offering—The Lord rejects him and chooses another captain over His people.

Saul reigned one year; and when he had reigned two years over Israel,

2 Saul chose him three thousand *men* of Israel; *whereof* two thousand were with Saul in Michmash and in mount Beth-el, and a thousand were with Jonathan in Gibeah of Benjamin: and the rest of the people he sent every man to his tent.

3 And Jonathan smote the garrison of the Philistines that *was* in Geba, and the Philistines heard *of it.* And Saul blew the trumpet throughout

11a Judg. 6:32 (14, 32).
 b Judg. 11:1 (1–11).
12a Hosea 13:10 (4–11);
 D&C 38:21.
 TG Governments.
14a TG Rebellion.
15a TG Disobedience.
 b Mosiah 7:29.
17a TG Kings, Earthly.
20a Ex. 32:30.
21a Eccl. 1:3 (2–3);
 Matt. 16:26.
22a Ps. 23:3;
 1 Jn. 2:12;
 1 Ne. 20:9.
23a 1 Kgs. 8:36 (33–36);
 John 14:6.
24a TG Reverence.
 b TG Commitment.
 c Mosiah 2:20 (20–21).

all the land, saying, Let the Hebrews hear.

4 And all Israel heard say *that* Saul had smitten a garrison of the Philistines, and *that* Israel also was had in abomination with the Philistines. And the people were called together after Saul to Gilgal.

5 ¶ And the Philistines gathered themselves together to fight with Israel, thirty thousand chariots, and six thousand horsemen, and people as the sand which *is* on the sea shore in multitude: and they came up, and pitched in Michmash, eastward from Beth-aven.

6 When the men of Israel saw that they were in a strait, (for the people were distressed,) then the people did *a*hide themselves in *b*caves, and in thickets, and in rocks, and in high places, and in pits.

7 And *some of* the *a*Hebrews went over Jordan to the land of Gad and Gilead. As for Saul, he *was* yet in Gilgal, and all the people followed him trembling.

8 ¶ And he tarried seven days, according to the set time that Samuel *had appointed:* but Samuel came not to Gilgal; and the people were scattered from him.

9 And *a*Saul said, Bring hither a burnt offering to me, and peace offerings. And he *b*offered the *c*burnt offering.

10 And it came to pass, that as soon as he had made an end of offering the burnt offering, behold, Samuel came; and Saul went out to meet him, that he might *a*salute him.

11 ¶ And Samuel said, What hast thou done? And Saul said, Because I saw that the people were scattered from me, and *that* thou camest not within the days appointed, and *that* the Philistines gathered themselves together at Michmash;

12 Therefore said I, The Philistines will come down now upon me to Gilgal, and I have not made supplication unto the LORD: I *a*forced myself therefore, and offered a burnt offering.

13 And Samuel said to Saul, Thou hast done foolishly: thou hast not kept the commandment of the LORD thy God, which he commanded thee: for now would the LORD have established thy kingdom upon Israel for ever.

14 But now thy *a*kingdom shall not continue: the LORD hath *b*sought him a *c*man after his own *d*heart, and the LORD hath commanded him *to be* captain over his people, because thou hast not kept *that* which the LORD commanded thee.

15 And Samuel arose, and gat him up from Gilgal unto Gibeah of Benjamin. And Saul numbered the people *that were* present with him, about six hundred men.

16 And Saul, and Jonathan his son, and the people *that were* present with them, abode in Gibeah of Benjamin: but the Philistines encamped in Michmash.

17 ¶ And the spoilers came out of the camp of the Philistines in three companies: one company turned unto the way *that leadeth to* Ophrah, unto the land of Shual:

18 And another company turned the way *to* Beth-horon: and another company turned *to* the way of the border that looketh to the valley of Zeboim toward the wilderness.

19 ¶ Now there was no *a*smith found throughout all the land of Israel: for the Philistines said, Lest the Hebrews make *them* swords or spears:

20 But all the Israelites went down to the Philistines, to sharpen every man his *a*share, and his *b*coulter, and his axe, and his mattock.

---

13 6*a* 1 Sam. 14:11.
　　b 1 Sam. 14:22.
　　7*a* 1 Sam. 14:21.
　　9*a* TG Unrighteous
　　　　Dominion.
　　b TG Priesthood,
　　　　Authority.

　　c 1 Sam. 10:8.
　10*a* Judg. 18:15.
　12*a* TG Priesthood,
　　　　Qualifying for.
　14*a* 1 Sam. 15:28 (23–29).
　　b TG Called of God.
　　c 1 Chr. 10:14.

　　d TG Heart.
　19*a* 2 Kgs. 24:14.
　20*a* OR plowshare.
　　b IE a cutter on a plow to
　　　　cut the turf.

21 Yet they had a file for the *mattocks, and for the coulters, and for the forks, and for the axes, and to sharpen the goads.

22 So it came to pass in the day of battle, that there was neither sword nor spear found in the hand of any of the people that *were* with Saul and Jonathan: but with Saul and with Jonathan his son was there found.

23 And the garrison of the Philistines went out to the *passage of Michmash.

CHAPTER 14

Jonathan smites the garrison of the Philistines—Saul instructs the people to eat no food until evening—Unaware of the oath, Jonathan eats, and Saul decrees his death—He is rescued by the people —Saul vexes his enemies on every hand.

Now it came to pass upon a day, that Jonathan the son of Saul said unto the young man that bare his armour, Come, and let us go over to the Philistines' garrison, that *is* on the other side. But he told not his father.

2 And Saul tarried in the uttermost part of Gibeah under a pomegranate tree which *is* in Migron: and the people that *were* with him *were* about six hundred men;

3 And Ahiah, the son of Ahitub, I-chabod's brother, the son of Phinehas, the son of Eli, the LORD's priest in Shiloh, wearing an *ephod. And the people knew not that Jonathan was gone.

4 ¶ And between the *passages, by which Jonathan sought to go over unto the Philistines' garrison, *there was* a sharp rock on the one side, and a sharp rock on the other side: and the name of the one *was* Bozez, and the name of the other Seneh.

5 The forefront of the one *was* situate northward over against Michmash, and the other southward over against Gibeah.

6 And Jonathan said to the young man that bare his armour, Come, and let us go over unto the garrison of these uncircumcised: it may be that the LORD will work for us: for *there is* no *restraint to the LORD to save by many or by *few.

7 And his armourbearer said unto him, Do all that *is* in thine heart: *turn thee; behold, I *am* with thee according to thy heart.

8 Then said Jonathan, Behold, we will pass over unto *these* men, and we will discover ourselves unto them.

9 If they say thus unto us, Tarry until we come to you; then we will stand still in our place, and will not go up unto them.

10 But if they say thus, Come up unto us; then we will go up: for the LORD hath delivered them into our hand: and this *shall be* a sign unto us.

11 And both of them *discovered themselves unto the garrison of the Philistines: and the Philistines said, Behold, the Hebrews come forth out of the *holes where they had hid themselves.

12 And the men of the garrison answered Jonathan and his armourbearer, and said, Come up to us, and we will shew you a thing. And Jonathan said unto his armourbearer, Come up after me: for the LORD hath *delivered them into the hand of Israel.

13 And Jonathan climbed up upon his hands and upon his feet, and his armourbearer after him: and they fell before Jonathan; and his armourbearer slew after him.

14 And that first slaughter, which Jonathan and his armourbearer made, was about twenty men, within as it were an half acre of land, *which* a yoke *of oxen might plow.*

15 And there was trembling in the

21a ᴵᴱ an implement for digging and grubbing; a grubbing hoe.
23a 1 Sam. 14:4.
14 3a Ex. 28:4 (2–4);

1 Sam. 2:28; 22:18.
4a 1 Sam. 13:23.
6a ᵀᴳ God, Power of.
   b Judg. 7:4 (4–7).
7a ᴵᴱ turn thee to it.

11a ᴼᴿ showed, disclosed.
   b 1 Sam. 13:6.
12a 3 Ne. 3:21.

host, in the field, and among all the people: the garrison, and the spoilers, they also trembled, and the earth quaked: so it was a very great trembling.

16 And the watchmen of Saul in Gibeah of Benjamin looked; and, behold, the multitude melted away, and they went on beating down *one another*.

17 Then said Saul unto the people that *were* with him, Number now, and see who is gone from us. And when they had numbered, behold, Jonathan and his armourbearer *were* not *there*.

18 And Saul said unto Ahiah, Bring hither the ark of God. For the *ᵃ*ark of God was at that time with the children of Israel.

19 ¶ And it came to pass, while Saul talked unto the priest, that the noise that *was* in the host of the Philistines went on and increased: and Saul said unto the priest, Withdraw thine hand.

20 And Saul and all the people that *were* with him assembled themselves, and they came to the battle: and, behold, every man's sword was against his *ᵃ*fellow, *and there was* a very great *ᵇ*discomfiture.

21 Moreover the *ᵃ*Hebrews *that* were with the Philistines before that time, which went up with them into the camp *from the country* round about, even they also *turned* to be with the Israelites that *were* with Saul and Jonathan.

22 Likewise all the men of Israel which had *ᵃ*hid themselves in mount Ephraim, *when* they heard that the Philistines fled, even they also followed hard after them in the battle.

23 So the LORD saved Israel that day: and the battle passed over unto Beth-aven.

24 ¶ And the men of Israel were distressed that day: for Saul had adjured the people, saying, Cursed *be* the man that eateth *any* food until

evening, that I may be avenged on mine enemies. So none of the people tasted *any* food.

25 And all *they of* the land came to a wood; and there was honey upon the ground.

26 And when the people were come into the wood, behold, the honey dropped; but no man put his hand to his mouth: for the people feared the oath.

27 But Jonathan heard not when his father charged the people with the oath: wherefore he put forth the end of the rod that *was* in his hand, and dipped it in an honeycomb, and put his hand to his mouth; and his eyes were *ᵃ*enlightened.

28 Then answered one of the people, and said, Thy father *ᵃ*straitly charged the people with an oath, saying, Cursed *be* the man that eateth *any* food this day. And the people were faint.

29 Then said Jonathan, My father hath troubled the land: see, I pray you, how mine eyes have been enlightened, because I tasted a little of this honey.

30 How much more, if *ᵃ*haply the people had eaten freely to day of the spoil of their enemies which they found? for had there not been now a much greater slaughter among the Philistines?

31 And they smote the Philistines that day from Michmash to Aijalon: and the people were very faint.

32 And the people flew upon the spoil, and took sheep, and oxen, and calves, and slew *them* on the ground: and the people did eat *them* with the blood.

33 ¶ Then they told Saul, saying, Behold, the people sin against the LORD, in that they eat with the blood. And he said, Ye have transgressed: roll a great stone unto me this day.

34 And Saul said, Disperse yourselves among the people, and say

---

18*a* Ex. 25:10 (10–16).
20*a* Judg. 7:22;
    2 Chr. 20:23.
   b OR panic, confusion.

21*a* 1 Sam. 13:7.
22*a* 1 Sam. 13:6.
27*a* IE refreshed from being
    tired.

28*a* OR strictly.
30*a* IE perchance.

unto them, Bring me hither every man his ox, and every man his sheep, and slay *them* here, and eat; and sin not against the Lord in eating with the ^ablood. And all the people brought every man his ox with him that night, and slew *them* there.

35 And Saul built an altar unto the Lord: the same was the first altar that he built unto the Lord.

36 ¶ And Saul said, Let us go down after the Philistines by night, and spoil them until the morning light, and let us not leave a man of them. And they said, Do whatsoever seemeth good unto thee. Then said the priest, Let us draw near hither unto God.

37 And Saul asked counsel of God, Shall I go down after the Philistines? wilt thou deliver them into the hand of Israel? But he ^aanswered him not that day.

38 And Saul said, Draw ye near hither, all the chief of the people: and know and see wherein this sin hath been this day.

39 For, *as* the Lord liveth, which saveth Israel, though it be in Jonathan my son, he shall surely die. But *there was* not a man among all the people *that* answered him.

40 Then said he unto all Israel, Be ye on one side, and I and Jonathan my son will be on the other side. And the people said unto Saul, Do what seemeth good unto thee.

41 Therefore Saul said unto the Lord God of Israel, ^aGive a perfect *lot*. And Saul and Jonathan were taken: but the people escaped.

42 And Saul said, Cast *lots* between me and Jonathan my son. And Jonathan was taken.

43 Then Saul said to Jonathan, Tell me what thou hast done. And Jonathan told him, and said, I did but taste a little honey with the end of the rod that *was* in mine hand, *and,* lo, I must die.

44 And Saul answered, God do so and more also: for thou shalt surely die, Jonathan.

45 And the ^apeople said unto Saul, Shall Jonathan die, who hath wrought this great salvation in Israel? God forbid: *as* the Lord liveth, there shall not one hair of his head fall to the ground; for he hath wrought with God this day. So the people rescued Jonathan, that he died not.

46 Then Saul went up from following the Philistines: and the Philistines went to their own place.

47 ¶ So Saul took the kingdom over Israel, and fought against all his enemies on every side, against Moab, and against the children of Ammon, and against Edom, and against the kings of Zobah, and against the Philistines: and whithersoever he turned himself, he vexed *them.*

48 And he gathered an host, and smote the Amalekites, and delivered Israel out of the hands of them that spoiled them.

49 Now the sons of ^aSaul were Jonathan, and Ishui, and Melchishua: and the names of his two daughters *were these;* the name of the firstborn ^bMerab, and the name of the younger ^cMichal:

50 And the name of Saul's wife *was* ^aAhinoam, the daughter of Ahimaaz: and the name of the captain of his host *was* ^bAbner, the son of Ner, Saul's uncle.

51 And ^aKish *was* the father of Saul; and Ner the father of Abner *was* the son of Abiel.

52 And there was ^asore war against the Philistines all the days of Saul: and when Saul saw any strong man, or any valiant man, he took him unto him.

34*a* TG Blood, Eating of.
37*a* 1 Sam. 28:6.
41*a* IE Bring forth right.
45*a* TG Common Consent.
49*a* 1 Chr. 8:33.

b 1 Sam. 18:17 (17–19).
c 1 Sam. 18:27 (20–27);
   2 Sam. 3:14 (13–16);
   6:20 (20–23).
50*a* 2 Sam. 3:2.

b 2 Sam. 2:8.
51*a* 1 Sam. 9:1.
52*a* HEB strong or intense.

CHAPTER 15

Saul is commanded to smite and destroy the Amalekites and all that they have—He saves some animals to sacrifice—Saul is rejected as king and told that to obey is better than sacrifice—Samuel destroys Agag.

SAMUEL also said unto Saul, The LORD sent me to *a*anoint thee *to be* king over his people, over Israel: now therefore hearken thou unto the voice of the words of the LORD.

2 Thus saith the LORD of hosts, I remember *that* which *a*Amalek did to Israel, how he laid *wait* for him in the way, when he came up from Egypt.

3 Now go and smite Amalek, and utterly *a*destroy all that they have, and spare them not; but slay both man and woman, infant and suckling, ox and sheep, camel and ass.

4 And Saul gathered the people together, and numbered them in Telaim, two hundred thousand footmen, and ten thousand men of Judah.

5 And Saul came to a city of Amalek, and laid wait in the valley.

6 ¶ And Saul said unto the *a*Kenites, Go, depart, get you down from among the Amalekites, lest I destroy you with them: for ye shewed kindness to all the children of Israel, when they came up out of Egypt. So the Kenites departed from among the Amalekites.

7 And Saul smote the Amalekites from Havilah *until* thou comest to *a*Shur, that *is* over against Egypt.

8 And he took *a*Agag the king of the Amalekites alive, and utterly destroyed all the people with the edge of the sword.

9 But Saul and the people spared Agag, and the best of the sheep, and of the oxen, and of the fatlings, and the lambs, and all *that was* good, and would not utterly destroy them:

but every thing *that was* vile and refuse, that they destroyed utterly.

10 ¶ Then came the word of the LORD unto Samuel, saying,

11 *a*It *b*repenteth me that I have set up Saul *to be* king: for he is turned back from following me, and hath not performed my commandments. And it grieved Samuel; and he cried unto the LORD all night.

12 And when Samuel rose early to meet Saul in the morning, it was told Samuel, saying, Saul came to Carmel, and, behold, he set him up a place, and is gone about, and passed on, and gone down to Gilgal.

13 And Samuel came to Saul: and Saul said unto him, Blessed *be* thou of the LORD: I have performed the commandment of the LORD.

14 And Samuel said, What *meaneth* then this bleating of the sheep in mine ears, and the lowing of the oxen which I hear?

15 And Saul said, They have brought them from the Amalekites: for the people spared the best of the sheep and of the oxen, to sacrifice unto the LORD thy God; and the rest we have utterly destroyed.

16 Then Samuel said unto Saul, Stay, and I will tell thee what the LORD hath said to me this night. And he said unto him, Say on.

17 And Samuel said, When thou *wast* little in thine own sight, *wast* thou not *made* the head of the tribes of Israel, and the LORD *a*anointed thee king over Israel?

18 And the LORD sent thee on a journey, and said, Go and utterly destroy the sinners the Amalekites, and fight against them until they be consumed.

19 Wherefore then didst thou not obey the voice of the LORD, but didst fly upon the spoil, and didst evil in the sight of the LORD?

20 And Saul said unto Samuel, Yea,

---

15 1*a* TG Anointing.
 2*a* Ex. 17:8 (8–16).
 3*a* Deut. 2:34.
 6*a* Judg. 1:16.
 7*a* Gen. 25:18.
 8*a* Esth. 3:1.

11*a* JST 1 Sam. 15:11 I have set up Saul to be *a* king, *and he repenteth not that he hath sinned,* for he is . . .
 b The Hebrew root means

"to sigh," therefore "to feel sorrow."
 Gen. 6:6;
 2 Sam. 24:16;
 Joel 2:13.
17*a* TG Called of God.

I have obeyed the voice of the LORD, and have gone the way which the LORD sent me, and have brought Agag the king of Amalek, and have utterly destroyed the Amalekites.

21 But the people took of the spoil, sheep and oxen, the chief of the things which should have been utterly destroyed, to sacrifice unto the LORD thy God in Gilgal.

22 And Samuel said, Hath the LORD *as great* ᵃdelight in burnt offerings and sacrifices, as in obeying the ᵇvoice of the LORD? Behold, to ᶜobey *is* better than ᵈsacrifice, *and* to hearken than the fat of ᵉrams.

23 For ᵃrebellion *is as* the sin of witchcraft, and ᵇstubbornness *is as* iniquity and idolatry. Because thou hast ᶜrejected the word of the LORD, he hath also ᵈrejected thee from *being* king.

24 ¶ And Saul said unto Samuel, I have ᵃsinned: for I have ᵇtransgressed the commandment of the LORD, and thy words: because I ᶜfeared the people, and obeyed their voice.

25 Now therefore, I pray thee, pardon my sin, and turn again with me, that I may worship the LORD.

26 And Samuel said unto Saul, I will not return with thee: for thou hast rejected the word of the LORD, and the LORD hath rejected thee from being king over Israel.

27 And as Samuel turned about to go away, he laid hold upon the skirt of his mantle, and it ᵃrent.

28 And Samuel said unto him, The LORD hath rent the ᵃkingdom of Israel from thee this day, and hath ᵇgiven it to a ᶜneighbour of thine, *that is* better than thou.

29 And also ᵃthe Strength of Israel will not lie nor repent: for he *is* not a man, that he should repent.

30 Then he said, I have sinned: *yet* honour me now, I pray thee, before the elders of my people, and before Israel, and turn again with me, that I may worship the LORD thy God.

31 So Samuel turned again after Saul; and Saul worshipped the LORD.

32 ¶ Then said Samuel, Bring ye hither to me Agag the king of the Amalekites. And Agag came unto him delicately. And Agag said, Surely the bitterness of death is past.

33 And Samuel said, As thy sword hath made women childless, so shall thy mother be childless among women. And Samuel hewed Agag in pieces before the LORD in Gilgal.

34 ¶ Then Samuel went to Ramah; and Saul went up to his house to Gibeah of Saul.

35 And Samuel came no more to see Saul until the day of his death: nevertheless Samuel mourned for Saul: and ᵃthe LORD repented that he had made Saul king over Israel.

CHAPTER 16

The Lord chooses David of Bethlehem as king—He is anointed by Samuel—Saul chooses David as his companion and armor bearer.

AND the LORD said unto Samuel, How long wilt thou mourn for Saul, seeing I have rejected him from reigning over Israel? fill thine horn with oil, and go, I will send thee to ᵃJesse the ᵇBeth-lehemite: for I have provided me a ᶜking among his sons.

2 And Samuel said, How can I go? if Saul hear *it,* he will kill me. And the LORD said, Take an heifer with thee, and say, I am come to sacrifice to the LORD.

22a Ps. 40:6 (6–8);
   69:31 (30–31); Isa. 1:11.
 b TG God, Will of.
 c TG Duty; Obedience.
 d Ps. 51:16; Prov. 21:3;
   Heb. 10:6 (4–6).
   TG Sacrifice.
 e Micah 6:7.
23a TG Rebellion.
 b TG Stubbornness.

 c TG Disobedience.
 d Hosea 13:11 (9–14).
24a TG Confession.
 b 2 Sam. 12:13 (9–14).
 c TG Peer Influence.
27a OR was torn.
28a 1 Sam. 28:17 (17–18).
 b 1 Sam. 13:14 (13–14).
 c 2 Sam. 3:9.
29a IE the Lord.

35a JST 1 Sam. 15:35 . . . the
   Lord *rent the kingdom
   from Saul whom he had
   made king over Israel.*
16 1a TG Jesus Christ,
   Davidic Descent of.
 b Micah 5:2; Luke 2:4;
   John 7:42 (41–44).
 c 1 Kgs. 8:16;
   1 Chr. 11:3; 28:4.

3 And call Jesse to the sacrifice, and I will shew thee what thou shalt do: and thou shalt ^aanoint unto me *him* whom I name unto thee.

4 And Samuel did that which the LORD spake, and came to Beth-lehem. And the elders of the town trembled at his coming, and said, Comest thou peaceably?

5 And he said, Peaceably: I am come to sacrifice unto the LORD: ^asanctify yourselves, and come with me to the sacrifice. And he sanctified Jesse and his sons, and called them to the sacrifice.

6 ¶ And it came to pass, when they were come, that he looked on ^aEliab, and said, Surely the LORD's anointed *is* before him.

7 But the LORD said unto Samuel, Look not on his countenance, or on the height of his stature; because I have refused him: for *the LORD* ^a*seeth* not as ^bman seeth; for man looketh on the outward ^cappearance, but the ^dLORD looketh on the ^eheart.

8 Then Jesse called Abinadab, and made him pass before Samuel. And he said, Neither hath the LORD chosen this.

9 Then Jesse made Shammah to pass by. And he said, Neither hath the LORD chosen this.

10 Again, Jesse made seven of his sons to pass before Samuel. And Samuel said unto Jesse, The LORD hath not chosen these.

11 And Samuel said unto Jesse, Are here all *thy* children? And he said, There remaineth yet the youngest, and, behold, he keepeth the sheep. And Samuel said unto Jesse, Send and fetch him: for we will not sit down till he come hither.

12 And he sent, and brought him in. Now he *was* ruddy, *and* withal of a ^abeautiful countenance, and goodly to look to. And the LORD said, Arise, anoint him: for this *is* he.

13 Then Samuel took the horn of oil, and ^aanointed him in the midst of his brethren: and the ^bSpirit of the LORD came upon ^cDavid from that day forward. So Samuel rose up, and went to Ramah.

14 ¶ But the ^aSpirit of the LORD ^bdeparted from Saul, and an evil spirit ^cfrom the LORD troubled him.

15 And Saul's servants said unto him, Behold now, an evil spirit ^afrom God troubleth thee.

16 Let our lord now command thy servants, *which are* before thee, to seek out a man, *who is* a cunning player on an harp: and it shall come to pass, when the evil spirit ^afrom God is upon thee, that he shall play with his hand, and thou shalt be well.

17 And Saul said unto his servants, Provide me now a man that can play well, and bring *him* to me.

18 Then answered one of the servants, and said, Behold, I have seen a son of Jesse the Beth-lehemite, *that is* cunning in playing, and a mighty valiant man, and a man of war, and ^aprudent in matters, and a comely person, and the LORD *is* with him.

19 ¶ Wherefore Saul sent messengers unto Jesse, and said, Send me David thy son, which *is* with the sheep.

20 And Jesse took an ass *laden* with bread, and a bottle of wine, and a kid, and sent *them* by David his son unto Saul.

21 And David came to Saul, and stood before him: and he loved him greatly; and he became his armourbearer.

3*a* TG Called of God.
5*a* Ex. 19:10.
6*a* 1 Sam. 17:13;
   1 Chr. 2:13;
   2 Chr. 11:18.
7*a* Job 10:4.
  b Isa. 55:8 (8–9).
  c 2 Cor. 10:7.
  TG Discernment,
  Spiritual.

d TG God, Omniscience of.
  e TG Heart; Judgment.
12*a* TG Beauty.
13*a* Ps. 89:20.
  b TG Holy Ghost, Gift of;
  Holy Ghost, Mission of.
  c 1 Sam. 17:12;
  1 Chr. 2:15;
  Ps. 78:70.
14*a* TG Holy Ghost, Loss of.

b 1 Sam. 28:15 (15–16);
  Hosea 9:12.
c JST 1 Sam. 16:14 . . .
  which was not of the
  Lord . . .
15*a* JST 1 Sam. 16:15 . . .
  which is not of God . . .
16*a* JST 1 Sam. 16:16 . . .
  which is not of God . . .
18*a* TG Prudence.

22 And Saul sent to Jesse, saying, Let David, I pray thee, stand before me; for he hath found favour in my sight.

23 And it came to pass, when the ᵃevil spirit ᵇfrom God was upon Saul, that David took an harp, and played with his hand: so Saul was refreshed, and was well, and the evil spirit departed from him.

CHAPTER 17

Israel and the Philistines engage in war—Goliath of Gath, a giant, defies Israel and challenges any Israelite to personal combat—David goes against him in the name of the Lord—David slays Goliath with a sling and a stone—Israel defeats the Philistines.

Now the Philistines gathered together their armies to battle, and were gathered together at Shochoh, which *belongeth* to Judah, and pitched between Shochoh and Azekah, in Ephes-dammim.

2 And Saul and the men of Israel were gathered together, and pitched by the valley of Elah, and set the battle in array against the Philistines.

3 And the Philistines stood on a mountain on the one side, and Israel stood on a mountain on the other side: and *there was* a valley between them.

4 ¶ And there went out a champion out of the camp of the Philistines, named Goliath, of ᵃGath, whose height *was* six ᵇcubits and a span.

5 And *he had* an helmet of brass upon his head, and he *was* armed with a coat of mail; and the weight of the coat *was* five thousand shekels of brass.

6 And *he had* ᵃgreaves of brass upon his legs, and ᵇa target of brass between his shoulders.

7 And the ᵃstaff of his spear *was* like a weaver's beam; and his spear's head *weighed* six hundred shekels of iron: and one bearing a shield went before him.

8 And he stood and cried unto the armies of Israel, and said unto them, Why are ye come out to set *your* battle in array? *am* not I a Philistine, and ye servants to Saul? choose you a man for you, and let him come down to me.

9 If he be able to fight with me, and to kill me, then will we be your servants: but if I prevail against him, and kill him, then shall ye be our servants, and serve us.

10 And the Philistine said, I defy the armies of Israel this day; give me a man, that we may fight together.

11 When Saul and all Israel heard those words of the Philistine, they were dismayed, and greatly afraid.

12 ¶ Now ᵃDavid *was* the son of that Ephrathite of Beth-lehem-judah, whose name *was* Jesse; and he had eight sons: and the man went among men *for* an old man in the days of Saul.

13 And the three eldest sons of Jesse went *and* followed Saul to the battle: and the names of his three sons that went to the battle *were* ᵃEliab the firstborn, and next unto him Abinadab, and the third Shammah.

14 And David *was* the youngest: and the three eldest followed Saul.

15 But David went and returned from Saul to feed his father's sheep at Beth-lehem.

16 And the Philistine drew near morning and evening, and presented himself forty days.

17 And Jesse said unto David his son, Take now for thy brethren an ephah of this parched *corn*, and these ten loaves, and run to the camp to thy brethren;

23a TG Spirits, Evil or
    Unclean.
  b JST 1 Sam. 16:23 . . .
    which was not of God . . .
17 4a Josh. 11:22;
    1 Sam. 5:8;
    2 Sam. 21:20;

1 Chr. 18:1;
    Micah 1:10.
  b Deut. 3:11.
 6a IE shin armor.
  b IE armor protecting the
    neck (Targum).
 7a 2 Sam. 21:19.

12a 1 Sam. 16:13 (11–13);
    1 Chr. 2:15.
    TG Jesus Christ, Davidic
    Descent of.
13a 1 Sam. 16:6;
    1 Chr. 2:13.

18 And carry these ten cheeses unto the captain of *their* thousand, and look how thy brethren fare, and take their pledge.

19 Now Saul, and they, and all the men of Israel, *were* in the valley of Elah, fighting with the Philistines.

20 ¶ And David rose up early in the morning, and left the sheep with a keeper, and took, and went, as Jesse had commanded him; and he came to the trench, as the host was going forth to the fight, and shouted for the battle.

21 For Israel and the Philistines had put the battle in array, army against army.

22 And David left his *a*carriage in the hand of the keeper of the carriage, and ran into the army, and came and saluted his brethren.

23 And as he talked with them, behold, there came up the champion, the Philistine of Gath, Goliath by name, out of the armies of the Philistines, and spake according to the same words: and David heard *them.*

24 And all the men of Israel, when they saw the man, fled from him, and were sore afraid.

25 And the men of Israel said, Have ye seen this man that is come up? surely to defy Israel is he come up: and it shall be, *that* the man who killeth him, the king will enrich him with great riches, and will give him his daughter, and make his father's house free in Israel.

26 And David spake to the men that stood by him, saying, What shall be done to the man that killeth this Philistine, and taketh away the reproach from Israel? for who *is* this uncircumcised Philistine, that he should defy the armies of the *a*living God?

27 And the people answered him after this manner, saying, So shall it be done to the man that killeth him.

28 ¶ And Eliab his eldest brother heard when he spake unto the men; and Eliab's anger was kindled against David, and he said, Why camest thou down hither? and with whom hast thou left those few sheep in the wilderness? I know thy pride, and the naughtiness of thine heart; for thou art come down that thou mightest see the battle.

29 And David said, What have I now done? *Is there* not a cause?

30 ¶ And he turned from him toward another, and spake after the same manner: and the people answered him again after the former manner.

31 And when the words were heard which David spake, they rehearsed *them* before Saul: and he sent for him.

32 ¶ And David said to Saul, Let no man's heart fail because of him; thy servant *a*will go and *b*fight with this Philistine.

33 And Saul said to David, Thou art not able to go against this Philistine to fight with him: for thou *art but* a *a*youth, and he a man of war from his youth.

34 And David said unto Saul, Thy servant kept his father's sheep, and there came a lion, and a bear, and took a lamb out of the flock:

35 And I went out after him, and smote him, and delivered *it* out of his mouth: and when he arose against me, I caught *him* by his beard, and smote him, and slew him.

36 Thy servant slew both the lion and the bear: and this uncircumcised Philistine shall be as one of them, seeing he hath defied the armies of the living God.

37 David said moreover, The LORD that *a*delivered me out of the paw of the lion, and out of the paw of the bear, he will *b*deliver me out of the hand of this Philistine. And Saul said unto David, Go, and the LORD be with thee.

38 ¶ And Saul armed David with his armour, and he put an helmet of

---

22a OR baggage.
26a Alma 5:13;
　　Morm. 9:28;
　　D&C 14:9.

32a 1 Ne. 3:7;
　　D&C 124:90.
　b TG Courage.
33a 1 Chr. 29:1;

JS—H 1:22 (21–25).
37a TG Deliver.
　b TG God, Power of.

brass upon his head; also he armed him with a coat of mail.

39 And David girded his sword upon his armour, and he assayed to go; for he had not proved *it*. And David said unto Saul, I cannot go with these; for I have not proved *them*. And David put them off him.

40 And he took his staff in his hand, and chose him five smooth stones out of the brook, and put them in a shepherd's bag which he had, even in a scrip; and his sling *was* in his hand: and he drew near to the Philistine.

41 And the Philistine came on and drew near unto David; and the man that bare the shield *went* before him.

42 And when the Philistine looked about, and saw David, he disdained him: for he was *but* a youth, and ruddy, and of a fair countenance.

43 And the Philistine said unto David, *Am* I a ªdog, that thou comest to me with staves? And the Philistine cursed David by his gods.

44 And the Philistine said to David, Come to me, and I will give thy flesh unto the fowls of the air, and to the beasts of the field.

45 Then said David to the Philistine, Thou comest to me with a sword, and with a spear, and with a shield: but I come to thee in the ªname of the LORD of hosts, the God of the armies of Israel, whom thou hast defied.

46 This day will the LORD ªdeliver thee into mine hand; and I will smite thee, and take thine head from thee; and I will give the carcases of the host of the Philistines this day unto the fowls of the air, and to the wild beasts of the earth; that all the earth may ᵇknow that there is a God in Israel.

47 And all this assembly shall know that the LORD saveth not with sword and spear: for the ªbattle *is* the LORD's, and he will give you into our hands.

48 And it came to pass, when the Philistine arose, and came and drew nigh to meet David, that David hasted, and ran toward the army to meet the Philistine.

49 And David put his hand in his bag, and took thence a stone, and slang *it,* and smote the Philistine in his forehead, that the stone sunk into his forehead; and he fell upon his face to the earth.

50 So David prevailed over the Philistine with a sling and with a stone, and smote the Philistine, and slew him; but *there was* no sword in the hand of David.

51 Therefore David ran, and stood upon the Philistine, and took his sword, and drew it out of the sheath thereof, and slew him, and cut off his head therewith. And when the Philistines saw their champion was dead, they fled.

52 And the men of Israel and of Judah arose, and shouted, and pursued the Philistines, until thou come to the valley, and to the gates of Ekron. And the wounded of the Philistines fell down by the way to Shaaraim, even unto Gath, and unto Ekron.

53 And the children of Israel returned from chasing after the Philistines, and they spoiled their tents.

54 And David took the head of the Philistine, and brought it to Jerusalem; but he put his armour in his tent.

55 ¶ And when Saul saw David go forth against the Philistine, he said unto Abner, the captain of the host, ªAbner, whose son *is* this youth? And Abner said, *As* thy soul liveth, O king, I cannot tell.

56 And the king said, Inquire thou whose son the ªstripling *is*.

57 And as David returned from the slaughter of the Philistine, Abner took him, and brought him before Saul with the head of the Philistine in his hand.

43a 2 Sam. 3:8.
45a TG Name; Testimony.
46a TG God, Power of.

b D&C 20:17.
47a 2 Chr. 20:15;
        D&C 105:14.

55a 2 Sam. 2:8.
56a HEB young man.
        1 Sam. 16:22.

58 And Saul said to him, Whose son *art* thou, *thou* young man? And David answered, *I am* the son of thy servant Jesse the Beth-lehemite.

CHAPTER 18

Jonathan loves David—Saul sets David over his armies—David is honored by the people, and Saul becomes jealous—David marries Michal, a daughter of Saul.

AND it came to pass, when he had made an end of speaking unto Saul, that the soul of Jonathan was *a*knit with the soul of David, and Jonathan loved him as his own soul.

2 And Saul took him that day, and would let him go no more home to his father's house.

3 Then Jonathan and David made a *a*covenant, because he loved him as his own soul.

4 And Jonathan stripped himself of the robe that *was* upon him, and gave it to David, and his garments, even to his sword, and to his bow, and to his girdle.

5 ¶ And David went out whithersoever Saul sent him, *and* behaved himself wisely: and Saul set him over the men of war, and he was accepted in the sight of all the people, and also in the sight of Saul's servants.

6 And it came to pass as they came, when David was returned from the slaughter of the Philistine, that the *a*women came out of all cities of Israel, singing and dancing, to meet king Saul, with tabrets, with joy, and with *b*instruments of musick.

7 And the women answered *one another* as they played, and said, *a*Saul hath slain his thousands, and David his ten thousands.

8 And Saul was very wroth, and the saying displeased him; and he said, They have ascribed unto David ten thousands, and to me they have ascribed *but* thousands: and *what* can he have more but the kingdom?

9 And Saul eyed David from that day and forward.

10 ¶ And it came to pass on the morrow, that the evil spirit *a*from God came upon Saul, and he prophesied in the midst of the house: and David played with his hand, as at other times: and *there was* a javelin in Saul's hand.

11 And Saul cast the javelin; for he said, I will smite David even to the wall *with it.* And David avoided out of his presence twice.

12 ¶ And Saul was afraid of David, because the LORD was with him, and was *a*departed from Saul.

13 Therefore Saul removed him from him, and made him his captain over a thousand; and he went out and came in before the people.

14 And David behaved himself wisely in all his ways; and the LORD *was* with him.

15 Wherefore when Saul saw that he behaved himself very wisely, he was afraid of him.

16 But all Israel and *a*Judah loved David, because he went out and came in before them.

17 ¶ And Saul said to David, Behold my elder daughter *a*Merab, her will I give thee to wife: only be thou valiant for me, and fight the LORD's battles. For Saul said, Let not mine hand be upon him, but let the hand of the Philistines be upon him.

18 And David said unto Saul, Who *am* I? and what *is* my life, *or* my father's family in Israel, that I should be son in law to the king?

19 But it came to pass at the time when Merab Saul's daughter should have been given to David, that she was given unto Adriel the Meholathite to wife.

20 And Michal Saul's daughter loved David: and they told Saul, and the thing pleased him.

---

18 1*a* Gen. 44:30;
    1 Sam. 20:4 (4, 41);
    Mosiah 4:15; 18:21;
    D&C 88:123.
    TG Friendship.

3*a* 2 Sam. 9:1.
6*a* Judg. 11:34.
  b Ex. 15:20 (20–21).
7*a* 1 Sam. 29:5.
10*a* JST 1 Sam. 18:10 . . .

which was not of God . . .
12*a* D&C 121:37.
16*a* 2 Sam. 2:4.
17*a* 1 Sam. 14:49.

21 And Saul said, I will give him her, that she may be a snare to him, and that the hand of the Philistines may be against him. Wherefore Saul said to David, Thou shalt this day be my son in law *a*in *the one of* the twain.

22 ¶ And Saul commanded his servants, *saying,* Commune with David secretly, and say, Behold, the king hath delight in thee, and all his servants love thee: now therefore be the king's son in law.

23 And Saul's servants spake those words in the ears of David. And David said, Seemeth it to you a *a*light *thing* to be a king's son in law, seeing that I *am* a poor man, and lightly esteemed?

24 And the servants of Saul told him, saying, On this manner spake David.

25 And Saul said, Thus shall ye say to David, The king desireth not any dowry, but an hundred foreskins of the Philistines, to be avenged of the king's enemies. But Saul thought to make David fall by the hand of the Philistines.

26 And when his servants told David these words, it pleased David well to be the king's son in law: and the days were not expired.

27 Wherefore David arose and went, he and his men, and slew of the Philistines two hundred men; and David brought their foreskins, and they gave them in *a*full tale to the king, that he might be the king's son in law. And Saul gave him *b*Michal his daughter to wife.

28 ¶ And Saul saw and knew that the LORD *was* with David, and *that* Michal Saul's daughter loved him.

29 And Saul was yet the more afraid of David; and Saul became David's enemy continually.

30 Then the princes of the Philistines went forth: and it came to pass, after they went forth, *that* David behaved himself more wisely than all the servants of Saul; so that his name was much *a*set by.

CHAPTER 19

Saul seeks to kill David—Michal saves David by artifice—David joins Samuel and the company of prophets.

AND Saul spake to Jonathan his son, and to all his servants, that they should kill David.

2 But Jonathan Saul's son delighted much in David: and Jonathan told David, saying, Saul my father seeketh to kill thee: now therefore, I pray thee, take heed to thyself until the morning, and abide in a secret *place,* and hide thyself:

3 And I will go out and stand beside my father in the field where thou *art,* and I will commune with my father of thee; and what I see, that I will tell thee.

4 ¶ And Jonathan spake good of David unto Saul his father, and said unto him, Let not the king sin against his servant, against David; because he hath not sinned against thee, and because his works *have been* to thee-ward very good:

5 For he did put his life in his hand, and slew the Philistine, and the LORD wrought a great salvation for all Israel: thou sawest *it,* and didst rejoice: wherefore then wilt thou sin against innocent blood, to slay David without a cause?

6 And Saul hearkened unto the voice of Jonathan: and Saul sware, *As* the LORD liveth, he shall not be slain.

7 And Jonathan called David, and Jonathan shewed him all those things. And Jonathan brought David to Saul, and he was in his presence, as in times past.

8 ¶ And there was war again: and David went out, and fought with the Philistines, and slew them with a great slaughter; and they fled from him.

9 And the evil spirit *a*from the LORD was upon Saul, as he sat in his house with his javelin in his hand: and David played with *his* hand.

10 And Saul sought to smite David

21*a* IE by one of my two daughters.
23*a* IE insignificant.

27*a* IE full number.
  b 1 Sam. 14:49.
30*a* OR adored.

19 9*a* JST 1 Sam. 19:9 . . .
  which was not of the
  Lord . . .

even to the wall with the javelin; but he slipped away out of Saul's presence, and he smote the javelin into the wall: and David fled, and escaped that night.

11 Saul also sent messengers unto David's house, to watch him, and to slay him in the morning: and Michal David's wife told him, saying, If thou save not thy life to night, to morrow thou shalt be slain.

12 ¶ So Michal let David down through a window: and he went, and fled, and escaped.

13 And Michal took an ªimage, and laid *it* in the bed, and put a pillow of goats' *hair* for his bolster, and covered *it* with a cloth.

14 And when Saul sent messengers to take David, she said, He *is* sick.

15 And Saul sent the messengers *again* to see David, saying, Bring him up to me in the bed, that I may slay him.

16 And when the messengers were come in, behold, *there was* an image in the bed, with a pillow of goats' *hair* for his bolster.

17 And Saul said unto Michal, Why hast thou deceived me so, and sent away mine enemy, that he is escaped? And Michal answered Saul, He said unto me, Let me go; why should I kill thee?

18 ¶ So David fled, and escaped, and came to Samuel to Ramah, and told him all that Saul had done to him. And he and Samuel went and dwelt in Naioth.

19 And it was told Saul, saying, Behold, David *is* at Naioth in Ramah.

20 And Saul sent messengers to take David: and when they saw the company of the ªprophets prophesying, and Samuel standing *as* appointed over them, the Spirit of God was upon the messengers of Saul, and they also prophesied.

21 And when it was told Saul, he sent other messengers, and they prophesied likewise. And Saul sent messengers again the third time, and they prophesied also.

22 Then went he also to Ramah, and came to a great well that *is* in Sechu: and he asked and said, Where *are* Samuel and David? And one said, Behold, *they be* at Naioth in Ramah.

23 And he went thither to Naioth in Ramah: and the Spirit of God was upon him also, and he went on, and prophesied, until he came to Naioth in Ramah.

24 And he stripped off his clothes also, and prophesied before Samuel in like manner, and lay down naked all that day and all that night. Wherefore they say, Is Saul also among the ªprophets?

CHAPTER 20

David and Jonathan make a covenant of friendship and peace—They take leave of each other.

AND David fled from Naioth in Ramah, and came and said before Jonathan, What have I done? what *is* mine iniquity? and what *is* my sin before thy father, that he seeketh my life?

2 And he said unto him, God forbid; thou shalt not die: behold, my father will do nothing either great or small, but that he will shew it me: and why should my father hide this thing from me? it *is* not *so.*

3 And David sware moreover, and said, Thy father certainly knoweth that I have found grace in thine eyes; and he saith, Let not Jonathan know this, lest he be grieved: but truly *as* the LORD liveth, and *as* thy soul liveth, *there is* but a step between me and death.

4 Then said Jonathan unto David, Whatsoever thy soul ªdesireth, I will even do *it* for thee.

5 And David said unto Jonathan, Behold, to morrow *is* the new ªmoon, and I should not fail to sit with the king at meat: but let me go, that I may hide myself in the field unto the third *day* at even.

6 If thy father at all miss me, then

13a Judg. 17:5.
20a 1 Sam. 10:10.

24a 1 Sam. 10:12 (11–13).
20 4a 1 Sam. 18:1;

D&C 88:123.
5a TG Astronomy.

say, David earnestly asked *leave* of me that he might run to Bethlehem his city: for *there is* a yearly sacrifice there for all the family.

7 If he say thus, *It is* well; thy servant shall have peace: but if he be very wroth, *then* be sure that evil is determined by him.

8 Therefore thou shalt deal kindly with thy servant; for thou hast brought thy servant into a ᵃcovenant of the Lᴏʀᴅ with thee: notwithstanding, if there be in me iniquity, slay me thyself; for why shouldest thou bring me to thy father?

9 And Jonathan said, Far be it from thee: for if I knew certainly that evil were determined by my father to come upon thee, then would not I tell it thee?

10 Then said David to Jonathan, Who shall tell me? or what *if* thy father answer thee roughly?

11 ¶ And Jonathan said unto David, Come, and let us go out into the field. And they went out both of them into the field.

12 And Jonathan said unto David, O Lᴏʀᴅ God of Israel, when I have sounded my father about to morrow any time, *or* the third *day,* and, behold, *if there be* good toward David, and I then send not unto thee, and shew it thee;

13 The Lᴏʀᴅ do so and much more to Jonathan: but if it please my father *to do* thee evil, then I will shew it thee, and send thee away, that thou mayest go in peace: and the Lᴏʀᴅ be with thee, as he hath been with my father.

14 And thou shalt not only while yet I live shew me the ᵃkindness of the Lᴏʀᴅ, that I die not:

15 But *also* thou shalt not cut off thy kindness from my house for ever: no, not when the Lᴏʀᴅ hath cut off the enemies of David every one from the face of the earth.

16 So Jonathan made *a covenant* with the house of David, *saying,* Let the Lᴏʀᴅ even require *it* at the hand of David's enemies.

17 And Jonathan caused David to swear again, because he loved him: for he loved him as he loved his own soul.

18 Then Jonathan said to David, To morrow *is* the new moon: and thou shalt be missed, because thy seat will be empty.

19 And *when* thou hast stayed three days, *then* thou shalt go down quickly, and come to the place where thou didst hide thyself when the business was *in hand,* and shalt remain by the stone Ezel.

20 And I will shoot three arrows on the side *thereof,* as though I shot at a mark.

21 And, behold, I will send a lad, *saying,* Go, find out the arrows. If I expressly say unto the lad, Behold, the arrows *are* on this side of thee, take them; then come thou: for *there is* peace to thee, and no hurt; *as* the Lᴏʀᴅ liveth.

22 But if I say thus unto the young man, Behold, the arrows *are* beyond thee; go thy way: for the Lᴏʀᴅ hath sent thee away.

23 And *as touching* the matter which thou and I have spoken of, behold, the Lᴏʀᴅ *be* between thee and me for ever.

24 ¶ So David hid himself in the field: and when the new moon was come, the king sat him down to eat meat.

25 And the king sat upon his seat, as at other times, *even* upon a seat by the wall: and Jonathan arose, and Abner sat by Saul's side, and David's place was empty.

26 Nevertheless Saul spake not any thing that day: for he thought, Something hath befallen him, he *is* not clean; surely he *is* not clean.

27 And it came to pass on the morrow, *which was* the second *day* of the month, that David's place was empty: and Saul said unto Jonathan his son, Wherefore cometh not the son of Jesse to meat, neither yesterday, nor to day?

28 And Jonathan answered Saul,

8*a* 2 Sam. 21:7. 14*a* 2 Sam. 9:1.

David earnestly asked *leave* of me *to go* to Beth-lehem:

29 And he said, Let me go, I pray thee; for our family hath a sacrifice in the city; and my brother, he hath commanded me *to be there:* and now, if I have found favour in thine eyes, let me get away, I pray thee, and see my brethren. Therefore he cometh not unto the king's table.

30 Then Saul's *a*anger was kindled against Jonathan, and he said unto him, Thou son of the perverse rebellious *woman,* do not I know that thou hast chosen the son of Jesse to thine own confusion, and unto the confusion of thy mother's nakedness?

31 For as long as the son of Jesse liveth upon the ground, thou shalt not be *a*established, nor thy kingdom. Wherefore now send and fetch him unto me, for he shall surely die.

32 And Jonathan answered Saul his father, and said unto him, Wherefore shall he be slain? what hath he done?

33 And Saul cast a javelin at him to smite him: whereby Jonathan knew that it was determined of his father to slay David.

34 So Jonathan arose from the table in fierce anger, and did eat no meat the second day of the month: for he was grieved for David, because his father had done him shame.

35 ¶ And it came to pass in the morning, that Jonathan went out into the field at the time appointed with David, and a little lad with him.

36 And he said unto his lad, Run, find out now the arrows which I shoot. *And* as the lad ran, he shot an arrow beyond him.

37 And when the lad was come to the place of the arrow which Jonathan had shot, Jonathan cried after the lad, and said, *Is* not the arrow beyond thee?

38 And Jonathan cried after the lad, Make speed, haste, stay not. And Jonathan's lad gathered up the arrows, and came to his master.

39 But the lad knew not any thing: only Jonathan and David knew the matter.

40 And Jonathan gave his artillery unto his lad, and said unto him, Go, carry *them* to the city.

41 ¶ *And* as soon as the lad was gone, David arose out of *a place* toward the south, and fell on his face to the ground, and bowed himself three times: and they kissed one another, and wept one with another, until David exceeded.

42 And *a*Jonathan said to David, Go in peace, forasmuch as we have sworn both of us in the name of the Lord, saying, The Lord be between me and thee, and between my seed and thy seed for ever. And he arose and departed: and Jonathan went into the city.

CHAPTER 21

David gets help from Ahimelech the priest—He eats the shewbread—He goes to Gath, where he pretends madness.

Then came David to *a*Nob to Ahimelech the priest: and Ahimelech was afraid at the meeting of David, and said unto him, Why *art* thou alone, and no man with thee?

2 And David said unto Ahimelech the priest, The king hath commanded me a business, and hath said unto me, Let no man know any thing of the business whereabout I send thee, and what I have commanded thee: and I have appointed *my* servants to such and such a place.

3 Now therefore what is under thine hand? give *me* five *loaves of* bread in mine hand, or what there is present.

4 And the priest answered David, and said, *There is* no common bread under mine hand, but there is *a*hallowed *b*bread; if the young men have kept themselves at least from women.

5 And David answered the priest, and said unto him, Of a truth women

---

30*a* TG Anger.
31*a* 1 Sam. 23:17.

42*a* 1 Sam. 23:16.
21 1*a* 1 Sam. 22:9.

4*a* Moro. 4:3.
b TG Bread, Shewbread.

have been kept from us about these three days, since I came out, and the vessels of the young men are holy, and *the bread is* in a manner common, yea, though it were sanctified this day in the vessel.

6 So the priest gave him ªhallowed *bread:* for there was no bread there but the ᵇshewbread, that was taken from before the Lᴏʀᴅ, to put hot bread in the day when it was taken away.

7 Now a certain man of the servants of Saul *was* there that day, detained before the Lᴏʀᴅ; and his name *was* ªDoeg, an Edomite, the chiefest of the herdmen that *belonged* to Saul.

8 ¶ And David said unto Ahimelech, And is there not here under thine hand spear or sword? for I have neither brought my sword nor my weapons with me, because the king's business required haste.

9 And the priest said, The sword of Goliath the Philistine, whom thou slewest in the valley of Elah, behold, it *is here* wrapped in a cloth behind the ephod: if thou wilt take that, take *it:* for *there is* no other save that here. And David said, *There is* none like that; give it me.

10 ¶ And David arose, and fled that day for fear of Saul, and went to Achish the king of Gath.

11 And the servants of Achish said unto him, *Is* not this David the king of the land? did they not ªsing one to another of him in dances, saying, Saul hath slain his thousands, and David his ten thousands?

12 And David laid up these words in his heart, and was sore afraid of Achish the king of Gath.

13 And he changed his behaviour before them, and feigned himself mad in their hands, and scrabbled on the doors of the gate, and let his ªspittle fall down upon his beard.

14 Then said Achish unto his servants, Lo, ye see the man is mad: wherefore *then* have ye brought him to me?

15 Have I need of mad men, that ye have brought this *fellow* to play the mad man in my presence? shall this *fellow* come into my house?

CHAPTER 22

David gains followers—He goes from one place to another, fleeing from Saul—Saul slays the priests who showed kindness to David.

Dᴀᴠɪᴅ therefore departed thence, and escaped to the cave Adullam: and when his brethren and all his father's house heard *it,* they went down thither to him.

2 And every one *that was* in distress, and every one *that was* in debt, and every one *that was* discontented, gathered themselves unto him; and he became a captain over them: and there were with him about four hundred men.

3 ¶ And David went thence to Mizpeh of Moab: and he said unto the king of Moab, Let my father and my mother, I pray thee, come forth, *and be* with you, till I know what God will do for me.

4 And he brought them before the king of Moab: and they dwelt with him all the while that David was in the hold.

5 ¶ And the prophet ªGad said unto David, Abide not in the hold; depart, and get thee into the land of Judah. Then David departed, and came into the forest of Hareth.

6 ¶ When Saul heard that David was discovered, and the men that *were* with him, (now Saul ªabode in Gibeah under a tree in Ramah, having his spear in his hand, and all his servants *were* standing about him;)

7 Then Saul said unto his servants that stood about him, Hear now, ye Benjamites; will the son of Jesse give every one of you fields and vineyards, *and* make you all captains

---

6a Matt. 12:3 (3–4).
  b Luke 6:4 (3–4).
7a 1 Sam. 22:9.

11a TG Singing.
13a HEB saliva.
22 5a BD Gad.

6a OR was sitting.

of thousands, and captains of hundreds;

8 That all of you have ^aconspired against me, and *there is* none that sheweth me that my son hath made a ^bleague with the son of Jesse, and *there is* none of you that is sorry for me, or sheweth unto me that my son hath stirred up my servant against me, to lie in wait, as at this day?

9 ¶ Then answered ^aDoeg the Edomite, which was set over the servants of Saul, and said, I saw the son of Jesse coming to ^bNob, to Ahimelech the son of Ahitub.

10 And he inquired of the LORD for him, and gave him ^avictuals, and gave him the sword of Goliath the Philistine.

11 Then the king sent to call Ahimelech the priest, the son of Ahitub, and all his father's house, the priests that *were* in Nob: and they came all of them to the king.

12 And Saul said, Hear now, thou son of Ahitub. And he answered, Here I *am,* my lord.

13 And Saul said unto him, Why have ye conspired against me, thou and the son of Jesse, in that thou hast given him bread, and a sword, and hast inquired of God for him, that he should rise against me, to lie in wait, as at this day?

14 Then Ahimelech answered the king, and said, And who *is so* faithful among all thy servants as David, which is the king's son in law, and goeth at thy bidding, and is honourable in thine house?

15 Did I then begin to inquire of God for him? be it far from me: let not the king impute *any* thing unto his servant, *nor* to all the house of my father: for thy servant knew nothing of all this, less or more.

16 And the king said, Thou shalt surely die, Ahimelech, thou, and all thy father's house.

17 ¶ And the king said unto the footmen that stood about him, Turn, and slay the priests of the LORD; because their hand also *is* with David, and because they knew when he fled, and did not shew it to me. But the servants of the king would not put forth their hand to fall upon the priests of the LORD.

18 And the king said to Doeg, Turn thou, and fall upon the priests. And Doeg the Edomite turned, and he fell upon the priests, and slew on that day fourscore and five persons that did wear a linen ^aephod.

19 And Nob, the city of the priests, smote he with the edge of the sword, both men and women, children and sucklings, and oxen, and asses, and sheep, with the edge of the sword.

20 ¶ And one of the sons of Ahimelech the son of Ahitub, named ^aAbiathar, escaped, and fled after David.

21 And Abiathar shewed David that Saul had slain the LORD's priests.

22 And David said unto Abiathar, I knew *it* that day, when Doeg the Edomite *was* there, that he would surely tell Saul: I have occasioned *the death* of all the persons of thy father's house.

23 Abide thou with me, fear not: for he that seeketh my life seeketh thy life: but with me thou *shalt be* in safeguard.

CHAPTER 23

David smites the Philistines and saves Keilah—He continues to flee from Saul—Jonathan comforts him in Ziph.

THEN they told David, saying, Behold, the Philistines fight against ^aKeilah, and they rob the threshingfloors.

2 Therefore David ^ainquired of the LORD, saying, Shall I go and smite these Philistines? And the LORD

8*a* TG Conspiracy.
  b OR covenant,
     agreement.
9*a* 1 Sam. 21:7.

b 1 Sam. 21:1.
10*a* HEB goods, provisions.
18*a* Ex. 28:4 (2–4);
     1 Sam. 2:28; 14:3.

20*a* 2 Sam. 15:24;
     1 Kgs. 2:26.
23 1*a* Josh. 15:44.
2*a* 2 Ne. 32:9.

said unto David, Go, and smite the Philistines, and save Keilah.

3 And David's men said unto him, Behold, we be afraid here in Judah: how much more then if we come to Keilah against the armies of the Philistines?

4 Then David inquired of the LORD yet again. And the LORD answered him and said, Arise, go down to Keilah; for I will deliver the Philistines into thine hand.

5 So David and his men went to Keilah, and fought with the Philistines, and brought away their cattle, and *smote them with a great slaughter. So David saved the inhabitants of Keilah.

6 And it came to pass, when Abiathar the son of Ahimelech fled to David to Keilah, *that* he came down *with* an ephod in his hand.

7 ¶ And it was told Saul that David was come to Keilah. And Saul said, God hath delivered him into mine hand; for he is shut in, by entering into a town that hath gates and bars.

8 And Saul called all the people together to war, to go down to Keilah, to besiege David and his men.

9 ¶ And David knew that Saul secretly practised mischief against him; and he said to Abiathar the priest, Bring hither the ephod.

10 Then said David, O LORD God of Israel, thy servant hath certainly heard that Saul seeketh to come to Keilah, to destroy the city for my sake.

11 Will the men of Keilah deliver me up into his hand? will Saul come down, as thy servant hath heard? O LORD God of Israel, I beseech thee, tell thy servant. And the LORD said, He will come down.

12 Then said David, Will the men of Keilah deliver me and my men into the hand of Saul? And the LORD said, They will deliver *thee* up.

13 ¶ Then David and his *a*men, *which were* about six hundred, arose

and departed out of Keilah, and went whithersoever they could go. And it was told Saul that David was escaped from Keilah; and he forbare to go forth.

14 And David abode in the wilderness in strong holds, and remained in a mountain in the wilderness of Ziph. And Saul sought him every day, but God delivered him not into his hand.

15 And David saw that Saul was come out to seek his life: and David *was* in the wilderness of Ziph in a *a*wood.

16 ¶ And *a*Jonathan Saul's son arose, and went to David into the wood, and strengthened his hand in God.

17 And he said unto him, Fear not: for the hand of Saul my father shall not find thee; and thou shalt be king over Israel, and I shall be next unto thee; and that also Saul my father *a*knoweth.

18 And they two made a covenant before the LORD: and David abode in the wood, and Jonathan went to his house.

19 ¶ Then came up the Ziphites to Saul to Gibeah, saying, Doth not David hide himself with us in strong holds in the wood, in the hill of Hachilah, which *is* on the south of Jeshimon?

20 Now therefore, O king, come down according to all the desire of thy soul to come down; and our part *shall be* to deliver him into the king's hand.

21 And Saul said, Blessed *be* ye of the LORD; for ye have compassion on me.

22 Go, I pray you, prepare yet, and know and see his place where *a*his haunt is, *and* who hath seen him there: for it is told me *that* he dealeth very subtilly.

23 See therefore, and take knowledge of all the lurking places where he hideth himself, and come ye again to me with the certainty, and I

5*a* Mosiah 10:20.
13*a* 2 Sam. 2:3; 19:41.
15*a* OR forest (also vv. 16,
18–19).
16*a* 1 Sam. 20:42 (41–42).
17*a* 1 Sam. 20:31 (30–31).
22*a* HEB his foot; i.e., his customary walk.

will go with you: and it shall come to pass, if he be in the land, that I will search him out throughout all the thousands of Judah.

24 And they arose, and went to Ziph before Saul: but David and his men *were* in the wilderness of Maon, in the plain on the south of Jeshimon.

25 Saul also and his men went to seek *him*. And they told David: wherefore he came down into a rock, and abode in the wilderness of Maon. And when Saul heard *that,* he pursued after David in the wilderness of Maon.

26 And Saul went on this side of the mountain, and David and his men on that side of the mountain: and David made haste to get away for fear of Saul; for Saul and his men compassed David and his men round about to take them.

27 ¶ But there came a messenger unto Saul, saying, Haste thee, and come; for the Philistines have invaded the land.

28 Wherefore Saul returned from pursuing after David, and went against the Philistines: therefore they called that place *a*Sela-hammahlekoth.

29 ¶ And David went up from thence, and dwelt in *a*strong holds at En-gedi.

CHAPTER 24

David finds Saul in a cave and spares his life—Saul confesses that David is more righteous than he—David swears that he will not cut off the seed of Saul.

AND it came to pass, when Saul was returned from following the Philistines, that it was told him, saying, Behold, David *is* in the wilderness of En-gedi.

2 Then Saul took three thousand chosen men out of all Israel, and went to seek David and his men upon the rocks of the wild goats.

3 And he came to the *a*sheepcotes by the way, where *was* a cave; and Saul went in to cover his feet: and David and his men remained in the *b*sides of the cave.

4 And the men of David said unto him, Behold the day of which the LORD said unto thee, Behold, I will deliver thine enemy into thine hand, that thou mayest do to him as it shall seem good unto thee. Then David arose, and cut off the *a*skirt of Saul's robe *b*privily.

5 And it came to pass afterward, that David's heart smote him, because he had cut off Saul's skirt.

6 And he said unto his men, The LORD forbid that I should do this thing unto my master, the LORD's anointed, to stretch forth mine hand against him, seeing he *is* the *a*anointed of the LORD.

7 So David stayed his servants with these words, and suffered them not to rise against Saul. But Saul rose up out of the cave, and went on *his* way.

8 David also arose afterward, and went out of the cave, and cried after Saul, saying, My lord the king. And when Saul looked behind him, David stooped with his face to the earth, and bowed himself.

9 ¶ And David said to Saul, Wherefore hearest thou men's words, saying, Behold, David seeketh thy hurt?

10 Behold, this day thine eyes have seen how that the LORD had delivered thee to day into mine hand in the cave: and *some* bade *me* kill thee: but *mine eye* *a*spared thee; and I said, I will not put forth mine hand against my lord; for he *is* the *b*LORD's anointed.

11 Moreover, my father, see, yea, see the skirt of thy robe in my hand: for in that I cut off the skirt of thy

---

28*a* IE The rock of divisions.
29*a* 1 Sam. 24:22.
24 3*a* OR sheepfolds; shelters, probably caves with stone walls about the

entrance.
b OR innermost part.
4*a* OR hem, corner, border which signifies the portion that symbolized his authority (also

vv. 5, 11).
b OR secretly.
6*a* TG Anointing.
10*a* TG Benevolence.
b 1 Sam. 26:9.

robe, and killed thee not, know thou and see that *there is* neither evil nor transgression in mine hand, and I have not sinned against thee; yet thou huntest my soul to take it.

12 The LORD ^ajudge between me and thee, and the LORD avenge me of thee: but mine hand shall not be upon thee.

13 As saith the proverb of the ancients, ^aWickedness proceedeth from the wicked: but mine hand shall not be upon thee.

14 After whom is the king of Israel come out? after whom dost thou pursue? after a dead dog, after a flea.

15 The LORD therefore be judge, and judge between me and thee, and see, and plead my cause, and deliver me out of thine hand.

16 ¶ And it came to pass, when David had made an end of speaking these words unto Saul, that Saul said, *Is* this thy voice, my son David? And Saul lifted up his voice, and wept.

17 And he said to David, Thou *art* more righteous than I: for thou hast rewarded me ^agood, whereas I have rewarded thee evil.

18 And thou hast shewed this day how that thou hast dealt well with me: forasmuch as when the LORD had delivered me into thine hand, thou killedst me not.

19 For if a man find his enemy, will he let him go well away? wherefore the LORD ^areward thee good for that thou hast done unto me this day.

20 And now, behold, I know well that thou shalt surely be king, and that the kingdom of Israel shall be established in thine hand.

21 Swear now therefore unto me by the LORD, that thou wilt not cut off my seed after me, and that thou wilt not destroy my name out of my father's house.

22 And David sware unto Saul. And Saul went home; but David and his men gat them up unto the ^ahold.

CHAPTER 25

Samuel dies—Nabal rebuffs David and refuses to give him food—Abigail intercedes, saves Nabal, and gives David a present—David is pacified, Nabal dies, and David marries Abigail.

AND Samuel died; and all the Israelites were gathered together, and lamented him, and buried him in his house at Ramah. And David arose, and went down to the wilderness of Paran.

2 And *there was* a man in Maon, whose possessions *were* in Carmel; and the man *was* very great, and he had three thousand sheep, and a thousand goats: and he was shearing his sheep in Carmel.

3 Now the name of the man *was* Nabal; and the name of his wife Abigail: and *she was* a woman of good understanding, and of a beautiful countenance: but the man *was* ^achurlish and evil in his doings; and he *was* of the house of Caleb.

4 ¶ And David heard in the wilderness that Nabal did shear his sheep.

5 And David sent out ten young men, and David said unto the young men, Get you up to Carmel, and go to Nabal, and greet him in my name:

6 And thus shall ye say to him that liveth *in prosperity*, ^aPeace *be* both to thee, and ^bpeace *be* to thine house, and peace *be* unto all that thou hast.

7 And now I have heard that thou hast shearers: now thy shepherds which were with us, we hurt them not, neither was there ought missing unto them, all the while they were in Carmel.

8 Ask thy young men, and they will shew thee. Wherefore let the young men find favour in thine eyes: for we come in a good day: give, I pray thee, whatsoever cometh to thine hand unto thy servants, and to thy son David.

9 And when David's young men

12a D&C 64:11.
13a TG Wickedness.
17a TG Reconciliation.
19a TG Reward.

22a 1 Sam. 23:29;
     Alma 58:6;
     3 Ne. 4:1.
25 3a OR rude, rough, "hard."

6a Ps. 122:8.
 b Luke 10:5.

came, they spake to Nabal according to all those words in the name of David, and ceased.

10 ¶ And Nabal answered David's servants, and said, Who *is* David? and who *is* the son of Jesse? there be many servants now a days that break away every man from his master.

11 Shall I then take my bread, and my water, and my flesh that I have killed for my shearers, and give *it* unto men, whom I know not whence they *be?*

12 So David's young men turned their way, and went again, and came and told him all those sayings.

13 And David said unto his men, Gird ye on every man his sword. And they girded on every man his sword; and David also girded on his sword: and there went up after David about four hundred men; and two hundred abode by the stuff.

14 ¶ But one of the young men told Abigail, Nabal's wife, saying, Behold, David sent messengers out of the wilderness to ᵃsalute our master; and he ᵇrailed on them.

15 But the men *were* very good unto us, and we were not hurt, neither missed we any thing, as long as we were conversant with them, when we were in the fields:

16 They were a wall unto us both by night and day, all the while we were with them keeping the sheep.

17 Now therefore know and consider what thou wilt do; for evil is determined against our master, and against all his household: for he *is such* a son of Belial, that *a man* cannot speak to him.

18 ¶ Then Abigail made haste, and took two hundred loaves, and two bottles of wine, and five sheep ready dressed, and five measures of parched *corn*, and an hundred clusters of raisins, and two hundred cakes of figs, and laid *them* on asses.

19 And she said unto her servants, Go on before me; behold, I come after you. But she told not her husband Nabal.

20 And it was *so, as* she rode on the ass, that she came down ᵃby the covert of the hill, and, behold, David and his men came down against her; and she met them.

21 Now David had said, Surely in vain have I kept all that this *fellow* hath in the wilderness, so that nothing was missed of all that *pertained* unto him: and he hath ᵃrequited me evil for good.

22 So and more also do God unto the enemies of David, if I leave of all that *pertain* to him by the morning light ᵃany that pisseth against the wall.

23 And when Abigail saw David, she hasted, and lighted off the ass, and fell before David on her face, and bowed herself to the ground,

24 And fell at his feet, and said, Upon me, my lord, *upon* me *let this* iniquity *be:* and let thine handmaid, I pray thee, speak in thine audience, and hear the words of thine handmaid.

25 Let not my lord, I pray thee, regard this man of Belial, *even* ᵃNabal: for as his name *is,* so *is* he; Nabal *is* his name, and folly *is* with him: but I thine handmaid saw not the young men of my lord, whom thou didst send.

26 Now therefore, my lord, *as* the LORD liveth, and *as* thy soul liveth, seeing the LORD hath withholden thee from coming to *shed* blood, and from avenging thyself with thine own hand, now let thine enemies, and they that seek evil to my lord, be as Nabal.

27 And now this blessing which thine handmaid hath brought unto my lord, let it even be given unto the young men that follow my lord.

28 I pray thee, forgive the trespass

14a HEB bless or greet.
  b HEB swooped upon (as a bird attacking).
20a OR concealed by the hill.

21a OR returned.
22a What follows is a derisive term for "any male" (also v. 34).
25a IE Fool (insensitive,

churlish person). Such a name must have been given him by those who knew him.

of thine handmaid: for the LORD will certainly make my lord a *a*sure *b*house; because my lord fighteth the battles of the LORD, and evil hath not been found in thee *all* thy days.

29 Yet a man is risen to pursue thee, and to seek thy soul: but the soul of my lord shall be bound in the bundle of life with the LORD thy God; and the souls of thine enemies, them shall he sling out, *as out* of the middle of a sling.

30 And it shall come to pass, when the LORD shall have done to my lord according to all the good that he hath spoken concerning thee, and shall have appointed thee ruler over Israel;

31 That this shall be no grief unto thee, nor offence of heart unto my lord, either that thou hast shed blood causeless, or that my lord hath avenged himself: but when the LORD shall have dealt well with my lord, then remember thine handmaid.

32 ¶ And David said to Abigail, Blessed *be* the LORD God of Israel, which sent thee this day to meet me:

33 And blessed *be* thy advice, and blessed *be* thou, which hast kept me this day from coming to *shed* blood, and from avenging myself with mine own hand.

34 For in very deed, *as* the LORD God of Israel liveth, which hath kept me back from hurting thee, except thou hadst hasted and come to meet me, surely there had not been left unto Nabal by the morning light any that pisseth against the wall.

35 So David received of her hand *that* which she had brought him, and said unto her, Go up in peace to thine house; see, I have hearkened to thy voice, and have accepted thy person.

36 ¶ And Abigail came to Nabal; and, behold, he held a feast in his house, like the feast of a king; and Nabal's heart *was* merry within him,

for he *was* very drunken: wherefore she told him nothing, less or more, until the morning light.

37 But it came to pass in the morning, when the wine was gone out of Nabal, and his wife had told him these things, that his heart died within him, and he became *as* a stone.

38 And it came to pass about ten days *after*, that the LORD *a*smote Nabal, that he died.

39 ¶ And when David heard that Nabal was dead, he said, Blessed *be* the LORD, that hath pleaded the cause of my reproach from the hand of Nabal, and hath kept his servant from evil: for the LORD hath returned the wickedness of Nabal upon his own head. And David sent and communed with Abigail, to take her to him to wife.

40 And when the servants of David were come to Abigail to Carmel, they spake unto her, saying, David sent us unto thee, to take thee to him to wife.

41 And she arose, and bowed herself on *her* face to the earth, and said, Behold, *let* thine handmaid *be* a servant to wash the feet of the servants of my lord.

42 And Abigail hasted, and arose, and rode upon an ass, with five damsels of hers that went after her; and she went after the messengers of David, and became his wife.

43 David also took *a*Ahinoam of Jezreel; and they were also both of them his *b*wives.

44 ¶ But Saul had given Michal his daughter, David's wife, to *a*Phalti the son of Laish, which *was* of Gallim.

CHAPTER 26

David again spares Saul's life—He again refuses to stretch forth his hand against the Lord's anointed—Saul and David separate.

28*a* OR firm house; an assurance of descendants.
 b 1 Sam. 2:35.

38*a* 2 Chr. 13:20; Abr. 1:20.
43*a* 2 Sam. 3:2.
 b 1 Sam. 30:5;

 2 Sam. 2:2; Jacob 1:15; D&C 132:38 (37–39).
44*a* 2 Sam. 3:15.

AND the Ziphites came unto Saul to Gibeah, saying, Doth not David hide himself in the hill of Hachilah, *which is* before Jeshimon?

2 Then Saul arose, and went down to the wilderness of Ziph, having three thousand chosen men of Israel with him, to seek David in the wilderness of Ziph.

3 And Saul pitched in the hill of Hachilah, which *is* before Jeshimon, by the way. But David abode in the wilderness, and he saw that Saul came after him into the wilderness.

4 David therefore sent out spies, and understood that Saul was come in very deed.

5 ¶ And David arose, and came to the place where Saul had pitched: and David beheld the place where Saul lay, and Abner the son of Ner, the captain of his host: and Saul lay in the *ª*trench, and the people pitched round about him.

6 Then answered David and said to Ahimelech the Hittite, and to Abishai the son of Zeruiah, brother to Joab, saying, Who will go down with me to Saul to the camp? And *ª*Abishai said, I will go down with thee.

7 So David and Abishai came to the people by night: and, behold, Saul lay sleeping within the trench, and his spear stuck in the ground at *ª*his bolster: but Abner and the people lay round about him.

8 Then said Abishai to David, God hath delivered thine enemy into thine hand this day: now therefore let me smite him, I pray thee, with the spear even to the earth at once, and I will not *smite* him the second time.

9 And David said to Abishai, Destroy him not: for *ª*who can stretch forth his hand against the LORD's anointed, and be guiltless?

10 David said furthermore, *As* the LORD liveth, the LORD shall smite him; or his day shall come to *ª*die;

or he shall descend into battle, and perish.

11 The LORD forbid that I should stretch forth mine hand against the LORD's anointed: but, I pray thee, take thou now the spear that *is* at his bolster, and the cruse of water, and let us go.

12 So David took the spear and the cruse of water from Saul's bolster; and they gat them away, and no man saw *it,* nor knew *it,* neither awaked: for they *were* all asleep; because a *ª*deep sleep from the LORD was fallen upon them.

13 ¶ Then David went over to the other side, and stood on the top of an hill afar off; a great space *being* between them:

14 And David cried to the people, and to Abner the son of Ner, saying, Answerest thou not, Abner? Then Abner answered and said, Who *art* thou *that* criest to the king?

15 And David said to Abner, *Art* not thou a *valiant* man? and who *is* like to thee in Israel? wherefore then hast thou not kept thy lord the king? for there came one of the people in to destroy the king thy lord.

16 This thing *is* not good that thou hast done. *As* the LORD liveth, ye *are* worthy to die, because ye have not kept your master, the LORD's anointed. And now see where the king's spear *is,* and the cruse of water that *was* at his bolster.

17 And Saul knew David's voice, and said, *Is* this thy voice, my son David? And David said, *It is* my voice, my lord, O king.

18 And he said, Wherefore doth my lord thus pursue after his servant? for what have I done? or what evil *is* in mine hand?

19 Now therefore, I pray thee, let my lord the king hear the words of his servant. If the LORD have stirred thee up against me, let him accept an offering: but if *they be* the children of men, cursed *be* they before the LORD; for they have driven me

---

26 5*a* IE barricade.
  6*a* 2 Sam. 2:18.
  7*a* IE the place of his

head.
  9*a* 1 Sam. 24:10.
  10*a* 1 Sam. 31:5.

12*a* Mosiah 24:19;
  Alma 55:15 (15–16).

out this day from abiding in the inheritance of the LORD, saying, Go, serve other gods.

20 Now therefore, let not my blood fall to the earth before the face of the LORD: for the king of Israel is come out to seek a flea, as when one doth hunt a partridge in the mountains.

21 ¶ Then said Saul, I have sinned: return, my son David: for I will no more do thee harm, because my soul was *a*precious in thine eyes this day: behold, I have played the fool, and have erred exceedingly.

22 And David answered and said, Behold the king's spear! and let one of the young men come over and fetch it.

23 The LORD render to every man his *a*righteousness and his faithfulness: for the LORD delivered thee into *my* hand to day, but I would not stretch forth mine hand *b*against the LORD's anointed.

24 And, behold, as thy life was much set by this day in mine eyes, so let my life be much set by in the eyes of the LORD, and let him deliver me out of all *a*tribulation.

25 Then Saul said to David, Blessed *be* thou, my son David: thou shalt both do great *things,* and also shalt still prevail. So David went on his way, and Saul returned to his place.

CHAPTER 27

David flees to Achish at Gath—He dwells among the Philistines for sixteen months.

AND David said in his heart, I shall now perish one day by the hand of Saul: *there is* nothing better for me than that I should speedily escape into the land of the Philistines; and Saul shall despair of me, to seek me any more in any coast of Israel: so shall I escape out of his hand.

2 And *a*David arose, and he passed over with the six hundred men that *were* with him unto *b*Achish, the son of Maoch, king of Gath.

3 And David dwelt with Achish at Gath, he and his men, every man with his household, *even* David with his two *a*wives, Ahinoam the Jezreelitess, and Abigail the Carmelitess, Nabal's wife.

4 And it was told Saul that David was fled to Gath: and he sought no more again for him.

5 ¶ And David said unto Achish, If I have now found grace in thine eyes, let them give me a place in some town in the country, that I may dwell there: for why should thy servant dwell in the royal city with thee?

6 Then Achish gave him Ziklag that day: wherefore Ziklag pertaineth unto the kings of Judah unto this day.

7 And the time that David dwelt in the country of the Philistines was a full year and four months.

8 ¶ And David and his men went up, and invaded the Geshurites, and the Gezrites, and the Amalekites: for those *nations were* of old the inhabitants of the land, as thou goest to Shur, even unto the land of Egypt.

9 And David smote the land, and left neither man nor woman alive, and took away the sheep, and the oxen, and the asses, and the camels, and the apparel, and returned, and came to Achish.

10 And Achish said, Whither have ye made a *a*road to day? And David said, Against the south of Judah, and against the south of the Jerahmeelites, and against the south of the Kenites.

11 And David saved neither man nor woman alive, to bring *tidings* to Gath, saying, Lest they should tell on us, saying, So did David, and so *will be* his manner all the while he dwelleth in the country of the Philistines.

12 And Achish believed David, saying, He hath made his people Israel utterly to abhor him; therefore he shall be my servant for ever.

21*a* TG Life, Sanctity of.
23*a* TG Righteousness.
  b TG Benevolence.
24*a* TG Tribulation.
27 2*a* 2 Sam. 2:3.
  b 1 Kgs. 2:39.
3*a* 2 Sam. 2:2;
    D&C 132:39.
10*a* HEB raid.

CHAPTER 28

Saul inquires of the witch of Endor for revelation—She foretells his death, the death of his sons, and the defeat of Israel by the Philistines.

AND it came to pass in those days, that the Philistines gathered their armies together for warfare, to fight with Israel. And Achish said unto David, Know thou assuredly, that thou shalt go out with me to battle, thou and thy men.

2 And David said to Achish, Surely thou shalt know what thy servant can do. And Achish said to David, Therefore will I make thee ªkeeper of mine head for ever.

3 ¶ Now Samuel was dead, and all Israel had lamented him, and buried him in Ramah, even in his own city. And Saul had ªput away those that had ᵇfamiliar spirits, and the wizards, out of the land.

4 And the Philistines gathered themselves together, and came and pitched in Shunem: and Saul gathered all Israel together, and they pitched in Gilboa.

5 And when Saul saw the host of the Philistines, he was afraid, and his heart greatly trembled.

6 And when Saul inquired of the LORD, the LORD ªanswered him not, neither by ᵇdreams, nor by ᶜUrim, nor by prophets.

7 ¶ Then said Saul unto his servants, Seek me a woman that hath a ªfamiliar spirit, that I may go to her, and inquire of her. And his servants said to him, Behold, *there is* a woman that hath a familiar spirit at En-dor.

8 And Saul disguised himself, and put on other raiment, and he went, and two men with him, and they came to the woman by night: and

he said, I pray thee, divine unto me by the familiar spirit, and bring me *him* up, whom I shall name unto thee.

9 And the woman said unto him, Behold, thou knowest what Saul hath done, how he hath cut off those that have familiar spirits, and the wizards, out of the land: wherefore then layest thou a snare for my life, to cause me to die?

10 And Saul sware to her by the LORD, saying, *As* the LORD liveth, there shall no punishment happen to thee for this thing.

11 Then said the woman, Whom shall I bring up unto thee? And he said, Bring me up Samuel.

12 And when the woman saw Samuel, she cried with a loud voice: and the woman spake to Saul, saying, Why hast thou deceived me? for thou *art* Saul.

13 And the king said unto her, Be not afraid: for what sawest thou? And the woman said unto Saul, I saw gods ascending out of the earth.

14 And he said unto her, What form *is* he of? And she said, ªAn old man cometh up; and he *is* covered with a mantle. And Saul perceived that it *was* Samuel, and he stooped with *his* face to the ground, and bowed himself.

15 ¶ And Samuel said to Saul, Why hast thou disquieted me, to bring me up? And Saul answered, I am sore distressed; for the Philistines make war against me, and God is ªdeparted from me, and answereth me no more, neither by prophets, nor by dreams: therefore I have called thee, that thou mayest make known unto me what I shall do.

16 Then said Samuel, Wherefore

---

28 2a IE captain of the bodyguard.
  3a IE he had banished spiritualists as required by Lev. 20:27; Deut. 18:9–11.
    b TG Sorcery.
  6a 1 Sam. 14:37; Mosiah 11:24 (23–24);

D&C 101:7 (7–8).
    b TG Dream.
    c TG Urim and Thummim.
  7a TG Spirits, Evil or Unclean; Superstitions.
  14a This cannot be a bona fide vision from God, brought about by a

spiritualist medium. See v. 15. Its effect was to destroy all hope. See v. 20; 31:1–4.
  15a See JST 1 Sam. 16:14–16, 23 (1 Sam. 16:14–16, 23 notes).
    Hosea 9:12;
    D&C 1:33.

then dost thou ask of me, seeing the LORD is departed from thee, and is become thine enemy?

17 And the LORD hath done to him, as he spake by me: for the LORD hath rent the ªkingdom out of thine hand, and given it to thy neighbour, *even* to David:

18 Because thou ªobeyedst not the voice of the LORD, nor executedst his fierce wrath upon Amalek, therefore hath the LORD done this thing unto thee this day.

19 Moreover the LORD will also deliver Israel with thee into the hand of the Philistines: and to morrow *shalt* thou and thy sons *be* with me: the LORD also shall deliver the host of Israel into the hand of the Philistines.

20 Then ªSaul fell straightway all along on the earth, and was sore afraid, because of the words of Samuel: and there was no strength in him; for he had eaten no bread all the day, nor all the night.

21 ¶ And the woman came unto Saul, and saw that he was sore troubled, and said unto him, Behold, thine handmaid hath obeyed thy voice, and I have put my life in my hand, and have hearkened unto thy words which thou spakest unto me.

22 Now therefore, I pray thee, hearken thou also unto the voice of thine handmaid, and let me set a morsel of bread before thee; and eat, that thou mayest have strength, when thou goest on thy way.

23 But he refused, and said, I will not eat. But his servants, together with the woman, compelled him; and he hearkened unto their voice. So he arose from the earth, and sat upon the bed.

24 And the woman had a fat calf in the house; and she hasted, and killed it, and took flour, and kneaded *it*, and did bake ªunleavened bread thereof:

25 And she brought *it* before Saul,

and before his servants; and they did eat. Then they rose up, and went away that night.

CHAPTER 29

Israel and the Philistines gather for war—The Philistine princes send David away.

Now the Philistines gathered together all their armies to Aphek: and the Israelites pitched by a ªfountain which *is* in Jezreel.

2 And the lords of the Philistines passed on by hundreds, and by thousands: but David and his men passed on ªin the rearward with Achish.

3 Then said the princes of the Philistines, What *do* these Hebrews *here*? And Achish said unto the princes of the Philistines, *Is* not this David, the servant of Saul the king of Israel, which hath been with me these days, or these years, and I have found no fault in him since he fell *unto me* unto this day?

4 And the princes of the Philistines were wroth with him; and the princes of the Philistines said unto him, Make this fellow return, that he may go again to his place which thou hast appointed him, and let him not go down with us to battle, lest in the battle he be an ªadversary to us: for wherewith should he ᵇreconcile himself unto his master? *should it* not *be* with the heads of these men?

5 *Is* not this David, of whom they sang one to another in dances, saying, ªSaul slew his thousands, and David his ten thousands?

6 ¶ Then Achish called David, and said unto him, Surely, *as* the LORD liveth, thou hast been upright, and thy going out and thy coming in with me in the host *is* good in my sight: for I have not found evil in thee since the day of thy coming unto me unto this day: nevertheless the lords favour thee not.

7 Wherefore now return, and go in

17*a* 1 Sam. 15:28.
18*a* D&C 58:32.
20*a* IE Saul collapsed.

24*a* TG Bread, Unleavened.
29 1*a* OR spring.
2*a* IE at the rear.

4*a* 1 Chr. 12:19.
   b TG Reconciliation.
5*a* 1 Sam. 18:6.

peace, that thou displease not the lords of the Philistines.

8 ¶ And David said unto Achish, But what have I done? and what hast thou found in thy servant so long as I have been with thee unto this day, that I may not go fight against the enemies of my lord the king?

9 And Achish answered and said to David, I know that thou *art* good in my sight, as an *a*angel of God: notwithstanding the princes of the Philistines have said, He shall not go up with us to the battle.

10 Wherefore now rise up early in the morning with thy master's servants that are come with thee: and as soon as ye be up early in the morning, and have light, depart.

11 So David and his men rose up early to depart in the morning, to return into the land of the Philistines. And the Philistines went up to Jezreel.

CHAPTER 30

The Amalekites spoil Ziklag and the borders of Judah—David smites Amalek and regains and divides the spoil.

AND it came to pass, when David and his men were come to Ziklag on the third day, that the Amalekites had invaded the south, and Ziklag, and smitten Ziklag, and burned it with fire;

2 And had taken the women captives, that *were* therein: they slew not any, either great or small, but carried *them* away, and went on their way.

3 ¶ So David and his men came to the city, and, behold, *it was* burned with fire; and their wives, and their sons, and their daughters, were taken captives.

4 Then David and the people that *were* with him lifted up their voice and wept, until they had no more power to weep.

5 And David's two *a*wives were taken captives, Ahinoam the Jez-reelitess, and Abigail the wife of Nabal the Carmelite.

6 And David was greatly distressed; for the people spake of stoning him, because the soul of all the people was grieved, every man for his sons and for his daughters: but David *a*encouraged himself in the LORD his God.

7 And David said to Abiathar the priest, Ahimelech's son, I pray thee, bring me hither the ephod. And Abiathar brought thither the ephod to David.

8 And David inquired at the LORD, saying, Shall I pursue after this troop? shall I overtake them? And he answered him, Pursue: for thou shalt surely overtake *them*, and without fail recover *all*.

9 So David went, he and the six hundred men that *were* with him, and came to the brook Besor, where those that were left behind stayed.

10 But David pursued, he and four hundred men: for two hundred abode behind, which were so faint that they could not go over the brook Besor.

11 ¶ And they found an Egyptian in the field, and brought him to David, and gave him bread, and he did eat; and they made him drink water;

12 And they gave him a piece of a cake of figs, and two clusters of raisins: and when he had eaten, his spirit came again to him: for he had eaten no bread, nor drunk *any* water, three days and three nights.

13 And David said unto him, To whom *belongest* thou? and whence *art* thou? And he said, I *am* a young man of Egypt, servant to an Amalekite; and my master left me, because three days agone I fell sick.

14 We made an invasion *upon* the south of the *a*Cherethites, and upon *the coast* which *belongeth* to Judah, and upon the south of Caleb; and we burned Ziklag with fire.

15 And David said to him, Canst thou bring me down to this company?

9*a* TG Angels.
30 5*a* 1 Sam. 25:43;

Jacob 2:24.
6*a* Ps. 56:3 (3–4).

14*a* 1 Kgs. 1:38.

And he said, Swear unto me by God, that thou wilt neither kill me, nor deliver me into the hands of my ^amaster, and I will bring thee down to this company.

16 ¶ And when he had brought him down, behold, *they were* spread abroad upon all the earth, eating and drinking, and dancing, because of all the great spoil that they had taken out of the land of the Philistines, and out of the land of Judah.

17 And David smote them from the twilight even unto the evening of the next day: and there escaped not a man of them, save four hundred young men, which rode upon camels, and fled.

18 And David recovered all that the ^aAmalekites had carried away: and David rescued his two wives.

19 And there was nothing lacking to them, neither small nor great, neither sons nor daughters, neither spoil, nor any *thing* that they had taken to them: David recovered all.

20 And David took all the flocks and the herds, *which* they drave before those *other* cattle, and said, This *is* David's spoil.

21 ¶ And David came to the two hundred men, which were so faint that they could not follow David, whom they had made also to abide at the brook Besor: and they went forth to meet David, and to meet the people that *were* with him: and when David came near to the people, he saluted them.

22 Then answered all the wicked men and *men* of Belial, of those that went with David, and said, Because they went not with us, we will not give them *ought* of the spoil that we have recovered, save to every man his wife and his children, that they may lead *them* away, and depart.

23 Then said David, Ye shall not do so, my brethren, with that which the LORD hath given us, who hath preserved us, and delivered the company that came against us into our hand.

24 For who will hearken unto you in this matter? but as his part *is* that goeth down to the battle, so *shall* his part *be* that tarrieth by the stuff: they ^ashall part alike.

25 And it was *so* from that day forward, that he made it a statute and an ordinance for Israel unto this day.

26 ¶ And when David came to Ziklag, he sent of the spoil unto the elders of Judah, *even* to his friends, saying, Behold a present for you of the spoil of the enemies of the LORD;

27 To *them* which *were* in Beth-el, and to *them* which *were* in south Ramoth, and to *them* which *were* in Jattir,

28 And to *them* which *were* in Aroer, and to *them* which *were* in Siphmoth, and to *them* which *were* in Eshtemoa,

29 And to *them* which *were* in Rachal, and to *them* which *were* in the cities of the Jerahmeelites, and to *them* which *were* in the cities of the Kenites,

30 And to *them* which *were* in Hormah, and to *them* which *were* in Chor-ashan, and to *them* which *were* in Athach,

31 And to *them* which *were* in Hebron, and to all the places where David himself and his men ^awere wont to haunt.

CHAPTER 31

The Philistines defeat Israel—Saul and his three sons are slain—Their bodies are retrieved by the Gileadites and burned.

Now the ^aPhilistines fought against Israel: and the men of Israel fled from before the Philistines, and fell down slain in mount Gilboa.

2 And the Philistines followed hard upon Saul and upon his sons; and the Philistines slew Jonathan, and Abinadab, and Malchi-shua, Saul's sons.

15*a* Deut. 23:15.
18*a* 2 Sam. 8:12.
24*a* IE shall divide it

equally.
31*a* IE where they usually went.

31 1*a* 1 Chr. 10:1 (1–12).

3 And the battle went sore against Saul, and the archers hit him; and he was sore wounded of the archers.

4 Then said Saul unto his armourbearer, Draw thy sword, and thrust me through therewith; lest these uncircumcised come and thrust me through, and abuse me. But his armourbearer would not; for he was sore afraid. Therefore Saul took a sword, and *a*fell upon it.

5 And when his armourbearer saw that *a*Saul was dead, he fell likewise upon his sword, and died with him.

6 So Saul died, and his three sons, and his armourbearer, and all his men, that same day together.

7 ¶ And when the men of Israel that *were* on the other side of the valley, and *they* that *were* on the other side Jordan, saw that the men of Israel fled, and that Saul and his sons were dead, they forsook the cities, and fled; and the Philistines came and dwelt in them.

8 And it came to pass on the morrow, when the Philistines came to strip the slain, that they found Saul and his three sons fallen in mount Gilboa.

9 And they cut off his head, and stripped off his armour, and sent into the land of the Philistines round about, to publish *it* in the house of their idols, and among the people.

10 And they put his armour in the house of Ashtaroth: and they fastened his *a*body to the wall of Beth-shan.

11 ¶ And when the inhabitants of *a*Jabesh-gilead heard of that which the Philistines had done to Saul;

12 All the valiant men arose, and went all night, and took the body of Saul and the bodies of his sons from the wall of Beth-shan, and came to Jabesh, and burnt them there.

13 And they took their bones, and buried *them* under a tree at Jabesh, and fasted seven days.

THE SECOND BOOK OF

SAMUEL

OTHERWISE CALLED
THE SECOND BOOK OF THE KINGS

CHAPTER 1

David learns of the death of Saul and Jonathan—He slays the Amalekite who claims to have killed Saul—David laments the passing of Saul and Jonathan with a song.

NOW it came to pass after the death of Saul, when David was returned from the slaughter of the Amalekites, and David had abode two days in Ziklag;

2 It came even to pass on the third day, that, behold, a man came out of the camp from Saul with his clothes rent, and earth upon his head: and *so* it was, when he came to David, that he fell to the earth, and did obeisance.

3 And David said unto him, From whence comest thou? And he said unto him, Out of the camp of Israel am I escaped.

4 And David said unto him, How

4*a* 2 Sam. 1:10 (1–16).
5*a* 1 Sam. 26:10.
10*a* 1 Chr. 10:10.
11*a* 2 Sam. 2:4.

went the matter? I pray thee, tell me. And he answered, That the people are fled from the battle, and many of the people also are fallen and dead; and Saul and Jonathan his son are dead also.

5 And David said unto the young man that told him, How knowest thou that Saul and Jonathan his son be dead?

6 And the young man that told him said, As I happened by chance upon mount Gilboa, behold, Saul leaned upon his spear; and, lo, the chariots and horsemen followed hard after him.

7 And when he looked behind him, he saw me, and called unto me. And I answered, Here *am* I.

8 And he said unto me, Who *art* thou? And I answered him, I *am* an Amalekite.

9 He said unto me again, Stand, I pray thee, upon me, and slay me: for anguish is come upon me, because my life *is* yet whole in me.

10 So I stood upon him, and *a*slew him, because I was sure that he could not live after that he was fallen: and I took the crown that *was* upon his head, and the bracelet that *was* on his arm, and have brought them hither unto my lord.

11 Then David took hold on his clothes, and rent them; and likewise all the men that *were* with him:

12 And they mourned, and wept, and fasted until even, for Saul, and for Jonathan his son, and for the people of the LORD, and for the house of Israel; because they were fallen by the sword.

13 ¶ And David said unto the young man that told him, Whence *art* thou? And he answered, I *am* the son of a stranger, an Amalekite.

14 And David said unto him, How wast thou not afraid to stretch forth thine hand to *a*destroy the LORD's *b*anointed?

15 And David called one of the young men, and said, Go near, *and* fall upon him. And he smote him that he died.

16 And David said unto him, Thy blood *be* upon thy head; for thy mouth hath testified against thee, saying, I have slain the LORD's anointed.

17 ¶ And David lamented with this lamentation over Saul and over Jonathan his son:

18 (Also he bade them *a*teach the children of Judah *the use of* the bow: behold, *it is* written in the book of *b*Jasher.)

19 The beauty of Israel is slain upon thy high places: how are the mighty fallen!

20 Tell *it* not in Gath, publish *it* not in the streets of Askelon; lest the daughters of the Philistines rejoice, lest the daughters of the uncircumcised triumph.

21 Ye mountains of Gilboa, *let there be* no dew, neither *let there be* rain, upon you, nor fields of offerings: for there the shield of the mighty is vilely cast away, the shield of Saul, *as though he had* not *been* anointed with oil.

22 From the blood of the slain, from the fat of the mighty, the bow of Jonathan turned not back, and the sword of Saul returned not empty.

23 Saul and Jonathan *were* lovely and pleasant in their lives, and in their death they were not *a*divided: they were swifter than eagles, they were stronger than lions.

24 Ye daughters of Israel, weep over Saul, who clothed you in scarlet, with *other* delights, who put on ornaments of gold upon your *a*apparel.

25 How are the mighty fallen in the midst of the battle! O Jonathan, *thou wast* slain in thine high places.

26 I am distressed for thee, my brother Jonathan: very pleasant hast thou been unto me: thy *a*love to me

1 10*a* 1 Sam. 31:4 (1–4);
    1 Chr. 10:4 (4–5).
14*a* 2 Sam. 4:10.
    b TG Anointing.
18*a* This verse appears to

be a superscription like
the one appearing at
the beginning of
Psalm 60.
    b TG Scriptures, Lost.

23*a* D&C 135:3.
24*a* TG Prosperity.
26*a* Alma 20:26;
    D&C 88:133.

was wonderful, passing the love of women.

27 How are the mighty fallen, and the weapons of ᵃwar perished!

CHAPTER 2

David is anointed king over the house of Judah—Ishbosheth becomes the king of Israel—David's followers defeat Abner and the men of Israel.

AND it came to pass after this, that David inquired of the LORD, saying, Shall I go up into any of the cities of Judah? And the LORD said unto him, Go up. And David said, Whither shall I go up? And he said, Unto Hebron.

2 So David went up thither, and his two ᵃwives also, Ahinoam the Jezreelitess, and Abigail Nabal's wife the Carmelite.

3 And his ᵃmen that *were* with him did David bring up, every man with his household: and they dwelt in the cities of Hebron.

4 And the men of Judah came, and there they anointed ᵃDavid king over the house of ᵇJudah. And they told David, saying, *That* the men of ᶜJabesh-gilead *were they* that buried Saul.

5 ¶ And David sent messengers unto the men of Jabesh-gilead, and said unto them, Blessed *be* ye of the LORD, that ye have shewed this kindness unto your lord, *even* unto Saul, and have buried him.

6 And now the LORD shew kindness and truth unto you: and I also will ᵃrequite you this kindness, because ye have done this thing.

7 Therefore now let your hands be strengthened, and be ye ᵃvaliant: for your master Saul is dead, and also the house of Judah have anointed me king over them.

8 ¶ But ᵃAbner the son of Ner, captain of Saul's host, took Ish-bosheth the son of Saul, and brought him over to Mahanaim;

9 And made him king over Gilead, and over the Ashurites, and over Jezreel, and over Ephraim, and over Benjamin, and over all Israel.

10 Ish-bosheth Saul's son *was* forty years old when he began to reign over Israel, and reigned two years. But the house of Judah followed David.

11 And the time that David was ᵃking in Hebron over the house of ᵇJudah was seven years and six months.

12 ¶ And Abner the son of Ner, and the servants of Ish-bosheth the son of Saul, went out from Mahanaim to Gibeon.

13 And Joab the son of Zeruiah, and the servants of David, went out, and met together by the pool of Gibeon: and they sat down, the one on the one side of the pool, and the other on the other side of the pool.

14 And Abner said to Joab, Let the young men now arise, and play before us. And Joab said, Let them arise.

15 Then there arose and went over by number twelve of Benjamin, which *pertained* to Ish-bosheth the son of Saul, and twelve of the servants of David.

16 And they caught every one his fellow by the head, and *thrust* his sword in his fellow's side; so they fell down together: wherefore that place was called ᵃHelkath-hazzurim, which *is* in Gibeon.

17 And there was a very sore battle that day; and Abner was beaten, and the men of Israel, before the servants of David.

18 ¶ And there were three sons of Zeruiah there, ᵃJoab, and ᵇAbishai, and Asahel: and ᶜAsahel *was as* light of foot as ᵈa wild roe.

19 And Asahel pursued after Abner;

27a TG War.
2 2a 1 Sam. 25:43 (42–43);
  27:3;
  D&C 132:39.
  3a 1 Sam. 23:13; 27:2 (2–3);
  2 Sam. 19:41.
  4a 2 Sam. 5:3 (1–3);
  1 Chr. 12:23.

  b 1 Sam. 18:16;
  2 Sam. 5:5.
  c 1 Sam. 31:11 (11–13).
  6a OR do, recompense.
  7a TG Courage.
  8a 1 Sam. 14:50; 17:55;
  2 Sam. 3:6; 1 Chr. 26:28.
  11a 2 Sam. 5:5; 1 Chr. 3:4.

  b TG Israel, Judah,
  People of.
  16a IE Field of foes.
  18a 1 Chr. 2:16.
  b 1 Sam. 26:6;
  1 Chr. 2:13–16; 11:20.
  c 1 Chr. 11:26.
  d OR a deer in the field.

and in going he turned not to the right hand nor to the left from following Abner.

20 Then Abner looked behind him, and said, *Art* thou Asahel? And he answered, I *am.*

21 And Abner said to him, Turn thee aside to thy right hand or to thy left, and lay thee hold on one of the young men, and take thee his armour. But Asahel would not turn aside from following of him.

22 And Abner said again to Asahel, Turn thee aside from following me: wherefore should I smite thee to the ground? how then should I hold up my face to Joab thy brother?

23 Howbeit he refused to turn aside: wherefore Abner with the hinder end of the spear smote him under the *a*fifth *rib,* that the spear came out behind him; and he fell down there, and died in the same place: and it came to pass, *that* as many as came to the place where *b*Asahel fell down and died stood still.

24 Joab also and Abishai pursued after Abner: and the sun went down when they were come to the hill of Ammah, that *lieth* before Giah by the way of the wilderness of Gibeon.

25 ¶ And the children of Benjamin gathered themselves together after Abner, and became one troop, and stood on the top of an hill.

26 Then Abner called to Joab, and said, Shall the sword devour for ever? knowest thou not that it will be bitterness in the latter end? how long shall it be then, ere thou bid the people return from following their brethren?

27 And Joab said, *As* God liveth, unless thou hadst spoken, surely then in the morning the people had gone up every one from following his brother.

28 So Joab blew a trumpet, and all the people stood still, and pursued after Israel no more, neither fought they any more.

29 And Abner and his men walked all that night through the plain, and passed over Jordan, and went through all Bithron, and they came to Mahanaim.

30 And Joab returned from following Abner: and when he had gathered all the people together, there lacked of David's servants nineteen men and Asahel.

31 But the servants of David had smitten of Benjamin, and of Abner's men, *so that* three hundred and threescore men died.

32 ¶ And they took up Asahel, and buried him in the sepulchre of his father, which *was in* Beth-lehem. And Joab and his men went all night, and they came to Hebron at break of day.

CHAPTER 3

The houses of David and Saul engage in a long war—David grows stronger—Abner joins David but is slain by Joab—David mourns for Abner.

NOW there was long war between the house of Saul and the house of David: but David waxed stronger and stronger, and the house of Saul waxed weaker and weaker.

2 ¶ And unto *a*David were sons born in Hebron: and his firstborn was Amnon, of *b*Ahinoam the Jezreelitess;

3 And his second, Chileab, of Abigail the wife of Nabal the Carmelite; and the third, *a*Absalom the son of Maacah the daughter of Talmai king of *b*Geshur;

4 And the fourth, *a*Adonijah the son of Haggith; and the fifth, Shephatiah the son of Abital;

5 And the sixth, Ithream, by Eglah David's wife. These were born to David in Hebron.

6 ¶ And it came to pass, while there was war between the house of Saul and the house of David, that *a*Abner

---

23a 2 Sam. 20:10.
  b 2 Sam. 3:27.
3 2a 2 Sam. 5:13;
    1 Chr. 3:1 (1–4).

  b 1 Sam. 14:50; 25:43.
3a 2 Sam. 13:1.
  b Deut. 3:14;
    2 Sam. 14:32 (23, 32);

    15:8.
4a 1 Kgs. 1:5.
6a 2 Sam. 2:8.

made himself strong for the house of Saul.

7 And Saul had a concubine, whose name was *a*Rizpah, the daughter of Aiah: and *Ish-bosheth* said to Abner, Wherefore hast thou gone in unto my father's concubine?

8 Then was Abner very wroth for the words of Ish-bosheth, and said, *Am* I a *a*dog's head, which against Judah do shew kindness this day unto the house of Saul thy father, to his brethren, and to his friends, and have not delivered thee into the hand of David, that thou chargest me to day with a fault concerning this woman?

9 So do God to Abner, and more also, except, as the LORD hath sworn to *a*David, even so I do to him;

10 To *a*translate the kingdom from the house of Saul, and to set up the throne of David over Israel and over Judah, from Dan even to Beer-sheba.

11 And he could not answer Abner a word again, because he feared him.

12 ¶ And Abner sent messengers to David on his behalf, saying, Whose *is* the land? saying *also,* Make thy *a*league with me, and, behold, my hand *shall be* with thee, to bring about all Israel unto thee.

13 ¶ And he said, Well; I will make a league with thee: but one thing I require of thee, that is, Thou shalt not see my face, except thou first bring Michal Saul's daughter, when thou comest to see my face.

14 And David sent messengers to Ish-bosheth Saul's son, saying, Deliver *me* my wife *a*Michal, which I espoused to me for an hundred foreskins of the Philistines.

15 And Ish-bosheth sent, and took her from *her* husband, *even* from *a*Phaltiel the son of Laish.

16 And her husband went with her along weeping behind her to Bahurim. Then said Abner unto him, Go, return. And he returned.

17 ¶ And Abner had communica-tion with the elders of Israel, saying, Ye sought for David in times past *to be* king over you:

18 Now then do *it:* for the LORD hath spoken of David, saying, By the hand of my servant David I will save my people Israel out of the hand of the Philistines, and out of the hand of all their enemies.

19 And Abner also spake in the ears of Benjamin: and Abner went also to speak in the ears of David in Hebron all that seemed good to Israel, and that seemed good to the whole house of Benjamin.

20 So Abner came to David to Hebron, and twenty men with him. And David made Abner and the men that *were* with him a feast.

21 And Abner said unto David, I will arise and go, and will gather all Israel unto my lord the king, that they may make a league with thee, and that thou mayest reign over all that thine heart desireth. And David sent Abner away; and he went in peace.

22 ¶ And, behold, the servants of David and Joab came from *pursuing* a troop, and brought in a great spoil with them: but Abner *was* not with David in Hebron; for he had sent him away, and he was gone in peace.

23 When Joab and all the host that *was* with him were come, they told Joab, saying, Abner the son of Ner came to the king, and he hath sent him away, and he is gone in peace.

24 Then Joab came to the king, and said, What hast thou done? behold, Abner came unto thee; why *is* it *that* thou hast sent him away, and he is quite gone?

25 Thou knowest Abner the son of Ner, that he came to deceive thee, and to know thy going out and thy coming in, and to know all that thou doest.

26 And when Joab was come out from David, he sent messengers after Abner, which brought him

---

7*a* 2 Sam. 21:8 (8, 10).
8*a* 1 Sam. 17:43.
9*a* 1 Sam. 15:28.
10*a* OR transfer.
12*a* OR covenant (also v. 13).
14*a* 1 Sam. 14:49;
18:27 (25–27).
15*a* 1 Sam. 25:44.

again from the well of Sirah: but David knew *it* not.

27 And when *a*Abner was returned to Hebron, Joab took him aside in the gate to speak with him quietly, and smote him there under the fifth *rib,* that he died, for the blood of *b*Asahel his brother.

28 ¶ And afterward when David heard *it,* he said, I and my kingdom *are* guiltless before the LORD for ever from the blood of Abner the son of Ner:

29 Let it rest on the head of *a*Joab, and on all his father's house; and let there not fail from the house of Joab one that hath an issue, or that is a leper, or that leaneth on a staff, or that falleth on the sword, or that lacketh bread.

30 So Joab and Abishai his brother slew Abner, because he had slain their brother Asahel at Gibeon in the battle.

31 ¶ And David said to Joab, and to all the people that *were* with him, Rend your clothes, and gird you with sackcloth, and mourn before Abner. And king David *himself* followed the bier.

32 And they buried Abner in Hebron: and the king lifted up his voice, and wept at the grave of Abner; and all the people wept.

33 And the king lamented over Abner, and said, Died Abner as a fool dieth?

34 Thy hands *were* not bound, nor thy feet put into fetters: as a man falleth before wicked men, *so* fellest thou. And all the people wept again over him.

35 And when all the people came to cause David to eat meat while it was yet day, David sware, saying, So do God to me, and more also, if I taste bread, or ought else, till the sun be down.

36 And all the people took notice *of it,* and it pleased them: as whatsoever the king did pleased all the people.

37 For all the people and all Israel understood that day that it was not of the king to slay Abner the son of Ner.

38 And the king said unto his servants, Know ye not that there is a prince and a great man fallen this day in Israel?

39 And I *am* this day weak, though anointed king; and these men the sons of Zeruiah *be* too hard for me: the LORD shall *a*reward the doer of evil according to his wickedness.

CHAPTER 4

Two of Saul's captains slay Ishbosheth—They take his head to David, who has them slain for killing a righteous person.

AND when Saul's son heard that Abner was dead in Hebron, his hands were feeble, and all the Israelites were troubled.

2 And Saul's son had two men *that were* captains of bands: the name of the one *was* Baanah, and the name of the other Rechab, the sons of Rimmon a Beerothite, of the children of Benjamin: (for Beeroth also was reckoned to Benjamin:

3 And the Beerothites fled to Gittaim, and were *a*sojourners there until this day.)

4 And *a*Jonathan, Saul's son, had a son *that was* lame of *his* feet. He was five years old when the tidings came of Saul and Jonathan out of Jezreel, and his nurse took him up, and fled: and it came to pass, as she made haste to flee, that he fell, and became lame. And his name *was* Mephibosheth.

5 And the sons of Rimmon the Beerothite, Rechab and Baanah, went, and came about the heat of the day to the house of Ish-bosheth, who lay on a bed at noon.

6 And they came thither into the midst of the house, *as though* they would have fetched wheat; and they smote him under the fifth *rib:* and

---

27*a* 1 Kgs. 2:5, 32.
  b 2 Sam. 2:23.
29*a* 1 Kgs. 2:33 (32–33).

39*a* TG Reward.
4 3*a* OR temporary dwellers; alien new-comers (no

inherited rights).
4*a* 2 Sam. 9:3.

Rechab and Baanah his brother escaped.

7 For when they came into the house, he lay on his bed in his bedchamber, and they smote him, and slew him, and beheaded him, and took his head, and gat them away through the plain all night.

8 And they brought the head of Ish-bosheth unto David to Hebron, and said to the king, Behold the head of Ish-bosheth the son of Saul thine enemy, which sought thy life; and the LORD hath avenged my lord the king this day of Saul, and of his seed.

9 ¶ And David answered Rechab and Baanah his brother, the sons of Rimmon the Beerothite, and said unto them, *As* the LORD liveth, who hath redeemed my soul out of all adversity,

10 When one told me, saying, Behold, *a*Saul is *b*dead, thinking to have brought good tidings, I took hold of him, and slew him in Ziklag, who *thought* that I would have given him a reward for his tidings:

11 How much more, when wicked men have slain a righteous person in his own house upon his bed? shall I not therefore now require his blood of your hand, and take you away from the earth?

12 And David commanded his young men, and they slew them, and cut off their hands and their feet, and hanged *them* up over the pool in Hebron. But they took the head of Ish-bosheth, and buried *it* in the sepulchre of Abner in Hebron.

CHAPTER 5

All Israel anoints David king—He takes Jerusalem and is blessed of the Lord— He conquers the Philistines.

THEN came all the tribes of Israel to *a*David unto Hebron, and spake, saying, Behold, we *are* thy bone and thy flesh.

2 Also in time past, when Saul was king over us, thou wast he that leddest out and broughtest in Israel: and the LORD said to thee, Thou shalt feed my people Israel, and thou shalt be a captain over Israel.

3 So all the elders of Israel came to the king to Hebron; and king David made a league with them in Hebron before the LORD: and they *a*anointed *b*David *c*king over Israel.

4 ¶ David *was* thirty years old when he began to *a*reign, *and* he *b*reigned forty years.

5 In Hebron he reigned over *a*Judah seven years and six months: and in Jerusalem he *b*reigned thirty and three years over all Israel and Judah.

6 ¶ And the king and his men went to Jerusalem unto the *a*Jebusites, the inhabitants of the land: which spake unto David, saying, Except thou take away the blind and the lame, thou shalt not come in hither: thinking, David cannot come in hither.

7 Nevertheless David took the strong hold of *a*Zion: the same *is* the *b*city of David.

8 And David said on that day, Whosoever getteth up to the gutter, and smiteth the *a*Jebusites, and the lame and the blind, *that are* hated of David's soul, *he shall be chief and captain*. Wherefore they said, The blind and the lame shall not come into the house.

9 So David dwelt in the fort, and called it the *a*city of David. And David built round about from *b*Millo and inward.

10 And David went on, and grew great, and the LORD God of hosts *was* with him.

10*a* 1 Chr. 10:13 (3–14).
　b 2 Sam. 1:14 (13–15).
5 1*a* 1 Chr. 11:1 (1–9).
　3*a* 1 Chr. 14:8.
　b 2 Sam. 2:4 (3–4);
　　1 Chr. 12:23.
　c TG Kings, Earthly.
　4*a* 1 Chr. 11:3.

　b 2 Sam. 8:15; 1 Kgs. 2:11;
　　1 Chr. 29:27.
5*a* 2 Sam. 2:4.
　b 2 Sam. 2:11; 1 Chr. 3:4.
6*a* Josh. 15:63; Judg. 1:21.
7*a* TG Zion.
　b 1 Kgs. 2:10.
8*a* 1 Chr. 11:4.

9*a* 1 Chr. 11:7.
　b The Hebrew root word
　　suggests a fill, terrace, or
　　elevation as part of the
　　defense bastion.
　　1 Kgs. 9:15 (15, 24); 11:27;
　　2 Kgs. 12:20;
　　2 Chr. 32:5.

11 ¶ And *a*Hiram king of Tyre sent messengers to David, and cedar trees, and carpenters, and masons: and they built David an house.

12 And David perceived that the LORD had established him king over Israel, and that he had exalted his kingdom for his people Israel's sake.

13 ¶ And David took *him* more concubines and *a*wives out of Jerusalem, after he was come from Hebron: and there were yet *b*sons and daughters born to David.

14 And these *be* the names of those that were born unto him in Jerusalem; Shammua, and Shobab, and Nathan, and Solomon,

15 Ibhar also, and Elishua, and Nepheg, and Japhia,

16 And Elishama, and Eliada, and Eliphalet.

17 ¶ But when the Philistines heard that they had anointed David king over Israel, all the Philistines came up to seek David; and David heard *of it,* and went down to the *a*hold.

18 The Philistines also came and spread themselves in the valley of Rephaim.

19 And David inquired of the LORD, saying, Shall I go up to the Philistines? wilt thou deliver them into mine hand? And the LORD said unto David, Go up: for I will doubtless deliver the Philistines into thine hand.

20 And David came to *a*Baal-perazim, and David smote them there, and said, The LORD hath broken forth upon mine enemies before me, as the *b*breach of waters. Therefore he called the name of that place Baal-perazim.

21 And there they left their *a*images, and David and his men *b*burned them.

22 ¶ And the *a*Philistines came up yet again, and spread themselves in the valley of Rephaim.

23 And when David inquired of the LORD, he said, Thou shalt not go up; *but* fetch a compass behind them, and come upon them over against the mulberry trees.

24 And let it be, when thou hearest the sound of a going in the tops of the mulberry trees, that then thou shalt bestir thyself: for then shall the LORD go out before thee, to smite the host of the Philistines.

25 And David did so, as the LORD had commanded him; and smote the *a*Philistines from Geba until thou come to Gazer.

CHAPTER 6

David takes the ark to the city of David—Uzzah is smitten for steadying the ark and dies—David dances before the Lord, causing a breach between him and Michal.

AGAIN, David *a*gathered together all *the* chosen *men* of Israel, thirty thousand.

2 And David arose, and went with all the people that *were* with him from Baale of Judah, to bring up from thence the *a*ark of God, whose name is called by the name of the LORD of hosts that dwelleth *between* the *b*cherubims.

3 And they set the ark of God upon a new cart, and brought it out of the house of Abinadab that *was* in Gibeah: and Uzzah and Ahio, the sons of Abinadab, drave the new cart.

4 And they brought it out of the house of Abinadab which *was* at Gibeah, accompanying the ark of God: and Ahio went before the ark.

5 And David and all the house of Israel played before the LORD on all manner of *instruments made of* fir wood, even on *a*harps, and on

---

11*a* 1 Kgs. 5:1.
13*a* Deut. 17:17 (14–17);
    Jacob 2:24 (23–24);
    3:5 (5–7);
    D&C 132:38 (38–39).
  b 2 Sam. 3:2.
17*a* OR stronghold.

20*a* 1 Chr. 14:11 (10–11);
    Isa. 28:21.
  b OR bursting-forth.
21*a* 1 Chr. 14:12.
  b HEB carried them away.
22*a* 1 Chr. 14:13 (13–16).
25*a* 2 Sam. 8:12.

6 1*a* 1 Chr. 13:5.
  2*a* 1 Chr. 13:13 (6–14).
  b TG Cherubim.
  5*a* Gen. 31:27;
    1 Chr. 15:16;
    Dan. 3:5 (5, 7, 10, 15).

psalteries, and on timbrels, and on cornets, and on cymbals.

6 ¶ And when they came to Na-chon's threshingfloor, Uzzah put forth *his hand* to the [a]ark of God, and took hold of it; for the oxen shook *it.*

7 And the anger of the LORD was kindled against [a]Uzzah; and God [b]smote him there for *his* error; and there he died by the ark of God.

8 And David was displeased, be-cause the LORD had made a breach upon Uzzah: and he called the name of the place [a]Perez-uzzah to this day.

9 And David was afraid of the LORD that day, and said, How shall the ark of the LORD come to me?

10 So David would not remove the ark of the LORD unto him into the city of David: but David carried it aside into the house of Obed-edom the Gittite.

11 And the ark of the LORD con-tinued in the house of Obed-edom the Gittite three months: and the LORD blessed Obed-edom, and all his household.

12 ¶ And it was told king David, saying, The LORD hath blessed the house of Obed-edom, and all that *pertaineth* unto him, because of the [a]ark of God. So David went and brought up the ark of God from the house of Obed-edom into the city of David with gladness.

13 And it was *so,* that when they that bare the ark of the LORD had gone six paces, he [a]sacrificed oxen and fatlings.

14 And David [a]danced before the LORD with all *his* might; and David *was* girded with a linen ephod.

15 So David and all the house of Israel brought up the ark of the LORD with shouting, and with the sound of the trumpet.

16 And as the ark of the LORD came into the city of David, Michal Saul's daughter looked through a window, and saw king David leaping and dancing before the LORD; and she despised him in her heart.

17 ¶ And they brought in the [a]ark of the LORD, and set it in his place, in the midst of the tabernacle that David had pitched for it: and David offered burnt offerings and peace offerings before the LORD.

18 And as soon as David had made an end of offering burnt offerings and peace offerings, he [a]blessed the people in the name of the LORD of hosts.

19 And he dealt among all the peo-ple, *even* among the whole multitude of Israel, as well to the women as men, to every one a cake of bread, and a good piece *of flesh,* and [a]a flagon *of wine.* So all the people departed every one to his house.

20 ¶ Then David returned to [a]bless his household. And [b]Michal the daughter of Saul came out to meet David, and said, How glorious was the king of Israel to day, who [c]un-covered himself to day in the eyes of the handmaids of his servants, as one of the vain fellows shame-lessly uncovereth himself!

21 And David said unto Michal, *It was* before the LORD, which chose me before thy father, and before all his house, to appoint me ruler over the people of the LORD, over Israel: therefore will I play before the LORD.

22 And I will yet be more vile than thus, and will be base in mine own sight: and of the maidservants which thou hast spoken of, of them shall I be had in honour.

23 Therefore Michal the daughter of Saul had no child unto the day of her death.

6a D&C 85:8.
7a 1 Chr. 15:2.
  b Num. 1:51;
     1 Sam. 6:19.
8a IE Breach of Uzzah.
12a TG Ark of the
     Covenant.

13a 1 Chr. 15:26 (25–28).
14a D&C 136:28.
17a 1 Kgs. 3:15.
18a 1 Kgs. 8:14 (14–15);
     1 Chr. 16:2.
19a HEB (perhaps) a
     raisin-cake.

20a 1 Chr. 16:43.
  b 1 Sam. 14:49.
  c IE In his joyful dancing,
     more of his body was
     exposed than she
     believed proper.

CHAPTER 7

David offers to build a house for the Lord—The Lord, through Nathan, says He has not asked David to do so—The Lord will establish David's house and kingdom forever—David offers a prayer of thanksgiving.

AND it came to pass, when the king sat in his house, and the LORD had given him ªrest round about from all his enemies;

2 That the king said unto Nathan the prophet, See now, I dwell in an house of cedar, but the ark of God dwelleth within ªcurtains.

3 And Nathan said to the king, Go, do all that *is* in thine ªheart; for the LORD *is* with thee.

4 ¶ And it came to pass that night, that the word of the LORD came unto ªNathan, saying,

5 Go and tell my servant David, Thus saith the LORD, Shalt thou build me an ªhouse for me to dwell in?

6 Whereas I have not dwelt in *any* house since the time that I brought up the children of Israel out of Egypt, even to this day, but have walked in a tent and in a tabernacle.

7 In all *the places* wherein I have walked with all the children of Israel spake I a word with any of the tribes of Israel, whom I commanded to feed my people Israel, saying, Why build ye not me an ªhouse of cedar?

8 Now therefore so shalt thou say unto my servant David, Thus saith the LORD of hosts, I took thee from the ªsheepcote, from following the sheep, to be ruler over my people, over Israel:

9 And I was with thee whithersoever thou wentest, and have cut off all thine enemies out of thy sight, and have made thee a great name, like unto the name of the great *men* that *are* in the earth.

10 Moreover I will appoint a place for my people Israel, and will plant them, that they may dwell in a place of their own, and move no more; neither shall the children of wickedness afflict them any more, as beforetime,

11 And as since the time that I commanded ªjudges *to be* over my people Israel, and have caused thee to ᵇrest from all thine enemies. Also the LORD telleth thee that he will make thee an ᶜhouse.

12 ¶ And when thy days be fulfilled, and thou shalt sleep with thy fathers, I will set up thy ªseed after thee, which shall proceed out of thy bowels, and I will establish his kingdom.

13 He shall ªbuild an house for my name, and I will ᵇstablish the throne of his kingdom for ever.

14 I will be his ªfather, and he shall be my ᵇson. If he commit iniquity, I will ᶜchasten him with the rod of men, and with the stripes of the children of men:

15 But my mercy shall not depart away from him, as I took *it* from Saul, whom I put away before thee.

16 And thine ªhouse and thy kingdom shall be established for ever before thee: thy ᵇthrone shall be established for ever.

17 According to all these words, and according to all this vision, so did Nathan speak unto David.

18 ¶ Then went king David in, and sat before the LORD, and he said, Who *am* I, O Lord GOD? and what *is* my house, that thou hast brought me hitherto?

19 And this was yet a small thing in thy sight, O Lord GOD; but thou hast spoken also of thy servant's

---

7 1ª 2 Sam. 7:11.
  2ª 2 Sam. 11:11.
  3ª 1 Chr. 22:7.
  4ª 2 Sam. 12:1.
  5ª TG Temple.
  7ª 1 Chr. 17:6.
  8ª IE sheepfold.
 11ª Judg. 2:16 (14–16).
  b 2 Sam. 7:1.

  c Ex. 1:21 (15–22);
    1 Sam. 2:35 (35–36).
 12ª 1 Kgs. 2:4; 8:19 (19–20);
    2 Chr. 23:3.
 13ª 1 Kgs. 6:12; 8:13.
  b TG Jesus Christ, Davidic
    Descent of.
 14ª Heb. 1:5.
  b Mosiah 5:7;

    27:25 (24–26);
    Moses 6:68 (64–68).
  c Ps. 89:32 (30–33);
    D&C 95:1 (1–2);
    101:4 (4–5).
 16ª 2 Kgs. 8:19 (18–19).
  b 1 Kgs. 9:5;
    Luke 1:33;
    John 12:34.

house for a great while to come. And *is* this the manner of man, O Lord GOD?

20 And what can David say more unto thee? for thou, Lord GOD, *a*knowest thy servant.

21 For thy word's sake, and according to thine own heart, hast thou done all these *a*great things, to make thy servant know *them.*

22 Wherefore thou art great, O LORD God: for *there is* none *a*like thee, neither *is there any* God beside thee, according to all that we have heard with our ears.

23 And what one *a*nation in the earth *is* like thy people, *even* like Israel, whom God went to redeem for a people to himself, and to make him a name, and to do for you great things and terrible, for thy land, before thy people, which thou redeemedst to thee from Egypt, *from* the nations and their gods?

24 For thou hast *a*confirmed to thyself thy people *b*Israel *to be* a people unto thee for ever: and thou, LORD, art become their God.

25 And now, O LORD God, the word that thou hast spoken concerning thy servant, and concerning his house, *a*establish *it* for ever, and do as thou hast said.

26 And let thy name be magnified for ever, saying, The LORD of hosts *is* the God over Israel: and let the house of thy servant David be established before thee.

27 For thou, O LORD of hosts, God of Israel, hast revealed to thy servant, saying, I will build thee an house: therefore hath thy servant found in his heart to pray this prayer unto thee.

28 And now, O Lord GOD, thou *art* that God, and thy words be *a*true, and thou hast promised this goodness unto thy servant:

29 Therefore now let it please thee to bless the house of thy servant, that it may continue for ever before thee: for thou, O Lord GOD, hast spoken *it:* and with thy blessing let the house of thy servant be blessed for ever.

CHAPTER 8

David defeats and subjects many nations—The Lord is with him—He executes judgment and justice unto all his people.

AND after this it came to pass, that David *a*smote the Philistines, and subdued them: and David took Metheg-ammah out of the hand of the Philistines.

2 And he smote *a*Moab, and *b*measured them with a line, casting them down to the ground; even with two lines measured he to put to death, and with one full line to keep alive. And *so* the *c*Moabites became David's servants, *and* brought gifts.

3 ¶ David smote also Hadadezer, the son of Rehob, king of Zobah, as he went to recover his border at the river Euphrates.

4 And David took from him a thousand *chariots,* and seven hundred horsemen, and twenty thousand footmen: and David houghed all the chariot *horses,* but reserved of them *for* an hundred chariots.

5 And when the *a*Syrians of Damascus came to succour Hadadezer king of Zobah, David slew of the Syrians two and twenty thousand men.

6 Then David put garrisons in Syria of Damascus: and the Syrians became servants to David, *and* brought gifts. And the LORD preserved David whithersoever he went.

7 And David took the *a*shields of gold that were on the servants of

---

20*a* Ps. 139:1 (1–4);
    Morm. 6:22;
    D&C 6:16.
21*a* 1 Chr. 17:19.
22*a* Ex. 8:10 (8–10); 15:11;
    1 Kgs. 8:23.
23*a* Deut. 4:7; 1 Kgs. 3:8;
    2 Ne. 29:8; Alma 9:20;
    Abr. 2:9.

24*a* Jacob 6:4.
  b D&C 38:33.
25*a* Ps. 119:38.
28*a* John 17:17; 2 Ne. 31:15;
    Alma 38:9; Ether 4:12;
    D&C 20:11; 66:11.
8 1*a* 1 Chr. 18:1 (1–17).
  2*a* Num. 24:17.
  b IE He apparently

determined their size
and put the taller,
stronger to death.
  c 2 Kgs. 1:1; 3:5.
5*a* HEB Aram; i.e.,
    Arameans. They were
    later called "Syrians" by
    Greek peoples.
7*a* 2 Kgs. 11:10.

Hadadezer, and brought them to Jerusalem.

8 And from Betah, and from Berothai, cities of Hadadezer, king David took exceeding much brass.

9 ¶ When Toi king of Hamath heard that David had smitten all the host of Hadadezer,

10 Then Toi sent Joram his son unto king David, to salute him, and to bless him, because he had fought against Hadadezer, and smitten him: for Hadadezer had wars with Toi. And *Joram* brought with him vessels of silver, and vessels of gold, and vessels of brass:

11 Which also king David did *a*dedicate unto the LORD, with the silver and gold that he had dedicated of all nations which he subdued;

12 Of Syria, and of Moab, and of the children of *a*Ammon, and of the *b*Philistines, and of *c*Amalek, and of the spoil of Hadadezer, son of Rehob, king of Zobah.

13 And David gat *him* a name when he returned from smiting of the Syrians in the valley of *a*salt, *being* eighteen thousand *men*.

14 ¶ And he put garrisons in Edom; throughout all Edom put he garrisons, and all they of *a*Edom became David's servants. And the LORD preserved David whithersoever he went.

15 And David *a*reigned over all Israel; and David executed judgment and justice unto all his people.

16 And *a*Joab the son of Zeruiah *was* over the host; and Jehoshaphat the son of Ahilud *was* recorder;

17 And *a*Zadok the son of Ahitub, and Ahimelech the son of Abiathar, *were* the priests; and Seraiah *was* the *b*scribe;

18 And *a*Benaiah the son of Jehoiada

was over both the Cherethites and the *b*Pelethites; and David's sons were *c*chief rulers.

CHAPTER 9

David seeks to honor the house of Saul—He finds Mephibosheth, the son of Jonathan, to whom he restores all the land of Saul.

AND David said, Is there yet any that is left of the house of Saul, that I may shew him *a*kindness for *b*Jonathan's sake?

2 And *there was* of the house of Saul a servant whose name *was* *a*Ziba. And when they had called him unto David, the king said unto him, *Art* thou Ziba? And he said, Thy servant *is* he.

3 And the king said, *Is* there not yet any of the house of Saul, that I may shew the kindness of God unto him? And Ziba said unto the king, *a*Jonathan hath yet a son, *which is* lame on *his* feet.

4 And the king said unto him, Where *is* he? And Ziba said unto the king, Behold, he *is* in the house of Machir, the son of Ammiel, in Lo-debar.

5 ¶ Then king David sent, and fetched him out of the house of Machir, the son of Ammiel, from Lo-debar.

6 Now when *a*Mephibosheth, the son of Jonathan, the son of Saul, was come unto David, he fell on his face, and did reverence. And David said, Mephibosheth. And he answered, Behold thy servant!

7 ¶ And David said unto him, Fear not: for I will surely shew thee kindness for Jonathan thy father's sake, and will restore thee all the land of

11*a* 1 Kgs. 7:51;
   1 Chr. 26:27 (26–27).
12*a* 2 Sam. 10:14 (6–14).
   b 2 Sam. 5:25 (17–25).
   c Ex. 17:14;
   1 Sam. 30:18 (1–20).
13*a* 2 Kgs. 14:7.
14*a* Gen. 27:37 (29–40);
   Num. 24:18;
   2 Kgs. 3:9;

Ps. 60:8.
15*a* 2 Sam. 5:4.
16*a* 2 Sam. 20:23 (23–26).
17*a* 2 Sam. 15:24;
   1 Kgs. 2:35;
   1 Chr. 6:8; 24:3.
   b TG Scribe.
18*a* 1 Kgs. 2:25.
   b 1 Kgs. 1:38.
   c HEB priests; apparently,

in this case, civil
   ministers.
9 1*a* TG Kindness.
   b 1 Sam. 18:3 (1–3);
   20:14 (14–17);
   Prov. 27:10.
2*a* 2 Sam. 16:1.
3*a* 2 Sam. 4:4.
6*a* 2 Sam. 19:24 (24–25).

Saul thy father; and thou shalt ^aeat bread at my table continually.

8 And he bowed himself, and said, What *is* thy servant, that thou shouldest look upon such a ^adead dog as I *am*?

9 ¶ Then the king called to Ziba, Saul's servant, and said unto him, I have given unto thy master's son all that pertained to Saul and to all his house.

10 Thou therefore, and thy sons, and thy servants, shall till the land for him, and thou shalt bring in *the fruits,* that thy master's son may have food to eat: but Mephibosheth thy master's son shall eat bread alway at my table. Now Ziba had fifteen sons and twenty servants.

11 Then said Ziba unto the king, According to all that my lord the king hath commanded his servant, so shall thy servant do. As for Mephibosheth, *said the king,* he shall eat at my table, as one of the king's sons.

12 And Mephibosheth had a young son, whose name *was* Micha. And all that dwelt in the house of Ziba *were* ^aservants unto Mephibosheth.

13 So Mephibosheth dwelt in Jerusalem: for he did eat continually at the king's table; and was lame on both his feet.

CHAPTER 10

David's messengers are abused by the Ammonites—Israel defeats the Ammonites and Syrians.

AND it came to pass after this, that the king of the children of ^aAmmon died, and Hanun his son reigned in his stead.

2 Then said David, I will shew kindness unto Hanun the son of Nahash, as his father shewed kindness unto me. And David sent to comfort him by the hand of his servants for his father. And David's servants came into the land of the children of Ammon.

3 And the princes of the children of Ammon said unto Hanun their lord, Thinkest thou that David doth honour thy father, that he hath sent comforters unto thee? hath not David *rather* sent his servants unto thee, to search the city, and to spy it out, and to overthrow it?

4 Wherefore Hanun took David's servants, and shaved off the one half of their beards, and cut off their garments in the middle, *even* to their buttocks, and sent them away.

5 When they told *it* unto David, he sent to meet them, because the men were greatly ashamed: and the king said, Tarry at Jericho until your beards be grown, and *then* return.

6 ¶ And when the children of Ammon saw that they stank before David, the children of Ammon sent and hired the Syrians of Bethrehob, and the Syrians of Zoba, twenty thousand footmen, and of king Maacah a thousand men, and of ^aIsh-tob twelve thousand men.

7 And when David heard of *it,* he sent Joab, and all the host of the mighty men.

8 And the children of Ammon came out, and put the battle in array at the entering in of the gate: and the Syrians of Zoba, and of Rehob, and Ish-tob, and Maacah, *were* by themselves in the field.

9 When Joab saw that the front of the battle was against him before and behind, he chose of all the choice *men* of Israel, and put *them* in array against the Syrians:

10 And the rest of the people he delivered into the hand of Abishai his brother, that he might put *them* in array against the children of Ammon.

11 And he said, If the Syrians be too strong for me, then thou shalt help me: but if the children of Ammon be too strong for thee, then I will come and help thee.

12 Be of good courage, and let us play the ^amen for our people, and

---

7a 2 Sam. 19:28.
8a 2 Sam. 16:9.
12a 2 Sam. 19:26 (24–29).

10 1a 1 Chr. 19:1 (1–19).
6a HEB Men of Tob (a land mentioned in

Judg. 11:3).
12a 1 Sam. 4:9;
Alma 46:12.

for the cities of our God: and the LORD do that which seemeth him good.

13 And Joab drew nigh, and the people that *were* with him, unto the battle against the Syrians: and they fled before him.

14 And when the children of *ª*Ammon saw that the Syrians were fled, then fled they also before Abishai, and entered into the city. So Joab returned from the children of Ammon, and came to Jerusalem.

15 ¶ And when the Syrians saw that they were smitten before Israel, they gathered themselves together.

16 And Hadarezer sent, and brought out the Syrians that *were* beyond the river: and they came to Helam; and Shobach the captain of the host of Hadarezer *went* before them.

17 And when it was told David, he gathered all Israel together, and passed over Jordan, and came to Helam. And the Syrians set themselves in array against David, and fought with him.

18 And the Syrians fled before Israel; and David slew *the men of* seven hundred chariots of the Syrians, and forty thousand horsemen, and smote Shobach the captain of their host, who died there.

19 And when all the kings *that were* servants to Hadarezer saw that they were smitten before Israel, they made peace with Israel, and served them. So the Syrians feared to help the children of Ammon any more.

CHAPTER 11

David lies with Bathsheba, and she conceives—He then arranges for the death in battle of her husband, Uriah.

AND it came to pass, after the year was expired, at the time when kings go forth *to battle*, that David sent *ª*Joab, and his servants with him,

and all Israel; and they destroyed the children of Ammon, and besieged Rabbah. But David tarried still at Jerusalem.

2 ¶ And it came to pass in an eveningtide, that David arose from off his bed, and walked upon the roof of the king's house: and from the roof he *ª*saw a woman washing herself; and the woman *was* very beautiful to *ᵇ*look upon.

3 And David sent and inquired after the woman. And *one* said, *Is* not this *ª*Bath-sheba, the daughter of Eliam, the wife of *ᵇ*Uriah the Hittite?

4 And David sent messengers, and took her; and she came in unto him, and he *ª*lay with her; for she was purified from her uncleanness: and she returned unto her house.

5 And the woman conceived, and sent and told David, and said, I *am* with child.

6 ¶ And David sent to Joab, *saying*, Send me Uriah the Hittite. And Joab sent Uriah to David.

7 And when Uriah was come unto him, David demanded *of him* how Joab did, and how the people did, and how the war prospered.

8 And David said to Uriah, Go down to thy house, and wash thy feet. And Uriah departed out of the king's house, and there followed him *ª*a mess *of meat* from the king.

9 But Uriah slept at the door of the king's house with all the servants of his lord, and went not down to his house.

10 And when they had told David, saying, Uriah went not down unto his house, David said unto Uriah, Camest thou not from *thy* journey? why *then* didst thou not go down unto thine house?

11 And Uriah said unto David, The ark, and Israel, and Judah, abide in *ª*tents; and my lord Joab, and the servants of my lord, are encamped

---

14*a* 2 Sam. 8:12.
11 1*a* 1 Chr. 20:1.
   2*a* TG Covet.
    b D&C 42:23.
   3*a* HEB Daughter of the

covenant. 1 Chr. 3:5.
  b HEB Jehovah is my
   light. 1 Kgs. 15:5;
   1 Chr. 11:41.
4*a* D&C 132:39 (38–39).

TG Sensuality.
8*a* IE a present of a portion
  of food.
  Gen. 43:34.
11*a* 2 Sam. 7:2 (2–6).

in the open fields; shall I then go into mine house, to eat and to drink, and to lie with my wife? *as* thou livest, and *as* thy soul liveth, I will not do this thing.

12 And David said to Uriah, Tarry here to day also, and to morrow I will let thee depart. So Uriah abode in Jerusalem that day, and the morrow.

13 And when David had called him, he did eat and drink before him; and he made him drunk: and at even he went out to lie on his bed with the servants of his lord, but went not down to his house.

14 ¶ And it came to pass in the morning, that David wrote a letter to Joab, and sent *it* by the hand of Uriah.

15 And he wrote in the letter, saying, Set ye Uriah in the forefront of the hottest battle, and retire ye from him, that he may be *a*smitten, and die.

16 And it came to pass, when Joab observed the city, that he assigned Uriah unto a place where he knew that valiant men *were*.

17 And the men of the city went out, and fought with Joab: and there fell *some* of the people of the servants of David; and Uriah the Hittite died also.

18 ¶ Then Joab sent and told David all the things concerning the war;

19 And charged the messenger, saying, When thou hast made an end of telling the matters of the war unto the king,

20 And if so be that the king's *a*wrath arise, and he say unto thee, Wherefore approached ye so nigh unto the city when ye did fight? knew ye not that they would shoot from the wall?

21 Who smote *a*Abimelech the son of Jerubbesheth? did not a woman cast a piece of a millstone upon

him from the wall, that he died in Thebez? why went ye nigh the wall? then say thou, Thy servant Uriah the Hittite is dead also.

22 ¶ So the messenger went, and came and shewed David all that Joab had sent him for.

23 And the messenger said unto David, Surely the men prevailed against us, and came out unto us into the field, and we were upon them even unto the entering of the gate.

24 And the shooters shot from off the wall upon thy servants; and *some* of the king's servants be dead, and thy servant Uriah the Hittite is dead also.

25 Then David said unto the messenger, Thus shalt thou say unto Joab, Let not this thing displease thee, for the sword devoureth one as well as another: make thy battle more strong against the city, and overthrow it: and encourage thou him.

26 ¶ And when the wife of Uriah heard that Uriah her husband was dead, she mourned for her husband.

27 And when the mourning was past, David sent and fetched her to his house, and she became his *a*wife, and bare him a son. But the thing that David had done *b*displeased the LORD.

CHAPTER 12

Nathan tells David the parable of the ewe lamb—The Lord gave many wives to David, who is now cursed for taking Bathsheba—David fasts and prays for his son, but the Lord takes him—Solomon is born—David conquers the royal city of the Ammonites.

AND the LORD sent *a*Nathan unto David. And he came unto him, and said unto him, There were two men in one city; the one rich, and the other poor.

15a 2 Sam. 12:9.
20a Joab had not followed the king's plan (see v. 15) but sent Uriah and his men right up to the city gate and wall.

He feared David might be angry because so many were killed with Uriah.
21a Judg. 9:53 (1–57).
27a 2 Sam. 12:9.

b 2 Sam. 12:11 (1–25);
1 Chr. 21:8 (1–8);
Ps. 88:14 (6–8, 14–18);
D&C 132:39.
12 1a 2 Sam. 7:4 (2–17);
2 Chr. 29:25.

2 The rich *man* had exceeding many flocks and herds:

3 But the poor *man* had nothing, save one little ewe lamb, which he had bought and nourished up: and it grew up together with him, and with his children; it did eat of his own meat, and drank of his own cup, and lay in his bosom, and was unto him as a daughter.

4 And there came a traveller unto the rich man, and he spared to take of his own flock and of his own herd, to dress for the wayfaring man that was come unto him; but took the poor man's lamb, and dressed it for the man that was come to him.

5 And David's anger was greatly kindled against the man; and he said to Nathan, *As* the Lord liveth, the man that hath done this *thing* shall surely die:

6 And he shall restore the lamb ^afourfold, because he did this thing, and because he had no pity.

7 ¶ And Nathan said to David, Thou *art* the man. Thus saith the Lord God of Israel, I ^aanointed thee king over Israel, and I delivered thee out of the hand of Saul;

8 And I gave thee thy master's house, and thy master's wives into thy bosom, and gave thee the house of Israel and of Judah; and if *that had been* too little, I would moreover have given unto thee such and such things.

9 Wherefore hast thou ^adespised the commandment of the Lord, to do evil in his sight? thou hast ^bkilled ^cUriah the Hittite with the sword, and hast taken his ^dwife *to be* thy wife, and hast slain him with the sword of the children of Ammon.

10 Now therefore the sword shall never depart from thine house; be-

cause thou hast ^adespised me, and hast taken the wife of Uriah the Hittite to be thy wife.

11 Thus saith the Lord, Behold, I will raise up ^aevil against thee out of thine own house, and I will take thy wives before thine eyes, and give *them* unto thy neighbour, and he shall lie with thy wives in the sight of this sun.

12 For thou didst *it* secretly: but I will ^ado this thing before all Israel, and before the sun.

13 And David said unto Nathan, I have ^asinned against the Lord. And Nathan said unto David, The Lord also ^bhath put away thy sin; thou shalt not die.

14 Howbeit, because by this deed thou hast given great occasion to the enemies of the Lord to ^ablaspheme, the child also *that is* born unto thee shall surely die.

15 ¶ And Nathan departed unto his house. And the Lord struck the child that Uriah's wife bare unto David, and it was very sick.

16 David therefore besought God for the child; and David ^afasted, and went in, and lay all night upon the earth.

17 And the elders of his house arose, *and went* to him, to raise him up from the earth: but he would not, neither did he eat bread with them.

18 And it came to pass on the seventh day, that the child died. And the servants of David feared to tell him that the child was dead: for they said, Behold, while the child was yet alive, we spake unto him, and he would not hearken unto our voice: how will he then vex himself, if we tell him that the child is dead?

19 But when David saw that his servants whispered, David perceived

6*a* Ex. 22:1;
    Luke 19:8.
7*a* TG Anointing.
9*a* Num. 15:31 (30–31);
    2 Ne. 15:24;
    D&C 3:7.
  b 2 Sam. 11:15 (15–17);
    2 Ne. 9:35; Alma 39:6;
    D&C 42:18.
  c D&C 132:39 (38–39).
  d 2 Sam. 11:27.

10*a* Mosiah 14:3;
    15:26 (26–27).
11*a* 2 Sam. 11:27 (1–27);
    15:2 (1–14);
    1 Chr. 21:8 (1–8);
    Ps. 88:14 (6–8, 14–18).
12*a* 2 Sam. 16:22.
13*a* Gen. 39:9;
    1 Sam. 15:24; Ps. 51:4.
    TG Sin.
  b HEB hath caused to pass;

i.e., he was not punished immediately by death; but he did not escape punishment. See D&C 132:39.
JST 2 Sam. 12:13 . . . hath *not* put away thy sin *that* thou shalt not die. 2 Ne. 9:35.
14*a* Alma 39:11 (3–11).
16*a* TG Fast, Fasting.

that the child was dead: therefore David said unto his servants, Is the child dead? And they said, He is dead.

20 Then David arose from the earth, and washed, and anointed *himself,* and changed his ^aapparel, and came into the house of the LORD, and worshipped: then he came to his own house; and when he required, they set bread before him, and he did eat.

21 Then said his servants unto him, What thing *is* this that thou hast done? thou didst ^afast and weep for the child, *while it was* alive; but when the child was dead, thou didst rise and eat bread.

22 And he said, While the child was yet alive, I fasted and wept: for I said, Who can tell *whether* GOD will be gracious to me, that the child may live?

23 But now he is dead, wherefore should I fast? can I bring him back again? I shall go to him, but he shall not return to me.

24 ¶ And David ^acomforted Bath-sheba his wife, and went in unto her, and lay with her: and she bare a son, and he called his name ^bSolomon: and the LORD loved him.

25 And he sent by the hand of Nathan the prophet; and he called his name Jedidiah, because of the LORD.

26 ¶ And ^aJoab fought against Rabbah of the children of Ammon, and took the royal city.

27 And Joab sent messengers to David, and said, I have fought against Rabbah, and have taken the city of waters.

28 Now therefore gather the rest of the people together, and encamp against the city, and take it: lest I take the city, and it be called after my name.

29 And David gathered all the people together, and went to Rabbah, and fought against it, and took it.

30 And he took their king's ^acrown from off his head, the weight whereof *was* a talent of gold with the precious stones: and it was *set* on David's head. And he brought forth the spoil of the city in great abundance.

31 And he brought forth the people that *were* therein, and put *them* under ^asaws, and under harrows of iron, and under axes of iron, and made them pass through the brick-kiln: and thus did he unto all the cities of the children of Ammon. So David and all the people returned unto Jerusalem.

CHAPTER 13

Amnon desires Tamar, his sister, and forces her—He is slain by Absalom's command—Absalom flees to Geshur.

AND it came to pass after this, that ^aAbsalom the son of David had a fair sister, whose name *was* ^bTamar; and Amnon the son of David loved her.

2 And Amnon was so vexed, that he fell sick for his sister Tamar; for she *was* a virgin; and Amnon thought it hard for him to do any thing to her.

3 But Amnon had a friend, whose name *was* ^aJonadab, the son of Shimeah David's brother: and Jonadab *was* a very subtil man.

4 And he said unto him, Why *art* thou, *being* the king's son, lean from day to day? wilt thou not tell me? And Amnon said unto him, I love ^aTamar, my brother Absalom's sister.

5 And Jonadab said unto him, Lay thee down on thy bed, and make thyself sick: and when thy father cometh to see thee, say unto him, I pray thee, let my sister Tamar come, and give me meat, and dress the meat in my sight, that I may see *it,* and eat *it* at her hand.

6 ¶ So Amnon lay down, and made

20*a* TG Apparel.	Matt. 1:6.	**13** 1*a* 2 Sam. 3:3 (2–3).
21*a* TG Fast, Fasting.	26*a* 1 Chr. 20:1.	*b* 1 Chr. 3:9.
24*a* 1 Kgs. 1:17.	30*a* Ps. 21:3.	3*a* 2 Sam. 13:32.
b 1 Chr. 22:9;	31*a* 1 Chr. 20:3.	4*a* D&C 63:16.

himself sick: and when the king was come to see him, Amnon said unto the king, I pray thee, let Tamar my sister come, and make me a couple of cakes in my sight, that I may eat at her hand.

7 Then David sent home to Tamar, saying, Go now to thy brother Amnon's house, and dress him meat.

8 So Tamar went to her brother Amnon's house; and he was laid down. And she took flour, and kneaded *it,* and made cakes in his sight, and did bake the cakes.

9 And she took a pan, and poured *them* out before him; but he refused to eat. And Amnon said, Have out all men from me. And they went out every man from him.

10 And Amnon said unto Tamar, Bring the meat into the chamber, that I may eat of thine hand. And Tamar took the cakes which she had made, and brought *them* into the chamber to Amnon her brother.

11 And when she had brought *them* unto him to eat, he *a*took hold of her, and said unto her, Come lie with me, my sister.

12 And she answered him, Nay, my brother, do not *a*force me; for no such thing ought to be done in Israel: do not thou this *b*folly.

13 And I, whither shall I cause my *a*shame to go? and as for thee, thou shalt be as one of the fools in Israel. Now therefore, I pray thee, speak unto the king; for he will not withhold me from thee.

14 Howbeit he would not hearken unto her voice: but, being stronger than she, forced her, and lay with her.

15 ¶ Then Amnon hated her exceedingly; so that the hatred wherewith he hated her *was* greater than the love wherewith he had loved her. And Amnon said unto her, Arise, be gone.

16 And she said unto him, *There is* no cause: this evil in sending me away *is* greater than the other that thou didst unto me. But he would not hearken unto her.

17 Then he called his servant that ministered unto him, and said, Put now this *woman* out from me, and bolt the door after her.

18 And *she had* a garment of divers colours upon her: for with such robes were the king's daughters *that were* virgins apparelled. Then his servant brought her out, and bolted the door after her.

19 ¶ And Tamar put ashes on her head, and rent her garment of divers colours that *was* on her, and laid her hand on her head, and went on crying.

20 And Absalom her brother said unto her, Hath Amnon thy brother been with thee? but hold now thy peace, my sister: he *is* thy brother; regard not this thing. So Tamar remained desolate in her brother Absalom's house.

21 ¶ But when king David heard of all these things, he was very wroth.

22 And Absalom spake unto his brother Amnon neither good nor bad: for Absalom hated Amnon, because he had forced his sister Tamar.

23 ¶ And it came to pass after two full years, that Absalom had sheepshearers in Baal-hazor, which *is* beside Ephraim: and Absalom invited all the king's sons.

24 And Absalom came to the king, and said, Behold now, thy servant hath sheepshearers; let the king, I beseech thee, and his servants go with thy servant.

25 And the king said to Absalom, Nay, my son, let us not all now go, lest we be chargeable unto thee. And he pressed him: howbeit he would not go, but blessed him.

26 Then said Absalom, If not, I pray thee, let my brother Amnon go with us. And the king said unto him, Why should he go with thee?

27 But Absalom pressed him, that he let Amnon and all the king's sons go with him.

28 ¶ Now Absalom had commanded his servants, saying, Mark ye now when Amnon's heart is

---

11*a* TG Sensuality.
12*a* TG Sexual Immorality.
b Lev. 18:9 (6–22).
13*a* TG Shame.

merry with wine, and when I say unto you, Smite Amnon; then kill him, fear not: have not I commanded you? be "courageous, and be valiant.

29 And the servants of Absalom did unto Amnon as Absalom had commanded. Then all the king's sons arose, and every man gat him up upon his mule, and fled.

30 ¶ And it came to pass, while they were in the way, that tidings came to David, saying, Absalom hath slain all the king's sons, and there is not one of them left.

31 Then the king arose, and tare his garments, and lay on the earth; and all his servants stood by with their clothes rent.

32 And "Jonadab, the son of Shimeah David's brother, answered and said, Let not my lord suppose *that* they have slain all the young men the king's sons; for Amnon only is dead: for by the appointment of Absalom this hath been determined from the day that he forced his sister Tamar.

33 Now therefore let not my lord the king take the thing to his heart, to think that all the king's sons are dead: for Amnon only is dead.

34 But Absalom fled. And the young man that kept the watch lifted up his eyes, and looked, and, behold, there came much people by the way of the hill side behind him.

35 And Jonadab said unto the king, Behold, the king's sons come: as thy servant said, so it is.

36 And it came to pass, as soon as he had made an end of speaking, that, behold, the king's sons came, and lifted up their voice and wept: and the king also and all his servants wept very sore.

37 ¶ But Absalom fled, and went to Talmai, the son of Ammihud, king of "Geshur. And *David* mourned for his son every day.

38 So Absalom fled, and went to Geshur, and was there three years.

39 And *the soul of* king David longed to go forth unto Absalom: for he was comforted concerning Amnon, seeing he was dead.

CHAPTER 14

Joab arranges by artifice to bring Absalom home after three years—After two more years, Absalom sees the king, and they are reconciled.

Now Joab the son of Zeruiah perceived that the king's heart *was* toward Absalom.

2 And Joab sent to Tekoah, and fetched thence a wise woman, and said unto her, I pray thee, feign thyself to be a mourner, and put on now mourning apparel, and anoint not thyself with oil, but be as a woman that had a long time mourned for the dead:

3 And come to the king, and speak on this manner unto him. So Joab put the words in her mouth.

4 ¶ And when the woman of Tekoah spake to the king, she fell on her face to the ground, and did obeisance, and said, Help, O king.

5 And the king said unto her, What aileth thee? And she answered, I *am* indeed a widow woman, and mine husband is dead.

6 And thy handmaid had two sons, and they two strove together in the field, and *there was* none to part them, but the one smote the other, and slew him.

7 And, behold, the whole family is risen against thine handmaid, and they said, Deliver him that smote his brother, that we may kill him, for the life of his brother whom he slew; and we will destroy the heir also: and so they shall quench my coal which is left, and shall not leave to my husband *neither* name nor remainder upon the earth.

8 And the king said unto the woman, Go to thine house, and I will give charge concerning thee.

9 And the woman of Tekoah said unto the king, My lord, O king, the iniquity *be* on me, and on my father's

---

28*a* TG Hypocrisy. | 32*a* 2 Sam. 13:3. | 37*a* 2 Sam. 3:3.

house: and the king and his throne *be* guiltless.

10 And the king said, Whosoever saith *ought* unto thee, bring him to me, and he shall not touch thee any more.

11 Then said she, I pray thee, let the king remember the Lord thy God, that thou wouldest not suffer the *a*revengers of blood to destroy any more, lest they destroy my son. And he said, *As* the Lord liveth, there shall not one hair of thy son fall to the earth.

12 Then the woman said, Let thine handmaid, I pray thee, speak *one* word unto my lord the king. And he said, Say on.

13 And the woman said, Wherefore then hast thou thought such a thing against the people of God? for the king doth speak this thing as one which is faulty, in that the king doth not fetch home again his banished.

14 For we must needs die, and *are* as water spilt on the ground, which cannot be gathered up again; neither doth God respect *any* person: yet doth he devise means, that his banished be not *a*expelled from him.

15 Now therefore that I am come to speak of this thing unto my lord the king, *it is* because the people have made me afraid: and thy handmaid said, I will now speak unto the king; it may be that the king will perform the request of his handmaid.

16 For the king will hear, to deliver his handmaid out of the hand of the man *that would* destroy me and my son together out of the inheritance of God.

17 Then thine handmaid said, The word of my lord the king shall now be comfortable: for as an angel of God, so *is* my lord the king to discern good and bad: therefore the Lord thy God will be with thee.

18 Then the king answered and said unto the woman, Hide not from me, I pray thee, the thing that I shall ask thee. And the woman said, Let my lord the king now speak.

19 And the king said, *Is not* the hand of Joab with thee in all this? And the woman answered and said, *As* thy soul liveth, my lord the king, none can turn to the right hand or to the left from ought that my lord the king hath spoken: for thy servant Joab, he bade me, and he put all these words in the mouth of thine handmaid:

20 To fetch about this form of speech hath thy servant Joab done this thing: and my lord *is* wise, according to the wisdom of an angel of God, to know all *things* that *are* in the earth.

21 ¶ And the king said unto Joab, Behold now, I have done this thing: go therefore, bring the young man Absalom again.

22 And Joab fell to the ground on his face, and bowed himself, and *a*thanked the king: and Joab said, To day thy servant knoweth that I have found grace in thy sight, my lord, O king, in that the king hath fulfilled the request of his servant.

23 So Joab arose and went to Geshur, and brought Absalom to Jerusalem.

24 And the king said, Let him turn to his own house, and let him not see my face. So Absalom returned to his own house, and saw not the king's face.

25 ¶ But in all Israel there was none to be so much praised as Absalom for his beauty: from the sole of his foot even to the crown of his head there was no blemish in him.

26 And when he polled his head, (for it was at every year's end that he polled *it:* because *the hair* was heavy on him, therefore he polled it:) he weighed the hair of his head at two hundred shekels after the king's weight.

27 And unto Absalom there were born three *a*sons, and one daughter, whose name *was* Tamar: she was a woman of a fair countenance.

28 ¶ So Absalom dwelt two full

---

14 11*a* Num. 35:19 (19, 21).
   14*a* TG God, Mercy of.
22*a* HEB blessed.
27*a* 2 Sam. 18:18.

years in Jerusalem, and saw not the king's face.

29 Therefore Absalom sent for Joab, to have sent him to the king; but he would not come to him: and when he sent again the second time, he would not come.

30 Therefore he said unto his servants, See, Joab's field is near mine, and he hath barley there; go and set it on fire. And Absalom's servants set the field on fire.

31 Then Joab arose, and came to Absalom unto *his* house, and said unto him, Wherefore have thy servants set my field on fire?

32 And Absalom answered Joab, Behold, I sent unto thee, saying, Come hither, that I may send thee to the king, to say, Wherefore am I come from ᵃGeshur? *it had been* good for me *to have been* there still: now therefore let me see the king's face; and if there be *any* iniquity in me, let him kill me.

33 So Joab came to the king, and told him: and when he had called for Absalom, he came to the king, and bowed himself on his face to the ground before the king: and the king kissed Absalom.

CHAPTER 15

Absalom conspires against David and gains the support of the people—David flees, and Absalom enters Jerusalem.

AND it came to pass after this, that Absalom prepared him chariots and horses, and fifty men to run before him.

2 And ᵃAbsalom rose up early, and stood beside the way of the gate: and it was *so,* that when any man that had a controversy came to the king for judgment, then Absalom called unto him, and said, Of what city *art* thou? And he said, Thy servant *is* of one of the tribes of Israel.

3 And Absalom said unto him, See, thy matters *are* good and right; but

there *is* no man *deputed* of the king to hear thee.

4 Absalom said moreover, Oh that I were made judge in the land, that every man which hath any suit or cause might come unto me, and I would do him justice!

5 And it was *so,* that when any man came nigh *to him* to do him obeisance, he put forth his hand, and took him, and kissed him.

6 And on this manner did Absalom to all Israel that came to the king for judgment: so ᵃAbsalom stole the hearts of the men of Israel.

7 ¶ And it came to pass after forty years, that Absalom said unto the king, I pray thee, let me go and pay my vow, which I have vowed unto the LORD, in Hebron.

8 For thy servant vowed a vow while I abode at ᵃGeshur in Syria, saying, If the LORD shall bring me again indeed to Jerusalem, then I will serve the LORD.

9 And the king said unto him, Go in peace. So he arose, and went to Hebron.

10 ¶ But Absalom sent spies throughout all the tribes of Israel, saying, As soon as ye hear the sound of the trumpet, then ye shall say, Absalom reigneth in Hebron.

11 And with Absalom went two hundred men out of Jerusalem, *that were* called; and they went in their simplicity, and they knew not any thing.

12 And Absalom sent for ᵃAhithophel the Gilonite, David's ᵇcounsellor, from his city, *even* from ᶜGiloh, while he offered sacrifices. And the ᵈconspiracy was strong; for the people increased continually with Absalom.

13 ¶ And there came a messenger to David, saying, The hearts of the men of Israel are after Absalom.

14 And David said unto all his servants that *were* with him at Jerusalem, Arise, and let us ᵃflee; for we

---

32a 2 Sam. 3:3.
15 2a 2 Sam. 12:11.
  6a 1 Chr. 3:2.
  8a 2 Sam. 3:3.

12a 2 Sam. 16:23;
    1 Chr. 27:33.
  b TG Counselor.
  c 2 Sam. 17:23.

d TG Conspiracy.
14a 2 Sam. 17:27 (27–29);
    Ps. 3:1.

shall not *else* escape from Absalom: make speed to depart, lest he overtake us suddenly, and bring evil upon us, and smite the city with the edge of the sword.

15 And the king's servants said unto the king, Behold, thy servants *are ready to do* whatsoever my lord the king shall appoint.

16 And the king went forth, and all his household after him. And the king left ten women, *which were* ᵃconcubines, to keep the house.

17 And the king went forth, and all the people after him, and tarried in a place that was far off.

18 And all his servants passed on beside him; and all the Cherethites, and all the Pelethites, and all the Gittites, six hundred men which came after him from Gath, passed on before the king.

19 ¶ Then said the king to Ittai the Gittite, Wherefore goest thou also with us? return to thy place, and abide with the king: for thou *art* a stranger, and also an exile.

20 Whereas thou camest *but* yesterday, should I this day make thee go up and down with us? seeing I go whither I may, return thou, and take back thy brethren: mercy and truth *be* with thee.

21 And Ittai answered the king, and said, *As* the LORD liveth, and *as* my lord the king liveth, surely in what place my lord the king shall be, whether in death or life, even there also will thy servant be.

22 And David said to Ittai, Go and pass over. And Ittai the Gittite passed over, and all his men, and all the little ones that *were* with him.

23 And all the country wept with a loud voice, and all the people passed over: the king also himself passed over the brook Kidron, and all the people passed over, toward the way of the wilderness.

24 ¶ And lo ᵃZadok also, and all the Levites *were* with him, bearing the ark of the covenant of God:

and they set down the ark of God; and ᵇAbiathar went up, until all the people had done passing out of the city.

25 And the king said unto Zadok, Carry back the ark of God into the city: if I shall find favour in the eyes of the LORD, he will bring me again, and shew me *both* it, and his habitation:

26 But if he thus say, I have no delight in thee; behold, *here am* I, let him do to me as seemeth good unto him.

27 The king said also unto Zadok the priest, *Art not* thou a ᵃseer? return into the city in peace, and your two sons with you, Ahimaaz thy son, and ᵇJonathan the son of Abiathar.

28 See, I will tarry in the plain of the wilderness, until there come word from you to certify me.

29 Zadok therefore and Abiathar carried the ark of God again to Jerusalem: and they tarried there.

30 ¶ And David went up by the ascent of *mount* Olivet, and wept as he went up, and had his ᵃhead covered, and he went barefoot: and all the people that *was* with him covered every man his head, and they went up, weeping as they went up.

31 ¶ And *one* told David, saying, Ahithophel *is* among the conspirators with Absalom. And David said, O LORD, I pray thee, turn the ᵃcounsel of Ahithophel into foolishness.

32 ¶ And it came to pass, that *when* David was come to the top *of the mount,* where he worshipped God, behold, Hushai the Archite came to meet him with his coat rent, and earth upon his head:

33 Unto whom David said, If thou passest on with me, then thou shalt be a burden unto me:

34 But if thou return to the city, and say unto Absalom, I will be thy servant, O king; *as* I *have been* thy father's servant hitherto, so *will* I now also *be* thy servant: then mayest

16a 2 Sam. 16:21.
24a 2 Sam. 8:17; 19:11.
  b 1 Sam. 22:20 (20, 23);

1 Kgs. 2:26.
27a TG Seer.
  b 1 Kgs. 1:42.

30a Esth. 6:12.
31a 2 Sam. 17:14.

thou for me defeat the counsel of Ahithophel.

35 And *hast thou* not there with thee Zadok and Abiathar the priests? therefore it shall be, *that* what thing soever thou shalt hear out of the king's house, thou shalt tell *it* to Zadok and Abiathar the priests.

36 Behold, *they have* there with them their two sons, Ahimaaz Zadok's *son,* and Jonathan Abiathar's *son;* and by them ye shall send unto me every thing that ye can hear.

37 So Hushai David's friend came into the city, and Absalom came into Jerusalem.

CHAPTER 16

Mephibosheth is alleged to be seeking to be king—Shimei, of the house of Saul, curses David—Ahithophel counsels Absalom, and Absalom takes his father's concubines.

AND when David was a little past the top *of the hill,* behold, [a]Ziba the servant of Mephibosheth met him, with a couple of asses saddled, and upon them two hundred *loaves* of bread, and an hundred bunches of raisins, and an hundred of summer fruits, and a bottle of wine.

2 And the king said unto Ziba, What meanest thou by these? And Ziba said, The asses *be* for the king's household to ride on; and the bread and summer fruit for the young men to eat; and the wine, that such as be faint in the wilderness may drink.

3 And the king said, And where *is* thy master's son? And Ziba said unto the king, Behold, he abideth at Jerusalem: for he said, To day shall the house of Israel restore me the kingdom of my father.

4 Then said the king to Ziba, Behold, thine *are* all that *pertained* unto Mephibosheth. And Ziba said, I humbly beseech thee *that* I may find grace in thy sight, my lord, O king.

5 ¶ And when king David came to Bahurim, behold, thence came out a man of the family of the house of Saul, whose name *was* [a]Shimei, the son of Gera: he came forth, and [b]cursed still as he came.

6 And he cast stones at David, and at all the servants of king David: and all the people and all the mighty men *were* on his right hand and on his left.

7 And thus said Shimei when he cursed, Come out, come out, thou bloody man, and thou [a]man of Belial:

8 The LORD hath returned upon thee all the blood of the house of Saul, in whose stead thou hast reigned; and the LORD hath delivered the kingdom into the hand of Absalom thy son: and, behold, thou *art taken* in thy mischief, because thou *art* a bloody man.

9 ¶ Then said Abishai the son of Zeruiah unto the king, Why should this [a]dead dog curse my lord the king? let me go over, I pray thee, and take off his head.

10 And the king said, What have I to do with you, ye sons of Zeruiah? so let him curse, because the LORD hath said unto him, Curse David. Who shall then say, Wherefore hast thou done so?

11 And David said to Abishai, and to all his servants, Behold, my son, which came forth of my bowels, seeketh my life: how much more now *may this* Benjamite *do it?* let him alone, and let him curse; for the LORD hath bidden him.

12 It may be that the LORD will look on mine affliction, and that the LORD will [a]requite me good for his cursing this day.

13 And as David and his men went by the way, Shimei went along on the hill's side over against him, and cursed as he went, and threw stones at him, and cast dust.

14 And the king, and all the people

---

16 1*a* 2 Sam. 9:2 (2–12).
   5*a* 2 Sam. 19:16 (16, 19);
     1 Kgs. 2:8 (8–9).
    b 1 Kgs. 2:44.

7*a* HEB man of worthlessness; idiom of terrible insult. Deut. 13:13.

9*a* 2 Sam. 9:8.
12*a* Morm. 3:15; D&C 82:23; 98:23.

that *were* with him, came weary, and refreshed themselves there.

15 ¶ And Absalom, and all the people the men of Israel, came to Jerusalem, and Ahithophel with him.

16 And it came to pass, when Hushai the Archite, David's friend, was come unto Absalom, that Hushai said unto Absalom, *a*God save the king, God save the king.

17 And Absalom said to Hushai, *Is* this thy kindness to thy friend? why wentest thou not with thy friend?

18 And Hushai said unto Absalom, Nay; but whom the LORD, and this people, and all the men of Israel, choose, his will I be, and with him will I abide.

19 And again, whom should I serve? *should* I not *serve* in the presence of his son? as I have served in thy father's presence, so will I be in thy presence.

20 ¶ Then said Absalom to Ahithophel, Give counsel among you what we shall do.

21 And Ahithophel said unto Absalom, Go in unto thy father's *a*concubines, which he hath left to keep the house; and all Israel shall hear that thou art abhorred of thy father: then shall the hands of all that *are* with thee be strong.

22 So they spread Absalom a tent upon the top of the house; and *a*Absalom went in unto his father's concubines in the sight of all Israel.

23 And the counsel of *a*Ahithophel, which he counselled in those days, *was* as if a man had inquired at the *b*oracle of God: so *was* all the counsel of Ahithophel both with David and with Absalom.

CHAPTER 17

Ahithophel's counsel is overthrown by Hushai's—David is warned and flees over the Jordan—Ahithophel hangs himself—The people prepare for war.

MOREOVER Ahithophel said unto Absalom, Let me now choose out twelve thousand men, and I will arise and pursue after David this night:

2 And I will come upon him while he *is* weary and weak handed, and will make him afraid: and all the people that *are* with him shall flee; and I will smite the king only:

3 And I will bring back all the people unto thee: the man whom thou seekest *is* as if all returned: *so* all the people shall be in peace.

4 And the saying pleased Absalom well, and all the *a*elders of Israel.

5 Then said Absalom, Call now Hushai the Archite also, and let us hear likewise what he saith.

6 And when Hushai was come to Absalom, Absalom spake unto him, saying, Ahithophel hath spoken after this manner: shall we do *after* his saying? if not; speak thou.

7 And Hushai said unto Absalom, The counsel that Ahithophel hath given *is* not good at this time.

8 For, said Hushai, thou knowest thy father and his men, that they *be* mighty men, and they *be* *a*chafed in their minds, as a bear robbed of her whelps in the field: and thy father *is* a man of war, and will not lodge with the people.

9 Behold, he is hid now in some pit, or in some *other* place: and it will come to pass, when some of them be overthrown at the first, that whosoever heareth it will say, There is a slaughter among the people that follow Absalom.

10 And he also *that is* valiant, whose heart *is* as the heart of a lion, shall utterly melt: for all Israel knoweth that thy father *is* a mighty man, and *they* which *be* with him *are* valiant men.

11 Therefore I counsel that all Israel be generally gathered unto thee, from Dan even to Beer-sheba, as the sand that *is* by the sea for multitude; and that thou go to battle in thine own person.

12 So shall we come upon him in

16a HEB Let the king live, let the king live!
21a 2 Sam. 15:16.
22a 2 Sam. 12:12.
23a 2 Sam. 15:12.
    b HEB word of God.
17 4a TG Elder.
   8a HEB bitter in their soul.

some place where he shall be found, and we will light upon him as the dew falleth on the ground: and of him and of all the men that *are* with him there shall not be left so much as one.

13 Moreover, if he be gotten into a city, then shall all Israel bring ropes to that city, and we will draw it into the river, until there be not one small stone found there.

14 And Absalom and all the men of Israel said, The counsel of Hushai the Archite *is* better than the counsel of Ahithophel. For the LORD had *a*appointed to defeat the good *b*counsel of Ahithophel, to the intent that the LORD might bring evil upon Absalom.

15 ¶ Then said Hushai unto Zadok and to Abiathar the priests, Thus and thus did Ahithophel counsel Absalom and the *a*elders of Israel; and thus and thus have I counselled.

16 Now therefore send quickly, and tell David, saying, Lodge not this night in the plains of the wilderness, but speedily pass over; lest the king be swallowed up, and all the people that *are* with him.

17 Now *a*Jonathan and Ahimaaz stayed by En-rogel; for they might not be seen to come into the city: and a wench went and told them; and they went and told king David.

18 Nevertheless a lad saw them, and told Absalom: but they went both of them away quickly, and came to a man's house in Bahurim, which had a well in his court; whither they went down.

19 And the woman took and spread a covering over the well's mouth, and spread ground corn thereon; and the thing was not known.

20 And when Absalom's servants came to the woman to the house, they said, Where *is* Ahimaaz and Jonathan? And the woman said unto them, They be gone over the brook of water. And when they had sought and could not find *them*, they returned to Jerusalem.

21 And it came to pass, after they were departed, that they came up out of the well, and went and told king David, and said unto David, Arise, and pass quickly over the water: for thus hath Ahithophel counselled against you.

22 Then David arose, and all the people that *were* with him, and they passed over Jordan: by the morning light there lacked not one of them that was not gone over Jordan.

23 ¶ And when Ahithophel saw that his counsel was not followed, he saddled *his* ass, and arose, and gat him home to his house, to his *a*city, and put his household in order, and hanged himself, and died, and was buried in the sepulchre of his father.

24 Then David came to Mahanaim. And Absalom passed over Jordan, he and all the men of Israel with him.

25 ¶ And Absalom made *a*Amasa captain of the host instead of *b*Joab: which Amasa *was* a man's son, whose name *was* Ithra an Israelite, that went in to Abigail the daughter of Nahash, sister to Zeruiah Joab's mother.

26 So Israel and Absalom pitched in the land of Gilead.

27 ¶ And it came to pass, when David was *a*come to Mahanaim, that Shobi the son of Nahash of Rabbah of the children of Ammon, and Machir the son of Ammiel of Lodebar, and *b*Barzillai the Gileadite of Rogelim,

28 Brought beds, and basins, and earthen vessels, and wheat, and barley, and flour, and parched *corn*, and beans, and lentiles, and parched *pulse*,

29 And *a*honey, and butter, and sheep, and cheese of *b*kine, for David, and for the people that *were* with him, to eat: for they said, The people *is* hungry, and weary, and thirsty, in the wilderness.

14*a* OR ordered, ordained.
  b 2 Sam. 15:31.
15*a* 1 Ne. 4:22.
17*a* 1 Kgs. 1:42.
23*a* 2 Sam. 15:12.
25*a* 2 Sam. 19:13;
  1 Chr. 12:18.
  b 1 Kgs. 2:28.
27*a* 2 Sam. 15:14; Ps. 3:1.
  b 2 Sam. 19:32 (32–38).
29*a* 2 Ne. 17:15.
  b OR cattle.

CHAPTER 18

The Israelites are smitten in the woods of Ephraim—Joab slays Absalom—Tidings of his death are taken to David, who mourns for his son.

AND David numbered the people that *were* with him, and set captains of thousands and captains of hundreds over them.

2 And David sent forth a third part of the people under the hand of Joab, and a third part under the hand of Abishai the son of Zeruiah, Joab's brother, and a third part under the hand of Ittai the Gittite. And the king said unto the people, I will surely go forth with you myself also.

3 But the people answered, Thou shalt not *a*go forth: for if we flee away, they will not care for us; neither if half of us die, will they care for us: but now *thou art* worth ten thousand of us: therefore now *it is* better that thou *b*succour us out of the city.

4 And the king said unto them, What seemeth you best I will do. And the king stood by the gate side, and all the people came out by hundreds and by thousands.

5 And the king commanded *a*Joab and Abishai and Ittai, saying, *b*Deal gently for my sake with the young man, *even* with Absalom. And all the people heard when the king gave all the captains charge concerning Absalom.

6 ¶ So the people went out into the field against Israel: and the battle was in the *a*wood of Ephraim;

7 Where the people of Israel were slain before the servants of David, and there was there a great slaughter that day of twenty thousand *men.*

8 For the battle was there scattered over the face of all the country: and the wood devoured more people that day than the sword devoured.

9 ¶ And Absalom met the servants of David. And Absalom rode upon a mule, and the mule went under the thick boughs of a great oak, and his head caught hold of the oak, and he was taken up between the heaven and the earth; and the mule that *was* under him went away.

10 And a certain man saw *it,* and told Joab, and said, Behold, I saw Absalom hanged in an oak.

11 And Joab said unto the man that told him, And, behold, thou sawest *him,* and why didst thou not smite him there to the ground? and I would have given thee ten *shekels* of silver, and a girdle.

12 And the man said unto Joab, Though I should receive a thousand *shekels* of silver in mine hand, *yet* would I not put forth mine hand against the king's son: for in our hearing the king *a*charged thee and Abishai and Ittai, saying, Beware that none *touch* the young man Absalom.

13 Otherwise I should have wrought falsehood against mine own life: for there is no matter hid from the king, and thou thyself wouldest have set thyself against *me.*

14 Then said Joab, I may not tarry thus with thee. And he took three darts in his hand, and thrust them through the heart of Absalom, while he *was* yet alive in the midst of the oak.

15 And ten young men that bare Joab's armour compassed about and smote Absalom, and slew him.

16 And Joab blew the trumpet, and the people returned from pursuing after Israel: for Joab held back the people.

17 And they took Absalom, and cast him into a great pit in the wood, and laid a very great heap of stones upon him: and all Israel fled every one to his tent.

18 ¶ Now Absalom in his lifetime had taken and reared up for himself a pillar, which *is* in the *a*king's dale: for he said, I have no *b*son to keep my name in remembrance: and he called the pillar after his own name: and it

---

18 3*a* 2 Sam. 21:17.
 b HEB help us.
 5*a* 1 Kgs. 2:5.

b 2 Sam. 18:12.
6*a* Josh. 17:18 (15–18).
12*a* 2 Sam. 18:5.

18*a* Gen. 14:17.
 b 2 Sam. 14:27.

is called unto this day, Absalom's ᶜplace.

19 ¶ Then said Ahimaaz the son of Zadok, Let me now run, and bear the king tidings, how that the LORD hath avenged him of his enemies.

20 And Joab said unto him, Thou shalt not bear tidings this day, but thou shalt bear tidings another day: but this day thou shalt bear no tidings, because the king's son is dead.

21 Then said Joab to Cushi, Go tell the king what thou hast seen. And Cushi bowed himself unto Joab, and ran.

22 Then said Ahimaaz the son of Zadok yet again to Joab, But howsoever, let me, I pray thee, also run after Cushi. And Joab said, Wherefore wilt thou run, my son, seeing that thou hast no tidings ready?

23 But howsoever, *said he,* let me run. And he said unto him, Run. Then Ahimaaz ran by the way of the plain, and overran Cushi.

24 And David sat between the two gates: and the watchman went up to the roof over the gate unto the wall, and lifted up his eyes, and looked, and behold a man running alone.

25 And the watchman cried, and told the king. And the king said, If he *be* alone, *there is* tidings in his mouth. And he came apace, and drew near.

26 And the watchman saw another man running: and the watchman called unto the porter, and said, Behold *another* man running alone. And the king said, He also bringeth tidings.

27 And the watchman said, Me thinketh the running of the foremost is like the running of Ahimaaz the son of Zadok. And the king said, He *is* a good man, and cometh with good tidings.

28 And Ahimaaz called, and said unto the king, All is well. And he fell down to the earth upon his face before the king, and said, Blessed *be* the LORD thy God, which hath delivered up the men that lifted up their hand against my lord the king.

29 And the king said, *Is* the young man Absalom safe? And Ahimaaz answered, When Joab sent the king's servant, and *me* thy servant, I saw a great tumult, but I knew not what *it was.*

30 And the king said *unto him,* Turn aside, *and* stand here. And he turned aside, and stood still.

31 And, behold, Cushi came; and Cushi said, Tidings, my lord the king: for the LORD hath avenged thee this day of all them that rose up against thee.

32 And the king said unto Cushi, *Is* the young man Absalom safe? And Cushi answered, The enemies of my lord the king, and all that rise against thee to do *thee* hurt, be as *that* young man *is.*

33 ¶ And the king was much moved, and went up to the chamber over the gate, and wept: and as he went, thus he said, O my son Absalom, my son, my son Absalom! would God I had died for thee, O Absalom, my son, my son!

CHAPTER 19

Joab rebukes David for favoring his enemies instead of his friends—David replaces Joab with Amasa—Shimei, who cursed David, is pardoned—Mephibosheth pledges allegiance to David—The men of Judah take David back to Jerusalem.

AND it was told Joab, Behold, the king weepeth and mourneth for Absalom.

2 And the victory that day was *turned* into mourning unto all the people: for the people heard say that day how the king was grieved for his son.

3 And the people gat them by stealth that day into the city, as people being ashamed steal away when they flee in battle.

4 But the king covered his face, and the king cried with a loud voice, O my son Absalom, O Absalom, my son, my son!

5 And Joab came into the house to

18c OR monument.

the king, and said, Thou hast shamed this day the faces of all thy servants, which this day have saved thy life, and the lives of thy sons and of thy daughters, and the lives of thy wives, and the lives of thy concubines;

6 In that thou lovest thine enemies, and hatest thy friends. For thou hast declared this day, that thou regardest neither princes nor servants: for this day I perceive, that if Absalom had lived, and all we had died this day, then it had pleased thee well.

7 Now therefore arise, go forth, and *a*speak comfortably unto thy servants: for I swear by the LORD, if thou go not forth, there will not tarry one with thee this night: and that will be worse unto thee than all the evil that befell thee from thy youth until now.

8 Then the king arose, and sat in the gate. And they told unto all the people, saying, Behold, the king doth sit in the gate. And all the people came before the king: for Israel had fled every man to his tent.

9 ¶ And all the people were at *a*strife throughout all the tribes of Israel, saying, The king saved us out of the hand of our enemies, and he delivered us out of the hand of the Philistines; and now he is fled out of the land for Absalom.

10 And Absalom, whom we anointed over us, is dead in battle. Now therefore why speak ye not a word of bringing the king back?

11 ¶ And king David sent to *a*Zadok and to Abiathar the priests, saying, Speak unto the elders of Judah, saying, Why are ye the last to bring the king back to his house? seeing the speech of all Israel is come to the king, *even* to his house.

12 Ye *are* my *a*brethren, ye *are* my bones and my flesh: wherefore then are ye the last to bring back the king?

13 And say ye to *a*Amasa, *Art* thou not of my bone, and of my flesh? God do so to me, and more also, if thou be not captain of the host before me continually in the room of Joab.

14 And he bowed the heart of all the men of Judah, even as *the heart of* one man; so that they sent *this word* unto the king, Return thou, and all thy servants.

15 So the king returned, and came to Jordan. And Judah came to *a*Gilgal, to go to meet the king, to conduct the king over Jordan.

16 ¶ And *a*Shimei the son of Gera, a Benjamite, which *was* of Bahurim, hasted and came down with the men of Judah to meet king David.

17 And *there were* a thousand men of Benjamin with him, and Ziba the servant of the house of Saul, and his fifteen sons and his twenty servants with him; and they went over Jordan before the king.

18 And there went over a ferry boat to carry over the king's household, and to do what he thought good. And Shimei the son of Gera fell down before the king, as he was come over Jordan;

19 And said unto the king, Let not my lord impute iniquity unto me, neither do thou remember that which thy servant did perversely the day that my lord the king went out of Jerusalem, that the king should take it to his heart.

20 For thy servant doth know that I have sinned: therefore, behold, I am come the first this day of all the house of Joseph to go down to meet my lord the king.

21 But Abishai the son of Zeruiah answered and said, Shall not Shimei be put to death for this, because he *a*cursed the LORD's *b*anointed?

22 And David said, What have I to do with you, ye sons of Zeruiah, that ye should this day be adversaries unto me? shall there any man be put to

---

19 7*a* HEB speak to the heart; i.e., show appreciation.
9*a* TG Strife.
11*a* 2 Sam. 15:24 (24–29).
12*a* 2 Sam. 19:42.
13*a* 2 Sam. 17:25; 20:4.
15*a* Josh. 5:9.
16*a* 2 Sam. 16:5.
21*a* Ex. 22:28; D&C 121:16.
b TG Anointing.

death this day in Israel? for do not I know that I *am* this day king over Israel?

23 Therefore the king said unto Shimei, Thou shalt not die. And the king sware unto him.

24 ¶ And *a*Mephibosheth the son of Saul came down to meet the king, and had neither dressed his feet, nor trimmed his beard, nor washed his clothes, from the day the king departed until the day he came *again* in peace.

25 And it came to pass, when he was come to Jerusalem to meet the king, that the king said unto him, Wherefore wentest not thou with me, Mephibosheth?

26 And he answered, My lord, O king, my *a*servant deceived me: for thy servant said, I will saddle me an ass, that I may ride thereon, and go to the king; because thy servant *is* lame.

27 And he hath slandered thy servant unto my lord the king; but my lord the king *is* as an angel of God: do therefore *what is* good in thine eyes.

28 For all *of* my father's house were but dead men before my lord the king: yet didst thou set thy servant among them that did *a*eat at thine own table. What right therefore have I yet to cry any more unto the king?

29 And the king said unto him, Why speakest thou any more of thy matters? I have said, Thou and Ziba divide the land.

30 And Mephibosheth said unto the king, Yea, let him take all, forasmuch as my lord the king is come again in peace unto his own house.

31 ¶ And *a*Barzillai the Gileadite came down from Rogelim, and went over Jordan with the king, to conduct him over Jordan.

32 Now *a*Barzillai was a very aged man, *even* fourscore years old: and he had provided the king of sustenance while he lay at Mahanaim; for he *was* a very great man.

33 And the king said unto Barzillai, Come thou over with me, and I will feed thee with me in Jerusalem.

34 And Barzillai said unto the king, How long have I to live, that I should go up with the king unto Jerusalem?

35 I *am* this day fourscore years old: *and* can I discern between good and evil? can thy servant taste what I eat or what I drink? can I hear any more the voice of singing men and singing women? wherefore then should thy servant be yet a burden unto my lord the king?

36 Thy servant will go a little way over Jordan with the king: and why should the king recompense it me with such a reward?

37 Let thy servant, I pray thee, turn back again, that I may die in mine own city, *and be buried* by the grave of my father and of my mother. But behold thy servant Chimham; let him go over with my lord the king; and do to him what shall seem good unto thee.

38 And the king answered, Chimham shall go over with me, and I will do to him that which shall seem good unto thee: and whatsoever thou shalt require of me, *that* will I do for thee.

39 And all the people went over Jordan. And when the king was come over, the king kissed Barzillai, and blessed him; and he returned unto his own place.

40 Then the king went on to Gilgal, and Chimham went on with him: and all the people of Judah conducted the king, and also half the people of Israel.

41 ¶ And, behold, all the men of Israel came to the king, and said unto the king, Why have our brethren the men of Judah stolen thee away, and have brought the king, and his household, and all David's *a*men with him, over Jordan?

42 And all the men of Judah answered the men of Israel, Because

---

24*a* 2 Sam. 9:6 (3, 6).
26*a* 2 Sam. 9:12 (9–13).
28*a* 2 Sam. 9:7 (7, 10, 13).

31*a* 1 Kgs. 2:7.
32*a* 2 Sam. 17:27.
41*a* 1 Sam. 23:13;

2 Sam. 2:3.

the king *is* near of *ᵃ*kin to us: wherefore then be ye angry for this matter? have we eaten at all of the king's *cost?* or hath he given us any gift?

43 And the men of Israel answered the men of Judah, and said, We have ten parts in the king, and we have also more *right* in David than ye: why then did ye despise us, that our advice should not be first had in bringing back our king? And the words of the men of Judah were fiercer than the words of the men of Israel.

CHAPTER 20

Sheba leads the tribes of Israel away from David—Joab slays Amasa and pursues Sheba—A wise woman intercedes—The death of Sheba ends the insurrection.

AND there happened to be there a man of *ᵃ*Belial, whose name *was* Sheba, the son of Bichri, a Benjamite: and he blew a trumpet, and said, We have no part in David, neither have we inheritance in the son of Jesse: every man to his tents, O Israel.

2 So every man of Israel went up from after David, *and* followed Sheba the son of Bichri: but the men of Judah clave unto their king, from Jordan even to Jerusalem.

3 ¶ And David came to his house at Jerusalem; and the king took the ten women *his* *ᵃ*concubines, whom he had left to keep the house, and put them in ward, and fed them, but went not in unto them. So they were shut up unto the day of their death, living in widowhood.

4 ¶ Then said the king to *ᵃ*Amasa, Assemble me the men of Judah within three days, and be thou here present.

5 So Amasa went to assemble *the men of* Judah: but he tarried longer than the set time which he had appointed him.

6 And David said to Abishai, Now shall Sheba the son of Bichri do us more harm than *did* Absalom: take thou thy lord's servants, and pursue after him, lest he get him *ᵃ*fenced cities, and escape us.

7 And there went out after him Joab's men, and the Cherethites, and the Pelethites, and all the mighty men: and they went out of Jerusalem, to pursue after Sheba the son of Bichri.

8 When they *were* at the great stone which *is* in Gibeon, Amasa went before them. And Joab's garment that he had put on was girded unto him, and upon it a girdle *with* a sword fastened upon his loins in the sheath thereof; and as he went forth it fell out.

9 And Joab said to Amasa, *Art* thou in health, my brother? And Joab took Amasa by the beard with the right hand to *ᵃ*kiss him.

10 But *ᵃ*Amasa took no heed to the sword that *was* in Joab's hand: so he smote him therewith in the *ᵇ*fifth *rib,* and shed out his bowels to the ground, and struck him not again; and he died. So Joab and Abishai his brother pursued after Sheba the son of Bichri.

11 And one of Joab's men stood by him, and said, He that favoureth Joab, and he that *is* for David, *let him go* after Joab.

12 And Amasa wallowed in blood in the midst of the highway. And when the man saw that all the people stood still, he removed Amasa out of the highway into the field, and cast a cloth upon him, when he saw that every one that came by him stood still.

13 When he was removed out of the highway, all the people went on after Joab, to pursue after Sheba the son of Bichri.

14 ¶ And he went through all the tribes of Israel unto Abel, and to Beth-maachah, and all the Berites: and they were gathered *ᵃ*together, and went also after him.

42*a* 2 Sam. 19:12.
20 1*a* Deut. 13:13.
   3*a* Jacob 1:15.

4*a* 2 Sam. 19:13.
6*a* IE fortified.
9*a* Prov. 27:6.

10*a* 1 Kgs. 2:5 (5, 32).
   b 2 Sam. 2:23.
14*a* Alma 46:21 (19–21).

15 And they came and besieged him in Abel of Beth-maachah, and they cast up a bank against the city, and it stood in the trench: and all the people that *were* with Joab battered the wall, to throw it down.

16 ¶ Then cried a wise woman out of the city, Hear, hear; say, I pray you, unto Joab, Come near hither, that I may speak with thee.

17 And when he was come near unto her, the woman said, *Art* thou Joab? And he answered, I *am* he. Then she said unto him, Hear the words of thine handmaid. And he answered, I do hear.

18 Then she spake, saying, They were wont to speak in old time, saying, They shall surely ask *counsel* at Abel: and so they ended *the matter.*

19 I *am one of them that are* peaceable *and* faithful in Israel: thou seekest to destroy a city and a mother in Israel: why wilt thou swallow up the inheritance of the LORD?

20 And Joab answered and said, Far be it, far be it from me, that I should swallow up or *ᵃ*destroy.

21 The matter *is* not so: but a man of mount Ephraim, Sheba the son of Bichri by name, hath lifted up his hand against the king, *even* against David: deliver him only, and I will depart from the city. And the woman said unto Joab, Behold, his head shall be thrown to thee over the wall.

22 Then the woman went unto all the people in her wisdom. And they cut off the head of Sheba the son of Bichri, and cast *it* out to Joab. And he blew a trumpet, and they retired from the city, every man to his tent. And Joab returned to Jerusalem unto the king.

23 ¶ Now ᵃJoab *was* over all the host of Israel: and Benaiah the son of Jehoiada *was* over the Cherethites and over the Pelethites:

24 And Adoram *was* over the tribute: and Jehoshaphat the son of Ahilud *was* recorder:

25 And Sheva *was* scribe: and Zadok and Abiathar *were* the priests:

26 And Ira also the Jairite was a chief ruler about David.

CHAPTER 21

The Lord sends a famine—David understands that the famine came because Saul smote the Gibeonites, contrary to the oath of Israel—David delivers up seven sons of Saul to be hanged by the Gibeonites—Israel and the Philistines continue their wars.

THEN there was a famine in the days of David three years, year after year; and David inquired of the LORD. And the LORD answered, *It is* for Saul, and for *his* bloody house, because he slew the Gibeonites.

2 And the king called the Gibeonites, and said unto them; (now the ᵃGibeonites *were* not of the children of Israel, but of the remnant of the Amorites; and the children of Israel had sworn unto them: and Saul sought to slay them in his zeal to the children of Israel and Judah.)

3 Wherefore David said unto the Gibeonites, What shall I do for you? and wherewith shall I make the atonement, that ye may bless the inheritance of the LORD?

4 And the Gibeonites said unto him, We will have no silver nor gold of Saul, nor of his house; neither for us shalt thou kill any man in Israel. And he said, What ye shall say, *that* will I do for you.

5 And they answered the king, The man that consumed us, and that devised against us *that* we should be destroyed from remaining in any of the ᵃcoasts of Israel,

6 Let seven men of his ᵃsons be delivered unto us, and we will hang them up unto the LORD in ᵇGibeah of Saul, *whom* the LORD did choose. And the king said, I will give *them.*

7 But the king spared Mephibosheth, the son of Jonathan the son of Saul, because of the LORD's ᵃoath

---

20a D&C 109:43.
23a 2 Sam. 8:16 (16–18).
21 2a Josh. 9:17 (3–17).

5a OR territory.
6a Deut. 24:16;
Hel. 11:9.

b Josh. 18:28.
7a 1 Sam. 20:8;
1 Ne. 4:33 (30–35).

that *was* between them, between David and Jonathan the son of Saul.

8 But the king took the two sons of *a*Rizpah the daughter of Aiah, whom she bare unto Saul, Armoni and Mephibosheth; and the five sons of Michal the daughter of Saul, whom she brought up for Adriel the son of Barzillai the Meholathite:

9 And he delivered them into the hands of the Gibeonites, and they hanged them in the hill before the Lord: and they fell *all* seven together, and were put to death in the days of harvest, in the first *days*, in the beginning of barley harvest.

10 ¶ And Rizpah the daughter of Aiah took *a*sackcloth, and spread it for her upon the rock, from the beginning of harvest until water dropped upon them out of heaven, and suffered neither the birds of the air to rest on them by day, nor the beasts of the field by night.

11 And it was told David what Rizpah the daughter of Aiah, the concubine of Saul, had done.

12 ¶ And David went and took the bones of Saul and the bones of Jonathan his son from the men of Jabesh-gilead, which had stolen them from the street of Beth-shan, where the Philistines had hanged them, when the Philistines had slain Saul in Gilboa:

13 And he brought up from thence the bones of Saul and the bones of Jonathan his son; and they gathered the bones of them that were hanged.

14 And the bones of Saul and Jonathan his son buried they in the country of Benjamin in Zelah, in the sepulchre of Kish his father: and they performed all that the king commanded. And after that God was entreated for the land.

15 ¶ Moreover the Philistines had yet war again with Israel; and David went down, and his servants with him, and fought against the Philistines: and David waxed faint.

16 And Ishbi-benob, which *was* of the sons of the giant, the weight of whose spear *weighed* three hundred *shekels* of brass in weight, he being girded with a new *sword,* thought to have slain David.

17 But Abishai the son of Zeruiah *a*succoured him, and smote the Philistine, and killed him. Then the men of David sware unto him, saying, Thou shalt *b*go no more out with us to battle, that thou quench not the light of Israel.

18 And it came to pass after this, that there was again a *a*battle with the Philistines at Gob: then Sibbechai the Hushathite slew Saph, which *was* of the sons of the giant.

19 And there was again a battle in Gob with the Philistines, where Elhanan the son of Jaare-oregim, a Beth-lehemite, slew *the brother of* Goliath the Gittite, the *a*staff of whose spear *was* like a weaver's beam.

20 And there was yet a battle in *a*Gath, where was a man of *great* stature, that had on every hand six fingers, and on every foot six toes, four and twenty in number; and he also was born to the giant.

21 And when he defied Israel, Jonathan the son of Shimea the brother of David slew him.

22 These four were born to the giant in Gath, and fell by the hand of David, and by the hand of his servants.

CHAPTER 22

David praises the Lord in a psalm of thanksgiving—The Lord is his fortress and savior, He is mighty and powerful in deliverance, He rewards men according to their righteousness, He shows mercy to the merciful, His way is perfect, He lives, and blessed is He.

AND David spake unto the Lord the words of this *a*song in the day *that* the Lord had delivered him out of the hand of all his enemies, and out of the hand of Saul:

8*a* 2 Sam. 3:7 (7–8).
10*a* Mosiah 11:25.
17*a* HEB aided.

b 2 Sam. 18:3 (3–4).
18*a* 1 Chr. 20:4 (4–8).
19*a* 1 Sam. 17:7.

20*a* 1 Sam. 17:4.
22 1*a* 1 Chr. 16:7.
TG Singing.

2 And he said, The LORD *is* my
*a*rock, and my fortress, and my deliverer;

3 The God of my rock; in him
will I *a*trust: *he is* my *b*shield, and
the horn of my salvation, my high
*c*tower, and my *d*refuge, my saviour;
thou savest me from violence.

4 I will call on the LORD, *who is*
worthy to be praised: so shall I be
saved from mine enemies.

5 When the waves of death *a*compassed me, the floods of ungodly
men made me afraid;

6 The sorrows of *a*hell compassed
me about; the snares of death prevented me;

7 In my *a*distress I called upon the
LORD, and cried to my God: and he
did hear my voice out of his *b*temple,
and my cry *did enter* into his ears.

8 Then the earth shook and trembled; the foundations of heaven
moved and shook, because he was
wroth.

9 There went up a smoke out of
his nostrils, and fire out of his
mouth devoured: coals were kindled
by it.

10 He bowed the heavens also,
and came down; and darkness *was*
under his feet.

11 And he rode upon a *a*cherub,
and did fly: and he was seen upon
the wings of the wind.

12 And he made *a*darkness pavil-
ions round about him, dark waters,
and thick clouds of the skies.

13 Through the brightness before
him were coals of fire kindled.

14 The LORD thundered from
heaven, and the most High uttered
his voice.

15 And he sent out arrows, and
scattered them; lightning, and *a*discomfited them.

16 And the channels of the sea
appeared, the foundations of the
world were discovered, at the rebuking of the LORD, at the blast of
the breath of his nostrils.

17 He sent from above, he took me;
he drew me out of many waters;

18 He delivered me from my strong
enemy, *and* from them that hated
me: for they were too strong for me.

19 They prevented me in the day
of my calamity: but the LORD was
my stay.

20 He brought me forth also into
a *a*large place: he delivered me, because he delighted in me.

21 The LORD *a*rewarded me according to my righteousness: according
to the *b*cleanness of my hands hath
he recompensed me.

22 For I have kept the ways of
the LORD, and have not wickedly
departed from my God.

23 For all his *a*judgments *were* before me: and *as for* his statutes, I did
not depart from them.

24 I was also upright before him,
and have kept myself from mine
iniquity.

25 Therefore the LORD hath recompensed me according to my
righteousness; according to my
cleanness in his eye sight.

26 With the merciful thou wilt
shew thyself merciful, *and* with
the upright man thou wilt shew
thyself upright.

27 With the pure thou wilt shew
thyself pure; and with the *a*froward
thou wilt shew thyself unsavoury.

28 And the *a*afflicted people thou
wilt save: but thine eyes *are* upon
the *b*haughty, *that* thou mayest bring
them down.

29 For thou *art* my *a*lamp, O LORD:
and the LORD will lighten my
darkness.

30 For by thee I have run through
a troop: by my God have I leaped
over a wall.

2*a* TG Rock.
3*a* TG Faith; Trust in God.
  b Deut. 20:1; D&C 35:14.
  c Prov. 18:10;
      D&C 97:20.
  d TG Refuge.
5*a* OR enclosed.
6*a* TG Damnation.

7*a* D&C 136:29.
  b D&C 121:4 (1–4).
11*a* TG Cherubim.
12*a* OR darkness His
      covering.
15*a* HEB scattered.
20*a* Ps. 118:5.
21*a* TG Reward.

  b TG Cleanliness.
23*a* Deut. 7:12.
27*a* OR deceitful, perverted,
      crooked.
28*a* Ps. 18:27; Isa. 49:13;
      1 Ne. 21:13.
  b TG Haughtiness.
29*a* D&C 14:9.

31 *As for* God, his way *is* ^aperfect; the ^bword of the LORD *is* tried: he *is* a buckler to all them that trust in him.

32 For who *is* God, save the LORD? and who *is* a ^arock, save our God?

33 God *is* my ^astrength *and* ^bpower: and he maketh my way ^cperfect.

34 He maketh my feet like hinds' *feet:* and setteth me upon my high places.

35 He teacheth my hands to ^awar; so that a bow of ^bsteel is broken by mine arms.

36 Thou hast also given me the shield of thy salvation: and thy gentleness hath made me great.

37 Thou hast enlarged my steps under me; so that my feet did not slip.

38 I have pursued mine enemies, and destroyed them; and turned not again until I had consumed them.

39 And I have consumed them, and wounded them, that they could not arise: yea, they are fallen under my feet.

40 For thou hast girded me with strength to battle: them that rose up against me hast thou subdued under me.

41 Thou hast also given me the ^anecks of mine enemies, that I might destroy them that hate me.

42 They looked, but *there was* none to save; *even* unto the LORD, but he answered them not.

43 Then did I beat them as small as the dust of the earth, I did stamp them as the mire of the street, *and* did spread them abroad.

44 Thou also hast delivered me from the strivings of my people, thou hast kept me *to be* head of the heathen: a people *which* I knew not shall serve me.

45 Strangers shall submit themselves unto me: as soon as they hear, they shall be obedient unto me.

46 Strangers shall fade away, and they shall be afraid out of their close places.

47 The LORD ^aliveth; and blessed *be* my rock; and ^bexalted be the God of the ^crock of my salvation.

48 It *is* God that ^aavengeth me, and that bringeth down the people under me,

49 And that bringeth me forth from mine enemies: thou also hast lifted me up on high above them that rose up against me: thou hast delivered me from the violent man.

50 Therefore I will give ^athanks unto thee, O LORD, among the heathen, and I will sing praises unto thy name.

51 *He is* the tower of salvation for his king: and sheweth mercy to his anointed, unto David, and to his seed for evermore.

CHAPTER 23

David speaks by the power of the Holy Ghost—Rulers must be just, ruling in the fear of God—David's mighty men are named and their deeds extolled.

Now these *be* the last words of David. David the son of Jesse said, and the man *who was* raised up on high, the anointed of the God of Jacob, and the sweet psalmist of Israel, said,

2 The ^aSpirit of the LORD ^bspake by me, and his word *was* in my tongue.

3 The God of Israel said, the ^aRock of Israel spake to me, He that ^bruleth over men *must be* just, ruling in the ^cfear of God.

4 And *he shall be* as the light of the morning, *when* the sun riseth, *even* a morning without clouds; *as* the tender grass *springing* out of the earth by clear shining after rain.

---

31 a TG God, Perfection of;
	Perfection.
	b Ps. 12:6 (6–7); 18:30.
32 a Deut. 32:31.
33 a TG Strength.
	b TG God, Power of;
	Priesthood, Power of.
	c Job 22:3.
35 a Ps. 144:1 (1–15).
	b 1 Ne. 16:18.

41 a Gen. 49:8.
47 a D&C 76:22 (22–23).
	b Ex. 15:2.
	c Ps. 89:26; 95:1.
48 a Morm. 3:15.
50 a TG Thanksgiving.
23 2 a TG God, Spirit of;
	Teaching with the
	Spirit.
	b TG Delegation of

Responsibility;
	Prophecy;
	Scriptures, Writing of.
3 a TG Rock.
	b Mosiah 29:12 (10–36);
	D&C 98:9.
	c Ex. 18:21;
	Mosiah 4:1 (1–3).

5 Although my house *be* not so with God; yet he hath made with me an *a*everlasting covenant, ordered in all *things,* and sure: for *this is* all my salvation, and all *my* desire, although he make *it* not to grow.

6 ¶ But *the sons* of Belial *shall be* all of them as thorns thrust away, because they cannot be taken with hands:

7 But the man *that* shall touch them must be *a*fenced with iron and the staff of a spear; and they shall be utterly burned with fire in the *same* place.

8 ¶ These *be* the names of the *a*mighty men whom David had: The Tachmonite that sat in the seat, chief among the captains; the same *was* Adino the Eznite: *he lift up his spear* against eight hundred, whom he slew at one time.

9 And after him *was* Eleazar the son of Dodo the Ahohite, *one* of the three mighty men with David, when they defied the Philistines *that* were there gathered together to battle, and the men of Israel were gone away:

10 He arose, and smote the Philistines until his hand was weary, and his hand clave unto the sword: and the LORD wrought a great victory that day; and the people returned after him only to spoil.

11 And after him *was* Shammah the son of Agee the Hararite. And the Philistines were gathered together into a troop, where was a piece of ground full of lentiles: and the people fled from the Philistines.

12 But he stood in the midst of the ground, and defended it, and slew the Philistines: and the LORD wrought a great victory.

13 And three of the thirty chief went down, and came to David in the harvest time unto the cave of Adullam: and the troop of the Philistines pitched in the valley of Rephaim.

14 And David *was* then in an hold, and the garrison of the Philistines *was* then *in* Beth-lehem.

15 And David longed, and said, Oh that one would give me drink of the water of the well of Beth-lehem, which *is* by the gate!

16 And the three mighty men brake through the host of the Philistines, and drew water out of the well of Beth-lehem, that *was* by the gate, and took *it,* and brought *it* to David: nevertheless he would not drink thereof, but poured it out unto the LORD.

17 And he said, Be it far from me, O LORD, that I should do this: *is not this* the blood of the men that went in jeopardy of their lives? therefore he would not drink it. These things did these three mighty men.

18 And Abishai, the brother of Joab, the son of Zeruiah, was chief among three. And he lifted up his spear against three hundred, *and* slew *them,* and had the name among three.

19 Was he not most *a*honourable of three? therefore he was their captain: howbeit he attained not unto the *first* three.

20 And *a*Benaiah the son of Jehoiada, the son of a valiant man, of Kabzeel, who had done many acts, he slew two lionlike men of Moab: he went down also and slew a lion in the midst of a pit in time of snow:

21 And he slew an Egyptian, a goodly man: and the Egyptian had a spear in his hand; but he went down to him with a staff, and plucked the spear out of the Egyptian's hand, and slew him with his own spear.

22 These *things* did Benaiah the son of Jehoiada, and had the name among three mighty men.

23 He was more honourable than the thirty, but he attained not to the *first* three. And David set him over his guard.

24 Asahel the brother of Joab *was* one of the thirty; Elhanan the son of Dodo of Beth-lehem,

25 Shammah the Harodite, Elika the Harodite,

5*a* D&C 49:9.
7*a* OR equipped.
8*a* 1 Chr. 11:10 (10–41).
19*a* 1 Chr. 11:20.
20*a* 1 Chr. 27:6.

26 Helez the Paltite, Ira the son of Ikkesh the Tekoite,

27 Abiezer the Anethothite, Mebunnai the Hushathite,

28 Zalmon the Ahohite, Maharai the Netophathite,

29 Heleb the son of Baanah, a Netophathite, Ittai the son of Ribai out of Gibeah of the children of Benjamin,

30 Benaiah the Pirathonite, Hiddai of the brooks of Gaash,

31 Abi-albon the Arbathite, Azmaveth the Barhumite,

32 Eliahba the Shaalbonite, of the sons of Jashen, Jonathan,

33 Shammah the Hararite, Ahiam the son of Sharar the Hararite,

34 Eliphelet the son of Ahasbai, the son of the Maachathite, Eliam the son of Ahithophel the Gilonite,

35 Hezrai the Carmelite, Paarai the Arbite,

36 Igal the son of Nathan of Zobah, Bani the Gadite,

37 Zelek the Ammonite, Naharai the Beerothite, armourbearer to Joab the son of Zeruiah,

38 Ira an Ithrite, Gareb an Ithrite,

39 Uriah the Hittite: thirty and seven in all.

CHAPTER 24

David sins in numbering Israel and Judah—The men of war total 1,300,000—The Lord destroys 70,000 men by pestilence—David sees an angel, offers sacrifice, and the plague is stayed.

AND again the anger of the LORD was kindled against Israel, and *a*he moved David against them to say, Go, *b*number Israel and Judah.

2 For the king said to Joab the captain of the host, which *was* with him, Go now through all the tribes of Israel, from Dan even to Beer-sheba, and number ye the people, that I may know the number of the people.

3 And Joab said unto the king,

Now the LORD thy God add unto the people, how many soever they be, an hundredfold, and that the eyes of my lord the king may see *it:* but why doth my lord the king delight in this thing?

4 Notwithstanding the king's word prevailed against Joab, and against the captains of the host. And Joab and the captains of the host went out from the presence of the king, to number the people of Israel.

5 ¶ And they passed over Jordan, and pitched in Aroer, on the right side of the city that *lieth* in the midst of the river of Gad, and toward Jazer:

6 Then they came to Gilead, and to the land of Tahtim-hodshi; and they came to Dan-jaan, and about to Zidon,

7 And came to the strong hold of Tyre, and to all the cities of the Hivites, and of the Canaanites: and they went out to the south of Judah, *even* to Beer-sheba.

8 So when they had gone through all the land, they came to Jerusalem at the end of nine months and twenty days.

9 And Joab gave up the sum of the *a*number of the people unto the king: and there were in Israel *b*eight hundred thousand valiant men that drew the sword; and the men of Judah *were* five hundred thousand men.

10 ¶ And David's heart smote him after that he had numbered the people. And David said unto the LORD, I have sinned greatly in that I have done: and now, I beseech thee, O LORD, take away the iniquity of thy servant; for I have done very foolishly.

11 For when David was up in the morning, the word of the LORD came unto the *a*prophet Gad, David's *b*seer, saying,

12 Go and say unto David, Thus saith the LORD, I offer thee three

24 1*a* Apparently something is missing, and "Satan" should be the antecedent of "he." See

1 Chr. 21:1.
b Num. 1:19;
1 Chr. 21:1 (1–28).
9*a* 1 Chr. 7:2 (1–13).

b 1 Chr. 21:5.
11*a* Amos 3:7.
b TG Seer.

things; choose thee one of them, that I may *do it* unto thee.

13 So Gad came to David, and told him, and said unto him, Shall seven years of ªfamine come unto thee in thy land? or wilt thou flee three months before thine enemies, while they pursue thee? or that there be three days' pestilence in thy land? now advise, and see what answer I shall return to him that sent me.

14 And David said unto Gad, I am in a great strait: let us fall now into the hand of the LORD; for his ªmercies *are* great: and let me not fall into the hand of man.

15 ¶ So the LORD sent a pestilence upon Israel from the morning even to the time appointed: and there died of the people from Dan even to Beer-sheba seventy thousand men.

16 And when the angel stretched out his hand upon Jerusalem to destroy it, ªthe LORD repented him of the evil, and said to the angel that destroyed the people, It is enough: ᵇstay now thine hand. And the angel of the LORD was by the threshingplace of Araunah the Jebusite.

17 And David spake unto the LORD when he saw the angel that smote the people, and said, Lo, I have sinned, and I have done wickedly: but these sheep, what have they done? let thine hand, I pray thee, be against me, and against my father's house.

18 ¶ And Gad came that day to David, and said unto him, Go up, rear an ªaltar unto the LORD in the threshingfloor of Araunah the Jebusite.

19 And David, according to the saying of Gad, went up as the LORD commanded.

20 And Araunah looked, and saw the king and his servants coming on toward him: and Araunah went out, and bowed himself before the king on his face upon the ground.

21 And Araunah said, Wherefore is my lord the king come to his servant? And David said, To buy the threshingfloor of thee, to build an altar unto the LORD, that the plague may be stayed from the people.

22 And Araunah said unto David, Let my lord the king take and offer up what *seemeth* good unto him: behold, *here be* oxen for burnt sacrifice, and threshing instruments and *other* instruments of the oxen for wood.

23 All these *things* did Araunah, *as* a king, give unto the king. And Araunah said unto the king, The LORD thy God accept thee.

24 And the king said unto Araunah, Nay; but I will surely buy *it* of thee at a price: neither will I offer burnt offerings unto the LORD my God of that which doth cost me nothing. So David bought the threshingfloor and the oxen for ªfifty shekels of silver.

25 And David built there an ªaltar unto the LORD, and offered burnt offerings and peace ᵇofferings. So the LORD was entreated for the land, and the plague was stayed from Israel.

13ª 1 Chr. 21:12.
14ª TG God, Mercy of.
16ª The Hebrew root means "to sigh," therefore "to feel sorrow."
  Gen. 6:6;
  1 Sam. 15:11;
  Joel 2:13.
  See also 1 Chr. 21:15.
  JST 2 Sam. 24:16 . . .

the Lord *said unto him, Stay now thine hand, it is enough; for the people repented, and the Lord stayed the hand of the angel, that he destroyed not the people . . .*
b Alma 10:23;
  Moro. 9:14;
  D&C 38:22 (22, 33);

39:16;
  Moses 7:51.
18ª Gen. 22:2;
  1 Chr. 22:1 (1–2);
  2 Chr. 3:1.
24ª 1 Chr. 21:25.
25ª 1 Chr. 21:26.
  b TG Sacrifice.

THE FIRST BOOK OF THE
KINGS

COMMONLY CALLED
THE THIRD BOOK OF THE KINGS

CHAPTER 1

Abishag cherishes David in his extreme age—Adonijah aspires to be king—Bathsheba and Nathan advise David of Adonijah's plotting—David names Solomon as king, and he is anointed by Zadok—Adonijah's cause fails.

NOW king David was old *and* stricken in years; and they covered him with clothes, but he gat no heat.

2 Wherefore his servants said unto him, Let there be sought for my lord the king a young virgin: and let her stand before the king, and let her *a*cherish him, and let her lie in thy bosom, that my lord the king may get heat.

3 So they sought for a fair damsel throughout all the *a*coasts of Israel, and found *b*Abishag a Shunammite, and brought her to the king.

4 And the damsel *was* very fair, and cherished the king, and ministered to him: but the king knew her not.

5 Then *a*Adonijah the son of Haggith exalted himself, saying, I will be king: and he prepared him chariots and horsemen, and fifty men to run before him.

6 And his father had not displeased him at any time in saying, Why hast thou done so? and he also *was* a very *a*goodly *man;* and *his mother* bare him after *b*Absalom.

7 And he conferred with Joab the son of Zeruiah, and with *a*Abiathar the priest: and they following *b*Adonijah helped *him.*

8 But Zadok the priest, and Benaiah the son of Jehoiada, and Nathan the prophet, and Shimei, and Rei, and the mighty men which *belonged* to David, were not with Adonijah.

9 And Adonijah slew sheep and oxen and fat cattle by the stone of Zoheleth, which *is* by En-rogel, and called all his brethren the king's sons, and all the men of Judah the king's servants:

10 But Nathan the prophet, and Benaiah, and the mighty men, and Solomon his brother, he called not.

11 ¶ Wherefore Nathan spake unto Bath-sheba the mother of Solomon, saying, Hast thou not heard that Adonijah the son of Haggith doth reign, and David our lord knoweth *it* not?

12 Now therefore come, let me, I pray thee, give thee counsel, that thou mayest save thine own life, and the life of thy son Solomon.

13 Go and get thee in unto king David, and say unto him, Didst not thou, my lord, O king, swear unto thine handmaid, saying, Assuredly *a*Solomon thy son shall reign after me, and he shall sit upon my throne? why then doth Adonijah reign?

14 Behold, while thou yet talkest there with the king, I also will come in after thee, and confirm thy words.

15 ¶ And Bath-sheba went in unto the king into the chamber: and the king was very old; and Abishag the

---

1 2 *a* IE wait upon.
3 *a* OR borders.
 b 1 Kgs. 2:17.

5 *a* 2 Sam. 3:4.
6 *a* HEB handsome.
 b 1 Kgs. 2:22.

7 *a* 1 Kgs. 2:22.
 b 1 Kgs. 2:28.
13 *a* 1 Chr. 22:9.

Shunammite ministered unto the king.

16 And Bath-sheba bowed, and did obeisance unto the king. And the king said, What wouldest thou?

17 And she said unto him, My lord, thou ^aswarest by the LORD thy God unto thine handmaid, *saying,* Assuredly Solomon thy son shall reign after me, and he shall sit upon my throne.

18 And now, behold, Adonijah reigneth; and now, my lord the king, thou knowest *it* not:

19 And he hath slain oxen and fat cattle and sheep in abundance, and hath called all the sons of the king, and Abiathar the priest, and Joab the captain of the host: but Solomon thy servant hath he not called.

20 And thou, my lord, O king, the eyes of all Israel *are* upon thee, that thou shouldest tell them who shall sit on the throne of my lord the king after him.

21 Otherwise it shall come to pass, when my lord the king shall sleep with his fathers, that I and my son Solomon shall be counted offenders.

22 ¶ And, lo, while she yet talked with the king, Nathan the prophet also came in.

23 And they told the king, saying, Behold Nathan the prophet. And when he was come in before the king, he bowed himself before the king with his face to the ground.

24 And Nathan said, My lord, O king, hast thou said, Adonijah shall reign after me, and he shall sit upon my throne?

25 For he is gone down this day, and hath slain oxen and fat cattle and sheep in abundance, and hath called all the king's sons, and the captains of the host, and Abiathar the priest; and, behold, they eat and drink before him, and say, ^aGod save king Adonijah.

26 But me, *even* me thy servant, and Zadok the priest, and Benaiah

the son of Jehoiada, and thy servant Solomon, hath he not called.

27 Is this thing done by my lord the king, and thou hast not shewed *it* unto thy servant, who should sit on the throne of my lord the king after him?

28 ¶ Then king David answered and said, Call me Bath-sheba. And she came into the king's presence, and stood before the king.

29 And the king sware, and said, As the LORD liveth, that hath redeemed my soul out of all distress,

30 Even as I sware unto thee by the LORD God of Israel, saying, Assuredly Solomon thy son shall reign after me, and he shall sit upon my throne in my stead; even so will I certainly do this day.

31 Then Bath-sheba bowed with *her* face to the earth, and did reverence to the king, and said, Let my lord king David live for ever.

32 ¶ And king David said, Call me Zadok the priest, and Nathan the prophet, and Benaiah the son of Jehoiada. And they came before the king.

33 The king also said unto them, Take with you the servants of your lord, and cause Solomon my son to ride upon mine own mule, and bring him down to ^aGihon:

34 And let Zadok the priest and Nathan the prophet ^aanoint him there ^bking over Israel: and blow ye with the trumpet, and say, ^cGod save king Solomon.

35 Then ye shall come up after him, that he may come and sit upon my throne; for he shall be king in my stead: and I have appointed him to be ruler over Israel and over Judah.

36 And Benaiah the son of Jehoiada answered the king, and said, Amen: the LORD God of my lord the king say so *too.*

37 As the LORD hath been with my lord the king, even so be he with Solomon, and make his throne

---

17*a* 2 Sam. 12:24 (15–25).
25*a* HEB May King Adonijah live (long)!
33*a* 2 Chr. 32:30.

34*a* 1 Sam. 10:1;
1 Kgs. 2:15;
1 Chr. 29:22.
b 1 Chr. 23:1.

c HEB Let King Solomon live!

greater than the throne of my lord king David.

38 So Zadok the priest, and Nathan the prophet, and Benaiah the son of Jehoiada, and the ^aCherethites, and the ^bPelethites, went down, and caused Solomon to ride upon king David's mule, and brought him to Gihon.

39 And Zadok the priest took an horn of ^aoil out of the ^btabernacle, and anointed Solomon. And they blew the trumpet; and all the people said, God save king Solomon.

40 And all the people came up after him, and the people piped with pipes, and rejoiced with great joy, so that the earth rent with the sound of them.

41 ¶ And Adonijah and all the guests that *were* with him heard *it* as they had made an end of eating. And when Joab heard the sound of the trumpet, he said, Wherefore *is this* noise of the city being in an uproar?

42 And while he yet spake, behold, ^aJonathan the son of Abiathar the priest came: and Adonijah said unto him, Come in; for thou *art* a valiant man, and bringest good tidings.

43 And Jonathan answered and said to Adonijah, Verily our lord king David hath made Solomon king.

44 And the king hath sent with him Zadok the priest, and Nathan the prophet, and Benaiah the son of Jehoiada, and the Cherethites, and the Pelethites, and they have caused him to ride upon the king's mule:

45 And Zadok the priest and Nathan the prophet have anointed him king in Gihon: and they are come up from thence rejoicing, so that the city rang again. This *is* the noise that ye have heard.

46 And also Solomon sitteth on the throne of the kingdom.

47 And moreover the king's servants came to bless our lord king David, saying, God make the name of Solomon better than thy name, and make his throne greater than thy throne. And the king bowed himself upon the ^abed.

48 And also thus said the king, Blessed *be* the Lᴏʀᴅ God of Israel, which hath given *one* to sit on my throne this day, mine eyes even seeing *it*.

49 And all the guests that *were* with Adonijah were afraid, and rose up, and went every man his way.

50 ¶ And Adonijah feared because of Solomon, and arose, and went, and caught hold on the ^ahorns of the altar.

51 And it was told Solomon, saying, Behold, Adonijah feareth king Solomon: for, lo, he hath caught hold on the horns of the altar, saying, Let king Solomon swear unto me to day that he will not slay his servant with the sword.

52 And Solomon said, If he will shew himself a worthy man, there shall not an hair of him fall to the earth: but if wickedness shall be found in him, he shall die.

53 So king Solomon sent, and they brought him down from the altar. And he came and bowed himself to king Solomon: and Solomon said unto him, Go to thine house.

CHAPTER 2

David charges Solomon to keep the commandments and walk in the ways of the Lord—King David dies and Solomon reigns—Adonijah, Joab, and Shimei are put to death, and Abiathar is rejected as high priest—The kingdom is established with Solomon.

Now the days of David drew nigh that he should die; and he charged ^aSolomon his son, saying,

2 I go the ^away of all the earth: be thou strong therefore, and shew thyself a ^bman;

38*a* 1 Sam. 30:14.
  b 2 Sam. 8:18.
39*a* Ex. 30:25 (23–32).
  b TG Temple.
42*a* 2 Sam. 15:27 (27, 36);

17:17.
47*a* Gen. 47:31.
50*a* Ex. 27:2; 1 Kgs. 2:28.
2 1*a* See a poetic version
    of David's prayer

for Solomon on this
    occasion in Psalm 72.
2*a* Josh. 23:14; 2 Ne. 1:14.
  b 2 Ne. 1:21;
    Alma 48:17 (17–18).

3 And keep the charge of the LORD thy God, to ^awalk in his ways, to keep his statutes, and his ^bcommandments, and his judgments, and his testimonies, as it is written in the law of Moses, that thou mayest ^cprosper in all that thou doest, and whithersoever thou turnest thyself:

4 That the LORD may continue his word which he spake concerning me, saying, If thy ^achildren take ^bheed to their way, to walk before me in truth with all their ^cheart and with all their soul, there shall not fail thee (said he) a man on the ^dthrone of Israel.

5 Moreover thou knowest also what ^aJoab the son of Zeruiah did to me, *and* what he did to the two captains of the hosts of Israel, unto ^bAbner the son of Ner, and unto ^cAmasa the son of Jether, whom he slew, and shed the blood of war in peace, and put the blood of war upon his girdle that *was* about his loins, and in his shoes that *were* on his feet.

6 Do therefore according to thy wisdom, and let not his hoar head go down to the grave in peace.

7 But shew kindness unto the sons of ^aBarzillai the Gileadite, and let them be of those that eat at thy table: for so they came to me when I fled because of Absalom thy brother.

8 And, behold, *thou hast* with thee ^aShimei the son of Gera, a Benjamite of Bahurim, which cursed me with a grievous curse in the day when I went to Mahanaim: but he came down to meet me at Jordan, and I sware to him by the LORD, saying, I will not put thee to death with the sword.

9 Now therefore hold him not guiltless: for thou *art* a wise man, and knowest what thou oughtest to do unto him; but his hoar head bring thou down to the grave with blood.

10 So David slept with his fathers, and was ^aburied in the ^bcity of David.

11 And the days that David ^areigned over Israel *were* forty years: seven years reigned he in Hebron, and thirty and three years reigned he in Jerusalem.

12 ¶ Then sat ^aSolomon upon the throne of David his father; and his kingdom was established greatly.

13 ¶ And Adonijah the son of Haggith came to Bath-sheba the mother of Solomon. And she said, Comest thou peaceably? And he said, Peaceably.

14 He said moreover, I have somewhat to say unto thee. And she said, Say on.

15 And he said, Thou knowest that the ^akingdom was mine, and *that* all Israel set their faces on me, that I should reign: howbeit the kingdom is turned about, and is become my brother's: for it was his from the LORD.

16 And now I ask one petition of thee, deny me not. And she said unto him, Say on.

17 And he said, Speak, I pray thee, unto Solomon the king, (for he will not say thee nay,) that he give me ^aAbishag the Shunammite to wife.

18 And Bath-sheba said, Well; I will speak for thee unto the king.

19 ¶ Bath-sheba therefore went unto king Solomon, to speak unto him for Adonijah. And the king rose up to meet her, and bowed himself unto her, and sat down on his throne, and caused a seat to be set for the king's mother; and she sat on his right hand.

20 Then she said, I desire one small petition of thee; *I pray thee,* say me not nay. And the king said unto her, Ask on, my mother: for I will not say thee nay.

21 And she said, Let Abishag the

3*a* TG Walking with God.
  b 1 Ne. 17:15 (3, 15).
  c Deut. 29:9;
     1 Ne. 17:35 (35–38).
4*a* Ps. 132:12.
  b D&C 84:43 (43–44).
  c D&C 64:34.

d 2 Sam. 7:12.
5*a* 2 Sam. 18:5.
  b 2 Sam. 3:27 (27, 39).
  c 2 Sam. 20:10.
7*a* 2 Sam. 19:31 (31–38).
8*a* 2 Sam. 16:5;
     1 Kgs. 2:36 (36, 44).

10*a* Acts 2:29.
   b 2 Sam. 5:7; 1 Kgs. 3:1.
11*a* 2 Sam. 5:4 (4–5).
12*a* 1 Chr. 29:23.
15*a* 1 Kgs. 1:34 (11–46);
     1 Chr. 22:10 (9–10).
17*a* 1 Kgs. 1:3 (3–4).

Shunammite be given to Adonijah thy brother to wife.

22 And king Solomon answered and said unto his mother, And why dost thou ask Abishag the Shunammite for Adonijah? ask for him the kingdom also; for he *is* mine elder [a]brother; even for him, and for [b]Abiathar the priest, and for Joab the son of Zeruiah.

23 Then king Solomon sware by the LORD, saying, God do so to me, and more also, if Adonijah have not spoken this word against his own life.

24 Now therefore, *as* the LORD liveth, which hath established me, and set me on the throne of David my father, and who hath made me an house, as he promised, Adonijah shall be put to [a]death this day.

25 And king Solomon sent by the hand of [a]Benaiah the son of Jehoiada; and he fell upon him that he died.

26 ¶ And unto [a]Abiathar the priest said the king, Get thee to [b]Anathoth, unto thine own fields; for thou *art* worthy of death: but I will not at this time put thee to death, because thou barest the ark of the Lord GOD before David my father, and because thou hast been afflicted in all wherein my father was afflicted.

27 So Solomon thrust out [a]Abiathar from being priest unto the LORD; that he might [b]fulfil the word of the LORD, which he spake concerning the house of Eli in Shiloh.

28 ¶ Then tidings came to [a]Joab: for Joab had turned after [b]Adonijah, though he turned not after Absalom. And Joab fled unto the tabernacle of the LORD, and caught hold on the [c]horns of the altar.

29 And it was told king Solomon that Joab was fled unto the tabernacle of the LORD; and, behold, *he is* by the altar. Then Solomon sent Benaiah the son of Jehoiada, saying, Go, fall upon him.

30 And Benaiah came to the tabernacle of the LORD, and said unto him, Thus saith the king, Come forth. And he said, Nay; but I will die here. And Benaiah brought the king word again, saying, Thus said Joab, and thus he answered me.

31 And the king said unto him, Do as he hath said, and fall upon him, and bury him; that thou mayest take away the [a]innocent blood, which Joab shed, from me, and from the house of my father.

32 And the LORD shall return his blood upon his own head, who fell upon two men more righteous and better than he, and slew them with the sword, my father David not knowing *thereof, to wit,* [a]Abner the son of Ner, captain of the host of Israel, and Amasa the son of Jether, captain of the host of Judah.

33 Their blood shall therefore return upon the head of [a]Joab, and upon the head of his seed for ever: but upon David, and upon his seed, and upon his house, and upon his throne, shall there be peace for ever from the LORD.

34 So Benaiah the son of Jehoiada went up, and fell upon him, and slew him: and he was buried in his own house in the wilderness.

35 ¶ And the king put [a]Benaiah the son of Jehoiada in his room over the [b]host: and [c]Zadok the [d]priest did the king put in the room of Abiathar.

36 ¶ And the king sent and called for [a]Shimei, and said unto him, Build thee an house in Jerusalem, and dwell there, and go not forth thence any whither.

37 For it shall be, *that* on the day thou goest out, and passest over the brook Kidron, thou shalt know for certain that thou shalt surely die:

22a 1 Kgs. 1:6;
       1 Chr. 3:2 (2, 5).
   b 1 Kgs. 1:7.
24a TG Capital Punishment.
25a 2 Sam. 8:18.
26a 1 Sam. 22:20 (20, 23);
       2 Sam. 15:24 (24, 29).
   b Josh. 21:18.

27a 1 Kgs. 4:4.
   b 1 Sam. 2:31 (31–35).
28a 2 Sam. 17:25.
   b 1 Kgs. 1:7.
   c Ex. 21:13 (13–14);
       1 Kgs. 1:50.
31a Deut. 19:13.
32a 2 Sam. 3:27.

33a 2 Sam. 3:29.
35a 1 Kgs. 4:4.
   b OR army.
   c 2 Sam. 8:17;
       1 Chr. 6:8 (1–12).
   d 1 Sam. 2:35;
       1 Chr. 29:22.
36a 1 Kgs. 2:8.

thy blood shall be upon thine own head.

38 And Shimei said unto the king, The saying *is* good: as my lord the king hath said, so will thy servant do. And Shimei dwelt in Jerusalem many days.

39 And it came to pass at the end of three years, that two of the servants of Shimei ran away unto *a*Achish son of Maachah king of Gath. And they told Shimei, saying, Behold, thy servants *be* in Gath.

40 And Shimei arose, and saddled his ass, and went to Gath to Achish to seek his servants: and Shimei went, and brought his servants from Gath.

41 And it was told Solomon that Shimei had gone from Jerusalem to Gath, and was come again.

42 And the king sent and called for Shimei, and said unto him, Did I not make thee to swear by the LORD, and *a*protested unto thee, saying, Know for a certain, on the day thou goest out, and walkest abroad any whither, that thou shalt surely die? and thou saidst unto me, The word *that* I have heard *is* good.

43 Why then hast thou not kept the oath of the LORD, and the commandment that I have charged thee with?

44 The king said moreover to Shimei, Thou knowest all the *a*wickedness which thine heart *b*is privy to, that thou didst to David my father: therefore the LORD shall return thy wickedness upon thine own head;

45 And king Solomon *shall be* blessed, and the throne of David shall be established before the LORD for ever.

46 So the king commanded Benaiah the son of Jehoiada; which went out, and fell upon him, that he *a*died. And the kingdom was established in the hand of Solomon.

CHAPTER 3

Solomon loves the Lord and keeps His commandments—The Lord appears to Solomon and promises him a wise and an understanding heart—He judges between two harlots and determines who is the mother of a child.

AND Solomon made *a*affinity with *b*Pharaoh king of Egypt, and took Pharaoh's daughter, and brought her into the *c*city of David, until he had made an end of building his own *d*house, and the house of the LORD, and the *e*wall of Jerusalem round about.

2 Only the people sacrificed in high places, because there was no *a*house built unto the name of the LORD, until those days.

3 And Solomon loved the LORD, walking in the *a*statutes of David his father: only he *b*sacrificed and burnt incense in high places.

4 And the king went to *a*Gibeon to sacrifice there; for that *was* the great *b*high place: a thousand burnt offerings did Solomon offer upon that altar.

5 ¶ In *a*Gibeon the LORD *b*appeared to Solomon in a *c*dream by night: and God said, Ask what I shall give thee.

6 And Solomon said, Thou hast shewed unto thy servant David my father great mercy, according as he walked before thee in truth, and in righteousness, and in uprightness of heart with thee; and thou hast kept for him this great kindness, that thou hast given him a son to sit on his throne, as *it is* this day.

7 And now, O LORD my God, thou hast made thy servant king instead of David my father: and I *am but* a *a*little child: I know not *how* to go out or come in.

39*a* 1 Sam. 27:2.
42*a* OR solemnly warned thee.
44*a* 2 Sam. 16:5.
  b HEB knew.
46*a* Alma 62:10.
3 1*a* HEB a marriage alliance.
  b 1 Kgs. 7:8;
    9:16 (16, 24); 11:1.

c 1 Kgs. 2:10.
d 1 Kgs. 7:1.
e 1 Kgs. 9:15 (15, 19).
2*a* D&C 124:28 (25–48).
3*a* D&C 136:2.
  b 1 Ne. 5:9; 7:22.
4*a* Josh. 9:3;
    1 Chr. 21:29.
  b 1 Chr. 16:39.

5*a* 1 Kgs. 9:2.
  b 1 Kgs. 11:9;
    2 Chr. 1:7 (7–12);
    D&C 110:8 (7–8).
  c TG Dream.
7*a* 1 Chr. 22:5; 29:1;
    3 Ne. 9:22; 11:37 (37–38).

8 And thy servant *is* in the midst of thy people which thou hast chosen, a ^agreat people, that cannot be ^bnumbered nor counted for multitude.

9 Give therefore thy servant an ^aunderstanding ^bheart to judge thy people, that I may ^cdiscern between good and bad: for who is able to judge this thy so great a people?

10 And the speech pleased the Lord, that Solomon had asked this thing.

11 And God said unto him, Because thou hast asked this thing, and hast not asked for thyself long life; neither hast asked ^ariches for thyself, nor hast asked the life of thine ^benemies; but hast asked for thyself ^cunderstanding to discern judgment;

12 Behold, I have done according to thy words: lo, I have ^agiven thee a ^bwise and an understanding heart; so that there was none like thee before thee, neither after thee shall any arise like unto thee.

13 And I have also given thee that which thou hast not asked, both ^ariches, and honour: so that there shall not be any among the kings like unto thee all thy days.

14 And if thou wilt walk in my ways, to keep my statutes and my ^acommandments, as thy father David did walk, then I will lengthen thy days.

15 And Solomon awoke; and, behold, *it was* a dream. And he came to Jerusalem, and stood before the ^aark of the covenant of the LORD, and offered up burnt offerings, and offered peace ^bofferings, and made a feast to all his servants.

16 ¶ Then came there two women, *that were* harlots, unto the king, and stood before him.

17 And the one woman said, O my lord, I and this woman dwell in one house; and I was delivered of a child with her in the house.

18 And it came to pass the third day after that I was delivered, that this woman was delivered also: and we *were* together; *there was* no stranger with us in the house, save we two in the house.

19 And this woman's child died in the night; because she ^aoverlaid it.

20 And she arose at midnight, and took my son from beside me, while thine handmaid slept, and laid it in her bosom, and laid her dead child in my bosom.

21 And when I rose in the morning to give my child suck, behold, it was dead: but when I had considered it in the morning, behold, it was not my son, which I did bear.

22 And the other woman said, Nay; but the living *is* my son, and the dead *is* thy son. And this said, No; but the dead *is* thy son, and the living *is* my son. Thus they spake before the king.

23 Then said the king, The one saith, This *is* my son that liveth, and thy son *is* the dead: and the other saith, Nay; but thy son *is* the dead, and my son *is* the living.

24 And the king said, Bring me a sword. And they brought a sword before the king.

25 And the king said, Divide the living child in two, and give half to the one, and half to the other.

26 Then spake the woman whose the living child *was* unto the king, for her bowels yearned upon her son, and she said, O my lord, give her the living child, and in no wise slay it. But the other said, Let it be neither mine nor thine, *but* divide *it*.

27 Then the king answered and said, Give her the living child, and in no wise slay it: she *is* the mother thereof.

8*a* 2 Sam. 7:23.
  b Gen. 13:16;
     Abr. 3:14.
9*a* TG Understanding.
  b TG Heart.
  c TG Discernment,
     Spiritual.
11*a* Jacob 2:18 (18–19);

Alma 39:14;
  D&C 6:7 (6–7); 11:7.
  b D&C 98:23.
  c 2 Ne. 21:2.
12*a* TG Guidance, Divine.
  b 1 Kgs. 4:29 (29–31); 5:12;
     2 Ne. 28:15; Jacob 6:12;
     Mosiah 29:11;

Morm. 9:28;
  JS—H 1:11 (11–13).
13*a* 1 Kgs. 10:23 (23, 25);
     Matt. 6:33.
14*a* D&C 54:6.
15*a* 2 Sam. 6:17; 2 Chr. 1:4.
  b TG Sacrifice.
19*a* OR laid upon it.

28 And all Israel heard of the judgment which the king had judged; and they feared the king: for they saw that the ^awisdom of God *was* in him, to do judgment.

CHAPTER 4

The officers in Solomon's court are listed—Solomon reigns in peace and prosperity over a large kingdom—His wisdom and understanding exceed that of all men.

So king Solomon was king over all Israel.

2 And these *were* the princes which he had; Azariah the son of Zadok the priest,

3 Elihoreph and Ahiah, the sons of Shisha, ^ascribes; Jehoshaphat the son of Ahilud, the ^brecorder.

4 And ^aBenaiah the son of Jehoiada *was* over the host: and Zadok and ^bAbiathar *were* the priests:

5 And Azariah the son of Nathan *was* over the ^aofficers: and Zabud the son of Nathan *was* principal officer, *and* the king's friend:

6 And Ahishar *was* over the household: and ^aAdoniram the son of Abda *was* over the ^btribute.

7 ¶ And Solomon had twelve ^aofficers over all Israel, which ^bprovided victuals for the king and his household: each man his month in a year made provision.

8 And these *are* their names: The son of Hur, in mount Ephraim:

9 The son of Dekar, in Makaz, and in Shaalbim, and Beth-shemesh, and Elon-beth-hanan:

10 The son of Hesed, in Aruboth; to him *pertained* Sochoh, and all the land of Hepher:

11 The son of Abinadab, in all the region of Dor; which had Taphath the daughter of Solomon to wife:

12 Baana the son of Ahilud; *to him pertained* Taanach and Megiddo, and all Beth-shean, which *is* by Zartanah beneath Jezreel, from Beth-shean to Abel-meholah, *even* unto *the place that is* beyond Jokneam:

13 The son of Geber, in Ramoth-gilead; to him *pertained* the towns of Jair the son of Manasseh, which *are* in Gilead; to him *also pertained* the region of Argob, which *is* in Bashan, threescore great cities with walls and brasen bars:

14 Ahinadab the son of Iddo *had* Mahanaim:

15 Ahimaaz *was* in Naphtali; he also took Basmath the daughter of Solomon to wife:

16 Baanah the son of Hushai *was* in Asher and in Aloth:

17 Jehoshaphat the son of Paruah, in Issachar:

18 Shimei the son of Elah, in Benjamin:

19 Geber the son of Uri *was* in the country of Gilead, *in* the country of Sihon king of the Amorites, and of Og king of Bashan; and *he was* the only officer which *was* in the land.

20 ¶ Judah and Israel *were* many, as the ^asand which *is* by the sea in multitude, eating and drinking, and making merry.

21 And Solomon ^areigned over all kingdoms from ^bthe river unto the land of the Philistines, and unto the border of Egypt: they brought presents, and served Solomon all the days of his life.

22 ¶ And Solomon's ^aprovision for one day was thirty measures of fine flour, and threescore measures of meal,

23 Ten fat oxen, and twenty oxen out of the pastures, and an hundred sheep, beside harts, and roebucks, and fallowdeer, and fatted fowl.

24 For he had ^adominion over all *the region* on this side the river, from Tiphsah even to ^bAzzah, over all the

---

28*a* 2 Ne. 21:2.
4 3*a* TG Scribe.
  b D&C 127:6; 128:2.
  4*a* 1 Kgs. 2:35.
  b 1 Kgs. 2:27.
  5*a* 1 Kgs. 4:27; 5:16; 9:23.
  6*a* 1 Kgs. 5:14; 12:18.

  b IE conscripted labor.
  7*a* TG Delegation of
    Responsibility.
  b 1 Kgs. 12:4.
  20*a* Gen. 22:17 (17–18);
    1 Ne. 12:1.
  21*a* 2 Chr. 9:26.

  b IE the Euphrates.
    Gen. 15:18.
  22*a* 1 Sam. 8:15 (10–22).
  24*a* Ex. 23:31 (31–33).
  b OR Gaza.

kings on this side the river: and he had ^cpeace on all sides round about him.

25 And Judah and Israel dwelt ^asafely, every man under his ^bvine and under his fig tree, from Dan even to Beer-sheba, all the days of Solomon.

26 ¶ And Solomon had forty ^athousand stalls of ^bhorses for his chariots, and twelve thousand horsemen.

27 And those ^aofficers provided victual for king Solomon, and for all that came unto king Solomon's table, every man in his month: they lacked nothing.

28 Barley also and straw for the horses and ^adromedaries brought they unto the place where *the officers* were, every man according to his charge.

29 ¶ And God ^agave Solomon ^bwisdom and ^cunderstanding exceeding much, and largeness of heart, even as the sand that *is* on the sea shore.

30 And Solomon's wisdom excelled the wisdom of all the children of the east country, and all the wisdom of Egypt.

31 For he was wiser than all men; than Ethan the Ezrahite, and Heman, and Chalcol, and Darda, the sons of Mahol: and his fame was in all nations round about.

32 And he spake three thousand ^aproverbs: and his ^bsongs were a thousand and five.

33 And he spake of trees, from the cedar tree that *is* in Lebanon even unto the hyssop that springeth out of the wall: he spake also of beasts, and of fowl, and of creeping things, and of fishes.

34 And there came of all people to hear the wisdom of Solomon, from ^aall kings of the earth, which had heard of his wisdom.

CHAPTER 5

Solomon solicits and gains Hiram's help in getting timber to build the temple—The Israelites hew stones and cut timber for the temple.

AND ^aHiram king of Tyre sent his servants unto Solomon; for he had heard that they had anointed him king in the room of his father: for Hiram was ever a ^blover of David.

2 And Solomon sent to ^aHiram, saying,

3 Thou knowest how that David my father could not build an ^ahouse unto the name of the LORD his God for the wars which were about him on every side, until the ^bLORD put them under the soles of his feet.

4 But now the LORD my God hath given me ^arest on every side, *so that there is* neither adversary nor evil occurrent.

5 And, behold, I purpose to build an house unto the name of the LORD my God, as the LORD spake unto David my father, saying, Thy son, whom I will set upon thy throne in thy room, he shall build an ^ahouse unto my name.

6 Now therefore command thou that they hew me ^acedar trees out of Lebanon; and my servants shall be with thy servants: and unto thee will I give hire for thy servants according to all that thou shalt appoint: for thou knowest that *there is* not among us any that ^bcan skill to hew timber like unto the Sidonians.

7 ¶ And it came to pass, when

24c 1 Kgs. 5:4;
    1 Chr. 22:9.
25a HEB confidently,
    securely.
  b Micah 4:4.
26a 1 Kgs. 10:26;
    2 Chr. 1:14.
  b Deut. 17:16;
    2 Chr. 9:25.
27a 1 Kgs. 4:5.
28a OR fast steeds.
29a TG Guidance, Divine.

  b 1 Kgs. 3:12.
    TG God, Wisdom of.
  c TG Understanding.
32a Prov. 1:1; 10:1; 25:1.
  b Song 1:1.
34a 2 Chr. 9:23.
5 1a 2 Sam. 5:11.
  b The Hebrew term here
    expresses the affection
    held by one friend for
    another;
    1 Sam. 16:21; 18:1, 3.

2a 2 Chr. 2:3 (3–16).
3a TG Temple.
  b Alma 46:7.
4a 1 Kgs. 4:24 (24–25);
    1 Chr. 22:9.
5a 2 Ne. 5:16;
    D&C 84:31;
    88:119 (119–20);
    97:12 (10–17).
6a 1 Chr. 22:4; Ezra 3:7;
    2 Ne. 19:10.
  b HEB know how.

Hiram heard the words of Solomon, that he rejoiced greatly, and said, ^aBlessed *be* the Lord this day, which hath given unto David a wise son over this great people.

8 And Hiram sent to Solomon, saying, I have considered the things which thou sentest to me for: *and* I will do all thy desire concerning timber of cedar, and concerning timber of ^afir.

9 My servants shall bring *them* down from Lebanon unto the sea: and I will convey them by sea in floats unto the place that thou shalt appoint me, and will cause them to be discharged there, and thou shalt receive *them:* and thou shalt accomplish my desire, in giving food for my household.

10 So Hiram gave Solomon cedar trees and fir trees *according to* all his desire.

11 And Solomon gave Hiram twenty thousand measures of wheat *for* food to his household, and twenty measures of pure oil: thus gave Solomon to Hiram year by year.

12 And the Lord gave Solomon ^awisdom, as he promised him: and there was peace between Hiram and Solomon; and they two made a ^bleague together.

13 ¶ And king Solomon raised a ^alevy out of all Israel; and the ^blevy was thirty thousand men.

14 And he sent them to Lebanon, ten thousand a month by courses: a month they were in Lebanon, *and* two months at home: and ^aAdoniram *was* over the levy.

15 And Solomon had threescore and ten thousand that bare ^aburdens, and fourscore thousand ^bhewers in the mountains;

16 Beside the chief of Solomon's ^aofficers which *were* over the work, three thousand and three hundred, which ^bruled over the people that wrought in the work.

17 And the king commanded, and they brought great stones, ^acostly stones, *and* hewed ^bstones, to lay the foundation of the house.

18 And Solomon's builders and Hiram's builders did hew *them,* and the ^astonesquarers: so they prepared timber and stones to build the house.

CHAPTER 6

Solomon builds the temple—The Lord promises to dwell among the Israelites if they are obedient—The ornaments of the temple are described.

And it came to pass in the four hundred and eightieth year after the children of Israel were come out of the land of Egypt, in the ^afourth year of Solomon's reign over Israel, in the month Zif, which *is* the second month, that he began to ^bbuild the ^chouse of the Lord.

2 And the ^ahouse which king ^bSolomon built for the Lord, the length thereof *was* threescore cubits, and the ^cbreadth thereof twenty *cubits,* and the height thereof thirty cubits.

3 And the ^aporch before the temple of the house, twenty cubits *was* the length thereof, according to the breadth of the house; *and* ten cubits *was* the breadth thereof before the house.

4 And for the house he made ^awindows of narrow lights.

5 ¶ And against the wall of the house he built ^achambers round about, *against* the walls of the house

7 *a* 1 Kgs. 10:9.
8 *a* 1 Kgs. 6:34.
12 *a* 1 Kgs. 3:12;
　　D&C 46:17.
　b HEB covenant, pact.
13 *a* 1 Kgs. 12:4.
　b 1 Kgs. 9:15.
14 *a* 1 Kgs. 4:6; 12:18.
15 *a* 1 Kgs. 9:21 (20–22).
　b IE hewers of stone.
16 *a* 1 Kgs. 4:5.

　b 1 Kgs. 9:23.
17 *a* 2 Ne. 5:16.
　b 1 Kgs. 6:7;
　　2 Ne. 19:10.
18 *a* HEB *Givlim;* i.e., Giblites,
　　or inhabitants of Gebal.
　　Josh. 13:5.
6 1 *a* 1 Kgs. 6:37.
　b 2 Chr. 3:1 (1–17).
　　TG Skill.
　c D&C 88:119;

　　124:27 (26–27).
2 *a* 2 Chr. 3:3 (3–4);
　　D&C 95:13.
　b 2 Ne. 5:16.
　c Ezek. 41:2.
3 *a* Ezek. 8:16; 40:49;
　　John 10:23;
　　Acts 3:11.
4 *a* OR recessed and latticed
　　windows.
5 *a* Ezek. 41:6 (5–9, 11).

round about, *both* of the temple and of the *b*oracle: and he made chambers round about:

6 The nethermost chamber *was* five cubits broad, and the middle *was* six cubits broad, and the third *was* seven cubits broad: for without in the wall of the house he made narrowed rests round about, that *the beams* should not be fastened in the walls of the house.

7 And the house, when it was in building, was built of *a*stone made ready before it was brought thither: so that there was neither hammer nor axe *nor* any tool of iron heard in the house, while it was in building.

8 The door for the middle chamber *was* in the right side of the house: and they went up with winding stairs into the middle *chamber,* and out of the middle into the third.

9 So he built the house, and finished it; and covered the house with beams and boards of cedar.

10 And *then* he built chambers against all the house, five cubits high: and they rested on the house with timber of cedar.

11 ¶ And the word of the LORD came to Solomon, saying,

12 *Concerning* this house which thou art in building, if thou wilt *a*walk in my statutes, and execute my judgments, and keep all my commandments to walk in them; then will I perform my *b*word with thee, which I spake unto David thy father:

13 And I will *a*dwell among the children of Israel, and will not *b*forsake my people Israel.

14 So Solomon built the house, and finished it.

15 And he built the walls of the house within with boards of cedar, both the floor of the house, and the walls of the ceiling: *and* he covered

them on the inside with wood, and covered the floor of the house with planks of fir.

16 And he built twenty cubits on the sides of the house, both the floor and the walls with boards of cedar: he even built *them* for it within, *even* for the *a*oracle, *even* for the most *b*holy *place.*

17 And the house, that *is,* the temple before it, was forty cubits *long.*

18 And the cedar of the house within *was* carved with knops and open flowers: all *was* cedar; there was no stone seen.

19 And the oracle he prepared in the house within, to set there the ark of the covenant of the LORD.

20 And the oracle in the forepart *was* twenty cubits in length, and twenty cubits in breadth, and twenty cubits in the height thereof: and he overlaid it with pure gold; and *so* covered the altar *which was of* cedar.

21 So Solomon overlaid the house within with pure *a*gold: and he made a partition by the chains of gold before the oracle; and he overlaid it with gold.

22 And the whole house he overlaid with gold, until he had finished all the house: also the whole *a*altar that *was* by the oracle he *b*overlaid with gold.

23 ¶ And within the oracle he *a*made two *b*cherubims *of* olive tree, *each* ten cubits high.

24 And five cubits *was* the one wing of the cherub, and five cubits the other wing of the cherub: from the uttermost part of the one wing unto the uttermost part of the other *were* ten cubits.

25 And the other cherub *was* ten cubits: both the cherubims *were* of one measure and one size.

26 The height of the one cherub *was*

5*b* 1 Kgs. 7:49; 8:8 (6, 8);
      D&C 124:39.
7*a* 1 Kgs. 5:17.
12*a* 1 Kgs. 9:4;
      D&C 124:55.
   b 2 Sam. 7:13; 1 Chr. 22:10.
13*a* Ex. 25:8;
      D&C 124:24, 27.

   b Deut. 31:6 (6, 8);
      Josh. 1:5; Heb. 13:5.
16*a* IE innermost room of
      the temple of Solomon;
      the Holy of Holies.
   b Ex. 26:33;
      1 Kgs. 7:50; 8:6;
      2 Chr. 3:8;

      Ezek. 41:4 (1–4);
      D&C 124:39.
21*a* 2 Ne. 5:15;
      D&C 124:26 (26–27).
22*a* Ex. 30:1.
   b Ex. 30:3.
23*a* TG Art.
   b TG Cherubim.

ten cubits, and so *was it* of the other cherub.

27 And he set the cherubims within the inner house: and they stretched forth the wings of the *a*cherubims, so that the wing of the one touched the *one* wall, and the wing of the other cherub touched the other wall; and their wings touched one another in the midst of the house.

28 And he overlaid the cherubims with gold.

29 And he carved all the walls of the house round about with carved figures of *a*cherubims and palm trees and open flowers, within and without.

30 And the floor of the house he overlaid with gold, within and without.

31 ¶ And for the entering of the oracle he made *a*doors *of* olive tree: the lintel *and* side posts *were* a fifth part *of the wall*.

32 The two doors also *were* of olive tree; and he carved upon them carvings of cherubims and palm trees and open flowers, and overlaid *them* with gold, and spread gold upon the cherubims, and upon the palm trees.

33 So also made he for the door of the temple posts *of* olive tree, a fourth part *of the wall*.

34 And the two doors *were* of *a*fir tree: the two leaves of the one door *were* folding, and the two leaves of the other door *were* folding.

35 And he carved *thereon* cherubims and palm trees and open flowers: and covered *them* with gold fitted upon the carved work.

36 ¶ And he built the inner *a*court with three rows of *b*hewed stone, and a row of cedar beams.

37 ¶ In the *a*fourth year was the foundation of the house of the LORD laid, in the month Zif:

38 And in the eleventh year, in the month Bul, which *is* the eighth month, was the house finished

throughout all the parts thereof, and according to all the fashion of it. So was he seven years in building it.

CHAPTER 7

Solomon builds himself a house—Hiram of Tyre makes the two pillars, the molten sea, the ten bases, the ten lavers, and all the vessels for the temple—The molten sea (baptismal font) rests on the backs of twelve oxen.

BUT Solomon was *a*building his own *b*house thirteen years, and he finished all his house.

2 ¶ He built also the *a*house of the forest of Lebanon; the length thereof *was* an hundred cubits, and the breadth thereof fifty cubits, and the height thereof thirty cubits, upon four rows of cedar pillars, with cedar beams upon the pillars.

3 And *it was* covered with cedar above upon the beams, that *lay* on forty five pillars, fifteen *in* a row.

4 And *there were* windows *in* three rows, and light *was* against light *in* three ranks.

5 And all the doors and posts *were* square, with the windows: and light *was* against light *in* three ranks.

6 ¶ And he made a porch of pillars; the length thereof *was* fifty cubits, and the breadth thereof thirty cubits: and the porch *was* before them: and the *other* pillars and the thick *a*beam *were* before them.

7 ¶ Then he made a porch for the throne where he might judge, *even* the porch of judgment: and *it was* covered with cedar from one side of the floor to the other.

8 ¶ And his house where he dwelt *had* another court within the porch, *which* was of the like work. Solomon made also an house for *a*Pharaoh's daughter, whom he had taken *to* wife, like unto this porch.

9 All these *were* of costly stones, according to the measures of hewed

---

27a Alma 42:3 (2–3).
29a 1 Kgs. 7:36;
    Ezek. 41:18.
31a Ezek. 41:23.
34a 1 Kgs. 5:8.

36a 2 Kgs. 21:5; Ezek. 8:16;
    D&C 94:4 (4–5).
  b 1 Kgs. 7:11.
37a 1 Kgs. 6:1.
7 1a Eccl. 2:4.

  b 1 Kgs. 3:1; 9:1.
2a Isa. 22:8.
6a Ezek. 41:25.
8a 1 Kgs. 3:1; 9:16 (16–24);
    11:1 (1–3).

stones, sawed with saws, within and without, even from the foundation unto the coping, and *so* on the outside toward the great court.

10 And the foundation *was of* costly stones, even great stones, stones of ten cubits, and stones of eight cubits.

11 And above *were* costly stones, after the measures of *a*hewed stones, and cedars.

12 And the great *a*court round about *was* with three rows of hewed stones, and a row of cedar beams, both for the inner court of the house of the LORD, and for the porch of the house.

13 ¶ And king Solomon sent and fetched *a*Hiram out of Tyre.

14 He *was* a widow's son of the tribe of Naphtali, and his father *was* a man of Tyre, a worker in brass: and he was filled with *a*wisdom, and understanding, and cunning to work all works in brass. And he came to king Solomon, and *b*wrought all his work.

15 For he cast two *a*pillars of brass, of eighteen cubits high apiece: and a line of twelve *b*cubits did compass either of them about.

16 And he made two *a*chapiters *of* molten brass, to set upon the tops of the pillars: the height of the one chapiter *was* five cubits, and the height of the other chapiter *was* five cubits:

17 *And* nets of checker work, and wreaths of chain work, for the chapiters which *were* upon the top of the pillars; seven for the one chapiter, and seven for the other chapiter.

18 And he made the pillars, and two rows round about upon the one network, to cover the chapiters that *were* upon the top, with pomegranates: and so did he for the other chapiter.

19 And the chapiters that *were* upon the top of the pillars *were* of lily work in the porch, four cubits.

20 And the chapiters upon the two pillars *had pomegranates* also above, over against the belly which *was* by the network: and the pomegranates *were* *a*two hundred in rows round about upon the other chapiter.

21 And he set up the *a*pillars in the porch of the temple: and he set up the right pillar, and called the name thereof Jachin: and he set up the left pillar, and called the name thereof Boaz.

22 And upon the top of the pillars *was* lily work: so was the work of the pillars finished.

23 ¶ And he made a molten *a*sea, ten cubits from the one brim to the other: *it was* round all about, and his height *was* five cubits: and a line of thirty cubits did compass it round about.

24 And under the brim of it round about *there were* knops compassing it, ten in a cubit, compassing the sea round about: the knops *were* cast in two rows, when it was cast.

25 It stood upon *a*twelve oxen, three looking toward the north, and three looking toward the west, and three looking toward the south, and three looking toward the east: and the sea *was set* above upon them, and all their hinder parts *were* inward.

26 And it *was* an hand breadth thick, and the brim thereof was wrought like the brim of a cup, with flowers of lilies: it contained two *a*thousand baths.

27 ¶ And he made ten *a*bases of brass; four cubits *was* the length of one base, and four cubits the breadth thereof, and three cubits the height of it.

28 And the work of the bases *was* on this *manner:* they had borders, and the borders *were* between the ledges:

29 And on the borders that *were* between the ledges *were* lions, oxen,

11*a* 1 Kgs. 6:36.
12*a* 2 Kgs. 21:5.
13*a* 2 Chr. 2:13 (13–14).
14*a* Ex. 35:35; 36:1 (1–2).
    b TG Skill.
15*a* 2 Kgs. 25:13.

b Jer. 52:21.
16*a* IE the decorative carved head of a pillar.
20*a* Jer. 52:23 (22–23).
21*a* Ezek. 40:49.
23*a* 2 Kgs. 16:17;

1 Chr. 18:8.
TG Baptism.
25*a* Jer. 52:20.
26*a* 2 Chr. 4:5.
27*a* 2 Kgs. 25:13.

and cherubims: and upon the ledges *there was* a base above: and beneath the lions and oxen *were* certain additions made of thin work.

30 And every base had four brasen wheels, and plates of brass: and the four corners thereof had undersetters: under the laver *were* undersetters molten, at the side of every addition.

31 And the mouth of it within the chapter and above *was* a cubit: but the mouth thereof *was* round *after* the work of the base, a cubit and an half: and also upon the mouth of it *were* gravings with their borders, foursquare, not round.

32 And under the borders *were* four wheels; and the axletrees of the wheels *were joined* to the base: and the height of a wheel *was* a cubit and half a cubit.

33 And the work of the wheels *was* like the work of a chariot wheel: their axletrees, and their naves, and their felloes, and their spokes, *were* all molten.

34 And *there were* four undersetters to the four corners of one base: *and* the undersetters *were* of the very base itself.

35 And in the top of the base *was there* a round compass of half a cubit high: and on the top of the base the ledges thereof and the borders thereof *were* of the same.

36 For on the plates of the ledges thereof, and on the borders thereof, he graved *a*cherubims, lions, and palm trees, according to the proportion of every one, and additions round about.

37 After this *manner* he made the ten bases: all of them had one casting, one measure, *and* one size.

38 ¶ Then made he ten *a*lavers of brass: one laver contained forty baths: *and* every laver was four cubits: *and* upon every one of the ten bases one laver.

39 And he put five bases on the right side of the house, and five on the left side of the house: and he set the *a*sea on the right side of the house eastward over against the south.

40 ¶ And Hiram made the *a*lavers, and the shovels, and the basins. So Hiram made an end of doing all the work that he made king Solomon for the house of the LORD:

41 The two pillars, and the *two* bowls of the chapiters that *were* on the top of the two pillars; and the two networks, to cover the two bowls of the chapiters which *were* upon the top of the pillars;

42 And four hundred pomegranates for the two networks, *even* two rows of pomegranates for one network, to cover the two bowls of the chapiters that *were* upon the pillars;

43 And the ten bases, and ten lavers on the bases;

44 And one sea, and twelve oxen under the sea;

45 And the pots, and the shovels, and the basins: and all these vessels, which Hiram made to king Solomon for the house of the LORD, *were of* bright brass.

46 In the plain of Jordan did the king cast them, in the clay ground between Succoth and Zarthan.

47 And Solomon left all the *a*vessels *unweighed*, because they were exceeding many: neither was the weight of the brass found out.

48 And *a*Solomon made all the vessels that *pertained* unto the house of the LORD: the *b*altar of gold, and the *c*table of gold, whereupon the *d*shewbread *was*,

49 And the *a*candlesticks of pure gold, five on the right *side*, and five on the left, before the *b*oracle, with the flowers, and the lamps, and the tongs *of* gold,

50 And the bowls, and the *a*snuffers, and the basins, and the spoons, and the censers *of* pure gold; and the

---

36*a* 1 Kgs. 6:29 (29, 32, 35); Ezek. 41:18.
38*a* 2 Chr. 4:6.
39*a* 2 Chr. 4:10.
40*a* OR washbasins.

47*a* 2 Kgs. 25:16.
48*a* 2 Kgs. 24:13.
  b Ex. 37:25.
  c Ex. 37:10.
  d Ex. 25:30.

49*a* Ex. 25:31 (31–38).
  b 1 Kgs. 6:5.
50*a* 2 Kgs. 25:14.

hinges *of* gold, *both* for the doors of the inner house, the most *b*holy *place, and* for the doors of the house, *to wit,* of the temple.

51 So was ended all the work that king Solomon made for the *a*house of the LORD. And Solomon brought in the things which David his father had *b*dedicated; *even* the silver, and the gold, and the vessels, did he put among the treasures of the house of the LORD.

CHAPTER 8

The ark, containing the two tablets of stone, is placed in the holy of holies—The glory of the Lord fills the temple—Solomon offers the dedicatory prayer—He asks for temporal and spiritual blessings upon repentant and prayerful Israel—The people sacrifice and worship for fourteen days.

THEN Solomon assembled the *a*elders of Israel, and all the heads of the tribes, the *b*chief of the fathers of the children of Israel, unto king Solomon in Jerusalem, that they might bring up the ark of the covenant of the LORD out of the city of David, which *is* Zion.

2 And all the men of Israel assembled themselves unto king Solomon at the *a*feast in the month Ethanim, which *is* the seventh month.

3 And all the elders of Israel came, and the *a*priests took up the ark.

4 And they brought up the ark of the LORD, and the tabernacle of the congregation, and all the holy vessels that *were* in the tabernacle, even those did the priests and the Levites bring up.

5 And king Solomon, and all the congregation of Israel, that were assembled unto him, *were* with him before the ark, sacrificing sheep and oxen, that could not be told nor numbered for multitude.

6 And the priests brought in the *a*ark of the covenant of the LORD unto his place, into the oracle of the house, to the most *b*holy *place, even* under the wings of the cherubims.

7 For the *a*cherubims spread forth *their* two wings over the place of the ark, and the cherubims covered the ark and the staves thereof above.

8 And they drew out the *a*staves, that the ends of the staves were seen out in the holy *place* before the *b*oracle, and they were not seen without: and there they are unto this day.

9 *There was* nothing in the *a*ark save the two *b*tables of stone, which Moses put there at *c*Horeb, when the LORD made *a covenant* with the children of Israel, when they came out of the land of Egypt.

10 And it came to pass, when the priests were come out of the holy *place,* that the *a*cloud filled the house of the LORD,

11 So that the priests could not stand to minister because of the cloud: for the *a*glory of the LORD had filled the house of the LORD.

12 ¶ Then spake *a*Solomon, The LORD said that he would dwell in the thick *b*darkness.

13 I have surely *a*built thee an *b*house to dwell in, a settled place for thee to *c*abide in for ever.

14 And the king turned his face about, and *a*blessed all the congregation of Israel: (and all the congregation of Israel stood;)

15 And he said, Blessed *be* the LORD God of Israel, which spake with his

---

50*b* 1 Kgs. 6:16.
51*a* TG Temple.
  b 2 Sam. 8:11 (10–11).
8 1*a* 2 Chr. 5:2 (2–10, 14).
  b HEB princes, leaders.
2*a* Lev. 23:34; 1 Kgs. 8:65;
    2 Chr. 7:8 (8–10).
3*a* Num. 4:15;
    2 Chr. 5:5 (4–5).
6*a* Ex. 26:33 (33–34).
  b 1 Kgs. 6:16.

7*a* TG Cherubim.
8*a* Ex. 25:15.
  b 1 Kgs. 6:5.
9*a* TG Ark of the Covenant.
  b Ex. 25:21; 40:20;
    1 Kgs. 8:21.
    TG Law of Moses; Scriptures, Preservation of.
  c Ex. 3:12 (1, 12);
    Deut. 1:6 (5–8);
    4:10 (10–13).

10*a* D&C 84:5.
    TG God, Manifestations of.
11*a* Ezek. 43:5; 44:4;
    D&C 94:8; 109:12.
12*a* 2 Chr. 6:1 (1–42).
  b Ps. 97:2.
13*a* 2 Sam. 7:13.
  b D&C 109:12.
  c Ex. 15:17.
14*a* 2 Sam. 6:18.

mouth unto David my father, and hath with his hand fulfilled *it,* saying,

16 Since the day that I brought forth my people Israel out of Egypt, I chose no city out of all the tribes of Israel to build an house, that my name might be therein; but I chose *a*David to be over my people Israel.

17 And it was in the heart of David my father to build an *a*house for the name of the LORD God of Israel.

18 And the LORD said unto David my father, Whereas it was in thine heart to build an *a*house unto my name, thou didst well that it was in thine heart.

19 Nevertheless thou shalt not build the house; but thy *a*son that shall come forth out of thy loins, he shall build the house unto my name.

20 And the LORD hath performed his word that he spake, and I am risen up in the room of David my father, and sit on the throne of Israel, as the LORD promised, and have built an house for the name of the LORD God of Israel.

21 And I have set there a place for the ark, wherein *is* the *a*covenant of the LORD, which he made with our fathers, when he brought them out of the land of Egypt.

22 ¶ And Solomon stood before the altar of the LORD in the presence of all the congregation of Israel, and *a*spread forth his hands toward heaven:

23 And he said, *a*LORD God of Israel, *there is* no *b*God like thee, in heaven above, or on earth beneath, who *c*keepest covenant and mercy with thy servants that *d*walk before thee with all their heart:

24 Who hast kept with thy servant David my father that thou promisedst him: thou spakest also with thy mouth, and hast fulfilled *it* with thine hand, as *it is* this day.

25 Therefore now, LORD God of Israel, keep with thy servant David my father that thou promisedst him, saying, There shall not fail thee a man in my sight to sit on the throne of Israel; *a*so that thy children take heed to their way, that they walk before me as thou hast walked before me.

26 And now, O God of Israel, let thy word, I pray thee, be verified, which thou spakest unto thy servant David my father.

27 But will God indeed dwell on the earth? behold, the heaven and *a*heaven of heavens cannot contain thee; how much less this house that I have builded?

28 Yet have thou respect unto the prayer of thy servant, and to his supplication, O LORD my God, to hearken unto the cry and to the prayer, which thy servant prayeth before thee to day:

29 That thine eyes may be open toward this *a*house night and day, *even* toward the *b*place of which thou hast said, My *c*name shall be there: that thou mayest hearken unto the *d*prayer which thy servant shall make toward this place.

30 And hearken thou to the supplication of thy servant, and of thy people Israel, when they shall pray toward this place: and hear thou in heaven thy dwelling place: and when thou hearest, forgive.

31 ¶ If any man trespass against his neighbour, and *a*an oath be laid upon him to cause him to swear, and the oath come before thine altar in this house:

32 Then hear thou in heaven, and

16a 1 Sam. 16:1.
17a D&C 109:8.
18a D&C 124:22.
19a 2 Sam. 7:12 (12–13).
21a Deut. 31:26;
   1 Kgs. 8:9.
22a Ex. 9:29 (29–33).
23a 2 Chr. 6:14 (12–42);
   D&C 109:1 (1–80).
   b Deut. 4:39;

   1 Sam. 2:2 (1–10);
   2 Sam. 7:22;
   Ps. 71:19.
   c Deut. 7:9;
   D&C 54:6; 82:10.
   d TG Walking with God.
25a HEB if only thy . . .
27a 2 Chr. 2:6.
29a 2 Kgs. 19:1.
   b Deut. 12:5 (5–28); 15:20;

   17:8 (8–17); 26:2 (1–11);
   2 Chr. 7:12.
   c 2 Kgs. 21:4;
   D&C 18:40 (21–41);
   20:36; 97:15 (15–17);
   109:26 (16–26).
   d D&C 109:8.
31a OR he require an oath
   of him.
   Ex. 22:11.

do, and judge thy servants, condemning the wicked, to bring his way upon his head; and justifying the righteous, to give him according to his ^arighteousness.

33 ¶ When thy people Israel be ^asmitten down before the enemy, because they have ^bsinned against thee, and shall turn again to thee, and confess thy name, and pray, and make supplication unto thee in this house:

34 Then hear thou in heaven, and forgive the sin of thy people Israel, and bring them again unto the land which thou gavest unto their fathers.

35 ¶ When heaven is ^ashut up, and there is no ^brain, because they have sinned against thee; if they pray toward this place, and confess thy name, and turn from their sin, when thou afflictest them:

36 Then hear thou in heaven, and forgive the sin of thy servants, and of thy people Israel, that thou ^ateach them the good way wherein they should ^bwalk, and give rain upon thy land, which thou hast given to thy people for an inheritance.

37 ¶ If there be in the land famine, if there be pestilence, blasting, mildew, locust, or if there be caterpiller; if their enemy besiege them in ^athe land of their cities; whatsoever plague, whatsoever ^bsickness there be;

38 What prayer and supplication soever be made by any man, or by all thy people Israel, which shall know every man the plague of his own heart, and spread forth his hands toward this house:

39 Then hear thou in heaven thy dwelling place, and forgive, and do, and give to every man according to his ways, whose heart thou knowest; (for thou, even thou only, knowest the ^ahearts of all the children of men;)

40 That they may ^afear thee all the days that they live in the land which thou gavest unto our fathers.

41 Moreover concerning a ^astranger, that is not of thy people Israel, but cometh out of a far ^bcountry for thy name's sake;

42 (For they shall hear of thy great name, and of thy strong ^ahand, and of thy stretched out arm;) when he shall come and pray toward this house;

43 Hear thou in heaven thy dwelling place, and do according to all that the stranger calleth to thee for: that all people of the earth may ^aknow thy name, to ^bfear thee, as do thy people Israel; and that they may know that this house, which I have builded, is called by thy name.

44 ¶ If thy people go out to battle against their enemy, whithersoever thou shalt ^asend them, and shall pray unto the LORD toward the city which thou hast chosen, and toward the house that I have built for thy name:

45 Then hear thou in heaven their prayer and their supplication, and maintain their cause.

46 If they sin against thee, (for there is no man that ^asinneth not,) and thou be angry with them, and ^bdeliver them to the enemy, so that they carry them away captives unto the land of the ^cenemy, far or near;

47 Yet if they shall ^abethink themselves in the land whither they were carried captives, and repent, and make supplication unto thee in the land of them that carried them captives, saying, We have ^bsinned, and

32a TG Righteousness.
33a Lev. 26:17.
  b D&C 103:8.
35a Deut. 11:17 (10–18);
  Ether 4:9;
  D&C 77:8.
  b Hel. 11:4 (3–5).
36a Ps. 27:11; 86:11;
  2 Ne. 25:28; 33:10.
  b 1 Sam. 12:23 (16–23).
37a Septuagint: any of their cities.
  b TG Sickness.
39a D&C 6:16.
40a Ps. 130:4.
41a TG Stranger.
  b Isa. 2:2 (2–4);
  D&C 64:42 (42–43).
42a Deut. 3:24.
43a Josh. 4:24.
  TG Israel, Mission of; Name.
  b D&C 64:43.
44a D&C 98:33.
46a TG Sin.
  b Mosiah 12:2 (2–9).
  c Lev. 26:44.
47a IE consider it in their heart.
  b 1 Sam. 7:6; Dan. 9:5.

have done perversely, we have committed wickedness;

48 And *so* ^areturn unto thee with all their heart, and with all their soul, in the land of their enemies, which led them away captive, and pray unto thee toward their ^bland, which thou gavest unto their fathers, the city which thou hast chosen, and the house which I have built for thy name:

49 Then ^ahear thou their prayer and their supplication in ^bheaven thy dwelling place, and maintain their cause,

50 And forgive thy people that have sinned against thee, and all their transgressions wherein they have transgressed against thee, and give them compassion before them who carried them captive, that they may have compassion on them:

51 For they *be* thy ^apeople, and thine ^binheritance, which thou broughtest forth out of Egypt, from the midst of the furnace of iron:

52 That thine eyes may be open unto the supplication of thy servant, and unto the supplication of thy people Israel, to hearken unto them in all that they call for unto thee.

53 For thou didst ^aseparate them from among all the people of the earth, *to be* ^bthine inheritance, as thou spakest by the hand of Moses thy servant, when thou broughtest our fathers out of Egypt, O Lord GOD.

54 And it was *so*, that when Solomon had made an end of ^apraying all this prayer and supplication unto the LORD, he arose from before the altar of the LORD, from kneeling on his knees with his hands spread up to heaven.

55 And he stood, and blessed all the congregation of Israel with a loud voice, saying,

56 Blessed *be* the LORD, that hath given rest unto his people Israel, according to all that he promised: there hath not ^afailed one ^bword of all his good ^cpromise, which he promised by the hand of Moses his servant.

57 The LORD our God be with us, as he was with our fathers: let him not leave us, nor forsake us:

58 That he may incline our hearts unto him, to walk in all his ways, and to keep his commandments, and his statutes, and his judgments, which he commanded our fathers.

59 And let these my words, wherewith I have made supplication before the LORD, be nigh unto the LORD our God day and night, that he maintain the cause of his servant, and the cause of his people Israel at all times, as the matter shall require:

60 That all the people of the earth may ^aknow that the LORD *is* ^bGod, *and that there is* ^cnone else.

61 Let your ^aheart therefore be ^bperfect with the LORD our God, to walk in his statutes, and to keep his commandments, as at this day.

62 ¶ And the king, and all Israel with him, ^aoffered sacrifice before the LORD.

63 And Solomon offered a ^asacrifice of peace offerings, which he offered unto the LORD, two and twenty thousand oxen, and an hundred and twenty thousand sheep. So the king and all the children of Israel ^bdedicated the house of the LORD.

64 The same day did the king hallow the middle of the court that *was* before the house of the LORD: for

48*a* Jer. 29:12 (12–14).
  b Ps. 5:7; Dan. 6:10.
49*a* Mosiah 21:15.
  b TG Heaven.
51*a* Ex. 33:13;
    2 Ne. 3:9; 8:16; 29:14;
    3 Ne. 16:8 (8–15);
    20:21 (15–21, 39);
    21:23 (12–24).
  b TG Inheritance.
53*a* Ex. 33:16; Lev. 20:24;

    John 17:6 (6–22);
    3 Ne. 15:19 (19–20).
  b Moses 1:26.
54*a* 2 Chr. 7:1 (1–3);
    D&C 109:4 (1–80).
56*a* Josh. 21:45; Matt. 24:35;
    1 Ne. 20:14; 2 Ne. 10:17;
    D&C 1:38; 64:31; 76:3;
    101:64.
  b 2 Ne. 9:16;
    Moses 4:30.

  c TG Promise.
60*a* TG Israel, Mission of.
  b Deut. 4:35 (35, 39).
  c Mosiah 5:8; D&C 76:1;
    Moses 1:6.
61*a* Moses 7:18.
  b 1 Chr. 28:9.
62*a* 2 Chr. 7:4 (4–10);
    Moses 5:5.
63*a* TG Sacrifice.
  b TG Dedication.

there he offered burnt offerings, and meat offerings, and the fat of the peace offerings: because the ^abrasen altar that *was* before the LORD *was* too little to receive the burnt offerings, and meat offerings, and the fat of the peace offerings.

65 And at that time Solomon held a ^afeast, and all Israel with him, a great congregation, from the ^bentering in of Hamath unto the river of Egypt, before the LORD our God, seven days and seven days, *even* fourteen days.

66 On the ^aeighth day he sent the people away: and they blessed the king, and went unto their tents joyful and glad of heart for all the goodness that the LORD had done for David his servant, and for Israel his people.

CHAPTER 9

The Lord again appears to Solomon—The Lord promises great blessings if the Israelites are obedient and great cursings if they forsake Him—Solomon reigns in splendor, levies tribute upon the non-Israelites, and builds a navy of ships.

AND it came to pass, when Solomon had ^afinished the building of the ^bhouse of the LORD, and the ^cking's house, and all Solomon's desire which he was pleased to do,

2 That the LORD ^aappeared to Solomon the second time, as he had appeared unto him at ^bGibeon.

3 And the LORD said unto him, I have heard thy ^aprayer and thy supplication, that thou hast made before me: I have hallowed this house, which thou hast built, to put my ^bname there for ever; and mine eyes and mine heart shall be there perpetually.

4 And if thou wilt ^awalk before me, as ^bDavid thy father walked, in ^cintegrity of heart, and in uprightness, to do according to all that I have commanded thee, *and* wilt keep my statutes and my judgments:

5 Then I will establish the ^athrone of thy kingdom upon Israel for ever, as I promised to David thy father, saying, There shall not fail thee a man upon the throne of Israel.

6 *But* if ye shall at all turn from following me, ye or your children, and will not keep my commandments *and* my statutes which I have set before you, but go and serve ^aother gods, and worship them:

7 Then will I ^acut off Israel out of the ^bland which I have given them; and this house, which I have hallowed for my name, will I cast out of my sight; and Israel shall be a proverb and a ^cbyword among all people:

8 And at this house, *which* is high, every one that passeth by it shall be astonished, and shall hiss; and they shall say, Why hath the LORD ^adone thus unto this land, and to this house?

9 And they shall answer, Because they forsook the LORD their God, who brought forth their fathers out of the land of Egypt, and have taken hold upon other gods, and have worshipped them, and served them: therefore hath the LORD brought upon them all this evil.

10 ¶ And it came to pass at the end of twenty years, when Solomon had built the two houses, the house of the LORD, and the king's house,

11 (Now Hiram the king of Tyre had furnished Solomon with cedar trees and fir trees, and with gold, according to all his desire,) that then king Solomon gave Hiram twenty cities in the land of Galilee.

12 And Hiram came out from Tyre to see the cities which Solomon had given him; and they pleased him not.

64a 2 Chr. 4:1.
65a Lev. 23:34;
    1 Kgs. 8:2.
  b IE approach, entrance.
66a 2 Chr. 7:9 (8–10).
9 1a 2 Chr. 7:11 (11–22).
  b 2 Ne. 5:16;
    D&C 109:4 (1–80).
c 1 Kgs. 7:1.
2a 1 Kgs. 11:9.
  b 1 Kgs. 3:5.
3a D&C 67:1.
  b 2 Kgs. 21:4.
4a 1 Kgs. 6:12.
  b 1 Kgs. 15:5.
  c TG Integrity.
5a 2 Sam. 7:16 (12, 16);
    Ps. 132:12.
6a 1 Kgs. 11:10.
7a 2 Kgs. 17:23.
  b TG Israel, Land of.
  c 1 Ne. 19:14 (13–14).
8a Deut. 29:24 (24–26);
    Jer. 22:8 (8–9).

13 And he said, What cities *are* these which thou hast given me, my brother? And he called them the land of *ªCabul unto this day.

14 And Hiram sent to the king sixscore talents of gold.

15 ¶ And this *is* the reason of the *ªlevy which king Solomon raised; for to build the house of the LORD, and his own house, and *ᵇMillo, and the *ᶜwall of Jerusalem, and Hazor, and Megiddo, and Gezer.

16 *For* *ªPharaoh king of Egypt had gone up, and taken Gezer, and burnt it with fire, and slain the Canaanites that dwelt in the city, and given it *for* a present unto his *ᵇdaughter, Solomon's wife.

17 And Solomon built Gezer, and Beth-horon the nether,

18 And Baalath, and Tadmor in the wilderness, in the land,

19 And all the cities of store that Solomon had, and cities for his chariots, and cities for his horsemen, and that which Solomon desired to build in Jerusalem, and in Lebanon, and in all the land of his dominion.

20 *And* all the people *that were* left of the Amorites, Hittites, Perizzites, Hivites, and Jebusites, which *were* not of the children of Israel,

21 Their *ªchildren that were left after them in the land, whom the children of Israel also were not able utterly to destroy, upon those did Solomon levy a tribute of *ᵇbondservice unto this day.

22 But of the children of Israel did Solomon make no bondmen: but they *were* men of war, and his servants, and his princes, and his captains, and rulers of his chariots, and his horsemen.

23 These *were* the chief of the *ªofficers that *were* over Solomon's work, five hundred and fifty, which bare

rule over the people that wrought in the work.

24 ¶ But Pharaoh's daughter came up out of the city of David unto her house which *Solomon* had built for her: then did he build Millo.

25 ¶ And *ªthree times in a year did Solomon *ᵇoffer burnt offerings and peace offerings upon the altar which he built unto the LORD, and he burnt incense upon the altar that *was* before the LORD. So he finished the house.

26 ¶ And king Solomon made a navy of ships in *ªEzion-geber, which *is* beside *ᵇEloth, on the shore of the Red sea, in the land of Edom.

27 And *ªHiram sent in the navy his servants, shipmen that had knowledge of the sea, with the servants of Solomon.

28 And they came to *ªOphir, and fetched from thence *ᵇgold, four hundred and twenty talents, and brought *it* to king Solomon.

CHAPTER 10

The queen of Sheba visits Solomon—His wealth and wisdom exceed that of all the kings of the earth.

AND when the *ªqueen of Sheba heard of the fame of Solomon concerning the name of the LORD, she came to *ᵇprove him with hard questions.

2 And she came to Jerusalem with a very great train, with camels that bare spices, and very much gold, and precious stones: and when she was come to Solomon, she communed with him of all that was in her heart.

3 And Solomon told her all her *ªquestions: there was not *any* thing hid from the king, which he told her not.

4 And when the queen of Sheba had

13*a* ɪᴇ Displeasing or Dirty.
15*a* 1 Kgs. 5:13.
   b 2 Sam. 5:9;
    1 Kgs. 11:27;
    2 Kgs. 12:20;
    2 Chr. 32:5.
   c 1 Kgs. 3:1.
16*a* 1 Kgs. 3:1.

   b 1 Kgs. 7:8; 11:1 (1–3).
21*a* 1 Chr. 22:2.
   b 1 Kgs. 5:15.
23*a* 1 Kgs. 4:5; 5:16.
25*a* 2 Chr. 8:13 (12–13).
   b ᴛɢ Sacrifice.
26*a* Num. 33:36;
    1 Kgs. 22:48.

   b 2 Kgs. 14:22.
27*a* 1 Kgs. 10:11.
28*a* Job 28:16.
   b Eccl. 2:8.
10 1*a* Matt. 12:42;
    Luke 11:31.
   b ᴛɢ Test.
3*a* ʜᴇʙ matters, concerns.

seen all Solomon's wisdom, and the house that he had built,

5 And the *a*meat of his table, and the sitting of his servants, and the attendance of his ministers, and their apparel, and his cupbearers, and his *b*ascent by which he went up unto the house of the LORD; there was no more spirit in her.

6 And she said to the king, It was a true report that I heard in mine own land of thy acts and of thy wisdom.

7 Howbeit I believed not the words, until I came, and mine eyes had seen *it:* and, behold, the half was not told me: thy wisdom and prosperity exceedeth the fame which I heard.

8 Happy *are* thy men, happy *are* these thy servants, which *a*stand continually before thee, *and* that hear thy wisdom.

9 *a*Blessed be the LORD thy God, which delighted in thee, to set thee on the throne of Israel: because the LORD loved Israel for ever, therefore made he thee king, to do judgment and justice.

10 And she gave the king an hundred and twenty talents of *a*gold, and of spices very great store, and precious stones: there came no more such abundance of spices as these which the queen of Sheba gave to king Solomon.

11 And the *a*navy also of Hiram, that brought gold from Ophir, brought in from Ophir great plenty of almug trees, and precious stones.

12 And the king made of the almug trees pillars for the house of the LORD, and for the king's house, harps also and psalteries for singers: there came no such almug trees, nor were seen unto this day.

13 And king Solomon gave unto the queen of Sheba all her desire, whatsoever she asked, beside *that* which Solomon gave her of his royal bounty. So she turned and went to her own country, she and her servants.

14 ¶ Now the weight of gold that came to Solomon in one year was six hundred threescore and six talents of gold,

15 Beside *that he had* of the merchantmen, and of the traffick of the spice merchants, and of all the kings of Arabia, and of the governors of the country.

16 ¶ And king Solomon made two hundred *a*targets *of* beaten gold: six hundred *shekels* of gold went to one target.

17 And *he made* three hundred shields *of* beaten gold; three pound of gold went to one shield: and the king put them in the house of the forest of Lebanon.

18 ¶ Moreover the king made a great throne of ivory, and overlaid it with the best gold.

19 The throne had six steps, and the top of the throne *was* round behind: and *there were* *a*stays on either side on the place of the seat, and two lions stood beside the stays.

20 And twelve lions stood there on the one side and on the other upon the six steps: there was not the like made in any kingdom.

21 ¶ And all king Solomon's drinking vessels *were of* gold, and all the vessels of the house of the forest of Lebanon *were of* pure gold; none *were of* silver: it was nothing accounted of in the days of Solomon.

22 For the king had at sea a navy of *a*Tharshish with the navy of Hiram: once in three years came the navy of Tharshish, bringing gold, and silver, ivory, and apes, and peacocks.

23 So king Solomon exceeded all the kings of the earth for *a*riches and for wisdom.

24 ¶ And all the earth sought to Solomon, to hear his wisdom, which God had put in his heart.

25 And they brought every man his

5*a* HEB food.
  b HEB burnt offerings which he offered in the house of the LORD.
8*a* Dan. 1:5.

9*a* 1 Kgs. 5:7.
10*a* Eccl. 2:8.
11*a* 1 Kgs. 9:27.
16*a* HEB shields or breastplates.

19*a* HEB armrests.
22*a* Ezek. 27:12; 38:13.
23*a* 1 Kgs. 3:13.

present, vessels of silver, and vessels of gold, and garments, and armour, and spices, horses, and mules, a rate year by year.

26 ¶ And Solomon gathered together chariots and horsemen: and he had a ªthousand and four hundred chariots, and twelve thousand horsemen, whom he bestowed in the cities for chariots, and with the king at Jerusalem.

27 And the king ªmade silver *to be* in Jerusalem as stones, and cedars made he *to be* as the sycomore trees that *are* in the vale, for abundance.

28 ¶ And Solomon had horses brought out of Egypt, and ªlinen yarn: the king's merchants received the linen yarn at a price.

29 And a chariot came up and went out of Egypt for six hundred *shekels* of silver, and an horse for an hundred and fifty: and so for all the kings of the Hittites, and for the kings of Syria, did they bring *them* out by their means.

CHAPTER 11

Solomon marries non-Israelite women, and his wives turn his heart to the worship of false gods—The Lord stirs up adversaries against him, including Jeroboam, the son of Nebat—Ahijah promises Jeroboam that he will be the king of the ten tribes—Solomon dies and Rehoboam reigns in his stead.

BUT king ªSolomon loved many ᵇstrange ᶜwomen, together with the ᵈdaughter of ᵉPharaoh, women of the Moabites, Ammonites, Edomites, Zidonians, *and* Hittites;

2 Of the nations *concerning* which the LORD said unto the children of Israel, Ye shall not go in to them, neither shall they come in unto you: *for* surely they will ªturn away your heart after their gods: Solomon clave unto these in love.

3 And he had seven hundred wives, princesses, and three hundred concubines: and his ªwives turned away his heart.

4 For it came to pass, when Solomon was old, *that* his ªwives turned away his heart after other gods: and his heart was not perfect with the LORD his God, ᵇas *was* the heart of David his father.

5 For Solomon went after Ashtoreth the goddess of the Zidonians, and after Milcom the abomination of the Ammonites.

6 And ªSolomon did evil in the sight of the LORD, ᵇand went not fully after the LORD, as *did* David his father.

7 Then did Solomon build an high place for ªChemosh, the abomination of Moab, in the ᵇhill that *is* before Jerusalem, and for Molech, the abomination of the children of Ammon.

8 And likewise did he for all his strange wives, which burnt incense and sacrificed unto their gods.

9 ¶ And the LORD was angry with Solomon, because his heart was ªturned from the LORD God of Israel, which had ᵇappeared unto him twice,

10 And had commanded him concerning this thing, that he should not go after ªother gods: but he kept not that which the LORD commanded.

11 Wherefore the LORD said unto Solomon, Forasmuch as this is done

---

26a 1 Kgs. 4:26.
27a HEB gave, put.
28a HEB from Kue (Cilicia). The name of this country is mistakenly translated to be "linen yarn."
11 1a Jacob 2:24 (23–24); D&C 132:38.
   b Deut. 17:17; Neh. 13:26.

c TG Woman.
d 1 Kgs. 7:8; 9:16 (16–24).
e 1 Kgs. 3:1.
2a TG Apostasy of Israel.
3a Jer. 44:9.
4a TG Marriage, Interfaith.
   b JST 1 Kgs. 11:4 . . . *and it became* as the heart . . .
6a TG Ingratitude.
   b JST 1 Kgs. 11:6 . . . *as David his father, and*

went not fully after the Lord.
7a Num. 21:29.
   b 2 Kgs. 23:13.
9a TG Apostasy of Individuals.
   b 1 Kgs. 3:5; 9:2.
   TG God, Privilege of Seeing.
10a 1 Kgs. 9:6 (6–7).

of thee, and thou hast not kept my [a]covenant and my statutes, which I have commanded thee, I will surely rend the [b]kingdom from thee, and will give it to thy servant.

12 Notwithstanding in thy days I will not do it for David thy father's sake: but I will rend it out of the hand of thy son.

13 Howbeit I will not rend away all the kingdom; but will give [a]one tribe to thy son for David my servant's sake, and for Jerusalem's sake which I have chosen.

14 ¶ And the LORD stirred up an [a]adversary unto Solomon, Hadad the Edomite: he was of the king's seed in Edom.

15 For it came to pass, when David was in [a]Edom, and Joab the captain of the host was gone up to bury the slain, after he had smitten every male in Edom;

16 (For six months did Joab remain there with all Israel, until he had cut off every male in Edom:)

17 That Hadad fled, he and certain Edomites of his father's servants with him, to go into Egypt; Hadad being yet a little child.

18 And they arose out of Midian, and came to Paran: and they took men with them out of Paran, and they came to Egypt, unto Pharaoh king of Egypt; which gave him an house, and appointed him victuals, and gave him land.

19 And Hadad found great favour in the sight of Pharaoh, so that he gave him to wife the sister of his own wife, the sister of Tahpenes the queen.

20 And the sister of Tahpenes bare him Genubath his son, whom Tahpenes weaned in Pharaoh's house: and Genubath was in Pharaoh's household among the sons of Pharaoh.

21 And when Hadad heard in Egypt that David slept with his fathers, and that Joab the captain of the host was dead, Hadad said to Pharaoh, Let me depart, that I may go to mine own country.

22 Then Pharaoh said unto him, But what hast thou lacked with me, that, behold, thou seekest to go to thine own country? And he answered, Nothing: howbeit let me go in any wise.

23 ¶ And God stirred him up another adversary, Rezon the son of Eliadah, which fled from his lord Hadadezer king of Zobah:

24 And he gathered men unto him, and became captain over a band, when David slew them of Zobah: and they went to Damascus, and dwelt therein, and reigned in Damascus.

25 And he was an adversary to Israel all the days of Solomon, beside the mischief that Hadad did: and he abhorred Israel, and reigned over Syria.

26 ¶ And Jeroboam the son of Nebat, an Ephrathite of Zereda, Solomon's servant, whose mother's name was Zeruah, a widow woman, even he lifted up his hand against the king.

27 And this was the cause that he lifted up his hand against the king: Solomon built [a]Millo, and repaired the breaches of the city of David his father.

28 And the man Jeroboam was a mighty man of valour: and Solomon seeing the young man that he was industrious, he made him ruler over all the charge of the house of Joseph.

29 And it came to pass at that time when Jeroboam went out of Jerusalem, that the prophet [a]Ahijah the Shilonite found him in the way; and he had clad himself with a new garment; and they two were alone in the field:

30 And [a]Ahijah caught the new garment that was on him, and rent it in twelve pieces:

31 And he said to Jeroboam, Take

11a TG Covenants.
  b 1 Kgs. 12:16 (15–16).
13a 1 Kgs. 12:20.
14a Hel. 12:3 (2–3).

15a 1 Chr. 18:13 (12–13).
27a 2 Sam. 5:9;
      1 Kgs. 9:15 (15, 24);
      2 Kgs. 12:20;

      2 Chr. 32:5.
29a 1 Kgs. 14:2.
30a 1 Kgs. 12:15.

thee ten pieces: for thus saith the LORD, the God of Israel, Behold, I will rend the kingdom out of the hand of Solomon, and will give ^aten tribes to thee:

32 (But he shall have ^aone tribe for my servant David's sake, and for Jerusalem's sake, the city which I have chosen out of all the tribes of Israel:)

33 Because that they have ^aforsaken me, and have worshipped Ashtoreth the goddess of the Zidonians, Chemosh the god of the Moabites, and ^bMilcom the god of the children of Ammon, and have not walked in my ways, to do *that which is* right in mine eyes, and *to keep* my statutes and my judgments, ^cas *did* David his father.

34 Howbeit I will not take the whole kingdom out of his hand: but I will make him prince all the days of his life for David my servant's sake, whom I chose, because he kept my commandments and my statutes:

35 But I will take the kingdom out of his son's hand, and will give it unto thee, *even* ten tribes.

36 And unto his son will I give ^aone ^btribe, that David my servant may have a light alway before me in Jerusalem, the city which I have ^cchosen me to put my name there.

37 And I will take thee, and thou shalt reign according to all that thy soul ^adesireth, and shalt be king over Israel.

38 And it shall be, if thou wilt hearken unto all that I command thee, and wilt ^awalk in my ways, and do *that is* right in my sight, to keep my statutes and my command-

ments, as David my servant ^bdid; that I will be with thee, and build thee a sure ^chouse, as I built for David, and will give Israel unto thee.

39 ^aAnd I will for this afflict the seed of ^bDavid, but not for ever.

40 Solomon sought therefore to kill Jeroboam. And Jeroboam arose, and fled into Egypt, unto ^aShishak king of Egypt, and was in Egypt until the death of Solomon.

41 ¶ And the rest of the acts of Solomon, and all that he did, and his wisdom, *are* they not written in the ^abook of the acts of Solomon?

42 And the time that Solomon reigned in Jerusalem over all Israel *was* forty years.

43 And Solomon slept with his fathers, and was buried in the city of David his father: and ^aRehoboam his son reigned in his stead.

CHAPTER 12

Rehoboam seeks to impose greater burdens upon the people—The ten tribes revolt and turn to Jeroboam—Jeroboam turns to idolatry and worships false gods.

AND ^aRehoboam went to Shechem: for all Israel were come to Shechem to make him king.

2 And it came to pass, when Jeroboam the son of Nebat, who was yet in Egypt, heard *of it*, (for he was fled from the presence of king Solomon, and Jeroboam dwelt in Egypt;)

3 That they sent and called him. And Jeroboam and all the congregation of Israel came, and spake unto Rehoboam, saying,

4 Thy father made our ^ayoke grievous: now therefore make thou the

---

31a TG Israel, Ten Lost
   Tribes of.
32a Septuagint: two tribes.
33a TG Apostasy of Israel.
   b Zeph. 1:5.
   c JST 1 Kgs. 11:33 . . . *and
      his heart is become* as
      David his father; *and he
      repenteth not as did David
      his father, that I may
      forgive him.*

36a Septuagint: two tribes.
   b 1 Kgs. 12:17.
   c Deut. 12:5.
37a Alma 29:4.
38a TG Walking with God.
   b JST 1 Kgs. 11:38 . . . *did
      in the day that I blessed
      him;* I will be . . .
   c 1 Sam. 2:35.
39a JST 1 Kgs. 11:39 *And for
      the transgression of*

   *David, and also for the
   people, I have rent the
   kingdom, and for this I
   will afflict . . .*
   b D&C 109:63 (63–64).
40a 1 Kgs. 14:25.
41a TG Scriptures, Lost.
43a 1 Chr. 3:10.
12 1a 2 Chr. 10:1 (1–19).
   4a 1 Kgs. 4:7; 5:13.
      TG Bondage, Physical.

grievous service of thy father, and his heavy yoke which he put upon us, lighter, and we will serve thee.

5 And he said unto them, Depart yet *for* three days, then come again to me. And the people departed.

6 ¶ And king Rehoboam consulted with the *a*old men, that stood before Solomon his father while he yet lived, and said, How do ye advise that I may answer this people?

7 And they spake unto him, saying, If thou wilt be a *a*servant unto this people this day, and wilt serve them, and answer them, and speak good words to them, then they will be thy servants for ever.

8 But he forsook the counsel of the *a*old men, which they had given him, and consulted with the young men that were grown up with him, *and* which stood before him:

9 And he said unto them, What counsel give ye that we may answer this people, who have spoken to me, saying, Make the yoke which thy father did put upon us lighter?

10 And the young men that were grown up with him spake unto him, saying, Thus shalt thou speak unto this people that spake unto thee, saying, Thy father made our yoke heavy, but make thou *it* lighter unto us; thus shalt thou say unto them, My little *finger* shall be thicker than my father's loins.

11 And now whereas my father did lade you with a heavy *a*yoke, I will add to your yoke: my father hath chastised you with whips, but I will chastise you with *b*scorpions.

12 ¶ So Jeroboam and all the people came to Rehoboam the third day, as the king had appointed, saying, Come to me again the third day.

13 And the king answered the people roughly, and forsook the *a*old men's counsel that they gave him;

14 And spake to them after the counsel of the young men, saying, My father made your yoke heavy, and I will add to your yoke: my father *also* chastised you with whips, but I will chastise you with scorpions.

15 Wherefore the king hearkened not unto the people; for the *a*cause was from the LORD, that he might perform his saying, which the LORD spake by *b*Ahijah the Shilonite unto Jeroboam the son of Nebat.

16 ¶ So when all Israel saw that the king hearkened not unto them, the people answered the king, saying, What portion have we in David? neither *have we* inheritance in the son of Jesse: to your tents, O Israel: now see to thine own house, David. So Israel *a*departed unto their tents.

17 But *as for* the children of Israel which dwelt in the cities of *a*Judah, Rehoboam reigned over them.

18 Then king Rehoboam sent *a*Adoram, who *was* over the tribute; and all Israel stoned him with stones, that he died. Therefore king Rehoboam made speed to get him up to his chariot, to flee to Jerusalem.

19 So *a*Israel *b*rebelled against the house of David unto this day.

20 And it came to pass, when all Israel heard that Jeroboam was come again, that they sent and called him unto the congregation, and made him king over all Israel: there was none that *a*followed the house of David, but the tribe of *b*Judah only.

21 ¶ And when *a*Rehoboam was come to Jerusalem, he assembled all the house of Judah, with the tribe of Benjamin, an hundred and fourscore thousand chosen men, which were warriors, to fight against the house of Israel, to bring the kingdom again to Rehoboam the son of Solomon.

6a OR elders.
7a Alma 1:26.
   TG Kings, Earthly;
   Service.
8a TG Old Age.
11a TG Governments.
  b HEB stinging whips.
13a OR elders'.

15a HEB turn of affairs.
  b 1 Kgs. 11:30 (30–31).
16a 1 Kgs. 11:11.
17a 1 Kgs. 11:36.
18a 1 Kgs. 4:6; 5:14.
19a TG Israel, Ten Lost
   Tribes of.
  b TG Rebellion.

20a TG Israel, Ten Lost
   Tribes of.
  b Septuagint: Judah and
   Benjamin.
   1 Kgs. 11:13.
21a 2 Chr. 11:1 (1–17).

22 But the word of God came unto ªShemaiah the man of God, saying,

23 Speak unto Rehoboam, the son of Solomon, king of Judah, and unto all the house of Judah and Benjamin, and to the remnant of the people, saying,

24 Thus saith the LORD, Ye shall not go up, nor fight against your ªbrethren the children of Israel: return every man to his house; for this thing is from me. They hearkened therefore to the word of the LORD, and returned to depart, according to the word of the LORD.

25 ¶ Then Jeroboam built Shechem in mount Ephraim, and dwelt therein; and went out from thence, and built Penuel.

26 And Jeroboam said in his heart, Now shall the kingdom return to the house of David:

27 If this people ªgo up to do sacrifice in the house of the LORD at Jerusalem, then shall the heart of this people turn again unto their lord, *even* unto Rehoboam king of Judah, and they shall kill me, and go again to Rehoboam king of Judah.

28 Whereupon the king took counsel, and ªmade two ᵇcalves *of* gold, and said unto them, It is too much for you to go up to Jerusalem: behold thy ᶜgods, O Israel, which brought thee up out of the land of Egypt.

29 And he set the one in Beth-el, and the other put he in ªDan.

30 And this thing became a sin: for the people went *to worship* before the one, *even* unto Dan.

31 And he made an ªhouse of high places, and made ᵇpriests of the lowest of the people, which were not of the sons of Levi.

32 And Jeroboam ordained a feast in the eighth month, on the fifteenth day of the month, like unto the ªfeast that *is* in Judah, and he offered upon the altar. So did he in Beth-el, sacrificing unto the calves that he had made: and he placed in Beth-el the ᵇpriests of the high places which he had made.

33 So he offered upon the altar which he had made in Beth-el the fifteenth day of the eighth month, *even* in the month which he had devised of his own heart; and ordained a feast unto the children of Israel: and he offered upon the altar, and burnt incense.

CHAPTER 13

Jeroboam is smitten and then healed by a prophet from Judah—The prophet delivers his message, is led astray by a prophet from Bethel, and is slain by a lion for his disobedience—Jeroboam continues false worship in Israel.

AND, behold, there came a man of God out of Judah by the word of the LORD unto Beth-el: and Jeroboam stood by the altar to burn incense.

2 And he cried against the altar in the word of the LORD, and said, O altar, altar, thus saith the LORD; Behold, a child shall be born unto the house of David, Josiah by name; and upon thee shall he offer the priests of the ªhigh places that burn incense upon thee, and men's bones shall be ᵇburnt upon thee.

3 And he gave a sign the same day, saying, This *is* the sign which the LORD hath spoken; Behold, the altar shall be ªrent, and the ashes that *are* upon it shall be poured out.

4 And it came to pass, when king Jeroboam heard the saying of the man of God, which had cried against the altar in Beth-el, that he put forth his hand from the altar, saying, Lay hold on him. And his hand, which he put forth against him,

---

22*a* 2 Chr. 12:15 (5, 7, 15).
24*a* TG Brotherhood and Sisterhood.
27*a* Deut. 12:5 (5–7).
28*a* 2 Kgs. 23:15.
   b 2 Kgs. 10:29; 17:16;

Hosea 8:5 (5–7); 10:5.
   c TG Idolatry.
29*a* Amos 8:14.
31*a* 2 Kgs. 17:29.
   b TG False Priesthoods.
32*a* Lev. 23:34 (33–34).

b TG Apostasy of Israel.
13 2*a* 2 Kgs. 23:20 (16–20).
   b 2 Chr. 34:5.
3*a* OR torn down.

dried up, so that he could not pull it in again to him.

5 The altar also was rent, and the ashes poured out from the altar, according to the sign which the man of God had given by the word of the LORD.

6 And the king answered and said unto the man of God, Entreat now the face of the LORD thy God, and pray for me, that my hand may be restored me again. And the man of God besought the LORD, and the king's hand was restored him again, and became as *it was* before.

7 And the king said unto the man of God, Come home with me, and refresh thyself, and I will give thee a reward.

8 And the man of God said unto the king, If thou wilt give me half thine house, I will not go in with thee, neither will I eat bread nor drink water in this place:

9 For so was it charged me by the word of the LORD, saying, Eat no bread, nor drink water, nor turn again by the same way that thou camest.

10 So he went another way, and returned not by the way that he came to Beth-el.

11 ¶ Now there dwelt an old prophet in Beth-el; and his sons came and told him all the works that the man of God had done that day in Beth-el: the words which he had spoken unto the king, them they told also to their father.

12 And their father said unto them, What way went he? For his sons had seen what way the man of God went, which came from Judah.

13 And he said unto his sons, Saddle me the ass. So they saddled him the ass: and he rode thereon,

14 And went after the man of God, and found him sitting under an oak: and he said unto him, *Art* thou the man of God that camest from Judah? And he said, I *am.*

15 Then he said unto him, Come home with me, and eat bread.

16 And he said, I may not return with thee, nor go in with thee: neither will I eat bread nor drink water with thee in this place:

17 For it was said to me by the word of the LORD, Thou shalt eat no bread nor drink water there, nor turn again to go by the way that thou camest.

18 He said unto him, I *am* a prophet also as thou *art;* and an *ª*angel spake unto me by the word of the LORD, saying, Bring him back with thee into thine house, that he may eat bread and *ᵇ*drink water. *But* he lied unto him.

19 So he went back with him, and did eat bread in his house, and drank water.

20 ¶ And it came to pass, as they sat at the table, that the word of the LORD came unto the prophet that brought him back:

21 And he cried unto the man of God that came from Judah, saying, Thus saith the LORD, Forasmuch as thou hast *ª*disobeyed the mouth of the LORD, and hast not kept the commandment which the LORD thy God commanded thee,

22 But camest back, and hast eaten bread and drunk water in the place, of the which *the* LORD did say to thee, Eat no bread, and drink no water; thy carcase shall not come unto the sepulchre of thy fathers.

23 ¶ And it came to pass, after he had eaten bread, and after he had drunk, that he saddled for him the ass, *to wit,* for the prophet whom he had brought back.

24 And when he was gone, a lion met him by the way, and slew him: and his carcase was cast in the way, and the ass stood by it, the lion also stood by the carcase.

25 And, behold, men passed by, and saw the carcase cast in the way, and the lion standing by the carcase: and they came and told *it* in the city where the old prophet dwelt.

26 And when the prophet that brought him back from the way

18*a* TG Angels.
  b JST 1 Kgs. 13:18 . . . drink water, *that I may prove him; and* he lied *not* unto him.
21*a* TG Disobedience.

heard *thereof*, he said, It *is* the man of God, who was disobedient unto the word of the LORD: therefore the LORD hath delivered him unto the lion, which hath torn him, and slain him, according to the word of the LORD, which he spake unto him.

27 And he spake to his sons, saying, Saddle me the ass. And they saddled *him*.

28 And he went and found his carcase cast in the way, and the ass and the lion standing by the carcase: the lion had not eaten the carcase, nor torn the ass.

29 And the prophet took up the carcase of the man of God, and laid it upon the ass, and brought it back: and the old prophet came to the city, to mourn and to bury him.

30 And he laid his carcase in his own ªgrave; and they mourned over him, *saying*, Alas, my brother!

31 And it came to pass, after he had buried him, that he spake to his sons, saying, When I am dead, then bury me in the sepulchre wherein the man of God *is* buried; lay my bones beside his bones:

32 For the saying which he cried by the word of the LORD against the altar in Beth-el, and against all the houses of the high places which *are* in the cities of Samaria, shall surely come to pass.

33 ¶ After this thing Jeroboam returned not from his evil way, but made again of the lowest of the people priests of the high places: whosoever would, he consecrated him, and he became *one* of the priests of the high places.

34 And this thing became ªsin unto the house of Jeroboam, even to cut *it* off, and to destroy *it* from off the face of the earth.

CHAPTER 14

Ahijah foretells the ruin of Jeroboam's house, the death of his child, and the scattering of the Israelites because of their idolatry—Jeroboam dies and Nadab reigns—Judah, under Rehoboam, turns to wickedness—Shishak of Egypt takes treasures from the temple—Rehoboam dies and Abijam reigns.

AT that time Abijah the son of Jeroboam fell sick.

2 And Jeroboam said to his wife, Arise, I pray thee, and disguise thyself, that thou be not known to be the wife of Jeroboam; and get thee to Shiloh: behold, there *is* ªAhijah the prophet, which told me that I *should be* king over this people.

3 And take with thee ten loaves, and ªcracknels, and a cruse of honey, and go to him: he shall tell thee what shall become of the child.

4 And Jeroboam's wife did so, and arose, and went to Shiloh, and came to the house of Ahijah. But Ahijah could not see; for his eyes were set by reason of his age.

5 ¶ And the LORD said unto Ahijah, Behold, the wife of Jeroboam cometh to ask a thing of thee for her son; for he *is* sick: thus and thus shalt thou say unto her: for it shall be, when she cometh in, that she shall feign herself *to be* another *woman*.

6 And it was *so*, when Ahijah heard the sound of her feet, as she came in at the door, that he said, Come in, thou wife of Jeroboam; why feignest thou thyself *to be* another? for I *am* sent to thee *with* heavy *tidings*.

7 Go, tell ªJeroboam, Thus saith the LORD God of Israel, Forasmuch as I exalted thee from among the people, and made thee prince over my people Israel,

8 And rent the kingdom away from the house of David, and gave it thee: and *yet* thou hast not been as my servant ªDavid, who kept my commandments, and who followed me with all his heart, to do *that* only which *was* right in mine eyes;

9 But hast done ªevil above all that

30a 2 Kgs. 23:17.
34a TG Apostasy of Israel.
14 2a 1 Kgs. 11:29 (29–31).

3a OR cakes.
7a 1 Kgs. 16:26;
    2 Kgs. 3:3.

8a 1 Kgs. 15:5.
9a TG Unrighteous
    Dominion.

were before thee: for thou hast gone and made thee other gods, and molten images, to provoke me to anger, and hast cast me behind thy back:

10 Therefore, behold, I will bring evil upon the house of ᵃJeroboam, and will cut off from Jeroboam him that pisseth against the wall, *and* him that is shut up and left in Israel, and will ᵇtake away the remnant of the house of ᶜJeroboam, as a man taketh away dung, till it be all gone.

11 Him that dieth of Jeroboam in the city shall the dogs eat; and him that dieth in the field shall the fowls of the air eat: for the LORD hath spoken *it*.

12 Arise thou therefore, get thee to thine own house: *and* when thy feet enter into the city, the child shall die.

13 And all Israel shall mourn for him, and bury him: for he only of Jeroboam shall come to the grave, because in him there is found *some* good thing toward the LORD God of Israel in the house of Jeroboam.

14 Moreover the LORD shall raise him up a king over Israel, who shall cut off the house of Jeroboam that day: but what? even now.

15 For the LORD shall smite Israel, as a reed is shaken in the water, and he shall root up ᵃIsrael out of this ᵇgood land, which he gave to their fathers, and shall scatter them beyond ᶜthe river, because they have made their ᵈgroves, ᵉprovoking the LORD to anger.

16 And he shall give Israel up because of the sins of ᵃJeroboam, who did sin, and who made Israel to sin.

17 ¶ And Jeroboam's wife arose, and departed, and came to Tirzah: *and* when she came to the threshold of the door, the child died;

18 And they buried him; and all Israel mourned for him, according to the word of the LORD, which he spake by the hand of his servant Ahijah the prophet.

19 And the rest of the acts of Jeroboam, how he warred, and how he reigned, behold, they *are* written in the ᵃbook of the ᵇchronicles of the kings of Israel.

20 And the days which Jeroboam reigned *were* two and twenty years: and he slept with his fathers, and Nadab his son reigned in his stead.

21 ¶ And Rehoboam the son of Solomon reigned in Judah. Rehoboam *was* forty and one years old when he began to reign, and he reigned seventeen years in Jerusalem, the city which the LORD did choose out of all the tribes of Israel, to put his name there. And his mother's name *was* Naamah an Ammonitess.

22 And Judah did ᵃevil in the sight of the LORD, and they ᵇprovoked him to jealousy with their sins which they had committed, above all that their fathers had done.

23 For they also built them ᵃhigh places, and ᵇimages, and groves, on every high hill, and under every green tree.

24 And there were also ᵃsodomites in the land: *and* they did according to all the abominations of the nations which the LORD cast out before the children of Israel.

25 ¶ And it came to pass in the fifth year of king Rehoboam, *that*

10a 2 Kgs. 9:9.
  b HEB burn, consume, destroy.
  c 1 Kgs. 15:29 (25–30).
15a TG Israel, Ten Lost Tribes of.
  b Josh. 23:16 (15–16).
  c IE the Euphrates.
  d HEB *asherim*; i.e., idolatrous, wooden poles, pillars, or trees. Deut. 16:21.

e TG Provoking.
16a 2 Kgs. 10:29; 13:2 (1–2, 11); 14:24; 15:9 (9, 18, 24).
19a It is significant that the kings of Israel and Judah kept official records; these records are no longer extant; they were used as source books by the author(s) of our books

of Kings; they are not our books of Chronicles.
  b 1 Chr. 27:24.
22a TG Apostasy of Israel.
  b TG Provoking.
23a 2 Kgs. 16:4 (2–4); Isa. 57:5.
  b 2 Chr. 24:18.
24a HEB male prostitutes; devotees of idolatrous, paganistic fertility worship.

ªShishak king of Egypt came up against Jerusalem:

26 And he took away the treasures of the house of the LORD, and the treasures of the king's house; he even took away all: and he took away all the shields of gold which Solomon had made.

27 And king Rehoboam made in their stead brasen shields, and committed *them* unto the hands of the chief of the guard, which kept the door of the king's house.

28 And it was *so*, when the king went into the house of the LORD, that the guard bare them, and brought them back into the guard chamber.

29 ¶ Now the rest of the acts of Rehoboam, and all that he did, *are* they not written in the book of the chronicles of the kings of Judah?

30 And there was war between Rehoboam and Jeroboam all *their* days.

31 And Rehoboam slept with his fathers, and was buried with his fathers in the city of David. And his mother's name *was* Naamah an Ammonitess. And ªAbijam his son reigned in his stead.

CHAPTER 15

Abijam reigns in wickedness and then Asa reigns in righteousness in Judah—Nadab and then Baasha reign in wickedness in Israel—Baasha destroys the house of Jeroboam.

Now in the eighteenth year of king Jeroboam the son of Nebat reigned Abijam over Judah.

2 Three years reigned he in Jerusalem. And his mother's name *was* ªMaachah, the daughter of Abishalom.

3 And he walked in all the sins of his father, which he had done before him: and his heart was not

perfect with the LORD his God, ªas the heart of David his father.

4 Nevertheless for David's sake did the LORD his God give him a lamp in Jerusalem, to set up his son after him, and to establish Jerusalem:

5 Because ªDavid did *that which was* right in the eyes of the LORD, and ᵇturned not aside from any *thing* that he commanded him all the days of his life, save only in the matter of ᶜUriah the Hittite.

6 And there was war between Rehoboam and Jeroboam all the days of his life.

7 Now the rest of the acts of Abijam, and all that he did, *are* they not written in the book of the chronicles of the kings of Judah? And there was war between Abijam and Jeroboam.

8 And Abijam slept with his fathers; and they buried him in the city of David: and Asa his son reigned in his stead.

9 ¶ And in the twentieth year of Jeroboam king of Israel reigned Asa over Judah.

10 And forty and one years reigned he in Jerusalem. And his ªmother's name *was* Maachah, the daughter of Abishalom.

11 And Asa did *that which was* right in the eyes of the LORD, ªas *did* David his father.

12 And he took away the sodomites out of the land, and removed all the idols that his fathers had made.

13 And also Maachah his mother, even her he removed from *being* queen, because she had made an idol ªin a grove; and Asa destroyed her idol, and burnt *it* by the brook Kidron.

14 But the high places were not removed: nevertheless Asa's heart was ªperfect with the LORD all his days.

25ª 1 Kgs. 11:40.
31ª OR Abijah (see 2 Chr. 12:16) or Abia (see Matt. 1:7).
15 2ª 2 Chr. 11:20.
3ª JST 1 Kgs. 15:3 . . . as the *Lord commanded* David

his father.
5ª 1 Kgs. 9:4.
   ᵇ Deut. 17:20.
   ᶜ 2 Sam. 11:3 (3–15); 1 Kgs. 14:8; D&C 132:39.
10ª IE grandmother's name

(vv. 2, 13; 2 Kgs. 8:26).
11ª JST 1 Kgs. 15:11 . . . as *he commanded* David his father.
13ª IE for Asherah (Canaanite goddess).
14ª Mosiah 29:13.

15 And he brought in the things which his father had dedicated, and the things which himself had dedicated, into the house of the LORD, silver, and gold, and vessels.

16 ¶ And there was war between Asa and Baasha king of Israel all their days.

17 And Baasha king of Israel went up against Judah, and built Ramah, that he might not suffer any to go out or come in to Asa king of Judah.

18 Then Asa took all the *a*silver and the gold *that were* left in the treasures of the house of the LORD, and the treasures of the king's house, and delivered them into the hand of his servants: and king Asa sent them to *b*Ben-hadad, the son of Tabrimon, the son of Hezion, king of *c*Syria, that dwelt at Damascus, saying,

19 *There is* a league between me and thee, *and* between my father and thy father: behold, I have sent unto thee a present of silver and gold; come and break thy league with Baasha king of Israel, that he may depart from me.

20 So Ben-hadad hearkened unto king Asa, and sent the captains of the hosts which he had against the cities of Israel, and smote Ijon, and Dan, and Abel-beth-maachah, and all Cinneroth, with all the land of Naphtali.

21 And it came to pass, when Baasha heard *thereof,* that he left off building of Ramah, and dwelt in Tirzah.

22 Then king Asa made a proclamation throughout all Judah; none *was* exempted: and they took away the stones of Ramah, and the timber thereof, wherewith Baasha had builded; and king Asa built with them Geba of Benjamin, and Mizpah.

23 The rest of all the acts of Asa, and all his might, and all that he did, and the cities which he built, *are* they not written in the book of the chronicles of the kings of Judah? Nevertheless in the time of his old age he was diseased in his feet.

24 And Asa slept with his fathers, and was buried with his fathers in the city of David his father: and *a*Jehoshaphat his son reigned in his stead.

25 ¶ And Nadab the son of Jeroboam began to reign over Israel in the second year of Asa king of Judah, and reigned over Israel two years.

26 And he did *a*evil in the sight of the LORD, and walked in the way of his father, and in his *b*sin wherewith he made Israel to sin.

27 ¶ And Baasha the son of Ahijah, of the house of Issachar, conspired against him; and Baasha smote him at Gibbethon, which *belonged* to the Philistines; for Nadab and all Israel laid siege to Gibbethon.

28 Even in the third year of Asa king of Judah did Baasha slay him, and reigned in his stead.

29 And it came to pass, when he reigned, *that* he smote all the house of *a*Jeroboam; he left not to Jeroboam any that breathed, until he had destroyed him, according unto the saying of the LORD, which he spake by his servant Ahijah the Shilonite:

30 Because of the sins of Jeroboam which he sinned, and which he made Israel sin, by his provocation wherewith he provoked the LORD God of Israel to *a*anger.

31 ¶ Now the rest of the acts of Nadab, and all that he did, *are* they not written in the book of the chronicles of the kings of Israel?

32 And there was war between Asa and Baasha king of Israel all their days.

33 In the third year of Asa king of Judah began Baasha the son of Ahijah to reign over all Israel in Tirzah, twenty and four years.

34 And he did *a*evil in the sight of

18*a* 2 Kgs. 12:18.
  b 2 Chr. 16:7 (7–9).
  c HEB Aram.
24*a* 2 Kgs. 3:7.

26*a* TG Unrighteous Dominion.
  b Mosiah 11:29 (27–29).
29*a* 1 Kgs. 14:10 (1–18).

30*a* TG Anger.
34*a* TG Unrighteous Dominion.

the Lord, and walked in the way of Jeroboam, and in his sin wherewith he made Israel to sin.

CHAPTER 16

Jehu prophesies evil upon Baasha and his house—Elah, Zimri, Omri, and Ahab reign in wickedness—Zimri destroys the house of Baasha—Ahab marries Jezebel, worships Baal, and provokes the Lord to anger.

THEN the word of the Lord came to Jehu the son of Hanani against Baasha, saying,

2 Forasmuch as I exalted thee out of the dust, and made thee prince over my people Israel; and thou hast walked in the way of Jeroboam, and hast made my people Israel to *a*sin, to provoke me to anger with their sins;

3 Behold, I will take away the posterity of *a*Baasha, and the posterity of his house; and will make thy house like the house of Jeroboam the son of Nebat.

4 Him that dieth of Baasha in the city shall the dogs eat; and him that dieth of his in the fields shall the fowls of the air eat.

5 Now the rest of the acts of Baasha, and what he did, and his might, *are* they not written in the book of the chronicles of the kings of Israel?

6 So Baasha slept with his fathers, and was buried in Tirzah: and Elah his son reigned in his stead.

7 And also by the hand of the prophet Jehu the son of Hanani came the word of the Lord against Baasha, and against his house, even for all the evil that he did in the sight of the Lord, in *a*provoking him to anger with the work of his hands, in being like the house of Jeroboam; and because he killed him.

8 ¶ In the twenty and sixth year of Asa king of Judah began Elah the son of Baasha to reign over Israel in Tirzah, two years.

9 And his servant Zimri, captain of half *his* chariots, conspired against him, as he was in Tirzah, drinking himself drunk in the house of Arza steward of *his* house in Tirzah.

10 And *a*Zimri went in and smote him, and killed him, in the twenty and seventh year of Asa king of Judah, and reigned in his stead.

11 ¶ And it came to pass, when he began to reign, as soon as he sat on his throne, *that* he slew all the house of Baasha: he left him not one that pisseth against a wall, neither of his kinsfolks, nor of his friends.

12 Thus did Zimri destroy all the house of Baasha, according to the word of the Lord, which he spake against Baasha by Jehu the prophet,

13 For all the sins of Baasha, and the sins of Elah his son, by which they sinned, and by which they *a*made Israel to sin, in provoking the Lord God of Israel to anger with their vanities.

14 Now the rest of the acts of Elah, and all that he did, *are* they not written in the book of the chronicles of the kings of Israel?

15 ¶ In the twenty and seventh year of Asa king of Judah did Zimri reign seven days in Tirzah. And the people *were* encamped against Gibbethon, which *belonged* to the Philistines.

16 And the people *that were* encamped heard say, Zimri hath conspired, and hath also slain the king: wherefore all Israel made Omri, the captain of the host, king over Israel that day in the camp.

17 And Omri went up from Gibbethon, and all Israel with him, and they besieged Tirzah.

18 And it came to pass, when Zimri saw that the city was taken, that he went into the palace of the king's house, and burnt the king's house over him with fire, and died,

19 For his sins which he sinned in doing evil in the sight of the Lord, in walking in the way of Jeroboam, and in his sin which he did, to make Israel to sin.

---

16 2*a* D&C 121:39.
3*a* 2 Kgs. 9:9.

7*a* TG Provoking.
10*a* 2 Kgs. 9:31.

13*a* TG Unrighteous Dominion.

20 Now the rest of the acts of Zimri, and his treason that he wrought, *are* they not written in the book of the chronicles of the kings of Israel?

21 ¶ Then were the people of Israel *a*divided into two parts: half of the people followed Tibni the son of Ginath, to make him king; and half followed Omri.

22 But the people that followed Omri prevailed against the people that followed Tibni the son of Ginath: so Tibni died, and Omri reigned.

23 ¶ In the thirty and first year of Asa king of Judah began Omri to reign over Israel, twelve years: six years reigned he in Tirzah.

24 And he bought the hill *a*Samaria of Shemer for two talents of silver, and built on the hill, and called the name of the city which he built, after the name of Shemer, owner of the hill, Samaria.

25 ¶ But *a*Omri wrought *b*evil in the eyes of the LORD, and did worse than all that *were* before him.

26 For he walked in all the way of *a*Jeroboam the son of Nebat, and in his sin wherewith he made Israel to *b*sin, to provoke the LORD God of Israel to anger with their vanities.

27 Now the rest of the acts of Omri which he did, and his might that he shewed, *are* they not written in the book of the chronicles of the kings of Israel?

28 So Omri slept with his fathers, and was buried in Samaria: and Ahab his son reigned in his stead.

29 ¶ And in the thirty and eighth year of Asa king of Judah began Ahab the son of Omri to reign over Israel: and Ahab the son of Omri

reigned over Israel in Samaria twenty and two years.

30 And *a*Ahab the son of Omri did *b*evil in the sight of the LORD above all that *were* before him.

31 And it came to pass, as if it had been a light thing for him to walk in the sins of Jeroboam the son of Nebat, that he took to *a*wife *b*Jezebel the daughter of Ethbaal king of the Zidonians, and went and served *c*Baal, and worshipped him.

32 And he reared up an altar for *a*Baal in the *b*house of Baal, which he had built in Samaria.

33 And *a*Ahab made a *b*grove; and Ahab did more to *c*provoke the LORD God of Israel to anger than all the kings of Israel that were before him.

34 ¶ In his days did Hiel the Beth-elite build *a*Jericho: he laid the foundation thereof in Abiram his firstborn, and set up the gates thereof in his youngest *son* Segub, according to the word of the LORD, which he spake by Joshua the son of *b*Nun.

CHAPTER 17

Elijah seals the heavens and is fed by the ravens—At his command the barrel of flour and the jar of oil of the widow of Zarephath never become empty—He raises her son from death.

AND *a*Elijah the Tishbite, *who was* *b*of the inhabitants of Gilead, said unto Ahab, *As* the LORD God of Israel liveth, before whom I stand, there shall not be dew nor *c*rain these years, but according to my *d*word.

2 And the word of the LORD came unto him, saying,

3 Get thee hence, and turn thee

21*a* Alma 51:6 (4–7).
24*a* 2 Kgs. 3:1.
25*a* Micah 6:16.
  b TG Unrighteous
      Dominion.
26*a* 1 Kgs. 14:7 (7–11);
      2 Kgs. 3:3.
  b Mosiah 29:17.
30*a* 2 Chr. 21:6; 22:3.
  b TG Unrighteous
      Dominion.
31*a* Ex. 34:16.

  b 1 Kgs. 18:4;
      2 Kgs. 9:34.
  c 2 Kgs. 10:18.
32*a* 2 Kgs. 3:2.
  b 2 Kgs. 10:27 (21–28).
33*a* 2 Kgs. 3:2.
  b Ex. 34:13;
      2 Kgs. 21:3;
      3 Ne. 21:18.
  c 2 Kgs. 13:6 (5–7);
      Jacob 1:8; Alma 12:36.
34*a* Josh. 6:26; 2 Kgs. 2:4.

  b Ex. 33:11;
      Num. 11:28;
      Neh. 8:17.
17 1*a* HEB *Eliyahu* or *Eliyah*;
        Greek: *Helias* (Elias).
        Matt. 17:3 (1–4);
        Luke 4:25;
        D&C 110:13 (13–16).
   b OR from Tishbe in
       Gilead.
   c TG Drought; Famine.
   d Hel. 10:5 (3–7).

eastward, and *a*hide thyself by the brook Cherith, that *is* *b*before Jordan.

4 And it shall be, *that* thou shalt drink of the brook; and I have commanded the ravens to feed thee there.

5 So he went and did according unto the word of the LORD: for he went and dwelt by the brook Cherith, that *is* before Jordan.

6 And the ravens brought him bread and flesh in the morning, and bread and flesh in the evening; and he drank of the brook.

7 And it came to pass after a while, that the brook dried up, because there had been no rain in the land.

8 ¶ And the word of the LORD came unto him, saying,

9 Arise, get thee to Zarephath, which *belongeth* to Zidon, and dwell there: behold, I have commanded a *a*widow woman there to sustain thee.

10 So he arose and went to Zarephath. And when he came to the gate of the city, behold, the widow woman *was* there gathering of sticks: and he called to her, and said, Fetch me, I pray thee, a little water in a vessel, that I may drink.

11 And as she was going to fetch *it,* he called to her, and said, Bring me, I pray thee, a morsel of *a*bread in thine hand.

12 And she said, *As* the LORD thy God liveth, I have not a cake, but an handful of meal in a barrel, and a little oil in a cruse: and, behold, I *am* gathering two sticks, that I may go in and dress it for me and my son, that we may eat it, and die.

13 And Elijah said unto her, Fear not; go *and* do as thou hast said: but make me thereof a little cake first, and bring *it* unto me, and after make for thee and for thy son.

14 For thus saith the LORD God of Israel, The barrel of meal shall not

waste, neither shall the cruse of oil fail, until the day *that* the LORD sendeth rain upon the earth.

15 And she *a*went and did according to the saying of Elijah: and she, and he, and her house, did eat *many* days.

16 *And* the barrel of meal wasted not, neither did the cruse of oil fail, according to the word of the LORD, which he spake by Elijah.

17 ¶ And it came to pass after these things, *that* the son of the woman, the mistress of the house, fell sick; and his *a*sickness was so sore, that there was no breath left in him.

18 And she said unto Elijah, What have I to do with thee, O thou man of God? art thou come unto me to call my *a*sin to remembrance, and to slay my son?

19 And he said unto her, Give me thy son. And he took him out of her bosom, and carried him up into a loft, where he abode, and laid him upon his own bed.

20 And he cried unto the LORD, and said, O LORD my God, hast thou also brought evil upon the widow with whom I sojourn, by slaying her son?

21 And he *a*stretched himself upon the child three times, and cried unto the LORD, and said, O LORD my God, I pray thee, let this child's *b*soul come into him again.

22 And the LORD heard the voice of Elijah; and the soul of the child came into him again, and he *a*revived.

23 And Elijah took the child, and brought him down out of the chamber into the house, and delivered him unto his mother: and Elijah said, See, thy *a*son liveth.

24 ¶ And the woman said to Elijah, Now by this I know that thou *art* a man of God, *and* that the word of the LORD in thy mouth *is* truth.

3*a* 1 Ne. 3:27;
  Mosiah 17:4 (1–4);
  Ether 13:13 (13, 22).
  TG Prophets,
  Rejection of.
  b OR east of (also v. 5).
9*a* Luke 4:25 (25–26);

  Mosiah 21:10 (10, 17);
  Moro. 9:16.
11*a* Alma 8:20.
15*a* 1 Ne. 3:7.
17*a* TG Sickness.
18*a* Job 13:26.
21*a* 2 Kgs. 4:34;

  Acts 20:10.
  TG Administrations to
    the Sick.
  b TG Spirit Body.
22*a* TG Death, Power over.
23*a* 2 Kgs. 4:37.

CHAPTER 18

Elijah is sent to meet Ahab—Obadiah saves a hundred prophets and meets Elijah—Elijah challenges the prophets of Baal to call down fire from heaven—They fail—He calls down fire, slays the prophets of Baal, and opens the heavens for rain.

AND it came to pass *after* many days, that the word of the LORD came to Elijah in the third year, saying, Go, shew thyself unto Ahab; and I will send rain upon the earth.

2 And Elijah went to shew himself unto Ahab. And *there was* a sore famine in Samaria.

3 And Ahab called Obadiah, which *was* the governor of *his* house. (Now Obadiah ªfeared the LORD greatly:

4 For it was *so,* when ªJezebel ᵇcut off the prophets of the LORD, that Obadiah took an hundred prophets, and hid them by fifty in a cave, and fed them with bread and water.)

5 And Ahab said unto Obadiah, Go into the land, unto all fountains of water, and unto all brooks: peradventure we may find grass to save the horses and mules alive, that we lose not all the beasts.

6 So they divided the land between them to pass throughout it: Ahab went one way by himself, and Obadiah went another way by himself.

7 ¶ And as Obadiah was in the way, behold, Elijah met him: and he knew him, and fell on his face, and said, *Art* thou that my lord Elijah?

8 And he answered him, I *am:* go, tell thy lord, Behold, Elijah *is here.*

9 And he said, What have I sinned, that thou wouldest deliver thy servant into the hand of Ahab, to slay me?

10 *As* the LORD thy God liveth, there is no nation or kingdom, whither my lord hath not sent to seek thee: and when they said, *He is* not *there;* he took an oath of the kingdom and nation, that they found thee not.

11 And now thou sayest, Go, tell thy lord, Behold, Elijah *is here.*

12 And it shall come to pass, *as soon as* I am gone from thee, that the Spirit of the LORD shall ªcarry thee whither I know not; and *so* when I come and tell Ahab, and he cannot find thee, he shall slay me: but I thy servant fear the LORD from my youth.

13 Was it not told my lord what I did when Jezebel ªslew the prophets of the LORD, how I hid an hundred men of the LORD's prophets by fifty in a cave, and fed them with bread and water?

14 And now thou sayest, Go, tell thy lord, Behold, Elijah *is here:* and he shall slay me.

15 And Elijah said, *As* the LORD of hosts liveth, before whom I stand, I will surely shew myself unto him to day.

16 So Obadiah went to meet Ahab, and told him: and Ahab went to meet Elijah.

17 ¶ And it came to pass, when Ahab saw Elijah, that ªAhab said unto him, *Art* thou he that troubleth Israel?

18 And he answered, I have not troubled Israel; but thou, and thy father's house, in that ye have ªforsaken the commandments of the LORD, and thou hast followed Baalim.

19 Now therefore send, *and* gather to me all Israel unto mount Carmel, and the ªprophets of Baal four hundred and fifty, and the prophets of the groves four hundred, which eat at Jezebel's table.

20 So Ahab sent unto all the children of Israel, and gathered the ªprophets together unto mount Carmel.

21 And Elijah came unto all the people, and said, How long halt ye between ªtwo opinions? if the LORD

---

18 3a D&C 76:5.
    4a 1 Kgs. 16:31.
     b 2 Kgs. 6:32; 9:7.
    12a Ezek. 37:1;
        1 Ne. 11:29 (19, 29);

14:30;
        Moses 6:64.
    13a TG Martyrdom.
    17a TG Prophets,
        Rejection of.

18a D&C 3:4 (4–7).
    19a 1 Kgs. 22:6.
    20a TG False Prophets.
    21a Hosea 10:2;
        James 1:8.

be God, *b*follow him: but if Baal, *then* follow him. And the people answered him not a word.

22 Then said Elijah unto the people, I, *even* I only, remain a prophet of the LORD; but Baal's prophets *are* four hundred and fifty men.

23 Let them therefore give us two bullocks; and let them choose one bullock for themselves, and cut it in pieces, and lay *it* on wood, and put no fire *under:* and I will dress the other bullock, and lay *it* on wood, and put no fire *under:*

24 And call ye on the name of your gods, and I will call on the name of the LORD: and the God that answereth by fire, let him be God. And all the people answered and said, It is well spoken.

25 And Elijah said unto the prophets of Baal, Choose you one bullock for yourselves, and dress *it* first; for ye *are* many; and call on the name of your *a*gods, but put no fire *under.*

26 And they took the bullock which was given them, and they dressed *it,* and called on the name of Baal from morning even until noon, saying, O Baal, hear us. But *there was* no voice, nor any that answered. And they leaped upon the altar which was made.

27 And it came to pass at noon, that Elijah mocked them, and said, Cry aloud: for he *is* a god; either he is talking, or he is *a*pursuing, or he is in a journey, *or* peradventure he sleepeth, and must be awaked.

28 And they cried aloud, and *a*cut themselves after their manner with knives and lancets, till the blood gushed out upon them.

29 And it came to pass, when midday was past, and they prophesied until the *time* of the offering of the *evening* sacrifice, that *there was* neither voice, nor any to answer, nor any that regarded.

30 And Elijah said unto all the people, Come near unto me. And all the people came near unto him. And he repaired the altar of the LORD *that was* broken down.

31 And Elijah took *a*twelve stones, according to the number of the tribes of the sons of Jacob, unto whom the word of the LORD came, saying, *b*Israel shall be thy name:

32 And with the stones he built an altar in the name of the LORD: and he made a trench about the altar, as great as would contain two measures of seed.

33 And he put the wood in order, and cut the bullock in pieces, and laid *him* on the wood, and said, Fill four *a*barrels with water, and pour *it* on the burnt sacrifice, and on the wood.

34 And he said, Do *it* the second time. And they did *it* the second time. And he said, Do *it* the third time. And they did *it* the third time.

35 And the water ran round about the altar; and he filled the trench also with water.

36 And it came to pass at *the time of* the offering of the *a*evening sacrifice, that Elijah the prophet came near, and said, LORD God of Abraham, Isaac, and of Israel, let it be known this day that thou *art* God in Israel, and *that* I *am* thy servant, and *that* I have done all these things at thy word.

37 Hear me, O LORD, hear me, that this people may know *a*that thou *art* the LORD God, and *that* thou hast turned their *b*heart back again.

38 Then the *a*fire of the LORD fell, and consumed the burnt sacrifice, and the wood, and the stones, and the dust, and licked up the water that *was* in the trench.

39 And when all the people saw *it,* they fell on their faces: and they said, The LORD, he *is* the God; the LORD, he *is* the God.

21*b* TG Agency.
25*a* TG Idolatry.
27*a* OR gone aside, or withdrawn.
28*a* Lev. 19:28;

Deut. 14:1.
31*a* Josh. 4:3 (1–9).
  b 2 Kgs. 17:34.
33*a* HEB jars.
36*a* Dan. 9:21.

37*a* OR that thou, Jehovah, art the God.
  b 1 Ne. 2:16;
     Alma 5:7.
38*a* D&C 133:41.

40 And Elijah said unto them, Take the prophets of Baal; let not one of them escape. And they took them: and Elijah brought them down to the brook Kishon, and slew them there.

41 ¶ And Elijah said unto Ahab, Get thee up, eat and drink; for *there is* a sound of abundance of rain.

42 So Ahab went up to eat and to drink. And Elijah went up to the top of Carmel; and he cast himself down upon the earth, and put his face between his knees,

43 And said to his servant, Go up now, look toward the sea. And he went up, and looked, and said, *There is* nothing. And he said, Go again seven times.

44 And it came to pass at the seventh time, that he said, Behold, there ariseth a little cloud out of the sea, like a man's hand. And he said, Go up, say unto Ahab, Prepare *thy chariot,* and get thee down, that the rain stop thee not.

45 And it came to pass in the mean while, that the heaven was black with clouds and wind, and there was a great rain. And Ahab rode, and went to Jezreel.

46 And the *a*hand of the LORD was on Elijah; and he *b*girded up his loins, and ran before Ahab to the entrance of Jezreel.

CHAPTER 19

Jezebel seeks the life of Elijah—An angel sends him to Horeb—The Lord speaks to Elijah, not in the wind nor the earthquake nor the fire, but in a still, small voice—Elisha joins Elijah.

AND Ahab told Jezebel all that Elijah had done, and withal how he had slain all the prophets with the sword.

2 Then Jezebel sent a messenger unto Elijah, saying, So let the *a*gods do *to me,* and more also, if I make not thy life as the life of one of them by to morrow about this time.

3 And when he saw *that,* he arose, and went for his life, and came to Beer-sheba, which *belongeth* to Judah, and left his servant there.

4 ¶ But he himself went a day's journey into the wilderness, and came and sat down under a *a*juniper tree: and he requested for himself that he might die; and said, It is enough; now, O LORD, take away my life; for I *am* not better than my fathers.

5 And as he lay and slept under a juniper tree, behold, then an *a*angel touched him, and said unto him, Arise *and* eat.

6 And he looked, and, behold, *there was* a cake baken on the coals, and a cruse of water at his head. And he did eat and drink, and laid him down again.

7 And the angel of the LORD came again the second time, and touched him, and said, Arise *and* eat; because the journey *is* too great for thee.

8 And he arose, and did eat and drink, and went in the strength of that *a*meat *b*forty days and forty nights unto *c*Horeb the *d*mount of God.

9 ¶ And he came thither unto a cave, and lodged there; and, behold, the word of the LORD *came* to him, and he said unto him, What doest thou here, Elijah?

10 And he said, I have been very jealous for the LORD God of hosts: for the children of Israel have forsaken thy covenant, thrown down thine altars, and slain thy prophets with the sword; and I, *even* I only, am left; and they *a*seek my life, to take it away.

11 And he said, Go forth, and stand upon the mount before the LORD. And, behold, the LORD passed by, and a great and strong wind rent

---

46a 2 Kgs. 3:15;
   D&C 43:2.
   b 2 Kgs. 4:29.
19 2a 1 Kgs. 20:10.
   4a HEB broom-bush (a

desert shrub); so also
   in v. 5.
5a TG Angels.
8a HEB food.
   b TG Fast, Fasting.

c Ex. 3:1;
   3 Ne. 25:4.
d Ex. 4:27.
10a TG Prophets,
   Rejection of.

the mountains, and brake in pieces the rocks before the LORD; *but* the LORD *was* not in the wind: and after the wind an earthquake; *but* the LORD *was* not in the earthquake:

12 And after the earthquake a fire; *but* the LORD *was* not in the fire: and after the fire a *a*still small *b*voice.

13 And it was *so,* when Elijah heard *it,* that he wrapped his face in his mantle, and went out, and stood in the entering in of the cave. And, behold, *there came* a voice unto him, and said, What doest thou here, Elijah?

14 And he said, I have been very *a*jealous for the LORD God of hosts: because the children of Israel have forsaken thy covenant, thrown down thine altars, and slain thy prophets with the sword; and I, *even* I only, am *b*left; and they seek my life, to take it away.

15 And the LORD said unto him, Go, return on thy way to the wilderness of Damascus: and when thou comest, anoint Hazael *to be* *a*king over Syria:

16 And Jehu the son of Nimshi shalt thou *a*anoint *to be* king over Israel: and *b*Elisha the son of Shaphat of Abel-meholah shalt thou *c*anoint *to be* prophet in thy room.

17 And it shall come to pass, *that* him that escapeth the sword of Hazael shall Jehu slay: and him that escapeth from the sword of Jehu shall Elisha slay.

18 Yet I have left *me* seven thousand in Israel, all the knees which have not bowed unto Baal, and every mouth which hath not kissed him.

19 ¶ So he departed thence, and found Elisha the son of Shaphat, who *was* plowing *with* twelve yoke *of oxen* before him, and he with the twelfth: and Elijah passed by him, and cast his *a*mantle upon him.

20 And he left the oxen, and ran after Elijah, and said, Let me, I pray thee, kiss my father and my mother, and *then* I will *a*follow thee. And he said unto him, Go back again: for what have I done to thee?

21 And he returned back from him, and took a yoke of oxen, and slew them, and boiled their flesh with the instruments of the oxen, and gave unto the people, and they did eat. Then he arose, and went after Elijah, and ministered unto him.

CHAPTER 20

Benhadad of Syria makes war with Israel—The Syrians are defeated twice—Ahab lets Benhadad go free, contrary to the will of the Lord.

AND Ben-hadad the king of Syria gathered all his host together: and *there were* thirty and two kings with him, and horses, and chariots: and he went up and besieged Samaria, and warred against it.

2 And he sent messengers to Ahab king of Israel into the city, and said unto him, Thus saith *a*Ben-hadad,

3 Thy *a*silver and thy gold *is* mine; thy wives also and thy children, *even* the goodliest, *are* mine.

4 And the king of Israel answered and said, My lord, O king, according to thy saying, I *am* thine, and all that I have.

5 And the messengers came again, and said, Thus speaketh Ben-hadad, saying, Although I have sent unto thee, saying, Thou shalt deliver me thy silver, and thy gold, and thy wives, and thy children;

6 Yet I will send my servants unto thee to morrow about this time, and they shall search thine house, and the houses of thy servants; and it shall be, *that* whatsoever is pleasant in *a*thine eyes, they shall put *it* in their hand, and take *it* away.

12*a* Job 4:16 (12–21);
   Hel. 5:30; 3 Ne. 11:3;
   D&C 20:35; 52:1 (1–2).
  b TG Inspiration;
   Revelation.
14*a* OR zealous.

  b Rom. 11:3 (3–4).
15*a* 2 Kgs. 8:13.
16*a* D&C 68:20; 109:35.
  b 2 Kgs. 2:1.
  c TG Called of God.
19*a* 2 Kgs. 2:8.

20*a* Luke 9:61.
20 2*a* 2 Kgs. 6:24.
  3*a* Alma 54:7 (5–11);
   3 Ne. 3:12.
  6*a* Greek, Vulgate, and
   Syriac: their.

7 Then the king of Israel called all the elders of the land, and said, Mark, I pray you, and see how this *man* ^aseeketh mischief: for he sent unto me for my wives, and for my children, and for my silver, and for my gold; and I denied him not.

8 And all the elders and all the people said unto him, Hearken not *unto him,* nor consent.

9 Wherefore he said unto the messengers of Ben-hadad, Tell my lord the king, All that thou didst send for to thy servant at the first I will do: but this thing I may not do. And the messengers departed, and brought him word again.

10 And Ben-hadad sent unto him, and said, The ^agods do so unto me, and more also, if the dust of Samaria shall suffice for handfuls for all the people that follow me.

11 And the king of Israel answered and said, Tell *him,* Let not him that girdeth on *his* ^a*harness* ^bboast himself as he that putteth it off.

12 And it came to pass, when *Ben-hadad* heard this message, as he *was* drinking, he and the kings in the ^apavilions, that he said unto his servants, Set *yourselves in array.* And they set *themselves in array* against the city.

13 ¶ And, behold, there came a prophet unto Ahab king of Israel, saying, Thus saith the LORD, Hast thou seen all this great multitude? behold, I will deliver it into thine hand this day; and thou shalt know that I *am* the LORD.

14 And Ahab said, By whom? And he said, Thus saith the LORD, *Even* by the ^ayoung men of the princes of the ^bprovinces. Then he said, Who shall order the battle? And he answered, Thou.

15 Then he ^anumbered the young men of the princes of the provinces, and they were two hundred and thirty two: and after them he numbered all the people, *even* all the children of Israel, *being* seven thousand.

16 And they went out at noon. But Ben-hadad *was* drinking himself drunk in the ^apavilions, he and the kings, the thirty and two kings that helped him.

17 And the young men of the princes of the provinces went out first; and Ben-hadad sent out, and they told him, saying, There are men come out of Samaria.

18 And he said, Whether they be come out for peace, take them alive; or whether they be come out for war, take them alive.

19 So these young men of the princes of the provinces came out of the city, and the army which followed them.

20 And they slew every one his man: and the Syrians fled; and Israel pursued them: and Ben-hadad the king of Syria escaped on an horse with the horsemen.

21 And the king of Israel went out, and smote the horses and chariots, and slew the Syrians with a great slaughter.

22 ¶ And the prophet came to the king of Israel, and said unto him, Go, strengthen thyself, and mark, and see what ^athou doest: for at the return of the year the king of Syria will come up against thee.

23 And the servants of the king of Syria said unto him, Their gods *are* gods of the hills; therefore they were stronger than we; but let us fight against them in the plain, and surely we shall be stronger than they.

24 And do this thing, Take the kings away, every man out of his place, and put captains in their rooms:

25 And number thee an army, like the army that thou hast lost, horse for horse, and chariot for chariot: and we will fight against them in the

---

7a 2 Kgs. 5:7 (5–7).
10a 1 Kgs. 19:2.
11a OR armor.
  b TG Boast.

12a HEB booths, shelters.
14a Alma 56:46 (43–49).
  b Eccl. 2:8.
15a OR mustered.

16a HEB booths, tents.
22a OR thou shouldest do.

plain, *and* surely we shall be stronger than they. And he hearkened unto their voice, and did so.

26 And it came to pass at the return of the year, that Ben-hadad numbered the Syrians, and went up to Aphek, to fight against Israel.

27 And the children of Israel were numbered, and *a*were all present, and went against them: and the children of Israel pitched before them like two little flocks of kids; but the Syrians filled the country.

28 ¶ And there came a man of God, and spake unto the king of Israel, and said, Thus saith the LORD, Because the Syrians have said, The LORD *is* God of the hills, but he *is* not God of the valleys, therefore will I deliver all this great multitude into thine hand, and ye shall know that I *am* the LORD.

29 And they pitched one over against the other seven days. And *so* it was, that in the seventh day the battle was joined: and the children of Israel slew of the Syrians an hundred thousand footmen in one day.

30 But the rest fled to Aphek, into the city; and *there* a wall fell upon twenty and seven thousand of the men *that were* left. And Ben-hadad fled, and came into the city, into an inner chamber.

31 ¶ And his servants said unto him, Behold now, we have heard that the kings of the house of Israel *are* merciful kings: let us, I pray thee, put sackcloth on our loins, and ropes upon our heads, and go out to the king of Israel: peradventure he will save thy life.

32 So they girded sackcloth on their loins, and *put* ropes on their heads, and came to the king of Israel, and said, Thy servant Ben-hadad saith, I pray thee, let me live. And he said, Is he yet alive? he *is* my brother.

33 Now the men did diligently observe whether *any thing would come* from him, and did hastily catch *it:* and they said, Thy brother Ben-hadad. Then he said, Go ye, bring him. Then Ben-hadad came forth to him; and he caused him to come up into the chariot.

34 And *Ben-hadad* said unto him, The cities, which my father took from thy father, I will restore; and thou shalt make *a*streets for thee in Damascus, as my father made in Samaria. Then *said Ahab,* I will send thee away with this covenant. So he made a covenant with him, and sent him away.

35 ¶ And a certain man of the *a*sons of the prophets said unto his neighbour in the word of the LORD, Smite me, I pray thee. And the man refused to smite him.

36 Then said he unto him, Because thou hast not obeyed the voice of the LORD, behold, as soon as thou art departed from me, a lion shall slay thee. And as soon as he was departed from him, a lion found him, and slew him.

37 Then he found another man, and said, Smite me, I pray thee. And the man smote him, so that in smiting he wounded *him.*

38 So the prophet departed, and waited for the king by the way, and disguised himself with *a*ashes upon his face.

39 And as the king passed by, he cried unto the king: and he said, Thy servant went out into the midst of the battle; and, behold, a man turned aside, and brought a man unto me, and said, Keep this man: if by any means he be missing, then shall thy life be for his life, or else thou shalt pay a talent of silver.

40 And as thy servant was busy here and there, he was gone. And the king of Israel said unto him, So *shall* thy judgment *be;* thyself hast decided *it.*

41 And he hasted, and took the ashes away from his face; and the king of Israel discerned him that he *was* of the prophets.

27*a* HEB were supplied with food.
34*a* IE bazaars, trading centers.
35*a* 2 Kgs. 2:3 (3, 5, 7, 15).
38*a* HEB headband over his eyes (also v. 41).

42 And he said unto him, Thus saith the LORD, Because thou hast let go out of *thy* hand a man whom I appointed to utter destruction, therefore thy *ª*life shall go for his life, and thy people for his people.

43 And the king of Israel went to his house heavy and displeased, and came to Samaria.

CHAPTER 21

Ahab desires the vineyard of Naboth— Jezebel arranges for false witnesses, and Naboth is stoned for blasphemy—Elijah prophesies that Ahab and Jezebel and their house will be destroyed.

AND it came to pass after these things, *that* Naboth the Jezreelite had a vineyard, which *was* in Jezreel, hard by the palace of Ahab king of Samaria.

2 And Ahab spake unto Naboth, saying, Give me thy vineyard, that I may have it for a garden of herbs, because it *is* near unto my house: and I will give thee for it a better vineyard than it; *or,* if it seem good to thee, I will give thee the worth of it in money.

3 And Naboth said to Ahab, The LORD forbid it me, that I should give the *ª*inheritance of my fathers unto thee.

4 And Ahab came into his house heavy and displeased because of the word which Naboth the Jezreelite had spoken to him: for he had said, I will not give thee the inheritance of my fathers. And he laid him down upon his bed, and turned away his face, and would eat no bread.

5 ¶ But Jezebel his wife came to him, and said unto him, Why is thy spirit so sad, that thou eatest no bread?

6 And he said unto her, Because I spake unto Naboth the Jezreelite, and said unto him, Give me thy vineyard for money; or else, if it please thee, I will give thee *another* vineyard for it: and he answered, I will not give thee my vineyard.

7 And Jezebel his wife said unto him, Dost thou now govern the kingdom of Israel? arise, *and* eat bread, and let thine heart be merry: I will give thee the vineyard of Naboth the Jezreelite.

8 So she wrote letters in Ahab's name, and sealed *them* with his *ª*seal, and sent the letters unto the elders and to the nobles that *were* in his city, dwelling with Naboth.

9 And she wrote in the letters, saying, Proclaim a *ª*fast, and set Naboth on high among the people:

10 And set two men, sons of Belial, before him, to bear witness *ª*against him, saying, Thou didst *ᵇ*blaspheme God and the king. And *then* carry him out, and stone him, that he may die.

11 And the men of his city, *even* the elders and the nobles who were the inhabitants in his city, did as Jezebel had sent unto them, *and* as it *was* written in the letters which she had sent unto them.

12 They proclaimed a fast, and set Naboth on high among the people.

13 And there came in two men, children of Belial, and sat before him: and the men of Belial witnessed against him, *even* against Naboth, in the presence of the people, saying, Naboth did blaspheme God and the king. Then they carried him forth out of the city, and stoned him with stones, that he died.

14 Then they sent to Jezebel, saying, Naboth is stoned, and is dead.

15 ¶ And it came to pass, when Jezebel heard that Naboth was stoned, and was dead, that Jezebel said to Ahab, Arise, take *ª*possession of the vineyard of Naboth the Jezreelite, which he refused to give thee for money: for Naboth is not alive, but dead.

16 And it came to pass, when Ahab heard that Naboth was dead, that Ahab rose up to go down to the vineyard of Naboth the Jezreelite, to take possession of it.

42*a* 1 Kgs. 22:37 (34–40);
　　2 Kgs. 10:24.
21 3*a* TG Inheritance.

8*a* TG Seal.
9*a* TG Fast, Fasting.
10*a* TG Tyranny.

b TG Blaspheme.
15*a* TG Selfishness.

17 ¶ And the word of the LORD came to Elijah the Tishbite, saying,

18 Arise, go down to meet Ahab king of Israel, which *is* in Samaria: behold, *he is* in the vineyard of Naboth, whither he is gone down to possess it.

19 And thou shalt speak unto him, saying, Thus saith the LORD, Hast thou killed, and also taken possession? And thou shalt speak unto him, saying, Thus saith the LORD, In the place where dogs licked the blood of Naboth shall dogs lick thy blood, even thine.

20 And Ahab said to Elijah, Hast thou found me, O mine enemy? And he answered, I have found *thee:* because thou hast sold thyself to work evil in the sight of the LORD.

21 Behold, I will bring evil upon thee, and will take away thy ᵃposterity, and will cut off from Ahab him that pisseth against the wall, and him that is shut up and left in Israel,

22 And will make thine house like the house of Jeroboam the son of Nebat, and like the house of Baasha the son of Ahijah, for the provocation wherewith thou hast provoked *me* to anger, and made Israel to sin.

23 And of Jezebel also spake the LORD, saying, The ᵃdogs shall eat Jezebel by the wall of Jezreel.

24 Him that dieth of Ahab in the city the dogs shall eat; and him that dieth in the field shall the fowls of the air eat.

25 ¶ But there was none like unto Ahab, which did sell himself to work wickedness in the sight of the LORD, whom Jezebel his wife stirred up.

26 And he did very ᵃabominably in following idols, according to all *things* as did the Amorites, whom the LORD cast out before the children of Israel.

27 And it came to pass, when Ahab heard those words, that he ᵃrent his clothes, and put sackcloth upon his flesh, and fasted, and lay in sackcloth, and went ᵇsoftly.

28 And the word of the LORD came to Elijah the Tishbite, saying,

29 Seest thou how Ahab humbleth himself before me? because he humbleth himself before me, I will not bring the evil in his days: *but* in his son's days will I bring the evil upon his house.

CHAPTER 22

Jehoshaphat of Judah and Ahab of Israel join forces against Syria—Ahab's prophets foretell success—Micaiah foretells the defeat and death of Ahab—Ahab is slain and dogs lick up his blood—Jehoshaphat reigns in righteousness in Judah—Ahaziah reigns in Israel and serves Baal.

AND they continued three years without war between Syria and Israel.

2 And it came to pass in the third year, that Jehoshaphat the king of Judah came down to the king of Israel.

3 And the king of Israel said unto his servants, Know ye that Ramoth in Gilead *is* ours, and we *be* still, *and* take it not out of the hand of the king of Syria?

4 And he said unto Jehoshaphat, Wilt thou go with me to battle to Ramoth-gilead? And Jehoshaphat said to the king of Israel, ᵃI *am* as thou *art*, my people as thy people, my horses as thy horses.

5 And Jehoshaphat said unto the king of Israel, Inquire, I pray thee, at the word of the LORD to day.

6 Then the king of Israel gathered the ᵃprophets together, about four hundred men, and said unto them, Shall I go against Ramoth-gilead to battle, or shall I forbear? And they said, Go up; for the Lord shall deliver *it* into the hand of the king.

7 And Jehoshaphat said, *Is there* not here a prophet of the LORD besides, that we might inquire of him?

21*a* 2 Kgs. 9:8.
23*a* 2 Kgs. 9:36.
26*a* 2 Kgs. 21:11.

27*a* 2 Kgs. 6:30.
   b OR dejectedly.
22 4*a* 2 Kgs. 3:7.

6*a* 1 Kgs. 18:19.

8 And the king of Israel said unto Jehoshaphat, *There is* yet one man, Micaiah the son of Imlah, by whom we may inquire of the LORD: but I ^ahate him; for he doth not prophesy good concerning me, but evil. And Jehoshaphat said, Let not the king say so.

9 Then the king of Israel called an officer, and said, Hasten *hither* Micaiah the son of Imlah.

10 And the king of Israel and Jehoshaphat the king of Judah sat each on his throne, having put on their robes, in a ^avoid place in the entrance of the gate of Samaria; and all the prophets prophesied before them.

11 And Zedekiah the son of Chenaanah made him horns of iron: and he said, Thus saith the LORD, With these shalt thou push the Syrians, until thou have consumed them.

12 And all the prophets prophesied so, saying, Go up to Ramoth-gilead, and prosper: for the LORD shall deliver *it* into the king's hand.

13 And the messenger that was gone to call Micaiah spake unto him, saying, Behold now, the words of the prophets *declare* good unto the king with one mouth: let thy word, I pray thee, be like the word of one of them, and speak *that which is* good.

14 And Micaiah said, *As* the LORD liveth, what the LORD saith unto me, that will I speak.

15 ¶ So he came to the king. And the king said unto him, Micaiah, shall we go against Ramoth-gilead to battle, or shall we forbear? And he answered him, Go, and prosper: for the LORD shall deliver *it* into the hand of the king.

16 And the king said unto him, How many times shall I adjure thee that thou tell me nothing but *that which is* true in the name of the LORD?

17 And he said, I saw all Israel ^ascattered upon the hills, as ^bsheep that have not a shepherd: and the LORD said, These have no master:

let them return every man to his house in peace.

18 And the king of Israel said unto Jehoshaphat, Did I not tell thee that he would prophesy no good concerning me, but evil?

19 And he said, Hear thou therefore the word of the LORD: I saw the LORD sitting on his throne, and all the host of heaven standing by him on his right hand and on his left.

20 And the LORD said, Who shall persuade Ahab, that he may go up and fall at Ramoth-gilead? And one said on this manner, and another said on that manner.

21 And there came forth a spirit, and stood before the LORD, and said, I will persuade him.

22 And the LORD said unto him, Wherewith? And he said, I will go forth, and I will be a ^alying spirit in the mouth of all his prophets. And he said, Thou shalt persuade *him*, and prevail also: go forth, and do so.

23 Now therefore, behold, the LORD hath put a ^alying spirit in the mouth of all these thy prophets, and the LORD hath spoken evil concerning thee.

24 But Zedekiah the son of Chenaanah went near, and smote Micaiah on the cheek, and said, Which way went the Spirit of the LORD from me to speak unto thee?

25 And Micaiah said, Behold, thou shalt see in that day, when thou shalt go into an inner chamber to hide thyself.

26 And the king of Israel said, Take Micaiah, and carry him back unto Amon the governor of the city, and to Joash the king's son;

27 And say, Thus saith the king, Put this *fellow* in the prison, and feed him with bread of affliction and with water of affliction, until I come in peace.

28 And Micaiah said, If thou return at all in peace, the LORD hath not spoken by me. And he said, Hearken, O people, every one of you.

8a TG Hate.
10a HEB threshing floor.
17a TG Israel, Scattering of.

b TG Sheep; Shepherd.
22a See JST 2 Chr. 18:22
   (2 Chr. 18:22 note a).

Isa. 19:14 (11–14).
23a 2 Chr. 18:22.

29 So the king of Israel and Jehoshaphat the king of Judah went up to Ramoth-gilead.

30 And the king of Israel said unto Jehoshaphat, I will disguise myself, and enter into the battle; but put thou on thy robes. And the king of Israel disguised himself, and went into the battle.

31 But the king of Syria commanded his thirty and two captains that had rule over his chariots, saying, Fight neither with small nor great, save only with the king of Israel.

32 And it came to pass, when the captains of the chariots saw Jehoshaphat, that they said, Surely it *is* the king of Israel. And they turned aside to fight against him: and Jehoshaphat cried out.

33 And it came to pass, when the captains of the chariots perceived that it *was* not the king of Israel, that they turned back from pursuing him.

34 And a *certain* man drew a bow at a venture, and smote the king of Israel *a*between the joints of the harness: wherefore he said unto the driver of his chariot, Turn thine hand, and carry me out of the host; for I am wounded.

35 And the battle increased that day: and the king was *a*stayed up in his chariot against the Syrians, and died at even: and the blood ran out of the wound into the midst of the chariot.

36 And there went a proclamation throughout the host about the going down of the sun, saying, Every man to his city, and every man to his own country.

37 ¶ So the king *a*died, and was brought to Samaria; and they buried the king in Samaria.

38 And *one* washed the chariot in the pool of Samaria; and the dogs licked up his blood; and they washed his armour; according unto the word of the LORD which he spake.

39 Now the rest of the acts of Ahab, and all that he did, and the *a*ivory house which he made, and all the cities that he built, *are* they not written in the book of the chronicles of the kings of Israel?

40 So Ahab slept with his fathers; and Ahaziah his son reigned in his stead.

41 ¶ And Jehoshaphat the son of Asa began to reign over Judah in the fourth year of Ahab king of Israel.

42 Jehoshaphat *was* thirty and five years old when he began to reign; and he reigned twenty and five years in Jerusalem. And his mother's name *was* Azubah the daughter of Shilhi.

43 And he walked in all the ways of Asa his father; he turned not aside from it, doing *that which was* right in the eyes of the LORD: nevertheless the high places were not taken away; *for* the people offered and burnt incense yet in the high places.

44 And Jehoshaphat made peace with the king of Israel.

45 Now the rest of the acts of Jehoshaphat, and his might that he shewed, and how he warred, *are* they not written in the book of the chronicles of the kings of Judah?

46 And the remnant of the *a*sodomites, which remained in the days of his father Asa, he took out of the land.

47 *There was* then no *a*king in Edom: a deputy *was* king.

48 Jehoshaphat made ships of Tharshish to go to Ophir for gold: but they went not; for the ships were broken at *a*Ezion-geber.

49 Then said Ahaziah the son of Ahab unto Jehoshaphat, Let my servants go with thy servants in the ships. But Jehoshaphat would not.

50 ¶ And Jehoshaphat slept with his fathers, and was buried with his fathers in the city of David his

---

34*a* HEB between the armor and the breastplate.
35*a* IE propped up.
37*a* 1 Kgs. 20:42.

39*a* Amos 3:15.
46*a* IE cultic male prostitutes.
47*a* 2 Kgs. 3:9.

48*a* Num. 33:36; 1 Kgs. 9:26.

father: and Jehoram his son reigned in his stead.

51 ¶ Ahaziah the son of Ahab began to reign over Israel in Samaria the seventeenth year of Jehoshaphat king of Judah, and reigned two years over Israel.

52 And he did evil in the sight of the LORD, and walked in the way of his father, and in the way of his mother, and in the way of Jeroboam the son of Nebat, who made Israel to sin:

53 For he served Baal, and worshipped him, and provoked to anger the LORD God of Israel, according to all that his father had done.

THE SECOND BOOK OF THE
KINGS

COMMONLY CALLED
THE FOURTH BOOK OF THE KINGS

CHAPTER 1

Ahaziah turns to Baalzebub to learn if he will live—Elijah prophesies Ahaziah's death—Elijah calls down fire from heaven to consume the soldiers sent to apprehend him.

THEN ᵃMoab rebelled against Israel after the death of Ahab.

2 And Ahaziah fell down through a lattice in his upper chamber that *was* in Samaria, and was sick: and he sent messengers, and said unto them, Go, inquire of ᵃBaalzebub the god of Ekron whether I shall recover of this disease.

3 But the angel of the LORD said to Elijah the Tishbite, Arise, go up to meet the messengers of the king of Samaria, and say unto them, *Is it* not because *there is* not a God in Israel, *that* ye go to inquire of Baalzebub the god of Ekron?

4 Now therefore thus saith the LORD, Thou shalt not come down from that bed on which thou art gone up, but shalt surely ᵃdie. And Elijah departed.

5 ¶ And when the messengers turned back unto him, he said unto them, Why are ye now turned back?

6 And they said unto him, There came a man up to meet us, and said unto us, Go, turn again unto the king that sent you, and say unto him, Thus saith the LORD, *Is it* not because *there is* not a God in Israel, *that* thou sendest to inquire of Baalzebub the god of Ekron? therefore thou shalt not come down from that bed on which thou art gone up, but shalt surely die.

7 And he said unto them, What manner of man *was he* which came up to meet you, and told you these words?

8 And they answered him, *He was* an ᵃhairy man, and girt with a girdle of leather about his loins. And he said, It *is* Elijah the Tishbite.

9 Then the king sent unto him a captain of fifty with his fifty. And he went up to him: and, behold, he sat on the top of an hill. And he spake unto him, Thou man of God, the king hath said, Come down.

---

1 1ᵃ 2 Sam. 8:2 (1–2); 2 Kgs. 3:4–5.
2ᵃ Matt. 12:24.
4ᵃ 2 Kgs. 1:17.
8ᵃ Mark 1:6.

10 And Elijah answered and said to the captain of fifty, If I *be* a man of God, then let ^afire come down from heaven, and consume thee and thy fifty. And there came down fire from heaven, and consumed him and his fifty.

11 Again also he sent unto him another captain of fifty with his fifty. And he answered and said unto him, O man of God, thus hath the king said, Come down quickly.

12 And Elijah answered and said unto them, If I *be* a man of God, let fire come down from heaven, and consume thee and thy fifty. And the fire of God came down from heaven, and consumed him and his fifty.

13 ¶ And he sent again a captain of the third fifty with his fifty. And the third captain of fifty went up, and came and fell on his knees before Elijah, and besought him, and said unto him, O man of God, I pray thee, let my life, and the life of these fifty thy servants, be precious in thy sight.

14 Behold, there came fire down from heaven, and burnt up the two captains of the former fifties with their fifties: therefore let my life now be precious in thy sight.

15 And the ^aangel of the Lord said unto Elijah, Go down with him: be not afraid of him. And he arose, and went down with him unto the king.

16 And he said unto him, Thus saith the Lord, Forasmuch as thou hast sent messengers to inquire of Baal-zebub the god of Ekron, *is it* not because *there is* no God in Israel to inquire of his word? therefore thou shalt not come down off that bed on which thou art gone up, but shalt surely die.

17 ¶ So he ^adied according to the word of the Lord which Elijah had spoken. And ^bJehoram reigned in his stead in the second year of Jehoram the son of Jehoshaphat king of Judah; because he had no son.

18 Now the rest of the acts of Ahaziah which he did, *are* they not written in the book of the chronicles of the kings of Israel?

CHAPTER 2

Elisha and the prophets know that Elijah is to be translated—Elijah divides the waters of the Jordan and is taken up into heaven in a whirlwind—The mantle of Elijah falls on Elisha, who also divides the waters of the Jordan—Elisha heals the waters of Jericho—Youths are torn by bears for mocking Elisha.

AND it came to pass, when the Lord would take up Elijah into heaven by a whirlwind, that Elijah went with ^aElisha from ^bGilgal.

2 And ^aElijah said unto Elisha, Tarry here, I pray thee; for the Lord hath sent me to ^bBeth-el. And Elisha said *unto him*, As the Lord liveth, and *as* thy soul liveth, I will not ^cleave thee. So they went down to Beth-el.

3 And the ^asons of the prophets that *were* at Beth-el came forth to Elisha, and said unto him, Knowest thou that the Lord will take away thy master from thy head to day? And he said, Yea, I know *it*; hold ye your peace.

4 And Elijah said unto him, Elisha, tarry here, I pray thee; for the Lord hath sent me to ^aJericho. And he said, *As* the Lord liveth, and *as* thy soul liveth, I will not leave thee. So they came to Jericho.

5 And the sons of the prophets that *were* at Jericho came to Elisha, and said unto him, Knowest thou that the Lord will take away thy master from thy head to day? And he answered, Yea, I know *it*; hold ye your peace.

6 And Elijah said unto him, Tarry,

10*a* Luke 9:54 (54–56);
　　 Hel. 13:13;
　　 3 Ne. 9:11.
15*a* TG Angels.
17*a* 2 Kgs. 1:4 (1–4).
　 b 2 Kgs. 3:1.

2 1*a* 1 Kgs. 19:16 (16–17).
　 b Josh. 5:9 (9–10);
　　 2 Kgs. 4:38.
2*a* 3 Ne. 25:5 (5–6);
　　 D&C 110:14 (13–16);
　　 128:17 (17–18).

　 b Gen. 12:8 (7–8);
　　 28:19 (16–19);
　　 Josh. 16:2 (1–2).
　 c Ruth 1:16 (16–17).
3*a* 1 Kgs. 20:35.
4*a* 1 Kgs. 16:34.

I pray thee, here; for the LORD hath sent me to Jordan. And he said, As the LORD liveth, and as thy soul liveth, I will not leave thee. And they two went on.

7 And fifty men of the sons of the prophets went, and stood to view afar off: and they two stood by Jordan.

8 And Elijah took his *a*mantle, and wrapped it together, and smote the *b*waters, and they were divided hither and thither, so that they two went over on dry ground.

9 ¶ And it came to pass, when they were gone over, that Elijah said unto Elisha, Ask what I shall do for thee, before I be taken away from thee. And Elisha said, I pray thee, let a *a*double portion of thy spirit be upon me.

10 And he said, Thou hast asked a hard thing: nevertheless, if thou see me when I am taken from thee, it shall be so unto thee; but if not, it shall not be so.

11 And it came to pass, as they still went on, and talked, that, behold, there appeared a *a*chariot of fire, and horses of fire, and parted them both asunder; and *b*Elijah went up by a *c*whirlwind into heaven.

12 ¶ And Elisha saw it, and he cried, My father, my father, the chariot of Israel, and the horsemen thereof. And he saw him no more: and he took hold of his own clothes, and rent them in two pieces.

13 He took up also the mantle of Elijah that fell from him, and went back, and stood by the bank of Jordan;

14 And he took the mantle of Elijah that fell from him, and smote the waters, and said, Where is the LORD God of Elijah? and when he also had smitten the waters, they *a*parted hither and thither: and Elisha went over.

15 And when the sons of the prophets which were to view at Jericho saw him, they said, The spirit of *a*Elijah doth *b*rest on Elisha. And they came to meet him, and bowed themselves to the ground before him.

16 ¶ And they said unto him, Behold now, there be with thy servants fifty strong men; let them go, we pray thee, and seek thy master: lest peradventure the *a*Spirit of the LORD hath taken him up, and cast him upon some mountain, or into some valley. And he said, Ye shall not send.

17 And when they urged him till he was ashamed, he said, Send. They sent therefore fifty men; and they sought three days, but found him not.

18 And when they came again to him, (for he tarried at Jericho,) he said unto them, Did I not say unto you, Go not?

19 ¶ And the men of the city said unto Elisha, Behold, I pray thee, the situation of this city is pleasant, as my lord seeth: but the water is naught, and the ground barren.

20 And he said, Bring me a new *a*cruse, and put salt therein. And they brought it to him.

21 And he went forth unto the spring of the waters, and cast the *a*salt in there, and said, Thus saith the LORD, I have healed these *b*waters; there shall not be from thence any more death or *c*barren land.

22 So the waters were healed unto this day, according to the saying of Elisha which he spake.

23 ¶ And he went up from thence unto Beth-el: and as he was going up by the way, there came forth *a*little children out of the city, and *b*mocked him, and said unto him, Go up, thou *c*bald head; go up, thou bald head.

8a 1 Kgs. 19:19.
  b Ex. 14:21;
    Josh. 3:16 (14–17).
9a Deut. 21:17.
11a Abr. 2:7.
  b TG Translated Beings.
  c Ezek. 1:4.
14a Ex. 14:21 (21–22).

15a D&C 2:2 (1–3); 27:9.
  b TG Priesthood,
    Ordination.
16a 1 Ne. 11:1;
    Alma 45:19 (18–19);
    Moses 6:64.
20a HEB dish, bowl.
21a 2 Kgs. 4:41.

  b Ex. 15:25;
    Ezek. 47:8 (8–9).
  c TG Barren.
23a HEB youths (not little
    children).
  b TG Mocking.
  c Lam. 4:16 (16–17).

24 And he turned back, and looked on them, and cursed them in the name of the LORD. And there came forth two she bears out of the wood, and tare forty and two children of them.

25 And he went from thence to mount *a*Carmel, and from thence he returned to Samaria.

CHAPTER 3

Jehoram of Israel and Jehoshaphat of Judah join forces against Moab—Elisha promises them water for their animals and victory in the war—The Moabites are defeated.

NOW *a*Jehoram the son of Ahab began to reign over Israel in *b*Samaria the eighteenth year of Jehoshaphat king of Judah, and reigned twelve years.

2 And he wrought *a*evil in the sight of the LORD; but not like his *b*father, and like his mother: for he put away the *c*image of *d*Baal that his father had made.

3 Nevertheless he cleaved unto the sins of *a*Jeroboam the son of Nebat, which made Israel to sin; he departed not therefrom.

4 ¶ And Mesha king of *a*Moab was a sheepmaster, and *b*rendered unto the king of Israel an hundred thousand lambs, and an hundred thousand rams, with the wool.

5 But it came to pass, when Ahab was dead, that the king of *a*Moab *b*rebelled against the king of Israel.

6 ¶ And king Jehoram went out of Samaria the same time, and numbered all Israel.

7 And he went and sent to *a*Jehoshaphat the king of Judah, saying, The king of Moab hath rebelled against me: wilt thou go with me against Moab to battle? And he said, I will go up: *b*I *am* as thou *art*, my people as thy people, *and* my horses as thy horses.

8 And he said, Which way shall we go up? And he answered, The way through the wilderness of Edom.

9 So the king of Israel went, and the king of Judah, and the *a*king of *b*Edom: and they *c*fetched a compass of seven days' journey: and there was no water for the host, and for the cattle that followed them.

10 And the king of Israel said, Alas! that the LORD hath called these three kings together, to deliver them into the hand of Moab!

11 But Jehoshaphat said, *Is there* not here a prophet of the LORD, that we may inquire of the LORD by him? And one of the king of Israel's servants answered and said, Here *is* Elisha the son of Shaphat, which poured water on the hands of Elijah.

12 And Jehoshaphat said, The word of the LORD is with him. So the king of Israel and Jehoshaphat and the king of Edom went down to him.

13 And Elisha said unto the king of Israel, What have I to do with *a*thee? *b*get thee to the prophets of thy father, and to the prophets of thy mother. And the king of Israel said unto him, Nay: for the LORD hath called these three kings together, to deliver them into the hand of Moab.

14 And Elisha said, *As* the LORD of hosts liveth, before whom I stand, surely, were it not that I regard the presence of Jehoshaphat the king of Judah, I would not look toward thee, nor see thee.

15 But now bring me a *a*minstrel.

25*a* 2 Kgs. 4:25.
3 1*a* 2 Kgs. 1:17.
  b 1 Kgs. 16:24.
  2*a* Alma 40:13;
    Abr. 1:6.
  b 1 Kgs. 16:33.
  c Mosiah 13:12 (12–13).
  d Judg. 6:25 (25–35);
    1 Kgs. 16:32 (31–33).
  3*a* 1 Kgs. 14:7 (7–11); 16:26.

4*a* Gen. 19:37 (31–37);
    2 Sam. 8:14.
  b Mosiah 7:22.
  5*a* 2 Sam. 8:2 (1–2);
    2 Kgs. 1:1.
  b Mosiah 10:6;
    Ether 10:3 (2–3).
  7*a* 1 Kgs. 15:24.
  b 1 Kgs. 22:4.
  9*a* 1 Kgs. 22:47.

  b Gen. 36:43;
    2 Sam. 8:14.
  c OR made a circuit.
  13*a* Ezek. 14:3;
    2 Cor. 6:14 (14–16).
  b Judg. 10:14 (13–14);
    Prov. 1:28 (27–28);
    Jer. 2:28 (26–37).
  15*a* 1 Sam. 10:5 (5–6);
    Eph. 5:19.

And it came to pass, when the minstrel played, that the [b]hand of the LORD came upon him.

16 And he said, Thus saith the LORD, Make this valley full of ditches.

17 For thus saith the LORD, Ye shall not see wind, neither shall ye see rain; yet that valley shall be filled with water, that ye may drink, both ye, and your cattle, and your beasts.

18 And this is *but* a [a]light thing in the sight of the LORD: he will [b]deliver the [c]Moabites also into your hand.

19 And ye shall smite every fenced city, and every choice city, and shall fell every good tree, and stop all wells of water, and mar every good piece of land with stones.

20 And it came to pass in the morning, when the meat [a]offering was offered, that, behold, there came water by the way of Edom, and the country was filled with water.

21 ¶ And when all the Moabites heard that the kings were come up to fight against them, they gathered all that were able to put on armour, and upward, and stood in the border.

22 And they rose up early in the morning, and the sun shone upon the water, and the Moabites saw the water on the other side *as* red as blood:

23 And they said, This *is* blood: the kings are surely slain, and they have smitten one another: now therefore, Moab, to the spoil.

24 And when they came to the camp of Israel, the Israelites rose up and smote the Moabites, so that they fled before them: but they went forward smiting the Moabites, even in *their* country.

25 And they beat down the cities, and on every good piece of land cast every man his stone, and filled it;

and they stopped all the wells of water, and felled all the good trees: only in [a]Kir-haraseth left they the stones thereof; howbeit the slingers went about *it*, and smote it.

26 ¶ And when the king of Moab saw that the battle was too sore for him, he took with him seven hundred men that drew swords, to break through *even* unto the king of Edom: but they could not.

27 Then he took his eldest son that should have reigned in his stead, and offered him *for* a burnt offering upon the wall. And there was great indignation against Israel: and they departed from him, and returned to *their own* land.

CHAPTER 4

Elisha multiplies the widow's oil—He promises a son to a Shunammite woman—The child dies and is raised to life by Elisha—He makes the poisonous food harmless—Bread and grain are multiplied for the people to eat.

NOW there cried a certain woman of the wives of the sons of the prophets unto Elisha, saying, Thy servant my husband is dead; and thou knowest that thy servant did fear the LORD: and the [a]creditor is come to take unto him my two sons to be [b]bondmen.

2 And Elisha said unto her, What shall I do for thee? tell me, what hast thou in the house? And she said, Thine handmaid hath not any thing in the house, save a pot of oil.

3 Then he said, Go, borrow thee vessels abroad of all thy neighbours, *even* empty vessels; borrow not a few.

4 And when thou art come in, thou shalt shut the door upon thee and upon thy sons, and shalt pour out into all those vessels, and thou shalt set aside that which is full.

5 So she went from him, and shut the door upon her and upon her

15b 1 Kgs. 18:46;
   Ezek. 1:3.
18a 1 Ne. 21:6.
   b 1 Ne. 3:29;

   3 Ne. 3:21.
   c Judg. 3:30 (28–30).
20a Ex. 29:39 (39–40);
   Mosiah 2:3.

25a Isa. 16:7.
4 1a TG Debt.
   b Matt. 18:25.

sons, who brought *the vessels* to her; and she poured out.

6 And it came to pass, when the vessels were full, that she said unto her son, Bring me yet a vessel. And he said unto her, *There is* not a vessel more. And the oil *a*stayed.

7 Then she came and told the man of God. And he said, Go, sell the oil, and pay thy debt, and live thou and thy children of the rest.

8 ¶ And it fell on a day, that Elisha passed to *a*Shunem, where *was* a great *b*woman; and she constrained him to eat bread. And *so* it was, *that* as oft as he passed by, he turned in thither to eat bread.

9 And she said unto her husband, Behold now, I perceive that this *is* an holy man of God, which passeth by us continually.

10 Let us make a little chamber, I pray thee, on the wall; and let us set for him there a bed, and a table, and a stool, and a candlestick: and it shall be, when he cometh to us, that he shall turn in thither.

11 And it fell on a day, that he came thither, and he turned into the chamber, and lay there.

12 And he said to Gehazi his servant, Call this Shunammite. And when he had called her, she stood before him.

13 And he said unto him, Say now unto her, Behold, thou hast been careful for us with all this care; what *is* to be done for thee? wouldest thou be spoken for to the king, or to the captain of the host? And she answered, I dwell among mine own people.

14 And he said, What then *is* to be done for her? And Gehazi answered, Verily she hath no child, and her husband is old.

15 And he said, Call her. And when he had called her, she stood in the door.

16 And he said, About this season, according to the *a*time of life, thou shalt embrace a son. And she said,

Nay, my lord, *thou* man of God, do not lie unto thine handmaid.

17 And the *a*woman conceived, and bare a son at that season that Elisha had said unto her, according to the time of life.

18 ¶ And when the child was grown, it fell on a day, that he went out to his father to the reapers.

19 And he said unto his father, My head, my head. And he said to a lad, Carry him to his mother.

20 And when he had taken him, and brought him to his mother, he sat on her knees till noon, and *then* died.

21 And she went up, and laid him on the bed of the man of God, and shut *the door* upon him, and went out.

22 And she called unto her husband, and said, Send me, I pray thee, one of the young men, and one of the asses, that I may run to the man of God, and come again.

23 And he said, Wherefore wilt thou go to him to day? *it is* neither new moon, nor sabbath. And she said, *It shall be* well.

24 Then she saddled an ass, and said to her servant, Drive, and go forward; slack not *thy* riding for me, except I bid thee.

25 So she went and came unto the man of God to mount *a*Carmel. And it came to pass, when the man of God saw her afar off, that he said to Gehazi his servant, Behold, *yonder is* that Shunammite:

26 Run now, I pray thee, to meet her, and say unto her, *Is it* well with thee? *is it* well with thy husband? *is it* well with the child? And she answered, *It is* well.

27 And when she came to the man of God to the hill, she caught him by the feet: but Gehazi came near to thrust her away. And the man of God said, Let her alone; for her soul *is* vexed within her: and the LORD hath *a*hid *it* from me, and hath not told me.

6*a* HEB stopped.
8*a* Josh. 19:18.
  b TG Woman.

16*a* Gen. 18:14.
17*a* TG Marriage, Motherhood.

25*a* 2 Kgs. 2:25.
27*a* D&C 6:16.

28 Then she said, Did I desire a son of my lord? did I not say, Do not deceive me?

29 Then he said to Gehazi, *a*Gird up thy loins, and take my staff in thine hand, and go thy way: if thou meet any man, *b*salute him not; and if any salute thee, answer him not again: and lay my *c*staff upon the face of the child.

30 And the mother of the child said, *As* the LORD liveth, and *as* thy soul liveth, I will not leave thee. And he arose, and followed her.

31 And Gehazi passed on before them, and laid the staff upon the face of the child; but *there was* neither voice, nor hearing. Wherefore he went again to meet him, and told him, saying, The child is not *a*awaked.

32 And when Elisha was come into the house, behold, the child was dead, *and* laid upon his bed.

33 He went in therefore, and *a*shut the door upon them twain, and prayed unto the LORD.

34 And he went up, and lay upon the child, and put his mouth upon his mouth, and his eyes upon his eyes, and his *a*hands upon his hands: and he *b*stretched himself upon the child; and the flesh of the child waxed warm.

35 Then he returned, and walked in the house to and fro; and went up, and stretched himself upon him: and the child sneezed seven times, and the child *a*opened his eyes.

36 And he called Gehazi, and said, Call this Shunammite. So he called her. And when she was come in unto him, he said, Take up thy son.

37 Then she went in, and fell at his feet, and bowed herself to the ground, and took up her *a*son, and went out.

38 ¶ And Elisha came again to *a*Gilgal: and *there was* a *b*dearth in the land; and the sons of the prophets *were* sitting before him: and he said unto his servant, Set on the great pot, and seethe pottage for the sons of the prophets.

39 And one went out into the field to gather herbs, and found a wild vine, and gathered thereof wild gourds his lap full, and came and shred *them* into the pot of pottage: for they knew *them* not.

40 So they poured out for the men to eat. And it came to pass, as they were eating of the pottage, that they cried out, and said, O *thou* man of God, *there is* death in the pot. And they could not eat *thereof.*

41 But he said, Then bring meal. And he cast *it* into the *a*pot; and he said, Pour out for the people, that they may eat. And there was no harm in the pot.

42 ¶ And there came a man from Baal-shalisha, and *a*brought the man of God bread of the firstfruits, twenty loaves of barley, and full ears of corn in the husk thereof. And he said, Give unto the people, that they may eat.

43 And his servitor said, What, should I set this before an hundred men? He said again, Give the people, that they may eat: for thus saith the LORD, They shall eat, and shall leave *thereof.*

44 So he set *it* before them, and they did eat, and *a*left *thereof,* according to the word of the LORD.

CHAPTER 5

Naaman, the Syrian, comes to Elisha to be healed of leprosy—He rejects the prophet's instruction at first but relents and dips himself in the Jordan seven times; he is healed—Elisha refuses to accept a reward—Gehazi accepts a gift from Naaman and is cursed with leprosy.

Now Naaman, captain of the host

29*a* 1 Kgs. 18:46.
 b Luke 10:4.
 c Acts 19:12.
31*a* John 11:11.
33*a* Matt. 6:6;
 3 Ne. 13:6.

34*a* TG Administrations to the Sick.
 b 1 Kgs. 17:21.
35*a* 2 Kgs. 8:1.
 TG Death, Power over.
37*a* 1 Kgs. 17:23.

38*a* 2 Kgs. 2:1.
 b OR famine.
41*a* 2 Kgs. 2:21.
42*a* 1 Sam. 9:7.
44*a* Matt. 14:20 (19–21);
 15:37 (36–38).

of the king of Syria, was a great man with his master, and honourable, because by him the LORD had given deliverance unto Syria: he was also a mighty man in valour, *but he was* a [a]leper.

2 And the Syrians had gone out by companies, and had brought away captive out of the land of Israel a little maid; and she waited on Naaman's wife.

3 And she said unto her mistress, Would God my lord *were* with the prophet that *is* in Samaria! for he would recover him of his leprosy.

4 And *one* went in, and told his lord, saying, Thus and thus said the maid that *is* of the land of Israel.

5 And the king of Syria said, Go to, go, and I will send a letter unto the king of Israel. And he departed, and [a]took with him ten talents of silver, and six thousand *pieces* of gold, and ten changes of raiment.

6 And he brought the letter to the king of Israel, saying, Now when this letter is come unto thee, behold, I have *therewith* sent Naaman my servant to thee, that thou mayest recover him of his leprosy.

7 And it came to pass, when the king of Israel had read the letter, that he rent his clothes, and said, *Am* I [a]God, to kill and to make alive, that this man doth send unto me to recover a man of his leprosy? wherefore consider, I pray you, and see how he [b]seeketh a quarrel against me.

8 ¶ And it was *so*, when Elisha the man of God had heard that the king of Israel had rent his clothes, that he sent to the king, saying, Wherefore hast thou rent thy clothes? let him come now to me, and he shall know that there is a [a]prophet in Israel.

9 So Naaman came with his horses and with his chariot, and stood at the door of the house of Elisha.

10 And Elisha sent a messenger unto him, saying, Go and [a]wash in Jordan seven times, and thy flesh shall come again to thee, and thou shalt be [b]clean.

11 But Naaman was wroth, and went away, and said, Behold, I thought, He will surely come out to me, and stand, and call on the name of the LORD his God, and strike his hand over the place, and recover the leper.

12 *Are* not Abana and Pharpar, rivers of Damascus, better than all the waters of Israel? may I not wash in them, and be clean? So he turned and went away in a rage.

13 And his servants came near, and spake unto him, and said, My father, *if* the prophet had bid thee *do some* [a]great thing, wouldest thou not have done *it*? how much rather then, when he saith to thee, Wash, and be clean?

14 Then went he down, and dipped himself seven times in Jordan, [a]according to the saying of the man of God: and his [b]flesh came again like unto the [c]flesh of a little child, and he was [d]clean.

15 ¶ And he returned to the man of God, he and all his company, and came, and stood before him: and he said, Behold, now I [a]know that *there is* no [b]God in all the earth, but in Israel: now therefore, I pray thee, take a [c]blessing of thy servant.

16 But he said, *As* the LORD liveth, before whom I stand, I will [a]receive [b]none. And he urged him to take *it*; but he refused.

17 And Naaman said, Shall there not then, I pray thee, be given to thy servant two mules' burden of earth? for thy servant will henceforth offer neither burnt offering nor sacrifice unto other gods, but unto the LORD.

18 In this thing the LORD pardon thy servant, *that* when my master

---

5 1a TG Leprosy.
  5a 1 Sam. 9:7.
  7a Gen. 30:2.
    b 1 Kgs. 20:7.
  8a Alma 17:29 (29–30).
 10a John 9:11 (8–11).
    TG Wash.

     b TG Purification.
 13a 1 Ne. 16:29;
     Alma 37:7 (6–8), 41;
     D&C 64:33.
 14a 2 Ne. 31:7.
    b Job 33:25.
    c Luke 4:27.

     d TG Administrations to
       the Sick; Heal.
 15a Alma 24:27.
    b Dan. 2:47.
    c Gen. 14:21 (21–24).
 16a Mosiah 2:12 (11–12).
    b Dan. 5:17.

goeth into the house of ^aRimmon to worship there, and he leaneth on my hand, and I bow myself in the house of Rimmon: when I bow down myself in the house of Rimmon, the LORD pardon thy servant in this thing.

19 And he said unto him, Go in peace. So he departed from him a little way.

20 ¶ But Gehazi, the servant of Elisha the man of God, said, Behold, my master hath spared Naaman this Syrian, in not receiving at his hands that which he brought: but, *as* the LORD liveth, I will run after him, and take somewhat of him.

21 So Gehazi followed after Naaman. And when Naaman saw *him* running after him, he lighted down from the chariot to meet him, and said, *Is* all well?

22 And he said, All *is* well. My master hath sent me, saying, Behold, even now there be come to me from mount Ephraim two young men of the sons of the prophets: give them, I pray thee, a talent of silver, and two changes of garments.

23 And Naaman said, Be content, take two talents. And he urged him, and bound two talents of silver in two bags, with two changes of garments, and laid *them* upon two of his servants; and they bare *them* before him.

24 And when he came to the tower, he took *them* from their hand, and bestowed *them* in the house: and he let the men go, and they departed.

25 But he went in, and stood before his master. And Elisha said unto him, Whence *comest thou,* Gehazi? And he said, Thy servant went no whither.

26 And he said unto him, Went not mine heart *with thee,* when the man turned again from his chariot to meet thee? *Is it* a time to receive money, and to receive garments, and oliveyards, and vineyards, and sheep, and oxen, and menservants, and maidservants?

27 The ^aleprosy therefore of Naaman shall cleave unto thee, and unto thy seed for ever. And he went out from his presence a leper *as white as snow.*

CHAPTER 6

Elisha causes an ax to float—He reveals to the king how to conduct a war with Syria—Horses and chariots of fire protect Elisha—The Syrians are smitten with blindness—Benhadad besieges Samaria, and foodstuff sells for a great price.

AND the sons of the prophets said unto Elisha, Behold now, the place where we dwell with thee is too ^astrait for us.

2 Let us go, we pray thee, unto Jordan, and take thence every man a beam, and let us make us a place there, where we may dwell. And he answered, Go ye.

3 And one said, Be content, I pray thee, and go with thy servants. And he answered, I will go.

4 So he went with them. And when they came to Jordan, they cut down wood.

5 But as one was felling a beam, the axe head fell into the water: and he cried, and said, Alas, master! for it was ^aborrowed.

6 And the man of God said, Where fell it? And he shewed him the place. And he cut down a stick, and cast *it* in thither; and the iron did swim.

7 Therefore said he, Take *it* up to thee. And he put out his hand, and took it.

8 ¶ Then the king of Syria warred against Israel, and took counsel with his servants, saying, In such and such a place *shall be* my camp.

9 And the man of God sent unto the king of Israel, saying, Beware that thou pass not such a place; for thither the Syrians are come down.

10 And the king of Israel sent to the place which the man of God told him and warned him of, and saved himself there, not once nor twice.

18*a* IE a Syrian god of wind, rain, and storm.   27*a* TG Leprosy.   **6** 1*a* OR narrow.   5*a* TG Borrow.

11 Therefore the heart of the king of Syria was sore troubled for this thing; and he called his servants, and said unto them, Will ye not shew me which of us *is* for the king of Israel?

12 And one of his servants said, None, my lord, O king: but Elisha, the prophet that *is* in Israel, telleth the king of Israel the words that thou speakest in thy bedchamber.

13 ¶ And he said, Go and spy where he *is*, that I may send and fetch him. And it was told him, saying, Behold, *he is* in Dothan.

14 Therefore sent he thither horses, and chariots, and a great host: and they came by night, and compassed the city about.

15 And when the servant of the man of God was risen early, and gone forth, behold, an host compassed the city both with horses and chariots. And his servant said unto him, Alas, my master! how shall we do?

16 And he answered, Fear not: for they that *be* with us *are* more than they that *be* with them.

17 And Elisha prayed, and said, LORD, I pray thee, open his *a*eyes, that he may see. And the LORD opened the eyes of the young man; and he saw: and, behold, the mountain *was* full of horses and *b*chariots of fire round about Elisha.

18 And when they came down to him, Elisha prayed unto the LORD, and said, Smite this people, I pray thee, with *a*blindness. And he smote them with blindness according to the word of Elisha.

19 ¶ And Elisha said unto them, This *is* not the way, neither *is* this the city: follow me, and I will bring you to the man whom ye seek. But he led them to Samaria.

20 And it came to pass, when they were come into Samaria, that Elisha said, LORD, open the eyes of these *men*, that they may see. And the LORD *a*opened their eyes, and they saw; and, behold, *they were* in the midst of Samaria.

21 And the king of Israel said unto Elisha, when he saw them, My father, shall I smite *them*? shall I smite *them*?

22 And he answered, Thou shalt not smite *them:* wouldest thou *a*smite those whom thou hast taken captive with thy sword and with thy bow? set bread and water before them, that they may eat and drink, and go to their master.

23 And he prepared great provision for them: and when they had eaten and drunk, he sent them away, and they went to their master. So the bands of Syria came no more into the land of Israel.

24 ¶ And it came to pass after this, that *a*Ben-hadad king of Syria gathered all his host, and went up, and besieged Samaria.

25 And there was a great famine in Samaria: and, behold, they besieged it, until an ass's head was *sold* for fourscore *pieces* of silver, and the fourth part of a cab of dove's dung for five *pieces* of silver.

26 And as the king of Israel was passing by upon the wall, there cried a woman unto him, saying, Help, my lord, O king.

27 And he said, If the LORD do not help thee, whence shall I help thee? out of the barnfloor, or out of the winepress?

28 And the king said unto her, What aileth thee? And she answered, This woman said unto me, Give thy son, that we may eat him to day, and we will eat my son to morrow.

29 So we boiled my son, and did *a*eat him: and I said unto her on the next day, Give thy son, that we may eat him: and she hath hid her son.

30 ¶ And it came to pass, when the king heard the words of the woman, that he *a*rent his clothes; and he passed by upon the wall, and the

---

17*a* Num. 22:23.
  b 2 Kgs. 7:6 (5–6).
18*a* Gen. 19:11.

20*a* Gen. 21:19.
22*a* Rom. 12:20.
24*a* 1 Kgs. 20:2.

29*a* Deut. 28:53 (52–53).
30*a* 1 Kgs. 21:27.

people looked, and, behold, *he had* sackcloth within upon his flesh.

31 Then he said, God do so and more also to me, if the head of Elisha the son of Shaphat shall stand on him this day.

32 But Elisha sat in his house, and the elders sat with him; and *the king* sent a man from before him: but ere the messenger came to him, he said to the elders, See ye how this son of a *ᵃ*murderer hath sent to take away mine head? look, when the messenger cometh, shut the door, and hold him fast at the door: *is* not the sound of his master's feet behind him?

33 And while he yet talked with them, behold, the messenger came down unto him: and he said, Behold, this evil *is* of the LORD; what should I wait for the LORD any longer?

CHAPTER 7

Elisha prophesies incredible plenty in Samaria—The Syrian hosts flee at a noise of battle and leave their possessions—Israel takes spoil from the Syrians.

THEN Elisha said, Hear ye the word of the LORD; Thus saith the LORD, To morrow about this time *shall* a measure of fine flour *be sold* for a shekel, and two measures of barley for a shekel, in the gate of Samaria.

2 Then a *ᵃ*lord on whose hand the king leaned answered the man of God, and said, Behold, *if* the LORD would make *ᵇ*windows in heaven, might this thing be? And he said, Behold, thou shalt see *it* with thine eyes, but shalt not eat thereof.

3 ¶ And there were four leprous men at the entering in of the gate: and they said one to another, Why sit we here until we die?

4 If we say, We will enter into the city, then the famine *is* in the city, and we shall die there: and if we sit still here, we die also. Now therefore come, and let us fall unto the host of the Syrians: if they save us alive, we shall live; and if they kill us, we shall but die.

5 And they rose up in the twilight, to go unto the camp of the Syrians: and when they were come to the uttermost part of the camp of Syria, behold, *there was* no man there.

6 For the Lord had made the host of the Syrians to hear a noise of *ᵃ*chariots, and a noise of horses, *even* the noise of a great host: and they said one to another, Lo, the king of Israel hath hired against us the kings of the Hittites, and the kings of the Egyptians, to come upon us.

7 Wherefore they arose and fled in the twilight, and left their tents, and their horses, and their asses, even the camp as it *was*, and fled for their life.

8 And when these lepers came to the uttermost part of the camp, they went into one tent, and did eat and drink, and carried thence silver, and gold, and raiment, and went and hid *it*; and came again, and entered into another tent, and carried thence *also*, and went and hid *it*.

9 Then they said one to another, We do not well: this day *is* a day of good tidings, and we hold our peace: if we tarry till the morning light, some mischief will come upon us: now therefore come, that we may go and tell the king's household.

10 So they came and called unto the porter of the city: and they told them, saying, We came to the camp of the Syrians, and, behold, *there was* no man there, neither voice of man, but horses tied, and asses tied, and the tents as they *were*.

11 And he called the porters; and they told *it* to the king's house within.

12 ¶ And the king arose in the night, and said unto his servants, I will now shew you what the Syrians have done to us. They know that we *be* hungry; therefore are they gone out of the camp to hide themselves in the field, saying, When they come out of the city, we shall catch them alive, and get into the city.

13 And one of his servants

32*a* 1 Kgs. 18:4.
7 2*a* OR officer, aide.
b Mal. 3:10.
6*a* 2 Kgs. 6:17.

answered and said, Let *some* take, I pray thee, five of the horses that remain, which are left in the city, (behold, they *are* as all the multitude of Israel that are left in it: behold, *I say,* they *are* even as all the multitude of the Israelites that are consumed:) and let us send and see.

14 They took therefore two chariot horses; and the king sent after the host of the Syrians, saying, Go and see.

15 And they went after them unto Jordan: and, lo, all the way *was* full of garments and vessels, which the Syrians had cast away in their haste. And the messengers returned, and told the king.

16 And the people went out, and spoiled the tents of the Syrians. So a measure of fine flour was *sold* for a shekel, and two measures of barley for a shekel, according to the word of the LORD.

17 ¶ And the king appointed the lord on whose hand he leaned to have the charge of the gate: and the people trode upon him in the gate, and he died, as the man of God had said, who spake when the king came down to him.

18 And it came to pass as the man of God had spoken to the king, saying, Two measures of barley for a shekel, and a measure of fine flour for a shekel, shall be to morrow about this time in the gate of Samaria:

19 And that lord answered the man of God, and said, Now, behold, *if* the LORD should make windows in heaven, might such a thing be? And he said, Behold, thou shalt see it with thine eyes, but shalt not eat thereof.

20 And so it fell out unto him: for the people trode upon him in the gate, and he died.

CHAPTER 8

Elisha prophesies a seven-year famine— The Shunammite woman is preserved through the famine—Jehoram and then Ahaziah reign in wickedness in Judah.

THEN spake Elisha unto the woman, whose son he had [a]restored to life, saying, Arise, and go thou and thine household, and sojourn wheresoever thou canst sojourn: for the LORD hath called for a [b]famine; and it shall also come upon the land seven years.

2 And the woman arose, and did after the saying of the man of God: and she went with her household, and sojourned in the land of the Philistines seven years.

3 And it came to pass at the seven years' end, that the woman returned out of the land of the Philistines: and she went forth to cry unto the king for her house and for her land.

4 And the king talked with Gehazi the servant of the man of God, saying, Tell me, I pray thee, all the great things that Elisha hath done.

5 And it came to pass, as he was telling the king how he had restored a dead body to life, that, behold, the woman, whose son he had restored to life, cried to the king for her house and for her land. And Gehazi said, My lord, O king, this *is* the woman, and this *is* her son, whom Elisha restored to life.

6 And when the king asked the woman, she told him. So the king appointed unto her a certain officer, saying, Restore all that *was* hers, and all the fruits of the field since the day that she left the land, even until now.

7 ¶ And Elisha came to Damascus; and Ben-hadad the king of Syria was sick; and it was told him, saying, The man of God is come hither.

8 And the king said unto Hazael, Take a present in thine hand, and go, meet the man of God, and inquire of the LORD by him, saying, Shall I recover of this disease?

---

8 1a 2 Kgs. 4:35 (32–35); | John 11:44 (43–44). | b TG Famine.

9 So Hazael went to meet him, and took a present with him, even of every good thing of Damascus, forty camels' burden, and came and stood before him, and said, Thy son Ben-hadad king of Syria hath sent me to thee, saying, Shall I recover of this disease?

10 And Elisha said unto him, Go, say unto him, Thou mayest certainly recover: howbeit the LORD hath shewed me that he shall surely die.

11 And he settled his countenance steadfastly, until he was ashamed: and the man of God wept.

12 And ªHazael said, Why weepeth my lord? And he answered, Because I know the evil that thou wilt do unto the children of Israel: their strong holds wilt thou set on fire, and their young men wilt thou slay with the sword, and wilt dash their children, and rip up their women with child.

13 And Hazael said, But what, is thy servant a dog, that he should do this great thing? And Elisha answered, The LORD hath shewed me that thou shalt be ªking over Syria.

14 So he departed from Elisha, and came to his master; who said to him, What said Elisha to thee? And he answered, He told me that thou shouldest surely recover.

15 And it came to pass on the morrow, that he took a thick cloth, and dipped it in water, and spread it on his face, so that he died: and Hazael reigned in his stead.

16 ¶ And in the fifth year of Joram the son of Ahab king of Israel, Jehoshaphat being then king of Judah, Jehoram the son of Jehoshaphat king of Judah began to reign.

17 Thirty and two years old was he when he began to reign; and he reigned eight years in Jerusalem.

18 And he walked in the way of the kings of Israel, as did the house of Ahab: for the daughter of Ahab was his wife: and he did evil in the sight of the LORD.

19 Yet the LORD would not ªdestroy Judah for ᵇDavid his servant's sake, as he promised him to give him alway a light, and to his children.

20 ¶ In his days Edom ªrevolted from under the ᵇhand of Judah, and made a king over themselves.

21 So Joram went over to Zair, and all the chariots with him: and he rose by night, and smote the Edomites which compassed him about, and the captains of the chariots: and the people fled into their tents.

22 Yet Edom revolted from under the hand of Judah unto this day. Then Libnah revolted at the same time.

23 And the rest of the acts of Joram, and all that he did, are they not written in the book of the chronicles of the kings of Judah?

24 And Joram slept with his fathers, and was buried with his fathers in the city of David: and Ahaziah his son reigned in his stead.

25 ¶ In the twelfth year of Joram the son of Ahab king of Israel did Ahaziah the son of Jehoram king of Judah begin to reign.

26 Two and twenty years old was ªAhaziah when he began to reign; and he reigned one year in Jerusalem. And his mother's name was Athaliah, the daughter of Omri king of Israel.

27 And he walked in the way of the house of Ahab, and did evil in the sight of the LORD, as did the house of Ahab: for he was the son in law of the house of Ahab.

28 ¶ And he went with ªJoram the son of Ahab to the war against Hazael king of Syria in Ramoth-gilead; and the Syrians wounded Joram.

29 And king Joram went back to be healed in Jezreel of the wounds which the Syrians had given him at Ramah, when he fought against Hazael king of Syria. And Ahaziah the son of Jehoram king of Judah went down to see Joram the son of Ahab in Jezreel, because he was sick.

12a 2 Kgs. 10:32; 13:3;
    Amos 1:4 (3–4).
13a 1 Kgs. 19:15.

19a 2 Chr. 21:7 (5–10).
  b 2 Sam. 7:16 (11–17).
20a Gen. 27:40.

  b TG Bondage, Physical.
26a 2 Chr. 22:2.
28a 2 Chr. 22:5 (5–6).

CHAPTER 9

A prophet anoints Jehu king over Israel and prophesies the destruction of the house of Ahab and the death of Jezebel—Jehu kills Joram in the field of Naboth—Jezebel is killed by Jehu and is eaten by dogs.

AND Elisha the prophet called one of the children of the prophets, and said unto him, Gird up thy loins, and take this box of oil in thine hand, and go to Ramoth-gilead:

2 And when thou comest thither, look out there Jehu the son of Jehoshaphat the son of Nimshi, and go in, and make him arise up from among his brethren, and carry him to an inner chamber;

3 Then take the box of oil, and pour *it* on his head, and say, Thus saith the LORD, I have anointed thee king over Israel. Then open the door, and flee, and tarry not.

4 ¶ So the young man, *even* the young man the prophet, went to Ramoth-gilead.

5 And when he came, behold, the captains of the host *were* sitting; and he said, I have an errand to thee, O captain. And Jehu said, Unto which of all us? And he said, To thee, O captain.

6 And he arose, and went into the house; and he poured the ªoil on his head, and said unto him, Thus saith the LORD God of Israel, I have anointed thee king over the people of the LORD, *even* over Israel.

7 And thou shalt ªsmite the house of Ahab thy master, that I may avenge the blood of my servants the prophets, and the blood of all the servants of the LORD, at the hand of ᵇJezebel.

8 For the whole house of ªAhab shall perish: and I will cut off from Ahab him that pisseth against the wall, and him that is shut up and left in Israel:

9 And I will make the house of Ahab like the house of ªJeroboam the son of Nebat, and like the house of ᵇBaasha the son of Ahijah:

10 And the ªdogs shall eat Jezebel in the portion of Jezreel, and *there shall be* none to bury *her*. And he opened the door, and fled.

11 ¶ Then Jehu came forth to the servants of his lord: and *one* said unto him, Is all well? wherefore came this mad *fellow* to thee? And he said unto them, Ye know the man, and his communication.

12 And they said, *It is* false; tell us now. And he said, Thus and thus spake he to me, saying, Thus saith the LORD, I have anointed thee king over Israel.

13 Then they hasted, and took every man his garment, and put *it* under him on the top of the stairs, and blew with trumpets, saying, Jehu is king.

14 So Jehu the son of Jehoshaphat the son of Nimshi conspired against Joram. (Now Joram had kept Ramoth-gilead, he and all Israel, because of Hazael king of Syria.

15 But king Joram was returned to be healed in Jezreel of the wounds which the Syrians had given him, when he fought with Hazael king of Syria.) And Jehu said, If it be your minds, *then* let none go forth *nor* escape out of the city to go to tell *it* in Jezreel.

16 So Jehu rode in a chariot, and went to Jezreel; for Joram lay there. And Ahaziah king of Judah was come down to see Joram.

17 And there stood a watchman on the tower in Jezreel, and he spied the company of Jehu as he came, and said, I see a company. And Joram said, Take an horseman, and send to meet them, and let him say, *Is it* peace?

18 So there went one on horseback to meet him, and said, Thus saith the king, *Is it* peace? And Jehu said, What hast thou to do with peace? turn thee behind me. And the watchman told, saying,

---

9 6a 2 Chr. 22:7 (7–9).
　7a 2 Kgs. 9:24 (21–25),
　　 33 (30–37); 10:8 (8–11).
　　　　　b 1 Kgs. 18:4.
　　　　　8a 1 Kgs. 21:21;
　　　　　　 2 Kgs. 10:17.
　　　　　　　　9a 1 Kgs. 14:10.
　　　　　　　　　b 1 Kgs. 16:3 (3, 11).
　　　　　　　　10a 2 Kgs. 9:36 (35–36).

The messenger came to them, but he cometh not again.

19 Then he sent out a second on horseback, which came to them, and said, Thus saith the king, *Is it* peace? And Jehu answered, What hast thou to do with peace? turn thee behind me.

20 And the watchman told, saying, He came even unto them, and cometh not again: and the driving *is* like the driving of Jehu the son of Nimshi; for he driveth furiously.

21 And Joram said, Make ready. And his chariot was made ready. And Joram king of Israel and Ahaziah king of Judah went out, each in his chariot, and they went out against Jehu, and met him in the portion of Naboth the Jezreelite.

22 And it came to pass, when Joram saw Jehu, that he said, *Is it* peace, Jehu? And he answered, What peace, so long as the whoredoms of thy mother Jezebel and her witchcrafts *are so* many?

23 And Joram turned his hands, and fled, and said to Ahaziah, *There is* treachery, O Ahaziah.

24 And Jehu drew a bow with his full strength, and ^asmote Jehoram between his arms, and the arrow went out at his heart, and he sunk down in his chariot.

25 Then said *Jehu* to Bidkar his captain, Take up, *and* cast him in the portion of the field of Naboth the Jezreelite: for remember how that, when I and thou rode together after Ahab his father, the LORD laid this burden upon him;

26 Surely I have seen yesterday the blood of Naboth, and the blood of his sons, saith the LORD; and I will requite thee in this plat, saith the LORD. Now therefore take *and* cast him into the plat *of ground*, according to the word of the LORD.

27 ¶ But when Ahaziah the king of Judah saw *this*, he fled by the way of the garden house. And Jehu followed after him, and said, ^aSmite him also in the chariot. *And they did*

so at the going up to Gur, which *is* by Ibleam. And he fled to Megiddo, and died there.

28 And his servants carried him in a chariot to Jerusalem, and buried him in his sepulchre with his fathers in the city of David.

29 And in the eleventh year of Joram the son of Ahab began Ahaziah to reign over Judah.

30 ¶ And when Jehu was come to Jezreel, Jezebel heard *of it*; and she painted her face, and ^atired her head, and looked out at a window.

31 And as Jehu entered in at the gate, she said, Had ^aZimri peace, who slew his master?

32 And he lifted up his face to the window, and said, Who *is* on my side? who? And there looked out to him two *or* three eunuchs.

33 And he said, Throw her down. So they ^athrew her down: and *some* of her blood was sprinkled on the wall, and on the horses: and he trode her under foot.

34 And when he was come in, he did eat and drink, and said, Go, see now this cursed *woman,* and bury her: for she *is* a king's ^adaughter.

35 And they went to bury her: but they found no more of her than the skull, and the feet, and the palms of *her* hands.

36 Wherefore they came again, and told him. And he said, This *is* the word of the LORD, which he spake by his servant Elijah the Tishbite, saying, In the portion of Jezreel shall ^adogs eat the flesh of Jezebel:

37 And the carcase of Jezebel shall be as dung upon the face of the field in the portion of Jezreel; *so* that they shall not say, This *is* Jezebel.

CHAPTER 10

Ahab's seventy sons are slain—Jehu destroys the house of Ahab and all the worshippers of Baal, but he continues to worship the golden calves in Bethel and Dan.

24*a* 2 Kgs. 9:7 (1–7).
27*a* 2 Chr. 22:9.
30*a* HEB adorned.

31*a* 1 Kgs. 16:10 (9–10).
33*a* 2 Kgs. 9:7 (1–7).
34*a* 1 Kgs. 16:31.

36*a* 1 Kgs. 21:23;
      2 Kgs. 9:10.

AND Ahab had seventy sons in Samaria. And Jehu wrote letters, and sent to Samaria, unto the rulers of Jezreel, to the elders, and to them that brought up Ahab's *children,* saying,

2 Now as soon as this letter cometh to you, seeing your master's sons *are* with you, and *there are* with you chariots and horses, a fenced city also, and armour;

3 Look even out the best and meetest of your master's sons, and set *him* on his father's throne, and fight for your master's house.

4 But they were exceedingly afraid, and said, Behold, two kings stood not before him: how then shall we stand?

5 And he that *was* over the house, and he that *was* over the city, the elders also, and the bringers up *of the children,* sent to Jehu, saying, We *are* thy servants, and will do all that thou shalt bid us; we will not make any king: do thou *that which is* good in thine eyes.

6 Then he wrote a letter the second time to them, saying, If ye *be* mine, and *if* ye will hearken unto my voice, take ye the heads of the men your master's sons, and come to me to Jezreel by to morrow this time. Now the king's sons, *being* seventy persons, *were* with the great men of the city, which brought them up.

7 And it came to pass, when the letter came to them, that they took the king's sons, and slew seventy persons, and put their heads in baskets, and sent him *them* to Jezreel.

8 ¶ And there came a messenger, and told him, saying, They have brought the ᵃheads of the king's sons. And he said, Lay ye them in two heaps at the entering in of the gate until the morning.

9 And it came to pass in the morning, that he went out, and stood, and said to all the people, Ye *be* righteous: behold, I ᵃconspired against my master, and slew all these?

10 Know now that there shall ᵃfall unto the earth nothing of the word of the LORD, which the LORD spake concerning the house of Ahab: for the LORD hath done *that* which he spake by his servant Elijah.

11 So ᵃJehu slew all that remained of the house of Ahab in Jezreel, and all his great men, and his kinsfolks, and his priests, until he left him none remaining.

12 ¶ And he arose and departed, and came to Samaria. *And* as he *was* at the shearing house in the way,

13 Jehu met with the brethren of Ahaziah king of Judah, and said, Who *are* ye? And they answered, We *are* the brethren of Ahaziah; and we go down to salute the children of the king and the children of the queen.

14 And he said, Take them alive. And they took them alive, and slew them at the pit of the shearing house, *even* two and forty men; neither left he any of them.

15 ¶ And when he was departed thence, he lighted on ᵃJehonadab the son of ᵇRechab *coming* to meet him: and he saluted him, and said to him, Is thine heart right, as my heart *is* with thy heart? And Jehonadab answered, It is. If it be, give *me* thine hand. And he gave *him* his hand; and he took him up to him into the chariot.

16 And he said, Come with me, and see my zeal for the LORD. So they made him ride in his chariot.

17 And when he came to Samaria, he slew all that remained unto ᵃAhab in Samaria, till he had destroyed him, according to the saying of the LORD, which he spake to Elijah.

18 ¶ And Jehu gathered all the people together, and said unto them, ᵃAhab served Baal a little; *but* Jehu shall serve him much.

19 Now therefore call unto me all the prophets of Baal, all his

---

10 8*a* 2 Kgs. 9:7 (1–7).
9*a* TG Conspiracy.
10*a* 1 Sam. 3:19;

Alma 37:17; D&C 1:38.
11*a* Hosea 1:4.
15*a* Jer. 35:6.

b 1 Chr. 2:55; Jer. 35:2.
17*a* 2 Kgs. 9:8.
18*a* 1 Kgs. 16:31 (31–33).

servants, and all his priests; let none be wanting: for I have a great sacrifice *to do* to Baal; whosoever shall be wanting, he shall not live. But Jehu did *it* in subtilty, to the intent that he might destroy the worshippers of Baal.

20 And Jehu said, Proclaim a ᵃsolemn assembly for Baal. And they proclaimed *it*.

21 And Jehu sent through all Israel: and all the worshippers of Baal came, so that there was not a man left that came not. And they came into the house of Baal; and the house of Baal was full from one end to another.

22 And he said unto him that *was* over the vestry, Bring forth ᵃvestments for all the worshippers of Baal. And he brought them forth vestments.

23 And Jehu went, and Jehonadab the son of Rechab, into the house of Baal, and said unto the worshippers of Baal, Search, and look that there be here with you none of the servants of the LORD, but the worshippers of Baal only.

24 And when they went in to offer sacrifices and burnt offerings, Jehu appointed fourscore men without, and said, *If* any of the men whom I have brought into your hands escape, *he that letteth him go*, his ᵃlife *shall be* for the life of him.

25 And it came to pass, as soon as he had made an end of offering the burnt offering, that Jehu said to the guard and to the captains, Go in, *and* slay them; let none come forth. And they smote them with the edge of the sword; and the guard and the captains cast *them* out, and went to the city of the house of Baal.

26 And they brought forth the images out of the house of Baal, and burned them.

27 And they brake down the image of Baal, and brake down the ᵃhouse of Baal, and made it a draught house unto this day.

28 Thus Jehu destroyed Baal out of Israel.

29 ¶ Howbeit *from* the sins of ᵃJeroboam the son of Nebat, who made Israel to ᵇsin, Jehu departed not from after them, *to wit*, the golden ᶜcalves that *were* in Beth-el, and that *were* in Dan.

30 And the LORD said unto Jehu, Because thou hast done well in executing *that which is* right in mine eyes, *and* hast done unto the house of Ahab according to all that *was* in mine heart, thy children of the fourth *generation* shall sit on the ᵃthrone of Israel.

31 But Jehu took no heed to ᵃwalk in the law of the LORD God of Israel with all his heart: for he departed not from the sins of Jeroboam, which made Israel to sin.

32 ¶ In those days the LORD began to cut Israel short: and ᵃHazael smote them in all the coasts of Israel;

33 From Jordan eastward, all the land of Gilead, the Gadites, and the Reubenites, and the Manassites, from ᵃAroer, which *is* by the river Arnon, even Gilead and Bashan.

34 Now the rest of the acts of Jehu, and all that he did, and all his might, *are* they not written in the book of the chronicles of the kings of Israel?

35 And Jehu slept with his fathers: and they buried him in Samaria. And Jehoahaz his son reigned in his stead.

36 And the time that Jehu reigned over Israel in Samaria *was* twenty and eight years.

CHAPTER 11

Athaliah destroys the royal family in Judah and reigns herself in Judah—Joash is preserved and crowned king when seven years old—Jehoiada the priest destroys the house of Baal.

20*a* TG Solemn Assembly.
22*a* IE ceremonial robes.
24*a* 1 Kgs. 20:42.
27*a* 1 Kgs. 16:32 (31–33).
29*a* 1 Kgs. 14:16;

2 Kgs. 13:2 (1–2, 11); 14:24; 15:9 (9, 18, 24).
b Alma 46:9 (8–9).
c 1 Kgs. 12:28 (28–29).
30*a* 2 Kgs. 15:12.

31*a* TG Walking in Darkness.
32*a* 2 Kgs. 8:12; 13:3; Amos 1:4 (3–4).
33*a* Deut. 2:36.

AND when ^aAthaliah the mother of Ahaziah saw that her son was dead, she arose and destroyed all the seed royal.

2 But Jehosheba, the daughter of king Joram, sister of Ahaziah, took Joash the son of Ahaziah, and stole him from among the king's sons *which were* slain; and they hid him, *even* him and his nurse, in the bedchamber from Athaliah, so that he was not slain.

3 And he was with her hid in the house of the LORD six years. And Athaliah did reign over the land.

4 ¶ And the seventh year Jehoiada sent and fetched the rulers over hundreds, with the captains and the guard, and brought them to him into the house of the LORD, and made a ^acovenant with them, and took an oath of them in the house of the LORD, and shewed them the king's son.

5 And he commanded them, saying, This *is* the thing that ye shall do; A third part of you that enter in on the ^asabbath shall even be keepers of the watch of the king's house;

6 And a third part *shall be* at the ^agate of Sur; and a third part at the gate behind the guard: so shall ye keep the watch of the house, that it be not broken down.

7 And two parts of all you that go forth on the sabbath, even they shall keep the watch of the house of the LORD about the king.

8 And ye shall compass the king round about, every man with his weapons in his hand: and he that cometh within the ranges, let him be slain: and be ye with the king as he goeth out and as he cometh in.

9 And the captains over the hundreds did according to all *things* that Jehoiada the priest commanded: and they took every man his men that were to come in on the sabbath, with them that should go out on the sabbath, and came to Jehoiada the priest.

10 And to the captains over hundreds did the priest give king David's spears and ^ashields, that *were* in the temple of the LORD.

11 And the guard stood, every man with his weapons in his hand, round about the king, from the right corner of the temple to the left corner of the temple, *along* by the altar and the temple.

12 And he brought forth the king's son, and put the crown upon him, and *gave him* the ^atestimony; and they made him king, and anointed him; and they clapped their hands, and said, ^bGod save the king.

13 ¶ And when Athaliah heard the noise of the guard *and* of the people, she came to the people into the temple of the LORD.

14 And when she looked, behold, the king stood by a ^apillar, as the manner *was*, and the princes and the trumpeters by the king, and all the people of the land rejoiced, and blew with trumpets: and Athaliah rent her clothes, and cried, Treason, Treason.

15 But Jehoiada the priest commanded the captains of the hundreds, the officers of the host, and said unto them, Have her forth without the ranges: and him that followeth her kill with the sword. For the priest had said, Let her not be slain in the house of the LORD.

16 And they laid hands on her; and she went by the way by the which the ^ahorses came into the king's house: and there was she slain.

17 ¶ And Jehoiada made a covenant between the LORD and the king and the people, that they should be the LORD's people; between the king also and the people.

18 And all the people of the land went into the house of Baal, and brake it down; his altars and his images brake they in pieces thoroughly, and slew Mattan the priest of Baal before the altars. And the priest appointed officers over the house of the LORD.

---

11 1*a* 2 Chr. 22:10 (10–12).
4*a* 2 Chr. 23:1.
5*a* 1 Chr. 9:25.

6*a* 2 Chr. 23:5.
10*a* 2 Sam. 8:7.
12*a* Ex. 25:16.

b HEB May the king live!
14*a* 2 Kgs. 23:3.
16*a* 2 Chr. 23:15.

19 And he took the rulers over hundreds, and the captains, and the guard, and all the people of the land; and they brought down the king from the house of the LORD, and came by the way of the gate of the guard to the king's house. And he sat on the throne of the kings.

20 And all the people of the land rejoiced, and the city was in quiet: and they slew Athaliah with the sword *beside* the king's house.

21 Seven years old *was* Jehoash when he began to reign.

CHAPTER 12

Jehoash (Joash) reigns in righteousness—The breaches in the temple are repaired—The safety of Jerusalem is purchased with the hallowed things in the temple—Joash is slain and Amaziah reigns.

IN the seventh year of Jehu Jehoash began to reign; and forty years reigned he in Jerusalem. And his mother's name *was* Zibiah of Beersheba.

2 And Jehoash did *that which was* right in the sight of the LORD all his days wherein Jehoiada the priest instructed him.

3 But the ^ahigh places were not taken away: the people still sacrificed and burnt incense in the high places.

4 ¶ And Jehoash said to the priests, All the ^amoney of the dedicated things that is brought into the house of the LORD, *even* the money of every one that passeth *the account,* the money that every man is set at, *and* all the money that cometh into any man's heart to bring into the house of the LORD,

5 Let the priests take *it* to them, every man of his acquaintance: and let them repair the breaches of the house, wheresoever any breach shall be found.

6 But it was *so, that* in the three and twentieth year of king Jehoash the priests had not repaired the ^abreaches of the house.

7 Then king Jehoash called for Jehoiada the priest, and the *other* priests, and said unto them, Why repair ye not the breaches of the house? now therefore receive no *more* money of your acquaintance, but deliver it for the breaches of the house.

8 And the priests consented to receive no *more* money of the people, neither to repair the breaches of the house.

9 But Jehoiada the priest took a chest, and bored a hole in the lid of it, and set it beside the altar, on the right side as one cometh into the house of the LORD: and the priests that kept the door put therein all the money *that was* brought into the house of the LORD.

10 And it was *so,* when they saw that *there was* much money in the chest, that the king's scribe and the high priest came up, and they put up in bags, and told the ^amoney that was found in the house of the LORD.

11 And they gave the money, being told, into the hands of them that did the work, that had the oversight of the house of the LORD: and they laid it out to the carpenters and builders, that wrought upon the house of the LORD,

12 And to masons, and hewers of stone, and to buy timber and hewed stone to repair the breaches of the house of the LORD, and for all that was laid out for the house to repair *it.*

13 Howbeit there were not made for the house of the LORD ^abowls of silver, snuffers, basins, trumpets, any vessels of gold, or vessels of silver, of the money *that was* brought into the house of the LORD:

14 But they gave that to the workmen, and repaired therewith the house of the LORD.

15 Moreover they ^areckoned not with the men, into whose hand they

---

12 3*a* Deut. 12:2 (2–3).
4*a* Ex. 30:12;
2 Kgs. 22:4 (4–7).
6*a* OR gaps, holes.
10*a* 2 Chr. 24:11.
13*a* 2 Chr. 24:14.
15*a* 2 Kgs. 22:7 (6–7).

delivered the money to be bestowed on workmen: for they dealt faithfully.

16 The [a]trespass money and [b]sin money was not brought into the house of the LORD: it was the priests'.

17 ¶ Then Hazael king of Syria went up, and fought against Gath, and took it: and Hazael set his face to go up to Jerusalem.

18 And Jehoash king of Judah took all the hallowed things that Jehoshaphat, and Jehoram, and Ahaziah, his fathers, kings of Judah, had dedicated, and his own [a]hallowed things, and all the gold *that was* found in the treasures of the house of the LORD, and in the king's house, and sent *it* to Hazael king of Syria: and he went away from Jerusalem.

19 ¶ And the rest of the acts of Joash, and all that he did, *are* they not written in the book of the chronicles of the kings of Judah?

20 And his servants arose, and made a conspiracy, and [a]slew Joash in the house of [b]Millo, which goeth down to Silla.

21 For Jozachar the son of Shimeath, and Jehozabad the son of Shomer, his servants, smote him, and he died; and they buried him with his fathers in the city of David: and Amaziah his son reigned in his stead.

CHAPTER 13

Jehoahaz and his successors reign in wickedness in Israel—Elisha prophesies that Joash will defeat Syria—Elisha dies—A dead Israelite is restored to life after touching Elisha's bones.

IN the three and twentieth year of Joash the son of Ahaziah king of Judah Jehoahaz the son of Jehu began to reign over Israel in Samaria, *and reigned* seventeen years.

2 And he did *that which was* evil in the sight of the LORD, and followed the sins of [a]Jeroboam the son of Nebat, which made Israel to sin; he departed not therefrom.

3 ¶ And the [a]anger of the LORD was kindled against Israel, and he delivered them into the hand of [b]Hazael king of Syria, and into the hand of Ben-hadad the son of Hazael, all *their* days.

4 And Jehoahaz [a]besought the LORD, and the LORD hearkened unto him: for he saw the [b]oppression of Israel, because the king of Syria oppressed them.

5 (And the LORD gave Israel a [a]saviour, so that they went out from under the hand of the Syrians: and the children of Israel dwelt in their tents, as beforetime.

6 Nevertheless they departed not from the [a]sins of the house of Jeroboam, who made Israel sin, *but* walked therein: and there remained the grove also in Samaria.)

7 Neither did he leave of the people to Jehoahaz but fifty horsemen, and ten chariots, and ten thousand footmen; for the king of Syria had destroyed them, and had made them like the dust by [a]threshing.

8 ¶ Now the rest of the acts of Jehoahaz, and all that he did, and his might, *are* they not written in the book of the chronicles of the kings of Israel?

9 And Jehoahaz slept with his fathers; and they buried him in Samaria: and Joash his son reigned in his stead.

10 ¶ In the thirty and seventh year of Joash king of Judah began Jehoash the son of Jehoahaz to reign over Israel in Samaria, *and reigned* sixteen years.

16a Lev. 5:15 (15–16).
  b Lev. 4:23 (22–26); 7:7.
18a 1 Kgs. 15:18 (18–22).
20a 2 Kgs. 14:5 (5–6).
  b 2 Sam. 5:9;
    1 Kgs. 9:15 (15, 24);
    11:27;

2 Chr. 32:5.
13 2a 1 Kgs. 14:16;
    2 Kgs. 10:29; 14:24;
    15:9 (9, 18, 24).
  3a TG God, Indignation of.
  b 2 Kgs. 8:12; 10:32;

Amos 1:4 (3–4).
4a 1 Ne. 18:20 (18–20).
  b TG Oppression.
5a OR deliverer.
6a 1 Kgs. 16:33.
7a Amos 1:3.

11 And he did *that which was* evil in the sight of the LORD; he departed not from all the sins of Jeroboam the son of Nebat, who made Israel sin: *but* he walked therein.

12 And the rest of the acts of Joash, and all that he did, and his might wherewith he fought against Amaziah king of Judah, *are* they not written in the book of the chronicles of the kings of Israel?

13 And Joash slept with his fathers; and Jeroboam sat upon his throne: and Joash was buried in Samaria with the kings of Israel.

14 ¶ Now Elisha was fallen sick of his sickness whereof he died. And Joash the king of Israel came down unto him, and wept over his face, and said, O my father, my father, the chariot of Israel, and the horsemen thereof.

15 And Elisha said unto him, Take bow and arrows. And he took unto him bow and arrows.

16 And he said to the king of Israel, Put thine hand upon the bow. And he put his hand *upon it:* and Elisha put his hands upon the king's hands.

17 And he said, Open the window eastward. And he opened *it*. Then Elisha said, Shoot. And he shot. And he said, The arrow of the LORD's deliverance, and the arrow of deliverance from Syria: for thou shalt smite the Syrians in Aphek, till thou have consumed *them*.

18 And he said, Take the arrows. And he took *them*. And he said unto the king of Israel, Smite upon the ground. And he smote thrice, and [a]stayed.

19 And the man of God was wroth with him, and said, Thou shouldest have smitten five or six times; then hadst thou smitten Syria till thou hadst consumed *it*: whereas now thou shalt smite Syria *but* thrice.

20 ¶ And Elisha died, and they buried him. And the bands of the Moabites invaded the land at the coming in of the year.

21 And it came to pass, as they were burying a man, that, behold, they spied a band *of men;* and they cast the man into the sepulchre of Elisha: and when the man was let down, and touched the bones of Elisha, he revived, and stood up on his feet.

22 ¶ But Hazael king of Syria oppressed Israel all the days of Jehoahaz.

23 And the LORD was gracious unto them, and had [a]compassion on them, and had respect unto them, because of his [b]covenant with Abraham, Isaac, and Jacob, and would not destroy them, neither cast he them from his presence as yet.

24 So Hazael king of Syria died; and Ben-hadad his son reigned in his stead.

25 And Jehoash the son of Jehoahaz took again out of the hand of Ben-hadad the son of Hazael the cities, which he had taken out of the hand of Jehoahaz his father by war. Three times did Joash beat him, and recovered the cities of Israel.

CHAPTER 14

Amaziah reigns well in Judah—Israel defeats Judah in battle—Jeroboam reigns in wickedness in Israel.

IN the second year of Joash son of Jehoahaz king of Israel reigned Amaziah the son of Joash king of Judah.

2 He was twenty and five years old when he began to reign, and reigned twenty and nine years in Jerusalem. And his mother's name *was* Jehoaddan of Jerusalem.

3 And he did *that which was* right in the sight of the LORD, yet not like David his father: he did according to all things as Joash his father did.

4 Howbeit the high places were not taken away: as yet the people did sacrifice and burnt incense on the high places.

5 ¶ And it came to pass, as soon as the kingdom was confirmed in his hand, that he slew his servants

---

18*a* HEB ceased, stopped. | 23*a* TG Compassion. | *b* Ex. 32:13.

which had ^aslain the king his father.

6 But the children of the murderers he slew not: according unto that which is written in the book of the law of Moses, wherein the LORD commanded, saying, The fathers shall not be put to death for the children, nor the children be put to death for the fathers; but every man shall be put to ^adeath for his ^bown ^csin.

7 He slew of Edom in the valley of ^asalt ten thousand, and took Selah by war, and called the name of it Joktheel unto this day.

8 ¶ Then Amaziah sent messengers to Jehoash, the son of Jehoahaz son of Jehu, king of Israel, saying, Come, let us look one another in the face.

9 And Jehoash the king of Israel sent to Amaziah king of Judah, saying, The thistle that *was* in Lebanon sent to the cedar that *was* in Lebanon, saying, Give thy daughter to my son to wife: and there passed by a wild beast that *was* in Lebanon, and trode down the thistle.

10 Thou hast indeed smitten Edom, and thine heart hath ^alifted thee up: glory *of this*, and tarry at home: for why shouldest thou meddle to *thy* hurt, that thou shouldest fall, *even* thou, and Judah with thee?

11 But Amaziah would not hear. Therefore Jehoash king of Israel went up; and he and Amaziah king of Judah looked one another in the face at Beth-shemesh, which *belongeth* to Judah.

12 And Judah was put to the worse before Israel; and they fled every man to their tents.

13 And Jehoash king of Israel took Amaziah king of Judah, the son of Jehoash the son of Ahaziah, at Beth-shemesh, and came to Jerusalem, and brake down the wall of Jerusalem from the gate of Ephraim unto the corner gate, four hundred cubits.

14 And he took all the gold and silver, and all the vessels that were found in the house of the LORD, and in the treasures of the king's house, and hostages, and returned to Samaria.

15 ¶ Now the rest of the acts of Jehoash which he did, and his might, and how he fought with Amaziah king of Judah, *are* they not written in the book of the chronicles of the kings of Israel?

16 And Jehoash slept with his fathers, and was buried in Samaria with the kings of Israel; and Jeroboam his son reigned in his stead.

17 ¶ And Amaziah the son of Joash king of Judah lived after the death of Jehoash son of Jehoahaz king of Israel fifteen years.

18 And the rest of the acts of Amaziah, *are* they not written in the book of the chronicles of the kings of Judah?

19 Now they made a conspiracy against him in Jerusalem: and he fled to Lachish; but they sent after him to Lachish, and slew him there.

20 And they brought him on horses: and he was buried at Jerusalem with his fathers in the city of David.

21 ¶ And all the people of Judah took Azariah, which *was* sixteen years old, and made him king instead of his father Amaziah.

22 He built ^aElath, and restored it to Judah, after that the king slept with his fathers.

23 ¶ In the fifteenth year of Amaziah the son of Joash king of Judah Jeroboam the son of Joash king of Israel began to reign in Samaria, *and reigned* forty and one years.

24 And he did *that which was* evil in the sight of the LORD: he departed not from all the sins of ^aJeroboam the son of Nebat, who made Israel to sin.

25 He restored the coast of Israel from the entering of Hamath unto the sea of the plain, according to the

---

14 5*a* 2 Kgs. 12:20.
  6*a* TG Punish.
    b TG Accountability.
    c TG Sin.

7*a* 2 Sam. 8:13.
10*a* Deut. 8:14; Jacob 2:13;
    Alma 1:32; 31:25;
    Morm. 8:28.

22*a* 1 Kgs. 9:26.
24*a* 1 Kgs. 14:16;
    2 Kgs. 10:29; 13:2
    (1–2, 11); 15:9 (9, 18, 24).

word of the L ORD God of Israel, which he spake by the hand of his servant *Jonah, the son of Amittai, the prophet, which *was* of Gath-hepher.

26 For the L ORD saw the affliction of Israel, *that it was* very bitter: for *there was* not any shut up, nor any left, nor any helper for Israel.

27 And the L ORD said not that he would blot out the name of Israel from under heaven: but he saved them by the hand of Jeroboam the son of Joash.

28 ¶ Now the rest of the acts of Jeroboam, and all that he did, and his might, how he warred, and how he recovered Damascus, and Hamath, *which belonged* to Judah, for Israel, *are* they not written in the book of the chronicles of the kings of Israel?

29 And Jeroboam slept with his fathers, *even* with the kings of Israel; and Zachariah his son reigned in his stead.

CHAPTER 15

Many kings reign in Israel and in Judah—Their wickedness, wars, conspiracies, and evils are described—Much of Israel is carried captive to Assyria by Tiglath-pileser.

I N the twenty and seventh year of Jeroboam king of Israel began Azariah son of Amaziah king of Judah to reign.

2 Sixteen years old was he when he began to reign, and he reigned two and fifty years in Jerusalem. And his mother's name *was* Jecholiah of Jerusalem.

3 And he did *that which was* right in the sight of the L ORD, according to all that his father Amaziah had done;

4 Save that the high places were not removed: the people sacrificed and burnt incense still on the high places.

5 ¶ And the L ORD smote the king, so that he was a *leper unto the day of his death, and dwelt in a *several house. And *Jotham the king's son *was* over the house, judging the people of the land.

6 And the rest of the acts of Azariah, and all that he did, *are* they not written in the book of the chronicles of the kings of Judah?

7 So Azariah slept with his fathers; and they buried him with his fathers in the city of David: and Jotham his son reigned in his stead.

8 ¶ In the thirty and eighth year of Azariah king of Judah did Zachariah the son of Jeroboam reign over Israel in Samaria six months.

9 And he did *that which was* evil in the sight of the L ORD, as his fathers had done: he departed not from the sins of *Jeroboam the son of Nebat, who made Israel to sin.

10 And Shallum the son of Jabesh conspired against him, and *smote him before the people, and slew him, and reigned in his stead.

11 And the rest of the acts of Zachariah, behold, they *are* written in the book of the chronicles of the kings of Israel.

12 This *was* the word of the L ORD which he spake unto *Jehu, saying, Thy sons shall sit on the *throne of Israel unto the fourth *generation.* And so it came to pass.

13 ¶ Shallum the son of Jabesh began to reign in the nine and thirtieth year of *Uzziah king of Judah; and he reigned a full month in Samaria.

14 For Menahem the son of Gadi went up from Tirzah, and came to Samaria, and smote Shallum the son of Jabesh in Samaria, and slew him, and reigned in his stead.

15 And the rest of the acts of Shallum, and his conspiracy which he made, behold, they *are* written in the book of the chronicles of the kings of Israel.

16 ¶ Then Menahem smote Tiphsah, and all that *were* therein, and

---

25*a* Jonah 1:1.
15 5*a* TG Leprosy.
　b OR separate.
　　Lev. 13:46 (43–46).

c 1 Chr. 5:17 (10–17).
9*a* 1 Kgs. 14:16;
　2 Kgs. 10:29;
　13:2 (1–2, 11); 14:24.

10*a* Amos 7:9 (7–9).
12*a* Hosea 1:4.
　b 2 Kgs. 10:30.
13*a* Isa. 1:1.

the coasts thereof from Tirzah: because they opened not *to him*, therefore he smote *it; and* all the women therein that were with child he ripped up.

17 In the nine and thirtieth year of Azariah king of Judah began Menahem the son of Gadi to reign over Israel, *and reigned* ten years in Samaria.

18 And he did *that which was* evil in the sight of the LORD: he departed not all his days from the sins of Jeroboam the son of Nebat, who made Israel to sin.

19 *And* Pul the king of *a*Assyria came against the land: and Menahem gave Pul a thousand talents of silver, that his hand might be with him to confirm the kingdom in his hand.

20 And Menahem exacted the money of Israel, *even* of all the mighty men of wealth, of each man fifty shekels of silver, to give to the king of Assyria. So the king of Assyria turned back, and stayed not there in the land.

21 ¶ And the rest of the acts of Menahem, and all that he did, *are* they not written in the book of the chronicles of the kings of Israel?

22 And Menahem slept with his fathers; and Pekahiah his son reigned in his stead.

23 ¶ In the fiftieth year of Azariah king of Judah Pekahiah the son of Menahem began to reign over Israel in Samaria, *and reigned* two years.

24 And he did *that which was* evil in the sight of the LORD: he departed not from the sins of Jeroboam the son of Nebat, who made Israel to sin.

25 But *a*Pekah the son of Remaliah, a captain of his, conspired against him, and smote him in Samaria, in the palace of the king's house, with Argob and Arieh, and with him fifty men of the Gileadites: and he killed him, and reigned in his room.

26 And the rest of the acts of Pekahiah, and all that he did, behold, they *are* written in the book of the chronicles of the kings of Israel.

27 ¶ In the two and fiftieth year of Azariah king of Judah *a*Pekah the son of Remaliah began to reign over Israel in Samaria, *and reigned* twenty years.

28 And he did *that which was* evil in the sight of the LORD: he departed not from the sins of Jeroboam the son of Nebat, who made Israel to sin.

29 In the days of Pekah king of Israel came *a*Tiglath-pileser king of Assyria, and *b*took Ijon, and Abel-beth-maachah, and Janoah, and Kedesh, and Hazor, and Gilead, and Galilee, all the land of Naphtali, and *c*carried them captive to *d*Assyria.

30 And Hoshea the son of Elah made a conspiracy against Pekah the son of Remaliah, and smote him, and slew him, and reigned in his stead, in the twentieth year of *a*Jotham the son of Uzziah.

31 And the rest of the acts of Pekah, and all that he did, behold, they *are* written in the book of the chronicles of the kings of Israel.

32 ¶ In the second year of Pekah the son of Remaliah king of Israel began *a*Jotham the son of Uzziah king of Judah to reign.

33 Five and twenty years old was he when he began to reign, and he reigned sixteen years in Jerusalem. And his mother's name *was* Jerusha, the daughter of Zadok.

34 And he did *that which was* right in the sight of the LORD: he did according to all that his father Uzziah had done.

35 ¶ Howbeit the high places were not removed: the people sacrificed and burned incense still in the high

---

19*a* 2 Kgs. 17:6 (3–6);
    Ezek. 23:5;
    Hosea 8:9.
25*a* 2 Ne. 17:1 (1–13).
27*a* 2 Chr. 28:6;
    Isa. 7:1 (1–16).

29*a* 2 Kgs. 16:7;
    1 Chr. 5:6.
  b Isa. 8:4 (1–4).
  c 1 Chr. 5:26;
    Hosea 1:5.
  d TG Israel, Bondage of, in

Other Lands;
    Israel, Scattering of.
30*a* Isa. 1:1.
32*a* 1 Chr. 5:17;
    2 Ne. 17:1 (1–13).

places. He built the higher ^agate of the house of the LORD.

36 ¶ Now the rest of the acts of Jotham, and all that he did, *are* they not written in the book of the chronicles of the kings of Judah?

37 In those days the LORD began to send against Judah ^aRezin the king of Syria, and Pekah the son of Remaliah.

38 And ^aJotham slept with his fathers, and was buried with his fathers in the city of David his father: and Ahaz his son reigned in his stead.

CHAPTER 16

Ahaz reigns in wickedness in Judah—He offers his son in heathen sacrifice—He makes a new altar, destroys the brazen sea, and changes the method for sacrificing in the temple.

IN the seventeenth year of Pekah the son of Remaliah ^aAhaz the son of Jotham king of Judah began to reign.

2 Twenty years old *was* Ahaz when he began to reign, and reigned sixteen years in Jerusalem, and did not *that which was* right in the sight of the LORD his God, like David his father.

3 But he walked in the way of the kings of Israel, yea, and made his son to pass through the ^afire, according to the abominations of the ^bheathen, whom the LORD cast out from before the children of Israel.

4 And he sacrificed and burnt incense in the ^ahigh places, and on the hills, and under every green tree.

5 ¶ Then ^aRezin king of Syria and Pekah son of Remaliah king of Israel came up to Jerusalem to war: and they besieged Ahaz, but could not overcome *him.*

6 At that time Rezin king of Syria recovered Elath to Syria, and drave the Jews from Elath: and the Syrians came to Elath, and dwelt there unto this day.

7 So Ahaz sent messengers to ^aTiglath-pileser king of ^bAssyria, saying, I *am* thy servant and thy son: come up, and ^csave me out of the hand of the king of Syria, and out of the hand of the king of Israel, which rise up against me.

8 And Ahaz ^atook the silver and gold that was found in the house of the LORD, and in the treasures of the king's house, and sent *it for* a present to the king of Assyria.

9 And the king of Assyria hearkened unto him: for the king of Assyria went up against Damascus, and took it, and carried *the people of* it captive to Kir, and slew Rezin.

10 ¶ And king Ahaz went to Damascus to meet Tiglath-pileser king of Assyria, and saw an altar that *was* at Damascus: and king Ahaz sent to Urijah the priest the fashion of the altar, and the pattern of it, according to all the workmanship thereof.

11 And Urijah the priest built an altar according to all that king Ahaz had sent from Damascus: so Urijah the priest made *it* against king Ahaz came from Damascus.

12 And when the king was come from Damascus, the king saw the altar: and the king approached to the altar, and offered thereon.

13 And he burnt his burnt offering and his meat offering, and poured his drink offering, and sprinkled the blood of his peace offerings, upon the altar.

14 And he brought also the brasen altar, which *was* before the LORD, from the forefront of the house, from between the altar and the house of the LORD, and put it on the north side of the altar.

15 And king Ahaz commanded Urijah the priest, saying, Upon the

---

35*a* 2 Chr. 27:3;
    Ezek. 9:2.
37*a* 2 Kgs. 16:5 (1–6);
    Isa. 7:1;
    2 Ne. 17:1 (1–13).
38*a* Isa. 1:1.
16 1*a* Micah 1:1.

3*a* Lev. 18:21;
    2 Kgs. 17:17.
  b TG Heathen.
4*a* 1 Kgs. 14:23 (22–23);
    Isa. 57:5.
5*a* 2 Kgs. 15:37 (36–38);
    Isa. 7:1.

7*a* 2 Kgs. 15:29;
    1 Chr. 5:6.
  b 2 Kgs. 28:16 (16–21);
    Ezek. 16:28; 23:12;
    2 Ne. 18:4 (4–7); 20:12.
  c Isa. 10:20 (20–23).
8*a* 2 Chr. 28:21.

great altar burn the morning burnt offering, and the evening meat offering, and the king's burnt sacrifice, and his meat offering, with the burnt offering of all the people of the land, and their meat offering, and their drink offerings; and sprinkle upon it all the blood of the burnt offering, and all the blood of the sacrifice: and the brasen altar shall be for me to inquire *by*.

16 Thus did Urijah the priest, according to all that king Ahaz commanded.

17 ¶ And king Ahaz cut off the borders of the bases, and removed the laver from off them; and took down the *a*sea from off the brasen oxen that *were* under it, and put it upon a pavement of stones.

18 And the covert for the sabbath that they had built in the house, and the king's entry without, turned he from the *a*house of the LORD for the king of Assyria.

19 ¶ Now the rest of the acts of Ahaz which he did, *are* they not written in the book of the chronicles of the kings of Judah?

20 And *a*Ahaz slept with his fathers, and was buried with his fathers in the city of David: and Hezekiah his son reigned in his stead.

CHAPTER 17

Hoshea reigns in Israel and is subject to the Assyrians—The Israelites forsake the Lord, worship idols, serve Baal, and reject all that the Lord has given them— The ten tribes are carried away captive by the kings of Assyria—The land of Israel (Samaria) is repopulated by other people—Many forms of false worship are found among the Samaritans.

IN the twelfth year of Ahaz king of Judah began Hoshea the son of Elah to reign in Samaria over Israel nine years.

2 And he did *that which was* evil in the sight of the LORD, but not as the kings of Israel that were before him.

3 ¶ Against him came up *a*Shalmaneser king of Assyria; and Hoshea became his servant, and gave him presents.

4 And the king of Assyria found *a*conspiracy in Hoshea: for he had sent messengers to So king of Egypt, and brought no present to the king of Assyria, as *he had done* year by year: therefore the king of Assyria shut him up, and bound him in prison.

5 ¶ Then the king of *a*Assyria came up throughout all the land, and went up to Samaria, and besieged it three years.

6 ¶ In the ninth year of Hoshea the king of Assyria took *a*Samaria, and *b*carried *c*Israel away into *d*Assyria, and placed them in Halah and in Habor *by* the river of Gozan, and in the cities of the Medes.

7 For *so* it was, that the children of Israel had *a*sinned against the LORD their God, which had brought them up out of the land of Egypt, from under the hand of Pharaoh king of Egypt, and had feared other gods,

8 And walked in the statutes of the *a*heathen, whom the LORD cast out from before the children of Israel, and of the kings of Israel, which they had made.

9 And the children of Israel did secretly *those* things that *were* not right against the LORD their God, and they built them high places in all their cities, from the tower of the watchmen to the fenced city.

10 And they set them up images and *a*groves in every high hill, and under every green tree:

11 And there they burnt incense in all the high places, as *did* the heathen whom the LORD carried away before them; and wrought wicked

---

17*a* 1 Kgs. 7:23 (23–26).
18*a* TG Temple.
20*a* Isa. 1:1; 14:28.
17 3*a* Hosea 10:14 (13–14).
4*a* TG Conspiracy.
5*a* Hosea 1:4 (1–11); 7:16;

8:3 (1–14);
Micah 1:6 (1–16).
6*a* Hosea 13:16; 2 Ne. 18:4.
b TG Israel, Scattering of.
c TG Israel, Joseph, People of; Israel, Ten Lost

Tribes of.
d 2 Kgs. 15:19;
Ezek. 23:5; Hosea 8:9.
7*a* TG Apostasy of Israel.
8*a* TG Heathen.
10*a* Ex. 34:13.

things to provoke the Lᴏᴏ to anger:

12 For they served idols, whereof the Lord had said unto them, Ye shall ^anot do this thing.

13 Yet the Lord ^atestified against Israel, and against Judah, by all the ^bprophets, *and by* all the ^cseers, saying, Turn ye from your evil ways, and keep my commandments *and* my statutes, according to all the law which I commanded your fathers, and which I sent to you by my servants the prophets.

14 Notwithstanding they would ^anot hear, but ^bhardened their necks, like to the neck of their fathers, that did not ^cbelieve in the Lord their God.

15 And they rejected his statutes, and his covenant that he made with their fathers, and his testimonies which he testified against them; and they followed vanity, and became ^avain, and went after the heathen that *were* round about them, *concerning* whom the Lord had charged them, that they should not do like them.

16 And they left all the commandments of the Lord their God, and made them molten images, *even* two ^acalves, and made a ^bgrove, and worshipped all the ^chost of heaven, and served ^dBaal.

17 And they caused their sons and their daughters to pass through the ^afire, and used ^bdivination and enchantments, and sold themselves to do ^cevil in the sight of the Lord, to provoke him to anger.

18 Therefore the Lord was very angry with Israel, and ^aremoved them out of his sight: there was none left but the tribe of ^bJudah only.

19 Also Judah kept not the commandments of the Lord their God, but walked in the statutes of Israel which they made.

20 And the Lord ^arejected all the seed of Israel, and afflicted them, and delivered them into the hand of spoilers, until he had cast them out of his sight.

21 For he rent Israel from the house of David; and they made Jeroboam the son of Nebat king: and Jeroboam drave Israel from following the Lord, and made them sin a great sin.

22 For the children of Israel walked in all the sins of Jeroboam which he did; they departed not from them;

23 Until the Lord removed Israel out of his sight, as he had said by all his servants the ^aprophets. So was ^bIsrael ^ccarried away out of their own ^dland to Assyria unto this day.

24 ¶ And the king of Assyria ^abrought *men* from Babylon, and from Cuthah, and from Ava, and from Hamath, and from Sepharvaim, and placed *them* in the cities of Samaria instead of the children of Israel: and they possessed Samaria, and dwelt in the cities thereof.

25 And *so* it was at the beginning of their dwelling there, *that* they feared not the Lord: therefore the Lord sent lions among them, which slew *some* of them.

26 Wherefore they spake to the king of Assyria, saying, The nations which thou hast removed, and placed in the cities of Samaria, know not the manner of the God of the land: therefore he hath sent lions among them, and, behold, they slay

12*a* Ex. 20:4;
   Mosiah 13:12 (12–13).
13*a* Neh. 9:30; 1 Ne. 10:5;
   Hel. 8:24 (19–24).
   TG Preaching.
  b TG Authority;
   Prophets, Mission of.
  c TG Seer.
14*a* TG Prophets,
   Rejection of.
  b Deut. 9:13.

   TG Doubt.
  c TG Faith; Unbelief.
15*a* Rom. 1:21.
16*a* 1 Kgs. 12:28.
  b Deut. 16:21.
  c 2 Kgs. 21:3.
  d Hosea 11:2 (1–4).
17*a* 2 Kgs. 16:3.
  b TG Sorcery.
  c TG Evil.
18*a* 2 Kgs. 23:27; 2 Ne. 16:12.

  b TG Israel, Judah,
   People of.
20*a* TG God, Indignation of;
   Israel, Ten Lost
   Tribes of.
23*a* 1 Kgs. 9:7 (1–7).
  b TG Israel, Ten Lost
   Tribes of.
  c Hosea 1:6.
  d TG Israel, Land of.
24*a* Ezra 4:2 (2, 9–10).

them, because they know not the manner of the God of the land.

27 Then the king of Assyria commanded, saying, Carry thither one of the priests whom ye brought from thence; and let them go and dwell there, and let him teach them the manner of the God of the land.

28 Then one of the priests whom they had carried away from Samaria came and dwelt in Beth-el, and taught them how they should fear the LORD.

29 Howbeit every nation made gods of their own, and put *them* in the *a*houses of the high places which the *b*Samaritans had made, every nation in their cities wherein they dwelt.

30 And the men of Babylon made Succoth-benoth, and the men of Cuth made Nergal, and the men of Hamath made Ashima,

31 And the Avites made Nibhaz and Tartak, and the Sepharvites burnt their *a*children in fire to Adrammelech and Anammelech, the gods of Sepharvaim.

32 So they feared the LORD, and made unto themselves of the lowest of them priests of the high places, which sacrificed for them in the houses of the high places.

33 They feared the LORD, and served their own gods, after the manner of the nations whom they carried away from thence.

34 Unto this day they do after the former manners: they fear not the LORD, neither do they after their statutes, or after their ordinances, or after the law and commandment which the LORD commanded the children of Jacob, whom he named *a*Israel;

35 With whom the LORD had made a covenant, and charged them, saying, Ye shall not *a*fear other *b*gods, nor bow yourselves to them, nor serve them, nor sacrifice to them:

36 But the LORD, who brought you up out of the land of Egypt with great power and a stretched out arm, him shall ye fear, and him shall ye worship, and to him shall ye do sacrifice.

37 And the statutes, and the *a*ordinances, and the law, and the commandment, which he wrote for you, ye shall observe to do for evermore; and ye shall not fear other gods.

38 And the covenant that I have made with you ye shall not *a*forget; neither shall ye fear other gods.

39 But the LORD your God ye shall fear; and he shall *a*deliver you out of the hand of all your enemies.

40 Howbeit they did not hearken, but they did after their former manner.

41 So these nations feared the LORD, and served their graven images, both their children, and their children's children: as did their fathers, so do they unto this day.

CHAPTER 18

Hezekiah reigns in righteousness in Judah—He destroys idolatry and breaks the brazen serpent made by Moses because the children of Israel burn incense to it—Sennacherib, king of Assyria, invades Judah—In a blasphemous speech, Rabshakeh asks Jerusalem to surrender to the Assyrians.

Now it came to pass in the third year of Hoshea son of Elah king of Israel, *that* *a*Hezekiah the son of Ahaz king of Judah began to reign.

2 Twenty and five years old was he when he began to *a*reign; and he reigned twenty and nine years in Jerusalem. His mother's name also *was* Abi, the daughter of Zachariah.

3 And he did *that which was* right in the sight of the LORD, according to all that David his father did.

4 ¶ He removed the *a*high places,

29*a* 1 Kgs. 12:31.
  b John 4:9.
31*a* Morm. 4:21.
34*a* 1 Kgs. 18:31.
  TG Israel, Origins of.
35*a* Judg. 6:10.

  b Deut. 7:16 (16–18).
37*a* TG Ordinance.
38*a* Deut. 4:23;
  1 Ne. 21:15;
  Alma 46:8;
  D&C 133:2.

39*a* 2 Ne. 6:17;
  Alma 58:37;
  D&C 105:8; 108:8.
18 1*a* Micah 1:1.
  2*a* 2 Chr. 29:1 (1–29).
  4*a* 2 Kgs. 21:3.

and brake the ᵇimages, and ᶜcut down the groves, and brake in pieces the brasen ᵈserpent that Moses had made: for unto those days the children of Israel did burn incense to it: and he called it Nehushtan.

5 He ᵃtrusted in the LORD God of Israel; so that after him was none like him among all the kings of Judah, nor *any* that were before him.

6 For he ᵃclave to the LORD, *and* departed not from following him, but kept his commandments, which the LORD commanded Moses.

7 And the LORD was with him; *and* he prospered whithersoever he went forth: and he rebelled against the king of Assyria, and served him not.

8 He smote the Philistines, *even* unto Gaza, and the borders thereof, from the tower of the watchmen to the fenced city.

9 ¶ And it came to pass in the fourth year of king Hezekiah, which *was* the seventh year of Hoshea son of Elah king of Israel, *that* Shalmaneser king of Assyria came up against Samaria, and besieged it.

10 And at the end of three years they took it: *even* in the sixth year of Hezekiah, that *is* the ninth year of Hoshea king of Israel, Samaria was taken.

11 And the king of Assyria did carry away ᵃIsrael unto Assyria, and put them in Halah and in Habor *by* the river of Gozan, and in the cities of the Medes:

12 Because they ᵃobeyed not the voice of the LORD their God, but transgressed his covenant, *and* all that Moses the servant of the LORD commanded, and would not hear *them,* nor do *them.*

13 ¶ Now in the ᵃfourteenth year of king Hezekiah did Sennacherib king of Assyria come up against all the fenced cities of Judah, and took them.

14 And Hezekiah king of Judah sent to the king of Assyria to Lachish, saying, I have offended; return from me: that which thou puttest on me will I bear. And the king of Assyria appointed unto Hezekiah king of Judah three hundred talents of silver and thirty talents of gold.

15 And ᵃHezekiah gave *him* all the silver that was found in the house of the LORD, and in the treasures of the king's house.

16 At that time did Hezekiah cut off *the gold from* the doors of the temple of the LORD, and *from* the pillars which Hezekiah king of Judah had overlaid, and gave it to the king of Assyria.

17 ¶ And the king of Assyria ᵃsent ᵇTartan and Rabsaris and Rabshakeh from Lachish to king Hezekiah with a great host against Jerusalem. And they went up and came to Jerusalem. And when they were come up, they came and stood by the ᶜconduit of the upper pool, which *is* in the highway of the fuller's field.

18 And when they had called to the king, there came out to them ᵃEliakim the son of Hilkiah, which *was* over the household, and Shebna the scribe, and Joah the son of Asaph the recorder.

19 And Rab-shakeh said unto them, Speak ye now to Hezekiah, Thus saith the great king, the king of Assyria, What confidence *is* this wherein thou trustest?

20 Thou sayest, (but *they are but* vain words,) *I have* counsel and strength for the war. Now on whom dost thou trust, that thou rebellest against me?

21 Now, behold, thou trustest upon the staff of this bruised ᵃreed, *even* upon Egypt, on which if a man lean, it will go into his hand, and pierce it: so *is* Pharaoh king of Egypt unto all that trust on him.

22 But if ye say unto me, We trust

---

4 *b* Isa. 26:13.
  c Judg. 6:25;
     2 Kgs. 23:14.
  d 2 Ne. 25:20.
     TG Symbolism.
5 *a* 2 Kgs. 23:25.

6 *a* Josh. 23:8; Jacob 6:5.
11 *a* TG Israel, Ten Lost
      Tribes of.
12 *a* TG Disobedience.
13 *a* Isa. 36:1 (1–22).
15 *a* Isa. 39:2.

17 *a* 2 Chr. 32:9 (5–26).
   b Isa. 20:1.
   c OR ditch, aqueduct.
18 *a* Isa. 22:20.
21 *a* Isa. 36:6;
      Ezek. 29:6 (6–16).

in the LORD our God: *is* not that he, whose high places and whose altars Hezekiah hath taken away, and hath said to Judah and Jerusalem, Ye shall worship before this altar in Jerusalem?

23 Now therefore, I pray thee, give pledges to my lord the king of Assyria, and I will deliver thee two thousand horses, if thou be able on thy part to set riders upon them.

24 How then wilt thou turn away the face of one captain of the least of my master's servants, and put thy trust on Egypt for chariots and for horsemen?

25 Am I now come up without the LORD against this place to destroy it? The LORD said to me, Go up against this land, and destroy it.

26 Then said Eliakim the son of Hilkiah, and Shebna, and Joah, unto Rab-shakeh, Speak, I pray thee, to thy servants in the Syrian language; for we understand *it:* and talk not with us in the Jews' language in the ears of the people that *are* on the wall.

27 But Rab-shakeh said unto them, Hath my master sent me to thy master, and to thee, to speak these words? *hath he* not *sent me* to the men which sit on the wall, that they may eat their own dung, and drink their own piss with you?

28 Then Rab-shakeh stood and cried with a loud voice in the Jews' ªlanguage, and spake, saying, Hear the word of the great king, the king of Assyria:

29 Thus saith the king, Let not Hezekiah deceive you: for he shall not be able to deliver you out of his hand:

30 Neither let Hezekiah make you trust in the LORD, saying, The LORD will surely deliver us, and this city shall not be delivered into the hand of the king of Assyria.

31 Hearken not to Hezekiah: for thus saith the king of Assyria, Make *an agreement* with me by a present, and come out to me, and *then* eat ye every man of his own vine, and every one of his fig tree, and drink ye every one the waters of his cistern:

32 Until I come and take you away to a land like your own land, a land of corn and wine, a land of bread and vineyards, a land of oil olive and of honey, that ye may live, and not die: and hearken not unto Hezekiah, when he persuadeth you, saying, The LORD will deliver us.

33 Hath any of the gods of the nations delivered at all his land out of the hand of the king of Assyria?

34 Where *are* the gods of Hamath, and of Arpad? where *are* the gods of Sepharvaim, Hena, and Ivah? have they delivered Samaria out of mine hand?

35 Who *are* they among all the gods of the countries, that have delivered their country out of mine hand, that the LORD should deliver Jerusalem out of mine hand?

36 But the people held their peace, and answered him not a word: for the king's commandment was, saying, Answer him not.

37 Then came Eliakim the son of Hilkiah, which *was* over the household, and Shebna the scribe, and Joah the son of Asaph the recorder, to Hezekiah with *their* clothes rent, and told him the words of Rab-shakeh.

CHAPTER 19

Hezekiah seeks counsel from Isaiah to save Jerusalem—Isaiah prophesies the defeat of the Assyrians and the death of Sennacherib—Hezekiah prays for deliverance—Sennacherib sends a blasphemous letter—Isaiah prophesies that the Assyrians will be destroyed and that a remnant of Judah will flourish—An angel slays 185,000 Assyrians—Sennacherib is slain by his sons.

AND it came to pass, when king Hezekiah heard *it,* that he rent his clothes, and covered himself with sackcloth, and went into the ªhouse of the LORD.

---

28 *a* 2 Chr. 32:18 (5–26). | **19** 1 *a* 1 Kgs. 8:29 (29–30); | Ps. 73:17 (16–17).

2 And he sent Eliakim, which *was* over the household, and Shebna the ^ascribe, and the elders of the priests, covered with sackcloth, to Isaiah the prophet the son of Amoz.

3 And they said unto him, Thus saith Hezekiah, This day *is* a day of trouble, and of rebuke, and blasphemy: for the children are come to the birth, and *there is* not strength to bring forth.

4 It may be the Lord thy God will hear all the words of Rab-shakeh, whom the king of Assyria his master hath sent to reproach the living God; and will reprove the words which the Lord thy God hath heard: wherefore lift up *thy* ^aprayer for the ^bremnant that are left.

5 So the servants of king Hezekiah came to Isaiah.

6 ¶ And ^aIsaiah said unto them, Thus shall ye say to your master, Thus saith the Lord, Be not afraid of the words which thou hast heard, with which the servants of the king of Assyria have blasphemed me.

7 Behold, I will send a blast upon him, and he shall hear a rumour, and shall return to his own land; and I will cause him to fall by the sword in his own land.

8 ¶ So Rab-shakeh returned, and found the king of Assyria warring against Libnah: for he had heard that he was departed from Lachish.

9 And when he heard say of Tirhakah king of Ethiopia, Behold, he is come out to fight against thee: he sent messengers again unto Hezekiah, saying,

10 Thus shall ye speak to Hezekiah king of Judah, saying, Let not thy God in whom thou trustest ^adeceive thee, saying, Jerusalem shall not be delivered into the hand of the king of Assyria.

11 Behold, thou hast heard what the kings of Assyria have done to all lands, by destroying them utterly: and shalt thou be delivered?

12 Have the gods of the nations delivered them which my fathers have destroyed; *as* Gozan, and Haran, and Rezeph, and the children of Eden which *were* in Thelasar?

13 Where *is* the king of Hamath, and the king of Arpad, and the king of the city of Sepharvaim, of Hena, and Ivah?

14 ¶ And Hezekiah received the letter of the hand of the messengers, and read it: and Hezekiah went up into the house of the Lord, and spread it before the Lord.

15 And Hezekiah prayed before the Lord, and said, O Lord God of Israel, which dwellest *between* the ^acherubims, thou art the ^bGod, *even* thou alone, of all the kingdoms of the earth; thou hast ^cmade heaven and earth.

16 Lord, bow down thine ear, and hear: open, Lord, thine eyes, and see: and hear the words of Sennacherib, which hath sent him to reproach the living God.

17 Of a truth, Lord, the kings of Assyria have destroyed the nations and their lands,

18 And have cast their gods into the fire: for they *were* no gods, but the work of men's hands, wood and stone: therefore they have destroyed them.

19 Now therefore, O Lord our God, I beseech thee, save thou us out of his hand, that all the kingdoms of the earth may know that thou *art* the Lord God, *even* thou only.

20 ¶ Then Isaiah the son of Amoz sent to Hezekiah, saying, Thus saith the Lord God of Israel, *That* which thou hast ^aprayed to me against Sennacherib king of Assyria I have heard.

21 This *is* the word that the Lord hath spoken concerning him; The ^avirgin the daughter of Zion hath despised thee, *and* ^blaughed thee to scorn; the daughter of Jerusalem hath shaken her head at thee.

22 Whom hast thou reproached

2*a* TG Scribe.
4*a* TG Prayer.
  b TG Israel, Remnant of.
6*a* Isa. 37:6 (1–38).

10*a* Enos 1:6;
    Ether 3:12.
15*a* Ex. 25:22.
  b Neh. 9:6.

c TG Jesus Christ, Creator.
20*a* TG Prayer.
21*a* Lam. 2:13.
  b TG Laughter.

and blasphemed? and against whom hast thou exalted *thy* voice, and lifted up thine eyes on high? *even* against the Holy *One* of Israel.

23 By thy messengers thou hast reproached the Lord, and hast said, With the *a*multitude of my chariots I am come up to the height of the mountains, to the sides of Lebanon, and will cut down the tall cedar trees thereof, *and* the choice fir trees thereof: and I will enter into the lodgings of his borders, *and into* the forest of his Carmel.

24 I have digged and drunk strange waters, and with the sole of my feet have I dried up all the rivers of besieged places.

25 Hast thou not heard long ago *how* I have done it, *and* of ancient times that I have formed it? now have I brought it to pass, that thou shouldest be to lay waste fenced cities *into* ruinous heaps.

26 Therefore their inhabitants were of small power, they were dismayed and confounded; they were *as* the *a*grass of the field, and *as* the green herb, *as* the grass on the housetops, and *as corn* blasted before it be grown up.

27 But I know thy abode, and thy going out, and thy coming in, and thy rage against me.

28 Because thy rage against me and thy tumult is come up into mine ears, therefore I will put my hook in thy nose, and my bridle in thy lips, and I will turn thee back by the way by which thou camest.

29 And this *shall be* a sign unto thee, Ye shall eat this year such things as grow of themselves, and in the second year that which springeth of the same; and in the third year sow ye, and reap, and plant vineyards, and eat the fruits thereof.

30 And the *a*remnant that is escaped of the house of Judah shall yet again take root downward, and bear fruit upward.

31 For out of Jerusalem shall go forth a remnant, and they that escape out of mount Zion: the *a*zeal of the LORD *of hosts* shall do this.

32 Therefore thus saith the LORD concerning the king of Assyria, He shall not come into this city, nor shoot an arrow there, nor come before it with shield, nor cast a bank against it.

33 By the way that he came, by the same shall he return, and shall not come into this city, saith the LORD.

34 For I will *a*defend this city, to save it, for mine own sake, and for my servant David's sake.

35 ¶ And it came to pass that night, that the *a*angel of the LORD went out, and *b*smote in the camp of the *c*Assyrians an hundred fourscore and five thousand: and when they arose early in the morning, behold, they *were* all dead corpses.

36 So Sennacherib king of Assyria departed, and went and returned, and dwelt at Nineveh.

37 And it came to pass, as he was worshipping in the house of Nisroch his god, that Adrammelech and Sharezer his sons smote him with the sword: and they escaped into the land of Armenia. And Esarhaddon his son reigned in his stead.

CHAPTER 20

Hezekiah is told he will die and pleads with the Lord; his life is lengthened fifteen years—The shadow goes back ten degrees on the sundial of Ahaz—Isaiah prophesies the Babylonian captivity of Judah.

IN those days was *a*Hezekiah sick unto death. And the prophet Isaiah the son of Amoz came to him, and said unto him, Thus saith the LORD, Set thine house in order; for thou shalt *b*die, and not live.

2 Then he turned his face to the wall, and prayed unto the LORD, saying,

---

23*a* Isa. 10:13 (12–14).
26*a* Ps. 129:6.
30*a* TG Israel, Remnant of.
31*a* TG Zeal.

34*a* Hosea 1:7.
35*a* 2 Chr. 32:21 (5–26).
　b Isa. 10:12 (12–34).
　c Isa. 14:25 (24–28);

37:36 (33–38).
20 1*a* Isa. 38:1 (1–8).
　b Eccl. 3:2;
　　　D&C 42:48.

3 I beseech thee, O LORD, remember now how I have walked before thee in truth and with a perfect heart, and have done *that which is* good in thy sight. And Hezekiah wept sore.

4 And it came to pass, afore Isaiah was gone out into the middle court, that the word of the LORD came to him, saying,

5 Turn again, and tell Hezekiah the captain of my people, Thus saith the LORD, the God of David thy father, I have heard thy prayer, I have seen thy tears: behold, I will ᵃheal thee: on the third day thou shalt go up unto the house of the LORD.

6 And I will add unto thy ᵃdays fifteen years; and I will deliver thee and this city out of the hand of the king of Assyria; and I will defend this city for mine own sake, and for my servant David's sake.

7 And Isaiah said, Take a lump of figs. And they took and laid *it* on the boil, and he recovered.

8 ¶ And Hezekiah said unto Isaiah, What *shall be* the ᵃsign that the LORD will heal me, and that I shall go up into the house of the LORD the third day?

9 And Isaiah said, This sign shalt thou have of the LORD, that the LORD will do the thing that he hath spoken: shall the ᵃshadow go forward ten degrees, or go back ten degrees?

10 And Hezekiah answered, It is a light thing for the ᵃshadow to go down ten degrees: nay, but let the shadow return backward ten degrees.

11 And Isaiah the prophet cried unto the LORD: and he brought the shadow ten degrees ᵃbackward, by which it had gone down in the dial of Ahaz.

12 ¶ At that time ᵃBerodach-baladan, the son of Baladan, king of Babylon, sent letters and a present unto Hezekiah: for he had heard that Hezekiah had been sick.

13 And Hezekiah hearkened unto them, and shewed them all the house of his precious things, the silver, and the gold, and the spices, and the precious ointment, and *all* the house of his armour, and all that was found in his ᵃtreasures: there was nothing in his house, nor in all his dominion, that Hezekiah shewed them not.

14 ¶ Then came Isaiah the prophet unto king Hezekiah, and said unto him, What said these men? and from whence came they unto thee? And Hezekiah said, They are come from a far country, *even* from Babylon.

15 And he said, What have they seen in thine house? And Hezekiah answered, All *the things* that *are* in mine house have they seen: there is nothing among my treasures that I have not shewed them.

16 And Isaiah said unto Hezekiah, Hear the word of the LORD.

17 Behold, the days come, that all that *is* in thine house, and that which thy fathers have laid up in store unto this day, shall be ᵃcarried into Babylon: nothing shall be left, saith the LORD.

18 And of thy ᵃsons that shall issue from thee, which thou shalt beget, shall they take away; and they shall be ᵇeunuchs in the palace of the king of Babylon.

19 Then said Hezekiah unto Isaiah, Good *is* the word of the LORD which thou hast spoken. And he said, *Is it* not *good*, if peace and truth be in my days?

20 ¶ And the rest of the acts of Hezekiah, and all his might, and how he made a ᵃpool, and a conduit, and brought water into the city, *are* they not written in the book of the chronicles of the kings of Judah?

5a TG Heal.
6a TG Time.
8a Gen. 15:8 (7–9).
9a Hel. 12:14 (14–15).
10a 2 Chr. 32:24 (5–26);
    Isa. 38:8.

11a Josh. 10:12 (12–14).
12a Isa. 39:1.
13a TG Treasure.
17a 2 Kgs. 24:13 (12–14);
    1 Ne. 1:13.
18a Isa. 39:7 (3–7);

Dan. 1:3 (1–3).
    b OR officers.
20a 2 Chr. 32:30;
    Isa. 22:9.

21 And Hezekiah slept with his fathers: and Manasseh his son reigned in his stead.

CHAPTER 21

Manasseh turns Judah to idolatry, even sacrificing a son to a heathen god—Prophets foretell the destruction of Judah and Jerusalem—Wickedness continues under Amon.

[a]MANASSEH *was* twelve years old when he began to reign, and reigned fifty and five years in Jerusalem. And his mother's name *was* Hephzibah.

2 And he did *that which was* [a]evil in the sight of the LORD, after the [b]abominations of the heathen, whom the LORD cast out before the children of Israel.

3 For he built up again the [a]high places which Hezekiah his father had destroyed; and he reared up altars for Baal, and made a [b]grove, as did Ahab king of Israel; and worshipped all the [c]host of heaven, and served them.

4 And he built [a]altars in the [b]house of the LORD, of which the LORD said, In Jerusalem will I put my [c]name.

5 And he built altars for all the host of heaven in the two [a]courts of the house of the LORD.

6 And he made his son pass through the [a]fire, and observed times, and used [b]enchantments, and dealt with [c]familiar spirits and wizards: he wrought much wickedness in the sight of the LORD, to provoke *him* to anger.

7 And he set a graven [a]image of the grove that he had made in the house, of which the LORD said to David, and to Solomon his son, In this house, and in Jerusalem, which I have chosen out of all tribes of Israel, will I put my name for ever:

8 Neither will I make the feet of Israel move any more out of the land which I gave their fathers; only if they will observe to do according to all that I have commanded them, and according to all the law that my servant Moses commanded them.

9 But they hearkened not: and Manasseh seduced them to do more [a]evil than did the nations whom the LORD destroyed before the children of Israel.

10 ¶ And the LORD spake by his servants the prophets, saying,

11 Because [a]Manasseh king of Judah hath done these [b]abominations, *and* hath done [c]wickedly above all that the Amorites did, which *were* before him, and hath made Judah also to sin with his idols:

12 Therefore thus saith the LORD God of Israel, Behold, I *am* bringing *such* evil upon Jerusalem and Judah, that whosoever heareth of it, both his ears shall [a]tingle.

13 And I will stretch over Jerusalem the line of Samaria, and the plummet of the house of Ahab: and I will wipe Jerusalem as *a man* wipeth a dish, wiping *it*, and turning *it* upside down.

14 And I will forsake the remnant of mine inheritance, and [a]deliver them into the hand of their enemies; and they shall become a prey and a spoil to all their enemies;

15 Because they have done *that which was* evil in my sight, and have provoked me to anger, since the day their fathers came forth out of Egypt, even unto this day.

16 Moreover Manasseh [a]shed innocent [b]blood very much, till he had filled Jerusalem from one end to another; beside his sin wherewith he

---

21 1a 2 Chr. 33:1 (1–20).
2a TG Sin.
　b TG Apostasy of Israel.
3a 2 Kgs. 18:4.
　b 1 Kgs. 16:33 (32–33).
　c 2 Kgs. 17:16 (15–17).
4a Jer. 7:30 (29–31).
　TG Idolatry.
　b Ezek. 23:39.

c 1 Kgs. 8:29; 9:3 (1–4).
5a 1 Kgs. 6:36; 7:12.
6a Lev. 18:21;
　2 Chr. 28:3; 33:6;
　Ezek. 20:26.
　TG Superstitions.
　b Lev. 19:26.
　c TG Spirits, Evil or Unclean.

7a TG Idolatry.
9a TG Tyranny.
11a Jer. 15:4.
　b 2 Kgs. 24:3 (3–4).
　c 1 Kgs. 21:26; 2 Kgs. 23:26.
12a 1 Sam. 3:11; Jer. 19:3.
14a 2 Kgs. 24:2.
16a 2 Kgs. 24:4.
　b TG Blood, Shedding of.

made Judah to sin, in doing *that which was* evil in the sight of the LORD.

17 ¶ Now the rest of the acts of *a*Manasseh, and all that he did, and his sin that he sinned, *are* they not written in the book of the chronicles of the kings of Judah?

18 And Manasseh slept with his fathers, and was buried in the garden of his own house, in the garden of Uzza: and Amon his son reigned in his stead.

19 ¶ *a*Amon *was* twenty and two years old when he began to reign, and he reigned two years in Jerusalem. And his mother's name *was* Meshullemeth, the daughter of Haruz of Jotbah.

20 And he did *that which was* evil in the sight of the LORD, as his father Manasseh did.

21 And he walked in all the way that his father walked in, and served the idols that his father served, and worshipped them:

22 And he forsook the LORD God of his fathers, and walked not in the way of the LORD.

23 ¶ And the servants of Amon conspired against him, and slew the king in his own house.

24 And the people of the land slew all them that had conspired against king Amon; and the people of the land made *a*Josiah his son king in his stead.

25 Now the rest of the acts of Amon which he did, *are* they not written in the book of the chronicles of the kings of Judah?

26 And he was buried in his sepulchre in the garden of Uzza: and Josiah his son reigned in his stead.

CHAPTER 22

Josiah reigns in righteousness in Judah—Hilkiah repairs the temple and finds the book of the law—Josiah sorrows because of the wickedness of his fathers—Huldah prophesies wrath upon the people but blessings upon Josiah.

*a*JOSIAH *was* eight years old when he began to reign, and he reigned thirty and one years in Jerusalem. And his mother's name *was* Jedidah, the daughter of Adaiah of Boscath.

2 And he did *that which was* right in the sight of the LORD, and walked in all the way of David his father, and turned not aside to the right hand or to the left.

3 ¶ And it came to pass in the eighteenth year of king Josiah, *that* the king sent Shaphan the son of Azaliah, the son of Meshullam, the scribe, to the house of the LORD, saying,

4 Go up to *a*Hilkiah the high priest, that he may sum the *b*silver which is brought into the house of the LORD, which the keepers of the door have gathered of the people:

5 And let them deliver it into the hand of the doers of the work, that have the oversight of the house of the LORD: and let them give it to the doers of the work which *is* in the house of the LORD, to repair the *a*breaches of the house,

6 Unto carpenters, and builders, and masons, and to buy timber and hewn stone to repair the house.

7 Howbeit there was no *a*reckoning made with them of the money that was delivered into their hand, because they dealt faithfully.

8 ¶ And Hilkiah the high priest said unto Shaphan the scribe, I have found the *a*book of the law in the house of the LORD. And Hilkiah gave the book to Shaphan, and he read it.

9 And Shaphan the scribe came to the king, and brought the king word again, and said, Thy servants have gathered the money that was found in the house, and have delivered it into the hand of them that do the work, that have the oversight of the house of the LORD.

17*a* 2 Chr. 33:18 (11–19).
19*a* 2 Chr. 33:21 (21–25).
24*a* Zeph. 1:1.
22 1*a* 2 Chr. 34:1 (1–33).

4*a* 1 Chr. 6:13;
      Ezra 7:1.
b 2 Kgs. 12:4.
5*a* OR holes, broken areas.

7*a* 2 Kgs. 12:15.
8*a* TG Scriptures,
      Preservation of.

10 And Shaphan the scribe shewed the king, saying, Hilkiah the priest hath delivered me a book. And Shaphan read it before the king.

11 And it came to pass, when the king had heard the *words of the book of the law, that he rent his clothes.

12 And the king commanded Hilkiah the priest, and *Ahikam the son of Shaphan, and Achbor the son of Michaiah, and Shaphan the scribe, and Asahiah a servant of the king's, saying,

13 Go ye, inquire of the LORD for me, and for the people, and for all Judah, concerning the words of this book that is found: for great *is* the *wrath of the LORD that is kindled against us, because our fathers have not hearkened unto the words of this book, to *do according unto all that which is written concerning us.

14 So Hilkiah the priest, and Ahikam, and Achbor, and Shaphan, and Asahiah, went unto Huldah the prophetess, the wife of Shallum the son of Tikvah, the son of Harhas, keeper of the wardrobe; (now she dwelt in Jerusalem in the *college;) and they communed with her.

15 ¶ And she said unto them, Thus saith the LORD God of Israel, Tell the man that sent you to me,

16 Thus saith the LORD, Behold, I will bring evil upon this place, and upon the inhabitants thereof, *even* all the words of the *book which the king of Judah hath read:

17 Because they have forsaken me, and have burned incense unto other gods, that they might *provoke me to anger with all the works of their hands; therefore my wrath shall be kindled against this place, and shall not be quenched.

18 But to the king of Judah which sent you to inquire of the LORD, thus shall ye say to him, Thus saith the LORD God of Israel, *As touching* the words which thou hast heard;

19 Because thine heart was tender, and thou hast *humbled thyself before the LORD, when thou heardest what I spake against this place, and against the inhabitants thereof, that they should become a *desolation and a *curse, and hast rent thy clothes, and wept before me; I also have heard *thee,* saith the LORD.

20 Behold therefore, I will gather thee unto thy fathers, and thou shalt be gathered into thy grave in *peace; and thine eyes shall not see all the evil which I will bring upon this place. And they brought the king word again.

CHAPTER 23

Josiah reads the book of the covenant to the people—They covenant to keep the commandments—Josiah overturns the worship of false gods, removes the sodomites, and puts down idolatry—Idolatrous priests are slain—Judah holds a solemn Passover—Egypt subjects the land of Judah.

AND the king sent, and they gathered unto him all the elders of Judah and of Jerusalem.

2 And the king went up into the house of the LORD, and all the men of Judah and all the inhabitants of Jerusalem with him, and the priests, and the prophets, and all the people, both small and great: and he *read in their ears all the words of the book of the covenant which was found in the house of the LORD.

3 ¶ And the king stood by a *pillar, and made a *covenant before the LORD, to *walk after the LORD, and to keep his commandments and his testimonies and his statutes with all *their* heart and all *their* soul, to perform the words of this covenant that were written in this book. And all the people stood to the covenant.

11*a* Alma 31:5.
12*a* Jer. 26:24.
13*a* TG God, Indignation of.
  b TG Obedience.
14*a* IE one of two geographical sections of Jerusalem.
16*a* 2 Chr. 34:24 (14–27).
17*a* Jer. 44:8.
19*a* Alma 32:14 (14–15).
  b Lev. 26:33 (31–35).
  c TG Curse.
20*a* Alma 7:27; 40:12; D&C 19:23; 45:46.
23 2*a* TG Scriptures, Study of.
  3*a* 2 Kgs. 11:14.
    b TG Commitment.
    c Jer. 36:7.
    TG Walking with God.

4 And the king commanded Hilkiah the high priest, and the *a*priests of the second order, and the *b*keepers of the door, to bring forth out of the temple of the LORD all the vessels that were made for Baal, and for the grove, and for all the host of heaven: and he burned them without Jerusalem in the fields of Kidron, and carried the ashes of them unto Beth-el.

5 And he put down the idolatrous *a*priests, whom the kings of Judah had ordained to burn incense in the high places in the cities of Judah, and in the places round about Jerusalem; them also that burned incense unto Baal, to the sun, and to the moon, and to the planets, and to all the host of heaven.

6 And he brought out the *a*grove from the house of the LORD, without Jerusalem, unto the brook Kidron, and burned it at the brook Kidron, and stamped *it* small to powder, and cast the powder thereof upon the graves of the children of the people.

7 And he brake down the houses of the *a*sodomites, that *were* by the house of the LORD, where the women wove hangings for the grove.

8 And he brought all the priests out of the cities of Judah, and defiled the high places where the priests had burned incense, from Geba to Beer-sheba, and brake down the high places of the gates that *were* in the entering in of the gate of Joshua the governor of the city, which *were* on a man's left hand at the gate of the city.

9 Nevertheless the priests of the high places *a*came not up to the altar of the LORD in Jerusalem, but they did eat of the *b*unleavened bread among their brethren.

10 And he defiled *a*Topheth, which *is* in the valley of the children of *b*Hinnom, that no man might make his son or his daughter to pass through the fire to *c*Molech.

11 And he took away the horses that the kings of Judah had given to the sun, at the entering in of the house of the LORD, by the chamber of Nathan-melech the chamberlain, which *was* in the suburbs, and burned the chariots of the sun with fire.

12 And the altars that *were* on the top of the *a*upper chamber of Ahaz, which the kings of Judah had made, and the altars which Manasseh had made in the two courts of the house of the LORD, did the king beat down, and brake *them* down from thence, and cast the dust of them into the brook Kidron.

13 And the *a*high places that *were* before Jerusalem, which *were* on the right hand of the mount of corruption, which Solomon the king of Israel had builded for Ashtoreth the abomination of the Zidonians, and for Chemosh the abomination of the Moabites, and for Milcom the abomination of the children of Ammon, did the king defile.

14 And he brake in pieces the images, and *a*cut down the groves, and filled their places with the bones of men.

15 ¶ Moreover the altar that *was* at Beth-el, *and* the high place which Jeroboam the son of Nebat, who *a*made Israel to sin, had made, both that *b*altar and the high place he *c*brake down, and burned the high place, *and* stamped *it* small to powder, and burned the grove.

16 And as Josiah turned himself, he spied the sepulchres that *were* there in the mount, and sent, and took the bones out of the sepulchres, and burned *them* upon the altar, and

4a TG Priest, Aaronic Priesthood. BD Priests.
b 2 Kgs. 25:18.
5a TG False Priesthoods.
6a IE Asherah, a fertility goddess. 2 Chr. 34:4.
7a Deut. 23:17 (17–18).
9a Ezek. 44:13 (10–14).
b TG Bread, Unleavened.
10a Isa. 30:33; Jer. 7:31 (31–33); 19:6 (6, 12).
b Josh. 18:16.
c Lev. 18:21.
12a Jer. 19:13; 32:29; Zeph. 1:5.
13a 1 Kgs. 11:7.
14a 2 Kgs. 18:4.
15a 1 Kgs. 12:28 (28–33).
b TG Apostasy of Israel.
c Amos 3:14.

polluted it, according to the word of the LORD which the man of God proclaimed, who proclaimed these words.

17 Then he said, What title *is* that that I see? And the men of the city told him, *It is* the ªsepulchre of the man of God, which came from Judah, and proclaimed these things that thou hast done against the altar of Beth-el.

18 And he said, Let him alone; let no man move his bones. So they let his bones alone, with the bones of the prophet that came out of Samaria.

19 And all the houses also of the high places that *were* in the cities of Samaria, which the kings of Israel had made to provoke *the* LORD to anger, Josiah took away, and did to them according to all the acts that he had done in Beth-el.

20 And he slew all the priests of the ªhigh places that *were* there upon the altars, and ᵇburned men's bones upon them, and returned to Jerusalem.

21 ¶ And the king commanded all the people, saying, Keep the ªpassover unto the LORD your God, as *it is* written in the book of this covenant.

22 Surely there was not holden such a ªpassover from the days of the judges that judged Israel, nor in all the days of the kings of Israel, nor of the kings of Judah;

23 But in the eighteenth year of king Josiah, *wherein* this passover was holden to the LORD in Jerusalem.

24 ¶ Moreover the ªworkers with ᵇfamiliar spirits, and the wizards, and the images, and the idols, and all the abominations that were spied in the land of Judah and in Jerusalem, did Josiah put away, that he might perform the words of the law which were written in the book

that Hilkiah the priest found in the house of the LORD.

25 And like unto him was there no ªking before him, that ᵇturned to the LORD with all his heart, and with all his soul, and with all his might, according to all the law of Moses; neither after him arose there *any* like him.

26 ¶ Notwithstanding the LORD turned not from the fierceness of his great wrath, wherewith his anger was kindled against Judah, because of all the provocations that Manasseh had ªprovoked him withal.

27 And the LORD said, I will ªremove Judah also out of my sight, as I have ᵇremoved Israel, and will cast off this city ᶜJerusalem which I have chosen, and the house of which I said, My name shall be there.

28 Now the rest of the acts of Josiah, and all that he did, *are* they not written in the book of the chronicles of the kings of Judah?

29 ¶ In his days ªPharaoh-nechoh king of Egypt went up against the king of Assyria to the river Euphrates: and king ᵇJosiah went against him; and he slew him at Megiddo, when he had seen him.

30 And his servants carried him in a chariot dead from Megiddo, and brought him to Jerusalem, and buried him in his own sepulchre. And the people of the land took ªJehoahaz the son of Josiah, and anointed him, and made him king in his father's stead.

31 ¶ Jehoahaz *was* twenty and three years old when he began to reign; and he reigned three months in Jerusalem. And his mother's name *was* Hamutal, the daughter of Jeremiah of Libnah.

32 And he did *that which was* evil in the sight of the LORD, according to all that his fathers had done.

17a 1 Kgs. 13:30 (1, 29–30).
20a 1 Kgs. 13:2.
   b 2 Chr. 34:5.
21a Deut. 16:2;
   2 Chr. 35:1 (1–19).
22a 2 Chr. 35:18 (18–19).
24a Deut. 18:9 (9–14).

   b TG Sorcery;
      Spirits, Evil or Unclean.
25a Jer. 22:15.
   b Deut. 6:5;
      2 Kgs. 18:5.
26a 2 Kgs. 21:11.
27a 2 Kgs. 24:2.

   b 2 Kgs. 17:18 (18, 20).
   c 1 Ne. 1:13 (4, 13).
29a Jer. 46:2.
   b 2 Chr. 35:22 (20–23).
30a 2 Chr. 36:1 (1–4).

33 And Pharaoh-nechoh put him in ^abands at Riblah in the land of Hamath, that he might not reign in Jerusalem; and put the land to a tribute of an hundred talents of silver, and a talent of gold.

34 And Pharaoh-nechoh made Eliakim the son of Josiah king in the room of Josiah his father, and turned his name to ^aJehoiakim, and took Jehoahaz away: and he came to Egypt, and died there.

35 And Jehoiakim gave the silver and the gold to Pharaoh; but he taxed the land to give the money according to the commandment of Pharaoh: he exacted the silver and the gold of the people of the land, of every one according to his taxation, to give *it* unto Pharaoh-nechoh.

36 ¶ Jehoiakim *was* twenty and five years old when he began to reign; and he reigned eleven years in Jerusalem. And his mother's name *was* Zebudah, the daughter of Pedaiah of Rumah.

37 And he did *that which was* ^aevil in the sight of the LORD, according to all that his fathers had done.

CHAPTER 24

Jerusalem is besieged and taken by Nebuchadnezzar—Many of the people of Judah are carried captive into Babylon—Zedekiah becomes king in Jerusalem—He rebels against Babylon.

IN his days ^aNebuchadnezzar king of Babylon came up, and Jehoiakim became his servant three years: then he turned and rebelled against him.

2 And the LORD sent ^aagainst him bands of the ^bChaldees, and bands of the Syrians, and bands of the Moabites, and bands of the children of Ammon, and sent them against Judah to ^cdestroy it, according to

the ^dword of the LORD, which he spake by his servants the prophets.

3 Surely at the commandment of the LORD came *this* upon Judah, to remove *them* out of his sight, for the ^asins of ^bManasseh, according to all that he did;

4 And also for the innocent blood that he ^ashed: for he filled Jerusalem with innocent blood; which the LORD would not pardon;

5 ¶ Now the rest of the acts of ^aJehoiakim, and all that he did, *are* they not written in the book of the chronicles of the kings of Judah?

6 So ^aJehoiakim slept with his fathers: and Jehoiachin his son reigned in his stead.

7 And the king of Egypt came not again any more out of his land: for the king of Babylon had taken from the river of Egypt unto the river Euphrates all that pertained to the king of Egypt.

8 ¶ Jehoiachin *was* ^aeighteen years old when he began to reign, and he reigned in Jerusalem three months. And his mother's name *was* Nehushta, the daughter of Elnathan of Jerusalem.

9 And he did *that which was* evil in the sight of the LORD, according to all that his father had done.

10 ¶ At that time the servants of Nebuchadnezzar king of Babylon came up against Jerusalem, and the city was ^abesieged.

11 And ^aNebuchadnezzar king of Babylon came against the city, and his servants did besiege it.

12 And ^aJehoiachin the king of Judah went out to the king of ^bBabylon, he, and his mother, and his servants, and his princes, and his officers: and the king of Babylon took him in the eighth year of his reign.

13 And he ^acarried out thence all the ^btreasures of the house of the

33*a* 2 Kgs. 25:6; Ezek. 19:4.
34*a* 2 Chr. 36:5.
37*a* Jer. 22:13 (13–14).
24 1*a* 2 Chr. 36:6 (6–10);
　　　Dan. 1:1 (1–2).
　2*a* Ezek. 19:8.
　　b Job 1:17.
　　c Jer. 25:9 (9–11).

d 2 Kgs. 21:14 (12–16);
　　23:27;
　　1 Ne. 1:13.
3*a* 2 Kgs. 21:11.
　b Jer. 15:4.
4*a* 2 Kgs. 21:16.
5*a* 2 Chr. 36:8.
6*a* 1 Chr. 3:16;

　Jer. 22:24.
8*a* 2 Chr. 36:9.
10*a* 1 Ne. 7:13 (13–15).
11*a* Ezek. 17:12.
12*a* Ezek. 1:2 (1–2).
　b Jer. 20:5.
13*a* 2 Kgs. 20:17 (17–18).
　b Dan. 1:2.

LORD, and the treasures of the king's house, and cut in pieces all the ᶜvessels of gold which ᵈSolomon king of Israel had made in the temple of the LORD, as the LORD had said.

14 And he ᵃcarried away all Jerusalem, and all the princes, and all the mighty men of valour, *even* ten thousand captives, and all the craftsmen and ᵇsmiths: none remained, save the poorest sort of the people of the land.

15 And he carried away ᵃJehoiachin to Babylon, and the king's mother, and the king's wives, and his officers, and the ᵇmighty of the land, *those* carried he into ᶜcaptivity from Jerusalem to ᵈBabylon.

16 And all the men of might, *even* seven thousand, and craftsmen and smiths a thousand, all *that were* strong *and* apt for war, even them the king of Babylon brought captive to Babylon.

17 ¶ And the king of Babylon made ᵃMattaniah his father's brother king in his stead, and changed his name to ᵇZedekiah.

18 ᵃZedekiah *was* twenty and one years old when he began to reign, and he reigned eleven years in Jerusalem. And his mother's name *was* Hamutal, the daughter of Jeremiah of Libnah.

19 And he did *that which was* ᵃevil in the sight of the LORD, according to all that Jehoiakim had done.

20 For through the anger of the LORD it came to pass in Jerusalem and Judah, until he had cast them out from his presence, that ᵃZedekiah ᵇrebelled against the king of Babylon.

CHAPTER 25

Nebuchadnezzar again besieges Jerusalem—Zedekiah is captured, Jerusalem and the temple are destroyed, and most of the people of Judah are carried into Babylon—Gedaliah, left to govern the remnant, is slain—The remnant flee to Egypt—Jehoiachin is shown favor in Babylon.

AND it came to pass in the ᵃninth year of his reign, in the tenth month, in the tenth *day* of the month, *that* ᵇNebuchadnezzar king of Babylon came, he, and all his host, against Jerusalem, and pitched against it; and they ᶜbuilt forts against it round about.

2 And the city was besieged unto the eleventh year of king Zedekiah.

3 And on the ninth *day* of the *fourth* month the famine prevailed in the city, and there was no bread for the people of the land.

4 ¶ And the ᵃcity was ᵇbroken up, and all the men of war *fled* by night by the way of the gate between two walls, which *is* by the king's garden: (now the Chaldees *were* against the city round about:) and *the king* went the way toward the plain.

5 And the army of the Chaldees ᵃpursued after the king, and overtook him in the plains of Jericho: and all his army were ᵇscattered from him.

6 So they took the ᵃking, and brought him up to the king of ᵇBabylon to Riblah; and they gave ᶜjudgment upon him.

7 And they slew the ᵃsons of Zedekiah before his eyes, and put out the eyes of Zedekiah, and bound him

13c 2 Chr. 36:7;
       Jer. 27:16.
   d 1 Kgs. 7:48 (48–50).
14a 2 Kgs. 25:11 (1–12);
       Esth. 2:6;
       Jer. 13:19 (19, 24);
       1 Ne. 1:13;
       2 Ne. 6:8; 25:10;
       Omni 1:15.
   b 1 Sam. 13:19.
15a Jer. 29:2.
   b Ezek. 17:13.
   c TG Israel, Bondage of,
       in Other Lands.

   d Jer. 24:1;
       Ezek. 19:13.
17a 2 Chr. 36:10;
       Jer. 37:1.
   b 1 Chr. 3:15.
18a Jer. 52:1; 1 Ne. 1:4;
       Omni 1:15;
       Hel. 8:21.
19a Jer. 13:27;
       1 Ne. 1:13.
20a 2 Chr. 36:13;
       Jer. 52:3;
       Ezek. 17:15.
   b Jer. 27:11; 32:2 (1–5).

25 1a Jer. 39:1; 52:4;
         Ezek. 24:1.
     b Jer. 21:2.
     c Ezek. 4:2 (2–3).
   4a TG Jerusalem.
     b HEB penetrated,
         opened up.
   5a Jer. 52:8 (3–15).
     b Ezek. 12:14.
   6a Ezek. 17:12;
         Omni 1:15.
     b 2 Kgs. 23:33.
     c Ezek. 23:24.
   7a Hel. 8:21.

with fetters of brass, and *b*carried him to *c*Babylon.

8 ¶ And in the fifth month, on the seventh *day* of the month, which *is* the nineteenth year of king Nebuchadnezzar king of Babylon, came *a*Nebuzar-adan, captain of the guard, a servant of the king of Babylon, unto Jerusalem:

9 And he *a*burnt the *b*house of the LORD, and the king's house, and all the houses of Jerusalem, and every great *man's* house *c*burnt he with fire.

10 And all the army of the Chaldees, that *were with* the captain of the guard, brake down the walls of Jerusalem round about.

11 Now the rest of the people *that were* left in the city, and the fugitives that fell away to the king of Babylon, with the remnant of the multitude, did Nebuzar-adan the captain of the guard *a*carry away.

12 But the captain of the guard left of the *a*poor of the land *to be* vinedressers and husbandmen.

13 And the *a*pillars of brass that *were* in the house of the LORD, and the *b*bases, and the brasen *c*sea that *was* in the house of the LORD, did the Chaldees break in pieces, and carried the brass of them to *d*Babylon.

14 And the *a*pots, and the shovels, and the *b*snuffers, and the spoons, and all the vessels of brass wherewith they ministered, took they away.

15 And the firepans, and the bowls, *and* such things as *were* of gold, *in* gold, and of silver, *in* silver, the captain of the guard took away.

16 The two pillars, one sea, and the bases which Solomon had made for the house of the LORD; the brass of all these *a*vessels was without weight.

17 The height of the one pillar *was*

eighteen cubits, and the chapiter upon it *was* brass: and the height of the chapiter three cubits; and the wreathen work, and pomegranates upon the chapiter round about, all of brass: and like unto these had the second pillar with wreathen work.

18 ¶ And the captain of the guard took *a*Seraiah the chief priest, and Zephaniah the second priest, and the *b*three keepers of the door:

19 And out of the city he took an officer that was set over the *a*men of war, and five men of them that were in the king's presence, which were found in the city, and the principal scribe of the host, which mustered the people of the land, and threescore men of the people of the land *that were* found in the city:

20 And Nebuzar-adan captain of the guard took these, and brought them to the king of Babylon to Riblah:

21 And the king of Babylon smote them, and *a*slew them at Riblah in the land of Hamath. So Judah was carried away out of their land.

22 ¶ And *as for* the people that remained in the land of Judah, whom Nebuchadnezzar king of Babylon had left, even over them he made *a*Gedaliah the son of Ahikam, the son of Shaphan, ruler.

23 And when all the captains of the armies, they and their men, heard that the king of Babylon had made Gedaliah governor, there came to Gedaliah to Mizpah, even Ishmael the son of Nethaniah, and Johanan the son of Careah, and Seraiah the son of Tanhumeth the Netophathite, and Jaazaniah the son of a Maachathite, they and their men.

24 And Gedaliah sware to them, and to their men, and said unto

---

7*b* TG Israel, Scattering of.
  c TG Israel, Bondage of,
     in Other Lands.
8*a* Jer. 43:6.
9*a* Isa. 64:11;
     Jer. 39:8; 52:13;
     Ezek. 16:41.
  b TG Temple.
  c Ps. 79:1;
     Hosea 8:14.

11*a* 2 Kgs. 24:14 (10–16);
     Jer. 13:19 (19, 24);
     2 Ne. 6:8.
12*a* Jer. 40:7.
13*a* 1 Kgs. 7:15.
  b 1 Kgs. 7:27.
  c Jer. 27:19.
  d Jer. 20:5.
14*a* Ex. 27:3.
  b IE devices for

     extinguishing.
     1 Kgs. 7:50.
16*a* 1 Kgs. 7:47.
18*a* 1 Chr. 6:14.
  b 2 Kgs. 23:4.
19*a* Jer. 52:25.
21*a* Jer. 39:6; 52:10;
     Ezek. 11:10.
22*a* Jer. 40:5 (1–6); 43:6.

them, Fear not to be the servants of the Chaldees: dwell in the land, and serve the king of Babylon; and it shall be well with you.

25 But it came to pass in the seventh month, that Ishmael the son of Nethaniah, the son of Elishama, of the seed royal, came, and ten men with him, and smote Gedaliah, that he died, and the Jews and the Chaldees that were with him at Mizpah.

26 And all the people, both small and great, and the captains of the armies, arose, and came to Egypt: for they were afraid of the Chaldees.

27 ¶ And it came to pass in the seven and thirtieth year of the captivity of Jehoiachin king of Judah, in the twelfth month, on the seven and twentieth *day* of the month, *that* Evil-merodach king of Babylon in the year that he began to reign did lift up the head of Jehoiachin king of Judah out of prison;

28 And he spake ^akindly to him, and set his throne above the throne of the kings that *were* with him in Babylon;

29 And changed his prison garments: and he did eat bread continually before him all the days of his life.

30 And his allowance *was* a continual allowance given him of the king, a daily rate for every day, all the days of his life.

THE FIRST BOOK OF THE
CHRONICLES

CHAPTER 1

The genealogies and family ties from Adam to Abraham are given—The posterity of Abraham is listed.

^aADAM, Sheth, Enosh, 2 Kenan, Mahalaleel, Jered, 3 Henoch, ^aMethuselah, Lamech,

4 Noah, ^aShem, Ham, and Japheth.

5 ¶ The sons of Japheth; Gomer, and Magog, and Madai, and Javan, and Tubal, and Meshech, and Tiras.

6 And the sons of Gomer; Ashchenaz, and Riphath, and Togarmah.

7 And the sons of ^aJavan; Elishah, and Tarshish, Kittim, and Dodanim.

8 ¶ The sons of ^aHam; Cush, and Mizraim, Put, and Canaan.

9 And the sons of Cush; Seba, and Havilah, and Sabta, and Raamah, and Sabtecha. And the sons of Raamah; Sheba, and Dedan.

10 And Cush begat ^aNimrod: he began to be mighty upon the earth.

11 And ^aMizraim begat Ludim, and Anamim, and Lehabim, and Naphtuhim,

12 And Pathrusim, and Casluhim, (of whom came the ^aPhilistines,) and Caphthorim.

13 And Canaan begat Zidon his firstborn, and Heth,

14 The Jebusite also, and the Amorite, and the Girgashite,

15 And the Hivite, and the Arkite, and the Sinite,

28a Jer. 52:32 (31–34).

[1 CHRONICLES]

1 1a TG Adam.

3a Moses 8:2.
4a Moses 8:12.
7a Gen. 10:4 (2–5).
8a Gen. 10:6 (6–8).

10a Gen. 10:8 (8–9);
    Ether 2:1.
11a Gen. 10:13 (13–18).
12a Gen. 10:14.

16 And the Arvadite, and the Zemarite, and the Hamathite.

17 ¶ The sons of [a]Shem; Elam, and Asshur, and Arphaxad, and Lud, and Aram, and Uz, and Hul, and Gether, and Meshech.

18 And Arphaxad begat Shelah, and Shelah begat Eber.

19 And unto Eber were born two sons: the name of the one was Peleg; because in his days the earth was [a]divided: and his brother's name was Joktan.

20 And Joktan begat Almodad, and Sheleph, and Hazarmaveth, and Jerah,

21 Hadoram also, and Uzal, and Diklah,

22 And Ebal, and Abimael, and Sheba,

23 And Ophir, and Havilah, and Jobab. All these were the sons of Joktan.

24 ¶ Shem, Arphaxad, Shelah,

25 Eber, Peleg, Reu,

26 Serug, Nahor, [a]Terah,

27 Abram; the same is [a]Abraham.

28 The sons of Abraham; Isaac, and [a]Ishmael.

29 ¶ These are their generations: The firstborn of [a]Ishmael, Nebaioth; then Kedar, and Adbeel, and Mibsam,

30 Mishma, and Dumah, Massa, Hadad, and Tema,

31 Jetur, Naphish, and Kedemah. These are the sons of Ishmael.

32 ¶ Now the sons of [a]Keturah, Abraham's concubine: she bare Zimran, and Jokshan, and Medan, and [b]Midian, and Ishbak, and Shuah. And the sons of Jokshan; Sheba, and Dedan.

33 And the sons of Midian; Ephah, and Epher, and Henoch, and Abida, and Eldaah. All these are the sons of Keturah.

34 And Abraham begat Isaac. The sons of Isaac; Esau and Israel.

35 ¶ The sons of [a]Esau; Eliphaz, Reuel, and Jeush, and Jaalam, and Korah.

36 The sons of Eliphaz; Teman, and Omar, Zephi, and Gatam, Kenaz, and Timna, and Amalek.

37 The sons of Reuel; Nahath, Zerah, Shammah, and Mizzah.

38 And the sons of [a]Seir; Lotan, and Shobal, and Zibeon, and Anah, and Dishon, and Ezer, and Dishan.

39 And the sons of Lotan; Hori, and Homam: and Timna was Lotan's sister.

40 The sons of Shobal; Alian, and Manahath, and Ebal, Shephi, and Onam. And the sons of Zibeon; Aiah, and Anah.

41 The sons of Anah; Dishon. And the sons of Dishon; Amram, and Eshban, and Ithran, and Cheran.

42 The sons of Ezer; Bilhan, and Zavan, and Jakan. The sons of Dishan; Uz, and Aran.

43 ¶ Now these are the kings that reigned in the land of [a]Edom before any king reigned over the children of Israel; Bela the son of Beor: and the name of his city was Dinhabah.

44 And when Bela was dead, Jobab the son of Zerah of Bozrah reigned in his stead.

45 And when Jobab was dead, Husham of the land of the Temanites reigned in his stead.

46 And when Husham was dead, Hadad the son of Bedad, which smote Midian in the field of Moab, reigned in his stead: and the name of his city was Avith.

47 And when Hadad was dead, Samlah of Masrekah reigned in his stead.

48 And when Samlah was dead, Shaul of Rehoboth by the river reigned in his stead.

49 And when Shaul was dead, Baal-hanan the son of Achbor reigned in his stead.

50 And when Baal-hanan was dead, Hadad reigned in his stead: and the name of his city was Pai;

17a Gen. 10:22 (22–25).
19a TG Earth, Dividing of.
26a Abr. 2:1.
27a Gen. 17:5.

28a Gen. 16:15 (11, 15); 21:3 (2–3).
29a Gen. 25:13 (13–16).
32a Gen. 25:4 (1–4).

b Gen. 25:2.
35a Gen. 36:9 (9–13).
38a Gen. 36:20 (20–28).
43a Gen. 36:31 (31–43).

and his wife's name *was* Mehetabel, the daughter of Matred, the daughter of Mezahab.

51 ¶ Hadad died also. And the dukes of Edom were; duke Timnah, duke Aliah, duke Jetheth,

52 Duke Aholibamah, duke Elah, duke Pinon,

53 Duke Kenaz, duke Teman, duke Mibzar,

54 Duke Magdiel, duke Iram. These *are* the dukes of Edom.

CHAPTER 2

The descendants of Israel, Judah, Jesse, Caleb, and others are listed.

THESE *are* the sons of Israel; *a*Reuben, Simeon, Levi, and Judah, Issachar, and Zebulun,

2 *a*Dan, Joseph, and Benjamin, Naphtali, Gad, and Asher.

3 ¶ The sons of Judah; *a*Er, and *b*Onan, and Shelah: *which* three were born unto him of the daughter of Shua the Canaanitess. And Er, the firstborn of Judah, was evil in the sight of the LORD; and he slew him.

4 And Tamar his daughter in law bare him *a*Pharez and Zerah. All the sons of Judah *were* five.

5 The sons of Pharez; Hezron, and Hamul.

6 And the sons of Zerah; Zimri, and Ethan, and Heman, and Calcol, and Dara: five of them in all.

7 And the sons of Carmi; Achar, the troubler of Israel, who transgressed in the thing *a*accursed.

8 And the sons of Ethan; Azariah.

9 The sons also of *a*Hezron, that were born unto him; Jerahmeel, and Ram, and Chelubai.

10 And Ram begat Amminadab; and Amminadab begat Nahshon, prince of the children of Judah;

11 And Nahshon begat Salma, and Salma begat Boaz,

12 And Boaz begat Obed, and Obed begat Jesse,

13 ¶ And Jesse begat his firstborn *a*Eliab, and Abinadab the second, and Shimma the third,

14 Nethaneel the fourth, Raddai the fifth,

15 Ozem the sixth, *a*David the seventh:

16 Whose sisters *were* Zeruiah, and Abigail. And the sons of Zeruiah; Abishai, and *a*Joab, and Asahel, three.

17 And Abigail bare Amasa: and the father of Amasa *was* Jether the Ishmeelite.

18 ¶ And Caleb the son of Hezron begat *children* of Azubah *his* wife, and of Jerioth: her sons *are* these; Jesher, and Shobab, and Ardon.

19 And when Azubah was dead, Caleb took unto him Ephrath, which bare him Hur.

20 And Hur begat Uri, and Uri begat Bezaleel.

21 ¶ And afterward Hezron went in to the daughter of Machir the father of Gilead, whom he married when he *was* threescore years old; and she bare him Segub.

22 And Segub begat Jair, who had three and twenty cities in the land of Gilead.

23 And he took Geshur, and Aram, with the towns of Jair, from them, with Kenath, and the towns thereof, *even* threescore cities. All these *belonged to* the sons of Machir the father of Gilead.

24 And after that Hezron was dead in Caleb-ephratah, then Abiah Hezron's wife bare him Ashur the father of Tekoa.

25 ¶ And the sons of Jerahmeel the firstborn of Hezron were, Ram the firstborn, and Bunah, and Oren, and Ozem, *and* Ahijah.

26 Jerahmeel had also another wife, whose name *was* Atarah; she *was* the mother of Onam.

27 And the sons of Ram the firstborn of Jerahmeel were, Maaz, and Jamin, and Eker.

---

2 1*a* Gen. 29:32 (32–35).
  2*a* Gen. 30:6 (5–13).
  3*a* Gen. 38:3 (3–5).
    b Gen. 46:12.

4*a* Ruth 4:18;
    Matt. 1:3 (3–6).
7*a* Josh. 6:18; 7:1.
9*a* Matt. 1:3 (3–4).

13*a* 1 Sam. 16:6; 17:13.
15*a* 1 Sam. 16:13 (11–13);
    17:12.
16*a* 2 Sam. 2:18.

28 And the sons of Onam were, Shammai, and Jada. And the sons of Shammai; Nadab, and Abishur.

29 And the name of the wife of Abishur *was* Abihail, and she bare him Ahban, and Molid.

30 And the sons of Nadab; Seled, and Appaim: but Seled died without children.

31 And the sons of Appaim; Ishi. And the sons of Ishi; Sheshan. And the children of Sheshan; Ahlai.

32 And the sons of Jada the brother of Shammai; Jether, and Jonathan: and Jether died without children.

33 And the sons of Jonathan; Peleth, and Zaza. These were the sons of Jerahmeel.

34 ¶ Now Sheshan had no sons, but daughters. And Sheshan had a servant, an Egyptian, whose name *was* Jarha.

35 And Sheshan gave his daughter to Jarha his servant to wife; and she bare him Attai.

36 And Attai begat Nathan, and Nathan begat Zabad,

37 And Zabad begat Ephlal, and Ephlal begat Obed,

38 And Obed begat Jehu, and Jehu begat Azariah,

39 And Azariah begat Helez, and Helez begat Eleasah,

40 And Eleasah begat Sisamai, and Sisamai begat Shallum,

41 And Shallum begat Jekamiah, and Jekamiah begat Elishama.

42 ¶ Now the sons of Caleb the brother of Jerahmeel *were,* Mesha his firstborn, which *was* the father of Ziph; and the sons of Mareshah the father of Hebron.

43 And the sons of Hebron; Korah, and Tappuah, and Rekem, and Shema.

44 And Shema begat Raham, the father of Jorkoam: and Rekem begat Shammai.

45 And the son of Shammai *was* Maon: and Maon *was* the father of Beth-zur.

46 And Ephah, Caleb's concubine, bare Haran, and Moza, and Gazez: and Haran begat Gazez.

47 And the sons of Jahdai; Regem, and Jotham, and Geshan, and Pelet, and Ephah, and Shaaph.

48 Maachah, Caleb's concubine, bare Sheber, and Tirhanah.

49 She bare also Shaaph the father of Madmannah, Sheva the father of Machbenah, and the father of Gibea: and the daughter of Caleb *was* Achsah.

50 ¶ These were the sons of Caleb the son of Hur, the firstborn of Ephratah; Shobal the father of Kirjath-jearim,

51 Salma the father of Beth-lehem, Hareph the father of Beth-gader.

52 And Shobal the father of Kirjath-jearim had sons; Haroeh, *and* half of the Manahethites.

53 And the families of Kirjath-jearim; the Ithrites, and the Puhites, and the Shumathites, and the Mishraites; of them came the Zareathites, and the Eshtaulites.

54 The sons of Salma; Beth-lehem, and the Netophathites, Ataroth, the house of Joab, and half of the Manahethites, the Zorites.

55 And the families of the *ª*scribes which dwelt at Jabez; the Tirathites, the Shimeathites, *and* Suchathites. These *are* the *ᵇ*Kenites that came of Hemath, the father of the house of *ᶜ*Rechab.

CHAPTER 3

David's sons are named—The successors of Solomon to Jeconiah and beyond are listed.

Now these were the *ª*sons of David, which were born unto him in Hebron; the firstborn Amnon, of Ahinoam the Jezreelitess; the second Daniel, of Abigail the Carmelitess:

2 The third, *ª*Absalom the son of Maachah the daughter of Talmai king of Geshur: the fourth, *ᵇ*Adonijah the son of Haggith:

3 The fifth, Shephatiah of Abital: the sixth, Ithream by Eglah his wife.

4 *These* six were born unto him in Hebron; and there he [a]reigned seven years and six months: and in Jerusalem he reigned thirty and three years.

5 And these were born unto him in Jerusalem; Shimea, and Shobab, and Nathan, and [a]Solomon, four, of [b]Bath-shua the daughter of [c]Ammiel:

6 Ibhar also, and Elishama, and Eliphelet,

7 And Nogah, and Nepheg, and Japhia,

8 And Elishama, and Eliada, and Eliphelet, nine.

9 *These were* all the sons of David, beside the sons of the [a]concubines, and [b]Tamar their sister.

10 ¶ And Solomon's son *was* [a]Rehoboam, Abia his son, Asa his son, Jehoshaphat his son,

11 Joram his son, Ahaziah his son, Joash his son,

12 Amaziah his son, Azariah his son, Jotham his son,

13 Ahaz his son, Hezekiah his son, Manasseh his son,

14 Amon his son, Josiah his son.

15 And the sons of Josiah *were*, the firstborn Johanan, the second Jehoiakim, the third [a]Zedekiah, the fourth [b]Shallum.

16 And the sons of [a]Jehoiakim: Jeconiah his son, Zedekiah his son.

17 ¶ And the sons of Jeconiah; Assir, Salathiel his son,

18 Malchiram also, and Pedaiah, and Shenazar, Jecamiah, Hoshama, and Nedabiah.

19 And the sons of Pedaiah *were*, [a]Zerubbabel, and Shimei: and the sons of Zerubbabel; Meshullam, and Hananiah, and Shelomith their sister:

20 And Hashubah, and Ohel, and Berechiah, and Hasadiah, Jushab-hesed, five.

21 And the sons of Hananiah; Pelatiah, and Jesaiah: the sons of Rephaiah, the sons of Arnan, the sons of Obadiah, the sons of Shechaniah.

22 And the sons of Shechaniah; Shemaiah: and the sons of Shemaiah; Hattush, and Igeal, and Bariah, and Neariah, and Shaphat, six.

23 And the sons of Neariah; Elioenai, and Hezekiah, and Azrikam, three.

24 And the sons of Elioenai *were*, Hodaiah, and Eliashib, and Pelaiah, and Akkub, and Johanan, and Dalaiah, and Anani, seven.

CHAPTER 4

The families and descendants of Judah, Simeon, and others are chronicled—Various princes in their families are named.

THE sons of Judah; Pharez, Hezron, and Carmi, and Hur, and Shobal.

2 And Reaiah the son of Shobal begat Jahath; and Jahath begat Ahumai, and Lahad. These *are* the families of the Zorathites.

3 And these *were of* the father of Etam; Jezreel, and Ishma, and Idbash: and the name of their sister *was* Hazelelponi:

4 And Penuel the father of Gedor, and Ezer the father of Hushah. These *are* the sons of Hur, the firstborn of Ephratah, the father of Bethlehem.

5 ¶ And Ashur the father of Tekoa had two wives, Helah and Naarah.

6 And Naarah bare him Ahuzam, and Hepher, and Temeni, and Haahashtari. These *were* the sons of Naarah.

7 And the sons of Helah *were*, Zereth, and Jezoar, and Ethnan.

4a 2 Sam. 2:11; 5:5.
5a Matt. 1:6.
  b 2 Sam. 11:3.
  c Bath-shua is Bathsheba; and the name Eliam is the same as Ammiel with its syllables transposed.
9a Jacob 1:15.

10a 1 Kgs. 11:43.
15a 2 Kgs. 24:17.
  b Jer. 22:11.
16a 2 Kgs. 24:6; Jer. 22:24.
19a According to these verses, Zerubbabel was the grandson

of Jeconiah through Pedaiah; elsewhere he is called the son of Shealtiel.
Ezra 3:2; 5:2;
Hag. 1:1;
Matt. 1:12.

8 And Coz begat Anub, and Zobebah, and the families of Aharhel the son of Harum.

9 ¶ And Jabez was more honourable than his brethren: and his mother called his name Jabez, saying, Because I bare him with sorrow.

10 And Jabez called on the God of Israel, saying, Oh that thou wouldest bless me indeed, and enlarge my ᵃcoast, and that thine hand might be with me, and that thou wouldest keep *me* from evil, that it may not grieve me! And God granted him that which he requested.

11 ¶ And Chelub the brother of Shuah begat Mehir, which *was* the father of Eshton.

12 And Eshton begat Beth-rapha, and Paseah, and Tehinnah the father of Ir-nahash. These *are* the men of Rechah.

13 And the sons of Kenaz; Othniel, and Seraiah: and the sons of Othniel; Hathath.

14 And Meonothai begat Ophrah: and Seraiah begat Joab, the father of the valley of Charashim; for they were craftsmen.

15 And the sons of Caleb the son of Jephunneh; Iru, Elah, and Naam: and the sons of Elah, even Kenaz.

16 And the sons of Jehaleleel; Ziph, and Ziphah, Tiria, and Asareel.

17 And the sons of Ezra *were*, Jether, and Mered, and Epher, and Jalon: and she bare Miriam, and Shammai, and Ishbah the father of Eshtemoa.

18 And his wife Jehudijah bare Jered the father of Gedor, and Heber the father of Socho, and Jekuthiel the father of Zanoah. And these *are* the sons of Bithiah the daughter of Pharaoh, which Mered took.

19 And the sons of *his* wife Hodiah the sister of Naham, the father of Keilah the Garmite, and Eshtemoa the Maachathite.

20 And the sons of Shimon *were*, Amnon, and Rinnah, Ben-hanan, and Tilon. And the sons of Ishi *were*, Zoheth, and Ben-zoheth.

21 ¶ The sons of Shelah the son of Judah *were*, Er the father of Lecah, and Laadah the father of Mareshah, and the families of the house of them that wrought fine linen, of the house of Ashbea,

22 And Jokim, and the men of Chozeba, and Joash, and Saraph, who had the dominion in Moab, and Jashubi-lehem. And *these are* ancient things.

23 These *were* the potters, and those that dwelt among plants and hedges: there they dwelt with the king for his work.

24 ¶ The sons of Simeon *were*, Nemuel, and Jamin, Jarib, Zerah, *and* Shaul:

25 Shallum his son, Mibsam his son, Mishma his son.

26 And the sons of Mishma; Hamuel his son, Zacchur his son, Shimei his son.

27 And Shimei had sixteen sons and six daughters; but his brethren had not many children, neither did all their family multiply, like to the children of Judah.

28 And they dwelt at Beer-sheba, and Moladah, and Hazar-shual,

29 And at Bilhah, and at Ezem, and at Tolad,

30 And at Bethuel, and at Hormah, and at Ziklag,

31 And at Beth-marcaboth, and Hazar-susim, and at Beth-birei, and at Shaaraim. These *were* their cities unto the reign of David.

32 And their villages *were*, Etam, and Ain, Rimmon, and Tochen, and Ashan, five cities:

33 And all their villages that *were* round about the same cities, unto Baal. These *were* their habitations, and their genealogy.

34 And Meshobab, and Jamlech, and Joshah the son of Amaziah,

35 And Joel, and Jehu the son of Josibiah, the son of Seraiah, the son of Asiel,

36 And Elioenai, and Jaakobah, and Jeshohaiah, and Asaiah, and Adiel, and Jesimiel, and Benaiah,

37 And Ziza the son of Shiphi, the

4 10*a* Deut. 19:8.

son of Allon, the son of Jedaiah, the son of Shimri, the son of Shemaiah;

38 These mentioned by *their* names *were* princes in their families: and the house of their fathers increased greatly.

39 ¶ And they went to the entrance of Gedor, *even* unto the east side of the valley, to seek pasture for their flocks.

40 And they found fat pasture and good, and the land *was* wide, and quiet, and peaceable; for *they* of Ham had dwelt there of old.

41 And these written by name came in the days of Hezekiah king of Judah, and smote their tents, and the habitations that were found there, and destroyed them utterly unto this day, and dwelt in their rooms: because *there was* pasture there for their flocks.

42 And *some* of them, *even* of the sons of Simeon, five hundred men, went to mount Seir, having for their captains Pelatiah, and Neariah, and Rephaiah, and Uzziel, the sons of Ishi.

43 And they smote the rest of the Amalekites that were escaped, and dwelt there unto this day.

CHAPTER 5

The sons of Joseph received Reuben's birthright—Judah and his descendants became rulers in Israel—The line of Reuben down to the captivity is given—The Assyrians carry the Reubenites, Gadites, and half of Manasseh into captivity.

Now the sons of ᵃReuben the firstborn of Israel, (for he *was* the firstborn; but, forasmuch as he defiled his father's ᵇbed, his birthright was given unto the ᶜsons of ᵈJoseph the son of Israel: and the genealogy is not to be reckoned after the birthright.

2 For ᵃJudah prevailed above his brethren, and of him *came* the chief ᵇruler; but the ᶜbirthright *was* Joseph's:)

3 The sons, *I say*, of ᵃReuben the firstborn of Israel *were*, Hanoch, and Pallu, Hezron, and Carmi.

4 The sons of Joel; Shemaiah his son, Gog his son, Shimei his son,

5 Micah his son, Reaia his son, Baal his son,

6 Beerah his son, whom ᵃTilgath-pilneser king of Assyria carried away *captive:* he *was* prince of the Reubenites.

7 And his brethren by their families, when the genealogy of their generations was reckoned, *were* the chief, Jeiel, and Zechariah,

8 And Bela the son of Azaz, the son of Shema, the son of Joel, who dwelt in Aroer, even unto Nebo and ᵃBaal-meon:

9 And eastward he inhabited unto the entering in of the wilderness from the river Euphrates: because their cattle were multiplied in the land of ᵃGilead.

10 And in the days of Saul they made war with the Hagarites, who fell by their hand: and they dwelt in their tents throughout all the east *land* of Gilead.

11 ¶ And the children of Gad dwelt over against them, in the land of Bashan unto Salchah:

12 Joel the chief, and Shapham the next, and Jaanai, and Shaphat in Bashan.

13 And their brethren of the house of their fathers *were*, Michael, and Meshullam, and Sheba, and Jorai, and Jachan, and Zia, and Heber, seven.

14 These *are* the children of Abihail the son of Huri, the son of Jaroah, the son of Gilead, the son of Michael, the son of Jeshishai, the son of Jahdo, the son of Buz;

15 Ahi the son of Abdiel, the son of Guni, chief of the house of their fathers.

---

5 1a Gen. 29:32; 49:3 (3–4);
　　Deut. 33:6.
　b TG Sexual Immorality.
　c Josh. 14:4.
　d TG Israel, Joseph,
　　People of.

2a TG Israel, Judah,
　　People of.
　b Micah 5:2;
　　Matt. 2:6;
　　John 7:42.
　c TG Birthright;

　　Priesthood, History of.
3a Josh. 22:1 (1–6);
　　Ezek. 48:31 (6–7, 31).
6a 2 Kgs. 15:29; 16:7.
8a Ezek. 25:9.
9a Josh. 22:9 (9–12).

16 And they dwelt in Gilead in Bashan, and in her towns, and in all the suburbs of Sharon, upon their borders.

17 All these were reckoned by genealogies in the days of ^aJotham king of Judah, and in the days of Jeroboam king of Israel.

18 ¶ The sons of Reuben, and the Gadites, and half the tribe of Manasseh, of valiant men, men able to bear buckler and sword, and to shoot with bow, and skilful in war, *were* four and forty thousand seven hundred and threescore, that went out to the war.

19 And they made war with the Hagarites, with Jetur, and Nephish, and Nodab.

20 And they were ^ahelped against them, and the Hagarites were delivered into their hand, and all that *were* with them: for they cried to God in the battle, and he was ^bentreated of them; because they put their ^ctrust in him.

21 And they took away their cattle; of their camels fifty thousand, and of sheep two hundred and fifty thousand, and of asses two thousand, and of men an hundred thousand.

22 For there fell down many slain, because the war *was* of God. And they dwelt in their steads until the captivity.

23 ¶ And the children of the half tribe of Manasseh dwelt in the land: they increased from Bashan unto Baal-hermon and Senir, and unto mount Hermon.

24 And these *were* the heads of the house of their fathers, even Epher, and Ishi, and Eliel, and Azriel, and Jeremiah, and Hodaviah, and Jahdiel, mighty men of valour, famous men, *and* heads of the house of their fathers.

25 ¶ And they transgressed against the God of their fathers, and went a whoring after the gods of the people of the land, whom God destroyed before them.

26 And the God of Israel stirred up the spirit of Pul king of Assyria, and the spirit of Tilgath-pilneser king of Assyria, and he ^acarried them away, even the Reubenites, and the ^bGadites, and the half tribe of Manasseh, and brought them unto Halah, and Habor, and Hara, and to the river Gozan, unto this day.

CHAPTER 6

The sons of Levi, including David's singers, are listed—The responsibilities of Aaron and his descendants are given—Levite cities are designated in the areas of the various tribes.

THE sons of ^aLevi; Gershon, Kohath, and Merari.

2 And the sons of Kohath; Amram, Izhar, and Hebron, and Uzziel.

3 And the children of Amram; Aaron, and Moses, and Miriam. The sons also of Aaron; Nadab, and Abihu, Eleazar, and Ithamar.

4 ¶ Eleazar begat Phinehas, Phinehas begat Abishua,

5 And Abishua begat Bukki, and Bukki begat Uzzi,

6 And Uzzi begat Zerahiah, and Zerahiah begat Meraioth,

7 Meraioth begat Amariah, and Amariah begat Ahitub,

8 And Ahitub begat ^aZadok, and Zadok begat Ahimaaz,

9 And Ahimaaz begat Azariah, and Azariah begat Johanan,

10 And Johanan begat ^aAzariah, (he *it is* that executed the priest's office in the temple that Solomon built in Jerusalem:)

11 And Azariah begat Amariah, and Amariah begat Ahitub,

12 And Ahitub begat Zadok, and Zadok begat Shallum,

13 And Shallum begat ^aHilkiah, and Hilkiah begat Azariah,

17*a* 2 Kgs. 15:5 (1–7), 32.
20*a* Alma 57:26 (25–27).
    b Gen. 25:21.
    c TG Trust in God.
26*a* 2 Kgs. 15:29.

    b Gen. 49:19.
6 1*a* Gen. 46:11;
      Mal. 3:3 (2–3);
      D&C 84:34 (31–43).
8*a* 2 Sam. 8:17;

1 Kgs. 2:35;
1 Chr. 24:3.
10*a* 2 Chr. 26:17 (16–23).
13*a* 2 Kgs. 22:4 (4–14);
      Ezra 7:1.

14 And Azariah begat ^aSeraiah, and Seraiah begat Jehozadak,

15 And Jehozadak went *into captivity,* when the LORD carried away ^aJudah and Jerusalem by the hand of Nebuchadnezzar.

16 ¶ The sons of ^aLevi; Gershom, ^bKohath, and Merari.

17 And these *be* the names of the sons of Gershom; Libni, and Shimei.

18 And the sons of Kohath *were,* Amram, and Izhar, and Hebron, and Uzziel.

19 The sons of ^aMerari; Mahli, and Mushi. And these *are* the families of the Levites according to their fathers.

20 Of Gershom; Libni his son, Jahath his son, Zimmah his son,

21 Joah his son, Iddo his son, Zerah his son, Jeaterai his son.

22 The sons of Kohath; Amminadab his son, Korah his son, Assir his son,

23 ^aElkanah his son, and Ebiasaph his son, and Assir his son,

24 Tahath his son, Uriel his son, Uzziah his son, and Shaul his son.

25 And the sons of Elkanah; Amasai, and Ahimoth.

26 *As for* Elkanah: the sons of Elkanah; Zophai his son, and Nahath his son,

27 Eliab his son, Jeroham his son, Elkanah his son.

28 And the sons of ^aSamuel; the firstborn Vashni, and Abiah.

29 The sons of Merari; Mahli, Libni his son, Shimei his son, Uzza his son,

30 Shimea his son, Haggiah his son, Asaiah his son.

31 And these *are they* whom David set over the service of ^asong in the house of the LORD, after that the ark had rest.

32 And they ^aministered before the dwelling place of the tabernacle of the congregation with ^bsinging, until Solomon had built the house of the LORD in Jerusalem: and *then* they waited on their office ^caccording to their ^dorder.

33 And these *are* they that waited with their children. Of the sons of the Kohathites: Heman a singer, the son of Joel, the son of Shemuel,

34 The son of Elkanah, the son of Jeroham, the son of Eliel, the son of Toah,

35 The son of Zuph, the son of Elkanah, the son of Mahath, the son of Amasai,

36 The son of Elkanah, the son of Joel, the son of Azariah, the son of Zephaniah,

37 The son of Tahath, the son of Assir, the son of Ebiasaph, the son of Korah,

38 The son of Izhar, the son of Kohath, the son of Levi, the son of Israel.

39 And his brother ^aAsaph, who stood on his right hand, *even* Asaph the son of Berachiah, the son of Shimea,

40 The son of Michael, the son of Baaseiah, the son of Malchiah,

41 The son of Ethni, the son of Zerah, the son of Adaiah,

42 The son of Ethan, the son of Zimmah, the son of Shimei,

43 The son of Jahath, the son of Gershom, the son of Levi.

44 And their brethren the sons of Merari *stood* on the left hand: Ethan the son of Kishi, the son of Abdi, the son of Malluch,

45 The son of Hashabiah, the son of Amaziah, the son of Hilkiah,

46 The son of Amzi, the son of Bani, the son of Shamer,

47 The son of Mahli, the son of Mushi, the son of Merari, the son of Levi.

48 Their brethren also the ^aLevites *were* appointed unto all manner of service of the tabernacle of the house of God.

14a 2 Kgs. 25:18.
15a TG Israel, Judah, People of.
16a Ex. 6:16 (16–19).
  b 1 Chr. 15:5.
19a 1 Chr. 23:21.

23a 1 Sam. 1:1 (1–2).
28a 1 Sam. 8:1 (1–2).
31a 1 Chr. 9:33; 25:6 (1–7).
32a TG Priest, Aaronic Priesthood.

BD Priests.
  b Ezek. 40:44.
  c D&C 94:6.
  d TG Order.
39a 1 Chr. 25:1.
48a D&C 13.

49 ¶ But *a*Aaron and his *b*sons offered upon the altar of the burnt offering, and on the altar of incense, *and were appointed* for all the work of the *place* most holy, and to make an *c*atonement for Israel, according to all that Moses the *d*servant of God had commanded.

50 And these *are* the sons of *a*Aaron; Eleazar his son, Phinehas his son, Abishua his son,

51 Bukki his son, Uzzi his son, Zerahiah his son,

52 Meraioth his son, Amariah his son, Ahitub his son,

53 Zadok his son, Ahimaaz his son.

54 ¶ Now these *are* their dwelling places throughout their castles in their coasts, of the sons of Aaron, of the families of the *a*Kohathites: for theirs was the lot.

55 And they gave them Hebron in the land of Judah, and the suburbs thereof round about it.

56 But the fields of the city, and the villages thereof, they gave to Caleb the son of Jephunneh.

57 And to the sons of *a*Aaron they gave the cities of Judah, *namely*, Hebron, *the city* of refuge, and Libnah with her suburbs, and Jattir, and Eshtemoa, with their suburbs,

58 And Hilen with her suburbs, Debir with her suburbs,

59 And Ashan with her suburbs, and Beth-shemesh with her suburbs:

60 And out of the tribe of Benjamin; Geba with her suburbs, and Alemeth with her suburbs, and Anathoth with her suburbs. All their cities throughout their families *were* thirteen cities.

61 And unto the sons of Kohath, *which were* left of the family of that tribe, *were cities given* out of the half tribe, *namely, out of* the half *tribe* of Manasseh, by lot, ten cities.

62 And to the sons of Gershom throughout their families out of the tribe of Issachar, and out of the tribe of Asher, and out of the tribe of Naphtali, and out of the tribe of Manasseh in Bashan, thirteen cities.

63 Unto the sons of Merari *were given* by lot, throughout their families, out of the tribe of Reuben, and out of the tribe of Gad, and out of the tribe of Zebulun, twelve cities.

64 And the children of Israel gave to the Levites *these* cities with their suburbs.

65 And they gave by lot out of the tribe of the children of Judah, and out of the tribe of the children of Simeon, and out of the tribe of the children of Benjamin, these cities, which are called by *their* names.

66 And *the residue* of the families of the sons of *a*Kohath had cities of their coasts out of the tribe of Ephraim.

67 And they gave unto them, *of* the cities of refuge, Shechem in mount Ephraim with her suburbs; *they gave* also Gezer with her suburbs,

68 And Jokmeam with her suburbs, and Beth-horon with her suburbs,

69 And Aijalon with her suburbs, and Gath-rimmon with her suburbs:

70 And out of the half tribe of Manasseh; Aner with her suburbs, and Bileam with her suburbs, for the family of the remnant of the sons of Kohath.

71 Unto the sons of Gershom *were given* out of the family of the half tribe of Manasseh, Golan in Bashan with her suburbs, and Ashtaroth with her suburbs:

72 And out of the tribe of Issachar; Kedesh with her suburbs, Daberath with her suburbs,

73 And Ramoth with her suburbs, and Anem with her suburbs:

74 And out of the tribe of Asher; Mashal with her suburbs, and Abdon with her suburbs,

75 And Hukok with her suburbs, and Rehob with her suburbs:

76 And out of the tribe of Naphtali; Kedesh in Galilee with her suburbs,

---

49a Lev. 1:9.
  b D&C 84:34 (33–41).
  c Ex. 30:10 (1–10);
    Lev. 4:20;
        Alma 34:10 (10–15);
          Moses 5:7 (6–7).
  d TG Servant.
50a Num. 3:32.
54a Josh. 21:4.
57a Josh. 21:13 (11–19).
66a Josh. 21:20 (20–26).

and Hammon with her suburbs, and Kirjathaim with her suburbs.

77 Unto the rest of the children of ^aMerari *were given* out of the tribe of Zebulun, Rimmon with her suburbs, Tabor with her suburbs:

78 And on the other side Jordan by Jericho, on the east side of Jordan, *were given them* out of the tribe of Reuben, Bezer in the wilderness with her suburbs, and Jahzah with her suburbs,

79 Kedemoth also with her suburbs, and Mephaath with her suburbs:

80 And out of the tribe of Gad; Ramoth in Gilead with her suburbs, and Mahanaim with her suburbs,

81 And Heshbon with her suburbs, and Jazer with her suburbs.

CHAPTER 7

The sons and families are named for Issachar, Benjamin, Naphtali, Manasseh, Ephraim, and Asher.

Now the sons of ^aIssachar *were,* Tola, and Puah, Jashub, and Shimron, four.

2 And the sons of Tola; Uzzi, and Rephaiah, and Jeriel, and Jahmai, and Jibsam, and Shemuel, heads of their father's house, *to wit,* of Tola: *they were* valiant men of might in their generations; whose ^anumber *was* in the days of David two and twenty thousand and six hundred.

3 And the sons of Uzzi; Izrahiah: and the sons of Izrahiah; Michael, and Obadiah, and Joel, Ishiah, five: all of them chief men.

4 And with them, by their generations, after the house of their fathers, *were* bands of soldiers for war, six and thirty thousand *men:* for they had many wives and sons.

5 And their brethren among all the families of Issachar *were* valiant men of might, reckoned in all by their genealogies fourscore and seven thousand.

6 ¶ *The sons* of ^aBenjamin; Bela, and Becher, and Jediael, three.

7 And the sons of Bela; Ezbon, and Uzzi, and Uzziel, and Jerimoth, and Iri, five; heads of the house of *their* fathers, mighty men of valour; and were reckoned by their genealogies twenty and two thousand and thirty and four.

8 And the sons of Becher; Zemira, and Joash, and Eliezer, and Elioenai, and Omri, and Jerimoth, and Abiah, and Anathoth, and Alameth. All these *are* the sons of Becher.

9 And the number of them, after their genealogy by their generations, heads of the house of their fathers, mighty men of valour, *was* twenty thousand and two hundred.

10 The sons also of Jediael; Bilhan: and the sons of Bilhan; Jeush, and Benjamin, and Ehud, and Chenaanah, and Zethan, and Tharshish, and Ahishahar.

11 All these the sons of Jediael, by the heads of their fathers, mighty men of valour, *were* seventeen thousand and two hundred *soldiers,* fit to go out for war *and* battle.

12 Shuppim also, and Huppim, the children of Ir, *and* Hushim, the sons of Aher.

13 ¶ The sons of Naphtali; Jahziel, and Guni, and Jezer, and Shallum, the sons of Bilhah.

14 ¶ The sons of ^aManasseh; Ashriel, whom she bare: (*but his* concubine the Aramitess bare Machir the father of Gilead:

15 And Machir took to wife *the sister* of Huppim and Shuppim, whose sister's name *was* Maachah;) and the name of the second *was* Zelophehad: and Zelophehad had daughters.

16 And Maachah the wife of Machir bare a son, and she called his name Peresh; and the name of his brother *was* Sheresh; and his sons *were* Ulam and Rakem.

17 And the sons of Ulam; Bedan. These *were* the sons of Gilead, the son of Machir, the son of Manasseh.

77a Josh. 21:34 (34–39).
7 1a Gen. 46:13;
      Num. 1:28 (28–29);
26:23 (23–26).
2a 2 Sam. 24:9 (1–2, 9).
6a Gen. 46:21;
Num. 26:38.
14a Num. 26:29 (29–33);
       Alma 10:3.

18 And his sister Hammoleketh bare Ishod, and Abiezer, and Mahalah.

19 And the sons of Shemida were, Ahian, and Shechem, and Likhi, and Aniam.

20 ¶ And the sons of Ephraim; Shuthelah, and Bered his son, and Tahath his son, and Eladah his son, and Tahath his son,

21 ¶ And Zabad his son, and Shuthelah his son, and Ezer, and Elead, whom the men of Gath *that were* born in *that* land slew, because they came down to take away their cattle.

22 And Ephraim their father mourned many days, and his brethren came to comfort him.

23 ¶ And when he went in to his wife, she conceived, and bare a son, and he called his name Beriah, because it went evil with his house.

24 (And his daughter *was* Sherah, who built Beth-horon the [a]nether, and the upper, and Uzzen-sherah.)

25 And Rephah *was* his son, also Resheph, and Telah his son, and Tahan his son,

26 Laadan his son, Ammihud his son, Elishama his son,

27 Non his son, [a]Jehoshua his son.

28 ¶ And their possessions and habitations *were*, Beth-el and the towns thereof, and eastward Naaran, and westward Gezer, with the towns thereof; Shechem also and the towns thereof, unto Gaza and the towns thereof:

29 And by the borders of the children of Manasseh, Beth-shean and her towns, Taanach and her towns, Megiddo and her towns, Dor and her towns. In these dwelt the children of [a]Joseph the son of Israel.

30 ¶ The sons of Asher; Imnah, and Isuah, and Ishuai, and Beriah, and Serah their sister.

31 And the sons of Beriah; Heber, and Malchiel, who *is* the father of Birzavith.

32 And Heber begat Japhlet, and Shomer, and Hotham, and Shua their sister.

33 And the sons of Japhlet; Pasach, and Bimhal, and Ashvath. These *are* the children of Japhlet.

34 And the sons of Shamer; Ahi, and Rohgah, Jehubbah, and Aram.

35 And the sons of his brother Helem; Zophah, and Imna, and Shelesh, and Amal.

36 The sons of Zophah; Suah, and Harnepher, and Shual, and Beri, and Imrah,

37 Bezer, and Hod, and Shamma, and Shilshah, and Ithran, and Beera.

38 And the sons of Jether; Jephunneh, and Pispah, and Ara.

39 And the sons of Ulla; Arah, and Haniel, and Rezia.

40 All these *were* the children of Asher, heads of *their* father's house, choice *and* mighty men of valour, chief of the princes. And the number throughout the genealogy of them that were apt to the war *and* to battle *was* twenty and six thousand men.

CHAPTER 8

The sons and chief men of Benjamin are named.

Now Benjamin begat Bela his firstborn, Ashbel the second, and Aharah the third,

2 Nohah the fourth, and Rapha the fifth.

3 And the sons of Bela were, Addar, and Gera, and Abihud,

4 And Abishua, and Naaman, and Ahoah,

5 And Gera, and Shephuphan, and Huram.

6 And these *are* the sons of Ehud: these are the heads of the fathers of the inhabitants of Geba, and they removed them to Manahath:

7 And Naaman, and Ahiah, and Gera, he removed them, and begat Uzza, and Ahihud.

8 And Shaharaim begat *children* in the country of Moab, after he had sent them away; Hushim and Baara *were* his wives.

9 And he begat of Hodesh his wife,

24a HEB below, underneath.
27a Num. 11:28; 13:16.
29a TG Israel, Joseph, People of.

Jobab, and Zibia, and Mesha, and Malcham,

10 And Jeuz, and Shachia, and Mirma. These *were* his sons, heads of the fathers.

11 And of Hushim he begat Abitub, and Elpaal.

12 The sons of Elpaal; Eber, and Misham, and Shamed, who built Ono, and Lod, with the towns thereof:

13 Beriah also, and Shema, who *were* heads of the fathers of the inhabitants of Aijalon, who drove away the inhabitants of Gath:

14 And Ahio, Shashak, and Jeremoth,

15 And Zebadiah, and Arad, and Ader,

16 And Michael, and Ispah, and Joha, the sons of Beriah;

17 And Zebadiah, and Meshullam, and Hezeki, and Heber,

18 Ishmerai also, and Jezliah, and Jobab, the sons of Elpaal;

19 And Jakim, and Zichri, and Zabdi,

20 And Elienai, and Zilthai, and Eliel,

21 And Adaiah, and Beraiah, and Shimrath, the sons of Shimhi;

22 And Ishpan, and Heber, and Eliel,

23 And Abdon, and Zichri, and Hanan,

24 And Hananiah, and Elam, and Antothijah,

25 And Iphedeiah, and Penuel, the sons of Shashak;

26 And Shamsherai, and Shehariah, and Athaliah,

27 And Jaresiah, and Eliah, and Zichri, the sons of Jeroham.

28 These *were* heads of the fathers, by their generations, chief *men.* These dwelt in Jerusalem.

29 And at Gibeon dwelt the father of Gibeon; whose wife's name *was* Maachah:

30 And his firstborn son Abdon, and Zur, and Kish, and Baal, and Nadab,

31 And Gedor, and Ahio, and Zacher.

32 And Mikloth begat Shimeah. And these also dwelt with their brethren in Jerusalem, over against them.

33 ¶ And Ner begat ªKish, and Kish begat Saul, and ᵇSaul begat Jonathan, and Malchi-shua, and Abinadab, and Esh-baal.

34 And the son of Jonathan *was* Merib-baal; and Merib-baal begat Micah.

35 And the sons of Micah *were,* Pithon, and Melech, and Tarea, and Ahaz.

36 And Ahaz begat Jehoadah; and Jehoadah begat Alemeth, and Azmaveth, and Zimri; and Zimri begat Moza,

37 And Moza begat Binea: Rapha *was* his son, Eleasah his son, Azel his son:

38 And Azel had six sons, whose names *are* these, Azrikam, Bocheru, and Ishmael, and Sheariah, and Obadiah, and Hanan. All these *were* the sons of Azel.

39 And the sons of Eshek his brother *were,* Ulam his firstborn, Jehush the second, and Eliphelet the third.

40 And the sons of Ulam were mighty men of valour, archers, and had many sons, and sons' sons, an hundred and fifty. All these *are* of the sons of Benjamin.

CHAPTER 9

The inhabitants of Jerusalem are listed—The responsibilities of the Levites and the areas where they are to serve are listed—The family of Saul is named.

So all Israel were reckoned by ªgenealogies; and, behold, they *were* written in the ᵇbook of the kings of Israel and Judah, *who* were carried away to Babylon for their ᶜtransgression.

2 ¶ Now the first inhabitants that *dwelt* in their possessions in their cities *were,* the Israelites, the priests, Levites, and the ªNethinims.

---

8 33a 1 Sam. 9:1.
  b 1 Sam. 14:49.
9 1a TG Genealogy and

Temple Work.
  b 1 Ne. 5:12 (11–14).
  c TG Transgress.

2a Ezra 2:43; 7:24; 8:20.

3 And in Jerusalem dwelt of the children of Judah, and of the children of Benjamin, and of the children of Ephraim, and *a*Manasseh;

4 Uthai the son of Ammihud, the son of Omri, the son of Imri, the son of Bani, of the children of Pharez the son of Judah.

5 And of the Shilonites; Asaiah the firstborn, and his sons.

6 And of the sons of Zerah; Jeuel, and their brethren, six hundred and ninety.

7 And of the sons of Benjamin; Sallu the son of Meshullam, the son of Hodaviah, the son of Hasenuah,

8 And Ibneiah the son of Jeroham, and Elah the son of Uzzi, the son of Michri, and Meshullam the son of Shephathiah, the son of Reuel, the son of Ibnijah;

9 And their brethren, according to their generations, nine hundred and fifty and six. All these men *were* chief of the fathers in the house of their fathers.

10 ¶ And of the *a*priests; Jedaiah, and Jehoiarib, and Jachin,

11 And Azariah the son of Hilkiah, the son of Meshullam, the son of Zadok, the son of Meraioth, the son of Ahitub, the ruler of the house of God;

12 And Adaiah the son of Jeroham, the son of Pashur, the son of Malchijah, and Maasiai the son of Adiel, the son of Jahzerah, the son of Meshullam, the son of Meshillemith, the son of Immer;

13 And their brethren, heads of the house of their fathers, a thousand and seven hundred and threescore; very able men for the work of the service of the house of God.

14 And of the Levites; Shemaiah the son of Hasshub, the son of Azrikam, the son of Hashabiah, of the sons of Merari;

15 And Bakbakkar, Heresh, and Galal, and Mattaniah the son of Micah, the son of Zichri, the son of Asaph;

16 And Obadiah the son of Shemaiah, the son of Galal, the son of Jeduthun, and Berechiah the son of Asa, the son of Elkanah, that dwelt in the villages of the Netophathites.

17 And the porters *were*, Shallum, and Akkub, and Talmon, and Ahiman, and their brethren: Shallum *was* the chief;

18 Who hitherto *waited* in the king's *a*gate eastward: they *were* porters in the companies of the children of Levi.

19 And Shallum the son of Kore, the son of Ebiasaph, the son of Korah, and his brethren, of the house of his father, the Korahites, *were* over the work of the service, keepers of the gates of the tabernacle: and their fathers, *being* over the *a*host of the LORD, *were* keepers of the entry.

20 And Phinehas the son of Eleazar was the ruler over them in time past, *and* the LORD *was* with him.

21 *And* Zechariah the son of Meshelemiah *was* porter of the door of the tabernacle of the congregation.

22 All these *which were* chosen to be porters in the gates *were* two hundred and twelve. These were reckoned by their genealogy in their villages, whom David and Samuel the *a*seer did *b*ordain in their set office.

23 So they and their children *had* the oversight of the gates of the house of the LORD, *namely,* the house of the tabernacle, by wards.

24 In four quarters were the porters, toward the east, west, north, and south.

25 And their brethren, *which were* in their villages, *were* to come after *a*seven days from time to time with them.

26 For these Levites, the four chief porters, were in *their* set office, and were over the chambers and treasuries of the house of God.

27 ¶ And they lodged round about the house of God, because the charge

---

3*a* Alma 10:3.
10*a* Neh. 11:10.
18*a* Ezek. 46:1 (1–2).

19*a* HEB encampment.
22*a* TG Seer.
   b TG Priesthood,

Ordination.
25*a* 2 Kgs. 11:5.

was upon them, and the opening thereof every morning *pertained* to them.

28 And *certain* of them had the charge of the ministering vessels, that they should bring them in and out by tale.

29 *Some* of them also *were* appointed to oversee the vessels, and all the instruments of the sanctuary, and the fine flour, and the wine, and the oil, and the frankincense, and the spices.

30 And *some* of the sons of the priests made the ointment of the spices.

31 And Mattithiah, *one* of the Levites, who *was* the firstborn of Shallum the Korahite, had the set office over the things that were made in the pans.

32 And *other* of their brethren, of the sons of the Kohathites, *were* over the shewbread, to prepare *it* every sabbath.

33 And these *are* the ᵃsingers, chief of the fathers of the Levites, *who remaining* in the chambers *were* free: for they were employed in *that* work day and ᵇnight.

34 These chief fathers of the Levites *were* chief throughout their generations; these dwelt at Jerusalem.

35 ¶ And in Gibeon dwelt the father of Gibeon, Jehiel, whose wife's name *was* Maachah:

36 And his firstborn son Abdon, then Zur, and Kish, and Baal, and Ner, and Nadab,

37 And Gedor, and Ahio, and Zechariah, and Mikloth.

38 And Mikloth begat Shimeam. And they also dwelt with their brethren at Jerusalem, over against their brethren.

39 And Ner begat Kish; and Kish begat Saul; and Saul begat Jonathan, and Malchi-shua, and Abinadab, and Esh-baal.

40 And the son of Jonathan *was* Merib-baal: and Merib-baal begat Micah.

41 And the sons of Micah *were,* Pithon, and Melech, and Tahrea, *and Ahaz.*

42 And Ahaz begat Jarah; and Jarah begat Alemeth, and Azmaveth, and Zimri; and Zimri begat Moza;

43 And Moza begat Binea; and Rephaiah his son, Eleasah his son, Azel his son.

44 And Azel had six sons, whose names *are* these, Azrikam, Bocheru, and Ishmael, and Sheariah, and Obadiah, and Hanan: these *were* the sons of Azel.

CHAPTER 10

The Philistines defeat Israel—Saul dies for his transgressions.

Now the ᵃPhilistines fought against Israel; and the men of Israel fled from before the Philistines, and fell down slain in mount Gilboa.

2 And the Philistines followed hard after Saul, and after his sons; and the Philistines slew Jonathan, and Abinadab, and Malchi-shua, the sons of Saul.

3 And the battle went sore against Saul, and the archers hit him, and he was wounded of the archers.

4 Then said Saul to his armourbearer, Draw thy sword, and thrust me through therewith; lest these uncircumcised come and abuse me. But his armourbearer would not; for he was sore afraid. So ᵃSaul took a sword, and fell upon it.

5 And when his armourbearer saw that Saul was dead, he fell likewise on the sword, and died.

6 So Saul died, and his three sons, and all his house died together.

7 And when all the men of Israel that *were* in the valley saw that they fled, and that Saul and his sons were dead, then they forsook their cities, and fled: and the Philistines came and dwelt in them.

8 ¶ And it came to pass on the morrow, when the Philistines came to strip the slain, that they found

---

33*a* 1 Chr. 6:31; 25:6 (1–7).
  b Ps. 134:1 (1–3).

10 1*a* 1 Sam. 31:1 (1–13).
  4*a* 2 Sam. 1:10 (1–16).

Saul and his sons fallen in mount Gilboa.

9 And when they had stripped him, they took his head, and his armour, and sent into the land of the Philistines round about, to carry tidings unto their idols, and to the people.

10 And they put his armour in the house of their gods, and fastened his *head in the temple of Dagon.

11 ¶ And when all Jabesh-gilead heard all that the Philistines had done to Saul,

12 They arose, all the valiant men, and took away the body of Saul, and the bodies of his sons, and brought them to Jabesh, and buried their bones under the oak in Jabesh, and fasted seven days.

13 ¶ So *Saul died for his *transgression which he committed against the LORD, *even* against the word of the LORD, which he kept not, and also for asking *counsel* of *one that had* a *familiar spirit, to inquire *of it*;

14 And inquired not of the LORD: therefore he slew him, and turned the kingdom unto *David the son of Jesse.

CHAPTER 11

David is anointed king in Hebron—He takes Zion, the City of David—His valiant warriors are named and their deeds recounted.

THEN all Israel gathered themselves to *David unto Hebron, saying, Behold, we *are* thy bone and thy flesh.

2 And moreover in time past, even when Saul was king, thou *wast* he that leddest out and broughtest in Israel: and the LORD thy God said unto thee, Thou shalt feed my people Israel, and thou shalt be ruler over my people Israel.

3 Therefore came all the elders of Israel to the king to Hebron; and David made a covenant with them in Hebron before the LORD; and they anointed *David *king over Israel, according to the word of the LORD by Samuel.

4 ¶ And David and all Israel went to Jerusalem, which *is* Jebus; where the *Jebusites *were*, the inhabitants of the land.

5 And the inhabitants of Jebus said to David, Thou shalt not come hither. Nevertheless David took the castle of Zion, which *is* the city of David.

6 And David said, Whosoever smiteth the Jebusites first shall be chief and captain. So Joab the son of Zeruiah went first up, and was chief.

7 And David dwelt in the castle; therefore they called it the *city of David.

8 And he built the city round about, even from Millo round about: and Joab repaired the rest of the city.

9 So David waxed greater and greater: for the LORD of hosts *was* with him.

10 ¶ These also *are* the chief of the *mighty men whom David had, who strengthened themselves with him in his kingdom, *and* with all Israel, to make him king, according to the word of the LORD concerning Israel.

11 And this *is* the number of the mighty men whom David had; Jashobeam, an Hachmonite, the chief of the captains: he lifted up his spear against three hundred slain *by him* at one time.

12 And after him *was* Eleazar the son of Dodo, the Ahohite, who *was* one of the three *mighties.

13 He was with David at Pasdammim, and there the Philistines were gathered together to battle, where was a parcel of ground full of barley; and the people fled from before the Philistines.

10a 1 Sam. 31:10.
13a 2 Sam. 4:10.
   b TG Transgress.
   c TG Spirits, Evil or Unclean; Superstitions.

14a 1 Sam. 13:14.
11 1a 2 Sam. 5:1 (1–3, 6–10).
   3a 1 Sam. 16:1.
   b 2 Sam. 5:4 (3–5).
   4a Ex. 3:17; Josh. 15:63;

Judg. 1:21;
   2 Sam. 5:8 (6–8).
7a 2 Sam. 5:9.
10a 2 Sam. 23:8 (8–39).
12a OR mighty men.

14 And they set themselves in the midst of *that* parcel, and delivered it, and slew the Philistines; and the LORD saved *them* by a great deliverance.

15 ¶ Now three of the thirty captains went down to the rock to David, into the cave of Adullam; and the host of the Philistines encamped in the valley of Rephaim.

16 And David *was* then in the hold, and the Philistines' garrison *was* then at Beth-lehem.

17 And David longed, and said, Oh that one would give me drink of the water of the well of Beth-lehem, that *is* at the gate!

18 And the three brake through the host of the Philistines, and drew water out of the well of Beth-lehem, that *was* by the gate, and took *it,* and brought *it* to David: but David would not drink *of* it, but poured it out to the LORD,

19 And said, My God forbid it me, that I should do this thing: shall I drink the blood of these men that have put their lives in jeopardy? for with *the jeopardy of* their lives they brought it. Therefore he would not drink it. These things did these three mightiest.

20 ¶ And *a*Abishai the brother of Joab, he was chief of the three: for lifting up his spear against three hundred, he slew *them,* and had a *b*name among the three.

21 Of the three, he was more honourable than the two; for he was their captain: howbeit he attained not to the *first* three.

22 Benaiah the son of Jehoiada, the son of a valiant man of Kabzeel, who had done many acts; he slew two lionlike men of Moab: also he went down and slew a lion in a pit in a snowy day.

23 And he slew an Egyptian, a man of *great* stature, five cubits high; and in the Egyptian's hand *was* a spear like a weaver's beam; and he went down to him with a staff, and plucked the spear out of the Egyptian's hand, and slew him with his own spear.

24 These *things* did Benaiah the son of Jehoiada, and had the name among the three mighties.

25 Behold, he was honourable among the thirty, but attained not to the *first* three: and David set him over his guard.

26 ¶ Also the valiant men of the armies *were,* *a*Asahel the brother of Joab, Elhanan the son of Dodo of Beth-lehem,

27 Shammoth the Harorite, Helez the Pelonite,

28 Ira the son of Ikkesh the Tekoite, Abi-ezer the Antothite,

29 Sibbecai the Hushathite, Ilai the Ahohite,

30 Maharai the Netophathite, Heled the son of Baanah the Netophathite,

31 Ithai the son of Ribai of Gibeah, *that pertained* to the children of Benjamin, Benaiah the Pirathonite,

32 Hurai of the brooks of Gaash, Abiel the Arbathite,

33 Azmaveth the Baharumite, Eliahba the Shaalbonite,

34 The sons of Hashem the Gizonite, Jonathan the son of Shage the Hararite,

35 Ahiam the son of Sacar the Hararite, Eliphal the son of Ur,

36 Hepher the Mecherathite, Ahijah the Pelonite,

37 Hezro the Carmelite, Naarai the son of Ezbai,

38 Joel the brother of Nathan, Mibhar the son of Haggeri,

39 Zelek the Ammonite, Naharai the Berothite, the armourbearer of Joab the son of Zeruiah,

40 Ira the Ithrite, Gareb the Ithrite,

41 *a*Uriah the Hittite, Zabad the son of Ahlai,

42 Adina the son of Shiza the Reubenite, a captain of the Reubenites, and thirty with him,

43 Hanan the son of Maachah, and Joshaphat the Mithnite,

44 Uzzia the Ashterathite, Shama

20*a* 2 Sam. 2:18.
  b 2 Sam. 23:19.

26*a* 2 Sam. 2:18 (18–23);
      1 Chr. 27:7.

41*a* 2 Sam. 11:3;
      D&C 132:39.

and Jehiel the sons of Hothan the Aroerite,

45 Jediael the son of Shimri, and Joha his brother, the Tizite,

46 Eliel the Mahavite, and Jeribai, and Joshaviah, the sons of Elnaam, and Ithmah the Moabite,

47 Eliel, and Obed, and Jasiel the Mesobaite.

CHAPTER 12

David's mighty men are cataloged—The armies of the tribes of Israel join David at Hebron—Israel rejoices because of King David.

Now these *are* they that came to David to Ziklag, while he yet kept himself ^aclose because of Saul the son of Kish: and they *were* among the mighty men, helpers of the war.

2 *They were* armed with bows, and could use both the right hand and the ^aleft in *hurling* stones and *shooting* arrows out of a bow, *even* of Saul's brethren of Benjamin.

3 The chief *was* Ahiezer, then Joash, the sons of Shemaah the Gibeathite; and Jeziel, and Pelet, the sons of Azmaveth; and Berachah, and Jehu the Antothite,

4 And Ismaiah the Gibeonite, a mighty man among the thirty, and over the thirty; and Jeremiah, and Jahaziel, and Johanan, and Josabad the Gederathite,

5 Eluzai, and Jerimoth, and Bealiah, and Shemariah, and Shephatiah the Haruphite,

6 Elkanah, and Jesiah, and Azareel, and Joezer, and Jashobeam, the Korhites,

7 And Joelah, and Zebadiah, the sons of Jeroham of Gedor.

8 And of the Gadites there separated themselves unto David into the hold to the wilderness men of might, *and* men of war *fit* for the battle, that could handle shield and buckler, whose faces *were* like the faces of lions, and *were* as swift as the roes upon the mountains;

9 Ezer the first, Obadiah the second, Eliab the third,

10 Mishmannah the fourth, Jeremiah the fifth,

11 Attai the sixth, Eliel the seventh,

12 Johanan the eighth, Elzabad the ninth,

13 Jeremiah the tenth, Machbanai the eleventh.

14 These *were* of the sons of Gad, captains of the host: one of the least *was* over an hundred, and the greatest over a thousand.

15 These *are* they that went over Jordan in the first month, when it had overflown all his banks; and they put to flight all *them* of the valleys, *both* toward the east, and toward the west.

16 And there came of the children of Benjamin and Judah to the hold unto David.

17 And David went out to meet them, and answered and said unto them, If ye be come peaceably unto me to help me, mine heart shall be knit unto you: but if *ye be come* to betray me to mine enemies, seeing *there is* no wrong in mine hands, the God of our fathers look *thereon,* and rebuke *it.*

18 Then the spirit came upon ^aAmasai, *who was* chief of the captains, *and he said,* Thine *are we,* David, and on thy side, thou son of Jesse: peace, peace *be* unto thee, and peace *be* to thine helpers; for thy God helpeth thee. Then David received them, and made them captains of the band.

19 And there fell *some* of Manasseh to David, when he came with the Philistines against Saul to battle: but they helped them not: for the lords of the Philistines upon advisement sent him away, saying, He will ^afall to his master Saul to *the jeopardy of* our heads.

20 As he went to Ziklag, there fell to him of Manasseh, Adnah, and Jozabad, and Jediael, and Michael, and Jozabad, and Elihu, and Zilthai, captains of the thousands that *were* of Manasseh.

---

12 1*a* OR confined.   18*a* 2 Sam. 17:25.
    2*a* Judg. 20:16.   19*a* 1 Sam. 29:4.

21 And they helped David against the band *of the rovers:* for they *were* all mighty men of valour, and were captains in the host.

22 For at *that* time day by day there came to David to help him, until *it was* a great host, like the host of God.

23 ¶ And these *are* the numbers of the bands *that were* ready armed to the war, *and* came to ªDavid to Hebron, to turn the kingdom of Saul to him, according to the word of the LORD.

24 The children of Judah that bare shield and spear *were* six thousand and eight hundred, ready armed to the war.

25 Of the children of Simeon, mighty men of valour for the war, seven thousand and one hundred.

26 Of the children of Levi four thousand and six hundred.

27 And Jehoiada *was* the leader of the Aaronites, and with him *were* three thousand and seven hundred;

28 And Zadok, a young man mighty of valour, and of his father's house twenty and two captains.

29 And of the children of Benjamin, the kindred of ªSaul, three thousand: for hitherto the greatest part of them had kept the ward of the house of Saul.

30 And of the children of Ephraim twenty thousand and eight hundred, mighty men of valour, famous throughout the house of their fathers.

31 And of the half tribe of Manasseh eighteen thousand, which were expressed by name, to come and make David king.

32 And of the children of Issachar, *which were men* that had understanding of the ªtimes, to know what Israel ought to do; the heads of them *were* two hundred; and all their brethren *were* at their commandment.

33 Of Zebulun, such as went forth to battle, expert in war, with all instruments of war, fifty thousand, which could keep rank: *they were* not of double heart.

34 And of Naphtali a thousand captains, and with them with shield and spear thirty and seven thousand.

35 And of the Danites expert in war twenty and eight thousand and six hundred.

36 And of Asher, such as went forth to battle, expert in war, forty thousand.

37 And on the other side of Jordan, of the Reubenites, and the Gadites, and of the half tribe of Manasseh, with all manner of instruments of war for the battle, an hundred and twenty thousand.

38 All these men of war, that could keep rank, came with a perfect heart to Hebron, to make David king over all Israel: and all the rest also of Israel *were* of one heart to make David king.

39 And there they were with David three days, eating and drinking: for their brethren had prepared for them.

40 Moreover they that were nigh them, *even* unto Issachar and Zebulun and Naphtali, brought bread on asses, and on camels, and on mules, and on oxen, *and* meat, meal, cakes of figs, and bunches of raisins, and wine, and oil, and oxen, and sheep abundantly: for *there was* joy in Israel.

CHAPTER 13

David fetches the ark from Kirjath-jearim—Uzza is slain by the Lord when he steadies the ark—The house of Obed-edom prospers because they care for the ark.

AND David consulted with the captains of thousands and hundreds, *and* with every leader.

2 And David said unto all the congregation of Israel, If *it seem* good unto you, and *that it be* of the LORD our God, let us send abroad unto our brethren every where, *that are* left in all the land of Israel, and with

---

23a 2 Sam. 2:4 (3–4); 5:3 (1–3).
29a 1 Sam. 9:2 (1–2).
32a Esth. 1:13.

them *also* to the priests and Levites *which are* in their cities *and* suburbs, that they may gather themselves unto us:

3 And let us bring again the *a*ark of our God to us: for we inquired not at it in the days of Saul.

4 And all the *a*congregation said that they would do so: for the thing was right in the eyes of all the people.

5 So David *a*gathered all Israel together, from *b*Shihor of Egypt even unto the entering of Hemath, to bring the ark of God from Kirjath-jearim.

6 And David went up, and all Israel, to Baalah, *that is,* to Kirjath-jearim, which *belonged* to Judah, to bring up thence the ark of God the LORD, that dwelleth *between* the cherubims, whose name is called *on it.*

7 And they carried the ark of God in a new cart out of the house of Abinadab: and Uzza and Ahio drave the cart.

8 And David and all Israel played before God with all *their* might, and with *a*singing, and with harps, and with psalteries, and with timbrels, and with cymbals, and with trumpets.

9 ¶ And when they came unto the threshingfloor of Chidon, Uzza put forth his hand to hold the ark; for the oxen stumbled.

10 And the anger of the LORD was kindled against Uzza, and he smote him, because he put his *a*hand to the *b*ark: and there he died before God.

11 And David was displeased, because the LORD had made a *a*breach upon Uzza: wherefore that place is called Perez-uzza to this day.

12 And David was afraid of God that day, saying, How shall I bring the ark of God *home* to me?

13 So David brought not the *a*ark *home* to himself to the city of David, but carried it aside into the house of Obed-edom the Gittite.

14 And the ark of God remained with the family of Obed-edom in his house three months. And the LORD *a*blessed the house of Obed-edom, and all that he had.

CHAPTER 14

David marries wives, begets children, and defeats the Philistines; his fame spreads to all nations.

Now Hiram king of Tyre sent messengers to David, and timber of cedars, with masons and carpenters, to build him an house.

2 And David perceived that the LORD had confirmed him king over Israel, for his kingdom was lifted up on high, because of his people Israel.

3 ¶ And David took more *a*wives at Jerusalem: and David begat more sons and daughters.

4 Now these *are* the names of *his* children which he had in Jerusalem; Shammua, and Shobab, Nathan, and Solomon,

5 And Ibhar, and Elishua, and Elpalet,

6 And Nogah, and Nepheg, and Japhia,

7 And Elishama, and Beeliada, and Eliphalet.

8 ¶ And when the Philistines heard that David was *a*anointed king over all Israel, all the Philistines went up to seek David. And David heard *of it,* and went out against them.

9 And the Philistines came and spread themselves in the valley of Rephaim.

10 And David inquired of God, saying, Shall I go up against the Philistines? and wilt thou deliver them into mine hand? And the LORD said unto him, Go up; for I will deliver them into thine hand.

11 So they came up to *a*Baal-

---

13 3*a* 1 Sam. 5:1 (1–12).
    TG Ark of the
    Covenant.
  4*a* D&C 26:2.
  5*a* 2 Sam. 6:1.
   b Isa. 23:3.

  8*a* D&C 25:12.
 10*a* Num. 4:15.
   b 1 Chr. 15:2;
    D&C 85:8.
 11*a* 1 Chr. 15:13.
 13*a* 2 Sam. 6:2 (1–11).

 14*a* 1 Chr. 26:5 (4–5).
14 3*a* Jacob 2:24 (23–24);
    D&C 132:39 (38–39).
  8*a* 2 Sam. 5:3.
 11*a* 2 Sam. 5:20 (19–20);
    Isa. 28:21.

perazim; and David smote them there. Then David said, God hath broken in upon mine enemies by mine hand like the breaking forth of waters: therefore they called the name of that place Baal-perazim.

12 And when they had left their *gods there, David gave a commandment, and they were burned with fire.

13 And the *Philistines yet again spread themselves abroad in the valley.

14 Therefore David inquired again of God; and God said unto him, Go not up after them; turn away from them, and come upon them over against the mulberry trees.

15 And it shall be, when thou shalt hear a sound of going in the tops of the mulberry trees, *that* then thou shalt go out to battle: for God is gone forth before thee to smite the host of the Philistines.

16 David therefore did as God commanded him: and they smote the host of the Philistines from Gibeon even to Gazer.

17 And the fame of David went out into all lands; and the LORD brought the fear of him upon all nations.

CHAPTER 15

David prepares a place for the ark—The Levites bring the ark to Jerusalem—They sing and minister before the Lord.

AND *David* made him houses in the city of David, and prepared a place for the *ark of God, and pitched for it a tent.

2 Then David said, None ought to *carry the *ark of God but the *Levites: for them hath the LORD chosen to carry the ark of God, and to minister unto him for ever.

3 And David gathered all Israel together to Jerusalem, to bring up the ark of the LORD unto his place, which he had prepared for it.

4 And David assembled the *children of Aaron, and the Levites:

5 Of the sons of *Kohath; Uriel the chief, and his brethren an hundred and twenty:

6 Of the sons of Merari; Asaiah the chief, and his brethren two hundred and twenty:

7 Of the sons of Gershom; Joel the chief, and his brethren an hundred and thirty:

8 Of the sons of Elizaphan; Shemaiah the chief, and his brethren two hundred:

9 Of the sons of Hebron; Eliel the chief, and his brethren fourscore:

10 Of the sons of Uzziel; Amminadab the chief, and his brethren an hundred and twelve.

11 And David called for Zadok and Abiathar the priests, and for the Levites, for Uriel, Asaiah, and Joel, Shemaiah, and Eliel, and Amminadab,

12 And said unto them, Ye *are* the chief of the fathers of the Levites: sanctify yourselves, *both* ye and your brethren, that ye may bring up the ark of the LORD God of Israel unto *the place that* I have prepared for it.

13 For because ye *did it* not at the first, the LORD our God made a *breach upon us, for that we sought him not after the due *order.

14 So the priests and the Levites sanctified themselves to bring up the ark of the LORD God of Israel.

15 And the children of the Levites bare the *ark of God upon their shoulders with the staves thereon, as Moses commanded according to the word of the LORD.

16 And David spake to the chief of the Levites to appoint their brethren *to be* the singers with instruments of musick, psalteries and *harps and cymbals, sounding, by lifting up the voice with joy.

17 So the Levites appointed Heman the son of Joel; and of his

---

12*a* 2 Sam. 5:21.
13*a* 2 Sam. 5:22 (22–25).
15 1*a* TG Ark of the Covenant.
  2*a* Num. 4:15 (2–15);

Deut. 10:8.
  b 1 Chr. 13:10 (9–10).
  c 2 Sam. 6:7 (6–7).
  4*a* 1 Chr. 23:6.
  5*a* 1 Chr. 6:16.

13*a* 1 Chr. 13:11 (10–11).
  b D&C 107:84 (84, 99).
15*a* Ex. 25:14.
16*a* 2 Sam. 6:5;
    Dan. 3:5 (5, 7, 10, 15).

brethren, Asaph the son of Berechiah; and of the sons of Merari their brethren, Ethan the son of Kushaiah;

18 And with them their brethren of the second *degree*, Zechariah, Ben, and Jaaziel, and Shemiramoth, and Jehiel, and Unni, Eliab, and Benaiah, and Maaseiah, and Mattithiah, and Elipheleh, and Mikneiah, and Obed-edom, and Jeiel, the porters.

19 So the singers, Heman, Asaph, and Ethan, *were appointed* to sound with cymbals of brass;

20 And Zechariah, and Aziel, and Shemiramoth, and Jehiel, and Unni, and Eliab, and Maaseiah, and Benaiah, with psalteries on Alamoth;

21 And Mattithiah, and Elipheleh, and Mikneiah, and Obed-edom, and Jeiel, and Azaziah, with harps on the Sheminith to excel.

22 And Chenaniah, chief of the Levites, *was* for song: he instructed about the song, because he *was* skilful.

23 And Berechiah and Elkanah *were* doorkeepers for the ark.

24 And Shebaniah, and Jehoshaphat, and Nethaneel, and Amasai, and Zechariah, and Benaiah, and Eliezer, the priests, did blow with the *a*trumpets before the ark of God: and Obed-edom and Jehiah *were* doorkeepers for the ark.

25 ¶ So David, and the elders of Israel, and the captains over thousands, went to bring up the ark of the covenant of the LORD out of the house of Obed-edom with joy.

26 And it came to pass, when God helped the Levites that bare the ark of the covenant of the LORD, that they *a*offered *b*seven bullocks and seven rams.

27 And David *was* clothed with a robe of fine linen, and all the Levites that bare the ark, and the singers, and Chenaniah the master of the song with the singers: David also *had* upon him an ephod of linen.

28 Thus all Israel brought up the ark of the covenant of the LORD with shouting, and with sound of the cornet, and with trumpets, and with cymbals, making a noise with psalteries and harps.

29 ¶ And it came to pass, *as* the ark of the covenant of the LORD came to the city of David, that Michal the daughter of Saul looking out at a window saw king David dancing and playing: and she despised him in her heart.

CHAPTER 16

People offer sacrifices and praise the Lord—David delivers a psalm of thanksgiving—He praises the Lord—Asaph, Obed-edom, Zadok, and others minister before the Lord.

So they brought the *a*ark of God, and set it in the midst of the tent that David had pitched for it: and they offered burnt sacrifices and peace offerings before God.

2 And when David had made an end of offering the burnt offerings and the peace offerings, he *a*blessed the people in the name of the LORD.

3 And he dealt to every one of Israel, both man and woman, to every one a loaf of bread, and a good piece of flesh, and a flagon *of wine*.

4 ¶ And he appointed *certain* of the *a*Levites to minister before the ark of the LORD, and to *b*record, and to *c*thank and praise the LORD God of Israel:

5 Asaph the chief, and next to him Zechariah, Jeiel, and Shemiramoth, and Jehiel, and Mattithiah, and Eliab, and Benaiah, and Obed-edom: and Jeiel with psalteries and with harps; but Asaph made a sound with cymbals;

6 Benaiah also and Jahaziel the priests with trumpets continually before the ark of the covenant of God.

7 ¶ Then on that day David delivered first *this* *a*psalm to *b*thank the

---

24*a* Num. 10:8.
26*a* 2 Sam. 6:13 (12–15).
 b Num. 23:1.
16 1*a* TG Ark of the
  Covenant.
2*a* 2 Sam. 6:18.
4*a* 2 Chr. 29:25.
 b TG Record Keeping.
 c TG Thanksgiving.
7*a* 2 Sam. 22:1.
 b TG Thanksgiving.

LORD into the hand of Asaph and his brethren.

8 Give *a*thanks unto the LORD, *b*call upon his name, make known his *c*deeds among the people.

9 *a*Sing unto him, sing psalms unto him, *b*talk ye of all his *c*wondrous works.

10 Glory ye in his holy name: let the heart of them rejoice that seek the LORD.

11 *a*Seek the LORD and his strength, seek his face continually.

12 Remember his marvellous *a*works that he hath done, his wonders, and the judgments of his mouth;

13 O ye seed of Israel his servant, ye children of Jacob, his chosen ones.

14 He *is* the LORD our God; his judgments *are* in all the earth.

15 Be ye mindful always of his covenant; the word *which* he commanded to a thousand generations;

16 *Even of the* *a*covenant which he made with Abraham, and of his oath unto Isaac;

17 And hath confirmed the same to Jacob for a law, *and* to Israel *for* an *a*everlasting covenant,

18 Saying, Unto thee will I give the *a*land of Canaan, the lot of your inheritance;

19 When ye were but few, even a few, and strangers in it.

20 And *when* they went from nation to nation, and from *one* kingdom to another people;

21 He suffered no man to do them wrong: yea, he *a*reproved kings for their sakes,

22 *Saying,* Touch not mine anointed, and do my prophets no harm.

23 *a*Sing unto the LORD, all the earth; shew forth from day to day his salvation.

24 *a*Declare his glory among the heathen; his marvellous *b*works among all nations.

25 For *a*great *is* the LORD, and greatly to be praised: he also *is* to be feared above all gods.

26 For all the gods of the people *are* *a*idols: but the LORD made the heavens.

27 Glory and honour *are* in his *a*presence; strength and gladness *are* in his place.

28 Give unto the LORD, ye kindreds of the people, give unto the LORD glory and strength.

29 Give unto the LORD the glory *due* unto his name: bring an offering, and come before him: *a*worship the LORD in the *b*beauty of *c*holiness.

30 Fear before him, all the earth: the world also shall be stable, that it be not moved.

31 Let the heavens be glad, and let the earth rejoice: and let *men* say among the nations, The LORD *a*reigneth.

32 Let the sea roar, and the fulness thereof: let the fields rejoice, and all that *is* therein.

33 Then shall the *a*trees of the wood sing out at the presence of the LORD, because he cometh to *b*judge the *c*earth.

34 O give *a*thanks unto the LORD; for *he is* *b*good; for his mercy endureth for ever.

35 And say ye, Save us, O God of our salvation, and gather us together, and deliver us from the heathen, that we may give thanks to thy holy name, *and* glory in thy praise.

8a Mosiah 2:19 (19–21);
    Alma 37:37;
    Ether 6:9;
    D&C 46:32; 109:1.
  b Gen. 4:26;
    Ps. 116:17;
    D&C 65:4.
  c Ps. 145:12.
9a Ps. 95:1 (1–2);
    D&C 25:12.
  b Deut. 6:7 (6–9).
  c Ps. 9:1; 26:7;

    D&C 76:114.
11a Amos 5:6 (6, 14).
12a Ps. 111:3.
16a Neh. 9:8.
17a Ps. 105:10 (9–10).
18a TG Israel, Land of;
    Promised Lands.
21a Gen. 12:17.
23a Ps. 96:1.
24a TG Preaching.
  b D&C 65:4.
25a Ps. 95:3.

26a TG Idolatry.
27a TG God, Presence of.
29a TG Assembly for
    Worship.
  b TG Beauty.
  c TG Holiness.
31a Ps. 97:1.
33a Isa. 55:12.
  b TG Jesus Christ, Judge.
  c TG Earth, Destiny of.
34a D&C 98:1.
  b Ezra 3:11.

36 Blessed *be* the Lord God of Israel for ever and ever. And all the people said, Amen, and praised the Lord.

37 ¶ So he left there before the ark of the covenant of the Lord Asaph and his brethren, to minister before the ark continually, as every day's work required:

38 And Obed-edom with their brethren, threescore and eight; Obed-edom also the son of Jeduthun and Hosah *to be* porters:

39 And Zadok the priest, and his brethren the priests, before the tabernacle of the Lord in the ᵃhigh place that *was* at ᵇGibeon,

40 To ᵃoffer burnt offerings unto the Lord upon the altar of the burnt offering continually morning and evening, and *to do* according to all that is written in the law of the Lord, which he commanded Israel;

41 And with them Heman and Jeduthun, and the rest that were chosen, who were expressed by name, to give ᵃthanks to the Lord, because his ᵇmercy *endureth* for ever;

42 And with them Heman and Jeduthun with trumpets and cymbals for those that should make a sound, and with musical instruments of God. And the sons of Jeduthun *were* porters.

43 And all the people departed every man to his house: and David returned to ᵃbless his house.

CHAPTER 17

Nathan first approves David's building of a house of the Lord, then restrains him—David's son will build the temple—The triumph of Israel is foretold—David thanks the Lord for His goodness to Israel.

Now it came to pass, as David sat in his house, that David said to Nathan the prophet, Lo, I dwell in an house of cedars, but the ark of the covenant of the Lord *remaineth* under curtains.

2 Then Nathan said unto David, Do all that *is* in thine heart; for God *is* with thee.

3 ¶ And it came to pass the same night, that the word of God came to Nathan, saying,

4 Go and tell David my servant, Thus saith the Lord, Thou shalt not build me an house to dwell in:

5 For I have not dwelt in an house since the day that I brought up Israel unto this day; but have gone from tent to tent, and from *one* tabernacle *to another*.

6 Wheresoever I have walked with all Israel, spake I a word to any of the judges of Israel, whom I commanded to feed my people, saying, Why have ye not built me an ᵃhouse of cedars?

7 Now therefore thus shalt thou say unto my servant David, Thus saith the Lord of hosts, I took thee from the sheepcote, *even* from following the sheep, that thou shouldest be ruler over my people Israel:

8 And I have been with thee whithersoever thou hast walked, and have cut off all thine enemies from before thee, and have made thee a name like the name of the great men that *are* in the earth.

9 Also I will ordain a place for my people Israel, and will plant them, and they shall dwell in their place, and shall be moved no more; neither shall the children of wickedness waste them any more, as at the beginning,

10 And since the time that I commanded judges *to be* over my people Israel. Moreover I will subdue all thine ᵃenemies. Furthermore I tell thee that the Lord will build thee an house.

11 ¶ And it shall come to pass, when thy days be expired that thou must go *to be* with thy fathers, that I will raise up thy seed after thee,

39*a* 1 Kgs. 3:4;
   2 Chr. 1:3.
 b 1 Chr. 21:29.
40*a* Ex. 29:38 (38–39).

41*a* 2 Chr. 5:13;
   Ezra 3:11.
 b Neh. 9:17.
43*a* 2 Sam. 6:20 (20–23).

17 6*a* 2 Sam. 7:7.
  10*a* Ps. 89:10;
   Micah 4:10;
   D&C 65:6.

which shall be of thy sons; and I will establish his kingdom.

12 He shall build me an house, and I will stablish his throne for ever.

13 I will be his *a*father, and he shall be my son: and I will not take my mercy away from him, as I took *it* from *him* that was before thee:

14 But I will settle him in mine *a*house and in my kingdom for ever: and his throne shall be established for evermore.

15 According to all these words, and according to all this vision, so did Nathan speak unto David.

16 ¶ And David the king came and sat before the LORD, and said, Who *am* I, O LORD God, and what *is* mine house, that thou hast brought me hitherto?

17 And *yet* this was a small thing in thine eyes, O God; for thou hast *also* spoken of thy servant's house for a great while to come, and hast regarded me according to the estate of a man of high degree, O LORD God.

18 What can David *speak* more to thee for the honour of thy servant? for thou knowest thy servant.

19 O LORD, for thy servant's sake, and according to thine own heart, hast thou done all this *a*greatness, in making known all *these* great things.

20 O LORD, *there is* none like thee, neither *is there any* God beside thee, according to all that we have heard with our ears.

21 And what one nation in the earth *is* like thy people Israel, whom God went to redeem *to be* his own people, to make thee a name of greatness and terribleness, by driving out nations from before thy people, whom thou hast redeemed out of Egypt?

22 For thy people Israel didst thou make thine own people for ever; and thou, LORD, becamest their God.

23 Therefore now, LORD, let the thing that thou hast spoken concerning thy servant and concerning his house be established for ever, and do as thou hast said.

24 Let it even be established, that thy name may be magnified for ever, saying, The LORD of hosts *is* the God of Israel, *even* a God to Israel: and *let* the house of David thy servant *be* established before thee.

25 For thou, O my God, hast told thy servant that thou wilt build him an house: therefore thy servant hath found *in his heart* to pray before thee.

26 And now, LORD, thou art God, and hast promised this goodness unto thy servant:

27 Now therefore let it please thee to bless the house of thy servant, that it may be before thee for ever: for thou blessest, O LORD, and *it shall be* blessed for ever.

CHAPTER 18

David subdues all the adversaries of Israel and reigns in justice over the people.

Now after this it came to pass, that David *a*smote the Philistines, and subdued them, and took *b*Gath and her towns out of the hand of the Philistines.

2 And he smote Moab; and the Moabites became David's servants, *and* brought gifts.

3 ¶ And David smote Hadarezer king of Zobah unto Hamath, as he went to stablish his dominion by the river Euphrates.

4 And David took from him a thousand chariots, and seven thousand horsemen, and twenty thousand footmen: David also houghed all the chariot *horses,* but reserved of them an hundred chariots.

5 And when the Syrians of Damascus came to help Hadarezer king of Zobah, David slew of the Syrians two and twenty thousand men.

6 Then David put *garrisons* in Syriadamascus; and the Syrians became David's servants, *and* brought gifts. Thus the LORD preserved David whithersoever he went.

13*a* Heb. 1:5 (5–6).
14*a* Jer. 23:11;

D&C 124:145.
19*a* 2 Sam. 7:21.

18 1*a* 2 Sam. 8:1 (1–18).
  b 1 Sam. 17:4.

7 And David took the shields of gold that were on the servants of Hadarezer, and brought them to Jerusalem.

8 Likewise from Tibhath, and from Chun, cities of Hadarezer, brought David very much brass, wherewith *a*Solomon made the brasen *b*sea, and the pillars, and the vessels of brass.

9 ¶ Now when Tou king of Hamath heard how David had smitten all the host of Hadarezer king of Zobah;

10 He sent Hadoram his son to king David, to inquire of his welfare, and to congratulate him, because he had fought against Hadarezer, and smitten him; (for Hadarezer had war with Tou;) and *with him* all manner of vessels of gold and silver and brass.

11 ¶ Them also king David dedicated unto the LORD, with the silver and the gold that he brought from all *these* nations; from Edom, and from Moab, and from the children of Ammon, and from the Philistines, and from Amalek.

12 Moreover Abishai the son of Zeruiah slew of the Edomites in the valley of salt eighteen thousand.

13 ¶ And he put garrisons in Edom; and all the *a*Edomites became David's servants. Thus the LORD preserved David whithersoever he went.

14 ¶ So David reigned over all Israel, and executed judgment and justice among all his people.

15 And Joab the son of Zeruiah *was* over the host; and Jehoshaphat the son of Ahilud, recorder.

16 And Zadok the son of Ahitub, and Abimelech the son of Abiathar, *were* the priests; and Shavsha was scribe;

17 And Benaiah the son of Jehoiada *was* over the Cherethites and the Pelethites; and the sons of David *were* chief about the king.

CHAPTER 19

The Ammonites insult David's messengers and plan war against Israel—

David defeats the Ammonites and the Syrians.

NOW it came to pass after this, that Nahash the king of the children of *a*Ammon died, and his son reigned in his stead.

2 And David said, I will shew kindness unto Hanun the son of Nahash, because his father shewed kindness to me. And David sent messengers to comfort him concerning his father. So the servants of David came into the land of the children of Ammon to Hanun, to comfort him.

3 But the princes of the children of Ammon said to Hanun, Thinkest thou that David doth honour thy father, that he hath sent comforters unto thee? are not his servants come unto thee for to search, and to overthrow, and to spy out the land?

4 Wherefore Hanun took David's servants, and shaved them, and cut off their garments in the midst hard by their buttocks, and sent them away.

5 Then there went *certain,* and told David how the men were served. And he sent to meet them: for the men were greatly ashamed. And the king said, Tarry at Jericho until your beards be grown, and *then* return.

6 ¶ And when the children of Ammon saw that they had made themselves odious to David, Hanun and the children of Ammon sent a thousand talents of silver to hire them chariots and horsemen out of Mesopotamia, and out of Syriamaachah, and out of Zobah.

7 So they hired thirty and two thousand chariots, and the king of Maachah and his people; who came and pitched before *a*Medeba. And the children of Ammon gathered themselves together from their cities, and came to battle.

8 And when David heard *of it,* he sent Joab, and all the host of the mighty men.

9 And the children of Ammon came

8*a* 2 Ne. 5:16.
  b 1 Kgs. 7:23;

2 Chr. 4:15 (12–16).
13*a* 1 Kgs. 11:15.

19 1*a* 2 Sam. 10:1 (1–19).
  7*a* Josh. 13:9 (9, 16).

out, and put the battle in array before the gate of the city: and the kings that were come *were* by themselves in the field.

10 Now when Joab saw that the battle was set against him before and behind, he chose out of all the choice of Israel, and put *them* in array against the Syrians.

11 And the rest of the people he delivered unto the hand of Abishai his brother, and they set *themselves* in array against the children of Ammon.

12 And he said, If the Syrians be too strong for me, then thou shalt help me: but if the children of Ammon be too strong for thee, then I will help thee.

13 Be of good courage, and let us behave ourselves valiantly for our people, and for the cities of our God: and let the LORD do *that which is* good in his sight.

14 So Joab and the people that *were* with him drew nigh before the Syrians unto the battle; and they fled before him.

15 And when the children of Ammon saw that the Syrians were fled, they likewise fled before Abishai his brother, and entered into the city. Then Joab came to Jerusalem.

16 ¶ And when the Syrians saw that they were put to the worse before Israel, they sent messengers, and drew forth the Syrians that *were* beyond the river: and Shophach the captain of the host of Hadarezer *went* before them.

17 And it was told David; and he gathered all Israel, and passed over Jordan, and came upon them, and set *the battle* in array against them. So when David had put the battle in array against the Syrians, they fought with him.

18 But the Syrians fled before Israel; and David slew of the Syrians seven thousand *men which fought in* chariots, and forty thousand footmen, and killed Shophach the captain of the host.

19 And when the servants of Hadarezer saw that they were put to the worse before Israel, they made peace with David, and became his servants: neither would the Syrians help the children of Ammon any more.

CHAPTER 20

The Ammonites are overcome—Israel defeats the Philistines.

AND it came to pass, that after the year was expired, at the time that kings go out *to battle,* [a]Joab led forth the power of the army, and wasted the country of the children of Ammon, and came and besieged Rabbah. But David tarried at Jerusalem. And Joab smote Rabbah, and destroyed it.

2 And David took the crown of their king from off his head, and found it to weigh a talent of gold, and *there were* precious stones in it; and it was set upon David's head: and he brought also exceeding much spoil out of the city.

3 And he brought out the people that *were* in it, and [a]cut *them* with saws, and with harrows of iron, and with axes. Even so dealt David with all the cities of the children of Ammon. And David and all the people returned to Jerusalem.

4 ¶ And it came to pass after this, that there arose [a]war at Gezer with the Philistines; at which time Sibbechai the Hushathite slew Sippai, *that was* of the children of the giant: and they were subdued.

5 And there was war again with the Philistines; and Elhanan the son of Jair slew Lahmi the brother of Goliath the Gittite, whose spear staff *was* like a weaver's beam.

6 And yet again there was war at Gath, where was a man of *great* stature, whose fingers and toes *were* four and twenty, six *on each hand,* and six *on each foot:* and he also was the son of the giant.

7 But when he defied Israel,

---

20 1a 2 Sam. 11:1; 12:26.
  3a 2 Sam. 12:31.

TG Cruelty.
4a 2 Sam. 21:18.

Jonathan the son of Shimea David's brother slew him.

8 These were born unto the giant in Gath; and they fell by the hand of David, and by the hand of his servants.

CHAPTER 21

David sins by numbering Israel—The Lord sends pestilence upon the people—David offers sacrifices and the plague is stayed.

AND ^aSatan stood up against Israel, and ^bprovoked David to number Israel.

2 And David said to Joab and to the rulers of the people, Go, number Israel from Beer-sheba even to Dan; and bring the number of them to me, that I may know *it*.

3 And Joab answered, The LORD make his people an hundred times so many more as they *be*: but, my lord the king, *are* they not all my lord's servants? why then doth my lord require this thing? why will he be a cause of trespass to Israel?

4 Nevertheless the king's word prevailed against Joab. Wherefore Joab departed, and went throughout all Israel, and came to Jerusalem.

5 ¶ And Joab gave the sum of the number of the people unto David. And all *they of* Israel were a ^athousand thousand and an hundred thousand men that drew sword: and Judah *was* four hundred three-score and ten thousand men that drew sword.

6 But Levi and Benjamin counted he not among them: for the king's word was abominable to Joab.

7 And God was displeased with this thing; therefore he ^asmote Israel.

8 And David said unto God, I have ^asinned greatly, because I have done this thing: but now, I beseech thee, do away the iniquity of thy servant; for I have done very foolishly.

9 ¶ And the LORD spake unto Gad, David's ^aseer, saying,

10 Go and tell David, saying, Thus saith the LORD, I offer thee three *things:* choose thee one of them, that I may do *it* unto thee.

11 So Gad came to David, and said unto him, Thus saith the LORD, Choose thee

12 Either ^athree years' famine; or three months to be destroyed before thy foes, while that the sword of thine enemies overtaketh *thee;* or else three days the sword of the LORD, even the pestilence, in the land, and the angel of the LORD destroying throughout all the coasts of Israel. Now therefore advise thyself what word I shall bring again to him that sent me.

13 And David said unto Gad, I am in a great strait: let me fall now into the hand of the LORD; for very great *are* his mercies: but let me not fall into the hand of man.

14 ¶ So the LORD sent pestilence upon Israel: and there fell of Israel seventy thousand men.

15 ^aAnd God sent an angel unto Jerusalem to destroy it: and as he was destroying, the LORD beheld, and he repented him of the evil, and said to the angel that destroyed, It is enough, stay now thine hand. And the angel of the LORD stood by the threshingfloor of Ornan the Jebusite.

16 And David lifted up his eyes, and saw the angel of the LORD stand between the earth and the heaven, having a drawn sword in his hand stretched out over Jerusalem. Then David and the elders *of Israel, who were* clothed in sackcloth, fell upon their faces.

17 And David said unto God, *Is it* not I *that* commanded the people to be numbered? even I it is that have sinned and done evil indeed; but *as for* these sheep, what have they

---

21 1*a* TG Devil.
  b 2 Sam. 24:1 (1–25).
  5*a* 2 Sam. 24:9.
  7*a* 1 Chr. 27:24.
  8*a* 2 Sam. 11:27 (1–27);

12:11 (1–25);
Ps. 88:14 (6–8, 14–18).
9*a* TG Seer.
12*a* 2 Sam. 24:13;
  2 Ne. 1:18;

Mosiah 1:17;
Hel. 11:4;
Abr. 2:1.
15*a* JST 1 Chr. 21:15
  (Appendix).

done? let thine hand, I pray thee, O LORD my God, be on me, and on my father's house; but not on thy people, that they should be plagued.

18 ¶ Then the [a]angel of the LORD commanded Gad to say to David, that David should go up, and set up an altar unto the LORD in the [b]threshingfloor of Ornan the Jebusite.

19 And David went up at the saying of Gad, which he spake in the name of the LORD.

20 And Ornan turned back, and saw the angel; and his four sons with him hid themselves. Now Ornan was threshing wheat.

21 And as David came to Ornan, Ornan looked and saw David, and went out of the threshingfloor, and bowed himself to David with *his* face to the ground.

22 Then David said to Ornan, Grant me the place of *this* threshingfloor, that I may build an altar therein unto the LORD: thou shalt grant it me for the full price: that the plague may be stayed from the people.

23 And Ornan said unto David, Take *it* to thee, and let my lord the king do *that which is* good in his eyes: lo, I give *thee* the oxen *also* for burnt offerings, and the threshing instruments for wood, and the wheat for the meat offering; I give it all.

24 And king David said to Ornan, Nay; but I will verily buy it for the full price: for I will not take *that* which *is* thine for the LORD, nor offer burnt offerings without cost.

25 So David gave to Ornan for the place [a]six hundred shekels of gold by [b]weight.

26 And David built there an [a]altar unto the LORD, and offered burnt offerings and peace offerings, and called upon the LORD; and he answered him from heaven by [b]fire upon the altar of burnt offering.

27 And the LORD commanded the angel; and he put up his sword again into the sheath thereof.

28 ¶ At that time when David saw that the LORD had answered him in the threshingfloor of Ornan the Jebusite, then he sacrificed there.

29 For the [a]tabernacle of the LORD, which Moses made in the wilderness, and the altar of the burnt offering, *were* at that season in the high place at [b]Gibeon.

30 But David could not go before it to inquire of God: for he was afraid because of the sword of the angel of the LORD.

CHAPTER 22

David prepares gold, silver, brass, iron, stone, and cedar wood for the temple— He charges Solomon to do the work of building it.

THEN David said, This *is* the [a]house of the LORD God, and this *is* the [b]altar of the burnt offering for Israel.

2 And David commanded to gather together the [a]strangers that *were* in the [b]land of Israel; and he set masons to hew wrought stones to build the house of God.

3 And David prepared iron in abundance for the nails for the doors of the gates, and for the joinings; and brass in abundance without weight.

4 Also cedar trees in abundance: for the Zidonians and they of Tyre brought much [a]cedar wood to David.

5 And David said, Solomon my son *is* [a]young and tender, and the house *that is* to be builded for the LORD *must be* exceeding magnifical, of fame and of glory throughout all countries: I will *therefore* now make preparation for it. So David prepared abundantly before his death.

6 ¶ Then he called for Solomon his

18a Mosiah 4:1.
    b 2 Chr. 3:1 (1–2).
25a 2 Sam. 24:24.
    b Gen. 23:16.
26a 2 Sam. 24:25.
    b Lev. 9:24;

2 Chr. 7:1.
29a 1 Chr. 16:39.
    b 1 Kgs. 3:4.
22 1a 2 Chr. 3:1.
    b 2 Sam. 24:18.
2a 1 Kgs. 9:21.

b TG Israel, Land of.
4a 1 Kgs. 5:6.
5a 1 Kgs. 3:7;
    1 Chr. 29:1.

son, and charged him to build an *a*house for the LORD God of Israel.

7 And David said to Solomon, My son, as for me, it was in my *a*mind to build an *b*house unto the name of the LORD my God:

8 But the word of the LORD came to me, saying, Thou hast shed blood abundantly, and hast made great wars: thou shalt not build an house unto my name, because thou hast shed much blood upon the earth in my sight.

9 Behold, a son shall be born to thee, who shall be a man of rest; and I will give him *a*rest from all his enemies round about: for his name shall be *b*Solomon, and I will give peace and quietness unto Israel in his days.

10 He shall *a*build an house for my name; and he shall be my son, and I *will be* his father; and I will establish the throne of his *b*kingdom over Israel for ever.

11 Now, my son, the LORD be with thee; and prosper thou, and build the house of the LORD thy God, as he hath said of thee.

12 Only the LORD give thee wisdom and understanding, and give thee charge concerning Israel, that thou mayest keep the law of the LORD thy God.

13 Then shalt thou prosper, if thou takest heed to fulfil the statutes and judgments which the LORD charged Moses with concerning Israel: be strong, and of good *a*courage; dread not, nor be dismayed.

14 Now, behold, in my trouble I have prepared for the house of the LORD an hundred thousand *a*talents of gold, and a thousand thousand talents of silver; and of brass and iron without weight; for it is in abundance: timber also and stone have I prepared; and thou mayest add thereto.

15 Moreover *there are* workmen with thee in abundance, hewers and workers of stone and timber, and all manner of cunning men for every manner of work.

16 Of the gold, the silver, and the brass, and the iron, *there is* no number. Arise *therefore*, and be doing, and the LORD be with thee.

17 ¶ David also commanded all the princes of Israel to help Solomon his son, *saying*,

18 *Is* not the LORD your God with you? and hath he *not* given you rest on every side? for he hath given the inhabitants of the land into mine hand; and the land is subdued before the LORD, and before his people.

19 Now set your heart and your soul to seek the LORD your God; arise therefore, and build ye the sanctuary of the LORD God, to bring the *a*ark of the covenant of the LORD, and the holy vessels of God, into the house that is to be built to the name of the LORD.

CHAPTER 23

Solomon is made king—The Levites are numbered and assigned their various religious duties.

So when David was old and full of days, he made *a*Solomon his son king over Israel.

2 ¶ And he gathered together all the princes of Israel, with the priests and the Levites.

3 Now the Levites were numbered from the age of *a*thirty years and upward: and their *b*number by their polls, man by man, was thirty and eight thousand.

4 Of which, twenty and four thousand *were* to set forward the work of the house of the LORD; and six thousand *were* officers and *a*judges:

5 Moreover four thousand *were* *a*porters; and four thousand praised the LORD with the *b*instruments

---

6*a* TG Temple.	10*a* 1 Kgs. 6:12.	1 Chr. 29:22.
7*a* 2 Sam. 7:3 (3–5).	*b* 1 Kgs. 2:15.	3*a* Num. 4:3.
b Ps. 132:5 (1–5).	13*a* TG Courage.	*b* 1 Chr. 23:24.
9*a* 1 Kgs. 4:24 (24–25); 5:4.	14*a* 1 Chr. 29:4.	4*a* Deut. 16:18.
b 2 Sam. 12:24 (24–25);	19*a* TG Ark of the Covenant.	5*a* 1 Chr. 26:1.
1 Kgs. 1:13 (11–14).	**23** 1*a* 1 Kgs. 1:34 (33–39);	*b* Neh. 12:36; Amos 6:5.

which I made, *said David*, to ^cpraise *therewith.*

6 And David divided them into ^acourses among the sons of Levi, *namely*, Gershon, Kohath, and Merari.

7 ¶ Of the Gershonites *were*, Laadan, and Shimei.

8 The sons of Laadan; the chief *was* Jehiel, and Zetham, and Joel, three.

9 The sons of Shimei; Shelomith, and Haziel, and Haran, three. These *were* the chief of the fathers of Laadan.

10 And the sons of Shimei *were*, Jahath, Zina, and Jeush, and Beriah. These four *were* the sons of Shimei.

11 And Jahath was the chief, and Zizah the second: but Jeush and Beriah had not many sons; therefore they were in one reckoning, according to *their* father's house.

12 ¶ The sons of Kohath; Amram, Izhar, Hebron, and Uzziel, four.

13 The sons of ^aAmram; Aaron and Moses: and ^bAaron was ^cseparated, that he should sanctify the most holy things, he and his sons for ever, to burn ^dincense before the LORD, to minister unto him, and to ^ebless in his name for ever.

14 Now *concerning* ^aMoses the man of God, his ^bsons were named of the tribe of Levi.

15 The sons of Moses *were*, ^aGershom, and Eliezer.

16 Of the sons of Gershom, Shebuel *was* the chief.

17 And the sons of Eliezer *were*, Rehabiah the chief. And Eliezer had none other sons; but the sons of Rehabiah were very many.

18 Of the sons of Izhar; Shelomith the chief.

19 Of the sons of Hebron; Jeriah the first, Amariah the second, Jahaziel the third, and Jekameam the fourth.

20 Of the sons of Uzziel; Michah the first, and Jesiah the second.

21 ¶ The sons of ^aMerari; Mahli, and Mushi. The sons of Mahli; Eleazar, and Kish.

22 And Eleazar died, and had no sons, but daughters: and their brethren the sons of Kish took them.

23 The sons of Mushi; Mahli, and Eder, and Jeremoth, three.

24 ¶ These *were* the sons of ^aLevi after the house of their fathers; *even* the chief of the fathers, as they were counted by ^bnumber of names by their ^cpolls, that did the work for the service of the house of the LORD, from the age of twenty years and upward.

25 For David said, The LORD God of Israel hath given ^arest unto his people, that they may dwell in Jerusalem for ever:

26 And also unto the Levites; they shall no *more* carry the tabernacle, nor any vessels of it for the service thereof.

27 For by the last words of David the Levites *were* numbered from twenty years old and above:

28 Because their ^aoffice *was* to wait on the sons of Aaron for the service of the house of the LORD, in the courts, and in the chambers, and in the purifying of all holy things, and the work of the service of the house of God;

29 Both for the shewbread, and for the fine flour for meat offering, and for the unleavened cakes, and for *that which is baked in* the pan, and for that which is fried, and for all manner of measure and size;

30 And to stand every morning to ^athank and praise the LORD, and likewise at even; .

31 And to offer all burnt ^asacrifices unto the LORD in the sabbaths, in the new moons, and on the set

---

5c D&C 136:28.
6a 1 Chr. 15:4 (4–11);
   2 Chr. 8:14;
   31:2 (2–19); 35:4;
   Ezra 6:18.
13a Ex. 6:20.
  b Ex. 28:1.
  c TG Setting Apart.

d Rev. 5:8.
e Num. 6:23.
14a Deut. 33:1;
    D&C 84:31 (31–34).
  b 1 Chr. 26:24 (20–25).
15a Ex. 2:22; 18:3 (3–4).
21a 1 Chr. 6:19 (19, 29).
24a Num. 3:2 (1–39);

10:17 (17–21);
D&C 13; 124:39; 128:24.
  b 1 Chr. 23:3.
  c Num. 1:22.
25a D&C 84:24.
28a 2 Chr. 23:6.
30a TG Thanksgiving.
31a Isa. 1:13 (13–14).

[b]feasts, by number, according to the order commanded unto them, continually before the LORD:

32 And that they should keep the charge of the [a]tabernacle of the congregation, and the charge of the holy *place*, and the charge of the sons of [b]Aaron their brethren, in the service of the house of the LORD.

CHAPTER 24

The sons of Aaron and the rest of the sons of Levi are divided into groups and assigned their duties by lot.

NOW *these are* the [a]divisions of the sons of Aaron. The [b]sons of Aaron; Nadab, and Abihu, Eleazar, and Ithamar.

2 But Nadab and Abihu [a]died before their father, and had no children: therefore Eleazar and Ithamar executed the priest's office.

3 And David distributed them, both [a]Zadok of the sons of Eleazar, and Ahimelech of the sons of Ithamar, according to their offices in their service.

4 And there were more chief men found of the sons of Eleazar than of the sons of Ithamar; and *thus* were they divided. Among the sons of Eleazar *there were* sixteen chief men of the house of *their* fathers, and eight among the sons of Ithamar according to the house of their fathers.

5 Thus were they divided by [a]lot, one sort with another; for the governors of the sanctuary, and governors *of the house* of God, were of the sons of Eleazar, and of the sons of Ithamar.

6 And Shemaiah the son of Nethaneel the scribe, *one* of the Levites, wrote them before the king, and the princes, and Zadok the priest, and Ahimelech the son of Abiathar, and *before* the chief of the fathers of the priests and Levites: one principal household being taken for Eleazar, and *one* taken for Ithamar.

7 Now the first lot came forth to Jehoiarib, the second to Jedaiah,

8 The third to Harim, the fourth to Seorim,

9 The fifth to Malchijah, the sixth to Mijamin,

10 The seventh to Hakkoz, the eighth to [a]Abijah,

11 The ninth to Jeshua, the tenth to Shecaniah,

12 The eleventh to Eliashib, the twelfth to Jakim,

13 The thirteenth to Huppah, the fourteenth to Jeshebeab,

14 The fifteenth to Bilgah, the sixteenth to [a]Immer,

15 The seventeenth to Hezir, the eighteenth to Aphses,

16 The nineteenth to Pethahiah, the twentieth to Jehezekel,

17 The one and twentieth to Jachin, the two and twentieth to Gamul,

18 The three and twentieth to Delaiah, the four and twentieth to Maaziah.

19 These *were* the orderings of them in their service to come into the house of the LORD, according to their manner, under Aaron their father, as the LORD God of Israel had commanded him.

20 ¶ And the rest of the sons of Levi *were these:* Of the sons of Amram; Shubael: of the sons of Shubael; Jehdeiah.

21 Concerning Rehabiah: of the sons of Rehabiah, the first *was* Isshiah.

22 Of the Izharites; Shelomoth: of the sons of Shelomoth; Jahath.

23 And the sons of [a]Hebron; Jeriah *the first*, Amariah the second, Jahaziel the third, Jekameam the fourth.

24 *Of* the sons of Uzziel; Michah: of the sons of Michah; Shamir.

25 The brother of Michah *was* Isshiah: of the sons of Isshiah; Zechariah.

26 The sons of Merari *were* Mahli

---

31 *b* Num. 29:39.
32 *a* Num. 1:50 (50–53).
  b Num. 3:9 (6–9).
24 1 *a* 2 Chr. 35:4.

  b Ex. 28:1.
2 *a* Lev. 10:2 (1–2).
3 *a* 2 Sam. 8:17;
  1 Chr. 6:8.

5 *a* 1 Chr. 24:31.
10 *a* Luke 1:5.
14 *a* Jer. 20:1.
23 *a* 1 Chr. 26:31.

and Mushi: the sons of Jaaziah; Beno.

27 ¶ The sons of Merari by Jaaziah; Beno, and Shoham, and Zaccur, and Ibri.

28 Of Mahli *came* Eleazar, who had no sons.

29 Concerning Kish: the son of Kish *was* Jerahmeel.

30 The sons also of Mushi; Mahli, and Eder, and Jerimoth. These *were* the sons of the Levites after the house of their fathers.

31 These likewise cast ᵃlots over against their brethren the sons of Aaron in the presence of David the king, and Zadok, and Ahimelech, and the chief of the fathers of the priests and Levites, even the principal fathers over against their younger brethren.

CHAPTER 25

The Levite singers and musicians are assigned their duties by lot.

MOREOVER David and the captains of the host ᵃseparated to the ᵇservice of the sons of ᶜAsaph, and of Heman, and of Jeduthun, who should prophesy with harps, with psalteries, and with cymbals: and the number of the workmen according to their service was:

2 Of the sons of Asaph; Zaccur, and Joseph, and Nethaniah, and Asarelah, the sons of Asaph under the hands of Asaph, which prophesied according to the order of the king.

3 Of Jeduthun: the sons of Jeduthun; Gedaliah, and Zeri, and Jeshaiah, Hashabiah, and Mattithiah, six, under the hands of their father Jeduthun, who prophesied with a harp, to give thanks and to praise the LORD.

4 Of Heman: the sons of Heman; Bukkiah, Mattaniah, Uzziel, Shebuel, and Jerimoth, Hananiah, Hanani, Eliathah, Giddalti, and Romamti-ezer, Joshbekashah, Mallothi, Hothir, *and* Mahazioth:

5 All these *were* the sons of Heman the king's ᵃseer in the words of God, to lift up the horn. And God gave to Heman fourteen sons and three daughters.

6 All these *were* under the hands of their father for ᵃsong *in* the house of the LORD, with cymbals, psalteries, and harps, for the service of the house of God, according to the king's order to Asaph, Jeduthun, and Heman.

7 So the number of them, with their brethren that were instructed in the ᵃsongs of the LORD, *even* all that were ᵇcunning, was two hundred fourscore and eight.

8 ¶ And they cast ᵃlots, ward against *ward*, as well the small as the great, the teacher as the scholar.

9 Now the first lot came forth for Asaph to Joseph: the second to Gedaliah, who with his brethren and sons *were* twelve:

10 The third to Zaccur, *he*, his sons, and his brethren, *were* twelve:

11 The fourth to Izri, *he*, his sons, and his brethren, *were* twelve:

12 The fifth to Nethaniah, *he*, his sons, and his brethren, *were* twelve:

13 The sixth to Bukkiah, *he*, his sons, and his brethren, *were* twelve:

14 The seventh to Jesharelah, *he*, his sons, and his brethren, *were* twelve:

15 The eighth to Jeshaiah, *he*, his sons, and his brethren, *were* twelve:

16 The ninth to Mattaniah, *he*, his sons, and his brethren, *were* twelve:

17 The tenth to Shimei, *he*, his sons, and his brethren, *were* twelve:

18 The eleventh to Azareel, *he*, his sons, and his brethren, *were* twelve:

19 The twelfth to Hashabiah, *he*, his sons, and his brethren, *were* twelve:

20 The thirteenth to Shubael, *he*, his sons, and his brethren, *were* twelve:

31a 1 Chr. 24:5; 25:8 (8–31); 26:13 (13–14).
25 1a TG Setting Apart.
  b Num. 3:8 (5–8).
c 1 Chr. 6:39.
5a TG Seer.
6a 1 Chr. 6:31; 9:33.
7a 2 Chr. 23:13.
b TG Talents.
8a 1 Chr. 24:31; 26:13.

21 The fourteenth to Mattithiah, *he*, his sons, and his brethren, *were* twelve:

22 The fifteenth to Jeremoth, *he*, his sons, and his brethren, *were* twelve:

23 The sixteenth to Hananiah, *he*, his sons, and his brethren, *were* twelve:

24 The seventeenth to Joshbekashah, *he*, his sons, and his brethren, *were* twelve:

25 The eighteenth to Hanani, *he*, his sons, and his brethren, *were* twelve:

26 The nineteenth to Mallothi, *he*, his sons, and his brethren, *were* twelve:

27 The twentieth to Eliathah, *he*, his sons, and his brethren, *were* twelve:

28 The one and twentieth to Hothir, *he*, his sons, and his brethren, *were* twelve:

29 The two and twentieth to Giddalti, *he*, his sons, and his brethren, *were* twelve:

30 The three and twentieth to Mahazioth, *he*, his sons, and his brethren, *were* twelve:

31 The four and twentieth to Romamti-ezer, *he*, his sons, and his brethren, *were* twelve.

CHAPTER 26

The Levites are assigned as porters— They have charge of the treasures, serve as officers and judges, and conduct the outward business pertaining to the Israelites.

CONCERNING the *a*divisions of the *b*porters: Of the Korhites *was* Meshelemiah the son of Kore, of the sons of Asaph.

2 And the sons of Meshelemiah *were*, Zechariah the firstborn, Jediael the second, Zebadiah the third, Jathniel the fourth,

3 Elam the fifth, Jehohanan the sixth, Elioenai the seventh.

4 Moreover the sons of Obed-edom *were*, Shemaiah the firstborn, Jehozabad the second, Joah the third, and Sacar the fourth, and Nethaneel the fifth,

5 Ammiel the sixth, Issachar the seventh, Peulthai the eighth: for God *a*blessed him.

6 Also unto Shemaiah his son were sons born, that ruled throughout the house of their father: for they *were* mighty men of valour.

7 The sons of Shemaiah; Othni, and Rephael, and Obed, Elzabad, whose brethren *were* strong men, Elihu, and Semachiah.

8 All these of the sons of Obed-edom: they and their sons and their brethren, able men for strength for the service, *were* threescore and two of Obed-edom.

9 And Meshelemiah had sons and brethren, strong men, eighteen.

10 Also Hosah, of the children of Merari, had sons; Simri the chief, (for *though* he was not the firstborn, yet his father made him the chief;)

11 Hilkiah the second, Tebaliah the third, Zechariah the fourth: all the sons and brethren of Hosah *were* thirteen.

12 Among these *were* the divisions of the porters, *even* among the chief men, *having* wards one against another, to minister in the house of the LORD.

13 ¶ And they cast *a*lots, as well the small as the great, according to the house of their fathers, for every gate.

14 And the lot eastward fell to Shelemiah. Then for Zechariah his son, a wise counsellor, they cast lots; and his lot came out northward.

15 To Obed-edom southward; and to his sons the house of Asuppim.

16 To Shuppim and Hosah *the lot came forth* westward, with the gate Shallecheth, by the causeway of the going up, ward against ward.

17 Eastward *were* six Levites, northward four a day, southward four a day, and toward Asuppim two *and* two.

18 At Parbar westward, four at the causeway, *and* two at Parbar.

19 These *are* the divisions of the

---

26 1*a* 2 Chr. 35:4.
    b 1 Chr. 23:5.

5*a* 1 Chr. 13:14.
13*a* 1 Chr. 24:31; 25:8.

porters among the sons of Kore, and among the sons of Merari.

20 ¶ And of the Levites, Ahijah *was* over the treasures of the house of God, and over the treasures of the dedicated things.

21 *As concerning* the sons of Laadan; the sons of the Gershonite Laadan, chief fathers, *even* of Laadan the Gershonite, *were* Jehieli.

22 The sons of Jehieli; Zetham, and Joel his brother, *which were* over the treasures of the house of the Lord.

23 Of the Amramites, *and* the Izharites, the Hebronites, *and* the Uzzielites:

24 And Shebuel the son of [a]Gershom, the son of Moses, *was* ruler of the treasures.

25 And his brethren by Eliezer; Rehabiah his son, and Jeshaiah his son, and Joram his son, and Zichri his son, and Shelomith his son.

26 Which Shelomith and his brethren *were* over all the treasures of the dedicated things, which David the king, and the chief fathers, the captains over thousands and hundreds, and the captains of the host, had dedicated.

27 Out of the spoils won in battles did they [a]dedicate to maintain the house of the Lord.

28 And all that Samuel the [a]seer, and Saul the son of Kish, and [b]Abner the son of Ner, and Joab the son of Zeruiah, had dedicated; *and* whosoever had dedicated *any thing, it was* under the hand of Shelomith, and of his brethren.

29 ¶ Of the Izharites, Chenaniah and his sons *were* for the outward [a]business over Israel, for officers and judges.

30 *And* of the Hebronites, Hashabiah and his brethren, men of valour, a thousand and seven hundred, *were* officers among them of Israel on this side Jordan westward in all the business of the Lord, and in the service of the king.

31 Among the [a]Hebronites *was* Jerijah the chief, *even* among the Hebronites, according to the generations of his fathers. In the fortieth year of the reign of David they were sought for, and there were found among them mighty men of valour at Jazer of Gilead.

32 And his brethren, men of valour, *were* two thousand and seven hundred chief fathers, whom king David made rulers over the Reubenites, the Gadites, and the half tribe of Manasseh, for every matter pertaining to God, and affairs of the king.

CHAPTER 27

The officers who serve the king are named—The princes of the tribes of Israel are set forth.

Now the children of Israel after their number, *to wit,* the chief fathers and [a]captains of thousands and hundreds, and their officers that served the king in any matter of the courses, which came in and went out month by month throughout all the months of the year, of every course *were* twenty and four thousand.

2 Over the first course for the first month *was* Jashobeam the son of Zabdiel: and in his course *were* twenty and four thousand.

3 Of the children of Perez *was* the chief of all the captains of the host for the first month.

4 And over the course of the second month *was* Dodai an Ahohite, and of his course *was* Mikloth also the ruler: in his course likewise *were* twenty and four thousand.

5 The third captain of the host for the third month *was* Benaiah the son of Jehoiada, a chief priest: and in his course *were* twenty and four thousand.

6 This *is* that [a]Benaiah, *who was* mighty *among* the thirty, and above the thirty: and in his course *was* Ammizabad his son.

7 The fourth *captain* for the fourth month *was* [a]Asahel the brother of

---

24a 1 Chr. 23:14.
27a 2 Sam. 8:11 (10–11).
28a TG Seer.

b 2 Sam. 2:8.
29a Neh. 11:16.
31a 1 Chr. 24:23.

27 1a 1 Chr. 28:1.
6a 2 Sam. 23:20 (20–23).
7a 1 Chr. 11:26.

Joab, and Zebadiah his son after him: and in his course *were* twenty and four thousand.

8 The fifth captain for the fifth month *was* Shamhuth the Izrahite: and in his course *were* twenty and four thousand.

9 The sixth *captain* for the sixth month *was* Ira the son of Ikkesh the Tekoite: and in his course *were* twenty and four thousand.

10 The seventh *captain* for the seventh month *was* Helez the Pelonite, of the children of Ephraim: and in his course *were* twenty and four thousand.

11 The eighth *captain* for the eighth month *was* Sibbecai the Hushathite, of the Zarhites: and in his course *were* twenty and four thousand.

12 The ninth *captain* for the ninth month *was* Abiezer the Anetothite, of the Benjamites: and in his course *were* twenty and four thousand.

13 The tenth *captain* for the tenth month *was* Maharai the Netophathite, of the Zarhites: and in his course *were* twenty and four thousand.

14 The eleventh *captain* for the eleventh month *was* Benaiah the Pirathonite, of the children of Ephraim: and in his course *were* twenty and four thousand.

15 The twelfth *captain* for the twelfth month *was* Heldai the Netophathite, of Othniel: and in his course *were* twenty and four thousand.

16 ¶ Furthermore over the tribes of Israel: the ᵃruler of the Reubenites *was* Eliezer the son of Zichri: of the Simeonites, Shephatiah the son of Maachah:

17 Of the Levites, Hashabiah the son of Kemuel: of the Aaronites, Zadok:

18 Of Judah, Elihu, *one* of the brethren of David: of Issachar, Omri the son of Michael:

19 Of Zebulun, Ishmaiah the son of Obadiah: of Naphtali, Jerimoth the son of Azriel:

20 Of the children of Ephraim, Hoshea the son of Azaziah: of the half tribe of Manasseh, Joel the son of Pedaiah:

21 Of the half *tribe* of Manasseh in Gilead, Iddo the son of Zechariah: of Benjamin, Jaasiel the son of Abner:

22 Of Dan, Azareel the son of Jeroham. These *were* the princes of the tribes of Israel.

23 ¶ But David took not the number of them from twenty years old and under: because the Lᴏʀᴅ had said he would increase Israel like to the ᵃstars of the heavens.

24 Joab the son of Zeruiah began to number, but he finished not, because there fell ᵃwrath for it against Israel; neither was the number put in the account of the ᵇchronicles of king David.

25 ¶ And over the king's ᵃtreasures *was* Azmaveth the son of Adiel: and over the storehouses in the fields, in the cities, and in the villages, and in the castles, *was* Jehonathan the son of Uzziah:

26 And over them that did the work of the field for tillage of the ground *was* Ezri the son of Chelub:

27 And over the vineyards *was* Shimei the Ramathite: over the increase of the vineyards for the wine cellars *was* Zabdi the Shiphmite:

28 And over the olive trees and the sycomore trees that *were* in the low plains *was* Baal-hanan the Gederite: and over the cellars of oil *was* Joash:

29 And over the herds that fed in Sharon *was* Shitrai the Sharonite: and over the herds *that were* in the valleys *was* Shaphat the son of Adlai:

30 Over the camels also *was* Obil the Ishmaelite: and over the asses *was* Jehdeiah the Meronothite:

31 And over the flocks *was* Jaziz the Hagerite. All these *were* the rulers of the substance which *was* king David's.

16a 1 Chr. 28:1.
23a Gen. 15:5;
        D&C 132:30 (30–31).
24a 1 Chr. 21:7 (1–7).
    b 1 Kgs. 14:19;
        Esth. 10:2.
25a 1 Chr. 28:1.

32 Also Jonathan David's uncle was a ^acounsellor, a wise man, and a scribe: and Jehiel the son of Hachmoni *was* with the king's sons:

33 And ^aAhithophel *was* the king's counsellor: and Hushai the Archite *was* the king's companion:

34 And after Ahithophel *was* Jehoiada the son of Benaiah, and Abiathar: and the general of the king's army *was* Joab.

CHAPTER 28

David assembles the leaders of Israel—Solomon is appointed to build the temple—David exhorts Solomon and the people to keep the commandments—David gives Solomon the pattern and materials for the temple.

AND David assembled all the ^aprinces of Israel, the princes of the tribes, and the ^bcaptains of the companies that ministered to the king by course, and the captains over the thousands, and captains over the hundreds, and the stewards over all the ^csubstance and possession of the king, and of his sons, with the officers, and with the mighty men, and with all the valiant men, unto Jerusalem.

2 Then David the king stood up upon his feet, and said, Hear me, my brethren, and my people: *As for me,* I *had* in mine heart to build an house of ^arest for the ark of the covenant of the LORD, and for the ^bfootstool of our God, and had made ready for the building:

3 But God said unto me, Thou shalt not build an house for my name, because thou *hast been* a man of ^awar, and hast shed blood.

4 Howbeit the LORD God of Israel chose me before all the house of my father to be king over Israel for ever: for he hath chosen ^aJudah *to be* the ruler; and of the house of Judah,

the house of my father; and among the sons of my father he liked me to make *me* ^bking over all Israel:

5 And of all my sons, (for the LORD hath given me many sons,) he hath chosen Solomon my son to sit upon the throne of the kingdom of the LORD over Israel.

6 And he said unto me, Solomon thy son, he shall build my ^ahouse and my courts: for I have chosen him *to be* my son, and I will be his father.

7 Moreover I will establish his kingdom for ever, if he be constant to do my commandments and my judgments, as at this day.

8 Now therefore in the sight of all Israel the congregation of the LORD, and in the audience of our God, keep and seek for all the commandments of the LORD your God: that ye may possess this good ^aland, and leave *it* for an inheritance for your children after you for ever.

9 ¶ And thou, Solomon my son, know thou the God of thy father, and serve him with a ^aperfect heart and with a willing mind: for the LORD ^bsearcheth all hearts, and ^cunderstandeth all the imaginations of the thoughts: if thou ^dseek him, he will be found of thee; but if thou forsake him, he will cast thee off for ever.

10 Take heed now; for the LORD hath chosen thee to build an house for the sanctuary: be strong, and do *it.*

11 ¶ Then David gave to Solomon his son the pattern of the porch, and of the houses thereof, and of the treasuries thereof, and of the upper chambers thereof, and of the inner parlours thereof, and of the place of the mercy seat,

12 And the pattern of all that he had by the ^aspirit, of the courts of the house of the LORD, and of all the chambers round about, of the

---

32a TG Counselor.
33a 2 Sam. 15:12.
28 1a 1 Chr. 27:16 (16–22).
   b 1 Chr. 27:1 (1–15).
   c 1 Chr. 27:25 (25–31).
2a 2 Chr. 6:41.
   b Ps. 99:5;

Lam. 2:1.
3a 2 Ne. 13:2 (1–2).
4a TG Israel, Judah,
   People of.
   b 1 Sam. 16:1.
6a TG Temple.
8a 1 Ne. 2:20;

Moses 7:17 (17–18).
9a 1 Kgs. 8:61.
   b TG God, Omniscience of.
   c D&C 6:16.
   d D&C 88:63.
12a 1 Ne. 17:8 (8, 18).

treasuries of the house of God, and of the treasuries of the dedicated things:

13 Also for the courses of the priests and the Levites, and for all the work of the service of the house of the LORD, and for all the vessels of service in the house of the LORD.

14 *He gave* of gold by weight for *things* of gold, for all instruments of all manner of service; *silver also* for all instruments of silver by weight, for all instruments of every kind of service:

15 Even the weight for the candlesticks of gold, and for their *a*lamps of gold, by weight for every candlestick, and for the lamps thereof: and for the candlesticks of silver by weight, *both* for the candlestick, and *also* for the lamps thereof, according to the use of every candlestick.

16 And by weight *he gave* gold for the tables of shewbread, for every table; and *likewise* silver for the tables of silver:

17 Also pure gold for the fleshhooks, and the bowls, and the cups: and for the golden basins *he gave gold* by weight for every basin; and *likewise silver* by weight for every basin of silver:

18 And for the altar of incense refined gold by weight; and gold for the pattern of the chariot of the cherubims, that spread out *their wings,* and covered the ark of the covenant of the LORD.

19 All *this, said David,* the LORD made me understand in writing by *his* hand upon me, *even* all the works of this *a*pattern.

20 And David said to Solomon his son, Be strong and of good *a*courage, and do *it:* fear not, nor be dismayed: for the LORD God, *even* my God, *will be* with thee; he will not fail thee, nor forsake thee, until thou hast finished all the work for the service of the house of the LORD.

21 And, behold, the courses of the priests and the Levites, *even they shall be with thee* for all the service of the house of God: and *there shall be* with thee for all manner of workmanship every willing skilful man, for any manner of service: also the princes and all the people *will be* wholly at thy commandment.

CHAPTER 29

All Israel makes a liberal offering for the temple—David blesses and praises the Lord and instructs the people—David dies—Solomon reigns as king—The books of Nathan and Gad are mentioned.

FURTHERMORE David the king said unto all the congregation, Solomon my son, whom alone God hath chosen, *is* yet *a*young and tender, and the work *is* great: for the palace *is* not for man, but for the LORD God.

2 Now I have prepared with all my might for the house of my God the gold for *things to be made* of gold, and the silver for *things* of silver, and the brass for *things* of brass, the iron for *things* of iron, and wood for *things* of wood; onyx stones, and *stones* to be set, glistering stones, and of divers colours, and all manner of precious stones, and marble stones in abundance.

3 Moreover, because I have set my affection to the house of my God, I have of mine own proper good, of gold and silver, *which* I have given to the house of my God, over and above all that I have prepared for the holy house,

4 *Even* three thousand *a*talents of gold, of the gold of Ophir, and seven thousand talents of refined silver, to overlay the walls of the houses *withal:*

5 The gold for *things* of gold, and the silver for *things* of silver, and for all manner of work *to be made* by the hands of artificers. And who *then* is willing to consecrate his service this day unto the LORD?

15*a* Ex. 25:37.
19*a* Num. 8:4;
    Acts 7:44.
20*a* TG Courage.

29 1*a* 1 Sam. 17:33 (32–51);
    1 Kgs. 3:7;
    1 Chr. 22:5;
    1 Ne. 7:8 (8–18);

D&C 1:19 (19, 23);
    JS—H 1:22 (21–25).
4*a* 1 Chr. 22:14.

6 ¶ Then the chief of the fathers and princes of the tribes of Israel, and the captains of thousands and of hundreds, with the rulers of the king's work, offered willingly,

7 And gave for the service of the house of God of gold five thousand talents and ten thousand drams, and of silver ten thousand talents, and of brass eighteen thousand talents, and one hundred thousand talents of iron.

8 And they with whom *precious* stones were found gave *them* to the treasure of the ^ahouse of the LORD, by the hand of Jehiel the Gershonite.

9 Then the people rejoiced, for that they offered ^awillingly, because with perfect heart they offered ^bwillingly to the LORD: and David the king also rejoiced with great joy.

10 ¶ Wherefore David blessed the LORD before all the congregation: and David said, Blessed *be* thou, LORD God of Israel our ^afather, for ever and ever.

11 Thine, O LORD, *is* the greatness, and the power, and the ^aglory, and the victory, and the majesty: for all *that is* in the heaven and in the earth *is thine*; thine *is* the ^bkingdom, O LORD, and thou art exalted as head above all.

12 Both ^ariches and honour ^bcome of thee, and thou reignest over all; and in thine hand *is* power and might; and in thine hand *it is* to make great, and to give strength unto all.

13 Now therefore, our God, we ^athank thee, and praise thy glorious name.

14 But who *am* I, and what *is* my people, that we should be able to offer so willingly after this sort? for all things ^acome of thee, and of thine own have we given thee.

15 For we *are* ^astrangers before thee, and sojourners, as *were* all our fathers: our days on the earth *are* as a ^bshadow, and *there is* none abiding.

16 O LORD our God, all this store that we have prepared to build thee an house for thine holy name *cometh* of thine hand, and *is* all thine own.

17 I know also, my God, that thou ^atriest the heart, and hast pleasure in uprightness. As for me, in the uprightness of mine heart I have willingly offered all these things: and now have I seen with joy thy people, which are present here, to offer willingly unto thee.

18 O LORD God of Abraham, Isaac, and of Israel, our fathers, keep this for ever in the imagination of the thoughts of the heart of thy people, and prepare their heart unto thee:

19 And give unto Solomon my son a perfect ^aheart, to keep thy commandments, thy testimonies, and thy statutes, and to do all *these things,* and to build the palace, *for* the which I have made provision.

20 ¶ And David said to all the congregation, Now bless the LORD your God. And all the ^acongregation blessed the LORD God of their fathers, and bowed down their heads, and worshipped the LORD, and the king.

21 And they sacrificed sacrifices unto the LORD, and offered burnt offerings unto the LORD, on the morrow after that day, *even* a thousand bullocks, a thousand rams, *and* a thousand lambs, with their drink offerings, and sacrifices in abundance for all Israel:

22 And did eat and drink before the LORD on that day with great gladness. And they made ^aSolomon the son of David king the second time, and ^banointed *him* unto the LORD *to be* the chief governor, and Zadok *to be* ^cpriest.

---

8 a D&C 97:12 (10–17).
9 a Moro. 7:8;
     D&C 64:34.
   b TG Initiative.
10 a Deut. 32:6;
      Isa. 63:16; 64:8.
11 a Matt. 6:13 (9–13);
      D&C 65:6.
   b Ps. 22:28;

D&C 6:13.
12 a TG Treasure.
   b Mosiah 2:25; 4:22.
13 a TG Thanksgiving.
14 a Ps. 24:1;
      Mal. 3:8 (8–12).
15 a TG Stranger.
   b Ps. 102:11; 144:4;
      Jacob 7:26.

17 a TG Test.
19 a Deut. 5:29.
20 a TG Assembly for
      Worship.
22 a 1 Chr. 23:1.
   b 1 Kgs. 1:34 (33–39).
   c 1 Sam. 2:35;
      1 Kgs. 2:35.

23 Then *a*Solomon sat on the throne of the LORD as king instead of David his father, and prospered; and all Israel obeyed him.

24 And all the princes, and the mighty men, and all the sons likewise of king David, submitted themselves unto Solomon the king.

25 And the LORD *a*magnified Solomon exceedingly in the sight of all Israel, and bestowed upon him *such* royal majesty as had not been on any king before him in Israel.

26 ¶ Thus David the son of Jesse reigned over all Israel.

27 And the time that he *a*reigned over Israel *was* forty years; seven years reigned he in Hebron, and thirty and three *years* reigned he in Jerusalem.

28 And he died in a good old age, full of days, riches, and honour: and Solomon his son reigned in his stead.

29 Now the acts of David the king, first and last, behold, they *are* written in the book of Samuel the seer, and in the book of *a*Nathan the prophet, and in the book of Gad the *b*seer,

30 With all his reign and his might, and the times that went over him, and over Israel, and over all the kingdoms of the countries.

THE SECOND BOOK OF THE
CHRONICLES

CHAPTER 1

The Lord honors Solomon before all Israel—The Lord appears to him—Solomon chooses and is given wisdom—His kingdom is blessed with splendor and riches.

AND Solomon the son of David was strengthened in his kingdom, and the LORD his God *was* with him, and magnified him exceedingly.

2 Then Solomon spake unto all Israel, to the captains of thousands and of hundreds, and to the judges, and to every governor in all Israel, the chief of the fathers.

3 So Solomon, and all the congregation with him, went to the *a*high place that *was* at Gibeon; for there was the *b*tabernacle of the congregation of God, which Moses the servant of the LORD had made in the wilderness.

4 But the *a*ark of God had David brought up from Kirjath-jearim to *the place which* David had prepared for it: for he had pitched a tent for it at Jerusalem.

5 Moreover the *a*brasen altar, that Bezaleel the son of Uri, the son of Hur, had made, he put before the tabernacle of the LORD: and Solomon and the congregation sought unto *b*it.

6 And Solomon went up thither to the brasen altar before the LORD, which *was* at the tabernacle of the congregation, and offered a thousand burnt offerings upon it.

23a 1 Kgs. 2:12.
25a Josh. 3:7.
27a 2 Sam. 5:4 (4–5).
29a TG Scriptures, Lost.
    b TG Seer.

[2 CHRONICLES]
1 3a 1 Chr. 16:39.
    b HEB tent of meeting (also v. 13).

TG Temple.
4a 1 Kgs. 3:15.
5a Ex. 38:2 (1–2).
    b OR Him, i.e., the Lord.

7 ¶ In that night did God ^aappear unto Solomon, and said unto him, ^bAsk what I shall give thee.

8 And Solomon said unto God, Thou hast shewed great mercy unto David my father, and hast made me to reign in his stead.

9 Now, O LORD God, let thy promise unto David my father be established: for thou hast made me king over a people like the dust of the earth in multitude.

10 Give me now wisdom and ^aknowledge, that I may go out and come in before this people: for who can ^bjudge this thy people, *that is so* great?

11 And God said to Solomon, Because this was in thine heart, and thou hast not asked riches, wealth, or honour, nor the life of thine enemies, neither yet hast asked long life; but hast asked wisdom and knowledge for thyself, that thou mayest judge my people, over whom I have made thee king:

12 Wisdom and knowledge *is* granted unto thee; and I will give thee riches, and wealth, and honour, such as none of the kings have had that *have been* before thee, neither shall there any after thee have the like.

13 ¶ Then Solomon came *from his journey* to the high place that *was* at Gibeon to Jerusalem, from before the tabernacle of the congregation, and reigned over Israel.

14 And Solomon gathered chariots and horsemen: and he had a ^athousand and four hundred chariots, and twelve thousand horsemen, which he placed in the chariot cities, and with the king at Jerusalem.

15 And the king made silver and gold at Jerusalem *as plenteous* as stones, and cedar trees made he as the sycomore trees that *are* in the vale for abundance.

16 And Solomon had horses brought out of Egypt, and ^alinen yarn: the king's merchants received the linen yarn at a price.

17 And they fetched up, and brought forth out of Egypt a chariot for six hundred *shekels* of silver, and an horse for an hundred and fifty: and so brought they out *horses* for all the kings of the Hittites, and for the kings of ^aSyria, by their means.

CHAPTER 2

Solomon engages Huram of Tyre to supply timber for the temple—Laborers are organized to do the work.

AND Solomon determined to build an ^ahouse for the name of the LORD, and an house for his kingdom.

2 And Solomon told out threescore and ten thousand men to bear burdens, and fourscore thousand ^ato hew in the mountain, and three thousand and six hundred to oversee them.

3 ¶ And Solomon sent to ^aHuram the king of Tyre, saying, As thou didst deal with David my father, and didst send him cedars to build him an house to dwell therein, *even so deal with me.*

4 Behold, I ^abuild an house to the name of the LORD my God, to dedicate *it* to him, *and* to burn before him sweet incense, and for the continual ^bshewbread, and for the burnt offerings morning and evening, on the sabbaths, and on the new moons, and on the solemn feasts of the LORD our God. This *is an ordinance* for ever to Israel.

5 And the house which I build *is* great: for great *is* our God above all gods.

6 But who is able to build him an house, seeing the heaven and ^aheaven of heavens cannot contain him? who *am* I then, that I should build

---

7*a* 1 Kgs. 3:5 (5–14).
  b 3 Ne. 28:1 (1–12);
     D&C 7:1 (1–8).
10*a* TG Knowledge.
  b OR rule (also v. 11).
     Mosiah 29:12 (12–13).

14*a* 1 Kgs. 4:26.
16*a* 1 Kgs. 10:28.
17*a* HEB Aram.
2 1*a* TG Temple.
  2*a* IE to quarry stone.
  3*a* OR Hiram.

1 Kgs. 5:2 (2–11).
4*a* D&C 97:15 (13–15).
  b TG Bread, Shewbread.
6*a* 1 Kgs. 8:27.

him an house, save only to burn sacrifice before him?

7 Send me now therefore a man cunning to work in gold, and in silver, and in brass, and in iron, and in purple, and crimson, and blue, and that can skill to grave with the cunning men that *are* with me in Judah and in Jerusalem, whom David my father did provide.

8 Send me also cedar trees, fir trees, and algum trees, out of Lebanon: for I know that thy servants can skill to cut timber in Lebanon; and, behold, my servants *shall be* with thy servants,

9 Even to prepare me timber in abundance: for the house which I am about to build *shall be* wonderful great.

10 And, behold, I will give to thy servants, the hewers that cut timber, twenty thousand measures of beaten wheat, and twenty thousand measures of barley, and twenty thousand baths of wine, and twenty thousand baths of oil.

11 ¶ Then Huram the king of Tyre answered in writing, which he sent to Solomon, Because the LORD hath loved his people, he hath made thee king over them.

12 Huram said moreover, Blessed *be* the LORD God of Israel, that made heaven and earth, who hath given to David the king a wise son, endued with *a*prudence and understanding, that might build an house for the LORD, and an house for his kingdom.

13 And now I have sent a cunning man, endued with understanding, of *a*Huram my father's,

14 The son of a woman of the daughters of Dan, and his father *was* a man of Tyre, skilful to work in gold, and in silver, in brass, in iron, in stone, and in timber, in purple, in blue, and in fine linen, and in crimson; also to grave any manner of graving, and *a*to find out every device which shall be put to him, with thy cunning men, and with the cunning men of my lord David thy father.

15 Now therefore the wheat, and the barley, the oil, and the wine, which my lord hath spoken of, let him send unto his servants:

16 And we will cut wood out of Lebanon, as much as thou shalt need: and we will bring it to thee in floats by sea to Joppa; and thou shalt carry it up to Jerusalem.

17 ¶ And Solomon numbered all the *a*strangers that *were* in the land of Israel, after the numbering wherewith David his father had numbered them; and they were found an hundred and fifty thousand and three thousand and six hundred.

18 And he set threescore and ten thousand of them *to be* bearers of burdens, and fourscore thousand *to be* hewers in the mountain, and three thousand and six hundred overseers to set the people a work.

CHAPTER 3

Solomon begins to build the temple— He makes the veil and the pillars, and uses much gold and many precious stones.

THEN Solomon began to *a*build the house of the LORD at Jerusalem in mount *b*Moriah, where *the* LORD appeared unto David his father, in the place that David had prepared in the *c*threshingfloor of *d*Ornan the Jebusite.

2 And he began to build in the second *day* of the second month, in the fourth year of his reign.

3 ¶ Now these *are the things wherein* Solomon was instructed for the building of the *a*house of God. The length by cubits after the *b*first

---

12a TG Prudence.
13a 1 Kgs. 7:13 (13–51).
14a OR to execute any design.
17a TG Stranger.
3 1a 1 Kgs. 6:1 (1–38);
    1 Chr. 22:1;

2 Ne. 5:16 (15–17);
    D&C 84:5 (5, 31);
    124:31 (25–55).
b Gen. 22:2.
c 2 Sam. 24:18;
    1 Chr. 21:18 (18–27).

d OR Araunah; see also
    2 Sam. 24:18;
    1 Chr. 21:18; 22:1.
3a 1 Kgs. 6:2;
    D&C 119:2 (1–2).
b OR ancient measure.

measure *was* threescore cubits, and the breadth twenty cubits.

4 And the porch that *was* in the front *of the house*, the length *of it was* according to the breadth of the house, twenty cubits, and the height *was* an hundred and twenty: and he overlaid it within with pure gold.

5 And the greater house he ceiled with fir tree, which he overlaid with fine gold, and set thereon palm trees and chains.

6 And he garnished the house with precious stones for *a*beauty: and the gold *was* gold of Parvaim.

7 He overlaid also the house, the beams, the posts, and the walls thereof, and the doors thereof, with gold; and graved cherubims on the walls.

8 And he made the most *a*holy house, the length whereof *was* according to the breadth of the house, twenty cubits, and the breadth thereof twenty cubits: and he overlaid it with fine gold, *amounting* to six hundred talents.

9 And the weight of the nails *was* fifty shekels of gold. And he overlaid the upper chambers with gold.

10 And in the most holy house he made two *a*cherubims of image work, and overlaid them with gold.

11 ¶ And the wings of the cherubims *were* twenty cubits long: one wing *of the one cherub was* five cubits, reaching to the wall of the house: and the other wing *was likewise* five cubits, reaching to the wing of the other cherub.

12 And *one* wing of the other cherub *was* five cubits, reaching to the wall of the house: and the other wing *was* five cubits *also*, joining to the wing of the other cherub.

13 The wings of these cherubims spread themselves forth twenty cubits: and they stood on their feet, and their faces *were* inward.

14 ¶ And he made the veil *of* blue, and purple, and crimson, and fine linen, and wrought cherubims thereon.

15 Also he made before the house two pillars of thirty and five cubits high, and the chapiter that *was* on the top of each of them *was* five cubits.

16 And he made chains, *as* in the *a*oracle, and put *them* on the heads of the pillars; and made an hundred pomegranates, and put *them* on the chains.

17 And he reared up the pillars before the temple, one on the right hand, and the other on the left; and called the name of that on the right hand Jachin, and the name of that on the left Boaz.

CHAPTER 4

Solomon makes a basin and places it on twelve oxen—The altar, basins, pots, and various items are made.

MOREOVER he made an altar of *a*brass, twenty cubits the length thereof, and twenty cubits the breadth thereof, and ten cubits the height thereof.

2 ¶ Also he made a molten *a*sea of ten cubits from brim to brim, round in *b*compass, and five cubits the height thereof; and a line of thirty cubits did compass it round about.

3 And under it *was* the similitude of oxen, which did compass it round about: ten in a cubit, compassing the sea round about. Two rows of oxen *were* cast, when it was cast.

4 It stood upon twelve oxen, three looking toward the north, and three looking toward the west, and three looking toward the south, and three looking toward the east: and the sea *was set* above upon them, and all their hinder parts *were* inward.

5 And the thickness of it *was* an handbreadth, and the brim of it like the work of the brim of a cup, with flowers of lilies; *and* it received and held three *a*thousand baths.

6*a* TG Beauty.
8*a* 1 Kgs. 6:16;
   D&C 96:2.

10*a* TG Cherubim.
16*a* OR inner sanctuary.
4 1*a* 1 Kgs. 8:64.

2*a* TG Baptism; Temple.
  b IE shape.
5*a* 1 Kgs. 7:26.

6 ¶ He made also ten *a*lavers, and put five on the right hand, and five on the left, to *b*wash in them: such things as they offered for the burnt offering they *c*washed in them; but the sea *was* for the priests to wash in.

7 And he made ten *a*candlesticks of gold according to their form, and set *them* in the temple, five on the right hand, and five on the left.

8 He made also ten tables, and placed *them* in the temple, five on the right side, and five on the left. And he made an hundred basins of gold.

9 ¶ Furthermore he made the court of the priests, and the great court, and doors for the court, and overlaid the doors of them with brass.

10 And he set the *a*sea on the right side of the east end, over against the south.

11 And Huram made the pots, and the shovels, and the basins. And Huram finished the work that he was to make for king Solomon for the house of God;

12 *To wit,* the two pillars, and the pommels, and the chapiters *which were* on the top of the two pillars, and the two wreaths to cover the two pommels of the chapiters which *were* on the top of the pillars;

13 And four hundred pomegranates on the two wreaths; two rows of pomegranates on each wreath, to cover the two pommels of the chapiters which *were* upon the pillars.

14 He made also bases, and *a*lavers made he upon the bases;

15 One *a*sea, and twelve oxen under it.

16 The pots also, and the shovels, and the fleshhooks, and all their instruments, did Huram his father make to king Solomon for the house of the LORD of *a*bright brass.

17 In the plain of Jordan did the king cast them, in the clay ground between Succoth and Zeredathah.

18 Thus Solomon made all these vessels in great abundance: for the weight of the brass could not be found out.

19 ¶ And Solomon made all the vessels that *were for* the house of God, the golden altar also, and the tables whereon the shewbread *was set;*

20 Moreover the candlesticks with their lamps, that they should burn after the manner before the oracle, of pure gold;

21 And the flowers, and the lamps, and the tongs, *made he of* gold, *and* that perfect gold;

22 And the snuffers, and the basins, and the spoons, and the censers, *of* pure gold: and the entry of the house, the inner doors thereof for the most holy *place,* and the doors of the house of the temple, *were of* gold.

CHAPTER 5

The temple is finished, and the ark of the covenant is placed in the holy of holies—The glory of the Lord fills the temple.

THUS all the work that Solomon made for the house of the LORD was finished: and Solomon brought in *all* the things that David his father had dedicated; and the silver, and the gold, and all the instruments, put he among the treasures of the house of God.

2 ¶ Then Solomon assembled the *a*elders of Israel, and all the heads of the tribes, the chief of the fathers of the children of Israel, unto Jerusalem, to bring up the *b*ark of the covenant of the LORD out of the city of David, which *is* Zion.

3 Wherefore all the men of Israel assembled themselves unto the king in the feast which *was* in the seventh month.

4 And all the elders of Israel came; and the Levites took up the ark.

5 And they brought up the ark, and

6*a* 1 Kgs. 7:38.
　b TG Wash.
　c Ezek. 40:38.
7*a* HEB *menoroth;*

lampstands.
10*a* 1 Kgs. 7:39.
14*a* IE washbasins.
15*a* 1 Chr. 18:8.

16*a* OR polished bronze.
5 2*a* 1 Kgs. 8:1 (1–11).
　b TG Ark of the Covenant.

the tabernacle of the congregation, and all the holy vessels that *were* in the tabernacle, these did the *a*priests *and* the Levites bring up.

6 Also king Solomon, and all the congregation of Israel that were assembled unto him before the ark, sacrificed sheep and oxen, which could not be told nor numbered for multitude.

7 And the priests brought in the ark of the covenant of the LORD unto his place, to the *a*oracle of the house, into the most holy *place, even* under the wings of the cherubims:

8 For the *a*cherubims spread forth *their* *b*wings over the place of the ark, and the cherubims covered the ark and the staves thereof above.

9 And they drew out the staves *of the ark,* that the ends of the staves were seen from the ark before the oracle; but they were not seen without. And there it is unto this day.

10 *There was* nothing in the ark save the two tables which Moses put *therein* at Horeb, when the LORD made *a covenant* with the children of Israel, when they came out of Egypt.

11 ¶ And it came to pass, when the priests were come out of the holy *place:* (for all the priests *that were* present were sanctified, *and* did not *then* wait by course:

12 Also the Levites *which were* the singers, all of them of Asaph, of Heman, of Jeduthun, with their sons and their brethren, *being* arrayed in white *a*linen, having cymbals and *b*psalteries and harps, stood at the east end of the altar, and with them an hundred and twenty priests sounding with trumpets:)

13 It came even to pass, as the trumpeters and singers *were* as one, to make one sound to be heard in praising and *a*thanking the LORD; and when they lifted up *their* voice with the trumpets and cymbals and instruments of musick, and praised the LORD, *saying,* For *he is* good; for his mercy *endureth* for ever: that *then* the house was filled with a cloud, *even* the house of the LORD;

14 So that the priests could not stand to minister by reason of the *a*cloud: for the *b*glory of the LORD had filled the house of God.

CHAPTER 6

Solomon blesses the congregation of Israel—He offers the dedicatory prayer for the temple—He prays for mercy and blessings for penitent Israel.

THEN said *a*Solomon, The LORD hath said that he would dwell in the thick darkness.

2 But I have built an house of habitation for thee, and a place for thy dwelling for ever.

3 And the king turned his face, and blessed the whole congregation of Israel: and all the congregation of Israel stood.

4 And he said, Blessed *be* the LORD God of Israel, who hath with his hands fulfilled *that* which he spake with his mouth to my father David, saying,

5 Since the day that I brought forth my people out of the land of Egypt I chose no city among all the tribes of Israel to build an house in, that my name might be there; neither chose I any man to be a ruler over my people Israel:

6 But I have chosen *a*Jerusalem, that my name might be there; and have chosen David to be over my people Israel.

7 Now it was in the heart of David my father to build an house for the name of the LORD God of Israel.

8 But the LORD said to David my father, Forasmuch as it was in thine heart to build an house for my name,

5a 1 Kgs. 8:3.
7a OR inner sanctuary.
8a TG Cherubim.
  b D&C 77:4.
12a TG Apparel.
  b OR lyres.

13a 1 Chr. 16:41;
     Ezra 3:11;
     D&C 97:13; 136:28.
14a 3 Ne. 18:38;
     D&C 84:5.
  b Num. 9:15;

2 Chr. 7:2 (2–3);
     D&C 97:15.
6 1a 1 Kgs. 8:12 (12–52).
6a 2 Chr. 12:13;
     D&C 133:21 (21–24).

thou didst well in that it was in thine heart:

9 Notwithstanding thou shalt not build the house; but thy son which shall come forth out of thy loins, he shall build the house for my name.

10 The LORD therefore hath performed his word that he hath spoken: for I am risen up in the room of David my father, and am set on the throne of Israel, as the LORD promised, and have built the house for the name of the LORD God of Israel.

11 And in it have I put the ark, wherein *is* the covenant of the LORD, that he made with the children of Israel.

12 ¶ And he stood before the altar of the LORD in the presence of all the congregation of Israel, and spread forth his hands:

13 For Solomon had made a brasen scaffold, of five cubits long, and five cubits broad, and three cubits high, and had set it in the midst of the court: and upon it he stood, and kneeled down upon his knees before all the congregation of Israel, and spread forth his hands toward heaven,

14 And said, O *ª*LORD God of Israel, *there is* no God like thee in the heaven, nor in the earth; which keepest covenant, and *shewest* mercy unto thy servants, that *ᵇ*walk before thee with all their hearts:

15 Thou which hast kept with thy servant David my father that which thou hast promised him; and spakest with thy mouth, and hast fulfilled *it* with thine hand, as *it is* this day.

16 Now therefore, O LORD God of Israel, keep with thy servant David my father that which thou hast promised him, saying, There shall not fail thee a man in my sight to sit upon the throne of Israel; *ª*yet so that thy children take heed to their way to walk in my law, as thou hast walked before me.

17 Now then, O LORD God of Israel, let thy word be verified, which thou hast spoken unto thy servant David.

18 But will God in very deed dwell with men on the earth? behold, heaven and the heaven of heavens cannot contain thee; how much less this house which I have built!

19 Have respect therefore to the prayer of thy servant, and to his supplication, O LORD my God, to hearken unto the cry and the prayer which thy servant prayeth before thee:

20 That thine eyes may be open upon this house day and night, upon the place whereof thou hast said that thou wouldest put thy name there; to hearken unto the prayer which thy servant prayeth toward this place.

21 Hearken therefore unto the supplications of thy servant, and of thy people Israel, which they shall make toward this place: hear thou from thy dwelling place, *even* from heaven; and when thou hearest, forgive.

22 ¶ If a man sin against his neighbour, and an oath be laid upon him to make him swear, and the oath come before thine altar in this house;

23 Then hear thou from heaven, and do, and judge thy servants, by requiting the wicked, by recompensing his way upon his own head; and by justifying the righteous, by giving him according to his *ª*righteousness.

24 ¶ And if thy people Israel be *ª*put to the worse before the enemy, because they have sinned against thee; and shall *ᵇ*return and confess thy name, and pray and make supplication before thee in this house;

25 Then hear thou from the heavens, and forgive the sin of thy people Israel, and bring them again unto the land which thou gavest to them and to their fathers.

26 ¶ When the heaven is shut up, and there is no rain, because they have sinned against thee; *yet* if they pray toward this place, and confess

---

14*a* 1 Kgs. 8:23 (22–61).
  b TG Walking with God.

16*a* OR if only.
23*a* TG Righteousness.

24*a* HEB smitten.
  b OR repent.

thy name, and turn from their sin, when thou dost afflict them;

27 Then hear thou from heaven, and forgive the sin of thy servants, and of thy people Israel, when thou hast taught them the good way, wherein they should walk; and send rain upon thy land, which thou hast given unto thy people for an inheritance.

28 ¶ If there be dearth in the land, if there be pestilence, if there be ªblasting, or mildew, locusts, or caterpillers; if their enemies besiege them in the cities of their land; whatsoever ᵇsore or whatsoever sickness *there be:*

29 *Then* what prayer *or* what supplication soever shall be made of any man, or of all thy people Israel, when every one shall know his own sore and his own grief, and shall spread forth his hands in this house:

30 Then hear thou from heaven thy dwelling place, and forgive, and render unto every man according unto all his ways, whose heart thou knowest; (for thou only ªknowest the hearts of the children of men:)

31 That they may fear thee, to walk in thy ways, so long as they live in the land which thou gavest unto our fathers.

32 ¶ Moreover concerning the stranger, which is not of thy people Israel, but is come from a far country for thy great name's sake, and thy mighty hand, and thy stretched out arm; if they come and pray ªin this house;

33 Then hear thou from the heavens, *even* from thy dwelling place, and do according to all that the stranger calleth to thee for; that all people of the earth may know thy name, and fear thee, as *doth* thy people Israel, and may know that this house which I have built is called by thy name.

34 If thy people go out to war against their enemies by the way that thou shalt send them, and they pray unto thee toward this city which thou hast chosen, and the house which I have built for thy name;

35 Then hear thou from the heavens their prayer and their supplication, and maintain their cause.

36 If they sin against thee, (for *there is* no man which sinneth not,) and thou be angry with them, and deliver them over before *their* enemies, and they carry them away captives unto a land far off or near;

37 Yet *if* they ªbethink themselves in the land whither they are carried captive, and turn and pray unto thee in the land of their captivity, saying, We have sinned, we have done amiss, and have dealt wickedly;

38 If they return to thee with all their heart and with all their soul in the land of their captivity, whither they have carried them captives, and pray toward their land, which thou gavest unto their fathers, and *toward* the city which thou hast chosen, and toward the house which I have built for thy name:

39 Then hear thou from the heavens, *even* from thy dwelling place, their prayer and their supplications, and maintain their cause, and forgive thy people which have sinned against thee.

40 Now, my God, let, I beseech thee, thine eyes be open, and *let* thine ears *be* attent unto the prayer *that is made* in this place.

41 Now therefore arise, O Lᴏʀᴅ God, into thy ªresting place, thou, and the ark of thy strength: let thy priests, O Lᴏʀᴅ God, be clothed with salvation, and let thy saints rejoice in goodness.

42 O Lᴏʀᴅ God, turn not away the face of thine anointed: ªremember the mercies of David thy servant.

CHAPTER 7

Fire comes down from heaven and consumes the sacrifices and burnt offerings—The Lord appears to Solomon

---

28a ᴏʀ blight.
  b ʜᴇʙ stroke, plague (also v. 29).
30a ᴛɢ God, Omniscience of.
32a ʜᴇʙ toward.
37a ɪᴇ recall in their mind.
41a 1 Chr. 28:2.
42a Ps. 132:1.

and promises to bless the people—The Israelites will prosper if they keep the commandments.

Now when Solomon had made an end of ᵃpraying, the ᵇfire came down from heaven, and consumed the burnt offering and the sacrifices; and the glory of the LORD filled the house.

2 And the priests could not enter into the house of the LORD, because the ᵃglory of the LORD had filled the LORD's house.

3 And when all the children of Israel saw how the fire came down, and the glory of the LORD upon the house, they bowed themselves with their faces to the ground upon the pavement, and ᵃworshipped, and praised the LORD, *saying,* For *he is* good; for his mercy *endureth* for ever.

4 ¶ Then the king and all the people ᵃoffered sacrifices before the LORD.

5 And king Solomon offered a sacrifice of twenty and two thousand oxen, and an hundred and twenty thousand sheep: so the king and all the people ᵃdedicated the house of God.

6 And the priests waited on their offices: the Levites also with instruments of musick of the LORD, which David the king had made to praise the LORD, because his mercy *endureth* for ever, when David praised by their ministry; and the priests sounded trumpets before them, and all Israel stood.

7 Moreover Solomon hallowed the middle of the court that *was* before the house of the LORD: for there he offered burnt offerings, and the fat of the peace offerings, because the brasen altar which Solomon had made was not able to receive the burnt offerings, and the meat offerings, and the fat.

8 ¶ Also at the same time Solomon kept the ᵃfeast seven days, and all Israel with him, a very great congregation, from the entering in of Hamath unto the ᵇriver of Egypt.

9 And in the ᵃeighth day they made a ᵇsolemn assembly: for they kept the dedication of the altar seven days, and the feast seven days.

10 And on the three and twentieth day of the seventh month he sent the people away into their tents, glad and merry in heart for the goodness that the LORD had shewed unto David, and to Solomon, and to Israel his people.

11 Thus Solomon ᵃfinished the house of the LORD, and the king's house: and all that came into Solomon's heart to make in the house of the LORD, and in his own house, he prosperously effected.

12 ¶ And the LORD appeared to Solomon by night, and said unto him, I have heard thy prayer, and have chosen this ᵃplace to myself for an house of sacrifice.

13 ᵃIf I shut up heaven that there be no rain, or if I command the locusts to devour the land, or if I send pestilence among my people;

14 If my people, which are called by my name, shall ᵃhumble themselves, and ᵇpray, and seek my ᶜface, and turn from their wicked ways; then will I hear from heaven, and will forgive their sin, and will heal their land.

15 Now mine eyes shall be open, and mine ears attent unto the prayer *that is made* in this place.

16 For now have I ᵃchosen and ᵇsanctified this house, that my name may be there for ever: and mine eyes and mine heart shall be there perpetually.

---

7 1*a* 1 Kgs. 8:54.
  b Lev. 9:24;
    1 Chr. 21:26.
2*a* 2 Chr. 5:14 (13–14);
    D&C 84:5; 109:12, 37.
3*a* TG Assembly for
    Worship.
4*a* 1 Kgs. 8:62 (62–66).
5*a* TG Dedication.

8*a* 1 Kgs. 8:2.
  b HEB Wadi of Egypt;
    modern Wadi El Arish;
    Gen. 15:18.
9*a* 1 Kgs. 8:66 (65–66).
  b TG Solemn Assembly.
11*a* 1 Kgs. 9:1 (1–9).
12*a* Deut. 12:5 (5–28);
    16:2 (2–17); 18:6 (6–8);

31:11 (9–13);
    1 Kgs. 8:29 (26–30).
13*a* Hel. 12:3.
14*a* TG Humility.
  b TG Prayer.
  c D&C 101:38.
16*a* D&C 110:7; 124:51.
  b TG Dedication;
    Sacred.

17 And as for thee, if thou wilt *a*walk before me, as David thy father walked, and do according to all that I have commanded thee, and shalt observe my statutes and my judgments;

18 Then will I stablish the throne of thy kingdom, according as I have covenanted with David thy father, saying, There shall not fail thee a man *to be* ruler in Israel.

19 But if ye turn away, and forsake my statutes and my commandments, which I have set before you, and shall go and serve other gods, and worship them;

20 Then will I pluck them up by the *a*roots out of my land which I have given them; and this house, which I have sanctified for my name, will I cast out of my sight, and will make it *to be* a proverb and a byword among all nations.

21 And this house, which is high, shall be an astonishment to every one that passeth by it; so that he shall say, Why hath the Lord done thus unto this land, and unto this house?

22 And it shall be answered, Because they forsook the Lord God of their fathers, which brought them forth out of the land of Egypt, and laid hold on other gods, and worshipped them, and served them: therefore hath he brought all this *a*evil upon them.

CHAPTER 8

Solomon builds cities—He offers sacrifices according to the law of Moses—Priests and Levites are appointed to serve the Lord.

And it came to pass at the end of twenty years, wherein Solomon had built the house of the Lord, and his own house,

2 That the cities which *a*Huram had *b*restored to Solomon, Solomon built them, and caused the children of Israel to dwell there.

3 And Solomon went to Hamathzobah, and prevailed against it.

4 And he built Tadmor in the wilderness, and all the store cities, which he built in Hamath.

5 Also he built Beth-horon the upper, and Beth-horon the *a*nether, *b*fenced cities, with walls, gates, and bars;

6 And Baalath, and all the store cities that Solomon had, and all the chariot cities, and the cities of the horsemen, and all that Solomon desired to build in Jerusalem, and in Lebanon, and throughout all the land of his dominion.

7 ¶ *As for* all the people *that were* left of the Hittites, and the Amorites, and the Perizzites, and the Hivites, and the Jebusites, which *were* not of Israel,

8 *But* of their children, who were left after them in the land, whom the children of Israel consumed not, them did Solomon make to *a*pay tribute until this day.

9 But of the children of Israel did Solomon make no servants for his work; but they *were* men of war, and chief of his captains, and captains of his chariots and horsemen.

10 And these *were* the chief of king Solomon's officers, *even* two hundred and fifty, that bare rule over the people.

11 ¶ And Solomon brought up the daughter of Pharaoh out of the city of David unto the house that he had built for her: for he said, *a*My wife shall not dwell in the house of David king of Israel, because *the places are* holy, whereunto the ark of the Lord hath come.

12 ¶ Then Solomon offered burnt offerings unto the Lord on the altar of the Lord, which he had built before the porch,

13 Even after a certain rate *a*every day, offering according to the commandment of Moses, on the sabbaths, and on the new moons, and on

---

17a TG Walking with God.
20a Deut. 29:28 (26–28).
22a IE calamity.
8 2a OR Hiram.

b HEB given (see 1 Kgs. 9:12–13).
5a OR lower.
b OR fortified cities.

8a IE provide labor.
11a HEB No wife of mine shall dwell.
13a Ex. 29:38 (38–39).

the solemn feasts, *b*three times in the year, *even* in the feast of unleavened bread, and in the feast of weeks, and in the feast of tabernacles.

14 ¶ And he appointed, according to the *a*order of David his father, the *b*courses of the priests to their service, and the Levites to their charges, to praise and minister before the priests, as the *c*duty of every day required: the porters also by their courses at every gate: for so had David the man of God commanded.

15 And they departed not from the commandment of the king unto the priests and Levites concerning any matter, or concerning the treasures.

16 Now all the work of Solomon was prepared *a*unto the day of the foundation of the house of the LORD, and until it was finished. *So the* house of the LORD was *b*perfected.

17 ¶ Then went Solomon to Eziongeber, and to Eloth, at the sea side in the land of Edom.

18 And Huram sent him by the hands of his servants ships, and servants that had knowledge of the sea; and they went with the servants of Solomon to Ophir, and took thence four hundred and fifty talents of gold, and brought *them* to king Solomon.

CHAPTER 9

The queen of Sheba visits Solomon—He excels in wisdom, wealth, and magnificence—After reigning forty years, Solomon dies, and Rehoboam becomes king.

AND when the queen of Sheba heard of the fame of Solomon, she came to prove Solomon with hard questions at Jerusalem, with a very great company, and camels that bare spices, and gold in abundance, and precious stones: and when she was come to Solomon, she communed with him of all that was in her heart.

2 And Solomon told her all her questions: and there was nothing hid from Solomon which he told her not.

3 And when the queen of Sheba had seen the wisdom of Solomon, and the house that he had built,

4 And the meat of his table, and the sitting of his servants, and the attendance of his ministers, and their apparel; his cupbearers also, and their apparel; and his ascent by which he went up into the house of the LORD; there was no more spirit in her.

5 And she said to the king, *It was* a true report which I heard in mine own land of thine *a*acts, and of thy wisdom:

6 Howbeit I believed not their words, until I came, and mine eyes had seen *it:* and, behold, the one half of the greatness of thy wisdom was not told me: *for* thou exceedest the fame that I heard.

7 Happy *are* thy men, and happy *are* these thy servants, which stand continually before thee, and hear thy wisdom.

8 Blessed be the LORD thy God, which delighted in thee to set thee on his throne, *to be* king for the LORD thy God: because thy God loved Israel, to establish them for ever, therefore made he thee king over them, to do judgment and justice.

9 And she gave the king an hundred and twenty talents of gold, and of spices great abundance, and precious stones: neither was there any such spice as the queen of Sheba gave king Solomon.

10 And the servants also of Huram, and the servants of Solomon, which brought gold from Ophir, brought algum trees and precious stones.

11 And the king made *of* the algum trees terraces to the house of the LORD, and to the king's palace, and harps and psalteries for singers: and there were none such seen before in the land of Judah.

12 And king Solomon gave to the queen of Sheba all her desire,

---

13 *b* Deut. 16:16 (16–17);
    1 Kgs. 9:25.
14 *a* 2 Chr. 35:4.

b 1 Chr. 23:6;
    Ezra 6:18.
c TG Duty.

16 *a* Septuagint: from.
  b IE completed.
9 5 *a* OR sayings.

whatsoever she asked, beside *that* which she had brought unto the king. So she turned, and went away to her own land, she and her servants.

13 ¶ Now the weight of gold that came to Solomon in one year was six hundred and threescore and six talents of gold;

14 Beside *that which* ᵃchapmen and merchants brought. And all the kings of Arabia and governors of the country brought gold and silver to Solomon.

15 ¶ And king Solomon made two hundred ᵃtargets *of* beaten gold: six hundred *shekels* of beaten gold went to one target.

16 And three hundred shields *made he of* beaten gold: three hundred *shekels* of gold went to one shield. And the king put them in the house of the forest of Lebanon.

17 Moreover the king made a great throne of ivory, and overlaid it with pure gold.

18 And *there were* six steps to the throne, with a footstool of gold, *which were* fastened to the throne, and ᵃstays on each side of the sitting place, and two lions standing by the stays:

19 And twelve lions stood there on the one side and on the other upon the six steps. There was not the like made in any kingdom.

20 ¶ And all the drinking vessels of king Solomon *were of* gold, and all the vessels of the house of the forest of Lebanon *were of* pure gold: none *were of* silver; it was *not* any thing accounted of in the days of Solomon.

21 For the king's ships went to Tarshish with the servants of Huram: every three years once came the ships of Tarshish bringing gold, and silver, ivory, and apes, and peacocks.

22 And king Solomon passed all the kings of the earth in riches and wisdom.

23 ¶ And ᵃall the kings of the earth sought the presence of Solomon, to hear his wisdom, that God had put in his heart.

24 And they brought every man his present, vessels of silver, and vessels of gold, and raiment, harness, and spices, horses, and mules, a rate year by year.

25 ¶ And Solomon had four thousand stalls for ᵃhorses and chariots, and twelve thousand horsemen; whom he bestowed in the chariot cities, and with the king at Jerusalem.

26 ¶ And he ᵃreigned over all the kings from ᵇthe river even unto the land of the Philistines, and to the border of Egypt.

27 And the king made silver in Jerusalem as stones, and cedar trees made he as the sycomore trees that *are* in the low plains in abundance.

28 And they brought unto Solomon ᵃhorses out of Egypt, and out of all lands.

29 ¶ Now the rest of the acts of Solomon, first and last, *are* they not written in the book of ᵃNathan the prophet, and in the prophecy of Ahijah the Shilonite, and in the visions of Iddo the ᵇseer against Jeroboam the son of Nebat?

30 And Solomon reigned in Jerusalem over all Israel forty years.

31 And Solomon slept with his fathers, and he was buried in the city of David his father: and Rehoboam his son reigned in his stead.

CHAPTER 10

The people request relief, but Rehoboam promises to increase the burdens upon the people—Israel rebels and the kingdom is divided.

AND ᵃRehoboam went to Shechem: for to Shechem were all Israel come to make him king.

2 And it came to pass, when Jeroboam the son of Nebat, who *was* in Egypt, whither he had fled from the

---

14a ɪᴇ traders.
15a ɪᴇ large shields.
18a ɪᴇ armrests.
23a 1 Kgs. 4:34.

25a 1 Kgs. 4:26.
26a 1 Kgs. 4:21.
  b ɪᴇ the Euphrates.
28a Deut. 17:16.

29a ᴛɢ Scriptures, Lost.
  b ᴛɢ Seer.
10 1a 1 Kgs. 12:1 (1–20).

presence of Solomon the king, heard *it,* that Jeroboam returned out of Egypt.

3 And they sent and called him. So Jeroboam and all Israel came and spake to Rehoboam, saying,

4 Thy father made our yoke grievous: now therefore ease thou somewhat the grievous servitude of thy father, and his heavy yoke that he put upon us, and we will serve thee.

5 And he said unto them, Come again unto me after three days. And the people departed.

6 ¶ And king Rehoboam took counsel with the old men that had stood before Solomon his father while he yet lived, saying, What counsel give ye *me* to return answer to this people?

7 And they spake unto him, saying, If thou be kind to this people, and please them, and speak good words to them, they will be thy servants for ever.

8 But he forsook the counsel which the old men gave him, and took counsel with the young men that were brought up with him, that stood before him.

9 And he said unto them, What advice give ye that we may return answer to this people, which have spoken to me, saying, Ease somewhat the yoke that thy father did put upon us?

10 And the young men that were brought up with him spake unto him, saying, Thus shalt thou answer the people that spake unto thee, saying, Thy father made our yoke heavy, but make thou *it* somewhat lighter for us; thus shalt thou say unto them, My little *finger* shall be thicker than my father's loins.

11 For whereas my father put a heavy yoke upon you, I will put more to your yoke: my father chastised you with whips, but I *will chastise you* with scorpions.

12 So Jeroboam and all the people came to Rehoboam on the third day,

as the king bade, saying, Come again to me on the third day.

13 And the king answered them roughly; and king Rehoboam forsook the counsel of the old men,

14 And answered them after the advice of the young men, saying, My father made your yoke heavy, but I will add thereto: my father chastised you with whips, but I *will chastise you* with scorpions.

15 So the king hearkened not unto the people: for the cause was of God, that the Lord might perform his word, which he spake by the hand of Ahijah the Shilonite to Jeroboam the son of Nebat.

16 ¶ And when all Israel *saw* that the king would not hearken unto them, the people answered the king, saying, What portion have we in David? and *we have* none inheritance in the son of Jesse: every man to your tents, O Israel: *and* now, David, see to thine own house. So all Israel went to their tents.

17 But *as for* the children of Israel that dwelt in the cities of Judah, Rehoboam reigned over them.

18 Then king Rehoboam sent Hadoram that *was* over the tribute; and the children of Israel stoned him with stones, that he died. But king Rehoboam made speed to get him up to *his* chariot, to flee to Jerusalem.

19 And Israel rebelled against the house of David unto this day.

CHAPTER 11

Rehoboam strengthens the kingdom of Judah but is forbidden to subdue Israel—Jeroboam leads the kingdom of Israel into idolatry—Rehoboam takes many wives and concubines.

AND when [a]Rehoboam was come to Jerusalem, he gathered of the house of Judah and Benjamin an hundred and fourscore thousand chosen *men,* which were warriors, to fight against Israel, that he might bring the kingdom again to Rehoboam.

---

11 1*a* 1 Kgs. 12:21 (21–33).

2 But the word of the LORD came to Shemaiah the man of God, saying,

3 Speak unto Rehoboam the son of Solomon, king of Judah, and to all Israel in Judah and Benjamin, saying,

4 Thus saith the LORD, Ye shall not go up, nor fight against your brethren: return every man to his house: for this thing is done of me. And they obeyed the words of the LORD, and returned from going against Jeroboam.

5 ¶ And Rehoboam dwelt in Jerusalem, and built cities for ᵃdefence in Judah.

6 He built even Beth-lehem, and Etam, and Tekoa,

7 And Beth-zur, and Shoco, and Adullam,

8 And Gath, and Mareshah, and Ziph,

9 And Adoraim, and Lachish, and Azekah,

10 And Zorah, and Aijalon, and Hebron, which *are* in Judah and in Benjamin fenced cities.

11 And he fortified the strong holds, and put captains in them, and store of victual, and of oil and wine.

12 And in every several city *he put* shields and spears, and made them exceeding strong, having Judah and Benjamin on his side.

13 ¶ And the priests and the Levites that *were* in all Israel ᵃresorted to him out of all their ᵇcoasts.

14 For the Levites left their ᵃsuburbs and their ᵇpossession, and came to Judah and Jerusalem: for Jeroboam and his sons had ᶜcast them off from executing the priest's office unto the LORD:

15 And he ordained him ᵃpriests for the high places, and for the ᵇdevils, and for the calves which he had made.

16 And after them out of all the tribes of Israel such as set their hearts to seek the LORD God of Israel came to Jerusalem, to sacrifice unto the LORD God of their fathers.

17 So they strengthened the kingdom of Judah, and made Rehoboam the son of Solomon strong, three years: for three years they walked in the way of David and Solomon.

18 ¶ And Rehoboam took him Mahalath the daughter of Jerimoth the son of David to wife, *and* Abihail the daughter of ᵃEliab the son of Jesse.

19 Which bare him children; Jeush, and Shamariah, and Zaham.

20 And after her he took ᵃMaachah the daughter of Absalom; which bare him Abijah, and Attai, and Ziza, and Shelomith.

21 And Rehoboam loved Maachah the daughter of Absalom above all his wives and his concubines: (for he took eighteen wives, and threescore concubines; and begat twenty and eight sons, and threescore daughters.)

22 And Rehoboam made Abijah the son of Maachah the chief, *to be* ruler among his brethren: for *he thought* to make him king.

23 And he dealt wisely, and dispersed of all his ᵃchildren throughout all the countries of Judah and Benjamin, unto every fenced city: and he gave them victual in abundance. And he ᵇdesired many wives.

CHAPTER 12

Rehoboam forsakes the law of the Lord—The Egyptians plunder Jerusalem and take the treasures of the house of the Lord—The people repent and receive partial deliverance—Rehoboam dies.

AND it came to pass, when Rehoboam had established the kingdom, and had strengthened himself, he forsook the law of the LORD, and all Israel with him.

5a 2 Chr. 12:4.
13a IE took their stand on his side.
   b IE borders.
14a IE the open land surrounding the forty-eight Levite cities.

Lev. 25:34;
Num. 35:2 (2–7).
   b Josh. 21:41 (1–3, 41).
   c 2 Chr. 13:9 (9–10).
15a TG Apostasy of Israel; Idolatry.
   b HEB satyrs, demons (an

epithet for idols).
18a 1 Sam. 16:6.
20a 1 Kgs. 15:2.
23a HEB sons.
   b OR sought for them many wives.

2 And it came to pass, *that* in the fifth year of king Rehoboam Shishak king of Egypt came up against Jerusalem, because they had transgressed against the LORD,

3 With twelve hundred chariots, and threescore thousand horsemen: and the people *were* without number that came with him out of Egypt; the *a*Lubims, the Sukkiims, and the *b*Ethiopians.

4 And he took the *a*fenced cities which *pertained* to Judah, and came to Jerusalem.

5 ¶ Then came Shemaiah the prophet to Rehoboam, and *to* the princes of Judah, that were gathered together to Jerusalem because of Shishak, and said unto them, Thus saith the LORD, Ye have forsaken me, and therefore have I also left you in the hand of Shishak.

6 Whereupon the princes of Israel and the king humbled themselves; and they said, The LORD *is* righteous.

7 And when the LORD saw that they humbled themselves, the word of the LORD came to Shemaiah, saying, They have humbled themselves; *therefore* I will not destroy them, but I will grant them some deliverance; and my wrath shall not be poured out upon Jerusalem by the hand of Shishak.

8 Nevertheless they shall be his servants; that they may know my service, and the service of the kingdoms of the countries.

9 So Shishak king of Egypt came up against Jerusalem, and took away the treasures of the house of the LORD, and the treasures of the king's house; he took all: he carried away also the shields of gold which Solomon had made.

10 Instead of which king Rehoboam made shields of brass, and committed *them* to the hands of the chief of the guard, that kept the entrance of the king's house.

11 And when the king entered into the house of the LORD, the guard came and fetched them, and brought them again into the guard chamber.

12 And when he humbled himself, the wrath of the LORD turned from him, that he would not destroy *him* altogether: and also in Judah things went well.

13 ¶ So king Rehoboam strengthened himself in Jerusalem, and reigned: for Rehoboam *was* one and forty years old when he began to reign, and he reigned seventeen years in *a*Jerusalem, the city which the LORD had chosen out of all the tribes of Israel, to put his name there. And his mother's name *was* Naamah an Ammonitess.

14 And he did evil, because he prepared not his heart to seek the LORD.

15 Now the acts of Rehoboam, first and last, *are* they not written in the book of *a*Shemaiah the prophet, and of Iddo the *b*seer concerning genealogies? And *there were* wars between Rehoboam and Jeroboam continually.

16 And Rehoboam slept with his fathers, and was buried in the city of David: and *a*Abijah his son reigned in his stead.

CHAPTER 13

Abijah reigns in Judah—He defeats Jeroboam and the armies of Israel—The Lord strikes Jeroboam, and he dies.

Now in the eighteenth year of king Jeroboam began Abijah to reign over Judah.

2 He reigned three years in Jerusalem. His mother's name also *was* Michaiah the daughter of Uriel of Gibeah. And there was war between Abijah and Jeroboam.

3 And Abijah set the battle in array with an army of valiant men of war, *even* four hundred thousand chosen men: Jeroboam also set the battle in array against him with eight

---

12 3*a* IE Libyans.
  Nahum 3:9.
  b HEB Cushites, Nubians.
4*a* 2 Chr. 11:5 (5–12).

13*a* 2 Chr. 6:6.
15*a* 1 Kgs. 12:22.
  TG Scriptures, Lost.
  b TG Seer.

16*a* OR Abijam (see
  1 Kgs. 14:31).

hundred thousand chosen men, *being* mighty men of valour.

4 ¶ And Abijah stood up upon mount Zemaraim, which *is* in mount Ephraim, and said, Hear me, thou Jeroboam, and all Israel;

5 Ought ye not to know that the Lord God of Israel gave the kingdom over Israel to David for ever, *even* to him and to his sons by a ªcovenant of ᵇsalt?

6 Yet Jeroboam the son of Nebat, the servant of Solomon the son of David, is risen up, and hath rebelled against his lord.

7 And there are gathered unto him vain men, the ªchildren of Belial, and have strengthened themselves against Rehoboam the son of Solomon, when Rehoboam was young and tenderhearted, and could not withstand them.

8 And now ye think to withstand the kingdom of the Lord in the hand of the sons of David; and ye *be* a great multitude, and *there are* with you golden calves, which Jeroboam made you for gods.

9 Have ye not ªcast out the priests of the Lord, the sons of Aaron, and the Levites, and have made you priests after the manner of the nations of *other* lands? so that whosoever cometh to consecrate himself with a young ᵇbullock and seven rams, *the same* may be a priest of *them that are* no gods.

10 But as for us, the Lord *is* our God, and we have not forsaken him; and the priests, which minister unto the Lord, *are* the sons of Aaron, and the Levites *wait* upon *their* business:

11 And they burn unto the Lord every morning and every evening burnt sacrifices and sweet incense: the shewbread also *set they in order* upon the pure table; and the candlestick of gold with the lamps thereof, to burn every evening: for we keep the charge of the Lord our God; but ye have forsaken him.

12 And, behold, God himself *is* with us for *our* captain, and his priests with sounding trumpets to cry alarm against you. O children of Israel, fight ye not against the Lord God of your fathers; for ye shall not prosper.

13 ¶ But Jeroboam caused an ambushment to come about behind them: so they were before Judah, and the ambushment *was* behind them.

14 And when Judah looked back, behold, the battle *was* before and behind: and they cried unto the Lord, and the priests sounded with the trumpets.

15 Then the men of Judah gave a shout: and as the men of Judah shouted, it came to pass, that God smote Jeroboam and all Israel before Abijah and Judah.

16 And the children of Israel fled before Judah: and God delivered them into their hand.

17 And Abijah and his people slew them with a great slaughter: so there fell down slain of Israel five hundred thousand chosen men.

18 Thus the children of Israel were brought under at that time, and the children of Judah prevailed, because they ªrelied upon the Lord God of their fathers.

19 And Abijah pursued after Jeroboam, and took cities from him, Beth-el with the towns thereof, and Jeshanah with the towns thereof, and Ephrain with the towns thereof.

20 Neither did Jeroboam recover strength again in the days of Abijah: and the Lord ªstruck him, and he died.

21 ¶ But Abijah waxed mighty, and married fourteen wives, and begat twenty and two sons, and sixteen daughters.

22 And the rest of the acts of Abijah, and his ways, and his sayings, *are* written in the story of the prophet ªIddo.

13 5*a* Num. 18:19;
　　　 3 Ne. 12:13.
　　b TG Salt.
　 7*a* HEB sons of worthless-
　　　 ness; scoundrels.
　 9*a* 2 Chr. 11:14;
　　　 Alma 10:23.
　　b Ex. 29:1 (1–6).
　18*a* TG Trust in God.
　20*a* 1 Chr. 11:14;
　　　 Alma 30:52 (1–60).
　22*a* TG Scriptures, Lost.

CHAPTER 14

Asa reigns in Judah, rebuilds the cities, and defeats and plunders the Ethiopians, who attack Judah.

So Abijah slept with his fathers, and they buried him in the city of David: and Asa his son reigned in his stead. In his days the land was quiet ten years.

2 And *a*Asa did *that which was* good and right in the eyes of the LORD his God:

3 For he took away the altars of the strange *gods*, and the high places, and brake down the images, and cut down the *a*groves:

4 And commanded Judah to seek the LORD God of their fathers, and to do the law and the commandment.

5 Also he took away out of all the cities of Judah the high places and the images: and the kingdom was quiet before him.

6 ¶ And he built fenced cities in Judah: for the land had rest, and he had no war in those years; because the LORD had given him rest.

7 Therefore he said unto Judah, Let us build these cities, and make about *them* walls, and towers, gates, and bars, *while* the land *is* yet before us; because we have sought the LORD our God, we have sought *him*, and he hath given us rest on every side. So they built and prospered.

8 And Asa had an army *of men* that bare *a*targets and spears, out of Judah three hundred thousand; and out of Benjamin, that bare shields and drew bows, two hundred and fourscore thousand: all these *were* mighty men of valour.

9 ¶ And there came out against them Zerah the Ethiopian with an host of a thousand thousand, and three hundred chariots; and came unto Mareshah.

10 Then Asa went out against him, and they set the battle in array in the valley of Zephathah at Mareshah.

11 And Asa cried unto the LORD his God, and said, LORD, *it is* nothing with thee to help, whether with many, or with them that have no power: help us, O LORD our God; for we rest on thee, and in thy name we go against this multitude. O LORD, thou *art* our God; let not man prevail against thee.

12 So the LORD smote the Ethiopians before Asa, and before Judah; and the Ethiopians fled.

13 And Asa and the people that *were* with him pursued them unto Gerar: and the Ethiopians were overthrown, that they could not recover themselves; for they were destroyed before the LORD, and before his host; and they carried away very much spoil.

14 And they smote all the cities round about Gerar; for the fear of the LORD came upon them: and they spoiled all the cities; for there was exceeding much spoil in them.

15 They smote also the tents of cattle, and carried away sheep and camels in abundance, and returned to Jerusalem.

CHAPTER 15

Azariah prophesies that Judah will prosper if the people keep the commandments—Asa does away with false worship in Judah—Many from Ephraim, Manasseh, and Simeon migrate to Judah—The people covenant to serve the Lord and are blessed.

AND the Spirit of God came upon Azariah the son of Oded:

2 And he went out to meet Asa, and said unto him, Hear ye me, Asa, and all Judah and Benjamin; The LORD *is* with you, while ye be with him; and if ye seek him, he will be found of you; but if ye forsake him, he will forsake you.

3 Now for a long season Israel *hath been* without the true God, and without a *a*teaching priest, and without law.

---

14 2*a* 2 Chr. 21:12.
   3*a* IE idolatrous wooden objects associated with

fertility worship.
8*a* OR large shields.
15 3*a* Deut. 33:10;

2 Chr. 17:9;
2 Ne. 9:48.
TG Teacher.

4 But when they in their ^atrouble did turn unto the LORD God of Israel, and ^bsought him, he was found of them.

5 And in those times *there was* no peace to him that went out, nor to him that came in, but great vexations *were* upon all the inhabitants of the countries.

6 And nation was destroyed of nation, and city of city: for God did vex them with all adversity.

7 Be ye strong therefore, and let not your hands be weak: for your ^awork shall be rewarded.

8 And when Asa heard these words, and the prophecy of Oded the prophet, he took courage, and put away the abominable idols out of all the land of Judah and Benjamin, and out of the cities which he had taken from mount Ephraim, and renewed the altar of the LORD, that *was* before the porch of the LORD.

9 And he gathered all Judah and Benjamin, and the ^astrangers with them out of Ephraim and Manasseh, and out of Simeon: for they fell to him out of Israel in abundance, when they saw that the LORD his God *was* with him.

10 So they gathered themselves together at Jerusalem in the third month, in the fifteenth year of the reign of Asa.

11 And they offered unto the LORD the same time, of the spoil *which* they had brought, seven hundred oxen and seven thousand sheep.

12 And they entered into a ^acovenant to seek the LORD God of their fathers with all their heart and with all their soul;

13 That whosoever would not seek the LORD God of Israel should be put to death, whether small or great, whether man or woman.

14 And they sware unto the LORD with a loud voice, and with shouting, and with trumpets, and with ^acornets.

15 And all Judah rejoiced at the oath: for they had sworn with all their heart, and sought him with their whole desire; and he was ^afound of them: and the LORD gave them rest round about.

16 ¶ And also *concerning* Maachah the ^amother of Asa the king, he removed her from *being* queen, because she had made an idol in a grove: and Asa cut down her idol, and stamped *it,* and burnt *it* at the brook Kidron.

17 But the high places were not taken away out of Israel: nevertheless the heart of Asa was perfect all his days.

18 ¶ And he brought into the house of God the things that his father had dedicated, and that he himself had dedicated, silver, and gold, and vessels.

19 And there was no *more* war unto the five and thirtieth year of the reign of Asa.

CHAPTER 16

Asa employs Syria to defeat Israel—Hanani the seer reproves Asa for lack of faith—Asa suffers from disease and dies.

IN the six and thirtieth year of the reign of Asa Baasha king of Israel came up against Judah, and built Ramah, to the intent that he might let none go out or come in to Asa king of Judah.

2 Then Asa brought out silver and gold out of the treasures of the house of the LORD and of the king's house, and sent to Ben-hadad king of Syria, that dwelt at Damascus, saying,

3 *There is* a league between me and thee, as *there was* between my father and thy father: behold, I have sent thee silver and gold; go, break thy league with Baasha king of Israel, that he may depart from me.

4 And Ben-hadad hearkened unto king Asa, and sent the captains of his armies against the cities of Israel; and they smote Ijon, and

---

4a TG Adversity.
  b TG God, Access to.
7a TG Good Works.

9a IE foreigners.
   Alma 10:3.
12a Mosiah 5:5 (2, 5).

14a HEB *shofarim;* horns.
15a D&C 88:63.
16a IE grandmother.

Dan, and Abel-maim, and all the store cities of Naphtali.

5 And it came to pass, when Baasha heard *it,* that he left off building of Ramah, and let his work cease.

6 Then Asa the king took all Judah; and they carried away the stones of Ramah, and the timber thereof, wherewith Baasha was building; and he built therewith Geba and Mizpah.

7 ¶ And at that time Hanani the *a*seer came to Asa king of Judah, and said unto him, Because thou hast relied on the *b*king of Syria, and not *c*relied on the LORD thy God, therefore is the host of the king of *d*Syria escaped out of thine hand.

8 Were not the Ethiopians and the Lubims a huge host, with very many chariots and horsemen? yet, because thou didst rely on the LORD, he delivered them into thine hand.

9 For the eyes of the LORD run to and fro throughout the whole earth, to shew himself strong in the behalf of *them* whose heart *is* perfect toward him. Herein thou hast done foolishly: therefore from henceforth thou shalt have wars.

10 Then Asa was wroth with the seer, and put him in *a*a prison house; for *he was* in a rage with him because of this *thing.* And Asa oppressed *some* of the people the same time.

11 ¶ And, behold, the acts of Asa, first and last, lo, they *are* written in the book of the kings of Judah and Israel.

12 And Asa in the thirty and ninth year of his reign was diseased in his feet, until his disease *was* exceeding *great:* yet in his disease he sought not to the LORD, but to the physicians.

13 ¶ And Asa slept with his fathers, and died in the one and fortieth year of his reign.

14 And they buried him in his own sepulchres, which he had made for himself in the city of David, and laid him in the bed which was filled with sweet odours and divers kinds

of spices prepared by the apothecaries' art: and they made a very great *a*burning for him.

CHAPTER 17

Jehoshaphat reigns well and prospers in Judah—Priests travel and teach out of the book of the law of the Lord.

AND Jehoshaphat his son reigned in his stead, and strengthened himself against Israel.

2 And he placed forces in all the fenced cities of Judah, and set garrisons in the land of Judah, and in the cities of Ephraim, which Asa his father had taken.

3 And the LORD was with Jehoshaphat, because he walked in the first ways of his father David, and sought not unto Baalim;

4 But sought to the LORD God of his father, and walked in his commandments, and not after the doings of Israel.

5 Therefore the LORD stablished the kingdom in his hand; and all Judah brought to Jehoshaphat presents; and he had riches and honour in abundance.

6 And his heart was lifted up in the ways of the LORD: moreover he took away the high places and groves out of Judah.

7 ¶ Also in the third year of his reign he sent to his princes, *even* to Ben-hail, and to Obadiah, and to Zechariah, and to Nethaneel, and to Michaiah, to teach in the cities of Judah.

8 And with them *he sent* Levites, *even* Shemaiah, and Nethaniah, and Zebadiah, and Asahel, and Shemiramoth, and Jehonathan, and Adonijah, and Tobijah, and Tob-adonijah, Levites; and with them Elishama and Jehoram, priests.

9 And they taught in Judah, and *had* the book of the law of the LORD with them, and went about throughout all the cities of Judah, and *a*taught the people.

---

16 7*a* TG Seer.
     b 1 Kgs. 15:18.
     c D&C 30:1.
     d Septuagint: Israel.

10*a* OR stocks.
14*a* IE of the spices, as incense.
     2 Chr. 21:19.

17 9*a* Deut. 33:10;
     2 Chr. 15:3 (1–4);
     2 Ne. 9:48.

10 ¶ And the fear of the LORD fell upon all the kingdoms of the lands that *were* round about Judah, so that they made no war against Jehoshaphat.

11 Also *some* of the Philistines brought Jehoshaphat presents, and tribute silver; and the Arabians brought him flocks, seven thousand and seven hundred rams, and seven thousand and seven hundred he goats.

12 ¶ And Jehoshaphat waxed great exceedingly; and he built in Judah *a*castles, and cities of store.

13 And he had much business in the cities of Judah: and the men of war, mighty men of valour, *were* in Jerusalem.

14 And these *are* the numbers of them according to the house of their fathers: Of Judah, the captains of thousands; Adnah the chief, and with him mighty men of valour three hundred thousand.

15 And next to him *was* Jehohanan the captain, and with him two hundred and fourscore thousand.

16 And next him *was* Amasiah the son of Zichri, who willingly offered himself unto the LORD; and with him two hundred thousand mighty men of valour.

17 And of Benjamin; Eliada a mighty man of valour, and with him armed men with bow and shield two hundred thousand.

18 And next him *was* Jehozabad, and with him an hundred and fourscore thousand ready prepared for the war.

19 These waited on the king, beside *those* whom the king put in the fenced cities throughout all Judah.

CHAPTER 18

Jehoshaphat of Judah joins Ahab of Israel to fight Syria—Ahab's false prophets foretell victory—Micaiah prophesies the fall and death of Ahab—The Syrians slay Ahab.

NOW Jehoshaphat had riches and honour in abundance, and *a*joined affinity with Ahab.

2 And after *certain* years he went down to Ahab to Samaria. And Ahab killed sheep and oxen for him in abundance, and for the people that *he had* with him, and persuaded him to go up *with him* to Ramoth-gilead.

3 And Ahab king of Israel said unto Jehoshaphat king of Judah, Wilt thou go with me to Ramoth-gilead? And he answered him, I *am* as thou *art,* and my people as thy people; and *we will be* with thee in the war.

4 ¶ And Jehoshaphat said unto the king of Israel, *a*Inquire, I pray thee, at the word of the LORD to day.

5 Therefore the king of Israel gathered together of prophets four hundred men, and said unto them, Shall we go to Ramoth-gilead to battle, or shall I forbear? And they said, Go up; for God will deliver *it* into the king's hand.

6 But Jehoshaphat said, *Is there* not here a prophet of the LORD besides, that we might inquire of him?

7 And the king of Israel said unto Jehoshaphat, *There is* yet one man, by whom we may *a*inquire of the LORD: but I hate him; for he never prophesied good unto me, but always evil: the same *is* Micaiah the son of Imla. And Jehoshaphat said, Let not the king say so.

8 And the king of Israel called for one *of his* officers, and said, Fetch quickly Micaiah the son of Imla.

9 And the king of Israel and Jehoshaphat king of Judah sat either of them on his throne, clothed in *their* robes, and they sat in a void place at the entering in of the gate of Samaria; and all the prophets prophesied before them.

10 And Zedekiah the son of Chenaanah had made him *a*horns of iron, and said, Thus saith the LORD, With these thou shalt push Syria until they be consumed.

11 And all the prophets prophesied

12*a* IE fortifications.
18 1*a* IE allied himself by marriage.

4*a* Ether 1:38 (34–39).
7*a* Hel. 13:26 (26–28).
10*a* IE an emblem of

military might.

so, saying, Go up to Ramoth-gilead, and prosper: for the LORD shall deliver *it* into the hand of the king.

12 And the messenger that went to call Micaiah spake to him, saying, Behold, the words of the prophets *declare* good to the king with one assent; let thy word therefore, I pray thee, be like one of theirs, and speak thou good.

13 And Micaiah said, *As* the LORD liveth, even what my God saith, that will I speak.

14 And when he was come to the king, the king said unto him, Micaiah, shall we go to Ramoth-gilead to battle, or shall I forbear? And he said, Go ye up, and prosper, and they shall be delivered into your hand.

15 And the king said to him, How many times shall I adjure thee that thou say nothing but the truth to me in the name of the LORD?

16 Then he said, I did see all Israel scattered upon the mountains, as sheep that have no shepherd: and the LORD said, These have no master; let them return *therefore* every man to his house in peace.

17 And the king of Israel said to Jehoshaphat, Did I not tell thee *that* he would not prophesy good unto me, but evil?

18 Again he said, Therefore hear the word of the LORD; I saw the LORD sitting upon his throne, and all the host of heaven standing on his right hand and *on* his left.

19 And the LORD said, Who shall entice Ahab king of Israel, that he may go up and fall at Ramoth-gilead? And one spake saying after this manner, and another saying after that manner.

20 Then there came out a *a*spirit, and stood before the LORD, and said, I will entice him. And the LORD said unto him, Wherewith?

21 And he said, I will go out, and be a lying spirit in the mouth of all his prophets. And *the* LORD said,

Thou shalt entice *him*, and thou shalt also prevail: go out, and do *even* *a*so.

22 Now therefore, behold, the LORD hath *a*put a lying spirit in the mouth of these thy prophets, and the LORD hath spoken evil against thee.

23 Then Zedekiah the son of Chenaanah came near, and smote Micaiah upon the cheek, and said, Which way went the Spirit of the LORD from me to speak unto thee?

24 And Micaiah said, Behold, thou shalt see on that day when thou shalt go into an inner chamber to hide thyself.

25 Then the king of Israel said, Take ye Micaiah, and carry him back to Amon the governor of the city, and to Joash the king's son;

26 And say, Thus saith the king, Put this *fellow* in the prison, and feed him with bread of affliction and with water of affliction, until I return in peace.

27 And Micaiah said, If thou certainly return in peace, *then* hath not the LORD spoken by me. And he said, Hearken, all ye people.

28 So the king of Israel and Jehoshaphat the king of Judah went up to Ramoth-gilead.

29 And the king of Israel said unto Jehoshaphat, I will disguise myself, and will go to the battle; but put thou on thy robes. So the king of Israel disguised himself; and they went to the battle.

30 Now the king of Syria had commanded the captains of the chariots that *were* with him, saying, Fight ye not with small or great, save only with the king of Israel.

31 And it came to pass, when the captains of the chariots saw Jehoshaphat, that they said, It *is* the king of Israel. Therefore they compassed about him to fight: but Jehoshaphat cried out, and the LORD helped him; and God moved them *to depart* from him.

32 For it came to pass, that, when the captains of the chariots

---

20*a* JST 2 Chr. 18:20 . . . *lying spirit* . . .
21*a* JST 2 Chr. 18:21 . . . *so;*

for all these have sinned against me.

22*a* JST 2 Chr. 18:22 . . . *found* . . .

perceived that it was not the king of Israel, they turned back again from pursuing him.

33 And a *certain* man drew a bow at a venture, and smote the king of Israel between the joints of the harness: therefore he said to his chariot man, Turn thine hand, that thou mayest carry me out of the host; for I am wounded.

34 And the battle increased that day: howbeit the king of Israel stayed *himself* up in *his* chariot against the Syrians until the even: and about the time of the sun going down he died.

CHAPTER 19

Jehoshaphat is rebuked for helping ungodly Ahab—He helps the people return to the Lord, sets up judges, and administers justice.

AND Jehoshaphat the king of Judah returned to his house in peace to Jerusalem.

2 And Jehu the son of Hanani the *ª*seer went out to meet him, and said to king Jehoshaphat, Shouldest thou help the ungodly, and love them that hate the LORD? therefore *is* wrath upon thee from before the LORD.

3 Nevertheless there are good things found in thee, in that thou hast taken away the groves out of the land, and hast prepared thine heart to seek God.

4 And Jehoshaphat dwelt at Jerusalem: and he went out *ª*again through the people from Beer-sheba to mount Ephraim, and brought them back unto the LORD God of their fathers.

5 ¶ And he set *ª*judges in the land throughout all the fenced cities of Judah, city by city,

6 And said to the judges, Take heed what ye do: for ye judge not for man, but for the LORD, who *is* with you in the *ª*judgment.

7 Wherefore now let the fear of the LORD be upon you; take heed and do *it:* for *there is* no iniquity with the LORD our God, nor *ª*respect of persons, nor taking of *b*gifts.

8 ¶ Moreover in Jerusalem did Jehoshaphat set of the Levites, and *of* the priests, and of the chief of the fathers of Israel, for the judgment of the LORD, and for controversies, when they returned to Jerusalem.

9 And he charged them, saying, Thus shall ye do in the *ª*fear of the LORD, faithfully, and with a perfect heart.

10 And what *ª*cause soever shall come to you of your brethren that dwell in their cities, between blood and blood, between law and commandment, statutes and judgments, ye shall even *b*warn them that they trespass not against the LORD, and *so* wrath come upon you, and upon your brethren: this do, and ye shall not trespass.

11 And, behold, Amariah the chief *ª*priest *is* over you in all matters of the LORD; and Zebadiah the son of Ishmael, the ruler of the house of Judah, for all the king's matters: also the Levites *shall be* officers before you. Deal *b*courageously, and the LORD shall be with the good.

CHAPTER 20

The Ammonites and others attack Judah—Jehoshaphat and all the people fast and pray—Jahaziel prophesies the deliverance of Judah—Judah's attackers war among and destroy themselves.

IT came to pass after this also, *that* the children of Moab, and the children of Ammon, and with them *other* beside the Ammonites, came against Jehoshaphat to battle.

2 Then there came some that told Jehoshaphat, saying, There cometh a great multitude against thee from beyond the sea on this side Syria;

---

19 2*a* TG Seer.
  4*a* OR repeatedly.
  5*a* Ex. 18:21.
  6*a* TG Judgment.

7*a* Deut. 10:17.
  b Ex. 18:21 (21–22).
  9*a* Ex. 18:21.
  10*a* HEB dispute.

b TG Warn.
  11*a* D&C 107:87 (87–88).
  b TG Courage.

and, behold, they *be* in Hazazon-tamar, which *is* En-gedi.

3 And Jehoshaphat feared, and set himself to seek the LORD, and proclaimed a ᵃfast throughout all Judah.

4 And Judah gathered themselves together, to ask *help* of the LORD: even out of all the cities of Judah they came to seek the LORD.

5 ¶ And Jehoshaphat stood in the congregation of Judah and Jerusalem, in the house of the LORD, before the new court,

6 And said, O LORD God of our fathers, *art* not thou God in heaven? and rulest *not* thou over all the kingdoms of the heathen? and in thine hand *is there not* power and might, so that none is able to withstand thee?

7 *Art* not thou our God, *who* didst drive out the inhabitants of this land before thy people Israel, and gavest it to the ᵃseed of Abraham thy friend for ever?

8 And they dwelt therein, and have built thee a sanctuary therein for thy name, saying,

9 If, *when* evil cometh upon us, *as* the sword, judgment, or pestilence, or famine, we stand before this house, and in thy presence, (for thy name *is* in this house,) and cry unto thee in our ᵃaffliction, then thou wilt hear and help.

10 And now, behold, the children of Ammon and Moab and mount Seir, whom thou wouldest not let Israel invade, when they came out of the land of Egypt, but they turned from them, and destroyed them not;

11 Behold, *I say, how* they reward us, to come to cast us out of thy possession, which thou hast given us to inherit.

12 O our God, wilt thou not judge them? for we have no might against this great company that cometh against us; neither ᵃknow we what to do: but our eyes *are* upon thee.

13 And all Judah stood before the LORD, with their little ones, their wives, and their children.

14 ¶ Then upon Jahaziel the son of Zechariah, the son of Benaiah, the son of Jeiel, the son of Mattaniah, a Levite of the sons of Asaph, came the Spirit of the LORD in the midst of the congregation;

15 And he said, Hearken ye, all Judah, and ye inhabitants of Jerusalem, and thou king Jehoshaphat, Thus saith the LORD unto you, Be not afraid nor dismayed by reason of this great multitude; for the ᵃbattle *is* not yours, but God's.

16 To morrow go ye down against them: behold, they come up by the ᵃcliff of Ziz; and ye shall find them at the end of the ᵇbrook, ᶜbefore the wilderness of Jeruel.

17 Ye shall not *need* to fight in this *battle:* set yourselves, stand ye *still,* and see the ᵃsalvation of the LORD with you, O Judah and Jerusalem: fear not, nor be dismayed; to morrow go out against them: for the LORD *will be* with you.

18 And Jehoshaphat bowed his head with *his* face to the ground: and all Judah and the inhabitants of Jerusalem fell before the LORD, worshipping the LORD.

19 And the Levites, of the children of the Kohathites, and of the children of the Korhites, stood up to praise the LORD God of Israel with a loud voice on high.

20 ¶ And they rose early in the morning, and went forth into the wilderness of Tekoa: and as they went forth, Jehoshaphat stood and said, Hear me, O Judah, and ye inhabitants of Jerusalem; ᵃBelieve in the LORD your God, so shall ye be established; ᵇbelieve his prophets, so shall ye ᶜprosper.

21 And when he had consulted with the people, he appointed singers unto the LORD, and that should praise

20 3a TG Fast, Fasting.
  7a TG Seed of Abraham.
  9a TG Affliction.
 12a Heb. 11:8;
    1 Ne. 4:6.

15a 1 Sam. 17:47;
    D&C 105:14.
16a HEB ascent.
  b OR wadi, valley.
  c OR east of.

17a OR deliverance.
20a TG Faith.
  b OR Sustaining Church
    Leaders.
  c TG Abundant Life.

the beauty of holiness, as they went out before the army, and to say, Praise the LORD; for his mercy *en-dureth* for ever.

22 ¶ And when they began to sing and to praise, the LORD set ambushments against the children of Ammon, Moab, and mount Seir, which were come against Judah; and they *a*were smitten.

23 For the children of Ammon and Moab stood up against the inhabitants of mount Seir, utterly to slay and destroy *them:* and when they had made an end of the inhabitants of Seir, every one helped to destroy *a*another.

24 And when Judah came toward the watch tower in the wilderness, they looked unto the multitude, and, behold, they *were* dead bodies fallen to the earth, and none escaped.

25 And when Jehoshaphat and his people came to take away the spoil of them, they found among them in abundance both riches with the dead bodies, and precious jewels, which they stripped off for themselves, more than they could carry away: and they were three days in gathering of the spoil, it was so much.

26 ¶ And on the fourth day they assembled themselves in the valley of Berachah; for there they blessed the LORD: therefore the name of the same place was called, The valley of *a*Berachah, unto this day.

27 Then they returned, every man of Judah and Jerusalem, and Jehoshaphat in the forefront of them, to go again to Jerusalem with joy; for the LORD had made them to rejoice over their enemies.

28 And they came to Jerusalem with psalteries and harps and trumpets unto the house of the LORD.

29 And the fear of God was on all the kingdoms of *those* countries, when they had heard that the LORD fought against the enemies of Israel.

30 So the realm of Jehoshaphat was quiet: for his God gave him rest round about.

31 ¶ And Jehoshaphat reigned over Judah: *he was* thirty and five years old when he began to reign, and he reigned twenty and five years in Jerusalem. And his mother's name *was* Azubah the daughter of Shilhi.

32 And he walked in the way of Asa his father, and departed not from it, doing *that which was* right in the sight of the LORD.

33 Howbeit the high places were not taken away: for as yet the people had not prepared their hearts unto the God of their fathers.

34 Now the rest of the acts of Jehoshaphat, first and last, behold, they *are* written in the book of *a*Jehu the son of Hanani, who *is* mentioned in the book of the kings of Israel.

35 ¶ And after this did Jehoshaphat king of Judah join himself with Ahaziah king of Israel, who did very wickedly:

36 And he joined himself with him to make ships to go to Tarshish: and they made the ships in Ezion-geber.

37 Then Eliezer the son of Dodavah of Mareshah prophesied against Jehoshaphat, saying, Because thou hast joined thyself with Ahaziah, the LORD hath broken thy works. And the ships were broken, that they were not able to go to Tarshish.

CHAPTER 21

Jehoram slays his brothers, marries Ahab's daughter, and reigns in wickedness—Elijah prophesies a plague upon the people and the death of Jehoram—The Philistines and others war against Judah—Jehoram dies of sore diseases.

Now Jehoshaphat slept with his fathers, and was buried with his fathers in the city of David. And Jehoram his son reigned in his stead.

2 And he had brethren the sons of Jehoshaphat, Azariah, and Jehiel, and Zechariah, and Azariah, and

---

22*a* OR smote one another.
23*a* Judg. 7:22;

1 Sam. 14:20.
26*a* IE Blessing.

34*a* TG Scriptures, Lost.

Michael, and Shephatiah: all these *were* the sons of Jehoshaphat king of Israel.

3 And their father gave them great gifts of silver, and of gold, and of precious things, with ªfenced cities in Judah: but the kingdom gave he to Jehoram; because he *was* the firstborn.

4 Now when Jehoram was risen up to the kingdom of his father, he strengthened himself, and slew all his brethren with the sword, and *divers* also of the princes of Israel.

5 ¶ Jehoram *was* thirty and two years old when he began to reign, and he reigned eight years in Jerusalem.

6 And he walked in the way of the kings of Israel, like as did the house of ªAhab: for he had the daughter of Ahab to wife: and he wrought *that which was* evil in the eyes of the LORD.

7 Howbeit the LORD would not ªdestroy the house of David, because of the covenant that he had made with David, and as he promised to give a light to him and to his sons for ever.

8 ¶ In his days the Edomites revolted from under the dominion of Judah, and made themselves a king.

9 Then Jehoram went forth with his princes, and all his chariots with him: and he rose up by night, and smote the Edomites which ªcompassed him in, and the captains of the chariots.

10 So the Edomites revolted from under the hand of Judah unto this day. The same time *also* did Libnah revolt from under his hand; because he had forsaken the LORD God of his fathers.

11 Moreover he made high places in the mountains of Judah, and caused the inhabitants of Jerusalem to ªcommit fornication, and ᵇcompelled Judah *thereto*.

12 ¶ And there came a writing to

him from Elijah the prophet, saying, Thus saith the LORD God of David thy father, Because thou hast not walked in the ways of Jehoshaphat thy father, nor in the ways of ªAsa king of Judah,

13 But hast walked in the way of the kings of Israel, and hast made Judah and the inhabitants of Jerusalem to go a whoring, like to the whoredoms of the house of Ahab, and also hast slain thy brethren of thy father's house, *which were* better than thyself:

14 Behold, with a great ªplague will the LORD smite thy people, and thy children, and thy wives, and all thy goods:

15 And thou *shalt have* great sickness by disease of thy bowels, until thy bowels fall out by reason of the sickness day by day.

16 ¶ Moreover the LORD stirred up against Jehoram the spirit of the Philistines, and of the ªArabians, that *were* near the Ethiopians:

17 And they came up into Judah, and brake into it, and carried away all the substance that was found in the king's house, and his sons also, and his wives; so that there was never a son left him, save ªJehoahaz, the youngest of his sons.

18 ¶ And after all this the LORD smote him in his bowels with an incurable disease.

19 And it came to pass, that in process of time, after the end of two years, his bowels fell out by reason of his sickness: so he died of sore diseases. And his people made no ªburning for him, like the burning of his fathers.

20 Thirty and two years old was he when he began to reign, and he reigned in Jerusalem eight years, and departed without being desired. Howbeit they buried him in the city of David, but not in the ªsepulchres of the kings.

---

21 3*a* OR fortified.
  6*a* 1 Kgs. 16:30 (30–33);
    2 Chr. 22:3.
  7*a* 2 Kgs. 8:19 (16–19).
  9*a* OR surrounded.

11*a* IE be unfaithful to the
    Lord.
  b OR seduced.
12*a* 2 Chr. 14:2.
14*a* TG Plague.

16*a* 2 Chr. 22:1.
17*a* OR Ahaziah (see 2 Chr.
    22:1).
19*a* 2 Chr. 16:14.
20*a* 2 Chr. 28:27.

CHAPTER 22

Ahaziah reigns in wickedness and is slain by Jehu; his mother, Athaliah, reigns in his stead.

AND the inhabitants of Jerusalem made Ahaziah his youngest son king in his stead: for the band of men that came with the *a*Arabians to the camp had slain all the eldest. So Ahaziah the son of Jehoram king of Judah reigned.

2 *a*Forty and two years old *was* *b*Ahaziah when he began to reign, and he reigned one year in Jerusalem. His mother's name also *was* Athaliah the *c*daughter of Omri.

3 He also walked in the ways of the house of *a*Ahab: for his *b*mother was his counsellor to do wickedly.

4 Wherefore he did evil in the sight of the LORD like the house of Ahab: for they were his counsellors after the death of his father to his destruction.

5 ¶ He walked also after their counsel, and went with *a*Jehoram the son of Ahab king of Israel to war against Hazael king of Syria at Ramoth-gilead: and the Syrians smote Joram.

6 And he returned to be healed in Jezreel because of the wounds which were given him at Ramah, when he fought with Hazael king of Syria. And *a*Azariah the son of Jehoram king of Judah went down to see Jehoram the son of Ahab at Jezreel, because he was sick.

7 And the destruction of Ahaziah was of God by coming to Joram: for when he was come, he went out with Jehoram against Jehu the son of Nimshi, whom the LORD had *a*anointed to cut off the house of Ahab.

8 And it came to pass, that, when Jehu was executing judgment upon the house of Ahab, and found the princes of Judah, and the sons of the brethren of Ahaziah, that ministered to Ahaziah, he slew them.

9 And he sought Ahaziah: and they caught him, (for he was hid in Samaria,) and brought him to Jehu: and when they had *a*slain him, they buried him: Because, said they, he *is* the *b*son of Jehoshaphat, who sought the LORD with all his heart. So the house of Ahaziah had no power to keep still the kingdom.

10 ¶ But when *a*Athaliah the mother of Ahaziah saw that her son was dead, she arose and destroyed all the seed royal of the house of Judah.

11 But Jehoshabeath, the daughter of the king, took Joash the son of Ahaziah, and stole him from among the king's sons that were slain, and put him and his nurse in a bedchamber. So Jehoshabeath, the daughter of king Jehoram, the wife of Jehoiada the priest, (for she was the sister of Ahaziah,) hid him from Athaliah, so that she slew him not.

12 And he was with them hid in the house of God six years: and Athaliah reigned over the land.

CHAPTER 23

Jehoiada the priest makes Joash king—Athaliah is slain—Worship of the Lord is restored, and the priest of Baal is slain.

AND in the seventh year Jehoiada strengthened himself, and took the captains of hundreds, Azariah the son of Jeroham, and Ishmael the son of Jehohanan, and Azariah the son of Obed, and Maaseiah the son of Adaiah, and Elishaphat the son of Zichri, into *a*covenant with him.

2 And they went about in Judah, and gathered the Levites out of all the cities of Judah, and the chief of the fathers of Israel, and they came to Jerusalem.

---

22 1*a* 2 Chr. 21:16 (16–17).
  2*a* OR Twenty-two; see
    2 Kgs. 8:26.
    JST 2 Chr. 22:2 Two and
    twenty . . .
    b 2 Kgs. 8:26.
    c OR granddaughter; see

    2 Kgs. 8:26–27;
    2 Chr. 21:6.
  3 *a* 1 Kgs. 16:30 (30–33);
    2 Chr. 21:6.
    b TG Marriage, Motherhood.
  5 *a* 2 Kgs. 8:28.
  6 *a* OR Ahaziah (see vv. 7, 11)

    or Jehoahaz (see 2 Chr.
    21:17).
  7 *a* 2 Kgs. 9:6 (5–10).
  9 *a* 2 Kgs. 9:27.
    b OR grandson.
  10 *a* 2 Kgs. 11:1 (1–12).
23 1 *a* 2 Kgs. 11:4 (4–8).

3 And all the congregation made a covenant with the king in the house of God. And he said unto them, Behold, the king's son shall reign, as the LORD hath said of the sons of *a*David.

4 This *is* the thing that ye shall do; A third part of you entering on the sabbath, of the priests and of the Levites, *shall be* porters of the doors;

5 And a third part *shall be* at the king's house; and a third part at the *a*gate of the foundation: and all the people *shall be* in the courts of the house of the LORD.

6 But let none come into the house of the LORD, save the priests, and they that *a*minister of the Levites; they shall go in, for they *are* holy: but all the people shall keep the watch of the LORD.

7 And the Levites shall compass the king round about, every man with his weapons in his hand; and whosoever *else* cometh into the house, he shall be put to death: but be ye with the king when he cometh in, and when he goeth out.

8 So the Levites and all Judah did according to all things that Jehoiada the priest had commanded, and took every man his men that were to come in on the sabbath, with them that were to go *out* on the sabbath: for Jehoiada the priest dismissed not the courses.

9 Moreover Jehoiada the priest delivered to the captains of hundreds spears, and bucklers, and shields, that *had been* king David's, which *were* in the house of God.

10 And he set all the people, every man having his weapon in his hand, from the right side of the temple to the left side of the temple, along by the altar and the temple, by the king round about.

11 Then they brought out the king's son, and put upon him the crown, and *gave him* the *a*testimony, and made him king. And Jehoiada and his sons anointed him, and said, God save the king.

12 ¶ Now when Athaliah heard the noise of the people running and praising the king, she came to the people into the house of the LORD:

13 And she looked, and, behold, the king stood at his pillar at the entering in, and the princes and the trumpets by the king: and all the people of the land rejoiced, and sounded with trumpets, also the singers with instruments of musick, and such as taught to *a*sing praise. Then Athaliah rent her clothes, and said, Treason, Treason.

14 Then Jehoiada the priest brought out the captains of hundreds that were set over the host, and said unto them, Have her forth *a*of the ranges: and whoso followeth her, let him be slain with the sword. For the priest said, Slay her not in the house of the LORD.

15 So they laid hands on her; and when she was come to the entering of the *a*horse gate by the king's house, they slew her there.

16 ¶ And Jehoiada made a covenant between him, and between all the people, and between the king, that they should be the LORD's people.

17 Then all the people went to the house of Baal, and brake it down, and brake his altars and his images in pieces, and slew Mattan the priest of Baal before the altars.

18 Also Jehoiada appointed the offices of the house of the LORD by the hand of the priests the Levites, whom David had distributed in the house of the LORD, to offer the *a*burnt offerings of the LORD, as *it is* written in the law of Moses, with rejoicing and with singing, *as it was ordained* by David.

19 And he set the porters at the gates of the house of the LORD, that none *which was* unclean in any thing should enter in.

3*a* 2 Sam. 7:12.
5*a* 2 Kgs. 11:6.
6*a* 1 Chr. 23:28 (27–29); D&C 84:26 (25–27).
11*a* IE divine charge; see Deut. 17:14–20.
13*a* 1 Chr. 25:7.
14*a* OR between the ranks.
15*a* 2 Kgs. 11:16.
18*a* Mosiah 2:3.

20 And he took the captains of hundreds, and the nobles, and the governors of the people, and all the people of the land, and brought down the king from the house of the LORD: and they came through the high gate into the king's house, and set the king upon the throne of the kingdom.

21 And all the people of the land rejoiced: and the city was quiet, after that they had slain Athaliah with the sword.

CHAPTER 24

Joash and Jehoiada receive contributions and repair the house of the Lord—Jehoiada dies—Joash falls into idolatry, slays a prophet named Zechariah, and is himself slain in a conspiracy.

JOASH *was* seven years old when he began to reign, and he reigned forty years in Jerusalem. His mother's name also *was* Zibiah of Beer-sheba.

2 And Joash did *that which was* right in the sight of the LORD all the days of Jehoiada the priest.

3 And Jehoiada took for him two wives; and he begat sons and daughters.

4 ¶ And it came to pass after this, *that* Joash was minded to repair the house of the LORD.

5 And he gathered together the priests and the Levites, and said to them, Go out unto the cities of Judah, and gather of all Israel money to repair the house of your God from year to year, and see that ye hasten the matter. Howbeit the Levites hastened *it* not.

6 And the king called for Jehoiada the chief, and said unto him, Why hast thou not required of the Levites to bring in out of Judah and out of Jerusalem the *a*collection, *according to the commandment* of Moses the servant of the LORD, and of the congregation of Israel, for the *b*tabernacle of witness?

7 For the sons of Athaliah, that

wicked woman, had broken up the house of God; and also all the dedicated things of the house of the LORD did they bestow upon Baalim.

8 And at the king's commandment they made a chest, and set it without at the gate of the house of the LORD.

9 And they made a proclamation through Judah and Jerusalem, to bring in to the LORD the collection *that* Moses the servant of God *laid* upon Israel in the wilderness.

10 And all the princes and all the people rejoiced, and brought in, and cast into the chest, until they had made an end.

11 Now it came to pass, that at what time the chest was brought unto the king's office by the hand of the Levites, and when they saw that *there was* much *a*money, the king's scribe and the high priest's officer came and emptied the chest, and took it, and carried it to his place again. Thus they did day by day, and gathered money in abundance.

12 And the king and Jehoiada gave it to such as did the work of the service of the house of the LORD, and hired masons and carpenters to repair the house of the LORD, and also such as wrought iron and brass to mend the house of the LORD.

13 So the workmen wrought, and the work was perfected by them, and they set the house of God in his state, and strengthened it.

14 And when they had finished *it,* they brought the rest of the money before the king and Jehoiada, whereof were made *a*vessels for the house of the LORD, *even* vessels to minister, and to offer *withal,* and spoons, and vessels of gold and silver. And they offered burnt offerings in the house of the LORD continually all the days of Jehoiada.

15 ¶ But Jehoiada waxed old, and was full of days when he died; an hundred and thirty years old *was he* when he died.

16 And they buried him in the city

24 6*a* Ex. 30:16 (12–16).   11*a* 2 Kgs. 12:10.
    b Num. 1:53 (50–53).   14*a* 2 Kgs. 12:13.

of David among the kings, because he had done good in Israel, both toward God, and toward his house.

17 Now after the death of Jehoiada came the princes of Judah, and made obeisance to the king. Then the king hearkened unto them.

18 And they left the house of the LORD God of their fathers, and served groves and ^aidols: and wrath came upon Judah and Jerusalem for this their trespass.

19 Yet he ^asent ^bprophets to them, to bring them again unto the LORD; and they ^ctestified against them: but they would not give ear.

20 And the ^aSpirit of God came upon Zechariah the son of Jehoiada the priest, which stood above the people, and said unto them, Thus saith God, Why transgress ye the commandments of the LORD, that ye cannot ^bprosper? because ye have forsaken the LORD, he hath also forsaken you.

21 And they conspired against him, and ^astoned him with stones at the commandment of the king in the court of the house of the LORD.

22 Thus Joash the king remembered not the kindness which Jehoiada his father had done to him, but slew his son. And when he died, he said, The LORD look upon *it*, and require *it*.

23 ¶ And it came to pass at the end of the year, *that* the host of Syria came up against him: and they came to Judah and Jerusalem, and destroyed all the princes of the people from among the people, and sent all the spoil of them unto the king of Damascus.

24 For the army of the Syrians came with a small company of men, and the LORD delivered a very great host into their hand, because they had forsaken the LORD God of their fathers. So they executed judgment against Joash.

25 And when they were departed from him, (for they left him ^ain great diseases,) his own servants conspired against him for the blood of the sons of Jehoiada the priest, and slew him on his bed, and he died: and they buried him in the city of David, but they buried him not in the ^bsepulchres of the kings.

26 And these are they that conspired against him; ^aZabad the son of Shimeath an Ammonitess, and Jehozabad the son of Shimrith a Moabitess.

27 ¶ Now *concerning* his sons, and the greatness of the burdens *laid* upon him, and the repairing of the house of God, behold, they *are* written in the story of the book of the kings. And Amaziah his son reigned in his stead.

CHAPTER 25

Amaziah reigns, smites the Edomites, and worships false gods—A prophet foretells Amaziah's destruction—Judah is defeated by Israel, and Amaziah is slain in a conspiracy.

AMAZIAH *was* twenty and five years old *when* he began to reign, and he reigned twenty and nine years in Jerusalem. And his mother's name *was* Jehoaddan of Jerusalem.

2 And he did *that which was* right in the sight of the LORD, but not ^awith a perfect heart.

3 ¶ Now it came to pass, when the kingdom was established to him, that he slew his servants that had killed the king his father.

4 But he slew not their children, but *did* as *it is* written in the law in the book of Moses, where the LORD commanded, saying, The fathers shall not die for the children, neither shall the children die for the fathers, but every man shall die for his own ^asin.

5 ¶ Moreover Amaziah gathered

18*a* 1 Kgs. 14:23.
19*a* TG Authority.
   b 2 Ne. 27:5.
   c TG Preaching.
20*a* TG God, Spirit of.

   b Mosiah 7:29 (29–31).
21*a* TG Martyrdom;
     Prophets, Rejection of.
25*a* IE severely wounded.
   b 2 Chr. 28:27.

26*a* OR Jozachar (see
    2 Kgs. 12:21).
25 2*a* OR wholeheartedly.
  4*a* TG Accountability.

Judah together, and made them captains over thousands, and captains over hundreds, according to the houses of *their* fathers, throughout all Judah and Benjamin: and he numbered them from twenty years old and above, and found them three hundred thousand choice *men, able* to go forth to war, that could handle spear and shield.

6 He hired also an hundred thousand mighty men of valour out of Israel for an hundred talents of silver.

7 But there came a man of God to him, saying, O king, let not the army of Israel go with thee; for the LORD *is* not with Israel, *to wit, with* all the children of Ephraim.

8 But if thou wilt go, do *it,* be strong for the battle: God shall make thee fall before the enemy: for God hath *a*power to help, and to cast down.

9 And Amaziah said to the man of God, But what shall we do for the hundred talents which I have given to the army of Israel? And the man of God answered, The LORD is able to give thee much more than this.

10 Then Amaziah separated them, *to wit,* the army that was come to him out of Ephraim, to go home again: wherefore their anger was greatly kindled against Judah, and they returned home in great anger.

11 ¶ And Amaziah strengthened himself, and led forth his people, and went to the *a*valley of salt, and smote of the children of Seir ten thousand.

12 And *other* ten thousand *left* alive did the children of Judah carry away captive, and brought them unto the top of the rock, and cast them down from the top of the rock, that they all were broken in pieces.

13 ¶ But the soldiers of the army which Amaziah sent back, that they should not go with him to battle, fell upon the cities of Judah, from Samaria even unto Beth-horon, and smote three thousand of them, and took much spoil.

14 ¶ Now it came to pass, after that Amaziah was come from the slaughter of the Edomites, that he brought the gods of the children of Seir, and set them up *to be* his gods, and bowed down himself before them, and burned incense unto them.

15 Wherefore the *a*anger of the LORD was kindled against Amaziah, and he sent unto him a prophet, which said unto him, Why hast thou sought after the gods of the people, which could not deliver their own people out of thine hand?

16 And it came to pass, as he talked with him, that *the king* said unto him, *a*Art thou made of the king's counsel? forbear; why shouldest thou be smitten? Then the prophet forbare, and said, I know that God hath determined to destroy thee, because thou hast done this, and hast not hearkened unto my counsel.

17 ¶ Then Amaziah king of Judah took advice, and sent to Joash, the son of Jehoahaz, the son of Jehu, king of Israel, saying, Come, *a*let us see one another in the face.

18 And Joash king of Israel sent to Amaziah king of Judah, saying, The thistle that *was* in Lebanon sent to the cedar that *was* in Lebanon, saying, Give thy daughter to my son to wife: and there passed by a wild beast that *was* in Lebanon, and trode down the thistle.

19 Thou sayest, Lo, thou hast smitten the Edomites; and thine heart lifteth thee up to boast: abide now at home; why shouldest thou meddle to *thine* hurt, that thou shouldest fall, *even* thou, and Judah with thee?

20 But Amaziah would not hear; for it *came* of God, that he might deliver them into the hand *of their enemies,* because they sought after the gods of Edom.

21 So Joash the king of Israel went up; and they saw one another in the

---

8*a* D&C 60:4.
11*a* IE by the Dead Sea.
15*a* 2 Ne. 9:37.

16*a* HEB Have we made you a royal counselor?
17*a* IE let us face each other

on the battlefield;
2 Sam. 2:12–16.

face, *both* he and Amaziah king of Judah, at Beth-shemesh, which *belongeth* to Judah.

22 And Judah was put to the worse before Israel, and they fled every man to his tent.

23 And Joash the king of Israel took Amaziah king of Judah, the son of Joash, the son of Jehoahaz, at Beth-shemesh, and brought him to Jerusalem, and brake down the *a*wall of Jerusalem from the gate of Ephraim to the corner gate, four hundred cubits.

24 And *he took* all the gold and the silver, and all the vessels that were found in the house of God with Obed-edom, and the treasures of the king's house, the hostages also, and returned to Samaria.

25 ¶ And Amaziah the son of Joash king of Judah lived after the death of Joash son of Jehoahaz king of Israel fifteen years.

26 Now the rest of the acts of Amaziah, first and last, behold, *are* they not written in the book of the kings of Judah and Israel?

27 ¶ Now after the time that Amaziah did turn away from following the LORD they made a conspiracy against him in Jerusalem; and he fled to Lachish: but they sent to Lachish after him, and slew him there.

28 And they brought him upon horses, and buried him with his fathers in the city of Judah.

CHAPTER 26

Uzziah reigns and prospers as long as he keeps the commandments—He transgresses, attempts to burn incense upon the altar, and is cursed with leprosy.

THEN all the people of Judah took *a*Uzziah, who *was* sixteen years old, and made him king in the room of his father Amaziah.

2 He built Eloth, and restored it to Judah, after that the king slept with his fathers.

3 Sixteen years old *was* Uzziah when he began to reign, and he reigned fifty and two years in Jerusalem. His mother's name also *was* Jecoliah of Jerusalem.

4 And he did *that which was* right in the sight of the LORD, according to all that his father Amaziah did.

5 And he sought God in the days of Zechariah, who had understanding in the *a*visions of God: and as long as he sought the LORD, God made him to *b*prosper.

6 And he went forth and warred against the Philistines, and brake down the wall of Gath, and the wall of Jabneh, and the wall of Ashdod, and built cities about Ashdod, and among the Philistines.

7 And God helped him against the Philistines, and against the Arabians that dwelt in Gur-baal, and the Mehunims.

8 And the Ammonites gave gifts to Uzziah: and his name spread abroad *even* to the entering in of Egypt; for he strengthened *himself* exceedingly.

9 Moreover Uzziah built towers in Jerusalem at the corner gate, and at the valley gate, and at the turning *of the wall,* and fortified them.

10 Also he built towers in the desert, and digged many wells: for he had much cattle, both in the low country, and in the plains: husbandmen *also,* and vine dressers in the mountains, and in *a*Carmel: for he loved *b*husbandry.

11 Moreover Uzziah had an host of fighting men, that went out to war by bands, according to the number of their account by the hand of Jeiel the scribe and Maaseiah the ruler, under the hand of Hananiah, *one* of the king's captains.

12 The whole number of the chief of the fathers of the mighty men of valour *were* two thousand and six hundred.

13 And under their hand *was* an army, three hundred thousand and

---

23*a* 2 Chr. 32:5 (5–26).
26 1*a* OR Azariah (see
2 Kgs. 14:21; 15:1).
5*a* 2 Ne. 4:23.
b Hel. 12:1 (1–2).
10*a* OR fruitful fields.
b HEB the soil.

seven thousand and five hundred, that made war with mighty power, to help the king against the enemy.

14 And Uzziah prepared for them throughout all the host shields, and spears, and helmets, and *haber-geons, and bows, and slings *to cast* stones.

15 And he made in Jerusalem en-gines, invented by cunning men, to be on the towers and upon the bulwarks, to shoot arrows and great stones withal. And his name spread far abroad; for he was marvellously helped, till he was strong.

16 ¶ But when he was strong, his heart was lifted up to *his* destruc-tion: for he transgressed against the LORD his God, and went into the temple of the LORD to burn incense upon the altar of incense.

17 And *Azariah the priest went in after him, and with him four-score priests of the LORD, *that were* valiant men:

18 And they withstood Uzziah the king, and said unto him, It *apper-taineth *not unto thee, Uzziah, to *burn incense unto the LORD, but to the priests the sons of *Aaron, that are consecrated to burn *incense: go out of the sanctuary; for thou hast trespassed; neither *shall it be* for thine honour from the LORD God.

19 Then Uzziah was wroth, and *had* a censer in his hand to burn incense: and while he was wroth with the priests, the leprosy even rose up in his forehead before the priests in the house of the LORD, from beside the incense altar.

20 And Azariah the chief priest, and all the priests, looked upon him, and, behold, he *was* leprous in his forehead, and they thrust him out from thence; yea, himself hasted also to go out, because the LORD had *smitten him.

21 And Uzziah the king was a *leper unto the day of his death, and dwelt in a *several house, *being* a leper; for he was cut off from the house of the LORD: and Jotham his son *was* over the king's house, judg-ing the people of the land.

22 ¶ Now the rest of the acts of Uzziah, first and last, did Isaiah the prophet, the son of Amoz, *write.

23 So Uzziah slept with his fathers, and they buried him with his fa-thers in the field of the burial which *belonged* to the kings; for they said, He *is* a leper: and Jotham his son reigned in his stead.

CHAPTER 27

Jotham reigns, builds up the kingdom, and subdues the Ammonites.

JOTHAM *was* *twenty and five years old when he began to reign, and he reigned sixteen years in Jerusalem. His mother's name also *was* Jeru-shah, the daughter of Zadok.

2 And he did *that which was* right in the sight of the LORD, according to all that his father Uzziah did: howbeit he entered not into the temple of the LORD. And the peo-ple did yet corruptly.

3 He built the high *gate of the house of the LORD, and on the wall of Ophel he built much.

4 Moreover he built cities in the mountains of Judah, and in the forests he built *castles and towers.

5 ¶ He fought also with the king of the Ammonites, and prevailed against them. And the children of Ammon gave him the same year an hundred talents of silver, and ten thousand measures of wheat, and ten thousand measures of barley. So much did the children of Ammon pay unto him, both the second year, and the third.

6 So Jotham became mighty, be-cause he *prepared his ways before the LORD his God.

14a HEB armor.
17a 1 Chr. 6:10.
18a TG Priesthood,
   Authority.
  b TG Priesthood,
   Qualifying for.
  c Num. 16:40.

d D&C 84:18 (18–27);
   107:13 (13–14).
  e Ex. 30:7 (7–8).
20a TG Punish.
21a TG Leprosy.
  b HEB separate.
22a TG Scribe;

   Scriptures, Writing of.
27 1a Morm. 2:2.
  3a 2 Kgs. 15:35; Ezek. 9:2.
  4a OR forts.
  6a HEB ordered; i.e.,
   maintained a steady
   course.

7 ¶ Now the rest of the acts of Jotham, and all his wars, and his ways, lo, they *are* written in the book of the kings of Israel and Judah.

8 He was five and twenty years old when he began to reign, and reigned sixteen years in Jerusalem.

9 ¶ And Jotham slept with his fathers, and they buried him in the city of David: and Ahaz his son reigned in his stead.

CHAPTER 28

Ahaz reigns in wickedness and practices idolatry; his people are defeated by Israel—The captives are freed by the command of a prophet—The Edomites and Philistines attack Judah—Ahaz continues his idolatrous ways.

AHAZ *was* twenty years old when he began to reign, and he reigned sixteen years in Jerusalem: but he did not *that which was* right in the sight of the LORD, like David his father:

2 For he walked in the ways of the kings of Israel, and made also molten ᵃimages for Baalim.

3 Moreover he burnt incense in the valley of the son of Hinnom, and burnt his children in the ᵃfire, after the abominations of the heathen whom the LORD had cast out before the children of Israel.

4 He sacrificed also and burnt incense in the high places, and on the hills, and under every green tree.

5 Wherefore the LORD his God delivered him into the hand of the ᵃking of Syria; and they smote him, and carried away a great multitude of them captives, and brought *them* to Damascus. And he was also delivered into the hand of the king of Israel, who smote him with a great slaughter.

6 ¶ For ᵃPekah the son of Remaliah slew in Judah an hundred and twenty thousand in one day, *which were* all valiant men; because they had forsaken the LORD God of their fathers.

7 And Zichri, a mighty man of Ephraim, slew Maaseiah the king's son, and Azrikam the governor of the house, and Elkanah *that was* next to the king.

8 And the children of Israel carried away captive of their brethren two hundred thousand, women, sons, and daughters, and took also away much spoil from them, and brought the spoil to Samaria.

9 But a prophet of the LORD was there, whose name *was* Oded: and he went out before the host that came to Samaria, and said unto them, Behold, because the LORD God of your fathers was wroth with Judah, he hath delivered them into your hand, and ye have slain them in a rage *that* reacheth up unto heaven.

10 And now ye purpose to ᵃkeep under the children of Judah and Jerusalem for bondmen and bondwomen unto you: *but are there* not with you, even with you, sins against the LORD your God?

11 Now hear me therefore, and deliver the ᵃcaptives again, which ye have taken captive of your brethren: for the fierce wrath of the LORD *is* upon you.

12 Then certain of the heads of the children of Ephraim, Azariah the son of Johanan, Berechiah the son of Meshillemoth, and Jehizkiah the son of Shallum, and Amasa the son of Hadlai, stood up against them that came from the war,

13 And said unto them, Ye shall not bring in the captives hither: for whereas we have ᵃoffended against the LORD *already,* ye intend to add *more* to our sins and to our trespass: for our trespass is great, and *there is* fierce wrath against Israel.

14 So the armed men left the captives and the spoil before the princes and all the congregation.

15 And the men which were expressed by name rose up, and took the captives, and with the spoil clothed all that were naked among

---

28 2*a* Ex. 34:17.
3*a* 2 Kgs. 21:6; 2 Chr. 33:6; Ezek. 20:26.
5*a* Isa. 7:1.
6*a* 2 Kgs. 15:27 (27–28).
10*a* OR subjugate.
11*a* 1 Ne. 17:25; Mosiah 11:21; D&C 101:79.
13*a* TG Offense.

them, and arrayed them, and shod them, and gave them to *a*eat and to drink, and anointed them, and carried all the feeble of them upon asses, and brought them to Jericho, the city of palm trees, to their brethren: then they returned to Samaria.

16 ¶ At that time did king Ahaz send unto the kings of *a*Assyria to help him.

17 For again the Edomites had come and smitten Judah, and carried away captives.

18 The Philistines also had invaded the cities of the low country, and of the south of Judah, and had taken Beth-shemesh, and Ajalon, and Gederoth, and Shocho with the villages thereof, and Timnah with the villages thereof, Gimzo also and the villages thereof: and they dwelt there.

19 For the LORD brought Judah low because of Ahaz king of Israel; for he made Judah *a*naked, and transgressed sore against the LORD.

20 And Tilgath-pilneser king of Assyria came unto him, and distressed him, but strengthened him not.

21 For Ahaz *a*took away a portion *out* of the house of the LORD, and *out* of the house of the king, and of the princes, and gave *it* unto the king of Assyria: but he helped him not.

22 ¶ And in the time of his distress did he trespass yet more against the LORD: this *is that* king Ahaz.

23 For he sacrificed unto the gods of Damascus, which smote him: and he said, Because the gods of the kings of Syria help them, *therefore* will I sacrifice to them, that they may help me. But they were the *a*ruin of him, and of all Israel.

24 And Ahaz gathered together the vessels of the house of God, and cut in pieces the vessels of the house of God, and shut up the doors of the house of the LORD, and he made him altars in every corner of Jerusalem.

25 And in every *a*several city of Judah he made high places to burn incense unto other gods, and provoked to anger the LORD God of his fathers.

26 ¶ Now the rest of his acts and of all his ways, first and last, behold, they *are* written in the book of the kings of Judah and Israel.

27 And Ahaz slept with his fathers, and they buried him in the city, *even* in Jerusalem: but they brought him not into the *a*sepulchres of the kings of Israel: and Hezekiah his son reigned in his stead.

CHAPTER 29

Hezekiah reigns in righteousness and restores the worship of Jehovah—The Levites cleanse and sanctify the house of the Lord—The priests offer sacrifices and make reconciliation and atonement for the people—Hezekiah and all the people worship the Lord and praise His name.

HEZEKIAH began to *a*reign *when he was* five and twenty years old, and he reigned nine and twenty years in Jerusalem. And his mother's name *was* Abijah, the daughter of Zechariah.

2 And he did *that which was* right in the sight of the LORD, according to all that David his father had done.

3 ¶ He in the first year of his reign, in the first month, opened the doors of the house of the LORD, and repaired them.

4 And he brought in the priests and the Levites, and gathered them together into the east street,

5 And said unto them, Hear me, ye Levites, *a*sanctify now yourselves, and sanctify the house of the LORD God of your fathers, and carry forth the *b*filthiness out of the holy *place.*

6 For our fathers have *a*trespassed, and done *that which was* evil in the eyes of the LORD our God, and have forsaken him, and have turned away their faces from the habitation of the LORD, and turned *their* backs.

15*a* Prov. 25:21 (21–22).
16*a* 2 Kgs. 16:7 (7–18);
    Ezek. 16:28; 23:12.
19*a* Ex. 32:25.

21*a* 2 Kgs. 16:8 (8–9).
23*a* Alma 30:60.
25*a* IE single.
27*a* 2 Chr. 21:20; 24:25.

29 1*a* 2 Kgs. 18:2 (1–3).
  5*a* 2 Chr. 35:6.
    b TG Filthiness.
  6*a* Mosiah 26:30.

7 Also they have shut up the doors of the porch, and put out the lamps, and have not burned incense nor offered burnt offerings in the holy *place* unto the God of Israel.

8 Wherefore the wrath of the LORD was upon Judah and Jerusalem, and he hath delivered them to trouble, to astonishment, and to hissing, as ye see with your eyes.

9 For, lo, our fathers have fallen by the sword, and our sons and our daughters and our wives *are* in captivity for this.

10 Now *it is* in mine heart to make a covenant with the LORD God of Israel, that his fierce wrath may turn away from us.

11 My sons, be not now negligent: for the LORD hath *a*chosen you to stand before him, to serve him, and that ye should minister unto him, and burn incense.

12 ¶ Then the Levites arose, Mahath the son of Amasai, and Joel the son of Azariah, of the sons of the Kohathites: and of the sons of Merari, Kish the son of Abdi, and Azariah the son of Jehalelel: and of the Gershonites; Joah the son of Zimmah, and Eden the son of Joah:

13 And of the sons of Elizaphan; Shimri, and Jeiel: and of the sons of Asaph; Zechariah, and Mattaniah:

14 And of the sons of Heman; Jehiel, and Shimei: and of the sons of Jeduthun; Shemaiah, and Uzziel.

15 And they gathered their brethren, and sanctified themselves, and came, according to the commandment of the king, by the words of the LORD, to cleanse the house of the LORD.

16 And the priests went into the inner part of the house of the LORD, to cleanse *it,* and brought out all the uncleanness that they found in the temple of the LORD into the court of the house of the LORD. And the Levites took *it,* to carry *it* out abroad into the brook Kidron.

17 Now they began on the first *day* of the first month to sanctify, and on the eighth day of the month came they to the porch of the LORD: so they sanctified the house of the LORD in eight days; and in the sixteenth day of the first month they made an end.

18 Then they went in to Hezekiah the king, and said, We have cleansed all the house of the LORD, and the altar of burnt offering, with all the vessels thereof, and the shewbread table, with all the vessels thereof.

19 Moreover all the vessels, which king Ahaz in his reign did cast away in his transgression, have we prepared and sanctified, and, behold, they *are* before the altar of the LORD.

20 ¶ Then Hezekiah the king rose early, and gathered the rulers of the city, and went up to the house of the LORD.

21 And they brought seven bullocks, and seven rams, and seven lambs, and seven he goats, for a *a*sin offering for the kingdom, and for the sanctuary, and for Judah. And he commanded the priests the sons of Aaron to offer *them* on the altar of the LORD.

22 So they killed the bullocks, and the priests received the blood, and *a*sprinkled *it* on the altar: likewise, when they had killed the rams, they sprinkled the blood upon the altar: they killed also the lambs, and they sprinkled the blood upon the altar.

23 And they brought forth the he goats *for* the sin offering before the king and the congregation; and they laid their hands upon them:

24 And the priests killed them, and they made *a*reconciliation with their blood upon the altar, to make an *b*atonement for all Israel: for the king commanded *that* the burnt offering and the sin offering *should be made* for all Israel.

25 And he set the *a*Levites in the house of the LORD with cymbals, with psalteries, and with harps, according to the commandment of

---

11*a* TG Priesthood, Aaronic.
21*a* Lev. 4:14 (13–21).
22*a* Lev. 8:24 (14–15, 19, 24).

24*a* TG Reconciliation.
   b Lev. 1:4; 4:26;
     Num. 15:25.

25*a* 1 Chr. 16:4.

David, and of Gad the king's ᵇseer, and ᶜNathan the prophet: for *so was* the commandment of the LORD by his prophets.

26 And the Levites stood with the ᵃinstruments of David, and the priests with the trumpets.

27 And Hezekiah commanded to offer the burnt offering upon the altar. And when the burnt offering began, the song of the LORD began *also* with the trumpets, and with the instruments *ordained* by David king of Israel.

28 And all the ᵃcongregation worshipped, and the singers sang, and the trumpeters sounded: *and* all *this continued* until the burnt offering was finished.

29 And when they had made an end of offering, the king and all that were present with him bowed themselves, and worshipped.

30 Moreover Hezekiah the king and the princes commanded the Levites to sing praise unto the LORD with the words of David, and of Asaph the ᵃseer. And they sang praises with gladness, and they bowed their heads and worshipped.

31 Then Hezekiah answered and said, Now ye have consecrated yourselves unto the LORD, come near and bring sacrifices and ᵃthank offerings into the house of the LORD. And the congregation brought in sacrifices and thank offerings; and as many as were of a ᵇfree heart burnt offerings.

32 And the number of the burnt offerings, which the congregation brought, was threescore and ten bullocks, an hundred rams, *and* two hundred lambs: all these *were* for a burnt offering to the LORD.

33 And the consecrated things *were* six hundred oxen and three thousand sheep.

34 But the ᵃpriests were too few, so that they could not flay all the burnt offerings: wherefore their brethren the Levites did help them, till the work was ended, and until the *other* priests had ᵇsanctified themselves: for the Levites *were* more upright in heart to sanctify themselves than the priests.

35 And also the burnt offerings *were* in abundance, with the fat of the peace ᵃofferings, and the drink ᵇofferings for *every* burnt offering. So the service of the house of the LORD was set in ᶜorder.

36 And Hezekiah rejoiced, and all the people, that God had prepared the people: for the thing was *done* suddenly.

CHAPTER 30

Hezekiah invites all Israel to a solemn Passover in Jerusalem—Some accept the call; others laugh him to scorn—The faithful Israelites worship the Lord in Jerusalem.

AND Hezekiah sent to all Israel and Judah, and wrote letters also to Ephraim and Manasseh, that they should come to the house of the LORD at Jerusalem, to keep the passover unto the LORD God of Israel.

2 For the king had taken counsel, and his princes, and all the congregation in Jerusalem, to keep the passover in the ᵃsecond month.

3 For they could not keep it at ᵃthat time, because the priests had not sanctified themselves sufficiently, neither had the people gathered themselves together to Jerusalem.

4 And the thing pleased the king and all the congregation.

5 So they established a decree to make proclamation throughout all Israel, from Beer-sheba even to Dan, that they should come to keep the passover unto the LORD God of Israel at Jerusalem: for they had not done *it* ᵃof a long *time in such sort* as it was written.

25ᵇ TG Seer.
  c 2 Sam. 12:1.
26ᵃ Amos 6:5.
28ᵃ TG Assembly for Worship; Church.
30ᵃ TG Seer.

31ᵃ Lev. 7:12 (12, 16, 33).
  b OR willing, generous.
34ᵃ TG Priest, Aaronic Priesthood.
  BD Priests.
  b 2 Chr. 30:24 (3, 24).
35ᵃ Lev. 3:1.

  b Num. 15:5 (5, 7, 10).
  c TG Order.
30 2ᵃ Num. 9:11 (10–11).
  3ᵃ IE in the first month, as required.
  5ᵃ OR in such great numbers.

6 So the *posts went with the letters from the king and his princes throughout all Israel and Judah, and according to the commandment of the king, saying, Ye children of Israel, *turn again unto the LORD God of Abraham, Isaac, and Israel, and he will return to the remnant of you, that are escaped out of the hand of the kings of Assyria.

7 And be not ye like your *fathers, and like your brethren, which trespassed against the LORD God of their fathers, *who* therefore gave them up to desolation, as ye see.

8 Now be ye not *stiffnecked, as your fathers *were, but* *yield yourselves unto the LORD, and enter into his sanctuary, which he hath sanctified for ever: and serve the LORD your God, that the fierceness of his wrath may turn away from you.

9 For if ye *turn again unto the LORD, your brethren and your children *shall find* compassion before them that lead them captive, so that they shall come again into this land: for the LORD your God *is* gracious and *merciful, and will not turn away *his* face from you, if ye return unto him.

10 So the posts passed from city to city through the country of Ephraim and Manasseh even unto Zebulun: but they laughed them to scorn, and *mocked them.

11 Nevertheless *divers of Asher and Manasseh and of Zebulun humbled themselves, and came to Jerusalem.

12 Also in Judah the hand of God was to give them *one heart to do the commandment of the king and of the princes, by the word of the LORD.

13 ¶ And there assembled at Jerusalem much people to keep the feast of *unleavened bread in the second month, a very great congregation.

14 And they arose and took away the altars that *were* in Jerusalem, and all the altars for incense took they away, and cast *them* into the brook Kidron.

15 Then they killed the passover on the fourteenth *day* of the second month: and the priests and the Levites were ashamed, and sanctified themselves, and brought in the burnt offerings into the house of the LORD.

16 And they stood in their place after their manner, according to the law of Moses the man of God: the priests sprinkled the *blood, *which they received* of the hand of the Levites.

17 For *there were* many in the congregation that were not sanctified: therefore the Levites had the charge of the killing of the passovers for every one *that was* not clean, to sanctify *them* unto the LORD.

18 For a multitude of the people, *even* many of Ephraim, and Manasseh, Issachar, and Zebulun, had not *cleansed themselves, yet did they eat the passover otherwise than it was written. But Hezekiah prayed for them, saying, The good LORD pardon every one

19 *That* prepareth his heart to seek God, the LORD God of his fathers, though *he be* not *cleansed* according to the purification of the sanctuary.

20 And the LORD hearkened to Hezekiah, and *healed the people.

21 And the children of Israel that were present at Jerusalem kept the feast of unleavened bread seven days with great gladness: and the Levites and the priests praised the LORD day by day, *singing* with loud instruments unto the LORD.

22 And Hezekiah spake *comfortably unto all the Levites that taught the good knowledge of the LORD:

6a IE couriers, runners (also v. 10).
b Isa. 10:21 (21–23); Joel 2:12 (12–13).
7a TG Traditions of Men.
8a TG Stiffnecked.
b Mosiah 3:19; Hel. 3:35.
9a TG Israel, Restoration of.
b TG Mercy.
10a Luke 8:53; Alma 26:23.
11a IE some.
12a Moses 7:18.
13a TG Bread, Unleavened;
Passover.
16a Ex. 12:22 (21–22).
18a TG Purification.
20a TG Heal.
22a HEB to the heart; i.e., encouragingly, intimately.

and they did eat throughout the feast seven days, offering peace offerings, and making [b]confession to the LORD God of their fathers.

23 And the whole assembly took counsel to keep other seven days: and they kept *other* seven days with gladness.

24 For Hezekiah king of Judah did give to the congregation a thousand bullocks and seven thousand sheep; and the princes gave to the congregation a thousand bullocks and ten thousand sheep: and a great number of priests [a]sanctified themselves.

25 And all the congregation of Judah, with the priests and the Levites, and all the congregation that came out of Israel, and the strangers that came out of the land of Israel, and that dwelt in Judah, rejoiced.

26 So there was great joy in Jerusalem: for since the time of Solomon the son of David king of Israel *there was* not the like in Jerusalem.

27 ¶ Then the priests the Levites arose and [a]blessed the people: and their voice was heard, and their prayer came *up* to his holy dwelling place, *even* unto heaven.

CHAPTER 31

The faithful Israelites overthrow false worship among them—The people pay tithes and offerings—The Levites administer in temporal matters—Hezekiah serves faithfully.

NOW when all this was finished, all Israel that were present went out to the cities of Judah, and brake the [a]images in pieces, and cut down the [b]groves, and threw down the [c]high places and the altars out of all Judah and Benjamin, in Ephraim also and Manasseh, until they had utterly destroyed them all. Then all the children of Israel returned, every man to his possession, into their own cities.

2 ¶ And Hezekiah appointed the [a]courses of the priests and the Levites after their courses, every man according to his service, the priests and Levites for burnt offerings and for peace offerings, to minister, and to give thanks, and to praise in the gates of the [b]tents of the LORD.

3 *He appointed* also the king's portion of his substance for the burnt offerings, *to wit,* for the morning and evening burnt [a]offerings, and the burnt offerings for the [b]sabbaths, and for the [c]new moons, and for the set [d]feasts, as *it is* written in the law of the LORD.

4 Moreover he commanded the people that dwelt in Jerusalem to give the portion of the priests and the Levites, that they might be encouraged in the law of the LORD.

5 ¶ And as soon as the commandment came abroad, the children of Israel brought in abundance the firstfruits of corn, wine, and oil, and honey, and of all the increase of the field; and the [a]tithe of all *things* brought they in abundantly.

6 And *concerning* the children of Israel and Judah, that dwelt in the cities of Judah, they also brought in the tithe of oxen and sheep, and the tithe of holy things which were consecrated unto the LORD their God, and laid *them* by heaps.

7 In the third month they began to lay the foundation of the heaps, and finished *them* in the seventh month.

8 And when Hezekiah and the princes came and saw the heaps, they blessed the LORD, and his people Israel.

9 Then Hezekiah questioned with the priests and the Levites concerning the heaps.

10 And Azariah the chief priest of the house of Zadok answered him, and said, Since *the people* began to bring the offerings into the house of the LORD, we have had enough to

---

22b Lev. 5:5 (1–6).
24a 2 Chr. 29:34.
27a Num. 6:23 (23–27).
31 1a HEB pillars; i.e.,
    idolatrous symbols.

b HEB Asherahs; i.e.,
    fertility cult objects.
c 2 Chr. 32:12 (5–26).
2a 1 Chr. 23:6.
b HEB camps.

3a Num. 28:3 (3–8).
b Num. 28:10 (9–10).
c Num. 28:11 (11–15).
d Num. 28:17 (16–31).
5a TG Tithing.

eat, and have left plenty: for the LORD hath blessed his people; and that which is left *is* this great store.

11 ¶ Then Hezekiah commanded to prepare *a*chambers in the house of the LORD; and they prepared *them,*

12 And brought in the offerings and the tithes and the dedicated *things* faithfully: over which Cononiah the Levite *was* ruler, and Shimei his brother *was* the next.

13 And Jehiel, and Azaziah, and Nahath, and Asahel, and Jerimoth, and Jozabad, and Eliel, and Ismachiah, and Mahath, and Benaiah, *were* overseers under the hand of Cononiah and Shimei his brother, at the commandment of Hezekiah the king, and Azariah the ruler of the house of God.

14 And Kore the son of Imnah the Levite, the porter toward the east, *was* over the freewill offerings of God, to distribute the *a*oblations of the LORD, and the most holy things.

15 And *a*next him *were* Eden, and Miniamin, and Jeshua, and Shemaiah, Amariah, and Shecaniah, in the *b*cities of the priests, in *their* set office, to give to their brethren by courses, as well to the great as to the small:

16 Beside their genealogy of males, from *a*three years old and upward, *even* unto every one that entereth into the house of the LORD, his daily *b*portion for their service in their charges according to their courses;

17 Both to the genealogy of the priests by the house of their fathers, and the Levites from twenty years old and upward, in their charges by their courses;

18 And to the genealogy of all their little ones, their wives, and their sons, and their daughters, through all the congregation: for in their set office they sanctified themselves in holiness:

19 Also of the sons of Aaron the priests, *which were* in the *a*fields of the *b*suburbs of their cities, in every several city, the men that were expressed by name, to give portions to all the males among the priests, and to all that were reckoned by genealogies among the Levites.

20 ¶ And thus did Hezekiah throughout all Judah, and wrought *that which was* good and right and truth before the LORD his God.

21 And in every work that he began in the service of the house of God, and in the law, and in the commandments, to seek his God, he did *it* with all his heart, and prospered.

CHAPTER 32

Sennacherib invades Judah and besieges the cities—He rails against the Lord—Isaiah and Hezekiah pray, and an angel destroys the leaders of the Assyrian armies—Hezekiah reigns in righteousness despite some pride in his heart.

AFTER these things, and the establishment thereof, Sennacherib king of Assyria came, and entered into Judah, and encamped against the fenced cities, and thought to win them for himself.

2 And when Hezekiah saw that Sennacherib was come, and that he was purposed to fight against Jerusalem,

3 He took counsel with his princes and his mighty men to stop the waters of the fountains which *were* without the city: and they did help him.

4 So there was gathered much people together, who stopped all the fountains, and the brook that ran through the midst of the land, saying, Why should the kings of Assyria come, and find much water?

5 Also he strengthened himself, and built up all the *a*wall that was broken, and raised *it* up to the towers, and another wall without, and repaired *b*Millo *in* the city of David,

---

11*a* IE storerooms.
14*a* OR contributions.
15*a* OR assisting him.
  b Josh. 21:9 (9–19).
16*a* IE probably thirty (see

1 Chr. 23:3).
  b Dan. 1:5.
19*a* Lev. 25:34 (32–34).
  b OR open land.
32 5*a* 2 Chr. 25:23.

  b 2 Sam. 5:9;
   1 Kgs. 9:15 (15, 24);
   11:27;
   2 Kgs. 12:20.

and made ᶜdarts and shields in abundance.

6 And he set captains of war over the people, and gathered them together to him in the street of the gate of the city, and spake comfortably to them, saying,

7 Be strong and courageous, be not afraid nor dismayed for the king of Assyria, nor for all the multitude that *is* with him: for *there be* more with us than with him:

8 With him *is* an arm of ᵃflesh; but with us *is* the LORD our God to help us, and to fight our battles. And the people ᵇrested themselves upon the words of Hezekiah king of Judah.

9 ¶ After this did Sennacherib king of Assyria ᵃsend his servants to Jerusalem, (but he *himself laid siege* against Lachish, and all his power with him,) unto Hezekiah king of Judah, and unto all Judah that *were* at Jerusalem, saying,

10 Thus saith Sennacherib king of Assyria, Whereon do ye trust, that ye abide in the siege in Jerusalem?

11 Doth not Hezekiah persuade you to give over yourselves to die by famine and by thirst, saying, The LORD our God shall deliver us out of the hand of the king of Assyria?

12 Hath not the same Hezekiah taken away his ᵃhigh places and his altars, and commanded Judah and Jerusalem, saying, Ye shall worship before one altar, and burn incense upon it?

13 Know ye not what I and my fathers have done unto all the people of *other* lands? were the gods of the nations of those lands any ways able to deliver their lands out of mine hand?

14 Who *was there* among all the gods of those nations that my fathers utterly destroyed, that could deliver his people out of mine hand, that your God should be able to deliver you out of mine hand?

15 Now therefore let not Hezekiah deceive you, nor persuade you on this manner, neither yet believe him: for no god of any nation or kingdom was able to deliver his people out of mine hand, and out of the hand of my fathers: how much less shall your God deliver you out of mine hand?

16 And his servants spake yet *more* against the LORD God, and against his servant Hezekiah.

17 He wrote also letters to rail on the LORD God of Israel, and to speak against him, saying, As the gods of the nations of *other* lands have not delivered their people out of mine hand, so shall not the God of Hezekiah deliver his people out of mine hand.

18 Then they cried with a loud voice in the Jews' ᵃspeech unto the people of Jerusalem that *were* on the wall, to affright them, and to trouble them; that they might take the city.

19 And they spake against the God of Jerusalem, as against the gods of the people of the earth, *which were* the work of the hands of man.

20 And for this *cause* Hezekiah the king, and the prophet Isaiah the son of Amoz, prayed and cried to heaven.

21 ¶ And the LORD sent an ᵃangel, which cut off all the mighty men of valour, and the leaders and captains in the camp of the king of Assyria. So he returned with shame of face to his own land. And when he was come into the house of his god, they that came forth of his own bowels slew him there with the sword.

22 Thus the LORD saved Hezekiah and the inhabitants of Jerusalem from the hand of Sennacherib the king of Assyria, and from the hand of all *other*, and guided them on every side.

23 And many brought gifts unto the LORD to Jerusalem, and presents to Hezekiah king of Judah: so that he was magnified in the sight of all nations from thenceforth.

5c OR weapons.
8a TG Trust Not in the Arm of Flesh.

b OR relied upon.
9a 2 Kgs. 18:17 (17–19, 37).
12a 2 Chr. 31:1.

18a 2 Kgs. 18:28 (28–35).
21a 2 Kgs. 19:35 (35–37).

24 ¶ In those days Hezekiah was sick to the death, and prayed unto the LORD: and he spake unto him, and he gave him a *a*sign.

25 But Hezekiah rendered not again according to the benefit *done* unto him; for his heart was lifted up: therefore there was wrath upon him, and upon Judah and Jerusalem.

26 Notwithstanding Hezekiah humbled himself for the pride of his heart, *both* he and the inhabitants of Jerusalem, so that the wrath of the LORD came not upon them in the days of Hezekiah.

27 ¶ And Hezekiah had exceeding much riches and honour: and he made himself treasuries for silver, and for gold, and for precious stones, and for spices, and for shields, and for all manner of *a*pleasant jewels;

28 Storehouses also for the increase of *a*corn, and wine, and oil; and stalls for all manner of beasts, and cotes for flocks.

29 Moreover he provided him cities, and possessions of flocks and herds in abundance: for God had given him substance very much.

30 This same Hezekiah also stopped the upper *a*watercourse of *b*Gihon, and brought it straight down to the west side of the city of David. And Hezekiah prospered in all his works.

31 ¶ Howbeit in *the business of* the ambassadors of the princes of Babylon, who sent unto him to inquire of the wonder that was *done* in the land, God left him, to *a*try him, that he might know all *that was* in his heart.

32 ¶ Now the rest of the acts of *a*Hezekiah, and his goodness, behold, they *are* written in the vision of Isaiah the prophet, the son of Amoz, *and* in the book of the kings of Judah and Israel.

33 And Hezekiah slept with his fathers, and they buried him in the chiefest of the sepulchres of the sons of David: and all Judah and the inhabitants of Jerusalem did him honour at his death. And Manasseh his son reigned in his stead.

CHAPTER 33

Manasseh reigns in wickedness and worships false gods—He is taken captive into Assyria—He repents and serves the Lord—Amon reigns in unrighteousness and is slain.

*a*MANASSEH *was* twelve years old when he began to reign, and he reigned fifty and five years in Jerusalem:

2 But did *that which was* evil in the sight of the LORD, like unto the abominations of the heathen, whom the LORD had cast out before the children of Israel.

3 ¶ For he built again the *a*high places which Hezekiah his father had broken down, and he reared up altars for *b*Baalim, and made *c*groves, and worshipped all the host of heaven, and served them.

4 Also he built altars in the house of the LORD, whereof the LORD had said, In Jerusalem shall my name be for ever.

5 And he built altars for all the host of heaven in the two courts of the house of the LORD.

6 And he caused his children to pass through the *a*fire in the valley of the son of Hinnom: also he *b*observed times, and used enchantments, and used *c*witchcraft, and *d*dealt with a *e*familiar spirit, and with wizards: he wrought much evil in the sight of the LORD, to provoke him to anger.

7 And he set a carved image, the idol which he had made, in the house of God, of which God had said to

---

24*a* 2 Kgs. 20:10 (8–11).
27*a* HEB desirable articles.
28*a* OR grain.
30*a* 2 Kgs. 20:20 (20–21).
  b 1 Kgs. 1:33.
31*a* Deut. 8:2 (2–6).
32*a* Isa. 38:1 (1–22).

33 1*a* 2 Kgs. 21:1 (1–9).
  3*a* 2 Chr. 34:3 (3–7).
  b Jer. 9:14.
  c HEB *asheroth*—fertility worship symbols.
  6*a* 2 Kgs. 21:6; 2 Chr. 28:3; Ezek. 20:26.

  b IE practiced soothsaying.
  c Deut. 18:12 (10–14).
  d IE practiced spiritualism.
  e TG Spirits, Evil or Unclean.

David and to Solomon his son, In this house, and in Jerusalem, which I have chosen before all the tribes of Israel, will I put my name for ever:

8 Neither will I any more remove the foot of Israel from out of the land which I have appointed for your fathers; so that they will take heed to do all that I have commanded them, according to the whole law and the statutes and the ordinances by the hand of Moses.

9 So Manasseh made Judah and the inhabitants of Jerusalem to err, *and* to do ^aworse than the ^bheathen, whom the LORD had destroyed before the children of Israel.

10 And the LORD spake to Manasseh, and to his people: but they would not ^ahearken.

11 ¶ Wherefore the LORD brought upon them the captains of the host of the king of Assyria, which took Manasseh ^aamong the thorns, and bound him with fetters, and carried him to Babylon.

12 And when he was in ^aaffliction, he ^bbesought the LORD his God, and ^chumbled himself greatly before the God of his fathers,

13 And prayed unto him: and he was ^aentreated of him, and heard his supplication, and brought him again to Jerusalem into his kingdom. Then ^bManasseh knew that the LORD he *was* God.

14 Now after this he built a wall without the city of David, on the west side of Gihon, in the valley, even to the entering in at the fish ^agate, and compassed about Ophel, and raised it up a very great height, and put captains of war in all the ^bfenced cities of Judah.

15 And he took away the strange gods, and the idol out of the house of the LORD, and all the altars that he had built in the mount of the house of the LORD, and in Jerusalem, and cast *them* out of the city.

16 And he repaired the altar of the LORD, and sacrificed thereon peace offerings and thank offerings, and commanded Judah to serve the LORD God of Israel.

17 Nevertheless the people did sacrifice still in the high places, *yet* unto the LORD their God only.

18 ¶ Now the rest of the acts of ^aManasseh, and his prayer unto his God, and the words of the ^bseers that spake to him in the name of the LORD God of Israel, behold, they *are written* in the book of the kings of Israel.

19 His prayer also, and *how God* was entreated of him, and all his sin, and his trespass, and the places wherein he built high places, and set up groves and graven images, before he was humbled: behold, they *are* written among the ^asayings of the seers.

20 ¶ So Manasseh slept with his fathers, and they buried him in his own house: and Amon his son reigned in his stead.

21 ¶ ^aAmon *was* two and twenty years old when he began to reign, and reigned two years in Jerusalem.

22 But he did *that which was* evil in the sight of the LORD, as did Manasseh his father: for Amon sacrificed unto all the carved images which Manasseh his father had made, and served them;

23 And humbled not himself before the LORD, as Manasseh his father had humbled himself; but Amon trespassed more and more.

24 And his servants conspired against him, and slew him in his own house.

25 ¶ But the people of the land slew all them that had conspired against king Amon; and the people of the land made Josiah his son king in his stead.

9a Alma 24:30.
  b TG Heathen.
10a Alma 5:37; 10:6 (5–6).
11a HEB with hooks.
12a TG Affliction.

b D&C 101:8 (7–9).
c Alma 32:12 (6, 12–16).
13a Gen. 25:21.
  b Hel. 12:3 (2–3).
14a Zeph. 1:10.

b OR fortified.
18a 2 Kgs. 21:17.
  b TG Seer.
19a TG Scriptures, Lost.
21a 2 Kgs. 21:19 (19–24).

CHAPTER 34

*Josiah destroys idolatry in Judah—
The people of Judah repair the house
of the Lord—Hilkiah finds a book of
the law—Huldah the prophetess reveals
the desolations to come upon the people—Josiah and the people covenant to
serve the Lord.*

^aJOSIAH *was* eight years old when he began to reign, and he reigned in Jerusalem one and thirty years.

2 And he did *that which was* right in the sight of the LORD, and walked in the ways of David his father, and declined *neither* to the right hand, nor to the left.

3 ¶ For in the eighth year of his reign, while he was yet young, he began to ^aseek after the God of David his father: and in the twelfth year he began to ^bpurge Judah and Jerusalem from the high places, and the groves, and the carved images, and the molten images.

4 And they brake down the altars of Baalim in his presence; and the ^aimages, that *were* on high above them, he cut down; and the groves, and the carved images, and the molten images, he brake in pieces, and made dust *of them,* and strowed *it* upon the graves of them that had sacrificed unto them.

5 And he ^aburnt the bones of the priests upon their altars, and cleansed Judah and Jerusalem.

6 And *so did he* in the cities of Manasseh, and Ephraim, and Simeon, even unto Naphtali, with their mattocks round about.

7 And when he had broken down the altars and the groves, and had beaten the graven images into powder, and cut down all the idols throughout all the land of Israel, he returned to Jerusalem.

8 ¶ Now in the eighteenth year of his reign, when he had purged the land, and the house, he sent ^aShaphan the son of Azaliah, and

Maaseiah the governor of the city, and Joah the son of Joahaz the recorder, to repair the house of the LORD his God.

9 And when they came to Hilkiah the high priest, they delivered the money that was brought into the house of God, which the Levites that kept the doors had gathered of the hand of Manasseh and Ephraim, and of all the remnant of Israel, and of all Judah and Benjamin; and they returned to Jerusalem.

10 And they put *it* in the hand of the workmen that had the oversight of the house of the LORD, and they gave it to the workmen that wrought in the house of the LORD, to repair and amend the house:

11 Even to the artificers and builders gave they *it,* to buy hewn stone, and timber for couplings, and to floor the houses which the kings of Judah had destroyed.

12 And the men did the work faithfully: and the overseers of them *were* Jahath and Obadiah, the Levites, of the sons of Merari; and Zechariah and Meshullam, of the sons of the Kohathites, to set *it* forward; and *other of* the Levites, all that could skill of instruments of musick.

13 Also *they were* over the bearers of burdens, and *were* overseers of all that wrought the work in any manner of service: and of the Levites *there were* ^ascribes, and officers, and porters.

14 ¶ And when they brought out the money that was brought into the house of the LORD, Hilkiah the priest found a book of the law of the LORD *given* by Moses.

15 And Hilkiah answered and said to Shaphan the scribe, I have found the ^abook of the law in the house of the LORD. And Hilkiah delivered the book to Shaphan.

16 And Shaphan carried the book to the king, and brought the king

---

34 1*a* 2 Kgs. 22:1 (1–20).
   3*a* D&C 88:63 (63–67).
    b 2 Chr. 33:3 (3–22).
   4*a* OR sun images.

      2 Kgs. 23:6.
   5*a* 1 Kgs. 13:2;
      2 Kgs. 23:20.
   8*a* Jer. 26:24.

  13*a* TG Scribe.
  15*a* TG Scriptures,
      Preservation of.

word back again, saying, All that was committed to thy servants, they do *it.*

17 And they have gathered together the money that was found in the house of the LORD, and have delivered it into the hand of the overseers, and to the hand of the workmen.

18 Then Shaphan the scribe told the king, saying, Hilkiah the priest hath given me a book. And Shaphan read it before the king.

19 And it came to pass, when the king had heard the words of the law, that he rent his clothes.

20 And the king commanded Hilkiah, and Ahikam the son of Shaphan, and Abdon the son of Micah, and Shaphan the scribe, and Asaiah a servant of the king's, saying,

21 Go, inquire of the LORD for me, and for them that are left in Israel and in Judah, concerning the words of the book that is found: for great *is* the wrath of the LORD that is poured out upon us, because our fathers have not kept the word of the LORD, to do after all that is written in this *ª*book.

22 And Hilkiah, and *they* that the king *had appointed,* went to Huldah the prophetess, the wife of Shallum the son of Tikvath, the son of Hasrah, keeper of the wardrobe; (now she dwelt in Jerusalem in the *ª*college:) and they spake to her to that *effect.*

23 ¶ And she answered them, Thus saith the LORD God of Israel, Tell ye the man that sent you to me,

24 Thus saith the LORD, Behold, I will bring evil upon this place, and upon the inhabitants thereof, *even* all the *ª*curses that are written in the *b*book which they have read before the king of Judah:

25 Because they have forsaken me, and have burned incense unto other gods, that they might provoke me to anger with all the works of their hands; therefore my wrath shall be poured out upon this place, and shall not be quenched.

26 And as for the king of Judah, who sent you to inquire of the LORD, so shall ye say unto him, Thus saith the LORD God of Israel *concerning* the words which thou hast heard;

27 Because thine heart was tender, and thou didst humble thyself before God, when thou heardest his words against this place, and against the inhabitants thereof, and humbledst thyself before me, and didst rend thy clothes, and weep before me; I have even heard *thee* also, saith the LORD.

28 Behold, I will gather thee to thy fathers, and thou shalt be gathered to thy grave in peace, neither shall thine eyes see all the evil that I will bring upon this place, and upon the inhabitants of the same. So they brought the king word again.

29 ¶ Then the king sent and gathered together all the elders of Judah and Jerusalem.

30 And the king went up into the house of the LORD, and all the men of Judah, and the inhabitants of Jerusalem, and the priests, and the Levites, and all the people, great and small: and he *ª*read in their ears all the words of the book of the covenant that was found in the house of the LORD.

31 And the king stood in his place, and made a *ª*covenant before the LORD, to *b*walk after the LORD, and to keep his commandments, and his testimonies, and his statutes, with all his heart, and with all his soul, to perform the words of the covenant which are written in this book.

32 And he caused all that were present in Jerusalem and Benjamin to stand *to it.* And the inhabitants of Jerusalem did according to the covenant of God, the God of their fathers.

33 And Josiah took away all the

21*a* Deut. 6:6 (6–8);
   1 Ne. 15:24 (23–24);
   Mosiah 1:5.
22*a* HEB second section.
24*a* TG Curse.
  b 2 Kgs. 22:16 (8–20).
30*a* Mosiah 2:1 (1–41).
31*a* TG Covenants.
  b TG Walking with God.

abominations out of all the countries that *pertained* to the children of Israel, and made all that were present in Israel to serve, *even* to serve the LORD their God. *And* all his days they departed not from following the LORD, the God of their fathers.

CHAPTER 35

Josiah and all Judah keep a most solemn Passover—Josiah is mortally wounded by the Egyptians at Megiddo.

MOREOVER Josiah kept a *ª*passover unto the LORD in Jerusalem: and they killed the passover on the *ᵇ*fourteenth *day* of the first month.

2 And he set the priests in their charges, and encouraged them to the service of the house of the LORD,

3 And said unto the Levites that *ª*taught all Israel, which were holy unto the LORD, Put the holy ark in the house which Solomon the son of David king of Israel did build; *it shall* not *be* a burden upon *your* shoulders: serve now the LORD your God, and his people Israel,

4 And prepare *yourselves* by the *ª*houses of your fathers, after your courses, *ᵇ*according to the *ᶜ*writing of David king of Israel, and according to the writing of Solomon his son.

5 And *ª*stand in the holy *place* according to the divisions of the families of the fathers of your brethren the people, and *after* the division of the families of the Levites.

6 So kill the passover, and *ª*sanctify yourselves, and *ᵇ*prepare your brethren, that *they* may do according to the word of the LORD by the hand of Moses.

7 And Josiah gave to the people, of the flock, lambs and kids, all for the passover offerings, for all that were present, to the number of thirty thousand, and three thousand

bullocks: these *were* of the king's substance.

8 And his princes gave willingly unto the people, to the priests, and to the Levites: Hilkiah and Zechariah and Jehiel, rulers of the house of God, gave unto the priests for the passover offerings two thousand and six hundred *small cattle,* and three hundred oxen.

9 Conaniah also, and Shemaiah and Nethaneel, his brethren, and Hashabiah and Jeiel and Jozabad, chief of the Levites, gave unto the Levites for passover offerings five thousand *small cattle,* and five hundred oxen.

10 So the service was prepared, and the priests stood in their place, and the Levites in their courses, according to the king's commandment.

11 And they killed the passover, and the *ª*priests sprinkled *the* *ᵇ*blood from their hands, and the Levites *ᶜ*flayed *them.*

12 And they removed the burnt offerings, that they might give according to the divisions of the families of the people, to offer unto the LORD, as *it is* written in the book of Moses. And so *did they* with the oxen.

13 And they roasted the passover with fire according to the ordinance: but the *other* holy *offerings* *ª*sod they in pots, and in caldrons, and in pans, and divided *them* speedily among all the people.

14 And afterward they made ready for themselves, and for the priests: because the priests the sons of Aaron *were busied* in offering of burnt offerings and the fat until night; therefore the Levites prepared for themselves, and for the priests the sons of Aaron.

15 And the singers the sons of Asaph *were* in their place, according to the commandment of David, and Asaph, and Heman, and Jeduthun the king's *ª*seer; and the porters

35 1*a* 2 Kgs. 23:21 (21–23).
   b Ex. 12:6 (3–17).
  3*a* Deut. 33:10 (8–11).
  4*a* 1 Chr. 26:1 (1–32).
   b 1 Chr. 23:6 (1–32);
     24:1 (1–31).
   c 2 Chr. 8:14 (14–16).

  5*a* D&C 45:32; 87:8;
     101:22 (21–22).
  6*a* 2 Chr. 29:5 (3–11);
     D&C 88:74; 133:62.
   b Alma 4:19; 16:16;
     D&C 108:7.
 11*a* TG Priest, Aaronic

     Priesthood.
     BD Priests.
   b Ex. 12:22 (21–22).
   c OR skinned.
 13*a* IE boiled.
 15*a* TG Seer.

waited at every gate; they might not depart from their service; for their brethren the Levites prepared for them.

16 So all the service of the LORD was prepared the same day, to keep the passover, and to offer burnt offerings upon the altar of the LORD, according to the commandment of king Josiah.

17 And the children of Israel that were present kept the passover at that time, and the feast of unleavened bread seven days.

18 And there was no *a*passover like to that kept in Israel from the days of Samuel the prophet; neither did all the kings of Israel keep such a passover as Josiah kept, and the priests, and the Levites, and all Judah and Israel that were present, and the inhabitants of Jerusalem.

19 In the eighteenth year of the reign of Josiah was this passover kept.

20 ¶ After all this, when Josiah had prepared the temple, Necho king of Egypt came up to fight against Carchemish by Euphrates: and Josiah went out against him.

21 But he sent ambassadors to him, saying, What have I to do with thee, thou king of Judah? *I come* not against thee this day, but against the house wherewith I have war: for God commanded me to make haste: forbear thee from *meddling with* God, who *is* with me, that he destroy thee not.

22 Nevertheless *a*Josiah would not turn his face from him, but disguised himself, that he might fight with him, and hearkened not unto the words of Necho from the mouth of God, and came to fight in the valley of Megiddo.

23 And the archers shot at king Josiah; and the king said to his servants, Have me away; for I am sore wounded.

24 His servants therefore took him out of that chariot, and put him in the second chariot that he had; and they brought him to Jerusalem, and he died, and was buried in *one of* the sepulchres of his fathers. And all Judah and Jerusalem mourned for Josiah.

25 ¶ And Jeremiah *a*lamented for Josiah: and all the singing men and the singing women spake of Josiah in their lamentations to this day, and made them an ordinance in Israel: and, behold, they *are* written in the lamentations.

26 Now the rest of the acts of Josiah, and his goodness, according to *that which was* written in the law of the LORD,

27 And his deeds, first and last, behold, they *are* written in the book of the kings of Israel and Judah.

CHAPTER 36

Various kings rule in Judah—Nebuchadnezzar overruns Judah and makes Zedekiah king—Zedekiah rebels, the people reject the prophets, and the Chaldeans burn the temple and destroy Jerusalem—Cyrus of Persia decrees the building of the temple.

THEN the people of the land took *a*Jehoahaz the son of Josiah, and made him *b*king in his father's stead in Jerusalem.

2 Jehoahaz *was* twenty and three years old when he began to reign, and he reigned three months in Jerusalem.

3 And the king of Egypt *a*put him down at Jerusalem, and *b*condemned the land in an hundred talents of silver and a talent of gold.

4 And the king of Egypt made Eliakim his brother king over Judah and Jerusalem, and turned his name to Jehoiakim. And Necho took Jehoahaz his brother, and carried him to *a*Egypt.

5 ¶ *a*Jehoiakim *was* twenty and five years old when he began to reign, and he reigned eleven years in

---

18*a* 2 Kgs. 23:22.
22*a* 2 Kgs. 23:29.
25*a* Lam. 4:20.

36 1*a* 2 Kgs. 23:30 (28–30).
  b Ezek. 19:3.
3*a* OR deposed him.

b HEB fined.
4*a* Ezek. 19:4.
5*a* 2 Kgs. 23:34 (34, 36).

Jerusalem: and he did *that which was* evil in the sight of the LORD his God.

6 Against him came up ᵃNebuchadnezzar king of Babylon, and bound him in ᵇfetters, to carry him to Babylon.

7 Nebuchadnezzar also carried of the ᵃvessels of the house of the LORD to Babylon, and put them in his temple at Babylon.

8 Now the rest of the acts of ᵃJehoiakim, and his abominations which he did, and that which was found in him, behold, they *are* written in the book of the kings of Israel and Judah: and ᵇJehoiachin his son reigned in his stead.

9 ¶ Jehoiachin *was* ᵃeight years old when he began to reign, and he reigned three months and ten days in Jerusalem: and he did *that which was* evil in the sight of the LORD.

10 And when the year was expired, king Nebuchadnezzar sent, and brought him to ᵃBabylon, with the goodly vessels of the house of the LORD, and made ᵇZedekiah his brother king over Judah and Jerusalem.

11 ¶ ᵃZedekiah *was* one and twenty years old when he began to reign, and reigned eleven years in Jerusalem.

12 And he did *that which was* ᵃevil in the sight of the LORD his God, *and* humbled not himself before ᵇJeremiah the prophet *speaking* from the mouth of the LORD.

13 And he also ᵃrebelled against king Nebuchadnezzar, who had made him ᵇswear by God: but he ᶜstiffened his neck, and ᵈhardened his heart from turning unto the LORD God of Israel.

14 ¶ Moreover all the chief of the priests, and the people, transgressed very much after all the ᵃabominations of the heathen; and polluted the house of the LORD which he had hallowed in Jerusalem.

15 And the LORD God of their fathers ᵃsent to them by his ᵇmessengers, rising up ᶜbetimes, and sending; because he had compassion on his people, and on his dwelling place:

16 But they ᵃmocked the messengers of God, and despised his words, and misused his ᵇprophets, until the wrath of the LORD arose against his people, till *there was* no remedy.

17 Therefore he brought upon them the king of the Chaldees, who ᵃslew their young men with the sword in the house of their sanctuary, and had no compassion upon young man or maiden, old man, or him that stooped for age: he gave *them* all into his hand.

18 And all the vessels of the house of God, great and small, and the treasures of the house of the LORD, and the treasures of the king, and of his princes; all *these* he brought to Babylon.

19 And they burnt the house of God, and brake down the wall of ᵃJerusalem, and burnt all the palaces thereof with fire, and destroyed all the goodly vessels thereof.

20 And them that had escaped from the sword carried he away to ᵃBabylon; where they were servants to him and his sons until the reign of the kingdom of Persia:

21 To fulfil the word of the LORD by

6a 2 Kgs. 24:1 (1–16);
    Dan. 1:1 (1–2).
  b Ezek. 19:9.
7a 2 Kgs. 24:13.
8a 2 Kgs. 24:5.
  b OR Jeconiah (see
    1 Chr. 3:16) or
    Coniah (see Jer. 22:24).
9a OR eighteen; see
    2 Kgs. 24:8, 15.
10a TG Israel, Bondage of, in
    Other Lands.
  b 2 Kgs. 24:17;

    Jer. 52:1 (1–2);
    1 Ne. 1:4; Omni 1:15.
11a Jer. 37:1.
12a Ezek. 21:25.
  b Jer. 21:1 (1–7).
13a 2 Kgs. 24:20;
    Jer. 52:3; Ezek. 17:15.
  b Ezek. 17:13.
  c TG Stiffnecked.
  d TG Hardheartedness.
14a 1 Ne. 1:13 (13, 19).
15a Jer. 44:4 (4–5);
    D&C 133:71.

  b 1 Ne. 1:4 (4, 18).
    TG Prophets, Mission of.
  c HEB early, promptly.
16a Dan. 9:6.
    TG Apostasy of Israel;
    Mocking; Persecution;
    Prophets, Rejection of.
  b Hel. 13:24 (24–30).
17a Lam. 2:21.
19a TG Jerusalem.
20a Ezek. 19:12.
    TG Israel, Bondage of, in
    Other Lands.

the mouth of Jeremiah, until the land had enjoyed her sabbaths: *for as long as she lay desolate she kept* [a]sabbath, to fulfil [b]threescore and ten years.

22 ¶ Now in the first year of Cyrus king of Persia, that the word of the LORD *spoken* by the mouth of Jeremiah might be accomplished, the LORD stirred up the spirit of Cyrus king of Persia, that he made a proclamation throughout all his kingdom, and *put it* also in writing, saying,

23 Thus saith Cyrus king of Persia, All the kingdoms of the earth hath the LORD God of heaven given me; and he hath charged me to build him an [a]house in Jerusalem, which *is* in Judah. Who *is there* among you of all his people? The LORD his God *be* with him, and let him go up.

EZRA

CHAPTER 1

King Cyrus of Persia lets the Jews go back to Jerusalem to build the temple— Cyrus returns the vessels of the house of the Lord taken by Nebuchadnezzar.

NOW in the first year of Cyrus king of Persia, that the word of the LORD by the mouth of [a]Jeremiah might be fulfilled, the LORD stirred up the spirit of [b]Cyrus king of Persia, that he made a proclamation throughout all his kingdom, and *put it* also in writing, saying,

2 Thus saith [a]Cyrus king of Persia, The LORD God of heaven hath given me all the kingdoms of the earth; and he hath charged me to build him an [b]house at Jerusalem, which *is* in Judah.

3 Who *is there* among you of all his people? his God be with him, and let him go up to Jerusalem, which *is* in Judah, and build the house of the LORD God of Israel, (he *is* the God,) which *is* in Jerusalem.

4 And whosoever remaineth in any place where he sojourneth, let the men of his place help him with silver, and with gold, and with goods, and with beasts, beside the freewill offering for the house of God that *is* in Jerusalem.

5 ¶ Then rose up the chief of the fathers of Judah and Benjamin, and the priests, and the Levites, with all *them* whose spirit God had raised, to go up to build the house of the LORD which *is* in Jerusalem.

6 And all they that *were* about them [a]strengthened their hands with vessels of silver, with gold, with goods, and with beasts, and with precious things, beside all *that* was willingly offered.

7 ¶ Also Cyrus the king brought forth the vessels of the house of the LORD, which Nebuchadnezzar had [a]brought forth out of Jerusalem, and had put them in the house of his gods;

8 Even those did Cyrus king of Persia bring forth by the hand of Mithredath the treasurer, and numbered them unto Sheshbazzar, the prince of Judah.

9 And this *is* the number of them:

21a TG Sabbatical Year.
  b Jer. 25:12;
    Dan. 9:2.
23a Ezra 1:2 (1–3);
    Isa. 44:28.

[EZRA]
1 1a 1 Ne. 5:13; 7:14;
    Hel. 8:20.
  b Dan. 6:28.

2a Ezra 3:7.
  b 2 Chr. 36:23 (22–23);
    Isa. 44:28.
6a IE assisted them.
7a Jer. 27:22.

thirty [a]chargers of gold, a thousand chargers of silver, nine and twenty knives,

10 Thirty basins of gold, silver basins of a second *sort* four hundred and ten, *and* other vessels a thousand.

11 All the vessels of gold and of silver *were* five thousand and four hundred. All *these* did Sheshbazzar bring up with *them of* the [a]captivity that were brought up from Babylon unto Jerusalem.

CHAPTER 2

The descendants of the Jews taken captive who return to Jerusalem and to Judah are listed—The children of priests whose genealogy is lost are denied the priesthood—Faithful people contribute to the building of the temple.

Now these *are* the [a]children of the province that went up out of the captivity, of those which had been carried away, whom Nebuchadnezzar the king of Babylon had carried away unto [b]Babylon, and came again unto Jerusalem and Judah, every one unto his city;

2 [a]Which came with [b]Zerubbabel: Jeshua, Nehemiah, Seraiah, Reelaiah, Mordecai, Bilshan, Mispar, Bigvai, Rehum, Baanah. The number of the men of the people of Israel:

3 The children of Parosh, two thousand an hundred seventy and two.

4 The children of Shephatiah, three hundred seventy and two.

5 The children of Arah, seven hundred seventy and five.

6 The children of Pahath-moab, of the children of Jeshua *and* Joab, two thousand eight hundred and twelve.

7 The children of Elam, a thousand two hundred fifty and four.

8 The children of Zattu, nine hundred forty and five.

9 The children of Zaccai, seven hundred and threescore.

10 The children of [a]Bani, six hundred forty and two.

11 The children of Bebai, six hundred twenty and three.

12 The children of Azgad, a thousand two hundred twenty and two.

13 The children of Adonikam, six hundred sixty and six.

14 The children of Bigvai, two thousand fifty and six.

15 The children of Adin, four hundred fifty and four.

16 The children of Ater of Hezekiah, ninety and eight.

17 The children of Bezai, three hundred twenty and three.

18 The children of Jorah, an hundred and twelve.

19 The children of Hashum, two hundred twenty and three.

20 The children of Gibbar, ninety and five.

21 The children of Beth-lehem, an hundred twenty and three.

22 The men of Netophah, fifty and six.

23 The men of Anathoth, an hundred twenty and eight.

24 The children of Azmaveth, forty and two.

25 The children of Kirjath-arim, Chephirah, and Beeroth, seven hundred and forty and three.

26 The children of Ramah and Gaba, six hundred twenty and one.

27 The men of Michmas, an hundred twenty and two.

28 The men of Beth-el and Ai, two hundred twenty and three.

29 The children of Nebo, fifty and two.

30 The children of Magbish, an hundred fifty and six.

31 The children of the other Elam, a thousand two hundred fifty and four.

32 The children of Harim, three hundred and twenty.

33 The children of Lod, Hadid, and Ono, seven hundred twenty and five.

9*a* OR basins.
11*a* OR exiles.
2 1*a* Neh. 7:6 (6–73); 12:1.
   b 1 Ne. 1:13; 10:3;

Omni 1:15.
2*a* Neh. 7:7.
  b 1 Chr. 3:19 (17–19);
    Hag. 1:1;

Matt. 1:12 (11–13).
10*a* Neh. 7:15.

34 The children of Jericho, three hundred forty and five.

35 The children of Senaah, three thousand and six hundred and thirty.

36 ¶ The priests: the children of Jedaiah, of the house of Jeshua, nine hundred seventy and three.

37 The children of Immer, a thousand fifty and two.

38 The children of Pashur, a thousand two hundred forty and seven.

39 The children of Harim, a thousand and seventeen.

40 ¶ The Levites: the children of Jeshua and Kadmiel, of the children of Hodaviah, seventy and four.

41 ¶ The singers: the children of Asaph, an hundred twenty and eight.

42 ¶ The children of the porters: the children of Shallum, the children of Ater, the children of Talmon, the children of Akkub, the children of Hatita, the children of Shobai, *in* all an hundred thirty and nine.

43 ¶ The [a]Nethinims: the children of Ziha, the children of Hasupha, the children of Tabbaoth,

44 The children of Keros, the children of Siaha, the children of Padon,

45 The children of Lebanah, the children of Hagabah, the children of Akkub,

46 The children of Hagab, the children of Shalmai, the children of Hanan,

47 The children of Giddel, the children of Gahar, the children of Reaiah,

48 The children of Rezin, the children of Nekoda, the children of Gazzam,

49 The children of Uzza, the children of Paseah, the children of Besai,

50 The children of Asnah, the children of Mehunim, the children of Nephusim,

51 The children of Bakbuk, the children of Hakupha, the children of Harhur,

52 The children of Bazluth, the children of Mehida, the children of Harsha,

53 The children of Barkos, the children of Sisera, the children of Thamah,

54 The children of Neziah, the children of Hatipha.

55 ¶ The children of Solomon's servants: the children of Sotai, the children of Sophereth, the children of Peruda,

56 The children of Jaalah, the children of Darkon, the children of Giddel,

57 The children of Shephatiah, the children of Hattil, the children of Pochereth of Zebaim, the children of Ami.

58 All the Nethinims, and the children of Solomon's servants, *were* three hundred ninety and two.

59 And these *were* they which went up from Tel-melah, Tel-harsa, Cherub, Addan, *and* Immer: but they could not [a]shew their father's house, and their seed, whether they *were* of Israel:

60 The children of Delaiah, the children of Tobiah, the children of Nekoda, six hundred fifty and two.

61 ¶ And of the [a]children of the priests: the children of Habaiah, the children of Koz, the children of Barzillai; which took a wife of the daughters of Barzillai the Gileadite, and was called after their name:

62 These sought their [a]register *among* those that were [b]reckoned by [c]genealogy, but they were not found: therefore were they, as [d]polluted, [e]put from the [f]priesthood.

63 And the Tirshatha said unto them, that they should not eat of the most [a]holy things, till there stood

---

43a HEB servants of the temple (who attended the Levites in their sacred service).
1 Chr. 9:2;
Ezra 7:24; 8:20.
59a HEB tell, declare (their

lineage).
61a Neh. 7:63 (63–64);
D&C 85:12 (11–12).
62a OR record.
  b HEB they that traced their genealogy.
  c TG Book of Remem-

brance; Genealogy and Temple Work.
  d TG Worthiness.
  e OR excluded.
  f TG Priesthood, Qualifying for.
63a Lev. 22:2 (2, 10, 15–16).

up a priest with [b]Urim and with Thummim.

64 ¶ The whole congregation together *was* forty and two thousand three hundred *and* threescore,

65 Beside their servants and their maids, of whom *there were* seven thousand three hundred thirty and seven: and *there were* among them two hundred singing men and singing women.

66 Their horses *were* seven hundred thirty and six; their mules, two hundred forty and five;

67 Their camels, four hundred thirty and five; *their* asses, six thousand seven hundred and twenty.

68 ¶ And *some* of the chief of the fathers, when they came to the [a]house of the LORD which *is* at Jerusalem, offered freely for the house of God to set it up in his place:

69 They gave after their ability unto the treasure of the work threescore and one thousand drams of gold, and five thousand pound of silver, and one hundred priests' garments.

70 So the priests, and the Levites, and *some* of the people, and the singers, and the porters, and the Nethinims, dwelt in their cities, and all Israel in their cities.

CHAPTER 3

The altar is rebuilt—Regular sacrifices are reinstituted—The foundations of the temple are laid amid great rejoicing.

AND when the seventh month was come, and the children of Israel *were* in the cities, the people gathered themselves together as one man to Jerusalem.

2 Then stood up Jeshua the son of Jozadak, and his brethren the priests, and Zerubbabel the son of Shealtiel, and his brethren, and builded the altar of the God of Israel, to offer burnt [a]offerings thereon,

as *it is* written in the law of Moses the [b]man of God.

3 And they set the altar upon his bases; for fear *was* upon them because of the people of those countries: and they offered burnt offerings thereon unto the LORD, *even* burnt offerings morning and evening.

4 They kept also the [a]feast of tabernacles, as *it is* written, and *offered* the daily burnt offerings by number, according to the custom, as the duty of every day required;

5 And afterward *offered* the continual burnt offering, both of the new moons, and of all the set [a]feasts of the LORD that were consecrated, and of every one that [b]willingly offered a freewill offering unto the LORD.

6 From the first day of the seventh month began they to offer burnt offerings unto the LORD. But the foundation of the temple of the LORD was not *yet* laid.

7 They gave money also unto the masons, and to the carpenters; and meat, and drink, and oil, unto them of Zidon, and to them of Tyre, to bring [a]cedar trees from Lebanon to the sea of Joppa, according to the grant that they had of [b]Cyrus king of Persia.

8 ¶ Now in the second year of their coming unto the house of God at Jerusalem, in the second month, began Zerubbabel the son of Shealtiel, and Jeshua the son of Jozadak, and the remnant of their brethren the priests and the Levites, and all they that were come out of the captivity unto Jerusalem; and appointed the Levites, from twenty years old and upward, to set forward the work of the house of the LORD.

9 Then stood Jeshua *with* his sons and his brethren, Kadmiel and his sons, the sons of Judah, together, to set forward the workmen in the

---

63*b* TG Urim and Thummim.
68*a* Ps. 122:1;
    Mosiah 1:18;
    D&C 88:137.
3 2*a* Deut. 12:6 (5–6);

1 Ne. 5:9;
    Mosiah 2:3.
  b Deut. 33:1.
4*a* Lev. 23:34;
    Zech. 14:16.

5*a* Num. 29:39.
  b Ex. 25:2 (1–7).
7*a* 1 Kgs. 5:6.
  b Ezra 1:2 (2–3); 4:3.

house of God: the sons of Henadad, *with* their sons and their brethren the Levites.

10 And when the builders laid the foundation of the temple of the LORD, they set the priests in their apparel with trumpets, and the Levites the sons of Asaph with cymbals, to praise the LORD, after the ordinance of David king of Israel.

11 And they sang together by course in praising and giving *a*thanks unto the LORD; because *he is* *b*good, for his mercy *endureth* for ever toward Israel. And all the people shouted with a great shout, when they *c*praised the LORD, because the foundation of the house of the LORD was laid.

12 But many of the priests and Levites and chief of the fathers, *who were* *a*ancient men, that had seen the first house, when the foundation of this house was laid before their eyes, *b*wept with a loud voice; and many shouted aloud for joy:

13 So that the people could not discern the noise of the shout of joy from the noise of the weeping of the people: for the people shouted with a loud shout, and the noise was heard afar off.

CHAPTER 4

The Samaritans offer help, then hinder the work—The building of the temple and of the walls of Jerusalem ceases.

Now when the *a*adversaries of Judah and Benjamin heard that the children of the captivity builded the temple unto the LORD God of Israel;

2 Then they came to Zerubbabel, and to the chief of the fathers, and said unto them, Let us build with you: for we seek your God, as ye *do*; and we do sacrifice unto him since the days of Esar-haddon king of Assur, which *a*brought us up hither.

3 But Zerubbabel, and Jeshua, and the rest of the chief of the fathers of Israel, said unto them, Ye have nothing to do with us to build an house unto our God; but we ourselves together will build unto the LORD God of Israel, as *a*king Cyrus the king of Persia hath commanded us.

4 Then the people of the land *a*weakened the hands of the people of Judah, and troubled them in building,

5 And hired counsellors against them, to frustrate their purpose, all the days of Cyrus king of Persia, even until the reign of *a*Darius king of Persia.

6 And in the reign of *a*Ahasuerus, in the beginning of his reign, wrote they *unto him* an accusation against the inhabitants of Judah and Jerusalem.

7 ¶ And in the days of Artaxerxes wrote Bishlam, Mithredath, Tabeel, and the rest of their companions, unto Artaxerxes king of Persia; and the writing of the letter *was* written in the *a*Syrian tongue, and interpreted in the Syrian tongue.

8 Rehum the chancellor and Shimshai the scribe wrote a letter against Jerusalem to Artaxerxes the king in this sort:

9 Then *wrote* Rehum the chancellor, and Shimshai the scribe, and the rest of their companions; the Dinaites, the Apharsathchites, the Tarpelites, the Apharsites, the Archevites, the Babylonians, the Susanchites, the Dehavites, *and* the Elamites,

10 And the rest of the nations whom the great and noble Asnappar brought over, and set in the cities of Samaria, and the rest *that are* *a*on this side the river, and at such a time.

11*a* 1 Chr. 16:41; 2 Chr. 5:13;
  Alma 37:37; D&C 59:7.
  b 1 Chr. 16:34 (34, 41);
  Alma 5:40;
  D&C 50:44.
  c 1 Ne. 18:16; 2 Ne. 9:49;
  Alma 36:28;

  D&C 109:79; 136:28.
12*a* OR old.
  b Hag. 2:3 (3–9).
4 1*a* D&C 123:1 (1–17).
  2*a* 2 Kgs. 17:24.
  3*a* Ezra 3:7.
  4*a* IE discouraged the

  people.
  5*a* Dan. 6:28.
  6*a* Esth. 1:1.
  7*a* HEB Aramaic.
10*a* IE on the west side of
  the Euphrates River
  (also vv. 11, 16).

11 ¶ This *is* the copy of the letter that they sent unto him, *even* unto Artaxerxes the king; Thy servants the men on this side the river, and at such a time.

12 Be it known unto the king, that the Jews which came up from thee to us are come unto Jerusalem, building the rebellious and the bad city, and have set up the walls *thereof,* and joined the foundations.

13 Be it known now unto the king, that, if this city be builded, and the walls set up *again, then* will they not pay toll, tribute, and custom, and *so* thou shalt endamage the revenue of the kings.

14 Now because ^awe have maintenance from *the king's* palace, and it was not meet for us to see the king's dishonour, therefore have we sent and certified the king;

15 That search may be made in the ^abook of the records of thy fathers: so shalt thou find in the ^bbook of the records, and know that this city *is* a rebellious city, and hurtful unto kings and provinces, and that they have moved sedition within the same of old time: for which cause was this city destroyed.

16 We certify the king that, if this city be builded *again,* and the walls thereof set up, by this means thou shalt have no portion on this side the river.

17 ¶ *Then* sent the king an answer unto Rehum the chancellor, and *to* Shimshai the scribe, and *to* the rest of their companions that dwell in Samaria, and *unto* the rest beyond the river, Peace, and at such a time.

18 The letter which ye sent unto us hath been plainly read before me.

19 And I commanded, and search hath been made, and it is found that this city of old time hath made insurrection against kings, and *that* rebellion and sedition have been made therein.

20 There have been mighty kings also over Jerusalem, which have ^aruled over all *countries* beyond the river; and toll, tribute, and custom, was paid unto them.

21 Give ye now commandment to cause these men to ^acease, and that this city be not builded, until *another* commandment shall be given from me.

22 Take heed now that ye fail not to do this: why should damage grow to the hurt of the kings?

23 ¶ Now when the copy of king Artaxerxes' letter *was* read before Rehum, and Shimshai the scribe, and their companions, they went up in haste to Jerusalem unto the Jews, and made them to cease by force and power.

24 Then ceased the work of the house of God which *is* at Jerusalem. So it ceased unto the second year of the reign of Darius king of Persia.

CHAPTER 5

Haggai and Zechariah prophesy—Zerubbabel renews the building of the temple—The Samaritans challenge the Jews' right to continue their building work.

THEN the ^aprophets, ^bHaggai the prophet, and ^cZechariah the son of Iddo, prophesied unto the Jews that *were* in Judah and Jerusalem in the name of the God of Israel, *even* unto them.

2 Then rose up Zerubbabel the son of Shealtiel, and Jeshua the son of Jozadak, and began to build the house of God which *is* at Jerusalem: and with them *were* the prophets of God helping them.

3 ¶ At the same time came to them Tatnai, governor ^aon this side the river, and Shethar-boznai, and their companions, and said thus unto them, Who hath commanded you to build this house, and to make up this wall?

14a IE we are dependent on.
15a TG Record Keeping.
  b TG Scriptures,
      Writing of.
20a Lam. 1:1.

21a D&C 124:49.
5 1a Zech. 8:9.
  b Ezra 6:14.
  c Zech. 1:1.
3a IE on the west side of

the Euphrates River, including Syria and Cilicia.

4 Then said we unto them after this manner, What are the names of the men that make this building?

5 But the eye of their God was upon the elders of the Jews, that they could not cause them to cease, till the matter came to Darius: and then they returned answer by letter concerning this *matter*.

6 ¶ The copy of the letter that Tatnai, governor on this side the river, and Shethar-boznai, and his companions the Apharsachites, which *were* on this side the river, sent unto Darius the king:

7 They sent a letter unto him, wherein was written thus; Unto Darius the king, all peace.

8 Be it known unto the [a]king, that we went into the province of Judea, to the house of the great God, which is builded with great stones, and timber is laid in the walls, and this work goeth fast on, and prospereth in their hands.

9 Then asked we those elders, *and* said unto them thus, Who commanded you to build this house, and to make up these walls?

10 We asked their names also, to certify thee, that we might write the names of the men that *were* the chief of them.

11 And thus they returned us answer, saying, We are the servants of the God of heaven and earth, and build the house that was builded these many years ago, which a great king of Israel builded and set up.

12 But after that our fathers had provoked the God of heaven unto wrath, he gave them into the hand of Nebuchadnezzar the king of Babylon, the Chaldean, who destroyed this house, and carried the people away into Babylon.

13 But in the first year of Cyrus the king of Babylon *the same* king [a]Cyrus made a decree to build this house of God.

14 And the vessels also of gold and silver of the house of God, which Nebuchadnezzar took out of the temple that *was* in Jerusalem, and brought them into the temple of Babylon, those did Cyrus the king take out of the temple of Babylon, and they were delivered unto *one*, whose name *was* Sheshbazzar, whom he had made governor;

15 And said unto him, Take these vessels, go, carry them into the temple that *is* in Jerusalem, and let the house of God be builded in his place.

16 Then came the same Sheshbazzar, *and* laid the foundation of the house of God which *is* in Jerusalem: and since that time even until now hath it been in building, and *yet* it is not finished.

17 Now therefore, if *it seem* good to the king, let there be search made in the king's treasure house, which *is* there at Babylon, whether it be *so*, that a decree was made of Cyrus the king to build this house of God at Jerusalem, and let the king send his pleasure to us concerning this matter.

CHAPTER 6

Darius renews the decree of Cyrus to build the temple—It is finished and dedicated, and sacrifices and feasts commence again.

THEN Darius the king made a decree, and search was made in the house of the [a]rolls, where the treasures were laid up in Babylon.

2 And there was found at Achmetha, in the palace that *is* in the province of the Medes, a [a]roll, and therein *was* a record thus written:

3 In the first year of Cyrus the king *the same* Cyrus the king made a decree *concerning* the house of God at Jerusalem, Let the [a]house be builded, the place where [a]they offered sacrifices, and let the foundations thereof be strongly laid; the height thereof threescore cubits, *and* the breadth thereof threescore cubits;

4 With three rows of great stones, and a row of new timber: and let the expenses be given out of the king's house:

8a D&C 123:6.
13a Ezra 6:14.

6 1a OR books, archives.
2a Jer. 36:2 (2, 4);

Ezek. 2:9.
3a Hag. 1:8.

5 And also let the golden and silver vessels of the house of God, which Nebuchadnezzar took forth out of the temple which *is* at Jerusalem, and brought unto Babylon, be restored, and brought again unto the temple which *is* at Jerusalem, *every one* to his place, and place *them* in the house of God.

6 Now *therefore*, Tatnai, governor ^abeyond the river, Shethar-boznai, and your companions the Apharsachites, which *are* beyond the river, be ye far from thence:

7 Let the work of this house of God alone; let the governor of the Jews and the elders of the Jews build this house of God in his place.

8 Moreover I make a decree what ye shall do to the elders of these Jews for the building of this house of God: that of the king's goods, *even* of the tribute beyond the river, forthwith expenses be given unto these men, that they be not hindered.

9 And that which they have need of, both young bullocks, and rams, and lambs, for the burnt offerings of the God of heaven, wheat, salt, wine, and oil, according to the appointment of the priests which *are* at Jerusalem, let it be given them day by day without fail:

10 That they may offer ^asacrifices of sweet savours unto the God of heaven, and ^bpray for the life of the king, and of his sons.

11 Also I have made a decree, that whosoever shall alter this word, let timber be pulled down from his house, and being set up, let him be hanged thereon; and let his house be made a dunghill for this.

12 And the God that hath caused his name to dwell there destroy all kings and people, that shall put to their hand to alter *and* to destroy this house of God which *is* at Jeru-

salem. I Darius have made a decree; let it be done with speed.

13 ¶ Then Tatnai, governor ^aon this side the river, Shethar-boznai, and their companions, according to that which Darius the king had sent, so they did speedily.

14 And the elders of the Jews builded, and they prospered through the prophesying of ^aHaggai the prophet and Zechariah the son of Iddo. And they builded, and finished *it*, according to the commandment of the God of Israel, and according to the commandment of ^bCyrus, and Darius, and Artaxerxes king of Persia.

15 And this house was finished on the third day of the month ^aAdar, which was in the sixth year of the reign of Darius the king.

16 ¶ And the children of Israel, the priests, and the Levites, and the rest of the children of the captivity, kept the ^adedication of this house of God with joy,

17 And offered at the dedication of this house of God an hundred bullocks, two hundred rams, four hundred lambs; and for a sin offering for all Israel, twelve he goats, according to the number of the tribes of Israel.

18 And they set the ^apriests in their divisions, and the Levites in their ^bcourses, for the ^cservice of God, which *is* at Jerusalem; as it is written in the book of Moses.

19 And the children of the captivity kept the ^apassover upon the ^bfourteenth *day* of the first month.

20 For the priests and the Levites were purified together, all of them *were* pure, and killed the passover for all the children of the captivity, and for their brethren the priests, and for themselves.

21 And the children of Israel, which were come again out of captivity, and all such as had ^aseparated themselves

---

6a IE on the west side of
   the Euphrates River.
10a Mosiah 2:3.
  b Alma 6:6.
13a IE on the west side of
   the Euphrates River.
14a Ezra 5:1.

b Ezra 5:13;
  Dan. 6:28.
15a Esth. 3:7 (7, 13).
16a TG Dedication.
18a D&C 20:46 (46–49).
  b 1 Chr. 23:6;
   2 Chr. 8:14.

c Mosiah 2:17.
19a TG Passover.
  b Ex. 12:6 (3–17).
21a Neh. 10:28 (28–31);
   Alma 5:57;
   D&C 133:5 (5, 14).

unto them from the *b*filthiness of the *c*heathen of the land, to seek the Lord God of Israel, did eat,

22 And kept the feast of unleavened bread seven days with joy: for the Lord had made them joyful, and turned the heart of the king of Assyria unto them, *a*to strengthen their hands in the work of the house of God, the God of Israel.

CHAPTER 7

Ezra goes up to Jerusalem—Artaxerxes provides for beautifying the temple and sustains the Jews in their worship.

Now after these things, in the reign of Artaxerxes king of Persia, Ezra the son of Seraiah, the son of Azariah, the son of *a*Hilkiah,

2 The son of Shallum, the son of Zadok, the son of Ahitub,

3 The son of Amariah, the son of Azariah, the son of Meraioth,

4 The son of Zerahiah, the son of Uzzi, the son of Bukki,

5 The son of Abishua, the son of Phinehas, the son of Eleazar, the son of Aaron the chief priest:

6 This Ezra went up from Babylon; and he *was* a ready *a*scribe in the law of Moses, which the Lord God of Israel had given: and the king granted him all his request, according to the *b*hand of the Lord his God upon him.

7 And there went up *some* of the children of Israel, and of the priests, and the Levites, and the singers, and the porters, and the Nethinims, unto Jerusalem, in the seventh year of Artaxerxes the king.

8 And he came to Jerusalem in the fifth month, which *was* in the seventh year of the king.

9 For upon the first *day* of the first month began he to go up from Babylon, and on the first *day* of the fifth month came he to Jerusalem,

according to the good *a*hand of his God upon him.

10 For Ezra had *a*prepared his *b*heart to seek the law of the Lord, and to do *it*, and to teach in Israel *c*statutes and judgments.

11 ¶ Now this *is* the copy of the letter that the king Artaxerxes gave unto Ezra the priest, the scribe, *even* a *a*scribe of the words of the commandments of the Lord, and of his statutes to Israel.

12 Artaxerxes, king of kings, unto Ezra the priest, a scribe of the law of the God of heaven, perfect *peace*, and at such a time.

13 I make a decree, that all they of the people of Israel, and *of* his priests and Levites, in my realm, which are minded of their own freewill to go up to Jerusalem, go with thee.

14 Forasmuch as thou art sent of the king, and of his seven counsellors, to inquire concerning Judah and Jerusalem, according to the law of thy God which *is* in thine hand;

15 And to carry the silver and gold, which the king and his counsellors have freely offered unto the God of Israel, whose habitation *is* in Jerusalem,

16 And all the silver and gold that thou canst find in all the province of Babylon, with the freewill offering of the people, and of the priests, offering willingly for the house of their God which *is* in Jerusalem:

17 That thou mayest buy speedily with this money bullocks, rams, lambs, with their meat offerings and their drink offerings, and offer them upon the altar of the house of your God which *is* in Jerusalem.

18 And whatsoever shall seem good to thee, and to thy brethren, to do with the rest of the *a*silver and the gold, that do after the will of your God.

19 The vessels also that are given

---

21 *b* TG Filthiness.
  c TG Heathen.
22 *a* OR to assist them.
7 1 *a* 2 Kgs. 22:4 (4–14);
    1 Chr. 6:13.
  6 *a* Neh. 8:1.

    b Ezra 7:9 (9, 28); 8:18.
  9 *a* Ezra 7:6.
10 *a* 3 Ne. 17:3;
    D&C 29:8; 58:6; 78:7;
    132:3.
    TG Priesthood,

    Qualifying for.
    b TG Heart.
    c Neh. 8:3 (1–8).
11 *a* TG Scribe.
18 *a* Ex. 12:35 (33–36).

thee for the service of the house of thy God, *those* deliver thou before the God of Jerusalem.

20 And whatsoever more shall be needful for the house of thy God, which thou shalt have occasion to bestow, bestow *it* out of the king's treasure house.

21 And I, *even* I Artaxerxes the king, do make a decree to all the treasurers which *are* beyond the river, that whatsoever Ezra the priest, the scribe of the law of the God of heaven, shall require of you, it be done speedily,

22 Unto an hundred talents of silver, and to an hundred measures of wheat, and to an hundred baths of wine, and to an hundred baths of oil, and salt without prescribing *how much.*

23 Whatsoever is commanded by the God of heaven, let it be diligently done for the house of the God of heaven: for why should there be wrath against the realm of the king and his sons?

24 Also we *a*certify you, that touching any of the priests and Levites, singers, porters, *b*Nethinims, or ministers of this house of God, it shall not be lawful to impose toll, tribute, or custom, upon them.

25 And thou, Ezra, after the wisdom of thy God, that *is* in thine hand, set magistrates and *a*judges, which may judge all the people that *are* *b*beyond the river, all such as know the *c*laws of thy God; and *d*teach ye them that know *them* not.

26 And whosoever will not do the law of thy God, and the law of the king, let judgment be executed speedily upon him, whether *it be* unto *a*death, or to banishment, or to confiscation of goods, or to imprisonment.

27 ¶ Blessed *be* the LORD God of

our fathers, which hath put *such a thing* as this in the king's heart, to *a*beautify the house of the LORD which *is* in Jerusalem:

28 And hath extended mercy unto me before the king, and his counsellors, and before all the king's mighty princes. And I was strengthened as the hand of the LORD my God *was* upon me, and I gathered together out of Israel chief men to go up with me.

CHAPTER 8

Those who go up from Babylon to Jerusalem are listed—The Levites are called to accompany them—Ezra and the people fast and pray for and gain guidance and protection in going to Jerusalem.

THESE *are* now the *a*chief of their fathers, and *this is* the genealogy of them that went up with me from Babylon, in the reign of Artaxerxes the king.

2 Of the sons of Phinehas; Gershom: of the sons of Ithamar; Daniel: of the sons of David; Hattush.

3 Of the sons of Shechaniah, of the sons of Pharosh; Zechariah: and with him were reckoned by genealogy of the males an hundred and fifty.

4 Of the sons of Pahath-moab; Elihoenai the son of Zerahiah, and with him two hundred males.

5 Of the sons of Shechaniah; the son of Jahaziel, and with him three hundred males.

6 Of the sons also of Adin; Ebed the son of Jonathan, and with him fifty males.

7 And of the sons of Elam; Jeshaiah the son of Athaliah, and with him seventy males.

8 And of the sons of Shephatiah; Zebadiah the son of Michael, and with him fourscore males.

9 Of the sons of Joab; Obadiah the

24a OR inform.
  b 1 Chr. 9:2;
    Ezra 2:43; 8:20.
25a Ex. 18:13;
    Deut. 19:18 (16–19);
    Mosiah 29:11 (11, 25, 39);

D&C 134:3.
  b IE on the west side of
    the Euphrates River.
  c TG God, Law of.
  d Ex. 18:20;
    D&C 88:81.

26a TG Capital Punishment.
27a TG Beauty.
8 1a HEB heads of their
    fathers; i.e., patriarchal
    leaders.

son of Jehiel, and with him two hundred and eighteen males.

10 And of the sons of Shelomith; the son of Josiphiah, and with him an hundred and threescore males.

11 And of the sons of Bebai; Zechariah the son of Bebai, and with him twenty and eight males.

12 And of the sons of Azgad; Johanan the son of Hakkatan, and with him an hundred and ten males.

13 And of the last sons of Adonikam, whose names *are* these, Eliphelet, Jeiel, and Shemaiah, and with them threescore males.

14 Of the sons also of Bigvai; Uthai, and Zabbud, and with them seventy males.

15 ¶ And I gathered them together to the river that runneth to Ahava; and there abode we in tents three days: and I viewed the people, and the priests, and found there none of the sons of Levi.

16 Then sent I for Eliezer, for Ariel, for Shemaiah, and for Elnathan, and for Jarib, and for Elnathan, and for Nathan, and for Zechariah, and for ᵃMeshullam, chief men; also for Joiarib, and for Elnathan, men of understanding.

17 And I sent them with commandment unto Iddo the chief at the place Casiphia, and I told them what they should say unto Iddo, *and* to his brethren the Nethinims, at the place Casiphia, that they should bring unto us ministers for the house of our God.

18 And by the good ᵃhand of our God upon us they brought us a man of understanding, of the sons of Mahli, the son of Levi, the son of Israel; and Sherebiah, with his sons and his brethren, eighteen;

19 And Hashabiah, and with him Jeshaiah of the sons of Merari, his brethren and their sons, twenty;

20 Also of the ᵃNethinims, whom David and the princes had appointed for the service of the Levites, two hundred and twenty Nethinims: all of them were expressed by name.

21 ¶ Then I proclaimed a ᵃfast there, at the river of Ahava, that we might ᵇafflict ourselves before our God, to seek of him a right way for us, and for our little ones, and for all our substance.

22 For I was ashamed to require of the king a band of soldiers and horsemen to help us against the enemy in the way: because we had spoken unto the king, saying, The hand of our God *is* upon all them for ᵃgood that ᵇseek him; but his power and his wrath *is* against all them that forsake him.

23 So we ᵃfasted and besought our God for this: and he was ᵇentreated of us.

24 ¶ Then I ᵃseparated twelve of the chief of the priests, Sherebiah, Hashabiah, and ten of their brethren with them,

25 And weighed unto them the silver, and the gold, and the vessels, *even* the offering of the house of our God, which the king, and his counsellors, and his lords, and all Israel *there* present, had offered:

26 I even weighed unto their hand six hundred and fifty talents of silver, and silver vessels an hundred talents, *and* of gold an hundred talents;

27 Also twenty basins of gold, of a thousand drams; and two vessels of ᵃfine copper, precious as gold.

28 And I said unto them, Ye *are* holy unto the LORD; the vessels *are* holy also; and the silver and the gold *are* a freewill offering unto the LORD God of your fathers.

29 Watch ye, and keep *them*, until ye weigh *them* before the chief of the priests and the Levites, and chief of

---

16*a* Neh. 6:18.
18*a* Ezra 7:6.
20*a* 1 Chr. 9:2;
    Ezra 2:43; 7:24.
21*a* Omni 1:26;
    Alma 5:46 (45–46); 6:6.

b OR humble.
22*a* Rom. 8:28;
    D&C 6:13; 90:24.
 b 1 Ne. 17:3 (1–3);
    2 Ne. 1:5 (5–6);
    Ether 12:41;

    D&C 88:63.
23*a* TG Fast, Fasting.
 b Gen. 25:21.
24*a* TG Setting Apart.
27*a* OR shining brass.

the fathers of Israel, at Jerusalem, in the chambers of the house of the Lord.

30 So took the priests and the Levites the weight of the silver, and the gold, and the vessels, to bring *them* to Jerusalem unto the house of our God.

31 ¶ Then we departed from the river of Ahava on the twelfth *day* of the first month, to go unto Jerusalem: and the hand of our God was upon us, and he delivered us from the hand of the enemy, and of such as lay in wait by the way.

32 And we came to Jerusalem, and abode there three days.

33 ¶ Now on the fourth day was the silver and the gold and the vessels weighed in the house of our God by the hand of Meremoth the son of Uriah the priest; and with him *was* Eleazar the son of Phinehas; and with them *was* Jozabad the son of Jeshua, and Noadiah the son of Binnui, Levites;

34 By number *and* by weight of every one: and all the weight was written at that time.

35 *Also* the children of those that had been carried away, which were come out of the captivity, offered burnt offerings unto the God of Israel, twelve bullocks for all Israel, ninety and six rams, seventy and seven lambs, twelve he goats *for a* sin offering: all *this was* a burnt offering unto the Lord.

36 ¶ And they delivered the king's commissions unto the king's lieutenants, and to the governors *a*on this side the river: and they *b*furthered the people, and the house of God.

CHAPTER 9

Many Jews intermarry with the Canaanites and others and follow their abominations—Ezra prays and confesses the sins of all the people.

Now when these things were done,

the *a*princes came to me, saying, The people of Israel, and the priests, and the Levites, have not *b*separated themselves from the people of the lands, *doing* according to their *c*abominations, *even* of the Canaanites, the Hittites, the Perizzites, the Jebusites, the Ammonites, the Moabites, the Egyptians, and the Amorites.

2 For they have taken of their *a*daughters for themselves, and for their sons: so that the *b*holy seed have mingled themselves with the people of *those* lands: yea, the hand of the princes and rulers hath been chief in this trespass.

3 And when I heard this thing, I *a*rent my garment and my mantle, and plucked off the hair of my head and of my beard, and sat down astonied.

4 Then were assembled unto me every one that *a*trembled at the words of the God of Israel, because of the transgression of those that had been carried away; and I sat astonied until the evening sacrifice.

5 ¶ And at the evening sacrifice I arose up from my heaviness; and having rent my garment and my mantle, I fell upon my knees, and spread out my hands unto the Lord my God,

6 And said, O my God, I am ashamed and blush to lift up my face to thee, my God: for our iniquities are increased over *our* head, and our trespass is grown up unto the heavens.

7 Since the days of our fathers *have* we *been* in a great trespass unto this day; and for our iniquities have we, our kings, *and* our priests, been delivered into the hand of the kings of the lands, to the sword, to captivity, and to a spoil, and to *a*confusion of face, as *it is* this day.

8 And now for a little space *a*grace hath been *shewed* from the Lord our God, to leave us a remnant to escape, and to give us a *b*nail in his holy

---

36a IE on the west side of
   the Euphrates River.
  b OR raised, promoted.
9 1a IE officials.
  b Alma 5:57.

c Deut. 12:31 (30–31);
   D&C 3:18.
2a TG Marriage, Interfaith.
  b Deut. 7:6.
3a Job 1:20;

Alma 46:12.
4a Ps. 119:53; D&C 1:7.
7a HEB shame.
8a TG Grace.
  b Isa. 22:23 (23, 25).

place, that our God may ^clighten our eyes, and give us a little reviving in our bondage.

9 For we *were* bondmen; yet our God hath not forsaken us in our ^abondage, but hath extended mercy unto us in the sight of the kings of Persia, to give us a reviving, to set up the house of our God, and to repair the desolations thereof, and to give us a wall in Judah and in Jerusalem.

10 And now, O our God, what shall we say after this? for we have forsaken thy commandments,

11 Which thou hast commanded by thy servants the prophets, saying, The land, unto which ye go to possess it, is an unclean land with the ^afilthiness of the people of the lands, with their abominations, which have filled it from one end to another with their uncleanness.

12 Now therefore give not your daughters unto their sons, neither take their daughters unto your sons, nor seek their peace or their wealth for ever: that ye may be strong, and eat the good of the land, and leave *it* for an inheritance to your children for ever.

13 And after all that is come upon us for our ^aevil deeds, and for our great trespass, seeing that thou our God hast punished us less than our ^biniquities *deserve*, and hast given us *such* deliverance as this;

14 Should we again break thy commandments, and join in affinity with the people of these abominations? wouldest not thou be angry with us till thou hadst consumed *us*, so that *there should be* no remnant nor escaping?

15 O LORD God of Israel, thou *art* ^arighteous: for we remain yet escaped, as *it is* this day: behold, we *are* before thee in our trespasses: for we cannot stand before thee because of this.

CHAPTER 10

The Jews covenant to put away their wives taken from the Canaanites and others—Ezra assembles the people at Jerusalem—The Levites who married non-Israelite women are listed.

NOW when Ezra had prayed, and when he had ^aconfessed, weeping and casting himself down before the house of God, there assembled unto him out of Israel a very great congregation of men and women and children: for the people wept very sore.

2 And Shechaniah the son of Jehiel, *one* of the sons of Elam, answered and said unto Ezra, We have trespassed against our God, and have taken ^astrange wives of the people of the land: yet now there is hope in Israel concerning this thing.

3 Now therefore let us make a covenant with our God to put away all the wives, and such as are born of them, according to the counsel of my lord, and of those that tremble at the commandment of our God; and let it be done according to the law.

4 Arise; for *this* matter *belongeth* unto thee: we also *will be* with thee: be of good ^acourage, and do *it*.

5 Then arose Ezra, and made the chief priests, the Levites, and all Israel, to swear that they should do according to this word. And they sware.

6 ¶ Then Ezra rose up from before the house of God, and went into the chamber of Johanan the son of Eliashib: and *when* he came thither, he did eat no bread, nor drink water: for he mourned because of the transgression of them that had been carried away.

7 And they made proclamation throughout Judah and Jerusalem unto all the children of the captivity, that they should gather themselves together unto Jerusalem;

8 And that whosoever would not

8c　3 Ne. 13:22;
　　D&C 88:11.
9a　TG Bondage, Physical.
11a　TG Filthiness.

13a　TG Evil.
　　b　TG Sin.
15a　Ps. 119:137.
10 1a　TG Confession.

2a　OR foreign wives (also vv. 11, 14, 17, 44).
4a　TG Courage.

come within three days, according to the counsel of the princes and the elders, all his substance should be forfeited, and himself separated from the congregation of those that had been carried away.

9 ¶ Then all the men of Judah and Benjamin gathered themselves together unto Jerusalem within three days. It *was* the ninth month, on the twentieth *day* of the month; and all the people sat in the street of the house of God, trembling because of *this* matter, and for the great rain.

10 And Ezra the priest stood up, and said unto them, Ye have transgressed, and have taken strange *a*wives, to increase the trespass of Israel.

11 Now therefore make *a*confession unto the LORD God of your fathers, and do his pleasure: and *b*separate yourselves from the people of the land, and from the strange wives.

12 Then all the congregation answered and said with a loud voice, As thou hast said, so must we *a*do.

13 But the people *are* many, and *it is* a time of much rain, and we are not able to stand without, neither *is this* a work of one day or two: for we are many that have transgressed in this thing.

14 Let now our rulers of all the congregation stand, and let all them which have taken strange wives in our cities come at appointed times, and with them the elders of every city, and the judges thereof, until the fierce wrath of our God for this matter be turned from us.

15 ¶ Only Jonathan the son of Asahel and Jahaziah the son of Tikvah *a*were employed about this *matter:* and Meshullam and Shabbethai the Levite helped them.

16 And the children of the captivity did so. And Ezra the priest, *with* certain chief of the fathers, after the house of their fathers, and all of them by *their* names, were separated, and sat down in the first day of the tenth month to examine the matter.

17 And they made an end with all the men that had taken strange wives by the first day of the first month.

18 ¶ And among the sons of the priests there were found that had taken strange wives: *namely,* of the sons of Jeshua the son of Jozadak, and his brethren; Maaseiah, and Eliezer, and Jarib, and Gedaliah.

19 And they gave their hands that they would put away their wives; and *being* *a*guilty, *they offered* a ram of the flock for their trespass.

20 And of the sons of Immer; Hanani, and Zebadiah.

21 And of the sons of Harim; Maaseiah, and Elijah, and Shemaiah, and Jehiel, and Uzziah.

22 And of the sons of Pashur; Elioenai, Maaseiah, Ishmael, Nethaneel, Jozabad, and Elasah.

23 Also of the Levites; Jozabad, and Shimei, and Kelaiah, (the same *is* Kelita,) Pethahiah, Judah, and Eliezer.

24 Of the singers also; Eliashib: and of the porters; Shallum, and Telem, and Uri.

25 Moreover of Israel: of the sons of Parosh; Ramiah, and Jeziah, and Malchiah, and Miamin, and Eleazar, and Malchijah, and Benaiah.

26 And of the sons of Elam; Mattaniah, Zechariah, and Jehiel, and Abdi, and Jeremoth, and Eliah.

27 And of the sons of Zattu; Elioenai, Eliashib, Mattaniah, and Jeremoth, and Zabad, and Aziza.

28 Of the sons also of Bebai; Jehohanan, Hananiah, Zabbai, *and* Athlai.

29 And of the sons of Bani; Meshullam, Malluch, and Adaiah, Jashub, and Sheal, and Ramoth.

30 And of the sons of Pahathmoab; Adna, and Chelal, Benaiah, Maaseiah, Mattaniah, Bezaleel, and Binnui, and Manasseh.

31 And *of* the sons of Harim;

10*a* TG Marriage, Interfaith.
11*a* TG Repent.
  b TG Separation.

12*a* Mosiah 5:5 (1–5).
15*a* HEB (probably) stood up against this.

19*a* TG Guilt.

Eliezer, Ishijah, Malchiah, Shemaiah, Shimeon,

32 Benjamin, Malluch, *and* Shemariah.

33 Of the sons of Hashum; Mattenai, Mattathah, Zabad, Eliphelet, Jeremai, Manasseh, *and* Shimei.

34 Of the sons of Bani; Maadai, Amram, and Uel,

35 Benaiah, Bedeiah, Chelluh,

36 Vaniah, Meremoth, Eliashib,

37 Mattaniah, Mattenai, and Jaasau,

38 And Bani, and Binnui, Shimei,

39 And Shelemiah, and Nathan, and Adaiah,

40 Machnadebai, Shashai, Sharai,

41 Azareel, and Shelemiah, Shemariah,

42 Shallum, Amariah, *and* Joseph.

43 Of the sons of Nebo; Jeiel, Mattithiah, Zabad, Zebina, Jadau, and Joel, Benaiah.

44 All these had taken strange wives: and *some* of them had wives by whom they had children.

THE BOOK OF
NEHEMIAH

CHAPTER 1

Nehemiah mourns, fasts, and prays for the Jews in Jerusalem.

THE words of Nehemiah the son of Hachaliah. And it came to pass in the month ᵃChisleu, in the twentieth year, as I was in ᵇShushan the palace,

2 That ᵃHanani, one of my brethren, came, he and *certain* men of Judah; and I asked them concerning the Jews that had escaped, which were left of the captivity, and concerning Jerusalem.

3 And they said unto me, The ᵃremnant that are left of the captivity there in the province *are* in great affliction and reproach: the wall of Jerusalem also *is* broken down, and the gates thereof are burned with fire.

4 ¶ And it came to pass, when I heard these words, that I sat down and wept, and mourned *certain* days, and ᵃfasted, and prayed before the God of heaven,

5 And said, I beseech thee, O LORD God of heaven, ᵃthe great and terrible God, that ᵇkeepeth covenant and mercy for them that love him and observe his commandments:

6 Let thine ear now be attentive, and thine eyes open, that thou mayest hear the prayer of thy servant, which I pray before thee now, day and night, for the children of Israel thy servants, and ᵃconfess the sins of the children of Israel, which we have sinned against thee: both I and my father's house have sinned.

7 We have dealt very corruptly against thee, and have not kept the commandments, nor the statutes, nor the judgments, which thou commandedst thy servant Moses.

8 Remember, I beseech thee, the word that thou commandedst thy

---

1 1a IE the ninth of the Hebrew months, beginning at the new moon of December.
b OR Susa (the chief city of all Persia).
Esth. 1:2.
2a Neh. 7:2.
3a TG Israel, Remnant of.
4a TG Fast, Fasting.
5a HEB the God, the great, and the revered.
b Deut. 7:9; Dan. 9:4.
6a TG Confession.

servant Moses, saying, *If* ye transgress, I will *ª*scatter you abroad among the nations:

9 But *if* ye turn unto me, and keep my commandments, and do them; though there were of you cast out unto the uttermost part of the heaven, *yet* will I *ª*gather them from thence, and will bring them unto the place that I have chosen to set my name there.

10 Now these *are* thy servants and thy *ª*people, whom thou hast redeemed by thy great power, and by thy strong hand.

11 O Lord, I beseech thee, let now thine ear be attentive to the prayer of thy servant, and to the prayer of thy servants, who desire to *ª*fear thy name: and *ᵇ*prosper, I pray thee, thy servant this day, and grant him mercy in the sight of this man. For I was the king's cupbearer.

CHAPTER 2

Artaxerxes sends Nehemiah to Jerusalem—Sanballat and others oppose Nehemiah in rebuilding the walls and gates of Jerusalem.

AND it came to pass in the month Nisan, in the twentieth year of Artaxerxes the king, *that* wine *was* before him: and I took up the wine, and gave *it* unto the king. Now I had not been *beforetime* sad in his presence.

2 Wherefore the king said unto me, Why *is* thy countenance sad, seeing thou *art* not sick? this *is* nothing *else* but sorrow of heart. Then I was very sore afraid,

3 And said unto the king, Let the king live for ever: why should not my countenance be *ª*sad, when the city, the place of my fathers' sepulchres, *lieth* waste, and the gates thereof are consumed with fire?

4 Then the king said unto me, For what dost thou make request? So I prayed to the God of heaven.

5 And I said unto the king, If it please the king, and if thy servant have found favour in thy sight, that thou wouldest send me unto Judah, unto the city of my fathers' sepulchres, that I may build it.

6 And the king said unto me, (the queen also sitting by him,) For how long shall thy journey be? and when wilt thou return? So it pleased the king to send me; and I set him a time.

7 Moreover I said unto the king, If it please the king, let letters be given me to the governors *ª*beyond the river, that they may convey me over till I come into Judah;

8 And a letter unto Asaph the keeper of the king's forest, that he may give me timber to make beams for the gates of the palace which *appertained* to the house, and for the wall of the city, and for the house that I shall enter into. And the king granted me, according to the good hand of my God upon me.

9 ¶ Then I came to the governors beyond the river, and gave them the king's letters. Now the king had sent captains of the army and horsemen with me.

10 When *ª*Sanballat the Horonite, and *ᵇ*Tobiah the servant, the Ammonite, heard *of it,* it grieved them exceedingly that there was come a man to seek the welfare of the children of Israel.

11 So I came to Jerusalem, and was there three days.

12 ¶ And I arose in the night, I and some few men with me; neither told I *any* man what my God had put in my heart to do at Jerusalem: neither *was there any* beast with me, save the beast that I rode upon.

13 And I went out by night by

8*a* 1 Ne. 22:3 (3–5);
   2 Ne. 25:15 (14–16);
   D&C 45:19 (16–25).
9*a* Deut. 30:3 (1–5);
   Micah 7:12 (11–12);
   1 Ne. 22:12 (10–12);
   2 Ne. 21:12 (11–16);

   D&C 45:25 (24–25).
10*a* Ex. 33:13;
   2 Ne. 29:4;
   D&C 86:11;
   109:59 (59–67).
11*a* OR reverence.
  b Gen. 24:12.

2 3*a* Ps. 137:4.
 7*a* IE on the west side of
   the Euphrates River.
10*a* Neh. 4:1 (1–8);
   6:1 (1–14).
  b Neh. 6:16.

the ᵃgate of the ᵇvalley, even before the ᶜdragon well, and to the ᵈdung port, and viewed the walls of Jerusalem, which were broken down, and the gates thereof were consumed with fire.

14 Then I went on to the ᵃgate of the fountain, and to the king's pool: but *there was* no place for the beast *that was* under me to pass.

15 Then went I up in the night by the brook, and viewed the wall, and turned back, and entered by the gate of the valley, and *so* returned.

16 And the rulers knew not whither I went, or what I did; neither had I as yet told *it* to the Jews, nor to the priests, nor to the nobles, nor to the rulers, nor to the rest that did the work.

17 ¶ Then said I unto them, Ye see the distress that we *are* in, how Jerusalem *lieth* ᵃwaste, and the gates thereof are burned with fire: come, and let us build up the wall of Jerusalem, that we be no more a reproach.

18 Then I told them of the hand of my God which was good upon me; as also the king's words that he had spoken unto me. And they said, Let us rise up and build. So they strengthened their hands for *this* good *work.*

19 But when Sanballat the Horonite, and Tobiah the servant, the Ammonite, and Geshem the Arabian, heard *it,* they ᵃlaughed us to ᵇscorn, and despised us, and said, What *is* this thing that ye do? will ye rebel against the king?

20 Then answered I them, and said unto them, The God of heaven, he will prosper us; therefore we his servants will arise and build: but ye have no portion, nor right, nor memorial, in Jerusalem.

CHAPTER 3

The names and order of those who help to build the walls and gates of Jerusalem are listed.

THEN Eliashib the ᵃhigh priest rose up with his brethren the priests, and they builded the ᵇsheep gate; they sanctified it, and set up the doors of it; even unto the tower of Meah they sanctified it, unto the tower of Hananeel.

2 And next unto him builded the men of Jericho. And next to them builded Zaccur the son of Imri.

3 But the ᵃfish gate did the sons of Hassenaah build, who *also* laid the beams thereof, and set up the doors thereof, the locks thereof, and the bars thereof.

4 And next unto them repaired Meremoth the son of Urijah, the son of Koz. And next unto them repaired Meshullam the son of Berechiah, the son of Meshezabeel. And next unto them repaired Zadok the son of Baana.

5 And next unto them the Tekoites repaired; but their nobles put not their necks to the work of their Lord.

6 Moreover the old gate repaired Jehoiada the son of Paseah, and Meshullam the son of Besodeiah; they laid the beams thereof, and set up the doors thereof, and the locks thereof, and the bars thereof.

7 And next unto them repaired Melatiah the Gibeonite, and Jadon the Meronothite, the men of Gibeon,

---

13*a* IE the name of a gate in the wall of Jerusalem, approx. modern Jaffa gate.
  b Neh. 3:13.
  c OR fountain of the jackals—a well located near Jerusalem.
  d IE another gate in the wall of Jerusalem at approx. junction of Hinnom and Tyropoeon

valleys.
  Neh. 3:13; 12:31.
14*a* Perhaps a gate near En-rogel. The king's pool could be Siloam.
  Neh. 3:15; 12:37.
17*a* Ezek. 5:14.
19*a* TG Laughter.
  b Ps. 123:4;
  1 Ne. 8:33;
  Alma 26:23.
3 1*a* TG Priesthood, Aaronic.

  b A gate probably in the northeast wall of Jerusalem near the temple, for access of sacrificial animals.
3*a* Probably a northwestern gate, with access to the merchants' quarter; perhaps where Damascus gate now is.
  Neh. 12:39.

and of Mizpah, unto the throne of the governor [a]on this side the river.

8 Next unto him repaired Uzziel the son of Harhaiah, of the goldsmiths. Next unto him also repaired Hananiah the son of *one of* the [a]apothecaries, and they fortified Jerusalem unto the broad wall.

9 And next unto them repaired Rephaiah the son of Hur, the ruler of the half part of Jerusalem.

10 And next unto them repaired Jedaiah the son of Harumaph, even over against his house. And next unto him repaired Hattush the son of Hashabniah.

11 Malchijah the son of Harim, and Hashub the son of Pahath-moab, repaired the other piece, and the tower of the furnaces.

12 And next unto him repaired Shallum the son of Halohesh, the ruler of the half part of Jerusalem, he and his daughters.

13 The [a]valley gate repaired Hanun, and the inhabitants of Zanoah; they built it, and set up the doors thereof, the locks thereof, and the bars thereof, and a thousand cubits on the wall unto the dung gate.

14 But the dung gate repaired Malchiah the son of Rechab, the ruler of part of Beth-haccerem; he built it, and set up the doors thereof, the locks thereof, and the bars thereof.

15 But the [a]gate of the fountain repaired Shallun the son of Colhozeh, the ruler of part of Mizpah; he built it, and covered it, and set up the doors thereof, the locks thereof, and the bars thereof, and the wall of the pool of [b]Siloah by the king's garden, and unto the stairs that go down from the city of David.

16 After him repaired Nehemiah the son of Azbuk, the ruler of the half part of Beth-zur, unto *the place* over against the sepulchres of David, and to the pool that was made, and unto the house of the mighty.

17 After him repaired the Levites, Rehum the son of Bani. Next unto him repaired Hashabiah, the ruler of the half part of Keilah, in his part.

18 After him repaired their brethren, Bavai the son of Henadad, the ruler of the half part of Keilah.

19 And next to him repaired Ezer the son of Jeshua, the ruler of Mizpah, another piece over against the going up to the armoury at the turning *of the wall.*

20 After him Baruch the son of Zabbai earnestly repaired the other piece, from the turning *of the wall* unto the door of the house of Eliashib the high priest.

21 After him repaired Meremoth the son of Urijah the son of Koz another piece, from the door of the house of Eliashib even to the end of the house of Eliashib.

22 And after him repaired the priests, the men of the plain.

23 After him repaired Benjamin and Hashub over against their house. After him repaired Azariah the son of Maaseiah the son of Ananiah by his house.

24 After him repaired Binnui the son of Henadad another piece, from the house of Azariah unto the turning *of the wall,* even unto the corner.

25 Palal the son of Uzai, over against the turning *of the wall,* and [a]the tower which lieth out from the king's high house, that *was* by the court of the prison. After him Pedaiah the son of Parosh.

26 Moreover the [a]Nethinims dwelt in Ophel, unto *the place* over against the [b]water gate toward the east, and the tower that lieth out.

27 After them the Tekoites repaired another piece, over against the great tower that lieth out, even unto the wall of Ophel.

28 From above the [a]horse gate repaired the priests, every one over against his house.

7a ie on the west side of the Euphrates.

8a or perfumers, ointment makers.

13a Neh. 2:13.

15a Neh. 2:14.
b Isa. 8:6; John 9:7 (6–7).

25a or the upper tower that stands out from the king's house.

26a ie temple servants.
b Neh. 8:1.

28a Probably at southeast corner of temple area. Jer. 31:39.

29 After them repaired Zadok the son of Immer over against his house. After him repaired also Shemaiah the son of Shechaniah, the keeper of the ªeast gate.

30 After him repaired Hananiah the son of Shelemiah, and Hanun the sixth son of Zalaph, another piece. After him repaired Meshullam the son of Berechiah over against his chamber.

31 After him repaired Malchiah the goldsmith's son unto the place of the Nethinims, and of the merchants, over against the gate Miphkad, and ªto the going up of the corner.

32 And between the going up of the corner unto the sheep gate repaired the goldsmiths and the merchants.

CHAPTER 4

The Jews' enemies seek to prevent them from rebuilding the walls of Jerusalem— Nehemiah arms the laborers and keeps the work progressing.

BUT it came to pass, that when ªSanballat heard that we builded the wall, he was wroth, and took great indignation, and mocked the Jews.

2 And he spake before his brethren and the army of Samaria, and said, What do these feeble Jews? will they fortify themselves? will they sacrifice? will they make an end in a day? will they revive the stones out of the heaps of the rubbish which are burned?

3 Now Tobiah the Ammonite *was* by him, and he said, Even that which they build, if a fox go up, he shall even break down their stone wall.

4 Hear, O our God; for we are despised: and turn their reproach upon their own head, and give them for a prey in the land of captivity:

5 And cover not their iniquity, and let not their sin be blotted out from before thee: for they have provoked *thee* to anger before the builders.

6 So built we the wall; and all the wall was joined together unto the half thereof: for the ªpeople had a mind to ᵇwork.

7 ¶ But it came to pass, *that* when ªSanballat, and Tobiah, and the Arabians, and the Ammonites, and the Ashdodites, heard that the walls of Jerusalem were made up, *and* that the breaches began to be stopped, then they were very wroth,

8 And conspired all of them together to come *and* to fight against Jerusalem, and to hinder it.

9 Nevertheless we made our prayer unto our God, and set a watch against them day and night, because of them.

10 And Judah said, The strength of the bearers of burdens is decayed, and *there is* much rubbish; so that we are not able to build the wall.

11 And our adversaries said, They shall not know, neither see, till we come in the midst among them, and slay them, and cause the work to cease.

12 And it came to pass, that when the Jews which dwelt by them came, they said unto us ten times, From all places whence ye shall return unto us *they will be upon you.*

13 ¶ Therefore set I in the lower places behind the wall, *and* on the higher places, I even set the people after their families with their swords, their spears, and their bows.

14 And I looked, and rose up, and said unto the nobles, and to the rulers, and to the rest of the people, Be not ye ªafraid of them: remember the Lord, *which is* great and ᵇterrible, and ᶜfight for your brethren, your sons, and your daughters, your ᵈwives, and your houses.

15 And it came to pass, when our enemies heard that it was known unto us, and God had brought their ªcounsel to nought, that we returned

---

29a Probably the area of the "Golden Gate."
31a OR to the upper chamber of the corner.
4 1a Neh. 2:10 (10, 18–20).

6a TG Common Consent.
 b D&C 52:39; 75:3; 115:10.
7a Neh. 6:16.
14a D&C 98:14; 122:9.
 b OR feared, revered.

c TG War.
d Alma 46:12.
15a Ps. 33:10.

all of us to the wall, every one unto his work.

16 And it came to pass from that time forth, *that* the half of my servants wrought in the work, and the other half of them held both the spears, the shields, and the bows, and the *a*habergeons; and the rulers *were* behind all the house of Judah.

17 They which builded on the wall, and they that bare burdens, with those that laded, *every one* with one of his hands wrought in the work, and with the other *hand* held a weapon.

18 For the builders, every one had his sword girded by his side, and *so* builded. And he that sounded the trumpet *was* by me.

19 ¶ And I said unto the nobles, and to the rulers, and to the rest of the people, The work *is* great and large, and we are separated upon the wall, one far from another.

20 In what place *therefore* ye hear the sound of the trumpet, resort ye thither unto us: our God shall fight for us.

21 So we laboured in the work: and half of them held the spears from the rising of the morning till the stars appeared.

22 Likewise at the same time said I unto the people, Let every one with his servant lodge within Jerusalem, that in the night they may be a guard to us, and labour on the day.

23 So neither I, nor my brethren, nor my servants, nor the men of the guard which followed me, none of us put off our clothes, *saving that* every one put them off for washing.

CHAPTER 5

Many Jews are in bondage to their fellow Jews—At Nehemiah's direction they are freed, their lands are restored, and the taking of usury is discontinued.

AND there was a great cry of the people and of their wives against their brethren the Jews.

2 For there were that said, We, our sons, and our daughters, *are* many: therefore we take up corn *for them,* that we may eat, and live.

3 *Some* also there were that said, We have mortgaged our lands, vineyards, and houses, that we might buy corn, because of the *a*dearth.

4 There were also that said, We have *a*borrowed money for the king's tribute, *and that upon* our lands and vineyards.

5 Yet now our flesh *is* as the flesh of our brethren, our children as their children: and, lo, we bring into bondage our sons and our daughters to be servants, and *some* of our daughters are brought unto bondage *already:* neither *is it* in our power *to redeem them;* for other men have our lands and vineyards.

6 ¶ And I was very angry when I heard their cry and these words.

7 Then I consulted with myself, and I rebuked the nobles, and the rulers, and said unto them, Ye exact *a*usury, every one of his brother. And I set a great assembly against them.

8 And I said unto them, We after our ability have redeemed our brethren the Jews, which were sold unto the heathen; and will ye even sell your brethren? or shall they be sold unto us? Then held they their peace, and found nothing *to answer.*

9 Also I said, It *is* not good that ye do: ought ye not to *a*walk in the fear of our God because of the reproach of the *b*heathen our enemies?

10 I likewise, *and* my brethren, and my servants, might exact of them money and corn: I pray you, let us leave off this usury.

11 Restore, I pray you, to them, even this day, their lands, their vineyards, their oliveyards, and their houses, also *a*the hundredth *part* of the money, and of the corn, the wine, and the oil, that ye exact of them.

16*a* Probably armor of
    tough leather.
5 3*a* OR famine.

4*a* TG Borrow; Debt.
7*a* TG Usury.
9*a* TG Walking with God.

b TG Heathen.
11*a* OR the hundred pieces
    of silver.

12 Then said they, We will restore *them*, and will require nothing of them; so will we do as thou sayest. Then I called the priests, and took an oath of them, that they should do according to this promise.

13 Also I shook my lap, and said, So God shake out every man from his house, and from his labour, that performeth not this promise, even thus be he shaken out, and emptied. And all the congregation said, Amen, and praised the LORD. And the people did according to this promise.

14 ¶ Moreover from the time that I was appointed to be their governor in the land of Judah, from the twentieth year even unto the two and thirtieth year of Artaxerxes the king, *that is,* twelve years, I and my brethren *ª*have not eaten the *b*bread of the governor.

15 But the former governors that *had been* before me *ª*were chargeable unto the people, and had taken of them bread and wine, beside forty shekels of silver; yea, even their servants bare *b*rule over the people: but so did not I, because of the *c*fear of God.

16 Yea, also I continued in the work of this wall, neither bought we any land: and all my servants *were* gathered thither unto the work.

17 Moreover *there were* at my table an hundred and fifty of the Jews and rulers, beside those that came unto us from among the heathen that *are* about us.

18 Now *that* which was prepared *for me* daily *was* one ox *and* six choice sheep; also fowls were prepared for me, and once in ten days store of all sorts of wine: yet for all this required not I the bread of the governor, because the bondage was heavy upon this people.

19 Think upon me, my God, for good, *according* to all that I have done for this people.

CHAPTER 6

Sanballat engages in intrigue against Nehemiah and the building of the wall—The Jews finish the construction of the wall.

Now it came to pass, when *ª*Sanballat, and Tobiah, and Geshem the Arabian, and the rest of our enemies, heard that I had builded the wall, and *that* there was no breach left therein; (though at that time I had not set up the doors upon the gates;)

2 That Sanballat and Geshem sent unto me, saying, Come, let us meet together in *some one of* the villages in the plain of Ono. But they thought to do me *ª*mischief.

3 And I sent messengers unto them, saying, I *am* doing a great work, so that I cannot come down: why should the work cease, whilst I leave it, and come down to you?

4 Yet they sent unto me four times after this sort; and I answered them after the same manner.

5 Then sent Sanballat his servant unto me in like manner the fifth time with an open letter in his hand;

6 Wherein *was* written, It is reported among the heathen, and *ª*Gashmu saith *it, that* thou and the Jews think to rebel: for which cause thou buildest the wall, that thou mayest be their king, according to these words.

7 And thou hast also appointed prophets to preach of thee at Jerusalem, saying, *There is* a king in Judah: and now shall it be reported to the king according to these words. Come now therefore, and let us take counsel together.

8 Then I sent unto him, saying, There are no such things done as thou sayest, but thou *ª*feignest them out of thine own heart.

9 For they all made us afraid, saying, Their hands shall be weakened from the work, that it be not done. Now therefore, O *God*, strengthen my hands.

14a Mosiah 27:5.
  b Mosiah 2:14 (12, 14).
15a HEB laid a heavy
     burden upon the

people.
  b TG Authority.
  c TG Reverence.
6 1a Neh. 2:10 (10, 18–20).

2a D&C 10:23 (22–28).
6a OR Geshem.
8a Alma 55:1.

10 Afterward I came unto the house of Shemaiah the son of Delaiah the son of Mehetabeel, who *was* shut up; and he said, Let us meet together in the house of God, within the temple, and let us shut the doors of the temple: for they will come to slay thee; yea, in the night will they come to slay thee.

11 And I said, Should such a man as I flee? and who *is* *a*there, that, *being* as I *am,* would go into the temple to save his life? I will not go in.

12 And, lo, I perceived that God had not sent him; but that he pronounced this prophecy against me: for Tobiah and Sanballat had hired him.

13 Therefore *was* he hired, that I should be *a*afraid, and do so, and sin, and *that* they might have *matter* for an *b*evil report, that they might reproach me.

14 My God, think thou upon Tobiah and Sanballat according to these their works, and on the prophetess Noadiah, and the rest of the prophets, that would have put me in fear.

15 ¶ So the wall was finished in the twenty and fifth *day* of *the month* *a*Elul, in fifty and two days.

16 And it came to pass, that when all our *a*enemies heard *thereof,* and all the heathen that *were* about us saw *these things,* they were much cast down in their own eyes: for they perceived that this work was wrought of our God.

17 ¶ Moreover in those days the nobles of Judah sent many letters unto Tobiah, and *the letters* of Tobiah came unto them.

18 For *there were* many in Judah sworn unto him, because he *was* the son in law of Shechaniah the son of Arah; and his son Johanan had taken the daughter of *a*Meshullam the son of Berechiah.

19 Also they reported his good deeds before me, and uttered my words to him. *And* Tobiah sent letters to put me in fear.

CHAPTER 7

Provision is made to protect Jerusalem—The genealogy is given of the Jews who returned from Babylon—Priests without genealogical records are denied the priesthood.

NOW it came to pass, when the wall was built, and I had set up the doors, and the porters and the singers and the Levites were appointed,

2 That I gave my brother *a*Hanani, and Hananiah the ruler of the palace, charge over Jerusalem: for he *was* a *b*faithful man, and *c*feared God above many.

3 And I said unto them, Let not the gates of Jerusalem be opened until the sun be hot; and while they stand by, let them shut the doors, and bar *them:* and appoint watches of the inhabitants of Jerusalem, every one in his watch, and every one *to be* over against his house.

4 Now the city *was* large and great: but the people *were* few therein, and the houses *were* not builded.

5 ¶ And my God put into mine heart to gather together the nobles, and the rulers, and the people, that they might be reckoned by genealogy. And I found a *a*register of the *b*genealogy of them which came up at the first, and found written therein,

6 These *are* the *a*children of the province, that went up out of the *b*captivity, of those that had been carried away, whom Nebuchadnezzar the king of Babylon had carried away, and came again to Jerusalem and to Judah, every one unto his city;

7 *a*Who came with Zerubbabel,

11*a* JST Neh. 6:11 . . . *mine*
   enemy, that such a man
   as I would go . . .
13*a* D&C 3:7 (7–8).
  b TG Slander.
15*a* IE the sixth Hebrew
   month, from the new

moon of September to
  that of October.
16*a* Neh. 2:10; 4:7 (1, 7).
18*a* Ezra 8:16.
7 2*a* Neh. 1:2.
  b D&C 52:13; 132:53.
  c Ex. 18:21;

Mosiah 29:13.
5*a* TG Book of Life.
  b TG Book of
   Remembrance.
6*a* Ezra 2:1 (1–70).
  b OR exile.
7*a* Ezra 2:2.

Jeshua, Nehemiah, Azariah, Raamiah, Nahamani, Mordecai, Bilshan, Mispereth, Bigvai, Nehum, Baanah. The number, I *say*, of the men of the people of Israel *was this;*

8 The children of Parosh, two thousand an hundred seventy and two.

9 The children of Shephatiah, three hundred seventy and two.

10 The children of Arah, six hundred fifty and two.

11 The children of Pahath-moab, of the children of Jeshua and Joab, two thousand and eight hundred *and* eighteen.

12 The children of Elam, a thousand two hundred fifty and four.

13 The children of Zattu, eight hundred forty and five.

14 The children of Zaccai, seven hundred and threescore.

15 The children of ᵃBinnui, six hundred forty and eight.

16 The children of Bebai, six hundred twenty and eight.

17 The children of Azgad, two thousand three hundred twenty and two.

18 The children of Adonikam, six hundred threescore and seven.

19 The children of Bigvai, two thousand threescore and seven.

20 The children of Adin, six hundred fifty and five.

21 The children of Ater of Hezekiah, ninety and eight.

22 The children of Hashum, three hundred twenty and eight.

23 The children of Bezai, three hundred twenty and four.

24 The children of Hariph, an hundred and twelve.

25 The children of Gibeon, ninety and five.

26 The men of Beth-lehem and Netophah, an hundred fourscore and eight.

27 The men of Anathoth, an hundred twenty and eight.

28 The men of Beth-azmaveth, forty and two.

29 The men of Kirjath-jearim, Chephirah, and Beeroth, seven hundred forty and three.

30 The men of Ramah and Geba, six hundred twenty and one.

31 The men of Michmas, an hundred and twenty and two.

32 The men of Beth-el and Ai, an hundred twenty and three.

33 The men of the other Nebo, fifty and two.

34 The children of the other Elam, a thousand two hundred fifty and four.

35 The children of Harim, three hundred and twenty.

36 The children of Jericho, three hundred forty and five.

37 The children of Lod, Hadid, and Ono, seven hundred twenty and one.

38 The children of Senaah, three thousand nine hundred and thirty.

39 ¶ The priests: the children of Jedaiah, of the house of Jeshua, nine hundred seventy and three.

40 The children of Immer, a thousand fifty and two.

41 The children of Pashur, a thousand two hundred forty and seven.

42 The children of Harim, a thousand and seventeen.

43 ¶ The Levites: the children of Jeshua, of Kadmiel, *and* of the children of Hodevah, seventy and four.

44 ¶ The singers: the children of Asaph, an hundred forty and eight.

45 ¶ The porters: the children of Shallum, the children of Ater, the children of Talmon, the children of Akkub, the children of Hatita, the children of Shobai, an hundred thirty and eight.

46 ¶ The ᵃNethinims: the children of Ziha, the children of Hashupha, the children of Tabbaoth,

47 The children of Keros, the children of Sia, the children of Padon,

48 The children of Lebana, the children of Hagaba, the children of Shalmai,

49 The children of Hanan, the children of Giddel, the children of Gahar,

50 The children of Reaiah, the

15a Ezra 2:10.   46a OR temple servants.

children of Rezin, the children of Nekoda,

51 The children of Gazzam, the children of Uzza, the children of Phaseah,

52 The children of Besai, the children of Meunim, the children of Nephishesim,

53 The children of Bakbuk, the children of Hakupha, the children of Harhur,

54 The children of Bazlith, the children of Mehida, the children of Harsha,

55 The children of Barkos, the children of Sisera, the children of Tamah,

56 The children of Neziah, the children of Hatipha.

57 ¶ The children of Solomon's servants: the children of Sotai, the children of Sophereth, the children of Perida,

58 The children of Jaala, the children of Darkon, the children of Giddel,

59 The children of Shephatiah, the children of Hattil, the children of Pochereth of Zebaim, the children of Amon.

60 All the Nethinims, and the children of Solomon's servants, *were* three hundred ninety and two.

61 And these *were* they which went up *also* from Tel-melah, Tel-haresha, Cherub, Addon, and Immer: but they could not shew their father's house, nor their seed, whether they *were* of Israel.

62 The children of Delaiah, the children of Tobiah, the children of Nekoda, six hundred forty and two.

63 ¶ And of the priests: the *a*children of Habaiah, the children of Koz, the children of Barzillai, which took *one* of the daughters of Barzillai the Gileadite to wife, and was called after their name.

64 These sought their register *among* those that were reckoned by *a*genealogy, but it was not found:

therefore were they, as *b*polluted, put from the *c*priesthood.

65 And the *a*Tirshatha said unto them, that they should not eat of the most holy things, till there stood *up* a priest with *b*Urim and Thummim.

66 ¶ The whole congregation together *was* forty and two thousand three hundred and threescore,

67 Beside their manservants and their maidservants, of whom *there were* seven thousand three hundred thirty and seven: and they had two hundred forty and five singing men and singing women.

68 Their horses, seven hundred thirty and six: their mules, two hundred forty and five:

69 *Their* camels, four hundred thirty and five: six thousand seven hundred and twenty asses.

70 ¶ And some of the chief of the fathers *a*gave unto the work. The Tirshatha gave to the treasure a thousand drams of gold, fifty basins, five hundred and thirty priests' garments.

71 And *some* of the chief of the fathers gave to the treasure of the work twenty thousand drams of gold, and two thousand and two hundred pound of silver.

72 And *that* which the rest of the people gave *was* twenty thousand drams of gold, and two thousand pound of silver, and threescore and seven priests' garments.

73 So the priests, and the Levites, and the porters, and the singers, and *some* of the people, and the Nethinims, and all Israel, dwelt in their cities; and when the seventh month came, the children of Israel *were* in their cities.

CHAPTER 8

Ezra reads and interprets the law of Moses to the people—They keep the Feast of Tabernacles.

63*a* Ezra 2:61 (61–62); D&C 85:12 (11–12).
64*a* TG Genealogy and Temple Work.

b TG Worthiness.
c TG Priesthood, Qualifying for.
65*a* OR governor.

Neh. 8:9.
b TG Urim and Thummim.
70*a* D&C 109:5.

AND all the people gathered themselves together as one man into the street that *was* before the ^awater gate; and they spake unto ^bEzra the ^cscribe to bring the book of the law of Moses, which the LORD had commanded to Israel.

2 And Ezra the priest brought the ^alaw before the congregation both of men and women, and all that could hear with understanding, upon the first day of the seventh month.

3 And he read therein before the street that *was* before the water gate from the morning until midday, before the men and the women, and those that could understand; and the ears of all the people *were attentive* unto the ^abook of the law.

4 And Ezra the scribe stood upon a ^apulpit of wood, which they had made for the purpose; and beside him stood Mattithiah, and Shema, and Anaiah, and Urijah, and Hilkiah, and Maaseiah, on his right hand; and on his left hand, Pedaiah, and Mishael, and Malchiah, and Hashum, and Hashbadana, Zechariah, *and* Meshullam.

5 And Ezra opened the book in the sight of all the people; (for he was above all the people;) and when he opened it, all the people stood up:

6 And Ezra blessed the LORD, the great God. And all the people answered, Amen, Amen, with lifting up their hands: and they bowed their heads, and worshipped the LORD with *their* faces to the ground.

7 Also Jeshua, and Bani, and Sherebiah, Jamin, Akkub, Shabbethai, Hodijah, Maaseiah, Kelita, Azariah, Jozabad, Hanan, Pelaiah, and the Levites, caused the people to understand the law: and the people *stood* in their place.

8 So they read in the book in the ^alaw of God ^bdistinctly, and ^cgave the sense, and caused *them* to understand the reading.

9 ¶ And Nehemiah, which *is* the ^aTirshatha, and Ezra the priest the scribe, and the Levites that ^btaught the people, said unto all the people, This day *is* holy unto the LORD your God; ^cmourn not, nor weep. For all the people ^dwept, when they heard the words of the law.

10 Then he said unto them, Go your way, eat the fat, and drink the sweet, and send ^aportions unto them for whom nothing is prepared: for *this* ^bday *is* holy unto our Lord: neither be ye ^csorry; for the joy of the LORD is your ^dstrength.

11 So the Levites stilled all the people, saying, Hold your peace, for the day *is* holy; neither be ye grieved.

12 And all the people went their way to eat, and to drink, and to send portions, and to make great ^amirth, because they had ^bunderstood the words that were declared unto them.

13 ¶ And on the second day were gathered together the chief of the fathers of all the people, the priests, and the Levites, unto Ezra the scribe, even to ^aunderstand the words of the law.

14 And they found written in the law which the LORD had commanded by Moses, that ^athe children of Israel should dwell in booths in the ^bfeast of the seventh month:

15 And that they should publish and proclaim in all their cities, and in Jerusalem, saying, Go forth unto the mount, and fetch olive branches,

---

8 1*a* Neh. 3:26.
   b Ezra 7:6.
   c TG Scribe.
 2*a* Deut. 31:11.
 3*a* Ezra 7:10.
 4*a* Mosiah 2:7 (7–8).
 8*a* TG Scriptures, Study of.
   b Jacob 4:13 (13–14).
   c IE gave a commentary by the power of the

Holy Ghost.
Mosiah 1:2–5.
 9*a* Neh. 7:65.
   b TG Preaching.
   c TG Mourning.
   d Mosiah 4:1 (1–2).
10*a* Esth. 9:19.
   b D&C 59:12 (12–16).
   c 2 Ne. 4:15 (15–16).
   d TG Strength.

12*a* OR rejoicing.
   D&C 50:22 (17–22).
   b Mosiah 4:3.
13*a* TG Study.
14*a* This is the characteristic tradition of the feast of tabernacles.
   Lev. 23:43;
   Neh. 8:17 (16–17).
   b Zech. 14:16.

and pine branches, and myrtle branches, and palm branches, and branches of thick trees, to make booths, as *it is* written.

16 ¶ So the people went forth, and brought *them,* and made themselves booths, every one upon the roof of his house, and in their courts, and in the courts of the house of God, and in the street of the water gate, and in the street of the gate of ^aEphraim.

17 And all the congregation of them that were come again out of the captivity made ^abooths, and sat under the booths: for since the days of ^bJeshua the son of ^cNun unto that day had not the children of Israel done so. And there was very great gladness.

18 Also day by day, from the first day unto the last day, he ^aread in the book of the law of God. And they kept the feast seven days; and on the eighth day *was* a ^bsolemn assembly, according unto the manner.

CHAPTER 9

The Jews fast and confess their sins— The Levites bless and praise the Lord and recite His goodness toward Israel.

Now in the twenty and fourth day of this month the children of Israel were assembled with ^afasting, and with sackclothes, and earth upon them.

2 And the seed of Israel ^aseparated themselves from all ^bstrangers, and stood and ^cconfessed their sins, and the iniquities of their fathers.

3 And they stood up in their place, and read in the book of the law of the LORD their God *one* fourth part of the day; and *another* fourth part

they confessed, and worshipped the LORD their God.

4 ¶ Then stood up upon the stairs, of the Levites, Jeshua, and Bani, Kadmiel, Shebaniah, Bunni, Sherebiah, Bani, *and* Chenani, and cried with a loud voice unto the LORD their God.

5 Then the Levites, Jeshua, and Kadmiel, Bani, Hashabniah, Sherebiah, Hodijah, Shebaniah, *and* Pethahiah, said, Stand up *and* bless the LORD your God for ever and ever: and blessed be thy glorious name, which is exalted above all blessing and praise.

6 Thou, *even* thou, *art* ^aLORD alone; thou hast made ^bheaven, the heaven of heavens, with all their host, the earth, and all *things* that *are* therein, the seas, and all that *is* therein, and thou ^cpreservest them all; and the host of heaven worshippeth thee.

7 Thou *art* the LORD the God, who didst choose ^aAbram, and broughtest him forth out of ^bUr of the Chaldees, and gavest him the name of Abraham;

8 And foundest his heart faithful before thee, and madest a ^acovenant with him to give the land of the Canaanites, the Hittites, the Amorites, and the Perizzites, and the Jebusites, and the Girgashites, to give *it, I say,* to his seed, and hast performed thy words; for thou *art* ^brighteous:

9 And didst see the ^aaffliction of our fathers in Egypt, and heardest their cry by the ^bRed sea;

10 And shewedst signs and wonders upon Pharaoh, and on all his servants, and on all the people of his land: for thou knewest that they dealt proudly against them. So didst thou get thee a ^aname, as *it is* this day.

11 And thou didst ^adivide the sea

16a Neh. 12:39.
17a Neh. 8:14.
  b OR Joshua.
  c Ex. 33:11; Num. 11:28;
    1 Kgs. 16:34.
18a D&C 84:43 (43–44).
  b TG Solemn Assembly.
9 1a Jer. 36:6.
    TG Fast, Fasting.
  2a Alma 5:57.

  b OR foreigners.
  c TG Confession;
    Repent.
6a 2 Kgs. 19:15;
    Abr. 5:4 (1–5).
  b Rev. 14:7;
    Moses 3:4 (1–5).
  c Mosiah 2:21 (20–21).
7a Gen. 12:1.
  b Abr. 2:4 (3–4).

8a Gen. 12:7;
    1 Chr. 16:16.
  b D&C 3:2.
9a TG Affliction.
  b Hel. 8:11.
10a Ex. 7:5; 9:16.
11a Ex. 14:21;
    1 Ne. 4:2; 17:26;
    Mosiah 7:19;
    Hel. 8:11; D&C 8:3.

before them, so that they went through the midst of the sea on the dry land; and their persecutors thou threwest into the deeps, as a *b*stone into the mighty waters.

12 Moreover thou leddest them in the day by a cloudy *a*pillar; and in the night by a pillar of fire, to give them light in the way wherein they should go.

13 Thou camest down also upon mount Sinai, and spakest with them from heaven, and gavest them right judgments, and true laws, good *a*statutes and commandments:

14 And madest known unto them thy holy *a*sabbath, and commandedst them precepts, statutes, and laws, by the hand of Moses thy servant:

15 And gavest them *a*bread from heaven for their hunger, and broughtest forth *b*water for them out of the rock for their thirst, and promisedst them that they should go in to *c*possess the land which thou hadst sworn to give them.

16 But they and our fathers dealt proudly, and *a*hardened their necks, and hearkened not to thy commandments,

17 And refused to obey, neither were mindful of thy wonders that thou didst among them; but hardened their necks, and in their rebellion appointed a captain to *a*return to their bondage: but thou *art* a God ready to *b*pardon, gracious and *c*merciful, slow to *d*anger, and of great *e*kindness, and forsookest them not.

18 Yea, when they had made them a *a*molten *b*calf, and said, This *is* thy God that brought thee up out of Egypt, and had wrought great provocations;

19 Yet thou in thy manifold mercies *a*forsookest them not in the wilderness: the pillar of the cloud departed not from them by day, to lead them in the way; neither the pillar of fire by night, to shew them light, and the way wherein they should go.

20 Thou gavest also thy good *a*spirit to *b*instruct them, and withheldest not thy *c*manna from their mouth, and gavest them water for their thirst.

21 Yea, forty years didst thou sustain them in the wilderness, *so that* they lacked nothing; their clothes waxed not old, and their feet swelled not.

22 Moreover thou gavest them kingdoms and nations, and didst divide them into corners: so they possessed the land of Sihon, and the land of the king of Heshbon, and the land of Og king of Bashan.

23 Their children also *a*multipliedst thou as the stars of heaven, and broughtest them into the land, concerning which thou hadst promised to their fathers, that they should go in to possess *it*.

24 So the children went in and possessed the land, and thou subduedst before them the inhabitants of the land, the Canaanites, and gavest them into their hands, with their kings, and the people of the land, that they might do with them as they would.

25 And they took strong cities, and a *a*fat land, and possessed houses full of all goods, wells digged, vineyards, and oliveyards, and fruit trees in abundance: so they did eat, and were filled, and became fat, and delighted themselves in thy great goodness.

11*b* Ex. 15:5 (4–6).
12*a* Ex. 13:21; Deut. 1:33;
　　 Ps. 78:14.
13*a* Deut. 4:8;
　　 Ezek. 20:11;
　　 Mosiah 12:33;
　　 3 Ne. 25:4.
14*a* TG Sabbath.
15*a* Ex. 16:14.
　　 TG Bread.
　 b Ex. 17:6; 1 Ne. 17:29;

　　 2 Ne. 25:20.
　 c Deut. 1:8.
16*a* Jacob 4:14;
　　 Morm. 3:12 (11–12).
17*a* Num. 14:4.
　 b TG Forgive.
　 c 1 Chr. 16:41.
　 d TG Anger.
　 e TG Kindness.
18*a* Ex. 32:4.
　 b Deut. 9:16.

19*a* Jacob 6:4.
20*a* TG Teaching with the
　　 Spirit.
　 b TG Holy Ghost, Source
　　 of Testimony.
　 c Deut. 8:3;
　　 1 Ne. 17:28;
　　 Mosiah 7:19.
23*a* Gen. 15:5;
　　 D&C 132:30; Abr. 2:9.
25*a* Num. 13:27.

26 Nevertheless they were *a*disobedient, and *b*rebelled against thee, and cast thy law behind their backs, and *c*slew thy prophets which testified against them to turn them to thee, and they wrought great provocations.

27 Therefore thou deliveredst them into the hand of their *a*enemies, who *b*vexed them: and in the time of their *c*trouble, when they cried unto thee, thou heardest *them* from heaven; and according to thy manifold mercies thou gavest them *d*saviours, who saved them out of the hand of their enemies.

28 But after they had rest, they did evil again before thee: therefore leftest thou them in the hand of their enemies, so that they had the dominion over them: yet when they returned, and cried unto thee, thou heardest *them* from heaven; and many times didst thou deliver them according to thy mercies;

29 And testifiedst against them, that thou mightest bring them again unto thy law: yet they dealt proudly, and hearkened not unto thy commandments, but sinned against thy judgments, (which if a man do, he shall live in them;) and withdrew the shoulder, and hardened their neck, and would not hear.

30 Yet many years didst thou *a*forbear them, and *b*testifiedst against them by thy *c*spirit in thy *d*prophets: yet would they not give ear: therefore gavest thou them into the hand of the people of the lands.

31 Nevertheless for thy great mercies' sake thou didst not utterly consume them, nor forsake them; for thou *art* a gracious and *a*merciful God.

32 Now therefore, our God, the great, the mighty, and the *a*terrible God, who *b*keepest covenant and mercy, let not all the trouble seem little before thee, that hath come upon us, on our kings, on our princes, and on our priests, and on our prophets, and on our fathers, and on all thy people, since the time of the kings of Assyria unto this day.

33 Howbeit thou *art* *a*just in all that is brought upon us; for thou hast done right, but we have done *b*wickedly:

34 Neither have our kings, our princes, our priests, nor our fathers, kept thy law, nor hearkened unto thy commandments and thy testimonies, wherewith thou didst testify against them.

35 For they have not served thee in their kingdom, and in thy great goodness that thou gavest them, and in the large and fat land which thou gavest before them, neither turned they from their wicked works.

36 Behold, we *are* servants this day, and *for* the land that thou gavest unto our fathers to eat the fruit thereof and the good thereof, behold, we *are* servants in it:

37 And it yieldeth much increase unto the kings whom thou hast set over us because of our sins: also they have dominion over our bodies, and over our cattle, at their pleasure, and we *are* in great distress.

38 And because of all this we make a sure *covenant,* and write *it;* and our princes, Levites, *and* priests, seal *unto it.*

CHAPTER 10

The people covenant not to marry outside of Israel—They also covenant to honor the Sabbath, to pay tithes, and to keep the commandments.

Now those that sealed *were,* Nehemiah, the *a*Tirshatha, the son of Hachaliah, and Zidkijah,

26*a* TG Disobedience.
  b TG Rebellion.
  c Hel. 13:24 (24–26).
27*a* Judg. 2:14.
  b Hel. 12:3 (2–3).
  c TG Tribulation.
  d Judg. 3:9.
30*a* TG Forbear.

  b 2 Kgs. 17:13.
  c Acts 7:51.
    TG Holy Ghost,
    Mission of.
  d TG Prophets, Mission of.
31*a* TG God, Mercy of;
    Mercy.
32*a* OR feared (revered) God.

  b Deut. 7:9.
33*a* TG God, Justice of.
  b Mosiah 13:29;
    Alma 46:8;
    D&C 101:8 (7–8).
10 1*a* OR governor.

2 Seraiah, Azariah, Jeremiah,
3 Pashur, Amariah, Malchijah,
4 Hattush, Shebaniah, Malluch,
5 Harim, Meremoth, Obadiah,
6 Daniel, Ginnethon, Baruch,
7 Meshullam, Abijah, Mijamin,
8 Maaziah, Bilgai, Shemaiah: these *were* the priests.
9 And the Levites: both Jeshua the son of Azaniah, Binnui of the sons of Henadad, Kadmiel;
10 And their brethren, Shebaniah, Hodijah, Kelita, Pelaiah, Hanan,
11 Micha, Rehob, Hashabiah,
12 Zaccur, Sherebiah, Shebaniah,
13 Hodijah, Bani, Beninu.
14 The chief of the people; Parosh, Pahath-moab, Elam, Zatthu, Bani,
15 Bunni, Azgad, Bebai,
16 Adonijah, Bigvai, Adin,
17 Ater, Hizkijah, Azzur,
18 Hodijah, Hashum, Bezai,
19 Hariph, Anathoth, Nebai,
20 Magpiash, Meshullam, Hezir,
21 Meshezabeel, Zadok, Jaddua,
22 Pelatiah, Hanan, Anaiah,
23 Hoshea, Hananiah, Hashub,
24 Hallohesh, Pileha, Shobek,
25 Rehum, Hashabnah, Maaseiah,
26 And Ahijah, Hanan, Anan,
27 Malluch, Harim, Baanah.
28 ¶ And the rest of the people, the priests, the Levites, the porters, the singers, the *a*Nethinims, and all they that had *b*separated themselves from the people of the lands unto the law of God, their wives, their sons, and their daughters, every one having *c*knowledge, and having understanding;
29 They clave to their brethren, their nobles, and entered into *a*a *b*curse, and into an *c*oath, to walk in God's *d*law, which was given by Moses the servant of God, and to observe and do all the command-

ments of the LORD *e*our Lord, and his judgments and his statutes;
30 And that we would not give our *a*daughters unto the people of the land, nor take their daughters for our sons:
31 And *if* the people of the land bring *a*ware or any *b*victuals on the *c*sabbath day to sell, *that* we would not buy it of them on the sabbath, or on the holy day: and *that* we would leave the *d*seventh year, and the exaction of every debt.
32 Also we made ordinances for us, to *a*charge ourselves yearly with the third part of a shekel for the *b*service of the house of our God;
33 For the *a*shewbread, and for the continual *b*meat offering, and for the continual burnt offering, of the sabbaths, of the new moons, for the set feasts, and for the holy *things*, and for the sin offerings to make an *c*atonement for Israel, and *for* all the work of the house of our God.
34 And we *a*cast the lots among the priests, the Levites, and the people, for the *b*wood offering, to bring *it* into the house of our God, after the houses of our fathers, at times appointed year by year, to burn upon the altar of the LORD our God, as *it is* written in the law:
35 And to bring the *a*firstfruits of our ground, and the firstfruits of all fruit of all trees, year by year, unto the house of the LORD:
36 Also the *a*firstborn of our sons, and of our cattle, as *it is* written in the law, and the firstlings of our herds and of our flocks, to bring to the house of our God, unto the priests that minister in the house of our God:
37 And *that* we should bring the firstfruits of our *a*dough, and our

28*a* OR temple servants.
  b Ezra 6:21.
  c Mosiah 18:26.
29*a* JST Neh. 10:29 . . . *an oath, that* a curse *should come upon them if they did not walk . . .*
  b D&C 132:4.
    TG Curse.
  c Mosiah 18:10 (8–11).

d Ps. 119:106.
e JST Neh. 10:29 . . . *their God* . . .
30*a* TG Marriage, Interfaith.
31*a* OR merchandise.
  b OR grain.
  c TG Sabbath.
  d TG Sabbatical Year.
32*a* Ex. 30:13 (11–16).
  b 3 Ne. 24:8.

33*a* TG Bread, Shewbread.
  b Num. 28:8 (1–8).
  c Lev. 1:4; 2 Ne. 9:26.
34*a* 1 Ne. 3:11.
  b Gen. 22:3 (3, 6–7, 9);
    Neh. 13:31.
35*a* Ex. 22:29; 34:26;
    Ezek. 44:30.
36*a* TG Firstborn.
37*a* Lev. 23:17.

offerings, and the fruit of all manner of trees, of wine and of oil, unto the priests, to the chambers of the house of our God; and the tithes of our ground unto the Levites, that the same Levites might have the tithes in all the cities of our tillage.

38 And the priest the son of Aaron shall be with the Levites, when the Levites take tithes: and the Levites shall bring up the *a*tithe of the tithes unto the house of our God, to the chambers, into the treasure house.

39 For the children of Israel and the children of Levi shall bring the offering of the corn, of the new wine, and the oil, unto the chambers, where *are* the vessels of the sanctuary, and the priests that minister, and the porters, and the singers: and we will not forsake the house of our God.

CHAPTER 11

The people and their overseers are elected by lot to dwell in Jerusalem and the other cities.

AND the rulers of the people dwelt at Jerusalem: the rest of the people also cast lots, to bring one of ten to dwell in Jerusalem the *a*holy *b*city, and nine parts *to dwell* in *other* cities.

2 And the people blessed all the men, that willingly offered themselves to dwell at Jerusalem.

3 ¶ Now these *are* the chief of the province that dwelt in Jerusalem: but in the cities of Judah dwelt every one in his possession in their cities, *to wit*, Israel, the priests, and the Levites, and the *a*Nethinims, and the children of Solomon's servants.

4 And at Jerusalem dwelt *certain* of the children of Judah, and of the children of Benjamin. Of the children of Judah; Athaiah the son of Uzziah, the son of Zechariah, the son of Amariah, the son of Shephatiah, the son of Mahalaleel, of the children of Perez;

5 And Maaseiah the son of Baruch, the son of Col-hozeh, the son of Hazaiah, the son of Adaiah, the son of Joiarib, the son of Zechariah, the son of Shiloni.

6 All the sons of Perez that dwelt at Jerusalem *were* four hundred threescore and eight valiant men.

7 And these *are* the sons of Benjamin; Sallu the son of Meshullam, the son of Joed, the son of Pedaiah, the son of Kolaiah, the son of Maaseiah, the son of Ithiel, the son of Jesaiah.

8 And after him Gabbai, Sallai, nine hundred twenty and eight.

9 And Joel the son of Zichri *was* their overseer: and Judah the son of Senuah *was* second over the city.

10 Of the *a*priests: Jedaiah the son of Joiarib, Jachin.

11 Seraiah the son of Hilkiah, the son of Meshullam, the son of Zadok, the son of Meraioth, the son of Ahitub, *was* the ruler of the house of God.

12 And their brethren that did the work of the house *were* eight hundred twenty and two: and Adaiah the son of Jeroham, the son of Pelaliah, the son of Amzi, the son of Zechariah, the son of Pashur, the son of Malchiah,

13 And his brethren, chief of the fathers, two hundred forty and two: and Amashai the son of Azareel, the son of Ahasai, the son of Meshillemoth, the son of Immer,

14 And their brethren, mighty men of valour, an hundred twenty and eight: and their overseer *was* Zabdiel, the son of *one of* the great men.

15 Also of the Levites: Shemaiah the son of Hashub, the son of Azrikam, the son of Hashabiah, the son of Bunni;

16 And Shabbethai and Jozabad, of the *a*chief of the *b*Levites, *had* the *c*oversight of *d*the outward *e*business of the house of God.

17 And Mattaniah the son of Micha,

38*a* TG Tithing.
11 1*a* Matt. 4:5; 27:53;
　　　Rev. 11:2.
　　b Ezek. 48:31.
　3*a* OR temple servants.

10*a* 1 Chr. 9:10.
16*a* D&C 107:68 (68–69).
　　b TG Priest, Aaronic
　　　Priesthood.
　　　BD Priests.

c TG Bishop.
d OR outside work
　　connected with the
　　temple.
e 1 Chr. 26:29.

the son of Zabdi, the son of Asaph, *was* the principal to begin the thanksgiving in prayer: and Bakbukiah the second among his brethren, and Abda the son of Shammua, the son of Galal, the son of Jeduthun.

18 All the Levites in the holy city *were* two hundred fourscore and four.

19 Moreover the porters, Akkub, Talmon, and their brethren that kept the gates, *were* an hundred seventy and two.

20 ¶ And the residue of Israel, of the priests, *and* the Levites, *were* in all the cities of Judah, every one in his inheritance.

21 But the Nethinims dwelt in Ophel: and Ziha and Gispa *were* over the Nethinims.

22 The ^a^overseer also of the Levites at Jerusalem *was* Uzzi the son of Bani, the son of Hashabiah, the son of Mattaniah, the son of Micha. Of the sons of Asaph, the singers *were* over the business of the house of God.

23 For *it was* the king's commandment concerning them, that a certain portion should be for the singers, due for every day.

24 And Pethahiah the son of Meshezabeel, of the children of ^a^Zerah the son of Judah, *was* at the king's hand in all matters concerning the people.

25 And for the villages, with their fields, *some* of the children of Judah dwelt at Kirjath-arba, and *in* the villages thereof, and at Dibon, and *in* the villages thereof, and at Jekabzeel, and *in* the villages thereof,

26 And at Jeshua, and at Moladah, and at Beth-phelet,

27 And at Hazar-shual, and at Beersheba, and *in* the villages thereof,

28 And at Ziklag, and at Mekonah, and in the villages thereof,

29 And at En-rimmon, and at Zareah, and at Jarmuth,

30 Zanoah, Adullam, and *in* their villages, at Lachish, and the fields thereof, at Azekah, and *in* the villages thereof. And they dwelt from Beer-sheba unto the valley of Hinnom.

31 The children also of Benjamin from Geba *dwelt* at Michmash, and Aija, and Beth-el, and *in* their villages,

32 *And* at Anathoth, Nob, Ananiah,

33 Hazor, Ramah, Gittaim,

34 Hadid, Zeboim, Neballat,

35 Lod, and Ono, the valley of craftsmen.

36 And of the Levites *were* divisions *in* Judah, *and* in Benjamin.

CHAPTER 12

The priests and Levites who came up from Babylon are named—The walls of Jerusalem are dedicated—The offices of priests and Levites are appointed in the temple.

Now these *are* the ^a^priests and the Levites that went up with Zerubbabel the son of Shealtiel, and Jeshua: Seraiah, Jeremiah, Ezra,

2 Amariah, Malluch, Hattush,

3 Shechaniah, Rehum, Meremoth,

4 Iddo, Ginnetho, ^a^Abijah,

5 Miamin, Maadiah, Bilgah,

6 Shemaiah, and Joiarib, Jedaiah,

7 Sallu, Amok, Hilkiah, Jedaiah. These *were* the chief of the priests and of their brethren in the days of Jeshua.

8 Moreover the Levites: Jeshua, Binnui, Kadmiel, Sherebiah, Judah, *and* Mattaniah, *which was* over the thanksgiving, he and his brethren.

9 Also Bakbukiah and Unni, their brethren, *were* over against them in the watches.

10 ¶ And Jeshua begat Joiakim, Joiakim also begat Eliashib, and Eliashib begat Joiada,

11 And Joiada begat Jonathan, and Jonathan begat Jaddua.

12 And in the days of Joiakim were priests, the chief of the fathers: of Seraiah, Meraiah; of Jeremiah, Hananiah;

22*a* D&C 107:16 (13–17).
  TG Bishop.
24*a* Gen. 38:30.
12 1*a* Ezra 2:1 (1–2);
      1 Ne. 10:3.
  4*a* Luke 1:5.

13 Of Ezra, Meshullam; of Amariah, Jehohanan;

14 Of Melicu, Jonathan; of Shebaniah, Joseph;

15 Of Harim, Adna; of Meraioth, Helkai;

16 Of Iddo, Zechariah; of Ginnethon, Meshullam;

17 Of Abijah, Zichri; of Miniamin, of Moadiah, Piltai;

18 Of Bilgah, Shammua; of Shemaiah, Jehonathan;

19 And of Joiarib, Mattenai; of Jedaiah, Uzzi;

20 Of Sallai, Kallai; of Amok, Eber;

21 Of Hilkiah, Hashabiah; of Jedaiah, Nethaneel.

22 ¶ The Levites in the days of Eliashib, Joiada, and Johanan, and Jaddua, *were* recorded chief of the fathers: also the priests, to the reign of Darius the Persian.

23 The sons of Levi, the chief of the fathers, *were* written in the book of the chronicles, even until the days of Johanan the son of Eliashib.

24 And the chief of the Levites: Hashabiah, Sherebiah, and Jeshua the son of Kadmiel, with their brethren over against them, to praise *and* to give *ᵃ*thanks, according to the commandment of David the man of God, ward over against ward.

25 Mattaniah, and Bakbukiah, Obadiah, Meshullam, Talmon, Akkub, *were* porters keeping the ward at the *ᵃ*thresholds of the gates.

26 These *were* in the days of Joiakim the son of Jeshua, the son of Jozadak, and in the days of Nehemiah the governor, and of Ezra the priest, the scribe.

27 ¶ And at the dedication of the wall of Jerusalem they sought the Levites out of all their places, to bring them to Jerusalem, to keep the dedication with gladness, both with thanksgivings, and with singing, *with* cymbals, psalteries, and with harps.

28 And the sons of the singers gathered themselves together, both out of the plain country round about Jerusalem, and from the villages of Netophathi;

29 Also from the house of Gilgal, and out of the fields of Geba and Azmaveth: for the singers had builded them villages round about Jerusalem.

30 And the priests and the Levites *ᵃ*purified themselves, and purified the people, and the gates, and the wall.

31 Then I brought up the princes of Judah upon the wall, and appointed two great *companies of them that gave* thanks, *whereof one* went on the right hand upon the wall toward the *ᵃ*dung gate:

32 And after them went Hoshaiah, and half of the princes of Judah,

33 And Azariah, Ezra, and Meshullam,

34 Judah, and Benjamin, and Shemaiah, and Jeremiah,

35 And *certain* of the priests' sons with trumpets; *namely,* Zechariah the son of Jonathan, the son of Shemaiah, the son of Mattaniah, the son of Michaiah, the son of Zaccur, the son of Asaph:

36 And his brethren, Shemaiah, and Azarael, Milalai, Gilalai, Maai, Nethaneel, and Judah, Hanani, with the *ᵃ*musical instruments of David the man of God, and Ezra the scribe before them.

37 And at the *ᵃ*fountain gate, which was over against them, they went up by the stairs of the city of David, at the going up of the wall, above the house of David, even unto the water gate eastward.

38 And the other *company of them that gave* thanks went over against *them,* and I after them, and the half of the people upon the wall, from beyond the tower of the furnaces even unto the broad wall;

39 And from above the gate of *ᵃ*Ephraim, and above the old gate,

---

24*a* D&C 59:21.
25*a* OR storehouses.
30*a* Num. 8:7 (7–14);
   3 Ne. 19:28 (28–29);

D&C 50:29 (28–29);
   88:74 (74–75).
31*a* Neh. 2:13.
36*a* 1 Chr. 23:5.

37*a* Neh. 2:14.
39*a* Neh. 8:16.

and above the [b]fish gate, and the tower of Hananeel, and the tower of Meah, even unto the sheep gate: and they stood still in the prison gate.

40 So stood the two *companies of them that gave* thanks in the house of God, and I, and the half of the rulers with me:

41 And the priests; Eliakim, Maaseiah, Miniamin, Michaiah, Elioenai, Zechariah, *and* Hananiah, with trumpets;

42 And Maaseiah, and Shemaiah, and Eleazar, and Uzzi, and Jehohanan, and Malchijah, and Elam, and Ezer. And the singers sang loud, with Jezrahiah *their* overseer.

43 Also that day they offered great sacrifices, and rejoiced: for God had made them [a]rejoice with great joy: the wives also and the children rejoiced: so that the joy of Jerusalem was heard even afar off.

44 ¶ And at that time were some appointed over the chambers for the treasures, for the offerings, for the firstfruits, and for the [a]tithes, to gather into them out of the fields of the cities the portions of the law for the priests and Levites: for Judah rejoiced for the priests and for the Levites that waited.

45 And both the singers and the porters kept the [a]ward of their God, and the ward of the purification, according to the commandment of David, *and* of Solomon his son.

46 For in the days of David and Asaph of old *there were* chief of the singers, and songs of praise and thanksgiving unto God.

47 And all Israel in the days of Zerubbabel, and in the days of Nehemiah, gave the portions of the singers and the porters, every day his portion: and they sanctified *holy things* unto the Levites; and the Levites sanctified *them* unto the children of Aaron.

CHAPTER 13

The Ammonites and Moabites are denied a place in the congregation of God—Tobiah is ejected from his dwelling place in the temple—Nehemiah corrects abuses and reinstitutes Sabbath observance—Some Jews are rebuked for marrying non-Israelite women and defiling the priesthood.

ON that day they read in the [a]book of Moses in the audience of the people; and therein was found written, that the [b]Ammonite and the Moabite should not come into the congregation of God for ever;

2 Because they met not the children of Israel with bread and with water, but hired [a]Balaam against them, that he should curse them: howbeit our God turned the curse into a blessing.

3 Now it came to pass, when they had heard the law, that they separated from Israel all the [a]mixed multitude.

4 ¶ And before this, Eliashib the priest, having the oversight of the chamber of the house of our God, *was* allied unto Tobiah:

5 And he had prepared for him a great chamber, where aforetime they laid the meat offerings, the frankincense, and the vessels, and the tithes of the corn, the new wine, and the oil, which was commanded *to be given* to the Levites, and the singers, and the porters; and the offerings of the priests.

6 But in all this *time* was not I at Jerusalem: for in the two and thirtieth year of Artaxerxes king of Babylon came I unto the king, and after certain days obtained I leave of the king:

7 And I came to Jerusalem, and understood of the evil that Eliashib did for Tobiah, in preparing him a chamber in the courts of the house of God.

8 And it grieved me sore: therefore I cast forth all the household stuff of Tobiah out of the chamber.

39*b* Neh. 3:3.
43*a* Mosiah 2:20.
44*a* TG Tithing.

45*a* OR guard, watch.
13 1*a* Ex. 17:14;
    Moses 1:40.

b Deut. 23:3 (3–5).
2*a* Num. 22:5; 23:11.
3*a* Ex. 12:38.

9 Then I commanded, and they cleansed the chambers: and thither brought I again the vessels of the house of God, with the meat offering and the frankincense.

10 ¶ And I perceived that the portions of the Levites had not been given *them:* for the Levites and the singers, that did the work, were fled every one to his field.

11 Then contended I with the rulers, and said, Why is the house of God forsaken? And I gathered them together, and set them in their place.

12 Then brought all Judah the *a*tithe of the corn and the new wine and the oil unto the *b*treasuries.

13 And I made treasurers over the treasuries, Shelemiah the priest, and Zadok the scribe, and of the Levites, Pedaiah: and next to them *was* Hanan the son of Zaccur, the son of Mattaniah: for they were counted faithful, and their office *was* to distribute unto their brethren.

14 Remember me, O my God, concerning this, and wipe not out my good deeds that I have done for the house of my God, and for the offices thereof.

15 ¶ In those days saw I in Judah *some* treading wine presses on the *a*sabbath, and bringing in sheaves, and lading asses; as also wine, grapes, and figs, and all *manner of* burdens, which they brought into Jerusalem on the sabbath day: and I testified *against them* in the day wherein they sold *b*victuals.

16 There dwelt men of Tyre also therein, which brought fish, and all manner of ware, and sold on the sabbath unto the children of Judah, and in Jerusalem.

17 Then I contended with the nobles of Judah, and said unto them, What evil thing *is* this that ye do, and profane the sabbath day?

18 Did not your fathers thus, and did not our God bring all this evil upon us, and upon this city? yet ye bring more wrath upon Israel by profaning the sabbath.

19 And it came to pass, that when the gates of Jerusalem began to be dark before the sabbath, I commanded that the gates should be shut, and charged that they should not be opened till after the sabbath: and *some* of my servants set I at the gates, *that* there should no burden be brought in on the sabbath day.

20 So the merchants and sellers of all kind of ware lodged *a*without Jerusalem once or twice.

21 Then I testified against them, and said unto them, Why lodge ye about the wall? if ye do *so* again, I will lay hands on you. From that time forth came they no *more* on the sabbath.

22 And I commanded the Levites that they should cleanse themselves, and *that* they should come *and* keep the gates, to sanctify the sabbath day. Remember me, O my God, *concerning* this also, and spare me according to the greatness of thy mercy.

23 ¶ In those days also saw I Jews *that* had married wives of Ashdod, of Ammon, *and* of Moab:

24 And their children spake half in the speech of Ashdod, and could not speak in the Jews' *a*language, but according to the language of each people.

25 And I contended with them, and cursed them, and smote certain of them, and plucked off their hair, and made them swear by God, *saying,* Ye shall not *a*give your daughters unto *b*their sons, nor take their daughters unto your sons, or for yourselves.

26 Did not *a*Solomon king of Israel sin by these things? yet among many nations was there no king like him, who was beloved of his God, and God made him king over all Israel: nevertheless even him did outlandish women cause to sin.

27 Shall we then hearken unto you

12a TG Tithing.
  b OR storage houses.
15a TG Sabbath.
  b OR supplies.
20a OR outside of Jerusalem.
24a TG Language.
25a TG Marriage, Interfaith.
  b TG Gentiles.
26a 1 Kgs. 11:1;
    Jacob 2:24 (23–24).

to do all this great evil, to transgress against our God in marrying ^astrange wives?

28 And *one* of the sons of Joiada, the son of Eliashib the high priest, *was* son in law to Sanballat the Horonite: therefore I chased him from me.

29 Remember them, O my God, because they have defiled the ^apriesthood, and the ^bcovenant of the priesthood, and of the Levites.

30 Thus cleansed I them from all ^astrangers, and appointed the wards of the priests and the Levites, every one in his business;

31 And for the ^awood offering, at times appointed, and for the firstfruits. Remember me, O my God, for good.

THE BOOK OF
ESTHER

CHAPTER 1

Ahasuerus of Persia and Media makes royal feasts—Vashti disobeys the king and is deposed as queen.

NOW it came to pass in the days of ^aAhasuerus, (this *is* Ahasuerus which reigned, from India even unto Ethiopia, *over* an hundred and seven and twenty ^bprovinces:)

2 *That* in those days, when the king Ahasuerus sat on the throne of his kingdom, which *was* in ^aShushan the palace,

3 In the third year of his reign, he made a ^afeast unto all his princes and his servants; the power of Persia and Media, the nobles and princes of the provinces, *being* before him:

4 When he shewed the ^ariches of his glorious kingdom and the honour of his excellent majesty many days, *even* an hundred and fourscore days.

5 And when these days were expired, the king made a feast unto all the people that were present in Shushan the palace, both unto great and small, seven days, in the court of the ^agarden of the king's palace;

6 *Where were* white, green, and blue, *hangings,* fastened with cords of fine linen and purple to silver rings and pillars of marble: the beds *were of* gold and silver, upon a pavement of red, and blue, and white, and black, marble.

7 And they gave *them* drink in vessels of gold, (the vessels being diverse one from another,) and royal wine in abundance, according to the state of the king.

8 And the ^adrinking *was* according to the law; none did compel: for so the king had appointed to all the officers of his house, that they should do according to every man's ^bpleasure.

9 Also Vashti the queen made a feast for the women *in* the royal house which *belonged* to king Ahasuerus.

27a OR foreign wives.
29a TG Priesthood, Aaronic.
  b Mal. 2:8 (4–8).
    TG Priesthood, Oath and Covenant.
30a OR foreigners.
31a Neh. 10:34.

[ESTHER]
1 1a Ezra 4:6.
  b Esth. 9:30.
2a OR Susa; i.e., the capital of Persia.
    Neh. 1:1.

3a Alma 18:9.
4a Mosiah 11:8;
    Alma 4:6;
    Ether 10:7 (5–7).
5a Esth. 7:7.
8a 2 Ne. 15:22.
  b Alma 12:31.

10 ¶ On the seventh day, when the heart of the king was merry with wine, he commanded Mehuman, Biztha, ^aHarbona, Bigtha, and Abagtha, Zethar, and Carcas, the seven chamberlains that served in the presence of Ahasuerus the king,

11 To bring Vashti the queen before the king with the crown royal, to shew the people and the princes her beauty: for she *was* fair to look on.

12 But the queen Vashti refused to come at the king's commandment by *his* chamberlains: therefore was the king very ^awroth, and his anger burned in him.

13 ¶ Then the king said to the ^awise men, which knew the ^btimes, (for so *was* the king's manner toward all that knew law and judgment:

14 And the next unto him *was* Carshena, Shethar, Admatha, Tarshish, Meres, Marsena, *and* Memucan, the seven princes of Persia and Media, which saw the king's face, *and* which sat the first in the kingdom;)

15 What shall we do unto the queen Vashti according to law, because she hath not performed the commandment of the king Ahasuerus by the chamberlains?

16 And Memucan answered before the king and the princes, Vashti the queen hath not done wrong to the king only, but also to all the princes, and to all the people that *are* in all the provinces of the king Ahasuerus.

17 For *this* deed of the queen shall come abroad unto all women, so that they shall despise their husbands in their eyes, when it shall be reported, The king Ahasuerus commanded Vashti the queen to be brought in before him, but she came not.

18 *Likewise* shall the ladies of Persia and Media say this day unto all the king's princes, which have heard of the deed of the queen. Thus *shall*

there arise too much contempt and wrath.

19 If it please the king, let there go a royal commandment from him, and let it be written among the laws of the Persians and the Medes, that it be not ^aaltered, That Vashti come no more before king Ahasuerus; and let the king give her royal estate unto another that is better than she.

20 And when the king's decree which he shall make shall be published throughout all his empire, (for it is great,) all the ^awives shall give to their husbands honour, both to great and small.

21 And the saying pleased the king and the princes; and the king did according to the word of Memucan:

22 For he sent letters into all the king's provinces, into every province according to the writing thereof, and to every people after their ^alanguage, that every man should bear ^brule in his own house, and that *it* should be published according to the language of every people.

CHAPTER 2

Ahasuerus seeks a new queen—Mordecai presents Esther—Esther pleases the king and is chosen as queen—Mordecai exposes a plot against the king.

AFTER these things, when the wrath of king Ahasuerus was appeased, he remembered Vashti, and what she had done, and what was decreed against her.

2 Then said the king's servants that ministered unto him, Let there be fair young virgins sought for the king:

3 And let the king appoint officers in all the provinces of his kingdom, that they may gather together all the fair young virgins unto Shushan the palace, to the house of the women, unto the custody of Hege the king's chamberlain, keeper of the

---

10*a* Esth. 7:9.
12*a* Mosiah 17:3;
    Alma 47:3 (1–3).
13*a* Jer. 10:7.

b 1 Chr. 12:32;
    Matt. 16:3.
19*a* Esth. 8:8.
20*a* Eph. 5:22 (22–24).

22*a* Esth. 8:9.
  b 1 Tim. 3:5 (4–5);
    D&C 93:43 (41–43, 50).

women; and let their things for purification be given *them:*

4 And let the maiden which pleaseth the king be queen instead of Vashti. And the thing pleased the king; and he did so.

5 ¶ *Now* in Shushan the palace there was a certain Jew, whose name *was* Mordecai, the son of Jair, the son of Shimei, the son of Kish, a Benjamite;

6 Who had been *a*carried away from *b*Jerusalem with the captivity which had been carried away with Jeconiah king of Judah, whom Nebuchadnezzar the king of Babylon had carried away.

7 And he brought up Hadassah, that *is,* Esther, his uncle's daughter: for she had neither father nor mother, and the maid *was* fair and beautiful; whom Mordecai, when her father and mother were dead, took for his own daughter.

8 ¶ So it came to pass, when the king's commandment and his decree was heard, and when many maidens were gathered together unto Shushan the palace, to the custody of Hegai, that Esther was brought also unto the king's house, to the custody of Hegai, keeper of the women.

9 And the maiden pleased him, and she obtained kindness of him; and he speedily gave her her things for purification, with such things as belonged to her, and seven maidens, *which were* meet to be given her, out of the king's house: and he preferred her and her maids unto the best *place* of the house of the women.

10 Esther had not shewed her people nor her kindred: for Mordecai had *a*charged her that she should not shew *it.*

11 And Mordecai walked every day before the court of the women's house, to know how Esther did, and what should become of her.

12 ¶ Now when every maid's turn was come to go in to king Ahasuerus,

after that she had been twelve months, according to the manner of the women, (for so were the days of their *a*purifications accomplished, *to wit,* six months with oil of myrrh, and six months with sweet odours, and with *other* things for the purifying of the women;)

13 Then thus came *every* maiden unto the king; whatsoever she desired was given her to go with her out of the house of the women unto the king's house.

14 In the evening she went, and on the morrow she returned into the second house of the women, to the custody of Shaashgaz, the king's chamberlain, which kept the *a*concubines: she came in unto the king no more, except the king delighted in her, and that she were called by name.

15 ¶ Now when the turn of Esther, the *a*daughter of Abihail the uncle of Mordecai, who had taken her for his daughter, was come to go in unto the king, she required nothing but what Hegai the king's chamberlain, the keeper of the women, appointed. And Esther obtained favour in the sight of all them that looked upon her.

16 So Esther was taken unto king Ahasuerus into his house royal in the tenth month, which *is* the month Tebeth, in the seventh year of his reign.

17 And the king loved Esther above all the women, and she obtained grace and favour in his sight more than all the virgins; so that he set the royal crown upon her head, and made her queen instead of Vashti.

18 Then the king made a great feast unto all his princes and his servants, *even* Esther's feast; and he made a release to the provinces, and gave gifts, according to the state of the king.

19 And when the virgins were gathered together the second time, then Mordecai sat in the king's gate.

2 6a 2 Kgs. 24:14 (14–15).   Hel. 8:20 (20–21).   14a Ether 10:5.
    b 1 Ne. 10:3;   10a Esth. 8:1.   15a Esth. 9:29.
      2 Ne. 6:8;   12a TG Purification.

20 Esther had not *yet* shewed her kindred nor her people; as Mordecai had charged her: for Esther did the commandment of Mordecai, like as when she was brought up with him.

21 ¶ In those days, while Mordecai sat in the king's gate, two of the king's chamberlains, *a*Bigthan and Teresh, of those which kept the door, were wroth, and sought to *b*lay hand on the king Ahasuerus.

22 And the thing was known to *a*Mordecai, who told *it* unto Esther the queen; and Esther certified the king *thereof* in Mordecai's name.

23 And when inquisition was made of the matter, it was found out; therefore they were both hanged on a tree: and it was written in the *a*book of the chronicles before the king.

CHAPTER 3

Mordecai, the Jew, refuses to bow to Haman—Haman arranges a decree to kill all the Jews in the kingdom.

AFTER these things did king Ahasuerus *a*promote Haman the son of *b*Hammedatha the Agagite, and advanced him, and set his seat above all the princes that *were* with him.

2 And all the king's servants, that *were* in the king's gate, *a*bowed, and reverenced Haman: for the king had so commanded concerning him. But Mordecai bowed not, nor did *him* reverence.

3 Then the king's servants, which *were* in the king's gate, said unto Mordecai, Why transgressest thou the king's commandment?

4 Now it came to pass, when they spake daily unto him, and he hearkened not unto them, that they told Haman, to see whether Mordecai's matters would stand: for he had told them that he *was* a Jew.

5 And when Haman saw that Mordecai *a*bowed not, nor did him reverence, then was Haman full of *b*wrath.

6 And he thought scorn to lay hands on Mordecai alone; for they had shewed him the people of Mordecai: wherefore Haman sought to *a*destroy all the Jews that *were* throughout the whole kingdom of Ahasuerus, *even* the people of Mordecai.

7 ¶ In the first month, that *is*, the month Nisan, in the twelfth year of king Ahasuerus, they cast Pur, that *is*, the lot, before Haman from day to day, and from month to month, *to* the twelfth *month*, that *is*, the month *a*Adar.

8 ¶ And Haman said unto king Ahasuerus, There is a certain people scattered abroad and dispersed among the people in all the provinces of thy kingdom; and their laws *are* diverse from all people; neither keep they the king's laws: therefore it *is* not for the king's profit to suffer them.

9 If it please the king, let it be written that they may be *a*destroyed: and I will *b*pay ten thousand talents of silver to the hands of those that have the charge of the business, to bring *it* into the king's treasuries.

10 And the king took his *a*ring from his hand, and gave it unto Haman the son of Hammedatha the Agagite, the Jews' enemy.

11 And the king said unto Haman, The silver *is* given to thee, the people also, to do with them as it seemeth good to thee.

12 Then were the king's scribes called on the thirteenth day of the first month, and there was written according to all that Haman had commanded unto the king's lieutenants, and to the governors that *were* over every province, and to the rulers of every people of every province according to the writing thereof, and *to* every people after their

---

21*a* Esth. 6:2.
  b Ether 9:5.
22*a* Esth. 7:9.
23*a* Esth. 6:1.
3 1*a* Esth. 5:11.

  b 1 Sam. 15:8 (8–9).
2*a* Mosiah 7:12.
5*a* Esth. 5:9.
  b Prov. 27:3.
6*a* TG Tyranny.

7*a* Ezra 6:15.
9*a* Esth. 8:3; 9:24.
  b Esth. 7:4.
10*a* Gen. 41:42;
    Esth. 8:2.

language; in the *name of king Ahasuerus was it written, and *sealed
with the king's ring.

13 And the *letters were sent by
posts into all the king's provinces,
to destroy, to *kill, and to cause to
perish, all Jews, both young and old,
little children and women, in *one
day, *even* upon the thirteenth *day*
of the twelfth month, which *is* the
month Adar, and *to take* the spoil
of them for a prey.

14 The copy of the writing for a
commandment to be given in every
province was published unto all
people, that they should be ready
against that day.

15 The posts went out, being hastened by the king's commandment,
and the decree was given in Shushan
the palace. And the king and Haman sat down to drink; but the city
Shushan was perplexed.

CHAPTER 4

*Mordecai and the Jews mourn and fast
because of the king's decree—Esther, at
the peril of her life, prepares to go in
unto the king.*

WHEN Mordecai perceived all that
was done, Mordecai rent his clothes,
and put on sackcloth with ashes,
and went out into the midst of the
city, and cried with a loud and a
bitter cry;

2 And came even before the king's
gate: for none *might* enter into the
king's gate clothed with sackcloth.

3 And in every province, whithersoever the king's commandment
and his decree came, *there was* great
mourning among the Jews, and
*fasting, and weeping, and wail-
ing; and many lay in sackcloth and
ashes.

4 ¶ So Esther's maids and her
chamberlains came and told *it* her.
Then was the queen exceedingly
grieved; and she sent raiment to
clothe Mordecai, and to take away

his sackcloth from him: but he received *it* not.

5 Then called Esther for Hatach,
one of the king's chamberlains,
whom he had appointed to attend
upon her, and gave him a commandment to Mordecai, to know what it
was, and why it *was*.

6 So Hatach went forth to Mordecai
unto the street of the city, which
was before the king's gate.

7 And Mordecai told him of all that
had happened unto him, and of the
sum of the money that Haman had
promised to *pay to the king's treasuries for the Jews, to destroy them.

8 Also he gave him the copy of
the writing of the decree that was
given at Shushan to destroy them, to
shew *it* unto Esther, and to declare
it unto her, and to charge her that
she should go in unto the king, to
make supplication unto him, and
to make request before him for
her people.

9 And Hatach came and told Esther the words of Mordecai.

10 ¶ Again Esther spake unto
Hatach, and gave him commandment unto Mordecai;

11 All the king's servants, and
the people of the king's provinces,
do know, that whosoever, whether
man or woman, shall come unto
the king into the inner *court, who
is not called, *there is* one law of his
to put *him* to *death, except such to
whom the king shall hold out the
golden *sceptre, that he may live:
but I have not been called to come
in unto the king these thirty days.

12 And they told to Mordecai Esther's words.

13 Then Mordecai commanded to
answer Esther, Think not with thyself that thou shalt escape in the
king's house, more than all the Jews.

14 For if thou altogether holdest
thy peace at this time, *then* shall
there *enlargement and deliverance arise to the Jews from another

---

12a Esth. 8:10 (8–10).
  b TG Seal.
13a Esth. 9:1.
  b D&C 121:23.

c Esth. 8:12.
4 3a Esth. 9:31.
7a Esth. 7:4.
11a Esth. 6:4.

b TG Capital Punishment.
c Esth. 5:2; 8:4.
14a HEB breath; i.e., relief.

place; but thou and thy father's house shall be destroyed: and who knoweth whether thou art come to the kingdom for *such* a *b*time as this?

15 ¶ Then Esther bade *them* return Mordecai *this answer,*

16 Go, gather together all the Jews that are present in Shushan, and *a*fast ye for me, and neither eat nor drink three days, night or day: I also and my maidens will fast likewise; and so will I go in unto the king, which *is* not according to the law: and if I perish, I perish.

17 So Mordecai went his way, and did according to all that Esther had commanded him.

CHAPTER 5

The king receives Esther—She invites him and Haman to a banquet—Haman plans to have Mordecai hanged.

Now it came to pass on the third day, that Esther put on *her* royal *apparel,* and stood in the inner court of the king's house, over against the king's house: and the king sat upon his royal throne in the royal house, over against the gate of the house.

2 And it was so, when the king saw Esther the queen standing in the court, *that* she obtained favour in his sight: and the king held out to Esther the golden *a*sceptre that *was* in his hand. So Esther drew near, and touched the top of the sceptre.

3 Then said the king unto her, What wilt thou, queen Esther? and what *is* thy request? it shall be even given thee to the *a*half of the kingdom.

4 And Esther answered, If *it seem* good unto the king, let the king and Haman come this day unto the banquet that I have prepared for him.

5 Then the king said, Cause Haman to make haste, that he may do as Esther hath said. So the king and Haman came to the banquet that Esther had prepared.

6 ¶ And the king said unto Esther at the banquet of wine, What *is* thy *a*petition? and it shall be granted thee: and what *is* thy request? even to the half of the kingdom it shall be performed.

7 Then answered Esther, and said, My petition and my request *is;*

8 If I have found favour in the sight of the king, and if it please the king to grant my petition, and to perform my request, let the king and Haman come to the *a*banquet that I shall prepare for them, and I will do to morrow as the king hath said.

9 ¶ Then went Haman forth that day joyful and with a glad heart: but when Haman saw Mordecai in the king's gate, that he *a*stood not up, nor moved for him, he was full of indignation against Mordecai.

10 Nevertheless Haman refrained himself: and when he came home, he sent and called for his friends, and Zeresh his wife.

11 And Haman told them of the glory of his riches, and the multitude of his children, and all *the things* wherein the king had *a*promoted him, and how he had advanced him above the princes and servants of the king.

12 Haman said moreover, Yea, Esther the queen did let no man come in with the king unto the banquet that she had prepared but myself; and to morrow am I invited unto her also with the king.

13 Yet all this availeth me nothing, so long as I see Mordecai the Jew sitting at the king's gate.

14 ¶ Then said Zeresh his wife and all his friends unto him, Let a *a*gallows be made of fifty cubits high, and to morrow *b*speak thou unto the king that Mordecai may be hanged thereon: then go thou in merrily with the king unto the banquet. And the thing pleased Haman; and he caused the gallows to be made.

14*b* Gen. 45:7 (7–8).
16*a* TG Fast, Fasting.
5 2*a* Esth. 4:11.
  3*a* Mark 6:23.

6*a* Esth. 7:2.
8*a* Esth. 6:14.
9*a* Esth. 3:5.
11*a* Esth. 3:1.

14*a* Esth. 7:9.
  b Esth. 6:4.

CHAPTER 6

Mordecai receives great honors—Haman mourns and is counseled by his wife.

ON that night could not the king sleep, and he commanded to bring the book of [a]records of the [b]chronicles; and they were read before the king.

2 And it was found written, that Mordecai had told of [a]Bigthana and Teresh, two of the king's chamberlains, the keepers of the door, who sought to lay hand on the king Ahasuerus.

3 And the king said, What honour and dignity hath been done to Mordecai for this? Then said the king's servants that ministered unto him, There is nothing done for him.

4 ¶ And the king said, Who *is* in the court? Now Haman was come into the outward [a]court of the king's house, to [b]speak unto the king to hang Mordecai on the gallows that he had prepared for him.

5 And the king's servants said unto him, Behold, Haman standeth in the court. And the king said, Let him come in.

6 So Haman came in. And the king said unto him, What shall be done unto the man whom the king delighteth to honour? Now Haman thought in his heart, To whom would the king delight to do honour more than to myself?

7 And Haman answered the king, For the man whom the king delighteth to honour,

8 Let the royal apparel be brought which the king *useth* to wear, and the horse that the king rideth upon, and the crown royal which is set upon his head:

9 And let this apparel and horse be delivered to the hand of one of the king's most noble princes, that they may array the man *withal* whom the king delighteth to honour, and bring him on horseback through the street of the city, and proclaim before him, Thus shall it be done to the man whom the king delighteth to honour.

10 Then the king said to Haman, Make haste, *and* take the apparel and the horse, as thou hast said, and do even so to Mordecai the Jew, that sitteth at the king's gate: let nothing fail of all that thou hast spoken.

11 Then took Haman the apparel and the horse, and arrayed Mordecai, and brought him on horseback through the street of the city, and proclaimed before him, Thus shall it be done unto the man whom the king delighteth to honour.

12 ¶ And Mordecai came again to the king's gate. But Haman hasted to his house mourning, and having his [a]head covered.

13 And Haman told Zeresh his wife and all his friends every *thing* that had befallen him. Then said his wise men and Zeresh his wife unto him, If Mordecai *be* of the seed of the Jews, before whom thou hast begun to fall, thou shalt not prevail against him, but shalt surely fall before him.

14 And while they *were* yet talking with him, came the king's chamberlains, and hasted to bring Haman unto the [a]banquet that Esther had prepared.

CHAPTER 7

Esther reveals Haman's plot to destroy the Jews—He is hanged on his own gallows.

So the king and Haman came to banquet with Esther the queen.

2 And the king said again unto Esther on the second day at the banquet of wine, What *is* thy [a]petition, queen Esther? and it shall be granted thee: and what *is* thy request? and it shall be performed, *even* to the half of the kingdom.

3 Then Esther the queen answered

---

6 1*a* Esth. 2:23.
  b Esth. 10:2.
  2*a* Esth. 2:21 (21–23).

4*a* Esth. 4:11.
  b Esth. 5:14.
  12*a* 2 Sam. 15:30.

14*a* Esth. 5:8.
7 2*a* Esth. 5:6; 9:12.

and said, If I have found favour in thy sight, O king, and if it please the king, let my life be given me at my petition, and my people at my request:

4 For we are *a*sold, I and my people, to be destroyed, to be slain, and to perish. But if we had been sold for bondmen and bondwomen, I had held my tongue, *b*although the enemy could not countervail the king's damage.

5 ¶ Then the king Ahasuerus answered and said unto Esther the queen, Who is he, and where is he, that durst presume in his heart to do so?

6 And Esther said, The adversary and enemy *is* this wicked Haman. Then Haman was afraid before the king and the queen.

7 ¶ And the king arising from the banquet of wine in his wrath *went* into the palace *a*garden: and Haman stood up to make request for his life to Esther the queen; for he saw that there was evil determined against him by the king.

8 Then the king returned out of the palace garden into the place of the banquet of wine; and Haman was fallen upon the bed whereon Esther *was.* Then said the king, Will he force the queen also before me in the house? As the word went out of the king's mouth, they covered Haman's face.

9 And *a*Harbonah, one of the chamberlains, said before the king, Behold also, the *b*gallows fifty cubits high, which Haman had made for *c*Mordecai, who had spoken good for the king, standeth in the house of Haman. Then the king said, *d*Hang him thereon.

10 So they hanged Haman on the *a*gallows that he had prepared for Mordecai. Then was the king's wrath pacified.

CHAPTER 8

Mordecai is honored and placed over the house of Haman—Ahasuerus issues a decree to preserve the Jews.

ON that day did the king Ahasuerus give the house of Haman the Jews' enemy unto Esther the queen. And Mordecai came before the king; for Esther had told *a*what he *was* unto her.

2 And the king took off his *a*ring, which he had taken from Haman, and gave it unto Mordecai. And Esther set Mordecai over the house of Haman.

3 ¶ And Esther spake yet again before the king, and fell down at his feet, and besought him with tears to put away the mischief of Haman the Agagite, and his *a*device that he had devised against the Jews.

4 Then the king held out the golden *a*sceptre toward Esther. So Esther arose, and stood before the king,

5 And said, If it please the king, and if I have found favour in his sight, and the thing *seem* right before the king, and I *be* pleasing in his eyes, let it be written to reverse the letters devised by Haman the son of Hammedatha the Agagite, which he wrote to destroy the Jews which *are* in all the king's provinces:

6 For how can I endure to see the evil that shall come unto my people? or how can I endure to see the destruction of my kindred?

7 ¶ Then the king Ahasuerus said unto Esther the queen and to Mordecai the Jew, Behold, I have given Esther the house of Haman, and him they have hanged upon the gallows, because he laid his hand upon the Jews.

8 Write ye also for the Jews, as it liketh you, in the king's name, and seal *it* with the king's ring: for the

---

4*a* Esth. 3:9; 4:7.
  b HEB for that would
     not have damaged the
     king's interests.
7*a* Esth. 1:5.
9*a* Esth. 1:10.

b Esth. 5:14.
c Esth. 2:22 (21–22).
d Prov. 11:5 (5–6).
10*a* Matt. 7:2 (1–2);
    1 Ne. 14:3;
    D&C 10:26 (25–27).

8 1*a* Esth. 2:10 (7–20).
2*a* Gen. 41:42;
    Esth. 3:10.
3*a* Esth. 3:9 (8–11).
4*a* Esth. 4:11.

writing which is written in the king's name, and sealed with the king's ring, may no man *a*reverse.

9 Then were the king's scribes called at that time in the third month, that *is*, the month Sivan, on the three and twentieth *day* thereof; and it was written according to all that Mordecai commanded unto the Jews, and to the lieutenants, and the deputies and rulers of the provinces which *are* from India unto Ethiopia, an hundred twenty and seven provinces, unto every province according to the writing thereof, and unto every people after their language, and to the Jews according to their writing, and according to their *a*language.

10 And he wrote in the king Ahasuerus' *a*name, and sealed *it* with the king's ring, and sent *b*letters by posts on horseback, *and* riders on mules, camels, *and* young dromedaries:

11 Wherein the king granted the Jews which *were* in every city to *a*gather themselves together, and to stand for their life, to destroy, to slay, and to cause to perish, all the power of the people and province that would assault them, *both* little ones and women, and *to take* the spoil of them for a prey,

12 Upon *a*one day in all the provinces of king Ahasuerus, *namely,* upon the thirteenth *day* of the twelfth month, which *is* the month Adar.

13 The copy of the writing for a commandment to be given in every province *was* published unto all people, and that the Jews should be ready against that day to avenge themselves on their enemies.

14 *So* the posts that rode upon mules *and* camels went out, being hastened and pressed on by the king's commandment. And the decree was given at Shushan the palace.

15 ¶ And Mordecai went out from the presence of the king in royal *a*apparel of blue and white, and with a great crown of gold, and with a garment of fine linen and purple: and the city of Shushan rejoiced and was glad.

16 The Jews had light, and gladness, and joy, and honour.

17 And in every province, and in every city, whithersoever the king's commandment and his decree came, the Jews had joy and gladness, a feast and a good *a*day. And many of the people of the land became Jews; for the *b*fear of the Jews fell upon them.

CHAPTER 9

The Jews slay their enemies, including Haman's ten sons—The Feast of Purim is instituted to commemorate their deliverance and victory.

Now in the twelfth month, that *is,* the month Adar, on the thirteenth day of the same, when the king's *a*commandment and his decree drew near to be put in execution, in the day that the enemies of the Jews hoped to have power over them, (though it was turned to the contrary, that the Jews had rule over them that hated them;)

2 The Jews *a*gathered themselves together in their cities throughout all the provinces of the king Ahasuerus, to lay hand on such as sought their hurt: and no man could withstand them; for the *b*fear of them fell upon all people.

3 And all the rulers of the provinces, and the lieutenants, and the deputies, and officers of the king, helped the Jews; because the fear of Mordecai fell upon them.

4 For Mordecai *was* great in the king's house, and his fame went out throughout all the provinces: for this man Mordecai waxed greater and greater.

5 Thus the Jews smote all their enemies with the stroke of the sword,

---

8*a* Esth. 1:19.
9*a* Esth. 1:22.
10*a* Esth. 3:12 (12–13).
   b Esth. 9:29.

11*a* Esth. 9:2.
12*a* Esth. 3:13.
15*a* Gen. 41:42; Dan. 5:29.
17*a* Esth. 9:19 (19, 22).

  b Esth. 9:2.
9 1*a* Esth. 3:13 (12–13).
  2*a* Esth. 8:11.
   b Esth. 8:17.

and slaughter, and destruction, and did what they would unto those that hated them.

6 And in Shushan the palace the Jews slew and destroyed five hundred men.

7 And Parshandatha, and Dalphon, and Aspatha,

8 And Poratha, and Adalia, and Aridatha,

9 And Parmashta, and Arisai, and Aridai, and Vajezatha,

10 The ten sons of Haman the son of Hammedatha, the enemy of the Jews, slew they; but on the spoil laid they not their hand.

11 On that day the number of those that were slain in Shushan the palace was brought before the king.

12 ¶ And the king said unto Esther the queen, The Jews have slain and destroyed five hundred men in Shushan the palace, and the ten sons of Haman; what have they done in the rest of the king's provinces? now what *is* thy *a*petition? and it shall be granted thee: or what *is* thy request further? and it shall be done.

13 Then said Esther, If it please the king, let it be granted to the Jews which *are* in Shushan to do to morrow also according unto this day's decree, and let Haman's ten sons be hanged upon the gallows.

14 And the king commanded it so to be done: and the decree was given at Shushan; and they hanged Haman's ten sons.

15 For the Jews that *were* in Shushan gathered themselves together on the fourteenth day also of the month Adar, and slew three hundred men at Shushan; but on the prey they laid not their hand.

16 But the other Jews that *were* in the king's provinces gathered themselves together, and stood for their lives, and had rest from their enemies, and slew of their foes seventy and five thousand, but they laid not their hands on the prey,

17 On the thirteenth day of the month Adar; and on the fourteenth day of the same rested they, and made it a day of feasting and gladness.

18 But the Jews that *were* at Shushan assembled together on the thirteenth *day* thereof, and on the fourteenth thereof; and on the fifteenth *day* of the same they rested, and made it a day of feasting and gladness.

19 Therefore the Jews of the villages, that dwelt in the unwalled towns, made the fourteenth day of the month Adar *a day of* gladness and feasting, and a good *a*day, and of sending *b*portions one to another.

20 ¶ And Mordecai wrote these things, and sent letters unto all the Jews that *were* in all the provinces of the king Ahasuerus, *both* nigh and far,

21 To stablish *this* among them, that they should keep the fourteenth day of the month Adar, and the fifteenth day of the same, yearly,

22 As the days wherein the Jews rested from their enemies, and the month which was turned unto them from sorrow to joy, and from mourning into a good day: that they should make them days of feasting and joy, and of sending portions one to another, and gifts to the poor.

23 And the Jews undertook to do as they had begun, and as Mordecai had written unto them;

24 Because Haman the son of Hammedatha, the Agagite, the enemy of all the Jews, had *a*devised against the Jews to destroy them, and had cast Pur, that *is*, the lot, to consume them, and to destroy them;

25 But when *Esther* came before the king, he commanded by letters that his wicked device, which he devised against the Jews, should return upon his own head, and that he and his sons should be hanged on the gallows.

26 Wherefore they called these days Purim after the name of Pur.

12*a* Esth. 7:2.
19*a* Esth. 8:17.

b Neh. 8:10 (10, 12).
24*a* Esth. 3:9 (6–10).

Therefore for all the words of this letter, and *of that* which they had seen concerning this matter, and which had come unto them,

27 The Jews ordained, and took upon them, and upon their seed, and upon all such as joined themselves unto them, so as it should not fail, that they would keep these two days according to their writing, and according to their *appointed* time every year;

28 And *that* these days *should be* remembered and kept throughout every generation, every family, every province, and every city; and *that* these days of Purim should not fail from among the Jews, nor the memorial of them perish from their seed.

29 Then Esther the queen, the *a*daughter of Abihail, and Mordecai the Jew, wrote with all authority, to confirm this second *b*letter of Purim.

30 And he sent the letters unto all the Jews, to the hundred twenty and seven *a*provinces of the kingdom of Ahasuerus, *with* words of peace and truth,

31 To confirm these days of Purim in their times *appointed*, according as Mordecai the Jew and Esther the queen had enjoined them, and as they had decreed for themselves and for their seed, the matters of the *a*fastings and their cry.

32 And the decree of Esther confirmed these matters of Purim; and it was written in the book.

CHAPTER 10

Mordecai, the Jew, stands next to Ahasuerus in power and might.

AND the king Ahasuerus laid a tribute upon the land, and *upon* the isles of the sea.

2 And all the acts of his power and of his might, and the declaration of the greatness of Mordecai, whereunto the king *a*advanced him, *are* they not written in the book of the *b*chronicles of the kings of Media and Persia?

3 For Mordecai the *a*Jew *was* *b*next unto king Ahasuerus, and great among the Jews, and accepted of the multitude of his brethren, seeking the wealth of his people, and speaking peace to all his seed.

THE BOOK OF

JOB

CHAPTER 1

Job, a just and perfect man, is blessed with great riches—Satan obtains permission from the Lord to tempt and try Job—Job's property and children are destroyed, and yet he praises and blesses the Lord.

THERE was a man in the land of *a*Uz, whose name *was* *b*Job; and that man was *c*perfect and

---

29*a* Esth. 2:15.
  b Esth. 8:10 (8–12).
30*a* Esth. 1:1.
31*a* Esth. 4:3 (3, 16).
10 2*a* Dan. 3:30.

  b 1 Kgs. 14:19;
    1 Chr. 27:24;
    Esth. 6:1.
3*a* Dan. 6:3.
  b Gen. 41:40.

[JOB]
1 1*a* Gen. 10:23 (21–23);
    Lam. 4:21.
  b Ezek. 14:14; James 5:11.
  c TG Perfection.

ᵈupright, and one that ᵉfeared God, and eschewed evil.

2 And there were born unto him seven sons and three daughters.

3 His substance also was seven thousand sheep, and three thousand camels, and five hundred yoke of oxen, and five hundred she asses, and a very great household; so that this man was the greatest of all the men of the east.

4 And his ᵃsons went and feasted *in their* houses, every one his day; and sent and called for their three sisters to eat and to drink with them.

5 And it was so, when the days of *their* feasting were gone about, that Job sent and sanctified them, and rose up early in the morning, and offered burnt ᵃofferings *according* to the number of them all: for Job said, It may be that my ᵇsons have sinned, and ᶜcursed God in their hearts. Thus did Job continually.

6 ¶ Now there was a day when the ᵃsons of God came to present themselves before the Lᴏʀᴅ, and ᵇSatan came also among them.

7 And the Lᴏʀᴅ said unto Satan, Whence comest thou? Then Satan answered the Lᴏʀᴅ, and said, From going ᵃto and fro in the earth, and from walking up and down in it.

8 And the Lᴏʀᴅ said unto Satan, Hast thou considered my ᵃservant Job, that *there is* none like him in the earth, a perfect and an upright man, one that feareth God, and escheweth evil?

9 Then Satan answered the Lᴏʀᴅ, and said, Doth Job fear God for nought?

10 Hast not thou made an hedge about him, and about his house, and about all that he hath on every side? thou hast blessed the work of his hands, and his substance is increased in the land.

11 But put forth thine ᵃhand now, and touch all that he hath, and he will ᵇcurse thee to thy face.

12 And the Lᴏʀᴅ said unto Satan, Behold, all that he hath *is* in thy ᵃpower; only upon himself put not forth thine hand. So Satan went forth from the presence of the Lᴏʀᴅ.

13 ¶ And there was a day when his sons and his daughters *were* eating and drinking wine in their eldest brother's house:

14 And there came a messenger unto Job, and said, The oxen were plowing, and the asses feeding beside them:

15 And the Sabeans fell *upon them,* and took them away; yea, they have slain the servants with the edge of the sword; and I only am escaped alone to tell thee.

16 While he *was* yet speaking, there came also another, and said, The fire of God is fallen from heaven, and hath burned up the sheep, and the servants, and consumed them; and I only am escaped alone to tell thee.

17 While he *was* yet speaking, there came also another, and said, The ᵃChaldeans made out three bands, and fell upon the camels, and have carried them away, yea, and slain the servants with the edge of the sword; and I only am escaped alone to tell thee.

18 While he *was* yet speaking, there came also another, and said, Thy ᵃsons and thy daughters *were* eating and drinking wine in their eldest brother's house:

19 And, behold, there came a great wind from the wilderness, and smote the four corners of the house, and it fell upon the young men, and they

---

1d Job 4:6.
  e Deut. 5:29; Prov. 16:6;
    D&C 10:56 (55–56);
    45:39.
4a Job 1:18.
5a Job 42:8;
    1 Ne. 5:9 (8–9);
    3 Ne. 9:19.
  b 1 Ne. 1:1;

Mosiah 1:2 (2–3); 27:14;
3 Ne. 18:21 (20–21);
D&C 68:25 (25, 28).
  c TG Curse.
6a JST Job 1:6 . . .
    children . . .
    TG Sons and Daughters
    of God.
  b TG Devil.

7a D&C 10:27.
8a TG Servant.
11a Job 19:21.
  b TG Curse.
12a TG Probation.
17a Gen. 11:28;
    2 Kgs. 24:2;
    Abr. 1:30 (29–30).
18a Job 1:4.

are dead; and I only am escaped alone to tell thee.

20 Then Job arose, and ªrent his mantle, and shaved his head, and fell down upon the ground, and worshipped,

21 And said, ªNaked came I out of my mother's womb, and naked shall I return thither: the LORD gave, and the LORD hath ᵇtaken away; ᶜblessed be the name of the LORD.

22 In all this Job ªsinned not, nor charged God foolishly.

CHAPTER 2

Satan obtains permission from the Lord to afflict Job physically—Job is smitten with boils—Eliphaz, Bildad, and Zophar come to comfort him.

AGAIN there was a day when the ªsons of God came to present themselves before the LORD, and ᵇSatan came also among them to present himself before the LORD.

2 And the LORD said unto Satan, From whence comest thou? And Satan answered the LORD, and said, From going to and fro in the earth, and from walking up and down in it.

3 And the LORD said unto Satan, Hast thou considered my servant Job, that *there is* none like him in the earth, a ªperfect and an upright man, one that feareth God, and ᵇescheweth evil? and still he ᶜholdeth fast his ᵈintegrity, although thou movedst me against him, to destroy him without cause.

4 And Satan answered the LORD, and said, Skin for skin, yea, all that a man hath will he give for his ªlife.

5 But put forth thine hand now, and touch his bone and his flesh, and he will ªcurse thee to thy face.

6 And the LORD said unto Satan, Behold, he *is* in thine ªhand; but save his life.

7 ¶ So went Satan forth from the presence of the LORD, and smote Job with ªsore ᵇboils from the sole of his foot unto his crown.

8 And he took him a potsherd to scrape himself withal; and he sat down among the ªashes.

9 ¶ Then said his wife unto him, Dost thou still ªretain thine ᵇintegrity? ᶜcurse God, and die.

10 But he said unto her, Thou speakest as one of the foolish women speaketh. What? shall we receive ªgood at the hand of God, and shall we not receive ᵇevil? In all this did not Job ᶜsin with his lips.

11 ¶ Now when Job's three ªfriends heard of all this evil that was come upon him, they came every one from his own place; Eliphaz the Temanite, and Bildad the Shuhite, and Zophar the Naamathite: for they had made an appointment together to come to mourn with him and to comfort him.

12 And when they lifted up their eyes afar off, and knew him not, they lifted up their voice, and wept; and they rent every one his mantle, and sprinkled dust upon their heads toward heaven.

13 So they sat down with him upon the ground ªseven days and seven nights, and none spake a word unto him: for they saw that *his* ᵇgrief was very great.

CHAPTER 3

Job curses the circumstances of his birth—He asks, Why died I not from the womb?

20a Gen. 44:13;
   Ezra 9:3 (1–4).
21a Eccl. 5:15; 1 Tim. 6:7.
   b TG Patience; Suffering.
   c Gen. 14:20; D&C 36:3.
22a Job 2:10.
2 1a JST Job 2:1 . . .
   children . . .
   b TG Devil.
3a HEB blameless.
   TG Perfection.

b HEB turns from.
   c TG Perseverance.
   d TG Integrity.
4a TG Mortality.
5a TG Curse.
6a TG Probation.
7a TG Suffering.
   b Isa. 38:21.
8a Job 42:6; Matt. 11:21;
   Mosiah 11:25.
9a TG Perseverance.

b TG Steadfastness.
   c TG Blaspheme; Curse.
10a Matt. 5:45; 2 Ne. 2:11;
   D&C 29:39; 122:7 (5–9).
   TG Patience.
   b TG Evil; Suffering.
   c Job 1:22.
11a Job 4:1 (1–8).
13a Gen. 50:10.
   b Hel. 5:12;
   D&C 24:8; 122:7 (1–9).

AFTER this opened Job his mouth, and *a*cursed his day.

2 And Job spake, and said,

3 Let the day *a*perish wherein I was *b*born, and the night *in which* it was said, There is a man child conceived.

4 Let that day be darkness; let not God regard it from above, neither let the light shine upon it.

5 Let darkness and the *a*shadow of death stain it; let a cloud dwell upon it; let the blackness of the day terrify it.

6 *As for* that night, let darkness seize upon it; let it not be joined unto the days of the year, let it not come into the number of the months.

7 Lo, let that night be solitary, let no joyful voice come therein.

8 Let them curse it that curse the day, who are ready to raise up their mourning.

9 Let the stars of the twilight thereof be dark; let it look for light, but *have* none; neither let it see the dawning of the day:

10 Because it shut not up the doors of my *mother's* womb, nor hid sorrow from mine eyes.

11 Why *a*died I not from the womb? *why* did I *not* give up the ghost when I came out of the belly?

12 Why did the knees *a*prevent me? or why the breasts that I should suck?

13 For now should I have lain still and been quiet, I should have slept: then had I been at rest,

14 With kings and counsellors of the earth, *a*which built desolate places for themselves;

15 Or with princes that had gold, who filled their houses with silver:

16 Or as an hidden untimely birth I had not been; as infants *which* never saw light.

17 There the wicked cease *from* troubling; and there the weary be at *a*rest.

18 *There* the prisoners rest together; they hear not the voice of the oppressor.

19 The small and great are there; and the servant *is* free from his master.

20 Wherefore is *a*light given to him that is in *b*misery, and life unto the bitter *in* soul;

21 Which long for *a*death, but it *cometh* not; and dig for it more than for hid treasures;

22 Which rejoice exceedingly, *and* are glad, when they can find the grave?

23 *Why is light given* to a man whose way is hid, and whom God hath hedged in?

24 For my sighing cometh before I eat, and my roarings are poured out like the waters.

25 For the thing which I greatly feared is come upon me, and that which I was afraid of is come unto me.

26 I was not in safety, neither had I rest, neither was I quiet; yet trouble came.

CHAPTER 4

Eliphaz reproves Job, asking such questions as, Are the righteous cut off? Shall a man be more pure than his maker?

THEN *a*Eliphaz the Temanite answered and said,

2 *If* we assay to commune with thee, wilt thou be grieved? but who can withhold himself from speaking?

3 Behold, thou hast instructed many, and thou hast strengthened the weak hands.

4 Thy words have upholden him that was falling, and thou hast strengthened the feeble knees.

5 But now it is come upon thee, and thou faintest; it toucheth thee, and thou art troubled.

6 *Is* not *this* thy fear, thy *a*confidence, thy hope, and the *b*uprightness of thy ways?

---

3 1*a* TG Curse.
   3*a* TG Despair.
    b Jer. 20:14 (14–18).
   5*a* Ps. 23:4; 44:19;
       107:14 (10, 14);
       D&C 57:10.

11*a* Job 10:18 (18–19).
12*a* HEB receive.
14*a* HEB who rebuilt ruins.
17*a* TG Paradise.
20*a* D&C 88:67.
    b D&C 122:7 (1–7).

   TG Suffering.
21*a* Rev. 9:6.
 4 1*a* Job 2:11;
       D&C 121:10 (7–11).
   6*a* Prov. 3:26.
    b Job 1:1.

7 Remember, I pray thee, who *ever* perished, being ^ainnocent? or where were the righteous cut off?

8 Even as I have seen, they that plow iniquity, and ^asow wickedness, reap the same.

9 By the blast of God they perish, and by the breath of his nostrils are they consumed.

10 The roaring of the lion, and the voice of the fierce lion, and the ^ateeth of the young lions, are broken.

11 The old lion perisheth for lack of prey, and the stout lion's whelps are scattered abroad.

12 Now a thing was secretly brought to me, and mine ear received a little thereof.

13 In thoughts from the visions of the night, when deep sleep falleth on men,

14 Fear came upon me, and trembling, which made all my bones to shake.

15 Then a spirit passed before my face; the hair of my flesh stood up:

16 It stood still, but I could not discern the form thereof: an image *was* before mine eyes, *there was* ^asilence, and I heard a ^bvoice, *saying,*

17 Shall mortal man be more ^ajust than God? shall a man be more pure than his maker?

18 Behold, he put no trust in his servants; and his angels he charged with folly:

19 How much less *in* them that dwell in houses of ^aclay, whose foundation *is* in the dust, *which* are crushed before the moth?

20 They are destroyed from morning to evening: they perish for ever without any regarding *it.*

21 Doth not their excellency *which is* in them go away? they die, even without wisdom.

CHAPTER 5

Eliphaz counsels Job: Man is born unto

trouble, *seek unto God, and happy is the man whom God corrects.*

CALL now, if there be any that will answer thee; and to which of the ^asaints wilt thou turn?

2 For wrath killeth the foolish man, and envy slayeth the ^asilly one.

3 I have seen the foolish taking root: but suddenly I cursed his habitation.

4 His children are far from safety, and they are crushed in the gate, neither *is there* any to deliver *them.*

5 Whose harvest the hungry eateth up, and taketh it even out of the thorns, and the robber swalloweth up their substance.

6 Although affliction cometh not forth of the dust, neither doth trouble spring out of the ground;

7 Yet man is born unto ^atrouble, as the sparks fly upward.

8 I would seek unto God, and unto God would I commit my cause:

9 Which doeth great things and unsearchable; marvellous things without number:

10 Who giveth rain upon the earth, and sendeth waters upon the fields:

11 To set up on high those that be low; that those which ^amourn may be exalted to safety.

12 He disappointeth the devices of the crafty, so that their hands cannot perform *their* enterprise.

13 He taketh the wise in their own craftiness: and the counsel of the froward is carried headlong.

14 They meet with darkness in the daytime, and grope in the noonday as in the night.

15 But he saveth the poor from the sword, from their mouth, and from the hand of the mighty.

16 So the poor hath hope, and iniquity stoppeth her mouth.

17 Behold, ^ahappy *is* the man whom God correcteth: therefore

7a 1 Cor. 10:13;
  1 Ne. 22:19;
  Alma 14:11.
8a TG Harvest.
10a Ps. 58:6.
16a Hel. 5:30 (30–31);

D&C 85:6 (6–7).
  b 1 Kgs. 19:12 (11–13).
17a TG Justice.
19a TG Man, Physical
    Creation of.
5 1a HEB holy ones.

2a OR naive.
7a TG Adversity.
11a TG Mourning.
17a TG Happiness.

despise not thou the ^bchastening of the Almighty:

18 For he maketh sore, and bindeth up: he ^awoundeth, and his hands make whole.

19 He shall deliver thee in six troubles: yea, in seven there shall no evil touch thee.

20 In famine he shall redeem thee from death: and in war from the power of the sword.

21 Thou shalt be hid from the scourge of the tongue: neither shalt thou be ^aafraid of destruction when it cometh.

22 At destruction and famine thou shalt laugh: neither shalt thou be afraid of the beasts of the earth.

23 For thou shalt be in league with the stones of the field: and the ^abeasts of the field shall be at peace with thee.

24 And thou shalt know that thy tabernacle *shall be* in peace; and thou shalt visit thy habitation, and shalt not sin.

25 Thou shalt know also that thy seed *shall be* great, and thine offspring as the ^agrass of the earth.

26 Thou shalt come to *thy* grave in a full age, like as a shock of ^acorn cometh in in his season.

27 Lo this, we have searched it, so it *is*; hear it, and know thou *it* for thy good.

CHAPTER 6

Job bemoans his grief—He prays that God will grant his petitions—Those who are afflicted should be pitied—How forcible are right words!

BUT Job answered and said,

2 Oh that my ^agrief were throughly weighed, and my calamity laid in the balances together!

3 For now it would be heavier than the sand of the sea: therefore my words are swallowed up.

4 For the arrows of the Almighty *are* within me, the poison whereof

drinketh up my spirit: the terrors of God do set themselves in array against me.

5 Doth the wild ass bray when he hath grass? or loweth the ox over his fodder?

6 Can that which is unsavoury be eaten without salt? or is there *any* taste in the white of an egg?

7 The things *that* my soul refused to touch *are* as my sorrowful meat.

8 Oh that I might have my request; and that God would grant *me* the thing that I long for!

9 Even that it would please God to destroy me; that he would let loose his hand, and cut me off!

10 Then should I yet have comfort; yea, I would harden myself in sorrow: let him not spare; for I have not concealed the words of the Holy One.

11 What *is* my strength, that I should hope? and what *is* mine end, that I should prolong my life?

12 *Is* my strength the strength of stones? or *is* my flesh of brass?

13 *Is* not my help in me? and is wisdom driven quite from me?

14 To him that is afflicted ^apity *should be shewed* from his friend; but he forsaketh the fear of the Almighty.

15 My brethren have dealt deceitfully as a brook, *and* as the stream of brooks they pass away;

16 Which are blackish by reason of the ice, *and* wherein the snow is hid:

17 What time they wax warm, they vanish: when it is hot, they are consumed out of their place.

18 The paths of their way are turned aside; they go to nothing, and perish.

19 The ^atroops of Tema looked, the companies of Sheba waited for them.

20 They were confounded because they had hoped; they came thither, and were ashamed.

21 For now ye are nothing; ye see *my* casting down, and are afraid.

22 Did I say, ^aBring unto me? or,

17b TG Chastening.
18a HEB smites, bruises.
21a D&C 38:30.
23a Hosea 2:18.

25a Ps. 72:16.
26a OR grain.
6 2a TG Despair.
14a TG Compassion.

19a HEB caravans.
22a IE Bring gifts.

Give a reward for me of your substance?

23 Or, Deliver me from the enemy's hand? or, Redeem me from the hand of the mighty?

24 Teach me, and I will hold my tongue: and cause me to understand wherein I have erred.

25 How forcible are right words! but what doth your arguing reprove?

26 Do ye imagine to reprove words, and the speeches of one that is desperate, *which are* as wind?

27 Yea, ye overwhelm the fatherless, and ye dig a *ᵃpit* for your friend.

28 Now therefore be content, look upon me; for *it is* evident unto you if I lie.

29 Return, I pray you, let it not be iniquity; yea, return again, my righteousness *is* in it.

30 Is there iniquity in my tongue? cannot my taste discern perverse things?

CHAPTER 7

Job asks, Is there an appointed time for man on earth? What is man that Thou shouldst magnify him? Why dost Thou not pardon my transgression?

Is *there* not an *ᵃappointed* time to man upon earth? *are not* his days also like the days of an *ᵇhireling?*

2 As a servant earnestly desireth the shadow, and as an hireling looketh for *the reward of* his work:

3 So am I made to possess months of vanity, and wearisome nights are appointed to me.

4 When I lie down, I say, When shall I arise, and the night be gone? and I am full of tossings to and fro unto the dawning of the day.

5 My flesh is clothed with worms and clods of dust; my skin is broken, and become loathsome.

6 My *ᵃdays* are swifter than a weaver's shuttle, and are spent without hope.

7 O remember that my life *is* wind: mine eye shall no more see good.

8 The eye of him that hath seen me shall see me no *more:* thine eyes *are* upon me, and I *am* not.

9 *As* the cloud is consumed and vanisheth away: so he that goeth down to the grave shall come up no *more.*

10 He shall return no more to his house, neither shall his place know him any more.

11 Therefore I will not *ᵃrefrain* my mouth; I will speak in the anguish of my spirit; I will *ᵇcomplain* in the bitterness of my soul.

12 *Am* I a sea, or a whale, that thou settest a watch over me?

13 When I say, My bed shall comfort me, my couch shall ease my complaint;

14 Then thou scarest me with dreams, and terrifiest me through visions:

15 So that my soul chooseth strangling, *and* death rather than my life.

16 I loathe *it;* I would not live alway: let me alone; for my days *are* vanity.

17 What *is ᵃman,* that thou shouldest magnify him? and that thou shouldest set thine heart upon him?

18 And *that* thou shouldest visit him every morning, *and ᵃtry* him every moment?

19 How long wilt thou not depart from me, nor let me alone till I swallow down my spittle?

20 I have sinned; what shall I do unto thee, O thou preserver of men? why hast thou set me as a mark against thee, so that I am a burden to myself?

21 And why dost thou not pardon my transgression, and take away mine iniquity? for now shall I sleep in the dust; and thou shalt seek me in the morning, but I *shall* not *be.*

27a 2 Ne. 28:8.
7 1a Alma 12:27 (26–28);
    D&C 42:48; 121:25.
    b Job 14:6 (5–6).

6a Job 8:9; 10:20; 17:11.
11a OR restrain.
   b 1 Ne. 16:20;
    D&C 9:6.

17a Ps. 8:4 (1–9);
    144:3 (1–15).
18a TG Probation.

CHAPTER 8

Bildad asks, Doth God pervert judgment?—Bildad says, Our days upon earth are a shadow, and God will not cast away a perfect man.

THEN answered Bildad the Shuhite, and said,

2 How long wilt thou speak these *things?* and *how long shall* the words of thy mouth *be like* a strong wind?

3 Doth God pervert [a]judgment? or doth the Almighty pervert justice?

4 If thy children have sinned against him, and he have cast them away for their transgression;

5 If thou wouldest seek unto God betimes, and make thy supplication to the Almighty;

6 If thou *wert* pure and upright; surely now he would awake for thee, and make the habitation of thy righteousness prosperous.

7 Though thy beginning was small, yet thy latter end should greatly increase.

8 For inquire, I pray thee, of the former [a]age, and prepare thyself to the search of their fathers:

9 (For we *are but of* yesterday, and know nothing, because our [a]days upon earth *are* a shadow:)

10 Shall not they teach thee, *and* tell thee, and utter words out of their heart?

11 Can the rush grow up without mire? can the [a]flag grow without water?

12 Whilst it *is* yet in his greenness, *and* not cut down, it withereth before any *other* herb.

13 So *are* the paths of all that forget God; and the hypocrite's hope shall perish:

14 Whose hope shall be cut off, and whose trust *shall be* a spider's web.

15 He shall lean upon his house, but it shall not stand: he shall hold it fast, but it shall not endure.

16 He *is* [a]green before the sun, and his branch shooteth forth in his garden.

17 His roots are wrapped about the heap, *and* seeth the place of stones.

18 If he destroy him from his place, then *it* shall deny him, *saying,* I have not seen thee.

19 Behold, this *is* the joy of his way, and out of the earth shall others grow.

20 Behold, God will not cast away a perfect *man,* neither will he help the evil doers:

21 Till he fill thy mouth with laughing, and thy lips with rejoicing.

22 They that hate thee shall be clothed with [a]shame; and the dwelling place of the wicked shall come to nought.

CHAPTER 9

Job acknowledges the justice and greatness of God and concludes that man cannot contend against Him.

THEN Job answered and said,

2 I know *it is* so of a truth: but how should man be just [a]with God?

3 If he will [a]contend with him, he cannot answer him [b]one of a thousand.

4 *He is* wise in heart, and mighty in strength: who hath [a]hardened *himself* against him, and hath prospered?

5 [a]Which removeth the mountains, and they know not: which overturneth them in his anger.

6 Which shaketh the earth out of her place, and the pillars thereof tremble.

7 Which commandeth the sun, and it riseth not; and [a]sealeth up the stars.

8 Which alone [a]spreadeth out the heavens, and treadeth upon the waves of the sea.

9 Which maketh Arcturus, [a]Orion, and Pleiades, and the chambers of the south.

8 3*a* Alma 12:15.
  8*a* HEB generations.
  9*a* Job 7:6.
  11*a* OR reeds.
  16*a* HEB moist; i.e., thrives.
  22*a* TG Shame.

9 2*a* IE before.
  3*a* Eccl. 6:10;
    Isa. 45:9;
    Ether 4:8.
  b OR one time in.
  4*a* TG Hardheartedness.

5*a* OR Who.
7*a* IE hideth from view.
8*a* Ps. 104:2;
  Isa. 40:22;
  2 Ne. 8:13.
9*a* TG Astronomy.

10 Which doeth great things past finding out; yea, and wonders without number.

11 Lo, he goeth by me, and I see *him* not: he passeth on also, but I perceive him not.

12 Behold, he taketh away, who can hinder him? who will say unto him, What ᵃdoest thou?

13 *If* God will not withdraw his anger, the proud helpers do stoop under him.

14 How much less shall I answer him, *and* choose out my words *to reason* with him?

15 Whom, though I were righteous, *yet* would I not answer, *but* I would make supplication ᵃto my judge.

16 If I had called, and he had answered me; *yet* would I not believe that he had hearkened unto my voice.

17 For he breaketh me with a tempest, and multiplieth my wounds without cause.

18 He will not suffer me to take my breath, but filleth me with bitterness.

19 If *I speak* of strength, lo, *he is* strong: and if of judgment, who shall set me a time *to plead?*

20 If I justify myself, mine own mouth shall condemn me: *if I say,* I *am* perfect, it shall also prove me perverse.

21 *Though* I *were* perfect, ᵃyet would I not know my soul: I would despise my life.

22 This *is* one *thing*, therefore I said *it*, He ᵃdestroyeth the perfect and the wicked.

23 If the scourge slay suddenly, he will ᵃlaugh at the trial of the innocent.

24 The earth is given into the hand of the wicked: he covereth the faces of the judges thereof; if not, where, *and* who *is* he?

25 Now my days are swifter than a ᵃpost: they flee away, they see no good.

26 They are passed away as the swift ships: as the eagle *that* hasteth to the prey.

27 If I say, I will forget my complaint, I will leave off my heaviness, and comfort *myself:*

28 I am afraid of all my sorrows, I know that thou wilt not hold me innocent.

29 *If* I be wicked, why then labour I in vain?

30 If I wash myself with snow water, and make my hands never so clean;

31 Yet shalt thou plunge me in the ditch, and mine own clothes shall abhor me.

32 For *he is* not a man, as I *am, that* I should answer him, *and* we should come together in judgment.

33 Neither is there any ᵃdaysman betwixt us, *that* might lay his hand upon us both.

34 Let him take his rod away from me, and let not ᵃhis fear terrify me:

35 *Then* would I speak, and not fear him; but *it is* not so with me.

CHAPTER 10

Job is weary of life—He reasons with God about his afflictions—He asks, Why hast Thou brought me forth out of the womb?

MY soul is weary of my life; I will leave my complaint upon myself; I will speak in the ᵃbitterness of my soul.

2 I will say unto God, Do not condemn me; shew me wherefore thou contendest with me.

3 *Is it* good unto thee that thou shouldest oppress, that thou shouldest despise the work of thine hands, and shine upon the counsel of the wicked?

4 Hast thou eyes of flesh? or ᵃseest thou as man seeth?

5 *Are* thy days as the days of man? *are* thy years as man's days,

---

12a Rom. 9:20 (20–21); Moses 1:4.
15a OR before my accuser.
21a HEB I regard not myself.
22a Mal. 3:14 (14–18).

23a HEB mock.
25a HEB runner.
33a OR arbiter between.
34a HEB the dread of Him.
10 1a Isa. 38:15;

Moses 7:44 (42–44).
4a 1 Sam. 16:7; D&C 121:24.

6 That thou inquirest after mine iniquity, and searchest after my sin?

7 Thou knowest that I am not wicked; and *there is* none that can deliver out of thine hand.

8 Thine hands have *a*made me and fashioned me together round about; yet thou dost destroy me.

9 Remember, I beseech thee, that thou hast made me as the clay; and wilt thou bring me into *a*dust again?

10 Hast thou not poured me out as milk, and curdled me like cheese?

11 Thou hast clothed me with skin and flesh, and hast *a*fenced me with bones and sinews.

12 Thou hast granted me life and favour, and thy *a*visitation hath preserved my spirit.

13 And these *things* hast thou hid in thine heart: I know that this *is* with thee.

14 If I sin, then thou markest me, and thou wilt not acquit me from mine iniquity.

15 If I be wicked, woe unto me; and *if* I be righteous, *yet* will I not lift up my head. *I am* full of confusion; therefore see thou mine affliction;

16 For it increaseth. Thou huntest me as a fierce lion: and again thou shewest thyself marvellous upon me.

17 Thou renewest thy witnesses against me, and increasest thine indignation upon me; *a*changes and war *are* against me.

18 Wherefore then hast thou brought me forth out of the womb? Oh that I had given up the *a*ghost, and no eye had seen me!

19 I should have been as though I had not been; I should have been carried from the womb to the grave.

20 *Are* not my *a*days few? cease *then, and* let me alone, that I may take comfort a little,

21 Before I go *whence* I shall not return, *even* to the land of darkness and the shadow of *a*death;

22 A land of darkness, as darkness *itself; and* of the shadow of death, without any *a*order, and *where* the *b*light *is* as darkness.

CHAPTER 11

Zophar asks, Canst thou by searching find out God?—Zophar says that the hope of the wicked will fade away as though it had died.

THEN answered Zophar the Naamathite, and said,

2 Should not the multitude of words be answered? and should a man full of talk be justified?

3 Should thy lies make men hold their peace? and when thou mockest, shall no man make thee ashamed?

4 For thou hast said, My doctrine *is* *a*pure, and I am clean in thine eyes.

5 But oh that God would speak, and open his lips against thee;

6 And that he would shew thee the secrets of wisdom, that *they are* double to that which is! Know therefore that God *a*exacteth of thee *less* than thine iniquity *deserveth.*

7 Canst thou by searching find out God? canst thou find out the Almighty unto perfection?

8 *It is* as high as heaven; what canst thou do? deeper than hell; what canst thou know?

9 The measure thereof *is* longer than the earth, and broader than the sea.

10 If he cut off, and shut up, or gather together, then who can hinder him?

11 For he knoweth vain men: he seeth wickedness also; will he not then consider *it?*

12 For *a*vain man would be wise, though man be born *like* a wild ass's colt.

13 If thou prepare thine heart, and stretch out thine hands toward him;

8*a* TG Jesus Christ, Creator.
9*a* Gen. 3:19;
    Alma 42:30;
    Moses 4:25.
11*a* HEB covered, protected.

12*a* Moses 1:9 (9–10).
17*a* Ps. 55:19.
18*a* Job 3:11.
20*a* Job 7:6.
21*a* TG Death.

22*a* TG Order.
  b TG Light [noun].
11 4*a* 2 Ne. 9:47.
  6*a* D&C 38:14.
  12*a* 2 Ne. 9:28.

14 If iniquity *be* in thine hand, put it far away, and let not ªwickedness dwell in thy ᵇtabernacles.

15 For then shalt thou lift up thy ªface without spot; yea, thou shalt be steadfast, and shalt not fear:

16 Because thou shalt forget *thy* misery, *and* remember *it* as waters *that* pass away:

17 And *thine* age shall be clearer than the noonday; thou shalt shine forth, thou shalt be as the morning.

18 And thou shalt be secure, because there is hope; yea, thou shalt dig *about thee, and* thou shalt take thy rest in safety.

19 Also thou shalt lie down, and none shall make *thee* afraid; yea, many shall make suit unto thee.

20 But the eyes of the ªwicked shall fail, and they shall not escape, and their hope *shall be as* the giving up of the ghost.

CHAPTER 12

Job says, The souls of all things are in the hands of the Lord, with the ancient is wisdom, and the Lord governs in all things.

AND Job answered and said,

2 No doubt but ye *are* the people, and wisdom shall die with you.

3 But I have understanding as well as you; I *am* not inferior to you: yea, who knoweth not such things as these?

4 I am *as* one ªmocked of his neighbour, who calleth upon God, and he answereth him: the just upright *man is* laughed to scorn.

5 He that is ready to slip with *his* feet *is as* a lamp despised in the thought of him that is at ease.

6 The ªtabernacles of robbers ᵇprosper, and they that provoke God are secure; into whose hand God bringeth *abundantly.*

7 But ask now the beasts, and they shall teach thee; and the fowls of the air, and they shall tell thee:

8 Or speak to the ªearth, and it shall teach thee: and the fishes of the sea shall declare unto thee.

9 Who knoweth not in all these that the hand of the LORD hath wrought this?

10 In whose hand *is* the soul of every ªliving thing, and the ᵇbreath of all mankind.

11 Doth not the ear try words? and the mouth taste his meat?

12 With the ªancient *is* wisdom; and in length of days understanding.

13 With him *is* ªwisdom and ᵇstrength, he hath counsel and understanding.

14 Behold, he breaketh down, and it cannot be built again: he shutteth up a man, and there can be no opening.

15 Behold, he ªwithholdeth the waters, and they dry up: also he sendeth them out, and they overturn the earth.

16 With him *is* strength and wisdom: the deceived and the deceiver *are* his.

17 He leadeth counsellors away spoiled, and maketh the judges fools.

18 He looseth the bond of kings, and girdeth their loins with a girdle.

19 He leadeth princes away spoiled, and overthroweth the mighty.

20 He removeth away the speech of the trusty, and taketh away the understanding of the aged.

21 He poureth contempt upon ªprinces, and weakeneth the strength of the mighty.

22 He discovereth deep things out of darkness, and bringeth out to light the shadow of death.

23 He increaseth the nations, and destroyeth them: he enlargeth the nations, and straiteneth them *again.*

24 He taketh away the heart of

14a Alma 38:8.
  b HEB tents.
15a Job 22:26 (23, 26–27).
20a D&C 122:9.
12 4a TG Persecution.
  6a HEB tents.
  b Job 21:7;
       Ps. 73:12;
       Hel. 7:5 (5–6).
8a Alma 30:44.
10a TG Nature, Earth.
  b TG Breath of Life.
12a OR old men.
  TG Old Age.
13a 2 Ne. 9:8;
       Abr. 3:21.
  b TG Strength.
15a Deut. 11:17.
21a Isa. 40:23.

the chief of the people of the earth, and causeth them to ^awander in a wilderness *where there is* no way.

25 They grope in the dark without light, and he maketh them to stagger like *a* drunken *man.*

CHAPTER 13

Job testifies of his confidence in the Lord and says, Though He slay me, yet will I trust in Him, and He also will be my salvation.

LO, mine eye hath seen all *this,* mine ear hath heard and understood it.

2 What ye know, *the same* do I know also: I *am* not inferior unto you.

3 Surely I would speak to the Almighty, and I desire to reason with God.

4 But ye *are* forgers of lies, ye *are* all ^aphysicians of no value.

5 O that ye would altogether ^ahold your peace! and it should be your wisdom.

6 Hear now my reasoning, and hearken to the pleadings of my lips.

7 Will ye speak wickedly for God? and talk deceitfully for him?

8 Will ye accept his person? will ye contend for God?

9 Is it good that he should search you out? or as one man mocketh another, do ye *so* mock him?

10 He will surely reprove you, if ye do secretly accept persons.

11 Shall not his excellency make you afraid? and his dread fall upon you?

12 Your remembrances *are* like unto ashes, your bodies to bodies of clay.

13 Hold your peace, let me alone, that I may speak, and let come on me what *will.*

14 Wherefore do I take my flesh in my teeth, and put my life in mine hand?

15 Though he ^aslay me, yet will I ^btrust in him: but I will maintain mine own ways before him.

16 He also *shall be* my salvation: for an ^ahypocrite shall not come before him.

17 Hear diligently my speech, and my declaration with your ears.

18 Behold now, I have ordered *my* cause; I know that I shall be ^ajustified.

19 Who *is* he *that* will ^aplead with me? for now, if I hold my tongue, I shall give up the ghost.

20 Only do not two *things* unto me: then will I not hide myself from thee.

21 Withdraw thine hand far from me: and let not thy dread make me afraid.

22 Then call thou, and I will answer: or let me speak, and answer thou me.

23 How many *are* mine iniquities and sins? make me to ^aknow my transgression and my sin.

24 Wherefore hidest thou thy face, and holdest me for thine enemy?

25 Wilt thou break a leaf driven to and fro? and wilt thou pursue the dry stubble?

26 For thou writest bitter things against me, and makest me to possess the ^ainiquities of my youth.

27 Thou puttest my feet also in the stocks, and lookest narrowly unto all my paths; thou settest a print upon the heels of my feet.

28 And he, as a rotten thing, consumeth, as a garment that is moth eaten.

CHAPTER 14

Job testifies of the shortness of life, the certainty of death, and the guarantee of a resurrection—He asks, If a man die, will he live again?—Job answers that he will await the Lord's call to come forth from the grave.

^aMAN *that is* born of a woman *is* of few days, and full of trouble.

24*a* Amos 8:12 (11–13).
13 4*a* Job 16:2;
    D&C 121:10 (7–11).
  5*a* Prov. 17:28.
 15*a* TG Adversity.
   b D&C 42:46.

TG Faith; Trust in God.
16*a* TG Hypocrisy.
18*a* TG Justification.
19*a* HEB contend.
23*a* Alma 36:17 (12–19);
    D&C 18:44.

26*a* 1 Kgs. 17:18;
    Ps. 25:7;
    D&C 58:42.
14 1*a* 2 Ne. 2:21;
    Alma 12:24;
    Moses 4:23 (22–25).

2 He cometh forth like a flower, and is [a]cut down: he fleeth also as a shadow, and continueth not.

3 And dost thou open thine eyes upon such an one, and bringest me into judgment with thee?

4 Who can bring a clean *thing* out of an [a]unclean? not one.

5 Seeing his [a]days *are* determined, the number of his months *are* with thee, thou hast appointed his [b]bounds that he cannot pass;

6 Turn from him, that he may rest, till he shall accomplish, as an [a]hireling, his day.

7 For there is hope of a tree, if it be cut down, that it will sprout again, and that the tender branch thereof will not cease.

8 Though the root thereof wax old in the earth, and the stock thereof die in the ground;

9 *Yet* through the scent of water it will bud, and bring forth boughs like a plant.

10 But man [a]dieth, and wasteth away: yea, man giveth up the ghost, and where *is* he?

11 *As* the waters fail from the sea, and the flood decayeth and drieth up:

12 So man lieth down, and riseth not: till the heavens *be* no more, they shall not awake, nor be raised out of their sleep.

13 O that thou wouldest hide me in the grave, that thou wouldest keep me secret, until thy wrath be past, that thou wouldest appoint me a set time, and remember me!

14 If a man die, shall he [a]live *again?* all the days of my appointed time will I wait, till my change come.

15 Thou shalt call, and I will answer thee: thou wilt have a desire to the work of thine hands.

16 For now thou numberest my steps: dost thou not watch over my sin?

17 My transgression *is* sealed up in a bag, and thou sewest up mine iniquity.

18 And surely the mountain falling cometh to nought, and the rock is removed out of his place.

19 The waters wear the stones: thou washest away the things which grow *out* of the dust of the earth; and thou destroyest the hope of man.

20 Thou prevailest for ever against him, and he passeth: thou changest his countenance, and sendest him away.

21 His sons come to honour, and he knoweth *it* not; and they are brought low, but he perceiveth *it* not of them.

22 But his flesh upon him shall have [a]pain, and his soul within him shall mourn.

CHAPTER 15

Eliphaz sets forth the disquietude of wicked men—They do not believe they will return out of darkness and be resurrected.

THEN answered Eliphaz the Temanite, and said,

2 Should a wise man utter vain knowledge, and fill his belly with the east wind?

3 Should he reason with unprofitable talk? or with speeches wherewith he can do no good?

4 Yea, thou castest off fear, and restrainest prayer before God.

5 For thy mouth uttereth thine iniquity, and thou choosest the tongue of the crafty.

6 Thine own mouth condemneth thee, and not I: yea, thine own lips testify against thee.

7 *Art* thou the first man *that* was born? or wast thou made before the hills?

8 Hast thou heard the secret of God? and dost thou restrain wisdom to thyself?

9 What knowest thou, that we know not? *what* understandest thou, which *is* not in us?

10 With us *are* both the grayheaded

2a Isa. 38:12 (10–13).
4a TG Uncleanness.
5a TG Time.
  b Acts 17:26.

6a Job 7:1 (1–2).
10a Alma 11:45;
  40:11 (11–14);
  D&C 76:73 (71–74).

14a TG Resurrection.
22a TG Pain.

and very aged men, much elder than thy father.

11 *Are* the consolations of God small with thee? is there any secret thing with thee?

12 Why doth thine heart carry thee away? and what do thy eyes wink at,

13 That thou turnest thy spirit against God, and lettest *such* words go out of thy mouth?

14 What *is* man, that he should be ᵃclean? and *he which is* born of a woman, that he should be righteous?

15 Behold, ᵃhe putteth no trust in his saints; yea, the heavens are not clean in his sight.

16 How much more abominable and ᵃfilthy *is* man, which drinketh iniquity like water?

17 I will shew thee, hear me; and that *which* I have seen I will declare;

18 Which wise men have told from their fathers, and have not hid *it:*

19 Unto whom alone the earth was given, and no stranger passed among them.

20 The wicked man travaileth with pain all *his* days, and the number of years is hidden to the oppressor.

21 A dreadful sound *is* in his ears: in prosperity the destroyer shall come upon him.

22 He believeth not that he shall return out of darkness, and he is waited for of the sword.

23 He wandereth abroad for bread, *saying,* Where *is it?* he knoweth that the day of darkness is ready at his hand.

24 Trouble and anguish shall make him afraid; they shall prevail against him, as a king ready to the battle.

25 For he stretcheth out his hand against God, and strengtheneth himself against the Almighty.

26 He runneth upon him, *even* on his neck, upon the thick bosses of his bucklers:

27 Because he covereth his face with his fatness, and ᵃmaketh collops of fat on *his* flanks.

28 And he dwelleth in desolate cities, *and* in houses which no man inhabiteth, which are ready to become ᵃheaps.

29 He shall not be rich, neither shall his substance continue, neither shall he prolong the perfection thereof upon the earth.

30 He shall not depart out of darkness; the flame shall dry up his branches, and by the breath of his mouth shall he go away.

31 Let not him that is deceived trust in ᵃvanity: for vanity shall be his recompence.

32 It shall be accomplished before his time, and his branch shall not be green.

33 He shall shake off his unripe grape as the vine, and shall cast off his flower as the olive.

34 For the congregation of ᵃhypocrites *shall be* desolate, and fire shall consume the tabernacles of ᵇbribery.

35 They conceive ᵃmischief, and bring forth ᵇvanity, and their belly prepareth deceit.

CHAPTER 16

Job speaks against the wicked who oppose him—Though even his friends scorn him, he testifies that his witness is in heaven and his record is on high.

THEN Job answered and said,

2 I have heard many such things: miserable ᵃcomforters *are* ye all.

3 Shall vain words have an end? or what emboldeneth thee that thou answerest?

4 I also could speak as ye *do:* if your soul were in my soul's stead, I could heap up words against you, and shake mine head at you.

5 *But* I would strengthen you with my mouth, and the moving of my lips should assuage *your* grief.

---

15 14*a* Ether 12:37;
    D&C 38:42.
  15*a* IE God.
  16*a* TG Filthiness.
  27*a* OR has grown fat on

his loins.
  28*a* IE of ruins.
  31*a* TG Vanity.
  34*a* TG Hypocrisy.
    b TG Bribe.

35*a* Ps. 7:14;
    Isa. 59:4.
    b TG Vanity.
16 2*a* Job 13:4;
    D&C 121:10 (7–11).

6 Though I speak, my grief is not assuaged: and *though* I forbear, what am I eased?

7 But now he hath made me weary: thou hast made desolate all my company.

8 And thou hast filled me with wrinkles, *which* is a witness *against me:* and my leanness rising up in me beareth witness to my face.

9 He teareth *me* in his wrath, who hateth me: he gnasheth upon me with his teeth; mine enemy sharpeneth his eyes upon me.

10 They have gaped upon me with their mouth; they have smitten me upon the cheek *a*reproachfully; they have gathered themselves together against me.

11 God hath delivered me to the ungodly, and turned me over into the hands of the wicked.

12 I was at ease, but he hath broken me asunder: he hath also taken *me* by my neck, and shaken me to pieces, and set me up for his mark.

13 His archers compass me round about, he cleaveth my reins asunder, and doth not spare; he poureth out my gall upon the ground.

14 He breaketh me with breach upon breach, he runneth upon me like a *a*giant.

15 I have sewed sackcloth upon my skin, and *a*defiled my horn in the dust.

16 My face is foul with weeping, and on my eyelids *is* the shadow of death;

17 Not for *any* injustice in mine hands: also my prayer *is* pure.

18 O earth, cover not thou my blood, and let my cry have no place.

19 Also now, behold, my witness *is* in *a*heaven, and my record *is* on high.

20 My friends *a*scorn me: *but* mine eye poureth out *tears* unto God.

21 O that one might plead for a man with God, as a man *pleadeth* for his neighbour!

22 When a few years are come, then I shall go the *a*way *whence* I shall not return.

CHAPTER 17

Job speaks of the sorrow of death and of the grave in that day when the body returns to the dust.

MY *a*breath is corrupt, my days are extinct, the graves *are ready* for me.

2 *Are there* not mockers with me? and doth not mine eye continue in their provocation?

3 *a*Lay down now, put me in a surety with thee; who *is* he *that* will strike hands with me?

4 For thou hast hid their heart from understanding: therefore shalt thou not exalt *them.*

5 He that speaketh *a*flattery to *his* friends, even the eyes of his children shall fail.

6 He hath made me also a byword of the people; and *a*aforetime I was as a tabret.

7 Mine eye also is dim by reason of sorrow, and all my members *are* as a shadow.

8 Upright *men* shall be astonied at this, and the innocent shall stir up himself against the hypocrite.

9 The righteous also shall hold on his way, and he that hath *a*clean hands shall be stronger and stronger.

10 But as for you all, do ye return, and come now: for I cannot find *one* wise *man* among you.

11 My *a*days are past, my purposes are broken off, *even* the thoughts of my heart.

12 They change the night into day: the light *is* short because of darkness.

13 If I wait, the grave *is* mine *a*house: I have made my bed in the darkness.

14 I have said to corruption, Thou *art* my father: to the worm, *Thou art* my mother, and my sister.

10*a* TG Reproach.
14*a* HEB mighty man.
15*a* OR cast my strength.
19*a* TG Heaven.
20*a* Job 21:3 (1–3).
22*a* TG Death.

17 1*a* HEB spirit is consumed.
3*a* IE Lay down a pledge.
5*a* TG Flatter.
6*a* HEB I am as an abomination before men.

9*a* 2 Ne. 25:16;
     D&C 88:86.
11*a* Job 7:6.
13*a* Eccl. 12:5;
     Alma 40:11.

15 And where *is* now my hope? as for my hope, who shall see it?

16 They shall go down to the bars of the pit, when *our* rest together *is* in the dust.

CHAPTER 18

Bildad tells of the damned state of the wicked who know not God.

THEN answered Bildad the Shuhite, and said,

2 How long *will it be ere* ye make an end of words? mark, and afterwards we will speak.

3 Wherefore are we counted as beasts, *and* reputed vile in your sight?

4 He teareth himself in his anger: shall the earth be forsaken for thee? and shall the rock be removed out of his place?

5 Yea, the *a*light of the wicked shall be put out, and the spark of his fire shall not shine.

6 The light shall be dark in his *a*tabernacle, and his candle shall be put out with him.

7 The steps of his strength shall be straitened, and his own counsel shall cast him down.

8 For he is cast into a net by his own feet, and he walketh upon a snare.

9 The *a*gin shall take *him* by the heel, *and* the robber shall prevail against him.

10 The snare *is* laid for him in the ground, and a trap for him in the way.

11 Terrors shall make him afraid on every side, and shall drive him to his feet.

12 His strength shall be hungerbitten, and destruction *shall be* ready at his side.

13 It shall devour the strength of his skin: *even* the firstborn of death shall devour his strength.

14 His confidence shall be rooted out of his tabernacle, and it shall bring him to the king of terrors.

15 It shall dwell in his tabernacle, because *it is* none of his: brimstone shall be scattered upon his habitation.

16 His *a*roots shall be dried up beneath, and above shall his branch be cut off.

17 His remembrance shall perish from the earth, and he shall have no name in the street.

18 He shall be driven from light into darkness, and chased out of the world.

19 He shall neither have son nor nephew among his people, nor any remaining in his dwellings.

20 They that come after *him* shall be astonied at his day, as they that went before were affrighted.

21 Surely such *are* the dwellings of the wicked, and this *is* the place *of him that* knoweth not God.

CHAPTER 19

Job tells of the ills that have befallen him and then testifies, I know that my Redeemer lives—Job prophesies that he will be resurrected and that in his flesh he will see God.

THEN Job answered and said,

2 How long will ye vex my soul, and break me in pieces with words?

3 These ten times have ye reproached me: ye are not ashamed *that* ye make yourselves strange to me.

4 And be it indeed *that* I have erred, mine error remaineth with myself.

5 If indeed ye will magnify *yourselves* against me, and plead against me my reproach:

6 Know now that God hath overthrown me, and hath compassed me with his net.

7 Behold, I cry out of wrong, but I am not heard: I cry aloud, but *there is* no *a*judgment.

8 He hath fenced up my way that I cannot pass, and he hath set darkness in my paths.

---

18 5*a* Prov. 13:9; 20:20; 24:20.
6*a* HEB tent.

9*a* HEB trap.
16*a* Isa. 5:24 (24–25); 2 Ne. 15:24 (24–25);

D&C 133:64.
19 7*a* HEB justice.

9 He hath stripped me of my glory, and taken the crown *from* my head.

10 He hath destroyed me on every side, and I am gone: and mine hope hath he removed like a tree.

11 He hath also kindled his wrath against me, and he counteth me unto him as *one of* his enemies.

12 His troops come together, and raise up their way against me, and encamp round about my *a*tabernacle.

13 He hath put my brethren far from me, and mine acquaintance are verily estranged from me.

14 My kinsfolk have failed, and my familiar friends have *a*forgotten me.

15 They that dwell in mine house, and my maids, count me for a stranger: I am an alien in their sight.

16 I called my servant, and he gave *me* no answer; I entreated him with my mouth.

17 My *a*breath is strange to my wife, though I entreated for the children's *sake* of mine own body.

18 Yea, young children despised me; I arose, and they spake against me.

19 All my *a*inward friends abhorred me: and they whom I loved are turned against me.

20 My bone cleaveth to my skin and to my flesh, and I am escaped with the skin of my teeth.

21 Have pity upon me, have pity upon me, O ye my *a*friends; for the *b*hand of God hath touched me.

22 Why do ye persecute me as God, and are not satisfied with *a*my flesh?

23 Oh that my words were now written! oh that they were printed in a book!

24 That they were graven with an iron pen and lead in the rock for ever!

25 For I *a*know *that* my *b*redeemer liveth, and *that* *c*he shall *d*stand at the latter *day* upon the earth:

26 And *though* after my skin *worms* destroy this *a*body, yet in my *b*flesh shall I *c*see God:

27 Whom I shall see for myself, and mine eyes shall behold, and not another; *though* my reins be consumed within me.

28 But ye should say, Why persecute we him, seeing the root of the matter is found in me?

29 Be ye afraid of the sword: for wrath *bringeth* the punishments of the sword, that ye may know *there is* a judgment.

CHAPTER 20

Zophar shows the condition of the wicked—He says, The triumphing of the wicked is short, and the joy of the hypocrite is but for a moment.

THEN answered Zophar the Naamathite, and said,

2 Therefore do my thoughts cause me to answer, and for *this* I make haste.

3 I have heard the check of my reproach, and the spirit of my understanding causeth me to answer.

4 Knowest thou *not* this of old, since man was placed upon earth,

5 That the triumphing of the wicked *is* short, and the *a*joy of the hypocrite *but* for a moment?

6 Though his excellency mount up to the heavens, and his head reach unto the clouds;

7 *Yet* he shall perish for ever like his own dung: they which have seen him shall say, Where *is* he?

8 He shall fly away as a dream, and shall not be found: yea, he shall be chased away as a vision of the night.

9 The eye also *which* saw him shall *see him* no more; neither shall his place any more behold him.

12*a* HEB tent.
14*a* Ps. 31:11 (11–12).
17*a* OR spirit.
19*a* OR intimate.
21*a* TG Friendship.
  b Job 1:11.
22*a* IE the state of my body,

or suffering.
25*a* TG Loyalty; Testimony.
  b TG Jesus Christ,
    Foreordained;
    Jesus Christ, Redeemer.
  c TG Jesus Christ, Second
    Coming.

d TG Jesus Christ,
    Resurrection.
26*a* TG Mortality.
  b TG Flesh; Immortality;
    Resurrection.
  c 1 Jn. 3:2.
20 5*a* TG Joy.

10 His children shall seek to please the poor, and his hands shall restore their goods.

11 His bones are full *of the* ^a*sin* of his youth, which shall lie down with him in the dust.

12 Though wickedness be sweet in his mouth, *though* he hide it under his tongue;

13 *Though* he spare it, and forsake it not; but keep it still within his mouth:

14 *Yet* his meat in his bowels is turned, *it is* the gall of asps within him.

15 He hath swallowed down riches, and he shall vomit them up again: God shall cast them out of his belly.

16 He shall suck the poison of asps: the viper's tongue shall slay him.

17 He shall not see the rivers, the floods, the brooks of honey and butter.

18 That which he laboured for shall he restore, and shall not swallow *it* down: according to *his* substance *shall* the restitution *be,* and he shall not rejoice *therein.*

19 Because he hath oppressed *and* hath forsaken the poor; *because* he hath violently taken away an house which he builded not;

20 Surely he shall not feel quietness in his belly, he shall not save of that which he desired.

21 There shall none of his meat be left; therefore shall no man look for his goods.

22 In the fulness of his sufficiency he shall be in straits: every hand of the wicked shall come upon him.

23 *When* he is about to fill his belly, *God* shall cast the fury of his wrath upon him, and shall rain *it* upon him while he is eating.

24 He shall flee from the iron weapon, *and* the bow of steel shall strike him through.

25 It is drawn, and cometh out of the body; yea, the glittering sword cometh out of his gall: terrors *are* upon him.

26 All darkness *shall be* hid in his secret places: a fire not blown shall consume him; it shall go ill with him that is left in his tabernacle.

27 The heaven shall reveal his iniquity; and the earth shall rise up against him.

28 The increase of his house shall depart, *and his goods* shall flow away in the day of his wrath.

29 This *is* the portion of a wicked man from God, and the heritage appointed unto him by God.

CHAPTER 21

Job admits that the wicked sometimes prosper in this life—Then he testifies that their judgment will be hereafter in the day of wrath and destruction.

BUT Job answered and said,

2 Hear diligently my speech, and let this be your consolations.

3 Suffer me that I may speak; and after that I have spoken, ^amock on.

4 As for me, *is* my complaint to man? and if *it were so,* why should not my spirit be troubled?

5 Mark me, and be astonished, and lay *your* ^ahand upon *your* mouth.

6 Even when I remember I am afraid, and trembling taketh hold on my flesh.

7 Wherefore do the wicked live, become old, yea, are ^amighty in power?

8 Their seed is established in their sight with them, and their offspring before their eyes.

9 Their houses *are* safe from fear, neither *is* the rod of God upon them.

10 Their bull gendereth, and faileth not; their cow calveth, and casteth not her calf.

11 They send forth their little ones like a flock, and their children dance.

12 They take the timbrel and harp, and rejoice at the sound of the ^aorgan.

13 They spend their days in wealth, and in a moment go down to the grave.

14 Therefore they say unto God, Depart from us; for we desire not the knowledge of thy ways.

11*a* TG Carnal Mind.
21 3*a* Job 16:20 (10, 20).

5*a* Judg. 18:19.
7*a* Job 12:6; Hel. 7:5 (5–6).

TG Worldliness.
12*a* HEB flute.

15 What *is* the Almighty, that we should serve him? and what profit should we have, if we pray unto him?

16 Lo, their good *is* not in their hand: the counsel of the wicked is far from me.

17 How oft is the candle of the wicked put out! and *how oft* cometh their destruction upon them! *God* distributeth sorrows in his anger.

18 They are as stubble before the wind, and as *a*chaff that the storm carrieth away.

19 God layeth up his iniquity for his children: he *a*rewardeth him, and he shall know *it.*

20 His eyes shall see his destruction, and he shall *a*drink of the wrath of the Almighty.

21 For what pleasure *hath* he in his house after him, when the number of his months is cut off in the midst?

22 Shall *any* *a*teach God *b*knowledge? seeing he judgeth those that are high.

23 One dieth in his full strength, being wholly at ease and quiet.

24 His breasts are full of milk, and his bones are moistened with marrow.

25 And another dieth in the bitterness of his soul, and never eateth with pleasure.

26 They shall lie down alike in the *a*dust, and the worms shall cover them.

27 Behold, I know your thoughts, and the devices *which* ye wrongfully imagine against me.

28 For ye say, Where *is* the house of the prince? and where *are* the dwelling places of the wicked?

29 Have ye not asked them that go by the way? and do ye not know their tokens,

30 That the wicked is reserved to the day of destruction? they shall be brought forth to the day of wrath.

31 Who shall declare his way to his face? and who shall *a*repay him *what* he hath done?

32 Yet shall he be brought to the grave, and shall remain in the tomb.

33 The clods of the valley shall be sweet unto him, and every man shall draw after him, as *there are* innumerable before him.

34 How then comfort ye me in vain, seeing in your answers there remaineth *a*falsehood?

CHAPTER 22

Eliphaz accuses Job of various sins and exhorts him to repent.

THEN Eliphaz the Temanite answered and said,

2 Can a man be profitable unto God, as he that is wise may be profitable unto himself?

3 *Is it* any pleasure to the Almighty, that thou art *a*righteous? or *is it* gain *to him,* that thou makest thy ways *b*perfect?

4 Will he reprove thee for fear of thee? will he enter with thee into judgment?

5 *Is* not thy wickedness great? and thine iniquities infinite?

6 For thou hast taken a pledge from thy brother for nought, and stripped the naked of their clothing.

7 Thou hast not given water to the weary to drink, and thou hast withholden *a*bread from the *b*hungry.

8 But *as for* the mighty man, he had the earth; and the honourable man dwelt in it.

9 Thou hast sent widows away empty, and the arms of the *a*fatherless have been broken.

10 Therefore snares *are* round about thee, and sudden fear troubleth thee;

11 Or darkness, *that* thou canst not see; and abundance of waters cover thee.

18*a* Ps. 1:4.
19*a* TG Reward.
20*a* Ps. 75:8;
  Mosiah 3:18.
22*a* Isa. 40:13 (13–15).
  b TG God, Omniscience of.

26*a* TG Mortality.
31*a* TG Retribution.
34*a* TG False Doctrine.
22 3*a* Mosiah 2:21 (20–22).
  b 2 Sam. 22:33.
7*a* TG Bread.

b Matt. 25:42;
  Mosiah 4:26;
  Alma 4:12 (12–13).
9*a* Job 31:21 (21–22);
  James 1:27;
  3 Ne. 24:5.

12 *Is* not God in the height of heaven? and behold the height of the stars, how high they are!

13 And thou sayest, How doth God ^aknow? can he ^bjudge through the dark cloud?

14 Thick clouds *are* a covering to him, that he seeth not; and he walketh in the circuit of heaven.

15 Hast thou marked the old way which wicked men have trodden?

16 Which were cut down out of time, whose foundation was overflown with a flood:

17 Which said unto God, Depart from us: and what can the Almighty do for them?

18 Yet he filled their houses with good *things:* but the counsel of the wicked is far from me.

19 The righteous see *it,* and are glad: and the innocent laugh them to scorn.

20 Whereas our substance is not cut down, but the remnant of them the fire consumeth.

21 Acquaint now thyself with ^ahim, and be at ^bpeace: thereby good shall come unto thee.

22 Receive, I pray thee, the law from his mouth, and lay up his words in thine heart.

23 If thou return to the Almighty, thou shalt be ^abuilt up, thou shalt put away iniquity far from thy tabernacles.

24 Then shalt thou lay up gold as dust, and the *gold* of Ophir as the stones of the brooks.

25 Yea, the Almighty shall be thy defence, and thou shalt have plenty of silver.

26 For then shalt thou have thy delight in the Almighty, and shalt lift up thy ^aface unto God.

27 Thou shalt make thy prayer unto him, and he shall hear thee, and thou shalt pay thy ^avows.

28 Thou shalt also decree a thing, and it shall be established unto thee: and the light shall shine upon thy ways.

29 When *men* are cast down, then thou shalt say, *There is* lifting up; and he shall save the ^ahumble person.

30 He shall deliver the island of the innocent: and it is delivered by the pureness of thine hands.

CHAPTER 23

Job seeks the Lord and asserts his own righteousness—He says, When the Lord has tried me, I will come forth as gold.

THEN Job answered and said,

2 Even to day *is* my ^acomplaint bitter: my stroke is heavier than my groaning.

3 Oh that I knew where I might find him! *that* I might come *even* to his seat!

4 I would order *my* cause before him, and fill my mouth with arguments.

5 I would know the words *which* he would answer me, and understand what he would say unto me.

6 Will he plead against me with *his* great power? No; but he would put ^a*strength* in me.

7 There the righteous might ^adispute with him; so should I be ^bdelivered for ever from my judge.

8 Behold, I go forward, but he *is* not *there;* and backward, but I cannot perceive him:

9 On the left hand, where he doth work, but I cannot behold *him:* he hideth himself on the right hand, that I cannot see *him:*

10 But he ^aknoweth the way that I take: *when* he hath ^btried me, I shall come forth as gold.

11 My foot hath held his steps, his way have I kept, and not declined.

12 Neither have I gone back from

13a Ps. 73:11.
  b Ps. 94:9 (7–10);
    D&C 88:41.
21a IE God.
  b TG Peace of God.
23a 1 Ne. 17:3.

26a Job 11:15 (13–16, 18).
27a TG Vow.
29a TG Humility;
    Poor in Spirit.
23 2a Alma 34:41.
  6a 1 Ne. 17:3.

7a TG Disputations.
  b 2 Ne. 9:19 (18–19);
    D&C 108:8.
10a TG God, Omniscience of.
  b TG Test.

the commandment of his lips; I have esteemed the words of his mouth more than my necessary *food.*

13 But he *is* in one *mind,* and who can turn him? and *what* his soul desireth, even *that* he doeth.

14 For he performeth *the thing that is* appointed for me: and many such *things are* with him.

15 Therefore am I *a*troubled at his presence: when I consider, I am afraid of him.

16 For God maketh my heart soft, and the Almighty troubleth me:

17 Because I was not cut off before the darkness, *neither* hath he covered the darkness from my face.

CHAPTER 24

Murderers, adulterers, those who oppress the poor, and wicked people in general often go unpunished for a little while.

WHY, seeing times are not hidden from the Almighty, do they that know him not see his days?

2 *Some* remove the *a*landmarks; they violently take away flocks, and feed *thereof.*

3 They drive away the ass of the fatherless, they take the widow's ox for a pledge.

4 They turn the needy out of the way: the poor of the earth hide themselves together.

5 Behold, *as* wild asses in the desert, go they forth to their work; rising betimes for a prey: the wilderness *yieldeth* food for them *and* for *their* children.

6 They reap *every one* his *a*corn in the field: and they gather the vintage of the wicked.

7 They cause the naked to lodge without clothing, that *they have* no covering in the cold.

8 They are wet with the showers of the mountains, and embrace the rock for want of a shelter.

9 They pluck the fatherless from the breast, and take a pledge of the poor.

10 They cause *him* to go naked without clothing, and they take away the sheaf *from* the hungry;

11 *Which* make oil within their walls, *and* tread *their* winepresses, and suffer thirst.

12 Men groan from out of the city, and the soul of the wounded crieth out: yet God *a*layeth not folly *to them.*

13 They are of those that *a*rebel against the *b*light; they know not the ways thereof, nor abide in the paths thereof.

14 The murderer rising with the light killeth the poor and needy, and in the night is as a thief.

15 The eye also of the adulterer waiteth for the *a*twilight, saying, No eye shall see me: and disguiseth *his* face.

16 In the dark they dig through houses, *which* they had marked for themselves in the daytime: they know not the *a*light.

17 For the morning *is* to them even as the shadow of death: if *one* know *them,* they are in the terrors of the shadow of death.

18 He *is* swift as the waters; their portion is cursed in the earth: he beholdeth not the way of the vineyards.

19 *a*Drought and heat consume the snow waters: *so doth* the grave *those which* have sinned.

20 The womb shall forget him; the worm shall feed sweetly on him; he shall be no more remembered; and wickedness shall be broken as a tree.

21 He evil entreateth the barren *that* beareth not: and doeth not good to the widow.

22 He draweth also the mighty with his power: he riseth up, and no *man* is sure of life.

23 *Though* it be given him *to be* in

15*a* Gen. 45:3.
24 2*a* Deut. 19:14;
  Prov. 22:28;
  Hosea 5:10.
  6*a* HEB fodder.

12*a* OR does not give heed
  to their prayer.
13*a* 1 Ne. 2:23 (19–24);
  Mosiah 15:26;
  D&C 10:21 (20–22).

b Hel. 13:29.
15*a* Prov. 7:9 (9–10).
16*a* D&C 10:21.
19*a* TG Drought.

safety, whereon he resteth; yet his eyes *are* upon their ways.

24 They are exalted for a ᵃlittle while, but are gone and brought ᵇlow; they are taken out of the way as all *other,* and cut off as the ᶜtops of the ears of corn.

25 And if *it be* not *so* now, who will make me a liar, and make my speech nothing worth?

CHAPTER 25

Bildad bemoans the lowly state of man and classifies him as a worm.

THEN answered Bildad the Shuhite, and said,

2 Dominion and fear *are* with him, he maketh peace in his high places.

3 Is there any number of his armies? and upon whom doth not his light arise?

4 How then can man be ᵃjustified with God? or how can he be ᵇclean *that is* born of a woman?

5 Behold even to the moon, and it shineth not; yea, the stars are not pure in his sight.

6 How much less man, *that is* a worm? and the son of man, *which is* a worm?

CHAPTER 26

Job reproves Bildad's lack of empathy—He extols the power, greatness, and strength of the Lord.

BUT Job answered and said,

2 How hast thou helped *him that is* without power? how savest thou the arm *that hath* no strength?

3 How hast thou counselled *him that hath* no wisdom? and how hast thou plentifully declared the thing as it is?

4 To whom hast thou uttered words? and whose spirit came from thee?

5 Dead *things* are formed from under the waters, and the inhabitants thereof.

6 ᵃHell *is* naked before him, and destruction hath no covering.

7 He stretcheth out the north over the empty place, *and* hangeth the earth upon nothing.

8 He bindeth up the waters in his thick clouds; and the cloud is not rent under them.

9 He holdeth back the face of his throne, *and* spreadeth his cloud upon it.

10 He hath compassed the waters with bounds, until the day and night come to an end.

11 The pillars of heaven tremble and are astonished at his reproof.

12 He divideth the sea with his power, and by his understanding he smiteth through the proud.

13 By his ᵃspirit he hath ᵇgarnished the ᶜheavens; his hand hath formed the crooked ᵈserpent.

14 Lo, these *are* parts of his ways: but how little a portion is heard of him? but the thunder of his power who can understand?

CHAPTER 27

Job asserts his righteousness—When the wicked are buried in death, terrors will take hold of them.

MOREOVER Job continued his parable, and said,

2 *As* God liveth, *who* hath taken away my judgment; and the Almighty, *who* hath vexed my soul;

3 All the while my breath *is* in me, and the spirit of God *is* in my nostrils;

4 My lips shall not speak ᵃwickedness, nor my tongue utter ᵇdeceit.

5 God forbid that I should justify you: till I die I will not ᵃremove mine ᵇintegrity from me.

6 My ᵃrighteousness I hold fast,

24a Ps. 37:10 (10–11).
 b 2 Ne. 26:10.
 c HEB heads of grain.
25 4a TG Justification.
 b Ether 12:37;
   D&C 88:74 (74–75);
   135:5 (4–5).

26 6a Ps. 139:8 (1–16).
 13a 1 Ne. 19:12.
 b TG Jesus Christ,
   Creator.
 c TG Heaven.
 d Isa. 27:1.
27 4a Ps. 5:4 (4–12).

 b TG Deceit; Honesty.
 5a TG Perseverance.
 b Mosiah 24:15 (15–16);
   D&C 54:10.
   TG Integrity; Sincere;
   Steadfastness.
 6a TG Righteousness.

and will not let it go: my heart shall not *reproach me* so long as I live.

7 Let mine enemy be as the wicked, and he that riseth up against me as the unrighteous.

8 For what *is* the *hope of the hypocrite, though he hath *gained, when God taketh away his soul?

9 Will God *hear his *cry when trouble cometh upon him?

10 Will he delight himself in the *Almighty? will he always call upon God?

11 I will teach you by the hand of God: *that* which *is* with the Almighty will I not conceal.

12 Behold, all ye yourselves have seen *it;* why then are ye thus altogether vain?

13 This *is* the portion of a wicked man with God, and the heritage of *oppressors, *which* they shall receive of the Almighty.

14 If his *children be multiplied, *it is* for the sword: and his offspring shall not be satisfied with bread.

15 Those that remain of him shall be buried in death: and his widows shall not weep.

16 Though he heap up silver as the dust, and prepare *raiment as the clay;

17 He may prepare *it,* but the just shall put *it* on, and the innocent shall divide the silver.

18 He buildeth his house as a moth, and as a booth *that* the keeper maketh.

19 The rich man shall lie down, but he shall not be gathered: he openeth his eyes, and he *is* not.

20 Terrors take hold on him as waters, a tempest stealeth him away in the night.

21 The east wind carrieth him away, and he departeth: and as a storm hurleth him out of his place.

22 For *God* shall cast upon him, and not spare: he would fain flee out of his hand.

23 *Men* shall *clap their hands at him, and shall hiss him out of his place.

CHAPTER 28

Wealth comes out of the earth—Wisdom cannot be purchased—The fear of the Lord is wisdom, and to depart from evil is understanding.

SURELY there is a *vein for the silver, and a place for gold *where* they fine *it.*

2 Iron is taken out of the earth, and brass *is* molten *out of* the stone.

3 He setteth an end to darkness, and searcheth out all perfection: the stones of darkness, and the shadow of death.

4 The flood breaketh out from the inhabitant; *even the waters* forgotten of the foot: they are dried up, they are gone away from men.

5 *As for* the earth, out of it cometh bread: and under it is turned up as it were fire.

6 The stones of it *are* the place of sapphires: and it hath dust of gold.

7 *There is* a path which no fowl knoweth, and which the vulture's eye hath not seen:

8 The lion's whelps have not trodden it, nor the fierce lion passed by it.

9 He putteth forth his hand upon the rock; he overturneth the mountains by the roots.

10 He cutteth out rivers among the rocks; and his eye seeth every precious thing.

11 *He bindeth the floods from overflowing; and *the thing that is* hid bringeth he forth to light.

12 But where shall *wisdom be found? and where *is* the place of understanding?

13 Man knoweth not the price thereof; neither is it found in the land of the living.

6*b* Alma 29:5.
8*a* Alma 34:33 (33–35).
  b Matt. 16:26.
9*a* Prov. 1:28.
  b Mosiah 11:24 (21–25);
    21:14 (14–15).

TG God, Access to.
10*a* Mosiah 11:23.
13*a* TG Injustice;
    Oppression.
14*a* Deut. 28:41;
    2 Ne. 23:16 (15–16).

16*a* 3 Ne. 13:25.
23*a* Lam. 2:15.
28 1*a* OR mine.
11*a* HEB He restricts the
    rivers and streams.
12*a* TG God, Wisdom of.

14 The depth saith, It *is* not in me: and the sea saith, *It is* not with me.

15 It cannot be gotten for gold, neither shall silver be weighed *for* the price thereof.

16 It cannot be valued with the *a*gold of *b*Ophir, with the precious onyx, or the sapphire.

17 The gold and the crystal cannot equal it: and the exchange of it *shall not be for* jewels of fine gold.

18 No mention shall be made of coral, or of pearls: for the price of wisdom *is* above *a*rubies.

19 The topaz of Ethiopia shall not equal it, neither shall it be valued with pure gold.

20 Whence then cometh wisdom? and where *is* the place of understanding?

21 Seeing it is hid from the eyes of all living, and kept close from the fowls of the air.

22 Destruction and death say, We have heard the fame thereof with our ears.

23 God understandeth the way thereof, and he knoweth the place thereof.

24 For he looketh to the ends of the earth, *and* seeth under the whole heaven;

25 To make the weight for the winds; and he weigheth the waters by measure.

26 When he made a decree for the rain, and a way for the lightning of the thunder:

27 Then did he see it, and declare it; he prepared it, yea, and searched it out.

28 And unto man he said, Behold, the *a*fear of the Lord, that *is* *b*wisdom; and to depart from evil *is* *c*understanding.

CHAPTER 29

Job recalls his former prosperity and greatness—He was blessed because of his righteousness, his charity, and his good deeds.

MOREOVER Job continued his parable, and said,

2 Oh that I were as *in* months past, as *in* the days *when* God preserved me;

3 When his *a*candle shined upon my head, *and when* by his light I walked *through* darkness;

4 As I was in the days of my youth, when the *a*secret of God *was* upon my tabernacle;

5 When the Almighty *was* yet with me, *when* my children *were* about me;

6 When I washed my steps with butter, and the rock poured me out rivers of oil;

7 When I went out to the gate through the city, *when* I prepared my seat in the street!

8 The young men saw me, and hid themselves: and the aged arose, *and* stood up.

9 The princes refrained talking, and laid *their* hand on their mouth.

10 The nobles held their peace, and their tongue cleaved to the roof of their mouth.

11 When the ear heard *me*, then it blessed me; and when the eye saw *me*, it gave witness to me:

12 Because I delivered the *a*poor that cried, and the fatherless, and *him that had* none to help him.

13 The blessing of him that was ready to perish came upon me: and I caused the widow's heart to sing for joy.

14 I put on *a*righteousness, and it clothed me: my judgment *was* as a robe and a diadem.

15 I was eyes to the blind, and feet *was* I to the lame.

16 I *was* a father to the poor: and the cause *which* I knew not I searched out.

17 And I brake the jaws of the

16*a* Isa. 13:12.
  b 1 Kgs. 9:28.
18*a* Prov. 8:11 (10–11); 20:15.
28*a* TG Reverence.
  b TG God, the Standard of

Righteousness;
Wisdom.
  c TG Understanding.
29 3*a* OR lamp.
  4*a* OR friendship,

confidence.
12*a* Mosiah 4:26;
    D&C 42:31 (30–31);
    104:18.
14*a* TG Righteousness.

wicked, and plucked the spoil out of his teeth.

18 Then I said, I shall die in my nest, and I shall multiply *my* days as the sand.

19 My root *was* spread out by the waters, and the dew lay all night upon my branch.

20 My glory *was* fresh in me, and my bow was renewed in my hand.

21 Unto me *men* gave ear, and waited, and kept silence at my counsel.

22 After my words they spake not again; and my speech dropped upon them.

23 And they waited for me as for the rain; and they opened their mouth wide *as* for the latter rain.

24 *If* I laughed on them, they believed *it* not; and the light of my countenance they cast not down.

25 I chose out their way, and sat chief, and dwelt as a king in the army, as one *that* comforteth the mourners.

CHAPTER 30

Job is derided by the children of vile and base men—In his afflicted state, he cries to the Lord—Job says that he wept for those in trouble.

BUT now *they that are* younger than I have me in derision, whose fathers I would have disdained to have set with the dogs of my flock.

2 Yea, whereto *might* the strength of their hands *profit* me, in whom old age was perished?

3 For want and famine *they were* solitary; fleeing into the wilderness in former time desolate and waste.

4 Who cut up mallows by the bushes, and juniper roots *for* their meat.

5 They were driven forth from among *men*, (they cried after them as *after* a thief;)

6 To dwell in the clifts of the valleys, *in* caves of the earth, and *in* the rocks.

7 Among the bushes they brayed; under the nettles they were gathered together.

8 *They were* children of fools, yea, children of base men: they were viler than the earth.

9 And now am I their ªsong, yea, I am their byword.

10 They abhor me, they flee far from me, and spare not to spit in my face.

11 Because ªhe hath loosed my cord, and afflicted me, they have also let loose the bridle before me.

12 Upon *my* right *hand* rise the youth; they push away my feet, and they raise up against me the ways of their destruction.

13 They mar my path, they set forward my calamity, they have no helper.

14 They came *upon me* as a wide breaking in *of waters:* in the desolation they rolled themselves *upon me.*

15 Terrors are turned upon me: they pursue my soul as the wind: and my welfare passeth away as a cloud.

16 And now my soul is poured out upon me; the days of affliction have taken hold upon me.

17 My bones are pierced in me in the night season: and my sinews take no rest.

18 By the great force *of my disease* is my garment changed: it bindeth me about as the collar of my coat.

19 He hath cast me into the mire, and I am become like dust and ashes.

20 I cry unto thee, and thou dost not ªhear me: I stand up, and thou regardest me *not.*

21 Thou art become ªcruel to me: with thy strong hand thou opposest thyself against me.

22 Thou liftest me up to the wind; thou causest me to ride *upon it,* and dissolvest my substance.

23 For I know *that* thou wilt bring me *to* death, and *to* the house appointed for all living.

24 Howbeit he will not stretch out *his* hand to the grave, though they cry in his destruction.

---

30 9*a* Ps. 69:12.
11*a* OR God.

20*a* HEB answer.
21*a* TG Cruelty.

25 Did not I weep for him that was in trouble? was *not* my soul grieved for the poor?

26 When I looked for *a*good, then evil came *unto me:* and when I waited for light, there came darkness.

27 My bowels boiled, and rested not: the days of affliction prevented me.

28 I went mourning without the sun: I stood up, *and* I cried in the congregation.

29 I am a brother to dragons, and a companion to *a*owls.

30 My skin is black upon me, and my bones are burned with heat.

31 My harp also is *turned* to mourning, and my *a*organ into the voice of them that weep.

CHAPTER 31

Job invites judgment so that God may know his integrity—If he has done ill, Job welcomes the penalties for so doing.

I MADE a *a*covenant with mine eyes; why then should I think upon a maid?

2 For what portion of God *is there* from above? and *what* *a*inheritance of the Almighty from on high?

3 *Is* not destruction to the wicked? and a strange *punishment* to the workers of iniquity?

4 Doth not he see my ways, and count all my steps?

5 If I have walked with vanity, or if my foot hath *a*hasted to *b*deceit;

6 Let me be *a*weighed in an even balance, that God may know mine *b*integrity.

7 If my step hath turned out of the way, and mine heart *a*walked after mine eyes, and if any blot hath cleaved to mine hands;

8 *Then* let me sow, and let another eat; yea, let my offspring be rooted out.

9 If mine heart have been *a*deceived by a woman, or *if* I have laid wait at my neighbour's door;

10 *Then* let my wife grind unto another, and let others bow down upon her.

11 For this *is* an heinous crime; yea, it *is* an iniquity *to be punished by* the judges.

12 For it *is* a fire *that* consumeth to destruction, and would root out all mine increase.

13 If I did despise the cause of my manservant or of my maidservant, when they contended with me;

14 What then shall I do when God riseth up? and when he visiteth, what shall I answer him?

15 Did not he that made me in the womb make him? and did not one *a*fashion us in the womb?

16 If I have withheld the poor from *their* desire, or have caused the eyes of the widow to fail;

17 Or have eaten my morsel myself alone, and the fatherless hath not eaten thereof;

18 (For from my youth he was brought up with me, as *with* a father, and I have guided her from my mother's womb;)

19 If I have seen any perish for want of clothing, or any poor without covering;

20 If his loins have not blessed me, and *if* he were *not* warmed with the fleece of my sheep;

21 If I have lifted up my hand against the *a*fatherless, when I saw my help in the gate:

22 *Then* let mine arm fall from my shoulder blade, and mine arm be broken from the bone.

23 For destruction *from* God *was* a terror to me, and by reason of his highness I could not endure.

24 If I have made gold my hope, or have said to the fine gold, *Thou art* my confidence;

26a Jer. 8:15.
29a HEB ostriches.
31a HEB pipe, flute.
31 1a D&C 43:9.
　2a TG Inheritance.
　5a TG Rashness.

b TG Deceit.
6a Dan. 5:27.
　b TG Integrity.
7a Eccl. 11:9;
　Hel. 13:27 (26–27).
9a HEB enticed.

15a Mal. 2:10;
　Acts 17:26;
　Ether 3:15.
21a Job 22:9;
　James 1:27;
　3 Ne. 24:5.

25 If I rejoiced because my ^awealth *was* great, and because mine hand had gotten much;

26 If I beheld the sun when it shined, or the moon walking *in* brightness;

27 And my heart hath been secretly enticed, or my mouth hath kissed my hand:

28 This also *were* an iniquity *to be punished by* the judge: for I should have denied the God *that is* above.

29 If I ^arejoiced at the destruction of him that hated me, or lifted up myself when evil found him:

30 Neither have I suffered my mouth to sin by wishing a ^acurse to his soul.

31 If the men of my tabernacle said not, Oh that we had of his flesh! we cannot be satisfied.

32 The stranger did not lodge in the street: *but* I opened my doors to the traveller.

33 If I ^acovered my transgressions ^bas Adam, by hiding mine iniquity in my bosom:

34 Did I fear a great multitude, or did the contempt of families terrify me, that I kept silence, *and* went not out of the door?

35 Oh that one would hear me! behold, my desire *is, that* the Almighty would answer me, and *that* mine adversary had written a book.

36 Surely I would take it upon my shoulder, *and* bind it *as* a crown to me.

37 I would declare unto him the number of my steps; as a prince would I go near unto him.

38 If my land cry against me, or that the furrows likewise thereof complain;

39 If I have eaten the fruits thereof without money, or have caused the owners thereof to lose their life:

40 Let thistles grow instead of wheat, and ^acockle instead of barley. The words of Job are ended.

CHAPTER 32

Elihu, in anger, answers Job and his three friends—Elihu says, There is a spirit in man, and the inspiration of the Almighty gives understanding—He also says, Great men are not always wise.

So these three men ceased to answer Job, because he *was* righteous in his own eyes.

2 Then was kindled the wrath of Elihu the son of Barachel the Buzite, of the kindred of Ram: against Job was his wrath kindled, because he justified himself rather than God.

3 Also against his three friends was his wrath kindled, because they had found no answer, and *yet* had condemned Job.

4 Now Elihu had waited till Job had spoken, because they *were* elder than he.

5 When Elihu saw that *there was* no answer in the mouth of *these* three men, then his wrath was kindled.

6 And Elihu the son of Barachel the Buzite answered and said, I *am* young, and ye *are* very old; wherefore I was afraid, and durst not shew you mine opinion.

7 I said, Days should speak, and multitude of years should teach wisdom.

8 But *there is* a ^aspirit in man: and the ^binspiration of the Almighty giveth them ^cunderstanding.

9 Great men are not *always* wise: neither do the aged understand judgment.

10 Therefore I said, Hearken to me; I also will shew mine opinion.

11 Behold, I waited for your words; I gave ear to your reasons, whilst ye searched out what to say.

12 Yea, I attended unto you, and, behold, *there was* none of you that convinced Job, *or* that answered his words:

13 Lest ye should say, We have

25a Ps. 62:10;
    Alma 1:30 (30–31).
29a Prov. 17:5.
30a TG Curse.
33a Prov. 28:13.

b OR as some men do.
40a OR noxious weeds.
32 8a TG Man, a Spirit Child of Heavenly Father; Spirit Body;

Spirit Creation.
b TG Inspiration; Spirituality.
c TG Conscience; Understanding; Wisdom.

found out wisdom: God thrusteth him down, not man.

14 Now he hath not directed *his* words against me: neither will I answer him with your speeches.

15 They were amazed, they answered no more: they left off speaking.

16 When I had waited, (for they spake not, but stood still, *and* answered no more;)

17 *I said,* I will answer also my part, I also will shew mine opinion.

18 For I am full of matter, the spirit within me constraineth me.

19 Behold, my belly *is* as wine *which* hath no vent; it is ready to burst like new ᵃbottles.

20 I will speak, that I may be refreshed: I will open my lips and answer.

21 Let me not, I pray you, accept any man's person, neither let me give flattering titles unto man.

22 For I know not to give ᵃflattering titles; *in so doing* my maker would soon take me away.

CHAPTER 33

Elihu says, God is greater than man, He speaks to man in dreams and visions, He ransoms those cast into the pit, and He delivers their souls and gives them life.

WHEREFORE, Job, I pray thee, hear my speeches, and hearken to all my words.

2 Behold, now I have opened my mouth, my tongue hath spoken in my mouth.

3 My words *shall be of* the uprightness of my heart: and my lips shall utter knowledge clearly.

4 The ᵃSpirit of God hath made me, and the ᵇbreath of the Almighty hath given me life.

5 If thou canst answer me, set *thy words* in order before me, stand up.

6 Behold, I *am* according to thy wish in God's stead: I also am formed out of the clay.

7 Behold, my terror shall not make thee afraid, neither shall my hand be heavy upon thee.

8 Surely thou hast spoken in mine hearing, and I have heard the voice of *thy* words, *saying,*

9 I am clean without transgression, I *am* innocent; neither *is there* iniquity in me.

10 Behold, he findeth occasions against me, he counteth me for his enemy,

11 He putteth my feet in the stocks, he marketh all my paths.

12 Behold, *in* this thou art not just: I will answer thee, that God is ᵃgreater than man.

13 Why dost thou strive against him? for he giveth not account of any of his matters.

14 For God speaketh once, yea twice, *yet man* perceiveth it not.

15 In a ᵃdream, in a vision of the night, when deep sleep falleth upon men, in slumberings upon the bed;

16 Then he openeth the ears of men, and sealeth their instruction,

17 That he may withdraw man *from his* purpose, and hide pride from man.

18 He keepeth back his soul from the ᵃpit, and his life from perishing by the sword.

19 He is chastened also with pain upon his bed, and the multitude of his bones with strong *pain:*

20 So that his life abhorreth bread, and his soul dainty meat.

21 His flesh is consumed away, that it cannot be seen; and his bones *that* were not seen stick out.

22 Yea, his soul draweth near unto the grave, and his life to the destroyers.

23 If there be a messenger with him, an interpreter, one among a thousand, to shew unto man his uprightness:

24 Then he is gracious unto him, and saith, Deliver him from going

---

19*a* HEB wineskins.
22*a* TG Flatter.
33 4*a* TG God, Spirit of.

b TG Breath of Life; Man, a Spirit Child of Heavenly Father.

12*a* Isa. 55:9 (8–9).
15*a* TG Dream.
18*a* TG Hell.

down to the pit: I have found a ^aransom.

25 His ^aflesh shall be fresher than a child's: he shall return to the days of his youth:

26 He shall ^apray unto God, and he will be favourable unto him: and he shall see his face with joy: for he will render unto man his righteousness.

27 He looketh upon men, and *if any* say, I have sinned, and perverted *that which was* right, and it profited me not;

28 He will deliver his soul from going into the pit, and his life shall see the light.

29 Lo, all these *things* worketh God oftentimes with man,

30 To bring back his soul from the pit, to be enlightened with the light of the living.

31 Mark well, O Job, hearken unto me: hold thy peace, and I will speak.

32 If thou hast any thing to say, answer me: speak, for I desire to justify thee.

33 If not, hearken unto me: hold thy peace, and I shall teach thee wisdom.

CHAPTER 34

Elihu teaches, God cannot be unjust, commit iniquity, pervert judgment, or respect persons—Man should bear chastisement and do iniquity no more.

FURTHERMORE Elihu answered and said,

2 Hear my words, O ye wise *men;* and give ear unto me, ye that have knowledge.

3 For the ear trieth words, as the mouth tasteth meat.

4 Let us choose to us judgment: let us know among ourselves what *is* good.

5 For Job hath said, I am righteous: and God hath taken away my judgment.

6 Should I lie against my right? my wound *is* incurable without transgression.

7 What man *is* like Job, *who* drinketh up scorning like water?

8 Which goeth in company with the workers of iniquity, and walketh with wicked men.

9 For he hath said, It profiteth a man nothing that he should delight himself with God.

10 Therefore hearken unto me, ye men of understanding: far be it from God, *that he should do* wickedness; and *from* the Almighty, *that he should commit* iniquity.

11 For the ^awork of a man shall he render unto him, and cause every man to find according to *his* ways.

12 Yea, surely God will not do wickedly, neither will the Almighty pervert ^ajudgment.

13 Who hath given him a charge over the earth? or who hath disposed the whole world?

14 If he set his heart upon man, *if* he gather unto himself his spirit and his breath;

15 All flesh shall perish together, and man shall turn again unto ^adust.

16 If now *thou hast* understanding, hear this: hearken to the voice of my words.

17 Shall even he that hateth right govern? and wilt thou condemn him that is most just?

18 *Is it fit* to say to a king, *Thou art* wicked? *and* to princes, *Ye are* ungodly?

19 *How much less to him* that accepteth not the persons of princes, nor regardeth the rich more than the poor? for they all *are* the work of his hands.

20 In a moment shall they die, and the people shall be troubled at midnight, and pass away: and the mighty shall be taken away without hand.

21 For his eyes *are* upon the ways of man, and he seeth all his goings.

24a 1 Tim. 2:6.
25a 2 Kgs. 5:14.
26a 2 Ne. 32:9;
     D&C 75:11.

34 11a 2 Ne. 25:23;
         Alma 9:28;
         D&C 1:10; 6:33.
     12a Ps. 19:9;

2 Ne. 9:15; 30:9.
15a TG Death;
     Man, Physical
     Creation of.

22 *There is* no darkness, nor shadow of death, where the workers of iniquity may ᵃhide themselves.

23 For he will not lay upon man more *than right;* that he should enter into judgment with God.

24 He shall break in pieces mighty men without number, and set others in their stead.

25 Therefore he knoweth their works, and he overturneth *them* in the night, so that they are destroyed.

26 He striketh them as wicked men in the open sight of others;

27 Because they turned back from him, and would not consider any of his ways:

28 So that they cause the cry of the poor to come unto him, and he heareth the cry of the afflicted.

29 When he giveth ᵃquietness, who then can make trouble? and when he hideth *his* face, who then can behold him? whether *it be done* against a nation, or against a man only:

30 That the hypocrite reign not, lest the people be ensnared.

31 Surely it is meet to be said unto God, I have borne ᵃchastisement, I will not offend *any more:*

32 *That which* I see not teach thou me: if I have done iniquity, I will do no more.

33 *Should it be* according to thy mind? he will recompense it, whether thou refuse, or whether thou choose; and not I: therefore speak what thou knowest.

34 Let men of understanding tell me, and let a wise man hearken unto me.

35 Job hath spoken without knowledge, and his words *were* without wisdom.

36 My desire *is that* Job may be tried unto the end because of *his* answers for wicked men.

37 For he addeth rebellion unto his sin, he clappeth *his hands* among us, and multiplieth his words against God.

CHAPTER 35

Elihu contrasts the weakness of man and the power of God—Our wickedness hurts other men, and our righteousness helps them—Man should trust in the Lord.

ELIHU spake moreover, and said,

2 Thinkest thou this to be right, *that* thou saidst, My righteousness *is* more than God's?

3 For thou saidst, What advantage will it be unto thee? *and,* What profit shall I have, *if I be cleansed* from my sin?

4 I will answer thee, and thy companions with thee.

5 Look unto the heavens, and see; and behold the clouds *which* are higher than thou.

6 If thou sinnest, what doest thou against him? or *if* thy transgressions be multiplied, what doest thou unto him?

7 If thou be ᵃrighteous, what givest thou him? or what receiveth he of thine hand?

8 Thy wickedness *may hurt* a man as thou *art;* and thy righteousness *may profit* the son of man.

9 By reason of the multitude of oppressions they make *the oppressed* to cry: they cry out by reason of the arm of the mighty.

10 But none saith, Where *is* God my maker, who giveth ᵃsongs in the night;

11 Who teacheth us more than the beasts of the earth, and maketh us wiser than the fowls of heaven?

12 There they cry, but none giveth answer, because of the pride of evil men.

13 Surely God will not hear vanity, neither will the Almighty regard it.

14 Although thou sayest thou shalt not see him, *yet* judgment *is* before him; therefore trust thou in him.

15 But now, because *it is* not *so,* he hath visited in his anger; yet he knoweth *it* not in great extremity:

16 Therefore doth Job open his mouth in vain; he multiplieth words without knowledge.

22a Alma 12:14 (14–15);
    D&C 1:2.
29a TG Silence.
31a TG Chastening.
35 7a Prov. 9:12.
    10a Ps. 77:6.

CHAPTER 36

Elihu says, Those who are righteous are prospered—The wicked perish and die without knowledge—Elihu praises the greatness of God.

ELIHU also proceeded, and said,

2 Suffer me a little, and I will shew thee that I *have* yet to speak on God's behalf.

3 I will fetch my knowledge from afar, and will ascribe righteousness to my Maker.

4 For truly my words *shall* not *be* false: he that is perfect in knowledge *is* with thee.

5 Behold, God *is* mighty, and *ª*despiseth not *any: he is* mighty in strength *and* *b*wisdom.

6 He preserveth not the life of the wicked: but giveth right to the poor.

7 He withdraweth not his eyes from the righteous: but with kings *are they* on the throne; yea, he doth establish them for ever, and they are exalted.

8 And if *they be* bound in fetters, *and* be holden in cords of affliction;

9 Then he sheweth them their work, and their transgressions that they have exceeded.

10 He openeth also their ear to discipline, and commandeth that they return from iniquity.

11 If they obey and serve *him,* they shall spend their *ª*days in prosperity, and their years in *b*pleasures.

12 But if they *ª*obey not, they shall perish by the sword, and they shall die without knowledge.

13 But the hypocrites in heart heap up wrath: they cry not when he bindeth them.

14 They die in youth, and their life *is* among the unclean.

15 He *ª*delivereth the poor in his affliction, and openeth their ears in oppression.

16 Even so would he have removed thee out of the strait *into* a broad place, where *there is* no straitness; and that which should be set on thy table *should be* full of fatness.

17 But thou hast fulfilled the judgment of the wicked: judgment and justice take hold *on thee.*

18 Because *there is* wrath, *beware* lest he take thee away with *his* stroke: then a great ransom cannot deliver thee.

19 Will he esteem thy riches? *no,* not gold, nor all the forces of strength.

20 Desire not the night, when people are cut off in their place.

21 Take heed, regard not iniquity: for this hast thou chosen rather than affliction.

22 Behold, God exalteth by his power: who teacheth like him?

23 Who hath enjoined him his way? or who can say, Thou hast wrought iniquity?

24 Remember that thou magnify his work, which men behold.

25 Every man may see it; man may behold *it* afar off.

26 Behold, God *is* great, and we know *him* not, neither can the number of his years be searched out.

27 For he maketh small the drops of water: they pour down rain according to the vapour thereof:

28 Which the clouds do drop *and* distil upon man abundantly.

29 Also can *any* understand the spreadings of the clouds, *or* the noise of his tabernacle?

30 Behold, he spreadeth his light upon it, and covereth the bottom of the sea.

31 For by them judgeth he the people; he giveth meat in abundance.

32 With clouds he covereth the light; and commandeth it *not to shine* by *the cloud* that cometh betwixt.

33 The noise thereof sheweth concerning it, the cattle also concerning the vapour.

CHAPTER 37

Elihu concludes, saying, The Lord controls the laws of nature—God reigns in terrible majesty.

AT this also my heart trembleth, and is moved out of his place.

---

36 5*a* TG Hate.
  b TG God, Wisdom of.

11*a* TG Probation.
  b HEB pleasantness.

12*a* TG Disobedience.
15*a* TG Deliver.

2 Hear attentively the noise of his voice, and the sound *that* goeth out of his mouth.

3 He directeth it under the whole heaven, and his lightning unto the ends of the earth.

4 After it a voice roareth: he thundereth with the voice of his excellency; and he will not stay them when his voice is heard.

5 God thundereth marvellously with his voice; great things doeth he, which we cannot comprehend.

6 For he saith to the *a*snow, Be thou *on* the earth; likewise to the small rain, and to the great rain of his strength.

7 He sealeth up the hand of every man; that all men may know his work.

8 Then the beasts go into dens, and remain in their places.

9 Out of the south cometh the whirlwind: and cold out of the north.

10 By the breath of God frost is given: and the breadth of the waters is straitened.

11 Also by watering he wearieth the thick cloud: he scattereth his bright cloud:

12 And it is turned round about by his counsels: that they may do whatsoever he commandeth them upon the face of the world in the earth.

13 He causeth it to come, whether for correction, or for his land, or for mercy.

14 Hearken unto this, O Job: stand still, and *a*consider the wondrous *b*works of God.

15 Dost thou know when God disposed them, and caused the light of his cloud to shine?

16 Dost thou know the balancings of the clouds, the wondrous works of him which is perfect in *a*knowledge?

17 How thy garments *are* warm, when he quieteth the earth by the south *wind*?

18 Hast thou with him spread out the sky, *which is* strong, *and* as a molten looking glass?

19 Teach us what we shall say unto him; *for* we cannot order *our speech* by reason of darkness.

20 Shall it be told him that I speak? if a man speak, surely he shall be swallowed up.

21 And now *men* see not the bright light which *is* in the clouds: but the wind passeth, and cleanseth them.

22 Fair weather cometh out of the north: with God *is* terrible majesty.

23 *Touching* the Almighty, we cannot find him out: *he is* excellent in power, and in judgment, and in plenty of *a*justice: he will not *b*afflict.

24 Men do therefore fear him: he respecteth not any *that are* wise of heart.

CHAPTER 38

God asks Job where he was when the foundations of the earth were laid, when the morning stars sang together, and when all the sons of God shouted for joy—The phenomena of nature show the greatness of God and the weakness of man.

THEN the LORD answered Job out of the whirlwind, and said,

2 Who *is* this that darkeneth counsel by words without knowledge?

3 Gird up now thy loins like a man; for I will demand of thee, and answer thou me.

4 Where wast thou when I *a*laid the *b*foundations of the *c*earth? declare, if thou hast understanding.

5 Who hath *a*laid the measures thereof, if thou knowest? or who hath stretched the line upon it?

6 Whereupon are the foundations thereof fastened? or who laid the *a*corner stone thereof;

7 When the morning stars *a*sang

---

37 6*a* TG Nature, Earth.
  14*a* Ps. 46:10.
    b TG God, Works of.
  16*a* TG Knowledge.
  23*a* TG God, Justice of.

b 1 Cor. 10:13;
    Alma 13:28.
38 4*a* TG Jesus Christ,
      Creator.
    b TG Creation.

c TG Nature, Earth.
5*a* OR determined its
      measurements.
6*a* TG Cornerstone.
7*a* TG Singing.

together, and all the ^bsons of God shouted for ^cjoy?

8 Or *who* shut up the sea with doors, when it brake forth, *as if* it had issued out of the womb?

9 When I made the cloud the garment thereof, and thick darkness a swaddlingband for it,

10 And brake up for it my decreed *place,* and set bars and doors,

11 And said, Hitherto shalt thou come, but no further: and here shall thy proud waves be stayed?

12 Hast thou commanded the morning since thy days; *and* caused the dayspring to know his place;

13 That it might take hold of the ends of the earth, that the wicked might be shaken out of it?

14 It is turned as clay *to* the seal; and they stand as a garment.

15 And from the wicked their light is ^awithholden, and the high ^barm shall be broken.

16 Hast thou entered into the springs of the sea? or hast thou walked in the search of the depth?

17 Have the gates of death been opened unto thee? or hast thou seen the doors of the shadow of death?

18 Hast thou perceived the breadth of the earth? declare if thou knowest it all.

19 Where *is* the way *where* light dwelleth? and *as for* darkness, where *is* the place thereof,

20 That thou shouldest take it to the bound thereof, and that thou shouldest know the paths *to* the house thereof?

21 Knowest thou *it,* because thou wast then born? or *because* the number of thy days *is* great?

22 Hast thou entered into the ^atreasures of the snow? or hast thou seen the treasures of the hail,

23 Which I have reserved against the time of trouble, against the day of battle and war?

24 By what way is the light parted,

which scattereth the east wind upon the earth?

25 Who hath divided a watercourse for the overflowing of waters, or a way for the lightning of thunder;

26 To cause it to rain on the earth, *where* no man *is; on* the wilderness, wherein *there is* no man;

27 To satisfy the desolate and waste *ground;* and to cause the bud of the tender herb to spring forth?

28 Hath the rain a father? or who hath begotten the drops of dew?

29 Out of whose womb came the ice? and the hoary frost of heaven, who hath gendered it?

30 The waters are hid as *with* a stone, and the face of the deep is frozen.

31 Canst thou bind the sweet influences of Pleiades, or loose the bands of ^aOrion?

32 Canst thou bring forth Mazzaroth in his season? or canst thou guide Arcturus with his sons?

33 Knowest thou the ^aordinances of ^bheaven? canst thou set the dominion thereof in the earth?

34 Canst thou lift up thy voice to the clouds, that abundance of waters may cover thee?

35 Canst thou send lightnings, that they may go, and say unto thee, Here we *are?*

36 Who hath put wisdom in the inward parts? or who hath given understanding to the heart?

37 Who can number the clouds in wisdom? or who can stay the ^abottles of heaven,

38 When the dust groweth into hardness, and the clods cleave fast together?

39 Wilt thou hunt the prey for the lion? or fill the appetite of the young lions,

40 When they couch in *their* dens, *and* abide in the covert to lie in wait?

41 Who provideth for the ^araven

7*b* TG Council in Heaven; Man, Antemortal Existence of; Sons and Daughters of God.
  c TG Joy.

15*a* 2 Ne. 26:10; D&C 34:2.
  b Ps. 10:15; 2 Ne. 4:34; D&C 1:19.
22*a* OR storehouses.

31*a* TG Astronomy.
33*a* Jer. 31:35.
  b TG Heaven.
37*a* HEB waterskins.
41*a* Luke 12:24.

his food? when his young ones cry unto God, they wander for lack of meat.

CHAPTER 39

Man's weakness and ignorance are compared with God's mighty works— Does man even know how the laws of nature operate?

KNOWEST thou the time when the wild *a*goats of the rock bring forth? *or* canst thou mark when the hinds do calve?

2 Canst thou number the months *that* they fulfil? or knowest thou the time when they bring forth?

3 They bow themselves, they bring forth their young ones, they cast out their sorrows.

4 Their young ones are in good liking, they grow up with corn; they go forth, and return not unto them.

5 Who hath sent out the wild ass free? or who hath loosed the bands of the wild ass?

6 Whose house I have made the wilderness, and the barren land his dwellings.

7 He scorneth the multitude of the city, neither regardeth he the crying of the driver.

8 The range of the mountains *is* his pasture, and he searcheth after every green thing.

9 Will the *a*unicorn be willing to serve thee, or abide by thy crib?

10 Canst thou bind the unicorn with his band in the furrow? or will he harrow the valleys after thee?

11 Wilt thou trust him, because his strength *is* great? or wilt thou leave thy labour to him?

12 Wilt thou believe him, that he will bring home thy seed, and gather *it into* thy barn?

13 *Gavest thou* the goodly wings unto the peacocks? or wings and feathers unto the ostrich?

14 Which leaveth her eggs in the earth, and warmeth them in dust,

15 And forgetteth that the foot may crush them, or that the wild beast may break them.

16 She is *a*hardened against her young ones, as though *they were* not hers: her labour is in vain without fear;

17 Because God hath deprived her of wisdom, neither hath he imparted to her understanding.

18 What time she lifteth up herself on high, she scorneth the horse and his rider.

19 Hast thou given the horse strength? hast thou clothed his neck with thunder?

20 Canst thou make him afraid as a grasshopper? the glory of his nostrils *is* terrible.

21 He paweth in the valley, and rejoiceth in *his* strength: he goeth on to meet the armed men.

22 He mocketh at fear, and is not affrighted; neither turneth he back from the sword.

23 The quiver rattleth against him, the glittering spear and the shield.

24 He swalloweth the ground with fierceness and rage: neither believeth he that *it is* the sound of the trumpet.

25 He saith among the trumpets, Ha, ha; and he smelleth the battle afar off, the thunder of the captains, and the shouting.

26 Doth the hawk fly by thy wisdom, *and* stretch her wings toward the south?

27 Doth the eagle mount up at thy command, and make her nest on high?

28 She dwelleth and abideth on the rock, upon the crag of the rock, and the strong place.

29 From thence she seeketh the prey, *and* her eyes behold afar off.

30 Her young ones also suck up blood: and where the slain *are*, there *is* she.

CHAPTER 40

The Lord challenges Job, and Job replies humbly—The Lord speaks of His power to Job—He asks, Hast thou an arm like God?—He points to His power in the behemoth.

MOREOVER the LORD answered Job, and said,

---

39 1*a* TG Nature, Earth. | 9*a* HEB buffalo, bison. | 16*a* Lam. 4:3.

2 Shall he that contendeth with the Almighty instruct *him?* he that reproveth God, let him answer it.

3 ¶ Then Job answered the LORD, and said,

4 Behold, I am vile; what shall I answer thee? I will lay mine hand upon my mouth.

5 Once have I spoken; but I will not answer: yea, twice; but I will proceed no further.

6 ¶ Then answered the LORD unto Job out of the whirlwind, and said,

7 Gird up thy loins now like a man: I will demand of thee, and declare thou unto me.

8 Wilt thou also disannul my judgment? wilt thou condemn me, that thou mayest be righteous?

9 Hast thou an arm like God? or canst thou thunder with a voice like him?

10 Deck thyself now *with* majesty and excellency; and array thyself with glory and beauty.

11 Cast abroad the rage of thy wrath: and behold every one *that is* ªproud, and abase him.

12 Look on every one *that is* proud, *and* bring him low; and tread down the wicked in their place.

13 Hide them in the dust together; *and* bind their faces in secret.

14 Then will I also confess unto thee that thine own right hand can save thee.

15 ¶ Behold now behemoth, which I made with thee; he eateth grass as an ox.

16 Lo now, his strength *is* in his loins, and his force *is* in the navel of his belly.

17 He moveth his tail like a cedar: the sinews of his stones are wrapped together.

18 His bones *are as* strong pieces of brass; his bones *are* like bars of iron.

19 He *is* the chief of the ways of God: he that made him can make his sword to approach *unto him.*

20 Surely the mountains bring him forth food, where all the beasts of the field play.

21 He lieth under the shady trees, in the covert of the reed, and ªfens.

22 The shady trees cover him *with* their shadow; the willows of the brook compass him about.

23 Behold, he drinketh up a river, *and* hasteth not: he trusteth that he can draw up Jordan into his mouth.

24 He taketh it with his eyes: *his* nose pierceth through snares.

CHAPTER 41

The Lord points to His power in the leviathan—All things under the whole heaven are the Lord's.

CANST thou draw out leviathan with an hook? or his tongue with a cord *which* thou lettest down?

2 Canst thou put an hook into his nose? or bore his jaw through with a thorn?

3 Will he make many supplications unto thee? will he speak soft *words* unto thee?

4 Will he make a covenant with thee? wilt thou take him for a servant for ever?

5 Wilt thou play with him as *with* a bird? or wilt thou bind him for thy maidens?

6 Shall the companions make a banquet of him? shall they part him among the merchants?

7 Canst thou fill his skin with ªbarbed irons? or his head with fish spears?

8 Lay thine hand upon him, remember the battle, do no more.

9 Behold, the hope of him is in vain: shall not *one* be cast down even at the sight of him?

10 None *is so* fierce that dare stir him up: who then is able to stand before me?

11 Who hath prevented me, that I should repay *him? whatsoever is* under the whole heaven is mine.

12 I will not conceal his parts, nor his power, nor his comely proportion.

13 Who can discover the face of

---

40 11 *a* Isa. 2:12;
  2 Ne. 12:12; 23:11;
  D&C 64:24.
21 *a* HEB in marshes.

41 7 *a* OR harpoons.

his garment? *or* who can come *to him* with his double bridle?

14 Who can open the doors of his face? his teeth *are* terrible round about.

15 *His* scales *are his* pride, shut up together *as with* a close seal.

16 One is so near to another, that no air can come between them.

17 They are joined one to another, they stick together, that they cannot be sundered.

18 By his *a*neesings a light doth shine, and his eyes *are* like the eyelids of the morning.

19 Out of his mouth go burning lamps, *and* sparks of fire leap out.

20 Out of his nostrils goeth smoke, as *out* of a seething pot or caldron.

21 His breath kindleth coals, and a flame goeth out of his mouth.

22 In his neck remaineth strength, and sorrow is turned into joy before him.

23 The flakes of his flesh are joined together: they are firm in themselves; they cannot be moved.

24 His heart is as firm as a stone; yea, as hard as a piece of the nether *millstone.*

25 When he raiseth up himself, the mighty are afraid: by reason of breakings they purify themselves.

26 The sword of him that layeth at him cannot hold: the spear, the dart, nor the habergeon.

27 He esteemeth iron as straw, *and* brass as rotten wood.

28 The arrow cannot make him flee: slingstones are turned with him into stubble.

29 Darts are counted as stubble: he laugheth at the shaking of a spear.

30 Sharp stones *are* under him: he spreadeth sharp pointed things upon the mire.

31 He maketh the deep to boil like a pot: he maketh the sea like a pot of ointment.

32 He maketh a path to shine after him; *one* would think the deep *to be* hoary.

33 Upon earth there is not his like, who is made without fear.

34 He beholdeth all high *things:* he *is* a king over all the children of pride.

CHAPTER 42

Job repents in dust and ashes—He sees the Lord with his eyes—The Lord chastises Job's friends, accepts Job, blesses him, and makes his latter days greater than his beginning.

THEN Job answered the LORD, and said,

2 I know that thou canst *a*do *b*every *thing*, and *that* no thought can be withholden from thee.

3 Who *is* he that hideth counsel without knowledge? therefore have I uttered that I understood not; things too *a*wonderful for me, which I knew not.

4 Hear, I beseech thee, and I will speak: I will demand of thee, and declare thou unto me.

5 I have heard of thee by the hearing of the ear: but now mine eye seeth thee.

6 Wherefore I abhor *myself,* and repent in dust and *a*ashes.

7 ¶ And it was *so,* that after the LORD had spoken these words unto Job, the LORD said to Eliphaz the Temanite, My wrath is kindled against thee, and against thy two friends: for ye have not spoken of me *the thing that is* right, as my servant Job *hath.*

8 Therefore take unto you now seven bullocks and seven rams, and go to my servant Job, and offer up for yourselves a burnt *a*offering; and my servant Job shall *b*pray for you: for him will I accept: lest I deal with you *after your* folly, in that ye have not spoken of me *the thing which is* right, like my servant Job.

9 So Eliphaz the Temanite and Bildad the Shuhite *and* Zophar the Naamathite went, and did according as the LORD commanded them: the LORD also *a*accepted Job.

18*a* OR sneezings.
42 2*a* TG God, Works of.
   b Matt. 19:26.

3*a* Ps. 139:6.
6*a* Job 2:8; Matt. 11:21.
8*a* Job 1:5.

b Gen. 20:7.
9*a* Gen. 19:21.
   TG Probation.

10 And the Lord turned the captivity of Job, when he ^aprayed for his ^bfriends: also the Lord gave Job twice as much as he had before.

11 Then came there unto him all his brethren, and all his sisters, and all they that had been of his acquaintance before, and did eat bread with him in his house: and they bemoaned him, and comforted him over all the evil that the Lord had brought upon him: every man also gave him a piece of money, and every one an earring of gold.

12 So the Lord ^ablessed the latter end of Job more than his beginning: for he had fourteen thousand sheep, and six thousand camels, and a thousand yoke of oxen, and a thousand she asses.

13 He had also seven sons and three daughters.

14 And he called the name of the first, Jemima; and the name of the second, Kezia; and the name of the third, Keren-happuch.

15 And in all the land were no women found *so* fair as the daughters of Job: and their father gave them inheritance among their brethren.

16 After this lived Job an hundred and forty years, and saw his sons, and his sons' sons, *even* four generations.

17 So Job died, *being* old and full of days.

THE BOOK OF
PSALMS

PSALM 1

Blessed are the righteous—The ungodly will perish.

^aBLESSED *is* the man that ^bwalketh not in the ^ccounsel of the ungodly, nor standeth in the way of sinners, nor sitteth in the seat of the ^dscornful.

2 But his ^adelight *is* in the ^blaw of the Lord; and in his law doth he ^cmeditate day and night.

3 And he shall be like a ^atree planted by the rivers of water, that bringeth forth his fruit in his season; his leaf also shall not wither; and whatsoever he doeth shall ^bprosper.

4 The ungodly *are* not so: but *are* like the ^achaff which the wind driveth away.

5 Therefore the ungodly shall not stand in the judgment, nor sinners in the congregation of the righteous.

6 For the Lord knoweth the way of the ^arighteous: but the way of the ^bungodly shall perish.

PSALM 2

A messianic psalm—The heathen will rage against the Lord's anointed—The Lord speaks of His Son, whom He has begotten.

10a Matt. 5:44.
  b TG Friendship.
12a Gen. 26:12.

[Psalms]

1 1a TG Happiness.
  b Prov. 1:10 (10–19);
    Eph. 5:11 (8–13).
  c TG Counselor.

  d Ps. 26:4;
    Jer. 15:17.
2a TG Abundant Life.
  b HEB teaching, direction,
    doctrine.
    TG God, Law of.
  c TG Meditation.
3a Jer. 17:8 (7–8);
  b Gen. 39:3 (2–3);

    Mosiah 1:7;
    Alma 50:20; Hel. 12:1;
    D&C 9:13.
4a Job 21:18 (17–18);
    Ps. 83:13 (2, 13);
    Hosea 13:3 (1–4);
    Morm. 5:16 (16–18).
6a TG Righteousness.
  b TG Godliness.

WHY do the ᵃheathen rage, and the people imagine a vain thing?

2 The ᵃkings of the earth set themselves, and the rulers take ᵇcounsel together, against the Lᴏʀᴅ, and against his ᶜanointed, *saying,*

3 Let us break their bands asunder, and cast away their cords from us.

4 He that sitteth in the heavens shall ᵃlaugh: the Lord shall have them in derision.

5 Then shall he speak unto them in his wrath, and vex them in his sore displeasure.

6 Yet have I ᵃset my king upon my ᵇholy hill of Zion.

7 I will declare the decree: the Lᴏʀᴅ hath said unto me, Thou *art* my ᵃSon; this day have I begotten thee.

8 Ask of me, and I shall give *thee* the heathen *for* thine inheritance, and the uttermost parts of the earth *for* thy possession.

9 Thou shalt ᵃbreak them with a ᵇrod of iron; thou shalt ᶜdash them in pieces like a potter's vessel.

10 Be wise now therefore, O ye kings: be instructed, ye judges of the earth.

11 Serve the Lᴏʀᴅ with ᵃfear, and rejoice with trembling.

12 Kiss the Son, lest he be angry, and ye perish *from* the way, when his wrath is kindled but a little. ᵃBlessed *are* all they that put their ᵇtrust in him.

PSALM 3

David cries unto the Lord and is heard—Salvation is of the Lord.

A Psalm of David, when he fled from Absalom his son.

Lᴏʀᴅ, how are they increased that ᵃtrouble me! many *are* they that rise up against me.

2 Many *there be* which say of my soul, *There is* no help for him in God. Selah.

3 But thou, O Lᴏʀᴅ, *art* a ᵃshield for me; my glory, and the lifter up of mine head.

4 I cried unto the Lᴏʀᴅ with my voice, and he heard me out of his holy hill. Selah.

5 I laid me down and slept; I awaked; for the Lᴏʀᴅ sustained me.

6 I will not be afraid of ten thousands of people, that have set *themselves* against me round about.

7 Arise, O Lᴏʀᴅ; save me, O my God: for thou hast smitten all mine enemies *upon* the cheek bone; thou hast broken the teeth of the ungodly.

8 ᵃSalvation *belongeth* unto the Lᴏʀᴅ: thy blessing *is* upon thy people. Selah.

PSALM 4

David pleads for mercy—He counsels, Put your trust in the Lord.

To the chief Musician on Neginoth, A Psalm of David.

ᵃHEAR me when I call, O God of my ᵇrighteousness: thou hast enlarged me *when I was* in ᶜdistress; have mercy upon me, and hear my prayer.

2 O ye sons of men, how long *will ye turn* my glory into ᵃshame? *how long* will ye love ᵇvanity, *and* seek after leasing? Selah.

3 But know that the Lᴏʀᴅ hath ᵃset apart him that is ᵇgodly for himself: the Lᴏʀᴅ will hear when I call unto him.

---

2 1*a* ᴛɢ Heathen.
2*a* Acts 4:26 (25–27).
  b ᴛɢ Counsel.
  c ᴛɢ Anointing.
4*a* ᴛɢ Laughter.
6*a* ʜᴇʙ anointed my king.
  b Ps. 48:1; 99:9; Isa. 27:13.
7*a* ᴛɢ Jesus Christ, Divine Sonship; Jesus Christ, Prophecies about.
9*a* Isa. 11:4; 2 Ne. 21:4; D&C 19:15.

  b Rev. 2:27 (26–28).
  c Isa. 30:14 (13–14).
11*a* ᴛɢ Reverence.
12*a* ᴛɢ Blessing.
  b ᴛɢ Trust in God.
3 1*a* 2 Sam. 15:14; 17:27 (27–29).
3*a* ᴛɢ Protection, Divine.
8*a* ᴛɢ Salvation.
4 1*a* Ps. 34:4; Micah 7:7; 1 Jn. 5:14 (13–14); Mosiah 9:18;

Ether 1:40 (39–40).
  b Ps. 97:6 (5–6); Rom. 1:17; 2 Ne. 4:35; Ether 9:22; D&C 1:16.
  c Gen. 35:3; Ps. 118:5 (4–6); Isa. 25:4 (1, 4).
2*a* ᴛɢ Shame.
  b ᴛɢ Vanity.
3*a* ᴛɢ Setting Apart.
  b ᴛɢ Godliness.

4 Stand in awe, and sin not: commune with your own heart upon your bed, and be still. Selah.

5 Offer the ªsacrifices of righteousness, and put your trust in the LORD.

6 *There be* many that say, Who will shew us *any* good? LORD, lift thou up the light of thy ªcountenance upon us.

7 Thou hast put gladness in my heart, more than in the time *that* their ªcorn and their wine increased.

8 I will both lay me down in ªpeace, and sleep: for thou, LORD, only makest me dwell in safety.

PSALM 5

David asks the Lord to hear his voice—
The Lord hates workers of iniquity—
He blesses and shields the righteous.

To the chief Musician upon Nehiloth,
A Psalm of David.

GIVE ear to my words, O LORD, consider my ªmeditation.

2 Hearken unto the voice of my cry, my ªKing, and my God: for unto thee will I pray.

3 My voice shalt thou hear in the morning, O LORD; in the ªmorning will I direct *my prayer* unto thee, and will look up.

4 For thou *art* not a God that hath pleasure in ªwickedness: neither shall ᵇevil dwell with thee.

5 The foolish shall not stand in thy sight: thou hatest all ªworkers of iniquity.

6 Thou shalt destroy them that speak leasing: the LORD will abhor the bloody and deceitful man.

7 But as for me, I will come *into* thy house in the multitude of thy mercy: *and* in thy ªfear will I worship toward thy holy ᵇtemple.

8 Lead me, O LORD, in thy righteousness because of mine ªenemies; make thy way straight before my face.

9 For *there is* no faithfulness in their mouth; their ªinward part *is* very wickedness; their ᵇthroat *is* an open sepulchre; they ᶜflatter with their tongue.

10 Destroy thou them, O God; let them fall by their own counsels; cast them out in the multitude of their transgressions; for they have ªrebelled against thee.

11 But let all those that put their trust in thee rejoice: let them ever ªshout for joy, because thou defendest them: let them also that love thy name be joyful in thee.

12 For thou, LORD, wilt bless the ªrighteous; with favour wilt thou compass him as *with* a shield.

PSALM 6

David cries unto the Lord for mercy—
He asks to be healed and saved.

To the chief Musician on Neginoth
upon Sheminith, A Psalm of David.

O LORD, rebuke me not in thine anger, neither chasten me in thy hot displeasure.

2 Have mercy upon me, O LORD; for I *am* ªweak: O LORD, ᵇheal me; for my bones are vexed.

3 My soul is also sore vexed: but thou, O LORD, how long?

4 Return, O LORD, deliver my soul: oh save me for thy mercies' sake.

5 For in death *there is* no remembrance of thee: in the ªgrave who shall give thee thanks?

6 I am weary with my groaning; all the night make I my bed to swim; I water my couch with my ªtears.

5*a* TG Sacrifice.
6*a* Ps. 67:1; 119:135;
    Alma 5:14;
    3 Ne. 19:25 (24–25).
7*a* HEB grain.
8*a* TG Contentment.
5 1*a* TG Meditation.
2*a* Isa. 43:15.
3*a* Alma 37:37 (36–37).
4*a* Job 27:4 (4–5).
  b TG Evil.

5*a* Alma 5:32 (32–38).
7*a* OR reverence.
  b 1 Kgs. 8:48 (44–48);
    Dan. 6:10;
    Jonah 2:4.
8*a* TG Enemies.
9*a* Luke 11:44;
    Acts 23:3.
  b Rom. 3:13.
  c TG Flatter.
10*a* Mosiah 15:26 (26–27);

Hel. 8:25.
11*a* HEB sing.
12*a* 2 Ne. 9:18;
    Alma 40:12 (12–14);
    D&C 29:27 (27–28);
    88:26 (25–26).
6 2*a* HEB wretched, in
    misery.
  b TG Heal; Sickness.
5*a* Ps. 30:9.
6*a* 2 Ne. 33:3.

7 Mine eye is consumed because of grief; it waxeth old because of all mine enemies.

8 Depart from me, all ye workers of [a]iniquity; for the LORD hath heard the voice of my weeping.

9 The LORD hath heard my supplication; the LORD will receive my prayer.

10 Let all mine enemies be ashamed and sore vexed: let them return *and* be ashamed suddenly.

PSALM 7

David trusts in the Lord, who will judge the people—God is angry with the wicked.

Shiggaion of David, which he sang unto the LORD, concerning the words of Cush the Benjamite.

O LORD my God, in thee do I put my trust: save me from all them that persecute me, and deliver me:

2 Lest he tear my soul like a lion, rending *it* in pieces, while *there is* none to deliver.

3 O LORD my God, if I have done this; if there be iniquity in my hands;

4 If I have rewarded evil unto him that was at peace with me; (yea, I have delivered him that without cause is mine enemy:)

5 Let the enemy persecute my soul, and take *it*; yea, let him tread down my life upon the earth, and lay mine honour in the dust. Selah.

6 Arise, O LORD, in thine anger, lift up thyself because of the rage of mine enemies: and awake for me *to* the judgment *that* thou hast commanded.

7 So shall the congregation of the people compass thee about: for their sakes therefore return thou on high.

8 The LORD shall [a]judge the people: judge me, O LORD, according to my righteousness, and according to mine integrity *that is* in me.

9 Oh let the wickedness of the wicked come to an end; but establish the just: for the righteous God [a]trieth the hearts and reins.

10 My defence *is* of God, which saveth the upright in heart.

11 God judgeth the righteous, and God is [a]angry *with the wicked* every day.

12 If he turn not, he will whet his sword; he hath bent his bow, and made it ready.

13 He hath also prepared for him the instruments of death; he ordaineth his arrows against the persecutors.

14 Behold, he travaileth with iniquity, and hath conceived [a]mischief, and brought forth falsehood.

15 He made a pit, and digged it, and is [a]fallen into the ditch *which* he made.

16 His mischief shall [a]return upon his own head, and his violent dealing shall come down upon his own pate.

17 I will praise the LORD according to his righteousness: and will sing praise to the name of the LORD most high.

PSALM 8

A messianic psalm of David—He says that babes and children praise the Lord—He asks, What is man, that Thou art mindful of him?

To the chief Musician upon Gittith,
A Psalm of David.

O LORD our Lord, how excellent *is* thy name in all the earth! who hast set thy glory above the heavens.

2 Out of the mouth of [a]babes and sucklings hast thou ordained strength because of thine enemies, that thou mightest still the enemy and the avenger.

3 When I [a]consider thy [b]heavens,

8a TG Sin.
7 8a TG Jesus Christ, Judge.
  9a TG Test.
  11a TG God, Indignation of.
  14a Job 15:35;

Isa. 59:4.
15a 1 Ne. 14:3 (1–3);
    22:14 (13–14).
16a Ps. 9:16;
    Gal. 6:7;

Alma 3:26; 9:28;
D&C 6:33.
8 2a TG Children.
  3a TG Beauty.
  b TG Heaven.

the ᶜwork of thy fingers, the ᵈmoon and the stars, which thou hast ordained;

4 What is ᵃman, that thou art mindful of him? and the son of man, that thou ᵇvisitest him?

5 For thou hast made him a little ᵃlower than the ᵇangels, and hast crowned him with glory and honour.

6 Thou madest him to have ᵃdominion over the works of thy hands; thou hast put all *things* under his feet:

7 All ᵃsheep and oxen, yea, and the beasts of the field;

8 The fowl of the air, and the fish of the sea, *and whatsoever* passeth through the paths of the seas.

9 O LORD our Lord, how excellent *is* thy name in all the earth!

PSALM 9

A messianic psalm of David—He praises the Lord for rebuking the nations— The Lord will judge the world in righteousness—He will dwell in Zion—The wicked will be sent to hell.

To the chief Musician upon Muth-labben, A Psalm of David.

I WILL praise *thee*, O LORD, with my whole heart; I will shew forth all thy ᵃmarvellous works.

2 I will be glad and rejoice in thee: I will sing praise to thy name, O thou most High.

3 When mine enemies are turned back, they shall fall and perish at thy presence.

4 For thou hast maintained my right and my cause; thou satest in the throne judging right.

5 Thou hast rebuked the heathen, thou hast destroyed the wicked, thou hast ᵃput out their name for ever and ever.

6 O thou enemy, destructions are come to a perpetual end: and thou hast destroyed cities; their memorial is perished with them.

7 But the LORD shall endure for ever: he hath prepared his throne for ᵃjudgment.

8 And he shall ᵃjudge the world in ᵇrighteousness, he shall minister judgment to the people in uprightness.

9 The LORD also will be a ᵃrefuge for the ᵇoppressed, a refuge in times of trouble.

10 And they that know thy ᵃname will put their ᵇtrust in thee: for thou, LORD, hast not forsaken them that seek thee.

11 Sing praises to the LORD, which dwelleth in Zion: ᵃdeclare among the people his doings.

12 When he ᵃmaketh ᵇinquisition for blood, he remembereth them: he forgetteth not the cry of the ᶜhumble.

13 Have mercy upon me, O LORD; consider my trouble *which I suffer* of them that hate me, thou that liftest me up from the gates of death:

14 That I may shew forth all thy praise in the gates of the daughter of Zion: I will rejoice in thy ᵃsalvation.

15 The heathen are sunk down in the pit *that* they made: in the ᵃnet which they hid is their own foot taken.

16 The LORD is known *by* the judgment *which* he executeth: the wicked is ᵃsnared in the work of his own hands. Higgaion. Selah.

3c TG God, Works of.
d TG Astronomy.
4a Job 7:17 (17–18); Ps. 144:3 (1–15); Heb. 2:6 (6–8). TG Mortality.
b 1 Ne. 2:16; 19:11; Alma 17:10; D&C 5:16.
5a HEB less than the gods.
b TG Man, Potential to Become like Heavenly Father; Worth of Souls.
6a TG Man, Potential to Become like Heavenly Father.
7a TG Sheep.
9 1a 1 Chr. 16:9 (8–9); Ps. 26:7; D&C 76:114.
5a Deut. 9:14 (13–14); Mosiah 26:36.
7a TG Judgment, the Last.
8a TG Jesus Christ, Judge.
b TG Righteousness.
9a TG Refuge.
b TG Oppression.
10a Acts 4:12 (10–12).
b TG Trust in God.
11a TG Preaching.
12a HEB avenges.
b Gen. 9:5.
c TG Humility.
14a 1 Sam. 2:1 (1–10).
15a Ps. 25:15; 31:4; 57:6.
16a Ps. 7:16.

17 The wicked shall be turned into ^ahell, *and* all the nations that ^bforget God.

18 For the needy shall not alway be forgotten: the expectation of the poor shall *not* perish for ever.

19 Arise, O LORD; let not man prevail: let the heathen be judged in thy sight.

20 Put them in fear, O LORD: *that* the nations may know themselves *to be but* men. Selah.

PSALM 10

David speaks of various acts of the wicked—God is not in their thoughts—But the Lord is King forever and ever—He will judge the fatherless and oppressed.

WHY standest thou ^aafar off, O LORD? *why* ^bhidest thou *thyself* in times of trouble?

2 The wicked in *his* pride doth persecute the poor: let them be taken in the devices that they have imagined.

3 For the wicked ^aboasteth of his heart's desire, and blesseth the covetous, *whom* the LORD abhorreth.

4 The wicked, through the pride of his countenance, will not seek *after* God: ^aGod *is* ^bnot in all his thoughts.

5 His ways are always grievous; thy judgments *are* far above out of his sight: *as for* all his enemies, he puffeth at them.

6 He hath said in his heart, I shall not be moved: for *I shall* never *be* in adversity.

7 His mouth is full of ^acursing and deceit and ^bfraud: under his tongue *is* mischief and vanity.

8 He sitteth in the lurking places of the villages: in the secret places doth he murder the innocent: his eyes are privily set against the poor.

9 He lieth in wait secretly as a lion in his den: he lieth in wait to catch the poor: he doth catch the poor, when he draweth him into his net.

10 He croucheth, *and* humbleth himself, that the poor may fall by his strong ones.

11 He hath said in his heart, God hath forgotten: he hideth his face; he will never see *it.*

12 Arise, O LORD; O God, lift up thine hand: forget not the ^ahumble.

13 Wherefore doth the wicked contemn God? he hath said in his heart, Thou wilt not require *it.*

14 Thou hast seen *it;* for thou beholdest mischief and spite, to requite *it* with thy hand: the poor committeth himself unto thee; thou art the helper of the ^afatherless.

15 Break thou the ^aarm of the wicked and the evil *man:* seek out his wickedness *till* thou find none.

16 The LORD *is* ^aKing for ever and ever: the heathen are perished out of his land.

17 LORD, thou hast heard the desire of the humble: thou wilt prepare their heart, thou wilt cause thine ear to hear:

18 To judge the fatherless and the oppressed, that the man of the earth may no more oppress.

PSALM 11

David rejoices that the Lord is in His holy temple—The Lord tests the righteous and hates the wicked.

To the chief Musician, A *Psalm* of David.

^aIN the LORD put I my trust: how say ye to my soul, Flee *as* a bird to your mountain?

2 For, lo, the wicked bend *their* bow, they make ready their arrow upon the string, that they may privily ^ashoot at the upright in heart.

17*a* TG Hell.
   b Ps. 50:22.
10 1*a* TG Despair.
   b Prov. 15:29;
     Mosiah 11:24 (23–24);
     D&C 101:7.
3*a* TG Boast.
4*a* Ps. 14:1.

  b Alma 30:53.
7*a* TG Curse.
  b TG Fraud.
12*a* HEB afflicted, humbled.
    TG Contrite Heart;
    Humility.
14*a* Ps. 68:5;
    Hosea 14:3 (1–3);

    James 1:27; 3 Ne. 24:5.
15*a* Job 38:15;
    D&C 1:19.
16*a* TG Kingdom of God, in
    Heaven.
11 1*a* JST Ps. 11:1–5
    (Appendix).
2*a* Ps. 64:4 (1–6).

3 If the *a*foundations be destroyed, what can the righteous do?

4 The LORD *is* in his holy temple, the LORD's *a*throne *is* in *b*heaven: his eyes behold, his eyelids try, the children of men.

5 The LORD *a*trieth the righteous: but the wicked and him that loveth violence his soul hateth.

6 Upon the *a*wicked he shall rain snares, fire and brimstone, and an horrible tempest: *this shall be* the portion of their cup.

7 For the righteous LORD loveth *a*righteousness; *b*his countenance doth behold the upright.

PSALM 12

David decries flattering lips and proud tongues—He says, The words of the Lord are pure words.

To the chief Musician upon Sheminith,
A Psalm of David.

HELP, LORD; for the godly man ceaseth; for the faithful fail from among the children of men.

2 They speak vanity every one with his neighbour: *with* flattering lips *and* with a *a*double heart do they speak.

3 The LORD shall cut off all *a*flattering lips, *and* the tongue that speaketh proud things:

4 Who have said, With our tongue will we prevail; our lips *are* our own: who *is* lord over us?

5 For the oppression of the poor, for the sighing of the needy, now will I arise, saith the LORD; I will set *him* in safety *from him that* puffeth at him.

6 The *a*words of the LORD *are* *b*pure words: *as* silver tried in a furnace of earth, purified seven times.

7 Thou shalt keep them, O LORD, thou shalt preserve them from this generation for ever.

8 The wicked walk on every side, when the vilest men are exalted.

PSALM 13

David trusts in the Lord's mercy and rejoices in His salvation.

To the chief Musician, A Psalm of David.

How long wilt thou *a*forget me, O LORD? for ever? how long wilt thou *b*hide thy face from me?

2 How long shall I take counsel in my soul, *having* *a*sorrow in my heart daily? how long shall mine enemy be exalted over me?

3 Consider *and* *a*hear me, O LORD my God: lighten mine eyes, lest I sleep the *sleep of* death;

4 Lest mine enemy say, I have prevailed against him; *and* those that trouble me rejoice when I am moved.

5 But I have trusted in thy mercy; my heart shall rejoice in thy *a*salvation.

6 I will sing unto the LORD, because he hath dealt bountifully with me.

PSALM 14

David says, The fool has said in his heart, there is no God—Israel will rejoice in the day of restoration.

To the chief Musician, A *Psalm* of David.

*a*THE *b*fool hath said in his heart, *There is* *c*no *d*God. They are *e*corrupt, they have done abominable works, *there is* *f*none that doeth good.

2 The LORD looked down from heaven upon the children of men, to see if there were any that did understand, *and* seek God.

3*a* TG Cornerstone.	3*a* TG Flatter.	(Appendix).
4*a* TG Kingdom of God, in Heaven.	6*a* 2 Sam. 22:31; Ps. 18:30.	*b* Ps. 53:1 (1–6); Prov. 10:21.
b TG Heaven.	*b* Ps. 19:8.	*c* Ps. 10:4 (2–11).
5*a* TG Test.	13 1*a* TG Despair.	*d* Alma 30:40 (37–41).
6*a* Isa. 3:11 (9–11).	*b* D&C 121:1 (1–2).	*e* Gen. 6:5 (5–6);
7*a* TG Righteousness.	2*a* TG Suffering.	2 Tim. 3:8;
b OR the upright shall behold His face.	3*a* Ps. 55:17 (16–18).	D&C 10:21 (20–23); 112:23 (23–24).
12 2*a* James 1:8.	5*a* 1 Sam. 2:1 (1–10).	*f* Rom. 3:10 (10–12).
	14 1*a* JST Ps. 14:1–7	

3 They are all gone aside, they are *all* together become *ᵃfilthy: there is ᵇ*none that doeth good, no, not one.

4 Have all the workers of iniquity no knowledge? who eat up my people *as* they eat bread, and call not upon the LORD.

5 There were they in great fear: for God *is* in the generation of the righteous.

6 Ye have *ᵃ*shamed the counsel of the poor, because the LORD *is* his refuge.

7 Oh that the salvation of Israel *were come* out of Zion! when the LORD bringeth back the *ᵃ*captivity of his people, Jacob shall rejoice, *and* Israel shall be glad.

PSALM 15

David asks, Who will dwell in the Lord's holy hill?—He answers, The righteous, the upright, and those with integrity.

A Psalm of David.

LORD, who shall *ᵃ*abide in thy tabernacle? who shall dwell in thy holy *ᵇ*hill?

2 He that *ᵃ*walketh uprightly, and worketh righteousness, and speaketh the truth in his heart.

3 *He that ᵃ*backbiteth not with his tongue, nor doeth evil to his *ᵇ*neighbour, nor taketh up a reproach against his neighbour.

4 In whose eyes a vile person is contemned; but he honoureth them that fear the LORD. *He that* sweareth to *his own* hurt, and changeth not.

5 *He that* putteth not out his money to *ᵃ*usury, nor taketh *ᵇ*reward against the innocent. He that doeth these *things* shall never be moved.

PSALM 16

A messianic psalm of David—He rejoices in the Saints who are on the earth, in his own future redemption from hell, in the fact that God will not suffer His Holy One (the Messiah) to see corruption, and in the fulness of joy that is found in the Lord's presence.

Michtam of David.

PRESERVE me, O God: for in thee do I put my *ᵃ*trust.

2 O *my soul,* thou hast said unto the LORD, Thou *art* my Lord: *ᵃ*my goodness *extendeth* not to thee;

3 *But* to the saints that *are* in the earth, and *to* the excellent, in whom *is* all my delight.

4 Their sorrows shall be multiplied *that* hasten *after* another *ᵃ*god: their drink offerings of blood will I not offer, nor take up their names into my lips.

5 The LORD *is* the *ᵃ*portion of mine *ᵇ*inheritance and of my cup: thou *ᶜ*maintainest my lot.

6 The lines are fallen unto me in pleasant *places;* yea, I have a goodly heritage.

7 I will bless the LORD, who hath given me counsel: my reins also instruct me in the night seasons.

8 I have set the *ᵃ*LORD always before me: because *he is* at my *ᵇ*right hand, I shall not be moved.

9 Therefore my heart is glad, and my glory rejoiceth: my *ᵃ*flesh also shall rest in hope.

10 For thou wilt not *ᵃ*leave my *ᵇ*soul in *ᶜ*hell; neither wilt thou

---

3*a* TG Filthiness.
  b Mosiah 16:3 (3–5).
  6*a* TG Shame.
  7*a* Zeph. 2:7.
15 1*a* Ps. 24:3 (3–5);
      1 Ne. 15:33 (33–36);
      Mosiah 15:23 (19–26);
      D&C 76:62 (50–70);
      Moses 6:57 (55–59).
  b JST Ps. 15:1 . . . hill *of* Zion?
  2*a* TG Walking with God.

3*a* TG Backbiting;
      Gossip.
  b TG Neighbor.
  5*a* TG Usury.
  b OR a bribe.
16 1*a* TG Trust in God.
  2*a* HEB I have no good apart from Thee.
  4*a* Ex. 34:14 (13–17);
      2 Ne. 9:37 (37–38);
      Alma 7:6;
      D&C 124:84;

Abr. 1:11 (11–12, 15).
5*a* Ps. 73:26; 119:57.
  b Deut. 18:2.
  c HEB holdest my fate.
8*a* Acts 2:25 (25–31).
  b Ps. 109:31.
9*a* TG Resurrection.
10*a* 2 Ne. 4:31 (31–32).
  b Ps. 30:3.
  c TG Damnation;
      Hell;
      Spirits in Prison.

suffer thine *d*Holy One to see corruption.

11 Thou wilt shew me the path of life: in thy *a*presence *is* *b*fulness of *c*joy; at thy right hand *there are* *d*pleasures for evermore.

PSALM 17

David pleads with the Lord to hear his voice and to preserve him from men of the world—David hopes to behold the Lord's face in righteousness.

A Prayer of David.

HEAR the right, O LORD, attend unto my cry, give ear unto my prayer, *that goeth* not out of feigned lips.

2 Let my sentence come forth from thy presence; let thine eyes behold the things that are equal.

3 Thou hast *a*proved mine heart; thou hast visited *me* in the night; thou hast tried me, *and* shalt find nothing; I am purposed *that* my mouth shall not transgress.

4 Concerning the works of men, by the word of thy lips I have kept *me from* the paths of the destroyer.

5 *a*Hold up my goings in thy paths, *that* my footsteps slip not.

6 I have called upon thee, for thou wilt hear me, O God: incline thine ear unto me, *and* *a*hear my speech.

7 Shew thy marvellous lovingkindness, O thou that savest by thy right hand them which put their trust *in thee* from those that rise up *against them.*

8 Keep me as the apple of the eye, hide me under the shadow of thy wings,

9 From the wicked that oppress me, *from* my deadly enemies, *who* compass me about.

10 They are inclosed in their own fat: with their mouth they speak proudly.

11 They have now compassed us in our steps: they have set their eyes *a*bowing down to the earth;

12 Like as a lion *that* is greedy of his prey, and as it were a young lion lurking in secret places.

13 Arise, O LORD, disappoint him, cast him down: deliver my soul from the wicked, *a*which is thy sword:

14 From men *a*which are thy hand, O LORD, from men of the world, which have their *b*portion in *this* life, and whose belly thou fillest with thy hid *treasure:* they are full of children, and leave the rest of their *substance* to their babes.

15 As for me, I will behold thy face in *a*righteousness: I shall be satisfied, when I *b*awake, with thy likeness.

PSALM 18

David praises the Lord for His greatness and preserving care—The Lord's way is perfect—The Lord has given marvelous blessings—David testifies, The Lord lives, and blessed be my Rock.

To the chief Musician, A *Psalm* of David, the servant of the LORD, who spake unto the LORD the words of this song in the day *that* the LORD delivered him from the hand of all his enemies, and from the hand of Saul: And he said,

I WILL *a*love thee, O LORD, my strength.

2 The LORD *is* my *a*rock, and my *b*fortress, and my deliverer; my God, my *c*strength, in whom I will *d*trust; my buckler, and the horn of my salvation, *and* my high tower.

3 I will call upon the LORD, *who is* *a*worthy to be praised: so shall I be saved from mine enemies.

4 The sorrows of death compassed me, and the floods of ungodly men made me afraid.

10*d* TG Jesus Christ, Resurrection.
11*a* TG God, Presence of.
  b TG Exaltation.
  c TG Joy.
  d Ps. 36:8.
17 3*a* TG Test.
  5*a* Ps. 119:133.

6*a* OR answer.
11*a* OR to cast us to earth.
13*a* OR by.
14*a* OR by.
  b Ps. 73:12.
15*a* TG Righteousness.
  b TG Resurrection.
18 1*a* Alma 13:29;

D&C 20:31; 76:116.
2*a* TG Comfort; Rock.
  b TG Protection, Divine.
  c TG Strength.
  d Heb. 2:13.
3*a* TG Worthiness.

5 The sorrows of hell compassed me about: the snares of death ᵃprevented me.

6 In my ᵃdistress I called upon the LORD, and cried unto my God: he heard my voice out of his ᵇtemple, and my cry came before him, *even* into his ears.

7 Then the earth shook and trembled; the foundations also of the hills moved and were shaken, because he was wroth.

8 There went up a smoke out of his nostrils, and fire out of his mouth devoured: coals were kindled by it.

9 He bowed the heavens also, and came down: and darkness *was* under his feet.

10 And he rode upon a cherub, and did fly: yea, he did fly upon the wings of the wind.

11 He made darkness his secret place; his pavilion round about him *were* dark waters *and* thick clouds of the skies.

12 At the brightness *that was* before him his thick clouds passed, hail *stones* and coals of fire.

13 The LORD also thundered in the heavens, and the Highest gave his voice; hail *stones* and coals of fire.

14 Yea, he sent out his arrows, and scattered them; and he shot out lightnings, and discomfited them.

15 Then the channels of waters were seen, and the foundations of the world were discovered at thy rebuke, O LORD, at the blast of the breath of thy nostrils.

16 He sent from above, he took me, he drew me out of many waters.

17 He delivered me from my strong enemy, and from them which hated me: for they were too strong for me.

18 They prevented me in the day of my calamity: but the LORD was my stay.

19 He brought me forth also into a large place; he delivered me, because he delighted in me.

20 The LORD rewarded me according to my righteousness; according to the cleanness of my hands hath he recompensed me.

21 For I have kept the ways of the LORD, and have not wickedly departed from my God.

22 For all his judgments *were* before me, and I did not put away his statutes from me.

23 I was also upright before him, and I kept myself from mine iniquity.

24 Therefore hath the LORD recompensed me according to my righteousness, according to the ᵃcleanness of my hands in his eyesight.

25 With the merciful thou wilt shew thyself merciful; with an upright man thou wilt shew thyself upright;

26 With the pure thou wilt shew thyself pure; and ᵃwith the froward thou wilt shew thyself froward.

27 For thou wilt save the ᵃafflicted people; but wilt bring down ᵇhigh looks.

28 For thou wilt light my ᵃcandle: the LORD my God will ᵇenlighten my darkness.

29 For by thee I have run through a troop; and by my God have I leaped over a wall.

30 *As for* God, his way *is* ᵃperfect: the ᵇword of the LORD is tried: he *is* a buckler to all those that trust in him.

31 For who *is* God save the LORD? or who *is* a ᵃrock save our God?

32 *It is* ᵃGod that girdeth me with strength, and maketh my way perfect.

33 He maketh my feet like hinds' *feet*, and setteth me upon my high places.

34 He teacheth my hands to war, so that a bow of steel is broken by mine arms.

5a HEB confronted.
6a TG Suffering.
  b Jonah 2:7.
24a TG Cleanliness.
26a OR with the twisted thou wilt be subtile.
27a 2 Sam. 22:28;
  Isa. 49:13;
  1 Ne. 21:13.
  b 2 Ne. 20:33;
  3 Ne. 25:1; D&C 29:9.
28a OR lamp.
  b TG Edification.
30a TG God, Perfection of.
  b 2 Sam. 22:31;
  Ps. 12:6 (6–7).
31a TG Rock.
32a 1 Ne. 7:12; Alma 26:12.

35 Thou hast also given me the shield of thy salvation: and thy right hand hath holden me up, and thy gentleness hath made me great.

36 Thou hast enlarged my steps under me, that my feet did not slip.

37 I have pursued mine enemies, and overtaken them: neither did I turn again till they were consumed.

38 I have wounded them that they were not able to rise: they are fallen under my feet.

39 For thou hast girded me with strength unto the battle: thou hast subdued under me those that rose up against me.

40 Thou hast also given me the necks of mine enemies; that I might destroy them that hate me.

41 They *cried, but *there was* none to save *them: even* unto the LORD, but he answered them not.

42 Then did I beat them small as the dust before the wind: I did cast them out as the dirt in the streets.

43 Thou hast delivered me from the strivings of the people; *and* thou hast made me the head of the *heathen: a people *whom* I have not known shall serve me.

44 As soon as they hear of me, they shall obey me: the strangers shall submit themselves unto me.

45 The strangers shall fade away, and be afraid out of their close places.

46 The LORD *liveth; and blessed *be* my *rock; and let the God of my salvation be exalted.

47 *It is* God that avengeth me, and *subdueth the people under me.

48 He delivereth me from mine enemies: yea, thou liftest me up above those that rise up against me: thou hast delivered me from the violent man.

49 Therefore will I give thanks unto thee, O LORD, among the *heathen, and sing praises unto thy name.

50 Great deliverance giveth he to his king; and sheweth mercy to his *anointed, to David, and to his seed for evermore.

PSALM 19

David testifies, The heavens declare the glory of God, the law of the Lord is perfect, and the judgments of the Lord are true and righteous altogether.

To the chief Musician, A Psalm of David.

THE *heavens *declare the *glory of God; and the firmament sheweth his *handywork.

2 Day unto day uttereth speech, and night unto night sheweth knowledge.

3 *There is* no speech nor *language, *where* their voice is not heard.

4 Their line is gone out through all the earth, and their *words to the end of the world. In them hath he set a tabernacle for the sun,

5 Which *is* as a bridegroom coming out of his chamber, *and* rejoiceth as a strong man to run a race.

6 His going forth *is* from the end of the heaven, and his circuit unto the ends of it: and there is nothing hid from the heat thereof.

7 The *law of the LORD *is* *perfect, *converting the soul: the *testimony of the LORD *is* *sure, making *wise the *simple.

8 The statutes of the LORD *are* right, *rejoicing the heart: the commandment of the LORD *is* *pure, *enlightening the eyes.

9 The fear of the LORD *is* clean,

41*a* Jer. 11:11 (10–11);
　　Mosiah 21:15;
　　D&C 101:7.
43*a* HEB nations.
46*a* Deut. 5:24.
　b TG Rock.
47*a* Ps. 47:3.
49*a* Rom. 15:9.
50*a* Ps. 20:6;
　　D&C 109:80.

19 1*a* TG Heaven;
　　Nature, Earth.
　b Ps. 50:6.
　c TG Glory; God, Glory of.
　d D&C 104:14.
　3*a* TG Language.
　4*a* Rom. 10:18;
　　2 Ne. 31:15; D&C 64:31.
　7*a* TG Abundant Life;
　　God, Law of.

　b TG Perfection.
　c TG Conversion;
　　Scriptures, Value of.
　d TG Testimony.
　e Alma 32:34 (32–34).
　f TG Wisdom.
　g Ps. 116:6.
8*a* TG Cheerful.
　b Ps. 12:6.
　c TG Edification.

enduring for ever: the *judgments of the LORD *are* *true *and* righteous altogether.

10 More to be *desired *are they* than *gold, yea, than much fine gold: sweeter also than honey and the honeycomb.

11 Moreover by them is thy servant *warned: *and* in *keeping of them *there is* great reward.

12 Who can understand *his* errors? *cleanse thou me from *secret *faults.*

13 Keep back thy servant also from presumptuous *sins; let them not have *dominion over me: then shall I be upright, and I shall be innocent from the great *transgression.

14 Let the words of my mouth, and the *meditation of my heart, be acceptable in thy sight, O LORD, my *strength, and my redeemer.

PSALM 20

David prays that the Lord will hear in time of trouble—The Lord saves His anointed.

To the chief Musician, A Psalm of David.

THE LORD hear thee in the day of trouble; the name of the God of Jacob defend thee;

2 Send thee help from the *sanctuary, and strengthen thee out of Zion;

3 Remember all thy offerings, and accept thy burnt sacrifice; Selah.

4 Grant thee according to thine own heart, and fulfil all thy counsel.

5 We will rejoice in thy salvation, and in the name of our God we will set up *our* banners: the LORD fulfil all thy petitions.

6 Now know I that the LORD saveth his *anointed; he will hear him from his holy heaven with the saving strength of his right hand.

7 Some *trust in chariots, and some in horses: but we will remember the name of the LORD our God.

8 They are brought down and fallen: but we are risen, and stand upright.

9 Save, LORD: let the king hear us when we call.

PSALM 21

A messianic psalm of David—He tells of the glory of the great King—The King will triumph over all His enemies—Their evil designs will fail.

To the chief Musician, A Psalm of David.

THE king shall joy in thy strength, O LORD; and in thy salvation how greatly shall he rejoice!

2 Thou hast given him his heart's *desire, and hast not withholden the request of his lips. Selah.

3 For *thou preventest him with the blessings of goodness: thou settest a *crown of pure gold on his head.

4 He asked life of thee, *and* thou gavest *it* him, *even* length of days for ever and ever.

5 His *glory *is* great in thy salvation: honour and majesty hast thou laid upon him.

6 For thou hast made him most blessed for ever: thou hast made him exceeding glad with thy countenance.

7 For the king trusteth in the LORD, and through the mercy of the most High he shall not be moved.

8 Thine hand shall find out all thine enemies: thy right hand shall find out those that hate thee.

9 Thou shalt make them as a *fiery

9*a* Job 34:12;
   2 Ne. 9:15; 30:9.
b TG Truth.
10*a* Ps. 119:127.
b Ps. 119:72.
11*a* TG Warn.
b Mosiah 2:22;
   D&C 14:7; 58:2.
12*a* TG Purification.

b Ps. 90:8; D&C 1:3.
13*a* JST Ps. 19:13 . . . *acts* . . .
b Ps. 119:133.
c TG Transgress.
14*a* TG Meditation.
b TG Strength.
20 2*a* Ps. 73:17.
6*a* Ps. 18:50;
   D&C 109:80.

7*a* Isa. 31:1.
21 2*a* Alma 29:4.
3*a* HEB thou wilt meet him.
b 2 Sam. 12:30.
5*a* Ps. 45:3.
9*a* Mal. 4:1;
   1 Ne. 22:15;
   3 Ne. 25:1;
   D&C 29:9; 133:64.

oven in the time of thine anger: the LORD shall swallow them up in his wrath, and the fire shall devour them.

10 Their fruit shalt thou destroy from the earth, and their [a]seed from among the children of men.

11 For they intended evil against thee: they imagined a mischievous device, *which* they are not able *to perform.*

12 Therefore shalt thou make them turn their back, *when* thou shalt make ready *thine arrows* upon thy strings against the face of them.

13 Be thou exalted, LORD, in thine own strength: *so* will we sing and praise thy power.

PSALM 22

A messianic psalm of David—He foretells events in the Messiah's life—The Messiah will say, My God, my God, why hast Thou forsaken me?—They will pierce His hands and feet—He will yet govern among all nations.

To the chief Musician upon Aijeleth Shahar, A Psalm of David.

[a]MY God, my God, why hast thou [b]forsaken me? *why art thou so* far from helping me, *and from* [c]the words of my roaring?

2 O my God, I cry in the daytime, but thou hearest not; and in the night season, and am not silent.

3 But thou *art* holy, O *thou* that inhabitest the praises of Israel.

4 Our fathers [a]trusted in thee: they trusted, and thou didst deliver them.

5 They cried unto thee, and were delivered: they trusted in thee, and were not confounded.

6 But I *am* a worm, and no man; a [a]reproach of men, and [b]despised of the people.

7 All they that see me laugh me to [a]scorn: they shoot out the lip, they shake the head, *saying,*

8 He [a]trusted on the LORD *that* he would deliver him: let him deliver him, seeing he delighted in him.

9 But thou *art* he that took me out of the womb: thou didst make me hope *when I was* upon my mother's breasts.

10 I was cast upon thee from the womb: thou *art* my God from my mother's belly.

11 Be not far from me; for trouble *is* near; for *there is* none to help.

12 Many bulls have compassed me: strong *bulls* of Bashan have beset me round.

13 They gaped upon me *with* their mouths, *as* a ravening and a roaring lion.

14 I am poured out like water, and all my bones are out of joint: my [a]heart is like wax; it is melted in the midst of my bowels.

15 My strength is dried up like a potsherd; and my tongue cleaveth to my jaws; and thou hast brought me into the dust of death.

16 For dogs have compassed me: the assembly of the [a]wicked have inclosed me: they [b]pierced my hands and my feet.

17 I may tell all my bones: they look *and* stare upon me.

18 They part my [a]garments among them, and cast lots upon my vesture.

19 But be not thou far from me, O LORD: O my strength, [a]haste thee to help me.

20 Deliver my soul from the sword; [a]my darling from the power of the dog.

21 Save me from the lion's mouth: for thou hast heard me from the horns of the [a]unicorns.

10*a* Ps. 37:28; 109:13;
    2 Ne. 24:20.
22 1*a* Matt. 27:46.
  b TG Despair; Jesus
    Christ, Crucifixion
    of; Jesus Christ,
    Prophecies about.
  c IE my cry of distress.
  4*a* TG Trust in God.

6*a* TG Reproach.
  b Isa. 53:3;
    1 Ne. 19:14;
    Mosiah 14:3 (3–6).
7*a* Luke 23:35.
8*a* Matt. 27:43.
14*a* Jer. 23:9.
16*a* TG Jesus Christ,
    Betrayal of.

  b TG Jesus Christ,
    Crucifixion of; Jesus
    Christ, Prophecies
    about; Suffering.
18*a* Matt. 27:35; Mark 15:24;
    Luke 23:34; John 19:24.
19*a* TG Haste.
20*a* IE my life (idiom).
21*a* HEB bison, wild ox.

22 I will declare thy ^aname unto my brethren: in the midst of the congregation will I praise thee.

23 Ye that fear the LORD, praise him; all ye the seed of Jacob, glorify him; and fear him, all ye the seed of Israel.

24 For he hath not despised nor abhorred the affliction of the afflicted; neither hath he hid his face from him; but when he cried unto him, he heard.

25 My praise *shall be* of thee in the great ^acongregation: I will pay my vows before them that fear him.

26 The meek shall eat and be satisfied: they shall praise the LORD that seek him: your heart shall live for ever.

27 All the ends of the ^aworld shall remember and turn unto the LORD: and all the kindreds of the nations shall worship before thee.

28 For the ^akingdom *is* the LORD's: and he *is* the ^bgovernor among the nations.

29 All *they that be* fat upon earth shall eat and worship: all they that go down to the dust shall bow before him: and none can keep alive his own ^asoul.

30 A seed shall serve him; it shall be accounted to the Lord for a generation.

31 They shall come, and shall ^adeclare his righteousness unto a people that shall be born, that he hath done *this*.

PSALM 23

David declares, The Lord is my shepherd.

A Psalm of David.

THE LORD *is* my ^ashepherd; I shall not ^bwant.

2 He maketh me to lie down in green pastures: he ^aleadeth me beside the still waters.

3 He restoreth my soul: he leadeth me in the paths of ^arighteousness for his ^bname's sake.

4 Yea, though I ^awalk through the ^bvalley of the ^cshadow of ^ddeath, I will fear no ^eevil: for thou *art* with me; thy rod and thy staff they ^fcomfort me.

5 Thou preparest a table before me in the presence of mine enemies: thou ^aanointest my head with oil; my cup runneth over.

6 Surely ^agoodness and mercy shall follow me all the days of my life: and I will dwell in the house of the LORD for ever.

PSALM 24

David testifies, The earth is the Lord's and the fulness thereof, he who has clean hands and a pure heart will ascend unto the hill of the Lord, and the Lord of Hosts is the King of Glory.

A Psalm of David.

THE ^aearth *is* the ^bLORD's, and the fulness thereof; the world, and they that dwell therein.

2 For he hath founded it upon the seas, and established it upon the floods.

3 Who shall ^aascend into the hill of the LORD? or who shall stand in his ^bholy place?

4 He that hath ^aclean ^bhands, and a ^cpure ^dheart; who hath not lifted up

---

22 *a* Heb. 2:12.
25 *a* TG Assembly for
    Worship.
27 *a* TG World.
28 *a* 1 Chr. 29:11;
    Obad. 1:21; D&C 6:13.
    b TG Governments.
29 *a* TG Soul.
31 *a* TG Preaching.
23 1 *a* TG Jesus Christ, Good
    Shepherd; Shepherd.
    b Matt. 6:8; Philip. 4:19.
    TG Contentment.
  2 *a* TG Guidance, Divine.

3 *a* TG Righteousness.
   b 1 Sam. 12:22;
    Ps. 31:3; 109:21;
    1 Jn. 2:12; 1 Ne. 20:9.
4 *a* TG Walking with God.
   b Ps. 138:7;
    D&C 127:2 (1–2).
   c Job 3:5.
   d TG Death.
   e TG Evil.
   f TG Comfort.
5 *a* TG Anointing.
6 *a* TG Peace of God.
24 1 *a* Ex. 9:29; Deut. 10:14;

    Ps. 89:11;
    1 Cor. 10:26.
    TG Nature, Earth.
   b 1 Chr. 29:14.
3 *a* Ps. 15:1 (1–5);
    1 Ne. 15:33 (33–36);
    Mosiah 15:23 (19–26);
    D&C 76:62 (50–70);
    Moses 6:57 (55–59).
   b TG Holiness; Temple.
4 *a* TG Chastity; Cleanliness.
   b 1 Tim. 2:8.
   c TG Purity; Virtue.
   d TG Heart.

his soul unto *vanity, nor *sworn *deceitfully.

5 He shall receive the blessing from the LORD, and righteousness from the God of his salvation.

6 This *is* the generation of them that seek him, that seek thy face, *O Jacob. Selah.

7 *Lift up your heads, O ye gates; and be ye lift up, ye everlasting doors; and the King of glory shall *come in.

8 Who *is* this *King of *glory? The LORD strong and mighty, the LORD mighty in battle.

9 Lift up your heads, O ye gates; even lift *them* up, ye everlasting doors; and the King of glory shall come in.

10 Who is this *King of glory? The LORD of hosts, he *is* the King of glory. Selah.

PSALM 25

David pleads for truth and asks for pardon—Mercy and truth are for those who keep the commandments.

A *Psalm* of David.

UNTO thee, O LORD, do I *lift up my soul.

2 O my God, I *trust in thee: let me not be *ashamed, let not mine enemies triumph over me.

3 Yea, let none that wait on thee be *ashamed: let them be ashamed which transgress without cause.

4 Shew me thy *ways, O LORD; teach me thy paths.

5 *Lead me in thy truth, and teach me: for thou *art* the God of my salvation; on thee do I *wait all the day.

6 Remember, O LORD, thy tender *mercies and thy lovingkindnesses; for they *have been* ever of old.

7 Remember not the *sins of my youth, nor my transgressions: according to thy *mercy remember thou me for thy goodness' sake, O LORD.

8 Good and upright *is* the LORD: therefore will he *teach sinners in the way.

9 The meek will he *guide in judgment: and the meek will he teach his way.

10 All the paths of the LORD *are* mercy and truth unto such as keep his covenant and his testimonies.

11 For thy *name's sake, O LORD, pardon mine iniquity; for it *is* great.

12 What man *is* he that feareth the LORD? him shall he teach in the way *that* he shall choose.

13 His soul shall dwell at ease; and his seed shall inherit the *earth.

14 The *secret of the LORD *is* with them that *fear him; and he will shew them his covenant.

15 Mine *eyes *are* ever toward the LORD; for he shall pluck my feet out of the *net.

16 Turn thee unto me, and have *mercy upon me; for I *am* desolate and afflicted.

17 The troubles of my heart are enlarged: O bring thou me out of my distresses.

18 Look upon mine affliction and my *pain; and forgive all my sins.

19 Consider mine enemies; for they are many; and they hate me with *cruel hatred.

20 O keep my soul, and deliver me:

4e TG Vanity.
  f TG Swearing.
  g TG Deceit; Honesty.
6a OR even Jacob.
7a JST Ps. 24:7–10 (Appendix).
  b TG Jesus Christ, Second Coming.
8a TG Kingdom of God, in Heaven.
  b Alma 5:50.
10a TG Jesus Christ, Prophecies about.
25 1a Ps. 86:4; 143:8.
  2a TG Faith; Trust in God.

  b TG Shame.
3a TG Worthiness.
4a Ex. 33:13 (12–13); Ps. 143:8 (5–12); John 14:6; D&C 50:17 (17–20); 76:2 (1–5); 79:2.
5a TG Guidance, Divine; Leadership.
  b Gen. 49:18; Prov. 20:22; Isa. 40:31; 2 Ne. 6:13 (7, 13).
6a TG God, Mercy of.
7a Job 13:26; D&C 20:5; 58:42;

  JS—H 1:28 (28–29).
  b Ps. 51:1.
8a TG Education.
9a TG Guidance, Divine.
11a Ps. 109:21.
13a TG Earth, Destiny of.
14a TG Mysteries of Godliness.
  b TG Reverence.
15a Ps. 141:8; D&C 4:5.
  b Ps. 9:15; 31:4.
16a TG God, Mercy of.
18a TG Pain.
19a TG Cruelty.

let me not be ^aashamed; for I put my ^btrust in thee.

21 Let integrity and uprightness preserve me; for I wait on thee.

22 ^aRedeem Israel, O God, out of all his troubles.

PSALM 26

David says that he has walked in integrity and obedience—He loves the Lord's house.

A *Psalm* of David.

JUDGE me, O LORD; for I have walked in mine integrity: I have ^atrusted also in the LORD; *therefore* I shall not slide.

2 Examine me, O LORD, and ^aprove me; try my reins and my heart.

3 For thy lovingkindness *is* before mine eyes: and I have walked in thy truth.

4 I have not sat with ^avain persons, neither will I go in with dissemblers.

5 I have ^ahated the congregation of ^bevil doers; and will not sit with the wicked.

6 I will ^awash mine hands in innocency: so will I compass thine altar, O LORD:

7 That I may publish with the voice of thanksgiving, and tell of all thy ^awondrous works.

8 LORD, I have loved the habitation of thy house, and the place where thine ^ahonour dwelleth.

9 Gather not my soul with sinners, nor my life with ^abloody men:

10 In whose hands *is* mischief, and their right hand is full of ^abribes.

11 But as for me, I will walk in mine integrity: redeem me, and be merciful unto me.

12 My foot standeth in an even place: in the ^acongregations will I bless the LORD.

PSALM 27

David says, The Lord is my light and my salvation—He desires to dwell in the house of the Lord forever—He counsels, Wait on the Lord and be of good courage.

A *Psalm* of David.

THE LORD *is* my ^alight and my ^bsalvation; whom shall I ^cfear? the LORD *is* the ^dstrength of my life; of whom shall I be afraid?

2 When the wicked, *even* mine enemies and my foes, came upon me to eat up my flesh, they stumbled and fell.

3 Though an host should encamp against me, my heart shall not fear: though war should rise against me, in this *will* I *be* confident.

4 One *thing* have I desired of the LORD, that will I seek after; that I may ^adwell in the ^bhouse of the LORD all the days of my life, to behold the ^cbeauty of the LORD, and to ^dinquire in his temple.

5 For in the time of trouble he shall hide me in his ^apavilion: in the secret of his tabernacle shall he hide me; he shall set me up upon a ^brock.

6 And now shall mine head be lifted up above mine enemies round about me: therefore will I offer in his tabernacle sacrifices of joy; I will sing, yea, I will sing praises unto the LORD.

7 Hear, O LORD, *when* I cry with my voice: have mercy also upon me, and answer me.

20*a* TG Shame.
  b TG Trust in God.
22*a* Deut. 21:8;
  Ps. 130:8;
  D&C 84:99 (99–100).
26 1*a* TG Trust in God.
2*a* TG Test.
4*a* Ps. 1:1;
  Jer. 15:17;
  Rom. 12:9;
  D&C 38:42.
5*a* TG Hate.
  b D&C 68:1.

6*a* TG Wash.
7*a* 1 Chr. 16:9;
  Ps. 9:1;
  D&C 76:114.
8*a* OR glory, presence.
9*a* IE bloodguilty.
10*a* TG Bribe.
12*a* TG Assembly for
  Worship.
27 1*a* TG Jesus Christ, Light
  of the World; Light
  [noun]; Light of Christ.
  b TG Jesus Christ, Savior;

Salvation;
  Salvation, Plan of.
  c D&C 3:7 (5–9).
  d TG Strength.
4*a* 1 Ne. 10:21;
  Morm. 7:7;
  D&C 76:62 (50–62);
  Moses 6:57.
  b Ps. 65:4; Matt. 21:13.
  c TG Beauty.
  d OR contemplate.
5*a* Ps. 31:20.
  b Ps. 40:2.

8 *When thou saidst,* ªSeek ye my ᵇface; my heart said unto thee, Thy face, LORD, will I seek.

9 Hide not thy face *far* from me; put not thy servant away in anger: thou hast been my help; leave me not, neither forsake me, O God of my salvation.

10 When my father and my mother forsake me, then the LORD will take me up.

11 ªTeach me thy way, O LORD, and ᵇlead me in a plain path, because of mine enemies.

12 Deliver me not over unto the will of mine enemies: for ªfalse witnesses are risen up against me, and such as breathe out ᵇcruelty.

13 *I had fainted,* unless I had believed to see the goodness of the LORD in the ªland of the living.

14 ªWait on the LORD: be of good ᵇcourage, and he shall strengthen thine heart: ᶜwait, I say, on the LORD.

PSALM 28

David pleads with the Lord to hear his voice and grant his petitions—David prays, Save Thy people and bless Thine inheritance.

A *Psalm* of David.

UNTO thee will I cry, O LORD my rock; be not silent to me: lest, *if* thou be ªsilent to me, I become like them that go down into the ᵇpit.

2 Hear the voice of my supplications, when I cry unto thee, when I lift up my hands toward thy holy ªoracle.

3 Draw me not away with the wicked, and with the workers of iniquity, which ªspeak ᵇpeace to their neighbours, but ᶜmischief *is* in their hearts.

4 Give them according to their ªdeeds, and according to the wickedness of their endeavours: give them after the work of their hands; render to them their ᵇdesert.

5 Because they regard not the ªworks of the LORD, nor the operation of his hands, he shall destroy them, and not build them up.

6 Blessed *be* the LORD, because he hath heard the voice of my supplications.

7 The LORD *is* my strength and my shield; my heart ªtrusted in him, and I am helped: therefore my heart greatly rejoiceth; and with my song will I praise him.

8 The LORD *is* their strength, and he *is* the saving strength of his anointed.

9 Save thy people, and bless thine inheritance: feed them also, and lift them up for ever.

PSALM 29

David counsels, Worship the Lord in the beauty of holiness—David sets forth the wonder and power of the voice of the Lord.

A Psalm of David.

GIVE unto the LORD, O ye mighty, give unto the LORD glory and strength.

2 Give unto the LORD the glory due unto his name; worship the LORD in the ªbeauty of holiness.

3 The voice of the LORD *is* upon the ªwaters: the God of glory thundereth: the LORD *is* upon many waters.

4 The voice of the LORD *is* powerful; the voice of the LORD *is* full of majesty.

5 The voice of the LORD breaketh the cedars; yea, the LORD breaketh the cedars of Lebanon.

8a Ether 12:41;
      D&C 101:38.
   b TG God, Privilege of
      Seeing.
11a 1 Kgs. 8:36.
   b TG Guidance, Divine.
12a Matt. 15:19 (19–20);
      Hel. 7:21 (21–22).
   b TG Cruelty.
13a Ps. 116:9; D&C 81:3.

14a Ps. 37:34;
      Prov. 20:22;
      D&C 98:2 (2–3).
   b TG Courage.
   c TG Faith.
28 1a Ps. 83:1.
   b Ps. 88:4; 143:7;
      Prov. 1:12; 1 Ne. 14:3;
      2 Ne. 24:15.
   2a D&C 90:4 (1–5); 124:39

   (38–39), 126 (125–26).
   3a Prov. 26:25.
   b TG Peace.
   c TG Guile; Hypocrisy.
   4a TG Good Works.
   b OR due reward.
   5a Isa. 5:12 (11–12).
   7a TG Faith.
29 2a TG Beauty.
   3a TG Nature, Earth.

6 He maketh them also to skip like a calf; Lebanon and Sirion like a young ^aunicorn.

7 The voice of the LORD ^adivideth the flames of fire.

8 The voice of the LORD shaketh the wilderness; the LORD shaketh the wilderness of Kadesh.

9 The voice of the LORD maketh the hinds to calve, and discovereth the forests: and in his temple doth every one speak of *his* glory.

10 The LORD sitteth upon the ^aflood; yea, the LORD sitteth ^bKing for ever.

11 The LORD will give ^astrength unto his people; the LORD will bless his people with ^bpeace.

PSALM 30

David sings praises and gives thanks to the Lord—David pleads for mercy.

A Psalm *and* Song *at* the dedication of the house of David.

I WILL extol thee, O LORD; for thou hast lifted me up, and hast not made my foes to rejoice over me.

2 O LORD my God, I cried unto thee, and thou hast ^ahealed me.

3 O LORD, thou hast ^abrought up my ^bsoul from the grave: thou hast kept me alive, that I should not go down to the pit.

4 Sing unto the LORD, O ye saints of his, and give thanks at the remembrance of his holiness.

5 ^aFor his anger *endureth but* a moment; in his favour *is* life: weeping may endure for a night, but ^bjoy *cometh* in the morning.

6 And in my prosperity I said, I shall never be moved.

7 LORD, by thy favour thou hast made my mountain to stand strong: thou didst hide thy ^aface, *and* I was troubled.

8 I cried to thee, O LORD; and unto the LORD I made supplication.

9 ^aWhat profit *is there* in my ^bblood, when I go down to the pit? Shall the ^cdust praise thee? shall it declare thy truth?

10 Hear, O LORD, and have mercy upon me: LORD, be thou my helper.

11 Thou hast turned for me my ^amourning into dancing: thou hast put off my sackcloth, and girded me with ^bgladness;

12 To the end that *my* glory may sing praise to thee, and not be silent. O LORD my God, I will give thanks unto thee for ever.

PSALM 31

David trusts in the Lord and rejoices in His mercy—Speaking as the Messiah he says, Into Thine hand I commit my spirit—He counsels, O love the Lord, all ye His Saints, for the Lord preserves the faithful.

To the chief Musician, A Psalm of David.

IN thee, O LORD, do I put my ^atrust; let me never be ^bashamed: deliver me in thy ^crighteousness.

2 Bow down thine ear to me; deliver me speedily: be thou my strong rock, for an house of defence to save me.

3 For thou *art* my rock and my fortress; therefore for thy ^aname's sake lead me, and guide me.

4 Pull me out of the ^anet that they have laid ^bprivily for me: for thou *art* my strength.

6a HEB bison, buffalo.
7a OR speaks in.
10a TG Flood.
  b TG Kingdom of God, in Heaven.
11a TG Strength.
  b TG Peace.
30 2a TG Heal.
  3a Ps. 86:13;
     Acts 2:34;
     D&C 132:39.
  b Ps. 16:10.
  5a JST Ps. 30:5 For his anger *kindleth against*

the wicked; they repent, and in a moment it is turned away, and they are in his favor, and he giveth them life; therefore, weeping may . . .
  b TG Joy.
  7a Ps. 104:29;
     D&C 84:23 (21–23).
  9a JST Ps. 30:9 When I go down to the pit, my blood shall return to the dust. I will praise thee; my soul shall declare thy truth;

for what profit am I, if I do it not?
  b IE death.
  c Ps. 6:5.
11a Jer. 31:13.
  b Isa. 61:3.
31 1a TG Trust in God.
  b TG Shame.
  c Dan. 9:16.
  3a Ps. 23:3; 109:21.
  4a Ps. 9:15; 25:15.
  b OR secretly.

5 Into thine hand I commit my ^aspirit: thou hast redeemed me, O LORD God of truth.

6 I have hated them that regard lying vanities: but I trust in the LORD.

7 I will be glad and rejoice in thy mercy: for thou hast considered my trouble; thou hast known my soul in adversities;

8 And hast not shut me up into the hand of the enemy: thou hast set my feet in a large room.

9 Have mercy upon me, O LORD, for I am in trouble: mine eye is consumed with grief, *yea,* my soul and my ^abelly.

10 For my life is spent with grief, and my years with sighing: my strength faileth because of mine iniquity, and my bones are consumed.

11 I was a reproach among all mine enemies, but especially among my neighbours, and a fear to mine acquaintance: they that did see me without ^afled from me.

12 I am ^aforgotten as a dead man out of mind: I am like a broken ^bvessel.

13 For I have heard the ^aslander of many: fear *was* on every side: while they took counsel together against me, they devised to take away my life.

14 But I ^atrusted in thee, O LORD: I said, Thou *art* my God.

15 My times *are* in thy hand: deliver me from the hand of mine enemies, and from them that persecute me.

16 Make thy face to ^ashine upon thy servant: save me for thy mercies' sake.

17 Let me not be ^aashamed, O LORD; for I have called upon thee:

let the wicked be ashamed, *and* let them be silent in the grave.

18 Let the ^alying lips be put to ^bsilence; which speak grievous things proudly and contemptuously against the righteous.

19 *Oh* how great *is* thy ^agoodness, which thou hast laid up for them that fear thee; *which* thou hast wrought for them that trust in thee before the sons of men!

20 Thou shalt hide them in the secret of thy presence from the pride of man: thou shalt keep them secretly in a ^apavilion from the ^bstrife of tongues.

21 Blessed *be* the LORD: for he hath shewed me his marvellous kindness in a strong city.

22 For I said in my ^ahaste, I am cut off from before thine eyes: nevertheless thou heardest the voice of my supplications when I cried unto thee.

23 O ^alove the LORD, all ye his saints: *for* the LORD ^bpreserveth the ^cfaithful, and plentifully ^drewardeth the proud doer.

24 Be of good ^acourage, and he shall strengthen your heart, all ye that ^bhope in the LORD.

PSALM 32

David says, Blessed is the man unto whom the Lord imputes not iniquity— David acknowledges his sin—He recommends that the righteous be glad in the Lord and rejoice.

A *Psalm* of David, Maschil.

^aBLESSED *is he whose* ^btransgression *is* ^cforgiven, *whose* sin *is* covered.

5*a* Luke 23:46.
9*a* OR body.
11*a* Job 19:14 (14–15);
     Ps. 64:8.
12*a* Ps. 88:5 (4–5).
   b Jer. 22:28; 48:38;
     Hosea 8:8;
     Rev. 2:27 (26–27);
     D&C 76:33 (31–33).
13*a* Jer. 20:10.
    TG Slander.
14*a* TG Faith.
16*a* Num. 6:25.

17*a* TG Shame.
18*a* TG Honesty;
     Lying.
   b TG Silence.
19*a* TG Reward.
20*a* Ps. 27:5.
   b TG Gossip;
     Strife.
22*a* TG Haste; Rashness.
23*a* TG God, Love of.
   b TG Protection, Divine.
   c Mosiah 2:41;
     Ether 4:19;

     D&C 6:13; 61:10; 63:47;
     66:8.
   d TG Reward.
24*a* TG Courage.
   b OR wait for.
32 1*a* JST Ps. 32:1 Blessed
     are they whose
     transgressions are
     forgiven, *and who have*
     no sins to be covered.
     Rom. 4:7 (7–8).
   b TG Sin; Transgress.
   c TG Remission of Sins.

2 Blessed *is* the man unto whom the Lord imputeth not iniquity, and in whose spirit *there is* no ᵃguile.

3 When I kept silence, my bones waxed old through my roaring all the day long.

4 For day and night thy hand was heavy upon me: my ᵃmoisture is turned into the drought of summer. Selah.

5 I acknowledged my sin unto thee, and mine iniquity have I not hid. I said, I will ᵃconfess my ᵇtransgressions unto the Lord; and thou ᶜforgavest the iniquity of my sin. Selah.

6 For this shall every one that is ᵃgodly pray unto thee in a time when thou mayest be found: surely in the floods of great waters they shall not come nigh unto him.

7 Thou *art* my ᵃhiding place; thou shalt preserve me from trouble; thou shalt compass me about with songs of deliverance. Selah.

8 I will instruct thee and ᵃteach thee in the way which thou shalt go: I will guide thee with mine eye.

9 Be ye not as the horse, *or* as the mule, *which* have no understanding: whose mouth must be held in with bit and bridle, lest they come near unto thee.

10 Many ᵃsorrows *shall be* to the wicked: but he that ᵇtrusteth in the Lord, mercy shall compass him about.

11 Be glad in the Lord, and rejoice, ye righteous: and shout for joy, all *ye that are* upright in heart.

PSALM 33

Rejoice in the Lord—Sing unto Him a new song—He loves righteousness and

judgment—Blessed is the nation whose God is the Lord.

Rejoice in the Lord, O ye righteous: *for* ᵃpraise is comely for the upright.

2 Praise the Lord with harp: sing unto him with the psaltery *and* an instrument of ten strings.

3 Sing unto him a ᵃnew song; play skilfully with a loud noise.

4 For the ᵃword of the Lord *is* right; and all his works *are done* in truth.

5 He loveth ᵃrighteousness and ᵇjudgment: the earth is ᶜfull of the goodness of the Lord.

6 By the ᵃword of the Lord were the ᵇheavens made; and all the host of them by the breath of his mouth.

7 He gathereth the waters of the sea together as an heap: he layeth up the depth in storehouses.

8 Let all the earth fear the Lord: let all the inhabitants of the world stand in awe of him.

9 For he ᵃspake, and it was *done*; he commanded, and it stood fast.

10 The Lord bringeth the ᵃcounsel of the ᵇheathen to nought: he maketh the devices of the people of none effect.

11 The ᵃcounsel of the Lord standeth for ever, the thoughts of his heart to all generations.

12 Blessed *is* the nation whose God *is* the Lord; *and* the people *whom* he hath ᵃchosen for his own inheritance.

13 The Lord looketh from heaven; he beholdeth all the sons of men.

14 From the place of his habitation he ᵃlooketh upon all the inhabitants of the earth.

2a TG Guile; Sincere.
4a IE strength dried up as.
5a TG Confession.
  b TG Transgress.
  c TG Forgive.
6a TG Godliness.
7a Ps. 91:1; 119:114.
8a TG Teaching.
10a Prov. 13:21; Rom. 2:9;
  Alma 41:10; D&C 1:3.
  TG Despair.
  b TG Trust in God.
33 1a Ps. 147:1; Alma 26:8;

D&C 136:28 (28–29).
3a IE raise also fresh, new praises and thanks to God for His ever-new blessings.
  Ps. 40:3; D&C 25:12.
4a D&C 84:45.
5a TG Righteousness.
  b HEB justice.
  c Ps. 119:64.
6a See JST John 1:1–16 (Appendix).
  TG Jesus Christ, Creator.

  b TG Heaven.
9a Gen. 1:3;
  Ps. 148:5 (5–6);
  2 Cor. 4:6; D&C 38:3;
  Moses 2:5 (4–5).
10a Neh. 4:15.
  b HEB nations, Gentiles.
  TG Heathen.
11a 2 Ne. 9:16;
  D&C 1:38 (37–39);
  Moses 1:4.
12a Moses 1:26 (25–26).
14a Isa. 63:15.

15 He fashioneth their hearts alike; he considereth all their *a*works.

16 There is no king *a*saved by the multitude of an host: a mighty man is not delivered by much strength.

17 An *a*horse *is* a vain thing for safety: neither shall he *b*deliver *any* by his great strength.

18 Behold, the *a*eye of the LORD *is* upon them that fear him, upon them that hope in his mercy;

19 To deliver their soul from death, and to keep them alive in *a*famine.

20 Our soul waiteth for the LORD: he *is* our help and our *a*shield.

21 For our heart shall rejoice in him, because we have trusted in his holy name.

22 Let thy mercy, O LORD, be upon us, according as we *a*hope in thee.

PSALM 34

David blesses the Lord at all times—He counsels, Keep your tongue from evil; do good and seek peace—He says that not one of the Messiah's bones will be broken.

A *Psalm* of David, when he changed his behaviour before Abimelech; who drove him away, and he departed.

I WILL *a*bless the LORD at all times: his praise *shall* continually *be* in my mouth.

2 My soul shall make her boast in the LORD: the humble shall hear *thereof,* and be glad.

3 O *a*magnify the LORD with me, and let us exalt his name together.

4 I *a*sought the LORD, and he *b*heard me, and delivered me from all my fears.

5 They looked unto him, and were *a*lightened: and their faces were not ashamed.

6 This poor man cried, and the LORD heard *him,* and saved him out of all his troubles.

7 The *a*angel of the LORD encampeth round about them that fear him, and delivereth them.

8 O *a*taste and see that the LORD *is* *b*good: blessed *is* the man *that* trusteth in him.

9 O fear the LORD, ye his saints: for *there is* no want to them that fear him.

10 The young lions do lack, and suffer hunger: but they that seek the LORD shall not *a*want any good *thing.*

11 Come, ye children, hearken unto me: I will teach you the fear of the LORD.

12 What man *is he that* desireth life, *and* loveth *many* days, that he may see good?

13 Keep thy *a*tongue from evil, and thy lips from speaking *b*guile.

14 Depart from evil, and do *a*good; seek *b*peace, and pursue it.

15 The *a*eyes of the LORD *are* upon the *b*righteous, and his ears *are open* unto their cry.

16 The face of the LORD *is* against them that do evil, to cut off the remembrance of them from the earth.

17 *The righteous* cry, and the LORD heareth, and *a*delivereth them out of all their troubles.

18 The LORD *is* nigh unto them that are of a broken heart; and

15a 1 Ne. 15:33 (26–36);
    3 Ne. 27:25 (23–27).
16a Ps. 44:6;
    2 Ne. 4:34.
17a Prov. 21:31.
  b Amos 2:15.
18a Ps. 34:15;
    1 Pet. 3:12;
    D&C 1:1; 38:7 (7–8).
19a Ps. 37:19 (18–19).
20a Deut. 33:29 (26–29);
    D&C 35:14 (13–14).
22a TG Hope.
34 1a Mosiah 2:20 (20–21);

    Ether 6:9;
    D&C 46:7; 59:7; 78:19.
3a Philip. 1:20 (18–30).
4a Lam. 3:25;
    Heb. 11:6;
    Alma 37:37 (36–37).
  b Ps. 4:1 (1, 3).
5a TG Light of Christ.
7a TG Angels.
8a Mosiah 4:11;
    Alma 36:24 (24–26);
    Morm. 1:15.
  b Lam. 3:25;
    Nahum 1:7;

    D&C 70:18 (17–18).
10a Prov. 13:25.
13a TG Gossip; Profanity.
  b TG Guile; Honesty;
    Sincere.
14a Eccl. 3:12.
  b TG Peace;
    Peacemakers.
15a Ps. 33:18;
    Amos 9:8;
    D&C 67:2.
  b D&C 76:5.
17a 1 Cor. 10:13 (12–14);
    Alma 36:27 (26–27).

*saveth such as be *of a contrite spirit.

19 Many *are* the *afflictions of the righteous: but the LORD delivereth him out of them all.

20 He keepeth all his bones: not one of them is *broken.

21 Evil shall slay the wicked: and they that hate the righteous shall be desolate.

22 The LORD redeemeth the soul of his servants: and none of them that *trust in him shall be desolate.

PSALM 35

David complains of his enemies and their wrong dealings—He asks the Lord to judge him according to his righteousness.

A *Psalm* of David.

*PLEAD *my cause,* O LORD, with them that strive with me: *fight against them that fight against me.

2 Take hold of shield and buckler, and stand up for mine help.

3 Draw out also the spear, and stop *the way* against them that persecute me: say unto my soul, I *am* thy salvation.

4 Let them be confounded and put to shame that seek after my soul: let them be turned back and brought to confusion that devise my hurt.

5 Let them be as chaff before the wind: and let the angel of the LORD chase *them.*

6 Let their way be dark and slippery: and let the angel of the LORD *persecute them.

7 For without cause have they hid for me their net *in* a pit, *which* without cause they have digged for my soul.

8 Let destruction come upon him at unawares; and let his net that he hath hid catch himself: into that very destruction let him fall.

9 And my soul shall be *joyful in the LORD: it shall rejoice in his *salvation.

10 All my bones shall say, LORD, who *is* like unto thee, which *deliverest the *poor from him that is too strong for him, yea, the poor and the needy from him that spoileth him?

11 *False witnesses did rise up; they laid to my charge *things* that I knew not.

12 They *rewarded me evil for good *to* the spoiling of my soul.

13 But as for me, when they were *sick, my clothing *was* sackcloth: I humbled my soul with *fasting; and my prayer returned into mine own bosom.

14 I behaved myself as though *he had been* my friend *or* *brother: I bowed down heavily, as one that mourneth *for his* mother.

15 But in mine *adversity they rejoiced, and gathered themselves together: *yea,* the abjects gathered themselves together against me, and I knew *it* not; they did tear *me,* and ceased not:

16 With hypocritical *mockers in feasts, they gnashed upon me with their teeth.

17 Lord, how *long wilt thou look on? rescue my soul from their destructions, my *darling from the lions.

18 I will give thee thanks in the great congregation: I will praise thee among much people.

19 Let not them that are mine enemies wrongfully rejoice over me: *neither* let them wink with the eye that *hate me without a cause.

18a TG Remission of Sins.
  b HEB crushed in spirit.
    TG Contrite Heart;
    Meek;
    Poor in Spirit.
19a 2 Tim. 3:12.
    TG Affliction.
20a TG Jesus Christ,
    Prophecies about.
22a TG Faith;
    Trust in God.

35 1a D&C 121:5 (1–6).
  b Isa. 49:25;
    D&C 98:37; 105:14.
6a HEB pursue.
9a TG Joy.
  b TG Salvation.
10a Prov. 22:23.
  b Isa. 25:4;
    D&C 56:18 (18–19).
11a TG Slander.
12a Ps. 38:20.

13a TG Sickness.
  b TG Fast, Fasting.
14a TG Brotherhood and
    Sisterhood.
15a TG Adversity.
16a TG Mocking.
17a D&C 121:2 (1–6).
  b HEB only life.
19a TG Hate.

20 For they speak not peace: but they devise deceitful matters against *them that are* quiet in the land.

21 Yea, they opened their mouth wide against me, *and* said, Aha, aha, our eye hath seen *it.*

22 *This* thou hast seen, O LORD: keep not silence: O Lord, be not far from me.

23 Stir up thyself, and *a*awake to my judgment, *even* unto my cause, my God and my Lord.

24 Judge me, O LORD my God, according to thy righteousness; and let them not rejoice over me.

25 Let them not say in their hearts, Ah, so would we have it: let them not say, We have swallowed him up.

26 Let them be ashamed and brought to confusion together that rejoice at mine hurt: let them be clothed with shame and dishonour that magnify *themselves* against me.

27 Let them shout for joy, and be glad, that favour my righteous cause: yea, let them say continually, Let the LORD be magnified, which hath *a*pleasure in the prosperity of his servant.

28 And my tongue shall speak of thy righteousness *and* of thy praise all the day long.

PSALM 36

David praises the Lord for His mercy, His righteousness, and His loving kindness—The fountain of life is with the Lord.

To the chief Musician, A *Psalm* of David the servant of the LORD.

THE transgression of the wicked saith within my heart, *that there* is no *a*fear of God before his eyes.

2 For he flattereth himself in his own eyes, until his iniquity be found to be hateful.

3 The words of his mouth *are* iniquity and *a*deceit: he hath left off to be wise, *and* to do good.

4 He deviseth mischief upon his bed; he setteth himself in a way *that is* not good; he abhorreth not evil.

5 Thy *a*mercy, O LORD, *is* in the *b*heavens; *and* thy faithfulness reacheth unto the clouds.

6 Thy *a*righteousness *is* like the great mountains; thy judgments *are* a great deep: O LORD, thou preservest man and beast.

7 How excellent *is* thy lovingkindness, O God! therefore the children of men put their *a*trust under the shadow of thy wings.

8 They shall be abundantly satisfied with the fatness of thy house; and thou shalt make them drink of the river of thy *a*pleasures.

9 For with thee *is* the fountain of life: in thy light shall we see *a*light.

10 O continue thy lovingkindness unto them that know thee; and thy righteousness to the upright in heart.

11 Let not the foot of pride come against me, and let not the hand of the wicked remove me.

12 There are the workers of *a*iniquity fallen: they are cast down, and shall not be able to rise.

PSALM 37

David counsels, Trust in the Lord and do good—Rest in the Lord and wait patiently for Him—Cease from anger and forsake wrath—The meek will inherit the earth—The Lord loves justice and does not forsake His Saints.

A *Psalm* of David.

FRET not thyself because of evildoers, neither be thou *a*envious against the workers of iniquity.

2 For they shall soon be *a*cut down

23*a* Ps. 59:4.
27*a* TG Pleasure.
36 1*a* TG Courage;
　　　Fearful.
3*a* TG Deceit.
5*a* Alma 26:16;
　　Morm. 6:22;
　　D&C 97:2, 6.

b Ps. 71:19;
　Moses 6:42;
　Abr. 2:7 (7–8).
6*a* Dan. 9:16.
7*a* 2 Ne. 22:2;
　　Mosiah 4:6;
　　Hel. 12:1.
8*a* Ps. 16:11.

9*a* TG Light [noun].
12*a* Alma 5:57 (57–58);
　　　D&C 1:9 (9–10);
　　　JS—M 1:55 (31, 55).
37 1*a* TG Worldliness.
2*a* Alma 50:20;
　　D&C 1:14; 29:9 (9–12).

like the grass, and wither as the green herb.

3 *a*Trust in the LORD, and do good; *so* shalt thou dwell in the land, and verily thou shalt be fed.

4 Delight thyself also in the LORD; and he shall give thee the *a*desires of thine heart.

5 *a*Commit thy *b*way unto the LORD; trust also in him; and he shall bring *it* to pass.

6 And he shall *a*bring forth thy righteousness as the light, and thy judgment as the noonday.

7 Rest in the LORD, and wait *a*patiently for him: fret not thyself because of him who prospereth in his way, because of the man who bringeth wicked devices to pass.

8 *a*Cease from *b*anger, and forsake wrath: fret not thyself in any wise to do evil.

9 For evildoers shall be *a*cut off: but those that wait upon the LORD, they shall inherit the *b*earth.

10 For yet a *a*little while, and the wicked *shall* not *be:* yea, thou shalt diligently consider his place, and it *shall* not *be.*

11 But the *a*meek shall inherit the *b*earth; and shall *c*delight themselves in the abundance of peace.

12 The wicked plotteth against the just, and gnasheth upon him with his teeth.

13 The Lord shall *a*laugh at him: for he seeth that his day is coming.

14 The wicked have drawn out the sword, and have bent their bow, to cast down the poor and needy, *and* to slay such as be of upright conversation.

15 Their sword shall enter into their own heart, and their bows shall be broken.

16 A *a*little that a *b*righteous man hath *is* better than the *c*riches of many wicked.

17 For the arms of the wicked shall be broken: but the LORD upholdeth the righteous.

18 The LORD knoweth the days of the upright: and their *a*inheritance shall be for ever.

19 They shall not be ashamed in the evil time: and in the days of *a*famine they shall be satisfied.

20 But the wicked shall perish, and the enemies of the LORD *shall be* as the fat of lambs: they shall consume; into smoke shall they consume away.

21 The wicked *a*borroweth, and payeth not again: but the righteous sheweth mercy, and giveth.

22 For *such as be* blessed of him shall inherit the *a*earth; and *they that be* *b*cursed of him shall be cut off.

23 The steps of a *good* man are ordered by the LORD: and he delighteth in his way.

24 Though he fall, he shall not be utterly cast down: for the LORD upholdeth *him with* his hand.

25 I have been young, and *now* am old; yet have I not seen the *a*righteous forsaken, nor his seed begging bread.

26 *He is* ever merciful, and lendeth; and his seed *is* blessed.

27 Depart from evil, and do good; and dwell for evermore.

28 For the LORD loveth *a*judgment, and forsaketh not his saints; they are preserved for ever: but the *b*seed of the wicked shall be cut off.

29 The righteous shall inherit the land, and dwell therein for ever.

30 The mouth of the *a*righteous

3*a* TG Trust in God.
4*a* Enos 1:12; Alma 29:4.
5*a* TG Commitment;
      Dedication.
   b Alma 37:36 (35–37).
6*a* Jer. 51:10.
7*a* TG Patience.
8*a* TG Self-Mastery.
   b TG Anger.
9*a* TG Death, Spiritual,
      First.

b TG Earth, Destiny of.
10*a* Job 24:24.
11*a* TG Meek.
   b TG Earth, Destiny of.
   c TG Joy.
13*a* TG Laughter.
16*a* Prov. 15:16.
   b TG Righteousness.
   c TG Treasure.
18*a* TG Inheritance.
19*a* Ps. 33:19.

21*a* TG Borrow; Debt.
22*a* TG Earth, Destiny of.
   b TG Curse.
25*a* Matt. 10:31 (29–31);
      1 Ne. 17:3 (1–5, 12–14);
      Mosiah 2:41.
28*a* HEB justice.
   b Ps. 21:10 (10–11); 109:13;
      2 Ne. 24:20;
      D&C 121:15 (11–22).
30*a* Prov. 10:11.

speaketh wisdom, and his tongue talketh of judgment.

31 The *a*law of his God *is* in his *b*heart; none of his steps shall slide.

32 The wicked watcheth the righteous, and seeketh to slay him.

33 The Lord will not leave him in his hand, nor condemn him when he is judged.

34 *a*Wait on the Lord, and keep his way, and he shall exalt thee to inherit the land: when the wicked are cut off, thou shalt see *it*.

35 I have seen the wicked in great power, and spreading himself like a green bay tree.

36 Yet he passed away, and, lo, he *was* not: yea, I sought him, but he could not be found.

37 Mark the *a*perfect *man*, and behold the upright: for the end of *that* man *is* *b*peace.

38 But the transgressors shall be destroyed together: the *a*end of the wicked shall be cut off.

39 But the *a*salvation of the righteous *is* of the Lord: *he is* their strength in the time of trouble.

40 And the Lord shall help them, and deliver them: he shall deliver them from the wicked, and save them, because they trust in him.

PSALM 38

David sorrows for his sins—They rest as a disease upon him—He asks the Lord to be compassionate.

A Psalm of David, to bring to remembrance.

O Lord, rebuke me not in thy wrath: neither chasten me in thy hot displeasure.

2 For thine arrows stick fast in me, and thy hand presseth me sore.

3 *There is* no soundness in my flesh because of thine anger; neither *is there any* rest in my bones because of my sin.

4 For mine iniquities are gone over mine head: as an heavy burden they are too heavy for me.

5 My wounds stink *and* are corrupt because of my foolishness.

6 I am troubled; I am bowed down greatly; I go mourning all the day long.

7 For my loins are filled with a loathsome *disease:* and *there is* no soundness in my flesh.

8 I am feeble and sore broken: I *a*have roared by reason of the disquietness of my heart.

9 Lord, all my desire *is* before thee; and my groaning is not hid from thee.

10 My heart panteth, my strength faileth me: as for the light of mine *a*eyes, it also is gone from me.

11 My *a*lovers and my friends stand aloof from my sore; and my kinsmen stand afar off.

12 They also that seek after my life lay snares *for me:* and they that seek my hurt speak mischievous things, and imagine *a*deceits all the day long.

13 But I, as a deaf *man*, heard not; and *I was* as a dumb man *that* openeth not his mouth.

14 Thus I was as a man that heareth not, and in whose mouth *are* no reproofs.

15 For in thee, O Lord, do I hope: thou wilt hear, O Lord my God.

16 For I said, *Hear me*, lest *otherwise* they should rejoice over me: when my foot slippeth, they magnify *themselves* against me.

17 For I *am* ready to halt, and my sorrow *is* continually before me.

18 For I will *a*declare mine iniquity; I will be *b*sorry for my sin.

19 But mine enemies *are* lively, *and* they are strong: and they that hate me wrongfully are multiplied.

20 They also that *a*render evil for good are mine adversaries; because I follow *the thing that* good *is*.

31*a* Ps. 119:11;
    D&C 88:62.
  b TG Heart.
34*a* Ps. 27:14;
    D&C 98:2 (2–3).
37*a* TG Perfection.

  b TG Peace.
38*a* HEB future.
39*a* TG Salvation.
38 8*a* OR groaned.
10*a* Ps. 88:9.
11*a* HEB friends and

    neighbors.
12*a* TG Deceit.
18*a* TG Confession.
  b TG Repent.
20*a* Ps. 35:12.

21 Forsake me not, O Lord: O my God, be not far from me.

22 Make haste to help me, O Lord my salvation.

PSALM 39

David seeks to control his tongue—Man is altogether vanity—He is a stranger and a sojourner on the earth.

To the chief Musician, *even* to Jeduthun, A Psalm of David.

I said, I will take heed to my ways, that I sin not with my ^atongue: I will keep my ^bmouth with a bridle, while the wicked is before me.

2 I was dumb with silence, I held my peace, *even* from good; and my sorrow was stirred.

3 My heart was ^ahot within me, while I was musing the fire burned: *then* spake I with my tongue,

4 Lord, make me to know mine end, and the ^ameasure of my days, what it *is; that* I may know how frail I *am.*

5 Behold, thou hast made my days *as* an handbreadth; and mine age *is* as nothing before thee: verily every man at his best state *is* altogether ^avanity. Selah.

6 Surely every man walketh in a vain shew: surely they are disquieted in vain: he heapeth up ^ariches, and knoweth not who shall gather them.

7 And now, Lord, what wait I for? my hope *is* in thee.

8 ^aDeliver me from all my ^btransgressions: make me not the reproach of the foolish.

9 I was dumb, I opened not my mouth; because thou didst *it.*

10 Remove thy stroke away from me: I am consumed by the blow of thine hand.

11 When thou with rebukes dost ^acorrect man for iniquity, thou makest his beauty to consume away like a moth: surely every man *is* ^bvanity. Selah.

12 Hear my prayer, O Lord, and give ear unto my cry; hold not thy peace at my tears: for I *am* a ^astranger with thee, *and* a ^bsojourner, as all my fathers *were.*

13 O spare me, that I may recover strength, before I go hence, and be no more.

PSALM 40

A messianic psalm of David—The Messiah will come and preach righteousness— He will declare salvation—The righteous will say, The Lord be magnified.

To the chief Musician, A Psalm of David.

I ^awaited patiently for the Lord; and he inclined unto me, and heard my cry.

2 He brought me up also out of an horrible pit, out of the miry clay, and set my feet upon a ^arock, *and* established my goings.

3 And he hath put a ^anew ^bsong in my mouth, *even* praise unto our God: many shall see *it,* and fear, and shall trust in the Lord.

4 Blessed *is* that man that maketh the Lord his trust, and respecteth not the proud, nor such as turn aside to lies.

5 Many, O Lord my God, *are* thy wonderful ^aworks *which* thou hast done, and thy thoughts *which are* to us-ward: they cannot be reckoned up in order unto thee: *if* I would declare and speak *of them,* they are more than can be numbered.

6 Sacrifice and offering thou didst not ^adesire; mine ears hast thou opened: burnt offering and sin offering hast thou not required.

7 Then said I, Lo, I come: in the volume of the book *it is* written of me,

8 I delight to ^ado thy ^bwill, O my

---

39 1*a* James 3:2 (1–13).
  b Ps. 141:3.
  3*a* Jer. 20:9.
  4*a* Ps. 119:84.
  5*a* Isa. 40:15; Dan. 4:35.
  6*a* TG Treasure.
  8*a* TG Deliver.
  b TG Transgress.

11*a* OR chasten.
  b TG Vanity.
  12*a* TG Stranger.
  b Gen. 26:3.
40 1*a* Ps. 130:5;
    D&C 98:2 (2–3).
  2*a* Ps. 27:5.
  3*a* Ps. 33:3.

  b TG Singing.
  5*a* Ps. 92:5;
    Morm. 9:16 (16–20);
    D&C 76:114;
    Moses 1:4 (3–5).
  6*a* 1 Sam. 15:22.
  8*a* TG Objectives.
  b TG God, Will of.

God: yea, thy law *is* within my heart.

9 I have preached righteousness in the great congregation: lo, I have not refrained my lips, O LORD, thou knowest.

10 I have not hid thy righteousness within my heart; I have declared thy faithfulness and thy salvation: I have not concealed thy lovingkindness and thy truth from the great congregation.

11 Withhold not thou thy tender ^amercies from me, O LORD: let thy lovingkindness and thy truth continually preserve me.

12 For innumerable evils have compassed me about: mine iniquities have taken hold upon me, so that I am not able to look up; they are more than the hairs of mine head: therefore my heart ^afaileth me.

13 Be pleased, O LORD, to deliver me: O LORD, make haste to help me.

14 Let them be ashamed and confounded together that seek after my soul to destroy it; let them be driven backward and put to shame that wish me evil.

15 Let them be desolate for a reward of their ^ashame that say unto me, Aha, aha.

16 Let all those that seek thee rejoice and be glad in thee: let such as love thy salvation say continually, The LORD be magnified.

17 But I *am* poor and needy; *yet* the Lord thinketh upon me: thou *art* my help and my deliverer; ^amake no tarrying, O my God.

PSALM 41

A messianic psalm of David—Blessed is he who considers the poor—The treachery of Judas is foretold.

To the chief Musician, A Psalm of David.

BLESSED *is* he that considereth the ^apoor: the LORD will deliver him in time of trouble.

2 The LORD will ^apreserve him, and keep him alive; *and* he shall be blessed upon the earth: and thou wilt not deliver him unto the will of his enemies.

3 The LORD will strengthen him upon the bed of languishing: thou wilt ^amake all his bed in his ^bsickness.

4 I said, LORD, be merciful unto me: ^aheal my soul; for I have sinned against thee.

5 Mine enemies speak evil of me, When shall he die, and his name perish?

6 And if he come to see *me,* he speaketh vanity: his heart gathereth iniquity to itself; *when* he goeth abroad, he telleth *it.*

7 All that hate me whisper together against me: against me do they devise my hurt.

8 An evil disease, *say they,* cleaveth fast unto him: and *now* that he lieth he shall rise up no more.

9 Yea, mine own familiar ^afriend, in whom I trusted, which did eat of my bread, hath lifted up *his* ^bheel against me.

10 But thou, O LORD, be merciful unto me, and raise me up, that I may requite them.

11 By this I know that thou favourest me, because mine enemy doth not triumph over me.

12 And as for me, thou upholdest me in mine integrity, and settest me before thy face for ever.

13 ^aBlessed *be* the LORD God of Israel from everlasting, and to everlasting. Amen, and Amen.

PSALM 42

The souls of the righteous thirst for God—The wicked say, Where is your God?

To the chief Musician, Maschil, for the sons of Korah.

As the hart panteth after the water brooks, so panteth my soul after thee, O God.

11*a* Ps. 61:7.
12*a* Ps. 73:26.
15*a* TG Shame.
17*a* OR do not delay.
41 1*a* TG Poor.

2*a* Deut. 6:24.
3*a* IE heal all his infirmities when he is sick.
b TG Sickness.
4*a* Mosiah 4:10 (10–11);

D&C 61:2.
9*a* Acts 1:16 (16–17).
b TG Jesus Christ, Betrayal of.
13*a* Ps. 72:18; Alma 26:8.

2 My soul ^athirsteth for God, for the ^bliving God: when shall I come and appear before God?

3 My tears have been my meat day and night, while they continually say unto me, Where *is* thy God?

4 When I remember these *things*, I pour out my soul in me: for I had gone with the multitude, I went with them to the house of God, with the voice of joy and praise, with a multitude that kept holyday.

5 Why art thou cast down, O my soul? and *why* art thou disquieted in me? hope thou in God: for I shall yet praise him *for* the help of his countenance.

6 O my God, my soul is cast down within me: therefore will I remember thee from the land of Jordan, and of the Hermonites, from the hill Mizar.

7 Deep calleth unto deep at the noise of thy waterspouts: all thy waves and thy billows are gone over me.

8 *Yet* the LORD will command his lovingkindness in the daytime, and in the ^anight his song *shall be* with me, *and* my prayer unto the God of my life.

9 I will say unto God my rock, Why hast thou forgotten me? why go I mourning because of the oppression of the enemy?

10 *As* with a sword in my bones, mine enemies reproach me; while they say daily unto me, Where *is* thy God?

11 Why art thou ^acast down, O my soul? and why art thou disquieted within me? ^bhope thou in God: for I shall yet praise him, *who is* the health of my countenance, and my God.

PSALM 43

The righteous praise God and cry, Send out Thy light and Thy truth.

^aJUDGE me, O God, and plead my cause against an ungodly nation: O deliver me from the ^bdeceitful and unjust man.

2 For thou *art* the God of my strength: why dost thou cast me off? why go I ^amourning because of the oppression of the enemy?

3 O send out thy ^alight and thy truth: let them lead me; let them bring me unto thy holy hill, and to thy ^btabernacles.

4 Then will I go unto the altar of God, unto God my exceeding joy: yea, upon the harp will I praise thee, O God my God.

5 Why art thou cast down, O my soul? and why art thou disquieted within me? hope in God: for I shall yet praise him, *who is* the health of my countenance, and my God.

PSALM 44

The Saints praise the Lord and boast in His name forever—They are persecuted, maligned, and considered as sheep for the slaughter.

To the chief Musician
for the sons of Korah, Maschil.

WE have heard with our ears, O God, our ^afathers have ^btold us, *what* work thou didst in their days, in the times of old.

2 *How* thou didst drive out the heathen with thy hand, and plantedst them; *how* thou didst afflict the people, and cast them out.

3 For they got not the ^aland in possession by their own ^bsword, neither did their own arm save them: but thy right hand, and thine arm, and the light of thy countenance,

---

42 2*a* Ps. 63:1; 143:6 (5–12);
    Isa. 55:1 (1–3);
    John 4:14 (13–15);
    7:37 (37–39).
  b Josh. 3:10;
    Hosea 1:10;
    Alma 5:13;

    D&C 20:19.
  8*a* Ps. 63:6.
  11*a* 2 Ne. 4:28 (17–31).
    b TG Hope.
43 1*a* OR Vindicate.
    b TG Deceit.
  2*a* TG Mourning.

  3*a* TG Light [noun].
    b OR dwelling places.
44 1*a* TG Marriage,
    Fatherhood.
    b Deut. 32:7.
  3*a* Deut. 2:36.
    b Josh. 24:12.

because thou hadst a favour unto them.

4 Thou art my *a*King, O God: command deliverances for Jacob.

5 Through thee will we push down our enemies: through thy name will we tread them under that rise up against us.

6 For I will not *a*trust in my bow, neither shall my sword save me.

7 But thou hast saved us from our enemies, and hast put them to shame that hated us.

8 In God we *a*boast all the day long, and praise thy name for ever. Selah.

9 But thou hast cast off, and put us to shame; and goest not forth with our armies.

10 Thou makest us to turn back from the enemy: and they which hate us spoil for themselves.

11 Thou hast given us like sheep *appointed* for meat; and hast *a*scattered us among the heathen.

12 Thou sellest thy people for nought, and dost not increase *thy wealth* by their price.

13 Thou makest us a *a*reproach to our neighbours, a scorn and a *b*derision to them that are round about us.

14 Thou makest us a byword among the heathen, a shaking of the head among the people.

15 My confusion *is* continually before me, and the shame of my face hath covered me,

16 For the voice of him that reproacheth and blasphemeth; by reason of the enemy and avenger.

17 All this is come upon us; yet have we not forgotten thee, neither have we dealt falsely in thy covenant.

18 Our heart is not turned back, neither have our steps declined from thy way;

19 Though thou hast sore broken us in the place of *a*dragons, and covered us with the *b*shadow of death.

20 If we have forgotten the name of our God, or stretched out our hands to a strange god;

21 Shall not God search this out? for he *a*knoweth the secrets of the heart.

22 Yea, for thy sake are we *a*killed all the day long; we are counted as *b*sheep for the slaughter.

23 Awake, why sleepest thou, O Lord? arise, cast *us* not off for ever.

24 Wherefore hidest thou thy face, *and* forgettest our affliction and our oppression?

25 For our soul is bowed down to the *a*dust: our belly cleaveth unto the earth.

26 Arise for our help, and redeem us for thy mercies' sake.

PSALM 45

A messianic psalm—The Messiah is fairer than the children of men—He is anointed with the oil of gladness above His fellows—His name will be remembered in all generations.

To the chief Musician upon Shoshannim, for the sons of Korah, Maschil, A Song of loves.

MY heart is *a*inditing a good matter: I speak of the things which I have made touching the king: my tongue *is* the pen of a ready writer.

2 Thou art fairer than the children of men: *a*grace is poured into thy lips: therefore God hath blessed thee for ever.

3 Gird thy sword upon *thy* thigh, O *most* mighty, with thy *a*glory and thy majesty.

4 And in thy majesty ride prosperously because of truth and meekness *and* *a*righteousness; and thy

---

4*a* Ps. 74:12;
  2 Ne. 10:14;
  Alma 5:50;
  D&C 38:21 (21–22).
6*a* Ps. 33:16 (16–18);
  2 Ne. 4:34; 28:31;
  D&C 1:19 (19–20).
8*a* 2 Ne. 33:6;

Alma 26:16 (10–16);
  D&C 76:61.
11*a* TG Israel, Scattering of.
13*a* TG Reproach.
  b Ezek. 36:4.
19*a* HEB jackals.
  b Job 3:5.
21*a* TG God, Omniscience of.

22*a* Rom. 8:36.
  b TG Sheep.
25*a* Ps. 119:25.
45 1*a* HEB stirred over.
  2*a* Luke 4:22.
  3*a* Ps. 21:5.
  4*a* TG Righteousness.

right hand shall teach thee terrible things.

5 Thine arrows *are* sharp in the heart of the king's enemies; *whereby* the people fall under thee.

6 Thy *a*throne, O God, *is* for ever and ever: the sceptre of thy kingdom *is* a right sceptre.

7 Thou lovest righteousness, and hatest wickedness: therefore God, thy God, hath anointed thee with the oil of *a*gladness above thy fellows.

8 All thy garments *smell* of *a*myrrh, and aloes, *and* cassia, out of the ivory palaces, whereby they have made thee glad.

9 Kings' daughters *were* among thy honourable women: upon thy right hand did stand the queen in gold of Ophir.

10 Hearken, O daughter, and consider, and incline thine ear; *forget* also thine own people, and thy father's house;

11 So shall the king greatly desire thy beauty: for he *is* thy Lord; and worship thou him.

12 And the daughter of Tyre *shall be there* with a gift; *even* the rich among the people shall entreat thy favour.

13 The king's daughter *is* all glorious within: her *a*clothing *is* of wrought gold.

14 She shall be brought unto the king in raiment of needlework: the virgins her companions that follow her shall be brought unto thee.

15 With gladness and rejoicing shall they be brought: they shall enter into the king's palace.

16 Instead of thy fathers shall be thy children, whom thou mayest make princes in all the earth.

17 I will make thy name to be remembered in all generations: therefore shall the people praise thee for ever and ever.

PSALM 46

God is our refuge and strength—He dwells in His city, does marvelous things, and says, Be still and know that I am God.

To the chief Musician for the sons of Korah,
A Song upon Alamoth.

GOD *is* our *a*refuge and strength, a very present help in trouble.

2 Therefore will not we fear, though the earth be removed, and though the mountains be carried into the midst of the sea;

3 *Though* the waters thereof roar *and* be troubled, *though* the mountains shake with the swelling thereof. Selah.

4 *There is* a river, the streams whereof shall make glad the city of God, the holy *place* of the tabernacles of the most High.

5 God *is* in the *a*midst of her; she shall not be moved: God shall help her, *and that* right early.

6 The heathen raged, the kingdoms were moved: he uttered his voice, the earth melted.

7 The *a*LORD of hosts *is* with us; the God of Jacob *is* our refuge. Selah.

8 Come, behold the works of the LORD, what desolations he hath made in the earth.

9 He maketh *a*wars to cease unto the end of the earth; he breaketh the bow, and cutteth the spear in sunder; he burneth the chariot in the fire.

10 Be *a*still, and *b*know that I *am* God: I will be *c*exalted among the heathen, I will be exalted in the earth.

11 The LORD of hosts *is* with us; the God of Jacob *is* our refuge. Selah.

6a TG Kingdom of God, in Heaven.
7a TG Cheerful.
8a John 19:39.
13a TG Apparel.

46 1a TG Refuge.
5a Deut. 23:14;
  Isa. 12:6.
7a Isa. 8:10 (8, 10).
9a TG Peace.

10a TG Silence.
  b Job 37:14;
    D&C 101:16.
  c Isa. 2:11 (11, 17).

PSALM 47

The Lord is King over all the earth—
Sing praises to His name, for He reigns
over all.

To the chief Musician,
A Psalm for the sons of Korah.

O CLAP your hands, all ye people; shout unto God with the voice of triumph.

2 For the LORD most high *is* ^aterrible; *he is* a great King over all the earth.

3 He shall ^asubdue the people under us, and the nations under our feet.

4 He shall choose our inheritance for us, the excellency of Jacob whom he loved. Selah.

5 God is gone up with a shout, the LORD with the sound of a trumpet.

6 Sing praises to God, sing praises: sing praises unto our King, sing praises.

7 For God *is* the ^aKing of all the earth: sing ye praises with understanding.

8 God reigneth over the ^aheathen: God ^bsitteth upon the ^cthrone of his holiness.

9 The princes of the people are gathered together, *even* the people of the God of Abraham: for the ^ashields of the earth *belong* unto God: he is greatly exalted.

PSALM 48

Zion, the city of God, the joy of the
whole earth, will be established forever.

A Song *and* Psalm for the sons of Korah.

GREAT *is* the LORD, and greatly to be praised in the city of our God, in ^athe ^bmountain of his ^choliness.

2 ^aBeautiful for situation, the ^bjoy of the whole earth, *is* mount ^cZion, *on* the sides of the ^dnorth, the ^ecity of the great King.

3 God is known in her palaces for a refuge.

4 For, lo, the kings were assembled, they passed by together.

5 They saw *it, and* so they marvelled; they were troubled, *and* hasted away.

6 Fear took hold upon them there, *and* pain, as of a ^awoman in travail.

7 Thou breakest the ^aships of Tarshish with an east wind.

8 As we have heard, so have we seen in the city of the LORD of hosts, in the city of our God: God will establish it for ever. Selah.

9 We have thought of thy lovingkindness, O God, in the midst of thy temple.

10 According to thy ^aname, O God, so *is* thy praise unto the ends of the earth: thy right hand is full of righteousness.

11 Let mount Zion rejoice, let the ^adaughters of Judah be glad, because of thy judgments.

12 Walk about Zion, and go round about her: tell the towers thereof.

13 Mark ye well her bulwarks, consider her palaces; that ye may tell *it* to the ^ageneration following.

14 For this God *is* our God for ^aever and ever: he will be our guide *even* unto death.

---

47 2*a* Deut. 7:21;
     D&C 1:9 (9–10).
   3*a* Ps. 18:47.
   7*a* Zech. 14:9.
   8*a* HEB nations, Gentiles.
     b Rev. 7:15;
     D&C 88:13.
     c TG Kingdom of God, in
     Heaven.
   9*a* Ps. 89:18.
48 1*a* OR His holy mountain.

     b Isa. 2:3 (2–5).
     c Ps. 2:6.
   2*a* TG Beauty.
     b Lam. 2:15;
     Ezek. 20:6.
     c TG Zion.
     d There was in various
     lands a concept that the
     dwelling place of Deity
     was in the "north."
     Isa. 14:13.

     e Matt. 5:35.
   6*a* TG Woman.
   7*a* Isa. 2:16;
     Ezek. 27:25.
  10*a* Deut. 28:58.
  11*a* Ps. 97:8.
  13*a* Ps. 102:18.
  14*a* D&C 20:12;
     Abr. 1:19.

PSALM 49

Men cannot be ransomed or redeemed by wealth—God alone can redeem a soul from the grave—The glory of a rich man ceases with his death.

To the chief Musician,
A Psalm for the sons of Korah.

HEAR this, all *ye* people; give *a*ear, all *ye* inhabitants of the world:

2 Both low and high, rich and poor, together.

3 My mouth shall speak of wisdom; and the meditation of my heart *shall be* of understanding.

4 I will incline mine ear to a parable: I will *a*open my dark saying upon the harp.

5 Wherefore should I fear in the days of evil, *when* the iniquity of my *a*heels shall compass me about?

6 They that trust in their *a*wealth, and boast themselves in the multitude of their riches;

7 None *of them* can by any means redeem his brother, nor give to God a ransom for him:

8 (For the redemption of their *a*soul *is* precious, and it ceaseth for ever:)

9 That he should still *a*live for ever, *and* not see corruption.

10 For he seeth *that* wise men *a*die, likewise the fool and the brutish person perish, and leave their wealth to others.

11 Their inward thought *is, that* their houses *shall continue* for ever, *and* their dwelling places to all generations; they call *their* lands after their own *a*names.

12 Nevertheless man *being* in honour abideth not: he is like the beasts *that* perish.

13 This their way *is* their folly: yet their posterity approve their sayings. Selah.

14 Like sheep they are laid in the grave; death shall feed on them; and the upright shall have *a*dominion over them in the morning; and their beauty shall consume in the grave from their dwelling.

15 But God will *a*redeem my soul from the power of the grave: for he shall *b*receive me. Selah.

16 Be not thou afraid when one is made rich, when the glory of his house is increased;

17 For when he dieth he shall carry nothing away: his glory shall not descend after him.

18 Though while he lived he *a*blessed his soul: and *men* will praise thee, when thou doest well to thyself.

19 He shall go to the generation of his fathers; they shall never see light.

20 Man *that is* in honour, and understandeth not, is like the beasts *that* perish.

PSALM 50

Asaph speaks of the Second Coming— The Lord accepts the sacrifices of the righteous and will deliver them—Those whose conduct is right will see the salvation of God.

A Psalm of Asaph.

THE mighty God, *even* the LORD, hath spoken, and called the earth from the rising of the sun unto the going down thereof.

2 Out of Zion, the *a*perfection of *b*beauty, God hath *c*shined.

3 Our God shall come, and shall not keep silence: a *a*fire shall devour before him, and it shall be very tempestuous round about him.

4 He shall call to the *a*heavens from above, and to the earth, that he may *b*judge his people.

5 Gather my *a*saints together unto

---

49 1*a* Ps. 78:1.
    4*a* TG Problem-Solving.
    5*a* IE persecutors.
    6*a* TG Treasure.
    8*a* TG Worth of Souls.
    9*a* Ps. 89:48.
    10*a* Eccl. 2:16.
    11*a* Gen. 4:17.

14*a* Mal. 4:3 (2–3);
    Rev. 2:26.
15*a* Hosea 13:14;
    Mosiah 27:24 (24–26);
    D&C 93:38;
    Moses 5:9;
    A of F 1:3.
    b TG Eternal Life.

18*a* Deut. 29:19 (18–20).
50 2*a* Lam. 2:15.
    b TG Beauty.
    c Deut. 33:2.
    3*a* TG World, End of.
    4*a* Deut. 4:26.
    b TG Judgment, the Last.
    5*a* TG Saints.

me; those that have made a [b]cov-
enant with me by [c]sacrifice.

6 And the heavens shall [a]declare
his [b]righteousness: for God is [c]judge
himself. Selah.

7 Hear, O my people, and I will
speak; O Israel, and I will testify
against thee: I am [a]God, even thy
God.

8 I will not reprove thee for thy
sacrifices or thy burnt offerings,
to have been continually before me.

9 I will take no bullock out of thy
house, nor he goats out of thy folds.

10 For every beast of the forest is
mine, and the cattle upon a thousand hills.

11 I know all the fowls of the
mountains: and the wild beasts of
the field are mine.

12 If I were hungry, I would not
tell thee: for the [a]world is mine, and
the fulness thereof.

13 Will I eat the flesh of bulls, or
drink the blood of goats?

14 Offer unto God [a]thanksgiving;
and pay thy [b]vows unto the most
High:

15 And [a]call upon me in the day
of [b]trouble: I will deliver thee, and
thou shalt glorify me.

16 But unto the wicked God saith,
[a]What hast thou to do to declare my
statutes, or that thou shouldest take
my covenant in thy mouth?

17 Seeing thou hatest instruction,
and castest my words behind thee.

18 When thou sawest a thief, then
thou consentedst with him, and
hast been partaker with adulterers.

19 Thou givest thy mouth to evil,
and thy tongue frameth [a]deceit.

20 Thou sittest and speakest against
thy brother; thou [a]slanderest thine
own mother's son.

21 These things hast thou done,
and I kept silence; thou thoughtest
that I was altogether such an one as
thyself: but I will reprove thee, [a]and
set them in order before thine eyes.

22 Now consider this, ye that [a]for-
get God, lest I tear you in pieces, and
there be none to deliver.

23 Whoso offereth [a]praise glorifi-
eth me: and to him that ordereth
his conversation aright will I shew
the salvation of God.

PSALM 51

David pleads for forgiveness after he
went in to Bathsheba—He pleads, Create in me a clean heart, and renew a
right spirit within me.

To the chief Musician, A Psalm of David,
when Nathan the prophet came unto him,
after he had gone in to Bath-sheba.

HAVE [a]mercy upon me, O God, according to thy [b]lovingkindness:
according unto the multitude of
thy tender mercies [c]blot out my
[d]transgressions.

2 Wash me throughly from mine
iniquity, and [a]cleanse me from
my sin.

3 For I [a]acknowledge my transgressions: and my [b]sin is ever before me.

4 Against thee, thee only, have I
[a]sinned, and done this evil in thy
sight: that thou mightest be [b]jus-
tified when thou speakest, and be
clear when thou judgest.

5 Behold, I was shapen in iniquity; and in sin did my mother
[a]conceive me.

6 Behold, thou desirest truth in
the inward parts: and in the hidden
part thou shalt make me to know
wisdom.

5b TG Covenants.
  c TG Sacrifice.
6a Ps. 19:1; 97:6.
  b 2 Ne. 21:4;
    Mosiah 29:12.
  c TG Jesus Christ, Judge.
7a Ex. 20:2.
12a TG God, Works of;
    Stewardship.
14a TG Thanksgiving.
  b TG Vow.

15a Alma 38:5 (4–5);
    D&C 100:17.
  b Ps. 81:7.
16a OR What authority
    have you.
19a TG Deceit.
20a TG Slander.
21a JST Ps. 50:21 . . . and set
    covenants in order . . .
22a Ps. 9:17.
23a Ps. 61:8.

51 1a Ps. 25:7.
    b TG Kindness.
    c Acts 3:19.
    d TG Sin.
  2a Mosiah 26:29 (29–30).
    TG Purification.
  3a TG Confession.
    b TG Sin.
  4a 2 Sam. 12:13 (9–14).
    b Rom. 3:4; D&C 97:2.
  5a TG Conceived in Sin.

7 Purge me with ^ahyssop, and I shall be clean: wash me, and I shall be whiter than snow.

8 Make me to hear joy and gladness; *that* the bones *which* thou hast broken may rejoice.

9 Hide thy face from my sins, and blot out all mine iniquities.

10 Create in me a ^aclean heart, O God; and ^brenew a right spirit within me.

11 Cast me not away from thy ^apresence; and take not thy ^bholy spirit from me.

12 Restore unto me the joy of thy salvation; and uphold me *with thy* free spirit.

13 *Then* will I teach transgressors thy ways; and sinners shall be ^aconverted unto thee.

14 ^aDeliver me from bloodguiltiness, O God, thou God of my salvation: *and* my tongue shall sing aloud of thy righteousness.

15 O Lord, open thou my lips; and my mouth shall shew forth thy praise.

16 For thou desirest not ^asacrifice; else would I give *it:* thou delightest not in burnt offering.

17 The ^asacrifices of God *are* a broken spirit: a broken and a ^bcontrite heart, O God, thou wilt not despise.

18 Do good in thy good ^apleasure unto Zion: build thou the walls of Jerusalem.

19 Then shalt thou be pleased with the sacrifices of righteousness, with burnt offering and whole burnt offering: then shall they offer bullocks upon thine altar.

PSALM 52

David says that wicked tongues devise mischief and the wicked trust in riches—The Saints trust in the mercy of God forever.

To the chief Musician, Maschil, A *Psalm* of David, when Doeg the Edomite came and told Saul, and said unto him, David is come to the house of Ahimelech.

WHY boastest thou thyself in mischief, O mighty man? the goodness of God *endureth* continually.

2 Thy ^atongue deviseth mischiefs; like a sharp razor, working deceitfully.

3 Thou lovest evil more than good; *and* lying rather than to speak righteousness. Selah.

4 Thou lovest all devouring words, O *thou* deceitful tongue.

5 God shall likewise destroy thee for ever, he shall take thee away, and ^apluck thee out of *thy* dwelling place, and root thee out of the land of the living. Selah.

6 The righteous also shall see, and fear, and shall ^alaugh at him:

7 Lo, *this is* the man *that* made not God his strength; but trusted in the abundance of his riches, *and* strengthened himself in his wickedness.

8 But I *am* like a ^agreen olive tree in the house of God: I trust in the mercy of God for ever and ever.

9 I will praise thee for ever, because thou hast done *it:* and I will wait on thy name; for *it is* good before thy saints.

PSALM 53

David says, The fool says there is no God—There is none who does good—Gathered Israel will rejoice.

To the chief Musician upon Mahalath, Maschil, A *Psalm* of David.

THE ^afool hath said in his heart, *There is* no God. Corrupt are they, and have done abominable iniquity: *there is* ^bnone that doeth good.

2 God looked down from heaven

7*a* Num. 19:18.
10*a* TG Cleanliness;
      Purification; Repent.
   b Lam. 5:21.
11*a* TG Death, Spiritual,
      First.
   b TG Holy Ghost, Loss of.
13*a* TG Conversion.

14*a* TG Deliver.
16*a* 1 Sam. 15:22.
17*a* Hosea 14:2 (1–3);
      3 Ne. 9:20 (19–20).
   b TG Contrite Heart.
18*a* TG Pleasure.
52 2*a* Ps. 57:4;
        2 Ne. 13:8.

5*a* Prov. 2:22;
     Mosiah 16:2;
     D&C 63:54.
6*a* TG Laughter.
8*a* Ps. 92:12 (12–13);
     Jer. 11:16; D&C 35:24.
53 1*a* Ps. 14:1 (1–7).
       b Rom. 3:10 (10–12).

upon the children of men, to see if there were *any* that did understand, that did seek God.

3 Every one of them is gone back: they are altogether become filthy; *there is* none that doeth good, no, not one.

4 Have the workers of iniquity no knowledge? who eat up my people *as* they eat bread: they have not called upon God.

5 There were they in great fear, *where* no fear was: for God hath *a*scattered the bones of him that encampeth *against* thee: thou hast put *them* to shame, because God hath *b*despised them.

6 Oh that the salvation of Israel *were come* out of Zion! When God *a*bringeth back the captivity of his people, Jacob shall rejoice, *and* Israel shall be glad.

PSALM 54

David pleads for salvation and promises to serve God.

To the chief Musician on Neginoth, Maschil, A *Psalm* of David, when the Ziphims came and said to Saul, Doth not David hide himself with us?

SAVE me, O God, by thy name, and judge me by thy strength.

2 Hear my prayer, O God; give ear to the words of my mouth.

3 For *a*strangers are risen up against me, and oppressors seek after my soul: they have not set God before them. Selah.

4 Behold, *a*God *is* mine helper: the Lord *is* with them that uphold my soul.

5 He shall reward evil unto mine enemies: cut them off in thy truth.

6 I will freely sacrifice unto thee: I will praise thy name, O LORD; for *it is* good.

7 For he hath *a*delivered me out of all trouble: and mine eye hath seen *his* *b*desire upon mine enemies.

PSALM 55

David prays morning, noon, and night— He seeks protection and help against his enemies.

To the chief Musician on Neginoth, Maschil, A *Psalm* of David.

GIVE ear to my prayer, O God; and hide not thyself from my supplication.

2 Attend unto me, and hear me: I mourn in my complaint, and *a*make a noise;

3 Because of the voice of the enemy, because of the oppression of the wicked: for they cast iniquity upon me, and in wrath they hate me.

4 My heart is sore *a*pained within me: and the terrors of death are fallen upon me.

5 Fearfulness and trembling are come upon me, and horror hath overwhelmed me.

6 And I said, Oh that I had wings like a dove! *for then* would I fly away, and be at rest.

7 Lo, *then* would I wander far off, *and* remain in the wilderness. Selah.

8 I would hasten my escape from the windy storm *and* tempest.

9 Destroy, O Lord, *and* divide their tongues: for I have seen violence and *a*strife in the city.

10 Day and night they go about it upon the walls thereof: mischief also and sorrow *are* in the midst of it.

11 Wickedness *is* in the midst thereof: deceit and *a*guile depart not from her streets.

12 For *it was* not an enemy *that* reproached me; then I could have borne *it:* neither *was it* he that hated me *that* did magnify *himself* against me; then I would have hid myself from him:

13 But *it was* thou, a man mine equal, my guide, and mine acquaintance.

5*a* Lev. 26:17.
  b OR rejected.
6*a* OR delivers His people
  from captivity.
54 3*a* Ps. 86:14.

4*a* Ps. 118:7.
7*a* TG Deliver.
  b Ps. 118:7.
55 2*a* OR moan.
4*a* TG Pain.

9*a* TG Strife.
11*a* TG Guile;
  Sincere.

14 We took sweet counsel together, *and* walked unto the house of God in *a*company.

15 Let death seize upon them, *and* let them go down quick into *a*hell: for wickedness *is* in their dwellings, *and* among them.

16 As for me, I will call upon God; and the Lord shall save me.

17 Evening, and morning, and at noon, will I *a*pray, and cry aloud: and he shall *b*hear my voice.

18 He hath delivered my soul in peace from the battle *that was* against me: for there were many with me.

19 God shall hear, and *a*afflict them, even he that abideth of old. Selah. Because they have no *b*changes, therefore they fear not God.

20 He hath put forth his hands against such as be at peace with him: he hath broken his covenant.

21 *The words* of his mouth were smoother than butter, but war *was* in his heart: his words were softer than oil, yet *were* they drawn swords.

22 *a*Cast thy burden upon the Lord, and he shall sustain thee: he shall never suffer the *b*righteous to be moved.

23 But thou, O God, shalt bring them down into the pit of destruction: bloody and deceitful men shall not live out half their days; but I will trust in thee.

PSALM 56

David seeks mercy, trusts in and praises the Lord, and thanks Him for deliverance.

To the chief Musician upon Jonath-elem-rechokim, Michtam of David, when the Philistines took him in Gath.

BE merciful unto me, O God: for man would *a*swallow me up; he fighting daily oppresseth me.

2 Mine enemies would daily swallow *me* up: for *they be* many that fight against me, O thou most High.

3 What time I am afraid, I will *a*trust in thee.

4 In God I will praise his word, in God I have put my *a*trust; I will not *b*fear what flesh can do unto me.

5 Every day they wrest my words: all their thoughts *are* against me for evil.

6 They gather themselves together, they hide themselves, they mark my steps, when they *a*wait for my soul.

7 Shall they escape by iniquity? in *thine* anger cast down the people, O God.

8 Thou tellest my wanderings: put thou my tears into thy bottle: *are they* not in thy *a*book?

9 When I cry *unto thee*, then shall mine enemies turn back: this I know; for God *is* for me.

10 In God will I praise *his* word: in the Lord will I praise *his* word.

11 In God have I put my trust: I will not be afraid what man can do unto me.

12 Thy *a*vows *are* upon me, O God: I will render praises unto thee.

13 For thou hast delivered my *a*soul from death: *wilt* not *thou deliver* my feet from falling, that I may *b*walk before God in the light of the living?

PSALM 57

David pleads for mercy and acclaims the glory and exaltation of God.

To the chief Musician, Al-taschith, Michtam of David, when he fled from Saul in the cave.

BE merciful unto me, O God, be merciful unto me: for my soul

14*a* OR fellowship.
15*a* Num. 16:30.
17*a* TG Prayer.
  b Ps. 13:3.
19*a* OR humble.
  b Job 10:17.
22*a* Prov. 16:3;
    Matt. 6:25; 11:28 (28–30);

Philip. 4:6.
  b 1 Ne. 17:35 (33–38);
    22:17.
56 1*a* Ps. 124:3.
  3*a* 1 Sam. 30:6.
  4*a* TG Trust in God.
  b Ps. 118:6;
    Isa. 51:12;

2 Ne. 8:7 (7, 12);
    D&C 122:9.
6*a* OR hope to take my life.
8*a* TG Book of
    Remembrance.
12*a* TG Vow.
13*a* Ps. 116:8.
  b TG Walking with God.

trusteth in thee: yea, in the shadow of thy *a*wings will I make my refuge, until *these* calamities be overpast.

2 I will cry unto God most high; unto God that performeth *all things* for me.

3 He shall send from heaven, and save me *from* the reproach of him that would swallow me up. Selah. God shall send forth his mercy and his truth.

4 My soul *is* among lions: *and* I lie *even among* them that are set on fire, *even* the sons of men, whose *a*teeth *are* spears and arrows, and their *b*tongue a sharp *c*sword.

5 Be thou exalted, O God, above the heavens; *let* thy glory *be* above all the earth.

6 They have prepared a *a*net for my steps; my soul is bowed down: they have *b*digged a *c*pit before me, into the midst whereof they are fallen *themselves*. Selah.

7 My heart is *a*fixed, O God, my heart is fixed: I will *b*sing and give praise.

8 Awake up, my glory; awake, psaltery and harp: I *myself* will awake early.

9 I will praise thee, O Lord, among the people: I will sing unto thee among the nations.

10 For thy mercy *is* great unto the heavens, and thy truth unto the clouds.

11 Be thou exalted, O God, above the heavens: *let* thy glory *be* above all the earth.

PSALM 58

David reproves wicked judges—They go astray and speak lies.

To the chief Musician, Al-taschith, Michtam of David.

Do ye indeed speak righteousness, O congregation? do ye *a*judge up-rightly, O ye sons of men?

2 Yea, in heart ye work wicked-ness; ye weigh the violence of your hands in the earth.

3 The wicked are estranged from the *a*womb: they go *b*astray as soon as they be born, speaking lies.

4 Their poison *is* like the poison of a serpent: *they are* like the deaf adder *that* stoppeth her ear;

5 Which will not hearken to the voice of charmers, charming never so wisely.

6 Break their teeth, O God, in their mouth: break out the great *a*teeth of the young lions, O LORD.

7 Let them melt away as waters *which* run continually: *when* he bendeth *his bow to shoot* his arrows, let them be as cut in pieces.

8 As a snail *which* melteth, let *every one of them* pass away: *like* the un-timely birth of a woman, *that* they may not see the sun.

9 Before your pots can feel the thorns, he shall take them away as with a whirlwind, both living, and in *his* wrath.

10 The righteous shall rejoice when he seeth the vengeance: he shall wash his feet in the *a*blood of the wicked.

11 So that a man shall say, Verily *there is* a *a*reward for the righteous: verily he is a God that *b*judgeth in the earth.

PSALM 59

David prays to be delivered from his enemies—God rules in Jacob unto the ends of the earth.

To the chief Musician, Al-taschith, Michtam of David; when Saul sent, and they watched the house to kill him.

DELIVER me from mine enemies, O my God: defend me from them that rise up against me.

2 *a*Deliver me from the workers of iniquity, and save me from *b*bloody men.

---

57 1*a* Ruth 2:12.
  4*a* Prov. 30:14.
    b Ps. 52:2; 64:3.
    c Ps. 59:7; Prov. 25:18.
  6*a* Ps. 9:15 (15–16).
    b Ps. 119:85.
    c 1 Ne. 14:3.

  7*a* OR steadfast.
    b Ps. 108:1 (1–5);
      2 Ne. 22:5 (5–6);
      Alma 26:8;
      D&C 136:28.
58 1*a* Mosiah 29:11.
  3*a* Isa. 48:8.

    b TG Conceived in Sin.
  6*a* Job 4:10.
  10*a* Ps. 68:23.
  11*a* TG Reward.
    b TG Jesus Christ, Judge.
59 2*a* D&C 10:5.
    b OR bloodthirsty.

3 For, lo, they lie in wait for my soul: the mighty are gathered against me; not *for* my transgression, nor *for* my sin, O Lord.

4 They run and prepare themselves *ª*without *my* fault: *ᵇ*awake to help me, and behold.

5 Thou therefore, O Lord God of hosts, the God of Israel, awake to visit all the heathen: be not merciful to any wicked transgressors. Selah.

6 They return at evening: they make a noise like a dog, and go round about the city.

7 Behold, they belch out with their mouth: *ª*swords *are* in their lips: for who, *say they,* doth hear?

8 But thou, O Lord, shalt laugh at them; thou shalt have all the heathen in derision.

9 *Because of* his strength will I wait upon thee: for God *is* my defence.

10 *ª*The God of my mercy shall prevent me: God shall let me see *my desire* upon mine enemies.

11 Slay them not, lest my people forget: scatter them by thy power; and bring them down, O Lord our shield.

12 *For* the sin of their mouth *and* the words of their lips let them even be taken in their pride: and for cursing and lying *which* they speak.

13 Consume *them* in wrath, consume *them,* that they *may* not *be:* and let them know that God ruleth in Jacob unto the ends of the earth. Selah.

14 And at evening let them return; *and* let them make a noise like a dog, and go round about the city.

15 Let them wander up and down for meat, and grudge if they be not satisfied.

16 But I will sing of thy power; yea, I will sing aloud of thy mercy in the morning: for thou hast been my defence and refuge in the day of my *ª*trouble.

17 Unto thee, O my strength, will I sing: for God *is* my defence, *and* the God of my mercy.

PSALM 60

David says that the Lord has scattered His people—The Lord places Ephraim at the head and makes Judah His lawgiver.

To the chief Musician upon Shushaneduth, Michtam of David, to teach; when he strove with Aram-naharaim and with Aramzobah, when Joab returned, and smote of Edom in the valley of salt twelve thousand.

O God, thou hast cast us off, thou hast *ª*scattered us, thou hast been displeased; O turn thyself to us again.

2 Thou hast made the earth to tremble; thou hast broken it: heal the breaches thereof; for it shaketh.

3 Thou hast shewed thy people hard things: thou hast made us to drink the wine of *ª*astonishment.

4 Thou hast given a *ª*banner to them that fear thee, that it may be displayed because of the truth. Selah.

5 That thy *ª*beloved may be *ᵇ*delivered; save *with* thy right hand, and hear me.

6 God hath spoken in his holiness; I will rejoice, I will divide Shechem, and mete out the valley of *ª*Succoth.

7 Gilead *is* mine, and Manasseh *is* mine; Ephraim also *is* the strength of mine head; Judah *is* my *ª*lawgiver;

8 Moab *is* my washpot; over *ª*Edom will I cast out my shoe: *ᵇ*Philistia, triumph thou because of me.

4*a* OR for no guilt of mine.
   b Ps. 35:23.
   7*a* Ps. 57:4.
  10*a* HEB My God, in His loving kindness, shall go before me.
  16*a* TG Adversity.

60 1*a* 1 Ne. 10:14;
      2 Ne. 25:15 (14–18);
      D&C 101:13.
   3*a* HEB staggering.
   4*a* 2 Ne. 29:2.
   5*a* IE beloved people.
    b Ps. 108:6 (6–13).

6*a* Gen. 33:17.
7*a* Gen. 49:10.
8*a* 2 Sam. 8:14.
 b OR over Philistia will I triumph. See Ps. 108:9.

9 Who will bring me *into* the strong city? who will lead me into Edom?

10 *Wilt* not thou, O God, *which* hadst cast us off? and *thou*, O God, *which* didst not go out with our armies?

11 Give us help from trouble: for vain *is* the help of man.

12 Through God we shall do valiantly: for he *it is that* shall tread down our enemies.

PSALM 61

David finds shelter in the Lord, abides in the Lord's presence, and keeps his own vows.

To the chief Musician upon Neginah,
A *Psalm* of David.

HEAR my cry, O God; attend unto my prayer.

2 From the end of the earth will I cry unto thee, when my heart is overwhelmed: lead me to the *rock *that* is higher than I.

3 For thou hast been a shelter for me, *and* a strong *tower from the enemy.

4 I will abide in thy tabernacle for ever: I will trust in the covert of thy wings. Selah.

5 For thou, O God, hast heard my *vows: thou hast given *me* the heritage of those that fear thy name.

6 Thou wilt prolong the king's life: *and* his years as many generations.

7 He shall abide before God for ever: O prepare *mercy and truth, *which* may preserve him.

8 So will I sing *praise unto thy name for ever, that I may daily perform my vows.

PSALM 62

David praises God as his defense, his rock, and his salvation—The Lord judges men according to their works.

To the chief Musician, to Jeduthun,
A Psalm of David.

TRULY my soul waiteth upon God: from him *cometh* my salvation.

2 He only *is* my rock and my *salvation; *he is* my defence; I shall not be greatly moved.

3 How long will ye imagine mischief against a man? ye shall be slain all of you: as a bowing wall *shall ye be, and as* a tottering fence.

4 They only consult to cast *him* down from his excellency: they delight in lies: they bless with their mouth, but they *curse inwardly. Selah.

5 My soul, wait thou only upon God; for my expectation *is* from him.

6 He only *is* my *rock and my salvation: *he is* my defence; I shall not be moved.

7 In God *is* my salvation and my *glory: the rock of my strength, *and* my *refuge, *is* in God.

8 *Trust in him at all times; ye people, pour out your heart before him: God *is* a refuge for us. Selah.

9 Surely men of low degree *are* vanity, *and* men of high degree *are* a lie: to be laid in the balance, they *are* altogether *lighter* than *vanity.

10 Trust not in *oppression, and become not vain in robbery: if *riches increase, set not your *heart *upon them.

11 God hath spoken once; twice have I heard this; that power *belongeth* unto God.

12 Also unto thee, O Lord, *belongeth* *mercy: for thou renderest to every man according to his *work.

---

61 2a TG Rock.
  3a Prov. 18:10.
  5a TG Vow.
  7a Ps. 40:11.
  8a Ps. 50:23.
62 2a TG Salvation.
  4a TG Curse.
  6a TG Rock.

7a TG Glory.
  b TG Refuge.
8a TG Trust in God.
9a TG Vanity.
10a OR extortion.
  b Job 31:25;
    Luke 12:15;
    Alma 5:53 (53–56);

Hel. 12:2 (1–5);
    D&C 56:16 (16–18).
  c Jacob 2:19 (18–19).
12a Ps. 86:15.
  b TG Good Works;
    Justice.

PSALM 63

David thirsts for God, whom he praises with joyful lips.

A Psalm of David, when he was
in the wilderness of Judah.

O GOD, thou *art* my God; [a]early will I seek thee: my soul [b]thirsteth for thee, my flesh longeth for thee in a dry and [c]thirsty land, where no water is;

2 To see thy power and thy glory, so *as* I have seen thee in the sanctuary.

3 Because thy lovingkindness *is* [a]better than life, my lips shall praise thee.

4 Thus will I bless thee while I live: I will lift up my [a]hands in thy name.

5 My soul shall be satisfied as *with* marrow and fatness; and my mouth shall praise *thee* with joyful lips:

6 When I remember thee upon my [a]bed, *and* [b]meditate on thee in the *night* watches.

7 Because thou hast been my help, therefore in the shadow of thy wings will I rejoice.

8 My soul followeth hard after thee: thy right hand upholdeth me.

9 But those *that* seek my soul, to destroy *it*, shall go into the lower parts of the earth.

10 They shall fall by the sword: they shall be a portion for [a]foxes.

11 But the king shall rejoice in God; every one that sweareth by him shall glory: but the mouth of them that speak lies shall be stopped.

PSALM 64

David prays for safety—The righteous will be glad in heart.

To the chief Musician, A Psalm of David.

HEAR my voice, O God, in my prayer:
preserve my life from fear of the enemy.

2 Hide me from the secret counsel of the wicked; from the insurrection of the workers of iniquity:

3 Who whet their [a]tongue like a sword, *and* bend *their bows to shoot* their arrows, *even* [b]bitter words:

4 That they may [a]shoot in secret at the perfect: suddenly do they shoot at him, and fear not.

5 They encourage themselves *in* an evil matter: they commune of laying snares [a]privily; they say, Who shall [b]see them?

6 They search out [a]iniquities; they accomplish a diligent search: both the inward *thought* of every one *of them*, and the heart, *is* deep.

7 But God shall shoot at them *with* an arrow; suddenly shall they be wounded.

8 So they shall make their own tongue to [a]fall upon themselves: all that see them shall [b]flee away.

9 And all men shall fear, and shall declare the [a]work of God; for they shall wisely consider of his doing.

10 The righteous shall be glad in the LORD, and shall [a]trust in him; and all the upright in heart shall glory.

PSALM 65

David speaks of the blessedness of God's chosen—The Lord sends rain and good things upon the earth.

To the chief Musician,
A Psalm *and* Song of David.

PRAISE waiteth for thee, O God, in Sion: and unto thee shall the vow be performed.

2 O thou that hearest prayer, unto thee shall [a]all flesh [b]come.

3 Iniquities prevail against me: *as*

---

63 1*a* Isa. 26:9.
  b Ps. 42:2.
  c Ps. 143:6 (5–12).
  3*a* D&C 25:10 (10, 16).
  4*a* Ps. 119:48; 134:2 (1–3).
  6*a* Ps. 42:8; 119:55; 149:5.
  b TG Meditation.
  10*a* OR jackals.

64 3*a* Ps. 57:4.
  b Jer. 9:3.
  4*a* Ps. 11:2.
  5*a* TG Secret
    Combinations.
  b Alma 37:25;
    D&C 88:108 (108–9).
  6*a* D&C 10:25 (22–28).

  8*a* Prov. 18:7.
  b Ps. 31:11.
  9*a* TG God, Works of.
  10*a* TG Trust in God.
65 2*a* 2 Ne. 2:10;
    D&C 1:2.
  b Ps. 86:9.

for our transgressions, thou shalt ^apurge them away.

4 Blessed *is the man whom* thou choosest, and causest to approach *unto thee, that* he may dwell in thy ^acourts: we shall be satisfied with the goodness of thy house, *even* of thy holy temple.

5 *By* terrible things in righteousness wilt thou answer us, O God of our salvation; *who art* the confidence of all the ends of the earth, and of them that are afar off *upon* the sea:

6 Which by his strength setteth fast the mountains; *being* girded with power:

7 Which ^astilleth the noise of the seas, the noise of their waves, and the tumult of the people.

8 They also that dwell in the uttermost parts are afraid at thy ^atokens: thou makest the outgoings of the morning and evening to rejoice.

9 Thou visitest the earth, and waterest it: thou greatly enrichest it with the river of God, *which* is full of water: thou preparest them ^acorn, when thou hast so provided for it.

10 Thou waterest the ridges thereof abundantly: thou settlest the furrows thereof: thou makest it soft with showers: thou blessest the ^aspringing thereof.

11 Thou crownest the year with thy goodness; and thy paths drop fatness.

12 They drop *upon* the pastures of the wilderness: and the little hills rejoice on every side.

13 The pastures are clothed with flocks; the valleys also are covered over with corn; they shout for joy, they also sing.

PSALM 66

Praise and worship the Lord—He tests and tries men—Sacrifices are to be offered in His house.

To the chief Musician, A Song *or* Psalm.

MAKE a ^ajoyful noise unto God, all ye lands:

2 Sing forth the honour of his name: make his praise glorious.

3 Say unto God, How terrible *art thou in* thy works! through the greatness of thy power shall thine enemies ^asubmit themselves unto thee.

4 All the earth shall ^aworship thee, and shall sing unto thee; they shall sing *to* thy name. Selah.

5 Come and see the works of God: *he is* terrible *in his* doing toward the children of men.

6 He turned the ^asea into dry *land:* they went through the ^bflood on foot: there did we rejoice in him.

7 He ruleth by his power for ever; his eyes behold the nations: let not the rebellious exalt themselves. Selah.

8 O bless our God, ye people, and make the voice of his praise to be heard:

9 Which holdeth our soul in life, and suffereth not our ^afeet to ^bbe moved.

10 For thou, O God, hast ^aproved us: thou hast tried us, as silver is tried.

11 Thou broughtest us into the net; thou laidst ^aaffliction upon our loins.

12 Thou hast caused men to ride over our heads; we went through fire and through ^awater: but thou ^bbroughtest us out into a ^cwealthy *place.*

13 I will go into thy house with burnt offerings: I will pay thee my vows,

---

3*a* D&C 1:32.
4*a* Ps. 27:4;
    Enos 1:27;
    D&C 59:2.
7*a* Ps. 89:9;
    Matt. 8:26 (23–27).
8*a* OR signs.
9*a* HEB grain.
10*a* OR growth.

66 1*a* Ps. 95:1.
3*a* D&C 49:6; 76:61.
4*a* 2 Ne. 21:9;
    D&C 88:104.
6*a* Josh. 3:17 (14–17);
    Ps. 74:15.
    TG Israel,
    Deliverance of.
b HEB river.

9*a* Ps. 121:3.
b OR slip.
10*a* TG Test.
11*a* Lev. 26:21 (14–33);
    Deut. 9:8 (7–29).
12*a* Isa. 43:2.
b Lev. 26:6 (3–13).
c HEB bountiful.

14 Which my lips have uttered, and my mouth hath spoken, when I was in trouble.

15 I will offer unto thee burnt sacrifices of fatlings, with the incense of rams; I will offer bullocks with goats. Selah.

16 Come *and* hear, all ye that fear God, and I will declare what he hath done for my soul.

17 I cried unto him with my mouth, and he was extolled with my tongue.

18 If I regard iniquity in my heart, the Lord will not *a*hear *me:*

19 *But* verily God hath heard *me;* he hath attended to the voice of my prayer.

20 Blessed *be* God, which hath not turned away my prayer, nor his mercy from me.

PSALM 67

A messianic psalm—The Lord will cause His face to shine upon men—He will judge and govern in righteousness.

To the chief Musician on Neginoth, A Psalm *or* Song.

GOD be *a*merciful unto us, and bless us; *and* cause his face to *b*shine upon us; Selah.

2 That thy way may be known upon earth, thy *a*saving health among all nations.

3 Let the people praise thee, O God; let all the people praise thee.

4 O let the nations be glad and sing for joy: for thou shalt judge the people righteously, and govern the nations upon earth. Selah.

5 Let the people praise thee, O God; let all the people praise thee.

6 *Then* shall the *a*earth yield her *b*increase; *and* God, *even* our own God, shall bless us.

7 God shall bless us; and all the ends of the earth shall fear him.

PSALM 68

A messianic psalm of David—He extols JAH—The Lord gave the word—He takes captivity captive—He delivers us from death—Sing praises unto the Lord.

To the chief Musician, A Psalm *or* Song of David.

LET God arise, let his enemies be *a*scattered: let them also that *b*hate him flee before him.

2 As smoke is driven away, *so* drive *them* away: as *a*wax melteth before the fire, *so* let the wicked perish at the *b*presence of God.

3 But let the *a*righteous be glad; let them rejoice before God: yea, let them exceedingly rejoice.

4 Sing unto God, sing praises to his name: extol him that rideth upon the heavens by his name *a*JAH, and rejoice before him.

5 A father of the *a*fatherless, and a *b*judge of the widows, *is* God in his holy habitation.

6 God setteth the solitary in families: he bringeth out those which are bound with chains: but the *a*rebellious dwell in a dry *land.*

7 O God, when thou wentest forth before thy people, when thou didst *a*march through the wilderness; Selah:

8 The earth shook, the heavens also *a*dropped at the presence of God: *even* *b*Sinai itself *was moved* at the presence of God, the God of Israel.

9 Thou, O God, didst send a plentiful *a*rain, whereby thou didst confirm thine inheritance, when it was weary.

10 Thy congregation hath dwelt therein: thou, O God, hast prepared of thy goodness for the poor.

11 The Lord gave the word: great *was* the company of those that published *it.*

18*a* Prov. 1:28 (24–29).
67 1*a* D&C 50:16.
　　b Ps. 4:6.
　2*a* Luke 2:30 (30–31);
　　　Mosiah 15:28;
　　　D&C 133:37 (36–37).
　6*a* 2 Ne. 1:20.
　　b TG Earth, Renewal of.

68 1*a* Num. 10:35.
　　b TG Hate.
　2*a* Ps. 97:5;
　　　Micah 1:4.
　　b TG God, Presence of.
　3*a* Matt. 13:43.
　4*a* TG Jesus Christ,
　　　Jehovah.

5*a* Ps. 10:14; 3 Ne. 24:5;
　　D&C 136:8.
　b OR defender, defense.
6*a* TG Rebellion.
7*a* Judg. 5:4.
8*a* IE rained.
　b Judg. 5:5.
9*a* Ezek. 22:24; 34:26.

12 Kings of armies did flee apace: and she that tarried at home divided the spoil.

13 Though ye have lien among the pots, *yet shall ye be as* the wings of a dove covered with silver, and her feathers with yellow gold.

14 When the Almighty scattered kings in it, it was *white* as snow in Salmon.

15 The hill of God *is as* the hill of Bashan; an high hill *as* the hill of Bashan.

16 Why leap ye, ye high hills? *this is* the hill *which* God desireth to dwell in; yea, the Lord will dwell *in it* for ever.

17 The chariots of God *are* twenty thousand, *even* thousands of angels: the Lord *is* among them, *as in* Sinai, in the holy *place.*

18 Thou hast *ª*ascended on high, thou hast led *ᵇ*captivity captive: thou hast received gifts for men; yea, *for* the rebellious also, that the Lord God might dwell *among them.*

19 Blessed *be* the Lord, *who* daily loadeth us *with benefits, even* the God of our salvation. Selah.

20 *He that is* our God *is* the God of *ª*salvation; and unto God the Lord *belong* the issues from *ᵇ*death.

21 But God shall *ª*wound the head of his enemies, *and* the hairy scalp of such an one as goeth on still in his trespasses.

22 The Lord said, I will bring again from Bashan, I will bring *my people* again from the depths of the sea:

23 That thy foot may be dipped in the *ª*blood of *thine* enemies, *and* the tongue of thy dogs in the same.

24 They have seen thy goings, O God; *even* the goings of my God, my King, in the sanctuary.

25 The singers went before, the players on instruments *followed* after; among *them were* the damsels playing with timbrels.

26 Bless ye God in the congregations, *even* the Lord, *ª*from the fountain of Israel.

27 *ª*There *is* little Benjamin *with* their ruler, the princes of Judah *and* their council, the princes of Zebulun, *and* the princes of Naphtali.

28 Thy God hath commanded thy strength: strengthen, O God, that which thou hast wrought for us.

29 Because of thy temple at Jerusalem shall kings bring *ª*presents unto thee.

30 Rebuke the *ª*company of spearmen, the multitude of the bulls, with the calves of the people, *till every one* submit himself with pieces of silver: scatter thou the people *that* delight in war.

31 Princes shall come out of *ª*Egypt; Ethiopia shall soon stretch out her hands unto God.

32 Sing unto God, ye kingdoms of the earth; O sing praises unto the Lord; Selah:

33 To him that rideth upon the heavens of heavens, *which were* of old; lo, he doth send out his voice, *and that* a mighty voice.

34 Ascribe ye strength unto God: his excellency *is* over Israel, and his strength *is* in the clouds.

35 O God, *thou art* terrible out of thy holy places: the God of Israel *is* he that giveth strength and power unto *his* people. Blessed *be* God.

PSALM 69

A messianic psalm of David—The zeal of the Lord's house has eaten Him up— Reproach has broken His heart—He is given gall and vinegar to drink—He is persecuted—He will save Zion.

To the chief Musician upon Shoshannim, A Psalm of David.

Save me, O God; for the waters are come in unto *my* soul.

18*a* Acts 1:9; Eph. 4:8;
    D&C 88:6.
  b TG Jesus Christ,
    Prophecies about.
20*a* Isa. 17:10.
  b Deut. 32:39.

21*a* Hab. 3:13;
    Moses 4:21 (20–21).
23*a* Ps. 58:10.
26*a* IE you who are the
    offspring of.
27*a* HEB There is Benjamin,

    the youngest, leading
    them.
29*a* Ps. 76:11.
30*a* HEB beasts that dwell
    among reeds.
31*a* Isa. 19:21.

2 I sink in deep mire, where *there is* no standing: I am come into ^adeep waters, where the floods overflow me.

3 I am weary of my crying: my throat is dried: mine eyes fail while I wait for my God.

4 They that ^ahate me without a cause are more than the hairs of mine head: they that would destroy me, *being* mine enemies wrongfully, are mighty: then I restored *that* which I took not away.

5 O God, thou knowest my ^afoolishness; and my sins are not hid from thee.

6 Let not them that wait on thee, O Lord GOD of hosts, be ashamed for my sake: let not those that seek thee be confounded for my sake, O God of Israel.

7 Because for thy sake I have borne reproach; shame hath covered my face.

8 I am become a stranger unto my brethren, and an alien unto my mother's children.

9 For the ^azeal of thine house hath eaten me up; and the ^breproaches of them that reproached thee are fallen upon me.

10 When I wept, *and chastened* my soul with ^afasting, that was to my reproach.

11 I made sackcloth also my garment; and I became a proverb to them.

12 They that sit in the gate speak against me; and I *was* the ^asong of the drunkards.

13 But as for me, my prayer *is* unto thee, O LORD, *in* an acceptable time: O God, in the multitude of thy mercy hear me, in the truth of thy salvation.

14 Deliver me out of the mire, and let me not sink: let me be delivered from them that hate me, and out of the deep waters.

15 Let not the waterflood overflow me, neither let the deep swallow me up, and let not the ^apit shut her mouth upon me.

16 Hear me, O LORD; for thy lovingkindness *is* good: turn unto me according to the multitude of thy tender ^amercies.

17 And hide not thy face from thy servant; for I am in trouble: hear me speedily.

18 Draw ^anigh unto my soul, *and* redeem it: deliver me because of mine enemies.

19 Thou hast known my ^areproach, and my ^bshame, and my dishonour: mine adversaries *are* all before thee.

20 Reproach hath broken my heart; and I am full of ^aheaviness: and I looked *for some* to take pity, but *there was* none; and for comforters, but I found none.

21 They gave me also gall for my meat; and in my thirst they gave me ^avinegar to drink.

22 Let their table become a ^asnare before them: and *that which should have been* for *their* welfare, *let it become* a trap.

23 Let their eyes be darkened, that they ^asee not; and make their loins continually to shake.

24 Pour out thine indignation upon them, and let thy wrathful anger take hold of them.

25 Let their habitation be ^adesolate; *and* let none dwell in their tents.

26 For they persecute *him* whom thou hast smitten; and they talk to the grief of those whom thou hast wounded.

---

69 2 a Ps. 130:1;
　　　 D&C 122:7 (7–8).
　 4 a TG Hate.
　 5 a TG Foolishness.
　 9 a John 2:17 (14–17).
　　　 TG Jesus Christ, Prophecies about; Zeal.
　　 b TG Reproach.
　10 a TG Fast, Fasting.
　12 a Job 30:9.
　15 a Num. 16:33 (31–33).

16 a TG God, Mercy of.
18 a James 4:8 (7–8);
　　　 D&C 88:63.
19 a TG Reproach.
　 b TG Shame.
20 a Mark 14:33 (32–41).
　　　 TG Despair; Jesus Christ, Prophecies about.
21 a Matt. 27:34;
　　　 Mark 15:36;
　　　 Luke 23:36;

John 19:29 (28–29).
　　　 TG Jesus Christ, Prophecies about.
22 a Isa. 8:14 (13–15);
　　　 Rom. 11:9 (9–12);
　　　 2 Ne. 18:14 (13–15);
　　　 D&C 10:26.
23 a TG Spiritual Blindness.
25 a Jer. 12:7; 22:5;
　　　 Matt. 23:38;
　　　 Acts 1:20 (16–20).

27 Add ªiniquity unto their iniquity: and let them not come into thy righteousness.

28 Let them be blotted out of the ªbook of the living, and not be written with the righteous.

29 But I *am* poor and sorrowful: let thy salvation, O God, set me up on high.

30 I will praise the name of God with a song, and will magnify him with ªthanksgiving.

31 *This* also shall ªplease the LORD better than an ox *or* bullock that hath horns and hoofs.

32 The humble shall see *this, and* be glad: and your heart shall live that ªseek God.

33 For the LORD heareth the poor, and despiseth not ªhis prisoners.

34 Let the heaven and earth praise him, the seas, and every thing that moveth therein.

35 For God will save ªZion, and will ᵇbuild the cities of Judah: that they may dwell there, and have it in possession.

36 The seed also of his servants shall inherit it: and they that love his name shall dwell therein.

PSALM 70

David proclaims, Let God be magnified.

To the chief Musician, A *Psalm* of David,
to bring to remembrance.

MAKE *haste,* O God, to deliver me; make haste to help me, O LORD.

2 Let them be ashamed and confounded that seek after my soul: let them be turned backward, and put to confusion, that desire my hurt.

3 Let them be turned back for a reward of their shame that say, Aha, aha.

4 Let all those that seek thee rejoice and be glad in thee: and let such as love thy salvation say continually, Let God be magnified.

5 But I *am* poor and needy: make ªhaste unto me, O God: thou *art* my help and my deliverer; O LORD, make no tarrying.

PSALM 71

David praises God with thanksgiving—Who is like unto the Lord!

IN thee, O LORD, do I put my trust: let me never be put to confusion.

2 Deliver me in thy righteousness, and cause me to escape: incline thine ear unto me, and save me.

3 Be thou my strong habitation, whereunto I may continually resort: thou hast given commandment to save me; for thou *art* my ªrock and my fortress.

4 Deliver me, O my God, out of the hand of the wicked, out of the hand of the unrighteous and ªcruel man.

5 For thou *art* my hope, O Lord GOD: *thou art* my trust from my youth.

6 By thee have I been holden up from the womb: thou art he that took me out of my mother's bowels: my praise *shall be* continually of thee.

7 I am as a wonder unto many; but thou *art* my strong refuge.

8 Let my mouth be filled *with* thy praise *and with* thy honour all the day.

9 Cast me not off in the time of ªold age; forsake me not when my strength faileth.

10 For mine enemies speak against me; and they that lay wait for my soul take counsel together,

11 Saying, God hath forsaken him: persecute and take him; for *there is* none to deliver *him.*

12 O God, be not far from me: O my God, make haste for my help.

13 Let them be confounded *and* consumed that are adversaries to my soul; let them be covered *with* ªreproach and dishonour that seek my hurt.

27ª Matt. 27:25 (24–25).
28ª TG Book of Life; Record Keeping.
30ª Alma 34:38; D&C 46:7.
31ª 1 Sam. 15:22.

32ª D&C 101:38.
33ª OR those that are in bonds for His sake.
35ª Isa. 65:9.
    b OR rebuild.
70 5ª Ps. 141:1.

71 3ª Ps. 78:35; Hel. 5:12; D&C 6:34; Moses 7:53.
4ª TG Cruelty.
9ª TG Old Age.
13ª Ps. 109:29.

14 But I will hope continually, and will yet praise thee more and more.

15 My mouth shall shew forth thy righteousness *and* thy salvation all the day; for I know not the numbers *thereof.*

16 I will go in the ^astrength of the Lord GOD: I will make mention of thy righteousness, *even* of thine only.

17 O God, thou hast taught me from my youth: and hitherto have I declared thy wondrous works.

18 Now also when I am old and grayheaded, O God, forsake me not; until I have shewed thy strength unto *this* generation, *and* thy power to every one *that* is to come.

19 Thy ^arighteousness also, O God, *is* very ^bhigh, who hast done great things: O God, who *is* ^clike unto thee!

20 *Thou,* which hast shewed me great and sore troubles, shalt ^aquicken me again, and shalt bring me up again from the depths of the earth.

21 Thou shalt increase my greatness, and ^acomfort me on every side.

22 I will also praise thee with the psaltery, *even* thy truth, O my God: unto thee will I sing with the harp, O thou Holy One of Israel.

23 My lips shall greatly rejoice when I sing unto thee; and my soul, which thou hast redeemed.

24 My tongue also shall talk of thy righteousness all the day long: for they are confounded, for they are brought unto ^ashame, that seek my hurt.

PSALM 72

David speaks of Solomon, who is made a type of the Messiah—He will have dominion—His name will endure forever—All nations will call him blessed—

The whole earth will be filled with the glory of the Lord.

A *Psalm* for Solomon.

GIVE the king thy judgments, O God, and thy righteousness unto the king's son.

2 He shall ^ajudge thy people with righteousness, and thy poor with judgment.

3 The mountains shall bring peace to the people, and the little hills, by righteousness.

4 He shall judge the poor of the people, he shall save the children of the needy, and shall break in pieces the ^aoppressor.

5 They shall fear thee as long as the sun and moon ^aendure, throughout all generations.

6 He shall come down like rain upon the mown grass: as showers *that* water the earth.

7 In his days shall the ^arighteous flourish; and abundance of ^bpeace so long as the moon endureth.

8 He shall have ^adominion also from sea to sea, and from the river unto the ends of the earth.

9 They that dwell in the wilderness shall ^abow before him; and his enemies shall lick the dust.

10 The kings of Tarshish and of the isles shall ^abring presents: the kings of Sheba and ^bSeba shall offer gifts.

11 Yea, all kings shall fall down before him: all nations shall serve him.

12 For he shall deliver the needy when he crieth; the poor also, and *him* that hath no helper.

13 He shall spare the poor and needy, and shall save the souls of the needy.

14 He shall ^aredeem their soul from deceit and violence: and ^bprecious shall their blood be in his sight.

15 And he shall live, and to him shall be given of the gold of Sheba:

16a TG Strength.
19a TG God, Perfection of.
  b Ps. 36:5.
  c 1 Kgs. 8:23;
    Jer. 10:6.
20a D&C 33:16.
21a TG Comfort.

24a TG Shame.
72 2a TG Jesus Christ, Judge;
    Judgment.
  4a D&C 101:24 (23–24).
  5a Ps. 89:36 (36–37).
  7a TG Righteousness.
    b D&C 45:66; 54:10.

8a Zech. 9:10.
9a D&C 88:104 (104–6).
10a OR render tribute.
  b Isa. 43:3.
14a TG Redemption.
  b TG Life, Sanctity of.

prayer also shall be made for him continually; *and* daily shall he be praised.

16 There shall be an handful of corn in the earth upon the top of the mountains; the fruit thereof shall shake like Lebanon: and *they* of the city shall flourish like ªgrass of the earth.

17 His name shall endure for ever: his name shall be continued as long as the sun: and *men* shall be blessed in him: all nations shall call him ªblessed.

18 ªBlessed *be* the Lord God, the God of Israel, who only doeth wondrous things.

19 And blessed *be* his glorious name for ever: and let the whole earth be ªfilled *with* his ᵇglory; Amen, and Amen.

20 The prayers of David the son of Jesse are ended.

PSALM 73

God is good to Israel—The wicked and ungodly prosper in this world—They will be consumed with terrors hereafter—Those who trust in the Lord will be received up unto glory.

A Psalm of Asaph.

Truly God *is* good to Israel, *even* to such as are of a ªclean heart.

2 But as for me, my feet were almost gone; my steps had well nigh slipped.

3 For I was ªenvious at the foolish, *when* I saw the prosperity of the wicked.

4 For *there are* no bands in their death: but their strength *is* firm.

5 They *are* not in trouble *as other* men; neither are they plagued like *other* men.

6 Therefore pride compasseth them about as a ªchain; violence covereth them *as* a garment.

7 Their eyes stand out with ªfatness: they have more than heart could wish.

8 They are corrupt, and speak wickedly *concerning* oppression: they ªspeak loftily.

9 They set their mouth against the heavens, and their tongue walketh through the earth.

10 Therefore his people return hither: and waters of a full *cup* are wrung out to them.

11 And they say, How doth God ªknow? and is there knowledge in the most High?

12 Behold, these *are* the ungodly, who ªprosper in the ᵇworld; they increase *in* riches.

13 Verily I have cleansed my heart *in* vain, and ªwashed my hands in innocency.

14 For all the day long have I been plagued, and chastened every morning.

15 If I say, I will speak thus; behold, I should offend *against* the generation of thy children.

16 When I thought to know this, it *was* too painful for me;

17 Until I went into the ªsanctuary of God; *then* understood I their ᵇend.

18 Surely thou didst set them in slippery places: thou castedst them down into destruction.

19 How are they *brought* into desolation, as in a moment! they are utterly consumed with terrors.

20 As a dream when *one* awaketh; *so*, O Lord, when thou ªawakest, thou shalt ᵇdespise their image.

21 Thus my heart was grieved, and I was ªpricked in my reins.

22 So foolish *was* I, and ignorant: I was *as* a ªbeast before thee.

23 Nevertheless I *am* continually

16a Job 5:25.
17a Luke 1:48 (46–48).
18a Ps. 41:13; 106:48.
19a Num. 14:21;
   D&C 65:2.
   b 1 Ne. 22:24 (22–24);
   Alma 5:50;
   3 Ne. 26:3; D&C 7:3.
73 1a TG Purity.

3a TG Envy.
6a OR necklace.
7a D&C 68:31.
8a 2 Pet. 2:18 (10–19).
11a Job 22:13.
12a Job 12:6; Ps. 17:14;
   Hel. 7:5 (4–6).
   b TG Worldliness.
13a TG Wash.

17a 2 Kgs. 19:1;
   Ps. 20:2.
   b 2 Ne. 30:10;
   D&C 29:17;
   JS—M 1:55.
20a Ps. 78:65 (65–66).
   b 2 Ne. 9:42 (41–42).
21a TG Conscience.
22a Eccl. 3:18.

with thee: thou hast holden *me* by my right hand.

24 Thou shalt ªguide me with thy ᵇcounsel, and afterward receive me to ᶜglory.

25 Whom have I in heaven *but thee?* and *there is* none upon earth *that* I desire beside thee.

26 My ªflesh and my heart ᵇfaileth: *but* God *is* the ᶜstrength of my heart, and my ᵈportion for ever.

27 For, lo, they that are far from thee shall perish: thou hast destroyed all them that go a whoring from thee.

28 But *it is* good for me to draw near to God: I have put my trust in the Lord Gᴏᴅ, that I may declare all thy works.

PSALM 74

O God, remember Thy chosen congregation—The wicked destroy the sanctuary and burn the synagogues—O God, remember them for their deeds, and save Thy people.

Maschil of Asaph.

O Gᴏᴅ, why hast thou ªcast *us* off for ever? *why* doth thine anger smoke against the sheep of thy pasture?

2 Remember thy congregation, *which* thou hast ªpurchased of old; the rod of thine inheritance, *which* thou hast redeemed; this mount Zion, wherein thou hast dwelt.

3 Lift up thy feet unto the perpetual desolations; *even* all *that* the enemy hath done wickedly in the sanctuary.

4 Thine enemies roar in the midst of thy congregations; they set up their ªensigns *for* signs.

5 A *man* was famous according as he had lifted up axes upon the thick trees.

6 But now they break down the carved work thereof at once with axes and hammers.

7 They have cast fire into thy sanctuary, they have defiled *by casting down* the dwelling place of thy name to the ground.

8 They said in their hearts, Let us ªdestroy them together: they have burned up all the ᵇsynagogues of God in the land.

9 We see not our signs: *there is* ªno more any ᵇprophet: neither *is there* among us any that knoweth how long.

10 O God, how long shall the adversary reproach? shall the enemy ªblaspheme thy name for ever?

11 Why ªwithdrawest thou thy hand, even thy right hand? pluck *it* out of thy bosom.

12 For God *is* my ªKing of old, working salvation in the midst of the earth.

13 Thou didst divide the sea by thy strength: thou brakest the heads of the ªdragons in the waters.

14 Thou brakest the heads of leviathan in pieces, *and* gavest him *to be* meat to the people inhabiting the wilderness.

15 Thou didst ªcleave the fountain and the flood: thou ᵇdriedst up mighty rivers.

16 The day *is* thine, the night also *is* thine: thou hast prepared the light and the sun.

17 Thou hast set all the borders of the earth: thou hast made ªsummer and winter.

18 Remember this, *that* the enemy hath reproached, O Lᴏʀᴅ, and *that* the foolish people have blasphemed thy name.

19 O deliver not the soul of thy turtledove unto the multitude *of the wicked:* forget not the congregation of thy poor for ever.

24a ᴛɢ Conscience.
  b ᴛɢ Counsel.
  c ᴛɢ Eternal Life.
26a ᴛɢ Flesh and Blood.
  b Ps. 40:12 (12–13).
  c ᴛɢ Strength.
  d Ps. 16:5.
74 1a 1 Ne. 19:16 (15–16);
    D&C 35:25;

JS—M 1:27 (27, 37).
2a Ex. 15:16.
4a ᴛɢ Ensign.
8a Ps. 83:4.
  b ʜᴇʙ assembly places.
9a Amos 8:11 (11–12).
  b 1 Sam. 3:1;
    Lam. 2:9.
10a D&C 105:15;

112:26 (24–26).
11a Lam. 2:3.
12a Ps. 44:4;
    Alma 5:50.
13a Isa. 27:1; 51:9.
15a Ex. 17:6.
  b Josh. 3:17 (14–17);
    Ps. 66:6.
17a ᴛɢ Nature, Earth.

20 Have respect unto the ᵃcovenant: for the dark places of the earth are full of the habitations of ᵇcruelty.

21 O let not the oppressed return ashamed: let the poor and needy praise thy name.

22 Arise, O God, plead thine own cause: remember how the foolish man reproacheth thee daily.

23 Forget not the voice of thine enemies: the tumult of those that rise up against thee increaseth continually.

PSALM 75

The righteous praise and thank the God of Jacob—They will be exalted— God is the judge, and the wicked will be condemned.

To the chief Musician, Al-taschith,
A Psalm *or* Song of Asaph.

UNTO thee, O God, do we give thanks, *unto thee* do we give thanks: for *that* thy name is near thy wondrous works declare.

2 When I shall receive the congregation I will judge uprightly.

3 The earth and all the inhabitants thereof are dissolved: I bear up the ᵃpillars of it. Selah.

4 I said unto the ᵃfools, Deal not foolishly: and to the wicked, Lift not up the horn:

5 Lift not up your horn on high: speak *not with* a ᵃstiff neck.

6 For ᵃpromotion *cometh* neither from the east, nor from the west, nor from the south.

7 But God *is* the ᵃjudge: he putteth ᵇdown one, and setteth up another.

8 For in the hand of the LORD *there is* a ᵃcup, and the wine is red; it is full of mixture; and he poureth out of the same: but the dregs thereof, all the wicked of the earth shall wring *them* out, *and* ᵇdrink *them*.

9 But I will declare for ever; I will sing praises to the God of Jacob.

10 All the ᵃhorns of the wicked also will I cut off; *but* the horns of the righteous shall be exalted.

PSALM 76

God is known in Judah and dwells in Zion—He will save the meek of the earth.

To the chief Musician on Neginoth,
A Psalm *or* Song of Asaph.

IN Judah *is* God known: his name *is* great in Israel.

2 In Salem also is his tabernacle, and his dwelling place in Zion.

3 There brake he the arrows of the bow, the shield, and the sword, and the battle. Selah.

4 Thou *art* more glorious *and* excellent than the mountains of prey.

5 The stouthearted are spoiled, they have slept their sleep: and none of the men of might have found their hands.

6 At thy rebuke, O God of Jacob, both the chariot and horse are cast into a dead sleep.

7 Thou, *even* thou, *art* to be feared: and who may ᵃstand in thy sight when once thou art angry?

8 Thou didst cause judgment to be heard from heaven; the earth feared, and was still,

9 When God arose to judgment, to save all the ᵃmeek of the earth. Selah.

10 Surely the wrath of man shall praise thee: the remainder of wrath shalt thou ᵃrestrain.

11 ᵃVow, and pay unto the LORD your God: let all that be round about him bring ᵇpresents unto him that ought to be feared.

12 He shall cut off the spirit of princes: *he is* terrible to the kings of the earth.

20a Ps. 106:45;
　　D&C 1:22; 49:9.
　b TG Cruelty.
75 3a 1 Sam. 2:8.
　4a Hel. 9:21.
　5a TG Stiffnecked.
　6a Jer. 27:5 (5–6);

Dan. 2:21; 5:20 (18–20).
7a Mosiah 29:12;
　　D&C 64:11; Moses 6:57.
　b 1 Sam. 2:7.
8a Mosiah 3:26 (24–26);
　　Alma 40:26.
　b Job 21:20.

10a 1 Sam. 2:1; Jer. 48:25.
76 7a Ps. 130:3;
　　Rev. 6:17.
　9a Zeph. 2:3 (1–3).
10a TG Self-Mastery.
11a TG Vow.
　b Ps. 68:29.

PSALM 77

The righteous cry unto the Lord—They remember the wonders of old, how He redeemed the sons of Jacob and led Israel like a flock.

To the chief Musician, to Jeduthun, A Psalm of Asaph.

I CRIED unto God with my voice, *even* unto God with my voice; and he gave ear unto me.

2 In the day of my trouble I *ᵃ*sought the Lord: my sore ran in the night, and ceased not: my soul refused to be *ᵇ*comforted.

3 I remembered God, and was troubled: I *ᵃ*complained, and my spirit was *ᵇ*overwhelmed. Selah.

4 Thou holdest mine eyes waking: I am so troubled that I cannot speak.

5 I have considered the days of old, the years of ancient times.

6 I call to remembrance my *ᵃ*song in the night: I commune with mine own heart: and my spirit made diligent search.

7 Will the Lord cast off for ever? and will he be favourable no more?

8 Is his mercy clean gone for ever? doth *his* promise fail for evermore?

9 Hath God forgotten to be gracious? hath he in anger shut up his tender mercies? Selah.

10 And I said, This *is* my infirmity: *but I will remember* the years of the right hand of the most High.

11 I will remember the works of the LORD: surely I will remember thy wonders of old.

12 I will *ᵃ*meditate also of all thy work, and talk of thy doings.

13 Thy way, O God, *is* *ᵃ*in the sanctuary: who *is so* great a God as *our* God?

14 Thou *art* the God that doest *ᵃ*wonders: thou hast declared thy strength among the people.

15 Thou hast with *thine* arm redeemed thy people, the sons of Jacob and *ᵃ*Joseph. Selah.

16 The *ᵃ*waters saw thee, O God, the waters saw thee; they were afraid: the depths also were troubled.

17 The clouds poured out water: the skies sent out a sound: thine arrows also went abroad.

18 The voice of thy thunder *was* in the heaven: the lightnings *ᵃ*lightened the world: the earth trembled and shook.

19 Thy way *is* in the sea, and thy path in the great waters, and thy footsteps are not known.

20 Thou *ᵃ*leddest thy people like a flock by the hand of *ᵇ*Moses and Aaron.

PSALM 78

The Israelites are to teach the Lord's law to their children—Disobedient Israel provoked the Lord in the wilderness—The Egyptian plagues are recounted—The Lord chooses and blesses Judah and David.

Maschil of Asaph.

GIVE *ᵃ*ear, O my people, *to* my law: incline your ears to the words of my mouth.

2 I will open my mouth in a *ᵃ*parable: I will utter dark sayings of old:

3 Which we have heard and known, and our *ᵃ*fathers have told us.

4 We will not *ᵃ*hide *them* from their children, *ᵇ*shewing to the generation to come the praises of the LORD, and his strength, and his wonderful works that he hath done.

5 For he established a testimony in Jacob, and appointed a law in Israel, which he commanded our

---

77 2*a* Ps. 86:7.
  b Gen. 37:35;
     Moses 7:44.
  3*a* OR meditated.
  b Ps. 142:3 (1–3).
  6*a* Job 35:10.
  12*a* TG Meditation.
  13*a* HEB holy, sanctified.

14*a* TG Miracle.
15*a* 2 Ne. 3:4; 25:21;
     D&C 90:10.
16*a* Ex. 14:21.
18*a* Ps. 97:4.
20*a* Ex. 15:13.
  b Isa. 63:12 (11–12).
78 1*a* Ps. 49:1; 2 Ne. 9:31;

     Mosiah 26:28;
     D&C 1:14 (2, 11, 14);
     Moses 6:27.
2*a* Matt. 13:35; Luke 8:10.
3*a* Deut. 4:9;
     Ps. 145:4 (1–21).
4*a* D&C 68:25.
  b Isa. 38:19.

fathers, that they should make them known to their ªchildren:

6 That the generation to come might know *them, even* the children *which* should be born; *who* should arise and declare *them* to their children:

7 That they might set their hope in God, and not forget the works of God, but keep his commandments:

8 And might not be as their ªfathers, a ᵇstubborn and ᶜrebellious generation; a generation *that* set not their heart aright, and whose spirit was not steadfast with God.

9 The children of Ephraim, *being* armed, *and* carrying bows, turned back in the day of battle.

10 They kept not the ªcovenant of God, and refused to walk in his law;

11 And forgat his works, and his wonders that he had shewed them.

12 ªMarvellous things did he in the sight of their fathers, in the land of Egypt, *in* the field of ᵇZoan.

13 He ªdivided the sea, and caused them to pass through; and he made the waters to stand as an heap.

14 In the daytime also he led them with a ªcloud, and all the night with a light of fire.

15 He ªclave the rocks in the wilderness, and gave *them* drink as *out of* the great depths.

16 He brought streams also out of the rock, and caused waters to run down like rivers.

17 And they sinned yet more against him by provoking the most High in the wilderness.

18 And they tempted God in their heart by asking ªmeat for their ᵇlust.

19 Yea, they spake against God; they said, Can God furnish a ªtable in the wilderness?

20 Behold, he smote the rock, that the waters gushed out, and the streams overflowed; can he give bread also? can he provide flesh for his people?

21 Therefore the LORD heard *this,* and was wroth: so a ªfire was kindled against Jacob, and anger also came up against Israel;

22 Because they ªbelieved not in God, and ᵇtrusted not in his salvation:

23 Though he had commanded the clouds from above, and opened the doors of heaven,

24 And had rained down manna upon them to eat, and had given them of the ªcorn of heaven.

25 Man did eat ªangels' food: he sent them meat to the full.

26 He caused an ªeast wind to blow in the heaven: and by his power he brought in the south wind.

27 He rained flesh also upon them as dust, and feathered ªfowls like as the sand of the sea:

28 And he let *it* fall in the midst of their camp, round about their habitations.

29 So they did eat, and were well filled: for he gave them their own desire;

30 They were not estranged from their ªlust. But while their meat *was* yet in their mouths,

31 The wrath of God came upon them, and slew the fattest of them, and smote down the chosen *men* of Israel.

32 For all this they sinned still, and believed not for his wondrous works.

33 Therefore their days did he consume in ªvanity, and their years in trouble.

34 When he ªslew them, then they

5a TG Family, Children, Responsibilities toward.	Isa. 63:12.	22a TG Faith.
8a Zech. 1:4.	14a Ex. 13:21 (21–22); Neh. 9:12 (12, 19); Ps. 99:7.	b TG Trust in God.
b TG Stubbornness.		24a John 6:31.
c Jer. 5:23.	15a Ex. 17:6;	25a TG Angels.
10a Ex. 34:28.	Num. 20:11 (7–11).	26a Gen. 41:23; Ezek. 27:26.
12a TG Miracle.	18a Ex. 16:3 (2–3).	27a Ex. 16:13.
b Num. 13:22.	b TG Carnal Mind.	30a TG Lust.
13a Ex. 14:21 (21–22); Ps. 114:3;	19a Ex. 16:3 (3–5).	33a TG Vanity.
	21a Num. 11:1 (1, 10).	34a Hel. 12:3.

sought him: and they [b]returned and [c]inquired early after God.

35 And they remembered that God *was* their [a]rock, and the high God their redeemer.

36 Nevertheless they did [a]flatter him with their mouth, and they [b]lied unto him with their tongues.

37 For their [a]heart was not right with him, neither were they [b]steadfast in his covenant.

38 But he, *being* full of compassion, forgave *their* iniquity, and destroyed *them* not: yea, many a time turned he his anger away, and did not stir up all his wrath.

39 For he remembered that they *were but* [a]flesh; a wind that passeth away, and cometh not again.

40 How oft did they [a]provoke him in the wilderness, *and* grieve him in the desert!

41 Yea, they turned back and tempted God, and limited the Holy One of Israel.

42 They remembered not his hand, *nor* the day when he delivered them from the enemy.

43 How he had wrought his signs in Egypt, and his wonders in the field of Zoan:

44 And had turned their rivers into blood; and their [a]floods, that they could not drink.

45 He sent divers sorts of flies among them, which devoured them; and frogs, which destroyed them.

46 He gave also their increase unto the caterpiller, and their labour unto the [a]locust.

47 He destroyed their vines with [a]hail, and their sycomore trees with frost.

48 He gave up their cattle also to the hail, and their flocks to hot thunderbolts.

49 He cast upon them the fierceness of his anger, wrath, and indignation, and trouble, by sending [a]evil angels *among them.*

50 He made a way to his anger; he spared not their soul from death, but gave their life over to the pestilence;

51 And smote all the [a]firstborn in Egypt; the chief of *their* strength in the [b]tabernacles of [c]Ham:

52 But made his own people to go forth like sheep, and guided them in the wilderness like a flock.

53 And he led them on safely, so that they feared not: but the [a]sea overwhelmed their enemies.

54 And he brought them [a]to the border of his sanctuary, *even to* this mountain, *which* his right hand had purchased.

55 He cast out the heathen also before them, and divided them an inheritance by line, and made the tribes of Israel to dwell in their tents.

56 Yet they tempted and provoked the most high God, and kept not his testimonies:

57 But turned back, and dealt unfaithfully like their fathers: they were turned aside like a [a]deceitful bow.

58 For they [a]provoked him to anger with their high places, and moved him to jealousy with their graven images.

59 When God heard *this*, he was wroth, and greatly abhorred Israel:

60 So that he forsook the tabernacle of [a]Shiloh, the tent *which* he placed among men;

61 And delivered his strength into captivity, and his glory into the enemy's hand.

62 He gave his people over also unto the sword; and was wroth with his inheritance.

63 The fire consumed their young men; and their maidens were not given to marriage.

34b OR repented.
  c OR earnestly sought.
35a Ps. 71:3; 92:15;
      Moses 7:53.
36a TG Flatter.
  b Isa. 57:11.
37a TG Heart.
  b TG Steadfastness.

39a TG Mortality.
40a TG Provoking.
44a HEB streams.
46a Ex. 10:14 (12–15).
47a Ex. 9:25 (23–25).
49a TG Spirits, Evil or
      Unclean.
51a TG Firstborn.

  b HEB tents, dwellings.
  c Abr. 1:21 (21–25).
53a Ex. 14:28 (27–28).
54a OR into His holy land.
57a Hosea 7:16 (14–16).
58a Deut. 32:16.
60a Judg. 18:31.

64 Their priests fell by the sword; and their widows made no lamentation.

65 Then the Lord *awaked as one out of sleep, *and* like a mighty man that shouteth by reason of wine.

66 And he smote his enemies in the hinder parts: he put them to a perpetual reproach.

67 Moreover he refused the tabernacle of Joseph, and chose not the tribe of Ephraim:

68 But chose the tribe of Judah, the mount Zion which he loved.

69 And he built his sanctuary like high *palaces,* like the earth which he hath established for *ever.

70 He chose *David also his servant, and took him from the sheepfolds:

71 From following the ewes great with young he brought him to feed Jacob his people, and Israel his inheritance.

72 So he fed them according to the *integrity of his heart; and guided them by the skilfulness of his hands.

PSALM 79

The heathen nations destroy Jerusalem and defile the temple—Israel pleads for forgiveness and deliverance.

A Psalm of Asaph.

O GOD, the *heathen are come into thine inheritance; thy holy *temple have they defiled; they have laid Jerusalem on *heaps.

2 The dead bodies of thy servants have they given *to be* meat unto the fowls of the heaven, the flesh of thy saints unto the beasts of the earth.

3 Their blood have they *shed like water round about Jerusalem; and *there was* none to *bury *them.*

4 We are become a reproach to our neighbours, a scorn and derision to them that are round about us.

5 How long, LORD? wilt thou be *angry for ever? shall thy jealousy burn like fire?

6 Pour out thy wrath upon the heathen that have not known thee, and upon the kingdoms that have not called upon thy name.

7 For they have devoured Jacob, and laid waste his dwelling place.

8 O remember not against us former iniquities: let thy tender mercies speedily *prevent us: for we are brought very low.

9 Help us, O God of our salvation, for the glory of thy name: and deliver us, and purge away our sins, for thy name's sake.

10 Wherefore should the heathen say, Where *is* their God? let him be known among the heathen in our sight *by* the revenging of the blood of thy servants *which is* shed.

11 Let the sighing of the prisoner come before thee; according to the greatness of thy power preserve thou those that are appointed to die;

12 And render unto our neighbours sevenfold into their bosom their reproach, wherewith they have reproached thee, O Lord.

13 So we thy *people and *sheep of thy pasture will give thee thanks for ever: we will shew forth thy praise to all generations.

PSALM 80

Israel pleads with the Shepherd of Israel for deliverance, for salvation, and for His face to shine upon them.

To the chief Musician upon Shoshannim-Eduth, A Psalm of Asaph.

GIVE ear, O *Shepherd of Israel, thou that leadest Joseph like a flock; thou that dwellest *between* the *cherubims, shine forth.

2 Before Ephraim and Benjamin and Manasseh stir up thy strength, and come *and* save us.

65*a* Ps. 73:20.
69*a* TG Earth, Purpose of.
70*a* 1 Sam. 16:13 (11–13).
72*a* TG Sincere.
79 1*a* Lam. 5:2.
   b Lam. 1:10.

c 2 Kgs. 25:9.
3*a* 1 Ne. 1:4 (4, 18);
   D&C 45:19 (16–21).
b Jer. 14:16.
5*a* 2 Ne. 25:17 (15–18).
8*a* HEB come to us.

13*a* Isa. 64:9.
   b Alma 5:41 (38–42).
80 1*a* TG Jesus Christ, Good
      Shepherd;
      Shepherd.
   b TG Cherubim.

3 ^aTurn us again, O God, and cause thy face to shine; and we shall be saved.

4 O L<small>ORD</small> God of hosts, how long wilt thou be angry against the prayer of thy people?

5 Thou feedest them with the bread of tears; and givest them tears to drink in great measure.

6 Thou makest us a ^astrife unto our neighbours: and our enemies laugh among themselves.

7 Turn us again, O God of hosts, and cause thy face to shine; and we shall be saved.

8 Thou hast brought a ^avine out of ^bEgypt: thou hast ^ccast out the heathen, and planted it.

9 Thou preparedst *room* before it, and didst cause it to take deep root, and it filled the land.

10 The hills were ^acovered with the shadow of it, and the boughs thereof *were like* the goodly cedars.

11 She sent out her boughs unto the sea, and her branches unto the river.

12 Why hast thou *then* ^abroken down her hedges, so that all they which pass by the way do pluck her?

13 The boar out of the wood doth waste it, and the wild beast of the field doth devour it.

14 Return, we beseech thee, O God of hosts: look down from heaven, and behold, and visit this vine;

15 And the vineyard which thy right hand hath planted, and the branch *that* thou madest strong for thyself.

16 *It is* burned with fire, *it is* cut down: they perish at the rebuke of thy countenance.

17 Let thy hand be upon the man of thy right hand, upon the son of man *whom* thou madest strong for thyself.

18 So will not we ^ago back from thee: quicken us, and we will call upon thy name.

19 ^aTurn us again, O L<small>ORD</small> God of hosts, cause thy face to shine; and we shall be saved.

PSALM 81

Israel is commanded to sing praises to God—If the Israelites had walked in the Lord's ways, they would have triumphed over their enemies.

To the chief Musician upon Gittith,
A *Psalm* of Asaph.

S<small>ING</small> aloud unto God our strength: make a joyful noise unto the God of Jacob.

2 Take a psalm, and bring hither the timbrel, the pleasant harp with the psaltery.

3 Blow up the ^atrumpet in the new moon, in the time appointed, on our solemn feast day.

4 For this *was* a statute for Israel, *and* a law of the God of Jacob.

5 This he ordained in Joseph *for* a testimony, when he went out through the land of Egypt: *where* I heard a ^alanguage *that* I understood not.

6 I removed his shoulder from the ^aburden: his hands were delivered from the pots.

7 Thou calledst in ^atrouble, and I delivered thee; I answered thee in the secret ^bplace of thunder: I ^cproved thee at the waters of ^dMeribah. Selah.

8 Hear, O my people, and I will testify unto thee: O Israel, if thou wilt hearken unto me;

9 There shall no strange god be in thee; neither shalt thou worship any strange god.

10 I *am* the L<small>ORD</small> thy God, which brought thee out of the land of Egypt: open thy mouth wide, and I will fill it.

11 But my people would not

3*a* Lam. 5:21.
6*a* TG Strife.
8*a* TG Vineyard of the Lord.
  b Ex. 20:2;
     1 Ne. 17:23 (23–25);
     Moses 1:26.
  c Num. 21:3 (1–3);
     Acts 13:19 (17–19).

10*a* Gen. 13:16 (14–16).
12*a* Rom. 11:20 (15–24).
18*a* OR turn away.
19*a* 1 Ne. 22:12; D&C 35:25.
81 3*a* Lev. 23:24;
     Num. 10:10.
  5*a* TG Language.
  6*a* Ex. 1:11; 6:6 (6–7);

Mosiah 24:21 (14–21);
     D&C 109:48 (47–48).
7*a* Ps. 50:15;
   Alma 9:17; 38:5;
   D&C 3:8.
  b Ex. 19:18 (18–19).
  c HEB tested.
  d Ex. 17:7 (6–7).

hearken to my voice; and Israel would none of me.

12 So I ^agave them up unto their own hearts' ^blust: *and* they walked in their own counsels.

13 Oh that my people had ^ahearkened unto me, *and* Israel had walked in my ways!

14 I should soon have subdued their enemies, and turned my hand against their adversaries.

15 The haters of the LORD should have ^asubmitted themselves unto him: but their time should have endured for ever.

16 He should have fed them also with the finest of the wheat: and with honey out of the rock should I have satisfied thee.

PSALM 82

Thus says the Lord, Ye are gods and children of the Most High.

A Psalm of Asaph.

GOD ^astandeth in the congregation of the mighty; he judgeth among the gods.

2 How long will ye judge unjustly, and accept the ^apersons of the wicked? Selah.

3 Defend the poor and fatherless: do ^ajustice to the afflicted and needy.

4 Deliver the poor and needy: rid *them* out of the hand of the wicked.

5 They know not, neither will they understand; they ^awalk on in darkness: all the foundations of the earth are out of course.

6 I have said, Ye *are* gods; and all of you *are* ^achildren of the most High.

7 But ye shall ^adie like men, and fall like one of the princes.

8 Arise, O God, ^ajudge the earth: for thou shalt inherit all nations.

PSALM 83

God is asked to confound the enemies of His people—Jehovah is the Most High over all the earth.

A Song *or* Psalm of Asaph.

KEEP not thou ^asilence, O God: hold not thy peace, and be not still, O God.

2 For, lo, thine enemies make a tumult: and they that hate thee have lifted up the head.

3 They have taken crafty counsel against thy people, and consulted against thy hidden ones.

4 They have said, Come, and let us ^acut them off from *being* a nation; that the name of Israel may be no more in remembrance.

5 For they have consulted together with one consent: they are confederate against thee:

6 The ^atabernacles of Edom, and the Ishmaelites; of Moab, and the Hagarenes;

7 Gebal, and Ammon, and Amalek; the Philistines with the inhabitants of Tyre;

8 Assur also is joined with them: they have holpen the children of Lot. Selah.

9 Do unto them as *unto* the Midianites; as *to* ^aSisera, as *to* Jabin, at the brook of Kison:

10 *Which* perished at En-dor: they became *as* dung for the earth.

11 Make their nobles like Oreb, and like Zeeb: yea, all their princes as ^aZebah, and as Zalmunna:

12 Who said, Let us take to ourselves the ^ahouses of God in possession.

13 O my God, make them like a ^awheel; as the ^bstubble before the wind.

12a Acts 7:42;
    Rom. 1:28.
  b HEB stubbornness.
    TG Lust.
13a Deut. 32:29.
15a TG Submissiveness.
82 1a TG God, Access to.
  2a Prov. 18:5.
  3a TG Citizenship.
  5a TG Walking in
    Darkness.

6a TG Man, a Spirit Child
    of Heavenly Father;
    Man, Potential to
    Become like Heavenly
    Father;
    Sons and Daughters
    of God;
    Spirit Creation.
  7a 1 Cor. 15:22.
  8a TG Jesus Christ, Judge.
83 1a Ps. 28:1.

4a Ps. 74:8;
    Jer. 11:19.
  6a HEB tents.
  9a Judg. 4:15.
11a Judg. 8:5.
12a HEB pastures; i.e., the
    land of Israel.
13a Isa. 17:13.
  b Ps. 1:4.

14 As the fire burneth a *a*wood, and as the flame setteth the mountains on fire;

15 So persecute them with thy tempest, and make them afraid with thy storm.

16 Fill their faces with shame; that they may seek thy name, O LORD.

17 Let them be confounded and troubled for ever; yea, let them be put to shame, and *a*perish:

18 That *men* may know that thou, whose name alone is *a*JEHOVAH, *art* the most *b*high over all the earth.

PSALM 84

The righteous cry unto the living God—It is better to be a doorkeeper in the house of the Lord than to dwell in the tents of wickedness—No good thing is withheld from those who walk uprightly.

To the chief Musician upon Gittith,
A Psalm for the sons of Korah.

How *a*amiable *are* thy tabernacles, O LORD of hosts!

2 My soul longeth, yea, even *a*fainteth for the courts of the LORD: my heart and my flesh crieth out for the living God.

3 Yea, the sparrow hath found an house, and the swallow a nest for herself, where she may lay her young, *even* thine altars, O LORD of hosts, my King, and my God.

4 Blessed *are* they that dwell in thy house: they will be still praising thee. Selah.

5 Blessed *is* the man whose *a*strength *is* in thee; in whose heart *are* the ways *of them.*

6 *Who* passing through the valley of Baca make it a well; the rain also filleth the pools.

7 They go from strength to strength,

every one *of them* in Zion *a*appeareth before God.

8 O LORD God of hosts, hear my prayer: give ear, O God of Jacob. Selah.

9 Behold, O God our shield, and look upon the face of thine anointed.

10 For a day in thy courts *is* better than *a*a thousand. I had rather be a doorkeeper in the house of my God, than to dwell in the tents of wickedness.

11 For the LORD God *is* a *a*sun and *b*shield: the LORD will give *c*grace and glory: no good *thing* will he *d*withhold from them that *e*walk uprightly.

12 O LORD of hosts, blessed *is* the man that trusteth in thee.

PSALM 85

The Lord speaks peace to His people—Truth will spring out of the earth (the Book of Mormon), and righteousness will look down from heaven.

To the chief Musician,
A Psalm for the sons of Korah.

LORD, thou hast been *a*favourable unto thy land: thou hast brought back *b*the captivity of Jacob.

2 Thou hast forgiven the iniquity of thy people, thou hast covered all their sin. Selah.

3 Thou hast taken away all thy wrath: thou hast turned *thyself* from the fierceness of thine anger.

4 Turn us, O God of our salvation, and cause thine *a*anger toward us to cease.

5 Wilt thou be angry with us for ever? wilt thou draw out thine anger to all generations?

6 Wilt thou not revive us again: that thy people may rejoice in thee?

7 Shew us thy mercy, O LORD, and grant us thy salvation.

14*a* HEB forest.
17*a* 2 Ne. 25:14;
   D&C 71:7;
   Moses 7:15 (14–16).
18*a* TG Jesus Christ,
   Jehovah.
   b Ps. 97:9.
84 1*a* HEB lovely is Thy

dwelling place.
2*a* Ps. 119:81.
5*a* TG Strength.
7*a* Deut. 16:16.
10*a* IE a thousand
   elsewhere.
11*a* 3 Ne. 25:2.
   b Prov. 30:5.

c TG Grace.
d Rev. 21:7;
   D&C 76:59 (50–64).
e TG Walking with God.
85 1*a* Deut. 32:43.
   b OR Jacob out of
   captivity.
4*a* TG Anger.

8 I will hear what God the LORD will speak: for he will speak ᵃpeace unto his people, and to his saints: but let them not turn ᵇagain to folly.

9 Surely his ᵃsalvation *is* nigh them that fear him; that glory may dwell in our land.

10 Mercy and truth are met together; righteousness and peace have kissed *each other*.

11 ᵃTruth shall spring out of the ᵇearth; and righteousness shall look down from heaven.

12 Yea, the LORD shall give *that which is* ᵃgood; and our land shall yield her increase.

13 Righteousness shall go before him; and shall set *us* in the way of his steps.

PSALM 86

David implores God for mercy and is saved from the lowest hell—The Lord is good and generous in mercy—All nations will worship before Him.

A Prayer of David.

ᵃBow down thine ear, O LORD, hear me: for I *am* ᵇpoor and needy.

2 Preserve my ᵃsoul; for I *am* holy: O thou my God, save thy servant that trusteth in thee.

3 Be merciful unto me, O Lord: for I cry unto thee daily.

4 Rejoice the soul of thy servant: for unto thee, O Lord, do I ᵃlift up my soul.

5 For thou, Lord, *art* good, and ready to ᵃforgive; and plenteous in mercy unto all them that call upon thee.

6 Give ear, O LORD, unto my prayer; and attend to the voice of my supplications.

7 In the day of my trouble I will

ᵃcall upon thee: for thou wilt answer me.

8 Among the ᵃgods *there is* none like unto thee, O Lord; neither *are there any works* like unto thy works.

9 ᵃAll ᵇnations whom thou hast made shall ᶜcome and worship before thee, O Lord; and shall glorify thy name.

10 For thou *art* great, and doest wondrous things: thou *art* God alone.

11 ᵃTeach me thy way, O LORD; I will walk in thy truth: unite my heart to fear thy name.

12 I will praise thee, O Lord my God, with all my heart: and I will glorify thy name for evermore.

13 For great *is* thy mercy toward me: and thou hast ᵃdelivered my soul from the lowest hell.

14 O God, the ᵃproud are risen against me, and the assemblies of violent *men* have sought after my soul; and have not set thee before them.

15 But thou, O ᵃLord, *art* a God full of ᵇcompassion, and gracious, longsuffering, and plenteous in ᶜmercy and truth.

16 O turn unto me, and have mercy upon me; give thy strength unto thy servant, and save the son of thine handmaid.

17 Shew me a token for good; that they which hate me may see *it*, and be ashamed: because thou, LORD, hast holpen me, and comforted me.

PSALM 87

The Lord loves the gates of Zion, and He Himself will establish Zion.

A Psalm *or* Song for the sons of Korah.

HIS ᵃfoundation *is* in the holy mountains.

2 The LORD loveth the ᵃgates of

8a TG Peace of God.
  b 2 Pet. 2:20;
    D&C 42:26.
  9a Isa. 46:13; 51:5.
  11a TG Truth.
    b TG Book of Mormon.
  12a James 1:17; Alma 5:40.
86 1a HEB Incline.
    b Ps. 109:16 (15–16);

    3 Ne. 12:3;
      D&C 56:18 (17–18).
  2a OR life.
  4a Ps. 25:1; 143:8.
  5a TG Forgive.
  7a Ps. 77:2.
  8a Ex. 15:11.
  9a Isa. 66:18 (18–19).
    b D&C 88:104.

    c Ps. 65:2.
  11a 1 Kgs. 8:36.
  13a Ps. 30:3; Acts 2:34.
  14a Ps. 54:3.
  15a Num. 14:18; Ps. 103:8.
    b Ps. 145:8.
    c Ps. 62:12.
87 1a Isa. 28:16.
    2a IE cities.

^bZion more than all the dwellings of Jacob.

3 Glorious things are spoken of thee, O city of God. Selah.

4 I will make mention of Rahab and Babylon to them that know me: behold Philistia, and Tyre, with Ethiopia; this *man* was born there.

5 And of Zion it shall be said, This and that man was born in her: and the highest himself shall establish her.

6 The LORD shall count, when he writeth up the people, *that* this *man* was born there. Selah.

7 As well the singers as the players on instruments *shall be there:* all my ^asprings *are* in thee.

PSALM 88

A prayer of one who feels forsaken and who asks whether the Lord's loving kindness will be declared in the grave.

A Song *or* Psalm for the sons of Korah, to the chief Musician upon Mahalath Leannoth, Maschil of Heman the Ezrahite.

O LORD God of my salvation, I have cried day *and* night before thee:

2 Let my prayer come before thee: incline thine ear unto my cry;

3 For my soul is full of troubles: and my life draweth nigh unto the grave.

4 I am counted with them that go down into the ^apit: I am as a man *that hath* no strength:

5 Free among the dead, like the slain that lie in the grave, whom thou ^arememberest no more: and they are cut off from thy hand.

6 Thou hast laid me in the lowest pit, in darkness, in the deeps.

7 Thy wrath lieth hard upon me, and thou hast afflicted *me* with all thy waves. Selah.

8 Thou hast put away mine acquaintance far from me; thou hast made me an abomination unto them: *I am* shut up, and I cannot come forth.

9 Mine ^aeye mourneth by reason of ^baffliction: LORD, I have called daily upon thee, I have stretched out my hands unto thee.

10 Wilt thou shew wonders to the dead? shall the dead arise *and* praise thee? Selah.

11 Shall thy lovingkindness be declared in the grave? *or* thy faithfulness in destruction?

12 Shall thy wonders be known in the dark? and thy righteousness in the land of forgetfulness?

13 But unto thee have I cried, O LORD; and in the morning shall my prayer ^aprevent thee.

14 LORD, why castest thou off my soul? *why* ^ahidest thou thy face from me?

15 I *am* afflicted and ready to die from *my* youth up: *while* I suffer thy terrors I am distracted.

16 Thy fierce wrath goeth over me; thy terrors have cut me off.

17 They came round about me daily like water; they compassed me about together.

18 Lover and friend hast thou put far from me, *and* mine acquaintance into darkness.

PSALM 89

A messianic psalm—A song setting forth the mercy, greatness, justice, and righteousness of the Holy One of Israel— The Lord will establish David's seed and throne forever—God's Firstborn will be made higher than the kings of the earth.

Maschil of Ethan the Ezrahite.

I WILL sing of the mercies of the LORD for ever: with my mouth will I make known thy ^afaithfulness to all generations.

2 For I have said, Mercy shall be

2b TG Zion.
7a OR sources; i.e., of joy, happiness, etc.
88 4a Ps. 28:1; 143:7; 2 Ne. 24:15.

5a Ps. 31:12.
9a Ps. 38:10.
  b TG Affliction.
13a HEB come before Thy face.

14a 2 Sam. 11:27 (1–27); 12:11 (1–25); 1 Chr. 21:8 (1–8).
89 1a Ps. 119:90.

built up for ever: thy faithfulness shalt thou establish in the very heavens.

3 I have made a covenant with my ^achosen, I have sworn unto David my servant,

4 Thy seed will I ^aestablish for ever, and build up thy ^bthrone to all generations. Selah.

5 And the heavens shall praise thy wonders, O LORD: thy faithfulness also in the ^acongregation of the saints.

6 For who in the heaven can be compared unto the LORD? *who* among the sons of the mighty can be ^alikened unto the LORD?

7 God is greatly to be feared in the assembly of the ^asaints, and to be had in reverence of all *them that are* about him.

8 O LORD God of hosts, who *is* a strong LORD like unto thee? ^aor to thy faithfulness round about thee?

9 Thou rulest the raging of the sea: when the waves thereof arise, thou ^astillest them.

10 Thou hast broken Rahab in pieces, as one that is slain; thou hast scattered thine ^aenemies with thy strong arm.

11 The heavens *are* thine, the earth also *is* thine: *as for* the ^aworld and the fulness thereof, thou hast founded them.

12 The north and the south thou hast created them: Tabor and Hermon shall rejoice in thy name.

13 Thou hast a mighty arm: strong is thy hand, *and* high is thy right hand.

14 ^aJustice and ^bjudgment *are* the habitation of thy throne: mercy and truth shall go before thy face.

15 Blessed *is* the people that know the joyful sound: they shall walk, O LORD, in the light of thy countenance.

16 In thy name shall they rejoice all the day: and in thy righteousness shall they be exalted.

17 For thou *art* the glory of their strength: and in thy favour our ^ahorn shall be exalted.

18 For the LORD *is* our ^adefence; and the Holy One of Israel *is* our ^bking.

19 Then thou spakest in vision to thy holy one, and saidst, I have laid help upon *one that is* mighty; I have exalted *one* chosen out of the people.

20 I have found David my servant; with my holy oil have I ^aanointed him:

21 With whom my hand shall be established: mine arm also shall strengthen him.

22 The enemy shall not exact upon him; nor the son of wickedness afflict him.

23 And I will beat down his foes before his face, and plague them that hate him.

24 But my faithfulness and my mercy *shall be* with him: and in my name shall his horn be exalted.

25 I will set his hand also in the sea, and his right hand in the rivers.

26 He shall cry unto me, Thou *art* my father, my God, and the ^arock of my salvation.

27 Also I will make him *my* ^afirstborn, higher than the kings of the earth.

28 My mercy will I keep for him for evermore, and my covenant shall stand fast with him.

29 His ^aseed also will I make *to endure* for ever, and his throne as the days of heaven.

3*a* Hag. 2:23.
4*a* TG Jesus Christ, Davidic Descent of.
  b TG Jesus Christ, Millennial Reign; Kingdom of God, on Earth.
5*a* TG Church.
6*a* Jer. 10:7.
7*a* TG Saints.
8*a* HEB with Thy faithfulness.
9*a* Ps. 65:7; Matt. 8:26 (23–27); Mark 4:39 (37–41).
10*a* 1 Chr. 17:10; Micah 4:10; D&C 65:6.
11*a* Ps. 24:1.
14*a* TG God, Justice of; Justice.
  b TG Judgment.
17*a* 1 Sam. 2:1 (1–10).
18*a* Ps. 47:9.
  b TG Kingdom of God, in Heaven.
20*a* 1 Sam. 16:13.
26*a* 2 Sam. 22:47; Ps. 95:1.
27*a* TG Firstborn; Jesus Christ, Davidic Descent of; Jesus Christ, Firstborn.
29*a* Deut. 11:21.

30 If his children forsake my law, and walk not in my judgments;

31 If they break my statutes, and keep not my commandments;

32 Then will I visit their ᵃtransgression with the ᵇrod, and their iniquity with stripes.

33 Nevertheless my lovingkindness will I not utterly take from him, nor suffer my faithfulness to fail.

34 My covenant will I not break, nor alter the thing that is gone out of my lips.

35 Once have I ᵃsworn by my ᵇholiness that I will not lie unto David.

36 His seed shall ᵃendure for ever, and his throne as the sun before me.

37 It shall be established for ever as the moon, and as a faithful witness in heaven. Selah.

38 But thou hast cast off and abhorred, thou hast been wroth with thine anointed.

39 Thou hast made void the covenant of thy servant: thou hast profaned his crown by ᵃcasting it to the ground.

40 Thou hast broken down all his hedges; thou hast brought his strong holds to ruin.

41 All that pass by the way spoil him: he is a reproach to his neighbours.

42 Thou hast set up the right hand of his adversaries; thou hast made all his enemies to rejoice.

43 Thou hast also turned the edge of his sword, and hast not made him to stand in the battle.

44 Thou hast made his glory to cease, and cast his throne down to the ground.

45 The days of his youth hast thou shortened: thou hast covered him with ᵃshame. Selah.

46 How long, Lᴏʀᴅ? wilt thou hide thyself for ever? shall thy wrath burn like fire?

47 Remember how short my ᵃtime is: wherefore hast thou made all men in vain?

48 What man is he that ᵃliveth, and shall not see death? shall he deliver his soul from the hand of the grave? Selah.

49 Lord, where are thy former lovingkindnesses, which thou swarest unto David in thy truth?

50 Remember, Lord, the reproach of thy servants; how I do bear in my bosom the reproach of all the mighty people;

51 Wherewith thine enemies have reproached, O Lᴏʀᴅ; wherewith they have reproached the footsteps of thine anointed.

52 Blessed be the Lᴏʀᴅ for evermore. Amen, and Amen.

PSALM 90

A prayer of Moses, the man of God—God is from everlasting to everlasting—Man's days last but seventy years—Moses implores the Lord to give mercy and blessings to His people.

A Prayer of Moses the man of God.

Lᴏʀᴅ, thou hast been our dwelling place in all generations.

2 Before the mountains were brought forth, or ever thou hadst ᵃformed the earth and the world, even from ᵇeverlasting to everlasting, thou art God.

3 Thou ᵃturnest man to destruction; and sayest, Return, ye children of men.

4 For a thousand ᵃyears in thy sight are but as yesterday when it is past, and as a watch in the night.

5 Thou carriest them away as with a flood; they are as a sleep: in the morning they are like ᵃgrass which groweth up.

6 In the morning it flourisheth, and groweth up; in the evening it is cut down, and withereth.

32a TG Transgress.
  b 2 Sam. 7:14.
35a 3 Ne. 21:4.
  b Amos 4:2.
36a Ps. 72:5.
39a D&C 132:39 (37–39).

45a TG Shame.
47a TG Time.
48a Ps. 49:9.
90 2a D&C 38:1.
  b TG Eternity; God, Eternal

Nature of.
3a HEB returnest man to dust.
4a TG Time.
5a D&C 124:7.

7 For we are consumed by thine anger, and by thy wrath are we troubled.

8 Thou hast set our ^ainiquities before thee, our ^bsecret *sins* in the light of thy countenance.

9 For all our days are passed away in thy wrath: we spend our years as a tale *that is told.*

10 The ^adays of our years *are* threescore years and ten; and if by reason of strength *they be* fourscore years, yet *is* their strength labour and sorrow; for it is soon cut off, and we fly away.

11 Who knoweth the power of thine anger? even according to thy fear, *so is* thy wrath.

12 So teach *us* to number our days, that we may apply *our* hearts unto wisdom.

13 Return, O LORD, how long? and ^alet it repent thee concerning thy servants.

14 O satisfy us early with thy mercy; that we may rejoice and be glad all our days.

15 Make us glad according to the days *wherein* thou hast afflicted us, *and* the years *wherein* we have seen evil.

16 Let thy ^awork appear unto thy servants, and thy glory unto their children.

17 And let the ^abeauty of the LORD our God be upon us: and establish thou the work of our hands upon us; yea, the work of our hands establish thou it.

PSALM 91

A messianic psalm—The Lord will deliver the Messiah from terror, pestilence, and war—The Lord will give His angels charge over the Messiah and deliver Him and honor Him.

HE that dwelleth in the ^asecret place of the most High shall abide under the ^bshadow of the Almighty.

2 I will say of the LORD, *He is* my refuge and my fortress: my God; in him will I ^atrust.

3 Surely he shall deliver thee from the ^asnare of the fowler, *and* from the noisome pestilence.

4 He shall cover thee with his feathers, and under his wings shalt thou trust: his truth *shall be thy* ^ashield and ^bbuckler.

5 Thou shalt not be afraid for the ^aterror by night; *nor* for the arrow *that* flieth by day;

6 *Nor* for the pestilence *that* walketh in darkness; *nor* for the ^adestruction *that* wasteth at noonday.

7 A thousand shall fall at thy side, and ten thousand at thy right hand; *but* it shall not come nigh thee.

8 Only with thine eyes shalt thou behold and see the reward of the ^awicked.

9 Because thou hast made the LORD, *which is* my refuge, *even* the most High, thy habitation;

10 There shall no evil befall thee, neither shall any plague come nigh thy dwelling.

11 For he shall give his ^aangels charge over thee, to keep thee in all thy ways.

12 They shall bear thee up in *their* hands, lest thou dash thy foot against a stone.

13 Thou shalt ^atread upon the lion and adder: the young lion and the ^bdragon shalt thou trample under feet.

14 Because he hath set his love upon me, therefore will I deliver him: I will set him on high, because he hath known my name.

15 He shall call upon me, and I will answer him: I *will be* with him in trouble; I will deliver him, and honour him.

16 With long life will I satisfy him, and shew him my salvation.

8*a* Ps. 130:3; Jer. 16:17.
  b Ps. 19:12.
10*a* OR years of our life.
13*a* HEB have pity on Thy servants.
16*a* Moses 1:39.
17*a* TG Beauty.

91 1*a* Ps. 32:7.
  b Ps. 121:5.
  2*a* TG Trust in God.
  3*a* Ps. 124:7.
  4*a* Eph. 6:11; D&C 35:14.
  b Prov. 2:7.
  5*a* Isa. 43:2.

6*a* Dan. 3:25.
8*a* Mosiah 16:2;
   D&C 1:9 (9–10).
11*a* Luke 4:10 (10–11).
   TG Angels.
13*a* Luke 10:19.
  b OR serpent.

PSALM 92

*A psalm or song for the Sabbath day—
Give thanks unto the Lord—His enemies will perish—The righteous will
flourish—There is no unrighteousness
in the Lord.*

A Psalm *or* Song for the sabbath day.

IT *is a* good *thing* to give ªthanks
unto the LORD, and to sing praises
unto thy name, O most High:

2 To shew forth thy lovingkindness
in the morning, and thy faithfulness every night,

3 Upon an instrument of ten
strings, and upon the psaltery; upon
the harp with a solemn sound.

4 For thou, LORD, hast made me
glad through thy work: I will triumph in the works of thy hands.

5 O LORD, how great are thy
ªworks! *and* thy thoughts are very
deep.

6 A brutish man knoweth not;
neither doth a fool understand
this.

7 When the wicked spring as the
grass, and when all the workers of
iniquity do flourish; *it is* that they
shall be destroyed for ever:

8 But thou, LORD, *art most* high
for evermore.

9 For, lo, thine enemies, O LORD,
for, lo, thine enemies shall perish;
all the workers of iniquity shall be
scattered.

10 But my horn shalt thou exalt
like *the horn of* ªan unicorn: I shall
be anointed with fresh oil.

11 Mine eye also shall see *my desire* on mine enemies, *and* mine ears
shall hear *my desire* of the wicked
that rise up against me.

12 The righteous shall ªflourish
like the palm tree: he shall grow
like a cedar in Lebanon.

13 Those that be planted in the
house of the LORD shall flourish in
the courts of our God.

14 They shall still bring forth fruit
in ªold age; they shall be fat and
flourishing;

15 To shew that the LORD *is* upright: *he is* my ªrock, and *there is* no
ᵇunrighteousness in him.

PSALM 93

*The Lord reigns—He is from everlast-
ing—Holiness adorns the house of the
Lord forever.*

THE LORD reigneth, he is ªclothed
with majesty; the LORD is clothed
with strength, *wherewith* he hath
girded himself: the world also is
stablished, that it cannot be moved.

2 Thy throne *is* established of old:
thou *art* from ªeverlasting.

3 The ªfloods have lifted up, O
LORD, the floods have lifted up their
voice; the floods lift up their waves.

4 The LORD on high *is* mightier
than the noise of many waters, *yea,
than* the mighty waves of the sea.

5 Thy testimonies are very sure:
holiness becometh thine house, O
LORD, for ever.

PSALM 94

*The Lord will judge the earth and all
men—Blessed is he whom the Lord
teaches and chastens—The Lord will
not forsake His people, but He will cut
off the wicked.*

O LORD God, to whom ªvengeance
belongeth; O God, to whom vengeance belongeth, shew thyself.

2 Lift up thyself, thou ªjudge of
the earth: render a ᵇreward to the
proud.

3 LORD, how long shall the wicked,
how long shall the wicked ªtriumph?

4 *How long* shall they utter *and*
speak hard things? *and* all the workers of iniquity boast themselves?

5 They break in pieces thy people,
O LORD, and afflict thine heritage.

---

92 1a D&C 59:7.
    5a Ps. 40:5; Morm. 9:16;
        D&C 76:114;
        Moses 1:4.
    10a HEB a buffalo, bison.
    12a Ps. 52:8.

14a TG Old Age.
15a Ps. 78:35.
    b Rom. 9:14.
93 1a D&C 65:5.
    2a TG God, Eternal
        Nature of.

3a HEB rivers, streams.
94 1a TG Vengeance.
    2a TG Jesus Christ, Judge.
    b TG Reward.
    3a Alma 40:26;
        D&C 29:41; 121:8 (1–8).

6 They ^aslay the widow and the stranger, and murder the fatherless.

7 Yet they say, The LORD shall not see, neither shall the God of Jacob regard *it*.

8 Understand, ye brutish among the people: and *ye* fools, when will ye be wise?

9 He that planted the ear, shall he not ^ahear? he that formed the eye, shall he not see?

10 He that chastiseth the heathen, shall not he correct? he that teacheth man knowledge, *shall not he know?*

11 The LORD ^aknoweth the ^bthoughts of man, that they *are* ^cvanity.

12 Blessed *is* the man whom thou ^achastenest, O LORD, and teachest him out of thy law;

13 That thou mayest give him rest from the days of adversity, until the pit be digged for the wicked.

14 For the LORD will not cast off his people, neither will he ^aforsake his inheritance.

15 But judgment shall return unto righteousness: and all the upright in heart shall follow it.

16 Who will rise up for me against the evildoers? or who will stand up for me against the workers of iniquity?

17 Unless the LORD *had been* my help, my soul had almost dwelt in silence.

18 When I said, My foot slippeth; thy mercy, O LORD, held me up.

19 In the multitude of my thoughts within me thy comforts delight my soul.

20 Shall the throne of iniquity have fellowship with thee, which frameth ^amischief by a law?

21 They gather themselves together against the soul of the righteous, and condemn the innocent blood.

22 But the LORD is my defence; and my God *is* the rock of my refuge.

23 And he shall bring upon them their own iniquity, and shall cut them off in their own wickedness; *yea*, the LORD our God shall cut them off.

PSALM 95

Let us sing unto the Lord—Let us worship and bow down before Him—Israel provoked the Lord and failed to enter into His rest.

O COME, let us ^asing unto the LORD: let us make a ^bjoyful noise to the ^crock of our salvation.

2 Let us come before his presence with ^athanksgiving, and make a joyful noise unto him with psalms.

3 For the LORD *is* a ^agreat God, and a great ^bKing above all gods.

4 In his hand *are* the deep places of the earth: the strength of the hills *is* his also.

5 The sea *is* his, and he made it: and his hands formed the dry *land*.

6 O come, let us ^aworship and bow down: let us kneel before the LORD our ^bmaker.

7 For he *is* our God; and we *are* the people of his pasture, and the ^asheep of his hand. ^bTo day if ye will ^chear his ^dvoice,

8 ^aHarden not your heart, as ^bin the ^cprovocation, *and as in* the day of ^dtemptation in the wilderness:

9 When your fathers tempted me, ^aproved me, and saw my work.

10 ^aForty years long was I ^bgrieved with *this* ^cgeneration, and said, It *is*

6a 3 Ne. 24:5.
9a Job 22:13 (13–14); D&C 88:41.
11a TG God, Omniscience of.
  b Ezek. 20:32.
  c TG Vanity.
12a TG Chastening.
14a Deut. 31:6; 3 Ne. 22:10 (7–10); D&C 35:25.
20a TG Injustice.

95 1a 1 Chr. 16:9.
  b Ps. 66:1.
  c 2 Sam. 22:47; Ps. 89:26.
2a TG Thanksgiving.
3a 1 Chr. 16:25.
  b TG Kingdom of God, in Heaven.
6a TG Worship.
  b Ps. 149:2.
7a TG Jesus Christ, Good Shepherd; Sheep.

  b Heb. 3:7 (7–11).
  c Heb. 4:7.
  d D&C 88:66.
8a TG Hardheartedness.
  b HEB at Meribah.
  c TG Provoking.
  d TG Test.
9a TG Test.
10a Num. 14:33; Deut. 2:14 (14–15).
  b Ps. 119:158.
  c Prov. 30:12 (11–14).

a people that do err in their heart, and they have not known my ways:

11 Unto whom I sware in my wrath that they should not ªenter into my ᵇrest.

PSALM 96

Sing praises unto the Lord—Declare His name among the nations—Worship the Lord in the beauty of holiness—He comes to judge His people and the world.

O ªSING unto the LORD a new ᵇsong: sing unto the LORD, all the earth.

2 Sing unto the LORD, bless his name; shew forth his ªsalvation from day to day.

3 Declare his glory among the heathen, his wonders among all people.

4 For the LORD *is* great, and greatly to be praised: he *is* to be feared above all gods.

5 For all the gods of the nations *are* ªidols: but the LORD made the heavens.

6 ªHonour and majesty *are* before him: strength and beauty *are* in his sanctuary.

7 Give unto the LORD, O ye kindreds of the people, give unto the LORD glory and strength.

8 Give unto the LORD the ªglory *due unto* his name: bring an offering, and come into his ᵇcourts.

9 O worship the LORD in the beauty of ªholiness: fear before him, all the earth.

10 Say among the heathen *that* the LORD reigneth: the world also shall be established that it shall not be moved: he shall ªjudge the people righteously.

11 Let the heavens rejoice, and let the earth be glad; let the sea roar, and the fulness thereof.

12 Let the field be ªjoyful, and all that *is* therein: then shall all the trees of the wood rejoice

13 Before the ªLORD: for he cometh, for he cometh to judge the earth: he shall judge the world with righteousness, and the people with his truth.

PSALM 97

The Lord reigns in millennial glory— The hills melt at His presence—Those who love the Lord hate evil.

THE LORD ªreigneth; let the earth rejoice; let the multitude of isles be glad *thereof.*

2 Clouds and ªdarkness *are* round about him: righteousness and judgment *are* the habitation of his throne.

3 A fire goeth before him, and burneth up his enemies round about.

4 His lightnings ªenlightened the world: the earth saw, and trembled.

5 The hills ªmelted like ᵇwax at the presence of the LORD, at the presence of the Lord of the whole earth.

6 The heavens ªdeclare his ᵇrighteousness, and all the people see his glory.

7 ªConfounded be all they that serve graven ᵇimages, that boast themselves of idols: worship him, all *ye* gods.

8 Zion heard, and was glad; and the ªdaughters of Judah rejoiced because of thy judgments, O LORD.

9 For thou, LORD, *art* ªhigh above all the earth: thou art exalted far above all gods.

10 Ye that love the LORD, ªhate ᵇevil: he ᶜpreserveth the souls of his saints; he delivereth them out of the hand of the wicked.

11a Heb. 3:11.
  b TG God, Privilege of
    Seeing; Rest.
96 1a 1 Chr. 16:23.
  b D&C 25:12;
    84:98 (97–102).
  2a TG Salvation.
  5a TG Idolatry.
  6a TG Honor.
  8a Moses 4:2.
  b Ps. 116:19.

9a TG Holiness.
10a TG Jesus Christ, Judge.
12a Isa. 35:1.
13a TG Jesus Christ,
    Jehovah.
97 1a 1 Chr. 16:31.
  2a 1 Kgs. 8:12.
  4a Ps. 77:18.
  5a Judg. 5:5;
    Nahum 1:5.
  b Ps. 68:2; Micah 1:4.

6a Ps. 50:6.
  b Ps. 4:1.
7a Jacob 7:8 (6–15).
  b Ex. 20:4.
8a Ps. 48:11.
9a Ps. 83:18.
10a TG Hate.
  b TG Evil.
  c Ps. 121:7; 145:20 (1–21);
    1 Ne. 17:35 (33–35);
    D&C 82:10 (8–10).

11 ^aLight is sown for the righteous, and gladness for the upright in heart.

12 ^aRejoice in the LORD, ye righteous; and give ^bthanks at the remembrance of his holiness.

PSALM 98

Sing unto the Lord—All the ends of the earth will see His salvation—He comes to judge all men with equity and righteousness.

A Psalm.

O ^aSING unto the LORD a new song; for he hath done marvellous things: his right ^bhand, and his holy arm, hath gotten him the victory.

2 The LORD hath made ^aknown his salvation: his righteousness hath he openly shewed in the ^bsight of the ^cheathen.

3 He hath remembered his ^amercy and his truth toward the house of Israel: all the ends of the earth have seen the ^bsalvation of our God.

4 Make a joyful noise unto the LORD, all the earth: ^amake a loud noise, and rejoice, and sing praise.

5 Sing unto the LORD with the harp; with the harp, and the voice of a psalm.

6 With trumpets and sound of cornet make a joyful noise before the LORD, the King.

7 Let the sea roar, and the fulness thereof; the world, and they that dwell therein.

8 Let the floods clap *their* hands: let the hills be joyful together

9 Before the LORD; for he cometh to ^ajudge the earth: with righteousness shall he judge the ^bworld, and the people with equity.

PSALM 99

The Lord is great in Zion—Exalt the Lord and worship at His footstool, for He is holy.

THE LORD reigneth; let the people tremble: he sitteth *between* the ^acherubims; let the earth be moved.

2 The LORD *is* great in Zion; and he *is* high above all the people.

3 Let them praise thy great and terrible ^aname; *for it is* ^bholy.

4 The king's strength also loveth judgment; thou dost establish equity, thou executest judgment and righteousness in Jacob.

5 Exalt ye the LORD our God, and worship at his ^afootstool; *for he is* holy.

6 Moses and Aaron among his priests, and Samuel among them that call upon his name; they called upon the LORD, and he answered them.

7 He spake unto them in the ^acloudy pillar: they kept his testimonies, and the ordinance *that* he gave them.

8 Thou answeredst them, O LORD our God: thou wast a God that forgavest them, though thou tookest vengeance of their inventions.

9 Exalt the LORD our God, and ^aworship at his ^bholy hill; for the LORD our God *is* holy.

PSALM 100

Serve the Lord with gladness, all who are His people—Be thankful unto Him and bless His name.

A Psalm of praise.

MAKE a joyful noise unto the LORD, all ye lands.

2 Serve the LORD with ^agladness: come before his presence with ^bsinging.

11a D&C 50:24.
12a TG Joy.
 b D&C 59:21.
98 1a TG Singing.
 b Ex. 15:6 (1–12).
2a Isa. 62:2.
 b Lev. 26:45.
 c 1 Ne. 15:13;
  D&C 90:10 (10–11).
3a Gen. 24:27;

3 Ne. 5:21 (21–26).
 b TG Salvation.
4a HEB burst into song.
9a 1 Ne. 22:21 (21–24);
  Moses 6:57.
 b TG World.
99 1a TG Cherubim.
3a Rev. 15:4.
 b Luke 1:49.
5a 1 Chr. 28:2.

7a Ex. 33:9;
  Num. 14:14;
  Ps. 78:14; 105:39;
  1 Cor. 10:1.
9a TG Worship.
 b Ps. 2:6.
100 2a TG Cheerful.
 b TG Singing.

3 Know ye that the LORD he *is* God: *it is* he *that* hath ᵃmade us, and not we ourselves; *we are* his people, and the ᵇsheep of his pasture.

4 Enter into his gates with ᵃthanksgiving, *and* into his ᵇcourts with praise: be thankful unto him, *and* bless his name.

5 For the LORD *is* good; his mercy *is* everlasting; and his truth *endureth* to all generations.

PSALM 101

David sings of mercy and justice—He will forsake the company of evildoers.

A Psalm of David.

I WILL sing of mercy and judgment: unto thee, O LORD, will I sing.

2 I will behave myself ᵃwisely in a perfect way. O when wilt thou come unto me? I will walk within my house with a perfect heart.

3 I will set no wicked thing before mine eyes: I hate the work of them that turn aside; *it* shall not cleave to me.

4 A ᵃfroward heart shall depart from me: I will not ᵇknow a wicked *person.*

5 Whoso privily ᵃslandereth his neighbour, him will I cut off: him that hath an high look and a proud heart will not I ᵇsuffer.

6 Mine eyes *shall be* upon the faithful of the land, that they may dwell with me: he that ᵃwalketh in a ᵇperfect way, he shall serve me.

7 He that worketh ᵃdeceit shall not dwell within my house: he that telleth ᵇlies shall not tarry in my sight.

8 I will early destroy all the wicked of the land; that I may cut off all wicked doers from the city of the LORD.

PSALM 102

The psalmist offers a prayer of the afflicted—Zion will be built up when the Lord appears in His glory—Though the heaven and earth perish, the Lord who created them will endure forever.

A Prayer of the afflicted, when he is overwhelmed, and poureth out his complaint before the LORD.

HEAR my prayer, O LORD, and let my cry come unto thee.

2 ᵃHide not thy face from me in the day *when* I am in trouble; incline thine ear unto me: in the day *when* I call answer me speedily.

3 For my days are consumed like smoke, and my bones are burned as an hearth.

4 My heart is smitten, and withered like grass; so that I forget to eat my bread.

5 By reason of the voice of my groaning my bones cleave to my skin.

6 I am like a ᵃpelican of the wilderness: I am like an owl of the desert.

7 I watch, and am as a sparrow alone upon the house top.

8 Mine enemies reproach me all the day; *and* they that are mad against me are sworn against me.

9 For I have eaten ashes like bread, and mingled my drink with weeping,

10 Because of thine indignation and thy wrath: for thou hast lifted me up, and cast me down.

11 My days *are* like a ᵃshadow that declineth; and I am withered like ᵇgrass.

12 But thou, O LORD, shalt endure for ᵃever; and thy remembrance unto all generations.

13 Thou shalt arise, *and* have ᵃmercy upon ᵇZion: for the time to favour her, yea, the set time, is come.

3a Eph. 2:10.
  b TG Sheep.
4a TG Thanksgiving.
  b Ps. 116:19.
101 2a Jacob 6:12 (11–12).
  4a HEB perverse.
     Prov. 11:20; 17:20.
  b Matt. 7:23.

5a TG Backbiting;
   Slander.
  b Isa. 1:13.
6a TG Walking with
   God.
  b TG Perfection.
7a TG Deceit.
  b TG Honesty; Lying.

102 2a D&C 121:1 (1–8).
  6a HEB vulture, hawk.
  11a 1 Chr. 29:15;
     Ps. 144:4.
  b Isa. 40:6 (6–8).
  12a TG Immortality.
  13a Isa. 14:1.
  b TG Zion.

14 For thy servants take pleasure in her stones, and favour the dust thereof.

15 So the heathen shall fear the name of the LORD, and all the kings of the earth thy glory.

16 When the LORD shall build up Zion, he shall *appear in his glory.

17 He will regard the *prayer of the destitute, and not despise their prayer.

18 This shall be *written for the *generation to come: and the people which shall be created shall praise the LORD.

19 For he hath looked down from the height of his sanctuary; from heaven did the LORD behold the earth;

20 To hear the groaning of the prisoner; to loose those that are appointed to death;

21 To declare the name of the LORD in Zion, and his praise in Jerusalem;

22 When the people are gathered together, and the kingdoms, to serve the LORD.

23 He weakened my strength in the way; he shortened my days.

24 I said, O my God, take me not away in the midst of my days: thy years *are* throughout all generations.

25 Of old hast thou laid the foundation of the *earth: and the heavens *are* the work of thy hands.

26 They shall *perish, but thou shalt endure: yea, all of them shall wax old like a garment; as a vesture shalt thou change them, and they shall be changed:

27 But thou *art* the *same, and thy years shall have no *end.

28 The children of thy servants shall continue, and their *seed shall be established before thee.

PSALM 103

David exhorts the Saints to bless the Lord for His mercy—The Lord is merciful unto those who keep His commandments.

A *Psalm* of David.

BLESS the LORD, O my soul: and all that is within me, *bless* his holy name.

2 Bless the LORD, O my soul, and forget not all his benefits:

3 Who *forgiveth all thine iniquities; who healeth all thy *diseases;

4 Who *redeemeth thy life from destruction; who crowneth thee with lovingkindness and tender mercies;

5 Who satisfieth thy mouth with good *things; so that* thy youth is renewed like the *eagle's.

6 The LORD executeth righteousness and judgment for all that are oppressed.

7 He made known his ways unto Moses, his acts unto the children of Israel.

8 The *LORD *is* *merciful and gracious, slow to *anger, and plenteous in mercy.

9 He will not always chide: neither will he keep *his *anger for ever.

10 He hath not dealt with us after our sins; nor rewarded us according to our iniquities.

11 For as the heaven is high above the earth, *so* great is his mercy toward them that fear him.

12 As far as the east is from the west, *so* far hath he removed our transgressions from us.

13 Like as a father *pitieth *his *children, so* the LORD pitieth them that fear him.

14 For he knoweth our frame; he remembereth that we *are* *dust.

16a TG Jesus Christ, Second Coming.
17a Ezek. 36:37.
18a TG Scriptures, Writing of.
   b Ps. 48:13.
25a TG Creation.
26a Isa. 34:4; 51:6;
   2 Pet. 3:10 (10–12).

27a TG God, Eternal Nature of.
   b TG Eternity.
28a 2 Ne. 29:14;
   D&C 132:30;
   Moses 7:52 (50–53).
103 3a TG Forgive.
   b TG Sickness.
   4a TG Redemption.

5a Isa. 40:31.
8a Ps. 86:15.
   b Gen. 19:16; D&C 76:5.
   c TG Anger.
9a TG God, Indignation of.
13a Ezek. 24:21; Mal. 3:17.
   TG God, Mercy of.
   b TG Family.
14a TG Mortality.

15 *As for* man, his days *are* as grass: as a flower of the field, so he flourisheth.

16 For the wind passeth over it, and it is gone; and the place thereof shall know it no more.

17 But the *a*mercy of the LORD *is* from everlasting to everlasting upon them that fear him, and his righteousness unto children's children;

18 To such as keep his covenant, and to those that remember his commandments to do them.

19 The LORD hath prepared his throne in the heavens; and his kingdom ruleth over all.

20 Bless the LORD, ye his angels, that excel in strength, that do his commandments, hearkening unto the voice of his word.

21 Bless ye the LORD, all *ye* his hosts; *ye* ministers of his, that do his *a*pleasure.

22 Bless the LORD, all his works in all places of his dominion: bless the LORD, O my soul.

PSALM 104

The Lord is clothed with honor and majesty—He makes His angels spirits and His ministers a flaming fire—Through His providence He sustains all forms of life—His glory endures forever.

BLESS the LORD, O my soul. O LORD my God, thou art very great; thou art *a*clothed with honour and majesty.

2 Who coverest *thyself* with light as *with* a garment: who *a*stretchest out the *b*heavens like a curtain:

3 Who layeth the beams of his chambers in the waters: who maketh the *a*clouds his chariot: who walketh upon the wings of the wind:

4 Who maketh *a*his angels spirits; his ministers a flaming fire:

5 *Who* laid the foundations of the earth, *that* it should not be removed for ever.

6 Thou coveredst it with the deep as *with* a garment: the *a*waters stood above the mountains.

7 At thy rebuke they fled; at the voice of thy thunder they hasted away.

8 They go up by the mountains; they go down by the valleys unto the place which thou hast founded for them.

9 Thou hast set a bound that they may not pass over; that they turn not again to *a*cover the earth.

10 He sendeth the *a*springs into the valleys, *which* run among the hills.

11 They give drink to every beast of the field: the wild asses quench their thirst.

12 By them shall the fowls of the heaven have their habitation, *which* sing among the branches.

13 He watereth the hills from his chambers: the earth is satisfied with the fruit of thy works.

14 He causeth the grass to grow for the cattle, and herb for the service of man: that he may bring forth food out of the earth;

15 And wine *that* maketh glad the heart of man, *and* oil to make *his* face to shine, and bread *which* strengtheneth man's heart.

16 The *a*trees of the LORD are full *of sap*; the cedars of Lebanon, which he hath planted;

17 Where the birds make their nests: *as for* the stork, the fir trees *are* her house.

18 The high hills *are* a refuge for the wild goats; *and* the rocks for the *a*conies.

19 He appointed the *a*moon *b*for seasons: the sun knoweth his going down.

20 Thou makest darkness, and it is night: wherein all the beasts of the forest do creep *forth*.

17*a* TG God, Mercy of.
21*a* TG Pleasure.
104 1*a* Prov. 31:25.
   2*a* Job 9:8; Isa. 40:22.
    b TG Heaven.
   3*a* Isa. 19:1.

4*a* OR the winds His messengers.
   TG Angels.
6*a* Gen. 7:19.
9*a* Moses 7:51 (50–52).
10*a* TG Nature, Earth.

16*a* Num. 24:6.
18*a* OR rock badgers.
19*a* Gen. 1:14;
   Moses 2:14 (3–5, 14).
   b IE to indicate the time of month and year.

21 The young lions roar after their prey, and seek their meat from God.

22 The sun ariseth, they gather themselves together, and lay them down in their dens.

23 Man goeth forth unto his work and to his labour until the evening.

24 O LORD, how manifold are thy works! in wisdom hast thou made them all: the earth is full of thy ^ariches.

25 *So is* this great and wide sea, wherein *are* things creeping innumerable, both small and great beasts.

26 There go the ships: *there is* that leviathan, *whom* thou hast made to play therein.

27 These wait all upon thee; that thou mayest give *them* their meat in due season.

28 *That* thou givest them they gather: thou openest thine hand, they are filled with good.

29 Thou hidest thy ^aface, they are troubled: thou takest away their ^bbreath, they die, and return to their ^cdust.

30 Thou sendest forth thy spirit, they are created: and thou renewest the face of the earth.

31 The glory of the LORD shall endure for ever: the LORD shall rejoice in his works.

32 He looketh on the earth, and it trembleth: he toucheth the hills, and they smoke.

33 I will sing unto the LORD as long as I live: I will sing praise to my God while I have my being.

34 My ^ameditation of him shall be sweet: I will be glad in the LORD.

35 Let the sinners be consumed out of the earth, and let the wicked be no more. Bless thou the LORD, O my soul. ^aPraise ye the LORD.

PSALM 105

Make the Lord's doings known among all men—Show His covenant with Abraham and His dealings with Israel—Touch not His anointed, and do His prophets no harm—Israel is to ob serve His statutes and keep His laws.

O GIVE ^athanks unto the LORD; call upon his name: ^bmake known his deeds among the people.

2 Sing unto him, sing psalms unto him: ^atalk ye of all his wondrous works.

3 Glory ye in his holy name: let the heart of them rejoice that seek the LORD.

4 Seek the LORD, and his strength: seek his face evermore.

5 Remember his marvellous works that he hath done; his wonders, and the judgments of his mouth;

6 O ye seed of Abraham his servant, ye children of Jacob his chosen.

7 He *is* the LORD our God: his judgments *are* in all the earth.

8 He hath remembered his ^acovenant for ever, the word *which* he commanded to a thousand generations.

9 Which ^a*covenant* he made with Abraham, and his ^boath unto Isaac;

10 And confirmed the same unto Jacob for a law, *and* to Israel *for* an ^aeverlasting covenant:

11 Saying, Unto thee will I give the ^aland of Canaan, the lot of your inheritance:

12 When they were *but* a few men in number; yea, very few, and strangers in it.

13 When they went from one nation to another, from *one* kingdom to another people;

14 He suffered no man to do them wrong: yea, he ^areproved kings for their sakes;

15 *Saying,* Touch not mine ^aan-

24a HEB creations.
  TG Treasure.
29a Ps. 30:7.
  b TG Breath of Life.
  c Moses 4:25.
34a TG Meditation.
35a HEB *Hallelu-yah*

(Hallelujah), Praise
  ye Jehovah!
105 1a TG Thanksgiving.
  b TG Preaching.
2a D&C 19:37.
8a Ex. 2:24.
9a TG Covenants.

b Gen. 22:16 (16–18).
10a 1 Chr. 16:17 (16–17);
  Morm. 5:20;
  Abr. 2:9 (6–11).
11a TG Promised Lands.
14a Gen. 12:17; 20:3.
15a D&C 121:16.

ointed, and do my *b*prophets no harm.

16 Moreover he called for a *a*famine upon the land: he brake the whole *b*staff of bread.

17 He *a*sent a man before them, *even* Joseph, *who* was *b*sold for a servant:

18 Whose feet they hurt with *a*fetters: he was laid in iron:

19 Until the time that his *a*word came: the word of the LORD tried him.

20 The *a*king sent and loosed him; *even* the ruler of the people, and let him go free.

21 He made him *a*lord of his house, and ruler of all his substance:

22 To bind his princes at his pleasure; and teach his *a*senators wisdom.

23 Israel also came into *a*Egypt; and Jacob sojourned in the land of *b*Ham.

24 And he *a*increased his people greatly; and made them stronger than their enemies.

25 He turned their heart to hate his people, to deal *a*subtilly with his servants.

26 He sent Moses his servant; *and* Aaron whom he had chosen.

27 They shewed his signs among them, and wonders in the land of Ham.

28 He sent darkness, and made it dark; and they rebelled not against his word.

29 He turned their waters into *a*blood, and slew their fish.

30 Their land brought forth *a*frogs in abundance, in the chambers of their kings.

31 He spake, and there came divers sorts of flies, *and* *a*lice in all their *b*coasts.

32 He gave them *a*hail for rain, *and* flaming fire in their land.

33 He smote their vines also and their fig trees; and brake the trees of their coasts.

34 He spake, and the *a*locusts came, and caterpillers, and that without number,

35 And did eat up all the herbs in their land, and devoured the fruit of their ground.

36 He smote also all the *a*firstborn in their land, the chief of all their strength.

37 He brought *a*them forth also with *b*silver and gold: and *there was* not one feeble *person* among their tribes.

38 Egypt was *a*glad when they departed: for the fear of them fell upon them.

39 He spread a *a*cloud for a covering; and fire to give light in the night.

40 *The people* asked, and he brought *a*quails, and satisfied them with the bread of heaven.

41 He opened the rock, and the waters gushed out; they ran in the dry places *like* a river.

42 For he remembered his holy *a*promise, *and* Abraham his servant.

43 And he brought forth his *a*people with joy, *and* his chosen with gladness:

44 And gave them the lands of the heathen: and they inherited the labour of the people;

45 That they might observe his statutes, and keep his laws. Praise ye the LORD.

15b 2 Ne. 26:5 (3, 5).
16a TG Famine.
  b Lev. 26:26.
17a Gen. 45:5.
  b Gen. 37:36 (28, 36).
18a Gen. 39:20.
19a Gen. 40:8.
20a Gen. 41:14.
21a Gen. 41:40.
22a HEB elders.
23a Gen. 46:6; Ex. 1:1.
  b Abr. 1:23 (20–25).
24a Ex. 1:7.
25a Ex. 1:10 (8–10).
29a Ex. 7:20.
30a Ex. 8:6.
31a Ex. 8:17 (16–20).
  b HEB lands, territory.
32a Ex. 9:23 (22–26).
34a Ex. 10:4 (1–12).
36a Ex. 12:29 (27–31).
37a IE Israel.
  b Ex. 12:35.
38a Ex. 12:33.
39a Ex. 13:21; Ps. 99:7.
40a Ex. 16:13 (12–13).
42a TG Promise.
43a TG Seed of Abraham.

PSALM 106

Praise the Lord for His mercy and mighty works—Israel rebelled and did wickedly—Moses mediated between Israel and the Lord—Israel was scattered and slain for worshipping false gods.

[a]PRAISE ye the LORD. O give thanks unto the LORD; for *he is* [b]good: for his mercy *endureth* for ever.

2 Who can utter the mighty [a]acts of the LORD? *who* can shew forth all his praise?

3 Blessed *are* they that keep judgment, *and* he that doeth righteousness at all times.

4 Remember me, O LORD, with the favour *that thou bearest unto* thy people: O visit me with thy salvation;

5 That I may see the good of thy chosen, that I may rejoice in the gladness of thy nation, that I may glory with thine inheritance.

6 We have [a]sinned with our fathers, we have committed iniquity, we have done wickedly.

7 Our fathers understood not thy wonders in Egypt; they remembered not the multitude of thy mercies; but [a]provoked *him* at the sea, *even* at the [b]Red sea.

8 Nevertheless he saved them for his [a]name's sake, that he might make his mighty [b]power to be known.

9 He [a]rebuked the [b]Red sea also, and it was dried up: so he led them through the depths, as through the wilderness.

10 And he saved them from the hand of him that hated *them,* and redeemed them from the hand of the enemy.

11 And the waters covered their enemies: there was not [a]one of them left.

12 Then believed they his words; they sang his praise.

13 They soon forgat his works; they waited not for his counsel:

14 But [a]lusted exceedingly in the wilderness, and tempted God in the desert.

15 And he gave them their request; but sent leanness into their soul.

16 They [a]envied Moses also in the camp, *and* Aaron the saint of the LORD.

17 The earth [a]opened and swallowed up Dathan, and covered the company of Abiram.

18 And a [a]fire was kindled in their company; the flame burned up the wicked.

19 They made a calf in Horeb, and worshipped the [a]molten image.

20 Thus they changed their glory into the similitude of an ox that eateth grass.

21 They forgat God their saviour, which had done great things in Egypt;

22 Wondrous works in the land of Ham, *and* terrible things by the Red sea.

23 Therefore he said that he would [a]destroy them, had not Moses his chosen stood before him in the breach, to turn away his wrath, lest he should destroy *them.*

24 Yea, they despised the pleasant land, they [a]believed not his word:

25 But [a]murmured in their tents, *and* hearkened not unto the voice of the LORD.

26 Therefore he lifted up his hand against them, to overthrow them in the wilderness:

27 To overthrow their seed also among the nations, and to scatter them in the lands.

28 They joined themselves also unto [a]Baal-peor, and [b]ate the sacrifices [c]of the dead.

29 Thus they provoked *him* to

---

106 1*a* HEB *Hallelu-yah*
  (Hallelujah).
  b Ps. 119:68.
  2*a* Jacob 4:8.
  6*a* Jer. 14:20;
  Dan. 9:5 (5–6).
  7*a* Ex. 14:11 (11–12).
  b HEB Reed Sea.
  8*a* Ex. 9:16;

  Isa. 63:14;
  Ezek. 20:9; 36:22.
  b Ex. 18:1.
  9*a* 2 Ne. 7:2.
  b Ex. 14:21 (1–31).
  11*a* Ex. 14:28.
  14*a* TG Lust.
  16*a* TG Envy.
  17*a* Num. 16:32 (30–35).

  18*a* Num. 16:35.
  19*a* Ex. 32:4.
  23*a* Ex. 32:10 (10–11, 32).
  24*a* TG Unbelief.
  25*a* TG Murmuring.
  28*a* Hosea 9:10.
  b Ex. 34:15.
  c IE offered to.

anger with their ^ainventions: and the plague brake in upon them.

30 Then stood up ^aPhinehas, and executed judgment: and *so* the plague was stayed.

31 And that was counted unto him for righteousness unto all generations for evermore.

32 They angered *him* also at the waters of ^astrife, so that it went ill with Moses for their ^bsakes:

33 Because they provoked his spirit, so that he ^aspake unadvisedly with his lips.

34 They did not ^adestroy the nations, concerning whom the LORD commanded them:

35 But were ^amingled among the heathen, and learned their works.

36 And they served their ^aidols: which were a snare unto them.

37 Yea, they sacrificed their sons and their daughters unto devils,

38 And shed innocent ^ablood, *even* the blood of their sons and of their daughters, whom they sacrificed unto the ^bidols of Canaan: and the land was polluted with blood.

39 Thus were they defiled with their own works, and went a whoring with their own inventions.

40 Therefore was the ^awrath of the LORD kindled against his people, insomuch that he abhorred his own inheritance.

41 And he gave them into the hand of the heathen; and they that hated them ruled over them.

42 Their ^aenemies also ^boppressed them, and they were brought into subjection under their hand.

43 Many times did he deliver them; but they provoked *him* with their counsel, and were brought low for their iniquity.

44 Nevertheless he regarded their affliction, when he heard their cry:

45 And he remembered for them his ^acovenant, and ^brepented according to the multitude of his mercies.

46 He made them also to be pitied of all those that carried them captives.

47 Save us, O LORD our God, and gather us from among the heathen, to give thanks unto thy holy name, *and* to triumph in thy praise.

48 ^aBlessed *be* the LORD God of Israel from everlasting to everlasting: and let all the people say, Amen. Praise ye the LORD.

PSALM 107

The people of Israel are to praise and thank the Lord when they are gathered and redeemed—Oh, that men would praise the Lord!—The Lord's providences prevail in the lives of men.

O GIVE thanks unto the LORD, for *he is* good: for his mercy *endureth* for ever.

2 Let the redeemed of the LORD say *so*, whom he hath ^aredeemed from the hand of the enemy;

3 And gathered them out of the lands, from the east, and from the west, from the north, and from the south.

4 They ^awandered in the ^bwilderness in a solitary way; they found no city to dwell in.

5 Hungry and thirsty, their soul fainted in them.

6 Then they ^acried unto the LORD in their ^btrouble, *and* he delivered them out of their distresses.

7 And he led them forth by the right way, that they might go to a city of habitation.

8 Oh that *men* would praise the LORD *for* his goodness, and *for* his wonderful works to the children of men!

29*a* HEB doings.
30*a* Num. 25:7 (7–8).
32*a* Ezek. 47:19.
  TG Strife.
  b Deut. 1:37; 3:26.
33*a* Num. 20:10.
34*a* Judg. 1:21 (21, 27–36).
35*a* Judg. 3:5 (5–6);
  Isa. 2:6.

36*a* TG Apostasy of Israel.
38*a* Jer. 2:34 (31–37).
  b TG Idolatry.
40*a* Moses 7:34.
42*a* Lev. 26:38.
  b Judg. 4:3.
45*a* Ps. 74:20;
  Jer. 14:21.
  b HEB relented.

Judg. 2:18;
  Moses 8:25.
48*a* Ps. 72:18.
107 2*a* Deut. 7:8 (7–8);
  3 Ne. 9:17 (15–17).
  4*a* Jer. 2:6.
  b 1 Ne. 22:4.
  6*a* Jonah 2:7.
  b TG Adversity.

9 For he satisfieth the longing soul, and filleth the hungry soul with goodness.

10 Such as sit in ^adarkness and in the shadow of death, *being* bound in affliction and iron;

11 Because they ^arebelled against the words of God, and contemned the counsel of the most High:

12 Therefore he brought down their heart with labour; they fell down, and *there was* none to help.

13 Then they cried unto the LORD in their trouble, *and* he saved them out of their distresses.

14 He brought them out of darkness and the ^ashadow of death, and brake their bands in sunder.

15 Oh that *men* would praise the LORD *for* his goodness, and *for* his wonderful works to the children of men!

16 For he hath ^abroken the gates of brass, and cut the bars of iron in sunder.

17 Fools because of their transgression, and because of their iniquities, are afflicted.

18 Their soul abhorreth all manner of ^ameat; and they draw near unto the gates of death.

19 Then they cry unto the LORD in their trouble, *and* he saveth them out of their distresses.

20 He sent his word, and healed them, and delivered *them* from their destructions.

21 Oh that *men* would praise the LORD *for* his goodness, and *for* his wonderful works to the children of men!

22 And let them sacrifice the sacrifices of ^athanksgiving, and declare his works with ^brejoicing.

23 They that go down to the sea in ships, that do business in great waters;

24 These see the works of the LORD, and his wonders in the deep.

25 For he commandeth, and raiseth the stormy wind, which lifteth up the waves thereof.

26 They mount up to the heaven, they go down again to the depths: their soul is melted because of trouble.

27 They reel to and fro, and stagger like a drunken ^aman, and are at their wits' end.

28 Then they cry unto the LORD in their trouble, and he bringeth them out of their distresses.

29 He ^amaketh the storm a calm, so that the waves thereof are still.

30 Then are they glad because they be quiet; so he bringeth them unto their desired haven.

31 Oh that *men* would praise the LORD *for* his goodness, and *for* his wonderful works to the children of men!

32 Let them exalt him also in the ^acongregation of the people, and praise him in the assembly of the elders.

33 He turneth rivers into a wilderness, and the watersprings into dry ground;

34 A fruitful land into barrenness, for the ^awickedness of them that dwell therein.

35 He turneth the ^awilderness into a standing water, and dry ground into watersprings.

36 And there he maketh the hungry to dwell, that they may prepare a city for habitation;

37 And sow the fields, and plant vineyards, which may yield fruits of increase.

38 He blesseth them also, so that they are multiplied greatly; and suffereth not their cattle to decrease.

39 Again, they are ^aminished and brought low through oppression, affliction, and sorrow.

40 He poureth contempt upon princes, and causeth them to wander in the wilderness, *where there is* no way.

10*a* TG Darkness, Spiritual.
11*a* TG Rebellion.
14*a* Job 3:5.
16*a* Isa. 45:2.
18*a* HEB food.

22*a* Lev. 7:12.
   b TG Cheerful.
27*a* 2 Ne. 28:14.
29*a* Matt. 8:26 (24–27).
32*a* TG Church.

34*a* Ezek. 12:19.
35*a* TG Earth, Renewal of.
39*a* OR diminished.

41 Yet setteth he the poor on high from affliction, and maketh *him* families like a flock.

42 The righteous shall see *it,* and rejoice: and all iniquity shall stop her mouth.

43 Whoso *is* ᵃwise, and will observe these *things,* even they shall understand the lovingkindness of the LORD.

PSALM 108

David praises and exalts God—Judah is the Lord's lawgiver.

A Song *or* Psalm of David.

O GOD, my heart is fixed; I will ᵃsing and give praise, even with my glory.

2 Awake, psaltery and harp: I *myself* will awake early.

3 I will praise thee, O LORD, among the people: and I will sing praises unto thee among the nations.

4 For thy mercy *is* great above the heavens: and thy truth *reacheth* unto the clouds.

5 Be thou exalted, O God, above the heavens: and thy glory above all the earth;

6 That thy ᵃbeloved may be ᵇdelivered: save *with* thy right hand, and answer me.

7 God hath spoken ᵃin his holiness; I will rejoice, I will divide Shechem, and mete out the valley of Succoth.

8 Gilead *is* mine; Manasseh *is* mine; Ephraim also *is* the strength of mine head; Judah *is* my lawgiver;

9 Moab *is* my washpot; over Edom will I cast out my shoe; over Philistia will I triumph.

10 Who will bring me into the strong city? who will lead me into Edom?

11 *Wilt* not *thou,* O God, *who* hast cast us off? and wilt not thou, O God, go forth with our hosts?

12 Give us help from trouble: for vain *is* the help of man.

13 Through God we shall do valiantly: for he *it is that* shall tread down our enemies.

PSALM 109

David speaks of the cursings due to the wicked and deceitful—He prays that his enemies will be confounded.

To the chief Musician, A Psalm of David.

HOLD not thy peace, O God of my praise;

2 For the mouth of the wicked and the mouth of the deceitful are opened against me: they have spoken against me with a ᵃlying tongue.

3 They compassed me about also with words of hatred; and fought against me without a cause.

4 ᵃFor my love they are my adversaries: but I *give myself unto* prayer.

5 And they have rewarded me evil for good, and ᵃhatred for my love.

6 Set thou a wicked man over him: and let ᵃSatan stand at his right hand.

7 When he shall be ᵃjudged, let him be condemned: and let his ᵇprayer become sin.

8 Let his days be few; *and* let another take his ᵃoffice.

9 Let his children be fatherless, and his wife a widow.

10 Let his children be continually vagabonds, and beg: let them seek *their bread* also out of their desolate places.

11 Let the ᵃextortioner catch all that he hath; and let the strangers spoil his labour.

12 Let there be none to extend mercy unto him: neither let there be any to favour his fatherless children.

43a Hosea 14:9 (8–9).
108 1a Ps. 57:7 (7–11);
     2 Ne. 22:5; Alma 26:8;
     D&C 136:28.
   6a IE beloved people.
     b Ps. 60:5 (5–12).
   7a OR in His sanctuary.
109 2a D&C 109:30 (29–30).

4a JST Ps. 109:4 *And,*
   notwithstanding my love,
   they are my adversaries;
   yet I *will continue in*
   prayer *for them.*
5a 1 Jn. 3:15.
6a HEB an adversary,
   accuser.

    Zech. 3:1.
7a James 2:13; Hel. 8:25;
   D&C 10:23 (20–23);
   121:24 (23–25).
  b Prov. 28:9;
   Mosiah 11:25 (24–25).
8a Acts 1:20 (16–20).
11a OR creditors seize.

13 Let his ^aposterity be cut off; *and* in the generation following let their name be ^bblotted out.

14 Let the ^ainiquity of his fathers be remembered with the LORD; and let not the sin of his mother be blotted out.

15 Let them be before the LORD continually, that he may cut off the memory of them from the earth.

16 Because that he remembered not to shew mercy, but persecuted the ^apoor and needy man, that he might even slay the broken in heart.

17 As he loved cursing, so let it come unto him: as he delighted not in blessing, so let it be far from him.

18 As he clothed himself with cursing like as with his garment, so let it come into his bowels like water, and like oil into his bones.

19 Let it be unto him as the garment *which* covereth him, and for a girdle wherewith he is girded continually.

20 *Let* this *be* the reward of mine adversaries from the LORD, and of them that speak evil against my soul.

21 But do thou for me, O GOD the Lord, for thy ^aname's sake: because thy mercy *is* good, deliver thou me.

22 For I *am* poor and needy, and my heart is wounded within me.

23 I am gone like the shadow when it declineth: I am tossed up and down as the locust.

24 My knees are weak through fasting; and my flesh faileth of fatness.

25 I became also a reproach unto them: *when* they looked upon me they shaked their heads.

26 Help me, O LORD my God: O save me according to thy mercy:

27 That they may know that this is thy hand; *that* thou, LORD, hast done it.

28 Let them ^acurse, but bless thou: when they arise, let them be ashamed; but let thy servant rejoice.

29 Let mine adversaries be clothed with ^ashame, and let them cover themselves with their own confusion, as with a mantle.

30 I will greatly praise the LORD with my mouth; yea, I will praise him among the multitude.

31 For he shall stand at the ^aright hand of the ^bpoor, to save *him* from those that condemn his soul.

PSALM 110

A messianic psalm of David—Christ will sit on the Lord's right hand—He will be a priest forever after the order of Melchizedek.

A Psalm of David.

THE ^aLORD said unto my ^bLord, Sit thou at my ^cright ^dhand, until I make thine ^eenemies thy footstool.

2 The LORD shall send the ^arod of thy strength out of Zion: rule thou in the midst of thine enemies.

3 Thy people *shall be* willing in the day of thy power, in the beauties of holiness from the womb of the morning: thou hast the dew of thy youth.

4 The LORD hath ^asworn, and will not ^brepent, Thou *art* a ^cpriest for ever after the order of ^dMelchizedek.

5 The Lord at thy right hand shall strike through kings in the day of his wrath.

6 He shall judge among the heathen, he shall fill *the places* with the dead bodies; he shall wound the heads over many countries.

13a Ps. 21:10 (10–11); 37:28;
   Isa. 14:20; 2 Ne. 24:20;
   D&C 121:15 (13–15).
   b Mosiah 26:36;
   Alma 5:57 (56–58);
   D&C 20:83.
14a Ex. 20:5.
16a Ps. 86:1;
   Alma 5:55 (54–56);
   Hel. 6:39 (39–40);
   D&C 56:16.

21a Ps. 23:3; 25:11; 31:3.
28a TG Curse.
29a Ps. 71:13.
31a Ps. 16:8.
   b D&C 56:18 (15–18).
110 1a Mark 12:36.
   Luke 20:42.
   b Acts 2:34.
   c Heb. 1:13.
   d TG Celestial Glory.
   e TG Enemies.

2a Isa. 11:1; 53:2 (1–3);
   D&C 113:3 (3–4).
4a TG Oath.
   b 1 Sam. 15:35; Ps. 135:14.
   c TG High Priest, Melchizedek Priesthood;
   Jesus Christ, Prophecies about; Priesthood, Melchizedek.
   d TG Jesus Christ, Types of, in Anticipation.

7 He shall drink of the brook in the way: therefore shall he lift up the head.

PSALM 111

The Lord is gracious and full of compassion—Holy and reverend is His name—The fear of the Lord is the beginning of wisdom.

PRAISE ye the LORD. I will praise the LORD with *my* whole heart, in the *a*assembly of the upright, and *in* the congregation.

2 The works of the LORD *are* great, sought out of all them that have pleasure therein.

3 His *a*work *is* *b*honourable and glorious: and his righteousness endureth for ever.

4 He hath made his wonderful works to be remembered: the LORD *is* gracious and full of compassion.

5 He hath given meat unto them that fear him: he will ever be mindful of his covenant.

6 He hath shewed his people the power of his works, that he may give them the heritage of the *a*heathen.

7 The works of his hands *are* verity and judgment; all his commandments *are* sure.

8 They *a*stand fast for ever and ever, *and are* done in truth and uprightness.

9 He sent redemption unto his people: he hath commanded his covenant for ever: holy and *a*reverend *is* his name.

10 The fear of the LORD *is* the beginning of *a*wisdom: a good *b*understanding have all they that do *his* commandments: his praise endureth for ever.

PSALM 112

Blessed is the man who fears the Lord—The righteous will be remembered always.

PRAISE ye the LORD. Blessed *is* the man *that* *a*feareth the LORD, *that* *b*delighteth greatly in his *c*commandments.

2 His *a*seed shall be mighty upon earth: the generation of the upright shall be blessed.

3 Wealth and *a*riches *shall be* in his house: and his righteousness endureth for ever.

4 Unto the upright there ariseth *a*light in the darkness: *he is* gracious, and full of compassion, and righteous.

5 A good man sheweth favour, and lendeth: he will guide his affairs with discretion.

6 Surely he shall not be moved for ever: the righteous shall be in everlasting remembrance.

7 He shall not be afraid of evil tidings: his *a*heart is fixed, trusting in the LORD.

8 His heart *is* established, he shall not be afraid, until he see *his desire* upon his enemies.

9 He hath dispersed, he hath *a*given to the poor; his righteousness endureth for ever; his horn shall be exalted with honour.

10 The wicked shall see *it,* and be grieved; he shall gnash with his teeth, and melt away: the desire of the wicked shall perish.

PSALM 113

Blessed be the name of the Lord—Who is like unto the Lord our God?

PRAISE ye the LORD. Praise, O ye servants of the LORD, praise the name of the LORD.

2 Blessed be the name of the LORD from this time forth and for evermore.

3 From the rising of the sun unto the going down of the same the LORD's name *is* to be praised.

---

111 1*a* TG Assembly for Worship.
  3*a* 1 Chr. 16:12.
   b TG Honor.
  6*a* TG Heathen.
  8*a* 1 Ne. 14:7;
     D&C 29:33;

Moses 1:4.
9*a* TG Reverence.
10*a* TG Learn;
     Wisdom.
   b TG Understanding.
112 1*a* TG Reverence.
    b Ps. 119:35.

c TG Children of Light.
2*a* D&C 104:33.
3*a* TG Abundant Life.
4*a* TG Light [noun].
7*a* TG Commitment.
9*a* TG Almsgiving;
     Generosity.

4 The LORD *is* high above all nations, *and* his glory above the heavens.

5 Who *is* like unto the LORD our God, who dwelleth on high,

6 Who *a*humbleth *himself* to behold *the things that are* in heaven, and in the earth!

7 He *a*raiseth up the poor out of the dust, *and* lifteth the needy out of the dunghill;

8 That he may set *him* with princes, *even* with the princes of his people.

9 He maketh the *a*barren woman to keep house, *and to be* a joyful *b*mother of *c*children. Praise ye the LORD.

PSALM 114

The Lord governs the sea and the land for the blessing of His people.

WHEN Israel went out of *a*Egypt, the house of Jacob from a people of strange language;

2 Judah was his sanctuary, *and* Israel his dominion.

3 The sea saw *it,* and *a*fled: Jordan was driven back.

4 The mountains skipped like rams, *and* the little hills like lambs.

5 What *ailed* thee, O thou sea, that thou fleddest? thou Jordan, *that* thou wast driven back?

6 Ye mountains, *that* ye skipped like rams; *and* ye little hills, like lambs?

7 Tremble, thou earth, at the presence of the Lord, at the presence of the God of Jacob;

8 Which turned the rock *into* a standing water, the flint into a fountain of *a*waters.

PSALM 115

Our God is in the heavens—Idols are false gods—Trust in the Lord.

NOT unto us, O LORD, not unto us, but unto thy *a*name give glory, for thy mercy, *and* for thy truth's sake.

2 Wherefore should the heathen say, Where *is* now their God?

3 But our God *is* in the heavens: he hath done whatsoever he hath pleased.

4 Their *a*idols *are* silver and gold, the *b*work of men's hands.

5 They have mouths, but they *a*speak not: eyes have they, but they *b*see not:

6 They have ears, but they hear not: noses have they, but they smell not:

7 They have hands, but they handle not: feet have they, but they walk not: neither speak they through their throat.

8 They that make them are like unto them; *so is* every one that trusteth in them.

9 O Israel, *a*trust thou in the LORD: he *is* their help and their shield.

10 O house of Aaron, trust in the LORD: he *is* their help and their shield.

11 Ye that fear the LORD, trust in the LORD: he *is* their help and their shield.

12 The LORD hath been mindful of us: he will bless *us;* he will bless the house of Israel; he will bless the house of Aaron.

13 He will bless them that fear the LORD, *both* small and great.

14 The LORD shall *a*increase you more and more, you and your children.

15 Ye *are* *a*blessed of the LORD which made heaven and earth.

16 The heaven, *even* the heavens, are the LORD's: but the earth hath he given to the children of men.

17 The *a*dead praise not the LORD, neither any that go down into silence.

18 But we will bless the LORD from this time forth and for evermore. Praise the LORD.

---

113 6*a* TG Jesus Christ, Condescension of.
  7*a* 1 Sam. 2:8 (1–10).
  9*a* TG Barren.
    b TG Birth Control; Family, Love within; Marriage, Motherhood.

  c TG Family.
114 1*a* Ex. 13:3.
  3*a* Ex. 14:21 (21–22); Ps. 78:13.
  8*a* Ex. 17:6.
115 1*a* Isa. 48:11.
  4*a* Ex. 20:4.

  b Jer. 10:9.
  5*a* Isa. 46:7.
    b Isa. 44:9.
  9*a* TG Trust in God.
  14*a* Deut. 1:11.
  15*a* Gen. 24:31.
  17*a* D&C 128:22.

PSALM 116

Gracious is the Lord, and righteous—
Precious in the sight of the Lord is the
death of His Saints.

I ^aLOVE the LORD, because he hath heard my voice *and* my supplications.

2 Because he hath inclined his ear unto me, therefore will I call upon *him* as long as I live.

3 The sorrows of death compassed me, and the ^apains of ^bhell gat hold upon me: I found trouble and sorrow.

4 Then called I upon the name of the LORD; O LORD, I beseech thee, deliver my soul.

5 Gracious *is* the LORD, and righteous; yea, our God *is* ^amerciful.

6 The LORD preserveth the ^asimple: I was brought low, and he helped me.

7 Return unto thy rest, O my soul; for the LORD hath dealt bountifully with thee.

8 For thou hast ^adelivered my ^bsoul from death, mine eyes from tears, *and* my feet from falling.

9 I will walk before the LORD in the ^aland of the living.

10 I believed, therefore have I spoken: I was greatly afflicted:

11 I said in my ^ahaste, All men *are* liars.

12 What shall I ^arender unto the LORD *for* all his benefits toward me?

13 I will take the cup of salvation, and call upon the name of the LORD.

14 I will pay my vows unto the LORD now in the presence of all his people.

15 Precious in the sight of the LORD *is* the ^adeath of his saints.

16 O LORD, truly I *am* thy ^aservant; I *am* thy servant, *and* the son of thine handmaid: thou hast loosed my bonds.

17 I will offer to thee the sacrifice of thanksgiving, and will ^acall upon the name of the LORD.

18 I will pay my vows unto the LORD now in the presence of all his people,

19 In the ^acourts of the LORD's house, in the midst of thee, O Jerusalem. Praise ye the LORD.

PSALM 117

Praise the Lord for His mercy and truth.

O PRAISE the LORD, all ye nations: praise him, all ye people.

2 For his merciful kindness is great toward us: and the ^atruth of the LORD *endureth* for ever. Praise ye the LORD.

PSALM 118

A messianic psalm—Let all Israel say of
the Lord, His mercy endures forever—
The Stone that the builders refused is
become the headstone of the corner—
Blessed is he who comes in the name
of the Lord.

O GIVE thanks unto the LORD; for *he is* good: because his mercy *endureth* for ever.

2 Let Israel now say, that his mercy *endureth* for ever.

3 Let the house of Aaron now say, that his mercy *endureth* for ever.

4 Let them now that fear the LORD say, that his mercy *endureth* for ever.

5 I called upon the LORD in ^adistress: the LORD answered me, *and set me* in a ^blarge place.

6 The LORD *is* on my side; I will not ^afear: what can man do unto me?

7 The ^aLORD taketh my part with them that help me: therefore shall I see *my* ^bdesire upon them that hate me.

8 *It is* better to ^atrust in the LORD than to put ^bconfidence in man.

116 1*a* TG Love.
  3*a* TG Pain.
    b TG Damnation.
  5*a* TG God, Mercy of.
  6*a* Ps. 19:7.
  8*a* TG Deliver.
    b Ps. 56:13.
  9*a* Ps. 27:13.
 11*a* TG Rashness.

 12*a* TG Reward.
 15*a* TG Death.
 16*a* Ps. 119:125.
 17*a* Gen. 4:26;
      1 Chr. 16:8;
      D&C 65:4.
 19*a* Ps. 96:8; 100:4.
117 2*a* D&C 84:45; 93:24.
118 5*a* Ps. 4:1.

    b 2 Sam. 22:20.
  6*a* Ps. 56:4 (4, 11);
      2 Ne. 8:7 (7–8);
      D&C 122:9.
  7*a* Ps. 54:4.
    b Ps. 54:7.
  8*a* TG Trust in God.
    b TG Dependability.

9 *It is* better to trust in the LORD than to put confidence in princes.

10 All nations compassed me about: but in the name of the LORD will I destroy them.

11 They compassed me about; yea, they compassed me about: but in the name of the LORD I will destroy them.

12 They compassed me about like *a*bees; they are quenched as the fire of thorns: for in the name of the LORD I will destroy them.

13 Thou hast thrust sore at me that I might fall: but the LORD helped me.

14 The LORD *is* my *a*strength and song, and is become my *b*salvation.

15 The voice of rejoicing and salvation *is* in the *a*tabernacles of the righteous: the right hand of the LORD doeth valiantly.

16 The right *a*hand of the LORD is exalted: the right hand of the LORD doeth valiantly.

17 I shall not die, but live, and declare the works of the LORD.

18 The LORD hath chastened me sore: but he hath not given me over unto death.

19 Open to me the gates of righteousness: I will go into them, *and* I will praise the LORD:

20 This gate of the LORD, into which the righteous shall enter.

21 I will praise thee: for thou hast heard me, and art become my salvation.

22 The *a*stone *which* the builders refused is become the head *stone* of the *b*corner.

23 This is the LORD's doing; it *is* marvellous in our eyes.

24 This *is* the day *which* the LORD hath made; we will *a*rejoice and be glad in it.

25 Save now, I beseech thee, O LORD: O LORD, I beseech thee, send now prosperity.

26 *a*Blessed *be* he that cometh in the name of the LORD: we have blessed you out of the house of the LORD.

27 God *is* the LORD, which hath shewed us light: bind the sacrifice with cords, *even* unto the horns of the altar.

28 Thou *art* my God, and I will praise thee: *thou art* my God, I will exalt thee.

29 O give thanks unto the LORD; for *he is* good: for his mercy *endureth* for ever.

PSALM 119

א ALEPH

Blessed are they who keep the commandments.

*a*BLESSED *are* the undefiled in the way, who walk in the law of the LORD.

2 Blessed *are* they that keep his testimonies, *and that* *a*seek him with the whole heart.

3 They also do no iniquity: they walk in his ways.

4 Thou hast commanded *us* to keep thy precepts *a*diligently.

5 O that my ways were directed to keep thy statutes!

6 Then shall I not be ashamed, when I have respect unto all thy commandments.

7 I will praise thee with uprightness of heart, when I shall have learned thy righteous judgments.

8 I will keep thy statutes: O forsake me not utterly.

ב BETH

Ponder the precepts and ways of the Lord.

9 Wherewithal shall a young man *a*cleanse his way? by taking heed *thereto* according to thy word.

10 With my whole *a*heart have I sought thee: O let me not wander from thy commandments.

12*a* Deut. 1:44.
14*a* TG Strength.
  b TG Salvation.
15*a* HEB tents, dwellings.
16*a* Ex. 15:6 (6–7).
22*a* TG Cornerstone;

Jesus Christ, Prophecies about; Rock.
  b Zech. 10:4.
24*a* TG Joy.
26*a* Matt. 21:9 (1–11); 23:39; Mark 11:9; Luke 13:35.

119 1*a* TG Blessing.
  2*a* TG Children of Light.
  4*a* TG Dedication; Diligence.
  9*a* TG Purification.
  10*a* TG Commitment.

11 Thy ᵃword have I hid in mine heart, that I might not sin against thee.

12 Blessed *art* thou, O LORD: teach me thy statutes.

13 With my lips have I declared all the judgments of thy mouth.

14 I have rejoiced in the way of thy testimonies, as *much as* in all riches.

15 I will ᵃmeditate in thy precepts, and have respect unto thy ways.

16 I will delight myself in thy statutes: I will not forget thy word.

ג GIMEL

O Lord, open our eyes, that we may behold wondrous things out of Thy law.

17 Deal bountifully with thy servant, *that* I may live, and keep thy word.

18 Open thou mine eyes, that I may behold wondrous things out of thy law.

19 I *am* a ᵃstranger in the earth: hide not thy commandments from me.

20 My soul breaketh for the longing *that it hath* unto thy judgments at all times.

21 Thou hast rebuked the proud *that are* cursed, which do err from thy commandments.

22 Remove from me reproach and contempt; for I have kept thy testimonies.

23 Princes also did sit *and* speak against me: *but* thy servant did meditate in thy statutes.

24 Thy ᵃtestimonies also *are* my delight *and* my counsellors.

ד DALETH

O Lord, grant us Thy law, and make us to understand Thy precepts.

25 My soul cleaveth unto the ᵃdust: ᵇquicken thou me according to thy word.

26 I have declared my ways, and thou heardest me: teach me thy statutes.

27 Make me to ᵃunderstand the way of thy precepts: so shall I talk of thy wondrous works.

28 My soul melteth for heaviness: strengthen thou me according unto thy ᵃword.

29 Remove from me the way of lying: and grant me thy law graciously.

30 I have chosen the way of truth: thy judgments have I laid *before me.*

31 I have stuck unto thy testimonies: O LORD, put me not to shame.

32 I will run the way of thy commandments, when thou shalt ᵃenlarge my ᵇheart.

ה HE

O Lord, teach us Thy statutes, Thy law, and Thy commandments.

33 ᵃTeach me, O LORD, the way of thy statutes; and I shall keep it *unto* the end.

34 Give me ᵃunderstanding, and I shall keep thy law; yea, I shall observe it with *my* whole heart.

35 Make me to go in the path of thy commandments; for therein do I ᵃdelight.

36 Incline my heart unto thy testimonies, and not to ᵃcovetousness.

37 Turn away mine eyes from beholding ᵃvanity; *and* quicken thou me in thy way.

38 ᵃStablish thy word unto thy servant, who *is devoted* to thy fear.

39 Turn away my reproach which I fear: for thy ᵃjudgments *are* good.

40 Behold, I have longed after thy precepts: quicken me in thy righteousness.

11a Ps. 37:31.
15a TG Meditation.
19a HEB sojourner; i.e., not of this world.
  TG Stranger.
24a 2 Ne. 4:15.
25a Ps. 44:25.

b D&C 88:49.
27a D&C 50:12.
28a Jacob 6:7.
32a 2 Cor. 6:11 (11, 13).
  b IE understanding.
33a Ex. 33:13.
34a TG Understanding.

35a Ps. 112:1.
36a Ezek. 33:31 (30–33);
  Luke 12:15 (15–21);
  1 Tim. 6:10.
37a TG Vanity.
38a 2 Sam. 7:25.
39a 1 Ne. 22:21.

ו VAU

O Lord, give us mercy, truth, and salvation.

41 Let thy mercies come also unto me, O LORD, *even* thy salvation, according to thy word.

42 So shall I have wherewith to answer him that reproacheth me: for I trust in thy word.

43 And take not the word of truth utterly out of my mouth; for I have hoped in thy judgments.

44 So shall I keep thy law continually for ever and ever.

45 And I will walk at ^aliberty: for I seek thy precepts.

46 I will speak of thy testimonies also before ^akings, and will not be ^bashamed.

47 And I will delight myself in thy commandments, which I have loved.

48 My ^ahands also will I ^blift up unto thy commandments, which I have loved; and I will meditate in thy statutes.

ז ZAIN

The Lord's statutes and judgments comfort us during our pilgrimage.

49 Remember the word unto thy servant, upon which thou hast caused me to hope.

50 This *is* my ^acomfort in my ^baffliction: for thy word hath quickened me.

51 The proud have had me greatly in derision: *yet* have I not declined from thy law.

52 I remembered thy judgments of old, O LORD; and have comforted myself.

53 ^aHorror hath taken hold upon me because of the wicked that forsake thy law.

54 Thy statutes have been my songs in the house of my ^apilgrimage.

55 I have ^aremembered thy name, O LORD, in the ^bnight, and have kept thy law.

56 This I had, because I kept thy precepts.

ח CHETH

Make faithful people our companions.

57 *Thou art* my ^aportion, O LORD: I have said that I would keep thy words.

58 I entreated thy favour with *my* whole heart: be merciful unto me according to thy word.

59 I ^athought on my ways, and turned my feet unto thy testimonies.

60 I made haste, and ^adelayed not to keep thy commandments.

61 The bands of the wicked have robbed me: *but* I have not forgotten thy law.

62 At ^amidnight I will rise to give thanks unto thee because of thy righteous judgments.

63 I *am* a companion of all *them* that fear thee, and of them that keep thy precepts.

64 The earth, O LORD, is ^afull of thy mercy: teach me thy statutes.

ט TETH

O Lord, teach us Thy statutes.

65 Thou hast dealt well with thy servant, O LORD, according unto thy word.

66 Teach me good judgment and knowledge: for I have believed thy commandments.

67 ^aBefore I was ^bafflicted I went astray: but now have I kept thy word.

68 Thou *art* ^agood, and doest good; teach me thy statutes.

69 The proud have forged a lie against me: *but* I will keep thy precepts with *my* whole heart.

45*a* TG Liberty.
46*a* Matt. 10:18;
 Acts 9:15;
 D&C 1:23;
 124:3 (3, 16, 107).
 b Rom. 1:16.
48*a* Ps. 63:4.
 b Ezek. 47:14.

50*a* TG Comfort.
 b TG Affliction.
53*a* Ezra 9:4 (1–4).
54*a* Gen. 47:9.
55*a* Mosiah 5:12 (11–13).
 b Ps. 63:6.
57*a* Ps. 16:5;
 Lam. 3:24.

59*a* Luke 15:17.
60*a* TG Procrastination.
62*a* Acts 16:25.
64*a* Ps. 33:5.
67*a* Jer. 31:19 (18–19).
 b Alma 36:17 (12–21);
 D&C 101:2.
68*a* Ps. 106:1.

70 Their heart is as fat as grease; *but* I delight in thy law.

71 *It is* good for me that I have been *a*afflicted; that I might *b*learn thy statutes.

72 The law of thy mouth *is* better unto me than *a*thousands of *b*gold and silver.

׳ JOD

O Lord, let Thy tender mercies come upon us.

73 Thy hands have made me and fashioned me: give me understanding, that I may learn thy commandments.

74 They that fear thee will be glad when they see me; because I have hoped in thy word.

75 I know, O LORD, that thy judgments *are* right, and *that* thou in faithfulness hast afflicted me.

76 Let, I pray thee, thy merciful kindness be for my comfort, according to thy word unto thy servant.

77 Let thy tender mercies come unto me, that I may live: for thy law *is* my delight.

78 Let the proud be *a*ashamed; for they dealt perversely with me without a cause: *but* I will meditate in thy precepts.

79 Let those that fear thee turn unto me, and those that have known thy testimonies.

80 Let my heart be sound in thy statutes; that I be not ashamed.

⊃ CAPH

All the Lord's commandments are faithful.

81 My soul *a*fainteth for thy salvation: *but* I hope in thy word.

82 Mine eyes fail for thy word, saying, When wilt thou comfort me?

83 For I am become like a *a*bottle in the smoke; *yet* do I not forget thy statutes.

84 How *a*many *are* *b*the days of thy servant? when wilt thou execute *c*judgment on them that persecute me?

85 The proud have *a*digged pits for me, which *are* not after thy law.

86 All thy commandments *are* faithful: they persecute me wrongfully; help thou me.

87 They had almost consumed me upon earth; but I forsook not thy precepts.

88 Quicken me after thy lovingkindness; so shall I keep the testimony of thy mouth.

ל LAMED

O Lord, save us, for we have sought Thy precepts.

89 For ever, O LORD, thy *a*word is settled in heaven.

90 Thy *a*faithfulness *is* unto all generations: thou hast established the earth, and it abideth.

91 They continue this day according to thine ordinances: for all *are* thy servants.

92 Unless thy law *had been* my delights, I should then have perished in mine affliction.

93 I will never forget thy precepts: for with them thou hast quickened me.

94 I *am* thine, save me; for I have sought thy precepts.

95 The wicked have waited for me to destroy me: *but* I will consider thy testimonies.

96 I have seen an end of all perfection: *but* thy commandment *is* exceeding broad.

מ MEM

The Lord's law and His testimonies should be our meditation all the day.

97 O how love I thy law! it *is* my meditation all the day.

98 Thou through thy commandments hast made me wiser than

71a TG Chastening.
  b TG Learn.
72a IE thousands of pieces.
  b Ps. 19:10 (9–10).
78a TG Shame.

81a Ps. 84:2.
83a OR waterskin.
84a Ps. 39:4.
  b IE of affliction.
  c D&C 121:5 (1–6).

85a Ps. 57:6.
89a Ps. 148:6;
    1 Pet. 1:25;
    D&C 1:38.
90a Ps. 89:1.

mine enemies: for they *are* ever with me.

99 I have more *a*understanding than all my teachers: for thy testimonies *are* my *b*meditation.

100 I understand more than the *a*ancients, because I keep thy precepts.

101 I have *a*refrained my feet from every evil way, that I might keep thy word.

102 I have not departed from thy judgments: for thou hast taught me.

103 How sweet are thy words unto my taste! *yea, sweeter* than honey to my mouth!

104 Through thy precepts I get understanding: therefore I hate every false way.

נ NUN

The Lord's word is a lamp unto our feet.

105 Thy *a*word *is* a *b*lamp unto my feet, and a *c*light unto my path.

106 I have sworn, and I will perform *it*, that I will keep thy righteous *a*judgments.

107 I am afflicted very much: quicken me, O LORD, according unto thy word.

108 Accept, I beseech thee, the freewill *a*offerings of my mouth, O LORD, and teach me thy judgments.

109 My *a*soul *is* continually in my hand: yet do I not forget thy law.

110 The wicked have laid a snare for me: yet I erred not from thy precepts.

111 Thy testimonies have I taken as an heritage for ever: for they *are* the *a*rejoicing of my heart.

112 I have inclined mine heart to perform thy statutes alway, *even unto* the end.

ס SAMECH

Depart from evildoers and keep the commandments of God.

113 I hate *vain* thoughts: but thy law do I love.

114 Thou *art* my *a*hiding place and my shield: I hope in thy word.

115 *a*Depart from me, ye evildoers: for I will keep the commandments of my God.

116 Uphold me according unto thy word, that I may live: and let me not be ashamed of my *a*hope.

117 Hold thou me up, and I shall be *a*safe: and I will have respect unto thy statutes continually.

118 Thou hast trodden down all them that err from thy statutes: for their deceit *is* falsehood.

119 Thou puttest away all the wicked of the earth *like a*dross: therefore I love thy testimonies.

120 My flesh trembleth for fear of thee; and I am afraid of thy judgments.

ע AIN

O Lord, we are Thy servants; give us understanding.

121 I have done judgment and justice: leave me not to mine oppressors.

122 Be surety for thy servant for good: let not the proud oppress me.

123 Mine eyes fail for thy salvation, and for the word of thy righteousness.

124 Deal with thy servant according unto thy mercy, and teach me thy statutes.

125 I *am* thy *a*servant; give me understanding, that I may know thy testimonies.

126 *It is* time for *thee*, LORD, to work: *for* they have made void thy law.

127 Therefore I *a*love thy commandments above gold; yea, above fine gold.

128 Therefore I esteem all *thy* precepts *concerning* all *things to be* right; *and* I hate every false way.

99*a* TG Understanding.
  b TG Meditation.
100*a* HEB aged, elders.
101*a* TG Self-Mastery.
105*a* Alma 37:44 (38–46).
  b Prov. 6:23.
  c TG Light [noun].

106*a* Neh. 10:29.
108*a* Heb. 13:15.
109*a* Judg. 12:3 (1–3).
111*a* TG Cheerful.
114*a* Ps. 32:7.
115*a* Matt. 7:23;
     3 Ne. 14:23.

116*a* Rom. 5:5;
     Philip. 1:20.
117*a* Ezek. 34:27.
119*a* Ezek. 22:18 (17–22).
125*a* Ps. 116:16.
127*a* Ps. 19:10 (9–10).

ּפ PE

The Lord's testimonies are wonderful.

129 Thy testimonies *are* wonderful: therefore doth my soul keep them.

130 The entrance of thy words giveth light; it giveth ^aunderstanding unto the simple.

131 I opened my mouth, and panted: for I longed for thy commandments.

132 Look thou upon me, and be ^amerciful unto me, as thou usest to do unto those that love thy name.

133 ^aOrder my steps in thy word: and let not any iniquity have ^bdominion over me.

134 Deliver me from the ^aoppression of man: so will I keep thy precepts.

135 Make thy face to ^ashine upon thy servant; and teach me thy statutes.

136 Rivers of waters run down mine eyes, because they keep not thy law.

צ TZADDI

The Lord's law is the truth.

137 ^aRighteous *art* thou, O LORD, and upright *are* thy judgments.

138 Thy testimonies *that* thou hast commanded *are* ^arighteous and very faithful.

139 My ^azeal hath consumed me, because mine enemies have forgotten thy words.

140 Thy word *is* very pure: therefore thy servant loveth it.

141 I *am* small and despised: *yet* do not I forget thy precepts.

142 Thy righteousness *is* an everlasting righteousness, and thy law *is* the ^atruth.

143 Trouble and ^aanguish have taken hold on me: *yet* thy commandments *are* my delights.

144 The righteousness of thy testimonies *is* everlasting: give me understanding, and I shall live.

ק KOPH

O Lord, hear the voice of Thy servants according to Thy loving kindness.

145 I cried with *my* whole heart; hear me, O LORD: I will keep thy statutes.

146 I cried unto thee; save me, and I shall keep thy testimonies.

147 ^aI prevented the dawning of the morning, and cried: I hoped in thy word.

148 ^aMine eyes prevent the *night* watches, that I might meditate in thy word.

149 Hear my voice according unto thy lovingkindness: O LORD, quicken me according to thy judgment.

150 They draw nigh that follow after mischief: they are far from thy law.

151 Thou *art* ^anear, O LORD; and all thy commandments *are* truth.

152 Concerning thy testimonies, I have known of old that thou hast founded them for ever.

ר RESH

Great are Thy tender mercies, O Lord.

153 Consider mine affliction, and deliver me: for I do not forget thy law.

154 Plead my cause, and deliver me: quicken me according to thy word.

155 Salvation *is* far from the wicked: for they seek not thy statutes.

156 Great *are* thy tender mercies, O LORD: quicken me according to thy judgments.

157 Many *are* my persecutors and

130*a* TG Understanding.
132*a* TG God, Mercy of.
133*a* Ps. 17:5.
　b Ps. 19:13.
134*a* TG Oppression.
135*a* Num. 6:25;
　Ps. 4:6.

137*a* Ezra 9:15.
138*a* Isa. 45:19;
　D&C 67:9.
139*a* TG Zeal.
142*a* John 17:17.
143*a* TG Pain.
147*a* HEB I arose before the

dawning.
148*a* HEB Mine eyes were awake before the night watch.
151*a* Ps. 145:18.

mine enemies; *yet* do I not decline from thy testimonies.

158 I beheld the transgressors, and was [a]grieved; because they kept not thy word.

159 Consider how I love thy precepts: quicken me, O Lord, according to thy lovingkindness.

160 Thy word *is* true *from* the beginning: and every one of thy righteous judgments *endureth* for ever.

ש SCHIN

Those who love the Lord's law have peace.

161 Princes have persecuted me without a cause: but my heart standeth in awe of thy word.

162 I [a]rejoice at thy word, as one that findeth great spoil.

163 I hate and abhor lying: *but* thy law do I love.

164 Seven times a day do I praise thee because of thy righteous judgments.

165 Great [a]peace have they which love thy law: and nothing shall offend them.

166 Lord, I have hoped for thy salvation, and done thy commandments.

167 My soul hath kept thy testimonies; and I love them exceedingly.

168 I have kept thy precepts and thy testimonies: for all my [a]ways *are* before thee.

ת TAU

All the Lord's commandments are righteousness.

169 Let my cry come near before thee, O Lord: give me [a]understanding according to thy word.

170 Let my supplication come before thee: deliver me according to thy word.

171 My lips shall utter praise, when thou hast taught me thy statutes.

172 My tongue shall speak of thy word: for all thy commandments *are* righteousness.

173 Let thine hand help me; for I have chosen thy precepts.

174 I have longed for thy salvation, O Lord; and thy law *is* my delight.

175 Let my soul live, and it shall praise thee; and let thy judgments help me.

176 I have gone astray like a lost [a]sheep; seek thy servant; for I do not forget thy commandments.

PSALM 120

Call upon the Lord when in distress.

A Song of degrees.

In my distress I cried unto the Lord, and he heard me.

2 Deliver my soul, O Lord, from lying lips, *and* from a [a]deceitful tongue.

3 What shall be given unto thee? or what shall be done unto thee, thou false tongue?

4 Sharp arrows of the mighty, with coals of juniper.

5 Woe is me, that I sojourn in [a]Mesech, *that* I dwell in the [b]tents of [c]Kedar!

6 My soul hath long dwelt with him that hateth peace.

7 I *am for* peace: but when I speak, they *are* for [a]war.

PSALM 121

Help comes from the Lord—He is the guardian of Israel.

A Song of degrees.

I will [a]lift up mine eyes unto the hills, from whence cometh my help.

2 My [a]help *cometh* from the Lord, which made heaven and earth.

3 He will not suffer thy [a]foot to be

158a Ps. 95:10.
162a Isa. 9:3.
165a TG Peace;
    Peace of God.
168a Prov. 5:21.
169a TG Understanding.

176a TG Sheep.
120 2a TG Deceit.
   5a Gen. 10:2;
    Ezek. 27:13.
    b Jer. 49:29 (28–29).
    c Isa. 60:7.

7a TG War.
121 1a Ps. 123:1.
   2a Ps. 124:8.
   3a Ps. 66:9.

moved: he that *b*keepeth thee will not slumber.

4 Behold, he that keepeth Israel shall neither slumber nor sleep.

5 The LORD *is* thy *a*keeper: the LORD *is* thy *b*shade upon thy right hand.

6 The *a*sun shall not smite thee by day, nor the moon by night.

7 The LORD shall preserve thee from all evil: he shall *a*preserve thy soul.

8 The LORD shall preserve thy going out and thy *a*coming in from this time forth, and even for evermore.

PSALM 122

David says, Go into the house of the Lord—Give thanks unto Him.

A Song of degrees of David.

I WAS glad when they said unto me, Let us go into the *a*house of the LORD.

2 Our feet shall stand within thy gates, O Jerusalem.

3 Jerusalem is builded as a city that is compact together:

4 Whither the tribes go up, the tribes of the LORD, *a*unto the testimony of Israel, to give thanks unto the name of the LORD.

5 For there are set thrones of judgment, the thrones of the house of David.

6 Pray for the *a*peace of Jerusalem: they shall *b*prosper that love thee.

7 Peace be within thy walls, *and* prosperity within thy palaces.

8 For my brethren and companions' sakes, I will now say, *a*Peace *be* within thee.

9 Because of the house of the LORD our God I will seek thy good.

PSALM 123

Lift up your eyes unto the Lord, and plead with Him for mercy.

A Song of degrees.

UNTO thee *a*lift I up mine eyes, O thou that dwellest in the heavens.

2 Behold, as the eyes of servants *look* unto the hand of their masters, *and* as the eyes of a maiden unto the hand of her mistress; so our eyes *wait* upon the LORD our God, until that he have mercy upon us.

3 Have mercy upon us, O LORD, have mercy upon us: for we are exceedingly filled with contempt.

4 Our soul is exceedingly filled with the *a*scorning of those that are at ease, *and* with the contempt of the proud.

PSALM 124

David says, Israel's help is in the name of the Lord.

A Song of degrees of David.

IF *it had* not *been* the LORD who was on our side, now may Israel say;

2 If *it had* not *been* the LORD who was on our side, when men rose up against us:

3 Then they had *a*swallowed us up quick, when their wrath was kindled against us:

4 Then the waters had overwhelmed us, the stream had gone over our soul:

5 Then the proud waters had gone over our soul.

6 Blessed *be* the LORD, who hath not given us *as* a prey to their teeth.

7 Our soul is escaped as a bird out of the *a*snare of the fowlers: the snare is broken, and we are escaped.

8 Our *a*help *is* in the name of the LORD, who made heaven and earth.

---

3 *b* Ps. 127:1.
5 *a* OR watchman.
  b Ps. 91:1.
6 *a* Isa. 49:10;
    Rev. 7:16.
7 *a* Ps. 97:10;
    D&C 45:46.
8 *a* Deut. 28:6.
122 1 *a* Ezra 2:68;

2 Ne. 12:3 (2–3);
    D&C 133:13 (12–14).
    TG Genealogy and
    Temple Work.
4 *a* OR as a testimony for.
6 *a* TG Peace.
  b Jarom 1:9;
    Mosiah 1:7;
    Alma 37:13.

8 *a* 1 Sam. 25:6.
123 1 *a* Ps. 121:1;
    Ezek. 18:6.
4 *a* Neh. 2:19;
    Amos 6:1.
124 3 *a* Ps. 56:1 (1–2);
    Prov. 1:12.
7 *a* Ps. 91:3.
8 *a* Ps. 121:2.

PSALM 125

Blessed are they who trust in the Lord—
Peace will be upon Israel.

A Song of degrees.

THEY that ^atrust in the LORD *shall be* as mount Zion, *which* cannot be removed, *but* ^babideth for ever.

2 *As* the mountains *are* round about Jerusalem, so the LORD *is* round about his people from henceforth even for ever.

3 For the rod of the ^awicked shall not rest upon the lot of the righteous; lest the righteous put forth their hands unto ^ainiquity.

4 Do good, O LORD, unto *those that be* good, and to *them that are* upright in their hearts.

5 As for such as turn aside unto their crooked ways, the LORD shall lead them forth with the workers of iniquity: *but* ^apeace *shall be* upon Israel.

PSALM 126

The Lord has done great things for His people, Israel.

A Song of degrees.

WHEN the LORD turned again the captivity of Zion, we were like them that dream.

2 Then was our mouth filled with laughter, and our tongue with singing: then said they among the heathen, The LORD hath ^adone great ^bthings for them.

3 The LORD hath done great things for us; *whereof* we are glad.

4 ^aTurn again our captivity, O LORD, as the streams in the south.

5 They that sow in tears shall reap in ^ajoy.

6 He that goeth forth and weepeth,

bearing precious ^aseed, shall doubtless come again with rejoicing, bringing his ^bsheaves *with him.*

PSALM 127

Children are a heritage from the Lord.

A Song of degrees for Solomon.

EXCEPT the LORD build the house, they ^alabour in vain that build it: except the LORD ^bkeep the city, the watchman waketh *but* in vain.

2 *It is* vain for you to rise up early, to sit up late, to eat the bread of sorrows: *for* so he giveth his beloved ^asleep.

3 Lo, ^achildren *are* an ^bheritage of the LORD: *and* the fruit of the womb *is his* ^creward.

4 As arrows *are* in the hand of a mighty man; so *are* children of the youth.

5 ^aHappy *is* the man that hath his quiver full of them: they shall not be ashamed, but they shall speak with the enemies in the gate.

PSALM 128

Blessed are those who fear the Lord and walk in His ways.

A Song of degrees.

BLESSED *is* every one that feareth the LORD; that ^awalketh in his ways.

2 For thou shalt ^aeat the ^blabour of thine hands: ^chappy *shalt* thou *be,* and *it shall be* ^dwell with thee.

3 Thy ^awife *shall be* as a fruitful vine by the sides of thine house: thy children like olive plants round about thy table.

4 Behold, that thus shall the man be blessed that feareth the LORD.

5 The LORD shall ^abless thee out of

---

125 1a TG Trust in God.
  b 1 Jn. 2:17.
  3a TG Wickedness.
  5a Ps. 128:6;
     Gal. 6:16.
126 2a Ezek. 36:36.
  b Luke 1:49.
  4a OR Restore us from.
  5a TG Joy.
  6a D&C 75:5.

  b D&C 31:5; 33:9.
127 1a TG Labor.
  b Ps. 121:3.
  2a TG Sleep.
  3a TG Birth Control;
     Family, Patriarchal.
  b TG Marriage,
     Fatherhood.
  c TG Reward.
  5a TG Family, Love

  within;
  Happiness.
128 1a TG Righteousness.
  2a 2 Ne. 13:10.
  b Isa. 3:10.
  c TG Happiness.
  d TG Health.
  3a TG Marriage,
     Husbands.
  5a Ps. 134:3.

*b*Zion: and thou shalt see the good of Jerusalem all the days of thy life.

6 Yea, thou shalt see thy children's children, *and* *a*peace upon Israel.

PSALM 129

The Lord is righteous—Let those be confounded who hate Zion.

A Song of degrees.

MANY a time have they afflicted me from my youth, may Israel now say:

2 Many a time have they afflicted me from my youth: yet they have not *a*prevailed against me.

3 The plowers plowed upon my back: they made long their furrows.

4 The LORD *is* righteous: he hath cut asunder the cords of the wicked.

5 Let them all be confounded and turned back that hate Zion.

6 Let them be as the *a*grass *upon* the housetops, which withereth afore it groweth up:

7 Wherewith the *a*mower filleth not his hand; nor he that bindeth sheaves his bosom.

8 Neither do they which go by say, The blessing of the LORD *be* upon you: we bless you in the name of the LORD.

PSALM 130

O Lord, hear our prayers, forgive iniquity, and redeem Israel.

A Song of degrees.

OUT of the *a*depths have I cried unto thee, O LORD.

2 Lord, hear my voice: let thine ears be attentive to the voice of my supplications.

3 If thou, LORD, shouldest mark *a*iniquities, O Lord, who shall *b*stand?

4 But *there is* *a*forgiveness with thee, that thou mayest be *b*feared.

5 I *a*wait for the LORD, my soul doth wait, and in his word do I hope.

6 My soul *waiteth* for the Lord more than they that watch for the morning: *I say, more than* they that watch for the morning.

7 Let Israel hope in the LORD: for with the LORD *there is* mercy, and with him *is* plenteous *a*redemption.

8 And he shall *a*redeem Israel from all his iniquities.

PSALM 131

David says, Let Israel hope in the Lord forever.

A Song of degrees of David.

LORD, my heart is not *a*haughty, nor mine *b*eyes lofty: neither do I exercise myself in great matters, or in things too high for me.

2 Surely I have behaved and quieted myself, as a child that is weaned of his mother: my soul *is* even as a weaned child.

3 Let Israel hope in the LORD from henceforth and for ever.

PSALM 132

A messianic psalm—Of the fruit of David's loins will the Lord set One upon His throne—The Lord will bless Zion, and her Saints will shout for joy.

A Song of degrees.

LORD, *a*remember David, *and* all his afflictions:

2 How he sware unto the LORD, *and* *a*vowed unto the *b*mighty *God* of Jacob;

3 Surely I will not come into the tabernacle of my house, nor go up into my bed;

4 I will not give sleep to mine eyes, *or* slumber to mine eyelids,

5 Until I find out a place for the LORD, an *a*habitation for the mighty *God* of Jacob.

5*b* TG Zion.
6*a* Ps. 125:5.
129 2*a* 2 Cor. 4:9 (8–10).
6*a* 2 Kgs. 19:26.
7*a* HEB reaper.
130 1*a* Ps. 69:2.
3*a* Ps. 90:8.

b Ps. 76:7.
4*a* TG Forgive.
b 1 Kgs. 8:40 (39–40).
5*a* Ps. 40:1.
7*a* Isa. 55:7.
8*a* Ps. 25:22.
131 1*a* TG Haughtiness.

b Prov. 30:13.
132 1*a* 2 Chr. 6:42.
2*a* TG Vow.
b Isa. 49:26.
5*a* 1 Chr. 22:7.

6 Lo, we heard of it at Ephratah: we found it in the fields of ^athe wood.

7 We will go into his tabernacles: we will worship at his footstool.

8 Arise, O LORD, into thy rest; thou, and the ark of thy strength.

9 Let thy ^apriests be clothed with ^brighteousness; and let thy saints shout for joy.

10 For thy servant David's sake turn not away the face of thine anointed.

11 The LORD hath sworn *in* truth unto ^aDavid; he will not turn from it; Of the ^bfruit of thy body will I set upon thy ^cthrone.

12 If thy ^achildren will keep my ^bcovenant and my ^ctestimony that I shall teach them, their children shall also sit upon thy ^dthrone for evermore.

13 For the LORD hath chosen ^aZion; he hath desired *it* for his habitation.

14 This *is* my rest for ever: here will I dwell; for I have desired it.

15 I will abundantly bless her provision: I will satisfy her ^apoor with bread.

16 I will also ^aclothe her priests with salvation: and her saints shall ^bshout aloud for joy.

17 There will I make the ^ahorn of ^bDavid to bud: I have ordained a lamp for mine anointed.

18 His enemies will I clothe with ^ashame: but upon himself shall his crown flourish.

PSALM 133

David says, It is pleasant for brethren to dwell together in unity!

A Song of degrees of David.

BEHOLD, how good and how pleasant *it is* for ^abrethren to dwell together in ^bunity!

2 *It is* like the precious ointment upon the head, that ran down upon the beard, *even* Aaron's beard: that went down to the ^askirts of his garments;

3 As the dew of ^aHermon, *and as the dew* that descended upon the mountains of Zion: for there the LORD ^bcommanded the blessing, *even* life for evermore.

PSALM 134

Bless the Lord, and He will bless you.

A Song of degrees.

BEHOLD, bless ye the LORD, all *ye* servants of the LORD, which by ^anight stand in the house of the LORD.

2 Lift up your ^ahands *in* the sanctuary, and bless the LORD.

3 The LORD that made heaven and earth ^abless thee out of Zion.

PSALM 135

Praise and bless the Lord—Our Lord is above all gods; idols cannot see, hear, or speak.

PRAISE ye the LORD. Praise ye the name of the LORD; praise *him*, O ye servants of the LORD.

2 Ye that stand in the house of the LORD, in the courts of the house of our God,

3 Praise the LORD; for the LORD *is* good: sing praises unto his name; for *it is* pleasant.

4 For the LORD hath chosen ^aJacob unto himself, *and* Israel for his ^bpeculiar ^ctreasure.

6a HEB Ya'ar (a place).
9a TG Priesthood, Magnifying Callings within.
  b TG Righteousness.
11a Luke 1:55 (54–55);
    Gal. 3:16.
  b TG Jesus Christ, Davidic Descent of.
  c TG Jesus Christ, Millennial Reign.
12a 1 Kgs. 2:4.
  b D&C 90:24.
  c TG Testimony.

d 1 Kgs. 9:5.
13a TG Zion.
15a D&C 58:8 (8–11).
16a Isa. 61:10.
  b D&C 109:80.
17a TG Jesus Christ, Prophecies about.
  b TG Jesus Christ, Davidic Descent of.
18a TG Shame.
133 1a TG Family, Love within.
  b TG Common Consent;

Unity.
2a OR collar.
3a Deut. 3:9 (8–9).
  b Deut. 28:8 (1–9).
134 1a 1 Chr. 9:33.
2a Ps. 63:4 (2–4).
3a Ps. 128:5.
135 4a Gen. 32:28 (24–32);
    3 Ne. 5:21 (21–26);
    D&C 49:24 (23–25);
    52:2 (1–3).
  b TG Peculiar People.
  c TG Treasure.

5 For I know that the LORD *is* great, and *that* our Lord *is* above all gods.

6 Whatsoever the LORD pleased, *that* did he in heaven, and in earth, in the seas, and all deep places.

7 He causeth the *a*vapours to ascend from the ends of the earth; he maketh lightnings for the rain; he bringeth the wind out of his treasuries.

8 Who smote the firstborn of Egypt, both of man and beast.

9 *Who* sent tokens and wonders into the midst of thee, O Egypt, upon Pharaoh, and upon all his servants.

10 Who smote great nations, and slew mighty kings;

11 *a*Sihon king of the Amorites, and *b*Og king of Bashan, and all the *c*kingdoms of Canaan:

12 And gave their land *for* an *a*heritage, an heritage unto Israel his people.

13 Thy *a*name, O LORD, *endureth* for ever; *and* thy memorial, O LORD, throughout all generations.

14 For the LORD will judge his people, and he will *a*repent himself concerning his servants.

15 The *a*idols of the *b*heathen *are* silver and gold, the work of men's hands.

16 They have mouths, but they speak not; eyes have they, but they see not;

17 They have ears, but they hear not; neither is there *any* breath in their mouths.

18 They that make them are like unto them: *so is* every one that trusteth in them.

19 Bless the LORD, O house of Israel: bless the LORD, O house of Aaron:

20 Bless the LORD, O house of Levi: ye that fear the LORD, bless the LORD.

21 Blessed be the LORD out of Zion, which dwelleth at Jerusalem. Praise ye the LORD.

PSALM 136

Give thanks unto God for all things, for His mercy endures forever.

O GIVE *a*thanks unto the LORD; for *he is* good: for his mercy *endureth* for ever.

2 O give thanks unto the *a*God of gods: for his mercy *endureth* for ever.

3 O give thanks to the Lord of lords: for his mercy *endureth* for ever.

4 To him who alone doeth great wonders: for his mercy *endureth* for ever.

5 To him that by *a*wisdom made the heavens: for his mercy *endureth* for ever.

6 To him that stretched out the *a*earth above the waters: for his mercy *endureth* for ever.

7 To him that made great lights: for his mercy *endureth* for ever:

8 The *a*sun to rule by day: for his mercy *endureth* for ever:

9 The moon and stars to rule by night: for his mercy *endureth* for ever.

10 To him that smote Egypt in their firstborn: for his mercy *endureth* for ever:

11 And brought out *a*Israel from among them: for his mercy *endureth* for ever:

12 With a *a*strong hand, and with a stretched out arm: for his mercy *endureth* for ever.

13 To him which divided the Red sea into parts: for his mercy *endureth* for ever:

14 And made Israel to pass through the midst of it: for his mercy *endureth* for ever:

15 But *a*overthrew Pharaoh and

7*a* IE clouds to ascend.
11*a* Num. 21:24 (21–26);
    Ps. 136:19.
  b Num. 21:35 (33–35);
    Ps. 136:20.
  c Josh. 12:7 (7–24).
12*a* Josh. 13:6; Ps. 136:22.

13*a* Ex. 3:15.
14*a* Ps. 110:4;
    Joel 2:13.
15*a* TG Idolatry.
  b TG Heathen.
136 1*a* TG Thanksgiving.
    2*a* Deut. 10:17 (17–21).

5*a* TG God, Wisdom of.
6*a* TG Creation.
8*a* TG Astronomy.
11*a* Ex. 12:42 (41–42);
    13:18 (3–22).
12*a* Deut. 4:34 (33–35).
15*a* Hel. 8:11 (11–13).

his host in the Red sea: for his mercy *endureth* for ever.

16 To him which led his people through the wilderness: for his mercy *endureth* for ever.

17 To him which smote great kings: for his mercy *endureth* for ever:

18 And slew famous kings: for his mercy *endureth* for ever:

19 ᵃSihon king of the Amorites: for his mercy *endureth* for ever:

20 And ᵃOg the king of Bashan: for his mercy *endureth* for ever:

21 And gave their land for an heritage: for his mercy *endureth* for ever:

22 *Even* an ᵃheritage unto Israel his servant: for his mercy *endureth* for ever.

23 Who remembered us in our low estate: for his mercy *endureth* for ever:

24 And hath redeemed us from our enemies: for his mercy *endureth* for ever.

25 Who giveth ᵃfood to all ᵇflesh: for his mercy *endureth* for ever.

26 O give thanks unto the God of heaven: for his mercy *endureth* for ever.

PSALM 137

While in captivity, the Jews wept by the rivers of Babylon—Because of sorrow, they could not bear to sing the songs of Zion.

BY the rivers of Babylon, there we sat down, yea, we wept, when we remembered Zion.

2 We hanged our harps upon the willows in the midst thereof.

3 For there they that carried us away captive required of us a song; and they that wasted us *required of us* mirth, *saying,* Sing us *one* of the songs of Zion.

4 How shall we ᵃsing the LORD's song in a strange land?

5 If I forget thee, O Jerusalem, let my right hand forget *her cunning.*

6 If I do not remember thee, let my tongue cleave to the roof of my mouth; if I prefer not Jerusalem above my chief joy.

7 Remember, O LORD, the children of ᵃEdom in the day of Jerusalem; who said, ᵇRase *it,* rase *it, even* to the foundation thereof.

8 O daughter of ᵃBabylon, who art to be destroyed; happy *shall he be,* that rewardeth thee as thou hast served us.

9 Happy *shall he be,* that taketh and dasheth thy little ones against the stones.

PSALM 138

David praises the Lord for His loving kindness and truth—He worships toward the holy temple.

A *Psalm* of David.

I WILL praise thee with my whole heart: before the gods will I sing praise unto thee.

2 I will ᵃworship toward thy holy temple, and praise thy name for thy lovingkindness and for thy truth: for thou hast magnified thy word above all thy name.

3 In the day when I ᵃcried thou answeredst me, *and* strengthenedst me *with* strength in my soul.

4 All the ᵃkings of the earth shall praise thee, O LORD, when they hear the words of thy mouth.

5 Yea, they shall ᵃsing in the ways of the LORD: for great *is* the glory of the LORD.

6 Though the LORD *be* high, yet hath he respect unto the lowly: but the proud he knoweth afar off.

7 Though I walk in the midst of ᵃtrouble, thou wilt revive me: thou shalt stretch forth thine hand against the wrath of mine enemies, and thy right hand shall save me.

19a Ps. 135:11 (10–11).
20a Ps. 135:11.
22a Ps. 135:12.
25a D&C 104:17 (15–18);
    Moses 2:29 (28–30).
  b TG Flesh and Blood.

137 4a Neh. 2:3.
  7a Ezek. 25:12 (12–14).
   b Ezek. 35:5 (1–15).
  8a Isa. 47:1.
138 2a TG Worship.
  3a Enos 1:4 (1–11).

4a D&C 124:3 (2–11).
5a TG Singing.
7a Ps. 23:4 (1–6);
   D&C 127:2 (1–2).

8 *a*The LORD will perfect *that which* concerneth me: thy mercy, O LORD, *endureth* for ever: forsake not the *b*works of thine own hands.

PSALM 139

David says that the Lord knows all man's thoughts and doings—He asks, Where can man go to escape from the spirit and presence of the Lord?—Man is fearfully and wonderfully made.

To the chief Musician, A Psalm of David.

O LORD, thou hast *a*searched me, and *b*known *me.*

2 Thou knowest my downsitting and mine uprising, thou understandest my *a*thought afar off.

3 Thou compassest my path and my lying down, and art *a*acquainted *with* all my ways.

4 For *there is* not a word in my tongue, *but,* lo, O LORD, thou knowest it altogether.

5 Thou hast beset me behind and before, and laid thine hand upon me.

6 *Such a*knowledge *is* too *b*wonderful for me; it is high, I cannot *attain* unto it.

7 Whither shall I go from thy *a*spirit? or whither shall I flee from thy *b*presence?

8 If I ascend up into heaven, thou *art* there: if I make my bed in *a*hell, behold, thou *art there.*

9 *If* I take the wings of the morning, *and* dwell in the uttermost parts of the sea;

10 Even there shall thy hand lead me, and thy right hand shall hold me.

11 If I say, Surely the darkness shall cover me; even the night shall be light about me.

12 Yea, the darkness hideth not from thee; but the night shineth as the day: the darkness and the light *are* both alike *to thee.*

13 For thou hast *a*possessed my reins: thou hast *b*covered me in my mother's womb.

14 I will praise thee; for I am fearfully *and* wonderfully made: marvellous *are* thy works; and *that* my soul knoweth right well.

15 My substance was not hid from thee, when I was made in secret, *and* curiously wrought in the lowest parts of the earth.

16 Thine eyes did see my substance, yet being unperfect; and in thy *a*book all *my members* were written, *which* in continuance were fashioned, when *as yet there was* none of them.

17 How precious also are thy *a*thoughts unto me, O God! how great is the sum of them!

18 *If* I should count them, they are more in number than the sand: when I awake, I am still with thee.

19 Surely thou wilt *a*slay the wicked, O God: depart from me therefore, ye bloody men.

20 For they *a*speak against thee wickedly, *and* thine enemies take *thy name* in *b*vain.

21 Do not I hate them, O LORD, that hate thee? and am not I grieved with those that rise up against thee?

22 I hate them with perfect hatred: I count them mine enemies.

23 Search me, O God, and know my heart: *a*try me, and know my thoughts:

8*a* JST Ps. 138:8 The Lord will perfect *me in knowledge, concerning his kingdom. I will praise thee* O Lord, forever; *for thou art merciful, and wilt not* forsake the works of thine own hands.
  b Isa. 64:8.
139 1*a* D&C 121:24 (23–24).
  b 2 Sam. 7:20.
2*a* Amos 4:13;
    Matt. 12:25;
    Mosiah 24:12;
    D&C 6:16.
3*a* TG God, Omniscience of.
6*a* TG God, Intelligence of.
  b Job 42:3.
7*a* Jer. 23:24 (23–24).
  b Jonah 1:3.
8*a* Job 26:6 (1–9);
    Amos 9:2 (2–4).
13*a* HEB created my inward parts.
  b OR formed.
16*a* Ex. 32:32;
    Rev. 17:8.
17*a* Isa. 55:9 (8–9).
19*a* Isa. 11:4 (3–4);
    D&C 63:33 (29–37).
20*a* Jude 1:15 (14–16).
  b Matt. 5:33.
23*a* TG Test.

24 And see if *there be any* wicked way in me, and lead me in the way everlasting.

PSALM 140

David prays for deliverance from his enemies—The Lord maintains the cause of the poor and afflicted.

To the chief Musician, A Psalm of David.

*a*DELIVER me, O LORD, from the evil man: preserve me from the violent man;

2 Which imagine mischiefs in *their* heart; continually are they gathered together *for* war.

3 They have sharpened their tongues like a serpent; adders' *a*poison *is* under their lips. Selah.

4 Keep me, O LORD, from the hands of the wicked; preserve me from the violent man; who have purposed to overthrow my goings.

5 The proud have hid a *a*snare for me, and cords; they have spread a net by the wayside; they have set *b*gins for me. Selah.

6 I said unto the LORD, Thou *art* my God: hear the voice of my supplications, O LORD.

7 O GOD the Lord, the strength of my salvation, thou hast covered my head in the day of battle.

8 Grant not, O LORD, the desires of the wicked: further not his wicked device; *lest* they exalt themselves. Selah.

9 *As for* the head of those that compass me about, let the mischief of their own lips cover them.

10 Let burning coals fall upon them: let them be cast into the fire; into deep pits, that they rise not up again.

11 Let not an evil speaker be established in the earth: evil shall hunt the violent man to overthrow *him.*

12 I know that the LORD will maintain the cause of the afflicted, *and* the right of the poor.

13 Surely the righteous shall give thanks unto thy name: the upright shall dwell in thy *a*presence.

PSALM 141

David pleads with the Lord to hear his prayers—The reproof of the righteous is a kindness.

A Psalm of David.

LORD, I cry unto thee: make *a*haste unto me; give ear unto my voice, when I cry unto thee.

2 Let my *a*prayer be set forth before thee as *b*incense; *and* the lifting up of my hands *as* the *c*evening sacrifice.

3 Set a watch, O LORD, before my *a*mouth; keep the door of my lips.

4 Incline not my heart to *any* evil thing, to practise wicked works with men that work iniquity: and let me not eat of their dainties.

5 *a*Let the righteous *b*smite me; *it shall be* a *c*kindness: and let him reprove me; *it shall be* an excellent oil, *which* shall not break my head: for yet my prayer also *shall be* in their calamities.

6 When their judges are overthrown in stony places, *a*they shall hear my words; for they are sweet.

7 Our *a*bones are scattered at the grave's mouth, as when one cutteth and cleaveth *wood* upon the earth.

8 But mine *a*eyes *are* unto thee, O GOD the Lord: in thee is my trust; leave not my soul destitute.

9 Keep me from the snares *which* they have laid for me, and the gins of the workers of iniquity.

---

140 1*a* TG Deliver.
  3*a* Rom. 3:13 (9–18).
  5*a* Ps. 142:3.
    b OR traps.
  13*a* TG God, Presence of.
141 1*a* Ps. 70:5.
  2*a* Rev. 5:8 (1–10).
    b Ex. 30:7; 37:29.
    c Ex. 29:41 (38–42).

3*a* Ps. 39:1.
5*a* JST Ps. 141:5 *When the righteous smite me with the word of the Lord it is a kindness; and when they reprove me, it shall be an excellent oil, and shall not destroy my faith; for yet my prayer also*

shall be *for them. I delight not in their calamities.*
    b Prov. 27:6.
    c Prov. 9:8.
  6*a* IE the righteous.
  7*a* Ezek. 6:5.
  8*a* Ps. 25:15;
      D&C 4:5.

10 Let the wicked fall into their own nets, whilst that I withal escape.

PSALM 142

David prays for preservation from his persecutors.

Maschil of David;
A Prayer when he was in the cave.

I CRIED unto the LORD with my voice; with my voice unto the LORD did I make my supplication.

2 I poured out my complaint before him; I shewed before him my trouble.

3 When my spirit was *a*overwhelmed within me, then thou knewest my path. In the way wherein I walked have they privily laid a *b*snare for me.

4 I looked on *my* right hand, and beheld, but *there was* no man that would know me: refuge failed me; no man *a*cared for my soul.

5 I cried unto thee, O LORD: I said, Thou *art* my refuge *and* my portion in the land of the living.

6 Attend unto my cry; for I am brought very low: deliver me from my persecutors; for they are stronger than I.

7 Bring my *a*soul out of prison, that I may praise thy name: the righteous shall compass me about; for thou shalt deal bountifully with me.

PSALM 143

David prays for favor in judgment— He meditates on the Lord's works and trusts in Him.

A Psalm of David.

HEAR my prayer, O LORD, give ear to my supplications: in thy *a*faithfulness answer me, *and* in thy righteousness.

2 And enter not into judgment with thy servant: for in thy sight shall no man living be *a*justified.

3 For the enemy hath persecuted my soul; he hath smitten my life down to the ground; he hath made me to dwell in darkness, as those that have been long dead.

4 Therefore is my spirit overwhelmed within me; my heart within me is desolate.

5 I remember the days of old; I *a*meditate on all thy works; I muse on the work of thy hands.

6 I stretch forth my hands unto thee: my soul *a*thirsteth after thee, as a *b*thirsty land. Selah.

7 Hear me speedily, O LORD: my spirit faileth: hide not thy face from me, lest I be like unto them that go down into the *a*pit.

8 Cause me to hear thy lovingkindness in the morning; for in thee do I trust: cause me to know the *a*way wherein I should walk; for I *b*lift up my soul unto thee.

9 Deliver me, O LORD, from mine enemies: I flee unto thee to hide me.

10 Teach me to do thy *a*will; for thou *art* my God: thy *b*spirit *is* good; lead me into the land of uprightness.

11 Quicken me, O LORD, for thy name's sake: for thy righteousness' sake bring my soul out of trouble.

12 And of thy mercy cut off mine enemies, and destroy all them that afflict my soul: for I *am* thy servant.

PSALM 144

David blesses the Lord for deliverance and temporal prosperity—Happy is that people whose God is the Lord.

A *Psalm* of David.

BLESSED *be* the LORD my strength, which teacheth my hands to *a*war, *and* my fingers to fight:

---

142 3*a* Ps. 77:3.
  b Ps. 140:5.
  4*a* TG Apathy;
    Compassion.
  7*a* TG Spirits,
    Disembodied.
143 1*a* D&C 11:12 (10–12).
  2*a* TG Justification.

5*a* TG Meditation.
6*a* Ps. 42:2 (1–3);
    Isa. 55:1 (1–3);
    John 4:14 (13–15);
    7:37 (37–39).
  b Ps. 63:1.
7*a* Ps. 28:1; 88:4.
8*a* Ex. 33:13 (12–13);

Ps. 25:4 (1–5).
  b Ps. 25:1; 86:4;
    Lam. 3:41.
10*a* TG God, Will of.
  b TG God, Spirit of.
144 1*a* 2 Sam. 22:35 (32–36).

2 My goodness, and my fortress; my high tower, and my deliverer; my shield, and *he* in whom I trust; who subdueth my people under me.

3 LORD, what *is* ^aman, that thou takest knowledge of him! *or* the son of man, that thou makest account of him!

4 Man is like to ^avanity: his days *are* as a ^bshadow that passeth away.

5 Bow thy heavens, O LORD, and come down: touch the mountains, and they shall smoke.

6 Cast forth lightning, and scatter them: shoot out thine arrows, and destroy them.

7 Send thine hand from above; rid me, and deliver me out of great waters, from the hand of ^astrange children;

8 Whose mouth speaketh vanity, and their right hand *is* a right hand of ^afalsehood.

9 I will ^asing a new song unto thee, O God: upon a psaltery *and* an instrument of ten strings will I sing praises unto thee.

10 *It is he* that giveth ^asalvation unto kings: who delivereth David his servant from the hurtful sword.

11 Rid me, and deliver me from the hand of strange children, whose mouth speaketh ^avanity, and their right hand *is* a right hand of falsehood:

12 That our sons *may be* as plants grown up in their youth; *that* our daughters *may be* as corner stones, polished *after* the similitude of a palace:

13 *That* our garners *may be* full, affording all manner of store: *that* our sheep may bring forth thousands and ten thousands in our streets:

14 *That* our oxen *may be* strong to labour; *that there be* no breaking in, nor going out; that *there be* no complaining in our streets.

15 ^aHappy *is that* people, that is in such a case: *yea,* happy *is that* people, whose God *is* the LORD.

PSALM 145

David proclaims the greatness and majesty of God—The Lord is good to all—His kingdom is an everlasting kingdom—He is near to all who call upon Him, and He preserves those who love Him.

David's *Psalm* of praise.

I WILL extol thee, my God, O king; and I will bless thy name for ever and ever.

2 Every day will I bless thee; and I will praise thy name for ever and ever.

3 Great *is* the LORD, and greatly to be praised; and his greatness *is* unsearchable.

4 One ^ageneration shall praise thy works to another, and shall declare thy mighty acts.

5 I will speak of the glorious honour of thy majesty, and of thy wondrous works.

6 And *men* shall speak of the might of thy ^aterrible acts: and I will declare thy greatness.

7 They shall abundantly utter the memory of thy great goodness, and shall sing of thy righteousness.

8 The LORD *is* ^agracious, and full of ^bcompassion; slow to anger, and of great mercy.

9 The LORD *is* good to all: and his tender mercies *are* over all his works.

10 All thy works shall praise thee, O LORD; and thy ^asaints shall bless thee.

11 They shall speak of the glory of thy kingdom, and talk of thy power;

12 To make known to the sons of men his mighty ^aacts, and the glorious majesty of his kingdom.

13 Thy kingdom *is* an ^aeverlasting

3*a* Job 7:17 (17–18);
   Ps. 8:4 (1–9).
4*a* TG Vanity.
  b 1 Chr. 29:15;
   Ps. 102:11;
   Jacob 7:26.
7*a* HEB alien.
8*a* Isa. 44:20.

9*a* TG Singing.
10*a* OR victory.
11*a* TG Vanity.
15*a* TG Abundant Life;
   Happiness.
145 4*a* Deut. 4:9;
   Ps. 78:3 (3–4);
   Isa. 38:19.

6*a* Ex. 34:10.
8*a* Ex. 34:6.
  b Ps. 86:15.
10*a* TG Mission of Early
   Saints.
12*a* 1 Chr. 16:8.
13*a* TG Immortality.

kingdom, and thy dominion *endureth* throughout all generations.

14 The LORD upholdeth all that fall, and raiseth up all *those that be* bowed down.

15 The eyes of all wait upon thee; and thou givest them their meat in due season.

16 Thou openest thine hand, and satisfiest the desire of every living thing.

17 The LORD *is* ªrighteous in all his ways, and holy in all his works.

18 The LORD *is* ªnigh unto all them that call upon him, to all that call upon him in *b*truth.

19 He will fulfil the ªdesire of them that fear him: he also will hear their cry, and will save them.

20 The LORD ªpreserveth all them that love him: but all the wicked will he destroy.

21 My mouth shall speak the praise of the LORD: and let all flesh bless his holy name for ever and ever.

PSALM 146

Happy are they whose hope is in the Lord—The Lord frees the prisoners, loves the righteous, and reigns forever.

ªPRAISE ye the LORD. Praise the LORD, O my soul.

2 While I live will I praise the LORD: I will sing praises unto my God while I have any being.

3 Put not your ªtrust in princes, *nor* in the son of man, in whom *there is* no help.

4 His ªbreath goeth forth, he returneth to his earth; in that very day his thoughts perish.

5 ªHappy *is he* that *hath* the God of Jacob for his help, whose hope *is* in the LORD his God:

6 Which made heaven, and earth, the sea, and all that therein *is:* which keepeth truth for ever:

7 Which executeth judgment for the ªoppressed: which giveth food to the hungry. The LORD looseth the prisoners:

8 The LORD openeth *the* ªeyes *of* the *b*blind: the LORD raiseth them that are bowed down: the LORD loveth the righteous:

9 The LORD preserveth the strangers; he relieveth the ªfatherless and *b*widow: but the way of the wicked he turneth upside down.

10 The LORD shall reign for ªever, *even* thy God, O Zion, unto all generations. Praise ye the LORD.

PSALM 147

Praise the Lord for His power—His understanding is infinite—He sends His commandments, His word, His statutes, and His judgments unto Israel.

ªPRAISE ye the LORD: for *it is* good to sing praises unto our God; for *it* is pleasant; *and* praise is comely.

2 The LORD doth build up Jerusalem: he ªgathereth together the *b*outcasts of Israel.

3 He healeth the broken in heart, and bindeth up their wounds.

4 He telleth the number of the ªstars; he calleth them all by *their* *b*names.

5 Great *is* our Lord, and of great power: his ªunderstanding *is* infinite.

6 The LORD lifteth up the meek: he casteth the wicked down to the ground.

7 Sing unto the LORD with ªthanksgiving; sing praise upon the harp unto our God:

17*a* TG Righteousness.
18*a* Ps. 119:151.
  b John 4:23 (22–24);
    Moro. 10:4.
19*a* 1 Jn. 5:15 (14–15).
20*a* Ps. 97:10;
    1 Ne. 17:35 (33–35);
    D&C 82:10 (8–10).
    TG Protection,
    Divine.
146 1*a* HEB *Hallelu-yah.*

3*a* TG Trust Not in the
    Arm of Flesh.
4*a* TG Breath of Life.
5*a* TG Happiness.
7*a* TG Oppression.
8*a* Matt. 9:30 (27–31).
  b Isa. 42:7;
    Matt. 11:5.
9*a* James 1:27 (25–27);
    D&C 136:8 (7–9).
  b Prov. 15:25.

10*a* TG God, Eternal
    Nature of.
147 1*a* Ps. 33:1.
2*a* Deut. 30:3 (1–3).
  b Matt. 24:31.
4*a* TG Astronomy.
  b Isa. 40:26.
5*a* TG God, Omni-
    science of;
    Understanding.
7*a* TG Thanksgiving.

8 Who covereth the heaven with clouds, who prepareth rain for the earth, who maketh [a]grass to grow upon the mountains.

9 He giveth to the beast his food, *and* to the young ravens which cry.

10 He delighteth not in the strength of the horse: he taketh not pleasure in the legs of a man.

11 The LORD taketh [a]pleasure in them that fear him, in those that hope in his mercy.

12 Praise the LORD, O Jerusalem; praise thy God, O Zion.

13 For he hath strengthened the bars of thy gates; he hath blessed thy children within thee.

14 He maketh peace *in* thy borders, *and* filleth thee with the finest of the wheat.

15 He sendeth forth his commandment *upon* earth: his word runneth very swiftly.

16 He giveth snow like wool: he scattereth the hoarfrost like ashes.

17 He casteth forth his ice like morsels: who can stand before his cold?

18 He sendeth out his word, and melteth them: he causeth his wind to blow, *and* the waters flow.

19 He sheweth his word unto Jacob, his statutes and his judgments unto Israel.

20 He hath not dealt so with any nation: and *as for his* judgments, they have not [a]known them. Praise ye the LORD.

PSALM 148

Let all things praise the Lord: men and angels, the heavenly bodies, the elements and the earth, and all things thereon.

PRAISE ye the LORD. Praise ye the LORD from the heavens: praise him in the heights.

2 Praise ye him, all his angels: praise ye him, all his hosts.

3 Praise ye him, sun and moon: praise him, all ye stars of light.

4 Praise him, ye heavens of heavens, and ye [a]waters that *be* above the heavens.

5 Let them praise the name of the LORD: for he [a]commanded, and they were [b]created.

6 He hath also stablished them for ever and ever: he hath made a [a]decree which shall not pass.

7 Praise the LORD from the earth, ye [a]dragons, and all deeps:

8 Fire, and hail; snow, and vapour; stormy [a]wind fulfilling his word:

9 Mountains, and all hills; fruitful trees, and all cedars:

10 Beasts, and all cattle; creeping things, and flying fowl:

11 Kings of the earth, and all people; princes, and all [a]judges of the earth:

12 Both young men, and maidens; old men, and children:

13 Let them praise the name of the LORD: for his name alone is excellent; his [a]glory *is* above the earth and heaven.

14 He also exalteth the horn of his people, the praise of all his saints; *even* of the children of Israel, a people near unto him. Praise ye the LORD.

PSALM 149

Praise the Lord in the congregation of the Saints—He will beautify the meek with salvation.

PRAISE ye the LORD. Sing unto the LORD a new song, *and* his praise in the congregation of [a]saints.

2 Let Israel rejoice in him that [a]made him: let the children of [b]Zion be joyful in their [c]King.

3 Let them praise his name in the dance: let them sing praises unto him with the timbrel and harp.

4 For the LORD taketh pleasure in his people: he will [a]beautify the meek with salvation.

8*a* TG Nature, Earth.
11*a* TG Pleasure.
20*a* Amos 3:2 (1–2).
148 4*a* Gen. 1:7.
   5*a* Ps. 33:9.
    b TG Creation.

6*a* Ps. 119:89.
7*a* HEB sea monsters.
8*a* TG Nature, Earth.
11*a* OR rulers.
13*a* TG Celestial Glory.
149 1*a* TG Saints.

2*a* Ps. 95:6.
  b Joel 2:23;
    D&C 84:56.
  c Alma 5:50.
4*a* TG Beauty.

5 Let the saints be joyful in ᵃglory: let them ᵇsing aloud upon their ᶜbeds.

6 *Let* the high *praises* of God *be* in their mouth, and a ᵃtwoedged sword in their hand;

7 To execute vengeance upon the heathen, *and* punishments upon the people;

8 To bind their kings with chains, and their nobles with fetters of iron;

9 To execute upon them the judgment written: this honour have all his saints. Praise ye the Lᴏʀᴅ.

PSALM 150

Praise God in His sanctuary—Let everything that has breath praise the Lord.

Pʀᴀɪsᴇ ye the Lᴏʀᴅ. Praise God in his ᵃsanctuary: praise him in the firmament of his power.

2 Praise him for his mighty acts: praise him according to his excellent greatness.

3 Praise him with the sound of the trumpet: praise him with the psaltery and harp.

4 Praise him with the timbrel and dance: praise him with stringed instruments and ᵃorgans.

5 Praise him upon the loud cymbals: praise him upon the high sounding cymbals.

6 Let every thing that hath breath praise the Lᴏʀᴅ. Praise ye the Lᴏʀᴅ.

THE PROVERBS

CHAPTER 1

The fear of the Lord is the beginning of knowledge—If sinners entice you, do not consent—Those who hearken to wisdom will dwell safely.

THE ᵃproverbs of Solomon the son of David, king of Israel;

2 To know wisdom and instruction; to perceive the words of understanding;

3 To receive the ᵃinstruction of wisdom, justice, and judgment, and equity;

4 To give subtilty to the ᵃsimple, to the young man knowledge and discretion.

5 A wise *man* will hear, and will increase ᵃlearning; and a man of understanding shall attain unto wise counsels:

6 To understand a proverb, and the interpretation; the words of the wise, and their ᵃdark sayings.

7 ¶ The ᵃfear of the Lᴏʀᴅ *is* the beginning of ᵇknowledge: *but* fools despise ᶜwisdom and ᵈinstruction.

8 My son, hear the ᵃinstruction of thy father, and forsake not the law of thy ᵇmother:

9 For they *shall be* an ᵃornament of ᵇgrace unto thy head, and chains about thy neck.

10 ¶ My son, if sinners ᵃentice thee, ᵇconsent thou not.

11 If they say, Come with us, let us

5a TG Glory.
  b TG Singing.
  c Ps. 63:6.
6a D&C 6:2.
150 1a Alma 15:17.
  4a HEB pipes, flutes.

[PROVERBS]
1 1a 1 Kgs. 4:32;
  Prov. 10:1; 25:1.

3a TG Edification;
  Teachable.
4a Prov. 8:5.
5a TG Education; Learn.
6a OR riddles.
7a OR reverence of the
  LORD.
  TG Reverence.
  b TG Discernment,
  Spiritual; Knowledge.

c TG Wisdom.
d TG Problem-Solving.
8a TG Education.
  b TG Family, Children,
  Duties of.
9a Prov. 25:12.
  b Prov. 3:22.
10a TG Temptation.
  b Ps. 1:1 (1–2);
  Eph. 5:11 (8–13).

lay wait for blood, let us ^alurk privily for the innocent without cause:

12 Let us ^aswallow them up alive as the grave; and whole, as those that go down into the ^bpit:

13 We shall find all precious substance, we shall fill our houses with spoil:

14 Cast in thy lot among us; let us all have one purse:

15 My son, walk not thou in the way with them; ^arefrain thy foot from their path:

16 For their feet run to ^aevil, and make haste to shed blood.

17 Surely in vain the net is spread in the sight of any bird.

18 And they lay wait for their *own* blood; they lurk privily for their *own* lives.

19 So *are* the ways of every one that is ^agreedy of gain; *which* taketh away the life of the owners thereof.

20 ¶ Wisdom crieth without; she uttereth her voice in the streets:

21 She crieth in the chief place of concourse, in the openings of the gates: in the city she uttereth her words, *saying*,

22 How long, ye simple ones, will ye love simplicity? and the scorners delight in their ^ascorning, and fools ^bhate ^cknowledge?

23 Turn you at my reproof: behold, I will ^apour out my spirit unto you, I will make known my words unto you.

24 ¶ Because I have called, and ye ^arefused; I have stretched out my hand, and no man regarded;

25 But ye have set at ^anought all my ^bcounsel, and would none of my reproof:

26 I also will laugh at your calamity; I will mock when your fear cometh;

27 When your fear cometh as desolation, and your destruction cometh as a whirlwind; when distress and anguish cometh upon you.

28 Then shall they ^acall upon me, but I will not ^banswer; they shall seek me early, but they shall not find me:

29 For that they hated knowledge, and did not ^achoose the fear of the Lord:

30 They would none of my counsel: they despised all my ^areproof.

31 Therefore shall they eat of the ^afruit of their own way, and be filled with their own devices.

32 For the turning away of the simple shall slay them, and the prosperity of fools shall destroy them.

33 But whoso hearkeneth unto me shall dwell safely, and shall be quiet from fear of evil.

CHAPTER 2

The Lord gives wisdom, knowledge, and understanding—Walk in the way of good men.

My son, if thou wilt receive my words, and ^ahide my commandments with thee;

2 So that thou incline thine ear unto wisdom, *and* apply thine ^aheart to understanding;

3 Yea, if thou criest after knowledge, *and* liftest up thy voice for understanding;

4 If thou seekest her as silver, and searchest for her as *for* hid treasures;

5 Then shalt thou understand the ^afear of the Lord, and find the ^bknowledge of God.

6 For the Lord giveth ^awisdom: out of his mouth *cometh* knowledge and ^bunderstanding.

---

11 *a* OR ambush, lie in wait.
12 *a* Ps. 124:3.
　b Ps. 28:1.
15 *a* TG Abstain;
　　Self-Mastery.
16 *a* Isa. 59:7; 2 Ne. 19:17;
　　D&C 64:16.
19 *a* TG Selfishness.
22 *a* TG Malice.
　b TG Hate.
　c TG Knowledge.

23 *a* Isa. 42:1;
　　D&C 19:38; 95:4.
24 *a* TG Disobedience.
25 *a* Hel. 4:21.
　b TG Counsel.
28 *a* TG God, Access to.
　b Judg. 10:14 (13–14);
　　2 Kgs. 3:13; Job 27:9;
　　Ps. 66:18;
　　Jer. 2:28 (26–37);
　　D&C 101:7.

29 *a* TG Agency.
30 *a* TG Reproof.
31 *a* Jer. 6:19 (18–25).
2 1 *a* OR treasure.
　　Prov. 4:21.
2 *a* 2 Ne. 16:10; 3 Ne. 19:33.
5 *a* Alma 36:7.
　b TG Knowledge.
6 *a* TG God, Wisdom of;
　　Wisdom.
　b TG Understanding.

7 He layeth up sound wisdom for the righteous: *he is* a ^abuckler to them that ^bwalk uprightly.

8 He keepeth the paths of judgment, and preserveth the way of his saints.

9 Then shalt thou ^aunderstand righteousness, and judgment, and equity; *yea*, every good path.

10 ¶ When wisdom entereth into thine heart, and knowledge is pleasant unto thy soul;

11 ^aDiscretion shall preserve thee, understanding shall keep thee:

12 To deliver thee from the way of the evil *man*, from the man that speaketh froward things;

13 Who leave the paths of uprightness, to ^awalk in the ways of darkness;

14 Who rejoice to do evil, *and* delight in the ^afrowardness of the wicked;

15 Whose ways *are* crooked, and *they* froward in their paths:

16 To deliver thee from the ^astrange woman, *even* from the stranger *which* flattereth with her words;

17 Which forsaketh the guide of her youth, and forgetteth the covenant of her God.

18 For her house inclineth unto death, and her paths unto the dead.

19 None that go unto her ^areturn again, neither take they hold of the paths of life.

20 That thou mayest walk in the way of good *men*, and keep the paths of the righteous.

21 For the ^aupright shall dwell in the land, and the perfect shall remain in it.

22 But the wicked shall be ^acut off from the earth, and the transgressors shall be rooted out of it.

CHAPTER 3

Write mercy and truth upon the tablet of your heart—Trust in the Lord—Honor Him with your substance—Whom the Lord loves He corrects—Happy is the man who finds wisdom.

MY son, forget not my law; but let thine heart keep my commandments:

2 For length of days, and ^along life, and ^bpeace, shall they add to thee.

3 Let not mercy and ^atruth forsake thee: ^bbind them about thy neck; write them upon the ^ctable of thine ^dheart:

4 So shalt thou find ^afavour and good understanding in the sight of God and man.

5 ¶ ^aTrust in the LORD with all thine ^bheart; and lean not unto thine ^cown ^dunderstanding.

6 In all thy ways ^aacknowledge him, and he shall ^bdirect thy ^cpaths.

7 ¶ Be not ^awise in thine own eyes: ^bfear the LORD, and depart from evil.

8 It shall be ^ahealth to thy navel, and marrow to thy bones.

9 ^aHonour the LORD with thy ^bsubstance, and with the ^cfirstfruits of all thine increase:

10 So shall thy barns be filled with ^aplenty, and thy presses shall burst out with new wine.

11 ¶ My son, despise not the ^achastening of the LORD; neither be weary of his correction:

7a Ps. 91:4.
  b TG Walking with God.
9a 2 Ne. 28:30.
11a TG Rashness.
13a TG Walking in Darkness.
14a OR perverseness.
16a OR alien woman; unchaste women were often so called. Prov. 5:3 (3, 20). TG Adulterer.
19a Eccl. 7:26.
21a Prov. 10:30.
22a Ps. 52:5.

3 2a D&C 5:33.
  b TG Peace of God.
3a TG Truth.
  b Deut. 6:8 (4–10).
  c 2 Cor. 3:3 (2–3).
  d TG Heart.
4a 1 Sam. 2:26.
5a TG Faith; Trust in God; Trustworthiness.
  b TG Heart.
  c TG Trust Not in the Arm of Flesh.
  d TG Intelligence; Understanding.

6a TG Humility.
  b TG Guidance, Divine; Problem-Solving.
  c TG Walking with God.
7a 2 Ne. 15:21; 28:15.
  b TG Reverence.
8a TG Health; Word of Wisdom.
9a TG Honor.
  b TG Tithing.
  c Ex. 22:29.
10a TG Abundant Life; Blessing.
11a TG Chastening.

12 For whom the Lᴏʀᴅ loveth he ^acorrecteth; even as a ^bfather the son *in whom* he delighteth.

13 ¶ ^aHappy *is* the man *that* findeth ^bwisdom, and the man *that* getteth ^cunderstanding.

14 For the merchandise of it *is* better than the merchandise of silver, and the gain thereof than fine gold.

15 She *is* more precious than rubies: and all the things thou canst desire are not to be compared unto her.

16 Length of days *is* in her right hand; *and* in her left hand ^ariches and honour.

17 Her ways *are* ways of pleasantness, and all her paths *are* peace.

18 She *is* a tree of ^alife to them that lay hold upon her: and happy *is every one* that retaineth her.

19 The Lᴏʀᴅ by wisdom hath ^afounded the earth; by ^bunderstanding hath he established the heavens.

20 By his knowledge the depths are ^abroken up, and the clouds drop down the dew.

21 ¶ My son, let not them depart from thine eyes: keep sound wisdom and discretion:

22 So shall they be life unto thy soul, and ^agrace to thy neck.

23 Then shalt thou walk in thy way safely, and thy foot shall not stumble.

24 When thou liest down, thou shalt not be afraid: yea, thou shalt lie down, and thy sleep shall be sweet.

25 Be not afraid of sudden fear, neither of the desolation of the wicked, when it cometh.

26 For the Lᴏʀᴅ shall be thy ^aconfidence, and shall keep thy foot from being taken.

27 ¶ ^aWithhold not ^bgood from them to whom it is due, when it is in the power of thine hand to do *it*.

28 Say not unto thy neighbour, Go, and come again, and to morrow I will give; when thou hast it by thee.

29 ^aDevise not evil against thy ^bneighbour, seeing he dwelleth securely by thee.

30 ¶ ^aStrive not with a man without cause, if he have done thee no harm.

31 ¶ Envy thou not the ^aoppressor, and choose none of his ways.

32 For the ^afroward *is* abomination to the Lᴏʀᴅ: but his secret *is* with the righteous.

33 ¶ The ^acurse of the Lᴏʀᴅ *is* in the house of the wicked: but he blesseth the habitation of the just.

34 Surely he scorneth the scorners: but he giveth ^agrace unto the ^blowly.

35 The ^awise shall inherit glory: but ^bshame shall be the promotion of fools.

CHAPTER 4

Keep the commandments and live— With all your getting, get understanding—Go not in the way of evil men.

Hᴇᴀʀ, ye children, the ^ainstruction of a father, and attend to know understanding.

2 For I give you good doctrine, forsake ye not my law.

3 For I was my father's son, tender and only *beloved* in the sight of my mother.

4 He taught me also, and said unto me, Let thine heart retain my words: keep my commandments, and live.

5 Get wisdom, get understanding:

12a Hel. 15:3.
  b ᴛɢ Marriage, Fatherhood.
13a ᴛɢ Happiness.
  b ᴛɢ Wisdom.
  c ᴛɢ Study; Understanding.
16a Prov. 8:18 (12–18).
18a Eccl. 7:12.
19a Abr. 4:1.
  b ᴛɢ Understanding.

20a Gen. 7:11.
22a Prov. 1:9.
26a Job 4:6; Alma 7:27 (26–27). ᴛɢ Dependability.
27a Prov. 21:26 (25–26); Luke 6:30.
  b Gal. 6:10 (9–10).
29a D&C 42:27.
  b Prov. 21:10.
30a Prov. 25:8;

Rom. 12:18 (17–18).
31a ᴛɢ Oppression.
32a ᴏʀ perverse.
33a ᴛɢ Curse.
34a ᴛɢ Grace.
  b ᴏʀ humble.
35a ᴛɢ Wisdom.
  b ᴛɢ Shame.
4 1a Eph. 6:4 (1–4).

forget *it* not; neither decline from the words of my mouth.

6 Forsake her not, and she shall preserve thee: love her, and she shall keep thee.

7 [a]Wisdom *is* the principal thing; *therefore* get wisdom: and with all thy getting get [b]understanding.

8 Exalt her, and she shall promote thee: she shall bring thee to honour, when thou dost embrace her.

9 She shall give to thine head an [a]ornament of grace: a crown of [b]glory shall she deliver to thee.

10 Hear, O my son, and receive my sayings; and the [a]years of thy life shall be many.

11 I have taught thee in the way of wisdom; I have [a]led thee in right paths.

12 When thou goest, thy steps shall not be [a]straitened; and when thou [b]runnest, thou shalt not stumble.

13 Take fast [a]hold of [b]instruction; let *her* not go: keep her; for she *is* thy life.

14 ¶ Enter not into the [a]path of the wicked, and go not in the way of evil *men*.

15 Avoid it, pass not by it, turn from it, and pass away.

16 For they sleep not, except they have done mischief; and their sleep is taken away, unless they cause *some* to fall.

17 For they eat the bread of wickedness, and drink the wine of violence.

18 But the [a]path of the [b]just *is* as the shining [c]light, that [d]shineth more and more unto the perfect day.

19 The way of the wicked *is* as [a]darkness: they know not at what they stumble.

20 ¶ My son, attend to my words; incline thine ear unto my sayings.

21 Let them not depart from thine [a]eyes; [b]keep them in the midst of thine heart.

22 For they *are* [a]life unto those that find them, and health to all their flesh.

23 ¶ Keep thy heart with all diligence; for out of it *are* the issues of life.

24 Put away from thee a [a]froward mouth, and perverse lips put far from thee.

25 Let thine [a]eyes look right on, and let thine eyelids look straight before thee.

26 [a]Ponder the path of thy feet, and let all thy ways be established.

27 Turn not to the right hand nor to the left: remove thy foot from evil.

CHAPTER 5

Those who associate with immoral women will go down to hell—Rejoice with the wife of your youth.

MY son, attend unto my wisdom, *and* bow thine ear to my understanding:

2 That thou mayest regard discretion, and *that* thy lips may keep knowledge.

3 ¶ For the [a]lips of a [b]strange woman drop *as* an honeycomb, and her mouth *is* smoother than oil:

4 But her [a]end is [b]bitter as wormwood, sharp as a twoedged sword.

5 Her feet go down to [a]death; her steps take hold on [b]hell.

6 Lest thou shouldest ponder the path of life, her ways are moveable, *that* thou canst not know *them*.

7 Hear me now therefore, O ye

7a TG Wisdom.
 b TG Learn;
   Problem-Solving;
   Understanding.
9a TG Beauty.
 b TG Glory.
10a Ex. 20:12.
11a TG Leadership.
12a OR distressed,
   hampered.
 b D&C 89:20 (19–20).
13a 1 Ne. 15:24 (23–24).
 b TG Education.

14a 1 Ne. 12:17 (16–18).
18a 2 Ne. 31:18 (17–21).
 b TG Righteousness.
 c TG Example;
   Light [noun].
 d TG Discernment,
   Spiritual.
19a TG Darkness, Spiritual.
21a Prov. 4:25;
   Morm. 8:15;
   D&C 82:19.
 b Prov. 2:1.
22a Matt. 19:17.

24a OR perverse.
   D&C 50:33 (32–33);
   84:73; 105:24.
25a Prov. 4:21.
26a TG Meditation.
 5 3a TG Lust.
 b Prov. 2:16;
   Alma 39:3.
 4a Prov. 7:27;
   Jacob 2:35 (27–35).
 b Eccl. 7:26.
 5a TG Sexual Immorality.
 b TG Damnation.

children, and depart not from the words of my mouth.

8 ªRemove thy way far from her, and come not nigh the door of her house:

9 Lest thou give thine honour unto others, and thy years unto the cruel:

10 Lest strangers be filled with thy ªwealth; and thy labours *be* in the house of a stranger;

11 And thou mourn at the last, when thy flesh and thy body are consumed,

12 And say, How have I hated ªinstruction, and my heart despised reproof;

13 And have not ªobeyed the voice of my ᵇteachers, nor inclined mine ear to them that instructed me!

14 I was almost in all evil in the midst of the congregation and assembly.

15 ¶ Drink waters out of thine own cistern, and running waters out of thine own well.

16 Let thy fountains be dispersed abroad, *and* rivers of waters in the streets.

17 Let them be only thine own, and not strangers' with thee.

18 Let thy fountain be blessed: and rejoice with the ªwife of thy youth.

19 *Let her be as* the loving hind and pleasant roe; let her breasts satisfy thee at all times; and be thou ravished always with her ªlove.

20 And why wilt thou, my son, be ravished with a strange woman, and embrace the bosom of a stranger?

21 For the ªways of man *are* before the ᵇeyes of the LORD, and he ᶜpondereth all his goings.

22 ¶ His own ªiniquities shall take the wicked himself, and he shall be holden with the ᵇcords of his sins.

23 He shall die without instruction; and in the greatness of his folly he shall go astray.

CHAPTER 6

Six things that the Lord hates are named—Those who commit adultery destroy their own souls.

MY son, if thou ªbe surety for thy friend, *if* thou hast stricken thy hand with a stranger,

2 Thou art snared with the words of thy mouth, thou art taken with the words of thy mouth.

3 Do this now, my son, and deliver thyself, when thou art come into the hand of thy friend; go, ªhumble thyself, and make sure thy friend.

4 Give not sleep to thine eyes, nor slumber to thine eyelids.

5 Deliver thyself as a roe from the hand *of the hunter,* and as a bird from the hand of the fowler.

6 ¶ Go to the ªant, thou ᵇsluggard; consider her ways, and be wise:

7 Which having no guide, overseer, or ruler,

8 Provideth her meat in the summer, *and* gathereth her food in the harvest.

9 How long wilt thou ªsleep, O sluggard? when wilt thou arise out of thy sleep?

10 *Yet* a little sleep, a little slumber, a little folding of the hands to sleep:

11 So shall thy poverty come as one that travelleth, and thy want as an armed man.

12 ¶ A naughty person, a wicked man, walketh with a ªfroward mouth.

13 He winketh with his eyes, he speaketh with his feet, he teacheth with his fingers;

14 Frowardness *is* in his heart, he deviseth mischief continually; he soweth discord.

15 Therefore shall his calamity come suddenly; suddenly shall he be broken without ªremedy.

8*a* Alma 39:9 (9–11).
10*a* OR strength.
12*a* D&C 101:5 (1–5).
13*a* TG Disobedience.
    b TG Teacher.
18*a* TG Family, Love within;
    Marriage, Husbands.
19*a* D&C 42:22.
21*a* Ps. 119:168.

b Heb. 4:13.
c 2 Ne. 9:20;
    D&C 38:2 (1–2).
22*a* Hosea 7:2.
    b Alma 12:11 (10–11);
        36:18;
        Moses 7:26.
6 1*a* IE promise to discharge
        an obligation if the

debtor defaults.
    Prov. 11:15; 22:26.
3*a* D&C 67:10.
6*a* Prov. 30:25.
    TG Work, Value of.
    b TG Apathy; Laziness.
9*a* TG Sleep.
12*a* OR perverse.
15*a* Prov. 29:1.

16 ¶ These six *things* doth the Lord
*a*hate: yea, seven *are* an abomination unto him:

17 A *a*proud look, a lying tongue,
and hands that shed innocent blood,

18 An *a*heart that deviseth wicked
imaginations, feet that be swift in
running to mischief,

19 A *a*false witness *that* speaketh
*b*lies, and he that soweth *c*discord
among brethren.

20 ¶ My son, keep thy *a*father's
commandment, and forsake not the
law of thy mother:

21 *a*Bind them continually upon
thine heart, *and* tie them about
thy neck.

22 When thou goest, it shall lead
thee; when thou sleepest, it shall
keep thee; and *when* thou awakest,
it shall talk with thee.

23 For the commandment *is* a *a*lamp;
and the law *is* light; and reproofs of
instruction *are* the way of life:

24 To keep thee from the *a*evil
*b*woman, from the flattery of the
tongue of a strange woman.

25 *a*Lust not after her beauty in
thine heart; neither let her take
thee with her eyelids.

26 For by means of a whorish
woman *a man is brought* to a piece
of bread: and the adulteress will
hunt for the precious life.

27 Can a man take fire in his bosom, and his clothes not be burned?

28 Can one go upon hot coals, and
his feet not be burned?

29 So he that goeth in to his neighbour's wife; whosoever toucheth her
shall not be innocent.

30 *Men* do not despise a thief, if he
*a*steal to satisfy his soul when he
is hungry;

31 But *if* he be found, he shall

*a*restore sevenfold; he shall give all
the substance of his house.

32 *But* whoso committeth *a*adultery
with a woman lacketh *b*understanding: he *that* doeth it destroyeth his
own soul.

33 A wound and *a*dishonour shall
he get; and his reproach shall not
be wiped away.

34 For *a*jealousy *is* the rage of a
man: therefore he will not spare
in the day of vengeance.

35 He will not regard any ransom;
neither will he rest content, though
thou givest many gifts.

CHAPTER 7

*An immoral woman leads a man to
destruction as an ox to the slaughter—
The house of an adulterous woman is
the way to hell.*

My son, keep my words, and lay
up my commandments with thee.

2 Keep my *a*commandments, and
live; and my law as the *b*apple of
thine eye.

3 *a*Bind them upon thy fingers, write
them upon the table of thine *b*heart.

4 Say unto *a*wisdom, Thou *art* my
sister; and call *b*understanding *thy*
kinswoman:

5 That they may keep thee from the
strange woman, from the stranger
which *a*flattereth with her words.

6 ¶ For at the window of my house
I looked through my casement,

7 And beheld among the simple
ones, I discerned among the youths,
a young man void of understanding,

8 Passing through the street near
her corner; and he went the way
to her house,

9 In the *a*twilight, in the evening,
in the black and *b*dark night:

16 *a* TG Hate.
17 *a* TG Haughtiness; Pride.
18 *a* TG Hardheartedness.
19 *a* TG Slander.
   b TG Gossip;
      Honesty;
      Lying.
   c TG Disputations.
20 *a* TG Family, Children,
      Duties of.
21 *a* Deut. 6:8 (4–10).

23 *a* Ps. 119:105.
24 *a* TG Adulterer.
   b TG Woman.
25 *a* TG Chastity; Lust;
      Sexual Immorality.
30 *a* TG Stealing.
31 *a* Ex. 22:4 (1–4).
32 *a* TG Adulterer.
   b Prov. 9:6 (4–6).
33 *a* D&C 42:24 (24–26).
34 *a* TG Jealous.

7 2 *a* 1 Ne. 17:15 (3, 15);
      D&C 14:7.
   b Deut. 32:10 (7–10).
3 *a* Deut. 6:8.
   b Jer. 31:33.
4 *a* Alma 37:35.
   b TG Understanding.
5 *a* 2 Ne. 28:22 (20–23).
9 *a* Job 24:15.
   b Alma 10:25; 14:6;
      Moses 6:27; 7:26.

10 And, behold, there met him a woman *with* the attire of an ^aharlot, and subtil of heart.

11 (She *is* loud and ^astubborn; her feet abide not in her house:

12 Now *is she* without, now in the streets, and lieth in wait at ^aevery corner.)

13 So she caught him, and kissed him, *and* with an impudent face said unto him,

14 ^aI have peace offerings with me; this day have I payed my vows.

15 Therefore came I forth to meet thee, diligently to seek thy face, and I have found thee.

16 I have decked my bed with coverings of tapestry, with carved *works,* with fine linen of Egypt.

17 I have perfumed my bed with myrrh, ^aaloes, and cinnamon.

18 Come, let us take our fill of love until the morning: let us solace ourselves with loves.

19 For the goodman *is* not at home, he is gone a long journey:

20 He hath taken a bag of money with him, *and* will come home at the day appointed.

21 With her much fair speech she caused him to yield, with the flattering of her lips she forced him.

22 He goeth after her ^astraightway, as an ox goeth to the ^bslaughter, or as a fool to the correction of the stocks;

23 Till a dart strike through his liver; as a bird hasteth to the ^asnare, and knoweth not that it *is* for his life.

24 ¶ Hearken unto me now therefore, O ye children, and attend to the words of my mouth.

25 Let not thine ^aheart decline to her ways, go not astray in her paths.

26 For she hath cast down many wounded: yea, many strong *men* have been slain by her.

27 Her ^ahouse *is* the way to ^bhell, going down to the chambers of death.

CHAPTER 8

Wisdom is greatly to be desired—The Lord and the sons of men possessed wisdom in the premortal life.

DOTH not wisdom ^acry? and understanding put forth her voice?

2 She standeth in the top of high places, by the way in the places of the paths.

3 She crieth at the gates, at the entry of the city, at the coming in at the doors.

4 Unto you, O men, I call; and my voice *is* to the sons of man.

5 O ye ^asimple, understand wisdom: and, ye fools, be ye of an understanding ^bheart.

6 Hear; for I will speak of excellent things; and the opening of my lips *shall be* right things.

7 For my mouth shall ^aspeak ^btruth; and wickedness *is* an abomination to my lips.

8 All the words of my mouth *are* in righteousness; *there is* nothing froward or perverse in them.

9 They *are* all plain to him that ^aunderstandeth, and right to them that find ^bknowledge.

10 Receive my instruction, and not silver; and knowledge rather than choice gold.

11 For ^awisdom *is* better than ^brubies; and all the things that may be desired are not to be compared to it.

12 I wisdom dwell with ^aprudence, and find out knowledge of witty inventions.

10*a* TG Lust; Sexual Immorality.	*b* TG Fornication.	5*a* Prov. 1:4.
11*a* TG Stubbornness.	23*a* Eccl. 9:12.	*b* Mosiah 2:9; 12:27; 3 Ne. 19:33.
12*a* D&C 10:27 (26–27).	25*a* Alma 5:41.	7*a* TG Communication.
14*a* IE She cynically suggests her piety.	27*a* TG Whore. *b* Prov. 5:4; Jacob 2:35 (27–35).	*b* TG Truth. 9*a* 2 Ne. 32:4.
17*a* The Hebrew probably indicates a fragrant wood.	TG Damnation. 8 1*a* IE to make her availability and values known.	*b* Prov. 14:6. 11*a* TG Wisdom. *b* Job 28:18.
22*a* OR suddenly; all at once.		12*a* TG Prudence.

13 The ^afear of the Lord *is* to ^bhate evil: pride, and arrogancy, and the evil way, and the froward mouth, do I hate.

14 Counsel *is* mine, and sound wisdom: I *am* understanding; I have strength.

15 By me ^akings reign, and princes decree justice.

16 By me princes rule, and nobles, *even* all the judges of the earth.

17 I ^alove them that love me; and those that seek me early shall find me.

18 Riches and honour *are* with me; *yea,* durable ^ariches and righteousness.

19 My fruit *is* better than gold, yea, than fine gold; and my revenue than choice silver.

20 I lead in the way of righteousness, in the midst of the paths of judgment:

21 That I may cause those that love me to inherit substance; and I will fill their treasures.

22 The Lord possessed me in the beginning of his way, before his ^aworks of old.

23 I was set up from ^aeverlasting, from the ^bbeginning, or ever the earth was.

24 When *there were* no depths, I was brought forth; when *there were* no fountains abounding with water.

25 Before the mountains were settled, before the hills was I brought forth:

26 While as yet he had not made the earth, nor the fields, nor ^athe highest part of the dust of the world.

27 When he prepared the heavens, I *was* there: when he set a ^acompass upon the face of the depth:

28 When he established the clouds above: when he strengthened the fountains of the deep:

29 When he gave to the sea his decree, that the waters should not pass his commandment: when he appointed the foundations of the earth:

30 Then I was by him, *as* one brought up *with him:* and I was daily *his* delight, rejoicing always before him;

31 Rejoicing in the habitable part of his earth; and my delights *were* with the sons of men.

32 Now therefore hearken unto me, O ye children: for blessed *are they that* keep my ways.

33 Hear instruction, and be wise, and refuse it not.

34 Blessed *is* the man that heareth me, watching daily at my gates, waiting at the posts of my doors.

35 For whoso findeth me findeth ^alife, and shall obtain favour of the Lord.

36 But he that sinneth against me wrongeth his own soul: all they that hate me love ^adeath.

CHAPTER 9

Rebuke a wise man and he will love you—The fear of the Lord is the beginning of wisdom—The guests of an immoral woman are in the depths of hell.

^aWisdom hath builded her house, she hath hewn out her seven pillars:

2 She hath killed her beasts; she hath mingled her wine; she hath also furnished her table.

3 She hath sent forth her maidens: she crieth upon the highest places of the city,

4 Whoso *is* ^asimple, let him turn in hither: *as for* him that wanteth understanding, she saith to him,

5 ^aCome, eat of my bread, and drink of the wine *which* I have mingled.

13a TG Reverence.
  b Alma 13:12 (12–13).
15a Prov. 21:1.
17a D&C 76:5 (5–10).
18a Prov. 3:16.
22a TG Creation.
23a TG Eternity.

  b D&C 93:29.
26a HEB the head (or first) of the dust (or elements) of the earth.
27a OR circle; i.e., delimiting bounds, as in Job 26:10.
35a Prov. 21:21.

36a TG Death;
    Death, Spiritual, First.
9 1a Alma 26:35.
  4a D&C 1:23.
  5a Wisdom prepares her feast and invites participants.

6 Forsake the *foolish, and live; and go in the way of *understanding.

7 He that reproveth a scorner getteth to himself shame: and he that rebuketh a wicked *man getteth* himself a blot.

8 *Reprove not a scorner, lest he hate thee: rebuke a wise man, and he will *love thee.

9 Give *instruction* to a wise *man,* and he will be yet wiser: *teach a just *man,* and he will *increase in *learning.

10 The *fear of the LORD *is the beginning of *wisdom: and the *knowledge of the *holy *is *understanding.

11 For by me thy *days shall be multiplied, and the years of thy life shall be increased.

12 If thou be *wise, thou shalt be wise for thyself: but *if* thou scornest, thou alone shalt *bear *it.*

13 ¶ A foolish *woman *is* clamorous: she *is* simple, and knoweth nothing.

14 For she sitteth at the door of her house, on a seat in the high places of the city,

15 To call passengers who go right on their ways:

16 Whoso *is* simple, let him turn in hither: and *as for* him that wanteth understanding, she saith to him,

17 Stolen waters are sweet, and bread *eaten* in secret is pleasant.

18 But he knoweth not that the dead *are* there; *and that* her guests *are* in the depths of *hell.

CHAPTER 10

A wise son makes a glad father—The mouth of a righteous man is a well of life—He who utters slander is a fool—The desire of the righteous will be granted.

THE *proverbs of Solomon. A *wise son maketh a *glad *father: but a *foolish son *is* the *heaviness of his *mother.

2 *Treasures of wickedness profit nothing: but *righteousness delivereth from death.

3 The LORD will not suffer the soul of the righteous to famish: but he casteth away the substance of the wicked.

4 He becometh poor that dealeth *with* a *slack hand: but the hand of the *diligent maketh rich.

5 He that gathereth in summer *is* a wise son: *but* he that sleepeth in harvest *is* a son that causeth shame.

6 *Blessings *are* upon the head of the just: but violence covereth the mouth of the wicked.

7 The memory of the just *is* blessed: but the name of the *wicked shall *rot.

8 The wise in heart will receive commandments: but a prating fool shall fall.

9 He that *walketh *uprightly walketh surely: but he that perverteth his ways shall be known.

10 He that winketh with the eye causeth sorrow: but a prating fool shall fall.

11 The mouth of a *righteous *man* is a *well of life: but violence covereth the mouth of the wicked.

6a D&C 66:10.
 b Prov. 6:32.
8a TG Chastening.
 b Ps. 141:5.
9a TG Teaching.
 b Matt. 13:12 (11–12);
  D&C 88:118.
 c TG Learn.
10a TG Reverence.
 b TG Wisdom.
 c Prov. 30:3.
 d TG Holiness.
 e TG Understanding.
11a 1 Ne. 17:55;
  Mosiah 14:10.
12a Job 35:7 (6–8).

 b Gal. 6:5 (4–5).
13a TG Woman.
18a Alma 12:11;
  D&C 29:38;
  76:84 (84–86).
10 1a 1 Kgs. 4:32;
  Prov. 1:1; 25:1.
 b Prov. 17:21.
 c TG Happiness.
 d TG Marriage,
  Fatherhood.
 e Prov. 15:5, 20.
 f OR sorrow.
 g TG Family, Children,
  Duties of;
  Marriage, Motherhood.

2a TG Treasure.
 b TG Righteousness.
4a TG Laziness.
 b TG Dedication;
  Diligence.
6a D&C 39:8.
7a TG Wickedness.
 b Isa. 14:22;
  Jer. 51:62 (61–62).
9a TG Walking with God.
 b Prov. 28:6.
11a Ps. 37:30;
  Alma 36:26;
  D&C 108:7.
 b Prov. 13:14.

12 ^aHatred stirreth up ^bstrifes: but love covereth all sins.

13 In the lips of him that hath understanding wisdom is found: but a ^arod *is* for the back of him that is void of understanding.

14 Wise *men* lay up knowledge: but the ^amouth of the foolish *is* near destruction.

15 The rich man's ^awealth *is* his strong city: the destruction of the poor *is* their poverty.

16 The ^alabour of the righteous *tendeth* to ^blife: the fruit of the wicked to sin.

17 He *is in* the way of life that keepeth ^ainstruction: but he that refuseth ^breproof erreth.

18 He that hideth ^ahatred *with* lying lips, and he that uttereth a ^bslander, *is* a fool.

19 In the multitude of ^awords there wanteth not sin: but he that ^brefraineth his lips *is* wise.

20 The tongue of the just *is as* choice silver: the heart of the wicked *is* little worth.

21 The lips of the righteous feed many: but ^afools die for want of wisdom.

22 The blessing of the LORD, it maketh ^arich, and he addeth no sorrow with it.

23 *It is* as sport to a fool to do mischief: but a man of understanding hath wisdom.

24 The fear of the wicked, it shall come upon him: but the desire of the righteous shall be granted.

25 As the whirlwind passeth, so *is* the wicked no *more:* but the righteous *is* an everlasting foundation.

26 As vinegar to the teeth, and as smoke to the eyes, so *is* the sluggard to them that send him.

27 The ^afear of the LORD prolongeth days: but the years of the wicked shall be shortened.

28 The ^ahope of the righteous *shall be* gladness: but the expectation of the wicked shall perish.

29 The way of the LORD *is* ^astrength to the upright: but destruction *shall be* to the workers of iniquity.

30 The ^arighteous shall never be ^bremoved: but the wicked shall not inhabit the earth.

31 The mouth of the just bringeth forth wisdom: but the ^afroward tongue shall be cut out.

32 The lips of the righteous know what is acceptable: but the ^amouth of the wicked *speaketh* frowardness.

CHAPTER 11

The state and rewards of the righteous and the wicked are contrasted—When a wicked man dies, his expectations perish—He who wins souls is wise.

^aA FALSE ^bbalance *is* abomination to the LORD: but a just weight *is* his delight.

2 *When* ^apride cometh, then cometh ^bshame: but with the lowly *is* wisdom.

3 The ^aintegrity of the upright shall guide them: but the perverseness of transgressors shall destroy them.

4 ^aRiches profit not in the day of ^bwrath: but righteousness delivereth from death.

5 The ^arighteousness of the perfect shall direct his way: but the wicked shall ^bfall by his own wickedness.

6 The righteousness of the upright

12*a* TG Hate;
　　Malice.
　b TG Contention.
13*a* Prov. 19:29.
14*a* Prov. 18:7.
15*a* Prov. 18:11.
16*a* TG Labor;
　　Work, Value of.
　b Prov. 19:23.
17*a* TG Teachable.
　b TG Chastening;
　　Reproof.

18*a* TG Hate.
　b TG Slander.
19*a* TG Boast.
　b Prov. 17:27.
21*a* Ps. 14:1 (1–7).
22*a* TG Treasure.
27*a* TG Reverence.
28*a* TG Hope.
29*a* TG Strength.
30*a* Prov. 2:21 (21–22).
　b Lam. 1:8.
31*a* OR perverse.

32*a* Eccl. 10:12.
11 1*a* OR Deceptive scales
　　(i.e., made to deceive).
　b Amos 8:5.
2*a* 2 Ne. 26:20 (20–22);
　　D&C 38:39.
　b TG Shame.
3*a* TG Integrity.
4*a* TG Treasure.
　b D&C 1:9 (8–10).
5*a* Prov. 13:6.
　b Esth. 7:9.

shall deliver them: but transgressors shall be taken in *their own* naughtiness.

7 When a wicked man dieth, *his* expectation shall perish: and the hope of unjust *men* perisheth.

8 The righteous is delivered out of trouble, and the wicked cometh in his stead.

9 An ᵃhypocrite with *his* mouth destroyeth his neighbour: but through knowledge shall the ᵇjust be delivered.

10 When it goeth well with the ᵃrighteous, the city rejoiceth: and when the wicked perish, *there is* shouting.

11 By the blessing of the upright the city is exalted: but it is overthrown by the mouth of the wicked.

12 He that is void of wisdom despiseth his ᵃneighbour: but a man of understanding holdeth his peace.

13 A ᵃtalebearer revealeth secrets: but he that is of a faithful spirit concealeth the matter.

14 Where no ᵃcounsel *is,* the people fall: but in the ᵇmultitude of ᶜcounsellors *there is* safety.

15 He that is ᵃsurety for a stranger shall smart *for it:* and he that hateth suretiship is sure.

16 A gracious ᵃwoman retaineth honour: and strong *men* retain riches.

17 The merciful man doeth good to his own soul: but *he that is* ᵃcruel troubleth his own flesh.

18 The wicked worketh a ᵃdeceitful work: but to him that soweth ᵇrighteousness *shall be* a sure ᶜreward.

19 As righteousness *tendeth* to ᵃlife: so he that pursueth evil *pursueth it* to his own death.

20 They that are ᵃof a ᵇfroward heart *are* abomination to the LORD: but *such as are* upright in *their* way *are* his delight.

21 *Though* hand *join* in hand, the wicked shall not be unpunished: but the seed of the righteous shall be delivered.

22 *As* a jewel of gold in a swine's snout, *so is* a fair woman which is without discretion.

23 The desire of the righteous *is* only good: *but* the expectation of the wicked *is* wrath.

24 There is that scattereth, and yet ᵃincreaseth; and *there is* that withholdeth more than is meet, but *it tendeth* to poverty.

25 The liberal soul shall be made fat: and he that ᵃwatereth shall be watered also himself.

26 He that withholdeth corn, the people shall curse him: but blessing *shall be* upon the head of him that selleth *it.*

27 He that diligently seeketh good procureth favour: but he that seeketh mischief, it shall come unto him.

28 He that ᵃtrusteth in his riches shall fall: but the righteous shall flourish as a branch.

29 He that troubleth his own ᵃhouse shall inherit the wind: and the fool *shall be* servant to the wise of heart.

30 The fruit of the righteous *is* a ᵃtree of life; and he that winneth souls *is* wise.

31 Behold, the righteous shall be ᵃrecompensed in the earth: much more the wicked and the sinner.

CHAPTER 12

A virtuous woman is a crown to her husband—The way of a fool is right in his own eyes—Lying lips are an abomination to the Lord.

WHOSO loveth ᵃinstruction loveth

9a D&C 50:7 (7–8).
  b D&C 51:19.
10a Prov. 28:12.
12a D&C 59:6.
13a TG Gossip.
14a TG Counsel.
  b Prov. 24:6.
  c TG Counselor.
15a Prov. 6:1; 22:26.

16a TG Woman.
17a TG Cruelty.
18a TG Deceit.
  b TG Righteousness.
  c TG Reward; Wages.
19a Prov. 19:23;
    2 Ne. 9:39.
20a Prov. 21:8.
  b Ps. 101:4.

24a Prov. 13:7.
25a Matt. 7:2.
28a TG Trustworthiness.
29a TG Marriage,
    Fatherhood.
30a 1 Ne. 11:25.
31a D&C 1:10; 56:19.
12 1a TG Edification;
    Teachable.

knowledge: but he that hateth [b]reproof *is* brutish.

2 A good *man* obtaineth [a]favour of the LORD: but a man of wicked devices will he condemn.

3 A man shall not be established by wickedness: but the root of the righteous shall not be moved.

4 A [a]virtuous [b]woman *is* a crown to her [c]husband: but she that maketh ashamed *is* as rottenness in his bones.

5 The thoughts of the righteous *are* right: *but* the [a]counsels of the wicked *are* [b]deceit.

6 The words of the wicked *are* to lie in wait for blood: but the mouth of the upright shall deliver them.

7 The [a]wicked are [b]overthrown, and *are* not: but the house of the righteous shall stand.

8 A man shall be commended according to his wisdom: but he that is of a perverse heart shall be despised.

9 *He that is* despised, and hath a servant, *is* better than he that [a]honoureth himself, and lacketh bread.

10 A righteous *man* regardeth the life of his [a]beast: but the tender mercies of the wicked *are* [b]cruel.

11 He that tilleth his land shall be satisfied with bread: but he that followeth vain *persons is* void of understanding.

12 The wicked desireth the net of evil *men:* but the root of the righteous yieldeth *fruit.*

13 The wicked is snared by the [a]transgression of *his* [b]lips: but the just shall come out of trouble.

14 A man shall be satisfied with good by the fruit of *his* [a]mouth: and the recompence of a man's hands shall be rendered unto him.

15 The way of a [a]fool *is* right in his own eyes: but he that hearkeneth unto [b]counsel *is* wise.

16 A fool's wrath is presently known: but a [a]prudent *man* covereth shame.

17 *He that* speaketh truth sheweth forth righteousness: but a false witness deceit.

18 There is that speaketh like the piercings of a sword: but the tongue of the wise *is* health.

19 The lip of truth shall be established for ever: but a lying tongue *is* but for a moment.

20 Deceit *is* in the heart of them that imagine evil: but to the counsellors of peace *is* joy.

21 There shall no evil happen to the just: but the wicked shall be filled with mischief.

22 [a]Lying lips *are* abomination to the LORD: but they that deal [b]truly *are* his [c]delight.

23 A [a]prudent man concealeth [b]knowledge: but the heart of fools proclaimeth [c]foolishness.

24 The hand of the [a]diligent shall bear rule: but the [b]slothful shall be under tribute.

25 Heaviness in the heart of man maketh it stoop: but a good word maketh it glad.

26 The righteous *is* more excellent than his neighbour: but the way of the wicked seduceth them.

27 The [a]slothful *man* roasteth not that which he took in hunting: but the substance of a [b]diligent man *is* precious.

28 In the way of [a]righteousness *is* life; and *in* the pathway *thereof there is* no death.

---

1 b TG Chastening.
2 a D&C 82:10.
4 a Ruth 3:11.
   TG Chastity; Virtue.
  b TG Marriage, Wives;
    Woman.
  c TG Marriage, Husbands.
5 a TG Counselor.
  b TG Deceit.
7 a Prov. 15:25.
  b 3 Ne. 14:25 (24–27).
9 a Prov. 26:1 (1–10).

10 a Gen. 1:26;
    D&C 29:24 (24–25);
    49:19 (18–21); 77:2;
    Moses 3:19.
  b TG Cruelty.
13 a TG Transgress.
  b James 3:13 (2–14).
   TG Communication.
14 a TG Communication.
15 a TG Problem-Solving.
  b D&C 124:90 (89–90).
16 a TG Prudence.

22 a TG Lying.
  b TG Honesty.
  c TG God, the Standard of
    Righteousness.
23 a TG Prudence.
  b TG Knowledge.
  c TG Foolishness.
24 a TG Diligence.
  b TG Laziness.
27 a TG Laziness.
  b TG Diligence.
28 a TG Righteousness.

CHAPTER 13

The way of the transgressor is hard—
Evil pursues sinners—He who does
not discipline his children hates them.

A WISE son *heareth* his father's instruction: but a scorner heareth not rebuke.

2 A man shall eat good by the fruit of *his* mouth: but the soul of the transgressors *shall eat* violence.

3 He that keepeth his ªmouth keepeth his life: *but* he that openeth wide his ᵇlips shall have destruction.

4 The soul of the ªsluggard desireth, and *hath* nothing: but the soul of the diligent shall be made fat.

5 A righteous *man* ªhateth lying: but a wicked *man* is loathsome, and cometh to shame.

6 ªRighteousness keepeth *him that is* upright in the way: but wickedness overthroweth the sinner.

7 There is that maketh himself ªrich, yet *hath* nothing: *there is* that maketh himself poor, yet *hath* great ᵇriches.

8 The ransom of a man's life *are* his riches: but the poor heareth not rebuke.

9 The light of the righteous rejoiceth: but the ªlamp of the wicked shall be put out.

10 Only by ªpride cometh ᵇcontention: but with the well advised *is* wisdom.

11 ªWealth *gotten* by ᵇvanity shall be diminished: but he that gathereth by ᶜlabour shall increase.

12 Hope deferred maketh the heart sick: but *when* the desire cometh, *it is* a tree of life.

13 Whoso ªdespiseth the word shall be destroyed: but he that feareth the commandment shall be ᵇrewarded.

14 The law of the wise *is* a ªfountain of life, to depart from the snares of death.

15 Good understanding giveth favour: but the way of transgressors *is* hard.

16 Every ªprudent *man* dealeth with knowledge: but a fool layeth open *his* folly.

17 A wicked messenger falleth into mischief: but a faithful ambassador *is* health.

18 Poverty and ªshame *shall be to* him that refuseth ᵇinstruction: but he that regardeth ᶜreproof shall be honoured.

19 The desire accomplished is sweet to the soul: but *it is* abomination to fools to depart from evil.

20 He that walketh with wise *men* shall be wise: but a companion of fools shall be destroyed.

21 ªEvil pursueth sinners: but to the righteous good shall be repayed.

22 A good *man* leaveth an inheritance to his children's children: and the wealth of the sinner *is* laid up for the ªjust.

23 Much food *is in* the tillage of the poor: but there is *that is* destroyed for want of judgment.

24 He that spareth his ªrod hateth his son: but he that loveth him ᵇchasteneth him betimes.

25 The righteous eateth to the ªsatisfying of his soul: but the belly of the wicked shall want.

CHAPTER 14

Go from the presence of a foolish
man—A true witness delivers souls—
Righteousness exalts a nation.

---

13 3*a* TG Silence.
   b TG Gossip.
   4*a* TG Apathy; Laziness.
   5*a* TG Hate.
   6*a* Prov. 11:5 (3–6);
      D&C 133:44.
   7*a* Prov. 11:24; Matt. 16:26.
   b D&C 6:7.
   9*a* Job 18:5;
      Prov. 24:20.
   10*a* Prov. 28:25.

   b TG Contention.
   11*a* Hel. 13:19.
   b TG Vanity.
   c TG Industry; Labor.
   13*a* Prov. 19:16;
      Morm. 9:26.
   b TG Reward.
   14*a* Prov. 10:11; Moro. 7:11.
   16*a* TG Prudence.
   18*a* TG Shame.
   b Prov. 15:5.

   c D&C 95:1; 121:43.
   21*a* Ps. 32:10.
   22*a* Eccl. 2:26.
   24*a* Prov. 29:15.
   b Mosiah 4:14;
      D&C 68:28.
   TG Chastening;
      Family, Children,
      Responsibilities toward.
   25*a* Ps. 34:10;
      2 Ne. 9:51 (50–51).

EVERY wise ªwoman buildeth her house: but the foolish plucketh it down with her hands.

2 He that ªwalketh in his uprightness feareth the LORD: but *he that is* perverse in his ways despiseth him.

3 In the mouth of the foolish *is* a rod of pride: but the lips of the wise shall preserve them.

4 Where no oxen *are*, the crib *is* clean: but much increase *is* by the strength of the ox.

5 A faithful witness will not lie: but a false witness will utter lies.

6 A scorner seeketh wisdom, and *findeth it* not: but ªknowledge *is* easy unto him that understandeth.

7 Go from the presence of a foolish man, when thou perceivest not *in him* the lips of knowledge.

8 The ªwisdom of the prudent *is* to understand his way: but the folly of fools *is* ᵇdeceit.

9 ªFools make a mock at sin: but among the righteous *there is* favour.

10 The heart knoweth his own bitterness; and a stranger doth not intermeddle with his joy.

11 The ªhouse of the wicked shall be overthrown: but the ᵇtabernacle of the upright shall flourish.

12 There is a ªway which seemeth right unto a man, but the end thereof *are* the ways of ᵇdeath.

13 Even in ªlaughter the heart is sorrowful; and the end of that ᵇmirth *is* heaviness.

14 The backslider in heart shall be filled with his own ways: and a good man *shall be satisfied* from himself.

15 The simple believeth every word: but the ªprudent *man* looketh well to his going.

16 A wise *man* feareth, and departeth from evil: but the fool rageth, and is ªconfident.

17 *He that is* soon ªangry dealeth foolishly: and a man of wicked devices is hated.

18 The simple inherit folly: but the ªprudent are crowned with ᵇknowledge.

19 The evil bow before the good; and the wicked at the gates of the righteous.

20 The ªpoor is hated even of his own neighbour: but the rich *hath* many ᵇfriends.

21 He that despiseth his neighbour sinneth: but he that hath mercy on the ªpoor, ᵇhappy *is* he.

22 Do they not err that devise evil? but mercy and truth *shall be* to them that devise good.

23 In all ªlabour there is profit: but the ᵇtalk of the lips *tendeth* only to penury.

24 The crown of the wise *is* their riches: *but* the ªfoolishness of fools *is* folly.

25 A true witness delivereth souls: but a deceitful *witness* speaketh lies.

26 In the ªfear of the LORD *is* strong confidence: and his children shall have a place of refuge.

27 The fear of the LORD *is* a fountain of life, to depart from the snares of death.

28 In the multitude of people *is* the king's honour: but in the want of people *is* the destruction of the prince.

29 *He that is* ªslow to ᵇwrath *is* of great ᶜunderstanding: but *he that is* ᵈhasty of spirit exalteth folly.

30 A sound heart *is* the life of the

14 1a TG Woman.
  2a TG Walking with God.
  6a Prov. 8:9; 15:14; 17:24;
     2 Ne. 9:28.
  8a 2 Ne. 28:30.
   b TG Deceit.
  9a Ether 12:26.
 11a Matt. 7:27 (24–27).
   b HEB tent.
 12a Isa. 55:8 (8–9).
   b Prov. 15:10.
 13a TG Laughter.

   b Eccl. 2:1.
 15a TG Prudence.
 16a 2 Ne. 4:34;
     Morm. 3:9; 4:8.
 17a TG Anger.
 18a TG Prudence.
   b TG Knowledge.
 20a D&C 56:16.
   b Prov. 19:4.
 21a D&C 52:40; 104:18.
   b TG Happiness.
 23a TG Labor;

     Work, Value of.
   b TG Communication.
 24a TG Foolishness.
 26a TG Reverence.
 29a TG Self-Mastery.
   b Prov. 15:18;
     D&C 60:14.
     TG Patience.
   c TG Understanding.
   d IE quick-tempered.
     TG Haste;
     Rashness.

flesh: but ᵃenvy the rottenness of the bones.

31 He that ᵃoppresseth the poor reproacheth his Maker: but he that honoureth him hath mercy on the poor.

32 The wicked is driven away in his wickedness: but the righteous hath hope in his ᵃdeath.

33 Wisdom resteth in the heart of him that hath understanding: but *that which is* in the midst of fools is made known.

34 ᵃRighteousness exalteth a nation: but sin *is* a reproach to any people.

35 The king's favour *is* toward a wise servant: but his wrath is *against* him that causeth shame.

CHAPTER 15

A soft answer turns away wrath—A wise son makes a glad father—The thoughts of the wicked are an abomination to the Lord—Before honor comes humility.

A ᵃSOFT ᵇanswer turneth away ᶜwrath: but grievous words stir up anger.

2 The ᵃtongue of the wise useth knowledge aright: but the mouth of fools poureth out ᵇfoolishness.

3 The ᵃeyes of the LORD *are* in every place, beholding the evil and the good.

4 A wholesome ᵃtongue *is* a tree of life: but perverseness therein *is* a breach in the spirit.

5 A ᵃfool despiseth his father's ᵇinstruction: but he that regardeth reproof is prudent.

6 In the house of the righteous *is* much ᵃtreasure: but in the revenues of the wicked is trouble.

7 The ᵃlips of the wise disperse knowledge: but the heart of the foolish *doeth* not so.

8 The ᵃsacrifice of the wicked *is* an abomination to the LORD: but the prayer of the upright *is* his delight.

9 The way of the wicked *is* an abomination unto the LORD: but he loveth him that followeth after ᵃrighteousness.

10 ᵃCorrection *is* grievous unto him that forsaketh the way: *and* he that hateth ᵇreproof shall ᶜdie.

11 Hell and destruction *are* before the LORD: how much more then the hearts of the children of men?

12 A scorner loveth not one that reproveth him: neither will he go unto the wise.

13 A ᵃmerry ᵇheart maketh a ᶜcheerful countenance: but by ᵈsorrow of the heart the spirit is broken.

14 The heart of him that hath ᵃunderstanding seeketh ᵇknowledge: but the mouth of fools feedeth on ᶜfoolishness.

15 All the days of the afflicted *are* evil: but he that is of a merry heart *hath* a continual feast.

16 Better *is* ᵃlittle with the fear of the LORD than great treasure and trouble therewith.

17 Better *is* a dinner of herbs where ᵃlove is, than a ᵇstalled ox and hatred therewith.

18 A ᵃwrathful man stirreth up ᵇstrife: but *he that is* slow to ᶜanger appeaseth ᵈstrife.

19 The way of the ᵃslothful *man is*

30a TG Envy.
31a Deut. 24:14 (14–15); Prov. 17:5; Matt. 25:45; D&C 56:16.
    TG Oppression.
32a TG Jesus Christ, Death of.
34a 4 Ne. 1:16 (15–17).
    TG Righteousness.
15 1a TG Patience; Self-Mastery.
   b TG Communication.
   c Gen. 26:22 (17–22).
2a TG Communication.
   b TG Foolishness; Gossip.
3a TG God, Omniscience of.

4a TG Honesty; Profanity.
5a Prov. 10:1; D&C 68:31.
   b Prov. 13:18.
6a TG Treasure.
7a TG Communication.
8a Gen. 4:5; Moro. 7:8 (5–11).
   TG Sacrifice.
9a TG Righteousness.
10a 1 Ne. 16:2; 2 Ne. 1:26; 9:40; Mosiah 13:7.
    b TG Reproof.
    c Prov. 14:12.
13a TG Happiness.
    b Prov. 17:22.

   c TG Cheerful.
   d TG Sorrow.
14a TG Understanding.
    b Prov. 14:6.
    TG Knowledge.
    c TG Foolishness.
16a Ps. 37:16; Eccl. 4:6; James 2:5 (1–9).
17a Prov. 17:1.
    TG Love.
    b IE fattened ox.
18a Prov. 14:29.
    b TG Strife.
    c TG Anger.
    d TG Contention.
19a TG Laziness.

as an hedge of thorns: but the way of the righteous *is* made plain.

20 A wise son maketh a glad father: but a *a*foolish man despiseth his *b*mother.

21 Folly *is* joy to *him that is* destitute of wisdom: but a man of *a*understanding walketh uprightly.

22 Without *a*counsel purposes are disappointed: but in the multitude of counsellors they are established.

23 A man hath joy by the answer of his mouth: and a *a*word *spoken* in due *b*season, how good *is it!*

24 The way of life *is* *a*above to the wise, that he may depart from hell beneath.

25 The LORD will destroy the house of the *a*proud: but he will establish the border of the *b*widow.

26 The thoughts of the wicked *are* an abomination to the LORD: but *the words* of the pure *are* pleasant words.

27 He that is greedy of gain troubleth his own house; but he that hateth gifts shall live.

28 The heart of the righteous *a*studieth to *b*answer: but the mouth of the wicked poureth out evil things.

29 The LORD *is* *a*far from the *b*wicked: but he heareth the prayer of the righteous.

30 The light of the eyes rejoiceth the heart: *and* a good report maketh the bones fat.

31 The ear that heareth the reproof of life abideth among the wise.

32 He that refuseth instruction despiseth his own soul: but he that *a*heareth reproof getteth *b*understanding.

33 The *a*fear of the LORD *is* the instruction of wisdom; and before *b*honour *is* *c*humility.

CHAPTER 16

It is better to get wisdom than gold—Pride goes before destruction—The gray hair of the righteous person is a crown of glory.

THE *a*preparations of the heart in man, and the answer of the *b*tongue, *is* from the LORD.

2 All the ways of a man *are* *a*clean in his *b*own eyes; but the LORD weigheth the spirits.

3 *a*Commit thy works unto the LORD, and thy *b*thoughts shall be established.

4 The LORD hath made all *things* for himself: yea, even the wicked for the day of evil.

5 Every one *that is* *a*proud in heart *is* an abomination to the LORD: *though* hand *join* in hand, he shall not be unpunished.

6 By mercy and truth iniquity is purged: and by the *a*fear of the LORD men *b*depart from *c*evil.

7 When a man's ways please the LORD, he maketh even his *a*enemies to be at *b*peace with him.

8 *a*Better *is* a little with righteousness than great revenues without right.

9 A man's heart *a*deviseth his way: but the LORD directeth his steps.

10 A divine sentence *is* in the lips of the king: his mouth transgresseth not in judgment.

11 A just weight and balance *are*

20*a* Prov. 10:1.
  b TG Marriage, Motherhood.
21*a* TG Understanding.
22*a* 2 Ne. 9:28;
   Jacob 4:10;
   Alma 37:12;
   D&C 105:37; 122:2.
23*a* Prov. 25:11.
  b Eccl. 3:1 (1–8).
24*a* Col. 3:2;
   2 Ne. 9:39.
25*a* Prov. 12:7;
   D&C 64:24.
  b Ps. 146:9.
28*a* TG Study.
  b TG Communication.

29*a* Ps. 10:1.
  b Mosiah 11:24 (23–25);
   21:15;
   D&C 101:7.
32*a* OR obeys.
  b TG Understanding.
33*a* TG Reverence.
  b TG Honor.
  c TG Humility.
16 1*a* Alma 16:16 (16–17);
   32:6.
  b D&C 100:5 (5–8).
2*a* Prov. 30:12.
  b Judg. 17:6;
   Prov. 21:2.
3*a* Ps. 55:22;

   Matt. 6:25;
   Philip. 4:6.
  b TG Motivations.
5*a* D&C 42:40.
6*a* Ex. 1:17 (16–17);
   Job 1:1.
  b 3 Ne. 20:26.
  c D&C 136:21.
7*a* Ex. 34:24.
  b Dan. 1:9.
   TG Peace;
   Peace of God.
8*a* Alma 32:12 (12–13).
9*a* Ether 2:16 (16–25).

the LORD's: all the weights of the bag *are* his work.

12 *It is* an abomination to kings to commit ^awickedness: for the throne is established by righteousness.

13 ^aRighteous ^blips *are* the delight of kings; and they love him that speaketh right.

14 The wrath of a king *is as* messengers of death: but a wise man will pacify it.

15 In the light of the king's countenance *is* life; and his favour *is* as a cloud of the latter rain.

16 How much better *is it* to get ^awisdom than gold! and to get ^bunderstanding rather to be chosen than silver!

17 The highway of the upright *is* to depart from evil: he that keepeth his way preserveth his soul.

18 ^aPride *goeth* before destruction, and an ^bhaughty spirit before a fall.

19 Better *it is to be* of an ^ahumble spirit with the lowly, than to divide the spoil with the proud.

20 He that ^ahandleth a matter wisely shall find good: and whoso ^btrusteth in the LORD, ^chappy *is* he.

21 The wise in heart shall be called ^aprudent: and the sweetness of the lips increaseth learning.

22 Understanding *is* a wellspring of life unto him that hath it: but the instruction of fools *is* folly.

23 The heart of the wise teacheth his mouth, and addeth learning to his lips.

24 Pleasant words *are as* an honeycomb, sweet to the soul, and health to the bones.

25 There is a ^away that seemeth right unto a man, but the end thereof *are* the ways of death.

26 He that laboureth laboureth for himself; for his mouth craveth it of him.

27 An ungodly man diggeth up evil: and in his lips *there is* as a burning ^afire.

28 A froward man soweth ^astrife: and a whisperer separateth chief friends.

29 A violent man enticeth his neighbour, and leadeth him into the way *that is* not good.

30 He shutteth his eyes to devise froward things: moving his lips he bringeth evil to pass.

31 ^aThe hoary head *is* a crown of glory, *if* it be found in the way of righteousness.

32 *He that is* slow to ^aanger *is* better than the mighty; and he that ruleth his spirit than he that taketh a city.

33 The ^alot is cast into the lap; but the whole disposing thereof *is* of the LORD.

CHAPTER 17

He who is glad at calamities will be punished—A friend loves at all times—Even a fool, when he holds his peace, is counted wise.

BETTER *is* a dry morsel, and ^aquietness therewith, than an house full of sacrifices *with* ^bstrife.

2 A wise ^aservant shall have rule over a son that causeth shame, and shall have part of the inheritance among the brethren.

3 The ^afining pot *is* for silver, and the furnace for gold: but the LORD ^btrieth the ^chearts.

4 A wicked doer giveth heed to false lips; *and* a liar giveth ear to a naughty tongue.

5 Whoso ^amocketh the ^bpoor reproacheth his Maker: *and* he that

---

12*a* Mosiah 23:9 (8–10);
   29:17 (17–19).
13*a* TG Honesty.
   b TG Communication.
16*a* TG Objectives.
   b TG Understanding.
18*a* TG Pride.
   b TG Haughtiness.
19*a* TG Contrite Heart;
   Poor in Spirit.
20*a* D&C 58:27 (27–28).
   b TG Trust in God.

c TG Happiness.
21*a* TG Prudence.
25*a* 2 Ne. 28:7 (7–9);
   Alma 30:17 (17–18).
27*a* James 3:6 (1–13).
28*a* TG Strife.
31*a* IE The gray hair of
   old age.
   Prov. 20:29.
32*a* TG Anger.
33*a* Prov. 18:18;
   1 Ne. 3:11;

D&C 102:34.
17 1*a* Prov. 15:17.
   b TG Strife.
2*a* TG Servant.
3*a* Mal. 3:3 (2–3);
   D&C 128:24.
   b TG Test.
   c Jer. 17:10.
5*a* Prov. 14:31;
   Mosiah 4:17 (16–18).
   TG Mocking.
   b TG Poor.

is ^cglad at calamities shall not be unpunished.

6 ^aChildren's children *are* the ^bcrown of old men; and the ^cglory of ^dchildren *are* their fathers.

7 Excellent ^aspeech becometh not a fool: much less do lying lips a prince.

8 A gift *is as* a precious stone in the eyes of him that hath it: whithersoever it turneth, it prospereth.

9 He that ^acovereth a transgression ^bseeketh ^clove; but he that repeateth a matter separateth *very* friends.

10 A ^areproof entereth more into a wise man than an hundred stripes into a fool.

11 An evil *man* seeketh only ^arebellion: therefore a cruel messenger shall be sent against him.

12 Let a ^abear robbed of her whelps meet a man, rather than a fool in his folly.

13 Whoso ^arewardeth ^bevil for good, evil shall not depart from his house.

14 The beginning of ^astrife *is as* when one letteth out water: therefore leave off ^bcontention, before it be meddled with.

15 He that ^ajustifieth the ^bwicked, and he that condemneth the just, even they both *are* abomination to the LORD.

16 Wherefore *is there* a price in the hand of a fool to get wisdom, seeing *he hath* no heart *to it?*

17 A ^afriend loveth at all times, and a ^bbrother is born for adversity.

18 A man void of understanding striketh hands, *and* becometh surety in the presence of his friend.

19 He loveth transgression that loveth strife: *and* he that ^aexalteth his gate seeketh destruction.

20 He that hath a ^afroward heart findeth no good: and he that hath a perverse tongue falleth into mischief.

21 He that begetteth a ^afool *doeth it* to his sorrow: and the father of a fool hath no joy.

22 A ^amerry ^bheart doeth good *like* a medicine: but a broken spirit drieth the bones.

23 A wicked *man* taketh a ^agift out of the bosom to pervert the ways of judgment.

24 Wisdom *is* before him that hath ^aunderstanding; but the ^beyes of a fool *are* in the ends of the earth.

25 A ^afoolish son *is* a grief to his father, and bitterness to her that bare him.

26 Also to punish the just *is* not good, *nor* to strike princes for equity.

27 He that hath knowledge ^aspareth his words: *and* a man of ^bunderstanding ^cis of an excellent spirit.

28 Even a fool, when he ^aholdeth his peace, is counted wise: *and* he that ^bshutteth his lips *is esteemed* a man of understanding.

CHAPTER 18

A fool's mouth is his destruction—Whoever obtains a wife obtains a good thing—A man who has friends must show himself friendly.

THROUGH desire a man, having separated himself, seeketh *and* intermeddleth with all wisdom.

5c Job 31:29 (28–29);
    Prov. 24:17;
    Obad. 1:12.
6a TG Family, Love within;
    Family, Patriarchal.
  b TG Family, Children,
    Duties of;
    Marriage, Fatherhood.
  c TG Glory.
  d TG Children.
7a TG Communication.
9a IE forgives a
    transgression.
  b IE promotes a loving
    relationship.
  c D&C 64:9 (9–10).

10a TG Reproof.
11a TG Rebellion.
12a Hosea 13:8.
13a TG Reward.
  b TG Evil.
14a Prov. 25:8.
  b D&C 136:23 (23–34).
15a TG Injustice.
  b Prov. 24:24;
    Isa. 5:23.
17a TG Friendship.
  b TG Brotherhood and
    Sisterhood.
19a Prov. 29:23.
20a Ps. 101:4.
21a Prov. 10:1; 17:25.

22a TG Cheerful.
  b Prov. 15:13;
    D&C 59:15 (14–16).
23a TG Bribe.
24a Prov. 14:6.
  b Eccl. 2:14.
25a Prov. 17:21.
27a Prov. 10:19;
    James 1:19.
  b TG Understanding.
  c HEB is cool of spirit (i.e.,
    reserved).
28a Job 13:5.
  b Prov. 29:11;
    Amos 5:13.

2 A fool hath no delight in understanding, but that his heart may discover itself.

3 When the wicked cometh, *then* cometh also contempt, and with ignominy reproach.

4 The words of a man's mouth *are* as deep *a*waters, *and* the wellspring of wisdom *as* a flowing brook.

5 *It is* not good to accept the *a*person of the wicked, to overthrow the righteous in judgment.

6 A fool's lips enter into *a*contention, and his mouth calleth for strokes.

7 A fool's *a*mouth *is* his *b*destruction, and his lips *are* the snare of his soul.

8 The words of a *a*talebearer *are* as wounds, and they go down into the innermost parts of the belly.

9 He also that is *a*slothful in his work is brother to him that is a great *b*waster.

10 The name of the LORD *is* a strong *a*tower: the righteous runneth into it, and is safe.

11 The *a*rich man's *b*wealth *is* his strong city, and as an high wall in his own conceit.

12 Before destruction the heart of man is *a*haughty, and before honour *is* *b*humility.

13 He that *a*answereth a matter before he heareth *it*, it *is* folly and shame unto him.

14 The spirit of a man will sustain his infirmity; but a wounded spirit who can bear?

15 The heart of the *a*prudent getteth *b*knowledge; and the ear of the wise seeketh knowledge.

16 A man's gift maketh room for him, and bringeth him before great men.

17 *He that is* *a*first in his own cause *seemeth* just; but his neighbour cometh and searcheth him.

18 The *a*lot causeth contentions to cease, and parteth between the mighty.

19 A *a*brother *b*offended *is harder to be won* than a strong city: and *their* *c*contentions *are* like the bars of a castle.

20 A man's belly shall be satisfied with the fruit of his mouth; *and* with the increase of his lips shall he be filled.

21 Death and life *are* in the power of the *a*tongue: and they that love it shall eat the fruit thereof.

22 *a*Whoso findeth a *b*wife findeth a good *thing,* and obtaineth favour of the LORD.

23 The *a*poor useth *b*entreaties; but the rich answereth roughly.

24 A man *that hath* friends must shew himself friendly: and there is a *a*friend *that* sticketh closer than a *b*brother.

CHAPTER 19

A prudent wife is from the Lord—He who lends to the poor lends to the Lord—It is better to be a poor man than to be a liar.

BETTER *is* the *a*poor that walketh in his *b*integrity, than *he that is* perverse in his lips, and is a fool.

2 Also, *that* the soul *be* without *a*knowledge, *it is* not good; and he that *b*hasteth with *his* feet sinneth.

---

18 4*a* Prov. 20:5.
  5*a* Ps. 82:2.
  6*a* TG Contention.
  7*a* Prov. 10:14.
    b Ps. 64:8.
  8*a* OR slanderer.
    TG Gossip; Honesty.
  9*a* TG Laziness.
    b TG Waste.
  10*a* 2 Sam. 22:3;
    Ps. 61:3.
  11*a* Matt. 19:24 (16–24).
    b Prov. 10:15.
  12*a* Prov. 29:23.
    b Alma 7:23 (23–24);

D&C 112:10.
  13*a* TG Rashness.
  15*a* TG Prudence.
    b TG Knowledge.
  17*a* Mark 9:35.
  18*a* Prov. 16:33.
  19*a* TG Brotherhood and Sisterhood.
    b TG Offense.
    c TG Contention.
  21*a* Matt. 12:37 (34–37);
    Alma 12:14.
  22*a* JST Prov. 18:22 Whoso findeth a *good* wife *hath obtained* favor

of the Lord.
    b TG Marriage, Wives.
  23*a* Prov. 19:7.
    b Alma 32:5 (1–5).
  24*a* Prov. 27:10.
    TG Friendship.
    b TG Brotherhood and Sisterhood.
19 1*a* D&C 88:17; 104:16.
    b Prov. 28:6;
    Alma 27:27;
    D&C 124:20 (15, 20).
  2*a* D&C 42:61;
    Abr. 1:2.
    b TG Haste.

3 The ªfoolishness of man perverteth his way: and his heart fretteth against the Lord.

4 Wealth maketh many ªfriends; but the poor is separated from his neighbour.

5 A false ªwitness shall not be unpunished, and *he that* speaketh ᵇlies shall not escape.

6 Many will entreat the ªfavour of the prince: and every man *is* a ᵇfriend to him that giveth gifts.

7 All the brethren of the ªpoor do hate him: how much more do his friends go far from him? he pursueth *them with* words, *yet* they *are* wanting *to him*.

8 He that getteth wisdom loveth his own soul: he that keepeth ªunderstanding shall find good.

9 A false witness shall not be ªunpunished, and *he that* speaketh ᵇlies shall perish.

10 Delight is not seemly for a fool; much less for a ªservant to have rule over princes.

11 The ªdiscretion of a man deferreth his ᵇanger; and *it is* his ᶜglory to pass over a ᵈtransgression.

12 The king's wrath *is* as the ªroaring of a lion; but his favour *is* as dew upon the grass.

13 A foolish son *is* the calamity of his ªfather: and the contentions of a ᵇwife *are* a ᶜcontinual dropping.

14 House and riches *are* the inheritance of fathers: and a ªprudent wife *is* from the Lord.

15 ªSlothfulness casteth into a deep sleep; and an ᵇidle soul shall suffer hunger.

16 He that ªkeepeth the commandment keepeth his own soul; *but* he that despiseth his ways shall die.

17 He that hath ªpity upon the ᵇpoor lendeth unto the Lord; and that which he hath given will he pay him again.

18 ªChasten thy son while there is hope, and let not thy soul spare for his crying.

19 A man of great ªwrath shall suffer punishment: for if thou deliver *him*, yet thou must do it again.

20 Hear counsel, and receive ªinstruction, that thou mayest be wise in thy latter end.

21 *There are* many devices in a man's heart; nevertheless the ªcounsel of the Lord, that shall stand.

22 The desire of a man *is* his ªkindness: and a poor man *is* better than a ᵇliar.

23 The ªfear of the Lord *tendeth* to ᵇlife: and *he that hath it* shall abide satisfied; he shall not be visited with evil.

24 A ªslothful *man* hideth his hand in *his* bosom, and will not so much as bring it to his mouth again.

25 Smite a ªscorner, and the simple will beware: and reprove one that hath understanding, *and* he will understand knowledge.

26 He that wasteth *his* ªfather, *and* chaseth away *his* mother, *is* a son that causeth shame, and bringeth reproach.

27 Cease, my son, to ªhear the instruction *that causeth* to err from the words of knowledge.

28 An ungodly witness scorneth

3 *a* TG Foolishness.
4 *a* Prov. 14:20.
5 *a* Mosiah 13:23.
  b TG Lying.
6 *a* Prov. 29:26;
    Alma 47:35.
  b Matt. 5:46.
7 *a* Prov. 18:23.
8 *a* TG Understanding.
9 *a* TG Punish.
  b 2 Ne. 9:34.
10 *a* Prov. 30:22 (21–22);
    Eccl. 10:7 (6–7).
11 *a* TG Rashness.
  b TG Anger.
  c TG Glory.

d TG Transgress.
12 *a* Prov. 20:2.
13 *a* TG Marriage,
    Fatherhood.
  b Prov. 21:9.
  c Prov. 27:15.
14 *a* TG Prudence.
15 *a* TG Laziness;
    Procrastination.
  b TG Idleness.
16 *a* Prov. 13:13;
    Luke 11:28;
    D&C 1:32.
17 *a* TG Compassion;
    Generosity.
  b Mosiah 4:16 (16–18).

18 *a* TG Chastening.
19 *a* Morm. 8:21.
20 *a* TG Edification.
21 *a* Isa. 46:10.
22 *a* TG Kindness.
  b TG Lying.
23 *a* TG Reverence.
  b Prov. 10:16; 11:19.
24 *a* TG Laziness.
25 *a* Prov. 21:11.
26 *a* Prov. 20:20;
    Mosiah 13:20.
27 *a* 1 Ne. 8:34 (33–34);
    Mosiah 2:37 (33, 37).

judgment: and the mouth of the wicked devoureth iniquity.

29 Judgments are prepared for scorners, and [a]stripes for the back of fools.

CHAPTER 20

Wine is a mocker, and strong drink is raging—Turn to the Lord, and He will save you.

[a]WINE is a [b]mocker, strong drink *is* raging: and whosoever is deceived thereby is not wise.

2 The fear of a king *is* as the [a]roaring of a lion: *whoso* provoketh him to [b]anger sinneth *against* his own soul.

3 *It is* an honour for a man to cease from [a]strife: but every [b]fool will be [c]meddling.

4 The [a]sluggard will not plow by reason of the [b]cold; *therefore* shall he beg in harvest, and *have* nothing.

5 [a]Counsel in the [b]heart of man *is like* deep [c]water; but a man of understanding will draw it out.

6 Most men will proclaim every one his own goodness: but a faithful man who can find?

7 The just *man* [a]walketh in his [b]integrity: his [c]children *are* blessed after him.

8 A king that sitteth in the throne of judgment [a]scattereth away all evil with his eyes.

9 Who can say, I have made my heart [a]clean, I am pure from my [b]sin?

10 Divers weights, *and* divers measures, both of them *are* alike abomination to the LORD.

11 Even a child is known by his [a]doings, whether his [b]work *be* pure, and whether *it be* right.

12 The hearing ear, and the seeing eye, the LORD hath made even both of them.

13 Love not [a]sleep, lest thou come to poverty; open thine eyes, *and* thou shalt be satisfied with bread.

14 *It is* naught, *it is* naught, saith the buyer: but when he is gone his way, then he [a]boasteth.

15 There is gold, and a multitude of rubies: but the lips of knowledge *are* a precious [a]jewel.

16 Take his [a]garment that is surety *for* a stranger: and take a pledge of him for a strange woman.

17 [a]Bread of [b]deceit *is* sweet to a man; but afterwards his mouth shall be filled with gravel.

18 *Every* purpose is established by [a]counsel: and with good [b]advice make [c]war.

19 He that goeth about *as* a [a]talebearer revealeth secrets: therefore meddle not with him that [b]flattereth with his lips.

20 Whoso curseth his [a]father or his mother, his [b]lamp shall be put out in obscure [c]darkness.

21 An inheritance *may be* gotten hastily at the beginning; but the end thereof shall not be blessed.

22 Say not thou, I will [a]recompense evil; *but* [b]wait on the LORD, and he shall save thee.

23 Divers weights *are* an abomination unto the LORD; and [a]a false balance *is* not good.

29a IE flogging.
  Prov. 10:13.
20 1a TG Drunkenness;
  Temperance;
  Word of Wisdom.
  b TG Mocking.
2a Prov. 19:12.
  b Mosiah 17:12.
3a TG Strife.
  b Ether 12:26.
  c IE fomenting trouble.
4a TG Apathy; Idleness.
  b HEB winter; i.e., after
  the autumn harvest.
5a D&C 78:2.
  b D&C 11:26.

c Prov. 18:4.
7a TG Walking with God.
  b TG Integrity.
  c TG Family.
8a Prov. 25:5.
9a Rom. 3:23.
  b D&C 49:8; 109:34.
11a Matt. 7:16 (16–20).
  b TG Work, Value of.
13a TG Laziness.
14a TG Boast.
15a Job 28:18 (12–19).
16a Prov. 27:13.
17a IE Food gained by
  fraudulent means.
  b TG Deceit.

18a D&C 69:4.
  b Luke 14:31.
  c Prov. 24:6.
19a TG Gossip.
  b TG Flatter.
20a Prov. 19:26; 1 Ne. 2:11;
  Mosiah 13:20.
  b Job 18:5.
  c Alma 26:15.
22a TG Forbear; Retribution.
  b Ps. 25:5; 27:14;
  Isa. 40:31;
  2 Ne. 6:13 (7, 13);
  D&C 98:2.
23a OR deceptive scales (i.e.,
  made to deceive).

24 Man's ^agoings *are* of the LORD; how can a man then understand his own way?

25 *It is* a snare to the man *who* devoureth *that which is* holy, and after vows to make inquiry.

26 A wise ^aking scattereth the wicked, and bringeth the wheel over them.

27 The spirit of man *is* the candle of the LORD, searching all the inward parts of the belly.

28 Mercy and truth preserve the king: and his throne is upholden by mercy.

29 The ^aglory of young men *is* their strength: and the ^bbeauty of ^cold men *is* the ^dgray head.

30 The blueness of a wound cleanseth away evil: so *do* ^astripes the inward parts of the belly.

CHAPTER 21

Do righteousness and justice—Follow after righteousness and mercy—Safety comes from the Lord.

THE ^aking's heart *is* in the hand of the LORD, *as* the rivers of water: he turneth it whithersoever he will.

2 Every way of a man *is* right in his ^aown eyes: but the LORD ^bpondereth the ^chearts.

3 To do justice and judgment *is* more acceptable to the LORD than ^asacrifice.

4 ^aAn high look, and a ^bproud heart, *and* ^cthe plowing of the wicked, *is* sin.

5 The thoughts of the diligent *tend* only to plenteousness; but of every one *that is* ^ahasty only to want.

6 The getting of ^atreasures by a lying tongue *is* a ^bvanity tossed to and fro of them that seek death.

7 The robbery of the wicked shall destroy them; because they refuse to do judgment.

8 ^aThe way of man *is* froward and strange: but *as for* the pure, his work *is* right.

9 *It is* better to dwell in a corner of the housetop, ^athan with a brawling ^bwoman in a ^cwide house.

10 The soul of the wicked desireth evil: his ^aneighbour findeth no favour in his eyes.

11 When the ^ascorner is punished, the simple is made wise: and when the wise is instructed, he receiveth knowledge.

12 The righteous *man* wisely considereth the house of the ^awicked: *but God* overthroweth the wicked for *their* wickedness.

13 Whoso stoppeth his ears at the cry of the ^apoor, he also shall cry himself, but shall not be heard.

14 A gift in secret pacifieth ^aanger: and a reward in the bosom strong wrath.

15 *It is* joy to the just to do judgment: but destruction *shall be* to the workers of ^ainiquity.

16 The man that ^awandereth out of the way of understanding shall remain in the congregation of the dead.

17 He that loveth ^apleasure *shall be* a poor man: he that loveth wine and oil shall not be ^brich.

18 The wicked *shall be* a ^aransom for the righteous, and the transgressor for the upright.

24*a* Jer. 10:23.
26*a* TG Kings, Earthly.
29*a* TG Glory.
 b TG Beauty.
 c TG Old Age.
 d Lev. 19:32;
   Prov. 16:31.
30*a* IE flogging, strokes,
   blows.
21 1*a* Prov. 8:15.
 2*a* Prov. 16:2.
 b Prov. 24:12.
 c Luke 16:15.
 3*a* 1 Sam. 15:22.

4*a* OR Haughty eyes.
 b 2 Ne. 28:14.
 c OR the cultivating of
   wickedness.
5*a* TG Haste.
6*a* TG Treasure.
 b TG Vanity.
8*a* OR Perverse is the way
   of a man of crime.
   Prov. 11:20.
9*a* IE than with a
   contentious wife as a
   companion.
 b Prov. 19:13.

 c Prov. 25:24.
10*a* Prov. 3:29.
11*a* Prov. 19:25.
12*a* 2 Ne. 23:11.
13*a* Mosiah 4:16 (16–18).
14*a* TG Anger.
15*a* TG Injustice.
16*a* Isa. 53:6;
   2 Pet. 2:15 (12–15).
17*a* TG Pleasure.
 b TG Treasure.
18*a* Isa. 43:3 (1–4).

19 *It is* better to ^adwell in the wilderness, than with a ^bcontentious and an angry woman.

20 *There is* ^atreasure to be desired and oil in the dwelling of the wise; but a foolish man ^bspendeth it up.

21 He that followeth after ^arighteousness and mercy findeth ^blife, righteousness, and honour.

22 A ^awise *man* scaleth the city of the mighty, and casteth down the strength of the confidence thereof.

23 Whoso keepeth his ^amouth and his ^btongue keepeth his soul from troubles.

24 Proud *and* haughty scorner *is* his name, who dealeth in proud wrath.

25 The desire of the ^aslothful killeth him; for his hands refuse to ^blabour.

26 He ^acoveteth greedily all the day long: but the righteous ^bgiveth and spareth not.

27 The sacrifice of the wicked *is* abomination: how much more, *when* he bringeth it with a wicked mind?

28 A false witness shall perish: but the man that heareth speaketh constantly.

29 A wicked man ^ahardeneth his face: but *as for* the upright, he directeth his way.

30 *There is* no wisdom nor ^aunderstanding nor counsel against the LORD.

31 The ^ahorse *is* prepared against the day of battle: but ^bsafety *is* of the LORD.

CHAPTER 22

A good name is better than riches—
Train up a child in the way he should go.

A GOOD ^aname *is* rather to be chosen than great ^briches, *and* loving favour rather than silver and gold.

2 The ^arich and poor meet together: the LORD *is* the maker of them all.

3 A ^aprudent *man* foreseeth the evil, and hideth himself: but the simple pass on, and are punished.

4 By ^ahumility *and* the ^bfear of the LORD *are* riches, and honour, and life.

5 Thorns *and* snares *are* in the way of the ^afroward: he that doth keep his soul shall be far from them.

6 ^aTrain up a ^bchild in the way he should go: and when he is old, he will not depart from it.

7 The ^arich ruleth over the poor, and the ^bborrower *is* ^cservant to the lender.

8 He that ^asoweth iniquity shall ^breap vanity: and the rod of his anger shall fail.

9 He that hath a bountiful eye shall be blessed; for he giveth of his ^abread to the ^bpoor.

10 Cast out the scorner, and ^acontention shall go out; yea, ^bstrife and reproach shall cease.

11 He that loveth pureness of heart, *for* the grace of his lips the king *shall be* his friend.

12 The eyes of the LORD preserve knowledge, and he overthroweth the words of the transgressor.

13 The slothful *man* saith, *There is*

19*a* Prov. 25:24.
  b Prov. 27:15 (15–16);
    3 Ne. 11:29.
20*a* TG Treasure.
  b TG Waste.
21*a* Matt. 6:33;
    3 Ne. 12:6.
  b Prov. 8:35.
22*a* Eccl. 7:19.
23*a* James 3:2.
  b TG Gossip.
25*a* TG Apathy; Laziness.
  b TG Labor.
26*a* TG Covet.
  b Prov. 3:27 (27–28);
    Luke 6:30;

Eph. 4:28.
29*a* TG Hardheartedness.
30*a* TG Understanding.
31*a* Ps. 33:17.
  b OR victory.
22 1*a* Eccl. 7:1; 1 Ne. 1:1.
  b TG Treasure.
  2*a* Mosiah 4:19.
  3*a* TG Prudence.
  4*a* TG Humility.
  b OR reverence of the
    LORD.
    2 Ne. 1:20;
    Mosiah 2:24 (21–25).
    TG Reverence.
  5*a* OR perverse.

6*a* Eph. 6:4 (1–4).
    TG Education;
    Family, Children,
    Responsibilities toward;
    Marriage, Fatherhood;
    Teaching.
  b TG Children.
7*a* D&C 19:35.
  b TG Borrow; Debt.
  c TG Servant.
8*a* 2 Ne. 9:16.
  b TG Harvest.
9*a* TG Bread.
  b TG Almsgiving.
10*a* TG Contention.
  b TG Strife.

a lion without, I shall be slain in the streets.

14 The mouth of *strange women *is* a deep pit: he that is abhorred of the Lord shall fall therein.

15 Foolishness *is* bound in the heart of a child; *but* the rod of correction shall drive it far from him.

16 He that *oppresseth the poor to increase his *riches, *and* he that giveth to the rich, *shall* surely *come* to want.

17 Bow down thine ear, and hear the words of the wise, and apply thine heart unto my knowledge.

18 For *it is* a pleasant thing if thou keep them within thee; they shall withal be fitted in thy lips.

19 That thy trust may be in the Lord, I have made known to thee this day, even to thee.

20 Have not I written to thee excellent things in counsels and knowledge,

21 That I might make thee know the certainty of the *words of truth; that thou mightest answer the words of truth to them that send unto thee?

22 Rob not the *poor, because he *is* poor: neither oppress the afflicted in the gate:

23 For the Lord will *plead their *cause, and spoil the soul of those that spoiled them.

24 Make no *friendship with an *angry man; and with a furious man thou shalt not go:

25 Lest thou learn his ways, and get a snare to thy soul.

26 Be not thou *one* of them that *strike hands, *or* of them that are *sureties for debts.

27 If thou hast nothing to pay, why should he take away thy bed from under thee?

28 Remove not the ancient *landmark, which thy fathers have set.

29 Seest thou a man *diligent in his business? he shall stand before kings; he shall not stand before *mean *men.*

CHAPTER 23

Labor not to be rich—As a man thinks in his heart, so is he—Withhold not correction from a child—Be not among drunkards.

WHEN thou sittest to eat with a ruler, consider diligently what *is* before thee:

2 And put a knife to thy throat, if thou *be* a man given to *appetite.

3 Be not desirous of his *dainties: for they *are* deceitful meat.

4 Labour not to be *rich: cease from thine own *wisdom.

5 Wilt thou set thine eyes upon that which is not? for *riches* certainly make themselves wings; they fly away as an eagle toward heaven.

6 Eat thou not the bread of *him that hath* an evil eye, neither desire thou his dainty meats:

7 For as he *thinketh in his *heart, so *is* he: Eat and drink, saith he to thee; but his heart *is* not with thee.

8 The morsel *which* thou hast eaten shalt thou vomit up, and lose thy sweet words.

9 Speak not in the ears of a *fool: for he will despise the wisdom of thy words.

10 Remove not the old *landmark; and enter not into the fields of the fatherless:

11 For their redeemer *is* mighty; he shall *plead their cause with thee.

12 Apply thine heart unto *instruc-

14a TG Fornication.
16a TG Oppression.
  b TG Treasure.
21a D&C 18:3; 98:11.
22a Zech. 7:10.
23a Ps. 35:10;
  Prov. 23:11.
  b D&C 124:75.
24a TG Friendship.
  b TG Anger.
26a IE shake hands, showing

agreement.
  b Prov. 6:1; 11:15.
28a Deut. 19:14; Job 24:2;
  Prov. 23:10;
  Hosea 5:10.
29a TG Diligence.
  b OR obscure, or wicked
  (men).
23 2a TG Word of Wisdom.
  3a OR delicacies.
  4a Jacob 2:19 (18–19).

TG Treasure.
  b 2 Ne. 9:28 (28, 42).
7a TG Motivations.
  b TG Heart.
9a Prov. 24:7; Matt. 7:6;
  15:26 (26–28);
  D&C 6:12 (10–12);
  10:37 (36–37).
10a Prov. 22:28.
11a Prov. 22:23.
12a D&C 88:118 (118–22).

tion, and thine ears to the words of knowledge.

13 Withhold not [a]correction from the child: for *if* thou beatest him with the rod, he shall not die.

14 Thou shalt beat him with the rod, and shalt deliver his soul from hell.

15 My son, if thine heart be wise, my heart shall rejoice, even mine.

16 Yea, my reins shall rejoice, when thy lips speak right things.

17 Let not thine heart envy [a]sinners: but *be thou* in the fear of the LORD all the day long.

18 For surely there is an end; and thine expectation shall not be cut off.

19 Hear thou, my son, and be wise, and guide thine heart in the way.

20 Be not among [a]winebibbers; among [b]riotous eaters of flesh:

21 For the [a]drunkard and the glutton shall come to poverty: and drowsiness shall clothe *a man* with rags.

22 [a]Hearken unto thy father that begat thee, and despise not thy mother when she is old.

23 Buy the [a]truth, and sell *it* not; *also* wisdom, and instruction, and understanding.

24 The father of the righteous shall greatly rejoice: and he that begetteth a wise *child* shall have joy of him.

25 Thy father and thy mother shall be glad, and she that bare thee shall rejoice.

26 My son, give me thine heart, and let thine eyes [a]observe my ways.

27 For a [a]whore *is* a deep ditch; and a strange woman *is* a narrow pit.

28 She also lieth in wait as *for a* prey, and increaseth the transgressors among men.

29 Who hath woe? who hath sorrow? who hath [a]contentions? who hath babbling? who hath wounds without cause? who hath redness of eyes?

30 They that tarry long at the [a]wine; they that go to seek mixed wine.

31 Look not thou upon the [a]wine when it is red, when it giveth his colour in the cup, *when* it moveth itself aright.

32 At the last it biteth like a serpent, and stingeth like an [a]adder.

33 Thine eyes shall behold [a]strange women, and thine heart shall utter perverse things.

34 Yea, thou shalt be as he that lieth down in the midst of the sea, or as he that lieth upon the top of a mast.

35 They have stricken me, *shalt thou say, and* I was not sick; they have beaten me, *and* I felt *it* not: when shall I awake? I will seek it yet again.

CHAPTER 24

In a multitude of counselors there is safety—Fret not yourself because of evil men—It is not good to show partiality in judgment.

BE not thou [a]envious against [b]evil men, neither desire to be with them.

2 For their heart studieth destruction, and their lips talk of mischief.

3 Through wisdom is an house builded; and by understanding it is established:

4 And by knowledge shall the chambers be filled with all precious and pleasant riches.

5 A wise man *is* [a]strong; yea, a man of knowledge increaseth strength.

6 For by wise counsel thou shalt make thy [a]war: and in [b]multitude of [c]counsellors *there is* safety.

13a TG Chastening; Family, Children, Responsibilities toward.
17a Prov. 24:1, 19.
20a HEB imbibers of wine.
   b OR gluttonous eaters of meat.
   TG Rioting and Reveling.
21a TG Temperance;

Word of Wisdom.
22a TG Family, Children, Duties of.
23a TG Truth.
26a TG Watch.
27a D&C 42:23 (23–24).
29a TG Contention.
30a TG Temperance.
31a TG Drunkenness.

32a IE a kind of poisonous snake.
33a OR foreign women.
24 1a TG Envy.
   b Prov. 23:17.
5a Eccl. 7:19.
6a Prov. 20:18.
   b Prov. 11:14.
   c TG Counselor.

7 Wisdom *is* too high for a ^afool: he openeth not his mouth in the gate.

8 He that deviseth to do evil shall be called a mischievous person.

9 The thought of ^afoolishness *is* sin: and the scorner *is* an abomination to men.

10 *If* thou ^afaint in the day of adversity, thy strength *is* small.

11 If thou forbear to deliver *them that are* drawn unto death, and *those that are* ready to be slain;

12 If thou sayest, Behold, we knew it not; doth not he that ^apondereth the heart consider *it*? and he that keepeth thy soul, doth *not* he know *it*? and shall *not* he render to *every* man according to his ^bworks?

13 My son, eat thou ^ahoney, because *it is* good; and the honeycomb, *which is* sweet to thy taste:

14 So *shall* the knowledge of wisdom *be* unto thy soul: when thou hast found *it*, then there shall be a reward, and thy expectation shall not be cut off.

15 Lay not wait, O wicked *man*, against the dwelling of the righteous; spoil not his resting place:

16 For a just *man* falleth seven times, and ^ariseth up again: but the wicked shall fall into mischief.

17 Rejoice not when thine ^aenemy falleth, and let not thine heart be glad when he stumbleth:

18 Lest the LORD see *it*, and it displease him, and he turn away his wrath from him.

19 Fret not thyself because of evil *men*, neither be thou ^aenvious at the wicked;

20 For there shall be no reward to the evil *man*; the ^acandle of the wicked shall be put out.

21 My son, ^afear thou the LORD and the king: *and* meddle not with them that are given to change:

22 For their calamity shall rise suddenly; and who knoweth the ruin of them both?

23 These *things* also *belong* to the wise. *It is* not good to have ^arespect of persons in judgment.

24 He that saith unto the ^awicked, Thou *art* righteous; him shall the people curse, nations shall abhor him:

25 But to them that rebuke *him* shall be delight, and a good blessing shall come upon them.

26 *Every man* shall kiss *his* lips that giveth a right answer.

27 ^aPrepare thy work without, and make it fit for thyself in the field; and afterwards build thine house.

28 Be not a ^awitness against thy neighbour without cause; and ^bdeceive *not* with thy lips.

29 Say not, I will ^ado so to him as he hath done to me: I will render to the man according to his work.

30 I went by the field of the ^aslothful, and by the vineyard of the man void of understanding;

31 And, lo, it was all grown over with thorns, *and* nettles had covered the face thereof, and the stone ^awall thereof was broken down.

32 Then I saw, *and* considered *it* well: I looked upon *it*, *and* received instruction.

33 *Yet* a little ^asleep, a little slumber, a little folding of the hands to sleep:

34 So shall thy poverty come *as* one ^athat travelleth; and thy want as an armed man.

7a Prov. 23:9.
9a TG Foolishness.
10a 1 Ne. 4:2;
    D&C 89:20 (20–21).
12a Prov. 21:2.
  b Matt. 16:27;
    James 2:20 (14–20);
    D&C 1:10.
13a Prov. 25:16.
16a D&C 20:37.
17a Prov. 17:5;
    3 Ne. 12:44;

Morm. 3:15; 8:20.
    TG Enemies.
19a Prov. 23:17.
20a Job 18:5;
    Prov. 13:9.
21a 1 Pet. 2:17.
23a Deut. 1:17;
    Prov. 28:21;
    Matt. 22:16;
    D&C 1:35.
24a Prov. 17:15;
    D&C 121:20.

27a Luke 14:28.
28a Mosiah 13:23.
  b TG Honesty;
    Lying.
29a Matt. 7:12.
    TG Forbear.
30a TG Idleness;
    Laziness.
31a Isa. 5:5.
33a TG Sleep.
34a HEB marching (i.e., like
    a soldier).

CHAPTER 25

Boast not of false gifts—Give food and drink to your enemy.

THESE *are* also ᵃproverbs of Solomon, which the men of Hezekiah king of Judah copied out.

2 *It is* the glory of God to ᵃconceal a thing: but the honour of kings *is* to search out a matter.

3 The heaven for height, and the earth for depth, and the heart of kings *is* unsearchable.

4 Take away the ᵃdross from the silver, and there shall come forth a vessel for the finer.

5 ᵃTake away the wicked *from* before the ᵇking, and his throne shall be established in righteousness.

6 Put not forth thyself in the presence of the king, and stand not in the place of great *men:*

7 For better *it is* that it be said unto thee, ᵃCome up hither; than that thou shouldest be put lower in the presence of the prince whom thine eyes have seen.

8 Go not forth hastily to ᵃstrive, lest *thou know not* what to do in the end thereof, when thy neighbour hath put thee to shame.

9 Debate thy cause with thy neighbour *himself;* and ᵃdiscover not a secret to another:

10 Lest he that heareth *it* put thee to shame, and thine infamy turn not away.

11 A ᵃword fitly spoken *is like* apples of gold in pictures of silver.

12 *As* an earring of gold, and an ᵃornament of fine gold, *so is* a wise ᵇreprover upon an obedient ear.

13 As the cold of snow in the time of harvest, *so is* a faithful messenger to them that send him:

for he refresheth the soul of his masters.

14 Whoso ᵃboasteth himself of a false gift *is like* clouds and wind without rain.

15 By long ᵃforbearing is a prince ᵇpersuaded, and a soft tongue breaketh the bone.

16 Hast thou found ᵃhoney? eat so much as is sufficient for thee, lest thou be filled therewith, and vomit it.

17 Withdraw thy foot from thy neighbour's house; lest he be weary of thee, and *so* hate thee.

18 A man that ᵃbeareth ᵇfalse witness against his neighbour *is* a ᶜmaul, and a ᵈsword, and a sharp arrow.

19 Confidence in an unfaithful man in time of trouble *is like* a broken tooth, and a foot out of joint.

20 *As* he that taketh away a garment in cold weather, *and as* vinegar upon nitre, so *is* he that singeth songs to an heavy heart.

21 If thine ᵃenemy be ᵇhungry, give him bread to eat; and if he be thirsty, give him water to drink:

22 For thou shalt heap coals of fire upon his head, and the LORD shall ᵃreward thee.

23 The north wind driveth away rain: so *doth* an angry countenance a ᵃbackbiting tongue.

24 *It is* better to ᵃdwell in the corner of the housetop, than with a brawling woman and in a wide house.

25 *As* cold waters to a thirsty soul, so *is* good news from a far country.

26 A righteous man falling down before the wicked *is as* ᵃa troubled fountain, and a corrupt spring.

27 *It is* not good to eat much honey: so *for men* to search their own ᵃglory *is not* glory.

---

25 1a 1 Kgs. 4:32;
     Prov. 1:1; 10:1.
  2a Rom. 11:33; D&C 5:3.
  4a HEB waste, impurities.
  5a Prov. 20:8.
   b Mosiah 29:21 (21–24).
  7a Luke 14:10 (7–14).
  8a Prov. 3:30; 17:14.
  9a OR do not reveal.
 11a Prov. 15:23;
     Isa. 50:4.

 12a Prov. 1:9.
   b TG Chastening.
 14a TG Boast.
 15a TG Forbear.
   b D&C 121:41 (41–44).
 16a Prov. 24:13.
 18a TG Gossip.
   b Matt. 19:18;
     Mosiah 13:23.
   c HEB scatterer; i.e., some
     sort of war club.

   d Ps. 57:4.
 21a 3 Ne. 12:44 (43–45).
     TG Enemies.
   b 2 Chr. 28:15.
 22a TG Reward.
 23a TG Backbiting.
 24a Prov. 21:9, 19.
 26a HEB a trampled spring;
     i.e., ruined by wading
     into it. See Ezek. 34:18.
 27a TG Glory.

28 He that *hath* no ^arule over his own spirit *is like* a city *that is* broken down, *and* without walls.

CHAPTER 26

Honor is not fitting for a fool—Answer not a fool according to his folly—Where there is no talebearer, the strife ceases.

As snow in summer, and as rain in harvest, so ^ahonour is not seemly for a fool.

2 As the bird by wandering, as the swallow by flying, so the curse causeless shall not come.

3 A whip for the horse, a bridle for the ass, and a rod for the fool's back.

4 Answer not a fool according to his folly, lest thou also be like unto him.

5 ^aAnswer a fool according to his folly, lest he be wise in his ^bown conceit.

6 He that sendeth a message by the hand of a fool cutteth off the feet, *and* drinketh ^adamage.

7 The legs of the lame are not equal: so *is* a parable in the mouth of fools.

8 As he that bindeth a stone in a sling, so *is* he that giveth honour to a fool.

9 *As* a thorn goeth up into the hand of a drunkard, so *is* a parable in the mouth of fools.

10 The great *God* that formed all *things* both ^arewardeth the fool, and rewardeth transgressors.

11 As a dog returneth to his ^avomit, so a fool returneth to his folly.

12 Seest thou a man wise in his own ^aconceit? *there is* more hope of a ^bfool than of him.

13 The ^aslothful *man* saith, *There is* a lion in the way; a lion *is* in the streets.

14 *As* the door turneth upon his hinges, so *doth* the slothful upon his bed.

15 The slothful hideth his hand in *his* bosom; it grieveth him to bring it again to his mouth.

16 The sluggard *is* wiser in his own conceit than seven men that can render a reason.

17 He that passeth by, *and* meddleth with strife *belonging* not to him, *is* like one that ^ataketh a dog by the ears.

18 As a mad *man* who casteth firebrands, arrows, and death,

19 So *is* the man *that* ^adeceiveth his neighbour, and saith, Am not I in sport?

20 Where no wood is, *there* the fire goeth out: so where *there is* no ^atalebearer, the ^bstrife ceaseth.

21 *As* coals *are* to burning coals, and wood to fire; so *is* a ^acontentious man to kindle strife.

22 The words of a talebearer *are* as wounds, and they go down into the innermost parts of the belly.

23 Burning lips and a wicked heart *are like* a ^apotsherd covered with silver dross.

24 He that ^ahateth dissembleth with his lips, and layeth up ^bdeceit within him;

25 When he ^aspeaketh fair, believe him not: for *there are* seven abominations in his heart.

26 *Whose* hatred is covered by deceit, his wickedness shall be ^ashewed before the *whole* congregation.

27 Whoso diggeth a ^apit shall fall therein: and he that rolleth a stone, it will return upon him.

28*a* TG Self-Mastery.
26 1*a* Prov. 12:9;
    D&C 121:35.
  5*a* Matt. 16:2 (1–4).
    b OR own eyes (also
        vv. 12, 16).
  6*a* OR violence, injury.
  10*a* TG Reward.
  11*a* 2 Pet. 2:22;
      3 Ne. 7:8.
  12*a* Rom. 11:25; 12:16.

    b Prov. 29:20.
  13*a* TG Laziness.
  17*a* Dogs were not pets in
      Israel, but typically ran
      wild; one seized by the
      ears would certainly
      bite its attacker.
  19*a* D&C 10:25 (25–28).
  20*a* TG Gossip.
    b Alma 4:9 (8–9); 16:18.
  21*a* TG Contention.

  23*a* IE a broken piece of an
      earthen vessel.
  24*a* TG Hate.
    b TG Deceit.
  25*a* Ps. 28:3;
      Isa. 9:17.
  26*a* Alma 14:3 (2–3); 37:21.
  27*a* Prov. 28:10;
      1 Ne. 14:3; 22:14;
      2 Ne. 28:8;
      D&C 109:25.

28 A *a*lying tongue hateth *those that are* afflicted by it; and a *b*flattering mouth worketh ruin.

CHAPTER 27

Let another man praise you—A prudent man foresees evil—Hell and destruction are never full.

*a*BOAST not thyself of to *b*morrow; for thou knowest not what a day may bring forth.

2 Let another man *a*praise thee, and not thine own mouth; a stranger, and not thine own lips.

3 A stone *is* heavy, and the sand weighty; but a fool's *a*wrath *is* heavier than them both.

4 Wrath *is* *a*cruel, and *b*anger *is* outrageous; but who *is* able to stand before envy?

5 Open *a*rebuke *is* better than secret love.

6 Faithful *are* the *a*wounds of a *b*friend; but the *c*kisses of an enemy *are* *d*deceitful.

7 The full soul loatheth an honeycomb; but to the hungry soul every bitter thing is sweet.

8 As a bird that wandereth from her nest, so *is* a man that wandereth from his place.

9 Ointment and perfume rejoice the heart: so *doth* the sweetness of a man's friend by hearty counsel.

10 Thine own *a*friend, and thy father's friend, forsake not; neither go into thy brother's house in the day of thy calamity: *for better is* a *b*neighbour *that is* near than a brother far off.

11 My son, be wise, and make my heart glad, that I may answer him that reproacheth me.

12 A prudent *man* foreseeth the evil, *and* hideth himself; *but* the simple pass on, *and* are punished.

13 Take his *a*garment that is surety for a stranger, and take a pledge of him for a *b*strange woman.

14 He that blesseth his friend with a loud voice, rising early in the morning, it shall be counted a *a*curse to him.

15 A *a*continual dropping in a very rainy day and a *b*contentious woman are alike.

16 Whosoever hideth her hideth the wind, and the ointment of his right hand, *which* bewrayeth *itself.*

17 Iron sharpeneth iron; so a man sharpeneth the countenance of his *a*friend.

18 Whoso keepeth the fig tree shall *a*eat the fruit thereof: so he that *b*waiteth on his master shall be honoured.

19 As in water face answereth to face, so the heart of man to man.

20 *a*Hell and destruction are never full; so the eyes of man are never *b*satisfied.

21 *As* the fining pot for silver, and the furnace for gold; so *is* a man to his praise.

22 Though thou shouldest *a*bray a fool in a mortar among wheat with a pestle, *yet* will not his foolishness depart from him.

23 Be thou diligent to know the state of thy *a*flocks, *and* look well to thy herds.

24 For *a*riches *are* not for ever: and doth the crown *endure* to every generation?

28*a* TG Gossip.
  b TG Flatter.
27 1*a* TG Boast.
  b James 4:13 (13–14).
 2*a* TG Boast;
    Humility.
 3*a* Esth. 3:5.
 4*a* TG Cruelty.
  b TG Anger.
 5*a* Prov. 28:23.
 6*a* Ps. 141:5;
    D&C 121:43 (43–44).
  b TG Friendship.

  c 2 Sam. 20:9;
    Luke 22:48 (47–48).
  d TG Deceit.
10*a* 2 Sam. 9:1.
  b Prov. 18:24.
    TG Neighbor.
13*a* Prov. 20:16.
  b OR foreign woman.
14*a* TG Curse.
15*a* Prov. 19:13.
  b Prov. 21:19;
    3 Ne. 11:29.
17*a* TG Friendship.

18*a* 1 Cor. 9:7.
  b 1 Ne. 21:23;
    2 Ne. 6:13;
    D&C 133:11 (10–11).
20*a* IE The spirit world,
    place of the dead, is
    never filled up.
  b Eccl. 1:8.
22*a* OR pound, rub.
23*a* Alma 5:59 (37–60);
    D&C 20:53 (38–60).
24*a* 2 Ne. 9:30;
    Jacob 2:18 (18–19).

25 The hay appeareth, and the tender grass sheweth itself, and herbs of the mountains are gathered.

26 The lambs *are* for thy clothing, and the goats *are* the price of the field.

27 And *thou shalt have* goats' milk enough for thy food, for the food of thy household, and *for* the maintenance for thy maidens.

CHAPTER 28

The wicked flee when no man pursues—Whoever walks uprightly will be saved—A faithful man will abound with blessings.

THE wicked *a*flee when no man pursueth: but the *b*righteous are bold as a lion.

2 For the transgression of a land many *are* the princes thereof: but by a man of understanding *and* knowledge the state *thereof* shall be prolonged.

3 A poor man that *a*oppresseth the poor *is like* a sweeping rain which leaveth no food.

4 They that forsake the law praise the wicked: but such as keep the law contend with them.

5 Evil men *a*understand not judgment: but they that seek the LORD understand all *things*.

6 Better *is* the poor that walketh in his *a*uprightness, than *he that is* perverse *in his* ways, though he *be* rich.

7 Whoso keepeth the law *is* a wise son: but he that is a companion of *a*riotous *men* *b*shameth his father.

8 He that by *a*usury and unjust gain *b*increaseth his substance, he shall gather it for him that will pity the poor.

9 He that turneth away his ear from hearing the *a*law, even his *b*prayer *shall be* abomination.

10 Whoso causeth the righteous to go astray in an evil way, he shall *a*fall himself into his own *b*pit: but the upright shall have good *c*things in possession.

11 The rich man *is* wise in his own conceit; but the *a*poor that hath understanding searcheth him out.

12 When *a*righteous *men* do rejoice, *there is* great glory: but when the wicked rise, a man is hidden.

13 He that *a*covereth his sins shall not prosper: but whoso *b*confesseth and *c*forsaketh *them* shall have mercy.

14 Happy *is* the man that *a*feareth alway: but he that *b*hardeneth his heart shall fall into mischief.

15 As a *a*roaring lion, and a ranging bear; *so is* a wicked ruler over the poor people.

16 The prince that wanteth understanding *is* also a great oppressor: *but* he that hateth *a*covetousness shall prolong *his* days.

17 A man that doeth violence to the *a*blood of *any* person shall *b*flee to the pit; let no man stay him.

18 Whoso *a*walketh uprightly shall be saved: but *he that is* perverse *in his* ways shall fall at once.

19 He that tilleth his land shall have plenty of bread: but he that followeth after vain *persons* shall have poverty enough.

20 A faithful man shall abound with blessings: but he that maketh *a*haste to be *b*rich shall not be innocent.

---

28 1*a* Lev. 26:17;
  Amos 9:1.
  b 2 Ne. 9:40.
 3*a* TG Oppression.
 5*a* D&C 88:67.
 6*a* Prov. 10:9; 19:1.
 7*a* OR gluttonous.
  Luke 15:13 (12–13).
  TG Rioting and
  Reveling.
  b TG Shame.
 8*a* TG Usury.
  b Alma 11:20.
 9*a* Prov. 29:18;

D&C 88:35 (34–35).
  b Ps. 109:7;
  Moro. 7:6 (6–7).
10*a* TG Justice.
  b Prov. 26:27;
  1 Ne. 22:14.
  c Gen. 24:1;
  Matt. 6:33.
11*a* Alma 32:12 (12–13);
  D&C 104:16.
12*a* Prov. 11:10.
13*a* Job 31:33;
  Luke 12:2 (1–3);
  1 Jn. 1:10;

D&C 1:3; 121:37 (36–38).
  b TG Confession.
  c TG Repent.
14*a* TG Reverence.
  b TG Hardheartedness.
15*a* Ezek. 22:25.
16*a* TG Covet.
17*a* Alma 1:13 (13–14).
  b OR flee to the sepulchre
  (grave); i.e., flee to
  death.
18*a* TG Walking with God.
20*a* TG Haste.
  b TG Treasure.

21 To have [a]respect of persons *is* not good: for for a [b]piece of [c]bread *that* man will transgress.

22 He that hasteth to be rich *hath* an evil eye, and considereth not that poverty shall come upon him.

23 He that [a]rebuketh a man afterwards shall find more favour than he that [b]flattereth with the tongue.

24 Whoso robbeth his father or his mother, and saith, *It is* no transgression; the same *is* the companion of a destroyer.

25 He that is of a [a]proud heart stirreth up [b]strife: but he that putteth his [c]trust in the LORD shall be [d]made fat.

26 He that [a]trusteth in his own heart is a fool: but whoso walketh wisely, he shall be delivered.

27 He that giveth unto the [a]poor shall not lack: but he that hideth his eyes shall have many a curse.

28 When the [a]wicked rise, men hide themselves: but when they perish, the righteous increase.

CHAPTER 29

When the wicked rule, the people mourn—The righteous consider the cause of the poor—A fool speaks all that is in his mind—Where there is no vision, the people perish.

HE, that being often reproved hardeneth *his* neck, shall suddenly be destroyed, and that without [a]remedy.

2 When the [a]righteous are in [b]authority, the people [c]rejoice: but when the [d]wicked beareth [e]rule, the people [f]mourn.

3 Whoso loveth wisdom rejoiceth his father: but he that keepeth company with harlots [a]spendeth *his* substance.

4 The king by judgment establisheth the land: but he that receiveth gifts overthroweth it.

5 A man that [a]flattereth his neighbour spreadeth a net for his feet.

6 In the [a]transgression of an evil man *there is* a [b]snare: but the righteous doth sing and rejoice.

7 The righteous considereth the cause of the poor: *but* the wicked regardeth not to know *it*.

8 Scornful men bring a city into a snare: but wise *men* turn away wrath.

9 *If* a wise man contendeth with a foolish man, whether he rage or laugh, *there is* no rest.

10 The [a]bloodthirsty hate the upright: but the just seek his soul.

11 A fool [a]uttereth all his [b]mind: but a [c]wise *man* keepeth it in till afterwards.

12 If a ruler hearken to lies, all his servants *are* wicked.

13 The poor and the deceitful man meet together: the LORD lighteneth both their eyes.

14 The [a]king that faithfully judgeth the poor, his throne shall be established for ever.

15 The [a]rod and [b]reproof give wisdom: but a [c]child left *to himself* bringeth his [d]mother to [e]shame.

16 When the wicked are multiplied, transgression increaseth: but the righteous shall see their fall.

17 Correct thy son, and he shall

21 *a* Prov. 24:23;
    James 2:9.
  b Ezek. 13:19.
  c TG Bread.
23 *a* Prov. 27:5.
  b TG Flatter.
25 *a* Prov. 13:10;
    2 Ne. 28:12 (12–13).
  b TG Strife.
  c D&C 11:12; 84:116.
  d IE prosperous.
26 *a* TG Trust Not in the
    Arm of Flesh.
27 *a* TG Almsgiving;
    Poor; Welfare.

28 *a* D&C 98:9.
29 1 *a* Prov. 16:2;
  2 *a* TG Righteousness.
  b TG Governments.
  c Mosiah 5:4.
  d TG Wickedness.
  e TG Authority;
    Leadership;
    Tyranny.
  f Mosiah 7:23 (22–23);
    D&C 98:9.
  3 *a* Mosiah 11:4 (2–4).
  5 *a* Alma 46:5 (4–35).
  6 *a* TG Transgress.
  b Alma 12:6;

    D&C 10:26.
10 *a* Hel. 16:2;
    Ether 13:22 (13–15, 22).
11 *a* D&C 63:64.
  b TG Mind.
  c Prov. 17:28 (27–28).
14 *a* TG Kings, Earthly.
15 *a* Prov. 13:24.
  b TG Chastening;
    Reproof.
  c TG Family, Children,
    Responsibilities toward.
  d TG Marriage,
    Motherhood.
  e TG Shame.

give thee rest; yea, he shall give delight unto thy soul.

18 Where *there is* no ^avision, the people ^bperish: but he that ^ckeepeth the ^dlaw, ^ehappy *is* he.

19 A servant will not be corrected by words: for though he understand he will not answer.

20 Seest thou a man *that is* ^ahasty in his words? *there is* more hope of a ^bfool than of him.

21 He that delicately bringeth up his servant from a child shall have him become *his* son at the length.

22 An ^aangry man stirreth up ^bstrife, and a furious man aboundeth in transgression.

23 A man's ^apride shall bring him low: but honour shall uphold the ^bhumble in spirit.

24 Whoso is partner with a thief ^ahateth his own soul: he heareth cursing, and bewrayeth *it* not.

25 The ^afear of man bringeth a snare: but whoso putteth his ^btrust in the Lord shall be safe.

26 Many seek the ruler's ^afavour; but *every* man's judgment *cometh* from the Lord.

27 An unjust man *is* an abomination to the just: and *he that is* upright in the way *is* abomination to the ^awicked.

CHAPTER 30

Every word of God is pure—Give me neither poverty nor riches.

The words of Agur the son of Jakeh, *even* the prophecy: the man spake unto Ithiel, even unto Ithiel and Ucal,

2 Surely I *am* more brutish than *any* man, and have not the understanding of a man.

3 I neither learned wisdom, nor have the ^aknowledge of the holy.

4 Who hath ascended up into heaven, or descended? who hath gathered the wind in his fists? who hath bound the waters in a garment? who hath established all the ends of the earth? what *is* his name, and what *is* his son's name, if thou canst tell?

5 Every word of God *is* ^apure: he *is* a ^bshield unto them that put their trust in him.

6 ^aAdd thou not unto his words, lest he reprove thee, and thou be found a liar.

7 Two *things* have I required of thee; deny me *them* not before I die:

8 Remove far from me ^avanity and lies: give me neither poverty nor ^briches; feed me with ^cfood convenient for me:

9 Lest I be full, and ^adeny *thee*, and say, Who *is* the Lord? or lest I be poor, and steal, and take the name of my God *in vain*.

10 Accuse not a servant unto his master, lest he curse thee, and thou be found guilty.

11 *There is* a generation *that* curseth their father, and doth not bless their mother.

12 *There is* a ^ageneration *that are* ^bpure in their own eyes, and *yet* is not washed from their ^cfilthiness.

13 *There is* a generation, O how lofty are their ^aeyes! and their eyelids are lifted up.

14 *There is* a generation, whose ^ateeth *are as* swords, and their jaw teeth *as* knives, to devour the poor

18a TG Revelation; Vision.
  b TG Apostasy of Individuals.
  c Luke 11:28.
  d Prov. 28:9.
  e TG Happiness.
20a TG Haste; Rashness.
  b Prov. 26:12.
22a Eccl. 7:9; Matt. 5:22.
  b TG Strife.
23a Prov. 17:19; 18:12;

Hel. 12:5 (1–5).
  b TG Humility.
24a TG Hate.
25a John 12:42 (42–43); 19:38.
  TG Peer Influence.
  b TG Trust in God.
26a Prov. 19:6.
27a 1 Ne. 15:36.
30 3a Prov. 9:10.
  5a TG God, Perfection of.
  b Ps. 84:11.
  6a TG Scriptures,

Preservation of.
8a TG Vanity.
  b TG Treasure.
  c HEB bread of my portion; i.e., allotted food.
9a D&C 101:5.
12a Deut. 32:5; Ps. 95:10; Heb. 3:10.
  b Prov. 16:2.
  c TG Filthiness.
13a Ps. 131:1.
14a Ps. 57:4.

from off the earth, and the needy from *among* men.

15 The *a*horseleach hath two daughters, *crying*, Give, give. There are three *things that* are never satisfied, *yea*, four *things* say not, *It is* enough:

16 The grave; and the barren womb; the earth *that* is not filled with water; and the fire *that* saith not, *It is* enough.

17 The eye *that* mocketh at *his* father, and despiseth to obey *his* mother, the ravens of the valley shall pick it out, and the young eagles shall eat it.

18 There be three *things which* are too wonderful for me, yea, four which I know not:

19 The way of an eagle in the air; the way of a serpent upon a rock; the way of a ship in the midst of the sea; and the way of a man with a maid.

20 Such *is* the way of an adulterous woman; she eateth, and wipeth her *a*mouth, and saith, I have done no wickedness.

21 For three *things* the earth is disquieted, and for four *which* it cannot bear:

22 For a *a*servant when he reigneth; and a fool when he is filled with meat;

23 For an odious *woman* when she is married; and an handmaid that is heir to her mistress.

24 There be four *things which are* little upon the earth, but they *are* exceeding wise:

25 The *a*ants *are* a people not strong, yet they prepare their meat in the summer;

26 The *a*conies *are but* a feeble folk, yet make they their houses in the rocks;

27 The locusts have no king, yet go they forth all of them by bands;

28 The spider taketh hold with her hands, and is in kings' palaces.

29 There be three *things* which go well, yea, four are comely in going:

30 A lion *which is* strongest among beasts, and turneth not away for any;

31 A *a*greyhound; an he goat also; and a king, against whom *there is* no rising up.

32 If thou hast done foolishly in lifting up thyself, or if thou hast thought evil, *lay* thine hand upon thy mouth.

33 Surely the churning of milk bringeth forth butter, and the wringing of the nose bringeth forth blood: so the forcing of wrath bringeth forth *a*strife.

CHAPTER 31

Wine and strong drink are condemned— Plead the cause of the poor and needy—A virtuous woman is more precious than rubies.

THE words of king Lemuel, the prophecy that his *a*mother taught him.

2 What, my son? and what, the son of my womb? and what, the son of my vows?

3 Give not thy strength unto *a*women, nor thy ways to that which destroyeth kings.

4 *It is* not for kings, O Lemuel, *it is* not for kings to drink *a*wine; nor for princes strong drink:

5 Lest they drink, and forget the law, and pervert the judgment of any of the afflicted.

6 Give strong drink unto him that is ready to perish, and wine unto those that be of heavy hearts.

7 Let him drink, and forget his poverty, and remember his misery no more.

8 Open thy mouth for the dumb in the cause of all such as are appointed to destruction.

9 Open thy mouth, judge righteously, and plead the *a*cause of the poor and needy.

15*a* IE a blood-sucking parasite which is seemingly never satiated.
20*a* 1 Jn. 1:8 (8–10).
22*a* Prov. 19:10.

25*a* Prov. 6:6.
26*a* IE small animals, such as the rock badger.
31*a* Hebrew uncertain; perhaps "warhorse."
33*a* TG Strife.

31 1*a* TG Marriage, Motherhood.
3*a* TG Woman.
4*a* 2 Ne. 15:22 (22–23).
9*a* D&C 124:75, 89.

10 ¶ Who can find a ^avirtuous ^bwoman? for her price *is* far above rubies.

11 The heart of her husband doth safely ^atrust in her, so that he shall have no need of spoil.

12 She will do him good and not evil all the days of her life.

13 She seeketh wool, and flax, and worketh willingly with her ^ahands.

14 She is like the merchants' ships; she bringeth her food from afar.

15 She ^ariseth also while it is yet night, and giveth meat to her household, and a portion to her maidens.

16 She considereth a field, and buyeth it: with the fruit of her hands she planteth a vineyard.

17 She girdeth her loins with strength, and strengtheneth her arms.

18 She perceiveth that her merchandise *is* good: her candle goeth not out by night.

19 She layeth her hands to the spindle, and her hands hold the ^adistaff.

20 She stretcheth out her hand to the ^apoor; yea, she reacheth forth her hands to the needy.

21 She is not afraid of the snow for her household: for all her household *are* clothed with scarlet.

22 She maketh herself coverings of tapestry; her ^aclothing *is* silk and purple.

23 Her husband is known in the gates, when he sitteth among the elders of the land.

24 She maketh fine linen, and selleth *it*; and delivereth girdles unto the merchant.

25 Strength and honour *are* her ^aclothing; and she shall rejoice in time to come.

26 She openeth her mouth with wisdom; and in her tongue *is* the law of ^akindness.

27 She looketh well to the ways of her household, and eateth not the bread of ^aidleness.

28 Her children arise up, and call her blessed; her husband *also*, and he praiseth her.

29 Many daughters have done virtuously, but thou excellest them all.

30 Favour *is* deceitful, and ^abeauty *is* vain: *but* a woman *that* ^bfeareth the LORD, she shall be praised.

31 Give her of the fruit of her hands; and let her own works praise her in the gates.

ECCLESIASTES

OR, THE PREACHER

CHAPTER 1

Everything under the sun is vanity and vexation of spirit—He who increases in knowledge increases in sorrow.

THE words of the ^aPreacher, the son of David, king in Jerusalem.

2 ^aVanity of vanities, saith the Preacher, vanity of vanities; all *is* ^bvanity.

10*a* TG Chastity; Virtue.
  b TG Marriage, Marry; Marriage, Wives; Woman.
11*a* TG Dependability.
13*a* 1 Thes. 4:11; 2 Ne. 5:17.
15*a* D&C 88:124.
19*a* IE stick on which

spinning materials are wound.
20*a* D&C 42:30.
22*a* TG Apparel.
25*a* Ps. 104:1; 2 Ne. 9:14; D&C 88:125.
26*a* TG Kindness.
27*a* TG Idleness.

30*a* TG Beauty.
  b OR reveres the LORD.

[ECCLESIASTES]

1 1*a* Eccl. 7:27.
  2*a* TG Vanity.
  b IE empty, fleeting, unsubstantial.

3 What *profit hath a man of all his labour which he taketh under the sun?

4 *One* generation passeth away, and *another* generation cometh: but the *earth abideth for ever.

5 The sun also ariseth, and the sun goeth down, and hasteth to his place where he arose.

6 The wind goeth toward the south, and turneth about unto the north; it whirleth about continually, and the wind returneth again according to *his circuits.

7 All the rivers run into the sea; yet the sea *is* not full; unto the place from whence the rivers come, thither they return again.

8 All things *are* full of labour; man cannot utter *it:* the eye is not *satisfied with seeing, nor the ear filled with hearing.

9 The thing that hath been, it *is that* which shall be; and that which is done *is* that which shall be done: and *there is* no *new *thing* under the sun.

10 Is there *any* thing whereof it may be said, See, this *is* new? it hath been already of old time, which was before us.

11 *There is* no *remembrance of former *things*; neither shall there be *any* remembrance of *things* that are to come with *those* that shall come after.

12 ¶ I the Preacher was king over Israel in Jerusalem.

13 And I gave my heart to seek and search out by *wisdom concerning all *things* that are done under heaven: this *sore travail hath God given to the sons of man to be exercised therewith.

14 I have seen all the works that are done under the sun; and, behold, all *is *vanity and *vexation of spirit.

15 *That which is *crooked cannot be made straight: and that which is wanting cannot be numbered.

16 I communed with mine own heart, saying, Lo, *I am come to great estate, and have gotten more wisdom than all *they* that have been before me in Jerusalem: yea, my heart had great experience of wisdom and knowledge.

17 And I gave my *heart to know wisdom, and to know madness and folly: I perceived that this also is vexation of spirit.

18 For in much wisdom *is* much grief: and he that increaseth *knowledge increaseth *sorrow.

CHAPTER 2

All the riches and wealth of the king are vanity and vexation of spirit—Wisdom is better than folly—God gives wisdom, knowledge, and joy to man.

I SAID in mine heart, Go to now, I will prove thee with *mirth, therefore enjoy *pleasure: and, behold, this also *is* vanity.

2 I said of laughter, *It is* mad: and of mirth, What doeth it?

3 I sought in mine heart to give myself unto wine, yet acquainting mine heart with wisdom; and to lay hold on folly, till I might see what *was* that good for the sons of men, which they should do under the heaven all the days of their life.

4 I made me great works; I *builded me houses; I planted me vineyards:

5 I made me gardens and orchards, and I planted trees in them of all *kind of* fruits:

6 I made me pools of water, to water therewith the wood that bringeth forth trees:

3*a* 1 Sam. 12:21;
　　Matt. 16:26;
　　2 Ne. 9:51.
4*a* TG Earth, Destiny of.
6*a* OR its circuit.
8*a* Prov. 27:20.
9*a* Eccl. 3:15.
11*a* TG Veil.
13*a* D&C 97:1 (1–2).
　　b HEB (literally) "evil

business"; i.e., that which is of little profit.
　　Eccl. 4:8.
14*a* TG Vanity.
　　b HEB striving after wind; thus, frustration.
　　Eccl. 2:17 (17, 26);
　　4:4 (4, 6, 16); 6:9.
15*a* Eccl. 7:13.
16*a* HEB I have become

great.
17*a* Eccl. 7:25;
　　Mosiah 12:27.
18*a* TG Knowledge.
　　b TG Sorrow.
2 1*a* Prov. 14:13;
　　D&C 88:121.
　　b TG Pleasure;
　　Selfishness.
4*a* 1 Kgs. 7:1 (1–12).

7 I got *me* servants and maidens, and had servants born in my house; also I had great possessions of great and small cattle above all that were in Jerusalem before me:

8 I gathered me also silver and ^agold, and the peculiar treasure of kings and of the ^bprovinces: I gat me men singers and women singers, and the delights of the sons of men, *as* musical instruments, and that of all sorts.

9 So I was great, and increased more than all that were before me in Jerusalem: also my wisdom remained with me.

10 And whatsoever mine eyes desired I kept not from them, I withheld not my heart from any joy; for my heart rejoiced in all my labour: and this was my portion of all my ^alabour.

11 Then I looked on all the works that my hands had wrought, and on the labour that I had laboured to do: and, behold, all *was* vanity and vexation of spirit, and *there was* no profit under the sun.

12 ¶ And I turned myself to behold wisdom, and madness, and folly: for what *can* the man *do* that cometh after the king? *even* that which hath been already done.

13 Then I saw that wisdom excelleth folly, as far as light excelleth ^adarkness.

14 The wise man's eyes *are* in his head; but the fool walketh in ^adarkness: and I myself perceived also that one ^bevent happeneth to them all.

15 Then said I in my heart, As it happeneth to the fool, so it happeneth even to me; and why was I then more ^awise? Then I said in my heart, that this also *is* vanity.

16 For *there is* no ^aremembrance of the wise more than of the fool for ever; seeing that which now *is* in the days to come shall all be forgotten. And how ^bdieth the wise *man*? as the fool.

17 Therefore I hated life; because the work that is wrought under the sun *is* grievous unto me: for all *is* vanity and ^avexation of spirit.

18 ¶ Yea, I hated all my labour which I had taken under the sun: because I should leave it unto the man that shall be after me.

19 And who knoweth whether he shall be a wise *man* or a fool? yet shall he have rule over all my labour wherein I have laboured, and wherein I have shewed myself wise under the sun. This *is* also vanity.

20 Therefore I went about to cause my heart to ^adespair of all the labour which I took under the sun.

21 For there is a man whose labour *is* in wisdom, and in knowledge, and in ^aequity; yet to a man that hath not laboured therein shall he leave it *for* his portion. This also *is* ^bvanity and a great evil.

22 For what hath man of all his labour, and of the vexation of his heart, wherein he hath laboured under the sun?

23 For all his days *are* sorrows, and his travail grief; yea, his heart taketh not rest in the night. This is also vanity.

24 ¶ *There is* nothing better for a man, *than* that he should eat and drink, and *that* he should make his ^asoul enjoy good in his ^blabour. This also I saw, that it *was* from the hand of God.

25 For who can eat, or who else can hasten *hereunto*, more than I?

26 For *God* giveth to a man that *is* good in his sight wisdom, and knowledge, and joy: but to the sinner he giveth travail, to gather and to heap up, that he may give to *him that is* ^agood before God. This also *is* vanity and vexation of spirit.

8*a* 1 Kgs. 9:28;
    10:10 (10–14).
 b 1 Kgs. 20:14.
10*a* Eccl. 3:22; 5:18; 9:9.
13*a* TG Darkness, Spiritual.
14*a* Prov. 17:24.

b Eccl. 9:2.
15*a* Eccl. 6:11.
16*a* Eccl. 3:19.
 b Ps. 49:10.
17*a* Eccl. 1:14.
20*a* TG Despair.

21*a* OR propriety, skill.
 b TG Vanity.
24*a* Luke 12:19 (19–21).
 b TG Labor.
26*a* Prov. 13:22.

CHAPTER 3

To every thing there is a season—
Whatever God does, it will be forever—
God will judge the righteous and the
wicked.

To every *thing there is* a ªseason, and a ᵇtime to every purpose under the heaven:

2 A ªtime to be born, and a time to ᵇdie; a time to plant, and a time to pluck up *that which is* planted;

3 A time to kill, and a time to heal; a time to break down, and a time to build up;

4 A time to weep, and a time to ªlaugh; a time to ᵇmourn, and a time to dance;

5 A time to cast away stones, and a time to gather stones together; a time to embrace, and a time to refrain from embracing;

6 A time to ªget, and a time to lose; a time to keep, and a time to cast away;

7 A time to ªrend, and a time to sew; a time to keep ᵇsilence, and a time to speak;

8 A time to love, and a time to ªhate; a time of war, and a time of peace.

9 What profit hath he that worketh in that wherein he ªlaboureth?

10 I have seen the ªtravail, which God hath given to the sons of men to be ᵇexercised in it.

11 He hath made every *thing* ªbeautiful in his time: also ᵇhe hath set the world in their heart, so that no man can find out the ᶜwork that God maketh from the beginning to the end.

12 I know that *there is* no good in them, but for *a man* to rejoice, and to do ªgood in his life.

13 And also that every man should eat and drink, and enjoy the good of all his labour, it *is* the ªgift of God.

14 I know that, whatsoever God doeth, it shall be ªfor ᵇever: nothing can be put to it, nor any thing taken from it: and God doeth *it,* that *men* should ᶜfear before him.

15 That which hath been *is* ªnow; and that which is to be hath already been; and God requireth that which is past.

16 ¶ And moreover I saw under the sun the place of judgment, *that* ªwickedness *was* there; and the place of righteousness, *that* iniquity *was* there.

17 I said in mine heart, God shall ªjudge the righteous and the wicked: for *there is* a time there for every purpose and for every work.

18 I said in mine heart concerning the ªestate of the sons of men, that God might manifest them, and that they might see that they themselves are ᵇbeasts.

19 For that which ªbefalleth the sons of men befalleth beasts; even one thing befalleth them: as the one dieth, so dieth the other; yea, they have all one breath; so that a man hath no preeminence above a beast: for all *is* vanity.

20 All go unto one place; all are of the ªdust, and all turn to dust again.

21 Who knoweth the spirit of man that goeth upward, and the spirit of the beast that goeth downward to the earth?

22 Wherefore I perceive that *there is* nothing better, than that a man

---

3 1a Prov. 15:23.
   b TG Time.
  2a Acts 17:26;
    Alma 40:10;
    D&C 138:53 (53–56).
   b 2 Kgs. 20:1 (1–6);
    D&C 42:48.
  4a TG Laughter.
   b TG Mourning.
  6a OR seek.
  7a Gen. 44:13.
   b TG Silence.
  8a TG Hate.

9a Alma 29:15 (14–16).
10a OR business, work,
    occupation, task.
  b D&C 122:7 (5–7).
11a TG Beauty.
  b HEB He hath set the
    eternal in their heart
    without which man
    cannot find out the
    work that God hath
    done.
  c Eccl. 8:17.
12a Ps. 34:14.

13a TG God, Gifts of.
14a TG Marriage, Celestial.
  b 1 Ne. 10:18 (18–19).
  c Eccl. 5:7; Heb. 12:28;
    Mosiah 4:1.
15a Eccl. 1:9.
16a 4 Ne. 1:44.
17a TG Jesus Christ, Judge;
    Judgment, the Last.
18a OR affairs.
  b Ps. 73:22.
19a Eccl. 2:16.
20a Gen. 3:19.

should rejoice in his own [a]works; for that *is* his portion: for who shall bring him to see what shall be after him?

CHAPTER 4

Oppression and evil deeds are vanity—The strength of two is better than one—Better is a poor and wise child than an old and foolish king.

So I returned, and considered all the oppressions that are done under the sun: and behold the tears of *such as were* oppressed, and they had no comforter; and on the side of their oppressors *there was* power; but they had no comforter.

2 Wherefore I praised the dead which are already dead more than the living which are yet alive.

3 Yea, better *is he* than both they, which hath not yet been, who hath not seen the evil work that is done under the sun.

4 ¶ Again, I considered all travail, and every right work, that for this a man is [a]envied of his neighbour. This *is* also vanity and [b]vexation of spirit.

5 The [a]fool foldeth his hands together, and eateth his own flesh.

6 Better *is* an [a]handful *with* [b]quietness, than both the hands full *with* travail and vexation of spirit.

7 ¶ Then I returned, and I saw [a]vanity under the sun.

8 There is one *alone,* and *there is* not a second; yea, he hath neither child nor brother: yet *is there* no end of all his labour; neither is his eye satisfied with riches; neither *saith he,* For whom do I labour, and [a]bereave my soul of good? This *is* also vanity, yea, it *is* a [b]sore travail.

9 ¶ [a]Two *are* better than one; because they have a good [b]reward for their labour.

10 For if they fall, the one will lift up his fellow: but woe to him *that is* alone when he falleth; for *he hath* not another to help him up.

11 Again, if two lie together, then they have heat: but how can one be warm *alone?*

12 And if one prevail against him, two shall withstand him; and a threefold cord is not quickly broken.

13 ¶ Better *is* a [a]poor and a wise child than an old and foolish king, who will no more be [b]admonished.

14 For out of prison he cometh to reign; whereas also *he that is* born in his kingdom becometh poor.

15 I considered all the living which walk under the sun, with the second child that shall stand up in his stead.

16 *There is* no end of all the people, *even* of all that have been before them: they also that come after shall not rejoice in him. Surely this also *is* vanity and vexation of spirit.

CHAPTER 5

God is in heaven—A fool's voice is known by a multitude of words—Keep your vows—Riches and wealth are the gift of God.

[a]KEEP thy foot when thou goest to the house of God, and be more ready to hear, than to give the sacrifice of fools: for they consider not that they do evil.

2 Be not [a]rash with thy mouth, and let not thine heart be [b]hasty to [c]utter *any* thing before God: for God *is* in heaven, and thou upon earth: therefore let thy [d]words be few.

3 For a dream cometh through the multitude of business; and a fool's voice *is known* by multitude of words.

4 When thou vowest a vow unto God, defer not to pay it; for *he hath* no pleasure in fools: pay that which thou hast [a]vowed.

22*a* Eccl. 2:10.
4 4*a* Gen. 26:14.
  b Eccl. 1:14.
5*a* 2 Ne. 9:28.
6*a* Prov. 15:16.
  b TG Silence.
7*a* TG Vanity.

8*a* OR deprive myself.
  b Eccl. 1:13.
9*a* Moses 3:24.
  b TG Reward.
13*a* 3 Ne. 12:3.
  b TG Teachable;
  Warn.

5 1*a* TG Reverence.
2*a* TG Rashness.
  b TG Haste.
  c Matt. 12:36;
  Eph. 5:4.
  d Matt. 6:7.
4*a* Lev. 22:21.

5 Better *is it* that thou shouldest not vow, than that thou shouldest *a*vow and not pay.

6 Suffer not thy mouth to cause thy flesh to sin; neither say thou before the angel, that it *was* an error: wherefore should God be angry at thy voice, and destroy the work of thine hands?

7 For in the multitude of dreams and many words *there are* also *divers* *a*vanities: but *b*fear thou God.

8 ¶ If thou seest the *a*oppression of the poor, and violent perverting of *b*judgment and justice in a province, marvel not at the matter: for *he that is* higher than the highest regardeth; and *there be* higher than they.

9 ¶ Moreover the profit of the earth is for all: the king *himself* is served by the field.

10 He that loveth *a*silver shall not be satisfied with silver; nor he that loveth abundance with increase: this *is* also *b*vanity.

11 When goods increase, they are increased that eat them: and what good *is there* to the owners thereof, saving the beholding *of them* with their eyes?

12 The *a*sleep of a *b*labouring man *is* sweet, whether he eat little or much: but the abundance of the rich will not suffer him to sleep.

13 There is a *a*sore evil *which* I have seen under the sun, *namely,* riches kept for the owners thereof to their hurt.

14 But those riches perish by evil travail: and he begetteth a son, and *there is* nothing in his hand.

15 As he came forth of his mother's womb, *a*naked shall he return to go as he came, and shall take nothing of his labour, which he may carry away in his hand.

16 And this also *is* a sore evil, *that* in all points as he came, so shall he go: and what profit hath he that hath laboured for the wind?

17 All his days also he eateth in darkness, and *he hath* much sorrow and wrath with his sickness.

18 ¶ Behold *that* which I have seen: *it is* good and comely *for one* to eat and to drink, and to enjoy the good of all his *a*labour that he taketh under the sun all the days of his life, which God giveth him: for it *is* his *b*portion.

19 Every man also to whom God hath given *a*riches and wealth, and hath given him power to eat thereof, and to take his portion, and to rejoice in his *b*labour; this *is* the *c*gift of God.

20 For he shall not much remember the days of his life; because God answereth *him* in the joy of his heart.

CHAPTER 6

Unless a man's soul is filled with good, his riches, wealth, honor, and posterity are vanity.

THERE is an evil which I have seen under the sun, and it *is* common among men:

2 A man to whom God hath given riches, wealth, and honour, so that he wanteth nothing for his soul of all that he desireth, yet God giveth him not power to eat thereof, but a stranger eateth it: this *is* vanity, and it *is* an evil *a*disease.

3 ¶ If a man beget an hundred *children,* and live many years, so that the days of his years be many, and his soul be not filled with good, and also *that* he have no *a*burial; I say, *that* an untimely birth *is* better than he.

4 For he cometh in *a*with vanity, and departeth in darkness, and his name shall be covered with darkness.

5*a* TG Honesty.
7*a* TG Vanity.
  b OR revere thou God.
      Eccl. 3:14.
8*a* TG Oppression.
  b TG Judgment.
10*a* TG Treasure.

b TG Vanity.
12*a* TG Sleep.
  b TG Industry; Labor.
13*a* OR grievous.
15*a* Job 1:21.
18*a* TG Industry.
  b Eccl. 2:10.

19*a* TG Treasure.
  b TG Labor.
  c TG God, Gifts of.
6 2*a* OR affliction, sadness.
  3*a* Isa. 14:20;
      Jer. 22:19.
  4*a* OR in transitoriness.

5 Moreover he hath not seen the sun, nor known *any thing:* this hath more rest than the other.

6 ¶ Yea, though he live a thousand years twice *told,* yet hath he seen no good: do not all go to one place?

7 All the labour of man *is* for his mouth, and yet the appetite is not filled.

8 For what hath the wise more than the fool? what hath the poor, that knoweth to walk before the living?

9 ¶ Better *is* the "sight of the eyes than the wandering of the desire: this *is* also "vanity and "vexation of spirit.

10 That which hath been is named already, and it is known that it *is* man: neither may he "contend with him that is mightier than he.

11 ¶ Seeing there be many things that increase "vanity, what *is* man the "better?

12 For who knoweth what *is* good for man in *this* life, all the days of his vain life which he spendeth as a shadow? for who can tell a man what shall be after him under the sun?

CHAPTER 7

Wisdom gives life to them that have it—All men are sinners—God has made man upright.

A GOOD "name *is* better than precious ointment; and the day of death than the day of one's birth.

2 ¶ *It is* better to go to the house of "mourning, than to go to the house of feasting: for that *is* the end of all men; and the living will lay *it* to his heart.

3 Sorrow *is* better than laughter: for by the "sadness of the countenance the heart is made better.

4 The heart of the wise *is* in the house of mourning; but the heart of fools *is* in the house of mirth.

5 *It is* better to hear the "rebuke of the wise, than for a man to hear the song of fools.

6 For as the crackling of thorns under a pot, so *is* the "laughter of the fool: this also *is* "vanity.

7 ¶ Surely oppression maketh a wise man "mad; and a gift destroyeth the heart.

8 Better *is* the end of a thing than the beginning thereof: *and* the "patient in spirit *is* better than the proud in spirit.

9 Be not "hasty in thy spirit to be "angry: for "anger resteth in the bosom of fools.

10 Say not thou, What is *the cause* that the former days were better than these? for thou dost not inquire wisely concerning this.

11 ¶ Wisdom *is* good with an inheritance: and *by it there is* profit to them that see the sun.

12 For "wisdom *is* a "defence, *and* money *is* a defence: but the excellency of knowledge *is, that* wisdom giveth "life to them that have it.

13 Consider the work of God: for who can make *that* "straight, which he hath made crooked?

14 In the day of prosperity be joyful, but in the day of "adversity consider: God also hath set the one over against the other, to the end that man should find nothing after him.

15 All *things* have I seen in the days of my "vanity: there is a "just *man* that perisheth in his righteousness, and there is a wicked *man* that prolongeth *his life* in his wickedness.

16 Be not righteous over much; neither make thyself over wise: why shouldest thou destroy thyself?

17 Be not over much wicked,

9*a* TG Sight.
  b TG Vanity.
  c Eccl. 1:14.
10*a* Job 9:3 (1–4);
    Isa. 45:9.
11*a* TG Vanity.
  b Eccl. 2:15.
7 1*a* Prov. 22:1.
  2*a* TG Mourning.

3*a* 2 Cor. 7:10.
5*a* TG Reproof.
6*a* TG Laughter;
    Levity.
  b TG Vanity.
7*a* OR a fool (foolish).
8*a* TG Patience.
9*a* TG Rashness.
  b Prov. 29:22 (21–23).

  c TG Anger.
12*a* D&C 6:7.
  b HEB shade; i.e., a
    protection.
  c Prov. 3:18 (13–19).
13*a* Eccl. 1:15.
14*a* TG Adversity.
15*a* TG Vanity.
  b Eccl. 8:14.

neither be thou foolish: why shouldest thou die before thy time?

18 *It is* good that thou shouldest
take hold of this; yea, also from this
withdraw not thine hand: for he
that ^afeareth God shall come forth
of them all.

19 ^aWisdom ^bstrengtheneth the
wise more than ten mighty *men*
which are in the city.

20 For *there is* not a ^ajust man
upon earth, that doeth good, and
^bsinneth not.

21 Also take no heed unto all words
that are spoken; lest thou hear thy
servant curse thee:

22 For oftentimes also thine own
heart knoweth that thou thyself
likewise hast cursed others.

23 ¶ All this have I proved by wisdom: I said, I will be wise; but it
was far from me.

24 That which is far off, and exceeding deep, who can find it out?

25 I applied mine ^aheart to know,
and to search, and to seek out ^bwis-
dom, and the reason *of things,* and to
know the wickedness of folly, even
of foolishness *and* madness:

26 And I find more ^abitter than
death the ^bwoman, whose heart *is*
snares and nets, *and* her hands *as*
bands: whoso pleaseth God shall
escape from her; but the ^csinner
shall be ^dtaken by her.

27 Behold, this have I found, saith
the ^apreacher, *counting* one by one,
to find out the account:

28 Which yet my soul seeketh, but
I find not: one man among a thousand have I found; but a woman
among all those have I not found.

29 Lo, this only have I found, that
God hath made man upright; but
they have sought out many ^ain-
ventions.

CHAPTER 8

None have power to avoid death—It will
not be well with the wicked; he turns
to pleasure and cannot find wisdom.

WHO *is* as the wise *man?* and who
knoweth the interpretation of a
thing? a man's wisdom maketh his
face to ^ashine, and the boldness of
his face shall be changed.

2 I *counsel thee* to keep the ^aking's
commandment, and *that* in regard
of the oath of God.

3 Be not hasty to go out of his
sight: stand not in an evil thing; for
he doeth whatsoever pleaseth him.

4 Where the word of a king *is, there*
is power: and who may say unto
him, What doest thou?

5 Whoso keepeth the ^acommand-
ment shall feel no evil thing: and
a wise man's heart discerneth both
^btime and judgment.

6 ¶ Because to every purpose there
is time and judgment, therefore the
misery of man *is* great upon him.

7 For he knoweth not that which
shall be: for who can tell him when
it shall be?

8 *There is* no man that hath power
over the spirit to retain the spirit;
neither *hath he* power in the day of
^adeath: and *there is* no discharge in
that war; neither shall wickedness
^bdeliver those that are given to it.

9 All this have I seen, and applied
my heart unto every work that is
done under the sun: *there is* a time
wherein one man ruleth over another to his own hurt.

10 And so I saw the wicked buried, who had come and gone from
the place of the holy, and they were
forgotten in the city where they had
so done: this *is* also vanity.

11 Because sentence against an
evil work is not executed ^aspeedily,

18*a* OR reveres God.
19*a* Prov. 21:22;
　　Eccl. 9:16 (16–18);
　　D&C 52:17.
　 b Prov. 24:5.
20*a* D&C 33:4.
　 b TG Sin.
25*a* Eccl. 1:17;

Mosiah 12:27.
　 b D&C 42:68.
26*a* Prov. 5:4.
　 b TG Woman.
　 c 1 Ne. 22:15 (15–17).
　 d Prov. 2:19.
27*a* Eccl. 1:1.
29*a* OR devices, arts.

8 1*a* D&C 50:24; 84:45.
　 2*a* TG Citizenship;
　　　Governments.
　 5*a* 1 Ne. 20:18.
　 b TG Time.
　 8*a* 2 Ne. 9:6.
　 b TG Deliver.
　11*a* D&C 98:2.

therefore the heart of the sons of men is fully *b*set in them to do evil.

12 ¶ Though a sinner do evil an hundred times, and his *days* be prolonged, yet surely I know that it shall be *a*well with them that *b*fear God, which fear before him:

13 But it shall not be well with the wicked, neither shall he prolong *his* days, *which are* as a shadow; because he *a*feareth not before God.

14 There is a *a*vanity which is done upon the earth; that there be *b*just *men,* unto whom it happeneth according to the work of the wicked; again, there be wicked *men,* to whom it happeneth according to the work of the righteous: I said that this also *is* vanity.

15 Then I commended mirth, because a man hath no better thing under the sun, than to eat, and to drink, and to be merry: for that shall abide with him of his labour the days of his life, which God giveth him under the sun.

16 ¶ When I applied mine heart to know *a*wisdom, and to see the business that is done upon the earth: (for also *there is that* neither day nor night seeth sleep with his eyes:)

17 Then I beheld all the work of God, that a man cannot find out the *a*work that is done under the sun: because though a man labour to seek *it* out, yet he shall not find *it*; yea further; though a *b*wise *man* think to know *it*, yet shall he not be able to find *it*.

CHAPTER 9

God's providence rules over all—All men are subject to time and chance— Wisdom is better than strength—One sinner destroys much good.

FOR all this I considered in my heart even to declare all this, that the righteous, and the wise, and their works, *are* in the hand of God: no man knoweth either love or hatred by all *that is* before them.

2 All *things come* alike to all: *there is* one *a*event to the *b*righteous, and to the wicked; to the good and to the clean, and to the unclean; to him that sacrificeth, and to him that sacrificeth not: as *is* the good, so *is* the sinner; *and* he that *c*sweareth, as *he* that *d*feareth an oath.

3 This *is* an evil among all *things* that are done under the sun, that *there is* one event unto all: yea, also the heart of the sons of men is full of evil, and madness *is* in their heart while they live, and after that *they* go to the *a*dead.

4 ¶ For to him that is joined to all the living there is *a*hope: for a living dog is better than a dead lion.

5 For the living know that they shall die: but the dead know not any thing, neither have they any more a reward; for the memory of them is forgotten.

6 Also their love, and their hatred, and their envy, is now perished; neither have they any more a portion for ever in any *thing* that is done under the sun.

7 ¶ Go thy way, eat thy bread with joy, and drink thy wine with a *a*merry heart; for God now accepteth thy works.

8 Let thy garments be always *a*white; and let thy head lack no ointment.

9 Live *a*joyfully with the *b*wife whom thou *c*lovest all the days of the life of thy *d*vanity, which he hath given thee under the sun, all the days of thy vanity: for that *is* thy

11*b* Ex. 8:15 (13–15).
12*a* Ex. 1:20 (7–20);
         D&C 1:9.
      b Isa. 3:10.
         TG Reverence.
13*a* OR is not reverent
         before God.
         Jer. 44:10 (10–11);
         D&C 10:56.
14*a* TG Vanity.

      b Eccl. 7:15;
         Mal. 3:14 (14–18).
16*a* D&C 1:26; 42:68.
17*a* Eccl. 3:11.
      b 2 Ne. 9:28;
         D&C 76:9.
9 2*a* Eccl. 2:14.
      b Alma 12:8.
      c IE makes a covenant.
      d IE avoids committing

         himself.
3*a* Alma 40:11 (11–12).
4*a* TG Hope.
7*a* TG Cheerful.
8*a* Alma 5:21 (21, 24, 27).
9*a* TG Joy.
      b TG Marriage, Husbands;
         Marriage, Wives.
      c TG Family, Love within.
      d TG Vanity.

ᵉportion in *this* life, and in thy labour which thou takest under the sun.

10 Whatsoever thy hand findeth to do, do *it* with thy ᵃmight; for *there is* no work, nor device, nor ᵇknowledge, nor wisdom, in the ᶜgrave, whither thou goest.

11 ¶ I returned, and saw under the sun, that the race *is* not to the ᵃswift, nor the battle to the strong, neither yet bread to the wise, nor yet riches to men of understanding, nor yet favour to men of skill; but time and chance happeneth to them all.

12 For man also knoweth not his time: as the fishes that are taken in an evil net, and as the birds that are caught in the snare; so *are* the sons of men ᵃsnared in an evil time, when it falleth suddenly upon them.

13 ¶ This wisdom have I seen also under the sun, and it *seemed* great unto me:

14 *There was* a little city, and few men within it; and there came a great king against it, and besieged it, and built great bulwarks against it:

15 Now there was found in it a poor wise man, and he by his wisdom delivered the city; yet no man remembered that same poor man.

16 Then said I, ᵃWisdom *is* better than strength: nevertheless the poor man's ᵇwisdom *is* despised, and his words are not heard.

17 The words of wise *men are* heard in quiet more than the cry of him that ruleth among fools.

18 ᵃWisdom *is* better than weapons of war: but one ᵇsinner destroyeth much good.

CHAPTER 10

A little folly destroys the reputation of the wise and honorable—The words of a wise man's mouth are gracious—A fool is full of words.

DEAD flies cause the ointment of the ᵃapothecary to send forth a stinking savour: *so doth* a little ᵇfolly him that is in reputation for wisdom *and* honour.

2 A wise man's heart *is* at his right hand; but a fool's heart at his left.

3 Yea also, when he that is a fool walketh by the way, his wisdom faileth *him,* and he saith to every one *that* he *is* a fool.

4 If the spirit of the ruler rise up against thee, leave not thy place; for yielding pacifieth great offences.

5 There is an evil *which* I have seen under the sun, as an error *which* proceedeth from the ruler:

6 Folly is set in great dignity, and the rich sit in low place.

7 I have seen ᵃservants upon horses, and princes walking as servants upon the earth.

8 He that diggeth a pit shall ᵃfall into it; and whoso breaketh an hedge, a serpent shall bite him.

9 Whoso removeth stones shall be hurt therewith; *and* he that cleaveth wood shall be endangered thereby.

10 If the iron be blunt, and he do not whet the edge, then must he put to more strength: but wisdom *is* profitable to direct.

11 Surely the serpent will bite without enchantment; and a babbler is no better.

12 The ᵃwords of a wise man's mouth *are* gracious; but the lips of a ᵇfool will swallow up himself.

13 The beginning of the words of his mouth *is* foolishness: and the end of his talk *is* mischievous ᵃmadness.

14 A fool also is full of words: a man cannot tell what shall be; and what shall be after him, who can tell him?

15 The labour of the foolish wearieth every one of them, because he knoweth not how to go to the city.

9e Eccl. 2:10.
10a TG Industry.
  b 2 Ne. 9:13 (13–14);
    D&C 130:18.
  c Alma 34:33.
11a Amos 2:14 (14–15);
    Mosiah 4:27.
12a Prov. 7:23 (21–23).

16a Eccl. 7:19.
  b Mark 6:2 (2–3).
18a D&C 6:7.
  b Josh. 7:11 (1, 11–12);
    Eccl. 10:1.
10 1a OR perfumer
    (ointment maker).
  b Josh. 7:11 (1, 11–12);

Eccl. 9:18.
7a Prov. 19:10.
8a Alma 30:60.
12a Prov. 10:32.
  b 2 Ne. 9:28 (28–29); 19:17;
    D&C 35:7.
13a IE extreme folly.

16 ¶ Woe to thee, O land, when thy king is a ᵃchild, and thy princes eat in the morning!

17 Blessed art thou, O land, when thy king is the son of nobles, and thy princes eat in due season, for strength, and not for ᵃdrunkenness!

18 ¶ By much ᵃslothfulness the building decayeth; and through ᵇidleness of the hands the house droppeth through.

19 ¶ A feast is made for laughter, and wine maketh merry: but money answereth all things.

20 ¶ Curse not the ᵃking, no not in thy thought; and curse not the rich in thy bedchamber: for a bird of the air shall carry the voice, and that which hath wings shall tell the matter.

CHAPTER 11

Do good and give to them who need—God will bring all men to judgment.

CAST thy ᵃbread upon the waters: for thou shalt find it after many days.

2 Give a portion to seven, and also to eight; for thou ᵃknowest not what evil shall be upon the earth.

3 If the clouds be full of rain, they empty *themselves* upon the earth: and if the tree fall toward the south, or toward the north, in the place where the tree falleth, there it shall be.

4 He that observeth the wind shall not sow; and he that regardeth the clouds shall not ᵃreap.

5 As thou knowest not what is the way of the ᵃspirit, *nor* how the bones *do grow* in the womb of her that is with child: even so thou knowest not the works of God who ᵇmaketh all.

6 In the morning sow thy seed, and in the evening withhold not thine hand: for thou knowest not whether shall prosper, either this

or that, or whether they both *shall be* alike good.

7 ¶ Truly the ᵃlight is sweet, and a pleasant *thing it is* for the eyes to behold the sun:

8 But if a man live many years, *and* rejoice in them all; yet let him remember the days of ᵃdarkness; for they shall be many. All that cometh is ᵇvanity.

9 ¶ Rejoice, O young man, in thy youth; and let thy heart ᵃcheer thee in the days of thy youth, and ᵇwalk in the ways of thine heart, and in the sight of thine eyes: but know thou, that for all these *things* God will bring thee into ᶜjudgment.

10 Therefore remove sorrow from thy heart, and put away ᵃevil from thy flesh: for childhood and youth *are* ᵇvanity.

CHAPTER 12

At death the spirit will return to God who gave it—The words of the wise are as goads—The whole duty of man is to fear God and keep His commandments.

REMEMBER now thy Creator in the days of thy ᵃyouth, while the ᵇevil days come not, nor the years draw nigh, when thou shalt say, I have no pleasure in them;

2 While the sun, or the light, or the moon, or the stars, be not darkened, nor the clouds return after the rain:

3 In the day when the keepers of the house shall tremble, and the strong men shall bow themselves, and the grinders cease because they are few, and those that look out of the windows be darkened,

4 And the doors shall be shut in the streets, when the sound of the grinding is low, and he shall rise up at the voice of the bird, and all the daughters of musick shall be brought low;

5 Also *when* they shall be afraid of

16a Isa. 3:4 (4–5, 12).
17a TG Word of Wisdom.
18a TG Laziness.
  b TG Idleness.
20a TG Citizenship;
    Kings, Earthly.
11 1a TG Bread.

2a D&C 39:21.
4a TG Harvest.
5a John 3:8 (5–8).
  b TG Creation.
7a TG Light [noun].
8a Eccl. 12:1.
  b TG Vanity.

9a TG Happiness.
  b Job 31:7.
  c TG Judgment, the Last.
10a TG Carnal Mind.
  b TG Vanity.
12 1a Alma 37:35.
  b Eccl. 11:8.

that which is high, and fears *shall be* in the way, and the almond tree shall flourish, and the grasshopper shall be a burden, and desire shall fail: because man goeth to his long [a]home, and the mourners go about the streets:

6 Or ever the silver cord be loosed, or the golden bowl be broken, or the pitcher be broken at the fountain, or the wheel broken at the cistern.

7 Then shall the [a]dust return to the earth as it was: and the [b]spirit shall return unto God who [c]gave it.

8 ¶ Vanity of vanities, saith the preacher; all *is* vanity.

9 And moreover, because the preacher was wise, he still taught the people knowledge; yea, he gave good heed, and sought out, *and* set in order many proverbs.

10 The preacher sought to find out [a]acceptable words: and *that which was* written *was* upright, *even* words of truth.

11 The words of the wise *are* as [a]goads, and as nails fastened *by* the masters of assemblies, *which* are given from one shepherd.

12 And further, by these, my son, be admonished: of making many books *there is* no end; and much [a]study *is* a weariness of the flesh.

13 ¶ Let us hear the conclusion of the whole matter: [a]Fear God, and [b]keep his commandments: for this *is* the whole [c]duty of man.

14 For God shall bring every [a]work into [b]judgment, with every secret thing, whether *it be* good, or whether *it be* evil.

THE
SONG OF SOLOMON

CHAPTER 1

The poet sings of love and devotion.

THE [a]song of songs, which *is* Solomon's.

2 Let him kiss me with the kisses of his mouth: for thy love *is* better than wine.

3 Because of the savour of thy good ointments thy name *is as* ointment poured forth, therefore do the virgins love thee.

4 Draw me, we will run after thee: the king hath brought me into his chambers: we will be glad and rejoice in thee, we will remember thy love more than wine: the upright love thee.

5 I *am* black, but comely, O ye daughters of Jerusalem, as the tents of Kedar, as the curtains of Solomon.

6 Look not upon me, because I *am* black, because the sun hath looked upon me: my mother's children were angry with me; they made me

5 *a* Job 17:13;
    Alma 40:11.
7 *a* TG Man, Physical
    Creation of; Mortality.
  b TG Death; Man,
    Antemortal Existence
    of; Spirit Body;
    Spirit Creation;
    Spirits, Disembodied.
  c TG Man, a Spirit Child

of Heavenly Father.
10 *a* HEB words of delight.
11 *a* IE sharp-pointed sticks
    to spur oxen onward.
12 *a* TG Study.
13 *a* OR Revere God.
    TG Reverence.
  b TG Obedience.
  c TG Duty;
    Mission of Early Saints.

14 *a* TG Good Works.
  b TG Jesus Christ, Judge;
    Judgment, the Last.

[SONG OF SOLOMON]

Note: The JST manuscript
    states that "the Songs
    of Solomon are not
    inspired writings."

1 1 *a* 1 Kgs. 4:32.

the keeper of the vineyards; *but* mine own vineyard have I not kept.

7 Tell me, O thou whom my soul loveth, where thou feedest, where thou makest *thy flock* to rest at noon: for why should I be as one that turneth aside by the flocks of thy companions?

8 ¶ If thou know not, O thou fairest among women, go thy way forth by the footsteps of the flock, and feed thy kids beside the shepherds' tents.

9 I have compared thee, O my love, to a company of horses in Pharaoh's chariots.

10 Thy cheeks are comely with rows *of jewels,* thy neck with chains *of gold.*

11 We will make thee borders of gold with studs of silver.

12 ¶ While the king *sitteth* at his table, my *a*spikenard sendeth forth the smell thereof.

13 A bundle of myrrh *is* my wellbeloved unto me; he shall lie all night betwixt my breasts.

14 My beloved *is* unto me *as* a cluster of *a*camphire in the vineyards of En-gedi.

15 Behold, thou *art* fair, my love; behold, thou *art* fair; thou *hast* doves' eyes.

16 Behold, thou *art* fair, my beloved, yea, pleasant: also our bed *is* green.

17 The beams of our house *are* cedar, *and* our rafters of fir.

CHAPTER 2

Beloved ones are praised and described.

I AM the rose of Sharon, *and* the lily of the valleys.

2 As the lily among thorns, so *is* my love among the daughters.

3 As the apple tree among the trees of the wood, so *is* my beloved among the sons. I sat down under his shadow with great delight, and his fruit *was* sweet to my taste.

4 He brought me to the banqueting house, and his banner over me *was* love.

5 Stay me with flagons, *a*comfort me with apples: for I *am* sick of love.

6 His left hand *is* under my head, and his right hand doth embrace me.

7 I charge you, O ye daughters of Jerusalem, by the roes, and by the hinds of the field, that ye stir not up, nor awake *my* love, till he please.

8 ¶ The voice of my beloved! behold, he cometh leaping upon the mountains, skipping upon the hills.

9 My beloved is like a roe or a young *a*hart: behold, he standeth behind our wall, he looketh forth at the windows, shewing himself through the lattice.

10 My beloved spake, and said unto me, Rise up, my love, my fair one, and come away.

11 For, lo, the winter is past, the rain is over *and* gone;

12 The *a*flowers appear on the earth; the time of the singing *of birds* is come, and the voice of the *b*turtle is heard in our land;

13 The fig tree putteth forth her green figs, and the vines *with* the tender grape give a *good* smell. Arise, my love, my fair one, and come away.

14 ¶ O my dove, *that art* in the clefts of the rock, in the secret *places* of the stairs, let me see thy countenance, let me hear thy voice; for sweet *is* thy voice, and thy countenance *is* comely.

15 Take us the foxes, the little foxes, that spoil the vines: for our vines *have* tender grapes.

16 ¶ My beloved *is* mine, and I *am* his: he feedeth among the lilies.

17 Until the day break, and the shadows flee away, turn, my beloved, and be thou like a roe or a young hart upon the mountains of Bether.

12*a* IE a fragrant ointment.
  Song 4:13 (13–14).
14*a* OR henna (a shrub with

small white flowers).
2 5*a* IE refresh me.
9*a* OR gazelle, fawn.

12*a* TG Nature, Earth.
  b IE turtle-dove.
  Jer. 8:7.

CHAPTER 3

A love song concerning Solomon is presented.

BY night on my bed I sought him whom my soul loveth: I sought him, but I found him not.

2 I will rise now, and go about the city in the streets, and in the broad ways I will seek him whom my soul loveth: I sought him, but I found him not.

3 The watchmen that go about the city found me: *to whom I said,* Saw ye him whom my soul loveth?

4 *It was* but a little that I passed from them, but I found him whom my soul loveth: I held him, and would not let him go, until I had brought him into my mother's house, and into the chamber of her that conceived me.

5 I charge you, O ye daughters of Jerusalem, by the roes, and by the hinds of the field, that ye stir not up, nor awake *my* love, till he please.

6 ¶ Who *is* this that cometh out of the wilderness like pillars of smoke, perfumed with myrrh and frankincense, with all powders of the merchant?

7 Behold his bed, which *is* Solomon's; threescore valiant men *are* about it, of the valiant of Israel.

8 They all hold swords, *being* expert in war: every man *hath* his sword upon his thigh because of fear in the night.

9 King Solomon made himself a chariot of the wood of Lebanon.

10 He made the pillars thereof *of* silver, the bottom thereof *of* gold, the covering of it *of* purple, the midst thereof being paved *with* love, for the daughters of Jerusalem.

11 Go forth, O ye daughters of Zion, and behold king Solomon with the crown wherewith his mother crowned him in the day of his espousals, and in the day of the gladness of his heart.

CHAPTER 4

A song describes the beauty of the poet's beloved.

BEHOLD, thou *art* fair, my love; behold, thou *art* fair; thou *hast* doves' eyes within thy locks: thy hair *is* as a flock of goats, that appear from mount Gilead.

2 Thy teeth *are* like a flock *of sheep that are even* shorn, which came up from the washing; whereof every one bear twins, and none *is* barren among them.

3 Thy lips *are* like a thread of scarlet, and thy speech *is* comely: thy temples *are* like a piece of a pomegranate within thy locks.

4 Thy neck *is* like the tower of David builded for an armoury, whereon there hang a thousand bucklers, all shields of mighty men.

5 Thy two breasts *are* like two young roes that are twins, which feed among the lilies.

6 Until the day break, and the shadows flee away, I will get me to the mountain of myrrh, and to the hill of frankincense.

7 Thou *art* all fair, my love; *there is* no spot in thee.

8 ¶ Come with me from Lebanon, my [a]spouse, with me from Lebanon: look from the top of Amana, from the top of Shenir and Hermon, from the lions' dens, from the mountains of the leopards.

9 Thou hast ravished my heart, [a]my [b]sister, *my* spouse; thou hast ravished my heart with one of thine eyes, with one chain of thy neck.

10 How fair is thy love, my sister, *my* spouse! how much better is thy love than wine! and the smell of thine ointments than all spices!

11 Thy lips, O *my* spouse, drop *as* the honeycomb: honey and milk *are* under thy tongue; and the smell of thy garments *is* like the smell of Lebanon.

12 A garden inclosed *is* my sister,

---

4 8*a* Song 5:1.
9*a* This form of address is
an idiom to express tenderness. See also v. 12.
b Song 5:1.

my spouse; a spring shut up, a fountain sealed.

13 Thy plants *are* an orchard of pomegranates, with pleasant fruits; [a]camphire, with [b]spikenard,

14 Spikenard and saffron; calamus and cinnamon, with all trees of frankincense; myrrh and aloes, with all the chief spices:

15 A fountain of gardens, a well of living waters, and streams from Lebanon.

16 ¶ Awake, O north wind; and come, thou south; blow upon my garden, *that* the spices thereof may flow out. Let my beloved come into his garden, and eat his pleasant fruits.

CHAPTER 5

The song of love and affection continues.

I AM come into my garden, my [a]sister, *my* [b]spouse: I have gathered my myrrh with my spice; I have eaten my honeycomb with my honey; I have drunk my wine with my milk: eat, O friends; drink, yea, drink abundantly, O beloved.

2 ¶ I sleep, but my heart waketh: *it is* the voice of my beloved that knocketh, *saying*, Open to me, my sister, my love, my dove, my undefiled: for my head is filled with dew, *and* my locks with the drops of the night.

3 I have put off my coat; how shall I put it on? I have washed my feet; how shall I defile them?

4 My beloved put in his hand by the hole *of the door*, and my bowels were moved for him.

5 I rose up to open to my beloved; and my hands dropped *with* myrrh, and my fingers *with* sweet smelling myrrh, upon the handles of the lock.

6 I opened to my beloved; but my beloved had withdrawn himself, *and* was gone: my soul failed when he spake: I sought him, but I could not find him; I called him, but he gave me no answer.

7 The watchmen that went about the city found me, they smote me, they wounded me; the keepers of the walls took away my veil from me.

8 I charge you, O daughters of Jerusalem, if ye find my beloved, that ye tell him, that I *am* sick of love.

9 ¶ What *is* thy beloved more than *another* beloved, O thou fairest among women? what *is* thy beloved more than *another* beloved, that thou dost so charge us?

10 My beloved *is* white and ruddy, the chiefest among ten thousand.

11 His head *is as* the most fine gold, his locks *are* bushy, *and* black as a raven.

12 His eyes *are as the eyes* of doves by the rivers of waters, washed with milk, *and* fitly set.

13 His cheeks *are* as a bed of spices, *as* sweet flowers: his lips *like* lilies, dropping sweet smelling myrrh.

14 His hands *are as* gold rings set with the beryl: his belly *is as* bright ivory overlaid *with* sapphires.

15 His legs *are as* pillars of marble, set upon sockets of fine gold: his countenance *is* as Lebanon, excellent as the cedars.

16 His mouth *is* most sweet: yea, he *is* altogether lovely. This *is* my beloved, and this *is* my friend, O daughters of Jerusalem.

CHAPTER 6

The song of love continues.

WHITHER is thy beloved gone, O thou fairest among women? whither is thy beloved turned aside? that we may seek him with thee.

2 My beloved is gone down into his garden, to the beds of spices, to feed in the gardens, and to gather lilies.

3 I *am* my beloved's, and my beloved *is* mine: he feedeth among the lilies.

4 ¶ Thou *art* beautiful, O my love, as Tirzah, comely as Jerusalem, terrible as *an army* with banners.

5 Turn away thine eyes from me,

13*a* OR henna.
  b Song 1:12.

5 1*a* Song 4:9.
  b Song 4:8.

for they have overcome me: thy hair *is* as a flock of goats that appear from Gilead.

6 Thy teeth *are* as a flock of sheep which go up from the washing, whereof every one beareth twins, and *there is* not one barren among them.

7 As a piece of a pomegranate *are* thy temples within thy locks.

8 There are threescore queens, and fourscore concubines, and virgins without number.

9 My dove, my undefiled is *but* one; she *is* the *only* one of her mother, she *is* the choice *one* of her that bare her. The daughters saw her, and blessed her; *yea*, the queens and the concubines, and they praised her.

10 ¶ Who *is* she *that* looketh forth as the morning, fair as the moon, clear as the sun, *and* terrible as *an army* with banners?

11 I went down into the garden of nuts to see the fruits of the valley, *and* to see whether the vine flourished, *and* the pomegranates budded.

12 Or ever I was aware, my soul made me *like* the chariots of Amminadib.

13 Return, return, O Shulamite; return, return, that we may look upon thee. What will ye see in the Shulamite? As it were the company of two armies.

CHAPTER 7

The song of love continues.

How beautiful are thy feet with shoes, O prince's daughter! the joints of thy thighs *are* like jewels, the work of the hands of a cunning workman.

2 Thy navel *is like* a round goblet, *which* wanteth not liquor: thy belly *is like* an heap of wheat set about with lilies.

3 Thy two breasts *are* like two young roes *that are* twins.

4 Thy neck *is* as a tower of ivory; thine eyes *like* the fishpools in Heshbon, by the gate of Bath-rabbim: thy nose *is* as the tower of Lebanon which looketh toward Damascus.

5 Thine head upon thee *is* like Carmel, and the hair of thine head like purple; the king *is* held in the galleries.

6 How fair and how pleasant art thou, O love, for delights!

7 This thy stature is like to a palm tree, and thy breasts to clusters *of grapes.*

8 I said, I will go up to the palm tree, I will take hold of the boughs thereof: now also thy breasts shall be as clusters of the vine, and the smell of thy nose like apples;

9 And the roof of thy mouth like the best wine for my beloved, that goeth *down* sweetly, causing the lips of those that are asleep to speak.

10 ¶ I *am* my beloved's, and his desire *is* toward me.

11 Come, my beloved, let us go forth into the field; let us lodge in the villages.

12 Let us get up early to the vineyards; let us see if the vine flourish, *whether* the tender grape appear, *and* the pomegranates bud forth: there will I give thee my loves.

13 The mandrakes give a smell, and at our gates *are* all manner of pleasant *fruits,* new and old, *which* I have laid up for thee, O my beloved.

CHAPTER 8

Many waters cannot quench love.

O THAT thou *wert* as my brother, that sucked the breasts of my mother! *when* I should find thee without, I would kiss thee; yea, I should not be despised.

2 I would lead thee, *and* bring thee into my mother's house, *who* would instruct me: I would cause thee to drink of spiced wine of the juice of my pomegranate.

3 His left hand *should be* under my head, and his right hand should embrace me.

4 I charge you, O daughters of Jerusalem, that ye stir not up, nor awake *my* love, until he please.

5 Who *is* this that cometh up from the wilderness, leaning upon her beloved? I raised thee up under the

apple tree: there thy mother brought thee forth: there she brought thee forth *that* bare thee.

6 ¶ Set me as a seal upon thine heart, as a seal upon thine arm: for love *is* strong as death; jealousy *is* ^acruel as the grave: the coals thereof *are* coals of fire, *which hath* a most vehement flame.

7 Many waters cannot quench love, neither can the floods drown it: if a man would give all the substance of his house for love, it would utterly be contemned.

8 ¶ We have a little sister, and she hath no breasts: what shall we do for our sister in the day when she shall be spoken for?

9 If she *be* a wall, we will build upon her a palace of silver: and if she *be* a door, we will inclose her with boards of cedar.

10 I *am* a wall, and my breasts like towers: then was I in his eyes as one that found favour.

11 Solomon had a vineyard at Baal-hamon; he let out the vineyard unto keepers; every one for the fruit thereof was to bring a thousand *pieces* of silver.

12 My vineyard, which *is* mine, *is* before me: thou, O Solomon, *must have* a thousand, and those that keep the fruit thereof two hundred.

13 Thou that dwellest in the gardens, the companions hearken to thy voice: cause me to hear *it*.

14 ¶ Make haste, my beloved, and be thou like to a roe or to a young ^ahart upon the mountains of spices.

THE BOOK OF THE PROPHET
ISAIAH

CHAPTER 1

The people of Israel are apostate, rebellious, and corrupt; only a few remain faithful—The people's sacrifices and feasts are rejected—They are called upon to repent and work righteousness—Zion will be redeemed in the day of restoration.

THE ^avision of ^bIsaiah the son of Amoz, which he saw concerning ^cJudah and Jerusalem in the days of ^dUzziah, ^eJotham, ^fAhaz, *and* Hezekiah, kings of Judah.

2 ^aHear, O heavens, and give ear, O earth: for the Lord hath spoken, I have nourished and brought up children, and they have ^brebelled against me.

3 The ox knoweth his owner, and the ass his master's ^acrib: *but* Israel doth not ^bknow, my people doth not consider.

4 Ah ^asinful nation, a people laden with iniquity, a seed of evildoers, ^bchildren that are ^ccorrupters: they have forsaken the Lord, they have provoked the Holy One of Israel unto ^danger, they are gone away backward.

---

8 6a TG Cruelty.
14a OR gazelle, fawn.

[Isaiah]
1 1a TG Vision.
  b 1 Ne. 19:23 (23–24);
    3 Ne. 23:1.
  c TG Israel, Judah,
    People of.

d 2 Kgs. 15:13 (1–13);
  Hosea 1:1.
e 2 Kgs. 15:30, 38 (13–38);
  Micah 1:1.
f 2 Kgs. 16:20 (19–20).
2a Deut. 32:1;
  D&C 1:1 (1–2); 76:1.
  b Deut. 32:19.
3a HEB stall or manger.

b TG Apostasy of Israel;
  God, Knowledge about;
  Ignorance.
4a TG Man, Natural, Not
  Spiritually Reborn.
  b Isa. 57:4.
  c D&C 38:11 (10–12).
  d TG Anger.

5 ¶ Why should ye be ᵃstricken any more? ye will ᵇrevolt more and more: the whole head is sick, and the whole heart ᶜfaint.

6 From the sole of the foot even unto the head *there is* no soundness in it; *but* wounds, and bruises, and putrifying sores: they have not been ᵃclosed, neither bound up, neither ᵇmollified with ointment.

7 Your ᵃcountry *is* ᵇdesolate, your cities *are* burned with fire: your land, ᶜstrangers devour it in your presence, and *it is* desolate, as overthrown by strangers.

8 And the daughter of Zion is left as a cottage in a ᵃvineyard, as ᵇa lodge in a garden of cucumbers, as a besieged city.

9 Except the LORD of hosts had left unto us a very small ᵃremnant, we should have been as Sodom, *and* we should have been like unto Gomorrah.

10 ¶ Hear the word of the LORD, ye rulers of ᵃSodom; give ear unto the law of our God, ye people of Gomorrah.

11 To what purpose *is* the multitude of your ᵃsacrifices unto me? saith the LORD: I am full of the burnt offerings of rams, and the fat of fed beasts; and I ᵇdelight not in the blood of bullocks, or of lambs, or of he goats.

12 When ye come to appear before me, who hath required this at your hand, to tread my courts?

13 Bring no more ᵃvain ᵇoblations;

incense is an abomination unto me; the new moons and ᶜsabbaths, the calling of ᵈassemblies, I cannot ᵉaway with; *it is* ᶠiniquity, even the ᵍsolemn meeting.

14 Your new ᵃmoons and your appointed ᵇfeasts my soul hateth: they are a trouble unto me; I am ᶜweary to bear *them*.

15 And when ye spread forth your hands, I will hide mine eyes from you: yea, when ye make many ᵃprayers, I will not hear: your hands are full of ᵇblood.

16 ¶ ᵃWash you, make you ᵇclean; put away the ᶜevil of your doings from before mine eyes; ᵈcease to do evil;

17 ᵃLearn to do ᵇwell; seek ᶜjudgment, ᵈrelieve the oppressed, ᵉjudge the fatherless, plead for the ᶠwidow.

18 Come now, and let us ᵃreason together, saith the LORD: though your ᵇsins be as scarlet, they shall be as ᶜwhite as snow; though they be red like crimson, they shall be as wool.

19 If ye be ᵃwilling and ᵇobedient, ye shall eat the ᶜgood of the land:

20 But if ye refuse and ᵃrebel, ye shall be ᵇdevoured with the sword: for the mouth of the LORD hath spoken *it*.

21 ¶ How is the faithful city become an ᵃharlot! it was full of ᵇjudgment; righteousness lodged in it; but now murderers.

22 Thy silver is become ᵃdross, thy wine mixed with water:

23 Thy ᵃprinces *are* rebellious, and

5a HEB smitten.
  b TG Rebellion.
  c HEB diseased.
6a HEB squeezed out.
  b HEB softened.
7a Deut. 28:51 (51–52).
  b Jer. 9:11;
    Micah 3:12; 2 Ne. 13:8.
  c TG Israel, Scattering of.
8a TG Vineyard of the Lord.
  b IE a watchman's hut.
9a TG Israel, Remnant of.
10a Ezek. 16:46 (44–55).
11a TG Sacrifice.
  b 1 Sam. 15:22.
13a TG Hypocrisy.
  b 1 Chr. 23:31 (28–32).
  c Lam. 2:6.
  d Matt. 15:9.

  e HEB endure.
    Ps. 101:5.
  f Isa. 29:13.
  g TG Solemn Assembly.
14a Hosea 2:11.
  b Amos 5:21.
  c Isa. 43:24 (24–28).
15a 1 Sam. 8:18;
    D&C 101:7 (7–8).
    TG God, Access to.
  b HEB bloods; i.e.,
    bloodshed.
    Isa. 59:2 (2–3).
16a Jer. 7:3 (1–7).
    TG Baptism.
  b TG Cleanliness;
    Purification; Purity.
  c TG Evil.
  d TG Repent.

17a TG Learn.
  b TG Good Works.
  c HEB justice.
  d TG Charity.
  e IE give a just verdict to
    the fatherless.
  f TG Widows.
18a D&C 50:10.
  b TG Forgive; Sin.
  c TG Purification.
19a TG Teachable.
  b TG Obedience.
  c TG Abundant Life.
20a TG Rebellion.
  b TG Punish.
21a TG Apostasy of Israel.
  b OR justice.
22a TG Apostasy of Israel.
23a TG Kings, Earthly.

companions of thieves: every one loveth [b]gifts, and followeth after rewards: they [c]judge not the fatherless, neither doth the cause of the widow come unto them.

24 Therefore saith the Lord, the LORD of hosts, the mighty One of Israel, Ah, I will ease me of mine [a]adversaries, and avenge me of mine enemies:

25 ¶ And I will [a]turn my hand upon thee, and purely [b]purge away thy dross, and take away all thy tin:

26 And I will [a]restore thy judges as at the first, and thy [b]counsellors as at the beginning: afterward thou shalt be called, The [c]city of righteousness, the faithful city.

27 [a]Zion shall be redeemed with [b]judgment, and her [c]converts with righteousness.

28 ¶ And the destruction of the transgressors and of the sinners *shall be* together, and they that forsake the LORD shall be consumed.

29 For they shall be ashamed of the [a]oaks which ye have desired, and ye shall be confounded for the gardens that ye have chosen.

30 For ye shall be as an oak whose leaf fadeth, and as a garden that hath no water.

31 And the strong shall be [a]as tow, and the maker of it as a spark, and they shall both [b]burn together, and none shall quench *them.*

CHAPTER 2

Isaiah sees the latter-day temple, gathering of Israel, and millennial judgment and peace—The proud and wicked will be brought low at the Second Coming—Compare 2 Nephi 12.

THE word that [a]Isaiah the son of Amoz [b]saw concerning Judah and Jerusalem:

2 And it shall come to pass in the [a]last days, *that* the [b]mountain of the LORD's [c]house shall be [d]established in the top of the mountains, and shall be exalted above the hills; and all [e]nations shall flow unto it.

3 And many people shall go and say, Come ye, and let us [a]go up to the [b]mountain of the LORD, to the [c]house of the God of Jacob; and he will [d]teach us of his ways, and we will walk in his paths: for out of [e]Zion shall go forth the [f]law, and the word of the LORD from Jerusalem.

4 And he shall [a]judge among the nations, and shall rebuke many people: and they shall beat their swords into plowshares, and their spears into pruninghooks: nation shall not lift up sword against nation, neither shall they learn [b]war any more.

5 O house of Jacob, come ye, and let us [a]walk in the [b]light of the LORD.

6 ¶ Therefore thou hast forsaken

---

23 b IE bribes.
   Ezek. 22:12.
   TG Bribe.
 c HEB "do not do justice to."
   TG Judgment.
24 a D&C 101:58.
25 a HEB return; i.e.,
   repeatedly chastise.
 b Jer. 9:7;
   Mal. 3:3.
26 a Jer. 33:7 (7–8).
 b TG Counselor.
 c TG Jerusalem.
27 a TG Zion.
 b HEB justice.
 c TG Conversion.
29 a IE terebinth trees and
   gardens used in idol
   worship.
31 a IE as a tuft of
   inflammable fibers.
 b Isa. 9:16 (16–21).

2 1 a Isaiah chapters 2–14 are
   quoted from the brass
   plates by Nephi in 2 Ne.
   12–24; there are some
   differences in wording
   which should be noted.
 b HEB *khazah,* meaning
   "envisioned." It means
   Isaiah received his
   message through a
   vision from the Lord.
2 a TG Last Days.
 b Isa. 13:2;
   Micah 4:1 (1–3).
 c TG Jerusalem, New.
 d TG Dispensations;
   Restoration of the
   Gospel.
 e 1 Kgs. 8:41 (41–42).
   TG Israel, Mission of;
   Nations.
3 a TG Millennium,

   Preparing a People for.
 b Ps. 48:1;
   Isa. 30:29;
   3 Ne. 20:22;
   D&C 84:2 (2–4).
 c TG Temple.
 d TG Missionary Work;
   Teaching.
 e Isa. 33:20.
   TG Kingdom of God, on
   Earth;
   Zion.
 f HEB teaching, or
   doctrine.
   TG God, Law of; Mission
   of Latter-day Saints.
4 a TG Jesus Christ, Judge.
 b TG Millennium;
   Peace; War.
5 a TG Walking with God.
 b TG Jesus Christ, Light of
   the World.

thy people the house of Jacob, because they [a]be replenished from the east, and *are* [b]soothsayers like the Philistines, and they [c]please themselves in the children of strangers.

7 Their land also is full of silver and gold, neither *is there any* end of their treasures; their land is also full of horses, neither *is there any* end of their chariots:

8 Their land also is full of [a]idols; they [b]worship the work of their own hands, that which their own fingers have made:

9 And the [a]mean man [b]boweth down, and the great man humbleth himself: therefore forgive them not.

10 ¶ Enter into the rock, and hide thee in the dust, for fear of the LORD, and for the glory of his majesty.

11 The lofty looks of man shall be humbled, and the haughtiness of men shall be bowed down, and the LORD alone shall be [a]exalted in that [b]day.

12 For the [a]day of the LORD of hosts *shall be* upon every *one that is* [b]proud and lofty, and upon every *one that is* lifted up; and he shall be brought [c]low:

13 And upon all the [a]cedars of Lebanon, *that are* high and lifted up, and upon all the oaks of Bashan,

14 And upon all the high mountains, and upon all the hills *that are* lifted up,

15 And upon every high tower, and upon every fenced wall,

16 [a]And upon all the ships of Tarshish, and upon all pleasant pictures.

17 And the loftiness of man shall be bowed down, and the [a]haughtiness of men shall be made low: and the LORD alone shall be exalted in that day.

18 And the [a]idols he shall utterly abolish.

19 And they shall go into the [a]holes of the rocks, and into the caves of the earth, for [b]fear of the LORD, and for the glory of his majesty, when he ariseth to shake terribly the earth.

20 In that day a man shall [a]cast his idols of silver, and his idols of gold, which they made *each one* for himself to worship, to the moles and to the bats;

21 To go into the clefts of the rocks, and into the tops of the ragged rocks, for fear of the LORD, and for the glory of his majesty, when he ariseth to shake terribly the earth.

22 [a]Cease ye from man, whose breath *is* in his nostrils: for [b]wherein is he to be accounted of?

CHAPTER 3

Judah and Jerusalem will be punished for their disobedience—The Lord pleads for and judges His people—The daughters of Zion are cursed and tormented for their worldliness—Compare 2 Nephi 13.

[a]FOR, behold, the Lord, the LORD of hosts, doth take away from [b]Jerusalem and from Judah the stay and the staff, the whole stay of [c]bread, and the whole stay of water,

2 The mighty man, and the man of

6a IE are filled, supplied with teachings, alien beliefs.
   Ps. 106:35.
 b TG Sorcery.
 c HEB strike hands with, or make covenant with.
8a TG Apostasy of Israel; Idolatry.
 b TG Trust Not in the Arm of Flesh; Worship.
9a IE ordinary man.
 b 2 Ne. 12:9.
11a Ps. 46:10 (7–11); Isa. 28:5.

 b Isa. 52:6; Hosea 2:16 (14–23); Zech. 9:16.
12a TG Day of the Lord.
 b TG Pride.
 c Job 40:11.
13a Ezek. 31:3.
16a The Greek (Septuagint) version has one phrase that the Hebrew does not, and one phrase that the Greek does not; but 2 Ne. 12:16 has both. Ps. 48:7; Ezek. 27:25.

17a TG Haughtiness.
18a TG Idolatry.
19a Rev. 6:15.
 b TG Courage; Fearful.
20a HEB cast away.
22a IE Cease depending on mortal man; he is of little power compared to God.
   Moses 1:10.
 b TG Trust Not in the Arm of Flesh.
3 1a 2 Ne. 13:1 (1–26).
 b Lev. 26:32 (26–33).
 c Lam. 1:11.

war, the judge, and the prophet, and the prudent, and the *a*ancient,

3 The captain of fifty, and the honourable man, and the counsellor, and *a*the cunning artificer, and the *b*eloquent orator.

4 And I will give *a*children *to be* their princes, and babes shall rule over them.

5 And the people shall be oppressed, every one by another, and every one by his neighbour: the child shall behave himself proudly against the *a*ancient, and the base against the honourable.

6 When a man shall take hold of his brother of the house of his father, *saying,* Thou hast clothing, be thou our ruler, and *let* this *a*ruin *be* under thy hand:

7 In that day shall he swear, saying, I will not be *a*an healer; for in my house *is* neither bread nor clothing: make me not a ruler of the people.

8 For *a*Jerusalem is ruined, and Judah is *b*fallen: because their tongue and their doings *are* against the LORD, to provoke the eyes of his glory.

9 ¶ The shew of their countenance doth witness against them; and they declare their *a*sin as *b*Sodom, they hide *it* not. Woe unto their soul! for they have rewarded evil unto themselves.

10 Say ye to the *a*righteous, that *it*

shall be well *with him:* for they shall *b*eat the fruit of their doings.

11 Woe unto the *a*wicked! *it shall be* ill *with him:* for *b*the reward of his hands shall be given him.

12 ¶ As *for* my people, children *are* their oppressors, and *a*women rule over them. O my people, they which *b*lead thee cause *thee* to err, and destroy the way of thy paths.

13 The LORD standeth up to *a*plead, and standeth to judge the people.

14 The LORD will enter into *a*judgment with the *b*ancients of his people, and the *c*princes thereof: for ye have *d*eaten up the vineyard; the *e*spoil of the *f*poor *is* in your houses.

15 What mean ye *that* ye *a*beat my people to pieces, and grind the faces of the poor? saith the Lord GOD of hosts.

16 ¶ Moreover the LORD saith, Because the *a*daughters of Zion are *b*haughty, and *c*walk with stretched forth necks and *d*wanton eyes, walking and *e*mincing *as* they go, and making a tinkling with their feet:

17 Therefore the Lord will smite with a scab the crown of the head of the daughters of Zion, and the LORD will *a*discover their secret parts.

18 In that day the Lord will take away the bravery of *their* tinkling ornaments *about their feet,* and *their* *a*cauls, and *their* *b*round tires like the moon,

---

2*a* OR elder (also v. 5).
3*a* OR the wise man of magic arts.
  b HEB skillful enchanter.
4*a* Eccl. 10:16.
5*a* Deut. 28:50 (49–51);
    Lam. 4:16 (16–17).
6*a* 2 Ne. 13:6.
7*a* HEB a binder up (of a wound); i.e., I cannot solve your problems.
8*a* Micah 3:12.
  b Lam. 1:3 (1–3).
9*a* Gen. 19:5.
    TG Apostasy of Israel.
  b Gen. 13:10 (10–13);
    Deut. 32:32.
10*a* Eccl. 8:12.
    TG Righteousness.
  b Ps. 128:2.

11*a* Ps. 11:6.
  b IE the recompense of his deeds shall be done to him.
12*a* Isa. 3:16–4:1.
  b Isa. 1:13.
13*a* HEB contend.
    Micah 6:2.
14*a* TG Jesus Christ, Judge.
  b HEB elders.
  c HEB rulers or leaders.
  d HEB consumed or burned.
  e IE embezzled gain.
  f Ezek. 22:12 (6–13);
    Amos 3:10;
    Alma 4:12 (12–13).
15*a* Amos 2:6–7; 4:1;
    D&C 52:40.
16*a* TG Modesty.

  b TG Haughtiness; Vanity.
  c TG Walking in Darkness.
  d TG Carnal Mind.
  e IE walking with short, rapid steps in an affected manner.
17*a* HEB expose; idiom meaning "put them to shame."
18*a* Possibly hairnets. Authorities do not always agree on the nature of the female ornaments listed in vv. 18–23.
  b IE ornaments shaped like a crescent moon.

19 The chains, and the bracelets, and the ^amufflers,

20 The bonnets, and the ornaments of the legs, and the headbands, and the tablets, and the earrings,

21 The rings, and nose jewels,

22 The ^achangeable suits of ^bapparel, and the mantles, and the wimples, and the crisping pins,

23 The ^aglasses, and the fine linen, and the hoods, and the veils.

24 And it shall come to pass, *that* instead of sweet smell there shall be stink; and instead of a girdle ^aa rent; and instead of well set hair ^bbaldness; and instead of ^ca stomacher a girding of sackcloth; *and* ^dburning instead of ^ebeauty.

25 Thy ^amen shall fall by the sword, and thy mighty in the war.

26 And her ^agates shall ^blament and ^cmourn; and she *being* ^ddesolate shall sit upon the ^eground.

CHAPTER 4

Zion and her daughters will be redeemed and cleansed in the millennial day— Compare 2 Nephi 14.

AND in that day ^aseven women shall take hold of one ^bman, saying, We will eat our own bread, and wear our own apparel: only let us be called by thy ^cname, to take away our ^dreproach.

2 In that day shall the ^abranch of the LORD be ^bbeautiful and glorious, and the ^cfruit of the earth *shall be* excellent and comely for them that are ^descaped of Israel.

3 And it shall come to pass, *that* he that is ^aleft in ^bZion, and *he that* remaineth in ^cJerusalem, shall be called holy, *even* every one that is ^dwritten among the living in Jerusalem:

4 ^aWhen the Lord shall have ^bwashed away the filth of the daughters of Zion, and shall have ^cpurged the blood of Jerusalem from the midst thereof by the spirit of judgment, and by the spirit of ^dburning.

5 And the LORD will create upon every dwelling place of mount ^aZion, and upon her assemblies, a ^bcloud and smoke by day, and the shining of a flaming ^cfire by night: for upon all the glory *shall be* a defence.

6 And there shall be a tabernacle for a shadow in the daytime from the heat, and for a place of ^arefuge, and for a covert from storm and from rain.

CHAPTER 5

The Lord's vineyard (Israel) will become desolate, and His people will be scattered—Woes will come upon them in their apostate and scattered state— The Lord will lift an ensign and gather Israel—Compare 2 Nephi 15.

19*a* HEB veils.
22*a* HEB resplendent garments.
  b TG Apparel.
23*a* OR transparent garments.
24*a* HEB rags.
  b Isa. 15:2;
    Ezek. 7:18 (18–19);
    Amos 8:10.
  c OR a robe.
  d OR branding (a mark of slavery).
  e TG Beauty.
25*a* Isa. 4:1;
    Amos 4:10.
26*a* Lam. 2:9 (8–10).
  b Lam. 2:8.
  c Lam. 1:4 (4–6).
  d IE Jerusalem shall be emptied, cleaned out.
  e Lam. 2:10.

4 1*a* IE because of scarcity of men due to wars. See Isa. 3:25.
  b Isa. 3:25 (24–25).
  c TG Marriage, Marry.
  d IE the stigma of being unmarried and childless.
    TG Reproach.
2*a* Jer. 23:5 (5–6);
    2 Ne. 3:5;
    Jacob 2:25.
  b TG Beauty.
  c IE the earth will be renewed, and will be productive, prosperous, and beautiful.
  d Isa. 10:20;
    D&C 133:12 (11–13).
3*a* TG Israel, Restoration of.
  b TG Zion.

  c TG Jerusalem.
  d IE those saved by approval of the Messiah.
    TG Record Keeping.
4*a* IE When the Lord has cleansed the earth (v. 4), He will set up His dwelling and His protective presence here (vv. 5–6).
  b Mal. 3:2.
  c TG Millennium, Preparing a People for.
  d TG World, End of.
5*a* TG Zion.
  b Deut. 1:33.
    TG Protection, Divine.
  c TG God, Presence of.
6*a* D&C 45:66 (66–72).
    TG Refuge.

^aNow will I ^bsing to my wellbeloved a song of my beloved touching his ^cvineyard. My wellbeloved hath a vineyard ^din a very fruitful hill:

2 And he fenced it, and gathered out the stones thereof, and planted it with the choicest vine, and built a tower in the midst of it, and also made a winepress therein: and he looked that it should bring forth grapes, and it brought forth wild grapes.

3 And now, O inhabitants of Jerusalem, and men of Judah, judge, I pray you, betwixt me and my vineyard.

4 What could have been done more to my vineyard, that I have not done in it? wherefore, when I looked that it should bring forth grapes, brought it forth ^awild grapes?

5 And now go to; I will tell you what I will do to my ^avineyard: I will ^btake away the hedge thereof, and it shall be eaten up; *and* break down the ^cwall thereof, and it shall be trodden down:

6 And I will lay it waste: it shall not be pruned, nor digged; but there shall come up briers and thorns: I will also command the clouds that they rain no rain upon it.

7 For the ^avineyard of the Lord of hosts *is* the house of Israel, and the men of Judah his pleasant plant: and he looked for ^bjudgment, but behold oppression; for righteousness, but behold ^ca cry.

8 ¶ Woe unto them that ^ajoin ^bhouse to house, *that* lay field to field, till *there be* no place, that they may ^cbe placed alone in the midst of the earth!

9 In mine ears *said* the Lord of hosts, Of a truth many houses shall be desolate, *even* great and fair, without inhabitant.

10 Yea, ten acres of vineyard shall yield one ^abath, and the seed of an homer shall yield an ephah.

11 ¶ Woe unto them that rise up early in the morning, *that* they may follow strong drink; that continue until night, *till* ^awine inflame them!

12 And the harp, and the ^aviol, the ^btabret, and pipe, and wine, are in their feasts: but they ^cregard not the ^dwork of the Lord, neither consider the operation of his hands.

13 ¶ Therefore my people are gone into ^acaptivity, because *they have* no ^bknowledge: and their honourable men *are* famished, and their multitude dried up with thirst.

14 Therefore hell hath enlarged herself, and opened her mouth without measure: and their glory, and their multitude, and their ^apomp, and he that rejoiceth, shall descend into it.

15 And the mean man shall be brought down, and the mighty man shall be humbled, and the eyes of the ^alofty shall be humbled:

16 But the Lord of hosts shall be exalted in ^ajudgment, and God that is ^bholy shall be sanctified in righteousness.

17 Then shall the lambs feed after their manner, and the waste places of the fat ones shall strangers eat.

18 Woe unto them that ^adraw

---

5 1a 2 Ne. 15:1 (1–30).
  b IE The prophet composes a song or poetic parable of a vineyard, showing God's mercy and Israel's unresponsiveness.
  c D&C 101:44 (43–58).
  d IE in Israel.
4a TG Apostasy of Israel.
5a Matt. 21:43 (33–44).
  b D&C 24:19.
  c Prov. 24:31;
    Lam. 2:7 (6–7).

7a TG Vineyard of the Lord.
  b OR justice.
  c IE a riotous or raucous outcry.
8a TG Covet.
  b Micah 2:2.
  c IE be left to dwell alone. The wealthy landowners absorb the small farms of the poor.
10a Ezek. 45:11.
11a TG Drunkenness.
12a HEB lyre.

  b HEB drums.
  c TG Rebellion.
  d Ps. 28:5 (4–5).
13a TG Bondage, Spiritual.
  b TG God, Knowledge about;
    Knowledge.
14a HEB noise, or uproar.
15a OR haughty.
16a TG Jesus Christ, Judge.
  b Lev. 19:2;
    Josh. 24:19.
18a HEB entice, or pull.

iniquity with cords of [b]vanity, and sin [c]as it were with a cart rope:

19 That say, [a]Let him make [b]speed, *and* [c]hasten his work, that we may [d]see *it:* and let the counsel of the Holy One of Israel draw nigh and come, that we may know *it!*

20 ¶ Woe unto them that call [a]evil [b]good, and good evil; that put [c]darkness for [d]light, and light for darkness; that put bitter for sweet, and sweet for bitter!

21 Woe unto *them that are* [a]wise in their own [b]eyes, and [c]prudent in their own sight!

22 Woe unto *them that are* mighty to [a]drink [b]wine, and men of strength to mingle strong drink:

23 Which [a]justify the [b]wicked for reward, and [c]take away the righteousness of the righteous from him!

24 Therefore as the fire devoureth the [a]stubble, and the flame consumeth the chaff, *so* their [b]root shall be as rottenness, and their blossom shall go up as dust: because they have cast away the law of the LORD of hosts, and despised the word of the Holy One of Israel.

25 Therefore is the [a]anger of the LORD kindled against his people, and he hath [b]stretched forth his hand against them, and hath smitten them: and the hills did tremble, and their carcases *were* torn in the midst of the streets. For all this his anger is not turned away, but his hand *is* stretched out still.

26 ¶ And he will lift up an [a]ensign to the nations from far, and will [b]hiss unto them from the [c]end of the earth: and, behold, they shall [d]come with speed swiftly:

27 None shall be weary nor stumble among them; none shall slumber nor sleep; neither shall the girdle of their loins be loosed, nor the latchet of their shoes be broken:

28 Whose arrows *are* sharp, and all their bows bent, their horses' hoofs shall be counted like flint, and their wheels like a whirlwind:

29 Their roaring *shall be* like a lion, they shall roar like young [a]lions: yea, they shall roar, and lay hold of the [b]prey, and shall carry *it* away safe, and none shall deliver *it.*

30 And in that day they shall roar against them like the roaring of the sea: and if *one* look unto the land, behold darkness *and* sorrow, and the [a]light is [b]darkened in the heavens thereof.

CHAPTER 6

Isaiah sees the Lord—His sins are forgiven—He is called to prophesy—He prophesies of the Jews' rejection of Christ's teachings—A remnant will return—Compare 2 Nephi 16.

[a]IN the year that king Uzziah died I [b]saw also the [c]Lord sitting upon a [d]throne, high and lifted up, and [e]his train filled the temple.

2 Above it stood the [a]seraphims:

---

18 *b* TG Vanity.
  c IE they are tied to their sins like beasts to their burdens.
19 *a* IE They will not believe in the Messiah until they see Him.
  b Amos 5:18.
  c 2 Pet. 3:4 (3–4).
  d TG Sign Seekers.
20 *a* TG Evil.
  b TG Discernment, Spiritual; God, the Standard of Righteousness.
  c TG Darkness, Spiritual.
  d TG Light [noun].
21 *a* TG Wisdom.
  b TG Pride.

  c TG Prudence.
22 *a* TG Drunkenness.
  b TG Word of Wisdom.
23 *a* TG Injustice.
  b Prov. 17:15.
  c IE deprive him of his legal rights.
24 *a* Isa. 47:14.
  b Job 18:16.
25 *a* TG God, Indignation of.
  b TG God, Access to.
26 *a* TG Ensign; Millennium, Preparing a People for.
  b OR whistle; i.e., signal for the gathering. Isa. 7:18; 2 Ne. 29:2 (1–3).
  c Deut. 28:49.

  d TG Israel, Gathering of.
29 *a* TG Israel, Deliverance of.
  b 3 Ne. 21:12 (12–13).
30 *a* TG World, End of.
  b TG Darkness, Spiritual.
6 1 *a* 2 Ne. 16:1 (1–13).
  b TG Jesus Christ, Appearances, Antemortal.
  c TG Jesus Christ, Jehovah.
  d D&C 137:3. TG Kingdom of God, in Heaven.
  e IE the hem of His garment, or the skirts thereof.
2 *a* TG Cherubim; Symbolism.

each one had six wings; with twain he covered his face, and with twain he covered his feet, and with twain he did fly.

3 And one cried unto another, and said, Holy, holy, holy, *is* the [a]LORD of hosts: the whole earth *is* full of his [b]glory.

4 And the [a]posts of the door moved at the voice of him that cried, and the house was filled with [b]smoke.

5 ¶ Then said I, Woe *is* me! for I am [a]undone; because I *am* a man of [b]unclean lips, and I dwell in the midst of a people of unclean lips: for mine eyes have [c]seen the [d]King, the LORD of hosts.

6 Then flew one of the seraphims unto me, having a live [a]coal in his hand, *which* he had taken with the tongs from off the altar:

7 And he laid *it* upon my [a]mouth, and said, Lo, this hath touched thy lips; and thine iniquity is [b]taken away, and thy sin purged.

8 Also I heard the voice of the Lord, saying, Whom shall I [a]send, and who will go for us? Then said I, Here *am* I; [b]send me.

9 ¶ And he said, Go, and tell this people, [a]Hear ye indeed, but [b]understand not; and see ye indeed, but [c]perceive not.

10 Make the [a]heart of this people fat, and make their ears heavy, and [b]shut their eyes; lest they see with their eyes, and hear with their ears,

and understand with their heart, and convert, and be healed.

11 Then said I, Lord, [a]how long? And he answered, Until the cities be wasted without inhabitant, and the houses without man, and the land be utterly desolate,

12 And the LORD have removed men far away, and *there be* a great forsaking in the midst of the land.

13 ¶ But yet in it *shall be* a tenth, and [a]*it* shall return, and shall be eaten: as a teil tree, and as an oak, whose substance *is* in them, when they cast *their leaves:* so the holy seed *shall be* the [b]substance thereof.

CHAPTER 7

Ephraim and Syria wage war against Judah—Christ will be born of a virgin—Compare 2 Nephi 17.

[a]AND it came to pass in the days of Ahaz the son of Jotham, the son of Uzziah, king of Judah, *that* [b]Rezin the [c]king of Syria, and [d]Pekah the son of Remaliah, king of Israel, went up toward Jerusalem to war against it, but could not prevail against it.

2 And it was told the house of David, saying, Syria is confederate with [a]Ephraim. And his heart was moved, and the heart of his people, as the trees of the wood are moved with the wind.

3 Then said the LORD unto Isaiah, Go forth now to meet Ahaz, thou,

---

3a Ezek. 1:28 (9–11, 28);
   Rev. 4:8 (7–9).
 b TG Jesus Christ,
   Glory of.
4a HEB foundations of the
   thresholds trembled.
 b Ex. 19:18.
5a HEB cut off; i.e., he was
   overwhelmed by his
   consciousness of the
   sins of himself and his
   people.
 b TG Uncleanness.
 c TG God, Privilege
   of Seeing;
   Testimony.
 d Matt. 2:2;
   JST Matt. 3:2 (Matt. 2:2
   note a).
6a IE a symbol of

cleansing.
7a Jer. 1:9.
 b TG Forgive.
8a TG Authority;
   Called of God;
   Priesthood, Keys of;
   Prophets, Mission of;
   Teaching with the
   Spirit.
 b TG Priesthood,
   Ordination.
9a Matt. 13:14–15;
   Acts 28:26–27.
 b Luke 8:10;
   2 Ne. 16:9.
 c TG Unbelief.
10a TG Hardheartedness.
 b TG Spiritual Blindness.
11a The prophet wonders
   how long men will

be so, and the Lord
answers: until mortal
man is no more.
13a 2 Ne. 16:13.
 b IE like a tree, though
   its leaves be scattered,
   life and potential
   to produce seed yet
   remain in it.
7 1a 2 Ne. 17:1 (1–25).
 b 2 Kgs. 15:37 (36–38);
   16:5 (1–6);
   Isa. 8:6; 9:11.
 c 2 Chr. 28:5 (1–6).
 d 2 Kgs. 15:27 (27–37).
2a IE All northern Israel
   was called by the name
   of Ephraim, the leading
   northern tribe.

and *Shear-jashub thy son, at the end of the *conduit of the upper pool *in the highway of the fuller's field;

4 And say unto him, *Take heed, and be quiet; fear not, neither be fainthearted for the two tails of these smoking firebrands, for the fierce anger of Rezin with Syria, and of the son of Remaliah.

5 Because Syria, Ephraim, and the son of Remaliah, have taken evil counsel against thee, saying,

6 Let us go up against Judah, and vex it, and let us *make a breach therein for us, and set a king in the midst of it, *even* the son of Tabeal:

7 Thus saith the Lord GOD, It shall not stand, neither shall it come to pass.

8 For the head of Syria *is* *Damascus, and the head of Damascus *is* Rezin; and within threescore and five years shall *Ephraim be broken, that it be not a people.

9 And the head of Ephraim *is* Samaria, and the head of Samaria *is* Remaliah's son. *If ye will not believe, surely ye shall not be established.

10 ¶ Moreover the LORD spake again unto Ahaz, saying,

11 Ask thee a sign of the LORD thy God; ask it either in the depth, or in the height above.

12 But Ahaz said, I will not ask, neither will I *tempt the LORD.

13 And he said, Hear ye now, O house of David; *Is it* a small thing for you to weary men, but will ye weary my God also?

14 Therefore the Lord himself shall give you a *sign; *Behold, a *virgin shall conceive, and bear a *son, and shall call his name *Immanuel.

15 *Butter and honey shall he eat, that he may know to refuse the evil, and choose the good.

16 For *before the child shall know to refuse the *evil, and choose the good, the land that thou abhorrest shall be forsaken of both her kings.

17 ¶ *The LORD shall bring upon thee, and upon thy people, and upon thy father's house, days that have not come, from the day that *Ephraim departed from *Judah; *even* the king of Assyria.

18 And it shall come to pass in that day, *that* the LORD shall *hiss *for the fly that *is* in the uttermost part of the rivers of Egypt, and for the bee that *is* in the land of Assyria.

19 And they shall come, and shall rest all of them in the desolate valleys, and in the holes of the rocks, and upon all thorns, and upon all bushes.

20 In the same day shall the Lord *shave with a razor that is hired, *namely*, by them beyond the river, by the king of Assyria, the head, and the hair of the feet: and it shall also consume the beard.

21 And it shall come to pass in that day, *that* *a man shall nourish a young cow, and two sheep;

22 And it shall come to pass, for the abundance of milk *that* they

---

3*a* HEB The remnant shall return.
Isa. 8:3, 18 (17–18).
  b HEB canal, or tunnel.
Isa. 22:11.
  c IE by way of the launderers' field near the stream below the pool of Siloam.
4*a* IE Don't be alarmed by the attack; those two kings have little fire left.
6*a* HEB divide it up.
8*a* Isa. 17:1 (1, 3).
  b TG Israel, Joseph, People of; Israel, Ten Lost Tribes of.

9*a* IE If you lack faith, you will not be saved.
TG Faith.
12*a* OR test, try.
TG Test.
14*a* TG Signs.
  b Matt. 1:23.
  c TG Jesus Christ, Birth of; Jesus Christ, Prophecies about.
  d TG Jesus Christ, Divine Sonship.
  e HEB With us is God.
TG Foreordination.
15*a* OR Curd and honey— the only foods available to the poor at times.
16*a* IE before he is mature.

Isa. 8:4.
  b TG Evil.
17*a* IE The immediate danger is the threat of Assyria.
  b TG Israel, Joseph, People of.
  c TG Israel, Judah, People of.
18*a* OR whistle; i.e., signal, summon.
Isa. 5:26.
  b IE for attacking forces.
20*a* IE the land will be depopulated by a foreign invader.
21*a* IE only a few self-sustaining survivors shall remain.

shall give he shall eat butter: for ^abutter and honey shall every one eat that is left in the land.

23 And it shall come to pass in that day, *that* every place shall be, where there were a thousand vines at a thousand ^asilverlings, it shall *even* be for briers and thorns.

24 With arrows and with bows shall *men* come thither; because all the land shall become briers and thorns.

25 And *on* all hills that shall be ^adigged with the mattock, there shall not come thither the fear of briers and thorns: but it shall be for the sending forth of oxen, and for the treading of ^blesser cattle.

CHAPTER 8

Christ will be as a stone of stumbling and a rock of offense—Seek the Lord, not muttering wizards—Turn to the law and to the testimony for guidance— Compare 2 Nephi 18.

MOREOVER the LORD said unto me, Take thee a great ^aroll, and ^bwrite in it with ^ca man's pen concerning ^dMaher-shalal-hash-baz.

2 And I took unto me faithful witnesses to record, Uriah the priest, and Zechariah the son of Jeberechiah.

3 And I went unto ^athe prophetess; and she conceived, and bare a son. Then said the LORD to me, Call his name ^bMaher-shalal-hash-baz.

4 For ^abefore the child shall ^bhave knowledge to cry, My father, and my mother, the riches of Damascus and the spoil of ^cSamaria shall be ^dtaken away before the king of Assyria.

5 ¶ The LORD spake also unto me again, saying,

6 Forasmuch as this people refuseth the waters of ^aShiloah that go softly, and rejoice in ^bRezin and Remaliah's son;

7 Now therefore, behold, the Lord bringeth up upon ^athem the ^bwaters of the river, strong and many, *even* the king of ^cAssyria, and all his glory: and he shall come up over all his channels, and go over all his banks:

8 And he shall ^apass through Judah; he shall overflow and go over, he shall reach *even* to the ^bneck; and the stretching out of his wings shall fill the breadth of thy land, O ^cImmanuel.

9 ¶ ^aAssociate yourselves, O ye people, and ye shall be broken in pieces; and give ear, all ye of far countries: gird yourselves, and ye shall be broken in pieces; gird yourselves, and ye shall be broken in pieces.

10 Take ^acounsel together, and it shall come to nought; speak the word, and it shall not stand: for ^bGod *is* with us.

11 ¶ For the LORD spake thus to me ^awith a strong hand, and instructed me that I should not walk in the way of this people, saying,

12 Say ye not, A ^aconfederacy, to all *them to* whom this people shall say, A confederacy; neither fear ye their fear, nor be afraid.

13 Sanctify the LORD of hosts

22a HEB curd and honey; i.e., typical nomad staples.
23a OR pieces of silver.
25a HEB hoed with the hoe.
　b HEB sheep, or goats.
8 1a 2 Ne. 18:1 (1–22).
　b TG Scriptures, Writing of.
　c HEB an engraving tool of a man.
　d HEB To speed to the spoil, he hasteneth the prey.
3a IE his wife.

Alma 32:23.
　b Isa. 7:3; 8:18 (17–18).
4a Isa. 7:16.
　b 2 Ne. 18:4.
　c TG Israel, Ten Lost Tribes of.
　d 2 Kgs. 15:29.
6a Neh. 3:15; John 9:7.
　b Isa. 7:1 (1–6).
7a IE upon northern Israel first.
　b Jer. 46:7 (7–8).
　c Isa. 10:12.
8a IE Assyria will

penetrate Judah also.
　b Isa. 30:28.
　c IE the land of the future birth of Immanuel.
9a IE Form alliances.
10a D&C 1:19; 3:7 (6–11).
　b IE Judah (land of Immanuel) will be spared.
Ps. 46:7.
11a IE in power.
12a IE Judah should not rely on secret plots with others for safety.

himself; and ^alet him *be* your fear, and *let* him *be* your dread.

14 And he shall be for a ^asanctuary; but for a ^bstone of ^cstumbling and for a ^drock of ^eoffence to both the houses of Israel, for a gin and for a ^fsnare to the inhabitants of Jerusalem.

15 And many among them shall stumble, and fall, and be broken, and be snared, and be taken.

16 ^aBind up the testimony, ^bseal the ^claw among my disciples.

17 And I will wait upon the LORD, that ^ahideth his ^bface from the house of Jacob, and I will look for him.

18 Behold, I and the children whom the LORD hath given me *are* for ^asigns and for wonders in Israel from the LORD of hosts, which dwelleth in mount Zion.

19 ¶ And when they shall say unto you, Seek unto them that have ^afamiliar spirits, and unto ^bwizards that peep, and that mutter: should not a people seek unto their God? ^cfor the living to the dead?

20 To the ^alaw and to the testimony: if ^bthey speak not according to this word, *it is* because *there is* no ^clight in them.

21 And ^athey shall pass through it, hardly bestead and hungry: and it shall come to pass, that when they shall be hungry, they shall fret

themselves, and ^bcurse their king and their God, and look upward.

22 And they shall look unto the earth; and behold trouble and ^adarkness, ^bdimness of anguish; and *they shall be* driven to darkness.

CHAPTER 9

Isaiah speaks about the Messiah— The people in darkness will see a great Light—Unto us a Child is born— He will be the Prince of Peace and reign on David's throne—Compare 2 Nephi 19.

^aNEVERTHELESS the dimness *shall not be* such as *was* in her vexation, ^bwhen at the first he lightly afflicted the land of ^cZebulun and the land of Naphtali, and afterward did more grievously afflict *her by* the way of the sea, beyond Jordan, in Galilee of the nations.

2 The people that walked in ^adarkness have seen a great ^blight: they that dwell in the land of the shadow of death, upon them hath the light shined.

3 Thou hast ^amultiplied the ^bnation, ^cand not increased the joy: they joy before thee according to the joy in harvest, *and* as *men* ^drejoice when they divide the spoil.

4 For thou hast broken the ^ayoke of his ^bburden, and the staff of his

13*a* IE be reverent and humble before God.
14*a* IE security for those who trust Him, but dismay and suffering for unbelievers. Ezek. 11:16 (15–21).
  b TG Cornerstone.
  c Matt. 21:44 (43–45); Luke 2:34; Rom. 9:32 (28–33).
  d TG Rock.
  e Matt. 11:6; 24:10. TG Offense.
  f Ps. 69:22.
16*a* D&C 109:46.
  b TG Seal.
  c HEB teachings or doctrine.
17*a* Deut. 32:20.
  b Isa. 54:8 (4–10).
18*a* IE The names of Isaiah and his sons mean

respectively: "Jehovah saves"; "He hastens the prey"; and "A remnant shall return." Isa. 7:3; 8:3. TG Symbolism.
19*a* TG Sorcery; Spirits, Evil or Unclean.
  b IE sorcerers, soothsayers. TG Superstitions.
  c OR on behalf of.
20*a* TG Scriptures, Value of.
  b IE the spiritualist mediums (also in vv. 21–22).
  c TG Light [noun].
21*a* IE Israel would be taken into captivity because they would not hearken.
  b TG Blaspheme.
22*a* TG Darkness, Spiritual.
  b HEB dark affliction.
9 1*a* 2 Ne. 19:1 (1–21).
  b Rabbinical

commentators relate this to the attacks by Assyria under Tiglath-pileser and Sargon II.
  c Matt. 4:15 (14–16).
2*a* The "dimness" and "darkness" were apostasy and captivity (Isa. 8:20–22); the "great light" is Christ (Isa. 9:6–7). TG Darkness, Spiritual.
  b TG Jesus Christ, Light of the World; Light [noun].
3*a* Isa. 26:15.
  b Abr. 2:9.
  c The word *not* should be removed. 2 Ne. 19:3 (2–7).
  d Ps. 119:162.
4*a* TG Bondage, Spiritual.
  b Isa. 10:27 (24–27).

shoulder, the *c*rod of his oppressor, as *d*in the day of *e*Midian.

5 *a*For every battle of the warrior *is* with confused noise, and garments rolled in blood; but *this* shall be with *b*burning *and* fuel of fire.

6 For unto us a *a*child is *b*born, unto us a *c*son is given: and the *d*government shall be upon his shoulder: and his name shall be called Wonderful, *e*Counsellor, The *f*mighty *g*God, The *h*everlasting Father, The Prince of *i*Peace.

7 Of the increase of *his* *a*government and peace *there shall be* no *b*end, upon the throne of *c*David, and upon his kingdom, to order it, and to establish it with judgment and with *d*justice from henceforth even for ever. The *e*zeal of the LORD of hosts will perform this.

8 ¶ The Lord sent a word into Jacob, and it hath lighted upon *d*Israel.

9 And all the people shall know, *even* Ephraim and the inhabitant of Samaria, that say in the *a*pride and stoutness of heart,

10 The bricks are fallen down, but we will build with hewn stones: the sycomores are cut down, but we will change *them into* cedars.

11 Therefore the LORD shall set up the adversaries of *a*Rezin against him, and join his enemies together;

12 The Syrians *a*before, and the Philistines *b*behind; and they shall devour Israel with open mouth. For all this his *c*anger is not turned away, but *d*his hand *is* *e*stretched out still.

13 ¶ For the people *a*turneth not unto him that smiteth them, neither do they *b*seek the LORD of hosts.

14 Therefore the LORD will cut off from Israel head and tail, branch and rush, in one day.

15 The *a*ancient and honourable, he *is* the head; and the *b*prophet that teacheth lies, he *is* the tail.

16 For the *a*leaders of this people cause *them* to err; and *they that are* led of them *are* *b*destroyed.

17 Therefore the Lord shall have no joy in their young men, neither shall have mercy on their fatherless and widows: for every one *is* an *a*hypocrite and an evildoer, and every mouth *b*speaketh folly. For all this his anger is not turned away, but his hand *is* stretched out still.

18 ¶ For wickedness burneth as the fire: it shall devour the briers and *a*thorns, and shall kindle in the *b*thickets of the forest, and they shall mount up *like* the lifting up of smoke.

19 Through the wrath of the LORD of hosts is the land darkened, and

---

4*c* Isa. 14:5.
  d HEB was broken in the day of Midian.
  e Judg. 7:23 (19–23); Isa. 10:26.
5*a* HEB When the whole battle . . . was with confused noise, and . . . blood.
  b This "burning" is to be the cleansing of the earth by fire prior to the setting up of the messianic kingdom. 3 Ne. 25:1; D&C 64:23 (23–24); JS—H 1:37.
6*a* TG Jesus Christ, Prophecies about.
  b TG God, Manifestations of; Jesus Christ, Birth of.
  c TG Jesus Christ, Divine Sonship.

d TG Governments; Jesus Christ, Authority of; Jesus Christ, Millennial Reign; Jesus Christ, Mission of.
  e TG Counselor.
  f TG Jesus Christ, Power of.
  g Mosiah 7:27 (26–27).
  h TG Immortality.
  i TG Peace; Peace of God.
7*a* TG Governments; Kingdom of God, on Earth.
  b Luke 1:33 (32–33).
  c TG Jesus Christ, Davidic Descent of.
  d TG God, Justice of; Justice.
  e TG Zeal.
8*a* IE The prophetic message that follows (vv. 8–21) was a

warning to the northern ten tribes, called Israel.
9*a* 2 Ne. 9:28 (28–29).
11*a* Isa. 7:1.
12*a* IE on the east.
  b IE on the west.
  c Jer. 4:8.
  d IE In spite of all, the Lord is available if they will turn to Him (also vv. 17, 21).
  e TG God, Access to.
13*a* TG Rebellion.
  b Hosea 7:10.
15*a* OR elder and man of rank. 2 Ne. 19:15.
  b TG False Prophets.
16*a* TG Leadership.
  b Isa. 1:31.
17*a* TG Hypocrisy.
  b Prov. 26:25.
18*a* Isa. 10:17.
  b Isa. 10:34.

the people shall be as the fuel of the fire: no man shall ªspare his ᵇbrother.

20 And he shall snatch on the right hand, and be hungry; and he shall eat on the left hand, and they shall not be satisfied: they shall ªeat every man the ᵇflesh of his own arm:

21 Manasseh, Ephraim; and Ephraim, Manasseh: *and* they together *shall be* against Judah. For all this his anger is not turned away, but his hand *is* stretched out still.

CHAPTER 10

The destruction of Assyria is a type of the destruction of the wicked at the Second Coming—Few people will be left after the Lord comes again—The remnant of Jacob will return in that day—Compare 2 Nephi 20.

ªWOE unto them that decree ᵇunrighteous decrees, and that write grievousness *which* they have prescribed;

2 To turn aside the needy from ªjudgment, and to take away the right from the ᵇpoor of my people, that widows may be their prey, and *that* they may rob the fatherless!

3 And what will ye do in the day of ªvisitation, and in the desolation *which* shall come from far? to whom will ye flee for help? and where will ye leave your glory?

4 Without me they shall bow down under the prisoners, and they shall fall under the slain. For all this his anger is not turned away, but his hand *is* stretched out still.

5 ¶ O ªAssyrian, the rod of mine anger, and the staff in their hand is mine indignation.

6 I will send him against an ªhypocritical nation, and against the peo-

ple of my wrath will I give him a charge, to take the spoil, and to take the prey, and to tread them down like the mire of the streets.

7 Howbeit he meaneth not so, neither ªdoth his heart think so; but *it is* in his heart to destroy and cut off nations not a few.

8 For he saith, *Are* not my princes altogether kings?

9 *Is* not Calno as Carchemish? *is* not Hamath as Arpad? *is* not Samaria as Damascus?

10 As my hand hath found the kingdoms of the idols, and whose graven images did excel them of Jerusalem and of Samaria;

11 Shall I not, as I have done unto Samaria and her idols, so do to Jerusalem and her idols?

12 Wherefore it shall come to pass, *that* when the Lord hath performed his whole work upon mount Zion and on Jerusalem, I will ªpunish ᵇthe fruit of the stout heart of the king of ᶜAssyria, and the glory of his high looks.

13 For he saith, By the ªstrength of my hand I have done *it,* and by my wisdom; for I am prudent: and I have removed the bounds of the people, and have robbed their treasures, and I have put down the inhabitants like a valiant *man:*

14 And my hand hath found as a nest the riches of the people: and as one gathereth eggs *that are* left, have I gathered all the earth; and there was none that moved the wing, or opened the mouth, or peeped.

15 ªShall the axe ᵇboast itself against him that heweth therewith? or shall the saw magnify itself against him that ᶜshaketh it? as if the rod should shake *itself* against them

---

19a Mosiah 9:2;
  JS—M 1:30.
  b Ezek. 38:21;
  Micah 7:2 (2, 6).
20a Hag. 1:6.
  b Jer. 19:9.
10 1a 2 Ne. 20:1 (1–34).
  b TG Injustice.
2a OR justice.
  TG Judgment.
  b Mosiah 4:16 (16–18);

D&C 38:16.
3a IE punishment.
  Hosea 9:7;
  Luke 19:44.
5a OR Assyria is the rod of
  my anger, and my wrath
  is a staff in their hand.
  Ezek. 31:3.
6a TG Hypocrisy.
7a HEB did his heart
  intend it thus.

12a 2 Kgs. 19:35 (35–37).
  b IE the proud boasting.
  c Isa. 8:7.
13a 2 Kgs. 19:23.
15a All the metaphors in
  this verse ask the same
  question: Can man
  (e.g., the Assyrian king)
  prosper against God?
  b TG Boast.
  c HEB wields, moves.

that lift it up, *or* as if the staff should lift up *itself, as if it were* no wood.

16 Therefore shall the Lord, the Lord of hosts, send among his ^afat ones leanness; and under ^bhis glory he shall kindle a burning like the burning of a fire.

17 And the light of Israel shall be for a fire, and his Holy One for a flame: and it shall burn and devour his ^athorns and his briers in one day;

18 And shall consume the glory of his forest, and of his fruitful field, both ^asoul and body: and they shall be as when a standardbearer fainteth.

19 And the rest of the trees of his forest shall be few, that a child may write them.

20 ¶ And it shall come to pass in ^athat day, *that* the remnant of Israel, and such as are ^bescaped of the house of Jacob, shall no more again ^cstay upon him that smote them; but shall stay upon the LORD, the Holy One of Israel, in truth.

21 The ^aremnant shall ^breturn, *even* the remnant of Jacob, unto the mighty God.

22 For though thy people Israel be as the ^asand of the sea, *yet* a remnant of them shall ^breturn: ^cthe ^dconsumption ^edecreed shall overflow with righteousness.

23 For the Lord GOD of hosts shall ^amake a consumption, even determined, in the midst of all the land.

24 ¶ Therefore thus saith the Lord GOD of hosts, O my people that dwellest in Zion, be not afraid of the Assyrian: he shall ^asmite thee with a rod, and shall lift up his staff against thee, after the manner of ^bEgypt.

25 For yet a very little ^awhile, and the ^bindignation shall cease, and mine anger in their destruction.

26 And the LORD of hosts shall stir up a scourge for him according to the slaughter of ^aMidian at the rock of ^bOreb: and *as* his ^crod *was* upon the sea, so shall he lift it up after the manner of ^dEgypt.

27 And it shall come to pass in that day, *that* his ^aburden shall be taken away from off thy shoulder, and his yoke from off thy neck, and the ^byoke shall be destroyed because of the ^canointing.

28 ^aHe is come to Aiath, he is passed to Migron; at Michmash he hath laid up his carriages:

29 They are gone over the passage: they have taken up their lodging at Geba; Ramah is afraid; Gibeah of Saul is fled.

30 Lift up thy voice, O daughter of Gallim: cause it to be heard unto Laish, O poor Anathoth.

31 Madmenah is removed; the inhabitants of Gebim gather themselves to flee.

32 As yet shall he remain at Nob that day: he shall shake his hand *against* the mount of the daughter of Zion, the hill of Jerusalem.

33 Behold, the Lord, the LORD of hosts, shall lop the bough with ^aterror: and the high ones of stature

16a Ezek. 34:16;
   2 Ne. 15:17.
 b IE of the king of Assyria
   (also vv. 17–19).
17a Isa. 9:18.
18a IE Assyria will vanish
   completely.
20a This prophecy extends
   to the latter days in the
   succeeding verse.
 b Isa. 4:2.
 c OR lean, rely upon.
   2 Kgs. 16:7.
21a TG Israel, Remnant of.
 b 2 Chr. 30:6 (1–7);
   1 Ne. 10:3.
22a Rom. 9:27 (27–28).

 b TG Israel, Gathering of.
 c IE even when
   punishment comes,
   mercy is available.
 d TG World, End of.
 e Matt. 24:34;
   D&C 1:7.
23a IE cause the decreed
   destruction.
24a Isa. 30:31.
 b IE as the Egyptians did
   in earlier times.
25a Isa. 54:7.
 b Dan. 11:36;
   2 Ne. 20:25.
26a Isa. 9:4.
 b Judg. 7:25 (19–25).

 c Ex. 14:26 (26–27).
 d Ex. 14:27 (16–27).
27a Isa. 9:4 (3–4).
 b TG Bondage, Physical.
 c TG Jesus Christ,
   Messiah.
28a Progress of the
   Assyrian armies toward
   Jerusalem is traced;
   then (vv. 33–34) the
   Lord's action against
   them is figuratively
   described.
33a See Isa. 36–37 or
   2 Kgs. 18:13–19:37 for
   a fulfillment of this
   prophecy.

shall be hewn down, and the *b*haughty shall be humbled.

34 And he shall cut down the *a*thickets of the forest with iron, and Lebanon shall fall *b*by a mighty one.

CHAPTER 11

The stem of Jesse (Christ) will judge in righteousness—The knowledge about God will cover the earth in the Millennium—The Lord will raise an ensign and gather Israel—Compare 2 Nephi 21.

*a*AND there shall come forth a *b*rod out of the *c*stem of *d*Jesse, and a *e*Branch shall grow out of his roots:

2 And the *a*spirit of the LORD shall rest upon him, the spirit of *b*wisdom and *c*understanding, the spirit of *d*counsel and might, the spirit of knowledge and of the fear of the LORD;

3 And shall make him of quick understanding in the fear of the LORD: and he shall not *a*judge *b*after the sight of his eyes, neither reprove after the hearing of his ears:

4 But with righteousness shall *a*he *b*judge the poor, and *c*reprove with equity for the *d*meek of the earth: and he shall *e*smite the earth with the rod of his mouth, and with the

*f*breath of his lips shall he *g*slay the wicked.

5 And righteousness shall be the *a*girdle of his loins, and faithfulness the girdle of his *b*reins.

6 The *a*wolf also shall dwell with the lamb, and the leopard shall lie down with the kid; and the calf and the young lion and the fatling together; and a little child shall lead them.

7 And the cow and the bear shall feed; their young ones shall lie down together: and the lion shall eat straw like the ox.

8 And the sucking child shall play on the hole of *a*the asp, and the weaned child shall put his hand on the *b*cockatrice' den.

9 They shall not *a*hurt nor *b*destroy in all my holy *c*mountain: for the *d*earth shall be full of the *e*knowledge of the LORD, as the waters cover the sea.

10 ¶ And in *a*that day there shall be a *b*root of Jesse, which shall stand for an *c*ensign of the people; *d*to it shall the *e*Gentiles seek: and his *f*rest shall be glorious.

11 And it shall come to pass in that day, *that* the Lord shall set his hand again the *a*second time to *b*recover

---

33*b* TG Haughtiness.
34*a* Isa. 9:18.
  b Isa. 37:36.
11 1*a* 2 Ne. 21:1 (1–16);
    JS—H 1:40.
  b Ps. 110:2;
    D&C 113:3 (1–6).
  c D&C 113:1 (1–2).
    TG Jesus Christ,
    Messiah; Jesus Christ,
    Prophecies about.
  d Jesse was the father
    of David; reference
    is made to the royal
    Davidic genealogical
    line in which Jesus is
    eventually born.
    Micah 5:2;
    Heb. 7:14.
    TG Jesus Christ,
    Davidic Descent of.
  e Jer. 23:5.
2*a* TG God, Spirit of;
    Holy Ghost, Mission of.
  b TG Wisdom.
  c TG Understanding.

  d TG Counsel.
3*a* TG Jesus Christ,
    Millennial Reign.
  b IE by appearances and
    by hearsay.
    John 7:24.
    TG Discernment,
    Spiritual; Sight.
4*a* 2 Ne. 30:9 (8–15).
  b TG Jesus Christ,
    Authority of;
    Jesus Christ, Judge.
  c HEB decide with equity.
    TG Reproof.
  d TG Meek.
  e Ps. 2:9; 2 Ne. 7:8.
  f Isa. 30:28.
  g Ps. 139:19 (17–24);
    2 Ne. 30:10 (10–11);
    D&C 63:33 (29–37).
5*a* Ex. 12:11;
    Isa. 59:17 (16–17);
    Eph. 6:14;
    D&C 27:16 (16–17).
  b OR waist.
6*a* TG Nature, Earth.

8*a* OR the horned viper.
  b IE another venomous
    serpent.
9*a* Isa. 60:18;
    D&C 101:26.
  b TG Peace.
  c TG Zion.
  d Hab. 2:14.
    TG Earth, Renewal of.
  e TG God, Knowledge
    about; Knowledge;
    Millennium.
10*a* IE the latter days.
    JS—H 1:40.
  b Rev. 5:5;
    D&C 113:6 (5–6).
  c TG Ensign.
  d OR unto him.
  e TG Gentiles;
    Israel, Mission of.
  f TG Rest.
11*a* D&C 137:6.
  b TG Israel, Gathering of;
    Israel, Restoration of;
    Restoration of the
    Gospel.

the ^cremnant of his people, which shall be left, from Assyria, and from Egypt, and from Pathros, and from Cush, and from Elam, and from Shinar, and from Hamath, and from the ^dislands of the sea.

12 And he shall set up an ^aensign for the nations, and shall assemble the outcasts of Israel, and gather together the dispersed of Judah from the four corners of the earth.

13 The envy also of Ephraim shall depart, and the adversaries of Judah shall be cut off: Ephraim shall not ^aenvy ^bJudah, and Judah shall not vex Ephraim.

14 But they shall ^afly upon the ^bshoulders of the Philistines toward the west; ^cthey shall spoil them of the east together: they shall lay their hand upon Edom and Moab; and the children of Ammon shall obey them.

15 And the LORD shall utterly ^adestroy the tongue of the ^bEgyptian sea; and with his mighty wind shall he shake his hand over the river, and shall smite it in the seven streams, and make *men* go over dryshod.

16 And there shall be ^aan ^bhighway for the remnant of his people, which shall be left, from Assyria; like as it was to Israel in the day that he came up out of the land of Egypt.

CHAPTER 12

In the millennial day, all men will praise the Lord—He will dwell among them—Compare 2 Nephi 22.

^aAND ^bin that day thou shalt say, ^cO LORD, I will praise thee: though thou wast angry with me, thine anger is turned away, and thou comfortedst me.

2 Behold, God *is* my salvation; I will trust, and not be afraid: for the LORD ^aJEHOVAH *is* my ^bstrength and *my* song; he also is become my ^csalvation.

3 Therefore with ^ajoy shall ye draw water out of the wells of salvation.

4 And in that day shall ye say, ^aPraise the LORD, ^bcall upon his name, declare his doings among the people, make mention that his name is exalted.

5 ^aSing unto the LORD; for he hath done excellent things: this *is* known in all the earth.

6 Cry out and shout, thou ^ainhabitant of Zion: for great *is* the Holy One of Israel in the ^bmidst of thee.

CHAPTER 13

The destruction of Babylon is a type of the destruction at the Second Coming—It will be a day of wrath and vengeance—Babylon (the world) will fall forever—Compare 2 Nephi 23.

11c TG Israel, Ten Lost Tribes of.
  d 2 Ne. 10:20 (19–22); D&C 133:8.
12a TG Dispensations; Ensign; Kingdom of God, on Earth; Mission of Latter-day Saints.
13a The tribes led by Judah and Ephraim were historically adversaries (after events of 1 Kgs. 12:16–20). In the latter days this enmity will be healed.
  TG Envy.
  b TG Israel, Judah, People of.
14a HEB fly down on the shoulder; i.e., attack the western slopes

that were Philistine territory.
  b 2 Ne. 10:8 (8–9).
  c HEB together (i.e., Ephraim and Judah) they shall spoil.
15a Zech. 10:11.
  b IE facilitate the return, as in the days of Moses.
16a HEB a way, or road. See D&C 133:23–27.
  b Ex. 14:29; Isa. 19:23; 35:8 (8–10); 2 Ne. 21:16; D&C 133:27.
12 1a 2 Ne. 22:1 (1–6).
  b IE in the time of the events of the preceding chapter.
  c IE The people who are gathered will sing this song of praise.

2a This is one of the four times only that the name Jehovah is written out in full in the King James English Bible. See Ex. 6:3; Ps. 83:18; Isa. 26:4. In all other places LORD is used instead.
  TG Jesus Christ, Jehovah.
  b TG Priesthood, Power of; Strength.
  c TG Salvation.
3a TG Joy.
4a TG Thanksgiving.
  b OR proclaim.
5a TG Singing.
6a D&C 68:26.
  b Deut. 23:14; Ps. 46:5.

^aTHE ^bburden of ^cBabylon, which Isaiah the son of Amoz did see.

2 Lift ye up a ^abanner upon the high ^bmountain, ^cexalt the voice unto them, shake the hand, that they may go into the gates of the nobles.

3 I have commanded my ^asanctified ones, I have also called my ^bmighty ones for mine anger, *even* them that rejoice in my highness.

4 The noise of a multitude in the mountains, like as of a great people; a tumultuous noise of the ^akingdoms of nations gathered together: the LORD of hosts mustereth the host of the ^bbattle.

5 They come from a far country, from the end of heaven, *even* the LORD, and the weapons of his indignation, to ^adestroy the whole land.

6 ¶ ^aHowl ye; for the ^bday of the LORD *is* at hand; it shall come as a destruction from the Almighty.

7 Therefore shall all hands be faint, and every man's heart shall ^amelt:

8 And they shall be afraid: pangs and sorrows shall take hold of them; they shall be in ^apain as a woman that ^btravaileth: they shall be amazed one at another; their faces *shall be as* flames.

9 Behold, the day of the LORD cometh, cruel both with wrath and fierce anger, to lay the land desolate: and he shall ^adestroy the sinners thereof out of it.

10 For the stars of heaven and the constellations thereof shall not give their light: the sun shall be ^adarkened in his going forth, and the moon shall not cause her light to shine.

11 And I will ^apunish the ^bworld for *their* evil, and the wicked for their iniquity; and I will cause the arrogancy of the proud to cease, and will lay low the ^chaughtiness of the ^dterrible.

12 I will make a man more ^aprecious than fine gold; even a man than the ^bgolden wedge of Ophir.

13 Therefore I will ^ashake the heavens, and the ^bearth shall ^cremove out of her place, in the wrath of the LORD of hosts, and in the day of his fierce ^danger.

14 And it shall be as the ^achased roe, and as a sheep that ^bno man taketh up: they shall every man turn to his own ^cpeople, and flee every one into his own ^dland.

15 Every one that is found shall be ^athrust through; and every one that is joined *unto them* shall fall by the sword.

16 Their ^achildren also shall be dashed to pieces before their eyes; their ^bhouses shall be ^cspoiled, and their wives ravished.

17 Behold, I will stir up the ^aMedes against them, which shall not regard silver; and *as for* gold, they shall not delight in it.

---

13 1*a* 2 Ne. 23:1 (1–22).
   b "Burden" as used in Isaiah is a message of doom "lifted up" against a people. Isa. 14:28.
   c The historic destruction of wicked Babylon, prophesied in Isa. 13 and 14, is made typical of the ultimate destruction of the whole wicked world. D&C 133:14 (5, 7, 14).
  2*a* OR ensign.
   TG Ensign.
   b Isa. 2:2.
   c HEB raise.
  3*a* "Sanctified ones" and "saints" are synony-

mously translated from either of two Hebrew words in the Old Testament.
   b Joel 3:11.
  4*a* Zeph. 3:8.
   b TG War.
  5*a* Zech. 12:9 (4, 8–9).
  6*a* Isa. 14:31.
   b TG Day of the Lord.
  7*a* Moses 7:66.
  8*a* TG Pain.
   b Hosea 13:13.
  9*a* TG Earth, Cleansing of; World, End of.
 10*a* Ezek. 32:7 (7–8); Joel 2:10; Matt. 24:29.
 11*a* TG Punish.
   b TG World.
   c TG Haughtiness.

   d HEB tyrants.
 12*a* Isa. 24:6.
   TG Worth of Souls.
   b Job 28:16.
 13*a* Hag. 2:6;
   2 Ne. 8:6;
   3 Ne. 26:3.
   b Isa. 14:26 (22–26); 24:1; D&C 88:87 (87–92).
   c TG Earth, Renewal of.
   d Lam. 1:12.
 14*a* OR hunted deer.
   b HEB none gathers in.
   c Jer. 50:16.
   d TG Lands of Inheritance.
 15*a* OR pierced or stabbed.
 16*a* Nahum 3:10.
   b Zech. 14:2 (1–2).
   c OR plundered.
 17*a* Dan. 5:30–31.

18 *Their* bows also shall dash the young men to pieces; and they shall have no pity on the fruit of the womb; their eye shall not spare children.

19 ¶ And *ª*Babylon, the glory of kingdoms, the *ᵇ*beauty of the *ᶜ*Chaldees' excellency, shall be as when God *ᵈ*overthrew *ᵉ*Sodom and Gomorrah.

20 It shall never be *ª*inhabited, neither shall it be dwelt in from generation to generation: neither shall the Arabian pitch tent there; neither shall the shepherds make their fold there.

21 But *ª*wild beasts of the desert shall lie there; and their houses shall be full of doleful creatures; and owls shall dwell there, and *ᵇ*satyrs shall dance there.

22 And the wild beasts of the islands shall cry in their desolate *ª*houses, and *ᵇ*dragons in *their* pleasant palaces: and her time *is* near to come, and her days shall not be prolonged.

CHAPTER 14

Israel will be gathered and enjoy millennial rest—Lucifer was cast out of heaven for rebellion—Israel will triumph over Babylon (the world)—Compare 2 Nephi 24.

*ª*FOR the LORD will have *ᵇ*mercy on Jacob, and will yet *ᶜ*choose Israel, and set them in their own *ᵈ*land: and the *ᵉ*strangers shall be joined with them, and they shall cleave to the house of Jacob.

2 And the *ª*people shall take them, and *ᵇ*bring them to their place: and the house of Israel shall possess them in the land of the LORD for servants and handmaids: and they shall take them *ᶜ*captives, whose captives they were; and they shall *ᵈ*rule over their oppressors.

3 And it shall come to pass in the day that the LORD shall give thee rest from thy sorrow, and from thy fear, and from the hard bondage wherein thou wast made to serve,

4 ¶ That thou shalt take up this *ª*proverb against the king of *ᵇ*Babylon, and say, How hath the oppressor ceased! the *ᶜ*golden city ceased!

5 The LORD hath broken the *ª*staff of the *ᵇ*wicked, *and* the sceptre of the rulers.

6 He who smote the people in wrath with *ª*a continual stroke, he that ruled the nations in anger, is persecuted, *and* none hindereth.

7 The whole earth is at *ª*rest, *and* is quiet: they break forth into singing.

8 Yea, the *ª*fir trees rejoice at thee, *and* the cedars of Lebanon, *saying,* Since thou art *ᵇ*laid down, *ᶜ*no feller is come up against us.

9 *ª*Hell from beneath is moved for thee to meet *thee* at thy coming: it stirreth up the *ᵇ*dead for thee, *even* all the chief ones of the earth; it hath raised up from their thrones all the kings of the nations.

10 All they shall speak and say unto thee, Art thou also become weak as we? art thou become like unto us?

11 Thy pomp is brought down to *ª*the grave, *and* the noise of thy

---

19*a* TG Babylon.
 b HEB vainglorious grandeur of the Babylonians.
 c Isa. 23:13.
 d Jer. 20:16; Amos 4:11.
 e Gen. 19:24; Jer. 50:40.
20*a* Jer. 50:3.
21*a* Isa. 34:14 (11–15).
 b HEB he-goats, or demons.
22*a* HEB palaces.
 b HEB (perhaps) jackals,

or wild dogs.
14 1*a* 2 Ne. 24:1 (1–32).
 b Ps. 102:13.
 c Zech. 1:17.
 d TG Israel, Land of.
 e TG Conversion; Israel, Mission of; Stranger.
2*a* IE Other nations shall help Israel.
 b Isa. 60:9.
 c Ezek. 39:10.
 d TG Kingdom of God, on Earth.
4*a* IE a satirical song.

 b TG Babylon.
 c HEB (perhaps) insolent, or proud.
5*a* Isa. 9:4.
 b TG Wickedness.
6*a* OR constant blows.
7*a* TG Earth, Renewal of.
8*a* HEB cypress.
 b IE in death.
 c HEB the (tree) cutter has not come upon us.
9*a* TG Hell.
 b IE disembodied spirits.
11*a* HEB *sheol,* or the spirit world.

viols: the worm is spread under thee, and the worms cover thee.

12 How art thou *a*fallen from *b*heaven, O *c*Lucifer, son of the morning! *how* art thou cut down to the ground, which didst weaken the *d*nations!

13 For thou hast said in thine *a*heart, *b*I will ascend into heaven, I will *c*exalt my *d*throne above the stars of God: I will sit also upon the mount of the congregation, in the sides of the *e*north:

14 I will ascend above the heights of the clouds; I will be like the *a*most High.

15 Yet thou shalt be brought down to *a*hell, to the sides of the pit.

16 They that see *a*thee shall *b*narrowly look upon thee, *and* consider thee, *saying, Is* this the man that made the earth to tremble, that did shake kingdoms;

17 *That* made the world as a wilderness, and destroyed the cities thereof; *that* opened not the house of his prisoners?

18 All the kings of the nations, *even* all of them, lie in *a*glory, every one in *b*his own house.

19 But thou art cast out of thy grave like *a*an abominable branch, *and as* the raiment of those that are slain, thrust through with a sword, that go down to *b*the stones of the pit; as a carcase trodden under feet.

20 Thou shalt not be *a*joined with them in burial, because thou hast destroyed thy land, *and* slain thy people: the *b*seed of *c*evildoers shall never be renowned.

21 *a*Prepare slaughter for his children for the iniquity of their fathers; that they do not rise, nor possess the land, nor fill the face of the world with cities.

22 For I will rise up against them, saith the LORD of hosts, and *a*cut off from Babylon the name, and remnant, and son, and nephew, saith the LORD.

23 I will also make it a possession for the *a*bittern, and pools of water: and I will sweep it with the *b*besom of destruction, saith the LORD of hosts.

24 ¶ The LORD of hosts hath sworn, saying, Surely as I have thought, so shall it come to pass; and as I have purposed, *so* shall it stand:

25 That *a*I will break the Assyrian in my land, and upon *b*my mountains tread him under foot: then shall his *c*yoke depart from off them, and his burden depart from off their shoulders.

26 This *is* the purpose that is purposed upon the whole *a*earth: and this *is* the hand that is stretched out upon *b*all the nations.

27 For the LORD of hosts hath *a*purposed, and who shall disannul *it*? and his hand *is* stretched out, and who shall turn it back?

12*a* Rev. 8:10.
  b TG Heaven.
  c HEB morning star, son of dawn. The ruler of the wicked world (Babylon) is spoken of as Lucifer, the ruler of all wickedness. TG Devil.
  d TG Nations.
13*a* Ezek. 31:10.
  b Moses 4:1.
  c TG Selfishness.
  d TG Council in Heaven.
  e IE dwelling of the gods according to Babylonian belief. Ps. 48:2.
14*a* D&C 29:36 (36–37); 76:28 (25–29).
15*a* TG Damnation;

Death, Spiritual, First; Hell; Spirits in Prison.
16*a* IE the king of Babylon; the preceding verses, 12–15, applied to either Lucifer or the king.
  b HEB squint at thee and reflect upon thee.
18*a* Ezek. 32:27.
  b IE his family tomb.
19*a* IE a rejected branch, pruned off and discarded.
  b IE the very bottom.
20*a* Eccl. 6:3.
  b Ps. 109:13.
  c TG Wickedness.
21*a* IE Let not another evil generation arise and resume an evil regime.

Deut. 24:16.
22*a* Prov. 10:7; Jer. 51:62 (61–62).
23*a* Isa. 34:11 (11–15).
  b OR broom.
25*a* The subject shifts to Assyria's attack and downfall in Judah, 701 B.C. (vv. 24–27). 2 Kgs. 19:35 (32–37); Isa. 37:36 (33–38); Zech. 10:11.
  b IE the mountains of Judah.
  c TG Bondage, Physical.
26*a* Isa. 13:13 (4–13); D&C 88:87 (87–92).
  b IE Eventually all worldly nations will be overthrown thus.
27*a* TG God, Power of.

28 In the [a]year that king [b]Ahaz died was this [c]burden.

29 ¶ Rejoice not thou, whole [a]Palestina, because the rod of him that smote thee is broken: for out of the serpent's root shall come forth a cockatrice, and his fruit *shall be* a fiery flying serpent.

30 And the firstborn of the poor shall feed, and the needy shall lie down in safety: and I will kill thy root with famine, and he shall slay thy remnant.

31 [a]Howl, O gate; cry, O city; thou, whole [b]Palestina, *art* dissolved: for there shall come from the north a smoke, and none *shall be* alone in his appointed times.

32 What shall *one* then answer the messengers of the [a]nation? That the LORD hath founded [b]Zion, and the [c]poor of his people shall [d]trust in it.

CHAPTER 15

Moab will be laid waste, and her people will howl and weep.

THE [a]burden of [b]Moab. Because in the night [c]Ar of Moab is laid waste, *and* brought to silence; because in the night Kir of [d]Moab is laid waste, *and* brought to silence;

2 He is gone up to Bajith, and to Dibon, the high places, to weep: Moab shall howl over Nebo, and over Medeba: on all their heads *shall be* [a]baldness, *and* every beard [b]cut off.

3 In their streets they shall gird themselves with sackcloth: on the tops of their houses, and in their streets, every one shall howl, weeping abundantly.

4 And Heshbon shall [a]cry, and Elealeh: their voice shall be heard *even* unto Jahaz: therefore the armed soldiers of Moab shall cry out; his life shall be grievous unto him.

5 My [a]heart shall cry out for Moab; his fugitives *shall flee* unto Zoar, an [b]heifer of three years old: for by [c]the mounting up of Luhith with weeping shall they go it up; for in the way of [d]Horonaim they shall raise up a cry of destruction.

6 For the waters of Nimrim shall be desolate: for the hay is withered away, the grass faileth, there is no green thing.

7 Therefore the abundance they have gotten, and that which they have laid up, shall they carry away to the [a]brook of the willows.

8 For the cry is gone round about the borders of Moab; the howling thereof unto Eglaim, and the howling thereof unto [a]Beer-elim.

9 For the waters of Dimon shall be full of blood: for I will bring more upon Dimon, lions upon him that escapeth of Moab, and upon the remnant of the land.

CHAPTER 16

Moab is condemned, and her people will sorrow—The Messiah will sit on David's throne, seeking justice and hastening righteousness.

[a]SEND ye the lamb to the ruler of the land from Sela to the wilderness,

---

28a IE About 720 B.C., this burden or message of doom was prophesied about the Philistines, while Judah would be secure.
b 2 Kgs. 16:20.
c Isa. 13:1.
29a HEB Philistia (also v. 31).
31a Isa. 13:6.
b Jer. 47:1;
Ezek. 25:15 (15–16);
Amos 1:8.
32a IE Philistia.

b TG Zion.
c TG Poor.
d OR seek refuge in it.
15 1a IE a message of doom "lifted up" against Moab.
b Gen. 19:37 (30–37);
Ezek. 25:8.
c Deut. 2:9.
d Jer. 48:4 (1–47).
2a Isa. 3:24;
Jer. 48:37.
b IE in mourning over the destruction.
4a Jer. 48:34.

5a Isa. 16:11;
Jer. 48:36.
b IE Zoar should still have been young and vigorous.
c OR the ascent of Luhith.
d Jer. 48:3.
7a IE probably the border between Moab and Edom.
8a Num. 21:16 (16–18).
16 1a IE Send an appeal to the king of Judah, who then ruled also Edom.

unto the mount of the daughter of Zion.

2 For it shall be, *that*, as a wandering bird cast out of the nest, *so* the daughters of Moab shall be at the fords of ªArnon.

3 ªTake counsel, execute judgment; make thy shadow as the night in the midst of the noonday; hide the outcasts; bewray not him that wandereth.

4 ªLet mine ᵇoutcasts dwell with thee, Moab; be thou a covert to them from the face of the spoiler: for the extortioner is at an end, the spoiler ceaseth, the oppressors are consumed out of the land.

5 And in ªmercy shall the ᵇthrone be established: and he shall sit upon it in truth in the tabernacle of David, judging, and seeking judgment, and ᶜhasting ᵈrighteousness.

6 ¶ ªWe have heard of the ᵇpride of Moab; *he is* very proud: *even* of his haughtiness, and his pride, and his wrath: *but* his lies *shall* not *be* so.

7 Therefore shall Moab ªhowl for Moab, every one shall howl: for the foundations of ᵇKir-hareseth shall ye mourn; surely *they are* stricken.

8 For the fields of Heshbon languish, *and* the vine of Sibmah: the lords of the heathen have broken down the principal plants thereof, they are come *even* unto ªJazer, they wandered *through* the wilderness: her branches are stretched out, they are gone over the sea.

9 ¶ Therefore I will bewail with the weeping of Jazer the vine of Sibmah: I will water thee with my tears, O Heshbon, and Elealeh: for

the shouting for thy summer fruits and for thy harvest is fallen.

10 And ªgladness is taken away, and joy out of the plentiful field; and in the vineyards there shall be no singing, neither shall there be shouting: the treaders shall tread out no wine in *their* presses; I have made *their vintage* shouting to cease.

11 Wherefore my ªbowels shall sound like an harp for Moab, and mine inward parts for Kir-haresh.

12 ¶ And it shall come to pass, when it is seen that Moab is weary on the high place, that he shall come to his sanctuary to ªpray; but he shall not prevail.

13 This *is* the word that the LORD hath spoken concerning ªMoab since that time.

14 But now the LORD hath spoken, saying, Within three years, as the years of an hireling, and the glory of Moab shall be contemned, with all that great multitude; and the remnant *shall be* very small *and* feeble.

CHAPTER 17

Israel was scattered because she forgot God—Yet the nations that plunder her will be destroyed.

THE ªburden of ᵇDamascus. Behold, Damascus is taken away from *being* a city, and it shall be a ruinous heap.

2 The cities of Aroer *are* forsaken: they shall be for flocks, which shall lie down, and none shall make *them* afraid.

3 The fortress also shall cease from ªEphraim, and the kingdom from Damascus, and the remnant of Syria: they shall be as the glory of the

---

2 a Num. 21:13 (13–28).
3 a HEB Give counsel. This
  begins Moab's appeal to
  Judah (vv. 3–5).
4 a HEB Let mine outcasts
  dwell with thee; be thou
  a covert for Moab.
  b Mosiah 4:16.
5 a Jer. 48:47 (46–47).
  b TG Jesus Christ,
  Millennial Reign.
  c TG Haste.
  d Mosiah 2:11 (11–14).

6 a Beginning of Judah's
  reply, declining Moab's
  appeal.
  b TG Pride.
7 a Jer. 48:20 (20, 31).
  b 2 Kgs. 3:25.
8 a Num. 21:32.
10 a Jer. 48:33.
11 a Isa. 15:5;
  Jer. 48:36.
12 a D&C 101:7 (7–8).
13 a Amos 2:1 (1–3).
17 1 a IE a message of doom

"lifted up" against
Damascus.
  b Isa. 7:8.
3 a IE Syria and northern
  Israel (Ephraim) were
  allies, and both were
  soon to be conquered
  by Assyria.
  TG Israel, Joseph,
  People of;
  Israel, Ten Lost
  Tribes of.

children of Israel, saith the LORD of hosts.

4 And in that day it shall come to pass, *that* the glory of Jacob shall be made thin, and the fatness of his flesh shall wax lean.

5 And it shall be as when the harvestman gathereth the corn, and reapeth the ears with his arm; and it shall be as he that gathereth ears in the valley of Rephaim.

6 ¶ Yet *a*gleaning grapes shall be left in it, as the shaking of an olive tree, two *or* three berries in the top of the uppermost bough, four *or* five in the outmost fruitful branches thereof, saith the LORD God of Israel.

7 At that day shall a man look to his *a*Maker, and *b*his eyes shall have respect to the Holy One of Israel.

8 And he shall not look to the altars, the work of his hands, neither shall respect *that* which his fingers have made, either the *a*groves, or the images.

9 ¶ In that day shall his strong cities be as a forsaken bough, and an uppermost branch, which they left because of the children of Israel: and there shall be desolation.

10 Because *a*thou hast *b*forgotten the God of thy *c*salvation, and hast not been mindful of the *d*rock of thy strength, therefore *e*shalt thou plant pleasant plants, and shalt set it with strange slips:

11 In the day shalt thou make thy plant to grow, and in the morning shalt thou make thy seed to flourish: *but* the harvest *shall be* a heap in the day of grief and of desperate sorrow.

12 ¶ Woe to *a*the multitude of many people, *which* make a noise like the noise of the seas; and to the rushing of nations, *that* make a rushing like the rushing of mighty waters!

13 The nations shall rush like the rushing of many waters: but *God* shall rebuke them, and they shall flee far off, and shall be chased as the chaff of the mountains before the wind, and like a *a*rolling thing before the whirlwind.

14 And behold at eveningtide trouble; *and* before the morning he *is* not. This *is* the portion of them that *a*spoil us, and the lot of them that rob us.

CHAPTER 18

The Lord will raise the gospel ensign, send messengers to His scattered people, and gather them to Mount Zion.

*a*WOE to the land shadowing with wings, which *is* *b*beyond the rivers of *c*Ethiopia:

2 That sendeth ambassadors by the sea, even in vessels of *a*bulrushes upon the waters, *saying*, Go, ye swift messengers, to a nation scattered and peeled, to a people terrible from their beginning hitherto; a nation meted out and trodden down, whose land the rivers have *b*spoiled!

3 All ye inhabitants of the world, and dwellers on the earth, see ye, when he lifteth up an *a*ensign on the mountains; and when he bloweth a trumpet, hear ye.

4 For so the LORD said unto me, I will take my rest, and I will consider in my dwelling place like a clear heat upon herbs, *and* like a cloud of dew in the heat of harvest.

5 For afore the harvest, when the bud is perfect, and the sour grape is ripening in the flower, he shall both cut off the sprigs with pruning hooks, and take away *and* cut down the branches.

6*a* IE only a small remnant of Israel will be found after Assyria's conquest.
TG Israel, Remnant of.
7*a* Hosea 8:14.
  b IE In their bereavement they will begin to repent.
8*a* Micah 5:14.
10*a* IE Israel.

b Hel. 7:20 (17–22).
c Ps. 68:20 (19–20).
d TG Rock.
e HEB thou dost plant . . . ; i.e., practice idolatrous things.
12*a* IE the Assyrian empire of numerous nations (vv. 12–14).
13*a* Ps. 83:13.

14*a* Isa. 33:1 (1, 4).
18 1*a* HEB *hoy* (a form of greeting).
  b Zeph. 3:10 (8–10).
  c HEB Cush; a far distant land is suggested.
2*a* HEB reed or papyrus.
  b HEB cut up or divided.
3*a* TG Ensign.

6 They shall be left together unto the fowls of the mountains, and to the [a]beasts of the earth: and the fowls shall summer upon them, and all the beasts of the earth shall winter upon them.

7 ¶ In that time shall the present be brought unto the LORD of hosts of a people [a]scattered and peeled, and from a people terrible from their beginning hitherto; a nation meted out and trodden under foot, whose land the rivers have spoiled, to the place of the name of the LORD of hosts, the [b]mount Zion.

CHAPTER 19

The Lord will smite and destroy Egypt— Finally He will heal her, and Egypt and Assyria will be blessed with Israel.

THE [a]burden of [b]Egypt. Behold, the LORD rideth upon a swift [c]cloud, and shall come into Egypt: and the [d]idols of Egypt shall be moved at his presence, and the heart of Egypt shall melt in the midst of it.

2 And I will set the Egyptians against the Egyptians: and they shall fight every one against his brother, and every one against his neighbour; city against city, *and* kingdom against kingdom.

3 And the spirit of Egypt shall fail in the midst thereof; and I will destroy the counsel thereof: and they shall seek to the idols, and to the charmers, and to [a]them that have [b]familiar spirits, and to the wizards.

4 And the Egyptians will I give over into the hand of [a]a [b]cruel lord; and a fierce king shall rule over them, saith the Lord, the LORD of hosts.

5 And the waters shall [a]fail from the sea, and the river shall be wasted and [b]dried up.

6 And they shall turn the rivers far away; *and* the brooks of defence shall be emptied and dried up: the reeds and flags shall wither.

7 The paper reeds by the brooks, by the mouth of the brooks, and every thing sown by the brooks, shall wither, be driven away, and be no *more*.

8 The fishers also shall mourn, and all they that cast [a]angle into the brooks shall lament, and they that spread nets upon the waters shall languish.

9 Moreover they that work in fine flax, and they that weave [a]networks, shall be confounded.

10 And [a]they shall be broken in the purposes thereof, all that make sluices *and* ponds for fish.

11 ¶ Surely the princes of [a]Zoan *are* fools, the counsel of the wise counsellors of Pharaoh is become brutish: how say ye unto Pharaoh, I *am* the son of the wise, the son of ancient kings?

12 Where *are* they? where *are* thy wise *men*? and let them tell thee now, and let them know what the LORD of hosts hath purposed upon Egypt.

13 The princes of Zoan are become fools, the princes of [a]Noph are deceived; they have also seduced Egypt, *even they that are* the [b]stay of the tribes thereof.

14 The LORD hath mingled a [a]perverse spirit in the midst thereof: and they have caused Egypt to err in every work thereof, as a drunken *man* staggereth in his vomit.

15 Neither shall there be *any* work for Egypt, which [a]the head or tail, branch or rush, may do.

16 In that day shall [a]Egypt be like unto women: and it shall be afraid

6a D&C 29:20.
7a 1 Ne. 22:7 (6–8).
  b 3 Ne. 20:33 (29–34);
    D&C 84:2.
19 1a IE a message of doom
    "lifted up" against
    Egypt.
  b Jer. 25:19; 46:13 (13–26);
    Ezek. 29:2; 31:2; 32:2.
  c Ps. 104:3.

  d Ex. 12:12;
    Jer. 43:12.
3a HEB necromancers.
  b TG Sorcery.
4a OR hard masters.
  b Isa. 20:4.
5a HEB dry up.
  b Jer. 51:36;
    Ezek. 30:12.
8a OR fish hooks.

9a HEB fine linen.
10a HEB her foundations
    shall be crushed.
11a Num. 13:22.
13a Jer. 44:1.
  b IE cornerstones.
14a 1 Kgs. 22:22 (19–23).
15a IE the different levels of
    society.
16a Joel 3:19; Zech. 10:11.

and fear because of the shaking of the hand of the LORD of hosts, which he shaketh over it.

17 And the land of ᵃJudah shall be a terror unto Egypt, every one that maketh mention thereof shall be afraid in himself, because of the counsel of the LORD of hosts, which he hath determined against it.

18 ¶ In that day shall five cities in the land of Egypt speak the language of Canaan, and swear to the LORD of hosts; one shall be called, The city of ᵃdestruction.

19 In that day shall there be an altar to the LORD in the midst of the land of Egypt, and a pillar at the border thereof to the LORD.

20 And it shall be for a sign and for a witness unto the LORD of hosts in the land of Egypt: for they shall cry unto the LORD because of the oppressors, and he shall send them a saviour, and a great one, and he shall deliver them.

21 And the LORD shall be known to ᵃEgypt, and the Egyptians shall know the LORD in that day, and shall do sacrifice and oblation; yea, they shall vow a ᵇvow unto the LORD, and perform it.

22 And the LORD shall smite Egypt: he shall smite and heal it: and they shall ᵃreturn even to the LORD, and he shall be entreated of them, and shall heal them.

23 ¶ In that day shall there be a ᵃhighway out of Egypt to Assyria, and the Assyrian shall come into Egypt, and the Egyptian into Assyria, and the Egyptians shall serve with the Assyrians.

24 In that day shall ᵃIsrael be the third with Egypt and with Assyria, even a ᵇblessing in the midst of the land:

25 Whom the LORD of hosts shall bless, saying, Blessed be Egypt my people, and Assyria the work of my hands, and ᵃIsrael mine ᵇinheritance.

CHAPTER 20

Assyria will overrun Egypt and make her ashamed.

IN the ᵃyear that ᵇTartan came unto Ashdod, (when Sargon the king of Assyria sent him,) and fought against Ashdod, and took it;

2 At the same time spake the LORD by Isaiah the son of Amoz, saying, Go and loose the sackcloth from off thy loins, and put off thy shoe from thy foot. And he did so, walking ᵃnaked and barefoot.

3 And the LORD said, Like as my servant Isaiah hath walked naked and barefoot three years for a ᵃsign and wonder upon Egypt and upon Ethiopia;

4 So shall the ᵃking of Assyria lead away the Egyptians prisoners, and the ᵇEthiopians captives, young and old, naked and barefoot, even with their buttocks uncovered, to the shame of Egypt.

5 And ᵃthey shall be afraid and ashamed of Ethiopia their expectation, and of Egypt their glory.

6 And the inhabitant of this isle shall say in that day, Behold, such is our expectation, whither we flee for help to be delivered from the king of Assyria: and how shall we escape?

17a TG Last Days.
18a HEB *Heres;*
   possibly "of the sun";
   perhaps Heliopolis, one
   of the oldest cities of
   the Nile delta.
21a Ps. 68:31.
   b TG Vow.
22a TG Conversion.
23a Isa. 11:16;
   2 Ne. 21:16.

24a IE all three will be
   allied, with Israel as
   a blessing in the midst
   of them.
   b TG Israel, Mission of.
25a TG Israel, Remnant of.
   b Joel 3:2.
20 1a IE about 711 B.C.
   b 2 Kgs. 18:17.
2a IE without an upper
   garment, like a slave

or exile.
3a TG Signs.
4a Isa. 19:4.
   b Ezek. 30:9.
5a IE People of Judah
   shall be dismayed
   by Assyria's power,
   dispelling any hope of
   help from Egypt and
   Ethiopia.

CHAPTER 21

Babylon is fallen, is fallen!—Other nations also are destroyed.

THE [a]burden of the desert of the sea. As whirlwinds in [b]the south pass through; *so* it cometh from the desert, from a terrible land.

2 A grievous vision is declared unto me; the [a]treacherous dealer dealeth treacherously, and the spoiler spoileth. Go up, O [b]Elam: besiege, O Media; all the sighing thereof have I made to cease.

3 Therefore are my loins filled with pain: pangs have taken hold upon me, as the pangs of a woman that travaileth: I was bowed down at the hearing *of it;* I was [a]dismayed at the seeing *of it.*

4 My heart panted, fearfulness affrighted me: the night of my pleasure hath he turned into fear unto me.

5 Prepare the table, watch in the watchtower, eat, drink: arise, ye princes, *and* anoint the shield.

6 For thus hath the Lord said unto me, Go, set a watchman, let him [a]declare what he seeth.

7 And he saw a chariot *with* a couple of horsemen, a chariot of asses, *and* a chariot of camels; and he hearkened diligently with much heed:

8 And he cried, A lion: My lord, I stand continually upon the watchtower in the daytime, and I am set in my ward whole nights:

9 And, behold, here cometh a chariot of men, *with* a couple of horsemen. And he answered and said, [a]Babylon is fallen, is fallen; and all the graven images of her gods he hath broken unto the ground.

10 [a]O my threshing, and the corn of my floor: that which I have heard of the LORD of hosts, the God of Israel, have I declared unto you.

11 ¶ The [a]burden of Dumah. He calleth to me out of [b]Seir, Watchman, [c]what of the night? Watchman, what of the night?

12 The watchman said, [a]The morning cometh, and also the night: if ye will inquire, inquire ye: return, come.

13 ¶ The [a]burden upon Arabia. In the forest in Arabia shall ye lodge, O ye travelling companies of Dedanim.

14 The inhabitants of the land of Tema brought water to him that was thirsty, they prevented with their bread him that fled.

15 For they fled from the swords, from the drawn sword, and from the bent bow, and from the grievousness of war.

16 For thus hath the Lord said unto me, Within a year, according to the years of an hireling, and all the glory of [a]Kedar shall fail:

17 And the residue of the number of archers, the mighty men of the children of Kedar, shall be diminished: for the LORD God of Israel hath spoken *it.*

CHAPTER 22

Jerusalem will be attacked and scourged—The people will be carried captive—The Messiah will hold the key of the house of David, inherit

---

21 1*a* IE a message or prophecy of doom to Babylon.
  b OR the Negev desert.
  2*a* Isa. 33:1.
  b This prophecy was fulfilled in 538 B.C., about 200 years after Isaiah lived.
  3*a* IE Isaiah was astonished at the cataclysmic scene he saw in vision, even though an enemy was the nation destroyed.

6*a* TG Preaching.
9*a* Rev. 14:8 (8–11); D&C 1:16.
10*a* HEB O my threshed one and son of my threshing floor. (The prophet thus addressed the Israelites who will survive Babylon's downfall.)
11*a* IE a message of doom to the Edomites.
  b Gen. 36:8 (8–9); Ezek. 35:2.
  c IE How much is spent?

How long will darkness (i.e., oppression) last?
12*a* IE The end of Babylonian captivity approaches, but another oppressor follows; inquire again later.
13*a* Arabian caravans and camps would also suffer disruption and oppression by the Babylonian conquest (vv. 13–17).
16*a* Isa. 60:7.

glory, and be fastened as a nail in a sure place.

THE ^aburden of the valley of vision. What aileth thee now, that thou art wholly gone up to the housetops?

2 Thou that art full of ^astirs, a tumultuous city, a joyous city: thy slain *men are* not slain with the sword, nor dead in battle.

3 All thy rulers are fled together, they are bound by the archers: all that are found in thee are bound together, *which* have fled from far.

4 Therefore said I, Look away from me; I will ^aweep bitterly, labour not to comfort me, because of the spoiling of the daughter of my people.

5 For *it is* a day of ^atrouble, and of treading down, and of perplexity by the Lord GOD of hosts in the valley of vision, breaking down the walls, and of crying to the mountains.

6 And Elam bare the quiver with chariots of men *and* horsemen, and Kir uncovered the shield.

7 And it shall come to pass, *that* thy choicest valleys shall be full of chariots, and the horsemen shall set themselves in array at the gate.

8 ¶ And he ^adiscovered the covering of Judah, and thou didst look in that day to the armour of the ^bhouse of the forest.

9 Ye have seen also the ^abreaches of the city of David, that they are many: and ye gathered together the waters of the lower ^bpool.

10 And ye have numbered the houses of Jerusalem, and the houses have ye broken down to fortify the wall.

11 Ye made also a ^aditch between the two walls for the water of the old pool: but ye have not looked unto the ^bmaker thereof, neither had respect unto him that fashioned it long ago.

12 And in that day did the Lord GOD of hosts ^acall to ^bweeping, and to mourning, and to ^cbaldness, and to girding with sackcloth:

13 And behold ^ajoy and gladness, slaying oxen, and killing sheep, eating flesh, and drinking wine: let us ^beat and drink; for ^cto morrow we shall die.

14 And it was revealed in mine ears by the LORD of hosts, Surely this iniquity shall not be purged from you till ye die, saith the Lord GOD of hosts.

15 ¶ Thus saith the Lord GOD of hosts, Go, get thee unto this treasurer, *even* unto ^aShebna, which *is* over the house, *and say,*

16 What hast thou here? and whom hast thou here, that thou hast hewed thee out a sepulchre here, *as* he that heweth him out a sepulchre on high, *and* that graveth an habitation for himself in a rock?

17 Behold, the LORD will carry thee away with a mighty captivity, and will surely cover thee.

18 He will surely violently turn and toss thee *like* a ball into a large ^acountry: there shalt thou die, and there the chariots of thy glory *shall be* the shame of thy lord's house.

19 And I will drive thee from thy station, and from thy state shall he pull thee down.

20 ¶ And it shall come to pass in that day, that I will ^acall my servant ^bEliakim the son of Hilkiah:

---

22 1*a* IE a message of doom to Jerusalem.
2*a* OR noise.
4*a* TG Mourning.
5*a* Isa. 37:3.
8*a* HEB stripped off.
  b 1 Kgs. 7:2.
9*a* IE cracks, breaks in the wall.
  b 2 Kgs. 20:20.
11*a* Isa. 7:3.
  b IE you have not turned to the Lord.

12*a* IE call for repentance.
  b Joel 2:17;
    2 Cor. 7:10;
    James 4:9 (8–10).
  c Ezek. 7:18.
13*a* IE They went on with revelry as usual.
  b Luke 12:19;
    1 Cor. 15:32;
    2 Ne. 28:8.
  c TG Procrastination.
15*a* IE a personal warning to Shebna (vv. 15–19).

18*a* IE probably Assyria.
20*a* IE Eliakim shall replace Shebna. Moreover, the symbolic name "Eliakim" in ensuing verses becomes representative of the Messiah, the Savior, especially vv. 23–25. The name means "God shall cause to arise."
  b 2 Kgs. 18:18.

21 And I will clothe him with thy robe, and strengthen him with thy girdle, and I will commit thy *a*government into his hand: and he shall be a father to the inhabitants of Jerusalem, and to the house of Judah.

22 And the *a*key of the house of David will I lay upon his shoulder; so he shall open, and none shall shut; and he shall shut, and none shall open.

23 And I will fasten him *as* a *a*nail in a sure place; and he shall be for a glorious throne to his father's house.

24 And they shall hang upon him all the glory of his father's house, the offspring and the issue, all vessels of small quantity, from the vessels of cups, even to all the vessels of flagons.

25 In that day, saith the LORD of hosts, shall the nail that is fastened in the sure place be removed, and be cut down, and fall; and the burden that *was* upon it shall be cut off: for the LORD hath spoken *it*.

CHAPTER 23

Tyre will be overthrown.

THE *a*burden of *b*Tyre. Howl, ye ships of Tarshish; for it is laid waste, so that there is no house, no entering in: from the land of *c*Chittim it is revealed to them.

2 Be *a*still, ye inhabitants of the isle; thou whom the merchants of Zidon, that pass over the sea, have replenished.

3 And by great waters the *a*seed of *b*Sihor, the harvest of the river, *is* her revenue; and she is a mart of nations.

4 Be thou ashamed, O *a*Zidon: for the sea hath spoken, *even* the *b*strength of the sea, saying, I travail

not, nor bring forth children, neither do I nourish up young men, *nor* bring up virgins.

5 *a*As at the report concerning Egypt, *so* shall they be sorely pained at the report of Tyre.

6 Pass ye over to Tarshish; howl, ye inhabitants of the isle.

7 *Is* this your joyous *city,* whose antiquity *is* of ancient days? her own feet shall carry her afar off to sojourn.

8 Who hath taken this counsel against Tyre, the crowning *city,* whose merchants *are* *a*princes, whose *b*traffickers *are* the *c*honourable of the earth?

9 The LORD of hosts hath purposed it, to stain the pride of all glory, *and* to bring into contempt all the honourable of the earth.

10 Pass through thy land as a river, O daughter of Tarshish: *there is* no more strength.

11 He stretched out his hand over the sea, he shook the kingdoms: the LORD hath given a commandment *a*against the merchant *city,* to destroy the strong holds thereof.

12 And he said, Thou shalt no more rejoice, O thou oppressed virgin, daughter of Zidon: arise, pass over to Chittim; there also shalt thou have no rest.

13 Behold the land of the *a*Chaldeans; this people was not, *till* the Assyrian founded it for them that dwell in the wilderness: they set up the towers thereof, they raised up the palaces thereof; *and* he brought it to ruin.

14 Howl, ye ships of Tarshish: for your strength is laid waste.

15 And it shall come to pass in that day, that Tyre shall be forgotten seventy years, according to the days

---

21*a* TG Governments.
22*a* TG Priesthood,
   Keys of;
   Sealing.
23*a* Ezra 9:8;
   Zech. 10:4.
   TG Jesus Christ,
   Prophecies about.
23 1*a* IE a message of doom
   to the Phoenician city,

Tyre.
b Ezek. 26:2 (2–3);
   Amos 1:9.
c IE Cyprus. Refugees tell
   of destruction.
2*a* HEB silent, stunned.
3*a* IE grain from the Nile.
b 1 Chr. 13:5.
4*a* Jer. 25:22;
   Ezek. 28:21.

b Ezek. 26:17.
5*a* OR When the report is
   heard by Egypt.
8*a* Ezek. 26:16.
b IE traders.
c HEB ones honored, i.e.,
   famous.
11*a* OR concerning Canaan.
13*a* Isa. 13:19.

of one king: after the end of seventy years shall Tyre sing as an harlot.

16 Take an harp, go about the city, thou harlot that hast been forgotten; make sweet melody, sing many songs, that thou mayest be remembered.

17 ¶ And it shall come to pass after the end of seventy years, that the LORD will visit Tyre, and she shall ªturn to her hire, and shall commit ᵇfornication with all the kingdoms of the world upon the face of the earth.

18 And ªher merchandise and her ᵇhire shall be ᶜholiness to the LORD: it shall not be treasured nor laid up; for her merchandise shall be for them that dwell before the LORD, to eat sufficiently, and for durable clothing.

CHAPTER 24

Men will transgress the law and break the everlasting covenant—At the Second Coming, they will be burned, the earth will reel, and the sun will be ashamed— Then the Lord will reign in Zion and in Jerusalem.

BEHOLD, the LORD maketh the ªearth ᵇempty, and maketh it waste, and ᶜturneth it upside down, and scattereth abroad the inhabitants thereof.

2 And it shall be, as with the people, so with the priest; as with the servant, so with his master; as with the maid, so with her mistress; as with the ªbuyer, so with the seller; as with the lender, so with the borrower; as with ᵇthe taker of usury, so with the giver of usury to him.

3 The land shall be utterly emptied, and utterly spoiled: for the LORD hath spoken this word.

4 The earth ªmourneth *and* fadeth away, the world languisheth *and* fadeth away, ᵇthe haughty people of the earth do languish.

5 The earth also is defiled under the inhabitants thereof; because they have ªtransgressed the laws, ᵇchanged the ᶜordinance, ᵈbroken the ᵉeverlasting ᶠcovenant.

6 Therefore hath the ªcurse devoured the earth, and they that dwell therein are desolate: therefore the ᵇinhabitants of the earth are ᶜburned, and ᵈfew men left.

7 The new wine mourneth, the vine languisheth, all the merryhearted do sigh.

8 The mirth of ªtabrets ᵇceaseth, the noise of them that rejoice endeth, the joy of the harp ceaseth.

9 They shall not drink wine with a song; strong ªdrink shall be bitter to them that drink it.

10 The city of confusion is broken down: every house is shut up, that no man may come in.

11 *There is* a crying for wine in the streets; all ªjoy is darkened, the mirth of the land is gone.

12 In the city is left desolation, and the gate is smitten with destruction.

13 ¶ When thus it shall be in the midst of the land among the ªpeople, *there shall be* as the shaking of an olive tree, *and* as the gleaning grapes when the vintage is done.

14 ªThey shall lift up their voice, they shall sing for the majesty of the

---

17ª OR return.
  ᵇ Rev. 18:3 (3, 9).
18ª IE Any success she
     has will only be as
     permitted by the Lord.
  ᵇ TG Wages.
  ᶜ Jer. 2:3.
24 1ª Isa. 13:13.
  ᵇ D&C 5:19.
  ᶜ IE when the whole
     wicked world shall
     end.
 2ª Ezek. 7:12.
  ᵇ OR him who exacts
     payment, so with him

who makes payment.
  TG Usury.
 4ª TG Mourning.
  ᵇ OR the upper classes are
     despondent.
 5ª TG Disobedience.
  ᵇ D&C 1:15.
  ᶜ TG Ordinance.
  ᵈ TG Apostasy of
     Individuals;
     Apostasy of Israel;
     Apostasy of the Early
     Christian Church.
  ᵉ TG New and Everlasting
     Covenant.

 ᶠ TG Covenants.
 6ª TG Curse;
     Earth, Curse of.
  ᵇ Rev. 17:2;
     D&C 1:17.
  ᶜ TG Day of the Lord;
     Earth, Cleansing of.
  ᵈ Isa. 13:12.
 8ª HEB drums.
  ᵇ Hosea 2:11.
 9ª TG Word of Wisdom.
11ª Joel 1:12 (11–13).
13ª HEB peoples or nations.
14ª IE The righteous
     remnant.

LORD, they shall cry aloud from the sea.

15 Wherefore glorify ye the LORD in the *a*fires, *even* the name of the LORD God of Israel in the isles of the sea.

16 ¶ From the uttermost part of the earth have we heard songs, *even* glory to the righteous. But I said, *a*My leanness, my leanness, woe unto me! the treacherous dealers have dealt treacherously; yea, *b*the treacherous dealers have dealt very treacherously.

17 Fear, and the pit, and the snare, *are* upon thee, O inhabitant of the earth.

18 And it shall come to pass, *that* he who fleeth from the noise of the fear shall fall into the pit; and he that cometh up out of the midst of the pit shall be taken in the snare: for the windows from on high are open, and the foundations of the earth do shake.

19 The earth is utterly broken down, the earth is clean dissolved, the earth is *a*moved exceedingly.

20 The *a*earth shall reel to and fro like a drunkard, and shall be removed like a cottage; and the transgression thereof shall be heavy upon it; and it shall fall, and not rise again.

21 And it shall come to pass in that *a*day, *that* the LORD shall *b*punish the host of the high ones *that are* on high, and the kings of the earth upon the earth.

22 And they shall be gathered together, *as* *a*prisoners are gathered in the pit, and shall be shut up in the *b*prison, and after many days shall they be *c*visited.

23 Then the moon shall be con-founded, and the sun *a*ashamed, when the LORD of hosts shall reign in mount *b*Zion, and in Jerusalem, and before *c*his ancients gloriously.

CHAPTER 25

In Mount Zion the Lord will prepare a gospel feast of rich food—He will swallow up death in victory—It will be said, Lo, this is our God.

O LORD, thou *art* my God; I will exalt thee, I will praise thy name; for thou hast done wonderful *things*; *thy* counsels of old *are* faithfulness *and* truth.

2 For thou hast made of a city an heap; *of* a defenced city a ruin: a palace of strangers to be no city; it shall never be built.

3 Therefore shall the strong people glorify thee, the city of the terrible nations shall fear thee.

4 For thou hast been a strength to the *a*poor, a strength to the needy in his *b*distress, a *c*refuge from the storm, a shadow from the heat, when the blast of the terrible ones *is* as a storm *against* the wall.

5 Thou shalt bring down the noise of strangers, as the heat in a dry place; *even* the heat with the shadow of a cloud: the *a*branch of the terrible ones shall be brought low.

6 ¶ And in this mountain shall the LORD of hosts make unto all *a*people a feast of fat things, a feast of wines on the lees, of fat things full of marrow, of wines on the lees well refined.

7 And he will destroy in this mountain the face of the covering cast over all people, and the *a*veil that is spread over all nations.

8 He will swallow up *a*death in

15*a* HEB lights; or perhaps a scribal error for "islands."
16*a* HEB I waste away! Woe is me!
  b Despite the rejoicing of the remnant, the prophet laments the destruction of the many peoples who rejected righteousness (vv. 16–18).

19*a* TG Earth, Renewal of.
20*a* TG Last Days.
21*a* TG Day of the Lord.
  b TG Punish.
22*a* TG Spirits in Prison.
  b TG Hell;
     Salvation for the Dead.
  c John 5:25.
23*a* D&C 133:49.
  b TG Zion.
  c OR His elders in glory.

25 4*a* Ps. 35:10;
     D&C 56:18 (18–19).
  b Ps. 4:1.
  c TG Comfort; Refuge.
5*a* OR song of tyrants.
6*a* OR nations.
7*a* TG Veil.
8*a* John 20:9;
     1 Cor. 15:54.
  TG Jesus Christ, Death of; Resurrection.

*b*victory; and the Lord GOD will wipe away tears from off all faces; and the *c*rebuke of his people shall he take away from off all the earth: for the LORD hath spoken *it*.

9 ¶ And it shall be said in that day, Lo, this *is* our *a*God; we have waited for him, and he will save us: this *is* the LORD; we have *b*waited for him, we will be glad and rejoice in his *c*salvation.

10 For in this mountain shall the hand of the LORD rest, and Moab shall be trodden down under him, even as straw is trodden down for the dunghill.

11 And he shall spread forth his hands in the midst of them, as he that swimmeth spreadeth forth *his hands* to swim: and he shall bring down their pride together with the spoils of their hands.

12 And the fortress of the high fort of thy walls shall he bring down, lay low, *and* bring to the ground, *even* to the *a*dust.

CHAPTER 26

Trust in the Lord forever—Jehovah will die and be resurrected—All men will rise in the Resurrection.

IN that day shall this song be sung in the land of Judah; We have a strong city; salvation will *God* appoint *for* *a*walls and bulwarks.

2 Open ye the *a*gates, that the righteous nation which keepeth the truth may enter in.

3 Thou wilt keep *him* in perfect *a*peace, *whose* mind *is* stayed *on thee*: because he trusteth in thee.

4 Trust ye in the LORD for ever:

for in the LORD *a*JEHOVAH *is* *b*everlasting *c*strength:

5 ¶ For he bringeth down them that dwell on high; the lofty city, he layeth it low; he layeth it low, *even* to the ground; he bringeth it *even* to the dust.

6 The foot shall tread it down, *even* the feet of the poor, *and* the steps of the needy.

7 The way of the just *is* uprightness: thou, most *a*upright, dost weigh the path of the just.

8 Yea, in the way of thy judgments, O LORD, have we *a*waited for thee; the desire of *our* soul *is* to thy name, and to the remembrance of thee.

9 With my soul have I desired thee in the night; yea, with my spirit within me will I *a*seek thee *b*early: for when thy *c*judgments *are* in the earth, the inhabitants of the world will learn righteousness.

10 Let favour be shewed to the wicked, *yet* will he not learn righteousness: in the land of uprightness will he deal unjustly, and will not behold the majesty of the LORD.

11 LORD, *when* thy hand is lifted up, they will not see: *but* *a*they shall see, and be *b*ashamed for *their* envy at the people; yea, the fire of thine enemies shall devour them.

12 ¶ LORD, thou wilt ordain peace for us: for thou also hast wrought all our *a*works in us.

13 O LORD our God, *other* *a*lords beside thee have had dominion over us: *but* by thee only will we make mention of thy name.

14 *a*They are dead, they shall not live; *they are* deceased, they shall

---

8*b* TG Jesus Christ,
   Foreordained;
   Jesus Christ,
   Mission of;
   Jesus Christ,
   Resurrection.
c OR reproach of His
   people.
9*a* TG Jesus Christ,
   Prophecies about.
b TG Jesus Christ,
   Foreordained.

c TG Salvation.
12*a* 1 Ne. 22:14.
26 1*a* Isa. 60:18.
2*a* Hel. 3:28.
3*a* TG Contentment;
   Peace of God.
4*a* TG Jesus Christ, Jehovah.
b TG Eternity.
c TG Strength.
7*a* TG God, Justice of.
8*a* Isa. 33:2.
9*a* TG Prayer.

b Ps. 63:1.
c OR precepts.
11*a* OR let them see Thy zeal
   for Thy people, and be
   ashamed; yea, let fire
   destroy Thine enemies.
b Mosiah 27:31.
12*a* Alma 5:40 (40–41).
13*a* 2 Kgs. 18:4 (4–6).
14*a* IE the "other lords" of
   v. 13.

not rise: therefore hast thou visited and destroyed them, and made all their memory to perish.

15 Thou hast ªincreased the nation, O LORD, thou hast increased the nation: thou art glorified: thou hadst ᵇremoved *it* far *unto* all the ends of the earth.

16 LORD, in ªtrouble have they visited thee, they poured out a prayer *when* thy ᵇchastening *was* upon them.

17 Like as a woman with child, *that* draweth near the time of her delivery, is in pain, *and* crieth out in her pangs; so have we been in thy sight, O LORD.

18 We have been with child, we have been in pain, we have as it were brought forth wind; we have not wrought any deliverance in the earth; neither have the inhabitants of the world ªfallen.

19 Thy dead *men* shall ªlive, *together with* ᵇmy dead body shall they ᶜarise. Awake and sing, ye that dwell in dust: for thy dew *is as* the dew of herbs, and the earth shall cast out the dead.

20 ¶ Come, my people, enter thou into thy chambers, and shut thy doors about thee: hide thyself as it were for a little moment, ªuntil the indignation be overpast.

21 For, behold, the LORD cometh out of his place to punish the inhabitants of the earth for their iniquity: the earth also shall disclose her ªblood, and shall no more cover her slain.

CHAPTER 27

The people of Israel will blossom and bud and fill the earth with fruit—They will be gathered one by one and will worship the Lord.

IN that day the LORD with his ªsore and great and strong ᵇsword shall punish ᶜleviathan the piercing serpent, even leviathan that crooked ᵈserpent; and he shall slay the ᵉdragon that *is* in the sea.

2 In that day ªsing ye unto her, A vineyard of red wine.

3 I the LORD do keep it; I will water it every moment: lest *any* hurt it, I will keep it night and day.

4 Fury *is* not in me: who would set the briers *and* thorns against me in battle? I would go through them, I would burn them together.

5 Or let him take hold of my strength, *that* he may make peace with me; *and* he shall make peace with me.

6 He shall cause them that come of Jacob to take root: ªIsrael shall blossom and bud, and fill the face of the world with ᵇfruit.

7 ¶ Hath he smitten him, as he smote those that smote him? *or* is he slain according to the slaughter of them that are slain by him?

8 In measure, when it shooteth forth, thou wilt debate with it: he stayeth his rough wind in the day of the east wind.

9 By this therefore shall the iniquity of Jacob be ªpurged; and this *is* all the fruit to take away his sin; when he maketh all the stones of the

---

15ª Isa. 9:3;
   Abr. 2:9.
 ᵇ HEB expanded all the
   borders of the land.
16ª Israel recalls all the
   misery of the past days
   of exile, vv. 16–18.
 ᵇ TG Chastening.
18ª OR been brought low.
19ª TG Immortality.
 ᵇ TG Jesus Christ,
   Foreordained.
 ᶜ TG Jesus Christ,
   Mission of;
   Jesus Christ,
   Resurrection;

Resurrection.
20ª IE until the cleansing
   of the earth is over.
21ª HEB bloods; i.e., the
   bloodshed, crime, and
   violence committed
   will be exposed and
   recompensed.
27 1ª HEB hard.
 ᵇ Isa. 66:16.
 ᶜ IE a legendary sea
   monster representing
   the forces of chaos that
   opposed the Creator.
   See JST Rev. 12:1–17
   (Appendix).

ᵈ Job 26:13.
ᵉ Ps. 74:13;
   Isa. 51:9;
   Rev. 20:2.
2ª This song of the
   vineyard, about Israel,
   anticipates ultimate
   fulfillment of its
   destiny (vv. 2–6).
6ª Ether 13:11.
 ᵇ IE the blessings of
   salvation.
   TG Vineyard of the
   Lord.
9ª OR atoned for.

altar as chalkstones that are beaten in sunder, the groves and [b]images shall not stand up.

10 Yet the defenced city *shall be* desolate, *and* the habitation forsaken, and left like a wilderness: there shall the calf feed, and there shall he lie down, and consume the branches thereof.

11 When the [a]boughs thereof are withered, they shall be broken off: the women come, *and* set them on fire: for it *is* a people of no [b]understanding: therefore he that [c]made them will not have mercy on them, and he that formed them will shew them no favour.

12 ¶ And it shall come to pass in that day, *that* the LORD shall [a]beat off [b]from the channel of the river unto the stream of Egypt, and ye shall be [c]gathered one by one, O ye children of Israel.

13 And it shall come to pass in that day, *that* the [a]great trumpet shall be blown, and they shall come which were ready to perish in the land of Assyria, and the outcasts in the land of Egypt, and shall worship the LORD in the [b]holy mount at Jerusalem.

CHAPTER 28

Woe to the drunkards of Ephraim!— Revelation comes line upon line and precept upon precept—Christ, the sure foundation, is promised.

WOE to the crown of pride, to the [a]drunkards of [b]Ephraim, whose glorious beauty *is* a fading flower, which *are* on the head of [c]the fat

valleys of them that are overcome with wine!

2 Behold, the Lord hath a mighty and strong one, *which* as a [a]tempest of hail *and* a destroying [b]storm, as a flood of mighty waters overflowing, shall cast down to the earth with the hand.

3 The crown of pride, the drunkards of Ephraim, shall be trodden under feet:

4 And the glorious beauty, which *is* on the head of the fat valley, shall be a fading flower, *and* as the [a]hasty fruit before the summer; which *when* he that looketh upon it seeth, while it is yet in his hand he eateth it up.

5 ¶ In [a]that day shall the LORD of hosts be for a crown of [b]glory, and for a diadem of beauty, unto the residue of his people,

6 And for a spirit of judgment to him that sitteth in judgment, and for strength to them that turn the battle to the gate.

7 ¶ But [a]they also have [b]erred through [c]wine, and through strong drink are out of the way; the priest and the [d]prophet have erred through strong drink, they are swallowed up of wine, they are out of the way through strong drink; they err in vision, they stumble *in* judgment.

8 For all tables are full of vomit *and* [a]filthiness, *so that there is* no place *clean.*

9 ¶ Whom shall he teach [a]knowledge? and whom shall he make to understand doctrine? *them that are* [b]weaned from the [c]milk, *and* drawn from the breasts.

10 For precept *must be* upon precept, [a]precept upon precept; line

9 b TG Idolatry.
11 a Jacob 5:58 (58, 77).
  b TG Understanding.
  c Deut. 32:6.
12 a IE harvest, or glean.
  b IE from Mesopotamia.
  c TG Israel, Gathering of.
13 a HEB great *shophar*; i.e., the ram's horn used as a ceremonial trumpet. Matt. 24:31; D&C 49:23 (23–28).
  b Ps. 2:6.
28 1 a Hosea 12:1 (1–5).

b IE the leading tribe of the northern ten tribes of Israel about to be captured by Assyria in 722 B.C.
  c IE the valleys of rich produce.
2 a Isa. 30:30 (29–31).
  b Ezek. 38:9.
4 a HEB first or early fruit.
5 a IE a future day, after the scattering of Israel, in the time of preparation for final things.

b Isa. 2:11 (10–12).
7 a IE religious leaders of a later apostasy.
  b Isa. 56:10 (10–12).
  c TG Word of Wisdom.
  d TG False Prophets.
8 a TG Filthiness.
9 a TG Knowledge.
  b IE Instructions in righteousness must begin with the young.
  c D&C 19:22.
10 a D&C 98:12; 128:21.

upon line, line upon line; here a little, *and* there a little:

11 For with stammering lips and another tongue will he speak to this people.

12 To whom he said, This *is* the rest *wherewith* ye may cause the weary to rest; and this *is* the refreshing: yet they would not hear.

13 But the word of the LORD was unto them precept upon precept, *a*precept upon precept; line upon line, line upon line; here a little, *and* there a little; that they might go, and *b*fall backward, and be broken, and snared, and taken.

14 ¶ Wherefore hear the word of the LORD, ye scornful men, that rule this people which *is* in Jerusalem.

15 Because ye have said, We have made a covenant with death, and with hell are we at agreement; when the overflowing *a*scourge shall pass through, it shall not come unto us: for we have made lies our *b*refuge, and under falsehood have we hid ourselves:

16 ¶ Therefore thus saith the Lord GOD, Behold, I lay in Zion for a *a*foundation a *b*stone, a tried stone, a precious *c*corner *stone*, a sure foundation: he that believeth shall not make haste.

17 Judgment also will I lay to the line, and righteousness to the plummet: and the hail shall sweep away the refuge of lies, and the waters shall overflow the hiding place.

18 ¶ And *a*your covenant with death shall be disannulled, and your agreement with hell shall not stand; when the overflowing scourge shall pass through, then ye shall be trodden down by it.

19 From the time that it goeth forth it shall take you: for morning by morning shall it pass over, by day and by night: and it shall be a vexation only *to* understand the report.

20 For the bed is shorter than that *a man* can stretch himself *on it:* and the covering narrower than that he can wrap himself *in it.*

21 For the LORD shall rise up as *in* *a*mount Perazim, he shall be wroth as *in* the valley of *b*Gibeon, that he may do his work, his strange work; and bring to pass his act, his *c*strange act.

22 Now therefore be ye not mockers, lest your bands be made strong: for I have heard from the Lord GOD of hosts a *a*consumption, even determined upon the whole earth.

23 ¶ Give ye ear, and hear my voice; hearken, and hear my speech.

24 Doth the plowman plow all day to sow? doth he open and break the clods of his ground?

25 When he hath made plain the face thereof, doth he not cast abroad the fitches, and scatter the cummin, and cast in the principal wheat and the appointed barley and the rie in their place?

26 For his God doth instruct him to discretion, *and* doth teach him.

27 For the fitches are not threshed with a threshing instrument, neither is a cart wheel turned about upon the cummin; but the fitches are beaten out with a staff, and the cummin with a rod.

28 Bread *corn* is bruised; because he will not ever be threshing it, nor break *it with* the wheel of his cart, nor bruise it *with* his horsemen.

29 This also *a*cometh forth from the LORD of hosts, *which* is wonderful in counsel, *and* excellent in working.

13*a* 2 Ne. 28:30;
   D&C 50:24; 93:20.
  b IE In spite of the Lord's
   instructing Israel
   through prophets,
   many of the people
   apostatized.
15*a* D&C 45:31 (30–59).
  b TG Refuge; Trust Not in
   the Arm of Flesh.

16*a* Hel. 5:12.
  b Ps. 87:1;
   1 Pet. 2:6 (6–8).
   TG Jesus Christ,
   Prophecies about.
  c TG Cornerstone.
18*a* IE the evil and
   conspiring people's
   plans.
21*a* 2 Sam. 5:20 (19–20);

   1 Chr. 14:11 (10–11).
  b Josh. 10:10 (8–14).
  c D&C 95:4; 101:95.
22*a* Dan. 9:27.
   TG World, End of.
29*a* IE The reaping and
   threshing of the world
   (as on a farm, vv. 23–29)
   will be properly done
   by the Lord.

CHAPTER 29

A people (the Nephites) will speak as a voice from the dust—The Apostasy, restoration of the gospel, and coming forth of a sealed book (the Book of Mormon) are foretold—Compare 2 Nephi 27.

*a*WOE to *b*Ariel, to Ariel, the city *c*where David dwelt! add ye year to year; let them kill sacrifices.

2 Yet I will distress Ariel, and there shall be heaviness and *a*sorrow: and it shall be unto me as Ariel.

3 And I will *a*camp against thee round about, and will lay siege against thee with a mount, and I will raise forts against thee.

4 And thou shalt be brought down, *and* shalt speak out of the ground, and thy speech shall be low out of the *a*dust, and thy voice shall be, as of one that hath a familiar spirit, out of the *b*ground, and thy speech shall whisper out of the dust.

5 Moreover the multitude of thy strangers shall be like small dust, and the multitude of the terrible ones *shall be* as chaff that passeth away: yea, it shall be at an instant suddenly.

6 Thou shalt be visited of the LORD of hosts with thunder, and with earthquake, and great noise, with storm and tempest, and the flame of devouring *a*fire.

7 ¶ And the multitude of all the nations that fight against Ariel, even all that fight against her and her munition, and that distress her, shall be as a dream of a night vision.

8 It shall even be as when an hungry *man* dreameth, and, behold, he eateth; but he awaketh, and his soul is empty: or as when a thirsty man dreameth, and, behold, he drinketh; but he awaketh, and, behold, *he is* faint, and his soul hath appetite: so shall the multitude of all the nations be, that *a*fight against mount *b*Zion.

9 ¶ Stay yourselves, and wonder; cry ye out, and cry: they are *a*drunken, but not with wine; they stagger, but not with strong drink.

10 For the LORD hath poured out upon you the spirit of deep *a*sleep, and hath closed your *b*eyes: the *c*prophets and your rulers, the *d*seers hath he *e*covered.

11 And the vision of all is become unto you as the words of a *a*book that is *b*sealed, which *men* deliver to one that is learned, saying, Read this, I pray thee: and he saith, I cannot; for it *is* sealed:

12 And the book is delivered to *a*him that is not learned, saying, Read this, I pray thee: and he saith, I am not learned.

13 ¶ Wherefore the Lord said, Forasmuch as this people *a*draw near *me* with their *b*mouth, and with their lips do *c*honour me, but have *d*removed their *e*heart far from me, and their *f*fear toward me is taught by the *g*precept of men:

14 Therefore, behold, I will proceed to do a *a*marvellous *b*work among this people, *even* a marvellous work and a wonder: for the *c*wisdom of their wise *men* shall *d*perish, and

---

29 1*a* JST Isa. 29:1–8
   (Appendix).
   b HEB Hearth of God;
      i.e., the temple; translated as "the altar" in Ezek.
      43:15, second clause.
   c IE Jerusalem.
2*a* TG Sorrow.
3*a* 2 Ne. 26:15.
4*a* Moro. 10:27.
   b TG Book of Mormon.
6*a* D&C 97:26.
8*a* TG Protection, Divine.
   b TG Zion.
9*a* 2 Ne. 27:4.
10*a* Rom. 11:8 (7–8).
   b TG Spiritual Blindness.

c 2 Ne. 27:5.
d TG Seer.
e Micah 3:7.
11*a* TG Book of Mormon;
      Scriptures to Come Forth.
   b 2 Ne. 27:7 (6–26);
      JS—H 1:65 (63–65).
      TG Seal.
12*a* JS—H 1:59.
13*a* JS—H 1:19 (5–26).
   b Ezek. 33:31 (30–33).
      TG Apostasy of the Early
      Christian Church;
      Hypocrisy.
   c Isa. 48:1;
      Matt. 15:8 (7–9).
   d Isa. 1:13.

TG Apostasy of Israel.
e TG Hardheartedness;
   Heart;
   Worship.
f OR regard, reverence
   for me.
g TG Traditions of Men.
14*a* 1 Ne. 22:8;
   D&C 4:1.
   TG Book of Mormon;
   Restoration of the
   Gospel.
b TG God, Works of.
c TG Wisdom.
d D&C 76:9.

the *e*understanding of their *f*prudent *men* shall be hid.

15 Woe unto them that seek deep to hide their *a*counsel from the LORD, and their works are in the dark, and they say, Who *b*seeth us? and who knoweth us?

16 Surely your turning of things upside down shall be esteemed as the potter's clay: for shall the *a*work say of him that made it, He made me not? or shall the thing framed say of him that framed it, He had no understanding?

17 *Is* it not yet a very little while, and Lebanon shall be turned into a fruitful field, and the fruitful field shall be esteemed as a forest?

18 ¶ And in that *a*day shall the deaf hear the words of the *b*book, and the *c*eyes of the blind shall see out of *d*obscurity, and out of darkness.

19 The meek also shall increase *their* *a*joy in the LORD, and the *b*poor among men shall rejoice in the Holy One of Israel.

20 For the terrible one is brought to nought, and the scorner is consumed, and all that *a*watch for iniquity are *b*cut off:

21 That make a man an *a*offender for a word, and lay a snare for him that reproveth in *b*the gate, and *c*turn aside the just for a thing of nought.

22 Therefore thus saith the LORD, who redeemed Abraham, concerning the *a*house of Jacob, Jacob shall not now be ashamed, neither shall his face now wax pale.

23 But when he seeth his children,

the *a*work of mine hands, in the midst of him, they shall sanctify my name, and sanctify the Holy One of Jacob, and shall *b*fear the *c*God of Israel.

24 They also that *a*erred in spirit shall come to understanding, and they that murmured shall *b*learn doctrine.

CHAPTER 30

Israel is scattered for rejecting the seers and prophets—Israel's people will be gathered and blessed temporally and spiritually—The Lord will come in a day of apostasy to judge and destroy the wicked.

WOE to the *a*rebellious children, saith the LORD, that take *b*counsel, but not of me; and that cover with a covering, but not of my spirit, that they may add sin to sin:

2 That walk to go down into Egypt, and have not asked at my mouth; to strengthen themselves in the strength of *a*Pharaoh, and to trust *b*in the shadow of *c*Egypt!

3 Therefore shall the strength of Pharaoh be your shame, and the trust in the shadow of Egypt *your* confusion.

4 For his princes were at Zoan, and his ambassadors came to Hanes.

5 They *a*were all *b*ashamed of a people *that* could not profit them, nor be an help nor profit, but a shame, and also a reproach.

6 The *a*burden of the beasts of the *b*south: into the land of trouble and anguish, from whence *come* the

---

14*e* TG Knowledge;
    Understanding.
  f TG Prudence.
15*a* TG Counselor.
  b Isa. 47:10.
16*a* Isa. 45:9; 64:8.
18*a* TG Last Days.
  b TG Book of Mormon.
  c Isa. 32:3.
    TG Sight.
  d TG Darkness, Spiritual.
19*a* TG Joy.
  b TG Poor.
20*a* Rev. 12:10;
    D&C 88:124.
    TG Watch.

  b D&C 45:50.
21*a* TG Offense.
  b IE the place of public
    transactions.
  c Amos 5:12.
22*a* 1 Ne. 15:19 (19–20).
23*a* Isa. 45:11.
  b OR stand in awe of the
    God of Israel.
  c Isa. 45:3;
    3 Ne. 11:14;
    D&C 36:1; 127:3.
24*a* D&C 1:25.
  b TG Learn.
30 1*a* TG Rebellion;
    Stiffnecked.

  b TG Counselor.
2*a* TG Trust Not in the
    Arm of Flesh.
  b IE in an alliance with
    Egypt for protection
    against Assyria.
  c Jer. 2:18 (14–19).
5*a* OR will be.
  b Jer. 2:36.
6*a* IE a message of doom
    for those of Judah who
    travel with loads of
    gifts on animals toward
    Egypt (vv. 2–7).
  b HEB Negev; i.e., the
    southern desert.

young and old lion, the viper and fiery flying serpent, they will carry their riches upon the shoulders of young asses, and their treasures upon the bunches of camels, to a people *that* shall not profit *them*.

7 For the ^aEgyptians shall help in vain, and to no purpose: therefore have I cried concerning this, Their strength *is* to sit still.

8 ¶ Now go, ^awrite it before them in a table, and note it in a book, that it may be for the time to come for ever and ever:

9 That ^athis *is* a ^brebellious people, lying children, children *that* will not hear the law of the LORD:

10 Which say to the ^aseers, See not; and to the prophets, Prophesy not unto us right things, speak unto us ^bsmooth things, prophesy ^cdeceits:

11 Get you out of the way, turn aside out of the path, cause the Holy One of Israel to cease from before us.

12 Wherefore thus saith the Holy One of Israel, Because ye despise this word, and trust in oppression and perverseness, and stay thereon:

13 Therefore this iniquity shall be to you as a breach ready to fall, swelling out in a high wall, whose breaking cometh suddenly at an instant.

14 And he shall break it as the ^abreaking of the potters' vessel that is broken in pieces; he shall not spare: so that there shall not be found in the bursting of it a sherd to take fire from the hearth, or to take water *withal* out of the pit.

15 For thus saith the Lord GOD, the Holy One of Israel; In returning and rest shall ye be saved; in ^aquietness and in confidence shall be your strength: and ye would not.

16 But ye said, No; for we will flee upon ^ahorses; therefore shall ye flee: and, We will ride upon the swift; therefore shall they that pursue you be swift.

17 One thousand *shall flee* at the rebuke of one; at the rebuke of five shall ye flee: till ye be left as a beacon upon the top of a mountain, and as an ^aensign on an hill.

18 ¶ And therefore will the LORD ^await, that he may be gracious unto you, and therefore will he be exalted, that he may have mercy upon you: for the LORD *is* a God of ^bjudgment: blessed *are* all they that ^cwait for him.

19 For the people shall dwell in ^aZion at Jerusalem: thou shalt weep no more: he will be very gracious unto thee at the voice of thy cry; when he shall hear it, he will answer thee.

20 And *though* the Lord give you the bread of ^aadversity, and the water of affliction, yet shall not ^bthy teachers be removed into a corner any more, but thine eyes shall see thy ^cteachers:

21 And thine ears shall hear a word behind thee, saying, This *is* the way, ^awalk ye in it, when ye turn to the right hand, and when ye turn to the left.

22 Ye shall defile also the covering of thy graven images of silver, and the ornament of thy molten images of gold: thou shalt cast them away as a menstruous cloth; thou shalt say unto it, Get thee hence.

23 Then shall he give the rain ^aof thy seed, that thou shalt sow the ground withal; and bread of the increase of the earth, and it shall be fat and plenteous: in that day shall thy cattle feed in large pastures.

24 The oxen likewise and the young

7a Lam. 4:17.
8a TG Scriptures,
  Preservation of;
  Scriptures, Writing of.
9a IE the Israelite people
  who won't hearken to
  the prophets.
  b Hel. 13:26 (25–28).
10a TG Seer.
  b TG False Doctrine.

c TG Honesty.
14a Ps. 2:9.
15a TG Silence.
16a Isa. 31:1.
17a D&C 113:6.
18a IE The Lord will
  wait until the day of
  restoration to bless
  Israel with His presence.
  b HEB Justice.

TG Judgment.
  c D&C 98:2.
19a TG Zion.
20a TG Adversity.
  b HEB thy teacher; i.e.,
  the Lord.
  c TG Teacher.
21a TG Walking with God.
23a IE for thy seed.

asses that *ear the ground shall eat clean provender, which hath been winnowed with the shovel and with the fan.

25 And there shall be upon every high mountain, and upon every high hill, rivers *and* streams of waters in the *day of the great slaughter, when the towers fall.

26 Moreover the light of the moon shall be as the light of the sun, and the light of the sun shall be sevenfold, as the light of seven days, in the day that the LORD bindeth up the breach of his people, and *healeth the stroke of their wound.

27 ¶ Behold, the *name of the LORD cometh from far, burning with his *anger, and the burden *thereof is* heavy: his lips are full of indignation, and his tongue as a devouring fire:

28 And his *breath, as an overflowing stream, shall reach to the midst of the *neck, to sift the nations with the sieve of *vanity: and *there shall be* a bridle in the jaws of the people, causing *them* to err.

29 *Ye shall have a song, as in the night *when *a holy solemnity is kept; and gladness of heart, as when one goeth with a pipe to come into the *mountain of the LORD, to the *mighty One of Israel.

30 And the LORD shall cause his glorious voice to be heard, and shall shew the lighting down of his arm, with the indignation of *his* anger, and *with* the flame of a devouring fire, *with* scattering, and *tempest, and hailstones.

31 For through the voice of the LORD shall the *Assyrian be beaten down, *which *smote with a rod.

32 And *in* every place where the grounded staff shall pass, which the LORD shall lay upon him, *it* shall be with tabrets and harps: and *in battles of shaking will he fight *with it.

33 For *Tophet *is* ordained of old; yea, for the king it is prepared; he hath made *it* deep *and* large: the pile thereof *is* fire and much wood; the breath of the LORD, like a stream of brimstone, doth kindle it.

CHAPTER 31

Israel is reproved for turning to Egypt for help—When the Lord comes, He will defend and preserve His people.

WOE to them that go down to Egypt for *help; and *stay on *horses, and trust in chariots, because *they are* many; and in horsemen, because they are very strong; but they look not unto the Holy One of Israel, neither seek the LORD!

2 Yet he also *is* wise, and will bring *evil, and will not *call back his words: but will arise against the house of the evildoers, and against the help of them that work iniquity.

3 Now the Egyptians *are* men, and not *God; and their horses flesh, and not spirit. When the LORD shall stretch out his hand, both he that helpeth shall fall, and he that is *holpen shall fall down, and they all shall fail together.

4 For thus hath the LORD spoken unto me, Like as the *lion and the young lion roaring on his prey, when

---

24*a* HEB work the soil.
25*a* IE day of destruction of all enemies.
26*a* IE heals their affliction (after long exile).
27*a* IE A symbol of His power will come to destroy "Assyria" or wickedness (see v. 31).
  b TG God, Indignation of.
28*a* Isa. 11:4.
  b Isa. 8:8.
  c TG Vanity.
29*a* IE the righteous

survivors.
  b HEB the sanctifying of a feast day.
  c Isa. 2:3 (2–3); D&C 49:25.
  d HEB rock.
30*a* Isa. 28:2.
31*a* Isa. 37:36.
  b Isa. 10:24 (24–27).
32*a* HEB with waves of battles.
  b OR against them.
33*a* IE the place of burning. 2 Kgs. 23:10.

31 1*a* TG Trust Not in the Arm of Flesh.
  b OR rely. Ps. 20:7.
  c Isa. 30:16; Hosea 14:3 (1–3).
2*a* IE calamity upon evildoers.
  b Num. 23:19.
3*a* OR gods.
  b IE Both Egypt and they who trusted in Egypt shall fall.
4*a* Hosea 11:10; Amos 1:2.

a multitude of shepherds is called forth against him, *he* will not be afraid of their voice, nor abase himself for the noise of them: so shall the LORD of hosts come down to *b*fight for mount Zion, and for the hill thereof.

5 As birds *a*flying, so will the LORD of hosts *b*defend Jerusalem; defending also he will deliver *it; and* passing over he will preserve *it.*

6 ¶ Turn ye unto *him from* whom the children of Israel have deeply revolted.

7 For in that day every man shall cast away his idols of silver, and his idols of gold, which your own hands have made unto you *for* a sin.

8 ¶ Then shall the *a*Assyrian fall with the sword, not of a mighty man; and the sword, not of a mean man, shall devour him: but he shall flee from the sword, and his young men shall be discomfited.

9 And he shall pass over to his strong hold for fear, and his princes shall be afraid of the *a*ensign, saith the LORD, whose fire *is* in Zion, and his furnace in Jerusalem.

CHAPTER 32

A king (the Messiah) will reign in righteousness—The land of Israel will be a wilderness until the day of restoration and gathering.

BEHOLD, a *a*king shall reign in righteousness, and princes shall rule in *b*judgment.

2 And *a*a man shall be as an hiding place from the wind, and a covert from the tempest; as rivers of water in a dry place, as the shadow of a great rock in a weary land.

3 And the *a*eyes of them that see shall not be dim, and the ears of them that hear shall hearken.

4 The heart also of the rash shall understand knowledge, and the tongue of the stammerers shall be ready to speak plainly.

5 The vile person shall be no more called *a*liberal, nor the *b*churl said *to be* *c*bountiful.

6 For the vile person will speak *a*villany, and his heart will work iniquity, to practise *b*hypocrisy, and to utter error against the LORD, to make empty the soul of the hungry, and he will cause the drink of the thirsty to fail.

7 The instruments also of the churl *are* evil: he deviseth wicked devices to destroy the poor with *a*lying words, even when the needy speaketh right.

8 But the liberal deviseth liberal things; and by liberal things shall he stand.

9 ¶ Rise up, ye *a*women that are at ease; hear my voice, ye *b*careless daughters; give ear unto my speech.

10 Many days and years shall ye be troubled, ye careless women: for the vintage shall *a*fail, the gathering shall not come.

11 Tremble, ye women that are at ease; be troubled, ye careless ones: strip you, and make you bare, and gird *a*sackcloth upon *your* loins.

12 They shall *a*lament for the teats, for the pleasant fields, for the fruitful vine.

13 Upon the land of my people shall come up thorns *and* briers; yea, upon all the houses of joy *in* the joyous city:

14 Because the palaces shall be forsaken; the multitude of the city *a*shall be left; the forts and towers shall be for dens for ever, a joy of wild asses, a pasture of flocks;

4*b* Isa. 42:13.
5*a* IE hovering over their young.
  b Hosea 1:7.
8*a* IE Assyria shall fall by destruction from God. Isa. 37:36 (1–38).
9*a* D&C 45:68 (68–71).
32 1*a* Jer. 23:5 (5–6).
  TG Kings, Earthly.

  b OR justice.
2*a* IE the king mentioned in v. 1.
3*a* Isa. 29:18; 35:5.
5*a* HEB noble.
  b OR miser.
  c HEB a nobleman or wealthy.
6*a* HEB obscenity.
  b TG Hypocrisy.

7*a* TG Slander.
9*a* TG Woman.
  b HEB confident or secure (also vv. 10–11).
  TG Vanity.
10*a* Joel 1:5 (5–7).
11*a* TG Apparel.
12*a* HEB beat the breast (in mourning).
14*a* OR deserted.

15 Until the spirit be poured upon us from on high, and the wilderness be a *a*fruitful field, and the fruitful field be counted for a forest.

16 Then judgment shall dwell in the wilderness, and righteousness remain in the fruitful field.

17 And the work of righteousness shall be *a*peace; and the effect of righteousness quietness and *b*assurance for ever.

18 And my people shall dwell in a peaceable habitation, and in sure dwellings, and in quiet resting places;

19 When it shall *a*hail, coming down on the forest; and the *b*city shall be low in a low place.

20 Blessed *are* ye that sow beside all waters, that send forth *thither* the feet of the ox and the ass.

CHAPTER 33

Apostasy and wickedness will precede the Second Coming—The Lord will come with devouring fire—Zion and its stakes will be perfected—The Lord is our Judge, Lawgiver, and King.

WOE to thee that *a*spoilest, and thou *wast* not spoiled; and dealest *b*treacherously, and they dealt not treacherously with thee! when thou shalt cease to spoil, thou shalt be spoiled; *and* when thou shalt make an end to deal treacherously, they shall deal treacherously with thee.

2 O LORD, be gracious unto us; we have *a*waited for thee: be thou their *b*arm every morning, our salvation also in the time of trouble.

3 At the noise of the tumult the people fled; at the lifting up of thyself the nations were scattered.

4 And your spoil shall be gathered *like* the gathering of the caterpiller:

as the running to and fro of locusts shall he run upon them.

5 The LORD is exalted; for he dwelleth on high: he hath filled Zion with judgment and righteousness.

6 And wisdom and *a*knowledge shall be the stability of thy times, *and* strength of salvation: the fear of the LORD *is* his *b*treasure.

7 Behold, their valiant ones shall cry without: the ambassadors of peace shall weep bitterly.

8 The highways lie waste, the wayfaring man ceaseth: he hath *a*broken the covenant, he hath despised the cities, he regardeth no man.

9 The earth *a*mourneth *and* languisheth: Lebanon is ashamed *and* hewn down: Sharon is like a wilderness; and Bashan and Carmel shake off *their fruits.*

10 Now will I rise, saith the LORD; now will I be exalted; now will I lift up myself.

11 Ye shall conceive chaff, ye shall bring forth stubble: your breath, *as* fire, shall devour you.

12 And the people shall be *as* the burnings of lime: *as* thorns cut up shall they be burned in the fire.

13 ¶ Hear, ye *that are* far off, what I have done; and, ye *that are* near, acknowledge my might.

14 The sinners in Zion are afraid; fearfulness hath surprised the hypocrites. Who among us shall dwell with the devouring fire? who among us shall dwell with *a*everlasting *b*burnings?

15 He that *a*walketh righteously, and speaketh uprightly; he that despiseth *b*the gain of oppressions, that shaketh his hands from holding of *c*bribes, that stoppeth his ears from hearing of *d*blood, and shutteth his eyes *e*from seeing evil;

15*a* TG Earth, Renewal of.
17*a* TG Conscience;
  Peace; Peacemakers;
  Peace of God.
  b TG Happiness; Joy.
19*a* D&C 29:16.
  b IE The "forest" and
  "city" are probably "the
  proud and the wicked."
33 1*a* Isa. 17:14;

Hab. 2:8 (6–8).
  b Isa. 21:2.
2*a* Isa. 26:8.
  b Omni 1:13;
  Mosiah 12:24.
6*a* TG Knowledge.
  b TG Treasure.
8*a* OR annulled the treaty
  or contract.
9*a* D&C 123:7.

14*a* TG Eternal Life.
  b D&C 130:7 (6–7);
  137:2 (2–3).
15*a* TG Walking with God.
  b OR profit by extortion.
  c TG Bribe.
  d HEB bloods; i.e.,
  violence.
  e IE from being a
  participant in evils.

16 He shall dwell on high: his place of defence *shall be* the munitions of rocks: bread shall be given him; his waters *shall be* sure.

17 Thine eyes shall see the king in his *a*beauty: they shall behold the land that is very far off.

18 Thine heart shall meditate terror. Where *is* the *a*scribe? where *is* the receiver? where *is* he that counted the towers?

19 Thou shalt not see *a*a fierce people, a people of a deeper *b*speech than thou canst perceive; of a stammering tongue, *that thou canst* not understand.

20 Look upon *a*Zion, the city of our solemnities: thine eyes shall see Jerusalem a quiet habitation, a tabernacle *that* shall not be taken down; not one of the *b*stakes thereof shall ever be removed, neither shall any of the cords thereof be broken.

21 But there the glorious LORD *will be* *a*unto us a place of broad rivers *and* streams; wherein shall go no galley with oars, neither shall gallant ship pass thereby.

22 For the LORD *is* our *a*judge, the LORD *is* our *b*lawgiver, the LORD *is* our king; he will save us.

23 Thy tacklings are loosed; they could not well strengthen their mast, they could not spread the sail: then is the prey of a great spoil divided; the lame take the prey.

24 And the inhabitant shall not say, I am sick: the people that dwell therein *shall be* forgiven *their* iniquity.

CHAPTER 34

The Second Coming will be a day of vengeance and judgment—The indignation of the Lord will be upon all nations—His sword will fall upon the world.

COME near, ye nations, to hear; and hearken, ye people: let the earth hear, and all that is therein; the world, and all things that come forth of it.

2 For the indignation of the LORD *is* upon all nations, and *his* fury upon all their armies: he hath utterly destroyed them, he hath delivered them to the slaughter.

3 Their slain also shall be cast out, and their *a*stink shall come up out of their carcases, and the mountains shall be melted with their blood.

4 And all the host of heaven shall be *a*dissolved, and the heavens shall be rolled together as a *b*scroll: and all their host shall fall down, as the leaf falleth off from the vine, and as *c*a falling *fig* from the fig tree.

5 For my sword shall be bathed in heaven: behold, it shall come down upon *a*Idumea, and upon the people of my *b*curse, to judgment.

6 The sword of the LORD is filled with blood, it is made fat with fatness, *and* with the blood of lambs and goats, with the fat of the kidneys of rams: for the LORD hath a *a*sacrifice in Bozrah, and a great slaughter in the land of Idumea.

7 And the *a*unicorns shall come down with them, and the bullocks with the bulls; and their land shall be soaked with blood, and their dust made fat with fatness.

8 For *it is* the day of the LORD's *a*vengeance, *and* the year of recompences for the controversy of Zion.

9 And the streams *a*thereof shall be turned into pitch, and the dust

---

17*a* TG Beauty.
18*a* OR tallyman (i.e., of the former Assyrian conqueror).
19*a* IE any more foreign invaders.
   b Deut. 28:49;
      Jer. 5:15.
20*a* Isa. 2:3 (2–4).
   b TG Stake.
21*a* OR with us in majesty in a place.
22*a* TG Jesus Christ, Judge.

   b D&C 38:22.
34 3*a* Joel 2:20.
   4*a* Ps. 102:26;
      Luke 21:26.
   b Rev. 6:14;
      JST Rev. 6:14 (Rev. 6:14 note *a*).
   c HEB an unripe fruit.
   5*a* HEB Edom.
      Jer. 49:17 (7–22);
      Ezek. 25:14 (12–14);
      Amos 9:12;
      Obad. 1:18 (8, 18–19, 21).

      TG World, End of.
   b TG Curse.
   6*a* Jer. 46:10.
   7*a* JST Isa. 34:7 . . . *reem* . . . (*Re'em* is Hebrew for "wild ox.")
   8*a* Isa. 61:2;
      Mal. 4:1 (1, 3);
      3 Ne. 21:21 (20–21);
      D&C 97:26 (25–28).
   9*a* IE of Edom.

thereof into brimstone, and the land thereof shall become burning pitch.

10 It shall not be quenched night nor day; the smoke thereof shall go up for ever: from generation to generation it shall lie waste; none shall pass through it for ever and ever.

11 ¶ But the ^acormorant and the ^bbittern shall possess it; the owl also and the raven shall dwell in it: and he shall stretch out upon it the line of confusion, and the ^cstones of emptiness.

12 They shall call the nobles thereof to the kingdom, but none *shall be* there, and all her princes shall be nothing.

13 And thorns shall come up in her palaces, nettles and brambles in the fortresses thereof: and it shall be ^aan habitation of dragons, *and* a court for owls.

14 The ^awild beasts of the desert shall also meet with the wild beasts of the island, and the satyr shall cry to his fellow; the screech owl also shall rest there, and find for herself a place of rest.

15 There shall the great owl make her nest, and lay, and hatch, and gather under her shadow: there shall the vultures also be gathered, every one with her mate.

16 ¶ Seek ye out of the book of the LORD, and read: no one of these shall fail, none shall want her mate: for my mouth it hath ^acommanded, and his spirit it hath gathered them.

17 And he hath cast the lot for them, and his hand hath divided it unto them by line: they shall possess it for ever, from generation to generation shall they dwell therein.

CHAPTER 35

In the day of restoration, the desert will blossom, the Lord will come, Israel will be gathered, and Zion will be built up.

THE wilderness and the ^asolitary place shall be ^bglad for ^cthem; and the ^ddesert shall rejoice, and ^eblossom as the rose.

2 It shall blossom abundantly, and rejoice even with joy and singing: the glory of ^aLebanon shall be given unto it, the excellency of Carmel and Sharon, they shall see the ^bglory of the LORD, *and* the excellency of our God.

3 ¶ Strengthen ye the ^aweak hands, and confirm the ^bfeeble knees.

4 Say to them *that are* of a fearful heart, Be strong, fear not: behold, your God will come *with* ^avengeance, *even* God *with* a recompence; he will come and save you.

5 Then the ^aeyes of the ^bblind shall be opened, and the ears of the deaf shall be unstopped.

6 Then shall the lame *man* leap as an ^ahart, and the tongue of the dumb ^bsing: for in the wilderness shall waters break out, and streams in the desert.

7 And the ^aparched ground shall become a pool, and the thirsty land springs of water: in the ^bhabitation of dragons, where each lay, *shall be* grass with reeds and rushes.

8 And an ^ahighway shall be there, and a way, and it shall be called The way of ^bholiness; the ^cunclean shall not pass over it; but it *shall be* for those: the wayfaring men, though fools, shall not err *therein*.

9 No lion shall be there, nor *any* ravenous beast shall go up thereon,

---

11a Zeph. 2:14.
  b Isa. 14:23.
  c HEB plummet.
13a HEB the resort of jackals.
14a Isa. 13:21.
16a D&C 1:7 (7, 18, 37–38).
35 1a D&C 117:7.
  b Ps. 96:12.
  c IE the righteous who

return.
  d Ezek. 36:34.
  e TG Earth, Renewal of; Israel, Blessings of.
2a Isa. 60:13.
  b TG Millennium.
3a Rom. 14:1 (1–3).
  b Heb. 12:12; D&C 81:5.
4a Morm. 3:15.

5a Isa. 32:3.
  b TG Sight.
6a OR deer.
  b TG Singing.
7a D&C 133:29.
  b HEB resorts of jackals.
8a Isa. 11:16; 51:10 (10–11).
  b TG Holiness.
  c TG Chastity.

it shall not be found there; but the ^aredeemed shall walk *there:*

10 And the ransomed of the LORD shall ^areturn, and come to ^bZion with ^csongs and everlasting ^djoy upon their heads: they shall obtain joy and gladness, and ^esorrow and sighing shall flee away.

CHAPTER 36

The Assyrians war against Judah and blaspheme the Lord.

Now it came to pass in the ^afourteenth year of king Hezekiah, *that* Sennacherib king of ^bAssyria came up against all the defenced cities of Judah, and took them.

2 And the king of Assyria sent ^aRabshakeh from Lachish to Jerusalem unto king Hezekiah with a great army. And he stood by the conduit of the upper pool in the highway of the fuller's field.

3 Then came forth unto him Eliakim, Hilkiah's son, which was over the house, and Shebna the scribe, and Joah, Asaph's son, the recorder.

4 ¶ And Rabshakeh said unto them, Say ye now to Hezekiah, Thus saith the great king, the king of Assyria, What confidence *is* this wherein thou trustest?

5 I say, *sayest thou,* (but *they are but* vain words) *I have* counsel and strength for war: now on whom dost thou trust, that thou rebellest against me?

6 Lo, thou trustest in the staff of this broken ^areed, on ^bEgypt; whereon if a man lean, it will go into his hand, and pierce it: so *is* Pharaoh king of Egypt to all that trust in him.

7 But if thou say to me, We trust in the LORD our God: *is it* not he, whose ^ahigh places and whose altars Hezekiah hath taken away, and said

to Judah and to Jerusalem, Ye shall worship before this altar?

8 Now therefore give pledges, I pray thee, to my master the king of Assyria, and I will give thee two thousand horses, if thou be able on thy part to set riders upon them.

9 How then wilt thou turn away the face of one captain of the least of my master's servants, and put thy trust on Egypt for chariots and for horsemen?

10 And am I now come up without the LORD against this land to destroy it? the LORD said unto me, Go up against this land, and destroy it.

11 ¶ Then said Eliakim and Shebna and Joah unto Rabshakeh, Speak, I pray thee, unto thy servants in the ^aSyrian language; for we understand *it:* and speak not to us in the Jews' language, in the ears of the people that *are* on the wall.

12 ¶ But Rabshakeh said, Hath my master sent me to thy master and to thee to speak these words? *hath he* not *sent me* to the men that sit upon the wall, that they may eat their own dung, and drink their own piss with you?

13 Then Rabshakeh stood, and cried with a loud voice in the Jews' language, and said, Hear ye the words of the great king, the king of Assyria.

14 Thus saith the king, Let not Hezekiah deceive you: for he shall not be able to deliver you.

15 Neither let Hezekiah make you trust in the LORD, saying, The LORD will surely deliver us: this city shall not be delivered into the hand of the king of Assyria.

16 Hearken not to Hezekiah: for thus saith the king of Assyria, Make *an agreement* with me *by* a present, and come out to me: and eat ye every one of his vine, and every one

9 *a* Isa. 51:10 (10–11).
10 *a* TG Israel, Gathering of.
  b D&C 45:66 (66–71);
    109:39.
  c TG Singing.
  d Isa. 65:18.
  e TG Sorrow.

36 1 *a* 2 Kgs. 18:13 (11–37).
  b TG Israel, Scattering of.
  2 *a* HEB the Assyrian chief
    of the officers.
  6 *a* 2 Kgs. 18:21;
    Ezek. 29:6 (6–16).
  b TG Trust Not in the

Arm of Flesh.
7 *a* IE All outlying shrines
    had been eliminated, in
    favor of one temple, in
    Jerusalem.
11 *a* HEB Aramaic.

of his fig tree, and drink ye every one the waters of his own cistern;

17 Until I come and take you away to a land like your own land, a land of corn and wine, a land of bread and vineyards.

18 *Beware* lest Hezekiah persuade you, saying, The LORD will deliver us. Hath any of the gods of the nations delivered his land out of the hand of the king of Assyria?

19 Where *are* the gods of Hamath and Arphad? where *are* the gods of Sepharvaim? and have they delivered *a*Samaria out of my hand?

20 Who *are they* among all the gods of these lands, that have delivered their land out of my hand, that the LORD should deliver Jerusalem out of my hand?

21 But they *a*held their peace, and answered him not a word: for the king's commandment was, saying, Answer him not.

22 ¶ Then came Eliakim, the son of Hilkiah, that *was* over the household, and Shebna the scribe, and Joah, the son of Asaph, the recorder, to Hezekiah with *their* clothes rent, and told him the words of Rabshakeh.

CHAPTER 37

Hezekiah seeks counsel from Isaiah to save Jerusalem—Isaiah prophesies the defeat of the Assyrians and the death of Sennacherib—Hezekiah prays for deliverance—Sennacherib sends a blasphemous letter—Isaiah prophesies that the Assyrians will be destroyed and that a remnant of Judah will flourish—An angel slays 185,000 Assyrians—Sennacherib is slain by his sons.

AND it came to pass, when king Hezekiah heard *it*, that he rent his clothes, and covered himself with sackcloth, and went into the house of the LORD.

2 And he sent Eliakim, who *was* over the household, and Shebna the scribe, and the elders of the priests covered with sackcloth, unto Isaiah the prophet the son of Amoz.

3 And they said unto him, Thus saith Hezekiah, This day *is* a day of *a*trouble, and of rebuke, and of *b*blasphemy: for the children are come to *c*the birth, and *there is* not strength to bring forth.

4 It may be the LORD thy God will hear the words of Rabshakeh, whom the king of Assyria his master hath sent to reproach the living God, and will reprove the words which the LORD thy God hath heard: wherefore lift up *thy* prayer for the remnant that is left.

5 So the servants of king Hezekiah came to Isaiah.

6 ¶ And *a*Isaiah said unto them, Thus shall ye say unto your master, Thus saith the LORD, Be not afraid of the words that thou hast heard, wherewith the servants of the king of Assyria have blasphemed me.

7 Behold, I will *a*send a blast upon him, and he shall hear a *b*rumour, and return to his own land; and I will cause him to fall by the sword in his own land.

8 ¶ So Rabshakeh returned, and found the king of Assyria warring against Libnah: for he had heard that he was departed from Lachish.

9 And he heard say concerning Tirhakah king of Ethiopia, He is come forth to make war with thee. And when he heard *it*, he sent messengers to Hezekiah, saying,

10 Thus shall ye speak to Hezekiah king of Judah, saying, Let not thy God, in whom thou trustest, deceive thee, saying, Jerusalem shall not be given into the hand of the king of Assyria.

11 Behold, thou hast heard what the kings of Assyria have done to all lands by destroying them utterly; and shalt thou be delivered?

12 Have the gods of the nations delivered them which my fathers have destroyed, *as* Gozan, and Haran,

---

19*a* IE the capital of northern Israel (ten tribes), which had already been captured.

21*a* OR were silent.
37 3*a* Isa. 22:5.
    b OR provocation.
    c IE the crisis.

Hosea 13:13 (9–14).
6*a* 2 Kgs. 19:6 (6–37).
7*a* HEB put a spirit in him.
    b OR report or tidings.

and Rezeph, and the children of Eden which *were* in Telassar?

13 Where *is* the king of Hamath, and the king of Arphad, and the king of the city of Sepharvaim, Hena, and Ivah?

14 ¶ And Hezekiah received the letter from the hand of the messengers, and read it: and Hezekiah went up unto the house of the LORD, and spread it before the LORD.

15 And Hezekiah prayed unto the LORD, saying,

16 O LORD of hosts, God of Israel, that dwellest *between* the *a*cherubims, thou *art* the God, *even* thou alone, of all the kingdoms of the earth: thou hast made heaven and earth.

17 Incline thine ear, O LORD, and hear; open thine eyes, O LORD, and see: and hear all the words of Sennacherib, which hath sent to *a*reproach the living God.

18 Of a truth, LORD, the kings of Assyria have laid waste all the nations, and their *a*countries,

19 And have cast their gods into the fire: for they *were* no *a*gods, but the work of men's hands, wood and stone: therefore they have destroyed them.

20 Now therefore, O LORD our God, save us from his hand, that all the kingdoms of the earth may know that thou *art* the LORD, *even* thou only.

21 ¶ Then Isaiah the son of Amoz sent unto Hezekiah, saying, Thus saith the LORD God of Israel, Whereas thou hast prayed to me against Sennacherib king of Assyria:

22 This *is* the word which the LORD hath spoken concerning him; *a*The virgin, the daughter of Zion, hath despised thee, *and* laughed thee to scorn; the daughter of Jerusalem hath shaken her head at thee.

23 Whom hast thou reproached and blasphemed? and against whom hast thou exalted *thy* voice, and lifted up thine eyes on high? *even* against the Holy One of Israel.

24 By thy servants hast thou reproached the Lord, and hast said, By the multitude of my chariots am I come up to the height of the mountains, to the sides of Lebanon; and I will cut down the tall *a*cedars thereof, *and* the choice fir trees thereof: and I will enter into the height of his border, *and* the forest of his Carmel.

25 I have digged, and drunk water; and with the sole of my feet have I dried up all the rivers of the besieged places.

26 Hast thou not heard long ago, how *a*I have done it; *and* of ancient times, that I have formed it? now have I brought it to pass, that thou shouldest be to lay waste defenced cities *into* ruinous heaps.

27 Therefore their inhabitants *were* of small power, they were dismayed and confounded: they were *as* the grass of the field, and *as* the green herb, *as* the grass on the housetops, and *as corn* blasted before it be grown up.

28 But I know thy abode, and thy going out, and thy coming in, and thy rage against me.

29 Because thy rage against me, and thy tumult, is come up into mine ears, therefore will I put my hook in thy nose, and my bridle in thy lips, and I will turn thee back by the way by which thou camest.

30 And this *shall be* a sign unto *a*thee, Ye shall eat *this* year such as groweth of itself; and the second year that which springeth of the same: and in the third year sow ye, and reap, and plant vineyards, and eat the fruit thereof.

31 And the remnant that is escaped of the house of Judah shall again take root downward, and bear fruit upward:

32 For out of Jerusalem shall go forth a *a*remnant, and they that escape out of mount Zion: the *b*zeal of the LORD of hosts shall do this.

16*a* TG Cherubim.
17*a* HEB blaspheme.
18*a* OR lands.
19*a* TG Idolatry.
22*a* IE The unconquered

people of Jerusalem.
24*a* Jer. 22:7 (6–7).
26*a* IE The prophet speaks for the Lord who created everything.

30*a* IE Hezekiah, king of Judah.
32*a* TG Israel, Remnant of.
   b TG Zeal.

33 Therefore thus saith the LORD concerning the king of Assyria, He shall not come into this city, nor shoot an arrow there, nor come before it with shields, nor cast a *a*bank against it.

34 By the way that he came, by the same shall he return, and shall not come into this city, saith the LORD.

35 For I will *a*defend this city to save it for mine own sake, and for my servant David's sake.

36 Then the *a*angel of the LORD went forth, and smote in the camp of the *b*Assyrians a hundred and fourscore and five thousand: and when *c*they arose early in the morning, behold, they *were* all dead corpses.

37 ¶ So Sennacherib king of Assyria departed, and went and returned, and dwelt at Nineveh.

38 And it came to pass, as he was worshipping in the house of Nisroch his god, that Adrammelech and Sharezer his sons smote him with the sword; and they escaped into the land of Armenia: and Esarhaddon his son reigned in his stead.

CHAPTER 38

Hezekiah's life is lengthened fifteen years—The sun goes back ten degrees as a sign—Hezekiah praises and thanks the Lord.

IN those days was *a*Hezekiah sick unto death. And Isaiah the prophet the son of Amoz came unto him, and said unto him, Thus saith the LORD, Set thine house in order: for thou shalt die, and not live.

2 Then Hezekiah turned his face toward the wall, and prayed unto the LORD,

3 And said, Remember now, O LORD, I beseech thee, how I have walked before thee in truth and with a perfect heart, and have done that which is good in thy sight. And Hezekiah wept sore.

4 ¶ Then came the word of the LORD to Isaiah, saying,

5 Go, and say to Hezekiah, Thus saith the LORD, the God of David thy father, I have heard thy prayer, I have seen thy tears: behold, I will *a*add unto thy days fifteen years.

6 And I will deliver thee and this city out of the hand of the king of Assyria: and I will *a*defend this city.

7 And this *shall be* a sign unto thee from the LORD, that the LORD will do this thing that he hath spoken;

8 Behold, I will bring again the *a*shadow of the degrees, which is gone down in the sun dial of Ahaz, ten degrees backward. So the *b*sun returned ten degrees, by which degrees it was gone down.

9 ¶ The *a*writing of Hezekiah king of Judah, when he had been sick, and was recovered of his sickness:

10 I said in the cutting off of my days, I shall go to the gates of the grave: I am deprived of the residue of my years.

11 I said, I shall not see the LORD, *even* the LORD, in the land of the living: I shall behold man no more with the inhabitants of the world.

12 Mine age is departed, and is removed from me as a shepherd's tent: I have *a*cut off like a weaver my life: he will cut me off *b*with pining sickness: from day *even* to night wilt thou make an end of me.

13 I reckoned till morning, *that*, as a lion, so will he break all my bones: from day *even* to night wilt thou make an end of me.

14 Like a crane *or* a swallow, so did I chatter: I did mourn as a dove: mine eyes fail *with looking* upward: O LORD, I am oppressed; *a*undertake for me.

15 What shall I say? he hath both

33*a* Luke 19:43.
35*a* Isa. 38:6.
36*a* See JST 2 Sam. 24:16
  (2 Sam. 24:16 note *a*).
  Isa. 10:34.
  b 2 Kgs. 19:35 (32–37);
  Isa. 14:25 (24–28); 30:31;
  31:8 (7–9).

c IE those who were left.
38 1*a* 2 Kgs. 20:1 (1–6, 9–11);
  2 Chr. 32:32.
  5*a* D&C 42:48.
  TG Benevolence.
  6*a* Isa. 37:35.
  8*a* 2 Kgs. 20:10 (9–10).
  b Josh. 10:12 (12–14).

9 *a* TG Scriptures, Writing of.
12 *a* Job 14:2 (1–2).
  b OR as a dangling thread;
  i.e., when a weaver has
  finished weaving a piece
  of cloth, he rolls it up to
  cut it off the loom.
14 *a* HEB be my security.

spoken unto me, and himself hath done *it:* I shall go softly all my years in the ^abitterness of my soul.

16 O Lord, by these *things men* live, and in all these *things is* the life of my spirit: ^aso wilt thou recover me, and make me to live.

17 Behold, ^afor peace I had great bitterness: but thou hast in love to my soul ^b*delivered it* from the pit of corruption: for thou hast cast all my sins behind thy back.

18 For the grave cannot praise thee, death can *not* celebrate thee: they that go down into the pit cannot hope for thy truth.

19 The living, the living, he shall praise thee, as I *do* this day: the ^afather to the children shall make known thy ^btruth.

20 The LORD *was ready* to save me: therefore we will sing my songs to the stringed instruments all the days of our life in the house of the LORD.

21 For Isaiah had said, Let them take a lump of figs, and ^alay *it* for a plaster upon the ^bboil, and he shall recover.

22 Hezekiah also had said, What *is* the sign that I shall go up to the house of the LORD?

CHAPTER 39

Hezekiah reveals his wealth to Babylon—Isaiah prophesies the Babylonian captivity.

AT that time ^aMerodach-baladan, the son of Baladan, king of Babylon, sent letters and a present to Hezekiah: for he had heard that he had been sick, and was recovered.

2 And ^aHezekiah was glad of them, and shewed them the house of his precious things, the silver, and the gold, and the spices, and the precious ointment, and all the house

of his armour, and all that was found in his treasures: there was nothing in his house, nor in all his dominion, that Hezekiah shewed them not.

3 ¶ Then came Isaiah the prophet unto king Hezekiah, and said unto him, What said these men? and from whence came they unto thee? And Hezekiah said, They are come from a far country unto me, *even* from Babylon.

4 Then said he, What have they seen in thine house? And Hezekiah answered, All that *is* in mine house have they seen: there is nothing among my treasures that I have not shewed them.

5 Then said Isaiah to Hezekiah, ^aHear the word of the LORD of hosts:

6 Behold, the days come, that all that *is* in thine house, and *that* which thy fathers have laid up in store until this day, shall be carried to Babylon: nothing shall be left, saith the LORD.

7 And of thy ^asons that shall issue from thee, which thou shalt beget, shall they take away; and they shall be eunuchs in the palace of the king of Babylon.

8 Then said Hezekiah to Isaiah, Good *is* the word of the LORD which thou hast spoken. He said moreover, For there shall be peace and truth in my days.

CHAPTER 40

Isaiah speaks about the Messiah—Prepare ye the way of the Lord—He will feed His flock like a shepherd—Israel's God is incomparably great.

COMFORT ye, ^acomfort ye my people, saith your God.

2 Speak ye comfortably to Jerusalem, and cry unto her, that her ^awarfare is accomplished, that her iniquity is ^bpardoned: for she hath

15*a* Job 10:1;
    Moses 7:44 (42–44).
16*a* HEB restore me.
17*a* OR on my peace came
    great bitterness.
  b Mosiah 27:29 (28–30).
19*a* Ps. 145:4.

  b Ps. 78:4 (2–4).
21*a* HEB smear it on.
  b Job 2:7.
39 1*a* 2 Kgs. 20:12 (12–19).
  2*a* 2 Kgs. 18:15 (15–16).
  5*a* D&C 70:1.
  7*a* 2 Kgs. 20:18 (14–18);

    Dan. 1:3 (1–3).
40 1*a* TG Israel, Restoration of.
  2*a* OR time of service.
  b TG Forgive.

received of the LORD's hand ^cdouble for all her sins.

3 ¶ The ^avoice of him that crieth in the wilderness, ^bPrepare ye the ^cway of the LORD, make straight in the desert a ^dhighway for our God.

4 Every ^avalley shall be ^bexalted, and every ^cmountain and hill shall be made ^dlow: and the ^ecrooked shall be made straight, and ^fthe rough places plain:

5 And the ^aglory of the LORD shall be ^brevealed, and all flesh shall ^csee it together: for the mouth of the LORD hath spoken it.

6 The voice said, Cry. And he said, What shall I cry? All ^aflesh is ^bgrass, and all the goodliness thereof is as the flower of the field:

7 The grass withereth, the flower fadeth: because the spirit of the LORD bloweth upon it: surely the people is grass.

8 The grass withereth, the flower fadeth: but the ^aword of our God shall stand for ever.

9 ¶ O ^aZion, that bringest ^bgood ^ctidings, get thee up into the high mountain; O Jerusalem, that bringest good tidings, lift up thy voice with strength; lift it up, be not afraid; say unto the cities of ^dJudah, Behold your God!

10 Behold, the Lord GOD will come with strong hand, and his ^aarm shall rule for him: behold, his ^breward is with him, and his work before him.

11 He shall feed his ^aflock like a ^bshepherd: he shall gather the lambs with his arm, and carry them in his bosom, and shall gently lead those that are with young.

12 ¶ Who hath measured the waters in the hollow of his hand, and meted out heaven with the span, and comprehended the dust of the earth in a measure, and weighed the mountains in scales, and the hills in a balance?

13 Who hath ^adirected the ^bSpirit of the LORD, or being his ^ccounsellor hath taught him?

14 With whom took he ^acounsel, and who instructed him, and taught him in the path of ^bjudgment, and taught him knowledge, and shewed to him the way of understanding?

15 Behold, the ^anations are as a ^bdrop of a bucket, and are counted as the small dust of the balance: behold, he taketh up the ^cisles as a very little thing.

16 And Lebanon is not sufficient to burn, nor the beasts thereof sufficient for a burnt offering.

17 All nations before him are as nothing; and they are counted to him less than nothing, and ^avanity.

18 ¶ To whom then will ye ^aliken God? or what likeness will ye compare unto him?

19 The workman melteth a graven image, and the ^agoldsmith spreadeth it over with gold, and casteth silver chains.

20 He that is so impoverished that he hath no oblation chooseth a tree that will not rot; he seeketh unto him

---

2c Jer. 16:18; 17:18.
3a Matt. 3:3;
   D&C 88:66; 128:20.
 b Matt. 11:10 (7–10);
   1 Ne. 10:8;
   D&C 65:1.
   TG Foreordination.
 c TG Jesus Christ,
   Prophecies about.
 d TG Jesus Christ, Second
   Coming.
4a Luke 3:5;
   Hel. 14:23;
   D&C 109:74.
 b HEB lifted up or raised.
 c TG Earth, Renewal of.
 d Zech. 14:10.
 e Isa. 45:2.

 f HEB the mountains into
   a plain.
5a TG Jesus Christ, Glory of.
 b TG Jesus Christ, Second
   Coming.
 c D&C 101:23.
6a TG Mortality.
 b Ps. 102:11;
   D&C 124:7.
8a TG Jesus Christ, Messenger of the Covenant.
9a TG Jerusalem, New.
 b TG Gospel.
 c Isa. 52:7.
 d TG Israel, Judah,
   People of.
10a D&C 1:14 (13–14).
 b TG Reward.

11a TG Church; Sheep.
 b TG Jesus Christ, Good
   Shepherd; Jesus Christ,
   Millennial Reign;
   Shepherd.
13a Job 21:22.
 b TG God, Spirit of.
 c TG Counselor.
14a TG Counsel.
 b 1 Ne. 22:21 (20–22).
15a TG Nations.
 b Ps. 39:5;
   Dan. 4:35.
 c TG Earth, Dividing of.
17a TG Vanity.
18a Isa. 46:5 (5–11).
19a Isa. 44:12;
   Jer. 10:3 (3–5).

a cunning workman to prepare a graven image, *that* ^ashall not be moved.

21 Have ye not known? have ye not heard? hath it not been told you from the beginning? have ye not understood from the foundations of the earth?

22 *It is* he that sitteth upon the circle of the earth, and the inhabitants thereof *are* as grasshoppers; that ^astretcheth out the heavens as a curtain, and spreadeth them out as a tent to dwell in:

23 That bringeth the ^aprinces to nothing; he maketh the judges of the earth as vanity.

24 Yea, they shall not be planted; yea, they shall not be sown: yea, their stock shall not take root in the earth: and he shall also blow upon them, and they shall wither, and the whirlwind shall take them away as stubble.

25 To whom then will ye liken me, or shall I be equal? saith the Holy One.

26 Lift up your eyes on high, and behold who hath created these *things*, that bringeth out their host by number: he calleth them all by ^anames by the greatness of his might, for that *he is* strong in power; not one faileth.

27 Why sayest thou, O Jacob, and speakest, O Israel, My way is hid from the LORD, and my judgment is ^apassed over from my God?

28 ¶ Hast thou not known? hast thou not heard, *that* the ^aeverlasting God, the LORD, the ^bCreator of the ends of the earth, fainteth not, neither is weary? *there is* no ^csearching of his understanding.

29 He giveth power to the faint; and to *them that have* no might he increaseth strength.

30 Even the youths shall faint and be weary, and the young men shall utterly fall:

31 But they that ^await upon the LORD shall ^brenew *their* ^cstrength; they shall mount up with wings as ^deagles; they shall ^erun, and not be weary; *and* they shall walk, and not faint.

CHAPTER 41

To Israel the Lord says, Ye are my servants; I will preserve you—Idols are nothing—One will bring good tidings to Jerusalem.

KEEP ^asilence before me, O islands; and let the people ^brenew *their* strength: let them come near; then let them speak: let us come near ^ctogether to judgment.

2 Who raised up the righteous *man* from the ^aeast, called him to his foot, gave the nations before him, and made *him* ^brule over kings? he gave *them* as the dust to his sword, *and* as driven stubble to his bow.

3 He pursued them, *and* passed safely; *even* by the way *that* he had not gone with his feet.

4 Who hath wrought and done *it,* calling the generations from the beginning? I the LORD, the ^afirst, and with the last; I *am* he.

5 The isles saw *it,* and feared; the ends of the earth were afraid, drew near, and came.

6 They ^ahelped every one his neighbour; and *every one* said to his brother, Be of good courage.

7 So the carpenter encouraged the goldsmith, *and* he that smootheth *with* the hammer him that smote the anvil, saying, It *is* ready for the sodering: and he fastened it with nails, *that* it ^ashould not be moved.

8 But thou, Israel, *art* my servant,

20*a* Isa. 41:7.
22*a* Job 9:8;
    Ps. 104:2.
23*a* Job 12:21.
26*a* Ps. 147:4.
27*a* IE disregarded by.
28*a* Gen. 21:33.
   b TG Jesus Christ, Creator.
   c OR fathoming.
    Rom. 11:33.

31*a* HEB hope for or anticipate.
    Ps. 25:5;
    Prov. 20:22;
    2 Ne. 6:13 (7, 13).
   b Isa. 41:1.
   c TG Health; Strength.
   d Ps. 103:5.
   e D&C 89:20.
41 1*a* TG Silence.

   b Isa. 40:31.
   c D&C 50:10 (10–11).
2*a* Isa. 46:11.
   b Isa. 45:1;
    Dan. 5:30.
4*a* TG Jesus Christ, Firstborn;
    Jesus Christ, Jehovah.
6*a* TG Service.
7*a* Isa. 40:20.

Jacob whom I have ᵃchosen, the seed of Abraham my ᵇfriend.

9 *Thou* whom I have taken from the ends of the earth, and called thee from the chief men thereof, and said unto thee, Thou *art* my ᵃservant; I have chosen thee, and not cast thee away.

10 ¶ ᵃFear thou not; for I *am* with thee: be not dismayed; for I *am* thy God: I will strengthen thee; yea, I will help thee; yea, I will uphold thee with the right hand of my righteousness.

11 Behold, all they that were incensed against thee shall be ashamed and confounded: they shall be as nothing; and they that strive with thee shall ᵃperish.

12 Thou shalt seek them, and shalt not find them, *even* them that contended with thee: they that war against thee shall be as nothing, and as a thing of nought.

13 For I the Lᴏʀᴅ thy God will hold thy right hand, saying unto thee, Fear not; I will help thee.

14 Fear not, thou ᵃworm Jacob, *and* ye men of Israel; I will help thee, saith the ᵇLᴏʀᴅ, and thy ᶜredeemer, the ᵈHoly One of Israel.

15 Behold, I will make thee a new sharp threshing instrument having teeth: thou shalt thresh the ᵃmountains, and beat *them* small, and shalt make the hills as chaff.

16 Thou shalt ᵃfan them, and the wind shall carry them away, and the whirlwind shall scatter them: and thou shalt rejoice in the Lᴏʀᴅ, *and* shalt glory in the Holy One of Israel.

17 *When* the poor and needy seek water, and *there is* none, *and* their tongue faileth for thirst, I the Lᴏʀᴅ will hear them, *I* the God of Israel will not ᵃforsake them.

18 I will open ᵃrivers in high places, and fountains in the midst of the valleys: I will make the ᵇwilderness a pool of water, and the dry land springs of water.

19 I will plant in the wilderness the cedar, the ᵃshittah tree, and the myrtle, and the oil tree; I will set in the desert the ᵇfir tree, *and* the ᶜpine, and the box tree together:

20 That they may see, and know, and consider, and understand together, that the hand of the Lᴏʀᴅ hath done this, and the Holy One of Israel hath ᵃcreated it.

21 Produce your cause, saith the Lᴏʀᴅ; bring forth your ᵃstrong *reasons*, saith the King of Jacob.

22 Let them bring *them* forth, and shew us what shall happen: let them shew the former things, what they *be*, that we may consider them, and know the latter end of them; or declare us things for to come.

23 Shew the things that are to come hereafter, that we may know that ye *are* gods: yea, do good, or do evil, that we may be dismayed, and behold *it* together.

24 Behold, ye *are* of nothing, and your work of nought: an ᵃabomination *is he that* chooseth you.

25 I have raised up *one* from the north, and he shall come: from the rising of the sun shall he call upon my name: and he shall come upon princes as *upon* mortar, and as the potter treadeth clay.

26 Who hath ᵃdeclared from the beginning, that we may know? and beforetime, that we may say, *He is* righteous? yea, *there is* none that sheweth, yea, *there is* none that declareth, yea, *there is* none that heareth your words.

27 The first *shall say* to Zion,

8a ᴛɢ Peculiar People.
  b James 2:23.
9a ᴛɢ Israel, Mission of.
10a Gen. 26:24;
    Deut. 31:6 (6, 8);
    Isa. 43:5; 44:8;
    D&C 68:6.
11a 2 Ne. 10:16.
14a ɪᴇ meek and humble.
  b ᴛɢ Jesus Christ,

    Jehovah.
  c ᴛɢ Jesus Christ,
    Redeemer.
  d ᴛɢ Holiness.
15a ɪᴇ Israel's erstwhile
    strong enemies.
16a Jer. 51:2.
17a 1 Ne. 21:15 (14–15);
    D&C 61:36.
18a Isa. 43:19.

  b ᴛɢ Earth, Renewal of.
19a ᴏʀ acacia.
  b ᴏʀ cypress.
    Isa. 60:13.
  c ʜᴇʙ ash tree.
20a ᴛɢ Jesus Christ, Creator.
21a D&C 71:8 (7–10).
24a 2 Ne. 9:37.
26a ᴛɢ God, Omni-
    science of.

Behold, behold them: and I will give to Jerusalem one that bringeth good tidings.

28 For I beheld, and *there was* no man; even among them, and *there was* no counsellor, that, when I asked of them, could answer a word.

29 Behold, they *are* all *ᵃ*vanity; their works *are* nothing: their molten *ᵇ*images *are* wind and confusion.

CHAPTER 42

Isaiah speaks about the Messiah—The Lord will bring His law and His justice, be a light to the Gentiles, and free the prisoners—Praise the Lord.

BEHOLD my *ᵃ*servant, whom I uphold; mine *ᵇ*elect, *in whom* my soul delighteth; I have *ᶜ*put my *ᵈ*spirit upon him: he shall bring forth *ᵉ*judgment to the Gentiles.

2 He shall not cry, nor *ᵃ*lift up, nor cause his voice to be heard in the street.

3 *ᵃ*A bruised reed shall he not break, and the smoking flax shall he not quench: he shall bring forth judgment unto truth.

4 He shall not fail nor be discouraged, till he have set judgment in the earth: and the *ᵃ*isles shall wait for his law.

5 ¶ Thus saith God the LORD, he that *ᵃ*created the heavens, and stretched them out; he that spread forth the earth, and that which cometh out of it; he that giveth *ᵇ*breath unto the people upon it, and *ᶜ*spirit to them that *ᵈ*walk therein:

6 I the LORD have called thee in righteousness, and will hold thine hand, and will keep thee, and give thee for a *ᵃ*covenant of the people, for a *ᵇ*light of the *ᶜ*Gentiles;

7 To *ᵃ*open the *ᵇ*blind eyes, to bring out the *ᶜ*prisoners from the *ᵈ*prison, *and* them that sit in darkness out of the prison house.

8 I *am* the LORD: that *is* my name: and my glory will I not give to another, neither my praise to graven images.

9 Behold, the *ᵃ*former things are come to pass, and new things do I declare: before they spring forth I tell *ᵇ*you of them.

10 *ᵃ*Sing unto the LORD a new song, *and* his praise from the end of the earth, ye that go down to the sea, and all that is therein; the isles, and the inhabitants thereof.

11 Let the wilderness and the cities thereof lift up *their voice*, the villages *that* Kedar doth inhabit: let the inhabitants of the rock sing, let them shout from the top of the mountains.

12 Let them give glory unto the LORD, and declare his praise in the islands.

13 The LORD shall go forth as a mighty man, he shall stir up *ᵃ*jealousy like a man of *ᵇ*war: he shall cry, yea, roar; he shall prevail against his enemies.

14 I have long time holden my peace; I have been still, *and* *ᵃ*refrained myself: *now* will I cry like a travailing woman; I will *ᵇ*destroy and devour at once.

15 I will make waste mountains and hills, and dry up all their herbs; and I will make the rivers islands, and I will dry up the pools.

29*a* TG Vanity.
  b Isa. 44:9;
     3 Ne. 21:17 (17–19);
     D&C 1:16.
42 1*a* Matt. 12:18 (17–21).
     TG Servant;
     Witness of the Father.
  b TG Election.
  c Prov. 1:23.
  d TG God, Spirit of.
  e 1 Ne. 13:33 (33–34).
  2*a* IE the voice.
  3*a* IE He will not harm
     nor hurt the weakest.

4*a* 2 Ne. 10:20 (20–22).
5*a* TG Creation;
     Jesus Christ, Creator.
  b TG Breath of Life.
  c TG Man, a Spirit Child
     of Heavenly Father;
     Spirit Creation.
  d TG Mortality.
6*a* Isa. 49:8.
  b TG Light [noun].
  c D&C 45:9; 88:84 (84–85);
     JS—H 1:41.
7*a* TG Jesus Christ,
     Prophecies about.

  b Ps. 146:8;
     Matt. 11:5.
  c TG Genealogy and
     Temple Work;
     Salvation for the Dead.
  d TG Hell.
9*a* TG God, Foreknowl-
     edge of.
  b Amos 3:7.
10*a* TG Singing.
13*a* OR zeal, ardor.
  b Isa. 31:4.
14*a* Isa. 64:12.
  b Mosiah 12:8.

16 And I will bring the blind by a way *that* they knew not; I will lead them in paths *that* they have not known: I will make *a*darkness light before them, and crooked things straight. These things will I do unto them, and not forsake them.

17 ¶ They shall be turned back, they shall be greatly ashamed, that trust in graven images, that say to the molten images, Ye *are* our gods.

18 Hear, ye deaf; and look, ye blind, that ye may see.

19 *a*Who *is* blind, but my servant? or deaf, as my messenger *that* I sent? who *is* blind as *he that is* *b*perfect, and blind as the LORD's servant?

20 *a*Seeing many things, but thou observest not; opening the ears, but he heareth not.

21 The LORD is well pleased for his righteousness' sake; he will magnify the law, and make *it* *a*honourable.

22 But this *is* a *a*people robbed and spoiled; *they are* all of them snared in holes, and they are hid in prison houses: they are for a prey, and none delivereth; for a spoil, and none saith, *b*Restore.

23 Who among you will give ear to this? *who* will hearken and hear for the time to come?

24 Who gave Jacob for a spoil, and *a*Israel to the robbers? did not the LORD, he against whom we have sinned? for they would not *b*walk in his ways, neither were they *c*obedient unto his law.

25 Therefore he hath poured upon him the fury of his anger, and the strength of battle: and it hath set him on fire round about, yet he knew not; and it burned him, yet he laid *it* not to heart.

CHAPTER 43

To Israel the Lord says, I am your God; I will gather your descendants; beside me there is no Savior; you are my witnesses.

BUT now thus saith the LORD that created thee, O Jacob, and he that formed thee, O Israel, Fear not: for I have *a*redeemed thee, I have called *thee* by thy name; thou *art* mine.

2 When thou passest through the *a*waters, I *will be* with thee; and through the rivers, they shall not overflow thee: when thou walkest through the *b*fire, thou shalt not be *c*burned; neither shall the flame kindle upon thee.

3 For I *am* the LORD thy God, the *a*Holy One of Israel, thy *b*Saviour: I gave *c*Egypt *for* thy *d*ransom, Ethiopia and *e*Seba for thee.

4 Since thou wast *a*precious in my sight, thou hast been honourable, and I have loved thee: therefore will I give men for thee, and people for thy life.

5 *a*Fear not: for I *am* with thee: I will *b*bring thy seed from the east, and gather thee from the west;

6 I will say to the *a*north, *b*Give up; and to the south, Keep not back: bring my sons from far, and my daughters from the ends of the earth;

7 *Even* every one that is called by my name: for I have *a*created him for my glory, I have formed him; yea, I have made him.

8 ¶ Bring forth the blind people

16a 2 Ne. 3:5.
19a JST Isa. 42:19–23 (Appendix).
  b IE the ransomed and redeemed of Israel, who should also become the Lord's servants.
20a TG Spiritual Blindness.
21a TG Honor.
22a IE Israel of Isaiah's time (vv. 22–25).
  b 1 Ne. 15:19 (18–20).
24a TG Israel, Ten Lost

Tribes of.
  b TG Walking in Darkness.
  c TG Disobedience.
43 1a IE He will provide redemption in spite of the things told in Isa. 42:22–25.
  TG Redemption.
2a Ps. 66:12.
  b Dan. 3:27.
  c Ps. 91:5 (5–8).
3a TG Holiness.

  b TG Jesus Christ, Savior.
  c Isa. 45:14.
  d Prov. 21:18.
  e Ps. 72:10.
4a D&C 18:10.
5a Isa. 41:10 (10, 13).
  b TG Israel, Gathering of.
6a TG Israel, Ten Lost Tribes of.
  b OR Deliver up.
7a TG Man, New, Spiritually Reborn.

that have eyes, and the deaf that have ears.

9 Let all the nations be gathered together, and let the people be assembled: who among them can declare this, and shew us former things? let them bring forth their witnesses, that they may be justified: or let them hear, and say, *It is* truth.

10 *a*Ye *are* my *b*witnesses, saith the LORD, and my servant whom I have *c*chosen: that ye may know and *d*believe me, and understand that I *am* he: before me there was no God formed, neither shall there be after me.

11 I, *even* I, *am* the LORD; and *a*beside me *there is* no *b*saviour.

12 I have declared, and have saved, and I have shewed, when *there was* no strange *god* among you: therefore ye *are* my witnesses, saith the LORD, that I *am* God.

13 Yea, before the day *was* I *am* he; and *there is* none that can deliver out of my hand: I will work, and who shall *a*let it?

14 ¶ Thus saith the LORD, your *a*redeemer, the Holy One of Israel; For your sake I have sent to Babylon, and have brought down all their nobles, and the Chaldeans, whose cry *is* in the ships.

15 I *am* the LORD, your Holy One, the creator of Israel, your *a*King.

16 Thus saith the LORD, which *a*maketh a way in the sea, and a path in the mighty waters;

17 Which bringeth forth the chariot and horse, the army and the power; they shall *a*lie down together, they shall not rise: they are extinct, they are *b*quenched as tow.

18 ¶ Remember ye not the former things, neither consider the things of old.

19 Behold, I will do a new thing; now it shall spring forth; shall ye not know it? I will even make a way in the *a*wilderness, *and* *b*rivers in the desert.

20 The beast of the field shall honour me, the *a*dragons and the owls: because I give waters in the wilderness, *and* rivers in the desert, to give drink to my people, my chosen.

21 This *a*people have I formed for myself; they shall shew forth my praise.

22 ¶ But thou hast not called upon me, O Jacob; but thou hast been weary of me, O Israel.

23 Thou hast not brought me the *a*small cattle of thy burnt offerings; neither hast thou honoured me with thy sacrifices. I have not caused thee to serve with an offering, nor wearied thee with incense.

24 Thou hast bought me no *a*sweet cane with money, neither hast thou filled me with the fat of thy sacrifices: but thou hast *b*made me to serve with thy sins, thou hast *c*wearied me with thine iniquities.

25 I, *even* I, *am* he that *a*blotteth out thy *b*transgressions for mine own *c*sake, and will not remember thy sins.

26 Put me in remembrance: let us plead together: *a*declare thou, that thou mayest be justified.

27 Thy *a*first father hath sinned, and thy teachers have transgressed against me.

28 Therefore I have *a*profaned the *b*princes of the sanctuary, and have given Jacob to the curse, and Israel to reproaches.

10*a* IE Israel.
  b TG Israel, Mission of.
  c Hag. 2:23.
  d TG Faith.
11*a* Hosea 13:4; D&C 76:1.
  b TG Jesus Christ,
     Jehovah.
13*a* HEB turn it back.
14*a* TG Jesus Christ,
     Jehovah; Redemption.
15*a* Ps. 5:2.
16*a* Ex. 14:16 (16–22).

17*a* IE die.
  b OR extinguished as
     smoldering flax.
19*a* TG Earth, Renewal of.
  b Isa. 41:18.
20*a* HEB jackals and
     ostriches.
21*a* IE Israel.
23*a* HEB lambs or kids.
24*a* IE spices for the
     anointing oil. See
     Ex. 30:23.

  b OR burdened.
  c Isa. 1:14.
25*a* TG Forgive;
     Remission of Sins.
  b TG Transgress.
  c Isa. 48:11.
26*a* IE Confess.
27*a* IE early Israel; e.g., in
     the wilderness, under
     Moses.
28*a* IE dishonored.
  b OR ministers, priests.

CHAPTER 44

The Lord's Spirit will be poured out on the descendants of Israel—Idols of wood are as fuel for a fire—The Lord will gather, bless, and redeem Israel and rebuild Jerusalem.

YET now hear, O Jacob my [a]servant; and Israel, whom I have chosen:

2 Thus saith the LORD that made thee, and [a]formed thee from the womb, *which* will help thee; Fear not, O Jacob, my servant; and thou, [b]Jesurun, whom I have chosen.

3 For I will pour water upon [a]him that is [b]thirsty, and floods upon the dry ground: I will pour my [c]spirit upon thy seed, and my blessing upon thine offspring:

4 And they shall spring up *as* among the grass, as willows by the water courses.

5 One shall say, I *am* the [a]LORD's; and another shall call *himself* by the [b]name of Jacob; and another shall subscribe *with* his hand unto the LORD, and surname *himself* by the name of Israel.

6 Thus saith the LORD the [a]King of Israel, and his redeemer the LORD of hosts; I *am* the [b]first, and I *am* the last; and beside me *there is* no God.

7 And who, as I, shall call, and shall declare it, and set it in order for me, since I appointed the ancient people? and the things that are coming, and shall come, let them shew unto them.

8 [a]Fear ye not, neither be afraid: have not I told thee from that time, and have declared *it*? ye *are* even my witnesses. Is there a God beside me? yea, *there is* no [b]God; I know not *any*.

9 ¶ They that make a graven [a]image *are* all of them vanity; and their [b]delectable things shall not profit; and they *are* their own witnesses; they [c]see not, nor know; that they may be ashamed.

10 Who hath formed a god, or molten a graven [a]image *that is* profitable for nothing?

11 Behold, all his [a]fellows shall be ashamed: and the workmen, they *are* of men: let them all be gathered together, let them stand up; *yet* they shall fear, *and* they shall be ashamed together.

12 The [a]smith with the tongs both worketh in the coals, and fashioneth it with hammers, and worketh it with the strength of his arms: yea, he is hungry, and his strength faileth: he drinketh no water, and is faint.

13 The carpenter stretcheth out *his* rule; he marketh it out with a line; he fitteth it with planes, and he marketh it out with the compass, and maketh it after the figure of a man, according to the beauty of a man; that it may remain in the house.

14 He heweth him down cedars, and taketh the cypress and the oak, which he strengtheneth for himself among the trees of the forest: he planteth an ash, and the rain doth nourish *it*.

15 Then shall it be for a man to burn: for he will take thereof, and warm himself; yea, he kindleth *it*, and baketh bread; yea, he maketh a god, and worshippeth *it*; he maketh it a graven image, and falleth down thereto.

16 He burneth part thereof in the fire; with part thereof he eateth flesh; he roasteth roast, and is satisfied: yea, he warmeth *himself*, and

---

44 1*a* Isa. 44:21; 45:4;
  1 Ne. 20:20.
 2*a* Isa. 49:5;
  Jer. 1:5.
  b Deut. 33:26.
 3*a* OR that which is
  thirsty.
  b 2 Ne. 9:50 (50–51).
  c Ezek. 36:27 (26–27);
  Acts 2:17.
 5*a* TG Conversion;

  Israel, Mission of.
  b Abr. 2:10 (9–10).
 6*a* TG Kingdom of God,
  in Heaven.
  b TG Jesus Christ,
  Jehovah.
 8*a* Isa. 41:10.
  b Isa. 45:5 (5–22); 46:9;
  2 Ne. 6:7;
  3 Ne. 24:6;
  Moses 1:6.

 9*a* Isa. 41:29 (24, 29);
  3 Ne. 21:17 (17–19);
  D&C 1:16.
  b HEB beloved things; i.e.,
  their idols.
  c Ps. 115:5 (5, 8).
 10*a* Hab. 2:18.
 11*a* IE the fellow-
  worshippers of idols.
 12*a* Isa. 40:19 (19–20);
  Jer. 10:3 (3–5).

saith, Aha, I am warm, I have seen the fire:

17 And the residue thereof he maketh a god, *even* his graven image: he falleth down unto it, and worshippeth *it,* and prayeth unto it, and saith, Deliver me; for thou *art* my god.

18 They have not *a*known nor understood: for he hath *b*shut their eyes, that they cannot see; *and* their *c*hearts, that they cannot understand.

19 And none considereth in his heart, neither *is there* knowledge nor understanding to say, I have burned part of it in the fire; yea, also I have baked bread upon the coals thereof; I have roasted flesh, and eaten *it:* and shall I make the residue thereof an abomination? shall I fall down to the *a*stock of a tree?

20 He feedeth on ashes: a *a*deceived heart hath turned him aside, that he cannot deliver his soul, nor say, *Is there* not a *b*lie in my right hand?

21 ¶ Remember *a*these, O Jacob and Israel; for thou *art* my *b*servant: I have formed thee; thou *art* my servant: O Israel, thou shalt not be *c*forgotten of me.

22 I have blotted out, as a thick cloud, thy *a*transgressions, and, as a cloud, thy sins: return unto me; for I have redeemed thee.

23 *a*Sing, O ye heavens; for the LORD hath done *it:* shout, ye lower parts of the earth: break forth into *b*singing, ye mountains, O forest, and every tree therein: for the LORD hath *c*redeemed Jacob, and glorified himself in Israel.

24 Thus saith the LORD, thy *a*redeemer, and he that *b*formed thee

from the womb, I *am* the LORD that *c*maketh all *things;* that stretcheth forth the heavens alone; that spreadeth abroad the earth by myself;

25 That frustrateth the tokens of the liars, and maketh diviners mad; that turneth *a*wise *men* backward, and maketh their knowledge foolish;

26 That confirmeth the word of his servant, and performeth the counsel of his messengers; that saith to Jerusalem, Thou shalt be inhabited; and to the cities of Judah, Ye shall be built, and I will raise up the decayed places thereof:

27 That saith to the deep, Be dry, and I will *a*dry up thy rivers:

28 That saith of *a*Cyrus, *He is* my *b*shepherd, and shall perform all my *c*pleasure: even saying to Jerusalem, Thou shalt be *d*built; and to the *e*temple, Thy foundation shall be laid.

CHAPTER 45

Cyrus will free the captives of Israel from Babylon—Come unto Jehovah (Christ) and be saved—To Him every knee will bow and every tongue will take an oath.

THUS saith the LORD to his *a*anointed, to *b*Cyrus, whose right hand I have *c*holden, to *d*subdue nations before him; and I will loose the loins of kings, to open before him the *e*two leaved gates; and the gates shall not be shut;

2 I will go before thee, and make the *a*crooked places straight: I will *b*break in pieces the gates of brass, and cut in sunder the bars of iron:

18*a* Isa. 45:20.	23*a* Isa. 49:13.	*c* Isa. 46:10.
b Jacob 4:14.	*b* TG Singing.	*d* Isa. 45:13.
c 3 Ne. 19:33.	*c* TG Israel, Restora-	*e* 2 Chr. 36:23 (22–23);
19*a* TG Superstitions.	tion of.	Ezra 1:2 (1–3).
20*a* Hosea 4:12;	24*a* TG Jesus Christ,	**45** 1*a* TG Foreordination.
Rom. 1:21.	Jehovah.	*b* TG Governments.
b Ps. 144:8.	*b* 1 Ne. 21:5.	*c* OR strengthened.
21*a* IE these things.	*c* TG Jesus Christ, Creator.	*d* Isa. 41:2;
b Isa. 44:1 (1–2); 45:4;	25*a* 1 Cor. 1:20;	Dan. 5:30.
1 Ne. 20:20.	D&C 133:58.	*e* OR double doors.
c 3 Ne. 16:11 (10–12);	27*a* Jer. 50:38; 51:36.	2*a* Isa. 40:4.
20:29 (28–31).	28*a* TG Governments.	*b* Ps. 107:16.
22*a* TG Transgress.	*b* Jer. 50:44.	

3 And I will give thee the ^atreasures of darkness, and hidden riches of secret places, that thou mayest know that I, the LORD, which call *thee* by thy ^bname, *am* the ^cGod of Israel.

4 For Jacob my ^aservant's sake, and Israel mine ^belect, I have even ^ccalled thee by thy name: I have surnamed thee, though thou hast not known me.

5 ¶ ^aI *am* the LORD, and *there is* none else, *there is* no God beside me: I girded thee, though thou hast not known me:

6 That they may know from the ^arising of the sun, and from the west, that *there is* none beside me. I *am* the LORD, and *there is* none else.

7 I form the ^alight, and create darkness: I make peace, and create ^bevil: I the LORD do all these *things*.

8 Drop down, ye heavens, from above, and let the skies pour down ^arighteousness: let the earth open, and let ^bthem bring forth ^csalvation, and let righteousness spring up together; I the LORD have created it.

9 Woe unto him that ^astriveth with his ^bMaker! *Let* the potsherd *strive* with the potsherds of the earth. Shall the ^cclay say to him that fashioneth it, What makest thou? or thy work, He hath no hands?

10 Woe unto him that saith unto *his* father, What begettest thou? or to ^athe woman, What hast thou brought forth?

11 Thus saith the LORD, the Holy One of Israel, and his Maker, Ask me of things to come concerning my ^asons, and concerning the ^bwork of my hands ^ccommand ye me.

12 I have ^amade the earth, and ^bcreated man upon it: I, *even my* hands, have stretched out the heavens, and all their ^chost have I commanded.

13 I have raised ^ahim up in righteousness, and I will direct all his ways: he shall ^bbuild my city, and he shall let go my captives, not for ^cprice nor reward, saith the LORD of hosts.

14 Thus saith the LORD, The labour of ^aEgypt, and merchandise of Ethiopia and of the Sabeans, men of stature, shall come over unto thee, and they shall be thine: they shall come ^bafter thee; in chains they shall come over, and they shall fall down unto thee, they shall make supplication unto thee, *saying*, Surely God *is* in thee; and *there is* ^cnone else, *there is* no God.

15 Verily thou *art* a God that ^ahidest thyself, O God of Israel, the ^bSaviour.

16 They shall be ashamed, and also confounded, all of them: they shall go to confusion together *that are* makers of ^aidols.

17 *But* Israel shall be ^asaved in the ^bLORD with an everlasting ^csalvation: ye shall not be ashamed nor confounded world without end.

---

3 *a* OR hidden treasures (probably of Babylonia).
  Jer. 50:37; 51:13.
  b Ex. 33:12 (12, 17); JS—H 1:33 (17, 33, 49).
  c Isa. 29:23; 3 Ne. 11:14; D&C 36:1; 127:3.
4 *a* Isa. 44:1 (1–2), 21; 1 Ne. 20:20.
  b TG Election.
  c TG Governments.
5 *a* Isa. 44:8; 46:9; 2 Ne. 6:7; 3 Ne. 24:6; Moses 1:6.
6 *a* Mal. 1:11.
7 *a* TG Light [noun].
  b Amos 3:6;

Alma 5:40; Moro. 7:12.
8 *a* TG Righteousness.
  b IE the heavens and the earth.
  c TG Book of Mormon.
9 *a* Job 9:3 (1–4); Eccl. 6:10; Jacob 4:10.
  b Hosea 8:14.
  c Isa. 29:16; 64:8; Jer. 18:6; Rom. 9:21.
10 *a* IE his mother.
11 *a* TG Sons and Daughters of God.
  b Isa. 29:23.
  c IE ask me what you want to know.

12 *a* TG Jesus Christ, Creator.
  b TG Man, Physical Creation of.
  c Gen. 2:1.
13 *a* IE Cyrus.
  b Isa. 44:28.
  c Isa. 52:3.
14 *a* Isa. 43:3.
  b OR behind.
  c Moses 1:6.
15 *a* D&C 38:7 (7–8).
  b TG Jesus Christ, Savior; Salvation.
16 *a* TG Idolatry.
17 *a* D&C 35:25; 38:33.
  b TG Jesus Christ, Jehovah.
  c TG Salvation, Plan of.

18 For thus saith the LORD that ^acreated the heavens; God himself that formed the earth and made it; he hath established it, he created it not in vain, he formed it to be ^binhabited: I *am* the LORD; and *there is* none else.

19 I have not spoken in ^asecret, in a dark place of the earth: I said not unto the seed of Jacob, Seek ye me in vain: I the LORD speak ^brighteousness, I declare things that are ^cright.

20 ¶ Assemble yourselves and come; draw near together, ye *that are* ^aescaped of the ^bnations: they have no ^cknowledge that set up the wood of their graven image, and ^dpray unto a god *that* cannot save.

21 Tell ye, and bring *them* near; yea, let them take counsel together: who hath declared this from ancient time? *who* hath told it from that time? *have* not I the LORD? and *there is* no God else beside me; a ^ajust God and a ^bSaviour; *there is* none beside me.

22 ^aLook unto me, and be ye ^bsaved, all the ends of the earth: for I *am* God, and *there is* none else.

23 I have sworn by myself, the word is gone out of my mouth *in* righteousness, and shall not return, That unto me every ^aknee shall bow, every tongue shall ^bswear.

24 Surely, shall *one* say, in the LORD have I righteousness and ^astrength: *even* to him shall *men* come; and all that are incensed against him shall be ashamed.

25 In the LORD shall all the seed of Israel be ^ajustified, and shall glory.

CHAPTER 46

Idols are not to be compared with the Lord—He alone is God and will save Israel.

^aBEL boweth down, Nebo stoopeth, their idols were upon the beasts, and upon the cattle: your carriages *were* heavy loaden; *they are* a ^bburden to the weary *beast*.

2 ^aThey stoop, they bow down together; they could not deliver the burden, but themselves are gone into captivity.

3 ¶ Hearken unto me, O house of Jacob, and all the ^aremnant of the house of Israel, which are borne *by me* from the belly, which are carried from the womb:

4 And *even* to *your* ^aold age I *am* he; and *even* to ^bhoar hairs will I carry *you*: I have made, and I will bear; even I will ^ccarry, and will ^ddeliver *you*.

5 ¶ To whom will ye ^aliken me, and make *me* equal, and compare me, that we may be like?

6 They lavish gold out of the bag, and weigh silver in the balance, *and* hire a goldsmith; and he maketh it a god: they fall down, yea, they ^aworship.

7 They ^abear him upon the shoulder, they carry him, and set him in his place, and he standeth; from his place shall he not remove: yea, *one* shall ^bcry unto him, yet can he not answer, nor save him out of his trouble.

8 Remember this, and shew yourselves ^amen: bring *it* again to mind, O ye transgressors.

18a TG Jesus Christ, Creator.
  b TG Earth, Purpose of.
19a Isa. 48:16; D&C 1:34.
  b Ps. 119:138; D&C 67:9.
  c 2 Ne. 25:28 (28–29);
    D&C 3:2.
20a Isa. 46:3.
  b TG Conversion;
    Israel, Mission of.
  c Isa. 44:18 (18–19).
  d Isa. 46:7.
21a TG God, Justice of;
    Justice.
  b TG Jesus Christ,
    Jehovah;
    Remission of Sins.

22a D&C 6:36; 43:34.
  b TG Salvation, Plan of.
23a Rom. 14:11;
    Philip. 2:10.
    TG Jesus Christ,
    Second Coming.
  b OR take an oath, or
    covenant.
    Deut. 6:13.
24a 1 Ne. 17:3;
    Alma 26:12;
    D&C 113:8 (7–8).
25a TG Justification.
46 1a Bel and Nebo are
    idol-gods.
    Jer. 50:2.

  b IE Instead of idols
    helping man, man has
    to carry them.
2a IE the idols.
3a Isa. 45:20.
4a TG Old Age.
  b OR gray hairs.
  c Isa. 63:9.
  d TG Deliver.
5a Isa. 40:18 (18–26).
6a TG Worship.
7a Jer. 10:5 (3–6).
  b Ps. 115:5 (4–8);
    Isa. 45:20.
8a 1 Sam. 4:9;
    1 Cor. 16:13.

9 ^aRemember the ^bformer things of old: for ^cI *am* God, and *there is* none else; *I am* God, and *there is* ^dnone like me,

10 ^aDeclaring the ^bend from the beginning, and from ancient times *the things* that are not *yet* done, saying, My ^ccounsel shall stand, and I will do all my ^dpleasure:

11 Calling a ^aravenous bird from the ^beast, the man that executeth my counsel from a far country: yea, I have ^cspoken *it,* I will also bring it to pass; I have purposed *it,* I will also do it.

12 ¶ Hearken unto me, ye ^astouthearted, that *are* far from righteousness:

13 I bring near my righteousness; it shall not be far off, and my ^asalvation shall not ^btarry: and I will place salvation in Zion for Israel my glory.

CHAPTER 47

Babylon and Chaldea will be destroyed for their iniquities—No one will save them.

COME down, and sit in the dust, O virgin daughter of ^aBabylon, sit on the ground: *there is* no ^bthrone, O ^cdaughter of the Chaldeans: for thou shalt no more be called tender and delicate.

2 ^aTake the millstones, and grind meal: uncover thy locks, make bare the leg, uncover the thigh, ^bpass over the rivers.

3 Thy nakedness shall be uncovered, yea, thy shame shall be seen:

I will take vengeance, and ^aI will not meet *thee as* a man.

4 *As for* our redeemer, the LORD of hosts *is* his name, the Holy One of Israel.

5 Sit thou silent, and ^aget thee into darkness, O daughter of the Chaldeans: for thou shalt no more be called, The lady of kingdoms.

6 ¶ I was wroth with my people, I have polluted mine inheritance, and ^agiven them into thine hand: thou didst shew them no mercy; upon the ancient hast thou very heavily laid thy yoke.

7 ¶ And thou saidst, I shall be ^aa lady for ever: *so* that thou didst not lay these *things* to thy heart, neither didst remember the latter ^bend of it.

8 Therefore hear now this, *thou art* given to pleasures, that dwellest carelessly, that sayest in thine heart, I *am,* and none else beside me; I shall not sit *as* a ^awidow, neither shall I know the ^bloss of children:

9 But these two *things* shall come to thee in a moment in one day, the loss of children, and widowhood: they shall come upon thee ^ain their perfection for the multitude of thy sorceries, *and* for the great abundance of thine enchantments.

10 ¶ For thou hast trusted in thy wickedness: thou hast said, None ^aseeth me. Thy wisdom and thy knowledge, it hath perverted thee; and thou hast said in thine heart, I *am,* and none else beside me.

11 ¶ Therefore shall evil come upon thee; thou shalt not know from

9 a Deut. 32:7.
  b TG God, Foreknowledge of.
  c Isa. 44:8; 45:5 (5–22);
    2 Ne. 6:7;
    3 Ne. 24:6;
    Moses 1:6.
  d Ex. 8:10 (8–10).
10 a TG Foreordination;
    God, Intelligence of;
    God, Omniscience of.
  b OR latter things.
  c Prov. 19:21.
  d Isa. 44:28.
11 a HEB bird of prey; i.e., a
    symbol of Cyrus and
    his rapid conquest.

  b Isa. 41:2 (2, 25).
  c Num. 23:19.
12 a TG Hardheartedness.
13 a Ps. 85:9;
    Isa. 51:5; 62:11.
  b OR be tardy.
47 1 a Ps. 137:8.
  b IE Babylon was to
    be overthrown; this
    prophecy was fulfilled
    by Cyrus, 539 B.C.
  c HEB virgin daughter;
    i.e., the heretofore
    unconquered
    Babylonian empire.
2 a IE Prepare to become
    slaves.

  b IE on the way to exile.
3 a IE I will not negotiate
    or compromise in this
    matter.
5 a IE You are going into
    exile.
6 a IE Israel's Babylonian
    captivity is predicted.
7 a OR a mistress.
  b Lam. 1:9.
8 a Lam. 1:1.
  b IE Babylon will be
    depopulated and its
    king will be destroyed.
9 a IE on full measure.
10 a Isa. 29:15;
    Ezek. 9:9.

whence it riseth: and *a*mischief shall fall upon thee; thou shalt not be able to put it off: and *b*desolation shall come upon thee suddenly, *which* thou shalt not know.

12 Stand now with thine enchantments, and with the multitude of thy sorceries, wherein thou hast laboured from thy youth; if so be thou shalt be able to profit, if so be thou mayest prevail.

13 Thou art wearied in the multitude of thy counsels. Let now the *a*astrologers, the stargazers, the *b*monthly prognosticators, stand up, and save thee from *these things* that shall come upon thee.

14 Behold, they shall be as *a*stubble; the fire shall burn them; they shall not deliver themselves from the power of the flame: *there shall not be* a coal to warm at, *nor* fire to sit before it.

15 Thus shall they be unto thee with whom thou hast laboured, *even* thy merchants, from thy youth: they shall wander every one to his quarter; none shall save thee.

CHAPTER 48

The Lord reveals His purposes to Israel—Israel has been chosen in the furnace of affliction and is to depart from Babylon—Compare 1 Nephi 20.

HEAR ye this, O house of Jacob, which are called by the name of Israel, and are come forth out of the *a*waters of Judah, which *b*swear by the name of the LORD, and make *c*mention of the God of Israel, *but* not in truth, nor in righteousness.

2 For they call themselves of the *a*holy city, and *b*stay themselves upon the God of Israel; The LORD of hosts *is* his name.

3 I have *a*declared the *b*former things from the beginning; and they went forth out of my mouth, and I shewed them; I did *them* suddenly, and they came to pass.

4 Because I knew that *a*thou *art* *b*obstinate, and thy *c*neck *is* an iron sinew, and thy brow brass;

5 I have even from the beginning declared *it* to thee; before it came to pass I shewed *it* thee: lest thou shouldest say, Mine idol hath done them, and my graven image, and my molten image, hath commanded them.

6 Thou hast heard, see all this; and will not ye declare *it?* I have shewed thee new things from this time, even hidden things, and thou didst not know them.

7 They are created now, and not from the beginning; even before the day when thou heardest them not; lest thou shouldest say, Behold, I knew them.

8 Yea, thou heardest not; yea, thou knewest not; yea, from that time *that* thine ear was not opened: for I knew that thou wouldest deal very treacherously, and wast called a transgressor from the *a*womb.

9 ¶ For my *a*name's sake will I defer mine *b*anger, and for my praise will I refrain for thee, that I cut thee not off.

10 Behold, I have refined thee, but not with silver; I have chosen thee in the *a*furnace of *b*affliction.

11 For mine own *a*sake, *even* for mine own sake, will I do *it:* for how should *my* *b*name be polluted? and I will not *c*give my glory unto another.

12 ¶ Hearken unto me, O Jacob and Israel, my called; I *am* he; I *am* the first, I also *am* the last.

13 Mine hand also hath laid the

11*a* HEB ruin, or calamity.
  b D&C 29:8; 63:37.
13*a* TG Sorcery.
  b Lev. 19:26.
14*a* Ex. 15:7 (7–8);
    Isa. 5:24;
    Mal. 4:1.
48 1*a* 1 Ne. 20:1.
    TG Baptism.
  b TG Swearing.

  c Isa. 29:13.
2*a* TG Jerusalem.
  b IE pretend to rely upon.
3*a* TG God, Omniscience of.
  b TG God, Foreknowledge of.
4*a* IE Israel.
  b TG Stubbornness.
  c TG Stiffnecked.

8*a* Ps. 58:3.
9*a* Josh. 7:9.
  b TG Anger.
10*a* Ezek. 22:18 (18–22).
  b TG Affliction.
11*a* Ps. 115:1;
    Isa. 43:25;
    Ezek. 20:9.
  b TG Swearing.
  c Matt. 21:43.

foundation of the ^aearth, and my right hand hath spanned the heavens: *when* I call unto them, they stand up together.

14 All ye, assemble yourselves, and hear; which among them hath declared these *things?* The LORD hath loved him: he will do his ^apleasure on ^bBabylon, and his arm *shall be on* the Chaldeans.

15 I, *even* I, have spoken; yea, I have called him: I have brought him, and he shall make his way prosperous.

16 ¶ Come ye near unto me, hear ye this; I have not spoken in ^asecret from the beginning; from the time that it was, there *am* I: and now the Lord GOD, and his Spirit, hath ^bsent me.

17 Thus saith the LORD, thy Redeemer, the Holy One of Israel; I *am* the LORD thy God which teacheth thee to profit, which ^aleadeth thee by the way *that* thou shouldest go.

18 O that thou hadst hearkened to my commandments! then had thy ^apeace been as a river, and thy righteousness as the waves of the sea:

19 Thy ^aseed also had been as the sand, and the offspring of thy bowels like the gravel thereof; his name should not have been cut off nor destroyed from before me.

20 ¶ Go ye forth of ^aBabylon, flee ye from the ^bChaldeans, with a voice of singing declare ye, tell this, utter it *even* to the end of the earth; say ye, The LORD hath redeemed his servant Jacob.

21 And they thirsted not *when* he led them through the deserts: he caused the ^awaters to flow out of the rock for them: he clave the rock also, and the waters gushed out.

22 *There is* no ^apeace, saith the LORD, unto the wicked.

CHAPTER 49

The Messiah will be a light to the Gentiles and will free the prisoners—Israel will be gathered with power in the last days—Kings will be the nursing fathers of Israel—Compare 1 Nephi 21.

^aLISTEN, O isles, unto me; and ^bhearken, ye people, from far; The LORD hath ^ccalled me from the womb; from the bowels of my mother hath he made mention of my name.

2 And he hath made my mouth like a sharp ^asword; in the shadow of his hand hath he hid me, and made me a polished shaft; in his quiver hath he hid me;

3 And said unto me, Thou *art* my ^aservant, O Israel, in whom I will be ^bglorified.

4 Then I said, I have laboured in vain, I have spent my strength for nought, and in vain: *yet* surely my judgment *is* with the LORD, and my work with my God.

5 ¶ And now, saith the LORD that ^aformed me from the womb *to be* his servant, to bring Jacob again to him, Though Israel be not gathered, yet shall I be glorious in the eyes of the LORD, and my God shall be my strength.

6 And he said, It is a light thing that thou shouldest be my servant to raise up the tribes of Jacob, and to restore the preserved of Israel: I will also give thee for a ^alight to the ^bGentiles, that thou mayest be my ^csalvation unto the end of the earth.

13*a* TG Creation.
14*a* IE Cyrus will do his desire, or wish.
  b D&C 1:16; 64:24.
16*a* Isa. 45:19;
    2 Ne. 26:23 (23–28).
  b TG Authority.
17*a* TG Leadership.
18*a* TG Peace of God.
19*a* Gen. 22:17 (15–19);
    1 Ne. 20:19 (18–22).
20*a* Isa. 52:11.

  b TG Israel, Bondage of, in Other Lands.
21*a* Ex. 17:6;
    Num. 20:11.
22*a* TG Peace;
    Peace of God.
49 1*a* 1 Ne. 21:1 (1–26).
  b D&C 1:1.
  c Abr. 3:23 (22–24).
2*a* Heb. 4:12.
3*a* TG Israel, Restoration of; Servant.

  b John 15:8; Abr. 2:11.
5*a* Isa. 44:2 (2, 24);
    Jer. 1:5.
6*a* D&C 86:11 (8–11).
    TG Abrahamic Covenant; Election; Israel, Blessings of; Israel, Mission of; Missionary Work.
  b TG Gentiles; Nations.
  c TG Priesthood, Power of; Salvation, Plan of.

7 Thus saith the LORD, the Redeemer of Israel, *and* his Holy One, to him whom man despiseth, to him whom the nation abhorreth, to a servant of rulers, Kings shall see and arise, princes also shall worship, because of the LORD that is faithful, *and* the Holy One of Israel, and he shall choose thee.

8 Thus saith the LORD, In an acceptable *a*time have I heard thee, and in a day of salvation have I helped thee: and I will preserve thee, and give thee for a *b*covenant of the people, to establish the earth, to cause to *c*inherit the desolate heritages;

9 That thou mayest say to the *a*prisoners, Go forth; to them that *are* in darkness, Shew yourselves. They shall feed in the ways, and their pastures *shall be* in all high places.

10 They shall not hunger nor *a*thirst; neither shall the heat nor *b*sun smite them: for he that hath mercy on them shall lead them, even by the springs of water shall he guide them.

11 And I will make all my mountains a way, and my *a*highways shall be exalted.

12 Behold, these shall come from far: and, lo, these from the *a*north and from the west; and these from the land of Sinim.

13 ¶ *a*Sing, O heavens; and be joyful, O earth; and break forth into *b*singing, O mountains: for the LORD hath *c*comforted his people, and will have *d*mercy upon his *e*afflicted.

14 But Zion said, The LORD hath *a*forsaken me, and my Lord hath forgotten me.

15 Can a *a*woman forget her suck-ing child, that she should not have compassion on the son of her womb? yea, they may forget, yet will I not *b*forget thee.

16 Behold, I have graven thee upon the palms of *my* hands; thy walls *are* continually before me.

17 Thy children shall make haste; thy destroyers and they that made thee waste shall go forth of thee.

18 ¶ Lift up thine eyes round about, and behold: all these *a*gather themselves together, *and* come to thee. *As* I live, saith the LORD, thou shalt surely clothe thee with them all, as with an ornament, and bind them *on thee*, as a bride *doeth*.

19 For thy waste and thy desolate places, and the land of thy destruction, shall even now be too narrow by reason of the inhabitants, and they that swallowed thee up shall be far away.

20 The children which thou shalt have, after thou hast lost the other, shall say again in thine ears, The place *is* too *a*strait for me: give place to me that I may dwell.

21 Then shalt *a*thou say in thine heart, Who hath begotten me these, seeing I have lost my children, and am *b*desolate, a captive, and removing to and fro? and who hath brought up these? Behold, I was left alone; these, where *had* they *been*?

22 Thus saith the Lord GOD, Behold, I will *a*lift up mine hand to the *b*Gentiles, and set up my *c*standard to the people: and they shall bring thy *d*sons in *their* arms, and thy daughters shall be carried upon *their* shoulders.

23 And kings shall be thy *a*nursing

8*a* 2 Cor. 6:2.
b Isa. 42:6.
c Isa. 61:4.
9*a* TG Israel, Mission of;
  Salvation for the Dead;
  Spirits in Prison.
10*a* Rev. 7:16 (13–17).
  b Ps. 121:6.
11*a* TG Jesus Christ, Second
  Coming.
12*a* TG Israel, Ten Lost
  Tribes of.
13*a* Isa. 44:23.

b D&C 128:22.
c TG Comfort;
  Holy Ghost, Comforter.
d TG Compassion.
e 2 Sam. 22:28;
  Ps. 18:27;
  1 Ne. 21:13.
14*a* Ezek. 37:11.
15*a* TG Woman.
  b TG God, Mercy of.
18*a* TG Israel, Gathering of.
20*a* OR tight or narrow.
21*a* IE Zion.

b 3 Ne. 22:1.
22*a* TG Millennium,
  Preparing a People for.
  b Isa. 60:5;
  Rev. 21:24.
  c TG Ensign.
  d Isa. 60:4;
  1 Ne. 19:16 (16–17);
  A of F 1:10.
23*a* 1 Ne. 22:8 (1–9);
  2 Ne. 10:9 (5–9).

fathers, and their queens thy nursing [b]mothers: they shall [c]bow down to thee with *their* face toward the earth, and lick up the dust of thy feet; and thou shalt know that I *am* the LORD: for they shall not be [d]ashamed that wait for me.

24 ¶ Shall the prey be taken from the mighty, or the lawful captive delivered?

25 But thus saith the LORD, Even the captives of the mighty shall be taken away, and the prey of the terrible shall be delivered: for I will [a]contend with him that contendeth with thee, and I will save thy children.

26 And I will feed them that [a]oppress thee with their own flesh; and they shall be drunken with their own blood, as with sweet wine: and all flesh shall [b]know that I the LORD *am* thy [c]Saviour and thy [d]Redeemer, the [e]mighty One of Jacob.

CHAPTER 50

Isaiah speaks as the Messiah—He will have the tongue of the learned—He will give His back to the smiters—He will not be confounded—Compare 2 Nephi 7.

[a]THUS saith the LORD, Where *is* the bill of your mother's [b]divorcement, whom I have put away? or which of my creditors *is it* to whom I have sold you? Behold, for your [c]iniquities have ye sold yourselves, and for your transgressions is your [d]mother put away.

2 Wherefore, when I came, *was there* no man? when I called, *was there* none to answer? Is my [a]hand

shortened at all, that it cannot redeem? or have I no [b]power to deliver? behold, at my rebuke I [c]dry up the sea, I make the rivers a wilderness: their fish stinketh, because *there is* no water, and dieth for thirst.

3 I clothe the heavens with blackness, and I make sackcloth their covering.

4 The Lord GOD hath given me the tongue of the [a]learned, that I should know how to speak a [b]word in season to *him that is* weary: he wakeneth morning by morning, he wakeneth mine ear to hear as the learned.

5 ¶ The Lord GOD hath opened mine [a]ear, and I was not [b]rebellious, neither turned away back.

6 I [a]gave my [b]back to the [c]smiters, and my [d]cheeks to them that plucked off the hair: I [e]hid not my face from [f]shame and [g]spitting.

7 ¶ For the Lord GOD will help me; therefore shall I not be confounded: therefore have I set my face like a flint, and I know that I shall not be ashamed.

8 He is near that [a]justifieth me; who will contend with me? let us stand together: who *is* mine adversary? let him come near to me.

9 Behold, the Lord GOD will help me; who *is* he *that* shall condemn me? lo, they all shall wax [a]old as a garment; the [b]moth shall eat them up.

10 ¶ Who *is* among you that feareth the LORD, that obeyeth the [a]voice of his [b]servant, that walketh *in* [c]darkness, and hath no [d]light? let

23 b Isa. 60:16.
   c Isa. 60:14;
       Rev. 3:9.
   d TG Shame.
25 a Ps. 35:1;
       2 Ne. 6:16–17;
       D&C 98:37.
26 a TG Oppression.
   b D&C 63:6.
   c TG Jesus Christ,
       Jehovah.
   d TG Redemption.
   e Ps. 132:2.
50 1 a 2 Ne. 7:1 (1–11).
   b TG Abrahamic
       Covenant;

Divorce.
   c TG Apostasy of Israel.
   d Hosea 2:2.
 2 a Isa. 59:1;
       D&C 35:8.
   b D&C 133:67.
   c TG Drought.
 4 a Luke 21:15 (14–15).
   b Prov. 25:11.
 5 a D&C 58:1.
   b Matt. 26:39;
       Philip. 2:8.
 6 a TG Jesus Christ,
       Condescension of.
   b TG Jesus Christ,
       Prophecies about.

   c Isa. 53:4 (1–12);
       Matt. 27:26.
       TG Suffering.
   d Lam. 3:30.
   e TG Jesus Christ,
       Exemplar.
   f TG Shame.
   g Matt. 26:67.
 8 a Rom. 8:32 (32–34).
 9 a Isa. 51:6;
       D&C 1:16.
   b Isa. 51:8 (7–8).
10 a D&C 1:38.
   b TG Servant.
   c TG Darkness, Spiritual.
   d TG Light [noun].

him [e]trust in the name of the LORD, and [f]stay upon his God.

11 Behold, all ye that kindle a fire, that compass *yourselves* about with sparks: walk in the [a]light of your fire, and in the sparks *that* ye have kindled. This shall ye have of mine hand; ye shall lie down in [b]sorrow.

CHAPTER 51

In the last days, the Lord will comfort Zion and gather Israel—The redeemed will come to Zion amid great joy—Compare 2 Nephi 8.

[a]HEARKEN to me, ye that follow after righteousness, ye that seek the LORD: look unto the [b]rock *whence* ye are hewn, and to the hole of the pit *whence* ye are digged.

2 Look unto [a]Abraham your [b]father, and unto Sarah *that* bare you: for I called him [c]alone, and [d]blessed him, and increased him.

3 For the LORD shall [a]comfort [b]Zion: he will comfort all her waste places; and he will make her wilderness like [c]Eden, and her desert like the [d]garden of the LORD; joy and gladness shall be found therein, thanksgiving, and the voice of melody.

4 ¶ Hearken unto me, my people; and give ear unto me, O my nation: for a [a]law shall proceed from me, and I will make my judgment to rest for a light of the people.

5 My righteousness *is* near; my [a]salvation is gone forth, and mine arms shall [b]judge the people; the

[c]isles shall wait upon me, and on mine arm shall they trust.

6 Lift up your eyes to the heavens, and look upon the earth beneath: for the heavens shall [a]vanish away like smoke, and the earth shall [b]wax [c]old like a garment, and they that dwell therein shall die in like manner: but my salvation shall be for ever, and my righteousness shall not be abolished.

7 ¶ Hearken unto me, ye that know righteousness, the people in whose [a]heart *is* my law; [b]fear ye not the [c]reproach of [d]men, neither be ye afraid of their [e]revilings.

8 For the [a]moth shall eat them up like a garment, and the worm shall eat them like wool: but my righteousness shall be for ever, and my salvation from generation to generation.

9 ¶ Awake, awake, put on [a]strength, O arm of the LORD; awake, as in the ancient days, in the generations of old. *Art* thou not it that hath cut Rahab, *and* wounded the [b]dragon?

10 *Art* thou not it which hath [a]dried the sea, the waters of the great deep; that hath made the depths of the sea a [b]way for the [c]ransomed to pass over?

11 Therefore the [a]redeemed of the LORD shall [b]return, and come with singing unto Zion; and everlasting [c]joy *shall be* upon their head: they shall obtain gladness and joy; *and* sorrow and [d]mourning shall flee away.

10e D&C 84:116.
  f HEB be supported by.
11a TG Light [noun].
  b TG Sorrow.
51 1a 2 Ne. 8:1 (1–25).
  b IE These are defined in the next verse as Abraham and Sarah.
     TG Rock.
  2a 3 Ne. 20:27.
  b TG Family, Eternal.
  c Gen. 12:1;
     Abr. 1:16.
  d Gen. 24:1.
  3a Zech. 1:17 (14–17).
     TG Comfort.
  b TG Zion.
  c TG Earth, Destiny of;

Earth, Renewal of;
     Eden.
  d Ezek. 36:35.
  4a OR teaching, doctrine.
     TG God, Law of.
  5a Ps. 85:9;
     Isa. 46:13.
  b TG Jesus Christ, Judge.
  c Isa. 60:9;
     1 Ne. 22:4;
     2 Ne. 10:8,
     20 (20–22); 29:7;
     D&C 133:8.
  6a HEB be dispersed.
     Ps. 102:26 (25–27);
     2 Pet. 3:10 (10–12).
  b HEB decay.
  c Isa. 50:9.

7a TG Heart.
  b Matt. 10:28.
  c TG Reproach.
  d D&C 30:11.
  e TG Reviling.
8a Isa. 50:9.
9a TG Strength.
  b Ps. 74:13;
     Isa. 27:1.
10a Ex. 14:21.
  b Isa. 35:8 (8–10).
  c Isa. 35:9 (9–10).
11a TG Israel, Restoration of.
  b TG Israel, Gathering of.
  c TG Joy.
  d TG Mourning.

12 I, *even* I, *am* he that comforteth you: who *art* thou, that thou shouldest be ªafraid of a man *that* shall die, and of the son of man *which* shall be made *as* grass;

13 And ªforgettest the LORD thy maker, that hath stretched forth the heavens, and laid the foundations of the ᵇearth; and hast feared continually every day because of the fury of the oppressor, as if he were ready to destroy? and where *is* the fury of the oppressor?

14 The captive exile hasteneth that he may be loosed, and that he should not die in the ªpit, nor that his bread should fail.

15 But I *am* the LORD thy God, that divided the ªsea, whose waves roared: The LORD of hosts *is* his name.

16 And I have put my ªwords in thy mouth, and I have covered thee in the shadow of mine hand, that I may plant the heavens, and lay the foundations of the earth, and say unto Zion, Thou *art* my people.

17 ¶ Awake, awake, stand up, O Jerusalem, which hast drunk at the hand of the LORD the ªcup of his ᵇfury; thou hast drunken the dregs of the ᶜcup of trembling, *and* wrung *them* out.

18 *There is* none to guide her among all the sons *whom* she hath brought forth; neither *is there any* that taketh her by the hand of all the sons *that* she hath brought up.

19 These ªtwo *things* are come unto thee; who shall be sorry for thee? desolation, and destruction, and the famine, and the sword: by whom shall I comfort thee?

20 Thy sons have fainted, they lie at the head of all the streets, as a ªwild bull in a net: they are full of the fury of the LORD, the rebuke of thy God.

21 ¶ Therefore hear now this, thou afflicted, and drunken, but not with wine:

22 Thus saith thy Lord the LORD, and thy God *that* ªpleadeth the cause of his people, Behold, I have taken out of thine hand the cup of trembling, *even* the dregs of the cup of my fury; thou shalt no more drink it again:

23 But I will put it into the ªhand of them that ᵇafflict thee; which have said to thy soul, ᶜBow down, that we may go over: and thou hast laid thy body as the ground, and as the street, to them that went over.

CHAPTER 52

In the last days, Zion will return, and Israel will be redeemed—The Messiah will deal prudently and be exalted.

ªAWAKE, awake; put on thy ᵇstrength, O ᶜZion; put on thy ᵈbeautiful ᵉgarments, O ᶠJerusalem, the holy city: for henceforth there shall no more come into thee the uncircumcised and the unclean.

2 ªShake thyself from the dust; ᵇarise, *and* sit down, O Jerusalem: loose thyself from the ᶜbands of thy neck, O captive daughter of Zion.

3 For thus saith the LORD, Ye have ªsold yourselves for nought; and ye shall be redeemed without ᵇmoney.

4 For thus saith the Lord ªGOD, My people went down aforetime into ᵇEgypt to sojourn there; and the

---

12a Ps. 56:4;
  Jer. 1:8 (7–8).
13a TG Apathy.
  b TG Creation.
14a Zech. 9:11.
15a 1 Ne. 4:2.
16a 2 Ne. 33:10 (10–11);
  Moro. 10:27 (27–29);
  D&C 1:24.
17a Jer. 25:15.
  b TG God, Indignation of.
  c Zech. 12:2.
19a Zech. 4:14 (11–14);

Rev. 11:3 (3–12).
20a OR antelope.
22a Jer. 50:34.
23a Jer. 25:17.
  b 3 Ne. 20:28.
  c Isa. 52:2.
52 1a 3 Ne. 20:36 (36–38).
  b TG Israel, Restoration
  of; Mission of
  Latter-day Saints;
  Priesthood, Power of;
  Strength.
  c TG Zion.

d D&C 113:7–8.
  e D&C 82:14.
  f TG Jerusalem.
2a Isa. 51:23.
  b IE Arise from the dust
  and sit down in dignity,
  being redeemed at last.
  c D&C 113:10.
  TG Bondage, Spiritual.
3a TG Apostasy of Israel.
  b Isa. 45:13.
4a HEB Jehovah.
  b Gen. 46:6 (2–7).

Assyrian oppressed them without cause.

5 Now therefore, what have I here, saith the LORD, that my people is taken away for nought? they that rule over them make them to howl, saith the LORD; and my name continually every day is ªblasphemed.

6 Therefore my people shall know my name: therefore *they shall know* in that ªday that I *am* he that doth speak: behold, *it is* I.

7 ¶ How ªbeautiful upon the mountains are the feet of him that ᵇbringeth ᶜgood ᵈtidings, that ᵉpublisheth ᶠpeace; that bringeth good tidings of good, that publisheth salvation; that saith unto ᵍZion, Thy God reigneth!

8 Thy ªwatchmen shall lift up the voice; with the voice together shall they sing: for they shall ᵇsee eye to eye, when the LORD ᶜshall bring again ᵈZion.

9 ¶ Break forth into joy, sing together, ye ªwaste places of Jerusalem: for the LORD hath comforted his people, he hath redeemed Jerusalem.

10 The LORD hath made ªbare his holy ᵇarm in the eyes of all the nations; and all the ends of the earth shall ᶜsee the ᵈsalvation of our God.

11 ¶ Depart ye, depart ye, go ye ªout from thence, ᵇtouch no ᶜunclean *thing*; go ye ᵈout of the midst of her; be ye ᵉclean, that bear the vessels of the LORD.

12 For ye shall not go out with ªhaste, nor go by flight: for the LORD will go before you; and the God of Israel *will be* your ᵇrearward.

13 ¶ Behold, my ªservant shall deal ᵇprudently, he shall be exalted and extolled, and be very high.

14 As many were ªastonied at thee; his ᵇvisage was so marred more than any man, and his form more than the sons of men:

15 So shall he ªsprinkle many nations; the kings shall shut their mouths at him: for *that* which had not been ᵇtold them shall they see; and *that* which they had not heard shall they consider.

CHAPTER 53

Isaiah speaks about the Messiah—His humiliation and sufferings are described—He makes His soul an offering for sin and makes intercession for the transgressors—Compare Mosiah 14.

WHO hath ªbelieved our report? and to whom is the arm of the LORD revealed?

2 For he shall grow up before him as a tender ªplant, and as a ᵇroot out of a ᶜdry ground: he hath no form nor comeliness; and when we shall see him, *there is* no ᵈbeauty that we should desire him.

3 He is ªdespised and rejected of

5a TG Blaspheme.
6a Isa. 2:11;
   Hosea 2:16 (14–23);
   Zech. 9:16.
7a TG Beauty.
 b TG Dispensations.
 c TG Gospel.
 d Isa. 40:9;
   Mosiah 15:14 (13–18);
   D&C 128:19.
 e TG Missionary Work.
 f TG Peace; Peacemakers.
 g TG Zion.
8a TG Watchman.
 b D&C 84:98.
 c HEB returns to Zion,
   or restores Zion.
   TG Millennium,
   Preparing a People for.
 d D&C 12:6; 39:13.

9a OR ruins.
10a 1 Ne. 22:10 (10–11);
   D&C 133:3.
 b TG God, Power of.
 c TG Jesus Christ, Second
   Coming.
 d TG Salvation.
11a D&C 38:42.
 b 2 Tim. 2:21.
 c Isa. 48:20;
   2 Cor. 6:17 (14–17);
   Rev. 18:4.
 d TG Separation.
 e TG Chastity; Priesthood,
   Qualifying for; Purity.
12a TG Haste.
 b OR rearguard.
   D&C 49:27.
13a TG Servant.
 b TG Prudence.

14a OR astonished.
 b OR appearance.
15a JST Isa. 52:15 . . .
   gather . . .
   Ezek. 36:25;
   1 Pet. 1:2.
 b Rom. 15:21.
53 1a John 12:38;
   Rom. 10:16;
   Mosiah 14:1 (1–12).
2a Ps. 110:2.
 b Rev. 22:16.
 c TG Jesus Christ,
   Condescension of.
 d HEB it is not for His
   appearance.
3a Ps. 22:6;
   Mark 9:12;
   1 Pet. 2:23 (13–25).
   TG Malice.

men; a man of *b*sorrows, and acquainted with grief: and we hid as it were *our* faces from him; he was despised, and we *c*esteemed him not.

4 ¶ Surely he hath *a*borne our *b*griefs, and carried our sorrows: yet we did esteem him stricken, smitten of God, and afflicted.

5 But he *was* *a*wounded for our *b*transgressions, *he was* bruised for our iniquities: the chastisement of our peace *was* upon him; and with his *c*stripes we are *d*healed.

6 All we like *a*sheep have gone *b*astray; we have turned every one to his *c*own way; and the LORD hath laid on him the *d*iniquity of us all.

7 He was *a*oppressed, and he was *b*afflicted, yet he *c*opened not his mouth: he is brought as a *d*lamb to the *e*slaughter, and as a sheep before her shearers is dumb, so he openeth not his mouth.

8 He was taken from prison and from judgment: and who shall declare his *a*generation? for he was cut off out of the land of the living: for the *b*transgression of my people was he stricken.

9 And he made his grave with the *a*wicked, and with the rich in his *b*death; *c*because he had done no *d*violence, neither *was any* *e*deceit in his mouth.

10 ¶ Yet it pleased the LORD to *a*bruise him; he hath put *him* to grief: when thou shalt make his soul an *b*offering for sin, he shall see *his* *c*seed, he shall prolong *his* days, and the *d*pleasure of the LORD shall prosper in his hand.

11 He shall see of the travail of his soul, *and* shall be satisfied: by his *a*knowledge shall my righteous *b*servant *c*justify many; for he shall *d*bear their iniquities.

12 Therefore will I divide him *a portion* with the great, and he shall divide the spoil with the strong; because he hath poured out his soul unto *a*death: and he was numbered with the *b*transgressors; and he bare the sin of many, and made *c*intercession for the transgressors.

CHAPTER 54

In the last days, Zion and her stakes will be established, and Israel will be gathered in mercy and tenderness—Israel will triumph—Compare 3 Nephi 22.

*a*SING, O *b*barren, thou *that* didst not bear; break forth into singing, and cry aloud, thou *that* didst not travail with child: for more *are* the children of the desolate than the children of the married wife, saith the LORD.

2 Enlarge the place of thy tent, and let them stretch forth the curtains

---

3 *b* TG Sorrow.
  c Matt. 9:11 (10–13);
    John 1:10.
    TG Respect.
4 *a* Isa. 50:6;
    Philip. 2:7 (5–8).
  b TG Compassion;
    Jesus Christ, Redeemer.
5 *a* TG Jesus Christ,
    Mission of; Jesus Christ,
    Prophecies about;
    Salvation, Plan of.
  b Rom. 4:25.
    TG Redemption;
    Transgress.
  c 1 Pet. 2:24 (24–25).
  d TG Remission of Sins.
6 *a* TG Sheep.
  b Prov. 21:16;
    2 Pet. 2:15 (12–15).
  c 2 Ne. 12:5;
    D&C 1:16.
    TG Selfishness.

  d 2 Cor. 5:21.
    TG Jesus Christ,
    Atonement through;
    Sin.
7 *a* TG Oppression.
  b TG Affliction.
  c Mark 14:61; 15:3 (2–14).
  d Gen. 22:8 (8–14);
    Jer. 11:19;
    Mosiah 14:7 (6–8);
    D&C 135:4.
    TG Jesus Christ, Lamb
    of God;
    Jesus Christ, Trials of.
  e TG Persecution.
8 *a* Mosiah 15:10.
  b TG Remission of Sins;
    Transgress.
9 *a* Luke 23:32 (32–33).
  b TG Jesus Christ,
    Death of.
  c OR although.
  d 1 Pet. 2:22.

  e TG Deceit;
    Guile;
    Honesty.
10 *a* Gen. 3:15.
  b TG Self-Sacrifice.
  c Mosiah 15:10 (5–13).
    TG Sons and Daughters
    of God.
  d TG Pleasure.
11 *a* TG Knowledge.
  b TG Servant.
  c TG Justification.
  d TG Accountability.
12 *a* TG Jesus Christ,
    Crucifixion of;
    Jesus Christ, Death of;
    Martyrdom.
  b Mark 15:28;
    Luke 22:37.
  c Rom. 8:34.
54 1 *a* 3 Ne. 20:34.
  b 3 Ne. 22:1 (1–17).
    TG Barren.

of thine habitations: spare not, lengthen thy cords, and strengthen thy ^astakes;

3 For thou shalt break forth on the right hand and on the left; and thy seed shall inherit the Gentiles, and make the desolate cities to be inhabited.

4 Fear not; for thou shalt not be ashamed: neither be thou confounded; for thou shalt not be put to shame: for thou shalt forget the ^ashame of thy youth, and shalt not remember the ^breproach of thy widowhood any more.

5 For thy Maker *is* thine ^ahusband; the ^bLORD of hosts *is* his name; and thy ^cRedeemer the Holy One of Israel; The ^dGod of the whole earth shall he be called.

6 For the LORD hath called thee as a ^awoman ^bforsaken and grieved in spirit, and a ^cwife of youth, ^dwhen thou wast refused, saith thy God.

7 For a small ^amoment have I ^bforsaken thee; but with great mercies will I ^cgather thee.

8 In a little ^awrath I ^bhid my ^cface from thee for a moment; but with everlasting ^dkindness will I have ^emercy on thee, saith the LORD thy Redeemer.

9 For this *is as* the waters of Noah unto me: for *as* I have sworn that the ^awaters of Noah should no more go over the earth; so have I sworn that I would not be wroth with thee, nor rebuke thee.

10 For the ^amountains shall depart, and the hills be removed; but my kindness shall not depart from thee, neither shall the ^bcovenant of my peace be removed, saith the LORD that hath mercy on thee.

11 ¶ O thou afflicted, tossed with tempest, *and* not comforted, behold, I will lay thy ^astones with fair colours, and lay thy foundations with sapphires.

12 And I will make thy windows of agates, and thy gates of carbuncles, and all thy borders of pleasant stones.

13 And all thy ^achildren *shall be* ^btaught of the LORD; and great *shall be* the ^cpeace of thy children.

14 In righteousness shalt thou be established: thou shalt be far from oppression; for thou shalt not fear: and from terror; for it shall not come near thee.

15 Behold, they shall surely gather together, *but* not by me: whosoever shall gather together against thee shall fall for thy sake.

16 Behold, I have created the smith that bloweth the coals in the fire, and that bringeth forth an instrument for his work; and I have created the ^awaster to destroy.

17 ¶ No ^aweapon that is formed against thee shall prosper; and every ^btongue *that* shall rise against thee in judgment thou shalt condemn. This *is* the heritage of the ^cservants of the LORD, and their righteousness *is* of me, saith the LORD.

CHAPTER 55

Come and drink; salvation is free—
The Lord will make an everlasting
covenant with Israel—Seek the Lord
while He is near.

2*a* TG Stake.
4*a* TG Shame.
 b TG Reproach.
5*a* Jer. 51:5;
   Lam. 1:1;
   Rev. 19:7.
   TG Abrahamic
   Covenant.
 b TG Jesus Christ, Jehovah.
 c TG Jesus Christ,
   Redeemer.
 d Mosiah 15:1 (1–4).
6*a* TG Woman.
 b Isa. 60:15; 62:4.

 c Mal. 2:14 (14–15).
 d HEB because thou wast
   despised.
7*a* Isa. 10:25.
 b TG Chastening;
   Israel, Ten Lost
   Tribes of.
 c TG Israel, Gathering of.
8*a* Isa. 60:10.
 b Ezek. 39:29.
 c Isa. 8:17; 64:7.
 d TG Kindness.
 e TG God, Mercy of.
9*a* TG Earth, Cleansing of;

   Flood.
10*a* TG Earth, Renewal of.
 b Mal. 2:5.
11*a* TG Rock.
13*a* TG Children;
   Family, Children,
   Responsibilities toward.
 b TG Teachable;
   Teaching.
 c TG Israel, Restoration of.
16*a* IE God controls all.
17*a* TG Protection, Divine.
 b Acts 6:10.
 c TG Servant.

HO, every one that [a]thirsteth, come ye to the [b]waters, and he that hath no money; come ye, buy, and eat; yea, come, [c]buy wine and milk without money and without [d]price.

2 Wherefore do ye [a]spend money for *that which is* not bread? and your [b]labour for *that which* satisfieth not? hearken [c]diligently unto me, and eat ye *that which is* good, and let your soul delight itself in fatness.

3 Incline your ear, and [a]come unto me: hear, and your [b]soul shall live; and I will make an everlasting [c]covenant with you, *even the* [d]sure mercies of David.

4 Behold, I have given him *for a* [a]witness to the people, a [b]leader and commander to the people.

5 Behold, thou shalt call a nation *that* thou knowest not, and [a]nations *that* knew not thee shall run unto thee because of the LORD thy God, and for the Holy One of Israel; for he hath glorified thee.

6 ¶ [a]Seek ye the [b]LORD while he may be found, call ye upon him while he is near:

7 Let the wicked forsake his way, and the unrighteous man his thoughts: and let him [a]return unto the LORD, and he will have mercy upon him; and to our God, for he will abundantly [b]pardon.

8 ¶ For my [a]thoughts *are* not [b]your thoughts, neither *are* your [c]ways my [d]ways, saith the LORD.

9 For *as* the heavens are higher than the earth, so are my [a]ways

[b]higher than your ways, and my [c]thoughts than your thoughts.

10 For as the [a]rain cometh down, and the snow from heaven, and returneth not thither, but watereth the earth, and maketh it bring forth and bud, that it may give seed to the sower, and [b]bread to the eater:

11 So shall my [a]word be that goeth forth out of my mouth: it shall not return unto me void, but it shall accomplish that which I please, and it shall prosper *in the thing* whereto I sent it.

12 For ye shall go out with [a]joy, and be led forth with peace: the mountains and the hills shall break forth before you into singing, and all the [b]trees of the field shall clap *their* hands.

13 Instead of the thorn shall come up the [a]fir tree, and instead of the brier shall come up the myrtle tree: and it shall be to the LORD for a name, for an everlasting sign *that* shall not be cut off.

CHAPTER 56

All who keep the commandments will be exalted—Other people will join Israel—The Lord will gather others to the house of Israel.

THUS saith the LORD, Keep ye judgment, and do [a]justice: for my salvation *is* [b]near to come, and my righteousness to be revealed.

2 Blessed *is* the man *that* doeth this, and the son of man *that* layeth hold

55 1a Ps. 42:2 (1–3); 143:6 (5–12); Luke 6:21; John 4:14 (13–15); 7:37 (37–39); 2 Ne. 9:50 (50–51).
 b TG Living Water.
 c 2 Ne. 26:25.
 d Matt. 10:8.
 2a TG Waste.
 b TG Labor.
 c TG Diligence.
 3a Matt. 11:28 (28–30); John 6:44; Heb. 7:25; 3 Ne. 12:20 (19–20); D&C 45:46 (45–46); 132:12.
 b TG Soul.

 c TG New and Everlasting Covenant.
 d Acts 13:34 (26–41).
 4a TG Jesus Christ, Prophecies about.
 b Ezek. 34:23; John 10:3 (1–16); 18:37.
 5a Isa. 60:5; Zech. 2:11 (10–12). TG Israel, Mission of.
 6a TG God, Access to.
 b Luke 13:25 (24–27).
 7a TG Repent.
 b Ps. 130:7.
 8a TG God, Intelligence of; God, Will of; God, Wisdom of; Intelligence; Motivations.

 b 1 Sam. 16:7; Ezek. 28:2.
 c Prov. 14:12.
 d Jacob 4:8.
 9a TG Spirituality.
 b Job 33:12; Abr. 3:19.
 c Ps. 139:17 (17–24).
 10a TG Nature, Earth.
 b TG Bread.
 11a Deut. 32:2; Ezek. 12:25; D&C 121:45.
 12a TG Joy.
 b 1 Chr. 16:33 (31–33); D&C 128:23 (22–23).
 13a HEB cypress tree. TG Earth, Renewal of.
 56 1a TG Justice.
 b Ezek. 36:8 (8–15); Matt. 3:2; 4:17.

on it; that keepeth the ^asabbath from polluting it, and keepeth his hand from doing any ^bevil.

3 ¶ Neither let the ^ason of the ^bstranger, that hath joined himself to the LORD, speak, saying, The LORD hath utterly separated me from his people: neither let the eunuch say, Behold, I *am* a dry tree.

4 For thus saith the LORD unto the eunuchs that keep my sabbaths, and choose *the things* that please me, and take hold of my covenant;

5 Even unto them will I give in mine ^ahouse and within my walls a place and a name better than of ^bsons and of daughters: I will give them an everlasting name, that shall not be cut off.

6 Also the sons of the stranger, that join themselves to the LORD, to serve him, and to love the name of the LORD, to be his servants, every one that keepeth the sabbath from polluting it, and taketh hold of my covenant;

7 Even them will I bring to my holy ^amountain, and make them joyful in my ^bhouse of ^cprayer: their burnt offerings and their sacrifices *shall be* ^daccepted upon mine altar; for mine ^ehouse shall be called an house of prayer for ^fall ^gpeople.

8 The Lord GOD which ^agathereth the outcasts of Israel saith, Yet will I gather ^bothers to him, beside those that are gathered unto him.

9 ¶ ^aAll ye beasts of the field, come to devour, *yea,* all ye beasts in the forest.

10 His ^awatchmen *are* ^bblind: they are all ignorant, they *are* all dumb dogs, they cannot bark; sleeping, lying down, loving to slumber.

11 Yea, *they are* ^agreedy dogs *which* can never have enough, and they *are* ^bshepherds *that* cannot understand: they all look to their ^cown way, every one for his gain, from his quarter.

12 Come ye, *say they,* I will fetch wine, and we will fill ourselves with strong drink; and to morrow shall be as this day, *and* much more abundant.

CHAPTER 57

When the righteous die, they enter into peace—Mercy is promised to the penitent—There is no peace for the wicked.

THE righteous ^aperisheth, and no man layeth *it* to heart: and merciful men *are* taken away, none considering that the righteous is taken away from the evil *to come.*

2 He shall enter into ^apeace: they shall rest in their beds, *each one* walking *in* his uprightness.

3 ¶ But draw near hither, ye ^asons of the sorceress, the seed of the ^badulterer and the whore.

4 Against whom do ye sport yourselves? against whom make ye a wide mouth, *and* draw out the tongue? *are* ye not ^achildren of transgression, a seed of falsehood,

5 Enflaming yourselves with ^aidols under every green tree, ^bslaying the ^cchildren in the valleys under the clifts of the rocks?

6 Among the smooth *stones* of the stream *is* thy portion; they, they *are* thy lot: even to them hast thou poured a drink offering, thou hast

---

2*a* TG Sabbath.
  b D&C 133:5 (3–5).
3*a* Isa. 60:10.
  b Rom. 8:15.
5*a* TG Genealogy and Temple Work.
  b 1 Jn. 3:1 (1–2).
7*a* Ezek. 20:40.
  b TG Temple.
  c TG Prayer.
  d Isa. 60:7; Mal. 3:4.
  e Luke 19:46.
  f Alma 19:36;

D&C 38:16.
  g Mal. 1:11.
8*a* TG Israel, Gathering of.
  b TG Conversion;
    Israel, Mission of.
9*a* Here begins a short rebuke to the wicked of the time (vv. 9–12).
10*a* TG Watchman.
  b Isa. 28:7.
11*a* TG Covet.
  b Ezek. 34:2 (2–3).
  c TG Selfishness.

57 1*a* D&C 59:2 (1–2).
  2*a* TG Paradise.
  3*a* IE people affiliated with evil; see vv. 4–5.
    b TG Sexual Immorality.
  4*a* Isa. 1:4.
  5*a* 1 Kgs. 14:23 (22–23);
    2 Kgs. 16:4 (2–4).
    b IE participating in abominable cult sacrifices.
    Jer. 7:31; 32:35.
    c Ezek. 16:20.

offered a meat offering. Should I receive comfort in these?

7 Upon a lofty and high mountain hast thou set thy *a*bed: even thither wentest thou up to offer sacrifice.

8 Behind the doors also and the posts hast thou set up thy remembrance: for thou hast *a*discovered *thyself to* *b*another than me, and art gone up; thou hast enlarged thy bed, and made thee *a covenant* with them; thou lovedst their bed where thou sawest *it.*

9 And thou wentest to the *a*king with ointment, and didst increase thy perfumes, and didst send thy messengers far off, and didst debase *thyself even* unto hell.

10 Thou art wearied in the greatness of thy way; *yet* saidst thou not, There is no *a*hope: thou hast found the *b*life of thine hand; therefore thou wast not grieved.

11 And of whom hast thou been afraid or *a*feared, that thou hast *b*lied, and hast not remembered me, nor laid *it* to thy heart? have not I held my peace even of old, and thou fearest me not?

12 I will *a*declare thy righteousness, and thy works; for they shall not profit thee.

13 ¶ When thou criest, let thy companies deliver thee; but the wind shall carry them all away; vanity shall take *them:* but he that putteth his trust in me shall possess the land, and shall inherit my holy *a*mountain;

14 *a*And shall say, Cast ye up, cast ye up, *b*prepare the way, take up the *c*stumblingblock out of the way of my people.

15 For thus saith the high and lofty One that inhabiteth *a*eternity, whose name *is* *b*Holy; I dwell in the high and holy *place,* with him also *that is* of a *c*contrite and *d*humble spirit, to *e*revive the spirit of the *f*humble, and to revive the heart of the contrite ones.

16 For I will not *a*contend for ever, neither will I be always wroth: for the spirit should fail before me, and the *b*souls *which* I have made.

17 For the *a*iniquity of his *b*covetousness was I wroth, and smote him: I hid me, and was wroth, and he went on *c*frowardly in the way of his heart.

18 I have seen his ways, and will heal him: I will *a*lead him also, and restore *b*comforts unto him and to his *c*mourners.

19 I create the *a*fruit of the lips; Peace, peace to *him that is* *b*far off, and to *him that is* near, saith the LORD; and I will heal him.

20 But the *a*wicked *are* like the troubled sea, when it cannot rest, whose waters cast up mire and dirt.

21 *There is* no *a*peace, saith my God, to the wicked.

CHAPTER 58

The true law of the fast, with its purposes and attendant blessings, is set forth—The commandment to keep the Sabbath is given.

CRY aloud, *a*spare not, lift up thy *b*voice like a *c*trumpet, and *d*shew my people their *e*transgression, and the house of Jacob their sins.

7*a* IE as an altar for idolatrous use.
8*a* HEB exposed.
  b TG Idolatry.
9*a* HEB *melech* or *molech* (a horrible idol).
10*a* Jer. 18:12 (11–12).
  b IE renewal of strength.
11*a* D&C 3:7.
  b Ps. 78:36 (35–37).
12*a* D&C 1:3.
13*a* TG Lands of Inheritance.
14*a* HEB And he shall say.
  b Isa. 62:10.

  c Jacob 4:14 (13–14).
15*a* TG God, Eternal Nature of.
  b Luke 1:49.
  c TG Contrite Heart.
  d TG Humility.
  e Isa. 61:1.
  f TG Poor in Spirit.
16*a* Micah 7:18; D&C 1:33.
  b Moses 3:7.
17*a* D&C 63:32.
  b Ezek. 33:31.
  c HEB turning away.
18*a* D&C 112:10.
  b TG Comfort.

  c TG Sorrow.
19*a* IE speech.
    Heb. 13:15.
  b Acts 2:39.
20*a* TG Wickedness.
21*a* TG Conscience; Peace.
58 1*a* D&C 34:10.
  b TG Priesthood, Magnifying Callings within.
  c HEB ram's horn.
    Alma 29:1 (1–2);
    D&C 33:2; 42:6.
  d TG Prophets, Mission of.
  e TG Transgress.

2 *Yet they seek me daily, and delight to know my ways, as a nation that did righteousness, and forsook not the ordinance of their God: they ask of me the *ordinances of justice; they take delight in approaching to God.

3 ¶ *Wherefore have we fasted, *say they*, and thou seest not? *wherefore* have we afflicted our soul, and thou takest no knowledge? Behold, in the day of your *fast ye find *pleasure, and *exact all your labours.

4 Behold, ye fast for *strife and *debate, and to smite with the fist of wickedness: ye shall not *fast as *ye do this* day, to make your voice to be heard on high.

5 Is it such a fast that I have chosen? a day for a man to afflict his soul? *is it* to bow down his head as a bulrush, and to spread sackcloth and ashes *under him?* wilt thou call this a fast, and an acceptable day to the Lord?

6 *Is* not this the fast that I have chosen? to loose the *bands of wickedness, to undo the heavy burdens, and to let the oppressed go *free, and that ye break every yoke?

7 *Is it* not to deal thy bread to the *hungry, and that thou bring the *poor that are cast out to thy house? when thou seest the naked, that thou cover him; and that thou hide not thyself from *thine own flesh?

8 ¶ Then shall thy *light break forth as the morning, and thine *health shall spring forth speedily: and thy righteousness shall go before thee; the glory of the Lord shall be thy *rearward.

9 Then shalt thou *call, and the Lord shall answer; thou shalt cry, and he shall say, Here I *am.* If thou take away from the midst of thee the yoke, the *putting forth of the finger, and speaking vanity;

10 And *if* thou draw out thy soul to the *hungry, and satisfy the afflicted soul; then shall thy light *rise in obscurity, and thy darkness *be* as the noonday:

11 And the Lord shall *guide thee continually, and satisfy thy soul in *drought, and *make fat thy bones: and thou shalt be like a watered garden, and like a *spring of water, whose waters fail not.

12 And *they that shall be* of thee shall build the old waste places: thou shalt raise up the foundations of many generations; and thou shalt be called, The repairer of the breach, The restorer of paths to dwell in.

13 ¶ If thou turn away thy foot from the sabbath, *from* doing thy pleasure on my holy day; and call the *sabbath a delight, the holy of the Lord, honourable; and shalt honour him, not doing thine own ways, nor finding thine own pleasure, nor speaking *thine own* words:

14 Then shalt thou delight thyself in the Lord; and I will cause thee to ride upon the *high places of the earth, and feed thee with the heritage of Jacob thy father: for the mouth of the Lord hath spoken *it.*

2a IE They do all the rituals, but lack something yet.
 b TG Ordinance.
3a Mal. 3:14 (13–15); Alma 34:28.
 b TG Fast, Fasting.
 c TG Pleasure.
 d OR inflict travail on others.
4a TG Strife.
 b IE Fasting without spiritual motivation only engenders discomfort and

irritability.
 c TG Hypocrisy.
6a 2 Ne. 1:13; Mosiah 23:12 (12–13); 27:29 (28–29).
 b TG Liberty.
7a TG Almsgiving.
 b TG Poor; Welfare.
 c IE thy brother, or relative.
8a TG Light [noun].
 b TG Health.
 c OR rearguard.
9a Matt. 7:7 (7–8);

3 Ne. 18:20 (18–21); D&C 8:1.
 b IE pointing in a gesture of scorn.
10a Mosiah 4:26.
 b OR shine in the darkness.
11a TG Guidance, Divine.
 b TG Drought.
 c HEB strengthen.
 d TG Abundant Life.
13a TG Sabbath.
14a Deut. 32:13 (7–14).

CHAPTER 59

The people of Israel are separated from their God by iniquity—Their sins testify against them—The Messiah will intercede, come to Zion, and redeem the repentant.

BEHOLD, the LORD's ᵃhand is not ᵇshortened, that it cannot save; neither his ear heavy, that it cannot ᶜhear:

2 But your iniquities have ᵃseparated between you and your God, and your ᵇsins ᶜhave hid *his* face from you, that he will not ᵈhear.

3 For your hands are defiled with ᵃblood, and your fingers with iniquity; your lips have spoken lies, your tongue hath muttered perverseness.

4 None calleth for justice, nor *any* pleadeth for truth: they ᵃtrust in vanity, and speak lies; they conceive ᵇmischief, and bring forth iniquity.

5 They hatch cockatrice' eggs, and weave the spider's web: he that eateth of their eggs dieth, and that which is crushed breaketh out into a viper.

6 Their webs shall not become garments, neither shall they cover themselves with their works: their works *are* works of iniquity, and the act of violence *is* in their hands.

7 Their feet ᵃrun to ᵇevil, and they make ᶜhaste to ᵈshed innocent blood: their thoughts *are* thoughts of iniquity; wasting and destruction *are* in their paths.

8 The way of ᵃpeace they know not; and *there is* no ᵇjudgment in their goings: they have made them ᶜcrooked paths: whosoever goeth therein shall not know peace.

9 ¶ Therefore is judgment far from us, neither doth ᵃjustice overtake us: we wait for ᵇlight, but behold obscurity; for brightness, *but* we ᶜwalk in darkness.

10 We ᵃgrope for the wall like the blind, and we grope as if *we had* no eyes: we stumble at noonday as in the night; *we are* in desolate places as dead *men.*

11 We roar all like bears, and mourn sore like doves: we look for judgment, but *there is* none; for salvation, *but* it is far off from us.

12 For our transgressions are multiplied before thee, and our sins ᵃtestify against us: for our transgressions *are* with us; and *as for* our iniquities, we ᵇknow them;

13 In transgressing and lying against the LORD, and departing away from our God, speaking oppression and revolt, conceiving and uttering from the heart words of falsehood.

14 And judgment is turned away backward, and justice standeth afar off: for truth is fallen in the street, and ᵃequity cannot enter.

15 Yea, truth faileth; and he *that* departeth from evil maketh himself a prey: and the LORD saw *it,* and it displeased him that *there was* no judgment.

16 ¶ And he saw that *there was* ᵃno man, and wondered that *there was* no ᵇintercessor: therefore his ᶜarm ᵈbrought ᵉsalvation unto him; and his righteousness, it sustained him.

17 For he put on ᵃrighteousness

59 1 *a* Isa. 50:2.
  b D&C 35:8.
  c TG God, Omniscience of.
 2 *a* TG God, Access to; Separation.
  b Isa. 1:15.
  c OR have made Him hide.
  d Mosiah 11:25 (23–25); 21:15 (13–15); D&C 101:7.
 3 *a* Alma 5:22.
 4 *a* TG Trust Not in the Arm of Flesh.

  b Job 15:35; Ps. 7:14.
 7 *a* Hel. 12:4 (4–6).
  b Prov. 1:16 (10–19).
  c TG Rashness.
  d Rom. 3:15.
 8 *a* TG Peace of God.
  b OR equity, justice.
  c TG Wickedness.
 9 *a* OR charity, righteousness.
  b Jer. 8:15.
  c TG Walking in Darkness.
 10 *a* Deut. 28:29.

 12 *a* Alma 5:23 (22–23).
  b 2 Ne. 9:14.
 14 *a* OR honesty.
 16 *a* IE no one able to help.
  b Jer. 27:18; Heb. 7:25 (25–26); D&C 45:3 (3–5).
  c 2 Ne. 1:15; Jacob 6:5; Alma 5:33; 3 Ne. 9:14.
  d IE The Lord brought salvation to man.
  e Isa. 63:5.
 17 *a* D&C 27:18 (15–18).

as a *b*breastplate, and an helmet
of salvation upon his head; and he
put on the garments of vengeance
for clothing, and was clad with zeal
as a cloak.

18 According to *their* *a*deeds, ac-
cordingly he will *b*repay, fury to
his adversaries, *c*recompence to his
enemies; to the islands he will repay recompence.

19 So shall they *a*fear the *b*name
of the LORD from the west, and his
glory from the rising of the sun.
When the enemy shall come in like
a flood, the *c*Spirit of the LORD shall
lift up a standard against him.

20 ¶ And the *a*Redeemer shall
*b*come to *c*Zion, and unto them that
*d*turn from transgression in Jacob,
saith the LORD.

21 As for me, this *is* my *a*covenant
with them, saith the LORD; My spirit
that *is* upon thee, and my words
which I have put in thy mouth, shall
not depart out of thy mouth, nor
out of the mouth of thy seed, nor out
of the mouth of thy seed's seed,
saith the LORD, from henceforth and
for ever.

CHAPTER 60

*In the last days, Israel will rise again
as a mighty nation—The gentile peoples
will join with and serve Israel—Zion
will be established—Finally, Israel will
dwell in celestial splendor.*

*a*ARISE, shine; for thy *b*light is come,
and the glory of the LORD is risen
upon thee.

2 For, behold, the *a*darkness shall
cover the earth, and gross *b*darkness
the people: but the LORD shall *c*arise
upon thee, and his *d*glory shall be
seen upon thee.

3 And the *a*Gentiles shall come to
thy *b*light, and kings to the brightness of thy rising.

4 Lift up thine eyes round about,
and see: all they gather themselves
together, they come to thee: thy
*a*sons shall come from far, and thy
daughters shall be nursed at *thy* side.

5 Then thou shalt see, and *a*flow
together, and thine heart shall fear,
and be enlarged; because the *b*abundance of the sea shall be converted
unto thee, the *c*forces of the *d*Gentiles shall come unto thee.

6 The multitude of camels shall
cover thee, the dromedaries of Midian and Ephah; all they from Sheba
shall come: they shall bring *a*gold
and incense; and they shall shew
forth the praises of the LORD.

7 All the flocks of *a*Kedar shall be
gathered together unto thee, the
rams of Nebaioth shall minister
unto thee: they shall come up with
*b*acceptance on mine *c*altar, and I
will glorify the house of my *d*glory.

8 Who *are* *a*these *that* fly as a cloud,
and as the doves to their windows?

9 Surely the *a*isles shall wait for

17*b* Isa. 11:5; 61:10;
      Rom. 13:12;
      Eph. 6:14 (11, 13–17).
18*a* Alma 36:15;
      41:3 (2–5); 42:27;
      D&C 1:10 (9–10).
   b TG Punish.
   c TG Retribution.
19*a* OR stand in awe of or
      reverence.
   b Mal. 1:11.
   c TG God, Spirit of.
20*a* Rom. 11:26.
   b TG Jesus Christ,
      Prophecies about.
   c TG Zion.
   d D&C 100:15 (15–17).
21*a* Rom. 11:27;
      Heb. 10:16 (16–17);
      D&C 49:9 (5–9).
60 1*a* IE Zion is to arise and

      be a light unto the
      nations.
   b TG Light [noun];
      Light of Christ.
2*a* IE ignorance and
      wickedness.
      D&C 112:23.
      TG Apostasy of the
      Early Christian Church.
   b TG Darkness, Spiritual.
   c OR shine upon,
      illuminate thee.
      TG Jesus Christ, Second
      Coming.
   d TG Jesus Christ,
      Glory of.
3*a* TG Conversion;
      Gentiles.
   b TG Israel, Mission of;
      Light [noun].
4*a* Isa. 49:22 (20–22);

1 Ne. 19:16 (16–17);
      A of F 1:10.
5*a* OR be radiant.
   b HEB multitude.
   c HEB wealth of Gentiles.
      (See Isa. 61:6.)
   d Isa. 49:22; 55:5;
      Rev. 21:24.
6*a* Isa. 61:6;
      D&C 124:11 (3–11).
7*a* Ps. 120:5;
      Isa. 21:16 (16–17).
   b Isa. 56:7;
      Ezek. 20:40;
      Mal. 3:4.
   c Isa. 66:20.
   d Hag. 2:7 (7–9).
8*a* IE the people who flock
      in over the sea.
9*a* Isa. 51:5;
      D&C 64:42 (41–43).

me, and the ships of Tarshish first, to ᵇbring thy sons from far, their silver and their gold with them, unto the name of the LORD thy God, and to the Holy One of Israel, because he hath glorified thee.

10 And the ᵃsons of strangers shall ᵇbuild up thy walls, and their kings shall minister unto thee: for in my ᶜwrath I smote thee, but in my favour have I had mercy on thee.

11 Therefore thy ᵃgates shall be open continually; they shall not be shut day nor night; that *men* may bring unto thee the ᵇforces of the Gentiles, and *that* their kings *may be* brought.

12 For the ᵃnation and ᵇkingdom that will not serve thee shall ᶜperish; yea, *those* ᵈnations shall be utterly wasted.

13 The glory of ᵃLebanon shall come unto thee, the ᵇfir tree, the pine tree, and the box together, to ᶜbeautify the place of my sanctuary; and I will make the place of my ᵈfeet glorious.

14 The sons also of them that afflicted thee shall come bending unto thee; and all they that despised thee shall ᵃbow themselves down at the soles of thy feet; and they shall call thee, The city of the LORD, The Zion of the Holy One of Israel.

15 Whereas thou hast been ᵃforsaken and hated, so that no man went through *thee,* I will make thee an eternal excellency, a joy of many generations.

16 Thou shalt also suck the ᵃmilk of the Gentiles, and shalt suck the breast of ᵇkings: and thou shalt know that I the LORD *am* thy ᶜSaviour and thy Redeemer, the mighty One of Jacob.

17 For brass I will bring gold, and for iron I will bring silver, and for wood brass, and for stones iron: I will also make thy officers peace, and thine exactors righteousness.

18 ᵃViolence shall no more be heard in thy land, wasting nor destruction within thy borders; but thou shalt call thy ᵇwalls Salvation, and thy gates ᶜPraise.

19 The ᵃsun shall be no more thy light by day; neither for brightness shall the moon give light unto thee: but the LORD shall be unto thee an everlasting ᵇlight, and thy God thy glory.

20 Thy sun shall no more go down; neither shall thy moon withdraw itself: for the LORD shall be thine ᵃeverlasting light, and the days of thy ᵇmourning shall be ended.

21 Thy people also *shall be* all ᵃrighteous: they shall inherit the ᵇland for ᶜever, the ᵈbranch of my planting, the ᵉwork of my hands, that I may be glorified.

22 A ᵃlittle one shall become a thousand, and a small one a ᵇstrong nation: I the LORD will hasten it in ᶜhis time.

CHAPTER 61

Isaiah speaks about the Messiah—The Messiah will have the Spirit, preach the gospel, and proclaim liberty—In the last days, the Lord will call His

---

9b Isa. 14:2.
10a Isa. 56:3 (3–6).
  b Zech. 6:15.
  c Isa. 54:8 (7–8);
    D&C 98:22 (21–22);
    101:9.
11a Rev. 21:25 (23–26).
  b HEB wealth of Gentiles.
12a Jer. 12:17;
    Zech. 14:18 (17–18).
  b TG Kings, Earthly.
  c 1 Ne. 22:14;
    2 Ne. 10:13 (13–16).
  d Dan. 2:44;
    1 Cor. 15:24.
13a Isa. 35:2.

  b HEB cypress.
    Isa. 41:19.
  c TG Beauty.
  d Ezek. 43:7;
    Matt. 5:35.
14a Isa. 49:23; Rev. 3:9;
    D&C 49:10;
    64:43 (41–43);
    97:19 (19–20).
15a Isa. 54:6; 62:4.
16a Isa. 49:23.
  b 1 Ne. 21:23 (22–23);
    2 Ne. 6:7 (6–7).
  c TG Jesus Christ, Jehovah.
18a Isa. 11:9; 65:25 (17–25).
  b Isa. 26:1.

  c Isa. 61:11.
19a Rev. 21:23; 22:5.
  b TG Jesus Christ, Light of
    the World; Light [noun];
    Light of Christ.
20a TG Eternal Life.
  b TG Mourning.
21a TG Righteousness.
  b OR earth.
  c Ezek. 37:25.
  d TG Vineyard of the Lord.
  e Isa. 64:8;
    Eph. 2:10.
22a Matt. 13:31 (31–32).
  b D&C 133:58.
  c JST Isa. 60:22 . . . *my . . .*

ministers and make an everlasting covenant with the people.

THE ^aSpirit of the Lord ^bGOD *is* upon me; because the LORD hath ^canointed me to ^dpreach ^egood tidings unto the ^fmeek; he hath sent me to ^gbind up the brokenhearted, to ^hproclaim ⁱliberty to the ^jcaptives, and the opening of the ^kprison to *them that are* bound;

2 To proclaim the acceptable year of the LORD, and the day of ^avengeance of our God; to ^bcomfort all that ^cmourn;

3 To appoint unto them that mourn in Zion, to give unto them ^abeauty for ashes, the oil of ^bjoy for mourning, the garment of praise for the spirit of heaviness; that they might be called ^ctrees of ^drighteousness, the ^eplanting of the LORD, that he might be glorified.

4 ¶ And they shall ^abuild the old wastes, they shall raise up the former desolations, and they shall repair the waste cities, the desolations of many generations.

5 And strangers shall stand and feed your flocks, and the sons of the alien *shall be* your plowmen and your vinedressers.

6 But ye shall be named the ^aPriests of the LORD: *men* shall call you the Ministers of our God: ye shall eat the ^briches of the Gentiles, and in their glory shall ye boast yourselves.

7 ¶ For your shame *ye shall have* ^adouble; and *for* confusion they shall rejoice in their portion: therefore in their land they shall possess

^bthe double: everlasting joy shall be unto them.

8 For I the LORD love ^ajudgment, I hate robbery for burnt offering; and I will direct their work in truth, and I will make an everlasting ^bcovenant with them.

9 And their seed shall be known among the Gentiles, and their offspring among the people: all that see them shall acknowledge them, that they *are* the ^aseed *which* the LORD hath blessed.

10 I will greatly rejoice in the LORD, my soul shall be joyful in my God; for he hath ^aclothed me with the ^bgarments of salvation, he hath covered me with the robe of righteousness, as a bridegroom decketh *himself* with ornaments, and as a bride adorneth *herself* with her jewels.

11 For as the earth bringeth forth her bud, and as the garden causeth the things that are sown in it to spring forth; so the Lord GOD will cause righteousness and ^apraise to spring forth before all the nations.

CHAPTER 62

In the last days, Israel will be gathered— Zion will be established—Her watchmen will teach about the Lord—The gospel standard will be lifted up—The people will be called holy, the redeemed of the Lord.

FOR Zion's sake will I not hold my peace, and for Jerusalem's sake I will not rest, until the righteousness thereof go forth as brightness, and

---

61 1 a Luke 4:18 (18–19).
  TG God, Spirit of.
  b HEB Jehovah.
  c TG Anointing;
    Jesus Christ, Messiah;
    Jesus Christ,
    Prophecies about.
  d John 3:34.
    TG Jesus Christ, Mission
    of; Missionary Work;
    Preaching; Teaching.
  e TG Gospel.
  f TG Meek.
  g Isa. 57:15.
  h John 5:25.
  i TG Liberty.

  j TG Bondage, Spiritual.
  k D&C 138:8 (5–10),
    42 (31, 42).
    TG Spirits in Prison.
  2 a Isa. 34:8;
    Mal. 4:1 (1, 3);
    3 Ne. 21:21 (20–21);
    D&C 97:26 (25–28).
  b TG Comfort;
    Compassion.
  c TG Mourning; Sorrow.
  3 a TG Beauty.
  b Ps. 30:11 (10–12).
  c TG Vineyard of the Lord.
  d TG Israel, Mission of.
  e Ezek. 34:29 (20–31).

  4 a Isa. 49:8 (8–11);
    Ezek. 36:10 (8–15),
    34 (34–35).
  6 a Isa. 66:21.
  b Isa. 60:6;
    D&C 124:11 (3–11).
  7 a Zech. 9:12.
  b IE a double portion.
  8 a TG Judgment.
  b TG Covenants.
  9 a Isa. 65:23;
    Abr. 2:11 (8–11).
  10 a Ps. 132:16 (13–16).
  b Isa. 59:17;
    Eph. 6:14 (11, 13–17).
  11 a Isa. 60:18 (17–19).

the salvation thereof as a lamp *that* burneth.

2 And the Gentiles shall *a*see thy righteousness, and all kings thy glory: and thou shalt be called by a new *b*name, which the mouth of the Lord shall name.

3 Thou shalt also be a *a*crown of glory in the hand of the Lord, and a royal diadem in the hand of thy God.

4 Thou shalt no more be termed *a*Forsaken; neither shall thy *b*land any more be termed Desolate: but thou shalt be called *c*Hephzi-bah, and thy land *d*Beulah: for the Lord delighteth in thee, and thy land shall be married.

5 ¶ For *as* a young man marrieth a virgin, *so* shall thy sons marry thee: and *as* the bridegroom rejoiceth over the bride, *so* shall thy God *a*rejoice over thee.

6 I have set *a*watchmen upon thy walls, O Jerusalem, *which* shall never hold their peace day nor night: ye that make mention of the Lord, keep not silence,

7 And give him no rest, till he establish, and till he make Jerusalem a *a*praise in the earth.

8 The Lord hath sworn by his right hand, and by the arm of his strength, Surely I will no more give thy corn *to be* meat for thine enemies; and the sons of the stranger shall not drink thy wine, for the which thou hast laboured:

9 But they that have gathered it shall eat it, and praise the Lord; and they that have brought it together shall drink it in the courts of my *a*holiness.

10 ¶ Go through, go through the gates; *a*prepare ye the way of the people; cast up, cast up the *b*highway; gather out the stones; lift up a *c*standard for the people.

11 Behold, the Lord hath proclaimed unto the end of the *a*world, Say ye to the *b*daughter of Zion, Behold, thy *c*salvation cometh; behold, his *d*reward *is* with him, and his work before him.

12 And they shall call them, The holy people, The redeemed of the Lord: and thou shalt be called, Sought out, A city not forsaken.

CHAPTER 63

The Second Coming will be a day of vengeance and also the year of the redeemed of the Lord—Then the Saints will praise the Lord and acknowledge Him as their father.

Who *is* this that *a*cometh from *b*Edom, with dyed garments from Bozrah? this *that is* glorious in his apparel, travelling in the greatness of his strength? I that speak in righteousness, mighty to save.

2 Wherefore *art thou* *a*red in thine apparel, and thy garments like him that treadeth in the *b*winefat?

3 I have trodden the *a*winepress alone; and of the people *there was* none with me: for I will tread them in mine anger, and trample them in my fury; and their blood shall be *b*sprinkled upon my garments, and I will stain all my raiment.

4 For the day of *a*vengeance *is* in mine heart, and the year of my *b*redeemed is come.

---

62 2*a* Ps. 98:2 (1–3).
  b Isa. 65:15;
     Rev. 2:17;
     D&C 130:11 (10–11).
  3*a* Zech. 9:16;
     Mal. 3:17;
     D&C 66:12; 104:7.
  4*a* Isa. 54:6; 60:15.
     TG Israel, Restoration of.
  b TG Israel, Land of.
  c IE My desire is in her.
  d IE Married wife.
  5*a* Isa. 65:19.
  6*a* TG Watchman.
  7*a* Zeph. 3:20.

9*a* OR sanctuary.
10*a* Isa. 57:14.
   b D&C 133:27 (23–30).
   c TG Ensign.
11*a* TG World.
   b Zech. 9:9.
   c Isa. 46:13;
      Matt. 21:5.
   d TG Reward.
63 1*a* TG Jesus Christ, Second
      Coming.
   b IE the worldly nations;
      D&C 1:36.
2*a* Gen. 49:11 (11–12);
   Rev. 19:13 (13–15);

D&C 76:107;
   133:48 (46–50).
b HEB press; i.e., the
   winepress and the vat
   for collecting the juice
   of the grapes.
3*a* Rev. 14:19 (17–20);
   19:15;
   D&C 88:106.
b Lev. 8:30;
   D&C 133:51.
4*a* TG Vengeance.
b Zeph. 3:20;
   D&C 133:52.

5 And I looked, and *there was* none to help; and I wondered that *there was* none to uphold: therefore mine own arm brought *a*salvation unto me; and my fury, it upheld me.

6 And I will tread down the people in mine anger, and *a*make them drunk in my fury, and I will bring down their strength to the earth.

7 ¶ I will mention the *a*lovingkindnesses of the Lord, *and* the praises of the Lord, according to all that the Lord hath bestowed on us, and the great *b*goodness toward the house of Israel, which he hath bestowed on them according to his mercies, and according to the multitude of his lovingkindnesses.

8 For he said, Surely they *are* my people, children *that* will not lie: so he was their *a*Saviour.

9 In all their *a*affliction he was afflicted, and the *b*angel of his *c*presence saved them: in his *d*love and in his pity he *e*redeemed them; and he bare them, and *f*carried them all the days of old.

10 ¶ But they *a*rebelled, and *b*vexed his *c*holy Spirit: therefore he was turned to be their *d*enemy, *and* he fought against them.

11 Then *a*he remembered the days of old, Moses, *and* his people, *saying,* Where *is* he that brought them up out of the *b*sea with the *c*shepherd of his *d*flock? where *is* he that put his holy Spirit within *e*him?

12 That led *them* by the right hand of *a*Moses with his glorious arm, *b*dividing the water before them, to make himself an everlasting name?

13 That led them through the deep, as an horse in the wilderness, *that* they should not stumble?

14 *a*As a beast goeth down into the valley, the *b*Spirit of the Lord caused *c*him to rest: so didst thou lead thy people, to make thyself a glorious *d*name.

15 ¶ *a*Look down from heaven, and behold from the habitation of thy *b*holiness and of thy glory: where *is* thy zeal and thy strength, *c*the sounding of thy bowels and of thy mercies toward me? are they restrained?

16 Doubtless thou *art* our *a*father, though Abraham *b*be ignorant of us, and Israel acknowledge us not: thou, O Lord, *art* our father, our redeemer; thy name *is* from *c*everlasting.

17 ¶ O Lord, why hast thou *a*made us to err from thy ways, *and* *b*hardened our heart from thy fear? Return for thy servants' sake, the tribes of thine inheritance.

18 The *a*people of thy holiness have possessed *it* but a little while: our adversaries have *b*trodden down thy sanctuary.

19 We are *thine:* thou never barest rule over them; they were not called by thy *a*name.

---

5 *a* Isa. 59:16.
6 *a* OR break them in pieces (according to several Hebrew texts).
7 *a* TG Kindness.
  b D&C 133:52.
8 *a* TG Jesus Christ, Jehovah.
9 *a* D&C 133:53.
  TG Affliction; Compassion.
  b Ex. 23:20 (20–23).
  c Ex. 33:14.
  d TG Charity; Love.
  e D&C 138:3 (2–4).
  TG Jesus Christ, Atonement through; Jesus Christ, Redeemer.
  f Isa. 46:4 (3–4).
10 *a* Num. 14:11 (11–12).

b TG Holy Ghost, Loss of.
c TG Holiness.
d Lam. 2:4 (4–5).
11 *a* IE His people remembered.
  b TG Israel, Deliverance of.
  c OR shepherds.
  d TG Church.
  e OR them.
12 *a* Ps. 77:20.
  b Ex. 14:21; Ps. 78:13.
14 *a* OR As cattle go.
  b TG God, Spirit of.
  c OR them.
  d Ex. 9:16; Ps. 106:8; Ezek. 20:9.
15 *a* Deut. 26:15; Ps. 33:14.

b TG Holiness.
c IE the abundance of Thy tenderness.
16 *a* Deut. 32:6; 1 Chr. 29:10; Isa. 64:8.
  b IE Such forefathers as Abraham and Jacob, long dead, were not available to help.
  c TG God, Eternal Nature of.
17 *a* JST Isa. 63:17 . . . *suffered* us to err from thy ways, and *to harden* our heart . . .
  b TG Hardheartedness.
18 *a* Deut. 7:6.
  b Isa. 64:11.
19 *a* Isa. 65:1.

CHAPTER 64

The people of the Lord pray for the Second Coming and for the salvation that will then be theirs.

OH that thou wouldest *a*rend the heavens, that thou wouldest come down, that the *b*mountains might flow down at thy *c*presence,

2 As *when* the melting fire burneth, the fire causeth the waters to boil, to make thy name known to thine adversaries, *that* the nations may *a*tremble at thy presence!

3 When thou didst *a*terrible things *which* we looked not for, thou camest down, the *b*mountains flowed down at thy presence.

4 For since the beginning of the world *men* have not heard, nor perceived by the ear, neither hath the *a*eye seen, O God, beside thee, *what* he hath *b*prepared for him that waiteth for him.

5 Thou meetest him that rejoiceth and worketh righteousness, *those that* remember thee in thy ways: behold, thou art wroth; for we have sinned: in those is continuance, and we shall be saved.

6 But we are all as an *a*unclean *thing*, and all our righteousnesses *are* as *b*filthy rags; and we all do fade as a leaf; and our iniquities, like the wind, have taken us away.

7 And *there is* none that calleth upon thy name, that stirreth up himself to take hold of thee: for thou hast hid thy *a*face from us, and hast consumed us, because of our iniquities.

8 But now, O LORD, thou *art* our *a*father; we *are* the clay, and thou

our potter; and we all *are* the *b*work of thy hand.

9 ¶ Be not wroth very sore, O LORD, neither remember iniquity for ever: behold, see, we beseech thee, we *are* all thy *a*people.

10 Thy holy cities are a wilderness, Zion is a wilderness, Jerusalem a desolation.

11 Our holy and our *a*beautiful house, where our fathers praised thee, is *b*burned up with fire: and all our pleasant things are laid *c*waste.

12 Wilt thou *a*refrain thyself for these *things*, O LORD? wilt thou hold thy peace, and afflict us very sore?

CHAPTER 65

Ancient Israel was rejected for rejecting the Lord—The Lord's people will rejoice and triumph during the Millennium.

I AM *a*sought of *them that* asked not *for me*; I am found of *them that* sought me not: I said, Behold me, behold me, unto a nation *that* was not called by my *b*name.

2 I have spread out my hands all the day unto a *a*rebellious people, which walketh in a way *that was* not good, after their own thoughts;

3 A people that provoketh me to *a*anger continually to my face; that sacrificeth in gardens, and burneth incense upon altars of *b*brick;

4 *a*Which remain among the graves, and lodge in the monuments, which eat swine's flesh, and broth of abominable *things is in* their vessels;

5 Which say, Stand by thyself, come not near to me; for I am *a*holier than thou. These *are* a smoke in my nose, a fire that burneth all the day.

64 1*a* D&C 133:40.
  b Rev. 16:20 (17–21);
    D&C 133:22,
    40 (40–47).
  c TG God, Presence of.
2*a* D&C 34:8.
3*a* Ex. 34:10.
  b Micah 1:4.
4*a* 1 Cor. 2:9;
    D&C 76:10.
  b D&C 133:45.
    TG Reward.
6*a* TG Uncleanness.

  b TG Filthiness.
7*a* Isa. 54:8.
8*a* Deut. 32:6;
    1 Chr. 29:10;
    Isa. 63:16;
    Mosiah 15:2 (1–4);
    Alma 11:39 (38–40).
  b Ps. 138:8;
    Isa. 29:16; 45:9; 60:21.
    TG Creation.
9*a* Ps. 79:13.
11*a* TG Beauty.
  b 2 Kgs. 25:9.

  c Isa. 63:18.
12*a* Isa. 42:14.
65 1*a* Rom. 10:20.
  b Isa. 63:19.
2*a* Rom. 10:21;
    2 Ne. 1:2.
3*a* TG Anger.
  b Ex. 20:25 (24–25).
4*a* HEB Who sit.
5*a* Matt. 9:11 (10–12);
    Luke 18:11;
    Alma 31:16 (13–19).

6 Behold, *it is* written before me: I will not keep silence, but will ªrecompense, even recompense into their bosom,

7 Your iniquities, and the iniquities of your fathers together, saith the Lord, which have burned incense upon the mountains, and ªblasphemed me upon the hills: therefore will I measure their former work into their bosom.

8 ¶ Thus saith the Lord, As the ªnew wine is found in the cluster, and *one* saith, Destroy it not; for a blessing *is* in it: so will I do for my servants' sakes, that I may ᵇnot destroy them all.

9 And I will bring forth a seed out of Jacob, and out of ªJudah an inheritor of my mountains: and mine ᵇelect shall ᶜinherit it, and my servants shall dwell there.

10 And Sharon shall be a fold of flocks, and the valley of ªAchor a place for the herds to lie down in, for my people that have sought me.

11 ¶ But ye *are* they that forsake the Lord, that forget my holy mountain, that prepare a table for that ªtroop, and that furnish the drink offering unto that ᵇnumber.

12 Therefore will I number you to the sword, and ye shall all bow down to the slaughter: because when I ªcalled, ye did not answer; when I spake, ye did not hear; but did evil before mine eyes, and did choose *that* wherein I delighted not.

13 Therefore thus saith the Lord God, Behold, my servants shall eat, but ye shall be hungry: behold, my servants shall drink, but ye shall be thirsty: behold, my servants shall rejoice, but ye shall be ashamed:

14 Behold, my servants shall sing for joy of heart, but ye shall cry for sorrow of heart, and shall ªhowl for vexation of spirit.

15 And ye shall leave your name for a ªcurse unto my chosen: for the Lord God shall slay thee, and call his servants by another ᵇname:

16 That he who ªblesseth himself in the earth shall bless himself in the God of truth; and he that sweareth in the earth shall ᵇswear by the God of truth; because the former troubles are forgotten, and because they are hid from mine eyes.

17 ¶ For, behold, I ªcreate new ᵇheavens and a ᶜnew ᵈearth: and the ᵉformer shall not be remembered, nor come into mind.

18 But be ye glad and rejoice for ever *in that* which I create: for, behold, I create Jerusalem a ªrejoicing, and her people a joy.

19 And I will ªrejoice in Jerusalem, and joy in my people: and the voice of weeping shall be no more heard in her, nor the voice of crying.

20 There shall be no more thence an infant of days, nor an ªold man that hath not filled his days: for the ᵇchild shall die an hundred years old; but the sinner *being* an hundred years old shall be accursed.

21 And they shall build houses, and inhabit *them*; and they shall plant vineyards, and ªeat the fruit of them.

22 They shall not build, and another inhabit; they shall not plant, and another eat: for as the days of a ªtree *are* the days of my people, and mine elect shall long enjoy the work of their hands.

23 They shall not ªlabour in vain,

6a Jer. 16:18;
    Mosiah 12:1; D&C 1:10.
7a Ezek. 20:27.
8a OR grape juice.
  b Gen. 18:32 (23–32).
9a Ps. 69:35 (35–36).
  b TG Election.
  c Deut. 18:9.
10a Hosea 2:15.
11a HEB Gad (an idol of
    fortune).
  b HEB Meni (an idol

of fate).
12a Isa. 66:4.
14a Matt. 8:12.
15a Deut. 28:37.
  b Isa. 62:2; Rev. 2:17;
    D&C 130:11 (10–11).
16a IE invokes blessings in
    his own behalf.
  b IE make covenants
    through the power of
    God.
17a TG Jesus Christ, Creator.

b TG Heaven.
  c TG Earth, Renewal of;
    Millennium.
  d TG Earth, Destiny of.
  e TG World, End of.
18a Isa. 35:10.
19a Isa. 62:5.
20a TG Old Age.
  b D&C 101:30.
21a D&C 101:101.
22a D&C 101:30.
23a TG Labor.

nor bring forth for trouble; for they *are* the *b*seed of the blessed of the LORD, and their *c*offspring with them.

24 And it shall come to pass, that before they call, I will *a*answer; and while they are yet speaking, I will hear.

25 The *a*wolf and the lamb shall *b*feed together, and the lion shall eat straw like the bullock: and dust *shall be* the serpent's meat. They shall not *c*hurt nor destroy in all my holy mountain, saith the LORD.

CHAPTER 66

At the Second Coming, Israel, as a nation, will be born in a day; the wicked will be destroyed; and the Gentiles will hear the gospel.

THUS saith the LORD, The heaven *is* my *a*throne, and the earth *is* my footstool: where *is* the house that ye build unto me? and where *is* the place of my rest?

2 For all those *things* hath mine hand made, and all those *things* have been, saith the LORD: but to this *man* will I look, *even* to *him that is* poor and of a *a*contrite spirit, and trembleth at my word.

3 *a*He that killeth an ox *is as if* he slew a man; he that sacrificeth a lamb, *as if* he cut off a dog's neck; he that offereth an oblation, *as if he offered* swine's blood; he that burneth incense, *as if* he blessed an idol. Yea, they have chosen their own ways, and their soul delighteth in their abominations.

4 *a*I also will choose their delusions, and will bring their fears upon them; because when I *b*called, none did answer; when I spake, they did not hear: but they did evil before mine eyes, and chose *that* in which I delighted not.

5 ¶ Hear the word of the LORD, ye that tremble at his word; Your brethren that hated you, that *a*cast you out for my name's sake, said, Let the LORD be *b*glorified: but he shall appear to your joy, and they shall be ashamed.

6 A voice of noise from the city, a voice from the temple, a voice of the LORD that rendereth recompence to his enemies.

7 *a*Before she *b*travailed, she brought forth; before her pain came, she was delivered of a man *c*child.

8 Who hath heard such a thing? who hath seen such things? Shall the earth be made to bring forth in one day? *or* shall a nation be born at once? for as soon as Zion travailed, she brought forth her children.

9 Shall I bring to the birth, and not cause to bring forth? saith the LORD: shall I cause to bring forth, and shut *the* womb? saith thy God.

10 Rejoice ye with Jerusalem, and be glad with her, all ye that love her: rejoice for joy with her, all ye that mourn for her:

11 That ye may suck, and be satisfied with the breasts of her consolations; that ye may milk out, and be delighted with the abundance of her glory.

12 For thus saith the LORD, Behold, I will extend peace to her *a*like a river, and the glory of the *b*Gentiles like a flowing stream: then shall ye suck, ye shall be borne upon *her* sides, and be dandled upon *her* knees.

13 As one whom his *a*mother comforteth, so will I *b*comfort you; and ye shall be *c*comforted in Jerusalem.

23*b* Isa. 61:9.
   c TG Family, Eternal.
24*a* Alma 9:26.
25*a* TG Peace.
   b 2 Ne. 30:12 (12–15).
   c Isa. 60:18 (17–22).
66 1*a* Matt. 5:34.
   TG Kingdom of God, in Heaven.
  2*a* TG Contrite Heart.
  3*a* IE The same person

both sacrifices and yet sins;
   James 3:9–12.
4*a* IE The Lord will respond to their evils and punish them.
   b Isa. 65:12.
5*a* Luke 6:22.
   b 2 Thes. 1:10 (9–10).
7*a* IE Zion will suddenly be repopulated (vv. 7–9).

   b Micah 4:10.
   c Rev. 12:2 (1–5); JST Rev. 12:1–8 (Appendix).
12*a* IE abundantly.
   b D&C 35:7.
13*a* TG Marriage, Motherhood.
   b TG Comfort.
   c TG Israel, Restoration of.

14 And when ye see *this*, your heart shall rejoice, and your bones shall flourish like an herb: and the *a*hand of the Lord shall be known toward his servants, and *his* *b*indignation toward his enemies.

15 For, behold, the Lord will come with *a*fire, and with his *b*chariots like a whirlwind, to render his anger with fury, and his rebuke with flames of fire.

16 For by fire and by his *a*sword will *b*the Lord *c*plead with all flesh: and the *d*slain of the Lord shall be many.

17 They that sanctify themselves, and purify themselves in the gardens behind one *tree* in the midst, eating swine's flesh, and the *a*abomination, and the *b*mouse, shall be consumed together, saith the Lord.

18 For I *a*know their *b*works and their thoughts: it shall come, that I will gather *c*all nations and tongues; and they shall come, and see my glory.

19 And I will set a *a*sign among them, and I will send those that escape of them unto the nations, *to* Tarshish, Pul, and *b*Lud, that draw the bow, *to* Tubal, and Javan, *to* the isles afar off, that have not heard my fame, neither have seen my glory; and they shall *c*declare my glory among the *d*Gentiles.

20 And they shall bring all your brethren *for* an *a*offering unto the Lord out of all nations upon horses, and in chariots, and in litters, and upon mules, and upon swift beasts, to my holy mountain Jerusalem, saith the Lord, as the children of Israel bring an offering in a clean vessel into the house of the Lord.

21 And I will also take of them for *a*priests *and* for Levites, saith the Lord.

22 For as the *a*new heavens and the new earth, which I will make, shall remain before me, saith the Lord, so shall your *b*seed and your name remain.

23 And it shall come to pass, *that* from one new moon to another, and from one sabbath to another, shall all flesh come to *a*worship before me, saith the Lord.

24 And they shall go forth, and look upon the carcases of the men that have transgressed against me: for their *a*worm shall not die, neither shall their *b*fire be quenched; and they shall be an abhorring unto all flesh.

14a TG Protection, Divine.
 b TG God, Indignation of.
15a D&C 29:12 (12, 21, 28); 130:7; 133:41.
 b Abr. 2:7.
16a Deut. 32:41; Isa. 27:1. TG War.
 b HEB the Lord will judge all flesh.
 c Jer. 25:31; Ezek. 38:22;

Joel 3:2.
 d Jer. 25:33.
17a Several examples of forbidden practices are listed here.
 b Lev. 11:29.
18a TG God, Omniscience of.
 b Rev. 3:15 (15–16).
 c Ps. 86:9.
19a TG Ensign.
 b Jer. 46:9;

Ezek. 27:10; 30:5.
 c TG Israel, Mission of.
 d TG Gentiles.
20a Isa. 60:7.
21a Isa. 61:6.
22a TG Earth, Renewal of.
 b TG Israel, Blessings of.
23a Zech. 14:16.
24a Mark 9:48 (43–48); D&C 76:44.
 b TG Hell.

THE BOOK OF THE PROPHET

JEREMIAH

CHAPTER 1

Jeremiah was foreordained to be a prophet unto the nations—He is called as a mortal to declare the word of the Lord.

THE words of Jeremiah the son of Hilkiah, of the priests that *were* in ªAnathoth in the land of Benjamin:

2 To whom the word of the LORD came in the days of Josiah the son of Amon king of Judah, in the thirteenth ªyear of his reign.

3 It came also in the days of Jehoiakim the son of Josiah king of Judah, unto the end of the eleventh year of Zedekiah the son of Josiah king of Judah, unto the ªcarrying away of Jerusalem captive in the fifth month.

4 Then the word of the LORD came unto me, saying,

5 Before I ªformed thee in the belly I ᵇknew thee; and before thou camest forth out of the womb I ᶜsanctified thee, *and* I ᵈordained thee a prophet unto the ᵉnations.

6 Then said I, Ah, Lord GOD! behold, I cannot ªspeak: for I *am* a ᵇchild.

7 ¶ But the LORD said unto me, Say not, I *am* a child: for thou shalt go to all that I shall ªsend thee, and whatsoever I ᵇcommand thee thou shalt ᶜspeak.

8 Be not ªafraid of their faces: for I *am* with thee to deliver thee, saith the LORD.

9 Then the LORD put forth his hand, and touched my ªmouth. And the LORD said unto me, Behold, I have put my ᵇwords in thy ᶜmouth.

10 See, I have this day ªset thee over the nations and over the kingdoms, to root out, and to ᵇpull down, and to destroy, and to ᶜthrow down, to ᵈbuild, and to plant.

11 ¶ Moreover the word of the LORD came unto me, saying, Jeremiah, what ªseest thou? And I said, I see a rod of an almond tree.

12 Then said the LORD unto me, Thou hast well seen: for I will hasten my word to perform it.

13 And the word of the LORD came unto me the second time, saying, What seest thou? And I said, I see a ªseething ᵇpot; and the face thereof *is* toward the north.

14 Then the LORD said unto me, Out of the ªnorth an evil shall break forth upon all the inhabitants of the land.

15 For, lo, I will call all the families of the kingdoms of the north, saith the LORD; and they shall come, and

---

1 1*a* Jer. 29:27.
  2*a* Jer. 25:3; 36:2.
  3*a* Jer. 52:15.
  5*a* Isa. 44:2 (2, 24); 49:5.
    TG Man, Antemortal Existence of.
   b TG God, Foreknowledge of.
   c TG Birth Control; Sanctification.
   d TG Called of God; Foreordination; Priesthood, Keys of; Priesthood, Ordination.
   e Jer. 25:15 (15–29); 46:1.

6*a* Ex. 4:10;
   D&C 60:2 (2–3);
   Moses 6:31 (31–34).
 b HEB youth (also v. 7).
7*a* TG Priesthood, Magnifying Callings within.
 b Matt. 28:20;
   1 Ne. 3:7.
 c TG Prophets, Mission of; Teaching with the Spirit.
8*a* Isa. 51:12 (12–13);
   Ezek. 2:6;
   Matt. 10:28;

   D&C 3:1 (1–5).
9*a* Isa. 6:7.
 b TG Prophecy.
 c Ex. 4:12 (12–16).
10*a* TG Delegation of Responsibility.
 b Jer. 18:7.
 c Jer. 45:4.
 d TG Prophets, Mission of.
11*a* TG Vision.
13*a* OR boiling.
 b Ezek. 24:3 (3–5).
14*a* Jer. 4:6; 6:1; 10:22;
   Ezek. 26:7.

they shall set every one his throne at the entering of the ^{a}gates of Jerusalem, and against all the walls thereof round about, and against all the cities of Judah.

16 And I will utter my judgments against them touching all their wickedness, who have ^{a}forsaken me, and have burned incense unto other ^{b}gods, and worshipped the works of their own hands.

17 ¶ Thou therefore gird up thy loins, and arise, and speak unto them all that I command thee: be not dismayed at their faces, lest I confound thee before them.

18 For, behold, I have made thee this day a defenced city, and an iron pillar, and brasen walls against the whole land, against the kings of Judah, against the ^{a}princes thereof, against the priests thereof, and against the people of the land.

19 And they shall ^{a}fight against thee; but they shall not ^{b}prevail against thee; for I *am* with thee, saith the LORD, to deliver thee.

CHAPTER 2

The people of Judah forsook the Lord, the fountain of living waters—They worshipped idols and rejected the prophets.

MOREOVER the word of the LORD came to me, saying,

2 Go and cry in the ears of Jerusalem, saying, Thus saith the LORD; I remember thee, the kindness of thy youth, the love of thine espousals, ^{a}when thou wentest after me in the wilderness, in a land *that was* not sown.

3 Israel *was* ^{a}holiness unto the LORD, *and* the firstfruits of his increase: all that devour him shall offend; evil shall come upon them, saith the LORD.

4 Hear ye the word of the LORD, O house of Jacob, and all the families of the house of Israel:

5 ¶ Thus saith the LORD, What iniquity have your fathers found in me, that they are gone far from me, and have walked after vanity, and are become vain?

6 Neither said they, Where *is* the LORD that brought us up out of the land of Egypt, that ^{a}led us through the wilderness, through a land of deserts and of pits, through a land of drought, and of the shadow of death, through a land that no man passed through, and where no man dwelt?

7 And I brought you into a plentiful country, to eat the fruit thereof and the goodness thereof; but when ye entered, ye ^{a}defiled my ^{b}land, and made mine heritage an abomination.

8 The priests said not, Where *is* the LORD? and they that handle the law knew me not: the ^{a}pastors also transgressed against me, and the ^{b}prophets prophesied by Baal, and walked after *things that* do not profit.

9 ¶ Wherefore I will yet plead with you, saith the LORD, and with your children's children will I plead.

10 For pass ^{a}over the isles of Chittim, and see; and send unto Kedar, and consider diligently, and see if there be such a thing.

11 Hath a nation changed *their* ^{a}gods, which *are* yet no gods? but my people have changed their glory for *that which* doth not profit.

12 Be astonished, O ye heavens, at this, and be horribly afraid, be ye very desolate, saith the LORD.

13 For my people have committed two ^{a}evils; they have forsaken me the fountain of ^{b}living waters, *and* hewed them out cisterns, broken cisterns, that can hold no water.

14 ¶ *Is* Israel a ^{a}servant? *is* he a homeborn *slave*? why is he spoiled?

15a Jer. 39:3.
16a Jer. 19:4.
  b TG Idolatry.
18a OR rulers, or officers.
19a TG Prophets, Rejection of.
  b 1 Ne. 22:16;
    D&C 121:11 (7–15).

2 2a 1 Ne. 17:26 (26–29).
  3a Ex. 28:36;
    Isa. 23:18.
  6a Ps. 107:4.
  7a Jer. 16:18.
    TG Pollution.
    b Hosea 9:3.
  8a TG Shepherd.

  b TG False Prophets.
10a OR over to.
11a TG Idolatry.
13a TG Apostasy of Israel.
  b TG Living Water.
14a Ex. 4:22 (22–23).

15 The young lions roared upon him, *and* yelled, and they made his land waste: his cities are burned without inhabitant.

16 Also the children of Noph and *a*Tahapanes have broken the crown of thy head.

17 Hast thou not procured this unto thyself, in that thou hast *a*forsaken the LORD thy God, when he led thee by the way?

18 And now what hast thou to do in the way of *a*Egypt, to drink the waters of Sihor? or what hast thou to do in the way of Assyria, to drink the waters of *b*the river?

19 Thine own wickedness shall correct thee, and thy backslidings shall *a*reprove thee: know therefore and see that *it is* an evil *thing* and bitter, that thou hast forsaken the LORD thy God, and that my fear *is* not in thee, saith the Lord GOD of hosts.

20 ¶ For of old time I have broken thy yoke, *and* burst thy bands; and thou saidst, I will not transgress; when upon every high hill and under every green tree thou wanderest, playing the *a*harlot.

21 Yet I had planted thee a noble *a*vine, wholly a right seed: how then art thou turned into the degenerate plant of a strange vine unto me?

22 For though thou *a*wash thee with *b*nitre, and take thee much soap, *yet* thine iniquity is marked before me, saith the Lord GOD.

23 How canst thou say, I am not polluted, I have not gone after Baalim? see thy way in the valley, know what thou hast done: *thou art* a swift dromedary traversing her ways;

24 A wild ass used to the wilderness, *that* snuffeth up the wind at her pleasure; in her occasion who can turn her away? all they that seek her will not weary themselves; in her month they *a*shall find her.

25 Withhold thy foot from being unshod, and thy throat from thirst: but thou saidst, There is no *a*hope: no; for I have loved strangers, and after them will I go.

26 As the thief is *a*ashamed when he is found, so is the house of Israel ashamed; they, their kings, their princes, and their priests, and their prophets,

27 Saying to *a*a stock, Thou *art* my father; and to a stone, Thou hast brought me forth: for they have turned *their* *b*back unto me, and not *their* face: but in the *c*time of their trouble they will say, Arise, and save us.

28 But where *are* thy *a*gods that thou hast made thee? let them arise, if they can save thee in the time of thy trouble: for *according to* the number of thy cities are thy gods, O Judah.

29 Wherefore will ye *a*plead with me? ye all have transgressed against me, saith the LORD.

30 In vain have I smitten your children; they received no *a*correction: your own sword hath devoured your prophets, like a destroying lion.

31 ¶ O generation, see ye the word of the LORD. Have I been a wilderness unto Israel? a land of darkness? wherefore say my people, We are lords; we will come no more unto thee?

32 Can a maid forget her ornaments, *or* a bride her attire? yet my people have *a*forgotten me days without number.

33 Why trimmest thou thy way to

16*a* IE Tahapanhes, in
   Egypt, in the land of
   Goshen.
   Jer. 43:7 (7–8); 44:1.
17*a* TG Apostasy of Israel.
18*a* Isa. 30:2 (1–2).
   b IE the Euphrates.
19*a* TG Reproof.
20*a* TG Idolatry.
21*a* TG Vineyard of the

Lord.
22*a* TG Wash.
   b IE alkali; carbonate
   of soda.
24*a* JST Jer. 2:24 . . . shall
   not find her.
25*a* Jer. 18:12.
26*a* TG Shame.
27*a* OR wood; i.e., an idol.
   Jer. 3:9.

b Jer. 18:17; 32:33;
   Ezek. 8:16.
c Mosiah 11:24 (22–25);
   D&C 101:7 (7–9).
28*a* Judg. 10:14 (13–14);
   2 Kgs. 3:13;
   Prov. 1:28 (27–28).
29*a* HEB quarrel, contend.
30*a* TG Chastening.
32*a* Jer. 18:15.

seek love? therefore hast thou also taught the wicked ^aones thy ways.

34 Also in thy skirts is found the ^ablood of the souls of the poor innocents: I have not found it by secret search, but upon all ^bthese.

35 Yet thou sayest, Because I am ^ainnocent, surely his anger shall turn from me. Behold, I will plead with thee, because thou sayest, I have not sinned.

36 Why gaddest thou about so much to change thy way? thou also shalt be ^aashamed of Egypt, as thou wast ashamed of Assyria.

37 Yea, thou shalt go forth from him, and thine hands upon thine head: for the LORD hath rejected thy confidences, and thou shalt not prosper in them.

CHAPTER 3

Israel and Judah defiled and polluted the land through wickedness—In the last days, the Lord will gather the people of Israel, one from a city and two from a family, and bring them to Zion.

THEY say, If a man ^aput away his wife, and she go from him, and become another man's, shall he return unto her again? shall not that land be greatly ^bpolluted? but thou hast played the harlot with many lovers; yet return again to me, saith the LORD.

2 Lift up thine eyes unto the high places, and see where thou hast not been lien with. In the ways hast thou sat for them, as the Arabian in the wilderness; and thou hast polluted the land with thy ^awhoredoms and with thy wickedness.

3 Therefore the ^ashowers have been withholden, and there hath been no ^blatter ^crain; and thou hadst a

whore's forehead, thou refusedst to be ashamed.

4 Wilt thou not from this time cry unto me, My father, thou *art* the guide of my youth?

5 Will he reserve *his* ^aanger for ever? will he keep *it* to the end? Behold, thou hast spoken and done evil things as thou couldest.

6 ¶ The LORD said also unto me in the days of Josiah the king, Hast thou seen *that* which backsliding Israel hath done? she is gone up upon every high mountain and under every green tree, and there hath played the harlot.

7 And I said after she had done all these *things,* Turn thou unto me. But she returned not. And her treacherous ^asister Judah saw *it.*

8 And I saw, when for all the causes whereby backsliding Israel committed ^aadultery I had put her away, and given her a bill of ^bdivorce; yet her treacherous sister Judah feared not, but went and played the harlot also.

9 And it came to pass through the lightness of her whoredom, that she defiled the land, and ^acommitted adultery with ^bstones and with ^cstocks.

10 And yet for all this her treacherous sister Judah hath not turned unto me with her whole heart, but ^afeignedly, saith the LORD.

11 And the LORD said unto me, The backsliding Israel hath ^ajustified herself more than treacherous Judah.

12 ¶ Go and ^aproclaim these words toward the ^bnorth, and say, ^cReturn, thou backsliding Israel, saith the LORD; *and* I will not cause mine anger to fall upon you: for I *am* merciful, saith the LORD, *and* I will not keep *anger* for ever.

33*a* HEB women.
34*a* Ps. 106:38;
  Jer. 19:4.
  b IE their clothing.
35*a* Mosiah 12:14 (9–15);
  Alma 21:6.
36*a* Isa. 30:5 (3, 5).
3 1*a* TG Divorce.
  b TG Pollution.
2*a* Deut. 31:16.

3*a* Jer. 14:22; Amos 4:7.
  b OR spring rain.
  c Lev. 26:4 (3–4);
    Jer. 14:4.
5*a* Micah 7:18.
7*a* Ezek. 16:46 (45–46, 61);
    23:2.
8*a* TG Adulterer.
  b TG Divorce.
9*a* Lev. 17:7; 20:5;

    Ezek. 23:37.
  b TG Idolatry.
  c Jer. 2:27 (20–30).
10*a* JS—H 1:19.
11*a* Ezek. 16:51;
    D&C 88:39 (38–39).
12*a* D&C 30:9.
  b TG Israel, Ten Lost
    Tribes of.
  c TG Israel, Restoration of.

13 Only acknowledge thine iniquity, that thou hast transgressed against the LORD thy God, and hast scattered thy ways to the strangers under every green tree, and ye have not *a*obeyed my voice, saith the LORD.

14 Turn, O backsliding children, saith the LORD; for I am *a*married unto you: and I will take you one of a city, and two of a family, and I will *b*bring you to *c*Zion:

15 And I will give you *a*pastors according to mine heart, which shall feed you with *b*knowledge and understanding.

16 And it shall come to pass, when ye be multiplied and increased in the land, in those days, saith the LORD, they shall say no more, The *a*ark of the covenant of the LORD: neither shall it come to mind: neither shall they remember it; neither shall they visit *it*; neither shall *that* be done any more.

17 At that time they shall call *a*Jerusalem the throne of the LORD; and all the *b*nations shall be *c*gathered unto it, to the name of the LORD, to Jerusalem: neither shall they walk any more after the *d*imagination of their evil heart.

18 In those days the *a*house of Judah shall walk with the house of Israel, and they shall come together out of the *b*land of the *c*north to the land that I have given for an inheritance unto your fathers.

19 But I said, How shall I put thee among the children, and give thee a pleasant land, a goodly heritage of the hosts of nations? and I said, Thou shalt call me, My father; and shalt not turn away from me.

20 ¶ Surely *as* a wife treacherously *a*departeth from her husband, so have ye dealt treacherously with me, O house of Israel, saith the LORD.

21 A voice was heard upon the high places, weeping *and* supplications of the children of Israel: for they have perverted their way, *and* they have forgotten the LORD their God.

22 Return, ye backsliding children, *and* I will *a*heal your backslidings. Behold, we come unto thee; for thou *art* the LORD our God.

23 Truly in vain *is salvation hoped for* from the hills, *and from* the multitude of mountains: truly in the LORD our God *is* the salvation of Israel.

24 For shame hath devoured the labour of our fathers from our youth; their flocks and their herds, their sons and their daughters.

25 We lie down in our *a*shame, and our confusion covereth us: for we have *b*sinned against the LORD our God, we and our fathers, from our youth even unto this day, and have not obeyed the voice of the LORD our God.

CHAPTER 4

Israel and Judah are called to repentance—Jeremiah laments for the miseries of Judah.

IF thou wilt return, O Israel, saith the LORD, return unto me: and if thou wilt put away thine abominations out of my sight, then shalt thou not remove.

2 And thou shalt swear, The *a*LORD liveth, in truth, in judgment, and in righteousness; and the nations shall bless themselves in him, and in him shall they glory.

3 ¶ For thus saith the LORD to the men of Judah and Jerusalem, *a*Break up your fallow ground, and sow not among *b*thorns.

13*a* TG Disobedience.
14*a* TG Abrahamic
  Covenant.
  b TG Missionary Work.
  c TG Zion.
15*a* HEB shepherds.
  TG Bishop.
  b TG Knowledge.
16*a* TG Ark of the Covenant.

17*a* Joel 3:21 (18–21);
  Zech. 2:10 (10–12);
  Rev. 22:3 (3–4).
  b TG Nations.
  c TG Israel, Gathering of.
  d OR stubbornness.
18*a* 2 Ne. 29:14 (8, 14).
  b Jer. 16:15.
  c TG Israel, Ten Lost

  Tribes of.
20*a* TG Divorce.
22*a* 3 Ne. 9:13; 18:32.
25*a* TG Shame.
  b TG Apostasy of Israel.
4 2*a* Jer. 16:14.
  3*a* Hosea 10:12.
  b Matt. 13:7.

4 ªCircumcise yourselves to the LORD, and take away the foreskins of your heart, ye men of Judah and inhabitants of Jerusalem: lest my fury come forth like fire, and burn that none can quench it, because of the evil of your doings.

5 Declare ye in Judah, and publish in Jerusalem; and say, Blow ye the trumpet in the land: cry, gather together, and say, Assemble yourselves, and let us go into the defenced cities.

6 Set up the ªstandard toward ᵇZion: retire, stay not: for I will bring evil from the ᶜnorth, and a great destruction.

7 The ªlion is come up from his thicket, and the destroyer of the Gentiles is on his way; he is gone forth from his place to make thy ᵇland desolate; and thy cities shall be laid waste, without an inhabitant.

8 For this ªgird you with sackcloth, lament and howl: for the fierce ᵇanger of the LORD is not turned back from us.

9 And it shall come to pass at that day, saith the LORD, that the heart of the king shall perish, and the heart of the princes; and the priests shall be astonished, and the prophets shall wonder.

10 Then said I, Ah, Lord GOD! surely thou hast greatly deceived this people and Jerusalem, saying, Ye shall have peace; whereas the sword reacheth unto the soul.

11 At that time shall it be said to this people and to Jerusalem, A dry ªwind of the high places in the wilderness toward the daughter of my people, not to fan, nor to cleanse,

12 Even a full wind from those places shall come unto me: now also will I give sentence against them.

13 Behold, he shall come up as ªclouds, and his chariots shall be as a whirlwind: his horses are ᵇswifter than eagles. Woe unto us! for we are spoiled.

14 O Jerusalem, ªwash thine heart from wickedness, that thou mayest be saved. How long shall thy vain thoughts lodge within thee?

15 For a voice declareth from Dan, and publisheth affliction from mount Ephraim.

16 Make ye mention to the nations; behold, publish against Jerusalem, that watchers come from a far country, and give out their voice against the cities of Judah.

17 As keepers of a field, are they against her round about; because she hath been rebellious against me, saith the LORD.

18 Thy way and thy doings have procured these things unto thee; this is thy wickedness, because it is bitter, because it reacheth unto thine heart.

19 ¶ My ªbowels, my bowels! I am ᵇpained at my very heart; my heart maketh a noise in me; I cannot hold my peace, because thou hast heard, O my soul, the sound of the trumpet, the alarm of war.

20 ªDestruction upon destruction is cried; for the whole land is spoiled: suddenly are my ᵇtents spoiled, and my curtains in a moment.

21 How long shall I see the standard, and hear the sound of the trumpet?

22 For my people is ªfoolish, they have not ᵇknown me; they are sottish children, and they have none understanding: they are wise to do ᶜevil, but to do good they have no knowledge.

23 I beheld the earth, and, lo, it was ªwithout form, and ᵇvoid; and the heavens, and they had no light.

4a TG Circumcision.
6a TG Ensign.
 b TG Zion.
 c Jer. 1:14 (13–14); 6:1; 10:22.
7a Jer. 49:19.
 b TG Israel, Land of.
8a Joel 1:13 (1–13).

 b Isa. 9:12 (12, 17, 21).
11a Jer. 51:1 (1–2).
13a Ezek. 38:9.
 b Lam. 4:19.
14a TG Cleanliness; Purification; Purity.
19a Lam. 1:20.

 b TG Pain.
20a Ezek. 7:26.
 b Jer. 10:20.
22a TG Foolishness.
 b Mosiah 5:13.
 c Hel. 12:4 (1–7).
23a OR empty and desolate.
 b Moses 2:2 (2–26).

24 I beheld the mountains, and, lo, they trembled, and all the hills moved lightly.

25 I beheld, and, lo, *there was* no man, and all the birds of the heavens were fled.

26 I beheld, and, lo, the fruitful place *was* a wilderness, and all the cities thereof were broken down at the presence of the LORD, *and* by his fierce anger.

27 For thus hath the LORD said, The whole land shall be desolate; yet will I not make a full ªend.

28 For this shall the earth mourn, and the heavens above be black: because I have spoken *it*, I have purposed *it*, and will not ªrepent, neither will I turn back from it.

29 The whole city shall flee for the noise of the horsemen and bowmen; they shall go into thickets, and climb up upon the rocks: every city *shall be* ªforsaken, and not a man dwell therein.

30 And *when* thou *art* spoiled, what wilt thou do? Though thou clothest thyself with crimson, though thou deckest thee with ªornaments of gold, though thou ᵇrentest thy face with painting, in vain shalt thou make thyself fair; *thy* ᶜlovers will despise thee, they will seek thy life.

31 For I have heard a voice as of a woman in travail, *and* the anguish as of her that bringeth forth her first child, the voice of the daughter of ªZion, *that* bewaileth herself, *that* spreadeth her hands, *saying,* Woe is me now! for my soul is wearied because of murderers.

CHAPTER 5

Judgments will be poured out upon the people of Judah because of their sins— Their iniquities cause blessings to be withheld from them.

RUN ye to and fro through the streets of Jerusalem, and see now, and know, and seek in the broad places thereof, if ye can find a man, if there be *any* that ªexecuteth judgment, that seeketh the truth; and I will pardon it.

2 And though they say, The LORD liveth; surely they ªswear falsely.

3 O LORD, *are* not thine eyes upon the truth? thou hast stricken them, but they have not grieved; thou hast consumed them, *but* they have refused to receive correction: they have made their faces harder than a rock; they have refused to ªreturn.

4 Therefore I said, Surely these *are* poor; they are foolish: for they ªknow not the way of the LORD, *nor* the judgment of their God.

5 I will get me unto the great men, and will speak unto them; for they have known the way of the LORD, *and* the judgment of their God: but these have altogether broken the ªyoke, *and* burst the bonds.

6 Wherefore a lion out of the forest shall slay them, *and* a ªwolf of the ᵇevenings shall spoil them, a leopard shall watch over their cities: every one that goeth out thence shall be torn in pieces: because their ᶜtransgressions are many, *and* their backslidings are increased.

7 ¶ How shall I pardon thee for this? thy children have forsaken me, and sworn by *them that are* no gods: when I had fed them to the ªfull, they then committed ᵇadultery, and assembled themselves by troops in the harlots' houses.

8 They were *as* ªfed horses in the morning: every one neighed after his neighbour's wife.

9 Shall I not ªvisit for these *things?* saith the LORD: and shall not my soul be ᵇavenged on such a nation as this?

27a Jer. 5:10.
28a HEB relent.
29a TG Israel, Scattering of.
30a Hosea 2:13.
   b OR enlargest thine eyes.
   c HEB sensuous lovers.
31a Lam. 1:17.
5 1a OR does justly.

Gen. 18:26;
   Ezek. 22:30.
2a TG Swearing.
3a OR repent.
   Hag. 2:17.
4a TG Ignorance.
5a IE of the law and the
   covenants.

6a Zeph. 3:3.
   b OR plains, wilderness.
   c TG Wickedness.
7a Deut. 32:15.
   b TG Adulterer.
8a HEB lusty stallions.
9a OR punish (also v. 29).
   b Jer. 9:9; 44:22.

10 ¶ Go ye up upon her walls, and *a*destroy; but make not a full *b*end: take away her battlements; for they *are* not the LORD's.

11 For the house of Israel and the house of Judah have dealt very treacherously against me, saith the LORD.

12 They have belied the LORD, and said, *It is* not he; neither shall evil come upon us; neither shall we see *a*sword nor famine:

13 And the prophets shall become wind, and the word *is* not in them: thus shall it be done unto them.

14 Wherefore thus saith the LORD God of hosts, Because ye speak this word, behold, I will make my words in thy *a*mouth fire, and this people wood, and it shall devour them.

15 Lo, I will bring a nation upon you from far, O house of Israel, saith the LORD: it *is* a mighty nation, it *is* an ancient nation, a nation whose *a*language thou knowest not, neither understandest what they say.

16 Their quiver *is* as an open sepulchre, they *are* all mighty men.

17 And they shall *a*eat up thine harvest, and thy bread, *which* thy sons and thy daughters should eat: they shall eat up thy flocks and thine herds: they shall eat up thy vines and thy fig trees: they shall impoverish thy fenced cities, wherein thou trustedst, with the sword.

18 Nevertheless in those days, saith the LORD, I will not make a full end with you.

19 ¶ And it shall come to pass, when ye shall say, Wherefore doeth the LORD our God all these *things* unto us? then shalt thou answer them, Like as ye have *a*forsaken me, and served strange *b*gods in your land, so shall ye *c*serve *d*strangers in a land *that is* not yours.

20 Declare this in the house of Jacob, and publish it in Judah, saying,

21 Hear now this, O *a*foolish people, and without understanding; which have eyes, and *b*see not; which have ears, and *c*hear not:

22 Fear ye not me? saith the LORD: will ye not tremble at my presence, which have placed the sand *for* the bound of the sea by a perpetual decree, that it cannot pass it: and though the waves thereof toss themselves, yet can they not prevail; though they roar, yet can they not pass over it?

23 But this people hath a revolting and a *a*rebellious heart; they are revolted and gone.

24 Neither say they in their heart, Let us now fear the LORD our God, that giveth rain, both *a*the former and the latter, in his season: he reserveth unto us the appointed weeks of the harvest.

25 ¶ Your iniquities have turned away these *things*, and your sins have withholden good *things* from you.

26 For among my people are found *a*wicked *men:* they lay wait, as he that setteth snares; they set a trap, they *b*catch men.

27 As a cage is full of birds, so *are* their houses full of deceit: therefore they are become *a*great, and waxen rich.

28 They are waxen fat, they shine: yea, they overpass the deeds of the wicked: they *a*judge not the cause, the cause of the fatherless, yet they prosper; and the right of the needy do they not judge.

29 Shall I not visit for these *things*? saith the LORD: shall not my soul be avenged on such a nation as this?

30 ¶ A wonderful and *a*horrible thing is committed in the land;

31 The *a*prophets prophesy *b*falsely, and the *c*priests bear rule by their

---

10*a* Jer. 39:8 (8–10).
  b Jer. 4:27.
12*a* Jer. 14:13.
14*a* TG Prophets, Mission of.
15*a* Isa. 33:19.
17*a* Deut. 28:51 (31, 33, 51).
19*a* TG Apostasy of Israel.
  b TG Idolatry.

  c TG Israel, Scattering of.
  d TG Stranger.
21*a* TG Foolishness.
  b TG Watch.
  c Matt. 13:14.
23*a* Ps. 78:8.
24*a* IE winter and spring.
26*a* TG Wickedness.

  b D&C 10:13.
27*a* TG Worldliness.
28*a* TG Judgment.
30*a* Hosea 6:10.
31*a* TG False Prophets.
  b Jer. 7:8;
    Lam. 4:13.
  c TG Priestcraft.

means; and my people *d*love *to have it* so: and what will ye do in the end thereof?

CHAPTER 6

Jerusalem will be destroyed because of her iniquity—She will be overrun by a great and cruel nation.

O YE children of Benjamin, gather yourselves to flee out of the midst of Jerusalem, and blow the trumpet in Tekoa, and set up a sign of fire in Beth-haccerem: for evil appeareth out of the *a*north, and great destruction.

2 I have likened the daughter of Zion to a comely and delicate *woman*.

3 The shepherds with their flocks shall come unto her; they shall pitch *their* tents against her round about; they shall feed every one in his place.

4 Prepare ye war against her; arise, and let us go up at noon. Woe unto us! for the day goeth away, for the shadows of the evening are stretched out.

5 Arise, and let us go by night, and let us destroy her palaces.

6 ¶ For thus hath the LORD of hosts said, Hew ye down trees, and cast a *a*mount against Jerusalem: this *is* the city to be *b*visited; she *is* wholly oppression in the midst of her.

7 As a fountain casteth out her waters, so she casteth out her *a*wickedness: *b*violence and spoil is heard in her; before me continually *is* grief and wounds.

8 Be thou instructed, O Jerusalem, lest my soul depart from thee; lest I make thee desolate, a land not inhabited.

9 ¶ Thus saith the LORD of hosts, They shall *a*throughly glean the remnant of Israel as a vine: turn back thine hand as a grapegatherer *b*into the baskets.

10 To whom shall I speak, and give *a*warning, that they may hear? behold, their ear *is* *b*uncircumcised, and they cannot hearken: behold, the word of the LORD is unto them a reproach; they have no delight in it.

11 Therefore I am full of the fury of the LORD; I am weary with holding in: I will pour it out upon the children abroad, and upon the assembly of young men together: for even the husband with the wife shall be taken, the aged with *him that is* full of days.

12 And their houses shall be turned unto others, *with their* fields and wives together: for I will stretch out my hand upon the inhabitants of the land, saith the LORD.

13 For from the least of them even unto the greatest of them every one *is* given to *a*covetousness; and from the prophet even unto the *b*priest every one dealeth falsely.

14 They have healed also the hurt *of the daughter* of my people slightly, saying, *a*Peace, peace; when *there is* no peace.

15 Were they ashamed when they had committed abomination? nay, they were not at all ashamed, neither could they blush: therefore they shall fall among them that fall: at the time *that* I *a*visit them they shall be cast down, saith the LORD.

16 Thus saith the LORD, Stand ye in the ways, and see, and ask for the old *a*paths, where *is* the good way, and *b*walk therein, and ye shall find *c*rest for your souls. But they said, We will not walk *therein*.

17 Also I set *a*watchmen over you, *saying, *b*Hearken to the sound of the trumpet. But they said, We will not hearken.

18 ¶ Therefore hear, ye nations, and know, O congregation, what *is* among them.

19 Hear, O earth: behold, I will

31*d* Rom. 1:32.
6 1*a* Jer. 1:14; 4:6; 10:22.
　6*a* Ezek. 4:2.
　　b OR punished.
　7*a* TG Wickedness.
　　b Jer. 20:8.
　9*a* OR thoroughly.

b OR unto the new
　branches.
10*a* TG Warn.
　b Acts 7:51.
13*a* TG Covet.
　b TG Priestcraft.
14*a* TG Peace.

15*a* OR punish.
16*a* Jer. 18:15.
　b TG Walking with God.
　c TG Rest.
17*a* TG Watchman.
　b TG Obedience.

bring ^aevil upon this people, *even* the ^bfruit of their thoughts, because they have not hearkened unto my words, nor to my law, but rejected it.

20 To what purpose cometh there to me incense from Sheba, and the sweet cane from a far country? your burnt offerings *are* not ^aacceptable, nor your sacrifices sweet unto me.

21 Therefore thus saith the LORD, Behold, I will lay ^astumblingblocks before this people, and the fathers and the sons together shall fall upon them; the neighbour and his friend shall perish.

22 Thus saith the LORD, Behold, a people cometh from the ^anorth country, and a great nation shall be raised from the sides of the earth.

23 They shall lay hold on bow and spear; they *are* cruel, and have no mercy; their voice roareth like the sea; and they ride upon horses, set in array as men for war against thee, O daughter of Zion.

24 We have heard the fame thereof: our hands wax feeble: anguish hath taken hold of us, *and* pain, as of a woman in travail.

25 Go not forth into the field, nor walk by the way; for the sword of the enemy *and* fear *is* on every side.

26 ¶ O daughter of my people, gird *thee* with ^asackcloth, and wallow thyself in ashes: make thee mourning, *as for* an ^bonly son, most bitter lamentation: for the spoiler shall suddenly come upon us.

27 I have set thee *for* a tower *and* a fortress among my people, that thou mayest know and try their way.

28 They *are* all grievous revolters, walking with ^aslanders: *they are* brass and iron; they *are* all corrupters.

29 The bellows ^aare burned, the lead is consumed of the fire; ^bthe founder melteth in vain: for the wicked are not plucked away.

30 Reprobate silver shall *men* call them, because the LORD hath rejected them.

CHAPTER 7

If the people of Judah repent, they will be preserved—The temple has become a den of robbers—The Lord rejects that generation of the people of Judah for their idolatries—They offer their children as sacrifices.

THE word that came to Jeremiah from the LORD, saying,

2 Stand in the gate of the LORD's house, and proclaim there this word, and say, Hear the word of the LORD, all *ye of* Judah, that enter in at these gates to worship the LORD.

3 Thus saith the LORD of hosts, the God of Israel, ^aAmend your ways and your doings, and I will cause you to dwell in this place.

4 Trust ye not in lying words, saying, The temple of the LORD, The temple of the LORD, The temple of the LORD, *are* these.

5 For if ye ^athroughly amend your ways and your doings; if ye throughly execute judgment between a man and his neighbour;

6 *If* ye oppress not the ^astranger, the ^bfatherless, and the widow, and shed not innocent blood in this place, neither walk after other gods to your hurt:

7 Then will I cause you to dwell in this place, in the land that I gave to your fathers, for ever and ever.

8 ¶ Behold, ye ^atrust in ^blying words, that cannot profit.

9 Will ye steal, ^amurder, and commit adultery, and swear falsely, and burn incense unto Baal, and ^bwalk after other gods whom ye know not;

19*a* OR calamity.
  TG Evil.
  b Prov. 1:31.
20*a* TG Hypocrisy.
21*a* Ezek. 3:20;
  Mosiah 7:29.
22*a* Deut. 28:49;
  Jer. 50:41 (41–43).

26*a* TG Apparel.
  b Amos 8:10.
28*a* TG Slander.
29*a* OR blew the fire.
  b OR the smelting is
  in vain.
7 3*a* Isa. 1:16 (16–20).
  5*a* OR thoroughly.

6*a* Jer. 22:3.
  b TG Charity.
8*a* TG Trust Not in the
  Arm of Flesh.
  b Jer. 5:31.
9*a* TG Murder.
  b TG Walking in Darkness.

10 And come and ᵃstand before me in this house, which is called by my name, and say, We are delivered to do all these abominations?

11 Is this ᵃhouse, which is called by my name, become a ᵇden of ᶜrobbers in your eyes? Behold, even I have seen it, saith the LORD.

12 But go ye now unto my place which was in ᵃShiloh, where I set my name at the first, and see what I did to it for the wickedness of my people Israel.

13 And now, because ye have done all these works, saith the LORD, and I spake unto you, rising up early and speaking, but ye heard not; and I called you, but ye ᵃanswered not;

14 Therefore will I do unto this ᵃhouse, which is called by my name, wherein ye trust, and unto the place which I gave to you and to your fathers, as I have done to Shiloh.

15 And I will cast you out of my sight, as I have cast out all your brethren, even the whole seed of Ephraim.

16 Therefore pray not thou for this people, neither lift up cry nor prayer for them, neither make intercession to me: for I will not ᵃhear thee.

17 ¶ Seest thou not what they do in the cities of Judah and in the streets of Jerusalem?

18 The children gather wood, and the fathers kindle the fire, and the women knead their dough, to make cakes to ᵃthe queen of heaven, and to pour out drink offerings unto other gods, that they may provoke me to anger.

19 Do they provoke me to anger? saith the LORD: do they not provoke themselves ᵃto the confusion of their own faces?

20 Therefore thus saith the Lord GOD; Behold, mine ᵃanger and my fury shall be poured out upon this place, upon man, and upon beast, and upon the trees of the field, and upon the fruit of the ground; and it shall burn, and shall not be quenched.

21 ¶ Thus saith the LORD of hosts, the God of Israel; Put your burnt offerings unto your sacrifices, and eat flesh.

22 For I spake not unto your fathers, nor commanded them in the day that I brought them out of the land of Egypt, concerning burnt offerings or sacrifices:

23 But this thing commanded I them, saying, ᵃObey my ᵇvoice, and I will be your God, and ye shall be my people: and walk ye in all the ways that I have commanded you, that it may be well unto you.

24 But they hearkened not, nor inclined their ear, but walked in the counsels and in the ᵃimagination of their evil heart, and went ᵇbackward, and not forward.

25 Since the day that your fathers came forth out of the land of Egypt unto this day I have even ᵃsent unto you all my servants the ᵇprophets, daily rising up early and sending them:

26 Yet they hearkened not unto me, nor inclined their ear, but ᵃhardened their neck: they did ᵇworse than their fathers.

27 Therefore thou shalt speak all these words unto them; but they will not hearken to thee: thou shalt also call unto them; but they will not answer thee.

28 But thou shalt say unto them, This is a nation that ᵃobeyeth not the voice of the LORD their God, nor receiveth correction: truth is

---

10a D&C 88:134 (133–34).
11a TG Temple.
   b Matt. 21:13;
     Luke 19:46 (46–48).
   c TG Apostasy of Israel.
12a Josh. 18:1;
     1 Sam. 1:3;
     Jer. 26:6.
13a TG Apostasy of Israel.

14a Ezek. 7:22 (21–22); 24:21.
16a Jer. 11:14;
     Mosiah 21:15.
18a IE the fertility goddess,
     such as the Babylonian
     Ishtar.
19a HEB to their shame, or
     disgrace.
20a TG God, Indignation of.

23a TG Obedience.
   b D&C 1:38.
24a 1 Ne. 12:18.
   b TG Apostasy of Israel.
25a TG Authority.
   b TG Prophets, Mission of.
26a TG Hardheartedness.
   b Jer. 16:12.
28a TG Teachable.

perished, and is cut off from their mouth.

29 ¶ Cut off thine hair, O *Jerusalem*, and cast *it* away, and take up a *a*lamentation on high places; for the Lord hath rejected and forsaken the generation of his wrath.

30 For the children of Judah have done evil in my sight, saith the Lord: they have set their *a*abominations in the house which is called by my name, to *b*pollute it.

31 And they have built the high places of *a*Tophet, which *is* in the valley of the son of *b*Hinnom, to *c*burn their sons and their daughters in the *d*fire; which I commanded *them* not, neither came it into my heart.

32 ¶ Therefore, behold, the days come, saith the Lord, that it shall no more be called Tophet, nor the valley of the son of Hinnom, but the valley of slaughter: for they shall bury in Tophet, till there be no place.

33 And the *a*carcases of this people shall be meat for the fowls of the heaven, and for the beasts of the earth; and none shall fray *them* away.

34 Then will I cause to cease from the cities of Judah, and from the streets of Jerusalem, the voice of *a*mirth, and the *b*voice of gladness, the voice of the bridegroom, and the voice of the bride: for the land shall be *c*desolate.

CHAPTER 8

Calamities will befall the inhabitants of Jerusalem—For them the harvest is past, the summer is ended, and they are not saved.

At that time, saith the Lord, they shall bring out the bones of the kings of Judah, and the bones of his princes, and the bones of the priests, and the bones of the prophets, and the bones of the inhabitants of Jerusalem, out of their graves:

2 And they shall spread them before the sun, and the moon, and all the host of heaven, whom they have loved, and whom they have served, and after whom they have walked, and whom they have sought, and whom they have *a*worshipped: they shall not be gathered, nor be *b*buried; they shall be for dung upon the face of the earth.

3 And *a*death shall be *b*chosen rather than life by all the residue of them that remain of this evil family, which remain in all the places whither I have driven them, saith the Lord of hosts.

4 ¶ Moreover thou shalt say unto them, Thus saith the Lord; Shall they fall, and not arise? shall he turn away, and not return?

5 Why *then* is this people of Jerusalem slidden back by a perpetual *a*backsliding? they hold fast deceit, they refuse to return.

6 I hearkened and heard, *but* they spake not aright: no man repented him of his wickedness, saying, What have I done? every one turned to his course, as the horse rusheth into the battle.

7 Yea, the stork in the heaven knoweth her appointed times; and the *a*turtle and the crane and the swallow observe the time of their coming; but my people *b*know not the judgment of the Lord.

8 How do ye say, We are *a*wise, and the law of the Lord *is* with us? Lo, certainly in vain made he *it*; the pen of the scribes *is* in vain.

9 The wise *men* are ashamed, they are dismayed and taken: lo, they have *a*rejected the word of the Lord; and what wisdom *is* in them?

29*a* Ezek. 19:1 (1, 14).
30*a* 2 Kgs. 21:4 (4, 7).
  b TG Sacrilege.
31*a* 2 Kgs. 23:10.
  b Josh. 18:16.
  c TG Idolatry.
  d Lev. 18:21;
     Deut. 12:31; 18:10.
33*a* Jer. 9:22; 19:7;

Ether 9:34.
34*a* Jer. 16:9; 25:10;
     Hosea 2:11.
  b Rev. 18:23 (22–24).
  c Jer. 27:17; 44:2.
8 2*a* TG Idolatry.
  b Jer. 25:33.
3*a* Rev. 9:6.
  b TG Agency.

5*a* TG Apostasy of Israel.
7*a* HEB turtle-dove.
     Song 2:12 (10–12).
  b Hel. 12:6 (6–22).
8*a* 1 Cor. 1:20 (19–20);
     2 Ne. 9:28.
9*a* TG Apostasy of Israel;
     Disobedience.

10 Therefore will I give their wives unto others, *and* their fields to them that shall inherit *them:* for every one from the least even unto the greatest is given to covetousness, from the prophet even unto the priest every one dealeth falsely.

11 For they have healed the hurt of the daughter of my people slightly, saying, Peace, peace; when *there is* no peace.

12 Were they *a*ashamed when they had committed abomination? nay, they were not at all ashamed, neither could they blush: therefore shall they fall among them that fall: in the time of their visitation they shall be *b*cast down, saith the LORD.

13 ¶ I will surely *a*consume them, saith the LORD: *there shall be* no grapes on the vine, nor figs on the fig tree, and the leaf shall fade; and *the things that* I have given them shall pass away from them.

14 Why do we sit still? assemble yourselves, and let us enter into the *a*defenced cities, and let us be silent there: for the LORD our God hath put us to silence, and given us water of gall to drink, because we have sinned against the LORD.

15 We looked for *a*peace, but no good *came; and* for a time of health, and behold trouble!

16 The snorting of his horses was heard from Dan: the whole land trembled at the sound of the neighing of his *a*strong ones; for they are come, and have devoured the land, and all that is in it; the city, and those that dwell therein.

17 For, behold, I will send serpents, cockatrices, among you, which *will* not *be* charmed, and they shall bite you, saith the LORD.

18 ¶ When I would comfort myself against sorrow, my heart *is* faint in me.

19 Behold the voice of the cry of the daughter of my people because of them that dwell in a far country: *Is* not the LORD in Zion? *is* not her king in her? Why have they provoked me to *a*anger with their graven images, *and* with *b*strange vanities?

20 The *a*harvest is past, the summer is ended, and we are not saved.

21 For the hurt of the daughter of my people am I hurt; I am *a*black; astonishment hath taken hold on me.

22 *Is there* no *a*balm in Gilead; *is there* no physician there? why then is not the health of the daughter of my people recovered?

CHAPTER 9

Jeremiah sorrows greatly because of the sins of the people—They will be scattered among the nations and punished.

OH that my head were waters, and mine eyes a fountain of *a*tears, that I might *b*weep day and night for the slain of the daughter of my people!

2 Oh that I had in the wilderness a lodging place of wayfaring men; that I might leave my people, and go from them! for they *be* all adulterers, an assembly of treacherous men.

3 And they bend their tongues *like* their bow *for* *a*lies: but they are not valiant for the truth upon the earth; for they proceed from evil to evil, and they *b*know not me, saith the LORD.

4 Take ye heed every one of his neighbour, and *a*trust ye not in any brother: for every brother will *b*utterly supplant, and every neighbour will walk with *c*slanders.

5 And they will deceive every one his neighbour, and will not speak the

---

12*a* Alma 47:36.
  b TG Punish.
13*a* 2 Ne. 26:6;
    D&C 63:34.
14*a* OR fortified.
15*a* Job 30:26;
    Isa. 59:9;
    Jer. 14:19.
16*a* Lam. 1:15.
19*a* TG Anger.

  b OR foreign idols.
20*a* D&C 45:2; 56:16;
    76:79 (71–79).
21*a* Hebrew idiom meaning
    "gloomy."
    Joel 2:6;
    Nahum 2:10.
22*a* Jer. 46:11.
9 1*a* TG Mourning.
  b TG Despair;

    Suffering.
3*a* Ps. 64:3.
  b John 17:3;
    D&C 101:16.
4*a* Micah 7:5 (5–6);
    2 Ne. 28:31;
    D&C 1:19.
  b OR consistently deceive.
  c TG Slander.

truth: they have taught their tongue to speak *a*lies, *and* *b*weary themselves to commit iniquity.

6 Thine habitation *is* in the midst of deceit; through deceit they refuse to know me, saith the LORD.

7 Therefore thus saith the LORD of hosts, Behold, I will *a*melt them, and *b*try them; for how shall I do for the daughter of my people?

8 Their tongue *is as* an arrow shot out; it speaketh deceit: *one* speaketh peaceably to his neighbour with his mouth, but in *a*heart he layeth his wait.

9 ¶ Shall I not *a*visit them for these *things?* saith the LORD: shall not my soul be *b*avenged on such a nation as this?

10 For the mountains will I take up a weeping and wailing, and for the habitations of the wilderness a lamentation, because they are burned up, so that none can pass through *them;* neither can *men* hear the voice of the cattle; both the fowl of the heavens and the beast are fled; they are gone.

11 And I will make Jerusalem heaps, *and* a den of *a*dragons; and I will make the cities of Judah *b*desolate, without an inhabitant.

12 ¶ Who *is* the wise man, that may understand this? and *who is he* to whom the mouth of the LORD hath spoken, that he may declare it, for what the land perisheth *and* is burned up like a wilderness, that none passeth through?

13 And the LORD saith, Because they have forsaken my law which I set before them, and have not *a*obeyed my voice, neither walked therein;

14 But have walked after the *a*imagination of their own heart, and after *b*Baalim, which their fathers taught them:

15 Therefore thus saith the LORD of hosts, the God of Israel; Behold, I will feed them, *even* this people, with wormwood, and give them water of gall to drink.

16 I will *a*scatter them also among the *b*heathen, whom neither they nor their fathers have known: and I will send a sword after them, till I have consumed them.

17 ¶ Thus saith the LORD of hosts, Consider ye, and call for the mourning *a*women, that they may come; and send for cunning *women,* that they may come:

18 And let them make haste, and take up a wailing for us, that our eyes may run down with tears, and our eyelids gush out with waters.

19 For a voice of wailing is heard out of Zion, How are we spoiled! we are greatly confounded, because we have forsaken the land, because our dwellings have cast *us* out.

20 Yet hear the word of the LORD, O ye women, and let your ear receive the word of his mouth, and teach your daughters wailing, and every one her neighbour lamentation.

21 For death is come up into our windows, *and* is entered into our palaces, to cut off the children from without, *and* the young men from the streets.

22 Speak, Thus saith the LORD, Even the *a*carcases of men shall fall as dung upon the open field, and as the handful after the harvestman, and none shall gather *them.*

23 ¶ Thus saith the LORD, Let not the wise *man* glory in his wisdom, neither let the mighty *man* glory in his might, let not the rich *man* glory in his *a*riches:

24 But let him that glorieth *a*glory in this, that he understandeth and knoweth me, that I *am* the LORD

5*a* TG Lying.
  b OR are impatient.
7*a* 2 Ne. 23:7 (7–9);
  D&C 133:41.
  b Isa. 1:25 (25–26);
  Mal. 3:2 (2–3).
8*a* TG Hypocrisy.
9*a* Mosiah 12:1;

D&C 124:50.
  b Jer. 5:9 (9, 29); 44:22.
11*a* HEB jackals.
  b Isa. 1:7;
  2 Ne. 13:8.
13*a* TG Disobedience.
14*a* 1 Ne. 12:18.
  b 2 Chr. 33:3.

16*a* TG Israel, Scattering of.
  b TG Heathen.
17*a* TG Woman.
22*a* Jer. 7:33.
23*a* TG Treasure.
24*a* 1 Cor. 1:31;
  2 Cor. 10:17 (15–18);
  Alma 26:36 (36–37).

which exercise lovingkindness, judgment, and righteousness, in the earth: for in these *things* I *b*delight, saith the LORD.

25 ¶ Behold, the days come, saith the LORD, that I will punish all *them which are* *a*circumcised with the uncircumcised;

26 Egypt, and Judah, and Edom, and the children of Ammon, and Moab, and all *that are* in the *a*utmost corners, that dwell in the wilderness: for all *these* nations *are* uncircumcised, and all the house of Israel *are* uncircumcised in the heart.

CHAPTER 10

Learn not the way of other nations— Their gods are idols and molten images— The Lord is the true and living God.

HEAR ye the word which the LORD speaketh unto you, O house of Israel:

2 Thus saith the LORD, Learn not the way of the *a*heathen, and be not dismayed at the signs of heaven; for the heathen are dismayed at them.

3 For the *a*customs of the people *are* vain: for *one* cutteth a tree out of the forest, the work of the hands of the workman, with the axe.

4 They deck it with silver and with gold; they fasten it with nails and with hammers, that it move not.

5 They *are* upright as the palm tree, but speak not: they must needs be *a*borne, because they cannot go. Be not afraid of them; for they cannot do evil, neither also *is it* in them to do good.

6 Forasmuch as *there is* none *a*like unto thee, O LORD; thou *art* great, and thy name *is* great in might.

7 Who would not fear thee, O King of nations? for to thee doth it

appertain: forasmuch as among all the *a*wise *men* of the nations, and in all their kingdoms, *there is* none *b*like unto thee.

8 But they are altogether brutish and foolish: the stock *is* a doctrine of vanities.

9 Silver spread into plates is brought from Tarshish, and gold from Uphaz, the work of the workman, and of the hands of the founder: blue and purple *is* their clothing: they *are* all the *a*work of *b*cunning *men*.

10 But the LORD *is* the true *a*God, he *is* the *b*living God, and an everlasting *c*king: at his wrath the earth shall tremble, and the nations shall not be able to abide his *d*indignation.

11 Thus shall ye say unto them, The *a*gods that have not made the heavens and the earth, *even* they shall perish from the earth, and from under these heavens.

12 He hath made the earth by his power, he hath established the world by his wisdom, and hath stretched out the heavens by his discretion.

13 When he uttereth his voice, *there is* a multitude of waters in the heavens, and he causeth the vapours to ascend from the ends of the earth; he maketh lightnings with rain, and bringeth forth the wind out of his *a*treasures.

14 Every man is brutish in *his* knowledge: every founder is confounded by the graven *a*image: for his molten image *is* falsehood, and *there is* no breath in them.

15 They *are* vanity, *and* the work of *a*errors: in the time of their *b*visitation they shall perish.

16 The portion of Jacob *is* not like them: for he *is* the former of all *things*; and Israel *is* the rod of his

---

24*b* Micah 7:18.
25*a* TG Circumcision.
26*a* Jer. 25:23.
10 2*a* TG Heathen.
　3*a* Isa. 40:19 (19–20); 44:12.
　　 TG Traditions of Men.
　5*a* Isa. 46:7.
　6*a* Ps. 71:19.

7*a* Esth. 1:13.
　b Ex. 8:10 (8–10);
　　 Ps. 89:6.
9*a* Ps. 115:4.
　b D&C 124:84.
10*a* Josh. 22:34;
　　 D&C 76:1.
　b JS—H 1:17.

　c TG Kingdom of God,
　　 in Heaven.
　d TG God, Indignation of.
11*a* TG Idolatry.
13*a* HEB storehouses.
14*a* TG Idolatry.
15*a* HEB mockery.
　b D&C 56:1.

inheritance: The LORD of hosts *is* his name.

17 ¶ Gather up thy wares out of the land, O inhabitant of the fortress.

18 For thus saith the LORD, Behold, I will sling out the inhabitants of the land at this once, and will distress them, that they may find *it so.*

19 ¶ Woe is me for my hurt! my wound is grievous: but I said, Truly this *is* a grief, and I must bear it.

20 My ªtabernacle is spoiled, and all my cords are broken: my children are gone forth of me, and they *are* not: *there is* none to stretch forth my tent any more, and to set up my curtains.

21 For the ªpastors are become brutish, and have not sought the LORD: therefore they shall not prosper, and all their flocks shall be scattered.

22 Behold, the noise of the bruit is come, and a great commotion out of the ªnorth country, to make the cities of Judah desolate, *and* a den of ᵇdragons.

23 ¶ O LORD, I know that the ªway of man *is* not in himself: *it is* not in man that walketh to direct his steps.

24 O LORD, ªcorrect me, but with ᵇjudgment; not in thine anger, lest thou bring me to nothing.

25 Pour out thy fury upon the heathen that know thee not, and upon the ªfamilies that call not on thy name: for they have eaten up Jacob, and devoured him, and consumed him, and have made his habitation desolate.

CHAPTER 11

The people of Judah are cursed for breaking the covenant of obedience— The Lord will not hear their prayers.

THE word that came to Jeremiah from the LORD, saying,

2 Hear ye the words of this covenant, and speak unto the men of Judah, and to the inhabitants of Jerusalem;

3 And say thou unto them, Thus saith the LORD God of Israel; ªCursed *be* the man that ᵇobeyeth not the words of this ᶜcovenant,

4 Which I commanded your fathers in the day *that* I brought them forth out of the land of Egypt, from the iron furnace, saying, ªObey my voice, and do them, according to all which ᵇI command you: so shall ye be my people, and I will be your God:

5 That I may perform the ªoath which I have sworn unto your fathers, to give them a ᵇland ᶜflowing with milk and honey, as *it is* this day. Then answered I, and said, So be it, O LORD.

6 Then the LORD said unto me, Proclaim all these words in the cities of Judah, and in the streets of Jerusalem, saying, Hear ye the words of this covenant, and do them.

7 For I earnestly ªprotested unto your fathers in the day *that* I brought them up out of the land of Egypt, *even* unto this day, rising early and protesting, saying, Obey my voice.

8 Yet they obeyed not, nor inclined their ear, but walked every one in the imagination of their evil heart: therefore I ªwill bring upon them all the words of this covenant, which I commanded *them* to do; but they did *them* not.

9 And the LORD said unto me, A ªconspiracy is found among the men of Judah, and among the inhabitants of Jerusalem.

10 They are ªturned back to the iniquities of their forefathers, which refused to hear my words; and they went after other gods to ᵇserve them: the house of Israel and the

---

20*a* Jer. 4:20.
21*a* TG Shepherd.
22*a* Jer. 1:14; 4:6; 6:1.
  b HEB jackals.
23*a* Prov. 20:24.
24*a* TG Punish.
  b Ezek. 34:16;
    1 Ne. 22:21.

25*a* Eph. 6:4 (1–4).
11 3*a* TG Curse.
  b TG Disobedience.
  c Ex. 20:20 (1–26).
4*a* TG Obedience.
  b Alma 5:38 (37–41).
5*a* Deut. 7:12 (12–13);
    D&C 38:20.

  b TG Israel, Land of.
  c Ex. 3:8.
7*a* HEB witnessed.
8*a* OR brought.
9*a* TG Conspiracy.
10*a* Zeph. 1:6.
  b OR worship.

house of Judah have broken my covenant which I made with their fathers.

11 ¶ Therefore thus saith the LORD, Behold, I will bring *a*evil upon them, which they shall not be able to escape; and though they shall *b*cry unto me, I will not hearken unto them.

12 Then shall the cities of Judah and inhabitants of Jerusalem go, and cry unto the gods unto whom they offer incense: but they shall not save them at all in the time of their trouble.

13 For *according to* the number of thy cities were thy *a*gods, O Judah; and *according to* the number of the streets of Jerusalem have ye set up altars to *that* shameful thing, *even* *b*altars to burn incense unto Baal.

14 Therefore *a*pray not thou for this people, neither lift up a cry or prayer for them: for I will not hear *them* in the time that they cry unto me for their trouble.

15 What hath my beloved to do in mine house, *seeing* she hath wrought lewdness with many, and *a*the holy flesh is passed from thee? when thou doest evil, then thou rejoicest.

16 The LORD called thy name, A *a*green *b*olive tree, fair, *and* of goodly fruit: with the noise of a great tumult he hath kindled fire upon it, and the branches of it are broken.

17 For the LORD of hosts, that planted thee, hath pronounced evil against thee, for the evil of the house of Israel and of the house of Judah, which they have done against themselves to provoke me to anger in offering incense unto Baal.

18 ¶ And the LORD hath given me knowledge *of it*, and I know *it:* then thou shewedst me their doings.

19 But I *was* like a *a*lamb *or* an ox *that* is brought to the *b*slaughter; and I knew not that they had *c*devised *d*devices against me, *saying*, Let us destroy the tree with the fruit thereof, and let us *e*cut him off from the land of the living, that his name may be no more remembered.

20 But, O LORD of hosts, that judgest righteously, that *a*triest the reins and the *b*heart, let me see thy vengeance on them: for unto thee have I revealed my cause.

21 Therefore thus saith the LORD of the men of Anathoth, that seek thy *a*life, saying, Prophesy not in the name of the LORD, that thou die not by our hand:

22 Therefore thus saith the LORD of hosts, Behold, I will punish them: the young men shall die by the sword; their sons and their daughters shall die by famine:

23 And there shall be no remnant of them: for I will bring evil upon the men of Anathoth, *even* the year of their visitation.

CHAPTER 12

Jeremiah complains of the prosperity of the wicked—If other nations learn the ways of Israel, they will be numbered with Israel.

RIGHTEOUS *art* thou, O LORD, when I plead with thee: yet let me talk with thee of *thy* judgments: Wherefore doth the way of the *a*wicked prosper? *wherefore* are all they happy that deal very treacherously?

2 *a*Thou hast planted them, yea, they have taken root: they grow, yea, they bring forth fruit: thou *art* near in their mouth, and far from their reins.

3 But thou, O LORD, *a*knowest me:

11*a* TG Punish.
  b Ps. 18:41 (40–41);
    Mosiah 21:15;
    D&C 101:7.
    TG God, Access to.
13*a* TG Idolatry.
  b TG Apostasy of Israel.
14*a* Jer. 7:16; 14:11.
15*a* IE acceptable sacrifice
    has ceased.

16*a* Ps. 52:8.
  b TG Vineyard of the Lord.
19*a* Isa. 53:7; Mosiah 14:7;
    D&C 135:4.
  b TG Persecution.
  c TG Prophets, Rejection of.
  d Lam. 3:62 (60–62).
  e Ps. 83:4;
    1 Ne. 1:20.

20*a* TG Test.
  b D&C 64:34.
21*a* TG Prophets, Rejection of.
12 1*a* Mosiah 16:2;
    D&C 1:9.
    TG Wickedness.
2*a* Matt. 15:8.
3*a* TG God, Omniscience of.

thou hast seen me, and tried mine heart toward thee: pull them out like sheep for the slaughter, and prepare them for the day of slaughter.

4 How long shall the land mourn, and the herbs of every field wither, for the wickedness of them that dwell therein? the beasts are consumed, and the birds; because they said, He shall not see our last end.

5 ¶ If thou hast run with the footmen, and they have wearied thee, then how canst thou contend with horses? and *if* in the land of peace, *wherein* thou trustedst, *they wearied thee,* then how wilt thou do in the swelling of Jordan?

6 For even thy ^abrethren, and the house of thy father, even they have dealt treacherously with thee; yea, they have called a multitude after thee: believe them not, though they speak fair words unto thee.

7 ¶ I have ^aforsaken mine house, I have left mine heritage; I have given the dearly beloved of my soul into the hand of her enemies.

8 Mine heritage is unto me as a lion in the forest; it crieth out against me: therefore have I hated it.

9 Mine heritage *is* unto me *as* a speckled bird, the birds round about *are* against her; come ye, assemble all the ^abeasts of the field, come to devour.

10 Many ^apastors have destroyed my ^bvineyard, they have trodden my portion under foot, they have made my pleasant portion a desolate wilderness.

11 They have made it desolate, *and being* desolate it mourneth unto me; the whole land is made desolate, because no man ^alayeth *it* to heart.

12 The spoilers are come upon all high places through the wilderness: for the sword of the LORD shall devour from the *one* end of the land even to the *other* end of the land: no flesh shall have peace.

13 They have sown wheat, but shall reap thorns: they have ^aput themselves to pain, *but* shall not profit: and they shall be ashamed of your revenues because of the fierce anger of the LORD.

14 ¶ Thus saith the LORD against all mine evil neighbours, that touch the inheritance which I have caused my people Israel to inherit; Behold, I will pluck them out of their land, and pluck out the house of Judah from among them.

15 And it shall come to pass, after that I have plucked them out I will return, and have ^acompassion on them, and will ^bbring them again, every man to his heritage, and every man to his land.

16 And it shall come to pass, if they will diligently learn the ways of my people, to swear by my name, The LORD liveth; as they taught my people to swear by Baal; then shall they be built in the midst of my people.

17 But if they will not ^aobey, I will utterly pluck up and destroy that ^bnation, saith the LORD.

CHAPTER 13

Israel and Judah will be as a rotted and decayed belt—The people are commanded to repent—Judah will be taken captive and scattered as stubble.

THUS saith the LORD unto me, Go and get thee a linen girdle, and put it upon thy loins, and put it not in water.

2 So I got a girdle according to the word of the LORD, and put *it* on my loins.

3 And the word of the LORD came unto me the second time, saying,

4 Take the girdle that thou hast got, which *is* upon thy loins, and arise, go to Euphrates, and hide it there in a hole of the rock.

5 So I went, and hid it by Euphrates, as the LORD commanded me.

6a TG Prophets, Rejection of.
7a Ps. 69:25;
  Jer. 22:5;
  Matt. 23:38;
   Luke 13:35.
9a IE Babylon and others.
10a TG False Prophets.
  b Jacob 6:2.
11a IE pays attention.
13a OR taken pains.
15a Deut. 30:3.
  b TG Israel, Gathering of.
17a TG Disobedience.
  b Isa. 60:12.

6 And it came to pass after many days, that the LORD said unto me, Arise, go to Euphrates, and take the girdle from thence, which I commanded thee to hide there.

7 Then I went to Euphrates, and digged, and took the girdle from the place where I had hid it: and, behold, the girdle was marred, it was profitable for nothing.

8 Then the word of the LORD came unto me, saying,

9 Thus saith the LORD, After this manner will I mar the ᵃpride of Judah, and the great pride of Jerusalem.

10 This evil people, which refuse to hear my words, which walk in the ᵃimagination of their heart, and ᵇwalk after other gods, to serve them, and to worship them, shall even be as this girdle, which is good for nothing.

11 For as the girdle cleaveth to the loins of a man, so have I caused to cleave unto me the whole house of Israel and the whole house of Judah, saith the LORD; that they might be unto me for a people, and for a name, and for a praise, and for a glory: but they would not ᵃhear.

12 ¶ Therefore thou shalt speak unto them this word; Thus saith the LORD God of Israel, Every bottle shall be filled with wine: and they shall say unto thee, Do we not certainly know that every bottle shall be filled with wine?

13 Then shalt thou say unto them, Thus saith the LORD, Behold, I will fill all the inhabitants of this land, even the kings that sit upon David's throne, and the priests, and the prophets, and all the inhabitants of Jerusalem, with ᵃdrunkenness.

14 And I will dash them one against another, even the fathers and the sons together, saith the LORD:

I will not pity, nor spare, nor have mercy, but ᵃdestroy them.

15 ¶ Hear ye, and give ear; be not ᵃproud: for the LORD hath spoken.

16 Give glory to the LORD your God, before he cause ᵃdarkness, and before your feet stumble upon the dark mountains, and, while ye look for light, he turn it into the shadow of death, *and* make *it* gross darkness.

17 But if ye will not hear it, my soul shall weep in secret places for *your* pride; and mine eye shall weep sore, and run down with tears, because the LORD's ᵃflock is carried away captive.

18 Say unto the king and to the queen, Humble yourselves, sit down: for your principalities shall come down, *even* the crown of your glory.

19 The cities of the south shall be shut up, and none shall open *them:* Judah shall be ᵃcarried away captive all of it, it shall be wholly carried away captive.

20 Lift up your eyes, and behold them that come from the north: where *is* the flock *that* was given thee, thy beautiful flock?

21 What wilt thou say when he shall punish thee? for thou hast taught them *to be* captains, *and* as chief over thee: shall not sorrows take thee, as a woman in travail?

22 ¶ And if thou say in thine heart, Wherefore come these things upon me? For the greatness of thine iniquity are thy ᵃskirts ᵇdiscovered, *and* thy heels made bare.

23 Can the Ethiopian change his skin, or the leopard his spots? *then* may ye also do ᵃgood, that are accustomed to do evil.

24 Therefore will I ᵃscatter them as the stubble that passeth away by the wind of the wilderness.

25 This *is* thy lot, the portion of thy

---

13 9a TG Pride.
  10a HEB stubbornness.
    b TG Walking in Darkness.
  11a 1 Ne. 1:20.
  13a Ezek. 23:33.
  14a 1 Ne. 1:13 (4–13); 2:13.

15a TG Pride.
16a TG Darkness, Spiritual.
17a TG Church.
19a 2 Kgs. 24:14 (10–16); 25:11 (1–12); 2 Ne. 6:8.
22a Hosea 2:3.

  b HEB stripped off.
23a Alma 5:40; D&C 33:4.
24a 1 Ne. 10:12 (12–14); 22:3 (3–4).

measures from me, saith the LORD; because thou hast forgotten me, and trusted in falsehood.

26 Therefore will I discover thy skirts upon thy face, that thy shame may appear.

27 I have seen thine adulteries, and thy neighings, the lewdness of thy whoredom, *and* thine ᵃabominations on the hills in the fields. Woe unto thee, O Jerusalem! wilt thou not be made ᵇclean? when *shall it* once *be?*

CHAPTER 14

Jeremiah prays because of dearth and famine—The Lord will not hear because of the wickedness of His people.

THE word of the LORD that came to Jeremiah concerning the ᵃdearth.

2 Judah mourneth, and the gates thereof languish; they are ᵃblack unto the ground; and the cry of Jerusalem is gone up.

3 And their nobles have sent their little ones to the waters: they came to the pits, *and* found no water; they returned with their vessels empty; they were ashamed and confounded, and covered their heads.

4 Because the ground is chapt, for there was no ᵃrain in the earth, the plowmen were ashamed, they covered their heads.

5 Yea, the hind also calved in the field, and forsook *it,* because there was no grass.

6 And the wild asses did stand in the high places, they snuffed up the wind like ᵃdragons; their eyes did fail, because *there was* no grass.

7 ¶ O LORD, though our iniquities testify against us, do thou *it* for thy name's sake: for our backslidings are many; we have sinned against thee.

8 O the hope of Israel, the saviour thereof in time of trouble, why

shouldest thou be as a stranger in the land, and as a wayfaring man *that* turneth aside to tarry for a night?

9 Why shouldest thou be as a man astonied, as a mighty man *that* cannot save? yet thou, O LORD, *art* in the midst of us, and we are called by thy name; leave us not.

10 ¶ Thus saith the LORD unto this people, Thus have they loved to wander, they have not ᵃrefrained their feet, therefore the LORD doth not accept them; he will now remember their ᵇiniquity, and visit their sins.

11 Then said the LORD unto me, ᵃPray not for this people for *their* good.

12 When they fast, I will not ᵃhear their cry; and when they offer burnt offering and an oblation, I will not accept them: but I will ᵇconsume them by the sword, and by the famine, and by the pestilence.

13 ¶ Then said I, Ah, Lord GOD! behold, the prophets say unto them, Ye shall not see the ᵃsword, neither shall ye have famine; but I will give you assured peace in this place.

14 Then the LORD said unto me, The ᵃprophets prophesy ᵇlies in my name: I sent them not, neither have I commanded them, neither spake unto them: they prophesy unto you a false ᶜvision and divination, and a thing of nought, and the ᵈdeceit of their heart.

15 Therefore thus saith the LORD concerning the prophets that prophesy in my name, and I ᵃsent them not, yet they say, Sword and famine shall not be in this land; By sword and famine shall those prophets be ᵇconsumed.

16 And the people to whom they prophesy shall be cast out in the streets of Jerusalem because of

---

27a 2 Kgs. 24:19;
   1 Ne. 1:13.
  b Ezek. 24:13.
14 1a TG Famine.
  2a OR dejected.
  4a Jer. 3:3.
  6a HEB jackals.
  10a TG Abstain;

    Self-Mastery.
  b TG Apostasy of Israel.
11a Jer. 7:16; 11:14.
12a Mosiah 11:24 (23–25);
    21:15;
    D&C 101:7 (6–8).
  b Jer. 16:4.
13a Jer. 5:12.

14a TG False Prophets.
  b Jer. 27:10.
   TG False Doctrine.
  c TG Vision.
  d TG Deceit.
15a TG Authority.
  b Jer. 44:12.

the famine and the sword; and they shall have none to [a]bury them, them, their wives, nor their sons, nor their daughters: for I will pour their wickedness upon them.

17 ¶ Therefore thou shalt say this word unto them; Let mine eyes run down with tears night and day, and let them not cease: for the virgin daughter of my people is broken with a great breach, with a very grievous blow.

18 If I go forth into the field, then behold the [a]slain with the sword! and if I enter into the city, then behold them that are sick with famine! yea, both the prophet and the priest go about into a [b]land that they know not.

19 Hast thou utterly rejected Judah? hath thy soul lothed Zion? why hast thou smitten us, and *there is* no healing for us? we looked for [a]peace, and *there is* no good; and for the time of healing, and behold trouble!

20 We [a]acknowledge, O LORD, our wickedness, *and* the iniquity of our fathers: for we have [b]sinned against thee.

21 Do not abhor *us*, for thy name's sake, do not disgrace the throne of thy glory: remember, break not thy [a]covenant with us.

22 Are there *any* among the [a]vanities of the Gentiles that can cause rain? or can the heavens give [b]showers? *art* not thou he, O LORD our God? therefore we will wait upon thee: for thou hast [c]made all these *things*.

CHAPTER 15

The people of Judah will suffer death, the sword, famine, and captivity—They will be scattered into all the kingdoms of the earth—Jerusalem will be destroyed.

THEN said the LORD unto me, Though Moses and Samuel stood before me, *yet* my mind *could* not *be* toward this people: cast *them* out of my sight, and let them go forth.

2 And it shall come to pass, if they say unto thee, Whither shall we go forth? then thou shalt tell them, Thus saith the LORD; Such as *are* for death, to death; and such as *are* for the sword, to the sword; and such as *are* for the famine, to the famine; and such as *are* for the captivity, to the captivity.

3 And I will appoint over them four [a]kinds, saith the LORD: the sword to slay, and the dogs to tear, and the fowls of the heaven, and the beasts of the earth, to [b]devour and destroy.

4 And I will cause them to be removed into all kingdoms of the earth, because of [a]Manasseh the son of Hezekiah king of Judah, for *that* which he did in Jerusalem.

5 For who shall have pity upon thee, O Jerusalem? or who shall bemoan thee? or who shall go aside to ask how thou doest?

6 Thou hast forsaken me, saith the LORD, thou art gone backward: therefore will I stretch out my hand against thee, and destroy thee; I am weary with repenting.

7 And I will [a]fan them with a fan in the gates of the land; I will [b]bereave *them* of children, I will destroy my people, *since* they return not from their ways.

8 Their widows are increased to me above the sand of the seas: I have brought upon them against the mother of the young men a spoiler at noonday: I have caused *him* to fall upon it suddenly, and terrors upon the city.

9 She that hath borne seven languisheth: she hath given up the ghost; her sun is gone down while *it*

16a Ps. 79:3.
18a Lam. 2:21.
  b TG Israel, Scattering of.
19a Jer. 8:15.
20a TG Confession.
  b Ps. 106:6.
21a Ps. 106:45.

22a IE worthless idols of the nations.
  b Jer. 3:3 (1–5).
  c Mosiah 4:2;
    3 Ne. 9:15;
    D&C 14:9; 45:1.
15 3a HEB destroyers.

  b D&C 29:20.
4a 2 Kgs. 21:11; 24:3 (3–4).
7a IE scatter them.
    Jer. 51:2.
  b Ezek. 36:13 (8–15).

was yet day: she hath been ashamed and confounded: and the residue of them will I deliver to the sword before their enemies, saith the LORD.

10 ¶ *a*Woe is me, my mother, that thou hast borne me a man of *b*strife and a man of contention to the whole earth! I have neither lent on usury, nor men have lent to me on *c*usury; *yet* every one of them doth curse me.

11 The LORD said, Verily it shall be well with thy remnant; verily I will cause the enemy to entreat thee *well* in the time of evil and in the time of affliction.

12 Shall iron break the northern iron and the steel?

13 Thy substance and thy treasures will I give to the spoil without price, and *that* for all thy sins, even in all thy borders.

14 And I will make *thee* to pass with thine enemies into a *a*land *which* thou knowest not: for a fire is kindled in mine anger, *which* shall burn upon you.

15 ¶ O LORD, thou knowest: remember me, and *a*visit me, and revenge me of my persecutors; take me not away in thy longsuffering: know that for thy sake I have *b*suffered *c*rebuke.

16 Thy words were found, and I did *a*eat them; and thy word was unto me the joy and rejoicing of mine heart: for I am called by thy *b*name, O LORD God of hosts.

17 I sat not in the assembly of the *a*mockers, nor rejoiced; I sat alone because of thy hand: for thou hast filled me with indignation.

18 Why is my pain perpetual, and my wound incurable, *which* refuseth to be healed? wilt thou be altogether unto me as a liar, *and as* waters *that* fail?

19 ¶ Therefore thus saith the LORD, If thou *a*return, then will I bring thee again, *and* thou shalt stand before me: and if thou take forth the precious from the vile, thou shalt be as my mouth: let them return unto thee; but return not thou unto them.

20 And I will make thee unto this people a *a*fenced brasen wall: and they shall fight against thee, but they shall not prevail against thee: for I *am* with thee to *b*save thee and to deliver thee, saith the LORD.

21 And I will deliver thee out of the hand of the wicked, and I will redeem thee out of the hand of the terrible.

CHAPTER 16

The utter ruin of Judah is foreseen—Israel is rejected and scattered for serving false gods—Fishers and hunters will gather Israel again, and the people will serve the Lord—The gospel is to be restored.

THE word of the LORD came also unto me, saying,

2 Thou shalt not take thee a wife, neither shalt thou have sons or daughters in this place.

3 For thus saith the LORD concerning the sons and concerning the daughters that are born in this place, and concerning their mothers that bare them, and concerning their fathers that begat them in this land;

4 They shall die of grievous deaths; they shall not be *a*lamented; neither shall they be buried; *but* they shall be as dung upon the face of the earth: and they shall be *b*consumed by the sword, and by famine; and their *c*carcases shall be meat for the fowls of heaven, and for the beasts of the earth.

5 For thus saith the LORD, Enter not into the house of *a*mourning, neither go to lament nor bemoan them: for I have taken away my peace from this people, saith the LORD, *even* lovingkindness and mercies.

10*a* TG Despair.
  b TG Strife.
  c TG Usury.
14*a* Jer. 16:13; 17:4.
15*a* OR be mindful of me.
  b TG Suffering.
  c HEB taunts.

16*a* Ezek. 3:3 (1, 3);
    Rev. 10:10 (9–10).
  b D&C 18:27.
17*a* Ps. 1:1; 26:4.
19*a* OR repent.
20*a* HEB fortified wall of
    brass.

  b TG Protection, Divine.
16 4*a* TG Mourning.
  b Jer. 14:12.
  c Deut. 28:26.
  5*a* Ezek. 24:17.

6 Both the great and the small shall die in this land: they shall not be buried, neither shall *men* lament for them, *ª*nor cut themselves, nor make themselves bald for them:

7 Neither shall *men ª*tear *themselves* for them in mourning, to comfort them for the dead; neither shall *men* give them the cup of consolation to drink for their father or for their mother.

8 Thou shalt not also go into the house of feasting, to sit with them to eat and to drink.

9 For thus saith the LORD of hosts, the God of Israel; Behold, I will cause to cease out of this place in your eyes, and in your days, the voice of *ª*mirth, and the voice of gladness, the voice of the bridegroom, and the voice of the bride.

10 ¶ And it shall come to pass, when thou shalt shew this people all these words, and they shall say unto thee, *ª*Wherefore hath the LORD pronounced all this great evil against us? or what *is* our iniquity? or what *is* our sin that we have committed against the LORD our God?

11 Then shalt thou say unto them, Because your fathers have forsaken me, saith the LORD, and have walked after other gods, and have served them, and have worshipped them, and have forsaken me, and have not kept my law;

12 And ye have done *ª*worse than your *ᵇ*fathers; for, behold, ye walk every one after the *ᶜ*imagination of his evil heart, that they may not hearken unto me:

13 Therefore will I *ª*cast you out of this *ᵇ*land into a land that ye know not, *neither* ye nor your fathers; and there shall ye serve other *ᶜ*gods day and night; where I will not *ᵈ*shew you favour.

14 ¶ Therefore, behold, the days come, saith the LORD, that it shall no more be said, The *ª*LORD liveth, that brought up the children of Israel out of the land of Egypt;

15 But, The LORD liveth, that *ª*brought up the children of Israel from the land of the *ᵇ*north, and from all the *ᶜ*lands whither he had driven them: and I will *ᵈ*bring them again into their *ᵉ*land that I gave unto their fathers.

16 ¶ Behold, I will send for many *ª*fishers, saith the LORD, and they shall fish them; and after will I send for many hunters, and they shall hunt them from every mountain, and from every hill, and out of the holes of the rocks.

17 For mine eyes *are* upon all their ways: they are not hid from my face, neither is their *ª*iniquity hid from mine eyes.

18 And first I will *ª*recompense their iniquity and their sin *ᵇ*double; because they have *ᶜ*defiled my land, they have filled mine inheritance with the carcases of their detestable and abominable things.

19 O LORD, my strength, and my fortress, and my refuge in the day of affliction, the *ª*Gentiles shall come unto thee from the ends of the earth, and shall say, Surely our fathers have *ᵇ*inherited lies, vanity, and *things* wherein *there is* no profit.

20 Shall a man make *ª*gods unto himself, and they *are* no *ᵇ*gods?

21 Therefore, behold, I will this once cause them to know, I will cause them to know mine hand and my might; and they shall *ª*know that my *ᵇ*name *is* The LORD.

6*a* Deut. 14:1.
7*a* HEB break bread.
9*a* Jer. 7:34; 25:10.
10*a* Deut. 29:24.
12*a* Jer. 7:26.
  b TG Traditions of Men.
  c OR stubbornness.
13*a* TG Israel, Scattering of.
  b Jer. 15:14.
  c TG Idolatry.
  d HEB grant you amnesty

or clemency.
14*a* Jer. 4:2.
15*a* TG Israel, Gathering of.
  b TG Israel, Ten Lost Tribes of.
  c Jer. 3:18.
  d Jer. 24:6; 32:37.
  e TG Israel, Land of.
16*a* TG Missionary Work.
17*a* Ps. 90:8.
18*a* Isa. 65:6.

  b Isa. 40:2;
    Jer. 17:18.
  c Jer. 2:7.
    TG Pollution.
19*a* OR nations.
  b D&C 93:39.
20*a* TG Apostasy of Israel.
  b TG Idolatry.
21*a* TG Israel, Restoration of.
  b Ex. 6:3; 15:3;
    Abr. 1:16; 2:8.

CHAPTER 17

The captivity of Judah comes because of sin and forsaking the Lord—Hallow the Sabbath day; doing so will save the people; otherwise they will be destroyed.

THE sin of Judah *is* written with a pen of iron, *and* with the point of a diamond: *it is* ^agraven upon the table of their heart, and upon the ^bhorns of your altars;

2 Whilst their children remember their ^aaltars and their ^bgroves by the green trees upon the high hills.

3 O my ^amountain in the field, I will give thy substance *and* all thy treasures to the spoil, *and* thy high places for sin, throughout all thy borders.

4 And thou, even thyself, shalt discontinue from thine heritage that I gave thee; and I will cause thee to ^aserve thine enemies in the ^bland which thou knowest not: for ye have kindled a fire in mine anger, *which* shall burn for ever.

5 ¶ Thus saith the LORD; ^aCursed *be* the man that ^btrusteth in man, and maketh ^cflesh his arm, and whose heart ^ddeparteth from the LORD.

6 For he shall be like the ^aheath in the desert, and shall not see when good cometh; but shall inhabit the parched places in the wilderness, *in* a ^bsalt land and not inhabited.

7 Blessed *is* the man that ^atrusteth in the LORD, and whose ^bhope the LORD is.

8 For he shall be as a ^atree planted by the waters, and *that* spreadeth out her roots by the river, and shall

not ^bsee when heat cometh, but her leaf shall be green; and shall not be careful in the year of ^cdrought, neither shall cease from yielding fruit.

9 ¶ The heart *is* deceitful above all *things*, and desperately wicked: who can know it?

10 I the LORD ^asearch the ^bheart, I try the ^creins, even to give every man according to his ^dways, *and* according to the fruit of his doings.

11 *As* the partridge sitteth *on eggs*, and hatcheth *them* not; *so* he that getteth ^ariches, and not by right, shall leave them in the midst of his days, and at his end shall be a fool.

12 ¶ A glorious high throne from the beginning *is* the place of our sanctuary.

13 O LORD, the hope of Israel, all that ^aforsake thee shall be ashamed, *and* they that depart from me shall be written in the earth, because they have forsaken the LORD, the fountain of living waters.

14 ^aHeal me, O LORD, and I shall be healed; save me, and I shall be saved: for thou *art* my ^bpraise.

15 ¶ Behold, they say unto me, Where *is* the word of the LORD? let it ^acome now.

16 As for me, I have not hastened from *being* a pastor to follow thee: neither have I desired the woeful day; thou knowest: that which came out of my lips was *right* before thee.

17 Be not a terror unto me: thou *art* my ^ahope in the day of evil.

18 Let them be ^aconfounded that persecute me, but let not me be

17 1*a* 1 Ne. 3:3.
  b Ex. 27:2.
 2*a* 2 Ne. 9:37;
     Alma 31:1.
  b HEB *asherim;* i.e.,
     fertility idols.
     TG Idolatry.
 3*a* IE Jerusalem.
 4*a* TG Israel, Scattering of.
  b Jer. 15:14.
 5*a* TG Curse.
  b TG Trust Not in the
     Arm of Flesh.
  c D&C 1:19.

  d TG Apostasy of
     Individuals.
 6*a* HEB juniper tree.
     Jer. 48:6.
  b Deut. 29:23.
 7*a* TG Trust in God.
  b TG Hope.
 8*a* Ps. 1:3 (2–3);
     D&C 97:9 (8–9).
  b HEB fear.
  c TG Drought.
10*a* TG Judgment.
  b TG God, Omniscience of.

  c Prov. 17:3.
  d TG Good Works;
     Justice.
11*a* 2 Ne. 9:30;
     D&C 56:16.
13*a* Alma 46:21.
14*a* 3 Ne. 9:13.
  b Alma 26:8.
15*a* TG Sign Seekers.
17*a* 3 Ne. 4:10.
18*a* HEB ashamed or
     disappointed.

confounded: let them be dismayed, but let not me be dismayed: bring upon them the day of evil, and destroy them with *b*double destruction.

19 ¶ Thus said the LORD unto me; Go and stand in the gate of the children of the people, whereby the kings of Judah come in, and by the which they go out, and in all the gates of Jerusalem;

20 And say unto them, Hear ye the word of the LORD, ye kings of Judah, and all Judah, and all the inhabitants of Jerusalem, that enter in by these gates:

21 Thus saith the LORD; Take heed to yourselves, and bear no burden on the *a*sabbath day, nor bring *it* in by the gates of Jerusalem;

22 Neither carry forth a burden out of your houses on the sabbath day, neither do ye any work, but hallow ye the sabbath day, as I commanded your fathers.

23 But they obeyed not, neither inclined their ear, but made their neck *a*stiff, that they might not hear, nor receive instruction.

24 And it shall come to pass, if ye diligently hearken unto me, saith the LORD, to bring in no burden through the gates of this city on the sabbath day, but hallow the sabbath day, to do no work therein;

25 Then shall there enter into the gates of this city *a*kings and princes sitting upon the throne of David, riding in chariots and on horses, they, and their princes, the men of Judah, and the inhabitants of Jerusalem: and this city shall remain for ever.

26 And they shall come from the cities of Judah, and from the places about Jerusalem, and from the land of Benjamin, and from the plain, and from the mountains, and from the south, bringing burnt offerings, and sacrifices, and meat offerings, and incense, and bringing sacrifices of praise, unto the house of the LORD.

27 But if ye will not hearken unto me to hallow the *a*sabbath day, and not to bear a burden, even entering in at the gates of Jerusalem on the sabbath day; then will I kindle a fire in the gates thereof, and it shall devour the *b*palaces of Jerusalem, and it shall not be quenched.

CHAPTER 18

Israel is as potter's clay in the hands of the Lord—If nations repent, the Lord withholds the evil decreed against them—The people of Judah will be scattered.

THE word which came to Jeremiah from the LORD, saying,

2 Arise, and go down to the *a*potter's house, and there I will cause thee to hear my words.

3 Then I went down to the potter's house, and, behold, he wrought a work on the wheels.

4 And the vessel that he made of clay was marred in the hand of the potter: so he made it again another vessel, as seemed good to the potter to make *it*.

5 Then the word of the LORD came to me, saying,

6 O house of Israel, cannot I do with you as this *a*potter? saith the LORD. Behold, as the clay *is* in the potter's hand, so *are* ye in mine hand, O house of Israel.

7 At *what* instant I shall speak concerning a nation, and concerning a kingdom, to pluck up, and to *a*pull down, and to destroy *it*;

8 If that nation, against whom I have pronounced, *a*turn from their evil, I will *b*repent of the evil that I thought to do unto them.

9 And at *what* instant I shall speak concerning a nation, and concerning a kingdom, to build and to plant *it*;

10 If it do *a*evil in my sight, that it

18*b* Isa. 40:2; Jer. 16:18.
21*a* TG Sabbath.
23*a* TG Stiffnecked.
25*a* Jer. 22:4.
27*a* Ezek. 22:26; 44:24.
  b OR citadels or great

buildings.
18 2*a* Jer. 19:1 (1–2).
  6*a* Isa. 45:9;
    Rom. 9:21;
    2 Ne. 27:27.
  7*a* Jer. 1:10.

8*a* See JST Jer. 26:13, 19 (Jer.
    26:13 note *a*, 19 note *a*).
    TG Repent.
  b OR relent regarding the
    punishment.
10*a* Alma 9:12.

*b*obey not my voice, then I will *c*repent of the *d*good, wherewith I said I would benefit them.

11 ¶ Now therefore go to, speak to the men of Judah, and to the inhabitants of Jerusalem, saying, Thus saith the LORD; Behold, I frame evil against you, and devise a device against you: return ye now every one from his evil way, and make your ways and your doings good.

12 And they said, There is no *a*hope: but we will *b*walk after our own devices, and we will every one do the imagination of his evil heart.

13 Therefore thus saith the LORD; Ask ye now among the heathen, who hath heard such things: the virgin of Israel hath done a very horrible thing.

14 Will *a man* leave the snow of Lebanon *which cometh* from the rock of the field? *or* shall the cold flowing waters that come from another place be forsaken?

15 Because my people hath *a*forgotten me, they have burned incense to *b*vanity, and they have caused them to stumble in their ways *from* the ancient paths, to walk in *c*paths, *in* a way not cast up;

16 To make their land *a*desolate, *and* a perpetual hissing; every one that passeth thereby shall be astonished, and *b*wag his head.

17 I will scatter them as with an *a*east wind before the enemy; I will shew them the *b*back, and not *c*the face, in the day of their calamity.

18 ¶ Then said they, Come, and let us *a*devise devices against Jeremiah; for the law shall not perish from the priest, nor counsel from the wise, nor the word from the prophet. Come, and let us smite him with the tongue, and let us not give heed to any of his words.

19 Give heed to me, O LORD, and hearken to the voice of them that contend with me.

20 Shall evil be recompensed for good? for they have digged a pit for my soul. Remember that I stood before thee to speak good for them, *and* to turn away thy wrath from them.

21 Therefore deliver up their children to the famine, and pour out their *blood* by the force of the sword; and let their wives be bereaved of their children, and *be* widows; and let their men be put to death; *let* their young men *be* slain by the sword in battle.

22 Let a cry be heard from their houses, when thou shalt bring a troop suddenly upon them: for they have digged a pit to take me, and hid snares for my feet.

23 Yet, LORD, thou knowest all their counsel against me to slay *me:* forgive not their iniquity, neither blot out their sin from thy sight, but let them be overthrown before thee; deal *thus* with them in the time of thine anger.

CHAPTER 19

The Lord will bring evil upon Judah—They sacrifice their children to Baal—In the siege they will eat the flesh of their sons and daughters.

THUS saith the LORD, Go and get a *a*potter's earthen bottle, and *take* of the *b*ancients of the people, and of the ancients of the priests;

2 And go forth unto the valley of the son of *a*Hinnom, which *is* by the entry of the east gate, and proclaim there the words that I shall tell thee,

3 And say, Hear ye the word of the LORD, O kings of Judah, and inhabitants of Jerusalem; Thus saith the LORD of hosts, the God of Israel; Behold, I will bring evil upon this

---

10*b* TG Disobedience.
   c See JST Jer. 26:13, 19
     (Jer. 26:13 note *a*, 19
     note *a*).
   d D&C 56:4 (3–4);
     58:32 (31–33).
12*a* Isa. 57:10;
     Jer. 2:25.

  b TG Walking in Darkness.
15*a* Jer. 2:32.
  b OR idols.
  c Jer. 6:16.
16*a* Jer. 19:8;
     Micah 6:16.
  b Zeph. 2:15.
17*a* Ezek. 17:10; 27:26;

     Mosiah 7:31; 12:6.
  b Jer. 2:27.
  c OR my.
18*a* TG Prophets, Rejection of.
19 1*a* Jer. 18:2.
  b OR elders.
2*a* Josh. 18:16.

place, the which whosoever heareth, his ears shall ᵃtingle.

4 Because they have ᵃforsaken me, and have ᵇestranged this place, and have burned incense in it unto other ᶜgods, whom neither they nor their fathers have known, nor the kings of Judah, and have filled this place with the ᵈblood of innocents;

5 They have built also the high places of Baal, to burn their sons with ᵃfire *for* burnt offerings unto Baal, which I commanded not, nor spake *it*, neither came *it* into my mind:

6 Therefore, behold, the days come, saith the LORD, that this place shall no more be called ᵃTophet, nor The valley of the son of Hinnom, but The valley of slaughter.

7 And I will make void the counsel of Judah and Jerusalem in this place; and I will cause them to fall by the sword before their enemies, and by the hands of them that seek their lives: and their ᵃcarcases will I give to be meat for the fowls of the heaven, and for the beasts of the earth.

8 And I will make this city ᵃdesolate, and an hissing; every one that passeth thereby shall be astonished and hiss because of all the ᵇplagues thereof.

9 And I will cause them to ᵃeat the flesh of their sons and the ᵇflesh of their daughters, and they shall eat every one the flesh of his friend in the siege and straitness, wherewith their enemies, and they that seek their lives, shall ᶜstraiten them.

10 Then shalt thou break the bottle in the sight of the men that go with thee,

11 And shalt say unto them, Thus saith the LORD of hosts; Even so will I break this people and this city, as

one breaketh a potter's vessel, that cannot be made whole again: and they shall bury *them* in Tophet, till *there be* no place to bury.

12 Thus will I do unto this place, saith the LORD, and to the inhabitants thereof, and *even* make this city as Tophet:

13 And the houses of Jerusalem, and the houses of the kings of Judah, shall be defiled as the place of Tophet, because of all the houses upon whose ᵃroofs they have burned incense unto all the host of heaven, and have poured out drink offerings unto other gods.

14 Then came Jeremiah from Tophet, whither the LORD had sent him to prophesy; and he stood in the court of the LORD's house; and said to all the people,

15 Thus saith the LORD of hosts, the God of Israel; Behold, I will bring upon this city and upon all her towns all the evil that I have pronounced against it, because they have hardened their necks, that they might not hear my words.

CHAPTER 20

Jeremiah is smitten and put in the stocks—He prophesies that all Judah will be taken captive by Babylon.

Now ᵃPashur the son of ᵇImmer the priest, who *was* also ᶜchief governor in the house of the LORD, heard that Jeremiah prophesied these things.

2 Then Pashur ᵃsmote Jeremiah the prophet, and put him in the stocks that *were* in the high gate of Benjamin, which *was* by the house of the LORD.

3 And it came to pass on the morrow, that Pashur brought forth Jeremiah out of the stocks. Then

3*a* 1 Sam. 3:11;
    2 Kgs. 21:12.
4*a* Jer. 1:16.
  b OR alienated.
  c TG Idolatry.
  d Jer. 2:34 (31–37).
5*a* Lev. 18:21;
    Jer. 32:35;
    Morm. 4:14.
6*a* 2 Kgs. 23:10.

7*a* Jer. 7:33;
    Alma 16:10.
8*a* Jer. 18:16.
  b TG Plague.
9*a* Lev. 26:29;
    Deut. 28:53;
    Lam. 2:20;
    Ezek. 5:10.
  b Isa. 9:20;
    Lam. 4:10.

  c OR distress or afflict.
13*a* 2 Kgs. 23:12;
    Zeph. 1:5.
20 1*a* Jer. 21:1; 38:1.
   b 1 Chr. 24:14.
   c OR senior officer.
 2*a* 1 Ne. 16:2;
    Hel. 13:24 (24–27).

said Jeremiah unto him, The L<small>ORD</small> hath not called thy name Pashur, but *a*Magor-missabib.

4 For thus saith the L<small>ORD</small>, Behold, I will make thee a terror to thyself, and to all thy friends: and they shall fall by the sword of their enemies, and thine eyes shall behold *it:* and I will give all Judah into the hand of the king of Babylon, and he shall carry them *a*captive into Babylon, and shall slay them with the sword.

5 Moreover I will deliver all the *a*strength of this city, and all the labours thereof, and all the *b*precious things thereof, and all the treasures of the kings of Judah will I give into the hand of their enemies, which shall spoil them, and take them, and carry them to *c*Babylon.

6 And thou, Pashur, and all that dwell in thine house shall go into captivity: and thou shalt come to Babylon, and there thou shalt die, and shalt be buried there, thou, and all thy friends, to whom thou hast prophesied *a*lies.

7 ¶ O L<small>ORD</small>, thou hast *a*deceived me, and I was deceived: thou art stronger than I, and hast prevailed: I am in *b*derision daily, every one mocketh me.

8 For since I spake, I cried out, I cried *a*violence and spoil; because the word of the L<small>ORD</small> was made a reproach unto me, and a derision, daily.

9 Then I said, I will not make mention of him, nor speak any more in his name. But *his word* was in mine heart as a *a*burning fire shut up in my bones, and I was weary with forbearing, and I could not *b*stay.

10 ¶ For I heard the *a*defaming of many, fear on every side. Report, *say they,* and we will report it. All my *b*familiars watched for my halting, *saying,* Peradventure he will be enticed, and we shall prevail against him, and we shall take our revenge on him.

11 But the L<small>ORD</small> *is* with me as a mighty terrible one: therefore my persecutors shall stumble, and they shall not *a*prevail: they shall be greatly ashamed; for they shall not prosper: *their* everlasting *b*confusion shall never be forgotten.

12 But, O L<small>ORD</small> of hosts, that *a*triest the righteous, *and* seest the *b*reins and the heart, let me see thy vengeance on them: for unto thee have I opened my cause.

13 Sing unto the L<small>ORD</small>, praise ye the L<small>ORD</small>: for he hath delivered the soul of the poor from the hand of evildoers.

14 ¶ *a*Cursed *be* the day wherein I was born: let not the day wherein my mother bare me be blessed.

15 Cursed *be* the man who brought tidings to my father, saying, A man child is born unto thee; making him very glad.

16 And let that man be as the cities which the L<small>ORD</small> *a*overthrew, and repented not: and let him hear the cry in the morning, and the shouting at noontide;

17 Because he slew me not from the womb; or that my mother might have been my grave, and her womb *to be* always great *with me.*

18 Wherefore came I forth out of the womb to see labour and *a*sorrow, that my days should be consumed with shame?

CHAPTER 21

Jeremiah foretells the siege, captivity, and destruction of Jerusalem— Zedekiah is to be taken captive by Nebuchadrezzar.

T<small>HE</small> word which came unto *a*Jeremiah from the L<small>ORD</small>, when king

---

3*a* IE Terror all around.
4*a* 1 Ne. 1:13 (11–14).
5*a* HEB provision or goods.
 b Ezek. 22:25.
 c 2 Kgs. 24:12 (12–16);
  25:13 (13–17).
6*a* TG Lying.
7*a* HEB persuaded.

b Lam. 3:14.
 TG Despair;
 Suffering.
8*a* Jer. 6:7.
9*a* Ps. 39:3; 3 Ne. 11:3.
 b Acts 4:20; Ether 12:2.
10*a* Ps. 31:13.
 b OR familiar friends.

11*a* TG Protection, Divine.
 b OR disgrace.
12*a* TG Test.
 b HEB inward parts.
14*a* Job 3:3 (3–4).
16*a* Isa. 13:19 (19–20).
18*a* TG Sorrow.
21 1*a* 2 Chr. 36:12 (10–13).

Zedekiah sent unto him [b]Pashur the son of Melchiah, and Zephaniah the son of Maaseiah the priest, saying,

2 Inquire, I pray thee, of the LORD for us; for [a]Nebuchadrezzar king of Babylon maketh war against us; if so be that the LORD will deal with us according to all his wondrous works, that he may go up from us.

3 ¶ Then said Jeremiah unto them, Thus shall ye say to Zedekiah:

4 Thus saith the LORD God of Israel; Behold, I will turn back the weapons of war that *are* in your hands, wherewith ye fight against the king of Babylon, and *against* the Chaldeans, which besiege you [a]without the walls, and I will assemble them into the midst of this city.

5 And I myself will fight against you with an [a]outstretched hand and with a strong arm, even in anger, and in fury, and in great wrath.

6 And I will smite the inhabitants of this city, both man and beast: they shall die of a great pestilence.

7 And afterward, saith the LORD, I will deliver [a]Zedekiah king of Judah, and his servants, and the people, and such as are left in this city from the pestilence, from the sword, and from the famine, into the hand of Nebuchadrezzar king of [b]Babylon, and into the hand of their enemies, and into the hand of those that seek their life: and he shall smite them with the edge of the sword; he shall not [c]spare them, neither have pity, nor have mercy.

8 ¶ And unto this people thou shalt say, Thus saith the LORD; Behold, I set before you the way of [a]life, and the way of death.

9 He that abideth in this city shall die by the sword, and by the famine, and by the pestilence: but he that goeth out, and [a]falleth to the Chaldeans that besiege you, he shall live, and his [b]life shall be unto him for a prey.

10 For I have set my [a]face against this city for [b]evil, and not for good, saith the LORD: it shall be given into the hand of the king of [c]Babylon, and he shall burn it with fire.

11 ¶ And touching the house of the king of Judah, *say,* Hear ye the word of the LORD;

12 O house of David, thus saith the LORD; Execute judgment in the morning, and deliver *him that is* spoiled out of the hand of the oppressor, lest my fury go out like fire, and burn that none can quench *it,* because of the evil of your doings.

13 Behold, I *am* against thee, O inhabitant of the valley, *and* rock of the plain, saith the LORD; which say, [a]Who shall come down against us? or who shall enter into our habitations?

14 But I will punish you according to the fruit of your doings, saith the LORD: and I will kindle a fire in the forest thereof, and it shall devour all things round about it.

CHAPTER 22

David's throne stands or falls according to the obedience of the kings—The judgments of the Lord rest upon the kings of Judah.

THUS saith the LORD; Go down to the house of the king of Judah, and speak there this word,

2 And say, Hear the word of the LORD, O king of Judah, that sittest upon the throne of David, thou, and thy servants, and thy people that enter in by these gates:

3 Thus saith the LORD; Execute ye [a]judgment and righteousness, and deliver the spoiled out of the hand of the oppressor: and do no wrong, do no violence to the [b]stranger, the

---

1 b Jer. 20:1; 38:1.
2 a 2 Kgs. 25:1;
　　Jer. 43:10.
4 a OR outside.
5 a Deut. 4:34.
7 a 1 Ne. 1:4 (4, 13).
　　b TG Israel, Bondage of, in

Other Lands.
　c Deut. 28:50.
8 a Deut. 30:15;
　　Matt. 7:14 (13–14);
　　1 Ne. 14:7.
9 a OR surrenders.
　b Jer. 39:18; 45:5.

10 a Lev. 20:5;
　　Jer. 44:11.
　b Amos 9:4.
　c Jer. 34:2; 38:3; 52:13.
13 a 2 Ne. 28:21 (21–25).
22 3 a TG Justice.
　b Jer. 7:6.

fatherless, nor the widow, neither shed innocent ᶜblood in this place.

4 For if ye do this thing indeed, then shall there enter in by the gates of this house ᵃkings sitting upon the throne of David, riding in chariots and on horses, he, and his servants, and his people.

5 But if ye will not hear these words, I ᵃswear by myself, saith the LORD, that this house shall become a ᵇdesolation.

6 For thus saith the LORD unto the king's house of Judah; Thou *art* Gilead unto me, *and* the head of Lebanon: *yet* surely I will make thee a wilderness, *and* cities *which* are not inhabited.

7 And I will prepare destroyers against thee, every one with his weapons: and they shall cut down thy choice ᵃcedars, and cast *them* into the fire.

8 And many nations shall pass by this city, and they shall say every man to his neighbour, Wherefore hath the LORD ᵃdone thus unto this great city?

9 Then they shall answer, Because they have ᵃforsaken the covenant of the LORD their God, and worshipped other gods, and served them.

10 ¶ Weep ye not for the dead, neither bemoan him: *but* weep sore for him that goeth away: for he shall return no more, nor see his native country.

11 For thus saith the LORD touching ᵃShallum the son of Josiah king of Judah, which reigned instead of Josiah his father, which went forth out of this place; He shall not return thither any more:

12 But he shall die in the place whither they have led him captive, and shall see this land no more.

13 ¶ ᵃWoe unto him that buildeth his house by ᵇunrighteousness, and his chambers by wrong; *that* useth

his neighbour's service without ᶜwages, and giveth him not for his work;

14 That saith, I will build me a wide house and large chambers, and cutteth him out windows; and *it is* ceiled with cedar, and painted with vermilion.

15 Shalt thou reign, because thou closest *thyself* in cedar? did not thy ᵃfather eat and drink, and do judgment and justice, *and* then *it was* well with him?

16 He judged the cause of the poor and needy; then *it was* well *with him: was* not this to know me? saith the LORD.

17 But thine eyes and thine heart *are* not but for thy covetousness, and for to shed innocent blood, and for oppression, and for violence, to do *it*.

18 Therefore thus saith the LORD concerning Jehoiakim the son of Josiah king of Judah; They shall not lament for him, *saying*, Ah my brother! or, Ah sister! they shall not lament for him, *saying*, Ah lord! or, Ah his glory!

19 He shall be ᵃburied with the burial of an ass, drawn and cast forth beyond the gates of Jerusalem.

20 ¶ Go up to Lebanon, and cry; and lift up thy voice in Bashan, and cry from the passages: for all thy lovers are destroyed.

21 I spake unto thee in thy prosperity; *but* thou saidst, I will not hear. This *hath been* thy manner from thy youth, that thou ᵃobeyedst not my voice.

22 The wind shall eat up all thy pastors, and thy ᵃlovers shall go into captivity: surely then shalt thou be ashamed and confounded for all thy wickedness.

23 O inhabitant of Lebanon, that makest thy nest in the cedars, how ᵃgracious shalt thou be when pangs

3c D&C 132:19.
4a Jer. 17:25.
5a Amos 6:8.
  b Ps. 69:25;
    Jer. 12:7;
    Matt. 23:38;
    Luke 13:35.
7a Isa. 37:24.
8a 1 Kgs. 9:8.
9a Deut. 29:25.
11a 1 Chr. 3:15.
13a James 5:4 (1–6).
  b 2 Kgs. 23:37;
    Ezek. 19:6.
c TG Wages.
15a 2 Kgs. 23:25.
19a Eccl. 6:3.
21a TG Disobedience.
22a Lam. 1:2.
23a HEB pitied.

come upon thee, the pain as of a woman in travail!

24 *As* I live, saith the LORD, though ᵃConiah the son of ᵇJehoiakim king of Judah were the signet upon my right hand, yet would I pluck thee thence;

25 And I will ᵃgive thee into the hand of them that seek thy life, and into the hand *of them* whose face thou fearest, even into the hand of Nebuchadrezzar king of Babylon, and into the hand of the Chaldeans.

26 And I will cast thee out, and thy mother that bare thee, into another country, where ye were not born; and there shall ye die.

27 But to the land whereunto they desire to return, thither shall they not return.

28 *Is* this man Coniah a despised broken idol? *is he* a ᵃvessel wherein *is* no pleasure? wherefore are they cast out, he and his seed, and are cast into a land which they know not?

29 O earth, earth, earth, hear the ᵃword of the LORD.

30 Thus saith the LORD, ᵃWrite ye this man childless, a man *that* shall not prosper in his days: for no man of his seed shall prosper, sitting upon the throne of David, and ruling any more in Judah.

CHAPTER 23

The remnants of Israel will be gathered in the last days—The Branch, who is the King (the Messiah), will reign in righteousness—False prophets who teach lies will be cursed.

WOE be unto the ᵃpastors that destroy and scatter the sheep of my pasture! saith the LORD.

2 Therefore thus saith the LORD God of Israel against the pastors that feed my people; Ye have scattered my flock, and driven them away, and have not ᵃvisited them: behold, I will visit upon you the evil of your doings, saith the LORD.

3 And I will ᵃgather the ᵇremnant of my flock out of all countries whither I have driven them, and will bring them again to their folds; and they shall be fruitful and increase.

4 And I will set up ᵃshepherds over them which shall feed them: and they shall fear no more, nor be dismayed, neither shall they be lacking, saith the LORD.

5 ¶ Behold, the days come, saith the LORD, that I will raise unto ᵃDavid a righteous ᵇBranch, and a ᶜKing shall ᵈreign and prosper, and shall execute ᵉjudgment and ᶠjustice in the earth.

6 In his days Judah shall be saved, and Israel shall dwell ᵃsafely: and this *is* his name whereby he shall be called, THE LORD OUR ᵇRIGHTEOUSNESS.

7 Therefore, behold, the days come, saith the LORD, that they shall no more say, The LORD liveth, which brought up the children of Israel out of the land of Egypt;

8 But, The LORD liveth, which brought up and which led the seed of the house of Israel out of the ᵃnorth country, and from all countries whither I had driven them; and they shall dwell in their own land.

9 ¶ Mine ᵃheart within me is broken because of the prophets; all my bones shake; I am like a drunken man, and like a man whom wine

---

24a Jer. 37:1.
  b 2 Kgs. 24:6;
    1 Chr. 3:16.
25a Jer. 34:20.
28a Ps. 31:12; Jer. 48:38;
    Hosea 8:8.
29a D&C 1:2 (1–2).
30a TG Record Keeping.
23 1a Jer. 25:34;
    Zech. 11:17.
  2a IE been mindful of.
  3a TG Israel, Gathering of.

  b TG Israel, Remnant of.
4a TG Bishop; Shepherd.
5a TG Jesus Christ, Davidic
    Descent of.
  b Isa. 4:2; 11:1; 32:1;
    Jer. 30:9;
    Ezek. 34:24 (23–24).
    TG Jesus Christ,
    Prophecies about.
  c Matt. 2:2.
    TG Jesus Christ,
    Authority of.

  d TG Jesus Christ,
    Millennial Reign.
  e TG Jesus Christ, Judge;
    Judgment.
  f TG God, Justice of;
    Justice.
6a Deut. 33:28;
    Ezek. 28:26.
  b TG Righteousness.
8a TG Israel, Ten Lost
    Tribes of.
9a Ps. 22:14.

hath overcome, because of the Lord, and because of the words of his holiness.

10 For the land is full of ^aadulterers; for because of ^bswearing the land mourneth; the pleasant places of the wilderness are dried up, and their course is evil, and their force *is* not right.

11 For both ^aprophet and ^bpriest are ^cprofane; yea, in my ^dhouse have I found their wickedness, saith the Lord.

12 Wherefore their way shall be unto them as slippery *ways* in the darkness: they shall be driven on, and fall therein: for I will bring evil upon them, *even* the year of their ^avisitation, saith the Lord.

13 And I have seen folly in the prophets of Samaria; they prophesied in Baal, and caused my people Israel to err.

14 I have seen also in the prophets of Jerusalem an horrible thing: they commit ^aadultery, and walk in lies: they strengthen also the hands of evildoers, that none doth return from his ^bwickedness: they are all of them unto me as Sodom, and the inhabitants thereof as Gomorrah.

15 Therefore thus saith the Lord of hosts concerning the prophets; Behold, I will feed them with wormwood, and make them drink the water of gall: for from the prophets of Jerusalem is ^aprofaneness gone forth into all the land.

16 Thus saith the Lord of hosts, Hearken not unto the words of the prophets that ^aprophesy unto you: they make you vain: they speak a ^bvision of their own heart, *and* not out of the mouth of the Lord.

17 They say still unto them that despise me, The Lord hath said, Ye shall have peace; and they say unto every one that walketh after the imagination of his own heart, No evil shall come upon you.

18 For who hath stood in the counsel of the Lord, and hath perceived and heard his word? who hath marked his word, and heard *it?*

19 Behold, a ^awhirlwind of the Lord is gone forth in fury, even a grievous whirlwind: it shall fall grievously upon the head of the wicked.

20 The anger of the Lord shall not return, until he have executed, and till he have performed the thoughts of his heart: in the latter days ye shall consider it perfectly.

21 I have not ^asent these ^bprophets, yet they ran: I have not spoken to them, yet they prophesied.

22 But if they had stood in my counsel, and had caused my people to hear my words, then they should have turned them from their evil way, and from the evil of their doings.

23 *Am* I a God at hand, saith the Lord, and not a God afar off?

24 Can any ^ahide himself in secret places that I shall not see him? saith the Lord. Do not I ^bfill heaven and earth? saith the Lord.

25 I have heard what the prophets said, that ^aprophesy lies in my name, saying, I have dreamed, I have dreamed.

26 How long shall *this* be in the heart of the prophets that prophesy lies? yea, *they are* prophets of the deceit of their own heart;

27 Which think to cause my people to forget my name by their dreams which they tell every man to his neighbour, as their fathers have forgotten my name for Baal.

28 The prophet that hath a dream, let him tell a dream; and he that hath my word, let him speak my word faithfully. What *is* the chaff to the wheat? saith the Lord.

10a TG Apostasy of Israel.
  b OR cursing.
    TG Swearing.
11a TG False Prophets.
  b D&C 1:16 (15–16).
    TG Priestcraft.
  c OR irreligious.
  d 1 Chr. 17:14;

D&C 124:145.
12a OR punishment.
14a TG Adulterer.
  b Ezek. 16:50 (49–50).
15a OR ungodliness.
16a TG False Prophets.
  b TG False Doctrine.
19a 3 Ne. 21:21 (20–21).

21a TG Authority.
  b 2 Ne. 28:12 (9, 12, 15);
    3 Ne. 14:15.
    TG Superstitions.
24a Ps. 139:7 (1–16).
  b D&C 88:12 (7–13).
25a Matt. 7:22 (21–23).

29 *Is* not my word like as a fire? saith the LORD; and like a hammer *that* breaketh the rock in pieces?

30 Therefore, behold, I *am* against the prophets, saith the LORD, that steal my words every one from his neighbour.

31 Behold, I *am* against the prophets, saith the LORD, that use their tongues, and say, He saith.

32 Behold, I *am* against them that prophesy false [a]dreams, saith the LORD, and do tell them, and cause my people to err by their lies, and by their lightness; yet I sent them not, nor commanded them: therefore they shall not profit this people at all, saith the LORD.

33 ¶ And when this people, or the prophet, or a priest, shall ask thee, saying, What *is* the [a]burden of the LORD? thou shalt then say unto them, What burden? I will even forsake you, saith the LORD.

34 And *as for* the prophet, and the priest, and the people, that shall say, The burden of the LORD, I will even punish that man and his house.

35 Thus shall ye say every one to his neighbour, and every one to his brother, What hath the LORD answered? and, What hath the LORD spoken?

36 And the burden of the LORD shall ye mention no more: for every man's word shall be his burden; for ye have perverted the [a]words of the living God, of the LORD of hosts our God.

37 Thus shalt thou say to the prophet, What hath the LORD answered thee? and, What hath the LORD spoken?

38 But since ye say, The burden of the LORD; therefore thus saith the LORD; Because ye say this word, The burden of the LORD, and I have sent unto you, saying, Ye shall not say, The burden of the LORD;

39 Therefore, behold, I, even I, will utterly forget you, and I will forsake you, and the city that I gave you and your fathers, *and cast you* out of my presence:

40 And I will bring an everlasting [a]reproach upon you, and a perpetual shame, which shall not be forgotten.

CHAPTER 24

Zedekiah and the people of Judah will be cursed and scattered—Some will be gathered back from Chaldea to serve the Lord.

THE LORD shewed me, and, behold, two baskets of figs *were* set before the temple of the LORD, after that Nebuchadrezzar king of Babylon had carried away captive Jeconiah the son of [a]Jehoiakim king of Judah, and the [b]princes of Judah, with the carpenters and smiths, from Jerusalem, and had brought them to [c]Babylon.

2 One basket *had* very good figs, *even* like the [a]figs *that are* first ripe: and the other basket *had* very [b]naughty figs, which could not be eaten, they were so bad.

3 Then said the LORD unto me, What seest thou, Jeremiah? And I said, Figs; the good figs, very good; and the evil, very evil, that cannot be eaten, they are so evil.

4 ¶ Again the word of the LORD came unto me, saying,

5 Thus saith the LORD, the God of Israel; Like these good figs, so will I acknowledge them that are carried away captive of Judah, whom I have sent out of this place into the land of the Chaldeans for *their* [a]good.

6 For I will set mine eyes upon them for good, and I will [a]bring them again to this [b]land: and I will build them, and not pull *them* down; and I will [c]plant them, and not pluck *them* up.

7 And I will give them an [a]heart to

32*a* TG Dream.
33*a* OR prophecy.
36*a* D&C 50:1.
40*a* 3 Ne. 16:9.
24 1*a* Jer. 27:20.
　　b OR governors or

officers.
　　Jer. 29:2.
　c 2 Kgs. 24:15 (14–15).
2*a* Hosea 9:10.
　b HEB bad or corrupted.
5*a* D&C 122:7.

6*a* Jer. 16:15.
　b 2 Ne. 25:11 (11–17).
　c Jacob 5:56 (56–60).
7*a* TG Man, New,
　　Spiritually Reborn.

know me, that I *am* the LORD: and they shall be my people, and I will be their God: for they shall return unto me with their whole heart.

8 ¶ And as the evil figs, which cannot be eaten, they are so evil; surely thus saith the LORD, So will I give Zedekiah the king of Judah, and his princes, and the *ª*residue of Jerusalem, that remain in this land, and them that dwell in the land of Egypt:

9 And I will deliver them to be removed into all the kingdoms of the earth for *their* hurt, *to be* a *ª*reproach and a proverb, a taunt and a *ᵇ*curse, in all places whither I shall drive them.

10 And I will send the sword, the *ª*famine, and the pestilence, among them, till they be *ᵇ*consumed from off the land that I gave unto them and to their fathers.

CHAPTER 25

Captive Judah will serve Babylon for seventy years—Various nations will be overthrown—In the last days, all the inhabitants of the earth will be at war.

THE word that came to Jeremiah concerning all the people of Judah in the fourth year of Jehoiakim the son of Josiah king of Judah, that *was* the first year of Nebuchadrezzar king of Babylon;

2 The which Jeremiah the prophet spake unto all the people of Judah, and to all the inhabitants of Jerusalem, saying,

3 From the thirteenth *ª*year of Josiah the son of Amon king of Judah, even unto this day, that *is* the three and twentieth year, the word of the LORD hath come unto me, and I have spoken unto you, rising early and speaking; but ye have not hearkened.

4 And the LORD hath sent unto you all his servants the *ª*prophets, rising early and sending *them;* but ye have not hearkened, nor inclined your ear to hear.

5 They said, Turn ye again now every one from his evil way, and from the evil of your doings, and dwell in the land that the LORD hath given unto you and to your fathers for ever and ever:

6 And go not after other gods to serve them, and to worship them, and provoke me not to anger with the works of your hands; and I will do you no hurt.

7 Yet ye have not hearkened unto me, saith the LORD; that ye might provoke me to anger with the works of your hands to your own hurt.

8 ¶ Therefore thus saith the LORD of hosts; Because ye have not *ª*heard my words,

9 Behold, I will *ª*send and take all the families of the north, saith the LORD, and *ᵇ*Nebuchadrezzar the king of *ᶜ*Babylon, my servant, and will bring them against this land, and against the inhabitants thereof, and against all these nations round about, and will utterly *ᵈ*destroy them, and make them an astonishment, and an hissing, and perpetual desolations.

10 Moreover I will take from them the voice of *ª*mirth, and the voice of gladness, the voice of the bridegroom, and the voice of the bride, the sound of the millstones, and the light of the candle.

11 And this whole land shall be a desolation, *and* an astonishment; and these nations shall serve the *ª*king of Babylon *ᵇ*seventy years.

12 ¶ And it shall come to pass, when *ª*seventy years are accomplished, *that* I will *ᵇ*punish the king of Babylon, and that nation, saith

---

8*a* OR remnant.
9*a* Deut. 28:37;
  Ezek. 5:15 (14–15);
  Joel 2:17 (17–19);
  Micah 6:16;
  1 Ne. 19:14 (13–16).
  b Jer. 26:6.
10*a* D&C 43:25 (25–26).

b Micah 6:16.
25 3*a* Jer. 1:2; 36:2.
  4*a* Jer. 26:5;
    1 Ne. 1:19 (13–19).
  8*a* OR obeyed.
  9*a* IE send for.
    b Jer. 43:10.
    c TG Israel, Bondage of,

  in Other Lands.
  d 2 Kgs. 24:2.
10*a* Jer. 7:34; 16:9.
11*a* Jer. 28:14.
  b Jer. 29:10.
12*a* 2 Chr. 36:21;
  Dan. 9:2.
  b Dan. 5:26.

the LORD, for their iniquity, and the land of the Chaldeans, and will make it perpetual desolations.

13 And I will bring upon that land all my words which I have pronounced against it, *even* all that is written in this book, which Jeremiah hath prophesied against all the nations.

14 For many nations and great kings shall *a*serve themselves of them also: and I will recompense them according to their deeds, and according to the works of their own hands.

15 ¶ For thus saith the LORD God of Israel unto me; Take the wine *a*cup of this fury at my hand, and cause all the *b*nations, to whom I send thee, to drink it.

16 And they shall drink, and be moved, and be mad, because of the sword that I will send among them.

17 Then took I the *a*cup at the LORD's hand, and made all the nations to drink, unto whom the LORD had sent me:

18 *aTo wit,* Jerusalem, and the cities of Judah, and the kings thereof, and the princes thereof, to make them a desolation, an astonishment, an hissing, and a curse; as *it is* this day;

19 *a*Pharaoh king of *b*Egypt, and his servants, and his princes, and all his people;

20 And all the *a*mingled people, and all the kings of the land of Uz, and all the kings of the land of the *b*Philistines, and Ashkelon, and Azzah, and Ekron, and the remnant of Ashdod,

21 *a*Edom, and *b*Moab, and the children of Ammon,

22 And all the kings of *a*Tyrus, and all the kings of *b*Zidon, and the kings of the isles which *are* beyond the sea,

23 Dedan, and Tema, and Buz, and all *that are* in the *a*utmost corners,

24 And all the kings of Arabia, and all the kings of the mingled people that dwell in the desert,

25 And all the kings of Zimri, and all the kings of Elam, and all the kings of the Medes,

26 And all the kings of the *a*north, far and near, one with another, and all the kingdoms of the world, which *are* upon the face of the earth: and the king of *b*Sheshach shall drink after them.

27 Therefore thou shalt say unto them, Thus saith the LORD of hosts, the God of Israel; Drink ye, and be *a*drunken, and spue, and fall, and rise no more, because of the sword which I will send among you.

28 And it shall be, if they refuse to take the cup at thine hand to *a*drink, then shalt thou say unto them, Thus saith the LORD of hosts; Ye shall certainly drink.

29 For, lo, I *a*begin to bring evil on the city which is called by my name, and should ye be utterly unpunished? Ye shall not be unpunished: for I will call for a sword upon all the inhabitants of the earth, saith the LORD of hosts.

30 Therefore prophesy thou against them all these words, and say unto them, The LORD shall roar from on high, and utter his voice from his holy habitation; he shall mightily *a*roar upon his habitation; he shall give a shout, as they that tread *the grapes,* against all the inhabitants of the earth.

31 A noise shall come *even* to the ends of the earth; for the LORD hath a *a*controversy with the nations, he will *b*plead with all flesh; he will give them *that are* wicked to the sword, saith the LORD.

14a OR enslave them.
15a Isa. 51:17; Lam. 4:21;
    Ezek. 23:31;
    2 Ne. 8:17; Mosiah 3:26;
    D&C 29:17.
  b Jer. 1:5; 46:1.
17a Isa. 51:23.
18a OR Namely.
19a Jer. 46:25 (2, 25).

  b Isa. 19:1; Ezek. 29:2.
20a Jer. 50:37.
  b Jer. 47:1.
21a Jer. 9:26; 27:3; 49:7.
  b Jer. 48:1.
22a Jer. 47:4.
  b Isa. 23:4 (4–12);
    Ezek. 28:21.
23a Jer. 9:26.

26a Jer. 50:9.
  b Jer. 51:41.
27a Jer. 48:26.
28a Obad. 1:16.
29a Ezek. 9:6.
30a Joel 3:16; Amos 1:2.
31a Hosea 4:1.
  b Isa. 66:16;
    Ezek. 38:22; Joel 3:2.

32 Thus saith the LORD of hosts, Behold, evil shall go forth from nation to nation, and a great *a*whirlwind shall be raised up from the coasts of the earth.

33 And the *a*slain of the LORD shall be at that day from *one* end of the earth even unto the *other* end of the earth: they shall not be *b*lamented, neither gathered, nor *c*buried; they shall be dung upon the ground.

34 ¶ Howl, ye *a*shepherds, and cry; and wallow yourselves *in the ashes,* ye principal of the flock: for the days of your slaughter and of your *b*dispersions are accomplished; and ye shall fall like a pleasant vessel.

35 And the shepherds shall have no way to flee, nor the principal of the flock to escape.

36 A voice of the cry of the shepherds, and an howling of the principal of the flock, *shall be heard:* for the LORD hath spoiled their pasture.

37 And the peaceable habitations are cut down because of the fierce anger of the LORD.

38 He hath forsaken his covert, as the lion: for their land is desolate because of the fierceness of the oppressor, and because of his fierce anger.

CHAPTER 26

Jeremiah prophesies the destruction of the people—For this he is arraigned, tried, and then acquitted.

IN the beginning of the reign of *a*Jehoiakim the son of Josiah king of Judah came this word from the LORD, saying,

2 Thus saith the LORD; Stand in the court of the LORD's house, and speak unto all the cities of Judah, which come to worship in the LORD's house, all the words that I command thee to speak unto them; *a*diminish not a word:

3 If so be they will hearken, and turn every man from his evil way, that I may *a*repent me of the evil, which I purpose to do unto them because of the evil of their doings.

4 And thou shalt say unto them, Thus saith the LORD; If ye will not *a*hearken to me, to *b*walk in my *c*law, which I have set before you,

5 To hearken to the words of my servants the *a*prophets, whom I sent unto you, both rising up early, and sending *them,* but ye have not hearkened;

6 Then will I make this house like *a*Shiloh, and will make this city a *b*curse to all the nations of the *c*earth.

7 So the priests and the prophets and all the people heard Jeremiah speaking these words in the house of the LORD.

8 ¶ Now it came to pass, when Jeremiah had made an end of speaking all that the LORD had commanded *him* to speak unto all the people, that the priests and the prophets and all the people took him, saying, Thou shalt surely *a*die.

9 Why hast thou prophesied in the name of the LORD, saying, This house shall be like Shiloh, and this city shall be *a*desolate without an inhabitant? And all the people were gathered against Jeremiah in the house of the LORD.

10 ¶ When the *a*princes of Judah heard these things, then they came up from the king's house unto the house of the LORD, and sat down in the entry of the new gate of the LORD's *house.*

11 Then spake the priests and the

32*a* OR storm.
33*a* Isa. 66:16.
  b TG Mourning.
  c Jer. 8:2.
34*a* Jer. 23:1.
  b Ezek. 36:19.
26 1*a* Jer. 26:21; 27:1.
  2*a* D&C 28:3.
  3*a* HEB relent; i.e., change the decreed punish-

ment because of their changed behavior.
4*a* Lev. 26:14; Deut. 28:15; Alma 5:37 (37–38); D&C 5:5.
  b TG Walking with God.
  c D&C 41:5; 42:2; 130:20.
5*a* Jer. 25:4; 2 Ne. 27:5; Jacob 6:8; Ether 7:24.

6*a* Jer. 7:12.
  b Jer. 24:9; 1 Ne. 19:14.
  c JST Jer. 26:6 . . . earth; *for ye have not hearkened unto my servants the prophets.*
8*a* TG Prophets, Rejection of.
9*a* TG Apostasy of Israel.
10*a* HEB officers, or rulers.

prophets unto the princes and to all the people, saying, This man *is* worthy to die; for he hath *a*prophesied against this city, as ye have heard with your ears.

12 ¶ Then spake Jeremiah unto all the princes and to all the people, saying, The Lord sent me to prophesy against this house and against this city all the words that ye have heard.

13 Therefore now amend your ways and your doings, and obey the voice of the Lord your God; *a*and the Lord will repent him of the evil that he hath pronounced against you.

14 As for me, behold, I *am* in your *a*hand: do with me as seemeth good and meet unto you.

15 But know ye for certain, that if ye put me to death, ye shall surely bring *a*innocent blood upon yourselves, and upon this city, and upon the inhabitants thereof: for of a truth the Lord hath sent me unto you to speak all these words in your ears.

16 ¶ Then said the princes and all the people unto the priests and to the prophets; This man *is* not worthy to die: for he hath spoken to us in the name of the Lord our God.

17 Then rose up certain of the elders of the land, and spake to all the assembly of the people, saying,

18 *a*Micah the Morasthite prophesied in the days of Hezekiah king of Judah, and spake to all the people of Judah, saying, Thus saith the Lord of hosts; Zion shall be *b*plowed *like* a field, and *c*Jerusalem shall become heaps, and the mountain of the house as the high places of a forest.

19 Did Hezekiah king of Judah and all Judah put him at all to death?

did he not fear the Lord, *a*and besought the Lord, and the Lord repented him of the evil which he had pronounced against them? Thus might we procure great evil against our souls.

20 And there was also a man that prophesied in the name of the Lord, Urijah the son of Shemaiah of Kirjath-jearim, who *a*prophesied against this city and against this land according to all the words of Jeremiah:

21 And when *a*Jehoiakim the king, with all his mighty men, and all the princes, heard his words, the king sought to put him to death: but when Urijah heard it, he was afraid, and fled, and went into Egypt;

22 And Jehoiakim the king sent men into Egypt, *namely*, *a*Elnathan the son of Achbor, and *certain* men with him into Egypt.

23 And they fetched forth Urijah out of Egypt, and brought him unto Jehoiakim the king; who *a*slew him with the sword, and cast his dead body into the graves of the common people.

24 Nevertheless the hand of *a*Ahikam the son of *b*Shaphan was with Jeremiah, that they should not give him into the hand of the people to put him to death.

CHAPTER 27

The Lord sends word to many nations that they are to serve Babylon—The vessels of the Lord's house will go into Babylon.

In the beginning of the reign of *a*Jehoiakim the son of Josiah king of Judah came this word unto Jeremiah from the Lord, saying,

---

11a Jer. 38:4;
　　Mosiah 17:1.
13a JST Jer. 26:13 . . . *and*
　　repent, and the Lord will
　　turn away the evil . . .
14a Mosiah 13:10 (5–35).
15a Mosiah 17:10.
18a Micah 1:1.
　b Micah 3:12.
　c 1 Ne. 1:4 (4–18);

2 Ne. 1:4;
　　Hel. 8:20.
19a JST Jer. 26:19 . . .
　　and beseech the Lord
　　and repent? and the
　　Lord *turned away* the
　　evil which he had
　　pronounced against
　　them. Thus *by putting*
　　Jeremiah to death we

might procure great
　　evil against our souls.
20a 1 Ne. 1:4.
21a Jer. 26:1.
22a Jer. 36:12.
23a 1 Ne. 3:18 (17–18).
24a 2 Kgs. 22:12.
　b 2 Chr. 34:8;
　　Jer. 36:10.
27 1a Jer. 26:1 (1, 21).

2 Thus saith the LORD to me; Make thee bonds and *a*yokes, and put them upon thy neck,

3 And send them to the *a*king of *b*Edom, and to the king of Moab, and to the king of the Ammonites, and to the king of Tyrus, and to the king of *c*Zidon, by the hand of the messengers which come to Jerusalem unto Zedekiah king of Judah;

4 And command them to say unto their masters, Thus saith the LORD of hosts, the God of Israel; Thus shall ye say unto your masters;

5 I have made the *a*earth, the man and the beast that *are* upon the ground, by my great power and by my outstretched arm, and have *b*given it unto whom it seemed meet unto me.

6 And now have I *a*given all these lands into the hand of Nebuchadnezzar the king of Babylon, my servant; and the *b*beasts of the field have I given him also to serve him.

7 And all *a*nations shall serve him, and his son, and his son's son, until the very time of his land come: and then many nations and great kings shall *b*serve themselves of him.

8 And it shall come to pass, *that* the nation and kingdom which will not serve the same Nebuchadnezzar the king of Babylon, and that will not put their neck under the yoke of the king of Babylon, that nation will I punish, saith the LORD, with the sword, and with the famine, and with the pestilence, until I have consumed them by his hand.

9 Therefore hearken not ye to your prophets, nor to your *a*diviners, nor to your dreamers, nor to your enchanters, nor to your *b*sorcerers, which speak unto you, saying, Ye shall not serve the king of Babylon:

10 For they prophesy a *a*lie unto you, to remove you far from your land; and that I should drive you out, and ye should perish.

11 But the nations that bring their neck under the *a*yoke of the king of Babylon, and serve him, those will I let remain still in their own land, saith the LORD; and they shall till it, and dwell therein.

12 ¶ I spake also to Zedekiah king of Judah according to all these words, saying, Bring your necks under the yoke of the king of *a*Babylon, and serve him and his people, and live.

13 Why will ye die, thou and thy people, by the sword, by the famine, and by the pestilence, as the LORD hath spoken against the nation that will not serve the king of Babylon?

14 Therefore hearken not unto the words of the prophets that speak unto you, saying, Ye shall not serve the king of Babylon: for they prophesy a lie unto you.

15 For I have not sent them, saith the LORD, yet they *a*prophesy a lie in my name; that I might drive you out, and that ye might perish, ye, and the prophets that prophesy unto you.

16 Also I spake to the priests and to all this people, saying, Thus saith the LORD; Hearken not to the words of your prophets that prophesy unto you, saying, Behold, the *a*vessels of the LORD's house shall now shortly be brought again from Babylon: for they prophesy a lie unto you.

17 Hearken not unto them; serve the king of *a*Babylon, and live: wherefore should this city be laid *b*waste?

18 But if they *be* prophets, and if the word of the LORD be with them, let them now make *a*intercession to the LORD of hosts, that the vessels which are left in the house of the LORD, and *in* the house of the king of

2*a* Jer. 28:10 (10–13).
3*a* Jer. 52:32.
  b Jer. 25:21.
  c Ezek. 28:21.
5*a* 1 Ne. 17:36 (36–37).
  b Ps. 75:6 (6–7);
     Dan. 2:21; 5:20 (18–20).
6*a* D&C 134:1.

  b Jer. 28:14.
7*a* Dan. 4:22.
  b OR make him subservient.
9*a* Jer. 29:8.
  b TG Sorcery.
10*a* Jer. 14:14;
     Alma 30:42;

D&C 50:2.
11*a* 2 Kgs. 24:20.
12*a* Jer. 49:30 (30–33).
15*a* TG False Prophets.
16*a* 2 Kgs. 24:13.
17*a* Jer. 52:3.
  b Jer. 7:34; 44:2.
18*a* Isa. 59:16.

Judah, and at Jerusalem, go not to Babylon.

19 ¶ For thus saith the LORD of hosts concerning the [a]pillars, and concerning the [b]sea, and concerning the [c]bases, and concerning the residue of the vessels that remain in this city,

20 Which Nebuchadnezzar king of Babylon took not, when he carried away captive [a]Jeconiah the son of Jehoiakim king of Judah from Jerusalem to Babylon, and all the nobles of Judah and Jerusalem;

21 Yea, thus saith the LORD of hosts, the God of Israel, concerning the vessels that remain *in* the house of the LORD, and *in* the house of the king of Judah and of Jerusalem;

22 They shall be carried to Babylon, and there shall they be until the day that I visit them, saith the LORD; then will I [a]bring them up, and restore them to this place.

CHAPTER 28

Hananiah prophesies falsely that the Babylonian yoke will be broken.

AND it came to pass the same year, in the beginning of the reign of Zedekiah king of Judah, in the fourth year, *and* in the fifth month, *that* Hananiah the son of Azur the prophet, which *was* of Gibeon, spake unto me in the house of the LORD, in the presence of the priests and of all the people, saying,

2 Thus speaketh the LORD of hosts, the God of Israel, saying, I have broken the yoke of the king of Babylon.

3 Within two full years will I bring again into this place all the vessels of the LORD's house, that Nebuchadnezzar king of Babylon took away from this place, and carried them to Babylon:

4 And I will bring again to this place Jeconiah the son of Jehoiakim king of Judah, with all the captives of Judah, that went into Babylon, saith the LORD: for I will break the yoke of the king of Babylon.

5 ¶ Then the prophet Jeremiah said unto the prophet Hananiah in the presence of the priests, and in the presence of all the people that stood in the house of the LORD,

6 Even the prophet Jeremiah said, Amen: the LORD do so: the LORD perform thy words which thou hast prophesied, to bring again the vessels of the LORD's house, and all that is carried away captive, from Babylon into this place.

7 Nevertheless hear thou now this word that I speak in thine ears, and in the ears of all the people;

8 The prophets that have been before me and before thee of old prophesied both against many countries, and against great kingdoms, of war, and of evil, and of pestilence.

9 The prophet which [a]prophesieth of [b]peace, when the word of the prophet shall come to pass, *then* shall the [c]prophet be known, that the LORD hath truly sent him.

10 ¶ Then Hananiah the prophet took the [a]yoke from off the prophet Jeremiah's neck, and brake it.

11 And Hananiah spake in the presence of all the people, saying, Thus saith the LORD; Even so will I break the yoke of Nebuchadnezzar king of Babylon from the neck of all nations within the space of two full years. And the prophet Jeremiah went his way.

12 ¶ Then the word of the LORD came unto Jeremiah *the prophet*, after that Hananiah the prophet had broken the yoke from off the neck of the prophet Jeremiah, saying,

13 Go and tell Hananiah, saying, Thus saith the LORD; Thou hast broken the yokes of wood; but thou shalt make for them yokes of iron.

14 For thus saith the LORD of hosts,

19a Jer. 52:17 (12–22).
  b 2 Kgs. 25:13.
  c OR stands.
20a Jer. 24:1.

22a Ezra 1:7.
28 9a Deut. 18:22.
   b Ezek. 13:10 (9–10).
   c Deut. 18:21 (20–22);

Matt. 7:16 (15–18).
10a Jer. 27:2.

the God of Israel; I have put a ^ayoke of iron upon the neck of all these nations, that they may serve ^bNebuchadnezzar king of Babylon; and they shall serve him: and I have given him the ^cbeasts of the field also.

15 ¶ Then said the ^aprophet Jeremiah unto Hananiah the prophet, Hear now, Hananiah; The LORD hath not sent thee; but thou makest this people to trust in a ^blie.

16 Therefore thus saith the LORD; Behold, I will cast thee from off the face of the earth: this year thou shalt ^adie, because thou hast taught rebellion against the LORD.

17 So Hananiah the prophet died the same year in the seventh month.

CHAPTER 29

Jeremiah tells the Jews in Babylon to prepare for seventy years of captivity— Those remaining in Jerusalem will yet be scattered—Shemaiah prophesies falsely and is cursed.

Now these *are* the words of the letter that Jeremiah the prophet sent from Jerusalem unto the residue of the elders which were carried away captives, and to the priests, and to the prophets, and to all the people whom Nebuchadnezzar had carried away captive from Jerusalem to Babylon;

2 (After that ^aJeconiah the king, and the queen, and the ^beunuchs, the ^cprinces of Judah and Jerusalem, and the carpenters, and the smiths, were departed from Jerusalem;)

3 By the hand of Elasah the son of Shaphan, and Gemariah the son of Hilkiah, (whom Zedekiah king of Judah sent unto Babylon to Nebuchadnezzar king of Babylon) saying,

4 Thus saith the LORD of hosts, the God of Israel, unto all that are carried away captives, whom I have caused to be carried away from Jerusalem unto Babylon;

5 Build ye houses, and dwell *in them*; and plant ^agardens, and eat the fruit of them;

6 Take ye wives, and beget sons and daughters; and take wives for your sons, and give your daughters to husbands, that they may bear sons and daughters; that ye may be increased there, and not diminished.

7 And seek the ^apeace of the city whither I have caused you to be carried away captives, and pray unto the LORD for it: for in the peace thereof shall ye have peace.

8 ¶ For thus saith the LORD of hosts, the God of Israel; Let not your prophets and your ^adiviners, that be in the midst of you, deceive you, neither hearken to your ^bdreams which ye cause to be dreamed.

9 For they ^aprophesy falsely unto you in my name: I have not sent them, saith the LORD.

10 ¶ For thus saith the LORD, That after ^aseventy years be accomplished at Babylon I will visit you, and ^bperform my good word toward you, in causing you to ^creturn to this place.

11 For I know the thoughts that I think toward you, saith the LORD, thoughts of peace, and not of evil, to give you an expected ^aend.

12 Then shall ye ^acall upon me, and ye shall go and pray unto me, and I will ^bhearken unto you.

13 And ye shall ^aseek me, and find *me*, when ye shall ^bsearch for me with all your ^cheart.

14 And I will be found of you, saith the LORD: and I will turn away your

14*a* 1 Ne. 13:5 (4–9).
  b Jer. 25:11.
  c Jer. 27:6.
15*a* TG False Prophets.
  b Jer. 29:31.
    TG Lying.
16*a* Jacob 7:20 (1–20);
    Alma 30:59 (12–60).
29 2*a* 2 Kgs. 24:15.
  b OR officers or courtiers.

c OR ministers or
    officials.
    Jer. 24:1.
5*a* TG Nature, Earth.
7*a* TG Contentment.
8*a* Jer. 27:9.
  b TG Dream.
9*a* TG False Prophets.
10*a* Jer. 25:11.
  b Jer. 33:14.

c 1 Ne. 10:3;
    2 Ne. 6:9 (8–9).
11*a* Jer. 31:17.
12*a* 1 Kgs. 8:48.
  b HEB hear you.
13*a* TG God, Access to.
  b Ezek. 36:37.
  c James 5:16;
    1 Ne. 1:5 (5–8);
    3 Ne. 12:6.

captivity, and I will *a*gather you from all the nations, and from all the places whither I have driven you, saith the LORD; and I will bring you again into the place whence I caused you to be carried away captive.

15 ¶ Because ye have said, The LORD hath raised us up prophets in Babylon;

16 *Know* that thus saith the LORD of the king that sitteth upon the throne of David, and of all the people that dwelleth in this city, *and* of your brethren that are not gone forth with you into captivity;

17 Thus saith the LORD of hosts; Behold, I will send upon them the sword, the famine, and the pestilence, and will make them like vile figs, that cannot be eaten, they are so *a*evil.

18 And I will *a*persecute them with the sword, with the famine, and with the pestilence, and will deliver them to be *b*removed to all the kingdoms of the earth, to be a curse, and an astonishment, and an hissing, and a reproach, among all the nations whither I have driven them:

19 Because they have not hearkened to my words, saith the LORD, which I sent unto them by my servants the prophets, rising up early and sending *them*; but ye would not hear, saith the LORD.

20 ¶ Hear ye therefore the word of the LORD, all ye of the captivity, whom I have sent from Jerusalem to Babylon:

21 Thus saith the LORD of hosts, the God of Israel, of Ahab the son of Kolaiah, and of Zedekiah the son of Maaseiah, which prophesy a lie unto you in my name; Behold, I will deliver them into the hand of Nebuchadrezzar king of Babylon; and he shall slay them before your eyes;

22 And of them shall be taken up a curse by all the captivity of Judah which *are* in Babylon, saying,

The LORD make thee like Zedekiah and like Ahab, whom the king of Babylon roasted in the fire;

23 Because they have committed *a*villany in Israel, and have committed *b*adultery with their neighbours' wives, and have spoken lying words in my name, which I have not commanded them; even I know, and *am* a witness, saith the LORD.

24 ¶ *Thus* shalt thou also speak to Shemaiah the Nehelamite, saying,

25 Thus speaketh the LORD of hosts, the God of Israel, saying, Because thou hast sent letters in thy name unto all the people that *are* at Jerusalem, and to Zephaniah the son of Maaseiah the priest, and to all the priests, saying,

26 The LORD hath made thee priest in the stead of Jehoiada the priest, that ye should be officers in the house of the LORD, for every man *that is* mad, and maketh himself a prophet, that thou shouldest put him in prison, and in the stocks.

27 Now therefore why hast thou not reproved Jeremiah of *a*Anathoth, which maketh himself a prophet to you?

28 For therefore he sent unto us *in* Babylon, saying, This *captivity is* long: build ye houses, and dwell *in them*; and plant gardens, and eat the fruit of them.

29 And Zephaniah the priest read this letter in the ears of Jeremiah the prophet.

30 ¶ Then came the word of the LORD unto Jeremiah, saying,

31 Send to all them of the captivity, saying, Thus saith the LORD concerning Shemaiah the Nehelamite; Because that Shemaiah hath prophesied unto you, and I sent him not, and he caused you to trust in a *a*lie:

32 Therefore thus saith the LORD; Behold, I will punish Shemaiah the Nehelamite, and his seed: he shall not have a man to dwell among this people; neither shall he behold the

---

14*a* TG Israel, Gathering of; Israel, Judah, People of.
17*a* OR bad.
18*a* HEB pursue after.
 b TG Israel, Scattering of.
23*a* HEB vile deeds.
 b TG Adulterer.
27*a* Jer. 1:1.
31*a* Jer. 28:15.

good that I will do for my people, saith the LORD; because he hath taught rebellion against the LORD.

CHAPTER 30

In the last days, Judah and Israel will be gathered to their own lands—David, their king (the Messiah), will reign over them.

THE word that came to Jeremiah from the LORD, saying,

2 Thus speaketh the LORD God of Israel, saying, Write thee all the words that I have spoken unto thee in a book.

3 For, lo, the days come, saith the LORD, that I will bring again the captivity of my people *a*Israel and Judah, saith the LORD: and I will cause them to *b*return to the land that I gave to their fathers, and they shall possess it.

4 ¶ And these *are* the words that the LORD spake concerning Israel and concerning Judah.

5 For thus saith the LORD; We have heard a voice of trembling, of fear, and not of peace.

6 Ask ye now, and see whether a man doth travail with child? wherefore do I see every man with his hands on his loins, as a woman in travail, and all faces are turned into paleness?

7 Alas! for that *a*day *is* great, so that none *is* like it: it *is* even the time of Jacob's trouble; but he shall be saved out of it.

8 For it shall come to pass in that day, saith the LORD of hosts, *that* I will break his *a*yoke from off thy neck, and will burst thy bonds, and strangers shall no more *b*serve themselves of him:

9 But they shall serve the LORD their God, and *a*David their king, whom I will raise up unto them.

10 ¶ Therefore fear thou not, O my servant Jacob, saith the LORD; neither be dismayed, O Israel: for, lo, I will *a*save thee from afar, and thy seed from the land of their captivity; and Jacob shall return, and shall be in rest, and be quiet, and none shall make *him* afraid.

11 For I *am* with thee, saith the LORD, to save thee: though I make a full *a*end of all nations whither I have scattered thee, yet will I not make a full end of thee: but I will correct thee in measure, and will not leave thee altogether unpunished.

12 For thus saith the LORD, *a*Thy bruise *is* incurable, *and* thy wound *is* grievous.

13 *There is* none to plead thy cause, that thou mayest be bound up: thou hast no healing medicines.

14 All thy *a*lovers have forgotten thee; they seek thee not; for I have *b*wounded thee with the *c*wound of an enemy, with the chastisement of a *d*cruel one, for the multitude of thine *e*iniquity; *because* thy sins were increased.

15 Why criest thou for thine affliction? *a*thy *b*sorrow *is* incurable for the multitude of thine iniquity: *because* thy *c*sins were increased, I have done these things unto thee.

16 Therefore all they that devour thee shall be devoured; and all thine adversaries, every one of them, shall go into captivity; and they that spoil thee shall be a spoil, and all that prey upon thee will I give for a prey.

17 For I will restore *a*health unto

---

30 3 *a* TG Israel, Twelve Tribes of.
  b TG Israel, Gathering of.
7 *a* Joel 2:11;
    Mal. 4:5.
8 *a* TG Bondage, Physical; Bondage, Spiritual.
  b OR enslave, or exploit him.
9 *a* Jer. 23:5 (5–6); Ezek. 34:24 (23–24); 37:24 (24–25).

10 *a* Hosea 13:9;
      D&C 38:33; 136:22.
11 *a* Amos 9:8;
      D&C 101:9 (1–9).
   TG Israel, Scattering of.
12 *a* JST Jer. 30:12–13 . . . thy bruise is *not* incurable, *although* thy *wounds are* grievous. *Is there* none to plead thy cause, that thou mayest be bound up? *Hast thou* no

healing medicines?
14 *a* Lam. 1:2.
   b OR caused thee to be wounded.
   c Hosea 5:13.
   d TG Cruelty.
   e Lam. 1:5.
15 *a* JST Jer. 30:15 . . . Is thy sorrow incurable? . . .
   b Lam. 1:12.
   c D&C 101:2 (1–9).
17 *a* TG Health.

thee, and I will heal thee of thy wounds, saith the LORD; because they called thee an Outcast, *saying*, This *is* Zion, whom no man seeketh after.

18 ¶ Thus saith the LORD; Behold, I will bring again the captivity of Jacob's tents, and have *a*mercy on his dwellingplaces; and the city shall be builded upon her own heap, and *b*the palace shall remain after the manner thereof.

19 And out of them shall proceed thanksgiving and the voice of them that make merry: and I will *a*multiply them, and they shall not be few; I will also glorify them, and they shall not be *b*small.

20 Their children also shall be as aforetime, and their congregation shall be established before me, and I will punish all that oppress them.

21 And their nobles shall be of *a*themselves, and their governor shall proceed from the midst of them; and I will cause him to *b*draw near, and he shall approach unto me: for who *is* this that engaged his heart to approach unto me? saith the LORD.

22 And ye shall be my *a*people, and I will be your God.

23 Behold, the *a*whirlwind of the LORD goeth forth with fury, a continuing whirlwind: it shall fall with *b*pain upon the head of the wicked.

24 The fierce anger of the LORD shall not return, until he have done *it*, and until he have performed the intents of his heart: in the *a*latter days ye shall *b*consider it.

CHAPTER 31

In the last days, Israel will be gathered—The Lord declares that Ephraim has the birthright as the firstborn—The Lord

will make a new covenant with Israel, to be inscribed in the heart—Then all Israel will know the Lord.

AT the same time, saith the LORD, will I be the God of all the *a*families of Israel, and they shall be my people.

2 Thus saith the LORD, The people *which were* left of the sword found grace in the wilderness; *even* Israel, when I went to cause him to rest.

3 The LORD hath appeared *a*of old unto me, *saying*, Yea, I have *b*loved thee with an everlasting *c*love: therefore with lovingkindness have I *d*drawn thee.

4 Again I will build thee, and thou shalt be built, O virgin of Israel: thou shalt again be adorned with thy tabrets, and shalt go forth in the dances of them that make merry.

5 Thou shalt yet plant vines upon the mountains of Samaria: the planters shall plant, and shall eat *them* as common things.

6 For there shall be a day, *that* the *a*watchmen upon the mount Ephraim shall cry, Arise ye, and let us go up to *b*Zion unto the LORD our God.

7 For thus saith the LORD; Sing with gladness for Jacob, and shout among the chief of the nations: publish ye, praise ye, and say, O LORD, *a*save thy people, the remnant of Israel.

8 Behold, I will bring them from the *a*north country, and gather them from the *b*coasts of the earth, *and* with them the blind and the lame, the woman with child and her that travaileth with child together: a great company shall return thither.

9 They shall come with *a*weeping, and with supplications will I lead them: I will cause them to walk by the rivers of waters in a straight

---

18*a* D&C 101:9.
  b HEB the citadel shall stand in its right place.
19*a* D&C 45:58.
  b OR insignificant.
21*a* OR their own people.
  b TG God, Presence of.
22*a* Hosea 2:23; Zech. 13:9; D&C 84:101.

23*a* D&C 63:6.
  b TG Pain.
24*a* Ezek. 38:16.
  b HEB fully understand this. See 2 Ne. 25:8.
31 1*a* TG Family; Family, Eternal.
  3*a* HEB from afar.
  b TG Love.

  c TG God, Love of.
  d IE to me.
6*a* TG Watchman.
  b TG Zion.
7*a* D&C 38:33.
8*a* TG Israel, Ten Lost Tribes of.
  b HEB ends.
9*a* Jer. 50:4.

way, wherein they shall not stumble: for I am a *b*father to Israel, and *c*Ephraim *is* my *d*firstborn.

10 ¶ Hear the word of the LORD, O ye nations, and declare *it* in the isles afar off, and say, He that scattered Israel will *a*gather him, and keep him, as a shepherd *doth* his flock.

11 For the LORD hath redeemed Jacob, and *a*ransomed him from the hand of *him that was* stronger than he.

12 Therefore they shall come and sing in the height of Zion, and shall flow together to the goodness of the LORD, for wheat, and for wine, and for oil, and for the young of the flock and of the herd: and their soul shall be as a watered garden; and they shall not *a*sorrow any more at all.

13 Then shall the virgin rejoice in the dance, both young men and old together: for I will turn their *a*mourning into joy, and will comfort them, and make them rejoice from their sorrow.

14 And I will satiate the soul of the priests with fatness, and my people shall be satisfied with my *a*goodness, saith the LORD.

15 ¶ Thus saith the LORD; A voice was heard in *a*Ramah, lamentation, *and* bitter weeping; Rahel weeping for her children refused to be comforted for her children, because they *were* not.

16 Thus saith the LORD; Refrain thy voice from weeping, and thine eyes from tears: for thy work shall be *a*rewarded, saith the LORD; and they shall come again from the land of the enemy.

17 And there is hope *a*in thine *b*end, saith the LORD, that thy children shall come again to their own border.

18 ¶ I have surely heard Ephraim bemoaning himself *thus*; Thou hast chastised me, and I was chastised, as a bullock unaccustomed *to the yoke:* *a*turn thou me, and I shall be turned; for thou *art* the LORD my God.

19 Surely *a*after that I was turned, I repented; and after that I was instructed, I smote upon *my* thigh: I was ashamed, yea, even confounded, because I did bear the reproach of my youth.

20 *Is* Ephraim my dear son? *is he* *a*a pleasant child? for since I spake against him, I do earnestly remember him still: therefore my bowels are troubled for him; I will surely have mercy upon him, saith the LORD.

21 Set thee up waymarks, make thee *a*high heaps: set thine heart toward the highway, *even* the way *which* thou wentest: turn again, O virgin of Israel, turn again to these thy cities.

22 ¶ How long wilt thou go about, O thou *a*backsliding daughter? for the LORD hath created a new thing in the earth, A woman shall compass a man.

23 Thus saith the LORD of hosts, the God of Israel; As yet they shall use this speech in the land of Judah and in the cities thereof, when I shall bring again their captivity; The LORD bless thee, O habitation of justice, *and* mountain of holiness.

24 And there shall dwell in Judah itself, and in all the cities thereof together, husbandmen, and they *that* go forth with flocks.

25 For I have satiated the weary soul, and I have replenished every sorrowful soul.

26 Upon this I awaked, and beheld; and my sleep was sweet unto me.

27 ¶ Behold, the days come, saith the LORD, that I will sow the house of Israel and the house of Judah

---

9*b* 2 Cor. 6:18.
  c Gen. 48:20 (18–20);
       D&C 133:34.
  d TG Birthright;
       Firstborn.
10*a* TG Israel, Gathering of.
11*a* HEB delivered or freed.

12*a* TG Sorrow.
13*a* Ps. 30:11.
       TG Mourning.
14*a* Ex. 33:19.
15*a* Matt. 2:18.
16*a* TG Reward.
17*a* HEB for thy future.

  b Jer. 29:11.
18*a* Lam. 5:21.
19*a* Ps. 119:67.
20*a* OR a child in whom I
       delight.
21*a* HEB signposts.
22*a* HEB unruly or apostate.

with the seed of man, and with the seed of beast.

28 And it shall come to pass, *that* like as I have *a*watched over them, to *b*pluck up, and to *c*break down, and to throw down, and to destroy, and to afflict; so will I *d*watch over them, to build, and to plant, saith the LORD.

29 In those days they shall say no more, The fathers have eaten a sour *a*grape, and the children's teeth are set on edge.

30 But every one shall *a*die for his own *b*iniquity: every man that eateth the sour grape, his teeth shall be set on edge.

31 ¶ Behold, the days come, saith the LORD, that I will make a *a*new *b*covenant with the house of *c*Israel, and with the house of Judah:

32 Not according to the *a*covenant that I made with their fathers in the day *that* I took them by the hand to bring them out of the land of Egypt; which my covenant they brake, although I was an husband unto them, saith the LORD:

33 But this *shall be* the *a*covenant that I will make with the house of Israel; After those days, saith the LORD, I will put my *b*law in their inward parts, and write it in their *c*hearts; and will be their God, and they shall be my people.

34 And they shall teach no more every man his neighbour, and every man his brother, saying, Know the LORD: for they shall all *a*know me, from the least of them unto the greatest of them, saith the LORD: for I will forgive their *b*iniquity, and I will remember their sin no more.

35 ¶ Thus saith the LORD, which

giveth the *a*sun for a light by *b*day, *and* the *c*ordinances of the moon and of the stars for a light by night, which divideth the sea when the waves thereof roar; The LORD of hosts *is* his name:

36 If those *a*ordinances depart from before me, saith the LORD, *then* the seed of Israel also shall cease from being a nation before me for ever.

37 Thus saith the LORD; If heaven above can be measured, and the foundations of the earth searched out beneath, I will also cast off all the seed of Israel for all that they have done, saith the LORD.

38 ¶ Behold, the days come, saith the LORD, that the city shall be *a*built to the LORD from the tower of Hananeel unto the gate of the corner.

39 And the measuring *a*line shall yet go forth over against it upon the hill Gareb, and shall compass about to Goath.

40 And the whole valley of the dead bodies, and of the ashes, and all the fields unto the brook of Kidron, unto the corner of the horse gate toward the east, *shall be* *a*holy unto the LORD; it shall not be plucked up, nor thrown down any more for ever.

CHAPTER 32

Jeremiah is imprisoned by Zedekiah—The prophet purchases land to symbolize the return of Israel to their land—The Lord will gather Israel and make an everlasting covenant with them.

THE word that came to Jeremiah from the LORD in the tenth year of Zedekiah king of Judah, which

---

28a Jer. 44:27.
  b Jer. 45:4.
  c Dan. 9:14.
  d TG Watch.
29a Lam. 5:7;
     Ezek. 18:2.
30a TG Justice.
  b TG Accountability.
31a TG New and Everlasting
     Covenant; Restoration
     of the Gospel.
  b TG Abrahamic

Covenant; Covenants.
  c TG Israel, Judah,
     People of.
32a TG Covenants.
33a Hosea 2:18 (14–23);
     Morm. 5:20;
     D&C 45:9.
  b Rom. 2:15 (13–15).
     TG God, Law of.
  c Prov. 7:3; 2 Cor. 3:3;
     Heb. 8:10.
     TG Conversion.

34a TG God, Knowledge
     about; Millennium,
     Preparing a People for.
  b TG Sin.
35a TG Astronomy.
  b Gen. 1:18.
  c OR established courses.
     Job 38:33.
36a TG Ordinance.
38a Zech. 14:10.
39a Zech. 1:16.
40a D&C 63:49.

was the eighteenth year of Nebu-chadrezzar.

2 For then the king of Babylon's army ^abesieged Jerusalem: and Jeremiah the prophet was shut up in the court of the prison, which *was* in the king of Judah's house.

3 For Zedekiah king of Judah had shut him up, saying, Wherefore dost thou prophesy, and say, Thus saith the LORD, Behold, I will give this city into the hand of the king of Babylon, and he shall take it;

4 And Zedekiah king of Judah shall not escape out of the hand of the Chaldeans, but shall surely be delivered into the hand of the king of Babylon, and shall speak with him mouth to mouth, and his eyes shall behold his eyes;

5 And he shall lead Zedekiah to ^aBabylon, and there shall he be until I visit him, saith the LORD: though ye fight with the Chaldeans, ye shall not prosper?

6 ¶ And Jeremiah said, The word of the LORD came unto me, saying,

7 Behold, Hanameel the son of Shallum thine uncle shall come unto thee, saying, Buy thee my field that *is* in Anathoth: for the right of redemption *is* thine to buy *it*.

8 So Hanameel mine uncle's son came to me in the court of the prison according to the word of the LORD, and said unto me, Buy my field, I pray thee, that *is* in Anathoth, which *is* in the country of Benjamin: for the right of inheritance *is* thine, and the redemption *is* thine; buy *it* for thyself. Then I knew that this *was* the word of the LORD.

9 And I bought the field of Hanameel my uncle's son, that *was* in Anathoth, and ^aweighed him the money, *even* seventeen shekels of silver.

10 And I subscribed the evidence, and sealed *it*, and took witnesses, and weighed *him* the money in the balances.

11 So I took the evidence of the purchase, *both* that which was sealed *according* to the law and custom, and that which was open:

12 And I gave the evidence of the purchase unto ^aBaruch the son of Neriah, the son of Maaseiah, in the sight of Hanameel mine uncle's *son*, and in the presence of the witnesses that subscribed the ^bbook of the purchase, before all the Jews that sat in the court of the prison.

13 ¶ And I charged Baruch before them, saying,

14 Thus saith the LORD of hosts, the God of Israel; Take these ^aevidences, this evidence of the purchase, both which is sealed, and this evidence which is open; and put them in an earthen vessel, that they may continue many days.

15 For thus saith the LORD of hosts, the God of Israel; Houses and fields and vineyards shall be possessed again in this land.

16 ¶ Now when I had delivered the evidence of the purchase unto Baruch the son of Neriah, I prayed unto the LORD, saying,

17 Ah Lord GOD! behold, thou hast made the heaven and the earth by thy great power and stretched out arm, *and* there is nothing too ^ahard for thee:

18 Thou shewest lovingkindness unto thousands, and recompensest the iniquity of the fathers into the bosom of their children after them: the Great, the Mighty God, the LORD of hosts, *is* his name,

19 Great in counsel, and mighty in work: for thine eyes *are* open upon all the ways of the sons of men: to ^agive every one according to his ^bways, and according to the fruit of his doings:

20 Which hast set signs and wonders in the land of Egypt, *even* unto this day, and in Israel, and among *other* men; and hast made thee a name, as at this day;

---

32 2*a* 2 Kgs. 24:20.
   5*a* TG Israel, Bondage of, in Other Lands.
   9*a* Gen. 23:16.

12*a* Jer. 43:3.
   b OR deed.
14*a* OR documents.
17*a* TG God, Power of.

19*a* TG Reward.
   b TG Good Works; Justice.

21 And hast brought forth thy people Israel out of the land of Egypt with signs, and with wonders, and with a strong hand, and with a stretched out arm, and with great terror;

22 And hast given them this land, which thou didst swear to their fathers to give them, a land flowing with milk and honey;

23 And they came in, and possessed it; but they obeyed not thy voice, neither walked in thy law; they have done nothing of all that thou commandedst them to do: therefore thou hast caused all this evil to come upon them:

24 Behold the mounts, they are come unto the city to take it; and the city is given into the hand of the Chaldeans, that fight against it, because of the sword, and of the famine, and of the pestilence: and what thou hast spoken is come to pass; and, behold, thou seest *it*.

25 And thou hast said unto me, O Lord GOD, Buy thee the field for money, and take witnesses; for the city is given into the hand of the Chaldeans.

26 ¶ Then came the word of the LORD unto Jeremiah, saying,

27 Behold, I *am* the LORD, the God of all flesh: is there any thing too hard for me?

28 Therefore thus saith the LORD; Behold, I will give this city into the hand of the Chaldeans, and into the hand of Nebuchadrezzar king of Babylon, and he shall take it:

29 And the Chaldeans, that fight against this city, shall come and set fire on this city, and burn it with the houses, upon whose *a*roofs they have offered incense unto Baal, and poured out drink offerings unto other gods, to provoke me to anger.

30 For the children of Israel and the children of Judah have only done evil before me from their youth: for the children of Israel have only provoked me to *a*anger with the work of their hands, saith the LORD.

31 For this city hath been to me *as* a provocation of mine anger and of my fury from the day that they built it even unto this day; that I should remove it from before my face,

32 Because of all the evil of the children of Israel and of the children of Judah, which they have done to provoke me to anger, they, their kings, their princes, their priests, and their prophets, and the men of Judah, and the inhabitants of Jerusalem.

33 And they have turned unto me the *a*back, and not the face: though I taught them, rising up early and teaching *them*, yet they have not hearkened to receive instruction.

34 But they set their abominations in *a*the house, which is called by my name, to defile it.

35 And they built the high places of Baal, which *are* in the valley of the son of Hinnom, to cause their sons and their daughters to pass through the *a*fire unto Molech; which I commanded them not, neither came it into my mind, that they should do this abomination, to cause Judah to sin.

36 ¶ And now therefore thus saith the LORD, the God of Israel, concerning this city, whereof ye say, It shall be delivered into the hand of the king of Babylon by the sword, and by the famine, and by the pestilence;

37 Behold, I will *a*gather them out of all countries, whither I have driven them in mine anger, and in my fury, and in great wrath; and I will *b*bring them again unto this place, and I will cause them to dwell safely:

38 And they shall be my people, and I will be their God:

39 And I will give them one *a*heart, and one way, that they may fear me

---

29a 2 Kgs. 23:12.
30a TG Anger.
33a Jer. 2:27;
   Ezek. 8:16.
34a IE the temple.

35a Lev. 18:21;
   Jer. 19:5.
37a D&C 45:69.
   TG Israel, Gathering of.
   b Jer. 16:15.

39a TG Conversion;
   Man, New, Spiritually
   Reborn.

for ever, for the [b]good of them, and of their children after them:

40 And I will make an [a]everlasting [b]covenant with them, that I will not turn away from them, to do them good; but I will put my fear in their hearts, that they shall not depart from me.

41 Yea, I will rejoice over them to do them good, and I will plant them in this land assuredly with my whole heart and with my whole soul.

42 For thus saith the LORD; Like as I have brought all this great evil upon this people, so will I bring upon them all the good that I have promised them.

43 And fields shall be bought in this land, whereof ye say, It is desolate without man or beast; it is given into the hand of the Chaldeans.

44 Men shall buy fields for money, and subscribe evidences, and [a]seal them, and take witnesses in the land of Benjamin, and in the places about Jerusalem, and in the cities of Judah, and in the cities of the mountains, and in the cities of the [b]valley, and in the cities of the south: for I will cause their [c]captivity to return, saith the LORD.

CHAPTER 33

Judah and Israel will be gathered—The Branch of Righteousness (the Messiah) is promised—The Seed of David (the Messiah) will reign forever.

MOREOVER the word of the LORD came unto Jeremiah the second time, while he was yet shut up in the court of the prison, saying,

2 Thus saith the LORD the maker thereof, the LORD that formed it, to establish it; the LORD is his name;

3 Call unto me, and I will answer thee, and [a]shew thee great and mighty things, which thou knowest not.

4 For thus saith the LORD, the God of Israel, concerning the houses of this city, and concerning the houses of the kings of Judah, which are thrown down by the mounts, and by the sword;

5 They come to fight with the Chaldeans, but it is to fill them with the dead bodies of men, whom I have slain in mine anger and in my fury, and for all whose wickedness I have hid my face from this city.

6 Behold, I will bring it health and cure, and I will cure them, and will reveal unto them the abundance of peace and truth.

7 And I will cause the captivity of Judah and the captivity of Israel to [a]return, and will build them, as at the first.

8 And I will [a]cleanse them from all their iniquity, whereby they have sinned against me; and I will pardon all their iniquities, whereby they have sinned, and whereby they have transgressed against me.

9 ¶ And it shall be to me a name of joy, a [a]praise and an honour before all the nations of the earth, which shall hear all the good that I do unto them: and they shall fear and tremble for all the goodness and for all the prosperity that I procure unto it.

10 Thus saith the LORD; Again there shall be heard in this place, which ye say shall be desolate without man and without beast, even in the cities of Judah, and in the streets of Jerusalem, that are desolate, without man, and without inhabitant, and without beast,

11 The voice of joy, and the voice of gladness, the voice of the bridegroom, and the voice of the bride, the voice of them that shall say, Praise the LORD of hosts: for the LORD is good; for his mercy endureth for ever: and of them that shall bring the sacrifice of praise into the house of the LORD. For I will cause to

---

39 b Deut. 6:24; 10:13.
40 a TG New and Everlasting Covenant.
  b TG Covenants.
44 a TG Seal.

b HEB coastal plain.
c TG Israel, Ten Lost Tribes of.
33 3 a TG God, Omniscience of.

7 a Isa. 1:26.
8 a TG Forgive; Purification.
9 a Jer. 49:25.

return the captivity of the land, as at the first, saith the LORD.

12 Thus saith the LORD of hosts; Again in this place, which is desolate without man and without beast, and in all the cities thereof, shall be an habitation of shepherds causing *their* flocks to *a*lie down.

13 In the cities of the mountains, in the cities of the vale, and in the cities of the south, and in the land of Benjamin, and in the places about Jerusalem, and in the cities of Judah, shall the flocks pass again under the hands of him that *a*telleth *them*, saith the LORD.

14 Behold, the days come, saith the LORD, that I will *a*perform that good thing which I have *b*promised unto the house of Israel and to the house of Judah.

15 ¶ In those days, and at that time, will I cause the *a*Branch of righteousness to grow up unto *b*David; and he shall *c*execute judgment and righteousness in the *d*land.

16 In those days shall Judah be saved, and Jerusalem shall dwell safely: and this *is the name* wherewith she shall be called, The LORD our righteousness.

17 ¶ For thus saith the LORD; David shall never *a*want a man to sit upon the throne of the house of Israel;

18 Neither shall the priests the Levites want a man before me to offer burnt offerings, and to kindle meat offerings, and to do sacrifice continually.

19 ¶ And the word of the LORD came unto Jeremiah, saying,

20 Thus saith the LORD; If ye can break my covenant of the day, and my covenant of the night, and that there should not be day and *a*night in their season;

21 *Then* may also my covenant be broken with David my servant, that he should not have a son to reign upon his throne; and with the Levites the priests, my ministers.

22 As the host of heaven cannot be numbered, neither the sand of the sea measured: so will I multiply the seed of David my servant, and the Levites that minister unto me.

23 Moreover the word of the LORD came to Jeremiah, saying,

24 Considerest thou not what this people have spoken, saying, The two families which the LORD hath chosen, he hath even cast them off? thus they have despised my people, that they should be no more a nation before them.

25 Thus saith the LORD; If my covenant *be* not with day and night, *and if* I have not appointed the ordinances of heaven and earth;

26 Then will I cast away the seed of Jacob, and David my servant, *so* that I will not take *any* of his seed *to be* rulers over the seed of Abraham, Isaac, and Jacob: for I will cause their captivity to return, and have mercy on them.

CHAPTER 34

Jeremiah prophesies the captivity of Zedekiah—The people of Judah will be removed into all the kingdoms of the earth.

THE word which came unto Jeremiah from the LORD, when Nebuchadnezzar king of Babylon, and all his army, and all the kingdoms of the earth of his dominion, and all the people, fought against Jerusalem, and *a*against all the cities thereof, saying,

2 Thus saith the LORD, the God of Israel; Go and speak to Zedekiah king of Judah, and tell him, Thus saith the LORD; Behold, I will give this city into the hand of the king of *a*Babylon, and he shall burn it with fire:

3 And thou shalt not escape out of his hand, but shalt surely be taken,

---

12*a* Ezek. 34:14.
13*a* HEB counts.
14*a* Jer. 29:10.
  b TG Promise.
15*a* TG Jesus Christ,

Prophecies about.
  b TG Jesus Christ, Davidic Descent.
  c OR do justice.
  d OR earth.

17*a* OR lack.
20*a* Gen. 8:22.
34 1*a* Ezek. 26:3.
  2*a* Jer. 21:10; 38:3; 52:13.

and delivered into his hand; and thine eyes shall behold the eyes of the king of *Babylon, and he shall speak with thee mouth to mouth, and thou shalt go to Babylon.

4 Yet hear the word of the LORD, O Zedekiah king of Judah; Thus saith the LORD of thee, Thou shalt not die by the sword:

5 *But* thou shalt die in peace: and with the burnings of thy fathers, the former kings which were before thee, so shall they burn *odours* for thee; and they will lament thee, *saying,* Ah lord! for I have pronounced the word, saith the LORD.

6 Then Jeremiah the prophet spake all these words unto Zedekiah king of Judah in Jerusalem,

7 When the king of Babylon's army fought against Jerusalem, and against all the cities of Judah that were left, against Lachish, and against Azekah: for these defenced cities remained of the cities of Judah.

8 ¶ *This is* the word that came unto Jeremiah from the LORD, after that the king Zedekiah had made a covenant with all the people which *were* at Jerusalem, to proclaim *liberty unto them;

9 That every man should let his manservant, and every man his maidservant, *being* an Hebrew or an Hebrewess, go free; that none should *serve himself of them, *to wit,* of a Jew his brother.

10 Now when all the princes, and all the people, which had entered into the covenant, heard that every one should let his manservant, and every one his maidservant, go free, that none should serve themselves of them any more, then they obeyed, and let *them* go.

11 But afterward they *turned, and caused the servants and the handmaids, whom they had let go free, to return, and brought them into subjection for servants and for handmaids.

12 ¶ Therefore the word of the LORD came to Jeremiah from the LORD, saying,

13 Thus saith the LORD, the God of Israel; I made a covenant with your fathers in the day that I brought them forth out of the land of Egypt, out of the house of bondmen, saying,

14 At the end of *seven years let ye go every man his brother an Hebrew, which hath been sold unto thee; and when he hath served thee six years, thou shalt let him go free from thee: but your fathers hearkened not unto me, neither inclined their ear.

15 And ye were now turned, and had done right in my sight, in proclaiming liberty every man to his neighbour; and ye had made a covenant before me in the house which is called by my name:

16 But ye turned and *polluted my name, and caused every man his servant, and every man his handmaid, whom ye had set at liberty at their pleasure, to return, and brought them into subjection, to be unto you for servants and for handmaids.

17 Therefore thus saith the LORD; Ye have not hearkened unto me, in proclaiming *liberty, every one to his brother, and every man to his neighbour: behold, I proclaim a liberty for you, saith the LORD, to the sword, to the pestilence, and to the famine; and I will make you to be removed into all the kingdoms of the earth.

18 And I will give the men that have transgressed my covenant, which have not performed the words of the covenant which they had made before me, when they *cut the calf in twain, and *passed between the parts thereof,

19 The princes of Judah, and the princes of Jerusalem, the eunuchs, and the priests, and all the people of

---

3a TG Israel, Bondage of, in
    Other Lands.
8a TG Liberty.
9a OR enslave them.

11a IE turned back on their
    word.
14a TG Sabbatical Year.
16a HEB profaned.

   TG Pollution.
17a TG Liberty.
18a Gen. 15:10.
   b Gen. 15:17.

the land, which passed between the parts of the calf;

20 I will even ªgive them into the hand of their enemies, and into the hand of them that seek their life: and their dead bodies shall be for meat unto the fowls of the heaven, and to the beasts of the earth.

21 And Zedekiah king of Judah and his princes will I give into the hand of their enemies, and into the hand of them that seek their life, and into the hand of the king of Babylon's army, which are gone up from you.

22 Behold, I will command, saith the LORD, and cause them to return to this city; and they shall fight against it, and take it, and burn it with fire: and I will make the cities of Judah a desolation without an inhabitant.

CHAPTER 35

The Rechabites are commended and blessed for their obedience.

THE word which came unto Jeremiah from the LORD in the days of Jehoiakim the son of Josiah king of Judah, saying,

2 Go unto the house of the ªRechabites, and speak unto them, and bring them into the house of the LORD, into one of the chambers, and give them wine to drink.

3 Then I took Jaazaniah the son of Jeremiah, the son of Habaziniah, and his brethren, and all his sons, and the whole house of the Rechabites;

4 And I brought them into the house of the LORD, into the chamber of the sons of Hanan, the son of Igdaliah, a man of God, which *was* by the chamber of the princes, which *was* above the chamber of Maaseiah the son of Shallum, the keeper of the door:

5 And I set before the sons of the house of the Rechabites pots full of wine, and cups, and I said unto them, Drink ye wine.

6 But they said, We will drink no wine: for ªJonadab the son of Rechab our father commanded us, saying, Ye shall drink no wine, *neither* ye, nor your sons for ever:

7 Neither shall ye build house, nor sow seed, nor plant vineyard, nor have *any:* but all your days ye shall dwell in tents; that ye may live many days in the land where ye *be* strangers.

8 Thus have we obeyed the voice of Jonadab the son of Rechab our father in all that he hath charged us, to drink no wine all our days, we, our wives, our sons, nor our daughters;

9 Nor to build houses for us to dwell in: neither have we vineyard, nor field, nor seed:

10 But we have dwelt in tents, and have obeyed, and done according to all that Jonadab our father commanded us.

11 But it came to pass, when Nebuchadrezzar king of Babylon came up into the land, that we said, Come, and let us go to Jerusalem for fear of the army of the Chaldeans, and for fear of the army of the Syrians: so we dwell at Jerusalem.

12 ¶ Then came the word of the LORD unto Jeremiah, saying,

13 Thus saith the LORD of hosts, the God of Israel; Go and tell the men of Judah and the inhabitants of Jerusalem, Will ye not receive instruction to hearken to my words? saith the LORD.

14 The words of Jonadab the son of Rechab, that he commanded his sons not to drink wine, are performed; for unto this day they drink none, but obey their father's commandment: notwithstanding I have spoken unto you, rising early and speaking; but ye hearkened not unto me.

15 I have sent also unto you all my servants the ªprophets, rising up early and sending *them,* saying, ᵇReturn ye now every man from his evil way, and amend your doings, and go

---

20a Jer. 22:25.
35 2a 2 Kgs. 10:15;

1 Chr. 2:55.
6a 2 Kgs. 10:15.

15a D&C 98:17 (15–18).
  b TG Repent.

not after other gods to serve them, and ye shall dwell in the land which I have given to you and to your fathers: but ye have not inclined your ear, nor hearkened unto me.

16 Because the sons of Jonadab the son of Rechab have performed the commandment of their father, which he commanded them; but this people hath not hearkened unto me:

17 Therefore thus saith the LORD God of hosts, the God of Israel; Behold, I will bring upon Judah and upon all the inhabitants of Jerusalem all the evil that I have pronounced against them: because I have spoken unto them, but they have not *heard; and I have called unto them, but they have not answered.

18 ¶ And Jeremiah said unto the house of the Rechabites, Thus saith the LORD of hosts, the God of Israel; Because ye have obeyed the commandment of Jonadab your father, and kept all his precepts, and done according unto all that he hath commanded you:

19 Therefore thus saith the LORD of hosts, the God of Israel; Jonadab the son of Rechab shall not want a man to stand before me for ever.

CHAPTER 36

Baruch writes the prophecies of Jeremiah and reads them in the house of the Lord—Jehoiakim, the king, burns the book, and judgment comes upon him—Jeremiah dictates the prophecies again and adds many more.

AND it came to pass in the fourth year of Jehoiakim the son of Josiah king of Judah, *that* this word came unto Jeremiah from the LORD, saying,

2 Take thee a *roll of a book, and write therein all the words that I have spoken unto thee against Israel, and against Judah, and against all the nations, from the day I spake

unto thee, from the days of Josiah, even unto this *day.

3 It may be that the house of Judah will hear all the evil which I purpose to do unto them; that they may return every man from his evil way; that I may forgive their iniquity and their sin.

4 Then Jeremiah called Baruch the son of Neriah: and *Baruch *wrote from the mouth of Jeremiah all the words of the LORD, which he had spoken unto him, upon a roll of a book.

5 And Jeremiah commanded Baruch, saying, I *am* *shut up; I cannot go into the house of the LORD:

6 Therefore go thou, and read in the roll, which thou hast written from my mouth, the words of the LORD in the ears of the people in the LORD's house upon the *fasting day: and also thou shalt read them in the ears of all Judah that come out of their cities.

7 It may be they will present their supplication before the LORD, and will *return every one from his evil way: for great *is* the anger and the fury that the LORD hath pronounced against this people.

8 And Baruch the son of Neriah did according to all that Jeremiah the prophet commanded him, reading in the book the words of the LORD in the LORD's house.

9 And it came to pass in the fifth year of Jehoiakim the son of Josiah king of Judah, in the ninth month, *that* they proclaimed a fast before the LORD to all the people in Jerusalem, and to all the people that came from the cities of Judah unto Jerusalem.

10 Then read Baruch in the book the words of Jeremiah in the house of the LORD, in the chamber of Gemariah the son of *Shaphan the scribe, in the higher court, at the entry of the new gate of the LORD's house, in the ears of all the people.

17a OR obeyed.
36 2a Ezra 6:2; Ezek. 2:9.
　　b Jer. 1:2; 25:3.
　　4a Jer. 45:1.

b TG Scriptures,
　　Writing of.
5a HEB under arrest, or in
　　confinement.

D&C 122:6 (1–7).
6a Neh. 9:1 (1–3).
7a 2 Kgs. 23:3 (2–3).
10a Jer. 26:24.

11 ¶ When Michaiah the son of Gemariah, the son of Shaphan, had heard out of the book all the words of the LORD,

12 Then he went down into the king's house, into the scribe's chamber: and, lo, all the *a*princes sat there, *even* Elishama the scribe, and Delaiah the son of Shemaiah, and *b*Elnathan the son of Achbor, and Gemariah the son of Shaphan, and Zedekiah the son of Hananiah, and all the princes.

13 Then Michaiah declared unto them all the words that he had heard, when Baruch read the book in the ears of the people.

14 Therefore all the princes sent Jehudi the son of Nethaniah, the son of Shelemiah, the son of Cushi, unto Baruch, saying, Take in thine hand the roll wherein thou hast read in the ears of the people, and come. So Baruch the son of Neriah took the roll in his hand, and came unto them.

15 And they said unto him, Sit down now, and read it in our ears. So Baruch read *it* in their ears.

16 Now it came to pass, when they had heard all the words, they were *a*afraid both one and other, and said unto Baruch, We will surely tell the king of all these words.

17 And they asked Baruch, saying, Tell us now, How didst thou write all these words at his mouth?

18 Then Baruch answered them, He pronounced all these words unto me with his mouth, and I wrote *them* with ink in the book.

19 Then said the princes unto Baruch, Go, hide thee, thou and Jeremiah; and let no man know where ye be.

20 ¶ And they went in to the king into the court, but they laid up the roll in the chamber of Elishama the scribe, and told all the words in the ears of the king.

21 So the king sent Jehudi to fetch the roll: and he took it out of Elishama the scribe's chamber. And Jehudi read it in the ears of the king, and in the ears of all the princes which stood beside the king.

22 Now the king sat in the *a*winterhouse in the ninth month: and *there was a fire* on the hearth burning before him.

23 And it came to pass, *that* when Jehudi had read three or four leaves, he cut it with the penknife, and cast *it* into the fire that *was* on the hearth, until all the roll was consumed in the fire that *was* on the hearth.

24 Yet they were not afraid, nor rent their garments, *neither* the king, nor any of his servants that heard all these words.

25 Nevertheless Elnathan and Delaiah and Gemariah had made intercession to the king that he would not burn the roll: but he would not hear them.

26 But the king commanded Jerahmeel the son of *a*Hammelech, and Seraiah the son of Azriel, and Shelemiah the son of Abdeel, to take Baruch the scribe and Jeremiah the prophet: but the LORD *b*hid them.

27 ¶ Then the word of the LORD came to Jeremiah, after that the king had burned the roll, and the words which Baruch wrote at the mouth of Jeremiah, saying,

28 Take thee again another roll, and *a*write in it all the former words that were in the first roll, which Jehoiakim the king of Judah hath burned.

29 And thou shalt say to Jehoiakim king of Judah, Thus saith the LORD; Thou hast burned this roll, saying, Why hast thou written therein, saying, The king of Babylon shall certainly come and destroy this land, and shall cause to cease from thence man and beast?

30 Therefore thus saith the LORD of Jehoiakim king of Judah; He shall have none to sit upon the throne of David: and his dead body shall

---

12*a* OR officers or officials.
    b Jer. 26:22.
16*a* Mosiah 4:1 (1–2).

22*a* Amos 3:15.
26*a* HEB the king.
    b 1 Ne. 3:27.

28*a* TG Scriptures, Preservation of.

be cast out in the day to the heat, and in the night to the frost.

31 And I will punish him and his seed and his servants for their iniquity; and I will bring upon them, and upon the inhabitants of Jerusalem, and upon the men of Judah, all the evil that I have pronounced against them; but they hearkened not.

32 ¶ Then took Jeremiah another roll, and gave it to Baruch the *scribe, the son of Neriah; who wrote therein from the mouth of Jeremiah all the words of the book which Jehoiakim king of Judah had burned in the fire: and there were *added besides unto them many like words.

CHAPTER 37

Jeremiah prophesies that Egypt will not save Judah from Babylon—He is cast into a dungeon—Zedekiah transfers him to the court of the prison.

AND *king *Zedekiah the son of Josiah reigned instead of *Coniah the son of *Jehoiakim, whom Nebuchadrezzar king of Babylon made king in the land of Judah.

2 But neither he, nor his servants, nor the people of the land, did hearken unto the words of the LORD, which he spake by the prophet Jeremiah.

3 And Zedekiah the king sent Jehucal the son of Shelemiah and Zephaniah the son of Maaseiah the priest to the prophet Jeremiah, saying, Pray now unto the LORD our God for us.

4 Now Jeremiah came in and went out among the people: for they had not put him into prison.

5 Then Pharaoh's army was come forth out of Egypt: and when the Chaldeans that besieged Jerusalem heard tidings of them, they departed from Jerusalem.

6 ¶ Then came the word of the LORD unto the prophet Jeremiah, saying,

7 Thus saith the LORD, the God of Israel; Thus shall ye say to the king of Judah, that sent you unto me to inquire of me; Behold, Pharaoh's *army, which is come forth to help you, shall return to *Egypt into their own land.

8 And the Chaldeans shall come again, and fight against this city, and take it, and *burn it with fire.

9 Thus saith the LORD; Deceive not yourselves, saying, The Chaldeans shall surely depart from us: for they shall not depart.

10 For though ye had smitten the whole army of the Chaldeans that fight against you, and there remained *but* wounded men among them, *yet* should they rise up every man in his tent, and burn this city with fire.

11 ¶ And it came to pass, that when the army of the Chaldeans was broken up from Jerusalem for fear of Pharaoh's army,

12 Then Jeremiah went forth out of Jerusalem to go into the land of Benjamin, to separate himself thence in the midst of the people.

13 And when he was in the gate of Benjamin, a captain of the ward *was* there, whose name *was* Irijah, the son of Shelemiah, the son of Hananiah; and he took Jeremiah the prophet, saying, Thou *fallest away to the Chaldeans.

14 Then said Jeremiah, *It is* false; I fall not away to the Chaldeans. But he hearkened not to him: so Irijah took Jeremiah, and brought him to the princes.

15 Wherefore the princes were wroth with *Jeremiah, and smote him, and put him in prison in the house of Jonathan the scribe: for they had made that the *prison.

32*a* TG Scribe.
  b TG Scriptures, Preservation of.
37 1*a* 2 Chr. 36:11 (10–12).
  b 2 Kgs. 24:17 (17–18);
    1 Ne. 1:4; 5:13 (12–13);
      Omni 1:15.
  c Jer. 22:24.
  d Jer. 52:31.
7*a* Ezek. 17:17.
  b Lam. 4:17.
8*a* Jer. 52:13.
13*a* OR art deserting.
15*a* 2 Ne. 27:5.
  b TG Prophets, Rejection of.

16 ¶ When Jeremiah was entered into the dungeon, and into the ᵃcabins, and Jeremiah had remained there many days;

17 Then Zedekiah the king sent, and took him out: and the king asked him secretly in his house, and said, Is there *any* word from the LORD? And Jeremiah said, There is: for, said he, thou shalt be delivered into the hand of the king of Babylon.

18 Moreover Jeremiah said unto king Zedekiah, What have I offended against thee, or against thy servants, or against this people, that ye have put me in prison?

19 Where *are* now your prophets which prophesied unto you, saying, The king of Babylon shall not come against you, nor against this land?

20 Therefore hear now, I pray thee, O my lord the king: let my supplication, I pray thee, be accepted before thee; that thou cause me not to return to the house of Jonathan the scribe, lest I die there.

21 Then Zedekiah the king commanded that they should commit Jeremiah into the court of the prison, and that they should give him daily a piece of ᵃbread out of the bakers' street, until all the bread in the city were spent. Thus Jeremiah remained in the court of the prison.

CHAPTER 38

The rulers cast Jeremiah into a muddy dungeon—He is freed by Ebed-melech, an Ethiopian, and put in the court of the prison—Jeremiah counsels Zedekiah concerning the war.

THEN Shephatiah the son of Mattan, and Gedaliah the son of ᵃPashur, and Jucal the son of Shelemiah, and ᵇPashur the son of Malchiah, heard the words that Jeremiah had spoken unto all the people, saying,

2 Thus saith the LORD, He that remaineth in this city shall die by the sword, by the famine, and by the pestilence: but he that goeth forth to the Chaldeans shall live; for he shall have his life for a prey, and shall live.

3 Thus saith the LORD, This city shall surely be given into the hand of the king of ᵃBabylon's army, which shall take it.

4 Therefore the ᵃprinces said unto the king, We beseech thee, let this man be put to death: for thus he weakeneth the hands of the men of war that remain in this city, and the hands of all the people, in speaking such words unto them: for this man seeketh not the ᵇwelfare of this people, but the hurt.

5 Then Zedekiah the king said, Behold, he *is* in your hand: for the king ᵃis not *he that* can do *any* thing against you.

6 Then took they Jeremiah, and cast him into the dungeon of Malchiah the son of ᵃHammelech, that *was* in the court of the prison: and they let down Jeremiah with cords. And in the dungeon *there was* no water, but mire: so Jeremiah sunk in the mire.

7 ¶ Now when Ebed-melech the Ethiopian, one of the eunuchs which was in the king's house, heard that they had put Jeremiah in the dungeon; the king then sitting in the gate of Benjamin;

8 Ebed-melech went forth out of the king's house, and spake to the king, saying,

9 My lord the king, these men have done evil in all that they have done to Jeremiah the prophet, whom they have cast into the dungeon; and he is like to die for hunger in the place where he is: for *there is* no more ᵃbread in the city.

10 Then the king commanded Ebed-melech the Ethiopian, saying, Take from hence thirty men with

---

16*a* OR cells.
21*a* Jer. 38:9.
38 1*a* Jer. 21:1.
   b Jer. 20:1.

3*a* Jer. 21:10; 34:2; 52:13.
4*a* OR officers or rulers.
   b Jer. 26:11.
5*a* OR cannot prevail

against you in any matter.
6*a* HEB the king.
9*a* Jer. 37:21.

thee, and take up Jeremiah the prophet out of the dungeon, before he die.

11 So Ebed-melech took the men with him, and went into the house of the king under the treasury, and took thence *a*old cast clouts and old rotten rags, and let them down by cords into the dungeon to Jeremiah.

12 And Ebed-melech the Ethiopian said unto Jeremiah, Put now *these* old cast clouts and rotten rags under thine armholes under the cords. And Jeremiah did so.

13 So they drew up Jeremiah with cords, and took him up out of the dungeon: and Jeremiah remained in the court of the prison.

14 ¶ Then Zedekiah the king sent, and took Jeremiah the prophet unto him into the third entry that *is* in the house of the LORD: and the king said unto Jeremiah, I will ask thee a thing; hide nothing from me.

15 Then Jeremiah said unto Zedekiah, If I declare *it* unto thee, wilt thou not surely put me to death? and if I give thee counsel, wilt thou not hearken unto me?

16 So Zedekiah the king sware secretly unto Jeremiah, saying, *As* the LORD liveth, that made us this soul, I will not put thee to death, neither will I give thee into the hand of these men that seek thy life.

17 Then said Jeremiah unto Zedekiah, Thus saith the LORD, the God of hosts, the God of Israel; If thou wilt assuredly go forth unto the king of Babylon's princes, then thy soul shall live, and this city shall not be burned with fire; and thou shalt live, and thine house:

18 But if thou wilt not go forth to the king of Babylon's princes, then shall this city be given into the hand of the Chaldeans, and they shall burn it with fire, and thou shalt not escape out of their hand.

19 And Zedekiah the king said unto Jeremiah, I am afraid of the Jews that *a*are fallen to the Chaldeans, lest they deliver me into their hand, and they *b*mock me.

20 But Jeremiah said, They shall not deliver *thee*. Obey, I beseech thee, the voice of the LORD, which I speak unto thee: so it shall be well unto thee, and thy soul shall live.

21 But if thou refuse to go forth, this *is* the word that the LORD hath shewed me:

22 And, behold, all the women that are left in the king of Judah's house *shall be* brought forth to the king of Babylon's princes, and those *women* shall say, Thy friends have set thee on, and have prevailed against thee: thy feet are sunk in the mire, *and* they are turned away back.

23 So they shall bring out all thy wives and thy *a*children to the Chaldeans: and thou shalt not escape out of their hand, but shalt be taken by the hand of the king of Babylon: and thou shalt cause this city to be burned with fire.

24 ¶ Then said Zedekiah unto Jeremiah, Let no man know of these words, and thou shalt not die.

25 But if the princes hear that I have talked with thee, and they come unto thee, and say unto thee, Declare unto us now what thou hast said unto the king, hide it not from us, and we will not put thee to death; also what the king said unto thee:

26 Then thou shalt say unto them, I presented my supplication before the king, that he would not cause me to return to Jonathan's house, to die there.

27 Then came all the princes unto Jeremiah, and asked him: and he told them according to all these words that the king had commanded. So they left off speaking with him; for the matter was not perceived.

28 So Jeremiah abode in the court of the prison until the day that Jerusalem was taken: and he was *there* when Jerusalem was taken.

---

11 *a* HEB worn-out clothes.
19 *a* HEB have deserted to.
b HEB maltreat.
23 *a* Jer. 39:6.

CHAPTER 39

Jerusalem is taken, and the people are taken captive—Jeremiah and Ebed-melech, the Ethiopian, are preserved.

IN the ^aninth year of Zedekiah king of Judah, in the tenth month, came Nebuchadrezzar ^bking of Babylon and all his army against ^cJerusalem, and they besieged it.

2 And in the eleventh year of Zedekiah, in the fourth month, the ninth *day* of the month, the city was broken up.

3 And all the princes of the king of Babylon came in, and sat in the middle ^agate, *even* Nergal-sharezer, Samgar-nebo, Sarsechim, Rab-saris, Nergal-sharezer, Rab-mag, with all the residue of the princes of the king of Babylon.

4 ¶ And it came to pass, *that* when ^aZedekiah the king of Judah saw them, and all the men of war, then they fled, and went forth out of the city by night, by the way of the king's garden, by the gate betwixt the two walls: and he went out the way of the plain.

5 But the Chaldeans' army pursued after them, and overtook ^aZedekiah in the ^bplains of Jericho: and when they had taken him, they brought him up to Nebuchadnezzar king of Babylon to Riblah in the land of Hamath, where he ^cgave judgment upon him.

6 Then the king of Babylon ^aslew the ^bsons of Zedekiah in Riblah before his eyes: also the king of Babylon slew all the nobles of Judah.

7 Moreover he put out Zedekiah's ^aeyes, and bound ^bhim with chains, to carry him to Babylon.

8 ¶ And the ^aChaldeans ^bburned the king's house, and the houses of the people, with fire, and ^cbrake down the walls of Jerusalem.

9 Then Nebuzar-adan the captain of the guard carried away captive into Babylon the remnant of the people that remained in the city, and those that fell away, that ^afell to him, with the rest of the people that remained.

10 But ^aNebuzar-adan the captain of the guard left of the poor of the people, which had nothing, in the land of Judah, and gave them vineyards and fields at the same time.

11 ¶ Now Nebuchadrezzar king of Babylon gave charge concerning Jeremiah to Nebuzar-adan the captain of the guard, saying,

12 Take him, and ^alook well to him, and do him no harm; but do unto him even as he shall say unto thee.

13 So Nebuzar-adan the captain of the guard sent, and Nebushasban, Rab-saris, and Nergal-sharezer, Rab-mag, and all the king of Babylon's princes;

14 Even they sent, and took Jeremiah out of the court of the prison, and committed him unto ^aGedaliah the son of Ahikam the son of Shaphan, that he should carry him home: so he dwelt among the people.

15 ¶ Now the word of the LORD came unto Jeremiah, while he was shut up in the court of the prison, saying,

16 Go and speak to Ebed-melech the Ethiopian, saying, Thus saith the LORD of hosts, the God of Israel; Behold, I will bring my words upon this city for evil, and not for good; and they shall be *accomplished* in that day before thee.

17 But I will deliver thee in that day, saith the LORD: and thou shalt

---

39 1*a* 2 Kgs. 25:1;
  Jer. 52:4;
  Ezek. 24:1.
 b Ezek. 24:2.
 c TG Jerusalem.
3*a* Jer. 1:15.
4*a* Jer. 52:3 (3–15);
  Omni 1:15 (15–16).
5*a* Jer. 44:30.
 b Lam. 4:19.

 c OR pronounced
  sentence.
6*a* 2 Kgs. 25:21 (19–21);
  Jer. 52:10;
  Ezek. 11:10.
 b Jer. 38:23;
  Hel. 6:10; 8:21.
7*a* Jer. 52:11;
  Ezek. 12:13.
 b Lam. 4:20.

 8*a* Lam. 5:2.
 b 2 Kgs. 25:9;
  Jer. 52:13;
  Ezek. 16:41.
 c Jer. 5:10 (10–18).
9*a* OR had deserted.
10*a* Jer. 43:6.
12*a* HEB keep your eyes
  on him.
14*a* Jer. 43:6.

not be given into the hand of the men of whom thou *art* afraid.

18 For I will surely deliver thee, and thou shalt not fall by the sword, but thy *a*life shall be for a prey unto thee: because thou hast put thy trust in me, saith the LORD.

CHAPTER 40

The king of Babylon makes Gedaliah governor over the remnant left in Judah—Jeremiah is freed and dwells among them.

THE word that came to Jeremiah from the LORD, after that Nebuzaradan the captain of the guard had let him go from Ramah, when he had taken him being bound in chains among all that were carried away captive of Jerusalem and *a*Judah, which were carried away captive unto Babylon.

2 And the captain of the guard took Jeremiah, and said unto him, The LORD thy God hath pronounced this evil upon this place.

3 Now the LORD hath brought *it,* and done according as he hath said: because ye have *a*sinned against the LORD, and have not obeyed his voice, therefore this *b*thing is come upon you.

4 And now, behold, I loose thee this day from the chains which *were* upon thine hand. If it seem good unto thee to come with me into Babylon, come; and I will look well unto thee: but if it seem ill unto thee to come with me into Babylon, forbear: behold, all the land *is* before thee: whither it seemeth good and convenient for thee to go, thither go.

5 Now while he was not yet gone back, *he said,* Go back also to *a*Gedaliah the son of Ahikam the son of Shaphan, whom the king of Babylon hath made governor over the cities of Judah, and dwell with him among the people: or go wheresoever it seemeth convenient unto thee to go. So the captain of the guard gave him *b*victuals and a reward, and let him go.

6 Then went Jeremiah unto Gedaliah the son of Ahikam to Mizpah; and dwelt with him among the people that were left in the land.

7 ¶ Now when all the captains of the forces which *were* in the fields, *even* they and their men, heard that the king of Babylon had made Gedaliah the son of Ahikam governor in the land, and had committed unto him men, and women, and children, and of the *a*poor of the land, of them that were not carried away captive to Babylon;

8 Then they came to Gedaliah to Mizpah, even Ishmael the son of Nethaniah, and *a*Johanan and Jonathan the sons of Kareah, and Seraiah the son of Tanhumeth, and the sons of Ephai the Netophathite, and Jezaniah the son of a Maachathite, they and their men.

9 And Gedaliah the son of Ahikam the son of Shaphan sware unto them and to their men, saying, Fear not to serve the Chaldeans: dwell in the land, and serve the king of Babylon, and it shall be well with you.

10 As for me, behold, I will dwell at Mizpah to serve the Chaldeans, which will come unto us: but ye, gather ye wine, and summer fruits, and oil, and put *them* in your vessels, and dwell in your cities that ye have taken.

11 Likewise when all the Jews that *were* in Moab, and among the Ammonites, and in Edom, and that *were* in all the countries, heard that the king of Babylon had left a remnant of Judah, and that he had set over them Gedaliah the son of Ahikam the son of Shaphan;

12 Even all the Jews returned out of all places whither they were driven, and came to the land of Judah, to Gedaliah, unto Mizpah, and gathered wine and summer fruits very much.

13 ¶ Moreover Johanan the son of

18*a* Jer. 21:9; 45:5.
40 1*a* Matt. 2:18.
3*a* D&C 101:2 (1–9).

b Jer. 44:23.
5*a* 2 Kgs. 25:22 (22–26);
Jer. 43:6.

b HEB a food allowance.
7*a* 2 Kgs. 25:12.
8*a* Jer. 43:2.

Kareah, and all the *a*captains of the forces that *were* in the fields, came to Gedaliah to Mizpah,

14 And said unto him, Dost thou certainly know that Baalis the king of the Ammonites hath sent Ishmael the son of Nethaniah to slay thee? But Gedaliah the son of Ahikam believed them not.

15 Then Johanan the son of Kareah spake to Gedaliah in Mizpah secretly, saying, Let me go, I pray thee, and I will slay Ishmael the son of Nethaniah, and no man shall know *it:* wherefore should he slay thee, that all the Jews which are gathered unto thee should be scattered, and the remnant in Judah perish?

16 But Gedaliah the son of Ahikam said unto Johanan the son of Kareah, Thou shalt not do this thing: for thou speakest falsely of Ishmael.

CHAPTER 41

Ishmael kills Gedaliah and carries the people of Mizpah captive—They are rescued by Johanan.

Now it came to pass in the seventh month, *that* Ishmael the son of Nethaniah the son of Elishama, of the seed royal, and the princes of the king, even ten men with him, came unto Gedaliah the son of Ahikam to Mizpah; and there they did eat bread together in Mizpah.

2 Then arose Ishmael the son of Nethaniah, and the ten men that were with him, and smote Gedaliah the son of Ahikam the son of Shaphan with the sword, and slew him, whom the king of Babylon had made governor over the land.

3 Ishmael also slew all the Jews that were with him, *even* with Gedaliah, at Mizpah, and the Chaldeans that were found there, *and* the men of war.

4 And it came to pass the second day after he had slain Gedaliah, and no man knew *it,*

5 That there came certain from Shechem, from Shiloh, and from Samaria, *even* fourscore men, having their beards shaven, and their clothes rent, and having cut themselves, with offerings and incense in their hand, to bring *them* to the house of the LORD.

6 And Ishmael the son of Nethaniah went forth from Mizpah to meet them, weeping all along as he went: and it came to pass, as he met them, he said unto them, Come to Gedaliah the son of Ahikam.

7 And it was *so,* when they came into the midst of the city, that Ishmael the son of Nethaniah slew them, *and cast them* into the midst of the pit, he, and the men that *were* with him.

8 But ten men were found among them that said unto Ishmael, Slay us not: for we have treasures in the field, of wheat, and of barley, and of oil, and of honey. So he forbare, and slew them not among their brethren.

9 Now the pit wherein Ishmael had cast all the dead bodies of the men, whom he had slain because of Gedaliah, *was* it which Asa the king had made for fear of Baasha king of Israel: *and* Ishmael the son of Nethaniah filled it with *them that were* slain.

10 Then Ishmael carried away captive all the residue of the people that *were* in Mizpah, *even* the king's *a*daughters, and all the people that remained in Mizpah, whom Nebuzar-adan the captain of the guard had committed to Gedaliah the son of Ahikam: and Ishmael the son of Nethaniah carried them away captive, and departed to go over to the Ammonites.

11 ¶ But when Johanan the son of Kareah, and all the captains of the forces that *were* with him, heard of all the evil that Ishmael the son of Nethaniah had done,

12 Then they took all the men, and went to fight with Ishmael the son of Nethaniah, and found him by the *a*great waters that *are* in Gibeon.

13 Now it came to pass, *that* when all the people which *were* with

---

13*a* Jer. 43:4.   **41** 10*a* Jer. 43:6.   12*a* OR many pools.

Ishmael saw Johanan the son of Kareah, and all the captains of the forces that *were* with him, then they were glad.

14 So all the people that Ishmael had carried away captive from Mizpah *a*cast about and returned, and went unto Johanan the son of Kareah.

15 But Ishmael the son of Nethaniah escaped from Johanan with eight men, and went to the Ammonites.

16 Then took Johanan the son of Kareah, and all the captains of the forces that *were* with him, all the remnant of the people whom he had recovered from Ishmael the son of Nethaniah, from Mizpah, after *that* he had slain Gedaliah the son of Ahikam, *even* mighty men of war, and the women, and the children, and the *a*eunuchs, whom he had brought again from Gibeon:

17 And they departed, and dwelt in the habitation of Chimham, which is by Beth-lehem, to go to enter into Egypt,

18 Because of the Chaldeans: for they were afraid of them, because Ishmael the son of Nethaniah had slain Gedaliah the son of Ahikam, whom the king of Babylon made governor in the land.

CHAPTER 42

Jeremiah promises Johanan and the remnant of Judah peace and safety if they remain in Judah, but the sword, famine, and pestilence if they go to Egypt.

THEN all the captains of the forces, and Johanan the son of Kareah, and Jezaniah the son of Hoshaiah, and all the people from the least even unto the greatest, came near,

2 And said unto Jeremiah the prophet, Let, we beseech thee, our supplication be accepted before thee, and pray for us unto the LORD

thy God, *even* for all this remnant; (for we are left *but* a few of many, as thine eyes do behold us:)

3 That the LORD thy God may shew us the way wherein we may walk, and the thing that we may do.

4 Then Jeremiah the prophet said unto them, I have heard *you*; behold, I will *a*pray unto the LORD your God according to your words; and it shall come to pass, *that* whatsoever thing the LORD shall answer you, I will declare *it* unto you; I will keep nothing back from you.

5 Then they said to Jeremiah, The LORD be a true and *a*faithful witness between us, if we do not even according to all things for the which the LORD thy God shall send thee to us.

6 Whether *it be* good, or whether *it be* evil, we will obey the *a*voice of the LORD our God, to whom we send thee; that it may be well with us, when we obey the voice of the LORD our God.

7 ¶ And it came to pass after ten days, that the word of the LORD came unto Jeremiah.

8 Then called he Johanan the son of Kareah, and all the captains of the forces which *were* with him, and all the people from the least even to the greatest,

9 And said unto them, Thus saith the LORD, the God of Israel, unto whom ye sent me to present your supplication before him;

10 If ye will still abide in this land, then will I build you, and not pull *you* down, and I will plant you, and not pluck *you* up: *a*for I repent me of the evil that I have done unto you.

11 Be not afraid of the king of Babylon, of whom ye are afraid; be not afraid of him, saith the LORD: for I *am* with you to save you, and to deliver you from his hand.

12 And I will shew mercies unto

14*a* HEB turned around and came back.
16*a* OR courtiers or officials.
42 4*a* Num. 21:7; 1 Sam. 7:5;
2 Ne. 33:3; Enos 1:9.
5*a* Rev. 1:5; 3:14.
6*a* D&C 25:16.
10*a* IE I feel compassion regarding the
punishment I bring upon you.
JST Jer. 42:10 . . . *and I will turn away* the evil that I have done unto you.

you, that he may have mercy upon you, and cause you to return to your own land.

13 ¶ But if ye say, We will not dwell in this land, neither obey the voice of the LORD your God,

14 Saying, No; but we will go into the land of Egypt, where we shall see no war, nor hear the sound of the *a*trumpet, nor have hunger of bread; and there will we dwell:

15 And now therefore hear the word of the LORD, ye remnant of Judah; Thus saith the LORD of hosts, the God of Israel; If ye wholly set your *a*faces to enter into Egypt, and go to sojourn there;

16 Then it shall come to pass, *that* the sword, which ye feared, shall overtake you there in the land of Egypt, and the famine, whereof ye were afraid, shall follow close after you there in Egypt; and there ye shall die.

17 So shall it be with all the men that set their faces to go into Egypt to sojourn there; they shall die by the sword, by the famine, and by the pestilence: and none of them shall remain or escape from the evil that I will bring upon them.

18 For thus saith the LORD of hosts, the God of Israel; As mine anger and my fury hath been poured forth upon the inhabitants of Jerusalem; so shall my fury be poured forth upon you, when ye shall enter into Egypt: and ye shall be an *a*execration, and an astonishment, and a curse, and a reproach; and ye shall see this place no more.

19 ¶ The LORD hath said concerning you, O ye remnant of Judah; Go ye not into *a*Egypt: know certainly that I have admonished you this day.

20 For ye *a*dissembled in your hearts, when ye sent me unto the LORD your God, saying, Pray for us unto the LORD our God; and according unto all that the LORD our God shall say, so declare unto us, and we will do *it.*

21 And *now* I have this day declared *it* to you; but ye have not *a*obeyed the voice of the LORD your God, nor any *thing* for the which he hath sent me unto you.

22 Now therefore know certainly that ye shall die by the sword, by the famine, and by the pestilence, in the place whither ye desire to go *and* to sojourn.

CHAPTER 43

Johanan carries Jeremiah and the remnant of Judah into Egypt—Jeremiah prophesies that Babylon will conquer Egypt.

AND it came to pass, *that* when Jeremiah had made an end of speaking unto all the people all the words of the LORD their God, for which the LORD their God had sent him to them, *even* all these words,

2 Then spake Azariah the son of Hoshaiah, and *a*Johanan the son of Kareah, and all the proud men, saying unto Jeremiah, Thou speakest falsely: the LORD our God hath not sent thee to say, Go not into Egypt to sojourn there:

3 But *a*Baruch the son of Neriah setteth thee on against us, for to deliver us into the hand of the Chaldeans, that they might put us to death, and carry us away captives into Babylon.

4 So Johanan the son of Kareah, and all the *a*captains of the forces, and all the people, obeyed not the voice of the LORD, to dwell in the land of Judah.

5 But Johanan the son of Kareah, and all the captains of the forces, took all the remnant of Judah, that were returned from all nations, whither they had been driven, to dwell in the land of Judah;

6 *Even* men, and women, and children, and the king's *a*daughters, and

---

14*a* HEB *shofar* or alarm.
15*a* Jer. 44:12.
18*a* Jer. 44:12.
19*a* Deut. 17:16.

20*a* HEB have deceived your souls.
21*a* TG Disobedience.
43 2*a* Jer. 40:8.

3*a* Jer. 32:12.
4*a* Jer. 40:13.
6*a* Jer. 41:10.

every person that *b*Nebuzar-adan the captain of the guard had left with *c*Gedaliah the son of Ahikam the son of Shaphan, and Jeremiah the prophet, and Baruch the son of Neriah.

7 So they came into the land of *a*Egypt: for they obeyed not the voice of the LORD: thus came they *even* to *b*Tahpanhes.

8 ¶ Then came the word of the LORD unto Jeremiah in Tahpanhes, saying,

9 Take great stones in thine hand, and hide them in the clay in the brickkiln, which *is* at the entry of Pharaoh's house in Tahpanhes, in the sight of the men of Judah;

10 And say unto them, Thus saith the LORD of hosts, the God of Israel; Behold, I will send and take *a*Nebuchadrezzar the king of Babylon, my servant, and will set his throne upon these stones that I have hid; and he shall spread his royal pavilion over them.

11 And when he cometh, he shall *a*smite the land of Egypt, *and deliver* such *as are* for death to death; and such *as are* for captivity to captivity; and such *as are* for the sword to the sword.

12 And I will kindle a fire in the houses of the *a*gods of Egypt; and he shall burn them, and carry them away *b*captives: and he shall array himself with the land of Egypt, as a shepherd putteth on his garment; and he shall go forth from thence in peace.

13 He shall break also the images of Beth-shemesh, that *is* in the land of Egypt; and the houses of the gods of the Egyptians shall he burn with fire.

CHAPTER 44

Jeremiah prophesies that the Jews in Egypt, save a small remnant, will be destroyed because they worship false gods.

THE word that came to Jeremiah concerning all the Jews which dwell in the land of Egypt, which dwell at *a*Migdol, and at *b*Tahpanhes, and at *c*Noph, and in the country of Pathros, saying,

2 Thus saith the LORD of hosts, the God of Israel; Ye have seen all the *a*evil that I have brought upon Jerusalem, and upon all the cities of Judah; and, behold, this day they *are* a *b*desolation, and no man dwelleth therein,

3 Because of their wickedness which they have committed to provoke me to anger, in that they went to *a*burn incense, *and* to serve other *b*gods, whom they knew not, *neither* they, ye, nor your fathers.

4 Howbeit I *a*sent unto you all my servants the prophets, rising early and sending *them*, saying, Oh, do not this *b*abominable thing that I hate.

5 But they *a*hearkened not, nor inclined their ear to turn from their *b*wickedness, to burn no incense unto other gods.

6 Wherefore my fury and mine anger was poured forth, and was kindled in the cities of Judah and in the streets of Jerusalem; and they are wasted *and* desolate, as at this day.

7 Therefore now thus saith the LORD, the God of hosts, the God of Israel; Wherefore commit ye *this* great *a*evil against your souls, to cut off from you man and woman, child and suckling, out of Judah, to leave you none to remain;

6*b* 2 Kgs. 25:8 (8–20);
    Jer. 39:10.
  c 2 Kgs. 25:22 (22–26);
    Jer. 39:14; 40:5 (1–6).
7*a* Jer. 44:24.
  b Jer. 2:16; 46:14.
10*a* Jer. 21:2 (2, 7); 25:9.
11*a* Jer. 44:13;
    2 Ne. 9:33.
12*a* Ex. 12:12;

Isa. 19:1;
    Jer. 46:25;
    Ezek. 30:13.
  b Jer. 48:7.
44 1*a* Ex. 14:2;
    Jer. 46:14.
  b Jer. 2:16.
  c Isa. 19:13.
2*a* Jer. 7:34; 27:17.
  b 2 Ne. 1:4.

3*a* Morm. 5:15.
  b Gal. 4:8.
4*a* 2 Chr. 36:15;
    D&C 133:71.
  b Deut. 12:31.
5*a* TG Prophets, Rejection of.
  b Alma 45:16.
7*a* Num. 16:38.

8 In that ye *a*provoke me unto wrath with the *b*works of your hands, burning incense unto other gods in the land of Egypt, whither ye be gone to dwell, that ye might *c*cut yourselves off, and that ye might be a curse and a reproach among all the nations of the earth?

9 Have ye forgotten the wickedness of your fathers, and the wickedness of the kings of Judah, and the wickedness of their *a*wives, and your own wickedness, and the wickedness of your wives, which they have committed in the land of Judah, and in the streets of Jerusalem?

10 They are not *a*humbled *even* unto this day, neither have they *b*feared, nor walked in my law, nor in my statutes, that I set before you and before your fathers.

11 ¶ Therefore thus saith the LORD of hosts, the God of Israel; Behold, I will set my *a*face against you for evil, and to cut off all Judah.

12 And I will take the remnant of Judah, that have set their *a*faces to go into the land of Egypt to sojourn there, and they shall all be *b*consumed, *and* fall in the land of Egypt; they shall *even* be consumed by the sword *and* by the famine: they shall die, from the least even unto the greatest, by the sword and by the famine: and they shall be an *c*execration, *and* an astonishment, and a curse, and a reproach.

13 For I will *a*punish them that dwell in the land of Egypt, as I have punished Jerusalem, by the sword, by the famine, and by the pestilence:

14 So that none of the remnant of Judah, which are gone into the land of Egypt to sojourn there, shall escape or remain, that they should return into the land of Judah, to the which they have a desire to return to dwell there: for none shall return but such as shall escape.

15 ¶ Then all the men which knew that their wives had burned incense unto other gods, and all the women that stood by, a great multitude, even all the people that dwelt in the land of Egypt, in Pathros, answered Jeremiah, saying,

16 *As for* the word that thou hast spoken unto us in the name of the LORD, we will not *a*hearken unto thee.

17 But we will certainly do whatsoever thing goeth forth out of our *a*own mouth, to burn incense unto *b*the queen of heaven, and to pour out drink offerings unto her, as we have done, we, and our fathers, our kings, and our princes, in the cities of Judah, and in the streets of Jerusalem: for *then* had we plenty of *c*victuals, and were well, and saw no evil.

18 But since we left off to burn incense to the queen of heaven, and to pour out drink offerings unto her, we have *a*wanted all *things,* and have been consumed by the sword and by the famine.

19 And when we burned incense to the queen of heaven, and poured out drink offerings unto her, did we make her cakes to worship her, and pour out drink offerings unto her, without our men?

20 ¶ Then Jeremiah said unto all the people, to the men, and to the women, and to all the people which had given him *that* answer, saying,

21 The incense that ye burned in the cities of Judah, and in the streets of Jerusalem, ye, and your fathers, your kings, and your princes, and the people of the land, did not the LORD *a*remember them, and came it *not* into his mind?

22 So that the LORD could no longer bear, because of the evil of your

---

8*a* 2 Kgs. 22:17.
 b Acts 17:29.
 c 3 Ne. 21:20 (20–21).
9*a* 1 Kgs. 11:3 (1–3).
10*a* D&C 54:3.
 b Eccl. 8:13 (12–13);
  D&C 10:56.

11*a* Lev. 20:5; Jer. 21:10.
12*a* Jer. 42:15.
 b Jer. 14:15.
 c Jer. 42:18.
13*a* Jer. 43:11.
16*a* Mosiah 16:2;
  Ether 11:13.

17*a* D&C 1:16.
 b IE the fertility goddess, such as the Babylonian Ishtar.
 c Hosea 2:5.
18*a* HEB lacked.
21*a* D&C 121:24.

doings, *and* because of the abominations which ye have committed; therefore is your land a *a*desolation, and an astonishment, and a curse, without an inhabitant, as at this day.

23 Because ye have burned incense, and because ye have sinned against the LORD, and have not *a*obeyed the voice of the LORD, nor walked in his law, nor in his statutes, nor in his testimonies; therefore this *b*evil is happened unto you, as at this day.

24 Moreover Jeremiah said unto all the people, and to all the women, Hear the word of the LORD, all Judah that *are* in the land of *a*Egypt:

25 Thus saith the LORD of hosts, the God of Israel, saying; Ye and your wives have both spoken with your mouths, and fulfilled with your hand, saying, We will surely perform our vows that we have vowed, to burn incense to the queen of heaven, and to pour out drink offerings unto her: ye will surely accomplish your vows, and surely perform your vows.

26 Therefore hear ye the word of the LORD, all Judah that dwell in the land of Egypt; Behold, I have *a*sworn by my great *b*name, saith the LORD, that my name shall no more be named in the mouth of any man of Judah in all the land of Egypt, saying, The Lord GOD liveth.

27 Behold, I will *a*watch over them for evil, and not for good: and all the men of Judah that *are* in the land of Egypt shall be consumed by the sword and by the famine, until there be an end of them.

28 Yet a small number that *a*escape the sword shall return out of the land of Egypt into the land of Judah, and all the remnant of Judah, that are gone into the land of Egypt to sojourn there, shall know whose *b*words shall stand, mine, or theirs.

29 ¶ And this *shall be* a sign unto you, saith the LORD, that I will punish you in this place, that ye may know that my words shall surely stand against you for evil:

30 Thus saith the LORD; Behold, I will give *a*Pharaoh-hophra king of Egypt into the hand of his enemies, and into the hand of them that seek his life; as I gave *b*Zedekiah king of Judah into the hand of Nebuchadrezzar king of Babylon, his enemy, and that sought his life.

CHAPTER 45

Jeremiah promises Baruch that his life will be preserved.

THE word that Jeremiah the prophet spake unto *a*Baruch the son of Neriah, when he had written these words in a book at the mouth of Jeremiah, in the fourth year of Jehoiakim the son of Josiah king of Judah, saying,

2 Thus saith the LORD, the God of Israel, unto thee, O Baruch;

3 Thou didst say, Woe is me now! for the LORD hath added grief to my sorrow; I fainted in my sighing, and I find no *a*rest.

4 ¶ Thus shalt thou say unto him, The LORD saith thus; Behold, *that* which I have built will I *a*break down, and that which I have planted I will *b*pluck up, even *c*this whole land.

5 And *a*seekest thou great things for thyself? seek *them* not: for, behold, I will bring evil upon all flesh, saith the LORD: but thy *b*life will I give unto thee for a prey in all places whither thou goest.

22*a* Jer. 5:9; 9:9.
23*a* TG Disobedience.
　b Deut. 31:29;
　　Jer. 40:3.
24*a* Jer. 43:7.
26*a* Heb. 6:13.
　b 1 Ne. 20:11.
27*a* Jer. 31:28.

28*a* Ezek. 6:8; 7:16.
　b Moses 4:30.
30*a* Jer. 46:25;
　　Ezek. 17:17.
　b Jer. 39:5;
　　1 Ne. 1:4.
45 1*a* Jer. 36:4.
　3*a* Lam. 1:3.

4*a* Jer. 1:10.
　b Jer. 31:28.
　c Hebrew text adds: for it
　　is mine.
5*a* Mark 8:36 (36–37).
　b Jer. 21:9; 39:18.

CHAPTER 46

Jeremiah prophesies the conquest of Egypt by Babylon—Jacob will be saved and will return to his own land.

THE word of the LORD which came to Jeremiah the prophet against the *a*Gentiles;

2 Against Egypt, against the army of *a*Pharaoh-necho king of Egypt, which was by the river Euphrates in Carchemish, which Nebuchadrezzar king of Babylon smote in the fourth year of Jehoiakim the son of Josiah king of Judah.

3 Order ye the buckler and shield, and draw near to battle.

4 Harness the horses; and get up, ye horsemen, and stand forth with *your* helmets; furbish the spears, *and* put on the *a*brigandines.

5 Wherefore have I seen them dismayed *and* *a*turned away back? and their mighty ones are beaten down, and are fled apace, and look not back: *for* fear *was* round about, saith the LORD.

6 Let not the swift flee away, nor the mighty man escape; they shall stumble, and fall toward the north by the river Euphrates.

7 Who *is* this *that* cometh up as a *a*flood, whose waters are moved as the rivers?

8 Egypt riseth up like *a*a flood, and *his* waters are moved like the rivers; and he saith, I will go up, *and* will cover the earth; I will destroy the city and the inhabitants thereof.

9 Come up, ye horses; and rage, ye chariots; and let the mighty men come forth; the Ethiopians and the Libyans, that handle the shield; and the *a*Lydians, that handle *and* bend the bow.

10 For this *is* the *a*day of the Lord GOD of hosts, a day of vengeance,

that he may avenge him of his adversaries: and the sword shall devour, and it shall be *b*satiate and made drunk with their blood: for the Lord GOD of hosts hath a *c*sacrifice in the north country by the river Euphrates.

11 Go up into Gilead, and take *a*balm, O virgin, the daughter of Egypt: in vain shalt thou use many medicines; *for* thou shalt not be cured.

12 The nations have heard of thy *a*shame, and thy cry hath filled the land: for the mighty man hath stumbled against the mighty, *and* they are fallen both together.

13 ¶ The word that the LORD spake to Jeremiah the prophet, how Nebuchadrezzar king of Babylon should come *and* smite the land of *a*Egypt.

14 Declare ye in Egypt, and publish in *a*Migdol, and publish in Noph and in *b*Tahpanhes: say ye, Stand fast, and prepare thee; for the sword shall devour round about thee.

15 Why are thy *a*valiant *men* swept away? they stood not, because the LORD did drive them.

16 He made many to fall, yea, one fell upon another: and they said, Arise, and let us go again to our own people, and to the land of our nativity, from the oppressing sword.

17 They did cry there, Pharaoh king of Egypt *is but* a noise; he hath passed the time appointed.

18 *As* I live, saith the King, whose name *is* the LORD of hosts, Surely as Tabor *is* among the mountains, and as Carmel by the sea, *so* shall he come.

19 O thou daughter dwelling in Egypt, furnish thyself to go into *a*captivity: for Noph shall be waste and desolate without an inhabitant.

20 Egypt *is like* a very fair heifer,

---

46 1*a* Jer. 1:5; 25:15 (15–29).
  2*a* 2 Kgs. 23:29.
  4*a* OR armor.
  5*a* HEB retreating.
  7*a* Isa. 8:7 (7–8);
    Jer. 47:2;
    Dan. 11:22.
  8*a* HEB the river.

  9*a* Isa. 66:19;
    Ezek. 27:10; 30:5.
  10*a* Joel 1:15.
    b OR sated.
    c Isa. 34:6.
  11*a* Jer. 8:22; 51:8.
  12*a* TG Shame.
  13*a* Isa. 19:1 (1–22).

  14*a* Jer. 44:1.
    b Jer. 43:7.
  15*a* Mosiah 1:13;
    Hel. 4:24 (24, 26).
  19*a* Ezek. 29:12;
    30:23 (23, 26).

but destruction cometh; it cometh out of the north.

21 Also her hired men *are* in the midst of her like fatted bullocks; for they also are turned back, *and* are fled away together: they did not stand, because the day of their calamity was come upon them, *and* the time of their visitation.

22 The voice thereof shall go like a serpent; for they shall march with an army, and come against her with axes, as hewers of wood.

23 They shall cut down her forest, saith the LORD, though it cannot be searched; because they are more than the grasshoppers, and *are* innumerable.

24 The daughter of Egypt shall be confounded; she shall be delivered into the hand of the people of the north.

25 The *a*LORD of hosts, the God of Israel, saith; Behold, I will punish *b*the multitude of *c*No, and *d*Pharaoh, and Egypt, with their *e*gods, and their kings; even Pharaoh, and *all* them that trust in him:

26 And I will deliver them into the hand of those that seek their lives, and into the hand of Nebuchadrezzar king of Babylon, and into the hand of his servants: and afterward it shall be *a*inhabited, as in the days of old, saith the LORD.

27 ¶ But fear not thou, O my servant *a*Jacob, and be not dismayed, O Israel: for, behold, I will save thee from afar off, and thy seed from the land of their captivity; and Jacob shall return, and be in rest and at ease, and none shall make *him* afraid.

28 Fear thou not, O Jacob my servant, saith the LORD: for I *am* with thee; for I will make a full end of all the nations whither I have driven thee: but I will not make a full end of thee, but correct thee in measure; yet will I not leave thee wholly unpunished.

CHAPTER 47

Jeremiah foretells desolation and destruction upon the Philistines.

THE word of the LORD that came to Jeremiah the prophet against the *a*Philistines, before that Pharaoh smote Gaza.

2 Thus saith the LORD; Behold, *a*waters rise up out of the north, and shall be an overflowing flood, and shall overflow the land, and all that is therein; the city, and them that dwell therein: then the men shall cry, and all the inhabitants of the land shall howl.

3 At the noise of the stamping of the hoofs of his strong *horses*, at the rushing of his chariots, *and at* the rumbling of his wheels, the fathers shall not look back to *their* children for feebleness of hands;

4 Because of the day that cometh to spoil all the Philistines, *and* to cut off from *a*Tyrus and Zidon every helper that remaineth: for the LORD will spoil the Philistines, the remnant of the country of Caphtor.

5 Baldness is come upon Gaza; Ashkelon is cut off *with* the remnant of their valley: how long wilt thou cut thyself?

6 O thou sword of the LORD, how long *will it be* ere thou be quiet? put up thyself into thy scabbard, rest, and be still.

7 How can it be quiet, seeing the LORD hath given it a charge against Ashkelon, and against the sea shore? there hath he appointed it.

CHAPTER 48

Judgment and destruction will come upon the Moabites for their contempt of God.

AGAINST *a*Moab thus saith the LORD of hosts, the God of Israel; Woe unto Nebo! for it is spoiled: Kiriathaim is confounded *and* taken: Misgab is confounded and dismayed.

25*a* D&C 1:33.
  b HEB Amon of Thebes.
  c Ezek. 30:14; Nahum 3:8.
  d Jer. 25:19; 44:30.
  e Jer. 43:12.

26*a* Ezek. 29:13.
27*a* 3 Ne. 20:13 (11–13);
        22:7 (6–17).
47 1*a* Isa. 14:31 (29–32);
        Jer. 25:20;

    Ezek. 25:15 (15–16);
      Amos 1:8.
  2*a* Jer. 46:7 (7–8).
  4*a* Jer. 25:22.
48 1*a* Jer. 25:21.

2 *There shall be* no more praise of Moab: in Heshbon they have devised evil against it; come, and let us cut it off from *being* a nation. Also thou shalt be cut down, O Madmen; the sword shall pursue thee.

3 A voice of crying *shall be* from *a*Horonaim, spoiling and great destruction.

4 *a*Moab is destroyed; her little ones have caused a cry to be heard.

5 For in the going up of Luhith continual weeping shall go up; for in the going down of Horonaim the enemies have heard a cry of destruction.

6 Flee, save your lives, and be like the *a*heath in the wilderness.

7 ¶ For because thou hast trusted in thy *a*works and in thy treasures, thou shalt also be taken: and Chemosh shall go forth into *b*captivity *with* his priests and his princes together.

8 And the spoiler shall come upon every city, and no city shall escape: the valley also shall perish, and the plain shall be destroyed, as the LORD hath spoken.

9 Give wings unto Moab, that it may flee and get away: for the cities thereof shall be desolate, without any to dwell therein.

10 *a*Cursed *be* he that doeth the work of the LORD deceitfully, and cursed *be* he that keepeth back his sword from blood.

11 ¶ Moab hath been at ease from his youth, and he hath *a*settled on his *b*lees, and hath not been emptied from vessel to vessel, neither hath he gone into captivity: therefore his taste remained in him, and his scent is not changed.

12 Therefore, behold, the days come, saith the LORD, that I will send unto him *a*wanderers, that shall cause him to wander, and shall empty his vessels, and break their bottles.

13 And Moab shall be *a*ashamed of Chemosh, as the house of Israel was ashamed of Beth-el their confidence.

14 ¶ How say ye, We *are* mighty and strong men for the war?

15 Moab is spoiled, and gone up *out of* her cities, and his chosen young men are gone down to the slaughter, saith the King, whose name *is* the LORD of hosts.

16 The calamity of Moab *is* near to come, and his affliction hasteth fast.

17 All ye that are about him, bemoan him; and all ye that know his name, say, How is the strong staff broken, *and* the beautiful rod!

18 Thou daughter that dost inhabit Dibon, come down from *thy* glory, and sit in thirst; for the spoiler of Moab shall come upon thee, *and* he shall destroy thy strong holds.

19 O inhabitant of *a*Aroer, stand by the way, and espy; ask him that fleeth, and her that escapeth, *and* say, What is done?

20 Moab is confounded; for it is broken down: *a*howl and cry; tell ye it in Arnon, that Moab is spoiled,

21 And judgment is come upon the plain country; upon Holon, and upon Jahazah, and upon Mephaath,

22 And upon Dibon, and upon Nebo, and upon Beth-diblathaim,

23 And upon Kiriathaim, and upon Beth-gamul, and upon Beth-meon,

24 And upon *a*Kerioth, and upon *b*Bozrah, and upon all the cities of the land of Moab, far or near.

25 The *a*horn of Moab is cut off, and his arm is broken, saith the LORD.

26 ¶ Make ye him *a*drunken: for he magnified *himself* against the LORD: Moab also shall wallow in his vomit, and he also shall be in derision.

27 For was not Israel a derision unto thee? was he found among thieves? for since thou spakest of him, thou skippedst for joy.

3a Isa. 15:5.
4a Isa. 15:1.
6a Jer. 17:6.
7a Mosiah 12:29.
  b Jer. 43:12; 49:3.
10a TG Curse.

11a HEB relaxed his guard.
  b Zeph. 1:12.
12a HEB tilters (those who empty things out).
13a Hosea 10:6.
19a Deut. 2:36.

20a Isa. 16:7.
24a Jer. 48:41.
  b Jer. 49:13.
25a Ps. 75:10.
26a Jer. 25:27.

28 O ye that dwell in Moab, leave the cities, and dwell in the rock, and be like the dove *that* maketh her nest in the sides of the hole's mouth.

29 We have heard the *a*pride of Moab, (he is exceeding proud) his loftiness, and his arrogancy, and his pride, and the haughtiness of his heart.

30 I know his wrath, saith the LORD; but *it shall* not *be* so; his lies shall not so effect *it*.

31 Therefore will I howl for Moab, and I will cry out for all Moab; *mine heart* shall mourn for the men of Kir-heres.

32 O vine of Sibmah, I will weep for thee with the weeping of Jazer: thy *a*plants are gone over the sea, they reach *even* to the sea of Jazer: the spoiler is fallen upon thy summer fruits and upon thy vintage.

33 And joy and *a*gladness is taken from the plentiful field, and from the land of Moab; and I have caused wine to fail from the winepresses: none shall tread with shouting; *their* *b*shouting *shall be* no shouting.

34 From the cry of *a*Heshbon *even* unto Elealeh, *and even* unto Jahaz, have they uttered their voice, from Zoar *even* unto Horonaim, *as* an heifer of three years old: for the waters also of Nimrim shall be desolate.

35 Moreover I will cause to cease in Moab, saith the LORD, him that offereth in the high places, and him that burneth incense to his gods.

36 Therefore mine *a*heart shall sound for Moab like pipes, and mine heart shall sound like *b*pipes for the men of Kir-heres: because the *c*riches *that* he hath gotten are perished.

37 For every head *shall be* *a*bald, and every beard clipped: upon all the hands *shall be* cuttings, and upon the loins sackcloth.

38 *There shall be* lamentation generally upon all the housetops of Moab, and in the streets thereof: for I have broken Moab like a *a*vessel wherein *is* no pleasure, saith the LORD.

39 They shall howl, *saying*, How is it broken down! how hath Moab turned the back with shame! so shall Moab be a derision and a dismaying to all them about him.

40 For thus saith the LORD; Behold, he shall fly as an *a*eagle, and shall spread his wings over Moab.

41 *a*Kerioth is taken, and the strong holds are *b*surprised, and the mighty men's hearts in Moab at that day shall be as the heart of a woman in her pangs.

42 And Moab shall be destroyed from *being* a people, because he hath *a*magnified *himself* against the LORD.

43 Fear, and the pit, and the snare, *shall be* upon thee, O inhabitant of Moab, saith the LORD.

44 He that fleeth from the fear shall fall into the pit; and he that getteth up out of the pit shall be taken in the snare: for I will bring upon it, *even* upon Moab, the year of their visitation, saith the LORD.

45 They that fled stood under the shadow of Heshbon because of the force: but a fire shall come forth out of *a*Heshbon, and a flame from the midst of Sihon, and shall devour the corner of *b*Moab, and the crown of the head of the tumultuous ones.

46 Woe be unto thee, O Moab! the people of Chemosh perisheth: for thy sons are taken captives, and thy daughters captives.

47 ¶ Yet will I *a*bring again the captivity of *b*Moab in the latter days, saith the LORD. Thus far *is* the judgment of Moab.

29*a* TG Pride.
32*a* HEB branches.
33*a* Isa. 16:10.
  b OR cheering.
34*a* Isa. 15:4.
36*a* Isa. 15:5; 16:11.
  b OR flutes.

c Hel. 13:31 (18, 31, 33).
37*a* Isa. 15:2.
38*a* Ps. 31:12;
    Jer. 22:28;
    Hosea 8:8.
40*a* Ezek. 17:3.
41*a* Jer. 48:24.

b HEB captured.
42*a* Zeph. 2:8 (8, 10).
45*a* Num. 21:28.
  b Num. 24:17.
47*a* OR turn away, remove.
  b Isa. 16:5 (1–5).

CHAPTER 49

Judgment and destruction will come upon the people of Ammon, Edom, Kedar, Hazor, and Elam.

CONCERNING the Ammonites, thus saith the LORD; Hath Israel no sons? hath he no heir? why *then* doth their king inherit Gad, and his people dwell in his cities?

2 Therefore, behold, the days come, saith the LORD, that I will cause an alarm of war to be heard in *a*Rabbah of the *b*Ammonites; and it shall be a desolate heap, and her *c*daughters shall be burned with fire: then shall Israel be heir unto them that were his heirs, saith the LORD.

3 Howl, O Heshbon, for Ai is spoiled: cry, ye daughters of Rabbah, gird you with sackcloth; lament, and run to and fro by the hedges; for their king shall go into *a*captivity, *and* his priests and his princes together.

4 Wherefore gloriest thou in the valleys, thy flowing valley, O backsliding daughter? that trusted in her *a*treasures, *saying,* Who shall come unto me?

5 Behold, I will bring a fear upon thee, saith the Lord GOD of hosts, from all those that be about thee; and ye shall be driven out every man right forth; and none shall gather up him that wandereth.

6 And afterward I will *a*bring again the captivity of the children of Ammon, saith the LORD.

7 ¶ Concerning *a*Edom, thus saith the LORD of hosts; *Is* wisdom no more in Teman? is counsel perished from the *b*prudent? is their wisdom vanished?

8 Flee ye, turn back, dwell deep, O inhabitants of Dedan; for I will bring the calamity of Esau upon him, the time *that* I will visit him.

9 If grapegatherers come to thee, would they not leave *some* gleaning grapes? if *a*thieves by night, they will destroy till they have enough.

10 But I have made *a*Esau bare, I have uncovered his secret places, and he shall not be able to hide himself: his *b*seed is spoiled, and his brethren, and his neighbours, and he *is* not.

11 Leave thy fatherless children, I will preserve *them* alive; and let thy *a*widows trust in me.

12 For thus saith the LORD; Behold, they whose judgment *was* not to *a*drink of the cup have assuredly drunken; and *art* thou he *that* shall altogether go unpunished? thou shalt not go unpunished, but thou shalt surely drink *of it.*

13 For I have sworn by myself, saith the LORD, that *a*Bozrah shall become a desolation, a reproach, a waste, and a curse; and all the *b*cities thereof shall be perpetual wastes.

14 I have heard a *a*rumour from the LORD, and an ambassador is sent unto the *b*heathen, *saying,* Gather ye together, and come against her, and rise up to the battle.

15 For, lo, I will make thee small among the heathen, *and* despised among men.

16 Thy terribleness hath deceived thee, *and* the *a*pride of thine heart, O thou that dwellest in the clefts of the rock, that holdest the height of the hill: though thou shouldest make thy nest as high as the eagle, I will bring thee down from thence, saith the LORD.

17 Also *a*Edom shall be a desolation: every one that goeth by it shall be astonished, and shall hiss at all the plagues thereof.

---

49 2*a* Ezek. 21:20; 25:5 (4–5);
    Amos 1:14.
  b Ezek. 21:28.
  c OR villages.
 3*a* Jer. 48:7.
 4*a* Alma 7:6.
 6*a* OR turn away, remove.
 7*a* Gen. 36:1;
    Jer. 25:21;
    Lam. 4:21;

    Ezek. 25:13 (12–14);
    Amos 1:11;
    Obad. 1:1 (1–14).
  b TG Prudence.
 9*a* Obad. 1:5.
10*a* Gen. 36:43.
  b Mal. 1:3.
11*a* TG Widows.
12*a* Obad. 1:16.
13*a* Jer. 48:24.

  b Ezek. 35:9.
14*a* OR report.
  b HEB nations, or
    Gentiles.
16*a* Obad. 1:3 (1–4).
17*a* Isa. 34:5;
    Ezek. 25:14 (12–14);
    Amos 9:12;
    Obad. 1:18 (8, 18–19, 21).

18 As in the overthrow of ᵃSodom and Gomorrah and the neighbour *cities* thereof, saith the LORD, no man shall abide there, neither shall a son of man dwell in it.

19 Behold, he shall come up like a ᵃlion from the swelling of Jordan against the habitation of the strong: but I will suddenly make him run away from her: and who *is* a chosen *man, that* I may appoint over her? for who *is* like me? and who will appoint me the time? and who *is* that shepherd that will stand before me?

20 Therefore hear the counsel of the LORD, that he hath taken against Edom; and his purposes, that he hath purposed against the inhabitants of Teman: Surely the least of the flock shall draw them out: surely he shall make their habitations desolate with them.

21 The earth is ᵃmoved at the noise of their fall, at the cry the noise thereof was heard in the Red sea.

22 Behold, he shall come up and fly as the eagle, and spread his wings over Bozrah: and at that day shall the heart of the mighty men of Edom be as the heart of a woman in her pangs.

23 ¶ Concerning Damascus. Hamath is confounded, and Arpad: for they have heard evil tidings: they are fainthearted; *there is* sorrow on the sea; it cannot be quiet.

24 Damascus is waxed feeble, *and* turneth herself to flee, and fear hath seized on *her:* anguish and ᵃsorrows have taken her, as a woman in travail.

25 How is the city of ᵃpraise not ᵇleft, the city of my joy!

26 Therefore her young men shall fall in her streets, and all the men of war shall be cut off in that day, saith the LORD of hosts.

27 And I will kindle a fire in the wall of Damascus, and it shall consume the palaces of Ben-hadad.

28 ¶ Concerning ᵃKedar, and concerning the kingdoms of Hazor, which Nebuchadrezzar king of Babylon shall smite, thus saith the LORD; Arise ye, go up to Kedar, and spoil the men of the east.

29 Their ᵃtents and their flocks shall they take away: they shall take to themselves their ᵇcurtains, and all their vessels, and their camels; and they shall cry unto them, ᶜFear *is* on every side.

30 ¶ Flee, get you far off, dwell deep, O ye inhabitants of Hazor, saith the LORD; for ᵃNebuchadrezzar king of Babylon hath taken counsel against you, and hath conceived a purpose against you.

31 Arise, get you up unto the wealthy nation, that dwelleth without care, saith the LORD, which have neither gates nor bars, *which* dwell alone.

32 And their camels shall be a booty, and the multitude of their cattle a spoil: and I will scatter into all winds them *that are* in the utmost corners; and I will bring their calamity from all sides thereof, saith the LORD.

33 And Hazor shall be a dwelling for ᵃdragons, *and* a desolation for ever: there shall no man abide there, nor *any* son of man dwell in it.

34 ¶ The word of the LORD that came to Jeremiah the prophet against ᵃElam in the beginning of the reign of ᵇZedekiah king of Judah, saying,

35 Thus saith the LORD of hosts; Behold, I will break the bow of Elam, the chief of their might.

36 And upon Elam will I bring the four winds from the four ᵃquarters of heaven, and will scatter them toward all those winds; and there shall

---

18a Gen. 19:24.
19a Jer. 4:7.
21a Ezek. 26:15.
24a TG Sorrow.
25a Jer. 33:9.

b HEB forsaken.
28a IE Arabia.
29a Ps. 120:5.
  b OR tent-cloths.
  c Jer. 50:46.

30a Jer. 27:12.
33a HEB jackals.
34a Ezek. 32:24.
  b 1 Ne. 1:4.
36a HEB ends or extremities.

be no nation whither the outcasts of Elam shall not come.

37 For I will cause Elam to be dismayed before their enemies, and before them that seek their life: and I will bring *a*evil upon them, *even* my fierce anger, saith the LORD; and I will send the sword after them, till I have consumed them:

38 And I will set my throne in Elam, and will destroy from thence the king and the princes, saith the LORD.

39 ¶ But it shall come to pass in the latter days, *that* I will bring again the captivity of Elam, saith the LORD.

CHAPTER 50

Babylon will be destroyed and never rise again—The scattered people of Israel will be brought again into the lands of their inheritance.

THE *a*word that the LORD spake against Babylon *and* against the land of the Chaldeans by Jeremiah the prophet.

2 Declare ye among the nations, and publish, and set up a standard; publish, *and* conceal not: say, Babylon is taken, *a*Bel is confounded, Merodach is broken in pieces; her idols are confounded, her images are broken in pieces.

3 For out of the *a*north there cometh up a nation against her, which shall make her land desolate, and none shall *b*dwell therein: they shall remove, they shall depart, both man and beast.

4 ¶ In those days, and in that time, saith the LORD, the children of Israel shall *a*come, they and the children of Judah *b*together, going and *c*weeping: they shall go, and seek the LORD their God.

5 They shall ask the way to Zion with their faces thitherward, *saying,* Come, and let us join ourselves to the LORD in a *a*perpetual *b*covenant *that* shall not be forgotten.

6 My people hath been lost sheep: their *a*shepherds have caused them to go astray, they have turned them away *on* the mountains: they have gone from mountain to hill, they have forgotten their restingplace.

7 All that found them have devoured them: and their adversaries said, We *a*offend not, because they have sinned against the LORD, the habitation of justice, even the LORD, the hope of their fathers.

8 *a*Remove out of the midst of Babylon, and go forth out of the land of the *b*Chaldeans, and be as the he goats before the flocks.

9 ¶ For, lo, I will raise and cause to come up against Babylon an assembly of great nations from the *a*north country: and they shall set themselves in array against her; from thence she shall be taken: their *b*arrows *shall be* as of a mighty expert man; none shall return *c*in vain.

10 And Chaldea shall be a spoil: all that spoil her shall be satisfied, saith the LORD.

11 Because ye were glad, because ye rejoiced, O ye destroyers of mine heritage, because ye are grown fat as the heifer at grass, and bellow as bulls;

12 Your mother shall be sore confounded; she that bare you shall be ashamed: behold, the *a*hindermost of the nations *shall be* a wilderness, a dry land, and a desert.

13 Because of the wrath of the LORD it shall not be inhabited, but it shall be wholly desolate: every one that goeth by Babylon shall be astonished, and hiss at all her plagues.

14 Put yourselves in array against Babylon round about: all ye that

---

37*a* OR calamity or disaster.
50 1*a* Jer. 51:60.
  2*a* Isa. 46:1.
  3*a* Jer. 51:48.
   b Isa. 13:20.
  4*a* TG Israel, Gathering of.

 b Ezek. 37:22.
 c Jer. 31:9;
    Zech. 12:10.
5*a* OR everlasting.
 b TG Covenants.
6*a* 2 Ne. 28:12 (9–16).
7*a* HEB are not guilty.

8*a* TG Separation.
 b TG Israel, Bondage of, in Other Lands.
9*a* Jer. 25:26.
 b Num. 24:8.
 c HEB empty.
12*a* OR last.

bend the bow, shoot at her, spare no arrows: for she hath sinned against the LORD.

15 Shout against her round about: she hath *a*given her hand: her foundations are fallen, her walls are thrown down: for it *is* the vengeance of the LORD: take vengeance upon her; as she hath done, do unto her.

16 Cut off the sower from Babylon, and him that handleth the sickle in the time of harvest: for fear of the oppressing sword they shall turn every one to his *a*people, and they shall flee every one to his own *b*land.

17 ¶ Israel *is* a scattered sheep; the lions have driven *him* away: first the king of Assyria hath devoured him; and last this Nebuchadrezzar king of Babylon hath *a*broken his bones.

18 Therefore thus saith the LORD of hosts, the God of Israel; Behold, I will punish the king of Babylon and his land, as I have punished the king of Assyria.

19 And I will *a*bring Israel again to his habitation, and he shall feed on Carmel and Bashan, and his soul shall be satisfied upon mount Ephraim and Gilead.

20 In those days, and in that time, saith the LORD, the iniquity of Israel shall be sought for, and *there shall be* none; and the sins of Judah, and they shall not be found: for I will *a*pardon them whom I reserve.

21 ¶ Go up against the land of Merathaim, *even* against it, and against the inhabitants of Pekod: waste and utterly destroy after them, saith the LORD, and do according to all that I have commanded thee.

22 A sound of battle *is* in the land, and of great destruction.

23 How is the hammer of the whole earth cut asunder and broken! how is Babylon become a desolation among the nations!

24 I have laid a snare for thee, and thou art also taken, O Babylon, and thou wast not aware: thou art found, and also caught, because thou hast striven against the LORD.

25 The LORD hath opened his armoury, and hath brought forth the weapons of his indignation: for this *is* the work of the Lord GOD of hosts in the land of the Chaldeans.

26 Come against her from the utmost border, open her storehouses: cast her up as heaps, and destroy her utterly: let nothing of her be left.

27 Slay all her bullocks; let them go down to the slaughter: woe unto them! for their day is come, the time of their *a*visitation.

28 The voice of them that flee and escape out of the land of Babylon, to declare in Zion the vengeance of the LORD our God, the vengeance of his temple.

29 Call together the archers against Babylon: all ye that bend the bow, camp against it round about; let none thereof escape: recompense her according to her work; according to all that she hath done, do unto her: for she hath been proud against the LORD, against the Holy One of Israel.

30 Therefore shall her young men fall in the streets, and all her men of war shall be cut off in that day, saith the LORD.

31 Behold, I *am* against thee, O *thou* most proud, saith the Lord GOD of hosts: for thy day is come, the time *that* I will visit thee.

32 And the most proud shall stumble and fall, and none shall raise him up: and I will kindle a fire in his cities, and it shall devour all round about him.

33 ¶ Thus saith the LORD of hosts; The children of Israel and the children of Judah *were* oppressed together: and all that took them captives held them fast; they refused to let them go.

34 Their Redeemer *is* strong; the LORD of hosts *is* his name: he shall throughly *a*plead their cause, that he

---

15*a* IE submitted.
16*a* Isa. 13:14.
  b TG Lands of

Inheritance.
17*a* Num. 24:8.
19*a* TG Israel, Gathering of.

20*a* TG Forgive.
27*a* OR punishment.
34*a* Isa. 51:22.

may give rest to the land, and disquiet the inhabitants of Babylon.

35 ¶ A sword *is* upon the Chaldeans, saith the Lord, and upon the inhabitants of Babylon, and upon her princes, and upon her wise *men*.

36 A sword *is* upon the liars; and they shall dote: a sword *is* upon her mighty men; and they shall be dismayed.

37 A sword *is* upon their horses, and upon their chariots, and upon all the [a]mingled people that *are* in the midst of her; and they shall become as women: a sword *is* upon her [b]treasures; and they shall be robbed.

38 A [a]drought *is* upon her waters; and they shall be [b]dried up: for it *is* the land of graven images, and they are mad upon *their* idols.

39 Therefore the wild beasts of the desert with the wild beasts of the islands shall dwell *there*, and the [a]owls shall dwell therein: and it shall be no more inhabited for ever; neither shall it be dwelt in from generation to generation.

40 As God overthrew [a]Sodom and Gomorrah and the neighbour *cities* thereof, saith the Lord; *so* shall no man abide there, neither shall any son of man dwell therein.

41 Behold, a people shall come from the [a]north, and a great nation, and many kings shall be raised up from the [b]coasts of the earth.

42 They shall hold the bow and the lance: they *are* [a]cruel, and will not shew mercy: their voice shall roar like the sea, and they shall ride upon horses, *every one* put in array, like a man to the battle, against thee, O daughter of Babylon.

43 The king of Babylon hath heard the report of them, and his hands waxed feeble: anguish took hold of him, *and* pangs as of a woman in travail.

44 Behold, he shall come up like a lion from the swelling of Jordan unto the habitation of the strong: but I will make them suddenly run away from her: and who *is* a chosen *man, that* I may appoint over her? for who *is* like me? and who will appoint me the time? and who *is* that [a]shepherd that will stand before me?

45 Therefore hear ye the counsel of the Lord, that he hath taken against Babylon; and his purposes, that he hath purposed against the land of the Chaldeans: Surely the least of the flock shall draw them out: surely he shall make *their* habitation desolate with them.

46 At the noise of the taking of Babylon the earth is [a]moved, and the cry is heard among the nations.

CHAPTER 51

Judgment, destruction, and desolation will come upon Babylon for her sins—Israel is commanded, Flee from Babylon—Israel is the Lord's rod to destroy all kingdoms.

Thus saith the Lord; Behold, I will raise up against [a]Babylon, and against them that dwell in the midst of them that rise up against me, a destroying [b]wind;

2 And will send unto Babylon [a]fanners, that shall fan her, and shall empty her land: for in the day of trouble they shall be against her round about.

3 Against *him that* bendeth let the archer bend his bow, and against *him that* lifteth himself up in his brigandine: and spare ye not her young men; destroy ye utterly all her host.

4 Thus the slain shall fall in the land of the Chaldeans, and *they that are* thrust through in her streets.

5 For Israel *hath* not *been* [a]forsaken,

37a Jer. 25:20.
  b Isa. 45:3;
    Jer. 51:13.
38a TG Drought.
  b Isa. 44:27;
    Jer. 51:36.
39a HEB daughters of the ostrich.

40a Gen. 19:24;
    Isa. 13:19.
41a Jer. 6:22 (22–24).
  b HEB remote parts.
42a TG Cruelty.
44a Isa. 44:28.
46a Jer. 49:29.
51 1a TG Babylon.

  b Jer. 4:11 (11–13).
2a OR strangers who shall scatter her.
    Isa. 41:16;
    Jer. 15:7;
    Matt. 3:12.
5a Isa. 54:5 (5–8).

nor Judah of his God, of the Lord of hosts; though their land was filled with sin against the Holy One of Israel.

6 Flee *a*out of the midst of *b*Babylon, and deliver every man his soul: be not cut off in her iniquity; for this *is* the time of the Lord's vengeance; he will render unto her a recompence.

7 Babylon *hath been* a golden cup in the Lord's hand, that made all the earth drunken: the nations have drunken of her wine; therefore the nations are mad.

8 Babylon is suddenly fallen and destroyed: *a*howl for her; take *b*balm for her pain, if so be she may be healed.

9 We would have healed Babylon, but she is not healed: forsake her, and let us go every one into his own *a*country: for her *b*judgment reacheth unto heaven, and is lifted up *even* to the skies.

10 The Lord hath *a*brought forth our righteousness: come, and let us declare in Zion the work of the Lord our God.

11 Make bright the arrows; gather the shields: the Lord hath raised up the spirit of the kings of the Medes: for his device *is* against Babylon, to destroy it; because it *is* the vengeance of the Lord, the vengeance of his temple.

12 Set up the standard upon the walls of Babylon, make the watch strong, set up the watchmen, prepare the ambushes: for the Lord hath both devised and done that which he spake against the inhabitants of Babylon.

13 O thou that dwellest upon many *a*waters, abundant in *b*treasures, thine end is come, *and* the measure of thy covetousness.

14 The Lord of hosts hath *a*sworn by himself, *saying*, Surely I will fill thee with men, as with caterpillers; and they shall lift up a shout against thee.

15 He hath *a*made the earth by his *b*power, he hath established the world by his wisdom, and hath stretched out the heaven by his *c*understanding.

16 When he uttereth *his* voice, *there is* a multitude of waters in the heavens; and he causeth the vapours to ascend from the ends of the earth: he maketh lightnings with rain, and bringeth forth the wind out of his treasures.

17 Every man is brutish by *his* knowledge; every founder is confounded by the *a*graven image: for his molten image *is* falsehood, and *there is* no breath in them.

18 They *are* vanity, the work of errors: in the time of their visitation they shall perish.

19 The portion of Jacob *is* not like them; for he *is* the *a*former of all things: and *Israel is* the rod of his inheritance: the Lord of hosts *is* his name.

20 Thou *art* my battle axe *and* weapons of war: for with thee will I break in pieces the nations, and with thee will I destroy kingdoms;

21 And with thee will I break in pieces the horse and his rider; and with thee will I break in pieces the chariot and his rider;

22 With thee also will I break in pieces man and woman; and with thee will I break in pieces old and young; and with thee will I break in pieces the young man and the maid;

23 I will also break in pieces with thee the shepherd and his flock; and with thee will I break in pieces the husbandman and his yoke of oxen; and with thee will I break in pieces captains and rulers.

24 And I will render unto Babylon and to all the inhabitants of Chaldea

---

6*a* Gen. 19:14.
  b TG Babylon.
8*a* Rev. 18:9 (9–19).
  b Jer. 46:11.
9*a* TG Lands of
     Inheritance.

b Rev. 18:5 (4–5).
10*a* Ps. 37:6.
13*a* Rev. 17:1 (1–5);
      1 Ne. 14:11.
  b Isa. 45:3;
     Jer. 50:37.

14*a* Amos 6:8.
15*a* TG Jesus Christ, Creator.
  b TG God, Power of.
  c TG Understanding.
17*a* D&C 1:16.
19*a* OR creator.

all their *a*evil that they have done in Zion in your sight, saith the LORD.

25 Behold, I *am* against thee, O *a*destroying mountain, saith the LORD, which destroyest all the earth: and I will stretch out mine hand upon thee, and roll thee down from the rocks, and will make thee a burnt mountain.

26 And they shall not take of thee a stone for a corner, nor a stone for foundations; but thou shalt be desolate for ever, saith the LORD.

27 Set ye up a *a*standard in the land, blow the trumpet among the nations, prepare the nations against her, call together against her the kingdoms of Ararat, Minni, and Ashchenaz; appoint a captain against her; cause the horses to come up as the rough caterpillers.

28 Prepare against her the nations with the kings of the Medes, the captains thereof, and all the rulers thereof, and all the land of his dominion.

29 And the land shall tremble and sorrow: for every purpose of the LORD shall be performed against Babylon, to make the land of Babylon a desolation without an inhabitant.

30 The mighty men of Babylon have *a*forborn to fight, they have remained in *their* holds: their might hath failed; they became as *b*women: they have burned her dwellingplaces; her bars are broken.

31 One *a*post shall run to meet another, and one messenger to meet another, to *b*shew the king of *c*Babylon that his city is *d*taken at *one* end,

32 And that the passages are stopped, and the reeds they have burned with fire, and the men of war are affrighted.

33 For thus saith the LORD of hosts, the God of Israel; The daughter of Babylon *is* like a threshingfloor,

it is time to thresh her: yet a little while, and the time of her *a*harvest shall come.

34 Nebuchadrezzar the king of Babylon hath devoured me, he hath crushed me, he hath made me an empty vessel, he hath swallowed me up like a *a*dragon, he hath filled his belly with my delicates, he hath cast me out.

35 The violence done to me and to my flesh *be* upon Babylon, shall the inhabitant of Zion say; and my blood upon the inhabitants of Chaldea, shall Jerusalem say.

36 Therefore thus saith the LORD; Behold, I will plead thy cause, and take vengeance for thee; and I will *a*dry up her sea, and make her springs dry.

37 And *a*Babylon shall become heaps, a dwellingplace for *b*dragons, an astonishment, and an hissing, without an inhabitant.

38 They shall roar together like lions: they shall yell as lions' whelps.

39 In their heat I will make their feasts, and I will make them drunken, that they may rejoice, and sleep a perpetual sleep, and not wake, saith the LORD.

40 I will bring them down like lambs to the slaughter, like rams with he goats.

41 How is *a*Sheshach taken! and how is the praise of the whole earth surprised! how is Babylon become an astonishment among the nations!

42 The sea is come up upon Babylon: she is covered with the multitude of the waves thereof.

43 Her cities are a desolation, a dry land, and a wilderness, a land wherein no man dwelleth, neither doth *any* son of man pass thereby.

44 And I will punish Bel in Babylon, and I will bring forth out of his mouth that which he hath

---

24*a* 1 Ne. 14:3.
25*a* IE Babylon.
27*a* TG Ensign.
30*a* OR ceased.
  b Nahum 3:13.
31*a* HEB runner.

b HEB tell or inform.
c Dan. 5:30.
d OR captured completely.
33*a* TG Harvest.
34*a* HEB sea monster.
36*a* Isa. 19:5; 44:27;

Jer. 50:38;
  Ezek. 30:12.
37*a* TG Babylon.
  b HEB jackals.
41*a* Jer. 25:26.

swallowed up: and the nations shall not flow together any more unto him: yea, the wall of Babylon shall fall.

45 My people, go ye out of the midst of her, and deliver ye every man his soul from the fierce anger of the LORD.

46 And lest your heart faint, and ye fear for the rumour that shall be heard in the land; a rumour shall both come *one* year, and after that in *another* year *shall come* a rumour, and violence in the land, ruler against ruler.

47 Therefore, behold, the days come, that I will do judgment upon the graven images of Babylon: and her whole land shall be confounded, and all her slain shall fall in the midst of her.

48 Then the heaven and the earth, and all that *is* therein, shall ^asing for Babylon: for the spoilers shall come unto her from the ^bnorth, saith the LORD.

49 As Babylon *hath caused* the slain of Israel to fall, so at Babylon shall fall the slain of all the earth.

50 Ye that have escaped the sword, go away, stand not still: remember the LORD afar off, and let Jerusalem come into your mind.

51 We are ^aconfounded, because we have heard reproach: shame hath covered our faces: for strangers are come into the ^bsanctuaries of the LORD's house.

52 Wherefore, behold, the days come, saith the LORD, that I will do judgment upon her graven images: and through all her land the wounded shall groan.

53 Though Babylon should mount up to heaven, and though she should fortify the height of her strength, *yet* from me shall spoilers come unto her, saith the LORD.

54 A sound of a cry *cometh* from Babylon, and great destruction from the land of the Chaldeans:

55 Because the LORD hath spoiled Babylon, and destroyed out of her the great voice; when her waves do roar like great waters, a noise of their voice is uttered:

56 Because the spoiler is come upon her, *even* upon Babylon, and her mighty men are taken, every one of their bows is broken: for the LORD God of recompences shall surely requite.

57 And I will make drunk her princes, and her wise *men,* her captains, and her rulers, and her mighty men: and they shall sleep a perpetual sleep, and not wake, saith the King, whose name *is* the LORD of hosts.

58 Thus saith the LORD of hosts; The broad walls of Babylon shall be utterly broken, and her high gates shall be burned with fire; and the people shall labour in ^avain, and the folk in the fire, and they shall be weary.

59 ¶ The word which Jeremiah the prophet commanded Seraiah the son of Neriah, the son of Maaseiah, when he went with Zedekiah the king of Judah into Babylon in the fourth year of his reign. And *this* Seraiah *was* a ^aquiet prince.

60 So Jeremiah wrote in a book all the evil that should come upon Babylon, *even* all these ^awords that are written against Babylon.

61 And Jeremiah said to Seraiah, When thou comest to Babylon, and shalt see, and shalt read all these words;

62 Then shalt thou say, O LORD, thou hast spoken against this place, to ^acut it off, that none shall remain in it, neither man nor beast, but that it shall be ^bdesolate for ever.

63 And it shall be, when thou hast made an end of reading this book, *that* thou shalt bind a stone to it, and cast it into the midst of Euphrates:

64 And thou shalt say, Thus shall Babylon sink, and shall not rise from

---

48a OR be jubilant.
  b Jer. 50:3.
51a HEB ashamed.
  b Lam. 1:10;

Ezek. 23:38; 44:7.
58a Hab. 2:13.
59a OR quartermaster.
60a Jer. 50:1.

62a Prov. 10:7;
    Isa. 14:22.
  b D&C 35:11.

the evil that I will bring upon her: and they shall be weary. Thus far *are* the words of Jeremiah.

CHAPTER 52

Jerusalem is besieged and taken by the Chaldeans—Many people and the vessels of the house of the Lord are carried into Babylon.

^aZEDEKIAH *was* one and twenty years old when he began to reign, and he reigned eleven years in Jerusalem. And his mother's name *was* Hamutal the daughter of Jeremiah of Libnah.

2 And he did *that which was* evil in the eyes of the LORD, according to all that Jehoiakim had done.

3 For through the anger of the LORD it came to pass in Jerusalem and Judah, till he had cast them out from his presence, that ^aZedekiah rebelled against the king of Babylon.

4 ¶ And it came to pass in the ^aninth year of his reign, in the tenth month, in the tenth *day* of the month, *that* Nebuchadrezzar king of Babylon came, he and all his army, against Jerusalem, and pitched against it, and built ^bforts against it round about.

5 So the city was besieged unto the eleventh year of king Zedekiah.

6 And in the fourth month, in the ninth *day* of the month, the ^afamine was sore in the city, so that there was no ^bbread for the people of the land.

7 Then the ^acity was broken up, and all the men of war fled, and went forth out of the city by night by the way of the gate between the two walls, which *was* by the king's garden; (now the Chaldeans *were*

by the city round about:) and they went by the way of the plain.

8 ¶ But the army of the Chaldeans ^apursued after the king, and overtook Zedekiah in the plains of Jericho; and all his army was scattered from him.

9 Then they took the king, and carried him up unto the king of Babylon to Riblah in the land of Hamath; where he gave judgment upon him.

10 And the king of Babylon slew the ^asons of Zedekiah before his eyes: he ^bslew also all the princes of Judah in Riblah.

11 Then he put out the ^aeyes of Zedekiah; and the king of Babylon bound him in chains, and ^bcarried him to ^cBabylon, and put him in prison till the day of his death.

12 ¶ Now in the fifth month, in the tenth *day* of the month, which *was* the nineteenth year of Nebuchadrezzar king of Babylon, came Nebuzar-adan, captain of the guard, *which* served the king of Babylon, into Jerusalem,

13 And ^aburned the house of the LORD, and the king's house; and all the houses of Jerusalem, and all the houses of the great *men,* ^bburned he with fire:

14 And all the army of the Chaldeans, that *were* with the captain of the guard, brake down all the ^awalls of Jerusalem round about.

15 Then Nebuzar-adan the captain of the guard ^acarried away captive *certain* of the poor of the people, and the residue of the people that remained in the city, and those that ^bfell away, that fell to the king of Babylon, and the rest of the multitude.

---

52 1 *a* 2 Kgs. 24:18;
   2 Chr. 36:10 (10–13).
 3 *a* 2 Kgs. 24:20;
   2 Chr. 36:13;
   Jer. 27:17 (12, 16–17);
   39:4 (1–10);
   Ezek. 17:15;
   1 Ne. 1:4.
 4 *a* 2 Kgs. 25:1;
   Jer. 39:1;
   Ezek. 24:1.
  b OR siege-walls.

 6 *a* Lam. 4:4 (4, 8–10);
   Amos 4:6.
   TG Famine.
  b OR food.
 7 *a* TG Jerusalem.
 8 *a* 2 Kgs. 25:5 (1–27).
10 *a* Hel. 6:10; 8:21.
  b 2 Kgs. 25:21 (19–21);
   Jer. 39:6;
   Ezek. 11:10.
11 *a* Jer. 39:7; Ezek. 12:13.
  b Omni 1:15.

  c TG Israel, Bondage of,
   in Other Lands.
13 *a* 2 Kgs. 25:9;
   Jer. 39:8;
   Ezek. 16:41.
  b Jer. 21:10; 34:2;
   37:8; 38:3.
14 *a* Dan. 9:25.
15 *a* Jer. 1:3;
   1 Ne. 1:13; 10:13 (12–13);
   2 Ne. 25:10 (10–11).
  b OR had deserted.

16 But Nebuzar-adan the captain of the guard left *certain* of the poor of the land for vinedressers and for husbandmen.

17 Also the ᵃpillars of brass that *were* in the house of the LORD, and the bases, and the brasen ᵇsea that *was* in the house of the LORD, the Chaldeans brake, and carried all the brass of them to Babylon.

18 The ᵃcaldrons also, and the shovels, and the ᵇsnuffers, and the bowls, and the spoons, and all the vessels of brass wherewith they ministered, took they away.

19 And the basins, and the firepans, and the bowls, and the caldrons, and the candlesticks, and the spoons, and the cups; *that* which *was* of gold *in* gold, and *that* which *was* of silver *in* silver, took the captain of the guard away.

20 The two pillars, one ᵃsea, and ᵇtwelve brasen ᶜbulls that *were* under the bases, which king Solomon had made in the house of the LORD: the brass of all these vessels was without weight.

21 And *concerning* the pillars, the height of one pillar *was* eighteen cubits; and ᵃa fillet of twelve ᵇcubits did compass it; and the thickness thereof *was* four fingers: *it was* hollow.

22 And a ᵃchapiter of brass *was* upon it; and the height of one chapiter *was* five cubits, with network and pomegranates upon the chapiters round about, all *of* brass. The second pillar also and the pomegranates *were* like unto these.

23 And there were ᵃninety and six pomegranates on a side; *and* all the pomegranates upon the network *were* an hundred round about.

24 ¶ And the captain of the guard took Seraiah the chief priest, and Zephaniah the second priest, and the three keepers of the door:

25 He took also out of the city an ᵃeunuch, which had the charge of the men of war; and seven ᵇmen of them that were near the king's person, which were found in the city; and the principal scribe of the host, who mustered the people of the land; and threescore men of the people of the land, that were found in the midst of the city.

26 So Nebuzar-adan the captain of the guard took them, and brought them to the king of Babylon to Riblah.

27 And the king of Babylon smote them, and put them to death in Riblah in the land of Hamath. Thus Judah was carried away ᵃcaptive out of his own land.

28 This *is* the people whom Nebuchadrezzar carried away captive: in the seventh year three thousand Jews and three and twenty:

29 In the eighteenth year of Nebuchadrezzar he carried away captive from Jerusalem eight hundred thirty and two persons:

30 In the three and twentieth year of Nebuchadrezzar Nebuzar-adan the captain of the guard carried away ᵃcaptive of the Jews seven hundred forty and five persons: all the persons *were* four thousand and six hundred.

31 ¶ And it came to pass in the seven and thirtieth year of the captivity of Jehoiachin king of Judah, in the twelfth month, in the five and twentieth *day* of the month, *that* Evil-merodach king of Babylon in the *first* year of his reign lifted up the head of ᵃJehoiachin king of Judah, and brought him forth out of prison,

32 And spake ᵃkindly unto him, and set his throne above the throne of the ᵇkings that *were* with him in Babylon,

---

17a Jer. 27:19 (16–22).
  b TG Temple.
18a OR pans.
  b IE instruments to extinguish lamps.
20a TG Baptism.
  b 1 Kgs. 7:25.
  c TG Temple.

21a HEB a line; i.e., its circumference was 12 cubits, about 18 feet, or 5½ meters.
  b 1 Kgs. 7:15.
22a OR decorative head of column.
23a 1 Kgs. 7:20 (18–20).

25a OR officer.
  b 2 Kgs. 25:19.
27a Lam. 1:3 (1–3).
30a Dan. 9:11 (1–27).
31a Jer. 37:1.
32a 2 Kgs. 25:28 (27–30).
  b Jer. 27:3.

33 And changed his prison garments: and he did continually eat bread before him all the days of his life.

34 And *for* his diet, there was a continual *a*diet given him of the king of Babylon, every day a portion until the day of his death, all the days of his life.

THE

LAMENTATIONS

OF JEREMIAH

CHAPTER 1

Jeremiah laments the miserable condition of Jerusalem—Jerusalem herself complains of her deep sorrow.

HOW doth the city sit solitary, *that was* full of people! *how* is she become as a *a*widow! she *that was* great among the nations, *and* *b*princess among the provinces, *how* is she become tributary!

2 *a*She weepeth sore in the night, and her tears *are* on her cheeks: among all her *b*lovers she hath none to *c*comfort *her:* all her friends have dealt treacherously with her, they are become her enemies.

3 Judah is gone into *a*captivity because of affliction, and because of great servitude: she dwelleth among the heathen, she findeth no *b*rest: all her persecutors overtook her between the straits.

4 The ways of Zion do *a*mourn, because none come to the *b*solemn feasts: all her gates are desolate: her priests sigh, her virgins are afflicted, and she *is* in bitterness.

5 Her adversaries are the chief, her enemies prosper; for the LORD hath *a*afflicted her for the multitude of her *b*transgressions: her children are gone into captivity before the enemy.

6 And from the daughter of Zion all her *a*beauty is departed: her princes are become like harts *that* find no pasture, and they are gone without strength before the pursuer.

7 Jerusalem remembered in the days of her affliction and of her miseries all her pleasant things that she had in the days of old, when her people fell into the hand of the enemy, and none did help her: the adversaries saw her, *and* did *a*mock at her sabbaths.

8 *a*Jerusalem hath grievously sinned; therefore she is *b*removed: all that honoured her despise her, because they have seen her *c*nakedness: yea, she sigheth, and turneth backward.

34*a* OR allowance.

[LAMENTATIONS]

1 1*a* Isa. 47:8 (7–9); 54:5.
  b Ezra 4:20.
2*a* Zech. 7:13 (8–14).
  b Jer. 22:22; 30:14.
  c D&C 101:7 (7–9).
3*a* Isa. 3:8 (8–9);

Jer. 52:27;
  2 Ne. 13:8 (8–9);
  15:13 (13–15);
  25:10 (9–10).
  b Jer. 45:3.
4*a* Isa. 3:26 (16–26);
  2 Ne. 13:26 (16–26).
  b Hosea 2:11.
5*a* Mosiah 1:17; Hel. 12:3.

b Jer. 30:14 (14–17);
  D&C 101:2; 103:4;
  105:9 (2–10).
6*a* 2 Ne. 13:24 (16–26).
7*a* TG Mocking.
8*a* D&C 5:20 (19–20).
  b Prov. 10:30.
  c Ezek. 16:37;
  Hosea 2:10.

9 Her ^afilthiness *is* in her skirts; she remembereth not her last ^bend; therefore she came down wonderfully: she had no comforter. O LORD, behold my affliction: for the enemy hath magnified *himself.*

10 The adversary hath spread out his hand upon all her pleasant things: for she hath seen *that* the heathen entered into her ^asanctuary, whom thou didst command *that* they should not enter into thy ^bcongregation.

11 All her people sigh, they seek ^abread; they have given their pleasant things for meat to relieve the soul: see, O LORD, and consider; for I am become vile.

12 ¶ *Is it* nothing to you, all ye that pass by? behold, and see if there be any sorrow like unto my ^asorrow, which is done unto me, wherewith the LORD hath afflicted *me* in the day of his fierce ^banger.

13 From above hath he sent fire into my bones, and it prevaileth against them: he hath spread a ^anet for my feet, he hath turned me back: he hath made me desolate *and* faint all the day.

14 The yoke of my transgressions is bound by his hand: they are wreathed, *and* come up upon my neck: he hath made my strength to fall, the Lord hath delivered me into *their* hands, *from whom* I am not able to rise up.

15 The Lord hath trodden under foot all my mighty ^amen in the midst of me: he hath called an assembly against me to crush my young men: the Lord hath trodden the virgin, the daughter of Judah, *as* in a winepress.

16 For these *things* I weep; mine eye, mine eye runneth down with water, because the comforter that should relieve my soul is far from me: my children are desolate, because the enemy prevailed.

17 ^aZion spreadeth forth her hands, *and there is* none to comfort her: the LORD hath commanded concerning Jacob, *that* his adversaries *should be* round about him: Jerusalem is as a menstruous woman among them.

18 ¶ The LORD is righteous; for I have rebelled against his commandment: hear, I pray you, all people, and behold my sorrow: my virgins and my young men are gone into captivity.

19 I called for my lovers, *but they* deceived me: my priests and mine elders gave up the ghost in the city, while they sought their meat to relieve their souls.

20 Behold, O LORD; for I *am* in distress: my ^abowels are troubled; mine heart is turned within me; for I have grievously ^brebelled: abroad the ^csword bereaveth, at home *there is* as death.

21 They have heard that I sigh: *there is* none to comfort me: all mine enemies have heard of my trouble; they are glad that thou hast done *it:* thou wilt bring the day *that* thou hast called, and they shall be like unto me.

22 Let all their wickedness come before thee; and do unto them, as thou hast done unto me for all my transgressions: for my sighs *are* many, and my heart *is* faint.

CHAPTER 2

Misery, sorrow, and desolation prevail in Jerusalem.

How hath the Lord covered the daughter of Zion with a cloud in his anger, *and* cast down from heaven unto the earth the beauty of Israel, and remembered not his ^afootstool in the day of his anger!

2 The Lord hath swallowed up all the habitations of Jacob, and hath not ^apitied: he hath thrown down in his wrath the strong holds of the

---

9a TG Filthiness.
  b Deut. 32:29;
    Isa. 47:7.
10a Ps. 79:1;
    Jer. 51:51.
  b TG Church.
11a Isa. 3:1.

12a Jer. 30:15.
  b Isa. 13:13.
13a Ezek. 17:20 (13, 20).
15a Jer. 8:16.
17a Jer. 4:31.
20a Jer. 4:19 (19–20);
    Lam. 2:11.

  b Hel. 12:3.
  c Ezek. 7:15.
2 1a 1 Chr. 28:2;
    1 Ne. 17:39;
    D&C 38:17;
    Abr. 2:7.
  2a 2 Ne. 23:18.

daughter of Judah; he hath brought *them* down to the ground: he hath polluted the kingdom and the princes thereof.

3 He hath cut off in *his* fierce anger all the horn of Israel: he hath *a*drawn back his right hand from before the enemy, and he *b*burned against Jacob like a flaming fire, *which* devoureth round about.

4 He hath bent his bow like an *a*enemy: he stood with his right hand as an adversary, and slew all *that were* pleasant to the eye in the tabernacle of the daughter of Zion: he poured out his fury like fire.

5 The Lord was as an enemy: he hath swallowed up Israel, he hath swallowed up all her palaces: he hath destroyed his strong holds, and hath increased in the daughter of Judah *a*mourning and lamentation.

6 And he hath violently taken away his tabernacle, as *if it were of* a garden: he hath destroyed his places of the assembly: the LORD hath caused the solemn feasts and *a*sabbaths to be forgotten in Zion, and hath despised in the indignation of his anger the king and the priest.

7 The Lord hath cast off his altar, he hath abhorred his sanctuary, he hath given up into the hand of the enemy the *a*walls of her palaces; they have made a noise in the house of the LORD, as in the day of a solemn feast.

8 The LORD hath purposed to destroy the wall of the daughter of Zion: he hath stretched out a line, he hath not withdrawn his hand from destroying: therefore he made the rampart and the wall to *a*lament; they languished together.

9 Her *a*gates are sunk into the ground; he hath destroyed and broken her bars: her king and her princes *are* *b*among the Gentiles: the law *is* no *more*; her *c*prophets also find no *d*vision from the LORD.

10 The elders of the daughter of Zion sit upon the *a*ground, *and* keep *b*silence: they have cast up dust upon their heads; they have girded themselves with *c*sackcloth: the virgins of Jerusalem hang down their heads to the ground.

11 Mine eyes do fail with *a*tears, my *b*bowels are troubled, my liver is poured upon the earth, for the *c*destruction of the daughter of my people; because the children and the sucklings swoon in the streets of the city.

12 They say to their mothers, Where *is* corn and wine? when they swooned as the wounded in the streets of the city, when their soul was poured out into their mothers' bosom.

13 What thing shall I take to witness for thee? what thing shall I liken to thee, O daughter of Jerusalem? what shall I equal to thee, that I may comfort thee, O *a*virgin daughter of Zion? for thy breach *is* great like the sea: who can heal thee?

14 Thy *a*prophets have seen *b*vain and foolish things for thee: and they have not discovered thine iniquity, to turn away thy captivity; but have seen for thee false burdens and causes of banishment.

15 All that *a*pass by *b*clap *their* hands at thee; they hiss and wag their head at the daughter of Jerusalem, *saying, Is* this the city that *men* call The *c*perfection of *d*beauty, The *e*joy of the whole earth?

16 All thine *a*enemies have opened their mouth against thee: they *b*hiss

3*a* Ps. 74:11.
  b Jacob 5:26.
4*a* Isa. 63:10 (9–10).
5*a* TG Mourning.
6*a* Isa. 1:13 (13–14).
7*a* Isa. 5:5 (4–5).
8*a* Isa. 3:26.
9*a* Isa. 3:26.
  b 2 Ne. 23:15;
       Alma 59:6 (5–6).

  c Ps. 74:9.
  d TG Revelation.
10*a* Isa. 3:26 (24–26).
  b D&C 38:12 (11–12).
  c Ezek. 7:18.
11*a* Morm. 6:18 (17–22).
  b Lam. 1:20.
  c Lam. 3:48.
13*a* 2 Kgs. 19:21.
14*a* TG False Prophets.

  b Hel. 13:27 (27–29).
15*a* Ezek. 5:14.
  b Job 27:23.
  c Ps. 50:2;
       Ezek. 16:14.
  d Ezek. 27:3; 28:12.
  e Ps. 48:2.
16*a* Lam. 3:46 (46–51).
  b 3 Ne. 16:9.

and gnash the teeth: they say, We have swallowed *her* up: certainly this *is* the day that we looked for; we have found, we have seen *it*.

17 The Lord hath done *that* which he had *a*devised; he hath fulfilled his word that he had commanded in the days of old: he hath thrown down, and hath not pitied: and he hath caused *thine* enemy to rejoice over thee, he hath set up the horn of thine adversaries.

18 Their heart cried unto the Lord, O wall of the daughter of Zion, let tears run down like a river day and night: give thyself no rest; let not the apple of thine eye cease.

19 Arise, cry out in the night: in the beginning of the watches pour out thine heart like water before the face of the Lord: lift up thy hands toward him for the life of thy young children, that faint for hunger in the top of every street.

20 ¶ Behold, O Lord, and consider to whom thou hast done this. Shall the women *a*eat their fruit, *and* children of a span long? shall the priest and the prophet be slain in the sanctuary of the Lord?

21 The young and the old lie on the ground in the streets: my virgins and my young men are fallen by the sword; thou hast *a*slain *them* in the day of thine anger; thou hast killed, *and* not pitied.

22 Thou hast called as in a solemn day my terrors round about, so that in the day of the Lord's anger none escaped nor remained: those that I have swaddled and brought up hath mine enemy consumed.

CHAPTER 3

Jeremiah, speaking for Judah, laments the calamity but trusts in the Lord and prays for deliverance.

I AM the man *that* hath seen affliction by the rod of his wrath.

2 He hath led me, and brought *me into* darkness, but not *into* light.

3 Surely against me is he turned; he turneth his hand *against me* all the day.

4 My flesh and my skin hath he made old; he hath broken my bones.

5 He hath builded against me, and compassed *me* with gall and travail.

6 He hath set me in dark places, as *they that be* dead of old.

7 He hath *a*hedged me about, that I cannot get out: he hath made my chain heavy.

8 Also when I cry and shout, he shutteth out my prayer.

9 He hath inclosed my ways with hewn stone, he hath made my paths crooked.

10 He *was* unto me *as* a bear lying in wait, *and as* a lion in secret places.

11 He hath turned aside my ways, and pulled me in pieces: he hath made me desolate.

12 He hath bent his bow, and set me as a mark for the arrow.

13 He hath caused the arrows of his quiver to enter into my reins.

14 I was a *a*derision to all my people; *and* their song all the day.

15 He hath filled me with bitterness, he hath made me drunken with wormwood.

16 He hath also broken my teeth with gravel stones, he hath covered me with ashes.

17 And thou hast removed my soul far off from peace: I forgat prosperity.

18 And I said, My strength and my hope is perished from the Lord:

19 Remembering mine affliction and my misery, the wormwood and the gall.

20 My soul hath *them* still in remembrance, and is humbled in me.

21 This I recall to my mind, therefore have I hope.

22 ¶ *It is of* the Lord's mercies that we are not consumed, because his compassions fail not.

23 *They are* new every morning: great *is* thy faithfulness.

24 The Lord *is* my *a*portion, saith

17a Zech. 1:6.
20a Jer. 19:9;
   Ezek. 5:10.

21a 2 Chr. 36:17;
   Jer. 14:18; Lam. 3:43.
3 7a Hosea 2:6;

D&C 122:7.
14a Jer. 20:7 (7–8).
24a Ps. 119:57.

my soul; therefore will I hope in him.

25 The Lord is ᵃgood unto them that ᵇwait for him, to the soul *that* ᶜseeketh him.

26 *It is* good that *a man* should both ᵃhope and quietly wait for the salvation of the Lord.

27 *It is* good for a man that he ᵃbear the yoke in his ᵇyouth.

28 He sitteth alone and keepeth silence, because he hath borne *it* upon him.

29 He putteth his mouth in the dust; if so be there may be hope.

30 He giveth *his* ᵃcheek to him that smiteth him: he is filled full with ᵇreproach.

31 For the Lord will not cast off for ever:

32 But though he cause grief, yet will he have ᵃcompassion according to the multitude of his mercies.

33 For he doth not ᵃafflict willingly nor grieve the children of men.

34 To crush under his feet all the prisoners of the earth,

35 To turn aside the right of a man before the face of the most High,

36 To subvert a man in his cause, the Lord approveth not.

37 ¶ Who *is* he *that* saith, and it cometh to pass, *when* the Lord commandeth *it* not?

38 Out of the mouth of the most High proceedeth not evil and good?

39 Wherefore doth a living man complain, a man for the punishment of his sins?

40 Let us ᵃsearch and try our ways, and turn again to the Lord.

41 Let us ᵃlift up our heart with *our* hands unto God in the heavens.

42 We have transgressed and have rebelled: thou hast not pardoned.

43 Thou hast covered with anger, and persecuted us: thou hast ᵃslain, thou hast not pitied.

44 Thou hast covered thyself with a cloud, that *our* prayer should not pass through.

45 Thou hast made us *as* the offscouring and refuse in the midst of the people.

46 All our ᵃenemies have opened their mouths against us.

47 Fear and a snare is come upon us, desolation and destruction.

48 Mine eye runneth down with ᵃrivers of water for the ᵇdestruction of the daughter of my people.

49 Mine eye trickleth down, and ceaseth not, without any intermission,

50 Till the Lord look down, and behold from heaven.

51 Mine eye affecteth mine heart because of all the daughters of my city.

52 Mine enemies chased me sore, like a bird, without cause.

53 They have cut off my life in the dungeon, and cast a stone upon me.

54 Waters flowed over mine head; *then* I said, I am cut off.

55 ¶ I called upon thy name, O Lord, out of the low dungeon.

56 Thou hast heard my voice: hide not thine ear at my breathing, at my cry.

57 Thou ᵃdrewest near in the day *that* I called upon thee: thou saidst, Fear not.

58 O Lord, thou hast pleaded the causes of my soul; thou hast redeemed my life.

59 O Lord, thou hast seen my wrong: judge thou my cause.

60 Thou hast seen all their vengeance *and* all their imaginations against me.

61 Thou hast heard their reproach,

25a Ps. 34:8; Nahum 1:7; D&C 70:18 (17–18). b 2 Ne. 6:7; D&C 133:45. c Ps. 34:4 (4, 6, 10); Heb. 11:6; Alma 37:37 (36–37). 26a TG Hope. 27a Micah 7:9 (8–9); D&C 136:31. b Alma 37:35. 30a Isa. 50:6; Matt. 5:39; 3 Ne. 12:39. b TG Reproach. 32a TG Compassion. 33a D&C 133:53. 40a Luke 15:18. 41a Ps. 143:8; D&C 25:13; 27:15; 30:6; 31:3; 35:26. 43a Lam. 2:21. 46a Lam. 2:16. 48a TG Mourning. b Lam. 2:11. 57a D&C 88:63 (62–63).

O LORD, *and* all their imaginations against me;

62 The lips of those that rose up against me, and their *a*device against me all the day.

63 Behold their sitting down, and their rising up; I *am* their musick.

64 ¶ Render unto them a recompence, O LORD, according to the work of their hands.

65 Give them sorrow of heart, thy curse unto them.

66 Persecute and destroy them in anger from under the heavens of the LORD.

CHAPTER 4

The condition of Zion is pitiful because of sin and iniquity.

How is the gold become dim! *how* is the most fine gold changed! the stones of the sanctuary are poured out in the top of every street.

2 The precious sons of Zion, comparable to fine gold, how are they esteemed as earthen pitchers, the work of the hands of the potter!

3 Even the sea monsters draw out the breast, they give suck to their young ones: the daughter of my people *is* become *a*cruel, like the ostriches in the wilderness.

4 The tongue of the sucking child cleaveth to the roof of his mouth for thirst: the young children ask *a*bread, *and* no man breaketh *it* unto them.

5 They that did feed delicately are desolate in the streets: they that were brought up in scarlet embrace dunghills.

6 For the punishment of the iniquity of the daughter of my people is greater than the punishment of the sin of Sodom, that was overthrown as in a moment, and no hands stayed on her.

7 Her Nazarites were purer than snow, they were whiter than milk, they were more ruddy in body than rubies, their polishing *was* of sapphire:

8 Their visage is blacker than a coal; they are not known in the streets: their skin cleaveth to their bones; it is withered, it is become like a stick.

9 *They that be* slain with the sword are better than *they that be* slain with hunger: for these pine away, stricken through for *want of* the fruits of the field.

10 The hands of the pitiful *a*women have *b*sodden their own children: they were their *c*meat in the destruction of the daughter of my people.

11 The LORD hath accomplished his fury; he hath poured out his fierce anger, and hath kindled a fire in Zion, and it hath devoured the foundations thereof.

12 The kings of the earth, and all the inhabitants of the world, would not have believed that the adversary and the enemy should have entered into the gates of Jerusalem.

13 ¶ For the *a*sins of her prophets, *and* the iniquities of her priests, that have shed the blood of the *b*just in the midst of her,

14 They have wandered *as* blind *men* in the streets, they have polluted themselves with blood, so that men could not touch their garments.

15 They cried unto them, Depart ye; *it is* unclean; depart, depart, touch not: when they fled away and wandered, they said among the heathen, They shall no more sojourn *there*.

16 The anger of the LORD hath divided them; he will no more regard them: they respected not the persons of the priests, they favoured not the *a*elders.

17 As for us, our eyes as yet failed for our vain help: in our watching we have watched for a *a*nation *that* could not save *us*.

62*a* Jer. 11:19;
  Alma 10:13; 11:21.
4 3*a* Job 39:16 (13–16).
  TG Cruelty.
  4*a* Jer. 52:6.
  10*a* TG Woman.

b Lev. 26:29;
  Deut. 28:57 (56–57).
c Jer. 19:9.
13*a* Jer. 5:31;
  Hel. 13:27.
b Mosiah 17:10;

  Alma 14:11; 60:13.
16*a* Deut. 28:50 (49–51);
  2 Kgs. 2:23 (23–24);
  Isa. 3:5; 1 Ne. 2:12.
17*a* Isa. 30:7 (5, 7);
  Jer. 37:7.

18 They hunt our steps, that we cannot go in our streets: our end is near, our days are fulfilled; for our ^aend is come.

19 Our persecutors are ^aswifter than the eagles of the heaven: they pursued us upon the mountains, they laid wait for us in the wilderness.

20 The breath of our nostrils, the ^aanointed of the LORD, was taken in their ^bpits, of whom we said, Under his shadow we shall live among the heathen.

21 ¶ Rejoice and be glad, O daughter of ^aEdom, that dwellest in the land of ^bUz; the ^ccup also shall pass through unto thee: thou shalt be drunken, and shalt make thyself naked.

22 ¶ The punishment of thine iniquity is accomplished, O daughter of Zion; he will no more carry thee away into captivity: he will visit thine iniquity, O daughter of Edom; he will discover thy sins.

CHAPTER 5

Jeremiah recites in prayer the sorrowful condition of Zion.

REMEMBER, O LORD, what is come upon us: consider, and behold our reproach.

2 Our inheritance is turned to ^astrangers, our houses to aliens.

3 We are orphans and fatherless, our mothers *are* as widows.

4 We have drunken our water for money; our wood is sold unto us.

5 Our necks *are* under ^apersecution: we labour, *and* have no rest.

6 We have given the hand *to* the Egyptians, *and to* the Assyrians, to be satisfied with bread.

7 Our ^afathers have ^bsinned, *and are* not; and we have borne their iniquities.

8 Servants have ruled over us: *there is* none that doth deliver *us* out of their hand.

9 We gat our bread with *the peril of* our lives because of the sword of the wilderness.

10 Our skin was black like an oven because of the terrible famine.

11 They ravished the women in Zion, *and* the maids in the cities of Judah.

12 Princes are hanged up by their hand: the faces of elders were not honoured.

13 They took the young men to grind, and the children fell under the wood.

14 The elders have ceased from the gate, the young men from their musick.

15 The joy of our heart is ceased; our dance is turned into mourning.

16 The crown is fallen *from* our head: woe unto us, that we have sinned!

17 For this our heart is faint; for these *things* our eyes are dim.

18 Because of the mountain of Zion, which is desolate, the foxes walk upon it.

19 Thou, O LORD, remainest for ever; thy throne from generation to generation.

20 Wherefore dost thou forget us for ever, *and* forsake us so long time?

21 ^aTurn thou us unto thee, O LORD, and we shall be turned; renew our days as of old.

22 But thou hast utterly rejected us; thou art very wroth against us.

18a Ezek. 7:2 (2–3, 6).
19a Jer. 4:13; 39:5.
20a 2 Chr. 35:25;
    Jer. 39:7.
  b Ezek. 19:8 (4, 8);
    D&C 122:7 (5, 7).
21a Jer. 49:7;
    2 Ne. 21:14.
  b Job 1:1.

  c Jer. 25:15 (15–16);
    Mosiah 3:26;
    D&C 43:26 (24–26).
5 2a Ps. 79:1;
    Jer. 39:8.
  5a TG Persecution.
  7a TG Marriage,
    Fatherhood.
  b Jer. 31:29;

    Ezek. 18:2;
    Mosiah 13:13.
21a Ps. 51:10; 80:3;
    Jer. 31:18;
    Mosiah 7:33;
    Morm. 9:6;
    D&C 98:47.

THE BOOK OF THE PROPHET

EZEKIEL

CHAPTER 1

Ezekiel sees in vision four living creatures, four wheels, and the glory of God on His throne.

NOW it came to pass in the thirtieth year, in the fourth *month*, in the fifth *day* of the month, as I *was* among the *a*captives by the river of *b*Chebar, *that the* heavens were *c*opened, and I saw *d*visions of God.

2 In the fifth *day* of the month, which *was* the *a*fifth year of king *b*Jehoiachin's captivity,

3 The word of the LORD came expressly unto Ezekiel the priest, the son of Buzi, in the land of the Chaldeans by the river Chebar; and the *a*hand of the LORD was there upon him.

4 ¶ And I looked, and, behold, a *a*whirlwind came out of the north, a great cloud, and a *b*fire infolding itself, and a brightness *was* about it, and out of the midst thereof as the colour of amber, out of the midst of the fire.

5 Also out of the midst thereof *came* the likeness of four living *a*creatures. And this *was* their appearance; they had the likeness of a man.

6 And every one had four faces, and every one had four wings.

7 And their feet *were* straight feet; and the sole of their feet *was* like the sole of a calf's foot: and they sparkled like the colour of burnished *a*brass.

8 And *they had* the hands of a man under their wings on their four sides; and they four had their faces and their wings.

9 Their wings *were* joined one to another; they turned not when they went; they went every one *a*straight forward.

10 As for the likeness of their faces, they four had the face of a man, and the face of a lion, on the right side: and they four had the face of an ox on the left side; they four also had the face of an eagle.

11 Thus *were* their faces: and their *a*wings *were* stretched upward; two *wings* of every one *were* joined one to another, and two covered their bodies.

12 And they went every one straight forward: whither the spirit was to go, they went; *and* they turned not when they went.

13 As for the likeness of the living creatures, their appearance *was* like burning coals of fire, *and* like the appearance of *a*lamps: it went up and down among the living creatures; and the fire was bright, and out of the fire went forth lightning.

14 And the living creatures ran and returned as the appearance of a flash of lightning.

15 ¶ Now as I beheld the living creatures, behold one *a*wheel upon the earth by the living creatures, with his four faces.

16 The appearance of the *a*wheels and their work *was* like unto the colour of a beryl: and they four

---

1 1*a* HEB exiles.
    TG Israel, Bondage of, in Other Lands.
  b Ezek. 10:15.
  c Acts 7:56 (55–56);
    1 Ne. 1:8 (6–11); 11:14;
    D&C 107:19; 110:11.
  d Ezek. 8:3; 40:2; 43:3;

1 Ne. 1:16;
  JS—H 1:24 (21–25).
2*a* Ezek. 24:1; 26:1; 33:21.
  b 2 Kgs. 24:12 (12, 15).
3*a* 2 Kgs. 3:15;
  Ezek. 8:1; 33:22;
  37:1; 40:1.
4*a* 2 Kgs. 2:11.

  b IE continuous fire.
5*a* TG Symbolism.
7*a* Ezek. 40:3.
9*a* Ezek. 10:11.
11*a* D&C 77:4.
13*a* Ezek. 10:9.
15*a* Dan. 7:9.
16*a* Ezek. 10:9.

had one likeness: and their appearance and their work *was* as it were a wheel in the middle of a wheel.

17 When they [a]went, they went upon their four sides: *and* they turned not when they went.

18 As for their rings, they were so high that they were dreadful; and their rings *were* full of eyes round about them four.

19 And when the living creatures went, the wheels went by them: and when the living creatures were lifted up from the earth, the wheels were lifted up.

20 Whithersoever the [a]spirit was to go, they went, thither *was their* spirit to go; and the wheels were lifted up over against them: for the spirit of the living creature *was* in the wheels.

21 When those went, *these* went; and when those stood, *these* stood; and when those were lifted up from the earth, the wheels were lifted up over against them: for the spirit of the living creature *was* in the wheels.

22 And the likeness of the [a]firmament upon the heads of the [b]living creature *was* as the [c]colour of the terrible [d]crystal, stretched forth over their heads above.

23 And under the firmament *were* their wings straight, the one toward the other: every one had two, which covered on this side, and every one had two, which covered on that side, their bodies.

24 And when they went, I heard the noise of their wings, like the noise of great waters, as the [a]voice of the Almighty, the voice of speech, as the noise of an host: when they stood, they let down their wings.

25 And there was a voice from the firmament that *was* over their heads, when they stood, *and* had let down their wings.

26 ¶ And above the firmament that *was* over their heads *was* the likeness of a throne, as the appearance of a sapphire stone: and upon the likeness of the [a]throne *was* the likeness as the [b]appearance of a man above upon it.

27 And I saw as the colour of amber, as the appearance of [a]fire round about within it, from the appearance of his loins even upward, and from the appearance of his loins even downward, I saw as it were the appearance of fire, and it had brightness round about.

28 As the appearance of the [a]bow that is in the cloud in the day of rain, so *was* the appearance of the brightness round about. This *was* the [b]appearance of the likeness of the [c]glory of the [d]Lord. And when I saw *it*, I [e]fell upon my face, and I heard a voice of one that spake.

CHAPTER 2

Ezekiel is called to take the word of the Lord to Israel—He sees a book in which lamentations and mourning are written.

AND he said unto me, [a]Son of man, stand upon thy feet, and I will speak unto thee.

2 And the [a]spirit entered into me when he spake unto me, and set me upon my feet, that I heard him that spake unto me.

3 And he said unto me, Son of man, I [a]send thee to the children of Israel,

17a Ezek. 10:11.
20a Ezek. 10:17.
22a HEB expanse over.
　　Ezek. 10:1.
　b Ezek. 10:20.
　c HEB appearance of wonderful crystal.
　d Rev. 4:6;
　　D&C 77:1; 130:9 (7–9).
24a Ezek. 43:2; Rev. 1:15;
　　Hel. 12:9; 3 Ne. 11:3;
　　D&C 110:3.
26a Ezek. 10:1.

　b TG Jesus Christ, Appearances, Antemortal.
27a Ezek. 8:2.
28a Rev. 4:3.
　b TG God, Privilege of Seeing.
　c Ezek. 11:22.
　d Isa. 6:3 (2–3);
　　Rev. 4:8 (7–9).
　e Ezek. 3:23 (23–24); 44:4;
　　Acts 9:4 (3–5);
　　Ether 3:6 (6–8).

2 1a The expression "son of man" used in Ezekiel refers only to this prophet. As a Hebrew idiom it means simply "human." It is not to be confused with the title "Son of Man," which refers to Christ.
　2a TG Teaching with the Spirit.
　3a TG Priesthood, Keys of; Priesthood, Ordination.

to a *b*rebellious nation that hath rebelled against me: they and their fathers have transgressed against me, *even* unto this very day.

4 For *they are* impudent children and *a*stiffhearted. I do *b*send thee unto them; and thou shalt say unto them, Thus saith the Lord God.

5 And they, whether they will hear, or whether they will forbear, (for they *are* a *a*rebellious house,) *b*yet shall know that there hath been a prophet among them.

6 ¶ And thou, son of man, *a*be not *b*afraid of them, neither be afraid of their words, though briers and thorns *be* with thee, and thou dost *c*dwell among scorpions: be not afraid of their words, nor be dismayed at their looks, though they *be* a rebellious house.

7 And thou shalt *a*speak my words unto them, whether they will hear, or whether they will forbear: for they *are* most rebellious.

8 But thou, son of man, hear what I say unto thee; Be not thou rebellious like that rebellious house: open thy mouth, and *a*eat that I give thee.

9 ¶ And when I looked, behold, an hand *was* sent unto me; and, lo, a *a*roll of a *b*book *was* therein;

10 And he spread it before me; and it *was* written *a*within and without: and *there was* written therein lamentations, and mourning, and woe.

CHAPTER 3

Ezekiel is made a watchman unto the house of Israel—The blood of Israel is required at his hand unless he raises the warning voice.

Moreover he said unto me, Son of man, eat that thou findest; eat this *a*roll, and go speak unto the house of Israel.

2 So I opened my mouth, and he caused me to eat that roll.

3 And he said unto me, Son of man, cause thy belly to eat, and fill thy bowels with this roll that I give thee. Then did I *a*eat *it*; and it was in my mouth as honey for sweetness.

4 ¶ And he said unto me, Son of man, go, get thee unto the house of Israel, and speak with my words unto them.

5 For thou *art* not sent to a people of a strange speech and of an hard language, *but* to the house of Israel;

6 Not to many people of a strange speech and of an hard language, whose words thou canst not understand. Surely, had I sent thee to them, they would have *a*hearkened unto thee.

7 But the house of Israel will not hearken unto thee; for they will not hearken unto me: for all the house of Israel *are* impudent and *a*hardhearted.

8 Behold, I have made thy face strong against their faces, and thy forehead strong against their foreheads.

9 As an *a*adamant harder than flint have I made thy forehead: fear them not, neither be dismayed at their looks, though they *be* a rebellious house.

10 Moreover he said unto me, Son of man, all my words that I shall speak unto thee receive in thine heart, and hear with thine ears.

11 And go, get thee to them of the captivity, unto the children of thy people, and speak unto them, and tell them, Thus saith *a*the Lord God; whether they will hear, or whether they will forbear.

3*b* TG Apostasy of Israel;
   Rebellion.
4*a* TG Stiffnecked;
   Stubbornness.
 b TG Called of God.
5*a* Ezek. 12:2; 44:6.
 b Ezek. 33:33.
6*a* Jer. 1:8.
 b TG Peer Influence.
 c OR sit.

7*a* Num. 24:13.
   TG Authority;
   Prophets, Mission of.
8*a* Ezek. 3:3 (2–3);
   Rev. 10:10 (9–10).
9*a* HEB scroll.
   Ezra 6:2;
   Jer. 36:2 (2, 4).
 b Rev. 5:1; 10:2;
   D&C 77:6.

10*a* HEB front and back.
3 1*a* HEB scroll.
3*a* Jer. 15:16;
   Ezek. 2:8;
   Rev. 10:10 (9–10).
6*a* Matt. 11:21 (21, 23).
7*a* TG Hardheartedness;
   Stubbornness.
9*a* OR diamond.
11*a* HEB the Lord Jehovah.

12 Then the *spirit took me up, and I heard behind me a voice of a great rushing, *saying,* Blessed *be* the glory of the LORD from his place.

13 *I heard* also the *noise of the wings of the living creatures that touched one another, and the noise of the wheels over against them, and a noise of a great rushing.

14 So the spirit lifted me up, and took me away, and I went in bitterness, in the heat of my spirit; but the hand of the LORD was strong upon me.

15 ¶ Then I came to them of the captivity at Tel-abib, that dwelt by the river of Chebar, and I sat where they sat, and remained there astonished among them seven days.

16 And it came to pass at the end of seven days, that the word of the LORD came unto me, saying,

17 Son of man, I have made thee a *watchman unto the house of Israel: therefore hear the word at my mouth, and give them *warning from me.

18 When I say unto the wicked, Thou shalt surely *die; and thou givest him not *warning, nor speakest to warn the wicked from his wicked way, to save his life; the same wicked *man* shall *die in his *iniquity; but his blood will I *require at thine hand.

19 Yet if thou *warn the wicked, and he turn not from his wickedness, nor from his wicked way, he shall die in his iniquity; but thou hast delivered thy soul.

20 Again, When a *righteous *man* doth *turn from his *righteousness, and commit iniquity, and I lay a *stumblingblock before him, he shall die: because thou hast not given him warning, he shall die in

his sin, and his righteousness which he hath done shall not be remembered; but his blood will I require at thine hand.

21 Nevertheless if thou warn the righteous *man,* that the righteous sin not, and he doth not sin, he shall surely live, because he is *warned; also thou hast delivered thy soul.

22 ¶ And the hand of the LORD was there upon me; and he said unto me, Arise, go forth into the *plain, and I will there talk with thee.

23 Then I arose, and went forth into the plain: and, behold, the glory of the LORD stood there, as the glory which I saw by the river of Chebar: and I *fell on my face.

24 Then the spirit entered into me, and set me upon my feet, and spake with me, and said unto me, Go, shut thyself within thine house.

25 But thou, O son of man, behold, they shall put bands upon thee, and shall bind thee with them, and thou shalt not go out among them:

26 And I will make thy tongue cleave to the roof of thy mouth, that thou shalt be *dumb, and shalt not be to them a reprover: for they *are* a rebellious house.

27 But when I speak with thee, I will open thy *mouth, and thou shalt say unto them, Thus *saith the Lord GOD; He that heareth, let him hear; and he that forbeareth, let him forbear: for they *are* a rebellious house.

CHAPTER 4

Ezekiel symbolically illustrates the siege and famine that will befall Jerusalem.

THOU also, son of man, take thee *a tile, and lay it before thee, and

---

12a TG God, Spirit of; Guidance, Divine.
13a OR sound.
17a TG Delegation of Responsibility; Watchman.
  b TG Priesthood, Magnifying Callings within.
18a Ezek. 33:14.

  b TG Watch.
  c TG Justice.
  d TG Sin.
  e TG Accountability.
19a TG Prophets, Mission of; Warn.
20a Ezek. 18:24.
  b Ezek. 33:12 (12–13, 18).
  c TG Righteousness.
  d Jer. 6:21;

    Ezek. 14:4 (3–7);
    2 Ne. 26:20.
21a D&C 1:4.
22a Ezek. 8:4.
23a Ezek. 1:28.
26a Ezek. 24:27.
27a TG Prophecy; Teaching with the Spirit.
  b TG Prophets, Mission of.
4 1a IE a clay tablet.

*b*portray upon it the city, *even* Jerusalem:

2 And *a*lay siege against it, and *b*build a fort against it, and *c*cast a *d*mount against it; set the camp also against it, and set *e*battering rams against it round about.

3 Moreover take thou unto thee an iron pan, and set it *for* a wall of iron between thee and the city: and set thy face against it, and it shall be besieged, and thou shalt lay siege against it. This *shall be* a *a*sign to the house of Israel.

4 Lie thou also upon thy left side, and lay the iniquity of the house of Israel upon it: *according* to the number of the days that thou shalt lie upon it thou shalt bear their iniquity.

5 For I have laid upon thee the years of their iniquity, according to the number of the days, three hundred and ninety days: so shalt thou bear the iniquity of the house of Israel.

6 And when thou hast accomplished them, lie again on thy right side, and thou shalt bear the iniquity of the house of Judah forty days: I have appointed thee each day for a year.

7 Therefore thou shalt set thy face toward the siege of Jerusalem, and thine arm *shall be* uncovered, and thou shalt prophesy against it.

8 And, behold, I will lay bands upon thee, and thou shalt not turn thee from one side to another, till thou hast ended the days of thy siege.

9 ¶ Take thou also unto thee wheat, and barley, and beans, and lentiles, and millet, and *a*fitches, and put them in one vessel, and make thee bread thereof, *according* to the number of the days that thou shalt lie upon thy side, three hundred and ninety days shalt thou eat thereof.

10 And thy *a*meat which thou shalt eat *shall be* by weight, twenty shekels a day: from time to time shalt thou eat it.

11 Thou shalt drink also water by measure, the sixth part of an hin: from time to time shalt thou drink.

12 And thou shalt eat it *as* barley cakes, and thou shalt bake it with dung that cometh out of man, in their sight.

13 And the LORD said, Even thus shall the children of Israel eat their *a*defiled bread among the Gentiles, whither I will drive them.

14 Then said I, Ah Lord GOD! behold, my soul hath not been *a*polluted: for from my youth up even till now have I not eaten of that which *b*dieth of itself, or is *c*torn in pieces; neither came there *d*abominable flesh into my mouth.

15 Then he said unto me, Lo, I have given thee cow's dung for man's dung, and thou shalt prepare thy bread therewith.

16 Moreover he said unto me, Son of man, behold, I will break the staff of bread in Jerusalem: and they shall eat bread by weight, and with care; and they shall drink water by measure, and with *a*astonishment:

17 That they may want bread and water, and be *a*astonied one with another, and *b*consume away for their iniquity.

CHAPTER 5

The judgment of Jerusalem will include famine, pestilence, war, and the scattering of her inhabitants.

AND thou, son of man, take thee a sharp knife, take thee a barber's razor, and cause *it* to pass upon thine head and upon thy beard: then take thee balances to weigh, and divide the *hair*.

2 Thou shalt burn with fire a third

1*b* IE engrave or cut in it a representation of the city.
2*a* IE draw upon it the plan of the attack against the city.
  b 2 Kgs. 25:1.
  c OR build up a mound

or bank.
  d Jer. 6:6.
  e Ezek. 21:22.
3*a* 2 Ne. 25:9.
9*a* OR spelt (a type of wheat).
10*a* HEB food.
13*a* Hosea 9:3 (1–3).

14*a* TG Pollution.
  b Lev. 7:24.
  c Ex. 22:31.
  d Lev. 7:18; 19:7.
16*a* IE fearfulness, anxiety.
17*a* HEB appalled.
  b Hel. 12:3.

part in the midst of the city, when the days of the siege are fulfilled: and thou shalt take a third part, *and* smite about it with a knife: and a third part thou shalt scatter in the wind; and I will draw out a ^asword after them.

3 Thou shalt also take thereof a few in number, and bind them in thy skirts.

4 Then take of them again, and cast them into the midst of the fire, and burn them in the fire; *for* thereof shall a fire come forth into all the house of Israel.

5 ¶ Thus saith the Lord GOD; This *is* Jerusalem: I have set it in the ^amidst of the nations and countries *that are* round about her.

6 And she hath changed my judgments into ^awickedness more than the nations, and my statutes more than the countries that *are* round about her: for they have ^brefused my judgments and my statutes, they have not walked in them.

7 Therefore thus saith the Lord GOD; Because ye multiplied more than the nations that *are* round about you, *and* have not walked in my statutes, neither have kept my ^ajudgments, neither have done according to the judgments of the nations that *are* round about you;

8 Therefore thus saith the Lord GOD; Behold, I, even I, *am* against thee, and will execute judgments in the midst of thee in the ^asight of the nations.

9 And I will do in thee that which I have not ^adone, and whereunto I will not do any more the like, because of all thine ^babominations.

10 Therefore the fathers shall ^aeat the sons in the midst of thee, and the sons shall eat their fathers;

and I will execute judgments in thee, and the whole remnant of thee will I ^bscatter into all the winds.

11 Wherefore, *as* I live, saith the Lord GOD; Surely, because thou hast ^adefiled my sanctuary with all thy ^bdetestable things, and with all thine abominations, therefore will I also ^cdiminish *thee*; neither shall mine eye ^dspare, neither will I have any pity.

12 ¶ A third part of thee shall die with the pestilence, and with famine shall they be consumed in the midst of thee: and a third part shall fall by the sword round about thee; and I will scatter a third part into all the winds, and I will draw out a sword after them.

13 Thus shall mine anger be accomplished, and ^aI will cause my ^bfury to rest upon them, and I will be comforted: and they shall know that I the LORD have ^cspoken *it* in my zeal, when I have accomplished my fury in them.

14 Moreover I will make thee ^awaste, and a ^breproach among the nations that *are* round about thee, in the sight of all that ^cpass by.

15 So it shall be a ^areproach and a taunt, an instruction and an astonishment unto the nations that *are* round about thee, when I shall execute judgments in thee in anger and in fury and in furious rebukes. I the LORD have spoken *it*.

16 When I shall send upon them the evil arrows of famine, which shall be for *their* destruction, *and* which I will send to destroy you: and I will increase the famine upon you, and will break your staff of bread:

17 So will I send upon you famine and evil beasts, and they shall

5 2*a* Ezek. 12:14.
　5*a* 1 Ne. 21:6;
　　　 Alma 4:11; 39:11;
　　　 D&C 103:9 (8–9).
　6*a* Alma 24:30.
　　b 1 Ne. 1:19 (18–20);
　　　 2:13; 7:14.
　7*a* Ezek. 11:12.
　8*a* D&C 42:91.

　9*a* Dan. 9:12.
　　b D&C 29:21.
　10*a* Jer. 19:9;
　　　 Lam. 2:20.
　　b TG Israel, Scattering of.
　11*a* TG Sacrilege.
　　b TG Idolatry.
　　c Deut. 8:19 (18–20).
　　d Ezek. 7:4; 20:17.

　13*a* Ezek. 24:13 (13–14).
　　b Ezek. 21:17; 38:18.
　　c D&C 20:36.
　14*a* Lev. 26:31;
　　　 Neh. 2:17.
　　b Ezek. 22:4.
　　c Lam. 2:15.
　15*a* Jer. 24:9.

*a*bereave thee; and pestilence and blood shall pass through thee; and I will bring the *b*sword upon thee. I the LORD have spoken *it.*

CHAPTER 6

The people of Israel will be destroyed for their idolatry—A remnant only will be saved and scattered.

AND the word of the LORD came unto me, saying,

2 Son of man, set thy *a*face toward the *b*mountains of Israel, and prophesy against them,

3 And say, Ye mountains of Israel, hear the word of the Lord GOD; Thus saith the Lord GOD to the mountains, and to the hills, to the rivers, and to the valleys; Behold, I, *even* I, will bring a sword upon you, and I will destroy your high places.

4 And your altars shall be desolate, and your images shall be broken: and I will cast down your slain *men* before your idols.

5 And I will lay the dead *a*carcases of the children of Israel before their idols; and I will scatter your bones round about your altars.

6 In all your dwellingplaces the cities shall be laid waste, and the high places shall be desolate; that your altars may be laid waste and made desolate, and your idols may be broken and cease, and your images may be cut down, and your works may be abolished.

7 And the slain shall fall in the midst of you, and ye shall *a*know that I *am* the LORD.

8 ¶ Yet will I leave a *a*remnant, that ye may have *some* that shall *b*escape the sword among the nations, when ye shall be *c*scattered through the countries.

9 And they that escape of you shall remember me among the nations whither they shall be carried cap-

tives, because I am broken with their whorish heart, which hath departed from me, and with their eyes, which go a *a*whoring after their idols: and they shall *b*lothe themselves for the *c*evils which they have committed in all their abominations.

10 And they shall know that I *am* the LORD, *and that* I have not said in vain that I would do this evil unto them.

11 ¶ Thus saith the Lord GOD; Smite with thine hand, and stamp with thy foot, and say, Alas for all the evil abominations of the house of Israel! for they shall fall by the sword, by the famine, and by the pestilence.

12 He that is far off shall die of the pestilence; and he that is near shall fall by the sword; and he that remaineth and is besieged shall die by the famine: thus will I accomplish my fury upon them.

13 Then shall ye know that I *am* the LORD, when their slain *men* shall be among their idols round about their altars, upon every high hill, in all the tops of the mountains, and under every green tree, and under every thick oak, the place where they did offer sweet savour to all their *a*idols.

14 So will I stretch out my hand upon them, and make the land desolate, yea, more desolate than the wilderness toward Diblath, in all their habitations: and they shall know that I *am* the LORD.

CHAPTER 7

Desolation, war, pestilence, and destruction will sweep the land of Israel—The desolation of the people is foreseen.

MOREOVER the word of the LORD came unto me, saying,

2 Also, thou son of man, thus saith

17*a* IE deprive of children.
  Ezek. 36:13 (8–15).
  b Ezek. 14:21; 33:27;
    Rev. 6:8.
6 2*a* Ezek. 20:46; 35:2 (1–15).
  b Ezek. 36:1 (1–7).

5*a* Ps. 141:7.
7*a* TG God, Knowledge
    about.
8*a* TG Israel, Remnant of.
  b Jer. 44:28;
    Ezek. 7:16.

c TG Israel, Scattering of.
9*a* Ezek. 23:30.
  b TG Repent.
  c Ezek. 36:31.
13*a* TG Idolatry.

the Lord GOD unto the land of Israel; An ^aend, the end is come upon the four corners of the land.

3 Now *is* the end *come* upon thee, and I will send mine anger upon thee, and will ^ajudge thee according to thy ways, and will recompense upon thee all thine abominations.

4 And mine eye shall not ^aspare thee, neither will I have pity: but I will ^brecompense thy ways upon thee, and thine abominations shall be in the midst of thee: and ye shall ^cknow that I *am* the LORD.

5 Thus saith the Lord GOD; An evil, an ^aonly evil, behold, is ^bcome.

6 An end is come, the end is come: it watcheth for thee; behold, it is come.

7 The morning is come unto thee, O thou that dwellest in the land: the time is come, the day of trouble *is* near, and not the sounding again of the mountains.

8 Now will I shortly pour out my ^afury upon thee, and accomplish mine anger upon thee: and I will judge thee according to thy ways, and will recompense thee for all thine abominations.

9 And mine eye shall not spare, neither will I have pity: I will recompense thee according to thy ways and thine abominations *that* are in the midst of thee; and ye shall know that I *am* the LORD that smiteth.

10 Behold the day, behold, it is come: the morning is gone forth; the rod hath blossomed, pride hath budded.

11 Violence is risen up into a rod of wickedness: none of them *shall remain,* nor of their multitude, nor of any of theirs: neither *shall there be* ^awailing for them.

12 The time is come, the day

draweth near: let not the ^abuyer rejoice, nor the seller mourn: for wrath *is* upon all the multitude thereof.

13 For the seller shall not return to that which is sold, although they were yet alive: for the vision *is* touching the whole multitude thereof, *which* shall not return; neither shall any strengthen himself in the iniquity of his life.

14 They have blown the trumpet, even to make all ready; but none goeth to the battle: for my wrath *is* upon all the multitude thereof.

15 The ^asword *is* without, and the pestilence and the famine within: he that *is* in the field shall die with the sword; and he that *is* in the city, famine and pestilence shall devour him.

16 ¶ But they that ^aescape of them shall escape, and shall be on the mountains like doves of the valleys, all of them ^bmourning, every one for his iniquity.

17 All ^ahands shall be feeble, and all knees shall be weak *as* water.

18 They shall also gird *themselves* with ^asackcloth, and horror shall cover them; and ^bshame *shall be* upon all faces, and ^cbaldness upon all their heads.

19 They shall cast their silver in the streets, and their gold shall be removed: their silver and their gold shall not be able to deliver them in the day of the wrath of the LORD: they shall not satisfy their souls, neither fill their bowels: because it is the ^astumblingblock of their ^biniquity.

20 ¶ As for the beauty of his ornament, he set it in majesty: but they made the ^aimages of their abominations *and* of their detestable things therein: therefore have I set it far from them.

7 2*a* Lam. 4:18;
    Amos 8:2.
  3*a* 1 Sam. 3:13;
    Ezek. 18:30.
  4*a* Ezek. 5:11.
   b Ezek. 9:10; 11:21;
    16:43; 22:31;
    D&C 1:10.
   c TG God, Knowledge about.

  5*a* OR singular or unique.
   b OR coming.
  8*a* Ezek. 20:8.
  11*a* TG Mourning.
  12*a* Isa. 24:2 (1–3).
  15*a* Deut. 32:25;
    Lam. 1:20.
  16*a* Jer. 44:28;
    Ezek. 6:8.
   b TG Mourning.

  17*a* Ezek. 21:7.
  18*a* Lam. 2:10.
   b TG Shame.
   c Isa. 3:24 (1–26); 22:12.
  19*a* Zeph. 1:3;
    1 Ne. 14:1.
   b TG Wickedness.
  20*a* TG Idolatry.

21 And I will give it into the hands of the strangers for a prey, and to the wicked of the earth for a spoil; and they shall ^apollute it.

22 My face will I turn also from them, and they shall ^apollute my secret ^b*place:* for the robbers shall enter into it, and defile it.

23 ¶ Make a chain: for the land is full of ^abloody crimes, and the city is full of violence.

24 Wherefore I will bring the worst of the heathen, and they shall possess their houses: I will also make the pomp of the strong to cease; and their holy places shall be defiled.

25 Destruction cometh; and they shall seek peace, and *there shall be* none.

26 ^aMischief shall come upon mischief, and rumour shall be upon rumour; then shall they seek a vision of the prophet; but the ^blaw shall perish from the priest, and counsel from the ^cancients.

27 The king shall mourn, and the prince shall be clothed with desolation, and the hands of the people of the land shall be troubled: I will do unto them after their way, and according to their deserts will I judge them; and they shall ^aknow that I *am* the LORD.

CHAPTER 8

Ezekiel sees in vision the wickedness and abominations of the people of Judah in Jerusalem—He sees idolatry practiced in the temple itself.

AND it came to pass in the sixth year, in the sixth *month*, in the fifth *day* of the month, *as* I sat in mine house, and the ^aelders of Judah sat before me, that the ^bhand of the Lord GOD fell there upon me.

2 Then I beheld, and lo a likeness as the appearance of ^afire: from the appearance of his loins even downward, fire; and from his loins even upward, as the appearance of brightness, as the colour of amber.

3 And he put forth the form of an hand, and took me by a lock of mine head; and the ^aspirit lifted me up between the earth and the ^bheaven, and brought me in the ^cvisions of God to Jerusalem, to the door of the inner gate that looketh toward the north; where *was* the seat of the image of jealousy, which provoketh to jealousy.

4 And, behold, ^athe glory of the God of Israel *was* there, according to the vision that I saw in the ^bplain.

5 ¶ Then said he unto me, Son of man, lift up thine eyes now the way toward the north. So I lifted up mine eyes the way toward the north, and behold northward at the gate of the altar this image of jealousy in the entry.

6 He said furthermore unto me, Son of man, seest thou what they do? *even* the great abominations that the house of Israel committeth here, that I should go far off from my sanctuary? but turn thee yet again, *and* thou shalt see greater abominations.

7 ¶ And he brought me to the door of the court; and when I looked, behold a hole in the wall.

8 Then said he unto me, Son of man, dig now in the wall: and when I had digged in the wall, behold a door.

9 And he said unto me, Go in, and behold the wicked ^aabominations that they do here.

10 So I went in and saw; and behold every form of creeping things, and abominable beasts, and all the idols of the house of Israel, portrayed upon the wall round about.

11 And there stood before them ^aseventy men of the ^bancients of the

---

21 a Dan. 8:11; 11:31.
22 a TG Pollution.
  b Jer. 7:14;
    Ezek. 24:21.
23 a TG Blood, Shedding of.
26 a Jer. 4:20.
  b Mal. 2:7 (1–9).
  c HEB elders.

27 a TG God, Knowledge
    about.
8 1 a Ezek. 14:1.
    TG Elder.
  b Ezek. 1:3.
2 a Ezek. 1:27 (26–27).
3 a TG God, Spirit of.
  b TG Heaven.

c Ezek. 1:1; 40:2.
4 a TG God, Glory of.
  b Ezek. 3:22.
9 a TG Superstitions.
11 a TG Seventy.
  b HEB elders.

house of Israel, and in the midst of them stood Jaazaniah the son of Shaphan, with every man his censer in his hand; and a thick cloud of incense went up.

12 Then said he unto me, Son of man, hast thou seen what the ancients of the house of Israel do in the dark, every man in the chambers of his imagery? for they say, The LORD seeth us not; the LORD hath forsaken the earth.

13 ¶ He said also unto me, Turn thee yet again, *and* thou shalt see greater abominations that they do.

14 Then he brought me to the door of the gate of the LORD's house which *was* toward the north; and, behold, there sat women weeping for *a*Tammuz.

15 ¶ Then said he unto me, Hast thou seen *this*, O son of man? turn thee yet again, *and* thou shalt see greater abominations than these.

16 And he brought me into the inner *a*court of the LORD's house, and, behold, at the door of the temple of the LORD, between the *b*porch and the altar, *were* about five and twenty men, with their *c*backs toward the temple of the LORD, and their faces toward the east; and they worshipped *d*the sun toward the east.

17 ¶ Then he said unto me, Hast thou seen *this*, O son of man? Is it a light thing to the house of Judah that they commit the abominations which they commit here? for they have filled the land with violence, and have returned to provoke me to anger: and, lo, they put the branch to their nose.

18 Therefore will I also deal in fury: mine eye shall not spare, neither will I have pity: and though they cry in mine ears with a loud voice, *yet* will I not hear them.

CHAPTER 9

Ezekiel sees the marking of the righteous and the slaughter of all others, beginning at the Lord's sanctuary.

HE cried also in mine ears with a loud voice, saying, Cause them that have charge over the city to draw near, even every man *with* his destroying weapon in his hand.

2 And, behold, six men came from the way of the higher *a*gate, which lieth toward the north, and every man a slaughter weapon in his hand; and one man among them *was* *b*clothed with linen, with a *c*writer's *d*inkhorn by his side: and they went in, and stood beside the brasen *e*altar.

3 And the glory of the God of Israel was gone up from the *a*cherub, whereupon he was, to the threshold of the house. And he called to the man clothed with linen, which *had* the writer's inkhorn by his side;

4 And the LORD said unto him, Go through the midst of the city, through the midst of Jerusalem, and set a mark upon the *a*foreheads of the men that sigh and that cry for all the abominations that be done in the midst thereof.

5 ¶ And to the others he said in mine hearing, Go ye after him through the city, and smite: let not your eye spare, neither have ye pity:

6 Slay utterly old *and* young, both maids, and little children, and women: but come not near any man upon whom *is* the mark; and *a*begin at my sanctuary. Then they began at the *b*ancient men which *were* before the house.

7 And he said unto them, Defile the house, and fill the courts with the slain: go ye forth. And they went forth, and slew in the city.

8 ¶ And it came to pass, while they

14*a* IE Amorite idol.
16*a* 1 Kgs. 6:36.
  b 1 Kgs. 6:3.
  c Jer. 2:27; 32:33.
  d IE the sun god of
     Egyptians or father of
     the gods.

TG Idolatry.
9 2*a* 2 Kgs. 15:35;
     2 Chr. 27:3.
  b Dan. 12:6.
  c TG Scriptures,
     Writing of.
  d OR inkwell.

e Ex. 27:1 (1–8).
3*a* TG Cherubim.
4*a* D&C 77:9.
6*a* Jer. 25:29.
  b HEB elders.

were slaying them, and I was left, that I fell upon my face, and cried, and said, Ah Lord GOD! wilt thou destroy all the residue of Israel in thy pouring out of thy fury upon Jerusalem?

9 Then said he unto me, The iniquity of the house of Israel and Judah *is* exceeding great, and the land is full of blood, and the city full of perverseness: for they say, The LORD hath forsaken the earth, and the LORD *a*seeth not.

10 And as for me also, mine eye shall not spare, neither will I have pity, *but* I will *a*recompense their way upon their head.

11 And, behold, the man clothed with linen, which *had* the inkhorn by his side, reported the matter, saying, I have done as thou hast commanded me.

CHAPTER 10

He sees in vision, as before, the wheels, the cherubims, and the throne and the glory of God.

THEN I looked, and, behold, in the *a*firmament that was above the head of the cherubims there appeared over them as it were a sapphire stone, as the appearance of the likeness of a *b*throne.

2 And he spake unto the man clothed with linen, and said, Go in between the wheels, *even* under the cherub, and fill thine hand with coals of fire from between the cherubims, and *a*scatter *them* over the city. And he went in in my sight.

3 Now the cherubims stood on the right side of the house, when the man went in; and the cloud filled the inner court.

4 Then the glory of the LORD went up from the cherub, *and stood* over the threshold of the house; and the house was filled with the *a*cloud, and the court was full of the brightness of the LORD's glory.

5 And the sound of the cherubims' wings was heard *even* to the outer court, as the voice of the Almighty God when he speaketh.

6 And it came to pass, *that* when he had commanded the man clothed with linen, saying, Take fire from between the wheels, from between the cherubims; then he went in, and stood beside the wheels.

7 And *one* cherub stretched forth his hand from between the cherubims unto the fire that *was* between the cherubims, and took *thereof,* and put *it* into the hands of *him that was* clothed with linen: who took *it,* and went out.

8 ¶ And there appeared in the cherubims the form of a man's hand under their wings.

9 And when I looked, behold the four wheels by the cherubims, one wheel by one cherub, and another wheel by another cherub: and the appearance of the *a*wheels *was* as the colour of a beryl stone.

10 And *as for* their appearances, they four had one likeness, as if a wheel had been in the midst of a wheel.

11 When they *a*went, they went *b*upon their four sides; they turned not as they went, but to the place whither the *c*head looked they followed it; they turned not as they went.

12 And their whole body, and their backs, and their hands, and their wings, and the wheels, *were* full of eyes round about, *even* the wheels that they four had.

13 As for the wheels, it was cried unto them in my hearing, O wheel.

14 And every one had four faces: the first face *was* the face of a *a*cherub, and the second face *was* the face of a man, and the third the face of a lion, and the fourth the face of an eagle.

15 And the cherubims *a*were lifted

9*a* Isa. 47:10.
10*a* Ezek. 7:4.
10 1*a* Ezek. 1:22.
  b Ezek. 1:26.
2*a* Rev. 8:5.

4*a* TG God, Manifestations of.
9*a* Ezek. 1:16.
11*a* Ezek. 1:17.
  b IE towards any one of

their four directions.
  c Ezek. 1:9.
14*a* Ezek. 41:18 (18–19).
15*a* OR mounted.

up. This *is* the living creature that I saw by the river of *b*Chebar.

16 And when the cherubims went, the wheels went by them: and when the cherubims lifted up their wings to mount up from the earth, the same wheels also turned not from beside them.

17 When they stood, *these* stood; and when they were lifted up, *these* lifted up themselves *also*: for the *a*spirit of the living creature *was* in them.

18 Then the *a*glory of the LORD *b*departed from off the threshold of the house, and stood over the cherubims.

19 And the *a*cherubims lifted up their wings, and mounted up from the earth in my sight: when they went out, the wheels also *were* beside them, and *every one* stood at the door of the *b*east gate of the LORD's house; and the glory of the God of Israel *was* over them above.

20 This *is* the *a*living creature that I saw under the God of Israel by the river of Chebar; and I knew that they *were* the cherubims.

21 Every one had four faces apiece, and every one four wings; and the likeness of the hands of a man *was* under their wings.

22 And the likeness of their faces *was* the same faces which I saw by the river of Chebar, their appearances and themselves: they went every one straight forward.

CHAPTER 11

He sees in vision the destruction of Jerusalem and the captivity of the Jews— He prophesies the latter-day gathering of Israel.

MOREOVER the *a*spirit lifted me up, and brought me unto the *b*east gate of the LORD's house, which looketh eastward: and behold at the door of the gate five and twenty men; among whom I saw Jaazaniah the son of Azur, and Pelatiah the son of Benaiah, *c*princes of the people.

2 Then said he unto me, Son of man, these *are* the men that devise mischief, and give wicked counsel in this city:

3 Which say, *It is* not near; let us build houses: this *city is* the caldron, and we *be* the flesh.

4 ¶ Therefore prophesy against them, prophesy, O son of man.

5 And the *a*Spirit of the LORD fell upon me, and said unto me, Speak; Thus saith the LORD; Thus have ye said, O house of Israel: for I *b*know the things that come into your *c*mind, *every one of* them.

6 Ye have multiplied your *a*slain in this city, and ye have filled the streets thereof with the slain.

7 Therefore thus saith the Lord GOD; Your slain whom ye have laid in the midst of it, they *are* the flesh, and this *city is* the caldron: but I will bring you forth out of the midst of it.

8 Ye have feared the sword; and I will bring a sword upon you, saith the Lord GOD.

9 And I will bring you out of the midst thereof, and deliver you into the hands of *a*strangers, and will execute judgments among you.

10 Ye shall *a*fall by the sword; I will judge you in the border of Israel; and ye shall know that I *am* the LORD.

11 This *city* shall not be your caldron, neither shall ye be the flesh in the midst thereof; *but* I will judge you in the border of Israel:

12 And ye shall know that I *am* the LORD: for ye have not walked in my statutes, neither executed my *a*judgments, but have done after the *b*manners of the *c*heathen that *are* round about you.

15*b* Ezek. 1:1.
17*a* Ezek. 1:20.
18*a* TG God, Manifestations of.
  b Hosea 9:12.
19*a* TG Cherubim.
  b Ezek. 11:1.
20*a* Ezek. 1:22.

11 1*a* TG God, Spirit of; Guidance, Divine.
  b Ezek. 10:19.
  c OR leaders.
5*a* TG Holy Ghost, Mission of.
  b TG God, Omniscience of.

c Ezek. 20:32. TG Mind.
6*a* TG Blood, Shedding of.
9*a* OR foreigners.
10*a* 2 Kgs. 25:21 (19–21); Jer. 39:6; 52:10.
12*a* Ezek. 5:7.
  b TG Apostasy of Israel.
  c TG Heathen.

13 ¶ And it came to pass, when I prophesied, that Pelatiah the son of Benaiah died. Then fell I down upon my face, and cried with a loud voice, and said, Ah Lord GOD! wilt thou make a full end of the remnant of Israel?

14 Again the word of the LORD came unto me, saying,

15 Son of man, thy brethren, *even* thy brethren, *a*the men of thy kindred, and all the house of Israel wholly, *are* they unto whom the inhabitants of Jerusalem have said, Get you far from the LORD: unto us is this land given in possession.

16 Therefore say, Thus saith the Lord GOD; Although I have cast them far off among the heathen, and although I have scattered them among the countries, yet will I be to them as a little *a*sanctuary in the countries where they shall come.

17 Therefore say, Thus saith the Lord GOD; I will even *a*gather you from the *b*people, and assemble you out of the countries where ye have been scattered, and I will give you the *c*land of Israel.

18 And they shall come thither, and they shall take away all the detestable things thereof and all the abominations thereof from thence.

19 And I will *a*give them one *b*heart, and I will put a *c*new *d*spirit within you; and I will take the stony heart out of their flesh, and will give them an *e*heart of flesh:

20 That they may *a*walk in my statutes, and keep mine *b*ordinances, and do them: and they shall be my *c*people, and I will be their God.

21 But *as for them* whose heart *a*walketh after the heart of their detestable things and their abominations, I will *b*recompense their way upon their own heads, saith the Lord GOD.

22 ¶ Then did the cherubims lift up their wings, and the wheels beside them; and the *a*glory of the God of Israel *was* over them above.

23 And the *a*glory of the LORD went up from the midst of the city, and stood upon the mountain which *is* on the east side of the city.

24 ¶ Afterwards the *a*spirit took me up, and brought me in a vision by the Spirit of God into Chaldea, to them of the captivity. So the vision that I had seen went up from me.

25 Then I spake unto them of the captivity all the things that the LORD had shewed me.

CHAPTER 12

Ezekiel makes himself a symbol of the scattering of the people of Judah from Jerusalem—He then prophesies their scattering among all nations.

THE word of the LORD also came unto me, saying,

2 Son of man, thou dwellest in the midst of a *a*rebellious house, which have *b*eyes to see, and *c*see not; they have ears to hear, and hear not: for they *are* a rebellious house.

3 Therefore, thou son of man, prepare thee *a*stuff for *b*removing, and remove by day in their sight; and thou shalt remove from thy place to another place in their sight: it may be they will consider, though they *be* a rebellious house.

4 Then shalt thou bring forth thy stuff by day in their sight, as stuff for removing: and thou shalt go forth at even in their sight, as they that go forth into captivity.

5 Dig thou through the wall in their sight, and carry out thereby.

15*a* Septuagint and Syriac: thy fellow exiles.
16*a* Isa. 8:14.
  TG Refuge.
17*a* TG Israel, Gathering of.
  b HEB peoples or nations.
  c TG Israel, Land of.
19*a* TG God, Gifts of.
  b TG Conversion.
  c TG Man, New,

Spiritually Reborn.
  d TG Spirituality.
  e 2 Cor. 3:3 (2–3).
20*a* TG Walking with God.
  b TG Ordinance.
  c TG Israel, Mission of.
21*a* Deut. 28:15 (15–68).
  b Ezek. 7:4.
22*a* Ezek. 1:28.
23*a* Ezek. 43:2 (1–6).

24*a* TG God, Spirit of.
12 2*a* Ezek. 2:5; 44:6.
  b D&C 76:116 (116–18).
  c TG Spiritual Blindness; Watch.
3*a* HEB vessels or equipment.
  b HEB exile.

6 In their sight shalt thou bear *it* upon *thy* shoulders, *and* carry *it* forth in the twilight: thou shalt cover thy face, that thou see not the *a*ground: for I have set thee *for* a *b*sign unto the house of Israel.

7 And I did so as I was commanded: I brought forth my stuff by day, as stuff for captivity, and in the *a*even I digged through the wall with mine hand; I brought *it* forth in the twilight, *and* I bare *it* upon *my* shoulder in their sight.

8 ¶ And in the morning came the word of the LORD unto me, saying,

9 Son of man, hath not the house of Israel, the *a*rebellious house, said unto thee, *b*What doest thou?

10 Say thou unto them, Thus saith the Lord GOD; This burden *concerneth* the prince in Jerusalem, and all the house of Israel that *are* among them.

11 Say, I *am* your *a*sign: like as I have *b*done, so shall it be done unto them: they shall remove *and* go into captivity.

12 And the prince that *is* among them shall *a*bear upon *his* shoulder in the twilight, and shall go forth: they shall dig through the wall to carry out thereby: he shall cover his face, that he see not the ground with *his* eyes.

13 My *a*net also will I spread upon him, and he shall be taken in my snare: and I will bring him to *b*Babylon *to* the land of the Chaldeans; yet shall he not *c*see it, though he shall die there.

14 And I will *a*scatter toward every wind all that *are* about him to help him, and all his *b*bands; and I will draw out the *c*sword after them.

15 And they shall know that I *am* the LORD, when I shall *a*scatter them among the nations, and disperse them in the countries.

16 But I will leave a *a*few men of them from the sword, from the famine, and from the pestilence; that they may declare all their abominations among the heathen whither they come; and they shall know that I *am* the LORD.

17 ¶ Moreover the word of the LORD came to me, saying,

18 Son of man, eat thy bread with quaking, and drink thy water with trembling and with *a*carefulness;

19 And say unto the people of the land, Thus saith the Lord GOD of the inhabitants of Jerusalem, *and* of the land of Israel; They shall eat their bread with carefulness, and drink their water with *a*astonishment, that her land may be desolate from all that is therein, because of the *b*violence of all them that dwell therein.

20 And the cities that are inhabited shall be laid waste, and the land shall be desolate; and ye shall know that I *am* the LORD.

21 ¶ And the word of the LORD came unto me, saying,

22 Son of man, what *is* that proverb *that* ye have in the land of Israel, saying, The days are prolonged, and every vision faileth?

23 Tell them therefore, Thus saith the Lord GOD; I will make this proverb to cease, and they shall no more use it as a proverb in Israel; but say unto them, The days are at hand, and the *a*effect of every vision.

24 For there shall be no more any vain vision nor *a*flattering *b*divination within the house of Israel.

25 For I *am* the LORD: I will speak, and the *a*word that I shall speak shall come to pass; it shall be no

---

6a OR land.
  b Ezek. 24:24.
    TG Signs.
7a HEB evening.
9a Ezek. 17:12.
  b Ezek. 24:19; 37:18.
11a OR type (of things to come).
    TG Signs.
  b Ezek. 24:24.

12a IE the baggage of exile.
13a Ezek. 17:20; 32:3;
    Hosea 7:12.
  b TG Israel, Bondage of, in Other Lands.
  c Jer. 39:7; 52:11.
14a 2 Kgs. 25:5.
  b HEB troops.
    Ezek. 17:21.
  c Ezek. 5:2.

15a TG Israel, Scattering of.
16a TG Israel, Remnant of.
18a HEB apprehension or anxiety.
19a HEB dismay.
  b Ps. 107:34.
23a IE fulfillment.
24a TG Flatter.
  b TG Sorcery.
25a Isa. 55:11.

more prolonged: for in your days, O rebellious house, will I say the *b*word, and will perform it, saith the Lord GOD.

26 ¶ Again the word of the LORD came to me, saying,

27 Son of man, behold, *they of* the house of Israel say, The vision that he seeth *is* for many days *to come,* and he prophesieth of the times *that are ª*far off.

28 Therefore say unto them, Thus saith the Lord GOD; There shall none of my words be prolonged any more, but the word which I have spoken shall be done, saith the Lord GOD.

CHAPTER 13

Ezekiel reproves false prophets, both male and female, who speak lies, to whom God has not spoken.

AND the word of the LORD came unto me, saying,

2 Son of man, prophesy against the *ª*prophets of Israel that prophesy, and say thou unto them that prophesy out of their own hearts, Hear ye the word of the LORD;

3 Thus saith the Lord GOD; Woe unto the *ª*foolish prophets, that follow their own spirit, and have seen nothing!

4 O Israel, thy prophets are like the foxes in the deserts.

5 Ye have not gone up into the *ª*gaps, neither made up the hedge for the house of Israel to stand in the battle in the day of the LORD.

6 They have seen vanity and lying *ª*divination, saying, The LORD saith: and the LORD hath not sent them: and they have made *others* to hope that they would confirm the word.

7 Have ye not seen a vain vision, and have ye not spoken a lying divination, whereas ye say, The LORD saith *it; ª*albeit I have not spoken?

8 Therefore thus saith the Lord GOD; Because ye have spoken *ª*vanity, and seen *b*lies, therefore, behold, I *am* against you, saith the Lord GOD.

9 And mine hand shall be upon the prophets that see vanity, and that divine lies: they shall not be in the assembly of my people, neither shall they be written in the *ª*writing of the house of Israel, neither shall they *b*enter into the land of Israel; and ye shall know that I *am* the Lord GOD.

10 ¶ Because, even because they have seduced my people, saying, *ª*Peace; and *there was* no peace; and one built up a wall, and, lo, others daubed it with untempered *b*mortar:

11 Say unto them which daub *it* with untempered *mortar,* that it shall fall: there shall be an overflowing shower; and ye, O great hailstones, shall fall; and a stormy wind shall rend *it.*

12 Lo, when the wall is fallen, shall it not be said unto you, Where *is* the *ª*daubing wherewith ye have daubed *it?*

13 Therefore thus saith the Lord GOD; I will even rend *it* with a stormy wind in my fury; and there shall be an overflowing shower in mine anger, and great *ª*hailstones in *my* fury to consume *it.*

14 So will I break down the wall that ye have daubed with untempered *mortar,* and bring it down to the ground, so that the foundation thereof shall be discovered, and it shall fall, and ye shall be consumed in the midst thereof: and ye shall know that I *am* the LORD.

15 Thus will I accomplish my wrath upon the wall, and upon them that have daubed it with untempered *mortar,* and will say unto you, The wall *is* no *more,* neither they that daubed it;

25*b* TG Promise.
27*a* Amos 6:3.
13 2*a* TG False Prophets.
  3*a* Hosea 9:7 (7–9);
    2 Ne. 28:9; Hel. 13:29.
  5*a* IE breaks in the wall.
  6*a* TG Superstitions.

7*a* OR although.
8*a* OR folly.
  b TG Honesty.
9*a* TG Book of Life;
    Book of Remembrance;
    Record Keeping.
  b Ezek. 20:38.

10*a* Jer. 28:9 (8–9).
    TG Peace.
  b Ezek. 22:28.
12*a* OR plaster.
13*a* Rev. 11:19; 16:21;
    Mosiah 12:6;
    D&C 29:16.

16 *To wit,* the prophets of Israel which prophesy concerning Jerusalem, and which see visions of ªpeace for her, and *there is* no peace, saith the Lord GOD.

17 ¶ Likewise, thou son of man, set thy face against the daughters of thy people, which prophesy out of their own heart; and prophesy thou against them,

18 And say, Thus saith the Lord GOD; Woe to the *women* that sew ªpillows to all armholes, and make kerchiefs upon the head of every stature to hunt souls! Will ye hunt the souls of my people, and will ye save the souls alive *that come* unto you?

19 And will ye pollute me among my people for handfuls of barley and for ªpieces of bread, to slay the souls that should not die, and to save the souls alive that should not live, by your lying to my people that hear *your* lies?

20 Wherefore thus saith the Lord GOD; Behold, I *am* against your ªpillows, wherewith ye there hunt the souls to make *them* fly, and I will tear them from your arms, and will let the souls go, *even* the souls that ye hunt to make *them* ᵇfly.

21 Your kerchiefs also will I tear, and deliver my people out of your hand, and they shall be no more in your hand to be hunted; and ye shall know that I *am* the LORD.

22 Because with ªlies ye have made the heart of the righteous sad, whom I have not made sad; and strengthened the hands of the wicked, that he should not return from his wicked way, ᵇby promising him life:

23 Therefore ye shall see no more vanity, nor ªdivine ᵇdivinations: for I will deliver my people out of your hand: and ye shall know that I *am* the LORD.

CHAPTER 14

The Lord will not answer those who worship false gods and work iniquity—Ezekiel preaches repentance—The people would not be saved though Noah, Daniel, and Job ministered among them.

THEN came certain of the ªelders of Israel unto me, and sat before me.

2 And the word of the LORD came unto me, saying,

3 Son of man, these men have set up their idols in their heart, and put the stumblingblock of their ªiniquity before their face: should I be ᵇinquired of at all by ᶜthem?

4 Therefore speak unto them, and say unto them, Thus saith the Lord GOD; Every man of the house of Israel that setteth up his idols in his heart, and putteth the ªstumblingblock of his iniquity before his face, and cometh to the prophet; I the LORD will answer him that cometh according to the multitude of his idols;

5 That I may take the house of Israel in their own heart, because they are all estranged from me through their idols.

6 ¶ Therefore say unto the house of Israel, Thus saith the Lord GOD; Repent, and turn *yourselves* from your idols; and turn away your faces from all your abominations.

7 For every one of the house of Israel, or of the stranger that sojourneth in Israel, which separateth himself from me, and setteth up his idols in his heart, and putteth the stumblingblock of his iniquity before his face, and cometh to a prophet to inquire of him concerning me; I the LORD will answer him by myself:

8 And I will set my ªface against that man, and will make him a ᵇsign

---

16a TG Peace.
18a HEB bands or coverings to all elbows (trappings for magical arts).
19a Prov. 28:21.
20a HEB bands wherewith ye trap souls.
  b HEB free.

22a TG False Doctrine; Lying.
  b HEB to save his life.
23a Micah 3:6.
  b TG Sorcery.
14 1a Ezek. 8:1.
  3a TG Wickedness.
  b Ezek. 20:3; 36:37.

c 2 Kgs. 3:13; 2 Cor. 6:14 (14–16).
4a Ezek. 3:20; 2 Ne. 26:20.
8a Lev. 17:10.
  b Num. 26:10.

and a proverb, and I will cut him off from the midst of my people; and ye shall know that I *am* the LORD.

9 And if the prophet be deceived when he hath spoken a thing, *ᵃ*I the LORD have deceived that prophet, and I will stretch out my hand upon him, and will destroy him from the midst of my people Israel.

10 And they shall bear the *ᵃ*punishment of their iniquity: the punishment of the prophet shall be even as the punishment of him that seeketh *unto him;*

11 That the house of Israel may go no more astray from me, neither be polluted any more with all their transgressions; but that they may be my *ᵃ*people, and I may be their God, saith the Lord GOD.

12 ¶ The word of the LORD came again to me, saying,

13 Son of man, when the land sinneth against me by trespassing grievously, then will I stretch out mine hand upon it, and will *ᵃ*break the staff of the bread thereof, and will send famine upon it, and will cut off man and beast from it:

14 *ᵃ*Though these three men, *ᵇ*Noah, *ᶜ*Daniel, and *ᵈ*Job, were in it, they should deliver *but* their own souls by their righteousness, saith the Lord GOD.

15 ¶ If I cause *ᵃ*noisome beasts to pass through the land, and they spoil it, so that it be desolate, that no man may pass through because of the beasts:

16 *Though* these three men *were* in it, *as* I live, saith the Lord GOD, they shall deliver neither sons nor daughters; they only shall be delivered, but the land shall be desolate.

17 ¶ Or *if* I bring a *ᵃ*sword upon that land, and say, Sword, go through the land; so that I cut off man and beast from it:

18 Though these three men *were* in it, *as* I live, saith the Lord GOD,

they shall deliver neither sons nor daughters, but they only shall be delivered themselves.

19 ¶ Or *if* I send a pestilence into that land, and pour out my fury upon it in blood, to cut off from it man and beast:

20 Though Noah, Daniel, and Job, *were* in it, *as* I live, saith the Lord GOD, they shall deliver neither son nor daughter; they shall *but* deliver their own souls by their righteousness.

21 For thus saith the Lord GOD; How much more when I send my four sore judgments upon Jerusalem, the *ᵃ*sword, and the famine, and the noisome beast, and the pestilence, to cut off from it man and beast?

22 ¶ Yet, behold, therein shall be left a *ᵃ*remnant that shall be brought forth, *both* sons and daughters: behold, they shall come forth unto you, and ye shall see their way and their doings: and ye shall be comforted concerning the evil that I have brought upon Jerusalem, *even* concerning all that I have brought upon it.

23 And they shall comfort you, when ye see their ways and their doings: and ye shall know that I have not done without cause all that I have done in it, saith the Lord GOD.

CHAPTER 15

Jerusalem, as a useless vine, will be burned.

AND the word of the LORD came unto me, saying,

2 Son of man, What is the vine tree more than any tree, *or than* a branch which is among the trees of the forest?

3 Shall wood be taken thereof to do any work? or will *men* take a pin of it to hang any vessel thereon?

4 Behold, it is cast into the fire for fuel; the fire devoureth both the

9*a* JST Ezek. 14:9 . . . I the Lord have *not* deceived . . .
10*a* TG Punish.
11*a* TG Israel, Mission of.
13*a* Lev. 26:26.

14*a* Jer. 15:1.
   b Gen. 6:9.
   c Ezek. 28:3;
      Dan. 9:22 (22–23).
   d Job 1:1.
15*a* HEB wild or evil.

17*a* Lev. 26:25.
21*a* Ezek. 5:17; 33:27;
      Rev. 6:8.
22*a* TG Israel, Remnant of.

ends of it, and the midst of it is burned. Is it meet for *any* work?

5 Behold, when it was whole, it was meet for no work: how much less shall it be meet yet for *any* work, when the fire hath devoured it, and it is burned?

6 ¶ Therefore thus saith the Lord GOD; As the *a*vine tree among the trees of the forest, which I have given to the fire for fuel, so will I give the inhabitants of *b*Jerusalem.

7 And I will set my face against them; they shall go out from *one* fire, and *another* fire shall devour them; and ye shall know that I *am* the LORD, when I set my face against them.

8 And I will make the land desolate, because they have committed a trespass, saith the Lord GOD.

CHAPTER 16

Jerusalem has become as a harlot, reveling in her idols and worshipping false gods—She has partaken of all the sins of Egypt and the nations round about, and she is rejected—Yet in the last days, the Lord will again establish His covenant with her.

AGAIN the word of the LORD came unto me, saying,

2 Son of man, cause Jerusalem to know her *a*abominations,

3 And say, Thus saith the Lord GOD unto Jerusalem; Thy *a*birth and thy nativity *is* of the land of Canaan; thy father *was* an Amorite, and thy *b*mother an Hittite.

4 And *as for* thy nativity, in the day thou wast *a*born thy *b*navel was not cut, neither wast thou washed in water to *c*supple *thee*; thou wast not salted at all, nor swaddled at all.

5 None eye pitied thee, to do any of these unto thee, to have compassion upon thee; but thou wast cast out in the open field, to the lothing of thy person, in the day that thou wast born.

6 ¶ And when I passed by thee, and saw thee polluted in thine own blood, I said unto thee *when thou wast* in thy blood, Live; yea, I said unto thee *when thou wast* in thy blood, Live.

7 I have caused thee to multiply as the bud of the field, and thou hast increased and *a*waxen great, and thou art come to excellent ornaments: *thy* breasts are fashioned, and thine hair is grown, whereas thou *wast* *b*naked and bare.

8 Now when I passed by thee, and looked upon thee, behold, thy time *was* the time of *a*love; and I spread my skirt over thee, and covered thy nakedness: yea, I sware unto thee, and entered into a covenant with thee, saith the Lord GOD, and thou becamest mine.

9 Then washed I thee with water; yea, I throughly *a*washed away thy blood from thee, and I anointed thee with oil.

10 I clothed thee also with broidered work, and shod thee with badgers' skin, and I girded thee about with fine linen, and I covered thee with silk.

11 I decked thee also with ornaments, and I put bracelets upon thy hands, and a chain on thy neck.

12 And I put a jewel on thy *a*forehead, and earrings in thine ears, and a beautiful crown upon thine head.

13 Thus wast thou decked with gold and silver; and thy raiment *was* *of* fine linen, and silk, and broidered work; thou didst eat fine flour, and honey, and oil: and thou wast exceeding beautiful, and thou didst prosper into a kingdom.

14 And thy *a*renown went forth among the heathen for thy beauty: for it *was* perfect through my

15 6a TG Vineyard of the
　　Lord.
　　b 1 Ne. 1:13.
16 2a Ezek. 20:4;
　　D&C 88:81.
　　3a HEB origins.

b Ezek. 16:45.
4a Hosea 2:3.
　b IE umbilical cord.
　c HEB cleanse.
7a HEB grown large.
　b Hosea 2:3 (3, 8–12).

8a TG Love.
9a TG Remission of Sins.
12a HEB nose.
14a Lam. 2:15.

*b*comeliness, which I had put upon thee, saith the Lord GOD.

15 ¶ But thou didst trust in thine own beauty, and playedst the *a*harlot because of thy renown, and pouredst out thy fornications on every one that passed by; his it was.

16 And of thy garments thou didst take, and deckedst thy high places with divers colours, and playedst the harlot thereupon: *the like things shall not come, neither shall it be so.*

17 Thou hast also taken thy fair jewels of my gold and of my silver, which I had given thee, and madest to thyself *a*images of men, and didst commit whoredom with them,

18 And tookest thy broidered garments, and coveredst them: and thou hast set mine oil and mine incense before them.

19 My meat also which I gave thee, fine *a*flour, and oil, and honey, *wherewith* I fed thee, thou hast even set it before them for a sweet savour: and *thus* it was, saith the Lord GOD.

20 Moreover thou hast taken thy sons and thy daughters, whom thou hast borne unto me, and these hast thou *a*sacrificed unto them to be devoured. *Is this* of thy whoredoms a small matter,

21 That thou hast slain my children, and delivered them to cause them to pass through *the fire* for them?

22 And in all thine abominations and thy whoredoms thou hast not remembered the days of thy youth, when thou wast naked and bare, *and* wast polluted in thy blood.

23 And it came to pass after all thy wickedness, (woe, woe unto thee! saith the Lord GOD;)

24 *That* thou hast also built unto thee an eminent place, and hast made thee an high place in every street.

25 Thou hast built thy high place *a*at every head of the way, and hast made thy beauty to be abhorred, and hast opened thy feet to every one that passed by, and multiplied thy *b*whoredoms.

26 Thou hast also committed fornication with the Egyptians thy neighbours, great of flesh; and hast increased thy whoredoms, to provoke me to anger.

27 Behold, therefore I have stretched out my hand over thee, and have diminished *a*thine ordinary *food,* and delivered thee unto the will of them that hate thee, the daughters of the Philistines, which are ashamed of thy lewd way.

28 Thou hast played the whore also with the *a*Assyrians, because thou wast unsatiable; yea, thou hast played the harlot with them, and yet couldest not be satisfied.

29 Thou hast moreover multiplied thy fornication in the land of Canaan unto Chaldea; and yet thou wast not satisfied herewith.

30 How weak is thine heart, saith the Lord GOD, seeing thou doest all these *things,* the work of an imperious whorish woman;

31 In that thou buildest thine eminent place in the head of every way, and makest thine high place in every street; and hast not been as an harlot, in that thou scornest hire;

32 *But as* a wife that committeth adultery, *which* taketh strangers instead of her *a*husband!

33 They give gifts to all whores: but thou givest thy gifts to all thy lovers, and *a*hirest them, that they may come unto thee on every side for thy whoredom.

34 And the contrary is in thee from *other* women in thy whoredoms, whereas none followeth thee to commit whoredoms: and in that thou givest a reward, and no reward is given unto thee, therefore thou art contrary.

14*b* HEB splendor.
15*a* Hosea 4:15 (14–15).
17*a* TG Idolatry.
19*a* Hosea 2:8.
20*a* Isa. 57:5.

25*a* OR at the head of every street.
 b Jacob 2:33 (25–35).
27*a* HEB thine allotted portion.

28*a* 2 Kgs. 16:7 (7–18);
 2 Chr. 28:16 (16–21);
 Ezek. 23:12.
32*a* Hosea 2:7; Joel 1:8.
33*a* Hosea 8:9.

35 ¶ Wherefore, O harlot, hear the word of the LORD:

36 Thus saith the Lord GOD; Because thy *a*filthiness was poured out, and thy nakedness discovered through thy whoredoms with thy lovers, and with all the idols of thy *b*abominations, and by the blood of thy children, which thou didst give unto them;

37 Behold, therefore I will gather all thy lovers, with whom thou hast taken pleasure, and all *them* that thou hast loved, with all *them* that thou hast *a*hated; I will even gather them round about *b*against thee, and will discover thy *c*nakedness unto them, that they may see all thy nakedness.

38 And I will *a*judge thee, as women that break wedlock and shed blood are judged; and I will give thee blood in fury and jealousy.

39 And I will also give thee into their hand, and they shall throw down thine eminent place, and shall break down thy high places: they shall *a*strip thee also of thy clothes, and shall take thy fair jewels, and leave thee naked and bare.

40 They shall also bring up a company against thee, and they shall stone thee with stones, and thrust thee through with their swords.

41 And they shall *a*burn thine houses with fire, and execute judgments upon thee in the sight of many women: and I will cause thee to cease from playing the harlot, and thou also shalt give no hire any more.

42 So will I make my fury toward thee to rest, and my jealousy shall depart from thee, and I will be quiet, and will be no more angry.

43 Because thou hast not remembered the days of thy youth, but hast fretted me in all these *things*;

behold, therefore I also will *a*recompense thy way upon *thine* head, saith the Lord GOD: and thou shalt not commit this lewdness above all thine abominations.

44 ¶ Behold, every one that useth proverbs shall use *this* proverb against thee, saying, As *is* the mother, *so is* her daughter.

45 Thou *art* thy mother's daughter, that lotheth her husband and her children; and thou *art* the sister of thy sisters, which lothed their husbands and their children: your *a*mother *was* an Hittite, and your father an Amorite.

46 And thine elder *a*sister *is* Samaria, she and her daughters that dwell at thy left hand: and thy younger sister, that dwelleth at thy right hand, *is* *b*Sodom and her daughters.

47 Yet hast thou not walked after their ways, nor done after their abominations: but, as *if that were* a very little *thing*, thou wast corrupted more than they in all thy ways.

48 *As* I live, saith the Lord GOD, *a*Sodom thy sister hath not done, she nor her daughters, as thou hast done, thou and thy daughters.

49 Behold, this was the iniquity of thy sister *a*Sodom, *b*pride, fulness of bread, and abundance of *c*idleness was in her and in her daughters, neither did she strengthen the hand of the poor and needy.

50 And they were haughty, and committed *a*abomination before me: therefore I took them *b*away *c*as I saw good.

51 Neither hath Samaria committed half of thy sins; but thou hast multiplied thine abominations more than they, and hast *a*justified thy sisters in all thine abominations which thou hast done.

52 Thou also, which hast *a*judged

36*a* TG Filthiness.
  b Ezek. 36:18 (16–20).
37*a* Ezek. 23:28 (28–29).
  b Ezek. 23:22.
  c Lam. 1:8.
38*a* Ezek. 23:45.
39*a* Ezek. 23:26.
41*a* 2 Kgs. 25:9;
    Jer. 39:8; 52:13.

43*a* Ezek. 7:4.
45*a* Ezek. 16:3.
46*a* Jer. 3:7 (7–8, 10);
    Ezek. 23:2.
  b Isa. 1:10.
48*a* Matt. 10:15; 11:24.
49*a* Gen. 13:13.
  b TG Pride.
  c TG Idleness;

Laziness.
50*a* Jer. 23:14.
    TG Homosexual
    Behavior.
  b Gen. 19:24 (24–29).
  c HEB when I saw it.
51*a* Jer. 3:11.
52*a* Rom. 2:3.

thy sisters, bear thine own ^bshame for thy sins that thou hast committed more abominable than they: they are more righteous than thou: yea, be thou confounded also, and bear thy shame, in that thou hast justified thy sisters.

53 When I shall bring again their captivity, the captivity of Sodom and her daughters, and the captivity of Samaria and her daughters, then *will I* ^a*bring again* the captivity of thy captives in the midst of them:

54 That thou mayest bear thine own shame, and mayest be confounded in all that thou hast done, in that thou art a comfort unto them.

55 When thy sisters, Sodom and her daughters, shall return to their former ^aestate, and Samaria and her daughters shall return to their former estate, then thou and thy daughters shall return to your former estate.

56 For thy sister Sodom was not mentioned by thy mouth in the day of thy pride,

57 Before thy wickedness was discovered, as at the time of *thy* reproach of the daughters of ^aSyria, and all *that are* round about her, the daughters of the Philistines, which despise thee round about.

58 Thou hast borne thy lewdness and thine abominations, saith the LORD.

59 For thus saith the Lord GOD; I will even deal with thee as thou hast done, which hast despised the ^aoath in breaking the covenant.

60 ¶ Nevertheless I will remember my covenant with thee in the days of thy youth, and I will establish unto thee an everlasting ^acovenant.

61 Then thou shalt ^aremember thy ways, and be ^bashamed, when thou shalt receive thy sisters, thine elder and thy younger: and I will give them unto thee for daughters, but not by thy covenant.

62 And I will establish my covenant with thee; and thou shalt know that I *am* the LORD:

63 That thou mayest remember, and be confounded, and never open thy ^amouth any more because of thy shame, when I am pacified toward thee for all that thou hast done, saith the Lord GOD.

CHAPTER 17

Ezekiel shows in a parable how Israel, while subject to Babylon, wrongfully sought help from Egypt—Yet the Lord will bring forth in the last days a goodly tree from the cedars of Lebanon.

AND the word of the LORD came unto me, saying,

2 Son of man, put forth a riddle, and speak a parable unto the house of Israel;

3 And say, Thus saith the Lord GOD; A great ^aeagle with great wings, longwinged, full of feathers, which had divers colours, came unto Lebanon, and took the highest branch of the cedar:

4 He cropped off the top of his young twigs, and ^acarried it into a land of ^btraffick; he set it in a city of merchants.

5 He took also of the seed of the land, and ^aplanted it in a fruitful field; he placed *it* by great waters, *and* set it *as* a willow tree.

6 And it grew, and became a spreading ^avine of low stature, whose branches turned toward him, and the roots thereof were under him: so it became a vine, and brought forth branches, and shot forth sprigs.

7 There was also another great eagle with great wings and many feathers: and, behold, this vine did bend her roots toward him, and shot

---

52*b* TG Shame.
53*a* OR turn away.
55*a* Ezek. 36:11 (8–15).
57*a* HEB Aram.
59*a* D&C 84:40 (39–44).

60*a* TG Covenants.
61*a* Ezek. 36:31.
  b TG Repent.
63*a* Rom. 3:19.
17 3*a* Jer. 48:40.

4*a* TG Israel, Scattering of.
  b HEB trade or traders.
5*a* TG Israel, Scattering of.
6*a* TG Vineyard of the Lord.

forth her branches toward him, that he might water it by the furrows of her plantation.

8 It was planted in a *a*good soil by great waters, that it might bring forth branches, and that it might bear fruit, that it might be a goodly vine.

9 Say thou, Thus saith the Lord GOD; Shall it prosper? shall he not pull up the roots thereof, and cut off the fruit thereof, that it wither? it shall wither in all the leaves of her spring, even without great power or many people to pluck it up by the roots thereof.

10 Yea, behold, *being* planted, shall it prosper? shall it not utterly wither, when the *a*east *b*wind toucheth it? it shall wither in the furrows where it grew.

11 ¶ Moreover the word of the LORD came unto me, saying,

12 Say now to the *a*rebellious house, Know ye not what these *things mean?* tell *them*, Behold, the *b*king of Babylon is come to Jerusalem, and hath taken the king thereof, and the princes thereof, and led them with him to Babylon;

13 And hath taken of the king's *a*seed, and made a covenant with him, and hath taken an *b*oath of him: he hath also taken the *c*mighty of the land:

14 That the kingdom might be base, that it might not lift itself up, *but* that by keeping of his covenant it might stand.

15 But he *a*rebelled against him in sending his ambassadors into Egypt, that they might give him horses and much people. Shall he prosper? shall he escape that doeth such *things?* or shall he break the covenant, and be delivered?

16 *As* I live, saith the Lord GOD, surely in the place *where* the king *dwelleth* that made him king, whose oath he despised, and whose covenant he brake, *even* with him in the midst of *a*Babylon he shall die.

17 Neither shall *a*Pharaoh with *his* mighty *b*army and great company *c*make for him in the war, by casting up *d*mounts, and building forts, to cut off many persons:

18 Seeing he despised the oath by breaking the covenant, when, lo, he had given his hand, and hath done all these *things*, he shall not escape.

19 Therefore thus saith the Lord GOD; *As* I live, surely mine oath that he hath despised, and my covenant that he hath broken, even it will I recompense upon his own head.

20 And I will spread my *a*net upon him, and he shall be *b*taken in my snare, and I will bring him to *c*Babylon, and will *d*plead with him there for his trespass that he hath trespassed against me.

21 And all his fugitives with all his *a*bands shall fall by the sword, and they that remain shall be *b*scattered toward all winds: and ye shall know that I the LORD have spoken *it*.

22 ¶ Thus saith the Lord GOD; I will also take of the highest *a*branch of the high cedar, and will set *it*; I will crop off from the top of his young *b*twigs a tender one, and will *c*plant *it* upon an high mountain and eminent:

23 In the mountain of the height of Israel will I plant it: and it shall bring forth boughs, and bear fruit, and be a goodly cedar: and under it shall dwell all fowl of every wing; in the shadow of the branches thereof shall they dwell.

8*a* Jacob 5:25, 43.
10*a* Jer. 18:17.
  b Ezek. 19:12.
12*a* Ezek. 12:9.
  b 2 Kgs. 24:11 (11–12);
    25:6 (1–7);
    Omni 1:15.
13*a* Ezek. 19:14.
  b 2 Chr. 36:13.
  c 2 Kgs. 24:15.

15*a* 2 Kgs. 24:20;
    2 Chr. 36:13; Jer. 52:3.
16*a* TG Israel, Bondage of, in
    Other Lands.
17*a* Jer. 44:30.
  b Jer. 37:7.
  c OR help him.
  d OR siegeworks.
20*a* Lam. 1:13; Ezek. 12:13;
    Hosea 7:12.

  b Ezek. 21:23.
  c TG Israel, Bondage of, in
    Other Lands.
  d Ezek. 20:35.
21*a* Ezek. 12:14.
  b Zech. 2:6.
22*a* Omni 1:15 (14–17);
    Mosiah 25:2; Hel. 8:21.
  b Jacob 5:24 (22–24).
  c TG Israel, Scattering of.

24 And all the trees of the field shall know that I the LORD have brought down the high tree, have ^aexalted the low tree, have dried up the green tree, and have made the dry tree to flourish: I the LORD have spoken and have ^bdone *it*.

CHAPTER 18

Men will be punished for their own sins—Sinners will die, and the righteous will surely live—A righteous man who sins will be damned, and a sinner who repents will be saved.

THE word of the LORD came unto me again, saying,

2 What mean ye, that ye use this proverb concerning the land of Israel, saying, The fathers have eaten sour ^agrapes, and the children's teeth are set on edge?

3 *As* I live, saith the Lord GOD, ye shall not have *occasion* any more to use this proverb in Israel.

4 Behold, all souls are mine; as the soul of the father, so also the soul of the son is mine: the soul that ^asinneth, it shall ^bdie.

5 ¶ But if a man be ^ajust, and do that which is lawful and right,

6 *And* hath not eaten upon the mountains, neither hath ^alifted up his eyes to the ^bidols of the house of Israel, neither hath ^cdefiled his neighbour's wife, neither hath come near to a menstruous ^dwoman,

7 And hath not oppressed any, *but* hath restored to the debtor his ^apledge, hath spoiled none by violence, hath given his bread to the hungry, and hath covered the ^bnaked with a garment;

8 He *that* hath not given forth upon ^ausury, neither hath taken any increase, *that* hath withdrawn his hand from iniquity, hath exe-

cuted true judgment between man and man,

9 Hath walked in my statutes, and hath kept my judgments, to deal truly; he *is* just, he shall surely live, saith the Lord GOD.

10 ¶ If he beget a son *that is* a robber, a shedder of blood, and *that* doeth the like to *any* one of these *things,*

11 And that doeth not any of those *duties,* but even hath eaten upon the mountains, and defiled his ^aneighbour's wife,

12 Hath oppressed the ^apoor and needy, hath spoiled by violence, hath not restored the pledge, and hath lifted up his eyes to the idols, hath committed abomination,

13 Hath given forth upon usury, and hath taken increase: shall he then live? he shall not live: he hath done all these abominations; he shall surely die; his ^ablood shall be upon him.

14 ¶ Now, lo, *if* he beget a son, that seeth all his father's sins which he hath done, and considereth, and doeth not ^asuch like,

15 *That* hath not eaten upon the mountains, neither hath lifted up his eyes to the idols of the house of Israel, hath not defiled his neighbour's wife,

16 Neither hath oppressed any, hath not withholden the pledge, neither hath spoiled by violence, *but* hath given his bread to the hungry, and hath covered the naked with a garment,

17 *That* hath taken off his hand from the poor, *that* hath not received usury nor increase, hath executed my judgments, hath walked in my statutes; he shall not die for the iniquity of his father, he shall surely live.

18 *As for* his father, because he

24a 2 Ne. 20:33;
    D&C 112:8 (3–8).
  b Ezek. 36:36.
18 2a Jer. 31:29;
    Lam. 5:7.
  4a TG Justice; Sin.
    b TG Punish.
  5a Heb. 12:23;

D&C 76:69 (66–69).
  6a Ps. 123:1.
    b 2 Ne. 9:37.
    c D&C 42:24 (22–26).
    d Lev. 18:19.
  7a Ex. 22:26;
    Deut. 24:13;
    Ezek. 33:15.

  b Alma 34:28 (18–29).
  8a TG Usury.
 11a Lev. 20:10.
 12a 2 Ne. 13:14 (14–15);
    28:13 (12–13);
    Hel. 4:12 (11–13).
 13a Ezek. 33:4.
 14a HEB like them.

*a*cruelly oppressed, spoiled his brother by violence, and did *that* which *is* not good among his people, lo, even he shall die in his iniquity.

19 ¶ Yet say ye, Why? doth not the son bear the iniquity of the father? When the son hath done that which is lawful and right, *and* hath kept all my statutes, and hath done them, he shall surely live.

20 The soul that *a*sinneth, it shall die. The son shall not *b*bear the iniquity of the father, neither shall the father bear the iniquity of the son: the *c*righteousness of the righteous shall be upon him, and the wickedness of the wicked shall be upon him.

21 But if the wicked will *a*turn from all his sins that he hath committed, and keep all my statutes, and do that which is lawful and right, he shall surely live, he shall not die.

22 All his *a*transgressions that he hath committed, they shall not be mentioned unto him: in his righteousness that he hath done he shall live.

23 Have I any *a*pleasure at all that the wicked should die? saith the Lord GOD: *and* not that he should return from his ways, and live?

24 ¶ But when the *a*righteous *b*turneth away from his *c*righteousness, and committeth iniquity, *and* doeth according to all the abominations that the wicked *man* doeth, shall he live? All his righteousness that he hath done shall not be mentioned: in his trespass that he hath trespassed, and in his *d*sin that he hath sinned, in them he shall die.

25 ¶ Yet ye say, The *a*way of the Lord is not *b*equal. Hear now, O house of Israel; Is not my way equal? are not your ways unequal?

26 When a righteous *man* *a*turneth away from his righteousness, and committeth iniquity, and *b*dieth in them; for his iniquity that he hath done shall he die.

27 Again, when the wicked *man* *a*turneth away from his wickedness that he hath committed, and doeth that which is lawful and right, he shall save his soul alive.

28 Because he considereth, and turneth away from all his transgressions that he hath committed, he shall surely live, he shall not die.

29 Yet saith the house of Israel, The way of the Lord is not *a*equal. O house of Israel, are not my ways equal? are not your ways unequal?

30 Therefore I will *a*judge you, O house of Israel, every one according to his ways, saith the Lord GOD. Repent, and turn *yourselves* from all your *b*transgressions; so iniquity shall not be your ruin.

31 ¶ *a*Cast away from you all your transgressions, whereby ye have transgressed; and make you a new *b*heart and a *c*new spirit: for why will ye *d*die, O house of Israel?

32 For I have no pleasure in the death of him that dieth, saith the Lord GOD: wherefore turn *yourselves*, and live ye.

CHAPTER 19

Ezekiel laments for Israel because she has been taken captive by other nations and has become like a vine planted in dry and thirsty ground.

MOREOVER take thou up a *a*lamentation for the princes of Israel,

2 And say, What *is* thy mother?

18*a* TG Cruelty.
20*a* TG Sin.
  b TG Accountability;
    Punish.
  c TG Righteousness.
21*a* TG Repent.
22*a* TG Forgive;
    Transgress.
23*a* Ezek. 33:11;
    1 Tim. 2:4 (4, 6);
    2 Pet. 3:9.

    TG Pleasure.
24*a* Ezek. 3:20.
  b Ezek. 33:12 (12–13, 18).
  c TG Righteousness.
  d 2 Ne. 9:38.
25*a* Ezek. 33:17.
  b HEB right or just.
26*a* TG Apostasy of
    Individuals.
  b 1 Ne. 15:33 (32–33);
    Mosiah 15:26;

    Moro. 10:26.
27*a* Ezek. 33:14.
29*a* HEB right or just.
30*a* Ezek. 7:3 (3, 8); 33:20.
  b TG Transgress.
31*a* Ezek. 20:7.
  b TG Conversion; Heart.
  c TG Man, New,
    Spiritually Reborn.
  d Ezek. 33:11.
19 1*a* Jer. 7:29.

A *a*lioness: she lay down among lions, she nourished her whelps among young lions.

3 And she brought up one of her *a*whelps: it became a young lion, and it learned to catch the prey; it devoured men.

4 The nations also heard of him; he was taken in their pit, and they brought him with *a*chains unto the land of *b*Egypt.

5 Now when she saw that she had waited, *and* her hope was lost, then she took another of her whelps, *and* made him a young lion.

6 And he went up and down among the lions, he became a young lion, and learned to catch the prey, *and* *a*devoured men.

7 And he knew their desolate palaces, and he laid waste their cities; and the land was desolate, and the fulness thereof, by the noise of his roaring.

8 Then the nations set *a*against him on every side from the provinces, and spread their net over him: he was *b*taken in their *c*pit.

9 And they put him in ward in *a*chains, and brought him to the king of Babylon: they brought him into *b*holds, that his voice should no more be heard upon the mountains of Israel.

10 ¶ Thy mother *is* like a *a*vine *b*in thy blood, planted by the waters: she was fruitful and full of branches by reason of many waters.

11 And she had strong rods for the sceptres of them that bare rule, and her stature was exalted among the thick branches, and she appeared in her height with the multitude of her branches.

12 But she was plucked up in fury, she was cast down to the ground, and the *a*east *b*wind dried up her fruit: her strong rods were broken and withered; the fire consumed them.

13 And now she *is* planted in the *a*wilderness, in a dry and thirsty ground.

14 And *a*fire is gone out of a *b*rod of her branches, *which* hath devoured her fruit, so that she hath no strong rod *to be* a sceptre to rule. This *is* a lamentation, and shall be for a lamentation.

CHAPTER 20

From the time of their deliverance from Egypt to the day of Ezekiel, the people of Israel have rebelled and failed to keep the commandments—In the last days, the Lord will gather Israel and restore His gospel covenant.

AND it came to pass in the seventh *a*year, in the fifth *month*, the tenth *day* of the month, *that* certain of the *b*elders of Israel came to inquire of the LORD, and sat before me.

2 Then came the word of the LORD unto me, saying,

3 Son of man, speak unto the elders of Israel, and say unto them, Thus saith the Lord GOD; Are ye come to inquire of me? *As* I live, saith the Lord GOD, I will not be *a*inquired of by you.

4 Wilt thou judge them, son of man, wilt thou judge *them*? cause them to know the *a*abominations of their fathers:

5 ¶ And say unto them, Thus saith the Lord GOD; In the day when I *a*chose Israel, and *b*lifted up mine hand unto the seed of the house of Jacob, and made myself known unto them in the land of Egypt, when I lifted up mine hand unto them, saying, I *am* the *c*LORD your God;

2*a* Reference is to Judah, of which the royal house came. (Recall Gen. 49:8–12.)
3*a* 2 Chr. 36:1.
4*a* 2 Kgs. 23:33 (33–34).
  b 2 Chr. 36:4 (3–4).
6*a* Jer. 22:13 (13–18).
8*a* 2 Kgs. 24:2.
  b Hel. 4:26.

c Lam. 4:20.
9*a* 2 Chr. 36:6.
  b HEB strongholds.
10*a* TG Vineyard of the Lord.
  b HEB in thy likeness.
12*a* 2 Chr. 36:20 (17–20).
  b Ezek. 17:10.
13*a* 2 Kgs. 24:15 (12–16).
14*a* Judg. 9:15 (1–20).
  b Ezek. 17:13 (13–21).

20 1*a* Ezek. 33:21.
  b TG Elder.
3*a* 1 Sam. 8:18;
    Ezek. 14:3;
    Mosiah 21:15;
    D&C 101:7.
4*a* Ezek. 16:2.
5*a* TG Israel, Mission of.
  b OR covenanted.
  c Ex. 20:2.

6 In the day *that* I lifted up mine hand unto them, to ᵃbring them forth of the land of Egypt into a ᵇland that I had ᶜespied for them, flowing with milk and honey, which *is* the ᵈglory of all lands:

7 Then said I unto them, ᵃCast ye away every man the abominations of his eyes, and defile not yourselves with the idols of Egypt: I *am* the LORD your God.

8 But they rebelled against me, and would not hearken unto me: they did not every man cast away the abominations of their eyes, neither did they forsake the idols of Egypt: then I said, I will pour out my ᵃfury upon them, to accomplish my anger against them in the midst of the land of Egypt.

9 But I wrought for my ᵃname's sake, that it should not be polluted before the heathen, among whom they *were,* in whose sight I made myself known unto them, in bringing them forth out of the land of Egypt.

10 ¶ Wherefore I ᵃcaused them to go forth out of the land of Egypt, and brought them into the wilderness.

11 And I gave them my ᵃstatutes, and shewed them my judgments, which *if* a man do, he shall even ᵇlive in them.

12 Moreover also I gave them my ᵃsabbaths, to be a sign between me and them, that they might know that I *am* the LORD that ᵇsanctify them.

13 But the house of Israel ᵃrebelled against me in the wilderness: they walked not in my statutes, and they ᵇdespised my judgments, which *if* a man do, he shall even live in them; and my sabbaths they greatly polluted: then I said, I would pour out my fury upon them in the ᶜwilderness, to consume them.

14 But I wrought for my name's sake, that it should not be polluted before the heathen, in whose sight I brought them out.

15 Yet also I lifted up my hand unto them in the wilderness, that I would not bring them into the ᵃland which I had given *them,* flowing with milk and honey, which *is* the glory of all lands;

16 Because they despised my judgments, and walked not in my statutes, but polluted my sabbaths: for their ᵃheart went after their idols.

17 Nevertheless mine eye ᵃspared them from destroying them, neither did I make an end of them in the wilderness.

18 But I said unto their children in the wilderness, Walk ye not in the statutes of your ᵃfathers, neither observe their judgments, nor defile yourselves with their idols:

19 I *am* the LORD your God; walk in my ᵃstatutes, and keep my judgments, and do them;

20 And ᵃhallow my sabbaths; and they shall be a ᵇsign between me and you, that ye may know that I *am* the LORD your God.

21 Notwithstanding the children ᵃrebelled against me: they walked not in my statutes, neither kept my judgments to do them, which *if* a man do, he shall even live in them; they polluted my sabbaths: then I said, I would pour out my fury upon them, to accomplish my anger against them in the wilderness.

22 Nevertheless I withdrew mine hand, and wrought for my name's sake, that it should not be polluted in the sight of the heathen, in whose sight I brought them forth.

6a TG Israel, Deliverance of.
  b Abr. 2:6.
  c OR sought out.
  d Ps. 48:2.
7a Ezek. 18:31.
8a Ezek. 7:8.
9a Ex. 9:16;
    Ps. 106:8;
    Isa. 48:11; 63:14;
    Ezek. 36:21 (21–24).

10a Ex. 13:18 (18, 20).
11a Deut. 4:8;
    Neh. 9:13.
  b 2 Ne. 1:16 (16–17);
    5:10 (10–11).
12a TG Sabbath.
  b TG Sanctification.
13a 1 Cor. 10:5 (5–10).
  b 1 Ne. 17:30 (30–31);
    Jacob 4:14.

  c Num. 14:29; 26:65.
15a TG Israel, Land of.
16a TG Heart.
17a Ezek. 5:11.
18a Hel. 15:4;
    D&C 93:39.
19a Deut. 5:31; 6:1.
20a OR keep holy or sanctify.
  b TG Signs.
21a TG Rebellion.

23 I lifted up mine hand unto them also in the wilderness, that I would ^ascatter them among the heathen, and disperse them through the countries;

24 Because they had not executed my judgments, but had despised my statutes, and had polluted my sabbaths, and their eyes were after their fathers' idols.

25 Wherefore I gave them also statutes *that were* not good, and judgments whereby they should not live;

26 And I polluted them in their own gifts, in that they caused to pass ^athrough *the* ^b*fire* all that openeth the womb, that I might make them desolate, to the ^cend that they might ^dknow that I *am* the LORD.

27 ¶ Therefore, son of man, speak unto the house of Israel, and say unto them, Thus saith the Lord GOD; Yet in this your fathers have ^ablasphemed me, in that they have committed a trespass against me.

28 *For* when I had brought them into the land, *for* the which I lifted up mine hand to give it to them, then they saw every high hill, and all the thick trees, and they offered there their sacrifices, and there they presented the provocation of their offering: there also they made their sweet savour, and poured out there their drink offerings.

29 Then I said unto them, What *is* the high place whereunto ye go? And the name thereof is called Bamah unto this day.

30 Wherefore say unto the house of Israel, Thus saith the Lord GOD; Are ye polluted after the manner of your fathers? and commit ye whoredom after their abominations?

31 For when ye offer your gifts, when ye make your sons to pass through the fire, ye pollute yourselves with all your idols, even unto this day: and shall I be inquired of by you, O house of Israel? As I live, saith the Lord GOD, I will not be inquired of by you.

32 And that which cometh into your ^amind shall not be at all, that ye say, We will be as the ^bheathen, as the families of the countries, to serve ^cwood and stone.

33 ¶ As I live, saith the Lord GOD, surely with a mighty hand, and with a stretched out arm, and with fury poured out, will I rule over you:

34 And I will bring you out from the people, and will ^agather you out of the countries wherein ye are scattered, with a mighty hand, and with a stretched out arm, and with fury poured out.

35 And I will bring you into the ^awilderness of the people, and there will I ^bplead with you ^cface to face.

36 Like as I pleaded with your fathers in the wilderness of the land of Egypt, so will I plead with you, saith the Lord GOD.

37 And I will cause you ^ato pass under the ^brod, and I will bring you into the bond of the ^ccovenant:

38 And I will ^apurge out from among you the ^brebels, and them that transgress against me: I will bring them forth out of the country where they sojourn, and they shall not ^center into the ^dland of Israel: and ye shall know that I *am* the LORD.

39 As for you, O house of Israel, thus saith the Lord GOD; Go ye, serve ye every one his idols, and hereafter *also,* if ye will not hearken unto me: but ^apollute ye my holy name no more with your gifts, and with your ^bidols.

23a TG Israel, Scattering of.
26a IE as burnt sacrifices to Moloch.
  b 2 Kgs. 21:6; 2 Chr. 28:3; 33:6.
  c Hel. 12:3.
  d TG God, Knowledge about.
27a Isa. 65:7.
32a Ps. 94:11;

Ezek. 11:5.
  b TG Traditions of Men.
  c TG Idolatry.
34a Deut. 30:3 (1–5).
35a Hosea 2:14.
  b Ezek. 17:20.
  c TG God, Presence of.
37a IE to be numbered as the flock.
  b Lev. 27:32.

  c 3 Ne. 29:1 (1–3); Morm. 5:14 (14, 20).
38a Ezek. 34:17 (17, 20, 22).
  b TG Rebellion.
  c Ezek. 13:9.
  d TG Israel, Land of.
39a Ezek. 39:7; 43:7.
  b D&C 1:16.

40 For in mine holy ^amountain, in the mountain of the height of Israel, saith the Lord GOD, there shall all the house of ^bIsrael, all of them in the land, serve me: there will I ^caccept them, and there will I require your offerings, and the firstfruits of your oblations, with all your holy things.

41 I will accept you with your sweet savour, when I bring you out from the people, and ^agather you out of the countries wherein ye have been scattered; and I will be ^bsanctified in you before the heathen.

42 And ye shall ^aknow that I *am* the LORD, when I shall bring you into the land of Israel, into the country *for* the which I ^blifted up mine hand to give it to your fathers.

43 And there shall ye ^aremember your ways, and all your doings, wherein ye have been defiled; and ye shall lothe yourselves in your own sight for all your evils that ye have committed.

44 And ye shall know that I *am* the LORD, when I have wrought with you for my name's sake, not according to your wicked ways, nor according to your corrupt doings, O ye house of Israel, saith the Lord GOD.

45 ¶ Moreover the word of the LORD came unto me, saying,

46 Son of man, set thy ^aface toward the south, and ^bdrop *thy word* toward the south, and prophesy against the forest ^cof the south field;

47 And say to the forest of the south, Hear the word of the LORD; Thus saith the Lord GOD; Behold, I will kindle a fire in thee, and it shall devour every green tree in thee, and every dry tree: the flaming flame shall not be quenched, and all faces from the south to the north shall be burned therein.

48 And all flesh shall see that I the LORD have kindled it: it shall not be quenched.

49 Then said I, Ah Lord GOD! they ^asay of me, Doth he not speak parables?

CHAPTER 21

Both the righteous and the wicked in Jerusalem will be slain—Babylon will draw a sharp and bright sword against Israel and will prevail.

AND the word of the LORD came unto me, saying,

2 Son of man, set thy ^aface toward Jerusalem, and ^bdrop *thy word* toward the holy places, and prophesy against the ^cland of Israel,

3 And say to the land of Israel, Thus saith the LORD; Behold, I *am* against thee, and will draw forth my ^asword out of his sheath, and will cut off from thee the righteous and the wicked.

4 Seeing then that I will cut off from thee the righteous and the wicked, therefore shall my sword go forth out of his sheath against all flesh from the south to the north:

5 That all flesh may know that I the LORD have drawn forth my sword out of his sheath: it shall not ^areturn any more.

6 Sigh therefore, thou son of man, with the breaking of *thy* loins; and with bitterness sigh before their eyes.

7 And it shall be, when they say unto thee, Wherefore sighest thou? that thou shalt answer, For the tidings; because it cometh: and every heart shall melt, and all ^ahands shall be feeble, and every spirit shall faint, and all knees shall be weak *as* water: behold, it cometh, and shall be brought to pass, saith the Lord GOD.

8 ¶ Again the word of the LORD came unto me, saying,

40a Isa. 56:7.
  b TG Israel, Twelve
    Tribes of.
  c Isa. 60:7;
    Mal. 3:4.
41a TG Israel, Gathering of.
  b TG Sanctification.
42a 3 Ne. 16:4 (4–5); 20:13.

  b IE covenanted.
43a Mosiah 2:40;
    Alma 5:18 (7–18).
46a Ezek. 6:2; 21:2.
  b OR preach.
  c IE of the Negev.
49a TG Prophets,
    Rejection of.

21 2a Ezek. 20:46.
  b OR preach against.
  c TG Israel, Land of.
 3a D&C 1:13.
 5a IE be sheathed.
 7a Ezek. 7:17.

9 Son of man, prophesy, and say, Thus saith the LORD; Say, A sword, a sword is sharpened, and also ªfurbished:

10 It is sharpened to make a sore slaughter; it is furbished that it may glitter: should we then make mirth? it contemneth the rod of my son, *as* every tree.

11 And he hath given it to be furbished, that it may be ªhandled: this sword is sharpened, and it is furbished, to give it into the hand of the slayer.

12 Cry and howl, son of man: for it shall be upon my people, it *shall be* upon all the princes of Israel: terrors by reason of the sword shall be upon my people: smite therefore upon *thy* thigh.

13 Because *it is* a ªtrial, and what if *the sword* ᵇcontemn even the rod? it shall be no *more*, saith the Lord GOD.

14 Thou therefore, son of man, prophesy, and smite *thine* hands together, and let the sword be doubled the third time, the sword of the slain: it *is* the sword of the great *men that are* slain, which entereth into their privy chambers.

15 I have set the point of the sword against all their gates, that *their* heart may faint, and *their* ruins be multiplied: ah! *it is* made bright, *it is* wrapped up for the slaughter.

16 Go thee one way or other, *either* on the right hand, *or* on the left, whithersoever thy face *is* set.

17 I will also smite mine hands together, and I will cause my ªfury to rest: I the LORD have said *it*.

18 ¶ The word of the LORD came unto me again, saying,

19 Also, thou son of man, appoint thee two ways, that the sword of the king of Babylon may come: both twain shall come forth out of one land: and choose thou a place, choose *it* at the head of the way to the city.

20 Appoint a way, that the sword may come to ªRabbath of the Ammonites, and to Judah in Jerusalem the defenced.

21 For the king of Babylon stood at the parting of the way, at the head of the two ways, to use divination: he made *his* arrows bright, he consulted with images, he looked in the liver.

22 At his right hand was the divination for Jerusalem, to appoint captains, to open the mouth in the slaughter, to lift up the voice with shouting, to appoint ªbattering rams against the gates, to cast ᵇa mount, *and* to build ᶜa fort.

23 And it shall be unto them as a false divination in their sight, to them that have sworn oaths: but he will call to remembrance the iniquity, that they may be ªtaken.

24 Therefore thus saith the Lord GOD; Because ye have made your iniquity to be remembered, in that your ªtransgressions are discovered, so that in all your doings your sins do appear; because, *I say*, that ye are come to remembrance, ye shall be ᵇtaken with the hand.

25 ¶ And thou, profane ªwicked prince of Israel, whose ᵇday is come, when iniquity *shall have* an end,

26 Thus saith the Lord GOD; Remove the ªdiadem, and take off the crown: this *shall* not *be* the same: exalt *him that is* ᵇlow, and abase *him that is* high.

27 I will overturn, overturn, overturn, it: and it shall be no *more*, until he ªcome ᵇwhose ᶜright it is; and I will give it *him*.

28 ¶ And thou, son of man, prophesy and say, Thus saith the Lord

---

9a OR polished.
11a HEB seized by hand.
13a OR time of testing.
  b HEB reject.
17a Ezek. 5:13;
  3 Ne. 21:21.
20a Jer. 49:2;
  Ezek. 25:5 (4–5);
  Amos 1:14.

22a Ezek. 4:2.
  b OR siege mounds.
  c OR siegeworks.
23a Ezek. 17:20 (20, 24).
24a D&C 3:9.
  b IE captured.
25a 2 Chr. 36:12 (12–13).
  b Ezek. 22:3.
26a HEB headdress or miter.

  b Luke 1:52.
27a TG Jesus Christ, Second
    Coming.
  b The Hebrew word *shiloh*
    may be a short form of
    asher-lo, which can be
    rendered "whose right
    it is."
  c Gen. 49:10.

GOD concerning the [a]Ammonites, and concerning their reproach; even say thou, The sword, the sword *is* drawn: for the slaughter *it is* [b]furbished, to consume because of the glittering:

29 [a]Whiles they see vanity unto thee, whiles they divine a lie unto thee, to bring thee upon the necks of *them that are* slain, of the wicked, whose day is come, when their iniquity *shall have* an end.

30 Shall I cause *it* to return into his sheath? I will judge thee in the place where thou wast created, in the land of thy nativity.

31 And I will pour out mine [a]indignation upon thee, I will blow against thee in the [b]fire of my [c]wrath, and deliver thee into the hand of brutish men, *and* skilful to destroy.

32 Thou shalt be for fuel to the fire; thy blood shall be in the midst of the land; thou shalt be no *more* remembered: for I the LORD have spoken *it*.

CHAPTER 22

Ezekiel catalogs the sins of the people of Judah in Jerusalem—They will be scattered and destroyed for their iniquities.

MOREOVER the word of the LORD came unto me, saying,

2 Now, thou son of man, wilt thou judge, wilt thou judge the bloody city? yea, thou shalt shew her all her abominations.

3 Then say thou, Thus saith the Lord GOD, The city [a]sheddeth [b]blood in the midst of it, that her [c]time may come, and maketh idols against herself to defile herself.

4 Thou art become guilty in thy blood that thou hast shed; and hast defiled thyself in thine idols which thou hast made; and thou hast caused thy days to draw near, and art come *even* unto thy years: therefore have I made thee a [a]reproach unto the heathen, and a mocking to all countries.

5 *Those that be* near, and *those that be* far from thee, shall mock thee, *which art* infamous *and* much vexed.

6 Behold, the princes of Israel, every one were in thee to their power to shed blood.

7 In thee have they [a]set light by [b]father and mother: in the midst of thee have they dealt by [c]oppression with the [d]stranger: in thee have they vexed the fatherless and the [e]widow.

8 Thou hast despised mine holy things, and hast profaned my sabbaths.

9 In thee are men that [a]carry tales to shed blood: and in thee they eat upon the mountains: in the midst of thee they commit [b]lewdness.

10 In thee have they discovered their fathers' [a]nakedness: in thee have they [b]humbled her that was set [c]apart for [d]pollution.

11 And one hath committed abomination with his neighbour's wife; and another hath lewdly defiled his daughter in law; and another in thee hath humbled his sister, his father's daughter.

12 In thee have they taken [a]gifts to shed blood; thou hast taken [b]usury and increase, and thou hast greedily gained of thy neighbours by extortion, and hast forgotten me, saith the Lord GOD.

13 ¶ Behold, therefore I have smitten mine hand at thy [a]dishonest gain which thou hast made, and at

---

28a Jer. 49:2 (1–2).
  b OR polished.
29a IE While they see false visions for you.
31a TG God, Indignation of.
  b Ezek. 22:21 (20–21).
  c D&C 43:26.
22 3a Ezek. 36:18 (16–20).
  b TG Blood, Shedding of.
  c Ezek. 21:25.
4a Ezek. 5:14.

7a HEB treated lightly or dishonored.
  b TG Honoring Father and Mother.
  c Zech. 7:10 (9–11).
  d TG Stranger.
  e Amos 5:12; Hel. 6:39 (37–40).
9a OR slander in order to.
  b TG Sensuality.
10a Lev. 18:7 (7–8).

  b HEB abused her who is unclean in her time of menstruation.
  c Lev. 18:19.
  d Ezek. 36:17 (16–20).
12a Deut. 27:25; Isa. 1:23.
  b Isa. 3:14; Amos 3:10; Alma 4:12 (12–13).
  TG Usury.
13a TG Honesty.

thy blood which hath been in the midst of thee.

14 Can thine heart endure, or can thine hands be strong, in the days that I shall deal with thee? I the Lord have spoken *it,* and will do *it.*

15 And I will ^ascatter thee among the heathen, and disperse thee in the countries, and will consume thy ^bfilthiness out of thee.

16 And thou shalt take thine inheritance in thyself in the sight of the heathen, and thou shalt know that I *am* the Lord.

17 And the word of the Lord came unto me, saying,

18 Son of man, the house of Israel is to me become ^adross: all they *are* brass, and tin, and iron, and lead, in the midst of the ^bfurnace; they are *even* the dross of silver.

19 Therefore thus saith the Lord God; Because ye are all become dross, behold, therefore I will gather you into the midst of Jerusalem.

20 *As* they gather silver, and brass, and iron, and lead, and tin, into the midst of the furnace, to blow the fire upon it, to melt *it;* so will I gather *you* in mine anger and in my fury, and I will leave *you there,* and melt you.

21 Yea, I will gather you, and blow upon you in the ^afire of my wrath, and ye shall be melted in the midst thereof.

22 As silver is melted in the midst of the furnace, so shall ye be melted in the midst thereof; and ye shall know that I the Lord have poured out my fury upon you.

23 ¶ And the word of the Lord came unto me, saying,

24 Son of man, say unto her, Thou *art* the land that is not cleansed, nor ^arained upon in the day of ^bindignation.

25 *There is* a ^aconspiracy of her ^bprophets in the midst thereof, like a ^croaring lion ravening the prey; they have devoured souls; they have taken the ^dtreasure and ^eprecious things; they have made her many widows in the midst thereof.

26 Her ^apriests have ^bviolated my law, and have profaned mine holy things: they have put no ^cdifference between the holy and profane, neither have they shewed *difference* between the unclean and the clean, and have hid their eyes from my ^dsabbaths, and I am ^eprofaned among them.

27 Her ^aprinces in the midst thereof *are* like wolves ravening the prey, to shed blood, *and* to destroy souls, to get dishonest ^bgain.

28 And her prophets have daubed them with untempered ^amortar, seeing vanity, and ^bdivining lies unto them, saying, Thus saith Lord God, when the Lord hath not spoken.

29 The people of the land have used oppression, and exercised robbery, and have vexed the ^apoor and needy: yea, they have oppressed the stranger wrongfully.

30 And I sought for a man among them, that should make up the hedge, and stand in the gap before me for the land, that I should not ^adestroy it: but I found none.

31 Therefore have I poured out mine indignation upon them; I have consumed them with the fire of my wrath: their own way have I ^arecompensed upon their heads, saith the Lord God.

15*a* TG Israel, Scattering of; Israel, Ten Lost Tribes of.
  b TG Filthiness.
18*a* Ps. 119:119.
  TG Apostasy of Israel; Wickedness.
  b Isa. 48:10.
21*a* Ezek. 21:31.
24*a* Ps. 68:9; Ezek. 34:26.

  b TG God, Indignation of.
25*a* TG Conspiracy.
  b TG False Prophets.
  c Prov. 28:15.
  d TG Treasure.
  e Jer. 20:5.
26*a* TG Apostasy of Israel.
  b Mal. 2:8.
  c Lev. 10:10; Ezek. 44:23.
  d Jer. 17:27 (22, 24, 27);

  Ezek. 44:24.
  e TG Profanity.
27*a* TG Kings, Earthly.
  b 2 Ne. 26:29; 4 Ne. 1:26.
28*a* Ezek. 13:10.
  b TG Superstitions.
29*a* TG Poor.
30*a* Gen. 18:26; Jer. 5:1.
31*a* Ezek. 7:4.

CHAPTER 23

Two sisters, Samaria and Jerusalem, committed whoredoms by worshipping idols—Both are destroyed for their lewdness.

THE word of the LORD came again unto me, saying,

2 Son of man, there were two women, the *a*daughters of one mother:

3 And they committed whoredoms in Egypt; they committed whoredoms in their youth: there were their breasts pressed, and there they bruised the teats of their virginity.

4 And the names of them *were* *a*Aholah the elder, and *b*Aholibah her sister: and they were mine, and they bare sons and daughters. Thus *were* their names; Samaria *is* Aholah, and Jerusalem Aholibah.

5 And Aholah played the harlot when she was mine; and she doted on her lovers, on the *a*Assyrians *her* neighbours,

6 *Which were* clothed with blue, captains and rulers, all of them desirable young men, horsemen riding upon horses.

7 Thus she committed her whoredoms with them, with all them *that were* the chosen men of Assyria, and with all on whom she doted: with all their idols she defiled herself.

8 Neither left she her whoredoms *brought* from Egypt: for in her youth they lay with her, and they bruised the breasts of her virginity, and poured their whoredom upon her.

9 Wherefore I have delivered her into the hand of her lovers, into the hand of the Assyrians, upon whom she doted.

10 These discovered her nakedness: they took her sons and her daughters, and slew her with the sword: and she became famous among women; for they had executed judgment upon her.

11 And when her sister Aholibah saw *this*, she was more corrupt in her inordinate love than she, and in her whoredoms more than her sister in *her* whoredoms.

12 She doted upon the *a*Assyrians *her* neighbours, captains and rulers clothed most gorgeously, horsemen riding upon horses, all of them desirable young men.

13 Then I saw that she was defiled, *that* they *took* both one way,

14 And *that* she increased her whoredoms: for when she saw men portrayed upon the wall, the images of the Chaldeans portrayed with vermilion,

15 Girded with girdles upon their loins, exceeding in dyed attire upon their heads, all of them princes to look to, after the manner of the Babylonians of Chaldea, the land of their nativity:

16 And as soon as she saw them with her eyes, she doted upon them, and sent messengers unto them into Chaldea.

17 And the Babylonians came to her into the bed of love, and they defiled her with their whoredom, and she was *a*polluted with them, and her mind was alienated *b*from them.

18 So she discovered her whoredoms, and discovered her nakedness: then my mind was alienated from her, like as my mind was alienated from her sister.

19 Yet she multiplied her whoredoms, in calling to remembrance the days of her youth, wherein she had played the harlot in the land of Egypt.

20 For she doted upon their paramours, whose flesh *is as* the flesh of asses, and whose issue *is like* the issue of horses.

21 Thus thou calledst to remembrance the lewdness of thy youth, in bruising thy teats by the Egyptians for the paps of thy youth.

---

23 2*a* Jer. 3:7 (7–8, 10);
     Ezek. 16:46 (45–46, 61).
   4*a* HEB A tent.
     b HEB My tent is in her.

5*a* 2 Kgs. 15:19; 17:6 (3–6);
     Hosea 8:9.
12*a* 2 Kgs. 16:7 (7–18);
     2 Chr. 28:16 (16–21);

Ezek. 16:28.
17*a* TG Filthiness.
   b JST Ezek. 23:17 . . . from
     me by them.

22 ¶ Therefore, O Aholibah, thus saith the Lord GOD; Behold, I will raise up thy lovers against thee, [a]from whom thy mind is alienated, and I will bring them [b]against thee on every side;

23 The Babylonians, and all the Chaldeans, Pekod, and Shoa, and Koa, *and* all the Assyrians with them: all of them desirable young men, captains and rulers, great lords and renowned, all of them riding upon horses.

24 And they shall come against thee with chariots, wagons, and wheels, and with an assembly of people, *which* shall set against thee buckler and shield and helmet round about: and I will set judgment before them, and they shall [a]judge thee according to their judgments.

25 And I will set my jealousy against thee, and they shall deal furiously with thee: they shall take away thy nose and thine ears; and thy remnant shall [a]fall by the sword: they shall take thy sons and thy daughters; and thy residue shall be devoured by the fire.

26 They shall also [a]strip thee out of thy clothes, and take away thy fair jewels.

27 Thus will I make thy lewdness to cease from thee, and thy whoredom *brought* from the land of Egypt: so that thou shalt not lift up thine eyes unto them, nor remember Egypt any more.

28 For thus saith the Lord GOD; Behold, I will deliver thee into the hand *of them* whom thou [a]hatest, into the hand *of them* from whom thy mind is alienated:

29 And they shall deal with thee hatefully, and shall take away all thy labour, and shall leave thee naked and bare: and the nakedness of thy whoredoms shall be discovered, both thy lewdness and thy whoredoms.

30 I will do these *things* unto thee, because thou hast gone a [a]whoring after the heathen, *and* because thou art polluted with their idols.

31 Thou hast walked in the way of thy sister; therefore will I give her [a]cup into thine hand.

32 Thus saith the Lord GOD; Thou shalt drink of thy sister's cup deep and large: thou shalt be laughed to scorn and had in derision; it containeth much.

33 Thou shalt be filled with [a]drunkenness and sorrow, with the cup of astonishment and desolation, with the cup of thy sister Samaria.

34 Thou shalt even drink it and suck *it* out, and thou shalt break the sherds thereof, and pluck off thine own breasts: for I have spoken *it*, saith the Lord GOD.

35 Therefore thus saith the Lord GOD; Because thou hast [a]forgotten me, and cast me behind thy back, therefore [b]bear thou also thy lewdness and thy whoredoms.

36 ¶ The LORD said moreover unto me; Son of man, wilt thou judge Aholah and Aholibah? yea, declare unto them their abominations;

37 That they have committed [a]adultery, and blood *is* in their hands, and with their idols have they committed [b]adultery, and have also caused their sons, whom they bare unto me, to pass for them through *the fire*, to devour *them*.

38 Moreover this they have done unto me: they have [a]defiled my sanctuary in the same day, and have profaned my sabbaths.

39 For when they had slain their children to their idols, then they came the same day into my sanctuary to [a]profane it; and, lo, thus

---

22a JST Ezek. 23:22 . . . *by whom thy mind is alienated from me,* and I will . . .
   b Ezek. 16:37.
24a 2 Kgs. 25:6 (6–7).
25a 2 Ne. 6:8.

26a Ezek. 16:39.
28a Ezek. 16:37 (37–41).
30a Ezek. 6:9.
31a Jer. 25:15.
33a Jer. 13:13.
35a TG Unbelief.
   b IE bear the

consequences of.
37a TG Adulterer.
   b Lev. 17:7; 20:5;
      Jer. 3:9 (8–9).
38a Jer. 51:51;
      Ezek. 44:7.
39a TG Sacrilege.

have they done in the midst of mine ^bhouse.

40 And furthermore, that ye have sent for men to come from far, unto whom a messenger *was* sent; and, lo, they came: for whom thou didst wash thyself, paintedst thy eyes, and deckedst thyself with ^aornaments,

41 And satest upon a stately bed, and a table prepared before it, whereupon thou hast set mine incense and mine oil.

42 And a voice of a multitude being at ease *was* with her: and with the men of the common sort *were* brought ^aSabeans from the wilderness, which put bracelets upon their hands, and beautiful crowns upon their heads.

43 Then said I unto *her that was* old in adulteries, Will they now commit whoredoms with her, and she *with them?*

44 Yet they went in unto her, as they go in unto a woman that playeth the harlot: so went they in unto Aholah and unto Aholibah, the lewd women.

45 ¶ And the righteous men, they shall ^ajudge them after the manner of adulteresses, and after the manner of women that shed blood; because they *are* adulteresses, and blood *is* in their hands.

46 For thus saith the Lord GOD; I will bring up a company upon them, and will give them to be removed and spoiled.

47 And the company shall stone them with stones, and dispatch them with their swords; they shall slay their ^asons and their daughters, and burn up their houses with fire.

48 Thus will I cause lewdness to cease out of the land, that all women may be taught not to do after your lewdness.

49 And they shall recompense your lewdness upon you, and ye shall bear the sins of your ^aidols: and ye shall know that I *am* the Lord GOD.

CHAPTER 24

The irrevocable judgment of Jerusalem is foretold—As a sign to the Jews, Ezekiel does not weep at his wife's death.

AGAIN in the ^aninth year, in the tenth month, in the tenth *day* of the month, the word of the LORD came unto me, saying,

2 Son of man, write thee the name of the day, *even* of this same day: the ^aking of ^bBabylon set himself against Jerusalem this same day.

3 And utter a parable unto the ^arebellious house, and say unto them, Thus saith the Lord GOD; Set on a ^bpot, set *it* on, and also pour water into it:

4 Gather the pieces thereof into it, *even* every good piece, the thigh, and the shoulder; fill *it* with the choice bones.

5 Take the choice of the flock, and burn also the bones under it, *and* make it boil well, and let them seethe the bones of it therein.

6 ¶ Wherefore thus saith the Lord GOD; Woe to the ^abloody city, to the pot whose scum *is* therein, and whose ^bscum is not gone out of it! bring it out piece by piece; ^clet no lot fall upon it.

7 For her blood is in the midst of her; she set it upon the top of a rock; she poured it not upon the ground, to ^acover it with dust;

8 That it might cause fury to come up to take vengeance; I have set her blood upon the top of a rock, that it should not be covered.

9 Therefore thus saith the Lord GOD; Woe to the bloody city! I will even make the pile for fire great.

---

39 *b* 2 Kgs. 21:4;
   D&C 121:19.
40 *a* Hosea 2:13.
42 *a* HEB drunkards.
45 *a* Ezek. 16:38.
47 *a* Ezek. 24:21.
49 *a* TG Idolatry.

24 1 *a* 2 Kgs. 25:1;
   Jer. 39:1; 52:4;
   Ezek. 1:2; 33:21.
2 *a* Jer. 39:1.
   b 1 Ne. 10:3.
3 *a* Ezek. 44:6 (6–7).
   b Jer. 1:13 (13–14).

6 *a* TG Blood, Shedding of.
   b OR refuse or filth.
   c IE let none of the
   pieces be selected for
   consecration.
7 *a* Lev. 17:13.

10 Heap on wood, kindle the fire, consume the flesh, and spice it well, and let the bones be burned.

11 Then set it empty upon the coals thereof, that the brass of it may be hot, and may burn, and *that* the filthiness of it may be molten in it, *that* the scum of it may be consumed.

12 She hath wearied *herself* with lies, and her great scum went not forth out of her: her scum *shall be* in the fire.

13 In thy *a*filthiness *is* lewdness: because I have purged thee, and thou wast not purged, thou shalt not be *b*purged from thy filthiness any more, till *c*I have caused my fury to rest upon thee.

14 I the LORD have spoken *it*: it shall come to pass, and I will *a*do *it*; I will not go back, neither will I spare, neither will I repent; according to thy ways, and according to thy doings, shall they judge thee, saith the Lord GOD.

15 ¶ Also the word of the LORD came unto me, saying,

16 Son of man, behold, I take away from thee the desire of thine eyes with a stroke: yet neither shalt thou mourn nor weep, neither shall thy tears run down.

17 Forbear to cry, make no *a*mourning for the dead, bind the *b*tire of thine *c*head upon thee, and put on thy shoes upon thy feet, and *d*cover not *thy* lips, and eat not the bread of men.

18 So I spake unto the people in the morning: and at even my wife died; and I did in the morning as I was commanded.

19 ¶ And the people said unto me, Wilt thou not tell us *a*what these *things are* to us, that thou doest *so?*

20 Then I answered them, The word of the LORD came unto me, saying,

21 Speak unto the house of Israel, Thus saith the Lord GOD; Behold, I will profane my *a*sanctuary, the excellency of your strength, the desire of your eyes, and that which your soul *b*pitieth; and your *c*sons and your daughters whom ye have left shall fall by the sword.

22 And ye shall do as I have done: ye shall not cover *your* lips, nor eat the bread of men.

23 And your tires *shall be* upon your heads, and your shoes upon your feet: ye shall not mourn nor weep; but ye shall pine away for your iniquities, and *a*mourn one toward another.

24 Thus Ezekiel is unto you a *a*sign: according to all that he hath *b*done shall ye do: and when this cometh, ye shall know that I *am* the Lord GOD.

25 Also, thou son of man, *shall it* not *be* in the day when I take from them their strength, the joy of their glory, the desire of their eyes, and that whereupon they set their minds, their sons and their daughters,

26 *That* he that *a*escapeth in that day shall come unto thee, to cause *thee* to hear *it* with *thine* ears?

27 In that day shall thy mouth be opened to him which is escaped, and thou shalt speak, and be no more *a*dumb: and thou shalt be a sign unto them; and they shall know that I *am* the LORD.

CHAPTER 25

The Lord's vengeance will fall on the Ammonites, on the Moabites and Edomites, and on the Philistines.

THE word of the LORD came again unto me, saying,

2 Son of man, set thy face against the *a*Ammonites, and prophesy against them;

13*a* TG Filthiness.
　b Jer. 13:27;
　　　D&C 128:24.
　c Ezek. 5:13.
14*a* 2 Ne. 9:17.
17*a* Jer. 16:5 (5, 7).
　b HEB headdress (turban).
　　　Ex. 33:4.

　c Lev. 10:6.
　d Lev. 13:45.
19*a* Ezek. 12:9; 37:18.
21*a* Jer. 7:14;
　　　Ezek. 7:22 (21–22).
　b Ps. 103:13.
　c Ezek. 23:47.
23*a* Mosiah 7:24;

　　　Hel. 9:22.
24*a* Ezek. 12:6.
　b Ezek. 12:11.
26*a* Ezek. 33:21 (21–22).
27*a* Ezek. 3:26 (26–27);
　　　33:22.
25 2*a* Gen. 19:38 (36–38).

3 And say unto the Ammonites, Hear the word of the Lord GOD; Thus saith the Lord GOD; Because thou saidst, Aha, against my sanctuary, when it was profaned; and against the land of Israel, when it was desolate; and against the house of Judah, when they went into captivity;

4 Behold, therefore I will deliver thee to the men of the east for a possession, and they shall set their palaces in thee, and make their dwellings in thee: they shall eat thy fruit, and they shall drink thy milk.

5 And I will make *a*Rabbah a stable for camels, and the Ammonites a couchingplace for flocks: and ye shall know that I *am* the LORD.

6 For thus saith the Lord GOD; Because thou hast clapped *thine* hands, and stamped with the feet, and rejoiced in heart with all thy *a*despite against the land of Israel;

7 Behold, therefore I will stretch out mine hand upon thee, and will deliver thee for a spoil to the heathen; and I will cut thee off from the people, and I will cause thee to perish out of the countries: I will destroy thee; and thou shalt know that I *am* the LORD.

8 ¶ Thus saith the Lord GOD; Because that *a*Moab and *b*Seir do say, Behold, the house of Judah *is* like unto all the *c*heathen;

9 Therefore, behold, I will open the side of Moab from the cities, from his cities *which are* on his frontiers, the glory of the country, *a*Beth-jeshimoth, *b*Baal-meon, and Kiriathaim,

10 Unto the men of the east with the Ammonites, and will give them in possession, that the Ammonites may not be remembered among the nations.

11 And I will execute judgments upon Moab; and they shall know that I *am* the LORD.

12 ¶ Thus saith the Lord GOD; Because that *a*Edom hath dealt against the house of Judah by taking vengeance, and hath greatly offended, and revenged himself upon them;

13 Therefore thus saith the Lord GOD; I will also stretch out mine hand upon *a*Edom, and will cut off man and beast from it; and I will make it *b*desolate from Teman; and they of Dedan shall fall by the sword.

14 And I will lay my vengeance upon *a*Edom by the hand of my people Israel: and they shall do in Edom according to mine anger and according to my fury; and they shall know my vengeance, saith the Lord GOD.

15 ¶ Thus saith the Lord GOD; Because the *a*Philistines have dealt by revenge, and have taken vengeance with a despiteful heart, to destroy *it* for the old hatred;

16 Therefore thus saith the Lord GOD; Behold, I will stretch out mine hand upon the Philistines, and I will cut off the Cherethims, and destroy the remnant of the *a*sea coast.

17 And I will execute great vengeance upon them with furious rebukes; and they shall know that I *am* the LORD, when I shall lay my vengeance upon them.

CHAPTER 26

Because she rejoiced in the sorrows and fall of Jerusalem, Tyre will be destroyed.

AND it came to pass in the eleventh *a*year, in the first *day* of the month, *that* the word of the LORD came unto me, saying,

2 Son of man, because that *a*Tyrus hath said against *b*Jerusalem, Aha,

---

5*a* Jer. 49:2;
  Ezek. 21:20;
  Amos 1:14.
6*a* OR contempt (malice).
8*a* Isa. 15:1.
  b Ezek. 35:2 (1–15).
  c TG Heathen.
9*a* Josh. 12:3.

  b 1 Chr. 5:8.
12*a* Ps. 137:7.
13*a* Jer. 49:7.
  b Mal. 1:3.
14*a* Isa. 34:5;
    Jer. 49:17 (7–22);
    Amos 9:12;
    Obad. 1:18 (8, 18–19, 21).

15*a* Isa. 14:31 (29–32);
    Jer. 47:1;
    Amos 1:8.
16*a* Zeph. 2:5 (4–5).
26 1*a* Ezek. 1:2; 33:21.
  2*a* Isa. 23:1;
    Amos 1:9.
  b TG Jerusalem.

she is broken *that was* the gates of the people: she is turned unto me: I shall be replenished, *now* she is laid waste:

3 Therefore thus saith the Lord GOD; Behold, I *am* against thee, O Tyrus, and will cause many nations to come up *a*against thee, as the sea causeth his waves to come up.

4 And they shall destroy the walls of Tyrus, and break down her towers: I will also scrape her dust from her, and make her like the *a*top of a rock.

5 It shall be *a place for* the spreading of nets in the midst of the sea: for I have spoken *it,* saith the Lord GOD: and it shall become a spoil to the nations.

6 And her daughters which *are* in the field shall be slain by the sword; and they shall *a*know that I *am* the LORD.

7 ¶ For thus saith the Lord GOD; Behold, I will bring upon *a*Tyrus Nebuchadrezzar king of Babylon, a king of kings, from the *b*north, with horses, and with chariots, and with horsemen, and companies, and much people.

8 He shall slay with the sword thy daughters in the field: and he shall make a fort against thee, and cast a mount against thee, and lift up the *a*buckler against thee.

9 And he shall set *a*engines of war against thy walls, and with his axes he shall break down thy towers.

10 By reason of the abundance of his horses their dust shall cover thee: thy walls shall shake at the noise of the horsemen, and of the wheels, and of the chariots, when he shall enter into thy gates, as men enter into a city wherein is made a breach.

11 With the hoofs of his horses shall he tread down all thy streets: he shall slay thy people by the sword, and thy strong garrisons shall go down to the ground.

12 And they shall make a spoil of thy riches, and make a prey of thy merchandise: and they shall break down thy walls, and destroy thy pleasant houses: and they shall lay thy stones and thy timber and thy dust in the midst of the water.

13 And I will cause the noise of thy songs to cease; and the sound of thy harps shall be no more heard.

14 And I will make thee like the *a*top of a rock: thou shalt be *a place* to spread nets upon; thou shalt be built no more: for I the LORD have spoken *it,* saith the Lord GOD.

15 ¶ Thus saith the Lord GOD to Tyrus; Shall not the *a*isles *b*shake at the sound of thy fall, when the wounded cry, when the slaughter is made in the midst of thee?

16 Then all the *a*princes of the sea shall come down from their thrones, and lay away their robes, and put off their broidered garments: they shall clothe themselves with trembling; they shall sit upon the ground, and shall tremble at *every* moment, and be astonished at thee.

17 And they shall take up a lamentation for thee, and say to thee, How art thou destroyed, *that wast* inhabited of seafaring men, the renowned city, which wast *a*strong in the sea, she and her inhabitants, which cause their terror *to be* on all that haunt it!

18 Now shall the *a*isles tremble in the day of thy fall; yea, the isles that *are* in the sea shall be troubled at thy departure.

19 For thus saith the Lord GOD; When I shall make thee a *a*desolate city, like the cities that are not inhabited; when I shall bring up the *b*deep upon thee, and great waters shall cover thee;

20 When I shall bring thee down

3*a* Jer. 34:1.
4*a* Ezek. 26:14.
6*a* 1 Ne. 21:26 (25–26);
    Mosiah 11:22 (20–22);
    D&C 43:25.
7*a* Ezek. 29:18.
 b Jer. 1:14.

8*a* OR shield.
9*a* OR battering rams.
14*a* Ezek. 26:4.
15*a* Ezek. 26:18; 39:6;
    2 Ne. 10:20.
 b Jer. 49:21.
16*a* Isa. 23:8.

17*a* Isa. 23:4.
18*a* Ezek. 26:15.
19*a* 3 Ne. 10:7 (7–8).
 b Ezek. 27:34;
    3 Ne. 9:7 (7–8).

with them that descend into the pit, with the people of old time, and shall set thee in the low parts of the earth, in places desolate of old, with them that go down to the pit, that thou be not inhabited; and I shall set glory in the land of the living;

21 I will make thee a terror, and thou *shalt be* no *more:* though thou be sought for, yet shalt thou never be found again, saith the Lord GOD.

CHAPTER 27

Ezekiel laments the fall of Tyre and the loss of her riches and commerce.

THE word of the LORD came again unto me, saying,

2 Now, thou son of man, take up a *a*lamentation for Tyrus;

3 And say unto Tyrus, O thou that art situate at the entry of the sea, *which art* a merchant of the people for many isles, Thus saith the Lord GOD; O Tyrus, thou hast said, I *am* of perfect *a*beauty.

4 Thy borders *are* in the midst of the seas, thy builders have perfected thy beauty.

5 They have made all thy *ship* boards of fir trees of *a*Senir: they have taken cedars from Lebanon to make masts for thee.

6 *Of* the *a*oaks of Bashan have they made thine oars; the company of the Ashurites have made thy benches *of* ivory, *brought* out of the isles of Chittim.

7 Fine linen with broidered work from Egypt was that which thou spreadest forth to be thy sail; blue and purple from the isles of *a*Elishah was that which covered thee.

8 The inhabitants of Zidon and Arvad were thy mariners: thy wise *men*, O Tyrus, *that* were in thee, were thy pilots.

9 The ancients of Gebal and the

wise *men* thereof were in thee thy *a*calkers: all the ships of the sea with their mariners were in thee to *b*occupy thy merchandise.

10 They of Persia and of *a*Lud and of Phut were in thine army, thy men of war: they hanged the shield and helmet in thee; they set forth thy comeliness.

11 The men of Arvad with thine army *were* upon thy walls round about, and the Gammadims were in thy towers: they hanged their shields upon thy walls round about; they have made thy beauty perfect.

12 *a*Tarshish *was* thy merchant by reason of the multitude of all *kind of* riches; with silver, iron, tin, and lead, they traded in thy fairs.

13 Javan, Tubal, and *a*Meshech, they *were* thy merchants: they traded the persons of men and vessels of brass in thy market.

14 They of the house of *a*Togarmah traded in thy fairs with horses and horsemen and mules.

15 The men of Dedan *were* thy merchants; many *a*isles *were* the merchandise of thine hand: they brought thee *for* a present horns of ivory and ebony.

16 *a*Syria *was* thy merchant by reason of the multitude of the wares of thy making: they occupied in thy fairs with emeralds, purple, and broidered work, and fine linen, and coral, and agate.

17 Judah, and the *a*land of Israel, they *were* thy merchants: they traded in thy market wheat of *b*Minnith, and Pannag, and honey, and oil, and balm.

18 Damascus *was* thy merchant in the multitude of the wares of thy making, for the multitude of all riches; in the wine of Helbon, and white wool.

19 Dan also and Javan going to and

27 2*a* Ezek. 28:12 (11–12).
　3*a* Lam. 2:15;
　　　Ezek. 28:12.
　5*a* Deut. 3:9 (8–9).
　6*a* Zech. 11:2.
　7*a* Gen. 10:4.
　9*a* IE those who repair leaks in ships.

　　　b HEB trade or exchange.
10*a* Isa. 66:19;
　　　Jer. 46:9;
　　　Ezek. 30:5.
12*a* 1 Kgs. 10:22;
　　　Ezek. 38:13.
13*a* Gen. 10:2 (2–3);
　　　Ps. 120:5;

　　　Ezek. 38:2.
14*a* Gen. 10:3 (2–3);
　　　Ezek. 38:6.
15*a* Ezek. 30:5.
16*a* HEB Aram.
17*a* TG Israel, Land of.
　　　b Judg. 11:33.

fro occupied in thy fairs: bright iron, cassia, and calamus, were in thy market.

20 Dedan *was* thy merchant in precious clothes for chariots.

21 Arabia, and all the princes of Kedar, they *a*occupied with thee in lambs, and rams, and goats: in these *were they* thy merchants.

22 The merchants of Sheba and Raamah, they *were* thy merchants: they occupied in thy fairs with chief of all spices, and with all precious stones, and gold.

23 Haran, and Canneh, and Eden, the merchants of Sheba, Asshur, *and* Chilmad, *were* thy merchants.

24 These *were* thy merchants in all sorts *of things,* in blue clothes, and broidered work, and in chests of rich apparel, bound with cords, and made of cedar, among thy merchandise.

25 The *a*ships of Tarshish did sing of thee in thy market: and thou wast replenished, and made very glorious in the midst of the seas.

26 ¶ Thy rowers have brought thee into great waters: the *a*east wind hath broken thee in the midst of the seas.

27 Thy riches, and thy fairs, thy merchandise, thy mariners, and thy pilots, thy calkers, and the occupiers of thy merchandise, and all thy men of war, that *are* in thee, and in all thy company which *is* in the midst of thee, shall fall into the midst of the seas in the day of thy ruin.

28 The suburbs shall shake at the sound of the cry of thy pilots.

29 And all that handle the oar, the mariners, *and* all the pilots of the sea, shall come down from their ships, they shall stand upon the land;

30 And shall cause their voice to be heard against thee, and shall cry bitterly, and shall cast up *a*dust upon their heads, they shall wallow themselves in the ashes:

31 And they shall make themselves utterly bald for thee, and gird them with sackcloth, and they shall weep for thee with bitterness of heart *and* bitter wailing.

32 And in their wailing they shall take up a lamentation for thee, and lament over thee, *saying,* What *city is* like Tyrus, like the destroyed in the midst of the sea?

33 When thy wares went forth out of the seas, thou filledst many people; thou didst enrich the kings of the earth with the multitude of thy riches and of thy merchandise.

34 In the time *when* thou shalt be broken by the *a*seas in the depths of the waters thy merchandise and all thy company in the midst of thee shall fall.

35 All the inhabitants of the isles shall be astonished at thee, and their kings shall be sore afraid, they shall be troubled in *their* countenance.

36 The merchants among the people shall hiss at thee; thou shalt be a terror, and never *shalt be* any more.

CHAPTER 28

Tyre and Sidon will fall and be destroyed—The Lord will gather the people of Israel to their own land—They will then dwell safely.

THE word of the LORD came again unto me, saying,

2 Son of man, say unto the prince of Tyrus, Thus saith the Lord GOD; Because thine *a*heart *is* lifted up, and thou hast said, I *am* a God, I sit *in* the seat of God, in the midst of the seas; yet thou *art* a *b*man, and not God, though thou set thine heart as the heart of God:

3 Behold, thou *art* wiser than *a*Daniel; there is no secret that they can hide from thee:

4 With thy wisdom and with thine understanding thou hast gotten thee riches, and hast gotten gold and silver into thy treasures:

21*a* HEB traded.
25*a* Ps. 48:7; Isa. 2:16.
26*a* Gen. 41:23;
      Ps. 78:26;

Jer. 18:17;
      Mosiah 7:31; 12:6.
30*a* Rev. 18:19.
34*a* Ezek. 26:19.

28 2*a* TG Pride.
      b Isa. 55:8 (8–9).
3*a* Ezek. 14:14;
      Dan. 9:22 (22–23).

5 By thy great *a*wisdom *and* by thy traffick hast thou increased thy riches, and thine heart is lifted up because of thy riches:

6 Therefore thus saith the Lord GOD; Because thou hast set thine heart as the heart of God;

7 Behold, therefore I will bring strangers upon thee, the terrible of the nations: and they shall draw their *a*swords against the beauty of thy wisdom, and they shall defile thy brightness.

8 They shall bring thee down to the pit, and thou shalt die the deaths of *them that are* slain in the midst of the seas.

9 Wilt thou yet say before him that slayeth thee, I *am* God? but thou *shalt be* a man, and no God, in the hand of him that slayeth thee.

10 Thou shalt die the deaths of the uncircumcised by the hand of strangers: for I have spoken *it*, saith the Lord GOD.

11 ¶ Moreover the word of the LORD came unto me, saying,

12 Son of man, take up a *a*lamentation upon the king of Tyrus, and say unto him, Thus saith the Lord GOD; Thou sealest up the sum, full of wisdom, and perfect in *b*beauty.

13 Thou hast been in *a*Eden the garden of God; every precious stone *was* thy covering, the sardius, topaz, and the diamond, the beryl, the onyx, and the jasper, the sapphire, the emerald, and the carbuncle, and gold: the workmanship of thy tabrets and of thy pipes was prepared in thee in the day that thou wast created.

14 Thou *art* the anointed *a*cherub that covereth; and I have set thee *so:* thou wast upon the holy mountain of God; thou hast walked up and down in the midst of the stones of fire.

15 Thou *wast* perfect in thy ways from the day that thou wast created, till iniquity was found in thee.

16 By the multitude of thy merchandise they have filled the midst of thee with violence, and thou hast sinned: therefore I will cast thee as profane out of the mountain of God: and I will destroy thee, O covering cherub, from the midst of the stones of fire.

17 Thine *a*heart was lifted up because of thy beauty, thou hast corrupted thy wisdom by reason of thy brightness: I will cast thee to the ground, I will lay thee before kings, that they may behold thee.

18 Thou hast defiled thy sanctuaries by the multitude of thine iniquities, by the iniquity of thy *a*traffick; therefore will I bring forth a fire from the midst of thee, it shall devour thee, and I will bring thee to ashes upon the earth in the sight of all them that behold thee.

19 All they that know thee among the people shall be astonished at thee: thou shalt be a terror, and never *shalt* thou *be* any more.

20 ¶ Again the word of the LORD came unto me, saying,

21 Son of man, set thy face against *a*Zidon, and prophesy against it,

22 And say, Thus saith the Lord GOD; Behold, I *am* against thee, O Zidon; and I will be glorified in the midst of thee: and they shall know that I *am* the LORD, when I shall have executed judgments in her, and shall be sanctified in her.

23 For I will send into her pestilence, and blood into her streets; and the wounded shall *a*be judged in the midst of her by the sword upon her on every side; and they shall know that I *am* the LORD.

24 ¶ And there shall be no more a *a*pricking brier unto the house of

---

5*a* 2 Ne. 9:28 (28–29), 42;
  Hel. 1:16.
7*a* Ezek. 30:11.
12*a* Ezek. 27:2;
  Ether 15:16.
  b Lam. 2:15;
  Ezek. 27:3.

13*a* Ezekiel implies
  that Tyrus has been
  presumed to be an
  earthly paradise.
  Ezek. 31:9 (8–9).
14*a* TG Cherubim.
17*a* Ezek. 31:10.

18*a* HEB merchandise or
  business dealings.
21*a* Isa. 23:4 (4–12);
  Jer. 25:22; 27:3.
23*a* HEB fall.
24*a* Num. 33:55;
  Josh. 23:13.

Israel, nor *any* grieving thorn of all *that are* round about them, that despised them; and they shall know that I *am* the Lord GOD.

25 Thus saith the Lord GOD; When I shall have *a*gathered the house of *b*Israel from the people among whom they are scattered, and shall be sanctified in them in the sight of the *c*heathen, then shall they dwell in their *d*land that I have given to my servant Jacob.

26 And they shall dwell *a*safely therein, and shall build houses, and plant vineyards; yea, they shall dwell *b*with confidence, when I have executed judgments upon all those that despise them round about them; and they shall know that I *am* the LORD their God.

CHAPTER 29

Egypt will be overthrown by Babylon— When Egypt rises again, it will be the basest of kingdoms.

IN the tenth year, in the tenth *month*, in the twelfth *day* of the month, the word of the LORD came unto me, saying,

2 Son of man, set thy face against Pharaoh king of Egypt, and prophesy against him, and against all *a*Egypt:

3 Speak, and say, Thus saith the Lord GOD; Behold, I *am* against thee, Pharaoh king of Egypt, the great *a*dragon that lieth in the midst of his rivers, which hath said, *b*My river *is* mine own, and I have made *it* for myself.

4 But I will put *a*hooks in thy jaws, and I will cause the fish of thy rivers to stick unto thy scales, and I will bring thee up out of the midst of thy rivers, and all the fish of thy rivers shall stick unto thy scales.

5 And I will *a*leave thee *thrown* into the wilderness, thee and all the fish of thy rivers: thou shalt fall upon the open fields; thou shalt not be brought together, nor gathered: I have given thee for meat to the beasts of the field and to the fowls of the heaven.

6 And all the inhabitants of Egypt shall know that I *am* the LORD, because they have been a staff of *a*reed to the house of Israel.

7 When they took hold of thee by thy hand, thou didst break, and rend all their shoulder: and when they leaned upon thee, thou brakest, and madest all their loins to *a*be at a stand.

8 ¶ Therefore thus saith the Lord GOD; Behold, I will bring a sword upon thee, and cut off man and beast out of thee.

9 And the land of Egypt shall be desolate and waste; and they shall know that I *am* the LORD: because he hath said, The river *is* mine, and I have made *it*.

10 Behold, therefore I *am* against thee, and against thy rivers, and I will make the land of Egypt utterly waste *and* desolate, *a*from the tower of Syene even unto the border of *b*Ethiopia.

11 No foot of man shall pass through it, nor foot of beast shall pass through it, neither shall it be inhabited forty years.

12 And I will make the land of Egypt desolate in the midst of the countries *that are* desolate, and her cities among the cities *that are* laid waste shall be desolate forty years: and I will *a*scatter the Egyptians among the nations, and will disperse them through the countries.

13 ¶ Yet thus saith the Lord GOD; At the end of forty years will I *a*gather the Egyptians from the people whither they were scattered:

25*a* TG Israel, Gathering of.
　b TG Israel, Ten Lost Tribes of.
　c HEB nations or Gentiles.
　d Ezek. 36:28; 37:25.
26*a* Jer. 23:6;
　　Ezek. 34:28 (25, 28).
　b HEB in safety.

29 2*a* Isa. 19:1;
　　Jer. 25:19;
　　Joel 3:19.
3*a* 2 Ne. 8:9.
　b IE the Nile.
4*a* Ezek. 38:4.
5*a* HEB cast thee off.
6*a* 2 Kgs. 18:21;

　　Isa. 36:6.
7*a* OR come to a standstill.
10*a* HEB from Migdol to Syene.
　b HEB Cush.
12*a* Jer. 46:19;
　　Ezek. 30:23 (23, 26).
13*a* Jer. 46:26.

14 And I will ^abring again the captivity of Egypt, and will cause them to return *into* the land of Pathros, into the land of their ^bhabitation; and they shall be there a ^cbase kingdom.

15 It shall be the basest of the kingdoms; neither shall it exalt itself any more above the nations: for I will diminish them, that they shall no more rule over the nations.

16 And it shall be no more the confidence of the house of Israel, which bringeth *their* iniquity to remembrance, when they shall look after them: but they shall know that I *am* the Lord GOD.

17 ¶ And it came to pass in the seven and twentieth year, in the first *month,* in the first *day* of the month, the word of the LORD came unto me, saying,

18 Son of man, Nebuchadrezzar king of Babylon caused his army to serve a great service against ^aTyrus: every head *was* made bald, and every shoulder *was* peeled: yet had he no wages, nor his army, for Tyrus, for the service that he had served against it:

19 Therefore thus saith the Lord GOD; Behold, I will give the land of Egypt unto Nebuchadrezzar king of Babylon; and he shall take her multitude, and take her spoil, and take her prey; and it shall be the wages for his army.

20 I have given him the land of Egypt *for* his labour wherewith he served against it, because they wrought for me, saith the Lord GOD.

21 ¶ In that day will I cause the horn of the house of Israel to ^abud forth, and I will give thee the ^bopening of the mouth in the midst of them; and they shall know that I *am* the LORD.

CHAPTER 30

Egypt and its helpers will be made desolate by Babylon.

THE word of the LORD came again unto me, saying,

2 Son of man, prophesy and say, Thus saith the Lord GOD; Howl ye, ^aWoe worth the day!

3 For the day *is* near, even the day of the LORD *is* near, a ^acloudy day; it shall be the time of the heathen.

4 And the sword shall come upon Egypt, and great pain shall be in ^aEthiopia, when the slain shall fall in Egypt, and they shall take away her multitude, and her foundations shall be broken down.

5 ^aEthiopia, and ^bLibya, and ^cLydia, and all the mingled people, and Chub, and the men of the land that is in league, shall fall with them by the sword.

6 Thus saith the LORD; They also that uphold Egypt shall fall; and the pride of her power shall come down: ^afrom the tower of Syene shall they fall in it by the sword, saith the Lord GOD.

7 And they shall be desolate in the midst of the countries *that are* desolate, and her cities shall be in the midst of the cities *that are* wasted.

8 And they shall know that I *am* the LORD, when I have set a fire in Egypt, and *when* all her helpers shall be destroyed.

9 In that day shall messengers go forth from me in ships to make the careless ^aEthiopians afraid, and great pain shall come upon them, as in the day of Egypt: for, lo, it cometh.

10 Thus saith the Lord GOD; I will also make the multitude of Egypt to cease by the hand of Nebuchadrezzar king of Babylon.

11 He and his people with him,

14*a* HEB return from exile the Egyptians.
  b HEB origin.
  c OR lowly.
18*a* Ezek. 26:7.
21*a* Hebrew metaphor meaning power, capacity.

  b Hebrew idiom meaning "authority to speak."
30 2*a* HEB Alas for the day!
  3*a* Ezek. 34:12; D&C 109:61.
  4*a* HEB Cush.
  5*a* Zeph. 2:12.

  b HEB Phut or Put.
  c Isa. 66:19; Jer. 46:9; Ezek. 27:10.
  6*a* HEB from Migdol to Syene.
  9*a* Isa. 20:4.

the terrible of the nations, shall be brought to destroy the land: and they shall draw their [a]swords against Egypt, and fill the land with the slain.

12 And I will make the rivers [a]dry, and sell the land into the hand of the wicked: and I will make the land waste, and all that is therein, by the hand of strangers: I the LORD have spoken *it*.

13 Thus saith the Lord GOD; I will also destroy the [a]idols, and I will cause *their* images to cease out of [b]Noph; and there shall be no more a [c]prince of the land of Egypt: and I will put a fear in the land of Egypt.

14 And I will make Pathros desolate, and will set fire in Zoan, and will execute judgments in [a]No.

15 And I will pour my fury upon Sin, the strength of Egypt; and I will cut off the multitude of No.

16 And I will set fire in Egypt: Sin shall have great pain, and No shall be rent asunder, and Noph *shall have* distresses daily.

17 The young men of Aven and of Pi-beseth shall fall by the sword: and these *cities* shall go into captivity.

18 At Tehaphnehes also the day shall be darkened, when I shall break there the yokes of Egypt: and the pomp of her strength shall cease in her: as for her, a cloud shall cover her, and her daughters shall go into captivity.

19 Thus will I execute judgments in Egypt: and they shall know that I *am* the LORD.

20 ¶ And it came to pass in the eleventh year, in the first *month*, in the seventh *day* of the month, *that* the word of the LORD came unto me, saying,

21 Son of man, I have broken the arm of Pharaoh king of Egypt; and, lo, it shall not be bound up to be healed, to put a [a]roller to bind it, to make it strong to hold the sword.

22 Therefore thus saith the Lord GOD; Behold, I *am* against Pharaoh king of Egypt, and will break his arms, the strong, and that which was broken; and I will cause the sword to fall out of his hand.

23 And I will [a]scatter the Egyptians among the nations, and will disperse them through the countries.

24 And I will strengthen the arms of the king of Babylon, and put my sword in his hand: but I will break Pharaoh's arms, and he shall groan before him with the groanings of a deadly wounded *man*.

25 But I will strengthen the arms of the king of Babylon, and the arms of Pharaoh shall fall down; and they shall know that I *am* the LORD, when I shall put my sword into the hand of the king of Babylon, and he shall stretch it out upon the land of Egypt.

26 And I will scatter the Egyptians among the nations, and disperse them among the countries; and they shall know that I *am* the LORD.

CHAPTER 31

Pharaoh's glory and fall are compared to that of the Assyrians.

AND it came to pass in the eleventh year, in the third *month*, in the first *day* of the month, *that* the word of the LORD came unto me, saying,

2 Son of man, speak unto Pharaoh king of [a]Egypt, and to his multitude; Whom art thou like in thy greatness?

3 ¶ Behold, the [a]Assyrian *was* a [b]cedar in Lebanon with fair branches, and with a shadowing shroud, and of an high stature; and his top was among the thick boughs.

4 The waters made him great, the deep set him up on high with her rivers running round about his plants, and sent out her little rivers unto all the trees of the field.

---

11 *a* Ezek. 28:7.
12 *a* Isa. 19:5; Jer. 51:36.
13 *a* Jer. 43:12.
  b IE Memphis.
  c Zech. 10:11.

14 *a* IE Thebes.
  Jer. 46:25;
  Nahum 3:8.
21 *a* HEB bandage.
23 *a* Jer. 46:19;

Ezek. 29:12.
31 2 *a* Isa. 19:1;
  Ezek. 32:2.
3 *a* Isa. 10:5.
  b Isa. 2:13.

5 Therefore his height was exalted above all the trees of the field, and his boughs were multiplied, and his branches became long because of the multitude of waters, when he shot forth.

6 All the fowls of heaven made their nests in his boughs, and under his branches did all the beasts of the field bring forth their young, and under his shadow dwelt all great nations.

7 Thus was he fair in his greatness, in the length of his branches: for his root was by great waters.

8 The cedars in the garden of God could not hide him: the fir trees were not like his boughs, and the chestnut trees were not like his branches; nor any tree in the garden of God was like unto him in his beauty.

9 I have made him fair by the multitude of his branches: so that all the trees of *a*Eden, that *were* in the garden of God, envied him.

10 ¶ Therefore thus saith the Lord GOD; Because thou hast lifted up thyself in height, and he hath shot up his top among the thick boughs, and his *a*heart is lifted up in his height;

11 I have therefore delivered him into the hand of the mighty one of the heathen; he shall surely deal with him: I have driven him out for his wickedness.

12 And strangers, the terrible of the nations, have cut him off, and have left him: upon the mountains and in all the valleys his branches are fallen, and his boughs are broken by all the rivers of the land; and all the people of the earth are gone down from his shadow, and have left him.

13 Upon his ruin shall all the fowls of the heaven remain, and all the beasts of the field shall be upon his branches:

14 To the end that none of all the trees by the waters exalt themselves for their height, neither shoot up their top among the thick boughs, neither their trees stand up in their height, all that drink water: for they are all delivered unto death, to *a*the nether parts of the earth, in the midst of the children of men, with them that go down to the pit.

15 Thus saith the Lord GOD; In the day when he went down to the grave I caused a mourning: I covered the deep for him, and I restrained the floods thereof, and the great waters were stayed: and I caused Lebanon to mourn for him, and all the trees of the field fainted for him.

16 I made the nations to shake at the sound of his fall, when I cast him down to hell with them that descend into the pit: and all the trees of Eden, the choice and best of Lebanon, all that drink water, shall be comforted in the nether parts of the earth.

17 They also went down into hell with him unto *them that be* slain with the sword; and *they that were* his arm, *that* dwelt under his shadow in the midst of the heathen.

18 ¶ To whom art thou thus like in glory and in greatness among the trees of Eden? yet shalt thou be brought down with the trees of Eden unto the nether parts of the earth: thou shalt lie in the midst of the uncircumcised with *them that be* slain by the sword. This *is* Pharaoh and all his multitude, saith the Lord GOD.

CHAPTER 32

Ezekiel laments for the fearful fall of Pharaoh and of Egypt.

AND it came to pass in the twelfth year, in the twelfth month, in the first *day* of the month, *that* the word of the LORD came unto me, saying,

2 Son of man, take up a lamentation for Pharaoh king of *a*Egypt, and say unto him, Thou art like a young lion of the nations, and thou *art* as a

---

9*a* Ezek. 28:13.
10*a* Isa. 14:13 (13–15);
    Ezek. 28:17.

14*a* HEB the earth
    underneath; i.e., the
    grave.

32 2*a* Isa. 19:1;
    Ezek. 31:2.

*b*whale in the seas: and thou camest forth with thy rivers, and troubledst the waters with thy feet, and *c*fouledst their rivers.

3 Thus saith the Lord GOD; I will therefore *a*spread out my net over thee with a company of many people; and they shall bring thee up in my net.

4 Then will I leave thee upon the land, I will cast thee forth upon the open field, and will cause all the fowls of the heaven to remain upon thee, and I will fill the beasts of the whole earth with thee.

5 And I will lay thy flesh upon the mountains, and fill the valleys with thy *a*height.

6 *a*I will also water with thy blood the land wherein thou swimmest, *even* to the mountains; and the rivers shall be full of thee.

7 And when I shall *a*put thee out, I will *b*cover the heaven, and make the *c*stars thereof dark; I will cover the sun with a cloud, and the moon shall not give her light.

8 All the bright lights of heaven will I make dark over thee, and set darkness upon thy land, saith the Lord GOD.

9 I will also *a*vex the hearts of many people, when I shall bring thy destruction among the nations, into the countries which thou hast not known.

10 Yea, I will make many people amazed at thee, and their kings shall be horribly afraid for thee, when I shall brandish my sword before them; and they shall tremble at *every* moment, every man for his own life, in the day of thy fall.

11 ¶ For thus saith the Lord GOD; The sword of the king of Babylon shall come upon thee.

12 By the swords of the mighty will I cause thy multitude to fall, the terrible of the nations, all of them: and they shall spoil the pomp of Egypt, and all the multitude thereof shall be destroyed.

13 I will destroy also all the beasts thereof from beside the great waters; neither shall the foot of man trouble them any more, nor the hoofs of beasts trouble them.

14 Then will I make their waters deep, and cause their rivers to run like oil, saith the Lord GOD.

15 When I shall make the land of Egypt desolate, and the country shall be destitute of that whereof it was full, when I shall smite all them that dwell therein, then shall they know that I *am* the LORD.

16 This *is* the lamentation wherewith they shall lament her: the daughters of the nations shall lament her: they shall lament for her, *even* for Egypt, and for all her multitude, saith the Lord GOD.

17 ¶ It came to pass also in the twelfth year, in the fifteenth *day* of the month, *that* the word of the LORD came unto me, saying,

18 Son of man, wail for the multitude of Egypt, and cast them down, *even* her, and the daughters of the famous nations, unto the *a*nether parts of the earth, with *them* that go down into the pit.

19 Whom dost thou pass in beauty? go down, and be thou laid with the uncircumcised.

20 They shall fall in the midst of *them that are* slain by the sword: she is delivered to the sword: draw her and all her multitudes.

21 The strong among the mighty shall speak to him out of the midst of *a*hell with them that help him: they are gone down, they lie uncircumcised, slain by the sword.

22 Asshur *is* there and all her company: his graves *are* about him: all of them slain, fallen by the sword:

23 Whose graves are set in the sides of the pit, and her company is round about her grave: all of them slain,

---

2*b* HEB monster.
   c TG Pollution.
3*a* Ezek. 12:13.
5*a* IE heaps of corpses.
6*a* IE I will irrigate the

land of your flood
plains with your blood.
7*a* HEB extinguish thee.
   b Isa. 13:10;
   Joel 2:10;

Matt. 24:29.
   c JS—M 1:33.
9*a* JS—M 1:8.
18*a* TG Spirits in Prison.
21*a* TG Hell.

fallen by the sword, which caused terror in the land of the living.

24 There *is* [a]Elam and all her multitude round about her grave, all of them slain, fallen by the sword, which are gone down uncircumcised into the nether parts of the earth, which caused their terror in the land of the living; yet have they borne their [b]shame with them that go down to the pit.

25 They have set her a bed in the midst of the slain with all her multitude: her graves *are* round about him: all of them uncircumcised, slain by the sword: though their terror was caused in the land of the living, yet have they borne their shame with them that go down to the pit: he is put in the midst of *them that be* slain.

26 There *is* Meshech, Tubal, and all her multitude: her graves *are* round about him: all of them uncircumcised, slain by the sword, though they caused their terror in the land of the living.

27 And they shall not lie with the [a]mighty *that are* fallen of the uncircumcised, which are gone down to hell with their weapons of war: and they have laid their swords under their heads, but their [b]iniquities shall be upon their bones, though *they were* the terror of the mighty in the land of the living.

28 Yea, thou shalt be broken in the midst of the uncircumcised, and shalt lie with *them that are* slain with the sword.

29 There *is* Edom, her kings, and all her princes, which with their might are laid by *them that were* slain by the sword: they shall lie with the uncircumcised, and with them that go down to the pit.

30 There *be* the princes of the north, all of them, and all the Zidonians, which are gone down with the slain; with their terror they are ashamed of their might; and they lie uncir-

cumcised with *them that be* slain by the sword, and bear their shame with them that go down to the pit.

31 Pharaoh shall see them, and shall be comforted over all his multitude, *even* Pharaoh and all his army slain by the sword, saith the Lord GOD.

32 For I have caused my terror in the land of the living: and he shall be laid in the midst of the uncircumcised with *them that are* slain with the sword, *even* Pharaoh and all his multitude, saith the Lord GOD.

CHAPTER 33

Watchmen who raise the warning voice save their own souls—Repentant sinners are saved—The righteous who turn to sin are damned—The people of Judah in Jerusalem are destroyed because of their sins.

AGAIN the word of the LORD came unto me, saying,

2 Son of man, speak to the children of thy people, and say unto them, When I bring the sword upon a land, if the people of the land take a man of their coasts, and set him for their [a]watchman:

3 If when he seeth the sword come upon the land, he blow the trumpet, and [a]warn the people;

4 Then whosoever heareth the sound of the trumpet, and taketh not warning; if the sword come, and take him away, his [a]blood shall be upon his [b]own head.

5 He heard the sound of the trumpet, and took not warning; his blood shall be upon him. But he that taketh warning shall deliver his soul.

6 But if the watchman see the sword come, and blow not the trumpet, and the people be not [a]warned; if the sword come, and take *any* person from among them, he is taken away in his iniquity; but his blood will I [b]require at the watchman's hand.

24a Jer. 49:34 (34–39).
  b Ezek. 34:29; 36:6.
27a Isa. 14:18 (18–19).
  b Gal. 6:7.

33 2a 3 Ne. 16:18;
       D&C 101:45 (45, 53–54).
   3a TG Warn.
   4a Ezek. 18:13;

Acts 18:6.
  b TG Accountability.
6a D&C 88:81 (81–82).
  b TG Accountability.

7 ¶ So thou, O son of man, I have set thee a ᵃwatchman unto the house of Israel; therefore thou shalt hear the word at my mouth, and warn them from me.

8 When I say unto the wicked, O wicked *man*, thou shalt surely die; if thou dost not speak to warn the wicked from his way, that wicked *man* shall die in his iniquity; but his blood will I require at thine hand.

9 Nevertheless, if thou ᵃwarn the wicked of his way to turn from it; if he do not turn from his way, he shall die in his ᵇiniquity; but thou hast delivered thy soul.

10 Therefore, O thou son of man, speak unto the house of Israel; Thus ye speak, saying, If our transgressions and our sins *be* upon us, and we pine away in them, how should we then live?

11 Say unto them, *As* I live, saith the Lord GOD, I have no ᵃpleasure in the ᵇdeath of the wicked; but that the wicked turn from his way and live: turn ye, turn ye from your evil ways; for why will ye ᶜdie, O house of Israel?

12 Therefore, thou son of man, say unto the children of thy people, The righteousness of the righteous shall not deliver him in the day of his ᵃtransgression: as for the wickedness of the wicked, he shall not fall thereby in the day that he turneth from his wickedness; neither shall the righteous be able to live for his *righteousness* in the day that he sinneth.

13 When I shall say to the righteous, *that* he shall surely live; if he ᵃtrust to his own righteousness, and commit ᵇiniquity, all his righ-teousnesses shall not be remembered; but for his iniquity that he hath committed, he shall die for it.

14 Again, when I say unto the wicked, Thou shalt surely ᵃdie; if he ᵇturn from his sin, and do that which is lawful and right;

15 *If* the wicked ᵃrestore the ᵇpledge, give again that he had robbed, walk in the ᶜstatutes of life, without committing iniquity; he shall surely live, he shall not die.

16 None of his ᵃsins that he hath committed shall be mentioned unto him: he hath done that which is lawful and right; he shall surely live.

17 ¶ Yet the children of thy people say, The ᵃway of the Lord is not ᵇequal: but as for them, their way is not ᶜequal.

18 When the righteous ᵃturneth from his ᵇrighteousness, and committeth iniquity, he shall even die thereby.

19 But if the wicked turn from his wickedness, and do that which is lawful and right, he shall live thereby.

20 ¶ Yet ye say, The way of the Lord is not equal. O ye house of Israel, I will ᵃjudge you every one after his ways.

21 ¶ And it came to pass in the ᵃtwelfth year of our captivity, in the tenth *month*, in the fifth *day* of the month, *that* one that had ᵇescaped out of Jerusalem came unto me, saying, The ᶜcity is smitten.

22 Now the ᵃhand of the LORD was upon me in the evening, afore he that was escaped came; and had opened my mouth, until he came to me in the morning; and my mouth was opened, and I was no more ᵇdumb.

7a TG Leadership; Watchman.
9a TG Priesthood, Magnifying Callings within; Prophets, Mission of.
  b 1 Ne. 10:21.
11a Ezek. 18:23; Mosiah 26:30; 29:20; Moses 7:39.
  b TG God, Mercy of.
  c Ezek. 18:31.
12a Ezek. 3:20; 18:24.

13a TG Trustworthiness.
  b TG Apostasy of Individuals.
14a Ezek. 3:18.
  b Ezek. 18:27.
15a TG Reconciliation; Repent.
  b Ezek. 18:7.
  c Lev. 18:5.
16a TG Forgive.
17a Ezek. 18:25 (25, 27).
  b HEB right or just.

c TG Justice.
18a TG Apostasy of Individuals.
  b TG Righteousness.
20a Ezek. 18:30; 1 Ne. 10:20.
21a Ezek. 1:2; 20:1; 24:1; 26:1.
  b Ezek. 24:26.
  c TG Jerusalem.
22a Ezek. 1:3.
  b Ezek. 24:27.

23 Then the word of the LORD came unto me, saying,

24 Son of man, they that inhabit those ªwastes of the land of Israel speak, saying, Abraham was one, and he inherited the land: but we *are* many; the land is given us for inheritance.

25 Wherefore say unto them, Thus saith the Lord GOD; Ye eat with the ªblood, and lift up your eyes toward your idols, and shed blood: and shall ye possess the land?

26 Ye ªstand upon your sword, ye work abomination, and ye defile every one his neighbour's wife: and shall ye possess the land?

27 Say thou thus unto them, Thus saith the Lord GOD; *As* I live, surely they that *are* in the wastes shall fall by the ªsword, and him that *is* in the open field will I give to the beasts to be devoured, and they that *be* in the forts and in the caves shall die of the pestilence.

28 For I will lay the land most desolate, and the pomp of her strength shall cease; and the mountains of Israel shall be desolate, that none shall pass through.

29 Then shall they know that I *am* the LORD, when I have laid the land most desolate because of all their abominations which they have committed.

30 ¶ Also, thou son of man, the children of thy people still are talking against thee by the walls and in the doors of the houses, and speak one to another, every one to his brother, saying, Come, I pray you, and hear what is the word that cometh forth from the LORD.

31 And they come unto thee as the people cometh, and they sit before thee *as* my people, and they ªhear thy words, but they will not do them: for with their ᵇmouth they shew much love, *but* their heart goeth after their ᶜcovetousness.

32 And, lo, thou *art* unto them as a very lovely song of one that hath a pleasant voice, and can play well on an instrument: for they hear thy words, but they do them not.

33 And ªwhen this cometh to pass, (lo, it will come,) then shall they know that a prophet hath been among them.

CHAPTER 34

The Lord reproves those shepherds who do not feed the flock—In the last days, the Lord will gather the lost sheep of Israel—The Messiah will be their Shepherd—The Lord will make His gospel covenant with them.

AND the word of the LORD came unto me, saying,

2 Son of man, prophesy against the shepherds of Israel, prophesy, and say unto them, Thus saith the Lord GOD unto the shepherds; Woe *be* to the ªshepherds of Israel that do feed themselves! should not the shepherds ᵇfeed the flocks?

3 Ye eat the ªfat, and ye clothe you with the wool, ye kill them that are fed: *but* ye feed not the flock.

4 The diseased have ye not strengthened, neither have ye healed that which was ªsick, neither have ye bound up *that which was* broken, neither have ye brought again that which was driven away, neither have ye sought that which was lost; but with force and with ᵇcruelty have ye ruled them.

5 And they were scattered, because *there is* no shepherd: and they became meat to all the beasts of the field, when they were scattered.

6 My ªsheep wandered through all the mountains, and upon every high hill: yea, my flock was scattered

---

24a Ezek. 36:4.
25a TG Blood, Eating of.
26a IE resort to violence.
27a Ezek. 5:17; 14:21;
    Rev. 6:8.
31a Matt. 11:15;
    Heb. 5:11 (11–14);
    2 Ne. 9:31;

D&C 1:14.
  b Isa. 29:13;
    Matt. 15:8 (7–8);
    Luke 6:46;
    Alma 34:28; JS—H 1:19.
  c Ps. 119:36;
    Isa. 57:17.
33a Ezek. 2:5.

34 2a Isa. 56:11.
    TG Shepherd.
  b TG Priesthood, Magnifying Callings within.
3a 2 Ne. 26:29.
4a TG Sickness.
  b TG Cruelty.
6a TG Sheep.

upon all the face of the earth, and none did search or seek *after them.*

7 ¶ Therefore, ye shepherds, hear the word of the Lord;

8 *As* I live, saith the Lord God, surely because my flock became a prey, and my flock became meat to every beast of the field, because *there was* no shepherd, neither did my shepherds search for my flock, but the *a*shepherds *b*fed themselves, and fed not my flock;

9 Therefore, O ye shepherds, hear the word of the Lord;

10 Thus saith the Lord God; Behold, I *am* against the shepherds; and I will *a*require my flock at their hand, and cause them to *b*cease from feeding the flock; neither shall the shepherds feed themselves any more; for I will deliver my flock from their mouth, that they may not be meat for them.

11 ¶ For thus saith the Lord God; Behold, I, *even* I, will both *a*search my sheep, and seek them out.

12 As a *a*shepherd seeketh out his flock in the day that he is among his sheep *that are* scattered; so will I *b*seek out my *c*sheep, and will deliver them out of all places where they have been *d*scattered in the *e*cloudy and *f*dark day.

13 And I will *a*bring them out from the people, and *b*gather them from the countries, and will bring them to their own *c*land, and feed them upon the mountains of Israel by the rivers, and in all the inhabited places of the country.

14 I will feed them in a good pasture, and upon the high mountains of Israel shall their fold be: there shall they *a*lie in a good fold, and *in* a fat pasture shall they feed upon the mountains of Israel.

15 I will feed my flock, and I will cause them to lie down, saith the Lord God.

16 I will seek that which was *a*lost, and bring again that which was driven away, and will bind up *that which was* broken, and will strengthen that which was *b*sick: but I will destroy the *c*fat and the strong; I will feed them with *d*judgment.

17 And *as for* you, O my *a*flock, thus saith the Lord God; Behold, I *b*judge *c*between cattle and cattle, between the rams and the he goats.

18 *Seemeth it* a small thing unto you to have eaten up the good pasture, but ye must tread down with your feet the residue of your pastures? and to have drunk of the deep waters, but ye must *a*foul the residue with your feet?

19 And *as for* my flock, they eat that which ye have *a*trodden with your feet; and they drink that which ye have fouled with your feet.

20 ¶ Therefore thus saith the Lord God unto them; Behold, I, *even* I, will judge between the fat cattle and between the lean cattle.

21 Because ye have thrust with side and with shoulder, and pushed all the diseased with your horns, till ye have scattered them abroad;

22 Therefore will I save my *a*flock, and they shall no more be a prey; and I will judge between cattle and cattle.

23 And I will set up *a*one *b*shepherd over them, and he shall feed them, *even* my servant *c*David; he shall

---

8a TG Apostasy of Israel.
 b 2 Ne. 28:13 (9–16);
   Morm. 8:37 (37–41).
10a Jacob 1:19;
   D&C 72:3; 112:33.
 b D&C 107:100 (99–100).
11a TG Missionary Work.
12a TG Shepherd.
 b TG Israel, Gathering of.
 c TG Jesus Christ, Good
   Shepherd.
 d 2 Ne. 25:15 (11–19).
 e Ezek. 30:3.

 f Joel 2:2;
   Matt. 24:29.
13a Ezek. 38:8.
   TG Millennium,
   Preparing a People for.
 b D&C 33:6 (3–7).
 c Deut. 18:9.
14a Jer. 33:12.
16a Luke 15:4; 19:10.
 b TG Sickness.
 c Isa. 10:16.
 d Jer. 10:24.
17a TG Sheep.

 b Ezek. 20:38.
 c HEB between sheep and
   sheep; i.e., between one
   sheep and another.
18a TG Pollution.
19a 1 Ne. 19:7.
22a 2 Ne. 25:16 (15–18).
23a Ezek. 37:22.
 b Isa. 55:4.
   TG Shepherd.
 c Ezek. 37:24.
   TG Millennium.

feed them, and he shall be their shepherd.

24 And I *the LORD will be their *God, and my servant *David a *prince among them; I the LORD have spoken *it.*

25 And I will make with them a *covenant of peace, and will cause the evil beasts to cease out of the land: and they shall dwell *safely in the wilderness, and sleep in the woods.

26 And I will make them and the places round about my hill a blessing; and I will cause the *shower to come down in his season; there shall be showers of *blessing.

27 And the tree of the field shall yield her fruit, and the *earth shall yield her increase, and they shall be *safe in their land, and shall know that I *am* the LORD, when I have broken the bands of their *yoke, and delivered them out of the hand of those that *served themselves of them.

28 And they shall no more be a prey to the heathen, neither shall the beast of the land devour them; but they shall dwell *safely, and none shall make *them* afraid.

29 And I will raise up for them a *plant of renown, and they shall be no more consumed with hunger in the land, neither bear the *shame of the heathen any more.

30 Thus shall they know that I the LORD their God *am* with them, and *that* they, *even* the house of Israel, *are* my people, saith the Lord GOD.

31 And ye my *flock, the flock of my pasture, *are* men, *and* I *am* your God, saith the Lord GOD.

CHAPTER 35

Judgment will fall upon Mount Seir and all Idumea for their hatred of Israel.

MOREOVER the word of the LORD came unto me, saying,

2 Son of man, set thy *face against mount *Scir, and prophesy against it,

3 And say unto it, Thus saith the Lord GOD; Behold, O mount Seir, I *am* against thee, and I will stretch out mine hand against thee, and I will make thee most desolate.

4 I will lay thy cities waste, and thou shalt be desolate, and thou shalt know that I *am* the LORD.

5 Because thou hast had a perpetual *hatred, and hast shed *the blood of* the children of Israel by the force of the sword in the time of their calamity, in the time *that their* iniquity *had* an end:

6 Therefore, *as* I live, saith the Lord GOD, I will prepare thee unto blood, and blood shall pursue thee: *sith thou hast not hated blood, even blood shall pursue thee.

7 Thus will I make mount Seir most desolate, and cut off from it him that passeth out and him that returneth.

8 And I will fill his mountains with his *slain *men:* in thy hills, and in thy valleys, and in all thy *rivers, shall they fall that are slain with the sword.

9 I will make thee perpetual desolations, and thy *cities shall not return: and ye shall know that I *am* the LORD.

10 Because thou hast said, These two nations and these two countries shall be mine, and we will *possess it; whereas the LORD was there:

24*a* HEB Jehovah.
 b Ex. 29:45 (45–46);
  Lev. 26:12 (11–13);
  Ezek. 37:27 (22–28).
 c Jer. 23:5 (5–6); 30:9;
  Hosea 3:5.
 d Ezek. 37:25 (24–25); 44:3.
25*a* Ezek. 37:26.
 b Ezek. 38:8;
  D&C 45:68 (68–70).
26*a* Ps. 68:9;
  Ezek. 22:24.

 b TG Israel, Blessings of.
27*a* TG Earth, Destiny of.
 b Ps. 119:117.
 c TG Bondage, Physical;
  Bondage, Spiritual.
 d HEB enslaved them.
28*a* Ezek. 28:26.
29*a* Isa. 61:3.
 b Ezek. 32:24; 36:6.
  TG Shame.
31*a* TG Sheep.
35 2*a* Ezek. 6:2.

 b Gen. 32:3; 36:8 (8–9);
  Deut. 2:1;
  Isa. 21:11;
  Ezek. 25:8.
 5*a* Ps. 137:7;
  Ezek. 36:2 (1–7);
  Obad. 1:11 (10–11).
 6*a* OR since.
 8*a* Ether 14:21 (21–22).
 b HEB ravines.
 9*a* Jer. 49:13.
10*a* Ezek. 36:2 (1–7).

11 Therefore, *as* I live, saith the Lord GOD, I will even do according to thine anger, and according to thine envy which thou hast used out of thy hatred against them; and I will make myself known among them, when I have judged thee.

12 And thou shalt know that I *am* the LORD, *and that* I have heard all thy [a]blasphemies which thou hast spoken against the mountains of Israel, saying, They are laid desolate, they are given us to consume.

13 Thus with your mouth ye have [a]boasted against me, and have multiplied your words against me: I have heard *them.*

14 Thus saith the Lord GOD; When the whole earth rejoiceth, I will make thee desolate.

15 As thou didst rejoice at the inheritance of the house of Israel, because it was desolate, so will I [a]do unto thee: thou shalt be desolate, O mount Seir, and all [b]Idumea, *even* all of it: and they shall know that I *am* the LORD.

CHAPTER 36

In the last days, all the house of Israel will be gathered to their own lands— The Lord will give them a new heart and a new spirit—They will have His gospel law.

ALSO, thou son of man, prophesy unto the [a]mountains of Israel, and say, Ye mountains of Israel, hear the word of the LORD:

2 Thus saith the Lord GOD; Because the [a]enemy hath said against you, Aha, even the ancient high places are ours in [b]possession:

3 Therefore prophesy and say, Thus saith the Lord GOD; Because they have made *you* desolate, and swallowed you up on every side, that ye might be a possession unto the residue of the heathen, and ye are taken up in the lips of talkers, and *are* an infamy of the people:

4 Therefore, ye mountains of Israel, hear the word of the Lord GOD; Thus saith the Lord GOD to the mountains, and to the hills, to the [a]rivers, and to the valleys, to the desolate [b]wastes, and to the cities that are forsaken, which became a prey and [c]derision to the residue of the heathen that *are* round about;

5 Therefore thus saith the Lord GOD; Surely in the fire of my [a]jealousy have I spoken against the residue of the heathen, and against all [b]Idumea, which have appointed my land into their possession with the joy of all *their* heart, with despiteful minds, to cast it out for a prey.

6 Prophesy therefore concerning the land of Israel, and say unto the mountains, and to the hills, to the rivers, and to the valleys, Thus saith the Lord GOD; Behold, I have spoken in my jealousy and in my fury, because ye have borne the [a]shame of the heathen:

7 Therefore thus saith the Lord GOD; I have lifted up mine hand, Surely the heathen that *are* about you, they shall bear their shame.

8 ¶ But ye, O mountains of Israel, ye shall shoot forth your [a]branches, and yield your fruit to my people of Israel; for they are [b]at hand to come.

9 For, behold, I *am* for you, and I will [a]turn unto you, and ye shall be tilled and sown:

10 And I will multiply men upon you, all the house of Israel, *even* all of it: and the cities shall be [a]inhabited, and the [b]wastes shall be [c]builded:

11 And I will multiply upon you man and beast; and they shall increase and bring fruit: and I will

---

12*a* TG Blaspheme.
13*a* Hel. 4:13.
15*a* Obad. 1:15.
  b TG World, End of.
36 1*a* Ezek. 6:2.
 2*a* Ezek. 35:5.
  b Ezek. 35:10.

4*a* HEB ravines.
 b Ezek. 33:24.
 c Ps. 44:13.
5*a* Deut. 4:24.
 b HEB Edom.
6*a* Ezek. 32:24; 34:29.
8*a* Jacob 5:3 (3–77).

 b Isa. 56:1;
  D&C 4:4 (1–7).
9*a* D&C 88:63 (63–64).
10*a* Zech. 2:4.
  b Amos 9:14.
  c Isa. 61:4.

settle you after your old ªestates, and will do better *unto you* than at your beginnings: and ye shall know that I *am* the LORD.

12 Yea, I will cause men to walk upon you, *even* my people Israel; and they shall ªpossess thee, and thou shalt be their inheritance, and thou shalt no more henceforth bereave them *of men.*

13 Thus saith the Lord GOD; Because they say unto you, Thou *land* devourest up men, and hast ªbereaved thy nations;

14 Therefore thou shalt devour men no more, neither bereave thy nations any more, saith the Lord GOD.

15 Neither will I cause *men* to hear in thee the shame of the heathen any more, neither shalt thou bear the reproach of the people any more, neither shalt thou cause thy nations to fall any more, saith the Lord GOD.

16 ¶ Moreover the word of the LORD came unto me, saying,

17 Son of man, when the house of Israel dwelt in their own land, they ªdefiled it by their own way and by their doings: their way was before me as the ᵇuncleanness of a removed woman.

18 Wherefore I poured my fury upon them for the blood that they had ªshed upon the land, and for their ᵇidols *wherewith* they had ᶜpolluted it:

19 And I ªscattered them among the ᵇheathen, and they were ᶜdispersed through the countries: according to their way and ᵈaccording to their doings I judged them.

20 And when they entered unto the heathen, whither they went, they ªprofaned my holy name, when they said to them, These *are* the people of the LORD, and are gone forth ᵇout of his land.

21 ¶ But I had ªpity for mine holy ᵇname, which the house of Israel had profaned among the heathen, whither they went.

22 Therefore say unto the house of Israel, Thus saith the Lord GOD; I do not *this* for your ªsakes, O house of Israel, but for mine holy ᵇname's sake, which ye have profaned among the heathen, whither ye went.

23 And I will sanctify my great name, which was profaned among the ªheathen, which ye have profaned in the midst of them; and the heathen shall know that I *am* the LORD, saith the Lord GOD, when I shall be ᵇsanctified in you before their eyes.

24 For I will take you from among the heathen, and ªgather you out of all countries, and will bring you into your own ᵇland.

25 ¶ Then will I ªsprinkle clean water upon you, and ye shall be clean: from all your ᵇfilthiness, and from all your ᶜidols, will I cleanse you.

26 A ªnew ᵇheart also will I ᶜgive you, and a new ᵈspirit will I put within you: and I will take away the stony ᵉheart out of your flesh, and I will give you an heart of flesh.

27 And I will put my ªspirit within you, and cause you to walk in my statutes, and ye shall keep my judgments, and do *them.*

28 And ye shall dwell in the ªland that I gave to your fathers; and ye shall be my people, and I will be your God.

11a Ezek. 16:55.
12a 1 Ne. 10:3.
13a Jer. 15:7;
   Ezek. 5:17.
17a Lev. 18:25;
   2 Ne. 13:8; 25:14.
 b Ezek. 22:10.
18a Ezek. 22:3.
 b 2 Ne. 20:11.
 c Ezek. 16:36.
19a Hel. 3:16.
 b TG Heathen.
 c Jer. 25:34.

 d Ezek. 39:24.
20a TG Blaspheme.
 b JST Ezek. 36:20 . . . out
   of *this* land.
21a HEB concern.
 b Ezek. 20:9.
22a Deut. 9:5.
 b Ps. 106:8.
23a TG Conversion.
 b TG Sanctification.
24a TG Israel, Gathering of.
 b TG Israel, Land of.
25a Isa. 52:15; 3 Ne. 20:45.

 b TG Filthiness.
 c Ezek. 37:23.
26a TG Man, New,
   Spiritually Reborn.
 b 3 Ne. 10:6.
 c TG God, Gifts of.
 d TG Spirituality.
 e TG Conversion.
27a Isa. 44:3; Acts 2:17;
   D&C 46:28 (28, 30);
   84:46; 95:4.
28a Ezek. 28:25;
   37:12 (12–13), 25.

29 I will also save you from all your uncleannesses: and I will ^acall for the corn, and will increase it, and lay no famine upon you.

30 And I will multiply the fruit of the tree, and the increase of the field, that ye shall receive no more reproach of famine among the heathen.

31 Then shall ye ^aremember your own evil ways, and your doings that *were* not good, and shall lothe yourselves in your own sight for your ^biniquities and for your abominations.

32 Not for your sakes do I *this*, saith the Lord God, be it known unto you: be ashamed and confounded for your own ways, O house of Israel.

33 Thus saith the Lord God; In the day that I shall have cleansed you from all your iniquities I will also cause *you* to dwell in the cities, and the wastes shall be builded.

34 And the ^adesolate land shall be ^btilled, whereas it lay desolate in the sight of all that passed by.

35 And they shall say, This land that was desolate is become like the ^agarden of Eden; and the waste and desolate and ruined cities *are* become ^bfenced, *and* are inhabited.

36 Then the heathen that are left round about you shall know that I the Lord ^abuild the ruined *places, and* plant that that was desolate: I the Lord have spoken *it*, and I will ^bdo *it*.

37 Thus saith the Lord God; I will yet *for* this be ^ainquired of by the house of Israel, to do *it* for them; I will increase them with men like a flock.

38 As the ^aholy flock, as the flock of Jerusalem in her solemn feasts; so shall the waste cities be filled with flocks of men: and they shall know that I *am* the Lord.

CHAPTER 37

Ezekiel is shown the valley of dry bones—Israel will inherit the land in the Resurrection—The stick of Judah (the Bible) and the stick of Joseph (the Book of Mormon) will become one in the Lord's hand—The children of Israel will be gathered and cleansed—David (the Messiah) will reign over them—They will receive the everlasting gospel covenant.

THE ^ahand of the Lord was upon me, and ^bcarried me out in the ^cspirit of the Lord, and set me down in the midst of the valley which *was* full of bones,

2 And caused me to pass by them round about: and, behold, *there were* very many in the open valley; and, lo, *they were* very dry.

3 And he said unto me, Son of man, can these bones ^alive? And I answered, O Lord God, thou knowest.

4 Again he said unto me, Prophesy upon these bones, and say unto them, O ye dry bones, hear the word of the Lord.

5 Thus saith the Lord God unto these bones; Behold, I will cause ^abreath to enter into you, and ye shall live:

6 And I will lay sinews upon you, and will bring up flesh upon you, and cover you with skin, and put breath in you, and ye shall live; and ye shall know that I *am* the Lord.

7 So I prophesied as I was commanded: and as I prophesied, there was a noise, and behold a shaking, and the bones came together, ^abone to his bone.

8 And when I beheld, lo, the sinews and the flesh came up upon them, and the skin covered them above: but *there was* no breath in them.

9 Then said he unto me, Prophesy unto the ^awind, prophesy, son of man, and say to the wind, Thus saith

---

29a HEB summon the grain.
31a Ezek. 16:61.
  b Ezek. 6:9.
34a Isa. 35:1.
  b Isa. 61:4 (4–6).
35a Isa. 51:3.
  TG Millennium.
  b OR fortified.

36a Ps. 126:2;
    Ezek. 17:24.
  b D&C 62:6.
37a Ps. 102:17; Jer. 29:13;
    Ezek. 14:3;
    3 Ne. 13:8.
38a HEB flock for sacrifices.
37 1a Ezek. 1:3.

  b 1 Kgs. 18:12;
    Luke 4:1.
  c TG God, Spirit of.
3a OR resurrect.
5a TG Breath of Life.
7a D&C 138:17 (11–17, 43).
9a HEB spirit, breath, or wind.

the Lord GOD; Come from the four ^bwinds, O breath, and breathe upon these slain, that they may live.

10 So I prophesied as he commanded me, and the ^abreath came into them, and they lived, and stood up upon their feet, an exceeding great army.

11 ¶ Then he said unto me, Son of man, these bones are the whole house of Israel: behold, they say, Our bones are dried, and our hope is ^alost: we are cut off for our parts.

12 Therefore prophesy and say unto them, Thus saith the Lord GOD; Behold, O my people, I will open your ^agraves, and cause you to ^bcome up out of your graves, and ^cbring you into the ^dland of Israel.

13 And ye shall know that I *am* the LORD, when I have opened your graves, O my people, and brought you up out of your graves,

14 And shall put my ^aspirit in you, and ye shall live, and I shall place you in your own land: then shall ye know that I the LORD have spoken *it*, and performed *it*, saith the LORD.

15 ¶ The word of the LORD came again unto me, saying,

16 Moreover, thou son of man, take thee one ^astick, and ^bwrite upon it, For ^cJudah, and for the children of Israel his companions: then take another stick, and ^dwrite upon it, For ^eJoseph, the ^fstick of Ephraim, and *for* all the house of Israel his companions:

17 And join them one to another

into one stick; and they shall become ^aone in thine hand.

18 ¶ And when the children of thy people shall speak unto thee, saying, Wilt thou not shew us ^awhat thou *meanest* by these?

19 Say unto them, Thus saith the Lord GOD; Behold, I will take the stick of ^aJoseph, which *is* in the hand of Ephraim, and the tribes of Israel his fellows, and will put them with him, *even* with the stick of Judah, and make them one stick, and they shall be one in mine hand.

20 ¶ And the sticks whereon thou writest shall be in thine hand before their eyes.

21 And say unto them, Thus saith the Lord GOD; Behold, I will take the children of Israel from among the ^aheathen, whither they be gone, and will ^bgather them on every side, and bring them into their own land:

22 And I will make them ^aone ^bnation in the land upon the mountains of Israel; and ^cone king shall be king to them all: and they shall be no more ^dtwo nations, neither shall they be divided into two kingdoms any more at all:

23 Neither shall they defile themselves any more with their ^aidols, nor with their detestable things, nor with any of their transgressions: but I will ^bsave them out of all their dwellingplaces, wherein they have sinned, and will ^ccleanse them: so shall they be my people, and I will be their God.

24 And ^aDavid my servant *shall be*

9 b Dan. 11:4;
   Rev. 7:1.
10 a TG Breath of Life.
11 a Isa. 49:14.
12 a TG Jesus Christ,
     Prophecies about.
   b TG Resurrection.
   c TG Israel, Gathering of.
   d Ezek. 36:28 (24–28).
14 a Alma 40:23 (16–24);
     D&C 88:15 (15–17).
16 a HEB wood. Wooden
     writing tablets were in
     common use in Babylon
     in Ezekiel's day.
     Num. 17:2 (1–10).
     TG Scriptures to Come

   Forth.
   b TG Scriptures,
     Preservation of.
   c TG Israel, Judah,
     People of.
   d TG Scriptures,
     Writing of.
   e TG Israel, Joseph,
     People of.
   f D&C 27:5.
17 a 1 Ne. 13:41;
     2 Ne. 3:12.
18 a Ezek. 12:9; 24:19.
19 a TG Book of Mormon.
21 a HEB nations or Gentiles.
   b TG Israel, Gathering of.
22 a Jer. 50:4;

   John 10:16.
   TG Unity.
   b TG Israel, Restoration of.
   c Ezek. 34:23.
   d The tribes led by Judah
     and by Ephraim were
     historically adversaries
     (after events of 1 Kgs.
     12:16–20). In the latter
     days this enmity will be
     healed.
23 a Ezek. 36:25.
   b Zech. 9:16.
   c TG Purification.
24 a Jer. 30:9;
     Ezek. 34:23.

king over them; and they all shall have one [b]shepherd: they shall also walk in my judgments, and observe my statutes, and do them.

25 And they shall dwell in the [a]land that I have given unto Jacob my servant, wherein your fathers have dwelt; and they shall dwell therein, *even* they, and their children, and their children's children for [b]ever: and my servant David *shall be* their [c]prince for ever.

26 Moreover I will make a [a]covenant of peace with them; it shall be an [b]everlasting [c]covenant with them: and I will place them, and multiply them, and will set my [d]sanctuary in the midst of them for evermore.

27 My [a]tabernacle also shall be with them: yea, I will be their [b]God, and they shall be my people.

28 And the [a]heathen shall [b]know that I the Lord do [c]sanctify Israel, when my sanctuary shall be in the midst of them for evermore.

CHAPTER 38

The battle of Gog, from the land of Magog, against Israel will usher in the Second Coming—The Lord will come amid war and pestilence, and all men will shake at His presence.

And the word of the Lord came unto me, saying,

2 Son of man, set thy face against [a]Gog, the land of Magog, the chief prince of Meshech and Tubal, and prophesy against him,

3 And say, Thus saith the Lord God; Behold, I *am* against thee, O Gog, the chief prince of Meshech and Tubal:

4 And I will turn thee back, and put [a]hooks into thy jaws, and I will bring thee forth, and all thine army, horses and horsemen, all of them clothed with all sorts *of armour, even* a great company *with* bucklers and shields, all of them handling swords:

5 Persia, [a]Ethiopia, and Libya with them; all of them with shield and helmet:

6 [a]Gomer, and all his bands; the house of [b]Togarmah of the north quarters, and all his bands: *and* many people with thee.

7 Be thou prepared, and prepare for thyself, thou, and all thy company that are assembled unto thee, and be thou a guard unto them.

8 ¶ After many days thou shalt be [a]visited: in the latter years thou shalt come into the land *that is* brought back from the sword, *and is* [b]gathered out of many people, against the [c]mountains of Israel, which have been always waste: but it is brought forth out of the nations, and they shall dwell [d]safely all of them.

9 Thou shalt ascend and come like a [a]storm, thou shalt be like a [b]cloud to cover the land, thou, and all thy bands, and many people with thee.

10 Thus saith the Lord God; It shall also come to pass, *that* at the same time shall things come into thy [a]mind, and thou shalt think an evil thought:

11 And thou shalt say, I will go up to the land of unwalled villages; I will go to them that are at rest, that dwell safely, all of them dwelling without walls, and having neither bars nor gates,

12 To take a spoil, and to take a prey; to turn thine hand upon the desolate places *that are now*

24b TG Shepherd.
25a Ezek. 28:25; 36:28.
  b Isa. 60:21.
  c Ezek. 34:24; 44:3.
26a Ezek. 34:25.
  b TG New and Everlasting Covenant.
  c TG Restoration of the Gospel.
  d TG God, Presence of; Temple.

27a D&C 124:38 (37–40).
  b Ezek. 34:24 (20–31).
28a TG Heathen.
  b TG God, Knowledge about.
  c TG Sanctification.
38 2a Gen. 10:2 (2–3); Ezek. 27:13; 39:1; Rev. 20:8.
  4a Ezek. 29:4.
  5a HEB Cush and Phut.

6a Gen. 10:2 (2–3).
  b Gen. 10:3 (2–3); Ezek. 27:14.
8a OR mustered.
  b Ezek. 34:13.
  c D&C 133:13.
  d Ezek. 34:25.
9a Isa. 28:2.
  b Jer. 4:13.
10a TG Mind.

inhabited, and upon the people *that are* gathered out of the nations, which have gotten cattle and goods, that dwell in the midst of the land.

13 Sheba, and Dedan, and the merchants of ^aTarshish, with all the young lions thereof, shall say unto thee, Art thou come to take a spoil? hast thou gathered thy company to take a prey? to carry away silver and gold, to take away cattle and goods, to take a great spoil?

14 ¶ Therefore, son of man, prophesy and say unto Gog, Thus saith the Lord GOD; In that day when my people of Israel dwelleth safely, shalt thou not know *it*?

15 And thou shalt come from thy place out of the ^anorth parts, thou, and many people with thee, all of them riding upon horses, a great company, and a mighty army:

16 And thou shalt come up ^aagainst my people of Israel, as a cloud to cover the land; it shall be in the ^blatter days, and I will bring thee against my land, that the ^cheathen may know me, when I shall be sanctified ^din thee, O Gog, before their eyes.

17 Thus saith the Lord GOD; Art thou he of whom I have spoken in old time by my servants the prophets of Israel, which prophesied in those days *many* years that I would bring thee against them?

18 And it shall come to pass at the same time when Gog shall come against the land of Israel, saith the Lord GOD, *that* my ^afury shall come up in my face.

19 For in my jealousy *and* in the fire of my wrath have I spoken, Surely in that day there shall be a great ^ashaking in the land of Israel;

20 So that the fishes of the sea, and the fowls of the heaven, and the beasts of the field, and all creeping things that creep upon the earth, and all the men that *are* upon the face of the earth, shall shake at my presence, and the mountains shall be thrown down, and the steep places shall fall, and every wall shall fall to the ground.

21 And I will call for a sword against him throughout all my mountains, saith the Lord GOD: every man's sword shall be against his ^abrother.

22 And I will ^aplead against him with ^bpestilence and with blood; and I will rain upon him, and upon his bands, and upon the many people that *are* with him, an overflowing rain, and great ^chailstones, ^dfire, and brimstone.

23 Thus will I magnify myself, and ^asanctify myself; and I will be ^bknown in the eyes of many nations, and they shall know that I *am* the LORD.

CHAPTER 39

Gog and the land of Magog will be destroyed—For seven years the people in the cities of Israel will burn the weapons of war—For seven months they will bury the dead—Then will come the supper of the great God and the continued gathering of Israel.

THEREFORE, thou son of man, prophesy against ^aGog, and say, Thus saith the Lord GOD; Behold, I *am* against thee, O Gog, the chief prince of Meshech and Tubal:

2 And I will turn thee back, and leave but the sixth part of thee, and will cause thee to come up from the ^anorth parts, and will bring thee upon the mountains of Israel:

3 And I will ^asmite thy bow out of thy left hand, and will cause thine arrows to fall out of thy right hand.

4 Thou shalt fall upon the mountains of Israel, thou, and all thy bands, and the people that *is* with

---

13a 1 Kgs. 10:22;
    Ezek. 27:12.
15a Ezek. 39:2.
16a Luke 21:20 (20–24);
    Rev. 16:16.
  b Jer. 30:24.
  c TG Conversion.
  d HEB through thee.

18a Ezek. 5:13.
19a Hag. 2:6 (6–7).
21a Isa. 9:19.
22a Isa. 66:16; Jer. 25:31;
    Joel 3:2; Zech. 14:3.
  b TG Last Days.
  c Ex. 9:18 (13–35);
    Josh. 10:11; Rev. 16:21;

D&C 29:16.
  d Ezek. 39:6; D&C 29:21.
    TG World, End of.
23a TG Sanctification.
  b Ezek. 39:7.
39 1a Ezek. 38:2 (2–3).
  2a Ezek. 38:15.
  3a Joel 2:20; Zech. 12:9.

thee: I will give thee unto the ravenous birds of every sort, and *to* the beasts of the field to be devoured.

5 Thou shalt fall upon the open field: for I have spoken *it*, saith the Lord GOD.

6 And I will send a *ª*fire on Magog, and among them that dwell *ᵇ*carelessly in the *ᶜ*isles: and they shall know that I *am* the LORD.

7 So will I make my holy name *ª*known in the midst of my people Israel; and I will not *let them* *ᵇ*pollute my holy name any more: and the *ᶜ*heathen shall *ᵈ*know that I *am* the LORD, the Holy One in Israel.

8 ¶ Behold, it is come, and it is done, saith the Lord GOD; this *is* the day whereof I have spoken.

9 And they that dwell in the cities of Israel shall go forth, and shall set on fire and burn the weapons, both the shields and the bucklers, the bows and the arrows, and the handstaves, and the spears, and they shall burn them with fire seven years:

10 So that they shall take no wood out of the field, neither cut down *any* out of the forests; for they shall burn the weapons with fire: and they shall *ª*spoil those that spoiled them, and rob those that robbed them, saith the Lord GOD.

11 ¶ And it shall come to pass in that day, *that* I will give unto Gog a place there of graves in Israel, the valley of the *ª*passengers on the east of the sea: and it shall stop the *noses* of the passengers: and there shall they bury Gog and all his multitude: and they shall call *it* The valley of Hamon-gog.

12 And seven months shall the house of Israel be burying of them, that they may cleanse the land.

13 Yea, all the people of the land shall bury *them*; and it shall be to them *ª*a renown the day that I shall be glorified, saith the Lord GOD.

14 And they shall *ª*sever out men of continual employment, passing through the land to bury with the *ᵇ*passengers those that remain upon the face of the earth, to cleanse it: after the end of seven months shall they search.

15 And the passengers *that* pass through the land, when *any* seeth a man's bone, then shall he set up a sign by it, till the buriers have buried it in the valley of Hamon-gog.

16 And also the name of the city *shall be* Hamonah. Thus shall they cleanse the land.

17 ¶ And, thou son of man, thus saith the Lord GOD; Speak unto every feathered fowl, and to every *ª*beast of the field, Assemble yourselves, and come; gather yourselves on every side to my sacrifice that I do sacrifice for you, *even* a great sacrifice upon the mountains of Israel, that ye may eat flesh, and drink blood.

18 Ye shall eat the flesh of the mighty, and drink the blood of the princes of the earth, of rams, of lambs, and of goats, of bullocks, all of them fatlings of Bashan.

19 And ye shall eat fat till ye be full, and drink blood till ye be drunken, of my sacrifice which I have sacrificed for you.

20 Thus ye shall be filled at my table with horses and chariots, with mighty men, and with all men of war, saith the Lord GOD.

21 And I will set my glory among the *ª*heathen, and all the heathen shall see my judgment that I have executed, and my hand that I have laid upon them.

22 So the house of Israel shall know that I *am* the LORD their God from that day and forward.

6*a* Ezek. 38:22.
  b HEB securely, confidently, without care.
  c Ezek. 26:15;
     27:15 (3, 6–7, 15);
     2 Ne. 10:20.
7*a* TG God, Knowledge

about.
  b Ezek. 20:39; 43:7.
     TG Pollution.
  c TG Conversion.
  d Ezek. 38:23.
10*a* Isa. 14:2.
11*a* HEB travelers.

13*a* HEB a name; i.e.,
     famous.
14*a* HEB separate, set apart.
  b HEB travelers.
17*a* D&C 29:20 (17–20).
21*a* TG Conversion;
     Heathen.

23 ¶ And the *a*heathen shall know that the house of Israel went into captivity for their iniquity: because they trespassed against me, therefore *b*hid I my face from them, and gave them into the hand of their *c*enemies: so fell they all by the sword.

24 *a*According to their *b*uncleanness and according to their *c*transgressions have I done unto them, and hid my face from them.

25 Therefore thus saith the Lord GOD; Now will I *a*bring again the captivity of Jacob, and have mercy upon the whole house of *b*Israel, and will be jealous for my holy name;

26 After that they have borne their shame, and all their trespasses whereby they have trespassed against me, when they dwelt safely in their land, and none made *them* afraid.

27 When I have brought them again from the people, and *a*gathered them out of their enemies' lands, and am sanctified in them in the sight of many nations;

28 Then shall they know that I *am* the LORD their God, which caused them to be led into captivity among the heathen: but I have gathered them unto their own land, and have left none of them any more there.

29 Neither will I *a*hide my face any more from them: for I have *b*poured out my spirit upon the house of Israel, saith the Lord GOD.

CHAPTER 40

A heavenly messenger shows Ezekiel in vision a city where the temple is lo-cated—Ezekiel is shown the form and size of the temple and its courts.

IN the five and twentieth year of our captivity, in the beginning of the year, in the tenth *day* of the month, in the fourteenth year after that the city was smitten, in the selfsame day the *a*hand of the LORD was upon me, and brought me thither.

2 In the *a*visions of God brought he me into the land of Israel, and set me upon a very high *b*mountain, by which *was* as the frame of a city on the south.

3 And he brought me thither, and, behold, *there was* a man, whose appearance *was* like the appearance of *a*brass, with a line of flax in his hand, and a *b*measuring *c*reed; and he stood in the gate.

4 And the man said unto me, Son of man, behold with thine eyes, and hear with thine ears, and set thine *a*heart upon all that I shall shew thee; for to the intent that I might shew *them* unto thee *art* thou brought hither: *b*declare all that thou seest to the house of Israel.

5 And behold a wall on the outside of the *a*house round about, and in the man's hand a measuring reed of six *b*cubits *long c*by the cubit and an hand breadth: so he *d*measured the *e*breadth of the building, one reed; and the height, one reed.

6 ¶ Then came he unto the *a*gate which *b*looketh toward the east, and went up the stairs thereof, and measured the threshold of the gate, which *was* one reed broad; and the other threshold *of the gate, which was* one reed broad.

23a TG Conversion.
  b Deut. 31:17 (16–17).
  c Lev. 26:25.
24a Ezek. 36:19.
  b TG Uncleanness.
  c TG Transgress.
25a HEB restore Jacob from exile.
  b TG Israel, Twelve Tribes of.
27a TG Israel, Gathering of.
29a Isa. 54:8.
  b Zech. 12:10.
40 1a Ezek. 1:3.

2a Ezek. 1:1; 8:3.
  b Ezek. 43:12;
    Rev. 21:10;
    Moses 1:1.
3a Ezek. 1:7.
  b Ezek. 42:16 (16–19); 47:3;
    Rev. 11:1.
  c Ezek. 45:1.
4a D&C 8:2 (2–3).
  b Ezek. 43:10.
5a TG Temple.
  b Ezek. 41:8; 43:13.
  c IE six long cubits, of a cubit plus a

handbreadth each. Thus each would be about 21 inches or 53 centimeters; and the total length of the measuring reed is about 10½ feet or 3.2 meters.
  d Ezek. 42:20.
  e Rev. 21:16.
6a Ezek. 42:15; 43:1 (1–2); 44:1; 47:2.
  b OR faces.

7 And *every* little chamber *was* one reed long, and one reed broad; and between the little chambers *were* five cubits; and the threshold of the gate by the porch of the gate within *was* one reed.

8 He measured also the porch of the gate within, one reed.

9 Then measured he the porch of the gate, eight cubits; and the posts thereof, two cubits; and the porch of the gate *was* inward.

10 And the little chambers of the gate eastward *were* three on this side, and three on that side; they three *were* of one measure: and the posts had one measure on this side and on that side.

11 And he measured the breadth of the entry of the gate, ten cubits; *and* the ᵃlength of the gate, thirteen cubits.

12 The space also before the little chambers *was* one cubit *on this side,* and the space *was* one cubit on that side: and the little chambers *were* six cubits on this side, and six cubits on that side.

13 He measured then the gate from the roof of *one* little chamber to the roof of another: the breadth *was* five and twenty cubits, door against door.

14 He made also posts of threescore cubits, even unto the post of the court round about the gate.

15 And from the ᵃface of the gate of the entrance unto the face of the porch of the inner gate *were* fifty cubits.

16 And *there were* narrow windows to the little chambers, and to their posts within the gate round about, and likewise to the arches: and windows *were* round about inward: and upon *each* post *were* ᵃpalm trees.

17 Then brought he me into the outward court, and, lo, *there were* ᵃchambers, and a pavement made for the court round about: thirty chambers ᵇ*were* upon the pavement.

18 And the pavement by the side of the gates over against the length of the gates *was* the lower pavement.

19 Then he measured the breadth from the forefront of the lower gate unto the forefront of the inner court without, an hundred cubits eastward and northward.

20 ¶ And the gate of the ᵃoutward court that looked toward the ᵇnorth, he measured the length thereof, and the breadth thereof.

21 And the little chambers thereof *were* three on this side and three on that side; and the posts thereof and the arches thereof were after the measure of the first gate: the length thereof *was* fifty cubits, and the breadth five and twenty cubits.

22 And their windows, and their arches, and their palm trees, *were* after the measure of the gate that looketh toward the east; and they went up unto it by seven steps; and the arches thereof *were* before them.

23 And the gate of the inner court *was* ᵃover against the gate toward the north, and toward the east; and he measured from gate to gate an hundred cubits.

24 ¶ After that he brought me toward the south, and behold a gate toward the south: and he measured the posts thereof and the arches thereof according to these measures.

25 And *there were* windows in it and in the arches thereof round about, like those windows: the length *was* fifty cubits, and the breadth five and twenty cubits.

26 And *there were* seven steps to go up to it, and the arches thereof *were* before them: and it had palm trees, one on this side, and another on that side, upon the posts thereof.

27 And *there was* a gate in the inner court toward the south: and he measured from gate to gate toward the south an hundred cubits.

28 And he brought me to the inner court by the south gate: and he measured the south gate according to these measures;

11*a* OR height.
15*a* OR front.
16*a* Ezek. 41:18.

17*a* Ezek. 41:10; 42:4 (1, 4–5).
b HEB faced.
20*a* Ezek. 42:1.

b Ezek. 44:4.
23*a* OR opposite.

29 And the little chambers thereof, and the posts thereof, and the arches thereof, according to these measures: and *there were* windows in it and in the arches thereof round about: *it was* fifty cubits long, and five and twenty cubits broad.

30 And the arches round about *were* five and twenty cubits long, and five cubits broad.

31 And the arches thereof *were* toward the *a*utter court; and palm trees *were* upon the posts thereof: and the going up to it *had* eight steps.

32 ¶ And he brought me into the inner court toward the east: and he measured the gate according to these measures.

33 And the little chambers thereof, and the posts thereof, and the arches thereof, *were* according to these measures: and *there were* windows therein and in the arches thereof round about: *it was* fifty cubits long, and five and twenty cubits broad.

34 And the arches thereof *were* toward the outward court; and palm trees *were* upon the posts thereof, on this side, and on that side: and the going up to it *had* eight steps.

35 ¶ And he brought me to the north gate, and measured *it* according to these measures;

36 The little chambers thereof, the posts thereof, and the arches thereof, and the windows to it round about: the length *was* fifty cubits, and the breadth five and twenty cubits.

37 And the posts thereof *were* toward the utter court; and palm trees *were* upon the posts thereof, on this side, and on that side: and the going up to it *had* eight steps.

38 And the chambers and the entries thereof *were* by the posts of the gates, where they *a*washed the burnt *b*offering.

39 ¶ And in the porch of the gate *were* two tables on this side, and two tables on that side, to slay thereon the *a*burnt offering and the *b*sin offering and the *c*trespass offering.

40 And at the side without, as one goeth up to the entry of the north gate, *were* two tables; and on the other side, which *was* at the porch of the gate, *were* two tables.

41 Four tables *were* on this side, and four tables on that side, by the side of the gate; eight tables, whereupon they slew *their sacrifices.*

42 And the four tables *were* of hewn stone for the burnt offering, of a cubit and an half long, and a cubit and an half broad, and one cubit high: whereupon also they laid the instruments wherewith they slew the burnt offering and the sacrifice.

43 And within *were* hooks, an hand broad, fastened round about: and upon the tables *was* the flesh of the offering.

44 ¶ And *a*without the inner gate *were* the chambers of the *b*singers in the inner court, which *was* at the side of the north gate; and their prospect *was* toward the south: one at the side of the east gate *having* the prospect toward the north.

45 And he said unto me, This chamber, whose prospect *is* toward the south, *is* for the priests, the *a*keepers of the charge of the house.

46 And the chamber whose prospect *is* toward the north *is* for the *a*priests, the keepers of the *b*charge of the altar: these *are* the sons of *c*Zadok among the sons of Levi, which *d*come near to the LORD to minister unto him.

47 So he measured the court, an hundred cubits long, and an *a*hundred cubits broad, foursquare; and the altar *that was* before the house.

48 ¶ And he brought me to the porch of the house, and measured

---

31*a* OR outer.
38*a* 2 Chr. 4:6.
  b Ezek. 46:2.
39*a* Lev. 1:3 (3, 9, 13–14).
  b Lev. 4:3 (2–3);
    Ezek. 42:13.
  c Lev. 5:6 (5–6);

Ezek. 46:20.
44*a* OR outside.
  b 1 Chr. 6:32 (31–33).
45*a* Ezek. 44:14 (8, 14–16);
    48:11.
46*a* Ezek. 42:13.
  b Num. 18:5.

  c Ezek. 43:19.
  d Num. 16:5;
    Ezek. 44:15 (15–16);
    45:4.
47*a* Ezek. 41:13; 42:8.

each post of the porch, five cubits on this side, and five cubits on that side: and the breadth of the gate *was* three cubits on this side, and three cubits on that side.

49 The length of the ᵃporch *was* twenty cubits, and the breadth eleven cubits; and *he brought me* by the steps whereby they went up to it: and *there were* ᵇpillars by the posts, one on this side, and another on that side.

CHAPTER 41

Ezekiel sees the inner temple and the Holy of Holies, and he is shown their form and size.

AFTERWARD he brought me to the temple, and measured the posts, six cubits broad on the one side, and six cubits broad on the other side, *which was* the breadth of the tabernacle.

2 And the breadth of the ᵃdoor *was* ten cubits; and the sides of the door *were* five cubits on the one side, and five cubits on the other side: and he measured the length thereof, forty cubits: and the ᵇbreadth, twenty cubits.

3 Then went he inward, and measured the post of the door, two cubits; and the door, six cubits; and the breadth of the door, seven cubits.

4 So he measured the length thereof, twenty cubits; and the breadth, twenty cubits, before the temple: and he said unto me, This is the most ᵃholy *place.*

5 After he measured the wall of the ᵃhouse, six cubits; and the breadth of *every* side chamber, four cubits, round about the house on every side.

6 And the side chambers *were* three, one over another, and thirty in order; and they entered into the wall which *was* of the house for the side ᵃchambers round about, that they might have hold, but they had not hold in the wall of the house.

7 And *there was* an enlarging, and a winding about still upward to the side chambers: for the winding about of the house went still upward round about the house: therefore the breadth of the house *was still* upward, and so increased *from* the lowest *chamber* to the highest by the midst.

8 I saw also the height of the house round about: the foundations of the side chambers *were* a full reed of six great ᵃcubits.

9 The thickness of the wall, which *was* for the side chamber without, *was* five cubits: and *that* which *was* left *was* the place of the side chambers that *were* within.

10 And between the ᵃchambers *was* the wideness of twenty cubits round about the house on every side.

11 And the doors of the side chambers *were* toward *the place that was* left, one door toward the north, and another door toward the south: and the breadth of the place that *was* left *was* five cubits round about.

12 Now the building that *was* before the separate place at the end toward the west *was* seventy cubits broad; and the wall of the building *was* five cubits thick round about, and the length thereof ninety cubits.

13 So he measured the house, an hundred cubits long; and the separate place, and the building, with the walls thereof, an ᵃhundred cubits long;

14 Also the breadth of the face of the house, and of the separate place toward the east, an hundred cubits.

15 And he measured the length of the building ᵃover against the separate place which *was* behind it, and the galleries thereof on the one side and on the other side, an hundred cubits, with the inner temple, and the porches of the court;

16 The door posts, and the narrow windows, and the ᵃgalleries round

---

49a 1 Kgs. 6:3.
 b 1 Kgs. 7:21.
41 2a Ezek. 47:1.
 b 1 Kgs. 6:2.
 4a 1 Kgs. 6:16;

Ezek. 44:13; 45:3;
  D&C 124:39.
5a OR temple.
6a 1 Kgs. 6:5 (5, 8).
8a Ezek. 40:5; 43:13.

10a Ezek. 40:17;
  42:4 (1, 4–5).
13a Ezek. 40:47; 42:8.
15a OR facing or opposite.
16a Ezek. 42:3.

about on their three stories, over against the door, *b*ceiled with wood round about, and from the ground up to the windows, and the windows *were* covered;

17 To that above the door, even unto the inner house, and without, and by all the wall round about within and without, by measure.

18 And *it was* made with *a*cherubims and *b*palm trees, so that a *c*palm tree *was* between a cherub and a cherub; and *every* *d*cherub had two faces;

19 So that the face of a man *was* toward the palm tree on the one side, and the face of a young lion toward the palm tree on the other side: *it was* made through all the house round about.

20 From the ground unto above the door *were* cherubims and palm trees made, and *on* the wall of the temple.

21 The *a*posts of the temple *were* squared, *and* the face of the sanctuary; the appearance *of the one* as the appearance *of the other*.

22 The *a*altar of wood *was* three cubits high, and the length thereof two cubits; and the corners thereof, and the length thereof, and the walls thereof, *were* of wood: and he said unto me, This *is* the *b*table that *is* before the LORD.

23 And the temple and the sanctuary had two *a*doors.

24 And the doors had two leaves *apiece*, two turning leaves; two *leaves* for the one door, and two leaves for the other *door*.

25 And *there were* made on them, on the doors of the temple, cherubims and palm trees, like as *were* made upon the walls; and *there were* thick *a*planks upon the face of the porch without.

26 And *there were* narrow windows and palm trees on the one side and on the other side, on the sides of the porch, and *upon* the side chambers of the house, and thick planks.

CHAPTER 42

Ezekiel sees in the temple the chambers for the priests.

THEN he brought me forth into the *a*utter court, the way toward the north: and he brought me into the chamber that *was* *b*over against the separate place, and which *was* before the building toward the north.

2 Before the length of an hundred cubits *was* the north door, and the breadth *was* fifty cubits.

3 *a*Over against the twenty *cubits* which *were* for the inner court, and over against the pavement which *was* for the utter court, *was* *b*gallery against gallery in three *stories*.

4 And before the *a*chambers *was* a walk of ten cubits breadth inward, a way of one cubit; and their doors toward the north.

5 Now the upper chambers *were* shorter: for the galleries were higher than these, than the lower, and than the middlemost of the building.

6 For they *were* in three *stories*, but had not pillars as the pillars of the courts: therefore *the building* was straitened more than the lowest and the middlemost from the ground.

7 And the wall that *was* without over against the chambers, toward the *a*utter court on the forepart of the chambers, the length thereof *was* fifty cubits.

8 For the length of the chambers that *were* in the utter court *was* fifty cubits: and, lo, before the temple *were* an *a*hundred cubits.

9 And from under these chambers *was* the entry on the east side, as one goeth into them from the utter court.

---

16 *b* HEB paneled or veneered.
18 *a* 1 Kgs. 6:29 (29, 32, 35); 7:36.
 b Rev. 7:9.
 c Ezek. 40:16.
 d Ezek. 10:14.

21 *a* Ezek. 46:2.
22 *a* Ex. 30:1; Rev. 11:1.
 b Ezek. 44:16; Mal. 1:12 (7, 12).
23 *a* 1 Kgs. 6:31 (31–33).
25 *a* 1 Kgs. 7:6.

42 1 *a* Ezek. 40:20.
 b OR opposite.
3 *a* OR Adjoining.
 b Ezek. 41:16 (15–16).
4 *a* Ezek. 40:17; 41:10; 46:19.
7 *a* OR outer.
8 *a* Ezek. 40:47; 41:13.

10 The chambers *were* in the thickness of the wall of the court toward the east, over against the separate place, and over against the building.

11 And the way before them *was* like the appearance of the chambers which *were* toward the north, as long as they, *and* as broad as they: and all their goings out *were* both according to their fashions, and according to their doors.

12 And according to the doors of the chambers that *were* toward the south *was* a door in the head of the way, *even* the way directly before the wall toward the east, as one entereth into them.

13 ¶ Then said he unto me, The north chambers *and* the south chambers, which *are* before the separate place, they *be* holy chambers, where the ^apriests that approach unto the Lord shall ^beat the most holy things: there shall they lay the most holy things, and the ^cmeat offering, and the ^dsin offering, and the trespass offering; for the place *is* holy.

14 When the priests enter therein, then shall they not go out of the holy *place* into the utter court, but there they shall lay their ^agarments wherein they minister; for they *are* holy; and shall put on other garments, and shall approach to *those things* which *are* for the people.

15 Now when he had made an end of measuring the inner house, he brought me forth toward the ^agate whose prospect *is* toward the east, and measured it round about.

16 He measured the east side with the ^ameasuring reed, five hundred reeds, with the measuring reed round about.

17 He measured the north side, five hundred reeds, with the measuring reed round about.

18 He measured the south side, five hundred reeds, with the measuring reed.

19 ¶ He turned about to the west side, *and* measured five hundred reeds with the measuring reed.

20 He ^ameasured it by the four sides: it had a wall round about, ^bfive hundred *reeds* long, and five hundred broad, to make a separation between the sanctuary and the ^cprofane place.

CHAPTER 43

The glory of God fills the temple—His throne is there, and He promises to dwell in the midst of Israel forever—Ezekiel sees the altar and the ordinances of the altar.

Afterward he brought me to the gate, *even* the ^agate that ^blooketh toward the east:

2 And, behold, the ^aglory of the God of Israel came from the way of the ^beast: and his ^cvoice *was* like a noise of many ^dwaters: and the earth ^eshined with his ^fglory.

3 And *it was* according to the appearance of the vision which I saw, *even* according to the vision that I saw when I came to destroy the city: and the visions *were* like the ^avision that I saw by the river Chebar; and I fell upon my face.

4 And the glory of the Lord ^acame into the ^bhouse by the way of the gate ^cwhose prospect *is* toward the east.

5 So the ^aspirit took me up, and brought me into the inner court; and, behold, the ^bglory of the Lord filled the house.

6 And I heard *him* speaking unto

13a Ezek. 40:46.
  b Lev. 6:26 (16, 26); 10:13.
  c Lev. 2:1 (1, 3, 10).
  d Lev. 4:3 (2–3);
    Ezek. 40:39.
14a Ezek. 44:19.
15a Ezek. 40:6; 43:1 (1–2);
    44:1.
16a Ezek. 40:3.
20a Ezek. 40:5.

  b Ezek. 45:2.
  c OR common.
    Ezek. 45:6; 48:15.
43 1a Ezek. 40:6; 42:15; 44:1.
  b OR faces.
  2a Ezek. 11:23;
    Rev. 21:11.
  b Matt. 24:27.
  c Ezek. 1:24; Rev. 1:15;
    D&C 110:3.

  d D&C 133:22.
  e Rev. 18:1.
  f D&C 94:8; 101:25.
  3a Ezek. 1:1.
  4a Ezek. 44:2.
  b TG Temple.
  c OR which faces.
  5a TG God, Spirit of.
  b 1 Kgs. 8:11 (10–11);
    Ezek. 44:4.

me out of the house; and the man stood by me.

7 ¶ And he said unto me, Son of man, the place of my throne, and the place of the soles of my [a]feet, where I will dwell in the midst of the children of Israel for ever, and my holy name, shall the house of Israel no more [b]defile, *neither* they, nor their kings, by their whoredom, nor by the carcases of their kings in their high places.

8 In their setting of their threshold by my thresholds, and their post by my posts, and the wall between me and them, they have even defiled my holy [a]name by their abominations that they have committed: wherefore I have consumed them in mine anger.

9 Now let them put away their whoredom, and the carcases of their kings, far from me, and I will dwell in the midst of them for ever.

10 ¶ Thou son of man, [a]shew the house to the house of Israel, that they may be ashamed of their iniquities: and let them measure the [b]pattern.

11 And if they be ashamed of all that they have done, shew them the form of the [a]house, and the fashion thereof, and the goings out thereof, and the comings in thereof, and all the forms thereof, and all the ordinances thereof, and all the forms thereof, and all the laws thereof: and write *it* in their sight, that they may keep the whole form thereof, and all the [b]ordinances thereof, and do them.

12 This *is* the law of the house; Upon the top of the [a]mountain the whole limit thereof round about *shall be* most holy. Behold, this *is* the law of the house.

13 ¶ And these *are* the measures of the altar after the cubits: The cu-

bit *is* a [a]cubit and an hand breadth; even the bottom *shall be* a cubit, and the breadth a cubit, and the border thereof by the edge thereof round about *shall be* a span: and this *shall be* the higher place of the altar.

14 And from the bottom *upon* the ground *even* to the lower [a]settle *shall be* two cubits, and the breadth one cubit; and from the lesser settle *even* to the greater settle *shall be* four cubits, and the breadth *one* cubit.

15 So the altar *shall be* four cubits; and from the altar and upward *shall be* four horns.

16 And the altar *shall be* twelve *cubits* long, twelve broad, square in the four squares thereof.

17 And the settle *shall be* fourteen *cubits* long and fourteen broad in the four squares thereof; and the border about it *shall be* half a cubit; and the bottom thereof *shall be* a cubit about; and his stairs shall look toward the east.

18 ¶ And he said unto me, Son of man, thus saith the Lord GOD; These *are* the ordinances of the altar in the day when they shall make it, to offer burnt offerings thereon, and to [a]sprinkle blood thereon.

19 And thou shalt give to the [a]priests the Levites that be of the seed of [b]Zadok, which approach unto me, to minister unto me, saith the Lord GOD, a young [c]bullock for a [d]sin offering.

20 And thou shalt take of the blood thereof, and put *it* on the four horns [a]of it, and on the four corners of the settle, and upon the border round about: thus shalt thou cleanse and purge it.

21 Thou shalt take the bullock also of the sin offering, and [a]he shall [b]burn it in the appointed place of the house, [c]without the sanctuary.

22 And on the second day thou

7a Isa. 60:13;
    Matt. 5:35.
  b Ezek. 20:39; 39:7.
8a D&C 63:61 (60–64).
10a Ezek. 40:4.
  b OR arrangement, plan.
11a TG Genealogy and
    Temple Work;

    Temple.
  b TG Ordinance.
12a Ezek. 40:2.
13a Ezek. 40:5; 41:8.
14a OR ledge, border.
18a Lev. 1:5.
19a Deut. 17:9;
    Ezek. 44:15; 48:11.

  b Ezek. 40:46.
  c Ex. 29:10.
  d Lev. 8:14.
20a IE of the altar.
21a IE the officiating priest.
  b Ex. 29:14.
  c OR outside the Holy
    Place.

shalt offer a kid of the goats without blemish for a sin offering; and they shall cleanse the altar, as they did cleanse *it* with the bullock.

23 When thou hast made an end of cleansing *it,* thou shalt offer a young bullock without blemish, and a ram out of the flock without blemish.

24 And thou shalt offer them before the LORD, and the priests shall cast ᵃsalt upon them, and they shall offer them up *for* a burnt offering unto the LORD.

25 ᵃSeven days shalt thou prepare every day a goat *for* a sin offering: they shall also prepare a young bullock, and a ram out of the flock, without blemish.

26 Seven days shall they purge the altar and purify it; and they shall consecrate themselves.

27 And when these days are expired, it shall be, *that* upon the ᵃeighth day, and *so* forward, the priests shall make your burnt ᵇofferings upon the altar, and your peace offerings; and I will accept you, saith the Lord GOD.

CHAPTER 44

The glory of the Lord fills the house of the Lord—No strangers may enter the sanctuary—The services of the priests in the temple are explained.

THEN he brought me back the way of the ᵃgate of the outward sanctuary which looketh toward the east; and it *was* shut.

2 Then said the LORD unto me; This gate shall be shut, it shall not be opened, and no man shall enter in by it; because the LORD, the God of Israel, hath ᵃentered in by it, therefore it shall be shut.

3 *It is* for the ᵃprince; the prince, he shall sit in it to eat ᵇbread before

the LORD; he shall enter by the way of the porch of *that* gate, and shall go out by the way of the same.

4 ¶ Then brought he me the way of the ᵃnorth gate before the house: and I looked, and, behold, the ᵇglory of the LORD filled the house of the LORD: and I ᶜfell upon my face.

5 And the LORD said unto me, Son of man, mark well, and behold with thine eyes, and hear with thine ears all that I say unto thee concerning all the ordinances of the house of the LORD, and all the laws thereof; and mark well the entering in of the house, with every going forth of the sanctuary.

6 And thou shalt say to the ᵃrebellious, *even* to the house of Israel, Thus saith the Lord GOD; O ye house of Israel, let it suffice you of all your abominations,

7 In that ye have brought *into my sanctuary* ᵃstrangers, uncircumcised in heart, and uncircumcised in flesh, to be in my sanctuary, to ᵇpollute it, *even* my house, when ye offer my ᶜbread, the ᵈfat and the ᵉblood, and they have broken my ᶠcovenant because of all your abominations.

8 And ye have not kept the charge of mine holy things: but ye have set keepers of my charge in my sanctuary for yourselves.

9 ¶ Thus saith the Lord GOD; No stranger, ᵃuncircumcised in heart, nor uncircumcised in flesh, shall enter into my sanctuary, of any stranger that *is* among the children of Israel.

10 And the Levites that are gone away far from me, when Israel went astray, which went astray away from me after their idols; they shall even bear their ᵃiniquity.

11 Yet they shall be ministers in my ᵃsanctuary, *having* charge at the

24*a* TG Salt.
25*a* Ex. 29:35 (35–36);
    Lev. 8:33.
27*a* Lev. 9:1.
  b TG Sacrifice.
44 1*a* Ezek. 40:6; 42:15;
    43:1 (1–2).
2*a* Ezek. 43:4.
3*a* Ezek. 34:24;

    37:25 (24–25); 45:7; 48:21.
  b Gen. 31:54.
4*a* Ezek. 40:20 (17, 20).
  b Ex. 40:34 (34–35);
    1 Kgs. 8:11 (10–11);
    Ezek. 43:5.
  c Ezek. 1:28.
6*a* Ezek. 2:5; 12:2; 24:3.
7*a* Jer. 51:51;

    Ezek. 23:38.
  b TG Sacrilege.
  c Lev. 3:11.
  d Lev. 3:17 (16–17).
  e TG Blood, Eating of.
  f D&C 1:15.
9*a* TG Circumcision.
10*a* OR guilt.
11*a* TG Temple.

gates of the house, and *b*ministering to the house: they shall slay the
burnt offering and the sacrifice for
the people, and they shall stand before them to minister unto them.

12 Because they ministered unto
them before their idols, and caused
the house of Israel to fall into iniquity; therefore have I lifted up
mine hand against them, saith the
Lord GOD, and they shall bear their
iniquity.

13 And they shall not come *a*near
unto me, to do the office of a priest
unto me, nor to come near to any of
my holy things, in the most *b*holy
place: but they shall bear their
*c*shame, and their abominations
which they have committed.

14 But I will make them *a*keepers
of the charge of the house, for all
the service thereof, and for all that
shall be done therein.

15 ¶ But the *a*priests the *b*Levites, the sons of Zadok, that kept
the charge of my sanctuary when
the children of Israel went astray
from me, they shall *c*come near to
me to minister unto me, and they
shall stand before me to offer unto
me the fat and the blood, saith the
Lord GOD:

16 They shall enter into my sanctuary, and they shall come near to
my *a*table, to minister unto me, and
they shall keep my charge.

17 ¶ And it shall come to pass, *that*
when they *a*enter in at the gates of
the inner court, they shall be clothed
with *b*linen garments; and no wool
shall come upon them, whiles they
minister in the gates of the inner
court, and within.

18 They shall have linen *a*bonnets
upon their heads, and shall have
linen *b*breeches upon their loins;
they shall not gird *themselves* with
any thing that causeth sweat.

19 And when they go forth into
the utter court, *even* into the utter
court to the people, they shall put
off their *a*garments wherein they
ministered, and lay them in the
holy chambers, and they shall put
on other garments; and they shall
not sanctify the people with their
garments.

20 Neither shall they *a*shave their
heads, nor suffer their locks to grow
long; they shall only *b*poll their
heads.

21 Neither shall any *a*priest drink
*b*wine, when they enter into the inner court.

22 Neither shall they take for their
wives a *a*widow, nor her that is *b*put
away: but they shall take maidens
of the seed of the house of Israel,
or a widow that had a priest before.

23 And they shall *a*teach my people
the *b*difference between the *c*holy and
profane, and cause them to discern
between the *d*unclean and the clean.

24 And in *a*controversy they shall
stand in judgment; *and* they
shall *b*judge it according to my
*c*judgments: and they shall keep
my laws and my statutes in all mine
*d*assemblies; and they shall hallow
my *e*sabbaths.

25 And they shall come at no *a*dead
person to defile themselves: but for
father, or for mother, or for son, or
for daughter, for brother, or for sister
that hath had no husband, they
may defile themselves.

11*b* Ezek. 45:5; 46:24.
13*a* Num. 18:3; 2 Kgs. 23:9.
   b Ezek. 41:4 (1–4); 45:3.
   c TG Shame.
14*a* Ezek. 40:45; 48:11.
15*a* Deut. 17:9; Ezek. 43:19.
   TG Priest, Aaronic
   Priesthood.
   BD Priests.
   b Deut. 10:8.
   c Num. 16:5; Ezek. 40:46.
16*a* Ezek. 41:22;
   Mal. 1:12 (7, 12).
17*a* Ex. 28:43.

   b Ex. 28:39; 39:27.
18*a* Ex. 39:28.
   b Lev. 6:10.
19*a* Ezek. 42:14.
20*a* Lev. 21:5;
   1 Cor. 11:14.
   b OR cut, trim.
21*a* TG Priest, Aaronic
   Priesthood.
   BD Priests.
   b Lev. 10:9.
22*a* Lev. 21:14 (7, 13–14).
   b OR divorced.
   Matt. 5:32.

23*a* Mosiah 23:14.
   b Lev. 10:10;
   Ezek. 22:26.
   TG Discernment,
   Spiritual.
   c TG Sacred.
   d TG Uncleanness.
24*a* Deut. 17:8 (8–9).
   b Moro. 7:15 (15–18).
   c Deut. 25:1 (1–3).
   d TG Meetings.
   e Jer. 17:27 (22, 24, 27);
   Ezek. 22:26.
25*a* Lev. 21:1 (1–3).

26 And after he is *a*cleansed, they shall reckon unto him seven days.

27 And in the day that he goeth into the sanctuary, unto the inner court, to minister in the sanctuary, he shall offer his sin offering, saith the Lord GOD.

28 And *a*it shall be unto them for an *b*inheritance: I *am* their inheritance: and ye shall give them no possession in Israel: I *am* their possession.

29 They shall eat the *a*meat offering, and the sin offering, and the trespass offering; and every dedicated thing in Israel shall be theirs.

30 And the first of all the *a*firstfruits of all *things*, and every *b*oblation of all, of every *sort* of your oblations, shall be the priest's: ye shall also give unto the priest the first of your *c*dough, that he may cause the blessing to rest in thine house.

31 The priests shall not eat of any thing that is *a*dead of itself, or torn, whether it be fowl or beast.

CHAPTER 45

Portions of land will be provided for the sanctuary and the dwellings of the priests—The people are to offer their sacrifices and oblations and keep their feasts.

MOREOVER, when ye shall divide by lot the land for inheritance, ye shall offer an oblation unto the LORD, an holy portion of the land: the *a*length *shall be* the length of five and twenty thousand *b*reeds, and the breadth *shall be* ten thousand. This *shall be* holy in all the borders thereof round about.

2 Of this there shall be for the sanctuary five hundred *in length*, with five hundred *in breadth*, *a*square round about; and fifty cubits round about for the *b*suburbs thereof.

3 And of this measure shalt thou measure the length of five and twenty thousand, and the breadth of ten thousand: and in it shall be the *a*sanctuary *and* the most *b*holy place.

4 The holy *portion* of the land shall be for the *a*priests the ministers of the sanctuary, which shall *b*come near to minister unto the LORD: and it shall be a place for their houses, and an holy place for the sanctuary.

5 And the five and twenty thousand of length, and the ten thousand of breadth, shall also the *a*Levites, the *b*ministers of the house, have for themselves, for a possession for twenty chambers.

6 ¶ And ye shall appoint the possession of the *a*city five thousand broad, and five and twenty thousand long, over against the oblation of the holy *portion*: it shall be for the whole house of Israel.

7 ¶ And a *a*portion *shall be* for the prince on the one side and on the other side of the oblation of the holy *portion*, and of the possession of the city, before the oblation of the holy *portion*, and before the possession of the city, from the west side westward, and from the east side eastward: and the length *shall be* over against one of the portions, from the west border unto the east border.

8 *a*In the *b*land shall be his possession in Israel: and my *c*princes shall no more oppress my people; and *the rest of* the land shall they give to the house of Israel according to their *d*tribes.

9 ¶ Thus saith the Lord GOD; Let it suffice you, O princes of Israel:

26*a* Num. 19:11 (11–12).
28*a* IE the temple service.
  b Num. 18:20.
29*a* OR grain or flour.
  Lev. 6:14 (14–18, 25–29).
30*a* Ex. 22:29;
  Neh. 10:35.
  b OR offering.
  c Num. 15:20.
31*a* Lev. 22:8.

45 1*a* Ezek. 40:3.
  b Rev. 11:1.
2*a* Ezek. 42:20.
  b Ezek. 48:15.
3*a* Ezek. 48:10.
  b Ezek. 41:4; 44:13.
4*a* Ezek. 48:11 (11–12).
  b Ezek. 40:46.
5*a* Ezek. 48:13.
  b Ezek. 44:11; 46:24.

6*a* Ezek. 42:20; 48:15.
7*a* Ezek. 44:3; 48:21.
8*a* OR It shall be his
  possession in the land
  of Israel.
  b Ezek. 46:18.
  c TG Kings, Earthly.
  d TG Israel, Twelve
  Tribes of.

remove violence and spoil, and execute judgment and ^ajustice, take away your ^bexactions from my people, saith the Lord GOD.

10 Ye shall have just balances, and a just ^aephah, and a just bath.

11 The ephah and the ^abath shall be of one measure, that the bath may contain the tenth part of an ^bhomer, and the ephah the tenth part of an homer: the measure thereof shall be after the homer.

12 And the ^ashekel *shall be* twenty gerahs: twenty shekels, five and twenty shekels, fifteen shekels, shall be your maneh.

13 This *is* the ^aoblation that ye shall offer; the sixth part of an ephah of an homer of wheat, and ye shall give the sixth part of an ephah of an homer of barley:

14 Concerning the ordinance of oil, the bath of oil, *ye shall offer* the tenth part of a bath out of the cor, *which is* an homer of ten baths; for ten baths *are* an homer:

15 And one lamb out of the flock, out of two hundred, out of the fat pastures of Israel; for a meat offering, and for a burnt offering, and for peace offerings, to make reconciliation for them, saith the Lord GOD.

16 All the people of the land shall give this oblation for the prince in Israel.

17 And it shall be the prince's part *to give* burnt offerings, and meat offerings, and ^adrink offerings, in the feasts, and in the new ^bmoons, and in the sabbaths, in all ^csolemnities of the house of Israel: he shall prepare the ^dsin offering, and the meat offering, and the burnt offering, and the peace offerings, to make reconciliation for the house of Israel.

18 Thus saith the Lord GOD; In the first *month,* in the first *day* of the

month, thou shalt take a young bullock without blemish, and cleanse the sanctuary:

19 And the priest shall take of the blood of the sin offering, and put *it* upon the posts of the house, and upon the four corners of the settle of the altar, and upon the posts of the gate of the inner court.

20 And so thou shalt do the seventh *day* of the month for every one that ^aerreth, and for *him that is* simple: so shall ye ^breconcile the house.

21 In the first *month,* in the ^afourteenth day of the month, ye shall have the passover, a feast of seven days; ^bunleavened bread shall be eaten.

22 And upon that day shall the prince prepare for himself and for all the people of the land a bullock *for* a sin offering.

23 And seven days of the feast he shall prepare a burnt offering to the LORD, seven bullocks and seven rams without blemish daily the seven days; and a ^akid of the goats daily *for* a sin offering.

24 And he shall prepare a meat offering of an ephah for a bullock, and an ephah for a ram, and an hin of ^aoil for an ephah.

25 In the ^aseventh *month,* in the fifteenth day of the month, shall he do the like in the feast of the seven days, according to the sin offering, according to the burnt offering, and according to the meat offering, and according to the oil.

CHAPTER 46

The ordinances of worship and of sacrifice are explained.

THUS saith the Lord GOD; The ^agate of the inner court that ^blooketh toward the east shall be shut the six

---

9*a* TG Justice.
  b OR expropriations; i.e., illegal taking away of property or possessions.
10*a* Lev. 19:36;
    Deut. 25:15 (14–15);
    Amos 8:5.
11*a* Isa. 5:10 (8–10).
  b Lev. 27:16.

12*a* Gen. 23:15;
    Ex. 30:13.
13*a* TG Sacrifice.
17*a* Ex. 29:40.
  b Num. 28:11;
    Ezek. 46:1.
  c TG Solemn Assembly.
  d Lev. 14:19.
20*a* Lev. 4:27.

  b TG Reconciliation.
21*a* Lev. 23:5.
  b TG Bread, Unleavened.
23*a* Num. 28:15.
24*a* Ex. 29:40.
25*a* Lev. 23:34.
46 1*a* 1 Chr. 9:18.
  b OR faces.

working days; but on the ^csabbath it shall be opened, and in the day of the new ^dmoon it shall be opened.

2 And the prince shall enter by the way of the porch of *that* gate without, and shall stand by the ^apost of the gate, and the priests shall prepare his burnt ^boffering and his peace offerings, and he shall worship at the threshold of the gate: then he shall go forth; but the gate shall not be shut until the evening.

3 Likewise the people of the land shall worship at the door of this gate before the LORD in the sabbaths and in the new moons.

4 And the burnt offering that the prince shall offer unto the LORD in the ^asabbath day *shall be* six lambs without blemish, and a ram without blemish.

5 And the meat offering *shall be* an ephah for a ram, and the meat offering for the lambs as he shall be able to give, and an hin of oil to an ephah.

6 And in the day of the new moon *it shall be* a young bullock without blemish, and six lambs, and a ram: they shall be without blemish.

7 And he shall prepare a meat offering, an ephah for a bullock, and an ephah for a ram, and for the lambs according as his hand shall attain unto, and an hin of oil to an ephah.

8 And when the prince shall enter, he shall go in by the way of the porch of *that* gate, and he shall go forth by the way thereof.

9 ¶ But when the people of the land shall come before the LORD in the solemn ^afeasts, he that entereth in by the way of the north gate to worship shall go out by the way of the south gate; and he that entereth by the way of the south gate shall go forth by the way of the north gate: he shall not return by the way of the gate whereby he came in, but shall go forth over against it.

10 And the prince in the midst of them, when they go in, shall go in; and when they go forth, shall go forth.

11 And in the feasts and in the ^asolemnities the meat offering shall be an ephah to a bullock, and an ephah to a ram, and to the lambs as he is able to give, and an hin of oil to an ephah.

12 Now when the prince shall prepare a ^avoluntary burnt offering or peace ^bofferings ^cvoluntarily unto the LORD, *one* shall then open him the gate that looketh toward the east, and he shall prepare his burnt offering and his peace offerings, as he did on the sabbath day: then he shall go forth; and after his going forth *one* shall shut the gate.

13 Thou shalt ^adaily prepare a burnt offering unto the LORD *of* a lamb of the first year without blemish: thou shalt prepare it every morning.

14 And thou shalt prepare a meat offering for it every morning, the sixth part of an ephah, and the third part of an hin of oil, to ^atemper with the fine flour; a meat offering continually by a perpetual ordinance unto the LORD.

15 Thus shall they prepare the lamb, and the meat offering, and the oil, every morning *for* a continual burnt offering.

16 ¶ Thus saith the Lord GOD; If the prince give a gift unto any of his sons, the inheritance thereof shall be his sons'; it *shall be* their possession by inheritance.

17 But if he give a gift of his inheritance to one of his servants, then it shall be his to the year of ^aliberty; after it shall return to the prince: but his inheritance shall be his sons' for them.

18 Moreover the prince shall not take of the people's ^ainheritance by ^boppression, to thrust them out of

1*c* TG Sabbath.
  d Ezek. 45:17.
2*a* Ezek. 41:21.
  b Ezek. 40:38.
4*a* Num. 28:10 (9–10).
9*a* Ex. 23:14 (1–17);

Deut. 16:16.
11*a* TG Solemn Assembly.
12*a* D&C 58:26 (26–29).
  b TG Sacrifice.
  c Lev. 7:16; 22:23.
13*a* Ex. 29:38.

14*a* OR moisten, soften.
17*a* TG Liberty.
18*a* Ezek. 45:8.
  b Mosiah 2:14 (12–15).

their possession; *but* he shall give his sons inheritance out of his own possession: that my people be not scattered every man from his possession.

19 ¶ After he brought me through the entry, which *was* at the side of the gate, into the holy *a*chambers of the priests, which looked toward the north: and, behold, there *was* a place on the two sides westward.

20 Then said he unto me, This *is* the place where the priests shall boil the *a*trespass offering and the sin offering, where they shall *b*bake the meat offering; that they bear *them* not out into the utter court, to sanctify the people.

21 Then he brought me forth into the utter court, and caused me to pass by the four corners of the court; and, behold, in every corner of the court *there was* a court.

22 In the four corners of the court *there were* courts joined of forty *cubits* long and thirty broad: these four corners *were* of one measure.

23 And *there was* a row *of* *a*building round about in them, round about them four, and *it was* made with boiling places under the rows round about.

24 Then said he unto me, These *are* the places of them that boil, where the *a*ministers of the house shall boil the sacrifice of the people.

CHAPTER 47

Waters issue from the house of the Lord and heal the Dead Sea—The Lord shows the borders of the land.

AFTERWARD he brought me again unto the *a*door of the house; and, behold, *b*waters issued out from under the threshold of the house eastward: for the forefront of the house *stood toward* the east, and the waters came down from under from the right side of the *c*house, at the south *side* of the altar.

2 Then brought he me out of the way of the gate northward, and led me about the way without unto the utter *a*gate by the way that looketh eastward; and, behold, there ran out waters on the right side.

3 And when the man that had the *a*line in his hand went forth eastward, he measured a thousand cubits, and he brought me through the waters; the waters *were* to the ankles.

4 Again he measured a thousand, and brought me through the waters; the waters *were* to the knees. Again he measured a thousand, and brought me through; the waters *were* to the loins.

5 Afterward he measured a thousand; *and it was* a river that I could not pass over: for the waters were risen, waters to swim in, a river that could not be passed over.

6 ¶ And he said unto me, Son of man, hast thou seen *this*? Then he brought me, and caused me to return to the brink of the river.

7 Now when I had returned, behold, at the bank of the river *were* very many trees on the one side and on the other.

8 Then said he unto me, These waters issue out toward the east country, and go down into the desert, and go into the *a*sea: *which being* brought forth into the sea, the *b*waters shall be healed.

9 And it shall come to pass, *that* every thing that liveth, which moveth, whithersoever the rivers shall come, shall live: and there shall be a very great multitude of fish, because these waters shall come thither: for they shall be healed; and every thing shall live whither the river cometh.

10 And it shall come to pass, *that* the fishers shall stand *a*upon it from En-gedi even unto En-eglaim; they

---

19*a* Ezek. 42:4 (4–12).
20*a* Ezek. 40:39.
  b Lev. 2:4.
23*a* OR masonry.
24*a* Ezek. 44:11; 45:5.

47 1*a* Ezek. 41:2 (1–2).
  b Joel 3:18;
    Zech. 14:8; Rev. 22:1.
  c TG Temple.
2*a* Ezek. 40:6.

3*a* Ezek. 40:3;
  Zech. 2:1.
8*a* Deut. 3:17.
  b 2 Kgs. 2:21.
10*a* OR by it.

shall be a *place* to spread forth nets; their fish shall be according to their kinds, as the fish of the great sea, exceeding many.

11 But the miry places thereof and the marshes thereof shall not be healed; they shall be given to salt.

12 And by the river upon the bank thereof, on this side and on that side, shall grow all trees for meat, whose leaf shall not fade, neither shall the fruit thereof be consumed: it shall bring forth new fruit according to his months, because their waters they issued out of the sanctuary: and the fruit thereof shall be for meat, and the ᵃleaf thereof for ᵇmedicine.

13 ¶ Thus saith the Lord GOD; This *shall be* the border, whereby ye shall inherit the land according to the twelve ᵃtribes of Israel: ᵇJoseph *shall have two* portions.

14 And ye shall inherit it, one as well as another: *concerning* the which I ᵃlifted up mine hand to give it unto your fathers: and this land shall fall unto you for ᵇinheritance.

15 And this *shall be* the border of the land toward the north side, from the great sea, the way of Hethlon, as men go to Zedad;

16 Hamath, Berothah, Sibraim, which *is* between the border of Damascus and the border of Hamath; Hazar-hatticon, which *is* by the ᵃcoast of Hauran.

17 And the border from the sea shall be Hazar-enan, the border of Damascus, and the north northward, and the border of Hamath. And *this is* the north side.

18 And the east side ye shall measure from Hauran, and from Damascus, and from Gilead, and from the land of Israel *by* Jordan, from the border unto the ᵃeast sea. And *this is* the east side.

19 And the south side southward, from Tamar *even* to the waters of ᵃstrife *in* Kadesh, the river to the great sea. And *this is* the south side southward.

20 The west side also *shall be* the great sea from the border, till a man come over against Hamath. This *is* the west side.

21 So shall ye divide this land unto you according to the tribes of Israel.

22 ¶ And it shall come to pass, *that* ye shall ᵃdivide it by lot for an inheritance unto you, and to the strangers that sojourn among you, which shall beget children among you: and they shall be unto you as ᵇborn in the country among the children of Israel; they shall have inheritance with you among the tribes of Israel.

23 And it shall come to pass, *that* in what tribe the stranger sojourneth, there shall ye give *him* his inheritance, saith the Lord GOD.

CHAPTER 48

The portions of land for the tribes are named—The gates of the city bear the names of the tribes—The name of the city will be The Lord Is There.

Now these *are* the names of the ᵃtribes. From the north end to the coast of the way of Hethlon, as one goeth to Hamath, Hazar-enan, the border of Damascus northward, to the coast of Hamath; for these are his sides east *and* west; a *portion* for ᵇDan.

2 And by the border of Dan, from the east side unto the west side, a *portion for* Asher.

3 And by the border of Asher, from the east side even unto the west side, a *portion for* Naphtali.

4 And by the border of Naphtali,

12a Rev. 22:2.
  b Alma 46:40.
13a TG Israel, Twelve
     Tribes of.
  b Josh. 14:4;
     Ezek. 48:4 (4–5).
14a IE made an oath, or
     covenant.

Ps. 119:48 (44–48).
  b Num. 34:2 (2–15);
     Ezek. 48:29 (1–29);
     2 Ne. 10:7 (7–8).
16a HEB border.
18a Joel 2:20.
19a Num. 20:13;
     Deut. 33:8;

Ps. 106:32.
22a Josh. 1:6.
  b Ex. 12:48 (19, 48–49);
     Lev. 16:29.
48 1a TG Israel, Twelve
       Tribes of.
   b Num. 2:25 (25–31).

from the east side unto the west side, a *portion for* [a]Manasseh.

5 And by the border of Manasseh, from the east side unto the west side, a *portion for* [a]Ephraim.

6 And by the border of Ephraim, from the east side even unto the west side, a *portion for* Reuben.

7 And by the border of Reuben, from the east side unto the west side, a *portion for* Judah.

8 ¶ And by the border of Judah, from the east side unto the west side, shall be the offering which ye shall offer of five and twenty thousand *reeds in* breadth, and *in* length as one of the *other* parts, from the east side unto the west side: and the sanctuary shall be in the midst of it.

9 The oblation that ye shall offer unto the LORD *shall be* of five and twenty thousand in length, and of ten thousand in breadth.

10 And for them, *even* for the priests, shall be *this* holy oblation; toward the north five and twenty thousand *in length,* and toward the west ten thousand in breadth, and toward the east ten thousand in breadth, and toward the south five and twenty thousand in length: and the [a]sanctuary of the LORD shall be in the midst thereof.

11 *It shall be* for the [a]priests that are sanctified of the sons of Zadok; which have [b]kept my charge, which went not astray when the children of Israel went astray, as the Levites went astray.

12 And *this* oblation of the land that is offered shall be unto them a thing most holy by the border of the Levites.

13 And over against the border of the priests the [a]Levites *shall have* five and twenty thousand in length, and ten thousand in breadth: all the length *shall be* five and twenty thousand, and the breadth ten thousand.

14 And they shall not [a]sell of it, neither exchange, nor alienate the firstfruits of the land: for *it is* holy unto the LORD.

15 ¶ And the five thousand, that are left in the breadth over against the five and twenty thousand, shall be a [a]profane *place* for the city, for dwelling, and for [b]suburbs: and the city shall be in the midst thereof.

16 And these *shall be* the measures thereof; the north side four thousand and five hundred, and the south side four thousand and five hundred, and on the east side four thousand and five hundred, and the west side four thousand and five hundred.

17 And the suburbs of the city shall be toward the north two hundred and fifty, and toward the south two hundred and fifty, and toward the east two hundred and fifty, and toward the west two hundred and fifty.

18 And the residue in length over against the oblation of the holy *portion shall be* ten thousand eastward, and ten thousand westward: and it shall be over against the oblation of the holy *portion;* and the increase thereof shall be for food unto them that serve the city.

19 And they that serve the city shall serve it out of all the tribes of Israel.

20 All the oblation *shall be* five and twenty thousand by five and twenty thousand: ye shall offer the holy oblation foursquare, with the possession of the city.

21 ¶ And the [a]residue *shall be* for the prince, on the one side and on the other of the holy oblation, and of the possession of the city, over against the five and twenty thousand of the oblation toward the east border, and westward over against the five and twenty thousand toward the west border, over against the portions for the prince: and it shall be the holy

---

4a Ezek. 47:13.
5a Ether 13:6 (5–12).
10a Ezek. 45:3.
11a Ezek. 43:19; 45:4.
   b Ezek. 40:45;

44:14 (8, 14–16).
13a Ezek. 45:5.
14a Lev. 27:28 (10, 28, 33).
15a OR common.
   Ezek. 42:20; 45:6.

b Num. 35:2 (1–5);
   Ezek. 45:2.
21a Ezek. 44:3; 45:7.

oblation; and the sanctuary of the house *shall be* in the midst thereof.

22 Moreover from the possession of the Levites, and from the possession of the city, *being* in the midst *of that* which is the prince's, between the border of Judah and the border of Benjamin, shall be for the prince.

23 As for the rest of the tribes, from the east side unto the west side, Benjamin *shall have a portion.*

24 And by the border of Benjamin, from the east side unto the west side, Simeon *shall have a portion.*

25 And by the border of Simeon, from the east side unto the west side, Issachar a *portion.*

26 And by the border of Issachar, from the east side unto the west side, Zebulun a *portion.*

27 And by the border of Zebulun, from the east side unto the west side, Gad a *portion.*

28 And by the border of Gad, at the south side southward, the border shall be even from Tamar *unto* the waters of [a]strife *in* Kadesh, *and* to the river toward the great sea.

29 This *is* the land which ye shall divide by lot unto the tribes of Israel for [a]inheritance, and these *are* their portions, saith the Lord GOD.

30 ¶ And these *are* the goings out of the city on the north side, four thousand and five hundred measures.

31 And the [a]gates of the [b]city *shall be* after the names of the tribes of Israel: three gates northward; one gate of [c]Reuben, one gate of Judah, one gate of Levi.

32 And at the east side four thousand and five hundred: and three gates; and one gate of Joseph, one gate of Benjamin, one gate of Dan.

33 And at the south side four thousand and five hundred measures: and three gates; one gate of Simeon, one gate of Issachar, one gate of Zebulun.

34 At the west side four thousand and five hundred, *with* their three gates; one gate of Gad, one gate of Asher, one gate of Naphtali.

35 *It was* round about eighteen thousand *measures:* [a]and the name of the city from *that* day *shall be,* The LORD *is* there.

THE BOOK OF
DANIEL

CHAPTER 1

Daniel and certain Hebrews are trained in the court of Nebuchadnezzar—They eat plain food and drink no wine—God gives them knowledge and wisdom beyond all others.

IN the third year of the reign of [a]Jehoiakim king of Judah came [b]Nebuchadnezzar king of Babylon unto Jerusalem, and besieged it.

2 And the Lord gave Jehoiakim king of Judah into his hand, with

---

28a HEB Meribah.
   Num. 20:13.
29a Num. 34:2 (2–15);
   Ezek. 47:14 (14–21);
   2 Ne. 10:7 (7–8).
31a Rev. 21:12 (12–13).
   b Neh. 11:1 (1–2).
   c Deut. 33:6 (6–8);

1 Chr. 5:3 (1, 3, 18);
   Rev. 7:5.
35a JST Ezek. 48:35 . . . and
   the name of the city
   from that day shall be
   called, Holy; for the Lord
   shall be there.
   Rev. 21:3.

[DANIEL]

1 1a TG Israel, Bondage of, in
   Other Lands.
   b 2 Kgs. 24:1 (1–16);
   2 Chr. 36:6 (6–10).

part of the ªvessels of the house of God: which he carried into the land of ᵇShinar to the house of his god; and he brought the ᶜvessels into the treasure house of his god.

3 ¶ And the king spake unto Ashpenaz ªthe master of his eunuchs, that he should bring *certain* of the children of Israel, and of the king's ᵇseed, and of the princes;

4 Children in whom *was* no blemish, but ªwell favoured, and skilful in all wisdom, and cunning in knowledge, and understanding science, and such as *had* ability in them to stand in the king's palace, and whom they might teach the learning and the tongue of the Chaldeans.

5 And the king appointed them a daily ªprovision of the king's ᵇmeat, and of the wine which he drank: so nourishing them three years, that at the end thereof they might ᶜstand before the king.

6 Now among these were of the children of Judah, ªDaniel, ᵇHananiah, Mishael, and Azariah:

7 Unto whom the prince of the eunuchs gave ªnames: for he gave unto Daniel *the* ᵇ*name* of Belteshazzar; and to Hananiah, of Shadrach; and to Mishael, of Meshach; and to Azariah, of Abed-nego.

8 ¶ But Daniel ªpurposed in his heart that he would not ᵇdefile himself with the portion of the king's meat, nor with the ᶜwine which he drank: therefore he requested of the prince of the eunuchs that he might not defile himself.

9 Now God had brought Daniel into ªfavour and ᵇtender love with the prince of the eunuchs.

10 And the prince of the eunuchs said unto Daniel, I ªfear my lord the king, who hath appointed your meat and your drink: for why should he see your faces ᵇworse liking than the children which *are* of your ᶜsort? then shall ye make *me* endanger my head to the king.

11 Then said Daniel to ªMelzar, whom the prince of the eunuchs had set over Daniel, Hananiah, Mishael, and Azariah,

12 Prove thy servants, I beseech thee, ten days; and let them give us ªpulse to eat, and water to drink.

13 Then let our ªcountenances be looked upon before thee, and the countenance of the children that eat of the portion of the king's meat: and as thou seest, deal with thy servants.

14 So he consented to them in this matter, and proved them ten days.

15 And at the end of ten days their countenances appeared fairer and fatter in flesh than all the children which did eat the portion of the king's meat.

16 Thus Melzar took away the portion of their meat, and the wine that they should drink; and gave them pulse.

17 ¶ As for these four children, God gave them ªknowledge and skill in all ᵇlearning and wisdom: and Daniel had ᶜunderstanding in all ᵈvisions and dreams.

18 Now at the end of the days that the king had said he should bring them in, then the prince of the eunuchs brought them in before Nebuchadnezzar.

19 And the king communed with

2ª 2 Kgs. 24:13.
   b Gen. 11:2.
   c Dan. 5:2.
3ª OR chief of his officers.
   b 2 Kgs. 20:18 (14–18);
     Isa. 39:7 (3–7).
4ª HEB good in
     appearance.
5ª 2 Chr. 31:16.
   b HEB delicacies.
   c 1 Kgs. 10:8.
6ª Dan. 6:13.
   b Dan. 2:17.

7ª Dan. 2:26.
   b Dan. 5:12.
8ª TG Commitment.
   b Hosea 9:3 (1–3).
     TG Word of Wisdom.
   c TG Temperance.
9ª Prov. 16:7.
   b HEB compassion.
10ª TG Courage;
      Fearful.
   b IE less healthy.
   c OR age.
11ª HEB the steward.

12ª IE foods made of seeds,
      grains, etc.
      Mosiah 9:9 (8–9);
      D&C 89:14.
13ª D&C 89:18.
17ª Dan. 2:20 (20–22);
      Jacob 4:8;
      Alma 12:9 (9–11);
      D&C 89:19.
   b TG Education; Learn.
   c Gen. 41:15 (1–43);
      Dan. 10:1.
   d TG Vision.

them; and among them all was found none like Daniel, Hananiah, Mishael, and Azariah: therefore stood they before the king.

20 And in all matters of wisdom *and* understanding, that the king inquired of them, he found them ten times better than all the *a*magicians *and* astrologers that *were* in all his realm.

21 And Daniel continued *even* unto the first year of king Cyrus.

CHAPTER 2

Nebuchadnezzar's dream is revealed to Daniel—The king saw a great image, a stone cut from the mountain without hands destroyed the image, and the stone grew and filled the whole earth—The stone is the latter-day kingdom of God.

AND in the second year of the reign of Nebuchadnezzar Nebuchadnezzar dreamed *a*dreams, wherewith his spirit was *b*troubled, and his sleep brake from him.

2 Then the king commanded to call the *a*magicians, and the astrologers, and the sorcerers, and the Chaldeans, for to shew the king his dreams. So they came and stood before the king.

3 And the king said unto them, I have dreamed a dream, and my spirit was troubled to know the dream.

4 Then spake the Chaldeans to the king in *a*Syriack, O king, live for ever: tell thy servants the dream, and we will *b*shew the interpretation.

5 The king answered and said to the Chaldeans, The thing is *a*gone from me: if ye will not make known unto me the dream, with the interpretation thereof, ye shall be *b*cut in pieces, and your houses shall be made a dunghill.

6 But if ye shew the dream, and the interpretation thereof, ye shall receive of me gifts and rewards and great honour: therefore shew me the dream, and the interpretation thereof.

7 They answered again and said, Let the king tell his servants the dream, and we will shew the interpretation of it.

8 The king answered and said, I know of certainty that ye would gain the time, because ye see the thing is gone from me.

9 But if ye will not make known unto me the dream, *there is but* one decree for you: for ye have prepared lying and corrupt words to speak before me, *a*till the time be changed: therefore tell me the dream, and I shall know that ye can shew me the interpretation thereof.

10 ¶ The Chaldeans answered before the king, and said, There is not a man upon the earth that can shew the king's matter: therefore *there is* no king, lord, nor ruler, *that* asked such things at any magician, or astrologer, or Chaldean.

11 And *it is* a rare thing that the king requireth, and there is none other that can shew it before the king, except the *a*gods, whose dwelling is not with flesh.

12 For this cause the king was angry and very furious, and commanded to destroy all the wise *men* of Babylon.

13 And the decree went forth that the wise *men* should be slain; and they sought Daniel and his fellows to be slain.

14 ¶ Then Daniel answered with counsel and wisdom to Arioch the captain of the king's guard, which was gone forth to slay the wise *men* of Babylon:

15 He answered and said to Arioch the king's captain, Why *is* the decree *so* *a*hasty from the king? Then

---

20a TG Sorcery;
    Superstitions.
2 1a TG Dream.
    b Gen. 41:8 (1–8).
  2a Dan. 4:6.
  4a HEB Aramaic
    (a language related

to Hebrew).
    b OR reveal or tell.
5a Persian: sure with me;
    i.e., he knew his dream
    and desired to test
    them. See vv. 8–9.
    b Dan. 3:29.

9a IE till with time
    circumstance will
    change.
11a Dan. 4:8; 5:14 (11, 14).
15a TG Rashness.

Arioch made the thing known to Daniel.

16 Then Daniel went in, and desired of the king that he would give him time, and that he would shew the king the interpretation.

17 Then Daniel went to his house, and made the thing known to *a*Hananiah, Mishael, and Azariah, his companions:

18 That they would desire mercies of the God of heaven concerning this secret; that Daniel and his fellows should not perish with the rest of the wise *men* of Babylon.

19 ¶ Then was the *a*secret revealed unto Daniel in a night *b*vision. Then Daniel blessed the God of heaven.

20 Daniel answered and said, Blessed be the name of God for ever and ever: for *a*wisdom and might are his:

21 And he changeth the *a*times and the *b*seasons: he *c*removeth kings, and setteth up kings: he giveth *d*wisdom unto the wise, and *e*knowledge to them that know understanding:

22 He *a*revealeth the deep and secret things: he *b*knoweth what *is* in the darkness, and the *c*light dwelleth with him.

23 I thank thee, and praise thee, O thou God of my fathers, who hast given me wisdom and might, and hast made known unto me now what we desired of thee: for thou hast *now* made known unto us the king's matter.

24 ¶ Therefore Daniel went in unto Arioch, whom the king had ordained to destroy the wise *men* of Babylon: he went and said thus unto him; Destroy not the wise *men*

of Babylon: bring me in before the king, and I will shew unto the king the interpretation.

25 Then Arioch brought in Daniel before the king in haste, and said thus unto him, I have found a man of the captives of Judah, that will make known unto the king the interpretation.

26 The king answered and said to Daniel, whose *a*name *was* Belteshazzar, Art thou able to make *b*known unto me the dream which I have seen, and the interpretation thereof?

27 Daniel answered in the presence of the king, and said, The secret which the king hath demanded cannot the wise *men*, the *a*astrologers, the magicians, the soothsayers, shew unto the king;

28 But there is a God in heaven that *a*revealeth *b*secrets, and maketh known to the king Nebuchadnezzar what shall be in the latter days. Thy *c*dream, and the visions of thy head upon thy bed, are these;

29 As for thee, O king, thy thoughts came *into thy mind* upon thy bed, what should come to pass hereafter: and he that *a*revealeth secrets maketh known to thee what shall come to pass.

30 But as for me, this secret is not revealed to me for *any* *a*wisdom that I have more than any living, but *b*for *their* sakes that shall make known the interpretation to the king, and that thou mightest know the thoughts of thy heart.

31 ¶ Thou, O king, sawest, and behold a great *a*image. This great image, whose brightness *was* excellent,

17*a* Dan. 1:6.
19*a* Amos 3:7.
  b TG Dream.
20*a* Dan. 1:17.
21*a* Abr. 3:4.
  b Acts 1:7;
    D&C 88:42 (42–45);
    121:12.
  c Ps. 75:6 (6–7);
    Jer. 27:5 (5–6);
    Dan. 5:20 (18–20).
  d TG Wisdom.
  e Alma 12:10 (9–11);
    D&C 50:24.

    TG Knowledge.
22*a* Alma 26:22;
    D&C 124:5.
  b TG God, Intelligence of.
  c James 1:17;
    D&C 88:50 (49–50).
26*a* Dan. 1:7.
  b Dan. 5:16.
27*a* TG Sorcery;
    Superstitions.
28*a* TG God, Omniscience of;
    Holy Ghost, Gifts of.
  b Gen. 40:8;
    D&C 76:10.

    TG Mysteries of
    Godliness.
  c TG Dream.
29*a* TG Revelation.
30*a* Gen. 41:16;
    Acts 3:12;
    Alma 18:17 (16–34).
  b Aramaic: in order that
    the interpretation may
    be made known to the
    king.
31*a* TG Symbolism.

stood before thee; and [b]the form thereof *was* terrible.

32 This image's head *was* of fine gold, his breast and his arms of silver, his belly and his thighs of brass,

33 His legs of iron, his feet part of iron and part of clay.

34 Thou sawest till that a [a]stone was cut out [b]without hands, which smote the image upon his feet *that were* of iron and clay, and brake them to pieces.

35 Then was the iron, the clay, the brass, the silver, and the gold, broken to pieces together, and became like the chaff of the summer threshingfloors; and the wind carried them away, that no [a]place was found for them: and the [b]stone that smote the image became a great mountain, and filled the whole earth.

36 ¶ This *is* the dream; and we will tell the interpretation thereof before the king.

37 Thou, O king, *art* a king of kings: for the God of heaven hath given thee a [a]kingdom, power, and strength, and glory.

38 And wheresoever the children of men dwell, the beasts of the field and the fowls of the heaven hath he given into thine hand, and hath made thee ruler over them all. Thou *art* this [a]head of gold.

39 And after thee shall arise another [a]kingdom inferior to thee, and another third kingdom of brass, which shall bear [b]rule over all the earth.

40 And the fourth [a]kingdom shall be strong as iron: forasmuch as iron breaketh in pieces and subdueth all *things*: and as iron that breaketh

all these, shall it break in pieces and bruise.

41 And whereas thou sawest the feet and toes, part of potters' clay, and part of iron, the kingdom shall be divided; but there shall be in it of the strength of the [a]iron, forasmuch as thou sawest the iron mixed with miry clay.

42 And *as* the toes of the feet *were* part of iron, and part of clay, *so* the kingdom shall be partly strong, and partly broken.

43 And whereas thou sawest iron mixed with miry clay, they shall mingle themselves with the seed of men: but they shall not cleave one to another, even as iron is not mixed with clay.

44 And in the [a]days of these [b]kings shall the God of heaven [c]set up a [d]kingdom, which shall never be [e]destroyed: and the [f]kingdom shall not be left to other people, *but* it shall [g]break in pieces and [h]consume all these [i]kingdoms, and it shall stand for ever.

45 Forasmuch as thou sawest that the [a]stone was cut out of the mountain without hands, and that it brake in pieces the iron, the brass, the clay, the silver, and the gold; the great God hath made [b]known to the king what shall come to pass hereafter: and the dream *is* certain, and the interpretation thereof sure.

46 ¶ Then the king Nebuchadnezzar fell upon his face, and [a]worshipped Daniel, and commanded that they should offer an oblation and sweet odours unto him.

47 The king answered unto Daniel, and said, Of a truth *it is*, that your [a]God *is* a [b]God of gods, and a [c]Lord of

31*b* Aramaic: its appearance was frightening.
34*a* TG Rock.
  b Dan. 8:25.
35*a* Rev. 20:11.
  b TG Kingdom of God, on Earth; Mission of Latter-day Saints.
37*a* TG Governments.
38*a* Dan. 7:4.
39*a* Dan. 5:28; 7:5.
  b TG Authority.

40*a* Dan. 7:7.
41*a* Dan. 7:7.
44*a* TG Last Days.
  b TG Nations.
  c TG Millennium, Preparing a People for.
  d TG Dispensations; Jesus Christ, Millennial Reign; Kingdom of God, on Earth; Restoration of the Gospel.
  e Dan. 6:26; Matt. 21:43.

f D&C 138:44.
g Isa. 60:12; 1 Cor. 15:24.
h Hag. 2:22.
  TG Missionary Work.
i D&C 103:7.
45*a* D&C 65:2.
  b TG Revelation.
46*a* Acts 14:15 (11–15); 1 Ne. 17:55.
47*a* 1 Cor. 8:6 (5–6).
  b 2 Kgs. 5:15; Rev. 19:6.
  c Rev. 17:14.

kings, and a revealer of secrets, seeing thou couldest reveal this secret.

48 Then the king made Daniel a *a*great man, and gave him many great gifts, and made him ruler over the whole province of Babylon, and chief of the governors over all the wise *men* of Babylon.

49 Then Daniel requested of the king, and he *a*set Shadrach, Meshach, and Abed-nego, over the affairs of the province of Babylon: but Daniel *b*sat in the gate of the king.

CHAPTER 3

Nebuchadnezzar creates a golden image and commands all men to worship it—Shadrach, Meshach, and Abed-nego refuse and are cast into the fiery furnace—They are preserved and come out unharmed.

NEBUCHADNEZZAR the king made an image of gold, whose height *was* threescore cubits, *and* the breadth thereof six cubits: he set it up in the plain of Dura, in the province of Babylon.

2 Then Nebuchadnezzar the king sent to gather together the princes, the governors, and the captains, the judges, the treasurers, the counsellors, the sheriffs, and all the rulers of the provinces, to come to the dedication of the image which Nebuchadnezzar the king had set up.

3 Then the princes, the governors, and captains, the judges, the treasurers, the counsellors, the sheriffs, and all the rulers of the provinces, were gathered together unto the dedication of the image that Nebuchadnezzar the king had set up; and they stood before the image that Nebuchadnezzar had set up.

4 Then an herald cried aloud, To you it is commanded, O people, nations, and *a*languages,

5 *That* at what time ye hear the sound of the cornet, flute, *a*harp, *b*sackbut, psaltery, *c*dulcimer, and all kinds of musick, ye fall down and worship the golden image that Nebuchadnezzar the king hath set up:

6 And whoso falleth not down and worshippeth shall the same hour be *a*cast into the midst of a *b*burning fiery furnace.

7 Therefore at that time, when all the people heard the sound of the cornet, flute, harp, sackbut, psaltery, and all kinds of musick, all the people, the nations, and the languages, fell down *and* worshipped the golden image that Nebuchadnezzar the king had set up.

8 ¶ Wherefore at that time certain Chaldeans came near, and accused the Jews.

9 They spake and said to the king Nebuchadnezzar, O king, live for ever.

10 Thou, O king, hast made a decree, that every man that shall hear the sound of the cornet, flute, harp, sackbut, psaltery, and dulcimer, and all kinds of musick, shall fall down and worship the golden image:

11 And whoso falleth not down and worshippeth, *that* he should be cast into the midst of a burning fiery furnace.

12 There are certain Jews whom thou hast *a*set over the affairs of the province of Babylon, Shadrach, Meshach, and Abed-nego; these men, O king, have not regarded thee: they serve not thy gods, nor worship the golden image which thou hast set up.

13 ¶ Then Nebuchadnezzar in *his* rage and fury commanded to bring Shadrach, Meshach, and Abed-nego. Then they brought these men before the king.

14 Nebuchadnezzar spake and said unto them, *Is it* true, O Shadrach, Meshach, and Abed-nego, do not ye

---

48*a* Gen. 41:40.
49*a* Dan. 3:12.
  b OR remained at the king's court.
3 4*a* TG Language.

5*a* 2 Sam. 6:5;
  1 Chr. 15:16.
  b The Aramaic word denotes a triangular stringed instrument.

  c Aramaic: bagpipe.
6*a* TG Tyranny.
  b Mosiah 17:13 (13–20).
12*a* Dan. 2:49.

serve my gods, nor worship the golden image which I have set up?

15 Now if ye be ready that at what time ye hear the sound of the cornet, flute, harp, sackbut, psaltery, and dulcimer, and all kinds of musick, ye fall down and worship the image which I have made; *well:* but if ye worship not, ye shall be cast the same hour into the midst of a burning fiery furnace; and who *is* that God that shall deliver you out of my hands?

16 Shadrach, Meshach, and Abed-nego, answered and said to the king, O Nebuchadnezzar, we *are* not *a*careful to answer thee in this matter.

17 If it be *so,* our God whom we serve is able to *a*deliver us from the burning fiery furnace, and he will deliver *us* out of thine hand, O king.

18 But if not, be it known unto thee, O king, that we will not *a*serve thy gods, nor worship the golden image which thou hast set up.

19 ¶ Then was Nebuchadnezzar full of fury, and the *a*form of his visage was changed against Shadrach, Meshach, and Abed-nego: *therefore* he spake, and commanded that they should heat the furnace one seven times more than it was wont to be heated.

20 And he commanded the most mighty men that *were* in his army to bind Shadrach, Meshach, and Abed-nego, *and* to cast *them* into the burning fiery furnace.

21 Then these men were bound in their coats, their hosen, and their hats, and their *other* garments, and were cast into the midst of the burning fiery furnace.

22 Therefore because the king's commandment was urgent, and the furnace exceeding hot, the flame of the fire slew those men that took up Shadrach, Meshach, and Abed-nego.

23 And these three men, Shadrach, Meshach, and Abed-nego, fell down bound into the midst of the burning fiery furnace.

24 Then Nebuchadnezzar the king was astonied, and rose up in haste, *and* spake, and said unto his counsellors, Did not we cast three men bound into the midst of the fire? They answered and said unto the king, True, O king.

25 He answered and said, Lo, I see four men loose, walking in the midst of the fire, and they have no *a*hurt; and the form of the fourth is like the Son of God.

26 ¶ Then Nebuchadnezzar came near to the mouth of the burning fiery furnace, *and* spake, and said, Shadrach, Meshach, and Abed-nego, ye servants of the most high God, come forth, and come *hither.* Then Shadrach, Meshach, and Abed-nego, came forth of the midst of the fire.

27 And the princes, governors, and captains, and the king's counsellors, being gathered together, saw these men, upon whose bodies the *a*fire had no power, nor was an hair of their head singed, neither were their coats *b*changed, nor the smell of fire had passed on them.

28 *Then* Nebuchadnezzar spake, and said, Blessed *be* the God of Shadrach, Meshach, and Abed-nego, who hath sent his *a*angel, and delivered his servants that *b*trusted in him, and *c*have changed the king's word, and yielded their bodies, that they might not serve nor worship any god, except their own God.

29 Therefore I make a decree, That every people, nation, and language, which speak any thing amiss against the God of Shadrach, Meshach, and Abed-nego, shall be *a*cut in pieces, and their houses shall be made a dunghill: because there is no other God that can *b*deliver after this sort.

16a Matt. 10:19;
     Acts 20:24.
17a TG Deliver.
18a Ex. 1:17 (16–17).
19a OR expression of his
     countenance.
25a Ps. 91:6 (3–9);

3 Ne. 28:21.
27a Isa. 43:2;
     Heb. 11:34 (32–34);
     4 Ne. 1:32.
   b OR damaged.
28a TG Angels.
   b TG Trustworthiness.

c IE were successful
   in defying the king's
   decree.
29a Dan. 2:5.
   b Mark 9:23 (17–29).

30 Then the king ^apromoted Shadrach, Meshach, and Abed-nego, in the province of Babylon.

CHAPTER 4

Daniel interprets Nebuchadnezzar's dream of the great tree, describing the king's fall and madness—The king learns that the Most High rules and sets the basest of men over earthly kingdoms.

NEBUCHADNEZZAR the king, unto all people, nations, and languages, that dwell in all the earth; Peace be multiplied unto you.

2 I thought it good to shew the signs and wonders that the high God hath wrought toward me.

3 How great *are* his signs! and how mighty *are* his wonders! his ^akingdom *is* an everlasting kingdom, and his dominion *is* from generation to generation.

4 ¶ I Nebuchadnezzar was at rest in mine house, and ^aflourishing in my palace:

5 I saw a dream which made me afraid, and the thoughts upon my bed and the visions of my head troubled me.

6 Therefore made I a decree to bring in all the ^awise *men* of Babylon before me, that they might make known unto me the interpretation of the dream.

7 Then came in the ^amagicians, the astrologers, the Chaldeans, and the soothsayers: and I told the dream before them; but they did not make known unto me the interpretation thereof.

8 ¶ But at the last Daniel came in before me, whose name *was* Belteshazzar, according to the name of my god, and in whom *is* the spirit of the holy ^agods: and before him I told the dream, *saying,*

9 O Belteshazzar, master of the magicians, because I know that the spirit of the holy gods *is* in thee, and no secret troubleth thee, tell me the visions of my dream that I have seen, and the interpretation thereof.

10 Thus *were* the visions of mine head in my bed; I saw, and behold a tree in the midst of the earth, and the height thereof *was* great.

11 The tree grew, and was strong, and the height thereof reached unto heaven, and the sight thereof to the end of all the earth:

12 The leaves thereof *were* fair, and the fruit thereof much, and in it *was* meat for all: the beasts of the field had shadow under it, and the fowls of the heaven dwelt in the boughs thereof, and all flesh was fed of it.

13 I saw in the visions of my head upon my bed, and, behold, a watcher and an holy one came down from heaven;

14 He cried aloud, and said thus, Hew down the tree, and cut off his branches, shake off his leaves, and scatter his fruit: let the beasts get away from under it, and the fowls from his branches:

15 Nevertheless leave the stump of his roots in the earth, even with a band of iron and brass, in the tender grass of the field; and let it be wet with the dew of heaven, and *let* his portion *be* with the beasts in the grass of the earth:

16 Let his heart be changed from man's, and let a beast's heart be given unto him; and let seven ^atimes pass over him.

17 This matter *is* by the decree of the watchers, and the demand by the word of the holy ones: to the intent that the living may know that the most High ruleth in the kingdom of men, and giveth it to whomsoever he will, and setteth up over it the ^abasest of men.

18 This dream I king Nebuchadnezzar have seen. Now thou, O Belteshazzar, declare the interpretation thereof, forasmuch as all the wise *men* of my kingdom are not able to make known unto me the

---

interpretation: but thou *art* able; for the ᵃspirit of the ᵇholy gods *is* in thee.

19 ¶ Then Daniel, whose name *was* Belteshazzar, was astonied for one hour, and his thoughts troubled him. The king spake, and said, Belteshazzar, let not the dream, or the interpretation thereof, trouble thee. Belteshazzar answered and said, My lord, the dream *be* to them that hate thee, and the interpretation thereof to thine enemies.

20 The tree that thou sawest, which grew, and was strong, whose height reached unto the heaven, and the sight thereof to all the earth;

21 Whose leaves *were* fair, and the fruit thereof much, and in it *was* meat for all; under which the beasts of the field dwelt, and upon whose branches the fowls of the heaven had their habitation:

22 It *is* thou, O king, that art grown and become strong: for thy greatness is grown, and reacheth unto heaven, and thy ᵃdominion to the end of the earth.

23 And whereas the king saw a watcher and an holy one coming down from heaven, and saying, Hew the tree down, and destroy it; yet leave the stump of the roots thereof in the earth, even with a band of iron and brass, in the tender grass of the field; and let it be wet with the dew of heaven, and *let* his portion *be* with the beasts of the field, till seven times pass over him;

24 This *is* the interpretation, O king, and this *is* the decree of the most High, which is come upon my lord the king:

25 That they shall drive thee from men, and thy dwelling shall be with the beasts of the field, and they shall make thee to eat grass as oxen, and they shall wet thee with the dew of heaven, and seven times shall pass over thee, till thou know that the most High ruleth in the kingdom of men, and giveth it to whomsoever he will.

26 And whereas they commanded to leave the stump of the tree roots; thy kingdom shall be sure unto thee, after that thou shalt have known that the heavens do rule.

27 Wherefore, O king, let my counsel be acceptable unto thee, and break off thy sins by righteousness, and thine iniquities by shewing ᵃmercy to the poor; ᵇif it may be a lengthening of thy tranquillity.

28 ¶ All this came upon the king Nebuchadnezzar.

29 At the end of twelve months he walked in the palace of the kingdom of Babylon.

30 The king spake, and said, Is not this great Babylon, that I have built ᵃfor the house of the kingdom by the might of my power, and for the honour of my majesty?

31 While the word *was* in the king's mouth, there fell a voice from heaven, *saying*, O king Nebuchadnezzar, to thee it is spoken; The kingdom is ᵃdeparted from thee.

32 And they shall drive thee from men, and thy dwelling *shall be* with the beasts of the field: they shall make thee to eat grass as oxen, and seven times shall pass over thee, until thou know that the most High ruleth in the kingdom of men, and giveth it to whomsoever he will.

33 The same hour was the thing fulfilled upon Nebuchadnezzar: and he was driven from men, and did eat grass as oxen, and his body was wet with the dew of heaven, till his hairs were grown like eagles' *feathers*, and his nails like birds' *claws*.

34 And at the end of ᵃthe days I Nebuchadnezzar lifted up mine eyes unto heaven, and mine understanding returned unto me, and I blessed the most High, and I praised and honoured him that liveth for ever, whose dominion *is* an everlasting dominion, and his

---

18*a* TG God, Spirit of; Inspiration.
  b TG Holiness.
22*a* Jer. 27:7 (6–8).

27*a* Mosiah 4:21 (16–21); D&C 42:31 (30–39).
  b OR so that your prosperity may be long.

30*a* OR as a royal residence.
31*a* Dan. 5:20.
34*a* IE the seven years.

kingdom *is* from generation to generation:

35 And all the inhabitants of the earth *are* reputed as *a*nothing: and he doeth according to his *b*will in the army of heaven, and *among* the inhabitants of the earth: and none can *c*stay his hand, or say unto him, What doest thou?

36 At the same time my reason returned unto me; and for the glory of my kingdom, mine honour and brightness returned unto me; and my counsellors and my lords sought unto me; and I was established in my kingdom, and excellent majesty was added unto me.

37 Now I Nebuchadnezzar praise and extol and honour the King of heaven, all whose works *are* truth, and his ways *a*judgment: and those that *b*walk in pride he is able to *c*abase.

CHAPTER 5

Belshazzar and his revelers drink from the vessels of the temple—A hand writes upon the wall, telling of Belshazzar's downfall—Daniel interprets the words and reproves the king for pride and idolatry—That night Babylon is conquered.

BELSHAZZAR the king made a great feast to a thousand of his lords, and drank wine before the thousand.

2 Belshazzar, whiles he tasted the wine, commanded to bring the golden and silver *a*vessels which his father Nebuchadnezzar had taken out of the temple which *was* in Jerusalem; that the king, and his princes, his wives, and his concubines, might drink therein.

3 Then they brought the golden vessels that were taken out of the temple of the house of God which *was* at Jerusalem; and the king, and his princes, his wives, and his concubines, drank in them.

4 They drank wine, and praised the gods of gold, and of silver, of brass, of iron, of wood, and of stone.

5 ¶ In the same hour came forth fingers of a man's hand, and wrote *a*over against the candlestick upon the plaster of the wall of the king's palace: and the king saw the part of the *b*hand that wrote.

6 Then the king's *a*countenance was changed, and his thoughts *b*troubled him, so that *c*the joints of his loins were loosed, and his knees smote one against another.

7 The king cried aloud to bring in the *a*astrologers, the Chaldeans, and the soothsayers. *And* the king spake, and said to the wise *men* of Babylon, Whosoever shall read this writing, and shew me the interpretation thereof, shall be clothed with scarlet, and *have* a chain of gold about his neck, and shall be the third ruler in the kingdom.

8 Then came in all the king's wise *men:* but they could not read the writing, nor make known to the king the interpretation thereof.

9 Then was king Belshazzar greatly troubled, and his countenance was changed in him, and his lords were astonied.

10 ¶ *Now* the queen, by reason of the words of the king and his lords, came into the banquet house: *and* the queen spake and said, O king, live for ever: let not thy thoughts trouble thee, nor let thy countenance be changed:

11 There is a man in thy kingdom, in whom *is* the *a*spirit of the holy gods; and in the days of thy father light and understanding and wisdom, like the wisdom of the gods, was found in him; whom the king Nebuchadnezzar thy father, the king, *I say,* thy father, made master of the magicians, astrologers, Chaldeans, *and* soothsayers;

35*a* Ps. 39:5; Isa. 40:15;
   Hel. 12:7;
   Moses 1:10.
  b TG God, Will of.
  c D&C 38:33; 121:33.
37*a* OR justice.
  b TG Walking in

   Darkness.
  c OR humble.
5 2*a* Num. 18:3;
   Dan. 1:2.
  5*a* OR opposite the
   lampstand.
  b Ether 3:6;

   Abr. 3:12 (11–12).
  6*a* Alma 18:12.
  b Alma 42:29.
  c OR his hip joints.
  7*a* TG Sorcery.
  11*a* TG God, Spirit of;
   Inspiration.

12 Forasmuch as an excellent spirit, and knowledge, and understanding, interpreting of dreams, and shewing of hard sentences, and dissolving of doubts, were found in the same Daniel, whom the king [a]named Belteshazzar: now let Daniel be called, and he will shew the interpretation.

13 Then was Daniel brought in before the king. *And* the king spake and said unto Daniel, *Art* thou that Daniel, which *art* of the children of the captivity of Judah, whom the king my father brought out of Jewry?

14 I have even heard of thee, that the spirit of the [a]gods *is* in thee, and *that* light and understanding and excellent wisdom is found in thee.

15 And now the wise *men*, the [a]astrologers, have been brought in before me, that they should read this writing, and make known unto me the interpretation thereof: but they could not shew the interpretation of the thing:

16 And I have heard of thee, that thou canst make interpretations, and dissolve doubts: now if thou canst read the [a]writing, and make [b]known to me the interpretation thereof, thou shalt be clothed with scarlet, and *have* a chain of gold about thy neck, and shalt be the third ruler in the kingdom.

17 ¶ Then Daniel answered and said before the king, Let thy [a]gifts be to thyself, and give thy rewards to another; yet I will read the writing unto the king, and make known to him the interpretation.

18 O thou king, the most high God gave Nebuchadnezzar thy father a kingdom, and majesty, and glory, and honour:

19 And for the majesty that he gave him, all people, nations, and languages, trembled and feared before him: whom he would he slew; and whom he would he kept alive; and whom he would he set up; and whom he would he put down.

20 But when his [a]heart was lifted up, and his [b]mind hardened in pride, he was [c]deposed from his kingly throne, and they took his glory from him:

21 And he was driven [a]from the sons of men; and his heart was made like the beasts, and his dwelling *was* with the wild asses: they fed him with grass like oxen, and his body was wet with the dew of heaven; till he knew that the most high God ruled in the kingdom of men, and *that* he appointeth over it whomsoever he will.

22 And thou his son, O Belshazzar, hast not humbled thine heart, though thou knewest all this;

23 But hast lifted up thyself against the Lord of heaven; and they have brought the vessels of his house before thee, and thou, and thy lords, thy wives, and thy concubines, have drunk wine in them; and thou hast praised the [a]gods of silver, and gold, of brass, iron, wood, and stone, which see not, nor hear, nor know: and the God in whose hand thy breath *is*, and whose *are* all thy ways, hast thou not glorified:

24 Then was the part of the hand sent from him; and this writing was written.

25 ¶ And this *is* the writing that was written, MENE, MENE, TEKEL, UPHARSIN.

26 This *is* the interpretation of the thing: [a]MENE; God hath [b]numbered thy kingdom, and finished it.

27 [a]TEKEL; Thou art [b]weighed in the balances, and art found wanting.

28 [a]PERES; Thy kingdom is divided, and given to the Medes and [b]Persians.

12a Dan. 1:7.
14a Dan. 2:11.
15a TG Sorcery.
16a Alma 10:2.
  b Dan. 2:26;
    Mosiah 8:13 (13–18);
    D&C 8:1 (1–5).
17a 2 Kgs. 5:16.

20a TG Hardheartedness.
  b TG Mind.
  c Ps. 75:6 (6–7);
    Jer. 27:5 (5–6);
    Dan. 2:21; 4:31 (30–31).
21a Alma 30:56.
23a TG Idolatry.
26a Aramaic: numbered.

  b Jer. 25:12.
27a Aramaic: shekel, or
    weight.
  b Job 31:6.
28a Aramaic: division.
    JST Dan. 5:28
    UPHARSIN . . .
  b Dan. 2:39; 7:5.

29 Then commanded Belshazzar, and they *a*clothed Daniel with scarlet, and *put* a chain of gold about his neck, and made a proclamation concerning him, that he should be the third ruler in the kingdom.

30 ¶ In that night was Belshazzar the king of the *a*Chaldeans *b*slain.

31 And *a*Darius the Median took the kingdom, *being* about threescore and two years old.

CHAPTER 6

Darius makes Daniel the first of his presidents—Daniel worships the Lord in defiance of a decree of Darius—He is cast into the den of lions—His faith saves him, and Darius decrees that all people are to revere the God of Daniel.

IT pleased Darius to set over the kingdom an hundred and twenty princes, which should be over the whole kingdom;

2 And over these three presidents; of whom Daniel *was* *a*first: that the princes might give accounts unto them, and the king should have no damage.

3 Then this Daniel was preferred above the presidents and princes, because an excellent *a*spirit *was* in him; and the king thought to set him *b*over the whole realm.

4 ¶ Then the presidents and princes sought to find *a*occasion against Daniel concerning the kingdom; but they could find none occasion nor fault; forasmuch as he *was* faithful, neither was there any error or fault found in him.

5 Then said these men, We shall not find any occasion against this Daniel, except we find *it* against him concerning the law of his God.

6 Then these presidents and princes assembled together to the king, and said thus unto him, King Darius, live for ever.

7 All the presidents of the kingdom, the governors, and the princes, the counsellors, and the captains, have consulted together to establish a royal statute, and to make a firm decree, that whosoever shall ask a petition of any God or man for thirty days, save of thee, O king, he shall be *a*cast into the den of lions.

8 Now, O king, establish the decree, and sign the writing, that it be not changed, according to the law of the Medes and Persians, which *a*altereth not.

9 Wherefore king Darius signed the writing and the decree.

10 ¶ Now when Daniel knew that the writing was signed, he went into his house; and his windows being open in his chamber toward *a*Jerusalem, he kneeled upon his knees *b*three times a day, and *c*prayed, and gave *d*thanks before his God, as he did aforetime.

11 Then these men assembled, and found Daniel praying and making supplication before his God.

12 Then they came near, and spake before the king concerning the king's decree; Hast thou not signed a decree, that every man that shall ask *a petition* of any God or man within thirty days, save of thee, O king, shall be cast into the den of lions? The king answered and said, The thing *is* true, according to the law of the Medes and Persians, which altereth not.

13 Then answered they and said before the king, That *a*Daniel, which *is* of the children of the captivity of Judah, regardeth not thee, O king, nor the decree that thou hast signed, but maketh his petition three times a day.

14 Then the king, when he heard *these* words, was sore displeased with himself, and set *his* heart on

---

29*a* Gen. 41:42; Esth. 8:15.
30*a* Jer. 51:31 (31, 39).
　b Isa. 41:2; 45:1.
31*a* Dan. 11:1.
6 2*a* OR one.
　3*a* TG God, Spirit of.

　　b Gen. 41:41 (38–45);
　　　Esth. 10:3; Dan. 8:27.
4*a* D&C 64:8; 88:124.
7*a* TG Tyranny.
8*a* IE cannot be revoked,
　　once signed.

10*a* 1 Kgs. 8:48 (44–48);
　　Ps. 5:7.
　b Alma 34:21.
　c TG Prayer.
　d TG Thanksgiving.
13*a* Dan. 1:6.

Daniel to deliver him: and he laboured till the going down of the sun to deliver him.

15 Then these men assembled unto the king, and said unto the king, Know, O king, that the law of the Medes and Persians *is*, That no decree nor statute which the king establisheth may be changed.

16 Then the king commanded, and they brought Daniel, and cast *him* into the den of lions. *Now* the king spake and said unto Daniel, Thy God whom thou servest continually, he will deliver thee.

17 And a stone was brought, and laid upon the mouth of the den; and the king *a*sealed it with his own signet, and with the signet of his lords; that the purpose might not be changed concerning Daniel.

18 ¶ Then the king went to his palace, and passed the night fasting: neither were instruments of musick brought before him: and his sleep went from him.

19 Then the king arose very early in the morning, and went in haste unto the den of lions.

20 And when he came to the den, he cried with a lamentable voice unto Daniel: *and* the king spake and said to Daniel, O Daniel, *a*servant of the living God, is thy God, whom thou servest continually, able to deliver thee from the lions?

21 Then said Daniel unto the king, O king, live for ever.

22 My God hath sent his *a*angel, and hath shut the *b*lions' mouths, that they have not hurt me: forasmuch as before him innocency was found in me; and also before thee, O king, have I done no hurt.

23 Then was the king exceeding glad for him, and commanded that they should take Daniel up out of the den. So Daniel was taken up out of the den, and no manner of

hurt was found upon him, because he *a*believed in his God.

24 ¶ And the king commanded, and they brought those men which had accused Daniel, and they cast *them* into the den of lions, them, their children, and their wives; and the lions *a*had the mastery of them, and brake all their bones in pieces or ever they came at the bottom of the den.

25 ¶ Then king Darius wrote unto all people, nations, and languages, that dwell in all the earth; Peace be multiplied unto you.

26 I make a decree, That in every dominion of my kingdom men tremble and fear before the God of Daniel: for he *is* the *a*living God, and *b*steadfast for ever, and his kingdom *that* which shall not be *c*destroyed, and his dominion *shall be even* unto the end.

27 He *a*delivereth and rescueth, and he worketh signs and wonders in heaven and in earth, who hath *b*delivered Daniel from the power of the lions.

28 So this Daniel prospered in the reign of *a*Darius, and in the reign of *b*Cyrus the Persian.

CHAPTER 7

Daniel sees four beasts representing the kingdoms of men—He sees the ancient of days (Adam) to whom the Son of Man (Christ) will come—The kingdom will be given to the Saints forever.

IN the first year of Belshazzar king of Babylon Daniel had a *a*dream and visions of his head upon his bed: then he wrote the dream, *and* told the sum of the matters.

2 Daniel spake and said, I saw in my vision by night, and, behold, the four winds of the heaven strove upon the great sea.

3 And four great *a*beasts came up

17*a* TG Seal.
20*a* TG Servant.
22*a* TG Angels.
  b Heb. 11:33.
23*a* TG Faith.
24*a* OR overpowered them.

26*a* Alma 7:6;
    D&C 14:9; 20:19.
  b TG Steadfastness.
  c Dan. 2:44.
27*a* D&C 108:8.
  b TG Deliver.

28*a* Ezra 1:1 (1–2); 4:5.
  b Ezra 6:14 (14–15).
7 1*a* TG Dream.
  3*a* TG Symbolism.

from the *b*sea, diverse one from another.

4 The *a*first *was* like a lion, and had eagle's wings: I beheld till the wings thereof were plucked, and it was lifted up from the earth, and made stand upon the feet as a man, and a man's heart was given to it.

5 And behold another *a*beast, a second, like to a bear, and it raised up itself on one side, and *it had* three ribs in the mouth of it between the teeth of it: and they said thus unto it, Arise, devour much flesh.

6 After this I beheld, and lo another, like a leopard, which had upon the back of it four wings of a fowl; the beast had also four *a*heads; and dominion was given to it.

7 After this I saw in the night visions, and behold a fourth *a*beast, dreadful and terrible, and strong exceedingly; and it had great *b*iron teeth: it devoured and brake in pieces, and stamped the residue with the feet of it: and it *was* diverse from all the beasts that *were* before it; and it had *c*ten horns.

8 I considered the horns, and, behold, there came up among them another little *a*horn, before whom there were three of the first horns plucked up by the roots: and, behold, in this horn *were* eyes like the eyes of man, and a *b*mouth speaking great things.

9 ¶ I beheld till the *a*thrones were *b*cast down, and the *c*Ancient of days did sit, whose *d*garment *was* white as snow, and the hair of his head like the pure wool: his throne *was like* the fiery flame, *and* his *e*wheels *as* burning fire.

10 A fiery stream issued and came forth from before him: *a*thousand thousands ministered unto him, and ten thousand times ten thousand stood before him: the *b*judgment was set, and the *c*books were opened.

11 I beheld then because of the voice of the great words which the horn spake: I beheld *even* till the *a*beast was slain, and his body destroyed, and given to the burning *b*flame.

12 As concerning the rest of the beasts, they had their dominion taken away: yet their lives were prolonged for a season and time.

13 I saw in the night visions, and, behold, *one* like the *a*Son of man came with the *b*clouds of heaven, and came to the Ancient of days, and they brought him near before him.

14 And there was given him *a*dominion, and glory, and a *b*kingdom, that all people, nations, and languages, should serve him: his dominion *is* an *c*everlasting dominion, which shall not pass away, and his kingdom *that* which shall not be destroyed.

15 ¶ I Daniel was grieved in my spirit in the midst of *my* body, and the visions of my head troubled me.

16 I came near unto one of them that stood by, and asked him the truth of all this. So he told me, and made me know the interpretation of the things.

17 These great beasts, which are four, *are* four *a*kings, *which* shall arise out of the earth.

18 But the *a*saints of the most High shall take the kingdom, and possess

3*b* Rev. 13:1 (1–2);
     JST Rev. 13:1 (Rev. 13:1
     note *a*).
4*a* Dan. 2:38.
5*a* Dan. 2:39; 5:28.
6*a* Dan. 8:8; 11:4 (3–4).
7*a* Dan. 2:40.
   b Dan. 2:41.
   c Dan. 7:24 (20–24).
8*a* Dan. 8:9.
   b Rev. 13:5.
9*a* 1 Cor. 15:24.
     TG Kings, Earthly.
   b Aramaic: set up.

   c D&C 138:38.
     TG Adam.
   d TG Clothing.
   e Ezek. 1:15.
10*a* Rev. 5:11.
    b Rev. 11:18.
     TG Judgment, the Last.
    c Mal. 3:16; Rev. 20:12.
11*a* Rev. 19:20;
     D&C 76:36.
    b Rev. 20:10;
     D&C 29:28 (21, 26–30);
     43:33.
13*a* Rev. 11:15.

     TG Jesus Christ, Second
     Coming; Jesus Christ,
     Son of Man.
    b Luke 21:27.
14*a* TG Jesus Christ,
     Authority of;
     Jesus Christ, Judge;
     Judgment; Kingdom of
     God, on Earth.
    b TG Millennium.
    c TG Jesus Christ,
     Millennial Reign.
17*a* IE kingdoms.
18*a* TG Saints.

the kingdom for ever, even for ever and ever.

19 Then I would know the truth of the fourth beast, which was diverse from all the others, exceeding dreadful, whose teeth *were of* iron, and his nails *of* brass; *which* devoured, brake in pieces, and stamped the residue with his feet;

20 And of the ten horns that *were* in his head, and *of* the other which came up, and before whom three fell; even *of* that horn that had eyes, and a mouth that spake very great things, whose look *was* more stout than his fellows.

21 I beheld, and the same horn made ^awar with the saints, and prevailed against them;

22 Until the ^aAncient of days came, and ^bjudgment was given to the ^csaints of the most High; and the time came that the saints possessed the kingdom.

23 Thus he said, The fourth beast shall be the fourth kingdom upon earth, which shall be diverse from all kingdoms, and shall devour the whole earth, and shall tread it down, and break it in pieces.

24 And the ten ^ahorns out of this kingdom *are* ^bten kings *that* shall arise: and another shall rise after them; and he shall be diverse from the first, and he shall subdue three kings.

25 And he shall speak *great* words against the most High, and shall ^awear out the saints of the most High, and think to change times and laws: and they shall be given into his hand until a time and times and the dividing of time.

26 But the ^ajudgment shall sit, and they shall take away his dominion, to consume and to destroy *it* unto the end.

27 And the ^akingdom and dominion, and the greatness of the kingdom under the whole heaven, shall be ^bgiven to the people of the saints of the most High, whose kingdom *is* an ^ceverlasting kingdom, and all dominions shall serve and obey him.

28 Hitherto *is* the end of the matter. As for me Daniel, my ^acogitations much troubled me, and my countenance changed in me: but I kept the matter in my heart.

CHAPTER 8

Daniel sees in vision a ram (Media and Persia), a goat (Greece), four other kings, and then, in the last days, a fierce king who will destroy the holy people—This king will be broken when he stands up against the Prince of Princes.

IN the third year of the reign of king Belshazzar a vision appeared unto me, *even unto me* Daniel, after that which appeared unto me at the first.

2 And I saw in a vision; and it came to pass, when I saw, that I *was* at Shushan *in* the palace, which *is* in the province of Elam; and I saw in a vision, and I was by the ^ariver of Ulai.

3 Then I lifted up mine eyes, and saw, and, behold, there stood before the river a ^aram which had *two* horns: and the *two* horns *were* high; but one *was* higher than the other, and the higher came up last.

4 I saw the ram ^apushing westward, and northward, and southward; so that no beasts might stand before him, neither *was there any* that could deliver out of his hand; but he ^bdid according to his will, and became great.

5 And as I was considering, behold, an he ^agoat came from the west on the face of the whole earth, and touched not the ground: and the

---

21*a* Dan. 8:24;
      Rev. 12:17 (8–17).
   TG Last Days;
      War.
22*a* D&C 27:11; 116.
   b 1 Cor. 6:2;
      Rev. 20:4.
   TG Judgment.

c D&C 20:13.
24*a* Rev. 17:12.
   b Dan. 7:7.
25*a* Rev. 12:13 (13–17).
26*a* TG Judgment, the Last.
27*a* D&C 136:41 (41–42).
   b D&C 103:7 (7–8).
   c TG Eternity.

28*a* OR thoughts.
8 2*a* HEB water-course.
      Dan. 8:16;
      1 Ne. 11:1 (1–5).
3*a* Dan. 8:20.
4*a* Dan. 11:40.
   b Dan. 11:3.
5*a* Dan. 8:21.

goat *had* a notable horn between his eyes.

6 And he came to the ram that had *two* horns, which I had seen standing before the river, and ran unto him in the fury of his power.

7 And I saw him come close unto the ram, and he was ªmoved with ᵇcholer against him, and smote the ram, and brake his two horns: and there was no power in the ram to stand before him, but he cast him down to the ground, and stamped upon him: and there was none that could deliver the ram out of his hand.

8 Therefore the he goat waxed very great: and when he was strong, the great horn was broken; and ªfor it came up ᵇfour notable ones toward the four winds of heaven.

9 And out of one of them came forth a little ªhorn, which waxed exceeding great, toward the south, and toward the east, and toward the pleasant *land*.

10 And it waxed great, *even* ªto the host of heaven; and it cast down *some* of the host and of the stars to the ground, and stamped upon them.

11 Yea, he magnified *himself* even to the prince of the host, and by him the ªdaily ᵇsacrifice was taken away, and the place of his sanctuary was ᶜcast down.

12 And an host was given *him* against the daily *sacrifice* by reason of transgression, and it cast down the truth to the ground; and it practised, and prospered.

13 ¶ Then I heard one ªsaint speaking, and another saint said unto that certain *saint* which spake, How long *shall be* the vision *concerning* the daily *sacrifice*, and the transgression of desolation, to give both

the sanctuary and the host to be trodden under foot?

14 And he said unto me, Unto two thousand and three hundred days; then shall the sanctuary be cleansed.

15 ¶ And it came to pass, when I, *even* I Daniel, had seen the vision, and sought for the meaning, then, behold, there stood before me as the appearance of a man.

16 And I heard a man's voice between *the ªbanks of* Ulai, which called, and said, ᵇGabriel, make this *man* to understand the vision.

17 So he came near where I stood: and when he came, I was afraid, and fell upon my face: but he said unto me, Understand, O son of man: for at the time of the end *shall be* the vision.

18 Now as he was speaking with me, I was in a deep sleep on my face toward the ground: but he ªtouched me, and set me upright.

19 And he said, Behold, I will make thee know what shall be ªin the last end of the indignation: for at the time appointed the end *shall be.*

20 The ªram which thou sawest having *two* horns *are* the kings of Media and Persia.

21 And the rough ªgoat *is* the king of ᵇGrecia: and the great horn that *is* between his eyes *is* the first king.

22 Now that being ªbroken, whereas four stood up for it, four kingdoms shall stand up out of the nation, but not in his power.

23 And in the latter time of their kingdom, when the transgressors are come to the full, a king of fierce countenance, and understanding ªdark sentences, shall stand up.

24 And his power shall be mighty, but not by his own power: and he shall ªdestroy wonderfully, and shall prosper, and practise, and shall

---

7*a* HEB enraged.
  b Dan. 11:11.
8*a* HEB instead of it.
  b Dan. 7:6; 11:4 (3–4).
9*a* Dan. 7:8.
10*a* OR against.
11*a* Ex. 29:38.
  b Dan. 12:11.
  c Ezek. 7:21 (20–21);

Dan. 11:31.
13*a* TG Saints.
16*a* Dan. 8:2.
  b Dan. 9:21;
    Luke 1:19 (19, 26);
    D&C 128:21.
18*a* Dan. 9:21.
19*a* IE in the latter part
    of the period of

indignation, or in the
  last days.
20*a* Dan. 8:3.
21*a* Dan. 8:5.
  b Dan. 10:20; 11:2.
22*a* Dan. 11:4.
23*a* HEB riddles.
24*a* Dan. 7:21.

[b]destroy the mighty and the [c]holy people.

25 And through his policy also he shall cause craft to prosper in his hand; and he shall magnify *himself* in his heart, and [a]by peace shall destroy many: he shall also stand up against the Prince of princes; but he shall be broken [b]without hand.

26 And the vision of the evening and the morning which was told *is* true: wherefore shut thou up the vision; for it [a]*shall be* for many days.

27 And I Daniel fainted, and was sick *certain* days; afterward I rose up, and did the [a]king's business; and I was astonished at the vision, but none understood *it*.

CHAPTER 9

Daniel fasts, confesses, and prays for all Israel—Gabriel reveals the time of the coming of the Messiah, who will make reconciliation for iniquity—The Messiah will be cut off.

In the first year of [a]Darius the son of Ahasuerus, of the seed of the Medes, which was made king over the realm of the Chaldeans;

2 In the first year of his reign I Daniel understood by books the number of the years, whereof the word of the Lord came to Jeremiah the prophet, that he would accomplish [a]seventy years in the [b]desolations of Jerusalem.

3 ¶ And I set my face unto the Lord God, to [a]seek by prayer and supplications, with fasting, and [b]sackcloth, and ashes:

4 And I prayed unto the Lord my God, and made my [a]confession, and said, O Lord, the great and dreadful God, [b]keeping the covenant and [c]mercy to them that love him, and to them that keep his commandments;

5 We have [a]sinned, and have committed iniquity, and have done wickedly, and have rebelled, even by departing from thy precepts and from thy judgments:

6 Neither have we [a]hearkened unto thy servants the prophets, which spake in thy name to our kings, our princes, and our fathers, and to all the people of the land.

7 O Lord, [a]righteousness *belongeth* unto thee, but unto us [b]confusion of faces, as at this day; to the men of Judah, and to the inhabitants of Jerusalem, and unto all Israel, *that are* near, and *that are* far off, through all the countries whither thou hast driven them, because of their trespass that they have trespassed against thee.

8 O Lord, to us *belongeth* confusion of face, to our kings, to our princes, and to our fathers, because we have sinned against thee.

9 To the Lord our God *belong* mercies and [a]forgivenesses, though we have [b]rebelled against him;

10 Neither have we obeyed the voice of the Lord our God, to [a]walk in his laws, which he set before us by his servants the prophets.

11 Yea, all Israel have transgressed thy law, even by departing, that they might not [a]obey thy voice; therefore the [b]curse is poured upon us, and the oath that *is* written in the law of Moses the servant of God, because we have sinned against him.

12 And he hath confirmed his words, which he spake against us, and against our judges that judged us, by bringing upon us a great [a]evil: for under the whole heaven

---

24b Rev. 17:17.
  c Moses 7:26 (24–26).
25a OR in a time of peace.
  b Dan. 2:34;
    D&C 65:2.
26a IE pertains to many
    days hereafter.
27a Dan. 6:3.
9 1a Dan. 11:1.
2a 2 Chr. 36:21;
    Jer. 25:12.

  b TG Israel, Bondage of, in
    Other Lands.
3a Dan. 10:12.
  b TG Apparel.
4a TG Confession.
  b Deut. 7:9;
    Neh. 1:5.
  c D&C 109:1.
5a 1 Kgs. 8:47;
    Ps. 106:6.
6a 2 Chr. 36:16 (15–16).

7a TG Righteousness.
  b OR shamefacedness.
9a Alma 24:10;
    D&C 64:7 (6–7);
    84:61 (60–61).
  b TG Rebellion.
10a TG Walking with God.
11a TG Disobedience.
  b Jer. 52:30 (1–30).
    TG Curse.
12a OR calamity.

hath not been *b*done as hath been done upon Jerusalem.

13 As *it is* written in the *a*law of Moses, all this evil is come upon us: yet made we not our prayer before the LORD our God, that we might turn from our iniquities, and understand thy truth.

14 Therefore hath the LORD watched upon the *a*evil, and brought it upon us: for the LORD our God *is* righteous in all his works which he doeth: for we *b*obeyed not his voice.

15 And now, O Lord our God, that hast brought thy people forth out of the land of Egypt with a mighty hand, and hast gotten thee renown, as at this day; we have sinned, we have done wickedly.

16 ¶ O Lord, according to all thy *a*righteousness, I beseech thee, let thine anger and thy fury be turned away from thy city Jerusalem, thy holy *b*mountain: because for our sins, and for the iniquities of our fathers, Jerusalem and thy people *are become* a *c*reproach to all *that are* about us.

17 Now therefore, O our God, hear the prayer of thy servant, and his supplications, and cause thy face to *a*shine upon thy sanctuary that is desolate, for the Lord's sake.

18 O my God, incline thine ear, and hear; open thine eyes, and behold our desolations, and the city which is called by thy name: for we do not present our supplications before thee for our righteousnesses, but for thy great mercies.

19 O Lord, hear; O Lord, forgive; O Lord, hearken and do; defer not, for thine own sake, O my God: for thy city and thy people are called by thy name.

20 ¶ And whiles I *was* speaking, and praying, and confessing my sin and the sin of my people Israel, and presenting my supplication before the LORD my God for the holy mountain of my God;

21 Yea, whiles I *was* speaking in prayer, even the man *a*Gabriel, whom I had seen in the vision at the beginning, being caused to fly swiftly, *b*touched me about the time of the *c*evening oblation.

22 And he informed *me*, and talked with me, and said, O *a*Daniel, I am now come forth to give thee skill and understanding.

23 At the beginning of thy supplications the commandment came forth, and I am come to shew *thee*; for thou *art* greatly beloved: therefore understand the matter, and consider the vision.

24 Seventy weeks are determined upon thy people and upon thy holy city, to finish the transgression, and to make an end of sins, and to make *a*reconciliation for iniquity, and to bring in everlasting righteousness, and to seal up the vision and prophecy, and to anoint the most Holy.

25 Know therefore and understand, *that* from the going forth of the commandment to restore and to build Jerusalem unto the Messiah the Prince *shall be* seven weeks, and threescore and two weeks: the street shall be built again, and the *a*wall, even in troublous times.

26 And after threescore and two weeks shall *a*Messiah be cut off, but not for himself: and the people of the prince that shall come shall *b*destroy the city and the sanctuary; and the end thereof *shall be* with a flood, and unto the end of the war desolations are determined.

27 And he shall confirm the covenant with many for one week: and in the midst of the week he shall cause

12 *b* Ezek. 5:9.
13 *a* Lev. 26:14 (14–46).
14 *a* Jer. 31:28.
  b TG Disobedience.
16 *a* Ps. 31:1; 36:6;
  D&C 133:47 (46–47).
  b Dan. 11:45;
  Zech. 8:3.
  c TG Reproach.

17 *a* Num. 6:25;
  3 Ne. 19:25.
21 *a* Dan. 8:16.
  TG Angels.
  b Dan. 8:18.
  c 1 Kgs. 18:36.
22 *a* Ezek. 14:14; 28:3.
24 *a* TG Jesus Christ,
  Prophecies about;

  Reconciliation.
25 *a* Jer. 52:14.
26 *a* TG Jesus Christ,
  Atonement through;
  Jesus Christ, Crucifixion
  of; Jesus Christ,
  Messiah; Jesus Christ,
  Prophecies about.
  b Luke 19:44 (43–44).

the sacrifice and the oblation to cease, and for the overspreading of *a*abominations he shall make *it* *b*desolate, even until the *c*consummation, and that determined shall be poured upon the desolate.

CHAPTER 10

Daniel sees the Lord and others in a glorious vision—He is shown what is to be in the latter days.

IN the third year of Cyrus king of Persia a thing was revealed unto Daniel, whose name was called Belteshazzar; and the thing *was* true, but the time appointed *was* long: and he understood the thing, and had *a*understanding of the vision.

2 In those days I Daniel was *a*mourning three full weeks.

3 I ate no *a*pleasant bread, neither came flesh nor wine in my mouth, neither did I anoint myself at all, till three whole weeks were fulfilled.

4 And in the four and twentieth day of the first month, as I was by the side of the great river, which *is* *a*Hiddekel;

5 Then I lifted up mine eyes, and looked, and behold a certain man *a*clothed in linen, whose loins *were* girded with fine gold of Uphaz:

6 His body also *was* like the beryl, and his face as the appearance of lightning, and his eyes as lamps of fire, and his arms and his feet like in colour to polished brass, and the voice of his words like the voice of a multitude.

7 And I Daniel alone saw the *a*vision: for the men that were with me saw not the vision; but a great quaking fell upon them, so that they fled to hide themselves.

8 Therefore I was left alone, and saw this great vision, and there remained no *a*strength in me: for my comeliness was turned in me into corruption, and I retained no strength.

9 Yet heard I the voice of his words: and when I heard the voice of his words, then was I in a deep sleep on my face, and my face *a*toward the ground.

10 ¶ And, behold, an hand touched me, which set me upon my knees and *upon* the palms of my hands.

11 And he said unto me, O Daniel, a man greatly *a*beloved, understand the words that I speak unto thee, and stand upright: for unto thee am I now sent. And when he had spoken this word unto me, I stood trembling.

12 Then said he unto me, *a*Fear not, Daniel: for from the first day that thou didst *b*set thine heart to understand, and to *c*chasten thyself before thy God, thy words were *d*heard, and I am come for thy words.

13 But the prince of the kingdom of Persia withstood me one and twenty days: but, lo, *a*Michael, one of the chief princes, came to help me; and I remained there with the kings of Persia.

14 Now I am come to make thee understand what shall befall thy people in the latter days: for yet the vision *is* for *many* days.

15 And when he had spoken such words unto me, I set my face toward the ground, and I became *a*dumb.

16 And, behold, *one* like the similitude of the sons of men touched my lips: then I opened my mouth, and spake, and said unto him that stood before me, O my lord, by the vision my sorrows are turned upon me, and I have retained no strength.

27*a* TG Abomination of Desolation.
　b Luke 21:24 (20–24); D&C 88:85.
　c Isa. 28:22; Dan. 12:1; 2 Ne. 20:23.
10 1*a* Dan. 1:17 (6–20).
　2*a* Alma 17:3 (3, 9).
　3*a* HEB desirable foods.
　4*a* IE the Tigris.

5*a* Dan. 12:6; Rev. 1:13.
7*a* Acts 9:7 (3–7); Alma 36:11 (6–11).
8*a* 1 Ne. 17:47; 19:20; Alma 27:17; Moses 1:10 (9–10).
9*a* 1 Ne. 1:7; JS—H 1:20.
11*a* D&C 7:1 (1, 5).
12*a* Luke 1:13 (12–13);

Hel. 5:26; D&C 68:6; 98:1; JS—H 1:32.
　b Dan. 9:3.
　c HEB humble thyself.
　d Mosiah 9:18; 27:14; Abr. 1:16 (15–16).
13*a* TG Adam.
15*a* Luke 1:20 (20–22); Mosiah 27:19.

17 For how can the servant of this my lord talk with this my lord? for as for me, straightway there remained no strength in me, neither is there breath left in me.

18 Then there came again and touched me *one* like the appearance of a man, and he strengthened me,

19 And said, O man greatly beloved, fear not: peace *be* unto thee, be strong, yea, be strong. And when he had spoken unto me, I was strengthened, and said, Let my lord speak; for thou hast strengthened me.

20 Then said he, Knowest thou wherefore I come unto thee? and now will I return to fight with the prince of Persia: and when I am gone forth, lo, the prince of *a*Grecia shall come.

21 *a*But I will shew thee that which is noted in the scripture of truth: and *there is* none that holdeth with me in these things, but *b*Michael your prince.

CHAPTER 11

Daniel sees the successive kings and their wars, leagues, and conflicts that lead up to the Second Coming of Christ.

ALSO I in the first year of *a*Darius the Mede, *even* I, stood to confirm and to strengthen him.

2 And now will I shew thee the truth. Behold, there shall stand up yet three kings in Persia; and the fourth shall be far richer than *they* all: and by his strength through his riches he shall stir up all against the *a*realm of *b*Grecia.

3 And a mighty king shall stand up, that shall rule with great dominion, and do *a*according to his will.

4 And when he shall stand up, his kingdom shall be *a*broken, and shall be divided toward the *b*four *c*winds of heaven; and not to his posterity, nor according to his dominion which he ruled: for his kingdom shall be plucked up, even for others beside those.

5 ¶ And the king of the south shall be strong, and *one* of his princes; and he shall be strong above him, and have dominion; his dominion *shall be* a great dominion.

6 And in the end of years they shall join themselves together; for the king's daughter of the south shall come to the king of the north to make an agreement: but she shall not retain the power of the arm; neither shall he stand, nor his arm: but she shall be given up, and they that brought her, and he that begat her, and he that strengthened her in *these* times.

7 But out of a branch of her roots shall *one* stand up in his estate, which shall come with an army, and shall enter into the fortress of the king of the north, and shall deal against them, and shall prevail:

8 And shall also carry captives into Egypt their gods, with their *a*princes, *and* with their precious vessels of silver and of gold; and he shall continue *more* years than the king of the north.

9 So the king of the south shall come into *his* kingdom, and shall return into his own land.

10 But his sons shall be stirred up, and shall assemble a multitude of great forces: and *one* shall certainly come, and overflow, and pass through: then shall he return, and be stirred up, *even* to his fortress.

11 And the king of the south shall be moved with *a*choler, and shall come forth and fight with him, *even* with the king of the north: and he shall set forth a great multitude; but

20*a* Dan. 8:21.
21*a* IE But I will tell you what is inscribed in the writing of truth: No one supports me against them (Persia and Grecia, which is

Macedonia) except Michael your prince.
b TG Angels.
11 1*a* Dan. 5:31; 9:1.
2*a* IE kingdom of Macedonia.
b Dan. 8:21.

3*a* Dan. 8:4.
4*a* Dan. 8:22 (8–22).
b Dan. 7:6; 8:8.
c Ezek. 37:9;
Rev. 7:1.
8*a* HEB molten images.
11*a* Dan. 8:7.

the multitude shall be given into his hand.

12 *And* when he hath taken away the multitude, his heart shall be lifted up; and he shall cast down *many* ten thousands: but he shall not be strengthened *by it.*

13 For the king of the north shall return, and shall set forth a multitude greater than the former, and shall certainly come after certain years with a great army and with much riches.

14 And in those times there shall many stand up against the king of the south: also the *a*robbers of thy people shall exalt themselves to establish the vision; but they shall fall.

15 So the king of the north shall come, and cast up a *a*mount, and take the most fenced cities: and the arms of the south shall not withstand, neither his chosen people, neither *shall there be any* strength to withstand.

16 But he that cometh against him shall do according to his own will, and none shall stand before him: and he shall stand in the glorious land, which by his hand shall be consumed.

17 He shall also set his face to enter with the strength of his whole kingdom, and upright ones with him; thus shall he do: and he shall give him the daughter of women, corrupting her: but she shall not stand *on his side,* neither be for him.

18 After this shall he turn his face unto the isles, and shall take many: but a prince for his own behalf shall cause the reproach offered by him to cease; without his own reproach he shall cause *it* to turn upon him.

19 Then he shall turn his face toward the fort of his own land: but he shall stumble and fall, and not be found.

20 Then shall stand up in his estate a raiser of taxes *in* the glory of the kingdom: but within few days he shall be destroyed, neither in anger, nor in battle.

21 And in his estate shall stand up a vile person, to whom they shall not give the honour of the kingdom: but he shall come in peaceably, and obtain the kingdom by *a*flatteries.

22 And with the arms of a *a*flood shall they be overflown from before him, and shall be broken; yea, also the prince of the covenant.

23 And after the league *made* with him he shall work deceitfully: for he shall come up, and shall become strong with a small people.

24 He shall enter peaceably even upon the fattest places of the province; and he shall do *that* which his fathers have not done, nor his fathers' fathers; he shall scatter among them the prey, and spoil, and riches: *yea,* and he shall forecast his devices against the strong holds, even for a time.

25 And he shall stir up his power and his courage against the king of the south with a great army; and the king of the south shall be stirred up to battle with a very great and mighty army; but he shall not stand: for they shall forecast devices against him.

26 Yea, they that feed of the portion of his meat shall destroy him, and his army shall overflow: and many shall fall down slain.

27 And both these kings' hearts *shall be* to do mischief, and they shall speak lies at one table; but it shall not prosper: for yet the end *shall be* at the time appointed.

28 Then shall he return into his land with great riches; and his heart *shall be* against the holy covenant; and he shall do *exploits,* and return to his own land.

29 At the time appointed he shall return, and come toward the south; but it shall not be as the former, or as the latter.

30 ¶ For the ships of *a*Chittim shall come against him: therefore he shall be grieved, and return, and have indignation against the holy covenant: so shall he do; he shall even

---

14*a* HEB oppressors.
15*a* OR siegework.

21*a* TG Flatter.
22*a* Jer. 46:7 (7–8).

30*a* Num. 24:24.

return, and have intelligence with them that forsake the holy covenant.

31 And arms shall stand on his part, and they shall *a*pollute *b*the sanctuary of strength, and shall take away the daily *sacrifice,* and they shall place the *c*abomination that maketh desolate.

32 And such as do wickedly against the covenant shall he corrupt by flatteries: but the people that do know their God shall be strong, and do *exploits.*

33 And they that understand among the people shall instruct many: yet they shall fall by the sword, and by flame, by captivity, and by spoil, *many* days.

34 Now when they shall fall, they shall be holpen with a little help: but many shall cleave to them with flatteries.

35 And *some* of them of understanding shall fall, to *a*try them, and to purge, and to make *them* white, *even* to the time of the end: because *it is* yet for a time appointed.

36 And the king shall do according to his will; and he shall exalt himself, and magnify himself above every god, and shall speak marvellous things against the *a*God of gods, and shall prosper till the *b*indignation be accomplished: for that that is determined shall be done.

37 Neither shall he regard the God of his fathers, nor the desire of women, nor regard any god: for he shall magnify himself above all.

38 But in his estate shall he honour the God of forces: and a god whom his fathers knew not shall he honour with gold, and silver, and with precious stones, and pleasant things.

39 Thus shall he do in the most strong holds with a strange god, whom he shall acknowledge *and*

increase with glory: and he shall cause them to rule over many, and shall divide the land for gain.

40 And at the time of the end shall the king of the south push at him: and the king of the north shall come against him like a *a*whirlwind, with chariots, and with horsemen, and with many ships; and he shall *b*enter into the countries, and shall overflow and pass over.

41 He shall enter also into the glorious land, and many *countries* shall be overthrown: but these shall escape out of his hand, *even* Edom, and Moab, and the chief of the children of Ammon.

42 He shall stretch forth his hand also upon the countries: and the land of Egypt shall not escape.

43 But he shall have power over the treasures of gold and of silver, and over all the precious things of Egypt: and the Libyans and the Ethiopians *shall *a*be* at his steps.

44 But tidings out of the east and out of the north shall trouble him: therefore he shall go forth with great fury to destroy, and utterly to *a*make away many.

45 And he shall plant the tabernacles of his palace between the seas in the glorious holy *a*mountain; yet he shall come to his end, and none shall help him.

CHAPTER 12

In the last days, Michael will deliver Israel from their troubles—Daniel tells of the two resurrections—The wise will know the times and meanings of his visions.

AND at that time shall *a*Michael stand up, the great prince *b*which standeth for the children of thy people: and there shall be a time of *c*trouble, such as never was since

---

31*a* Ezek. 7:21 (20–21);
     Dan. 8:11.
  b IE the temple.
  c TG Abomination of
     Desolation.
35*a* Dan. 12:10; Zech. 13:9.
36*a* Deut. 10:17;
     D&C 121:32.

  b Isa. 10:25;
     2 Ne. 20:25.
40*a* Zech. 9:14;
     3 Ne. 8:16; D&C 63:6.
  b Dan. 8:4.
43*a* IE march with him.
44*a* HEB destroy.
45*a* Dan. 9:16;

     D&C 133:13.
12 1*a* TG Adam; Last Days.
   b OR who has charge
      over.
   c Dan. 9:27 (24–27);
      Rev. 16:18;
      JS—M 1:18
      (18–19, 32–36).

there was a nation *even* to that same time: and at that time thy people shall be delivered, every one that shall be found written in the *d*book.

2 And many of them that *a*sleep in the dust of the earth shall *b*awake, some to *c*everlasting life, and some to *d*shame *and* *e*everlasting contempt.

3 And they that be *a*wise shall *b*shine as the *c*brightness of the firmament; and they that turn many to *d*righteousness as the stars for ever and ever.

4 But thou, O Daniel, shut up the words, and *a*seal the *b*book, *even* to the *c*time of the end: many shall run to and fro, and *d*knowledge shall be increased.

5 ¶ Then I Daniel looked, and, behold, there stood other two, the one on this side of the bank of the river, and the other on that side of the bank of the river.

6 And *one* said to the man *a*clothed in linen, which *was* upon the waters of the river, How long *shall it be to* the end of these wonders?

7 And I heard the man clothed in linen, which *was* upon the waters of the river, when he held up his right hand and his left hand unto heaven, and *a*sware by him that liveth for ever that *it shall be* for a time, times, and an half; and when he shall have accomplished to *b*scatter the power of the holy people, all these *things* shall be finished.

8 And I heard, but I understood not: then said I, O my Lord, what *shall be* the *a*end of these *things*?

9 And he said, Go thy way, Daniel: for the words *are* closed up and *a*sealed till the time of the end.

10 Many shall be *a*purified, and made white, and *b*tried; but the *c*wicked shall do wickedly: and none of the wicked shall understand; but the wise shall *d*understand.

11 And from the time *that* the daily *a*sacrifice shall be taken away, and the *b*abomination that maketh desolate set up, *there shall be* a thousand two hundred and ninety days.

12 Blessed *is* he that waiteth, and cometh to the thousand three hundred and five and thirty days.

13 But go thou thy way till the end *be:* for thou shalt *a*rest, and *b*stand in thy lot at the end of the days.

1*d* TG Book of Life; Record Keeping.
2*a* John 5:28 (28–29); Morm. 9:13 (13–14); D&C 43:18.
 b TG Resurrection.
 c TG Eternal Life; Immortality.
 d TG Damnation; Hell; Shame.
 e TG Death, Spiritual, Second.
3*a* TG Wisdom.
 b Alma 40:25. TG Celestial Glory.
 c D&C 76:70 (51–71).

 d TG Righteousness.
4*a* TG Seal.
 b TG Scriptures to Come Forth.
 c D&C 38:5 (4–6).
 d D&C 121:33.
6*a* Ezek. 9:2; Dan. 10:5.
7*a* Rev. 10:6; D&C 88:110.
 b Luke 21:24; Rev. 12:13 (13–17); 1 Ne. 10:12 (12–14); 22:3 (3–8); D&C 45:17.
8*a* Moses 7:58 (54–67).
9*a* 1 Ne. 14:26;

 2 Ne. 27:10; Ether 4:5 (4–7); D&C 35:18; JS—H 1:65.
10*a* TG Purification.
 b Dan. 11:35; Zech. 13:9.
 c Rev. 22:11; Alma 41:13.
 d Matt. 13:10 (10–13); John 8:47.
11*a* Dan. 8:11.
 b TG Abomination of Desolation.
13*a* TG Paradise.
 b OR rise unto your destiny.

HOSEA

CHAPTER 1

Hosea and his family are a sign unto Israel—In the day of gathering, the people of Israel will become the sons of the living God.

THE word of the LORD that came unto Hosea, the son of Beeri, in the days of ᵃUzziah, Jotham, Ahaz, *and* Hezekiah, kings of Judah, and in the days of Jeroboam the son of Joash, king of Israel.

2 The beginning of the word of the LORD by Hosea. And the LORD said to Hosea, Go, take unto thee a ᵃwife of whoredoms and children of whoredoms: for the land hath committed great ᵇwhoredom, *departing* from the LORD.

3 So he went and took Gomer the daughter of Diblaim; which conceived, and bare him a son.

4 And the LORD said unto him, Call his name Jezreel; for yet a little *while*, and I will avenge the blood of Jezreel upon the house of ᵃJehu, and will cause to ᵇcease the kingdom of the house of Israel.

5 And it shall come to pass at that day, that I will ᵃbreak the bow of Israel in the valley of Jezreel.

6 ¶ And she conceived again, and bare a daughter. And *God* said unto him, Call her name ᵃLo-ruhamah: for I will ᵇno more have mercy upon the house of Israel; but I will utterly take them ᶜaway.

7 But I will have ᵃmercy upon the house of ᵇJudah, and will save them by the LORD their God, and will not save them by bow, nor by sword, nor by battle, by ᶜhorses, nor by horsemen.

8 ¶ Now when she had weaned Lo-ruhamah, she conceived, and bare a son.

9 Then said *God*, Call his name ᵃLo-ammi: for ye *are* not my people, and I will not be your *God*.

10 ¶ Yet the ᵃnumber of the children of Israel shall be as the ᵇsand of the sea, which cannot be measured nor numbered; and it shall come to pass, *that* in the place where it was said unto them, Ye *are* not my people, *there* it shall be said unto them, Ye *are* the ᶜsons of the ᵈliving God.

11 Then shall the children of Judah and the children of Israel be ᵃgathered together, and appoint themselves one head, and they shall come up out of the land: for great *shall be* the day of Jezreel.

CHAPTER 2

Worshipping false gods brings severe judgments upon Israel—In the last days, Israel will be reconciled to God and become His people.

SAY ye unto your brethren, ᵃAmmi; and to your sisters, ᵇRuhamah.

2 Plead with your ᵃmother, plead: for she *is* not my wife, neither *am* I

---

1 1*a* Isa. 1:1;
   Amos 1:1.
  2*a* Hosea 3:1 (1–3).
   b TG Idolatry;
    Whore.
  4*a* 2 Kgs. 10:11;
    15:12 (10–12).
   b 2 Kgs. 17:5 (1–6, 24).
  5*a* 2 Kgs. 15:29.
  6*a* IE Not having obtained
    mercy.
   b D&C 109:61 (60–62).

  c 2 Kgs. 17:23.
  7*a* 2 Kgs. 19:34 (34–35);
    Isa. 31:5.
   b D&C 109:64;
    133:35 (13, 35).
   c Hosea 14:3.
  9*a* IE Not my people.
 10*a* Gen. 32:12;
    D&C 132:30 (30–33);
    Abr. 3:14.
   b 1 Ne. 20:19.
   c TG Man, a Spirit Child

   of Heavenly Father;
    Sons and Daughters
    of God;
    Spirit Creation.
   d Josh. 3:10;
    Ps. 42:2.
 11*a* 2 Ne. 29:8 (8–9).
    TG Israel, Gathering of.
 2 1*a* IE My people.
   b IE Having obtained
    mercy.
  2*a* Isa. 50:1.

her husband: let her therefore put away her whoredoms out of her sight, and her adulteries from between her breasts;

3 Lest I ^astrip her ^bnaked, and set her as in the day that she was ^cborn, and make her as a wilderness, and set her like a dry land, and slay her with ^dthirst.

4 And I will not have mercy upon her children; for they *be* the children of whoredoms.

5 For their mother hath played the harlot: she that conceived them hath done ^ashamefully: for she said, I will go after my lovers, that give *me* my ^bbread and my water, my wool and my flax, mine oil and my drink.

6 ¶ Therefore, behold, I will ^ahedge up thy way with thorns, and make a wall, that she shall not find her paths.

7 And she shall follow after her lovers, but she shall not overtake them; and she shall seek them, but shall not find *them:* then shall she say, I will go and return to my first ^ahusband; for then *was it* better with me than now.

8 For she did not know that I gave her ^acorn, and wine, and oil, and multiplied her silver and gold, *which* they prepared for Baal.

9 Therefore will I return, and take away my corn in the time thereof, and my wine in the season thereof, and will recover my wool and my flax *given* to cover her nakedness.

10 And now will I discover her ^alewdness in the sight of her lovers, and none shall deliver her out of mine hand.

11 I will also cause all her ^amirth to ^bcease, her feast days, her new

^cmoons, and her ^dsabbaths, and all her ^esolemn feasts.

12 And I will destroy her vines and her fig trees, whereof she hath said, These *are* my rewards that my lovers have given me: and I will make them a forest, and the beasts of the field shall eat them.

13 And I will visit upon her the days of ^aBaalim, wherein she burned incense to them, and she decked herself with her ^bearrings and her jewels, and she went after her lovers, and forgat me, saith the LORD.

14 ¶ Therefore, behold, I will allure her, and bring her into the ^awilderness, and speak comfortably unto her.

15 And I will give her her vineyards from thence, and the valley of ^aAchor for a door of hope: and she shall ^bsing there, as in the days of her youth, and as in the day when she came up out of the land of Egypt.

16 And it shall be at that ^aday, saith the LORD, *that* thou shalt call me ^bIshi; and shalt call me no more ^cBaali.

17 For I will take away the names of ^aBaalim out of her mouth, and they shall no more be remembered by their name.

18 And in that day will I make a ^acovenant for them with the ^bbeasts of the field, and with the fowls of heaven, and *with* the creeping things of the ground: and I will break the bow and the sword and the battle out of the earth, and will make them to lie down ^csafely.

19 And I will ^abetroth thee unto me for ever; yea, I will betroth thee unto me in righteousness, and in

3a Jer. 13:22.
  b Ezek. 16:7 (7–15).
  c Ezek. 16:4.
  d Amos 8:11.
5a TG Shame.
  b Jer. 44:17 (15–17).
6a Lam. 3:7 (7–8).
7a Ezek. 16:32 (8, 32, 38).
8a HEB grain.
  Deut. 7:13;
  Ezek. 16:19 (17–19).
10a Lam. 1:8.

11a Jer. 7:34.
  b Isa. 24:8 (7–11).
  c Isa. 1:14 (10–15).
  d TG Sabbath.
  e Lam. 1:4.
13a Judg. 3:7;
  Hosea 11:2.
  b Jer. 4:30; Ezek. 23:40.
14a Ezek. 20:35.
15a IE Trouble.
  Josh. 7:26;
  Isa. 65:10.

  b Ex. 15:1 (1, 20).
16a Isa. 2:11; 52:6;
  Zech. 9:16.
  b IE My husband.
  c IE My master.
17a Ex. 23:13.
18a Jer. 31:33 (31–34);
  Morm. 5:20; D&C 45:9.
  b Job 5:23.
  c TG Millennium; Peace.
19a TG Abrahamic
  Covenant.

judgment, and in lovingkindness, and in mercies.

20 I will even betroth thee unto me in faithfulness: and thou shalt *a*know the LORD.

21 And it shall come to pass in that day, I will hear, saith the LORD, I will hear the heavens, and they shall hear the earth;

22 And the earth shall hear the corn, and the wine, and the oil; and they shall hear Jezreel.

23 And I will sow her unto me in the earth; and I will have mercy upon *a*her that had not obtained mercy; and I will say to *b*them which were not my *c*people, Thou *art* my *d*people; and they shall say, Thou art my God.

CHAPTER 3

Israel will seek the Lord, return to the Lord, and receive of His goodness in the latter days.

THEN said the LORD unto me, Go yet, love a woman beloved of *her* friend, yet an *a*adulteress, according to the love of the LORD toward the children of Israel, who look to other gods, and love *b*flagons of wine.

2 So I bought her to me for fifteen *pieces* of silver, and *for* an homer of barley, and an half homer of barley:

3 And I said unto her, Thou shalt abide for me many days; thou shalt not play the harlot, and thou shalt not be for *another* man: so *will* I also *be* for thee.

4 For the children of Israel shall abide many days without a king, and without a prince, and without a sacrifice, and without an image, and without an ephod, and *without* teraphim:

5 Afterward shall the children of Israel return, and *a*seek the LORD their God, and *b*David their king; and shall fear the LORD and his goodness in the *c*latter days.

CHAPTER 4

Israel loses all truth, mercy, and knowledge of God and goes whoring after false gods.

HEAR the word of the LORD, ye children of Israel: for the LORD hath a *a*controversy with the inhabitants of the land, because *there is* no *b*truth, nor mercy, nor *c*knowledge of God in the land.

2 By *a*swearing, and *b*lying, and killing, and *c*stealing, and committing adultery, they *d*break out, and *e*blood toucheth blood.

3 Therefore shall the *a*land mourn, and every one that dwelleth therein shall languish, with the beasts of the field, and with the fowls of heaven; yea, the fishes of the sea also shall be taken away.

4 Yet let no man *a*strive, nor reprove another: for thy people *are* as they that strive with the priest.

5 Therefore shalt thou fall in the day, and the *a*prophet also shall fall with thee in the night, and I will destroy thy mother.

6 ¶ My people are destroyed for lack of *a*knowledge: because thou hast *b*rejected *c*knowledge, I will also reject thee, that thou shalt be no priest to me: seeing thou hast forgotten the *d*law of thy God, I will also forget thy children.

7 As they were increased, so they sinned against me: *therefore* will I change their glory into *a*shame.

20*a* John 17:3.
23*a* HEB *lo-ruhamah.*
 b HEB *lo-ammi.*
 c Rom. 9:25.
 d Jer. 30:22; Zech. 13:9.
3 1*a* Hosea 1:2.
 TG Adulterer.
 b HEB raisin-cakes (used in fertility rites).
5*a* 2 Ne. 6:11; D&C 113:10.
 b Ezek. 34:24 (23–24).

 c Deut. 31:29 (28–29).
4 1*a* Jer. 25:31;
 Hosea 12:2 (1–2);
 Micah 6:2.
 b TG Truth.
 c TG God, Knowledge about.
2*a* TG Profanity; Swearing.
 b TG Lying.
 c TG Stealing.
 d IE break all bounds.

 e OR bloodshed leads to bloodshed.
3*a* Joel 1:10.
4*a* TG Contention; Strife.
5*a* TG False Prophets.
6*a* TG God, Knowledge about; Ignorance.
 b TG Disobedience.
 c TG Knowledge.
 d TG Apostasy of Israel.
7*a* TG Shame.

8 They eat up the sin of my people, and they set their heart on their iniquity.

9 And there shall be, like people, like priest: and I will punish them for their ways, and reward them their doings.

10 For they shall eat, and not have enough: they shall commit whoredom, and shall not increase: because they have left off to take heed to the LORD.

11 ^aWhoredom and wine and new wine take away the heart.

12 ¶ My people ask ^acounsel at their stocks, and their staff declareth unto them: for the ^bspirit of ^cwhoredoms hath caused *them* to err, and they have gone a whoring from under their God.

13 They sacrifice upon the tops of the mountains, and burn incense upon the hills, under oaks and poplars and elms, because the shadow thereof *is* good: therefore your daughters shall commit whoredom, and your spouses shall commit ^aadultery.

14 I will not punish your daughters when they commit whoredom, nor your spouses when they commit adultery: for themselves are separated with whores, and they sacrifice with harlots: therefore the people *that* doth not understand shall fall.

15 ¶ Though thou, Israel, play the ^aharlot, *yet* let not Judah offend; and come not ye unto Gilgal, neither go ye up to ^bBeth-aven, nor swear, The LORD liveth.

16 For Israel slideth back as a backsliding heifer: now the LORD will feed them as a lamb in a large place.

17 Ephraim *is* joined to ^aidols: let him alone.

18 Their drink is sour: they have committed whoredom continually: her rulers ^awith shame do love, Give ye.

19 The wind hath bound her up in her wings, and they shall be ashamed because of their sacrifices.

CHAPTER 5

The kingdoms of Judah and Israel will both fall because of their iniquities.

HEAR ye this, O priests; and hearken, ye house of Israel; and give ye ear, O house of the king; for judgment *is* toward you, because ye have been a snare on Mizpah, and a net spread upon Tabor.

2 And the revolters are profound to make slaughter, though I *have been* a rebuker of them all.

3 I know Ephraim, and Israel is not hid from me: for now, O Ephraim, thou committest ^awhoredom, *and* Israel is defiled.

4 ^aThey will not frame their doings to turn unto their God: for the spirit of whoredoms *is* in the midst of them, and they have not known the LORD.

5 And the pride of Israel doth testify to his face: therefore shall Israel and Ephraim fall in their iniquity; Judah also shall fall with them.

6 They shall go with their flocks and with their herds to seek the LORD; but they shall not find *him*; he hath ^awithdrawn himself from them.

7 They have dealt treacherously against the LORD: for they have begotten strange children: now shall a ^amonth devour them with their portions.

8 Blow ye the ^acornet in Gibeah, *and* the trumpet in Ramah: cry aloud *at* Beth-aven, after thee, O Benjamin.

9 Ephraim shall be desolate in the day of rebuke: among the tribes of Israel have I made known that which shall surely be.

11a TG Whore.
12a TG Superstitions.
   b Isa. 44:20;
     Rom. 1:21.
   c TG Whore.
13a TG Adulterer.
15a Ezek. 16:15 (15, 34).

  b Hosea 10:8 (7–8).
17a TG Apostasy of Israel.
18a OR deeply love
     dishonor.
5 3a Hosea 9:1.
  4a HEB Their behavior
     does not permit them to

   return to their God.
6a D&C 101:7 (7–8).
7a IE Within a month they
   and their property shall
   be destroyed.
8a HEB *shofar*, or ram's
   horn.

10 The princes of Judah were like them that remove the ^abound: *therefore* I will pour out my wrath upon them like water.

11 Ephraim *is* oppressed *and* broken in judgment, because he willingly walked ^aafter the commandment.

12 Therefore *will* I *be* unto Ephraim as a moth, and to the house of Judah as rottenness.

13 When Ephraim saw his sickness, and Judah *saw* his ^awound, then went ^bEphraim to the Assyrian, and sent to king ^cJareb: yet could he not ^dheal you, nor cure you of your wound.

14 For I *will be* unto Ephraim as a lion, and as a young lion to the house of Judah: I, *even* I, will tear and go away; I will take away, and none shall rescue *him*.

15 ¶ I will go *and* return to my place, till they ^aacknowledge their offence, and ^bseek my face: in their ^caffliction they will seek me early.

CHAPTER 6

Hosea calls Israel to return and serve the Lord—The mercy and knowledge of God are more important than ritualistic sacrifices.

COME, and let us return unto the LORD: for he hath torn, and he will ^aheal us; he hath smitten, and he will bind us up.

2 After two days will he ^arevive us: in the third day he will raise us up, and we shall live in his ^bsight.

3 Then shall we know, *if* we follow on to know the LORD: his going forth is prepared as the morning; and he shall come unto us as the rain, as the ^alatter *and* former rain unto the earth.

4 ¶ O Ephraim, what shall I do unto thee? O Judah, what shall I do unto thee? for your goodness *is* as a morning cloud, and as the early ^adew it goeth away.

5 Therefore have I hewed *them* by the prophets; I have ^aslain them by the words of my mouth: and thy judgments *are as* the light *that* goeth forth.

6 For ^aI desired ^bmercy, and not sacrifice; and the ^cknowledge of God more than burnt ^dofferings.

7 But they like ^amen have ^btransgressed the covenant: there have they dealt treacherously against me.

8 Gilead *is* a city of them that work iniquity, *and is* polluted with blood.

9 And as troops of robbers wait for a man, *so* the company of priests murder ^ain the way by consent: for they commit lewdness.

10 I have seen an ^ahorrible thing in the house of Israel: there *is* the whoredom of Ephraim, Israel is defiled.

11 Also, O Judah, he hath set an harvest for thee, when I returned the captivity of my people.

CHAPTER 7

Israel is reproved for her many sins—Ephraim is mixed among the people.

WHEN I would have healed Israel, then the iniquity of Ephraim was discovered, and the wickedness of Samaria: for they commit falsehood; and the thief cometh in, *and* the troop of robbers spoileth without.

2 And they consider not in their hearts *that* I remember all their wickedness: now their own ^adoings have beset them about; they are before my face.

10a HEB boundary marker.
   Deut. 19:14;
   Job 24:2;
   Prov. 22:28.
11a OR after filth.
13a Jer. 30:14.
   b Hosea 12:1 (1–2).
   c Hosea 10:6 (5–6).
   d Hosea 14:3 (1–3).
15a TG Confession.
   b D&C 101:8.

c TG Adversity;
   Affliction.
6 1a D&C 103:6 (4–8).
2a OR restore us to life; i.e.,
   resurrect us.
   b OR presence.
3a IE spring rain . . . winter
   rain.
4a Hosea 14:5.
5a Heb. 4:12.
6a Matt. 9:13.

b HEB charity, or
   lovingkindness.
   Matt. 12:7.
c TG Knowledge.
d TG Sacrifice.
7a OR Adam.
   b Hosea 8:1.
9a HEB on the road to
   Shechem.
10a Jer. 5:30 (30–31).
7 2a Prov. 5:22.

3 They make the king glad with their wickedness, and the princes with their lies.

4 They *are* all adulterers, as an oven heated by the baker, *who* ceaseth from raising after he hath kneaded the dough, until it be leavened.

5 In the day of our king the princes have made *him* sick with bottles of wine; he stretched out his hand with scorners.

6 For they have made ready their heart like an oven, whiles they lie in wait: their baker sleepeth all the night; in the morning it burneth as a flaming fire.

7 They are all hot as an oven, and have devoured their judges; all their kings are fallen: *there is* none among them that calleth unto me.

8 Ephraim, he hath ᵃmixed himself among the people; Ephraim is a ᵇcake not turned.

9 ᵃStrangers have devoured his strength, and he knoweth *it* not: yea, gray hairs are here and there upon him, yet he knoweth not.

10 And the pride of Israel testifieth to his face: and they do not ᵃreturn to the Lᴏʀᴅ their God, nor ᵇseek him for all this.

11 ¶ Ephraim also is like a silly dove without heart: they call to Egypt, they go to Assyria.

12 When they shall go, I will spread my ᵃnet upon them; I will bring them down as the fowls of the heaven; I will chastise them, as their congregation hath heard.

13 Woe unto them! for they have fled from me: ᵃdestruction unto them! because they have transgressed against me: though I ᵇhave ᶜredeemed them, yet they have spoken lies against me.

14 And they have not ᵃcried unto me with their heart, when they howled upon their beds: they assemble themselves for corn and wine, *and* they rebel against me.

15 Though I have ᵃbound *and* strengthened their arms, yet do they imagine mischief against me.

16 They return, *but* not to the ᵃmost High: they are like a ᵇdeceitful bow: their princes shall ᶜfall by the sword for the rage of their tongue: this *shall be* their derision in the land of Egypt.

CHAPTER 8

Both Israel and Judah have forsaken the Lord—The Lord has written the great things of His law to Ephraim.

Sᴇᴛ the ᵃtrumpet to thy mouth. *He shall come* as an ᵇeagle against the house of the Lᴏʀᴅ, because they have ᶜtransgressed my covenant, and trespassed against my law.

2 Israel shall cry unto me, My ᵃGod, we ᵇknow thee.

3 Israel hath cast off *the thing that is* good: the ᵃenemy shall pursue him.

4 They have set up kings, but not by me: they have made princes, and ᵃI knew *it* not: of their silver and their gold have they made them idols, that they may be cut off.

5 ¶ Thy ᵃcalf, O Samaria, hath cast *thee* off; mine anger is kindled against them: how long *will it be* ᵇere they attain to innocency?

6 For from Israel *was* it also: the workman made it; therefore it *is* not God: but the calf of Samaria shall be broken in pieces.

7 For they have sown the wind, and they shall ᵃreap the whirlwind: it hath no stalk: the bud shall yield no

---

8*a* TG Separation.
  b Lev. 24:5.
9*a* TG Stranger.
10*a* TG Rebellion.
  b Isa. 9:13.
12*a* Ezek. 12:13; 17:20.
13*a* 1 Ne. 17:43 (42–43).
  b OR would have redeemed them.
  c Micah 6:4.
14*a* Morm. 2:13 (11–13).

15*a* HEB trained.
16*a* Hosea 11:7.
  b Ps. 78:57.
  c 2 Kgs. 17:5 (1–6, 24).
8 1*a* HEB *shofar*, or ram's horn.
  b Deut. 28:49.
  c Hosea 6:7.
2*a* Matt. 7:21 (21–23); Luke 6:46; D&C 112:26.

  b Titus 1:16.
3*a* 2 Kgs. 17:5 (1–6, 24).
4*a* IE I acknowledged them not.
5*a* 1 Kgs. 12:28 (28–30); Acts 7:41.
  b OR before they become clean.
7*a* Mosiah 7:30; D&C 6:33.

meal: if so be it yield, the strangers shall swallow it up.

8 Israel is ᵃswallowed up: now shall they be among the Gentiles as a ᵇvessel wherein *is* no pleasure.

9 For they are gone up to ᵃAssyria, a wild ass alone by himself: Ephraim hath ᵇhired lovers.

10 Yea, though they have hired among the nations, now will I gather them, and they shall sorrow a little for the burden of the king of princes.

11 Because Ephraim hath made many ᵃaltars to ᵇsin, altars shall be unto him to sin.

12 I have ᵃwritten to him the great things of my ᵇlaw, *but* they were counted as a strange thing.

13 They sacrifice flesh *for* the sacrifices of mine offerings, and eat *it;* but the LORD ᵃaccepteth them not; now will he ᵇremember their iniquity, and visit their sins: they shall return to ᶜEgypt.

14 For Israel hath forgotten his ᵃMaker, and buildeth ᵇtemples; and Judah hath multiplied ᶜfenced cities: but I will send a ᵈfire upon his cities, and it shall devour the palaces thereof.

CHAPTER 9

The people of Israel are taken into captivity for their sins—Ephraim will be a wanderer among the nations.

REJOICE not, O Israel, for joy, as *other* people: for thou hast gone a ᵃwhoring from thy God, thou hast loved a ᵇreward upon every ᶜcornfloor.

2 The floor and the winepress shall not feed them, and the new wine shall fail in her.

3 They shall not dwell in the LORD's ᵃland; but Ephraim shall return to ᵇEgypt, and they shall eat ᶜunclean *things* in Assyria.

4 They shall not offer wine *offerings* to the LORD, neither shall they be pleasing unto him: their sacrifices *shall be* unto them as the bread of mourners; all that eat thereof shall be polluted: for their bread for their soul shall not come into the house of the LORD.

5 What will ye do in the solemn day, and in the day of the feast of the LORD?

6 For, lo, they are gone because of destruction: Egypt shall gather them up, Memphis shall bury them: the pleasant *places* for their silver, nettles shall possess them: thorns *shall be* in their ᵃtabernacles.

7 The days of ᵃvisitation are come, the days of recompence are come; Israel shall know *it:* the prophet *is* a ᵇfool, the spiritual man *is* mad, for the multitude of thine iniquity, and the great hatred.

8 The watchman of Ephraim *was* with my God: *but* the prophet *is* a snare of a fowler in all his ways, *and* hatred in the house of his God.

9 They have deeply ᵃcorrupted *themselves,* as in the days of ᵇGibeah: *therefore* he will remember their iniquity, he will visit their sins.

10 I found Israel like grapes in the wilderness; I saw your fathers as the firstripe in the ᵃfig tree at her first time: *but* they went to ᵇBaal-peor, and separated themselves unto *that*

8a 1 Ne. 10:12;
　　Jacob 5:13 (13–14).
　b Ps. 31:12;
　　Jer. 22:28; 48:38.
9a 2 Kgs. 15:19; 17:6 (3–6);
　　Ezek. 23:5.
　b Ezek. 16:33 (33, 41).
11a Ex. 34:13;
　　Hosea 10:1.
　b TG Hypocrisy.
12a TG Scriptures,
　　Writing of.
　b Deut. 4:1, 6 (1–2, 6–8).
13a Amos 5:22 (21–22).

　b Amos 8:7.
　c Deut. 28:68 (58–59, 68);
　　Hosea 9:3 (1–3); 11:5.
14a Isa. 17:7; 45:9.
　b OR palaces or great
　　buildings.
　c OR fortified.
　d 2 Kgs. 25:9.
9 1a Deut. 31:16;
　　Hosea 5:3.
　b OR harlot's hire.
　c OR threshing floor.
3a Jer. 2:7.
　b Hosea 8:13 (11–14).

　c Ezek. 4:13;
　　Dan. 1:8.
6a HEB tents.
7a HEB punishment.
　　Isa. 10:3;
　　D&C 56:1.
　b Ezek. 13:3.
9a Ex. 32:7;
　　D&C 38:11.
　b Judg. 19:14 (12–30);
　　Hosea 10:9.
10a Jer. 24:2.
　b Num. 25:3 (1–3);
　　Ps. 106:28.

shame; and *their* ^cabominations were according as they loved.

11 *As for* Ephraim, their glory shall fly away like a bird, from the birth, and from the womb, and from the conception.

12 Though they bring up their children, yet will I bereave them, *that there shall* not *be* a man *left:* yea, woe also to them when I ^adepart from them!

13 Ephraim, as I saw ^aTyrus, *is* planted in a pleasant place: but Ephraim shall bring forth his children to the murderer.

14 Give them, O LORD: what wilt thou give? give them a miscarrying womb and dry breasts.

15 All their wickedness *is* in ^aGilgal: for there I hated them: for the wickedness of their doings I will drive them out of mine house, I will love them no more: all their princes *are* revolters.

16 Ephraim is smitten, their root is dried up, they shall bear no fruit: yea, though they bring forth, yet will I slay *even* the beloved *fruit* of their womb.

17 My God will cast them away, because they did not hearken unto him: and they shall be ^awanderers among the nations.

CHAPTER 10

Israel has plowed wickedness and reaped iniquity—Hosea calls upon Israel to seek the Lord.

ISRAEL *is* an empty ^avine, he bringeth forth ^bfruit unto ^chimself: according to the multitude of his fruit he hath increased the ^daltars; according to the goodness of his land they have made goodly images.

2 Their heart is ^adivided; now shall they be found ^bfaulty: he shall break down their altars, he shall spoil their images.

3 For now they shall say, We have no king, because we feared not the LORD; what then should a king do to us?

4 They have spoken words, swearing falsely in making a ^acovenant: thus judgment springeth up as hemlock in the furrows of the field.

5 The inhabitants of Samaria shall fear because of the ^acalves of Bethaven: for the people thereof shall mourn over it, and the priests thereof *that* rejoiced on it, for the glory thereof, because it is departed from it.

6 It shall be also carried unto Assyria *for* a present to king ^aJareb: Ephraim shall receive ^bshame, and Israel shall be ^cashamed of his own ^dcounsel.

7 *As for* Samaria, her king is cut off as the foam upon the water.

8 The high places also of ^aAven, the sin of Israel, shall be destroyed: the thorn and the thistle shall come up on their altars; and they shall say to the ^bmountains, Cover us; and to the hills, Fall on us.

9 O Israel, thou hast ^asinned from the days of ^bGibeah: there they stood: the ^cbattle in Gibeah against the children of iniquity did not overtake them.

10 *It is* in my desire that I should chastise them; and the people shall be gathered against them, when they shall bind themselves in their two furrows.

11 And Ephraim *is as* an heifer *that is* taught, *and* loveth to tread out *the corn*; but I passed over upon her fair neck: I will make Ephraim to ride; Judah shall plow, *and* Jacob shall break his clods.

10c TG Sexual Immorality.
12a 1 Sam. 16:14;
    28:15 (15–16);
    Ezek. 10:18.
13a IE Tyre.
15a Hosea 12:11; Amos 4:4.
17a TG Israel, Scattering of.
10 1a TG Vineyard of the
    Lord.
    b Jacob 5:32 (1–77).

c Luke 12:21 (16–21).
d Hosea 8:11.
2a 1 Kgs. 18:21;
    James 1:8; 3 Ne. 13:24.
    b HEB guilty.
4a 3 Ne. 24:5;
    D&C 104:5 (4–5).
5a 1 Kgs. 12:28.
6a Hosea 5:13.
    b TG Shame.

c Jer. 48:13.
d Hosea 11:6 (5–7).
8a Hosea 4:15.
    b Luke 23:30 (26–33);
    Rev. 6:16 (14–17);
    2 Ne. 26:5;
    Alma 12:14.
9a Judg. 20:4 (1–48).
    b Hosea 9:9.
    c Judg. 20:19 (18–21).

12 Sow to yourselves in *righteousness, *reap in mercy; *break up your
fallow ground: for *it is* time to seek
the LORD, till he come and rain
righteousness upon you.

13 Ye have plowed *wickedness, ye
have reaped iniquity; ye have eaten
the fruit of lies: because thou didst
trust in thy way, in the multitude
of thy mighty men.

14 Therefore shall a tumult arise
among thy people, and all thy fortresses shall be spoiled, as *Shal-
man spoiled Beth-arbel in the day
of battle: the mother was *dashed
in pieces upon *her* children.

15 So shall Beth-el do unto you
because of your great wickedness:
in a morning shall the king of Israel utterly be cut off.

CHAPTER 11

*Israel, as a child, was called out of Egypt
in similitude of our Lord, as a child,
coming out of Egypt—But Ephraim
turns away from the Lord.*

WHEN Israel *was* a child, then I
*loved him, and called my *son out
of *Egypt.

2 As they called them, so they
went from them: they *sacrificed
unto *Baalim, and burned incense
to graven images.

3 I taught Ephraim also to go, taking them by their arms; but they
knew not that I *healed them.

4 I drew them with cords of a man,
with bands of *love: and I was to them
as they that take off the yoke on their
jaws, and I laid meat unto them.

5 ¶ He shall not return into the
land of *Egypt, but the Assyrian
shall be his king, because they refused to return.

6 And the sword shall abide on
his cities, and shall consume his
branches, and devour *them,* because
of their own *counsels.

7 And my people are bent to *backsliding from me: though they called
them to the *most High, none at all
would exalt *him.*

8 How shall I give thee up,
Ephraim? *how* shall I deliver thee,
Israel? how shall I make thee as *Admah? *how* shall I set thee as Zeboim?
mine heart is turned *within me,
my repentings are kindled together.

9 I will not execute the fierceness
of mine anger, I will not return
to destroy Ephraim: for I *am* God,
and not man; the Holy One in the
midst of thee: and I will not *enter
into the city.

10 They shall *walk after the LORD:
he shall roar like a *lion: when he
shall roar, then the children shall
tremble from the west.

11 They shall tremble as a bird
out of Egypt, and as a dove out of
the land of Assyria: and I will place
them in their houses, saith the LORD.

12 Ephraim compasseth me about
with lies, and the house of Israel
with deceit: but Judah yet *ruleth
with God, and is faithful with the
saints.

CHAPTER 12

*The Lord uses prophets, visions, and
similitudes to guide His people, but
they become rich and will not wait
on the Lord—Ephraim provokes Him
most bitterly.*

*EPHRAIM feedeth on wind, and
followeth after the east wind: he
daily increaseth lies and desolation;
and they do make a *covenant with

12*a* TG Righteousness.
  b TG Harvest.
  c Jer. 4:3.
13*a* TG Wickedness.
14*a* 2 Kgs. 17:3.
  b Hosea 13:16 (15–16).
11 1*a* TG God, Love of.
  b Ex. 4:22 (22–23).
  c TG Jesus Christ,
     Prophecies about.
2*a* Hosea 13:1 (1–4).

b 2 Kgs. 17:16 (15–16);
   Hosea 2:13.
3*a* 1 Ne. 17:41 (40–41);
   Alma 33:20 (18–23).
4*a* TG Love.
5*a* Hosea 8:13 (11–14).
6*a* Hosea 10:6.
7*a* TG Ingratitude.
  b Hosea 7:16 (14–16).
8*a* Gen. 19:24 (24–25);
   Deut. 29:23.

b JST Hosea 11:8 . . .
   *toward thee, and my
   mercies are extended to
   gather thee.*
9*a* OR come in anger.
10*a* TG Walking with God.
  b Isa. 31:4.
12*a* OR walks.
12 1*a* Isa. 28:1 (1–8).
  b Hosea 5:13.

the Assyrians, and oil is carried into Egypt.

2 The LORD hath also a ªcontroversy with Judah, and will punish Jacob according to his ways; according to his doings will he recompense him.

3 ¶ He took his brother by the ªheel in the womb, and by his strength he had power with God:

4 Yea, he had power over the ªangel, and ᵇprevailed: he wept, and made supplication unto him: he found him *in* ᶜBeth-el, and there he spake with ᵈus;

5 Even the LORD God of hosts; the LORD *is* his ªmemorial.

6 Therefore ªturn thou to thy God: keep mercy and judgment, and wait on thy God continually.

7 ¶ *He is* a merchant, the ªbalances of deceit *are* in his hand: he loveth to oppress.

8 And Ephraim said, Yet I am become rich, I have found me out substance: *in* all my labours they shall find none iniquity in me that *were* sin.

9 And I *that am* the LORD thy God from the land of Egypt will yet make thee to dwell in ªtabernacles, as in the days of the solemn feast.

10 I have also spoken by the prophets, and I have multiplied visions, and used similitudes, by the ministry of the prophets.

11 *Is there* iniquity *in* Gilead? surely they are vanity: they sacrifice bullocks in ªGilgal; yea, their altars *are* as heaps in the furrows of the fields.

12 And Jacob fled into the country of ªSyria, and Israel served for a ᵇwife, and for a wife he kept *sheep.*

13 And by a ªprophet the ᵇLORD

brought Israel out of Egypt, and by a prophet was he preserved.

14 Ephraim provoked *him* to anger most bitterly: therefore shall he leave his ªblood upon him, and his reproach shall his Lord return unto him.

CHAPTER 13

Ephraim's sins provoke the Lord— There is no Savior beside the Lord—He ransoms from the grave and redeems from death.

WHEN Ephraim spake trembling, he exalted himself in Israel; but when he ªoffended in Baal, he died.

2 And now they sin more and more, and have made them molten ªimages of their silver, *and* idols according to their own understanding, all of it the work of the craftsmen: they say of them, Let the men that sacrifice kiss the calves.

3 Therefore they shall be as the morning cloud, and as the early dew that passeth away, as the ªchaff *that* is driven with the whirlwind out of the floor, and as the smoke out of the chimney.

4 Yet I *am* the LORD thy God from the land of Egypt, and thou shalt know no ªgod but me: for *there is* no ᵇsaviour ᶜbeside me.

5 ¶ I did ªknow thee in the wilderness, in the land of great ᵇdrought.

6 According to their pasture, so were they ªfilled; they were filled, and their heart was exalted; therefore have they ᵇforgotten me.

7 Therefore I will be unto them as a lion: as a leopard by the way will I observe *them:*

8 I will meet them as a ªbear *that is*

---

2 a Hosea 4:1 (1–2).
3 a Gen. 25:26.
4 a TG Angels.
  b Gen. 32:28 (24–28).
  c Gen. 28:13 (10–16).
  d OR him.
5 a Ex. 3:15 (13–15).
6 a TG Conversion.
7 a Micah 6:11.
9 a OR tents.
    Lev. 23:34.
11 a Hosea 9:15 (13–15).

12 a Gen. 28:5;
      Deut. 26:5.
   b Gen. 29:20 (15–28).
13 a 1 Ne. 17:24 (24–26).
   b Ex. 12:50.
14 a IE guilt.
13 1 a Hosea 11:2.
2 a Deut. 27:15.
3 a Ps. 1:4;
    2 Ne. 26:18;
    Morm. 5:16 (16–18).
4 a Mosiah 12:35.

  b Acts 4:12; 2 Ne. 25:20.
    TG Jesus Christ, Jehovah;
    Jesus Christ, Redeemer.
  c Isa. 43:11;
    D&C 76:1.
5 a Deut. 2:7.
  b TG Drought.
6 a Deut. 8:16 (12, 16);
    1 Ne. 17:28 (26–29).
  b TG Apostasy of
    Individuals.
8 a Prov. 17:12.

bereaved *of her whelps,* and will rend the *b*caul of their heart, and there will I devour them like a lion: the wild beast shall tear them.

9 ¶ O Israel, thou hast *a*destroyed thyself; but in me *is* thine *b*help.

10 I will be thy *a*king: where *is any other* that may save thee in all thy cities? and thy judges of whom thou saidst, Give me a *b*king and princes?

11 I gave thee a king in mine *a*anger, and *b*took *him* away in my wrath.

12 The iniquity of Ephraim *is* bound up; his sin *is* hid.

13 The *a*sorrows of a *b*travailing woman shall come upon him: he *is* an unwise son; for he should not stay long in *the place of* the *c*breaking forth of children.

14 I will *a*ransom them from the power of the *b*grave; I will *c*redeem them from death: O *d*death, I will be thy *e*plagues; O grave, I will be thy destruction: *f*repentance shall be hid from mine eyes.

15 ¶ Though he be fruitful among *his* brethren, an east *a*wind shall come, the wind of the LORD shall come up from the wilderness, and his spring shall become dry, and his fountain shall be dried up: he shall spoil the treasure of all pleasant vessels.

16 *a*Samaria shall become desolate; for she hath rebelled against her God: they shall fall by the sword: their infants shall be *b*dashed in pieces, and their women with child shall be ripped up.

CHAPTER 14

In the last days, Ephraim will repent and return unto the Lord.

O ISRAEL, return unto the LORD thy God; for thou hast *a*fallen by thine iniquity.

2 Take with you words, and turn to the LORD: say unto him, Take away all iniquity, and receive *us* graciously: so will we *a*render the *b*calves of our lips.

3 *a*Asshur shall not *b*save us; we will not ride upon *c*horses: neither will we say any more to the work of our hands, *Ye are* our gods: for in thee the *d*fatherless findeth mercy.

4 ¶ I will heal their backsliding, I will *a*love them freely: for mine anger is turned away from him.

5 I will be as the *a*dew unto Israel: he shall grow as the lily, and cast forth his roots as Lebanon.

6 His branches shall spread, and his beauty shall be as the *a*olive tree, and his smell as Lebanon.

7 They that dwell under his shadow shall return; they shall revive *as* the corn, and grow as the vine: the scent thereof *shall be* as the wine of Lebanon.

8 Ephraim *shall say,* What have I to do any more with idols? I have heard *him,* and observed him: I *am* like a green fir tree. From me is thy fruit found.

9 Who *is* *a*wise, and he shall understand these *things? b*prudent, and he shall know them? for the *c*ways of the LORD *are* right, and the just shall *d*walk in them: but the transgressors shall fall therein.

8*b* IE chamber.
9*a* Hosea 14:1;
　　Mosiah 27:13.
　b Jer. 30:10;
　　D&C 38:33; 136:22.
10*a* 1 Sam. 12:12 (12–15).
　b 1 Sam. 8:5 (5, 19).
11*a* 1 Sam. 8:7.
　b 1 Sam. 15:23.
13*a* TG Sorrow.
　b Isa. 13:8.
　c Isa. 37:3.
14*a* Ps. 49:15.
　b TG Resurrection.
　c TG Jesus Christ,

　　Foreordained;
　　Jesus Christ,
　　Prophecies about;
　　Jesus Christ,
　　Resurrection.
　d TG Jesus Christ,
　　Death of.
　e TG Plague.
　f HEB compassion.
15*a* Gen. 41:23.
16*a* 2 Kgs. 17:6.
　b Hosea 10:14.
14 1*a* Hosea 13:9 (9–14).
　2*a* D&C 59:8.
　b Ps. 51:17.

3*a* IE Assyria.
　b Hosea 5:13.
　c Isa. 31:1;
　　Hosea 1:7.
　d Ps. 10:14.
4*a* TG Love.
5*a* Deut. 32:2;
　　Hosea 6:4;
　　D&C 128:19.
6*a* TG Vineyard of the Lord.
9*a* Ps. 107:43.
　b TG Prudence.
　c 2 Ne. 1:19; 31:19 (19–21).
　d TG Walking with God.

JOEL

CHAPTER 1

Call a solemn assembly and gather to the house of the Lord, for the day of the Lord is at hand.

THE word of the LORD that came to Joel the son of Pethuel.

2 Hear this, ye ᵃold men, and give ear, all ye ᵇinhabitants of the land. Hath this been in your days, or even in the days of your fathers?

3 Tell ye your children of it, and *let* your children *tell* their children, and their children another generation.

4 ᵃThat which the palmerworm hath left hath the ᵇlocust eaten; and that which the locust hath left hath the cankerworm eaten; and that which the cankerworm hath left hath the caterpiller eaten.

5 Awake, ye drunkards, and weep; and howl, all ye drinkers of wine, because of the new wine; for it is ᵃcut off from your mouth.

6 For a nation is come up upon my land, strong, and without ᵃnumber, whose ᵇteeth *are* the teeth of a lion, and he hath the cheek teeth of a great lion.

7 He hath laid my vine waste, and barked my fig tree: he hath made it clean bare, and cast *it* away; the branches thereof are made white.

8 ¶ Lament like a virgin girded with sackcloth for the ᵃhusband of her youth.

9 The meat offering and the drink offering is cut off from the house of the LORD; the priests, the LORD's ministers, mourn.

10 The field is wasted, the ᵃland mourneth; for the ᵇcorn is wasted: the new wine is dried up, the oil languisheth.

11 Be ye ashamed, O ye husbandmen; howl, O ye vinedressers, for the wheat and for the barley; because the harvest of the field is perished.

12 The vine is dried up, and the fig tree languisheth; the pomegranate tree, the palm tree also, and the apple tree, *even* all the trees of the field, are withered: because ᵃjoy is withered away from the sons of men.

13 ᵃGird yourselves, and lament, ye priests: howl, ye ministers of the altar: come, lie all night in sackcloth, ye ministers of my God: for the meat offering and the drink offering is withholden from the house of your God.

14 ¶ Sanctify ye a ᵃfast, call a ᵇsolemn assembly, gather the elders *and* all the inhabitants of the land *into* the house of the LORD your God, and cry unto the LORD,

15 Alas for the day! for the ᵃday of the LORD *is* at hand, and as a destruction from the Almighty shall it come.

16 Is not the ᵃmeat cut off before our eyes, *yea*, joy and gladness from the house of our God?

17 The seed is rotten under their clods, the ᵃgarners are laid desolate, the barns are broken down; for the corn is withered.

---

1 2*a* HEB elders.
  b D&C 1:6.
  4*a* IE The invading or conquering armies are compared to four varieties (or stages of growth) of locusts.
  b Lev. 26:24 (14–38).
  5*a* Isa. 32:10.

6*a* Rev. 9:16.
  b Rev. 9:8.
  8*a* Ezek. 16:32 (32–38).
  10*a* Hosea 4:3;
    D&C 43:25 (24–25);
    87:6 (1–8);
    JS—M 1:29.
  b OR grain.
  12*a* Isa. 24:11.

13*a* Jer. 4:8.
  14*a* TG Fast, Fasting.
  b TG Solemn Assembly.
  15*a* Jer. 46:10;
    Amos 5:18.
  TG Day of the Lord.
  16*a* OR food.
  17*a* OR storehouses.

18 How do the beasts groan! the herds of cattle are perplexed, because they have no pasture; yea, the flocks of sheep are made desolate.

19 O Lord, to thee will I cry: for the ^afire hath devoured the pastures of the wilderness, and the flame hath burned all the trees of the field.

20 The ^abeasts of the field cry also unto thee: for the rivers of waters are dried up, and the fire hath devoured the pastures of the wilderness.

CHAPTER 2

War and desolation will precede the Second Coming—The sun and the moon will be darkened—The Lord will pour out His Spirit upon all flesh—There will be dreams and visions.

Blow ye the ^atrumpet in Zion, and sound an alarm in my holy ^bmountain: let all the inhabitants of the land tremble: for the ^cday of the Lord cometh, for *it is* nigh at hand;

2 A day of ^adarkness and of gloominess, a day of clouds and of thick darkness, as the morning spread upon the mountains: a great people and a strong; there hath not been ever the like, neither shall be any more after it, *even* to the years of many generations.

3 A fire ^adevoureth before them; and behind them a flame burneth: the land *is* as the garden of ^bEden before them, and behind them a desolate wilderness; yea, and nothing shall escape them.

4 The appearance of them *is* as the appearance of horses; and as horsemen, so shall they run.

5 Like the ^anoise of chariots on the tops of mountains shall they leap, like the noise of a flame of fire that devoureth the ^bstubble, as a strong people set in battle array.

6 Before their face the people shall be much pained: all faces shall gather ^ablackness.

7 They shall run like mighty men; they shall climb the wall like men of war; and they shall march every one on his ways, and they shall not break their ranks:

8 Neither shall one thrust another; they shall walk every one in his path: and *when* they fall upon the sword, they shall not be wounded.

9 They shall run to and fro in the city; they shall run upon the wall, they shall climb up upon the houses; they shall enter in at the windows like a thief.

10 The ^aearth shall quake before them; the heavens shall ^btremble: the ^csun and the moon shall be ^ddark, and the stars shall withdraw their shining:

11 And the Lord shall utter his ^avoice before his army: for his camp *is* very great: for *he is* strong that executeth his word: for the ^bday of the Lord *is* ^cgreat and very terrible; and who can ^dabide it?

12 ¶ Therefore also now, saith the Lord, ^aturn ye *even* to me with all your ^bheart, and with ^cfasting, and with weeping, and with mourning:

13 And ^arend your heart, and not your garments, ^band turn unto the

---

19a Zeph. 1:18;
    2 Ne. 6:15 (14–15);
    Jacob 5:77; 6:3;
    D&C 29:21;
    45:41 (40–41);
    97:26 (25–26).
20a Joel 2:22 (21–22).
2 1a HEB *shofar*, or ram's horn.
  b Joel 3:17;
    2 Ne. 12:3 (2–4);
    30:15 (12–18).
  c TG Day of the Lord.
2a Ezek. 34:12 (11–19);
    Amos 5:18 (18–20).
3a D&C 29:21.
  b TG Eden.
5a Rev. 9:9.

b 1 Ne. 22:15 (15, 23);
  2 Ne. 15:24; 26:6 (4, 6);
  D&C 64:24 (23–24);
  133:64.
6a Hebrew idiom meaning "gloom."
  Jer. 8:21; Nahum 2:10.
10a TG Earth, Destiny of.
  b D&C 43:18; 84:118.
  c D&C 29:14; 45:42;
    88:87; 133:49;
    JS—M 1:33.
  d Isa. 13:10; Ezek. 32:7;
    Matt. 24:29.
11a D&C 35:21;
    43:18 (17–25); 88:90;
    133:50 (50–52).

b Jer. 30:7.
  c D&C 34:8.
  d Mal. 3:2.
12a 2 Chr. 30:6 (2–27).
  TG Conversion.
  b TG Commitment.
  c TG Fast, Fasting.
13a 3 Ne. 9:20;
    D&C 64:34.
  b JST Joel 2:13 . . . *and repent, and turn unto the Lord your God; for he is gracious and merciful, slow to anger, and of great kindness, and he will turn away the evil from you.*

LORD your God: for he *is* gracious and merciful, slow to anger, and of great ^ckindness, and ^drepenteth him of the evil.

14 ^aWho knoweth *if* he will return and repent, and leave a blessing behind him; *even* a meat offering and a drink offering unto the LORD your God?

15 ¶ Blow the trumpet in Zion, sanctify a fast, call a ^asolemn assembly:

16 Gather the people, sanctify the congregation, assemble the elders, gather the children, and those that suck the breasts: let the bridegroom go forth of his chamber, and the bride out of her ^acloset.

17 Let the priests, the ministers of the LORD, ^aweep between the porch and the altar, and let them say, Spare thy ^bpeople, O LORD, and give not thine heritage to ^creproach, that the heathen should rule over them: wherefore should they say among the people, Where *is* their God?

18 ¶ Then will the LORD be ^ajealous for his land, and ^bpity his people.

19 Yea, the LORD will answer and say unto his people, Behold, I will send you corn, and wine, and oil, and ye shall be satisfied therewith: and I will no more make you a reproach among the heathen:

20 But I will ^aremove far off from you the northern *army*, and will drive him into a land barren and desolate, with his face toward the ^beast sea, and his hinder part toward the utmost sea, and his

^cstink shall come up, and his ill savour shall come up, because he hath done great things.

21 ¶ Fear not, O land; be glad and rejoice: for the LORD will do great things.

22 Be not afraid, ye ^abeasts of the field: for the pastures of the wilderness do spring, for the tree beareth her fruit, the fig tree and the vine do yield their strength.

23 Be glad then, ye children of ^aZion, and rejoice in the LORD your God: for he hath given you the former rain moderately, and he will cause to come down for you the ^brain, the former rain, and the ^clatter rain in the first *month*.

24 And the floors shall be full of wheat, and the ^afats shall overflow with wine and oil.

25 And I will ^arestore to you the years that the locust hath eaten, the cankerworm, and the caterpiller, and the palmerworm, my great army which I sent among you.

26 And ye shall eat in plenty, and be satisfied, and praise the name of the LORD your God, that hath dealt wondrously with you: and my people shall never be ^aashamed.

27 And ye shall know that I *am* in the ^amidst of Israel, and *that* I *am* the LORD your God, and none else: and my people shall never be ashamed.

28 ¶ And it shall come to pass afterward, *that* I will ^apour out my ^bspirit upon all flesh; and your sons and your daughters shall ^cprophesy, your ^dold men shall ^edream dreams, your young men shall see ^fvisions:

13c TG Kindness.
d Gen. 6:6;
1 Sam. 15:11;
2 Sam. 24:16;
Ps. 135:14.
14a JST Joel 2:14 *Therefore repent, and* who knoweth *but* he will return and leave a blessing behind him; *that you may offer* a meat offering . . .
15a TG Solemn Assembly.
16a HEB wedding canopy.
17a TG Isa. 22:12;
2 Cor. 7:10;
James 4:9 (8–10).
b Ex. 33:13.
c Jer. 24:9;
1 Ne. 19:14;
3 Ne. 16:9 (8–9).
TG Reproach.
18a HEB zealous.
Zech. 1:14;
3 Ne. 20:46 (29–36, 46);
Ether 13:5 (5, 11).
b OR have compassion on.
20a Ezek. 39:3 (2–5).
b Ezek. 47:18.
c Isa. 34:3.
22a Joel 1:20.
23a Ps. 149:2;
D&C 84:56.
b Lev. 26:4 (3–4).
c Deut. 11:14; Zech. 10:1.
24a OR vats.
25a Lev. 26:3 (3–14);
2 Ne. 1:20.
26a 2 Ne. 6:13 (7, 13);
3 Ne. 22:4.
27a TG God, Presence of.
28a JS—H 1:41.
TG Dispensations;
Restoration of the Gospel.
b TG God, Spirit of;
Millennium, Preparing a People for.
c TG Holy Ghost, Gifts of.
d TG Old Age.
e TG Dream.
f TG Vision.

29 And also upon the servants and upon the handmaids in those days will I pour out my spirit.

30 And I will shew ^awonders in the ^bheavens and in the earth, blood, and ^cfire, and pillars of smoke.

31 The sun shall be turned into darkness, and the moon into ^ablood, before the great and the terrible ^bday of the LORD come.

32 And it shall come to pass, *that* whosoever shall ^acall on the name of ^bthe LORD shall be ^cdelivered: for in ^dmount ^eZion and in ^fJerusalem shall be ^gdeliverance, as the LORD hath said, and in the ^hremnant whom the LORD shall ⁱcall.

CHAPTER 3

All nations will be at war—Multitudes will stand in the valley of decision as the Second Coming draws near—The Lord will dwell in Zion.

FOR, behold, in those days, and in that time, when I shall ^abring again the captivity of Judah and Jerusalem,

2 I will also ^agather all nations, and will bring them down into the valley of Jehoshaphat, and will ^bplead with them there for my people and *for* my ^cheritage Israel, whom they have scattered among the nations, and parted my land.

3 And they have cast lots for my people; and have given a boy for an harlot, and sold a girl for wine, that they might drink.

4 Yea, and what have ye to do with me, O Tyre, and Zidon, and all the coasts of Palestine? will ye render me a recompence? and if ye

^arecompense me, swiftly *and* speedily will I return your ^brecompence upon your own head;

5 Because ye have taken my silver and my gold, and have carried into your temples my goodly pleasant things:

6 The children also of Judah and the children of Jerusalem have ye sold unto the Grecians, that ye might remove them far from their border.

7 Behold, I will raise them out of the place whither ye have sold them, and will return your recompence upon your own head:

8 And I will sell your sons and your daughters into the hand of the children of Judah, and they shall sell them to the Sabeans, to a people far off: for the LORD hath spoken *it*.

9 ¶ Proclaim ye this among the Gentiles; Prepare ^awar, wake up the mighty men, let all the men of war draw near; let them come up:

10 Beat your plowshares into swords, and your pruninghooks into spears: let the weak say, I *am* ^astrong.

11 Assemble yourselves, and come, all ye heathen, and gather yourselves together round about: thither cause thy ^amighty ones to come down, O LORD.

12 Let the ^aheathen be wakened, and come up to the valley of Jehoshaphat: for there will I sit to ^bjudge all the heathen round about.

13 Put ye in the ^asickle, for the ^bharvest is ripe: come, get you down; for the ^cpress is full, the ^dfats overflow; for their wickedness *is* great.

30a D&C 45:40.
   TG Last Days.
  b TG Astronomy;
   Heaven.
  c TG World, End of.
31a Rev. 6:12.
  b TG Day of the Lord.
32a D&C 93:1; 100:17.
   TG Prayer.
  b HEB Jehovah.
  c TG Jesus Christ, Savior;
   Salvation.
  d D&C 76:66.
  e TG Zion.

  f TG Jerusalem.
  g Obad. 1:17 (15–17).
  h TG Israel, Remnant of.
  i TG Israel, Gathering of.
3 1a HEB cause the return.
  2a Micah 4:11;
   Zeph. 3:8.
  b Isa. 66:16;
   Jer. 25:31;
   Ezek. 38:22.
  c Isa. 19:25.
  4a TG Reward.
  b Deut. 32:35.
  9a TG War.

10a 2 Cor. 12:10;
   Heb. 11:34;
   Ether 12:27;
   D&C 50:16.
11a Isa. 13:3.
12a TG Heathen.
  b TG Jesus Christ, Judge.
13a Alma 26:5;
   D&C 4:4.
  b D&C 6:3; 101:64.
  c Rev. 14:19;
   D&C 76:107.
  d OR vats.

14 Multitudes, ^amultitudes in the valley of decision: for the ^bday of the LORD *is* near in the valley of decision.

15 The ^asun and the moon shall be ^bdarkened, and the stars shall withdraw their shining.

16 The ^aLORD also shall ^broar out of ^cZion, and ^dutter his voice from Jerusalem; and the heavens and the earth shall ^eshake: but the LORD *will be* the ^fhope of his people, and the strength of the children of Israel.

17 So shall ye know that I *am* the LORD your God ^adwelling in Zion, my holy ^bmountain: then shall ^cJerusalem be holy, and there shall no ^dstrangers pass through her any more.

18 ¶ And it shall come to pass in that day, *that* the ^amountains shall drop down new wine, and the hills shall flow with milk, and all the rivers of Judah shall flow with waters, and a ^bfountain shall come forth of the house of the LORD, and shall water the valley of Shittim.

19 ^aEgypt shall be a desolation, and Edom shall be a desolate wilderness, for the violence *against* the children of Judah, because they have shed innocent blood in their land.

20 But Judah shall dwell for ever, and Jerusalem from generation to generation.

21 For I will cleanse their blood *that* I have not cleansed: for the LORD dwelleth in ^aZion.

AMOS

CHAPTER 1

Amos shows the Lord's judgments upon Syria, the Philistines, Tyre, Edom, and Ammon.

THE words of Amos, who was among the herdmen of Tekoa, which he saw concerning Israel in the days of ^aUzziah king of Judah, and in the days of ^bJeroboam the son of Joash king of Israel, two years before the ^cearthquake.

2 And he said, The LORD will ^aroar from Zion, and utter his voice from Jerusalem; and the ^bhabitations of the shepherds shall mourn, and the top of Carmel shall wither.

3 Thus saith the LORD; For three transgressions of Damascus, and for four, I will not turn away *the punishment* thereof; because they have ^athreshed Gilead with threshing instruments of iron:

4 But I will send a fire into the house of ^aHazael, which shall devour the palaces of Ben-hadad.

14a Zech. 14:2 (2–5);
  Rev. 16:16.
 b Obad. 1:15.
15a TG Last Days;
  World, End of.
 b 2 Ne. 23:10.
16a TG Jesus Christ, Second
  Coming.
 b Jer. 25:30.
 c TG Zion.
 d D&C 133:21.
 e D&C 21:6.
  TG Last Days.
 f TG Hope.

17a TG Millennium.
 b Joel 2:1;
  Zech. 8:3.
 c TG Jerusalem.
 d Zech. 14:21.
  TG Stranger.
18a TG Earth, Renewal of.
 b Ezek. 47:1;
  Zech. 14:8;
  Rev. 22:1.
19a Isa. 19:16 (11–25);
  Ezek. 29:2;
  Zech. 10:11.
21a Jer. 3:17;

  Zech. 2:10 (10–12);
  Rev. 22:3 (3–4).

[AMOS]

1 1a Hosea 1:1.
 b Amos 7:10.
 c Zech. 14:5.
2a Isa. 31:4;
  Jer. 25:30.
 b OR pastures.
3a 2 Kgs. 13:7.
4a 2 Kgs. 8:12; 10:32; 13:3.

5 I will break also the bar of Damascus, and cut off the inhabitant from the plain of Aven, and him that holdeth the sceptre from the house of Eden: and the people of Syria shall go into captivity unto Kir, saith the LORD.

6 ¶ Thus saith the LORD; For three transgressions of Gaza, and for four, I will not turn away *the punishment* thereof; because they carried away captive the whole captivity, to deliver *them* up to Edom:

7 But I will send a fire on the wall of Gaza, which shall devour the palaces thereof:

8 And I will cut off the inhabitant from *a*Ashdod, and him that holdeth the sceptre from Ashkelon, and I will turn mine hand against Ekron: and the remnant of the *b*Philistines shall perish, saith the Lord GOD.

9 ¶ Thus saith the LORD; For three transgressions of *a*Tyrus, and for four, I will not turn away *the punishment* thereof; because they delivered up the whole captivity to Edom, and remembered not the *b*brotherly covenant:

10 But I will send a fire on the wall of *a*Tyrus, which shall devour the palaces thereof.

11 ¶ Thus saith the LORD; For three transgressions of *a*Edom, and for four, I will not turn away *the punishment* thereof; because he did pursue his brother with the sword, and did cast off all pity, and his anger did tear perpetually, and he kept his wrath for ever:

12 But I will send a fire upon *a*Teman, which shall devour the palaces of Bozrah.

13 ¶ Thus saith the LORD; For three transgressions of the children of Ammon, and for four, I will not turn away *the punishment* thereof; because they have ripped up the women with child of Gilead, that they might enlarge their border:

14 But I will kindle a fire in the wall of *a*Rabbah, and it shall devour the palaces thereof, with shouting in the day of battle, with a tempest in the day of the whirlwind:

15 And their king shall go into captivity, he and his princes together, saith the LORD.

CHAPTER 2

The Lord will pour out judgments upon Moab, Judah, and Israel for their unrighteousness.

THUS saith the LORD; For three transgressions of *a*Moab, and for four, I will not turn away *the punishment* thereof; because he burned the bones of the king of Edom into lime:

2 But I will send a fire upon Moab, and it shall devour the palaces of Kerioth: and Moab shall die with tumult, with shouting, *and* with the sound of the trumpet:

3 And I will cut off the judge from the midst thereof, and will slay all the princes thereof with him, saith the LORD.

4 ¶ Thus saith the LORD; For three transgressions of Judah, and for four, I will not turn away *the punishment* thereof; because they have *a*despised the law of the LORD, and have not kept his commandments, and their lies caused them to err, after the which their fathers have walked:

5 But I will send a fire upon Judah, and it shall devour the palaces of Jerusalem.

6 ¶ Thus saith the LORD; For three transgressions of Israel, and for four, I will not turn away *the punishment* thereof; because they *a*sold the righteous for silver, and the poor for a pair of shoes;

7 That pant after the dust of the earth on the head of the poor, and turn aside the way of the meek: and

8a Amos 3:9.
  b Isa. 14:31 (29–32);
    Jer. 47:1;
    Ezek. 25:15 (15–16).
9a Isa. 23:1;
    Ezek. 26:2.

b TG Brotherhood and
    Sisterhood.
10a Zech. 9:3 (3–4).
11a Jer. 49:7.
12a Obad. 1:9 (9–10).
14a Jer. 49:2;

Ezek. 21:20; 25:5 (4–5).
2 1a Isa. 16:13.
4a Lev. 26:14 (14–15).
6a Amos 8:6.

a man and his father will go in unto the *same* maid, to ^aprofane my holy name:

8 And they lay *themselves* down upon clothes laid to pledge by every altar, and they drink the wine of the condemned *in* the house of their god.

9 ¶ Yet ^adestroyed I the Amorite before them, whose height *was* like the height of the cedars, and he *was* strong as the oaks; yet I destroyed his fruit from above, and his roots from beneath.

10 Also I ^abrought you up from the land of Egypt, and led you ^bforty years through the wilderness, to possess the land of the Amorite.

11 And I raised up of your sons for prophets, and of your young men for ^aNazarites. *Is it* not even thus, O ye children of Israel? saith the Lord.

12 But ye gave the Nazarites wine to drink; and commanded the prophets, saying, Prophesy not.

13 Behold, I am pressed under you, as a cart is pressed *that is* full of sheaves.

14 Therefore the ^aflight shall perish from the ^bswift, and the strong shall not strengthen his force, neither shall the mighty ^cdeliver himself:

15 Neither shall he stand that handleth the bow; and *he that is* swift of foot shall not deliver *himself*: neither shall he that rideth the horse ^adeliver himself.

16 And *he that is* courageous among the mighty shall flee away naked in that day, saith the Lord.

CHAPTER 3

The Lord reveals His secrets unto His servants the prophets—Because Israel rejects the prophets and follows evil, the nation is overwhelmed by an adversary.

Hear this word that the Lord hath spoken against you, O children of Israel, against the whole family which I ^abrought up from the land of Egypt, saying,

2 You ^aonly have I ^bknown of all the families of the earth: therefore I will ^cpunish you for all your iniquities.

3 Can two walk together, except they be ^aagreed?

4 Will a lion roar in the forest, when he hath no prey? will a young lion cry out of his den, if he have taken nothing?

5 Can a bird fall in a snare upon the earth, where no ^agin *is* for him? shall *one* take up a snare from the earth, and have taken nothing at all?

6 Shall a trumpet be blown in the city, and the people not be afraid? shall there be ^aevil in a city, and the Lord hath not ^bdone *it*?

7 Surely the Lord God will do nothing, ^abut he ^brevealeth his ^csecret unto his servants the ^dprophets.

8 The lion hath roared, who will not fear? the Lord God hath spoken, who can but ^aprophesy?

9 ¶ Publish in the palaces at ^aAshdod, and in the palaces in the land of Egypt, and say, Assemble yourselves upon the mountains of Samaria, and behold the great tumults

---

7a TG Sacrilege.
9a Num. 21:24 (21–25);
   Josh. 24:8.
10a Ex. 12:51;
   Amos 3:1.
  b Num. 14:33.
11a Num. 6:2 (2–21).
14a Amos 9:1.
  b Eccl. 9:11.
  c TG Deliver.
15a Ps. 33:17.
3 1a Amos 2:10;
   1 Ne. 5:15;
   D&C 136:22.
  2a TG Peculiar People.

  b Ps. 147:20 (19–20);
   Mosiah 26:24 (24–27);
   D&C 103:17 (7–18).
  c TG Accountability.
3a TG Unity.
5a IE bait, or lure.
6a Isa. 45:7;
   Alma 5:40;
   Moro. 7:12.
  b JST Amos 3:6 . . .
   known . . .
7a JST Amos 3:7 . . . until . . .
  b Ex. 18:15;
   D&C 132:7.
   TG Guidance, Divine;

   Revelation;
   Scriptures to Come
   Forth;
   Warn.
  c Dan. 2:19.
  d 2 Sam. 24:11;
   Isa. 42:9;
   Mosiah 8:16 (16–18);
   Alma 13:26.
   TG Prophecy;
   Prophets, Mission of;
   Restoration of the
   Gospel.
8a Acts 4:20.
9a Amos 1:8.

in the midst thereof, and the oppressed in the midst thereof.

10 For they know not to do right, saith the LORD, who store up *a*violence and robbery in their palaces.

11 Therefore thus saith the Lord GOD; An adversary *there shall be even* round about the land, and he shall bring down thy strength from thee, and thy palaces shall be spoiled.

12 Thus saith the LORD; As the shepherd taketh out of the mouth of the lion two legs, or a piece of an ear; so shall the children of Israel be taken out that dwell in Samaria in the corner of a bed, and in Damascus *in* a couch.

13 Hear ye, and testify in the house of Jacob, saith the Lord GOD, the God of hosts,

14 That in the day that I shall visit the transgressions of Israel upon him I will also visit the altars of *a*Beth-el: and the horns of the altar shall be cut off, and *b*fall to the ground.

15 And I will smite the *a*winter house with the summer house; and the houses of *b*ivory shall perish, and the great houses shall have an end, saith the LORD.

CHAPTER 4

The Lord withholds rain, sends famine and pestilence, and destroys gardens and vineyards as judgments upon His people, yet they do not return unto the Lord.

HEAR this word, ye *a*kine of Bashan, that *are* in the mountain of *b*Samaria, which oppress the *c*poor, which crush the needy, which say to their masters, Bring, and let us drink.

2 The Lord GOD hath sworn by his *a*holiness, that, lo, the days shall come upon you, that he will take you away with hooks, and your posterity with fishhooks.

3 And ye shall go out at the *a*breaches, every *cow at that which is* before her; and ye shall cast *them* into the palace, saith the LORD.

4 ¶ Come to Beth-el, and transgress, at *a*Gilgal multiply transgression; and bring your sacrifices every morning, *and* your *b*tithes after three *c*years:

5 And offer a sacrifice of *a*thanksgiving with *b*leaven, and proclaim *and* publish the *c*free offerings: for this liketh you, O ye children of Israel, saith the Lord GOD.

6 ¶ And I also have given you *a*cleanness of teeth in all your cities, and want of bread in all your places: yet have ye not *b*returned unto me, saith the LORD.

7 And also I have withholden the *a*rain from you, when *there were* yet three months to the harvest: and I caused it to rain upon one city, and caused it not to rain upon another city: one piece was rained upon, and the piece whereupon it rained not withered.

8 So two *or* three cities wandered unto one city, to drink water; but they were not satisfied: yet have ye not returned unto me, saith the LORD.

9 I have smitten you with blasting and mildew: when your gardens and your vineyards and your fig trees and your olive trees increased, the palmerworm devoured *them:* yet have ye not returned unto me, saith the LORD.

10 I have sent among you the pestilence after the manner of Egypt: your *a*young men have I slain with the sword, and have taken away your horses; and I have made the stink of your camps to come up unto

10*a* Isa. 3:14;
  Ezek. 22:12 (6–13);
  Alma 4:12 (12–13).
14*a* Amos 5:5 (5–6).
  b 2 Kgs. 23:15.
15*a* Jer. 36:22.
  b 1 Kgs. 22:39.
4 1*a* IE cows.
  b Amos 6:1.

c 2 Ne. 20:2.
2*a* Ps. 89:35.
3*a* OR broken places.
4*a* Hosea 9:15 (13–15).
  b Deut. 14:28;
    D&C 119:4 (4–5).
  c HEB days.
5*a* TG Thanksgiving.
  b TG Leaven.

c Lev. 22:18 (18–21).
6*a* Hag. 2:17;
  Hel. 12:3;
  D&C 43:22 (22–30).
7*a* Jer. 3:3.
10*a* Isa. 3:25;
  D&C 45:33.

your nostrils: yet have ye not returned unto me, saith the LORD.

11 I have overthrown *some* of you, as God [a]overthrew [b]Sodom and Gomorrah, and ye were as a [c]firebrand plucked out of the [d]burning: yet have ye not returned unto me, saith the LORD.

12 Therefore thus will I do unto thee, O Israel: *and* because I will do this unto thee, prepare to meet thy God, O Israel.

13 For, lo, he that [a]formeth the mountains, and createth the wind, and declareth unto man what *is* his [b]thought, that maketh the [c]morning [d]darkness, and treadeth upon the high places of the earth, The LORD, The God of hosts, *is* his name.

CHAPTER 5

The people of Israel are exhorted to seek the Lord and do good so that they may live—Their sacrifices to false gods are abhorrent.

HEAR ye this word which I take up against you, *even* a lamentation, O house of Israel.

2 The virgin of Israel is fallen; she shall no more rise: she is forsaken upon her land; *there is* none to raise her up.

3 For thus saith the Lord GOD; The city that went out *by* a thousand shall leave an hundred, and that which went forth *by* an hundred shall leave ten, to the house of Israel.

4 ¶ For thus saith the LORD unto the house of Israel, [a]Seek ye me, and ye shall live:

5 But seek not Beth-el, nor enter into Gilgal, and pass not to Beer-sheba: for Gilgal shall surely go into captivity, and [a]Beth-el shall come to nought.

6 [a]Seek the LORD, and ye shall live; lest he break out like fire in the house of Joseph, and devour *it*, and *there be* none to quench *it* in Beth-el.

7 Ye who turn judgment to wormwood, and leave off righteousness in the earth,

8 *Seek him* that maketh [a]the seven [b]stars and Orion, and turneth the shadow of death into the [c]morning, and maketh the day [d]dark with night: that calleth for the [e]waters of the sea, and poureth them out upon the face of the earth: [f]The LORD *is* his name:

9 That strengtheneth the spoiled against the strong, so that the spoiled shall come against the fortress.

10 They hate him that rebuketh in the [a]gate, and they abhor him that speaketh uprightly.

11 Forasmuch therefore as your treading *is* upon the poor, and ye take from him burdens of wheat: ye have [a]built houses of hewn stone, but ye shall not [b]dwell in them; ye have planted pleasant vineyards, but ye shall not drink wine of them.

12 For I know your manifold transgressions and your mighty sins: they afflict the just, they take a [a]bribe, and they [b]turn aside the [c]poor in the gate *from their right*.

13 Therefore the [a]prudent shall keep [b]silence in that time; for it *is* an evil time.

14 Seek [a]good, and not [b]evil, that ye may live: and so the LORD, the God of hosts, shall be with you, as ye have spoken.

15 Hate the evil, and [a]love the

11a Isa. 13:19.
  b Gen. 19:24.
  c Zech. 3:2.
  d Mal. 4:1; Jude 1:23.
13a TG Jesus Christ, Creator.
  b Ps. 139:2; Jacob 2:5;
    Alma 18:32;
    3 Ne. 28:6;
    D&C 33:1.
  c Amos 5:8.
  d Amos 8:9.
5 4a 2 Ne. 1:20;
    Mosiah 26:30.

5a Amos 3:14.
6a 1 Chr. 16:11;
    Alma 37:47;
    Ether 12:41;
    D&C 45:46; 88:63;
    101:38.
8a IE the Pleiades.
  b TG Astronomy.
  c Amos 4:13.
  d Amos 8:9.
  e Amos 9:6.
  f HEB Jehovah.
10a 2 Ne. 27:32.

11a Zeph. 1:13.
  b Deut. 28:30.
12a TG Bribe.
  b Isa. 29:21.
  c Ezek. 22:7 (7–13);
    Hel. 6:39 (37–40).
13a TG Prudence.
  b Prov. 17:28 (27–28).
14a Ether 4:12 (11–12);
    Moro. 7:16;
    D&C 6:13; 58:28 (26–33).
  b TG Evil.
15a TG Love.

good, and establish judgment in the gate: it may be that the LORD God of hosts will be gracious unto the remnant of [b]Joseph.

16 Therefore the LORD, the God of hosts, the Lord, saith thus; Wailing *shall be* in all streets; and they shall say in all the highways, Alas! alas! and they shall call the husbandman to mourning, and such as are skilful of lamentation to wailing.

17 And in all vineyards *shall be* wailing: for I will pass through thee, saith the LORD.

18 Woe unto you that [a]desire the [b]day of the LORD! to what end *is* it for you? the day of the LORD *is* [c]darkness, and not light.

19 As if a man did flee from a lion, and a bear met him; or went into the house, and leaned his hand on the wall, and a serpent bit him.

20 *Shall* not the day of the LORD *be* darkness, and not light? even very dark, and no brightness in it?

21 ¶ I hate, I despise your [a]feast days, and [b]I will not smell in your [c]solemn assemblies.

22 Though ye [a]offer me burnt offerings and your meat offerings, I will not [b]accept *them:* neither will I regard the peace [c]offerings of your fat beasts.

23 Take thou away from me the noise of thy songs; for I will not hear the melody of thy viols.

24 But let [a]judgment run down as waters, and [b]righteousness as a mighty stream.

25 Have ye offered unto me sacrifices and offerings in the wilderness forty years, O house of Israel?

26 But ye have borne the tabernacle of your [a]Moloch and Chiun your images, the star of your god, which ye made to yourselves.

27 Therefore will I cause you to go into captivity beyond Damascus, saith the LORD, whose name *is* The God of hosts.

CHAPTER 6

Woe to them who are at ease in Zion— Israel will be plagued with desolation.

WOE to them *that are* at [a]ease in Zion, and trust in the mountain of [b]Samaria, *which are* named chief of the nations, to whom the house of Israel came!

2 Pass ye unto Calneh, and see; and from thence go ye to Hamath the great: then go down to Gath of the Philistines: *be they* better than these kingdoms? or their border greater than your border?

3 Ye that put [a]far away the evil day, and cause the seat of violence to come near;

4 That lie upon beds of ivory, and stretch themselves upon their couches, and eat the lambs out of the flock, and the calves out of the midst of the stall;

5 That chant to the sound of the viol, *and* invent to themselves [a]instruments of [b]musick, like David;

6 That drink wine in bowls, and anoint themselves with the chief ointments: but they are not grieved for the affliction of Joseph.

7 ¶ Therefore now shall they go [a]captive with the first that go captive, and the [b]banquet of them that stretched themselves shall be removed.

8 The Lord GOD hath [a]sworn by himself, saith the LORD the God of hosts, I abhor the [b]excellency of Jacob, and hate his palaces: therefore will I deliver up the city with all that is therein.

15b 2 Ne. 3:4; 25:21;
   Jacob 2:25.
18a Isa. 5:19 (18–19).
  b Joel 1:15; 3 Ne. 21:20;
   D&C 45:39 (39–42).
  c Joel 2:2;
   D&C 133:49;
   JS—M 1:33 (32–34).
21a Isa. 1:14.
  b IE I will not take heed
   of your sacrifices,

incense, etc.
  c TG Solemn Assembly.
22a TG Hypocrisy.
  b Hosea 8:13; Mal. 1:10.
  c TG Sacrifice.
24a Amos 6:12; 2 Ne. 15:7.
  b TG Righteousness.
26a TG Apostasy of Israel.
6 1a Ps. 123:4;
   2 Ne. 28:24 (21–24).
  b Amos 4:1.

3a Ezek. 12:27.
5a 1 Chr. 23:5;
   2 Chr. 29:26 (25–28).
  b D&C 136:28.
7a TG Israel, Scattering of.
  b OR revelry.
8a Jer. 22:5; 51:14;
   Heb. 6:13;
   D&C 97:20.
  b HEB pride.
   Amos 8:7.

9 And it shall come to pass, if there remain ten *a*men in one house, that they shall die.

10 And a man's uncle shall take him up, and he that burneth him, to bring out the bones out of the house, and shall say unto him that *is* by the sides of the house, *Is there* yet *any* with thee? and he shall say, No. Then shall he say, Hold thy tongue: for we may not make mention of the name of the LORD.

11 For, behold, the LORD commandeth, and he will smite the great house with breaches, and the little house with clefts.

12 ¶ Shall horses run upon the rock? will *one* plow *there* with oxen? for ye have turned *a*judgment into gall, and the fruit of righteousness into hemlock:

13 Ye which *a*rejoice in a thing of nought, which say, Have we not taken to us horns by our own strength?

14 But, behold, I will raise up against you a nation, O house of Israel, saith the LORD the God of hosts; and they shall afflict you from the entering in of Hemath unto the river of the wilderness.

CHAPTER 7

Amos relates how he was called of God to be a prophet—He prophesies the captivity of Israel.

THUS hath the Lord GOD shewed unto me; and, behold, he formed grasshoppers in the beginning of the shooting up of the latter growth; and, lo, *it was* the latter growth after the king's mowings.

2 And it came to pass, *that* when they had made an end of eating the grass of the land, then I said, O Lord GOD, forgive, I beseech thee: by whom shall Jacob arise? for he *is* small.

3 *a*The LORD *b*repented for this: It shall not be, saith the LORD.

4 ¶ Thus hath the Lord GOD shewed unto me: and, behold, the Lord GOD called to contend by fire, and it devoured the great deep, and did eat up a part.

5 Then said I, O Lord GOD, cease, I beseech thee: by whom shall Jacob arise? for he *is* small.

6 *a*The LORD repented for this: This also shall not be, saith the Lord GOD.

7 ¶ Thus he shewed me: and, behold, the Lord stood upon a wall *made* by a plumbline, with a plumbline in his hand.

8 And the LORD said unto me, Amos, what seest thou? And I said, A plumbline. Then said the Lord, Behold, I will set a plumbline in the midst of my people Israel: I will not again *a*pass by them any more:

9 And the high places of Isaac shall be desolate, and the sanctuaries of Israel shall be laid waste; and I will rise against the *a*house of Jeroboam with the sword.

10 ¶ Then Amaziah the priest of Beth-el sent to *a*Jeroboam king of Israel, saying, Amos hath conspired against thee in the midst of the house of Israel: the land is not able to bear all his words.

11 For thus Amos saith, Jeroboam shall die by the sword, and Israel shall surely be led away captive out of their own land.

12 Also Amaziah said unto Amos, O thou *a*seer, go, flee thee away into the land of Judah, and there eat bread, and prophesy there:

13 But prophesy not again any more at Beth-el: for it *is* the king's *a*chapel, and it *is* the king's court.

14 ¶ Then answered Amos, and

9*a* OR people.
12*a* Amos 5:24.
13*a* Mosiah 11:19;
    D&C 3:4.
7 3*a* JST Amos 7:3 *And the Lord said, concerning Jacob, Jacob shall repent for this, therefore I will*

not utterly destroy him, saith the Lord.
b Gen. 6:6;
    Num. 23:19.
6*a* JST Amos 7:6 *And the Lord said, concerning Jacob, Jacob shall repent of his wickedness;*

therefore I will not utterly destroy him, saith the Lord God.
8*a* Amos 8:2.
9*a* 2 Kgs. 15:10 (8–12).
10*a* Amos 1:1.
12*a* TG Seer.
13*a* OR sanctuary.

said to Amaziah, I *was* no ᵃprophet, neither *was* I a prophet's son; but I *was* an herdman, and a gatherer of sycomore fruit:

15 And the LORD took me as I followed the flock, and the ᵃLORD said unto me, ᵇGo, ᶜprophesy unto my people Israel.

16 ¶ Now therefore hear thou the word of the LORD: Thou sayest, Prophesy not against Israel, and drop not *thy word* against the house of Isaac.

17 Therefore thus saith the LORD; Thy wife shall be an harlot in the city, and thy sons and thy daughters shall fall by the sword, and thy land shall be divided by line; and thou shalt die in a polluted land: and ᵃIsrael shall surely go into captivity forth of his land.

CHAPTER 8

Amos prophesies the downfall of Israel—There will be a famine of hearing the word of the Lord.

THUS hath the Lord GOD shewed unto me: and behold a basket of summer fruit.

2 And he said, Amos, what seest thou? And I said, A basket of summer fruit. Then said the LORD unto me, The ᵃend is come upon my people of Israel; I will not again ᵇpass by them any more.

3 And the songs of the temple shall be howlings in that day, saith the Lord GOD: *there shall be* many dead bodies in every place; they shall cast *them* forth with silence.

4 ¶ Hear this, O ye that swallow up the needy, even to make the poor of the land to fail,

5 Saying, When will the new moon be gone, that we may sell corn? and the ᵃsabbath, that we may set forth wheat, making the ᵇephah small, and the shekel great, and falsifying the ᶜbalances by deceit?

6 That we may ᵃbuy the poor for silver, and the needy for a pair of shoes; *yea*, and sell the refuse of the wheat?

7 The LORD hath sworn by the ᵃexcellency of Jacob, Surely I will never ᵇforget any of their works.

8 Shall not the land tremble for this, and every one ᵃmourn that dwelleth therein? and it shall rise up wholly as a flood; and it shall ᵇbe cast out and drowned, as *by* the flood of Egypt.

9 And it shall come to pass in that day, saith the Lord GOD, that I will cause the ᵃsun to go down at noon, and I will ᵇdarken the ᶜearth in the clear day:

10 And I will turn your feasts into mourning, and all your songs into ᵃlamentation; and I will bring up sackcloth upon all loins, and ᵇbaldness upon every head; and I will make it as the mourning of an ᶜonly *son*, and the end thereof as a bitter day.

11 ¶ Behold, the days come, saith the Lord GOD, that I will send a famine in the land, not a ᵃfamine of bread, nor a ᵇthirst for water, but of hearing the ᶜwords of the LORD:

12 And they shall wander from sea to sea, and from the north even to the east, they shall ᵃrun to and fro to seek the word of the LORD, and shall not find *it*.

13 In that day shall the fair virgins and young men faint for thirst.

14*a* JS—H 1:23 (22–23).
15*a* TG Called of God.
   b TG Priesthood, Keys of.
   c TG Prophecy;
     Prophets, Mission of.
17*a* TG Israel, Ten Lost
     Tribes of.
8 2*a* Ezek. 7:2.
   b Amos 7:8.
5*a* TG Sabbath.
  b Lev. 19:36;
    Deut. 25:15 (14–15);

    Ezek. 45:10.
   c Prov. 11:1.
6*a* Amos 2:6.
7*a* Amos 6:8.
  b Hosea 8:13.
8*a* Amos 9:5.
  b HEB overflow and recede
    like the river of Egypt.
9*a* Micah 3:6.
  b Amos 4:13; 5:8;
    Luke 23:44 (44–45).
  c TG Earth, Destiny of.

10*a* TG Mourning.
   b Isa. 3:24 (16–26).
   c Jer. 6:26;
    Zech. 12:10.
11*a* 1 Sam. 3:1;
    Ps. 74:9.
   TG Apostasy of Israel;
    Apostasy of the Early
    Christian Church.
   b Hosea 2:3.
   c Rev. 12:6.
12*a* Job 12:24 (24–25).

14 They that ^aswear by the sin of Samaria, and say, Thy god, O ^bDan, liveth; and, The manner of Beersheba liveth; even they shall fall, and never rise up again.

CHAPTER 9

Israel will be sifted among all nations— In the last days, the people of Israel will be gathered again into their own land, and it will become productive.

I SAW the Lord standing upon the altar: and he said, Smite the lintel of the door, that the posts may shake: and cut them in the head, all of them; and I will ^aslay the last of them with the sword: he that ^bfleeth of them shall not flee away, and he that escapeth of them shall not be delivered.

2 Though they dig into ^ahell, thence shall mine hand take them; though they climb up to heaven, thence will I bring them down:

3 And though they ^ahide themselves in the top of Carmel, I will search and take them out thence; and though they be hid from my sight in the bottom of the sea, thence will I command the serpent, and he shall bite them:

4 And though they go into captivity before their enemies, thence will I command the sword, and it shall slay them: and I will set mine eyes upon them for ^aevil, and not for good.

5 And the Lord GOD of hosts *is* he that toucheth the land, and it shall ^amelt, and all that dwell therein shall ^bmourn: and it shall rise up wholly like a flood; and shall be drowned, as *by* the flood of Egypt.

6 *It is* he that buildeth his ^astories in the heaven, and hath founded his troop in the earth; he that calleth for the ^bwaters of the sea, and poureth them out upon the face of the earth: The LORD *is* his name.

7 *Are* ye not as children of the Ethiopians unto me, O children of Israel? saith the LORD. Have not I brought up Israel out of the land of Egypt? and the Philistines from Caphtor, and the Syrians from Kir?

8 Behold, the ^aeyes of the Lord GOD *are* upon the sinful kingdom, and I will ^bdestroy it from off the face of the earth; saving that I will not utterly ^cdestroy the house of Jacob, saith the LORD.

9 For, lo, I will command, and I will ^asift the house of ^bIsrael among all nations, like as *corn* is sifted in a sieve, yet shall not the least grain ^cfall upon the earth.

10 All the sinners of my people shall die by the sword, which say, The evil shall not overtake nor ^aprevent us.

11 ¶ In that day will I raise up the ^atabernacle of David that is fallen, and close up the breaches thereof; and I will raise up his ruins, and I will build it as in the days of old:

12 That they may ^apossess the remnant of ^bEdom, and of all the ^cheathen, which are called by my name, saith the LORD that doeth this.

13 Behold, the days come, saith the LORD, that the plowman shall overtake the reaper, and the treader of grapes him that ^asoweth seed; and the mountains shall drop sweet wine, and all the hills shall ^bmelt.

14a TG Swearing.
  b 1 Kgs. 12:29 (28–30).
9 1a 3 Ne. 16:9.
  b Prov. 28:1;
    Amos 2:14.
2a Ps. 139:8 (8–9).
3a 2 Ne. 12:10;
    Alma 12:14.
4a Jer. 21:10.
5a D&C 101:25 (23–25).
  b Amos 8:8.
6a Moses 1:33.
  b Amos 5:8;

Moses 2:7 (6–7);
    Abr. 4:9 (9–10).
8a Ps. 34:15;
    D&C 1:1; 38:7; 67:2.
  b D&C 5:33.
  c Jer. 30:11;
    2 Ne. 3:3 (2–4);
    6:11 (10–11);
    20:20 (20–21).
9a TG Israel, Scattering of.
  b TG Israel, Ten Lost
    Tribes of.
  c Mal. 3:6.

10a HEB confront.
11a Acts 15:16 (15–17).
    TG Temple.
12a Obad. 1:17;
    2 Ne. 24:2 (1–2).
  b Isa. 34:5;
    Jer. 49:17 (7–22);
    Ezek. 25:14 (12–14);
    Obad. 1:18 (8, 18–19, 21).
  c TG Heathen.
13a Gen. 8:22.
  b 3 Ne. 26:3;
    Morm. 9:2.

14 And I will bring again the ^acaptivity of my people of ^bIsrael, and they shall ^cbuild the ^dwaste cities, and inhabit *them*; and they shall plant vineyards, and drink the wine thereof; they shall also make gardens, and eat the fruit of them.

15 And I will ^aplant them upon their ^bland, and they shall ^cno more be pulled up out of their land which I have given them, saith the LORD thy God.

OBADIAH

Obadiah prophesies the downfall of Edom—Saviors will stand upon Mount Zion.

THE vision of Obadiah. Thus saith the Lord GOD concerning ^aEdom; We have heard a rumour from the LORD, and an ambassador is sent among the heathen, Arise ye, and let us rise up against her in battle.

2 Behold, I have made thee small among the heathen: thou art greatly despised.

3 ¶ The ^apride of thine ^bheart hath deceived thee, thou that dwellest in the clefts of the rock, whose habitation *is* high; that saith in his heart, Who shall bring me down to the ground?

4 Though thou exalt *thyself* as the eagle, and though thou set thy nest among the stars, thence will I bring thee down, saith the LORD.

5 If ^athieves came to thee, if robbers by night, (how art thou cut off!) would they not have stolen till they had enough? if the grapegatherers came to thee, would they not leave *some* grapes?

6 How are *the things* of Esau searched out! *how* are his hidden things sought up!

7 All the men of thy confederacy have brought thee *even* to the border: the men that were at peace with thee have deceived thee, *and* prevailed against thee; *they that eat* thy bread have laid a wound under thee: *there is* none understanding in him.

8 Shall I not in ^athat day, saith the LORD, even destroy the wise *men* out of Edom, and understanding out of the mount of Esau?

9 And thy mighty *men*, O ^aTeman, shall be dismayed, to the end that every one of the mount of Esau may be ^bcut off by slaughter.

10 ¶ For *thy* violence against thy brother Jacob shame shall cover thee, and thou shalt be cut off for ever.

11 In the day that thou stoodest on the other side, in the day that the strangers carried away captive his forces, and foreigners entered into his gates, and cast lots upon Jerusalem, even thou *wast* as ^aone of them.

12 But thou shouldest not have looked on the day of thy brother in the day that he became a stranger;

14a Zeph. 2:7;
        3 Ne. 16:16 (11–20).
    b TG Israel, Gathering of.
    c D&C 77:15; 84:3 (2–5);
        101:18; 103:11.
    d Ezek. 36:10 (8–15).
15a D&C 55:5.
    b D&C 77:15.

    TG Promised Lands.
    c 3 Ne. 20:29.

[OBADIAH]
1 1a Gen. 36:1;
        Jer. 49:7 (7–22).
    3a Jer. 49:16 (14–16);
        2 Ne. 20:33;

    Hel. 4:12 (12–13);
        D&C 101:42.
    b TG Hardheartedness.
    5a Jer. 49:9.
    8a D&C 45:26.
    9a Amos 1:12.
    b D&C 56:3; 64:35 (35–36).
11a Ezek. 35:5 (1–15).

neither shouldest thou have ^arejoiced over the children of Judah in the day of their destruction; neither shouldest thou have spoken proudly in the day of distress.

13 Thou shouldest not have entered into the gate of my people in the day of their calamity; yea, thou shouldest not have looked on their affliction in the day of their calamity, nor have laid *hands* on their substance in the day of their calamity;

14 Neither shouldest thou have stood in the crossway, to cut off those of his that did escape; neither shouldest thou have delivered up those of his that did remain in the day of distress.

15 For the ^aday of the Lord *is* near upon all the ^bheathen: as thou hast ^cdone, it shall be done unto thee: thy ^dreward shall return upon thine own head.

16 For as ye have ^adrunk upon my holy mountain, *so* shall all the heathen drink continually, yea, they shall drink, and they shall swallow down, and they shall be as though they had not been.

17 ¶ But upon mount ^aZion shall be ^bdeliverance, and there shall be holiness; and the house of Jacob shall ^cpossess their possessions.

18 And the house of Jacob shall be a ^afire, and the house of Joseph a flame, and the house of ^bEsau for stubble, and they shall kindle in them, and devour them; and there shall not be *any* remaining of the house of Esau; for the Lord hath spoken *it.*

19 And *they of* the south shall possess the mount of Esau; and *they of* the plain the ^aPhilistines: and they shall possess the fields of Ephraim, and the fields of Samaria: and Benjamin *shall possess* Gilead.

20 And the captivity of this host of the children of Israel *shall possess* that of the Canaanites, *even* unto Zarephath; and the captivity of Jerusalem, which *is* in Sepharad, shall possess the cities of the south.

21 And ^asaviours shall come up on ^bmount Zion to ^cjudge the mount of Esau; and the ^dkingdom shall be the Lord's.

JONAH

CHAPTER 1

Jonah is sent to call Nineveh to repentance—He flees on a ship, is cast into the sea, and is swallowed by a great fish.

NOW the word of the Lord came unto ^aJonah the son of Amittai, saying,

2 Arise, go to Nineveh, that great city, and ^acry against it; for their ^bwickedness is come up before me.

12a Prov. 17:5.
15a Joel 3:14 (11–21).
  b TG Heathen.
  c Ezek. 35:15.
  d TG Reward.
16a Jer. 25:28 (15–33);
    49:12 (7–12).
17a TG Zion.
  b Joel 2:32.
    TG Deliver.
  c Amos 9:12.
18a Zech. 12:6;

2 Ne. 15:24; 20:17;
  3 Ne. 20:16.
  b Isa. 34:5;
    Jer. 49:17 (7–22);
    Ezek. 25:14 (12–14);
    Amos 9:12.
19a Zeph. 2:5 (5–7);
    2 Ne. 21:14.
21a D&C 103:9–10.
    TG Genealogy and
    Temple Work;
    Mission of Latter-day

Saints;
  Salvation for the Dead.
  b D&C 76:66.
  c D&C 64:37 (31–38).
  d Ps. 22:28;
    2 Ne. 33:12 (11–12).

[Jonah]

1 1a 2 Kgs. 14:25.
  2a TG Missionary Work;
    Prophets, Mission of.
    b D&C 56:14.

3 But Jonah rose up to *a*flee unto Tarshish from the *b*presence of the LORD, and went down to Joppa; and he found a ship going to Tarshish: so he paid the fare thereof, and went down into it, to go with them unto Tarshish from the presence of the LORD.

4 ¶ But the LORD sent out a great wind into the sea, and there was a mighty *a*tempest in the sea, so that the ship was like to be broken.

5 Then the mariners were afraid, and cried every man unto his god, and cast forth the wares that *were* in the ship into the sea, to lighten *it* of them. But Jonah was gone down into the sides of the ship; and he lay, and was fast asleep.

6 So the shipmaster came to him, and said unto him, What meanest thou, O sleeper? arise, *a*call upon thy God, if so be that God will think upon us, that we perish not.

7 And they said every one to his fellow, Come, and let us cast lots, that we may know for whose cause this evil *is* upon us. So they cast lots, and the lot fell upon Jonah.

8 Then said they unto him, Tell us, we pray thee, for whose cause this evil *is* upon us; What *is* thine occupation? and whence comest thou? what *is* thy country? and of what people *art* thou?

9 And he said unto them, I *am* an Hebrew; and I fear the *a*LORD, the God of heaven, which hath made the sea and the dry *land.*

10 Then were the men exceedingly afraid, and said unto him, Why hast thou done this? For the men knew that he fled from the presence of the LORD, because he had told them.

11 ¶ Then said they unto him, What shall we do unto thee, that the sea may be calm unto us? for the sea wrought, and was tempestuous.

12 And he said unto them, Take me up, and cast me forth into the sea; so shall the sea be calm unto you: for I know that for my sake this great tempest *is* upon you.

13 Nevertheless the men rowed hard to bring *it* to the land; but they could not: for the sea wrought, and was tempestuous against them.

14 Wherefore they cried unto the LORD, and said, We beseech thee, O LORD, we beseech thee, let us not perish for this man's life, and lay not upon us innocent blood: for thou, O LORD, hast done as it pleased thee.

15 So they took up Jonah, and cast him forth into the sea: and the sea ceased from her raging.

16 Then the men feared the LORD exceedingly, and offered a sacrifice unto the LORD, and made vows.

17 ¶ Now the LORD had prepared a great fish to swallow up Jonah. And Jonah was in the belly of the fish *a*three days and three nights.

CHAPTER 2

Jonah prays to the Lord, and the fish vomits him out on dry ground.

THEN Jonah prayed unto the LORD his God out of the fish's belly,

2 And said, I cried by reason of mine *a*affliction unto the LORD, and he heard me; out of the belly of *b*hell cried I, *and* thou heardest my voice.

3 For thou hadst cast me into the deep, in the midst of the seas; and the floods compassed me about: all thy billows and thy waves passed over me.

4 Then I said, I am cast out of thy sight; yet I will look again toward thy holy *a*temple.

5 The waters compassed me about, *a*even to the soul: the depth closed me round about, the weeds were wrapped about my head.

6 I went down to the bottoms of the mountains; the earth with her bars

---

3*a* TG Procrastination.
  b Ps. 139:7 (1–16);
     Moses 4:14.
4*a* Matt. 8:24;
     1 Ne. 18:13 (9–13).
6*a* 1 Ne. 18:21 (15–22).

9*a* TG Jesus Christ,
     Jehovah.
17*a* Matt. 16:4.
     TG Jesus Christ,
     Death of;
     Jesus Christ, Types of,

     in Anticipation.
2 2*a* TG Affliction.
     b Alma 36:18.
4*a* Ps. 5:7.
5*a* IE to the point of death.

was about me for ever: yet hast thou ᵃbrought up my life from corruption, O Lᴏʀᴅ my God.

7 When my soul fainted within me I ᵃremembered the Lᴏʀᴅ: and my ᵇprayer came in unto thee, into thine holy ᶜtemple.

8 They that observe ᵃlying vanities forsake their own mercy.

9 But I will sacrifice unto thee with the voice of thanksgiving; I will pay *that* that I have ᵃvowed. ᵇSalvation *is* of the Lᴏʀᴅ.

10 ¶ And the Lᴏʀᴅ spake unto the fish, and it vomited out Jonah upon the dry *land.*

CHAPTER 3

Jonah prophesies the downfall of Nineveh—The people repent, and the city is saved.

Aɴᴅ the word of the Lᴏʀᴅ came unto Jonah the second time, saying,

2 Arise, go unto Nineveh, that great city, and ᵃpreach unto it the preaching that I bid thee.

3 So Jonah arose, and went unto Nineveh, according to the word of the Lᴏʀᴅ. Now Nineveh was an ᵃexceeding great city of three days' ᵇjourney.

4 And Jonah began to enter into the city a day's journey, and he cried, and said, Yet forty days, and Nineveh shall be overthrown.

5 ¶ ᵃSo the people of ᵇNineveh believed God, and proclaimed a ᶜfast, and put on sackcloth, from the greatest of them even to the least of them.

6 For word came unto the king

of Nineveh, and he arose from his throne, and he laid his robe from him, and covered *him* with ᵃsackcloth, and sat in ashes.

7 And he caused *it* to be proclaimed and published through Nineveh by the decree of the king and his nobles, saying, Let neither man nor beast, herd nor flock, taste any thing: let them not feed, nor drink water:

8 But let man and beast be covered with sackcloth, and cry mightily unto God: yea, let them ᵃturn every one from his evil way, and from the violence that *is* in their hands.

9 Who can tell *if* ᵃGod will turn and repent, and turn away from his fierce anger, that we perish not?

10 ¶ And God ᵃsaw their works, that they ᵇturned from their ᶜevil way; and God repented of the evil, that he had said that he would do unto them; and he did *it* ᵈnot.

CHAPTER 4

Jonah is displeased with the Lord for His mercy upon the people—The Lord rebukes him.

Bᴜᴛ it displeased Jonah exceedingly, and he was very angry.

2 And he prayed unto the Lᴏʀᴅ, and said, I pray thee, O Lᴏʀᴅ, *was* not this my saying, when I was yet in my country? Therefore I fled before unto Tarshish: for I knew that thou *art* a gracious God, and ᵃmerciful, slow to anger, and of great kindness, and ᵇrepentest thee of the evil.

3 Therefore now, O Lᴏʀᴅ, take, I beseech thee, my life from me; for *it is* better for me to die than to live.

6*a* ᴛɢ Jesus Christ, Prophecies about.
7*a* Ps. 107:6 (5–6); Hel. 12:3.
  b ᴛɢ Prayer.
  c Ps. 18:6.
8*a* ᴛɢ Honesty.
9*a* ᴛɢ Vow.
  b ᴛɢ Salvation.
3 2*a* ᴛɢ Missionary Work; Preaching; Prophets, Mission of.
3*a* ʜᴇʙ great city to God.
  b ɪᴇ through greater Nineveh with its

environs.
5*a* Alma 31:5.
  b Matt. 12:41.
  c ᴛɢ Fast, Fasting.
6*a* Mosiah 11:25.
8*a* Alma 19:33; 3 Ne. 20:26.
9*a* ᴊsᴛ Jonah 3:9 . . . *we will repent, and turn unto God, but he will* turn away from *us his fierce anger* . . .
10*a* D&C 121:24.
  b ᴛɢ Repent.
  c ᴊsᴛ Jonah 3:10 . . . evil

way *and repented; and God turned away* the evil that he had said he would *bring upon them.*
  d D&C 56:4 (4–6).
4 2*a* ᴛɢ Mercy.
  b ʜᴇʙ relentest; i.e., Jonah knew that God could revoke the calamity decreed, but expected He would do so even without the repentance of the people.

4 ¶ Then said the LORD, Doest thou well to be angry?

5 So Jonah went out of the city, and sat on the east side of the city, and there made him a ^abooth, and sat under it in the shadow, till he might see what would become of the city.

6 And the LORD God prepared a ^agourd, and made *it* to come up over Jonah, that it might be a shadow over his head, to deliver him from his grief. So Jonah was exceeding glad of the gourd.

7 But God prepared a worm when the morning rose the next day, and it smote the gourd that it withered.

8 And it came to pass, when the sun did arise, that God prepared a vehement ^aeast wind; and the sun

beat upon the head of Jonah, that he fainted, and wished in himself to die, and said, *It is* better for me to die than to live.

9 And God said to Jonah, Doest thou well to be ^aangry for the gourd? And he said, I do well to be angry, *even* unto death.

10 Then said the LORD, Thou hast had pity on the gourd, for the which thou hast not laboured, neither madest it grow; which came up in a night, and perished in a night:

11 And should not I ^aspare Nineveh, that great city, wherein are more than sixscore thousand ^bpersons that cannot ^cdiscern between their right hand and their left hand; and *also* much cattle?

MICAH

CHAPTER 1

Micah prophesies the downfall of Samaria and Jerusalem.

THE word of the LORD that came to ^aMicah the Morasthite in the days of ^bJotham, ^cAhaz, and ^dHezekiah, kings of Judah, which he saw concerning Samaria and Jerusalem.

2 Hear, all ye people; hearken, O earth, and all that therein is: and let the Lord GOD be witness against you, the Lord from his holy temple.

3 For, behold, the ^aLORD ^bcometh forth out of his place, and will come down, and tread upon the high places of the earth.

4 And the ^amountains shall be molten under him, and the valleys shall be cleft, as ^bwax before the fire, *and* as the waters *that are* poured down a steep place.

5 For the ^atransgression of Jacob *is* all this, and for the sins of the house of Israel. What *is* the transgression of Jacob? *is it* not Samaria? and what *are* the high places of Judah? *are they* not Jerusalem?

6 Therefore I will make ^aSamaria as an heap of the field, *and* as plantings of a vineyard: and I will pour down the stones thereof into the valley, and I will ^bdiscover the foundations thereof.

7 And all the graven images thereof

5*a* OR shelter.
6*a* OR castor bean plant.
8*a* Mosiah 7:31; 12:6.
9*a* TG Anger.
11*a* 2 Ne. 26:33;
   Alma 26:37 (27, 37).
   TG Benevolence.
  b TG Worth of Souls.
  c TG Man, Natural, Not

Spiritually Reborn.

[MICAH]

1 1*a* Jer. 26:18.
  b Isa. 1:1.
  c 2 Kgs. 16:1 (1–3).
  d 2 Kgs. 18:1 (1–8).
 3*a* TG Jesus Christ, Second
     Coming.

 b TG Dispensations.
4*a* Judg. 5:5 (4–5);
   Isa. 64:3 (1–3);
   D&C 49:23.
 b Ps. 68:2; 97:5.
5*a* TG Apostasy of Israel.
6*a* 2 Kgs. 17:5 (1–6, 24).
 b HEB lay bare.

shall be beaten to pieces, and all the hires thereof shall be burned with the fire, and all the idols thereof will I lay desolate: for she gathered *it* of the hire of an harlot, and they shall return to the hire of an harlot.

8 Therefore I will wail and howl, I will go stripped and naked: I will make a wailing like the dragons, and mourning as the owls.

9 For her wound *is* incurable; for it is come unto Judah; he is come unto the gate of my people, *even* to Jerusalem.

10 ¶ Declare ye *it* not at *a*Gath, weep ye not at all: in the house of *b*Aphrah roll thyself in the dust.

11 Pass ye away, thou inhabitant of Saphir, having thy shame naked: the inhabitant of Zaanan came not forth in the mourning of Beth-ezel; he shall receive of you his standing.

12 For the inhabitant of Maroth waited carefully for good; but evil came down from the LORD unto the gate of Jerusalem.

13 O thou inhabitant of Lachish, bind the chariot to the swift beast: she *is* the beginning of the sin to the daughter of Zion: for the transgressions of Israel were found in thee.

14 Therefore shalt thou give presents to Moresheth-gath: the houses of Achzib *shall be* a lie to the kings of Israel.

15 Yet will I bring an heir unto thee, O inhabitant of Mareshah: he shall come unto Adullam the glory of Israel.

16 Make thee bald, and *a*poll thee for thy delicate children; enlarge thy baldness as the eagle; for they are gone into captivity from thee.

CHAPTER 2

The destruction of Israel is lamented— The Lord will gather the remnant of Israel.

WOE to them that devise iniquity, and work evil upon their beds! when the morning is light, they practise it, because it is in the power of their hand.

2 And they *a*covet *b*fields, and take *them* by violence; and houses, and take *them* away: so they oppress a man and his house, even a man and his heritage.

3 Therefore thus saith the LORD; Behold, against this family do I devise an evil, from which ye shall not remove your necks; neither shall ye go haughtily: for this time *is* evil.

4 ¶ In that day shall *one* take up a parable against you, and lament with a doleful lamentation, *and* say, We be utterly spoiled: he hath changed the portion of my people: how hath he removed *it* from me! turning away he hath divided our fields.

5 Therefore thou shalt have none that shall cast a cord by lot in the congregation of the LORD.

6 Prophesy ye not, *say they to them that* prophesy: they shall not prophesy to them, *that* they shall not take shame.

7 ¶ O *thou that art* named the house of Jacob, is the spirit of the LORD straitened? *are* these his doings? do not my *a*words do good to him that walketh uprightly?

8 Even of late my people is risen up as an enemy: ye pull off the robe with the garment from them that pass by securely as men *a*averse from war.

9 The women of my people have ye cast out from their pleasant houses; from their children have ye taken away my *a*glory for ever.

10 Arise ye, and depart; for this *is* not *your a*rest: because it is polluted, it shall destroy *you*, even with a sore destruction.

11 If a man walking in the spirit

10*a* 1 Sam. 17:4.
  b IE Dust or Ashes. (Each of the cities named in vv. 10–16 will meet a fate appropriate to the meaning of its name.)

16*a* OR cut off thy hair.
2 2*a* TG Covet.
  b Isa. 5:8 (8–9).
7*a* Jacob 2:8;
     Hel. 3:29 (29–30).
8*a* HEB returning.

9*a* Mosiah 4:12;
     D&C 81:4 (3–4);
     Moses 1:39.
10*a* D&C 84:24.

and ^afalsehood do lie, *saying,* I will prophesy unto thee of wine and of strong drink; he shall even be the ^bprophet of this people.

12 ¶ I will surely assemble, O Jacob, all of thee; I will surely ^agather the ^bremnant of Israel; I will put them together as the sheep of ^cBozrah, as the flock in the midst of their fold: they shall make great noise by reason of *the multitude of* men.

13 The breaker is come up before them: they have broken up, and have passed through the gate, and are gone out by it: and their ^aking shall pass before them, and the LORD on the head of them.

CHAPTER 3

Priests who teach for hire and prophets who divine for money bring a curse upon the people.

AND I said, Hear, I pray you, O heads of Jacob, and ye princes of the house of Israel; *Is it* not for you to know judgment?

2 Who hate the good, and love the evil; who pluck off their skin from off them, and their flesh from off their bones;

3 Who also eat the flesh of my people, and flay their skin from off them; and they break their bones, and chop them in pieces, as for the pot, and as flesh within the caldron.

4 Then shall they ^acry unto the LORD, but he will not hear them: he will even hide his face from them at that time, as they have behaved themselves ill in their doings.

5 ¶ Thus saith the LORD concerning the ^aprophets that make my people

err, that bite with their teeth, and cry, ^bPeace; and he that putteth not into their mouths, they even prepare ^cwar against him.

6 Therefore ^anight *shall be* unto you, that ye shall not have a vision; and it shall be dark unto you, that ye shall not ^bdivine; and the ^csun shall go down over the ^dprophets, and the day shall be dark over them.

7 Then shall the seers be ^aashamed, and the ^bdiviners confounded: yea, they shall all cover their lips; for *there is* ^cno answer of God.

8 ¶ But truly I am full of ^apower by the ^bspirit of the LORD, and of judgment, and of might, to declare unto Jacob his ^ctransgression, and to Israel his sin.

9 Hear this, I pray you, ye heads of the house of Jacob, and princes of the house of Israel, that abhor judgment, and pervert all equity.

10 They build up Zion with blood, and Jerusalem with iniquity.

11 The heads thereof judge for reward, and the priests thereof teach for hire, and the ^aprophets thereof divine for ^bmoney: yet will they lean upon the LORD, and say, *Is* not the LORD among us? none evil can come upon us.

12 Therefore shall Zion for your ^asake be ^bplowed *as* a field, and ^cJerusalem shall become ^dheaps, and the mountain of ^ethe house as the high places of the forest.

CHAPTER 4

In the last days, the temple will be built, Israel will gather to it, the millennial era will commence, and the Lord will reign in Zion.

11a TG Priestcraft.
  b Hel. 13:27.
12a D&C 33:6.
  b TG Israel, Remnant of.
  c HEB the sheepfold.
13a D&C 38:21.
3 4a Mosiah 11:24 (23–25).
    TG God, Access to.
  5a TG False Prophets.
  b TG Peace.
  c 1 Ne. 11:35 (34–36);
    D&C 121:38.

6a D&C 38:11 (11–12);
    112:23;
    Moses 7:61 (61–62).
  b Ezek. 13:23.
  c Amos 8:9.
  d Morm. 1:17 (13–17).
7a Zech. 13:4;
    2 Ne. 6:13 (7, 13);
    D&C 90:17.
  b TG Superstitions.
  c Isa. 29:10.
8a TG Priesthood, Power of.

  b TG God, Spirit of;
    Holy Ghost, Mission of.
  c Alma 24:9 (7–9);
    Hel. 13:26.
11a TG Apostasy of Israel;
    False Prophets.
  b TG Priestcraft.
12a Hel. 12:3.
  b Jer. 26:18.
  c Isa. 3:8.
  d Isa. 1:7.
  e IE the temple.

BUT in the last days it shall come to pass, *that* the ªmountain of the house of the LORD shall be ªestablished in the top of the mountains, and it shall be exalted above the hills; and people shall flow unto it.

2 And many nations shall come, and say, Come, and let us go up to the ªmountain of the LORD, and to the house of the God of Jacob; and he will teach us of his ways, and we will ªwalk in his paths: for the ªlaw shall go forth of ªZion, and the word of the LORD from ªJerusalem.

3 ¶ And he shall judge among many people, and rebuke strong nations afar off; and they shall beat their ªswords into plowshares, and their spears into pruninghooks: nation shall not lift up a sword against nation, neither shall they learn ªwar any more.

4 But they shall sit every man under his ªvine and under his fig tree; and none shall make *them* afraid: for the mouth of the LORD of hosts hath spoken *it*.

5 For all people will walk every one in the ªname of his god, and we will walk in the ªname of the LORD our God for ever and ever.

6 In that day, saith the LORD, will I assemble her that ªhalteth, and I will ªgather her that is driven out, and her that I have afflicted;

7 And I will make her that halted a remnant, and her that was cast far off a strong nation: and the LORD shall ªreign over them in mount ªZion from henceforth, even for ever.

8 ¶ And thou, O tower of the flock, the strong hold of the daughter of Zion, unto thee shall it come, even the first dominion; the kingdom shall come to the daughter of Jerusalem.

9 Now why dost thou cry out aloud? *is there* no king in thee? is thy counsellor perished? for pangs have taken thee as a woman in travail.

10 Be in pain, and labour to bring forth, O daughter of Zion, like a woman in ªtravail: for now shalt thou go forth out of the city, and thou shalt dwell in the field, and thou shalt go *even* to ªBabylon; there shalt thou be delivered; there the LORD shall redeem thee from the hand of thine ªenemies.

11 ¶ Now also many nations are ªgathered against thee, that say, Let her be defiled, and let our eye look upon Zion.

12 But they know not the thoughts of the LORD, neither understand they his counsel: for he shall gather them as the sheaves into the floor.

13 Arise and thresh, O daughter of Zion: for I will make thine horn iron, and I will make thy hoofs brass: and thou shalt ªbeat in pieces many people: and I will ªconsecrate their gain unto the LORD, and their substance unto the Lord of the whole earth.

CHAPTER 5

The Messiah will be born in Bethlehem—In the last days, the remnant of Jacob will triumph gloriously over the Gentiles.

Now gather thyself in troops, O daughter of troops: he hath laid siege against us: they shall smite the judge of Israel with a rod upon the cheek.

2 But thou, ªBeth-lehem Ephratah,

---

4 1a Isa. 2:2 (1–3).
  b TG Dispensations.
2a TG Zion.
  b TG Walking with God.
  c D&C 58:13.
  d TG Jerusalem, New.
  e TG Jerusalem.
3a TG Millennium.
  b TG War.
4a 1 Kgs. 4:25.
5a D&C 134:7 (4, 7);
  A of F 1:11.

b Zech. 10:12.
6a HEB is lame.
  b TG Israel, Gathering of.
7a Luke 1:33 (30–33);
    D&C 1:36;
    A of F 1:10.
  b TG Zion.
10a Isa. 66:7 (7–8).
  b 1 Ne. 1:13;
    Omni 1:15.
  c 1 Chr. 17:10;
    Ps. 89:10;

  D&C 65:6.
11a Joel 3:2 (1–2, 9–14);
    Zech. 12:3 (2–3).
13a 3 Ne. 20:19 (17–22).
  b 2 Ne. 2:2; 32:9;
    D&C 42:30.
5 2a 1 Sam. 16:1;
    Luke 2:4 (1–5);
    John 7:42 (41–44).
    TG Jesus Christ,
    Birth of; Jesus Christ,
    Prophecies about.

though thou be little among the thousands of *b*Judah, *yet* out of thee shall he come forth unto me *that is* to be *c*ruler in Israel; whose goings forth *have been* from of old, from *d*everlasting.

3 Therefore will he give them up, until the time *that* she which travaileth hath brought forth: then the *a*remnant of his brethren shall return unto the children of Israel.

4 ¶ And he shall stand and *a*feed in the *b*strength of the LORD, in the majesty of the name of the LORD his God; and they shall abide: for now shall he be great unto the ends of the earth.

5 And this *man* shall be the *a*peace, when the Assyrian shall come into our land: and when he shall tread in our palaces, then shall we raise against him seven shepherds, and eight principal men.

6 And they shall waste the land of Assyria with the sword, and the land of *a*Nimrod in the entrances thereof: thus shall he deliver *us* from the Assyrian, when he cometh into our land, and when he treadeth within our borders.

7 And the remnant of Jacob shall be in the midst of many people as a dew from the LORD, as the showers upon the grass, that tarrieth not for man, nor waiteth for the sons of men.

8 ¶ And the *a*remnant of Jacob shall be among the Gentiles in the midst of many people as a *b*lion among the beasts of the forest, as a young *c*lion among the flocks of *d*sheep: who, if he go through, both treadeth down, and teareth in pieces, and none can deliver.

9 Thine hand shall be lifted up upon thine adversaries, and all thine enemies shall be cut off.

10 And it shall come to pass in that day, saith the LORD, that I will cut off thy *a*horses out of the midst of thee, and I will destroy thy chariots:

11 And I will cut off the cities of thy land, and throw down all thy strong holds:

12 And I will cut off witchcrafts out of thine hand; and thou shalt have no *more* *a*soothsayers:

13 Thy graven images also will I cut off, and thy standing images out of the midst of thee; and thou shalt no more worship the work of thine hands.

14 And I will pluck up thy *a*groves out of the midst of thee: so will I destroy thy cities.

15 And I will execute vengeance in anger and fury upon the heathen, such as they have not heard.

CHAPTER 6

In spite of all His goodness to them, the people have not served the Lord in spirit and in truth—They must act righteously, love mercy, and walk humbly before Him.

HEAR ye now what the LORD saith; Arise, contend thou before the mountains, and let the hills hear thy voice.

2 Hear ye, O mountains, the LORD's *a*controversy, and ye strong foundations of the earth: for the LORD hath a controversy with his people, and he will *b*plead with Israel.

3 O my people, what have I done unto thee? and wherein have I wearied thee? testify against me.

4 For I brought thee up out of the land of Egypt, and *a*redeemed thee out of the house of servants; and I sent before thee Moses, Aaron, and Miriam.

5 O my people, remember now

2*b* Isa. 11:1;
  Heb. 7:14.
  c 1 Chr. 5:2;
    Matt. 2:6;
    JST Matt. 3:6 (Appendix).
  d TG Immortality.
3*a* D&C 113:10.
4*a* IE feed the flock.
  b TG Priesthood, Power of.

5*a* 2 Ne. 19:6;
    D&C 19:23; 27:16; 111:8.
6*a* Gen. 10:9 (9–10).
8*a* TG Israel, Remnant of.
  b TG Israel, Deliverance of.
  c 3 Ne. 16:15 (7–15);
    21:12 (12–21);
    D&C 87:5.
  d TG Sheep.

10*a* Hag. 2:22 (20–23);
     Zech. 9:10 (9–11).
12*a* TG Sorcery.
14*a* Isa. 17:8.
6 2*a* Hosea 4:1.
   b Isa. 3:13 (12–13).
  4*a* Hosea 7:13 (11–13);
     Alma 29:12.

what ᵃBalak king of Moab consulted, and what Balaam the son of Beor answered him from Shittim unto Gilgal; that ye may know the righteousness of the Lᴏʀᴅ.

6 ¶ Wherewith shall I come before the Lᴏʀᴅ, *and* bow myself before the high God? shall I come before him with burnt offerings, with calves of a year old?

7 Will the Lᴏʀᴅ be pleased with thousands of ᵃrams, *or* with ten thousands of rivers of oil? shall I give my ᵇfirstborn *for* my ᶜtransgression, the fruit of my body *for* the sin of my soul?

8 He hath shewed thee, O man, what *is* good; and what doth the Lᴏʀᴅ ᵃrequire of thee, but to do ᵇjustly, and to love ᶜmercy, and to ᵈwalk ᵉhumbly with thy God?

9 The Lᴏʀᴅ's voice crieth unto the city, and *the man of* wisdom shall see thy name: hear ye the rod, and who hath appointed it.

10 ¶ Are there yet the ᵃtreasures of wickedness in the house of the wicked, and the scant measure *that is* abominable?

11 Shall I count *them* ᵃpure with the wicked ᵇbalances, and with the bag of deceitful weights?

12 For the rich men thereof are full of ᵃviolence, and the inhabitants thereof have spoken lies, and their tongue *is* deceitful in their mouth.

13 Therefore also will I make *thee* sick in smiting thee, in making *thee* desolate because of thy sins.

14 Thou shalt eat, but not be ᵃsatisfied; and ᵇthy casting down *shall be* in the midst of thee; and thou shalt take hold, but shalt not deliver; and *that* which thou deliverest will I give up to the sword.

15 Thou shalt ᵃsow, but thou shalt not reap; thou shalt tread the olives, but thou shalt not anoint thee with oil; and sweet wine, but shalt not drink wine.

16 ¶ For the statutes of ᵃOmri are kept, and all the works of the house of Ahab, and ye walk in their counsels; that I should make thee a ᵇdesolation, and the inhabitants thereof an hissing: therefore ye shall bear the ᶜreproach of my people.

CHAPTER 7

Though the people of Israel have rebelled, yet in the last days the Lord will have mercy on them—He will have compassion and pardon their iniquities.

Wᴏᴇ is me! for I am as when they have gathered the summer fruits, as the grapegleanings of the vintage: *there is* no cluster to eat: my soul desired the firstripe fruit.

2 The good *man* is perished out of the earth: and *there is* none upright among men: they all lie in wait for blood; they hunt every man his ᵃbrother with a net.

3 ¶ That they may do evil with both hands earnestly, the prince asketh, and the judge *asketh* for a reward; and the great *man,* he uttereth his mischievous desire: so they wrap it up.

4 The best of them *is* as a brier: the most upright *is sharper* than a thorn hedge: the day of thy watchmen *and* thy ᵃvisitation cometh; now shall be their perplexity.

5 ¶ ᵃTrust ye not in a friend, put ye not confidence in a guide: keep the doors of thy mouth from her that lieth in thy bosom.

6 For the son dishonoureth the

5*a* Num. 22:2 (2–5).
7*a* 1 Sam. 15:22;
　　Heb. 10:6 (4–6).
　b ᴛɢ Firstborn.
　c ᴛɢ Transgress.
8*a* D&C 64:34 (22, 34).
　　ᴛɢ Duty;
　　God, the Standard of
　　Righteousness.
　b ᴛɢ Good Works;
　　Justice.

　c ᴛɢ Mercy.
　d ᴛɢ Walking with God.
　e ᴛɢ Children of Light;
　　Humility.
10*a* ᴛɢ Treasure.
11*a* Ex. 34:7.
　b Hosea 12:7.
12*a* Hab. 1:2.
14*a* Lev. 26:26.
　b ᴏʀ thy hunger shall be
　　in thy inward parts.

15*a* Deut. 28:38;
　　Hag. 1:6.
16*a* 1 Kgs. 16:25 (16, 25–26).
　b Jer. 18:16 (16–17); 24:10.
　c Jer. 24:9;
　　2 Ne. 29:5.
7 2*a* Isa. 9:19.
　4*a* ɪᴇ punishment.
　5*a* Jer. 9:4.
　　ᴛɢ Trust Not in the
　　Arm of Flesh.

father, the daughter riseth up against her mother, the daughter in law against her mother in law; a man's ^aenemies *are* the men of his own ^bhouse.

7 Therefore I will look unto the LORD; I will wait for the God of my salvation: my God will ^ahear me.

8 ¶ Rejoice not against me, O mine enemy: when I fall, I shall arise; when I sit in ^adarkness, the LORD *shall be* a ^blight unto me.

9 I will ^abear the indignation of the LORD, because I have sinned against him, until he plead my cause, and execute judgment for me: he will bring me forth to the ^blight, *and* I shall behold his righteousness.

10 Then *she that is* mine enemy shall see *it,* and shame shall cover her which said unto me, Where is the LORD thy God? mine eyes shall behold her: now shall she be ^atrodden down as the mire of the streets.

11 *In* the day that thy walls are to be built, *in* that day shall the decree be far removed.

12 *In* that day *also* he shall ^acome even to thee from Assyria, and *from* the fortified cities, and from the fortress even to the river, and from sea to sea, and *from* mountain to mountain.

13 Notwithstanding the land shall be desolate because of them that dwell therein, for the fruit of their doings.

14 ¶ Feed thy people with thy rod, the flock of thine heritage, which dwell solitarily *in* the wood, in the midst of Carmel: let them feed *in* Bashan and Gilead, as in the days of old.

15 According to the days of thy coming out of the land of Egypt will I shew unto him marvellous *things.*

16 ¶ The nations shall see and be confounded at all their might: they shall lay *their* hand upon *their* mouth, their ears shall be deaf.

17 They shall lick the dust like a serpent, they shall move out of their holes like worms of the earth: they shall be afraid of the LORD our God, and shall fear because of thee.

18 Who *is* a God like unto thee, that ^apardoneth iniquity, and passeth by the transgression of the remnant of his heritage? he retaineth not his ^banger for ever, because he ^cdelighteth in ^dmercy.

19 He will turn again, he will have ^acompassion upon us; he will subdue our iniquities; and thou wilt cast all their sins into the depths of the sea.

20 Thou wilt perform the truth to Jacob, *and* the mercy to ^aAbraham, which thou hast ^bsworn unto our fathers from the days of old.

NAHUM

CHAPTER 1

Nahum speaks of the burning of the earth at the Second Coming and of the mercy and power of the Lord.

THE burden of Nineveh. The book of the vision of Nahum the Elkoshite.

2 God *is* jealous, and the LORD revengeth; the LORD revengeth, and

---

6*a* Luke 12:53.
  TG Enemies.
 b Matt. 10:36 (35–36).
7*a* Ps. 4:1 (1, 3).
8*a* TG Darkness, Spiritual.
 b TG Jesus Christ, Light of
  the World.

9*a* Lam. 3:27 (24–27).
 b 3 Ne. 16:4 (4–5).
10*a* Mal. 4:3.
12*a* Neh. 1:9;
  D&C 101:13.
18*a* TG Forgive.
 b Isa. 57:16;

Jer. 3:5 (1–5).
 c Jer. 9:24.
 d TG God, Mercy of;
  Mercy.
19*a* D&C 64:2.
20*a* 2 Ne. 29:14.
 b Luke 1:55 (54–55), 72.

is furious; the LORD will take vengeance on his adversaries, and he reserveth *wrath* for his enemies.

3 The LORD *is* ªslow to anger, and great in power, and will not at all acquit *the* ᵇwicked: the LORD *hath* his way in the whirlwind and in the storm, and the clouds *are* the dust of his feet.

4 He rebuketh the sea, and maketh it dry, and drieth up all the rivers: Bashan languisheth, and Carmel, and the flower of Lebanon languisheth.

5 The mountains quake at him, and the hills ªmelt, and the earth is ᵇburned at his ᶜpresence, yea, the world, and all that dwell therein.

6 Who can stand before his ªindignation? and who can abide in the fierceness of his anger? his fury is poured out like fire, and the rocks are thrown down by him.

7 The LORD *is* ªgood, a strong hold in the day of trouble; and he knoweth them that ᵇtrust in him.

8 But with an overrunning flood he will make an utter end of the place thereof, and darkness shall pursue his enemies.

9 What do ye imagine against the LORD? he will make an utter end: affliction shall not rise up the second time.

10 For while *they be* folden together *as* thorns, and while they are drunken *as* drunkards, they shall be devoured as ªstubble fully dry.

11 There is *one* come out of thee, that imagineth evil against the LORD, a wicked counseller.

12 Thus saith the LORD; Though *they be* quiet, and likewise many, yet thus shall they be cut down, when he shall pass through. Though I have afflicted thee, I will afflict thee no more.

13 For now will I break his ªyoke

from off thee, and will burst thy bonds in sunder.

14 And the LORD hath given a commandment concerning thee, *that* no more of thy name be sown: out of the house of thy gods will I cut off the graven image and the molten image: I will make thy grave; for thou art vile.

15 Behold upon the mountains the ªfeet of him that bringeth good tidings, that publisheth peace! O Judah, keep thy solemn feasts, perform thy vows: for the wicked shall no more pass through thee; he is utterly cut off.

CHAPTER 2

Nineveh will be destroyed, which is a symbol of what will be in the latter days.

HE that dasheth in pieces is come up before thy face: keep the munition, ªwatch the way, make *thy* loins strong, fortify *thy* power mightily.

2 For the LORD hath turned away the excellency of Jacob, as the excellency of Israel: for the emptiers have emptied them out, and marred their vine branches.

3 The shield of his mighty men is made red, the valiant men *are* in scarlet: the chariots *shall be* with flaming torches in the day of his preparation, and the ªfir trees shall be terribly shaken.

4 The chariots shall rage in the streets, they shall justle one against another in the broad ways: they shall seem like torches, they shall run like the lightnings.

5 He shall recount his ªworthies: they shall stumble in their walk; they shall make haste to the wall thereof, and the defence shall be prepared.

6 The gates of the rivers shall be opened, and the palace shall be dissolved.

---

1 3*a* TG Forbear.
  b Ex. 34:7;
    Morm. 4:5;
    D&C 1:9.
  5*a* Ps. 97:5.
  b D&C 101:66.
    TG Earth, Cleansing of.
  c TG God, Presence of.

6*a* TG God, Indignation of.
7*a* Ps. 34:8;
    Lam. 3:25;
    D&C 70:18 (17–18).
  b TG Faith.
10*a* 2 Ne. 26:6 (4–6);
    D&C 29:9;
    JS—H 1:37.

13*a* TG Bondage, Physical.
15*a* Rom. 10:15;
    Mosiah 15:18 (13–18);
    3 Ne. 20:40;
    D&C 128:19.
2 1*a* TG Watch.
  3*a* Zech. 11:2.
  5*a* HEB nobles, leaders.

7 And ^aHuzzab shall be led away captive, she shall be brought up, and her maids shall lead *her* as with the voice of doves, tabering upon their breasts.

8 But Nineveh *is* of old like a pool of water: yet they shall flee away. Stand, stand, *shall they cry*; but none shall look back.

9 Take ye the spoil of silver, take the spoil of gold: for *there is* none end of the store *and* glory out of all the pleasant furniture.

10 She is empty, and void, and waste: and the heart melteth, and the knees smite together, and much pain *is* in all loins, and the faces of them all gather ^ablackness.

11 Where *is* the dwelling of the lions, and the feedingplace of the young lions, where the lion, *even* the old lion, walked, *and* the lion's whelp, and none made *them* afraid?

12 The lion did tear in pieces enough for his whelps, and strangled for his lionesses, and filled his holes with prey, and his dens with ^aravin.

13 Behold, I *am* against thee, saith the LORD of hosts, and I will burn her chariots in the smoke, and the sword shall devour thy young lions: and I will cut off thy prey from the earth, and the voice of thy messengers shall no more be heard.

CHAPTER 3

The miserable downfall of Nineveh is foretold.

WOE to the bloody city! it *is* all full of lies *and* robbery; the prey departeth not;

2 The noise of a whip, and the noise of the rattling of the wheels, and of the pransing horses, and of the jumping chariots.

3 The horseman lifteth up both the bright sword and the glittering spear: and *there is* a multitude of slain, and a great number of carcases; and *there is* none end of *their* corpses; they stumble upon their corpses:

4 Because of the multitude of the whoredoms of the wellfavoured harlot, the mistress of witchcrafts, that selleth nations through her whoredoms, and families through her witchcrafts.

5 Behold, I *am* against thee, saith the LORD of hosts; and I will discover thy skirts upon thy face, and I will shew the nations thy nakedness, and the kingdoms thy shame.

6 And I will cast abominable filth upon thee, and make thee vile, and will set thee as a gazingstock.

7 And it shall come to pass, *that* all they that look upon thee shall flee from thee, and say, Nineveh is laid waste: who will bemoan her? whence shall I seek comforters for thee?

8 Art thou better than ^apopulous No, that was situate among the rivers, *that had* the waters round about it, whose rampart *was* the sea, *and* her ^bwall *was* from the sea?

9 Ethiopia and Egypt *were* her strength, and *it was* ^ainfinite; ^bPut and ^cLubim were thy helpers.

10 Yet *was* she carried away, she went into captivity: her young ^achildren also were dashed in pieces at the top of all the streets: and they cast lots for her honourable men, and all her great men were bound in chains.

11 Thou also shalt be drunken: thou shalt be hid, thou also shalt seek strength because of the enemy.

12 All thy strong holds *shall be like* fig trees with the firstripe figs: if they be shaken, they shall even fall into the mouth of the eater.

13 Behold, thy people in the midst of thee *are* ^awomen: the gates of thy land shall be set wide open unto

---

7*a* OR the queen.
10*a* Hebrew idiom meaning "gloom."
    Jer. 8:21;
    Joel 2:6.
12*a* HEB torn flesh.

3 8*a* HEB No-amon; i.e., Thebes.
    Jer. 46:25;
    Ezek. 30:14 (14–16).
  b IE defense.
9*a* HEB without limit.

  b Gen. 10:6.
  c IE the Libyans.
    2 Chr. 12:3 (2–3).
10*a* Isa. 13:16.
13*a* Jer. 51:30.

thine enemies: the fire shall devour thy bars.

14 Draw thee waters for the siege, fortify thy strong holds: go into clay, and tread the mortar, make strong the brickkiln.

15 There shall the fire devour thee; the sword shall cut thee off, it shall eat thee up like the cankerworm: make thyself many as the cankerworm, make thyself many as the locusts.

16 Thou hast multiplied thy merchants above the stars of heaven: the cankerworm spoileth, and flieth away.

17 Thy crowned *are* as the locusts, and thy captains as the great grasshoppers, which camp in the hedges in the cold day, *but* when the sun ariseth they flee away, and their place is not known where they *are*.

18 Thy shepherds slumber, O king of Assyria: thy nobles shall dwell *in the dust:* thy people is scattered upon the mountains, and no man gathereth *them*.

19 *There is* no healing of thy bruise; thy wound is grievous: all that hear the *a*bruit of thee shall clap the hands over thee: for upon whom hath not thy wickedness passed continually?

HABAKKUK

CHAPTER 1

When Habakkuk learns that the Lord will raise up the Chaldeans to overrun the land of Israel, he is troubled that the wicked can be thus employed.

THE burden which Habakkuk the prophet did see.

2 O LORD, *a*how long shall I cry, and thou wilt not hear! *even* cry out unto thee *of* *b*violence, and thou wilt not save!

3 Why dost thou shew me iniquity, and cause *me* to behold grievance? for spoiling and violence *are* before me: and there are *that* raise up *a*strife and contention.

4 Therefore the law *a*is slacked, and judgment doth never go forth: for the wicked doth compass about the righteous; therefore wrong judgment proceedeth.

5 ¶ Behold ye among the heathen, and regard, and wonder marvel-lously: for *I* will work a *a*work in your days, *which* ye will not believe, though it be told *you*.

6 For, lo, I raise up the Chaldeans, *that* bitter and hasty nation, which shall march through the breadth of the land, to possess the dwelling-places *that are* not theirs.

7 They *are* terrible and dreadful: their judgment and their dignity *a*shall proceed of themselves.

8 Their horses also are swifter than the leopards, and are more fierce than the evening wolves: and their horsemen shall spread themselves, and their horsemen shall come from far; they shall fly as the eagle *that* hasteth to eat.

9 They shall come all for violence: their faces shall sup up *as* the east wind, and they shall gather *a*the captivity as the sand.

10 And they shall scoff at the kings, and the princes shall be a scorn unto them: they shall deride every strong

---

19*a* HEB report.

[HABAKKUK]

1 2*a* D&C 121:2 (1–3).

b Micah 6:12.
3*a* TG Strife.
4*a* HEB grows cold.
5*a* Acts 13:41 (40–41).

7*a* OR are of their own making.
9*a* OR captives.

hold; for they shall heap dust, and take it.

11 Then shall *his* ᵃmind change, and he shall pass over, and offend, *imputing* this his power unto his god.

12 ¶ *Art* thou not from everlasting, O Lᴏʀᴅ my God, mine Holy One? we shall not die. O Lᴏʀᴅ, thou hast ordained them for judgment; and, O mighty God, thou hast established them for correction.

13 *Thou art* of purer eyes than to behold evil, and canst not look on iniquity: wherefore lookest thou upon them that deal treacherously, *and* holdest thy tongue when the wicked devoureth *the man that is* more righteous than he?

14 And makest men as the fishes of the sea, as the creeping things, *that have* no ruler over them?

15 They take up all of them with the ᵃangle, they catch them in their net, and gather them in their ᵇdrag: therefore they rejoice and are glad.

16 Therefore they sacrifice unto their net, and burn incense unto their drag; because by them their portion *is* fat, and their meat plenteous.

17 Shall they therefore empty their net, and not spare continually to slay the nations?

CHAPTER 2

The Lord admonishes patience and promises that the just will live by faith— The earth will be filled with knowledge about God—Idols have no power.

I ᴡɪʟʟ stand upon my watch, and set me upon the tower, and will watch to see what he will say unto me, and what I shall answer when I am reproved.

2 And the Lᴏʀᴅ answered me, and said, ᵃWrite the vision, and make *it* plain upon tables, that he may run that readeth it.

3 For the vision *is* yet for an appointed time, but at the end it shall speak, and not lie: though it tarry, wait for it; because it will surely ᵃcome, it will not tarry.

4 Behold, his soul *which* is lifted up is not upright in him: but the just shall live by his ᵃfaith.

5 ¶ Yea also, because he transgresseth by wine, *he is* a proud man, neither keepeth at home, who enlargeth his desire as hell, and *is* as death, and cannot be satisfied, but gathereth unto him all nations, and heapeth unto him all people:

6 Shall not all these take up a parable against him, and a taunting proverb against him, and say, Woe to him that increaseth *that which is* not his! how long? and to him that ladeth himself with thick clay!

7 Shall they not rise up suddenly that shall bite thee, and awake that shall vex thee, and thou shalt be for ᵃbooties unto them?

8 Because thou hast ᵃspoiled many nations, all the remnant of the people shall spoil thee; because of men's blood, and *for* the violence of the land, of the city, and of all that dwell therein.

9 ¶ Woe to him that ᵃcoveteth an evil covetousness to his house, that he may set his nest on high, that he may be delivered from the power of evil!

10 Thou hast ᵃconsulted shame to thy house by cutting off many people, and hast sinned *against* thy soul.

11 For the stone shall cry out of the wall, and ᵃthe beam out of the timber shall answer it.

12 ¶ Woe to him that buildeth a town with ᵃblood, and stablisheth a city by iniquity!

13 Behold, *is it* not of the Lᴏʀᴅ of hosts that the people shall labour in

---

11a TG Mind.
15a OR hook.
  b OR net.
2 2a TG Scriptures,
    Preservation of.
  3a D&C 39:21.

4a HEB faithfulness,
    steadfastness.
   TG Faith; Perseverance.
7a OR plunder, spoil.
8a Isa. 33:1.
9a TG Covet.

10a OR devised.
11a OR a rafter out of the
    woodwork will
    witness it.
12a HEB bloodshed.
   TG Cruelty.

the very fire, and the people shall weary themselves for very ^avanity?

14 For the ^aearth shall be filled with the ^bknowledge of the glory of the LORD, as the waters cover the sea.

15 ¶ Woe unto him that giveth his neighbour drink, that puttest thy bottle to *him*, and makest *him* ^adrunken also, that thou mayest look on their nakedness!

16 Thou art filled ^awith shame for glory: drink thou also, and let thy foreskin be uncovered: the cup of the LORD's right hand shall be turned unto thee, and shameful spewing *shall be* on thy glory.

17 For the violence of Lebanon shall cover thee, and the spoil of beasts, *which* made them afraid, because of men's blood, and for the violence of the land, of the city, and of all that dwell therein.

18 ¶ What profiteth the graven ^aimage that the maker thereof hath graven it; the molten image, and a teacher of lies, that the maker of his work trusteth therein, to make dumb idols?

19 Woe unto him that saith to the wood, Awake; to the dumb stone, Arise, it shall teach! Behold, it *is* laid over with gold and silver, and *there is* no breath at all in the midst of it.

20 But the LORD *is* in his holy temple: let all the earth keep ^asilence before him.

CHAPTER 3

In his prayer Habakkuk trembles at the majesty of God.

A PRAYER of Habakkuk the prophet upon ^aShigionoth.

2 O LORD, I have heard thy speech, *and* was afraid: O LORD, revive thy work in the midst of the years, in the midst of the years make known; in wrath remember mercy.

3 God came from Teman, and the Holy One from mount ^aParan. Selah. His glory covered the heavens, and the earth was full of his praise.

4 And *his* brightness was as the light; ^ahe had horns *coming* out of his hand: and there *was* the hiding of his power.

5 Before him went the pestilence, and ^aburning coals went forth at his feet.

6 He stood, and measured the earth: he beheld, and drove asunder the nations; and the everlasting mountains were scattered, the perpetual ^ahills did bow: his ways *are* everlasting.

7 I saw the tents of ^aCushan in affliction: *and* the curtains of the land of ^bMidian did tremble.

8 Was the LORD displeased against the rivers? *was* thine anger against the rivers? *was* thy wrath against the sea, that thou didst ride upon thine horses *and* thy chariots of salvation?

9 Thy bow was made quite naked, *according* to the oaths of the tribes, *even thy* word. Selah. Thou didst cleave the earth with rivers.

10 The ^amountains saw thee, *and* they trembled: the overflowing of the water passed by: the deep uttered his voice, *and* lifted up his hands on high.

11 The ^asun *and* moon stood still in their habitation: at the light of thine arrows they went, *and* at the shining of thy glittering spear.

12 Thou didst march through the land in indignation, thou didst thresh the heathen in anger.

13*a* Jer. 51:58.
  TG Vanity.
14*a* Isa. 11:9.
  TG Earth, Destiny of.
  b TG God, Knowledge about;
  Knowledge.
15*a* TG Word of Wisdom.
16*a* OR more with shame than with glory.

TG Shame.
18*a* Isa. 44:10.
  TG Idolatry.
20*a* Zeph. 1:7.
3 1*a* A type of poetry.
  3*a* This alludes to historic occasions when the Lord miraculously delivered the people. Deut. 33:2 (2–3).

4*a* OR rays of light are at His side.
5*a* HEB a flame.
6*a* D&C 133:31.
7*a* Historic allusions as in v. 3. Judg. 3:10 (8–10).
  b Num. 31:2 (1–12).
10*a* Ex. 19:18 (16–18).
11*a* Josh. 10:12 (12–13); Hel. 12:15.

13 Thou wentest forth for the *a*salvation of thy people, *even* for salvation with thine anointed; thou *b*woundedst the head out of the house of the wicked, by discovering the foundation unto the neck. Selah.

14 Thou didst strike through with his staves the head of his villages: they came out as a whirlwind to scatter me: their rejoicing *was* as to devour the poor secretly.

15 Thou didst walk through the sea with thine horses, *through* the *a*heap of great waters.

16 When I heard, my belly trembled; my lips quivered at the voice: rottenness entered into my bones, and I trembled in myself, that I might rest in the day of trouble: when he cometh up unto the people, he will invade them with his troops.

17 ¶ Although the fig tree shall not blossom, neither *shall* fruit *be* in the vines; the labour of the olive shall fail, and the fields shall yield no meat; the flock shall be cut off from the fold, and *there shall be* no herd in the stalls:

18 Yet I will rejoice in the LORD, I will joy in the God of my salvation.

19 The LORD God *is* my *a*strength, and he will make my feet like hinds' *feet,* and he will make me to walk upon mine *b*high places. To the chief singer on my stringed instruments.

ZEPHANIAH

CHAPTER 1

The destruction of Judah is symbolic of the Second Coming—It is the day of the Lord's sacrifice, a day of wrath and trouble.

THE word of the LORD which came unto Zephaniah the son of Cushi, the son of Gedaliah, the son of Amariah, the son of Hizkiah, in the days of *a*Josiah the son of Amon, king of Judah.

2 I will utterly *a*consume all *things* from off the land, saith the LORD.

3 I will consume man and beast; I will consume the fowls of the heaven, and the fishes of the sea, and the *a*stumblingblocks with the wicked; and I will cut off man from off the land, saith the LORD.

4 I will also *a*stretch out mine hand upon Judah, and upon all the inhabitants of Jerusalem; and I will cut off the remnant of Baal from this place, *and* the name of the *b*Chemarims with the priests;

5 And them that worship the host of heaven upon the *a*housetops; and them that worship *and* that swear by the LORD, and that swear by *b*Malcham;

6 And them that are *a*turned back from the LORD; and *those* that have not sought the LORD, nor inquired for him.

7 *a*Hold thy peace at the presence of the Lord GOD: for the *b*day of the LORD *is* at hand: for the LORD hath prepared a sacrifice, he hath bid his guests.

13*a* TG Jesus Christ, Prophecies about; Jesus Christ, Redeemer; Jesus Christ, Savior; Remission of Sins; Salvation.
  b Ps. 68:21.
15*a* Josh. 3:16 (14–17).
19*a* TG Strength.

  b Deut. 32:13; 33:29.

[ZEPHANIAH]

1 1*a* 2 Kgs. 21:24.
  2*a* 1 Ne. 22:23;
      2 Ne. 26:6;
      D&C 101:24.
  3*a* OR idols.

      Ezek. 7:19.
4*a* 2 Ne. 19:21.
  b OR idolatrous priests.
5*a* 2 Kgs. 23:12; Jer. 19:13.
  b 1 Kgs. 11:33.
6*a* Jer. 11:10 (9–10).
7*a* Hab. 2:20.
  b TG Day of the Lord.

8 And it shall come to pass in the day of the LORD's sacrifice, that I will punish the princes, and the king's children, and all such as are clothed with strange *a*apparel.

9 In the same day also will I punish all those that leap *a*on the threshold, which fill their masters' houses with violence and deceit.

10 And it shall come to pass in that day, saith the LORD, *that there shall be* the noise of a cry from the fish *a*gate, and an howling from *b*the second, and a great crashing from the hills.

11 Howl, ye inhabitants of *a*Maktesh, for all the merchant people are cut down; all they that bear silver are cut off.

12 And it shall come to pass at that time, *that* I will search Jerusalem with candles, and punish the men that are *a*settled on their *b*lees: that say in their heart, The LORD will *c*not do good, neither will he do evil.

13 Therefore their goods shall become a booty, and their houses a desolation: they shall also *a*build houses, but not inhabit *them*; and they shall *b*plant vineyards, but not drink the wine thereof.

14 The *a*great day of the LORD *is* near, *it is* near, and hasteth greatly, *even* the voice of the day of the LORD: the mighty man shall cry there bitterly.

15 That day *is* a day of wrath, a day of trouble and distress, a day of wasteness and *a*desolation, a day of darkness and gloominess, a day of clouds and thick darkness,

16 A day of the *a*trumpet and alarm against the *b*fenced cities, and against the high towers.

17 And I will bring distress upon men, that they shall walk like blind men, because they have sinned against the LORD: and their blood shall be poured out as dust, and their flesh as the dung.

18 Neither their silver nor their gold shall be able to deliver them in the day of the LORD's wrath; but the whole land shall be devoured by the *a*fire of his jealousy: for he shall make even a speedy riddance of all them that dwell in the land.

CHAPTER 2

Seek righteousness; seek meekness—Judgment will come upon the Philistines, the Moabites, the children of Ammon, the Ethiopians, and the Assyrians.

GATHER yourselves together, yea, gather together, O nation not desired;

2 Before the decree bring forth, *before* the day pass as the chaff, before the fierce anger of the LORD come upon you, before the day of the LORD's anger come upon you.

3 Seek ye the LORD, all ye *a*meek of the earth, which have wrought his judgment; seek *b*righteousness, seek meekness: it may be ye shall be hid in the *c*day of the LORD's anger.

4 ¶ For Gaza shall be forsaken, and *a*Ashkelon a desolation: they shall drive out Ashdod at the noon day, and Ekron shall be rooted up.

5 Woe unto the inhabitants of the *a*sea coast, the nation of the Cherethites! the word of the LORD *is* against you; O Canaan, the land of the *b*Philistines, I will even destroy thee, that there shall be no inhabitant.

6 And the sea coast shall be

8*a* Morm. 8:36 (36–37).
9*a* OR over; i.e., to plunder and pillage.
10*a* 2 Chr. 33:14.
 b IE the second quarter, a district of Jerusalem.
11*a* IE a district of Jerusalem.
12*a* OR complacent, indifferent.

 b Jer. 48:11.
 c Mal. 3:14.
13*a* Amos 5:11.
 b Deut. 28:30 (30, 39).
14*a* Mal. 4:5;
  D&C 110:16.
15*a* TG World, End of.
16*a* HEB *shofar*, or ram's horn.
 b D&C 101:57.

18*a* Joel 1:19 (19–20).
2 3*a* Ps. 76:9;
  3 Ne. 12:5;
  D&C 88:17 (15–17).
 b TG Righteousness.
 c TG World, End of.
4*a* Zech. 9:5.
5*a* Ezek. 25:16.
 b Obad. 1:19.

[a]dwellings *and* cottages for shepherds, and folds for flocks.

7 And the coast shall be for the remnant of the house of Judah; they shall feed thereupon: in the houses of Ashkelon shall they lie down in the evening: for the Lord their God shall visit them, and turn away their [a]captivity.

8 ¶ I have heard the reproach of Moab, and the [a]revilings of the children of Ammon, whereby they have reproached my people, and [b]magnified *themselves* against their border.

9 Therefore *as* I live, saith the Lord of hosts, the God of Israel, Surely Moab shall be as [a]Sodom, and the children of Ammon as Gomorrah, *even* [b]the breeding of nettles, and saltpits, and a perpetual desolation: the residue of my people shall spoil them, and the remnant of my people shall possess them.

10 This shall they have for their pride, because they have reproached and magnified *themselves* against the people of the Lord of hosts.

11 The Lord *will be* [a]terrible unto them: for he will famish all the gods of the earth; and *men* shall [b]worship him, every one from his place, *even* all the isles of the [c]heathen.

12 ¶ Ye [a]Ethiopians also, ye *shall be* slain by my sword.

13 And he will stretch out his hand against the north, and destroy [a]Assyria; and will make Nineveh a desolation, *and* dry like a wilderness.

14 And flocks shall lie down in the midst of her, all the beasts of the nations: both the [a]cormorant and the bittern shall lodge in the upper lintels of it; *their* voice shall sing in the windows; desolation *shall be* in the thresholds: for he shall uncover the cedar work.

15 This *is* the rejoicing city that dwelt carelessly, that said in her heart, I *am*, and *there is* none beside me: how is she become a desolation, a place for beasts to lie down in! every one that passeth by her shall hiss, *and* [a]wag his hand.

CHAPTER 3

At the Second Coming, all nations will assemble to battle—Men will have a pure language—The Lord will reign in their midst.

Woe to her that is [a]filthy and polluted, to the oppressing city!

2 She [a]obeyed not the voice; she received not correction; she trusted not in the Lord; she drew not near to her God.

3 Her princes within her *are* roaring lions; her judges *are* evening [a]wolves; they gnaw not the bones till the morrow.

4 Her prophets *are* [a]light *and* treacherous persons: her priests have [b]polluted the sanctuary, they have done violence to the [c]law.

5 The just Lord *is* in the midst thereof; he will not do iniquity: every morning doth he bring his judgment to light, he faileth not; but the unjust knoweth no shame.

6 I have cut off the nations: their towers are desolate; I made their streets waste, that none passeth by: their cities are destroyed, so that there is no man, that there is none inhabitant.

7 I said, Surely thou wilt fear me, thou wilt receive instruction; so their dwelling should not be cut off, howsoever I punished them: but they rose early, *and* corrupted all their doings.

8 ¶ Therefore wait ye upon me, saith the Lord, until the day that I rise up to the prey: for my

---

6a OR pastures and
  meadows.
7a Deut. 30:3 (1–5);
  Ps. 14:7;
  Amos 9:14 (14–15);
  Zeph. 3:20.
8a TG Reviling.
  b Jer. 48:42 (29, 42).

9a Gen. 19:24.
  b IE occupied by weeds
    and salt pits.
11a D&C 45:74.
  b Mal. 1:11.
  c TG Heathen.
12a Ezek. 30:5 (4–5).
13a 2 Ne. 20:12 (12, 24–25).

14a Isa. 34:11 (10–11).
15a Jer. 18:16.
3 1a TG Filthiness.
2a TG Disobedience.
3a Jer. 5:6.
4a OR wanton.
  b TG Sacrilege.
  c HEB torah.

determination *is* ^ato gather the ^bnations, that I may assemble the kingdoms, to pour upon them mine indignation, *even* all my fierce anger: for all the ^cearth shall be devoured with the fire of my jealousy.

9 For then will I turn to the people a pure ^alanguage, that they may all call upon the name of the LORD, to serve him with one ^bconsent.

10 From ^abeyond the rivers of Ethiopia my suppliants, *even* the daughter of my dispersed, shall bring mine offering.

11 In that day shalt thou not be ashamed for all thy doings, wherein thou hast transgressed against me: for then I will take away out of the midst of thee them that rejoice in thy pride, and thou shalt no more be ^ahaughty ^bbecause of my holy mountain.

12 I will also leave in the midst of thee an afflicted and poor people, and they shall trust in the name of the LORD.

13 The remnant of Israel shall not do iniquity, nor speak ^alies; neither shall a deceitful tongue be found in their mouth: for they shall feed and lie down, and none shall make *them* afraid.

14 ¶ Sing, O daughter of Zion;

shout, O Israel; be glad and rejoice with all the heart, O daughter of Jerusalem.

15 The LORD hath taken away thy judgments, he hath cast out thine enemy: the king of Israel, *even* the LORD, *is* in the ^amidst of thee: thou shalt not see evil any more.

16 In that day it shall be said to Jerusalem, Fear thou not: *and to* Zion, Let not thine hands be slack.

17 The LORD thy God in the midst of thee *is* mighty; he will save, he will rejoice over thee with joy; he will rest in his love, he will joy over thee with singing.

18 I will gather *them that are* sorrowful for the solemn assembly, *who* are of thee, *to whom* the reproach of it *was* a burden.

19 Behold, at that time I will undo all that afflict thee: and I will save her that ^ahalteth, and ^bgather her that was driven out; and I will get them praise and fame in every land where they have been put to shame.

20 At that time will I bring you *again*, even in the time that I ^agather you: for I will make you a name and a ^bpraise among all people of the earth, when I turn back your ^ccaptivity before your eyes, saith the LORD.

8*a* Joel 3:2 (1–2).
  b Isa. 13:4.
  c TG Earth, Destiny of; World, End of.
9*a* TG Communication; Language.
  b TG Common Consent;

Unity.
10*a* Isa. 18:1.
11*a* TG Haughtiness.
  b HEB in.
13*a* TG Lying.
15*a* TG Jesus Christ, Millennial Reign.

19*a* OR is lame.
  b TG Israel, Gathering of.
20*a* Isa. 63:4.
  b Isa. 62:7.
  c Deut. 30:3 (1–5); Zeph. 2:7.

HAGGAI

CHAPTER 1

Haggai exhorts the people to build the temple.

IN ^athe second year of Darius the king, in the sixth ^bmonth, in the first day of the month, came the word of the LORD by Haggai the prophet unto ^cZerubbabel the son of Shealtiel, governor of Judah, and to Joshua the son of Josedech, the high priest, saying,

2 Thus speaketh the LORD of hosts, saying, This people say, The time is not come, the time that the LORD's house should be built.

3 Then came the word of the LORD by Haggai the prophet, saying,

4 *Is it* time for you, O ye, to dwell in your ^aceiled houses, and this house *lie* waste?

5 Now therefore thus saith the LORD of hosts; ^aConsider your ways.

6 Ye have ^asown much, and bring in little; ye ^beat, but ye have not enough; ye drink, but ye are not filled with drink; ye clothe you, but there is none warm; and he that ^cearneth wages earneth ^dwages *to put it* into a bag with ^eholes.

7 ¶ Thus saith the LORD of hosts; ^aConsider your ^bways.

8 Go up to the mountain, and bring wood, and build the ^ahouse; and I will take pleasure in it, and I will be glorified, saith the LORD.

9 Ye looked for much, and, lo, *it came* to little; and when ye brought *it* home, I did blow upon it. Why? saith the LORD of hosts. Because of mine house that *is* waste, and ye run every man unto his own house.

10 Therefore the heaven over you is stayed from dew, and the earth is stayed *from* her ^afruit.

11 And I called for a ^adrought upon the land, and upon the mountains, and upon the ^bcorn, and upon the new wine, and upon the oil, and upon *that* which the ground bringeth forth, and upon men, and upon cattle, and upon all the labour of the hands.

12 ¶ Then Zerubbabel the son of Shealtiel, and Joshua the son of Josedech, the high priest, with all the remnant of the people, obeyed the voice of the LORD their God, and the words of Haggai the prophet, as the LORD their God had ^asent him, and the people did fear before the LORD.

13 Then spake Haggai the LORD's messenger in the LORD's message unto the people, saying, I *am* with you, saith the LORD.

14 And the LORD stirred up the spirit of Zerubbabel the son of Shealtiel, governor of Judah, and the spirit of Joshua the son of Josedech, the high priest, and the spirit of all the remnant of the people; and they came and did work in the house of the LORD of hosts, their God,

15 In the four and twentieth day of the sixth month, in the second year of Darius the king.

---

1 1*a* Probably 520 B.C.
 Darius Hystaspes
 reigned 521–486 B.C.
 b Hag. 2:1, 10 (10, 20).
 c Grandson of Jehoiachin,
 former king of Judah.
 1 Chr. 3:19 (17–19);
 Ezra 2:2 (1–2);
 Matt. 1:12 (11–13).
 4*a* HEB paneled.

5*a* Hag. 2:18.
6*a* Deut. 28:38 (38–40);
 Micah 6:15.
 b Isa. 9:20.
 c TG Family, Managing
 Finances in.
 d TG Wages.
 e TG Waste.
7*a* TG Meditation.
 b 2 Pet. 2:15.

8*a* Ezra 6:3;
 D&C 88:119; 95:3.
10*a* Deut. 28:18.
11*a* TG Drought;
 Famine.
 b OR grain.
12*a* TG Priesthood,
 Authority.

CHAPTER 2

Haggai speaks about the Messiah—The Desire of All Nations will come—The Lord will give peace in His temple.

IN the seventh ^a*month*, in the one and twentieth *day* of the month, came the word of the LORD by the prophet Haggai, saying,

2 Speak now to Zerubbabel the son of Shealtiel, governor of Judah, and to Joshua the son of Josedech, the high priest, and to the residue of the people, saying,

3 Who *is* left among you that saw this ^ahouse in her first glory? and how do ye see it now? *is it* not in your eyes in comparison of it as nothing?

4 Yet now be strong, O Zerubbabel, saith the LORD; and be strong, O Joshua, son of Josedech, the high priest; and be ^astrong, all ye people of the land, saith the LORD, and work: for I *am* with you, saith the LORD of hosts:

5 *According to* the word that I covenanted with you when ye came out of Egypt, so my ^aspirit remaineth among you: fear ye not.

6 For thus saith the LORD of hosts; Yet once, it *is* a little while, and I will ^ashake the heavens, and the earth, and the sea, and the dry *land*;

7 And I will shake all nations, and the desire of all nations shall ^acome: and I will fill this house with ^bglory, saith the LORD of hosts.

8 The ^asilver *is* mine, and the gold *is* mine, saith the LORD of hosts.

9 The glory of this latter house shall be greater than of the former, saith the LORD of hosts: and in this place will I give ^apeace, saith the LORD of hosts.

10 ¶ In the four and twentieth *day* of the ninth ^amonth, in the second year of Darius, came the word of

the LORD by Haggai the prophet, saying,

11 Thus saith the LORD of hosts; Ask now the priests *concerning* the law, saying,

12 If one bear holy flesh in the skirt of his garment, and with his skirt do touch bread, or pottage, or wine, or oil, or any meat, shall it be holy? And the priests answered and said, No.

13 Then said Haggai, If *one that is* unclean by a dead body touch any of these, shall it be unclean? And the priests answered and said, It shall be unclean.

14 Then answered Haggai, and said, So *is* this people, and so *is* this nation before me, saith the LORD; and so *is* every work of their hands; and that which they offer there *is* unclean.

15 And now, I pray you, consider from this day and upward, from before a stone was laid upon a stone in the temple of the LORD:

16 Since those *days* were, when *one* came to an heap of twenty *measures,* there were *but* ten: when *one* came to the ^apressfat for to draw out fifty *vessels* out of the press, there were *but* twenty.

17 I ^asmote you with ^bblasting and with mildew and with hail in all the labours of your hands; yet ye ^c*turned* not to me, saith the LORD.

18 ^aConsider now from this day and upward, from the four and twentieth day of the ninth *month,* *even* from the day that the foundation of the LORD's temple was laid, consider *it.*

19 Is the seed yet in the barn? yea, as yet the vine, and the fig tree, and the pomegranate, and the olive tree, hath not brought forth: from this day will I bless *you.*

20 ¶ And again the word of the

---

2 1*a* Hag. 1:1.
   3*a* Ezra 3:12 (11–13).
   4*a* D&C 27:15 (15–18);
      75:22.
   5*a* Ex. 29:45 (41, 45).
   6*a* Isa. 13:13;
      Ezek. 38:19 (19–20).
      TG Last Days.

   7*a* TG Jesus Christ, Second
      Coming.
    b Ex. 40:34;
      Isa. 60:7;
      D&C 97:15.
   8*a* D&C 38:39.
   9*a* TG Peace;
      Peace of God.

  10*a* Hag. 1:1.
  16*a* IE winevat.
  17*a* Deut. 28:22.
    b IE rust, smut, or blight.
    c Jer. 5:3;
      Amos 4:6 (6–11).
  18*a* Hag. 1:5.

LORD came unto Haggai in the four and twentieth *day* of the month, saying,

21 Speak to Zerubbabel, governor of Judah, saying, I will shake the heavens and the *a*earth;

22 And I will *a*overthrow the throne of kingdoms, and I will destroy the strength of the kingdoms of the heathen; and I will overthrow the chariots, and those that ride in them; and the *b*horses and their riders shall come down, every one by the sword of his *c*brother.

23 In that day, saith the LORD of hosts, will I take thee, O Zerubbabel, my servant, the son of Shealtiel, saith the LORD, and will make thee as *a*a signet: for I have *b*chosen thee, saith the LORD of hosts.

ZECHARIAH

CHAPTER 1

Zechariah calls upon Judah to repent— He is shown in vision that the cities of Judah and the temple will be rebuilt.

IN the eighth month, in the second year of Darius, came the word of the LORD unto *a*Zechariah, the son of Berechiah, the son of Iddo the prophet, saying,

2 The LORD hath been sore displeased with your fathers.

3 Therefore say thou unto them, Thus saith the LORD of hosts; *a*Turn ye unto me, saith the LORD of hosts, and I will turn unto you, saith the LORD of hosts.

4 Be ye not as your *a*fathers, unto whom the former prophets have cried, saying, Thus saith the LORD of hosts; Turn ye now from your evil ways, and *from* your evil doings: but they did *b*not hear, nor *c*hearken unto me, saith the LORD.

5 Your fathers, where *are* they? and the prophets, do they live for ever?

6 But my words and my statutes, which I commanded my servants the prophets, did they not take hold of your fathers? and they returned and said, Like as the LORD of hosts *a*thought to do unto us, according to our ways, and according to our doings, so hath he dealt with us.

7 ¶ Upon the four and twentieth day of the eleventh month, which *is* the month Sebat, in the second year of Darius, came the word of the LORD unto Zechariah, the son of Berechiah, the son of Iddo the prophet, saying,

8 I saw by night, and behold a man riding upon a red horse, and he stood among the myrtle trees that *were* in the *a*bottom; and behind him *were there* red horses, speckled, and white.

9 Then said I, O my lord, what *are* these? And the *a*angel that talked with me said unto me, I will shew thee what these *be*.

10 And the man that stood among the myrtle trees answered and said, These *are they* whom the LORD hath sent to walk to and fro through the earth.

11 And they answered the angel of

21*a* TG Earth, Destiny of.
22*a* Dan. 2:44.
  b Micah 5:10.
  c Zech. 14:13.
23*a* IE one having authority.
  b Ps. 89:3;
    Isa. 43:10.

[ZECHARIAH]
1 1*a* Ezra 5:1.
  3*a* D&C 88:63.
    TG Repent.
  4*a* Ps. 78:8.
    b 2 Ne. 27:5;

Jacob 4:14;
D&C 136:36.
  c TG Hardheartedness.
6*a* Lam. 2:17.
8*a* IE of the valley.
9*a* TG Angels.

the LORD that stood among the myrtle trees, and said, We have walked to and fro through the earth, and, behold, all the earth sitteth still, and is at rest.

12 ¶ Then the angel of the LORD answered and said, O LORD of hosts, how long wilt thou not have mercy on Jerusalem and on the cities of Judah, against which thou hast had indignation these threescore and ten years?

13 And the LORD answered the angel that talked with me *with* good words *and* comfortable words.

14 So the angel that communed with me said unto me, Cry thou, saying, Thus saith the LORD of hosts; I am *ª*jealous for Jerusalem and for Zion with a great jealousy.

15 And I am very sore displeased with the heathen *that are* at ease: for I was but a little displeased, and they helped forward the affliction.

16 Therefore thus saith the LORD; I am returned to Jerusalem with mercies: my *ª*house shall be built in it, saith the LORD of hosts, and a *b*line shall be stretched forth upon Jerusalem.

17 Cry yet, saying, Thus saith the LORD of hosts; My cities through prosperity shall yet be spread abroad; and the LORD shall yet *ª*comfort Zion, and shall yet *b*choose Jerusalem.

18 ¶ Then lifted I up mine eyes, and saw, and behold four horns.

19 And I said unto the angel that talked with me, What *be* these? And he answered me, These *are* the horns which have scattered Judah, Israel, and Jerusalem.

20 And the LORD shewed me four *ª*carpenters.

21 Then said I, What come these to do? And he spake, saying, These *are* the horns which have scattered

Judah, so that no man did lift up his head: but these are come to *ª*fray them, to cast out the horns of the Gentiles, which lifted up *their* horn over the land of Judah to scatter it.

CHAPTER 2

In the last days, Judah will gather to Jerusalem—The people will come from the land of the north—The Lord will dwell among them.

I LIFTED up mine eyes again, and looked, and behold a man with a measuring *ª*line in his hand.

2 Then said I, Whither goest thou? And he said unto me, To measure Jerusalem, to see what *is* the breadth thereof, and what *is* the length thereof.

3 And, behold, the angel that talked with me went forth, and another angel went out to meet him,

4 And said unto him, Run, speak to this young man, saying, Jerusalem shall be *ª*inhabited *as* towns without walls for the multitude of men and cattle therein:

5 For I, saith the LORD, will be unto her a wall of *ª*fire round about, and will be the *b*glory in the midst of her.

6 ¶ Ho, ho, *come forth,* and flee from the land of the *ª*north, saith the LORD: for I have *b*spread you abroad as the *c*four winds of the heaven, saith the LORD.

7 *ª*Deliver thyself, O Zion, that dwellest *with* the daughter of Babylon.

8 For thus saith the LORD of hosts; After the glory hath he sent me unto the nations which spoiled you: for he that toucheth you toucheth the apple of his eye.

9 For, behold, I will shake mine hand upon them, and they shall be a spoil to their servants: and ye shall

---

14a HEB zealous.
  Joel 2:18;
  Zech. 8:2.
16a TG Last Days;
  Temple.
  b Jer. 31:39.
17a Isa. 51:3.
  b Isa. 14:1.
20a HEB craftsmen or

artisans.
21a HEB terrify.
2 1a Ezek. 47:3.
4a Ezek. 36:10.
5a TG God, Presence of;
  Protection, Divine.
  b TG Jesus Christ,
  Glory of.
6a TG Israel, Ten Lost

Tribes of.
  b Ezek. 17:21;
  1 Ne. 10:12 (12–13);
  22:4 (3–8);
  2 Ne. 25:15 (15–16);
  D&C 45:24 (19–25).
  c D&C 133:7 (6–8).
7a Rev. 18:4.

know that the LORD of hosts hath sent me.

10 ¶ Sing and rejoice, O daughter of Zion: for, lo, I come, and I will ^adwell in the midst of thee, saith the LORD.

11 And many ^anations shall be joined to the LORD in that day, and shall be my people: and I will dwell in the ^bmidst of thee, and thou shalt know that the LORD of hosts hath sent me unto thee.

12 And the LORD shall inherit ^aJudah his portion in the holy land, and shall choose Jerusalem again.

13 Be silent, O all flesh, before the LORD: for he is raised up out of his holy ^ahabitation.

CHAPTER 3

Zechariah speaks about the Messiah—The Branch will come—At the Second Coming, iniquity will be removed in one day.

AND he shewed me Joshua the high priest standing before the ^aangel of the LORD, and ^bSatan standing at his right hand to ^cresist him.

2 And the LORD said unto Satan, The LORD rebuke thee, O Satan; even the LORD that hath chosen Jerusalem rebuke thee: is not this a ^abrand plucked out of the fire?

3 Now Joshua was clothed with ^afilthy garments, and stood before the angel.

4 And he answered and spake unto those that stood before him, saying, Take away the filthy garments from him. And unto him he said, Behold, I have caused thine iniquity to pass from thee, and I will clothe thee with change of raiment.

5 And I said, Let them set ^aa fair mitre upon his head. So they set a fair mitre upon his head, and clothed him with garments. And the angel of the LORD stood by.

6 And the angel of the LORD protested unto Joshua, saying,

7 Thus saith the LORD of hosts; If thou wilt ^awalk in my ways, and if thou wilt keep my ^bcharge, then thou shalt also judge my house, and shalt also keep my courts, and I will give thee places to walk among ^cthese that stand by.

8 Hear now, O Joshua the high priest, thou, and thy fellows that sit before thee: for they *are* men wondered at: for, behold, I will bring forth my servant the ^aBRANCH.

9 For behold the stone that I have laid before Joshua; upon one stone *shall be* seven eyes: behold, I will engrave the graving thereof, saith the LORD of hosts, and I will remove the iniquity of that land in one day.

10 In that day, saith the LORD of hosts, shall ye call every man his neighbour under the vine and under the fig tree.

CHAPTER 4

Zerubbabel will lay the foundation of and finish the house of the Lord, the temple of Zerubbabel.

AND the angel that talked with me came again, and waked me, as a man that is wakened out of his sleep,

2 And said unto me, What seest thou? And I said, I have looked, and behold a ^acandlestick all *of* gold, with a bowl upon the top of it, and his seven lamps thereon, and seven

---

10*a* Lev. 26:12;
    Jer. 3:17;
    Joel 3:21 (18–21);
    Rev. 22:3 (3–4).
    TG Jesus Christ,
    Millennial Reign;
    Millennium.
11*a* Isa. 55:5;
    Zech. 8:22;
    D&C 45:69 (66–69);
    49:10; 97:19 (18–21).

    b D&C 1:36.
12*a* TG Israel, Judah,
    People of.
13*a* D&C 101:89.
3 1*a* TG Angels.
    b HEB the Adversary or
    Accuser (also v. 2).
    Ps. 109:6.
    c HEB accuse.
2*a* Amos 4:11.
3*a* TG Filthiness.

5*a* HEB a clean (pure) cap.
7*a* TG Walking with God.
    b Deut. 11:1.
    c IE the heavenly
    messengers.
8*a* TG Jesus Christ, Davidic
    Descent of;
    Jesus Christ, Prophecies
    about.
4 2*a* Ex. 37:17;
    Rev. 1:20.

pipes to the seven lamps, which *are* upon the top thereof:

3 And two olive trees by it, one upon the right *side* of the bowl, and the other upon the left *side* thereof.

4 So I answered and spake to the angel that talked with me, saying, What *are* these, my lord?

5 Then the angel that talked with me answered and said unto me, Knowest thou not what these be? And I said, No, my lord.

6 Then he answered and spake unto me, saying, This *is* the word of the LORD unto Zerubbabel, saying, Not by might, nor by power, but by my ªspirit, saith the LORD of hosts.

7 Who *art* thou, O great mountain? before Zerubbabel *thou shalt become* a plain: and he shall bring forth the headstone *thereof with* shoutings, *crying,* Grace, grace unto it.

8 Moreover the word of the LORD came unto me, saying,

9 The hands of Zerubbabel have laid the foundation of this house; his hands shall also finish it; and thou shalt know that the LORD of hosts hath sent me unto you.

10 For who hath despised the day of small things? for they shall rejoice, and shall see the plummet in the hand of Zerubbabel *with* those seven; they *are* the eyes of the LORD, which run to and fro through the whole earth.

11 ¶ Then answered I, and said unto him, What *are* these two olive trees upon the right *side* of the candlestick and upon the left *side* thereof?

12 And I answered again, and said unto him, What *be these* two olive branches which through the two golden pipes empty the golden *oil* out of themselves?

13 And he answered me and said, Knowest thou not what these *be?* And I said, No, my lord.

14 Then said he, These *are* the two ªanointed ones, that stand by the Lord of the whole earth.

CHAPTER 5

An angel reveals truths to Zechariah by the use of symbolic representations.

THEN I turned, and lifted up mine eyes, and looked, and behold a flying roll.

2 And he said unto me, What seest thou? And I answered, I see a flying roll; the length thereof *is* twenty cubits, and the breadth thereof ten cubits.

3 Then said he unto me, This *is* the curse that goeth forth over the face of the whole earth: for every one that ªstealeth shall be ᵇcut off *as* on this side according to it; and every one that sweareth shall be cut off *as* on that side according to it.

4 I will bring it forth, saith the LORD of hosts, and it shall enter into the house of the thief, and into the house of him that sweareth falsely by my name: and it shall remain in the midst of his house, and shall consume it with the timber thereof and the stones thereof.

5 ¶ Then the angel that talked with me went forth, and said unto me, Lift up now thine eyes, and see what *is* this that goeth forth.

6 And I said, What *is* it? And he said, This *is* an ephah that goeth forth. He said moreover, This *is* their resemblance through all the earth.

7 And, behold, there was lifted up a talent of lead: and this *is* a woman that sitteth in the midst of the ephah.

8 And he said, This *is* wickedness. And he cast it into the midst of the ephah; and he cast the weight of lead upon the mouth thereof.

9 Then lifted I up mine eyes, and looked, and, behold, there came out two women, and the wind *was* in their wings; for they had wings like the wings of a stork: and they lifted up the ephah between the earth and the heaven.

10 Then said I to the angel that talked with me, Whither do these bear the ephah?

6a TG God, Spirit of.
14a Isa. 51:19 (19–20);

Rev. 11:3 (1–14);
D&C 77:15.

5 3a TG Stealing.
  b D&C 42:20.

11 And he said unto me, To build it an house in the land of Shinar: and it shall be established, and set there upon her own base.

CHAPTER 6

Zechariah crowns Joshua, the high priest, in similitude of Christ, the Branch, who will come—Christ will be a priest upon His throne forever.

AND I turned, and lifted up mine eyes, and looked, and, behold, there came four chariots out from between two mountains; and the mountains *were* mountains of brass.

2 In the first chariot *were* red horses; and in the second chariot black horses;

3 And in the third chariot white horses; and in the fourth chariot grisled and bay horses.

4 Then I answered and said unto the angel that talked with me, What *are* these, my lord?

5 And the angel answered and said unto me, These *are* the four [a]spirits of the heavens, which go forth from standing before the Lord of all the earth.

6 The black horses which *are* therein go forth into the north country; and the white go forth after them; and the grisled go forth toward the south country.

7 And the bay went forth, and sought to go that they might walk to and fro through the earth: and he said, Get you hence, walk to and fro through the earth. So they walked to and fro through the earth.

8 Then cried he upon me, and spake unto me, saying, Behold, these that go toward the north country have quieted my spirit in the north country.

9 ¶ And the word of the LORD came unto me, saying,

10 Take of *them of* the captivity, *even* of Heldai, of Tobijah, and of Jedaiah, which are come from Babylon, and come thou the same day, and go into the house of Josiah the son of Zephaniah;

11 Then take silver and gold, and make crowns, and set *them* upon the head of Joshua the son of Josedech, the high priest;

12 And speak unto him, saying, Thus speaketh the LORD of hosts, saying, Behold the man [a]whose name *is* The [b]BRANCH; and he shall grow up out of his place, and he shall build the temple of the LORD:

13 Even he shall build the temple of the LORD; and he shall bear the glory, and shall sit and rule upon his throne; and he shall be a priest upon his throne: and the counsel of peace shall be between them both.

14 And the crowns shall be to Helem, and to Tobijah, and to Jedaiah, and to Hen the son of Zephaniah, for a memorial in the temple of the LORD.

15 And they *that are* far off shall come and [a]build in the temple of the LORD, and ye shall know that the LORD of hosts hath sent me unto you. And *this* shall come to pass, if ye will diligently [b]obey the voice of the LORD your God.

CHAPTER 7

The Lord reproves hypocrisy in fasts— He calls upon the people to show mercy and compassion and to live godly lives.

AND it came to pass in the fourth year of king Darius, *that* the word of the LORD came unto Zechariah in the fourth *day* of the ninth month, *even* in Chisleu;

2 When they had sent unto the house of God Sherezer and Regemmelech, and their men, to pray before the LORD,

3 *And* to speak unto the priests which *were* in the house of the LORD

---

6 5*a* Heb. 1:14 (7, 14).
12*a* HEB Branch is His name and from beneath Him one shall branch forth
and he shall build the temple of Jehovah.
b TG Jesus Christ, Davidic Descent of;
Jesus Christ, Prophecies about.
15*a* Isa. 60:10.
b TG Obedience.

of hosts, and to the prophets, saying, Should I weep in the fifth month, separating myself, as I have done these so many years?

4 ¶ Then came the word of the LORD of hosts unto me, saying,

5 Speak unto all the people of the land, and to the priests, saying, When ye fasted and mourned in the fifth and seventh *month*, even those seventy years, did ye at all *a*fast unto me, *even* to me?

6 And when ye did eat, and when ye did drink, did not ye eat *for yourselves*, and drink *for yourselves*?

7 *Should ye* not *hear* the words which the LORD hath cried by the *a*former prophets, when Jerusalem was inhabited and in prosperity, and the cities thereof round about her, when *men* inhabited the south and the plain?

8 ¶ And the word of the LORD came unto Zechariah, saying,

9 Thus speaketh the LORD of hosts, saying, Execute true *a*judgment, and shew *b*mercy and *c*compassions every man to his brother:

10 And *a*oppress not the widow, nor the fatherless, the stranger, nor the *b*poor; and let none of you imagine evil against his brother in your heart.

11 But they refused to hearken, and pulled away the shoulder, and stopped their ears, that they should not hear.

12 Yea, they made their hearts *as* an adamant *a*stone, lest they should hear the law, and the words which the LORD of hosts hath sent in his spirit by the former *b*prophets: therefore came a great wrath from the LORD of hosts.

13 Therefore it is come to pass, *that* as he cried, and they would not hear; so *a*they *b*cried, and I would not hear, saith the LORD of hosts:

14 But I *a*scattered them with a whirlwind among all the nations whom they knew not. Thus the land was desolate after them, that no man passed through nor returned: for they laid the pleasant land desolate.

CHAPTER 8

In the last days, Jerusalem will be restored, Judah will be gathered, and the Lord will bless His people beyond anything in the past.

AGAIN the word of the LORD of hosts came *to* me, saying,

2 Thus saith the LORD of hosts; I was jealous for Zion with great jealousy, and I was *a*jealous for her with great fury.

3 Thus saith the LORD; I am returned unto Zion, and will dwell in the midst of Jerusalem: and *a*Jerusalem shall be called a city of truth; and the *b*mountain of the LORD of hosts the holy mountain.

4 Thus saith the LORD of hosts; There shall yet *a*old men and old women dwell in the streets of Jerusalem, and every man with his staff in his hand for very age.

5 And the streets of the city shall be full of boys and girls playing in the streets thereof.

6 Thus saith the LORD of hosts; If it be marvellous in the eyes of the remnant of this people in these days, should it also be marvellous in mine eyes? saith the LORD of hosts.

7 Thus saith the LORD of hosts; Behold, I will *a*save my people from the east country, and from the west country;

8 And I will bring them, and they shall dwell in the midst of Jerusalem: and they shall be my *a*people, and I will be their God, in truth and in righteousness.

---

7 5*a* Matt. 6:16;
    3 Ne. 13:16 (16–18).
    TG Fast, Fasting.
   7*a* D&C 84:57 (14, 54–57).
   9*a* TG Justice.
    b TG Mercy.
    c TG Charity; Compassion.
  10*a* Ezek. 22:7 (7–14).
    TG Cruelty.
    b Prov. 22:22;

    Mosiah 4:26 (16–26);
    Hel. 4:12;
    D&C 42:30 (30–39, 71);
    83:6.
  12*a* Matt. 13:20.
    b Matt. 11:13;
    1 Ne. 3:20;
    Mosiah 15:13.
  13*a* Lam. 1:2 (1–3).
    b TG God, Access to.

  14*a* TG Israel, Ten Lost
    Tribes of.
  8 2*a* Zech. 1:14.
    3*a* TG Jerusalem.
    b Dan. 9:16;
    Joel 3:17.
    4*a* TG Old Age.
    7*a* JST Zech. 8:7 . . .
    gather . . .
    8*a* D&C 42:9.

9 ¶ Thus saith the LORD of hosts; Let your hands be strong, ye that hear in these days these words by the mouth of the ᵃprophets, which *were* in the day *that* the foundation of the house of the LORD of hosts was laid, that the temple might be built.

10 For before these days there was no hire for man, nor any hire for beast; neither *was there any* peace to him that went out or came in because of the affliction: for I set all men every one against his neighbour.

11 But now I *will* not *be* unto the residue of this people as in the former days, saith the LORD of hosts.

12 For the seed *shall be* prosperous; the vine shall give her fruit, and the ground shall give her increase, and the heavens shall give their dew; and I will cause the remnant of this people to possess all these *things*.

13 And it shall come to pass, *that* as ye were a ᵃcurse among the heathen, O house of Judah, and house of Israel; so will I ᵇsave you, and ye shall be a ᶜblessing: fear not, *but* let your hands be strong.

14 For thus saith the LORD of hosts; As I thought to punish you, when your fathers provoked me to wrath, saith the LORD of hosts, and I ᵃrepented not:

15 So again have I thought in these days to do well unto Jerusalem and to the house of Judah: fear ye not.

16 ¶ These *are* the things that ye shall do; Speak ye every man the ᵃtruth to his neighbour; execute the ᵇjudgment of truth and ᶜpeace in your gates:

17 And let none of you imagine evil in your hearts against his neighbour; and love no ᵃfalse oath: for all these *are things* that I hate, saith the LORD.

18 ¶ And the word of the LORD of hosts came unto me, saying,

19 Thus saith the LORD of hosts; The fast of the fourth *month,* and the fast of the fifth, and the fast of the seventh, and the fast of the tenth, shall be to the house of Judah joy and gladness, and cheerful feasts; therefore love the truth and peace.

20 Thus saith the LORD of hosts; *It shall* yet *come to pass,* that there shall come people, and the inhabitants of many cities:

21 And the inhabitants of one *city* shall go to another, saying, Let us go speedily to pray before the LORD, and to seek the LORD of hosts: I will go also.

22 Yea, many ᵃpeople and strong nations shall come to seek the LORD of hosts in Jerusalem, and to pray before the LORD.

23 Thus saith the LORD of hosts; In those days *it shall come to pass,* that ten men shall take hold out of all languages of the nations, even shall take hold of the skirt of him that is a Jew, saying, We will go with you: for we have heard *that* God *is* with ᵃyou.

CHAPTER 9

Zechariah speaks as the Messiah—The Messiah will come, having salvation, lowly and riding upon an ass—He will free the prisoners from the pit—Judah and Ephraim are instruments of the Lord.

THE burden of the word of the LORD in the land of Hadrach, and Damascus *shall be* the rest thereof: when the eyes of man, as of all the tribes of Israel, *shall be* toward the LORD.

2 And Hamath also shall border thereby; Tyrus, and Zidon, though it be very wise.

3 And ᵃTyrus did build herself a strong hold, and heaped up silver as the dust, and fine gold as the mire of the streets.

4 Behold, the Lord will cast her out, and he will smite her power in

---

9 *a* Ezra 5:1.
13 *a* TG Curse.
  b JST Zech. 8:13 . . .
    gather . . .
  c Gen. 18:18 (18–19).

TG Israel, Blessings of.
14 *a* HEB relented.
16 *a* TG Truth.
  b TG Justice.
  c TG Peacemakers.

17 *a* TG Lying.
22 *a* Zech. 2:11;
    2 Ne. 12:3.
23 *a* HEB you (plural).
9 3 *a* Amos 1:10 (9–10).

the sea; and she shall be devoured with fire.

5 ªAshkelon shall see *it,* and fear; Gaza also *shall see it,* and be very sorrowful, and Ekron; for her expectation shall be ashamed; and the king shall perish from Gaza, and Ashkelon shall not be inhabited.

6 And a bastard shall dwell in Ashdod, and I will cut off the pride of the Philistines.

7 And I will take away his blood out of his mouth, and his abominations from between his teeth: but he that remaineth, even he, *shall be* for our God, and he shall be as a governor in Judah, and Ekron as a ªJebusite.

8 And I will encamp about mine house because of the army, because of him that passeth by, and because of him that returneth: and no oppressor shall pass through them any more: for now have I seen with mine eyes.

9 ¶ Rejoice greatly, O ªdaughter of Zion; shout, O daughter of Jerusalem: behold, thy *b*King cometh unto thee: he *is* *c*just, and having salvation; lowly, and *d*riding upon an *e*ass, and upon a *f*colt the foal of an ass.

10 And I will cut off the chariot from Ephraim, and the ªhorse from Jerusalem, and the battle bow shall be cut off: and he shall speak peace unto the *b*heathen: and his *c*dominion *shall be* from sea *even* to sea, and from the river *even* to the ends of the earth.

11 As for thee also, by the ªblood of thy *b*covenant I have sent forth thy *c*prisoners out of the *d*pit wherein *is* no water.

12 ¶ Turn you to the strong hold,

ye prisoners of ªhope: even to day do I declare *that* I will *b*render *c*double unto thee;

13 When I have bent Judah for me, filled the bow with Ephraim, and raised up thy sons, O Zion, against thy sons, O Greece, and made thee as the sword of a mighty man.

14 And the LORD shall be seen over them, and his arrow shall go forth as the lightning: and the Lord GOD shall blow the trumpet, and shall go with ªwhirlwinds of the south.

15 The LORD of hosts shall defend them; and they shall devour, and subdue with sling stones; and they shall drink, *and* make a noise as through wine; and they shall be filled like bowls, *and* as the corners of the altar.

16 And the LORD their God shall ªsave them in that *b*day as the flock of his people: for *they shall be as* the *c*stones of a *d*crown, lifted up as an *e*ensign upon his land.

17 For how great *is* his goodness, and how great *is* his beauty! corn shall make the young men cheerful, and new wine the maids.

CHAPTER 10

Judah and Joseph will be scattered among the people in far countries—The Lord will hiss for them, gather them, and redeem them.

ASK ye of the LORD rain in the time of the ªlatter rain; *so* the LORD shall make bright clouds, and give them showers of rain, to every one grass in the field.

2 For the idols have spoken vanity, and the ªdiviners have seen a lie, and have told false *b*dreams; they

---

5 a Zeph. 2:4.
7 a Judg. 1:21.
9 a Isa. 62:11.
  b Matt. 21:5 (4–11);
    John 12:15 (12–16).
  c TG Justice.
  d TG Jesus Christ,
    Prophecies about.
  e Mark 11:7 (1–11).
  f Luke 19:35 (35–40).
10 a Micah 5:10.
  b TG Heathen.

c Ps. 72:8;
  D&C 58:22; 76:63.
11 a TG Jesus Christ,
    Atonement through;
    Redemption.
  b TG Covenants.
  c TG Genealogy and
    Temple Work;
    Salvation for the Dead.
  d Isa. 51:14.
12 a Moro. 7:41 (1, 3, 40–48).
  b HEB restore.

c Isa. 61:7.
14 a Dan. 11:40.
16 a Ezek. 37:23.
  b Isa. 2:11; 52:6;
    Hosea 2:16 (14–23).
  c Mal. 3:17; D&C 60:4.
  d Isa. 62:3.
  e TG Ensign.
10 1 a Deut. 11:14;
    Joel 2:23.
  2 a Deut. 18:20.
  b TG Dream.

comfort in vain: therefore they went their way as a flock, they were troubled, because *there was* no ᶜshepherd.

3 Mine anger was kindled against the shepherds, and I punished the goats: for the LORD of hosts hath visited his flock the house of Judah, and hath made them as his goodly horse in the battle.

4 Out of him came forth ᵃthe corner, out of him the ᵇnail, out of him the battle bow, out of him every oppressor together.

5 ¶ And they shall be as mighty *men*, which tread down *their enemies* in the mire of the streets in the battle: and they shall fight, because the LORD *is* with them, and the riders on horses shall be confounded.

6 And I will strengthen the house of Judah, and I will save the house of Joseph, and I will bring them again to place them; for I have mercy upon them: and they shall be as though I had not cast them off: for I *am* the LORD their God, and will ᵃhear them.

7 And *they of* ᵃEphraim shall be like a mighty *man*, and their heart shall rejoice as through wine: yea, their children shall see *it*, and be glad; their heart shall rejoice in the LORD.

8 I will hiss for them, and ᵃgather them; for I have redeemed them: and they shall increase as they have increased.

9 And I will ᵃsow them among the people: and they shall ᵇremember me in far countries; and they shall live with their children, and turn again.

10 I will bring them again also out of the land of Egypt, and gather them out of ᵃAssyria; and I will bring them into the land of Gilead

and Lebanon; and *place* shall not be found for them.

11 And he shall pass through the sea with affliction, and shall smite the waves in the sea, and all the deeps of the river shall dry up: and the pride of ᵃAssyria shall be brought down, and the ᵇsceptre of ᶜEgypt shall depart away.

12 And I will ᵃstrengthen them in the LORD; and they shall walk up and down in his ᵇname, saith the LORD.

CHAPTER 11

Zechariah speaks about the Messiah— The Messiah will be betrayed for thirty pieces of silver—They will be cast to the potter in the house of the Lord.

OPEN thy doors, O Lebanon, that the fire may devour thy cedars.

2 Howl, ᵃfir tree; for the cedar is fallen; because the mighty are spoiled: howl, O ye ᵇoaks of Bashan; for the forest of the vintage is come down.

3 ¶ *There is* a voice of the howling of the shepherds; for their glory is spoiled: a voice of the roaring of young lions; for the pride of Jordan is spoiled.

4 Thus saith the LORD my God; Feed the flock of the slaughter;

5 Whose possessors slay them, and hold themselves not ᵃguilty: and they that sell them say, Blessed *be* the LORD; for I am ᵇrich: and their own shepherds pity them not.

6 For I will no more pity the inhabitants of the land, saith the LORD: but, lo, I will deliver the men every one into his neighbour's hand, and into the hand of his king: and they shall smite the land, and out of their hand I will not deliver *them*.

7 And I will feed the flock of

2c TG Shepherd.
4a IE the cornerstone.
   Ps. 118:22 (21–22);
   Matt. 21:42 (42–46).
 b Isa. 22:23.
6a OR answer.
7a Gen. 48:14 (14–22);
   D&C 64:36 (33–36);
   109:60 (60–61);
   133:32 (16–35).

8a TG Israel, Gathering of.
9a Zech. 13:7 (7–9).
   TG Israel, Ten Lost
   Tribes of.
 b Deut. 30:2 (1–3).
10a TG Israel, Ten Lost
   Tribes of.
11a Isa. 14:25.
 b Isa. 11:15;
   Ezek. 30:13.

  c Isa. 19:16 (11–25);
    Joel 3:19.
12a D&C 31:8; 37:2.
  b Micah 4:5.
11 2a Nahum 2:3.
   b Ezek. 27:6.
 5a TG Guilt.
  b TG Treasure.

slaughter, *even* you, O poor of the flock. And I took unto me two staves; the one I called Beauty, and the other I called *a*Bands; and I fed the flock.

8 Three shepherds also I cut off in one month; and my soul lothed them, and their soul also abhorred me.

9 Then said I, I will not feed you: that that dieth, let it die; and that that is to be cut off, let it be cut off; and let the rest eat every one the flesh of another.

10 ¶ And I took my staff, *even* Beauty, and cut it asunder, that I might break my covenant which I had made with all the people.

11 And it was broken in that day: and so the poor of the flock *a*that waited upon me knew that it *was* the word of the LORD.

12 And I said unto them, If ye think good, give *me* my price; and if not, forbear. So they weighed for my price *a*thirty *pieces* of *b*silver.

13 And the LORD said unto me, Cast it unto the *a*potter: a goodly price that I was *b*prised at of them. And I took the thirty *pieces* of silver, and cast them to the potter in the house of the LORD.

14 Then I cut asunder mine other staff, *even* *a*Bands, that I might break the brotherhood between Judah and Israel.

15 ¶ And the LORD said unto me, Take unto thee yet the instruments of a foolish shepherd.

16 For, lo, I will raise up a shepherd in the land, *which* shall not visit those that be cut off, neither shall seek the young one, nor heal that that is broken, nor feed that that standeth still: but he shall eat the flesh of the fat, and tear their claws in pieces.

17 Woe to the idol *a*shepherd that

leaveth the flock! the sword *shall be* upon his arm, and upon his right eye: his arm shall be clean dried up, and his right eye shall be utterly darkened.

CHAPTER 12

In the final great war, all nations will be engaged at Jerusalem, but the Lord will defend His people—Then the Jews will look upon the Lord, whom they crucified, and there will be great mourning.

THE burden of the word of the LORD for Israel, saith the LORD, which stretcheth forth the heavens, and layeth the foundation of the *a*earth, and formeth the *b*spirit of man within him.

2 Behold, I will make Jerusalem a *a*cup of trembling unto all the *b*people round about, when they shall be in the siege both against Judah *and* against Jerusalem.

3 ¶ And in that day will I make Jerusalem a burdensome stone for all people: all that burden themselves with it shall be cut in pieces, though all the people of the earth be *a*gathered together against it.

4 In that day, saith the LORD, I will smite every horse with astonishment, and his rider with madness: and I will open mine eyes upon the house of Judah, and will smite every horse of the people with blindness.

5 And the governors of Judah shall say in their heart, The inhabitants of Jerusalem *shall be* my strength in the LORD of hosts their God.

6 ¶ In that day will I make the governors of Judah like an *a*hearth of fire among the wood, and like a torch of fire in a sheaf; and they shall devour all the *b*people round about, on the right hand and on the left: and *c*Jerusalem shall be

---

7*a* Zech. 11:14.
11*a* OR who watched for me.
12*a* TG Jesus Christ, Betrayal of.
  b Luke 22:5 (3–6).
13*a* Matt. 27:7 (3–10).

  b TG Jesus Christ, Prophecies about.
14*a* Zech. 11:7.
17*a* Jer. 23:1.
12 1*a* TG Creation.
  b TG Man, Antemortal Existence of.

2*a* Isa. 51:17 (17–23).
  b OR nations.
3*a* Micah 4:11;
    2 Ne. 23:4.
6*a* Obad. 1:18.
  b OR nations.
  c TG Jerusalem.

^dinhabited again in her own place, *even* in Jerusalem.

7 The LORD also shall save the tents of Judah first, that the glory of the house of ^aDavid and the glory of the inhabitants of Jerusalem do not magnify *themselves* against Judah.

8 In that day shall the LORD defend the inhabitants of Jerusalem; and he that is feeble among them at that day shall be as David; and the house of David *shall be* as God, as the angel of the LORD before them.

9 ¶ And it shall come to pass in that day, *that* I will seek to ^adestroy all the nations that come against ^bJerusalem.

10 And I will ^apour upon the house of David, and upon the inhabitants of Jerusalem, the spirit of ^bgrace and of supplications: and they shall ^clook upon me whom they have ^dpierced, and they shall ^emourn for him, as one mourneth for *his* ^fonly *son,* and shall be in bitterness for him, as one that is in bitterness for *his* firstborn.

11 In that day shall there be a great ^amourning in Jerusalem, as the mourning of Hadadrimmon in the valley of Megiddon.

12 And the land shall ^amourn, every family apart; the family of the house of David apart, and their wives apart; the family of the house of Nathan apart, and their wives apart;

13 The family of the house of Levi apart, and their wives apart; the family of Shimei apart, and their wives apart;

14 All the families that remain, every family apart, and their wives apart.

CHAPTER 13

The Jews will gain forgiveness at the Second Coming—They will ask the Lord, What are these wounds in Thine hands?—The remnant, tried and refined, will be His people.

IN that day there shall be a ^afountain opened to the house of David and to the inhabitants of Jerusalem for sin and for uncleanness.

2 ¶ And it shall come to pass in that day, saith the LORD of hosts, *that* I will cut off the names of the ^aidols out of the land, and they shall no more be remembered: and also I will cause the prophets and the unclean spirit to pass out of the land.

3 And it shall come to pass, *that* when any shall yet prophesy, then his father and his mother that begat him shall say unto him, Thou shalt not live; for thou speakest lies in the name of the LORD: and his father and his mother that begat him shall thrust him through when he prophesieth.

4 And it shall come to pass in that day, *that* the prophets shall be ^aashamed every one of his vision, when he hath prophesied; neither shall they wear a ^brough garment to deceive:

5 But he shall say, I *am* no prophet, I *am* an husbandman; for man taught me to keep cattle from my youth.

6 And *one* shall say unto him, What *are* these ^awounds in thine hands? Then he shall answer, *Those* with which I was ^bwounded *in* the house of my friends.

7 ¶ Awake, O sword, against my shepherd, and against the man ^a*that is* my fellow, saith the LORD of

---

6*d* D&C 109:64 (62–67).
  TG Israel, Gathering of.
7*a* TG Jesus Christ, Davidic
    Descent of.
9*a* Isa. 13:5;
    Ezek. 39:3 (2–5).
  b 1 Ne. 22:14 (14–19).
10*a* Ezek. 39:29 (28–29);
    D&C 105:12; 110:10.
  b TG Grace.
  c TG Jesus Christ, Second

Coming.
  d TG Jesus Christ,
    Crucifixion of.
  e Jer. 50:4.
  f Amos 8:10.
11*a* TG Mourning.
12*a* Matt. 24:30.
13 1*a* TG Baptism.
  2*a* TG Idolatry.
  4*a* Micah 3:7 (6–7).
  b Matt. 3:4.

6*a* TG Jesus Christ, Crucifixion of; Jesus Christ, Mission of; Jesus Christ, Second Coming.
  b D&C 45:52 (51–53).
    TG Jesus Christ, Betrayal of; Jesus Christ, Prophecies about; Martyrdom.
7*a* OR who stands next to me.

hosts: smite the [b]shepherd, and the [c]sheep shall be [d]scattered: and I will turn mine hand upon the little ones.

8 And it shall come to pass, *that* in all the land, saith the LORD, two parts therein shall be cut off *and* die; but the third shall be [a]left therein.

9 And I will bring the third part through the fire, and will [a]refine them as silver is refined, and will [b]try them as gold is [c]tried: they shall call on my name, and I will hear them: I will say, It *is* my [d]people: and they shall say, The LORD *is* my God.

CHAPTER 14

At His Second Coming, the Lord will fight for Israel—His feet will stand upon the Mount of Olives—He will be King over all the earth—Plagues will destroy the wicked.

BEHOLD, the [a]day of the LORD cometh, and thy spoil shall be divided in the midst of thee.

2 For I will gather all nations against Jerusalem to [a]battle; and the city shall be taken, and the [b]houses rifled, and the women ravished; and half of the city shall go forth into captivity, and the residue of the people shall not be cut off from the city.

3 Then shall the LORD go forth, and [a]fight against those nations, as when he fought in the day of battle.

4 ¶ And his [a]feet shall [b]stand in that day upon the [c]mount of Olives, which *is* before Jerusalem on the east, and the mount of Olives shall cleave in the midst thereof toward the east and toward the west, *and*

there shall be a very great valley; and half of the mountain shall remove toward the north, and half of it toward the south.

5 And ye shall flee *to* the valley of the mountains; for the valley of the mountains shall reach unto Azal: yea, ye shall flee, like as ye fled from before the [a]earthquake in the days of Uzziah king of Judah: and the LORD my God shall come, *and* all the [b]saints with thee.

6 And it shall come to pass in that day, *that* the [a]light shall not be clear, *nor* dark:

7 But it shall be one day which shall be known to the LORD, not day, nor night: but it shall come to pass, *that* at evening time it shall be light.

8 And it shall be in that day, *that* [a]living [b]waters shall go out from Jerusalem; half of them toward the former sea, and half of them toward the hinder sea: in summer and in winter shall it be.

9 And the LORD shall be [a]king over all the earth: in that day shall there be one LORD, and his name one.

10 All the land shall be turned as a [a]plain from Geba to Rimmon south of Jerusalem: and [b]it shall be lifted up, and inhabited in her [c]place, from Benjamin's gate unto the place of the first gate, unto the corner gate, and *from* the tower of Hananeel unto the king's winepresses.

11 And *men* shall dwell in it, and there shall be no more utter destruction; but Jerusalem shall be safely inhabited.

12 ¶ And this shall be the [a]plague wherewith the LORD will [b]smite all

7*b* Matt. 26:31;
    Mark 14:27 (27–31).
    TG Jesus Christ, Good
    Shepherd; Shepherd.
  c TG Sheep.
  d Zech. 10:9.
8*a* JS—M 1:44 (42–46).
9*a* 3 Ne. 24:2 (2–3);
    D&C 128:24.
    TG Suffering.
  b Dan. 12:10. TG Test.
  c Dan. 11:35.
  d Jer. 30:22; Hosea 2:23;
    Rom. 9:25.
14 1*a* D&C 1:14.

2*a* Joel 3:14 (9–14);
    Rev. 16:16.
    TG Last Days.
  b Isa. 13:16.
3*a* Ezek. 38:22.
4*a* TG God, Manifestations of.
  b TG Jesus Christ, Second
    Coming.
  c D&C 45:48 (47–53).
5*a* Amos 1:1.
  b 1 Thes. 4:14;
    JST 1 Thes. 4:17
    (1 Thes. 4:17 note *a*).
    TG Saints.

6*a* TG Light [noun].
8*a* TG Living Water.
  b Ezek. 47:1; Joel 3:18;
    Rev. 22:1.
9*a* Ps. 47:7;
    D&C 38:21; 41:4; 45:59.
    TG Jesus Christ,
    Authority of;
    Jesus Christ, Millennial
    Reign.
10*a* Isa. 40:4 (1–5).
   b HEB she; i.e., Jerusalem.
   c Jer. 31:38 (38–40).
12*a* D&C 29:18 (17–19).
   b TG Plague.

the people that have fought against Jerusalem; Their flesh shall consume away while they stand upon their feet, and their eyes shall consume away in their holes, and their tongue shall consume away in their mouth.

13 And it shall come to pass in that day, *that* a great tumult from the LORD shall be among them; and they shall lay hold every one on the hand of his neighbour, and his hand shall rise up against the hand of his ^aneighbour.

14 And Judah also shall fight at Jerusalem; and the wealth of all the ^aheathen round about shall be gathered together, gold, and silver, and apparel, in great abundance.

15 ^aAnd so shall be the plague of the horse, of the mule, of the camel, and of the ass, and of all the beasts that shall be in these ^btents, as this plague.

16 ¶ And it shall come to pass, *that* every one that is left of all the nations which came against Jerusalem shall even go up from year to year to ^aworship the ^bKing, the LORD of hosts, and to keep the ^cfeast of ^dtabernacles.

17 And it shall be, *that* whoso will not come up of *all* the families of the earth unto Jerusalem to worship the King, the LORD of hosts, even upon them shall be no rain.

18 And if the family of Egypt go not up, and come not, that *have* no *rain;* there shall be the plague, wherewith the LORD will smite the ^aheathen that come not up to keep the feast of tabernacles.

19 This shall be the punishment of Egypt, and the punishment of all nations that come not up to keep the feast of tabernacles.

20 ¶ In that day shall there be upon the bells of the horses, ^aHOLINESS UNTO THE LORD; and the pots in the LORD's house shall be like the bowls before the altar.

21 Yea, every pot in Jerusalem and in Judah shall be ^aholiness unto the LORD of hosts: and all they that sacrifice shall come and take of them, and ^bseethe therein: and in that day there shall be no more the ^cCanaanite in the house of the LORD of hosts.

MALACHI

CHAPTER 1

The Jews despise the Lord by offering polluted bread upon the altar and by sacrificing animals with blemishes— The Lord's name will be great among the Gentiles.

THE burden of the ^aword of the LORD to Israel by Malachi. 2 I have ^aloved you, saith the LORD. Yet ye say, Wherein hast thou loved us? *Was* not Esau Jacob's brother? saith the LORD: yet I ^bloved Jacob,

---

13a Hag. 2:22;
   D&C 45:68 (33, 68).
14a HEB nations or Gentiles.
15a IE The beasts also shall
   be smitten.
   b HEB camps.
16a Isa. 66:23;
   D&C 133:39 (37–40).

b 1 Tim. 6:15.
c Ezra 3:4;
   Neh. 8:14.
d Lev. 23:34.
18a Isa. 60:12.
20a Ex. 28:36.
21a OR sacred.
   b OR cook in them.

c Joel 3:17.

[MALACHI]

1 1a TG Priesthood, Keys of.
2a TG God, Love of; Love.
   b Rom. 9:13.

3 And I hated Esau, and laid his mountains and his ^aheritage ^bwaste for the ^cdragons of the wilderness.

4 Whereas Edom saith, We are impoverished, but we will return and build the desolate places; thus saith the LORD of hosts, They shall build, but I will throw down; and they shall call them, The border of wickedness, and, The people against whom the LORD hath indignation for ever.

5 And your eyes shall see, and ye shall say, The LORD will be magnified from the border of Israel.

6 ¶ A son ^ahonoureth *his* father, and a servant his master: if then I *be* a father, where *is* mine ^bhonour? and if I *be* a master, where *is* my fear? saith the LORD of hosts unto you, O priests, that despise my name. And ye say, Wherein have we despised thy name?

7 Ye offer polluted bread upon mine altar; and ye say, Wherein have we polluted thee? In that ye say, The table of the LORD *is* contemptible.

8 And if ye offer the ^ablind for ^bsacrifice, *is it* not evil? and if ye offer ^cthe lame and sick, *is it* not evil? offer it now unto thy governor; will he be pleased with thee, or accept thy person? saith the LORD of hosts.

9 And now, I pray you, beseech God that he will be gracious unto us: this hath been by your means: will he regard your persons? saith the LORD of hosts.

10 Who *is there* even among you that would shut the doors *for nought*? neither do ye kindle *fire* on mine altar for nought. I have no pleasure in you, saith the LORD of hosts, neither will I ^aaccept an offering at your hand.

11 For from the ^arising of the sun even unto the going down of the same my ^bname *shall be* great among the ^cGentiles; and in every place incense *shall be* offered unto my name, and a pure offering: for my name *shall be* great among the heathen, saith the LORD of hosts.

12 ¶ But ye have profaned it, in that ye say, The ^atable of the LORD *is* polluted; and the fruit thereof, *even* his meat, *is* contemptible.

13 Ye said also, Behold, what a weariness *is it!* and ye have ^asnuffed at it, saith the LORD of hosts; and ye brought *that which was* torn, and the ^blame, and the sick; thus ye brought an offering: should I ^caccept this of your hand? saith the LORD.

14 But ^acursed *be* the deceiver, which hath in his flock a male, and voweth, and sacrificeth unto the Lord a corrupt thing: for I *am* a great King, saith the LORD of hosts, and my name *is* ^bdreadful among the heathen.

CHAPTER 2

The priests are reproved for not keeping their covenants and not teaching the people—The Jews are condemned for dealing treacherously with one another and with their wives.

AND now, O ye priests, this commandment *is* for you.

2 If ye will not ^ahear, and if ye will not lay *it* to heart, to give glory unto my name, saith the LORD of hosts, I will even send a ^bcurse upon you, and I will curse your blessings: yea, I have cursed them already, because ye do not lay *it* to heart.

3 Behold, I will ^acorrupt your seed, and spread dung upon your faces, *even* the dung of your solemn feasts; and *one* shall take you away with it.

3a Jer. 49:10.
  b Ezek. 25:13.
  c HEB jackals.
6a TG Family, Children,
     Duties of.
  b TG Honoring Father and
     Mother.
8a Lev. 22:22.
  b TG Sacrifice.
  c IE lame or sick animals.

10a Amos 5:22 (21–22);
     3 Ne. 9:19 (19–20).
11a Isa. 45:6.
  b Isa. 59:19;
     Zeph. 2:11;
     Philip. 2:9 (5–12);
     D&C 18:23 (21–25);
     88:104.
  c Isa. 56:7.
     TG Gentiles.

12a Ezek. 41:22; 44:16.
13a OR belittled it.
  b Lev. 22:22 (22–25).
  c Lev. 22:20.
14a TG Curse.
  b D&C 45:70 (70–75).
2 2a Deut. 28:15.
  b TG Curse.
3a OR rebuke.

4 And ye shall know that I have sent this commandment unto you, that my *covenant might be with Levi, saith the LORD of hosts.

5 My *covenant was with him of life and peace; and I gave them to him *for* the fear wherewith he feared me, and was afraid before my name.

6 The law of *truth was in his mouth, and iniquity was not found in his lips: he walked with me in peace and equity, and did *turn many away from *iniquity.

7 For the priest's lips should keep *knowledge, and they should seek the *law at his mouth: for he *is* the *messenger of the LORD of hosts.

8 But ye are *departed out of the way; ye have caused many to *stumble at the law; ye have *corrupted the *covenant of Levi, saith the LORD of hosts.

9 Therefore have I also made you *contemptible and base before all the people, according as ye have not kept my ways, but have been partial in the law.

10 Have we not all one *father? hath not one God *created us? why do we deal treacherously every man against his brother, by *profaning the covenant of our fathers?

11 ¶ Judah hath dealt treacherously, and an abomination is committed in Israel and in Jerusalem; for Judah hath profaned the holiness of the LORD which he loved, and hath *married the daughter of a *strange god.

12 The LORD will *cut off the man that doeth this, the master and the scholar, out of the tabernacles of Jacob, and him that offereth an offering unto the LORD of hosts.

13 And this have ye done again, covering the altar of the LORD with tears, with weeping, and with crying out, insomuch that he regardeth not the offering any more, or receiveth *it* with good will at your hand.

14 ¶ Yet ye say, Wherefore? Because the LORD hath been witness between thee and the *wife of thy youth, against whom thou hast dealt treacherously: yet *is* she thy companion, and the wife of thy covenant.

15 And did not he make *one? Yet had he the residue of the spirit. And wherefore one? That he might seek a *godly *seed. Therefore take heed to your spirit, and let none deal treacherously against the *wife of his youth.

16 For the LORD, the God of Israel, saith that he hateth *putting away: for *one* covereth violence with his garment, saith the LORD of hosts: therefore take heed to your spirit, that ye deal not treacherously.

17 ¶ Ye have wearied the LORD with your words. Yet ye say, Wherein have we wearied *him?* When ye say, Every one that doeth *evil *is* good in the sight of the LORD, and he delighteth in them; or, Where *is* the God of *judgment?

CHAPTER 3

The Lord's messenger will prepare the way for the Second Coming—The Lord will sit in judgment—The people of Israel are commanded to pay tithes and offerings—They keep a book of remembrance.

4a TG Priesthood, Oath
  and Covenant.
5a Num. 25:12 (11–13);
  Isa. 54:10.
6a TG Honesty.
  b D&C 66:1.
  c Hel. 5:19 (17–19).
7a D&C 90:15 (14–15);
  107:99 (99–100); 131:6.
  b Ezek. 7:26.
  c TG Teacher.
8a Ezek. 22:26.
  b Mosiah 27:8 (8–9).

c 1 Sam. 2:17.
d Neh. 13:29.
9a 1 Sam. 2:30.
10a Eph. 4:6.
  TG God the Father,
  Elohim.
  b Job 31:15;
  Acts 17:26;
  D&C 76:24 (22–24).
  TG Man, Physical
  Creation of.
  c TG Profanity.
11a TG Marriage, Interfaith.

b TG Unbelief.
12a TG Excommunication.
14a Isa. 54:6.
  TG Marriage, Marry.
15a TG Unity.
  b TG Godliness.
  c Jacob 2:30.
  d TG Marriage, Husbands.
16a TG Divorce.
17a 2 Ne. 28:16 (7–8, 16).
  b Mal. 3:14 (14–15);
  2 Ne. 28:22 (16–22).

BEHOLD, I will ^asend my ^bmessenger, and he shall prepare the way before me: and the Lord, whom ye seek, shall suddenly ^ccome to his ^dtemple, even the ^emessenger of the covenant, whom ye delight in: behold, he shall come, saith the LORD of hosts.

2 But who may ^aabide the ^bday of his ^ccoming? and who shall ^dstand when he appeareth? for he *is* like a ^erefiner's ^ffire, and like fullers' ^gsoap:

3 And he shall sit *as* a ^arefiner and purifier of silver: and he shall ^bpurify the ^csons of ^dLevi, and purge them as gold and silver, that they may offer unto the LORD an ^eoffering in righteousness.

4 Then shall the offering of ^aJudah and Jerusalem be ^bpleasant unto the LORD, as in the days of old, and as in former years.

5 And I will come near to you to ^ajudgment; and I will be a swift witness against the ^bsorcerers, and against the ^cadulterers, and against ^dfalse swearers, and against those that ^eoppress the hireling in *his* ^fwages, the ^gwidow, and the fatherless, and that turn aside the ^hstranger *from his right,* and fear not me, saith the LORD of hosts.

6 For I *am* the LORD, I ^achange not; therefore ye sons of ^bJacob are not ^cconsumed.

7 ¶ Even from the days of your ^afathers ye are gone away from mine ^bordinances, and have not kept *them.* ^cReturn unto me, and I will return unto me, saith the LORD of hosts. But ye said, Wherein shall we return?

8 ¶ ^aWill a man ^brob God? Yet ye have robbed me. But ye say, Wherein have we robbed thee? In ^ctithes and offerings.

9 Ye *are* ^acursed with a curse: for ye have robbed me, *even* this whole nation.

10 Bring ye all the ^atithes into the storehouse, that there may be ^bmeat in mine house, and ^cprove me now herewith, saith the LORD of hosts, if I will not ^dopen you the ^ewindows of heaven, and pour you out a ^fblessing, that *there shall* not *be room* enough *to receive it.*

11 And I will ^arebuke the ^bdevourer for your sakes, and he shall not destroy the fruits of your ground; neither shall your vine cast her fruit before the time in the field, saith the LORD of hosts.

12 And all nations shall call you blessed: for ye shall be a delightsome land, saith the LORD of hosts.

13 ¶ Your words have been ^astout against me, saith the LORD. Yet ye say, What have we spoken *so much* against thee?

---

3 1*a* 3 Ne. 24:1 (1–18).
  b Matt. 11:10; Mark 1:2;
     1 Ne. 11:27;
     D&C 35:4; 45:9;
     JS—H 1:36.
     TG Last Days; Millennium, Preparing a People for; Restoration of the Gospel.
  c TG Jesus Christ, Prophecies about.
  d D&C 36:8; 42:36.
     TG Temple.
  e TG Jesus Christ, Messenger of the Covenant.
 2*a* Joel 2:11;
     D&C 35:21; 38:8; 128:24.
  b TG Day of the Lord.
  c TG Jesus Christ, Second Coming.
  d D&C 27:15 (15–18);
     87:8 (1–8).
  e Jer. 9:7;
     1 Cor. 3:13 (13–15).

 TG Suffering.
  f TG Earth, Cleansing of; World, End of.
  g Isa. 4:4 (3–4).
 3*a* Prov. 17:3.
  b Isa. 1:25.
     TG Purification.
  c 1 Chr. 6:1 (1–3);
     D&C 84:34 (31–43).
  d TG Priesthood, Aaronic.
  e TG Sacrifice.
 4*a* D&C 109:64 (64–67).
  b Isa. 56:7; 60:7;
     Ezek. 20:40.
 5*a* TG Judgment.
  b TG Sorcery.
  c TG Adulterer; Sexual Immorality.
  d D&C 121:18.
  e Eph. 6:9;
     Col. 4:1.
  f TG Wages.
  g D&C 83:6.
  h TG Stranger.
 6*a* TG God, Eternal Nature

 of; God, Perfection of.
  b D&C 109:67 (65–67).
  c Amos 9:9;
     D&C 5:19.
 7*a* Acts 7:51.
  b TG Ordinance.
  c TG Repent.
 8*a* TG Ingratitude.
  b 1 Chr. 29:14.
     TG Stealing.
  c TG Tithing.
 9*a* TG Curse.
10*a* Alma 13:15;
     D&C 64:23.
     TG Family, Managing Finances in.
  b TG Food; Meat; Welfare.
  c TG Test.
  d TG Generosity.
  e 2 Kgs. 7:2.
  f TG Blessing; Israel, Blessings of.
11*a* TG God, Power of.
  b D&C 85:3; 97:26.
13*a* OR strong.

14 Ye have said, It *is* ^avain to serve God: and what ^bprofit *is it* that we have kept his ordinance, and that we have walked mournfully before the LORD of hosts?

15 And now we call the ^aproud happy; yea, they that work ^bwickedness are set up; yea, *they that* tempt God are even delivered.

16 ¶ Then they that feared the LORD spake often one to another: and the LORD hearkened, and heard *it*, and a ^abook of ^bremembrance was written before him for them that feared the LORD, and that thought upon his name.

17 And they shall be ^amine, saith the LORD of hosts, in that day when I make up my ^bjewels; and I will ^cspare them, as a man spareth his own son that serveth him.

18 Then shall ye return, and ^adiscern between the righteous and the wicked, between him that serveth God and him that serveth him not.

CHAPTER 4

At the Second Coming, the proud and wicked will be burned as stubble—Elijah will return before that great and dreadful day.

^aFOR, behold, the ^bday cometh, that shall ^cburn as an oven; and all the ^dproud, yea, and all that do ^ewickedly, shall be ^fstubble: and the day that cometh shall burn them up, saith the LORD of hosts, that it shall leave them neither root nor ^gbranch.

2 ¶ But unto you that fear my name shall the ^aSun of righteousness ^barise with healing in his wings; and ye shall go forth, and grow up as calves of the ^cstall.

3 And ye shall ^atread down the wicked; for they shall be ashes under the soles of your feet in the day that I shall do *this*, saith the LORD of hosts.

4 ¶ Remember ye the law of Moses my servant, which I ^acommanded unto him in ^bHoreb for all Israel, *with* the statutes and judgments.

5 ¶ Behold, I will ^asend you ^bElijah the prophet ^cbefore the coming of the ^dgreat and dreadful ^eday of the LORD:

6 And he shall ^aturn the ^bheart of the ^cfathers to the ^dchildren, and the heart of the ^echildren to their fathers, lest I come and ^fsmite the ^gearth with a ^hcurse.

THE END OF THE PROPHETS*

14a Job 9:22; Isa. 58:3;
   Zeph. 1:12 (12–13);
   Mal. 2:17;
   3 Ne. 24:14 (14–18).
  b Eccl. 8:14.
15a D&C 64:24.
  b TG Worldliness.
16a Dan. 7:10.
  b TG Book of
   Remembrance.
17a D&C 101:3.
  b OR royal treasure.
   Isa. 62:3; Zech. 9:16;
   D&C 60:4.
  c Ps. 103:13;
   D&C 85:3.
18a D&C 101:95.
4 1a 3 Ne. 25:1 (1–6).
  b Isa. 34:8; 61:2;
   3 Ne. 21:21 (20–21);
   D&C 97:26 (25–28).
   TG Day of the Lord.
  c Ps. 21:9 (8–10);
   Amos 4:11; Jude 1:23.
   TG Earth, Cleansing of;
   World, End of.

  d TG Pride.
  e TG Sexual Immorality.
  f Isa. 47:14.
  g TG Vineyard of the Lord.
2a 3 Ne. 25:2.
  b 2 Ne. 25:13 (11–19).
  c 1 Ne. 22:24.
3a Ps. 49:14; Micah 7:10;
   Rev. 2:26;
   1 Ne. 14:3 (2–3);
   3 Ne. 21:12 (12–13).
4a Ex. 19:7 (7–8).
  b Deut. 4:10.
5a D&C 2:1.
  b John 1:21;
   JS—H 1:38 (38–39).
   TG Last Days;
   Millennium, Preparing a
   People for;
   Priesthood, Keys of.
  c D&C 77:13.
  d Zeph. 1:14 (14–18).
  e Jer. 30:7 (7–10);
   Hel. 12:25;
   3 Ne. 26:4; 28:31;
   Morm. 9:2;

   D&C 34:8 (6–9);
   43:17 (17–26); 112:24.
6a TG Restoration of the
   Gospel.
  b D&C 98:17 (16–17);
   138:47 (46–48).
   TG Heart.
  c TG Family, Eternal;
   Family, Love within;
   Genealogy and Temple
   Work; Honoring Father
   and Mother;
   Marriage, Fatherhood;
   Salvation for the Dead.
  d TG Family, Children,
   Responsibilities toward.
  e TG Children; Family,
   Children, Duties of.
  f 3 Ne. 25:6 (5–6);
   D&C 110:15 (13–16).
  g TG Earth, Destiny of.
  h TG Curse; Earth, Curse of.

* IE The end of the books
 of the prophets of the Old
 Testament.

SELECTIONS FROM THE
JOSEPH SMITH TRANSLATION

Following are excerpts from the Joseph Smith Translation of the Bible too lengthy for inclusion in the footnotes. For an explanation of this work, see "Joseph Smith Translation (JST)" in the Bible Dictionary. Joseph Smith's translation of the Bible has connections with or is mentioned in several sections of the Doctrine and Covenants (see sections 37, 45, 73, 76, 77, 86, 91, and 132). Also, the book of Moses and Joseph Smith—Matthew are excerpts from the Joseph Smith Translation.

JST, Genesis 1:1–8:18. Compare Genesis 1:1–6:13

This text of the Bible was restored by Joseph Smith and is published in the Pearl of Great Price as Selections from the Book of Moses.

JST, Genesis 9:4–6. Compare Genesis 8:20–22

4 And Noah builded an altar unto the Lord, and took of every clean beast, and of every clean fowl, and offered burnt offerings on the altar; *and gave thanks unto the Lord, and rejoiced in his heart.*

5 *And the Lord spake unto Noah, and he blessed him.* And *Noah* smelled a sweet savor, and *he* said in his heart;

6 *I will call on the name of the Lord, that he* will not again curse the ground any more for man's sake, for the imagination of man's heart is evil from his youth; *and that he* will *not* again smite any more every thing living, as *he* hath done, while the earth remaineth;

JST, Genesis 9:10–15. Compare Genesis 9:4–9

10 But, *the blood of all* flesh *which I have given you for meat, shall be shed upon the ground, which taketh life thereof, and the blood* ye shall not eat.

11 And surely, *blood shall not be shed, only for meat, to save your lives; and the blood* of every beast will I require *at your hands.*

12 *And* whoso sheddeth man's blood, by man shall his blood be shed; *for man shall not shed the blood of man.*

13 *For a commandment I give,* that every man's brother *shall preserve* the life of man, for in *mine own* image *have* I made man.

14 *And a commandment I give unto you,* Be ye fruitful and multiply; bring forth abundantly on the earth, and multiply therein.

15 And God spake unto Noah, and to his sons with him, saying, And I, behold, I *will* establish my covenant with you, *which I made unto your father Enoch, concerning* your seed after you.

JST, Genesis 9:21–25. Compare Genesis 9:16–17

21 And the bow shall be in the cloud; and I will look upon it, that I may remember the everlasting covenant, *which I made unto thy father Enoch; that, when men should keep all my commandments, Zion should again come on the earth, the city of Enoch which I have caught up unto myself.*

22 *And this is mine everlasting covenant, that when thy posterity shall embrace the truth, and look upward, then shall Zion look downward, and all the heavens shall shake with gladness, and the earth shall tremble with joy;*

23 *And the general assembly of the church of the firstborn shall come down out of heaven, and possess the earth, and shall have place until the end come. And this is mine everlasting covenant, which I made with thy father Enoch.*

24 *And the bow shall be in the cloud, and I will establish my covenant unto*

thee, which I have made between me and thee, for every living creature of all flesh that shall be upon the earth.

25 And God said unto Noah, This is the token of the covenant which I have established between me and thee; for all flesh that shall be upon the earth.

JST, Genesis 14:25–40. Compare Genesis 14:18–20

25 And Melchizedek lifted up his voice and blessed Abram.

26 Now Melchizedek was a man of faith, who wrought righteousness; and when a child he feared God, and stopped the mouths of lions, and quenched the violence of fire.

27 And thus, having been approved of God, he was ordained an high priest after the order of the covenant which God made with Enoch,

28 It being after the order of the Son of God; which order came, not by man, nor the will of man; neither by father nor mother; neither by beginning of days nor end of years; but of God;

29 And it was delivered unto men by the calling of his own voice, according to his own will, unto as many as believed on his name.

30 For God having sworn unto Enoch and unto his seed with an oath by himself; that every one being ordained after this order and calling should have power, by faith, to break mountains, to divide the seas, to dry up waters, to turn them out of their course;

31 To put at defiance the armies of nations, to divide the earth, to break every band, to stand in the presence of God; to do all things according to his will, according to his command, subdue principalities and powers; and this by the will of the Son of God which was from before the foundation of the world.

32 And men having this faith, coming up unto this order of God, were translated and taken up into heaven.

33 And now, Melchizedek was a priest of this order; therefore he obtained peace in Salem, and was called the Prince of peace.

34 And his people wrought righteousness, and obtained heaven, and sought for the city of Enoch which God had before taken, separating it from the earth, having reserved it unto the latter days, or the end of the world;

35 And hath said, and sworn with an oath, that the heavens and the earth should come together; and the sons of God should be tried so as by fire.

36 And this Melchizedek, having thus established righteousness, was called the king of heaven by his people, or, in other words, the King of peace.

37 And he lifted up his voice, and he blessed Abram, being the high priest, and the keeper of the storehouse of God;

38 Him whom God had appointed to receive tithes for the poor.

39 Wherefore, Abram paid unto him tithes of all that he had, of all the riches which he possessed, which God had given him more than that which he had need.

40 And it came to pass, that God blessed Abram, and gave unto him riches, and honor, and lands for an everlasting possession; according to the covenant which he had made, and according to the blessing wherewith Melchizedek had blessed him.

JST, Genesis 15:9–12. Compare Genesis 15:1–6

9 And Abram said, Lord God, how wilt thou give me this land for an everlasting inheritance?

10 And the Lord said, Though thou wast dead, yet am I not able to give it thee?

11 And if thou shalt die, yet thou shalt possess it, for the day cometh, that the Son of Man shall live; but how can he live if he be not dead? he must first be quickened.

12 And it came to pass, that Abram looked forth and saw the days of the Son of Man, and was glad, and his soul found rest, and he believed in the Lord; and the Lord counted it unto him for righteousness.

JST, Genesis 17:3–12. Compare Genesis 17:3–12

3 And *it came to pass, that* Abram fell on his face, *and called upon the name of the Lord.*

4 And God talked with him, saying, *My people have gone astray from my precepts, and have not kept mine ordinances, which I gave unto their fathers;*

5 *And they have not observed mine anointing, and the burial, or baptism wherewith I commanded them;*

6 *But have turned from the commandment, and taken unto themselves the washing of children, and the blood of sprinkling;*

7 *And have said that the blood of the righteous Abel was shed for sins; and have not known wherein they are accountable before me.*

8 *But as for thee,* behold, I *will* make my covenant with thee, and thou shalt be a father of many nations.

9 *And this covenant I make, that thy children may be known among all nations.* Neither shall thy name any more be called Abram, but thy name shall be called Abraham; for, a father of many nations have I made thee.

10 And I will make thee exceedingly fruitful, and I will make nations of thee, and kings shall come of thee, *and of thy seed.*

11 And I will establish *a covenant of circumcision with thee, and it shall be* my covenant between me and thee, and thy seed after thee, in their generations; *that thou mayest know forever that children are not accountable before me until they are eight years old.*

12 *And thou shalt observe to keep all my covenants wherein I covenanted with thy fathers; and thou shalt keep the commandments which I have given thee with mine own mouth, and I will be a God unto thee and thy seed after thee.*

JST, Genesis 17:23–24. Compare Genesis 17:17–18

23 Then Abraham fell on his face and *rejoiced,* and said in his heart, *There* shall a child be born unto him that is an hundred years old, and Sarah that is ninety years old *shall bear.*

24 And Abraham said unto God, Oh that Ishmael might live *uprightly* before thee!

JST, Genesis 19:9–15. Compare Genesis 19:8–10

9 And they said *unto him,* Stand back. *And they were angry with him.*

10 And they said *among themselves,* This one *man* came in to sojourn *among us,* and he will needs *now make himself to be* a judge; now we will deal worse with *him* than with them.

11 *Wherefore they said unto the man, We will have the men, and thy daughters also; and we will do with them as seemeth us good.*

12 *Now this was after the wickedness of Sodom.*

13 And Lot said, Behold now, I have two daughters which have not known man; let me, I pray you, *plead with my brethren that I may not* bring them out unto you; and ye *shall not* do unto them as seemeth good in your eyes;

14 *For God will not justify his servant in this thing; wherefore, let me plead with my brethren, this once only, that* unto these men ye do nothing, *that they may have peace in my house;* for therefore came they under the shadow of my roof.

15 *And they were angry with Lot* and came near to break the door, but the *angels of God, which were holy men,* put forth their hand and pulled Lot into the house unto them, and shut the door.

JST, Genesis 21:31–32. Compare Genesis 21:32–34

31 Then Abimelech, and Phicol,

the chief captain of his hosts, rose up, *and they planted a grove in Beersheba, and called there on the name of the Lord;* and they returned unto the land of the Philistines.

32 And Abraham *worshiped the everlasting God, and* sojourned in the land of the Philistines many days.

JST, Genesis 48:5–11. Compare Genesis 48:5–6

5 And now, of thy two sons, Ephraim and Manasseh, which were born unto thee in the land of Egypt, before I came unto thee into Egypt; *behold, they are mine, and the God of my fathers shall bless them; even* as Reuben and Simeon they *shall be blessed, for they are* mine; *wherefore they shall be called after my name. (Therefore they were called Israel.)*

6 And thy issue which thou begettest after them, shall be thine, and shall be called after the name of their brethren in their inheritance, *in the tribes; therefore they were called the tribes of Manasseh and of Ephraim.*

7 *And Jacob said unto Joseph, When the God of my fathers appeared unto me in Luz, in the land of Canaan; he sware unto me, that he would give unto me, and unto my seed, the land for an everlasting possession.*

8 *Therefore, O my son, he hath blessed me in raising thee up to be a servant unto me, in saving my house from death;*

9 *In delivering my people, thy brethren, from famine which was sore in the land; wherefore the God of thy fathers shall bless thee, and the fruit of thy loins, that they shall be blessed above thy brethren, and above thy father's house;*

10 *For thou hast prevailed, and thy father's house hath bowed down unto thee, even as it was shown unto thee, before thou wast sold into Egypt by the hands of thy brethren; wherefore thy brethren shall bow down unto thee, from generation to generation, unto the fruit of thy loins forever;*

11 *For thou shalt be a light unto my*

people, to deliver them in the days of their captivity, from bondage; and to bring salvation unto them, when they are altogether bowed down under sin.

JST, Genesis 50:24–38. Compare Genesis 50:24–26; 2 Nephi 3:4–22

24 And Joseph said unto his brethren, I die, *and go unto my fathers; and I go down to my grave with joy. The God of my father Jacob be with you, to deliver you out of affliction in the days of your bondage; for the Lord hath visited me, and I have obtained a promise of the Lord, that out of the fruit of my loins, the Lord God will raise up a righteous branch out of my loins; and unto thee, whom my father Jacob hath named Israel, a prophet; (not the Messiah who is called Shilo;) and this prophet shall deliver my people out of Egypt in the days of thy bondage.*

25 *And it shall come to pass that they shall be scattered again; and a branch shall be broken off, and shall be carried into a far country; nevertheless they shall be remembered in the covenants of the Lord, when the Messiah cometh; for he shall be made manifest unto them in the latter days, in the Spirit of power; and shall bring them out of darkness into light; out of hidden darkness, and out of captivity unto freedom.*

26 *A seer shall the Lord my God raise up, who shall be a choice seer unto the fruit of my loins.*

27 *Thus saith the Lord God of my fathers unto me, A choice seer will I raise up out of the fruit of thy loins, and he shall be esteemed highly among the fruit of thy loins; and unto him will I give commandment that he shall do a work for the fruit of thy loins, his brethren.*

28 *And he shall bring them to the knowledge of the covenants which I have made with thy fathers; and he shall do whatsoever work I shall command him.*

29 *And I will make him great in mine eyes, for he shall do my work; and he shall be great like unto him whom I have said I would raise up*

unto you, to deliver my people, O house of Israel, out of the land of Egypt; for a seer will I raise up to deliver my people out of the land of Egypt; and he shall be called Moses. And by this name he shall know that he is of thy house; for he shall be nursed by the king's daughter, and shall be called her son.

30 *And again, a seer will I raise up out of the fruit of thy loins, and unto him will I give power to bring forth my word unto the seed of thy loins; and not to the bringing forth of my word only, saith the Lord, but to the convincing them of my word, which shall have already gone forth among them in the last days;*

31 *Wherefore the fruit of thy loins shall write, and the fruit of the loins of Judah shall write; and that which shall be written by the fruit of thy loins, and also that which shall be written by the fruit of the loins of Judah, shall grow together unto the confounding of false doctrines, and laying down of contentions, and establishing peace among the fruit of thy loins, and bringing them to a knowledge of their fathers in the latter days; and also to the knowledge of my covenants, saith the Lord.*

32 *And out of weakness shall he be made strong, in that day when my work shall go forth among all my people, which shall restore them, who are of the house of Israel, in the last days.*

33 *And that seer will I bless, and they that seek to destroy him shall be confounded; for this promise I give unto you; for I will remember you from generation to generation; and his name shall be called Joseph, and it shall be after the name of his father; and he shall be like unto you; for the thing which the Lord shall bring forth by his hand shall bring my people unto salvation.*

34 *And the Lord sware unto Joseph that he would preserve his seed forever, saying, I will raise up Moses, and a rod shall be in his hand, and he shall gather together my people, and he shall lead them as a flock, and he shall smite the waters of the Red Sea with his rod.*

35 *And he shall have judgment, and shall write the word of the Lord. And he shall not speak many words, for I will write unto him my law by the finger of mine own hand. And I will make a spokesman for him, and his name shall be called Aaron.*

36 *And it shall be done unto thee in the last days also, even as I have sworn.* Therefore, Joseph said unto his brethren, God will surely visit you, and bring you out of this land, unto the land which he sware unto Abraham, and unto Isaac, and to Jacob.

37 And Joseph *confirmed many other things unto his brethren, and* took an oath of the children of Israel, saying unto them, God will surely visit you, and ye shall carry up my bones from hence.

38 So Joseph died *when he was* an hundred and ten years old; and they embalmed him, and *they* put him in a coffin in Egypt; *and he was kept from burial by the children of Israel, that he might be carried up and laid in the sepulchre with his father. And thus they remembered the oath which they sware unto him.*

JST, Exodus 4:24–27. Compare Exodus 4:24–27

24 And it came to pass, *that the Lord appeared unto him as he was in the way, by the inn. The Lord was angry with Moses, and his hand was about to fall upon him,* to kill him; *for he had not circumcised his son.*

25 Then Zipporah took a sharp stone and *circumcised* her son, and cast *the stone* at his feet, and said, Surely *thou art* a bloody husband unto me.

26 And the Lord spared Moses and let him go, *because Zipporah, his wife, circumcised the child.* And she said, Thou art a bloody husband. *And Moses was ashamed, and hid his face from the Lord, and said, I have sinned before the Lord.*

27 And the Lord said unto Aaron, Go into the wilderness to meet Moses, and he went and met him, in the mount of God; *in the mount*

where God appeared unto him; and Aaron kissed him.

JST, Exodus 32:14. Compare Exodus 32:14

14 And the Lord *said unto Moses, If they will repent of the evil which they have done, I will spare them, and turn away my fierce wrath; but, behold, thou shalt execute judgment upon all that will not repent of this evil this day. Therefore, see thou do this thing that I have commanded thee, or I will execute all that which I had* thought to do unto *my* people.

JST, Exodus 33:20, 23. Compare Exodus 33:20, 23

20 And he said *unto Moses,* Thou canst not see my face *at this time, lest mine anger be kindled against thee also, and I destroy thee, and thy people; for there shall no man among them* see me *at this time,* and live, *for they are exceeding sinful. And no sinful man hath at any time, neither shall there be any sinful man at any time, that shall see my face and live.*

23 And I will take away mine hand, and thou shalt see my back parts, but my face shall not be seen, *as at other times; for I am angry with my people Israel.*

JST, Exodus 34:1–2. Compare Exodus 34:1–2; D&C 84:21–26

1 And the Lord said unto Moses, Hew thee two *other* tables of stone, like unto the first, and I will write upon *them* also, the words *of the law, according as they were written at the* first *on the* tables which thou brakest; *but it shall not be according to the first, for I will take away the priesthood out of their midst; therefore my holy order, and the ordinances thereof, shall not go before them; for my presence shall not go up in their midst, lest I destroy them.*

2 *But I will give unto them the law as at the first, but it shall be after the law of a carnal commandment; for I have sworn in my wrath, that they shall not enter into my* presence, into my rest, in the days of their pilgrimage. Therefore do as I have commanded thee, and be ready in the morning, and come up in the morning unto mount Sinai, and present thyself there to me, in the top of the mount.

JST, 1 Chronicles 21:15. Compare 1 Chronicles 21:15

15 And God sent an angel unto Jerusalem to destroy it. *And the angel stretched forth his hand unto Jerusalem to destroy it; and God said to the angel, Stay now thine hand, it is enough; for as he was destroying,* the Lord beheld *Israel, that* he repented him of the evil; *therefore the Lord stayed* the angel that destroyed, *as he stood by the threshing floor of Ornan, the Jebusite.*

JST, Psalm 11:1–5. Compare Psalm 11:1–5

1 *In that day thou shalt come, O Lord; and* I will put my trust *in thee. Thou shalt say unto thy people, for mine ear hath heard thy voice; thou shalt say unto every soul, Flee unto my* mountain; *and the righteous shall flee like* a bird *that is let go from the snare of the fowler.*

2 For the wicked bend their bow; lo, they make ready their arrow upon the string, that they may privily shoot at the upright in heart, *to destroy their foundation.*

3 *But* the foundations *of the wicked shall* be destroyed, *and* what can *they* do?

4 *For* the Lord, *when he shall come into* his holy temple, *sitting upon God's* throne in heaven, his eyes *shall pierce the wicked.*

5 Behold his eyelids *shall* try the children of men, *and he shall redeem the righteous, and they shall be tried.* The Lord *loveth* the righteous, but the wicked, and him that loveth violence, his soul hateth.

JST, Psalm 14:1–7. Compare Psalm 14:1–7

1 The fool hath said in his heart,

There is no man that hath seen God. Because he showeth himself not unto us, therefore there is no God. *Be*hold, they are corrupt; they have done abominable works, *and none of them* doeth good.

2 *For* the Lord looked down from heaven upon the children of men, *and by his voice said unto his servant, Seek ye among the children of men,* to see if there *are* any that *do* understand God. *And he opened his mouth unto the Lord, and said, Behold, all these who say they are thine.*

3 *The Lord answered, and said,* They are all gone aside, they are together become filthy, *thou canst behold* none *of them* that *are doing* good, no, not one.

4 *All they have for their teachers are* workers of iniquity, *and there is* no knowledge *in them. They are they* who eat up my people. They eat bread and call not upon the Lord.

5 They *are* in great fear, for God *dwells* in the generation of the righteous. *He is the counsel of the poor, because they are ashamed of the wicked, and flee unto the Lord, for their refuge.*

6 *They are ashamed of* the counsel of the poor because the Lord is his refuge.

7 Oh that *Zion were established out of heaven,* the salvation of Israel. *O Lord, when wilt thou establish Zion?* When the Lord bringeth back the captivity of his people, Jacob shall rejoice, Israel shall be glad.

JST, Psalm 24:7–10. Compare Psalm 24:7–10

7 Lift up your heads, O ye *generations of Jacob;* and be ye lifted up; *and* the Lord strong and mighty; the Lord mighty in battle, who is the king of glory, *shall establish you forever.*

8 *And he will roll away the heavens; and will come down to redeem his people; to make you an everlasting name; to establish you upon his everlasting rock.*

9 Lift up your heads, O ye *generations of Jacob;* lift up *your heads,*

ye everlasting *generations,* and the *Lord of hosts, the king of kings;*

10 *Even* the king of glory shall come *unto you; and shall redeem his people, and shall establish them in righteousness.* Selah.

JST, Isaiah 29:1–8. Compare Isaiah 29:1–8

1 Woe to Ariel, to Ariel, the city where David dwelt! add ye year to year; let them kill sacrifices.

2 Yet I will distress Ariel, and there shall be heaviness and sorrow; *for thus hath the Lord said unto me,* It shall be unto Ariel;

3 *That I the Lord* will camp against *her* round about, and will lay siege against *her* with a mount, and I will raise forts against *her.*

4 And *she shall* be brought down, and *shall* speak out of the ground, and *her* speech shall be low out of the dust; and *her* voice shall be as of one that hath a familiar spirit, out of the ground, and *her* speech shall whisper out of the dust.

5 Moreover the multitude of *her* strangers shall be like small dust, and the multitude of the terrible ones shall be as chaff that passeth away; yea, it shall be at an instant suddenly.

6 For *they shall* be visited of the Lord of hosts with thunder, and with earthquake, and great noise, with storm and tempest, and the flame of devouring fire.

7 And the multitude of all the nations that fight against Ariel, even all that fight against her and her munition, and that distress her, shall be as a dream of a night vision.

8 *Yea,* it shall *be unto them even* as *unto* a hungry man *who* dreameth, and behold, he eateth, but he awaketh and his soul is empty; or *like unto* a thirsty man *who* dreameth, and behold, he drinketh, but he awaketh, and behold, he is faint, and his soul hath appetite. *Yea, even* so shall the multitude of all the nations be that fight against mount Zion.

JST, Isaiah 42:19–23. Compare Isaiah 42:19–22

19 For I will send my servant unto you who are blind; yea, a messenger to open the eyes of the blind, and unstop the ears of the deaf;

20 And they shall be made perfect notwithstanding their blindness, if they will hearken unto the messenger, the Lord's servant.

21 Thou art a people, seeing many things, but thou observest not; opening the ears to hear, but thou hearest not.

22 The Lord is not well pleased with such a people, but for his righteousness' sake he will magnify the law and make it honorable.

23 Thou art a people robbed and spoiled; thine enemies, all of them, have snared thee in holes, and they have hid thee in prison houses; they have taken thee for a prey, and none delivereth; for a spoil, and none saith, Restore.

JST, Matthew 3:4–6. Compare Matthew 2:4–6

4 And when he had gathered all the chief priests, and scribes of the people together, he demanded of them, saying, Where is the place that is written of by the prophets, in which Christ should be born? For he greatly feared, yet he believed not the prophets.

5 And they said unto him, It is written by the prophets, that he should be born in Bethlehem of Judea, for thus have they said,

6 The word of the Lord came unto us, saying, And thou Bethlehem, which lieth in the land of Judea, in thee shall be born a prince, which art not the least among the princes of Judea; for out of thee shall come the Messiah, who shall save my people Israel.

JST, Matthew 3:24–26. Compare Matthew 2:23

24 And it came to pass that Jesus grew up with his brethren, and waxed strong, and waited upon the Lord for the time of his ministry to come.

25 And he served under his father, and he spake not as other men, neither could he be taught; for he needed not that any man should teach him.

26 And after many years, the hour of his ministry drew nigh.

JST, Matthew 3:34–36. Compare Matthew 3:8–9

34 Why is it that ye receive not the preaching of him whom God hath sent? If ye receive not this in your hearts, ye receive not me; and if ye receive not me, ye receive not him of whom I am sent to bear record; and for your sins ye have no cloak.

35 Repent, therefore, and bring forth fruits meet for repentance;

36 And think not to say within yourselves, We are the children of Abraham, and we only have power to bring seed unto our father Abraham; for I say unto you that God is able of these stones to raise up children into Abraham.

JST, Matthew 3:38–40. Compare Matthew 3:11–12

38 I indeed baptize you with water, upon your repentance; and when he of whom I bear record cometh, who is mightier than I, whose shoes I am not worthy to bear, (or whose place I am not able to fill,) as I said, I indeed baptize you before he cometh, that when he cometh he may baptize you with the Holy Ghost and fire.

39 And it is he of whom I shall bear record, whose fan shall be in his hand, and he will thoroughly purge his floor, and gather his wheat into the garner; but in the fullness of his own time will burn up the chaff with unquenchable fire.

40 Thus came John, preaching and baptizing in the river of Jordan; bearing record, that he who was coming after him had power to baptize with the Holy Ghost and fire.

JST, Matthew 3:43–46. Compare Matthew 3:15–17

43 And Jesus, answering, said unto him, Suffer me to be baptized

of thee, for thus it becometh us to fulfill all righteousness. Then he suffered him.

44 *And John went down into the water and baptized him.*

45 And Jesus when he was baptized, went up straightway out of the water; *and John saw,* and lo, the heavens were opened unto him, and he saw the Spirit of God descending like a dove and lighting upon *Jesus.*

46 And lo, *he heard* a voice from heaven, saying, This is my beloved Son, in whom I am well pleased. *Hear ye him.*

JST, Matthew 5:21. Compare Matthew 5:19

21 Whosoever, therefore, shall break one of these least commandments, and shall teach men so *to do, he shall in no wise be saved in the kingdom of heaven;* but whosoever shall do and teach *these commandments of the law until it be fulfilled,* the same shall be called great, *and shall be saved* in the kingdom of heaven.

JST, Matthew 6:25–27. Compare Matthew 6:25; 10:10

25 *And, again, I say unto you, Go ye into the world, and care not for the world; for the world will hate you, and will persecute you, and will turn you out of their synagogues.*

26 *Nevertheless, ye shall go forth from house to house, teaching the people; and I will go before you.*

27 *And your heavenly Father will provide for you, whatsoever things ye need for food, what ye shall eat; and for raiment, what ye shall wear or put on.*

JST, Matthew 7:4–8. Compare Matthew 7:3–5

4 *And again, ye shall say unto them, Why is it that thou* beholdest the mote that is in thy brother's eye, but considerest not the beam that is in thine own eye?

5 Or how wilt thou say to thy brother, Let me pull out the mote out of thine eye; *and canst not behold* a beam in thine own eye?

6 *And Jesus said unto his disciples, Beholdest thou the scribes, and the Pharisees, and the priests, and the Levites? They teach in their synagogues, but do not observe the law, nor the commandments; and all have gone out of the way, and are under sin.*

7 *Go thou and say unto them, Why teach ye men the law and the commandments, when ye yourselves are the children of corruption?*

8 *Say unto them,* Ye hypocrites, first cast out the beam out of thine own eye; and then shalt thou see clearly to cast out the mote out of thy brother's eye.

JST, Matthew 7:9–11. Compare Matthew 7:6

9 *Go ye into the world, saying unto all, Repent, for the kingdom of heaven has come nigh unto you.*

10 *And the mysteries of the kingdom ye shall keep within yourselves; for it is not meet to* give that which is holy unto the dogs; neither cast ye your pearls *unto* swine, lest they trample them under their feet.

11 *For the world cannot receive that which ye, yourselves, are not able to bear; wherefore ye shall not give your pearls unto them, lest they* turn again and rend you.

JST, Matthew 7:12–17. Compare Matthew 7:7–8

12 *Say unto them, Ask of God;* ask, and it shall be given you; seek, and ye shall find; knock, and it shall be opened unto you.

13 For everyone that asketh, receiveth; and he that seeketh, findeth; and unto him that knocketh, it shall be opened.

14 *And then said his disciples unto him, They will say unto us, We ourselves are righteous, and need not that any man should teach us. God, we know, heard Moses and some of the prophets; but us he will not hear.*

15 *And they will say, We have the*

law for our salvation, and that is sufficient for us.

16 *Then Jesus answered, and said unto his disciples, Thus shall ye say unto them,*

17 *What man among you, having a son, and he shall be standing out, and shall say, Father, open thy house that I may come in and sup with thee, will not say, Come in, my son; for mine is thine, and thine is mine?*

JST, Matthew 9:18–21. Compare Matthew 9:16–17

18 *Then said the Pharisees unto him, Why will ye not receive us with our baptism, seeing we keep the whole law?*

19 *But Jesus said unto them, Ye keep not the law. If ye had kept the law, ye would have received me, for I am he who gave the law.*

20 *I receive not you with your baptism, because it profiteth you nothing.*

21 *For when that which is new is come, the old is ready to be put away.*

JST, Matthew 11:13–15. Compare Matthew 11:10–11, 13–14

13 *But the days will come, when the violent shall have no power; for all the prophets and the law prophesied that it should be thus until John.*

14 *Yea, as many as have prophesied have foretold of these days.*

15 *And if ye will receive it, verily, he was the Elias, who was for to come and prepare all things.*

JST, Matthew 12:37–38. Compare Matthew 12:43–44; see also JST, Luke 12:9–12

37 *Then came some of the scribes and said unto him, Master, it is written that, Every sin shall be forgiven; but ye say, Whosoever speaketh against the Holy Ghost shall not be forgiven. And they asked him, saying, How can these things be?*

38 *And he said unto them, When the unclean spirit is gone out of a man, he walketh through dry places, seeking rest and findeth none; but when a man speaketh*

against the Holy Ghost, then he saith, I will return into my house from whence I came out; and when he is come, he findeth him empty, swept and garnished; for the good spirit leaveth him unto himself.

JST, Matthew 13:39–44. Compare Matthew 13:39–42; see also D&C 86:1–7

39 *The harvest is the end of the world, or the destruction of the wicked.*

40 *The reapers are the angels, or the messengers sent of heaven.*

41 *As, therefore, the tares are gathered and burned in the fire, so shall it be in the end of this world, or the destruction of the wicked.*

42 *For in that day, before the Son of man shall come, he shall send forth his angels and messengers of heaven.*

43 *And they shall gather out of his kingdom all things that offend, and them which do iniquity, and shall cast them out among the wicked; and there shall be wailing and gnashing of teeth.*

44 *For the world shall be burned with fire.*

JST, Matthew 16:25–29. Compare Matthew 16:24–26

25 *Then said Jesus unto his disciples, If any man will come after me, let him deny himself, and take up his cross and follow me.*

26 *And now for a man to take up his cross, is to deny himself all ungodliness, and every worldly lust, and keep my commandments.*

27 *Break not my commandments for to save your lives; for whosoever will save his life in this world, shall lose it in the world to come.*

28 *And whosoever will lose his life in this world, for my sake, shall find it in the world to come.*

29 *Therefore, forsake the world, and save your souls; for what is a man profited, if he shall gain the whole world, and lose his own soul? Or what shall a man give in exchange for his soul?*

JST, Matthew 17:10–14. Compare Matthew 17:11–13

10 And Jesus answered and said unto them, Elias truly shall first come, and restore all things, *as the prophets have written.*

11 *And again* I say unto you that Elias has come already, *concerning whom it is written, Behold, I will send my messenger, and he shall prepare the way before me;* and they knew him not, and have done unto him, whatsoever they listed.

12 Likewise shall also the Son of man suffer of them.

13 *But I say unto you, Who is Elias? Behold, this is Elias, whom I send to prepare the way before me.*

14 Then the disciples understood that he spake unto them of John the Baptist, *and also of another who should come and restore all things, as it is written by the prophets.*

JST, Matthew 21:47–56. Compare Matthew 21:45–46

47 And when the chief priests and Pharisees had heard his parables, they perceived that he spake of them.

48 *And they said among themselves, Shall this man think that he alone can spoil this great kingdom? And they were angry with him.*

49 But when they sought to lay hands on him, they feared the multitude, because they *learned that the multitude* took him for a prophet.

50 *And now his disciples came to him, and Jesus said unto them, Marvel ye at the words of the parable which I spake unto them?*

51 *Verily, I say unto you, I am the stone, and those wicked ones reject me.*

52 *I am the head of the corner. These Jews shall fall upon me, and shall be broken.*

53 *And the kingdom of God shall be taken from them, and shall be given to a nation bringing forth the fruits thereof;* (meaning the Gentiles.)

54 *Wherefore, on whomsoever this stone shall fall, it shall grind him to powder.*

55 *And when the Lord therefore of the vineyard cometh, he will destroy those miserable, wicked men, and will let again his vineyard unto other husbandmen, even in the last days, who shall render him the fruits in their seasons.*

56 *And then understood they the parable which he spake unto them, that the Gentiles should be destroyed also, when the Lord should descend out of heaven to reign in his vineyard, which is the earth and the inhabitants thereof.*

JST, Matthew 26:22, 24–25. Compare Matthew 26:26–28; JST, Mark 14:20–25

22 And as they were eating, Jesus took bread and *brake it, and blessed* it, and gave to *his* disciples, and said, Take, eat; this is *in remembrance* of my body *which I give a ransom for you.*

24 For this is *in remembrance of* my blood of the new testament, which is shed for *as* many *as shall believe on my name,* for the remission of *their* sins.

25 *And I give unto you a commandment, that ye shall observe to do the things which ye have seen me do, and bear record of me even unto the end.*

JST, Mark 2:26–27. Compare Mark 2:27–28

26 *Wherefore the Sabbath was given unto man for a day of rest; and also that man should glorify God, and not that man should not eat;*

27 *For the Son of man made the Sabbath day,* therefore the Son of man is Lord also of the Sabbath.

JST, Mark 3:21–25. Compare Mark 3:28–30

21 *And then came certain men unto him, accusing him, saying, Why do ye receive sinners, seeing thou makest thyself the Son of God.*

22 *But he answered them and said,* Verily I say unto you, All sins which men have committed, when they repent, shall be forgiven *them; for I*

came to preach repentance unto the sons of men.

23 And blasphemies, wherewith soever they shall blaspheme, *shall be forgiven them that come unto me, and do the works which they see me do.*

24 *But there is a sin which shall not be forgiven.* He that shall blaspheme against the Holy Ghost, hath never forgiveness; but is in danger of *being cut down out of the world. And they shall inherit* eternal damnation.

25 *And this he said unto them* because they said, He hath an unclean spirit.

JST, Mark 7:10–12. Compare Mark 7:10

10 *Full well is it written of you, by the prophets whom ye have rejected.*

11 *They testified these things of a truth, and their blood shall be upon you.*

12 *Ye have kept not the ordinances of God;* for Moses said, Honor thy father and thy mother; and whoso curseth father or mother, let him die the death *of the transgressor, as it is written in your law; but ye keep not the law.*

JST, Mark 8:37–38. Compare Mark 8:35

37 For whosoever will save his life, shall lose it; *or whosoever will save his life, shall be willing to lay it down for my sake; and if he is not willing to lay it down for my sake, he shall lose it.*

38 But whosoever shall *be willing to* lose his life for my sake, and the gospel, the same shall save it.

JST, Mark 8:42–43. Compare Mark 8:38

42 *And they shall not have part in that resurrection when he cometh.*

43 *For verily I say unto you, That he shall come; and he that layeth down his life for my sake and the gospel's, shall come with him, and shall be clothed with his glory in the cloud, on the right hand of the Son of man.*

JST, Mark 9:40–48. Compare Mark 9:43–48

40 *Therefore, if thy hand offend thee, cut it off; or if thy brother offend thee and confess not and forsake not, he shall be cut off.* It is better for thee to enter into life maimed, than having two hands, to go into hell.

41 *For it is better for thee to enter into life without thy brother, than for thee and thy brother to be cast into hell;* into the fire that never shall be quenched, where their worm dieth not, and the fire is not quenched.

42 And *again,* if thy foot offend thee, cut it off; *for he that is thy standard, by whom thou walkest, if he become a transgressor, he shall be cut off.*

43 It is better for thee, to enter halt into life, than having two feet to be cast into hell; into the fire that never shall be quenched.

44 *Therefore, let every man stand or fall, by himself, and not for another; or not trusting another.*

45 *Seek unto my Father, and it shall be done in that very moment what ye shall ask, if ye ask in faith, believing that ye shall receive.*

46 And if thine eye *which seeth for thee, him that is appointed to watch over thee to show thee light, become a transgressor and* offend thee, pluck him out.

47 It is better for thee to enter into the kingdom of God, with one eye, than having two eyes to be cast into hell fire.

48 *For it is better that thyself should be saved, than to be cast into hell with thy brother,* where their worm dieth not, and where the fire is not quenched.

JST, Mark 14:20–26. Compare Mark 14:22–25

20 And as they did eat, Jesus took bread and blessed it, and brake, and gave to them, and said, Take *it, and eat.*

21 *Behold, this is for you to do in*

remembrance of my body; for as oft as ye do this ye will remember this hour that I was with you.

22 And he took the cup, and when he had given thanks, he gave it to them; and they all drank of it.

23 And he said unto them, This is *in remembrance of* my blood which is shed for many, *and the new testament which I give unto you; for of me ye shall bear record unto all the world.*

24 *And as oft as ye do this ordinance, ye will remember me in this hour that I was with you and drank with you of this cup, even the last time in my ministry.*

25 Verily I say unto you, *Of this ye shall bear record; for* I will no more drink of the fruit of the vine *with you,* until that day that I drink it new in the kingdom of God.

26 *And now they were grieved, and wept over him.*

JST, Mark 14:36–38. Compare Mark 14:32–34

36 And they came to a place which was named Gethsemane, *which was a garden; and the disciples began to be sore amazed, and to be very heavy, and to complain in their hearts, wondering if this be the Messiah.*

37 *And Jesus knowing their hearts, said* to his disciples, Sit ye here, while I shall pray.

38 And he taketh with him, Peter, and James, and John, *and rebuked them,* and said unto them, My soul is exceeding sorrowful, *even* unto death; tarry ye here and watch.

JST, Mark 16:3–6. Compare Mark 16:4–7; Luke 24:2–4

3 *But* when they looked, they saw that the stone was rolled away, (for it was very great,) *and two angels sitting thereon,* clothed in long white *garments;* and they were affrighted.

4 *But the angels said* unto them, Be not affrighted; ye seek Jesus of Nazareth, *who* was crucified; he is risen; he is not here; behold the place where they laid him;

5 *And* go your way, tell his disciples and Peter, that he goeth before you into Galilee; there shall ye see him as he said unto you.

6 *And they, entering into the sepulcher, saw the place where they laid Jesus.*

JST, Luke 3:4–11. Compare Luke 3:4–6

4 As it is written in the book of the *prophet* Esaias; *and these are the words,* saying, The voice of one crying in the wilderness, Prepare ye the way of the Lord, and make his paths straight.

5 *For behold, and lo, he shall come, as it is written in the book of the prophets, to take away the sins of the world, and to bring salvation unto the heathen nations, to gather together those who are lost, who are of the sheepfold of Israel;*

6 *Yea, even the dispersed and afflicted; and also to prepare the way, and make possible the preaching of the gospel unto the Gentiles;*

7 *And to be a light unto all who sit in darkness, unto the uttermost parts of the earth; to bring to pass the resurrection from the dead, and to ascend up on high, to dwell on the right hand of the Father,*

8 *Until the fullness of time, and the law and the testimony shall be sealed, and the keys of the kingdom shall be delivered up again unto the Father;*

9 *To administer justice unto all; to come down in judgment upon all, and to convince all the ungodly of their ungodly deeds, which they have committed; and all this in the day that he shall come;*

10 *For it is a day of power; yea,* every valley shall be filled, and every mountain and hill shall be brought low; the crooked shall be made straight, and the rough ways made smooth;

11 And all flesh shall see the salvation of God.

JST, Luke 3:19–20. Compare
Luke 3:10–13

19 *For it is well known unto you,
Theophilus, that after the manner of
the Jews, and according to the custom
of their law in receiving money into
the treasury, that out of the abundance which was received, was appointed unto the poor, every man his
portion;*
20 *And after this manner did the
publicans also, wherefore John* said
unto them, Exact no more than
that which is appointed you.

JST, Luke 6:29–30. Compare
Luke 6:29–30

29 And unto him who smiteth
thee on the cheek, offer also the
other; *or, in other words, it is better to offer the other, than to revile
again.* And him who taketh away
thy cloak, forbid not to take thy
coat also.
30 *For it is better that thou suffer
thine enemy to take these things, than
to contend with him. Verily I say unto
you, Your heavenly Father who seeth
in secret, shall bring that wicked one
into judgment.*

JST, Luke 9:24–25. Compare
Luke 9:24–25

24 For whosoever will save his
life, *must be willing to* lose it *for my
sake;* and whosoever will *be willing to* lose his life for my sake, the
same shall save it.
25 For what *doth it profit a man*
if he gain the whole world, *and yet
he receive him not whom God hath ordained, and he* lose *his own soul, and
he* himself be *a* castaway?

JST, Luke 12:9–12. Compare
Luke 12:9–10; see also JST, Matthew 12:37–38 and D&C 132:26–27

9 But he *who* denieth me before
men, shall be denied before the
angels of God.
10 *Now his disciples knew that he
said this, because they had spoken evil
against him before the people; for they
were afraid to confess him before men.*

11 *And they reasoned among themselves, saying, He knoweth our hearts,
and he speaketh to our condemna-
tion, and we shall not be forgiven.
But he answered them, and said unto
them,*
12 Whosoever shall speak a word
against the Son of man, *and repenteth,* it shall be forgiven him;
but unto him *who* blasphemeth
against the Holy Ghost, it shall not
be forgiven him.

JST, Luke 12:41–57. Compare
Luke 12:37–48

41 *For, behold, he cometh in the first
watch of the night, and he shall also
come in the second watch, and again
he shall come in the third watch.*
42 *And verily I say unto you, He
hath already come, as it is written of
him; and again when* he shall come
in the second watch, or come in
the third watch, blessed are those
servants *when he cometh, that he
shall* find so doing;
43 *For the Lord of those servants
shall gird himself, and make them to
sit down to meat, and will come forth
and serve them.*
44 *And now, verily I say these things
unto you, that ye may know this, that
the coming of the Lord is as a thief in
the night.*
45 *And it is like unto a man who is
an householder, who, if he watcheth
not his goods, the thief cometh in an
hour of which he is not aware, and
taketh his goods, and divideth them
among his fellows.*
46 *And they said among themselves,*
If the good man of the house had
known what hour the thief would
come, he would have watched, and
not have suffered his house to be
broken through *and the loss of his
goods.*
47 *And he said unto them, Verily I
say unto you, be ye therefore ready
also;* for the Son of man cometh at
an hour when ye think not.
48 Then Peter said unto him,
Lord, speakest thou this parable
unto us, or unto all?
49 And the Lord said, I *speak unto*

those whom the Lord shall make rulers over his household, to give his children their portion of meat in due season.

50 And they said, Who then is that faithful and wise servant?

51 And the Lord said unto them, It is that servant who watcheth, to impart his portion of meat in due season.

52 Blessed be that servant whom his Lord shall find, when he cometh, so doing.

53 Of a truth I say unto you, that he will make him ruler over all that he hath.

54 But the evil servant is he who is not found watching. And if that servant is not found watching, he will say in his heart, My Lord delayeth his coming; and shall begin to beat the menservants, and the maidens, and to eat, and drink, and to be drunken.

55 The Lord of that servant will come in a day he looketh not for, and at an hour when he is not aware, and will cut him down, and will appoint him his portion with the unbelievers.

56 And that servant who knew his Lord's will, and prepared not for his Lord's coming, neither did according to his will, shall be beaten with many stripes.

57 But he that knew not his Lord's will, and did commit things worthy of stripes, shall be beaten with few. For unto whomsoever much is given, of him shall much be required; and to whom the Lord has committed much, of him will men ask the more.

JST, Luke 14:35–37. Compare Luke 14:34

35 Then certain of them came to him, saying, Good Master, we have Moses and the prophets, and whosoever shall live by them, shall he not have life?

36 And Jesus answered, saying, Ye know not Moses, neither the prophets; for if ye had known them, ye would have believed on me; for to this intent they were written. For I am sent that

ye might have life. Therefore I will liken it unto salt which is good;

37 But if the salt has lost its savor, wherewith shall it be seasoned?

JST, Luke 16:16–23. Compare Luke 16:16–18

16 And they said unto him, We have the law, and the prophets; but as for this man we will not receive him to be our ruler; for he maketh himself to be a judge over us.

17 Then said Jesus unto them, The law and the prophets testify of me; yea, and all the prophets who have written, even until John, have foretold of these days.

18 Since that time, the kingdom of God is preached, and every man who seeketh truth presseth into it.

19 And it is easier for heaven and earth to pass, than for one tittle of the law to fail.

20 And why teach ye the law, and deny that which is written; and condemn him whom the Father hath sent to fulfill the law, that ye might all be redeemed?

21 O fools! for you have said in your hearts, There is no God. And you pervert the right way; and the kingdom of heaven suffereth violence of you; and you persecute the meek; and in your violence you seek to destroy the kingdom; and ye take the children of the kingdom by force. Woe unto you, ye adulterers!

22 And they reviled him again, being angry for the saying, that they were adulterers.

23 But he continued, saying, Whosoever putteth away his wife, and marrieth another, committeth adultery; and whosoever marrieth her who is put away from her husband, committeth adultery. Verily I say unto you, I will liken you unto the rich man.

JST, Luke 17:36–40. Compare Luke 17:37

36 And they answered and said unto him, Where, Lord, shall they be taken?

37 And he said unto them, Wheresoever the body is *gathered; or, in other words, whithersoever the saints are gathered*, thither will the eagles be gathered together; *or, thither will the remainder be gathered together.*

38 *This he spake, signifying the gathering of his saints; and of angels descending and gathering the remainder unto them; the one from the bed, the other from the grinding, and the other from the field, whithersoever he listeth.*

39 *For verily there shall be new heavens, and a new earth, wherein dwelleth righteousness.*

40 *And there shall be no unclean thing; for the earth becoming old, even as a garment, having waxed in corruption, wherefore it vanisheth away, and the footstool remaineth sanctified, cleansed from all sin.*

JST, Luke 21:24–26. Compare Luke 21:25–26

24 *Now these things he spake unto them, concerning the destruction of Jerusalem. And then his disciples asked him, saying, Master, tell us concerning thy coming?*

25 *And he answered them, and said, In the generation in which the times of the Gentiles shall be fulfilled,* there shall be signs in the sun, and in the moon, and in the stars; and upon the earth distress of nations with perplexity, *like* the sea and the waves roaring. *The earth also shall be troubled, and the waters of the great deep;*

26 Men's hearts failing them for fear, and for looking after those things which are coming on the earth. For the powers of heaven shall be shaken.

JST, Luke 24:2–4. Compare Luke 24:2–5

2 And they found the stone rolled away from the sepulcher, *and two angels standing by it in shining garments.*

3 And they entered *into the sepulcher, and not finding* the body of the Lord Jesus, they were much perplexed thereabout;

4 And were *affrighted*, and bowed down their faces to the earth. *But behold the angels* said unto them, Why seek ye the living among the dead?

JST, John 1:1–34. Compare John 1:1–34

1 In the beginning was the *gospel preached through the Son. And the gospel was the word*, and the *word* was with *the Son, and the Son was with* God, and the *Son* was *of* God.

2 The same was in the beginning with God.

3 All things were made by him; and without him was not anything made which was made.

4 In him was *the gospel*, and *the gospel was the life*, and the life was the light of men;

5 And the light shineth *in the world*, and the *world perceiveth* it not.

6 There was a man sent from God, whose name was John.

7 The same came *into the world* for a witness, to bear witness of the *light, to bear record of the gospel through the Son, unto all,* that through him *men* might believe.

8 He was not that *light*, but *came* to bear witness of that *light*,

9 Which was the true *light*, which lighteth every man *who* cometh into the world;

10 *Even the Son of God.* He *who* was in the world, and the world was made by him, and the world knew him not.

11 He came unto his own, and his own received him not.

12 But as many as received him, to them gave he power to become the sons of God; *only* to them who believe on his name.

13 *He was* born, not of blood, nor of the will of the flesh, nor of the will of man, but of God.

14 And the *same word* was made flesh, and dwelt among us, and we beheld his glory, the glory as of the Only Begotten of the Father, full of grace and truth.

15 John *bear* witness of him, and cried, saying, This *is* he of whom I spake; He who cometh after me, is preferred before me; for he was before me.

16 *For in the beginning was the Word, even the Son, who is made flesh, and sent unto us by the will of the Father. And as many as believe on his name shall receive of his fullness.* And of his fullness have all we received, *even immortality and eternal life, through his* grace.

17 For the law was given *through* Moses, but *life* and truth came *through* Jesus Christ.

18 *For the law was after a carnal commandment, to the administration of death; but the gospel was after the power of an endless life, through Jesus Christ, the Only Begotten Son, who is in the bosom of the Father.*

19 *And* no man hath seen God at any time, *except he hath borne record of the Son; for except it is through him no man can be saved.*

20 And this is the record of John, when the Jews sent priests and Levites from Jerusalem, to ask him; Who art thou?

21 And he confessed, and denied not *that he was Elias;* but confessed, *saying;* I am not the Christ.

22 And they asked him, *saying; How then art thou Elias?* And he said, I am not *that Elias who was to restore all things. And they asked him, saying,* Art thou that prophet? And he answered, No.

23 Then said they unto him, Who art thou? that we may give an answer to them that sent us. What sayest thou of thyself?

24 He said, I am the voice of one crying in the wilderness, Make straight the way of the Lord, as saith the prophet Esaias.

25 And they who were sent were of the Pharisees.

26 And they asked him, and said unto him; Why baptizest thou then, if thou be not the Christ, nor Elias *who was to restore all things,* neither that prophet?

27 John answered them, saying; I baptize with water, but there standeth one among you, whom ye know not;

28 He it is *of whom I bear record. He is that prophet, even Elias,* who, coming after me, is preferred before me, whose shoe's latchet I am not worthy to unloose, *or whose place I am not able to fill; for he shall baptize, not only with water, but with fire, and with the Holy Ghost.*

29 The next day John seeth Jesus coming unto him, and said; Behold the Lamb of God, who taketh away the sin of the world!

30 *And John bare record of him unto the people, saying,* This is he of whom I said; After me cometh a man who is preferred before me; for he was before me, and I knew him, *and* that he should be made manifest to Israel; therefore am I come baptizing with water.

31 And John bare record, saying; *When he was baptized of me,* I saw the Spirit descending from heaven like a dove, and it abode upon him.

32 And I knew him; *for* he who sent me to baptize with water, the same said unto me; Upon whom thou shalt see the Spirit descending, and remaining on him, the same is he who baptizeth with the Holy Ghost.

33 And I saw, and bare record that this is the Son of God.

34 *These things were done in Bethabara, beyond Jordan, where John was baptizing.*

JST, John 4:1–4. Compare John 4:1–2

1 When therefore the Pharisees had heard that Jesus made and baptized more disciples than John,

2 *They sought more diligently some means that they might put him to death; for many received John as a prophet, but they believed not on Jesus.*

3 *Now the Lord knew this, though he* himself baptized not *so many as* his disciples;

4 *For he suffered them for an example, preferring one another.*

JST, John 6:44. Compare John 6:44

44 No man can come unto me, except *he doeth the will of my* Father *who* hath sent me. *And this is the will of him who hath sent me, that ye receive the Son; for the Father beareth record of him; and he who receiveth the testimony, and doeth the will of him who sent me,* I will raise up *in the resurrection of the just.*

JST, John 13:8–10. Compare John 13:8–10

8 Peter saith unto him, Thou *needest not to* wash my feet. Jesus answered him, If I wash thee not, thou hast no part with me.
9 Simon Peter saith unto him, Lord, not my feet only, but also my hands and my head.
10 Jesus saith to him, He that *has* washed *his hands and his head,* needeth not save to wash his feet, but is clean every whit; and ye are clean, but not all. *Now this was the custom of the Jews under their law; wherefore, Jesus did this that the law might be fulfilled.*

JST, Acts 22:29–30. Compare Acts 22:29–30

29 Then straightway they departed from him which should have examined him, and the chief captain also was afraid after he knew that he was a Roman, because he had bound him, *and he loosed him from his bands.*
30 On the morrow, because he would have known the certainty wherefore he was accused of the Jews, *he* commanded the chief priests and all their council to appear, and brought Paul down, and set him before them.

JST, Romans 3:5–8. Compare Romans 3:5–8

5 But if *we remain in* our unrighteousness *and* commend the righteousness of God, *how dare* we say, God is unrighteous who taketh vengeance? (I speak as a man *who fears God,*)
6 God forbid; for then how shall God judge the world?
7 For if the truth of God hath more abounded through my lie, *(as it is called of the Jews,)* unto his glory; why yet am I also judged as a sinner? and not *received? Because* we *are* slanderously reported;
8 And some affirm that we say, *(whose damnation is just,)* Let us do evil that good may come. *But this is false.*

JST, Romans 4:2–5. Compare Romans 4:2–5

2 For if Abraham were justified by *the law of* works, he hath to glory *in himself;* but not *of* God.
3 For what saith the scripture? Abraham believed God, and it was counted unto him for righteousness.
4 Now to him *who is justified by the law of works,* is the reward reckoned, not of grace, but of debt.
5 But to him that *seeketh not to be justified by the law of works,* but believeth on him who justifieth *not* the ungodly, his faith is counted for righteousness.

JST, Romans 7:5–27. Compare Romans 7:5–25

5 For when we were in the flesh, the motions of sin, which were *not according to* the law, did work in our members to bring forth fruit unto death.
6 But now we are delivered from the law wherein we were held, *being dead to the law,* that we should serve in newness of spirit, and not in the oldness of the letter.
7 What shall we say then? Is the law sin? God forbid. Nay, I had not known sin, but by the law; for I had not known lust, except the law had said, Thou shalt not covet.
8 But sin, taking occasion by the commandment, wrought in me all manner of concupiscence. For without the law sin was dead.

9 For *once* I was alive without *transgression of* the law, but when the commandment *of Christ* came, sin revived, and I died.

10 And *when I believed not* the commandment *of Christ which came*, which was ordained to life, I found *it condemned me* unto death.

11 For sin, taking occasion, *denied* the commandment, *and* deceived me; and by it *I was slain.*

12 *Nevertheless, I found* the law *to be* holy, and the commandment *to be* holy, and just, and good.

13 Was then that which is good made death unto me? God forbid. But sin, that it might appear sin by that which is good working death in me; that sin, by the commandment, might become exceeding sinful.

14 For we know that the *commandment* is spiritual; but *when I was under the law, I was yet* carnal, sold under sin.

15 *But now I am spiritual;* for that which *I am commanded to do, I do; and that which I am commanded not to allow,* I allow not.

16 For what I *know is not right, I would* not *do; for that which is sin,* I hate.

17 If then I do *not* that which I would not *allow,* I consent unto the law, that it is good; *and I am not condemned.*

18 Now then, it is no more I that do *sin;* but I *seek to subdue that* sin which dwelleth in me.

19 For I know that in me, that is, in my flesh, dwelleth no good thing; for to will is present with me, *but to* perform that which is good I find not, *only in Christ.*

20 For the good that I would *have done when under the law, I find not to be good; therefore,* I do it not.

21 But the evil which I would not *do under the law, I find to be good;* that, I do.

22 Now if I do that, *through the assistance of Christ, I would not do under the law, I am not under the law; and it is no more that I seek to do*

wrong, but *to subdue* sin that dwelleth in me.

23 I find then *that under the* law, that when I would do good evil *was* present with me; for I delight in the law of God after the inward man.

24 *And now* I see another law, *even the commandment of Christ, and it is imprinted in my mind.*

25 *But* my members *are* warring against the law of my mind, and bringing me into captivity to the law of sin which is in my members.

26 *And if I subdue not the sin which is in me, but with the flesh serve the law of sin;* O wretched man that I am! who shall deliver me from the body of this death?

27 I thank God through Jesus Christ our Lord, *then, that so* with the mind I myself serve the law of God.

JST, Romans 8:29–30. Compare Romans 8:29–30

29 For *him* whom he did foreknow, he also did predestinate to be conformed to *his own* image, that he might be the firstborn among many brethren.

30 Moreover, *him* whom he did predestinate, *him* he also called; and *him* whom he called, *him* he also *sanctified;* and *him* whom he sanctified, *him* he also glorified.

JST, Romans 13:6–7. Compare Romans 13:6–7

6 For, for this cause pay ye *your consecrations* also *unto them;* for they are God's ministers, attending continually upon this very thing.

7 *But first,* render to all their dues, *according to custom,* tribute to whom tribute, custom to whom custom, *that your consecrations may be done in* fear *of him* to whom fear *belongs, and in* honor *of him* to whom honor *belongs.*

JST, 1 Corinthians 7:29–33, 38. Compare 1 Corinthians 7:29–38

29 But *I speak unto you who are*

called unto the ministry. For this I say, brethren, the time that remaineth is but short, that ye shall be sent forth unto the ministry. Even they who have wives, shall be as though they had none; for ye are called and chosen to do the Lord's work.

30 And it shall be with them who weep, as though they wept not; and them who rejoice, as though they rejoiced not, and them who buy, as though they possessed not;

31 And them who use this world, as not using it; for the fashion of this world passeth away.

32 But I would, brethren, that ye magnify your calling. I would have you without carefulness. For he who is unmarried, careth for the things that belong to the Lord, how he may please the Lord; therefore he prevaileth.

33 But he who is married, careth for the things that are of the world, how he may please his wife; therefore there is a difference, for he is hindered.

38 So then he that giveth himself in marriage doeth well; but he that giveth himself not in marriage doeth better.

JST, Galatians 3:19–20. Compare Galatians 3:19–20

19 Wherefore then, the law was added because of transgressions, till the seed should come to whom the promise was made in the law given to Moses, who was ordained by the hand of angels to be a mediator of this first covenant, (the law.)

20 Now this mediator was not a mediator of the new covenant; but there is one mediator of the new covenant, who is Christ, as it is written in the law concerning the promises made to Abraham and his seed. Now Christ is the mediator of life; for this is the promise which God made unto Abraham.

JST, Colossians 2:21–22. Compare Colossians 2:20–23

21 Which are after the doctrines and commandments of men, who teach you to touch not, taste not, handle not; all those things which are to perish with the using?

22 Which things have indeed a show of wisdom in will worship, and humility, and neglecting the body as to the satisfying the flesh, not in any honor to God.

JST, 2 Thessalonians 2:7–9. Compare 2 Thessalonians 2:7–9

7 For the mystery of iniquity doth already work, and he it is who now worketh, and Christ suffereth him to work, until the time is fulfilled that he shall be taken out of the way.

8 And then shall that wicked one be revealed, whom the Lord shall consume with the spirit of his mouth, and shall destroy with the brightness of his coming.

9 Yea, the Lord, even Jesus, whose coming is not until after there cometh a falling away, by the working of Satan with all power, and signs and lying wonders,

JST, 1 Timothy 2:4. Compare 1 Timothy 2:4

4 Who is willing to have all men to be saved, and to come unto the knowledge of the truth which is in Christ Jesus, who is the Only Begotten Son of God, and ordained to be a Mediator between God and man; who is one God, and hath power over all men.

JST, 1 Timothy 3:15–16. Compare 1 Timothy 3:15–16

Note: The subtle change in the following verses emphasizes that the "pillar and ground of the truth" is Jesus Christ.

15 But if I tarry long, that thou mayest know how thou oughtest to behave thyself in the house of God, which is the church of the living God.

16 The pillar and ground of the truth is, (and without controversy, great is the mystery of godliness,) God was manifest in the flesh, justified in the Spirit, seen of angels,

preached unto the Gentiles, believed on in the world, received up into glory.

JST, 1 Timothy 6:15–16.
Compare 1 Timothy 6:15–16

15 Which in his times he shall show, who is the blessed and only Potentate, the King of kings, and Lord of lords, *to whom be honor and power everlasting;*

16 *Whom no man hath seen, nor can see, unto whom no man can approach, only he who hath the light and the hope of immortality dwelling in him.*

JST, Hebrews 4:3. Compare Hebrews 4:3

3 For we who have believed do enter into rest, as he said, As I have sworn in my wrath, If they *harden their hearts* they shall *not* enter into my rest; *also, I have sworn, If they will not harden their hearts, they shall enter into my rest;* although the works of God were *prepared, (or finished,)* from the foundation of the world.

JST, Hebrews 6:3–10. Compare Hebrews 6:3–10

3 And *we will go on unto perfection* if God permit.

4 For *he hath made it* impossible for those who were once enlightened, and have tasted of the heavenly gift, and were made partakers of the Holy Ghost,

5 And have tasted the good word of God, and the powers of the world to come,

6 If they shall fall away, to *be renewed* again unto repentance; seeing they crucify unto themselves the Son of God afresh, and put him to an open shame.

7 For *the day cometh that* the earth which drinketh in the rain that cometh oft upon it, and bringeth forth herbs meet for them *who dwelleth thereon,* by whom it is dressed, *who now* receiveth blessings from God, *shall be cleansed with fire.*

8 *For* that which beareth thorns and briers is rejected, and is nigh unto cursing; *therefore they who bring not forth good fruits, shall be cast into the fire; for their* end is to be burned.

9 But, beloved, we are persuaded of better things of you, and things that accompany salvation, though we thus speak.

10 For God is not unrighteous, *therefore he will not* forget your work and labor of love, which ye have showed toward his name, in that ye have ministered to the saints, and do minister.

JST, Hebrews 7:3. Compare Hebrews 7:3

3 *For this Melchizedek was ordained a priest after the order of the Son of God, which order was* without father, without mother, without descent, having neither beginning of days, nor end of life. *And all those who are ordained unto this priesthood are* made like unto the Son of God, *abiding* a priest continually.

JST, Hebrews 7:19–21. Compare Hebrews 7:19–21

19 For the law *was administered without an oath and* made nothing perfect, but *was only* the bringing in of a better hope; by the which we draw nigh unto God.

20 Inasmuch as *this high priest was* not without an oath, *by so much was Jesus made the surety of a better testament.*

21 (For those priests were made without an oath; but this with an oath by him that said unto him, The Lord sware and will not repent, Thou art a priest forever after the order of Melchizedek;)

JST, Hebrews 7:25–26. Compare Hebrews 7:26–27

25 For such an high priest became us, who is holy, harmless, undefiled, separate from sinners, and made *ruler over* the heavens;

26 *And not* as those high priests *who* offered up sacrifice *daily,* first for *their* own sins, and then for the *sins of the people;* for *he needeth not offer sacrifice for his own sins, for he knew no sins; but for the sins of the people. And* this he did once, when he offered up himself.

JST, James 2:14–21. Compare James 2:14–22

14 What profit *is it,* my brethren, *for* a man *to* say he hath faith, and hath not works? can faith save him?

15 Yea, a man may say, I *will show thee I have faith without works; but I say,* Show me thy faith without works, and I will show thee my faith by my works.

16 *For* if a brother or sister be naked and destitute, and one of you say, Depart in peace, be warmed and filled; notwithstanding *he* give not those things which are needful to the body; what profit *is your faith unto such?*

17 Even so faith, if it *have* not works is dead, being alone.

18 *Therefore* wilt thou know, O vain man, that faith without works is dead *and cannot save you?*

19 Thou believest there is one God; thou doest well; the devils also believe, and tremble; *thou hast made thyself like unto them, not being justified.*

20 Was not Abraham our father justified by works, when he had offered Isaac his son upon the altar?

21 Seest thou how *works* wrought with his *faith,* and by works was faith made perfect?

JST, 2 Peter 3:3–13. Compare 2 Peter 3:3–13

3 Knowing this first, that *in the last days* there shall come scoffers, walking after their own lusts.

4 *Denying the Lord Jesus Christ,* and saying, Where is the promise of his coming? for since the fathers fell asleep, all things *must* continue as they *are, and have continued as they are* from the beginning of the creation.

5 For this they willingly are ignorant of, that *of old* the heavens, and the earth standing *in the water* and out of the water, *were created by the word of God;*

6 *And by the word of God,* the world that then was, being overflowed with water perished;

7 But the heavens, and the earth which are now, are kept in store *by the same word,* reserved unto fire against the day of judgment and perdition of ungodly men.

8 But *concerning the coming of the Lord,* beloved, *I would not have you* ignorant of this one thing, that one day is with the Lord as a thousand years, and a thousand years as one day.

9 The Lord is not slack concerning his promise *and coming,* as some men count slackness; but long-suffering *toward us,* not willing that any should perish, but that all should come to repentance.

10 But the day of the Lord will come as a thief in the night, in the which the heavens shall *shake, and the earth also shall tremble, and the mountains shall melt, and* pass away with a great noise, and the elements shall *be filled* with fervent heat; the earth also *shall be filled,* and the *corruptible* works *which* are therein shall be burned up.

11 *If* then all these things shall be *destroyed,* what manner of persons ought ye to be in holy *conduct* and godliness,

12 Looking *unto,* and *preparing for the day of* the coming of the Lord wherein the *corruptible things of the* heavens being on fire, shall be dissolved, and the *mountains* shall melt with fervent heat?

13 Nevertheless, *if we shall endure, we shall be kept* according to his promise. *And we* look for *a* new heavens, and a new earth wherein dwelleth righteousness.

JST, Revelation 1:1–8. Compare Revelation 1:1–8

1 The Revelation of *John, a servant of God,* which *was given* unto him *of Jesus Christ,* to show unto his servants things which must shortly come to pass, *that* he sent and signified by his angel unto his servant John,

2 Who *bore* record of the word of God, and of the testimony of Jesus Christ, and of all things that he saw.

3 Blessed *are they* who read, and they who hear *and understand* the words of this prophecy, and keep those things which are written therein, for the time *of the coming of the Lord draweth nigh.*

4 *Now this is the testimony of* John to *the seven servants who are over* the seven churches in Asia. Grace unto you, and peace from him *who* is, and *who* was, and *who* is to come; *who hath sent forth his angel from* before his throne, *to testify unto those who are the seven servants over the seven churches.*

5 *Therefore, I, John,* the faithful witness, *bear record of the things which were delivered me of the angel,* and from Jesus Christ the first begotten of the dead, and the *Prince* of the kings of the earth.

6 *And* unto him who loved us, *be glory; who* washed us from our sins in his own blood, and hath made us kings and priests unto God, his Father. To him be glory and dominion, forever and ever. Amen.

7 *For* behold, he cometh *in the* clouds *with ten thousands of his saints in the kingdom, clothed with the glory of his Father.* And every eye shall see him; and they who pierced him, and all kindreds of the earth shall wail because of him. Even so, Amen.

8 *For he saith,* I am Alpha and Omega, the beginning and the ending, the Lord, *who* is, and *who* was, and *who* is to come, the Almighty.

JST, Revelation 2:26–27. Compare Revelation 2:26–27

26 And *to him who* overcometh, and keepeth my *commandments* unto the end, will I give power over *many kingdoms;*

27 And he shall rule them with *the word of God; and they shall be in his hands* as the vessels *of clay in the hands* of a potter; *and he shall govern them by faith, with equity and justice,* even as I received of my Father.

JST, Revelation 12:1–17. Compare Revelation 12:1–17

Note the changed sequence of verses in the JST.

1 And there appeared a great *sign* in heaven, *in the likeness of things on the earth;* a woman clothed with the sun, and the moon under her feet, and upon her head a crown of twelve stars.

2 And *the woman* being with child, cried, travailing in birth, and pained to be delivered.

3 *And she brought forth a man child, who was to rule all nations with a rod of iron; and her child was caught up unto God and his throne.*

4 And there appeared another *sign* in heaven; and behold, a great red dragon, having seven heads and ten horns, and seven crowns upon his heads. And his tail drew the third part of the stars of heaven, and did cast them to the earth. And the dragon stood before the woman which was delivered, *ready* to devour her child *after* it was born.

5 And the woman fled into the wilderness, where she *had* a place prepared of God, that they should feed her there a thousand two hundred and threescore *years.*

6 And there was war in heaven; Michael and his angels fought against the dragon; and the dragon and his angels *fought against Michael;*

7 And *the dragon* prevailed not *against Michael, neither the child,*

nor the woman which was the church of God, who had been delivered of her pains, and brought forth the kingdom of our God and his Christ.

8 Neither was *there* place found in heaven *for* the great dragon, *who* was cast out; that old serpent called the devil, and *also called* Satan, which deceiveth the whole world; he was cast out into the earth; and his angels were cast out with him.

9 And I heard a loud voice saying in heaven, Now is come salvation, and strength, and the kingdom of our God, and the power of his Christ;

10 For the accuser of our brethren is cast down, which accused them before our God day and night.

11 *For* they *have overcome* him by the blood of the Lamb, and by the word of their testimony; *for* they loved not their own lives, *but kept the testimony even* unto death. Therefore, rejoice O heavens, and ye that dwell in them.

12 *And after these things I heard another voice saying,* Woe to the inhabiters of the earth, *yea,* and *they who dwell upon the islands* of the sea! for the devil is come down unto you, having great wrath, because he knoweth that he hath but a short time.

13 *For* when the dragon saw that he was cast unto the earth, he persecuted the woman which brought forth the man-child.

14 *Therefore,* to the woman were given two wings of a great eagle, that she might *flee* into the wilderness, into her place, where she is nourished for a time, and times, and half a time, from the face of the serpent.

15 And the serpent casteth out of his mouth water as a flood after the woman, that he might cause her to be carried away of the flood.

16 And the earth *helpeth* the woman, and the earth *openeth* her mouth, and *swalloweth* up the flood which the dragon *casteth* out of his mouth.

17 *Therefore,* the dragon was wroth with the woman, and went to make war with the remnant of her seed, which keep the commandments of God, and have the testimony of Jesus Christ.